Willings Volume 1
Section 1

UK Newspapers Index

This index cross-refers to all newspapers in Section 2

willings

Section 1 UK Newspapers Index

National Newspapers

1. London

2. South East:

Buckinghamshire, East Sussex, Hampshire, Kent, Oxfordshire, Surrey, West Sussex
Bracknell Forest UA, Brighton & Hove UA, Isle of Wight UA, Medway UA, Milton-Keynes UA, Portsmouth UA, Reading UA, Slough UA, Southampton UA, West Berkshire UA, Windsor & Maidenhead UA, Wokingham UA

3. East of England

Bedfordshire, Cambridgeshire, Essex, Hertfordshire, Norfolk, Suffolk
Luton UA, Peterborough UA, Southend on Sea UA, Thurrock UA

4. South West

Cornwall and Isles of Scilly, Devon, Dorset, Gloucestershire, Somerset, Wiltshire
Bath & North East Somerset UA, Bournemouth UA, City of Bristol UA, North Somerset UA, Plymouth UA, Poole UA, South Gloucestershire UA, Swindon UA, Torbay UA

5. East Midlands

Derbyshire, Leicestershire, Lincolnshire, Northamptonshire, Nottinghamshire
Derby UA, Leicester UA, Nottingham UA, Rutland UA

6. West Midlands

Shropshire, Staffordshire, Warwickshire, West Midlands, Worcestershire
Herefordshire UA, Stoke on Trent UA, Telford and Wrekin UA

7. Yorkshire & Humberside

North Yorkshire, South Yorkshire, West Yorkshire
York UA, City of Kingston upon Hull UA, East Riding of Yorkshire UA, North East Lincolnshire UA, North Lincolnshire UA

8. North East

Durham, Northumberland, Tyne & Wear
Darlington UA, Hartlepool UA, Middlesbrough UA, Redcar & Cleveland UA, Stockton-on-Tees UA

9. North West

Cheshire, Cumbria, Greater Manchester, Lancashire, Merseyside
Blackburn with Darwen UA, Blackpool UA, Halton UA, Warrington UA

10. Wales

11. Northern Ireland

12. Scotland

Counties & UAs

Non-Nationals

Section 1 UK Newspapers Index

Non-Nationals - England

Non-Nationals - England

Section 1 UK Newspapers Index

Non-Nationals - England

Anstey
MERCURY EXTRA 42

Ashby-de-la-Zouch
MERCURY EXTRA 42

Hinckley
THE HINCKLEY TIMES 38

Leicester
MELTON TIMES 42

Loughborough
LOUGHBOROUGH ECHO 41

Lutterworth
HARBOROUGH MAIL 37
MERCURY EXTRA 42

Market Harborough
HARBOROUGH MAIL 37

Melton Mowbray
MELTON TIMES 42
RUTLAND TIMES 48

Lincolnshire
GRIMSBY TELEGRAPH 36
HORNCASTLE NEWS 38
LINCOLNSHIRE FREE PRESS 41
SPALDING GUARDIAN 50

Alford
LOUTH LEADER 41

Barton-upon-Humber
SCUNTHORPE TELEGRAPH 49

Boston
BOSTON STANDARD 27

Bourne
LINCOLNSHIRE FREE PRESS 41
PETERBOROUGH TELEGRAPH 47
SPALDING GUARDIAN 50
STAMFORD MERCURY 51

Brigg
MARKET RASEN MAIL 42
SCUNTHORPE TELEGRAPH 49

Broughton
MERCURY EXTRA 42
PEEBLESSHIRE NEWS 46

Caistor
MARKET RASEN MAIL 42

Crowle
GAINSBOROUGH STANDARD 35
SCUNTHORPE TELEGRAPH 49

Gainsborough
GAINSBOROUGH STANDARD 35
LINCOLNSHIRE ECHO 41

Grantham
GRANTHAM JOURNAL 36
LINCOLNSHIRE ECHO 41

Horncastle
HORNCASTLE NEWS 38
LINCOLNSHIRE ECHO 41

Lincoln
LINCOLNSHIRE ECHO 41

Louth
LOUTH LEADER 41

Mablethorpe
LOUTH LEADER 41
MABLETHORPE & SUTTON ON SEA LEADER 42

Market Rasen
LINCOLNSHIRE ECHO 41
MARKET RASEN MAIL 42

Messingham
SCUNTHORPE TELEGRAPH 49

Scunthorpe
SCUNTHORPE TELEGRAPH 49

Sleaford
LINCOLNSHIRE ECHO 41
SLEAFORD STANDARD 49

Spalding
LINCOLNSHIRE FREE PRESS 41
PETERBOROUGH TELEGRAPH 47
SPALDING GUARDIAN 50

Stamford
PETERBOROUGH TELEGRAPH 47
RUTLAND TIMES 48
STAMFORD MERCURY 51

Sutton-on-Sea
LOUTH LEADER 41
MABLETHORPE & SUTTON ON SEA LEADER 42

Woodhall Spa
HORNCASTLE NEWS 38

London
BRENT & KILBURN TIMES 28
BRENTWOOD GAZETTE 28
CROYDON ADVERTISER 31
HACKNEY GAZETTE 37
HARROW TIMES 37
ISLINGTON GAZETTE 39
ISLINGTON TRIBUNE 39
LONDON EVENING STANDARD 41
ROMFORD RECORDER 48
THE SOUTH AFRICAN 23
SUTTON GUARDIAN 52
WALTHAM FOREST INDEPENDENT 53
WEST END EXTRA 54
THE WHARF 55
WIMBLEDON GUARDIAN 55

London - Barking & Dagenham Borough
EAST LONDON ENQUIRER 33
ESSEX ENQUIRER 34

Barking
EAST LONDON ENQUIRER 33
ESSEX ENQUIRER 34

Dagenham
EAST LONDON ENQUIRER 33
ESSEX ENQUIRER 34

London - Barnet Borough
LEICESTER MERCURY 41
SUNDAY MERCURY 51

London - Bexley Borough
BEXLEY TIMES 27

Bexley
BEXLEY TIMES 27

Bexleyheath
BEXLEY TIMES 27

Erith
BEXLEY TIMES 27

Sidcup
BEXLEY TIMES 27

Welling
BEXLEY TIMES 27

London - Brent Borough
HARROW TIMES 37

London - Bromley Borough
BROMLEY NEWS 28
BROMLEY TIMES 28
ORPINGTON NEWS 46

Beckenham
BROMLEY TIMES 28

Bromley
BROMLEY NEWS 28
BROMLEY TIMES 28

Chislehurst
BROMLEY TIMES 28

Orpington
BROMLEY TIMES 28
ORPINGTON NEWS 46

London - Camden Borough
CAMDEN NEW JOURNAL 29

London - City of
BRENT & KILBURN TIMES 28
ISLINGTON TRIBUNE 39
NEWHAM RECORDER 44
SUTTON GUARDIAN 52
WEST END EXTRA 54

London - Croydon Borough
CROYDON ADVERTISER 31
CROYDON GUARDIAN 31

Coulsdon
CROYDON ADVERTISER 31

Croydon
CROYDON ADVERTISER 31
CROYDON GUARDIAN 31

Kenley
CROYDON ADVERTISER 31

Purley
CROYDON ADVERTISER 31

London - Ealing Borough

Ealing
BRENT & KILBURN TIMES 28

London - Enfield Borough
ENFIELD INDEPENDENT 34
SOUTH WALES EVENING POST 50
WALES ON SUNDAY 53

Enfield
ENFIELD INDEPENDENT 34

Southgate
ENFIELD INDEPENDENT 34

London - Hackney Borough
HACKNEY CITIZEN 37

Hackney
HACKNEY CITIZEN 37
HACKNEY GAZETTE 37

Shoreditch
HACKNEY GAZETTE 37

London - Hammersmith & Fulham Borough

Fulham
BRENT & KILBURN TIMES 28

London - Haringey Borough

Crouch End
ISLINGTON GAZETTE 39

London - Harrow Borough
BRENT & KILBURN TIMES 28
HARROW TIMES 37

Harrow
BRENT & KILBURN TIMES 28
HARROW TIMES 37

London - Havering Borough
BRENTWOOD GAZETTE 28
EAST LONDON ENQUIRER 33
ESSEX ENQUIRER 34
ROMFORD RECORDER 48

Hornchurch
BRENTWOOD GAZETTE 28
EAST LONDON ENQUIRER 33
ESSEX ENQUIRER 34
ROMFORD RECORDER 48

Rainham
EAST LONDON ENQUIRER 33
ESSEX ENQUIRER 34

Section 1 UK Newspapers Index

Non-Nationals - England

Non-Nationals - England

Non-Nationals - England

Non-Nationals - England

Non-Nationals - Scotland

Section 1 UK Newspapers Index

Non-Nationals - Wales

Non-Nationals - Wales

Section 1 UK Newspapers Index

Non-Nationals - Wales

Willings Volume 1
Section 2

UK Newspapers

National & Regional Daily Newspapers listed A-Z
Regional & Local Weekly Newspapers listed A-Z
UK offices of Foreign News Media listed A-Z
Online newspapers listed A-Z

National & Regional Daily Newspapers

National & Regional Daily Newspapers (& Supplements)

Al Arab
995920
Editorial: 66 Hammersmith Road, London W14 8UD **Tel:** 44 02076 023999
Email: editor@alarab.co.uk
Web site: www.alarab.co.uk
Freq: WeeklyNot Audited
Editor: Mohamed Ahmed Hun Elhouni

Al Quds Al Arabi
995921
Editorial: 164-166 King Street, London W6 0QU **Tel:** 44 02087 418008
Email: alquds@alquds.co.uk
Web site: www.alquds.co.uk
Freq: Daily
Circ: 100000 Not Audited

Asian Leader
995952
Editorial: 187 Drake Street, Rochdale, Rochdale OL11 1EF **Tel:** 44 01706 670119
Email: newsdesk@asianleader.co.uk
Web site: http://asianleader.co.uk/
Freq: Bi-Weekly
Circ: 30000 Not Audited

Asian Lite
984756
Editorial: EMF House, 12 Charlotte Street, Manchester M1 4FL **Tel:** 44 01612 287362
Email: newsdesk@asianlite.com
Web site: www.asianlite.com
Freq: Weekly
Circ: 31000 Not Audited
Editor: Rafeek Ravuther
Profile: Newspaper covering news, social stories, entrepreneurs, immigration, parenting, campus, travel, food, Asian community related events, Bollywood, sport, fashion and lifestyle. Aimed at British Asian professionals and the business community.

Bangla Mirror
995280
Editorial: Unit 2, 60 Hanbury Street, London E1 5JL **Tel:** 44 02073 778966
Email: info@banglamirrornews.com
Web site: www.banglamirrornews.com
Freq: Weekly
Circ: 15000 Not Audited
Editor: Abdul Karim
Profile: Newspaper covering fashion, music, business, health, religion, legal advice, sports and culture. Aimed at British born Bangladeshis.
Ad Rate: Full Page Colour 1976.00

Bangla Post
1049243
Editorial: 10-14 Hollybush Gardens, London E2 9QP **Tel:** 44 02077 295295
Email: info@banglapost.co.uk
Web site: www.banglapost.co.uk
Freq: WeeklyNot Audited
Editor: Tareq Chowdhury
Profile: Newspaper with profiles of successful Bengalis in various professions, health, business, community focus covering issues relevant to British Bengalis and news from the sub-continent, events including films, theatre, meals, political events, shows and educations. Aimed at Bengali communities in the UK.
Ad Rate: Full Page Mono 1700.00
Ad Rate: Full Page Colour 2210.00

Big Print
985445
Editorial: PO Box 173, Peterborough PE2 6WS
Web site: www.rnib.org.uk
Freq: Weekly
Circ: 8000 Not Audited
Profile: National newspaper containing conventional news and reviews of national and international events. Aimed at those with failing eyesight.

Ad Rate: Full Page Mono 200.00

The Catholic Universe
982165
Editorial: Universe Media Ltd, Longbridge Road, Trafford Park, Manchester M17 1SN
Tel: 44 01619 085301
Web site: http://www.thecatholicuniverse.com/
Freq: Weekly
Circ: 25000 Not Audited
Profile: Founded in 1860, The Universe is a Catholic newspaper for the UK and Ireland. Its regular columnists include Lord Alton of Liverpool, Nobel-nominated human rights campaigner Father Shay Cullen, leading Labour MP and government advisor John Battle, and theologian Father Michael Buckley. Regular weekly news direct from Rome is supplied by Vatican Correspondent Gerry O'Connell.

Chinese People's Political Consultative Conference News
1061131
Tel: 44 86108 8146900
Email: zxb-tlb@vip.163.com
Web site: http://www.rmzxb.com.cn
Freq: Daily
Circ: 120003 Not Audited

Daily Ausaf
998819
Editorial: 595A Lea Bridge Road, London E10 6AJ **Tel:** 44 02085 218555
Email: news@dailyausaflondon.com
Web site: www.dailyausaf.com
Freq: Daily
Circ: 20000 Not Audited
Editor: Mohsin Khan

Daily Express
979794
Editorial: Northern & Shell Building, 10 Lower Thames Street, London EC3R 6EN
Tel: 44 02086 127000
Email: news.desk@express.co.uk
Web site: www.express.co.uk
Freq: Daily
Circ: 380632 Not Audited
Editor: Kelly Rose Bradford; **Editor:** Hugh Whittow
Profile: The Daily Express is a tabloid-sized newspaper covering culture, entertainment, national and international news, money, motoring, property, showbiz, sport and travel. Previous Title: The Express
Ad Rate: Full Page Colour 31360.00

Daily Mail
979795
Editorial: 3rd Floor, Northcliffe House, 2 Derry Street, London W8 5TT
Tel: 44 02079 386000
Email: news@dailymail.co.uk
Web site: www.dailymail.co.uk/news
Freq: Daily
Circ: 1443213 Not Audited
Editor: Paul Dacre
Profile: Tabloid sized daily newspaper that covers national and international news, business, finance, travel, sport, showbiz, science, technology and health stories. It has all the latest reviews across the arts and entertainment world as well as news, features and interviews. The Daily Mail first published in 1896 by Lord Northcliffe.The outlet offers RSS (Really Simple Syndication).
Ad Rate: Full Page Mono 32508.00
Ad Rate: Full Page Colour 45612.00

Daily Mirror
979796
Editorial: 1 Canada Square, Canary Wharf, London E14 5AP **Tel:** 44 02072 933000
Email: mirrornews@mirror.co.uk
Web site: www.mirror.co.uk
Freq: Daily
Circ: 625278 Not Audited
Editor: Geoff Hill; **Editor in Chief:** John Kierans
Profile: The Daily Mirror is a tabloid-sized daily newspaper covering national and international news stories, with articles on finance, entertainment, lifestyle, travel, television, show-biz and sport. The paper is available free on iPad to UK readers from Mondays to Fridays, as well as a full seven-day app.The paper was founded in 1903.
Ad Rate: Full Page Mono 29000.00
Ad Rate: Full Page Colour 36800.00

Daily Record
980056
Editorial: 1 Central Quay, Glasgow G3 8DA
Tel: 44 01413 093000
Email: reporters@dailyrecord.co.uk
Web site: www.dailyrecord.co.uk
Freq: Daily
Circ: 143635 Not Audited

Daily Star
980042
Editorial: Northern & Shell Building, 10 Lower Thames Street, London EC3R 6EN
Tel: 44 02086 127000
Email: news@dailystar.co.uk
Web site: www.dailystar.co.uk
Freq: Daily
Circ: 421812 Not Audited
Editor: Dawn Neesom
Profile: The Daily Star is a tabloid-sized newspaper covering the latest news, current affairs, sport, showbiz, entertainment and celebrities. The paper targets young readers interested in celebrities and entertainment.
Ad Rate: Full Page Colour 23765.00

Daily Star Sunday
982786
Editorial: Northern & Shell Building, 10 Lower Thames Street, London EC3R 6EN
Tel: 44 02086 127000
Email: sunday@dailystar.co.uk
Web site: www.dailystar.co.uk/sunday
Freq: Weekly
Circ: 259541 Not Audited
Editor: Stuart James
Profile: The Daily Star Sunday is a tabloid-sized Sunday newspaper covering the latest news, current affairs, sports, entertainment and showbiz.
Ad Rate: Full Page Colour 28420.00

The Daily Telegraph
979797
Editorial: 111 Buckingham Palace Road, London SW1W 0DT **Tel:** 44 02079 312000
Email: dtnews@telegraph.co.uk
Web site: www.telegraph.co.uk
Freq: Daily
Circ: 477927 Not Audited
Editor: Chris Evans
Profile: The Daily Telegraph is a daily, broadsheet newspaper providing national and international news, business, culture, comment, fashion, lifestyle, sport, technology and travel. The newspaper was founded in June 1855 as the Daily Telegraph and Courier.The Telegraph Magazine was awarded the Amnesty Human Rights Media Award for Photojournalism for Shannon Jensen's 'A Long Walk'.
Ad Rate: Full Page Mono 46000.00
Ad Rate: Full Page Colour 68000.00

Daily Wahdat
1061162
Tel: 44 92912 214154
Email: editorwahdat@gmail.com
Web site: http://dailywahdat.com.pk
Freq: Daily
Circ: 60002 Not Audited

Ecos de Quevedo
1060989
Email: diarioecosdequevedo@hotmail.com
Freq: DailyNot Audited

Financial Times
979819
Editorial: Number One, Southwark Bridge, London SE1 9HL **Tel:** 44 02078 733000
Email: main.news@ft.com
Web site: www.ft.com
Freq: Daily
Circ: 186018 Not Audited
Editor: Lionel Barber
Profile: Financial Times is a broadsheet newspaper covering business, finance, politics and technology. The weekday section provides features on business people, ideas and developments, delivering information on business and finance. FTfm section covers global fund management industry, prices and FT fund ratings, providing analysis and debate to asset managers and private investors. The newspaper was first published in 1888 and is published Monday to Saturday. This Outlet offer RSS (Really Simple Syndication).

Financial Times - Latvia, Riga Bureau
1072430
Not Audited

Financial Times - Philippines, Manila Bureau
1072439
Not Audited

First News
996009
Editorial: First Floor, 58 Southwark Bridge Road, London SE1 0AS
Tel: 44 02031 952000
Email: newsdesk@firstnews.co.uk
Web site: www.firstnews.co.uk
Freq: Weekly
Circ: 86413 Not Audited
Profile: First News is a newspaper with hard-hitting news as well as show-biz, movies, travel, computer games, sport, puzzles, health and competitions.
Ad Rate: Full Page Mono 1620.00
Ad Rate: Full Page Colour 1780.00

GSPC Property Guide
982569
Editorial: 12 Bothwell Street, Glasgow G2 6LU **Tel:** 44 01415 722400
Web site: www.gspc.co.uk
Freq: Bi-Weekly
Circ: 19000 Not Audited
Property Management & Maintenance, Residential Real Estate

The Guardian
979799
Editorial: Kings Place, 90 York Way, London N1 9GU **Tel:** 44 02033 532000
Email: national@theguardian.com
Web site: https://www.theguardian.com/uk
Freq: Daily
Circ: 149420 Not Audited
Profile: The Guardian is a national newspaper providing the latest UK and international news, sport, business, technology, fashion, comment, analysis and reviews. The news section of the Guardian provides coverage across a range of domestic and international current affairs. The Guardian was awarded National Newspaper in the British Press Awards. The Guardian website was awarded the best newspaper category and at the Media Awards it was awarded Website of the Year (Grand Prix), Best National News Site, Best Use of Social Media and Best Technical Innovation.The publication was founded in 1821 as a weekly newspaper in the liberal interest. This Outlet offer RSS (Really Simple Syndication).
Ad Rate: Full Page Mono 11400.00
Ad Rate: Full Page Colour 18000.00

The guardian weekly
981607
Editorial: Kings Place, 90 York Way, London N1 9GU **Tel:** 44 02033 532000
Email: weekly@guardian.co.uk
Web site: http://www.theguardian.com/weekly
Freq: Weekly
Circ: 56960 Not Audited
Editor: Abby Deveney
Profile: The Guardian Weekly is a newspaper containing a compilation of The Guardian and The Observer reviews and features, including extracts from Le Monde and The Washington Post; includes a section for ex-patriate readers.
Ad Rate: Full Page Mono 3750.00
Ad Rate: Full Page Colour 4500.00

The Hamodia
994647
Editorial: 113 Fairview Road, London N15 6TS **Tel:** 44 02084 427777
Email: editor@hamodia.co.uk
Web site: www.hamodia.co.uk
Freq: Weekly
Circ: 10000 Not Audited
Editor: Yeshua Jacob
Profile: Jewish orthodox newspaper covering news from Britain, America and Israel.
Ad Rate: Full Page Mono 800.00
Ad Rate: Full Page Colour 1200.00

Hemel Today
1096859
Profile: Website for local papers the Herald Express, the Hemel Hempstead Gazette and the Berkhamsted & Tring Gazette, providing local news for the area.

The Herald 979800
Editorial: 200 Renfield Street, Glasgow, Glasgow G2 3QB **Tel:** 44 01413 027000
Email: news@theherald.co.uk
Web site: www.heraldscotland.com
Freq: Daily
Circ: 28872 Not Audited
Profile: The Herald is a daily newspaper covering news, current affairs, business, entertainment and sports.
Ad Rate: Full Page Mono 10743.00
Ad Rate: Full Page Colour 12736.00

Hunan Economic Daily 1061802
Tel: 44 86731 4453570
Freq: 2 Times/Week
Circ: 100003 Not Audited

i 985772
Editorial: Northcliffe House, 2 Derry Street, London W8 5HF **Tel:** 44 02073 615678
Email: i@inews.co.uk
Web site: inews.co.uk
Freq: Daily
Circ: 267857 Not Audited
Editor: Oliver Duff
Profile: Online version of the i paper, covering all the latest on UK and international news, business, entertainment, politics and sport. The paper draws its content from the Independent, but the articles are shorter with a more populist approach.

International Casino Review 981618
Editorial: 20 New Road, Brighton BN1 1UF
Tel: 44 01257 277400
Email: ks@sjc.co.uk
Web site: https://www.casino-review.co/
Freq: Monthly
Circ: 5525 Not Audited
Profile: Magazine featuring coverage of International casinos, with news sections dedicated to Western, Central and Eastern Europe, Africa and the Middle East, Asia and Oceania, North America, South and Central America. Aimed at those in the gaming industry.
Computer & Video Games

Investment Adviser 979773
Editorial: Number One, Southwark Bridge, London SE1 9HL **Tel:** 44 02078 733000
Web site: www.ftadviser.com/ia
Freq: Weekly
Circ: 9229 Not Audited
Editor: Dan Jones
Profile: Newspaper providing objective information on investment funds and related products. Aimed at top financial intermediaries.
Ad Rate: Full Page Colour 5816.00
Fund Management

The Irish News 980739
Editorial: 113-117 Donegall Street, Belfast BT1 2GE **Tel:** 44 02890 322226
Email: newsdesk@irishnews.com
Web site: www.irishnews.com
Freq: Daily
Circ: 35523 Not Audited
Editor: Noel Doran
Profile: The Irish News is a regional daily newspaper covering regional news, sports, business and lifestyle for Northern Ireland.
Ad Rate: Full Page Mono 3600.00
Ad Rate: Full Page Colour 4303.00

The Irish Post 982137
Editorial: 88 Fenchurch Street, London EC3M 4BY **Tel:** 44 02089 004137
Email: editor@irishpost.co.uk
Web site: www.irishpost.co.uk
Freq: Weekly
Circ: 21000 Not Audited
Editor: Siobhan Breatnach
Profile: The Irish Post is a weekly, local newspaper published on Mondays, covering all the latest on Irish community news from across Britain with a focus on local news, business, entertainment and sport.
Ad Rate: Full Page Mono 3500.00
Ad Rate: Full Page Colour 3500.00

The Irish World 998761
Editorial: Irish World House, 934 North Circular Road, London NW2 7JR
Tel: 44 02084 537800
Email: admin@theirishworld.com
Web site: www.theirishworld.com
Freq: Weekly
Circ: 13107 Not Audited
Editor: Bernard Purcell
Profile: Website covering business, current affairs, Irish music, cinema, sport, humour, books, fashion and politics. Aimed at the Irish community living in Britain.

The Jewish Chronicle 982151
Editorial: 28 St Albans Lane, London NW11 7QE **Tel:** 44 02074 151500
Email: editorial@thejc.com
Web site: www.thejc.com
Freq: Weekly
Circ: 20512 Not Audited
Editor: Stephen Pollard
Profile: Magazine containing news and features of Jewish interest. Including news from Israel, fashion, motoring, food and wine, property and finance. The Jewish Chronicle states to be the world's oldest and most influential Jewish newspaper was founded in 184. The Jewish Chronicle has often known as The JC - has editorial independence and is guaranteed by the Jewish Chronicle Trust. Aimed at the Jewish community in the UK and throughout the world.
Ad Rate: Full Page Mono 5040.00
Ad Rate: Full Page Colour 6300.00

Lännen Media 1061106
Tel: 44 35810 6657770
Email: palaute@lannenmedia.fi
Freq: DailyNot Audited

Letters 1069768
Editorial: 1 Canada Square, Canary Wharf, London E14 5AP
Email: share@thenewday.co.uk

The Mail on Sunday 979811
Editorial: Northcliffe House, 2 Derry Street, London W8 5TT **Tel:** 44 02079 386000
Email: news@mailonsunday.co.uk
Web site: www.mailonsunday.co.uk
Freq: Weekly
Circ: 1232789 Not Audited
Editor: Geordie Greig
Profile: The Mail on Sunday is a Sunday newspaper that covers the latest UK and international news, sport, showbiz, science, travel and health stories from around the world. The newspaper was first published in 1982.
Ad Rate: Full Page Mono 39300.00
Ad Rate: Full Page Colour 55800.00

Metro 983521
Editorial: Northcliffe House, 2 Derry Street, London W8 5TT **Tel:** 44 02036 150600
Email: news.london@metro.co.uk
Web site: metro.co.uk
Freq: Daily
Circ: 1470715 Not Audited
Editor: Polly Humphris; **Editor:** Ted Young
Profile: The Metro is a free daily newspaper that covers UK and international news, sports, entertainment and lifestyle.
Ad Rate: Full Page Mono 28750.40
Ad Rate: Full Page Colour 36104.60

Midweek Sport 995031
Editorial: City View House, Union Street, Ardwick, Manchester M12 4JD
Tel: 44 01613 580381
Email: sportplus@sundaysport.co.uk
Web site: www.sundaysport.com
Freq: Weekly
Circ: 50000 Not Audited
Editor: Nick Appleyard; **Editor:** David Beevers

Morning Star 984428
Editorial: William Rust House, 52 Beachy Road, Bow, London E3 2NS
Tel: 44 02085 100815
Email: reception@peoples-press.com
Web site: www.morningstaronline.co.uk
Freq: Daily

Circ: 10000 Not Audited
Editor: Ben Chacko
Profile: Newspaper covering news and current affairs, with a focus on social and trade union issues. Aimed at the labour movement.
Ad Rate: Full Page Mono 1337.53
Ad Rate: Full Page Colour 1337.53

The Muslim News 983328
Editorial: PO Box 380, Harrow, London HA2 6LL **Tel:** 44 02088 638586
Email: info@muslimnews.co.uk
Web site: www.muslimnews.co.uk
Freq: Monthly
Circ: 21439 Not Audited
Editor: Ahmed Versi
Profile: Newspaper covering political and community affairs from the UK and abroad, education, social, ethical, legal, environment, science, cultural affairs and sports.
Ad Rate: Full Page Mono 2890.00
Ad Rate: Full Page Colour 2990.00

The Muslim Weekly 983327
Editorial: Suite 8, Montefiore Centre, Hanbury Street, London E1 5HZ
Email: suban@themuslimweekly.com
Web site: www.themuslimweekly.com
Freq: Weekly
Circ: 50000 Not Audited
Editor: Sabera Salam
Profile: Newspaper covering issues affecting Muslims in Britain and around the world with local and international news, current affairs, lifestyle, personalities, local communities and people, sport and Islamic art and culture all from an Islamic perspective. Aimed mainly at Muslims and other minority communities.
Ad Rate: Full Page Mono 1000.00
Ad Rate: Full Page Colour 1500.00

The National 988715
Editorial: 200 Renfield Street, Glasgow G2 3QB **Tel:** 44 01413 027000
Email: reporters@thenational.scot
Web site: www.thenational.scot/
Freq: Daily
Circ: 10380 Not Audited

The New European 1099575
Tel: 44 02070 466080
Email: theneweuropean@archant.co.uk
Web site: www.theneweuropean.co.uk
Freq: Weekly
Circ: 200000 Not Audited
Editor: Tom Armstrong; **Editor:** Dylan Jones

News Letter 981600
Editorial: 6-9 Donegall Square South, Belfast BT 1 5JA **Tel:** 44 02890 897700
Email: newsdesk@newsletter.co.uk
Web site: www.newsletter.co.uk
Freq: Daily
Circ: 15475 Not Audited
Editor: Alistair Bushe; **Editor:** Ruth Rodgers
Profile: The News Letter is a daily newspaper featuring the latest news, sport and entertainment from in and around Belfast.
Ad Rate: Full Page Mono 3029.40
Ad Rate: Full Page Colour 4241.16

The News Line 995370
Editorial: BCM Box 747, London WC1N 3XX
Tel: 44 02072 321101
Email: newsline@wrp.org.uk
Web site: www.wrp.org.uk
Freq: DailyNot Audited

The Observer 979813
Editorial: Kings Place, 90 York Way, London N1 9GU **Tel:** 44 02033 532000
Email: editor@observer.co.uk
Web site: https://www.theguardian.com/observer
Freq: Daily
Circ: 178545 Not Audited
Profile: The Observer is a Sunday newspaper focusing on in-depth analysis and comment on UK and world news, politics and entertainment. Offers a combination of main news and special interest supplements. The Observer attracts an audience that are interested in news,

current affairs, sport and cultural issues. The Observer was named national newspaper of the year at the British Press Awards. The newspaper was founded in 1791 by WS Bourne. Letters to the Editor should be sent to letters@observer.co.uk
Ad Rate: Full Page Mono 13933.00
Ad Rate: Full Page Colour 22000.00

Opinioneers 1065176

Pelita Brunei 1061186
Tel: 44 67323 83941
Email: pelita@brunet.bn
Web site: http://www.brunet.bn/news/pelita
Freq: Weekly
Circ: 25000 Not Audited

Pictures Desk 1065174
Email: pictures@thenewday.co.uk

Polish Express 998527
Editorial: Suite 161, 315 Chiswick High Road, London W4 4HH
Tel: 44 02030 266550
Email: editorial@polishexpress.co.uk
Web site: www.polishexpress.co.uk
Freq: Weekly
Circ: 75000 Not Audited
Profile: Newspaper covering culture, entertainment and life from a Polish perspective. Aimed at Polish communities in the UK.

Printed Circuit Information News 1060882
Tel: 44 86216 4139487
Email: newspaper@cpca.org.cn
Web site: http://www.cpca.org.cn
Circ: 5002 Not Audited

Pueblo 1060992
Tel: 44 52614 4103006
Email: reporteros2005@yahoo.com.mx
Web site: http://www.elpueblo.com
Freq: DailyNot Audited

Scotland on Sunday 979814
Editorial: Orchard Brae House (Level 7), 30 Queensferry Road, Edinburgh EH4 2HS
Tel: 44 01313 117311
Email: newsdeskts@scotsman.com
Web site: www.scotlandonsunday.com
Freq: Weekly
Circ: 16209 Not Audited
Profile: Scotland on Sunday is a broadsheet newspaper published every Sunday and covers Scottish and UK news, international news, arts, business, politics and sports.

The Scotsman 979802
Editorial: Orchard Brae House (Level 7), 30 Queensferry Road, Edinburgh EH4 2HS
Tel: 44 01313 117311
Email: newsdesks@scotsman.com
Web site: www.scotsman.com
Freq: Daily
Circ: 19449 Not Audited
Profile: The Scotsman is a daily newspaper covering all the latest Scottish, UK and international news, arts, business, education, environment, health, lifestyle, politics and transport.
Ad Rate: Full Page Mono 2735.64

Shopping 1070085
Editorial: 1 Canada Square, Canary Wharf, London E14 5AP **Tel:** 44 02072 933000
Web site: thenewday.co.uk
Freq: Daily

The South African 983411
Editorial: Riverbank House, 1 Putney Bridge Approach, Fulham, London SW6 3BQ
Tel: 44 08454 564910
Email: editor@thesouthafrican.com
Web site: www.thesouthafrican.com
Freq: Weekly
Circ: 25000 Not Audited
Editor: Deva Lee
Profile: Newspaper covering South African news as well as events, travel, recruitment, property, business and sport.
Ad Rate: Full Page Colour 750.00

National & Regional Daily Newspapers

Section 2 UK Newspapers

Sports Desk 1065175

The Sun 979803
Editorial: 1 London Bridge Street, London
SE1 9GF Tel: 44 02077 824104
Email: news@the-sun.co.uk
Web site: www.thesun.co.uk
Freq: Daily
Circ: 1568250 Not Audited
Profile: The Sun is a tabloid-sized
newspaper that covers national and
international news, business, finance, sports,
celebrities, entertainment, gossip, fashion
and television.
Ad Rate: Full Page Colour 55000.00

The Sun on Sunday 986658
Editorial: 1 London Bridge Street, London
SE1 9GF Tel: 44 02077 824000
Email: news@the-sun.co.uk
Web site: www.thesun.co.uk
Freq: Weekly
Circ: 1339583 Not Audited
Editor: Victoria Newton
Profile: The Sun on Sunday is a tabloid-
sized newspaper published on Sunday and
covers national and international news,
business, finance, sports, celebrities,
entertainment, gossip, fashion and
television.

Sunday Express 979815
Editorial: Northern & Shell Building, 10
Lower Thames Street, London EC3R 6EN
Tel: 44 02086 127000
Email: sundaynews@express.co.uk
Web site: www.express.co.uk
Freq: Weekly
Circ: 330816 Not Audited
Editor: Martin Townsend
Profile: The Sunday Express is a Sunday
newspaper that covers culture,
entertainment, national and international
news, money, motoring, property, showbiz,
sport and travel.
Ad Rate: Full Page Colour 40670.00

Sunday Herald 979816
Editorial: 200 Renfield Street, Glasgow,
Glasgow G2 3QB Tel: 44 01413 027000
Email: news@sundayherald.com
Web site: www.heraldscotland.com
Freq: Weekly
Circ: 21071 Not Audited
Profile: The Sunday Herald is regional paper
covering the latest news from Scotland, as
well as sport, politics, business and arts and
entertainment. The paper is owned by
Newsquest and was first published in 1999.
This outlet offers RSS (Really Simple
Syndication).
Ad Rate: Full Page Mono 3000.00
Ad Rate: Full Page Colour 3000.00

Sunday Mirror 980072
Editorial: 1 Canada Square, Canary Wharf,
London E14 5AP Tel: 44 02072 933000
Email: scoops@sundaymirror.co.uk
Web site: www.mirror.co.uk/
Freq: Weekly
Circ: 542823 Not Audited
Editor in Chief: John Kierans
Profile: The Sunday Mirror is the Sunday
edition of the Daily Mirror newspaper
covering national and international news
stories, with articles on finance,
entertainment, lifestyle, travel, television,
show-biz and sport. The newspaper was
founded in 1915.

Sunday People 980804
Editorial: 1 Canada Square, London E14
5AP Tel: 44 02072 933000
Web site: www.people.co.uk
Freq: Weekly
Circ: 214861 Not Audited
Profile: London Bureau for The Herald,
covering the latest business, politics, arts
and regional news in London for the
newspaper.

Sunday Sport 983212
Editorial: Floor 3 Maclaren House,
Lancastrian Office Centre, Talbot Road,
Manchester M32 0FP Tel: 44 08444 415141
Email: sportplus@sundaysport.co.uk

Web site: www.sundaysport.com/
Freq: Weekly
Circ: 70000 Not Audited
Editor: Nick Appleyard
Profile: The Sunday Sport is a tabloid
published by Sport Media Group. The
newspaper covers general interest news,
show-biz and sport, mixing them with sex
and humour. It was first published in 1986.
Ad Rate: Full Page Mono 2940.00
Ad Rate: Full Page Colour 4900.00

The Sunday Telegraph 979817
Editorial: 111 Buckingham Palace Road,
London SW1W 0DT Tel: 44 02079 312000
Email: stnews@telegraph.co.uk
Web site: www.telegraph.co.uk
Freq: Weekly
Circ: 351709 Not Audited
Profile: The Sunday Telegraph is a Sunday
newspaper covering news, current affairs,
business, culture, entertainment, jobs,
lifestyle, money, sport and travel. The paper
was awarded 'Front Page of the Year' at the
Press Awards.
Ad Rate: Full Page Mono 34000.00
Ad Rate: Full Page Colour 42000.00

The Sunday Times 979818
Editorial: 1 London Bridge Street, London
SE1 9GF Tel: 44 02077 825000
Email: newsdesk@sunday-times.co.uk
Web site: www.thesundaytimes.co.uk
Freq: Weekly
Circ: 765884 Not Audited
Editor: Martin Ivens
Profile: Broadsheet Sunday newspaper that
covers international and UK news, business,
and sport as well as comment and analysis.
The Sunday Times is read by 3.2 million
people every week.The Sunday Times
Business section analyses events of the
previous week and interviews key figures
from the business community. News Review
pulls together the news items from the week
that have caught the nation's interest and
raised important questions as well as
highlighting forthcoming events.The Sunday
Times Money section is a source of financial
market news and information. Culture is a
full-colour section for arts, books and
entertainment coverage, with reviews,
features, interviews, music section and
broadcast listings. Style focuses on fashion
and shopping, lifestyle and food,
relationships and health. Home is The
Sunday Times section with latest news and
trends in the property market in the UK and
abroad, and features on homes, interiors and
gardening. Travel covers hotel openings,
new trip launches, travel news and latest
trends. The Sunday Times Magazine is a
newspaper supplement with style reporting
and photography. Sundaytimes.co.uk was
awarded Best Campaigning/Investigative
Journalism and Best use of Photography at
the 2012 Online Media Awards. The Sunday
Times was founded in 1964.
Ad Rate: Full Page Mono 60690.00
Ad Rate: Full Page Colour 90090.00

Sur De Campeche 1061191
Email: elsur@elsur.com.mx
Web site: http://www.elsur.com.mx
Freq: Daily
Circ: 5000 Not Audited

Surma Newspaper 1057615
Editorial: Unit B, 10 Quaker Street, London
E1 6SZ Tel: 44 02073 779717
Email: news@surmanews.com
Web site: www.surmanews.com
Freq: Weekly
Circ: 15500 Not Audited
Editor: Sarz Mohammed

theSocialist 997313
Editorial: PO Box 24697, London E11 1YD
Tel: 44 02089 888777
Email: editors@socialistparty.org.uk
Web site: www.socialistparty.org.uk/
TheSocialistContents.htm
Freq: WeeklyNot Audited

The Times 979804
Editorial: 1 London Bridge Street, London
SE1 9GF Tel: 44 02077 825000
Email: home.news@thetimes.co.uk

Web site: www.thetimes.co.uk
Freq: Daily
Circ: 450064 Not Audited
Editor: John Witherow
Profile: Daily newspaper that covers UK and
world news, business and market news with
analysis, comment and opinion,
entertainment, technology, arts news, music
and film reviews, sports and jobs. The
Business section, which sits in the middle of
the newspaper, provides the editor's
commentary, analysis from specialist
correspondents and stock tips from the
Tempus column. The Times2 is The Times'
daily features section which includes health,
families, fashion, relationships and food.
Every Monday brings The Game, The Times'
weekly supplement dedicated to football.
From Tuesday to Saturday The Times brings
news, results and pictures of the world's
sporting events from the Melbourne Cup to
the Champions League to Wimbledon.
Bricks and Mortar is a supplement published
on Friday with property coverage. The
Times.co.uk was awarded Best Use of
Crowd Sourcing or Citizen Journalism at the
2012 Online Media Awards.The Times was
founded as The Daily Universal Register in
1785. Letter's to the Editor should be sent to
letters@thetimes.co.ukThe outlet offers RSS
(Really Simple Syndication).
Ad Rate: Full Page Mono 16645.00
Ad Rate: Full Page Colour 27195.00

The Voice 1060226
Editorial: The Elephant & Castle Shopping
Centre, Unit 236, London SE1 6TE
Tel: 44 02075 100340
Email: newsdesk@gvmedia.co.uk
Web site: www.voice-online.co.uk
Freq: Weekly
Circ: 30000 Not Audited
Profile: The Voice is a newspaper for the
UK's black community covering news,
entertainment and sport. The newspaper
was founded in 1982 and reports to have
'served the black community by giving them
a voice where other mainstream newspapers
have failed'.
Ad Rate: Full Page Mono 4428.00
Ad Rate: Full Page Colour 5757.00

**The Wall Street Journal
(Europe Edition)** 979805
Editorial: 1 London Bridge Street, London
SE1 9GF Tel: 44 02078 429200
Email: newseditors@wsj.com
Web site: http://www.wsj.com/europe
Freq: Daily
Circ: 58788 Not Audited
Editor: Thorold Barker

**The Wall Street Journal
(Europe Edition) - Nordic
Bureau Bureau** 1070567
Not Audited

Regional & Local Weekly Newspapers

Aberdeen Citizen 980625
Editorial: Lang Stracht, Mastrick, Aberdeen
AB15 6DF Tel: 44 01224 344150
Email: aberdeencitizenmail@ajl.co.uk
Web site: www.aberdeencitizen.co.uk
Freq: Weekly
Circ: 40536 Not Audited
Editor: Alan McCabe
Profile: Online version of the Aberdeen
Citizen covering local news for the
surrounding area of Aberdeen.

Abergavenny Chronicle 980615
Editorial: Tindle House, 13 Nevill Street,
Abergavenny NP7 5AA
Tel: 44 01873 852187

Email: newsdesk@tindlenews.co.uk
Web site: http://www.abergavennychronicle.
com/
Freq: Weekly
Circ: 5479 Not Audited
Editor: Liz Davies
Profile: Online version of the Abergavenny
Chronicle newspaper covering local news
and sports for the surrounding area.

Accrington Observer 980368
Editorial: Mitchell Henry House, Hollinwood
Avenue, Chadderton, Oldham OL9 8EF
Tel: 44 01612 112977
Email: accringtonobserver@menmedia.co.uk
Web site: www.accringtonobserver.co.uk
Freq: Weekly
Circ: 6178 Not Audited
Editor: Gareth Tidman
Profile: Online version of the Acrrington
Observer newspaper covering local news
and sports for the surrounding area of
Accrington.

The Advertiser (Waveney) 980537
Editorial: 1st floor, 36 North Quay, Great
Yarmouth NR30 1JE Tel: 44 01493 335000
Web site: www.waveneyadvertiser24.co.uk
Freq: Weekly
Circ: 42515 Not Audited

The advertiser series 998642
Editorial: Ribble House, Unit 10, Mandale
Business Park, Belmont, Durham DH1 1TH
Tel: 44 01325 381313
Email: newsdesk@nne.co.uk
Web site: www.theadvertiserseries.co.uk
Freq: Weekly
Circ: 128463 Not Audited

**Airdrie & Coatbridge
Advertiser** 980626
Editorial: 1 Central Quay, Glasgow G3 8DA
Tel: 44 01236 748648
Email: news@
airdrieandcoatbridgeadvertiser.co.uk
Web site: www.dailyrecord.co.uk/all-about/
airdrie-coatbridge
Freq: Weekly
Circ: 7086 Not Audited
Editor: Graham Miller
Profile: The Airdrie & Coatbridge Advertiser
is a weekly, local newspaper and covers
local news, sports and entertainment for the
surrounding area. The newspaper is
published on Wednesdays.
Ad Rate: Full Page Mono 3228.30
Ad Rate: Full Page Colour 4357.44

Al Hayat 994696
Editorial: 66 Hammersmith Road, London
W14 8UD Tel: 44 02076 052100
Email: information@alhayat.com
Web site: http://www.daralhayat.com/
Freq: Daily
Circ: 300000 Not Audited
Editor: Ghassan Charbel

Alderney Journal 984592
Editorial: 56 Victoria Street, Guernsey GY9
3UF Tel: 44 01481 823243
Email: editor@alderneyjournal.com
Web site: www.alderneyjournal.com
Freq: Bi-Weekly
Circ: 1400 Not Audited
Editor: Emma Pinch
Profile: Magazine covering community
news, what's on and the local history of
Alderney. Read by the residents of Alderney
Island.
Ad Rate: Full Page Mono 160.00

**Aldershot News and Mail
Series** 980309
Editorial: Stoke Mill, Woking Road,
Guildford, London GU1 1QA
Tel: 44 01483 508700
Email: aldershoteditorial@trinitymirror.com
Web site: www.gethampshire.co.uk
Freq: Weekly
Circ: 5457 Not Audited

Regional & Local Weekly Newspapers

Alfreton Chad - CEASED 2016
980480

Editorial: Sherwood Oaks Business Park, Southwell Road, Mansfield, Mansfield NG18 4TB
Web site: www.chad.co.uk/news/local/alfreton
Freq: Weekly
Circ: 12784 Not Audited
Profile: The Alfreton Chad is a weekly, local newspaper covering local news, sports and entertainment for the surrounding area. The newspaper is published on a Wednesday. The outlet offers RSS (Really Simple Syndication).

Alloa & Hillfoots Advertiser
980627

Editorial: 39 Drysdale Street, Alloa, Clackmannanshire, Clackmannan FK10 1JA
Tel: 44 01259 214416
Email: editorial@alloaadvertiser.co.uk
Web site: www.alloaadvertiser.com
Freq: Weekly
Circ: 5035 Not Audited

Alton Post Gazette
980310

Editorial: Tindle House, High Street, Bordon GU35 0AY **Tel:** 44 01420 477272
Web site: www.altonpostgazette.co.uk
Freq: Weekly
Circ: 8000 Not Audited
Editor: Paul Coates
Profile: The Alton Post Gazette is a weekly free local newspaper covering local news and sports for Alton and the surrounding area. The newspaper was first established in 1885.

Am Paipear
995942

Editorial: 41 Airport Road, Balivanich, Isle of Benbecula, Isle of Lewis HS7 5LA
Tel: 44 01870 603299
Email: editor@ampaipear.org.uk
Web site: www.ampaipear.org.uk
Freq: Monthly
Circ: 2000 Not Audited
Editor: Iain Morrison

Andersonstown News
983102

Editorial: Teach Basil, 2 Hannahstown Hill, Belfast BT17 0LT **Tel:** 44 02890 619000
Web site: www.belfastmediagroup.com/category/atown
Freq: Weekly
Circ: 8282 Not Audited
Editor: Anthony Neeson
Profile: The Andersonstown News is a weekly local newspaper and covers local news and sports for the surrounding area. The newspaper is published on a Thursday.
Ad Rate: Full Page Mono 1166.32
Ad Rate: Full Page Colour 1211.76

Andover Advertiser
980311

Editorial: Advertiser House, 24-32 London Street, Andover SP10 2PE
Tel: 44 01264 321205
Email: newsdesk@andoveradvertiser.co.uk
Web site: www.andoveradvertiser.co.uk
Freq: Weekly
Circ: 7602 Not Audited
Profile: Online version of the Andover Advertiser newspaper covering local news and sports for the surrounding area.

Annandale Series
994675

Editorial: 96 High Street, Annan, Annandale DG12 6EJ **Tel:** 44 01461 202078
Email: newsdesk@dngonline.co.uk
Web site: www.dng24.co.uk
Freq: Weekly
Circ: 3312 Not Audited
Editor: Bryan Armstrong

Arbroath Herald
980628

Editorial: 21 Market Place, Arbroath, Arbroath DD11 1HR **Tel:** 44 01241 435770
Email: news@arbroathherald.co.uk
Web site: www.arbroathherald.co.uk
Freq: Weekly
Circ: 4600 Not Audited
Profile: Online version of the Arbroath Herald newspaper covering local news, sports and lifestyle for the surrounding area.

Ardrossan & Saltcoats Herald
980629

Editorial: Ayrshire Weekly Press, Princes Street, Ardrossan, Ardrossan KA22 8BP
Tel: 44 01294 464321
Email: editorial@ardrossanherald.co.uk
Web site: www.ardrossanherald.com
Freq: Weekly
Circ: 6805 Not Audited
Editor: Caroline Patterson
Profile: Online version of the Ardrossan & Saltcoats Herald newspaper covering local news and sports for the surrounding area.

The Argus (Brighton)
980281

Editorial: Dolphin House, 2-5 Manchester Street, Brighton BN2 1TF
Tel: 44 01273 544544
Email: news@theargus.co.uk
Web site: www.theargus.co.uk
Freq: Daily
Circ: 11079 Not Audited

Argyllshire Advertiser
980630

Editorial: Argyll Street, Lochgilphead, Argyll PA31 8NB **Tel:** 44 01546 602345
Email: editor@argyllshireadvertiser.co.uk
Web site: www.argyllshireadvertiser.co.uk
Freq: Weekly
Circ: 5283 Not Audited
Profile: Online version of the Argyllshire Advertiser covering local news and sports for the surrounding area.

The Arran Banner
980631

Editorial: The Douglas Centre, Brodick, Isle Arran, Ardrossan KA27 8AJ
Tel: 44 01770 302142
Email: editor@arranbanner.co.uk
Web site: www.arranbanner.co.uk
Freq: Weekly
Circ: 2922 Not Audited
Editor: Hugh Boag
Profile: The Arran Banner is a weekly local newspaper covering the latest local news from the Isle of Arran.
Ad Rate: Full Page Mono 714.00
Ad Rate: Full Page Colour 928.00

Ashbourne News Telegraph
980245

Editorial: 6 Market Place, Ashbourne DE16 1ES **Tel:** 44 01335 300200
Email: editorial@ashbournenewstelegraph.co.uk
Web site: www.ashbournenewstelegraph.co.uk
Freq: Weekly
Circ: 4020 Not Audited
Profile: Online version of the Ashbourne News Telegraph newspaper covering local news and sports for the surrounding area.

Ashby Mail
998676

Editorial: Leicester Mercury Media Group, St George Street, Leicester LE1 9FQ
Tel: 44 01162 512512
Email: newsdesk@leicestermercury.co.uk
Web site: http://www.thisisleicestershire.co.uk
Freq: WeeklyNot Audited

Ashby, Coalville & Swadlincote Times Series
980380

Editorial: Bridge Road, Coalville, Leicester LE67 3QP **Tel:** 44 01530 813101
Email: editor@ashbytimes.com
Freq: Weekly
Circ: 7000 Not Audited
Editor: Ian Sleigh

The Ashford Advertiser
1050389

Editorial: Media House, 6 Stafford Close, Fairwood Business Estate, Ashford TN23 4TT **Tel:** 44 01233 660220
Email: atlanticprint1@aol.com
Web site: http://www.ashford247.co.uk
Freq: WeeklyNot Audited

Ashford Herald
988803

Editorial: Ashford Herald, Westcliffe House, West Cliff Gardens, Folkestone CT20 1SZ
Tel: 44 01303 850999

Email: newsdesk.folkestone@krnmedia.co.uk
Web site: http://www.ashfordherald.co.uk/
Freq: Weekly
Circ: 9917 Not Audited
Profile: Online version of the Ashford Herald newspaper covering local news and sports for the surrounding area. The outlet offers RSS (Really Simple Syndication).

Asian Image
995951

Editorial: Newspaper House, 1 High St, Blackburn BB1 1HT **Tel:** 44 01254 298372
Email: news@asianimage.co.uk
Web site: www.asianimage.co.uk
Freq: Monthly
Circ: 12000 Not Audited
Editor: Shuiab Khan
Profile: Website containing sport, sub-continent news, ethnic entertainment, recruitment, competitions and local issues.

Asian Sunday
996255

Editorial: Asian Sunday Newspaper, 1st Floor, 8 East Parade, Bradford BD1 5EE
Tel: 44 03335 770046
Email: newsdesk@asiansunday.co.uk
Web site: www.asiansunday.co.uk
Freq: Bi-Weekly
Circ: 85000 Not Audited

The Asian Today
995962

Editorial: 6a Olton Wharf, Richmond Road, Solihull, Solihull B92 7RN
Tel: 44 01213 142892
Email: info@theasiantoday.com
Web site: www.theasiantoday.com
Freq: Monthly
Circ: 80000 Not Audited
Editor: Anita Chumber
Profile: Newspaper covering the Asian community including news, lifestyle, fashion, entertainment and sport. Distributed freely in the Midlands including Birmingham, Leicester, Nottingham, Wolverhampton, Walsall and Coventry. First published in 2003. Aimed at the South Asian communities in the UK.
Ad Rate: Full Page Mono 840.00
Ad Rate: Full Page Colour 840.00

Asian Voice
982580

Editorial: Karma Yoga House, 12 Hoxton Market (off Coronet Street), London N1 6HW
Tel: 44 02077 494000
Email: aveditorial@abplgroup.com
Web site: www.asian-voice.com/
Freq: Weekly
Circ: 33000 Not Audited
Profile: Publication covering news from Britain and India for members of the Gujarat community. Includes features on cooking, beauty, health, finance and property. Read by students, teachers, professionals and those who are involved in charitable and community organisations.
Ad Rate: Full Page Mono 3132.00
Ad Rate: Full Page Colour 4104.00

asian world
986304

Editorial: Rapyal House, Unit 4B, Talbot Way, Smallheath Business Park, Birmingham B10 OHJ **Tel:** 44 0121 7 714545
Email: news@asianworldnews.co.uk
Web site: http://asianworldnews.co.uk/
Freq: Monthly
Circ: 60000 Not Audited
Editor: Sajad Hussain
Profile: Magazine covering local and global news issues, which affects the British Asian community.

Ayr Advertiser
980632

Editorial: Ayrshire Weekly Press, Princes Street, Ardrossan, Ardrossan KA22 8BP
Tel: 44 01292 267631
Email: editorial@ayradvertiser.co.uk
Web site: www.ayradvertiser.com
Freq: Weekly
Circ: 2273 Not Audited
Editor: Caroline Patterson
Profile: Online version of the Ayr Advertiser, Carrick Herald and the Troon & Prestwick Times newspapers covering local news and sports for the surrounding area.

Ayrshire Post
980633

Editorial: Nile Court, 154 High Street, Ayr KA7 1DH **Tel:** 44 01292 262200
Email: news@ayrshirepost.co.uk
Web site: http://www.ayrshirepost.net/
Freq: Weekly
Circ: 14207 Not Audited
Editor: Kenny Smith
Profile: Online version for the Ayrshire Post newspaper covering local news and sports for the surrounding area.

BALANCE
997421

Editorial: EMP Publishing Ltd, Central House, 1 Ballards Lane, London N3 1LQ
Tel: 44 02084 443401
Email: editor@balance.media
Web site: www.balance.media
Freq: Monthly
Circ: 201527 Not Audited
Editor: Sophie Scott
Profile: Health and lifestyle magazine published by Diabetes UK. Features the latest news and research on diabetes. There are celebrity interviews, personal experience and healthy lifestyle features, recipes, competitions and regular free supplements on hot topics.
Ad Rate: Full Page Colour 4945.00

Ballito: North Coast Courier
1060725

Tel: 44 27329 460276
Freq: Weekly
Circ: 27850 Not Audited

Ballymena & Antrim Times
984197

Tel: 44 02828 272303
Email: news@ballymenatimes.com
Web site: www.ballymenatimes.com
Freq: Weekly
Circ: 4000 Not Audited
Editor: Dessie Blackadder

Ballymena Guardian
983106

Editorial: 83-85 Wellington Street, Ballymena BT43 6AD **Tel:** 44 02825 641221
Email: editor@ballymenaguardian.co.uk
Web site: www.ballymenaguardian.co.uk
Freq: Weekly
Circ: 20000 Not Audited
Editor: Jim Flanagan
Profile: Online version of the Ballymena Guardian newspaper covering local news and sports for the surrounding area.

Ballymoney and Moyle Times
998509

Editorial: 5 Stone Row, Coleraine BT52 1EP
Tel: 44 02870 355260
Email: news@ballymoneytimes.co.uk
Web site: www.ballymoneytimes.co.uk
Freq: Weekly
Circ: 5960 Not Audited
Editor: Dessie Blackadder
Profile: Online version of the Ballymoney and Moyle Times covering local news, lifestyle and sports for the surrounding area. The outlet offers RSS (Really Simple Syndication).

Banbridge Chronicle
983111

Editorial: 11 Downshire Place, Co. Down, Banbridge BT32 3DF **Tel:** 44 02840 662322
Email: editor@thebanbridgechronicle.com
Web site: www.thebanbridgechronicle.com
Freq: Weekly
Circ: 3521 Not Audited
Editor: Bryan Hooks
Profile: Online version of the Banbridge Chronicle newspaper and covers local news and sports for the surrounding area.

The Banbridge Leader
983170

Tel: 44 02838 393939
Email: news@banbridgeleader.co.uk
Web site: www.banbridgeleader.co.uk
Freq: Weekly
Circ: 3110 Not Audited
Editor: Damian Wilson
Profile: This is the online version the Banbridge Leader, a weekly, local newspaper covering the latest news, sport

Regional & Local Weekly Newspapers

and lifestyle from Banbridge and the wider area.

Banbury Cake 980486
Editorial: Osney Mead, Oxford, Banbury OX2 0EJ **Tel:** 44 01865 425262
Email: banburycake@nqo.com
Web site: www.banburycake.co.uk
Freq: WeeklyNot Audited
Profile: Online version of the Banbury Cake newspaper covering local news and sports for the surrounding area. The outlet offers RSS (Really Simple Syndication).

Banbury Guardian 980487
Editorial: 7 North Bar, Banbury OX16 0TQ
Tel: 44 01295 227758
Email: editorial@banburyguardian.co.uk
Web site: http://www.banburyguardian.co.uk/
Freq: Weekly
Circ: 8841 Not Audited
Profile: Online version of the Banbury Guardian newspaper covering local news, sports and lifestyle.

Banffshire Advertiser 983649
Editorial: 13-15 West Church Street, Buckie AB56 1BN **Tel:** 44 01542 832265
Web site: www.banffshireadvertiser.co.uk
Freq: Weekly
Circ: 2226 Not Audited
Profile: Online version of the Banffshire Advertiser covering local news and sports for the surrounding area.

Banffshire Herald 980634
Editorial: 181 Mid Street, Keith AB55 5BL
Tel: 44 01542 886262
Web site: www.banffshireherald.co.uk
Freq: Weekly
Circ: 1473 Not Audited
Profile: The Banffshire Herald is a weekly local newspaper covering local news and sports for the surrounding area. The newspaper is published on a Friday.
Ad Rate: Full Page Mono 854.70
Ad Rate: Full Page Colour 1025.64

Banffshire Journal 983457
Editorial: Banffshire Journal, 22 Old Market Place, Banff AB45 1GE
Tel: 44 01261 812551
Email: editorial@banffshire-journal.co.uk
Web site: www.banffshire-journal.co.uk
Freq: Weekly
Circ: 2658 Not Audited
Profile: This is the online version of the Banffshire Journal, a weekly local newspaper covering all the latest on local news, lifestyle and sport in Banff, Buckie, Macduff and Turiff.

Barking & Dagenham Post 980290
Editorial: 7th Floor, Maritime House, 1 Linton Road, Barking IG11 8HG
Tel: 44 02084 784444
Email: postnewsdesk@archant.co.uk
Web site: www.bdpost.co.uk
Freq: Weekly
Circ: 4271 Not Audited

Barnet Press 982964
Web site: http://www.barnet-today.co.uk
Freq: Weekly
Circ: 77574 Not Audited

Barnsley Chronicle 980514
Editorial: 47 Church Street, Barnsley S70 2AS **Tel:** 44 01226 734262
Email: newsdesk@barnsley-chronicle.co.uk
Web site: www.barnsley-chronicle.co.uk
Freq: Weekly
Circ: 72359 Not Audited
Editor: Andrew Harrod
Profile: Online version of the Barnsley Chronicle newspaper covering local news, sports and features for the local area.

Barnsley Independent Today 980515
Tel: 44 01226 734262
Web site: http://www.barnsleyindependent.com/
Freq: Weekly
Circ: 45113 Not Audited

Barrhead News 980635
Editorial: 1st Floor, Carus House, 201 Dumbarton Road, Clydebank G81 4XJ
Tel: 44 01414 358888
Email: editorial@barrheadnews.co.uk
Web site: www.barrheadnews.com
Freq: Weekly
Circ: 3247 Not Audited
Profile: Online version of the Barrhead News newspaper covering local news and sports for the surrounding area.

Barrow Advertiser 994694
Editorial: Furness Newspapers, Abbey Road, Barrow-in-Furness LA14 5QS
Tel: 44 01229 821835
Email: news@nwemail.co.uk
Web site: www.nwemail.co.uk
Freq: Weekly
Circ: 32502 Not Audited

Barry & District News 980616
Editorial: Cardiff Road, Maesglas, Newport NP20 3QN **Tel:** 44 01633 777221
Email: barrynews@barryanddistrictnews.co.uk
Web site: www.barryanddistrictnews.co.uk
Freq: Weekly
Circ: 3229 Not Audited
Profile: Online version of the Barry & District News newspaper covering local news and sports for the surrounding area. The outlet offers RSS (Really Simple Syndication).

Basildon & Wickford Recorder 983087
Editorial: Newspaper House, Chester Hall Lane, Basildon SS14 3BL
Tel: 44 08444 774512
Email: echonews@newsquest.co.uk
Web site: www.basildonrecorder.co.uk
Freq: Weekly
Circ: 44121 Not Audited

Basingstoke Gazette 980312
Editorial: Gazette House, Pelton Road, Basingstoke RG21 6YD
Tel: 44 01256 461131
Email: newsdesk@basingstokegazette.co.uk
Web site: www.basingstokegazette.co.uk
Freq: Weekly
Circ: 8054 Not Audited
Profile: The Basingstoke Gazette is a twice-weekly local newspaper, published on Mondays and Thursdays, covering all the latest on local news, business, leisure and sport in Basingstoke and the surrounding areas of Hook, Tadley, Whitchurch, Southampton, Woking and Guildford. For the topic of leisure the coverage area extends further depending on the details of particular events.
Ad Rate: Full Page Mono 1377.00
Ad Rate: Full Page Colour 1377.00

Basingstoke Observer 980313
Editorial: Newspaper House, Hawksworth, Southmead Industrial Estate, Didcot OX11 7HR **Tel:** 44 01235 511700
Email: news@basingstokeobserver.co.uk
Web site: http://www.basingstokeobserver.co.uk
Freq: Weekly
Circ: 12500 Not Audited
Profile: Online version of the Basingstoke Observer covering local news and sports for the surrounding area.

The Bath Chronicle 980140
Editorial: Westpoint, James Street West, Bath BA1 2DA **Tel:** 44 01225 322322
Email: news@bathchron.co.uk
Web site: www.bathchronicle.co.uk
Freq: Weekly
Circ: 9435 Not Audited

Profile: Online version of The Bath Chronicle newspaper covering local news, sports and entertainment.

The Bath Echo 1053549
Tel: 44 01225 688688
Email: contact@bathecho.co.uk
Web site: www.bathecho.co.uk
Freq: Daily

Batley & Birstall News 980585
Editorial: c/o Floor 5, 26 Whitehall Road, Leeds LS12 1BE **Tel:** 44 01132 388950
Email: dewsbury.editorial@jpress.co.uk
Web site: http://www.batleynews.co.uk/
Freq: Weekly
Circ: 2000 Not Audited
Editor: John Kenealy
Profile: This is the online version of the Batley & Birstall News is a weekly, local newspaper covering all the latest on local news, sport, motors and property in Batley and Birstall.

The Beaver 981755
Editorial: LSE Students' Union, East Building, Houghton Street, London WC2A 2AE **Tel:** 44 02079 556705
Email: editor@thebeaveronline.co.uk
Web site: http://beaveronline.co.uk
Freq: Weekly
Circ: 2000 Not Audited
Profile: Magazine covering student issues, politics, the arts, what's on and events.
Ad Rate: Full Page Mono 949.00
Ad Rate: Full Page Colour 1249.00
Student Lifestyle

Beccles & Bungay Journal 980530
Editorial: 20 Blyburgate, Beccles NR34 9TB
Tel: 44 01502 712060
Email: newsdesk@archant.co.uk
Web site: www.becclesandbungayjournal.co.uk
Freq: Weekly
Circ: 4060 Not Audited

Bedford Times & Citizen 980188
Editorial: Northhouse, 3 Bond Avenue, Bletchley, Milton Keynes MK1 1SW
Tel: 44 01234 405060
Email: editorial@timesandcitizen.co.uk
Web site: www.bedfordtoday.co.uk
Freq: Weekly
Circ: 59648 Not Audited
Editor: Olga Norford
Profile: Bedford Times & Citizen is a free weekly paper published every Thursday throughout the Bedford Borough in Bedfordshire. The paper covers the latest local news and events from Bedford, Kempston and the surrounding local area.
Ad Rate: Full Page Colour 1294.38

Bedfordshire on Sunday 980189
Editorial: 22 Mill Street, Bedford, Bedford MK40 3HD **Tel:** 44 01234 369582
Email: editor@lsnmedia.co.uk
Web site: www.bedfordshire-news.co.uk
Freq: Weekly
Circ: 55595 Not Audited
Editor: Sarah Cox
Profile: Bedfordshire on Sunday is a regional newspaper covering regional news, business, lifestyle, general features and sport for Bedfordshire Borough and Central Bedfordshire. The outlet offers RSS (Really Simple Syndication).
Ad Rate: Full Page Mono 1050.00
Ad Rate: Full Page Colour 1050.00

The Beeston Express 996021
Editorial: PO Box 7440, Beeston, Nottingham NG9 1ZS **Tel:** 44 01159 228007
Email: enquiries@beestonexpress.co.uk
Web site: www.beestonexpress.co.uk
Freq: Bi-Weekly
Circ: 2000 Not Audited
Editor: Sheila Eden

Belfast News 983112
Editorial: Ground Floor, Metro Building, 6-9 Donegall Square South, Belfast BT1 5JA
Tel: 44 02838 393939

Email: newsdesk@newsletter.co.uk
Web site: http://www.newsletter.co.uk/
Freq: Weekly
Circ: 29000 Not Audited
Profile: The Belfast News is a free, weekly newspaper covering all the latest on news, sport and entertainment in Belfast.
Ad Rate: Full Page Mono 2034.90
Ad Rate: Full Page Colour 2848.86

Belfast Telegraph 980033
Editorial: 33 Clarendon Road, Clarendon Dock, Belfast BT1 3BG
Tel: 44 02890 264000
Email: newseditor@belfasttelegraph.co.uk
Web site: www.belfasttelegraph.co.uk
Freq: Daily
Circ: 40042 Not Audited
Editor: Gail Walker
Profile: The Belfast Telegraph is a daily regional newspaper and covers regional news, business, features and sports.
Ad Rate: Full Page Mono 12460.70
Ad Rate: Full Page Colour 15538.00

Bellshill Speaker 980636
Editorial: 29 Hope Street, Motherwell ML1 1BT **Tel:** 44 01698 264611
Email: editorial@bellshillspeaker.co.uk
Web site: www.bellshilltoday.co.uk
Freq: Weekly
Circ: 4065 Not Audited
Editor: Martin Clark
Profile: Bellshill Speaker is a weekly local newspaper covering local news, sports, lifestyle and community events for the surrounding area.

Belper News 980117
Editorial: 8 Heanor Road, Ilkeston DE7 6EP
Tel: 44 01246 504580
Email: editor@belpernews.co.uk
Web site: www.belpernews.co.uk
Freq: Weekly
Circ: 9365 Not Audited
Profile: Online version of the Belper News newspaper covering local news, sports and lifestyle for the surrounding area. This outlet offers RSS (Really Simple Syndication).

Ben Ledi View 998812
Editorial: c/o McLaren Community Leisure Centre, Mollands Road, Callander, Stirling FK17 8JP
Email: editor@benlediview.co.uk
Web site: www.benlediview.co.uk
Freq: Bi-Monthly
Circ: 1950 Not Audited

Berrow's Worcester Journal 983006
Editorial: Berrow's House, Hylton Road, Worcester WR2 5JX **Tel:** 44 01905 742244
Email: news@worcesternews.co.uk
Web site: www.berrowsjournal.co.uk
Freq: Weekly
Circ: 38713 Not Audited

The Berwick Advertiser 980475
Editorial: Boarding School Yard, 90 Marygate, Berwick upon Tweed, Berwick-upon-Tweed TD15 1BN
Tel: 44 01289 334686
Email: berwickadvertiser@jpress.co.uk
Web site: http://www.berwick-advertiser.co.uk/
Freq: Weekly
Circ: 4856 Not Audited
Editor: Paul Larkin
Profile: Online version of the Berwick Advertiser covering local news, sports and community events for the surrounding area.

The Berwickshire News 980637
Editorial: Boarding School Yard, 90 Marygate, Berwick upon Tweed, Berwick-upon-Tweed TD15 1BN
Tel: 44 01289 334681
Email: berwickshirenews@jpress.co.uk
Web site: http://www.berwickshire-news.co.uk/
Freq: Weekly
Circ: 3645 Not Audited
Profile: The Berwickshire News is the online version of the Berwickshire News and East

Lothian Herald and covers local news and sport for the surrounding area.

Bexhill Observer 980282
Editorial: Woods House, Telford Road, St Leonards, Hastings TN38 9LZ
Tel: 44 01424 730555
Email: bexobs@trbeckett.co.uk
Web site: www.bexhillobserver.net
Freq: Weekly
Circ: 5921 Not Audited

Bexley Times 980351
Editorial: Kent House, 81 Station Road, Ashford TN23 1PP **Tel:** 44 01233 653465
Email: feedback@bexleytimes.co.uk
Web site: www.bexleytimes.co.uk
Freq: Weekly
Circ: 15213 Not Audited
Profile: Online version of the Bexley Times newspaper covering local news and sports for the surrounding area. This outlet covers areas within the Borough of Bexley.

Bicester Advertiser 980488
Editorial: Newsquest Oxfordshire, Osney Mead, Oxford, Oxford OX2 0EJ
Tel: 44 01865 425262
Email: bicester@nqo.com
Web site: www.bicesteradvertiser.net
Freq: Weekly
Circ: 2770 Not Audited
Ad Rate: Full Page Mono 1193.40
Ad Rate: Full Page Colour 1491.75

Bicester Review 983008
Editorial: 61-62 Well Street, Buckingham MK18 1EN **Tel:** 44 01296 619779
Email: editorial@buckinghamadvertiser.co.uk
Web site: www.buckinghamtoday.co.uk
Freq: Weekly
Circ: 5081 Not Audited
Profile: The Bicester Review is a weekly, local newspaper covering all the latest on local news and sport in Bicester. The paper is published on Fridays.
Ad Rate: Full Page Mono 1242.36

Biggin Hill News 980352
Editorial: Winterton House, High Street, Westerham TN16 1AT **Tel:** 44 01959 564766
Email: bheditor@googlemail.com
Web site: www.biggin-hill-today.co.uk
Freq: Weekly
Circ: 3900 Not Audited
Editor: Luke King
Profile: Website for local paper the Biggin Hill News, covering the latest news and events from Biggin Hill. This outlet covers areas within the Borough of Bromley

Biggleswade Chronicle 980190
Editorial: 7 High Street, Biggleswade, Biggleswade SG18 0JB
Tel: 44 00158 2798514
Email: editorial@biggleswadechronicle.co.uk
Web site: www.biggleswadetoday.co.uk
Freq: Weekly
Circ: 7481 Not Audited
Editor: Olga Norford
Profile: The Biggleswade Chronicle is a weekly local newspaper covering local news, sports and lifestyle for the surrounding area. The newspaper is published on a Friday.This outlet offers RSS (Really simple syndication)
Ad Rate: Full Page Mono 1331.10
Ad Rate: Full Page Colour 1663.87

Birmingham Mail 979945
Editorial: Floor 6, Fort Dunlop, Fort Parkway, Birmingham B24 9FF
Tel: 44 01212 345536
Email: newsdesk@birminghammail.co.uk
Web site: www.birminghammail.co.uk
Freq: Daily
Circ: 19200 Not Audited
Profile: The Birmingham Mail is a regional daily newspaper covering the latest in regional news, sports and features for the surrounding area. This outlet offers RSS (Really simple syndication).
Ad Rate: Full Page Mono 6533.00
Ad Rate: Full Page Colour 8119.00

Birmingham Post 979807
Editorial: Floor 6, Fort Dunlop, Fort Parkway, Birmingham B24 9FF
Tel: 44 01212 363366
Web site: http://www.birminghampost.co.uk/
Freq: Weekly
Circ: 4132 Not Audited
Profile: Birmingham Post is a weekly tabloid-sized newspaper covering regional news, business and sports for the surrounding area. This outlet offers RSS (Really simple syndication).
Ad Rate: Full Page Mono 3932.00
Ad Rate: Full Page Colour 5308.00

The Birstall Post 980381
Editorial: Unit 109, Greenacres, The Sidings, Leicester LE4 3BR **Tel:** 44 01164 422067
Email: editor@birstallpost.co.uk
Web site: www.birstallpost.co.uk
Freq: Monthly
Circ: 5000 Not Audited
Editor: Jerry Jackson
Profile: Publication focussing on local and regional news and current affairs. PR Deadline: 18th of the month.
Ad Rate: Full Page Mono 350.00

Bishopston Voice 1057954
Editorial: Local Voice Network, 49 Dunkeld Vanue, Bristol BS34 7RQ
Tel: 44 01179 082121
Email: news@bishopstonvoice.co.uk
Web site: http://www.bishopstonvoice.co.uk/
Freq: Monthly
Circ: 11250 Not Audited

Blaby Courier 999159
Editorial: 4 Wynton Close, Blaby, Whetstone LE8 4HG **Tel:** 44 01162 771249
Email: blabycourier1@aol.com
Web site: http://www.blabycourier.org.uk
Freq: Monthly
Circ: 2600 Not Audited
Editor: Stuart Hook

Black Country Bugle 980563
Editorial: Black Country Bugle, Dudley Archives, Tipton Road, Dudley DY1 4SQ
Tel: 44 01384 889000
Email: editor@blackcountrybugle.co.uk
Web site: www.blackcountrybugle.co.uk
Freq: Weekly
Circ: 7713 Not Audited
Editor: John Butterworth
Profile: The Black Country Beagle is a magazine covering history, industrial heritage and legends for the surrounding area.

Blairgowrie Advertiser 980638
Editorial: 58 Watergate, Perth, Perth PH1 5TF **Tel:** 44 01738 493265
Email: news@blairgowrieadvertiser.co.uk
Web site: www.dailyrecord.co.uk/all-about/blairgowrie
Freq: Weekly
Circ: 1361 Not Audited
Profile: Website of the Blairgowrie Advertiser, a weekly newspaper covering news, sports and lifestyle for the local area.

Blits 1060499
Tel: 44 27219 177400
Email: mking@dieburger.co.za
Freq: Weekly
Circ: 80000 Not Audited

Blythe & Forsbrook Times 983524
Editorial: 18 Tape Street, Cheadle ST10 1BD **Tel:** 44 01538 752214
Email: news@timesandecho.co.uk
Web site: www.timesechoandlife.co.uk
Freq: Weekly
Circ: 8000 Not Audited
Profile: The Blythe & Forsbrook Times is a weekly newspaper covering local news, sports and leisure for the surrounding area. It is published every Wednesday. The company was established in 1896.
Ad Rate: Full Page Mono 725.00
Ad Rate: Full Page Colour 725.00

Bognor Regis Post 1074800
Tel: 44 01243 908506
Email: news@sussexpost.co.uk
Web site: http://postnewspapers.co.uk/
Freq: Weekly
Circ: 30000 Not Audited
Editor: Adam Cunard

Bolton Journal 979974
Editorial: The Wellsprings, The Civic Centre, Victoria Square, Bolton BL1 1AR
Tel: 44 01204 522345
Email: newsdesk@nqnw.co.uk
Web site: www.theboltonnews.co.uk
Freq: Weekly
Circ: 10172 Not Audited
Profile: Bolton Journal is a weekly local newspaper covering the latest in news, sports and business for the area. Previous title: Bolton Journal SeriesOnly JPEG attachments are accepted, no text attachments. Only one copy of press release required for the Bolton News and the Bolton Journal.
Ad Rate: Full Page Mono 1197.00
Ad Rate: Full Page Colour 1496.25

The Bolton News 979973
Editorial: The Wellsprings, The Civic Centre, Victoria Square, Bolton BL1 1AR
Tel: 44 01204 522345
Email: newsdesk@nqnw.co.uk
Web site: www.theboltonnews.co.uk
Freq: Daily
Circ: 9607 Not Audited
Profile: The Bolton News is a daily regional newspaper covering lifestyle, news and sport from Bolton and the surrounding area.
Ad Rate: Full Page Mono 1018.00
Ad Rate: Full Page Colour 1272.00

Bo'ness Journal 984767
Editorial: Unit 4A, Gateway Business Park, Beancross Road, Grangemouth FK3 8WX
Tel: 44 01324 690222
Email: editorial@journalandgazette.co.uk
Web site: www.linlithgowgazette.co.uk
Freq: Weekly
Circ: 2098 Not Audited
Editor: Jill Buchanan
Profile: The Bo'ness Journal is a weekly paper covering the latest news and events from Bo'ness and the surrounding area. The paper is distributed every Friday.

Border Telegraph 980639
Editorial: 32B Market Street, Galashiels TD1 3AA **Tel:** 44 01896 758395
Email: editorial@bordertelegraph.com
Web site: www.bordertelegraph.com
Freq: Weekly
Circ: 2777 Not Audited
Profile: Online version of the Border Telegraph newspaper covering local news and sports for the surrounding area.

Bordon Post 980314
Editorial: Borden Post, 33 High Street, Petersfield, Petersfield GU32 3JR
Tel: 44 01730 232600
Web site: http://www.bordonpost.co.uk/
Freq: Weekly
Circ: 652 Not Audited
Editor: Graeme Moir
Profile: The Bordon Post is a weekly paper published every Friday, covering the latest local news and events from Bordon.
Ad Rate: Full Page Mono 933.00
Ad Rate: Full Page Colour 1332.98

Borehamwood & Elstree Times 980337
Editorial: Observer House, Caxton Way, Watford, London WD18 8RJ
Tel: 44 01923 216216
Email: bwnews@london.newsquest.co.uk
Web site: www.borehamwoodtimes.co.uk
Freq: Weekly
Circ: 8721 Not Audited
Profile: Free online edition of the main weekly newspaper- Borehamwood & Elstree Times.

Boston Standard 980384
Editorial: 5-6 Church Lane, Boston, Boston PE21 6ND **Tel:** 44 01205 311433
Web site: www.bostonstandard.co.uk
Freq: Weekly
Circ: 5511 Not Audited
Profile: Online version of the Boston Standard covering local news and sports for the surrounding area.

Bournemouth Daily Echo 979081
Editorial: Richmond Hill, Bournemouth BH2 6HH **Tel:** 44 01202 554601
Email: newsdesk@bournemouthecho.co.uk
Web site: www.bournemouthecho.co.uk
Freq: Daily
Circ: 13579 Not Audited

Bracknell & Wokingham Weekender 983010
Editorial: Bowman House, 2-10 Bridge Street, Reading RG1 2LU
Tel: 44 01344 456611
Email: news@bracknellnews.co.uk
Web site: http://www.bracknellnews.co.uk/news/wokingham/
Freq: Weekly
Circ: 22391 Not Audited
Profile: Bracknell & Wokingham Weekender is a weekly local newspaper covering local news from the town of Bracknell and the surrounding area. The paper is published on a Thursday.
Ad Rate: Full Page Mono 2056.32

Bracknell News 982952
Editorial: Bowman House, 2-10 Bridge Street, Reading RG1 2LU
Tel: 44 01344 456611
Email: news@bracknellnews.co.uk
Web site: www.bracknellnews.co.uk
Freq: Weekly
Circ: 3027 Not Audited
Profile: Online version of the Bracknell News, Ascot News, Bracknell Midweek, Wokingham, Crowthorne & Sandhurst Newsweek and Business Review, covering the latest in local news, sports and business from the Berkshire region.

Bradley Stoke Journal 1074324
Tel: 44 01454 300400
Email: info@bradleystokejournal.co.uk
Web site: www.bradleystokejournal.co.uk
Freq: Monthly
Circ: 10200 Not Audited
Editor: Stephen Horton

Braintree and Witham Times 983012
Editorial: 76 High Street, Braintree, Braintree CM7 1JP **Tel:** 44 01376 343344
Email: bwtnews@newsquest.co.uk
Web site: www.braintreeandwithamtimes.co.uk
Freq: Weekly
Circ: 7494 Not Audited

The Bramley 998829
Editorial: 1 Appletree Close, Nottinghamshire, Southwell NG25 0AN
Tel: 44 01636 814477
Email: editor@bramleynewspaper.co.uk
Web site: www.bramleynewspaper.co.uk
Freq: Monthly
Circ: 11000 Not Audited

Brasil Observer 998366
Editorial: Unit 10, 43 Oswin Street, London SE11 4TF
Email: editor@brasilobserver.co.uk
Web site: www.brasilobserver.co.uk
Freq: MonthlyNot Audited

Brazilian News 997937
Editorial: Unit 8, Holles House, Overton Road, London SW9 7AP
Tel: 44 02077 387983
Email: editor@braziliannews.uk.com
Web site: www.braziliannews.uk.com
Freq: Weekly
Circ: 8000 Not Audited

Brechin Advertiser 980640
Editorial: 117/119 Castle Street, Forfar DD8 3AH **Tel:** 44 01307 474041
Email: news@brechinadvertiser.com

Web site: www.brechintoday.co.uk
Freq: Weekly
Circ: 1512 Not Audited
Profile: This is the online version of the Brechin Advertiser, a weekly, local newspaper covering all the latest on local news, sport and lifestyle in Brechin, Edzell and the surrounding area.

Brecon & Radnor Express
980617
Editorial: 11 The Bulwark, Brecon, Brecon LD3 7AE **Tel:** 44 01874 610111
Email: theeditor@brecon-radnor.co.uk
Web site: www.brecon-radnor-today.co.uk
Freq: Weekly
Circ: 7300 Not Audited
Editor: Eryl Jones
Profile: The Brecon & Radnor Express is a weekly local newspaper and covers local news and sports for the surrounding area. The newspaper is published on a Wednesday.
Ad Rate: Full Page Mono 2910.60
Ad Rate: Full Page Colour 3492.72

Brent & Kilburn Times 980413
Editorial: North West London Newspapers, Charles House, 108-110 Finchley Road, London NW3 5JJ **Tel:** 44 02074 330100
Email: times.series@archant.co.uk
Web site: www.kilburntimes.co.uk
Freq: Weekly
Circ: 14208 Not Audited
Profile: Online version of the Brent & Kilburn Times newspaper covering local news, sports and entertainment. This outlet covers areas within the Boroughs of Brent, Harrow and Camden.

Brentwood Gazette 980291
Editorial: First Floor, Kestrel House, Hedgerows Business Park, Springfield, Chelmsford CM2 5PF **Tel:** 44 01245 602776
Email: editorial@gazettenews.co.uk
Web site: www.brentwoodgazette.co.uk
Freq: Weekly
Circ: 8916 Not Audited
Profile: The Brentwood Gazette is a local weekly newspaper that covers news, sports and pictures for the surrounding area. This outlet covers areas within Havering Borough.

Bridgnorth Journal 980493
Editorial: 50a High Street, Bridgnorth, Bridgnorth WV16 4DX **Tel:** 44 01746 761411
Email: news@bridgnorthjournal.co.uk
Web site: www.bridgnorthjournal.co.uk
Freq: Weekly
Circ: 5250 Not Audited
Editor: Pete Carroll
Profile: Online version of the Bridgnorth Journal newspaper covering local news, sports and general features for the surrounding area.

Bridgwater Mercury 980500
Editorial: 1-4 St James Building, 44 St James Street, Taunton TA1 1JR
Tel: 44 01278 727960
Email: newsdesk@bridgwatermercury.co.uk
Web site: www.bridgwatermercury.co.uk
Freq: Weekly
Circ: 6988 Not Audited
Profile: Online version of the Bridgwater Mercury newspaper, covering all the latest local news, sport and entertainment for the surrounding area.

Bridlington Echo 1095948
Editorial: Unit A, Brett Street Business Park, Brett Street, Bridlington YO16 4LQ
Tel: 44 01262 310160
Web site: http://www.bridlingtonecho.co.uk/
Freq: Monthly
Circ: 12000 Not Audited

Bridlington Free Press 980457
Editorial: New Chase Court, Hopper Hill Road, Scarborough Business Park, Scarborough YO11 3YS
Tel: 44 01723 860100
Email: newsdesk@bridlingtonfreepress.co.uk
Web site: www.bridlingtonfreepress.co.uk
Freq: Weekly
Circ: 9070 Not Audited
Profile: Online version of the Bridlington Free Press newspaper covering local news and sports for the surrounding area.

Bridport News 980274
Editorial: Fleet House, Hampshire Road, Bridport DT4 9XD **Tel:** 44 01308 455904
Email: news@bridportnews.co.uk
Web site: http://www.bridportnews.co.uk/
Freq: Weekly
Circ: 5924 Not Audited
Profile: The Bridport News is a weekly, local newspaper covering all the latest on local news, sport and leisure in Bridport. The paper is published on Thursdays.

Brighouse Echo 980586
Editorial: The Fire Station, Dean Clough Mills, Halifax HX3 5AX **Tel:** 44 01484 714617
Email: brighouse.echo@brighouseecho.co.uk
Web site: www.brighouseecho.co.uk
Freq: Weekly
Circ: 4873 Not Audited
Profile: Online version of the Brighouse Echo covering local news and sports for the surrounding area. The outlet offers RSS (Really Simple Syndication).

Brighton & Hove Independent
987479
Editorial: Suite 225, Regency House, Brighton, Chichester BN1 2NW
Tel: 44 01273 358889
Email: news@brightonandhoveindependent.co.uk
Web site: www.brightonandhoveindependent.co.uk
Freq: Weekly
Circ: 13005 Not Audited
Profile: The Brighton & Hove Independent is a free weekly newspaper covering local news, business, sport and entertainment from the surrounding area. It is published every Friday.

Bristol Observer 980101
Editorial: Temple Way, Bristol BS2 0BY
Tel: 44 01179 343000
Email: epnews@bepp.co.uk
Web site: www.thisisbristol.co.uk
Freq: Weekly
Circ: 54972 Not Audited
Profile: The Bristol Observer is a weekly local newspaper covering the latest local news, sports and entertainment for the surrounding area. The newspaper is published on a Thursday. Community Newspaper editions:The Bristol Observer (East Kingswood & Keynsham) The Bristol Observer (South Gloucestershire)The Bristol Observer (South West)
Ad Rate: Full Page Mono 3902.40
Ad Rate: Full Page Colour 4878.00

Bristol Post 979905
Editorial: Temple Way, Bristol BS2 0BY
Tel: 44 01179 343331
Email: epnews@bepp.co.uk
Web site: www.bristolpost.co.uk
Freq: Daily
Circ: 17381 Not Audited

Brits Pos 1060581
Tel: 44 27122 524995
Email: tallie@britspos1.co.za
Freq: Weekly
Circ: 7743 Not Audited

Brixham News 980255
Editorial: Tindle House, 26 Warland, Totnes TQ9 5EL **Tel:** 44 01803 862585
Email: brixham.editorial@totnes-today.co.uk
Web site: www.totnes-today.co.uk
Freq: Weekly
Circ: 3500 Not Audited
Profile: The Brixham News is a free weekly local newspaper covering local news and sports for the surrounding area. The newspaper is published on Wednesday.
Ad Rate: Full Page Mono 1280.00
Ad Rate: Full Page Colour 1536.00

Brixton Bugle 986899
Web site: www.brixtonblog.com
Freq: Monthly
Circ: 10000 Not Audited
Editor: Zoe Jewell

Bromley News 980353
Editorial: Winterton House, High Street, Westerham TN16 1AT **Tel:** 44 01959 564766
Email: bheditor@gmail.com
Web site: www.bromley-today.co.uk
Freq: Weekly
Circ: 2000 Not Audited
Editor: Luke King
Profile: Website for local paper The Bromley News, covering the latest news and events from the London Borough of Bromley.

Bromley Times 980397
Editorial: Kent House, 81 Station Road, Ashford TN23 1PP **Tel:** 44 01233 653460
Email: feedback@bromleytimes.co.uk
Web site: www.bromleytimes.co.uk
Freq: Weekly
Circ: 4865 Not Audited
Profile: Online version of the Bromley Times newspaper covering local news, sports and entertainment for the surrounding area.

Bromsgrove Advertiser 980329
Editorial: St John's House, St John's Road, Stourbridge DY8 1EH **Tel:** 44 01384 358050
Email: yournews@bromsgroveadvertiser.co.uk
Web site: www.bromsgroveadvertiser.co.uk
Freq: Weekly
Circ: 37561 Not Audited
Profile: Online version of the Bromsgrove Advertiser newspaper covering local news and sports for the surrounding area. The outlet offers RSS (Really Simple Syndication).

Bromsgrove Standard 980330
Editorial: 44 High Street, Bromsgrove, Bromsgrove B61 8HQ **Tel:** 44 01527 574111
Email: editor@bromsgrovestandard.co.uk
Web site: www.bromsgrovestandard.co.uk
Freq: Weekly
Circ: 36967 Not Audited
Editor: Tristan Harris
Profile: Online version of the Bromsgrive Standard covering local news, sports and entertainment for the surrounding area.

Buchan Observer 980641
Editorial: 28-30 Seagate, Peterhead, Peterhead AB42 1JP **Tel:** 44 01779 871330
Email: news@buchanobserver.com
Web site: www.buchanobserver.co.uk
Freq: Weekly
Circ: 3884 Not Audited
Profile: Geographical Focus: Scotland
Ad Rate: Full Page Mono 820.00
Ad Rate: Full Page Colour 1066.00

Buckingham & Winslow Advertiser 982954
Editorial: Claydon House, 1 Edison Rd, Buckingham HP19 8TE
Tel: 44 01296 619779
Email: editorial@buckinghamadvertiser.co.uk
Web site: www.buckinghamtoday.co.uk
Freq: Weekly
Circ: 6730 Not Audited
Profile: The Buckingham & Winslow Advertiser is a weekly newspaper covering the latest in local news from the town of Buckingham and the surrounding area.
Ad Rate: Full Page Mono 1242.36

Buckinghamshire Advertiser
980198
Editorial: Trinity Mirror Southern, c/o Trinity Mirror Colour Print, St Albans Road, Watford Herts **Tel:** 44 01895 451000
Email: bucksnews@trinitysouth.co.uk
Web site: www.buckinghamshireadvertiser.co.uk
Freq: Weekly
Circ: 6084 Not Audited
Profile: The Buckinghamshire Advertiser is a weekly paper covering the latest in local news from the region of Buckinghamshire.

Buckinghamshire Examiner
980200
Editorial: Trinity Mirror Southern, c/o Trinity Mirror Colour Print, St Albans Road, Watford
Tel: 44 01895 451000
Email: bucksnews@trinitysouth.co.uk
Web site: http://www.getbucks.co.uk/
Freq: Weekly
Circ: 6084 Not Audited
Profile: The Buckinghamshire Examiner is a weekly paper covering the latest in local news and current affairs from the Buckinghamshire region.

Bucks Advertiser 980199
Editorial: Claydon House, 1 Edison Rd, Aylesbury, Aylesbury HP19 8TE
Tel: 44 01296 619735
Email: editorial@bucksherald.co.uk
Web site: www.bucksherald.co.uk
Freq: Weekly
Circ: 4616 Not Audited
Profile: The Bucks Advertiser is a free weekly paper with local news, sports, leisure and features from around Aylesbury. It is published every Friday.
Ad Rate: Full Page Mono 1141.38

Bucks Free Press 980201
Editorial: Loudwater Mill, Station Road, High Wycombe HP10 9TY **Tel:** 44 01494 755000
Email: bfpnews@london.newsquest.co.uk
Web site: www.bucksfreepress.co.uk
Freq: Weekly
Circ: 11625 Not Audited
Profile: Online version of the Bucks Free Press newspaper covering local news and sports for the surrounding area.

The Bucks Herald 980202
Editorial: Claydon House, 1 Edison Rd, Aylesbury HP19 8TE **Tel:** 44 01296 619735
Email: bucks.herald@jpress.co.uk
Web site: www.bucksherald.co.uk
Freq: Weekly
Circ: 10215 Not Audited
Profile: This is the online version of the Bucks Herald, a weekly local newspaper covering the latest on lifestyle, sport and news in Aylesbury and the surrounding areas.

Burnham & Highbridge Weekly News 980501
Editorial: 28 Angel Crescent, Bridgwater, Bridgwater TA6 3EW **Tel:** 44 01823 365151
Email: newsdesk@bridgwatermercury.co.uk
Web site: www.burnhamandhighbridgeweeklynews.co.uk
Freq: Weekly
Circ: 2205 Not Audited

Burnley Express 980370
Editorial: East Lancashire Newspapers, Bull Street, Burnley BB11 1DP
Tel: 44 01282 426161
Web site: www.burnleyexpress.net
Freq: 2 Times/Week
Circ: 15238 Not Audited
Profile: Online version of the Burnley Express newspaper, covering the latest local news, sports and lifestyle for the surrounding area.

Burton Mail 980118
Tel: 44 01283 245000
Email: editorial@burtonmail.co.uk
Web site: www.burtonmail.co.uk
Freq: Daily
Circ: 7806 Not Audited
Editor: Emma Turton
Profile: The Burton Mail is a daily regional newspaper and covers regional news, sports, business and entertainment. The newspaper was first launched in 1898. The outlet offers RSS (Really Simple Syndication)
Ad Rate: Full Page Colour 1070.00

Bury Free Press 980444
Editorial: King's Road, Bury St Edmunds, Bury St. Edmunds IP33 3ET
Tel: 44 01284 757857
Email: news@buryfreepress.co.uk
Web site: www.buryfreepress.co.uk
Freq: Weekly

Circ: 14150 Not Audited
Profile: This is the online version of the Bury Free Press covering news, sport, lifestyle and the local community for the surrounding area. Editions IncludeBury Free Press Town and Villages Edition Bury Free Press Stowmarket NewsBury Free Press Mildenhall Bury Free Press Thetford & Brandon News

Bury Times 980425
Editorial: The Wellsprings, The Civic Centre, Victoria Square, Bolton BL1 1AR
Tel: 44 01204 522345
Email: burynewsdesk@burytimes.co.uk
Web site: www.burytimes.co.uk
Freq: Weekly
Circ: 10426 Not Audited
Editor: Michael Crutchley
Profile: Online version of the Bury Times newspaper covering local news and sports for the surrounding area.

Business MK 981505
Editorial: 28 Linford Forum, Rockingham Drive, Linford Wood, Milton Keynes MK13 6LY **Tel:** 44 01908 394501
Email: news@businessmk.co.uk
Web site: www.businessmk.co.uk
Freq: Monthly
Circ: 5000 Not Audited
Editor: Andrew Gibbs
Profile: Business MK is a monthly magazine containing news on companies in Milton Keynes and North Buckinghamshire. Covers management, business developments and achievements, business start-ups, commercial property and investment property. The magazine is aimed at business people and Chamber of Commerce members in North Buckinghamshire.
Ad Rate: Full Page Colour 2275.00
Business

Business Times 981506
Editorial: 16 York Road, Northampton NN1 5QG **Tel:** 44 01604 259900
Email: news@business-times.co.uk
Web site: www.business-times.co.uk
Freq: Monthly
Circ: 9500 Not Audited
Editor: Judith Halliday
Profile: Business Times is a magazine containing news and information on business strategy in the area.
Ad Rate: Full Page Mono 1425.00

Business Weekly 980927
Editorial: St John's Innovation Centre, Cowley Road, Toft, Cambridge CB4 0WS
Tel: 44 01223 421865
Email: news@businessweekly.co.uk
Web site: www.businessweekly.co.uk
Freq: Weekly
Circ: 22500 Not Audited
Profile: Newspaper combining the latest business news including start-ups with in-depth reports and analysis on issues of importance to companies involved in manufacturing and services to industry. The publication also features lifestyle features and stories. Aimed at senior executives and decision makers in businesses throughout the East and South East of England.Previous title: Business Weekly Eastern England
Ad Rate: Full Page Mono 1380.00
Ad Rate: Full Page Colour 1560.00

Business2Business (UK) 998587
Editorial: 28 Linford Forum, Rockingham Drive, Linford Wood, Milton Keynes MK13 6LY **Tel:** 44 01908 394501
Email: news@businessmk.co.uk
Web site: www.businessmk.co.uk
Freq: Monthly
Circ: 4500 Not Audited
Editor: Andrew Gibbs
Business

The Buteman 980642
Editorial: 5 Victoria Street, Rothesay, Isle of Bute, Paisley PA20 OAJ
Tel: 44 01700 502931
Email: news@buteman.com
Web site: www.buteman.co.uk
Freq: Weekly
Circ: 2627 Not Audited

Profile: The Buteman is a weekly local newspaper covering all the latest local news, sport and lifestyle for the Isle of Bute.
Ad Rate: Full Page Mono 1200.00
Ad Rate: Full Page Colour 1500.00

Buxton Advertiser 980246
Editorial: 10 Scarsdale Place, Buxton SK17 6EG **Tel:** 44 01298 767080
Email: news@buxtonadvertiser.co.uk
Web site: www.buxtonadvertiser.co.uk
Freq: Weekly
Circ: 6995 Not Audited
Profile: Online version of the Buxton Advertiser newspaper covering local news, lifestyle and sports for the surrounding area. The outlet offers RSS (Really Simple Syndication).

Caernarfon & Denbigh Herald 980606
Editorial: Vale Road, Llandudno Junction, Conwy LL31 9SL **Tel:** 44 01286 671111
Email: caernarfon.herald@northwalesnews.co.uk
Web site: http://www.dailypost.co.uk/all-about/gwynedd
Freq: Weekly
Circ: 4863 Not Audited
Profile: The Caernarfon & Denbigh Herald is a weekly local newspaper covering local news for the surrounding area.
Ad Rate: Full Page Mono 1138.00
Ad Rate: Full Page Colour 1536.30

Caithness Courier 980643
Editorial: 42 Union Street, Wick, Caithness, Wick KW1 5ED **Tel:** 44 01955 602424
Email: editor@nosn.co.uk
Web site: www.johnogroat-journal.co.uk
Freq: Weekly
Circ: 4062 Not Audited
Editor: Iain Grant
Profile: The Caithness Courier is a weekly local newspaper covering local news and sports for the surrounding area.
Ad Rate: Full Page Mono 3080.00
Ad Rate: Full Page Colour 4000.00

Cambrian News 980618
Editorial: 7 Aberystwyth Science Park, Aberystwyth SY23 3AH
Tel: 44 01970 615000
Email: edit@cambrian-news.co.uk
Web site: www.cambrian-news.co.uk
Freq: Weekly
Circ: 19079 Not Audited
Profile: This is the online version of the Cambrian News, a weekly, local newspaper covering all the latest news, sport, lifestyle and property for the surrounding areas.

Cambridge News 980064
Editorial: Winship Road, Milton, Cambridge CB24 6BQ **Tel:** 44 01223 434434
Email: newsdesk@cambridge-news.co.uk
Web site: www.cambridge-news.co.uk
Freq: Daily
Circ: 12991 Not Audited
Profile: The Cambridge News is a daily regional newspaper covering all the latest entertainment, lifestyle, news and sport for the surrounding area. The outlet offers RSS (Really Simple Syndication).
Ad Rate: Full Page Mono 2952.00
Ad Rate: Full Page Colour 3838.00

Cambridge News & Crier - CEASED 980206
Editorial: Winship Road, Milton, Cambridge CB24 6PP **Tel:** 44 01223 434434
Web site: http://www.cambridge-news.co.uk
Freq: Weekly
Circ: 29000 Not Audited

Cambs Times 983013
Editorial: Audmoor House, 93 High Street, March, March PE15 9LH
Tel: 44 01354 661915
Email: news@cambs-times.co.uk
Web site: www.cambs-times.co.uk
Freq: Weekly
Circ: 12166 Not Audited
Editor: John Elworthy

Profile: The Cambs Times is a weekly local newspaper covering local news, sports and entertainment for the surrounding area. The newspaper is published on Fridays.

Camden Monthly 995369
Editorial: Unit 307, 203 Mare Studios, London E8 3QE **Tel:** 44 02070 182665
Email: editorial@camdenmonthly.com
Web site: www.camdenmonthly.com
Freq: Monthly
Circ: 65000 Not Audited

Camden New Journal 980398
Editorial: 40 Camden Road, London NW1 9DR **Tel:** 44 02074 199000
Email: editorial@camdennewjournal.co.uk
Web site: www.camdennewjournal.co.uk
Freq: Weekly
Circ: 47000 Not Audited
Editor: Eric Gordon
Profile: This is the online version of the Camden New Journal, a free, weekly, local newspaper covering all the latest on local news in the London borough of Camden.

Campaign Series 980619
Editorial: Cardiff Road, Maesglas, Newport, Newport NP20 3QN **Tel:** 44 01633 810000
Email: campaign.reporter@gwent-wales.co.uk
Web site: www.campaignseries.co.uk
Freq: Weekly
Circ: 20304 Not Audited

Campbeltown Courier 980644
Editorial: Main and Longrow South, Campbeltown, Argyll, Campbeltown PA28 6AE **Tel:** 44 01586 554646
Email: editor@campbeltowncourier.co.uk
Web site: www.campbeltowncourier.co.uk
Freq: Weekly
Circ: 5647 Not Audited
Editor: Mark Davey
Profile: Online version of the Cambeltown Courier newspaper covering local news and sports for the surrounding area.

Cannock Chronicle 980522
Editorial: 51-53 Queen Street, Wolverhampton WV1 1ES
Tel: 44 01543 465302
Email: cannock.chron@expressandstar.co.uk
Web site: https://www.expressandstar.com/free-editions/
Freq: Weekly
Circ: 50504 Not Audited
Profile: The Cannock Chronicle is a weekly, local newspaper covering all the latest on local news in Cannock. The paper is published on Thursdays

Canterbury Times 980350
Editorial: Kent Innovation Centre, Thanet Reach Business Park, Broadstairs, Broadstairs CT10 2QQ
Tel: 44 01843 609632
Email: newsdesk.times@krnmedia.co.uk
Web site: www.canterburytimes.co.uk
Freq: Weekly
Circ: 21940 Not Audited
Profile: Online version of the Canterbury Times newspaper covering local news, sports, entertainment and lifestyle for the surrounding area. The outlet offers RSS (Really Simple Syndication).

Canvey & Benfleet Times 1096034
Editorial: 106 The Broadway, Leigh-on-Sea, Southend, Southend-on-Sea SS9 1AB
Tel: 44 01702 477666
Email: ed@leightimes.co.uk
Web site: http://www.leightimes.co.uk/
Freq: Monthly
Circ: 14000 Not Audited
Editor: Michael Guy

Cardiff & South Wales Advertiser 980620
Editorial: Mackintosh House, 136 Newport Road, Cardiff, Cardiff CF24 1DJ
Tel: 44 02920 303900

Email: info@cardiffandsouthwalesadvertiser.com
Web site: www.cardiffandsouthwalesadvertiser.com
Freq: Bi-Weekly
Circ: 90000 Not Audited
Profile: The Cardiff & South Wales Advertiser is a free, glossy magazine covering all the latest on local news and entertainment in Cardiff and South Wales. The magazine is published fortnightly on Fridays.

Carletonville Herald 1060393
Tel: 44 27187 886693
Email: hstander@media24.com
Freq: Weekly
Circ: 5532 Not Audited

Carmarthen Journal 981673
Editorial: 18 King Street, Dyfed, Carmarthen, Carmarthen SA31 1BN
Tel: 44 01267 610467
Email: journal.star@swwmedia.co.uk
Web site: www.carmarthenjournal.co.uk
Freq: Weekly
Circ: 9759 Not Audited
Editor: Jonathan Roberts
Profile: The Carmarthen Journal is a weekly local newspaper covering local news, sport and leisure for the surrounding areas.

Carmarthenshire Herald 998285
Editorial: 44a Stepney Street, Llanelli SA15 3TR **Tel:** 44 01267 600500
Email: editor@herald.email
Web site: http://www.carmarthenshireherald.com/
Freq: Weekly
Circ: 14000 Not Audited

Carnoustie Guide and Gazette 995046
Editorial: 21 Market Place, Arbroath DD11 1HR **Tel:** 44 01241 435770
Email: news@arbroathherald.co.uk
Web site: www.guideandgazette.co.uk
Freq: Weekly
Circ: 3148 Not Audited

Carrick Gazette 980645
Editorial: 32 Dalrymple Street, Girvan, Ayrshire, Girvan KA26 9AE
Tel: 44 01465 712688
Email: editorial@carrickgazette.com
Web site: www.carricktoday.com
Freq: WeeklyNot Audited
Editor: David Walker
Profile: Online version of the Carrick Gazette newspaper covering local news, features and sports for the surrounding area.

Carrick Herald 983727
Editorial: Ayrshire Weekly Press, Princes Street, Ardrossan, Ardrossan KA22 8BP
Tel: 44 01292 267631
Email: editorial@ayradvertiser.com
Web site: www.carrickherald.com
Freq: Weekly
Circ: 5391 Not Audited
Editor: Caroline Patterson
Profile: Website of The Carrick Herald, a weekly local newspaper covering local news, sports and leisure for the surrounding area.

Carrick Times 984199
Editorial: 8 Dunluce Street, Larne BT40 1JG
Tel: 44 02828 272303
Email: news@carricktimes.co.uk
Web site: www.carrickfergustimes.co.uk
Freq: WeeklyNot Audited
Profile: This is the online version of the Carrick Times, a weekly, local newspaper covering all the latest on local news, sport, motors and property in Carrickfergus and the surrounding area.

Castle Point Rayleigh Standard 995774
Editorial: Newspaper House, Chester Hall Lane, Basildon, Basildon SS14 3BL
Tel: 44 01268 469875
Email: echonews@newsquest.co.uk
Web site: www.echo-news.co.uk
Freq: Weekly

Regional & Local Weekly Newspapers

Circ: 33781 Not Audited

The Caterham and District Independent
996616
Editorial: The Officers' Mess, Coldstream Road, Caterham, London CR3 5QX
Tel: 44 01883 346641
Email: info@caterham-independent.co.uk
Web site: www.caterham-independent.co.uk
Freq: Monthly
Circ: 26000 Not Audited
Editor: Julia Church

Central Fife Times & Advertiser
980646
Editorial: Pitreavie Business Park, Dunfermline, Dunfermline KY11 8QS
Tel: 44 01383 747500
Email: editorial@centralfifetimes.co.uk
Web site: www.centralfifetimes.com
Freq: Weekly
Circ: 3454 Not Audited
Editor: Jim Stark
Profile: Website of The Central Fife Times and Advertiser, a weekly newspaper covering local news, sports and leisure for the surrounding area.

The Ceredigion Herald
1068964
Tel: 44 01646 454545
Web site: http://ceredigionherald.com/
Freq: Weekly
Circ: 3300 Not Audited

The Challenge
980439
Editorial: The Foundry, 36 Henry Street, Liverpool L1 5BS Tel: 44 01517 067411
Email: thechallenge@merseymirror.com
Web site: www.thechallenge.co.uk
Freq: Monthly
Circ: 50000 Not Audited
Editor: Alan Birkett
Profile: The Challenge is a free, monthly, local newspaper covering all the latest on healthcare, lifestyle, news and sport for Knowsley and the surrounding area.
Ad Rate: Full Page Mono 910.00
Ad Rate: Full Page Colour 1137.50

Champion Newspapers
995948
Editorial: Clare House, 166 Lord Street, Southport PR9 0QA Tel: 44 01704 392392
Email: editorial@champnews.com
Web site: www.champnews.com
Freq: Weekly
Circ: 164336 Not Audited
Editor: Malcolm Hindle

Chard & Ilminster News
980503
Editorial: 44 St James Street, Taunton, Taunton TA1 1JR Tel: 44 01823 365104
Email: newsdesk@chardandilminsternews.co.uk
Web site: www.chardandilminsternews.co.uk
Freq: Weekly
Circ: 3644 Not Audited
Profile: This is the online version of the Chard and Ilminster News, covering news, sport and leisure for the surrounding area.

Cheadle & Tean Times
980523
Editorial: Times & Echo Office, 18 Tape Street, Cheadle, Cheadle ST10 1BD
Tel: 44 01538 752214
Email: news@timesandecho.co.uk
Web site: www.timesechoandlife.co.uk
Freq: Weekly
Circ: 6000 Not Audited
Profile: The Cheadle & Tean Times is a weekly newspaper covering local news, sports and leisure for the surrounding area. It is published every Wednesday. The company was established in 1896.
Ad Rate: Full Page Mono 725.00
Ad Rate: Full Page Colour 725.00

Cheadle Post & Times
980524
Editorial: 1 Market Place, Leek, Leek ST13 5HH Tel: 44 01538 714000
Email: newsdesk@thepostandtimes.co.uk
Web site: www.leek-news.co.uk/Cheadle-News/
Freq: Weekly

Circ: 1000 Not Audited
Editor: Stephen Houghton
Profile: Online version of the Cheadle Post and Times newspaper covering local news, sports and business for the surrounding area.

Cheddar Valley Gazette
984364
Editorial: Southover, Wells, Wells BA5 1UH
Tel: 44 01749 832300
Email: somersetlivenewsdesk@localworld.co.uk
Web site: www.somerlive.co.uk
Freq: Weekly
Circ: 13224 Not Audited
Editor: Tim Lethaby
Profile: Online version of the Cheddar Valley Gazette newspaper covering local news and sports for the surrounding area.

Chelmsford & Mid Essex Times
983014
Editorial: Newspaper House, Chester Hall Lane, Basildon, Basildon SS14 3BL
Web site: www.chelmsfordweeklynews.co.uk
Freq: Weekly
Circ: 39589 Not Audited
Editor: Gary Pearson
Profile: Online version of the Chelmsford Weekly News newspaper covering local news and sports for the surrounding area. The outlet offers RSS (Really Simple Syndication).

Cheshire Independent
982477
Editorial: 3 Bridgebank Industrial Estate, Taylor Street, Horwich, Horwich BL6 7PD
Tel: 44 01204 478813
Web site: www.cheshireindependent.co.uk
Freq: Monthly
Circ: 11000 Not Audited
Editor: John Henderson
Profile: This is the online version of the Cheshire Independent, a free, monthly, local paper covering the latest local news, sport and business in Cheshire, Macclesfield and the surrounding area.

Chester Chronicle
980215
Editorial: Maple House, Park West, Sealand Road, Chester CH1 4RN
Tel: 44 01244 606425
Email: cheshire.news@trinitymirror.com
Web site: www.chesterchronicle.co.uk
Freq: Weekly
Circ: 8334 Not Audited
Profile: Online version of the Chester Chronicle covering local news, sports and lifestyle for the surrounding area.

Chester Chronicle Xtra
999145
Editorial: Maple House, Park West, Sealand Road, Chester CH1 4RN
Tel: 44 01244 606425
Email: cheshire.news@trinitymirror.com
Web site: www.chesterchronicle.co.uk
Freq: Weekly
Circ: 20759 Not Audited

Chester Standard
980214
Editorial: 56 Watergate Street, Chester CH1 2LA Tel: 44 01244 304500
Email: news@chesterfirst.co.uk
Web site: www.chesterstandard.co.uk/
Freq: Weekly
Circ: 51218 Not Audited
Editor: Jonathan Barnett

Chew Valley Gazette
980504
Editorial: 5 South Parade, Chew Magna, Bristol BS40 8SH Tel: 44 01275 332266
Email: editorial@chewvalleygazette.co.uk
Web site: www.chewvalleygazette.co.uk
Freq: Monthly
Circ: 14500 Not Audited
Editor: Selina Cuff
Profile: Online version of the Chew Valley Gazette newspaper covering local news and sports for the surrounding area.

Chichester Herald
987691
Editorial: Suite 804, 26 The Hornet, Chichester, Chichester PO19 7BB

Email: news@chichesterherald.co.uk
Web site: www.chichesterherald.co.uk
Freq: Weekly

Chichester Observer
980576
Editorial: Suite 3 First Floor, City Gates, 2-4 Southgate, Chichester PO19 8DJ
Tel: 44 01243 531313
Email: news@chiobserver.co.uk
Web site: www.chichester.co.uk
Freq: Weekly
Circ: 27695 Not Audited
Profile: Online version of the Chichester Observer newspaper covering local news and sports for the surrounding area.

Chingford Times
986050
Editorial: Acorn House, Great Oaks, Basildon, Basildon SS14 1AH
Tel: 44 01268 503400
Email: news@chingfordtimes.co.uk
Web site: www.chingfordtimes.co.uk
Freq: Bi-WeeklyNot Audited
Profile: Website for local paper the Chingford Times covering the latest news and events from Chingford. This outlet covers areas within Waltham Forest Borough.

The Chiswick Herald
995395
Editorial: Unit 22, 295 Cheswick High Road, London W4 4HH Tel: 44 02036 230576
Email: newsdesk@chiswickherald.co.uk
Web site: www.chiswickherald.co.uk
Freq: Bi-Weekly
Circ: 10000 Not Audited

Chorley & Leyland Guardian
980372
Editorial: Oliver's Place, Fulwood, Preston PR2 9ZA Tel: 44 01772 838040
Email: guardian.newsdesk@jpress.co.uk
Web site: www.chorley-guardian.co.uk
Freq: Weekly
Circ: 6900 Not Audited

Chorley Citizen
980371
Editorial: 1 High Street, Newspaper House, Blackburn, Blackburn BB1 1HT
Tel: 44 01254 678678
Web site: www.chorleycitizen.co.uk
Freq: Weekly
Circ: 21423 Not Audited

The Chronicle (Newcastle)
980029
Editorial: NCJ Media, Groat Market, Newcastle upon Tyne NE1 1ED
Tel: 44 01912 327500
Email: ec.news@ncjmedia.co.uk
Web site: www.chroniclelive.co.uk
Freq: Daily
Circ: 26811 Not Audited
Profile: The Chronicle (Newcastle) is a regional daily newspaper covering regional news, sports and business for the surrounding area. The outlet offers RSS (Really Simple Syndication).
Ad Rate: Full Page Mono 6776.00
Ad Rate: Full Page Colour 8808.80

The Chronicle Series (Congleton)
980216
Editorial: 11 High St, Congleton, Congleton CW12 1BW Tel: 44 01260 273737
Email: chronicleseries@aol.com
Web site: www.chronicleseries.com
Freq: Weekly
Circ: 15000 Not Audited
Editor: Jeremy Condliffe

The Chronicle Series (Northern Ireland)
995927
Editorial: 20 Railway Road, Coleraine BT52 1PD Tel: 44 02870 343344
Email: editor@thechronicle.uk.com
Web site: www.ulsternet.co.uk
Freq: Weekly
Circ: 14841 Not Audited
Editor: John Fillis

The Circuit
1095728
Editorial: PO Box 939, Stockton-on-Tees TS19 1HY Tel: 44 01642 633866
Email: info@the-circuit.co.uk
Web site: http://www.the-circuit.co.uk
Freq: Monthly
Circ: 22000 Not Audited

City A.M.
982977
Editorial: 3rd Floor, Fountain House, 130 Fenchurch Street, London EC3M 5DJ
Tel: 44 02032 018900
Email: news@cityam.com
Web site: www.cityam.com
Freq: Daily
Circ: 90908 Not Audited
Editor: Christian May
Profile: City A.M is a free daily regional newspaper covering all the latest on business, company news, share tips and wealth management as well as features on the arts and sports. The outlet offers RSS (Really Simple Syndication).
Ad Rate: Full Page Mono 10535.00
Ad Rate: Full Page Colour 10535.00

Clacton Gazette
980292
Editorial: 28 Jackson Road, Clacton-on-Sea CO15 1QL Tel: 44 01255 221221
Email: cf.gazette@nqe.com
Web site: www.clactonandfrintongazette.co.uk
Freq: Weekly
Circ: 10506 Not Audited
Profile: Online version of the Clacton Gazette newspaper covering local news and sports for the surrounding area. The outlet offers RSS (Really Simple Syndication).

Cleethorpes Chronicle
984744
Tel: 44 01472 204020
Web site: http://www.cleethorpeschronicle.co.uk
Freq: Weekly
Circ: 19000 Not Audited
Profile: A weekly tabloid style newspaper sold in Cleethorpes and the surrounding area. It features a what's on section, including a 10-day guide, sport and seven-day TV listings.

Clitheroe Advertiser & Times
980098
Editorial: Fern Court Business Centre, Castlegate, Clitheroe BB7 1AZ
Tel: 44 01200 427667
Web site: www.clitheroeadvertiser.co.uk
Freq: Weekly
Circ: 5792 Not Audited

Clydebank Post
980647
Editorial: 1st Floor, Carus House, 201 Dumbarton Road, Clydebank G81 4XJ
Tel: 44 01414 358888
Email: editorial@clydebankpost.co.uk
Web site: www.clydebankpost.co.uk
Freq: Weekly
Circ: 4173 Not Audited
Profile: Online version of the Clydebank Post newspaper covering local news and sports for the surrounding area.

Coalville Mail
987751
Editorial: Leicester Mercury Media Group, St George Street, Leicester LE1 9FQ
Tel: 44 01162 512512
Email: newsdesk@leicestermercury.co.uk
Web site: www.thisisleicestershire.co.uk
Freq: WeeklyNot Audited

Coleraine Times
984220
Tel: 44 02870 355260
Email: news@colerainetimes.co.uk
Web site: www.colerainetimes.co.uk
Freq: Weekly
Circ: 2000 Not Audited
Editor: Dessie Blackadder
Profile: Online version of the Coleraine Times newspaper covering local news, sports and lifestyle for the surrounding area. The outlet offers RSS (Really Simple Syndication).

The Coleshill Post
996314
Editorial: Suite 3, Discovery Business Centre, Jubilee Works, Gorsey Lane, Coleshill B46 1JU **Tel:** 44 01675 238962
Email: editor@thecoleshillpost.co.uk
Web site: www.thecoleshillpost.co.uk
Freq: Monthly
Circ: 9000 Not Audited

The Comet Group
981645
Editorial: Bank House, Primett Road, Stevenage, Stevenage SG1 3EE
Tel: 44 01438 866000
Email: news@thecomet.net
Web site: www.thecomet.net
Freq: Weekly
Circ: 67054 Not Audited

concrete
981758
Editorial: Union of UEA Students, Union House, UEA, Norwich NR4 7TJ
Tel: 44 01603 593466
Email: concrete.editor@uea.ac.uk
Web site: www.concrete-online.co.uk
Freq: Bi-Weekly
Circ: 2600 Not Audited
Profile: Journal covering all matters related to concrete technology, design and construction of concrete structures. Read by consulting engineers, contractors, construction equipment and material manufacturers and suppliers.
Ad Rate: Full Page Colour 1650.00
Student Lifestyle

Corby Extra Local
1053347
Editorial: Ringstead Business Centre, 1-3 Spencer Street, Ringstead, Kettering NN14 4BX **Tel:** 44 01536 210223
Email: newsdesk@extranewspapers.co.uk
Web site: www.extranewspapers.co.uk/local/corby-local-news/
Freq: Bi-Weekly
Circ: 21000 Not Audited

Cornish & Devon Post Series
980230
Editorial: Tindle House, Westgate Street, Launceston PL15 7AL **Tel:** 44 01566 772424
Email: editor@thepost.uk.com
Web site: www.launceston-today.co.uk/
Freq: Weekly
Circ: 7279 Not Audited
Editor: Suzanne Cleave

Cornish Guardian
998506
Editorial: High Water House, City Wharf, Malpas Road, Truro TR1 1QH
Tel: 44 01872 271451
Email: cgedit@c-dm.co.uk
Web site: http://www.cornwalllive.com/
Freq: Weekly
Circ: 14286 Not Audited

Cornish Times
980232
Editorial: The Tindle Suite, Webbs House, Liskeard, Liskeard PL14 4AH
Tel: 44 01579 342174
Email: editorial@cornish-times.co.uk
Web site: www.cornish-times.co.uk
Freq: Weekly
Circ: 16000 Not Audited
Editor: Andrew Townsend
Profile: Online version of the Cornish Times newspaper covering local news, sports, lifestyle and business for the surrounding area of South East Cornwall. The outlet offers RSS (Really Simple Syndication).

The Cornishman
980231
Editorial: 13/14 Market Place, Penzance, Penzance TR18 2JB **Tel:** 44 01736 335512
Email: cornishman@c-dm.co.uk
Web site: http://www.cornwalllive.com/
Freq: Weekly
Circ: 10257 Not Audited
Profile: The Cornishman is a weekly, local newspaper covering all the latest on local news from Penzance, St Ives, Hayle, St Just and the Isles of Scilly.
Ad Rate: Full Page Mono 1123.20
Ad Rate: Full Page Colour 1516.32

County Antrim Post
999483
Tel: 44 02825 820888
Email: news@countyantrimpost.com
Freq: WeeklyNot Audited
Editor: Paul Ainsworth

County Border News Series
983625
Tel: 44 01959 564766
Web site: http://tindlenews.co.uk/
Freq: Weekly
Circ: 25000 Not Audited

County Derry Post
984911
Tel: 44 02877 743970
Email: editor@derrypost.com
Web site: http://www.derrynow.com/county-derry-post
Freq: Weekly
Circ: 4198 Not Audited
Editor: Orla McNicholl

County Down Spectator
983117
Editorial: Spectator Buildings, 91 Main Street, Bangor BT20 4AF
Tel: 44 02891 270270
Email: editor@spectatornewspapers.co.uk
Freq: Weekly
Circ: 8234 Not Audited
Editor: Paul Flowers; **Editor:** Paul Flowers; **Editor:** Paul Flowers

County Echo and St. Davids City Chronicle
983015
Editorial: Parc-y-Shwt, Fishguard, Fishguard SA65 9AP **Tel:** 44 01348 874445
Email: edit@countyecho.co.uk
Web site: http://www.countyecho.co.uk/
Freq: Weekly
Circ: 1918 Not Audited
Profile: This is the online version of the County Echo and St. Davids City Chronicle is a weekly, local newspaper covering all the latest on local news and sport in Cardigan, Fishguard, Haverfordwest and St David's.

County Times (Powys and Mid Wales)
998852
Editorial: 11c Broad Street, Welshpool, Powys, Welshpool SY21 7LE
Tel: 44 01938 553354
Email: news@countytimes.co.uk
Web site: www.countytimes.co.uk
Freq: Weekly
Circ: 12666 Not Audited
Editor: Nick Knight

The Courier (Dundee)
980028
Editorial: 80 Kingsway East, Dundee DD4 8SL **Tel:** 44 01382 575290
Email: news@thecourier.co.uk
Web site: www.thecourier.co.uk
Freq: Daily
Circ: 39324 Not Audited
Editor: Richard Neville

Coventry Observer
980554
Editorial: 45 The Parade, Leamington Spa, Leamington Spa CV32 4BL
Tel: 44 01926 451900
Email: editor@coventryobserver.co.uk
Web site: www.coventryobserver.co.uk
Freq: Weekly
Circ: 44420 Not Audited
Profile: Online version of the Coventry Observer newspaper covering local news and sports for the surrounding area.

Coventry Telegraph
979946
Editorial: Thomas Yeoman House, Leicester Row, Canal Basin, Coventry CV1 4LY
Tel: 44 02476 633633
Email: news@coventrytelegraph.net
Web site: www.coventrytelegraph.net
Freq: Daily
Circ: 15160 Not Audited
Editor: Keith Perry
Profile: The Coventry Telegraph is a regional daily newspaper and covers regional news, sports and entertainment for the surrounding area. This outlet offers RSS (Really Simple Syndication).
Ad Rate: Full Page Colour 3258.00

Cranbrook Herald
987552
Editorial: Fair Oak Close, Exeter Airport Business Park, Clyst Honiton, Exeter EX5 2UL **Tel:** 44 01392 888400
Web site: www.cranbrookherald.com
Freq: MonthlyNot Audited
Profile: Cranbrook Herald is a local newspaper covering the latest local news and events from Cranbrook, Devon.

Craven Herald & Pioneer
980099
Editorial: 38 High Street, Skipton BD23 1JU
Tel: 44 01756 792577
Email: news@cravenherald.co.uk
Web site: www.cravenherald.co.uk
Freq: Weekly
Circ: 9377 Not Audited
Profile: The Craven Herald Pioneer is a weekly local newspaper and covers local news, entertainment and sports for the surrounding area. The newspaper is published on a Thursday.
Ad Rate: Full Page Mono 1382.40
Ad Rate: Full Page Colour 1728.00

Crawley & Horley Observer
980008
Editorial: Springfield House, Springfield Road, Horsham, Crawley RH12 2RG
Tel: 44 01403 751200
Email: crawleyobserver@jpress.co.uk
Web site: http://www.crawleyobserver.co.uk/
Freq: Weekly
Circ: 6000 Not Audited

Crediton Courier
982485
Editorial: 102 High Street, Crediton, Crediton EX17 3LF **Tel:** 44 01363 774263
Email: editor@creditoncouriernewspaper.co.uk
Web site: www.creditoncouriernewspaper.co.uk
Freq: Weekly
Circ: 2373 Not Audited
Editor: Alan Quick

Crewe & Nantwich Guardian
980217
Editorial: Theatre Court, London Road, Northwich CW9 5HB **Tel:** 44 01606 813620
Email: crewe@guardiangrp.co.uk
Web site: www.creweguardian.co.uk
Freq: Weekly
Circ: 22025 Not Audited
Editor: Carla Flynn
Profile: The Crewe & Nantwich Guardian is a free weekly, local newspaper covering all the latest on local news and sport in Crewe. The paper is published on Thursdays.
Ad Rate: Full Page Colour 380.00

Crewe Chronicle
980218
Editorial: Maple House, Park West, Sealand Road, Chester CH1 4RN
Tel: 44 01244 606431
Email: crewe.news@trinitymirror.com
Web site: www.crewechronicle.co.uk
Freq: Weekly
Circ: 7830 Not Audited
Profile: Online version of the Crewe Chronicle newspaper covering local news and sports for the surrounding area. The outlet offers RSS (Really Simple Syndication).

Croydon Advertiser
980399
Editorial: Stoke Mill, Woking Road, Redhill, Guildford GU1 1QA **Tel:** 44 01737 783808
Email: newsdesk@croydonadvertiser.co.uk
Web site: www.croydonadvertiser.co.uk
Freq: Weekly
Circ: 6964 Not Audited
Profile: Online version of the Croydon Advertiser newspaper covering local news and sports for the surrounding area.

Croydon Guardian
980538
Editorial: Floors 9 & 10, Quadrant House, The Quadrant, Sutton SM2 5AS
Tel: 44 02087 226350
Email: newsdesk@croydonguardian.co.uk
Web site: www.croydonguardian.co.uk
Freq: Weekly
Circ: 55288 Not Audited

Profile: The Croydon Guardian is a weekly, local newspaper covering the latest local news, leisure and sport in Croydon. The paper is published on a Wednesday.
Ad Rate: Full Page Colour 1335.00

Cumberland & Westmorland Herald
980238
Editorial: 14 King Street, Penrith, Penrith CA11 7AH **Tel:** 44 01768 862313
Email: news@cwherald.com
Web site: www.cwherald.com
Freq: Weekly
Circ: 12930 Not Audited
Editor: Colin Maughan
Profile: Online version of the Cumberland & Westmorland Herald newspaper covering local news and sports for the surrounding area.

The Cumberland News
980239
Editorial: Newspaper House, Dalston Road, Carlisle CA2 5UA **Tel:** 44 01228 612600
Email: news@cumbrian-newspapers.co.uk
Web site: www.cumberlandnews.co.uk
Freq: Weekly
Circ: 18081 Not Audited
Profile: The Cumberland News is a weekly, local newspaper published on Fridays, covering all the latest on local news, business, farming and sport in Cumbria and southern Scotland.

Cumbernauld News & Kilsyth Chronicle
980648
Editorial: 10-12 Tay Walk, Glasgow G67 1BU **Tel:** 44 01236 725578
Email: editorial@cumbernauld-news.co.uk
Web site: www.cumbernauld-news.co.uk
Freq: Weekly
Circ: 7500 Not Audited
Editor: Martin Clark

Cumnock Chronicle
983016
Editorial: Dock Rd, Ardrossan, Ardrossan KA22 8DA **Tel:** 44 01290 421633
Email: editorial@cumnockchronicle.co.uk
Web site: www.cumnockchronicle.com
Freq: Weekly
Circ: 3948 Not Audited
Editor: Caroline Patterson
Profile: Online version of the Cumnock Chronicle covering local news and sports for the surrounding area.

Cynon Valley Leader
983017
Editorial: 6 Park Street, Cardiff CF10 1XR
Tel: 44 01443 629200
Email: cynon.valley.leader@mediawales.co.uk
Web site: www.walesonline.co.uk/all-about/cynon-valley
Freq: Weekly
Circ: 1975 Not Audited
Profile: The Cynon Valley Leader is a weekly paper covering the latest news and events from Cynon Valley. The paper is published every Wednesday.
Ad Rate: Full Page Mono 1466.08
Ad Rate: Full Page Colour 1979.21

Daily Gazette
982892
Editorial: Unit 1 Brunel Court, Brunel Way, Severalls Industrial Estate, Colchester, Colchester CO4 9XP **Tel:** 44 01206 506000
Email: gazette.newsdesk@newsquest.co.uk
Web site: http://www.gazette-news.co.uk
Freq: Daily
Circ: 9693 Not Audited
Profile: The Daily Gazette is a daily regional tabloid-sized newspaper and covers regional news, sports and entertainment for the surrounding area. This outlet offers RSS (Really Simple Syndication)
Ad Rate: Full Page Mono 622.10
Ad Rate: Full Page Colour 622.10

Daily Post (Wales)
980120
Editorial: Vale Road, Llandudno Junction, Conwy LL31 9SL **Tel:** 44 01492 574452
Email: welshnews@dailypost.co.uk
Web site: www.dailypost.co.uk
Freq: Daily
Circ: 22251 Not Audited
Editor: Andrew Campbell

Regional & Local Weekly Newspapers

Profile: Daily Post (Wales) is a daily regional newspaper covering the latest on regional news, business and sports for the surrounding area. This Outlet offer RSS (Really Simple Syndication)
Ad Rate: Full Page Mono 2992.00
Ad Rate: Full Page Colour 4039.00

Darlington & Stockton Times
980280
Editorial: PO Box 14, Priestgate, Darlington DL1 1NF **Tel:** 44 01325 381313
Email: newsdesk@dst.co.uk
Web site: www.dst.co.uk
Freq: Weekly
Circ: 15538 Not Audited
Profile: Online version of the Darlington & Stockton Times newspaper covering the latest local news, sports and business for the surrounding area. The outlet offers RSS (Really Simple Syndication).

Dartford and Gravesend Messenger Series
980354
Editorial: 7 High Street, London DA11 0BQ
Tel: 44 01474 564327
Web site: www.kentonline.co.uk
Freq: Weekly
Circ: 3725 Not Audited
Editor: Matthew Ramsden

Daventry Express
980473
Editorial: Albert House, Victoria Street, Northampton NN1 3NR
Tel: 44 01327 706712
Email: editorial@daventryexpress.co.uk
Web site: www.daventryonline.co.uk
Freq: Weekly
Circ: 6883 Not Audited
Editor: David Summers
Profile: Online version of the Daventry Express newspaper covering local news, sports, lifestyle and features for the surrounding area. The outlet offers RSS (Really Simple Syndication).

Dawlish Gazette & Teignmouth News
996019
Editorial: Tindle House, 6 Park Road, Dawlish EX7 9LQ **Tel:** 44 01626 864161
Email: editorial@dawlishnewspapers.co.uk
Web site: http://www.dawlishnewspapers.co.uk/
Freq: Weekly
Circ: 12144 Not Audited

Dawlish Post
987223
Editorial: The Old Manor House, 63 Wolborough Street, Newton Abbott, Newton Abbot TQ12 1NE **Tel:** 44 01626 353555
Email: editorial@middevonadvertiser.co.uk
Web site: http://www.dawlish-today.co.uk/
Freq: Weekly
Circ: 5200 Not Audited
Profile: Online version of the Dawlish Post newspaper covering local news and sports for the surrounding area. The outlet offers RSS (Really Simple Syndication).

Dearne Valley Weekender
980516
Editorial: 84 High Street, Mexborough S64 9AU **Tel:** 44 01709 768000
Email: newsdesk@rotherhamadvertiser.co.uk
Web site: http://www.rotherhamadvertiser.co.uk
Freq: Weekly
Circ: 47404 Not Audited
Editor: Andrew Mosley
Profile: The Dearne Valley Weekender is a free weekly local newspaper and covers local news, sports and entertainment for the surrounding area. The newspaper is published on a Thursday.
Ad Rate: Full Page Mono 1360.00
Ad Rate: Full Page Colour 1836.00

Deeside Piper
980649
Editorial: 1 Scott Skinner Square, Banchory, Banchory AB31 5SE **Tel:** 44 01330 826414
Email: news@deesidepiper.com
Web site: www.deesidepiper.com
Freq: Weekly
Circ: 3829 Not Audited

Profile: Online version of the Deeside Piper newspaper covering local news and sports for the surrounding area.

Denbighshire Free Press
980607
Editorial: Accent House, 23 Kinmel Street, Rhyl, Rhyl LL18 1AH **Tel:** 44 01352 707707
Email: editor@denbighshirefreepress.co.uk
Web site: www.denbighshirefreepress.co.uk
Freq: Weekly
Circ: 4464 Not Audited
Editor: Matt Warner

Derby Telegraph
979947
Editorial: 2 Siddalls Road, Derby DE1 2PB
Tel: 44 01332 411888
Email: newsdesk@derbytelegraph.co.uk
Web site: http://www.derbytelegraph.co.uk/home
Freq: Daily
Circ: 18903 Not Audited
Profile: The Derby Telegraph is a regional daily newspaper and covers regional news, sports, entertainment and business for the surrounding area.
Ad Rate: Full Page Mono 3441.60
Ad Rate: Full Page Colour 3441.60

Derbyshire Guardian
987684
Editorial: Sitwell House, 72 Wilson Street, Derby DE1 1PL **Tel:** 44 01332 650239
Web site: www.derbyshireguardian.co.uk
Freq: WeeklyNot Audited

Derbyshire Times
980247
Editorial: Spire Walk, off Derby Road, Chesterfield, Chesterfield S40 2WG
Tel: 44 01246 504578
Email: comment@derbyshiretimes.co.uk
Web site: www.derbyshiretimes.co.uk
Freq: Weekly
Circ: 19495 Not Audited
Profile: Online version of the Derbyshire Times covering local news and sports for the surrounding area.

Dereham Times
980445
Editorial: Bond House, 31 High Street, Dereham, Dereham NR19 1DZ
Tel: 44 01362 854700
Web site: www.derehamtimes.co.uk
Freq: Weekly
Circ: 4440 Not Audited

Derry Journal
983118
Tel: 44 02871 272200
Email: editorial@derryjournal.com
Web site: www.derryjournal.com
Freq: 3 Times/Week
Circ: 24078 Not Audited
Profile: Online version of the Derry Journal newspaper covering local news and sports for the surrounding area.

Derry News
983119
Tel: 44 02871 296600
Email: caroline@derrynews.net
Web site: www.derrynews.net
Freq: 2 Times/Week
Circ: 8553 Not Audited
Editor: Ciaran O'Neill
Profile: Derry News is a local, weekly newspaper covering all the latest on local news, features and sport for the surrounding area. The paper is published on Mondays and Thursdays.
Ad Rate: Full Page Mono 1600.00
Ad Rate: Full Page Colour 2200.00

Dewsbury Reporter
980587
Editorial: c/o Floor 5, 26 Whitehall Road, Leeds, Leeds LS12 1BE
Tel: 44 01924 433013
Email: dewsbury.editorial@jpress.co.uk
Web site: http://www.dewsburyreporter.co.uk/
Freq: Weekly
Circ: 5000 Not Audited
Editor: John Kenealy
Profile: This is the online version of the Dewsbury Reporter, a weekly local newspaper covering the latest on local news, lifestyle and sport in Dewsbury.

Die Afrikaner
1060694
Tel: 44 27123 358523
Email: redakteur@hnp.org.za
Web site: http://www.dieafrikaner.co.za
Circ: 10000 Not Audited

Diss Express
980446
Editorial: Norfolk and Suffolk House, Mere Street, Diss IP22 3AE **Tel:** 44 01379 642264
Email: editorial@dissexpress.co.uk
Web site: http://www.dissexpress.co.uk/
Freq: Weekly
Circ: 4090 Not Audited
Profile: Online version of the Diss Express with local news, sports and features for the surrounding area.

Diss Mercury
980447
Editorial: 26 Mere Street, Diss, Diss IP22 4AD **Tel:** 44 01379 644517
Email: edpnewsdesk@archant.co.uk
Web site: www.dissmercury.co.uk
Freq: Weekly
Circ: 15327 Not Audited
Editor: Anthony Carroll
Profile: The Diss Mercury is a weekly local newspaper covering local news for the surrounding area.

The District Post
986988
Editorial: First Floor, 7-8 Sterling Buildings, Carfax, Horsham RH12 1DR
Tel: 44 01403 793777
Email: newsdesk@thedistrictpost.co.uk
Web site: www.thedistrictpost.co.uk
Freq: Weekly
Circ: 24000 Not Audited

The Docklands and East London Advertiser
980402
Editorial: Maritime House, 7th Floor, 1 Linton Road, Barking IG11 8HG
Tel: 44 02084 773793
Email: ela.editorial@archant.co.uk
Web site: www.eastlondonadvertiser.co.uk
Freq: Weekly
Circ: 6181 Not Audited

Doncaster Free Press
980518
Editorial: 39 Printing Office Street, Doncaster DN1 1TP **Tel:** 44 01302 819111
Email: editorial@doncastertoday.co.uk
Web site: www.doncastertoday.co.uk
Freq: Weekly
Circ: 29176 Not Audited
Editor: Nancy Fielder
Profile: Online version of the Doncaster Free Press newspaper covering local news, sports and lifestyle for the surrounding area.

Donside Piper
980650
Editorial: 1 Scott Skinner Square, Banchory, Aberdeenshire, Banchory AB31 5SE
Tel: 44 01330 824955
Email: news@deesidepiper.com
Web site: www.donsidepiper.com
Freq: Weekly
Circ: 744 Not Audited

Dorking and Leatherhead Advertiser
980539
Editorial: Aquila House, 35 London Rd, Redhill RH1 1NJ **Tel:** 44 01737 305581
Email: editor@dorkingadvertiser.co.uk
Web site: www.dorkingandleatherheadadvertiser.co.uk
Freq: Weekly
Circ: 5907 Not Audited
Profile: This is the online version of the Dorking Advertiser and the Leatherhead Advertiser, covering news, sports and local community for the surrounding area.

Dorset Advertiser
998503
Editorial: Fleet House, Hampshire Road, Weymouth, Weymouth DT4 9XD
Tel: 44 01305 830930
Email: newsdesk@dorsetecho.co.uk
Web site: www.dorsetecho.co.uk
Freq: Weekly
Circ: 60497 Not Audited
Editor: Diarmuid MacDonagh

Dorset Echo
97998
Editorial: Fleet House, Hampshire Road, Weymouth, Weymouth DT4 9XD
Tel: 44 01305 830930
Email: newsdesk@dorsetecho.co.uk
Web site: www.dorsetecho.co.uk
Freq: Daily
Circ: 10196 Not Audited
Editor: Diarmuid MacDonagh
Profile: The Dorset Echo is a daily regional newspaper and covers regional news, sports, business and leisure.
Ad Rate: Full Page Mono 1775.5C
Ad Rate: Full Page Colour 1972.8C

Dover Express
987669
Editorial: Rear Suite, Westcliffe House, West Cliff Gardens, Folkestone CT20 1FH
Tel: 44 01303 851655
Email: newsdesk.doverexpress@krnmedia.co.uk
Web site: www.dover-express.co.uk
Freq: Weekly
Circ: 4706 Not Audited
Profile: Online version of the Dover Express newspaper covering local news and sports for the surrounding area.

Down Recorder
983143
Editorial: 2-4 Church Street, County Down, Downpatrick BT30 6EJ
Tel: 44 02844 613711
Email: editor@thedownrecorder.co.uk
Web site: www.thedownrecorder.co.uk
Freq: Weekly
Circ: 9000 Not Audited
Editor: Paul Symington
Profile: Online version of the Down Recorder newspaper covering local news, sports and general features for the surrounding area.

Downend Voice
1057950
Editorial: Local Voice Network, 49 Dunkeld Vanue, Bristol BS34 7RQ
Tel: 44 01179 078585
Email: news@downendvoice.co.uk
Web site: http://www.downendvoice.co.uk/
Freq: Monthly
Circ: 11500 Not Audited

Downs Mail
980355
Editorial: 2 Forge House, Bearsted Green Business Park, Bearsted, Maidstone ME14 4DT **Tel:** 44 01622 630330
Email: info@downsmail.co.uk
Web site: www.downsmail.co.uk
Freq: Monthly
Circ: 88000 Not Audited
Editor: Simon Finlay
Profile: This is the online version of the Downs Mail, a monthly newspaper with local news, sports and lifestyle for the Maidstone and Malling area.

Driffield & Wolds Weekly
1074322
Tel: 44 01377 232875
Email: news@driffieldwoldsweekly.co.uk
Freq: Weekly

Droitwich Spa Advertiser
980328
Editorial: Berrow's House, Hylton Road, Worcester WR2 5JX **Tel:** 44 01905 742253
Web site: www.droitwichadvertiser.co.uk
Freq: Weekly
Circ: 37561 Not Audited
Profile: Website covering Droitwich news.

Droitwich Standard
987816
Editorial: Webb House, Church Green East, Redditch B98 8BP **Tel:** 44 01527 588688
Email: editor@droitwichstandard.co.uk
Web site: www.droitwichstandard.co.uk
Freq: Weekly
Circ: 11975 Not Audited
Editor: Tristan Harris
Profile: This is the online version of the Droitwich Standard, a weekly local newspaper covering all the latest on local news, sport and entertainment in Droitwich.

Dromore Leader
987139
Editorial: 12A Bow Street, County Down, Lisburn BT28 1BN **Tel:** 44 02838 393939
Email: news@dromoreleader.co.uk
Web site: www.dromoreleader.co.uk

Freq: Weekly
Circ: 1489 Not Audited
Editor: Damian Wilson
Profile: Website for local paper the Dromore Leader covering the latest news and events from the town of Dromore and the surrounding local area.

Dudley Chronicle 980564
Editorial: 51-53 Queen Street, Wolverhampton WV1 1ES
Tel: 44 01384 353201
Email: dudley.chrons@expressandstar.co.uk
Web site: http://yourchronicle.com/
Freq: Weekly
Circ: 34968 Not Audited
Profile: The Dudley Chronicle is a weekly, local newspaper covering all the latest news and current affairs for the surrounding area.

Dudley News 980565
Editorial: St John's House, St John's Road, Stourbridge, Stourbridge DY8 1EH
Tel: 44 01384 358283
Email: newsgrouped@midlands.newsquest.co.uk
Web site: www.dudleynews.co.uk
Freq: Weekly
Circ: 20125 Not Audited
Profile: Online version of the Dudley News newspaper covering local news and sports for the surrounding area. The outlet offers RSS (Really Simple Syndication).

The Dulwich Diverter 1074308
Email: dulwichdiverter@gmail.com
Web site: http://dulwichdiverter.tumblr.com
Freq: Bi-Monthly
Circ: 8000 Not Audited

Dumbarton & Vale of Leven Reporter 980651
Editorial: 1st Floor, Carus House, 201 Dumbarton Road, Clydebank G81 4XJ
Tel: 44 01414 358888
Email: editorial@dumbartonreporter.co.uk
Web site: www.dumbartonreporter.co.uk
Freq: Weekly
Circ: 1928 Not Audited

Dumfries & Galloway Standard 980652
Editorial: 1 Park Lane, Dumfries DG1 2AX
Tel: 44 01387 240342
Email: dgnews@s-un.co.uk
Web site: www.dailyrecord.co.uk/all-about/dumfries-galloway
Freq: 2 Times/Week
Circ: 14921 Not Audited
Profile: Online version of the Dumfries and Galloway Standard newspaper covering local news and sports for the surrounding area.

Dumfries Courier 980653
Editorial: 96 High Street, Annan, Dumfries & Galloway, Annandale DG12 6EJ
Tel: 44 01461 202078
Email: newsdesk@dngonline.co.uk
Web site: www.dumfriescourier.co.uk
Freq: Weekly
Circ: 20220 Not Audited
Editor: Bryan Armstrong
Profile: Dumfries Courier is a weekly local newspaper covering local news and sports for the surrounding area. The newspaper is published on a Friday.

Dunfermline Press & West of Fife Advertiser 980654
Editorial: Forsyth House, Pitreavie Business Park, Pitreavie Industrial Estate, Dunfermline KY11 8US **Tel:** 44 01383 747500
Email: editorial@dunfermlinepress.co.uk
Web site: www.dunfermlinepress.com
Freq: Weekly
Circ: 10156 Not Audited

Dunmow Broadcast 980293
Editorial: 54 High Street, Saffron Walden, Saffron Walden CB10 1EE
Tel: 44 01799 513000
Email: editor@dunmow-broadcast.co.uk
Web site: http://www.dunmow-broadcast.co.uk

Freq: Weekly
Circ: 12251 Not Audited
Editor: Stefan Bartlett
Profile: Website covering news and sport from Dunmow, North West Essex, Cambridge and Stansted with property, jobs, cars and entertainment.

Dunoon Observer & Argyllshire Standard 980655
Editorial: Dunoon Observer and Argyllshire Standard, 84 John Street, Dunoon, Argyll PA23 7NS **Tel:** 44 01369 706854
Email: editorial@dunoon-observer.com
Web site: www.dunoon-observer.com
Freq: Weekly
Circ: 4328 Not Audited
Editor: Gordon Neish
Ad Rate: Full Page Mono 1020.00
Ad Rate: Full Page Colour 1272.00

Dunstable Gazette 988819
Editorial: Media House, 39 Upper George Street, Luton, Luton LU1 2RD
Tel: 44 01582 700600
Email: editorial@lutonnews.co.uk
Web site: www.dunstabletoday.co.uk
Freq: Weekly
Circ: 2229 Not Audited
Editor: Olga Norford
Profile: The Dunstable Gazette is a weekly local newspaper covering the local news and sports for the surrounding area. The outlet offers RSS (Really Simple Syndication).
Ad Rate: Full Page Colour 569.16

Durham Times 984286
Editorial: Ribbel House, Unit 10, Mandale Business Park, Durham DH1 1TF
Tel: 44 01913 842261
Email: newsdesknorth@nne.co.uk
Web site: www.durhamtimes.co.uk
Freq: Weekly
Circ: 5500 Not Audited
Profile: Online version of the Durham Times newspaper covering local news, sports and business for the surrounding area. The outlet offers RSS (Really Simple Syndication).

Dursley Gazette 983841
Editorial: Gazette Series, 6 Lansdown Road, Stroud, Dursley GL5 1BE
Tel: 44 01453 544000
Email: gazette.news@dursleygazette.co.uk
Web site: www.gazetteseries.co.uk
Freq: Weekly
Circ: 4370 Not Audited
Editor: Michael Purton

Ealing Gazette Series 980400
Editorial: Stoke Mill, Woking Road, London QU1 1QA **Tel:** 44 01483 508700
Web site: www.getwestlondon.com
Freq: Weekly
Circ: 22448 Not Audited

Easingwold Advertiser & Weekly News 980459
Editorial: The Advertiser Office, Market Place, Easingwold, York YO61 3AB
Tel: 44 01347 821329
Email: news@easingwoldadvertiser.com
Web site: www.easingwoldadvertiser.com
Freq: Weekly
Circ: 15000 Not Audited
Profile: Geographical Focus: English Counties
Ad Rate: Full Page Mono 382.20
Ad Rate: Full Page Colour 477.75

East Anglian Daily Times 980531
Editorial: Portman House, 120 Princes Street, Ipswich IP4 1RS
Tel: 44 01473 230023
Email: newsroom@archant.co.uk
Web site: www.eadt.co.uk
Freq: Daily
Circ: 15852 Not Audited
Profile: The East Anglian Daily Times is a daily regional newspaper covering business, entertainment, regional news and sport for the surrounding area. This outlet offers RSS (Really Simple Syndication).
Ad Rate: Full Page Mono 2880.00
Ad Rate: Full Page Colour 4032.00

East Fife Mail 980656
Editorial: 23 Kirk Wynd, Kirkcaldy, Kirkcaldy KY1 1EP **Tel:** 44 01592 645700
Email: ffpnews@fifetoday.co.uk
Web site: www.fifetoday.co.uk
Freq: Weekly
Circ: 5270 Not Audited
Editor: Jerzy Morkis
Profile: The East Fife Mail is a weekly paper published every Wednesday, covering the latest local news and events from North East Fife.
Ad Rate: Full Page Colour 1000.00

East Grinstead Courier 980577
Editorial: Aquila House, 35 London Road, Redhill, Redhill RH1 1NJ
Tel: 44 01737 305568
Email: editor@egcourier.co.uk
Web site: http://www.eastgrinsteadcourier.co.uk/
Freq: Weekly
Circ: 3339 Not Audited

East Kent Mercury 980357
Editorial: 13 Queen Street, Deal, Deal CT14 6EX **Tel:** 44 01304 365526
Email: mercurynews@thekmgroup.co.uk
Web site: www.kentonline.co.uk/east_kent_mercury/news.aspx
Freq: Weekly
Circ: 7701 Not Audited
Editor: Bob Bounds
Profile: Website covering East Kent Mercury online newspaper. The Mercury won best newspaper of the year. The site features articles on community, sport and local education.

East Kilbride News 980129
Editorial: One Central Quay, Glasgow G3 8DA **Tel:** 44 01698 283200
Email: news@eastkilbridenews.co.uk
Web site: http://www.dailyrecord.co.uk/all-about/east-kilbride
Freq: Weekly
Circ: 5067 Not Audited
Profile: Online version of the East Kilbride News newspaper covering local news, sports and lifestyle for the surrounding area. The outlet offers RSS (Really Simple Syndication).

East Kilbride Post 988806
Tel: 44 01355 458160
Email: editorial@eastkilbridepost.co.uk
Web site: www.eastkilbridepost.co.uk
Freq: Di-Weekly
Circ: 75000 Not Audited
Editor: Karen Kelly

East London Enquirer 980403
Editorial: Unit 1, Molyneux Court, Radford Way, Billericay, Billericay CM12 0BT
Tel: 44 01277 627300
Email: newsdesk@theenquirer.co.uk
Web site: www.theenquirer.co.uk
Freq: Weekly
Circ: 60000 Not Audited
Profile: The East London Enquirer is a weekly free paper distributed throughout Essex and parts of East London covering the latest local news and events in Essex, Thurrock and East London. This outlet covers areas within Havering Borough.
Ad Rate: Full Page Mono 3672.00
Ad Rate: Full Page Colour 4773.00

East Lothian Courier 980657
Editorial: 56 Court Street, Haddington, Haddington EH41 3AF **Tel:** 44 01620 822451
Email: editorial@eastlothiancourier.com
Web site: http://www.eastlothiancourier.com
Freq: Weekly
Circ: 10229 Not Audited
Profile: Website for local paper the East Lothian Courier, covering the latest local news and events from East Lothian.

Eastbourne Herald 980285
Editorial: Berkeley House, 26 Gildredge Road, Eastbourne BN21 4SA
Tel: 44 01323 414488
Email: eastbourne.herald@jpress.co.uk
Web site: www.eastbourneherald.co.uk

Freq: Weekly
Circ: 16000 Not Audited
Profile: Website for local papers The Eastbourne Herald and the Eastbourne Gazette, covering the latest local news and events from Eastbourne.

Eastern Daily Press 980443
Editorial: Prospect House, Rouen Road, Norwich NR1 1RE **Tel:** 44 01603 628311
Email: newsdesk@archant.co.uk
Web site: www.edp24.co.uk
Freq: Daily
Circ: 34438 Not Audited
Editor: Anthony Carroll; **Editor:** Andrew Papworth
Profile: The Eastern Daily Press is a regional daily newspaper covering regional news, business, lifestyle features and sport for the surrounding area.
Ad Rate: Full Page Colour 3569.28

Eastwood & Kimberley Advertiser 980481
Editorial: 8 Heanor Road, Ilkeston, Ilkeston DE7 8ER **Tel:** 44 01623 450307
Email: news@eastwoodadvertiser.co.uk
Web site: www.eastwoodtoday.co.uk
Freq: Weekly
Circ: 3166 Not Audited
Editor: Martin Hutton
Profile: Website for the Eastwood & Kimberley Advertiser covering the latest local news and events from Eastwood, Kimberley, Newthorpe and the surrounding area.

Echo (Essex) 995947
Editorial: Echo Newapapers, Newspaper House, Chester Hall Lane, Basildon SS14 3BL **Tel:** 44 01268 522792
Email: echonews@newsquest.co.uk
Web site: http://www.echo-news.co.uk
Freq: Daily
Circ: 56380 Not Audited
Editor: Gary Pearson

Edinburgh Evening News 980032
Editorial: Orchard Brae House (Level 7), 30 Queensferry Road, Edinburgh EH4 2HS
Tel: 44 01313 117311
Email: newsen@edinburghnews.com
Web site: www.edinburghnews.com
Freq: Daily
Circ: 18362 Not Audited
Profile: The Edinburgh Evening News is a daily regional newspaper and covers regional news, sports, business and lifestyle for the surrounding area. This outlet offers RSS (Really Simple Syndication).
Ad Rate: Full Page Mono 5067.36
Ad Rate: Full Page Colour 6334.88

Ellesmere Port Pioneer 980219
Editorial: Maple House, Park West, Sealand Road, Chester CH1 4RN
Tel: 44 01513 562345
Email: pioneer@cheshirenews.co.uk
Web site: www.chesterchronicle.co.uk/all-about/ellesmere-port
Freq: Weekly
Circ: 1143 Not Audited
Profile: The Ellesmere Port Pioneer is a local paper covering the latest local news from Ellesmere Port. The paper is distributed throughout Ellesmere Port and Neston and is priced at 70p.
Ad Rate: Full Page Mono 1381.76
Ad Rate: Full Page Colour 1865.38

Ellesmere Port Standard 980220
Editorial: 56 Watergate Street, Chester CH1 2LA **Tel:** 44 01244 304500
Email: news@chesterfirst.co.uk
Web site: www.chesterfirst.co.uk
Freq: Weekly
Circ: 24785 Not Audited
Editor: Jonathan Barnett

Ellon Advertiser 980659
Editorial: Bridge Street Shopping Centre, Ellon AB41 9AA **Tel:** 44 01467 624488
Email: newsdesk@wpeters.co.uk
Web site: www.wpeters.co.uk/newspaper.html
Freq: Weekly
Circ: 14000 Not Audited

Regional & Local Weekly Newspapers

Editor: Jan Mackie

Ellon Times
980660

Editorial: 28-30 Seagate, Peterhead, Ellon AB42 1JP Tel: 44 01779 871332
Email: news@ellontimes.co.uk
Web site: www.ellontimes.co.uk
Freq: Weekly
Circ: 1012 Not Audited
Profile: This is the online version of the Ellon Times & East Gordon Advertiser, a weekly, local newspaper published on Thursdays, covering all the latest on local news, lifestyle and sport in Ellon and the surrounding area.

Elmbridge Comet
987690

Editorial: Floors 9 & 10, Quadrant House, The Quadrant, London SM2 5AS
Tel: 44 02087 226368
Email: newsdesk@surreycomet.co.uk
Web site: www.surreycomet.co.uk/elmbridge/
Freq: Weekly
Circ: 5500 Not Audited
Profile: The Elmbridge Guardian is a free weekly paper covering the latest local news from the Elmbridge District in Surrey. The paper is published every Thursday and is distributed to Esher, Cobham, Oxshott, Walton, Weybridge, Hersham, Claygate, the Dittons, East and West Molesey.Editions include; The Elmbridge Guardian (Esher & Cobham Edition)The Elmbridge Guardian (Walton & Weybridge Edition)
Ad Rate: Full Page Mono 539.00
Ad Rate: Full Page Colour 700.00

Ely News
980208

Editorial: 27 Market Place, Ely, Cambridge CB7 4NP Tel: 44 01353 667916
Email: editorial@cambridge-news.co.uk
Web site: www.ely-news.co.uk
Freq: Weekly
Circ: 13643 Not Audited
Profile: Ely Weekly News is a weekly paper covering the latest local news and events from Ely and its surrounding villages. The paper is published every Thursday and is priced at 45p.

Ely Standard
980207

Editorial: Alexander House, Fore Hill, Ely, Ely CB7 4AF Tel: 44 01353 665521
Email: editor@ely-standard.co.uk
Web site: www.ely-standard.co.uk
Freq: Weekly
Circ: 5505 Not Audited
Editor: John Elworthy
Profile: The Ely Standard is a weekly paper covering the latest news from Ely and the surrounding area. The paper is published every Thursday and is distributed in Ely, Littleport and Soham. It it priced at 55p but is also available free. Editions Include:Ely Standard (Soham)
Ad Rate: Full Page Colour 1227.06

The Ems
995385

Editorial: Emsworth Community Association Building, North Street, Emsworth PO10 7DD
Tel: 44 01243 430462
Email: editor@emsworthresidents.co.uk
Web site: http://www.emsworthresidents.co.uk/the-ems/
Freq: Quarterly
Circ: 8900 Not Audited

Enfield Independent
980404

Editorial: Observer House, Caxton Way, Watford, London WD18 8RJ
Tel: 44 01923 216216
Email: enfieldletters@london.newsquest.co.uk
Web site: www.enfieldindependent.co.uk
Freq: Weekly
Circ: 50714 Not Audited
Profile: Website for local paper the Enfield Independent covering the latest local news and events from Enfield and the surrounding areas.

Epping Forest Independent
982960

Editorial: Guardian Series, Observer House, Caxton Way, Watford WD18 8RJ
Tel: 44 01992 572285
Web site: http://www.guardian-series.co.uk

Freq: Weekly
Circ: 8058 Not Audited

Epsom Guardian
985144

Editorial: Floors 9 & 10, Quadrant House, The Quadrant, Sutton SM2 5AS
Tel: 44 02087 226300
Email: newsdesk@epsomguardian.co.uk
Web site: www.epsomguardian.co.uk
Freq: Weekly
Circ: 34869 Not Audited
Profile: Online version of the Epsom Guardian covering local news and sports for the area of Epsom, Ewell, Banstead, Leatherhead and Ashtead.

Epworth Bells & Crowle Advertiser
980385

Editorial: 39 Printing Office Street, Doncaster DN1 1TN Tel: 44 01302 819111
Email: editorial@epworthtoday.co.uk
Web site: www.epworthbells.co.uk
Freq: Weekly
Circ: 2471 Not Audited
Profile: The Epworth Bells & Crowle Advertiser is a weekly, local newspaper published on Thursdays, covering all the latest on local news, lifestyle and sport in Epworth and the Isle of Axholme.
Ad Rate: Full Page Mono 197.92
Ad Rate: Full Page Colour 257.90

Eshowe Watch
1060688

Tel: 44 27354 741463
Email: eshowejourno@zululandobserver.co.za
Freq: Weekly
Circ: 6200 Not Audited

Eskdale and Liddesdale Advertiser
980661

Editorial: Commercial House, High Street, Langholm DG13 0JH Tel: 44 01387 380012
Email: eskdale.news@cumbrian-newspapers.co.uk
Web site: www.eladvertiser.co.uk
Freq: Weekly
Circ: 1333 Not Audited
Profile: This is the online version of the Eskdale and Liddesdale Advertiser, a weekly local newspaper covering all the latest news and events from Eskdale, Liddesdale, Langholm, Lockerbie and Hawick.

Espoo Esbo -lehti
1061001

Tel: 44 35894 2427330
Email: uutiset@espoo-lehti.fi
Web site: http://www.espoo.fi
Freq: Quarterly
Circ: 105000 Not Audited

The Essential Journal
1053622

Editorial: The Arts Village, Henry Street, Liverpool L1 5BL Tel: 44 01517 076759
Email: info@essentialjournal.co.uk
Web site: http://www.essentialjournal.co.uk/
Freq: Monthly
Circ: 50000 Not Audited

Art, Fashion, Literature, Men's Interests, Regional General Interest, Theater & Performing Arts, Visual Arts

Essex Chronicle
980294

Editorial: First Floor, Kestrel House, Hedgerows Business Park, Springfield, Chelmsford CM2 5PF Tel: 44 01245 602721
Email: newsdesk@essexchronicle.co.uk
Web site: www.essexchronicle.co.uk
Freq: Weekly
Circ: 16689 Not Audited
Profile: Online version of the Essex Chronicle covering the latest local news and sports from the surrounding area.

Essex County Standard
980296

Editorial: Unit 1 Brunel Court, Brunel Way, Severalls Industrial Estate, Colchester, Colchester CO4 9XP Tel: 44 01206 508288
Email: gazette.newsdesk@newsquest.co.uk
Web site: www.essexcountystandard.co.uk/
Freq: Weekly
Circ: 10549 Not Audited
Profile: Online version of the Essex County Standard newspaper covering local news and sports for the surrounding area.

Essex Enquirer
980295

Editorial: Independent House, Radford Business Centre, Billericay, Billericay CM12 0AA Tel: 44 01277 627300
Email: newsdesk@theenquirer.co.uk
Web site: www.theenquirer.co.uk
Freq: Weekly
Circ: 60000 Not Audited
Profile: The Essex Enquirer is a weekly free paper distributed throughout parts of Essex and London, covering the latest local news and events from the area. The paper is published every Thursday. This outlet covers areas within Havering Borough.
Ad Rate: Full Page Mono 3672.00
Ad Rate: Full Page Colour 4773.60

Evening Express (Aberdeen)
980009

Editorial: Lang stracht, Mastrick, Aberdeen AB15 6DF Tel: 44 01224 344150
Email: ee.news@ajl.co.uk
Web site: www.eveningexpress.co.uk
Freq: Daily
Circ: 25744 Not Audited
Editor: Alan McCabe

Evening Telegraph (Dundee)
980007

Editorial: 2 Albert Square, Dundee DD1 1DD
Tel: 44 01382 575879
Email: newsdesk@eveningtelegraph.co.uk
Web site: http://www.eveningtelegraph.co.uk/
Freq: Daily
Circ: 14971 Not Audited

Evening Times (Glasgow)
980030

Editorial: 200 Renfield Street, Glasgow G2 3QB Tel: 44 01413 027000
Email: news@eveningtimes.co.uk
Web site: www.eveningtimes.co.uk
Freq: Daily
Circ: 23696 Not Audited
Editor: Graham Shields
Profile: The Evening Times (Glasgow) is a daily regional newspaper and covers regional news, sports and business. The outlet offers RSS (Really Simple Syndication).
Ad Rate: Full Page Colour 1000.00

Evesham and Cotswold Journal
980331

Editorial: Evesham and Cotswold Journal, Berrows House, Hylton Road, Worcester WR2 5JX Tel: 44 01905 748200
Email: news@eveshamjournal.co.uk
Web site: www.eveshamjournal.co.uk
Freq: Weekly
Circ: 25032 Not Audited

Evesham Observer
984264

Editorial: 20a Webb House, Church Green East, Redditch B98 8BP
Tel: 44 01527 588688
Email: editor@eveshamobserver.co.uk
Web site: www.eveshamobserver.co.uk
Freq: Weekly
Circ: 13399 Not Audited
Editor: Rob George
Profile: Website for local paper the Evesham Observer covering the latest local news and events from Evesham and the surrounding area.

The Examiner
996566

Tel: 44 02830 868500
Email: editor@crossexaminer.co.uk
Web site: www.crossexaminer.co.uk
Freq: Weekly
Circ: 6500 Not Audited
Editor: Gerry Murray
Profile: The Examiner is a weekly, local newspaper covering all the latest on local news and entertainment for Crossmaglen, South Armagh, Newry and Down.
Ad Rate: Full Page Mono 360.00
Ad Rate: Full Page Colour 420.00

Exmouth Herald
980257

Editorial: Fair Oak Close, Exeter Airport Business Park, Clyst Honiton, Exeter EX5 2UL Tel: 44 01392 888400
Email: devon@archant.co.uk

Web site: www.exmouthherald.co.uk
Freq: Weekly
Circ: 14593 Not Audited
Profile: Website for local newspaper the Exmouth Herald, covering the latest local news and events from Exmouth and the surrounding local area.

Exmouth Journal
981512

Editorial: Archant South West, Fair Oak Close, Exeter Airport Business Park, Exeter EX5 2UL Tel: 44 01392 888400
Email: devon@archant.co.uk
Web site: www.exmouthjournal.co.uk
Freq: Weekly
Circ: 5461 Not Audited
Profile: The Exmouth Journal is a weekly local newspaper and covers local news and sports for the surrounding area. The newspaper is published on a Thursday.
Ad Rate: Full Page Mono 450.00

Express & Echo
980258

Editorial: Queens House, Little Queen Street, Exeter EX2 3LJ Tel: 44 01392 349000
Email: echonews@expressandecho.co.uk
Web site: www.devonlive.com/
Freq: 2 Times/Week
Circ: 12268 Not Audited
Editor: Jim Parker; Editor: Patrick Phelvin
Profile: Online version of the Express & Echo newspaper covering local news and sports for the surrounding area.

Express & Star
980011

Editorial: 51-53 Queen Street, Wolverhampton WV1 1ES
Tel: 44 01902 313131
Email: newsdesk@expressandstar.co.uk
Web site: www.expressandstar.com
Freq: Daily
Circ: 55373 Not Audited
Editor: Keith Harrison
Profile: The Express & Star is a daily regional newspaper covering regional news, sports and business for the surrounding area. The newspaper was first published in 1874. The outlet offers RSS (Really Simple Syndication).
Ad Rate: Full Page Mono 8034.00
Ad Rate: Full Page Colour 8034.00

Fakenham & Wells Times
986667

Editorial: 22 Norwich Street, Fakenham NR21 9AE Tel: 44 01328 862679
Web site: www.fakenhamtimes.co.uk
Freq: Weekly
Circ: 1735 Not Audited
Profile: Website covering news for Fakenham and Wells Times.

The Falkirk Herald
980662

Editorial: 4A Gateway Business Park, Beancross Road, Grangemouth FK3 8WX
Tel: 44 01324 690222
Email: editorial@falkirkherald.co.uk
Web site: www.falkirkherald.co.uk
Freq: Weekly
Circ: 19682 Not Audited
Editor: Jill Buchanan
Profile: Online version of the Falkirk Herald newspaper and covers local news, lifestyle and sports for the surrounding area.

The Farnham Herald Series
980540

Editorial: The Old Court House, Union Road, Farnham, Farnham GU9 7PT
Tel: 44 01252 725224
Email: news@farnhamherald.com
Web site: www.farnhamherald.com
Freq: Weekly
Circ: 20526 Not Audited
Editor: Tony Short

Faversham News
980358

Editorial: Gazette House, 5-8 Estuary View Business Park, Boorman Way, Whitstable CT5 3SE Tel: 44 01227 768181
Email: favershamnews@thekmgroup.co.uk
Web site: www.kentonline.co.uk
Freq: Weekly
Circ: 1893 Not Audited
Profile: The faversham News is a weekly paper covering the latest local news and

events from Faversham and the surrounding area. The paper is priced 95p.
Ad Rate: Full Page Mono 813.28
Ad Rate: Full Page Colour 1016.60

Faversham Times 983525
Editorial: Kent Innovation Centre, Thanet Reach Business Park, Broadstairs, Broadstairs CT10 2QQ
Tel: 44 01843 609637
Email: newsdesk.times@krnmedia.co.uk
Web site: www.canterburytimes.co.uk
Freq: Weekly
Circ: 21940 Not Audited
Profile: Website for local paper the Faversham Times, covering the latest news and events in Faversham.

Felix 981761
Editorial: Beit Quad, Prince Consort Road, London SW7 2BB **Tel:** 44 02075 948072
Email: felix@imperial.ac.uk
Web site: www.felixonline.co.uk
Freq: Weekly
Circ: 5000 Not Audited
Profile: Newspaper covering news and reviews, sport, competitions, topical and scientific features.
Ad Rate: Full Page Colour 1650.00
Student Lifestyle

Fenland Citizen 980209
Editorial: Limes House, Purfleet House, Kings Lynn, King's Lynn PE30 1HL
Tel: 44 01553 761188
Email: news@fenlandcitizen.co.uk
Web site: http://www.fenlandcitizen.co.uk/
Freq: Weekly
Circ: 31865 Not Audited
Editor: Mark Leslie
Profile: Website for weekly newspaper the Fenland Citizen covering the latest local news and events from Wisbech, March and Chatteris.

Fermanagh Herald 983125
Tel: 44 02866 322066
Email: editor@fermanaghherald.com
Web site: www.fermanaghherald.com
Freq: Weekly
Circ: 10254 Not Audited
Editor: Maurice Kennedy
Profile: Website of The Fermanagh Herald, a weekly newspaper covering local news, sports and events for the Fermanagh area.

Fife & Kinross Extra 980663
Editorial: Pitreavie Business Park, Dunfermline, Dunfermline KY11 8QS
Tel: 44 01383 747500
Email: editorial@dunfermlinepress.co.uk
Web site: www.dunfermlinepress.com
Freq: Weekly
Circ: 13241 Not Audited
Profile: The Fife & Kinross Extra is a weekly, local newspaper covering all the latest news and current affairs for the surrounding area.
Ad Rate: Full Page Mono 2041.00
Ad Rate: Full Page Colour 4082.00

Fife Free Press 980664
Editorial: 23 Kirk Wynd, Kirkcaldy, Kirkcaldy KY1 1EP **Tel:** 44 01592 645700
Email: ffpnews@fifetoday.co.uk
Web site: www.fifetoday.co.uk
Freq: Weekly
Circ: 11510 Not Audited
Editor: Allan Crow
Profile: Online version of the Fife Free Press newspaper covering local news and sports for the surrounding area.

Fife Herald 980665
Editorial: 23 Kirk Wynd, Kirkcaldy, Kirkcaldy KY1 1EP **Tel:** 44 01592 598808
Email: ffpnews@fifetoday.co.uk
Web site: www.fifetoday.co.uk
Freq: Weekly
Circ: 9129 Not Audited
Editor: Jerzy Morkis

Filey & Hunmanby Mercury 980461
Editorial: Newchase Court, Hopper Hill Road, Scarborough YO11 3YS
Tel: 44 01723 860100
Email: newsdesk@ymltd.co.uk
Web site: www.fileymercury.co.uk
Freq: Weekly
Circ: 35693 Not Audited
Profile: Website for local paper the Filey & Hunmanby Mercury, covering the latest news and events from Scarborough and the local area.

Filton Voice 986534
Tel: 44 07775 550607
Web site: www.filtonvoice.co.uk
Freq: Monthly
Circ: 7000 Not Audited

Fleetwood Weekly News 980373
Editorial: 168 Lord Street, Fleetwood FY7 6SR **Tel:** 44 01253 361721
Email: newsroom@fleetwoodweekly.co.uk
Web site: www.fleetwoodtoday.co.uk
Freq: Weekly
Circ: 3943 Not Audited
Profile: Website of The Fleetwood Weekly News, a weekly newspaper featuring local news, sports and lifestyle.

Flintshire Chronicle 980608
Editorial: Maple House, Park West, Sealand Road, Chester CH1 4RN
Tel: 44 01492 574452
Email: chroniclenews@cheshirenews.co.uk
Web site: www.flintshirechronicle.co.uk
Freq: Weekly
Circ: 4355 Not Audited
Profile: Flintshire Chronicle is a weekly local newspaper and covers local news and sports for the surrounding area. The newspaper is published on Thursdays.
Ad Rate: Full Page Mono 1185.92
Ad Rate: Full Page Colour 1600.92

Flintshire Standard 980609
Editorial: Mold Business Park, Wrexham Road, Mold, Mold CH7 1XY
Tel: 44 01352 707707
Email: news@leaderlive.co.uk
Web site: http://www.leaderlive.co.uk/
Freq: Weekly
Circ: 23756 Not Audited
Profile: The Flintshire Standard is a free weekly paper published every Wednesday covering the latest local news and events from Flintshire.
Ad Rate: Full Page Mono 1307.00
Ad Rate: Full Page Colour 1699.10

Focus Newspapers 998890
Editorial: PO Box 238, St Albans, London AL1 1WE **Tel:** 44 01727 757475
Email: editorial@focusnewspapers.co.uk
Web site: http://focusnewspapers.co.uk/
Freq: MonthlyNot Audited
Editor: Stefanie Hayes

Folkestone & Hythe Express 995926
Editorial: Express House, 34-36 North Street, Ashford, Ashford TN24 8JR
Tel: 44 01233 895801
Web site: www.kentonline.co.uk/folkestone
Freq: Weekly
Circ: 1560 Not Audited
Editor: Robert Barman

Folkestone Herald 980359
Editorial: Rear Suite, Westcliffe House, West Cliff Gardens, Folkestone CT20 1SZ
Tel: 44 01303 850999
Email: newsdesk.folkestone@krnmedia.co.uk
Web site: www.folkestoneherald.co.uk
Freq: Weekly
Circ: 12975 Not Audited
Editor: Lesley Finlay
Profile: Website for local paper the Folkestone Herald covering the latest news and events from the Shepway District in Kent.

Forest of Dean and Wye Valley Review 980302
Editorial: The Tindle Suite, Kings Building, Hill Street, Lydney GL15 5HE
Tel: 44 01594 841113
Email: revieweditor@theforestreview.co.uk
Web site: www.forest-and-wye-today.co.uk
Freq: Weekly
Circ: 46034 Not Audited
Editor: Mark Elson
Profile: Website covering news, sport, jobs, motors in Forest of Dean and Wye Valley areas.

The Forester 980303
Editorial: 43 High Street, Cinderford, Cinderford GL14 2SL
Web site: www.theforester.co.uk
Freq: Weekly
Circ: 8316 Not Audited
Editor: Andy Sherwill
Profile: Online version of the Forester, Cinderford Forester, Lydney Forester, Newent Forester and Coleford Forester, covering local news and sports for the surrounding areas. The outlet offers RSS (Really Simple Syndication).

Forfar Dispatch 980666
Editorial: 117-119 Castle Street, Forfar DD8 3AH **Tel:** 44 01307 464899
Email: news@forfardispatch.com
Web site: www.forfardispatch.co.uk
Freq: Weekly
Circ: 1652 Not Audited
Profile: This is the online version of the Forfar Dispatch, a weekly, local newspaper covering all the latest news, sport, lifestyle and community for the surrounding area.

Forres Gazette 980667
Editorial: 133-135 High Street, Forres, Forres IV36 1DX **Tel:** 44 01309 672615
Email: newsdesk@forres-gazette.co.uk
Web site: http://www.forres-gazette.co.uk
Freq: Weekly
Circ: 1999 Not Audited
Editor: Mike Collins; **Editor:** Tanya McLaren
Profile: This is the online version of the Forres Gazette, a weekly, local newspaper covering all the latest news, sport and property for the surrounding area.

Fraserburgh Herald 980668
Editorial: 60 High Street, Fraserburgh AB43 9HP **Tel:** 44 01346 513900
Email: news@fraserburghherald.com
Web site: www.fraserburghherald.co.uk
Freq: Weekly
Circ: 2962 Not Audited
Profile: The Fraserburgh Herald is a weekly, local newspaper, published on Thursdays, covering all the latest on local news, sport and lifestyle in Fraserburgh.
Ad Rate: Full Page Mono 618.00
Ad Rate: Full Page Colour 803.00

Frome Standard 981550
Editorial: 78b High Street, Midsomer Norton BA3 2DE **Tel:** 44 01761 417778
Email: editor@fromestandard.co.uk
Web site: www.somersetlive.co.uk
Freq: Weekly
Circ: 3915 Not Audited
Profile: Website of The Frome Standard, a weekly paper covering the latest local news and events from Frome and surrounding villages.

Frome Times 980505
Editorial: 31 Market Place, Melksham, Melksham SN12 6ES **Tel:** 44 01373 452109
Email: news@frometimes.co.uk
Web site: www.frometimes.co.uk
Freq: Bi-Weekly
Circ: 13050 Not Audited
Profile: Website for fortnightly publication, The Frome Times covering the latest local news and events from Frome.

Frome Valley Voice 1057949
Editorial: 33 Footes Lane, Frampton Cotterell, Bristol BS36 2JG
Tel: 44 01454 800120

Web site: http://www.fromevalleyvoice.co.uk/
Freq: Monthly
Circ: 7500 Not Audited
Editor: Richard Drew

Gainsborough Standard 980386
Editorial: Unit 1B Marshall's Yard, Beaumont Street, Gainsborough DN21 2NA
Tel: 44 01427 615323
Email: newsroom@gainsboroughstandard.co.uk
Web site: www.gainsboroughtoday.co.uk
Freq: Weekly
Circ: 2956 Not Audited
Profile: Website for local paper the Gainsborough Standard covering the latest news and events from Gainsborough and the surrounding local area.

Gairloch & District Times 998715
Editorial: Gairloch Community Hall, Achtercairn, Gairloch, Strathpeffer IV21 2BP
Tel: 44 01445 712856
Email: editor@gairlochtimes.co.uk
Web site: http://www.gairlochtimes.co.uk
Freq: Bi-Weekly
Circ: 2200 Not Audited
Editor: Phil Staton

The Galleon 998180
Editorial: Uni. of Portsmouth Student Union, The Student Centre, Cambridge Road, Portsmouth P01 2EP **Tel:** 44 02392 843657
Email: editor@galleonnews.com
Web site: www.galleonnews.com
Freq: Bi-Weekly
Circ: 3000 Not Audited
Student Lifestyle

Galloway Gazette 980669
Editorial: 71 Victoria Street, Newton Stewart, Wigtownshire, Galloway DG8 6NL
Email: editorial@gallowaygazette.com
Web site: www.gallowaygazette.com
Freq: Weekly
Circ: 12146 Not Audited
Editor: David Walker
Profile: Website for local paper the Galloway Gazette covering the latest local news and events from Galloway and the surrounding area.

The Galloway News 000070
Editorial: Park Lane, Dumfries DG1 2AX
Tel: 44 01387 255252
Email: gallowaynews@s-un.co.uk
Web site: www.dailyrecord.co.uk/all-about/dumfries-galloway
Freq: Weekly
Circ: 5252 Not Audited
Editor: Iain Pollock
Profile: This is the online version of the Galloway News, a weekly local paper covering the latest local news and events from Galloway and the surrounding area.

Garstang Courier 980374
Editorial: Oliver's Place, Fulwood, Preston PR1 9ZA **Tel:** 44 01772 838107
Email: garstang.courier@jpress.co.uk
Web site: www.garstangcourier.co.uk
Freq: Weekly
Circ: 4300 Not Audited
Profile: Online version of the Garstang Courier covering local news, lifestyle and sports for the surrounding area.

Gazette & Herald (Ryedale) 980470
Editorial: 22 Yorkersgate, Malton, Malton YO17 7AB **Tel:** 44 01904 567149
Email: gazette@gazetteherald.co.uk
Web site: www.gazetteherald.co.uk
Freq: Weekly
Circ: 7628 Not Audited
Profile: The Gazette and Herald is a weekly paper, published every Wednesday covering the latest local news from Ryedale and the surrounding area.
Ad Rate: Full Page Mono 2145.00
Ad Rate: Full Page Colour 2681.00

Regional & Local Weekly Newspapers

Section 2 UK Newspapers

The Gazette (Blackpool)   979963
Editorial: Avroe House, Avroe Crescent, Blackpool FY4 2DP **Tel:** 44 01253 400888
Email: editorial@blackpoolgazette.co.uk
Web site: www.blackpoolgazette.co.uk
Freq: Daily
Circ: 9537 Not Audited
Editor: Gillian Parkinson
Profile: The Gazette (Blackpool) is a regional daily newspaper distributed in the Blackpool and Fylde Coast area and covers regional news, sports and lifestyle from the area.
Ad Rate: Full Page Mono 420.00
Ad Rate: Full Page Colour 600.00

The Gazette (Johnstone & Renfrewshire)   980128
Editorial: 1st Floor, Carus House, 201 Dumbarton Road, Clydebank G81 4XJ
Tel: 44 01414 358888
Email: editorial@the-gazette.co.uk
Web site: www.the-gazette.co.uk
Freq: Weekly
Circ: 3247 Not Audited

The Gazette (Middlesbrough/Teesside)   979990
Editorial: Hudson Quay, The Halyard, Middlesbrough TS3 6RT
Tel: 44 01642 245401
Email: news@gazettemedia.co.uk
Web site: www.gazettelive.co.uk
Freq: Daily
Circ: 21174 Not Audited
Editor: Chris Styles

Glamorgan Gazette (Bridgend)   983021
Editorial: 6 Park Street, Cardiff CF10 1XR
Tel: 44 02920 243600
Email: glamorgan.gazette@walesonline.co.uk
Web site: www.walesonline.co.uk/all-about/bridgend
Freq: Weekly
Circ: 5637 Not Audited

Glamorgan Gem   998777
Editorial: Graig House, 53 Eastgate, Cowbridge CF71 7EL **Tel:** 44 01446 774484
Email: editorial@glamorgan-gem.co.uk
Web site: http://www.glamorgan-gem.co.uk/
Freq: Weekly
Circ: 46026 Not Audited
Editor: Caroline Attya

Glasgow South & Eastwood Extra   980671
Editorial: Park House, Academy Park, Gower Street, Glasgow G51 1PT
Tel: 44 01414 277878
Email: glasgow.editorial@jpress.co.uk
Web site: www.glasgowsouthandeastwoodextra.co.uk
Freq: Weekly
Circ: 25126 Not Audited

Glenfield Gazette   983115
Editorial: PO Box 9980, Glenfield, Leicester LE3 7DB **Tel:** 44 01162 874774
Email: glenfieldgazette@btinternet.com
Web site: www.glenfieldonline.co.uk
Freq: Monthly
Circ: 5000 Not Audited
Editor: Ken Russell
Profile: Local newspaper for the Glenfield area covering civic, social and industrial matters, women, health and beauty, radio and TV, children, toys, books, puzzles, entertainment, CDs, videos, travel and recreational activities.

Glenrothes Gazette   980673
Editorial: 23 Kirk Wynd, Kirkcaldy, Kirkcaldy KY1 1EP **Tel:** 44 01592 645700
Email: ffpnews@fifetoday.co.uk
Web site: http://www.fifetoday.co.uk/news/local-headlines/glenrothes
Freq: Weekly
Circ: 4530 Not Audited
Editor: Allan Crow

Glossop Chronicle   980250
Editorial: Quest Media Centre, Cavendish Mill Rear Entrance, Bank Street, Ashton-under-Lyne OL6 7DN **Tel:** 44 01613 312574
Email: editorial@reporterandchronicle.co.uk
Web site: www.tamesidereporter.com
Freq: Weekly
Circ: 32500 Not Audited
Editor: David Jones
Profile: The Glossop Chronicle is a weekly local newspaper covering local news and sports for the surrounding area.

Gloucester Citizen   980304
Editorial: Third Floor, St James' House, St James' Square, Cheltenham GL50 3PR
Tel: 44 01242 278000
Email: citizen.news@glosmedia.co.uk
Web site: http://www.gloucestershirelive.co.uk/
Freq: Daily
Circ: 8771 Not Audited
Editor: Jenny Eastwood
Profile: The Gloucester Citizen is a daily regional newspaper published from Monday to Saturday and covers regional news, sports, business and features for Gloucestershire.
Ad Rate: Full Page Mono 1904.00
Ad Rate: Full Page Colour 1999.20

Gloucester Review   987198
Editorial: The Tindle Suite, Kings Buildings, Hill Street, Lydney GL15 5HE
Tel: 44 01594 841113
Email: stories@glosnews.com
Web site: www.gloucesterreview.co.uk
Freq: Weekly
Circ: 10000 Not Audited
Editor: John Hawkins
Profile: The Gloucester News is a free weekly local newspaper covering local news and sports for the surrounding area.

Gloucestershire Echo   979982
Editorial: Third Floor, St James' House, St James' Square, Cheltenham GL50 3PR
Tel: 44 01242 278000
Email: echo.news@glosmedia.co.uk
Web site: http://www.gloucestershirelive.co.uk/
Freq: Daily
Circ: 13221 Not Audited
Editor: Matt Holmes
Profile: The Gloucestershire Echo is a daily regional newspaper covering regional news and sports for the surrounding area. The outlet offers RSS (Really Simple Syndication).
Ad Rate: Full Page Mono 2404.00
Ad Rate: Full Page Colour 2404.00

Gloucestershire Gazette Series   980305
Editorial: 6 Lansdown Road, Stroud GL5 1BE **Tel:** 44 01453 762412
Email: gazette.news@gazetteseries.co.uk
Web site: www.gazetteseries.co.uk
Freq: Weekly
Circ: 8094 Not Audited
Editor: Michael Purton

GO!   989271
Tel: 44 01892 681000
Email: whatson@courier.co.uk
Web site: www.courier.co.uk Not Audited

Good News Liverpool   1100051
Editorial: The Loft, Cotton Exchange, Bixteth Street, Liverpool L3 9LQ
Email: editorial@goodnewsliverpool.co.uk
Web site: http://www.goodnewsliverpool.co.uk/
Freq: Monthly
Circ: 15000 Not Audited
Editor: Rebecca Keegan

Goole Courier   998615
Editorial: 102 Boothferry Road, Goole, Goole DN14 6AE **Tel:** 44 01405 720110
Email: editorial@gooletimes.info
Freq: Weekly
Circ: 13186 Not Audited
Editor: Jane Rogers

Goole Times   980387
Editorial: 102 Boothferry Road, Goole, Goole DN14 6AE **Tel:** 44 01405 720110
Email: editorial@gooletimes.info
Web site: www.gooletimes.info
Freq: Weekly
Circ: 13750 Not Audited
Editor: Jane Rogers
Profile: Website for the Goole Times providing the latest local news and events from Goole and the surrounding villages.

Grange Now   982482
Tel: 44 01539 535453
Email: info@grangenow.co.uk
Web site: http://www.grangenow.co.uk/
Freq: Monthly
Circ: 7000 Not Audited
Profile: Magazine covering local news, issues, clubs and societies, schools, churches and local organisations.
Ad Rate: Full Page Mono 372.75

Grantham Journal   981547
Editorial: St Peter's Hill, St Peter's House, Grantham NG31 6QB **Tel:** 44 01476 562291
Email: comment@granthamjournal.co.uk
Web site: www.granthamjournal.co.uk
Freq: Weekly
Circ: 9066 Not Audited
Profile: Website for local paper the Grantham Journal providing the latest local news and events from Grantham and the surrounding villages.

Gravesend Reporter   983083
Editorial: Kent House, 81 Station Road, Ashford TN23 1PP **Tel:** 44 01233 653465
Email: feedback@gravesendreporter.co.uk
Web site: www.gravesendreporter.co.uk
Freq: Weekly
Circ: 27544 Not Audited
Profile: Website for local paper Gravesend Reporter providing the latest local news and events from Gravesend, Swanley and Dartford.

Great Yarmouth Mercury   980450
Editorial: 1st floor, 169 King Street, Great Yarmouth, Norwich NR30 2PA
Tel: 44 01493 847961
Web site: www.greatyarmouthmercury.co.uk
Freq: Weekly
Circ: 11305 Not Audited
Profile: The Great Yarmouth Mercury is a weekly local newspaper covering all the latest local news and sport for the borough of Great Yarmouth.
Ad Rate: Full Page Mono 1396.80
Ad Rate: Full Page Colour 1815.84

Greenock Telegraph   980674
Editorial: 2 Crawfurd Street, Greenock PA15 1LH **Tel:** 44 01475 726511
Email: editorial@greenocktelegraph.co.uk
Web site: www.greenocktelegraph.co.uk
Freq: Daily
Circ: 9555 Not Audited
Editor: Brian Hossack
Profile: The Greenock Telegraph is a regional daily newspaper covering regional news, sports and features for the surrounding area.
Ad Rate: Full Page Mono 5749.59
Ad Rate: Full Page Colour 5749.59

The Greenwich Visitor   999646
Web site: www.thegreenwichvisitor.com
Freq: Monthly
Circ: 40000 Not Audited

Grimsby & Cleethorpes Advertiser   983022
Editorial: 80 Cleethorpe Road, Grimsby DN31 3EH **Tel:** 44 01472 360360
Email: newsdesk@grimsbytelegraph.co.uk
Web site: www.grimsbytelegraph.co.uk
Freq: Weekly Not Audited

Grimsby Telegraph   980388
Editorial: First Floor, Heritage House, Fisherman's Wharf, Grimsby DN31 1SY
Tel: 44 01472 808000
Email: newsdesk@grimsbytelegraph.co.uk
Web site: www.grimsbytelegraph.co.uk
Freq: Daily
Circ: 16406 Not Audited
Profile: The Grimsby Telegraph is a daily newspaper providing the latest news, sport, business, entertainment and lifestyle articles. The publication is available around Grimsby, the towns of Immingham and Cleethorpes as well as in the region of North East Lincolnshire.
Ad Rate: Full Page Colour 2467.00

Grocotts Mail   1060358
Tel: 44 27466 227222
Freq: 2 Times/Week
Circ: 2348 Not Audited

Guardian Series (East London and West Essex)   995770
Editorial: Observer House, Caxton Way, Watford, London WD18 8RJ
Tel: 44 01923 216216
Web site: http://www.guardian-series.co.uk/
Freq: Weekly
Circ: 10051 Not Audited

The Guernsey Globe   984770
Editorial: PO Box 57, Braye Road, Saint Peter Port GY1 3BW **Tel:** 44 01481 240237
Email: newsroom@guernseypress.com
Web site: www.thisisguernsey.com
Freq: Weekly
Circ: 15000 Not Audited
Editor: Shaun Green
Profile: The Guernsey Globe is a free paper published every Wednesday covering the latest local news and events from Guernsey.
Ad Rate: Full Page Mono 1165.00
Ad Rate: Full Page Colour 2272.00

Guernsey Press and Star   981716
Editorial: PO Box 57, Braye Road, Vale, Guernsey GY1 3BW **Tel:** 44 01481 240240
Email: newsroom@guernseypress.com
Web site: http://guernseypress.com/
Freq: Daily
Circ: 12580 Not Audited
Editor: Shaun Green
Profile: The Guernsey Press and Star is the only daily newspaper published on the island of Guernsey. The paper provides local news and sport and features daily business pages that focus on the island's commercial and financial activities. There are also features on the island's daily life plus letters and commentary on the major issues of the day. This outlet offers RSS (Really Simple Syndication).
Ad Rate: Full Page Mono 1190.00
Ad Rate: Full Page Colour 2315.00

The Guide (Prestwich & Whitefield)   980430
Editorial: The Wellsprings, Civic Centre, Victoria Square, Bolton BL1 1AR
Tel: 44 01204 537274
Email: newsdesk@nqnw.co.uk
Web site: www.prestwichandwhitefieldguide.co.uk
Freq: Weekly
Circ: 1347 Not Audited
Editor: Michael Crutchley

Guth Bharraidh   995492
Editorial: Castlebay, Isle Of Barra, Isle of Lewis HS9 5XD **Tel:** 44 01871 810401
Email: barra.news@vabv.org.uk
Web site: www.isleofbarra.com
Freq: Weekly Not Audited
Editor: John MacNeil

Gwent Gazette   983023
Editorial: 6 Park Street, Cardiff CF10 1XR
Tel: 44 01685 789230
Email: gwent.gazette@walesonline.co.uk
Web site: www.walesonline.co.uk/all-about/blaenau%20gwent
Freq: Weekly
Circ: 1646 Not Audited
Profile: The Gwent Gazette is a weekly local newspaper covering all the latest news, sport and lifestyle for the surrounding area.
Ad Rate: Full Page Mono 1452.48
Ad Rate: Full Page Colour 1960.85

Hackney Citizen　　　　985624
Editorial: Unit 10, Celia Fiennes House, 8-20 Well Street, London E9 7PX
Tel: 44 02089 863010
Email: info@hackneycitizen.co.uk
Web site: www.hackneycitizen.co.uk
Freq: Monthly
Circ: 30000 Not Audited
Editor: Keith Magnum
Profile: Website for The Hackney Citizen, a free monthly newspaper covering local news, culture, sport and lifestyle for the Borough of Hackney.

Hackney Gazette　　　　980405
Editorial: Charles House, North West London Newspapers, 108-110 Finchley Road, London NW3 5JJ
Tel: 44 02084 784444
Email: gazette.news@archant.co.uk
Web site: www.hackneygazette.co.uk
Freq: Weekly
Circ: 1778 Not Audited
Editor: Ramzy Alwakeel
Profile: Website for weekly paper the Hackney Gazette, covering the latest news and events from the London Borough of Hackney.

Hackney Today　　　　984026
Editorial: Communications and Consultation, 1st Floor Maurice Bishop House, London E8 1HH
Tel: 44 02083 563275
Email: htnews@hackney.gov.uk
Web site: http://www.hackney.gov.uk/hackney-today
Freq: Monthly
Circ: 91687 Not Audited
Editor: Jane Young
Profile: Newspaper covering council and community news with a pull out listings guide.
Ad Rate: Full Page Colour 1735.00

Hale, Altrincham and Sale Independent　　　1094740
Tel: 44 01204 667345
Web site: www.independentnewspapers.com/hale
Freq: Monthly

Halesowen Chronicle　　　980567
Editorial: 51-53 Queen Street, Wolverhampton WV1 1ES
Tel: 44 01384 353201
Email: dudley.chrons@expressandstar.co.uk
Web site: http://yourchronicle.com/
Freq: Weekly
Circ: 27854 Not Audited
Profile: The Halesowen Chronicle is a weekly, local newspaper covering all the latest news and current affairs for the surrounding area.

Halesowen News　　　　980568
Editorial: St John's House, St John's Road, Stourbridge DY8 1EH **Tel:** 44 01384 358259
Email: newsgrouped@midlands.newsquest.co.uk
Web site: www.halesowennews.co.uk
Freq: Weekly
Circ: 32623 Not Audited
Profile: Online version of the Halesowen News newspaper covering local news and sports for the surrounding area.

Halifax Courier　　　　980588
Editorial: The Fire Station, Dean Clough Mills, Halifax HX3 5AX **Tel:** 44 01422 260200
Email: newsdesk@halifaxcourier.co.uk
Web site: www.halifaxcourier.co.uk
Freq: Weekly
Circ: 16747 Not Audited
Editor: John Kenealy
Profile: Online version of the Halifax Courier covering local news, business, sports and features for the surrounding area.

Halstead Gazette　　　　982959
Editorial: 76 High Street, Braintree CM7 1JP
Tel: 44 01376 343344
Email: hgnews@newsquest.co.uk
Web site: www.halsteadgazette.co.uk
Freq: Weekly

Circ: 3386 Not Audited
Profile: Website for local paper the Halstead Gazette covering the latest local news and events from the town of Halstead.

Ham & High (Broadway)　1075516
Editorial: Charles House, 108-110 Finchley Road, Hampstead, London NW3 5JJ
Tel: 44 02074 330100
Email: editorial@hamhigh.co.uk
Web site: http://www.hamhigh.co.uk/news/broadway
Freq: Weekly
Circ: 595 Not Audited

Ham & High (Express)　　980406
Editorial: Charles House, 108-110 Finchley Road, Hampstead, London NW3 5JJ
Tel: 44 02074 330100
Email: editorial@hamhigh.co.uk
Web site: www.hamhigh.co.uk
Freq: Weekly
Circ: 8492 Not Audited

Hamilton Advertiser　　　980675
Editorial: Press Building, Campbell Street, Hamilton ML3 6AX **Tel:** 44 01698 283200
Email: news@hamiltonadvertiser.co.uk
Web site: http://www.dailyrecord.co.uk/all-about/hamilton
Freq: Weekly
Circ: 9621 Not Audited
Editor: Robert Mitchell
Profile: Online version of the Hamilton Advertiser covering local news, sports and lifestyle for the surrounding area. The outlet offers RSS (Really Simple Syndication).

Hampshire Chronicle　　　980316
Editorial: 5 Upper Brook Street, Winchester, Winchester SO23 8AL **Tel:** 44 01962 861860
Email: news@hampshirechronicle.co.uk
Web site: www.hampshirechronicle.co.uk
Freq: Weekly
Circ: 7973 Not Audited

Hampshire Observer Series
　　　　　　　　　　　980322
Editorial: 20 Moorside Road, Winnall, Winchester SO23 7RX **Tel:** 44 01962 859559
Email: hampshiremedia@aol.com
Web site: www.hantsdirect.com
Freq: Weekly
Circ: 30719 Not Audited
Editor: Mark O'Connor

Harborough Mail　　　　980276
Editorial: Newspaper House, Ise Park, Rothwell Road, Kettering NN16 8GA
Tel: 44 01536 506100
Email: newsdesk@harboroughmail.co.uk
Web site: www.harboroughmail.co.uk
Freq: Weekly
Circ: 7932 Not Audited
Profile: This is the online version of the Harborough Mail, is a weekly, local newspaper published on Thursdays and covering all the latest on local news sport and lifestyle in Market Harborough and Lutterworth.

Harlow Star　　　　　980297
Editorial: The Media Centre, 40 Ware Road, Hertford, Hertford SG13 7HU
Tel: 44 01992 526666
Email: star@hertsessexnews.co.uk
Web site: www.harlowstar.co.uk
Freq: Weekly
Circ: 33000 Not Audited
Profile: Online version of the Harlow Star covering local news and sports for the surrounding area.

Harrogate Advertiser　　979971
Editorial: 1 Cardale Park, Harrogate HG3 1RZ **Tel:** 44 01423 707402
Email: news@harrogateadvertiser.co.uk
Web site: www.harrogateadvertiser.co.uk
Freq: Weekly
Circ: 15621 Not Audited
Profile: Website for local paper the Harrogate Advertiser covering the latest local news and events from Harrogate.

Harrow Times　　　　980408
Editorial: Observer House, Caxton Way, Watford, London WD18 8RJ
Tel: 44 01923 216216
Email: timesnews@london.newsquest.co.uk
Web site: www.harrowtimes.co.uk
Freq: Weekly
Circ: 49151 Not Audited
Profile: Website for local newspaper the Harrow Times, covering the latest news, sport and entertainment from Harrow and the surrounding area. This outlet covers areas within Harrow Borough.

Hartlepool Mail　　　　980227
Editorial: 15 Scarborough Street, Hartlepool TS24 7DA **Tel:** 44 01429 235197
Email: mail.news@northeast-press.co.uk
Web site: www.hartlepooltoday.co.uk
Freq: Daily
Circ: 5070 Not Audited
Profile: The Hartlepool Mail is a daily regional newspaper providing the latest news, sport, features and lifestyle articles in Hartlepool and Peterlee.
Ad Rate: Full Page Mono 1652.00
Ad Rate: Full Page Colour 2147.60

Harwich and Manningtree Standard　　　　982984
Editorial: 28 Jackson Road, Clacton-on-Sea CO15 1QL **Tel:** 44 01255 221221
Email: hms.news@nqe.com
Web site: www. harwichandmanningtreestandard.co.uk
Freq: Weekly
Circ: 4765 Not Audited
Profile: The Harwich and Manningtree Standard is a weekly, local newspaper covering all the latest news, sport and leisure for the surrounding area.
Ad Rate: Full Page Colour 405.00

Hastings & St Leonards Observer　　　　　980286
Editorial: Woods House, Telford Road, St Leonards-on-Sea, Hastings TN38 9LZ
Tel: 44 01424 854242
Email: hastings.observer@jpress.co.uk
Web site: www.hastingsobserver.co.uk
Freq: Weekly
Circ: 32853 Not Audited
Profile: Website for the Hastings & St Leonards Observer providing the latest local news coverage for the area.

Hastings Independent　　998310
Email: subs@hastingsindependentpress.co.uk
Web site: www.hastingsindependentpress.co.uk
Freq: Bi-Weekly
Circ: 7500 Not Audited

Haverhill Echo　　　　980533
Editorial: Groundkeeper's House, Castle Manor Academy, Eastern Avenue, Haverhill CB9 9JE **Tel:** 44 01440 706009
Email: news@haverhillecho.com
Web site: www.haverhilltoday.co.uk
Freq: Weekly
Circ: 3298 Not Audited
Profile: This is the online version of the Haverhill Echo, a weekly, local newspaper covering all the latest on local news, sport, motoring and property in Haverhill and surrounding villages.

Haverhill Weekly News　　982985
Editorial: Winship Road, Milton, Cambridge CB24 6BQ **Tel:** 44 01223 434434
Email: editorial@haverhillweeklynews.co.uk
Web site: http://www.cambridge-news.co.uk/haverhill
Freq: Weekly
Circ: 10946 Not Audited
Profile: Haverhill Weekly News is a weekly newspaper covering the latest in local news and events from the town of Haverhill.

Hawick News　　　　980676
Editorial: Tweed Mill Business Park, Dunsdale Road, Selkirk, Hawick TD7 5DU
Tel: 44 01750 725426
Email: hawicknews@jpress.co.uk
Web site: http://www.hawick-news.co.uk

Freq: Weekly
Circ: 4741 Not Audited
Profile: Website for weekly newspaper the Hawick News providing the latest local news coverage from town of Hawick and the surrounding area.

Hayling Islander　　　　980318
Editorial: 78 Elm Grove, Hayling Island PO11 9EH **Tel:** 44 02392 463473
Email: contactus@haylingislandtoday.co.uk
Web site: www.haylingtoday.co.uk
Freq: Monthly
Circ: 11500 Not Audited
Profile: Website covering news, sport, jobs, business, property of Hayling Island.

Heathrow Villager　　　　980409
Editorial: 260 Kingston Road, London TW18 1PG **Tel:** 44 01784 453196
Email: heathrow.villager@gmail.com
Web site: www.heathrowvillager.co.uk
Freq: Bi-Weekly
Circ: 42550 Not Audited
Editor: Ian West

Hebden Bridge Times & Todmorden News　　　980589
Editorial: The Fire Station, Dean Clough Mills, Halifax HX3 5AX **Tel:** 44 01422 260227
Email: hbtimes@hebdenbridgetimes.co.uk
Web site: www.hebdenbridgetimes.co.uk
Freq: Weekly
Circ: 5049 Not Audited

Helensburgh Advertiser　980677
Editorial: 1st Floor, Carus House, 201 Dumbarton Road, Clydebank G81 4XJ
Tel: 44 01414 358888
Email: editorial@helensburghadvertiser.co.uk
Web site: www.helensburghadvertiser.co.uk
Freq: Weekly
Circ: 3717 Not Audited
Profile: Website for local paper the Helensburgh Advertiser providing the latest local news coverage from Helensburgh and Arrochar.

Hemel Hempstead Gazette & Express　　　　　980338
Editorial: Bond Estate, 3 North House, Bond Avenue, Milton Keynes MK1 1SW
Tel: 44 01296 619700
Email: thegazette@jpress.co.uk
Web site: www.hemeltoday.co.uk
Freq: Weekly
Circ: 20000 Not Audited
Editor: David Summers
Profile: The Hemel Hempstead Gazette is a weekly paper covering the latest news and events from Hemel Hempstead and the surrounding local area.

Hemel Hempstead Herald Express　　　　　　998771
Editorial: Claydon House, 1 Edison Rd, Hemel Hempstead HP19 8TE
Tel: 44 01296 619700
Email: thegazette@jpress.co.uk
Web site: www.hemeltoday.co.uk
Freq: Weekly
Circ: 36068 Not Audited

Hemsworth & South Elmsall Express　　　　　980590
Editorial: First Floor, Bullring House, 23 Northgate, Wakefield, Wakefield WF1 3BJ
Tel: 44 01924 433029
Email: hemsworth@ywng.co.uk
Web site: www.hemsworthandsouthelmsallexpress.co.uk
Freq: Weekly
Circ: 2980 Not Audited
Editor: John Kenealy

Hendon Times Group　　980339
Editorial: Observer House, Caxton Way, Watford, London WD18 8RJ
Tel: 44 01923 216216
Email: timesnews@london.newsquest.co.uk
Web site: http://www.times-series.co.uk
Freq: Weekly
Circ: 57762 Not Audited

Henleaze & Westbury Voice
1057959

Editorial: Henleaze & Westbury Voice, 16 Chandag Road, Keynsham, Bristol BS31 1NR **Tel:** 44 01179 082121
Email: news@henleazeandwestburyvoice.co.uk
Web site: http://www.henleazeandwestburyvoice.co.uk/
Freq: Monthly
Circ: 9000 Not Audited

Henley Standard
998711

Editorial: Caxton House, 1 Station Road, Henley-on-Thames RG9 1AD
Tel: 44 01491 419444
Email: news@henleystandard.co.uk
Web site: www.henleystandard.co.uk
Freq: Weekly
Circ: 8998 Not Audited
Editor: Simon Bradshaw
Profile: Website for the Henley Standard covering the latest local news and events from Henley, Benson, Binfield Heath, Caversham, Goring, Shiplake, Sonning Common, Wargrave, Watlington, Whitchurch and Woodcote.

Herald & Post (Luton)
980192

Editorial: 39 Upper George Street, Luton LU1 2RD **Tel:** 44 01582 700600
Email: editorial@lutonnews.co.uk
Web site: www.lutontoday.co.uk
Freq: Weekly
Circ: 72001 Not Audited
Editor: Olga Norford

The Herald (Plymouth)
980256

Editorial: 3rd Floor, Studio 5-11, Millbay Road, Plymouth PL1 3LF
Tel: 44 01752 293000
Email: news@plymouthherald.co.uk
Web site: www.plymouthherald.co.uk
Freq: Daily
Circ: 16350 Not Audited
Editor: Paul Burton
Profile: The Herald (Plymouth) is a regional daily newspaper published from Monday to Saturday and covers regional news, sports, features, business and lifestyle.
Ad Rate: Full Page Mono 1500.00
Ad Rate: Full Page Colour 1500.00

Herald Express (Torquay)
980013

Editorial: Harmsworth House, Barton Hill Road, Torquay TQ2 8JN
Tel: 44 01803 676000
Email: newsdesk@heraldexpress.co.uk
Web site: www.devonlive.com/
Freq: Weekly
Circ: 16411 Not Audited
Editor: Jim Parker

Hereford Admag
995938

Editorial: 1a Red Barn Court, Hereford HR4 9QL **Tel:** 44 01432 376120
Email: hereford.reception@nwn.co.uk
Web site: www.herefordadmag.net
Freq: Weekly
Circ: 43522 Not Audited
Profile: The Hereford Admag is a weekly newspaper primarily featuring advertising for local businesses but also has a local entertainment section and feature articles on local topics.

Hereford Times
981596

Editorial: Holmer Road, Hereford, Hereford HR4 9UJ **Tel:** 44 01432 845873
Email: news@herefordtimes.com
Web site: www.herefordtimes.com
Freq: Weekly
Circ: 19747 Not Audited
Profile: Online version of the Hereford Times newspaper covering local news and sports for the surrounding area.

Herne Bay Gazette
983779

Editorial: Gazette House, 5-8 Boorman Way, Estuary View Business Park, Whitstable CT5 3SE **Tel:** 44 01227 768181
Email: hernebaygazette@thekmgroup.co.uk
Web site: www.kentonline.co.uk
Freq: Weekly
Circ: 1763 Not Audited

Profile: The Herne Bay Gazette is weekly paper published every Thursday covering the latest news and events from Herne Bay.
Ad Rate: Full Page Colour 1360.00

Herts & Essex Observer - MERGED with Hertfordshire Mercury Series
980342

Editorial: 12 North Street, Bishop's Stortford CM23 2LQ
Web site: www.hertsandessexobserver.co.uk
Freq: Weekly
Circ: 6909 Not Audited

Herts Advertiser
980343

Editorial: Town Hall Chambers, 35 Market Place, St Albans, London AL3 5DL
Tel: 44 01727 863332
Email: hertsad@archant.co.uk
Web site: www.hertsad.co.uk
Freq: Weekly
Circ: 37263 Not Audited
Profile: Online version of the Herts Advertiser newspaper covering local news and sports for the surrounding area.

Hexham Courant
980476

Editorial: Beaumont Street, Hexham NE46 3NA **Tel:** 44 01434 602351
Email: news.hx@hexham-courant.co.uk
Web site: http://www.hexham-courant.co.uk/
Freq: Weekly
Circ: 11111 Not Audited
Editor: Colin Tapping
Profile: Website for weekly paper the Hexham Courant covering the latest local news and events from Hexham, Alston, Corbridge, Haltwhistle and Prudhoe.

Heywood Advertiser
980426

Editorial: Mitchell Henry House, Chadderton, Oldham OL9 8EF
Tel: 44 01612 112326
Email: heywoodadvertiser@menmedia.co.uk
Web site: www.heywoodadvertiser.co.uk
Freq: Weekly
Circ: 1981 Not Audited
Profile: The Heywood Advertiser is a weekly paper published every Thursday covering the latest local news and events from the town of Heywood, Greater Manchester.
Ad Rate: Full Page Mono 595.00
Ad Rate: Full Page Colour 833.00

Highland News Group
998736

Editorial: New Century House, Stadium Road, Inverness IV1 1FG
Tel: 44 01463 233059
Email: newsdesk@spp-group.com
Web site: http://www.highland-news.co.uk/Home/
Freq: Weekly
Circ: 6061 Not Audited

Highvelder/Hoevelder
1060345

Tel: 44 27178 112221
Freq: Weekly
Circ: 17000 Not Audited

The Hinckley Times
980139

Editorial: Atkins Building, Lower Bond Street, Hinckley LE10 1QU
Tel: 44 01455 891965
Email: hinckleytimes@trinitymirror.com
Web site: www.hinckleytimes.net
Freq: Weekly
Circ: 8093 Not Audited
Editor: Simon Holden
Profile: This is the online version of the Hinckley Times, a weekly, local newspaper published on Thursdays and covering all the latest on local news, sport and lifestyle in Hinckley.

Holderness Gazette
980389

Editorial: 1 Seaside Road, Withernsea HU19 2DL **Tel:** 44 01964 611587
Email: news@holderness-gazette.co.uk
Web site: www.holderness-gazette.co.uk
Freq: Weekly
Circ: 7000 Not Audited
Profile: Website for local paper the Holderness Gazette covering the latest local

news and events from Holderness and the surrounding area.

Horncastle News
980390

Editorial: Church Lane, Horncastle LN9 5HW **Tel:** 44 01507 527530
Email: horncastle.news@jpress.co.uk
Web site: www.horncastletoday.co.uk
Freq: Weekly
Circ: 2860 Not Audited
Profile: Website for the Horncastle News covering the latest local news and events from Horncastle, Coningsby and Tattershall.

Horwich & Westhoughton Advertiser
982813

Editorial: Publishing House, 3 Bridgebank Industrial Estate, Taylor Street, Horwich BL6 7PD **Tel:** 44 01204 696916
Email: contact@horwichadvertiser.co.uk
Web site: www.horwichadvertiser.co.uk
Freq: Monthly
Circ: 16000 Not Audited
Editor: Mike Hulme

Hounslow Chronicle
980410

Editorial: Broadway Chambers, 14-26 Hammersmith Broadway, London W6 7AF
Tel: 44 02032 803201
Email: newshounslow@trinitysouth.co.uk
Web site: www.getwestlondon.co.uk/all-about/hounslow
Freq: Weekly
Circ: 18133 Not Audited
Profile: Online version of the Hounslow Chronicle newspaper covering local news and sports for the surrounding area.

Hucknall Dispatch
980123

Editorial: Sherwood Oaks Business Park, Southwell Road, Mansfield, Mansfield NG18 4TB **Tel:** 44 01623 456789
Email: newsdesk@hucknall-dispatch.co.uk
Web site: www.hucknalldispatch.co.uk
Freq: Weekly
Circ: 3728 Not Audited

The Huddersfield Daily Examiner
980591

Editorial: Pennine Business Park, Longbow Close, Bradley Road, Huddersfield HD2 1GQ
Tel: 44 01484 430000
Email: editorial@examiner.co.uk
Web site: www.examiner.co.uk
Freq: Daily
Circ: 12046 Not Audited
Editor: Henryk Zientek
Profile: The Huddersfield Daily Examiner is a regional daily newspaper providing the latest news, sports and features for the surrounding area.
Ad Rate: Full Page Mono 798.00
Ad Rate: Full Page Colour 1077.30

Hull Daily Mail
979969

Editorial: Blundell's Corner, Beverley Road, Hull HU3 1XS **Tel:** 44 01482 327111
Email: news@hulldailymail.co.uk
Web site: www.hulldailymail.co.uk/
Freq: Daily
Circ: 27054 Not Audited
Profile: The Hull Daily Mail is a regional daily newspaper that is available in Hull and the surrounding East Yorkshire region providing regional news, sports, features and events.
Ad Rate: Full Page Mono 4134.00
Ad Rate: Full Page Colour 5168.00

Huntly Express
980678

Editorial: 9 Gordon Street, Huntly AB54 8AJ
Tel: 44 01466 793622
Web site: www.huntlyexpress.co.uk
Freq: Weekly
Circ: 2036 Not Audited

The Hunts Post
980210

Editorial: 30 High Street, Huntingdon PE29 3TB **Tel:** 44 01480 411481
Email: news@huntspost.co.uk
Web site: www.huntspost.co.uk
Freq: Weekly
Circ: 39050 Not Audited
Editor: Stefan Bartlett

Profile: The Hunts Post is a weekly local newspaper covering all the latest on local news, sport and entertainment in Huntingdon and the surrounding area, including the towns of St.Neots and St.Ives.
Ad Rate: Full Page Mono 1188.00
Ad Rate: Full Page Colour 1485.00

The Ileach Newspaper
980685

Editorial: Main Street, Bowmore, Campbeltown PA43 7JH
Tel: 44 01496 810355
Email: ileach@ileach.co.uk
Web site: www.ileach.co.uk
Freq: Bi-Weekly
Circ: 2500 Not Audited

Ilford Recorder
980411

Editorial: 7th Floor, Maritime House, 1 Linton Road, Barking IG11 8HG
Tel: 44 02084 784444
Email: newsdesk@ilfordrecorder.co.uk
Web site: www.ilfordrecorder.co.uk
Freq: Weekly
Circ: 5130 Not Audited
Profile: This is the online version of the Ilford Recorder and Woodford Recorder, weekly, local newspapers published on Thursdays, covering all the latest on local news, sport and entertainment in Ilford and Woodford. This outlet covers areas within Redbridge Borough.

Ilkeston Advertiser
980252

Editorial: 8 Heanor Road, Ilkeston, Ilkeston DE7 8ER **Tel:** 44 01246 504536
Email: news@ilkestonadvertiser.co.uk
Web site: www.ilkestonadvertiser.co.uk
Freq: Weekly
Circ: 17316 Not Audited
Editor: Martin Hutton
Profile: Website for local paper the Ilkeston Advertiser covering the latest local news and events from Ilkeston.

Ilkley Gazette
980592

Editorial: 8 Wells Road, Ilkley LS29 9JD
Tel: 44 01943 607022
Web site: www.ilkleygazette.co.uk
Freq: Weekly
Circ: 3204 Not Audited
Profile: Online version of the Ilkley Gazette covering local news and sports for the surrounding area.

Impartial Reporter
983127

Tel: 44 02866 324422
Email: editorial@impartialreporter.com
Web site: www.impartialreporter.com
Freq: Weekly
Circ: 10762 Not Audited
Editor: Sarah Saunderson
Profile: Online version of the Impartial Reporter newspaper covering local news, sports, farming and entertainment for the surrounding area.

The Inverness Courier
980680

Editorial: New Century House, Stadium Road, Inverness IV1 1FG
Tel: 44 01463 233059
Email: newsdesk@spp-group.com
Web site: www.inverness-courier.co.uk
Freq: Weekly
Circ: 5960 Not Audited
Profile: Online version of the Inverness Courier newspaper covering local news and sports for the surrounding area.

Inverness Scene
980679

Editorial: New Century House, Stadium Road, Inverness IV1 1FF
Tel: 44 01463 732230
Email: newsdesk@highland-news.co.uk
Web site: http://www.highland-news.co.uk/
Freq: Weekly
Circ: 12965 Not Audited

Inverurie Advertiser
980681

Editorial: 35 High Street, Inverurie AB51 4XQ **Tel:** 44 01467 624849
Email: newsdesk@wpeters.co.uk
Web site: www.wpeters.co.uk/newspaper.html
Freq: Weekly

Circ: 14000 Not Audited
Editor: Jan Mackie
Profile: The Inverurie Advertiser is a weekly local newspaper covering local news and sports for the surrounding area.
Ad Rate: Full Page Mono 490.00

Inverurie Herald 980682
Editorial: 8 Bridge Street, Ellon, Ellon AB41 9AA **Tel:** 44 01779 871332
Email: heraldnews@inverurieherald.com
Web site: http://www.inverurieherald.co.uk/
Freq: Weekly
Circ: 696 Not Audited
Profile: This is the online version of the Inverurie Herald, a weekly local newspaper covering news, sport, lifestyle and community for the surrounding area.

Ipswich Star 980532
Editorial: Portman House, 120 Princes Street, Ipswich IP4 1RS
Tel: 44 01473 230023
Email: newsroom@archant.co.uk
Web site: www.ipswichstar.co.uk
Freq: Daily
Circ: 10138 Not Audited
Editor: Brad Jones
Profile: The Ipswich Star is a daily regional newspaper providing regional news, sports and features for the surrounding area.
Ad Rate: Full Page Mono 2339.04
Ad Rate: Full Page Colour 3274.66

Irvine Herald and Kilwinning Chronicle 980683
Editorial: 25 Portland Gate, Portland Street, Kilmarnock, Irvine KA7 1JN
Tel: 44 01563 557120
Email: news@irvineherald.co.uk
Web site: www.irvineherald.co.uk
Freq: Weekly
Circ: 3657 Not Audited

Irvine Times 980684
Editorial: Princes Street, Ardrossan, Ardrossan KA22 8BP **Tel:** 44 01294 273421
Email: editorial@irvinetimes.co.uk
Web site: www.irvinetimes.com
Freq: Weekly
Circ: 2073 Not Audited
Editor: Caroline Patterson
Profile: Online version of the Irvine Times newspaper covering local news and sports for the surrounding area.

Island News and Advertiser 986708
Editorial: Room 7, East Camp, Balivanich, Isle of Lewis HS7 5LA **Tel:** 44 07500 041671
Email: editor@islandnewsandadvertiser.co.uk
Web site: www.islandnewsandadvertiser.co.uk
Freq: Weekly
Circ: 1000 Not Audited

Isle of Man Courier 980347
Web site: www.iomtoday.co.im
Freq: Weekly
Circ: 39000 Not Audited
Profile: The Isle of Man Courier is a free weekly local newspaper covering local news and sports for the surrounding area. The newspaper is published on Friday.
Ad Rate: Full Page Mono 1793.16
Ad Rate: Full Page Colour 2689.70

Isle of Man Examiner 980348
Web site: www.iomtoday.co.im
Freq: Weekly
Circ: 10017 Not Audited
Profile: The Isle of Man Examiner is a weekly local newspaper covering local news and sports for the surrounding area. The newspaper is published on a Monday.
Ad Rate: Full Page Mono 1793.16
Ad Rate: Full Page Colour 2689.70

Isle of Thanet Gazette 980360
Editorial: Northcliffe House, 2 Derry Street, London W8 5TT **Tel:** 44 02037 631500
Email: newsdesk.thanet@krnmedia.co.uk
Web site: www.thanetgazette.co.uk
Freq: Weekly
Circ: 7810 Not Audited
Profile: This is the online version of the Isle of Thanet Gazette Gazette, a weekly, local newspaper covering all the latest on local news, sport and entertainment on the Isle of Thanet.

Isle of Wight County Press 980319
Tel: 44 01983 522210
Email: editor@iwcp.co.uk
Web site: www.iwcp.co.uk
Freq: Weekly
Circ: 25173 Not Audited
Editor: Alan Marriott
Profile: Online version of the Isle of Wight County Press covering local news and sports for the surrounding area. The outlet offers RSS (Really Simple Syndication).

Islington Gazette 980412
Editorial: Charles House, North West London Newspapers, 108-110 Finchley Road, Hampstead, London NW3 5JJ
Tel: 44 02084 784444
Email: gazette.news@archant.co.uk
Web site: www.islingtongazette.co.uk
Freq: Weekly
Circ: 6746 Not Audited
Editor: Ramzy Alwakeel
Profile: Website for local paper the Islington Gazette covering the latest news and events from Islington. This outlet covers areas within the Islington Borough.

Islington Tribune 984105
Editorial: 40 Camden Road, London NW1 9DR **Tel:** 44 02074 199000
Email: editorial@camdennewjournal.co.uk
Web site: www.islingtontribune.com
Freq: Weekly
Circ: 21443 Not Audited
Editor: Eric Gordon
Profile: Website for the Islington Tribune a free weekly paper covering the latest local news and events from Islington and the surrounding area. This outlet covers areas within Islington Borough.

Järvenpää-lehti 1061997
Tel: 44 35841 7540305
Email: toimitus@jarvenpaa-lehti.net
Web site: http://jarvenpaa-lehti.net/Not Audited

Jersey Evening Post 980740
Editorial: Guiton House, Five Oakes, Street Saviour, Jersey JE4 8XQ
Tel: 44 01534 611611
Email: news@jerseyeveningpost.com
Web site: http://jerseyeveningpost.com/
Freq: Daily
Circ: 13791 Not Audited
Editor: Andy Sibcy
Profile: The Jersey Evening Post is daily newspaper for the island of Jersey providing the latest in news, business and sports for the surrounding area.
Ad Rate: Full Page Mono 3409.00
Ad Rate: Full Page Colour 4223.00

Jewish News 982152
Editorial: PO Box 34296, London NW5 1YW
Tel: 44 02076 926929
Email: newsdesk@thejngroup.com
Web site: www.jewishnews.co.uk
Freq: Weekly
Circ: 23639 Not Audited
Profile: Newspaper covering restaurants, travel, films, fashion, books, property and motoring.
Ad Rate: Full Page Mono 3712.00
Ad Rate: Full Page Colour 4498.00

Jewish Telegraph (Manchester) 998892
Editorial: Telegraph House, 11 Park Hill, Bury Old Road, Manchester M25 0HH
Tel: 44 01617 409321
Email: pharris@jewishtelegraph.com
Web site: www.jewishtelegraph.com
Freq: Weekly
Circ: 16000 Not Audited

Jewish Tribune 985820
Editorial: 97 Stamford Hill, London N16 5DN
Tel: 44 02032 400100
Email: editor@jewishtribune.com
Freq: Weekly
Circ: 2500 Not Audited
Editor: Dan Levy
Profile: Publication covering news and current affairs. Aimed at the orthodox Jewish community.
Ad Rate: Full Page Mono 700.00
Ad Rate: Full Page Colour 875.00

John O'Groat Journal 980686
Editorial: 42 Union Street, Wick, Caithness, Wick KW1 5ED **Tel:** 44 01955 602424
Email: editor@nosn.co.uk
Web site: www.johnogroat-journal.co.uk
Freq: Weekly
Circ: 5397 Not Audited
Editor: Iain Grant
Profile: Online version of the John O'Groat Journal newspaper covering local news, sports and leisure for the surrounding area.

The Journal (Newcastle) 979988
Editorial: Thomson House, Groat Market, Newcastle upon Tyne NE1 1ED
Tel: 44 01912 327500
Email: ec.news@ncjmedia.co.uk
Web site: http://www.chroniclelive.co.uk/
Freq: Daily
Circ: 12587 Not Audited
Editor: Matt McKenzie
Profile: The Journal (Newcastle) is a regional daily newspaper and covers regional news, business and sports for the surrounding area. The outlet offers RSS (Really Simple Syndication).
Ad Rate: Full Page Mono 4570.00
Ad Rate: Full Page Colour 6169.50

Kayhan (London) 999013
Editorial: Kayhan London, P.O. Box 435, Old Brompton Road 2, London SW7 3DQ
Tel: 44 02036 333684
Email: info@kayhanlondon.net
Web site: www.kayhan.london
Freq: Weekly
Circ: 50000 Not Audited

KCW Today (Kensington, Chelsea and Westminster) 999200
Editorial: 80-100 Gwynne Road, London SW11 3UW **Tel:** 44 02077 382348
Email: news@kcwtoday.co.uk
Web site: www.kcwtoday.co.uk
Freq: Monthly
Circ: 25000 Not Audited
Editor: Kate Hawthorne

Keighley News 982886
Editorial: 80-86 North Street, Keighley, Keighley BD21 3AG **Tel:** 44 01535 606611
Email: alistair.shand@nqyne.co.uk
Web site: www.keighleynews.co.uk
Freq: Weekly
Circ: 7320 Not Audited
Profile: Online version of the Keighley News newspaper covering local news and sports for the surrounding area.

Kenilworth Weekly News 980555
Editorial: 32 Hamilton Terrace, Lemington Spa, Cambridge CB32 4LY
Tel: 44 01926 457737
Email: editorial@kenilworthweeklynews.co.uk
Web site: www.kenilworthonline.co.uk
Freq: Weekly
Circ: 43205 Not Audited
Profile: Website for local paper the Kenilworth Weekly News, covering the latest news, sports and entertainment from Kenilworth and the surrounding area.

Kensington and Chelsea Times 984669
Editorial: 9 Eardley Crescent, Earls Court, London SW5 9JS **Tel:** 44 02032 860102
Email: enquiries@kctimes.co.uk
Web site: www.kctimes.co.uk
Freq: Monthly
Circ: 10000 Not Audited

Kent and Sussex Courier 980361
Editorial: Courier House, Calverley Road, Tunbridge Wells, Tunbridge Wells TN1 2UN
Tel: 44 01892 239100
Email: editor@courier.co.uk
Web site: www.courier.co.uk
Freq: Weekly
Circ: 15806 Not Audited
Profile: The Kent and Sussex Courier is a weekly local newspaper covering local news and sports for the surrounding area. The paper is published on a Friday.

Kent Business 980004
Editorial: Medway House, Ginsbury Close, Sir Thomas Longley Road, Rochester ME2 4DU **Tel:** 44 01622 794680
Email: business@thekmgroup.co.uk
Web site: http://www.kentonline.co.uk/kent-business/
Freq: Monthly
Circ: 70786 Not Audited
Profile: Business newspaper covering county business and financial news.
Ad Rate: Full Page Colour 5984.00

Kent Messenger Group 980002
Editorial: 6&7 Middle Row, Maidstone, Kent, Maidstone ME14 1TG **Tel:** 44 01622 695666
Email: messengernews@thekmgroup.co.uk
Web site: www.kentonline.co.uk
Freq: Weekly
Circ: 69579 Not Audited
Editor: Denise Eaton

Kent on Sunday 980362
Editorial: Kent House, 81 Station Road, Ashford, Ashford TN23 1PP
Tel: 44 01233 653475
Email: editorial@kosmedia.co.uk
Web site: www.kentnews.co.uk
Freq: Weekly
Circ: 58436 Not Audited
Profile: Kent on Sunday is a weekly local newspaper distributed in Kent. It includes regional news, sports and events coverage.
Ad Rate: Full Page Mono 1782.00
Ad Rate: Full Page Colour 1782.00

Kentish Express Series 983047
Editorial: Express House, 34-36 North Street, Ashford TN24 8JR
Tel: 44 01233 623232
Email: kentishexpress@thekmgroup.co.uk
Web site: www.kentonline.co.uk/kentish_express/news.aspx
Freq: Weekly
Circ: 8856 Not Audited
Editor: Robert Barman

Kentish Gazette Series 980363
Editorial: Gazette House, 5-8 Estuary View Business Park, Boorman Way, Whitstable CT5 3SE **Tel:** 44 01227 768181
Email: kentishgazette@thekmgroup.co.uk
Web site: www.kentonline.co.uk
Freq: Weekly
Circ: 10769 Not Audited
Editor: Bob Bounds

Keswick Reminder 980240
Editorial: 32-34 Station Street, Keswick CA12 5HF **Tel:** 44 01768 772140
Email: news@keswickreminder.co.uk
Web site: www.keswickreminder.co.uk
Freq: Weekly
Circ: 3900 Not Audited
Editor: Jane Graves
Profile: The Keswick Reminder is a weekly, local newspaper published on Fridays and covering all the latest local news from the town of Keswick and the surrounding area.
Ad Rate: Full Page Mono 753.00

Kettering Extra Local 996433
Editorial: Ringstead Business Centre, 1-3 Spencer Street, Ringstead, Kettering NN14 4BX **Tel:** 44 08448 877770
Email: newsdesk@extranewspapers.co.uk
Web site: www.extranewspapers.co.uk/local/kettering-news/
Freq: Bi-Weekly
Circ: 21000 Not Audited

Regional & Local Weekly Newspapers

Keynsham Voice   988230
Editorial: 16 Chandag Road, Keynsham, Bristol BS31 1NR **Tel:** 44 01179 082121
Email: news@keynshamvoice.co.uk
Web site: www.keynshamvoice.co.uk
Freq: Monthly
Circ: 11500 Not Audited
Editor: Joni Mann

Kilmarnock Standard (Ayrshire Weekly News and Irvine Valley News)   980687
Editorial: 25 Portland Gate, Portland Street, Kilmarnock, Ayr KA7 1JN
Tel: 44 01563 545218
Email: news@kilmarnockstandard.co.uk
Web site: www.kilmarnockstandard.co.uk
Freq: Weekly
Circ: 8459 Not Audited
Editor: Clair Fullarton
Profile: Online version of the Kilmarnock Standard covering local news, sports, entertainment and lifestyle for the surrounding area. It also includes Kilmarnock-related content from the Daily Record and the Sunday Mail.

Kincardineshire Observer   980688
Editorial: 12 Ann Street, Stonehaven AB39 2ER **Tel:** 44 01569 762139
Email: news@mearnsleader.com
Web site: www.kincardineshiretoday.co.uk
Freq: Weekly
Circ: 927 Not Audited
Profile: Website of the Kincardineshire Observer local newspaper, covering news and events in Kincardineshire.

Kingston Guardian   980541
Editorial: Floors 9 & 10, Quadrant House, The Quadrant, Sutton SM2 5AS
Tel: 44 02087 226318
Email: newsdesk@kingstonguardian.co.uk
Web site: www.kingstonguardian.co.uk
Freq: Weekly
Circ: 30000 Not Audited
Profile: The Kingston Guardian is a weekly paper covering the latest news, sports and lifestyle from Kingston, Surbiton, Tolworth, New Malden, Chessington and Hook. This outlet covers areas within Kingston upon Thames Borough.
Ad Rate: Full Page Mono 519.48
Ad Rate: Full Page Colour 674.65

Kirkby Extra   1094455
Editorial: Admin Buildings, Admin Road, Kirkby L33 7TX **Tel:** 44 01515 472000
Freq: Monthly
Circ: 22600 Not Audited
Editor: Chris O'Shea

Kirkintilloch Herald   980689
Editorial: 11 Dalrymple Court, Kirkintilloch, East Dumbartonshire, Glasgow G66 3AA
Tel: 44 01417 750040
Email: kirkyherald@jnscotland.co.uk
Web site: www.kirkintillochtoday.co.uk
Freq: Weekly
Circ: 8010 Not Audited
Editor: Jim Holland
Profile: Online version of the Kirkintilloch Herald newspaper, a weekly local newspaper covering local news, lifestyle and sports for the surrounding area.

Kirklees Business News   983174
Editorial: Pennine Business Park, Longbow Close, Bradley Road, Huddersfield HD2 1GQ
Tel: 44 01484 430000
Email: henryk.zientek@examiner.co.uk
Web site: www.examiner.co.uk
Freq: Monthly
Circ: 12046 Not Audited
Editor: Henryk Zientek
Profile: Supplement included with Huddersfield Examiner on Tuesdays, covering transport, manufacturing and distribution industries and business service companies.
Ad Rate: Full Page Mono 1496.00
Ad Rate: Full Page Colour 2019.00

Kirriemuir Herald   980690
Editorial: 117-119 Castle Street, Forfar, Forfar DD8 3AH **Tel:** 44 01307 464899
Email: news@forfardispatch.com
Web site: www.kirriemuirherald.co.uk
Freq: Weekly
Circ: 600 Not Audited
Profile: This is the online version of the Kirriemuir Herald, a weekly, local newspaper covering all the latest news, sport, lifestyle and community for the surrounding area.

Klerksdorp Midweek Record   1060663
Tel: 44 27184 641911
Email: salome@klerksdorprecord.co.za
Freq: Weekly
Circ: 19500 Not Audited

Klerksdorp Record   1060535
Tel: 44 27184 641911
Email: salome@klerksdorprecord.co.za
Freq: Weekly
Circ: 14800 Not Audited

KM Extra (Ashford)   982969
Editorial: Express House, 34-36 North Street, Ashford, Ashford TN24 8JR
Tel: 44 01233 895801
Email: kentishexpress@thekmgroup.co.uk
Web site: www.kentonline.co.uk
Freq: Weekly
Circ: 8260 Not Audited
Editor: Robert Barman

KM Extra (Canterbury)   999132
Editorial: Gazette House, 5-8 Estuary View Business Park, Boorman Way, Whitstable CT5 3SE **Tel:** 44 01227 768181
Email: kentishgazette@thekmgroup.co.uk
Web site: www.kentonline.co.uk/canterbury/
Freq: Weekly
Circ: 20281 Not Audited

KM Extra (Folkestone and Hythe)   988847
Editorial: Express House, 34-36 North Street, Ashford TN24 8JR
Tel: 44 01233 895801
Email: folkestoneexpress@thekmgroup.co.uk
Web site: www.kentonline.co.uk/folkestone/
Freq: Weekly
Circ: 6777 Not Audited
Editor: Robert Barman

KM Extra (Maidstone)   988848
Editorial: 6-7 Middle Row, Maidstone ME14 1TG **Tel:** 44 01622 695666
Email: messengernews@thekmgroup.co.uk
Web site: www.kentonline.co.uk/maidstone/
Freq: Weekly
Circ: 8388 Not Audited
Editor: Denise Eaton

KM Extra (Medway)   998489
Editorial: Medway House, Ginsbury Close, Sir Thomas Longley Road, Rochester ME2 4DU **Tel:** 44 01634 227800
Email: medwaymessenger@thekmgroup.co.uk
Web site: www.kentonline.co.uk/medway
Freq: Weekly
Circ: 25663 Not Audited

KM Extra (Thanet)   982981
Editorial: 3 Margate Road, Ramsgate, Ramsgate CT11 7SP **Tel:** 44 01843 222777
Email: thanetextra@thekmgroup.co.uk
Web site: www.kentonline.co.uk/thanet
Freq: Weekly
Circ: 40969 Not Audited
Editor: Bob Bounds

Knaresborough Post   980462
Editorial: 1 Cardale Park, Beckwith Head Road, Harrogate HG3 1RZ
Tel: 44 01423 707402
Email: news@harrogateadvertiser.co.uk
Web site: www.harrogateadvertiser.co.uk/news/local/knaresborough
Freq: Weekly
Circ: 2064 Not Audited
Profile: The Knaresborough Post is a weekly local newspaper covering local news, sports, features and lifestyle for the community.

Knutsford Guardian   980221
Editorial: Theatre Court, London Road, Northwich, Northwich CW9 5HB
Tel: 44 01606 813600
Email: knutsford@guardiangrp.co.uk
Web site: www.knutsfordguardian.co.uk
Freq: Weekly
Circ: 4444 Not Audited
Editor: Carla Flynn
Profile: Website for local paper the Knutsford Guardian covering the latest in local news, entertainment and sports from Knutsford and the surrounding area.

Kurun Lehti   1061146
Tel: 44 35844 3430031
Email: toimitus@kurunlehti.fi
Web site: http://www.kurunlehti.fi
Freq: Bi-Weekly
Circ: 2800 Not Audited

Lakeland Life   1097902
Tel: 44 02866 324422
Email: editorial@impartialreporter.com
Web site: www.impartialreporter.com/supplements
Freq: Monthly
Circ: 11449 Not Audited
Editor: Sarah Saunderson

Lanark & Carluke Gazette   981494
Editorial: 5 Wellgate, Lanark, Clydebank ML11 9EG **Tel:** 44 07885 982384
Email: clgazette@jnscotland.co.uk
Web site: www.carlukegazette.co.uk
Freq: Weekly
Circ: 6826 Not Audited

Lancashire Evening Post   979954
Editorial: Oliver's Place, Fulwood, Preston, Preston PR2 9ZA **Tel:** 44 01772 254841
Email: lep.newsdesk@lep.co.uk
Web site: www.lep.co.uk
Freq: Daily
Circ: 10751 Not Audited
Editor: Gillian Parkinson
Profile: The Lancashire Evening Post is a daily, regional newspaper published from Monday to Saturday. It is owned by the Johnston Press and is based in the city of Preston. There are two editions of the paper, the County edition and the Chorley edition, for the town of Chorley based a few miles away from Preston. The paper covers the area of Lancashire including the towns of Wigan, Blackpool, Lancaster, Blackburn and Southport and features regional news, sport and entertainment coverage. This outlet offers RSS (Really Simple Syndication)Twitter handle:http://twitter.com/leponline
Ad Rate: Full Page Colour 1888.02

Lancashire Telegraph   979964
Editorial: 1 High Street, Blackburn, Blackburn BB1 1HT **Tel:** 44 01254 678678
Email: lt_editorial@nqnw.co.uk
Web site: www.lancashiretelegraph.co.uk
Freq: Daily
Circ: 11807 Not Audited
Profile: The Lancashire Telegraph is a daily newspaper distributed in East Lancashire, including the towns of Blackburn, Burnley, Accrington, Darwen, Nelson, Clitheroe, Colne, Rawtenstall and Ramsbottom. It is owned by Newsquest, and was previously known as the Lancashire Evening Telegraph, before it changed to its current name in 2006. The paper covers regional news, sport, business, features and entertainment news. This outlet offers RSS (Really Simple Syndication).
Ad Rate: Full Page Mono 1060.00
Ad Rate: Full Page Colour 1060.00

Lancaster Guardian   980375
Editorial: 41 Northgate, White Lund Industrial Estate, Morecambe, Morecambe LA3 3PA **Tel:** 44 01524 385929
Email: guardian@jpress.co.uk
Web site: www.lancasterguardian.co.uk
Freq: Weekly
Circ: 11198 Not Audited
Profile: Website for the Lancaster Guardian and the Morecambe Guardian covering news and sports for the surrounding area.

Lancing Herald   988853
Editorial: Cannon House, Chatsworth Road, Worthing BN11 1NA **Tel:** 44 01903 230051
Email: news@worthingherald.co.uk
Web site: www.worthingherald.co.uk
Freq: Weekly
Circ: 19901 Not Audited
Profile: The Lancing Herald is a weekly local newspaper covering local news, sport, lifestyle and community for the surrounding area.

Largs & Millport Weekly News   980691
Editorial: Herald Building, Dock Road, Ardrossan, Ardrossan KA22 8DA
Tel: 44 01475 689009
Email: editorial@largsnews.co.uk
Web site: www.largsandmillportnews.com
Freq: Weekly
Circ: 3339 Not Audited
Editor: Caroline Patterson
Profile: Online version of the Largs & Millport Weekly News covering local news and sports for the surrounding area.

Larne Times   983144
Tel: 44 02828 272303
Email: news@larnetimes.co.uk
Web site: www.larnetimes.co.uk
Freq: Weekly
Circ: 6715 Not Audited
Profile: This is the online version of the Larne Times, a weekly, local newspaper covering all the latest on local news, sport, motors and property in Larne and the surrounding areas of Newtownabbey, Carnlough, Greenisland, Mossley and Whitehead.

Launceston Journal Gazette   980233
Editorial: Tindle House, Westgate Street, Launceston PL15 7AL **Tel:** 44 01566 772424
Email: launceston@thepost.uk.com
Web site: www.launceston-today.co.uk
Freq: Weekly
Circ: 7990 Not Audited
Editor: Suzanne Cleave

Leader Series   998707
Editorial: Mold Business Park, Wrexham Road, Mold, Mold CH7 1XY
Tel: 44 01352 707707
Email: news@leaderlive.co.uk
Web site: www.leaderlive.co.uk
Freq: Daily
Circ: 13653 Not Audited
Editor: Jonathan Barnett

Leamington Spa Observer   994665
Editorial: 45 The Parade, Leamington Spa, Leamington Spa CV32 4BL
Tel: 44 01926 451900
Email: editor@leamingtonobserver.co.uk
Web site: www.leamingtonobserver.co.uk
Freq: Weekly
Circ: 17433 Not Audited
Editor: Ian Hughes

Leamington Spa The Courier   982988
Editorial: 32 Hamilton Terrace, Leamington Spa, Leamington Spa CV32 4LY
Tel: 44 01926 457737
Email: news@leamingtoncourier.co.uk
Web site: www.leamingtoncourier.co.uk
Freq: Weekly
Circ: 43205 Not Audited

Leatherhead Advertiser   980542
Editorial: Ground Floor Suite B, Regent House, 1 - 3 Queensway, Redhill RH1 1QT
Tel: 44 01737 783889
Email: editor@leatherheadadvertiser.co.uk
Web site: www.dorkingandleatherheadadvertiser.co.uk
Freq: Weekly

Circ: 7635 Not Audited
Profile: The Leatherhead Advertiser is a weekly local newspaper covering news, sports and local community for the surrounding area.
Ad Rate: Full Page Mono 2099.52

Leek Post & Times   980525
Editorial: 1 Market Place, Leek, Leek ST13 5HH **Tel:** 44 01538 714000
Email: newsdesk@thepostandtimes.co.uk
Web site: www.leek-news.co.uk
Freq: Weekly
Circ: 8448 Not Audited
Editor: Killoran Wills
Profile: Online version of the Leek Post and Times newspaper covering local news, sports, health and business for the surrounding area.

Leicester Mercury   979950
Editorial: 16 New Walk, Leicester LE1 6TF
Tel: 44 01162 512512
Email: newsdesk@leicestermercury.co.uk
Web site: www.leicestermercury.co.uk
Freq: Daily
Circ: 25859 Not Audited
Profile: The Leicester Mercury is a daily regional newspaper that covers the latest regional news, sports and business for the surrounding area.
Ad Rate: Full Page Mono 4896.00
Ad Rate: Full Page Colour 4896.00

Leigh Journal   980427
Editorial: 12-14 Bold Street, Leigh WN7 4AT
Tel: 44 01942 672241
Email: newsdesk@leighjournal.co.uk
Web site: www.leighjournal.co.uk
Freq: Weekly
Circ: 49449 Not Audited
Editor: Hayley Smith
Profile: This is the online version of the Leigh Journal, a weekly newspaper covering all the latest leisure, events, news and sport for the local area.

Leigh Observer   1073942
Editorial: Leigh Observer, Martland Mill, Wigan WN5 0LX **Tel:** 44 01942 228000
Email: newsroom@lancspublications.co.uk
Web site: http://www.leighobserver.co.uk/
Freq: WeeklyNot Audited

The Leigh Times   980298
Editorial: 106 Broadway, Leigh-on-Sea, Southend-on-Sea SS9 1AB
Tel: 44 01702 477666
Email: editor@leightimes.co.uk
Web site: www.leightimes.co.uk/
Freq: Bi-Weekly
Circ: 24000 Not Audited
Editor: Michael Guy

Leighton Buzzard Observer   980191
Editorial: 39 Upper George Street, Luton LU1 2RD **Tel:** 44 01582 700666
Email: news@lbobserver.co.uk
Web site: www.leightonbuzzardonline.co.uk
Freq: Weekly
Circ: 5131 Not Audited
Editor: Olga Norford
Profile: This is the online version of the Leighton Buzzard Observer, a weekly, local newspaper covering all the latest on local news, sport, motors and property in Leighton Buzzard and the surrounding areas of Eaton Bray, Linslade an Ivinghoe.

The Lennox Herald   980692
Editorial: 1 Central Quay, Glasgow G3 8DA
Tel: 44 01389 742299
Email: news@lennoxherald.co.uk
Web site: www.lennoxherald.co.uk
Freq: Weekly
Circ: 5633 Not Audited
Editor: Linzi Watson
Profile: Online version of the Lennox Herald newspaper covering local news and sports for the surrounding area.

Lentswe   1060548
Tel: 44 27184 641911
Email: salome@klerkdorprecord.co.za

Freq: Weekly
Circ: 13223 Not Audited

Letters to the Editor   1000944
Editorial: 15 Scarborough Street, Hartlepool TS24 7DA **Tel:** 44 01429 235197
Email: mail.news@northeast-press.co.uk
Web site: http://www.hartlepoolmail.co.uk/

Lewes and South Coast Argus   980288
Editorial: Dolphin House, 2-5 Manchester Street, Brighton BN2 1TF
Tel: 44 01273 544512
Email: jane.delaney@theargus.co.uk
Web site: www.theargus.co.uk
Freq: Weekly
Circ: 21630 Not Audited
Profile: The South Coast Leader is a weekly, local newspaper covering all the latest news and sport for the surrounding areas.
Ad Rate: Full Page Colour 1634.04

Lichfield Mercury   980526
Editorial: Ventura Park Road, Bitterscote, Tamworth B78 3LZ **Tel:** 44 01827 848586
Email: mercury.editorial@cintamworth.co.uk
Web site: www.lichfieldmercury.co.uk
Freq: Weekly
Circ: 29049 Not Audited
Profile: This is the online version of the Lichfield Mercury, a weekly, local newspaper covering all the latest on local news, sport and entertainment in Lichfield, Burntwood and the surrounding area.

Lincolnshire Echo   979948
Editorial: Ground Floor, Witham Wharf, Brayford Wharf East, Lincoln LN5 7AY
Tel: 44 01522 804300
Email: news@lincolnshireecho.co.uk
Web site: http://www.lincolnshirelive.co.uk/
Freq: Weekly
Circ: 14150 Not Audited
Profile: Online version of the Lincolnshire Echo covering local news, sports and entertainment for the surrounding area.

Lincolnshire Free Press   980391
Editorial: Priory House, The Crescent, Spalding PE11 1AB **Tel:** 44 01775 725021
Email: spaldingeditor@jpress.co.uk
Web site: www.spaldingtoday.co.uk
Freq: Weekly
Circ: 8292 Not Audited
Profile: Lincolnshire Free Press is a weekly local newspaper available on Tuesdays, covering local news for the surrounding area.
Ad Rate: Full Page Mono 1435.14

Linlithgow Gazette   980693
Editorial: Unit 4A, Gateway Business Park, Beancross Road, Grangemouth FK3 8WX
Tel: 44 01324 690222
Email: editorial@journalandgazette.co.uk
Web site: www.linlithgowtoday.co.uk
Freq: Weekly
Circ: 4579 Not Audited
Editor: Jill Buchanan
Profile: Website for local paper the Linlithgow Gazette covering the latest news, sport and entertainment from Linlithgow.

Littlehampton Gazette   980578
Editorial: Cannon House, Chatsworth Road, Worthing, Worthing BN11 1NA
Tel: 44 01903 714135
Email: letters@littlehamptongazette.co.uk
Web site: www.littlehamptontoday.co.uk
Freq: Weekly
Circ: 8988 Not Audited
Profile: Online version of the Littlehampton Gazette newspaper covering local news and sports for the surrounding area.

Liverpool Echo   979980
Editorial: PO Box 48, Old Hall Street, Liverpool L69 3EB **Tel:** 44 01514 722488
Email: news@liverpool.com
Web site: www.liverpoolecho.co.uk
Freq: Daily
Circ: 44427 Not Audited
Profile: The Liverpool Echo is a daily newspaper published by Trinity Mirror. It is published Monday to Saturday and covers

the latest regional news, sports, features, entertainment and business for the surrounding area.
Ad Rate: Full Page Mono 7344.00
Ad Rate: Full Page Colour 8160.00

Llanelli Herald   998335
Editorial: 44a Stepney Street, Llanelli SA15 3TR **Tel:** 44 01267 600500
Email: editor@herald.email
Web site: http://www.llanelliherald.com/
Freq: Weekly
Circ: 10000 Not Audited

Llanelli Star   982938
Editorial: 11 Cowell Street, Llanelli SA15 1UU **Tel:** 44 01554 745316
Web site: www.llanellistar.co.uk
Freq: Weekly
Circ: 7747 Not Audited
Profile: This is the online version of the Llanelli Star, a weekly local newspaper, covering all the latest news, sport and leisure for the surrounding area.

The Local   995261
Editorial: Cherryholt Road, Stamford, Stamford PE9 2EP **Tel:** 44 01780 758951
Email: news@bournelocal.co.uk
Web site: www.bournelocal.co.uk
Freq: WeeklyNot Audited
Profile: This is the online version of the Local (Bourne), a weekly, local newspaper covering all the latest on local news, sport and lifestyle in Bourne.

London Evening Standard   979798
Editorial: Northcliffe House, 2 Derry Street, London W8 5TT **Tel:** 44 02033 677000
Email: news@standard.co.uk
Web site: www.standard.co.uk
Freq: Daily
Circ: 899484 Not Audited
Profile: The London Evening Standard is a free, tabloid-sized, daily newspaper covering the arts, business, entertainment, fashion, lifestyle, regional and national news and travel for London and the South-East.
Ad Rate: Full Page Colour 57000.00

The London Jang   982935
Editorial: 1 Sanctuary Street, London SE1 1ED **Tel:** 44 02074 034122
Email: editorlondon@janggroup.com.pk
Web site: www.jang.com.pk
Freq: Daily
Circ: 2145 Not Audited
Editor: Istikhar Quisar

London Weekly News series   996043
Email: editorial@londonweeklynews.co.uk
Web site: http://www.londonweeklynews.co.uk/
Freq: Weekly
Circ: 24905 Not Audited

The Londonderry Sentinel   981662
Editorial: Suite 4 & 5, Spencer House, Spencer Road, Waterside, Londonderry BT47 6AA **Tel:** 44 02871 341175
Web site: www.londonderrysentinel.co.uk
Freq: Weekly
Circ: 3676 Not Audited
Editor: Peter Hutcheon
Profile: This is the online version of the Londonderry Sentinel, a weekly, local newspaper covering all the latest on local news, sport, property and motors in County Londonderry and the surrounding area.

Long Eaton & District Chronicle   995980
Editorial: 126 Derby Road, Long Eaton, Notts, Long Eaton NG10 4LS
Tel: 44 01159 461146
Email: newsdesk@longeatonchronicle.com
Web site: www.longeatonchronicle.com
Freq: Monthly
Circ: 15000 Not Audited
Editor: Bob Griffiths

Longridge & Ribble Valley News   980376
Editorial: Oliver's Place, Fulwood, Preston PR2 9ZA **Tel:** 44 01772 554547
Email: longridge.news@lep.co.uk
Web site: www.longridgetoday.co.uk
Freq: Weekly
Circ: 4769 Not Audited

Look Local   1076634
Editorial: 516 Manchester Road, Stocksbridge, Sheffield S36 2DU
Tel: 44 01142 831100
Email: news@looklocal.org.uk
Web site: www.looklocal.org.uk
Freq: Weekly
Circ: 27000 Not Audited
Editor: James Evans

Loughborough Echo   982965
Editorial: Princes' Court, Royal Way, Off Belton Road, Loughborough LE11 5XR
Tel: 44 01509 635802
Web site: www.loughboroughecho.net
Freq: Weekly
Circ: 9018 Not Audited
Profile: The Loughborough Echo is a weekly, local newspaper covering all the latest on local news, sport and lifestyle in Loughborough. The paper is published on a Thursday.
Ad Rate: Full Page Mono 1606.50

Louth Leader   980392
Editorial: Room 36, Fairfield Enterprise Centre, Lincoln Way, Louth LN11 0LS
Tel: 44 01507 353200
Email: louthleader@jpress.co.uk
Web site: www.louthleader.co.uk
Freq: Weekly
Circ: 7183 Not Audited
Profile: This is the online version of the Louth Leader, a weekly local newspaper covering local news for the surrounding area.

Lowestoft Journal   980534
Editorial: 147 London Road North, Lowestoft NR32 1NB **Tel:** 44 01502 525820
Email: lowestoft.journal@archant.co.uk
Web site: www.lowestoftjournal.co.uk
Freq: Weekly
Circ: 9559 Not Audited
Profile: Lowestoft Journal provides the latest local news and sports from Lowestoft, Southwold and Kessingland. The paper is available on Fridays.
Ad Rate: Full Page Mono 1417.02
Ad Rate: Full Page Colour 1700.42

Lowvelder/laevelder   1060536
Freq: Bi-Weekly
Circ: 17805 Not Audited

Ludlow & Tenbury Wells Advertiser   996026
Editorial: Hereford Times, Holmer Road, Hereford HR4 9UJ **Tel:** 44 01432 274413
Email: news@ludlowadvertiser.co.uk
Web site: www.ludlowadvertiser.co.uk
Freq: Weekly
Circ: 3166 Not Audited
Profile: This is the online version of the Ludlow Advertiser and Tenbury Wells advertiser, weekly, local newspapers covering all the latest on local news, sport and leisure in Ludlow, Tenbury and the surrounding areas.

Lurgan Mail   984218
Tel: 44 02838 327777
Email: editor@lurganmail.co.uk
Web site: www.lurgantoday.com
Freq: Weekly
Circ: 5522 Not Audited
Editor: Clint Aiken
Profile: Website of The Lurgan Mail, a weekly newspaper that covers local news, sports and lifestyle for the surrounding area.

Luton News   980193
Editorial: 39 Upper George Street, Luton LU1 2RD **Tel:** 44 01582 700600
Email: editorial@lutonnews.co.uk
Web site: www.lutontoday.co.uk

Regional & Local Weekly Newspapers

Freq: Weekly
Circ: 5488 Not Audited
Editor: Olga Norford
Profile: Luton News is a local weekly newspaper covering local news and sports for Luton, Barton-le-Clay, Toddington, Caddington and the surrounding area. The newspaper is published on a Wednesday.

Lynn News 980451
Editorial: Limes House, Purfleet Street, King's Lynn PE30 1HL **Tel:** 44 01553 761188
Email: newsdesk@lynnnews.co.uk
Web site: http://www.lynnnews.co.uk/
Freq: 2 Times/Week
Circ: 22142 Not Audited
Editor: Mark Leslie
Profile: Online version of the Lynn News covering local news and sports for the surrounding area.

Lytham St Annes Express 980377
Editorial: Avroe House, Avroe Crescent, Blackpool Business Park, Blackpool FY4 2DP **Tel:** 44 01253 361840
Email: news@lsaexpress.co.uk
Web site: www.lythamtoday.co.uk
Freq: Weekly
Circ: 4949 Not Audited

Mablethorpe & Sutton on Sea Leader 983739
Editorial: Room 36, Fairfield Enterprise Centre, Lincoln Way, Louth LN11 0LS
Tel: 44 01507 353200
Web site: www.louthleader.co.uk
Freq: Weekly
Circ: 1393 Not Audited
Profile: The Mablethorpe & Sutton on Sea Leader is a weekly local newspaper covering local news for the surrounding area.

Macclesfield Express 980222
Editorial: Office 1c, 11 Market Place, Macclesfield SK10 1EB
Tel: 44 01612 112985
Email: macclesfieldexpress@menmedia.co.uk
Web site: www.macclesfield-express.co.uk
Freq: Weekly
Circ: 7063 Not Audited
Editor: Gareth Tidman
Profile: Website for local paper the Macclefield Express providing the latest news, events and information from Macclesfield.

Maidenhead Advertiser 980195
Editorial: Newspaper House, 48 Bell Street, Maidenhead, Maidenhead SL6 1HX
Tel: 44 01628 680680
Email: news@baylismedia.co.uk
Web site: www.maidenhead-advertiser.co.uk
Freq: Weekly
Circ: 14506 Not Audited
Profile: Online version of the Maidenhead Advertiser covering local news and sports fro the surrounding area.

The Mail 979965
Editorial: Newspaper House, Abbey Road, Barrow in Furness, Barrow-in-Furness LA14 5QS **Tel:** 44 00122 9840100
Email: news@cnmedia.co.uk
Web site: www.nwemail.co.uk
Freq: Daily
Circ: 7744 Not Audited
Profile: Daily tabloid newspaper covering the latest in regional news, sports and business for the area of Barrow-in-Furness. This outlet offers RSS (Really simple syndication)
Ad Rate: Full Page Mono 1270.90
Ad Rate: Full Page Colour 1270.90

Mail Series (Bangor & Holyhead) 999163
Editorial: Vale Road, Llandudno Junction, Conwy LL31 9SL **Tel:** 44 01286 671111
Email: caernarfon.herald@northwalesnews.co.uk
Web site: www.dailypost.co.uk/all-about/bangor

Freq: Weekly
Circ: 4130 Not Audited

Maldon & Burnham Standard 986890
Editorial: 76 High Street, Braintree, Braintree CM7 1JP **Tel:** 44 01376 343344
Email: mbsdistrict@nqe.com
Web site: www.maldonandburnhamstandard.co.uk
Freq: Weekly
Circ: 5415 Not Audited
Profile: Online version of the Maldon Standard and the Burnham Standard newspapers covering local news and sports for the surrounding area. The outlet offers RSS (Really Simple Syndication).

Malvern Gazette 982978
Editorial: Berrow's House, Hylton Road, Worcester WR2 5JX **Tel:** 44 01905 748200
Email: news@malverngazette.co.uk
Web site: www.malverngazette.co.uk
Freq: Weekly
Circ: 8839 Not Audited
Profile: This is the online version of the Malvern Gazette, a weekly, local newspaper covering all the latest news, sport and leisure for the surrounding area.

Manchester Evening News 979864
Editorial: Mitchell Henry House, Hollinwood Avenue, Chadderton, Oldham OL9 8EF
Tel: 44 01618 327200
Email: newsdesk@men-news.co.uk
Web site: www.manchestereveningnews.co.uk
Freq: Daily
Circ: 47052 Not Audited
Profile: The Manchester Evening News is a regional daily newspaper providing the latest news, sport, business, entertainment and lifestyle news in the Greater Manchester area. The newspaper has two editions, Manchester Evening News (North) and Manchester Evening News (South).
Ad Rate: Full Page Mono 10434.00
Ad Rate: Full Page Colour 14608.44

Manchester Weekly News 988817
Editorial: Mitchell Henry House, Hollinwood Avenue, Chadderton, Oldham OL9 8EF
Tel: 44 01618 327200
Email: newsdesk@men-news.co.uk
Web site: www.manchestereveningnews.co.uk/
Freq: Weekly
Circ: 248264 Not Audited

Mansfield Chad 980010
Editorial: Unit 2A, Sherwood Oaks Business Park, Southwell Road, Mansfield, Mansfield NG18 4TB **Tel:** 44 01623 450307
Email: newsdesk@chad.co.uk
Web site: www.chad.co.uk/
Freq: Weekly
Circ: 18604 Not Audited
Profile: The Mansfield Chad is a weekly, local newspaper covering local news, sports and entertainment for the surrounding area. The newspaper is published on a Wednesday. The outlet offers RSS (Really Simple Syndication).
Ad Rate: Full Page Mono 2790.72

Mansfield, Ashfield and Warsop News Journal 1062753
Tel: 44 01623 707017
Email: info@news-journal.co.uk
Web site: http://www.news-journal.co.uk/
Freq: Monthly
Circ: 10000 Not Audited
Editor: Tim Morriss

Manx Independent 980349
Web site: www.iomtoday.co.im
Freq: Weekly
Circ: 8917 Not Audited
Profile: The Manx Independent is a weekly local newspaper covering local news and sports for the surrounding area. The newspaper is published on a Thursday.
Ad Rate: Full Page Mono 1793.16

Ad Rate: Full Page Colour 2689.70

Market Drayton Advertiser 980494
Editorial: 81 Shropshire Street, Market Drayton TF9 3DQ **Tel:** 44 01630 655295
Email: marketdrayton@shropshirestar.co.uk
Web site: www.marketdraytonadvertiser.com
Freq: Weekly
Circ: 4970 Not Audited
Profile: This is the online version of the Market Drayton Advertiser, a weekly, local newspaper covering all the latest on local news in Market Drayton.

Market Rasen Mail 980393
Editorial: Church Lane, Horncastle, Horncastle LN9 5HW **Tel:** 44 01673 844644
Email: rasenmail@jpress.co.uk
Web site: www.marketrasenmail.co.uk
Freq: Weekly
Circ: 2338 Not Audited
Profile: Website for local newspaper the Market Rasen Mail, covering the latest local news and events from Market Rasen and the surrounding local area.

Matlock Mercury 980253
Editorial: Spire Walk, Chesterfield, Chesterfield S40 2WG **Tel:** 44 01246 504536
Email: news@matlockmercury.co.uk
Web site: www.matlocktoday.co.uk
Freq: Weekly
Circ: 4364 Not Audited
Profile: Website of the Matlock Mercury, a weekly newspaper that serves the town of Matlock, Darley Dale, Wirksworth and Bakewell. The paper features a mix of local news and events, sport and lifestyle features.

Mearns Leader 980694
Editorial: 12 Ann Street, Stonehaven AB39 2ER **Tel:** 44 01569 762139
Email: news@mearnsleader.com
Web site: http://www.mearnsleader.com
Freq: Weekly
Circ: 1990 Not Audited
Profile: Website for the Mearns Leader covering the latest local news and events from Stonehaven and the surrounding area.

Medway Messenger 980364
Editorial: Medway House, Ginsbury Close, Sir Thomas Longely Road, Rochester ME2 4DU **Tel:** 44 01634 227803
Email: medwaymessenger@thekmgroup.co.uk
Web site: http://www.kentonline.co.uk/medway/
Freq: Weekly
Circ: 4197 Not Audited
Editor: Matthew Ramsden
Profile: The Medway Messenger is a weekly, local newspaper covering all the latest news and current affairs for the surrounding areas.
Ad Rate: Full Page Mono 1414.40
Ad Rate: Full Page Colour 1768.00

Melksham Independent News 980601
Editorial: 31 Market Place, Melksham SN12 6ES **Tel:** 44 01225 704761
Email: news@melkshamnews.co.uk
Web site: www.melkshamnews.com
Freq: Bi-Weekly
Circ: 13700 Not Audited
Profile: Online version of the Melksham Independent News newspaper covering local news for the surrounding area.

Melton Times 980382
Editorial: 49 Nottingham Street, Melton Mowbray LE13 1NT **Tel:** 44 01664 410041
Email: editor@meltontimes.co.uk
Web site: www.meltontimes.co.uk
Freq: Weekly
Circ: 18800 Not Audited
Editor: Mark Edwards
Profile: Website for the Melton Times, covering the latest local news and events from the Borough of Melton.

Meon Valley News 980321
Editorial: 3 Kingsbury Court, South Lane, Clanfield, Horndean PO8 0UX
Tel: 44 02392 572800
Email: editorial@meonvalleynews.com
Web site: www.meonvalleynews.com
Freq: Monthly
Circ: 52500 Not Audited
Profile: This is the online version of the Meon Valley News, a free, monthly, local newspaper covering all the latest on local news and features in the Meon Valley.

Mercury Extra 982989
Editorial: St George Street, Leicester LE1 9FQ **Tel:** 44 01162 512512
Email: newsdesk@leicestermercury.co.uk
Web site: www.leicestermercury.co.uk/
Freq: Weekly
Circ: 56383 Not Audited
Profile: The Mercury Extra is a free weekly newspaper using content from the Leicester Mercury. Editions Include:Mail (Leicester, Oadby and Wigston) Mail (Ashby and District)

The Mercury Newspaper 984201
Editorial: 4b Queens Road, Sheffield S2 4DG **Tel:** 44 01142 763633
Email: info@mercurynewspaper.co.uk
Web site: www.mercurynewspaper.co.uk
Freq: Weekly
Circ: 50000 Not Audited
Editor: David Platts
Ad Rate: Full Page Colour 350.00

Mercury Series 994653
Editorial: 2-4 Leigham Court Road, London SW16 2PD **Tel:** 44 02087 684900
Email: mercury@slp.co.uk
Web site: http://www.mercury-today.co.uk/
Freq: Weekly
Circ: 48812 Not Audited

Merthyr Express 982990
Editorial: 6 Park Cresent, Cardiff CF10 1XR
Tel: 44 01685 789230
Email: merthyr.express@mediawales.co.uk
Web site: http://www.walesonline.co.uk/all-about/merthyr-tydfil
Freq: Weekly
Circ: 3607 Not Audited
Profile: The Merthyr Express is a weekly, local newspaper covering all the latest news, sport and lifestyle for the surrounding area.
Ad Rate: Full Page Mono 1436.00
Ad Rate: Full Page Colour 1868.00

The Messenger 980543
Editorial: Tindle House, High Street, Bordon GU35 0AY **Tel:** 44 01420 477272
Email: messenger.editorial@tindlenews.co.uk
Web site: http://www.messenger-online.co.uk/
Freq: Weekly
Circ: 33000 Not Audited
Profile: Seventh Day Adventist news magazine.

Messenger Extra (Gravesend, Dartford and Swanley) 998535
Editorial: Messenger Extra (Gravesend, Dartford and Swanley), 7 High Street, Gravesend, London DA11 0BQ
Tel: 44 01474 564327
Email: gravesendmessenger@thekmgroup.co.uk
Web site: www.kentonline.co.uk
Freq: Weekly
Circ: 19471 Not Audited

Meyerton Star 1060508
Tel: 44 27169 507000
Email: rfitchat@media24.com
Freq: Weekly
Circ: 9257 Not Audited

Mid Bedfordshire Times & Citizen 997600
Editorial: Northhouse, 3 Bond Avenue, Bletchley, Milton Keynes MK1 1SW
Tel: 44 01234 405060
Email: editorial@timesandcitizen.co.uk
Web site: www.bedfordtoday.co.uk

Freq: Weekly
Circ: 16291 Not Audited
Editor: Olga Norford

Mid Cornwall Advertiser   980234
Editorial: Tindall House, 2 Trevanson Street, Wadebridge, Wadebridge PL27 7AW
Tel: 44 01208 815096
Email: editorial.nca@internet-today.co.uk
Web site: www.cornwalladvertisers.co.uk
Freq: Weekly
Circ: 51000 Not Audited
Profile: The Mid Cornwall Advertiser is a free local newspaper with local news, community events and features from the area. It is distributed in Truro, Newquay and St Austell as well as the surrounding Carrick district of Mid Cornwall.
Ad Rate: Full Page Mono 720.00
Ad Rate: Full Page Colour 795.00

Mid Devon Advertiser   980260
Editorial: Old Manor House, 63 Wolborough Street, Newton Abbot TQ12 1NE
Tel: 44 01626 353555
Email: editorial@middevonadvertiser.co.uk
Web site: http://www.middevonadvertiser.co.uk/
Freq: Weekly
Circ: 40000 Not Audited

Mid Devon Gazette (Series)   982991
Editorial: Raymond Penny House, Phoenix Lane, Tiverton EX16 6LU
Tel: 44 01884 258826
Email: news@middevongazette.co.uk
Web site: www.devonlive.com/
Freq: Weekly
Circ: 6943 Not Audited
Editor: Jim Parker; **Editor:** Patrick Phelvin

Mid Devon Star   980261
Tel: 44 01823 365210
Web site: http://www.middevonstar.co.uk
Freq: Weekly
Circ: 18165 Not Audited
Profile: The Mid Devon Star is a website for local paper The Star, covering the latest local news and events from Tiverton, Cullompton and the surrounding Mid Devon areas.

Mid Somerset Series   980502
Editorial: Southover, Wells BA5 1UH
Tel: 44 01740 832300
Web site: www.somersetlive.co.uk
Freq: Weekly
Circ: 12023 Not Audited
Editor: Tim Lethaby

Mid Sussex Citizen   996011
Editorial: 7-9 South Road, Haywards Heath RH16 4LE **Tel:** 44 01403 751200
Email: middy.news@sussexnewspapers.co.uk
Web site: www.midsussextimes.co.uk
Freq: WeeklyNot Audited

Mid Sussex Times   980580
Editorial: Springfield House, Springfield Road, Horsham RH12 2RG
Email: middy.news@sussexnewspapers.co.uk
Web site: www.midsussextimes.co.uk
Freq: WeeklyNot Audited
Profile: Website for local paper The Mid Sussex Times covering all the latest news, sport, lifestyle and community for the surrounding area.

Mid Ulster Mail   984191
Editorial: 52 Oldtown Street, Co. Tyrone, Cookstown BT80 8EF **Tel:** 44 02886 762288
Web site: www.midulstermail.co.uk
Freq: Weekly
Circ: 6534 Not Audited
Profile: Online version of the Mid Ulster Mail newspaper covering local news and sports for the surrounding area. The outlet offers RSS (Really Simple Syndication).

Mid Wales Journal   981671
Editorial: Marina Gallery, Middleton Street, Llandrindod Wells, Llandrindod Wells LD1 5ET **Tel:** 44 01597 828060
Web site: http://www.shropshirestar.com/mid-wales-journal/
Freq: Weekly
Circ: 5100 Not Audited
Editor: Mary Queally
Ad Rate: Full Page Mono 1033.20
Ad Rate: Full Page Colour 1033.20

Middleton Guardian   980429
Editorial: Mitchell Henry House, Hollinwood Avenue, Chadderton, Oldham OL9 8EF
Tel: 44 0161 2 112820
Email: middletonguardian@menmedia.co.uk
Web site: http://www.manchestereveningnews.co.uk/all-about/middleton
Freq: Weekly
Circ: 2583 Not Audited
Profile: This is the online version of the Middleton Guardian, a weekly, local newspaper covering all the latest on local news for the surrounding area. The paper is published on a Wednesday.

Midhurst and Petworth Observer   986295
Editorial: Capron House, North Street, Midhurst GU29 9DT **Tel:** 44 01730 816986
Email: midhurst@jpress.co.uk
Web site: www.midhurstandpetworth.co.uk
Freq: Weekly
Circ: 3500 Not Audited

Midlands Herald   1060456
Tel: 44 27333 306000
Email: alice@capro.com
Freq: Monthly
Circ: 8000 Not Audited

Midlothian Advertiser   980695
Editorial: 108 Holyrood Road, Edinburgh EH8 8AS **Tel:** 44 01313 117311
Email: midlothianadvertiser@jnlothian.co.uk
Web site: http://www.midlothianadvertiser.co.uk/
Freq: Weekly
Circ: 3531 Not Audited
Profile: Online version of the Midlothian Advertiser newspaper covering local news and sports for the surrounding area.

Midsomer Norton, Radstock & District Journal   981120
Editorial: Wans Dyke Business Centre, Unit 22, Midsomer Enterprise Park, Radstock Road, Midsomer Norton BA3 3BB
Tel: 44 01761 408160
Email: mnrjournal@btconnect.com
Web site: www.mnrjournal.co.uk
Freq: Weekly
Circ: 16000 Not Audited
Editor: Becky Brooks
Profile: The Midsomer Norton, Radstock & District Journal is a free weekly newspaper covering local news and sport. It includes regular features on dining out, gardening, motoring, health and beauty.
Ad Rate: Full Page Mono 335.00
Ad Rate: Full Page Colour 335.00

Midweek Herald   980262
Editorial: Fair Oak Close, Exeter Airport Business Park, Clyst Honiton, Exeter EX5 2UL **Tel:** 44 01392 888400
Email: midweek.editorial@archant.co.uk
Web site: www.midweekherald.co.uk
Freq: WeeklyNot Audited
Profile: Online version of the Midweek Herald covering local news and sports for the surrounding area.

Midweek Mercury   980512
Editorial: 32 Waterloo Street, Weston-super-Mare BS23 1LW
Tel: 44 01934 422622
Email: newsdesk@westonmercury.co.uk
Web site: www.westonmercury.co.uk
Freq: WeeklyNot Audited
Editor: Tom Wright
Profile: Midweek Mercury is a free weekly local newspaper and covers local news and

sports for the surrounding areas. The Newspaper is published on a Wednesday. The outlet offers RSS (Really Simple Syndication).
Ad Rate: Full Page Mono 994.50
Ad Rate: Full Page Colour 1243.10

Midweek Mercury   989266
Tel: 44 01992 526600
Email: mercury@hertsessexnews.co.uk
Web site: www.hertfordshiremercury.co.uk
Freq: WeeklyNot Audited
Profile: Midweek Mercury is a free weekly local newspaper and covers local news and sports for the surrounding areas. The Newspaper is published on a Wednesday. The outlet offers RSS (Really Simple Syndication).
Ad Rate: Full Page Mono 994.50
Ad Rate: Full Page Colour 1243.10

Midweek Mercury (North Herts)   994664
Editorial: Midweek Mercury, The Media Centre, 40 Ware Road, Hertford SG13 7HU
Tel: 44 01992 526625
Email: news@theadvertisergroup.co.uk
Web site: http://www.hertfordshiremercury.co.uk/
Freq: Weekly
Circ: 32478 Not Audited

Milford & West Wales Mercury   981357
Editorial: Western Telegraph office, Western Tangiers, Fishguard Road, Haverfordwest, Haverfordwest SA62 4BU
Tel: 44 01437 761764
Email: mercurynews@milfordmercury.co.uk
Web site: www.milfordmercury.co.uk
Freq: Weekly
Circ: 1814 Not Audited
Profile: Website of The Milford & West Wales Mercury, a weekly local newspaper covering all the latest news for the surrounding area.

Milngavie and Bearsden Herald   980696
Editorial: 11 Dalrymple Court, Glasgow G66 3AA **Tel:** 44 01417 750040
Email: mbherald@jnscotland.co.uk
Web site: www.milngavietoday.co.uk
Freq: Weekly
Circ: 12742 Not Audited
Editor: Jim Holland

Milton Keynes Citizen   980203
Editorial: North House, 3 Bond Avenue, Bletchley, Milton Keynes MK1 1SW
Tel: 44 01908 372279
Email: editorial@mkcitizen.co.uk
Web site: www.miltonkeynes.co.uk
Freq: Weekly
Circ: 92522 Not Audited
Editor: Olga Norford
Profile: Website for the Milton Keynes Citizen, Leighton-Linslade Citizen and Citizen First covering the latest in local news and current affairs, sport, entertainment and lifestyle features from Milton Keynes and the surrounding area.

Moffat News   980697
Editorial: 96 High Street, Annan, Annandale DG12 6EJ **Tel:** 44 01461 202078
Email: newsdesk@dngonline.co.uk
Web site: www.dng24.co.uk/news/regions/moffat
Freq: Weekly
Circ: 892 Not Audited
Editor: Bryan Armstrong
Profile: The Moffat News is a local weekly news paper covering local news and sports for the surrounding area.

Monmouthshire Beacon   982992
Editorial: Cornwall House, 56 Monnow Street, Monmouth NP25 3XJ
Tel: 44 01600 712142
Email: beaconnews@tindlenews.co.uk
Web site: www.monmouth-today.co.uk
Freq: Weekly
Circ: 5012 Not Audited
Editor: Victoria Hallifax

Profile: This is the online version of the Monmouthshire Beacon, a weekly local newspaper covering all the latest news, sport, features and events for the surrounding area.
Ad Rate: Full Page Mono 994.50
Ad Rate: Full Page Colour 1243.10

Montrose Review   980698
Editorial: 63 Murray Street, Angus, Montrose DD10 8JZ **Tel:** 44 01674 679030
Email: news@montrosereview.com
Web site: www.montrosereview.co.uk
Freq: Weekly
Circ: 2471 Not Audited
Profile: Website of local newspaper the Montrose Review, covering news and events in Montrose.

The Moorlander   1095953
Tel: 44 01647 432279
Email: editorial@themoorlander.co.uk
Web site: http://themoorlander.co.uk/
Freq: Bi-Weekly
Circ: 4000 Not Audited
Editor: Stuart Clarke

Morley Observer & Advertiser   980593
Editorial: Floor 5, 26 Whitehall Road, Leeds LS12 1BE **Tel:** 44 01924 433013
Email: editorial@morleytoday.co.uk
Web site: http://www.morleyobserver.co.uk/
Freq: Weekly
Circ: 4409 Not Audited
Editor: John Kenealy
Profile: This is the online version of the Morley Observer & Advertiser, a weekly local newspaper covering local news, lifestyle and sport in Morley. The paper was first published in 1871. This outlet offers RSS (Really Simple Syndication).

Morpeth Herald   980477
Editorial: Unit 15, Telford Court, Loansdean, Morpeth NE61 2DB **Tel:** 44 01670 516066
Email: morpeth.herald@jpress.co.uk
Web site: www.morpethherald.co.uk
Freq: Weekly
Circ: 1879 Not Audited
Editor: Paul Larkin
Profile: Website of the Morpeth Herald, a local, weekly paper that covers local news for the communities of Morpeth, Pegswood, Ponteland, Lynemouth and Ellington as well as outlying districts.

Motherwell Times   981492
Editorial: 29 Hope Street, Motherwell ML1 1BT **Tel:** 44 01698 242553
Email: motherwell.times@jnscotland.co.uk
Web site: www.motherwelltimes.co.uk
Freq: Weekly
Circ: 6382 Not Audited
Editor: Martin Clark
Profile: Online version of the Motherwell Times covering local news, sports, lifestyle and community events for the surrounding area.

Mountsorrel Post   1076217
Editorial: Unit 109, Greenacres, The Sidings, Leicester LE4 3BR **Tel:** 44 01164 422067
Email: editor@birstallpost.co.uk
Web site: www.birstallpost.co.uk
Freq: Quarterly
Circ: 3300 Not Audited
Editor: Jerry Jackson

Mourne Observer   983145
Editorial: Castlewellan Road, County Down, Newcastle BT33 0JX **Tel:** 44 02843 722666
Email: news@mourneobserver.com
Web site: www.mourneobserver.com
Freq: Weekly
Circ: 9768 Not Audited
Editor: Stephen Patton
Profile: Online version of the Mourne Observer newspaper covering local news for the surrounding area.

Musselburgh News   980699
Editorial: 108 Holyrood Road, Edinburgh EH8 8AS **Tel:** 44 01315 616600
Web site: www.eastlothiannews.co.uk/
Freq: Weekly

Regional & Local Weekly Newspapers

Circ: 1001 Not Audited
Profile: The Musselburgh News is a weekly paper covering the latest news and events from Musselburgh.

My Abbots News 987626
Editorial: Units 21-23, John Dickinson Enterprise Centre, Stationers Place, London Road, Apsley, London HP3 9QU
Tel: 44 01442 257015
Email: newseditor@mynewsmag.co.uk
Web site: www.mynewsmag.co.uk
Freq: MonthlyNot Audited

My Bushey News 987628
Editorial: Ground Floor, John Dickinson Enterprise Centre, Stationers Place, London Road, Apsley, London HP3 9QU
Tel: 44 01442 257015
Web site: www.mynewsmag.co.uk
Freq: Monthly
Circ: 6269 Not Audited

My Chorleywood News 987629
Editorial: Units 21-23, John Dickinson Enterprise Centre, Stationers Place, London Road, London HP3 9QU
Tel: 44 01442 257015
Web site: www.mynewsmag.co.uk
Freq: MonthlyNot Audited

My Croxley News 987630
Editorial: John Dickinson Enterprise Centre, Stationers Place, London Road, Apsley, London HP3 9QU **Tel:** 44 01442 257015
Web site: www.mynewsmag.co.uk
Freq: MonthlyNot Audited

My Garston News 987632
Editorial: Units 21-23, John Dickinson Enterprise Centre, Stationers Place, London Road, London HP3 9QU
Tel: 44 01442 257015
Web site: www.mynewsmag.co.uk
Freq: MonthlyNot Audited

My Kings News 987633
Editorial: John Dickinson Enterprise Centre, Stationers Place, London Road, Apsley, London HP3 9QU **Tel:** 44 01442 257015
Web site: www.mynewsmag.co.uk
Freq: MonthlyNot Audited

My Northwood News 987634
Editorial: Units 21-23, John Dickinson Enterprise Centre, Stationers Place, London Road, London HP3 9QU
Tel: 44 01442 257015
Web site: www.mynewsmag.co.uk
Freq: MonthlyNot Audited

My Radlett News 987636
Editorial: Units 21-23, John Dickinson Enterprise Centre, Stationers Place, London Road, London HP3 9QU
Tel: 44 01442 257015
Web site: www.mynewsmag.co.uk
Freq: MonthlyNot Audited

My Ricky News 987638
Editorial: John Dickinson Enterprise Centre, Stationers Place, London Road, Apsley, London HP3 9QU **Tel:** 44 01442 257015
Web site: www.mynewsmag.co.uk
Freq: MonthlyNot Audited

My Watford News 987639
Editorial: Units 21-23, John Dickinson Enterprise Centre, Stationers Place, London Road, Apsley, London HP3 9QU
Tel: 44 01442 257015
Web site: www.mynewsmag.co.uk
Freq: MonthlyNot Audited

Nairnshire Telegraph 983646
Editorial: 10 Leopold Street, Nairn IV12 4BG
Tel: 44 01667 453258
Email: ed@nairnshiretelegraph.com
Freq: WeeklyNot Audited
Editor: Iain Bain
Profile: The Nairnshire Telegraph is a local newspaper covering local news from the Nairn area.
Ad Rate: Full Page Mono 492.10

NAWA-I-JANG LONDON 999346
Editorial: 6 Globe House, 1 Bentinck Road, West Drayton UB7 7RQ
Tel: 44 02031 742057
Email: news@nawaijang.com
Web site: www.nawaijang.com
Freq: Weekly
Circ: 42000 Not Audited

New Forest Post 980323
Editorial: Newspaper House, Test Lane, Redbridge, Southampton SO16 9JX
Tel: 44 02380 424966
Email: newsdesk@dailyecho.co.uk
Web site: http://www.newforestpost.co.uk
Freq: Weekly
Circ: 24648 Not Audited
Profile: The New Forest Post is a weekly local newspaper covering local news and sports for the surrounding area.
Ad Rate: Full Page Mono 1490.40
Ad Rate: Full Page Colour 1656.00

New Milton Advertiser & Lymington Times 980320
Editorial: 66 Old Milton Road, New Milton, New Milton BH25 6DX **Tel:** 44 01425 613384
Email: news@adt.press
Web site: http://www.adt.press/
Freq: Weekly
Circ: 15590 Not Audited
Profile: Website for local paper's the New Milton Advertiser and the Lymington Times, covering the latest news from the New Forest.

New WORLD 995941
Editorial: 234 Holloway Road, London N7 8DA **Tel:** 44 02077 002673
Freq: Monthly
Circ: 10000 Not Audited
Profile: New World is a magazine featuring articles on topical issues relating to science, philosophy and culture.
Ad Rate: Full Page Mono 675.00
Ad Rate: Full Page Colour 850.00

Newark Advertiser 980482
Editorial: Unit 9 & 10 Halifax Court, Fernwood Business Park, Cross Lane, Newark NG24 3JP **Tel:** 44 01636 681234
Email: news@newarkadvertiser.co.uk
Web site: www.newarkadvertiser.co.uk
Freq: Weekly
Circ: 11786 Not Audited
Profile: Newark Advertiser is a weekly paper covering the latest news and events from Newark-on-Trent, Nottinghamshire and the surrounding local area.
Ad Rate: Full Page Mono 1790.10
Ad Rate: Full Page Colour 2040.10

Newark Trader Pictorial 982993
Editorial: Unit 9 & 10 Halifax Court, Fernwood Business Park, Cross Lane, Newark NG24 3JP **Tel:** 44 01636 681234
Email: news@newarkadvertiser.co.uk
Web site: www.newarkadvertiser.co.uk
Freq: Weekly
Circ: 15523 Not Audited

Newbury & Thatcham Advertiser 998675
Editorial: Newspaper House, Faraday Road, Newbury RG14 2DW **Tel:** 44 01635 524111
Email: newsdesk@newburynews.co.uk
Web site: www.newburytoday.co.uk
Freq: Weekly
Circ: 13135 Not Audited

Newbury & Thatcham Chronicle - CEASED 2016
980196
Editorial: Bowman House, Reading RG1 2LU
Web site: www. newburyandthatchamchronicle.co.uk
Freq: Weekly
Circ: 9895 Not Audited

Newbury & Thatcham Observer 1075505
Tel: 44 01235 516930
Email: news@observergroup.co.uk

Web site: http://newburyobserver.co.uk/
Freq: WeeklyNot Audited

Newbury Weekly News 979970
Editorial: Newspaper House, Faraday Road, Newbury RG14 2DW **Tel:** 44 01635 524111
Email: newsdesk@newburynews.co.uk
Web site: www.newburytoday.co.uk
Freq: Weekly
Circ: 13810 Not Audited
Profile: The Newbury Weekly News is a weekly newspaper covering the latest in local news for the town of Newbury and the surrounding area.
Ad Rate: Full Page Colour 850.00

Newham Recorder 980415
Editorial: 7th Floor Maritime House, 1 Linton Road, Barking IG11 8HG
Tel: 44 02084 784444
Email: newsdesk@newhamrecorder.co.uk
Web site: www.newhamrecorder.co.uk
Freq: Weekly
Circ: 17755 Not Audited
Profile: Website for local newspaper the Newham Recorder, covering the latest news, sport and entertainment news from the local area. This outlet covers areas within Newham Borough.

Newmarket Journal 980535
Editorial: Rookery House, Newmarket, Newmarket CB8 8SY
Web site: www.newmarkettoday.co.uk
Freq: Weekly
Circ: 7397 Not Audited
Profile: The Newmarket Journal is a weekly local newspaper covering local news for the surrounding area.

Newmarket News 982994
Editorial: Winship Road, Milton, Cambridge CB24 6PP **Tel:** 44 01638 662581
Email: editorial@newmarketweeklynews.co. uk
Web site: http://www.cambridge-news.co. uk/Newmarket/
Freq: Weekly
Circ: 9978 Not Audited

Newport Advertiser 982895
Editorial: Waterloo Road, Ketley, Telford TF1 5HU **Tel:** 44 01952 241456
Email: ketley.newsroom@shropshirestar.co. uk
Web site: www.newportadvertiser.co.uk
Freq: Weekly
Circ: 4970 Not Audited
Profile: The Newport Advertiser is a weekly local newspaper covering local news for the surrounding area.
Ad Rate: Full Page Mono 1092.00
Ad Rate: Full Page Colour 1135.00

Newquay Voice 982995
Editorial: 11A Trevena Terrace, Newquay TR7 1LJ **Tel:** 44 01637 878298
Email: editorial@newquayvoice.co.uk
Web site: www.newquayvoice.co.uk
Freq: Weekly
Circ: 5500 Not Audited
Editor: Simon Fearnley
Profile: The Newquay Voice is a weekly, local newspaper published on Wednesdays covering all the latest on local news and entertainment in Newquay.
Ad Rate: Full Page Colour 936.00

Newry Democrat 983146
Tel: 44 02830 251250
Email: editor@newrydemocrat.com
Web site: www.newrydemocrat.com
Freq: Weekly
Circ: 6000 Not Audited
Profile: Online version of the Newry Democrat newspaper covering local news and sports for the surrounding area.

Newry Reporter 983147
Tel: 44 02830 267633
Email: editor@newryreporter.com
Web site: www.newryreporter.com
Freq: Weekly
Circ: 8502 Not Audited
Editor: Paul Welsh

Profile: Online version of the Newry Advertiser newspaper covering local news, sports and community events for the surrounding area.

The News 980315
Editorial: 1000 Lakeside, North Harbour, Portsmouth PO6 3EN **Tel:** 44 02392 664488
Email: newsdesk@thenews.co.uk
Web site: www.portsmouth.co.uk
Freq: Daily
Circ: 24251 Not Audited

News & Star 979989
Editorial: Newspaper House, Dalston Road, Carlisle, Carlisle CA2 5UA
Tel: 44 01228 612600
Email: news@cumbrian-newspapers.co.uk
Web site: www.newsandstar.co.uk
Freq: Daily
Circ: 2664 Not Audited

The News (Portsmouth) 980308
Editorial: 1000 Lakeside, North Harbour, Western Road, Portsmouth PO6 3EN
Tel: 44 02392 622118
Email: newsdesk@thenews.co.uk
Web site: www.portsmouth.co.uk
Freq: Daily
Circ: 19797 Not Audited
Editor: Mark Waldron
Profile: The News is a regional daily newspaper covering regional news, sports, business and lifestyle for Portsmouth and the surrounding area. This Outlet offer RSS (Really Simple Syndication).
Ad Rate: Full Page Mono 4944.96
Ad Rate: Full Page Colour 6428.45

News Desk 1000935
Editorial: Maple House, Park West, Sealand Road, Chester CH1 4RN
Tel: 44 01270 502436
Email: crewe.news@trinitymirror.com
Web site: www.crewechronicle.co.uk

News Guardian 981356
Editorial: Unit 15, Telford Court, Loansdean, Morpeth NE61 2DB **Tel:** 44 01670 517171
Email: news.guardian@jpress.co.uk
Web site: www.newsguardian.co.uk
Freq: Weekly
Circ: 54979 Not Audited
Editor: Paul Larkin
Profile: This is the online version of the News Guardian, a weekly local newspaper covering local news, sports, lifestyle and community for the surrounding areas.

News Post Leader 980478
Editorial: Unit 15, Telford Court, Loansdean, Morpeth NE61 2DB **Tel:** 44 01670 517171
Email: news.leader@jpress.co.uk
Web site: http://www.newspostleader.co.uk
Freq: Weekly
Circ: 57906 Not Audited
Editor: Paul Larkin
Profile: This is the online version of the News Post Leader, a weekly local newspaper covering local news, sports, lifestyle and community for the surrounding area.

News Shopper Series 983007
Editorial: 5 Kingfisher House, Crayfields Business Park, New Mill Road, Orpington BR5 3QG **Tel:** 44 01689 885619
Email: newsroom@london.newsquest.co.uk
Web site: www.newsshopper.co.uk
Freq: Weekly
Circ: 273623 Not Audited

Newton News 982490
Editorial: St Cuthberts Way, Newton Aycliffe DL5 6DX **Tel:** 44 01325 300212
Web site: www.newtonnews.co.uk
Freq: Weekly
Circ: 15000 Not Audited
Editor: Syd Howarth
Profile: The Newton News is a weekly, local newspaper covering all the latest news, business and sport for the surrounding area.
Ad Rate: Full Page Colour 840.00

Newtownabbey Times 984216
Tel: 44 02828 272303
Email: news@newtownabbeytimes.co.uk
Web site: www.newtownabbeytoday.co.uk
Freq: Weekly
Circ: 9934 Not Audited
Profile: This is the online version of the Newtownabbey Times, a weekly local newspaper covering all the latest local news, sport, lifestyle and community for the surrounding area.

The Newtownards Chronicle 983134
Tel: 44 02891 813333
Email: news@ardschronicle.co.uk
Freq: Weekly
Circ: 8000 Not Audited
Editor: Mark Bain
Profile: Newtownards Chronicle is a local newspaper published on Thursdays covering all the local news and events from the Newtownards area.
Ad Rate: Full Page Mono 1152.00
Ad Rate: Full Page Colour 1440.00

Normanton Advertiser 995976
Editorial: 4 West Street, Normanton, Normanton WF6 2AP **Tel:** 44 01924 892117
Email: sales@normanton-advertiser.co.uk
Web site: http://www.normanton-advertiser.co.uk
Freq: Weekly
Circ: 8500 Not Audited
Editor: Peter Warrender

North Belfast News 983105
Tel: 44 02890 584444
Email: nbnjournalist@belfastmediagroup.com
Web site: www.belfastmediagroup.com
Freq: Weekly
Circ: 2626 Not Audited
Profile: The North Belfast News is a weekly newspaper published by the Belfast Media Group. Its coverage extends from Glengormley to Belfast city centre. The paper features a mix of local and community news, features and sports. The paper is available on Thursdays.
Ad Rate: Full Page Mono 843.48
Ad Rate: Full Page Colour 1096.52

North Cornwall Advertiser 980235
Editorial: Tindle House, 2 Trevanson Street, Wadebridge, Wadebridge PL27 7AW
Tel: 44 01208 815096
Email: enquiries@cornwalladvertisers.co.uk
Web site: www.cornwalladvertisers.co.uk
Freq: Monthly
Circ: 26000 Not Audited
Profile: North Cornwall Advertiser is a local paper covering local news and events in north Cornwall.
Ad Rate: Full Page Colour 795.00

North Devon Gazette 980263
Editorial: Unit 3, Old Station Road, Barnstaple EX32 8PB **Tel:** 44 01271 345056
Email: newsdesk@northdevongazette.co.uk
Web site: www.northdevongazette.co.uk
Freq: Weekly
Circ: 39542 Not Audited
Editor: Andy Keeble
Profile: Online version of the North Devon Gazette newspaper covering local news and sports for the surrounding area. The outlet offers RSS (Really Simple Syndication).

North Devon Journal 980264
Editorial: Avery House, Liberty Road, Barnstaple EX31 3TL **Tel:** 44 01271 343064
Email: editorial@northdevonjournal.co.uk
Web site: www.devonlive.com/
Freq: Weekly
Circ: 15761 Not Audited
Editor: Jim Parker
Profile: The North Devon Journal is a weekly local newspaper and covers local news and sports for the surrounding area. The newspaper is published on a Thursday.
Ad Rate: Full Page Mono 1754.40
Ad Rate: Full Page Colour 2193.00

North Norfolk & Broadland Town & Country News 995850
Editorial: Unit 5, Bank Street, Norwich NR12 9BA **Tel:** 44 01692 582287
Email: editorial@leisurepublishing.co.uk
Web site: www.townandcountrynews.co.uk
Freq: Monthly
Circ: 30000 Not Audited
Editor: Laurence Watts

North Norfolk News 980452
Editorial: 31 Church Street, Cromer NR27 9HG **Tel:** 44 01263 512732
Email: nnn.news@archant.co.uk
Web site: www.northnorfolknews.co.uk
Freq: Weekly
Circ: 4832 Not Audited
Editor: Ally McGilvray
Profile: The North Norfolk News is a weekly local newspaper covering local news for the surrounding area. First published: 1940.
Ad Rate: Full Page Mono 1362.24
Ad Rate: Full Page Colour 1770.92

North Somerset Times 980506
Editorial: 32 Waterloo Street, Weston Super Mare, Weston-super-Mare BS23 1LW
Tel: 44 01934 422522
Email: nstimes@archant.co.uk
Web site: www.northsomersettimes.co.uk
Freq: Weekly
Circ: 34149 Not Audited
Editor: Tom Wright
Profile: The North Somerset Times is a weekly paper covering the latest local news from North Somerset.
Ad Rate: Full Page Mono 1173.15
Ad Rate: Full Page Colour 1525.10

North Wales Chronicle 980610
Editorial: 302 High Street, Bangor LL57 1UL
Tel: 44 01248 387400
Email: news@northwaleschronicle.co.uk
Web site: www.northwaleschronicle.co.uk
Freq: Weekly
Circ: 30084 Not Audited
Editor: Andrew Martin
Profile: The North Wales Chronicle is a local newspapers featuring all the latest news and current affairs in the area. Regular features: Community Focus; Motoring; Property
Ad Rate: Full Page Mono 1718.28
Ad Rate: Full Page Colour 2061.60

North Wales Pioneer 980011
Editorial: 21 Penrhyn Road, Colwyn Bay LL29 8HY **Tel:** 44 01492 531188
Email: news@northwalespioneer.co.uk
Web site: www.northwalespioneer.co.uk
Freq: Weekly
Circ: 25295 Not Audited
Editor: Andrew Martin
Profile: This is the online version of the North Wales Pioneer, a weekly, local newspaper covering all the latest on local news, entertainment, property and sport in the borough of Conwy and the surrounding areas of Conwy Bay, Llandudno and Llandudno Junction. This outlet offers RSS (Really Simple Syndication).

North Wales Weekly News 980612
Editorial: Vale Road, Llandudno Junction, Conwy LL31 9SL **Tel:** 44 01492 574452
Email: news.desk@northwalesnews.co.uk
Web site: www.dailypost.co.uk/all-about/conwy
Freq: Weekly
Circ: 6408 Not Audited
Editor: Andrew Campbell
Profile: The North Wales Weekly News is a weekly local newspaper covering local news for the surrounding area.
Ad Rate: Full Page Mono 1912.16
Ad Rate: Full Page Colour 2294.59

North Watch 1060509
Tel: 44 27357 990500
Email: subeditor@zululandobserver.co.za
Freq: Weekly
Circ: 6000 Not Audited

North West Highlands Am Bratach 998495
Editorial: The Schoolhouse, Strathnaver by Kinbrace, Sutherland, Sutherland KW11 6UA
Tel: 44 01641 561214
Email: nwscca@yahoo.co.uk
Web site: www.bratach.co.uk
Freq: Monthly
Circ: 1000 Not Audited
Editor: Donald MacLeod

Northampton Chronicle & Echo 980471
Editorial: Albert House, Victoria Street, Northampton NN1 3NR
Tel: 44 01604 467000
Email: editor@northantsnews.co.uk
Web site: www.northamptonchron.co.uk
Freq: Weekly
Circ: 17283 Not Audited
Editor: David Summers
Profile: Online version of the Northampton Chronicle and Echo newspaper, covering local news, business and sports for the surrounding area. This outlet offers RSS (Really Simple Syndication).

Northamptonshire Telegraph 980472
Editorial: 10 Headlands, Kettering NN15 7HP **Tel:** 44 01536 506100
Email: nt.newsdesk@northantsnews.co.uk
Web site: www.northantstelegraph.co.uk/
Freq: Weekly
Circ: 19100 Not Audited
Editor: David Summers
Profile: The Northamptonshire Telegraph is a weekly local newspaper and covers local news and sports for the surrounding area. The newspaper is published on a Thursday. This outlet offers RSS (Really Simple Syndication).
Ad Rate: Full Page Mono 979.20
Ad Rate: Full Page Colour 979.20

Northern Cross 982154
Editorial: Northern Cross Trustees, St Anne's Presbytery, 43 Welbeck Avenue, Darlington DL1 2DR **Tel:** 44 01325 464008
Email: editor.norcross@btconnect.com
Web site: www.northerncross.org.uk
Freq: Monthly
Circ: 5600 Not Audited
Editor: Andrew Smith
Profile: Catholic newspaper for the RC Diocese of Hexham and Newcastle, linking 179 parishes and promoting Christian activities and opinions, with news and features on parish and diocesan events in the North East of England with interests in the rest of the Church in Britain and worldwide.
Ad Rate: Full Page Mono 520.00

The Northern Echo 979953
Editorial: Newsquest (North East) Ltd, PO Box 14, Priestgate, Darlington DL1 1NF
Tel: 44 01325 381313
Email: newsdesk@nne.co.uk
Web site: www.thenorthernecho.co.uk
Freq: Daily
Circ: 23971 Not Audited

The Northern Scot 980700
Editorial: 74-76 South Street, Elgin IV30 1JG
Tel: 44 01343 548777
Email: newsdesk@northern-scot.co.uk
Web site: www.northern-scot.co.uk
Freq: Weekly
Circ: 8948 Not Audited
Editor: Mike Collins
Profile: Online version of the Northern Scot newspaper and covers local news and sports for the surrounding area.

The Northern Times 980701
Editorial: Main Street, Golspie, Sutherland KW10 6RA **Tel:** 44 01408 633993
Email: editor@northern-times.co.uk
Web site: http://www.northern-times.co.uk
Freq: Weekly
Circ: 2767 Not Audited
Editor: Alison Cameron

Northumberland Gazette 980479
Editorial: 32 Bondgate Without, Alnwick NE66 1PN **Tel:** 44 01665 602234
Email: northumberland.gazette@northeast-press.co.uk
Web site: www.northumberlandgazette.co.uk
Freq: Weekly
Circ: 6710 Not Audited
Editor: Paul Larkin
Profile: Online version of the Northumberland Gazette newspaper covering local news and sports for the surrounding area.

Northwich Guardian 980223
Editorial: 3 Theatre Court, London Road, Northwich, Northwich CW9 5HB
Tel: 44 01606 813624
Email: northwich@guardiangrp.co.uk
Web site: www.northwichguardian.co.uk
Freq: Weekly
Circ: 9876 Not Audited
Editor: Carla Flynn
Profile: Website for the Northwich Guardian covering local news, sport and leisure for the surrounding area.

Norwich Evening News 980448
Editorial: Prospect House, Rouen Road, Norwich NR1 1RE **Tel:** 44 01603 628311
Email: newsdesk@archant.co.uk
Web site: www.eveningnews24.co.uk
Freq: Daily
Circ: 9172 Not Audited
Profile: The Norwich Evening News is a daily, regional newspaper published from Monday to Saturday and owned by Archant. The paper is distributed in the city of Norwich and the surrounding region. It covers local news stories from around the city, as well as sport, business, entertainment and human interest features.
Ad Rate: Full Page Mono 2251.00
Ad Rate: Full Page Colour 2251.00

Norwich Extra 1095955
Editorial: Prospect House, Rouen Road, Norwich NR1 1RE **Tel:** 44 01603 628311
Web site: http://www.eveningnews24.co.uk/home
Freq: Weekly
Circ: 59088 Not Audited

Noti-Arandas 1060859
Tel: 44 52348 7831371
Email: buzon@gruponotiarandas.com
Web site: http://www.notiarandas.com/
Circ: 1500 Not Audited

Nottingham Post 979949
Editorial: 3rd Floor City Gate, Toll House Hill, Nottingham NG1 5FS
Tel: 44 01159 482000
Email: newsdesk@nottinghampost.com
Web site: www.nottinghampost.com
Freq: Daily
Circ: 17524 Not Audited
Profile: The Nottingham Post is a regional, daily newspaper that covers regional news, sport, business and lifestyle for the surrounding area.
Ad Rate: Full Page Mono 4996.80
Ad Rate: Full Page Colour 5286.32

The Oban Times 980702
Editorial: P.O. Box 1, Oban, Argyll PA34 4HB **Tel:** 44 01631 568000
Email: editor@obantimes.co.uk
Web site: www.obantimes.co.uk
Freq: Weekly
Circ: 10802 Not Audited
Editor: Susan Windram

Okehampton Times 980265
Editorial: 8 East Street, Okehampton EX20 1AS **Tel:** 44 01822 613666
Email: editorial@okehampton-today.co.uk
Web site: www.okehampton-today.co.uk
Freq: Weekly
Circ: 13000 Not Audited
Profile: Website covering Okehampton news.

Regional & Local Weekly Newspapers

Olay Gazete
1097740
Editorial: 100 Green Lanes, Newington Green, London N16 9EH
Tel: 44 02079 239090
Email: info@olaygazete.co.uk
Web site: http://olaygazetesi.co.uk/
Freq: 2 Times/Week
Circ: 30000 Not Audited

Oldham Evening Chronicle
979972
Editorial: P.O. Box 47, 172 Union Street, Oldham OL1 1EQ **Tel:** 44 01616 332121
Email: editorial@oldham-chronicle.co.uk
Web site: www.oldham-chronicle.co.uk
Freq: Daily
Circ: 6812 Not Audited
Profile: The Oldham Evening Chronicle is a daily regional title that features the latest news, business, property and sport from around Oldham and the surrounding area. The paper also publishes the Oldham Extra and the Saddleworth Extra once a month, which include a round up of the month's news.
Ad Rate: Full Page Mono 1428.00
Ad Rate: Full Page Colour 1428.00

Orcadian
980703
Editorial: Hell's Half Acre, Crowness Crescent, Hatston Industrial Estate, Kirkwall, Orkney KW15 1GJ **Tel:** 44 01856 878000
Email: newsroom@orcadian.co.uk
Web site: www.orcadian.co.uk
Freq: Weekly
Circ: 7735 Not Audited
Editor: Sigurd Towrie
Profile: The Orcadian is a weekly, local newspaper published on Thursdays covering all the latest on local news in Orkney and the surrounding area.
Ad Rate: Full Page Mono 1188.00
Ad Rate: Full Page Colour 1620.00

Ormskirk Advertiser
982996
Editorial: PO Box 48, Old Hall Street, Liverpool L69 3EB **Tel:** 44 01704 398253
Email: newsdesk@ormskirkadvertiser.co.uk
Web site: http://www.southportvisiter.co.uk/all-about/ormskirk
Freq: Weekly
Circ: 2357 Not Audited
Editor: Andrew Brown
Profile: Ormskirk Advertiser is a weekly local newspaper covering local news and sports for the surrounding area.
Ad Rate: Full Page Mono 1893.12
Ad Rate: Full Page Colour 2555.00

Orpington News
1070431
Tel: 44 01959 564766
Email: bheditor@gmail.com
Web site: www.orpington-today.co.uk
Freq: Weekly
Editor: Luke King
Profile: The Orpington News is a weekly paper covering the latest news and events from the London Borough of Bromley.

Oswestry & Border Chronicle
985925
Editorial: 14 Salop Road, Oswestry SY11 2NU **Tel:** 44 01952 242424
Email: news@oswestrychronicle.co.uk
Web site: www.oswestrychronicle.com
Freq: Weekly
Circ: 11197 Not Audited

Oswestry & Border Counties Advertizer
980495
Tel: 44 01691 655321
Email: news@bordercountiesadvertiser.co.uk
Web site: www.bordercountiesadvertiser.co.uk
Freq: Weekly
Circ: 6654 Not Audited
Editor: Colin Channon
Profile: This is the online version of the Oswestry and Border Counties Advertizer, a weekly, local newspaper featuring a local mix of news and sport, community news and lifestyle features.

Our East End
980401
Editorial: Mulberry Place, 5 Clove Crescent, London E14 2BG **Tel:** 44 02073 643179
Web site: www.towerhamlets.gov.uk
Freq: Quarterly
Circ: 83395 Not Audited
Editor: Helen Watson

The Outlook
995281
Editorial: 8 Main Street, Rathfriland, Co Down, Newry BT34 5PF
Tel: 44 02840 630202
Email: news@outlooknews.co.uk
Web site: http://www.outlooknews.co.uk/
Freq: Weekly
Circ: 4500 Not Audited
Editor: Joanne Ross
Profile: Magazine covering lifestyle, personal finance and health issues.

Oxford Mail
980116
Editorial: Osney Mead, Oxford OX2 0EJ
Tel: 44 01865 425262
Email: news@nqo.com
Web site: www.oxfordmail.co.uk/
Freq: Daily
Circ: 10184 Not Audited
Profile: The Oxford Mail is a daily regional newspaper that is available in Oxford and the surrounding region including the towns of Bicester, Abingdon, Wantage, Didcot, Banbury and Witney. It covers regional news, sport, business, entertainment listings and lifestyle features.
Ad Rate: Full Page Mono 610.56
Ad Rate: Full Page Colour 763.20

The Oxford Student
981778
Editorial: 2 Worcester Street, Oxford OX1 2BX **Tel:** 44 01865 288467
Email: editor@oxfordstudent.com
Web site: www.oxfordstudent.com
Freq: Weekly
Circ: 15000 Not Audited
Profile: Magazine containing news, features, sport, letters, comment, drama, film, books, music, fashion and columns. Strong focus on Oxford-related news and features, with reviews of local and national arts and music.
Ad Rate: Full Page Colour 1150.00
Student Lifestyle

The Oxford Times
980489
Editorial: Osney Mead, Oxford OX2 0EJ
Tel: 44 01865 425262
Email: news@nqo.com
Web site: www.oxfordtimes.co.uk
Freq: Weekly
Circ: 8039 Not Audited
Profile: Website for local paper The Oxford Times covering the latest news from Oxford and the surrounding towns and villages.

Oxfordshire Guardian
980490
Editorial: Newspaper House, Hawksworth, Southmead Industrial Estate, Didcot OX11 7HR **Tel:** 44 01235 511700
Email: news@oxfordshireguardian.co.uk
Web site: www.oxfordshireguardian.co.uk
Freq: Weekly
Circ: 26500 Not Audited
Profile: Website for the Oxfordshire Guardian a weekly paper covering the latest news, sport and entertainment news from Oxfordshire.

Oxfordshire Herald Series
995934
Editorial: Osney Mead, Oxford OX2 0EJ
Tel: 44 01865 425262
Email: news@heraldseries.co.uk
Web site: www.heraldseries.co.uk
Freq: Weekly
Circ: 6487 Not Audited

The Packet Series
983019
Editorial: Falmouth Business Park, Bickland Water Road, Falmouth TR11 4SZ
Tel: 44 01326 213333
Email: editorial@packetseries.co.uk
Web site: http://www.falmouthpacket.co.uk/
Freq: Weekly
Circ: 16076 Not Audited
Editor: Paul Armstrong

Paisley Daily Express
980127
Editorial: 1 Central Quay, Glasgow G3 8DA
Tel: 44 01418 877911
Email: pde@trinitymirror.com
Web site: www.dailyrecord.co.uk/all-about/paisley
Freq: Daily
Circ: 4800 Not Audited
Editor: Cheryl McEvoy
Profile: The Paisley Daily Express is a daily Scottish paper published from Monday to Saturday and is distributed throughout the region of Renfrewshire. The paper covers the latest regional news stories, sports news and business news. The paper is currently owned by the Trinity Mirror group.
Ad Rate: Full Page Colour 1006.00

Paisley People
980704
Editorial: 1st Floor, Carus House, 201 Dumbarton Road, Clydebank G81 4XJ
Tel: 44 01414 358888
Email: editorial@the-gazette.co.uk
Web site: http://www.the-gazette.co.uk
Freq: Weekly
Circ: 2854 Not Audited
Profile: The Paisley People is a weekly local newspaper covering local news for the surrounding area.
Ad Rate: Full Page Mono 2481.00
Ad Rate: Full Page Colour 3225.30

Palatinate
998565
Editorial: Dunelm House, Durham, Durham DH1 3AN
Email: editor@palatinate.org.uk
Web site: www.palatinate.org.uk
Freq: Bi-Weekly
Circ: 4000 Not Audited
Student Lifestyle

Parikiaki
998759
Editorial: 140 Falkland Road, London N8 0NP **Tel:** 44 02083 415853
Email: english.section@parikiaki.com
Web site: www.parikiaki.com
Freq: Weekly
Circ: 7000 Not Audited
Editor: Andrea Georgiou
Profile: Parikiaki is a weekly publication covering news, arts, travel and sport. It is owned by Parikiaki Haravgi (U.K.) Ltd. First published in 1974. Parikiaki is aimed at the Cypriot community in London and throughout the UK.
Ad Rate: Full Page Mono 480.00
Ad Rate: Full Page Colour 590.00

Pateley Bridge & Nidderdale Herald
982909
Editorial: 1 Cardale Park, Beckwith Head Road, Harrogate HG3 1RZ
Tel: 44 01423 564321
Email: news@harrogateadvertiser.co.uk
Web site: www.harrogateadvertiser.co.uk/news/local/nidderdale
Freq: Weekly
Circ: 1700 Not Audited

Peak Advertiser
980254
Editorial: 1st Floor Offices, Orme Court, Granby Road, Bakewell DE45 1ES
Tel: 44 01629 812159
Email: editorial@peak-advertiser.co.uk
Web site: www.peak-advertiser.co.uk
Freq: Bi-Weekly
Circ: 30000 Not Audited
Editor: Steve Wilde
Profile: Peak Advertiser is a free monthly newspaper, providing local news and business news.
Ad Rate: Full Page Colour 675.00

The Peckham Peculiar
987660
Editorial: 106c Bushey Hill Road, London SE5 8QQ
Email: peckhampeculiar@gmail.com
Web site: http://peckhampeculiar.tumblr.com
Freq: Bi-Monthly
Circ: 8000 Not Audited
Editor: Mark McGinlay
Profile: Blog covering local news in Peckham. THE PECKHAM PECULIAR blog discusses anything from local news and events to culture and community. The blog has an archive dating back to January 2014.

Peeblesshire News
980705
Editorial: 72 High Street, Peebles EH45 8SW **Tel:** 44 01721 729481
Email: editorial@peeblesshirenews.com
Web site: www.peeblesshirenews.com
Freq: Weekly
Circ: 3345 Not Audited
Profile: Website of the Peeblesshire News, featuring a mix of local news and sport for the surrounding area.

Pembrokeshire Herald
987488
Editorial: 11 Hamilton Terrace, Milford Haven, Milford Haven SA73 3AL
Tel: 44 01646 454545
Email: editor@herald.email
Web site: www.pembrokeshireherald.com
Freq: Weekly
Circ: 10000 Not Audited
Profile: The Pembrokeshire Herald is a local newspaper covering the latest news and events from Pembrokeshire.

Penarth Times
981551
Editorial: Cardiff Road, Maesglas, Newport NP20 3QN **Tel:** 44 01633 777221
Email: penarthtimes@penarthtimes.co.uk
Web site: www.penarthtimes.co.uk
Freq: Weekly
Circ: 3313 Not Audited
Profile: Online version of the Penarth Times newspaper covering local news for the surrounding area. The outlet offers RSS (Really Simple Syndication).

People's Post: Athlone
1060453
Tel: 44 27217 139440
Email: adean@peoplespost.co.za
Web site: http://www.peoplespost.co.za
Freq: Weekly
Circ: 30427 Not Audited

People's Post: City Edition
1060449
Tel: 44 27217 139440
Email: adean@peoplespost.co.za
Web site: http://www.peoplespost.co.za
Freq: Weekly
Circ: 29421 Not Audited

People's Post: Claremont/Rondebosch
1060538
Tel: 44 27217 139440
Email: adean@peoplespost.co.za
Web site: http://www.peoplespost.co.za
Freq: Weekly
Circ: 32009 Not Audited

People's Post: Constantia/Wynberg
1060604
Tel: 44 27217 139440
Email: adean@peoplespost.co.za
Web site: http://www.peoplespost.co.za
Freq: Weekly
Circ: 30244 Not Audited

People's Post: False Bay
1060534
Tel: 44 27217 139440
Email: adean@peoplespost.co.za
Web site: http://www.peoplespost.co.za
Freq: Weekly
Circ: 31147 Not Audited

People's Post: Grassy Park
1060421
Tel: 44 27217 139440
Email: adean@peoplespost.co.za
Web site: http://www.peoplespost.co.za
Freq: Weekly
Circ: 22013 Not Audited

People's Post: Lansdowne
1060409
Tel: 44 27217 139440
Email: adean@peoplespost.co.za
Web site: http://www.peoplespost.co.za
Freq: Weekly
Circ: 21305 Not Audited

People's Post: Mitchell's Plain
1060646
Tel: 44 27217 139440
Email: adean@peoplespost.co.za
Web site: http://www.peoplespost.co.za
Freq: Weekly
Circ: 83837 Not Audited

People's Post: Retreat
1060633
Tel: 44 27217 139440
Email: adean@peoplespost.co.za
Web site: http://www.peoplespost.co.za
Freq: Weekly
Circ: 23598 Not Audited

People's Post: Woodstock/Maitland
1060674
Tel: 44 27217 139440
Email: adean@peoplespost.co.za
Freq: Weekly
Circ: 16391 Not Audited

Perthshire Advertiser
982997
Editorial: 58 Watergate, Perth, Perth PH1 5TS **Tel:** 44 01738 626211
Email: news@perthshireadvertiser.co.uk
Web site: www.perthshireadvertiser.co.uk
Freq: 2 Times/Week
Circ: 10056 Not Audited
Editor: Johnathon Menzies
Profile: Website of the Perthshire Advertiser, a newspaper featuring local news, sports and lifestyle for the surrounding area.

Peterborough Telegraph
980212
Editorial: Unex House - Suite B, Bourges Boulevard, Peterborough PE1 1NG
Tel: 44 01733 555111
Email: news@peterboroughtoday.co.uk
Web site: www.peterboroughtoday.co.uk
Freq: Weekly
Circ: 65900 Not Audited
Editor: Mark Edwards
Profile: Online version of the Peterborough Telegraph newspaper covering local news and sports for the surrounding area.

Petersfield Post
980324
Editorial: Petersfield Post, 33 High Street, Petersfield, Petersfield GU32 3JR
Tel: 44 01730 232600
Web site: www.petersfieldpost.co.uk
Freq: Weekly
Circ: 5922 Not Audited
Editor: Graeme Moir
Profile: Online version of the Petersfield Post covering local news, sport, jobs, property, cars and entertainment for the surrounding area.

The Phoenix
999193
Editorial: The Old Custom House, 1 Church Street, Stourbridge, Stourbridge DY8 1LT
Tel: 44 08000 096909
Email: newsdesk@thephoenixnewspaper.com
Web site: www.thephoenixnewspaper.com
Freq: Monthly
Circ: 40000 Not Audited
Profile: Magazine covering current affairs and business news, with political satire and gossip.
Ad Rate: Full Page Colour 4300.00

The Pigeon (Bristol)
1102796
Editorial: Monarch House, Smyth Road, Bedminster, Bristol BS3 2BX
Tel: 44 01173 224939
Email: news@the-pigeon.com
Web site: www.the-pigeon.com
Freq: Monthly
Circ: 10500 Not Audited
Editor: Matt Pawsey

Pocklington Post
980464
Editorial: Times House, Mill Street, Driffield YO25 6TN **Tel:** 44 01723 860100
Email: news@pocklingtontoday.co.uk
Web site: www.pocklingtontoday.co.uk
Freq: WeeklyNot Audited
Profile: Website for local paper the Pocklington Post covering the latest news and events from Pocklington and the surrounding area.

Pompey Chimes
985537
Editorial: First Floor, Peninsular House, Wharf Road, Portsmouth PO2 8HR
Tel: 44 02392 899673
Freq: Monthly
Circ: 8000 Not Audited
Editor: Neil Pugmire
Profile: A 16-page full colour newspaper distributed to 9,000 readers across 142 parishes in the diocese. Contains news, features, diary dates and information.

Pontefract & Castleford Express
980594
Editorial: First Floor, Bullring House, 23 Northgate, Wakefield WF1 3BJ
Tel: 44 01924 433029
Email: editorial@pandcexpress.co.uk
Web site: www.pontefractandcastlefordexpress.co.uk
Freq: Weekly
Circ: 10901 Not Audited
Editor: John Kenealy
Profile: The Pontefract & Castleford Express is a weekly local newspaper covering local news for the surrounding area.
Ad Rate: Full Page Mono 2126.70
Ad Rate: Full Page Colour 2126.70

Pontypridd & Llantrisant Observer
982909
Editorial: 10 Market Street, Pontypridd CF37 2ST **Tel:** 44 01443 629200
Email: pontypridd.observer@mediawales.uk
Web site: www.walesonline.co.uk/all-about/pontypridd
Freq: Weekly
Circ: 2024 Not Audited

Portadown Times
983110
Tel: 44 02838 395560
Email: editor@portadowntimes.co.uk
Web site: www.portadowntimes.co.uk
Freq: Weekly
Circ: 7764 Not Audited
Editor: Clint Aiken
Profile: Online version of the Portadown Times newspaper covering local news, sports and entertainment for the surrounding area.

Portsmouth View
996336
Editorial: 1000 Lakeside, North Harbour, Portsmouth PO6 3EN **Tel:** 44 02392 664488
Email: newsdesk@thenews.co.uk
Web site: www.portsmouth.co.uk/
Freq: Monthly
Circ: 50000 Not Audited

Post Lite
980483
Editorial: Nottingham Post Media Group, 3rd Floor City Gate, Tollhouse Hill, Nottingham NG1 5FS **Tel:** 44 01159 482000
Email: newsdesk@nottinghampost.com
Web site: www.nottinghampost.com/lite
Freq: Weekly
Circ: 63461 Not Audited
Editor: John Howorth

Potchefstroom Herald
1060435
Tel: 44 27182 930750
Email: hstander@media24.com
Freq: Weekly
Circ: 8787 Not Audited

PRAVÝ ZASTUPITEL
1060218
Freq: MonthlyNot Audited

The Press
995981
Editorial: 31 Branch Road, Batley, Batley WF17 5SB **Tel:** 44 01924 470296
Email: news@thepressnews.co.uk
Web site: www.thepressnewspaper.co.uk
Freq: Weekly
Circ: 14608 Not Audited
Editor: David Bentley
Profile: The Press is a daily regional newspaper covering regional news, features, sports and business for Yorkshire and surrounding areas.
Ad Rate: Full Page Mono 691.20
Ad Rate: Full Page Colour 1036.80

The Press (York)
980460
Editorial: PO Box 29, 84-86 Walmgate, York YO1 9YN **Tel:** 44 01904 567131
Email: newsdesk@thepress.co.uk
Web site: www.yorkpress.co.uk
Freq: Daily
Circ: 14608 Not Audited

The Press and Journal
979810
Editorial: PO Box 43, Lang Stracht, Mastrick, Aberdeen AB15 6DF
Tel: 44 01224 690222
Email: pj.newsdesk@ajl.co.uk
Web site: www.pressandjournal.co.uk
Freq: Daily
Circ: 51880 Not Audited

Pulse (Russian Focus)
996068
Editorial: 1007, 92 White Post Lane, London E0 5EN **Tel:** 44 02073 635370
Email: editor@pulse-uk.org.uk
Web site: http://www.pulse-uk.org.uk
Freq: Weekly
Circ: 20000 Not Audited
Editor: Tania Chuvatkina

Queensferry Gazette
986576
Editorial: Unit 4A, Gateway Business Park, Beancross Road, Grangemouth FK3 8WX
Tel: 44 01324 690222
Email: editorial@journalandgazette.co.uk
Web site: www.queensferrygazette.co.uk/
Freq: Weekly
Circ: 610 Not Audited
Editor: Jill Buchanan
Profile: The Queensferry Gazette is a weekly paper covering the latest news and events from Queensferry and the surrounding area. The paper is distributed every Friday.

Radcliffe Times
980431
Editorial: The Wellsprings, The Civic Centre, Victoria Square, Bolton BL1 1AR
Tel: 44 01204 522345
Email: newsdesk@nqnw.co.uk
Web site: www.burytimes.co.uk
Freq: Weekly
Circ: 9428 Not Audited
Editor: Michael Crutchley
Profile: The Radcliffe Times is a weekly paper covering the latest news and events from the town of Radcliffe.

Rayleigh Times
983095
Editorial: 106 Broadway, Leigh-On-Sea, Southend-on-Sea SS9 1AB
Tel: 44 01702 477666
Email: editor@leightimes.co.uk
Web site: http://www.leightimes.co.uk/
Freq: Monthly
Circ: 14000 Not Audited
Editor: Michael Guy

Reading Chronicle
979975
Editorial: Bowman House, 2-10 Bridge Street, Reading RG1 2LU
Tel: 44 01189 553324
Email: news@readingchronicle.co.uk
Web site: www.readingchronicle.co.uk
Freq: Weekly
Circ: 5528 Not Audited
Profile: Reading Chronicle is a website that features a mix of local news and sport, comment, entertainment and business news from around Reading and the surrounding area.

Reading Midweek
983000
Editorial: Reading Chronicle, Bowman House, 2-10 Bridge Street, Reading RG1 2LU **Tel:** 44 01189 553333
Email: news@readingchronicle.co.uk
Web site: www.readingchronicle.co.uk
Freq: Weekly
Circ: 5528 Not Audited
Profile: Reading Midweek is a weekly newspaper covering the latest in local news for Reading and the surrounding area.
Ad Rate: Full Page Mono 3092.64
Ad Rate: Full Page Colour 3865.80

Redditch & Alcester Advertiser
980333
Editorial: St John's House, St John's Road, Stourbridge DY8 1EH **Tel:** 44 01384 358059
Web site: www.redditchadvertiser.co.uk
Freq: Weekly
Circ: 38670 Not Audited
Profile: The Redditch & Alcester Advertiser is a weekly local newspaper covering local news for the surrounding area.

Retford Guardian
982915
Editorial: 21-27 Ryton Street, Worksop S80 2AY **Tel:** 44 01909 500500
Email: newsroom@worksop-guardian.co.uk
Web site: www.retfordtoday.co.uk
Freq: Weekly
Circ: 9255 Not Audited
Profile: Website covering news. The Retford Guardian website shares the latest news, events and sports news in the Retford area.

Retford Times
980484
Editorial: Chancery Court, 32 West Street, Retford DN22 6ES **Tel:** 44 01777 702275
Web site: http://www.lincolnshirelive.co.uk/retford
Freq: Weekly
Circ: 5562 Not Audited
Profile: Online version of the Retford & Gainsborough Times newspaper covering local news and sports for the surrounding area.

Rhondda Leader
982894
Editorial: 6 Park Crescent, Cardiff CF10 1XR
Tel: 44 01443 629200
Email: rhondda.leader@mediawales.co.uk
Web site: www.walesonline.co.uk/all-about/rhondda
Freq: Weekly
Circ: 2625 Not Audited
Profile: The Rhondda Leader is a weekly paid for local newspaper that is published by Media Wales on Wednesdays. The paper is available in the Rhondda Valley, covering the valleys of Rhondda Fawr and Rhondda Fach as well as the communities of Tonypandy, Ystrad, Treorchy and Ferndale.
Ad Rate: Full Page Mono 1017.28

Rhyl Prestatyn & Abergele Journal
980613
Editorial: Accent House, 23 Kinmel Street, Rhyl, Rhyl LL18 1AH **Tel:** 44 01492 531188
Email: editor@rhyljournal.co.uk
Web site: www.rhyljournal.co.uk
Freq: Weekly
Circ: 25857 Not Audited
Editor: Andrew Martin

Richmond & Twickenham Times
980416
Editorial: Floors 9 & 10, Quadrant House, The Quadrant, Sutton SM2 5AS
Tel: 44 02087 226328
Email: rtt@london.newsquest.co.uk
Web site: www.richmondandtwickenhamtimes.co.uk
Freq: WeeklyNot Audited
Profile: The Richmond & Twickenham Times is a weekly paper published every Friday, covering the latest news, sports and lifestyle from Richmond Upon Thames and the surrounding area. This outlet covers areas within Richmond upon Thames Borough

Ringwood and Fordingbridge News
999059
Editorial: 31 The Mount, Ringwood, Ringwood BH24 1XX **Tel:** 44 01425 479095
Freq: Bi-Weekly
Circ: 12000 Not Audited

Ripley & Heanor News
982975
Editorial: 8 Heanor Road, Heanor DE7 6EP
Tel: 44 01246 504536
Email: news@rhnews.co.uk
Web site: www.ripleytoday.co.uk
Freq: Weekly
Circ: 16997 Not Audited
Profile: Website for weekly paper Ripley and Heanor News covering the latest in local news for the surrounding area.

Regional & Local Weekly Newspapers

Ripon Gazette
980465
Editorial: 1 Cardale Park, Beckwithhead Road, Harrogate HG3 1RZ
Tel: 44 01423 707402
Email: news@harrogateadvertiser.co.uk
Web site: www.ripongazette.co.uk
Freq: Weekly
Circ: 3387 Not Audited
Profile: Website for the Ripon Gazette covering local news, sports and features for the local community.

Rising Sun
1060765
Tel: 44 13152 635978
Email: usag.japan@gmail.com
Web site: http://www.usagj.jp.pac.army.mil/news.aspx
Circ: 2000 Not Audited

Roar
1012049
Editorial: Kings College London Students Union, Macadam Building, Surrey Street, London WC2R 2NS **Tel:** 44 02078 482692
Email: editor@roarnews.co.uk
Web site: http://roarnews.co.uk/
Freq: Monthly
Circ: 1500 Not Audited
Student Lifestyle

Rochdale Observer
983001
Editorial: Mitchell Henry House, Hollinwood Avenue, Chadderton, Oldham OL9 8EF
Tel: 44 01618 327200
Email: rochdaleobserver@menmedia.co.uk
Web site: http://www.manchestereveningnews.co.uk/all-about/rochdale
Freq: 2 Times/Week
Circ: 13864 Not Audited
Profile: Online version of the Rochdale Observer newspaper covering local news and sports for the surrounding area.

Romford and Havering Post
980299
Editorial: 539 High Road, Ilford IG1 1UD
Tel: 44 02084 784444
Email: news.desk@romfordrecorder.co.uk
Web site: www.romfordrecorder.co.uk
Freq: Weekly
Circ: 16354 Not Audited

Romford Recorder
980300
Editorial: 539 High Road, Ilford, London IG1 1UD **Tel:** 44 02084 784444
Email: news.desk@romfordrecorder.co.uk
Web site: www.romfordrecorder.co.uk
Freq: Weekly
Circ: 11145 Not Audited
Profile: Website of the Romford Recorder, a weekly local newspaper covering local news for the surrounding area. This outlet covers areas within Havering Borough.

Romsey Advertiser
980325
Editorial: 21a Market Place, Romsey, Romsey SO51 8NA **Tel:** 44 01794 513396
Email: news@romseyadvertiser.co.uk
Web site: www.romseyadvertiser.co.uk
Freq: Weekly
Circ: 5054 Not Audited
Profile: Online version of the Romsey Advertiser newspaper covering local news and sports for the surrounding area.

The Ross Gazette
980335
Editorial: 54A Broad Street, Ross-on-Wye HR9 7DY **Tel:** 44 01989 562007
Email: editorial@rossgazette.com
Web site: http://www.ross-today.co.uk
Freq: Weekly
Circ: 4028 Not Audited
Editor: Jo Scriven
Profile: Regular features: Homes and Gardens; Motoring; Property
Ad Rate: Full Page Mono 1123.20

Rossendale Free Press
980379
Editorial: Mitchell Henry House, Hollinwood Avenue, Chadderton, Oldham OL9 8EF
Tel: 44 01612 112955
Email: freepressnews@menmedia.co.uk
Web site: www.rossendalefreepress.co.uk
Freq: Weekly

Circ: 6425 Not Audited
Editor: Gareth Tidman
Profile: Online version of the Rossendale Free Press covering local news and sports for the surrounding area.

Ross-shire Journal
980706
Editorial: Dochcarty Road, Dingwall, Dingwall IV15 9UG **Tel:** 44 01349 863436
Email: editor@rsjournal.co.uk
Web site: www.ross-shirejournal.co.uk
Freq: Weekly
Circ: 4731 Not Audited
Editor: Hector Mackenzie
Profile: This is the online version of the Ross-shire Journal, a weekly local newspaper covering all the latest news, sport, entertainment and weather for the surrounding area.

Rotherham Advertiser
980520
Editorial: 67 Wellgate Rotherham, Rotherham S60 2LT **Tel:** 44 01709 768000
Email: newsdesk@rotherhamadvertiser.co.uk
Web site: www.rotherhamadvertiser.com
Freq: Weekly
Circ: 20841 Not Audited
Editor: Andrew Mosley
Profile: Website for local papers the Rotherham Advertiser, Rotherham Record and the Dearne Valley Weekender, covering the latest local news, sports and entertainment news from Rotherham and the surrounding local area.

Rotherham Record
980521
Editorial: 67 Wellgate Rotherham, Rotherham S60 2LT **Tel:** 44 01709 768000
Email: newsdesk@rotherhamadvertiser.co.uk
Web site: www.rotherhamadvertiser.com
Freq: Weekly
Circ: 51851 Not Audited
Editor: Andrew Mosley
Profile: The Rotherham Record is a free weekly paper covering the latest news and events from Rotherham and the surrounding local area.
Ad Rate: Full Page Mono 1825.00
Ad Rate: Full Page Colour 2463.75

The Rothley Post
1076218
Editorial: Unit 109, Greenacres, The Sidings, Leicester LE4 3BR **Tel:** 44 01164 422067
Email: editor@birstallpost.co.uk
Web site: www.birstallpost.co.uk
Freq: Bi-Monthly
Circ: 2000 Not Audited
Editor: Jerry Jackson

Royal Sutton Coldfield Observer
980573
Editorial: Central Independent Newspapers, Ventura Park Road, Bitterscote, Tamworth B78 3LZ **Tel:** 44 01827 848586
Email: suttonobserver@cintamworth.co.uk
Web site: www.suttoncoldfieldobserver.co.uk
Freq: Weekly
Circ: 44180 Not Audited
Profile: The Royal Sutton Coldfield Observer is a free weekly local newspaper covering local news, sports and events for the surrounding area.
Ad Rate: Full Page Mono 1976.40

Royston Crow
982910
Editorial: 6 Melbourn Street, Royston SG8 7BX **Tel:** 44 01438 866200
Email: news@royston-crow.co.uk
Web site: www.royston-crow.co.uk
Freq: Weekly
Circ: 11872 Not Audited
Profile: Online version of the Royston Crow covering all the latest local news.

ROZMACH
1060160
Tel: 44 42055 6309004
Freq: Bi-Weekly
Circ: 200 Not Audited

Rugby Advertiser
980558
Editorial: 2 Albert Street, Rugby CV21 2RS
Tel: 44 01788 539999

Email: editorial@rugbyadvertiser.co.uk
Web site: www.rugbyadvertiser.co.uk
Freq: Weekly
Circ: 6532 Not Audited
Profile: Online version of the Rugby Advertiser covering local news, sports and entertainment for the surrounding area.

Rugby Observer
980559
Editorial: 45 The Parade, Leamington Spa, Leamington Spa CV32 4BL
Tel: 44 01926 451900
Email: editor@therugbyobserver.co.uk
Web site: https://rugbyobserver.co.uk/
Freq: Weekly
Circ: 20460 Not Audited
Editor: Ian Hughes
Profile: The Rugby Observer is a free, weekly, local newspaper published on Thursdays covering all the latest on local news, entertainment, property and sport in Rugby.
Ad Rate: Full Page Mono 1930.00
Ad Rate: Full Page Colour 2412.50

Runcorn & Widnes Weekly News
980224
Editorial: 2 Roberts Street, Widnes WA8 6LY **Tel:** 44 01514 223560
Email: runcornwidnesnews@trinitymirror.com
Web site: www.runcornandwidnesweeklynews.co.uk
Freq: Weekly
Circ: 5523 Not Audited
Profile: This is the online version of the Runcorn Weekly News and the Widnes Weekly News, covering all the latest on local news and the environment in Runcorn and Widnes.

Runcorn & Widnes World
982966
Editorial: The Academy, 138 Bridge Street, Warrington, Warrington WA1 2RU
Tel: 44 08456 037854
Email: newsroom@worldgroup.co.uk
Web site: www.runcornandwidnesworld.co.uk
Freq: Weekly
Circ: 21352 Not Audited
Editor: Hayley Smith
Profile: Website for local paper The Runcorn & Widnes World, covering the latest news, sport and entertainment news.

Rushden Extra Local
1053744
Editorial: Ringstead Business Centre, 1-3 Spencer Street, Ringstead, Kettering NN14 4BX **Tel:** 44 08448 877770
Email: newsdesk@extranewspapers.co.uk
Web site: www.extranewspapers.co.uk/local/rushden/
Freq: Bi-Weekly
Circ: 21000 Not Audited

Rutherglen Reformer
983002
Editorial: Campbell Street, Hamilton ML3 6AX **Tel:** 44 01698 283200
Email: news@rutherglenreformer.co.uk
Web site: www.rutherglenreformer.co.uk
Freq: Weekly
Circ: 2290 Not Audited
Editor: Douglas Dickie
Profile: The website of the Rutherglen Reformer, a weekly local newspaper covering the latest news, sports and lifestyle for the Rutherglen area.

Rutland Times
980383
Editorial: Woods House, Telford Road, Stamford, Stamford PE9 2EP **Tel:** 44 01780 758951
Email: rutland.editorial@jpress.co.uk
Web site: www.rutland-times.co.uk
Freq: Weekly
Circ: 1884 Not Audited
Profile: Online version of the Rutland Times newspaper covering local news, sports and lifestyle for the surrounding area.

Rye & Battle Observer
980287
Editorial: Woods House, Telford Road, Hastings TN38 9LZ **Tel:** 44 01424 854242
Email: rye.battle@jpress.co.uk
Web site: www.ryeandbattleobserver.co.uk
Freq: Weekly
Circ: 5921 Not Audited

Profile: Online version of the Rye and Battle Observer covering local news and sports for the surrounding area.

Saddleworth Independent
996491
Editorial: PO Box No 725, Greenfield, Oldham, Uppermill OL3 7XJ
Web site: www.saddind.co.uk
Freq: Monthly
Circ: 8000 Not Audited
Editor: Aimee Howarth

Saffron Walden Reporter
983092
Editorial: 54 High Street, Saffron Walden, Saffron Walden CB10 1EE
Tel: 44 01799 513000
Email: editor@saffronwalden-reporter.co.uk
Web site: www.saffronwaldenreporter.co.uk
Freq: Weekly
Circ: 16590 Not Audited
Editor: Stefan Bartlett
Profile: The Saffron Walden Reporter is a weekly local newspaper and covers local news and sports for the surrounding area. The newspaper is published on Thursdays.
Ad Rate: Full Page Mono 1188.00
Ad Rate: Full Page Colour 1485.00

Sale & Altrincham Messenger
980432
Editorial: 5 Washway Rd, Sale M33 7AD
Tel: 44 01619 083400
Email: sam.editorial@messengergrp.co.uk
Web site: www.messengernewspapers.co.uk
Freq: Weekly
Circ: 34783 Not Audited
Editor: Michael Crutchley
Profile: The Sale & Altrincham Messenger is a free weekly paper covering the latest local news and events from the Trafford area, including Sale, Altrincham, Hale, Bowdon, Stretford and Urmston.

Salisbury Advertiser
980317
Editorial: 8-12 Rollestone Street, Salisbury SP1 1DY **Tel:** 44 01722 412525
Email: newsdesk@salisburyjournal.co.uk
Web site: http://www.salisburyjournal.co.uk/salisbury_advertiser/
Freq: Weekly
Circ: 15144 Not Audited
Editor: Karen Bate
Profile: The Salisbury Advertiser is a free weekly, local newspaper and covers local news and sports. The newspaper is published on a Wednesday.

Salisbury Journal
980326
Editorial: 8-12 Rollerstone Street, Salisbury SP1 1DY **Tel:** 44 01722 426500
Email: editor@salisburyjournal.co.uk
Web site: www.salisburyjournal.co.uk
Freq: Weekly
Circ: 13858 Not Audited
Editor: Karen Bate
Profile: This is the online version of the Salisbury Journal and Forest Journal, weekly, local newspapers covering all the latest news, sport and leisure for Salisbury and the surrounding areas.

Sandwell Chronicle
980569
Editorial: 51-53 Queen Street, Wolverhampton WV1 1ES
Tel: 44 01384 353201
Email: sandwell.chronicle@expressandstar.co.uk
Web site: https://www.expressandstar.com/
Freq: Weekly
Circ: 43230 Not Audited
Editor: Charles Baker
Profile: Sandwell Chronicle is a free weekly local newspaper that is distributed in Sandwell Borough and covers local news and sports for the surrounding area. The newspaper is published on a Thursday.
Ad Rate: Full Page Mono 1909.44

Sasca News
998014
Email: info@sasca.org.uk
Web site: https://sascamanchester.wordpress.com/2015/04/23/welcome-to-sasca-news/
Freq: QuarterlyNot Audited

Editor: David Porter

The Scarborough News 980406
Editorial: Newchase Court, Hopper Hill Road, Scarborough YO11 3YS
Tel: 44 01723 860160
Email: newsdesk@jpress.co.uk
Web site: www.thescarboroughnews.co.uk/
Freq: Weekly
Circ: 35693 Not Audited
Profile: Online version of the Scarborough News newspaper covering local news and sports for the surrounding area.

Scarborough Review 087343
Editorial: Oaktree Farm, The Moor, Haxby, York YO32 2LH **Tel:** 44 01904 767881
Email: editor@thescarboroughreview.co.uk
Freq: Monthly
Circ: 14000 Not Audited
Editor: Dave Barry

Schellenberg meine gemeinde 1061897
Tel: 44 42339 92030
Email: gemeinde@schellenberg.li
Web site: http://www.schellenberg.li
Freq: 3 Times/Year
Circ: 550 Not Audited

Scunthorpe Telegraph 981656
Editorial: 4-5 Park Square, Laneham Street, Scunthorpe DN15 6JH **Tel:** 44 01724 273273
Email: newsdesk@scunthorpetelegraph.co.uk
Web site: http://www.scunthorpetelegraph.co.uk
Freq: Weekly
Circ: 14456 Not Audited
Profile: Online version of the Scunthorpe Telegraph covering local news and sports for the surrounding area.

The Sea (newspaper) 994617
Editorial: St Michael Paternoster Royal, College Hill, London EC4R 2RL
Tel: 44 02072 485202
Email: pr@missiontoseafarers.org
Web site: www.missiontoseafarers.org
Freq: Bi-Monthly
Circ: 28000 Not Audited
Editor: Carly Fields
Marine & Boat Trade, Shipping & Warehousing

Selby Times 980467
Editorial: Ground Floor, 11 The Crescent, Selby YO8 4PD **Tel:** 44 01757 291087
Email: editorial@selbytimes.info
Web site: https://www.gooletimes.info/
Freq: Weekly
Circ: 13750 Not Audited
Editor: Jane Rogers

Selkirk Weekend Advertiser 980707
Tel: 44 01750 505049
Email: southern-districtnews@jpress.co.uk
Web site: http://www.thesouthernreporter.co.uk/
Freq: Weekly
Circ: 900 Not Audited
Profile: This is the online version of the Selkirk Weekend Advertiser, a weekly local newspaper covering local news, sport and lifestyle for the surrounding area.

The Sentinel (Stoke) 979952
Editorial: Sentinel House, Bethesda Street, Hanley, Stoke-on-Trent ST1 3GN
Tel: 44 01782 864100
Email: newsdesk@thesentinel.co.uk
Web site: www.stokesentinel.co.uk
Freq: Daily
Circ: 26657 Not Audited

Seren 981772
Editorial: University of Wales Students Union, Deiniol Road, Gwynedd, Bangor LL57 2TH
Email: editor@seren.bangor.ac.uk
Web site: www.seren.bangor.ac.uk
Freq: MonthlyNot Audited

Profile: Students' Union newspaper of the University of Bangor.
Ad Rate: Full Page Colour 300.00
Student Lifestyle

Sevenoaks Chronicle 980365
Editorial: Courier House, 80-84 Calverley Road, Tunbridge Wells TN1 2UN
Tel: 44 01732 562921
Web site: www.kentlive.news
Freq: Weekly
Circ: 6760 Not Audited
Profile: Website for local paper the Sevenoaks Chronicle, covering the latest local news, sport and entertainment from Sevenoaks and the surrounding local area.

Shankill Extra 983837
Editorial: 177 Shankill Road, Belfast BT14 6RP **Tel:** 44 02890 325536
Email: news@shankillextra.co.uk
Freq: MonthlyNot Audited
Editor: John MacVicar
Profile: The Shankill Extra is a local newspaper covering all the local news from Shankill and North Belfast.
Ad Rate: Full Page Mono 932.40
Ad Rate: Full Page Colour 1398.60

Sheerness Times Guardian 980366
Editorial: 44 High Street, Sheerness ME12 1NL **Tel:** 44 01795 580300
Email: timesguardian@thekmgroup.co.uk
Web site: www.kentonline.co.uk/times_guardian/news.aspx
Freq: Weekly
Circ: 5061 Not Audited
Profile: Online version of the Sheerness Times Guardian covering local news and sports for the surrounding area.

Sheffield Telegraph 979968
Editorial: York Street, Sheffield S1 1PU
Tel: 44 01142 767676
Email: sheffieldtelegraph@sheffieldnewspapers.co.uk
Web site: www.sheffieldtelegraph.co.uk
Freq: Weekly
Circ: 10687 Not Audited
Editor: Nancy Fielder
Profile: Online version of the Sheffield Telegraph covering local news, sport, lifestyle and community events for the surrounding area.

The Shepway & Canterbury Advertiser 996571
Editorial: Ashford Advertiser Media Group, Media House, 6 Stafford Close, Fairwood Business Estate, Ashford TN23 4TT
Tel: 44 01233 000220
Web site: www.Shepway247.co.uk
Freq: Monthly
Circ: 90000 Not Audited

The Shepway Advertiser 998684
Editorial: Ashford Advertiser Media Group, Media House, 6 Stafford Close, Fairwood Business Estate, Ashford TN23 4TT
Circ: 90000 Not Audited

The Shetland Times 980709
Editorial: Gremista, Lerwick, Shetland ZE1 0PX **Tel:** 44 01595 742000
Email: editorial@shetlandtimes.co.uk
Web site: www.shetlandtimes.co.uk
Freq: Weekly
Circ: 9605 Not Audited
Editor: Adam Civico
Profile: The Shetland Times is a weekly local newspaper covering local news and sports for the surrounding area. The newspaper is published on a Friday.
Ad Rate: Full Page Mono 1233.60
Ad Rate: Full Page Colour 1665.60

The Shields Gazette 980777
Editorial: 7 Beach Row, South Shields, Newcastle upon Tyne, South Shields NE33 2QA **Tel:** 44 0191S 015800
Email: gazette.news@northeast-press.co.uk
Web site: www.shieldsgazette.com
Freq: Daily
Circ: 5584 Not Audited

Profile: The Shields Gazette is a daily regional newspaper and covers regional news, sports and lifestyle for South Shields and the surrounding area. This outlet offers RSS (Really Simple Syndication)
Ad Rate: Full Page Mono 945.50
Ad Rate: Full Page Colour 945.50

The Shire 995834
Editorial: Shirehampton Library, Shirehampton Public Hall, Station Road, Shirehampton, Bristol BS11 9TU
Tel: 44 07580 776199
Email: editor@shire.org.uk
Web site: www.shire.org.uk
Freq: Monthly
Circ: 5000 Not Audited

Shoreham Herald 980581
Editorial: Cannon House, Chatsworth Road, Worthing, Worthing BN11 1NA
Tel: 44 01903 282392
Email: letters@shorehamherald.co.uk
Web site: www.shorehamherald.co.uk
Freq: Weekly
Circ: 3749 Not Audited
Profile: This is the online version of the Shoreham Herald, a weekly local newspaper covering local news, sport, lifestyle and community for the surrounding area.

Shorelines 995169
Tel: 44 01243 379663
Freq: Monthly
Circ: 6500 Not Audited
Editor: Martin Shelley

Shrewsbury Chronicle 980497
Editorial: 7 Bellstone, Shrewsbury SY1 1HU
Tel: 44 01743 248248
Email: newsroom@shropshirestar.co.uk
Web site: www.shrewsburychronicle.co.uk
Freq: Weekly
Circ: 31421 Not Audited
Editor: Kim Bennett
Profile: This is the online version of the Shrewsbury Chronicle, a weekly local newspaper covering local news, sport and community for the surrounding area.

Shropshire Star 980492
Editorial: Waterloo Road, Ketley, Telford TF1 5HU **Tel:** 44 01952 242424
Email: newsroom@shropshirestar.co.uk
Web site: www.shropshirestar.com
Freq: Daily
Circ: 26752 Not Audited
Editor: Martin Wright
Profile: The Shropshire Star is a regional newspaper available in Shropshire, parts of Herefordshire, Worcestershire, Cheshire and Northern Powys and Llangollen in Wales. The paper covers the latest regional news, sport, business, entertainment, features and events in the region. The Weekend edition is 60p.
Ad Rate: Full Page Mono 3010.00
Ad Rate: Full Page Colour 3900.00

The Shuttle (Kidderminster) 980332
Editorial: St John's House, St John's Road, Stourbridge DY8 1EH **Tel:** 44 01384 358262
Email: editorial@kidderminstershuttle.co.uk
Web site: www.thisiskidderminster.co.uk
Freq: Weekly
Circ: 33389 Not Audited

Sichuan University Newspaper 1061536
Email: scdxxb@sina.comNot Audited

Sidmouth Herald 980266
Editorial: Fair Oak Close, Exeter Airport Business Park, Exeter EX5 2UL
Tel: 44 01392 888400
Email: sidmouth.editorial@archant.co.uk
Web site: www.sidmouthherald.co.uk
Freq: Weekly
Circ: 4984 Not Audited
Profile: Online version of the Sidmouth Herald newspaper covering local news and sports for the surrounding area. The outlet offers RSS (Really Simple Syndication).

Sittingbourne Messenger 983004
Editorial: 44 High Street, Sheerness ME12 1NL **Tel:** 44 01795 580300
Email: sittingbournekm@thekmgroup.co.uk
Web site: www.sittingbournemessenger.co.uk
Freq: WeeklyNot Audited
Profile: The Sittingbourne Messenger is a weekly paper published every Friday covering the latest local news and events from Sittingbourne and the surrounding local area.

Sittingbourne News Extra 986562
Editorial: 44 High Street, Sheerness, Sheerness ME12 1NL **Tel:** 44 01795 580300
Email: sittingbournekm@thekmgroup.co.uk
Web site: www.sittingbournemessenger.co.uk
Freq: Weekly
Circ: 4310 Not Audited
Profile: The Sittingbourne News Extra is a weekly newspaper covering all the local news in and around Sittingbourne.
Ad Rate: Full Page Mono 652.00
Ad Rate: Full Page Colour 816.00

Skegness Standard 980394
Editorial: 5 & 6 Church Lane, Boston PE21 6ND **Tel:** 44 01205 311433
Web site: www.skegnessstandard.co.uk
Freq: Weekly
Circ: 4500 Not Audited
Profile: Online version of the Skegness Standard newspaper covering local news, sports and lifestyle for the surrounding area.

Sleaford Standard 980395
Editorial: Unit 8, Sleaford Station Business Centre, Station Road, Sleaford, Sleaford NG34 7RG **Tel:** 44 01529 415981
Web site: www.sleafordtoday.co.uk
Freq: Weekly
Circ: 2178 Not Audited
Profile: Website of the Sleaford Standard, a weekly local newspaper covering local news for the surrounding area.

Slough & South Bucks Express 980197
Editorial: 48 Bell Street, Maidenhead, Maidenhead SL6 1HX **Tel:** 44 01628 680680
Email: news@baylismedia.co.uk
Web site: www.sloughexpress.co.uk
Freq: Weekly
Circ: 44461 Not Audited
Profile: Online version of the Slough & South Bucks Express newspaper covering local news, sports, entertainment and lifestyle.

Slough & South Bucks Observer 983005
Editorial: 3 Etongate, 112 Windsor Road, Slough, Slough SL1 2JA
Tel: 44 01753 627222
Email: newsroomslough@berksmedia.co.uk
Web site: www.sloughobserver.co.uk
Freq: Weekly
Circ: 4558 Not Audited
Profile: Website for local paper the Slough & South Bucks Observer featuring the latest news, sport, entertainment and community news from around the Slough, Windsor and South Buckinghamshire area.

Solihull News 980570
Editorial: Floor 6, Fort Dunlop, Birmingham B24 9FF **Tel:** 44 01212 345661
Email: solihullnews@trinitymirror.com
Web site: www.solihullnews.net
Freq: Weekly
Circ: 47431 Not Audited
Profile: The Solihull News is a free local weekly newspaper and covers local news and sports for the surrounding area. The newspaper is published on a Thursday.

Solihull Observer 981568
Editorial: 45 The Parade, Leamington Spa, Leamington Spa CV32 4BL
Tel: 44 01212 702291
Email: editor@solihullobserver.co.uk
Web site: www.solihullobserver.co.uk

Regional & Local Weekly Newspapers

Freq: Weekly
Circ: 49372 Not Audited
Profile: This it the online version of the Solihull Observer, Arden Observer and Shirley Observer, covering all the latest on local news, sport, business, entertainment and lifestyle in Solihull, Arden, Shirley, Henley-in-Arden, Balsall Common, Cheswick Green, Hall Green and Knowle.

Somerset County Gazette
980507
Editorial: 1-4 St James Building, 44 St James Street, Taunton TA1 1JR
Tel: 44 01823 365151
Email: newsdesk@countygazette.co.uk
Web site: www.somersetcountygazette.co.uk
Freq: Weekly
Circ: 12317 Not Audited
Profile: Online version of the Somerset County Gazette newspaper covering local news, sports and lifestyle for the surrounding area. The outlet offers RSS (Really Simple Syndication).

Somerset Guardian
980508
Editorial: Mid Somerset Series, Southover, Wells BA5 1UH **Tel:** 44 01749 832300
Email: editor@somersetguardian.co.uk
Web site: www.somersetlive.co.uk
Freq: Weekly
Circ: 4419 Not Audited
Profile: Website of the Somerset Guardian, a weekly paper covering the latest local news, sports and events from Midsomer Norton, Radstock, Peasedown St John, Paulton and surrounding villages.

South Belfast News
983108
Tel: 44 02890 584444
Email: m.mccourt@belfastmediagroup.com
Web site: www.belfastmediagroup.com
Freq: Weekly
Circ: 2500 Not Audited
Profile: The South Belfast News is a weekly paid for newspaper that comes out on Wednesday and is published by the Belfast Media Group. The paper is available in South Belfast, including the districts of Castlereagh, Bloomfield, Stormont, Rosetta, Ravenhill and Orangefield. The paper features a mix of local news and sport, community news and local entertainment listings.
Ad Rate: Full Page Mono 930.24
Ad Rate: Full Page Colour 1209.31

South Bristol Voice
1057945
Editorial: 18 Lilymead, Bristol BS4 2BX
Tel: 44 07811 766072
Email: paul@southbristolvoice.co.uk
Web site: http://www.southbristolvoice.co.uk/
Freq: Monthly
Circ: 8500 Not Audited
Editor: Paul Breeden

South Bucks Star
980205
Editorial: Bucks Free Press, Loudwater Mill, Station Road, High Wycombe HP10 9TY
Tel: 44 01494 755000
Web site: www.bucksfreepress.co.uk
Freq: Weekly
Circ: 12982 Not Audited
Profile: South Bucks Star is a free weekly tabloid published every Thursday and covers the latest in local news and current affairs.
Ad Rate: Full Page Colour 800.00

South Coast Herald
1060355
Email: candycek@dbn.caxton.co.za
Circ: 15730 Not Audited

South Devon & Plymouth Times
980267
Editorial: Tindle House, 26 Warland, Totnes, Newton Abbot TQ12 1NE
Tel: 44 01803 862585
Email: totnes.times@tindlenews.co.uk
Web site: www.totnes-today.co.uk
Freq: Weekly
Circ: 5000 Not Audited

South Hams Newspapers
980268
Editorial: 101-103 Fore Street, Kingsbridge, Kingsbridge TQ7 1AF **Tel:** 44 01548 856353
Email: editorial@southhams-today.co.uk
Web site: http://www.southhams-today.co.uk
Freq: Weekly
Circ: 39938 Not Audited

South London Press
980417
Editorial: 6th Floor, Yeoman House, 63 Croydon Road, London SE20 7TS
Tel: 44 02087 684932
Email: edit@londonnewsonline.co.uk
Web site: http://www.londonnewsonline.co.uk/
Freq: 2 Times/Week
Circ: 10797 Not Audited
Profile: Website for the South London Press including the titles Brixton & South London Press, Dulwich & South London Press, Streatham & South London Press, Streatham Today, Deptford & New Cross & South London Press, Forest Hill & Sydenham & South London Press, Wimbledon & South London Press, Wandsworth & South London Press, Bexley Mercury, Greenwich Mercury, Lewisham Mercury and the Lambeth Post. Covering the latest local news, sports and entertainment from South London. This outlet covers areas within the Boroughs of Bexley, Greenwich, Lambeth, Lewisham and Merton.

South Shropshire Journal
980498
Editorial: The Angel, Broad Street, Ludlow SY8 1NG **Tel:** 44 01584 876311
Email: ludlowreporters@shropshirestar.co.uk
Web site: www.southshropshirejournal.co.uk
Freq: Weekly
Circ: 5846 Not Audited
Editor: Mary Queally
Profile: The South Shropshire Journal is a free local weekly newspaper covering local news and sports for South Shropshire. The newspaper is published on a Friday.

South Wales Argus
979986
Editorial: Cardiff Road, Maes Glas, Newport, Newport NP20 3QN
Tel: 44 01633 810000
Email: newsdesk@southwalesargus.co.uk
Web site: www.southwalesargus.co.uk
Freq: Daily
Circ: 10808 Not Audited
Profile: South Wales Argus is a daily regional newspaper covering the latest news, sports and leisure. The newspaper is distributed in Newport and Monmouthshire and was first founded in 1892. It is owned by Newsquest.
Ad Rate: Full Page Mono 2016.00
Ad Rate: Full Page Colour 2016.00

South Wales Echo
979987
Editorial: 6 Park Street, Cardiff CF10 1XR
Tel: 44 02920 243630
Email: newsdesk@walesonline.co.uk
Web site: www.walesonline.co.uk
Freq: Daily
Circ: 15140 Not Audited
Editor: Paul Rowland; **Editor:** Tryst Williams
Profile: The South Wales Echo is a daily regional newspaper and is distributed throughout the South Wales region. The paper covers the latest regional news, sport and business news. It is published by Media Wales, part of Trinity Mirror.
Ad Rate: Full Page Mono 5801.76
Ad Rate: Full Page Colour 7832.37

South Wales Evening Post
979979
Editorial: South Wales Evening Post, Urban Village, 220 High Street, Swansea SA1 1NW
Tel: 44 01792 545500
Email: postnews@swwmedia.co.uk
Web site: http://www.walesonline.co.uk/all-about/swansea
Freq: Daily
Circ: 21031 Not Audited
Editor: Jonathan Roberts
Profile: The South Wales Evening Post is a daily regional newspaper that comes out from Monday to Saturday and covers the latest regional news from Swansea and the surrounding area. The paper also features a mix of sport, features, entertainment and business news.
Ad Rate: Full Page Mono 900.00
Ad Rate: Full Page Colour 990.00

South Wales Guardian
982939
Editorial: 37 Quay Street, Ammanford, Ammanford SA18 3BS **Tel:** 44 01269 592781
Web site: www.southwalesguardian.co.uk
Freq: Weekly
Circ: 4157 Not Audited
Profile: Online version of the South Wales Guardian covering local news and sports for the surrounding area.
Ad Rate: Full Page Mono 432.00

South Warrington News
982898
Editorial: 52 Walton Road, Stockton Heath, Warrington, Warrington WA4 6NL
Tel: 44 01925 600601
Email: editor@southwarringtonnews.co.uk
Web site: www.southwarringtonnews.com
Freq: MonthlyNot Audited
Editor: Brigid Hardman
Profile: This is the online version of the South Warrington News, a weekly local newspaper covering all the latest news for the surrounding area.

Southend Standard
982971
Editorial: 18 Clarence Road, Southend, Southend-on-Sea SS1 1AN
Tel: 44 08444 774512
Email: echonews@newsquest.co.uk
Web site: www.southendstandard.co.uk
Freq: Weekly
Circ: 38551 Not Audited
Profile: This is the online version of the Southend Standard, a weekly, local newspaper covering all the latest news, sport and leisure for the surrounding area.

Southern Daily Echo
979985
Editorial: Newspaper House, Test Lane, Redbridge, Southampton SO16 9JX
Tel: 44 02380 424777
Email: newsdesk@dailyecho.co.uk
Web site: www.dailyecho.co.uk
Freq: Daily
Circ: 16369 Not Audited
Editor: Lorraine Gourley

Southern Reporter
980710
Tel: 44 01750 724850
Email: southern-newsdesk@jpress.co.uk
Web site: www.thesouthernreporter.co.uk
Freq: Weekly
Circ: 12033 Not Audited
Profile: Website for local paper the Southern Reporter covering the latest local news and events from the Scottish Borders.

Southport Visiter
982972
Editorial: PO Box 48, Old Hall Street, Liverpool L69 3EB **Tel:** 44 01704 398249
Email: visiternews@southportvisiter.co.uk
Web site: www.southportvisiter.co.uk
Freq: Weekly
Circ: 4106 Not Audited
Editor: Andrew Brown
Profile: The Southport Visiter is a weekly, local newspaper covering all the latest news and current affairs for the surrounding areas.

Southwark News
982973
Editorial: Unit A302, Tower Bridge Business Complex, Clements Road, London SE16 4DG **Tel:** 44 02072 315258
Email: news@southwarknews.co.uk
Web site: www.southwarknews.co.uk
Freq: Weekly
Circ: 13000 Not Audited
Editor: John Kelly; **Editor:** Anthony Phillips
Profile: Website for the Southwark News, a weekly paper which covers local news, sports and lifestyle for the surrounding area. This outlet covers areas within Southwark Borough.

Southwell Advertiser
984585
Editorial: Unit 9 & 10 Halifax Court, Fernwood Business Park, Cross Lane, Newark NG24 3JP **Tel:** 44 01636 681234
Email: news@newarkadvertiser.co.uk
Web site: www.newarkadvertiser.co.uk/news/index.asp?c=southwell
Freq: Weekly
Circ: 42000 Not Audited
Profile: Southwell Advertiser is local weekly paper published every Thursday, covering the latest local news and events from Southwell and the surrounding local area.
Ad Rate: Full Page Mono 5171.40

Spalding and South Holland Voice
988053
Editorial: Units 1& 2 Winsover Centre, 14-16 Winsover Road, Spalding PE11 1EJ
Tel: 44 01775 768815
Email: news@spaldingvoice.co.uk
Web site: www.spaldingvoice.co.uk
Freq: Weekly
Circ: 14500 Not Audited
Editor: Rachel Mayfield

Spalding Guardian
980396
Editorial: Priory House, The Crescent, Spalding PE11 1AB **Tel:** 44 01775 725021
Email: spaldingeditor@jpress.co.uk
Web site: www.spaldingtoday.co.uk
Freq: Weekly
Circ: 6178 Not Audited
Profile: The Spalding Guardian is a local newspaper available on Thursdays, covering local news for the surrounding area.
Ad Rate: Full Page Mono 1196.46

Spenborough Guardian
980595
Editorial: Floor 5, 26 Whitehall Road, Leeds LS12 1BE **Tel:** 44 01924 433013
Email: spenborough.editorial@ywng.co.uk
Web site: http://www.spenboroughguardian.co.uk/
Freq: Weekly
Circ: 7227 Not Audited
Editor: John Kenealy
Profile: Website for local paper the Spenborough Guardian covering the latest local news and events from South Bradford.

Sports Mail
995470
Editorial: 1000 Lakeside, North Harbour, Portsmouth PO6 3EN **Tel:** 44 02392 664488
Email: sport@thenews.co.uk
Web site: www.portsmouth.co.uk/sport
Freq: Weekly
Circ: 20818 Not Audited

St Albans & Harpenden Review
980344
Editorial: Observor House, Caxton Way, Watford Business Park, London WD18 8RJ
Tel: 44 01923 216216
Web site: www.stalbansreview.co.uk
Freq: WeeklyNot Audited

St Andrews Citizen
983647
Editorial: 23 Kirk Wynd, Kirkcaldy, Kirkcaldy KY1 1EP **Tel:** 44 01592 645700
Email: ffpnews@fifetoday.co.uk
Web site: www.fifetoday.co.uk
Freq: Weekly
Circ: 4464 Not Audited
Editor: Jerzy Morkis

St Austell Voice
983459
Editorial: 5 Old Vicarage Place, St Austell, St. Austell PL25 5YY **Tel:** 44 01726 677222
Email: editorial@staustellvoice.co.uk
Web site: www.staustellvoice.co.uk
Freq: Weekly
Circ: 6300 Not Audited
Editor: Phillip Lamphee

St Helens Star
980440
Editorial: Unit 2, Catapult Too, Parade Street, St. Helens WA10 1LX
Tel: 44 01744 762766
Email: news@sthelensstar.co.uk
Web site: www.sthelensstar.co.uk
Freq: Weekly
Circ: 56119 Not Audited
Editor: Andrew Kilmurray
Profile: Online version of the St Helens Star newspaper covering local news and sports for the surrounding area.

St Ives Times & Echo 980236
Tel: 44 01736 795813
Email: times@stivesnews.co.uk
Web site: www.stivesnews.co.uk
Freq: Weekly
Circ: 3000 Not Audited
Editor: Toni Carver

**St. John Tradewinds
Newspaper** 1061810
Tel: 44 13407 766496
Email: info@tradewinds.vi
Web site: http://www.tradewinds.vi
Freq: Weekly
Circ: 3000 Not Audited

Staffordshire Newsletter 980527
Editorial: The Mills, Mill Bank, Stafford ST16
2QZ **Tel:** 44 01785 339600
Email: editor@staffordshirenewsletter.co.uk
Web site: www.staffordshirenewsletter.co.
uk
Freq: Weekly
Circ: 8461 Not Audited
Editor: Killoran Wills
Profile: Website of the Staffordshire
Newsletter, a weekly local newspaper
covering local news, sports and business.

Stamford Mercury 981658
Editorial: Cherryholt Road, Stamford,
Stamford PE9 2EP **Tel:** 44 01780 758951
Email: smeditor@stamfordmercury.co.uk
Web site: www.stamfordmercury.co.uk
Freq: Weekly
Circ: 17917 Not Audited
Profile: The Stamford Mercury is a weekly
local newspaper covering local news for the
surrounding area.
Ad Rate: Full Page Mono 1218.00
Ad Rate: Full Page Colour 1218.00

The Star (Doncaster) 980517
Editorial: The Star, York Street, Sheffield,
Sheffield S1 1PU **Tel:** 44 01142 767676
Email: news@thestar.co.uk
Web site: www.thestar.co.uk/news/local/
doncaster
Freq: Daily
Circ: 16708 Not Audited
Editor: Nancy Fielder

The Star (Sheffield) 979991
Editorial: York Street, Sheffield S1 1PU
Tel: 44 01142 767676
Email: news@thestar.co.uk
Web site: www.thestar.co.uk
Freq: Daily
Circ: 16708 Not Audited
Editor: Nancy Fielder

Star Courier 980548
Editorial: Stoke Mill, Woking Road, London
GU1 1QA **Tel:** 44 01483 508700
Email: aldershoteditorial@trinitymirror.com
Web site: www.gethampshire.co.uk/
starcourier
Freq: Weekly
Circ: 41382 Not Audited
Profile: Online version of the Star Courier
covering local news and sports for the
surrounding area.

Stirling News 980712
Editorial: 39 Drysdale Street, Alloa,
Clackmannanshire, Clackmannan FK10 1JA
Tel: 44 01259 214414
Email: editorial@stirlingnews.co.uk
Web site: www.stirlingnews.co.uk
Freq: Weekly
Circ: 14972 Not Audited
Profile: This is the online version of the
Stirling News, a weekly, local newspaper
covering the latest local news, entertainment
and sport in Stirling and the surrounding
area.

Stirling Observer 980713
Editorial: 34 Upper Craigs, Stirling,
Newcastle upon Tyne FK8 2DW
Tel: 44 01786 451110
Email: news@stirlingobserver.co.uk
Web site: http://www.dailyrecord.co.uk/all-
about/stirling

Freq: 2 Times/Week
Circ: 7499 Not Audited
Profile: Online version of the Stirling
Observer newspaper covering local news,
sports and community events for the
surrounding area.

Stockport Express 980433
Editorial: Mitchell Henry House, Hollinwood
Avenue, Chadderton, Oldham OL9 8EF
Tel: 44 01612 112956
Email: stockportexpress@menmedia.co.uk
Web site: www.stockportexpress.co.uk
Freq: Weekly
Circ: 6378 Not Audited
Profile: Website covering news. Stopckport
Express discusses anything from sport to
entertainment and jobs to property.

Stockport Independent 985384
Editorial: Publishing House, 3 Bridgebank
Industrial Estate, Taylor Street, Horwich BL6
7PD **Tel:** 44 01204 478813
Web site: www.independentnewspapers.co.
uk/stockport
Freq: Monthly
Circ: 11000 Not Audited
Editor: Mike Hulme

**Stockportmail Newspaper
Group** 1099573
Tel: 44 01614 912966
Email: stockportmail@aol.com
Web site: http://www.stockportmail.net/
Freq: MonthlyNot Audited

Stone & Eccleshall Gazette 995556
Tel: 44 01785 819919
Email: editorial@stonegazette.com
Web site: www.stonegazette.com
Freq: Monthly
Circ: 13400 Not Audited
Editor: Paul Mitchell

Stornoway Gazette 980714
Editorial: 10 Francis Street, Stornoway, Isle
of Lewis HS1 2XE **Tel:** 44 01851 702687
Email: news@stornowaygazette.co.uk
Web site: www.stornowaygazette.co.uk
Freq: Weekly
Circ: 8961 Not Audited
Editor: Melinda Gillen
Profile: Online version of the Stornoway
Gazette and West Coast Advertiser
newspaper covering local news and sports
for the surrounding area.

Stourbridge Chronicle 980571
Editorial: 51-53 Queen Street,
Wolverhampton WV1 1ES
Tel: 44 01384 353201
Email: dudley.chrons@expressandstar.co.uk
Web site: http://yourchronicle.com/
Freq: Weekly
Circ: 37902 Not Audited
Editor: Sarah Cowen
Profile: The Stourbridge Chronicle is a
weekly, local newspaper covering all the
latest news and current affairs for the
surrounding area.

Stourbridge News 980572
Editorial: St John's House, St John's Road,
Stourbridge DY8 1EH **Tel:** 44 01384 358050
Email: newsgrouped@midlands.newsquest.
co.uk
Web site: www.stourbridgenews.co.uk
Freq: Weekly
Circ: 45802 Not Audited
Profile: Online version of the Stourbridge
News newspaper covering local news and
sports for the surrounding area.

Strabane Chronicle 984223
Editorial: 15 Main Street, County Tyrone,
Strabane BT82 8AS **Tel:** 44 02871 882100
Email: editor@strabanechronicle.com
Web site: www.strabanechronicle.com
Freq: Weekly
Circ: 4491 Not Audited
Editor: Nigel McDonagh
Profile: Online version of the Strabane
Chronicle covering local news and sports.

Strabane Weekly News 981552
Tel: 44 02871 886869
Email: news@strabaneweekly.co.uk
Web site: www.strabaneweekly.co.uk
Freq: Weekly
Circ: 3500 Not Audited
Editor: Wesley Acheson
Profile: This is the online version of the
Strabane Weekly News, a weekly, local
newspaper covering all the latest news,
sports, entertainment, property and motors
for the surrounding areas.

**Stranraer & Wigtownshire
Free Press** 980715
Editorial: St Andrew Street, Stranraer,
Wigtown DG9 7EB **Tel:** 44 01776 702551
Email: news@stranraer-freepress.co.uk
Web site: www.stranraer-freepress.co.uk
Freq: Weekly
Circ: 5696 Not Audited
Editor: Alan Hall
Profile: This is the online version of the
Stranraer & Wigtownshire Free Press, a
weekly, local newspaper covering all the
latest on local news and sport in the
Stranraer, Wigtown and Newton Stewart.

Stratford Observer 980562
Editorial: 45 The Parade, Leamington Spa,
Leamington Spa CV32 4BL
Tel: 44 01789 293384
Email: editor@stratfordobserver.co.uk
Web site: http://www.stratfordobserver.co.
uk
Freq: Weekly
Circ: 13878 Not Audited
Editor: Ian Hughes

Stratford-upon-Avon Herald
980561
Editorial: York House, 17 Rother Street,
Stratford-upon-Avon CV37 6NB
Tel: 44 01789 266261
Email: news@stratford-herald.com
Web site: www.stratford-herald.com
Freq: Weekly
Circ: 10773 Not Audited
Editor: Amanda Chalmers
Profile: Online version of the Stratford-upon-
Avon Herald covering local news and sports
for the surrounding area.

**Stratford-Upon-Avon
Midweek** 980556
Editorial: York House, 17 Rother Street,
Stratford-upon-Avon CV37 6NB
Tel: 44 01789 266261
Email: news@stratford-herald.com
Web site: www.stratford-herald.com
Freq: Weekly
Circ: 50000 Not Audited
Editor: Amanda Chalmers

Strathallan Times 987550
Editorial: 39 Drysdale Street, Alloa,
Clackmannanshire, Clackmannan FK10 1JA
Tel: 44 01259 214416
Email: editorial@strathallantimes.co.uk
Web site: www.strathallantimes.co.uk
Freq: WeeklyNot Audited
Profile: Website for local paper the
Strathallan Times, a weekly paper covering
the latest local news, sports and events from
the Strathallan preserve, including
Auchterarder, Crieff, Comrie, Greenloaning,
Braco, Dunning and Blackford.

Strathearn Herald 980711
Editorial: 58 Watergate, Perth, Perth PH1
5TF **Tel:** 44 01738 493265
Email: news@strathearnherald.co.uk
Web site: www.dailyrecord.co.uk/all-about/
strathearn
Freq: Weekly
Circ: 1378 Not Audited
Editor: Johnathon Menzies
Profile: This is the online version of the
Strathearn Herald, a local weekly newspaper
covering news, sports, lifestyle and
comment for the local area.

**Strathspey & Badenoch
Herald** 982974
Editorial: 44 High Street, Granton on Spey,
Highlands, Badenoch PH26 3EH
Tel: 44 01479 872102
Email: editorial@sbherald.co.uk
Web site: www.strathspey-herald.co.uk
Freq: Weekly
Circ: 3166 Not Audited
Editor: Gavin Musgrove
Profile: This is the online version of the
Strathspey & Badenoch Herald, a weekly
local newspaper covering local news, sport,
motors and features for the surrounding
area.

Streeknuus 1060517
Tel: 44 27139 323031
Email: mail@streeknuus.co.za
Web site: http://www.streeknuus.co.za
Freq: Weekly
Circ: 3357 Not Audited

**Stretford & Urmston
Messenger** 980434
Editorial: 5 Washway Road, Sale M33 7AD
Tel: 44 01619 083400
Email: sam.editorial@messengergrp.co.uk
Web site: www.messengernewspapers.co.
uk
Freq: Weekly
Circ: 19205 Not Audited
Editor: Michael Crutchley
Profile: The Stretford & Urmston Messenger
is a weekly paper covering the latest news
and events from the Metropolitan Borough of
Trafford, in Greater Manchester.
Ad Rate: Full Page Mono 395.00

Stroud News & Journal 980306
Editorial: 6 Lansdown Road, Stroud GL5
1BE **Tel:** 44 01453 762412
Email: snjnews@stroudnewsandjournal.co.
uk
Web site: http://www.
stroudnewsandjournal.co.uk/
Freq: Weekly
Circ: 7555 Not Audited
Editor: Michael Purton
Profile: Online version of the Stroud News
and Journal covering local news and sports
for the surrounding area.

Suffolk Free Press 980536
Editorial: Borehamgate Precinct, Sudbury,
Sudbury CO10 2EE **Tel:** 44 01787 886911
Email: newsdesk@suffolkfreepress.co.uk
Web site: www.suffolkfreepress.co.uk
Freq: Weekly
Circ: 5439 Not Audited
Profile: Online version of the Suffolk Free
Press newspaper covering local news,
sports and lifestyle for the surrounding area.

Sunday Life 981598
Editorial: Belfast Telegraph, 124-144 Royal
Avenue, Belfast BT1 1EB
Tel: 44 02890 264000
Email: slnews@sundaylife.co.uk
Web site: www.sundaylife.co.uk
Freq: Weekly
Circ: 36467 Not Audited
Editor: Martin Breen

Sunday Mail 980624
Editorial: One Central Quay, Glasgow G3
8DA **Tel:** 44 01413 093000
Email: reporters@sundaymail.co.uk
Web site: http://www.dailyrecord.co.uk/all-
about/sunday%20mail
Freq: Weekly
Circ: 152892 Not Audited
Profile: The Sunday Mail is a regional
Sunday newspaper covering the latest in
regional news, business, entertainment,
lifestyle and sport. The outlet offers RSS
(Really Simple Syndication).
Ad Rate: Full Page Mono 17000.00
Ad Rate: Full Page Colour 22122.00

Sunday Mercury 981585
Editorial: Floor 6, Fort Dunlop, Fort
Parkway, Birmingham B24 9FF
Tel: 44 01212 363366
Email: sundaymercury@mrn.co.uk

Regional & Local Weekly Newspapers

Web site: www.birminghammail.co.uk/all-about/sunday-mercury
Freq: Weekly
Circ: 16234 Not Audited
Profile: The Sunday Mercury is a regional Sunday newspaper covering all the latest regional news, sports, lifestyle and entertainment. This outlet offers RSS (Really Simple Syndication).

The Sunday Post 980003
Editorial: 80 Kingsway East, Dundee DD4 8SL Tel: 44 01382 223131
Email: mail@sundaypost.com
Web site: https://www.sundaypost.com/
Freq: Weekly
Circ: 135181 Not Audited
Editor: Richard Prest
Profile: The Sunday Post is a regional Sunday newspaper covering regional news, sports, business and features for the surrounding area.
Ad Rate: Full Page Mono 10500.00
Ad Rate: Full Page Colour 12600.00

Sunday Sun (Newcastle) 980031
Editorial: Thomson House, Groat Market, Newcastle upon Tyne, Newcastle upon Tyne NE1 1ED Tel: 44 01912 327500
Email: ec.news@ncjmedia.co.uk
Web site: www.chroniclelive.co.uk/all-about/sunday-sun
Freq: Weekly
Circ: 23486 Not Audited
Editor: Matt McKenzie

Sunday World (Northern Ireland) 983179
Editorial: 124-144 Royal Ave, Belfast BT1 1DN Tel: 44 02890 238118
Email: news@sundayworld.com
Web site: www.sundayworld.com
Freq: Weekly
Circ: 162938 Not Audited
Editor: Richard Sullivan

Sunderland Echo 979967
Editorial: 1 Mandarin Road, Alexander House, Rainton Bridge, Houghton le Spring DH4 5RA Tel: 44 01915 015800
Email: echo.news@northeast-press.co.uk
Web site: www.sunderlandecho.com
Freq: Daily
Circ: 24994 Not Audited
Profile: The Sunderland Echo is an evening newspaper covering the latest news, sport, lifestyle and entertainment from Sunderland and the surrounding area. The Sunderland Echo is owned by Johnston Press and is published from Monday to Saturday. The paper was founded in 1873.
Ad Rate: Full Page Mono 4329.90
Ad Rate: Full Page Colour 5410.08

Surrey & Hants News 980546
Editorial: Tindle House, High Street, Bordon GU35 0AY Tel: 44 01420 477272
Email: surreyandhantsnews@tindlenews.co.uk
Web site: http://www.surreyandhantsnews.com/
Freq: Weekly
Circ: 56000 Not Audited
Profile: The Surrey & Hants News is a weekly paper covering the latest local news and events.
Ad Rate: Full Page Mono 1560.00
Ad Rate: Full Page Colour 1560.00

Surrey Advertiser 980024
Editorial: Stoke Mill, Woking Road, Guildford GU1 1QA Tel: 44 01483 508700
Email: tms-surreyadvertisereditorial@trinitymirror.com
Web site: http://www.getsurrey.co.uk/
Freq: Weekly
Circ: 16883 Not Audited
Profile: The Surrey Advertiser is a weekly local newspaper covering local news and sports for the surrounding area.
Ad Rate: Full Page Colour 2937.60

Surrey Comet 980547
Editorial: Floors 9 & 10, Quadrant House, The Quadrant, London SM2 5AS
Tel: 44 02087 226318

Email: newsdesk@surreycomet.co.uk
Web site: www.surreycomet.co.uk
Freq: Weekly
Circ: 5000 Not Audited
Profile: Online version the Surrey Comet, a weekly local newspaper covering local news, sports and lifestyle for the surrounding area.

Surrey Mirror 980549
Editorial: Aquila House, 35 London Rd, Redhill RH1 1NJ Tel: 44 01737 305581
Email: editor@surreymirror.co.uk
Web site: www.surreymirror.co.uk
Freq: Weekly
Circ: 8042 Not Audited
Profile: The Surrey Mirror is a weekly local newspaper covering local news for surrounding area.
Ad Rate: Full Page Mono 2099.52

Sussex Express Series 980289
Editorial: Berkeley House, 26 Gildredge Road, Eastbourne BN21 4SA
Tel: 44 01323 414488
Email: sussex.express@jpress.co.uk
Web site: www.sussexexpress.co.uk
Freq: Weekly
Circ: 7356 Not Audited

Sutton Guardian 982980
Editorial: Floors 9 & 10, Quadrant House, The Quadrant, Sutton SM2 5AS
Tel: 44 02087 226300
Email: newsdesk@suttonguardian.co.uk
Web site: www.suttonguardian.co.uk
Freq: Weekly
Circ: 39076 Not Audited
Profile: The Sutton Guardian is a weekly paper covering the latest news and current affairs from Sutton. This outlet covers areas within Hounslow Borough, Merton Borough, Sutton Borough and Kingston upon Thames Borough.
Ad Rate: Full Page Mono 555.17
Ad Rate: Full Page Colour 721.00

Swadlincote Post 986974
Web site: www.swadlincotepost.co.uk
Freq: Weekly
Circ: 10000 Not Audited
Profile: The Swadlincote Post is a free, weekly, local newspaper covering all the latest news and current affairs for the surrounding area.

Swanage & Wareham Voice 980278
Editorial: 21B Commercial Road, Swanage, Swanage BH19 1DF Tel: 44 01929 427428
Web site: http://www.swanageandwarehamvoice.co.uk/
Freq: Weekly
Circ: 8615 Not Audited
Profile: The Swanage & Wareham Advertiser is a free weekly local newspaper covering local news and sports for the surrounding area. The newspaper is published on a Thursday.
Ad Rate: Full Page Mono 1569.60
Ad Rate: Full Page Colour 1569.60

Swindon Advertiser 980600
Editorial: 100 Victoria Road, Swindon SN1 3BE Tel: 44 01793 528144
Email: newsdesk@swindonadvertiser.co.uk
Web site: www.swindonadvertiser.co.uk
Freq: Daily
Circ: 9562 Not Audited
Profile: The Swindon Advertiser is a daily tabloid newspaper published from Monday to Saturday and is owned by Newsquest. The newspaper covers news stories from around Swindon and the locality, as well as offering sport, business and features coverage.
Ad Rate: Full Page Mono 635.00
Ad Rate: Full Page Colour 770.00

Swindon Star 980602
Editorial: 100 Victoria Road, Swindon SN1 3BE Tel: 44 01793 528144
Email: newsdesk@swindonadvertiser.co.uk
Web site: www.swindonadvertiser.co.uk
Freq: Weekly
Circ: 25367 Not Audited

Profile: The Swindon Star is a free weekly local newspaper covering local news for the surrounding area. The newspaper is published every Thursday.
Ad Rate: Full Page Mono 2754.00

Tame Times- Bedfordview 1060647
Tel: 44 27118 628500
Web site: http://www.tametimes.co.za
Freq: Bi-Weekly
Circ: 63500 Not Audited

Tame Times- Joburg South 1060424
Tel: 44 27118 628500
Email: james@tametimes.co.za
Web site: www.tametimes.co.za
Freq: Bi-Weekly
Circ: 64500 Not Audited

Tameside Reporter 980435
Editorial: Quest Media Centre, Cavendish Mill Rear Entrance, Bank Street, Ashton-under-Lyne OL6 7DN Tel: 44 01613 312575
Email: editorial@reporterandchronicle.co.uk
Web site: www.tamesidereporter.com
Freq: Weekly
Circ: 30000 Not Audited
Editor: Nigel Skinner
Profile: The Tameside Reporter is a weekly local newspaper covering local news and sports for the surrounding area.

Tamworth Herald 980528
Editorial: Ventura Park Road, Bitterscote, Tamworth B78 3LZ Tel: 44 01827 848586
Email: tamworth.editorial@cintamworth.co.uk
Web site: www.thisistamworth.co.uk
Freq: Weekly
Circ: 11333 Not Audited
Profile: Website of the Tamworth Herald, a weekly local newspaper covering local news for the surrounding area.

Target Series 983551
Editorial: 16 Wide Bargate, Boston, Boston PE21 6SR Tel: 44 01205 315000
Email: news@targetseries.co.uk
Web site: http://www.bostontarget.co.uk/
Freq: Weekly
Circ: 18977 Not Audited
Editor: Adam Moss

Tarporley News 1104362
Email: info@tarporley.news
Web site: www.tarporley.news
Freq: Weekly

Tavistock Times Gazette 980270
Editorial: 14 Brook Street, Tavistock PL19 0HD Tel: 44 01822 613666
Email: editorial@tavistock-today.co.uk
Web site: http://www.tavistock-today.co.uk
Freq: Weekly
Circ: 8691 Not Audited
Profile: Online version of the Tavistock Times Gazette newspaper covering local news for the surrounding area.

Teesdale Mercury 983292
Editorial: 24 Market Place, Barnard Castle, Barnard Castle DL12 8NB
Tel: 44 01833 637140
Email: editor@teesdalemercury.co.uk
Web site: www.teesdalemercury.co.uk
Freq: Weekly
Circ: 6673 Not Audited
Editor: Trevor Brookes
Profile: Online version of the Teesdale Mercury, a weekly local newspaper covering news and events for the Teesdale area.

Teignmouth Post 980271
Editorial: The Old Manor House, 63 Wolborough Street, Newton Abbott, Newton Abbot TQ12 1NE Tel: 44 01626 353555
Email: editorial@middevonadvertiser.co.uk
Web site: http://www.teignmouth-today.co.uk/
Freq: Weekly
Circ: 12238 Not Audited

Profile: Website for local paper The Teignmouth Postcovering the latest news, sport and entertainment news from Teignmouth and the surrounding area.

Telegraph and Argus 979992
Editorial: Telegraph & Argus, Hall Ings, Bradford BD1 1JR Tel: 44 01274 729511
Email: newsdesk@telegraphandargus.co.uk
Web site: www.thetelegraphandargus.co.uk
Freq: Daily
Circ: 13951 Not Audited

Telford Journal 980499
Editorial: Waterloo Road, Ketley, Telford, Telford TF1 5HU Tel: 44 01952 242424
Email: tjnews@shropshirestar.co.uk
Web site: www.shropshirestar.com/telford-journal
Freq: Weekly
Circ: 41143 Not Audited
Editor: Pete Carroll
Profile: The Telford Journal is a weekly local newspaper available on Fridays covering all the latest on local news, sport, features and property for the surrounding area.
Ad Rate: Full Page Mono 1965.60
Ad Rate: Full Page Colour 2555.28

Tenby Observer 981655
Editorial: Tindle House, Warren Street, Tenby, Tenby SA70 7JY
Tel: 44 01834 843262
Email: editor@thetenbyobserver.co.uk
Web site: www.tenby-today.co.uk
Freq: Weekly
Circ: 8000 Not Audited
Editor: Neil Dickinson
Profile: This is the online version of the Tenby Observer, a weekly local paper covering the latest news, sport and events in Tenby and the surrounding Pembrokeshire area.

Thame Gazette 983215
Editorial: Claydon House, 1 Edison Rd, Aylesbury HP19 8TE Tel: 44 01296 619735
Email: editorial@bucksherald.co.uk
Web site: www.thametoday.co.uk
Freq: Weekly
Circ: 10670 Not Audited
Profile: This is the online version of the Thame Gazette, a free, weekly, local newspaper published on Fridays, covering all the latest on local news, lifestyle and sport in Thame and the surrounding areas of Aylesbury and Chinnor.

Thetford & Brandon Times 980454
Editorial: Prospect House, Rouen Road, Norwich NR1 1RE Tel: 44 01603 628311
Email: edpnewsdesk@archant.co.uk
Web site: www.thetfordandbrandontimes.co.uk/
Freq: Weekly
Circ: 18205 Not Audited

Thorne Times 996298
Editorial: Thorne Times, Gazette House, King Street, Doncaster DN8 5BA
Tel: 44 01405 947277
Email: newsdesk@thornetimes.co.uk
Web site: www.thornetimes.co.uk
Freq: Monthly
Circ: 16500 Not Audited

Three Counties Farmer 996242
Editorial: Newsquest (Hereford), Holmer Road, Hereford HR4 9UJ
Tel: 44 01432 274413
Email: editorial@threecountiesfarmer.co.uk
Web site: www.worcesternews.co.uk/tcf
Freq: Monthly
Circ: 7000 Not Audited
Animal Farming

Thurrock Enquirer 985897
Editorial: Independent House, Radford Way, Billericay CM12 0AA Tel: 44 01277 627300
Email: newsdesk@theenquirer.co.uk
Web site: www.theenquirer.co.uk
Freq: Weekly
Circ: 60000 Not Audited

Profile: The Thurrock Enquirer is a weekly local newspaper covering local news and sports for the surrounding area.

Thurrock Gazette
982870

Editorial: 91 Orsett Road, Grays, Grays RM17 5EX **Tel:** 44 01375 411514
Email: thurrockgazettenews@newsquest.co.uk
Web site: www.thurrockgazette.co.uk
Freq: Weekly
Circ: 44989 Not Audited
Editor: Gary Pearson
Profile: Online version of the Thurrock Gazette newspaper covering local news and sports for the surrounding area. The outlet offers RSS (Really Simple Syndication).

Times & Star
980241

Editorial: 21-27 Oxford Street, Workington CA14 2AN **Tel:** 44 01900 607600
Email: news.ts@timesandstar.co.uk
Web site: www.times-and-star.co.uk
Freq: Weekly
Circ: 9875 Not Audited
Editor: Deanne Shallcross
Profile: Online version of the Times & Star newspaper covering local news and sports for the surrounding area.

Times of Tunbridge Wells
988820

Editorial: 16 Lonsdale Gardens, Tunbridge Wells, Tunbridge Wells TN1 1NU
Tel: 44 01892 779650
Email: newsdesk@timesoftunbridgewells.co.uk
Web site: www.timesoftunbridgewells.co.uk
Freq: Weekly
Circ: 30000 Not Audited

Tivyside Advertiser
980621

Editorial: Creative Mwldan, Bath-house Road, Cardigan, Cardigan SA43 1JD
Tel: 44 01239 614343
Email: tivyside@tivysideadvertiser.co.uk
Web site: www.tivysideadvertiser.co.uk
Freq: Weekly
Circ: 4756 Not Audited

Totnes Times
980272

Editorial: Tindle House, 26 Warland, Totnes, Totnes TQ9 5EL **Tel:** 44 01803 862585
Email: editorial@totnes-today.co.uk
Web site: www.totnes-today.co.uk
Freq: Weekly
Circ: 12000 Not Audited
Profile: Website of The Totnes Times, a weekly local newspaper covering local news, sport and events for the surrounding area.

Tottenham and Wood Green Independent
981713

Editorial: Observer House, Caxton Way, Watford, London WD18 8RJ
Tel: 44 01923 216216
Email: haringeynews@london.newsquest.co.uk
Web site: www.haringeyindependent.co.uk
Freq: Weekly
Circ: 18154 Not Audited

Tribune & Courier Series
984438

Editorial: 46 High Street, West Mersea, Colchester CO5 8QA **Tel:** 44 01206 382935
Freq: Bi-Weekly Not Audited
Editor: Peter Headford

Troon Times
983728

Editorial: Ayrshire Weekly Press, Princes Street, Ardrossan, Ardrossan KA22 8BP
Tel: 44 01292 267631
Email: editorial@ayradvertiser.co.uk
Web site: www.troontimes.com
Freq: Weekly
Circ: 3491 Not Audited
Editor: Caroline Patterson

Turriff Advertiser
980716

Editorial: 16 High Street, Turriff AB53 4DT
Tel: 44 01888 563589
Email: newsdesk@wpeters.co.uk
Web site: www.wpeters.co.uk
Freq: Weekly
Circ: 14000 Not Audited

Editor: Jan Mackie

Tyrone Constitution
983148

Editorial: 25-27 High Street, Co Tyrone, Northern Ireland, Omagh BT78 1BD
Tel: 44 02882 242721
Email: news@tyronecon.co.uk
Web site: www.tyronecon.co.uk
Freq: Weekly
Circ: 9500 Not Audited
Editor: Wesley Acheson
Profile: This is the online version of the Tyrone Constitution, a weekly, local newspaper covering all the latest news, entertainment, property and motors for the surrounding areas.

Tyrone Courier
983135

Editorial: 58 Scotch Street, Co Tyrone, Dungannon BT70 1BD **Tel:** 44 02887 722271
Email: newsdesk@tyronecourier.com
Web site: www.tyronecourier.uk.com
Freq: Weekly
Circ: 14000 Not Audited
Editor: Ian Greer
Profile: Website of The Tyrone Courier, a weekly local newspaper covering all the latest news, sports and entertainment for the surrounding area.

The Tyrone Herald
987226

Editorial: 12-14 John Street, Co-Tyrone, Northern Ireland, Omagh BT78 1DW
Tel: 44 02882 243444
Email: editor@ulsterherald.com
Web site: www.ulsterherald.com
Freq: Weekly
Circ: 6531 Not Audited
Editor: Nigel McDonagh
Profile: The Tyrone Herald is a local weekly newspaper covering local news and sports for the area.
Ad Rate: Full Page Mono 1134.00
Ad Rate: Full Page Colour 1587.00

Tyrone Times
998720

Editorial: 52 Oldtown Street, Northern Ireland, Cookstown BT80 8EF
Tel: 44 02886 762288
Email: news@tyronetimes.co.uk
Web site: www.tyronetimes.co.uk
Freq: Weekly
Circ: 2226 Not Audited
Editor: Damian Wilson

Ulster Gazette
995961

Editorial: 56 Scotch Street, Armagh BT61 7DQ **Tel:** 44 02837 522099
Email: newsdesk@ulstergazette.co.uk
Web site: www.ulstergazette.co.uk
Freq: Weekly
Circ: 9109 Not Audited
Editor: John Hooks
Ad Rate: Full Page Mono 1047.55

The Ulster Herald
981661

Editorial: 12-14 John Street, Co-Tyrone, Northern Ireland, Omagh BT78 1DW
Tel: 44 02882 243444
Email: editor@ulsterherald.com
Web site: www.ulsterherald.com
Freq: Weekly
Circ: 12311 Not Audited
Editor: Nigel McDonagh
Profile: Website of the Ulster Herald newspaper, covering all the news, sports and events from Ulster.

Ulster Star
984217

Tel: 44 02838 393939
Email: news@ulsterstar.co.uk
Web site: www.lisburntoday.co.uk
Freq: Weekly
Circ: 5000 Not Audited
Editor: Damian Wilson
Profile: Online version of the Ulster Star and Lisburn Echo and covers local news and sports for the surrounding area.

Uttoxeter Advertiser
980529

Tel: 44 01283 524851
Email: editorial@uttoxeteradvertiser.co.uk
Web site: www.uttoxeteradvertiser.co.uk
Freq: Weekly
Circ: 2701 Not Audited

Editor: Emma Turton
Profile: This is the online version of the Uttoxeter Advertiser and the Uttoxeter Post & Times, featuring local news for the surrounding area

Uttoxeter Echo
981700

Editorial: 5 Church Street, Uttoxeter ST14 8AG **Tel:** 44 01538 753162
Email: news@timesandecho.co.uk
Web site: www.timesechoandlife.co.uk
Freq: Weekly
Circ: 10000 Not Audited
Profile: The Uttoxeter Echo is a weekly newspaper covering local news, sports and leisure for the surrounding area. It is published every Wednesday. The company was established in 1896.
Ad Rate: Full Page Mono 725.00
Ad Rate: Full Page Colour 725.00

Uxbridge Gazette Series
980420

Editorial: Trinity Mirror Southern, Stoke Mill, Woking Road, Guildford GU1 1QA
Tel: 44 01895 451000
Email: editorialuxbridge@trinitysouth.co.uk
Web site: www.getwestlondon.co.uk
Freq: Weekly
Circ: 25317 Not Audited

View From Axminster
983208

Editorial: Unit 3, St Michael's Business Centre, Church Street, Lyme Regis, Lyme Regis DT7 3DB **Tel:** 44 01297 631120
Email: edit@viewnews.co.uk
Web site: http://www.viewnews.co.uk/axminster/
Freq: Weekly
Circ: 800 Not Audited

View from Honiton and Ottery St Mary
980259

Editorial: Unit 3, St Michael's Business Centre, Church Street, Lyme Regis, Lyme Regis DT7 3DB **Tel:** 44 01297 446057
Email: edit@viewnews.co.uk
Web site: http://www.viewnews.co.uk/honiton/
Freq: Weekly
Circ: 6000 Not Audited

View From Seaton
984561

Editorial: Unit 3, St Michael's Business Centre, Church Street, Lyme Regis, Lyme Regis DT7 3DB **Tel:** 44 01297 631120
Email: edit@viewnews.co.uk
Web site: http://www.viewnews.co.uk/seaton/
Freq: Weekly
Circ: 22000 Not Audited

View from South Somerset
996238

Editorial: Unit 3, St Michael's Business Centre, Church Street, Lyme Regis, Lyme Regis DT7 3DB **Tel:** 44 01297 446057
Email: edit@viewnews.co.uk
Web site: https://www.viewnews.co.uk/category/south-somerset/
Freq: Weekly
Circ: 9000 Not Audited

The Villager
983204

Editorial: 3 Etongate, 112 Windsor Road, Slough, Slough SL1 2JA
Tel: 44 01189 553333
Email: villagernews@berksmedia.co.uk
Web site: www.thevillager.co.uk
Freq: Bi-Weekly
Circ: 10000 Not Audited
Profile: The Villager is a bi-weekly, free, local newspaper published on Fridays, covering all the latest on local news, business and entertainment in Ascot, Bagshot, Chobham, Egham, Englefield Green, Sunningdale, Sunninghill, Virginia Water and Windlesham.
Ad Rate: Full Page Colour 693.60

The Visitor (Morecambe)
980378

Editorial: White Lund Industrial Estate, 41 Northgate, Morecambe, Morecambe LA3 3PA **Tel:** 44 01524 385929
Email: visitor@jpress.co.uk
Web site: www.thevisitor.co.uk

Freq: Weekly
Circ: 21896 Not Audited

Wakefield Express
980597

Editorial: First Floor, Bullring House, 23 Northgate, Wakefield, Wakefield WF1 3BJ
Tel: 44 01924 375111
Email: editorial@wakefieldexpress.co.uk
Web site: www.wakefieldexpress.co.uk
Freq: Weekly
Circ: 21497 Not Audited
Editor: John Kenealy
Profile: Online version of the Wakefield Express covering local news and sports for the surrounding area.

Walden Local
980301

Editorial: 10 Emson Close, Saffron Walden CB10 1HL **Tel:** 44 01799 516161
Email: editor@waldenlocal.co.uk
Web site: www.waldenlocal.co.uk
Freq: Weekly
Circ: 30000 Not Audited
Editor: John Brooker
Profile: This is the online version of the Walden Local, a weekly, local newspaper published on Wednesdays covering all the latest on local news in Walden.

Wales on Sunday
979984

Editorial: Six Park Street, Cardiff CF10 1XR
Tel: 44 02920 243630
Email: newsdesk@walesonline.co.uk
Web site: www.walesonline.co.uk
Freq: Weekly
Circ: 11608 Not Audited
Editor: Paul Rowland
Profile: Wales on Sunday is a regional Sunday newspaper covering regional news, sports, business and lifestyle for the whole of Wales.
Ad Rate: Full Page Mono 4896.00
Ad Rate: Full Page Colour 5385.00

Walsall Advertiser incorporating the Great Barr Observer
980566

Editorial: Ventura Park Road, Bitterscote, Tamworth B78 3LZ **Tel:** 44 01827 848586
Email: greatbarrobserver@cintamworth.co.uk
Web site: http://www.walsalladvertiser.co.uk/
Freq: Weekly
Circ: 45703 Not Audited
Profile: The Great Barr Observer is a free weekly local newspaper covering local news, sports and events for the surrounding area.

Walsall Chronicle
981697

Editorial: 51-53 Queen Street, Wolverhampton WV1 1ES
Tel: 44 01543 5465305
Email: walsallchronicle@expressandstar.co.uk
Web site: http://yourchronicle.com/
Freq: Weekly
Circ: 43709 Not Audited
Editor: Leon Burakowski
Ad Rate: Full Page Mono 1230.00

Waltham Forest Echo
1053628

Editorial: Social Spider CIC, The Mill, 7-11 Coppermill Lane, Walthamstow, London E17 7HA **Tel:** 44 02085 217956
Email: wfecho@socialspider.com
Web site: http://walthamforestecho.co.uk/
Freq: Monthly
Circ: 20000 Not Audited
Editor: James Cracknell

Waltham Forest Independent
982968

Editorial: Guardian Series, Observer House, Caxton Way, Watford WD18 8RJ
Tel: 44 01992 572285
Web site: http://www.guardian-series.co.uk/news/wfnews/
Freq: Weekly
Circ: 14107 Not Audited
Profile: Waltham Forest Independent is a local freesheet covering the latest news from Waltham Forest. This outlet covers areas within Waltham Forest Borough.
Ad Rate: Full Page Mono 305.00

Regional & Local Weekly Newspapers

Ad Rate: Full Page Colour 305.00

Wandsworth Guardian   980421
Editorial: Floors 9 & 10, Quadrant House,
The Quadrant, Sutton SM2 5AS
Tel: 44 02087 226344
Email: newsdesk@wandsworthguardian.co.
uk
Web site: www.wandsworthguardian.co.uk
Freq: Weekly
Circ: 51309 Not Audited
Profile: The Wandsworth Guardian is a
weekly paper covering the latest news,
sports and entertainment from Wandsworth
Town, Putney, Battersea, Balham and
Tooting.
Ad Rate: Full Page Colour 463.50

Warminster Journal   980603
Editorial: 36 Market Place, Warminster
BA12 9AN **Tel:** 44 01985 213030
Email: news@warminsterjournal.co.uk
Web site: www.warminsterjournal.co.uk
Freq: Weekly
Circ: 3600 Not Audited
Profile: The Warminster Journal is a weekly
local newspaper covering local news and
sports for the surrounding area. The
newspaper is published on a Friday.

Warrington Guardian   980225
Editorial: Unit 4, Cygnet Court, Warrington
WA1 1PP **Tel:** 44 01925 596446
Email: editor@guardiangrp.co.uk
Web site: www.warringtonguardian.co.uk
Freq: Weekly
Circ: 14278 Not Audited
Editor: Hayley Smith
Profile: Online version of the Warrington
News newspaper covering local news and
sports for the surrounding area.

Warwick Courier   986291
Editorial: 32 Hamilton Terrace, Leamington
Spa CV32 4LY **Tel:** 44 01926 457737
Email: news@leamingtoncourier.co.uk
Web site: www.warwickcourier.co.uk
Freq: Weekly
Circ: 43205 Not Audited
Profile: Website of The Warwick Courier, a
weekly, local newspaper covering all the
latest news, sport, lifestyle and community
for the surrounding area.

Watford Free   980345
Editorial: Observer House, Caxton Way,
Watford, Watford WD18 8RJ
Tel: 44 01923 216216
Email: editor@watfordobserver.co.uk
Web site: www.watfordobserver.co.uk
Freq: Weekly
Circ: 32598 Not Audited
Profile: The Watford Free is a free weekly
local newspaper covering local news and
sports for Watford and the surrounding
areas. The newspaper is published on a
Thursday.
Ad Rate: Full Page Mono 1897.20

Watford Observer   983188
Editorial: Observer House, Caxton Way,
Watford Business Centre, Watford WD18
8RJ **Tel:** 44 01923 216216
Email: editor@watfordobserver.co.uk
Web site: www.watfordobserver.co.uk
Freq: Weekly
Circ: 9971 Not Audited
Profile: Online version of the Watford
Observer newspaper covering local news
and sports for the surrounding area.

Watton & Swaffham Times
984311
Editorial: Bond House, High Street,
Dereham NR19 1DZ **Tel:** 44 01362 854701
Email: edpnewsdesk@archant.co.uk
Web site: http://www.
wattonandswaffhamtimes.co.uk/home
Freq: Weekly
Circ: 7184 Not Audited

Wealden Advertiser   980367
Editorial: Cowden Close, Horns Road,
Cranbrook TN18 4QT **Tel:** 44 01580 753322
Web site: www.wealdenad.co.uk

Freq: WeeklyNot Audited
Profile: Magazine with adverts for vehicles,
property and situations vacant to plumbers,
builders and domestic appliances.
Ad Rate: Full Page Mono 515.00
Ad Rate: Full Page Colour 700.00

Weardale Gazette   983024
Editorial: 6 Market Place, Stanhope, Bishop
Auckland, Durham DL13 2UJ
Tel: 44 01388 527706
Web site: www.weardalegazette.co.uk
Freq: Bi-Weekly
Circ: 2000 Not Audited
Editor: Anita Atkinson
Profile: This is the online version of the
Weardale Gazette, a fortnightly, local
newspaper covering all the latest on local
news in Weardale.

Wellingborough Extra Local
1053747
Editorial: Ringstead Business Centre, 1-3
Spencer Street, Ringstead, Kettering NN14
4BX **Tel:** 44 08448 877770
Email: newsdesk@extranewspapers.co.uk
Web site: www.extranewspapers.co.uk/
local/wellingborough-news/
Freq: Bi-Weekly
Circ: 21000 Not Audited

Wellington Weekly News   980509
Editorial: 26 High Street, Wellington,
Wellington TA21 8RA **Tel:** 44 01823 662439
Email: edit@wellingtonweeklynews.co.uk
Web site: http://www.wellington-today.co.
uk
Freq: Weekly
Circ: 14000 Not Audited
Profile: This is the online version of the
Wellington Weekly News, a weekly, local
newspaper published in Wednesdays,
covering all the latest on local news,
entertainment and sport in Wellington.

Welwyn Hatfield Times   980346
Editorial: Campus West, The Campus,
Welwyn Garden City, Welwyn Garden City
AL8 6BX **Tel:** 44 01707 372370
Email: news@whtimes.co.uk
Web site: www.whtimes.co.uk
Freq: Weekly
Circ: 8589 Not Audited
Profile: Online version of the Welwyn
Hatfield Times newspaper covering local
news and sports for the surrounding area.

West & North Wiltshire Star
998552
Editorial: 15 Duke Street, Trowbridge BA14
8EF **Tel:** 44 01225 773600
Email: newsdesk@wiltshiretimes.co.uk
Web site: www.wiltshiretimes.co.uk
Freq: Weekly
Circ: 48399 Not Audited

West Briton   980237
Editorial: High Water House, City Wharf,
Malpas Road, Truro TR1 1QH
Tel: 44 01872 271451
Email: wbnews@c-dm.co.uk
Web site: http://www.cornwalllive.com/
Freq: Weekly
Circ: 18816 Not Audited
Profile: West Briton is a weekly, local
newspaper covering all the latest on local
news and sport in Cornwall. The paper is
available on Thursdays. Local Newspaper
EditionsWest Briton Falmouth & Penryn
Edition West Briton Helston & The Lizard
EditionWest Briton Truro & Mid Cornwall
Edition West Briton Camborne, Redruth &
Hayle Edition

West Highland Free Press
980717
Editorial: Pairc Nan Craobh, Broadford, Isle
of Skye IV49 9AP **Tel:** 44 01471 822464
Email: editor@whfp.com
Web site: www.whfp.com
Freq: Weekly
Circ: 6063 Not Audited
Editor: Ian McCormack
Profile: Online version of the West Highland
Free Press newspaper, covering local news

and sports for the local area of the Outer
Hebrides, Isle of Skye, Highlands & Islands,
Kyle of Lochalsh and Rosshire.

West Lothian Courier   980718
Editorial: 20-22 King Street, Bathgate,
Livingston EH54 9DX **Tel:** 44 01506 633544
Email: news@westlothiancourier.co.uk
Web site: www.westlothiancourier.co.uk
Freq: Weekly
Circ: 6410 Not Audited
Editor: Marjorie Kerr
Profile: This is the online version of the West
Lothian Courier, a weekly, local newspaper
newspaper covering all the latest on local
news, lifestyle and sport in the West Lothian
district of Scotland, including the towns of
Bathgate, Broxburn and Livingston. This
outlet offers RSS (Really Simple Syndication)

West Somerset Free Press
980510
Editorial: 5 Long Street, Williton, Taunton,
Williton TA4 4QN **Tel:** 44 01984 632731
Email: news@wsfp.co.uk
Web site: www.west-somerset-today.co.uk
Freq: Weekly
Circ: 9768 Not Audited
Editor: Gareth Purcell
Profile: This is the online version of the West
Somerset Free Press covering news, sports,
features and local community for the
surrounding area.

West Somerset News Trader
982967
Editorial: West Somerset Free Press Ltd, 5
Long Street, Williton, Williton TA4 4QN
Tel: 44 01984 632731
Email: news@wsfp.co.uk
Web site: www.west-somerset-today.co.uk
Freq: Weekly
Circ: 11163 Not Audited
Editor: Gareth Purcell
Profile: The West Somerset News Trader is
a weekly local newspaper covering news,
sports, features and local community for the
surrounding area.

West Sussex County Times
980583
Editorial: Springfield House, Springfield
Road, Horsham RH12 2RG
Tel: 44 01403 751200
Email: ct.news@jpress.co.uk
Web site: www.wscountytimes.co.uk
Freq: Weekly
Circ: 11541 Not Audited
Profile: This is the online version of the West
Sussex County Times, a weekly, local
newspaper published on Thursdays,
covering all the latest on local news, sport
and lifestyle for the West Sussex area. This
outlet offers RSS (Really Simple
Syndication).

West Sussex Gazette   998584
Editorial: Springfield House, Springfield
Road, Horsham RH12 2RG
Tel: 44 01403 751200
Web site: www.westsussextoday.co.uk
Freq: Weekly
Circ: 2675 Not Audited
Profile: Website for the West Sussex
Gazette covering the latest news and events
from the West Sussex County.

West Word   996150
Editorial: Morar Station Buildings, Morar,
Inverness - Shire, Auchterarder PH40 4NR
Tel: 44 01687 462720
Email: editor@westword.org.uk
Web site: www.westword.org.uk
Freq: Monthly
Circ: 1200 Not Audited
Editor: Ann Martin

Western Daily Press   980012
Editorial: Temple Way, Bristol BS99 7HD
Tel: 44 01179 343000
Email: wdnews@bepp.co.uk
Web site: http://www.somersetlive.co.uk/
Freq: Daily
Circ: 15544 Not Audited
Editor: Gavin Thompson

Profile: Western Daily Press is a regional
newspaper covering regional news, sports
and business for the surrounding area. This
Outlet offer RSS (Really Simple Syndication).
Ad Rate: Full Page Mono 2624.80
Ad Rate: Full Page Colour 2624.80

Western Gazette   980511
Editorial: Yeovil Innovation Centre, Barracks
Close, Copse Lane, Yeovil BA22 8RN
Tel: 44 01935 709700
Email: newsdesk@westgaz.co.uk
Web site: www.somersetlive.co.uk
Freq: Weekly
Circ: 10956 Not Audited
Editor: Emma Slee
Profile: Online version of the Western
Gazette covering local news and sports for
the surrounding area.

Western Mail   979808
Editorial: 6 Park Street, Cardiff CF10 1XR
Tel: 44 02920 243630
Email: newsdesk@walesonline.co.uk
Web site: www.walesonline.co.uk
Freq: Daily
Circ: 15697 Not Audited
Editor: Catrin Pascoe; **Editor:** Paul Rowland

Western Morning News   979809
Editorial: 3rd Floor, Studio 5-11, Millbay
Road, Plymouth PL1 3LF
Tel: 44 01752 293000
Email: wmnnewsdesk@
westernmorningnews.co.uk
Web site: http://www.devonlive.com/
Freq: Daily
Circ: 19842 Not Audited
Editor: Bill Martin
Profile: The Western Morning News is a
daily regional newspaper providing the latest
regional news, sports and business for the
surrounding area.
Ad Rate: Full Page Mono 2448.00
Ad Rate: Full Page Colour 3060.00

Western Telegraph   981705
Editorial: Western Tangiers, Fishguard
Road, Haverfordwest SA62 4BU
Tel: 44 01437 761786
Email: wtnews@westerntelegraph.co.uk
Web site: www.westerntelegraph.co.uk
Freq: Weekly
Circ: 11089 Not Audited
Profile: Online version of the Western
Telegraph covering local news,
entertainment and sport for the surrounding
area. This outlet offers RSS (Really Simple
Syndication).

Westminster Extra   980422
Editorial: 40 Camden Road, London NW1
9DR **Tel:** 44 02074 199000
Email: editorial@camdennewjournal.co.uk
Web site: www.westendextra.com
Freq: Weekly
Circ: 11500 Not Audited
Editor: Eric Gordon
Profile: Website for weekly paper the West
End Extra covering the latest news and
events from Westminster.

The Westmorland Gazette
980242
Editorial: 1 Wainwright's Yard,
Westmorland, Kendal LA9 4DP
Tel: 44 01539 790250
Email: newsdesk@newsquest.co.uk
Web site: www.thewestmorlandgazette.co.
uk
Freq: Weekly
Circ: 17724 Not Audited
Profile: The Westmorland Gazette is a
weekly, local newspaper published on
Thursdays, covering all the latest on local
news, leisure and sport in the Lake District,
South Cumbria, North Lancashire and the
Yorkshire Dales. The paper was established
in 1818.

Weston, Worle & Somerset
Mercury   981049
Editorial: 32 Waterloo Street, Weston-
super-Mare BS23 1LW
Tel: 44 01934 422522
Email: newsdesk@westonmercury.co.uk

Web site: www.thewestonmercury.co.uk
Freq: Weekly
Circ: 10809 Not Audited
Editor: Tom Wright
Profile: The Weston, Worle & Somerset Mercury is a weekly local newspaper covering local news and sports for the surrounding areas. The outlet offers RSS Really Simple Syndication).
Ad Rate: Full Page Mono 1088.00
Ad Rate: Full Page Colour 1414.40

Wetherby News
980468
Editorial: 1 Cardale Park, Harrogate HG3 1RZ Tel: 44 01423 707402
Email: news@harrogateadvertiser.co.uk
Web site: www.wetherbynews.co.uk
Freq: Weekly
Circ: 2666 Not Audited
Profile: This is the online version of the Wetherby News, a weekly, local newspaper published on Thursdays, covering all the latest on local news, lifestyle and sport om Wetherby and the surrounding area.

Weymouth & Dorchester Advertiser
980279
Editorial: Fleet House, Hampshire Road, Granby House, Weymouth DT4 9XD
Tel: 44 01305 830930
Email: newsdesk@dorsetecho.co.uk
Web site: www.dorsetecho.co.uk
Freq: Weekly
Circ: 16253 Not Audited
Editor: Diarmuid MacDonagh

The Wharf
980423
Editorial: 22nd Floor, One Canada Square, Canary Wharf, London E14 5AP
Tel: 44 02075 106306
Email: newsdesk@wharf.co.uk
Web site: www.wharf.co.uk
Freq: Weekly
Circ: 30000 Not Audited
Editor: Giles Broadbent
Profile: The Wharf is a free weekly, local newspaper published on Thursdays, covering all the latest on local news, business and lifestyle in Canary Wharf and the Docklands. This outlet covers areas within Tower Hamlets Borough.
Ad Rate: Full Page Mono 2312.00
Ad Rate: Full Page Colour 3005.00

Wharfedale & Aireborough Observer
980599
Editorial: 8 Wells Road, Ilkley LS29 9JD
Tel: 44 01943 607022
Web site: www.wharfedaleobserver.co.uk
Freq: Weekly
Circ: 2745 Not Audited
Profile: Online version of the Wharfedale & Aireborough Observer newspaper covering local news and sports for the surrounding area.

Whitby Gazette
980469
Editorial: St Hilda's Business Centre, The Ropery, Whitby YO22 4ET
Tel: 44 01723 860100
Email: editorial@whitbygazette.co.uk
Web site: www.whitbygazette.co.uk
Freq: WeeklyNot Audited
Profile: This is the online version of the Whitby Gazette, a weekly, local newspaper published on Fridays, covering all the latest on local news, lifestyle and sport in Whitby and the surrounding area. This outlet offers RSS (Really Simple Syndication).

Whitchurch Herald
983020
Tel: 44 01948 660350
Email: news@whitchurchherald.co.uk
Web site: www.whitchurchherald.co.uk
Freq: Weekly
Circ: 2838 Not Audited
Editor: Colin Channon
Profile: Online version of the Whitchurch Herald newspaper covering local news and sports for the surrounding area.

White Horse News
980604
Editorial: 31 Market Place, Melksham SN12 6ES Tel: 44 01225 704761
Email: news@whitehorsenews.co.uk
Web site: www.whitehorsenews.co.uk

Freq: Bi-Weekly
Circ: 10000 Not Audited
Profile: This is the online version of the White Horse News, a fortnightly, local newspaper published on Thursdays covering all the latest on local and entertainment in Wiltshire and Westbury.

Whitehaven News
980243
Editorial: 148 Queens Street, Whitehaven, Whitehaven CA28 7AZ Tel: 44 01946 595100
Email: news.wn@whitehaven-news.co.uk
Web site: www.whitehaven-news.co.uk
Freq: Weekly
Circ: 8361 Not Audited
Editor: Deanne Shallcross
Profile: The Whitehaven News is a weekly local newspaper covering local news and sport for Whitehaven and the surrounding area. The paper is available on Thursdays.
Ad Rate: Full Page Mono 3742.20
Ad Rate: Full Page Colour 3742.20

Whitstable Times
984928
Editorial: Suite 1, 3rd Floor, Mill Lane House, Mill Lane, Margate CT9 1JU
Tel: 44 01843 609632
Email: newsdesk.times@krnmedia.co.uk
Web site: http://www.canterburytimes.co.uk/
Freq: Weekly
Circ: 21940 Not Audited
Profile: This is the online version of the Whitstable Times, a weekly, local newspaper published on Thursdays, covering all the latest on local news, business and sport in Whitstable.

Wigan Evening Post
979966
Editorial: Martland Mill, Martland Mill Lane, Wigan WN5 0LX Tel: 44 01942 228000
Email: newsroom@lancspublications.co.uk
Web site: www.wigantoday.net
Freq: Daily
Circ: 2382 Not Audited
Editor: Janet Wilson
Profile: Wigan Evening Post is a daily regional newspaper covering regional news, sports, business and lifestyle for Wigan. The newspaper is published Monday to Saturday.This Outlet offer RSS'' (Really Simple Syndication).
Ad Rate: Full Page Mono 1217.88
Ad Rate: Full Page Colour 1582.00

Wigan Observer
980436
Editorial: Martland Mill, Martland Mill Lane, Wigan WN5 0LX Tel: 44 01942 228000
Email: newsroom@lancspublications.co.uk
Web site: http://www.wigantoday.net/
Freq: Weekly
Circ: 11504 Not Audited
Editor: Janet Wilson
Profile: The Wigan Observer is a weekly local newspaper covering all the latest on local news, lifestyle and sport in Wigan. The paper is available on Tuesdays.
Ad Rate: Full Page Colour 749.00

Wigan Reporter
980437
Tel: 44 01942 228000
Web site: http://www.wigantoday.net
Freq: Weekly
Circ: 28382 Not Audited
Profile: The Wigan Reporter is a weekly local newspaper covering all the latest on local news, lifestyle and sport in Wigan.

Wilmslow Guardian
988899
Editorial: Theatre Court, Northwich CW9 5HB Tel: 44 01606 813617
Email: wilmslow@guardiangrp.co.uk
Web site: www.wilmslowguardian.co.uk
Freq: Weekly
Circ: 1200 Not Audited
Editor: Carla Flynn

Wilts and Gloucestershire Standard
980307
Editorial: 74 Dyer Street, Cirencester, Cirencester GL7 2PW Tel: 44 01285 642642
Email: wgsnews@wiltsglosstandard.co.uk
Web site: www.wiltsglosstandard.co.uk
Freq: Weekly
Circ: 6799 Not Audited
Editor: Michael Purton

Profile: Online version of the Wilts & Gloucestershire Standard newspaper covering local news, sports and entertainment for the surrounding area.

Wiltshire Gazette and Herald
995788
Editorial: 15 Duke Street, Trowbridge BA14 8EF Tel: 44 01225 773600
Email: wtimes@newswilts.co.uk
Web site: www.gazetteandherald.co.uk
Freq: Weekly
Circ: 13396 Not Audited

Wiltshire Star
983935
Editorial: 15 Duke Street, Trowbridge, Trowbridge BA14 8EF Tel: 44 01225 773600
Email: wtimes@newswilts.co.uk
Web site: http://www.wiltshiretimes.co.uk/
Freq: Weekly
Circ: 23711 Not Audited
Profile: The Wiltshire Star is a weekly local newspaper covering local news for the surrounding area.

Wiltshire Times
980605
Editorial: 15 Duke Street, Trowbridge BA14 8EF Tel: 44 01225 773600
Email: wtimes@newswilts.co.uk
Web site: www.wiltshiretimes.co.uk
Freq: Weekly
Circ: 7688 Not Audited
Profile: Online version of the Wiltshire Times newspaper covering local news and sports for the surrounding area.

Wimbledon Guardian
980550
Editorial: Newsquest South & West London, Floors 9 & 10, Quadrant House, The Quadrant, Sutton SM2 5AS
Tel: 44 02087 226333
Email: newsdesk@wimbledonguardian.co.uk
Web site: www.wimbledonguardian.co.uk
Freq: Weekly
Circ: 29135 Not Audited
Profile: The Wimbledon Guardian is a weekly, local newspaper published on Thursdays covering all the latest on local news, sports and entertainment in Wimbledon, Balham, Tooting, Clapham and the surrounding area. This outlet covers areas within Merton Borough.
Ad Rate: Full Page Colour 794.90

Windsor, Ascot & Eton Express
987213
Editorial: 48 Bell Street, Maidenhead, Maidenhead SL61HX Tel: 44 01753 825111
Email: news@baylismedia.co.uk
Web site: www.windsorexpress.co.uk
Freq: Weekly
Circ: 11639 Not Audited
Profile: This is the online version of the Windsor, Ascot & Eton Express is a weekly, local newspaper published on Fridays, covering all the latest on local news, entertainment, lifestyle and sport in Windsor, Ascot & Eton.

Winsford & Middlewich Guardian
984864
Editorial: 3 Theatre Court, Northwich CW9 5HB Tel: 44 01606 813600
Email: winsford@guardiangrp.co.uk
Web site: www.winsfordguardian.co.uk
Freq: Weekly
Circ: 9083 Not Audited
Editor: Carla Flynn

Wirral Globe
980442
Editorial: Ground Floor, Haymarket Court, Hinson Street, Birkenhead CH41 5BX
Tel: 44 01516 494050
Email: globe.editorial@wirral-globe.co.uk
Web site: www.wirralglobe.co.uk
Freq: Weekly
Circ: 88204 Not Audited
Editor: Leigh Marles
Profile: This is the online version of the Wirral Globe, a weekly, local newspaper covering all the latest on local news and sport in the Wirral.

Wisbech Standard
980213
Editorial: 93 High Street, March, March PE15 9JJ Tel: 44 01354 661915
Email: editor@wisbechstandard.co.uk
Web site: www.wisbechstandard24.co.uk
Freq: Weekly
Circ: 9692 Not Audited
Editor: John Elworthy
Profile: The Wisbech Standard is a weekly, local newspaper covering all the latest on local news. entertainment and sport in the town of Wisbech and the surrounding area.
Ad Rate: Full Page Mono 1360.80
Ad Rate: Full Page Colour 1769.00

Wishaw Press
981493
Editorial: 1 Central Quay, Lanarkshire, Glasgow G3 8DA Tel: 44 01698 205205
Email: news@wishawpress.co.uk
Web site: www.wishawpress.co.uk
Freq: Weekly
Circ: 4942 Not Audited
Editor: Gary Fanning
Profile: This is the online version of the Wishaw Press, a weekly local newspaper covering all the latest on local news, sport and lifestyle in Hamilton, Wishaw and the surrounding area.

Witney Gazette
980491
Editorial: Osney Mead, Oxford OX2 0EJ
Tel: 44 01865 425262
Email: witney@nqo.com
Web site: www.witneygazette.co.uk
Freq: Weekly
Circ: 4736 Not Audited
Profile: Online version of the Witney Gazette newspaper covering local news and sports for the surrounding area.

Woking News & Mail
980551
Editorial: 16 Lower Guildford Road, Knaphill, Woking, London GU21 2EG
Tel: 44 01483 802700
Email: editor@wokingnewsandmail.org
Web site: www.wokingnewsandmail.co.uk
Freq: Weekly
Circ: 4000 Not Audited

The Wokingham Paper
997393
Editorial: Crown House, 231 Kings Road, Reading RG1 3LP Tel: 44 01183 272662
Email: news@wokinghampaper.co.uk
Web site: www.wokinghampaper.com
Freq: Weekly
Circ: 14000 Not Audited

Wolverhampton Chronicle
980575
Editorial: 51-53 Queen Street, Wolverhampton WV1 1ES
Tel: 44 01902 319363
Email: wolverhampton.chronicles@expressandstar.co.uk
Web site: http://yourchronicle.com/
Freq: Weekly
Circ: 47804 Not Audited
Editor: Sue Attwater
Profile: The Wolverhampton Chronicle is a weekly, local newspaper published on Tuesdays covering all the latest on local news in Wolverhampton.
Ad Rate: Full Page Mono 2521.50

Worcester & Malvern Observer
980336
Editorial: Webb House, Church Green East, Redditch, Redditch B98 8BP
Tel: 44 01905 670413
Email: editor@worcesterobserver.co.uk
Web site: www.worcesterobserver.co.uk
Freq: Weekly
Circ: 48778 Not Audited
Editor: Rob George

Worcester News
981687
Editorial: Berrow's House, Hylton Road, Worcester WR2 5JX Tel: 44 01905 748200
Email: news@worcesternews.co.uk
Web site: www.worcesternews.co.uk
Freq: Daily
Circ: 7130 Not Audited
Profile: The Worcester News is a daily regional newspaper and covers regional news, business and sports for the

Regional & Local Weekly Newspapers

surrounding area. This Outlet offer RSS (Really Simple Syndication)
Ad Rate: Full Page Mono 1282.50
Ad Rate: Full Page Colour 1425.00

Worksop Guardian   980485
Editorial: 21-27 Ryton Street, Worksop S80 2AY **Tel:** 44 01909 500500
Email: newsroom@worksop-guardian.co.uk
Web site: www.worksopguardian.co.uk
Freq: Weekly
Circ: 9176 Not Audited
Profile: Website of The Worksop Guardian, a local weekly newspaper covering local news, entertainment and sports for the surrounding area.

Worthing Advertiser   980584
Editorial: Cannon House, Chatsworth Road, Worthing BN11 1NA **Tel:** 44 01903 230051
Email: news@worthingherald.co.uk
Web site: www.worthingtoday.co.uk
Freq: Weekly
Circ: 19901 Not Audited
Profile: The Worthing Advertiser is a weekly, local newspaper published on Wednesdays, covering all the latest on local news, entertainment and sport in Worthing and the surrounding areas.
Ad Rate: Full Page Mono 2989.62
Ad Rate: Full Page Colour 2989.62

Worthing Herald   980582
Editorial: Cannon House, Chatsworth Road, Worthing BN11 1NA **Tel:** 44 01903 230051
Email: news@worthingherald.co.uk
Web site: www.worthingtoday.co.uk
Freq: Weekly
Circ: 19901 Not Audited
Profile: Online version of the Worthing Herald newspaper covering local news, sports and entertainment for the surrounding area.

Wrekin News   998538
Editorial: Bridge Road, Wellington, Telford, Telford TF1 1RY **Tel:** 44 01952 522562
Web site: www.wrekinnews.co.uk/

Freq: Monthly
Circ: 60000 Not Audited
Editor: James Baylis
Profile: News magazine for the Wrekin area in Shropshire.

Wrights Farming Register
                                        995889
Editorial: Kelsey Media, Cudham Tithe Barn, Berry's Hill, Cudham TN16 3AG
Tel: 44 01959 541444
Web site: www.wrightsregister.com
Freq: Monthly
Circ: 34000 Not Audited
Editor: Jeff Porter
Profile: Magazine focusing on all aspects of arable farming. Includes monthly editorial and features on farming and countryside topics including Rolling Back the Years which looks at pre-modern tractors, Landscape and Forestry, 4x4, Sports and Hobbies and a new Plant and Machinery section. In 'Down to Earth', Wrights looks at environmental and climate change issues, attracting contributions from respected figures in the agriculture, biofuel and conservation fields. Aimed at farmers and those involved within the agricultural industry. Regular features: 4x4; Down to earth Environment; Fresh in the Field New machinery, products and services.; Landscape and Forestry; Sports & Hobbies
Ad Rate: Full Page Colour 1202.00

Wymondham Mercury   980455
Editorial: 26 Mere Street, Diss IP22 4AD
Tel: 44 01379 644517
Email: edpnewsdesk@archant.co.uk
Web site: www.
wymondhamandattleboroughmercury.co.uk
Freq: Weekly
Circ: 13458 Not Audited
Editor: Anthony Carroll

Wythenshawe World   980438
Editorial: 24 Greek Street, Stockport, Manchester SK3 8AB **Tel:** 44 01619 984786
Email: stockportmail@gmail.com

Freq: Bi-Weekly
Circ: 27000 Not Audited
Profile: This is the online version of the Wythenshawe World, a bi-weekly, local newspaper published on alternate Fridays covering all the latest on local news and sport in Wythenshawe and the surrounding areas.

Y Cymro   980614
Editorial: 9 Bank Place, Porthmadog, Gwynedd, Porthmadog LL49 9AA
Tel: 44 01766 515514
Email: y-cymro@cambrian-news.co.uk
Web site: www.y-cymro.com
Freq: Weekly
Circ: 4082 Not Audited
Editor: Dylan Halliday

Yate & Sodbury Voice   1057957
Tel: 44 01454 800127
Email: contact@yateandsodburyvoice.co.uk
Web site: http://www.yateandsodburyvoice.co.uk/
Freq: Monthly
Circ: 9000 Not Audited
Editor: Richard Drew

Yellow Advertiser Series 998796
Editorial: Acorn House, Great Oaks Street, Basildon SS14 1AH **Tel:** 44 01268 503400
Web site: www.yellowadvertiser-today.co.uk
Freq: WeeklyNot Audited

Yorkshire Evening Post   979955
Tel: 44 01132 432701
Email: yep.newsdesk@ypn.co.uk
Web site: http://www.yorkshireeveningpost.co.uk/sport
Freq: Daily
Circ: 16108 Not Audited
Profile: The Yorkshire Evening Post is a daily regional newspaper and cover regional news, business, sports and lifestyle for Leeds and the surrounding area. This Outlet offer RSS (Really Simple Syndication)

Ad Rate: Full Page Mono 5700.0
Ad Rate: Full Page Colour 7411.0

The Yorkshire Post   97980
Editorial: PO Box 168, No1 Leeds, 26 Whitehall Road, Leeds LS12 1BE
Tel: 44 01132 432701
Email: yp.newsdesk@ypn.co.uk
Web site: www.yorkshirepost.co.uk
Freq: Daily
Circ: 25178 Not Audited
Editor: James Mitchinson
Profile: The Yorkshire Post is a daily regiona newspaper and covers regional news, business, lifestyle, motors, property, art, culture and sport for the surrounding area. This Outlet offer RSS (Really Simple Syndication)
Ad Rate: Full Page Mono 12179.30
Ad Rate: Full Page Colour 17399.00

Yorkshire Reporter   998205
Editorial: Yorkshire Reporter, Yorkshire House, 10 Hansby Close, Leeds LS14 6JX
Tel: 44 01132 735000
Email: newsdesk.lds@yorkshirereporter.co.uk
Web site: http://yorkshirereporter.co.uk
Freq: Monthly
Circ: 40000 Not Audited
Editor: Lesley Coates

Your Local Paper   987254
Editorial: 29 King Street, King's Lynn PE30 1ET **Tel:** 44 01553 611111
Email: news@yourlocalpaper.co.uk
Web site: www.yourlocalpaper.co.uk
Freq: Weekly
Circ: 22000 Not Audited
Profile: Your Local Paper is a local weekly newspaper and covers local news, sports, property, jobs and motoring. The newspaper is published on Friday.
Ad Rate: Full Page Mono 299.00
Ad Rate: Full Page Colour 299.00

Willings Volume 1
Section 3

UK Periodicals Index

This index cross-refers to all periodicals in Section 4.
The section is preceded by two summaries of categories, in A-Z order,
for business and consumer titles

Categories A-Z

Business

Business

Antique & Collectible Cars

Architecture & Design

Auto Aftermarket

Automakers

Aviation

Section 3 UK Periodicals Index

Business

Banking

Biotechnology

Bonds

Books

Branding

Broadcasting

Building & Construction

Business

Business

Carbon Emissions & Trading

Cardiology

Chemicals

Commercial Real Estate

Commodities

Community Care (UK)

Business

Company News & Appointments

Computers

Consumer Interest

Corporate Finance

Corporate Law

Corporate Management

Corporate Responsibility

Cosmetics

Section 3 UK Periodicals Index

Business

Credit Markets

Criminal Law

Data Management

Defense & National Security

Dentistry

Derivatives

Dermatology

Diabetes

Diagnostic Imaging

Disability

Displays

Displays, Graphics, & Imaging

Do-It-Yourself (DIY)

Economics

Education

Business

Environment

Equities

Family Law

Fashion

Finance

Financial Markets

Fitness & Exercise

Food

Foreign Exchange Market (FOREX)

Fund Management

Gardening

Gastroenterology

Genealogy

Geriatrics

Business

Golf

Government

Government Technology

Graphic Design

Section 3 UK Periodicals Index

Section 3 UK Periodicals Index

Business

Law

Legal Affairs

Legal Services

Lending

Litigation

Manufacturing

Marketing

Medical Technology

Medicine

Mergers & Acquisitions

Mining & Quarrying

Mobile Communications

Mobile Electronics

Nature & Wildlife

Neurology

News & Current Affairs

Nuclear Power

Business

Nursing/Nurses

Obstetrics & Gynecology (OB/GYN)

Occupational Therapy & Rehabilitation

Office Design

Office Supplies

Oil

Business

Oncology

Ophthalmology & Optometry

Orthopedics

Pain Management

Paper

Patient Support

Pediatrics

Pharmaceuticals

Business

Security & Security Systems

Sexual Health

Shipping & Warehousing

Small and Medium Business

Software

Sports Medicine

Steel

Students

Supply Chain Management (SCM)

Sustainable Development

Tax Law

Telecommunications/Electronic Communications

Tobacco

Toys

Travel

Travel Industry

Urban Planning & Development

Section 3 UK Periodicals Index

Consumer

Urology

Veterinary Medicine

Water & Sanitation

Women's Interests

Woodworking

Consumer

Accounting

Advertising Industry

Africa

AIDS/HIV

Airline Inflight

Consumer

Allergies

Alternative Medicine

Alcohol & Spirits

Section 3 UK Periodicals Index

Consumer

Consumer

Arts

Asia

Astrology & Parapsychology

Astronomy

Audio Video Trade

Australia

Auto Aftermarket

Automotive

Automakers

Consumer

Aviation

Banking

Bankruptcy

Bars, Clubs & Pubs

Section 3 UK Periodicals Index

Section 3 UK Periodicals Index

Bodybuilding

Bonds

Books

Bowling

Boxing

Consumer

Branding

Broadcasting

Consumer

Building & Construction

Business

Cameras

Camping and RV Travel

Consumer

Consumer

Chess

Children & Youth

Classical/Choral/Band Music

Comedy

Commercial Real Estate

Commodities

Community Care (UK)

Company News & Appointments

Computer & Video Games

Consumer

Computers

Consumer Affairs

Section 3 UK Periodicals Index

Consumer

Section 3 UK Periodicals Index

Consumer

Crafts

Crafts, Hobbies, & Collecting

Credit Markets

Cricket

Crime & Violence

Criminal Law

Section 3 UK Periodicals Index

Consumer

Dentistry

Derivatives

Dermatology

Diabetes

Diagnostic Imaging

Disability

Do-It-Yourself (DIY)

Consumer

Section 3 UK Periodicals Index

Consumer

Elementary School

Emerging Markets

Employment

EMS/Emergency Medical Services

Energy

Energy & Environment

Section 3 UK Periodicals Index

Consumer

Equities

Estate Planning

Ethical/Moral Issues

Ethnic & Multicultural

Europe

Expatriates

Extreme/Adventure Sports

Family & Parenting

Consumer

Family Law

Family Travel

Fashion

Section 3 UK Periodicals Index

Consumer

Federal Courts

Field Sports

Finance

Financial Markets

Fishing

Section 3 UK Periodicals Index

Fitness & Exercise

Food

Food & Drug Administration

Football (American)

Section 3 UK Periodicals Index

Consumer

Foreign Exchange Market (FOREX)

Fund Management

Games

Games, Competitions & Events

Gardening

Gastroenterology

Genealogy

Geriatrics

Golf

Government

Government Technology

Graphic Design

Grocery Stores

Gymnastics

Hair

Consumer

Health & Medicine

Health & Safety

Health Administration

Healthcare Industry

Hedge Funds

Hematology

Higher Education

History

Section 3 UK Periodicals Index

Consumer

Internet

Investment Banking

Jazz & Blues

Law

Legal Affairs

Legal Services

Leisure Activities

Lending

LGBT

Lifestyle

Literature

Consumer

Local Entertainment Guides

Luxury Goods

Consumer

Marine & Boat Trade

Manufacturing

Section 3 UK Periodicals Index

Consumer

Marketing

Martial Arts, MMA & Self-Defense

Media & Communications

Media Relations

Medical Technology

Medicine

Men's Interests

Consumer

Mergers & Acquisitions

Mining & Quarrying

Mobile Communications

Mobile Electronics

Section 3 UK Periodicals Index

Consumer

Motorcycles

Motorsports

Movies & Video

Consumer

Music

National News

Consumer

Nature & Wildlife

Neurology

News & Current Affairs

News & Current Affairs

Consumer

Obstetrics & Gynecology (OB/GYN)

Occupational Therapy & Rehabilitation

Off-road & 4-Wheel Drive Vehicles

Office Design

Office Supplies

Oil

Olympic Sports

Oncology

Ophthalmology & Optometry

Organic Food

Outdoor Recreation

Paper

Patient Support

Pediatrics

Personal Computers

Personal Finance

Personal Health & Wellness

Pets & Pet Products

Pharmaceuticals

Photography

Consumer

Plastic/Reconstructive/Cosmetic Surgery

Plastics

Poker

Politics

Pop Music

Consumer

Consumer

Rap & Hip Hop

R&B, Urban, World

Real Estate

Real Estate Law

Recruiting

Regional

Consumer

Students

Supply Chain Management (SCM)

Sustainable Development

Swimming/Watersports

Tax Law

Teachers

Teen/Young Adult

Consumer

Consumer

Travel Industry

Trucks & SUVs

Section 3 UK Periodicals Index

Consumer

Woodworking

Willings Volume 1
Section 4

UK Periodicals

UK Business Magazines listed A-Z
UK Consumer Magazines listed A-Z

Business Magazines

Business Magazines

(Perspective)　984034
Editorial: 10 Old Broad Street, London EC2N 1DW **Tel:** 44 02076 089000
Email: email@pendragon.co.uk
Web site: http://pendragon.info/perspective/
Freq: Daily
Circ: 129 Cision Digital Reach
Editor: Nina Savage
MAGAZINE (ONLINE)
Fund Management, Tax Law

*HE　997503
Editorial: Unit 111, Curtain House, 134-146 Curtain Road, London EC2A 3AR
Tel: 44 02072 166500
Email: news@researchresearch.com
Web site: http://info.researchprofessional.com/he/
Freq: Daily
Circ: 26171 Cision Digital Reach
MAGAZINE (ONLINE)
Higher Education

1000 Words Photography Magazine　998306
Editorial: 29 The Arthaus, 205 Richmond Road, London E8 3FF
Email: info@1000wordsmag.com
Web site: http://www.1000wordsmag.com/
Freq: Daily
Circ: 15422 Cision Digital Reach
MAGAZINE (ONLINE)
Photography

125 Magazine　983504
Editorial: 5 Calvert Avenue, London E2 7JP
Email: info@125magazine.com
Web site: www.125magazine.com
Freq: Semi-Annual
Circ: 65000 Not Audited
MAGAZINE
Photography

24housing　984760
Editorial: Unit 12, Whitestone Business Park, Whitestone, Hereford HR1 3SE
Tel: 44 08445 578324
Email: news@24publishing.co.uk
Web site: www.24housing.co.uk
Freq: Monthly
Circ: 29000 Not Audited
Editor: Chris Smith
Profile: Magazine focusing on social housing including in-depth reports, interviews and news about the sector. Aimed at housing professionals.
Ad Rate: Full Page Colour £2500.00
MAGAZINE
Public Sector, Residential Real Estate, Urban Planning & Development

2degrees　986930
Editorial: 228-240 Banbury Road, Oxford OX2 7BY **Tel:** 44 01865 597640
Web site: www.2degreesnetwork.com
Freq: Daily
Circ: 19482 Cision Digital Reach
MAGAZINE (ONLINE)
Environment

A Word About Wind　986577
Editorial: Hogrefe House, Albion Place, Oxford OX1 1QZ **Tel:** 44 02071 936013
Email: editorial@awordaboutwind.com
Web site: http://www.awordaboutwind.com/
Freq: 3 Times/Week
Circ: 14468 Cision Digital Reach
Editor: Richard Heap
MAGAZINE (ONLINE)
Alternative/Renewable Energy

A.M. Best Europe　998597
Editorial: 6th Floor, 12 Arthur Street, London EC4R 9AB **Tel:** 44 02076 266264
Web site: www.ambest.com
Freq: Daily
Circ: 152091 Cision Digital Reach
MAGAZINE (ONLINE)
Insurance

A1 Lighting　985683
Editorial: Unit 4, Fox and Pheasant Centre, Colchester Road, Colchester, Bures CO6 2PS **Tel:** 44 01787 222251
Email: enquiries@a1mediamagazines.com
Web site: www.a1lightingmagazine.com
Freq: Monthly
Circ: 3946 Not Audited
Profile: B2B magazine covering lighting industry. Published 11 times a year, provides news, projects, comments, coverage of industry events, exhibitions and awards.
Ad Rate: Full Page Colour £1800.00
MAGAZINE
Building & Construction

A1 Retail　985684
Editorial: Unit 4, Fox and Pheasant Centre, Colchester Road, Colchester, Bures CO6 2PS **Tel:** 44 01787 222251
Email: enquiries@a1mediamagazines.com
Web site: www.a1retailmagazine.com
Freq: Monthly
Circ: 6000 Not Audited
Profile: B2B publication published 12 times a year. Covers news, projects, comments from experts in retail, industry events, exhibitions and awards.
Ad Rate: Full Page Colour £1800.00
MAGAZINE
Retail Management

ABC&D　980851
Editorial: Unit 1 Sugar Brook Court, Aston Road, Worcestershire, Bromsgrove B60 3EX
Tel: 44 01527 834444
Email: claire.mackle@korumedia.co.uk
Web site: www.buildingtalk.com/abcd-magazine-products
Freq: Monthly
Circ: 15461 Not Audited
MAGAZINE
Architecture & Design, Building & Construction

Absolute UCITS　998999
Editorial: 4-8 Bouverie Street, London EC4Y 8AX **Tel:** 44 02077 797330
Email: info@hedgefundintelligence.com
Web site: www.hedgefundintelligence.com/UCITS.html
Freq: Daily
MAGAZINE (ONLINE)
Hedge Funds

Academy　986024
Editorial: 12 Deben Mill Business Centre, Melton, Woodbridge, Woodbridge IP12 1BL
Tel: 44 01394 389850
Email: editor@academymag.co.uk
Web site: http://academymag.co.uk
Freq: 3 Times/Year Not Audited
Editor: Caroline Whitty
MAGAZINE
Schools & Institutions

Academy Today　988920
Editorial: Unit 2.4 Paintworks, Arnos Vale, Bath Road, Bristol BS4 3EN
Tel: 44 01173 005526
Email: info@academytoday.co.uk
Web site: http://academytoday.co.uk/
Freq: Daily
Circ: 20078 Cision Digital Reach
Profile: Publication that covers all academy news. Including news on legal advice, teaching, money, facilities, school life, catering, innovation and sustainability.
MAGAZINE (ONLINE)
Higher Education, Students

Access All Areas　983909
Editorial: Second Floor, Apple Market House, 17 Union Street, Kingston upon Thames KT1 1RR **Tel:** 44 02084 811122
Web site: www.accessaa.co.uk
Freq: Monthly
Circ: 10300 Not Audited
Profile: Magazine covering the events industry and features news and legislative issues. Read by events organisers, council entertainment officers, marketing managers, promotion and production managers.
Ad Rate: Full Page Colour £2200.00
MAGAZINE
Marketing

Access International　987117
Editorial: Southfields, Southview Road, Wadhurst, Wadhurst TN5 6TP
Tel: 44 01892 784088
Email: info@khl.com
Web site: http://www.khl.com/magazines/access-international/
Freq: Bi-Monthly
Circ: 11241 Not Audited
Editor: Euan Youdale
Profile: Magazine covering the worldwide aerial work platform industry, focusing on the use of powered aerial work platforms and non-powered access equipment including scaffolding. Also the official magazine of the International Powered Access Federation (IPAF). Read by buyers and users of all types of access equipment, including powered aerial platforms and scaffolding.
Ad Rate: Full Page Colour £4800.00
MAGAZINE
Building & Construction

Accountancy　979891
Editorial: 145 London Road, Kingston upon Thames KT2 6SR **Tel:** 44 02082 471431
Email: accountancynews@wolterskluwer.co.uk
Web site: www.accountancylive.com/magazine
Freq: Monthly
Circ: 15000 Not Audited
Editor: Sara White
Profile: Magazine providing an in-depth insight and analysis of the major issues and technical developments affecting the UK accounting profession. The magazine is divided into four key categories; tax, accounting, audit and development. It covers a wide range of issues from technical accounting matters through to general business and careers features and provides articles on technical accounting, auditing, regulatory affairs and tax guidance. First published in 1889. Aimed at chartered accountants and finance professionals.
Ad Rate: Full Page Mono £4125.00
Ad Rate: Full Page Colour £4450.00
MAGAZINE
Accounting

Accountancy Age　979890
Editorial: 1 Hammersmith Broadway, London W6 9DL **Tel:** 44 02073 169032
Web site: www.accountancyage.com
Freq: Daily
Circ: 88865 Cision Digital Reach
Profile: Website covering business, financial and careers news for primarily UK based accountancy professionals. Aimed at part and fully qualified accountants throughout the UK.Alternative Title: Accountancy Age
MAGAZINE (ONLINE)
Accounting

The Accountant　979892
Editorial: 71-73 Carter Lane, London EC4V 5EQ **Tel:** 44 02079 366400
Email: vincent.huck@progressivemediagroup.com
Web site: www.theaccountant-online.com
Freq: Monthly Not Audited
Profile: Publication covering a mixture of news, analysis and interviews. Includes country surveys and reports on the development of accounting standards and practices worldwide. Average Pages per Issue: 20 Aimed at accountants.
MAGAZINE
Accounting

Accounting and Business　996003
Editorial: The Adelphi, 1-11 John Adam Street, London WC2N 6AU
Tel: 44 02070 595000
Web site: http://www.accaglobal.com/ab
Freq: Monthly
Circ: 159065 Not Audited
MAGAZINE
Accounting, Banking

Accounting Link　996296
Editorial: The Adelphi, 1-11 John Adam Street, London WC2N 6AU
Tel: 44 01415 822000
Web site: http://www.accaglobal.com/en/employer/accounting-link.html
Freq: Quarterly
Circ: 48077 Cision Digital Reach
MAGAZINE (ONLINE)
Accounting

Accounting Technician　982976
Editorial: 140 Aldersgate Street, London EC1A 4HY **Tel:** 44 02089 623020
Email: aat@aat.org.uk
Web site: www.aat.org.uk
Freq: No Frequency Established
Circ: 120000 Not Audited
Profile: Magazine covering business, accounting and training issues affecting accounting professionals. It contains practical information for students and practitioners. Read by members and students of the Association of Accounting Technicians.
Ad Rate: Full Page Colour £3950.00
MAGAZINE
Accounting

Accounting, Organizations and Society　998606
Editorial: The Boulevard, Langford Lane, Kidlington OX5 1GB **Tel:** 44 01865 843000
Web site: www.elsevier.com/wps/find/journaldescription.cws_home/486/description#description
Freq: Bi-Monthly Not Audited
MAGAZINE
Accounting

AccountingWEB.co.uk　980833
Editorial: 6th Floor, Bridge House, 48-52 Baldwin Street, Bristol BS1 1QB
Tel: 44 01179 153344
Email: editor@accountingweb.co.uk
Web site: http://www.accountingweb.co.uk/
Freq: Daily
Circ: 591046 Cision Digital Reach
Profile: Website covering accounting. The AccountingWeb is an professional online community covering tax, accountancy news, comment and technical data. It covers anything from taxes and financial reporting to technology and business.
MAGAZINE (ONLINE)
Accounting

ACNR (Advances in Clinical Neuroscience & Rehabilitation)　999322
Editorial: 1 The Lynch, Mere, Warminster BA12 6DQ **Tel:** 44 01747 860168
Email: anna@acnr.co.uk
Web site: www.acnr.co.uk
Freq: Bi-Monthly
Circ: 4500 Not Audited
MAGAZINE
Neurology

ACQ Magazine　985610
Editorial: 6th Floor, Davis House, 2 Robert Street, London CR0 1QQ
Tel: 44 08712 182470
Email: customerservice@acqmagazine.com
Web site: www.acq5.com
Freq: Monthly
Circ: 128000 Not Audited
Editor: Jake Robson
MAGAZINE
Mergers & Acquisitions, Private Equity

Acquisition International 985796
Editorial: Unit 10 Barton Marina, Barton Turn, Barton under Needwood, Burton on Trent, Barton-under-Needwood DE13 8AS
Tel: 44 07807 256842
Email: reception@acquisition-intl.com
Web site: www.acquisition-intl.com
Freq: Monthly
Circ: 108000 Not Audited
Editor: Charlotte Abbott
MAGAZINE
Mergers & Acquisitions

acquisitionsdaily.com 986448
Editorial: 2nd Floor, Waverley House, 7-12 Noel Street, London W1F 8GQ
Tel: 44 07867 425424
Email: info@acquisitionsdaily.com
Web site: www.acquisitionsdaily.com
Freq: Daily
Circ: 10038 Cision Digital Reach
MAGAZINE (ONLINE)
Mergers & Acquisitions

The ACR Journal 998578
Editorial: The Maltings, West Street, Bourne, Bourne PE10 9PH **Tel:** 44 01778 391000
Web site: www.acrjournal.uk
Freq: Monthly
Circ: 10000 Not Audited
Profile: Magazine containing news and information on a wide range of refrigeration and air conditioning topics. Aimed at air conditioning and refrigeration engineers, consultants, specifiers and end users.
Ad Rate: Full Page Mono £1515.00
Ad Rate: Full Page Colour £1590.00
MAGAZINE
Manufacturing

Activative Platform 995929
Editorial: New Hibernia House, Winchester Walk, London SE1 9AG
Tel: 44 02081 445345
Email: contact@activative.co.uk
Web site: www.activative.co.uk
Freq: Daily Not Audited
MAGAZINE
Marketing

Actuarial Post 985935
Editorial: Ellion House, 6 Alexandra Road, Tonbridge, Tonbridge TN9 2AA
Tel: 44 01732 359488
Email: pr@actuarialpost.co.uk
Web site: www.actuarialpost.co.uk
Freq: Daily
Circ: 16948 Cision Digital Reach
Editor: Ellie Burns
Profile: Website covering finance. The Actuarial Post discusses anything from pensions and investments to insurance.
MAGAZINE (ONLINE)
Insurance

The Actuary 980147
Editorial: 17 Britton Street, London EC1M 5TP **Tel:** 44 02078 806200
Email: news@theactuary.com
Web site: www.theactuary.com
Freq: Monthly
Circ: 27431 Not Audited
Profile: Magazine representing the actuarial profession within the UK. It covers commercial, financial, and technical advice underpinning the operation of insurance companies, pension funds and other institutions. Also covers wealth management. Read by members of the Faculty and Institute of Actuaries and those involved in the Staple Inn Actuarial Society.
Ad Rate: Full Page Colour £2520.00
MAGAZINE
Fund Management, Insurance

Ad Tech Daily 996809
Email: news@adoperationsonline.com
Web site: www.adtechdaily.com/
Freq: Daily
Circ: 58598 Cision Digital Reach
Editor: Otilia Otlacan
MAGAZINE (ONLINE)
Advertising Industry

Addiction 985410
Editorial: National Addiction Centre, P048, Institute of Psychiatry, 4 Windsor Walk, London SE5 8AF **Tel:** 44 02078 480452
Web site: www.addictionjournal.org
Freq: Monthly Not Audited
Profile: Journal covering all aspects of addiction. Read by scientists, practitioners and policy-makers.
Ad Rate: Full Page Mono £540.00
Ad Rate: Full Page Colour £1300.00
MAGAZINE
Neurology

Addiction Science & Clinical Practice 999649
Editorial: BioMed Central, 236 Gray's Inn Road, London WC1X 8HB
Tel: 44 02031 922009
Email: editorial@ascpjournal.org
Web site: www.springer.com/public+health/journal/13722
Freq: Semi-Annual Not Audited
MAGAZINE
Pharmaceuticals, Science

Additives for Polymers 984736
Editorial: Elsevier Ltd, Langford Lane, Kidlington OX5 1GB **Tel:** 44 01489 891447
Web site: www.additivesforpolymers.com
Freq: Monthly Not Audited
Editor: Caroline Edser
Profile: Newsletter containing details of relevant polymer additives materials and products, new applications, new research and technical developments, company news, market trends, legislation, environment, health and safety issues, new publications and related conferences.
MAGAZINE
Chemicals

The Adelphi Papers 996018
Editorial: Arundel House, 13-15 Arundel Street, Temple Place, London WC2R 3DX
Tel: 44 02073 797676
Web site: www.iiss.org/en/publications/adelphi
Freq: Bi-Monthly Not Audited
Editor: Nicholas Redman
MAGAZINE
Defense & National Security, Security & Security Systems

Adiona Magazine 994998
Editorial: Belvedere House, 2 Basing View, Basingstoke, Basingstoke RG21 4HG
Tel: 44 01256 313781
Email: info@adionamagazine.co.uk
Web site: www.adionamagazine.co.uk
Freq: Monthly Not Audited
MAGAZINE
Education, Human Resources, Recruiting

Admap 984005
Tel: 44 02074 678100
Web site: www.warc.com/admap
Freq: Monthly
Circ: 10000 Not Audited
Profile: Magazine containing marketing and advertising papers with a research and media bias, publishing original articles. Aimed at decision makers and managers in market research, advertising and marketing communications, and advertiser companies.
Ad Rate: Full Page Mono £1452.00
Ad Rate: Full Page Colour £2328.00
MAGAZINE
Advertising Industry, Marketing

ADS Advance 986430
Editorial: Rumsey House, Locks Hill, Rochford, Rochford SS4 1BB
Tel: 44 01702 530000
Web site: www.adsadvance.co.uk
Freq: Quarterly
Circ: 12500 Not Audited
MAGAZINE
Aviation

Advanced Composites Bulletin 984737
Editorial: 44 Friar Street, Droitwich, Droitwich WR9 8ED **Tel:** 44 08701 657211
Email: editor@intnews.com
Web site: www.performance-materials.net/htm/j20041027.154099.htm
Freq: Monthly Not Audited
Editor: James Bakewell
Profile: Subscription only monthly bulletin providing comprehensive coverage of international developments in composites. The bulletin contains worldwide coverage of advanced materials, new composite materials, processing, testing and applications. Nick Butler is the Editorial Director to whom press releases should be addressed.
MAGAZINE
Manufacturing, Plastics

Advances in Mental Health and Intellectual Disabilities 998982
Editorial: Howard House, Wagon Lane, Bingley BD16 1WA **Tel:** 44 01274 777700
Email: emerald@emeraldinsight.com
Web site: http://www.emeraldinsight.com/loi/amhid
Freq: Bi-Monthly Not Audited
Editor: Jean O'Hara
MAGAZINE
Neurology

AEC Magazine 982961
Editorial: Rooms 108–109, 4th Floor, 65 London Wall, London EC2M 5TU
Tel: 44 02033 557310
Web site: www.aecmag.com
Freq: Bi-Monthly
Circ: 10000 Not Audited
Profile: Independent magazine giving news, product reviews, user comments, case studies and buyers guides relating to IT and CAD in architecture, engineering and construction. Read by architects, engineers and construction managers.Previous title: CADDESK AEC.
Ad Rate: Full Page Colour £3000.00
MAGAZINE
Architecture & Design, Engineering, Graphic Design

The Aeronautical Journal 983643
Editorial: 4 Hamilton Place, London W1J 7BQ **Tel:** 44 02076 704352
Email: publications@aerosociety.com
Web site: www.aerosociety.com/News/Publications/Aero-Journal
Freq: Monthly
Circ: 800 Not Audited
Profile: Journal of the Royal Aeronautical Society. Publishes refereed technical and engineering papers on all aerospace sciences. The publication was first published in 1897 and has on average 60 pages per issue. Incorporating: The Aeronautical Quarterly Read by professionals in the aeronautical industry, research organisations and academia.The editor stresses the academic nature of the magazine and therefore, no PR materials should be sent to the magazine.
MAGAZINE
Aviation

Aeroplane 998482
Editorial: Aeroplane, PO Box 100, London PE9 1XQ **Tel:** 44 01780 755131
Web site: www.aeroplanemonthly.com
Freq: Monthly
Circ: 23585 Not Audited
Profile: Magazine featuring aviation history, preservation, nostalgia and personal recollections from pilots and ground crew. The publication was first published in 1973 and has on average 108 pages per issue. Aimed at enthusiasts of all ages.
Ad Rate: Full Page Colour £2149.00
MAGAZINE
Aviation

Aerospace 979956
Editorial: 4 Hamilton Place, London W1J 7BQ **Tel:** 44 02076 704300
Email: publications@aerosociety.com
Web site: www.aerosociety.com/News/Publications/Aerospace
Freq: Monthly
Circ: 20009 Not Audited
MAGAZINE
Aviation

Aerospace Manufacturing 983628
Editorial: Featherstone House, 375 High Street, Rochester, Chatham ME1 1DA
Tel: 44 01634 830566
Web site: www.aero-mag.com
Freq: Monthly
Circ: 15316 Not Audited
Editor: Mike Richardson
Profile: Publication covering the design, production and supply chain of the European civil and defence aerospace industries. Aimed at decision makers involved in design, production and procurement within the civil and defence aerospace industry.Digital images preferred. Regular features: Supply Chain Covers Supply chain management and associated issues.
Ad Rate: Full Page Colour £3500.00
MAGAZINE
Aviation, Engineering, Manufacturing

Aerospace Testing International 983731
Editorial: Abinger House, Church Street, Dorking, Dorking RH4 1DF
Tel: 44 01306 743744
Web site: http://www.aerospacetestinginternational.com
Freq: Quarterly
Circ: 9686 Not Audited
Profile: Magazine featuring news, features and technical articles covering every aspect of aerospace testing and test engineering. Aimed at aeronautical engineers and other aerospace professionals.
Ad Rate: Full Page Colour £4150.00
MAGAZINE
Aviation

aerospace-technology.com 984299
Editorial: John Carpenter House, John Carpenter Street, London EC4Y 0AN
Tel: 44 02079 366400
Email: onlineeditorial@kable.co.uk
Web site: http://www.aerospace-technology.com
Freq: Daily
Circ: 39038 Cision Digital Reach
Profile: Website covering aero technology. The aerospace-technology website shares information on international aerospace technology projects both in production and under development.
MAGAZINE (ONLINE)
Aviation

Aesthetic Dentistry Today 985246
Editorial: Hertford House, Farm Close, Shenley, Radlett WD7 9AB
Tel: 44 01923 851777
Email: info@fmc.co.uk
Web site: http://www.dentistry.co.uk/cosmetic-aesthetic-dental-news/
Freq: Quarterly
Circ: 1850 Not Audited
Profile: Magazine featuring clinical case articles written by aesthetic experts and practice management, marketing and technology features. Aimed at dentists already practicing or considering entering the field of aesthetic dentistry.
Ad Rate: Full Page Colour £2435.00
MAGAZINE
Dentistry

Aesthetic Medicine 1056758
Editorial: 1.17 The Plaza, 535 Kings Road, London SW10 0SZ **Tel:** 44 02073 510536
Email: info@aestheticmed.co.uk
Web site: aestheticmed.co.uk

Section 4 UK Periodicals Business

Business Magazines

Freq: Monthly
Circ: 6652 Not Audited
MAGAZINE
Plastic/Reconstructive/Cosmetic Surgery

Aesthetics   985934
Editorial: Holden House, 57 Rathbone Place, London W1T 1JU
Tel: 44 02071 481292
Email: editorial@aestheticsjournal.com
Web site: www.aestheticsjournal.com/
Freq: Monthly
Circ: 7467 Not Audited
Editor: Amanda Cameron
MAGAZINE
Plastic/Reconstructive/Cosmetic Surgery

Africa Fruit   1060682
Tel: 44 27118 278590
Freq: Quarterly
Circ: 5500 Not Audited
MAGAZINE
Animal Farming

Africa Power News   997387
Editorial: Global House, 13 Market Square, Horsham, Horsham RH12 1EU
Tel: 44 01403 220750
Email: powerl@gmp.uk.com
Web site: http://www.gmp.uk.com/africa-power-news/
Freq: Semi-Annual
Circ: 2535 Not Audited
MAGAZINE
Alternative/Renewable Energy, Carbon Emissions & Trading, Electricity, Energy, Nuclear Power, Oil, Water & Sanitation

African Banker   984519
Editorial: 7 Coldbath Square, London EC1R 4LQ **Tel:** 44 02078 413210
Email: editorial@icpublications.com
Web site: www.africanbusinessmagazine.com/african-banker
Freq: Quarterly
Circ: 20000 Not Audited
Editor: Lanre Akinola
Profile: Magazine covering news from the banking, finance, insurance, currency, direct and indirect financial investment sectors, as well as the stock markets and capital markets.
Ad Rate: Full Page Colour £6400.00
MAGAZINE
Banking, Emerging Markets

African Energy   983594
Editorial: 4 Bank Buildings, Station Road, Hastings, Hastings TN34 1NG
Tel: 44 01424 721667
Web site: www.africa-energy.com
Freq: Bi-Weekly Not Audited
Editor: Thalia Griffiths
Profile: African Energy is a monthly subscription only magazine providing independent and investigative analysis of the African continent's energy industries. The magazine covers developments and analysis of the energy sectors throughout Africa. It also focuses on emerging energy trends and political risks and factors related to the industry.
MAGAZINE
Alternative/Renewable Energy, Electricity, Nuclear Power, Oil, Water & Sanitation

African Journal of Midwifery and Women's Health   986292
Editorial: St Jude's Church, Dulwich Road, London SE24 0PB **Tel:** 44 02077 385454
Email: ajm@markallengroup.com
Web site: www.magonlinelibrary.com/r/ajmw
Freq: Quarterly Not Audited
MAGAZINE
Obstetrics & Gynecology (OB/GYN)

African Law & Business   996900
Editorial: 59 Tanner Street, London SE1 3PL
Tel: 44 02073 670720
Email: info@glgroup.com
Web site: http://www.africanlawbusiness.com

Freq: Daily
Circ: 15695 Cision Digital Reach
MAGAZINE (ONLINE)
Business, Corporate Law, Legal Services, Small and Medium Business

African Review of Business & Technology   980091
Editorial: University House, 11-13 Lower Grosvenor Place, London SW1W 0EX
Tel: 44 02078 347676
Email: post@alaincharles.com
Web site: www.africanreview.com
Freq: Monthly
Circ: 13000 Not Audited
MAGAZINE
Building & Construction, Business, Computers, Oil

African Security Review   1060730
Email: iss@issafrica.org Not Audited
MAGAZINE
Security & Security Systems

Ageing & Society   985715
Editorial: The Edinburgh Building, Shaftesbury Road, Cambridge CB2 8RU
Tel: 44 01223 326070
Email: ageingandsociety@yahoo.co.uk
Web site: https://www.cambridge.org/core/journals/ageing-and-society/article/index-to-ageing-and-society-vol-1
Freq: Monthly Not Audited
Editor: Christina Victor
MAGAZINE
Geriatrics

agendaNi   983863
Tel: 44 02892 619933
Email: info@agendani.com
Web site: www.agendani.co.uk
Freq: Bi-Monthly
Circ: 4844 Not Audited
Profile: Public affairs magazine covering public policy from health and education to the economy. Aimed at senior managers in the public, private and voluntary sectors.
Ad Rate: Full Page Colour £1495.00
MAGAZINE
Public Sector

Aggregates Business Europe
                                  986058
Editorial: Huntingdon House, 278-290 Huntingdon Street, London NG1 3LY
Tel: 44 01322 612055
Email: media@ropl.com
Web site: www.aggbusiness.com
Freq: Bi-Monthly
Circ: 9553 Not Audited
Editor: Guy Woodford
Profile: Magazine covering the quarrying sector and reports on quarrying best practice in both Europe and the rest of the world, new legislation and business news. The magazine also provides information on the latest equipment and systems available to quarry operators and features on innovative use of quarried material on the construction site. It provides in-depth quarry profiles looking at every aspect of operation at individual quarries as well as a series of reports on national aggregates markets. The magazine also includes news and information covering all aspects of quarrying from planning application, environmental issues and operation, through to the end use of aggregates, recycled aggregates and quarry restoration.
MAGAZINE
Mining & Quarrying

Aggregates Business International   988506
Editorial: Huntingdon House, 278-290 Huntingdon Street, London NG1 3LY
Tel: 44 01159 508098
Email: media@ropl.com
Web site: www.aggbusiness.com
Freq: Bi-Monthly
Circ: 9114 Not Audited
Editor: Guy Woodford
Profile: Magazine covering the aggregates markets of Asia, Africa and the Middle East.

Aimed at quarry owners, operators and managers who oversee and control the leading quarries, asphalt/ready-mixed concrete sites, precast concrete product lines and plant and machinery budgets across these regions.
MAGAZINE
Mining & Quarrying

Aging & Mental Health   995489
Editorial: Taylor & Francis Group, 2&4 Park Square, Milton Park, Abingdon OX14 4RN
Tel: 44 02070 177720
Email: amh@ucl.ac.uk
Web site: http://www.tandf.co.uk/journals/titles/13607863.asp
Freq: Monthly
Editor: Martin Orrell
MAGAZINE
Geriatrics, Neurology

The Aging Male   995815
Editorial: 4 Park Square, Milton Park, Abingdon OX14 4RN **Tel:** 44 02070 175544
Web site: http://www.tandfonline.com/action/journalInformation?show=editorialBoard&journalCode=itam20
Freq: Quarterly Not Audited
MAGAZINE
Diabetes, Geriatrics, Oncology, Sexual Health, Urology

Agra Europe   983588
Editorial: Christchurch Court, 10-15 Newgate Street, London EC1A 7AZ
Tel: 44 02070 177500
Email: agra@agra-net.com
Web site: https://www.agra-net.com/agra/agra-europe/
Freq: Weekly
Circ: 53251 Cision Digital Reach
Profile: Newsletter providing news, analysis and comment on European and international agricultural policy and trade. Read by food companies, agribusiness and governments.
MAGAZINE (ONLINE)
Animal Farming, Food

Agriculture & Food Security
                                  996444
Editorial: 236 Gray's Inn Road, London WC1X 8HB
Email: editorial@agricultureandfoodsecurity.com
Web site: www.agricultureandfoodsecurity.com
Freq: Daily Not Audited
MAGAZINE
Animal Farming, Food

Agrimoney   985340
Tel: 44 07920 545243
Email: newsdesk@agrimoney.com
Web site: www.agrimoney.com
Freq: Daily
Circ: 56015 Cision Digital Reach
Editor: Mike Verdin
MAGAZINE (ONLINE)
Animal Farming

AgriTrade News   984655
Email: editor@agritradenews.co.uk
Web site: www.agritradenews.co.uk
Freq: Weekly Not Audited
Profile: Magazine providing targeted news of interest to all those businesses that supply the UK farmer with essential inputs and buy commodities from the farm gate. The publication covers company news, people movements, new products, policy developments and events influencing markets. Aimed at Uk farmers and agricultural professionals.
MAGAZINE
Animal Farming

The Agronomist and Arable Farmer   981681
Editorial: Suite A, Arun House, Office Village, River Way, Uckfield TN22 1SL
Tel: 44 01825 983105
Web site: http://www.aafarmer.co.uk/
Freq: Bi-Monthly
Circ: 6000 Not Audited

Editor: Alistair Driver; **Editor:** Chris Lyddon
MAGAZINE
Animal Farming

Agrow   983392
Editorial: 5 Howick Place, London SW1P 1WG **Tel:** 44 02070 175000
Email: marketing@agra-net.com
Web site: www.agra-net.com/agra/agrow
Freq: Daily
MAGAZINE (ONLINE)
Animal Farming, Chemicals

ahcp voice   986360
Editorial: 4th Floor, Joynes House, New Road, Gravesend DA11 0AJ
Tel: 44 08455 006008
Email: ahcp@h2opublishing.co.uk
Web site: www.h2opublishing.co.uk/publications/healthcare-cleaning-hygiene/
Freq: Quarterly
Circ: 2488 Not Audited
Editor: Amanda Roberts
Profile: AHCP Voice is the official magazine for the Association of Healthcare Cleaning Professionals.
Ad Rate: Full Page Colour £1375.00
MAGAZINE
Health Administration

AIDS Care   985347
Editorial: 4 Park Square, Milton Park, Abingdon, Didcot OX14 4RN
Tel: 44 02070 176000
Email: authorqueries@tandf.co.uk
Web site: http://www.tandfonline.com/toc/caic20/current
Freq: Monthly Not Audited
Profile: Journal providing a forum for publishing in one authoritative source research and reports from the many complementary disciplines involved in the AIDS/HIV field. These include psychology, sociology, epidemiology, social work and anthropology, social aspects of medicine, nursing, education, health education, law, administration, counselling including various approaches such as behavioural therapy, psychotherapy and family therapy. Aimed at psychologists, sociologists, epidemiologists, social workers, anthropologists, medical practitioners, psychiatrists, nurses, health education teachers, public health specialists and counsellors.Only books for review and conference information would be considered for publication.
Ad Rate: Full Page Mono £300.00
MAGAZINE
AIDS/HIV

AIJ magazine   1065607
Editorial: 45 Clerkenwell Road, London EC1R 0EB **Tel:** 44 02074 905595
Web site: www.aijmagazine.co.uk
Freq: Quarterly
Editor: Nicky Roger
MAGAZINE
Architecture & Design

AIM Bulletin   987036
Editorial: Lindford Cottage, Church Lane, Cocking, Midhurst, Midhurst GU29 0HW
Tel: 44 01730 812419
Email: editor@heavyhorseworld.co.uk
Web site: www.aim-museums.co.uk
Freq: Bi-Monthly
Circ: 2600 Not Audited
Editor: Diana Zeuner
MAGAZINE
Genealogy

AIM Journal   995851
Web site: http://www.hubinvest.com/
Freq: Monthly
Circ: 18400 Not Audited
Editor: Andrew Hore
MAGAZINE
Fund Management, Investment Banking

Air Cargo Directory   996664
Editorial: First Floor, 131 Edgware Road, London W2 2HR **Tel:** 44 02077 243456
Email: directory@airtransportpubs.com

Web site: www.airtransportpubs.com/air-cargo-directory
Freq: Daily
Circ: 6 Cicion Digital Reach
MAGAZINE (ONLINE)
Aviation, Shipping & Warehousing

Air Cargo Eye
1052666
Editorial: 97 Judd Street, Bloomsbury, London WC1H 9JG
Circ: 9511 Cision Digital Reach
Editor: Thelma Etim
MAGAZINE (ONLINE)
Aviation, Shipping & Warehousing

Air Cargo News (U.K.)
979937
Editorial: 9 Sutton Court Road, Sutton, London SM1 4SZ **Tel:** 44 02087 228370
Web site: www.aircargonews.net
Freq: Bi-Weekly
Circ: 10983 Not Audited
Editor: Roger Hailey
MAGAZINE
Aviation, Shipping & Warehousing, Supply Chain Management (SCM)

Air Cargo Week
979936
Editorial: Robert Denholm House, Bletchingly Road, Nutfield, Redhill RH1 4HW
Tel: 44 01737 645777
Email: news@azurainternational.com
Web site: www.aircargoweek.com
Freq: Weekly
Circ: 8692 Not Audited
Editor: Justin Burns
MAGAZINE
Aviation, Shipping & Warehousing, Supply Chain Management (SCM)

Air Conditioning & Refrigeration News
998579
Editorial: 15A London Road, Maidstone, Maidstone ME16 8LY **Tel:** 44 01622 687031
Email: acreditorial@datateam.co.uk
Web site: http://www.acr-news.com
Freq: Monthly
Circ: 9629 Not Audited
Editor: Lynn Sencicle
MAGAZINE
Engineering

Air International
980119
Editorial: PO Box 100, Stamford PE9 1XQ
Tel: 44 01780 755131
Email: airint@keypublishing.com
Web site: www.airinternational.com
Freq: Monthly
Circ: 10841 Not Audited
Editor: Mark Ayton
Profile: Magazine covering news and features on civil and military aviation. The publication regularly visit aviation trade shows and major aircraft manufacturers to produce military and civil news, informed coverage of military aircraft and in-depth analysis of commercial operators and aircraft types. Covers mainly military air arms, commercial operators, airliners, aerospace companies and technology, plus future trends. Read by senior defence and aerospace executives.
Ad Rate: Full Page Colour £3620.00
MAGAZINE
Aviation

The Air League Newsletter
996013
Editorial: The Air League, Broadway House, Tothill Street, London SW1H 9NS
Tel: 44 02072 228463
Email: info@airleague.co.uk
Web site: www.airleague.co.uk
Freq: Bi-Monthly Not Audited
Editor: Richard Gardner
MAGAZINE
Aviation

Air Med & Rescue
985971
Editorial: 19 Lower Park Row, Bristol BS1 5BN **Tel:** 44 01179 226600
Email: editor@airmedandrescue.com
Web site: www.airmedandrescue.com

Freq: Monthly Not Audited
Editor: James Wallis; **Editor:** Sarah Watson
MAGAZINE
Aviation, EMS/Emergency Medical Services

Air Quality Bulletin
985015
Editorial: The Garth, Rockshaw Road, Merstham, Redhill RH1 3DB
Tel: 44 01737 642283
Email: enquiries@empublishing.co.uk
Web site: www.empublishing.co.uk/air/index.htm
Freq: Monthly Not Audited
Editor: Jack Pease
Profile: Air Quality Bulletin is a monthly newsletter covering all the latest on air quality management.
MAGAZINE
Environment

Air Traffic Technology International
984177
Editorial: Abinger House, Church Street, Dorking, Dorking RH4 1DF
Tel: 44 01306 743744
Email: airtraffic@ukipme.com
Web site: http://www.airtraffictechnologyinternational.com
Freq: Annual
Circ: 8500 Not Audited
Editor: Hazel King
Profile: Magazine focusing on the latest air traffic technology, products, services, simulation and training. Aimed at air traffic professionals, aviation authority managers and other aviation professionals.
Ad Rate: Full Page Colour £5450.00
MAGAZINE
Aviation

Aircraft Cabin Management
986639
Editorial: Suite E, 11 Bell Yard Mews, 175 Bermondsey Street, London SE1 3TN
Tel: 44 02077 243456
Email: info@airtransportpubs.com
Web site: www.aircraftcabinmanagement.com
Freq: Quarterly
Circ: 12000 Not Audited
Editor: Ian Harbison
Profile: Magazine covering commercial and business jet cabins. It analyses how the engineering behind products and layouts affects operators' economics.
Ad Rate: Full Page Colour £3250.00
MAGAZINE
Aviation, Manufacturing

Aircraft Commerce
004171
Editorial: West Point, 2nd Floor, Springfield Road, Horsham, Horsham RH12 2PD
Tel: 44 01403 230700
Web site: www.aircraft-commerce.com
Freq: Bi-Monthly
Circ: 10030 Not Audited
Profile: Magazine covering all aspects of the economics and management of air transport. First published in 1998. Aimed at decision makers and executives within the aircraft industry.
Ad Rate: Full Page Colour £8400.00
MAGAZINE
Aviation

Aircraft Interiors International
984469
Editorial: Abinger House, Church Street, Dorking, Dorking RH4 1DF
Tel: 44 01306 743744
Email: simon.hughes@ukipme.com
Web site: www.aircraftinteriorsinternational.com
Freq: Quarterly
Circ: 13652 Not Audited
Editor: Adam Gavine
Profile: Magazine containing world news, new product reviews, interviews, case studies on aircraft interior industry developments, systems appraisals and technology profiles. Aimed at designers, engineers, brand managers and department managers engaged in all aspects of aircraft

interior design and completion, including airlines, interior design consultants, aircraft manufacturers and completion centres.
Ad Rate: Full Page Colour £4225.00
MAGAZINE
Aviation

Aircraft Investor
1094462
Tel: 44 01737 910499
Web site: http://www.aircraftinvestor.com/
Freq: Daily
Circ: 12243 Cision Digital Reach
MAGAZINE (ONLINE)
Aviation

Aircraft Maintenance & Engineering Directory
984368
Editorial: Suite E, 11 Bell Yard Mews, 175 Bermondsey Street, London SE1 3TN
Tel: 44 02077 243456
Email: info@airtransportpubs.com
Web site: www.airtransportpubs.com/aircraft-maintenance-engineering-directory
Freq: Annual
Circ: 3500 Not Audited
Profile: Directory focusing on industry articles and statistics, and airline and world fleet data. Includes directories of airlines, third party services and manufacturers and suppliers of support equipment, systems and services. First published in 1997, the publication has an average of 376 pages per issue. Aimed at senior management within the airline and aircraft MRO industry worldwide.
MAGAZINE
Aviation

Aircraft Technology Engineering & Maintenance
980077
Editorial: 4th Floor, Tallis House, 2 Tallis Street, London EC4Y 0AB
Web site: www.mro-network.com
Freq: Bi-Monthly
Circ: 10000 Not Audited
Profile: International aviation magazine covering commercial aircraft design, manufacturing and maintenance (MRO) sectors. First published in 1992. Read by the management staff of aircraft and component manufacturers, airline manufacturers, airline management executives and MRO professionals working within the commercial aviation industry.
Ad Rate: Full Page Mono £3451.00
Ad Rate: Full Page Colour £5310.00
MAGAZINE
Aviation, Engineering

Aircraft Value News
998886
Editorial: Buckland House, Haydons Close, Chipping Campden, Chipping Campden GL55 6JN **Tel:** 44 02034 685594
Web site: http://www.aircraftvaluenews.com/
Freq: Bi-Weekly
Editor: Paul Leighton
MAGAZINE
Aviation

Airfinance Journal
979977
Editorial: 6-8 Bouverie Street, London EC4Y 8AX
Web site: www.airfinancejournal.com
Freq: Monthly
Circ: 3000 Not Audited
Profile: Journal covering corporate and asset financing within the commercial aerospace industry. Also cover wealth management. Incorporating Aircraft Economics, the publication was first published in 1980. Read by financiers, airline personnel, lawyers, manufacturers and insurers.
Ad Rate: Full Page Colour £7704.00
MAGAZINE
Aviation

AirForces Monthly
980086
Editorial: PO Box 100, Stamford PE9 1XQ
Tel: 44 01780 755131
Web site: www.airforcesmonthly.com
Freq: Monthly

Circ: 17518 Not Audited
Profile: Magazine containing news about modern military aircraft.
Ad Rate: Full Page Colour £1449.00
MAGAZINE
Aviation, Defense & National Security

airforce-technology.com
984634
Editorial: John Carpenter House, John Carpenter Street, London EC4Y 0AN
Tel: 44 02079 366400
Email: onlineeditorial@kable.co.uk
Web site: www.airforce-technology.com
Freq: Daily
Circ: 141096 Cision Digital Reach
Profile: Website covering air-force technology. "Airforce-technology.com attracts leading industry experts, keen to stay ahead of their field. Visitors hold a range of roles, from lead system and senior mechanical engineers to senior buyers, chiefs of weapon system divisions and logistics, weapons instructors and many more."
MAGAZINE (ONLINE)
Aviation, Defense & National Security

Airline Business
979913
Editorial: Quadrant House, London SM2 5AS **Tel:** 44 02086 523315
Web site: www.airlinebusiness.com
Freq: Monthly
Circ: 21000 Not Audited
Profile: Publication covering the financial and commercial aspects of airline management including corporate strategy, alliances, marketing, cost control, yields, financial performance and labour. The publication also covers mainline & national carriers, regional carriers, fleet air taxis, cargo carriers, charter carriers, low cost airlines & alliances. Read by senior management of the civil airline industry, plus associated finance, leasing, manufacturing and legal companies.
Ad Rate: Full Page Mono £5245.00
Ad Rate: Full Page Colour £6850.00
MAGAZINE
Aviation

Airline Cargo Management
984093
Editorial: Suite E, 11 Bell Yard Mews, 175 Bermondsey Street, London SE1 3TN
Tel: 44 02077 243456
Email: editor@airlinecargomanagement.com
Web site: www.airlinecargomanagement.com
Freq: Quarterly
Circ: 6000 Not Audited
Editor: Helen Massy-Beresford
Profile: Magazine focusing on international air cargo management issues. Aimed at senior airline and airport cargo managers and ground handling executives.
Ad Rate: Full Page Colour £2950.00
MAGAZINE
Aviation, Shipping & Warehousing, Supply Chain Management (SCM)

Airline Directory
995932
Editorial: First Floor, 131 Edgware Road, London W2 2HR **Tel:** 44 02077 243456
Email: directory@airtransportpubs.com
Web site: www.airtransportpubs.com
Freq: Annual
Circ: 3500 Not Audited
MAGAZINE
Aviation

Airline Economics
985939
Editorial: Suite 16745, 20-22 Wenlock Road, London N1 7GU **Tel:** 44 01630 647259
Email: news@aviationnews-online.com
Web site: www.aviationnews-online.com/airline-economics/
Freq: Bi-Monthly
Circ: 10000 Not Audited
MAGAZINE
Aviation

Airline Ground Services
997241
Editorial: Boswell Cottage, 19 South End, Croydon CR0 1BE **Tel:** 44 02082 534000
Email: editorial@evaint.com

Business Magazines

Web site: www.ags-airlinegroundservices.com
Freq: Semi-Annual
Circ: 10928 Not Audited
MAGAZINE
Aviation

Airliner World   981892
Editorial: PO Box 100, Stamford PE9 1XQ
Tel: 44 01780 755131
Email: airlinerworld@keypublishing.com
Web site: www.airlinerworld.com
Freq: Monthly
Circ: 31878 Not Audited
Editor: Craig West
Profile: The magazine covers world's airlines, airports and aircraft and all aspects of the commercial aviation scene including up-to-date airline, airport, aircraft and manufacturer information. Each month it provides comprehensive analysis of airlines and airports, including in-depth histories, and features articles on other aspects of the airline industry such as Air Traffic Control, Environment and Flight Safety, plus interviews with senior airline executives. Read in over 100 countries by Chief Executives of airlines and airports, ground staff, pilots, cabin crew, aviation-related professionals and well informed enthusiasts. Launched in 1999. Aimed at aircraft enthusiasts as well as industry professionals, airline and airport staff.Regular features: Aircraft Profiles of different aircraft used by the airline industry.; Airlines Profiles of airlines companies and their practices.; Airports Profile feature covering a different airport from around the world each issue.
Ad Rate: Full Page Colour £1680.00
MAGAZINE
Aviation

Airlines & Airliners   998550
Editorial: AJAviation, 2nd Floor Big North House, West Drayton, London UB7 8EJ
Tel: 44 01895 442123
Email: ajaviation@outlook.com
Web site: http://ajaviation.co.uk/airlines-airliners/
Freq: Annual Not Audited
Editor: Tony Eastwood
MAGAZINE
Aviation

Airlines International   984165
Editorial: 17 Britton Street, London EC1M 5TP **Tel:** 44 02073 242763
Email: airlineseditor@redactive.co.uk
Web site: www.airlines.iata.org
Circ: 8000 Not Audited
Editor: Graham Newton
MAGAZINE
Aviation

AirlineUpdate.com   999228
Editorial: 11 Heol y Parc, Pontyberem, Pontyberem SA15 5EA
Tel: 44 01269 871806
Email: info@airlineupdate.com
Web site: www.airlineupdate.com
Freq: Daily
Circ: 44345 Cision Digital Reach
MAGAZINE (ONLINE)
Aviation

Airmic News   998653
Editorial: AIRMIC Secretariat, 6 Lloyd's Avenue, London EC3N 3AX
Tel: 44 02076 803088
Email: enquiries@airmic.com
Web site: www.airmic.com
Freq: Daily
Circ: 16857 Cision Digital Reach
MAGAZINE (ONLINE)
Insurance

Airport Business (UK)   996551
Editorial: 3A Gatwick Metro Centre, Balcombe Road, Surrey, Horley RH6 9GA
Tel: 44 01293 783851
Email: post@pps-publications.com
Web site: www.airport-business.com
Freq: Quarterly

Circ: 10000 Not Audited
MAGAZINE
Aviation

Airport Directory   995532
Editorial: First Floor, 131 Edgware Road, London W2 2HR **Tel:** 44 02077 243456
Email: directory@airtransportpubs.com
Web site: www.airtransportpubs.com/airport-directory
Freq: Annual
Circ: 3500 Not Audited
MAGAZINE
Aviation

Airport Focus   987696
Editorial: Waterloo Chambers, 19 Waterloo Street, Glasgow G2 6AY
Tel: 44 01412 222100
Web site: http://airportfocusinternational.com
Freq: Bi-Monthly
Circ: 7100 Not Audited
MAGAZINE
Aviation

Airport Industry Review   985764
Editorial: John Carpenter House, John Carpenter Street, London EC4Y 0AN
Tel: 44 02079 366400
Email: onlinemags@nridigital.com
Web site: http://www.nridigital.com/airport-industry-review.html
Freq: Monthly
Circ: 9230 Cision Digital Reach
Profile: Website covering airport industry. Airport Industry Review is a digital magazine providing the latest news, trends and technological developments from the airport industry.
MAGAZINE (ONLINE)
Aviation, Shipping & Warehousing

The Airport Operator   983913
Editorial: 3 Birdcage Walk, London SW1H 9JJ **Tel:** 44 02077 993171
Email: info@aoa.org.uk
Web site: www.aoa.org.uk
Freq: Quarterly
Circ: 4000 Not Audited
Profile: Magazine covering the UK airport and aviation industry. Aimed at airport executives, legislators and relevant regulators.
MAGAZINE
Aviation

Airport World   983907
Editorial: 91 - 93 Windmill Road, Sunbury-on-Thames, London TW16 7EF
Web site: www.airport-world.com
Freq: Bi-Monthly
Circ: 7000 Not Audited
Profile: Magazine dealing with airport development and business strategies. Its primary aim is to provide a forum for airport-related management issues, a vehicle for airports to promote and market themselves, and a direct route for suppliers of products and services to airports. The publication was first published in 1996 and has on average 68 pages per issue. Aimed at airport senior and middle management. Primary circulation supplied by Airports Council International.
Ad Rate: Full Page Colour £4200.00
MAGAZINE
Aviation

Airports International   981321
Editorial: PO Box 100, Stamford, Peterborough PE9 1XQ
Tel: 44 01780 755131
Web site: www.airportsint.com
Freq: Bi-Monthly
Circ: 12054 Not Audited
Editor: Tom Allett
Profile: Magazine covering all aspects of ground based civil aviation operations. Features include buyers guides to equipment, airport safety and airport development. Aimed at airport directors and managers, operations directors, ground handling and ATC and ATM industry

personnel worldwide.Regular features: News Industry newsPress releases preferred by email. Pictures preferred in JPEG format.
Ad Rate: Full Page Colour £3939.00
MAGAZINE
Aviation

airport-technology.com   987717
Editorial: John Carpenter House, John Carpenter Street, London EC4Y 0AN
Tel: 44 02079 366400
Email: onlineeditorial@kable.co.uk
Web site: http://www.airport-technology.com
Freq: Daily
Circ: 49829 Cision Digital Reach
Profile: Website covering airport technology. The airport.technology.com website discusses projects both in production and under development to airport phone apps and innovation.
MAGAZINE (ONLINE)
Aviation

airqualitynews.com   1068848
Editorial: Elizabeth House, 39 York Road, London SE1 7NQ **Tel:** 44 02076 334500
Web site: www.airqualitynews.com
Freq: Daily
Circ: 12535 Cision Digital Reach
Editor: Steve Eminton
MAGAZINE (ONLINE)
Environment

Airside International   996842
Editorial: Boswell Cottage, 19 South End, London CR0 1BE **Tel:** 44 02082 534000
Email: editorial@evaint.com
Web site: evaint.com/our-publications/airside-international
Freq: Quarterly Not Audited
MAGAZINE
Aviation

Alcohol and Alcoholism   985322
Editorial: Oxford University Press, Great Clarendon Street, Oxford OX2 6DP
Tel: 44 01865 353907
Web site: alcalc.oxfordjournals.org
Freq: Bi-Monthly
MAGAZINE
Community Care (UK)

Alimentary Pharmacology & Therapeutics   996618
Web site: www.APandT.org
Freq: Bi-Weekly Not Audited
Editor: Roy Pounder
MAGAZINE
Gastroenterology

Allaboutrisk.com   984380
Tel: 44 02071 936737
Email: info@allaboutrisk.com
Web site: www.allaboutrisk.com
Freq: Daily
Circ: 6151 Cision Digital Reach
Editor: Jane Stoll
MAGAZINE (ONLINE)
Business, Corporate Responsibility, Insurance

Alpha Journal   988348
Editorial: 106 Lakeside, 82 Eaton Drive, London KT2 7RA
Email: editorial@alphajournal.com
Web site: www.alphajournal.com
Freq: Daily
Circ: 2429 Cision Digital Reach
Editor: Margie Lindsay
MAGAZINE (ONLINE)
Fund Management, Hedge Funds, Investment Banking

AlphaQ   997730
Editorial: First Floor, Liberation Station, St Helier, Jersey JE2 3AS
Tel: 44 01534 719780
Email: editorial@globalfundmedia.com
Web site: www.institutionalassetmanager.co.uk/special-reports/alphaq

Freq: Bi-Monthly Not Audited
MAGAZINE
Investment Banking

Alt Credit Intelligence   997905
Editorial: One London Wall, London EC2Y 5BD **Tel:** 44 02078 326632
Web site: https://hfm.global/altcreditintelligence/
Freq: Monthly
Profile: Magazine covering alternative credit. Aimed at alternative credit managers.
MAGAZINE (ONLINE)
Bonds, Corporate Finance, Corporate Management, Credit Markets, Emerging Markets, Government, Investment Banking, Lending, Public & Consumer Finance

AltAssets   979923
Editorial: WeWork 3026, 1 Fore Street, London EC2Y 5EJ **Tel:** 44 02077 491280
Email: editorial@altassets.net
Web site: https://www.altassets.net/
Freq: Daily
Circ: 95460 Cision Digital Reach
Profile: Website covering finance. The AltAssets provides the latest news, opinion and research on the private equity industry. The site is designed to serve the needs of professionals working in all parts of the industry, from the institutional investor to the venture-backed entrepreneur.
MAGAZINE (ONLINE)
Private Equity

AltFi   1066537
Editorial: Office 67, City Business Centre, 2 London Wall Buildings, London EC2M 5UU
Web site: www.altfi.com
Freq: Daily
Circ: 55504 Cision Digital Reach
Editor: Ryan Weeks
MAGAZINE (ONLINE)
Fund Management

Aluminium International Today   983746
Editorial: Quartz House, 20 Clarendon Road, Redhill RH1 1GX
Tel: 44 01737 855000
Email: aluminium@quartzltd.com
Web site: www.aluminiumtoday.com
Freq: Bi-Monthly
Circ: 5500 Not Audited
Editor: Nadine Bloxsome
Profile: Journal of aluminium production and processing. Includes industry news, technical features, products and services and diary of events. Aimed at production directors, metallurgists, works managers and quality control managers.Previous title: Aluminium Today
Ad Rate: Full Page Colour £3486.00
MAGAZINE
Manufacturing

Aluminium Times   984292
Editorial: Gresham House, 54 High Street, Shoreham-by-Sea, Shoreham-by-Sea BN43 5DB **Tel:** 44 01273 453033
Email: query@mmcpublications.co.uk
Web site: http://www.mmcpublications.co.uk/at.html
Freq: Bi-Monthly
Circ: 5200 Not Audited
Profile: Magazine covering news, product information, technical articles and profiles of companies and leading figures in the aluminium and light metals industry. Aimed at managers of companies in primary and secondary sectors, rolling mills and extruding aluminium works who are involved with the decision of purchasing consumables and equipment.
Ad Rate: Full Page Mono £1710.00
Ad Rate: Full Page Colour £1710.00
MAGAZINE
Manufacturing

Amateur Photographer   982025
Editorial: Pinehurst 2, Pinehurst Road, Farnborough Business Park, Farnborough, London GU14 7BF **Tel:** 44 01252 555000
Email: amateurphotographer@timeinc.com

Web site: www.amateurphotographer.co.uk
Freq: Weekly
Circ: 13673 Not Audited
Profile: Magazine containing news and product tests, plus interviews and articles about photographic techniques. Aimed at amateur photographers, semi-professionals and professionals.
Ad Rate: Full Page Mono £925.00
Ad Rate: Full Page Colour £1500.00
MAGAZINE
Photography

Ambulance Life   984503
Editorial: No 1The Colchester Business Centre, 1 George Williams Way, Colchester, Colchester CO1 2JS Tel: 44 01206 369448
Email: info@ambulance-life.co.uk
Web site: www.ambulance-life.co.uk
Freq: Monthly
Circ: 10000 Not Audited
Editor: Jill Bareham
Profile: Magazine covering new product reviews, personnel, special achievements, training and jobs within the UK ambulance service. Aimed at Ambulance personnel serving in the NHS Ambulance Service, the private Ambulance Service, Ambulance Associations plus St John and St Andrews Ambulance.
Ad Rate: Full Page Mono £2000.00
Ad Rate: Full Page Colour £2000.00
MAGAZINE
EMS/Emergency Medical Services, Hygiene, Security & Security Systems

Ambulance Today   984504
Editorial: 41 Canning Street, Liverpool L8 7NN Tel: 44 01517 088864
Email: editor@ambulancetoday.co.uk
Web site: www.ambulancetoday.co.uk
Freq: Quarterly
Circ: 380995 Not Audited
Editor: Declan Heneghan
Profile: Magazine covering all aspects of ambulance affairs, including good practice, health and safety, clinical governance, supplies and support. Also includes news and human interests stories. Aimed at ambulance staff and those working in the NHS, Red Cross and St John Ambulance.
Ad Rate: Full Page Colour £1500.00
MAGAZINE
Hygiene, Security & Security Systems

Ambulance UK   983923
Editorial: Media House, 48 High Street, Swanley, Swanley BR8 8BQ
Tel: 44 01322 660434
Email: info@mediapublishingcompany.com
Web site: www.ambulanceukonline.com
Freq: Bi-Monthly
Circ: 5144 Not Audited
Profile: Journal for the public and private sector ambulance services with articles on communications, training, vehicles, clothing and safety. Read by chief ambulance officers, chief executives, chairmen and other senior personnel of ambulance authorities and private ambulance stations.
Ad Rate: Full Page Mono £750.00
Ad Rate: Full Page Colour £1200.00
MAGAZINE
EMS/Emergency Medical Services

Americafruit   986654
Editorial: 132 Wandsworth Road, London SW8 2LB Tel: 44 02075 013700
Email: carl@fruitnet.com
Web site: http://www.fruitnet.com/americafruit/
Freq: Daily
Circ: 54 Cision Digital Reach
MAGAZINE (ONLINE)
Food, Supply Chain Management (SCM)

American Power News   985686
Editorial: Global House, 13 Market Square, Horsham, Horsham RH12 1EU
Tel: 44 01403 220750
Email: power@gmp.uk.com
Web site: www.gmp.uk.com/american-power-news
Freq: Semi-Annual
Circ: 14150 Not Audited

Profile: American Power News 'brings you the latest news and in-depth topical features on all aspects of the region's independent power generation market. With regular analysis of market trends, the latest contracts and new applications and product innovations.' American Power News is a quarterly subscription only magazine, published in A3 format.
Ad Rate: Full Page Mono £3083.00
Ad Rate: Full Page Colour £2410.00
MAGAZINE
Alternative/Renewable Energy, Carbon Emissions & Trading, Electricity, Energy, Nuclear Power, Oil, Water & Sanitation

Anaesthesia   983828
Tel: 44 01158 231895
Email: anaesthesia@aagbi.org
Web site: www.wiley.com/bw/journal.asp?ref=0003-2409&site=1
Freq: Monthly
Circ: 11224 Not Audited
Profile: Journal of the Association of Anaesthetists of Great Britain and Ireland.
Ad Rate: Full Page Mono £615.00
Ad Rate: Full Page Colour £1377.00
MAGAZINE
Anesthesiology

Anaesthesia and Intensive Care Medicine   985262
Editorial: The Boulevard, Langford Lane, Kidlington OX5 1GB Tel: 44 01865 843154
Email: anaesthesia@medicinepublishing.co.uk
Web site: www.anaesthesiajournal.co.uk/
Freq: Monthly Not Audited
MAGAZINE
Anesthesiology

The Analytical Scientist   988802
Editorial: Haig House, Haig Road, Knutsford, Knutsford WA16 8DX
Tel: 44 01565 745200
Email: info@texerepublishing.com
Web site: theanalyticalscientist.com
Freq: Monthly
Circ: 31000 Not Audited
Editor: Rich Whitworth
Profile: Magazine covering science. It features emerging technology, real lab problems and case studies illustrating innovative approaches to improve performance. It also contains profiles of the people driving the sector forward, and what these people think the future looks like, legislation and business perspectives from the many industries that rely on analytical science.
Ad Rate: Full Page Mono £6120.00
MAGAZINE
Science

Angel News   983096
Editorial: 6 Cholwell Cottages, Main Road, Temple Cloud, Bristol BS39 5DH
Tel: 44 07736 676212
Email: news@angelnews.co.uk
Web site: http://www.angelnewsletter.co.uk/
Freq: Daily
Circ: 14144 Cision Digital Reach
MAGAZINE (ONLINE)
Private Equity

Anglia Farmer   985968
Editorial: Countrywide Publications, Fountain Way, Reydon Business Park, Southwold IP18 6DH Tel: 44 01502 725800
Email: info@countrywidepublications.co.uk
Web site: www.angliafarmer.co.uk
Freq: Monthly
Circ: 7000 Not Audited
Editor: Johann Tasker
Profile: Journal covering items of agricultural relevance to East Anglia. Read by farmers and growers in the Eastern Counties, as well as allied trades and supply organisations. Previous title: Anglia Farmer and Contractor
Ad Rate: Full Page Colour £800.00
MAGAZINE
Animal Farming

Animal Pharm   983258
Editorial: Christchurch Court, 10 Newgate Street, London EC1A 7AZ
Tel: 44 02070 177500
Email: joseph.harvey@informa.com
Web site: https://www.agra-net.com/agra/animal-pharm/
Freq: Daily
Circ: 52271 Cision Digital Reach
Editor: Joseph Harvey
MAGAZINE (ONLINE)
Animal Farming

anna aero   987172
Editorial: 3a Gatwick Metro Centre, Balcombe Road, Horley, Horley RH6 9GA
Tel: 44 01530 271333
Web site: www.anna.aero
Freq: Weekly
Circ: 62474 Cision Digital Reach
Editor: Marc Watkins
MAGAZINE (ONLINE)
Aviation

Annals of Occupational and Environmental Medicine
                                    1006438
Tel: 44 02031 922009
Email: info@biomedcentral.com
Web site: www.aoemj.com
Freq: Daily Not Audited
MAGAZINE
Community Care (UK), Environment

Annals of the Rheumatic Diseases   998692
Editorial: Editorial Office, BMA House, Tavistock Square, London WC1H 9JR
Tel: 44 02073 836795
Email: ard@bmjgroup.com
Web site: http://ard.bmj.com
Freq: Monthly
Circ: 11660 Not Audited
Editor: Tore K Kvien
MAGAZINE
Rheumatology

Anti-Cancer Drugs   985343
Editorial: 250 Waterloo Road, London SE1 8RD Tel: 44 02079 810600
Web site: www.anti-cancerdrugs.com
Freq: Monthly Not Audited
MAGAZINE
Oncology, Pharmaceuticals

Anti-Corrosion Methods & Materials   981039
Editorial: Howard House, Wagon Lane, Bingley BD16 1WA Tel: 44 01274 777700
Email: emerald@emeraldinsight.com
Web site: http://emeraldgrouppublishing.com/products/journals/journals.htm?id=acmm
Freq: Bi-Monthly Not Audited
Profile: Journal covering all aspects of corrosion management, prevention and control. Read by production managers, works managers and researchers interested in, or having a responsibility for corrosion control and prevention.
MAGAZINE
Engineering

AOPA UK   994669
Editorial: Hangar 9 Redhill Aerodrome, Redhill RH1 5JY Tel: 44 01737 821409
Email: info@aopa.co.uk
Web site: http://www.iaopa.eu/home
Freq: Bi-Monthly
Circ: 6000 Not Audited
MAGAZINE
Aviation

APAC Insider   995019
Editorial: Unit 10, Barton Marina, Barton Turn, Barton under Needwood, Burton on Trent, Barton-under-Needwood DE13 8AS
Tel: 44 02037 256842
Web site: http://www.apacinsider.com/
Freq: Quarterly

Circ: 112000 Not Audited
MAGAZINE
Business, Corporate Responsibility, Financial Markets, Mergers & Acquisitions

APCJ   984706
Editorial: Quartz House, 20 Clarendon Road, Redhill, Redhill RH1 1QX
Tel: 44 01737 855000
Web site: www.asiapacificcoatingsjournal.com
Freq: Bi-Monthly
Circ: 10073 Not Audited
Editor: Chris Malthouse
MAGAZINE
Plastics

Applied Energy   1006760
Editorial: The Boulevard, Langford Lane, Oxford OX5 1GB Tel: 44 01865 843000
Email: appliedenergy@gmail.com
Web site: https://www.journals.elsevier.com/applied-energy/
Freq: Monthly Not Audited
Editor: S.K. Chou
MAGAZINE
Alternative/Renewable Energy, Electricity, Nuclear Power, Oil, Water & Sanitation

Apprentice Builder   986349
Editorial: Regal House, Regal Way, Watford, London WD24 4YF Tel: 44 01923 237799
Email: ab@hamerville.co.uk
Web site: www.apprenticebuilder.co.uk
Freq: Quarterly
Circ: 25000 Not Audited
Editor: Lee Jones
Profile: Magazine aimed at students undertaking apprenticeships within the building industry, including bricklaying, carpentry and joinery, painting and decorating, roofing, plastering and general building. It provides practical knowledge that enables students to understand their course content in more of a real life context.
Ad Rate: Full Page Colour £2270.00
MAGAZINE
Building & Construction, Commercial Real Estate, Education, Urban Planning & Development

Apprentice Eye   997743
Editorial: 1 Broadway, Hammersmith, London W6 9DL
Email: info@apprenticeeye.co.uk
Web site: www.apprenticeeye.co.uk
Freq: Daily
Circ: 14685 Cision Digital Reach
MAGAZINE (ONLINE)
Education

Appropriate Technology   988914
Editorial: Research Information Ltd, Grenville Court, Britwell Road, Burnham, Slough SL1 8DF Tel: 44 01628 600499
Email: info@researchinformation.co.uk
Web site: www.researchinformation.co.uk/apte.php
Freq: Quarterly Not Audited
Editor: David Dixon
Profile: International magazine communicating new practical technologies, policies and ideas addressing the elimination of poverty and hunger. Additional coverage includes: agriculture, water & sanitation, rural building and construction, sustainable & economic development projects and programmes, natural resource management, forestry, health, education & training, disaster and emergency relief management, micro-enterprises. Each issue has regular articles from Intermediate Technology Development Group (ITDG), Deutsche Gesellschaft fur Techische Zusammenarbeit, The Centre for Alternative Technology. Read by rural development field workers, projects/programme managers, extension officers and researchers working on behalf of NGO's, international aid agencies and co-ordinating bodies, government funded institutions, UN & intergovernment organization, research organizations. Launched in 1973.Read by fieldworkers, educators and policy makers.
Ad Rate: Full Page Mono £750.00

Business Magazines

Ad Rate: Full Page Colour £995.00
MAGAZINE
Animal Farming

Aquaculture Scoop   1054242
Web site: aquaculturedirectory.co.uk/
aquaculture-scoop
Freq: Quarterly
MAGAZINE
Animal Farming

Arab Banker   995955
Editorial: 43 Upper Grosvenor Street,
London W1K 2NJ **Tel:** 44 02076 594889
Web site: www.arab-bankers.co.uk
Freq: Annual
Circ: 4300 Not Audited
Profile: Magazine focusing on banking and
finance in the Middle East. Aimed at senior
banking personnel and government officials.
Ad Rate: Full Page Mono £3950.00
Ad Rate: Full Page Colour £4475.00
MAGAZINE
Banking

**Arabian Business - Editorial
(Arabic)**   1003006
Tel: 44 97144 443000
Web site: www.arabianbusiness.com
Freq: Monthly Not Audited
MAGAZINE
Business

Arable Farming   981148
Editorial: Unit 4, Fulwood Park, Caxton
Road, Preston PR2 9NZ
Tel: 44 01772 799429
Email: fgeditorial@fginsight.com
Web site: www.fginsight.com
Freq: Monthly
Circ: 8908 Not Audited
Editor: Teresa Rush
Profile: Magazine covering production,
marketing, distribution and selling of arable
crops.
MAGAZINE
Animal Farming

ArcheTech   987472
Editorial: 9 Upchurch Walk, Margate,
Margate CT9 3NT **Tel:** 44 01227 392031
Email: alex@archetechmag.co.uk
Web site: www.archetech.org.uk
Freq: Bi-Monthly
Circ: 30750 Not Audited
MAGAZINE
Architecture & Design

Architect Projects   988921
Editorial: Marlowe Innovation Centre,
Marlowe Way, Ramsgate, Ramsgate CT12
6FA **Tel:** 44 01843 598623
Email: editorial@architectprojects.co.uk
Web site: www.architectprojects.co.uk
Freq: Quarterly
Circ: 7892 Not Audited
Editor: Maria Still
Profile: Trade publication within the
architectural and construction industry
looking at current projects, new contracts
and upcoming projects, product launches,
discussions and interviews regarding
matters within the design and building
industry.
Ad Rate: Full Page Colour £1650.00
MAGAZINE
Architecture & Design, Building &
Construction

Architect's Choice   983564
Editorial: 1 Accent Park, Bakewell Road,
Orton Southgate, Peterborough PE2 6XS
Tel: 44 01733 385300
Email: ac@onecoms.co.uk
Web site: www.architectnews.co.uk
Freq: Bi-Monthly
Circ: 4000 Not Audited
Editor: Jade Tilley
Profile: Magazine covering products, news,
applications and features on architectural
projects. Provides features on large scale
projects, topical debates on worldwide
subjects in building and design and industry

happenings. First published in 1997, the
publication has an average of 36 pages per
issue. Read by designers and architects.
Ad Rate: Full Page Mono £720.00
Ad Rate: Full Page Colour £750.00
MAGAZINE
Architecture & Design

Architects Datafile   981084
Editorial: Cointronic House, Station Road,
Heathfield, Heathfield TN21 8DF
Tel: 44 01435 863500
Email: editorial@netmagmedia.eu
Web site: www.adfonline.eu
Freq: Monthly
Circ: 15000 Not Audited
Profile: Magazine focussing on architecture
and building design and covering projects,
new products and technical information.
Aimed at working architects.
Ad Rate: Full Page Mono £1425.00
Ad Rate: Full Page Colour £1425.00
MAGAZINE
Architecture & Design

Architects' Journal   979920
Editorial: 3 / 4th Floor, Telephone House,
69-77 Paul Street, London EC2A 4NQ
Tel: 44 02030 332600
Web site: www.architectsjournal.co.uk
Freq: Weekly
Circ: 6817 Not Audited
Profile: Journal covering British architecture
and British cities including in-depth weekly
news analysis, comprehensive building
studies, in-depth technical and practice
features and incisive commentary, and
forming opinions across the whole
construction industry on design-related
matters. Aimed at architects, technicians,
engineers and surveyors.
Ad Rate: Full Page Colour £3569.00
MAGAZINE
Architecture & Design

Architectural Design   984333
Editorial: The Atrium, Southern Gate,
Chichester PO19 8SQ
Email: cs-author@wiley.com
Web site: http://www.architectural-design-
magazine.com
Freq: Bi-Monthly
Circ: 4000 Not Audited
Editor: Helen Castle
Profile: Magazine covering architecture and
design. Aimed at architects and architectural
students. Helen Castle is the Executive
Commissioning Editor to whom press
releases should be addressed. Press
releases by post only.
MAGAZINE
Architecture & Design

The Architectural Review
                    981081
Editorial: 69-77 Paul Street, London EC2A
4NW **Tel:** 44 02030 332600
Email: editorial@architectural-review.com
Web site: https://www.architectural-review.
com/
Freq: Monthly
Circ: 10000 Not Audited
Profile: Magazine covering architecture
including design ideas and product
inspiration and critical vision of
contemporary architecture from around the
world. First published in 1896. Aimed at
architects, interior designers and landscape
architects.
Ad Rate: Full Page Colour £3660.00
MAGAZINE
Architecture & Design

**The Architectural
Technologists Book**   1052203
Editorial: Kingfishers Retreat, The Lodges,
Dunston Business Village, Stafford ST18
9AB **Tel:** 44 01785 711591
Email: james@l2media.uk
Web site: www.link2media.co.uk/#/the-
publications/atb/overview
Freq: Quarterly
Circ: 7000 Not Audited
MAGAZINE
Architecture & Design

**Architectural Technology
Magazine**   981569
Editorial: 397 City Road, London EC1V 1NH
Tel: 44 02072 782206
Email: editorial@ciat.org.uk
Web site: https://ciat.org.uk/
Freq: Quarterly
Circ: 10000 Not Audited
MAGAZINE
Architecture & Design

Architecture Today   981082
Editorial: 34 Pentonville Road, London N1
9HF **Tel:** 44 02078 370143
Email: editorial@architecturetoday.co.uk
Web site: www.architecturetoday.co.uk
Freq: Monthly
Circ: 12101 Not Audited
Editor: Chris Foges
Profile: Magazine focussing on architecture
and building design containing building
features, European news, practice articles
and special features. First published in 1989,
the publication has an average of 100 pages
per issue. PR Accepted in: English; French;
German Aimed at registered architects
practising in the UK.
Ad Rate: Full Page Mono £2140.00
Ad Rate: Full Page Colour £3110.00
MAGAZINE
Architecture & Design, Interior Design

Archives of Osteoporosis 995052
Editorial: 236 Gray's Inn Road, London
WC1X 8HB **Tel:** 44 20319 22000
Web site: http://www.springer.com/
medicine/orthopedics/journal/11657
Freq: Annual
MAGAZINE
Orthopedics

Arena   985042
Editorial: Usdaw Central Office, 188
Wilmslow Road, Manchester M14 6LJ
Tel: 44 01612 242804
Email: arena@usdaw.org.uk
Web site: www.usdaw.org.uk/Members/
Magazines
Freq: Quarterly
Circ: 365000 Not Audited
Profile: Magazine of the Union of Shop,
Distributive and Allied Workers. Read by
union members, Members of Parliament and
company managers.
Ad Rate: Full Page Colour £6950.00
MAGAZINE
Public Sector

Argent   998665
Editorial: 1st Floor, 251 Pentonville Road,
London N1 9NG **Tel:** 44 02074 499000
Email: info@thefsforum.co.uk
Web site: https://www.thefsforum.co.uk/
services/argent/
Freq: Semi-Annual
Circ: 1500 Not Audited
MAGAZINE
Banking, Marketing

army-technology.com   987718
Editorial: John Carpenter House, John
Carpenter Street, London EC4Y 0AN
Tel: 44 02079 366400
Email: onlineeditorial@kable.co.uk
Web site: www.army-technology.com
Freq: Daily
Circ: 127370 Cision Digital Reach
Profile: Website covering army technology.
"Army-technology.com brings you
up-to-date international news and features
on the defence industry, covering military
projects, trends, products, services and
more in the army sector."
MAGAZINE (ONLINE)
Defense & National Security

**Arrhythmia &
Electrophysiology Review**
                    997355
Editorial: 7/8 Woodlands Farm, Cookham
Dean, Cookham SL6 9PN
Email: managingeditor@radcliffecardiology.
com

Web site: www.radcliffecardiology.com/
journals/arrhythmia-electrophysiology-review
Freq: Quarterly
Circ: 10000 Not Audited
MAGAZINE
Cardiology

The Art of Design   984860
Editorial: St. Augustine's Business Centre,
125 Canterbury Road, Westgate-on-Sea,
Margate CT8 8NL **Tel:** 44 01843 830249
Email: rachel@artofdesignmagazine.com
Web site: www.theartofdesignmagazine.
com
Freq: Bi-Monthly
Circ: 15000 Not Audited
Editor: Rebecca Keating
Profile: Printed and interactive digital
magazine featuring the UK's leading
designers and manufactures within the
industry and looking at the latest news,
features and case studies for the whole
interior design industry.
Ad Rate: Full Page Colour £2250.00
MAGAZINE
Interior Design

Artemis.bm   996385
Email: press_submissions@artemis.bm
Web site: www.artemis.bm
Freq: Daily
Circ: 43567 Cision Digital Reach
MAGAZINE (ONLINE)
Insurance

Arthritis Research & Therapy
                    995912
Editorial: BioMed Central Floor 6, 236
Gray's Inn Road, London WC1X 8HL
Tel: 44 02031 922000
Email: editorial@arthritis-research.com
Web site: https://arthritis-research.
biomedcentral.com/
Freq: Bi-Monthly
Circ: 732148 Cision Digital Reach
MAGAZINE (ONLINE)
Rheumatology

Asia Oil & Gas   996695
Editorial: Ogilvie Publishing Ltd, 56
Aylesford Mews, Sunderland SR2 9HY
Tel: 44 01915 678497
Email: asia@ogilviepub.com
Web site: www.ogilviepub.com
Freq: Bi-Weekly Not Audited
Editor: Steve Hamlen
MAGAZINE
Oil

Asia Outlook   987433
Editorial: Outlook Publishing, 2nd Floor,
Woburn House, 84 St Benedicts Street,
Norwich NR2 4AB **Tel:** 44 01603 959655
Web site: www.asiaoutlookmag.com
Freq: Bi-Monthly
Circ: 190000 Not Audited
MAGAZINE
Business

Asia Pacific Baker & Biscuit
                    983435
Editorial: Chart House, 10 Western Road,
Borough Green, Sevenoaks, Tunbridge Wells
TN15 BAG **Tel:** 44 01883 734582
Email: editorial@mediatrade.ro
Web site: www.worldbakers.com/
Freq: Quarterly
Circ: 8156 Not Audited
Editor: Catalina Mihu
Profile: Magazine concerned with market
information, trends, technical and scientific
information within the Asia-Pacific bakery
industry. Aimed at producers of bread,
cakes, morning goods and other related
products across the Asia-Pacific rim.
Ad Rate: Full Page Colour £3700.00
MAGAZINE
Food

Asia Pacific Fire   986034
Editorial: The Abbey Manor Business
Centre, Preston Road, Yeovil, Yeovil BA20
2EN **Tel:** 44 01935 426428

Email: info@mdmpublishing.com
Web site: www.apfmag.mdmpublishing.com/
Freq: Quarterly
Circ: 7100 Not Audited
Editor: Neil Bibby
MAGAZINE
Security & Security Systems

Asia Research News 996488
Editorial: Lakin Rose Vision Park, Pioneer House, Cambridge CB24 9NL
Email: info@researchsea.com
Web site: www.researchsea.com
Circ: 10000 Not Audited
MAGAZINE

Asian Airlines and Airports (Singapore) 1060576
Web site: http://www.asianairlines-airports.com
Circ: 2865 Cision Digital Reach
MAGAZINE (ONLINE)
Aviation

Asian Restaurateur 1053811
Editorial: 6 Bute Crescent, Cardiff Bay, Cardiff Bay, Cardiff CF10 5AN
Tel: 44 02920 496725
Email: contact@asianrestaurateur.co.uk
Web site: www.asianrestaurateur.co.uk
Freq: Semi-Annual
Circ: 25000 Not Audited
MAGAZINE
Food

Asian Trader 980057
Editorial: Garavi Gujarat House, 1 Silex Street, London SE1 0DW
Tel: 44 02079 281234
Email: trader@gujarat.co.uk
Web site: www.asiantrader.biz
Freq: Bi-Weekly
Circ: 40275 Not Audited
Profile: Magazine covering the Asian community of retailers, convenience stores, grocers, newsagents and off-licenses. It provides information on issues of trading standards, regulations and opportunities and gives comprehensive coverage of the news and updates from the entire retail sector in the UK. Asian Trader features the latest in wholesale & retail, informative advertorials, market surveys, enlightening reports as well as new product launches. First published in 1985. Aimed at off-licences, grocers and newsagents.
Ad Rate: Full Page Colour £3300.00
MAGAZINE
Retail Management

Asia-Pacific Airports 999830
Editorial: 91 - 93 Windmill Road, Sunbury-on-Thames, London TW16 7EF
Tel: 44 02087 072743
Web site: www.aci-apa.com
Freq: Quarterly
Circ: 10000 Not Audited
MAGAZINE
News & Current Affairs

The Assessor 984465
Tel: 44 01296 642895
Email: editor@plenham.co.uk
Web site: www.iaea-online.org
Freq: Bi-Monthly
Circ: 1500 Not Audited
Editor: Ruth Draper
MAGAZINE
Engineering

Asset Finance International 990546
Editorial: 39 Manor Way, London SE3 9XG
Web site: www.assetfinanceinternational.com
Freq: Daily
Circ: 18640 Cision Digital Reach
Editor: Brian Rogerson
MAGAZINE (ONLINE)
Lending

Asset Servicing Times 985840
Editorial: 16 Bromley Road, Beckenham, London BR3 5JE
Web site: www.assetservicingtimes.com
Freq: Bi-Weekly
Circ: 15406 Cision Digital Reach
Editor: Mark Dugdale
Profile: Newsletter that covers the global asset servicing markets. It tracks US and international companies, providing insights into asset servicing operations around the world. It keeps keep senior executives abreast of the latest news in areas such as regulation, trends, data, technology, conferences and appointments.
MAGAZINE (ONLINE)
Fund Management

Assetman Insight Briefing 995478
Tel: 44 02073 623000
Email: pressreleases@assetman.net
Web site: www.assetman.net
Freq: Quarterly
Circ: 38000 Not Audited
MAGAZINE
Investment Banking

Assetman.net 988090
Tel: 44 02073 623000
Email: pressreleases@assetman.net
Web site: www.assetman.net
Freq: Daily
Circ: 4600 Cision Digital Reach
MAGAZINE (ONLINE)
Investment Banking

Assistive Technologies 983820
Editorial: 47 Church Street, Barnsley, Barnsley S70 2AS **Tel:** 44 01226 734639
Web site: www.assistivetechnologies.co.uk
Freq: Bi-Monthly
Circ: 9000 Not Audited
Profile: Assistive Technologies is a reference for healthcare professionals, experts and association businesses who have interests in assistive technologies, mobility improvement and disability sports. Aimed at workers in the health and medical industry and engineers in rehabilitation and mobility, along with mobility end users.
Ad Rate: Full Page Colour £1300.00
MAGAZINE
Health Administration, Medical Technology

Association Meetings International 983891
Editorial: Fairway House, Portland Road, East Grinstead, East Grinstead RH19 4ET
Tel: 44 01342 306700
Email: cat@cat-publications.com
Web site: www.meetpie.com
Freq: Bi-Monthly
Circ: 10082 Not Audited
Editor: James Lancaster
Profile: Magazine for those involved in planning and organising conferences and meetings for members of associations around the world. Aimed at organisers and association executives responsible for the planning and organisation of association conventions, congresses and meetings, both national and international.
Ad Rate: Full Page Colour £3195.00
MAGAZINE
Marketing

ATC Global Insight 999550
Editorial: Ludgate House, 245 Blackfriars Road, London SE1 9UY
Tel: 44 02079 215000
Web site: http://www.atcglobalhub.com
Freq: Daily
Circ: 5820 Cision Digital Reach
MAGAZINE (ONLINE)
Aviation

Atom Content Marketing 996705
Editorial: City Point, Temple Gate, Bristol BS1 6PL **Tel:** 44 01173 736160
Email: info@atomcontentmarketing.co.uk
Web site: http://atomcontentmarketing.co.uk/

Freq: Daily
Circ: 9459 Cision Digital Reach
MAGAZINE (ONLINE)
Business, Corporate Responsibility

Attendance Matters Magazine 998347
Editorial: Forum Business Media Ltd, 3rd Floor Regal House, 70 London Road, Twickenham TW1 3QS
Tel: 44 02089 418589
Web site: www.attendancemattersmagonline.co.uk
Freq: Quarterly Not Audited
MAGAZINE
Schools & Institutions

Audit & Risk 980956
Editorial: Unit G4, Harbour Yard, Chelsea Harbour, London SW10 0XD
Tel: 44 02070 457500
Email: auditandrisk@caspianmedia.com
Web site: www.auditandrisk.org.uk
Freq: Bi-Monthly
Circ: 8000 Not Audited
Editor: Ruth Prickett
MAGAZINE
Accounting

Auditoria 983360
Editorial: Abinger House, Church Street, Dorking, Dorking RH4 1DF
Tel: 44 01306 743744
Email: info@ukipme.com
Web site: www.ukipme.com/mag_auditoria.htm
Freq: Annual
Circ: 8000 Not Audited
Editor: Matt Ross
Profile: Magazine covering entertainment venue design, technology and operations. Includes views, surveys, interviews and market studies as well as security, ticketing, seating and lighting. Aimed at owners and operators of convention centres, concert halls, cinemas, arenas, concert halls and performing arts facilities.
Ad Rate: Full Page Colour £3950.00
MAGAZINE
Architecture & Design, Building & Construction

AuntMinnieEurope.com 986655
Editorial: 4 Upper Aston Hall Lane, Hawarden, Shotton CH5 3EN
Tel: 44 01244 538583
Email: editorial@auntminnieeurope.com
Web site: www.auntminnieeurope.com
Freq: Daily
Circ: 48873 Cision Digital Reach
Profile: Website covering radiology. The AuntMinnieEurope website shares the latest news and information about radiology imaging.
MAGAZINE (ONLINE)
Diagnostic Imaging, Health Administration

autism 995866
Editorial: Autism Research Group, Department of Psychology, City University, Northampton Square, London EC1V 0HB
Tel: 44 02070 408380
Email: katiemaras.autism@gmail.com
Web site: http://aut.sagepub.com/
Freq: Bi-Monthly Not Audited
MAGAZINE
Neurology

Automated Trader 983633
Editorial: Floor 28, 30 St Mary Axe, London EC3A 8EP **Tel:** 44 02073 376012
Email: press.releases@trader.news
Web site: www.automatedtrader.net
Freq: Quarterly
Circ: 20000 Not Audited
Profile: Automated Trader provides coverage of automated and algorithmic trading from both a technological and financial aspects. Published quarterly in January, April, July and October.
MAGAZINE
Computers, Financial Markets

Automation 981219
Editorial: 15a London Road, Maidstone, Maidstone ME16 8LY **Tel:** 44 01622 687031
Web site: www.connectingindustry.com/automation
Freq: Monthly
Circ: 11254 Not Audited
Profile: Magazine covering all aspects of automation in production and engineering. Aimed at manufacturing end users and machine designers.Alternative Title: Automation Previous title: Automation
Ad Rate: Full Page Colour £2200.00
MAGAZINE
Engineering, Manufacturing

Automation Update 997287
Editorial: The Mill, Spratling, St Manston, Manston CT12 5AN
Web site: http://automation-update.co.uk/
Freq: Monthly
Circ: 23000 Not Audited
Editor: Jenna Burridge
MAGAZINE
Engineering

Automotive Manufacturer 985587
Editorial: Cavendish Group Ltd, 5th Floor, Roman Wall House, 1-2 Crutched Friars, London EC3N 2NB **Tel:** 44 02037 944581
Email: editor@cavendishgroup.co.uk
Web site: www.automotivemanufacturer.net
Freq: Quarterly
Circ: 10000 Not Audited
Editor: Mark Bursa
Profile: Magazine covering information on European car manufacturing technologies. Aimed at chief engineers, manufacturing directors and car designers.Distributed in China only.
Ad Rate: Full Page Colour £5650.00
MAGAZINE
Manufacturing

Automotive Supply Chain 987414
Editorial: 286D Chase Road, London N14 6HF **Tel:** 44 01276 534640
Email: info@automotivesupplychain.org
Web site: www.automotivesupplychain.org
Freq: Quarterly
Circ: 10000 Not Audited
Editor: Sam Ogle
MAGAZINE
Supply Chain Management (SCM)

Autonomic Neuroscience: Basic and Clinical 999296
Editorial: The Boulevard, Langford Lane, Kidlington, Oxford OX5 1GB
Tel: 44 01865 843000
Email: autneu@elsevier.com
Web site: http://www.elsevier.com/wps/find/journaldescription.cws_home/506089/description#description
Freq: Monthly Not Audited
MAGAZINE
Neurology

AvBuyer 988454
Editorial: Trident Court, 1 Oak Croft Road, Chessington, London KT9 1BD
Tel: 44 02082 554000
Email: editorial@avbuyer.com
Web site: www.avbuyer.com
Freq: Monthly
Circ: 32000 Not Audited
Profile: Magazine covering articles and features on business configured aircraft and other material related to all aspects of avionics, engines, refurbishment, modifications and maintenance of business aircraft.
Ad Rate: Full Page Mono £2082.50
Ad Rate: Full Page Colour £2450.00
MAGAZINE
Aviation

The Aviation Historian 987103
Editorial: PO Box 962, Horsham RH12 9PP
Tel: 44 07572 237737
Web site: http://theaviationhistorian.com
Freq: Quarterly Not Audited

Business Magazines

Editor: Nick Stroud
Profile: Publication that features news and stories from aviation history.
MAGAZINE
Aviation

Aviation News 979938
Editorial: PO BOX 100, Stamford PE9 1XQ
Tel: 44 01780 755131
Email: dino.carrara@keypublishing.com
Web site: www.aviation-news.co.uk
Freq: Monthly
Circ: 20000 Not Audited
Editor: Dino Carrara
Profile: Magazine covering all aspects of the aircraft industry. Includes in-depth reports on airlines, staff and airports. Provides information on detailing airport movements, orders, leases and registrations. Read by RAF servicemen, aviators, enthusiasts and industry.
MAGAZINE
Aviation

Aviation Security International 984170
Editorial: 9 Marsh Brows, Formby, Liverpool L37 3PD **Tel:** 44 01704 621057
Email: info@asi-mag.com
Web site: www.asi-mag.com
Freq: Bi-Monthly
Circ: 8500 Not Audited
Profile: Magazine covering news, features and products on the security of the world's airlines and airports. Read by airline security managers, cabin crew trainers and director generals of civil aviation authorities.
Ad Rate: Full Page Colour £3495.00
MAGAZINE
Aviation, Defense & National Security

Aviation Strategy 984172
Editorial: Suite 102, Davina House, 137 Goswell Road, London EC1V 7ET
Tel: 44 07770 845979
Email: info@aviationstrategy.aero
Web site: http://www.aviationstrategy.aero/
Freq: Monthly
Editor: Keith McMullan
Profile: Journal covering detailed analysis and briefings on contemporary aviation issues, companies and markets. Also includes reports on aviation developments. Read by aviation executives, financiers and aerospace manufacturers.
MAGAZINE
Aviation

Aviation World 983664
Editorial: The Haven, Blacklands Lane, Sudbourne, Woodbridge IP12 2AX
Tel: 44 01394 450767
Web site: http://www.air-britain.com/avworld.html
Freq: Quarterly
Circ: 4500 Not Audited
Editor: Rod Simpson
Profile: Magazine covering contemporary and historical aviation subjects. Aimed at aircraft historians and spotters.Previous title: Air-Britain Aviation World
MAGAZINE
Aviation

Awards & Imaging 999207
Editorial: Marash House, 2-5 Brook Street, Tring, Tring HP23 5ED **Tel:** 44 01442 826826
Email: kyliegould@trophex.com
Web site: http://www.trophex.com/ten-magazine
Freq: Monthly
Profile: Specialist magazine for manufacturers and retailers of trophies, awards, engraving and personalisation products. The magazine provides regular news, information and articles on trophies and trophy components, awards, engraving and etching, sublimation, promotional items, signs, garments and allied products and services. The magazine was originally published under the title Trophy & Engraving News. Aimed at trophy retailers and people involved in the awards and engraving industry.
Ad Rate: Full Page Mono £756.00

Ad Rate: Full Page Colour £1129.00
MAGAZINE
Publishing

AWE International 984685
Editorial: 1 Oxford Court, The Granby, Weymouth DT4 9GH **Tel:** 44 01305 785199
Email: info@aweimagazine.com
Web site: www.aweimagazine.com
Freq: Quarterly
Circ: 6197 Not Audited
Editor: Kimberley de Selincourt
Profile: Magazine focusing on environmental monitoring and analysis and process emissions control including waste management. Topics covered include regulations, news, law and product reviews. Please send all press releases and trade news for the attention of advertising sales executive Sarah Thomas.
Ad Rate: Full Page Colour £2700.00
MAGAZINE
Environment

AZoMaterials 997374
Editorial: AZoNetwork UK Ltd., Studio F7, Battersea Studios, 80 Silverthorne Road, London SW8 3HE **Tel:** 44 02036 373970
Email: editorial@azom.com
Web site: www.azom.com
Freq: Daily
Circ: 192652 Cision Digital Reach
Editor: Stuart Milne
MAGAZINE (ONLINE)
Engineering

B&C Distributor 996589
Editorial: 71 Gloucester Place, London W1U 8JW **Tel:** 44 02073 161822
Web site: http://www. bridgingandcommercialdistributor.co.uk/
Freq: Daily
Circ: 1140 Cision Digital Reach
Editor: Beth Fisher
MAGAZINE (ONLINE)
Banking, Lending

B2B Marketing 983150
Editorial: Clover House, 147-149 Farringdon Road, London EC1R 3HN
Tel: 44 02074 381370
Email: editorial@b2bmarketing.net
Web site: www.b2bmarketing.net
Freq: Quarterly
Circ: 6000 Not Audited
Profile: Magazine covering all aspects of marketing to a business audience, with an emphasis on practical hands-on content aimed at helping practitioners improve their effectiveness. Aimed at senior marketing professionals and those working in the marketing services sector.
Ad Rate: Full Page Colour £3000.00
MAGAZINE
Marketing

B4 Magazine 984384
Editorial: PO Box 388, Kidlington, Oxford OX5 9EH **Tel:** 44 01865 742211
Email: editorial@b4-business.com
Web site: www.b4-business.com
Freq: Quarterly
Circ: 9000 Not Audited
Editor: Lorna Dodson
Profile: Online magazine covering Oxfords business community and showcasing what they do.
MAGAZINE
Business

BAGMA Bulletin 987800
Editorial: Middleton House, 2 Main Road, Middleton Cheney, Oxford OX17 2CN
Tel: 44 01295 713344
Email: info@birapublishing.co.uk
Web site: www.bagma.com
Freq: Bi-Monthly
Circ: 3000 Not Audited
Profile: Official journal of the British Agriculture and Garden Machinery Association containing news and features on all aspects of agricultural, garden and forestry machinery. Read by those involved in agriculture, gardening and forestry.

Ad Rate: Full Page Colour £1000.00
MAGAZINE
Commercial Real Estate

The Baltic Briefing 998334
Editorial: 38 St. Mary Axe, London EC3A 8BH **Tel:** 44 02072 839300
Email: editor@balticexchange.net
Web site: www.thebalticbriefing.com
Freq: Daily
Circ: 14080 Cision Digital Reach
Editor: Carly Fields
MAGAZINE (ONLINE)
Shipping & Warehousing

The Banker 979902
Editorial: Number One, Southwark Bridge, London SE1 9HL **Tel:** 44 02078 733000
Web site: www.thebanker.com
Freq: Monthly
Circ: 28430 Not Audited
Profile: Journal featuring articles on international banking, finance, economics, banking technology and capital markets. It combines in-depth regional and country coverage with reports on capital markets and structured finance, risk management, working capital management and securities services, environmental finance, trade and project finance, trading, technology and management and governance issues. First published in 1926. Aimed at senior bankers, corporate treasurers and financial directors of companies.
Ad Rate: Full Page Mono £9950.00
Ad Rate: Full Page Colour £13450.00
MAGAZINE
Banking

Banking Business Review 985383
Editorial: Banking Business Review, Progressive Trade Media Ltd., 40-42 Hatton Garden, London EC1N 8EB
Tel: 44 02079 366898
Email: news@industryreview.com
Web site: www.banking-business-review.com
Freq: Daily
Circ: 14700 Cision Digital Reach
MAGAZINE (ONLINE)
Banking

Banking Technology 979893
Editorial: Maple House, 149 Tottenham Court Road, London W1T 7AD
Tel: 44 02075 519010
Email: news@bankingtech.com
Web site: www.bankingtech.com
Freq: Monthly
Circ: 22000 Not Audited
Editor: Tanya Andreasyan
Profile: Magazine covering financial technology, systems, services and the latest developments. Includes coverage of transaction, investment and retail banking. First published in 1984. Aimed at senior executives in management in the financial services industry. Also marketing and data processing divisions of banks, savings banks and brokers.
Ad Rate: Full Page Colour £5577.00
MAGAZINE
Banking, Computers, Security & Security Systems

The Barrister 986305
Editorial: 21a-23a Dudden Hill Lane, London NW10 2ET **Tel:** 44 02035 070249
Email: admin@barristermagazine.com
Web site: www.barristermagazine.com
Freq: Quarterly
Circ: 7500 Not Audited
Editor: Nigel Simmonds
Profile: Magazine providing a topical review of legal and political issues. Includes articles on expert witnesses, legal and financial services, information technology, charitable trusts and education. Aimed at practising barristers in chambers.
Ad Rate: Full Page Colour £3950.00
MAGAZINE
Corporate Law, Criminal Law

Bathroom and Kitchen Update 984138
Editorial: 15A London Road, Maidstone, Maidstone ME16 8LY **Tel:** 44 01622 687031
Email: bathroom@datateam.co.uk
Web site: www.bathroomandkitchenupdate.com
Freq: Monthly
Circ: 13579 Not Audited
MAGAZINE
Interior Design

Bathroom Review 987131
Editorial: Bolney Place, Cowfold Road, Haywards Heath RH17 5QT
Tel: 44 01444 882732
Email: editorial@bathroom-review.co.uk
Web site: www.bathroom-review.co.uk
Freq: Daily
Circ: 9763 Cision Digital Reach
Editor: Diane Larner
MAGAZINE (ONLINE)
Interior Design

BD (Building Design) 980063
Editorial: 240 Blackfriars Road, London SE1 8BF **Tel:** 44 02079 215000
Email: bdonline@servicehelpline.co.uk
Web site: www.bdonline.co.uk
Freq: Daily
Circ: 160948 Cision Digital Reach
MAGAZINE (ONLINE)
Architecture & Design

Bdaily 985404
Editorial: Spaceworks, Benton Park Road, Wallsend, Newcastle upon Tyne NE7 7LX
Tel: 44 01912 236794
Email: editor@bdaily.co.uk
Web site: www.bdaily.co.uk
Freq: Daily
Circ: 168363 Cision Digital Reach
Editor: Jamie Hardesty
Profile: Website covering business. The BDaily website is an electronic publication covering business news, enterprise, culture, law, job vacancies, events and technology across the North East.
MAGAZINE (ONLINE)
Business, Corporate Responsibility

BDJ (British Dental Journal) 981179
Editorial: BDJ Editorial Office, The Macmillan Building, 4 Crinan Street, London N1 9XW **Tel:** 44 02078 434729
Email: bdj@bda.org
Web site: www.bdj.co.uk
Freq: Bi-Weekly
Circ: 18456 Not Audited
Editor: Kate Quinlan
MAGAZINE
Dentistry

BDJ In Practice 983257
Editorial: 64 Wimpole Street, London W1G 8YS **Tel:** 44 02079 350875
Email: bdjinpractice@bda.org
Web site: https://www.bda.org/bdjinpractice
Freq: Monthly
Circ: 18050 Not Audited
MAGAZINE
Dentistry

BDJ Student 998755
Editorial: The Macmillan Building, 4–6 Crinan Street, London N1 9XW
Tel: 44 02078 434724
Email: bdjstudent@bda.org
Web site: bdjstudent.co.uk
Freq: 3 Times/Year
Circ: 5500 Not Audited
MAGAZINE
Dentistry

BDJ Team 997385
Editorial: 4-6 Crinan Street, London N1 9XW
Tel: 44 02078 433680
Email: bdjteam@bda.org
Web site: www.nature.com/bdjteam
Freq: Monthly Not Audited

Editor: Kate Quinlan
MAGAZINE
Dentistry

The Beak Street Bugle 996316
Editorial: 47 Beak St, London W1F 9SE
Tel: 44 02074 342651
Email: editorial@beakstreetbugle.com
Web site: beakstreetbugle.com
Freq: Daily
Circ: 13182 Cision Digital Reach
MAGAZINE (ONLINE)
Advertising Industry

Bed & Breakfast News 986297
Editorial: Belfry House, Batts Field, Bruton
BA10 0DX **Tel:** 44 01749 814908
Email: info@bandbassociation.org
Web site: http://www.bandbassociation.org/
BandBnews.htm
Freq: Bi-Monthly
Circ: 3100 Not Audited
Editor: David Weston
Profile: Magazine containing industry
specific tourist industry news and products,
small business information and company
profiles. Aimed at bed and breakfast
proprietors, guest house and small hotels
with up to twelve bedrooms.
Ad Rate: Full Page Colour £600.00
MAGAZINE
Hotels/Motels

bellwether: Food Trends 996360
Editorial: 40 Bloomsbury Way, Lower
Ground Floor, London WC1A 2SE
Tel: 44 02034 755885
Email: enquiries@bellwetherft.com
Web site: www.bellwetherft.com
Freq: Annual Not Audited
MAGAZINE
Food

Benchmark 981035
Editorial: 46 Campbell Street, Hamilton,
Hamilton ML3 6AS **Tel:** 44 01355 225688
Web site: http://www.nafems.org/
publications/benchmark
Freq: Quarterly
Circ: 12000 Not Audited
Editor: David Quinn
Profile: Magazine covering independent
performance related testing of electronic
security systems.
Ad Rate: Full Page Colour £2100.00
MAGAZINE
Engineering

BENCHMARK 986344
Editorial: 3 High Street, Chislehurst, London
BR7 5AB **Tel:** 44 0282 958303
Web site: www.benchmarkmagazine.com
Freq: Monthly
Circ: 9500 Not Audited
Editor: Pete Conway
Profile: Magazine covering independent
performance related testing of electronic
security systems.
Ad Rate: Full Page Colour £2100.00
MAGAZINE
Security & Security Systems

Benefit 984599
Editorial: IRRV, 5th Floor, Northumberland
House, 303-306 High Holborn, London
WC1V 7JZ **Tel:** 44 02078 313505
Email: publications@irrv.org.uk
Web site: www.irrv.org.uk
Freq: Bi-Monthly
Circ: 1500 Not Audited
MAGAZINE
Business, Corporate Responsibility

Best Execution 984768
Editorial: 117 Waterloo Road, London SE1
8UL **Tel:** 44 02079 286796
Email: editorial@bestexecution.net
Web site: www.bestexecution.net
Freq: Quarterly
Circ: 7000 Not Audited
MAGAZINE
Financial Markets

Best Invest 980749
Editorial: 6 Chesterfield Gardens, Mayfair,
London W1J 5BQ **Tel:** 44 02031 316167
Email: best@bestinvest.co.uk
Web site: www.bestinvest.co.uk
Freq: Daily
Circ: 74306 Cision Digital Reach
MAGAZINE (ONLINE)
Banking

Best Practice & Research: Clinical Rheumatology 994700
Editorial: The Boulevard, Langford Lane,
Kidlington OX5 1GB **Tel:** 44 01865 843434
Email: berh@elsevier.com
Web site: http://www.elsevier.com/wps/
find/journaldescription.cws_home/623005/
description#descriptionhttp://ww
Freq: Bi-Monthly Not Audited
MAGAZINE
Rheumatology

Best Practice UK 985739
Editorial: Second Floor, Jago House,
Warwick Road, Solihull B91 3AB
Tel: 44 01217 112761
Email: bestpracticeuk@live.com
Web site: www.bestpracticeuk.co.uk
Freq: Monthly
Circ: 5000 Not Audited
MAGAZINE
Engineering, Health & Safety,
Manufacturing

BestAdvice 983671
Editorial: 19 Holydale Road, London SE15
2TE **Tel:** 44 02076 395120
Email: newsdesk@bestadvice.co.uk
Web site: http://www.bestadvice.co.uk/
Freq: Daily
Circ: 16911 Cision Digital Reach
Editor: Kevin Rose
MAGAZINE (ONLINE)
Finance, Legal Affairs

Better Wholesaling 986523
Editorial: 11 Angel Gate, City Road, London
EC1V 2SD **Tel:** 44 02076 890600
Email: betterwholesaling@newtrade.co.uk
Web site: www.betterwholesaling.com
Freq: Monthly
Circ: 4037 Not Audited
Editor: Martyn Fisher; **Editor:** Chris Gamm
Profile: Publication that gives advice to
grocery and foodservice wholesalers. It aims
to help and support its customers better by
promoting best practice examples from
leading wholesalers and suppliers across the
foodservice, cash & carry and delivered
sectors.
MAGAZINE
Food

Better Working World 1069278
Web site: www.betterworkingworld.ey.com/
Freq: Daily
Circ: 187902 Cision Digital Reach
MAGAZINE (ONLINE)
Business, Corporate Responsibility, Small
and Medium Business

beyondpositive 996713
Email: talk@beyondpositive.org
Web site: www.beyondpositive.org
Freq: Daily
Circ: 12940 Cision Digital Reach
MAGAZINE (ONLINE)
AIDS/HIV

BGS Newsletter 985189
Editorial: Marjory Warren House, 31 St
John's Square, London EC1M 4DN
Tel: 44 02076 081369
Email: bgs@bgsnet.org.uk
Web site: http://www.bgs.org.uk/index.php/
resources-6/newsletter
Freq: Bi-Monthly Not Audited
MAGAZINE
Geriatrics

BIFAlink 980998
Editorial: Redfern House, Browells Lane,
Feltham, London TW13 7EP
Tel: 44 02088 442266
Email: communications@bifa.org
Web site: http://www.bifa.org/bifalink
Freq: Monthly
Circ: 21000 Not Audited
Editor: Sharon Hammond
Profile: News from the British International
Freight Association. Aimed at BIFA
members.
Ad Rate: Full Page Colour £2195.00
MAGAZINE
Shipping & Warehousing, Supply Chain
Management (SCM)

Big Data Innovation 998086
Web site: www.channels.
theinnovationenterprise.com/big-data
Freq: Monthly Not Audited
MAGAZINE
Data Management

The Bill of Middlesex 987599
Editorial: 3tc House, 16 Crosby North Road,
Crosby, Liverpool L22 0NY
Tel: 44 01512 364141
Email: admin@benhampublishing.com
Web site: www.benhampublishing.com
Freq: Quarterly
Circ: 1700 Not Audited
MAGAZINE
Corporate Law, Government, Legal
Services

The Billboard 984917
Editorial: The Billboard, Goss Chambers,
Goss Street, Chester CH1 2BG
Tel: 44 01244 624022
Email: editor@thebillboard.co.uk
Web site: www.thebillboard.co.uk
Freq: Quarterly
Circ: 8000 Not Audited
Editor: Emma Harris
MAGAZINE
Security & Security Systems

BIM+ 1073939
Tel: 44 02074 905595
Web site: www.bimplus.co.uk
Freq: Daily
Circ: 78053 Cision Digital Reach
MAGAZINE (ONLINE)
Architecture & Design, Building &
Construction

Bio-Based World News 1068251
Tel: 44 02070 450900
Email: editor@biobasedworldnews.com
Web site: www.biobasedworldnews.com
Freq: Daily
Circ: 16232 Cision Digital Reach
MAGAZINE (ONLINE)
Alternative/Renewable Energy,
Biotechnology, Plastics

The Biochemist 981309
Editorial: Third floor, Charles Darwin House,
12 Roger Street, London WC1N 2JU
Tel: 44 02076 852410
Email: biochemist@portlandpress.com
Web site: http://www.biochemist.org/
Freq: Bi-Monthly
Circ: 6700 Not Audited
Profile: Journal of the Biochemical Society
containing interviews, features, application
stories, book reviews, comment, education
and policy. Read by biochemists, molecular
life scientists, students, research directors
and senior personnel in commercial and
academic life-science ventures.
Ad Rate: Full Page Mono £950.00
Ad Rate: Full Page Colour £1200.00
MAGAZINE
Biotechnology, Science

BioEnergy Insight 985903
Editorial: 124 Middleton Road, Morden,
London SM4 6RW **Tel:** 44 02086 874126
Web site: http://bioenergy-news.com/
Freq: Bi-Monthly
Circ: 3000 Not Audited

Editor: Liz Gyekye
Profile: Bioenergy Insight is a bi-monthly
magazine providing in-depth news, analysis
and developments from the biomass, biogas
and biopower sectors.
MAGAZINE
Alternative/Renewable Energy, Carbon
Emissions & Trading, Electricity, Energy,
Nuclear Power, Oil, Water & Sanitation

Biofuels 995711
Editorial: Mortimer House, 37-41 Mortimer
Street, London W1T 3JH
Tel: 44 02070 175544
Email: info@future-science.com
Web site: http://www.tandfonline.com/toc/
tbfu20/current
Freq: Bi-Monthly Not Audited
MAGAZINE
Alternative/Renewable Energy

Biofuels International 984156
Editorial: Marshall House, 124 Middleton
Road, Morden, London SM4 6RW
Tel: 44 02086 874126
Web site: http://www.biofuels-news.com
Freq: Bi-Monthly
Circ: 3000 Not Audited
Editor: Liz Gyekye
Profile: Magazine focusing on biofuels
including biodiesel, bioethanol and biomass.
Contains news and updates, country focus
reports, interviews, technology and details of
exhibitions and conferences. Every issue
includes in-depth analysis and features on
related subjects, including distribution,
handling, storage, equipment and second
generation technology, interviews with
leading biofuels producers, information on
the latest regulations and legislation and a
close examination of the biofuels sector in
particular regions. The magazine is issued bi
monthly.
Ad Rate: Full Page Colour £3600.00
MAGAZINE
Alternative/Renewable Energy

The Biologist 985690
Editorial: Capital House, 25 Chapel Street,
London NW1 5DH **Tel:** 44 02037 717200
Email: info@rsb.org.uk
Web site: https://thebiologist.rsb.org.uk/
biologist
Freq: Bi-Monthly Not Audited
Profile: Journal covering the diversity within
biological research today including
authoritative review articles on science
policy and new developments or
controversial issues. Aimed at professional
biologists, educators and students at all
levels, as well as the interested amateur.
Ad Rate: Full Page Mono £700.00
Ad Rate: Full Page Colour £850.00
MAGAZINE
Biotechnology, Science

Biomarkers in Medicine 998954
Editorial: Unitec House, 2 Albert Place,
London N3 1QB **Tel:** 44 02083 716080
Email: info@futuremedicine.com
Web site: www.futuremedicine.com/loi/
bmm
Freq: Bi-Monthly Not Audited
MAGAZINE
Biotechnology

The Biomedical Scientist 983213
Editorial: Institute of Biomedical Science, 12
Coldbath Square, London EC1R 5HL
Tel: 44 02077 130214
Email: biomedicalscientist@stepex.com
Web site: https://www.ibms.org/resources/
journals/the-biomedical-scientist/
Freq: Monthly
Circ: 20000 Not Audited
Editor: Brian Nation
Profile: Journal containing news on scientific
and management subjects, including
symposia reports. Published on behalf of the
Institute of Biomedical Science. Read by
biomedical scientists and clinical scientists.
Ad Rate: Full Page Colour £1545.00
MAGAZINE
Biotechnology, Science

Business Magazines

Section 4 UK Periodicals Business

Biometric Institute
997708

Editorial: 4th Floor, Imperial House, 15 Kingsway, London WC2B 6UN
Tel: 44 02075 814827
Email: manager@biometricsinstitute.org
Web site: www.biometricsinstitute.org
Freq: Daily
Circ: 12428 Cision Digital Reach
MAGAZINE (ONLINE)
Medical Technology

Biometric Technology Today
985334

Editorial: The Boulevard, Langford Lane, Kidlington OX5 1GB **Tel:** 44 01865 843239
Email: tracey.caldwell@btconnect.com
Web site: http://www.journals.elsevier.com/biometric-technology-today/
Freq: Monthly Not Audited
Profile: Journal covering automatic personal identification and verification technologies. Aimed at governments, retailers and those involved in the transport industry and financial sector. Also healthcare providers, computer manufacturers and systems integrators.
MAGAZINE
Science

BioNews
986939

Editorial: 140 Grays Inn Road, London WC1X 8AX **Tel:** 44 02072 787870
Email: admin@progress.org.uk
Web site: www.bionews.org.uk
Freq: Weekly
Circ: 43361 Cision Digital Reach
MAGAZINE (ONLINE)
Biotechnology, Obstetrics & Gynecology (OB/GYN), Science

BioPharma Asia
995315

Editorial: 6 Mitre Passage, Greenwich Peninsula, London SE10 0ER
Tel: 44 02034 407113
Email: admin@biopharma-asia.com
Web site: www.biopharma-asia.com
Freq: Bi-Monthly Not Audited
MAGAZINE
Pharmaceuticals

BioPharma Dealmakers
1068720

Tel: 44 02078 334000
Web site: biopharmadealmakers.nature.com
Freq: Quarterly
Editor: Raveena Bhambra
MAGAZINE
Science

BioPortfolio
984854

Editorial: Wessex Barn, Dorchester Road, Frampton, Boston DT2 9NB
Tel: 44 08435 574640
Email: prioritycontact2015@bioportfolio.com
Web site: www.bioportfolio.com
Freq: Daily
Circ: 194007 Cision Digital Reach
Profile: Website covering biotechnology. BioPortfolio provides the latest pharmaceutical news. "BioPortfolio is a news, information and knowledge resource covering the global life science industries impacted on by biotechnology".
MAGAZINE (ONLINE)
Biotechnology, Health Administration, Medical Technology, Pharmaceuticals

Bio-science Law Review
980869

Editorial: Office G18, Spinners Court, 55 West End, Witney OX28 1NH
Tel: 44 01993 706183
Email: ltp@lawtext.com
Web site: www.lawtext.com/lawtextweb/default.jsp?PageID=2
Freq: Bi-Monthly Not Audited
MAGAZINE
Biotechnology, Corporate Law, Intellectual Property

BioSocieties
996225

Editorial: 4 Crinan Street, London N1 9XW
Tel: 44 02078 334000
Email: biosoc@palgrave.com

Web site: http://www.palgrave-journals.com/biosoc
Freq: Quarterly Not Audited
Editor: Nikolas Rose; **Editor:** Ilina Singh;
Editor: Catherine Waldby
MAGAZINE
Science

Birmingham Business Post
986573

Editorial: Unit 9 Three Springs Unit, Three springs Trading Estate, Vincent Road, Worcester WR5 1BW **Tel:** 44 08000 807809
Email: hello@bbpmedia.co.uk
Web site: www.bbpmedia.co.uk/regions/midlands.html
Freq: Monthly
Circ: 31000 Not Audited
Editor: Diana White
Profile: Magazine covering business, start-ups and lifestyle.
MAGAZINE
Business

Birmingham Law Society Bulletin
980930

Editorial: Suite 101, Cheltenham House, 14-16 Temple Street, Birmingham B2 5BG
Tel: 44 01212 278704
Email: info@birminghamlawsociety.co.uk
Web site: www.birminghamlawsociety.co.uk
Freq: Monthly Not Audited
Editor: Judy Bonegal
Profile: Journal of the Birmingham Law Society containing news and features relating to the legal profession and the law.
Ad Rate: Full Page Colour £1339.00
MAGAZINE
Government

BitcoiNews
998342

Editorial: Cadogan House, Church Street, Reading RG1 2SB **Tel:** 44 07500 337002
Email: guydavies@bitcoinews.co.uk
Web site: http://bitcoinews.co.uk
Freq: Daily
Circ: 936 Cision Digital Reach
Editor: Guy Davies
MAGAZINE (ONLINE)
Foreign Exchange Market (FOREX)

BizJet Advisor
996251

Tel: 44 01778 440002
Web site: www.bizjetadvisor.com
Freq: Quarterly Not Audited
MAGAZINE
Aviation

BJA (British Journal of Anaesthesia)
985376

Editorial: Oxford University Press, Great Clarendon Street, Oxford OX2 6DP
Tel: 44 01865 353907
Email: bja@sheffield.ac.uk
Web site: bja.oxfordjournals.org/
Freq: Monthly Not Audited
MAGAZINE
Anesthesiology

BJA Education
995835

Editorial: Oxford University, Great Clarendon Street, Oxford OX2 6DP
Tel: 44 01865 353907
Email: bjaeducation@rcoa.ac.uk
Web site: www.bjaed.oxfordjournals.org
Freq: Bi-Monthly
Circ: 17800 Not Audited
MAGAZINE
Anesthesiology, Pain Management

BJOG: An International Journal of Obstetrics and Gynaecology
998785

Editorial: 27 Sussex Place, Regent's Park, London NW1 4RG **Tel:** 44 01865 778315
Email: bjog@editorialoffice.co.uk
Web site: www.bjog.org
Freq: Monthly Not Audited
MAGAZINE
Obstetrics & Gynecology (OB/GYN)

BJPsych Advances
996574

Editorial: BJPsych Advances, The Royal College of Psychiatrists, Publications and eLearning, 21 Prescot Street, London E1 8BB **Tel:** 44 02072 352351
Email: apt@rcpsych.ac.uk
Web site: http://apt.rcpsych.org
Freq: Bi-Monthly Not Audited
Editor: Patricia Casey
MAGAZINE
Neurology

BJPsych International
997079

Editorial: 21 Prescot Street, London E1 8BB
Tel: 44 02072 352351
Email: ip@rcpsych.ac.uk
Web site: www.rcpsych.ac.uk/publications/journals/ipinfo1.aspx
Freq: Quarterly
Circ: 15300 Not Audited
Editor: David Skuse
MAGAZINE
Neurology

BJU International
995861

Editorial: 9600 Garsington Road, Oxford OX4 2DQ **Tel:** 44 01865 476515
Email: editorial.office@bjui.info
Web site: www.bjui.org
Freq: Monthly
Circ: 5303 Not Audited
MAGAZINE
Urology

BL Magazine
1053087

Editorial: Floor One, Liberation Station, Esplanade, St Helier, Jersey JE2 3AS
Tel: 44 01534 615886
Email: news@blglobal.co.uk
Web site: www.blglobal.co.uk
Freq: Bi-Monthly
Circ: 12000 Not Audited
MAGAZINE
Banking, Business

Black + White Photography
982787

Editorial: 86 High Street, Lewes, Lewes BN7 1XN **Tel:** 44 01273 477374
Web site: http://www.blackandwhitephotographymag.co.uk/
Freq: Monthly Not Audited
Editor: Elizabeth Roberts
MAGAZINE
Photography

BLCC Construction News
985444

Editorial: Westwood House, Annie Med Lane, Brough HU15 2HG
Tel: 44 02071 274292
Email: construction@blcc.co.uk
Web site: www.blcc.co.uk
Freq: Daily
Circ: 6379 Cision Digital Reach
MAGAZINE (ONLINE)
Building & Construction

Blinds & Shutters
981102

Editorial: Cardinal Point, Park Road, Rickmansworth WD3 1RE
Tel: 44 01923 432705
Web site: www.blindsmagazine.co.uk
Freq: Quarterly
Circ: 5626 Not Audited
Editor: John Hatcher
Profile: Magazine containing news and views on the latest blinds, awnings and shutters and their many applications. Aimed at architects, specifiers, construction companies, facilities managers, designers, retailers, fitters, contractors and manufacturers.A charge may be made for colour separation.
Ad Rate: Full Page Colour £930.00
MAGAZINE
Interior Design

Blood Cancer Journal
996258

Editorial: The Macmillan Building, 4 Crinan Street, London N1 9XW
Tel: 44 02078 434870

Email: bcj@bcjnature.com
Web site: www.nature.com/bcj/index.html
Freq: Daily
Circ: 963 Cision Digital Reach
MAGAZINE (ONLINE)
Hematology, Oncology

Blood Pressure Monitoring
985942

Web site: http://journals.lww.com/bpmonitoring/pages/default.aspx
Freq: Bi-Monthly
Profile: Journal containing material covering all aspects of manual, automated and ambulatory monitoring of blood pressure and its variability including device technology and assessment, blood pressure variability, clinical pharmacology and therapeutics, clinical practice and epidemiology.
Ad Rate: Full Page Mono £765.00
Ad Rate: Full Page Colour £1645.00
MAGAZINE
Cardiology

Bloomberg New Energy Finance
983531

Editorial: City Gate House, 39-45 Finsbury Square, London EC2A 1QP
Tel: 44 02032 164700
Email: scocks@bloomberg.net
Web site: http://about.bnef.com/
Freq: Daily
Circ: 21031 Cision Digital Reach
MAGAZINE (ONLINE)
Alternative/Renewable Energy, Electricity, Nuclear Power, Oil, Water & Sanitation

Bloor Research
998243

Editorial: 2nd Floor, 145-157 St John Street, London EC1V 4PY **Tel:** 44 02070 439750
Email: info@bloor.eu
Web site: http://www.bloorresearch.com/
Freq: Daily
Circ: 13103 Cision Digital Reach
MAGAZINE (ONLINE)
Computers, Data Management, Software

Blue & Green Tomorrow
986610

Editorial: Landmark House, 1 Risenholme Road, Lincoln LN1 1RN
Email: editor@blueandgreentomorrow.com
Web site: www.blueandgreentomorrow.com
Freq: Daily
Circ: 40372 Cision Digital Reach
MAGAZINE (ONLINE)
Alternative/Renewable Energy, Environment

Blueprint
981116

Editorial: 7 Carmelite Street, Blackfriars, London EC4Y 0BS **Tel:** 44 02079 366400
Web site: www.designcurial.com/folksonomy/blueprint
Freq: Bi-Monthly
Circ: 6890 Not Audited
Editor: Johnny Tucker
Profile: Magazine for leading architects and designers. Read by architects, interior designers and those with a strong interest in design.
Ad Rate: Full Page Colour £4000.00
MAGAZINE
Architecture & Design

BlueSky
985602

Editorial: 38 Old Mill, Berkhampstead, Berkhamsted HP4 2NZ
Tel: 44 01442 300020
Email: editor@blueskynews.aero
Web site: www.blueskynews.aero
Freq: Weekly
Circ: 14329 Cision Digital Reach
MAGAZINE (ONLINE)
Aviation

BMC International Health & Human Rights
996536

Editorial: 236 Gray's Inn Road, London WC1X 8HB **Tel:** 44 02031 922000
Email: bmcinthealthhumrights@biomedcentral.com

Web site: http://bmcinthealthhumrights.biomedcentral.com/
Freq: Daily
Circ: 194383 Cision Digital Reach
MAGAZINE (ONLINE)
Health Administration

BMC Psychology
996248
Editorial: 236 Gray's Inn Road, London WC1X 8HB **Tel:** 44 02031 922009
Email: bmcpsychol@biomedcentral.com
Web site: http://bmcpsychology.biomedcentral.com/
Freq: Daily
Circ: 15243 Cision Digital Reach
MAGAZINE (ONLINE)
Neurology

BMI Research
994667
Editorial: 2 Broadgate Circle, London EC2M 2QS **Tel:** 44 02072 480468
Email: onquiry@bmirocoarch.oom
Web site: www.businessmonitor.com
Freq: Weekly Not Audited
Editor: David Snowdon
MAGAZINE
Banking, Business, Economics, Financial Markets, Foreign Exchange Market (FOREX), Government

BMJ Open Diabetes Research & Care
997140
Editorial: Editorial Office, BMA House, Tavistock Square, London WC1H 9JR
Email: info.bmjdrc@bmj.com
Web site: http://drc.bmj.com
Freq: Daily
Circ: 488 Cision Digital Reach
MAGAZINE (ONLINE)
Diabetes

bobsguide
983424
Editorial: One Hammersmith Broadway, Hammersmith, London W6 9LD
Tel: 44 02080 809167
Email: news@bobsguide.com
Web site: www.bobsguide.com
Freq: Daily
Circ: 140515 Cision Digital Reach
MAGAZINE (ONLINE)
Banking, Industry, Insurance

body language
985018
Editorial: 2D, Wimpole Street, London W1G 0EB **Tel:** 44 02075 145101
Email: info@faoo ltd.oom
Web site: www.bodylanguage.net
Freq: Monthly
Circ: 6000 Not Audited
Editor: Helen Unsworth
Profile: Magazine providing independent information on treatments and procedures within the cosmetic surgery sector. Aimed at practitioners.
Ad Rate: Full Page Colour £1995.00
MAGAZINE
Plastic/Reconstructive/Cosmetic Surgery

Bond Radar
998162
Editorial: 1 Bolt Court, 5th Floor, London EC4 3DQ **Tel:** 44 02078 320825
Email: newissues@bondradar.com
Web site: www.bondradar.com
Freq: Daily
Circ: 2815 Cision Digital Reach
MAGAZINE (ONLINE)
Bonds, Corporate Management, Emerging Markets, Government

Bonds & Loans
1068252
Editorial: 7-10 Chandos Street, London W1G 9DQ **Tel:** 44 02070 450920
Web site: www.globalfinancialconferences.com
Freq: Monthly
Circ: 30000 Not Audited
MAGAZINE
Lending

The Bone & Joint Journal
985201
Editorial: 22 Buckingham Street, London WC2N 6ET **Tel:** 44 02077 820010

Email: info@boneandjoint.org.uk
Web site: www.bjj.boneandjoint.org.uk
Freq: Monthly Not Audited
Profile: Official international journal covering all aspects of orthopaedics, sports injury and trauma.
Ad Rate: Full Page Mono £3060.00
Ad Rate: Full Page Colour £5235.00
MAGAZINE
Orthopedics

The Bookseller
979792
Editorial: Westminster Tower, Floor 10, 3 Albert Embankment, London SE1 7SP
Tel: 44 02033 580360
Web site: www.thebookseller.com
Freq: Weekly
Circ: 5620 Not Audited
Editor: Philip Jones
Profile: Magazine covering news and information on the book publishing trade Including opinion, blogs, author profiles and features about the book business. First published in 1858.Aimed at booksellers, librarians and publishers, reviewers, literary agents, authors and the media.
Ad Rate: Full Page Colour £2398.00
MAGAZINE
Books

Bookselling Essentials
984116
Editorial: 6 Bell Yard, London WC2A 2JR
Tel: 44 02074 214640
Email: mail@booksellers.org.uk
Web site: www.booksellers.org.uk
Freq: Quarterly
Circ: 2000 Not Audited
Editor: Meryl Halls
Profile: Official journal of the Booksellers Association. Gives news of the Association's services and activities and includes information about events and general developments in the book trade. Aimed at those within the industry.Alternative Title: Bookselling News Previous title: Bookselling
MAGAZINE
Books

BookTrade.info
982825
Editorial: P O Box 394, Harpenden, Harpenden AL5 1XJ
Email: newsdesk@booktrade.info
Web site: http://www.booktrade.info/
Freq: Daily
Circ: 57954 Cision Digital Reach
Editor: Steven Kelly
MAGAZINE (ONLINE)
Books

Boutique Hotel News
1054208
Editorial: 10-14 Accommodation Road, London NW11 8ED **Tel:** 44 02083 407989
Email: info@boutiquehotelnews.com
Web site: www.boutiquehotelnews.com
Freq: Daily
Circ: 15225 Cision Digital Reach
Editor: George Sell
MAGAZINE (ONLINE)
Hotels/Motels, Travel Industry

Boutique Hotelier
988355
Editorial: ITP Promedia, 16-25 Bastwick Street, London EC1V 3PS
Tel: 44 02031 764237
Web site: www.boutiquehotelier.com
Freq: Monthly
Circ: 3140 Not Audited
Editor: Zoe Monk
Profile: Magazine providing business intelligence for the owners, operators, key management personnel and decision makers in luxury boutique and lifestyle properties located throughout the UK. It contains news, interviews, comment and analysis, debate and examples of best practice and innovation within the boutique and lifestyle hotel industry.
Ad Rate: Full Page Mono £1950.00
MAGAZINE
Hotels/Motels

Bow Wave
999281
Editorial: North Court Farm, Main Road, Shorwell, Newport PO30 3JG
Tel: 44 07887 632503
Email: sam@wavyline.com
Web site: www.wavyline.com
Freq: Weekly
Circ: 2222 Cision Digital Reach
Editor: Sam Ignarski
MAGAZINE (ONLINE)
Shipping & Warehousing

Brain
983546
Editorial: Brain Editorial Office, Ormond House, 27 Boswell Street, London WC1N 3JZ **Tel:** 44 02032 903661
Email: brain@ucl.ac.uk
Web site: www.brain.oxfordjournals.org
Freq: Monthly
Circ: 400 Not Audited
Profile: Journal covering clinical neurology and related disciplines in the basic neurological sciences where relevant to clinical problems. Leading studies in neurological science are balanced with practical clinical articles.
Ad Rate: Full Page Mono £851.00
Ad Rate: Full Page Colour £1418.00
MAGAZINE
Neurology

Brand Quarterly
997906
Email: editorial@brandquarterly.com
Web site: http://www.brandquarterly.com/
Freq: Quarterly
Circ: 51487 Not Audited
MAGAZINE
Branding

Breast Cancer Management
996235
Editorial: Unitec House, 2 Albert Place, London N3 1QB **Tel:** 44 02083 716090
Email: info@futuremedicine.com
Web site: http://www.futuremedicine.com/loi/bmt
Freq: Bi-Monthly Not Audited
MAGAZINE
Oncology

Bridge Design & Engineering
983451
Editorial: 32 Vauxhall Bridge Road, London SW1V 2SS **Tel:** 44 02079 736400
Web site: www.bridgeweb.com
Freq: Quarterly
Circ: 4000 Not Audited
Editor: Helena Russell
Profile: Magazine containing international coverage of the design, construction, maintenance and management of bridges, with technical articles from industry experts and site reports. First Published in 1995. Aimed at designers, builders, architects and specialist manufacturers.
Ad Rate: Full Page Colour £2480.00
MAGAZINE
Architecture & Design, Building & Construction, Engineering

Bridgend & District Property News
982570
Editorial: Basepoint Business Centre, Crab Apple Way, Vale Park, Evesham WR11 1GP **Tel:** 44 01386 764918
Email: info@bridgendpropertynews.co.uk
Web site: www.bridgendpropertynews.co.uk
Freq: Bi-Weekly
Circ: 2881 Cision Digital Reach
Editor: Vernon Pethard
Profile: Newspaper covering local and national residential property including articles of interest and classified adds. Aimed at homebuyers and sellers in Bridgend, Maesteg, Porthcawl and surrounding areas.
MAGAZINE (ONLINE)
Property Management & Maintenance

Bridging & Commercial
987491
Editorial: 71 Gloucester Place, London W1U 8JW

Web site: http://www.bridgingandcommercial.co.uk/
Freq: Daily
Circ: 17955 Cision Digital Reach
Editor: Beth Fisher
Profile: Website covering commercial property. The Bridging & Commercial shares the latest news and information on commercial property and lending.
MAGAZINE (ONLINE)
Banking, Lending

Briefing
995038
Editorial: 20 Mortlake High Street, Mortlake, London SW14 8JN **Tel:** 44 08701 125058
Email: lsn@legalsupportnetwork.co.uk
Web site: www.legalsupportnetwork.co.uk
Freq: Monthly
Circ: 5100 Not Audited
Editor: Richard Brent
MAGAZINE
Legal Services

Bristol Business Post
986563
Editorial: Three Springs House, Three springs Trading Estate, Vincent, Worcester WR5 1BW **Tel:** 44 01905 723430
Email: newsdesk@bbpmedia.co.uk
Web site: www.bristolbusinesspost.co.uk
Freq: Bi-Monthly
Circ: 26000 Not Audited
Editor: Diana White
MAGAZINE
Business, Small and Medium Business

Bristol Property Live
985748
Editorial: Unit 2.4, Paintworks, Bristol BS4 3EN **Tel:** 44 01173 005526
Email: editor@bristolpropertylive.co.uk
Web site: www.bristolpropertylive.co.uk
Freq: Weekly
Circ: 20000 Not Audited
MAGAZINE
Property Management & Maintenance

British Association of Remote Sensing Companies
998895
Editorial: 2 Falcon Way, Shire Park, Welwyn Garden City, Welwyn Garden City AL7 1TW
Email: secretary@barsc.org.uk
Web site: www.barsc.org.uk
Freq: Semi-Annual Not Audited
MAGAZINE
Data Management, Industry, Science

British Baker
981278
Editorial: Broadfield Park, Crawley, Crawley RH11 9RT **Tel:** 44 01293 613400
Email: bb@wrbm.com
Web site: www.bakeryinfo.co.uk
Freq: Bi-Weekly
Circ: 6050 Not Audited
Profile: Magazine which covers all aspects of the baking and snack food industry in the UK including machinery, equipment, supermarkets, products reviews and industry news. First published in 1885, the publication has an average of 44 pages per issue. Press Day: Friday and Tuesday. Incorporating: Bake and Take. Read by plant bakers, supermarket in-store bakers, independent bakers and confectioners, manufacturers and suppliers of ingredients, plant and equipment and wholesale distributors.Regular features: Machinery and Equipment Focus Review of new products for the British baking industry.
Ad Rate: Full Page Colour £1925.00
MAGAZINE
Food

British Cinematographer
988917
Editorial: Pinewood Studios, Iver Heath, Iver Heath SL0 0NH **Tel:** 44 01753 650101
Web site: www.britishcinematographer.co.uk
Freq: Bi-Monthly Not Audited
Editor: Ron Prince
MAGAZINE
Photography

Business Magazines

British Dairying 981149
Tel: 44 01438 716220
Web site: www.britishdairying.co.uk
Freq: Monthly
Circ: 11900 Not Audited
Editor: Mike Green
Profile: Magazine covering technical and economic developments in the British dairy industry including news, independent business articles and technical information. Aimed at dairy farmers.
Ad Rate: Full Page Mono £1210.00
Ad Rate: Full Page Colour £1810.00
MAGAZINE
Animal Farming

British Farmer & Grower 981150
Tel: 44 02476 858500
Web site: http://www.nfuonline.com
Freq: Monthly
Circ: 48586 Not Audited
MAGAZINE
Animal Farming

British International Schools (BIS) 987544
Editorial: Pentastic Ltd, PO Box 4435, Cubbington, Leamington Spa CV31 9EA
Tel: 44 01926 339661
Web site: www.bismagazine.co.uk
Freq: 3 Times/Year
Circ: 3000 Not Audited
Editor: Andrew Maiden
MAGAZINE
Schools & Institutions

British Journal of Biomedical Science 985231
Editorial: Taylor & Francis Group, 2&4 Park Square, Milton Park, Abingdon OX14 4RN
Tel: 44 02070 177720
Email: sarahholman@ibms.org
Web site: http://www.tandfonline.com/toc/tbbs20/72/1?nav=tocList
Freq: Quarterly Not Audited
Profile: Journal containing articles and book reviews on all aspects of biomedical science. Aimed at scientists in universities and industry working in laboratory medicine in the NHS and around the world.
MAGAZINE
Biotechnology, Science

British Journal of Cancer 984566
Editorial: BJC Main Editorial Office, First floor, Angel Building, 407 St John Street, London EC1V 4AD Tel: 44 02034 696179
Email: bjc@bjcancer.net
Web site: www.nature.com/bjc
Freq: Bi-Weekly Not Audited
Profile: Journal on cancer.
MAGAZINE
Oncology

British Journal of Cardiac Nursing 984725
Editorial: St Jude's Church, Dulwich Road, London SE24 0PB Tel: 44 02077 385454
Email: bjcardn@markallengroup.com
Web site: http://www.magonlinelibrary.com/toc/bjca/current
Freq: Monthly Not Audited
Editor: Aysha Mendes
Profile: British Journal of Cardiac Nursing is the UK's quarterly journal dedicated to cardiac nursing. Contains clinical reviews, original research and professional articles available to cardiac nurses. Launched in January 2006. Targets nurses of cardiac specialty. Aimed at cardiac nurses.
Ad Rate: Full Page Colour £2200.00
MAGAZINE
Cardiology, Nursing/Nurses

The British Journal of Cardiology 983536
Editorial: 657 Fulham Road, London SW6 5PY Tel: 44 02077 314945
Email: editorial@bjcardio.co.uk
Web site: www.bjcardio.co.uk
Freq: Quarterly
Circ: 25000 Not Audited
Editor: Kim M Fox

Profile: Peer-reviewed journal linking primary and secondary care focusing on cardiovascular matters. Contains clinical reports, therapeutics, guidelines, policy, book reviews, case studies, news, analysis of new studies and features on cardiology practice. Aimed at hospital cardiologists and GPs with an interest in cardiology.
Ad Rate: Full Page Mono £1000.00
Ad Rate: Full Page Colour £1400.00
MAGAZINE
Cardiology

British Journal of Clinical Pharmacology 1054006
Email: bjcpedoffice@wiley.com
Web site: www.onlinelibrary.wiley.com
Freq: Monthly
MAGAZINE
Pharmaceuticals

British Journal of Clinical Psychology (BJCP) 995791
Editorial: The Atrium, Southern Gate, Chichester PO19 8SQ Tel: 44 01865 778315
Email: bjc@wiley.com
Web site: http://onlinelibrary.wiley.com/journal/10.1111/(ISSN)2044-8260;jsessionid=5A42909262FD0309668D122AF8
Freq: Quarterly Not Audited
MAGAZINE
Neurology

British Journal of Community Nursing 981615
Editorial: St Jude's Church, Dulwich Road, London SE24 0PB Tel: 44 02077 385454
Email: bjcn@markallengroup.co.uk
Web site: www.bjcn.co.uk
Freq: Monthly Not Audited
Profile: Clinical and professional Journal for the district nurse team. Aimed at district nurses and community staff nurses, and their team members.
Ad Rate: Full Page Colour £2000.00
MAGAZINE
Nursing/Nurses

British Journal of Developmental Psychology 998818
Editorial: The Atrium, Southern Gate, Chichester PO19 8QG Tel: 44 01162 529504
Email: bjdp@wiley.com
Web site: http://onlinelibrary.wiley.com/journal/10.1111/(ISSN)2044-835X
Freq: Quarterly Not Audited
Editor: Patrick Leman
MAGAZINE
Neurology

The British Journal of Diabetes & Vascular Disease 983537
Tel: 44 01675 477605
Email: editor@bjd-abcd.com
Web site: www.bjdvd.co.uk/index.php/bjdvd
Freq: Quarterly Not Audited
Profile: Journal focusing on diabetes and vascular disease, insulin resistance, hyperinsulinaemia, obesity, hypertension, dyslipidaemia, antherosclerosis, hyperglycaemia and thrombosis.
MAGAZINE
Diabetes

British Journal of Family Medicine 988590
Editorial: Rayford House, School Road, Hove BN3 5HX Tel: 44 01273 434943
Web site: www.bjfm.co.uk
Freq: Bi-Monthly Not Audited
MAGAZINE
Pharmaceuticals

British Journal of Health Psychology 999090
Editorial: The Atrium, Southern Gate, Chichester PO19 8QG Tel: 44 01162 529504
Email: bjhp-production@wiley.com
Web site: www.onlinelibrary.wiley.com/journal/10.1111/(ISSN)2044-8287

Freq: Quarterly Not Audited
MAGAZINE
Neurology

British Journal of Healthcare Assistants 984779
Editorial: St Jude's Church, Dulwich Road, London SE24 0PB Tel: 44 02077 385454
Email: bjhca@markallengroup.com
Web site: http://www.healthcare-assistants.co.uk
Freq: Monthly Not Audited
Editor: Peter Bradley
Profile: Journal for healthcare assistants and assistant practitioners who are interested in developing their own career, as well as providing the best possible support for the patients in their care. Each issue contains a wide range of evidence-based reviews providing positive examples of good practice. Articles highlight learning outcomes to support practitioners' on-going training and to help extend their knowledge and skills in all areas of practice. First published in 2007. Aimed at healthcare assistants and assistant practitioners.
Ad Rate: Full Page Colour £2000.00
MAGAZINE
Community Care (UK), Nursing/Nurses

British Journal of Healthcare Computing 984367
Editorial: Regent House, 13-15 Albert Street, Harrogate HG1 1JX
Tel: 44 01423 526971
Email: newsroom@bj-hc.co.uk
Web site: http://www.hitcentral.eu/british-journal-healthcare-computing
Freq: Daily
Circ: 281 Cision Digital Reach
Profile: Website covering health. The British Journal of Healthcare Computing website shares information on the latest health news, case studies, analysis and comment on healthcare informatics issues in the UK.
MAGAZINE (ONLINE)
Health Administration, Medical Technology

British Journal of Healthcare Management 980936
Editorial: St Judes Church, Dulwich Road, London SE24 0PB Tel: 44 02077 385454
Email: bjhcm@markallengroup.com
Web site: www.magonlinelibrary.com/toc/bjhc/current
Freq: Monthly
Circ: 7102 Not Audited
Profile: Journal containing peer reviewed management papers, practical advice for managers, analytical news features, policy analysis, political coverage and opinion features. Aimed at senior managers in healthcare and influential policy and political figures.A charge may be made for colour separation.
Ad Rate: Full Page Colour £1800.00
MAGAZINE
Health Administration

British Journal of Mental Health Nursing 986728
Editorial: St Jude's Church, Dulwich Road, London SE24 0PB Tel: 44 02077 385454
Email: bjmhn@markallengroup.com
Web site: www.bjmhn.co.uk
Freq: Bi-Monthly Not Audited
Profile: Journal covering mental health nursing.
MAGAZINE
Neurology, Nursing/Nurses

British Journal of Midwifery 981197
Editorial: St Jude's Church, Dulwich Road, London SE24 0PB Tel: 44 02077 385454
Email: bjm@markallengroup.com
Web site: www.magonlinelibrary.com/toc/bjom/current
Freq: Monthly
Circ: 2384 Not Audited
Profile: Journal promoting excellence in midwifery and women's health. Aimed at midwives.Previous title: BJM
Ad Rate: Full Page Mono £995.00

Ad Rate: Full Page Colour £1900.00
MAGAZINE
Obstetrics & Gynecology (OB/GYN)

British Journal of Neuroscience Nursing 985209
Editorial: St Jude's Church, Dulwich Road, London SE24 0PB Tel: 44 02077 385454
Email: bjnn@markallengroup.com
Web site: www.bjnn.co.uk
Freq: Bi-Monthly
Circ: 3500 Not Audited
Profile: British Journal of Neuroscience Nursing is a journal in the UK dedicated specifically to neuroscience nursing. Covers all aspects of clinical practice in neuroscience nursing including neurosurgery and critical care, and long-term neurological conditions.
Ad Rate: Full Page Colour £2200.00
MAGAZINE
Neurology, Nursing/Nurses

British Journal of Neurosurgery 995859
Editorial: 5 Howick Place, London SW1P 1WG Tel: 44 02070 175544
Email: ian.blackford@tandf.co.uk
Web site: http://www.tandfonline.com/loi/ibjn20#.Ve1wfZMeqWM
Freq: Bi-Monthly Not Audited
MAGAZINE
Neurology

British Journal of Nursing 981198
Editorial: St Jude's Church, Dulwich Road, London SE24 0PB Tel: 44 02077 385454
Email: bjn@markallengroup.com
Web site: www.britishjournalofnursing.com
Freq: Bi-Weekly
Circ: 1663 Not Audited
Profile: Clinical research based journal for all specialities of nursing. Read by nurses in hospitals and in the community.
Ad Rate: Full Page Colour £2000.00
MAGAZINE
Nursing/Nurses

British Journal of Occupational Therapy (BJOT) 985342
Editorial: College of Occupational Therapists, 106 - 114 Borough High Street, Southwark, London SE1 1LB
Tel: 44 02074 502313
Email: bjoteditorial@cot.co.uk
Web site: http://bjo.sagepub.com/
Freq: Monthly Not Audited
MAGAZINE
Occupational Therapy & Rehabilitation

British Journal of Pain 999396
Editorial: c/o The British Pain Society, Third Floor, Churchill House, 35 Red Lion Square, London WC1R 4SG Tel: 44 02072 697841
Web site: http://bjp.sagepub.com/
Freq: Quarterly Not Audited
MAGAZINE
Pain Management

British Journal of Photography 981260
Editorial: 9th Floor, Anchorage House, 2 Clove Crescent, London E14 2BE
Tel: 44 02071 932625
Email: bjp.reporter@bjphoto.co.uk
Web site: http://www.bjp-online.com
Freq: Monthly
Circ: 7601 Not Audited
Editor: Simon Bainbridge
Profile: Magazine covering the professional photographic market: social, press, commercial, documentary, fine art and scientific. Contains advanced technical reviews, technology reports, interviews, award winners and market reports. Read by full-time professional photographers, photography students and serious amateurs along with related occupations such as picture editors, art buyers and photo retailers.
Ad Rate: Full Page Mono £1025.00

Ad Rate: Full Page Colour £1300.00
MAGAZINE
Photography

British Journal of Primary Care Nursing
984427

Editorial: The British Journal of Primary Care Nursing - Cardiovascular Disease, Diabetes and Kidney Care, Minerva Mill Innovation Centre, Station Road, Alcester B49 5ET
Tel: 44 01789 766098
Email: production-cvd@bjpcn.com
Web site: http://www.bjpcn-cardiovascular.com/
Freq: Quarterly
Circ: 10000 Not Audited
MAGAZINE
Cardiology, Diabetes, Nursing/Nurses

The British Journal of Psychiatry
984446

Editorial: Royal College of Psychiatrists, 21 Prescot Street, London E1 8BB
Tel: 44 02037 012717
Email: bjp@rcpsych.ac.uk
Web site: www.rcpsych.ac.uk/publications/journals/bjpinfo1.aspx
Freq: Monthly
Circ: 17500 Not Audited
Editor: Kamaldeep Bhui
Profile: Journal of the Royal College of Psychiatrists. Containing research papers, small articles and reports on matters of clinical significance and all aspects of psychiatry and mental health. Aimed at psychiatrists, clinical psychologists and those within the mental health profession.
Ad Rate: Full Page Mono £825.00
Ad Rate: Full Page Colour £900.00
MAGAZINE
Neurology

British Journal of Psychology
985339

Editorial: The Atrium, Southern Gate, Chichester, Chichester PO19 8SQ
Tel: 44 01865 778315
Email: bjop@wiley.com
Web site: http://onlinelibrary.wiley.com/journal/10.1111/(ISSN)2044-8295
Freq: Quarterly Not Audited
MAGAZINE
Neurology

British Journal of Psychotherapy (BJP)
999427

Editorial: The Atrium, Southern Gate, Chichester PO19 8QG **Tel:** 44 01865 778315
Email: cs-journals@wiley.com
Web site: http://onlinelibrary.wiley.com/journal/10.1111/%28ISSN%291752-0118
Freq: Quarterly
Circ: 1858 Not Audited
MAGAZINE
Neurology

British Journal of Radiology
985385

Tel: 44 02036 682220
Email: publications@bir.org.uk
Web site: http://www.birpublications.org/toc/bjr/current
Freq: Monthly
Circ: 530 Not Audited
Profile: An international journal of radiology, radiation oncology and all related sciences.
MAGAZINE
Diagnostic Imaging

British Journal of School Nursing
984528

Editorial: St Jude's Church, Dulwich Road, London SE24 0PB **Tel:** 44 02075 016771
Email: bjsn@markallengroup.com
Web site: http://www.magonlinelibrary.com/toc/bjsn/current
Freq: Monthly
Circ: 2000 Not Audited
Editor: Caroline Voogd

Profile: Journal covering all aspects of children's and public health. Aimed at school nurses.
MAGAZINE
Nursing/Nurses

The British Journal of Social Work
984310

Editorial: Great Clarendon Street, Oxford OX2 6DP **Tel:** 44 01865 353907
Email: bjsw.editorialoffice@oup.com
Web site: www.bjsw.oxfordjournals.org
Freq: Bi-Monthly Not Audited
Editor: Malcolm Golightley
Profile: International journal of the British Association of Social Workers, covering research studies and theoretical articles. Read by social workers, administrators and social work educators.
Ad Rate: Full Page Mono £340.00
MAGAZINE
Community Care (UK)

British Journal of Visual Impairment
986865

Editorial: 1 Oliver's Yard, 55 City Road, London EC1Y 1SP **Tel:** 44 02073 248500
Web site: http://jvi.sagepub.com/
Freq: 3 Times/Year Not Audited
Editor: John Ravenscroft
Profile: Journal providing a national forum for all views on related subjects. Read by those professionally concerned with children and adults who have a visual impairment.
MAGAZINE
Ophthalmology & Optometry

British Journalism Review
981666

Editorial: 1 Oliver's Yard, 55 City Road, London EC1Y 1SP **Tel:** 44 02073 248500
Email: editor@bjr.org.uk
Web site: http://www.bjr.org.uk/
Freq: Quarterly
Circ: 1400 Not Audited
Editor: Kim Fletcher
Profile: Journal containing articles on current journalism issues in the print and broadcast media, plus research and analysis of media trends.
Ad Rate: Full Page Mono £5000.00
MAGAZINE
Publishing

British Plastics & Rubber
981250

Editorial: Carlton House, Sandpiper Way, Chester Business Park, Chester CH4 9QE
Tel: 44 01244 680222
Web site: www.britishplastics.co.uk
Freq: Bi-Monthly
Circ: 8000 Not Audited
Profile: Magazine covering technical news of the plastics, rubber and polymer processing industry. Read by managers with specifying and purchasing influence.
Ad Rate: Full Page Colour £1800.00
MAGAZINE
Plastics

British Plastics Federation Newsletter
997559

Editorial: 6 Bath Place, Rivington Street, London EC2A 3JE **Tel:** 44 02074 575000
Email: reception@bpf.co.uk
Web site: www.bpf.co.uk
Freq: Bi-Weekly Not Audited
MAGAZINE
Plastics

British Sugar Beet Review
984346

Editorial: British Sugar plc, Sugar Way, Peterborough PE2 9AY
Tel: 44 01733 422088
Email: beetreview@britishsugar.co.uk
Web site: www.beetreview.co.uk
Freq: Quarterly
Circ: 6600 Not Audited
Editor: Paul Simmonds
Profile: Journal covering sugar beet research, machine technology, and crop husbandry. Read by scientists and sugar beet growers.

Ad Rate: Full Page Mono £1961.00
Ad Rate: Full Page Colour £2226.00
MAGAZINE
Animal Farming

British Tax Review
982920

Editorial: 100 Avenue Road, London NW3 3PF **Tel:** 44 02073 937000
Email: btr@worc.ox.ac.uk
Web site: http://www.sweetandmaxwell.co.uk/Catalogue/ProductDetails.aspx?recordid=338&searchorigin=british+tax
Freq: Bi-Monthly Not Audited
Profile: British Tax Review provides analysis of tax law, examining changes and giving commentary for practitioners, academics and policy makers.
MAGAZINE
Tax Law

The Broker
983030

Editorial: 8th Floor, John Stow House, 18 Bevis Marks, London EC3A 7JB
Tel: 44 03447 700266
Email: enquiries@biba.org.uk
Web site: www.biba.org.uk
Freq: Quarterly
Circ: 5000 Not Audited
Editor: Pamela Quinn
Profile: Publication covering all matters relating to insurance broking. Read by members of BIBA only.
Ad Rate: Full Page Colour £1045.00
MAGAZINE
Insurance

Broker World
1054310

Tel: 44 01905 621444
Email: brokers@leasingworld.co.uk
Web site: http://www.broker-world.com/
Freq: Monthly
Circ: 450 Not Audited
Editor: Jan Szmigin
MAGAZINE
Banking

Brownfield Briefing
983720

Editorial: The Chapel, Wellington Road, London NW10 5LJ **Tel:** 44 02036 372192
Email: editorial@brownfieldbriefing.com
Web site: www.brownfieldbriefing.com
Freq: Monthly
Circ: 3000 Not Audited
Profile: Newsletter focusing on all aspects of previously developed land including contamination, remediation, regeneration and legal developments. Aimed at all those with an interest in the brownfield and remediation sector including environmental consultants, local authorities and developers, amongst others.
Ad Rate: Full Page Mono £1450.00
Ad Rate: Full Page Colour £1750.00
MAGAZINE
Building & Construction, Sustainable Development

Build
995516

Editorial: Floor 1, Suite F, The Maltsters, 1-2 Wetmore Road, Barton-under-Needwood DE14 1LS **Tel:** 44 02037 256841
Email: info@build-news.com
Web site: www.build-news.com
Freq: Quarterly
Circ: 110000 Not Audited
Editor: Jeremy Roe
MAGAZINE
Architecture & Design, Building & Construction, Commercial Real Estate, Interior Design, Office Design, Residential Real Estate, Retail, Sustainable Development, Travel Industry, Urban Planning & Development

The Builder
980067

Editorial: McDermott Chambers, 2 The Green, Kings Norton, Birmingham B38 8SD
Tel: 44 01214 513037
Web site: http://www.mcdermottpublishing.com/the-builder/
Freq: Monthly
Circ: 20564 Not Audited
Editor: David Steade

Profile: Magazine containing product information relating to the building trade. It is read by builders, developers and associated trade professionals who wants to keep up to date with new industry innovation and promotions. Aimed at builders, contractors, residential and light commercial property developers, architects, building and quantity surveyors.
Ad Rate: Full Page Colour £1695.00
MAGAZINE
Building & Construction

Builders Merchants Journal
981096

Editorial: 15A London Road, Maidstone, Maidstone ME16 8LY **Tel:** 44 01622 687031
Web site: www.buildersmerchantsjournal.net
Freq: Monthly
Circ: 7596 Not Audited
MAGAZINE
Building & Construction

Builders' Merchants News
980873

Editorial: 32 Vauxhall Bridge Road, London SW1V 2SS **Tel:** 44 02079 736400
Web site: www.buildersmerchantsnews.co.uk
Freq: Monthly
Circ: 7740 Not Audited
Editor: Nichola Farrugia
Profile: Magazine covering new products and developments in the building and construction industry including articles, features and products on workwear, PPE and water saving technologies. First published in 1977. Aimed at senior management in the building and construction industry.
Ad Rate: Full Page Colour £2670.00
MAGAZINE
Building & Construction

Building
979951

Editorial: 240 Blackfriars Road, London SE1 8BF **Tel:** 44 02079 215000
Email: newsdesk@ubm.com
Web site: www.building.co.uk
Freq: Weekly
Circ: 21271 Not Audited
Editor: Sarah Richardson
Profile: Magazine covering the construction industry. It provides a combination of news, interviews, analysis and hard industry data. It covers all levels of the specification chain, reaching an audience of contractors, housebuilders, architects, clients and surveyors. Aimed at senior managers and designers in the construction industry.
Ad Rate: Full Page Colour £3117.00
MAGAZINE
Architecture & Design, Building & Construction, Commercial Real Estate, Finance, Interior Design, Legal Affairs, Office Design, Property Management & Maintenance, Residential Real Estate, Retail

Building & Environment
980875

Editorial: The Boulevard, Langford Lane, Kidlington OX5 1GB **Tel:** 44 01865 843000
Email: bae2@elsevier.com
Web site: https://www.journals.elsevier.com/building-and-environment
Freq: Monthly Not Audited
MAGAZINE
Building & Construction

Building 4 Education
981562

Editorial: Unit 2.4 Paintworks, Arnos Vale, Bristol BS4 3EH **Tel:** 44 01173 005526
Email: info@b4ed.com
Web site: www.b4ed.com
Freq: Daily
Circ: 18286 Cision Digital Reach
Profile: Magazine covering building related matters that affect the education market place, including latest news, special features, case studies and new products and services. Aimed at a cross section in the education sector, including educational architects, independent and grant maintained schools, colleges and nurseries.

Business Magazines

Previous title: Educational Building A charge may be made for colour separation.Regular features: Case Studies; Latest News; New Products
Ad Rate: Full Page Colour £1200.00
MAGAZINE (ONLINE)
Architecture & Design, Legal Affairs, Sustainable Development, Urban Planning & Development

Building and Construction Review UK
1074314
Email: buildingandconstructionreviewuk@ live.com
Web site: bcruk.co.uk
Freq: Monthly
Circ: 5000 Not Audited
Editor: Ian Bird
MAGAZINE
Building & Construction

Building and Facilities News
985532
Editorial: 4th Floor, Maybrook House, Queensway, Halesowen B63 4AH
Tel: 44 01215 504593
Email: info@buildingandfacilitiesnews.co.uk
Web site: www.buildingandfacilitiesnews.co.uk
Freq: Monthly
Circ: 5000 Not Audited
Editor: Andre Laurent
Profile: Building and Facilities News is a magazine covering all the latest on building, building services, building products, facilities management, health and safety, lighting and interiors. The magazine is aimed at facilities managers, directors and senior buyers. Regular features: Cleaning; Doors and Windows; Facilities Management; Flooring; Green-energy, waste management, water, recycling; Health and Safety; Heating and Ventilating; Interior Design; Landscaping and external works; Roofing and Cladding
Ad Rate: Full Page Colour £2000.00
MAGAZINE
Building & Construction

Building Better Healthcare
985066
Editorial: Natraj Building, The Tanneries, 55 Bermondsey Street, London SE1 3XG
Tel: 44 02071 931279
Email: info@hpcimedia.com
Web site: http://www. buildingbetterhealthcare.co.uk/
Freq: Daily
Circ: 10000 Not Audited
Editor: Jo Makosinski
MAGAZINE
Health Administration

Building Construction Design
985805
Editorial: Cointronic House, Station Road, Heathfield, Heathfield TN21 8DF
Tel: 44 01435 863500
Email: editorial@netmagmedia.eu
Web site: http://www. buildingconstructiondesign.co.uk/
Freq: Bi-Monthly
Circ: 15673 Cision Digital Reach
MAGAZINE (ONLINE)
Building & Construction

Building Control Journal
984047
Editorial: Parliament Square, London SW1 3PD **Tel:** 44 02476 868555
Email: journals@rics.org
Web site: http://www.rics.org/uk/news/ journals/building-control-journal
Freq: Bi-Monthly
Circ: 1800 Not Audited
Editor: Barney Hatt
MAGAZINE
Architecture & Design, Urban Planning & Development

Building Design & Construction
997480
Editorial: 1st Floor, Turnbridge Mills, Quay Street, Huddersfield HD1 6QT
Tel: 44 02081 233414

Email: editor@ciaranjarosz.media
Web site: www.bdcmagazine.co.uk
Freq: Monthly
Circ: 14500 Not Audited
MAGAZINE
Building & Construction

Building Design News
984472
Editorial: Hill Farm Business Park, Linton Hill, Maidstone, Linton ME17 4AL
Tel: 44 01622 745333
Email: news@buildingdesign.co.uk
Web site: http://www.buildingdesign-news. co.uk
Freq: Daily
Circ: 13652 Cision Digital Reach
Editor: Penny Cooper
Profile: Website and newsletter covering all aspects of building design and construction projects. Aimed at building specifiers, buyers and end users including architects, contractors, facility managers, interior designers and building services engineers. Digital images preferred. PR by email only. Additional email: aja@buildingdesign.co.uk.
MAGAZINE (ONLINE)
Architecture & Design, Building & Construction, Interior Design, Residential Real Estate

Building Engineer
984023
Editorial: Lutyens House, Billing Brook Road, Northampton NN3 8NW
Tel: 44 01604 773948
Email: editor@cbuilde.com
Web site: www.cbuilde.com/resources/ building-engineer-journal/
Freq: Monthly
Circ: 7000 Not Audited
Editor: Carol Langham
Profile: Journal of The Association of Building Engineers covering all aspects of building regulations, products and technical articles. Read by building engineers, surveyors, architects and others involved in the technology of building.
Ad Rate: Full Page Mono £670.00
Ad Rate: Full Page Colour £1050.00
MAGAZINE
Architecture & Design, Building & Construction, Engineering

Building Innovations
984025
Editorial: Kingfisher's Retreat, Dunston Business Village, Stafford Road, Dunston, Stafford ST18 9AB **Tel:** 44 01785 711591
Email: james@l2media.uk
Web site: www.link2media.co.uk/#/the-publications/building-innovations/overview
Freq: Quarterly
Circ: 7000 Not Audited
Profile: Magazine covering the architectural and construction industry. Aimed at architects and technologists.
Ad Rate: Full Page Colour £795.00
MAGAZINE
Architecture & Design, Building & Construction

Building Law Monthly
998572
Editorial: 1-2 Bolt Court, London EC4A 3DQ
Web site: www.buildinglawmonthly.com
Freq: Monthly Not Audited
Profile: Newsletter providing updates on building regulations and case law. Aimed at law practitioners and legal buildings experts.
MAGAZINE
Real Estate Law

Building News
980876
Editorial: 2 The Green, Kings Norton, Birmingham B38 8SD **Tel:** 44 01214 513037
Web site: www.buildingnews.co.uk
Freq: Monthly
Circ: 14978 Not Audited
Editor: Lee Butler
Profile: Publication covering products, regulations, application and safety issues relevant to the building trade. Publication covering products, regulations, application and safety issues relevant to the building trade.
Ad Rate: Full Page Colour £1330.00
MAGAZINE
Building & Construction

Building Services and Environmental Engineer
995970
Editorial: 15a London Road, Maidstone, Maidstone ME16 8LY **Tel:** 44 01622 687031
Web site: www.bsee.co.uk
Freq: Monthly
Circ: 18681 Not Audited
MAGAZINE
Alternative/Renewable Energy, Building & Construction, Carbon Emissions & Trading, Electricity, Energy, Environment, Interior Design, Nuclear Power, Oil, Water & Sanitation

Building Surveying Journal
985654
Editorial: RICS, Parliament Square, London SW1P 3AD **Tel:** 44 02072 227000
Email: journals@rics.org
Web site: http://www.rics.org/uk/news/ journals/building-surveying-journal
Freq: Bi-Monthly
Circ: 19900 Not Audited
Editor: Barney Hatt
MAGAZINE
Architecture & Design, Legal Affairs, Urban Planning & Development

Building Worker
987535
Editorial: 177 Abbeville Road, London SW4 9RL **Tel:** 44 02076 222442
Email: buildingworker@ucatt.org.uk
Web site: www.ucatt.org.uk
Freq: Quarterly Not Audited
MAGAZINE
Building & Construction

Building4Change.com
985329
Editorial: Bucknalls Lane, Garston, Watford, London WD25 9XX **Tel:** 44 01923 664000
Email: building4change@bre.co.uk
Web site: http://www.building4change.com/
Freq: Daily
Circ: 18645 Cision Digital Reach
Editor: Damien Carr
MAGAZINE (ONLINE)
Environment, Property Management & Maintenance, Residential Real Estate

Buildingtalk.com
980877
Editorial: Unit 1, Sugarbrook Court, Aston Road, Bromsgrove B60 3EX
Tel: 44 01527 880806
Email: news@buildingtalk.com
Web site: http://www.buildingtalk.com
Freq: Daily
Circ: 15841 Cision Digital Reach
MAGAZINE (ONLINE)
Building & Construction

Bulk Distributor
980999
Editorial: Caledonian House, Tatton Street, Knutsford, Knutsford WA16 6AG
Tel: 44 01565 653283
Web site: www.Bulk-distributor.com
Freq: Bi-Monthly
Circ: 12000 Not Audited
Profile: Magazine covering the full distribution chain and all bulk commodities. Focusing on storage, transportation and handling. Read by shippers, their representatives and service providers to the bulk cargo industry.
Ad Rate: Full Page Colour £2850.00
MAGAZINE
Shipping & Warehousing, Supply Chain Management (SCM)

Bulk Materials International
981248
Editorial: Northbank House, 24 Bridge Street, Leatherhead, London KT22 8BX
Tel: 44 01372 375511
Email: info@wcnpublishing.com
Web site: www.bulkmaterialsinternational. com
Freq: Bi-Monthly
Circ: 6739 Not Audited
Editor: Benedict Young
Profile: News magazine reporting on the bulk handling, transport and storage of materials such as coal, fertilisers, animal feeds, ores, cement, aggregates and grain,

looking at it from a port and transport interface. First published in 1994. Aimed at companies involved in bulk handling of materials.
MAGAZINE
Shipping & Warehousing, Supply Chain Management (SCM)

Bulk Solids Today
983444
Editorial: 17 Whitley Close, Irthlingborough, Irthlingborough NN9 5GN
Tel: 44 01933 800294
Email: editorial@bulksolidstoday.co.uk
Web site: www.bulksolidstoday.co.uk
Freq: Bi-Monthly
Circ: 8500 Not Audited
Profile: Magazine covering the storage, movement, processing and control of powders and granular materials. Aimed at key buyers and specifiers of loose materials handling storage and processing equipment throughout the industry.
Ad Rate: Full Page Mono £650.00
Ad Rate: Full Page Colour £850.00
MAGAZINE
Engineering

The Bulletin
996467
Editorial: Charles Darwin House, 12 Roger Street, London WC1N 2JU
Tel: 44 02076 852500
Email: info@britishecologicalsociety.org
Web site: www.britishecologicalsociety.org/ publications/the-bulletin
Freq: Quarterly
Circ: 5000 Not Audited
Profile: Publication containing news and views from The British Ecological Society and informative features on ecological issues.
Ad Rate: Full Page Mono £450.00
Ad Rate: Full Page Colour £900.00
MAGAZINE
Environment

The Bulletin (BFFF)
985253
Editorial: Warwick House, Unit 7, Long Bennington Business Park, Main Road, Long Bennington, Newark NG23 5JR
Tel: 44 01400 283090
Email: bulletineditorial@bfff.co.uk
Web site: http://bfff.co.uk/about-bfff/ bulletin/
Freq: Bi-Monthly
Circ: 300 Not Audited
MAGAZINE
Food

BULLETIN for sports surface management
998765
Editorial: St Ives Estate, Bingley, Bradford BD16 1AU **Tel:** 44 01274 565131
Email: info@strigroup.com
Web site: strigroup.com
Freq: Quarterly
Circ: 6000 Not Audited
MAGAZINE
News & Current Affairs

Bunkerspot
984393
Editorial: Petrospot House, Somerville Court, Trinity Way, Adderbury, Banbury OX17 3SN **Tel:** 44 01295 814455
Email: news@petrospot.com
Web site: www.bunkerspot.com
Freq: Bi-Monthly
Circ: 7000 Not Audited
Editor: Lesley Bankes-Hughes
Profile: Magazine covering the bunker industry. It focuses on global marine fuels.
MAGAZINE
Shipping & Warehousing

Bureau of Freelance Photographers Market Newsletter
999199
Editorial: Vision House, Hatfield AL10 1FY
Tel: 44 01707 651450
Email: info@thebfp.com
Web site: www.thebfp.com
Freq: Monthly
Circ: 5000 Not Audited
MAGAZINE
Photography

The burning issue   984916

Editorial: Refuge House, 33-37 Watergate Row, Chester CH1 2LE
Tel: 44 01244 624022
Email: editor@theburningissue.co.uk
Web site: www.theburningissue.co.uk
Freq: Quarterly
Circ: 8000 Not Audited
Editor: Emma Harris
Profile: Publication that highlights the awareness campaigns of the Fire and Rescue Service and related organisations. Providing a forum for good practice within the services. Aimed at all employees of the Fire and Rescue Service nationwide.
Ad Rate: Full Page Colour £995.00
MAGAZINE
Security & Security Systems

The Bursar's Review   988759

Editorial: Bluett House, Unit 11-12 Manor Farm, Cliddesden, Basingstoke RG25 2JB
Tel: 44 01256 330369
Email: office@theisba.org.uk
Web site: http://www.theisba.org.uk
Freq: Quarterly Not Audited
Editor: Gillian Goode
Ad Rate: Full Page Colour £1250.00
MAGAZINE
Schools & Institutions

The Business (Dorset, West Hants and Salisbury)   998511

Editorial: 9 Gainsborough Road, Ashley Heath, Ringwood BH24 2HY
Tel: 44 01425 471500
Email: mail@bizmag.co.uk
Web site: www.bizmag.co.uk
Freq: Bi-Monthly
Circ: 4500 Not Audited
Editor: Gill Bevis
MAGAZINE
Business, Small and Medium Business

Business 365   985090

Editorial: Media House, Cronkbourne, Douglas, Isle of Man IM4 4SB
Tel: 44 01624 696565
Web site: http://www.business365.im/
Freq: Monthly
Circ: 9000 Not Audited
Editor: Simon Richardson
MAGAZINE
Business

Business Advice   995340

Editorial: Unit Q4, Harbour Yard, Chelsea Harbour, London SW10 0XD
Tel: 44 02070 457570
Email: editors@businessadvice.co.uk
Web site: www.businessadvice.co.uk
Freq: Daily
Circ: 79998 Cision Digital Reach
Editor: Hunter Ruthven
MAGAZINE (ONLINE)
Business, Corporate Responsibility, Small and Medium Business

Business Airport International   985463

Editorial: Abinger House, Church Street, Dorking, Dorking RH4 1DF
Tel: 44 01306 743744
Email: hazel.king@ukimediaevents.com
Web site: www.businessairportinternational. com
Freq: Quarterly
Circ: 8413 Not Audited
Editor: Hazel King
Profile: Magazine covering in-depth reviews of selected Fixed Base Operator (FBOs) and general and business aviation airports. It showcases airport location, terminal facilities, handling services, refueling, MRO facilities, passenger comforts and conveniences, corporate entertainment facilities, apron and runway facilities.
MAGAZINE
Aviation

Business and Industry Today   983995

Editorial: 4th Floor, Maybrook House, Queensway, Halesowen B63 1AH
Tel: 44 01215 507510
Email: info@businessandindustrytoday.co.uk
Web site: www.businessandindustrytoday. co.uk
Freq: Monthly
Circ: 5000 Not Audited
Editor: Andre Laurent
Profile: Magazine focusing on news, product reviews, company profiles, awards, appointments, exhibitions, start-ups and monthly themed features. Aimed at senior managers, purchasers and company directors.A charge may be made for colour separation.
Ad Rate: Full Page Mono £1500.00
Ad Rate: Full Page Colour £2016.00
MAGAZINE
Business

Business Brief   980924

Editorial: PO Box 582, Jersey JE4 8XQ
Tel: 44 01481 240240
Web site: http://www.briefci.com/
Freq: Monthly
Circ: 11000 Not Audited
Editor: James Falla
Profile: Magazine covering all aspects of industry, commerce and financial services in the Channel Islands.
Ad Rate: Full Page Mono £1200.00
Ad Rate: Full Page Colour £1200.00
MAGAZINE
Business

Business Bulletin   988928

Editorial: The Hub Exploration Drive, Aberdeen Energy Park, Bridge of Don, Aberdeen AB23 8GX **Tel:** 44 01224 343900
Email: business.bulletin@agcc.co.uk
Web site: http://www.agcc.co.uk/business-bulletin-contents/
Freq: Monthly
Circ: 1350 Not Audited
Editor: Joanna Fraser
MAGAZINE
Business, Small and Medium Business

Business Cornwall   984523

Editorial: Pool Innovation Centre, Trevenson Road, Redruth, Camborne TR15 3PL
Tel: 44 01209 718688
Email: info@businesscornwall.co.uk
Web site: www.businesscornwall.co.uk
Freq: Monthly
Circ: 4400 Not Audited
Profile: Magazine focusing on business issues, featuring key stories and analysis, information about people moves, interviews with major business people and profiles of upcoming business talent. Aimed at managers of SMEs in Cornwall.
Ad Rate: Full Page Colour £775.00
MAGAZINE
Business

Business Crowd UK   1052692

Email: team@businesscrowd.co.uk
Web site: www.businesscrowd.co.uk
Freq: Daily
Circ: 13069 Cision Digital Reach
MAGAZINE (ONLINE)
Business

Business Day Earth   1060482

Email: patrick@hsm.co.za
Freq: Quarterly
Circ: 30000 Not Audited
MAGAZINE
Business, Environment, Small and Medium Business

Business Day Empowerment   1060532

Email: patrick@hsm.co.za
Freq: Annual
Circ: 30000 Not Audited
MAGAZINE
Banking

The Business Economist   980148

Tel: 44 01264 737552
Email: journal@sbe.co.uk
Web site: http://www.sbe.co.uk/
Freq: Daily
Circ: 12467 Cision Digital Reach
Editor: Jim Hirst
Profile: Magazine covering developments in UK and world economics. Includes applied economic theory, and analysis of individual industries. First published in 1969, the publication has an average of 76 pages per issue. Read by accountants and business economists, financial institutions and governments.
Ad Rate: Full Page Mono £400.00
MAGAZINE (ONLINE)
Economics

Business Edge   983655

Editorial: Unit 4, Victoria Business Centre, 43 Victoria Road, Burgess Hill, Burgess Hill RH15 9LR **Tel:** 44 08458 842384
Email: enquiries@ sussexchamberofcommerce.co.uk
Web site: www.distinctivepublishing.co.uk/ publications/business-edge
Freq: Monthly
Circ: 3500 Not Audited
MAGAZINE
Business

Business Eye   981056

Editorial: 20 King's Road, Belfast BT5 6JJ
Tel: 44 02890 474490
Email: info@businesseye.co.uk
Web site: www.businesseye.co.uk
Freq: Monthly
Circ: 6000 Not Audited
Editor: Richard Buckley
Profile: Magazine covering training, leadership, start-ups and the latest developments within the business sector. Aimed at senior business managers and directors.
Ad Rate: Full Page Mono £1150.00
Ad Rate: Full Page Colour £1800.00
MAGAZINE
Business

Business First (Belfast)   996495

Editorial: Suite 60, Enterprise House, Balloo Avenue, Bangor BT19 7QT
Tel: 44 02891 472119
Email: gavin@businessfirstni.co.uk
Web site: www.businessfirstonline.co.uk
Freq: Bi-Monthly
Circ: 22500 Not Audited
MAGAZINE
Business, Corporate Responsibility, Small and Medium Business

Business Focus   996989

Editorial: Hart House Business Centre, Kimpton Road, Luton LU2 0LB
Tel: 44 01582 522448
Email: info@chamber-business.com
Web site: www.chamber-business.com/ focus_magazine.htm
Freq: Quarterly
Circ: 5500 Not Audited
Editor: Paula Devine
MAGAZINE
Business

Business Focus Magazine   997373

Editorial: Pure House, 64-66 Westwick Street, Norwich NR2 4SZ
Email: info@ceomediagroup.com
Web site: www.businessfocusmagazine. com
Freq: Monthly Not Audited
Editor: Chris Farnell
MAGAZINE
Business, Small and Medium Business

Business Franchise   984268

Editorial: 2-4 St Georges Road, Wimbledon, London SW19 4DP **Tel:** 44 02083 945215
Email: editor@businessfranchise.com
Web site: www.businessfranchise.com
Freq: Monthly
Circ: 12500 Not Audited
Profile: Official magazine of the British Franchise Association, covering all aspects of franchising as a method of starting your own business, including industry news, company profiles and legal & financial advice. First published in 1997, the publication has an average of 140 pages per issue. Aimed at those involved with franchising and those who want to know more.
Ad Rate: Full Page Colour £1760.00
MAGAZINE
Business, Corporate Responsibility

Business Grapevine   1101756

Email: editorialteam@executivegrapevine. com
Web site: http://www.businessgrapevine.co/
Freq: Daily
Circ: 18536 Cision Digital Reach
MAGAZINE (ONLINE)
Business, Small and Medium Business

Business in East Anglia   980925

Editorial: 21 Warrington Road, Ipswich IP1 3QU **Tel:** 44 01473 218633
Email: news@bizeast.com
Web site: www.bizea.co.uk
Freq: Bi-Monthly
Circ: 6500 Not Audited
Editor: Bill Fishlock
MAGAZINE
Business, Small and Medium Business

Business Intelligence   983964

Editorial: 34-38 Beverley Road, Hull HU3 1YE **Tel:** 44 01482 324976
Email: press@hull-humber-chamber.co.uk
Web site: www.hull-humber-chamber.co.uk
Freq: Bi-Monthly
Circ: 1400 Not Audited
Profile: Chamber of Commerce newsletter covering news and issues of interest to commerce and industry. Read by Chamber of Commerce Members in and around the Humber region.
Ad Rate: Full Page Mono £1777.00
Ad Rate: Full Page Colour £1777.00
MAGAZINE
Business, Small and Medium Business

Business Jet Interiors International   984470

Editorial: Abinger House, Church Street, Dorking, Dorking RH4 1DF
Tel: 44 01306 743744
Web site: www. businessjetinteriorsinternational.com
Freq: Quarterly
Circ: 8000 Not Audited
Editor: Izzy Kington
Profile: Magazine focusing on VIP and business jet interiors, covering aircraft designs, technologies, products and services, market trends and analysis, materials, craftsmanship, tailoring, concepts, seating, flooring, ambient lighting and bespoke fittings. Aimed at major and minor private charter operators, corporate fleet operators and multiple independent owners.
Ad Rate: Full Page Colour £3925.00
MAGAZINE
Aviation

Business Law International   981015

Editorial: 4th Floor, 10 St Bride Street, London EC4A 4AD **Tel:** 44 02078 420090
Email: editor@int-bar.org
Web site: http://www.ibanet.org/ Publications/business_law_international. aspx
Freq: 3 Times/Year
Circ: 14300 Not Audited
Profile: Magazine covering law journal devoted to issues of relevance to the international commercial, legal and academic community. The publication provide an in-depth discussion of current developments and timely issues, particularly those with a cross-border focus, and offer a survey of the law in areas of particular interest to our international readership. Aimed at international commercial lawyers.

Business Magazines

Ad Rate: Full Page Mono £1200.00
MAGAZINE
Corporate Law, Legal Services, Litigation, Tax Law

Business Leader   1100936
Editorial: 3 Bridgwater Court, Oldmixon Crescent, Weston-super-Mare BS24 9AY
Tel: 44 01934 428779
Email: editor@businessleader.uk.com
Web site: www.businessleader.uk.com
Freq: Quarterly
Circ: 10000 Not Audited
Editor: Oli Ballard
Profile: Web newsletter covering business. The Business Leader is a electronically delivered newsletter for the North London Chamber of Commerce containing a calendar of events, business news and company reviews.
MAGAZINE
Business, Small and Medium Business

Business Link   983658
Editorial: Armstrong House, Armstrong Street, Grimsby DN31 2QE
Tel: 44 01472 310310
Email: newsdesk@blmgroup.co.uk
Web site: www.blmforum.net
Freq: Monthly
Circ: 13000 Not Audited
MAGAZINE
Business

The Business Magazine   980775
Editorial: Howarth Lodge, 7 Reading Road, Pangbourne, Reading RG8 7LR
Tel: 44 0189 843509
Email: editorial@elcot.co.uk
Web site: www.businessmag.co.uk
Freq: Monthly
Circ: 4000 Not Audited
Profile: Magazine focussing on regional business-to-business news and analysis. The publication is used in a pro-active way by companies eager to find out what is happening in their locality and to follow up important sales, marketing and promotional leads that lie within its pages. Regular editorial features cover Wealth Management, Finance, Law, Accountancy, Technology, Deals, Property, People, Motoring, etc. Read by company directors, business executives and principles of owner managed businesses in the South East and South West of England.
Ad Rate: Full Page Colour £2400.00
MAGAZINE
Business

Business Matters   984267
Editorial: 17 Ensign House, Canary Wharf, London E14 9XQ **Tel:** 44 02078 637857
Email: editorial.bm@cbmeg.co.uk
Web site: www.bmmagazine.co.uk
Freq: Monthly
Circ: 47000 Not Audited
Editor: Paul Jones
Profile: Magazine containing news and briefings, details of government-led initiatives for small and medium businesses, high profile interviews, new software, best practice, advice, start-ups and tips. Also cover all aspects of wealth management. Aimed at owners and managers of small businesses and those hoping to start a new business.
Ad Rate: Full Page Colour £2540.00
MAGAZINE
Business, Corporate Responsibility

Business Money   980149
Editorial: Bowdens Business Centre, Hambridge, Taunton TA10 OBP
Tel: 44 01458 253536
Email: editor@business-money.com
Web site: http://www.business-money.com
Freq: Monthly
Circ: 14237 Not Audited
Editor: Robert Lefroy
Profile: Industry journal covering banking, finance, movers from within the fields of finance, SMEs, economics, politics and motoring. Aimed at accountants, legal practitioners, brokers and IFAs, as well as

major banks, factors, trade finance houses, all asset finance providers and commercial lenders.
Ad Rate: Full Page Colour £2090.00
MAGAZINE
Banking

Business Network   988841
Editorial: 11 The Swan Courtyard, Charles Edward Road, Yardley, Birmingham B26 1BU **Tel:** 44 01217 654144
Email: magazine@dnlcc.co.uk
Web site: http://www.emc-dnl.co.uk/news/19/business-network-magazine
Freq: Monthly
Circ: 5000 Not Audited
Profile: Business magazine containing news, features and company profiles. Distributed to business organisation members.
MAGAZINE
Business, Corporate Responsibility

Business News - Magazine
          995984
Tel: 44 01725 512200
Email: enquiries@phoenix-2.co.uk
Web site: http://www.phoenix-2.co.uk
Freq: Quarterly
Circ: 60000 Not Audited
Editor: Amanda Walker
MAGAZINE
Business

Business News Wales   1074321
Tel: 44 02920 376122
Email: contact@businessnewswales.com
Web site: businessnewswales.com
Freq: Daily
Circ: 16570 Cision Digital Reach
MAGAZINE (ONLINE)
Business, Small and Medium Business

Business Northants   1052653
Editorial: Woburn Media Ltd, 28 Linford Forum, Rockingham Drive, Milton Keynes MK14 6LY **Tel:** 44 01908 394501
Email: news@business-northants.co.uk
Web site: www.businessmk.co.uk
Freq: Monthly
Circ: 3500 Not Audited
Editor: Andrew Gibbs
MAGAZINE
Business

Business Quarter (BQ)   985114
Editorial: Spectrum 6, Spectrum Business Park, Seaham, Sunderland SR7 7TT
Tel: 44 01913 898468
Email: newsdesk@bq-magazine.co.uk
Web site: http://www.bqlive.co.uk/
Freq: Quarterly
Circ: 101096 Not Audited
Editor: Mike Hughes; **Editor:** Paul Robertson
MAGAZINE
Business, Corporate Responsibility

Business Report   985085
Editorial: Unit 7, Penderford Place, Pendeford Business Park, Wolverhampton, Wolverhampton WV9 5HA
Tel: 44 01902 255033
Web site: www.businessreport.co.uk
Freq: Daily
Circ: 1750 Cision Digital Reach
Profile: Website covering news and resources news from UK companies.
MAGAZINE (ONLINE)
Business, Small and Medium Business

Business Review Australia & Asia
          1074958
Editorial: 69-75 Thorpe Road, Norwich NR1 1UA **Tel:** 44 01603 217530
Web site: http://www.businessreviewaustralia.com/
Freq: Monthly
MAGAZINE
News & Current Affairs

Business Review Europe   985561
Editorial: 69-75 Thorpe Road, Norwich NR1 1UA **Tel:** 44 01603 217530
Web site: http://www.businessrevieweurope.eu/
Freq: Monthly
Circ: 33811 Cision Digital Reach
MAGAZINE (ONLINE)
Business, Small and Medium Business

Business Review Middle East
          1053052
Tel: 44 01603 217530
Web site: http://www.businessreviewmiddleeast.com/
Freq: Monthly
Circ: 15334 Cision Digital Reach
MAGAZINE (ONLINE)
Business, Small and Medium Business

Business Sale Report   983186
Editorial: 167 Oakhill Road, Putney, London SW15 2QW **Tel:** 44 02088 750200
Email: info@business-sale.com
Web site: www.business-sale.com
Freq: Monthly
Circ: 1500 Not Audited
MAGAZINE
Business

Business Scotland   986593
Editorial: Scottish Chambers of Commerce, 30 George Square, Glasgow G2 1EQ
Tel: 44 01412 048316
Email: admin@scottishchambers.org.uk
Web site: http://www.scottishchambers.org.uk/
Freq: Quarterly Not Audited
Profile: Magazine of the Scottish Chambers of Commerce. Publishes Chamber news, contacts and policy.
MAGAZINE
Business

Business Voice   980037
Editorial: CBI, Cannon Place, 78 Cannon Street, London EC4N 6HN
Tel: 44 02073 958264
Email: businessvoice@cbi.org.uk
Web site: www.cbi.org.uk/businessvoice
Freq: Daily
Circ: 2 Cision Digital Reach
Editor: Pip Brooking
Profile: Official magazine of the Thames Valley Chamber of Commerce covering business and economic issues.
MAGAZINE (ONLINE)
News & Current Affairs

Business Voice - Thames Valley Chamber of Commerce
          980926
Editorial: 150 Edinburgh Avenue, Slough, Slough SL1 4SS **Tel:** 44 01753 870500
Email: ginettegower@tvchamber.co.uk
Web site: www.thamesvalleychamber.co.uk
Freq: Bi-Monthly
Circ: 9000 Not Audited
Editor: Ginette Gower
MAGAZINE
Business

Business West Insight   999460
Editorial: Leigh Court, Abbots Leigh, Bristol BS8 3RA **Tel:** 44 01275 373373
Email: info@businesswest.co.uk
Web site: https://www.businesswest.co.uk/press-office/insight
Freq: Bi-Monthly
Circ: 2000 Not Audited
MAGAZINE
Business, Small and Medium Business

Business Works   996956
Editorial: First Floor, 28 Astwood Mews, London SW7 4DE **Tel:** 44 02078 350020
Email: info@biz-works.net
Web site: www.biz-works.net
Freq: Daily
Circ: 10056 Cision Digital Reach

Editor: Roger Prentis
MAGAZINE (ONLINE)
Business, Corporate Responsibility, Small and Medium Business

Business World (UK)   980151
Editorial: 2 Alliance trading Estate, Torrington Avenue, Coventry CV4 9BH
Tel: 44 02476 465000
Email: info@bizworldonline.com
Web site: www.bizworldonline.com
Freq: Monthly
Circ: 26428 Not Audited
Editor: Peter Marshall
MAGAZINE
Business, Corporate Responsibility

BusinessBecause.com   997088
Editorial: 107 Leadenhall Street, London EC3A 4AF
Email: info@businessbecause.com
Web site: www.businessbecause.com
Freq: Daily
Circ: 96472 Cision Digital Reach
Editor: Seb Murray
MAGAZINE (ONLINE)
Students

BusinessesForSale.com   986023
Editorial: Dynamis House, 6-8 Sycamore Street, London EC1Y 0SW
Tel: 44 02073 241940
Web site: www.businessesforsale.com
Freq: Daily
Circ: 1588814 Cision Digital Reach
Profile: Website covering all aspects of buying and selling a business including case studies of people who have already bought and sold businesses, general articles on business buying and relocation guides by country.
MAGAZINE (ONLINE)
Business, Small and Medium Business

BusinessGreen   984541
Editorial: Haymarket House, 28-29 Haymarket, London SW1Y 4RX
Tel: 44 02073 169000
Web site: www.businessgreen.com
Freq: Daily
Circ: 62028 Cision Digital Reach
Profile: Website covering green business and clean technology. businessGreen shares the latest news and analysis on green business and environment.
MAGAZINE (ONLINE)
Environment

Businessscotland.com   996726
Editorial: The Exchange, 29 Constitution Street, Edinburgh EH6 7BS
Tel: 44 01315 617287
Email: news@businessscotland.com
Web site: www.businessscotland.com
Freq: Daily
Circ: 760 Cision Digital Reach
MAGAZINE (ONLINE)
Business, Corporate Responsibility

Buying and Using Utilities
          983877
Editorial: PO Box 30, London W5 3ZT
Tel: 44 02089 973854
Web site: www.meuc.co.uk/publications
Freq: Quarterly
Circ: 6800 Not Audited
Editor: Peter Roper
Profile: Magazine covering energy, utilities and energy management. The magazine is published five times a year. Aimed at industrial and commercial buyers
MAGAZINE
Alternative/Renewable Energy, Carbon Emissions & Trading, Electricity, Energy, Nuclear Power, Oil, Water & Sanitation

The BUY-SIDE CLUB   997388
Tel: 44 02038 180006
Email: geraldine@thebuysideclub.com
Web site: www.thebuysideclub.com
Freq: Daily

Circ: 521 Cision Digital Reach
MAGAZINE (ONLINE)
Fund Management, Investment Banking

Bytestart
985348
Editorial: The Mount, Minsterley Road, Pontesbury, Shrewsbury SY5 0QJ
Email: editor@bytestart.co.uk
Web site: www.bytestart.co.uk
Freq: Daily
Circ: 92448 Cision Digital Reach
MAGAZINE (ONLINE)
Business, Corporate Responsibility

C & W In Business
983339
Editorial: Chamber House, Innovation Village, Cheetah Road, Coventry CV1 2TL
Tel: 44 02476 654321
Email: news@cw-chamber.co.uk
Web site: https://www.cw-chamber.co.uk/membership/essential-membership/raise-your-profile/cw in business magaz
Freq: Bi-Monthly
Circ: 8000 Not Audited
Profile: Regional business newspaper for the Central Midlands.
Ad Rate: Full Page Colour £1955.00
MAGAZINE
Business, Corporate Responsibility, Small and Medium Business

C+D (Chemist+Druggist)
980071
Editorial: 240 Blackfriars Road, London SE1 8BF **Tel:** 44 02079 218222
Email: haveyoursay@chemistanddruggist.co.uk
Web site: www.chemistanddruggist.co.uk
Freq: Weekly
Circ: 38165 Not Audited
Editor: James Waldron
MAGAZINE
Pharmaceuticals

The CA
980006
Editorial: Suite 2.3, Red Tree Business Suites, 33 Dalmarnock Road, Glasgow G40 4LA **Tel:** 44 01413 750504
Email: ca@thinkpublishing.co.uk
Web site: icas.org.uk/theCA
Freq: Monthly
Circ: 18337 Not Audited
Editor: Robert Outram
Profile: Journal of the Institute of Chartered Accountants of Scotland. Contains articles covering management, strategy, wealth management, finance and funding issues. It includes the latest trends in business practice as well as articles on human resources and IT and provides features on management, legal, IT and financial issues, ICAS membership news. First Published in 1897. Read by financial directors, managing directors, owner managers, chief executives, chairmen, lawyers, surveyors, stockbrokers and bankers.
Ad Rate: Full Page Colour £3066.00
MAGAZINE
Accounting, Banking, Business, Corporate Responsibility

Cabinet Maker
981099
Editorial: 1 Grain House, Mill Court, Great Shelford, Cambridge CB22 5LD
Tel: 44 01223 846825
Web site: www.cabinet-maker.co.uk
Freq: Weekly
Circ: 3000 Not Audited
Profile: Weekly trade news title for professionals working in the UK furniture market sector. With a comprehensive daily news website, Cabinet Maker is read by senior decision makers in furniture manufacturing, wholesale and retailing sectors.
Ad Rate: Full Page Colour £2975.00
MAGAZINE
Manufacturing, Woodworking

CAD User
981704
Editorial: 35 Station Square, London BR5 1LZ **Tel:** 44 01689 616000
Email: cad.user@btc.co.uk
Web site: www.caduser.com
Freq: Monthly

Circ: 15600 Not Audited
Editor: David Chadwick
Profile: Website focusing on construction related IT products and services.
MAGAZINE
Industry

Call Centre Helper
983003
Editorial: Trivethen, Dixton Road, Monmouth NP25 3PR **Tel:** 44 01600 714546
Email: newsdesk@callcentrehelper.com
Web site: www.callcentrehelper.com
Freq: Daily
Circ: 717467 Cision Digital Reach
Profile: Website covering the call centre industry and telecommunications.
MAGAZINE (ONLINE)
Education, Recruiting

Campaign
979854
Editorial: Bridge House, 69 London Road, Twickenham, London TW1 3QR
Tel: 44 02082 675000
Email: campaign@haymarket.com
Web site: www.campaignlive.co.uk
Freq: Weekly
Circ: 15000 Not Audited
Profile: Publication covering people and account moves, advertising campaigns, marketing strategies, finance management and the media. The publication has an average of 30 pages per issue and goes to press on Wednesday. Read by media owners, personnel in advertising agencies and marketing departments.
Ad Rate: Full Page Colour £7705.00
MAGAZINE
Advertising Industry, Branding, Marketing

CampdenFB
980846
Editorial: 30 Cannon Street, Lower Ground Floor, London EC4M 6XH
Tel: 44 02037 632800
Email: fb@campdenwealth.com
Web site: www.campdenfb.com
Freq: Quarterly
Circ: 10000 Not Audited
MAGAZINE
Business, Corporate Responsibility

CAMRADATA
997771
Editorial: Marlow House, Lloyd's Avenue, London EC3N 3AA **Tel:** 44 02033 275600
Email: info@camradata.com
Web site: camradata.com
Freq: Daily
Circ: 672 Cision Digital Reach
MAGAZINE (ONLINE)
Banking

Cancer Epidemiology
996066
Tel: 44 01392 285855
Email: cancerepi@elsevier.com
Web site: www.cancerepidemiology.net
Freq: Bi-Monthly Not Audited
MAGAZINE
Oncology

Cancer Investigation
995842
Editorial: 5 Howick Place, London SW1P 1WG **Tel:** 44 02070 177529
Email: enquiries@taylorandfrancis.com
Web site: http://informahealthcare.com/cnv
Freq: Daily
MAGAZINE
Oncology

Cancer Nursing Practice
981199
Editorial: The Heights, 59-65 Lowlands Road, Harrow, London HA1 3AE
Tel: 44 02084 231333
Web site: www.cancernursingpractice.co.uk
Freq: Monthly
Circ: 4922 Not Audited
Editor: Lisa Berry
Profile: The journal for practitioners and clinicians working within a range of specialties and caring for cancer patients.
Ad Rate: Full Page Colour £1880.00
MAGAZINE
Nursing/Nurses, Oncology

Cancer Treatment Reviews
983545
Editorial: The Boulevard, Langford Lane, Kidlington, Oxford OX5 1GB
Tel: 44 01865 843177
Email: ctr@elsevier.com
Web site: http://www.cancertreatmentreviews.com/
Freq: Bi-Monthly
Circ: 51 Not Audited
Editor: Nicholas Pavlidis
MAGAZINE
Oncology

The Canmaker
086011
Editorial: Durand House, Manor Royal, Crawley, Crawley RH10 9PY
Tel: 44 01293 435100
Email: canmaker@sayers-publishing.com
Web site: www.canmaker.com
Freq: Monthly
Circ: 3500 Not Audited
Editor: Mónica Higuera
Profile: Journal covering the worldwide metal packaging industry.
Ad Rate: Full Page Colour £2297.00
MAGAZINE
Manufacturing

CanTech International
983850
Editorial: The Maltings, 57 Bath Street, Gravesend, Dartford DA11 ODF
Tel: 44 01474 532202
Web site: www.cantechonline.com
Freq: Monthly
Circ: 3700 Not Audited
Editor: Alex Fordham
Profile: CanTech International is a magazine that provides the latest developments in the global metal packaging market, with legislation issues, technical articles, metal decorating, market information and product developments. It covers all aspects of metal packaging from the raw material supplier to the can maker and the filler, including news on the latest technologies and developments, 3D printing and digital printing, world news, plant and company profiles, machinery and equipment updates. Each issue includes a country or continent focus, as well as regular features covering all aspects of metal packaging. Read by top decision-makers in over 100 countries. Present at all the major exhibitions and conferences worldwide.
Ad Rate: Full Page Colour £4150.00
MAGAZINE
Manufacturing

Capital Insights
988935
Email: editor@capitalinsights.info
Web site: www.ey.com/gl/en/services/transactions/ey-capital-insights
Freq: Quarterly
Circ: 180000 Not Audited
Editor: Kate Jenkinson
MAGAZINE
Business, Corporate Responsibility, Fund Management

CapitalStructure
1062734
Editorial: Dukes House, 32-38 Dukes Place, London EC3A 7LP **Tel:** 44 02072 833820
Email: enquiries@capital-structure.com
Web site: http://www.capital-structure.com
Freq: Daily
Circ: 11587 Cision Digital Reach
MAGAZINE (ONLINE)
Bonds, Corporate Management, Lending

Captive Insurance Times
986990
Editorial: 16 Bromley Road, Beckenham, London BR3 5JE **Tel:** 44 02030 062710
Web site: www.captiveinsurancetimes.com
Freq: Bi-Weekly
Circ: 12867 Cision Digital Reach
Editor: Mark Dugdale
MAGAZINE (ONLINE)
Insurance

Captive Review
980967
Editorial: One London Wall, London EC2Y 5BD **Tel:** 44 02078 326500
Web site: www.captivereview.com

Freq: Monthly
Circ: 15000 Not Audited
Editor: Richard Cutcher
Profile: Magazine covering all aspects of the alternative risk transfer insurance market. Aimed at CEOs, CFOs and Risk Transfer Managers.
Ad Rate: Full Page Colour £3300.00
MAGAZINE
Insurance

Carbon Capture Journal
985633
Editorial: United House, North Road, London N7 9DP **Tel:** 44 02081 505295
Email: editor@carboncapturejournal.com
Web site: www.carboncapturejournal.com
Freq: Bi-Monthly
Circ: 3000 Not Audited
Editor: Keith Forward; **Editor:** Karl Jeffery
Profile: 'Carbon Capture Journal is specifically about industrial scale carbon capture and geological storage technology, with news about the major projects and development with government policy'.
Ad Rate: Full Page Colour £3995.00
MAGAZINE
Environment

Carbon Management
995449
Editorial: Taylor & Francis Group, 2&4 Park Square, Milton Park, London OX14 4RN
Tel: 44 02083 716090
Email: info@future-science.com
Web site: http://www.tandfonline.com/toc/tcmt20/current
Freq: Bi-Monthly Not Audited
MAGAZINE
Environment, Science

Carbon Pulse
988859
Email: news@carbon-pulse.com
Web site: www.carbon-pulse.com
Freq: Daily
Circ: 18433 Cision Digital Reach
MAGAZINE (ONLINE)
Carbon Emissions & Trading, Oil

Cardiac Rhythm News
986059
Editorial: 526 Fulham Road, London SW6 5NR **Tel:** 44 02077 368788
Email: info@bibamedical.com
Web site: https://cardiacrhythmnews.com
Freq: Quarterly
Circ: 5400 Not Audited
Profile: Cardiac Rhythm News is a quarterly newspaper providing latest news, features and important scientific information on preventing, diagnosing and treating heart failure, sudden cardiac death and bradycardia.
Ad Rate: Full Page Colour £3980.00
MAGAZINE
Cardiology

Cardiovascular News
998933
Editorial: 526 Fulham Road, London SW6 5NR **Tel:** 44 02077 368788
Email: publishing@bibamedical.com
Web site: www.cardiovascularnews.com/
Freq: Quarterly
Circ: 16117 Not Audited
Editor: Dawn Powell
MAGAZINE
Cardiology

Cards Insider
1066539
Editorial: One Lyric Square, London W6 0NB **Tel:** 44 02030 088415
Email: enquiries@lafferty.com
Web site: www.lafferty.com
Freq: Daily
Circ: 3416 Cision Digital Reach
MAGAZINE (ONLINE)
Banking, Retail Management

Care and Nursing Essentials
984708
Editorial: Rhone House, Canalside, Chorley PR6 0BU **Tel:** 44 01257 267677
Web site: http://www.careandnursing-magazine.co.uk
Freq: Bi-Monthly

Business Magazines

Circ: 7309 Not Audited
Profile: Magazine covering all aspects of healthcare management, including property, finance, training and recruitment, bathrooms and fittings, contract furnishing and flooring, laundries and sluice rooms, catering and kitchen equipment, cleaning and hygiene, bed and bedding, products and services, transport, mobility, holidays and days out.
Ad Rate: Full Page Colour £1200.00
MAGAZINE
Community Care (UK), Nursing/Nurses

Care Appointments   984205
Editorial: 70 West Regent Street, Glasgow G2 2QZ Tel: 44 01413 336665
Email: editorial@careappointments.co.uk
Web site: www.careappointments.co.uk
Freq: Daily
Circ: 17191 Cision Digital Reach
Editor: Laura McKellar
Profile: Magazine featuring jobs and opportunities, courses, training, advice, news, features and interviews.
Ad Rate: Full Page Mono £3295.00
Ad Rate: Full Page Colour £4495.00
MAGAZINE (ONLINE)
Community Care (UK)

Care Home Catering   988888
Editorial: 4th Floor, Joynes House, New Road, Gravesend DA11 0AJ
Tel: 44 03455 006008
Email: editor@carehomecatering.co.uk
Web site: www.carehomecatering.co.uk
Freq: Quarterly
Circ: 10720 Not Audited
Editor: Sue Dunk
MAGAZINE
Geriatrics

Care Home Management 981176
Editorial: Croham Lodge, Croham Road, Crowborough, Crowborough TN6 2RH
Tel: 44 01892 663350
Email: editorial@jnjmedia.co.uk
Web site: chmonline.co.uk
Freq: Bi-Monthly
Circ: 15991 Not Audited
Profile: Magazine covering topical issues within the care home industries including private, local authority and NHS, care homes, residential homes, NHS nursing homes and private nursing homes and suppliers to nursing homes. Aimed at group directors, managers and proprietors of care homes, facilities managers, special needs and disabled facilities staff.
Ad Rate: Full Page Colour £850.00
MAGAZINE
Geriatrics, Health Administration

Care Home Professional 1074320
Editorial: ITP Promedia, 16-25 Bastwick Street, London EC1V 3PS
Tel: 44 02031 764228
Email: b2bwebmaster@itppromedia.com
Web site: www.carehomeprofessional.com
Freq: Monthly
Circ: 3240 Not Audited
Editor: Andrew Seymour
MAGAZINE
Geriatrics

Care Industry News   986849
Tel: 44 01924 242156
Web site: http://careindustrynews.co.uk/
Freq: Daily
Circ: 19934 Cision Digital Reach
Profile: Website covering health. The care industry news website discusses anything from elderly care and events to health news.
MAGAZINE (ONLINE)
Community Care (UK), Geriatrics, Neurology

Care Management Matters
                                        981572
Editorial: 3 Valley Court, Lower Road, Croydon, Nr Royston, Croydon SG8 0HF
Tel: 44 01223 207770
Email: editor@caremanagementmatters.co.uk

Web site: www.caremanagementmatters.co.uk
Freq: Monthly
Circ: 16095 Not Audited
Profile: Magazine covering all aspects of senior management, finance, marketing, property, legal and training and recruiting matters for the UK care sector.
Ad Rate: Full Page Colour £1600.00
MAGAZINE
Community Care (UK), Geriatrics, Healthcare Industry

Care Talk   985832
Editorial: 2 King Street, Nottingham NG1 2AS
Email: editorial@caretalk.co.uk
Web site: www.caretalk.co.uk
Freq: Monthly
Circ: 24000 Not Audited
Editor: Lisa Carr
Profile: Magazine covering the care industry and social care sector. Aimed at those working within the industry.
Ad Rate: Full Page Colour £1200.00
MAGAZINE
Community Care (UK)

The Carer   995436
Editorial: Suite 4, Roddis House, Old Christchurch Road, Bournemouth, Bournemouth BH1 1LJ
Tel: 44 01202 552333
Email: editor@thecareruk.com
Web site: www.thecareruk.com
Freq: Quarterly
Circ: 15000 Not Audited
Profile: Magazine covering industry news, general news and new products.
Ad Rate: Full Page Colour £1300.00
MAGAZINE
Geriatrics

Cargo Airports & Airline Services   988199
Editorial: Boswell Cottage, 19 South End, Croydon CR0 1BE Tel: 44 02082 534000
Email: editorial@evaint.com
Web site: http://www.caasint.com/magazine
Freq: Quarterly
Circ: 6476 Not Audited
Editor: Will Waters
Profile: Aviation magazine covering cargo, airfreight, transport and logistics.
MAGAZINE
Aviation

Caring Times   981275
Editorial: Culvert House, Culvert Road, Battersea, London SW11 5DH
Tel: 44 02077 202108
Email: editor@caringtimes.plus.com
Web site: http://www.careinfo.org/caring-times.php
Freq: Monthly
Circ: 15566 Not Audited
Editor: Andrew Chapman; Editor: Geoff Hodgson
Profile: Magazine containing news, features and products for the long term social care sector.
Ad Rate: Full Page Mono £1925.00
Ad Rate: Full Page Colour £2485.00
MAGAZINE
Community Care (UK), Health Administration

Caring uk   983732
Editorial: 47 Church Street, Barnsley, Barnsley S70 2AS Tel: 44 01226 734639
Web site: http://www.caring-uk.co.uk
Freq: Monthly
Circ: 15617 Not Audited
Profile: Business to business magazine containing news, interviews, features, editorial insights and product information about the UK residential care and elderly nursing home sector, also covering sheltered housing and domiciliary care. Distributed to independent sector residential care and nursing specialist homes for older people, people with learning difficulties and the disabled; domiciliary care agencies, social services departments and health authorities.

Ad Rate: Full Page Colour £2340.00
MAGAZINE
Geriatrics, Health Administration

Cash & Treasury Management file   1060222
Editorial: 57 Broadway, Bramhall, Stockport SK7 3BU
Email: general@ctmfile.com
Web site: https://ctmfile.com/
Freq: Daily
Circ: 15141 Cision Digital Reach
MAGAZINE (ONLINE)
Banking, Foreign Exchange Market (FOREX), Investment Banking

Cast Metal & Diecasting Times   984298
Editorial: Gresham House, 54 High Street, Shoreham by Sea, Shoreham-by-Sea BN43 5DB Tel: 44 01273 453033
Freq: Bi-Monthly
Circ: 3300 Not Audited
Profile: Magazine reporting on new developments in the machinery field with company profiles, new contracts, news and up to date installation features.
Ad Rate: Full Page Colour £1350.00
MAGAZINE
Engineering, Manufacturing, Steel

CAT   984166
Editorial: Sentinel House, Harvest Crescent, Ancells Business Park, Fleet GU51 2UZ
Tel: 44 01252 532000
Email: cat@halldale.com
Web site: www.halldale.com/cat
Freq: Bi-Monthly
Circ: 18261 Not Audited
MAGAZINE
Aviation

Catering Insight   985165
Editorial: ITP Promedia, 16-25 Bastwick Street, London EC1V 3PS
Tel: 44 02031 764228
Web site: www.cateringinsight.com
Freq: Monthly
Circ: 4010 Not Audited
Editor: Clare Nicholls
Profile: Magazine covering catering equipment. It reports on the latest technological innovation and trends in catering equipment, and investigate the commercial opportunities this equipment presents to dealers, designers and specifiers.
MAGAZINE
Food

CCH Live News   997531
Editorial: 145 London Road, Kingston Upon Thames, London KT2 6SR
Tel: 44 08445 618166
Email: diane.tan@wolterskluwer.co.uk
Web site: http://www.cch.co.uk
Freq: Daily
Circ: 61049 Cision Digital Reach
MAGAZINE (ONLINE)
Accounting, Banking, Tax Law

CCH Tax News   997527
Editorial: 145 London Road, Kingston Upon Thames, London KT2 6SR
Circ: 4715 Cision Digital Reach
MAGAZINE (ONLINE)
Accounting

CCTime   1062134
Tel: 44 86108 7765777
Email: news@cctime.com
Web site: http://www.cctime.com
Circ: 547961 Cision Digital Reach
MAGAZINE (ONLINE)
Telecommunications/Electronic Communications

CD - corporate disputes   997434
Editorial: 23rd Floor, Alpha Tower, Suffolk Street, Queensway, Birmingham B1 1TT
Tel: 44 01216 005910
Email: corporatedisputes@financierworldwide.com

Web site: www.corporatedisputesmagazine.com
Freq: Quarterly Not Audited
MAGAZINE
Corporate Law

CDR (Commercial Dispute Resolution)   998881
Editorial: 59 Tanner Street, London SE1 3PL
Tel: 44 02073 670720
Email: info@glgroup.co.uk
Web site: www.cdr-news.com
Freq: Bi-Monthly
Circ: 25000 Not Audited
MAGAZINE
Corporate Law, Litigation

Cell & Gene Therapy Insights
                                        1075486
Editorial: 2 Brompton Mews, London N12 0BF Tel: 44 02084 463426
Email: info@insights.bio
Web site: http://insights.bio/cell-and-gene-therapy-insights/
Freq: Quarterly Not Audited
MAGAZINE
Biotechnology

Central & East Business Insider   996952
Editorial: Boulton House, 17-21 Chorlton Street, Manchester M1 3HY
Tel: 44 01619 079718
Email: insider@newsco.com
Web site: http://www.insidermedia.com/central_east
Freq: Daily
MAGAZINE (ONLINE)
Business, Corporate Responsibility, Finance, Mergers & Acquisitions, Small and Medium Business

Central Banking Journal 981008
Editorial: Haymarket House, 28-29 Haymarket, London SW1Y 4RX
Tel: 44 02074 849700
Email: info@centralbanking.com
Web site: www.centralbanking.com
Freq: Quarterly
Circ: 1100 Not Audited
MAGAZINE
Banking

CEO   981664
Editorial: John Carpenter House, John Carpenter Street, London EC4Y 0AN
Tel: 44 02079 366400
Email: info@theceomagazine.com
Web site: www.theceomagazine.com
Freq: Semi-Annual
Circ: 4791 Not Audited
MAGAZINE
Business, Company News & Appointments, Corporate Responsibility, Education, Health & Safety, Human Resources, Recruiting

CEO Magazine   997728
Editorial: Communications House, 26 York Street, London W1U 6PZ
Tel: 44 08700 672077
Email: info@ceo-mag.com
Web site: www.ceo-mag.com
Freq: Quarterly Not Audited
MAGAZINE
Business, Corporate Responsibility

Cereals and Oils Processing
                                        1062162
Tel: 44 86106 4882643
Email: cnlyjg@163.com
Freq: Monthly
Circ: 6503 Not Audited
MAGAZINE
Food

CERN Courier   988781
Editorial: IOP Publishing, Temple Circus, Temple Way, Bristol BS1 6HG
Tel: 44 01179 297481
Email: cern.courier@cern.ch

Web site: www.cerncourier.com/cws/latest/cern
Freq: Monthly
Editor: Antonella Del Rosso
Profile: International journal of high-energy physics. Contains product and technology news and views, and updates on software, hardware, components and inventions.
Ad Rate: Full Page Mono £3240.00
Ad Rate: Full Page Colour £4260.00
MAGAZINE
Nuclear Power

The Cerulli Edge - Europe Edition
996163
Editorial: Cerulli Associates Europe, 18 King William Street, London EC4N 7BP
Tel: 44 02035 851280
Email: info@cerulli.com
Web site: www.cerulli.com/research-products/cerulli-publications/edge-series/
Freq: Quarterly Not Audited
MAGAZINE
Fund Management

CFI.co
996049
Editorial: Meridien House, 69 – 71 Clarendon Road, Watford WD17 1DS
Tel: 44 02031 373679
Email: contact@cfi.co
Web site: http://cfi.co/
Freq: Quarterly
Circ: 38000 Not Audited
Editor: Wim Romeijn
MAGAZINE
Banking, Business, Financial Markets, Small and Medium Business

The Chamber
984354
Editorial: Unit 14a, Monument Way East, Woking, London GU21 5LY
Tel: 44 01483 735540
Web site: www.surrey-chambers.co.uk/the-chamber-magazine/
Freq: Bi-Monthly
Circ: 3000 Not Audited
Editor: Aisha Bennett
Profile: Official newspaper of Surrey Chambers of Commerce.
MAGAZINE
Business

Chamber Matters
996549
Editorial: Commerce House, Outer Circle Road, Lincoln LN2 4HY
Tel: 44 01622 523333
Email: enquiries@lincs-chamber.co.uk
Web site: www.lincs-chamber.co.uk
Freq: Bi-Monthly
Circ: 1500 Not Audited
MAGAZINE
Litigation

ChamberLink
983355
Editorial: Birmingham Chamber of Commerce, Chamber of Commerce House, 75 Harborne Road, Birmingham B15 3DH
Tel: 44 01214 546171
Web site: www.birmingham-chamber.com
Freq: Monthly
Circ: 5000 Not Audited
Editor: John Lamb
Profile: Publication for the Birmingham Chamber of Commerce and Industry and a business audience generally.
Ad Rate: Full Page Mono £1650.00
Ad Rate: Full Page Colour £1898.00
MAGAZINE
Business, Small and Medium Business

Chambers and Partners
995958
Editorial: 39-41 Parker Street, London WC2B 5PQ Tel: 44 02076 068844
Email: pressreleases@chambersandpartners.com
Web site: www.chambersandpartners.com
Freq: Annual Not Audited
MAGAZINE
Legal Services, Publishing

Changeboard
984859
Editorial: 20c Hillgate Place, Balham Hill, London SW12 9ER Tel: 44 02086 758851

Web site: www.changeboard.com
Freq: Quarterly
Circ: 85000 Not Audited
MAGAZINE
Recruiting

Channel Info
981059
Editorial: Pipers Business Centre, 220 Vale Road, Tonbridge, London GN9 1SP
Tel: 44 01732 441850
Web site: www.channelinfo.net
Freq: Monthly
Circ: 5936 Not Audited
Editor: Caron Bentley
Profile: Channel Info is a magazine covering the broad spectrum of the office market, including stationery, furniture, equipment, telecoms, supplies, IT products and services, 3D printing and digital printing. Contains industry news, case studies, profiles, new product information, market analysis, benchmarking, features and events coverage.
Ad Rate: Full Page Mono £1947.00
Ad Rate: Full Page Colour £1947.00
MAGAZINE
Auto Aftermarket, Office Supplies, Retail Management

Chart Breakout
985224
Editorial: 3 Campden House Court, 42 Gloucester Walk, London W8 4HU
Tel: 44 02079 377879
Web site: www.chartbreakout.co.uk
Freq: Monthly Not Audited
Editor: Quentin Lumsden
Profile: Journal covering the stock market covering fundamental and technical analysis and recommendations on shares. Read by private investors, asset management companies and bankers.
MAGAZINE
Financial Markets, Investment Banking

Charter Broker
1056762
Tel: 44 01279 714529
Email: info@charterbroker.aero
Web site: www.charterbroker.aero
Freq: Bi-Monthly
Circ: 14854 Not Audited
Editor: Caroline Hodge
MAGAZINE
Aviation

Chartered Banker
981009
Editorial: Drumsheugh House, 38b Drumsheugh Gardens, Edinburgh EH3 7SW
Tel: 44 01314 737777
Email: info@charteredbanker.com
Web site: www.charteredbanker.com
Freq: Bi-Monthly
Circ: 10500 Not Audited
Profile: Journal of the Chartered Institute of Banking in Scotland covering wealth management, banking and financial service practitioners' professional development. Previous title: The Scottish Banker Aimed at banking and finance professionals.
Ad Rate: Full Page Colour £1600.00
MAGAZINE
Banking

Chemical Communications
986547
Editorial: Royal Society of Chemistry, Thomas Graham House, Science Park, Milton Road, Cambridge CB4 0WF
Tel: 44 01223 420066
Web site: http://pubs.rsc.org/en/journals/journalissues/cc#!recentarticles&adv
Freq: 2 Times/Week Not Audited
Profile: Journal covering news and analysis on important developments within the chemical sciences.
Ad Rate: Full Page Colour £890.00
MAGAZINE
Chemicals, Science

The Chemical Engineer (tce)
980040
Editorial: Davis Building, 165-189 Railway Terrace, Rugby, Rugby CV21 3HQ
Tel: 44 01788 578214
Web site: www.tcetoday.com

Freq: Monthly
Circ: 29861 Not Audited
Editor: Adam Duckett
MAGAZINE
Chemicals, Engineering

Chemical Industries Association
1063452
Editorial: Kings Buildings, Smith Square, London SW1P 3JJ Tel: 44 02078 343399
Email: enquiries@cia.org.uk
Web site: www.cia.org.uk
Freq: Daily
Circ: 13634 Cision Digital Reach
MAGAZINE (ONLINE)
Chemicals

Chemical Watch
985221
Editorial: 140B Longden Coleham, Shrewsbury SY3 7DN Tel: 44 02036 032105
Email: news@chemicalwatch.com
Web site: www.chemicalwatch.com
Freq: Weekly
Circ: 45114 Cision Digital Reach
MAGAZINE (ONLINE)
Chemicals

chemicals-technology.com
985765
Editorial: John Carpenter House, John Carpenter Street, London EC4Y 0AN
Tel: 44 02079 366400
Email: onlineeditorial@kable.co.uk
Web site: www.chemicals-technology.com
Freq: Daily
Circ: 49240 Cision Digital Reach
MAGAZINE (ONLINE)
Chemicals

Chemistry & Industry
981077
Editorial: 14 - 15 Belgrave Square, London SW1X 8PS Tel: 44 01243 779777
Email: ci@wiley.com
Web site: www.soci.org/chemistryandindustry
Freq: Monthly
Circ: 2400 Not Audited
Editor: Neil Elsberg
Profile: Contains news and information on the fine chemicals, pharmaceutical, biotechnology and life science businesses. Includes articles on food, the environment, chemistry, water, biotechnology and energy. Read by chemical, pharmaceutical, biotechnology, life sciences industry executives, research managers, academics and government officials.
Ad Rate: Full Page Colour £2100.00
MAGAZINE
Chemicals, Science

Chemistry World
980179
Editorial: Thomas Graham House, Milton Road, Cambridge CB4 0WF
Tel: 44 01223 420066
Email: chemistryworld@rsc.org
Web site: www.rsc.org/chemistryworld
Freq: Monthly
Circ: 51375 Not Audited
Editor: Adam Brownsell
Profile: News magazine of the Royal Society of Chemistry covering global developments of the chemical sciences. Provides news and analysis, career development information, technology features and topical stories. Read by chemists and chemical scientists.
Ad Rate: Full Page Colour £5000.00
MAGAZINE
Chemicals, Science

Child: Care, Health and Development
999223
Editorial: 9600 Garsington Road, Oxford OX4 2DQ Tel: 44 01865 778315
Email: cs-author@wiley.com
Web site: http://onlinelibrary.wiley.com/journal/10.1111/(ISSN)1365-2214
Freq: Bi-Monthly Not Audited
Editor: Stuart Logan
MAGAZINE
Pediatrics

Children's Health Care
999681
Editorial: 4 Park Square, Milton Park, Abingdon, Didcot OX14 4RN
Tel: 44 02070 175544
Email: authorqueries@tandf.co.uk
Web site: http://www.tandfonline.com/toc/hchc20/current
Freq: Quarterly Not Audited
Editor: Kenneth Tarnowski
MAGAZINE
Pediatrics

China Agricultural Information
1061282
Tel: 44 86108 2109628
Email: zgnyxx001@126.com
Freq: Monthly
Circ: 10003 Not Audited
MAGAZINE
Animal Farming

China Fruit News
1061680
Tel: 44 86236 8349197
Email: tougao@southfruit.com.cn
Web site: http://gjyyrdgsxx.periodicals.net.cn
Freq: Monthly
Circ: 5001 Not Audited
MAGAZINE
Animal Farming

Chinese Journal of Atmospheric Sciences
1061398
Tel: 44 86108 2995051
Email: dqkx@mail.iap.ac.cn
Web site: http://www.iap.ac.cn
Freq: Bi-Monthly Not Audited
MAGAZINE
Science

Chinese Management Studies
995080
Editorial: Emerald Group Publishing Limited, Howard House, Wagon Lane, Bingley BD16 1WA Tel: 44 01274 777700
Web site: http://www.emeraldinsight.com/loi/CMS
Freq: Quarterly Not Audited
MAGAZINE
Business, Corporate Responsibility

Chinese Pharmaceutical Affairs
1061374
Tel: 44 86106 7095523
Email: zhongguoyaoshi@sina.com
Freq: Monthly
Circ: 10000 Not Audited
MAGAZINE
Pharmaceuticals

Chinwag
1066536
Editorial: PO Box 66046, London W3 3EP
Tel: 44 02071 832923
Email: editor@chinwag.com
Web site: www.chinwag.com
Freq: Daily
Circ: 39805 Cision Digital Reach
MAGAZINE (ONLINE)
Marketing

CHP Packer International
984410
Editorial: 53 Basepoint, Caxton Close, East Portway Industrial Estate, Andover SP10 3FG Tel: 44 01264 326480
Email: editorial@binstedgroup.com
Web site: www.binstedgroup.com/pubs/chp.html
Freq: Bi-Monthly
Circ: 4039 Not Audited
Editor: Ed Binsted
Profile: Magazine covering all aspects of packaging machinery and materials for the cosmetics, healthcare and pharmaceutical industries. Aimed at individuals responsible for purchasing, technical and production directors, packaging buyers and senior management.
Ad Rate: Full Page Colour £1535.00
MAGAZINE
Manufacturing

Business Magazines

Chromatography Today 986753
Editorial: Oak Court Business Centre, Sandridge Park, Porters Wood, St.Albans, London AL3 6PH **Tel:** 44 01727 858840
Email: info@labmate-online.com
Web site: www.chromatographytoday.com
Freq: Quarterly
Circ: 7563 Not Audited
Editor: Gwyneth Astles
Profile: Journal featuring in-depth articles and application notes exploring the most current issues within chromatography as well as industry news and information on the very latest products, training courses, exhibitions & conferences. News from the Chromatographic Society and biographies of ChromSoc medal winners are also included.
Ad Rate: Full Page Colour £2195.00
MAGAZINE
Science

Church Building & Heritage Review 983357
Editorial: Guardian Print Centre, Longbridge Road, Trafford Park, Manchester M17 1SN
Tel: 44 01619 085301
Email: editor@churchbuilding.co.uk
Web site: www.churchbuilding.co.uk
Freq: Bi-Monthly
Circ: 4000 Not Audited
MAGAZINE
Architecture & Design, Building & Construction, Interior Design

CIBSE Journal 983266
Editorial: 1 Cambridge Technopark, Newmarket Road, Cambridge CB5 8PE
Tel: 44 01223 378000
Email: editor@cibsejournal.com
Web site: www.cibsejournal.com
Freq: Monthly
Circ: 18625 Not Audited
Editor: Alex Smith
Profile: Magazine containing news and analysis, design, technical and practical guidance, new product information, continuous professional development content and legislation. Aimed at members of the Chartered Institution of Building Services Engineers as well as building engineers and their associates.
Ad Rate: Full Page Colour £3600.00
MAGAZINE
Architecture & Design, Building & Construction

CILEx Journal 998934
Editorial: Kempston Manor, Kempston, Bedford, Bedford MK42 7AB
Tel: 44 01234 845721
Web site: http://www.cilex.org.uk/cilex_ journal/journal_home.aspx
Freq: Monthly Not Audited
Editor: Val Williams
MAGAZINE
Criminal Law, Employment, Family Law, Litigation, Real Estate Law

CILIP Update 983294
Editorial: 7 Ridgmount Street, London WC1E 7AE **Tel:** 44 02072 550500
Email: info@cilip.org.uk
Web site: www.cilip.org.uk/update
Freq: Monthly
Circ: 12173 Not Audited
Profile: Update is the UK's practitioner journal for staff in public, academic and corporate sector libraries and information services. Update contains analysis and comment on relevant trends and developments in public policy, central and local government, education, law, business, management, information management, online media, cultural services and intellectual property. Update is read by opinion formers and senior and aspiring professionals in the educational, research, local and central government, health, corporate, professional services and voluntary sectors who specialize in information service delivery or information management.Aimed at those working in public libraries, academic libraries, the information technology sector and those in further and higher education.

Ad Rate: Full Page Colour £1180.00
MAGAZINE
Public Sector

CIMA Insight 982921
Editorial: 26 Chapter Street, London SW1P 4NP **Tel:** 44 02088 492323
Email: insight@cimaglobal.com
Web site: www.cimaglobal.com/insight
Freq: Monthly
Circ: 27172 Cision Digital Reach
Profile: Email newsletter covering accountancy in business. Includes articles on budgeting, forecasting, performance measurement, corporate governance and accounting standards. Aimed at professional accountants in business.
MAGAZINE (ONLINE)
Accounting

CIO UK 980863
Editorial: 7th Floor, Clifton House, 101 Euston Road, London NW1 2RA
Tel: 44 02077 562800
Web site: www.cio.co.uk
Freq: Monthly
Circ: 21000 Not Audited
Editor: Edward Qualtrough
MAGAZINE
Business, Corporate Responsibility, Data Management

Cities Today 999502
Editorial: Chester house, Fulham Green, 81-83 Fulham High Street, London SW6 3JA
Tel: 44 02071 938066
Email: editorial@cities-today.com
Web site: www.cities-today.com
Freq: Quarterly
Circ: 10000 Not Audited
Editor: Jonathan Andrews
MAGAZINE
Government, Public Sector

City Confidential 984723
Editorial: 1 Skipton Road, Ilkley, Ilkley LS29 9EH **Tel:** 44 01943 600644
Email: info@cityconfidential.co.uk
Web site: www.cityconfidential.co.uk
Freq: Bi-Weekly
Circ: 600 Not Audited
Editor: Simon Flather
MAGAZINE
Financial Markets

City Security Magazine 997504
Editorial: Northside House, Mount Pleasant, London EN4 9EB **Tel:** 44 02083 632813
Email: editorial@citysecuritymagazine.com
Web site: www.citysecuritymagazine.com
Freq: Quarterly
Circ: 11000 Not Audited
MAGAZINE
Security & Security Systems

Citywire 979849
Editorial: 1st Floor, 87 Vauxhall Walk, London SE11 5HJ **Tel:** 44 02078 402250
Email: news@citywire.co.uk
Web site: www.citywire.co.uk
Freq: Daily
Circ: 1003149 Cision Digital Reach
Profile: Website covering financial investment. An independent organization where the contributors discuss anything from taxes and retirement to savings and insurance.
MAGAZINE (ONLINE)
Fund Management

Civil Engineering (UK) 995987
Editorial: Institution of Civil Engineers, 1 Great George Street, London SW1P 3AA
Tel: 44 02076 652448
Email: editor@ice.org.uk
Web site: www.icevirtuallibrary.com/ content/serial/cien
Freq: Quarterly
Circ: 56000 Not Audited
Editor: Simon Fullalove
MAGAZINE
Engineering

Civil Engineering Surveyor 984088
Editorial: 2nd Floor Dominion House, Sibson Road, Sale, Sale M33 7PP
Tel: 44 01619 723100
Email: dsmart@cices.org
Web site: www.ices.org.uk
Freq: Monthly
Circ: 4000 Not Audited
Profile: Technical journal covering the civil engineering industry. Aimed at measurement engineers and quantity and land surveyors.
Ad Rate: Full Page Mono £1028.00
Ad Rate: Full Page Colour £1315.00
MAGAZINE
Building & Construction, Engineering, Real Estate Law

Civil Service World 982141
Editorial: Floor 11, The Shard, 32 London Bridge Street, London SE1 9SG
Tel: 44 02075 935501
Email: editorial@civilserviceworld.com
Web site: www.civilserviceworld.com/
Freq: Monthly
Circ: 7490 Not Audited
Editor: Jess Bowie
Profile: Magazine published for the upper ranks of the civil service, covering policy and management issues. Aimed at senior civil servants and MPs.
Ad Rate: Full Page Colour £6320.00
MAGAZINE
Government, Public Sector

CIWM Journal 980168
Editorial: 7-9 St Peter's Gardens, Marefair, Northampton NN1 1SX
Tel: 44 01604 620426
Web site: http://www.ciwm-journal.co.uk/
Freq: Monthly
Circ: 18000 Not Audited
Editor: Ben Wood
MAGAZINE
Hygiene

Claims Magazine (UK) 985110
Editorial: G1 - G6 East Wing, The Croft, Boroughbridge Road, Kirk Deighton, Harrogate LS22 5HG **Tel:** 44 01423 851150
Web site: www.claimsmag.co.uk
Freq: Bi-Monthly
Circ: 15653 Cision Digital Reach
Editor: Marek Handzel
MAGAZINE (ONLINE)
Insurance

Clapham Omnibus 996966
Editorial: 3tc House, 16 Crosby Road North, Crosby, Liverpool L22 0NY
Tel: 44 01512 364141
Email: admin@benhampublishing.com
Web site: www.benhampublishing.com
Freq: Quarterly
Circ: 1500 Not Audited
MAGAZINE
Corporate Law, Government, Legal Services

Classic Plant & Machinery 983726
Editorial: PO Box 13, Westerham, London TN16 3AG **Tel:** 44 01959 541444
Web site: http://tractormagazine.co.uk/ magazines/classic-plant-machinery/
Freq: Monthly
Circ: 14500 Not Audited
Profile: Magazine covering dump trucks, excavators, compressors, forklifts, mining machinery and road rollers. Includes news, restorations, auction reports, manufacturers' histories, finds and discoveries and events listings.
Ad Rate: Full Page Colour £485.00
MAGAZINE
Animal Farming, Engineering, Manufacturing

Clay Technology 984914
Editorial: 297 Euston Road, London NW1 3AQ **Tel:** 44 02074 517300
Email: ct@iom3.org

Web site: www.iom3.org/content/clay-technology-0
Freq: Quarterly
Circ: 650 Not Audited
Profile: Magazine of the Institute of Clay Technology. Contains matters affecting the construction products industries, especially heavy clay products. Aimed at members of the Institute of Clay Technology, managers and suppliers within the heavy clay sector.
Ad Rate: Full Page Mono £500.00
Ad Rate: Full Page Colour £882.00
MAGAZINE
Building & Construction

Clean Technology Business Review 987419
Editorial: Cleantechnology Business Review Progressive Trade Media Ltd., 40-42 Hatton Garden, London EC1N 8EB
Tel: 44 02079 366898
Email: news@industryreview.com
Web site: www.cleantechnology-business-review.com
Freq: Daily
Circ: 7519 Cision Digital Reach
Profile: Website covering clean technology. The Clean Technology Business Review features news, analysis and information on clean technology.
MAGAZINE (ONLINE)
Alternative/Renewable Energy, Environment

Cleaning & Maintenance 981279
Editorial: Quartz House, 20 Clarendon Road, Redhill, Redhill RH1 1GX
Tel: 44 01737 855041
Web site: www.cleaningmag.com
Freq: Monthly
Circ: 10501 Not Audited
Editor: Neil Nixon
Profile: Magazine providing news, articles and product information concerning the cleaning industry.
Ad Rate: Full Page Colour £2935.00
MAGAZINE
Hygiene

Cleaning Hygiene Today 998553
Editorial: Unit 5 Gateway, 20/25 Trading Estate London Road, Swanley, Swanley BR8 8DE **Tel:** 44 01322 662289
Web site: www.chtmag.com
Freq: Monthly
Circ: 11544 Not Audited
Profile: Magazine covering products, services, market trends, trade news and events relevant to the UK cleaning and hygiene industry. First published in 1989, the publication has an average of 90 pages per issue. Press day on the first week of month preceding the cover date. Aimed at personnel with purchasing and specifying authority for cleaning and hygiene equipment, supplies, services and those that have an interest in the cleaning industry, as well as executives working for the NHS within Estates & Facilities.
Ad Rate: Full Page Colour £1850.00
MAGAZINE
Hygiene

Cleaning Matters 981280
Editorial: Second Floor, North Suit, 13 - 21 Cantelupe Road, East Grinstead, East Grinstead RH19 3BE **Tel:** 44 01342 316390
Web site: www.cleaning-matters.com
Freq: Bi-Monthly
Circ: 12500 Not Audited
Editor: Catherine Hackett
Profile: Magazine covering news, views, features, new products, service information, testing and surveys. Aimed at buyers, specifiers manufacturers, distributors, cleaning and maintenance contractors, local authorities, facilities managers and those involved in cleaning products, services and equipment.A charge may be made for colour separation. Regular features: Access Equipment; Building Cleaning; Carpet & upholstery care; Chemicals and dosing; Cleaning equipment; Contract cleaning; Fire & flood restoration; Floorcare; Food hygiene; Graffiti gum and grime; Health and safety; Hospital hygiene; Pressure washers;

Scrubber dryers/burnishers; Training;
Washroom hygiene; Window cleaning;
Wipes & dispensers
Ad Rate: Full Page Mono £1470.00
Ad Rate: Full Page Colour £1070.00
MAGAZINE
Hygiene

Cleanroom Technology   986592
Editorial: Natraj Building, The Tanneries, 55
Bermondsey Street, London SE1 3XG
Tel: 44 02071 931279
Email: pharma@hpcimedia.com
Web site: www.cleanroom-technology.co.uk
Freq: Monthly
Circ: 7000 Not Audited
Editor: Susan Birks
Profile: European journal of contamination
control. Aimed at engineers, managers and
consultants in cleanroom and
contamination-control industries throughout
Europe.
Ad Rate: Full Page Colour £2275.00
MAGAZINE
Hygiene

Clearview   984711
Editorial: 2-3 Burleigh Court, Barnsley S70
1XY **Tel:** 44 01226 321450
Email: pr@clearview-uk.com
Web site: www.clearview-uk.com
Freq: Monthly
Circ: 14889 Not Audited
Editor: Becky Taylor
Profile: Magazine featuring specialist
solutions for the glass and glazing industry
including window, door, glass and
conservatory. Read by fabricators and
installers, architects, housing developers,
local authority professionals, shop fitters and
glass manufacturers.
Ad Rate: Full Page Colour £1195.00
MAGAZINE
Building & Construction

The Clerk   998872
Editorial: 8 The Crescent, Taunton, Taunton
TA1 4EA **Tel:** 44 01823 253646
Email: admin@slcc.co.uk
Web site: http://www.slcc.co.uk
Freq: Bi-Monthly
Circ: 4500 Not Audited
Editor: Richard Walden
Profile: Journal of the Society of Local
Council Clerks. Includes information and
news on new products, services and
equipment.
Ad Rate: Full Page Colour £625.00
MAGAZINE
Government

Clerks and Councils Direct
984796
Tel: 44 01359 254149
Email: clerkscouncils@btinternet.com
Web site: www.clerksandcouncilsdirect.co.
uk
Freq: Bi-Monthly
Circ: 10150 Not Audited
Profile: Magazine covering all matters
affecting town, parish and community
councils. Contains news, features and
information on products and services. Also
covers relations between all levels of local
government in England and Wales.
Ad Rate: Full Page Mono £1250.00
Ad Rate: Full Page Colour £1445.00
MAGAZINE
Business, Small and Medium Business

ClickZ UK   988313
Editorial: 1 Broadway, Hammersmith,
London W6 9DL
Email: editorial@clickz.com
Web site: www.clickz.com
Freq: Daily
Circ: 431103 Cision Digital Reach
MAGAZINE (ONLINE)
Marketing

Climate Action   1006440
Editorial: Climate Action, Floor 3, Two
America Square, London EC3N 2LU
Tel: 44 02078 710173
Email: info@climateactionprogramme.org

Web site: www.climateactionprogramme.
org
Freq: Annual
Circ: 10000 Not Audited
MAGAZINE
Energy & Environment, Environment

Clinica Medtech Intelligence
990360
Editorial: 10 Newgate Street, London EC1A
7AZ **Tel:** 44 02070 175000
Email: clinica.enquiry@informa.com
Web site: www.clinica.co.uk
Freq: Daily
Circ: 44663 Cision Digital Reach
Editor: Tina Tan
MAGAZINE (ONLINE)
Healthcare Industry, Medical Technology,
Science

Clinical & Experimental
Allergy   998877
Editorial: c/o John Wiley & Sons, Ltd, The
Atrium, Southern Gate, Chichester PO19
8QG **Tel:** 44 01865 778315
Web site: http://onlinelibrary.wiley.com/
journal/10.1111/(ISSN)1365-2222
Freq: Monthly Not Audited
Profile: Journal covering clinical and
experimental observations in disease in all
fields of medicine in which allergic
hypersensitivity plays a part. Aimed at allergy
practitioners and research scientists with an
interest in allergic diseases and
mechanisms.
MAGAZINE
Allergies

Clinical and Experimental
Dermatology   995870
Editorial: British Association of
Dermatologists, 4 Fitzroy Square, London
W1T 5HQ **Tel:** 44 02073 916346
Email: ced@wiley.com
Web site: http://onlinelibrary.wiley.com/
journal/10.1111/%28ISSN%291365-2230
Freq: Bi-Monthly Not Audited
Editor: George Millington
MAGAZINE
Dermatology

Clinical Endocrinology   995115
Editorial: The Atrium, Southern Gate,
Chichester PO19 8QG **Tel:** 44 01865 778315
Email: cenedoffice@wiley.com
Web site: http://onlinelibrary.wiley.com/
journal/10.1111/(ISSN)1365-2265
Freq: Monthly
MAGAZINE
Diabetes

Clinical Neurology and
Neurosurgery   995736
Editorial: The Boulevard, Langford Lane,
Kidlington, Oxford OX5 1GB
Tel: 44 01865 843434
Email: cnn@elsevier.com
Web site: http://www.clineu-journal.com/
Freq: Monthly Not Audited
Editor: Peter Paul De Deyn
MAGAZINE
Neurology

Clinical Oncology   983544
Tel: 44 01923 844568
Web site: www.clinicaloncologyonline.net/
Freq: Monthly
Circ: 1644 Not Audited
Profile: Journal covering all aspects of the
clinical management of cancer patients
including multidisciplinary approach to
therapy, articles on all types of malignant
disease and all modalities used in cancer
therapy.
Ad Rate: Full Page Mono £1116.00
Ad Rate: Full Page Colour £2028.00
MAGAZINE
Oncology

Clinical Pharmacist   981216
Editorial: 1 Lambeth High Street, London
SE1 7JN **Tel:** 44 08452 572570
Email: clinicalpharmacist@pharmj.org.uk

Web site: www.clinicalpharmacist.com
Freq: Monthly
Circ: 16698 Not Audited
Profile: Journal produced by PJ Publications
and published by Pharmaceutical Press, the
publishing division of the Royal
Pharmaceutical Society. It incorporates
Hospital Pharmacist, which was established
In 1994 for the publication of articles,
reviews, reports and papers about any
aspect of hospital pharmacy. Launched in
January 2009, Clinical Pharmacist has been
developed to support pharmacists working
in clinical roles in any sector of the
profession.Aimed at hospital pharmacists
and pharmaceutical advisers.
Ad Rate: Full Page Mono £3860.00
Ad Rate: Full Page Colour £5165.00
MAGAZINE
Pharmaceuticals

Clinical Rehabilitation   986866
Editorial: 1 Oliver's Yard, 55 City Road,
London EC1Y 1SP **Tel:** 44 02073 361244
Email: clinical.rehabilitation@sagepub.co.uk
Web site: http://cre.sagepub.com/
Freq: Monthly Not Audited
Profile: Academic publication providing a
forum for the exchange of ideas and
information for people concerned with
rehabilitation. The journal covers the whole
field of disability and rehabilitation.
Ad Rate: Full Page Mono £550.00
MAGAZINE
Occupational Therapy & Rehabilitation

Clinical Rheumatology   985146
Editorial: 236 Gray's Inn Road, 6th Floor,
London WC1X 8HB **Tel:** 44 02031 922762
Web site: www.springer.com/medicine/
rheumatology/journal/10067
Freq: Monthly
Circ: 2331 Not Audited
Profile: Journal containing original clinical
investigation and research in the general
field of rheumatology at postgraduate level.
MAGAZINE
Rheumatology

Clinical Risk   985150
Editorial: 1 Oliver's Yard, 55 City Road,
London EC1Y 1SP **Tel:** 44 02073 248500
Web site: http://cri.sagepub.com/
Freq: Bi-Monthly Not Audited
Profile: Clinical Risk is a bi-monthly
publication covering patient safety, risk
management and medical and legal issues.
Ad Rate: Full Page Mono £515.00
Ad Rate: Full Page Colour £1125.00
MAGAZINE
Health Administration

The Clinical Services Journal
984206
Editorial: Step House, North Farm Road,
Tunbridge Wells TN2 3DR
Tel: 44 01892 779999
Email: csj@stepcomms.com
Web site: www.clinicalservicesjournal.com
Freq: Monthly Not Audited
Profile: Journal covering healthcare and
clinical product news and developments as
well as technical articles based on the
application of products in clinical areas and
a look at clinical products used within.
Ad Rate: Full Page Colour £1915.00
MAGAZINE
Health Administration, Medical
Technology

Cloud Pro   985999
Editorial: CouldPro, 31 - 32 Alfred Place,
London WC1E 7DP **Tel:** 44 02079 076000
Web site: www.cloudpro.co.uk
Freq: Daily
Circ: 167998 Cision Digital Reach
MAGAZINE (ONLINE)
Computers

CML News & Views   985824
Editorial: 3rd Floor, North West Wing, Bush
House, Aldwych, London WC2B 4PJ
Tel: 44 02074 388923
Web site: https://www.cml.org.uk/news/
news-and-views/

Freq: Bi-Weekly
Circ: 19 Cision Digital Reach
Editor: Bernard Clarke
MAGAZINE (ONLINE)
Finance

CnFood.com   1062093
Web site: http://cnfood.com/
Circ: 648 Cision Digital Reach
MAGAZINE (ONLINE)
Food

CNS Oncology   1053755
Editorial: Unitec House, 2 Albert Place,
London N3 1QB **Tel:** 44 02083 716090
Email: info@futuremedicine.com
Web site: http://www.futuremedicine.com/
loi/cns
Freq: Bi-Monthly Not Audited
MAGAZINE
Oncology

Coaching at Work   983404
Editorial: 2nd Floor, 2 Walsworth Road,
Hitchin, Hitchin SG4 9SP
Tel: 44 08456 808185
Email: admin@coaching-at-work.com
Web site: www.coaching-at-work.com
Freq: Bi-Monthly
Circ: 2750 Not Audited
Editor: Liz Hall
Profile: Magazine covering coaching theory
and practical advice on coaching and
mentoring.
MAGAZINE
Company News & Appointments,
Education, Health & Safety, Human
Resources, Recruiting

Coal Daily International   994668
Editorial: Argus House, 175 St John Street,
London EC1V 4LW **Tel:** 44 02077 804200
Email: coal@argusmedia.com
Web site: http://www.argusmedia.com/coal/
argus-coal-daily-international/
Freq: Daily Not Audited
Editor: Dan Hayes
MAGAZINE
Nuclear Power, Oil

Coal International   983474
Editorial: 9 Storey Avenue, Gedling,
Nottingham NG4 4GN **Tel:** 44 01777 871007
Email: editor@mqworld.com
Web site: www.mqworld.com
Freq: Bi-Monthly
Circ: 5000 Not Audited
Profile: Bi-monthly publication providing
worldwide news and information on the coal
mining industry. It features the latest industry
news, case studies, new equipment and
technical articles.
Ad Rate: Full Page Colour £2400.00
MAGAZINE
Alternative/Renewable Energy, Nuclear
Power, Oil

Cobwebinfo.com   998542
Editorial: Unit 9 Bankside, The Watermark,
Gateshead NE11 9SY **Tel:** 44 01914 618000
Email: enquiries@cobwebinfo.com
Web site: www.cobwebinfo.com
Freq: Daily
Circ: 6533 Cision Digital Reach
MAGAZINE (ONLINE)
Business, Small and Medium Business

Cognition   995044
Editorial: 125 London Wall, London EC2Y
5AS **Tel:** 44 02074 244200
Email: cognition@elsevier.com
Web site: www.journals.elsevier.com/
cognition
Freq: Monthly Not Audited
MAGAZINE
Neurology

Cognitive Neuropsychiatry
995709
Editorial: Taylor & Francis Group, 2&4 Park
Square, Milton Park, Abingdon OX14 4RN
Tel: 44 02070 176000

Business Magazines

Email: support@tandfonline.com
Web site: http://www.tandf.co.uk/journals/pcnp
Freq: Bi-Monthly Not Audited
Editor: Anthony S. David
MAGAZINE
Neurology

Cognitive Neuropsychology
999240
Editorial: 2-4 Park Square, Milton Park, Abingdon OX14 4RN **Tel:** 44 02070 177720
Email: pcgn-peerreview@tandf.co.uk
Web site: www.tandfonline.com/loi/pcgn20#.UZuKRqJQH3U
Freq: Bi-Monthly Not Audited
Editor: Brenda Rapp
MAGAZINE
Neurology

Cold Chain News
983860
Editorial: 1 Wood Street, Dover CT16 1DZ
Tel: 44 01326 340263
Email: dean.stiles@coldchainnews.com
Web site: http://www.globalcoldchainnews.com/
Freq: Bi-Monthly
Circ: 1800 Not Audited
Editor: Dean Stiles
Profile: Journal focusing on the manufacture and operation of specialist equipment to store, transport and distribute temperature-sensitive products.
Ad Rate: Full Page Mono £1000.00
Ad Rate: Full Page Colour £1500.00
MAGAZINE
Shipping & Warehousing, Supply Chain Management (SCM)

Colorectal Cancer
996419
Editorial: Unitec House, 2 Albert Place, London N3 1QB **Tel:** 44 02083 716090
Email: info@futuremedicine.com
Web site: www.futuremedicine.com/loi/crc
Freq: Bi-Monthly Not Audited
MAGAZINE
Oncology

Colorectal Disease
998789
Editorial: John Wiley & Sons Inc, The Atrium, Southern Gate, Chichester PO19 8SQ **Tel:** 44 01865 476387
Email: miwillis@wiley.com
Web site: onlinelibrary.wiley.com/journal/10.1111/(ISSN)1463-1318
Freq: Monthly Not Audited
MAGAZINE
Gastroenterology

Commerce & Industry
984525
Editorial: 12-14 Hainton Avenue, Grimsby DN32 9BB **Tel:** 44 01472 359036
Web site: www.commerce-industry.co.uk
Freq: Monthly
Circ: 12500 Not Audited
Profile: Magazine featuring news of local company expansions, promotions and buy-outs. Also covers new products, legislative and parliamentary matters, EEC news, hotel and conference facilities and motoring.
Ad Rate: Full Page Mono £1498.00
Ad Rate: Full Page Colour £1834.00
MAGAZINE
Business, Corporate Responsibility

The Commercial Litigation Journal
1008428
Editorial: Legalease Ltd, 188-190 Fleet Street, London EC4A 2AG
Tel: 44 02073 969292
Email: office@helenswaffield.co.uk
Web site: http://www.legalease.co.uk/index.php/2014-06-27-10-00-49/2014-06-27-10-00-50/commercial-litigation
Freq: Bi-Monthly
MAGAZINE
Litigation

Commercial Micro Manufacturing International
996861
Editorial: 6 Lupin Drive, Huntington, Chester CH3 6SD **Tel:** 44 01244 680222
Web site: http://www.cmmmagazine.com
Freq: Bi-Monthly
Circ: 16300 Not Audited
Editor: Aleksandra Jones
MAGAZINE
Manufacturing

Commercial News Media
987357
Tel: 44 01278 760003
Email: news@commercialnewsmedia.co.uk
Web site: http://www.commercialnewsmedia.com
Freq: Daily
Circ: 17203 Cision Digital Reach
MAGAZINE (ONLINE)
Architecture & Design, Building & Construction, Commercial Real Estate, Finance, Interior Design, Legal Affairs, Office Design, Retail, Sustainable Development, Travel Industry

Commercial Property Monthly
980881
Editorial: Alpika House, 343 Eden Park Avenue, Beckenham BR3 3JN
Tel: 44 02079 936657
Email: carbonneutral@cpmonthly.com
Web site: www.commercialpropertymonthly.com
Freq: Bi-Monthly
Circ: 20000 Not Audited
Profile: Magazine covering retail, industrial and commercial property news.
Ad Rate: Full Page Mono £985.00
Ad Rate: Full Page Colour £1570.00
MAGAZINE
Architecture & Design, Building & Construction, Commercial Real Estate, Finance, Legal Affairs, Office Design, Residential Real Estate, Retail, Sustainable Development, Urban Planning & Development

Commercial Property Register Group
983929
Editorial: Suite 107, 5 Liberty Square, Kings Hill, West Malling ME19 4AU
Tel: 44 01322 387555
Email: info@southcoastpublishing.co.uk
Web site: www.compropregister.com
Freq: Daily
Circ: 2396 Cision Digital Reach
Editor: Clive Branson
MAGAZINE (ONLINE)
Architecture & Design, Building & Construction, Commercial Real Estate, Interior Design, Office Design, Residential Real Estate, Retail, Travel Industry

Commercial Risk Europe
985412
Editorial: 7 Granard Business Centre, Bunns Lane, Mill Hill, London NW7 2DQ
Tel: 44 02038 580192
Email: news@commercialriskeurope.com
Web site: www.commercialriskeurope.com
Freq: Monthly
Circ: 3717 Not Audited
MAGAZINE
Insurance

Commissioning
998338
Editorial: 10 Rose & Crown Yard, King Street, London SW1Y 6RE
Email: editorial@commissioningjournal.com
Web site: http://commissioningjournal.com
Freq: Monthly
Circ: 10000 Not Audited
MAGAZINE
Health Administration, Healthcare Industry

Commodities Now
979903
Tel: 44 01253 700502
Email: info@commodities-now.com
Web site: www.commodities-now.com
Freq: Quarterly
Circ: 8000 Not Audited

Profile: Magazine providing analysis and information on trends in the commodities markets. It covers power and energy including oil, metals and metal mining including precious metals and agricultural and environmental markets. Read by commodities specialists.
Ad Rate: Full Page Colour £3950.00
MAGAZINE
Alternative/Renewable Energy, Carbon Emissions & Trading, Commodities, Derivatives, Electricity, Energy, Mining & Quarrying, Nuclear Power, Oil, Steel

Comms Business
985667
Editorial: White House, Commercial Road, Tunbridge Wells, Tunbridge Wells TN1 2RR
Tel: 44 01892 538348
Web site: www.commsbusiness.co.uk
Freq: Monthly
Circ: 18130 Not Audited
Editor: Ian Hunter
Profile: Magazine covering essential news and analysis, themed features, opinion pieces, interviews, appointments and contract news.
Ad Rate: Full Page Colour £3575.00
MAGAZINE
Auto Aftermarket, Mobile Communications, Telecommunications/Electronic Communications

Comms Dealer
980860
Editorial: 3rd Floor, Armstrong House, 38 Market Square, Uxbridge, London UB8 1LH
Tel: 44 01895 454542
Email: info@bpl-business.com
Web site: http://www.comms-dealer.com
Freq: Monthly
Circ: 16020 Not Audited
Profile: Magazine covering industry news and information on telecommunications products.
Ad Rate: Full Page Colour £3190.00
MAGAZINE
Auto Aftermarket, Telecommunications/Electronic Communications

CommsBusiness (Online)
1055930
Editorial: Swink Media, White House, Commercial Road, Tunbridge Wells TN1 2RR **Tel:** 44 01892 538348
Email: mat@commsbusiness.co.uk
Web site: http://commsbusiness.co.uk
Freq: Daily
Circ: 80246 Cision Digital Reach
MAGAZINE (ONLINE)
Business, Data Management, Small and Medium Business, Telecommunications/Electronic Communications

Communicate (UK)
984873
Editorial: Unit 1G, 26-32 Voltaire Road, London SW4 6DH **Tel:** 44 02074 987008
Email: news@communicatemagazine.co.uk
Web site: www.communicatemagazine.co.uk
Freq: Monthly
Circ: 8000 Not Audited
Editor: Brittany Golob
MAGAZINE
Branding

Communications Africa
981079
Editorial: University House, 11-13 Lower Grosvenor Place, London SW1W 0EX
Tel: 44 02078 347676
Email: post@alaincharles.com
Web site: www.communicationsafrica.com
Freq: Bi-Monthly
Circ: 5068 Not Audited
Profile: Magazine covering telecommunications, electronics, world news and industry in Africa. The magazine is published bi-monthly.
Ad Rate: Full Page Mono £3550.00
Ad Rate: Full Page Colour £5220.00
MAGAZINE
Telecommunications/Electronic Communications

Communiqué
998577
Editorial: Mansard Group, Church Road, Little Bookham, London KT23 3JG
Tel: 44 01372 414200
Email: editor@pmlive.com
Web site: www.communiquelive.com
Freq: Semi-Annual
Circ: 5200 Not Audited
MAGAZINE
Pharmaceuticals

Community Care
981276
Editorial: Quadrant House, The Quadrant, Sutton, London SM2 5AS
Tel: 44 02086 523787
Email: communitycare@rbi.co.uk
Web site: www.communitycare.co.uk
Freq: Daily
Circ: 231182 Cision Digital Reach
Editor: Judy Cooper
Profile: Website covering the social care sector. The Community Care website shares the latest news, analysis, opinion and background information on social care.
MAGAZINE (ONLINE)
Community Care (UK)

Community Care Market News
983717
Editorial: 29 Angel Gate, City Road, London EC1V 2PT **Tel:** 44 02078 339123
Email: info@laingbuisson.com
Web site: http://www.laingbuisson.co.uk/Newsletters/CCMN.aspx
Freq: Monthly
Circ: 1000 Not Audited
Editor: Eleanore Robinson
Profile: Journal containing news, analysis and informed comment within the community care sector.
Ad Rate: Full Page Mono £1650.00
MAGAZINE
Community Care (UK), Geriatrics, Healthcare Industry

Community Practitioner
984374
Editorial: 17 Britton Street, London EC1M 5TP **Tel:** 44 02078 806200
Web site: http://www.communitypractitioner.co.uk/
Freq: Monthly
Circ: 19000 Not Audited
Profile: Official Journal of the Community Practitioners and Health Visitors Association. Includes professional reports and news features of people and events associated with community health and nursing.
Ad Rate: Full Page Mono £1390.00
Ad Rate: Full Page Colour £2310.00
MAGAZINE
Community Care (UK)

CompactNews
999093
Editorial: 78 York Street, London W1H 1DP
Tel: 44 02076 307775
Email: mail@compactnews.com
Web site: www.compactnews.com
Freq: Daily
Circ: 1748 Cision Digital Reach
MAGAZINE (ONLINE)
Telecommunications/Electronic Communications

Companion Animal
981168
Editorial: St Jude's Church, Dulwich Road, London SE24 0PB **Tel:** 44 02077 385454
Email: coan@markallengroup.com
Web site: http://magsubscriptions.com/healthcare/animalhealth/companion-print
Freq: Monthly
Circ: 6400 Not Audited
Editor: Debra Bourne
MAGAZINE
Veterinary Medicine

Comparative Immunology, Microbiology & Infectious Diseases
995888
Editorial: The Boulevard, Langford Lane, Kidlington OX5 1GB **Tel:** 44 01865 843000
Web site: http://www.journals.elsevier.com/comparative-immunology-microbiology-and-infectious-diseases/

Freq: Bi-Monthly
Circ: 17 Not Audited
MAGAZINE
Veterinary Medicine

Competition Law Insight 980809
Editorial: Christchurch Court, 10-15 Newgate Street, London EC1A 7AZ
Tel: 44 02070 177565
Web site: www.competitionlawinsight.com
Freq: Monthly Not Audited
Profile: Newsletter pinpointing the implications for business of key developments in community law.
MAGAZINE
Corporate Law

Competition Law International 997309
Editorial: 4th Floor, 10 St Bride Street, London EC4A 4AD **Tel:** 44 02078 420090
Email: editor@int-bar.org
Web site: http://www.ibanet.org/Publications/competition_law_international.aspx
Freq: Semi-Annual
Circ: 1600 Not Audited
MAGAZINE
Corporate Law

Completely London 985261
Editorial: Zetland House, Scrutton Street, London EC2A 4HJ **Tel:** 44 02077 493300
Web site: https://www.kfh.co.uk/press/completely-london-magazine
Freq: 3 Times/Year
Circ: 70000 Not Audited
Editor: Donna Hardie
Profile: Magazine covering London's culture, arts, people, design, property with photography. Distributed by Kinleigh Folkard & Hayward.
Ad Rate: Full Page Colour £1500.00
MAGAZINE
Property Management & Maintenance

Compounding World 999336
Editorial: 6 Pritchard Street, Bristol BS2 8RH **Tel:** 44 01179 249442
Web site: www.compoundingworld.com/
Freq: Monthly
Circ: 28122 Not Audited
Profile: Website covering polymer compounders and master batch producers. Compounding World discusses key technical developments, market trends, strategic business issues, legislative announcements, company profiles and new product launches.
Ad Rate: Full Page Colour £1500.00
MAGAZINE
Chemicals, Plastics

Computational Biology and Chemistry 996256
Editorial: Fac. of Creative Arts, Techn. and Sciences, University of Bedfordshire, Park Square, Luton LU1 3JU
Tel: 44 01582 489265
Web site: www.journals.elsevier.com/computational-biology-and-chemistry
Freq: Bi-Monthly Not Audited
Editor: James Crabbe
MAGAZINE
Biotechnology, Chemicals, Science

Computer and Telecommunications Law Review 982922
Editorial: Friars House, 160 Blackfriars Road, London SC1 8EZ
Tel: 44 02073 937000
Web site: www.sweetandmaxwell.co.uk
Freq: Bi-Monthly Not Audited
MAGAZINE
Computers, Corporate Law, Telecommunications/Electronic Communications

Computer Arts (UK) 981051
Editorial: Quay House, The Ambury, Bath BA1 1UA **Tel:** 44 01225 442244
Email: hello@computerarts.co.uk

Web site: www.creativebloq.com/computer-arts-magazine
Freq: Monthly
Circ: 12426 Not Audited
Editor: Nick Carson
MAGAZINE
Computers, Graphic Design, Software

Computer Fraud & Security 998764
Editorial: The Boulevard, Langford Lane, Kidlington, Oxford OX5 1GB
Tel: 44 01865 843687
Email: news@contrarisk.com
Web site: www.computerfraudandsecurity.com
Freq: Monthly Not Audited
Editor: Steve Mansfield-Devine
MAGAZINE
Computers, Security & Security Systems

Computers & Law 981050
Editorial: The Coach House, New Road, Studley, Calne SN11 9LT
Tel: 44 01249 822400
Email: lseastham@aol.com
Web site: www.scl.org
Freq: Bi-Monthly
Circ: 1600 Not Audited
Editor: Laurence Eastham
Profile: Journal for members of the Society for Computers & Law. Deals with IT applications of interest to lawyers and IT law and covers latest IT law news and trends.
Ad Rate: Full Page Colour £1100.00
MAGAZINE
Computers, Legal Services, Software

ComputerworldUK 984121
Editorial: 101 Euston Road, London NW1 2RA **Tel:** 44 02077 562800
Email: cwuknews@idg.co.uk
Web site: www.computerworlduk.com
Freq: Daily
Circ: 165027 Cision Digital Reach
Editor: Matthew Finnegan
MAGAZINE (ONLINE)
Computers

Computing Security 986941
Editorial: 35 Station Square, Petts Wood, Orpington BR5 1LZ **Tel:** 44 01689 616000
Web site: www.computingsecurity.co.uk
Freq: Bi-Monthly
Circ: 12000 Not Audited
Profile: Magazine dealing with the key issue that organisations face as they try to maintain secure networks in the face of new and old threats.
MAGAZINE
Computers, Security & Security Systems

Concrete 985707
Tel: 44 01276 607140
Email: editorial@concrete.org.uk
Web site: www.concrete.org.uk
Freq: Monthly
Circ: 3000 Not Audited
Editor: James Luckey
Profile: Journal covering all matters related to concrete technology, design and construction of concrete structures. Read by consulting engineers, contractors, construction equipment and material manufacturers and suppliers.
Ad Rate: Full Page Colour £1650.00
MAGAZINE
Engineering

Concrete Engineering International 988811
Editorial: Riverside House, 4 Meadows Business Park, Station Approach, Camberley GU17 9AB **Tel:** 44 01276 607140
Email: cei_editorial@concrete.org.uk
Web site: http://www.concrete.org.uk/magazine.asp
Freq: Semi-Annual
Circ: 4000 Not Audited
Editor: Helen Marney
MAGAZINE
Architecture & Design, Building & Construction

Concussion 1054119
Editorial: Unitec House, 2 Albert Place, London N3 1QB **Tel:** 44 02083 716090
Email: info@future-science-group.com
Web site: http://www.future-science-group.com/journalprofile/concussion/
Freq: No Frequency Established
Circ: 55 Cision Digital Reach
MAGAZINE (ONLINE)
Neurology

Confectionery Production 983695
Editorial: The Maltings, 57 Bath Street, Gravesend, London DA11 0DF
Tel: 44 01474 532202
Web site: www.confectioneryproduction.com
Freq: Monthly
Circ: 4100 Not Audited
Editor: Katie Smith
Profile: Publication covering machinery equipment, ingredients and packaging for the chocolate, bakery, ice cream and confectionery industries. Read by works, development engineers, technicians, sales personnel, managers and directors.
Ad Rate: Full Page Colour £2250.00
MAGAZINE
Food

Conference & Common Room 988560
Editorial: 63 Chapel Lane, Zeals, Warminster, Woodbridge BA12 6NP
Tel: 44 01394 389850
Email: enquiries@johncatt.com
Web site: www.candcr.co.uk
Freq: 3 Times/Year
Circ: 4000 Not Audited
Editor: Tom Wheare
Profile: Journal of the Headmasters' & Headmistresses' Conference (HMC) schools. It contains authoritative editorials of interest to all those who create and maintain the high standards associated with independent schools. Aimed at headteachers, bursars and the key teaching staff of these schools. The magazine is published three times a year, at the start of each school term, in September, January and April.
MAGAZINE
Education, Schools & Institutions, Students

Conference & Meetings World 985848
Editorial: 4th Floor, Sterling House, 6-10 St Georges Road, London SW19 4DP
Tel: 44 02084 811122
Email: info@mashmedia.net
Web site: http://www.c-mw.net
Freq: Quarterly
Circ: 5000 Not Audited
MAGAZINE
Marketing

Conference News 983734
Editorial: 4th Floor, Sterling House, 6-10 St Georges Road, London SW19 4DP
Tel: 44 02084 811122
Email: info@mashmedia.net
Web site: www.conference-news.co.uk
Freq: Monthly
Circ: 13811 Not Audited
Profile: Magazine featuring the latest conference news, interviews with key market figures and industry analysis. Aimed at organisers, venue owners and suppliers.
Ad Rate: Full Page Colour £2995.00
MAGAZINE
Marketing

Congress Times 1066028
Editorial: Olympus House, Werrington Centre, Werrington, Peterborough PE4 6NA
Tel: 44 01733 325522
Web site: www.vetsonline.com
Freq: Weekly
Circ: 19794 Not Audited
Editor: Rebecca Hubbard
MAGAZINE
Veterinary Medicine

Conservation and Utilization of Mineral Resouces 1061437
Tel: 44 86371 68632026
Email: kcbh@chinajournal.net.cn
Freq: Bi-Monthly
Circ: 1003 Not Audited
MAGAZINE
Environment, Mining & Quarrying, Steel

Construct UK 988750
Editorial: Marlowe Innovation Centre, Marlowe Way, Ramsgate, Ramsgate CT12 6FA **Tel:** 44 03301 330019
Email: info@constructuk.com
Web site: www.constructuk.com
Freq: Daily
Circ: 12529 Cision Digital Reach
MAGAZINE (ONLINE)
Advertising Industry, Branding, Building & Construction, Engineering, Marketing

Construction and Civil Engineering 998524
Editorial: Suite 10, Cringleford Business Centre, Intwood Road, Norwich NR4 6AU
Tel: 44 01603 274130
Web site: www.ccemagazine.com
Freq: Monthly
Circ: 85000 Not Audited
MAGAZINE
Building & Construction, Engineering

Construction Computing 987740
Editorial: 35 Station Square, Petts Wood, London BR5 1LZ **Tel:** 44 01689 616000
Web site: http://constructioncomputing.co.uk
Freq: Bi-Monthly
Circ: 15600 Not Audited
Editor: David Chadwick
Profile: Magazine focusing on construction related IT products and services, including case studies, product reviews, interviews, research, analysis and training. Provides in-depth discussions with key companies, associations and suppliers. Published six times a year and is combined with CAD User AEC Magazine. Aimed at IT professionals in construction, product, project and service companies.Alternative Title: CCO Previous title: Construction Computing OnlineOnly accepts digital images. First Published: 2005Average Pages per Issue: 36
Ad Rate: Full Page Colour £1850.00
MAGAZINE
Building & Construction, Computers

Construction Enquirer 985522
Editorial: 3 Brand Street, London SE10 8SP
Web site: www.constructionenquirer.com
Freq: Daily
Circ: 149844 Cision Digital Reach
Editor: Aaron Morby
Profile: Website covering construction. The Construction Enquirer website discusses anything from construction news.
MAGAZINE (ONLINE)
Building & Construction

Construction Europe 983692
Editorial: Southfields, Southview Road, Wadhurst, Wadhurst TN5 6TP
Tel: 44 01892 784088
Email: mail@khl.com
Web site: www.khl.com
Freq: Monthly
Circ: 16530 Not Audited
Editor: Sandy Guthrie
Profile: Magazine covering news and features for the construction industry in Europe including market insight, construction industry news, new equipment launches, business news and construction share trends. Read by contractors, consultants and international authorities.
Ad Rate: Full Page Colour £7100.00
MAGAZINE
Building & Construction

Business Magazines

Construction Forum Magazine 984124
Editorial: Bradford Buildings, 27 Mawdslay Street, Bolton BL1 1LN
Tel: 44 01204 238020
Web site: www.constructionforum.org
Freq: Monthly
Circ: 1172 Cision Digital Reach
Editor: John Morris
Profile: Magazine covering news and developments within the construction industry as well as construction reports and architectural and civil engineering projects throughout the UK and Ireland. Aimed at construction industry professionals, developers, main contractors, architects, consultants, local and central government, councils and housing associations, both in the UK and Ireland.
Ad Rate: Full Page Colour £1625.00
MAGAZINE (ONLINE)
Building & Construction

Construction Global 985689
Editorial: 69-75 Thorpe Road, Norwich NR1 1UA
Web site: www.constructionglobal.com
Freq: Monthly
MAGAZINE
Architecture & Design, Building & Construction, Finance, Interior Design, Legal Affairs, Residential Real Estate, Sustainable Development, Urban Planning & Development

The Construction Index 995848
Editorial: 85d High Street, March, March PE15 9LB **Tel:** 44 08451 685700
Email: editor@theconstructionindex.co.uk
Web site: www.theconstructionindex.co.uk
Freq: Monthly
Circ: 42723 Not Audited
Editor: David Taylor
Profile: Construction Index magazine includes construction news, analysis, market data, project reports, plant and equipment and product launches. Each month the magazine runs two specialist features. Targets specialist contractors and plant hirers, and organisations in the construction supply chain.
Ad Rate: Full Page Colour £1150.00
MAGAZINE
Building & Construction

Construction Industry Law Letter 980880
Editorial: 1-2 Bolt Court, London EC4A 3DQ
Tel: 44 02033 773976
Email: kate.clifton@informa.com
Web site: www.constructionindustrylaw.com
Freq: Monthly Not Audited
Profile: Newsletter summarising new developments in the law affecting the construction industry.
MAGAZINE
Building & Construction, Legal Affairs

Construction Industry News 984978
Editorial: Construction Industry News, The Old Church, 17 Old Leeds Road, Huddersfield HD1 1SG
Tel: 44 01484 441400
Email: editorial@codebluegroup.co.uk
Web site: http://cinmagazine.co.uk/
Freq: Monthly
Circ: 14500 Not Audited
Editor: Nigel Martin
Profile: Magazine covering all sectors of the building and construction industry.
Ad Rate: Full Page Mono £1395.00
Ad Rate: Full Page Colour £1965.00
MAGAZINE
Building & Construction

Construction Journal 996137
Editorial: RICS, Parliament Square, London SW1 3PD **Tel:** 44 02072 227000
Email: journals@rics.org
Web site: www.rics.org/constructionjournal
Freq: Bi-Monthly
Circ: 20000 Not Audited

Editor: Robert Mallett
MAGAZINE
Building & Construction, Finance, Legal Affairs, Urban Planning & Development

Construction Law 985997
Editorial: 7 Linden Close, Tunbridge Wells, Tunbridge Wells TN4 8HH
Tel: 44 01892 524455
Web site: www.constructionlaw.uk.com
Freq: Monthly Not Audited
Editor: Nick Barrett
Profile: Magazine covering the legal construction industry. It contains news and practical advice as well as issues affecting the industry. Aimed at people working in the public or private sector within the construction industry.
MAGAZINE
Real Estate Law

Construction Law Journal 983873
Editorial: The Articles Editor, Construction Law Journal, Atkin Building, Gray's Inn, London WC1R 5AT
Email: acbeurobranch@hotmail.com
Web site: http://www.sweetandmaxwell.co.uk/Catalogue/ProductDetails.aspx?productid=7248&recordid=509
Freq: Bi-Monthly Not Audited
Editor: Andrew Burr
MAGAZINE
Legal Affairs, Real Estate Law

Construction Law Review 980886
Editorial: Dominion House, Sibson Road, Sale, Sale M33 7PP **Tel:** 44 01619 723110
Web site: www.surco.uk.com/publications.php
Freq: Annual
Circ: 6000 Not Audited
Profile: Journal containing a major review of developments in construction law in the UK and overseas.
MAGAZINE
Real Estate Law

Construction Magazine 980884
Editorial: Planet Media & Design Ltd, 18F7 Brooke's Mill, Armitage Bridge, Huddersfield HD4 7NR **Tel:** 44 01484 321000
Email: construction@planet-media.co.uk
Web site: www.constructionmag.co.uk
Freq: Monthly
Circ: 15000 Not Audited
Profile: Magazine covering the construction industry, contains news, project and company features, product news and profiles. Aimed at the general construction industry.
Ad Rate: Full Page Mono £1535.00
Ad Rate: Full Page Colour £1925.00
MAGAZINE
Building & Construction

Construction Manager 980186
Editorial: 2nd Floor, 3 Waterhouse Square, 138 Holborn, London EC1N 2SW
Tel: 44 02074 905595
Email: construction-manager@atompublishing.co.uk
Web site: www.construction-manager.co.uk
Freq: Monthly
Circ: 31157 Not Audited
Editor: Denise Chevin
Profile: Magazine containing news and information about the building industry as well as articles about the C.I.O.B. Includes specification and re-specification of building products and services across the construction industry. Aimed at project managers, quantity surveyors, property developers, site managers, engineers, local authorities and architects.
Ad Rate: Full Page Colour £3117.00
MAGAZINE
Building & Construction

Construction National 984123
Editorial: Suite 2, 61 Lower Hillgate, Stockport SK1 3AW **Tel:** 44 01617 103881
Email: editorial@dmmonline.co.uk

Web site: www.constructionnational.co.uk
Freq: Quarterly
Circ: 18000 Not Audited
Profile: Magazine containing the latest news on the construction industry, construction housing, environmental issues, bio fuels, re-newable energy.
Ad Rate: Full Page Colour £1500.00
MAGAZINE
Building & Construction, Urban Planning & Development

Construction News 979869
Editorial: 3 / 4th Floor, Telephone House, 69-77 Paul Street, London EC2A 4NQ
Tel: 44 02030 332600
Email: cneditorial@emap.com
Web site: www.cnplus.co.uk
Freq: Weekly
Circ: 8595 Not Audited
Editor: Rebecca Evans
Profile: Construction News provides construction professionals with national news coverage affecting the future of their industry. It contains insight and analysis of the week's top news stories, industry jobs, features and special reports. First published in 1871. Aimed at building contractors, civil engineering contractors, sub-contractors, site managers, foremen, materials manufacturers and suppliers, plant manufacturers and suppliers and plant hire services to the construction industry.
Ad Rate: Full Page Colour £4300.00
MAGAZINE
Building & Construction

Construction Plant News 987303
Editorial: Regal House, Regal Way, Watford, London WD24 4YF **Tel:** 44 01923 237799
Web site: www.hamerville.co.uk/magazines/construction-plant-news/
Freq: Bi-Monthly
Circ: 8890 Not Audited
MAGAZINE
Building & Construction

Construction Plant World 984192
Editorial: 50 Queens Road, Buckhurst Hill, London IG9 5DD **Tel:** 44 02085 041661
Email: info@constructionplantworld.com
Web site: www.constructionplantworld.com
Freq: Bi-Weekly
Circ: 12000 Not Audited
Profile: Magazine covering machinery and plant for construction and related industries.
Ad Rate: Full Page Mono £160.00
Ad Rate: Full Page Colour £180.00
MAGAZINE
Building & Construction, Engineering, Manufacturing

Construction Update 996179
Editorial: The Mill, Spratling, St Manston, Manston CT12 5AN **Tel:** 44 01843 595818
Web site: www.construction-update.co.uk/
Freq: Monthly
Circ: 41095 Not Audited
Editor: David Stokes
MAGAZINE
Building & Construction, Engineering

Construction.co.uk 986652
Editorial: Flagship Media Group Ltd, Unit C3, 6 Westbank Drive, Belfast BT3 9LA
Tel: 44 02890 319008
Email: newscopy@construction.co.uk
Web site: www.construction.co.uk
Freq: Daily
Circ: 150206 Cision Digital Reach
MAGAZINE (ONLINE)
Building & Construction

ConstructionIreland.ie 986651
Editorial: Unit C3, 6 Westbank Drive, Belfast BT3 9LA **Tel:** 44 02890 319008
Web site: www.constructionireland.ie
Freq: Daily
Circ: 24775 Cision Digital Reach
MAGAZINE (ONLINE)
Building & Construction

Consultancy.uk 995173
Editorial: Flat 706, 109 Vernon House, Friar Lane, Nottingham NG1 6DQ
Tel: 44 01158 243666
Email: info@consultancy.uk
Web site: www.consultancy.uk
Freq: Daily
Circ: 161447 Cision Digital Reach
MAGAZINE (ONLINE)
Business, Corporate Responsibility

Contact (University of Dundee) 994654
Editorial: Press Office, Ground Floor Tower Building, University of Dundee, Dundee DD1 4HN **Tel:** 44 01382 384768
Email: press@dundee.ac.uk
Web site: www.dundee.ac.uk/externalrelations/pressoffice/contactmagazine/
Freq: Quarterly Not Audited
MAGAZINE
Education

Contact Centre NEWS 997891
Editorial: 132 Bromyard House, Bromyard Avenue, London W3 7BF
Email: sam.heggie-collins@oneweekmedia.co.uk
Web site: http://www.contactcentrenews.co.uk/
Freq: Daily
Circ: 16504 Cision Digital Reach
MAGAZINE (ONLINE)
Marketing, Telecommunications/Electronic Communications

Contact Centres 981684
Editorial: The Studio, 57 Cowper Road, Huntingdon PE29 1JH **Tel:** 44 02079 936325
Email: editor@contact-centres.com
Web site: http://www.contact-centres.com
Freq: Daily
Circ: 33112 Cision Digital Reach
Editor: Perry Sanger
MAGAZINE (ONLINE)
Data Management

Container Management 981001
Editorial: Marshall House, 124 Middleton Road, Morden, London SM4 6RW
Email: news@container-mag.com
Web site: www.container-mag.com
Freq: Bi-Monthly
Circ: 4177 Not Audited
Profile: Magazine focusing on container ports, shipping, intermodal operations and management, including container leasing and asset management, handling technology and issues and industry trends and developments.
Ad Rate: Full Page Colour £2400.00
MAGAZINE
Shipping & Warehousing, Supply Chain Management (SCM)

Container Shipping & Trade 987211
Editorial: Mitre House, 66 Abbey Road, Enfield EN1 2QN **Tel:** 44 02083 641551
Email: info@rivieramm.com
Web site: http://www.containerst.com/index.htm
Freq: Quarterly
Circ: 4000 Not Audited
Editor: Rebecca Moore
Profile: Publication that covers global shipping of containers, with the usual trade, ports and logistics aspects of this industry, but also reports on the ships themselves, the hugely expensive assets whose design and operation are so important to the future sustainability of the sector as it faces mounting economic and environmental pressures. This includes the technical aspects of the container ship fleet, covering topics such as power & propulsion, emissions, safety and much more.
MAGAZINE
Shipping & Warehousing

Containerisation International
982923

Editorial: Christchurch Court, 10 Newgate Street, London EC1A 7AZ
Tel: 44 02070 175000
Email: editorial@lloydslist.com
Web site: http://www.lloydslist.com/ll/sector/containers/
Freq: Monthly Not Audited
Profile: Magazine covering international authority on inter-modal container transportation, shipping, rail and trucking services, freighting policy, finance, insurance and leasing. Aimed at shippers, manufacturers, ports and terminals, leasing companies, research institutes, ocean carriers and financial institutions.
MAGAZINE
Shipping & Warehousing

Contaminated Land Bulletin
1051155

Editorial: 8A Stanthorpe Road, London SW16 2DX **Tel:** 44 02036 032100
Email: news@environment-analyst.com
Web site: https://environment-analyst.com/home
Freq: Monthly Not Audited
MAGAZINE
Environment

Context
984403

Editorial: Jubilee House, High Street, Tisbury, Shaftesbury SP3 6HA
Tel: 44 01747 873133
Email: editor@ihbc.org.uk
Web site: www.ihbc.org.uk/page55/context/index.html
Freq: Bi-Monthly
Circ: 2250 Not Audited
Profile: Journal of the Institute of Historic Building Conservation. Covers all aspects of conservation and repair of historic and listed buildings and gardens, new developments, urban design and architecture. Includes news, products, views and craft techniques.
Ad Rate: Full Page Colour £700.00
MAGAZINE
Architecture & Design, Building & Construction, Urban Planning & Development

Continuity
984679

Editorial: 10-11 Southview Park, Marsack Street, Caversham, Reading RG4 5AF
Tel: 44 01189 478215
Web site: http://www.thebci.org
Freq: Quarterly
Circ: 8900 Not Audited
Editor: Nigel Allen
MAGAZINE
Business, Corporate Responsibility

Continuity Insurance & Risk
981226

Editorial: Sixth Floor, 3 London Wall Buildings, London EC2M 5PD
Tel: 44 02075 622401
Email: deborah.ritchie@cirmagazine.com
Web site: www.cirmagazine.com
Freq: Bi-Monthly
Circ: 29000 Not Audited
Editor: Deborah Ritchie
MAGAZINE
Insurance

Contract Flooring Journal
981098

Editorial: Editorial Office, 102 Queens Road, Tunbridge Wells, Tunbridge Wells TN4 9JU
Tel: 44 01892 752400
Email: info@contractflooringjournal.co.uk
Web site: www.contractflooringjournal.co.uk
Freq: Monthly
Circ: 6546 Not Audited
Editor: David Strydom
MAGAZINE
Building & Construction

Contractor UK
984578

Editorial: 1 Northumberland Avenue, Trafalgar Square, London WC2N 5BW
Tel: 44 02078 725448
Email: editor@contractoruk.com
Web site: www.contractoruk.com
Freq: Daily
Circ: 135768 Cision Digital Reach
Editor: Anthony Sherick
Profile: Website providing a wide range of information and news related to the IT industry. Includes an IT directory, insurance, mortgages, income protection, tax advice and information about IT training. Delivers daily news articles, features and site guides, providing access to jobs and pensions, free banking deals, the forum for the contracting industry. The outlet offers RSS (Really Simple Syndication): http://www.contractoruk.com/rss.xml.
MAGAZINE (ONLINE)
Computers

Contractorcalculator.co.uk
985774

Editorial: 112C Roman Road, Basingstoke, Basingstoke RG23 8HE
Tel: 44 08712 185152
Email: press@contractorcalculator.co.uk
Web site: www.contractorcalculator.co.uk
Freq: Daily
Circ: 148639 Cision Digital Reach
Profile: Website covering business and finance. The CONTRACTORCALCULATOR.CO.UK website is the "leading website for contractors and freelancers". The website shares the latest news and information on insurance and mortgages to pensions and finances.
MAGAZINE (ONLINE)
Accounting, Business, Corporate Responsibility

Contractors World - International
997459

Editorial: CML House, 7 Bell Mead, Sawbridgeworth, London CM21 9ES
Email: infodesk@cwmags.com
Web site: http://cwmags.info/
Freq: Bi-Monthly
Circ: 99921 Not Audited
MAGAZINE
Architecture & Design, Building & Construction, Legal Affairs, Urban Planning & Development

Converting Today
981330

Editorial: John Carpenter House, John Carpenter Street, London EC4Y 0AN
Tel: 44 02079 366400
Email: matthew.rogerson@progressivemediagroup.com
Web site: www.convertingtoday.co.uk
Freq: Monthly
Circ: 5247 Not Audited
Profile: Magazine containing news and features of interest to management within the plastics, film, foil, paper and board converting industries including flexo printing, digital printing and 3D printing. Aimed at buyers and specifiers throughout Europe.
Ad Rate: Full Page Colour £3525.00
MAGAZINE
Paper, Plastics

COOConnect
985768

Editorial: Horatio House, 77-85 Fulham Palace Road, Hammersmith, London W6 8JA
Web site: www.cooconnect.com
Freq: Daily
Circ: 10760 Cision Digital Reach
MAGAZINE (ONLINE)
Hedge Funds, Investment Banking

The Cooling Post
988062

Editorial: 27 Old Gloucester Street, London WC1N 3AX **Tel:** 44 01883 622647
Email: info@coolingpost.com
Web site: www.coolingpost.com
Freq: Daily
Circ: 15479 Cision Digital Reach
Editor: Neil Everitt
Profile: Website covering the global air conditioning and refrigeration industry.
MAGAZINE (ONLINE)
Engineering

COPD: Journal of Chronic Obstructive Pulmonary Disease
995139

Editorial: Christchurch Court, 10 Newgate Street, London EC1A 7AZ
Tel: 44 02070 175000
Email: enquiries@taylorandfrancis.com
Web site: www.informahealthcare.com/loi/cop
Freq: Bi-Monthly
MAGAZINE
Respiratory Diseases

The CoQuo
1100044

Web site: http://www.thecoquo.com/
Freq: Daily
Circ: 521 Cision Digital Reach
MAGAZINE (ONLINE)
Economics, Financial Markets

Coronary Artery Disease
995757

Editorial: Wolters Kluwer, Citi Building, 41st Floor, 25 Canada Square, London E14 5LQ
Tel: 44 02079 810600
Email: lwweditorialoffice@wolterskluwer.com
Web site: http://journals.lww.com/coronary-artery/pages/default.aspx
Freq: Bi-Monthly Not Audited
MAGAZINE
Cardiology

CorpComms
981586

Editorial: 123 Blackstock Road, London N4 2JW **Tel:** 44 02073 593321
Email: queries@corpcommsmagazine.co.uk
Web site: www.corpcommsmagazine.co.uk
Freq: Monthly
Circ: 6500 Not Audited
Profile: Magazine covering advice on managing and communicating corporate image and identity.
Ad Rate: Full Page Colour £3850.00
MAGAZINE
Business, Corporate Responsibility

Corporate Citizenship Briefing
983138

Editorial: Holborn Gate, 26 Southampton Buildings, London WC2A 1PQ
Tel: 44 02078 611616
Email: editor@corporate-citizenship.com
Web site: http://ccbriefing.corporate-citizenship.com/
Freq: Daily
Circ: 5781 Cision Digital Reach
Profile: Magazine covering the latest news, developments and trends in corporate social responsibility, community affairs and the third sector.
MAGAZINE (ONLINE)
Business, Corporate Responsibility

Corporate Financier
980906

Editorial: Chartered Accountants' Hall, Moorgate Place, London EC2R 6EA
Tel: 44 02079 208100
Email: corpfinfac@icaew.com
Web site: http://www.icaew.com
Freq: Monthly
Circ: 6000 Not Audited
Editor: Marc Mullen
Profile: Magazine covering the developments in the corporate finance market including mergers and acquisitions, private equity, capital markets, HR, legal and regulatory issues.
Ad Rate: Full Page Colour £2250.00
MAGAZINE
Accounting, Investment Banking, Mergers & Acquisitions, Private Equity

Corporate Financing Week
980810

Editorial: Senator House, 85 Queen Victoria Street, London EC4V 4AB
Tel: 44 02072 480468
Email: editorial@corporatefinancingweek.com
Web site: www.corporatefinancingweek.com
Freq: Weekly
Circ: 190 Not Audited

Editor: David Snowdon
Profile: Publication covering mergers and acquisition activity in North America, Europe and emerging markets. Also includes features on IPOs and privatisations, equity and debt financing.
MAGAZINE
Bonds, Corporate Finance, Equities, Mergers & Acquisitions, Private Equity

Corporate Governance: An International Review
998648

Editorial: The Atrium, Southern Gate, Chichester PO19 8QG **Tel:** 44 01865 778315
Email: cgir@odu.edu
Web site: http://onlinelibrary.wiley.com/journal/10.1111/(ISSN)1467-8683
Freq: Bi-Monthly Not Audited
MAGAZINE
Business, Corporate Responsibility

Corporate Jet Investor
998945

Editorial: Hartland House, 45 Church Street, Reigate RH2 0AD **Tel:** 44 01737 844383
Web site: http://corporatejetinvestor.com/
Freq: Daily
Circ: 39375 Cision Digital Reach
Editor: Mike Halls
MAGAZINE (ONLINE)
Aviation

Corporate Rescue and Insolvency
985672

Editorial: Lexis House, 30 Farringdon Street, London EC4A 4HH **Tel:** 44 02074 002500
Web site: http://www.lexisnexis.co.uk/en-uk/products/corporate-rescue-and-insolvency.page
Freq: Bi-Monthly Not Audited
Profile: Journal featuring commentary and analysis on all areas of insolvency and restructuring law. Aimed at insolvency practitioners and professionals in related industries.
MAGAZINE
Corporate Law

Corporate Vision
997627

Editorial: Floor 1, Suite F, The Maltsters, 1-2 Wetmore Road, Barton-under-Needwood DE14 1LS **Tel:** 44 02037 256847
Email: info@corp-vis.com
Web site: http://www.mycorporatevision.com/
Freq: Monthly
Circ: 50000 Not Audited
MAGAZINE
Banking, Business, Small and Medium Business

The Costs Lawyers Magazine
995008

Web site: www.costslawyer.co.uk
Freq: Bi-Monthly
Circ: 940 Not Audited
Editor: Neil Rose
MAGAZINE
Litigation

Counter Terror Business
985402

Editorial: 226 High Road, Loughton, London IG10 1ET **Tel:** 44 02085 320055
Email: editorial@psigroupltd.co.uk
Web site: www.counterterrorbusiness.com
Freq: Quarterly
Circ: 10000 Not Audited
Profile: Magazine covering counter-terrorism. It features effective counter-terrorism strategies and the latest information from Government, emerging threats: CBRN, terrorism and organised crime and cyber-terrorism, best practices for effective inter-agency collaboration, policy and frameworks for emergency planning and crisis management, defence and emergency services procurement updates, specialist training, recruitment and HR management as well as security products for the armed forces, emergency services and private sector security operations. First published in 2009. Distributed to heads of security, intelligence officers, procurement officials and department heads in Government. Aimed at The Intelligence Services, Police,

Business Magazines

Home Office, MOD, Border Control, Customs, Aviation and Port Authorities in the UK and Europe, Heads of Private Sector organisations and others involved in security and defence.
MAGAZINE
Defense & National Security, Security & Security Systems

Countertrade & Offset   994708
Editorial: PO Box 5000, London N13 4GZ
Tel: 44 02088 865148
Email: editor@cto-offset.com
Web site: www.cto-offset.com
Freq: Bi-Weekly Not Audited
Editor: Lindsey Shanson
MAGAZINE
Defense & National Security

Countryside Voice   982124
Editorial: National Office, Campaign to Protect Rural England, 5-11 Lavington Street, London SE1 0NZ
Tel: 44 02079 812800
Email: info@cpre.org.uk
Web site: www.cpre.org.uk
Freq: 3 Times/Year
Circ: 35000 Not Audited
Editor: Claire Sargent
Profile: Magazine of the Campaign to Protect Rural England, covers recent stories and campaign updates, landscape protection, energy conservation and book reviews.
MAGAZINE
Environment

Courier (UK)   987369
Editorial: Studio 1, 88 Hanbury Street, London E1 5JL
Email: hello@wearecourier.com
Web site: www.courierpaper.com
Freq: Bi-Monthly
Circ: 20000 Not Audited
Editor: Soheb Panja
MAGAZINE
Business, Small and Medium Business

Courier News   983518
Editorial: Suite 4 Pentland House, Saltire Centre, Glenrothes, Glenrothes KY6 2AH
Tel: 44 01592 328199
Email: sales@newscast24.co.uk
Web site: www.couriernews.co.uk
Freq: Daily
Circ: 1005 Cision Digital Reach
Profile: Website covering transportation. The Delivery Magazine shares the latest information on transportation, cargo and freight news.
MAGAZINE (ONLINE)
Shipping & Warehousing, Supply Chain Management (SCM)

COVER   980832
Editorial: Haymarket House, 28-29 Haymarket, London SW1Y 4RX
Tel: 44 02073 169000
Web site: www.covermagazine.co.uk
Freq: Monthly
Circ: 83306 Cision Digital Reach
Editor: Fiona Murphy
Profile: Magazine covering health insurance policies. It features income protection, critical illness, PMI and long term care. It contains news and analysis on the key issues and products that matter to protection IFAs and health insurance brokers. Includes business protection, private medical insurance (PMI), international PMI and mortgage protection.
Ad Rate: Full Page Colour £5000.00
MAGAZINE (ONLINE)
Insurance

The Covered Bond Report   986026
Editorial: 37 Spectrum House, 32-34 Gordon House Road, London NW5 1LP
Email: editorial@coveredbondreport.com
Web site: www.coveredbondreport.com
Freq: Bi-Monthly Not Audited
MAGAZINE
Corporate Finance

CowManagement (UK)   998124
Tel: 44 01394 270587
Web site: http://www.cowmanagement.net/
Freq: Bi-Monthly
Circ: 11043 Not Audited
MAGAZINE
Animal Farming

CPD Specifier   986887
Editorial: The Oaks, Wesleyan Road, Ashley, Ashley TF9 4JT **Tel:** 44 01630 673000
Email: info@directcontactexhibitions.com
Web site: www.cpdspecifier.co.uk
Freq: 3 Times/Year
Circ: 9727 Not Audited
Profile: Magazine covering product reviews and services. Topics include civils & structurals, floors, hard landscaping, modern construction, parks & play provision, repair & refurb, roofs, soft landscaping, sustainability and walls.
Ad Rate: Full Page Colour £1395.00
MAGAZINE
Building & Construction

Cranes & Access   980969
Editorial: PO Box 6998, Brackley, Brackley NN13 5WY **Tel:** 44 08448 155900
Email: editor@vertikal.net
Web site: www.vertikal.net/en
Freq: Monthly
Circ: 8726 Not Audited
Editor: Mark Darwin; **Editor:** Mark Darwin
Profile: Magazine covering UK and Irish crane news and information on access equipment.
Ad Rate: Full Page Colour £2300.00
MAGAZINE
Building & Construction, Engineering

Creative Bloq   997229
Editorial: Quay House, The Ambury, Bath BA1 1UA **Tel:** 44 01225 442244
Email: contact@creativebloq.com
Web site: www.creativebloq.com
Freq: Daily
Circ: 10188248 Cision Digital Reach
MAGAZINE (ONLINE)
Graphic Design

Creative Teaching & Learning   985355
Editorial: 309 Scott House, Gibb Street, Birmingham B9 4DT **Tel:** 44 01212 247585
Email: enquiries@imaginativeminds.co.uk
Web site: www.teachingtimes.com/zone/creative-teaching.htm
Freq: Quarterly
Circ: 3000 Not Audited
Editor: Howard Sharron
MAGAZINE
Education, Schools & Institutions

creativematch   984259
Editorial: Wolsey House, 46 Highstreet, London KT10 9RB **Tel:** 44 08456 762250
Email: editor@creativematch.co.uk
Web site: www.creativematch.com
Freq: Daily
Circ: 9816 Cision Digital Reach
Editor: Mark Lesbirel
Profile: Website covering news on the UK creative industry.
MAGAZINE (ONLINE)
Education, Recruiting

Credit Collections & Risk   998437
Editorial: The Cellar, 81 Cambridge Road, Southend-on-Sea, Southend-on-Sea SS1 1EP **Tel:** 44 01206 212009
Web site: www.ccrmagazine.co.uk
Freq: Monthly
Circ: 10050 Not Audited
MAGAZINE
Corporate Management, Lending

Credit Collections & Risk - PublicSector   996401
Editorial: The Cellar, 81 Cambridge Rd, Southend-on-Sea SS1 1EP
Tel: 44 01206 212009
Web site: http://www.ccr-publicsector.com/

Freq: Monthly
Circ: 10050 Not Audited
MAGAZINE
Government, Public Sector

Credit Collections & Risk World   984209
Editorial: The Cellar, 81 Cambridge Road, Southend-on-Sea, Southend-on-Sea SS1 1EP **Tel:** 44 07766 416693
Web site: http://www.ccrworld.net/
Freq: Quarterly
Circ: 5500 Not Audited
MAGAZINE
Corporate Management, Lending

Credit Insurance News Digest   999691
Editorial: 27 Westmount Close, Worcester Park, London KT4 8FL **Tel:** 44 02083 372171
Web site: http://creditinsurancenews.com/
Freq: Monthly
Circ: 9979 Cision Digital Reach
MAGAZINE (ONLINE)
Corporate Finance

Credit Management   981060
Editorial: The Water Mill, Station Road, South Luffenham, Oakham LE15 8NB
Tel: 44 01780 722900
Email: info@cicm.com
Web site: www.icm.org.uk
Freq: Monthly
Circ: 7000 Not Audited
Profile: Journal of the Institute of Credit Management (ICM) covering developments in trade, retail and export credit including consumer and trade credit, export and company news, in-depth features, profiles and opinions as well as wealth management. First published in 1946, the publication has an average of 56 pages per issue. Aimed at credit professionals, influencers, decision makers and opinion formers in the industry.
Ad Rate: Full Page Colour £1550.00
MAGAZINE
Business

Credit Today   981712
Editorial: Axe & Bottle Court, 70 Newcomen Street, London SE1 1YT
Web site: www.credittoday.co
Freq: Monthly
Circ: 13430 Not Audited
MAGAZINE
Bonds, Corporate Finance, Corporate Management, Credit Markets, Emerging Markets, Government, Lending, Public & Consumer Finance

Creditflux   979904
Editorial: 10 Queen Street Place, 40 - 42 Charter House Street, London EC4R 1BE
Tel: 44 02037 411397
Email: editorial@creditflux.com
Web site: www.creditflux.com
Freq: Monthly
Circ: 1200 Not Audited
Profile: Journal covering news and analysis of the global credit derivatives market and structured credit markets. Aimed at derivatives dealers, investment managers, insurance companies, commercial banks, lawyers, consultants and recruiters.Regular features: Fishnife Peeling back the layers of the market.
Ad Rate: Full Page Colour £3500.00
MAGAZINE
Bonds, Corporate Finance, Corporate Management, Derivatives, Lending

CreditMan   984375
Editorial: Mariners House, 24 Nelsons Gardens, Hedge End, Southampton SO30 2NE **Tel:** 44 01489 787541
Email: info@creditman.co.uk
Web site: www.creditman.co.uk
Freq: Daily
Circ: 14093 Cision Digital Reach
Editor: John Arnold
Profile: Website covering credit cards. Business Credit Management UK discusses anything from business credit management

and debt information to credit reports and credit consultancy.
MAGAZINE (ONLINE)
Corporate Finance, Corporate Management, Lending

Criminal Law & Justice Weekly   986699
Editorial: Lexis House, 30 Farringdon Street, London EC4A 4HH
Web site: www.criminallawandjustice.co.uk
Freq: Weekly Not Audited
Editor: Diana Rose
Profile: Journal covering practice, criminal and local government law.
Ad Rate: Full Page Mono £900.00
Ad Rate: Full Page Colour £1050.00
MAGAZINE
Criminal Law, Human Rights

Crisis Response Journal   998847
Editorial: Crisis Response Journal, Sondes Place Farm, Westcott Road, Dorking RH4 3EB **Tel:** 44 07825 012516
Email: info@fire.org.uk
Web site: www.crisis-response.com/
Freq: Quarterly
Circ: 3500 Not Audited
MAGAZINE
Hygiene, Security & Security Systems

Critical Power   999437
Editorial: 70 Goring Road, Goring by Sea, Worthing, Worthing BN12 4AB
Tel: 44 08451 947338
Web site: http://bestmag.co.uk/criticalpower
Freq: Daily
Circ: 14 Cision Digital Reach
Editor: Gerry Woolf
MAGAZINE (ONLINE)
Alternative/Renewable Energy, Electricity, Engineering, Nuclear Power, Oil, Water & Sanitation

Critical Public Health   999282
Editorial: 4 Park Square, Milton Park, Abingdon OX14 4RN **Tel:** 44 02070 176000
Email: cph@lshtm.ac.uk
Web site: http://www.tandf.co.uk/journals/CCPH
Freq: Quarterly Not Audited
Editor: Judith Green
MAGAZINE
Health Administration

Criticaleye   999148
Editorial: 88 Kingsway, 6th Floor, Holborn, London WC2B 6AA **Tel:** 44 02077 267812
Email: info@criticaleye.net
Web site: http://www.criticaleye.com/
Freq: Daily
Circ: 11362 Cision Digital Reach
MAGAZINE (ONLINE)
Business, Corporate Responsibility

CRN (Computer Reseller News)   980843
Editorial: Haymarket House, 28-29 Haymarket, London SW1Y 4RX
Tel: 44 02073 169000
Web site: www.channelweb.co.uk
Freq: Bi-Weekly
Circ: 14000 Not Audited
MAGAZINE
Auto Aftermarket

Crop Production Magazine   986356
Editorial: White House Barn, Hanwood, Shrewsbury SY5 8LP **Tel:** 44 01743 861122
Email: angus@cpm-magazine.co.uk
Web site: http://www.cpm-magazine.co.uk
Freq: Monthly
Circ: 11500 Not Audited
Editor: Tom Allen-Stevens
MAGAZINE
Animal Farming

CRU 987686
Editorial: Chancery House, 53-64 Chancery Lane, London WC2A 1QS
Tel: 44 02079 032000
Web site: http://www.crugroup.com/
Freq: Daily
Circ: 38644 Cision Digital Reach
MAGAZINE (ONLINE)
Business, Corporate Responsibility

CSP Today 985359
Editorial: 7-9 Fashion Street, London E1 6PX **Tel:** 44 02073 757575
Email: editor@csptoday.com
Web site: http://analysis.newenergyupdate.com/csp-today
Freq: Daily
Profile: Website covering solar power. The CSP today website shares the latest news, events, reports, updates and information for the concentrated solar thermal power industry. The website also published a newsletter every Monday.
MAGAZINE (ONLINE)
Alternative/Renewable Energy

CTA Intelligence 987533
Editorial: One London Wall, London EC2Y 5BD **Tel:** 44 02078 326500
Email: news@hfmweek.com
Web site: www.ctaintelligence.com
Freq: Monthly Not Audited
MAGAZINE
Commodities, Financial Markets

Current Medical Research and Opinion 985233
Editorial: 69-77 Paul Street, London EC2A 4LQ
Email: info@cmrojournal.com
Web site: www.informahealthcare.com/loi/cmo
Freq: Monthly Not Audited
Profile: Peer-reviewed international journal for the rapid publication of original research on new and existing drugs, medical devices and therapies.
MAGAZINE
Science

Current Opinion in Cardiology 999530
Editorial: 250 Waterloo Road, London SE1 8RD **Tel:** 44 02079 810600
Web site: http://journals.lww.com/co-cardiology/pages/default.aspx
Freq: Bi-Monthly Not Audited
MAGAZINE
Cardiology

The Custodial Review 985974
Editorial: 53 Asgard Drive, Bedford MK40 3NF **Tel:** 44 01234 348878
Email: sales@custodialreview.co.uk
Web site: www.custodialreview.co.uk
Freq: Quarterly
Circ: 7500 Not Audited
Profile: Magazine dealing with security, communications, catering, building design and other subjects related to prisons, police custody, court custody, immigration custody, customs & excise custody and military custody. Read by people working, controlling and managing Custodial establishments.Aimed at Governors and Directors, Caterers, Heads of Security, Regimes PE and Works in Prisons. Chief constables, Custody managers and officers in the Police. Directors, caterers, Heads of works, security and PE in immigration centres.
Ad Rate: Full Page Colour £1095.00
MAGAZINE
Security & Security Systems

Customer Experience Magazine 987773
Editorial: Acacia Far, Lower Road, Royston, Croydon SG8 0EE **Tel:** 44 02071 932428
Web site: http://cxm.co.uk/
Freq: Monthly
Circ: 46000 Not Audited
Editor: Marija Pavlovic
Profile: Publication that looks at all aspects of customer service.
MAGAZINE
Business, Corporate Responsibility

Customer Insight Magazine 999005
Editorial: c/o The Leadership Factor, Taylor Hill Mill, Huddersfield HD4 6JA
Tel: 44 01484 467004
Email: uk@leadershipfactor.com
Web site: www.customer-insight.co.uk
Freq: Semi-Annual
Circ: 6000 Not Audited
MAGAZINE
Business

CWU Voice 985013
Editorial: 150 The Broadway, Wimbledon, London SW19 1RX **Tel:** 44 02089 717200
Email: info@cwu.org
Web site: www.cwu.org
Freq: Bi-Monthly
Circ: 220000 Not Audited
Editor: Simon Alford
Profile: Magazine covering issues related to the Post Office, British Telecom and engineering.
Ad Rate: Full Page Colour £9500.00
MAGAZINE
Banking, Telecommunications/Electronic Communications

CX Network 995311
Editorial: 129 Wilton Road, Pimlico, London SW1V 1JZ
Web site: http://www.cxnetwork.com/
Freq: Daily
Circ: 29007 Cision Digital Reach
Editor: Zarina de Ruiter
MAGAZINE (ONLINE)
Marketing

Cytotechnology 996649
Web site: springer.com/chemistry/biotechnology/journal/10616
Freq: Bi-Monthly Not Audited
MAGAZINE
Biotechnology, Science

DABS 983354
Editorial: McDermott Chambers, 2 The Green, Kings Norton, Birmingham B38 8SD
Tel: 44 01214 513037
Web site: www.mcdermottpublishing.com/dabs-2/
Freq: Monthly
Circ: 23466 Not Audited
Profile: Magazine containing information on building products and services including doors, windows, kitchens, bathrooms, refurbishment, new build, floors, walls, ceiling, safety, security, heating, plumbing, ventilation, roofing, cladding, insulation, external works, landscaping, drainage, design and interiors. Aimed at architects and specifiers, building contractors and developers, quantity surveyors and interior designers.
Ad Rate: Full Page Colour £1725.00
MAGAZINE
Architecture & Design, Building & Construction, Interior Design

Dairy Farmer 981152
Editorial: Unit 4, Fulwood Business Park, Caxton Road, Preston PR2 9NZ
Tel: 44 02073 322949
Email: peter.hollinshead@briefingmedia.com
Web site: http://www.fginsight.com/more-from-us/more-from-us/issues
Freq: Monthly
Circ: 8500 Not Audited
Editor: Peter Hollinshead
Profile: Website covering dairy farming. The Dairy Farmer is an online magazine covering technical articles on all aspects of dairy farming.
MAGAZINE
Animal Farming

Dairy Industries International 983862
Editorial: The Maltings, 57 Bath Street, Gravesend, London DA11 0DF
Tel: 44 01474 532202
Email: meganh@bellpublishing.com
Web site: www.dairyindustries.com
Freq: Monthly
Circ: 5000 Not Audited
Profile: Publication containing all aspects of dairy products processing and equipment worldwide.
Ad Rate: Full Page Mono £1565.00
Ad Rate: Full Page Colour £2059.00
MAGAZINE
Animal Farming

Dairy Industry Newsletter 983861
Editorial: PO Box 1215, Cambridge CB1 0UR **Tel:** 44 02037 738794
Web site: dairyindustrynewsletter.co.uk
Freq: Bi-Weekly
Circ: 800 Not Audited
Editor: Barry Wilson
Profile: Newsletter containing technical information, news and features about the dairy processing industry.
MAGAZINE
Animal Farming

Dam Engineering 1054504
Web site: http://www.waterpowermagazine.com/mediapacks/online/dam-engineering.html
Freq: Monthly
Editor: Carrieann Stocks
MAGAZINE
Water & Sanitation

darc 1101202
Editorial: Waterloo Place, Watson Square, Stockport, Manchester SK1 3AZ
Tel: 44 01614 768350
Web site: www.darcmagazine.com
Freq: Bi-Monthly
Circ: 12000 Not Audited
MAGAZINE
Architecture & Design, Interior Design

Data Centre Management 983635
Editorial: Suite 17, Exhibition House, Addison Bridge Place, London W14 8XP
Tel: 44 02073 485250
Web site: https://thestack.com/dcm/
Freq: Bi-Monthly
Circ: 6000 Not Audited
Editor: Heather Grimes
Profile: Magazine containing news, views, analysis and information for the management of data centres.
Ad Rate: Full Page Colour £2995.00
MAGAZINE
Data Management

Data Centre Solutions Europe 984184
Editorial: Hannay House, 39 Clarendon Road, Watford WD17 1JA
Tel: 44 01923 690200
Email: philip.alsop@angelbc.com
Web site: www.dcsuk.info
Freq: Monthly
Circ: 42453 Not Audited
MAGAZINE
Data Management

Data Centre Solutions UK 1052869
Editorial: Hannay House, 39 Clarendon Road, Watford WD17 1JA
Tel: 44 01923 690200
Email: philip.alsop@angelbc.com
Web site: www.dcsuk.info
Freq: Quarterly
Circ: 25673 Not Audited
MAGAZINE
Data Management

Data Economy 996947
Editorial: 12-13 Hatton Garden, London EC1N 8AN **Tel:** 44 02071 995730
Email: enquiries@data-economy.com
Web site: https://data-economy.com
Freq: Daily
Circ: 17134 Cision Digital Reach
MAGAZINE (ONLINE)
Data Management

Data Protection Leader 999588
Editorial: Cecile Park Media Ltd, 17 The Timber Yard, Drysdale Street, London N1 6ND **Tel:** 44 02070 121380
Email: alexis.kateifides@dataguidance.com
Web site: http://www.e-comlaw.com/data-protection-law-and-policy/
Freq: Monthly Not Audited
MAGAZINE
News & Current Affairs

Database Marketing 979995
Editorial: Waterloo Chambers, 2nd Floor, 19 Waterloo Street, Glasgow G2 6AY
Tel: 44 01412 222100
Web site: http://www.dbm.today
Freq: Monthly
Circ: 6000 Not Audited
Profile: Magazine covering database marketing management including campaign management, business and consumer data, customer relationship management strategy and software, profiling, segmentation and data warehousing as well as developments and ideas in customer management, target marketing and analytics through a mixture of features, news, columnists, in-depth case studies and software reviews. Launched in 1998. Aimed at database marketing managers, direct marketing managers, data planners, analysts, IT and marketing directors.
Ad Rate: Full Page Colour £1650.00
MAGAZINE
Data Management, Marketing, Software

DatacenterDynamics 983375
Editorial: 102-108 Clifton Street, London EC2A 4HW **Tel:** 44 02073 771907
Email: info@datacenterdynamics.com
Web site: www.datacenterdynamics.com
Freq: Bi-Monthly
Circ: 50000 Not Audited
MAGAZINE
Data Management

DataGuidance 997199
Editorial: Unit 17, The Timber Yard, Drysdale Street, London N1 6ND
Tel: 44 02070 121380
Email: info@dataguidance.com
Web site: www.dataguidance.com
Freq: Daily
Circ: 17199 Cision Digital Reach
MAGAZINE (ONLINE)
Intellectual Property

DataIQ 999607
Editorial: 2 Eastbourne Terrace, Paddington, London W2 6LG
Tel: 44 02038 291112
Email: editorial@dataiq.co.uk
Web site: http://www.dataiq.co.uk/
Freq: Quarterly
Circ: 18144 Cision Digital Reach
MAGAZINE (ONLINE)
Data Management

David Reviews 1062754
Editorial: Lovely Lenzie Ltd, Woodbourne House, Seven Sisters, Lenzie, Glasgow G66 3AW **Tel:** 44 0141 767766
Web site: www.davidreviews.com
Freq: Daily
Circ: 11772 Cision Digital Reach
Editor: Jason Stone
MAGAZINE (ONLINE)
Advertising Industry

DDN (Drink and Drugs News) 983442
Editorial: 57 High Street, Ashford, Ashford TN24 8SG **Tel:** 44 01233 633315

Business Magazines

Email: info@cjwellings.com
Web site: www.drinkanddrugsnews.com
Freq: Monthly
Circ: 11500 Not Audited
Editor: Claire Brown
MAGAZINE
Community Care (UK)

Dealer Support Magazine
981061

Editorial: One Tetbury Place, Business
Design Centre, 52 Upper Street, London N1
0QH Tel: 44 02037 948555
Email: editor@dealersupport.co.uk
Web site: www.dealersupport.co.uk
Freq: Monthly
Circ: 5300 Not Audited
Editor: Austin Clark
MAGAZINE
Office Supplies

Dealreporter
984326

Editorial: 10 Queen Street Place, London
EC4R 1BE Tel: 44 02037 411122
Web site: www.dealreporter.com
Freq: Daily
Circ: 12569 Cision Digital Reach
Profile: Website covering online news,
intelligence and data services and aimed at
the investment market. Ben Smith is the
Chief Content Editor to whom press releases
should be addressed.
MAGAZINE (ONLINE)
Hedge Funds, Mergers & Acquisitions

Decentralized Energy
983533

Editorial: The Water Tower, Gunpowder Mill,
Powdermill Lane, London EN9 1BN
Tel: 44 01992 656600
Web site: http://www.decentralized-energy.
com
Freq: Bi-Monthly
Circ: 15400 Not Audited
MAGAZINE
Alternative/Renewable Energy, Electricity,
Nuclear Power, Oil, Water & Sanitation

Decision
979998

Editorial: PO Box 49, Hayling Island PO11
9YJ Tel: 44 02392 465631
Email: mail@decisionmagazine.co.uk
Web site: www.decisionmagazine.co.uk
Freq: Quarterly
Circ: 16000 Not Audited
Profile: Management magazine with an
emphasis on strategy and corporate
leadership.
Ad Rate: Full Page Colour £2500.00
MAGAZINE
Business, Corporate Responsibility

Decision Marketing
985834

Editorial: 33 The Drive, Shoreham by Sea,
Shoreham-by-Sea BN43 5GB
Tel: 44 01273 278772
Email: news@decisionmarketing.co.uk
Web site: www.decisionmarketing.co.uk
Freq: Daily
Circ: 58913 Cision Digital Reach
MAGAZINE (ONLINE)
Data Management, Marketing

Decomworld
999052

Editorial: 7-9 Fashion Street, London E1
6PX Tel: 44 02074 224341
Email: info@decomworld.com
Web site: http://analysis.decomworld.com/
Freq: Daily
Circ: 3313 Cision Digital Reach
MAGAZINE (ONLINE)
Alternative/Renewable Energy, Carbon
Emissions & Trading, Electricity, Energy,
Nuclear Power, Oil, Water & Sanitation

Decorating Matters
985850

Editorial: 6th Floor, Manchester One, 53
Portland Street, Manchester M1 3LD
Tel: 44 01612 362782
Email: info@excelmediasolutions.co.uk
Web site: https://www.excelmediasolutions.
co.uk/portfolio-posts/decorating-matters-3/
Freq: Quarterly
Circ: 3500 Not Audited

Profile: Official magazine of the Scottish
Decorators Federation covering industry
news including employment and contractual
law, investment, vehicles, techniques,
applications and manufacturing news.
Ad Rate: Full Page Colour £750.00
MAGAZINE
Interior Design

The Decorator
986649

Editorial: 4 Kenwood Road, Sheffield S7
1NP
Web site: www.the-decorator.co.uk
Freq: Bi-Monthly
Circ: 2500 Not Audited
Profile: Official journal of the Painting and
Decoration Association. Contains articles on
decoration, architecture, finishing, paint and
varnish production.
Ad Rate: Full Page Colour £750.00
MAGAZINE
Interior Design

Deep Dive
1074959

Tel: 44 01932 339260
Email: editorial@pharmaphorum.com
Web site: http://www.pharmaphorum.com/
Freq: Quarterly Not Audited
MAGAZINE
Pharmaceuticals

Defaqto
995894

Tel: 44 01844 295454
Web site: www.defaqto.com
Freq: Daily
Circ: 23310 Cision Digital Reach
MAGAZINE (ONLINE)
Business

Defence & Security Systems
International
999844

Editorial: 40-42 Hatton Gardens, London
EC1N 8EB Tel: 44 02079 366400
Email: andrewhinton@globaltrademedia.
com
Web site: www.defence-and-security.com
Freq: Semi-Annual
Circ: 7683 Not Audited
MAGAZINE
Defense & National Security, Security &
Security Systems

Defence Analysis
980124

Editorial: PO Box 29478, London NW1 8GF
Email: info@defenceanalysis.com
Web site: www.defenceanalysis.com
Freq: Monthly Not Audited
Editor: Francis Tusa
Profile: Magazine containing independent
analysis of European military defences, also
covering the areas of the Middle East and
Asia.
MAGAZINE
Defense & National Security

Defence Contracts Bulletin
988544

Editorial: 60 Pacific Quay, Glasgow G51
1DZ Tel: 44 01413 328247
Web site: http://www.contracts.mod.uk/
publication
Freq: Bi-Weekly Not Audited
MAGAZINE
Defense & National Security

Defence Helicopter
980121

Editorial: 268 Bath Road, Slough SL1 4DX
Tel: 44 01753 727001
Email: news@shephardmedia.com
Web site: www.shephardmedia.com/
publications/magazine/defence-helicopter
Freq: Bi-Monthly
Circ: 9000 Not Audited
Profile: Journal containing the latest news
and in-depth coverage of military and public
service helicopters.
Ad Rate: Full Page Colour £7500.00
MAGAZINE
Aviation, Defense & National Security

Defence IQ
996377

Editorial: 129 Wilton Road, London SW1V
1JZ Tel: 44 02073 689368

Web site: www.defenceiq.com
Freq: Daily
Circ: 27285 Cision Digital Reach
MAGAZINE (ONLINE)
Defense & National Security

Defence News Analysis
998643

Editorial: 461 Harrow Road, London W10
4RG Tel: 44 02089 604488
Freq: Weekly Not Audited
Editor: Yvonne Headington
MAGAZINE
Defense & National Security

Defense & Security Analysis
998480

Editorial: 2-4 Park Square, Milton Park,
Abingdon OX14 4RN Tel: 44 02070 176000
Web site: www.tandfonline.com/toc/
cdan20/current#.U_M52cVdU8U
Freq: Quarterly Not Audited
MAGAZINE
Defense & National Security

Dementia
995713

Editorial: 1 Oliver's Yard, 55 City Road,
London EC1Y 1SP Tel: 44 02073 248500
Email: dem.pra@sagepub.com
Web site: http://dem.sagepub.com/
Freq: Bi-Monthly Not Audited
Editor: John Keady
MAGAZINE
Neurology

Demolition & Recycling
International
984203

Editorial: Southfields, Southview Road,
Wadhurst, Wadhurst TN5 6TP
Tel: 44 01892 784088
Web site: http://www.khl.com/magazines/
demolition-and-recycling-international/
Freq: Bi-Monthly
Circ: 10507 Not Audited
Editor: Steve Ducker
MAGAZINE
Building & Construction, Environment

Dental Health
983898

Editorial: Smile House, 2 East Union Street,
Rugby CV22 6JA Tel: 44 01788 575050
Email: enquiries@bsdht.org.uk
Web site: www.bsdht.org.uk/Default.aspx?
PageID=17338415&A=
SearchResult&SearchID=575420&ObjectID=
17338415&Objec
Freq: Bi-Monthly
Circ: 4000 Not Audited
Editor: Heather Lewis
Profile: Journal containing scientific articles
and news of interest to dental hygienists and
therapists, with features on dental health
education, prevention and periodontology,
oral health and paediatric dentistry.
Ad Rate: Full Page Mono £458.00
Ad Rate: Full Page Colour £899.00
MAGAZINE
Dentistry

Dental Insider
988224

Editorial: Mineral Lane, Chesham, Chesham
HP5 1NL Tel: 44 01494 782873
Email: admin@bdia.org.uk
Web site: www.bdia.org.uk/dental-insider.
html
Freq: Quarterly
Circ: 1200 Not Audited
Editor: Julian English
MAGAZINE
Dentistry

Dental Lab Journal
980979

Editorial: The DLA Office, Dental
Laboratories Association, 44-46 Wollaton
Road, Beeston, Beeston NG9 2NR
Tel: 44 01159 254888
Email: info@dla.org.uk
Web site: http://www.dla.org.uk/?q=
content/dental-lab-journal
Freq: Monthly
Circ: 2700 Not Audited

Editor: Richard Daniels
MAGAZINE
Dentistry

Dental Nursing
985471

Editorial: St Jude's Church, Dulwich Road,
London SE24 0PB
Email: dn@markallengroup.com
Web site: www.dental-nursing.co.uk
Freq: Monthly
Profile: Dental Nursing is a clinical and
professional journal for dental nurses.
Launched in 2005.
MAGAZINE
Dentistry, Nursing/Nurses

Dental Review News
1054413

Editorial: Elthorne Gate, 64 High Street,
Pinner, London HA5 5QA
Tel: 44 02080 043222
Email: newsdesk@dentalreview.news
Web site: www.dentalreview.news
Freq: Daily
Editor: Derek Pearson
MAGAZINE (ONLINE)
Dentistry

Dental Tribune UK
985200

Editorial: 535 Stillwater Drive 5, Manchester
M11 4TF Tel: 44 01612 231830
Email: newsroom@dental-tribune.com
Web site: http://www.dental-tribune.com
Freq: Bi-Weekly
Circ: 20000 Not Audited
MAGAZINE
Dentistry

Dental Update
981180

Editorial: Unit 2 Riverview Business Park,
Walnut Tree Close, Guildford, London GU1
4UX Tel: 44 01483 304944
Email: office@georgewarman.co.uk
Web site: www.dental-update.co.uk
Freq: Monthly
Circ: 7794 Not Audited
Profile: Journal of clinical reference with
review articles. Aimed at post-graduate
dental practitioners.
Ad Rate: Full Page Mono £600.00
Ad Rate: Full Page Colour £850.00
MAGAZINE
Dentistry

The Dentist
981182

Editorial: Unit 2 Riverview Business Park,
Walnut Tree Close, Guildford, London GU1
4UX Tel: 44 01483 304944
Email: the-dentist@georgewarman.co.uk
Web site: www.the-dentist.co.uk
Freq: Monthly
Circ: 17241 Not Audited
Editor: Eddie MacKenzie
Profile: Journal which concentrates on
practice management, with articles on
financial, legal and investment matters,
analysis pages, news, clinical management
and products.
Ad Rate: Full Page Mono £1100.00
Ad Rate: Full Page Colour £1675.00
MAGAZINE
Dentistry

Dentistry
981181

Editorial: Hertford House, Farm Close,
Shenley, Radlett WD7 9AB
Tel: 44 01923 851777
Email: newsdesk@dentistry.co.uk
Web site: www.dentistry.co.uk
Freq: Bi-Weekly
Circ: 20596 Not Audited
Editor: Julian English; Editor: Sebastian
Evans
Profile: Magazine covering all aspects of the
dental industry, including product updates
and practical information.
Ad Rate: Full Page Colour £3150.00
MAGAZINE
Dentistry

Dentistry Scotland
1052622

Tel: 44 01923 851777
Web site: http://www.dentistry.co.uk/
Freq: Quarterly
Circ: 2500 Not Audited

Editor: Sebastian Evans
Profile: Publication that looks at the Scottish dental market with news and clinical information.
MAGAZINE
Dentistry

DerivSource
996199
Email: editor@derivsource.com
Web site: www.derivsource.com
Freq: Daily
Circ: 14070 Cision Digital Reach
MAGAZINE (ONLINE)
Derivatives

desider
984624
Editorial: Press Office, Mailpoint 2032, Maple 0A, MOD Abbey Wood, Bristol BS34 8JH **Tel:** 44 01179 132483
Web site: https://www.gov.uk/government/collections/desider-magazine
Freq: Monthly
Circ: 14000 Not Audited
Editor: Tom Morris
Profile: Magazine covering stories and features about support to operations and equipment acquisition. Also covers the work of those in the DE&S and other corporate news and information.
Ad Rate: Full Page Mono £2967.00
Ad Rate: Full Page Colour £3376.00
MAGAZINE
Defense & National Security

Design & Build Review
1058243
Editorial: John Carpenter House, John Carpenter Street, London EC4Y 0AN
Tel: 44 02079 366400
Email: onlinemags@nridigital.com
Web site: http://www.nridigital.com/design-build-review.html
Freq: Monthly
Circ: 99 Cision Digital Reach
Editor: Lucy Ingham
MAGAZINE (ONLINE)
Architecture & Design

Design & Build UK
986863
Editorial: First Floor Office Suite 1, Caroline House, Bradshawgate, Bolton BL2 1BJ
Tel: 44 08444 170170
Web site: http://www.designandbuilduk.net
Freq: Daily
Circ: 12888 Cision Digital Reach
MAGAZINE (ONLINE)
Building & Construction, Interior Design

Design and Technology Education: An International Journal
981928
Editorial: 16 Wellesbourne House, Walton Road, Wellesbourne, Warwick Cv35 9JB
Tel: 44 01789 470007
Email: info@data.org.uk
Web site: www.data.org.uk
Freq: 3 Times/Year
Circ: 12285 Cision Digital Reach
Profile: Journal of the Design and Technology Association, which represents and supports all those involved in design and technology education. Covers a wide range of leading research into D&T: pedagogy, gender issues, academic reviews, classroom interaction, international comparisons. 3 issues per year. Linked to the annual D&T research conference. Launched in 1995. Read by members of the Design and Technology Association and teachers and trainee teachers of design and technology.
MAGAZINE (ONLINE)
Education, Higher Education, Schools & Institutions

Design Buy Build
984269
Editorial: St Augustines Business Centre, 125 Canterbury Road, Westgate-on-Sea, Margate CT8 8NL **Tel:** 44 01843 830249
Email: editorial@designbuybuild.co.uk
Web site: www.designbuybuild.co.uk
Freq: Bi-Monthly
Circ: 62000 Not Audited
Profile: Magazine covering new build projects including regulations, health and safety and products as well as information and news for all building industry professionals, specifiers and purchasers. Aimed at builders, interior designers, contractors, developers and specifiers.
Ad Rate: Full Page Colour £1495.00
MAGAZINE
Building & Construction, Interior Design

Design Exchange
984797
Editorial: LDI Media (UK), 366 Bethnal Green Road, London E2 0AH
Tel: 44 02071 184319
Email: editor@demagazine.co.uk
Web site: www.demagazine.co.uk
Freq: Semi-Annual
Circ: 15000 Not Audited
MAGAZINE
Architecture & Design, Commercial Real Estate, Interior Design, Office Design, Residential Real Estate, Retail, Travel Industry, Urban Planning & Development

Design Products & Applications
981239
Editorial: Blair House, 184/186 High Street, Tonbridge, Tonbridge TN9 1BQ
Tel: 44 01732 359990
Email: dpa@imlgroup.co.uk
Web site: http://www.dpaonthenet.net/
Freq: Monthly
Circ: 9966 Not Audited
Editor: Paige West
MAGAZINE
Engineering

Design Solutions
981240
Editorial: 15a London Road, Maidstone, Maidstone ME16 8LY **Tel:** 44 01622 699171
Web site: www.connectingindustry.com/DesignSolutions
Freq: Monthly
Circ: 12520 Not Audited
Editor: Rachael Morling; **Editor:** Lisa Peake
Profile: Magazine providing advice and information for solving design problems. Aimed at design engineers, OEMs, machine builders.Alternative Title: Design Solutions Previous title: CONNECTINGINDUSTRY.COM/oem design
Ad Rate: Full Page Colour £2200.00
MAGAZINE
Engineering

Design Week
979861
Editorial: Wells Point, 79 Wells Street, London W1T 3QN **Tel:** 44 02072 923703
Web site: http://www.designweek.co.uk/
Freq: Daily
Circ: 174371 Cision Digital Reach
Profile: Website covering design. Design Week shares the latest news on the design sector as interior, digital, furniture, packaging, graphic and print.
MAGAZINE (ONLINE)
Graphic Design

designbuild-network.com
987714
Editorial: John Carpenter House, John Carpenter Street, London EC4Y 0AN
Tel: 44 02079 366400
Email: onlineeditorial@kable.co.uk
Web site: www.designbuild-network.com
Freq: Daily
Circ: 31420 Cision Digital Reach
Profile: Magazine focusing on architecture, interior design and construction. Aimed at architects, building engineers, building surveyors, contractors and quantity surveyors.Alternative Title: idbi Previous title: Intelligent Design and Build InnovationsRegular features: Company A-Z; Features; Inside Architecture; New on this site; News & Updates; Projects; Speakers' Corner; White Papers
MAGAZINE (ONLINE)
Architecture & Design

DesignCurial
985105
Editorial: Progressive Trade Media Ltd., 7 Carmelite Street, Blackfriars, London EC4 Y0BS **Tel:** 44 02079 366400
Email: hello@designcurial.com
Web site: www.designcurial.com
Freq: Daily
Circ: 46625 Cision Digital Reach
MAGAZINE (ONLINE)
Interior Design

Designer Kitchen & Bathroom
984430
Tel: 44 01787 221396
Email: kbeye.editorial@propub.co.uk
Web site: www.designerkbmag.co.uk
Freq: Monthly
Circ: 11000 Not Audited
Editor: Martin Allen-Smith
Profile: Magazine covering interior designs and home decorating including products and design trends with particular reference to fitted kitchen and bathroom design. Aimed at professional designers working with kitchens and bathrooms, in particular architects, housebuilders, developers interior designers, specialist kitchen and bathroom designers, retailers and manufacturers.
Ad Rate: Full Page Colour £2300.00
MAGAZINE
Interior Design

Designing Techniques of Post and Telecommunications
1060863
Tel: 44 86216 637167975111
Email: dtptchina@dimpt.com
Web site: http://www.ydsjjs.com
Freq: Monthly
Circ: 25001 Not Audited
MAGAZINE
Mobile Communications

The DESK Magazine
1058391
Editorial: 117 Waterloo Road, London SE1 8UL **Tel:** 44 02079 286796
Email: contact@fi-desk.com
Web site: www.fi-desk.com
Freq: Quarterly
Circ: 5000 Not Audited
MAGAZINE
Equities, Financial Markets, Hedge Funds, Investment Banking

Develop
981608
Editorial: Saxon House, 6a St. Andrew Street, Hertford SG14 1JA
Tel: 44 01992 535646
Web site: www.develop-online.net
Freq: Monthly
Circ: 10000 Not Audited
Profile: Publication focused on the games development sector. International newsletter covering technical advice and coverage on business, political and educational issues affecting the interactive entertainment industry. Provides information on business, coding, art, sound and game design trends, and featuring interviews with the creative and commercial leaders in the field.
Ad Rate: Full Page Mono £1660.00
Ad Rate: Full Page Colour £1660.00
MAGAZINE
Software

DEVELOP3D
984826
Editorial: 465C Hornsey Road, 1st Floor, Room 7, Unit 2, London N19 4DR
Tel: 44 02033 557310
Web site: www.develop3d.com
Freq: Monthly
Circ: 15000 Not Audited
MAGAZINE
Graphic Design, Manufacturing

developer tech
987313
Email: enquiries@techforge.pub
Web site: www.developer-tech.com
Freq: Daily
Circ: 151017 Cision Digital Reach
Editor: Ryan Daws
MAGAZINE (ONLINE)
Mobile Communications

Developing Leaders
985847
Editorial: 42 Moray Place, Edinburgh EH3 6BT **Tel:** 44 02030 312900
Email: info@iedp.com
Web site: www.iedp.com/developing_leaders_magazine
Freq: Quarterly Not Audited
Editor: Roderick Millar
Profile: Magazine covering the strategies used by organisations to nurture leadership talent. Includes analysis of global executive development provision by top business schools and consultants.
MAGAZINE
Business, Corporate Responsibility

developingtelecoms.com
984974
Editorial: 60 Wood Vale, London SE23 3ED
Tel: 44 02086 936089
Email: editor@developingtelecoms.com
Web site: www.developingtelecoms.com
Freq: Daily
Circ: 24025 Cision Digital Reach
Editor: James Barton
MAGAZINE (ONLINE)
Telecommunications/Electronic Communications

Development Finance Today
997954
Editorial: 71 Gloucester Place, London W1U 8JW
Circ: 7938 Cision Digital Reach
Editor: Beth Fisher
MAGAZINE (ONLINE)
Finance, Lending

Developmental Medicine & Child Neurology
995036
Editorial: The Atrium, Southern Gate, Chichester PO19 8QG **Tel:** 44 01865 778315
Email: dmcn@editorialoffice.co.uk
Web site: http://onlinelibrary.wiley.com/journal/10.1111/%28ISSN%291469-8749
Freq: Monthly Not Audited
Editor: Bernard Dan
MAGAZINE
Neurology, Pediatrics

Diabetes & Primary Care
984676
Editorial: OmniaMed Ltd, 1.01 Cargo Works, 1-2 Hatfields, London SE1 9PG
Tel: 44 02037 358244
Email: dpc@omniamed.com
Web site: www.diabetesandprimarycare.co.uk
Freq: Bi-Monthly
Circ: 16000 Not Audited
Editor: Olivia Tamburello
MAGAZINE
Diabetes

Diabetes Care for Children & Young People
999507
Editorial: Unit 3.05 Enterprise House, 1/2 Hatfields, London SE1 9PG
Tel: 44 02076 271510
Email: dccyp@sbcommunicationsgroup.com
Web site: www.diabetescareforchildrenandyoungpeople.co.uk
Freq: Quarterly
Circ: 10000 Not Audited
MAGAZINE
Diabetes, Pediatrics

Diabetes Digest
984677
Editorial: 1.01 Cargo Works, 1-2 Hatfields, London SE1 9PG **Tel:** 44 02037 358244
Email: info@omniamed.com
Web site: www.diabetesdigestjournal.co.uk
Freq: Quarterly
Circ: 20000 Not Audited
MAGAZINE
Diabetes

Diabetes Research and Clinical Practice
999693
Editorial: The Boulevard, Langford Lane, Kidlington, Oxford OX5 1GB
Tel: 44 01865 843753
Email: diab@elsevier.com

Business Magazines

Web site: www.elsevier.com/wps/find/journaldescription.cws_home/505949/description
Freq: Monthly Not Audited
MAGAZINE
Diabetes

Diabetes Update 985839
Editorial: Macleod House, 10 Parkway, London NW1 7AA **Tel:** 44 02074 241000
Email: update@diabetes.org.uk
Web site: www.diabetes.org.uk/Professionals/Diabetes-Update/
Freq: Quarterly
Circ: 40000 Not Audited
MAGAZINE
Diabetes

Diabetes, Obesity and Metabolism 998607
Editorial: University of Nottingham School of of Medicine, The Medical School, Royal Derby Hospital, Uttoxeter Road, Derby DE22 3DT **Tel:** 44 01865 778315
Web site: http://onlinelibrary.wiley.com/journal/10.1111/%28ISSN%291463-1326
Freq: Monthly Not Audited
Editor: Richard Donnelly
MAGAZINE
Diabetes

The Diabetic Foot Journal 985227
Editorial: 1.03 Enterprise House, 1-2 Hatfields, London SE1 9PG
Tel: 44 02076 271510
Email: booking@sbcommsgroup.com
Web site: www.diabeticfootjournal.co.uk
Freq: Quarterly
Circ: 16000 Not Audited
Profile: The Diabetic Foot Journal is designed to provide healthcare professionals involved in the care of the diabetic foot topical, practical and relevant content relating to their field.
MAGAZINE
Diabetes

Diabetic Medicine 985455
Editorial: Diabetic Medicine, 9600 Garsington Road, Oxford OX4 2DQ
Tel: 44 01865 476542
Email: dme_editorial@wiley.com
Web site: http://onlinelibrary.wiley.com/journal/10.1111/%28ISSN%291464-5491
Freq: Monthly
Circ: 29227 Cision Digital Reach
Editor: Richard I.G Holt
MAGAZINE (ONLINE)
Diabetes

Diagnostic Imaging Europe 995047
Editorial: 2 Claridge Court, Lower Kings Road, Hertfordshire, Berkhamsted HP4 2AF
Tel: 44 01442 877777
Web site: www.dieurope.com
Freq: Bi-Monthly
Circ: 21058 Not Audited
Editor: Alan Barclay
MAGAZINE
Diagnostic Imaging, Medical Technology

Dialogue 987421
Editorial: The Loft, 19a Floral Street, Covent Garden, London WC2E 9DS
Web site: www.dialoguereview.com
Freq: Quarterly
Circ: 5000 Not Audited
Editor: Ben Walker
MAGAZINE
Business

Diesel Progress International 984300
Editorial: 40 Premier Avenue, Ashbourne, Ashbourne DE6 1LH **Tel:** 44 02031 792979
Email: info@dieselpub.com
Web site: http://www.dieselprogress.com/
Freq: Monthly
Circ: 10700 Not Audited

Profile: Diesel Progress International covers news, technology and products within the 'engine powered equipment and engine and component manufacturers in the on-highway, off-highway, stationary and marine markets; diesel, natural gas, gasoline or alternative fueled equipment'. The magazine has 9 issues a year.
Ad Rate: Full Page Colour £3075.00
MAGAZINE
Engineering

Digital Battlespace 985207
Editorial: 30 Saville Road, London W4 5HG
Tel: 44 02031 792570
Email: info@shephardmedia.com
Web site: http://www.digital-battlespace.com/
Freq: Bi-Monthly
Circ: 8800 Not Audited
Profile: Digital Battlespace covers the full spectrum of tri-service C4ISR issues from cyber warfare, through battlespace networking and command and control, to strategic and tactical communications.
MAGAZINE
Defense & National Security

Digital Business Lawyer 984016
Editorial: 17 The Timber Yard, Drysdale Street, London N1 6ND
Tel: 44 02070 121380
Web site: www.e-comlaw.com/e-commerce-law-and-policy/ Not Audited
Editor: Sophie Cameron
Profile: Journal focusing on the latest business, legal and regulatory developments in e-commerce. Aimed at lawyers and business people interested in e-commerce.
MAGAZINE
Consumer Interest, Corporate Law, Government, Intellectual Property, Legal Services, Tax Law

Digital by Default News 987427
Editorial: One Hammersmith Broadway, London W6 9DL **Tel:** 44 02080 809372
Email: info@digitalbydefaultnews.co.uk
Web site: www.digitalbydefaultnews.co.uk
Freq: Daily
Circ: 19079 Cision Digital Reach
MAGAZINE (ONLINE)
Government Technology

Digital Energy Journal 998588
Editorial: United House, North Road, London N7 9DP **Tel:** 44 02081 505292
Web site: www.digitalenergyjournal.com
Freq: Bi-Monthly
Circ: 8000 Not Audited
Editor: Karl Jeffery
MAGAZINE
Industry, Oil

Digital Health Legal 997799
Editorial: 17 The Timber Yard, Drysdale Street, London N1 6ND
Tel: 44 02070 121380
Web site: www.e-comlaw.com/ehealth-law-and-policy/index.asp Not Audited
Editor: Sophie Cameron
MAGAZINE
Consumer Interest, Healthcare Industry

Digital Health News 998510
Editorial: Southbank House, Black Prince Road, London SE1 7SJ
Tel: 44 02077 856900
Email: info@digitalhealth.net
Web site: www.digitalhealth.net
Freq: Daily
Circ: 97354 Cision Digital Reach
MAGAZINE (ONLINE)
Data Management, Software

Digital Labels & Packaging 985616
Editorial: 30 London Road, Southborough, Tunbridge Wells, Tunbridge Wells TN4 0RE
Tel: 44 01892 542099
Web site: http://www.paperandprint.com/digital-labels-and-packaging.aspx
Freq: Bi-Monthly
Circ: 5000 Not Audited

Editor: Neel Madsen
Profile: Magazine covering the digital labelling industry. Includes new technology as well as the latest news from the marketplace.
Ad Rate: Full Page Colour £1400.00
MAGAZINE
Graphic Design, Manufacturing, Publishing

Digital Look 985842
Editorial: Northern and Shell Building, 10 Lower Thames Street, London EC3R 6EN
Tel: 44 02036 577700
Email: londonnews@webfg.com
Web site: www.digitallook.com
Freq: Daily
Circ: 143062 Cision Digital Reach
Profile: The website Digital Look is a financial media and technology company providing online advertising opportunities and financial information solutions to leading organisations in the UK.
MAGAZINE (ONLINE)
Economics, Equities, Financial Markets

Digital Printer 984690
Editorial: 30 London Road, Southborough, Tunbridge Wells, Tunbridge Wells TN4 0RE
Tel: 44 01892 542099
Web site: www.digitalprintermag.co.uk
Freq: Monthly
Circ: 6895 Not Audited
Profile: Digital Printer is a magazine focusing on new developments in technology, featuring case studies from digital printers, publishing, printing and graphics and software as well as covering laser printing, inkjet, 3D printing, electron beam imaging, magnetography and digital duplicating.
Ad Rate: Full Page Mono £1400.00
Ad Rate: Full Page Colour £2200.00
MAGAZINE
Graphic Design, Publishing

digitalhealthage.com 988857
Tel: 44 01244 680222
Web site: www.digitalhealthage.com
Freq: Daily
Circ: 19561 Cision Digital Reach
MAGAZINE (ONLINE)
Medical Technology

Digitalisation World 1054168
Editorial: Hannay House, 39 Clarendon Road, Watford, London WD17 1JA
Email: philip.alsop@angelbc.com
Web site: https://digitalisationworld.com/
Freq: Monthly
Circ: 15827 Cision Digital Reach
MAGAZINE (ONLINE)
Data Management

Director 979958
Editorial: 3-7 Herbal Hill, London EC1R 5EJ
Tel: 44 02077 668950
Email: director.info@iod.com
Web site: www.director.co.uk
Freq: Monthly
Circ: 51085 Not Audited
Profile: Magazine covering leadership, wealth management, finance and business advice. Each issue focuses on the people running British business and contains features interviews with leading figures from across the full range of UK organisations. Aimed at members of the Institute of Directors (IoD) including CEOs of large corporations and entrepreneurial directors in start-up companies working within the media, manufacturing, e-business, public and voluntary sectors.
Ad Rate: Full Page Colour £7675.00
MAGAZINE
Business, Corporate Responsibility

Director of Finance 988573
Editorial: 13th floor, Portland House, Bressenden Place, London SW1E 5BH
Web site: www.dofonline.co.uk
Freq: Bi-Monthly
Circ: 28741 Cision Digital Reach
Editor: Katy Ward
Profile: Website covering finance. Director of Finance online shares information for

senior UK financial professionals covering accounting, governance, strategic finance, economy, management, business, taxes and lifestyle.
MAGAZINE (ONLINE)
Accounting, Banking

Director of Finance Online 984443
Editorial: Atalink Ltd, 1 New Oxford Street, High Holborn, London WC1A 1NU
Web site: www.dofonline.co.uk
Freq: Daily
Circ: 28741 Cision Digital Reach
MAGAZINE (ONLINE)
Accounting, Banking, Economics, Mergers & Acquisitions

Disability & Rehabilitation: Assistive Technology 995424
Editorial: Christchurch Court, 10 Newgate Street, London EC1A 7AZ
Tel: 44 02070 175544
Web site: www.tandfonline.com/toc/iidt20/current
Freq: Bi-Monthly Not Audited
Editor: Marcia J. Scherer
MAGAZINE
Medical Technology, Occupational Therapy & Rehabilitation

Disability and Rehabilitation 985386
Tel: 44 02070 175544
Web site: www.informahealthcare.com/loi/dre
Freq: Bi-Weekly
Circ: 895 Not Audited
Editor: Dave Müller
Profile: Journal covering the psycho-social aspects of disablement, clinical studies and related topics.
MAGAZINE
Occupational Therapy & Rehabilitation

Dispensing Optics 1056319
Tel: 44 07812 734717
Email: general@abdo.org.uk
Web site: http://www.abdo.org.uk/dispensing-optics/
Freq: Monthly
Circ: 9232 Not Audited
Profile: Journal of the Association of British Dispensing Opticians containing news, updates and product reviews. Read by dispensing opticians.
Ad Rate: Full Page Colour £1100.00
MAGAZINE
Medical Technology, Ophthalmology & Optometry

Dispute Resolution International 999357
Editorial: 4th Floor, 10 St Bride Street, London EC4A 4AD **Tel:** 44 02078 420090
Email: editor@int-bar.org
Web site: www.ibanet.org/Publications/publications_dispute_resolution_international.aspx
Freq: Semi-Annual
Circ: 4100 Not Audited
MAGAZINE
Legal Services, Litigation

Disrupts 996135
Editorial: DISRUPTS MEDIA LIMITED, 58 - 64 City Road, London EC1Y 2AL
Tel: 44 07535 670581
Email: editor@disrupts.co.uk
Web site: www.disrupts.co.uk
Freq: Monthly
Circ: 5000 Not Audited
MAGAZINE
Business, Small and Medium Business

Diversify Now 1073940
Tel: 44 01905 616665
Web site: www.diversify-now.com
Freq: Monthly
Circ: 10000 Not Audited
Editor: Emily Scaife
MAGAZINE
Animal Farming

DIY Week
981097

Editorial: 15A London Road, Maidstone, Maidstone ME16 8LY **Tel:** 44 01622 687031
Web site: www.diyweek.net
Freq: Bi-Weekly
Circ: 6960 Not Audited
Editor: Fiona Garcia
Profile: Magazine covering new products, promotions and news in the hardware, garden, housewares and DIY markets.
Ad Rate: Full Page Mono £2200.00
Ad Rate: Full Page Colour £2500.00
MAGAZINE
Building & Construction, Interior Design

DIYWEEK.net
984776

Editorial: 15A London Road, Maidstone, Maidstone ME16 8LY **Tel:** 44 01622 687031
Web site: www.diyweek.net
Freq: Daily
Circ: 14056 Cision Digital Reach
Editor: Fiona Garcia
MAGAZINE (ONLINE)
Do-It-Yourself (DIY), Gardening

The Door Industry Journal
1068721

Tel: 44 01444 464147
Email: mail@doorindustryjournal.co.uk
Web site: http://doorindustryjournal.co.uk/
Freq: 3 Times/Year
Circ: 17250 Not Audited
Profile: Journal of The Door & Hardware Federation covering garage doors, industrial doors, loading docks, dock levellers, sliding doors, entrance doors, timber doorsets, metal doorsets, fire doors, door and gate automation, access control, powered gates, barriers, CCTV, parking control, building hardware, ironmongery and locks. Further content covers business news, employment and legal, health and safety, product news, motoring and transport, computers and IT (also content from the US door and gate industries). Targets DHF members, garage door and industrial door specialists, automated gate installers and manufacturers, architects, facilities managers, specifiers, house-builders, developers, builders, contractors, architectural ironmongers, builders' merchants, locksmiths, housing associations, local authorities.
Ad Rate: Full Page Colour £1495.00
MAGAZINE
News & Current Affairs

Dorset Business
979997

Editorial: Chamber House, Acorn Office Park, Ling Road, Poole, Poole BH12 4NZ
Tel: 44 01202 714800
Email: contact@dorsetbusiness.net
Web site: www.businessdorset.co.uk
Freq: Monthly
Circ: 6000 Not Audited
Profile: Magazine of the Dorset Chamber of Commerce and Industry. Contains business news, profiles and sections on motoring, health and fitness.
Ad Rate: Full Page Colour £550.00
MAGAZINE
Business, Small and Medium Business

Downstream
981011

Editorial: Vienna House, International Square, Starley Way, Birmingham Int. Business Park, Bickenhill Lane, Solihull B37 7GN **Tel:** 44 01217 671319
Email: ds@fpsonline.co.uk
Freq: Quarterly
Circ: 2000 Not Audited
Profile: Magazine covering the downstream oil distribution industry including news, developments, legislation and environmental matters, tank and tanker manufacture and commercial vehicle updates.
Ad Rate: Full Page Mono £878.00
Ad Rate: Full Page Colour £1317.00
MAGAZINE
Oil

Drain Trader
983702

Editorial: The Runnings, Runnings Road, Cheltenham GL51 9NJ
Tel: 44 01242 576777

Email: info@draintraderltd.com
Web site: www.draintraderltd.com
Freq: Monthly
Circ: 4500 Not Audited
MAGAZINE
Engineering

Drewry Shipping Consultants
1064493

Editorial: 15-17 Christopher Street, London EC2A 2BS **Tel:** 44 02075 380191
Email: enquiries@drewry.co.uk
Web site: www.drewry.co.uk
Freq: Daily
Circ: 51635 Cision Digital Reach
Editor: Carly Fields
MAGAZINE (ONLINE)
Shipping & Warehousing

Drug Delivery Insight (DDI)
984474

Editorial: Senator House, 85 Queen Victoria Street, London EC4V 4AB
Tel: 44 02072 465170
Email: healthcare@espicom.com
Web site: http://store.bmiresearch.com/drug-delivery-insight.html
Freq: Bi-Weekly Not Audited
MAGAZINE
Medical Technology, Pharmaceuticals

Drug Discovery
998547

Editorial: Wood View, Unit 6, Bull Lane Industrial Estate, Sudbury, Acton CO10 0FD
Tel: 44 01787 319234
Web site: https://www.technologynetworks.com/drug-discovery/
Freq: Daily
Circ: 6 Cision Digital Reach
Editor: Ashley Board
MAGAZINE (ONLINE)
Biotechnology, Science

Drug Discovery Today
980770

Editorial: Gateway House, 28 The Quadrant, Richmond, London TW9 1DN
Tel: 44 02084 395525
Email: ddt@drugdiscoverytoday.com
Web site: www.drugdiscoverytoday.com
Freq: Monthly
Circ: 27019 Not Audited
Editor: Steve Carney
Profile: Drug Discovery Today covers drug discovery and development, with current reviews, the rapid scientific developments in drug discovery associated technologies, management, commercial and regulatory issues. Launched in 1996. Read by pharmaceutical research scientists, both in industry and academia, including medicinal chemists and molecular biologists.
Ad Rate: Full Page Colour £1585.00
MAGAZINE
Biotechnology, Medical Technology, Pharmaceuticals

Drug Discovery World
983911

Editorial: 39 Vineyard Path, Mortlake, London SW14 8ET **Tel:** 44 02084 875656
Email: robert@rjcoms.com
Web site: http://www.ddw-online.com
Freq: Quarterly
Circ: 15000 Not Audited
Profile: Magazine containing a business review of drug discovery and development. Aimed at pharmaceutical research and development professionals.
Ad Rate: Full Page Colour £4500.00
MAGAZINE
Healthcare Industry, Pharmaceuticals

Drug Resistance Updates
995723

Tel: 44 01865 843000
Web site: http://www.drupjournal.com/
Freq: Bi-Monthly
MAGAZINE
Infectious Diseases, Oncology, Pharmaceuticals

Drug Target Review
987984

Editorial: Court Lodge, Hogtrough Hill, Brasted, Westerham TN16 1NU
Tel: 44 01959 563311
Web site: www.drugtargetreview.com
Freq: Quarterly
Circ: 9077 Not Audited
Profile: Publication that covers the drug discovery industry.
MAGAZINE
Pharmaceuticals

drugdevelopment-technology.com
985366

Editorial: John Carpenter House, John Carpenter Street, London EC4Y 0AN
Tel: 44 02079 366400
Email: onlineeditorial@kable.co.uk
Web site: www.drugdevelopment-technology.com
Freq: Daily
Circ: 31401 Cision Digital Reach
MAGAZINE (ONLINE)
Biotechnology, Pharmaceuticals

Drugs & Dealers magazine
995341

Editorial: 40 Melton Street, London NW1 2FD **Tel:** 44 02071 939690
Email: info@biotechandmoney.com
Web site: http://www.biotechandmoney.com
Freq: Bi-Monthly
MAGAZINE
Healthcare Industry, Science

Drugs and Alcohol Today (DAT)
983917

Editorial: Howard House, Wagon Lane, Bingley BD16 1WA **Tel:** 44 01274 777700
Email: emerald@emeraldinsight.com
Web site: www.emeraldinsight.com/loi/dat
Freq: Quarterly Not Audited
Editor: Axel Klein
MAGAZINE
Community Care (UK)

Dry Bulk
1054095

Tel: 44 01252 718999
Web site: www.drybulkmagazine.com
Freq: Semi-Annual
Circ: 4003 Not Audited
MAGAZINE
Shipping & Warehousing

Dry Cargo International
984705

Editorial: Clover House, 24 Drury Road, Colchester, Colchester CO2 7UX
Tel: 44 01206 562560
Email: info@dc-int.com
Web site: www.dc-int.com
Freq: Monthly
Circ: 6600 Not Audited
Editor: Louise Dodds-Ely
Profile: Magazine covering the dry bulk industry. Aimed at senior executives and decision-makers in the industry.
MAGAZINE
Shipping & Warehousing

E&P Daily
980784

Editorial: Ogilvie Publishing Ltd, 56 Aylesford Mews, Sunderland SR2 9HY
Tel: 44 01915 678497
Email: epdaily@ogilviepub.com
Web site: www.ogilviepub.com
Freq: Daily
Circ: 6285 Cision Digital Reach
Editor: Steve Hamlen
MAGAZINE (ONLINE)
Oil

e-architect
987543

Editorial: 6 The Maltings, Haddington, Haddington EH41 4EF **Tel:** 44 01620 825722
Email: info@e-architect.co.uk
Web site: www.e-architect.co.uk
Freq: Daily
Circ: 229653 Cision Digital Reach
MAGAZINE (ONLINE)
Architecture & Design

Early Child Development and Care
995438

Editorial: 4 Park Square, Milton Park, Abingdon, Didcot OX14 4RN
Tel: 44 02070 176000
Web site: www.tandf.co.uk/journals/journal.asp?issn=0300-4430&linktype=1
Freq: Monthly Not Audited
Editor: Roy Evans
MAGAZINE
Pediatrics

Earthmovers
984834

Editorial: Sundial House, 17 Wickham Road, Beckenham, London BR3 5JS
Tel: 44 02086 394400
Email: editor@earthmoversmagazine.co.uk
Web site: www.earthmoversmagazine.co.uk
Freq: Monthly
Circ: 13500 Not Audited
Editor: Graham Black
Profile: Magazine covering the latest developments in earth moving machinery including site tests, buyers guides, fleet reviews and technical developments.
Ad Rate: Full Page Mono £1195.00
Ad Rate: Full Page Colour £1495.00
MAGAZINE
Building & Construction

East Midlands Business Link
987411

Editorial: Armstrong House, Armstrong Street, Grimsby, Grimsby DN31 2QE
Email: eastmidlands@blmgroup.co.uk
Web site: www.eastmidlandsbusinesslink.co.uk
Freq: Daily
Circ: 16935 Cision Digital Reach
Editor: Ian Evans
MAGAZINE (ONLINE)
Business, Small and Medium Business

Eastern Director
982904

Editorial: 14 Middletons Road, Yaxley, Peterborough PE7 3LR
Tel: 44 01733 242312
Email: news@pridepublications.co.uk
Web site: www.pridepublications.co.uk
Freq: Quarterly
Circ: 9000 Not Audited
Editor: Trevor Gehlcken
Profile: Independent business magazine for business leaders.
Ad Rate: Full Page Mono £675.00
Ad Rate: Full Page Colour £675.00
MAGAZINE
Business

e-bulletin
998817

Editorial: c/o General Optical Council, 41 Harley Street, London W1G 8DJ
Tel: 44 02075 803898
Email: bulletin@optical.org
Web site: www.optical.org/en/news_publications/Publications/ebulletin.cfm
Freq: Quarterly
MAGAZINE (ONLINE)
Ophthalmology & Optometry

ECA Today
985536

Editorial: 275 Newmarket Road, Cambridge CB5 8JE **Tel:** 44 01223 477411
Email: mail@ecatoday.co.uk
Web site: http://www.eca.co.uk/business-industry-support/eca-today
Freq: Quarterly
Profile: Journal of the Electrical Contractors' Association. It covers the electrical, property and building services sectors as well as the wider business environment. Aimed at members of the ECA, including the FSA and ELECSA as well as senior management within electrical contracting and fire and security systems installation companies.
Ad Rate: Full Page Colour £1995.00
MAGAZINE
Electricity

ecancermedicalscience
985210

Editorial: Cancer Intelligence, 154 Cheltenham Road, Bristol BS6 5RL
Tel: 44 01179 094608
Email: news@ecancer.org

Section 4 UK Periodicals Business

Business Magazines

Web site: http://ecancer.org/journal/journal.php
Freq: Daily
Circ: 488 Cision Digital Reach
MAGAZINE (ONLINE)
Oncology

Ecclesiastical and Heritage World
988219
Editorial: Suite 2, 61 Lower Hillgate, Stockport SK1 3AW **Tel:** 44 01617 103880
Web site: www.ecclesiasticalandheritageworld.co.uk
Freq: Quarterly Not Audited
Editor: Chris Stokes
Profile: Magazine covering the design, construction, refurbishment and maintenance of churches, their stonework, furnishings, museums, galleries and the heritage sector.
Ad Rate: Full Page Colour £1500.00
MAGAZINE
Property Management & Maintenance

Eco Building News
985461
Editorial: McDermott Chambers, 2 The Green, Kings Norton, Birmingham B38 8SD
Tel: 44 01214 513037
Web site: www.mcdermottpublishing.com/eco-building-news
Freq: Bi-Monthly
Circ: 12500 Not Audited
MAGAZINE
Sustainable Development

economia
986542
Editorial: 71-73 Carter Lane, London EC4V 5EQ **Tel:** 44 02030 962640
Email: economia@icaew.com
Web site: economia.icaew.com
Freq: Monthly
Circ: 130588 Not Audited
Editor: Amy Duff
Profile: Official magazine of the ICAEW. It provides commentary, intelligence and opinion across business, finance and accountancy. First published in February 2012. Aimed at accountants, finance leaders, decision makers and finance professionals.
MAGAZINE
Accounting

Economic and Labour Market Review
998540
Editorial: 4 Crinan Street, London N1 9XW
Tel: 44 02078 334000
Email: graeme.chamberlin@ons.gsi.gov.uk
Web site: www.palgrave-journals.com/elmr
Freq: Monthly
Circ: 700 Not Audited
MAGAZINE
Government, Human Resources

The Economist
979836
Editorial: The Adelphi Building, 1-11 John Adam Street, London WC2N 6HT
Tel: 44 02078 307000
Email: letters@economist.com
Web site: www.economist.com
Freq: Weekly
Circ: 248196 Not Audited
Editor In Chief: Zanny Minton Beddoes
Profile: The Economist is a weekly news and international affairs publication. It provides analysis of world business and current affairs, with authoritative insight and opinion on international news, world politics, business, finance, science and technology. It also features an overview of cultural trends and regular industry, business and country special reports. Established in 1843 by James Wilson. The Economist is written for a global audience of senior business, political and financial decision-makers. Its readership has grown to four million and includes many impressive names from among the world's opinion leaders. Readership includes senior figures in the world of politics and business.
Ad Rate: Full Page Mono £11900.00
Ad Rate: Full Page Colour £21300.00
MAGAZINE
Banking, Economics

Economist Intelligence Unit
987022
Editorial: 20 Cabot Square, Canary Wharf, London E14 4QW **Tel:** 44 02075 768181
Email: london@eiu.com
Web site: www.economistinsights.com
Freq: Daily
Circ: 34719 Cision Digital Reach
MAGAZINE (ONLINE)
Business, Economics, Small and Medium Business

Economy
1072719
Email: hello@ecnmy.org
Web site: www.ecnmy.org
Freq: Daily
Circ: 18415 Cision Digital Reach
MAGAZINE (ONLINE)
Economics

Ecoportal.net
1062078
Tel: 44 54115 3544256
Email: contenidos@ecoportal.net
Web site: http://mineria.ecoportal.net
Circ: 11 Cision Digital Reach
MAGAZINE (ONLINE)
Environment

eDelivery.net
997442
Editorial: 52-54 Gracechurch Street, London EC3V 0EH **Tel:** 44 02079 338999
Email: press@edelivery.net
Web site: www.edelivery.net
Freq: Quarterly
Circ: 55497 Cision Digital Reach
MAGAZINE (ONLINE)
Shipping & Warehousing, Supply Chain Management (SCM)

edie.net
981499
Editorial: Windsor Court, Wood Street, East Grinstead, East Grinstead RH19 1UZ
Tel: 44 01342 332000
Email: newsdesk@fav-house.com
Web site: www.edie.net
Freq: Daily
Circ: 108647 Cision Digital Reach
Editor: Luke Nicholls
MAGAZINE (ONLINE)
Alternative/Renewable Energy, Environment

Edit
1053889
Editorial: 10C Peckingham Street, West Midlands, Halesowen B63 3AW
Web site: http://retailbirmingham.com/projects/bid-edit-member-magazine/
Freq: Bi-Monthly Not Audited
MAGAZINE
Retail Management

EDUcatering
985375
Editorial: 4th Floor, Joynes House, New Road, Gravesend DA11 0AJ
Tel: 44 03455 006008
Web site: www.educateringmagazine.co.uk
Freq: Monthly
Circ: 4579 Not Audited
Editor: Morag Wilson
Profile: Trade publication covering catering within schools and contract catering.
MAGAZINE
Food, Schools & Institutions

Education Design & Build Magazine
985001
Editorial: SBC House, Restmor Way, Wallington, London SM6 7AH
Tel: 44 02082 881080
Email: info@educationdab.co.uk
Web site: www.educationdab.co.uk
Freq: Bi-Monthly
Circ: 8860 Not Audited
Editor: Richard Sutton
MAGAZINE
Building & Construction, Urban Planning & Development

Education for Primary Care
985211
Editorial: 2nd Floor, 5 Thomas More Square, London E1W 1YW **Tel:** 44 02079 543441
Web site: www.tandfonline.com/toc/tepc20/current
Freq: Bi-Monthly
Profile: Journal of the Association of Course Organisers, the National Association of Primary Care Educators UK and the World Organisation of Family Doctors (WONCA). The Journal aims to support vocational training and interprofessional development. Aimed at healthcare educators who are involved in organising and running educational activities across the primary care team.
MAGAZINE
Health Administration

Education in Chemistry
981522
Editorial: Thomas Graham House, Science Park, Milton Road, Cambridge CB4 0WF
Tel: 44 01223 420066
Email: eic@rsc.org
Web site: www.rsc.org/eic/
Freq: Bi-Monthly
Circ: 11000 Not Audited
Profile: Publication covering the whole spectrum of chemistry teaching, from balanced science in secondary schools to degrees.
Ad Rate: Full Page Mono £890.00
MAGAZINE
Higher Education, Schools & Institutions, Science

Education Technology
986669
Editorial: Unit 2.4, Paintworks, Bath Road, Bristol BS4 3EH **Tel:** 44 01173 005526
Web site: www.edtechnology.co.uk
Freq: Bi-Monthly
Circ: 7500 Not Audited
Profile: Magazine covering ICT developments that are relevant to the education sector, from primary schools to universities. It features technology news, reviews and features.
Ad Rate: Full Page Colour £1250.00
MAGAZINE
Computers, Schools & Institutions

Efficiency Exchange
997336
Editorial: Woburn House, 20 Tavistock Square, London WC1H 9HQ
Tel: 44 02074 195510
Email: rosie.niven@universitiesuk.ac.uk
Web site: http://www.efficiencyexchange.ac.uk
Freq: Daily
Circ: 16444 Cision Digital Reach
MAGAZINE (ONLINE)
Higher Education

EfficientEnergy.net
996458
Editorial: 38 West Street, Great Gransden, Sandy SG19 3AU **Tel:** 44 01892 542087
Email: editor@efficientenergy.net
Web site: http://efficientenergy.net/
Freq: Daily
Circ: 18000 Not Audited
Editor: David Keighley; **Editor:** Jonathan Severn
Profile: Business to business website providing a platform for suppliers to promote their products, equipment and services for energy efficient projects. Includes materials, components, products and systems.
MAGAZINE
Alternative/Renewable Energy, Building & Construction, Electricity, Engineering, Nuclear Power, Oil, Water & Sanitation

eFinancialCareers.com
984493
Editorial: Tabernacle Court, 16-28 Tabernacle Street, London EC2A 4DD
Tel: 44 02079 977900
Web site: www.efinancialcareers.com
Freq: Daily
Circ: 1540790 Cision Digital Reach
MAGAZINE (ONLINE)
Banking

e-Forex
980845
Editorial: Suite 10, 3 Edgar Buildings, George Street, Bath BA1 2FJ
Tel: 44 01179 875219
Web site: http://www.e-forex.net/
Freq: Quarterly
Circ: 25000 Not Audited
Editor: Charles Jago
Profile: Magazine devoted to online and electronic trading of foreign exchange and OTC financial instruments.
Ad Rate: Full Page Mono £2250.00
Ad Rate: Full Page Colour £2950.00
MAGAZINE
Financial Markets, Foreign Exchange Market (FOREX), Industry

EFORT Open Reviews
1055928
Editorial: 22 Buckingham Street, London WC2N 6ET **Tel:** 44 02077 820010
Email: openreviews@efort.org
Web site: www.efortopenreviews.org
Freq: Daily
Circ: 12007 Cision Digital Reach
MAGAZINE (ONLINE)
Orthopedics

EFT Businessweek
988448
Editorial: 1st Floor New Zealand House, 80 Hay Market, London SW1Y 4TE
Email: editor@exportft.com
Web site: www.exportft.com
Freq: Daily
Circ: 521 Cision Digital Reach
MAGAZINE (ONLINE)
Banking, Economics

EGR Marketing
1052539
Editorial: One London Wall, London EC2Y 5EA **Tel:** 44 02078 326500
Web site: http://egr.global/marketing/
Freq: Monthly Not Audited
MAGAZINE
Marketing

The EIC
988011
Editorial: 89 Albert Embankment, London SE1 7TP **Tel:** 44 02070 918600
Email: newsdesk@the-eic.com
Web site: http://www.the-eic.com
Freq: Daily
Circ: 36606 Cision Digital Reach
Profile: Website covering the energy sector. EIC shares the latest news on goods and services for energy industries worldwide.
MAGAZINE (ONLINE)
Alternative/Renewable Energy, Carbon Emissions & Trading, Electricity, Energy, Nuclear Power, Oil, Water & Sanitation

EJSO - European Journal of Surgical Oncology
995911
Editorial: EJSO Editorial Office, Health Sciences, Elsevier Ltd, The Boulevard, Langford Lane, Kidlington OX5 1GB
Tel: 44 01865 843753
Email: ejso@elsevier.com
Web site: http://www.journals.elsevier.com/ejso-european-journal-of-surgical-oncology
Freq: Monthly Not Audited
MAGAZINE
Oncology

EL Gazette
985745
Editorial: 14 Greville Stree, London EC1N 8SB **Tel:** 44 02037 359672
Email: editorial@elgazette.com
Web site: www.elgazette.com
Freq: Monthly
Circ: 2000 Not Audited
MAGAZINE
Education, Higher Education, Schools & Institutions, Students

Eldis Programme
995411
Editorial: Institute of Development Studies (IDS), Institute of Development Studies, University of Sussex, Brighton BN1 9RE
Tel: 44 01273 915776
Email: eldis@ids.ac.uk
Web site: www.eldis.org
Freq: Daily

Circ: 174684 Cision Digital Reach
MAGAZINE (ONLINE)
Government

Electrical Magazine 983159
Tel: 44 02892 612990
Email: elcctrical@kmpltd.co.uk
Web site: http://elecmagazine.com/
Freq: Bi-Monthly
Circ: 8100 Not Audited
Editor: Adam Hassin
MAGAZINE
Building & Construction

Electrical Portal 986494
Editorial: 11 Glenthorne Road, London W6 0LH
Web site: www.electricalportal.co.uk
Freq: Daily
Circ: 2002 Cision Digital Reach
MAGAZINE (ONLINE)
Electricity

Electro Optics 981635
Editorial: 4 Signet Court, Cambridge CB1 8LA Tel: 44 01223 211170
Email: editor.electro@europascience.com
Web site: www.electrooptics.com
Freq: Monthly
Circ: 14659 Not Audited
Profile: Magazine providing UK and European coverage of electro-optics, fibre-optics and image processing equipment and systems.
Ad Rate: Full Page Colour £3700.00
MAGAZINE
Science

Electronic Specifier Test & Measurement 998141
Editorial: Comice Place, Woodfalls Farm, Gravelly Ways, Maidstone ME18 6DA
Tel: 44 01622 871944
Email: editor@electronicspecifier.com
Web site: www.electronicspecifier.com
Freq: Quarterly
Circ: 13500 Not Audited
Editor: Mick Elliott
MAGAZINE
Engineering

ElectronicSpecifier Power 988682
Editorial: Comice Place, Woodfalls Farm, Gravelly Ways, Maidstone ME18 6DA
Tel: 44 01622 871944
Email: info@electronicspecifier.com
Web site: www.electronicspecifier.com
Freq: Bi-Monthly
Circ: 36700 Not Audited
MAGAZINE
Alternative/Renewable Energy, Carbon Emissions & Trading, Electricity, Energy, Engineering, Nuclear Power, Oil, Water & Sanitation

Elevation Magazine 984748
Editorial: 6 Butterly Avenue, Questor, Dartford, London DA1 1JG
Tel: 44 01322 626550
Web site: www.elevation.co.uk
Freq: Quarterly
Circ: 2000 Not Audited
Profile: Magazine covering all aspects of the UK lift industry.
Ad Rate: Full Page Mono £705.00
Ad Rate: Full Page Colour £1271.00
MAGAZINE
Engineering

Elite Business 987005
Editorial: Regency House, 16 Victoria Road, Chelmsford CM1 1NZ Tel: 44 01245 673700
Email: info@cemedia.co.uk
Web site: www.elitebusinessmagazine.co.uk
Freq: Monthly
Circ: 34000 Not Audited
MAGAZINE
Business, Corporate Responsibility

Elite Franchise 988421
Editorial: Regency House, 16 Victoria Road, Chelmsford CM1 1NZ Tel: 44 01245 673700
Email: editorial@cemedia.co.uk
Web site: http://elitefranchisemagazine.co.uk
Freq: Monthly Not Audited
MAGAZINE
Business, Retail Management, Small and Medium Business

EMEA Finance 984579
Editorial: 77 Leonard Street, London EC2A 4QS Tel: 44 02037 407117
Email: Info@emeafinance.com
Web site: www.emeafinance.com
Freq: Bi-Monthly
Circ: 10000 Not Audited
MAGAZINE
Banking, Financial Markets

Emergency Medicine Journal 984530
Editorial: BMA House, Tavistock Square, London WC1H 9JR Tel: 44 02071 111105
Email: editor.emj@bmj.com
Web site: www.emj.bmj.com
Freq: Monthly
Circ: 5560 Not Audited
Editor: Ellen Weber
Profile: Journal covering all aspects of emergency medicine.
Ad Rate: Full Page Mono £910.00
Ad Rate: Full Page Colour £1610.00
MAGAZINE
EMS/Emergency Medical Services

Emergency Nurse 981200
Editorial: The Heights, 59-65 Lowlands Road, Harrow, London HA1 3AE
Tel: 44 02084 231066
Web site: www.emergencynurse.co.uk
Freq: Monthly
Circ: 7808 Not Audited
Profile: Journal of the RCN Accident and Emergency Nursing Association. Covers news, products, views and issues. Aimed at accident and emergency nurses and nurses who work in minor injuries units, NHS direct and walk-in centres.
Ad Rate: Full Page Colour £1880.00
MAGAZINE
EMS/Emergency Medical Services, Nursing/Nurses

Emergency Services Times 983925
Editorial: Robert Denholm House, Bletchingley Road, Nutfield, Redhill RH1 4HW Tel: 44 01737 824010
Web site: www.emergencyservicestimes.com
Freq: Bi-Monthly
Circ: 6000 Not Audited
Profile: Publication covering news and developments within the emergency services.
Ad Rate: Full Page Mono £1400.00
Ad Rate: Full Page Colour £1400.00
MAGAZINE
EMS/Emergency Medical Services

Emerging Markets 994704
Editorial: 8 Bouverie Street, London EC4Y 8AX
Web site: www.emergingmarkets.org
Freq: Daily
Circ: 25000 Not Audited
Profile: Website covering economics. The Emerging Markets website provides a source of news, analysis and commentary on economic policy, international economics and global financial markets, with a special focus on the emerging world.
MAGAZINE
Banking, Bonds, Emerging Markets, Financial Markets, Government, Investment Banking, Lending

EMH (European Medical Hygiene) - SUSPENDED 996943
Editorial: 1 Oxford Court, The Granby, Weymouth, Weymouth DT4 9GH
Tel: 44 01305 785199

Email: info@emhmagazine.com
Freq: Quarterly
Circ: 5450 Not Audited
Editor: Kimberley de Selincourt
MAGAZINE
Health Administration

Employee Benefits 980156
Editorial: Wells Point, 79 Wells Street, London W1T 3QN Tel: 44 02079 704000
Email: eb.editorial@centaurmedia.com
Web site: www.employeebenefits.co.uk
Freq: Monthly
Circ: 9000 Not Audited
Editor: Debbie Lovewell-Tuck
Profile: Magazine covering all aspects of employee benefits. It discusses human resource news, including absence management and HR software. Read by personnel and finance directors, pension managers, compensation and benefit managers and those with responsibilities for buying and managing employee benefits.
Ad Rate: Full Page Colour £2920.00
MAGAZINE
Human Resources

Employers' Law 1074956
Editorial: Reed Business Information, Quadrant House, The Quadrant, Sutton SM2 5AS Tel: 44 02086 524669
Web site: https://subscribe.personneltoday.com/employerslaw/default.aspx?prom=WEB14
Freq: Monthly
Circ: 1565 Not Audited
Editor: Noel O'Reilly
MAGAZINE
Employment, Human Resources

Employment Law Journal 1052812
Tel: 44 02073 969292
Email: editorial@legal500.com
Web site: www.lawjournals.co.uk/journals/employment-law-journal
Freq: Monthly Not Audited
MAGAZINE
Employment

EmploymentSolicitor.com 1075966
Email: editor@marchmouse.co.uk
Web site: www.employmentsolicitor.com
Freq: Daily
Circ: 15968 Cision Digital Reach
Editor: Joanne O'Connell
MAGAZINE (ONLINE)
Business, Company News & Appointments, Education, Employment, Health & Safety, Human Resources, Recruiting, Small and Medium Business

Endodontic Practice 983900
Editorial: 1 Hertford House, Farm Close, Shenley, Radlett WD7 9AB
Tel: 44 01923 851777
Web site: www.dentistry.co.uk/endodontic-dental-news/
Freq: Quarterly
Circ: 3000 Not Audited
Profile: Endodontic Journal containing a variety of peer reviewed clinical articles and case studies to promote excellence within the profession, as well as practice management features, courses and product details.
Ad Rate: Full Page Colour £2275.00
MAGAZINE
Dentistry

ENDS Europe 981503
Editorial: Bridge House, 69 London Road, Twickenham, London TW1 3QR
Tel: 44 02082 678100
Email: news@endseurope.com
Web site: www.endseurope.com
Freq: Daily
Circ: 20587 Cision Digital Reach
Profile: Electronically delivered newsletter covering news and analysis on EU and

European environmental policy and legislation.
MAGAZINE (ONLINE)
Environment

The ENDS Report 980781
Editorial: Teddington Studios, Broom Road, Teddington, London TW11 9BE
Tel: 44 20826 74025
Email: news@ends.co.uk
Web site: www.endsreport.com
Freq: Monthly
Circ: 9000 Not Audited
Editor: Alison Carter
Profile: Magazine covering UK and EU environmental developments, including news and analysis of business and legislation and government policy. The publication also covers environmental policy and business, official reports and how environmental issues affect corporate strategy. First published in 1978. Aimed at environmental professionals in industry, consultancy, clean-up firms, government, regulatory authorities, environmental NGOs and academia.
Ad Rate: Full Page Colour £3500.00
MAGAZINE
Environment

Energy & Environment Management 985954
Editorial: Trelawney House, Chester Gate, Macclesfield SK11 6DW
Email: eet.editor@tenalpspublishing.com
Web site: www.eaem.co.uk
Freq: Daily
Circ: 14702 Cision Digital Reach
Editor: Marie Roberts
MAGAZINE (ONLINE)
Alternative/Renewable Energy, Carbon Emissions & Trading, Electricity, Energy, Environment, Nuclear Power, Oil, Water & Sanitation

Energy Business Review 984408
Editorial: Energy Business Review, Progressive Trade Media Ltd, 40-42 Hatton Garden, London EC1N 8EB
Tel: 44 02079 366898
Email: news@industryreview.com
Web site: http://www.energy-business-review.com
Freq: Daily
Circ: 7563 Cision Digital Reach
Profile: Website covering the energy industry. Energy Business Review features news, analysis and information about the energy industry.
MAGAZINE (ONLINE)
Alternative/Renewable Energy, Carbon Emissions & Trading, Electricity, Energy, Nuclear Power, Oil, Water & Sanitation

Energy Compass 980788
Editorial: Interpark House, 7 Down Street, 3rd Floor, London W1J 7AJ
Tel: 44 02075 182200
Web site: www.energyintel.com/Pages/About_ECW.aspx
Freq: Weekly Not Audited
Editor: Jill Junnola
MAGAZINE
Alternative/Renewable Energy, Electricity, Nuclear Power, Oil, Water & Sanitation

Energy Digital 1074961
Editorial: 69-75 Thorpe Road, Norwich NR1 1UA Tel: 44 01603 217530
Email: info@bizclikmedia.com
Web site: http://www.energydigital.com/
Freq: Monthly
MAGAZINE
Alternative/Renewable Energy, Carbon Emissions & Trading, Electricity, Energy, Nuclear Power, Oil, Water & Sanitation

Energy Engineering 983838
Editorial: Pure Offices, Plato Close, Leamington Spa CV34 6WE
Tel: 44 01926 671339
Email: info@energyengineering.co.uk
Web site: www.energyengineering.co.uk
Freq: Bi-Monthly

Business Magazines

Circ: 32000 Not Audited

Profile: Magazine that covers the products and processes, innovation, technology and management of renewable energy in all its forms.

Ad Rate: Full Page Colour £1945.00

MAGAZINE

Alternative/Renewable Energy

Energy in Buildings and Industry
981136

Editorial: PO Box 825, Guildford GU4 8WQ

Tel: 44 01483 452854

Email: mark.thrower@btinternet.com

Web site: www.energyzine.co.uk/

Freq: Monthly

Circ: 12035 Not Audited

MAGAZINE

Alternative/Renewable Energy, Carbon Emissions & Trading, Electricity, Energy, Nuclear Power, Oil, Water & Sanitation

The Energy Industry Times
985621

Editorial: 43 Woodend Road, London E17 4JS **Tel:** 44 02085 232573

Email: editorial@teitimes.com

Web site: www.mibmedia.com

Freq: Monthly

Circ: 8000 Not Audited

Profile: Monthly newspaper covering the power and energy industry.

MAGAZINE

Alternative/Renewable Energy, Carbon Emissions & Trading, Electricity, Energy, Nuclear Power, Oil, Water & Sanitation

Energy Intelligence Briefing
999121

Editorial: Interpark House, 7 Down Street, 3rd Floor, London W1J 7AJ

Tel: 44 02075 182200

Web site: http://www.energyintel.com/Pages/About_EIB.aspx

Freq: Weekly Not Audited

MAGAZINE

Alternative/Renewable Energy, Electricity, Nuclear Power, Oil, Water & Sanitation

Energy Intelligence Finance
1049244

Editorial: Interpark House, 7 Down Street, 3rd Floor, London W1J 7AJ

Tel: 44 02075 182200

Email: energyintelligence@energyintel.com

Web site: http://www.energyintel.com/pages/about_eif.aspx

Freq: Weekly

MAGAZINE

Oil

Energy Live News
985589

Editorial: 1 Dudrich House, Princes Lane, Muswell Hill, London N10 3LU

Tel: 44 02088 159222

Email: stories@energylivenews.com

Web site: www.energylivenews.com

Freq: Daily

Circ: 15803 Cision Digital Reach

Editor: Sumit Bose

Profile: Website providing energy news and information. It features articles on fossil fuels, renewables, nuclear and cleantech energy. The website is divided into eight sections; Energy Efficiency, Energy Policy, Gas, Nuclear Power, Oil & Petroleum, Power & Electricity, Sustainable Energy and Water & Environment.

MAGAZINE (ONLINE)

Alternative/Renewable Energy, Carbon Emissions & Trading, Electricity, Energy, Nuclear Power, Oil, Water & Sanitation

Energy Management
984896

Editorial: 15a London Road, Maidstone, Maidstone ME16 8LY **Tel:** 44 01622 699194

Web site: www.connectingindustry.com/EnergyManagement/

Freq: Quarterly

Circ: 4500 Not Audited

Editor: Michelle Lea; **Editor:** Michelle Winny

Profile: Magazine covering plant, works, maintenance processes, production and electrical engineering, buildings management, health and safety, materials handling.

MAGAZINE

Alternative/Renewable Energy, Carbon Emissions & Trading, Electricity, Energy, Nuclear Power, Oil, Water & Sanitation

Energy Manager Magazine
996053

Tel: 44 01933 316931

Email: ralph@energymanagermagazine.co.uk

Web site: www.energymanagermagazine.co.uk

Freq: Bi-Monthly

Circ: 8500 Not Audited

MAGAZINE

Environment, Government, Public Sector

Energy Now
984799

Editorial: New Venture House, Weir Lane, Worcester WR2 4AY **Tel:** 44 01905 616665

Email: info@energy-now.co.uk

Web site: www.energy-now.co.uk

Freq: Bi-Monthly

Circ: 20000 Not Audited

Editor: Emily Scaife

Profile: Magazine published every 2 months, focusing on the renewable energy options available to farmers and landowners. Features include news, interviews, case studies, company profiles, area reports, machinery, energy people and diary dates. Aimed at farmers and landowners.

Ad Rate: Full Page Colour £1386.00

MAGAZINE

Alternative/Renewable Energy

Energy Policy
981498

Editorial: The Boulevard, Langford Lane, Kidlington OX5 1GB **Tel:** 44 01865 843000

Email: energypolicy@elsevier.com

Web site: www.journals.elsevier.com/energy-policy

Freq: Monthly

Circ: 1784 Not Audited

Profile: Journal covering all aspects of energy supply, demand, utilisation and policy making, including information on pricing policy and energy efficiency potential in the domestic sector.

MAGAZINE

Alternative/Renewable Energy, Electricity, Nuclear Power, Oil, Water & Sanitation

Energy Procurement
997192

Editorial: PO Box 420, Reigate RH2 2DU

Tel: 44 02037 144450

Web site: www.theenergyst.com/category/energy-procurement/

Freq: Annual

Circ: 6800 Not Audited

Editor: Tim McManan-Smith

MAGAZINE

Alternative/Renewable Energy, Carbon Emissions & Trading, Electricity, Energy, Environment, Nuclear Power, Oil, Water & Sanitation

Energy Storage Journal
998251

Tel: 44 01243 782275

Email: sara@energystoragejournal.com

Web site: http://www.energystoragejournal.com/

Freq: Quarterly

Editor: Mike Halls

MAGAZINE

Alternative/Renewable Energy, Carbon Emissions & Trading, Electricity, Energy, Nuclear Power, Oil, Water & Sanitation

Energy World
980093

Editorial: 61 New Cavendish Street, London W1G 7AR **Tel:** 44 02074 677100

Email: eworld@energyinst.org

Web site: www.energyinst.org

Freq: Monthly

Circ: 5450 Not Audited

Editor: Steve Hodgson

Profile: Magazine of the Energy Institute, covering the international energy scene, focussing on alternative energies, climate change and energy security.

Ad Rate: Full Page Colour £3500.00

MAGAZINE

Alternative/Renewable Energy, Electricity, Nuclear Power, Oil, Water & Sanitation

Energy, Oil and Gas
984625

Editorial: Cringleford Business Centre, Suite 10, Intwood Road, Norwich NR4 6AU

Tel: 44 01603 274130

Web site: http://www.energy-oil-gas.com/

Freq: Monthly

Circ: 20000 Not Audited

Profile: European Oil & Gas magazine targets senior executives within the European Oil & Gas, and associated industries. Presents feature articles written by experts with technical, industrial or academic points of view. Includes latest solutions, best practices and industry trends and, case studies of companies in different sectors of the industry.

MAGAZINE

Oil

The Energyst
980900

Editorial: PO Box 420, Reigate RH2 2DU

Tel: 44 02037 144450

Web site: www.theenergyst.com

Freq: Bi-Monthly

Circ: 13145 Not Audited

Editor: Tim McManan-Smith

Profile: Magazine covering new products, technologies and trends in energy efficiency, environmental compliance and water use. Provides solutions to the problems of running an industrial location or commercial building.

Ad Rate: Full Page Mono £2585.00

Ad Rate: Full Page Colour £2985.00

MAGAZINE

Alternative/Renewable Energy, Electricity, Environment, Nuclear Power, Oil, Water & Sanitation

Engage Customer
995397

Tel: 44 01932 506300

Email: enquiries@ebm.media

Web site: www.engagecustomer.com

Freq: Daily

Circ: 30069 Cision Digital Reach

MAGAZINE (ONLINE)

Business

Engage Magazine
996099

Editorial: 4th Floor, Sterling House, 6-10 St George's Road, Wimbledon, London SW19 4DP **Tel:** 44 02089 718282

Email: info@mashmedia.net

Web site: www.engage-magazine.co.uk

Freq: Quarterly

Circ: 15000 Not Audited

MAGAZINE

Marketing

Engaged Investor
980962

Editorial: 120 Leman Street, London E1 8EU

Tel: 44 02076 183456

Web site: http://www.engagedinvestor.co.uk/

Freq: Bi-Monthly

Circ: 6984 Not Audited

Profile: Magazine designed to educate pension trustees about investment and long term financial planning. Aimed at pension fund trustees, charities and investment professionals.

Ad Rate: Full Page Colour £5402.00

MAGAZINE

Banking, Fund Management, Investment Banking

The Engineer
979868

Editorial: 79 Wells Street, London W1T 3QN

Tel: 44 02079 704000

Web site: www.theengineer.co.uk

Freq: Monthly

Circ: 28457 Not Audited

MAGAZINE

Engineering

Engineer Live
1102017

Editorial: Europa House, 13 - 17 Ironmonger Row, London EC1V 3QG

Tel: 44 02072 532545

Email: mail@setform.com

Web site: http://www.engineerlive.com/

Freq: Daily

Circ: 42008 Cision Digital Reach

MAGAZINE (ONLINE)

Engineering

Engineering
979930

Editorial: Pure Offices, Plato Close, Leamington Spa, Warwick CV34 6WE

Tel: 44 01926 671338

Email: info@engineeringnet.co.uk

Web site: www.engineeringmagazine.co.uk

Freq: Monthly

Circ: 16500 Not Audited

Profile: Magazine covering all aspects of the manufacturing industry. Includes articles covering concepts and innovations through the product lifecycle, from design to recycling.

Ad Rate: Full Page Colour £3460.00

MAGAZINE

Engineering

Engineering Capacity
981241

Editorial: Spinnaker House, Waterside Gardens, Fareham, Fareham PO16 8SD

Tel: 44 01329 825335

Email: editor@engineeringcapacity.com

Web site: www.engineeringcapacity.com

Freq: Monthly

Circ: 10100 Not Audited

Profile: News for UK manufacturing buyers about contract engineering/manufacturing services. In particular, news of the services offered by subcontract companies; their developments in core competences and performance improvements. Also, industry news of interest to UK manufacturers who outsource bespoke components and production services.

Ad Rate: Full Page Mono £1505.00

Ad Rate: Full Page Colour £2060.00

MAGAZINE

Engineering, Manufacturing

Engineering Integrity
981519

Tel: 44 01572 811315

Email: info@e-i-s.org.uk

Web site: www.e-i-s.org.uk

Freq: Semi-Annual

Circ: 1200 Not Audited

Profile: Journal of the Engineering Integrity Society containing technical articles, information on conferences and meetings, industry news and reports by the three groups within the Society.

Ad Rate: Full Page Mono £255.00

Ad Rate: Full Page Colour £445.00

MAGAZINE

Engineering

Engineering Maintenance Solutions
984848

Editorial: Cobalt House, Centre Court, Sir Thomas Longley Road, Rochester, Rochester ME2 4BQ **Tel:** 44 01634 731646

Email: editorial@engineeringmaintenance.info

Web site: http://www.engineeringmaintenance.info/

Freq: Bi-Monthly

Circ: 15000 Not Audited

MAGAZINE

Engineering

Engineering Specifier
1052942

Tel: 44 01622 871944

Email: editor@electronicspecifier.com

Web site: http://www.engineeringspecifier.com/

Freq: Daily

Circ: 13637 Cision Digital Reach

Editor: Joe Bush

MAGAZINE (ONLINE)

Engineering

Engineering Subcontractor
983336

Editorial: Enterprise House, Foundry Lane, Horsham, Horsham RH13 5PX

Tel: 44 01403 266022

Email: roger@rbpublishing.co.uk

Web site: www.rbpublishing.co.uk/engsubcon/index2.htm
Freq: Monthly
Circ: 10014 Not Audited
Editor: Roger Barber
Profile: Magazine covering the latest products and applications in order to increase productivity.
Ad Rate: Full Page Colour £1500.00
MAGAZINE
Engineering

Engineering Update   998286
Editorial: The Mill, Spratling, St Manston, Manston CT12 5AN
Web site: http://engineering-update.co.uk
Freq: Monthly
Circ: 73423 Not Audited
Editor: Jenna Burridge
Profile: Website covering engineering. The ENGINEERING UPDATE website shares the latest news and information on the engineering industry.
MAGAZINE
Engineering

EngineeringBecause.com
998935
Editorial: 107 Leadenhall Street, London EC3A 4AF
Email: info@engineeringbecause.com
Web site: www.engineeringbecause.com
Freq: Daily
Circ: 6437 Cision Digital Reach
MAGAZINE (ONLINE)
Engineering, Students

Engormix.com   1061873
Tel: 44 52442 2948138
Web site: http://www.engormix.com
Circ: 121354 Cision Digital Reach
MAGAZINE (ONLINE)
Animal Farming

Enterprise Mobility Exchange
1053339
Editorial: 2nd Floor, 129 Wilton Road, London SW1V 1JZ **Tel:** 44 02073 689484
Web site: http://www.enterprisemobilityexchange.com/
Freq: Daily
Circ: 42618 Cision Digital Reach
Editor: Zarina de Ruiter
MAGAZINE (ONLINE)
Business, Mobile Communications

Enterprise Nation   997089
Editorial: Enterprise Nation, Somerset House Exchange, The Strand, London WC2R 1LA **Tel:** 44 02072 579525
Email: media@enterprisenation.com
Web site: https://www.enterprisenation.com/blog
Freq: Daily
Circ: 242 Cision Digital Reach
MAGAZINE (ONLINE)
Business

Enterprise Risk   985203
Editorial: 2nd Floor, Sackville House, 143-149 Fenchurch Street, London EC3M 6BN
Tel: 44 02077 099808
Email: risk@sdw.co.uk
Web site: www.enterpriseriskmag.com/
Freq: Quarterly
Circ: 5500 Not Audited
Profile: Magazine covering all areas of risk management with a particular emphasis on enterprise risk.
Ad Rate: Full Page Colour £3500.00
MAGAZINE
Insurance

Enterprising Energy   984960
Editorial: 5 Station Road, Grangemouth, Falkirk FK3 8DG **Tel:** 44 01324 332034
Email: editorial@enterprisingenergy.org
Web site: http://www.enterprisingenergy.org/
Freq: Monthly
Circ: 20000 Not Audited

Profile: Enterprising Energy is a magazine reporting on developments and innovations within the offshore oil and gas, marine and renewable energy sectors worldwide. The magazine is primarily published in the UK but is also distributed throughout 'energy hotspots' worldwide.
Ad Rate: Full Page Mono £1465.00
MAGAZINE
Alternative/Renewable Energy, Carbon Emissions & Trading, Electricity, Energy, Nuclear Power, Oil, Water & Sanitation

Entertainment Law Review
980723
Editorial: The Hatchery, Hill Bank Lane, Mytholmroyd HX7 5HQ
Tel: 44 01422 888000
Web site: http://www.sweetandmaxwell.co.uk/Catalogue/ProductDetails.aspx?recordid=421&searchorigin=entertainme
Freq: Bi-Monthly Not Audited
Profile: Journal covering international developments in entertainment and media law, with particular emphasis on the legal protection and exploitation of creative talent. Aimed at legal professionals and those involved in the entertainment business.
MAGAZINE
Intellectual Property

Entrepreneur Handbook   997506
Tel: 44 02038 086102
Web site: www.entrepreneurhandbook.co.uk
Freq: Daily
Circ: 84382 Cision Digital Reach
MAGAZINE (ONLINE)
Business, Corporate Responsibility

EntrepreneurCountry Global
999006
Editorial: 17-19 Cockspur Street, London SW1Y 5BL **Tel:** 44 02030 211651
Email: entrepreneurcountry@ariadnecapital.com
Web site: www.entrepreneurcountryglobal.com
Freq: Daily
Circ: 7658 Cision Digital Reach
MAGAZINE (ONLINE)
Business, Corporate Responsibility

EnviroNews   1061053
Email: environewsph@gmail.com
MAGAZINE (ONLINE)
Alternative/Renewable Energy, Animal Farming, Carbon Emissions & Trading, Electricity, Energy, Environment, Nuclear Power, Oil, Water & Sanitation

Environment Analyst   984907
Editorial: Brownfield Briefing, The Chapel, Wellington Road, London NW10 5LJ
Tel: 44 02036 032100
Web site: https://environment-analyst.com/
Freq: Daily
Circ: 7604 Cision Digital Reach
Profile: Website covering environment. The Environment ANALYST is the website of a publishing and business research company of the same name, covering environmental news within the environmental services sector.
MAGAZINE (ONLINE)
Environment, Financial Markets

Environment Journal   1074631
Tel: 44 01625 614000
Email: hello@environmentjournal.online
Web site: http://environmentjournal.online/
Freq: Daily
Editor: Austin Macauley
MAGAZINE (ONLINE)
Alternative/Renewable Energy, Environment, Water & Sanitation

Environment Times   980842
Editorial: Victoria House, 2a Chapel Street, Adlington, Adlington PR7 4JL
Tel: 44 01257 474975
Web site: www.environmenttimes.co.uk
Freq: Quarterly Not Audited
Editor: Duncan Ashcroft

Profile: Magazine covering environmental topics, business information, legal comment and equipment guides.
Ad Rate: Full Page Colour £1890.00
MAGAZINE
Environment

Environmental Finance   980901
Editorial: 4th Floor, Thames House, 18 Park Street, London SE1 9EL
Tel: 44 02072 519151
Email: editorial@environmental-finance.com
Web site: www.environmental-finance.com
Freq: Daily
Circ: 18634 Cision Digital Reach
Editor: Peter Cripps
Profile: Magazine covering environmental risk and impact on companies including emissions trading, socially responsible investment, weather derivatives, renewable energy, and corporate social responsibility. Aimed at risk managers, insurance professionals, fund managers, brokers, environmental affairs managers and weather derivatives professionals.
Ad Rate: Full Page Colour £4995.00
MAGAZINE (ONLINE)
Carbon Emissions & Trading, Environment

Environmental Health News (U.K.)   980938
Editorial: Chadwick Court, 15 Hatfields, London SE1 8DJ **Tel:** 44 02078 275908
Email: ehn@cieh.org
Web site: www.ehn-online.com
Freq: Monthly
Circ: 10000 Not Audited
Editor: William Hatchett
MAGAZINE
Environment

Environmental Law and Management   982928
Editorial: Office G18, Spinners Court, 55 West End, Oxford OX28 1NH
Tel: 44 01993 706183
Email: ltp@lawtext.com
Web site: www.lawtext.com/lawtextweb/default.jsp?PageID=2
Freq: Bi-Monthly
Profile: Law report on land management and environmental law, covering developing issues, case law, statute policy and analysis.
MAGAZINE
Environment, Government

Environmental Law Monthly
988171
Editorial: The Ridge, South View Road, Pinner, London HA5 3YD
Tel: 44 02088 661934
Email: susan@singlelaw.com
Web site: www.singlelaw.com
Freq: Monthly Not Audited
Profile: Newsletter on major UK environmental legislation and regulation, EU developments and case law.
MAGAZINE
Environment

Environmental Science: Processes & Impacts   997115
Editorial: Thomas Graham House, Science Park, Milton Road, Cambridge CB4 0WF
Tel: 44 01223 432680
Web site: pubs.rsc.org/en/journals/journalissues/em#!recentarticles&adv
Freq: Monthly Not Audited
MAGAZINE
Environment

Environmental Scientist   998590
Editorial: 3rd Floor, 140 London, London EC2Y 5DN **Tel:** 44 02076 011920
Email: info@the-ies.org
Web site: www.ies-uk.org.uk
Freq: Quarterly
Circ: 1500 Not Audited
MAGAZINE
News & Current Affairs

The environmentalist   983453
Editorial: 17-18 Britton Street, Clerkenwell, London EC1M 5TP **Tel:** 44 02078 806200
Email: iema@redactive.co.uk
Web site: www.environmentalistonline.com
Freq: Monthly
Circ: 15000 Not Audited
Profile: Magazine of the Institute of Environmental Management & Assessment (IEMA). It contains news on current environmental issues including details of the latest regulations and consultations. Distributed to IEMA members.
Ad Rate: Full Page Mono £1295.00
MAGAZINE
Environment

Envirotec   981142
Editorial: Peebles Media Group, The Albus, 110 Brook Street, Glasgow G40 3AP
Tel: 44 01415 676000
Email: paul.marsh@peeblesmedia.com
Web site: www.envirotecmagazine.com
Freq: Bi-Monthly
Circ: 7943 Not Audited
Editor: Paul Marsh
Profile: Magazine covering water, waste, pollution technology, air quality, recycling and any industry subject concerned with environmental issues. Contains coverage of water waste treatment, contaminated land and landfill, waste management, atmospheric emissions and energy. Delivers comprehensive news and feature coverage of the environmental technology and services industries, land remediation, pipelines, waste disposal. Published to provide business opportunities for people in the environmental industry. Aimed at managers, departmental heads, key personnel in central and local government, water authorities, statutory and regulatory bodies and professional firms.
Ad Rate: Full Page Colour £1650.00
MAGAZINE
Environment

EP Vantage   984418
Editorial: 11-29 Fashion Street, London E1 6PX **Tel:** 44 02075 391819
Email: news@epvantage.com
Web site: www.epvantage.com
Freq: Daily
Circ: 15933 Cision Digital Reach
Editor: Lisa Urquhart
Profile: EP Vantage is a website providing news and analysis on the pharma and biotech industries. ' The website 'provides timely financial analysis of regulatory and patent decisions, marketing approvals, licensing deals, and M&A, giving fresh angles and insight to both current and future industry triggers'.
MAGAZINE (ONLINE)
Biotechnology, Healthcare Industry, Pharmaceuticals

EPDA   998697
Editorial: European Parkinson's Disease Association (EPDA), 1 Cobden Road, Sevenoaks TN13 3UB **Tel:** 44 02078 725510
Email: editorial@epda.eu.com
Web site: http://www.epda.eu.com
Freq: 3 Times/Year
Circ: 14473 Cision Digital Reach
MAGAZINE (ONLINE)
Neurology

ePHOTOzine   982829
Editorial: Unit 24 Evans Business Centre, Nobel Way, Dinnington, Sheffield S25 3QB
Tel: 44 01909 512111
Email: news@ephotozine.com
Web site: https://www.ephotozine.com/
Freq: Daily
Circ: 1590282 Cision Digital Reach
Profile: Website focusing on photography. ePHOTOzine website shares the latest information on photography including cameras, equipment reviews, photo galleries and daily news.
MAGAZINE (ONLINE)
Photography

Business Magazines

Epidemiology and Infection 996213
Editorial: Shaftesbury Road, Cambridge CB2 8RU **Tel:** 44 01223 358331
Email: journals@cambridge.org
Web site: http://journals.cambridge.org/action/displayJournal?jid=HYG
Freq: Monthly Not Audited
MAGAZINE
Infectious Diseases

Epilepsy Review 986039
Editorial: Epilepsy Society, Chesham Lane, Chalfont St Peter, Gerrards Cross SL9 0RJ
Tel: 44 01494 601300
Web site: www.epilepsysociety.org.uk
Freq: Quarterly
Circ: 2000 Not Audited
Editor: Nicola Swanborough
Profile: Magazine of the National Society for Epilepsy covering news, research, book reviews, letters to the Editor and fundraising.
MAGAZINE
Neurology

EPM (European Pharmaceutical Manufacturer) 984255
Tel: 44 01244 680222
Web site: www.epmmagazine.com
Freq: Bi-Monthly
Circ: 11000 Not Audited
MAGAZINE
Pharmaceuticals

eprivateclient 998440
Editorial: 107 Cheapside, London EC2V 6DN **Tel:** 44 02079 671601
Email: news@eprivateclient.com
Web site: www.eprivateclient.com
Freq: Daily
Circ: 10435 Cision Digital Reach
Editor: Will Sidery
MAGAZINE (ONLINE)
Tax Law

e-Protection Review 984366
Tel: 44 01451 821982
Email: info@andycouchman.com
Web site: www.protectionreview.co.uk
Freq: Monthly Not Audited
Editor: Andy Couchman
MAGAZINE
Insurance

Equestrian Business Monthly 998463
Editorial: The Old Dairy, Watton Road, Norwich NR9 4NN **Tel:** 44 01953 850678
Email: editorial@ebmonthly.co.uk
Web site: www.ebmonthly.co.uk
Freq: Monthly
Circ: 5500 Not Audited
Editor: Vanessa Britton
MAGAZINE
Animal Farming

Equine Veterinary Journal 985837
Tel: 44 01638 720250
Email: enquiries@evj.co.uk
Web site: onlinelibrary.wiley.com/journal/10.1001/(ISSN)2042-3306
Freq: Bi-Monthly Not Audited
Editor: Celia M. Marr
MAGAZINE
Veterinary Medicine

Equitywire 987526
Editorial: 10 Quarry Street, Guildford, London GU1 3UY **Tel:** 44 01483 573150
Email: info@equitywire.co.uk
Web site: equitywire.co.uk
Freq: Daily
Circ: 521 Cision Digital Reach
Editor: Matthew Clements
MAGAZINE (ONLINE)
Equities

e-reward.co.uk 983981
Editorial: 33 Denby Lane, Heaton Chapel, Stockport, Stockport SK4 2RA
Tel: 44 01614 322584
Email: paul@e-reward.co.uk
Web site: www.e-reward.co.uk
Freq: Daily
Circ: 13662 Cision Digital Reach
MAGAZINE (ONLINE)
Human Resources

eSociety 996280
Editorial: 10 Molasses Row, Plantation Wharf, York Road, London SW11 3UX
Tel: 44 02077 389383
Email: info@sbid.org
Web site: www.sbid.org
Freq: Semi-Annual
Circ: 5000 Not Audited
MAGAZINE
Building & Construction, Interior Design, Office Design, Residential Real Estate, Retail, Travel Industry

ESRF news 997394
Editorial: Temple Circus, Temple Way, Bristol BS1 6HG **Tel:** 44 01179 297481
Web site: http://www.esrf.eu/UsersAndScience/Publications/Newsletter/
Freq: 3 Times/Year
Circ: 10000 Not Audited
MAGAZINE
Science

The Essential Building Product Review 984903
Editorial: Kingfishers Retreat, The Lodges, Dunston Business Village, Stafford ST18 9AB **Tel:** 44 01785 711591
Email: james@l2media.uk
Web site: www.link2media.co.uk/#/the-publications/ebpr/overview
Freq: Quarterly
Circ: 7000 Not Audited
Profile: Magazine covering all aspects of the construction industry. Aimed at building specifiers and property owners in the commercial, retail, leisure, corporate and manufacturing sector.Previous title: Commercial and Industrial Buildings Product Review
Ad Rate: Full Page Colour £795.00
MAGAZINE
Architecture & Design, Building & Construction

Essential Kitchen & Bathroom Business 983718
Editorial: The Tower, Phoenix Square, Colchester, Colchester CO4 9HU
Tel: 44 01206 851117
Web site: www.kbbdaily.com/ekbbusiness.php
Freq: Monthly
Circ: 8933 Not Audited
Editor: Emma Hedges
Profile: Magazine covering news and design, kitchen sinks and taps, cooking, washing and cooling appliances, worktops, flooring, lighting and furniture, as well as bathroom suites, brassware, shower, tiles, accessories and lighting.
Ad Rate: Full Page Colour £3225.00
MAGAZINE
Interior Design

Essential Retail 987494
Editorial: 6 Morie Street, Wandsworth, London SW18 1SL
Web site: www.essentialretail.com
Freq: Daily
Circ: 52486 Cision Digital Reach
MAGAZINE (ONLINE)
Retail Management

Estate Agent Today 985039
Editorial: Angels House, 5 Albemarle Street, Beckenham, London BR3 5HZ
Tel: 44 08450 750152
Email: press@estateagenttoday.co.uk
Web site: www.estateagenttoday.co.uk
Freq: Daily

Circ: 163358 Cision Digital Reach
MAGAZINE (ONLINE)
Finance, Residential Real Estate, Retail, Travel Industry, Urban Planning & Development

Estates Gazette 979896
Editorial: Procter House, 110 High Holborn, London WC1V 6DW **Tel:** 44 02079 111701
Email: info@estatesgazette.com
Web site: http://www.estatesgazette.com/
Freq: Weekly
Circ: 16883 Not Audited
Editor: Damian Wild
Profile: Publication covering expert comment on the commercial, industrial, agricultural and residential property markets. Includes reports on market deals, and technical and legal issues. Contains investment opportunities, development prospects and auction listings, business and analysis, legal issues, property data, regional focus features, spotlight on current financial issues and the cost of money. First published in 1858. Aimed at estate agents, surveyors, property developers and construction companies. Also local authorities and government departments.
Ad Rate: Full Page Colour £3330.00
MAGAZINE
Architecture & Design, Building & Construction, Interior Design, Office Design, Residential Real Estate, Retail, Urban Planning & Development

ETF Strategy 986571
Editorial: Hamilton House, Mabledon Place, London WC1H 9BB
Email: press@etfstrategy.co.uk
Web site: www.etfstrategy.co.uk
Freq: Daily
Circ: 18122 Cision Digital Reach
Editor: Simon Smith
MAGAZINE (ONLINE)
Investment Banking

Ethical Boardroom 997756
Editorial: 86-90 Paul Street, London EC2A 4NE
Email: info@ethicalboard.com
Web site: www.ethicalboardroom.com
Freq: Quarterly
Circ: 48000 Not Audited
MAGAZINE
Business, Corporate Responsibility

Ethical Corporation 980185
Editorial: 7-9 Fashion Street, London E1 6PX **Tel:** 44 02073 757212
Web site: www.ethicalcorp.com
Freq: Monthly
Circ: 5000 Not Audited
Editor: Terry Slavin
Profile: Magazine providing companies around the world with practical advice and examples of how to successfully integrate responsible corporate practice into their management systems. Also covers the social and environmental challenges facing multinational organisations. Aimed at corporate, social and environmental responsibility managers, strategists and senior executives.
Ad Rate: Full Page Colour £1800.00
MAGAZINE
Business, Corporate Responsibility, Environment

Ethical Performance 980780
Editorial: Stodmarsh Enterprise Centre, Undertrees Centre, Stodmarsh, Canterbury CT3 4BE **Tel:** 44 01227 720900
Email: newsdesk@ethicalperformance.com
Web site: www.ethicalperformance.com
Freq: Monthly
Circ: 3500 Not Audited
Profile: Business newsletter focusing on corporate ethical performance. Covers social reporting, ethical codes of practice, community finance initiatives, ethical investments, corporate social responsibility, socially responsible investment and corporate governance.
MAGAZINE
Environment

EU Food Law 985167
Editorial: Christchurch Court, 10-15 Newgate Street, London EC1A 7AZ
Tel: 44 02070 176948
Web site: www.eurofoodlaw.com
Freq: Weekly Not Audited
Editor: Peter Rixon
MAGAZINE
Food

EUbusiness 988871
Editorial: 117 High Street, Chesham, Chesham HP5 1DE **Tel:** 44 02071 937242
Email: editor@eubusiness.com
Web site: http://www.eubusiness.com/
Freq: Daily
Circ: 153371 Cision Digital Reach
Profile: Website covering business. The EUbusiness website shares the latest business news and information about the European Union.
MAGAZINE (ONLINE)
Business, Small and Medium Business

eureka (Cat Lift Trucks) 1052682
Tel: 44 01252 856177
Email: more@gu9creative.com
Web site: http://www.eurekapub.eu/
Freq: 3 Times/Year Not Audited
MAGAZINE
Industry, Manufacturing, Supply Chain Management (SCM)

Eureka! 980079
Editorial: St Jude's Church, Dulwich Road, London SE24 0PB **Tel:** 44 01322 221144
Web site: www.eurekamagazine.co.uk
Freq: Monthly
Circ: 16963 Not Audited
Profile: Magazine bringing latest technology and innovation to UK design engineers and design management, with its regular news, features, in-depth cover stories and insightful analysis. It's focused on the latest design components and techniques, from 3D software to the latest materials, in industries ranging from automotive to medical. Aimed at engineers to help to improve their own designs.
Ad Rate: Full Page Colour £2850.00
MAGAZINE
Engineering

Euro Technology 988021
Tel: 44 01353 699456
Web site: www.eurotechnologymagazine.com
Freq: Daily Not Audited
Profile: Journal covering all aspects of industrial developments in Europe.
Ad Rate: Full Page Mono £1000.00
Ad Rate: Full Page Colour £1250.00
MAGAZINE
Manufacturing

euroasia industry 986343
Editorial: Wensum House, Prince of Wales Road, Norwich NR1 1DW
Tel: 44 01603 857651
Web site: www.euroasiaindustry.com
Freq: Monthly Not Audited
Editor: Sarah Pursey
Profile: Magazine focusing on news and articles on the major topics facing the European and Asian industries. Also covers in-depth business profiles of major European, Middle Eastern and Asian companies from across the manufacturing supply chain. Aimed at the senior representatives of many of the world's top global industrial companies, including chairpersons, CEOs, directors and senior management, as well as consultants, architects, researchers, marketers, journalists and senior analysts.
Ad Rate: Full Page Mono £3610.00
Ad Rate: Full Page Colour £5057.00
MAGAZINE
Alternative/Renewable Energy, Carbon Emissions & Trading, Electricity, Energy, Environment, Nuclear Power, Oil, Water & Sanitation

EuroChoices
995724

Editorial: 9600 Garsington Road, Oxford OX4 2DQ **Tel:** 44 01865 776868
Web site: http://onlinelibrary.wiley.com/journal/10.1111/(ISSN)1746-692X
Freq: 3 Times/Year Not Audited
Editor: John Davis
MAGAZINE
Animal Farming, Environment, Science

Eurofruit
1055306

Editorial: 132 Wandsworth Road, London SW8 2LB **Tel:** 44 02075 013700
Email: info@fruitnet.com
Web site: www.eurofruitmagazine.com
Freq: Monthly
Circ: 8000 Not Audited
Editor: Mike Knowles
Profile: Website covering Europe's leading fresh produce.
MAGAZINE
Food, Supply Chain Management (SCM)

Eurohedge
980043

Editorial: One London Wall, London EC2Y 5BD **Tel:** 44 02078 326500
Email: info@hedgefundintelligence.com
Web site: http://www.hedgefundintelligence.com/EuroHedge
Freq: Monthly
Circ: 1430 Not Audited
Profile: Newsletter providing news on all hedge fund managers based in Europe, an overview of the trends in the industry, names and strategies of promising new European funds as well as monitoring the performance of established managers and alerting service providers of potential business opportunities.
Ad Rate: Full Page Mono £5950.00
MAGAZINE
Hedge Funds

Europe & Middle East Outlook
986778

Editorial: Outlook Publishing, 2nd Floor, Woburn House, 84 St Benedicts Street, Norwich NR2 4AB **Tel:** 44 01603 959651
Web site: http://www.emeoutlookmag.com/
Freq: Bi-Monthly
Circ: 380000 Not Audited
MAGAZINE
Business

European Baker
983437

Editorial: Chart House, 10 Western Road, Borough Green, Sevenoaks, Tunbridge Wells TN15 BAG **Tel:** 44 01883 734582
Web site: www.worldbakers.com
Freq: Bi-Monthly
Circ: 0115 Not Audited
Editor: Catalina Mihu
Profile: Magazine concerned with market information, trends, technical and scientific information within the European bakery industry. Aimed at senior management, production managers, project managers and owners of larger bakeries across Europe.
Ad Rate: Full Page Colour £3700.00
MAGAZINE
Food, Manufacturing, Retail Management

European Biopharmaceutical Review (EBR)
998756

Editorial: First Floor, 131 Edgware Road, London W2 2HR **Tel:** 44 02077 243456
Web site: www.samedanltd.com/magazine/12
Freq: Quarterly
Circ: 15500 Not Audited
Editor: Deborah O'Neil
MAGAZINE
Biotechnology, Pharmaceuticals

European Business Air News
980122

Editorial: 134 South Street, Bishop's Stortford, Bishop's Stortford CM23 3BQ
Tel: 44 01279 714505
Email: newsdesk@ebanmagazine.com
Web site: www.ebanmagazine.com
Freq: Monthly
Circ: 36905 Not Audited

Profile: Magazine providing information on every aspect of business aircraft operation in Europe and monitors the market in order to reflect operators' opinions. Covers aircraft owners and operators, their current activities and plans for the future. Includes business aviation, privately-flown cabin-class piston twins, utility turbine helicopters, turboprops and business jets. Aimed at owners and operators of business aircraft and helicopters throughout Europe.
Ad Rate: Full Page Colour £10387.00
MAGAZINE
Aviation

European Cardiology Review
999155

Editorial: Radcliffe Cardiology, 7/8 Woodlands Farm, Cookham Dean, Cookham SL6 9PN
Email: editor@radcliffecardiology.com
Web site: http://www.radcliffecardiology.com/journals/european-cardiology-review
Freq: Semi-Annual
Circ: 10000 Not Audited
MAGAZINE
Cardiology

European CEO
982942

Editorial: 40 Compton Street, London EC1V 0BD **Tel:** 44 02072 535100
Email: enquiries@europeanceo.com
Web site: www.europeanceo.com
Freq: Quarterly
Circ: 54190 Not Audited
Profile: Magazine covering news, analysis and guidance on business matters affecting European business leaders. Aimed at CEOs, CFOs and Managing Directors.
Ad Rate: Full Page Colour £14850.00
MAGAZINE
Banking, Business, Corporate Responsibility

European Cleaning Journal
981361

Editorial: PO Box 299, Chesham, Chesham HP5 1FP **Tel:** 44 01494 791222
Email: info@europeancleaningjournal.com
Web site: www.europeancleaningjournal.com
Freq: Bi-Monthly
Circ: 22500 Not Audited
Editor: Michelle Marshall
Profile: Magazine carrying news, analysis and in-depth features on the European cleaning industry.
Ad Rate: Full Page Mono £2200.00
Ad Rate: Full Page Colour £3025.00
MAGAZINE
Hygiene

European Communications
980138

Editorial: 2nd Floor, 52-54 Gracechurch Street, London EC3V 0EH
Tel: 44 02079 338999
Web site: www.eurocomms.com
Freq: Quarterly
Circ: 28000 Not Audited
Profile: Magazine with news and information of the communications industry within Europe. Provides analysis of the latest technology, real-life applications, standards and legislative issues, key industry events and initiatives. Aimed at heads and deputies of PTTs, communication decision makers at government, OEMs, VARs and major end user companies.
Ad Rate: Full Page Colour £8950.00
MAGAZINE
Telecommunications/Electronic Communications

European Finance Director
998013

Tel: 44 02077 224334
Email: rands-editorial@analyticamedia.com
Web site: www.europeanfinancedirector.com
Freq: Bi-Weekly
Circ: 12500 Not Audited
MAGAZINE
Banking

The European Financial Review
995434

Editorial: 113 Sternhold Avenue, London SW2 4PF
Email: info@europeanfinancialreview.com
Web site: www.europeanfinancialreview.com
Freq: Bi-Monthly Not Audited
Editor: Elenora Elroy
MAGAZINE
Banking

European Heart Journal - Cardiovascular Imaging
995830

Editorial: Oxford University Press, Great Clarendon Street, Oxford OX2 6DP
Tel: 44 01865 353907
Email: ehjcimaging.editorialoffice@oup.com
Web site: http://ehjcimaging.oxfordjournals.org/
Freq: Monthly
Circ: 240 Not Audited
MAGAZINE
Cardiology, Diagnostic Imaging

The European Heart Journal: Acute Cardiovascular Care
996257

Editorial: SAGE Publications, 1 Oliver's Yard, 55 City Road, London EC1Y 1SP
Tel: 44 02073 248701
Web site: http://acc.sagepub.com/
Freq: Bi-Monthly Not Audited
MAGAZINE
Cardiology

European Intellectual Property Review
980724

Editorial: 5 Canada Square, Canary Wharf, London E14 5AQ **Tel:** 44 02073 937000
Web site: http://www.sweetandmaxwell.co.uk/catalogue/productdetails.aspx?productid=7061&recordid=460
Freq: Monthly Not Audited
MAGAZINE
Intellectual Property

European Journal of Cancer
994980

Editorial: The Boulevard, Langford Lane, Kidlington, Oxford OX5 1GB
Tel: 44 01865 843282
Email: ejcancer@elsevier.com
Web site: http://www.journals.elsevier.com/european-journal-of-cancer/
Freq: Monthly
MAGAZINE
Oncology

European Journal of Cancer Care
999140

Editorial: The Atrium, Southern Gate, Chichester PO19 8SQ **Tel:** 44 01865 476488
Email: eccedoffice@wiley.com
Web site: http://onlinelibrary.wiley.com/journal/10.1111/%28ISSN%291365-2354
Freq: Daily
Circ: 473 Cision Digital Reach
MAGAZINE (ONLINE)
Oncology

The European Journal of Emergency Medicine
999030

Editorial: Citi Building 41st Floor, 25 Canada Square, Canary Wharf, London E14 5LQ
Tel: 44 02031 976500
Email: ejem@lww.co.uk
Web site: http://journals.lww.com/euro-emergencymed/pages/default.aspx
Freq: Bi-Monthly Not Audited
Editor: Colin A. Graham
MAGAZINE
EMS/Emergency Medical Services

European Journal of Gastroenterology & Hepatology
985480

Editorial: 25 Canada Water, Canary Wharf, London E14 5LQ **Tel:** 44 02031 976693
Email: lwweditorialoffice@wolterskluwer.com

Web site: http://journals.lww.com/eurojgh/pages/default.aspx
Freq: Monthly Not Audited
Profile: European Journal of Gastroenterology & Hepatology publishes papers reporting original clinical and scientific research which contribute to the advancement of knowledge in the field of gastroenterology and hepatology. The journal publishes three types of manuscript: in-depth reviews (by invitation only), full papers and case reports. Aimed at the European Society of Gastroenterologists and Hepatologists and others. Phil Daly is the Publisher to whom enquiries should be addressed.
Ad Rate: Full Page Mono £750.00
Ad Rate: Full Page Colour £1610.00
MAGAZINE
Gastroenterology

European Journal of Haematology
995878

Editorial: Journals Customer Services, John Wiley & Sons, Ltd., The Atrium, Southern Gate, Chichester PO19 8QG
Tel: 44 01865 778315
Email: eur-j-haematology@wiley.com
Web site: http://onlinelibrary.wiley.com/journal/10.1111/%28ISSN%291600-0609/issues
Freq: Monthly Not Audited
MAGAZINE
Hematology

European Journal of Heart Failure
995913

Editorial: The Atrium, Southern Gate, Chichester PO19 8QG **Tel:** 44 01865 778315
Email: ejhf.editorialoffice@wiley.com
Web site: http://onlinelibrary.wiley.com/journal/10.1002/(ISSN)1879-0844/homepage/Contact.html
Freq: Monthly Not Audited
MAGAZINE
Cardiology

European Journal of Hospital Pharmacy: Science and Practice (EJHP)
986825

Editorial: BMA House, Tavistock Square, London WC1H 9JR **Tel:** 44 02073 836250
Email: info.ejhp@bmjgroup.com
Web site: http://ejhp.bmj.com
Freq: Bi-Monthly Not Audited
MAGAZINE
Health Administration, Pharmaceuticals

European Journal of Neuroscience
996598

Editorial: 9000 Garsington Road, Oxford OX4 2DQ **Tel:** 44 01865 776868
Email: editorial.office@ejneurosci.org
Web site: http://onlinelibrary.wiley.com/journal/10.1111/%28ISSN%291460-9568
Freq: Quarterly
Circ: 29 Not Audited
MAGAZINE
Neurology

European Journal of Obstetrics & Gynaecology and Reproductive Biology
995172

Editorial: The Boulevard, Langford Lane, Kidlington OX5 1GB **Tel:** 44 01865 843434
Email: eurosupport@elsevier.com
Web site: http://www.ejog.org/
Freq: Monthly
Circ: 21 Not Audited
MAGAZINE
Obstetrics & Gynecology (OB/GYN)

European Journal of Oncology Nursing
999026

Editorial: EJON Editorial Office, Stover Court, Bampfylde Street, Exeter, Exeter EX1 2AH **Tel:** 44 01392 285857
Email: ejon@elsevier.com
Web site: http://www.elsevier.com/wps/find/journaldescription.cws_home/623031/description#description

Business Magazines

Freq: Bi-Monthly Not Audited
MAGAZINE
Nursing/Nurses, Oncology

European Journal of Pain　998671
Editorial: The Atrium, Southern Gate, Chichester, Chichester PO19 8SQ
Tel: 44 01865 778315
Email: ejp@meditos.de
Web site: http://onlinelibrary.wiley.com/journal/10.1002/(ISSN)1532-2149/homepage/ForAuthors.html
Freq: Monthly Not Audited
MAGAZINE
Pain Management

European Journal of Palliative Care　985147
Editorial: The Pines Industrial Estate, Fordham Road, Newmarket CB8 7LG
Tel: 44 01638 723560
Email: edit@hayward.co.uk
Web site: http://www.haywardpublishing.co.uk/ejpc_.aspx
Freq: Bi-Monthly Not Audited
Editor: Julia Riley
Profile: Journal containing reports and articles on the latest treatments and developments within the field of palliative care.
Ad Rate: Full Page Colour £1950.00
MAGAZINE
Oncology

European Management Journal　995769
Editorial: The Boulevard, Langford Lane, Kidlington OX5 1GB **Tel:** 44 01865 843000
Web site: http://www.journals.elsevier.com/european-management-journal/
Freq: Bi-Monthly Not Audited
MAGAZINE
Business, Corporate Responsibility

European Offshore Petroleum Newsletter　980892
Editorial: Ogilvie Publishing Ltd, 56 Aylesford Mews, Sunderland SR2 9HY
Tel: 44 01915 678497
Email: eopn@ogilviepub.com
Web site: www.ogilviepub.com
Freq: Weekly Not Audited
Editor: Steve Hamlen
Profile: Newsletter covering offshore oil and gas activity in Europe and worldwide.
MAGAZINE
Oil

European Ophthalmic Review　999187
Editorial: The White House, Mill Road, Goring RG8 9DD **Tel:** 44 02071 933186
Email: editor@touchmedicalmedia.com
Web site: http://www.touchophthalmology.com/journals/european-ophthalmic-review
Freq: Semi-Annual
Circ: 10000 Not Audited
MAGAZINE
Ophthalmology & Optometry

European Pensions　984012
Editorial: Sixth Floor, 3 London Wall Buildings, London EC2M 5PD
Tel: 44 02075 622401
Web site: www.europeanpensions.net
Freq: Bi-Monthly
Circ: 8550 Not Audited
Editor: Laura Blows
Profile: Magazine featuring news analysis and features, pensions and investment news.
Ad Rate: Full Page Mono £11400.00
Ad Rate: Full Page Colour £11400.00
MAGAZINE
Fund Management

European Pharmaceutical Contractor　980929
Editorial: First Floor, 131 Edgware Road, London W2 2HR **Tel:** 44 02077 243456
Email: info@samedanltd.com
Web site: http://www.samedanltd.com/magazine/11

Freq: Quarterly Not Audited
Profile: Journal providing news and information about the Pan-European bio/pharmaceutical contract market.
Ad Rate: Full Page Colour £2850.00
MAGAZINE
Pharmaceuticals

European Pharmaceutical Review　980771
Editorial: Court Lodge, Hogtrough Hill, Brasted, Westerham TN16 1NU
Tel: 44 01959 563311
Web site: www.europeanpharmaceuticalreview.com
Freq: Bi-Monthly
Circ: 11999 Not Audited
Profile: Journal for the pharmaceutical industry. Features articles and news about the latest technologies in drug discovery and manufacturing. Covers business, manufacturing, processing, analysis and control, R and D, IT, outsourcing and packaging. Aimed at senior decision makers in the pharmaceutical industry across Europe.
Ad Rate: Full Page Colour £4937.00
MAGAZINE
Pharmaceuticals

European Plastic Product Manufacturer　998158
Editorial: Carlton House, Sandpiper Way, Chester Business Park, Chester CH4 9QE
Tel: 44 01244 680222
Web site: www.eppm.com
Freq: Bi-Monthly
Circ: 5500 Not Audited
Editor: Rose Brooke
MAGAZINE
Manufacturing, Plastics

European Reseller　981639
Editorial: 79 College Road, Harrow on the Hill, London HA1 1BD **Tel:** 44 02037 712617
Email: editor@europeanreseller.com
Web site: www.europeanreseller.com
Freq: Monthly
Circ: 15000 Not Audited
MAGAZINE
Auto Aftermarket

European Respiratory Journal　995853
Editorial: European Respiratory Society, 442 Glossop Road, Sheffield S10 2PX
Tel: 44 01142 672860
Email: info@ersj.org.uk
Web site: http://erj.ersjournals.com/
Freq: Monthly Not Audited
MAGAZINE
Respiratory Diseases

European Respiratory Review　998876
Editorial: European Respiratory Society, 442 Glossop Road, Sheffield S10 2PX
Tel: 44 01142 672860
Email: info@ersj.org.uk
Web site: http://err.ersjournals.com
Freq: Quarterly
Circ: 5000 Not Audited
Editor: Vincent Cottin
MAGAZINE
Respiratory Diseases

European Rubber Journal　983623
Editorial: Unit K, Venture House, Bone Lane, Newbury RG14 5SH **Tel:** 44 02082 539600
Email: editorial@european-rubber-journal.com
Web site: www.europeanrubberjournal.com
Freq: Bi-Monthly
Circ: 7155 Not Audited
Editor: Patrick Raleigh
Profile: Pan-European journal covering developments in the international rubber industry.
Ad Rate: Full Page Colour £3135.00
MAGAZINE
Manufacturing

European Science Editing　997412
Editorial: EASE Secretariat, West Trethellan, Trethellan Water, Redruth TR16 6BP
Tel: 44 01209 860450
Email: ese@ease.org.uk
Web site: europeanscienceediting.eu
Freq: Quarterly Not Audited
MAGAZINE
Science

European Urban and Regional Studies　983666
Editorial: 1 Oliver's Yard, 55 City Road, London EC1Y 1SP **Tel:** 44 02073 248500
Email: eurs@sagepub.co.uk
Web site: eur.sagepub.com
Freq: Quarterly Not Audited
Profile: International journal of research on European urban and regional development processes and policy issues. Read by academics and policy makers.
Ad Rate: Full Page Mono £500.00
MAGAZINE
Finance, Legal Affairs

European Urology　999699
Editorial: European Urology Editor Office, Academic Urology Unit - University of Sheffield, The Medical School Beech Hill Road, Sheffield S10 2RX
Email: platinum@europeanurology.com
Web site: www.europeanurology.com
Freq: Monthly Not Audited
MAGAZINE
Urology

EuroProperty　988373
Email: news@europroperty.com
Web site: www.europroperty.com
Freq: Monthly Not Audited
MAGAZINE
Finance, Legal Affairs, Sustainable Development, Urban Planning & Development

EVA　998659
Editorial: Boswell Cottage, 19 South End, Croydon, London CR0 1BE
Tel: 44 02082 534000
Web site: http://www.exviapaviationint.com/
Freq: Quarterly Not Audited
MAGAZINE
Aviation

Event　981251
Editorial: Bridge House, 69 London Road, Twickenham, London TW1 3QL
Tel: 44 02082 675000
Email: eventmagazine@haymarket.com
Web site: www.eventmagazine.co.uk
Freq: Bi-Monthly
Circ: 4982 Not Audited
Profile: Magazine aiming to convince marketers that successful events and exhibitions can bring brands and services to life. Read by decision-makers involved in all types of marketing activity.Previous title: Event Magazine
Ad Rate: Full Page Colour £3860.00
MAGAZINE
Marketing

eventindustrynews　987412
Editorial: 4 Glasby Square, Retford, Retford DN22 6EP **Tel:** 44 01777 802111
Email: editor@eventindustrynews.co.uk
Web site: www.eventindustrynews.co.uk
Freq: Daily
Circ: 80097 Cision Digital Reach
MAGAZINE (ONLINE)
Marketing

Every Investor　984017
Editorial: Fergusson House, 124 - 128 City road, London EC1V 2NJ
Email: editorial@everyinvestor.co.uk
Web site: www.everyinvestor.co.uk
Freq: Daily
Circ: 11698 Cision Digital Reach
MAGAZINE (ONLINE)
Equities

Evidence Based Midwifery　997060
Editorial: Royal College of Midwives, 15 Mansfield Street, St Marylebone, London W1G 9NH **Tel:** 44 03003 030444
Web site: https://www.rcm.org.uk/access-evidence-based-midwifery-journal
Freq: Quarterly Not Audited
Editor: Emma Godfrey-Edwards
MAGAZINE
Obstetrics & Gynecology (OB/GYN)

Evidence-Based Dentistry　996006
Editorial: c/o Rowena Milan, Nature Publishing Group, The Macmillan Building, 4 Crinan Street, London N1 9XW
Tel: 44 02078 434729
Email: ebd@nature.com
Web site: www.nature.com/ebd/
Freq: Quarterly
Circ: 20445 Not Audited
Editor: Derek Richards
MAGAZINE
Dentistry

Evidence-Based Mental Health　995040
Editorial: BMA House, Tavistock Square, London WC1H 9JR **Tel:** 44 02073 836270
Email: info.ebmh@bmjgroup.com
Web site: http://ebmh.bmj.com
Freq: Quarterly
Editor: Andrea Cipriani
MAGAZINE
Neurology

Evidence-Based Nursing　985212
Editorial: BMA House, Tavistock Square, London WC1H 9JR **Tel:** 44 02073 836250
Email: info.ebn@bmj.com
Web site: http://ebn.bmj.com
Freq: Quarterly
Circ: 8244 Not Audited
Editor: Alison Twycross
MAGAZINE
Nursing/Nurses

ExchangeWire　987743
Editorial: Smokehouse Yard, 44-46, St. John Street, London EC1M 4DF
Tel: 44 02072 533445
Email: press@exchangewire.com
Web site: www.exchangewire.com
Freq: Daily
Circ: 156982 Cision Digital Reach
Profile: Website covering technology, media industry and communication. The EXCHANGEWIRE website shares the latest information on data-driven display, media buying trends and the ad tech space in the EMEA and APAC regions.
MAGAZINE (ONLINE)
Advertising Industry

ExecReview　995039
Editorial: 86-90 Paul Street, London EC2A 4NE **Tel:** 44 02071 839010
Web site: www.execreview.com
Freq: Daily
Circ: 13645 Cision Digital Reach
MAGAZINE (ONLINE)
Banking

Executive Hire News　984369
Editorial: Castlemead, Lower Castle Street, Bristol BS1 3AG **Tel:** 44 01179 175444
Email: ehnteam@executivehirenews.co.uk
Web site: www.executivehirenews.co.uk
Freq: Bi-Monthly
Circ: 5379 Not Audited
Editor: Alan Guthrie
Profile: Magazine covering business information within the power tools, small plant and equipment hire industry. Aimed at hire company owners and management. Regular features: Equipment..... Suppliers of appropriate equipment; Serving..... Companies serving the grounds care hire market.
Ad Rate: Full Page Mono £1420.00

Ad Rate: Full Page Colour £1850.00
MAGAZINE
Building & Construction

Executive Magazine 983847
Editorial: New Century House, Stadium Road, Inverness IV1 1FG
Tel: 44 01463 732244
Email: business@spp-group.com
Freq: Monthly Not Audited
Profile: Business-to-business magazine covering regional news, business profiles and lifestyle.
Ad Rate: Full Page Colour £980.00
MAGAZINE
Business

Executive PA Magazine 983632
Editorial: 6 Snow Hill, London EC1A 2AY
Tel: 44 02070 027774
Email: editor@solutionspublish.co.uk
Web site: www.executivepa.com
Freq: Bi-Monthly
Circ: 15103 Not Audited
Profile: Magazine covering personnel, career development, training, business venues, technology, hospitality, travel, law and a broad spectrum of activities relevant to an office environment.
Ad Rate: Full Page Colour £3100.00
MAGAZINE
Human Resources

Executive Secretary Magazine 986290
Editorial: 17 Wood Road, Shepperton, London TW17 0DH
Circ: 5000 Not Audited
MAGAZINE
Education

Exhibition News 983668
Editorial: 2nd Floor, Apple Market House, 17 Union Street, Kingston upon Thames KT1 1RR **Tel:** 44 02084 811122
Email: exhibitionnews@mashmedia.net
Web site: www.exhibitionnews.co.uk
Freq: Monthly
Circ: 6000 Not Audited
Profile: Magazine covering all aspects of organising exhibitions. Features news, comment, interviews and personnel moves within major exhibition companies. Aimed at exhibition organisers, venues and suppliers.
Ad Rate: Full Page Colour £1700.00
MAGAZINE
Marketing

Exhibition World 986522
Editorial: 2nd Floor, Apple Market House, 16 Unity Road, Kingston upon Thames KT1 1RR
Tel: 44 02084 811122
Email: info@mashmedia.net
Web site: www.exhibitionworld.co.uk
Freq: Quarterly
Circ: 8000 Not Audited
Editor: Tom Hall
Profile: Magazine containing exhibition news and features from all over the world.
Ad Rate: Full Page Colour £2995.00
MAGAZINE
Marketing

Expert Investor 985032
Editorial: Fleet House, 1st Floor, 59-61 Clerkenwell Road, London EC1M 5LA
Tel: 44 02076 386354
Email: eieinfo@lastwordmedia.com
Web site: www.expertinvestoreurope.com
Freq: Quarterly
Circ: 3000 Not Audited
MAGAZINE
Fund Management

Expert Opinion on Drug Discovery 984208
Editorial: 5 Howick Place, London SW1P 1WG **Tel:** 44 02033 773712
Web site: www.informahealthcare.com/journal/edc
Freq: Monthly Not Audited
Profile: Review journal focusing on all the technology and disciplines involved in drug

discovery and the strategic planning behind it.
MAGAZINE
Pharmaceuticals

Expert Opinion on Orphan Drugs 1105189
Editorial: Christchurch Court, 10 Newgate Street, London EC1A 7AZ
Tel: 44 02070 174626
Email: subscriptions@informa.com
Web site: www.informahealthcare.com/journal/eod
Freq: Monthly Not Audited
MAGAZINE
Pharmaceuticals

Expert Opinion on Therapeutic Targets 996226
Editorial: Christchurch Court, 10 Newgate Street, London EC1A 7AZ
Tel: 44 02070 174626
Web site: www.informahealthcare.com/loi/ett
Freq: Monthly Not Audited
MAGAZINE
Pharmaceuticals, Science

Expert Review of Anticancer Therapy 996436
Editorial: 5 Howick Place, London SW1P 1WG **Tel:** 44 02070 175000
Web site: www.tandfonline.com/toc/iery20/current
Freq: Monthly Not Audited
MAGAZINE
Oncology

Expert Review of Anti-infective Therapy 996437
Editorial: 5 Howick Place, London SW1P 1WG **Tel:** 44 02070 177783
Email: mary.yianni@informa.com
Web site: www.tandfonline.com/toc/ierz20/current
Freq: Monthly Not Audited
MAGAZINE
Diagnostic Imaging

Expert Review of Cardiovascular Therapy 995756
Editorial: Informa House, 30-32 Mortimer Street, London W1W 7RE
Tel: 44 02070 175000
Web site: http://www.tandfonline.com/toc/ierk20/current
Freq: Monthly Not Audited
MAGAZINE
Cardiology

Expert Review of Clinical Immunology 995826
Editorial: Informa Healthcare, Christchurch Court, 10-15 Newgate Street, London EC1A 7AZ **Tel:** 44 02070 177720
Web site: http://informahealthcare.com/journal/erm
Freq: Bi-Monthly Not Audited
MAGAZINE
Allergies

Expert Review of Clinical Pharmacology 996440
Editorial: 4 Park Square, Milton Park, Abingdon OX14 4RN **Tel:** 44 02070 175544
Email: subscriptions@tandf.co
Web site: www.informahealthcare.com/journal/erj
Freq: Bi-Monthly Not Audited
MAGAZINE
Diagnostic Imaging, Infectious Diseases

Expert Review of Endocrinology & Metabolism 999535
Editorial: Christchurch Court, 10-15 Newgate Street, London EC1A 7AZ
Tel: 44 02070 176000
Web site: http://informahealthcare.com/journal/ere

Freq: Bi-Monthly Not Audited
MAGAZINE
Diabetes

Expert Review of Gastroenterology & Hepatology 999536
Editorial: Christchurch Court, 10-15 Newgate Street, London EC1A 7AZ
Tel: 44 02070 175000
Web site: www.informahealthcare.com/journal/erh
Freq: Bi-Monthly Not Audited
MAGAZINE
Gastroenterology

Expert Review of Hematology 999506
Editorial: 2&4 Park Square, Milton Park, Abingdon OX14 4RN **Tel:** 44 02070 175000
Email: enquiries@taylorandfrancis.com
Web site: http://www.tandfonline.com/toc/ierr20/current
Freq: Monthly Not Audited
MAGAZINE
Hematology

Expert Review of Medical Devices 997194
Editorial: Taylor & Francis Group, 2&4 Park Square, Milton Park, Abingdon OX14 4RN
Tel: 44 02070 176000
Email: enquiries@taylorandfrancis.com
Web site: http://www.tandfonline.com/toc/ierd20/current
Freq: Monthly Not Audited
MAGAZINE
Medical Technology

Expert Review of Molecular Diagnostics 997195
Editorial: Informa Healthcare, Christchurch Court, 10-15 Newgate Street, London EC1A 7AZ **Tel:** 44 02070 175000
Web site: www.informahealthcare.com/journal/ero
Freq: Monthly Not Audited
MAGAZINE
Diagnostic Imaging

Expert Review of Neurotherapeutics 999570
Editorial: Christchurch Court, 10 Newgate Street, London EC1A 7AZ
Email: info@expert-reviews.com
Web site: www.informahealthcare.com/journal/ern
Freq: Monthly
Circ: 32000 Not Audited
MAGAZINE
Pharmaceuticals

Expert Review of Ophthalmology 999572
Editorial: Christchurch Court, 10 Newgate Street, London EC1A 7AZ
Tel: 44 02070 174626
Web site: http://www.tandfonline.com/toc/ierl20/current
Freq: Bi-Monthly Not Audited
MAGAZINE
Ophthalmology & Optometry

Expert Review of Pharmacoeconomics & Outcomes Research 999832
Editorial: Christchurch Court, 10 Newgate Street, London EC1A 7AZ
Tel: 44 02070 175000
Web site: www.tandfonline.com/toc/ierp20/current
Freq: Bi-Monthly Not Audited
MAGAZINE
Healthcare Industry

Expert Review of Proteomics 999833
Editorial: Christchurch Court, 10 Newgate Street, London EC1A 7AZ
Tel: 44 02070 174626

Web site: http://informahealthcare.com/journal/eru
Freq: Bi-Monthly Not Audited
MAGAZINE
Biotechnology

Expert Review of Respiratory Medicine 999034
Editorial: Christchurch Court, 10 Newgate Street, London EC1A 7AZ
Web site: www.informahealthcare.com/journal/erx
Freq: Bi-Monthly Not Audited
MAGAZINE
Respiratory Diseases

Export and Freight 983156
Tel: 44 02892 688888
Email: info@4squaremedia.net
Web site: www.exportandfreight.com
Freq: Bi-Monthly
Circ: 9203 Not Audited
MAGAZINE
Shipping & Warehousing, Supply Chain Management (SCM)

Extralogistics Magazine 996051
Editorial: Cornwallis House, Pudding Lane, Maidstone, Maidstone ME14 1NH
Tel: 44 08456 066765
Email: contact@extralogisticsmagazine.co.uk
Web site: http://www.extralogisticsmagazine.co.uk/
Freq: Monthly Not Audited
Editor: Alan Ockelford
MAGAZINE
Shipping & Warehousing, Supply Chain Management (SCM)

Eye 998963
Editorial: Eye Editorial Office, Clinical Neurosciences, Mailpoint 806, Level D, Southampton General Hospital, Southampton SO16 6YD
Email: eye@rcophth.ac.uk
Web site: www.nature.com/eye/index.html
Freq: Monthly
Circ: 40000 Not Audited
Editor: Andrew Lotery
Profile: Magazine featuring a range of professional and practical articles. Topics include training, research, professional development, outdoor learning, in-depth analysis, focus on early years, foundation stage and reception year.
Ad Rate: Full Page Mono £995.00
Ad Rate: Full Page Colour £995.00
MAGAZINE
Ophthalmology & Optometry

eyeforpharma 986834
Editorial: 7-9 Fashion Street, London E1 6PX **Tel:** 44 02073 757575
Email: register@eyeforpharma.com
Web site: http://social.eyeforpharma.com/
Freq: Daily
Circ: 53759 Cision Digital Reach
Editor: Deirdre Coleman
Profile: Website covering pharmaceuticals. The eyeforpharma website discusses anything from the pharmaceutical industry and healthcare to patient services.
MAGAZINE (ONLINE)
Pharmaceuticals

eyenews 986656
Editorial: 9 Gayfield Square, Edinburgh EH1 3NT **Tel:** 44 01315 574184
Web site: www.eyenews.uk.com
Freq: Bi-Monthly
Circ: 3900 Not Audited
MAGAZINE
Ophthalmology & Optometry

Eyes 984511
Editorial: Unit 21, Highview, High Street, Bordon, Bordon GU35 0AX
Tel: 44 01420 473716
Email: bsaunders@rimsmedia.co.uk
Web site: http://eyesmagazine.co.uk/Home.html
Freq: Monthly

Business Magazines

Circ: 8000 Not Audited
Profile: Magazine focusing on the optical retail industry including industry news, product information, business and educational features plus eyewear fashion.
Ad Rate: Full Page Colour £1950.00
MAGAZINE
Ophthalmology & Optometry

eZonomics
996582
Editorial: ING Commercial Banking, 60 London Wall, London EC2M 5TQ
Tel: 44 02077 676656
Email: ezonomics@ing.com
Web site: www.ezonomics.com
Freq: Daily
Circ: 15424 Cision Digital Reach
MAGAZINE (ONLINE)
Banking

F.O. Licht's International Sugar & Sweetener Report
997670
Editorial: Christchurch Court, 10-15 Newgate Street, London EC1A 7AZ
Tel: 44 02070 177500
Web site: http://www.agra-net.com/agra/international-sugar-and-sweetener-report/
Freq: Daily
Circ: 463 Cision Digital Reach
Profile: Newsletter covering unique news and analysis on the world sugar and sweetener markets, with production, consumption and trade statistics.
MAGAZINE (ONLINE)
Food

F.O. Licht's World Biodiesel Price Report
998261
Editorial: 5 Howick Place, London SW1P 1WG Tel: 44 02070 175000
Web site: www.agra-net.net/agra/world-biodiesel-price-report
Freq: Weekly Not Audited
MAGAZINE
Oil

F.O. Licht's World Ethanol & Biofuels Report
983942
Editorial: Christchurch Court, 10-15 Newgate Street, London EC1A 7AZ
Tel: 44 02070 177497
Web site: https://www.agra-net.com/agra/world-ethanol-and-biofuels-report/
Freq: Monthly Not Audited
Profile: Newsletter covering news and analysis reporting on fuel ethanol, industrial and beverage alcohol with production, consumption and trade statistics.
MAGAZINE
Commodities

F.O. Licht's World Ethanol Price Report
998054
Editorial: Christchurch Court, 10-15 Newgate Street, London EC1A 7AZ
Tel: 44 02070 177500
Web site: www.agra-net.net/agra/world-ethanol-price-report/
Freq: Weekly Not Audited
MAGAZINE
Oil

F.O. Licht's World Molasses & Feed Ingredients Report
998053
Editorial: Christchurch Court, 10-15 Newgate Street, London EC1A 7AZ
Tel: 44 02070 176857
Email: marketing@agra-net.com
Web site: http://www.agra-net.com/agra/world-molasses-and-feed-ingredients-report/
Freq: Daily
Circ: 462 Cision Digital Reach
Profile: Newsletter covering news and analysis on molasses and special feed ingredients with production, consumption and trade statistics.
MAGAZINE (ONLINE)
Animal Farming

f2 Cameracarft
986390
Editorial: Maxwell Place, Maxwell Lane, Kelso, London TD5 7BB
Tel: 44 01573 226032
Email: iconmags@btconnect.com
Web site: www.iconpublications.com
Freq: Bi-Monthly
Circ: 3000 Not Audited
Profile: Magazine containing features, news, information, competitions and gallery exhibitions, trials, equipment tests, portfolios and profiles.
Ad Rate: Full Page Mono £600.00
Ad Rate: Full Page Colour £600.00
MAGAZINE
Photography

The Fabricator (UK)
996815
Editorial: The Studio, 47 Hillside Avenue, Elstree & Borehamwood, London WD6 1HQ
Tel: 44 02083 815511
Web site: www.profinder.eu
Freq: Monthly
Circ: 7200 Not Audited
MAGAZINE
Building & Construction, Interior Design

Facilities Management Journal
979933
Editorial: Unit 5 Gateway, 20-25 Trading Estate London Road, Swanley, Swanley BR8 8DE Tel: 44 01322 662289
Web site: www.fmj.co.uk
Freq: Monthly
Circ: 12500 Not Audited
MAGAZINE
Legal Affairs

Facilities Management UK (FMUK)
981070
Editorial: Chambers Business Centre, Chapel Road, Oldham, Oldham OL8 4QQ
Tel: 44 01616 838000
Web site: www.worldsfair.co.uk/index.php?option=com_content&view=article&id=19&Itemid=31
Freq: Bi-Monthly
Circ: 12000 Not Audited
Editor: Terry Ford
MAGAZINE
Legal Affairs

Facilities Management Update
998448
Editorial: 145 London Road, Kingston upon Thames KT2 6SR Tel: 44 02085 473333
Email: faca@wolterskluwer.co.uk
Web site: www.croner.co.uk
Freq: Monthly Not Audited
MAGAZINE
Alternative/Renewable Energy, Carbon Emissions & Trading, Electricity, Energy, Nuclear Power, Oil, Water & Sanitation

Factory Equipment
981220
Editorial: 15a London Road, Maidstone, Maidstone ME16 8LY Tel: 44 01622 687031
Email: feeditor@datateam.co.uk
Web site: http://www.connectingindustry.com/FactoryEquipment
Freq: Monthly
Circ: 14502 Not Audited
Editor: Jack Cheeseman
Profile: Publication which contains regular features on factory and warehouse equipment, industry comment, technologies and case studies, products and services. Aimed at purchasers and specifiers across all industrial sectors.Previous title: Factory Equipment News There may be a charge of GBP 99.00 for editorial production costs.
Ad Rate: Full Page Colour £2400.00
MAGAZINE
Manufacturing

Family Business United
997617
Editorial: The Cliftons, 49 Pendenza, Cobham, Cobham KT11 3BY
Tel: 44 07718 001179
Web site: http://www.familybusinessunited.com
Freq: Daily
Circ: 14946 Cision Digital Reach

Editor: Paul Andrews
MAGAZINE (ONLINE)
Business, Small and Medium Business

Family Capital
988605
Email: contact@famcap.com
Web site: www.famcap.com
Freq: Daily
Circ: 14564 Cision Digital Reach
MAGAZINE (ONLINE)
Business, Corporate Responsibility

Family Law
985640
Editorial: Castlemead Terrace Floor, Lower Castle Street, Bristol BS1 3AG
Tel: 44 01179 175076
Email: editor@familylaw.co.uk
Web site: www.familylaw.co.uk
Freq: Monthly
Circ: 2500 Not Audited
Profile: Journal reviewing all aspects of the law as it affects families. Includes case reports and analysis, details of forthcoming legislation, book reviews and conference reports.
Ad Rate: Full Page Mono £730.00
MAGAZINE
Family Law

Family Law Journal
985072
Editorial: 188-190 Fleet Street, London EC4A 2AG Tel: 44 02073 969292
Web site: www.legalease.co.uk/Family-Law-Journal.html
Freq: Monthly Not Audited
Editor: Geraldine Morris
Profile: Journal covering the full range of family law issues of interest to solicitors, barristers and those working for social services and charities. Provides concise digests of key developments in family law. Aimed at specialist lawyers and people concerned with family law.
Ad Rate: Full Page Mono £950.00
MAGAZINE
Family Law

FamilyOfficeGlobal
995016
Tel: 44 02073 210965
Email: info@gpfo.co.uk
Web site: www.the-globalpartnership.com
Freq: Quarterly
Circ: 1562 Not Audited
MAGAZINE
Business, Corporate Responsibility

Far Eastern Agriculture
981153
Editorial: University House, 11-13 Lower Grosvenor Place, London SW1W 0EX
Tel: 44 02078 347676
Email: post@alaincharles.com
Web site: www.fareasternagriculture.com
Freq: Bi-Monthly
Circ: 6000 Not Audited
Profile: Magazine covering all aspects of agriculture in Asia, including machinery, crop cultivation, livestock, feed, irrigation, agro-chemicals and biotechnology. Far Eastern Agriculture has been the region's agricultural magazine for over 24 years. FEAG also covers emerging market places in Indo-China, the sub-continent and the Russian Far East. Read by people involved in public and private sector agricultural production and related organisations in Asia.
Ad Rate: Full Page Mono £2400.00
Ad Rate: Full Page Colour £3530.00
MAGAZINE
Animal Farming

Farm Business
980075
Editorial: Hendal Oast, Hendal Farm, Groombridge, Hartfield TN3 9NU
Tel: 44 01892 861664
Email: info@ghpublishing.co.uk
Web site: http://www.farmbusiness.co.uk/
Freq: Bi-Weekly
Circ: 12500 Not Audited
Editor: Alistair Driver; Editor: Chris Lyddon
Profile: Magazine providing business information to assist farmers to produce food for the food chain.
Ad Rate: Full Page Colour £2530.00
MAGAZINE
Animal Farming

Farm Law
988168
Editorial: The Ridge, South View Road, Pinner, London HA5 3YD
Tel: 44 02088 661934
Web site: http://www.singlelaw.com/farm-law
Freq: Monthly Not Audited
Profile: Journal containing the latest legislation for agriculture and rural land with key extracts from legislation passed in Westminster, Brussels and Strasbourg. Also includes legal developments affecting all aspects of the business of food production and rural land use.
MAGAZINE
Animal Farming

Farmers Club Journal
983586
Editorial: 3 Whitehall Court, London SW1A 2EL Tel: 44 02079 303751
Email: editor@thefarmersclub.com
Web site: www.thefarmersclub.com
Freq: Bi-Monthly
Circ: 5500 Not Audited
Editor: Charles Abel; Editor: Charles Abel
Profile: Journal covering Club meetings and events, supplemented by technical articles from leading authorities on agricultural matters.
Ad Rate: Full Page Colour £480.00
MAGAZINE
Animal Farming

Farmers Guardian
980023
Editorial: Unit 4, Fulwood Park, Caxton Road, Preston PR2 9NZ
Tel: 44 01772 799429
Email: fgeditorial@farmersguardian.com
Web site: https://www.fginsight.com/news
Freq: Weekly
Circ: 32366 Not Audited
Editor: Ben Briggs
Profile: Magazine covering farming and agriculture. It addresses issues facing agriculture and provides business information and latest market prices. It features breaking news, details on legislation changes, disease outbreaks, business news and price movements. First published on 10 February 1844 as the Preston Guardian. Targets everyone in the farming industry.
Ad Rate: Full Page Colour £2566.00
MAGAZINE
Animal Farming

Farmers Guide
984348
Editorial: Parkside, London Road, Ipswich IP2 0SS Tel: 44 01473 691888
Web site: www.farmersguide.co.uk
Freq: Monthly
Circ: 27408 Not Audited
Editor: Jane Potts
Profile: Publication covering farm machinery (including comprehensive used machinery section). Also carries regular grain, fertiliser, seed and agrochemical articles, together with topical and company profiles.
Ad Rate: Full Page Colour £729.00
MAGAZINE
Animal Farming

Farmers Weekly
979909
Editorial: Quadrant House, The Quadrant, Sutton, London SM2 5AS
Tel: 44 02086 524911
Email: farmersweekly@proagrica.com
Web site: www.fwi.co.uk
Freq: Weekly
Circ: 53524 Not Audited
Editor: Karl Schneider
Profile: Magazine covering the agricultural industry and British agriculture. It provides the latest news, market trends and technical information to help farmers manage their businesses more effectively. It also contains business features, a weekly digest of facts and figures about British, European and world agriculture, Livestock, Arable and Machinery sections with reports on technical developments, farm sales and analysis of prices. Aimed at farmers, advertisers, distributors and manufacturers in the UK agricultural market.
Ad Rate: Full Page Colour £4134.00
MAGAZINE
Animal Farming

The FarmersMart   998828
Editorial: Unit 2 & 3, Burleigh Court, Burleigh Stree, Barnsley S70 1XY
Tel: 44 01226 321450
Email: pr@clearview-uk.com
Web site: www.farmers-mart.co.uk
Freq: Bi-Monthly
Circ: 8000 Not Audited
Editor: Patricia Gwynnette
MAGAZINE
Animal Farming

Farming Express   1099413
Email: info@farmingexpress.co.uk
Web site: http://www.farmingexpress.co.uk/
Freq: Weekly
Circ: 2189 Cision Digital Reach
Editor: Lorna Birch
MAGAZINE (ONLINE)
Animal Farming

Farming Life   983157
Editorial: 2 Esky Drive, Carn Industrial Estate, Portadown, Craigavon BT63 5YY
Tel: 44 02838 393939
Email: farminglife@jpress.co.uk
Web site: www.farminglife.com
Freq: 2 Times/Week
Circ: 50000 Not Audited
Editor: Ruth Rodgers
Profile: Magazine covering all aspects of the farming industry including development, news and advice.
Ad Rate: Full Page Mono £2999.00
Ad Rate: Full Page Colour £3748.50
MAGAZINE
Animal Farming

Farming Monthly National
983582
Editorial: 15-17 Dugdale Street, Nuneaton, Nuneaton CV11 5QJ **Tel:** 44 02476 353537
Email: sales@farmingmonthly.com
Web site: www.farmingmonthly.co.uk
Freq: Monthly
Circ: 20000 Not Audited
Editor: Andrew Poulton
Profile: Magazine covering all aspects of farming. Aimed at farmers and associated industries.Previous title: Farming Monthly Regular features: Farming Machinery Featuring farming machinery news and reviews.; Farming News Featuring news affecting the farming industry.; Forestry Featuring forestry machinery reviews.; Motors Featuring reviews of 4x4 and pick-up vehicles.; Show Report Featuring reviews of farming shows.
Ad Rate: Full Page Mono £740.00
Ad Rate: Full Page Colour £801.00
MAGAZINE
Animal Farming

Farming Online   983569
Editorial: PO Box 22, Telford TF13 9AD
Tel: 44 08709 090902
Email: content@farming.co.uk
Web site: www.farming.co.uk
Freq: Daily
Circ: 15013 Cision Digital Reach
Profile: Farming Online is a website covering all the latest on commercial farming news, tools and information.
MAGAZINE (ONLINE)
Animal Farming

Farming SA   1060659
Tel: 44 27214 063721
Email: mgwatyu@landbou.com
Web site: http://www.farmingsa.com
Circ: 10421 Not Audited
MAGAZINE
Animal Farming

Farming Scotland Magazine
985357
Editorial: Tolastadh House, 18 Corsie Drive, Kinnoull, Perth PH2 7BU
Tel: 44 01738 639747
Email: mail@farmingscotlandmagazine.com
Web site: www.farmingscotlandmagazine.com
Freq: Bi-Monthly

Circ: 5000 Not Audited
Profile: Publication covering arable, livestock and machinery farming news with advisory columns, topical features and company profiles. Aimed at the Scottish farming community.Digital images preferred.
Ad Rate: Full Page Mono £525.00
Ad Rate: Full Page Colour £675.00
MAGAZINE
Animal Farming

Farming UK   983590
Editorial: PO Box 75, Brighouse, Brighouse HD6 3WF **Tel:** 44 01484 400666
Email: info@farminguk.com
Web site: www.farminguk.com
Freq: Daily
Circ: 156305 Cision Digital Reach
Editor: Keith Wild
Profile: Website covering farming news, information, veterinary and husbandry news, with selected pages for regions of the UK.
MAGAZINE (ONLINE)
Animal Farming

Farming Wales   982810
Editorial: Agriculture House, Royal Welsh Showground, Builth Wells, Builth Wells LD2 3TU **Tel:** 44 01982 554200
Web site: www.nfu-cymru.org.uk
Freq: Monthly
Circ: 9000 Not Audited
MAGAZINE
Animal Farming

FarmWeek   981155
Editorial: 113 - 117 Donegall Street, Belfast BT1 2GE **Tel:** 44 02890 334480
Email: info@farmweek.com
Web site: www.farmweek.com
Freq: Weekly
Circ: 6733 Not Audited
Editor: Robert Irwin; **Editor:** Robert Irwin; **Editor:** Robert Irwin
Profile: Tabloid containing features on farming in Northern Ireland.
Ad Rate: Full Page Colour £3032.00
MAGAZINE
Animal Farming

FAST   988838
Editorial: Hawley Mill, Hawley Road, Dartford, Sutton at Hone DA2 7TJ
Tel: 44 01322 221144
Web site: www.fastening-solutions.co.uk
Freq: Quarterly
Circ: 7000 Not Audited
Editor: Brian Wall
Profile: Magazine dedicated to fastening, adhesives, assembly and joining technology to aid design and production personnel in choosing fastening methods and types in all areas of manufacture from concept to design and production. First published in 1995. Aimed at the manufacturing industry.
Ad Rate: Full Page Colour £1895.00
MAGAZINE
Engineering, Manufacturing

Fastener & Fixing Magazine
996756
Editorial: Romeland House, Romeland Hill, St Albans, London AL3 4ET
Tel: 44 01727 814400
Email: info@fastenerandfixing.com
Web site: www.fastenerandfixing.com
Freq: Bi-Monthly
Circ: 15000 Not Audited
MAGAZINE
Manufacturing

Fastener + Fixing Technology
999160
Editorial: Romeland House, Romeland Hill, St Albans, London AL3 4ET
Tel: 44 01727 814400
Email: editor@fastfixtechnology.com
Web site: www.fastfixtechnology.com
Freq: Daily
Circ: 4229 Cision Digital Reach
MAGAZINE (ONLINE)
Manufacturing

fDi Magazine   980840
Editorial: Number One, Southwark Bridge, London SE1 9HL **Tel:** 44 02078 733000
Web site: www.fDiIntelligence.com
Freq: Bi-Monthly
Circ: 15382 Not Audited
MAGAZINE
Banking, Economics, Emerging Markets, Financial Markets

FE Investegate   984058
Editorial: 2nd Floor, Golden House, 30 Great Pulteney Street, London W1F 9NN
Tel: 44 02075 347600
Email: editorial@financialexpress.net
Web site: www.investegate.co.uk
Freq: Daily
Circ: 916343 Cision Digital Reach
MAGAZINE (ONLINE)
Equities

FE News   985613
Editorial: 5 Harrington Lane, Pinhoe, Exeter EX4 8PF **Tel:** 44 08456 125750
Email: info@fenews.co.uk
Web site: www.fenews.co.uk
Freq: Daily
Circ: 15341 Cision Digital Reach
MAGAZINE (ONLINE)
Education

FE Trustnet   983026
Editorial: 2nd Floor, Golden House, 30 Great Pulteney Street, London W1F 9NN
Tel: 44 02075 347600
Email: editorial@financialexpress.net
Web site: www.trustnet.com
Freq: Daily
Circ: 656607 Cision Digital Reach
Editor: Gary Jackson; **Editor:** Anthony Luzio
MAGAZINE (ONLINE)
Fund Management

FE Week   986475
Editorial: 161-165 Greenwich High Road, London SE10 8JA **Tel:** 44 02081 234778
Email: news@feweek.co.uk
Web site: www.feweek.co.uk
Freq: Weekly
Circ: 3000 Not Audited
Editor: Nick Linford
Profile: Magazine covering the further education sector. Each issue features news, expert comment and technical information.
MAGAZINE
Education

The Fed   998748
Editorial: Yeoman House, Saltforda Street, London EC1R 0HF **Tel:** 44 02072 534225
Web site: www.nfmonline.com
Freq: Bi-Monthly
Circ: 16000 Not Audited
MAGAZINE
Retail Management

Feed Compounder   986625
Editorial: Pentlands Publishing Ltd, Plas Y Coed, Velfrey Road, Whitland SA34 0RA
Tel: 44 01994 240002
Email: mail@pentlandspublishing.com
Web site: http://feedcompounder.com/fc.htm
Freq: Bi-Monthly
Circ: 1200 Not Audited
Editor: Andrew Mounsey
Profile: Journal that covers all aspects of the animal feed industry. Includes economics, transport, health, nutrition, plant and equipment.
Ad Rate: Full Page Mono £850.00
Ad Rate: Full Page Colour £1350.00
MAGAZINE
Animal Farming

FeedNavigator.com   996356
Editorial: William Reed Business Media, Broadfield Park, Crawley RH11 9RT
Tel: 44 01293 613400
Web site: www.feednavigator.com
Freq: Daily

Circ: 15408 Cision Digital Reach
MAGAZINE (ONLINE)
Animal Farming

Fencing & Landscaping News
984394
Editorial: Office 1, 40 Stockhill Road, Greengates, Bradford BD10 9AX
Tel: 44 01274 610101
Web site: www.fencing-news.co.uk
Freq: Bi-Monthly
Circ: 10000 Not Audited
MAGAZINE
Animal Farming

Ferry & Cruise Review   983353
Editorial: PO Box 33, Ramsey, Isle of Man IM99 4LP **Tel:** 44 01624 898446
Email: ferrypubs@manx.net
Web site: www.ferrypubs.co.uk
Freq: Quarterly
Circ: 3500 Not Audited
Editor: John Hendy
Profile: Magazine focusing on the ferry industry, travel trade and shipping enthusiasts.
Ad Rate: Full Page Colour £300.00
MAGAZINE
Shipping & Warehousing

Fertilizer Focus   984496
Editorial: FMB House, 6 Windmill Road, Hampton Hill, London TW12 1RH
Tel: 44 02089 797866
Email: fertilizer@argusmedia.com
Web site: http://www.argusmedia.com/Fertilizer/Fertilizer-Focus
Freq: Bi-Monthly
Circ: 2100 Not Audited
Profile: Journal covering the fertilizer industry, production and use, technical and agronomic issues.
Ad Rate: Full Page Mono £1625.00
Ad Rate: Full Page Colour £2420.00
MAGAZINE
Animal Farming, Environment

Fertilizer International   984495
Editorial: Southbank House, Black Prince Road, London SE1 7SJ
Tel: 44 02077 932564
Web site: http://www.bcinsight.com/fertilizer_international.asp
Freq: Bi-Monthly Not Audited
Editor: Simon Inglethorpe
Profile: Journal analysing news in the world of fertilizer markets.
Ad Rate: Full Page Mono £1250.00
Ad Rate: Full Page Colour £2000.00
MAGAZINE
Animal Farming, Environment

Fertilizer Week   983502
Editorial: Chancery House, 53-64 Chancery Lane, London WC2A 1QS
Tel: 44 02079 032000
Web site: https://www.crugroup.com/prices/fertilizers/
Freq: Daily
Circ: 162 Cision Digital Reach
Profile: Newsletter focusing on industry news, markets and price information on global fertilizer trade. Aimed at executives, analysts and trade in all sectors of the fertilizer industry.
MAGAZINE (ONLINE)
Chemicals

Fetal & Pediatric Pathology
995425
Editorial: Christchurch Court, 10 Newgate Street, London EC1A 7AZ
Tel: 44 02070 175540
Web site: www.tandfonline.com/toc/ipdp20/current
Freq: Bi-Monthly Not Audited
MAGAZINE
Obstetrics & Gynecology (OB/GYN), Pediatrics

Business Magazines

Fibre Based Panels Bulletin
996599

Editorial: 2 Rothes Road, Dorking RH4 1JN
Tel: 44 01306 876709
Email: info@woodpanelsonline.com
Web site: www.woodpanelsonline.com
Freq: Bi-Monthly
Circ: 758 Cision Digital Reach
MAGAZINE (ONLINE)
Manufacturing

Fibre Systems
995918

Editorial: 4 Signet Court, Cambridge CB5
8LA **Tel:** 44 01223 221030
Email: editor.fibresystems@europascience.
com
Web site: http://www.fibre-systems.com/
Freq: Quarterly Not Audited
MAGAZINE
**Engineering, Telecommunications/
Electronic Communications**

FIDI Focus
996794

Editorial: 1 Cambridge Technopark,
Newmarket Road, Cambridge CB5 8PB
Tel: 44 01223 378000
Web site: www.fidi.org
Freq: Bi-Monthly
Circ: 1000 Not Audited
Editor: Rob Coston
MAGAZINE
Supply Chain Management (SCM)

Field Service News
988117

Email: editorial@fieldservicenews.com
Web site: http://fieldservicenews.com/
Freq: Quarterly
Circ: 5724 Not Audited
MAGAZINE
**Mobile Communications, Software,
Telecommunications/Electronic
Communications**

FierceWirelessEurope
986984

Email: info@fiercemarkets.com
Web site: http://www.fiercewireless.com/
europe
Freq: Daily
Circ: 12320 Cision Digital Reach
MAGAZINE (ONLINE)
**Mobile Communications,
Telecommunications/Electronic
Communications**

Figaro Digital
985356

Editorial: VHeaven Ltd, 4th Floor, 6 Aztec
Row Berners Road, London N1 0PW
Tel: 44 02078 703380
Email: editorial@figarodigital.co.uk
Web site: www.figarodigital.co.uk
Freq: Quarterly
Circ: 12000 Not Audited
Profile: A quarterly magazine for digital
people in brands and agencies.
MAGAZINE
Marketing

Film and Sheet Extrusion
999335

Editorial: 6 Pritchard Street, Bristol BS2
8RH **Tel:** 44 01179 249442
Web site: www.filmandsheet.com
Freq: Monthly
Circ: 20903 Not Audited
Editor: Lou Reade
Profile: Digital magazine featuring technical
developments, market trends, business
news and legislative announcements for the
producers of polymer film and sheets.
Ad Rate: Full Page Colour £1500.00
MAGAZINE
Plastics

Filtration + Separation
984301

Editorial: The Boulevard, Langford Lane,
Kidlington, Oxford OX5 1GB
Tel: 44 01865 843000
Email: fise@elsevier.com
Web site: www.filtsep.com
Freq: Bi-Monthly Not Audited
Editor: Alan Burrows
MAGAZINE
Engineering

Filtration Industry Analyst
984248

Editorial: The Boulevard, Langford Lane,
Kidlington, Oxford OX5 1GB
Tel: 44 01865 843695
Web site: www.elsevier.com/wps/find/
journaldescription.cws_home/600705/
description
Freq: Monthly Not Audited
Profile: Business newsletter containing
business information on the filtration and
separation industries worldwide.
MAGAZINE
Engineering

Finance and Management Magazine
990667

Tel: 44 01908 248250
Email: contactus@icaew.com
Web site: www.icaew.com/en/technical/
finance-and-management-faculty/finance-
and-management-faculty/finance-and
Freq: Monthly
Circ: 7200 Not Audited
MAGAZINE
**Accounting, Banking, Business,
Economics, Equities, Financial Markets,
Mergers & Acquisitions, Private Equity**

Finance Director Europe
980912

Editorial: John Carpenter House, John
Carpenter Street, London EC4Y 0AN
Tel: 44 02079 366400
Email: info@globaltrademedia.com
Web site: www.the-financedirector.com
Freq: Semi-Annual
Circ: 7338 Not Audited
Profile: Magazine covering all aspects of
corporate finance including commentary and
analysis from business leaders and articles
from financial journalists. Aimed at financial
directors and treasurers within Europe's
largest corporations and banks.
Ad Rate: Full Page Mono £7200.00
Ad Rate: Full Page Colour £720.00
MAGAZINE
Banking

Finance Monthly
985495

Editorial: Garrick House, 2 Queen Street,
Lichfield WS13 6QD **Tel:** 44 01543 255537
Email: info@finance-monthly.com
Web site: www.finance-monthly.com
Freq: Monthly
Circ: 195880 Not Audited
Editor: Emma Taylor
Profile: Magazine covering corporate
finance. It features global transaction news,
expert insight, company features, specialist
reviews and international transaction
reporting.
Ad Rate: Full Page Colour £1949.00
MAGAZINE
Banking

Financial Accountant
982931

Editorial: Quadrant House, The Quadrant,
Sutton SM2 5AS **Tel:** 44 02082 121948
Web site: www.ifa.org.uk
Freq: Bi-Monthly
Circ: 8000 Not Audited
Editor: Richard Curtis
MAGAZINE
Accounting

Financial Director
979832

Editorial: 1 Hammersmith Broadway,
London W6 9DL **Tel:** 44 02080 809375
Web site: www.financialdirector.co.uk
Freq: Monthly
Circ: 121952 Cision Digital Reach
Profile: Magazine covering financial
management including taxation, financial law
and regulation, procurement, corporate
finance and governance, wealth
management, financial services, IT strategy
and careers. The publication also provides
deep insights, informative reader surveys
and exclusive interviews that help Financial
Directors meet the challenges they face.
First published in 1984. Aimed at top-level
financial decision-makers in the UK,
including financial directors, chief financial
officers and financial controllers.

Ad Rate: Full Page Colour £4669.00
MAGAZINE (ONLINE)
Banking

Financial Management
980867

Editorial: 3-7 Herbal Hill, London EC1R 5EJ
Tel: 44 02077 757775
Email: editor@fm-magazine.com
Web site: www.fm-magazine.com
Freq: Monthly
Circ: 90666 Not Audited
Profile: Financial Management is CIMA's
official magazine covering IT solutions,
wealth management, financial services,
business services and products. Each issue
features an interview with a senior
management accountant who has made a
significant difference to their company or
sector, as well as regular pieces on
individuals at different stages in their careers
who are demonstrating entrepreneurial skills
or performing an unusual role under testing
circumstances. Aimed at part-qualified and
qualified members of the Chartered Institute
of Management Accountants.
Ad Rate: Full Page Colour £4900.00
MAGAZINE
**Accounting, Banking, Business,
Corporate Responsibility**

Financial Regulation International
983203

Editorial: 5 Howick Place, London SW1P
1WG **Tel:** 44 02070 177565
Web site: www.financialregulationintl.com
Freq: Monthly Not Audited
Editor: Dalvinder Singh
Profile: Publication reporting on worldwide
regulatory developments and their
implications for the financial services
industry.
MAGAZINE
Tax Law

Financial Regulatory Briefing
983503

Editorial: 2 Billing Place, London SW10 9UN
Tel: 44 02073 513926
Web site: www.frb.co.uk
Freq: Monthly Not Audited
Editor: Lance Poynter
Profile: Magazine focusing on factual
statements, regulatory information and
official pronouncements in the financial
services sector.
MAGAZINE
Banking

Financial Systems News
982933

Editorial: Clarendon House, 125 Shenley
Road, London WD6 1AG
Tel: 44 02084 452688
Email: editor@fsn.co.uk
Web site: www.fsn.co.uk
Freq: Daily
Circ: 13646 Cision Digital Reach
MAGAZINE (ONLINE)
**Banking, Business, Small and Medium
Business**

Financial Technologist
997400

Editorial: Harrington Starr Ltd, Vintners
Place, 68 Upper Thames Street, London
EC4V 3BJ **Tel:** 44 02035 877007
Email: info@harringtonstarr.co.uk
Web site: www.harringtonstarr.com
Freq: Quarterly
Circ: 60000 Not Audited
MAGAZINE
Banking

Financial World
980015

Editorial: 4-9 Burgate Lane, Canterbury CT1
2XJ **Tel:** 44 01227 818609
Web site: http://www.financialworld.co.uk/
Freq: Bi-Monthly
Circ: 12484 Not Audited
Editor: Ouida Taaffe
Profile: Magazine containing news, features,
interviews and case studies on the banking
and financial services sector.
Ad Rate: Full Page Colour £3950.00
MAGAZINE
Banking, Fund Management

Financier Worldwide Magazine
980166

Editorial: 23rd Floor Alpha Tower, Suffolk
Street, Queensway, Birmingham B1 1TT
Tel: 44 08453 450456
Email: info@financierworldwide.com
Web site: www.financierworldwide.com
Freq: Monthly
Circ: 50000 Not Audited
MAGAZINE
**Banking, Mergers & Acquisitions, Private
Equity**

FinBuzz
1053350

Editorial: Albert Buildings, 49 Queen Victoria
Street, London EC4N 4SA
Email: contact@finbuzz.com
Web site: http://finbuzz.com
Freq: Daily
Circ: 25891 Cision Digital Reach
MAGAZINE (ONLINE)
Business, Small and Medium Business

Fine Food Digest
983534

Editorial: Guild House, 23b Kingsmead
Business Park, Shaftesbury Road,
Gillingham SP8 5FB **Tel:** 44 01747 825200
Email: editorial@gff.co.uk
Web site: www.gff.co.uk/fine-food-digest-
online/
Freq: Monthly
Circ: 5500 Not Audited
Editor: Mick Whitworth
Profile: Business magazine for speciality
food and drink retailers, producers and
wholesalers in the UK. Fine Food Digest is
the magazine of The Guild of Fine Food.
Ad Rate: Full Page Colour £1430.00
MAGAZINE
Food

Finishing Magazine
996550

Editorial: Cardinal Point, Park Road,
Rickmansworth, London WD3 1RE
Tel: 44 01923 432705
Web site: www.finishingmagazine.co.uk
Freq: Bi-Monthly
Circ: 8000 Not Audited
Editor: John Hatcher
MAGAZINE
Manufacturing

Finn Niche
996325

Editorial: 149 Hammersmith Road, London
W14 0QL **Tel:** 44 02076 025405
Email: markku@finn-niche.com
Web site: http://www.finn-niche.com
Freq: Quarterly
Circ: 2500 Not Audited
MAGAZINE
Business

Fintech Finance
1054130

Editorial: Advertainment Media Ltd, 19
Greenwood Place, Kentish Town, London
NW5 1LB
Email: editorial@fintech.finance
Web site: www.fintech.finance/
Freq: Daily
Circ: 3023 Cision Digital Reach
MAGAZINE (ONLINE)
**Banking, Financial Markets, Investment
Banking**

FIRE
984963

Editorial: Rayford House, School Road,
Hove, Brighton BN3 5HX
Tel: 44 01273 434943
Email: info@pavpub.com
Web site: http://www.fire-magazine.com
Freq: Monthly
Circ: 3500 Not Audited
Profile: The Journal of the Fire Protection
and Firefighting Profession containing
columns from all main stakeholders, articles
on fire brigades, fire politics, operational
techniques, personnel moves, diary dates
and letters. A feature on one particular area
of fire safety is included in each issue.
Ad Rate: Full Page Mono £1576.00
Ad Rate: Full Page Colour £2392.00
MAGAZINE
Security & Security Systems

Fire & Rescue 981264
Editorial: 8 The Old Yarn Mills, Sherborne, Sherborne DT9 3RQ **Tel:** 44 01935 816030
Web site: www.hemmingfire.com
Freq: Quarterly
Circ: 10070 Not Audited
Editor: Ann-Marie Knegt
Profile: Magazine with worldwide coverage which reports on fire and rescue action, equipment, techniques, medical aspects and training issues for firefighters.
Ad Rate: Full Page Colour £2199.00
MAGAZINE
Security & Security Systems

Fire Risk Management 984897
Tel: 44 01608 812500
Email: frm@thefpa.co.uk
Web site: www.frmjournal.com
Freq: Monthly
Circ: 3000 Not Audited
Profile: Journal of the Fire Protection Association and The Institution of Fire Engineers. Includes guidance and feature articles on global fire industry, covering subjects such as fire engineering, risk management, fire service operations, new legislation, codes, standards and fire statistics.
Ad Rate: Full Page Colour £1600.00
MAGAZINE
Security & Security Systems

Fire Safety Journal 987330
Editorial: Elsevier Limited, The Boulevard, Langford Lane, Kidlington, Oxford OX5 1GB
Tel: 44 01865 843434
Web site: http://www.journals.elsevier.com/fire-safety-journal
Freq: Monthly Not Audited
MAGAZINE
Engineering, Security & Security Systems

Fire Times 984984
Editorial: Suite 7, Big Box Business Centre, Crowhurst Road, Brighton BN1 8AF
Tel: 44 01273 453033
Email: query@mmcpublications.co.uk
Web site: www.mmcpublications.co.uk/ft.html
Freq: Bi-Monthly
Circ: 5000 Not Audited
Profile: Magazine covering firefighting products and services and fire prevention within the fire brigade and industrial companies.
Ad Rate: Full Page Colour £1485.00
MAGAZINE
Security & Security Systems

Fireplace Specialist 985256
Editorial: 53 High Street, Arundel, Arundel BN18 9AJ **Tel:** 44 01903 889531
Email: editor@fireplacespecialist.com
Web site: www.fireplacespecialist.com
Freq: Bi-Monthly
Circ: 5500 Not Audited
Editor: Peddy Balfour
MAGAZINE
Interior Design

First 981616
Editorial: Local Government House, Smith Square, London SW1P 3HZ
Tel: 44 02076 643294
Email: first@local.gov.uk
Web site: www.local.gov.uk/first
Freq: Monthly
Circ: 18400 Not Audited
Editor: Karen Thornton
Profile: Magazine covering world politics and government policies affecting business. Aimed at business, financial and political leaders.
Ad Rate: Full Page Mono £12500.00
Ad Rate: Full Page Colour £15200.00
MAGAZINE
Government

First for Business 983944
Editorial: RMC House, 6 Broadfield Court, Broadfield Business Park, Sheffield S8 OXF
Tel: 44 01142 506300
Email: ffb@rmcmedia.co.uk

Web site: http://www.rmcmedia.co.uk/magazines/first-for-business/?cl=27
Freq: Monthly
Circ: 20000 Not Audited
Profile: Official bulletin of the Sheffield Chamber of Commerce and Industry and Sheffield First Partnership.
Ad Rate: Full Page Colour £1390.00
MAGAZINE
Business, Small and Medium Business

First Time Buyer 985008
Editorial: 37 Ivor Place, Marylebone, London NW1 6EA **Tel:** 44 02072 581777
Email: info@firsttimebuyermag.co.uk
Web site: www.firsttimebuyermag.co.uk
Freq: Monthly
Circ: 45000 Not Audited
Editor: Lynda Clark
Profile: Magazine dedicated to the world of affordable homes, tricks and tips on buying property and all the great deals out there. Contains news and views, expert opinion and up-to-date market information. Features latest developments, plus articles about architecture, interior design, finance and the law. Launched in December 2008. Facebook: http://www.facebook.com/pages/First-Time-Buyer-Magazine/38361178529.Twitter: http://twitter.com/ftbonline. Aimed at first time buyers or the parents of first time buyers trying to help their children onto the housing ladder.Lynda Clark is the Editor to whom all press-releases should be addressed.
MAGAZINE
Property Management & Maintenance

First Voice 980916
Editorial: Redactive Media Group, 17 Britton Street, London EC1M 5TP
Tel: 44 01536 747333
Email: editorial@firstvoice.co.uk
Web site: www.firstvoice.co.uk
Freq: Bi-Monthly
Circ: 160879 Not Audited
MAGAZINE
Business, Corporate Responsibility

FISH 984352
Editorial: IFM, PO Box 679, Hull HU5 9AX
Tel: 44 08453 887012
Email: info@ifm.org.uk
Web site: www.ifm.org.uk
Freq: Quarterly
Circ: 900 Not Audited
Editor: Lawrence Talks
Profile: Official magazine of the Institute of Fisheries Management and dedicated to the advancement of sustainable fisheries management. Aimed at members of the Institute, fisheries managers and interested anglers.
Ad Rate: Full Page Mono £175.00
MAGAZINE
Animal Farming

Fish Farmer 983707
Editorial: 496 Ferry Road, Edinburgh EH5 2DL **Tel:** 44 01315 511000
Email: editor@fishfarmer-magazine.com
Web site: http://www.fishupdate.com/category/aquaculture/fish-farmer-magazine/
Freq: Monthly
Circ: 18500 Not Audited
Editor: Jenny Hjul
Profile: International magazine featuring articles on marketing, feed, husbandry, research and development, plus management of all farmed fish and shellfish species. Also contains a website with daily news, events, buyers guides and web classifieds. Read by producers and suppliers of farmed seafood.
Ad Rate: Full Page Colour £1780.00
MAGAZINE
Animal Farming

Fish Friers Review 984351
Editorial: 4 Greenwood Mount, Leeds LS6 4LQ **Tel:** 44 01132 307044
Email: r.norris@federationoffishfriers.co.uk
Web site: www.federationoffishfriers.co.uk
Freq: Bi-Monthly
Circ: 5000 Not Audited

Profile: Magazine covering fish frying industry and containing information on pending legislation, trade trends, new products and promotions. Aimed at fish and chip shops throughout the UK.
Ad Rate: Full Page Colour £699.00
MAGAZINE
Food

Fishing News 981161
Editorial: Cudham Tithe Barn, Berry's Hill, Cudham TN16 3AG **Tel:** 44 01959 541444
Email: fishingnews.ed@kelsey.co.uk
Web site: fishingnews.co.uk
Freq: Weekly
Circ: 10795 Not Audited
Editor: David Linkie
Profile: News and comment on important developments in the UK and Ireland commercial fishing industry. Read by the commercial fishing industry.
Ad Rate: Full Page Colour £2601.00
MAGAZINE
Animal Farming

FISHupdate 983452
Editorial: 496 Ferry Road, Edinburgh EH5 2DL **Tel:** 44 01313 124550
Email: editor@fishfarmer-magazine.com
Web site: www.fishupdate.com
Freq: Daily
Circ: 17460 Cision Digital Reach
Editor: Jenny Hjul
MAGAZINE (ONLINE)
Animal Farming

Fitch Ratings 1063929
Editorial: Fitch Group Global HQ - London, 30 North Colonnade, London E14 5GN
Tel: 44 02035 301000
Web site: https://www.fitchratings.com/
Freq: Daily Not Audited
Editor: Brian Reid
MAGAZINE
Data Management, Financial Markets, Investment Banking

Flat Living 985321
Editorial: Sissons, Buntingford, Buntingford SG9 9LL
Email: info@flat-living.co.uk
Web site: http://www.flat-living.co.uk/advice/563-flat-living-mag
Freq: Quarterly
Circ: 14000 Not Audited
MAGAZINE
Residential Real Estate

Flavour and Fragrance Journal 984913
Editorial: The Atrium, Southern Gate, Chichester, Chichester PO19 8SQ
Tel: 44 01243 779777
Web site: http://onlinelibrary.wiley.com/journal/10.1002/(ISSN)1099-1026
Freq: Bi-Monthly
MAGAZINE
Chemicals

Fleet Street Publications 996005
Editorial: 8th Floor, Friars Bridge Court, 41-45 Blackfriars Road, London SE1 8NZ
Tel: 44 02076 333780
Web site: https://www.agorafinancial.co.uk/fleet-street-publications/
Freq: No Frequency Established
Circ: 45000 Not Audited
MAGAZINE
Equities

FlexoTech 985086
Editorial: 30 London Road, Southborough, Tunbridge Wells, Tunbridge Wells TN4 0RE
Tel: 44 01892 542099
Web site: www.paperandprint.com/flexotech.aspx/
Freq: Bi-Monthly
Circ: 5140 Not Audited
Editor: Neel Madsen
Profile: FlexoTech is a magazine covering the flexographic printing industry covering printing and finishing process of flexography

in Europe as well as digital printing, CAD and 3D printing.
Ad Rate: Full Page Colour £1995.00
MAGAZINE
Publishing

Flight Daily News 980068
Editorial: Quadrant House, Sutton SM2 5AS
Tel: 44 02086 523315
Email: flightdailynews@flightglobal.com
Web site: www.flightglobal.com/advertise/flight-daily-news/
Freq: No Frequency Established
Circ: 31603 Not Audited
MAGAZINE
Aviation

Flight International 979912
Editorial: Quadrant House, Sutton, London SM2 5AS **Tel:** 44 02086 523315
Email: marketing@flightglobal.com
Web site: https://www.flightglobal.com/products/flight-international/
Freq: Weekly
Circ: 53636 Not Audited
Editor: Craig Hoyle
Profile: Magazine covering aerospace industry news and features on commercial and military air transport. Aimed at managers in airlines, corporate aviation departments, manufacturers, governments and the armed forces.
Ad Rate: Full Page Mono £5770.00
Ad Rate: Full Page Colour £7790.00
MAGAZINE
Aviation, Defense & National Security, Engineering

Flight Safety 984388
Editorial: Rochester Airport, Chatham, Rochester ME5 9SD **Tel:** 44 01626 776199
Email: info@gen-av-safety.demon.co.uk
Web site: www.gasco.org.uk
Freq: Quarterly
Circ: 1500 Not Audited
Editor: Nigel Everett
Profile: Magazine covering general aviation flight safety (not including airline, airport or military flight safety), both in the air and on land. Includes Aviation Authority aircraft accident reports, summaries of safety leaflets and general aviation accident statistics.
Ad Rate: Full Page Mono £925.00
Ad Rate: Full Page Colour £1029.00
MAGAZINE
Aviation

Flightglobal Pro 994689
Editorial: Quadrant House, The Quadrant, Sutton, London SM2 5AS
Tel: 44 02086 523500
Email: commercialaviation@flightglobal.com
Web site: www.flightglobal.com
Freq: Daily
Circ: 431569 Cision Digital Reach
MAGAZINE (ONLINE)
Aviation

Flyer 981893
Editorial: Riverside Court, Lower Bristol Road, Bath BA2 3DZ **Tel:** 44 01225 481440
Web site: www.flyer.co.uk
Freq: Monthly
Circ: 18000 Not Audited
Editor: Ed Hicks
Profile: Magazine covering light aviation, aircraft reviews, destination reports and product news.
MAGAZINE
Aviation

FlyPast 981894
Editorial: P.O.Box 100, Stamford, Peterborough PE9 1XQ
Tel: 44 01780 755131
Email: flypast@keypublishing.com
Web site: www.flypast.com
Freq: Monthly
Circ: 40172 Not Audited
Editor: Chris Gilson
Profile: Magazine covering news and articles on preserved and vintage aircraft and modern airshows. Contains aircrew

Business Magazines

memories, researched features from 1914 into the 1960s, airshow news, product reviews, museum visits, restoration projects, in-detail surveys of famous aircraft as well as comprehensive news and photography from around the globe. Aimed at those with an interest in historic aviation.Regular features: Aviation History A look at different periods in aviation history.
Ad Rate: Full Page Colour £1815.00
MAGAZINE
Aviation

FM World
980805
Editorial: 17 Britton Street, London EC1M 5TP **Tel:** 44 02078 806229
Email: editorial@fm-world.co.uk
Web site: www.fm-world.co.uk
Freq: Monthly
Circ: 13626 Not Audited
Editor: Martin Read
Profile: Magazine covering all aspects of facilities management, includes news and views from a range of industry sectors. Aimed at facilities managers in large companies, corporations and the members of the British Institute of Facilities Management.Alternative Title: Facilities Management World
Ad Rate: Full Page Colour £2835.00
MAGAZINE
Hygiene, Security & Security Systems

FMO (Facilities Management Online)
980933
Editorial: Cefn Tew, Tynlon, Holyhead LL65 4UA **Tel:** 44 08454 688688
Email: info@fmonline.co.uk
Web site: www.fmonline.co.uk
Freq: Daily
Circ: 9929 Cision Digital Reach
Editor: James Brunson
MAGAZINE (ONLINE)
Architecture & Design, Building & Construction, Residential Real Estate

Focus and Self Storage Europe
1008434
Editorial: Priestley House, The Gullet, Nantwich, Nantwich CW5 5SZ
Tel: 44 01270 623150
Email: admin@ssauk.com
Web site: www.ssauk.com
Freq: Quarterly
Circ: 1500 Not Audited
Editor: Rennie Schafer
MAGAZINE
Interior Design

Focus on Commercial Aviation Safety
984175
Editorial: Graham Suite, Fairoaks Airport, Chobham GU24 8HX **Tel:** 44 01276 855193
Email: admin@ukfsc.co.uk
Web site: www.ukfsc.co.uk
Freq: Quarterly
Circ: 14500 Not Audited
Editor: Dai Whittingham
Profile: Official publication of The Flight Safety Committee. Covers news and articles on flight operations, air traffic control, simulators, meteorology and avionics.
Ad Rate: Full Page Colour £1500.00
MAGAZINE
Aviation

Focus on Surfactants
987906
Editorial: The Boulevard, Langford Lane, Kidlington OX5 1AS **Tel:** 44 01489 891447
Web site: www.elsevier.com/journals/focus-on-surfactants/1351-4210
Freq: Monthly Not Audited
Editor: Caroline Edser
Profile: International newsletter containing information on surface acting agents and their key market areas including detergents, toiletries and cosmetics.
MAGAZINE
Chemicals

Folding Carton Industry
985959
Editorial: 1 Salisbury Office Park, London Road, Salisbury, Salisbury SP1 3HP
Tel: 44 01722 337038

Email: publications@brunton.co.uk
Web site: http://www.thepackagingportal.com/digital-issues
Freq: Bi-Monthly
Circ: 7500 Not Audited
Profile: Magazine covering news on all aspects of carton manufacture including the latest techniques, new machinery and production data. Aimed at management in the folding carton industry.
Ad Rate: Full Page Colour £1680.00
MAGAZINE
Manufacturing, Paper

Food & Drink News
983578
Editorial: 18F7 Brooke's Mill, Armitage Bridge, Huddersfield HD4 7NR
Tel: 44 01484 321000
Web site: www.foodanddrinknews.co.uk
Freq: Monthly
Circ: 17500 Not Audited
Profile: Magazine providing up-to-date news and views on all aspects of the food and drink industry.
Ad Rate: Full Page Mono £1535.00
Ad Rate: Full Page Colour £1925.00
MAGAZINE
Food

Food Business Review
983526
Editorial: 40-42 Hatton Garden, Hatton Garden, London EC1N 8EB
Tel: 44 02079 366898
Email: news@industryreview.com
Web site: http://www.food-business-review.com
Freq: Daily
Circ: 13700 Cision Digital Reach
Profile: Website covering the food industry. The Food Business Review the latest news, comment and information from the food industry.
MAGAZINE (ONLINE)
Food, Retail Management

Food Contact World
998319
Editorial: Cleeve Road, Leatherhead, London KT22 7RU **Tel:** 44 01372 802000
Email: info@smitherspira.com
Web site: http://www.smitherspira.com/publications/subscriptions/food-contact-world
Freq: Bi-Weekly
Circ: 9 Cision Digital Reach
MAGAZINE (ONLINE)
Food, Manufacturing

Food Management Today
987302
Editorial: Food Management Today, PO Box 5116, Milton Keynes MK15 8ZQ
Tel: 44 01908 613323
Email: editorial@foodmanagement.today
Web site: http://www.foodmanagement.today/
Freq: Bi-Monthly
Circ: 4490 Not Audited
Editor: Emily Ansell Elfer
Profile: Business magazine covering the food processing and manufacturing sector. Features company profiles, retailing trends, leading industry interviews, political and legislative information and news, equipment and machinery, supply and raw materials, ingredients, R&D, chilled and frozen foods. Aimed at managers and senior executives within the industry.
MAGAZINE
Food

Food Manufacture
980017
Editorial: Broadfield Park, Crawley, Crawley RH11 9RT **Tel:** 44 01293 613400
Email: foodman@wrbm.com
Web site: www.foodmanufacture.co.uk
Freq: Monthly
Circ: 10678 Not Audited
Editor: Rick Pendrous
Profile: Publication covering ingredients, processing, machinery, packaging, handling and storage, process control and distribution. Provides latest industry news and analysis, latest rules, regulations and legislation, interviews with industry leaders, product innovations and new product development news.Read by directors and

senior management. Regular features:Ingredients - Insight on ingredients used in food manufacture Manufacturing - Analysis of food manufactureNew Product Development - Reviews and information regarding new products relevant to food manufacture Packaging - Insight on food packagingProcessing equipment Supply Chain - Logistics news relevant to the food manufacturing industry.
Ad Rate: Full Page Colour £2168.00
MAGAZINE
Food, Manufacturing

Food Packaging Bulletin
984044
Editorial: Grenville Court, Britwell Road, Burnham SL1 8DF **Tel:** 44 01628 600499
Email: info@researchinformation.co.uk
Web site: www.researchinformation.co.uk/fpbu.php
Freq: Monthly Not Audited
Editor: Bob Yorke
Profile: Newsletter covering all aspects of regulatory affairs in food packaging.
MAGAZINE
Food, Supply Chain Management (SCM)

Food Packer & Processor International
983940
Editorial: 53 Basepoint, Caxton Close, East Portway Industrial Estate, Andover SP10 3FG **Tel:** 44 01264 326480
Email: editorial@binstedgroup.com
Web site: http://www.binstedgroup.com/pubs/fppi.html
Freq: Bi-Monthly
Circ: 4892 Not Audited
Editor: Ed Binsted
Profile: Magazine covering primary and secondary packaging equipment and materials for the food industry. Aimed at those responsible for specifying and buying packaging materials.
Ad Rate: Full Page Mono £995.00
Ad Rate: Full Page Colour £1535.00
MAGAZINE
Supply Chain Management (SCM)

Food Processing (U.K.)
981285
Editorial: Blair House, 184/186 High Street, Tonbridge, Tonbridge TN9 1BQ
Tel: 44 01732 359990
Email: fp@imlgroup.co.uk
Web site: www.fponthenet.net
Freq: Monthly
Circ: 9000 Not Audited
Editor: Suzanne Gill
MAGAZINE
Food, Manufacturing

Food Science & Technology Journal
986010
Editorial: 5 Cambridge Court, 210 Shepherds Bush Road, London W6 7NJ
Email: fst-online@ifst.org
Web site: www.fstjournal.org
Freq: Quarterly Not Audited
MAGAZINE
Food

Food Trade Review
983579
Editorial: Normandie Lodge, 2 Chatsfield, Ewell, Epsom KT17 1QS
Tel: 44 02083 940238
Email: info@foodtradereview.com
Web site: www.ftrtoday.com
Freq: Monthly
Circ: 5000 Not Audited
Profile: Magazine containing news about the latest methods and techniques of food processing and manufacturing, as well as the latest trade news. It covers new machinery, equipment and services used in a food factory, new factories, ingredients and additives, appointments, new retail and catering products and packs.
Ad Rate: Full Page Mono £1250.00
Ad Rate: Full Page Colour £1400.00
MAGAZINE
Food, Manufacturing

FOODNEWS
9836
Editorial: Christchurch Court, 10 - 15 Newgate Street, London EC1A 7AZ
Tel: 44 02070 177500
Web site: https://www.agra-net.com/agra/foodnews/
Freq: Daily
Circ: 18962 Cision Digital Reach
Profile: Magazine covering weekly prices, production and trade news for the world markets for fruit juice and fruit juice concentrates, canned and frozen foods, tomato products, dairy products and dried fruit and nuts.
Ad Rate: Full Page Colour .... £2710.
MAGAZINE (ONLINE)
Food

foodprocessing-technology.com
9812
Editorial: John Carpenter House, John Carpenter Street, London EC4Y 0BS
Tel: 44 02079 366400
Email: onlineeditorial@kable.co.uk
Web site: http://www.foodprocessing-technology.com
Freq: Daily
Circ: 26861 Cision Digital Reach
MAGAZINE (ONLINE)
Food, Industry

Foodservice Equipment Journal
9888
Editorial: 16-25 Bastwick Street, London EC1V 3PS **Tel:** 44 02031 764228
Web site: www.foodserviceequipmentjournal.com
Freq: Monthly
Circ: 3030 Not Audited
Editor: Andrew Seymour; **Editor:** Andrew Seymour
MAGAZINE
Food

Ford & Fordson Tractors
986
Editorial: Cudham Tithe Barn, Berry's Hill, Cudham TN16 3AG **Tel:** 44 01959 541444
Web site: http://tractormagazine.co.uk/magazines/ford-fordson-tractors/
Freq: Bi-Monthly
Circ: 12700 Not Audited
Profile: Magazine featuring Ford and Fordson tractors.
MAGAZINE
Antique & Collectible Cars

Forecourt Trader
980
Editorial: Broadfield Park, Crawley, Crawl RH11 9RT **Tel:** 44 01293 613400
Email: merril.boulton@wrbm.com
Web site: www.forecourttrader.co.uk
Freq: Monthly
Circ: 10283 Not Audited
Editor: Merril Boulton
Profile: Publication containing the latest news, features, legal advice and the latest developments in products and equipment Read by retailers, major suppliers of forecourt equipment and oil company executives responsible for key purchasing decisions.
Ad Rate: Full Page Colour £2650
MAGAZINE
Carbon Emissions & Trading, Oil, Suppl Chain Management (SCM)

Forest Bioenergy Review
987
Editorial: Tralee, Hillcrest Road, Edenbrid Edenbridge TN8 6JS **Tel:** 44 01732 50572
Email: pulppaperlogistics@virginmedia.co
Web site: www.forestbioenergyreview.co
Freq: Quarterly
Circ: 13764 Not Audited
Editor: David Young
Profile: The magazine covering bio energ from forest biomass, pulp and paper industries.
Ad Rate: Full Page Colour £2000
MAGAZINE
Alternative/Renewable Energy

Forestry and Timber News
985526

Editorial: 59 George St, Edinburgh EH2 2JG
Tel: 44 01312 401410
Web site: www.confor.org.uk
Freq: Bi-Monthly
Circ: 3000 Not Audited
Editor: Stefanie Kaiser
MAGAZINE
Environment, Manufacturing

The Forestry Journal
981111

Editorial: PO Box 7570, Dumfries, Sanquhar DG2 8YD **Tel:** 44 01387 702272
Email: info@forestryjournal.co.uk
Web site: www.forestryjournal.co.uk
Freq: Monthly
Circ: 5500 Not Audited
Profile: Magazine covering a wide range of subjects including woodland and forestry equipment, arboriculture, estate and amenity work, timber harvesting and extraction, planting, chipping, shredding, ground preparation, road making, sawmilling and timber haulage.
Ad Rate: Full Page Mono £700.00
Ad Rate: Full Page Colour £1100.00
MAGAZINE
Animal Farming

forward
996767

Editorial: 2 Trueman Place, Oldbrook, Milton Keynes MK6 2HH **Tel:** 44 01908 604191
Email: sia@spinal.co.uk
Web site: www.spinal.co.uk/your-community/our-magazine
Freq: Bi-Monthly
Circ: 7300 Not Audited
MAGAZINE
Orthopedics

Foundry Trade Journal International
986006

Tel: 44 01544 340332
Web site: www.foundrytradejournal.com
Freq: Monthly
Circ: 4000 Not Audited
Profile: Magazine covering all aspects of the international ferrous and non-ferrous foundry industry, including greensand, chemical bonded, carbon dioxide silicate, shell moulding, diecasting (gravity, low pressure, high pressure), investment casting, centrifugal and continuous.
Ad Rate: Full Page Colour £2480.00
MAGAZINE
Engineering, Industry, Manufacturing, Steel

Fractional Trade
1064092

Editorial: 10-14 Accomodation Road, Golders Green, London NW11 8ED
Tel: 44 02083 407989
Email: info@fractionaltrade.com
Web site: www.fractionaltrade.com
Freq: Daily
Circ: 2222 Cision Digital Reach
MAGAZINE (ONLINE)
Finance, Property Management & Maintenance

Franchise International
986772

Editorial: Franchise House, 56 Surrey Street, Norwich NR1 3FD **Tel:** 44 01603 620301
Web site: http://www.internationalfranchisedirectory.net/
Freq: Daily
Circ: 7352 Cision Digital Reach
Profile: Website promoting the availability of master franchise rights worldwide.
MAGAZINE (ONLINE)
Business, Corporate Responsibility

The Franchise Magazine
983936

Editorial: 2nd Floor, 2-4 St Georges Road, London SW19 4DP **Tel:** 44 01603 620301
Web site: www.thefranchisemagazine.net
Freq: Daily
Circ: 9913 Cision Digital Reach
Profile: Journal promoting franchising in the UK.

Ad Rate: Full Page Colour £1875.00
MAGAZINE (ONLINE)
Business, Retail Management

Franchise World
983501

Editorial: Highland House, 165 The Broadway, Wimbledon, London SW19 1NE
Tel: 44 02086 052555
Email: info@franchiseworld.co.uk
Web site: www.franchiseworld.co.uk
Freq: Bi-Monthly
Circ: 10000 Not Audited
Editor: Nick Riding
Profile: Is a bi-monthly magazine that covers the latest news and developments on franchisors and franchisees as well as the service and product suppliers targeting existing franchisors. It also provides coverage of the British Franchise Association sponsored exhibitions.
Ad Rate: Full Page Colour £1425.00
MAGAZINE
Retail Management

Franchiseek
996063

Editorial: 129A High Street, Lymington, Hampshire, Lymington SO41 9AQ
Tel: 44 01323 332838
Web site: www.franchiseek.com
Freq: Daily
Circ: 7289 Cision Digital Reach
MAGAZINE (ONLINE)
Business, Corporate Responsibility

Franchisor News
1053996

Editorial: 2nd Floor, 2 -4 St Georges Road, Wimbledon, London SW19 4DP
Tel: 44 02083 945200
Email: annie.blinkhorn@vmgl.com
Web site: https://www.franchiseinfo.co.uk/info-franchisors/franchisor-news
Freq: Bi-Monthly Not Audited
MAGAZINE
Business

Franklin Templeton Investments
995270

Editorial: Cannon Place, 78 Cannon Street, London EC4N 6HL
Circ: 4093 Cision Digital Reach
MAGAZINE (ONLINE)
Investment Banking

Fraud Intelligence
983859

Editorial: 5 Howick Place, London SW1P 1WG **Tel:** 44 02070 174214
Web site: www.counter-fraud.com
Freq: Bi-Monthly Not Audited
Profile: Specialist newsletter giving practical and probing solutions to fraud and corruption in corporate and business operations, how to recognise it, defend yourself against it and how to deal with it. The publication also covers developments in case law and statute.
MAGAZINE
Corporate Law, Criminal Law, Litigation, Tax Law

Fraud Watch
983050

Editorial: 3A Market Place, Uppingham, Oakham LE15 9QH **Tel:** 44 01572 820088
Web site: www.fraudwatchonline.com
Freq: Bi-Monthly Not Audited
Profile: Publication dealing with fraud and compliance issues within financial services across the world. Includes payment cards, counterfeiting, money laundering and internal audit fraud.
Ad Rate: Full Page Colour £2000.00
MAGAZINE
Banking, Corporate Law, Tax Law

Freelancers In The UK
996986

Tel: 44 07748 804713
Email: nick@full-media.com
Web site: www.freelancersintheuk.co.uk
Freq: Daily
Circ: 1653 Cision Digital Reach
MAGAZINE (ONLINE)
Business

Freight & Logistics
979939

Editorial: Hermes House, St John's Road, Tunbridge Wells, Tunbridge Wells TN4 9UZ
Tel: 44 01892 552205
Web site: http://www.fta.co.uk/membership/member_information_services/freight-and-logistics-magazine/index.htm
Freq: Monthly
Circ: 9036 Not Audited
Profile: Journal for FTA members. Covers all modes of transport.
Ad Rate: Full Page Colour £2080.00
MAGAZINE
Shipping & Warehousing

Freight Business Journal
999219

Editorial: Station House, Mersey Road, Merseyside, Liverpool L17 6AG
Tel: 44 01514 276800
Email: info@fbj-online.com
Web site: www.fbj-online.com
Freq: Bi-Monthly
Circ: 8247 Not Audited
Editor: Chris Lewis
MAGAZINE
Shipping & Warehousing

Freight Industry Times
983651

Editorial: Zinc Media, Kings House, Royal Court Brook Street, Macclesfield SK11 7AE
Tel: 44 01625 613000
Web site: www.freight-online.co.uk
Freq: Quarterly
Circ: 5000 Not Audited
Editor: Michael Parry
Profile: Magazine providing news on all sectors of the freight industry including road, sea, air and rail.
Ad Rate: Full Page Colour £3675.00
MAGAZINE
Shipping & Warehousing

Freighters World
985813

Editorial: 7th Floor Chancery House, St Nicholas Way, Sutton SM1 1JB
Tel: 44 02087 228370
Email: editorial@aircargonews.net
Web site: http://www.aircargonews.net/freighters-world.html
Freq: Quarterly
Circ: 4367 Not Audited
Editor: Roger Hailey
Profile: Magazine covering all-cargo operations. Features editorial appraisal from freighter specialists around the world. It also analyses the latest news and trends, features interviews with leading industry figures and has comprehensive coverage of the varied world of dedicated all-cargo operators.
MAGAZINE
Aviation, Shipping & Warehousing

FreightWeek
1058388

Editorial: 143-145 Stanwell Road, Richmond TW15 3QN UK **Tel:** 44 07411 847547
Web site: www.freightweek.org
Freq: Monthly
Circ: 29000 Not Audited
Profile: Website covering freight. The freightweek website shares the latest news on sustainable business practices for the global logistics industry. The Freight Week newsletter, FW is distributed to '25,000 individuals worldwide'.
MAGAZINE
Business, Corporate Responsibility, Environment

Fresh Business Thinking
984059

Editorial: 9-11 Castle Street, Office Suite 2, Cardiff CF10 1BS **Tel:** 44 08455 000327
Email: editor@freshbusinessthinking.com
Web site: freshbusinessthinking.com
Freq: Daily
Circ: 59708 Cision Digital Reach
Editor: Jonathan Davies
MAGAZINE (ONLINE)
Business, Small and Medium Business

Frontera News
1064283

Editorial: 120 Pall Mall, London SW1Y 5ED
Tel: 44 02078 594185
Web site: https://fronteranews.com/

Freq: Daily
Circ: 16507 Cision Digital Reach
MAGAZINE (ONLINE)
Economics, Emerging Markets, Financial Markets, Fund Management

Frontier Energy
996392

Editorial: c/o Maynard Heady LLP, Matrix House, 12-16 Lionel Road, Canvey Island, Canvey Island SS8 9DE
Tel: 44 07710 122258
Email: editor@frontierenergy.info
Web site: www.frontierenergy.info
Freq: Quarterly
Circ: 5100 Not Audited
Editor: Martin Clark
MAGAZINE
Oil, Shipping & Warehousing

Frontline
984014

Editorial: 14 Bedford Row, London WC1R 4ED **Tel:** 44 02073 066666
Email: frontline@csp.org.uk
Web site: http://www.csp.org.uk/news-events/frontline-magazine
Freq: Bi-Weekly
Circ: 50000 Not Audited
Profile: Publication containing news and information about physiotherapy and chartered physiotherapists, physiotherapy assistants and students.
MAGAZINE
Occupational Therapy & Rehabilitation

Frontline Gastroenterology
999835

Editorial: BMA House, Tavistock Square, London WC1H 9JR **Tel:** 44 02073 836318
Email: info.fg@bmjgroup.com
Web site: http://fg.bmj.com/
Freq: Quarterly
Circ: 3700 Not Audited
Editor: Anton Emmanuel
MAGAZINE
Gastroenterology

Frozen & Chilled Foods
981287

Editorial: PO Box 88, Edenbridge, Edenbridge TN8 6ZW **Tel:** 44 01732 868288
Web site: www.frozenandchilledfoods.com
Freq: Bi-Monthly
Circ: 5500 Not Audited
Profile: Magazine covering every aspect of temperature controlled foods and their uses including company profiles, exhibition reviews and previews, hygiene and safety, packaging, transport, storage and distribution. Read by buyers, directors and product managers of manufacturers and processors of frozen and chilled foods, frozen food retail chains, multiple retail offices, symbol groups, cash and carries, co-operatives and wholesale distributors.
Ad Rate: Full Page Colour £1750.00
MAGAZINE
Food

The Fruit Grower
983852

Editorial: Lion House, Church Street, Maidstone, Maidstone ME14 1EN
Tel: 44 01622 695656
Email: fruit@actpub.co.uk
Web site: http://thefruitgrower.co.uk/
Freq: Monthly
Circ: 2300 Not Audited
Editor: Chris Tanton
Profile: Magazine covering all aspects of commercial fruit grown in the U.K, including machinery and equipment, planting, pruning pest control, harvesting and marketing.
Ad Rate: Full Page Mono £1065.00
Ad Rate: Full Page Colour £1465.00
MAGAZINE
Animal Farming

FRY Magazine.com
984050

Editorial: 196 Pettswood Road, Orpington, London BR5 1LG **Tel:** 44 01323 765472
Email: info@fry-online.co.uk
Web site: www.fry-online.co.uk
Freq: Daily
Circ: 10303 Cision Digital Reach

Business Magazines

Editor: Helen Edmonds
MAGAZINE (ONLINE)
Food

FSC Report 999061
Editorial: 30 Cannon Street, London EC4M 6XH **Tel:** 44 02037 632800
Email: enquiries@campdenwealth.com
Web site: http://www.campdenwealth.com/
Freq: Annual
Circ: 14000 Not Audited
MAGAZINE
Banking

FTSE Global Markets 980792
Editorial: 1st Floor, Rennie House, 57-60 Aldgate High Street, London EC3N 1AL
Tel: 44 02076 805151
Web site: www.ftseglobalmarkets.com
Freq: Bi-Monthly
Circ: 25000 Not Audited
Editor: Francesca Carnevale
Profile: Magazine covering financial markets including pension funds, mutual funds, stock exchanges, hedge funds, investment, brokerages, trading, wealth management as well as specialist data providers and comment or analysis on the world's equity and debt markets, specialist investment services and key corporates. First published in 2004, the publication has an average of 96 pages per issue. Aimed at fund and hedge fund managers, securities services providers, issuers, pension plan sponsors, investment bankers, brokers, stock exchanges and specialist financial data providers.
Ad Rate: Full Page Colour £7995.00
MAGAZINE
Bonds, Corporate Finance, Corporate Management, Equities, Fund Management, Lending

Fuel Cells Bulletin 980797
Editorial: Elsevier Limited, The Boulevard, Langford Lane, Kidlington, Oxford OX5 1GB
Tel: 44 01865 843239
Web site: https://www.journals.elsevier.com/fuel-cells-bulletin/
Freq: Monthly
Circ: 6000 Not Audited
Editor: Steve Barrett
MAGAZINE
Alternative/Renewable Energy, Electricity, Nuclear Power, Oil, Water & Sanitation

Fuel Oil News (UK) 981012
Editorial: Caledonian House, Tatton Street, Knutsford, Knutsford WA16 6AG
Tel: 44 01565 653283
Web site: http://fueloilnews.co.uk/
Circ: 1100 Not Audited
Editor: Jane Hughes
MAGAZINE
Oil, Shipping & Warehousing

FundEd 1057951
Tel: 44 01342 718679
Email: funded@communityinspired.co.uk
Web site: funded.org.uk
Freq: Quarterly
Circ: 10000 Not Audited
Editor: Nikki Burch
MAGAZINE
Higher Education, Schools & Institutions, Students

Funding for Independent Schools 983932
Editorial: 26 Red Lion Square, London WC1R 4HQ **Tel:** 44 02031 943000
Email: info@pentastic.co.uk
Web site: www.fismagazine.co.uk
Freq: 3 Times/Year
Circ: 4000 Not Audited
Editor: Andrew Maiden
Profile: Funding for Independent Schools improves the effective management of independent schools through coverage of financial, strategic and fundraising issues.
Ad Rate: Full Page Colour £1550.00
MAGAZINE
Schools & Institutions

Funds Europe 979779
Editorial: 288 Bishopsgate, London EC2M 4QP **Tel:** 44 02031 785872
Email: contact@funds-europe.com
Web site: www.funds-europe.com
Freq: Monthly
Circ: 10243 Not Audited
Profile: Magazine providing in-depth analysis of all issues pertaining to the construction of a cross-border funds business in Europe including developments in Europe's retail, institutional investment fund markets and wealth management.
Ad Rate: Full Page Colour £7250.00
MAGAZINE
Fund Management

Funds Global Asia 987136
Editorial: 288 Bishopsgate, London EC2M 4QP **Tel:** 44 02031 785872
Email: contact@fundsglobalasia.com
Web site: http://www.fundsglobalasia.com/
Freq: Quarterly
Circ: 4131 Not Audited
Profile: Publication that services the global asset management community and asset servicing communities by publishing in-depth reports containing commentary, interviews, roundtable discussions and analysis from regions which share fundamental interests and concerns with Europe.
Ad Rate: Full Page Colour £7450.00
MAGAZINE
Fund Management

Funds Global MENA 995415
Editorial: 288 Bishopsgate, London EC2M 4QP **Tel:** 44 02031 785878
Email: contact@fundsglobalmena.com
Web site: http://www.fundsglobalmena.com/
Freq: Quarterly
Circ: 14271 Not Audited
MAGAZINE
Fund Management

Funds-Axis 998566
Editorial: 31 Southampton Row, London WC1B 5HJ **Tel:** 44 02890 329736
Email: info@funds-axis.com
Web site: www.funds-axis.com
Freq: Daily
Circ: 3929 Cision Digital Reach
MAGAZINE (ONLINE)
Fund Management

FundServices.net 990678
Editorial: Cambrian House, Upper St Johns Road, Burgess Hill RH15 8HB
Tel: 44 02073 623000
Web site: www.fundservices.net
Freq: Daily
Circ: 11473 Cision Digital Reach
MAGAZINE (ONLINE)
Fund Management

FundStrategy 979772
Editorial: Wells Point, 79 Wells Street, London W1T 3QN **Tel:** 44 02079 438000
Web site: www.fundstrategy.co.uk
Freq: Monthly
Circ: 5500 Not Audited
Profile: Magazine covering investment fund industry news and analysis. Also covers multi-manager and fund distribution. Aimed at top end financial advisers in investment businesses, multi-managers and 'gatekeepers' in banks and other financial institutions.
Ad Rate: Full Page Colour £2200.00
MAGAZINE
Fund Management

Funeral Director Monthly 984502
Editorial: 618 Warwick Road, Solihull, Solihull B91 1AA **Tel:** 44 01217 11134320
Email: editor@nafd.org.uk
Web site: www.funeraldirectormonthly.org.uk
Freq: Monthly
Circ: 3586 Not Audited
Editor: Su Lewis
Profile: Official magazine of the National Association of Funeral Directors, designed to keep funeral directors abreast of important industry developments by highlighting new initiatives, carrying updates on UK, European and International issues and reporting on key business subjects, such as Health and Safety and Employment Law. Aimed at funeral directors, NAFD members and decision-makers in all areas of the business of providing services and products for funerals.
Ad Rate: Full Page Mono £460.00
Ad Rate: Full Page Colour £595.00
MAGAZINE
Hygiene, Security & Security Systems

Funeral Service Journal 984499
Editorial: The Media Centre, Garcia Estate, Canterbury Road, Worthing BN13 1AL
Tel: 44 01903 604335
Email: editorial@fsj.co.uk
Web site: www.fsj.co.uk
Freq: Monthly
Circ: 2800 Not Audited
Profile: Journal covering all aspects of undertaking and funeral direction.
Ad Rate: Full Page Mono £175.00
Ad Rate: Full Page Colour £377.00
MAGAZINE
Hygiene, Security & Security Systems

Funeral Service Times 985244
Editorial: Wellington House, 90-92 Butt Road, Colchester CO3 3DA
Tel: 44 02035 150208
Email: copy@funeralservicetimes.co.uk
Web site: www.funeralservicetimes.co.uk
Freq: Monthly
Circ: 5750 Not Audited
Editor: Sara Cork
Profile: Magazine covering issues of concern or interest to the sector of the funeral services.
Ad Rate: Full Page Colour £765.00
MAGAZINE
Hygiene, Security & Security Systems

The Furnishing Report 984865
Email: info@thefurnishingreport.com
Web site: www.thefurnishingreport.com
Freq: Daily
Circ: 12675 Cision Digital Reach
MAGAZINE (ONLINE)
Building & Construction

Furniture & Joinery Production 983132
Editorial: 4 Red Barn Mews, High Street Battle, Tunbridge Wells TN33 0AG
Tel: 44 01424 774982
Web site: www.furnitureproduction.net
Freq: Monthly
Circ: 7500 Not Audited
MAGAZINE
Interior Design, Manufacturing

Furniture News 981100
Editorial: 4 Red Barn Mews, High Street, Battle, Battle TN33 0AG
Tel: 44 01424 774982
Web site: www.furniturenews.net
Freq: Monthly
Circ: 7000 Not Audited
Profile: Publication containing news and analysis, editorial comment, show previews and reviews and features covering all domestic and contract interiors products.
Ad Rate: Full Page Colour £1569.00
MAGAZINE
Interior Design

Future Airport 981320
Editorial: John Carpenter House, John Carpenter Street, London EC4Y 0AN
Tel: 44 02079 366400
Web site: www.futureairport.com
Freq: Semi-Annual
Circ: 6677 Not Audited
Profile: Magazine covering all aspects of airport technology, including projects, long term views and reviews.
Ad Rate: Full Page Mono £5800.00

Ad Rate: Full Page Colour £6900.00
MAGAZINE
Aviation

Future Banking 983748
Editorial: John Carpenter House, John Carpenter Street, London EC4Y 0AN
Tel: 44 02079 366400
Email: info@globaltrademedia.com
Web site: www.banking-gateway.com
Freq: Semi-Annual
Circ: 4442 Not Audited
Profile: Magazine looking at merging trends and breakthrough technologies within the financial markets. Aimed at key decision makers working within Europe's leading financial services organisations.
MAGAZINE
Banking

Future Cardiology 998873
Editorial: Unitec House, 2 Albert Place, London N3 1QB **Tel:** 44 02083 716090
Email: info@futuremedicine.com
Web site: www.futuremedicine.com/loi/fca
Freq: Bi-Monthly Not Audited
MAGAZINE
Cardiology

Future Constructor & Architect (FC&A) 981698
Editorial: Pear Platt, Woodfalls Industrial Estate, Gravelly Way, Maidstone ME18 6DA
Tel: 44 01622 873229
Web site: http://www.fca-magazine.com
Freq: Monthly
Circ: 15000 Not Audited
MAGAZINE
Building & Construction, Engineering

Future Medicinal Chemistry 996253
Editorial: Unitec House, 2 Albert Place, London N3 1QB **Tel:** 44 02083 716090
Email: info@future-science.com
Web site: www.future-science.com/loi/fmc
Freq: Monthly Not Audited
MAGAZINE
Pharmaceuticals

Future Neurology 997118
Editorial: Unitec House, 2 Albert Place, London N3 1QB **Tel:** 44 02083 716090
Email: info@futuremedicine.com
Web site: www.futuremedicine.com/loi/fnl
Freq: Bi-Monthly Not Audited
MAGAZINE
Neurology

Future Oncology 997075
Editorial: Unitec House, 2 Albert Place, London N3 1QB **Tel:** 44 02083 716090
Email: info@futuremedicine.com
Web site: www.futuremedicine.com/loi/fon
Freq: Monthly Not Audited
MAGAZINE
Oncology

Future Power Technology 985661
Editorial: John Carpenter House, John Carpenter Street, London EC4Y 0AN
Tel: 44 02079 366400
Email: onlinemags@nridigital.com
Web site: www.nridigital.com/future-power.html
Freq: Monthly
Circ: 322 Cision Digital Reach
Profile: Website covering the power industry. The Future Power Technology is a digital magazine, providing 'in-depth coverage of developments in the power industry and the latest technology'.
MAGAZINE (ONLINE)
Alternative/Renewable Energy, Carbon Emissions & Trading, Electricity, Energy, Nuclear Power, Oil, Water & Sanitation

Future Science OA 1054534
Editorial: Unitec House, 2 Albert Place, London N3 1QB **Tel:** 44 02083 716090
Email: info@future-science.com

Web site: http://www.future-science.com/loi/fso
Freq: Semi-Annual
MAGAZINE
Biotechnology

Future Travel Experience
986803
Editorial: 3a Gatwick Metro Centre, Balcombe Road, Surrey, Horley RH6 9GA
Tel: 44 01293 783851
Email: post@pps-publications.com
Web site: www.FutureTravelExperience.com
Freq: Daily
Circ: 17902 Cision Digital Reach
Profile: Website covering the travel process. FUTURE TRAVEL EXPERIENCE shares the latest news, information or reviews on the travel industry and the travel process. The outlet offers RSS (Really Simple Syndication).
MAGAZINE (ONLINE)
Aviation

FX
983192
Editorial: 71-73 Carter Lane, London EC4V 5EQ **Tel:** 44 02079 366400
Web site: www.fxmagazine.co.uk
Freq: Monthly
Circ: 46463 Not Audited
Profile: Magazine focusing on design in the commercial sector. Includes articles on public sector, office, retail, hotel, lighting and leisure design.
Ad Rate: Full Page Colour £2500.00
MAGAZINE
Interior Design

FX Week
979840
Editorial: Haymarket House, 28-29 Haymarket, London SW1Y 4RX
Tel: 44 02074 849700
Web site: www.fxweek.com
Freq: Weekly
Circ: 2874 Not Audited
Editor: Eva Szalay
Profile: Newsletter that focuses exclusively on the business of foreign exchange and related short-term interest rate products.
Ad Rate: Full Page Mono £2475.00
Ad Rate: Full Page Colour £3250.00
MAGAZINE
Foreign Exchange Market (FOREX)

FX-MM
980844
Editorial: Court Lodge, Hogtrough Hill, Brasted, Westerham TN16 1NU
Tel: 44 01959 563311
Web site: www.fx-mm.com
Freq: Monthly
Circ: 21000 Not Audited
Editor: Peter Garnham
Profile: Journal covering all aspects of foreign exchange and trading instruments including political, economic and market conditions. Also covers treasury, technology as well as fund management and wealth management.
Ad Rate: Full Page Colour £3986.00
MAGAZINE
Derivatives, Foreign Exchange Market (FOREX), Fund Management

Gas International
984151
Tel: 44 01509 678182
Email: editor@igem.org.uk
Web site: www.igem.org.uk
Freq: Monthly
Circ: 4000 Not Audited
MAGAZINE
Engineering, Oil

Gas Matters
980890
Editorial: 10 St Brides Street, London EC4A 4AD **Tel:** 44 02073 329900
Email: info@gas-matters.com
Web site: www.gasstrategies.com/publications/gas-matters
Freq: Monthly Not Audited
Profile: Gas Matters is a subscription only digital magazine published 10 times a year. The magazine covers the latest business

news and industry information on the global gas and energy industries.
MAGAZINE
Carbon Emissions & Trading, Oil

Gas Matters Today
983790
Editorial: 10 St Brides Street, London EC4A 4AD **Tel:** 44 02073 329900
Email: info@gas-matters.com
Web site: http://www.gasstrategies.com/information-services/gas-matters-today
Freq: Daily
Circ: 327 Cision Digital Reach
MAGAZINE (ONLINE)
Carbon Emissions & Trading, Oil

Gas Purification
1061180
Tel: 44 86255 7057410
Email: qtjh@vip.163.com
Web site: http://cgvip.com/gk/86683x/200802
Freq: Bi-Monthly
Circ: 3001 Not Audited
MAGAZINE
Oil

Gas to Power Journal
987659
Editorial: 1st Floor, 30 Warner Street, London EC1R 5EX **Tel:** 44 02072 532700
Web site: www.gastopowerjournal.com
Freq: Weekly Not Audited
MAGAZINE
Alternative/Renewable Energy, Electricity, Oil

Gas Turbine Power Generation Technology
1062000
Tel: 44 86755 83680053
Email: csee_agtpg@126.com
Web site: http://www.agtpg.com
Freq: Quarterly
Circ: 3003 Not Audited
MAGAZINE
Alternative/Renewable Energy, Carbon Emissions & Trading, Electricity, Energy, Nuclear Power, Oil, Water & Sanitation

Gastroenterology Today
983833
Editorial: Media House, 48 High Street, Swanley, Swanley BR8 8BQ
Tel: 44 01322 660434
Email: info@mediapublishingcompany.com
Web site: http://www.gastroenterologytoday.com/
Freq: 3 Times/Year
Circ: 2211 Not Audited
Editor: Martin Goldman
Profile: Journal containing original papers, audits, reviews, case reports, meetings reports, news, updates and topical material. Aimed at hospital-based gastroenterologists at senior level plus all relevant major GI departments.
Ad Rate: Full Page Mono £800.00
Ad Rate: Full Page Colour £1200.00
MAGAZINE
Gastroenterology

gasworld magazine
999171
Tel: 44 01872 225031
Web site: www.gasworld.com
Freq: Monthly
Circ: 2500 Not Audited
MAGAZINE
Oil

Gateshead Council News
984489
Editorial: Gateshead Council, Civic Centre, Regent Street, Gateshead NE8 1HH
Tel: 44 01914 333444
Web site: www.gateshead.gov.uk/
Freq: Quarterly
Circ: 96000 Not Audited
Editor: Diane Brennan
Profile: Magazine covering local government issues including health, education, social services, art, sport and entertainment. Aimed at Gateshead residents, businesses and visitors.
MAGAZINE
Government

GC Magazine
988740
Tel: 44 02073 969292
Web site: http://www.legal500.com/assets/pages/qc/home.html
Freq: Quarterly
Circ: 190000 Not Audited
MAGAZINE
Legal Services

Generation
984061
Tel: 44 01732 220120
Email: press@familybusinessplace.com
Web site: www.familybusinessplace.com
Freq: Semi-Annual
Circ: 6000 Not Audited
Editor: Amalia Brightley-Gillott
MAGAZINE
Business

Generics Bulletin
984751
Editorial: 4 Poplar Road, Dorridge, Solihull, Solihull B93 8DB **Tel:** 44 01564 777550
Email: editor@generics-bulletin.com
Web site: www.generics-bulletin.com
Freq: Weekly
Circ: 8000 Not Audited
Editor: Aidan Fry
Profile: Newsletter covering commercial and regulatory information for the global generics industry.
Ad Rate: Full Page Mono £940.00
Ad Rate: Full Page Colour £1410.00
MAGAZINE
Biotechnology, Healthcare Industry, Pharmaceuticals

Genome Biology
999431
Editorial: BioMed Central, 236 Gray's Inn Road, London WC1X 8HB
Tel: 44 02031 922009
Email: editorial@genomebiology.com
Web site: http://genomebiology.com/
Freq: Monthly Not Audited
Editor: Louisa Flintoft
MAGAZINE
Biotechnology

Genome Medicine
996532
Editorial: BioMed Central, 236 Gray's Inn Road, London WC1X 8HD
Tel: 44 02031 922009
Email: editorial@genomemedicine.com
Web site: genomemedicine.com
Freq: Monthly Not Audited
MAGAZINE
Pharmaceuticals

GeoDrilling International
981355
Editorial: Aspermont Media, 4th Floor Vintners Place, 68 Upper Thames Street, London EC4V 3BJ **Tel:** 44 02072 166060
Email: nia.kajastie@aspermontmedia.com
Web site: www.geodrillinginternational.com
Freq: Monthly
Circ: 11692 Not Audited
Editor: Nia Kajastie
Profile: Publication covering all aspects of drilling in soils and rocks, including civil engineering, water well work, construction, piling, geotechnical, geothermal, coal bed methane, mineral resources exploration and environmental testing, quarrying, and open pit/underground mining. Aimed at manufacturers of equipment, geotechnical contracting and consulting companies, governmental users and academics.
Ad Rate: Full Page Colour £1641.00
MAGAZINE
Mining & Quarrying

Geography
984844
Editorial: Geographical Association, 160 Solly Street, Sheffield S1 4BF
Tel: 44 01142 960088
Email: info@geography.org.uk
Web site: www.geography.org.uk
Freq: 3 Times/Year
Circ: 4500 Not Audited
Profile: Journal covering all matters relating to research and teaching.
Ad Rate: Full Page Mono £390.00
Ad Rate: Full Page Colour £760.00
MAGAZINE
Schools & Institutions, Students

Geoscientist
984515
Editorial: The Geological Society, Burlington House, London W1J 0BG
Tel: 44 02074 349944
Web site: www.geolsoc.org.uk/geoscientist
Freq: Monthly
Circ: 11000 Not Audited
Editor: Ted Nield
Profile: Magazine covering news and developments in earth sciences.
Ad Rate: Full Page Mono £1320.00
Ad Rate: Full Page Colour £1980.00
MAGAZINE
Environment, Science

Glass & Glazing Products
981246
Editorial: The Manor, Nepicar House, Wrotham Heath, London Road, Sevenoaks, Sevenoaks TN15 7RS **Tel:** 44 01732 748000
Web site: www.ggpmag.com
Freq: Monthly
Circ: 10500 Not Audited
Editor: Luke Wood
Profile: Website about glass and glazing market, updated on a daily basis with the latest industry news and views as well as having a jam packed articles area and all the latest product information.
MAGAZINE
Building & Construction, Residential Real Estate

Glass International
985960
Editorial: Quartz House, 20 Clarendon Road, Redhill, Redhill RH1 1QX
Tel: 44 01737 855000
Email: gregmorris@quartzltd.com
Web site: http://www.glass-international.com
Freq: Monthly
Circ: 5500 Not Audited
Editor: Greg Morris
Profile: Magazine containing information on the latest technology in glass production and in-depth surveys on the location and activities of the glassmaking industries in countries around the world.
Ad Rate: Full Page Mono £2980.00
Ad Rate: Full Page Colour £3900.00
MAGAZINE
Manufacturing

glass news
986347
Editorial: 12 Sunderland Street, Tickhill, Harworth DN11 9QJ **Tel:** 44 07805 051322
Web site: www.glassnews.co.uk
Freq: Monthly
Circ: 14000 Not Audited
Editor: Chris Champion
Profile: Monthly newspaper delivered to 10,000 fabricators, installers, sealed unit manufacturers, glass processing and manufacture, profile system suppliers, machinery manufacturers, software (all glass and glazing associated companies).
MAGAZINE
Manufacturing

Glass Times
984144
Editorial: 9 Cornhill Road, Davyhulme, Manchester M41 5TJ **Tel:** 44 02084 441302
Email: bulletin@glasstimes.co.uk
Web site: www.glasstimes.co.uk
Freq: Monthly
Circ: 10535 Not Audited
Editor: Nathan Bushell
Profile: Journal covering all aspects of the glass industry, containing articles on glass and glazing, industry news and product information.
Ad Rate: Full Page Colour £1930.00
MAGAZINE
Manufacturing

Glass Worldwide
988905
Editorial: 1 Cantelupe Mews, Cantelupe Road, East Grinstead, East Grinstead RH19 3BG **Tel:** 44 01342 322133
Web site: http://www.cbm-ltd.com/home
Freq: Bi-Monthly
Circ: 9000 Not Audited
Profile: Magazine covering the unique forum for the exchange of production-related news and views between global glassmakers and

Business Magazines

their suppliers. The editorial profile is focusing on the identification of practical solutions to the everyday issues faced by professionals throughout the world.
MAGAZINE
Manufacturing

The Glazine   984710
Editorial: 47 Bucknalls Lane, London WD25 9NE Tel: 44 01923 461527
Email: news@the-glazine.com
Web site: http://www.the-glazine.com
Freq: Weekly
Circ: 7008 Cision Digital Reach
Profile: Website covering glass. THE GLAZINE website shares the latest news and information on glass, glazing and fenestration industries.
MAGAZINE (ONLINE)
Building & Construction

Global Accountant   987497
Editorial: South Bank Technopark, London SE1 6LN Tel: 44 02081 662662
Email: news@globalaccountantweb.com
Web site: www.globalaccountantweb.com
Freq: Daily
Circ: 15500 Cision Digital Reach
Profile: Global Accountant magazine covers, analyses and comments on recent news, technical knowledge and job skills that drive accountancy.
MAGAZINE (ONLINE)
Accounting

Global Arbitration Review (GAR)   983244
Editorial: 87 Lancaster Road, London W11 1QQ Tel: 44 02074 670175
Email: editorial@globalarbitrationreview.com
Web site: www.globalarbitrationreview.com
Freq: Bi-Monthly
Circ: 2000 Not Audited
Editor: Alison Ross
MAGAZINE
Litigation

Global Assets   981590
Editorial: Po Box 726, Greencliffe, St Helier, Jersey, St. Helier JE4 0XJ
Tel: 44 01534 859006
Email: ceo@financeoffshore.com
Web site: www.financeoffshore.com
Freq: Quarterly
Circ: 521 Cision Digital Reach
MAGAZINE (ONLINE)
Banking

Global Banking and Finance Review   986442
Editorial: Kemp House, 152-160 City Road, London EC1V 2NX Tel: 44 02081 443511
Web site: www.globalbankingandfinance.com
Freq: Daily
Circ: 561938 Cision Digital Reach
Editor: Wanda Rich
MAGAZINE (ONLINE)
Banking

Global Brands Magazine   995541
Editorial: Unit 4 Vista Place, Coy Pond Business PK Ingworth Road, Poole, Poole BH12 1JY Tel: 44 02081 333475
Email: info@gbrandsmag.com
Web site: www.globalbrandsmagazine.com
Freq: Daily
Circ: 100000 Not Audited
MAGAZINE
Branding

Global Cement Magazine   981086
Editorial: 1st Floor, Adelphi Court, 1 East Street, Epsom, London KT17 1BB
Tel: 44 01372 743837
Email: info@propubs.com
Web site: www.globalcement.com
Freq: Monthly
Circ: 4227 Not Audited
Profile: Journal containing research and comment on trade and production issues within the global cement industry, as well as

news and details of the latest technical advances in the field.
Ad Rate: Full Page Mono £2280.00
Ad Rate: Full Page Colour £3360.00
MAGAZINE
Building & Construction

Global Coal News and Analysis   997064
Tel: 44 01730 265095
Email: coalemea@ihs.com
Web site: https://www.ihs.com/products/global-coal-news-analysis.html
Freq: Monthly
Circ: 591 Cision Digital Reach
Editor: David Price
MAGAZINE (ONLINE)
Mining & Quarrying

Global Competition Review
                                          980721
Editorial: 87 Lancaster Road, London W11 1QQ Tel: 44 02079 089212
Email: editorial@globalcompetitionreview.com
Web site: www.globalcompetitionreview.com
Freq: Monthly
Circ: 7000 Not Audited
Profile: Magazine covering competition (antitrust) policy and regulation, including news stories, feature articles, high-profile interviews and special reports. Aimed at competition or antitrust lawyers, academics and enforcers worldwide.
Ad Rate: Full Page Colour £3000.00
MAGAZINE
Corporate Law

Global Construction Review
                                          988274
Editorial: Atom, 45-47 Clerkenwell Green, London EC1R 0EB Tel: 44 02074 905595
Web site: http://www.globalconstructionreview.com/
Freq: Daily
Circ: 55230 Cision Digital Reach
Editor: Rod Sweet
MAGAZINE (ONLINE)
Building & Construction

Global Convenience Store Focus   999531
Editorial: 2 Severn Street, Welshpool SY21 7AB Tel: 44 01938 556090
Email: info@insightresearch.co.uk
Web site: http://www.globalconveniencestorefocus.co.uk/
Freq: Monthly
Circ: 8288 Cision Digital Reach
Editor: Fiona Briggs
MAGAZINE (ONLINE)
Retail Management

Global Corporate Venturing
                                          985599
Editorial: 3-4 Doughty Street, London WC1N 2PN
Email: news@globalcorporateventuring.com
Web site: www.globalcorporateventuring.com
Freq: Monthly
Circ: 11000 Not Audited
Profile: Magazine focusing of a different economic sector each month, providing data and analysis of companies' activities in buying minority stakes in third party businesses. A news section covers the previous months deal activity, people moves and regulatory stories. The magazine also features comment from industry figures. Aimed at the in-house venture capital units of businesses.
MAGAZINE
Banking, Economics

Global Custodian   980055
Editorial: Upper Ground Floor, 200 Aldersgate Street, London EC1A 4HD
Tel: 44 02073 973800
Web site: www.globalcustodian.com
Freq: Bi-Monthly
Circ: 20383 Not Audited

Profile: Magazine covering the global securities services industry. It provides news, features and analysis of all of the operational and administrative aspects of the securities industry including payment systems, fund management, CSDs, CCPs, ICSDs, collateral management, custody, off shore administration, mutual fund administration, prime brokerage, hedge funds, private equity and derivatives.
Ad Rate: Full Page Colour £12350.00
MAGAZINE
Equities

Global Defence Technology
                                          983097
Editorial: John Carpenter House, John Carpenter Street, London EC4Y 0AN
Tel: 44 02079 366400
Email: onlinemags@nridigital.com
Web site: http://www.nridigital.com/global-defence-technology.html
Freq: Monthly
Circ: 1591 Cision Digital Reach
Profile: Website covering defence. Global Defence Technology is a digital magazine providing 'in-depth coverage of the latest defence technology and industry developments'.
MAGAZINE (ONLINE)
Defense & National Security

Global Energy News   995018
Editorial: Floor 1, Suite F, The Maltsters, 1-2 Wetmore Road, Burton on Trent, Barton-under-Needwood DE14 1LS
Tel: 44 02037 256841
Web site: http://www.globalenergy-news.com/
Freq: Quarterly
Circ: 70000 Not Audited
MAGAZINE
Business, Corporate Responsibility, Financial Markets, Small and Medium Business

Global Gypsum Magazine
                                          986301
Editorial: 1st Floor, Adelphi Court, 1 East Street, Epsom, London KT17 1BB
Tel: 44 01372 743837
Email: info@propubs.com
Web site: www.globalgypsum.com
Freq: Bi-Monthly
Circ: 2750 Not Audited
Profile: Magazine concentrating on the raw gypsum and plasterboard industry. Contains news, case studies, advances in technology, contract updates and conference and exhibition reports.
Ad Rate: Full Page Mono £2280.00
Ad Rate: Full Page Colour £3360.00
MAGAZINE
Building & Construction

Global Health & Pharma   998260
Tel: 44 02037 256840
Web site: www.ghp-magazine.com
Freq: Monthly
Circ: 260000 Not Audited
MAGAZINE
Healthcare Industry, Pharmaceuticals

The Global Innovation Report
                                          998283
Editorial: GDR Creative Intelligence, Dilke House, 1 Malet Street, London WC1E 7JN
Tel: 44 02075 805589
Email: info@gdruk.com
Web site: www.gdruk.com/index.html
Freq: Quarterly Not Audited
MAGAZINE
Branding, Graphic Design, Marketing, Retail, Retail Management

Global Investigations Review
                                          987727
Editorial: 87 Lancaster Road, London W11 1QQ Tel: 44 02079 081183
Web site: www.globalinvestigationsreview.com
Freq: Bi-Monthly Not Audited

Editor: David Vascott
MAGAZINE
Corporate Law, Legal Services, Tax Law

Global Investor Group   979778
Editorial: GlobalCapital, 8 Bouverie Street, London EC4Y 8AX Tel: 44 02077 798999
Web site: www.globalinvestorgroup.com
Freq: Bi-Monthly
Circ: 6350 Not Audited
MAGAZINE
Banking, Foreign Exchange Market (FOREX), Fund Management

The Global Legal Post   986716
Editorial: 86-90 Paul Street, London EC2A 4NE Tel: 44 02071 935342
Email: europe.editorial@globallegalpost.com
Web site: http://www.globallegalpost.com/
Freq: Daily
Circ: 57178 Cision Digital Reach
Profile: The Global Legal Post is a website that covers news, comment and analysis on the legal world.
MAGAZINE (ONLINE)
Corporate Law

Global Meat News   986864
Editorial: Broadfield Park, Crawley RH11 9RT Tel: 44 01293 613400
Web site: www.globalmeatnews.com
Freq: Daily
Circ: 50647 Cision Digital Reach
Editor: Rod Addy
MAGAZINE (ONLINE)
Animal Farming, Food

Global Mobile   980143
Editorial: Mortimer House, 37-41 Mortimer Street, London W1T 3JH
Tel: 44 02070 175000
Web site: https://tmt.knect365.com/
Freq: Bi-Weekly
Circ: 15398 Cision Digital Reach
Editor: Paul Lambert
MAGAZINE (ONLINE)
Telecommunications/Electronic Communications

Global Mobile Daily   983337
Editorial: Mortimer House, 37-41 Mortimer Street, London W1T 3JH
Tel: 44 02070 175000
Email: pr@ovum.com
Web site: http://www.telecomsmarketresearch.com/research/TMAAAQIB-Global-Mobile-Daily.shtml
Freq: Daily
Circ: 53 Cision Digital Reach
Editor: Paul Lambert
MAGAZINE (ONLINE)
Telecommunications/Electronic Communications

The Global Recruiter   981123
Editorial: 112-114 High Street, Rickmansworth, London WD3 1AQ
Tel: 44 08450 948022
Email: editorial@theglobalrecruiter.com
Web site: www.theglobalrecruiter.com
Freq: Monthly Not Audited
Editor: Simon Kent
Profile: Magazine covering all recruitment, staffing and HR issues.
Ad Rate: Full Page Colour £1760.00
MAGAZINE
Education, Health & Safety, Human Resources, Recruiting

Global Reinsurance   980782
Editorial: 120 Leman Street, London E1 8EU
Tel: 44 02076 183456
Web site: www.globalreinsurance.com
Freq: Quarterly
Circ: 7170 Not Audited
Editor: Samera Owusu-Tutu
MAGAZINE
Insurance

Global Restructuring Review
1052556

Editorial: 87 Lancaster Road, London W11 1QQ **Tel:** 44 02074 670170
Email: editorial@globalrestructuringreview. com
Web site: http://globalrestructuringreview. com/
Freq: Bi-Monthly Not Audited
MAGAZINE
Accounting, Corporate Law

Global Risk Regulator
980134

Editorial: Number One, Southwark Bridge, London SE1 9HL **Tel:** 44 02078 734240
Email: grr@ft.com
Web site: www.globalriskregulator.com
Freq: Monthly Not Audited
Profile: Website covering financial regulation, risk management, capital markets and news from regulators and participants in the banking, insurance and securities industries.
MAGAZINE
Bonds, Corporate Finance, Corporate Management, Derivatives, Emerging Markets, Government, Lending

Global Telecoms Business
980144

Editorial: 8 Bouverie Street, London EC4Y 8AX **Tel:** 44 02077 798888
Web site: www.globaltelecomsbusiness. com
Freq: Bi-Monthly Not Audited
Editor: Alan Burkitt-Gray
Profile: Global Telecoms Business is a magazine covering funding, investment, business strategy and regulation of the telecommunications industry.
Ad Rate: Full Page Colour £4500.00
MAGAZINE
Telecommunications/Electronic Communications

Global Telecoms Insight
985767

Editorial: St John Carpenter House, St John Carpenter Street, London EC4Y 0AN
Tel: 44 02079 366400
Web site: www.mobilecomms-technology. com
Freq: Daily
Circ: 5191 Cision Digital Reach
Editor: Andrew Tunnicliffe
MAGAZINE (ONLINE)
Telecommunications/Electronic Communications

Global Trade Review
981006

Editorial: 4 Hillgate Place, London SW12 9ER **Tel:** 44 02086 739666
Email: info@exportagroup.com
Web site: www.gtreview.com
Freq: Bi-Monthly
Circ: 10000 Not Audited
Profile: Magazine featuring the market's key banks, credit and political risk insurers, corporates, traders, law firms, brokers and consultants with news, leads and analysis on global emerging markets trade, commodity and export finance and risk. Aimed at bankers, trade financiers, credit and political risk insurers, corporates, traders, law firms, brokers and consultants.
MAGAZINE
Banking

Global Turnaround
980159

Editorial: The Stables, Charlcombe Lane, Bath BA1 8DS **Tel:** 44 01225 421273
Email: info@globalturnaround.com
Web site: www.globalturnaround.com
Freq: Monthly Not Audited
Profile: Global Turnaround is a monthly magazine for company rescue and bankruptcy specialists.
MAGAZINE
Corporate Management, Hedge Funds, Investment Banking, Private Equity

Global Water Intelligence
983235

Editorial: Kingsmead House, Oxpens Road, Oxford OX1 1XX **Tel:** 44 01865 204208

Web site: www.globalwaterintel.com
Freq: Monthly
Circ: 4500 Not Audited
Editor: Ian Elkins
Profile: Newsletter providing analysis and strategic data on the international water market.
Ad Rate: Full Page Colour £3300.00
MAGAZINE
Water & Sanitation

GlobalCapital
979838

Editorial: 8 Bouverie Street, London EC4Y 8AX **Tel:** 44 02077 798888
Web site: www.globalcapital.com
Freq: Weekly
Circ: 11570 Not Audited
Editor: Ralph Sinclair
Profile: Publication providing news on deals, people, and the driving forces behind international capital markets. Aimed at executives in the international capital markets.
Ad Rate: Full Page Colour £9250.00
MAGAZINE
Bonds, Corporate Finance, Corporate Management, Credit Markets, Derivatives, Emerging Markets, Equities, Foreign Exchange Market (FOREX), Government, Lending

GlobalCapital Derivatives
998146

Editorial: Nestor House, Playhouse Yard, London EC4V 5HX **Tel:** 44 02077 798888
Web site: www.globalcapital.com/ derivatives
Freq: Daily
Circ: 19227 Cision Digital Reach
MAGAZINE (ONLINE)
Derivatives

GlobalCapital Securitization
990359

Editorial: 8 Bouverie Street, London EC4Y 8AX **Tel:** 44 02077 798888
Web site: www.globalcapital.com/ securitization
Freq: Daily
Circ: 16428 Cision Digital Reach
MAGAZINE (ONLINE)
Bonds, Corporate Finance, Corporate Management, Lending

GlobalCustody.net
995783

Tel: 44 02073 623000
Web site: www.globalcustody.net
Freq: Daily
Circ: 15600 Cision Digital Reach
MAGAZINE (ONLINE)
Accounting, Banking

GlobalRMB
987896

Editorial: GlobalCapital RMB, 8 Bouverie Street, London EC4Y 8AX
Tel: 44 02077 798888
Web site: www.globalcapital.com/rmb
Freq: Daily
Circ: 353 Cision Digital Reach
MAGAZINE (ONLINE)
Financial Markets, Foreign Exchange Market (FOREX)

The Globe and Laurel
983175

Editorial: HMS Excellent, Whale Island, Portsmouth PO2 8ER **Tel:** 44 02392 547208
Email: royalsmag@btconnect.com
Web site: http://www.rmctf.org.uk/globe-laurel.php
Freq: Bi-Monthly
Circ: 12500 Not Audited
Editor: Graham Adcock RM
MAGAZINE
Defense & National Security

GM
994702

Editorial: Rayford House, School Road, Hove, Brighton BN3 5HX
Tel: 44 01273 434943
Email: info@pavpub.com
Web site: www.gmjournal.co.uk
Freq: Monthly

Circ: 23000 Not Audited
MAGAZINE
Geriatrics

GM Business Connect
997955

Editorial: 8 Eastway, Sale, Manchester M33 4DX **Tel:** 44 01619 698632
Email: editorial@gmbusinessconnect.co.uk
Web site: http://www.gmbusinessconnect. co.uk/
Freq: Bi-Monthly
Circ: 5000 Not Audited
MAGAZINE
Business, Small and Medium Business

GM2
988591

Editorial: Rayford House, School Road, Hove BN3 5HX **Tel:** 44 01273 434943
Email: info@pavpub.com
Web site: www.gmjournal.co.uk
Freq: Monthly Not Audited
Profile: Journal covering specific therapy areas, with each issue looking at a different theme, including heart and diabetes, neurology and psychiatry, gender and oncology and palliative care.
MAGAZINE
News & Current Affairs

GMA Talkback
998645

Editorial: 127 Gloucester Road, Brighton BN1 4AF
Web site: www.the-gma.com
Freq: Bi-Monthly
Circ: 24000 Not Audited
Editor: Sally Hooton
MAGAZINE
Marketing

Go!Public
984163

Editorial: Kingfishers Retreat, The Lodges, Dunston Business Village, Stafford ST18 9AB **Tel:** 44 1785 711591
Email: james@l2media.co.uk
Web site: http://link2media.co.uk/
Freq: Quarterly
Circ: 7000 Not Audited
MAGAZINE
Architecture & Design, Building & Construction

The Good Property Guide
985902

Editorial: 23 Austin Friars, London EC2N 2QP **Tel:** 44 02035 863353
Web site: www.thegoodpropertyguide.com
Freq: Bi-Monthly
Circ: 320000 Not Audited
Profile: Magazine covering property, featuring a regular celebrity interview, up to date property and travel news with homes for sale or rent from around the world. Aimed at affluent individuals with a high disposable income.
MAGAZINE
Residential Real Estate, Travel Industry

Gorkana News
996004

Editorial: 5 Churchill Place, Canary Wharf, London E14 5HU **Tel:** 44 02076 740200
Email: communityteam@gorkana.com
Web site: http://www.gorkana.com/news/? nav_location=main_menu
Freq: Daily
Circ: 18 Cision Digital Reach
MAGAZINE (ONLINE)
Branding, Marketing, Publishing

GOVERNANCE
985817

Editorial: Governance Publishing & Information Services Ltd, The Old Stables, Market Street, Burnham-on-Sea TA9 3BP
Tel: 44 01278 793300
Email: info@governance.co.uk
Web site: www.governance.co.uk
Freq: Monthly
Circ: 360 Not Audited
Profile: Magazine covering all aspects of charity governance including model documents, legal, financial and charity commission updates, legal and financial matters and practical advice.
MAGAZINE
Business, Small and Medium Business

Governance + Compliance
981076

Editorial: Saffron House, 6-10 Kirby Street, London EC1N 8TS **Tel:** 44 02075 804741
Web site: www.icsa.org.uk/knowledge/ governance-and-compliance
Freq: Monthly
Circ: 12800 Not Audited
Profile: Magazine containing features and news of interest to chartered and company secretaries and other business professionals in company, charity and local government administration. Focusing on corporate governance, legal compliance and business law and ethics. Read by chartered and company secretaries, company directors and senior managers, local government and charity managers and administration workers and other business professionals in all sectors.Digital images only.
Ad Rate: Full Page Colour £3510.00
MAGAZINE
Business, Corporate Responsibility, Human Resources

Government Business
981599

Editorial: 226 High Road, Loughton, London IG10 1ET **Tel:** 44 02085 320055
Email: editorial@psigroupltd.co.uk
Web site: www.governmentbusiness.co.uk
Freq: Bi-Monthly
Circ: 10345 Not Audited
Profile: Journal covering public sector and privatised utility financial and administrative issues. Aimed at chief executives, finance directors, facilities managers and other senior executives within local and central government, health service and other regulated utilities.
Ad Rate: Full Page Colour £2495.00
MAGAZINE
Government, Public Sector

Government Opportunities (GO)
981514

Editorial: Medius, 60 Pacific Quay, Glasgow G51 1DZ **Tel:** 44 01412 707379
Email: feedback@govopps.co.uk
Web site: www.govopps.co.uk
Freq: Daily
Circ: 14023 Cision Digital Reach
MAGAZINE (ONLINE)
Government

GPAUK Magazine
996290

Editorial: 49 Greek Street, London W1D 4EG **Tel:** 44 02038 718878
Email: contact@gpa-uk.org
Web site: www.gpa-uk.org
Freq: Monthly
Circ: 30000 Not Audited
MAGAZINE
Company News & Appointments, Human Resources, Recruiting

Graduate Recruiter
996262

Editorial: 6 Bath Place, Rivington Street, London EC2A 3JE **Tel:** 44 02070 332460
Email: info@agr.org.uk
Web site: www.agr.org.uk
Freq: Bi-Monthly
Circ: 800 Not Audited
Editor: Tej Rai
MAGAZINE
Education, Higher Education, Students

Greater Manchester Business Week
985818

Editorial: Mitchell Henry House, Hollinwood Avenue, Chadderton, Oldham OL9 8EF
Tel: 44 01618 327200
Email: businessdesk@men-news.co.uk
Web site: www.gmbw.co.uk
Freq: Weekly
Circ: 12500 Not Audited
MAGAZINE
Business

Green Building
983356

Editorial: PO Box 32, Llandysul, Llandysul SA44 5ZA **Tel:** 44 01559 370798
Email: editor@greenbuildingpress.co.uk
Web site: www.greenbuildingpress.co.uk

Business Magazines

Freq: Quarterly
Circ: 5000 Not Audited
Editor: Keith Hall
Profile: Supplement of Renewable Energy Focus.
MAGAZINE
Sustainable Development

Green Chemistry　986653
Editorial: Royal Society of Chemistry, Thomas Graham House, Science Park, Milton Road, Cambridge CB4 0WF
Tel: 44 01223 420066
Email: green@rsc.org
Web site: pubs.rsc.org/en/journals/journalissues/gc
Freq: Monthly Not Audited
Profile: Journal assessing the surge in research and development of clean technology systems. Includes items on the design of more eco-friendly chemicals, materials and technologies, measurement analysis systems, waste reduction options and news and legislative matters.
Ad Rate: Full Page Mono £890.00
MAGAZINE
Chemicals, Environment, Science

Green Print　1053545
Email: hello@earthisland.co.uk
Web site: www.earthisland.co.uk/#!greenprint/cjij
Freq: Quarterly
Circ: 6800 Not Audited
MAGAZINE
Environment, Publishing

GREEN.TV　986783
Editorial: Salter Brothers, Folly Bridge, Oxford OX1 4LB Tel: 44 01865 236167
Email: contact@green.tv
Web site: www.green.tv
Freq: Daily
Circ: 6603 Cision Digital Reach
MAGAZINE (ONLINE)
Environment

GreenAir　997575
Editorial: 4 Loveday Road, London W13 9JS
Email: editorial@greenaironline.com
Web site: www.greenaironline.com
Freq: Daily
Circ: 33218 Cision Digital Reach
Editor: Christopher Surgenor
MAGAZINE (ONLINE)
Aviation, Environment

GreenHotelier　984027
Editorial: c/o Business in the Community, 137 Shepherdess Walk, London N1 7RQ
Tel: 44 02075 666664
Email: info@greenhotelier.org
Web site: www.greenhotelier.org
Freq: Daily
Circ: 25277 Cision Digital Reach
MAGAZINE (ONLINE)
Environment, Hotels/Motels

Greenkeeping　1006321
Editorial: Unit 122, 30 Great Guilford Street, London SE1 0HS Tel: 44 02078 032420
Email: info@unionpress.co.uk
Web site: http://www.greenkeepingeu.com
Freq: Monthly
Circ: 9000 Not Audited
Editor: Alistair Dunsmuir
MAGAZINE
Fitness & Exercise, Golf

GreenPort　999123
Editorial: Spinnaker House, Waterside Gardens, Fareham PO16 8SD
Tel: 44 01329 825335
Email: editor@greenport.com
Web site: www.greenport.com
Freq: Quarterly
Circ: 5504 Not Audited
MAGAZINE
Environment, Shipping & Warehousing

Greetings Today　981293
Editorial: Naishville, 1 Churchgates, The Wilderness, Berkhamsted, Berkhamsted HP4 2UB Tel: 44 01442 289930
Web site: http://www.greetingstoday.co.uk/
Freq: Monthly
Circ: 6093 Not Audited
Editor: Tracey Bearton
Profile: Greetings Today is a magazine covering news, developments and in-depth features on the greetings card industry, including 3D printing.
Ad Rate: Full Page Colour £1375.00
MAGAZINE
Office Supplies

Grinding & Surface Finishing Magazine　983335
Editorial: Enterprise House, Foundry Lane, Horsham, Horsham RH13 5PX
Tel: 44 01403 266022
Email: roger@rbpublishing.co.uk
Web site: http://www.rbpublishing.co.uk/grindsurf/
Freq: Bi-Monthly
Circ: 10000 Not Audited
Editor: Roger Barber
MAGAZINE
Engineering

The Grocery Trader　983073
Editorial: 12 Kings Park, Primrose Hill, Kings Langley, London WD4 8ST
Tel: 44 01923 272960
Email: grocery@flame1.com
Web site: www.grocerytrader.co.uk
Freq: Monthly
Circ: 5086 Not Audited
Profile: Newsletter covering all aspects of the UK grocery trade including product information, market news and company news from retailers and suppliers.
Ad Rate: Full Page Colour £1690.00
MAGAZINE
Food

Ground Engineering　983090
Editorial: 3 / 4th Floor, Telephone House, 69-77 Paul Street, London EC2A 4NQ
Tel: 44 02030 332818
Web site: www.geplus.co.uk
Freq: Monthly
Circ: 3000 Not Audited
Editor: Claire Smith
Profile: Journal of the British Geotechnical Association. Concerned with the practical application of soil and rock mechanics in the construction of foundations, underground chambers and tunnels and engineering geology.
Ad Rate: Full Page Colour £2285.00
MAGAZINE
Building & Construction, Engineering, Sustainable Development

Ground Handling International　981344
Editorial: The Stables, Willow Lane, Paddock Wood, Maidstone TN12 6PF
Tel: 44 01322 221144
Web site: www.groundhandling.com
Freq: Bi-Monthly
Circ: 8417 Not Audited
Editor: Alwyn Brice
Profile: Magazine concentrating on the international ground handling industry. Covers handling issues including, health and safety, technology, legislation, new products and interviews with senior industry figures.
Ad Rate: Full Page Mono £5100.00
Ad Rate: Full Page Colour £6675.00
MAGAZINE
Aviation

Growing Business　980016
Editorial: Block C, Imperial Works, Perren St, London NW5 3ED Tel: 44 02071 833932
Email: hello@startups.co.uk
Web site: http://startups.co.uk/growingbusiness/
Freq: Daily
Circ: 63412 Cision Digital Reach

Editor: Lucy Wayment
MAGAZINE (ONLINE)
Business, Corporate Responsibility

Growth Company Investor　980776
Editorial: Vitesse Media Plc, 5th Floor, 14 Bonhill Street, London EC2A 4BX
Tel: 44 02072 507010
Email: gci@vitessemedia.co.uk
Web site: www.growthcompany.co.uk
Freq: Monthly
Circ: 800 Not Audited
Editor: David Thornton
MAGAZINE
Equities, Financial Markets

GrowthBusiness.co.uk　983346
Editorial: Vitesse Media Plc, 5th Floor, 14 Bonhill Street, London EC2A 4BX
Tel: 44 02072 507010
Web site: www.growthbusiness.co.uk
Freq: Daily
Circ: 165125 Cision Digital Reach
Editor: Praseeda Nair
Profile: Website covering business. The growbusiness.co.uk provides news and analysis for entrepreneurs investing in a growth company.
MAGAZINE (ONLINE)
Business, Corporate Responsibility

Gulf Fire　1054156
Tel: 44 01935 426428
Email: duncan.white@mdmpublishing.com
Web site: www.gulffire.mdmpublishing.com/
Freq: Quarterly
Circ: 8000 Not Audited
MAGAZINE
Health & Safety, Security & Security Systems

guru3d.com　995012
Email: news@guru3d.com
Web site: www.guru3d.com
Freq: Daily
Circ: 3802060 Cision Digital Reach
MAGAZINE (ONLINE)
Computers

Gut　999102
Editorial: BMJ Journals Department, BMA House, Tavistock Square, London WC1H 9JR Tel: 44 02073 836318
Email: info.gut@bmj.com
Web site: gut.bmj.com/
Freq: Monthly
Circ: 2950 Not Audited
Editor: Emad El-Omar
MAGAZINE
Gastroenterology

Gwlad　983573
Editorial: Welsh Government, Cathays Park, Cardiff CF10 3NQ Tel: 44 02920 823787
Email: gwlad@wales.gsi.gov.uk
Web site: www.gwladonline.org
Freq: Bi-Monthly
Circ: 38000 Not Audited
Profile: Provides agricultural and rural affairs information from the Welsh Assembly Government.
MAGAZINE
Animal Farming

H&V News　981113
Editorial: 3 / 4th Floor, Telephone House, 69-77 Paul Street, London EC2A 4NQ
Tel: 44 02030 332600
Email: hvneditorial@emap.com
Web site: www.hvnplus.co.uk
Freq: Bi-Weekly
Circ: 10450 Not Audited
Profile: Magazine covering all aspects of heating, ventilating and air conditioning. Aimed at people working in the industry.
Ad Rate: Full Page Colour £2640.00
MAGAZINE
Building & Construction

Hali　98324
Editorial: HALI Publications Ltd, 8 Ability Plaza, Arbutus Street, London E8 4DT
Tel: 44 02037 274940
Email: hali.admin@hali.com
Web site: www.hali.com
Freq: Quarterly
Circ: 5000 Not Audited
Editor: Ben Evans; Editor: Lucy Upward
Profile: Magazine focusing on international carpet, textile and Islamic art. Aimed at professional traders, academics, museum curators, collectors, amateur enthusiasts and designers.
Ad Rate: Full Page Colour £1570.00
MAGAZINE
Interior Design

Hampshire Chamber Business News　996477
Editorial: Southampton Solent University, Sir James Matthews Building, 157-187 Above Bar Street, Southampton SO14 7NH
Tel: 44 02380 206150
Web site: www.hampshirechamber.co.uk/events-and-news/news/magazine/
Freq: Monthly
Circ: 4500 Not Audited
Editor: Lorraine Gourley
MAGAZINE
Business

Hampshire Legal　999611
Editorial: 3tc House, 16 Crosby North Road, Crosby, Crosby L22 0NY
Tel: 44 01512 364141
Email: admin@benhampublishing.com
Web site: www.benhampublishing.com
Freq: Quarterly
Circ: 1200 Not Audited
MAGAZINE
Corporate Law, Government, Legal Services

Handling & Storage Solutions　981326
Editorial: 2nd Floor - North Suite, Kings House, 13-21 Cantelupe Road, East Grinstead, East Grinstead RH19 3BE
Tel: 44 01342 314300
Web site: www.hsssearch.com
Freq: Monthly
Circ: 16000 Not Audited
Editor: Simon Duddy
Profile: Magazine covering products and services related to materials, handling, storage, conveying, packaging, health and safety and premises management.
Ad Rate: Full Page Mono £1935.00
Ad Rate: Full Page Colour £1935.00
MAGAZINE
Supply Chain Management (SCM)

Handy Shipping Guide　990676
Tel: 44 01702 421188
Email: newsdesk@handyshippingguide.com
Web site: www.handyshippingguide.com
Freq: Daily
Circ: 31509 Cision Digital Reach
Profile: Website covering reasonable amount of information on any freight linked company completely free of charge in an effort to extend and improve the value of the guide to all interested parties.
MAGAZINE (ONLINE)
Shipping & Warehousing, Supply Chain Management (SCM)

HardCopy　981643
Editorial: Prigg Meadow, Ashburton, Ashburton TQ13 7DF Tel: 44 01364 654100
Email: maildesk@greymatter.com
Web site: www.greymatter.com/corporate/hardcopy
Freq: 3 Times/Year
Circ: 9000 Not Audited
Editor: Matt Nicholson
Profile: Grey Matter customer magazine that focuses on software development including product reviews. Established in 1999, HardCopy Magazine is independently written for IT professionals featuring interviews, reviews and news from the world of IT. Provides articles and Buyers Guides offering

advice on a wide range of topics designed to keep you up to date with the latest software offerings, news on products, software and licensing, interviews with leading publishers and competitions. HardCopy is sent in printed format to 18,000 customers who have requested the magazine. Grey Matter has been publishing HardCopy since January 2000, and in November 2010 they will be publishing the 50th issue.Aimed at software professionals.
Ad Rate: Full Page Colour £3200.00
MAGAZINE
Data Management, Software

The HARLEY STREET JOURNAL
998291
Editorial: The Custard Factory, 231 Zellig Building, Birmingham B9 4AA
Web site: theharleystreetjournal.co.uk
Freq: Bi-Monthly Not Audited
Editor: Laura Casewell
MAGAZINE
Plastic/Reconstructive/Cosmetic Surgery

Hays Journal
995100
Editorial: 5th Floor, Drury House, 34-43 Russell Street, London WC2B 5HA
Tel: 44 02070 100999
Email: haysjournal@hays.com
Web site: http://www.hays.co.uk/hays-journal/index.htm
Freq: Semi-Annual
Circ: 25000 Not Audited
MAGAZINE
Recruiting

HazardEx
983194
Editorial: Blair House, 184/186 High Street, Tonbridge, Tonbridge TN9 1BQ
Tel: 44 01732 359990
Email: hazardex@imlgroup.co.uk
Web site: www.hazardexonthenet.net
Freq: Monthly
Circ: 40000 Not Audited
Editor: Alan Franck
MAGAZINE
Engineering

Hazardous Cargo Bulletin
981013
Editorial: Cargo Media Ltd, Marlborough House, 298 Regents Park Road, London N3 2SZ **Tel:** 44 02083 714000
Web site: www.hazardouscargo.com
Freq: Monthly
Circ: 7000 Not Audited
Profile: International journal dealing with the handling, storage and transport of hazardous materials by all modes.
Ad Rate: Full Page Colour £2925.00
MAGAZINE
Shipping & Warehousing

Hazards
980940
Editorial: PO Box 4042, Sheffield S8 2DG
Tel: 44 01142 014265
Email: editor@hazards.org
Web site: www.hazards.org
Freq: Quarterly
Circ: 9000 Not Audited
Editor: Rory O'Neill
Profile: Magazine focusing on workplace health and safety. Targets workplace unions providing the information and resources to make the unions job easier.
Ad Rate: Full Page Mono £850.00
MAGAZINE
Health & Safety

headoftrading.com
995148
Editorial: 31 -35 Kirby Street, London EC1N 8TE **Tel:** 44 02074 921957
Email: editor@headoftrading.com
Web site: www.headoftrading.com
Freq: Daily
Circ: 13173 Cision Digital Reach
MAGAZINE (ONLINE)
Commodities, Derivatives, Financial Markets

Health & Safety International
985263
Editorial: 1 Oxford Court, The Granby, Weymouth, Weymouth DT4 0GH
Tel: 44 01305 785199
Email: info@hsimagazine.com
Web site: www.hsimagazine.com
Freq: Bi-Monthly
Circ: 8263 Not Audited
Editor: Kimberley de Selincourt
MAGAZINE
Health & Safety

Health & Safety Matters
981126
Editorial: Second Floor, North Suit, 13 - 21 Cantelupe Road, East Grinstead, East Grinstead RH19 3BE **Tel:** 44 01342 314300
Email: admin@western-bp.co.uk
Web site: www.hsmsearch.com
Freq: Bi-Monthly
Circ: 18000 Not Audited
Editor: Catherine Hackett; **Editor:** Chris Shaw
Profile: Magazine containing product news and features on all matters relating to health and safety in the industrial manufacturing workplace. The magazine provides product and service solutions as well as industry guidance and opinions. It looks at the sourcing of health and safety products, services and solutions. Aimed at those with specific health and safety responsibility such as health and safety managers and those who find health and safety part of their overall responsibility.Alternative Title: HSM
Ad Rate: Full Page Colour £1950.00
MAGAZINE
Health & Safety

Health & Safety Middle East
985831
Editorial: 1 Oxford Court, The Granby, Weymouth, Weymouth DT4 9GH
Tel: 44 01305 785199
Email: info@hsmemagazine.com
Web site: www.hsmemagazine.com
Freq: Bi-Monthly
Circ: 7282 Not Audited
Editor: Kimberley de Selincourt
MAGAZINE
Health & Safety

Health & Social Care in the Community
998704
Editorial: 9600 Garsington Road, Oxford OX4 2DQ
Email: hsc@wiley.com
Web site: onlinelibrary.wiley.com/journal/10.1111/(ISSN)1365-2524;jsessionid=6459AD6DE0673B4924892BD3AAADC17C
Freq: Bi-Monthly Not Audited
Editor: Karen Luker
MAGAZINE
Community Care (UK)

Health and Safety at Work
981125
Editorial: 13th Floor, Quadrant House, Brighton Road, Sutton SM6 5AS
Email: healthandsafety@lexisnexis.co.uk
Web site: www.healthandsafetyatwork.com
Freq: Monthly
Circ: 18593 Not Audited
Profile: Magazine containing coverage of occupational health and safety in all public and private sectors, including working environment matters in the UK and Europe. Features incisive news reports and insight into topical occupational health and safety issues. It provides need-to-know information on prosecutions as well as information on how to stay compliant. The magazine was first published in 1978. This outlet offers RSS (Really Simple Syndication).Read by health and safety managers, consultants, safety representatives and facilities/environment managers. Alternative Title: HSW magazinePhotographs are preferred in digital format.
Ad Rate: Full Page Mono £1755.00
Ad Rate: Full Page Colour £1840.00
MAGAZINE
Health & Safety

Health and Safety Bulletin
997930
Web site: https://store.lexisnexis.co.uk/categories/legal/health-amp-safety-38/health-and-safety-bulletin-skuu
Freq: Monthly Not Audited
MAGAZINE
Health & Safety

Health Business
980992
Editorial: 226 High Road, Loughton, London IG10 1ET **Tel:** 44 02085 320055
Email: editorial@psigroupltd.co.uk
Web site: www.healthbusinessuk.com
Freq: Bi-Monthly
Circ: 7162 Not Audited
MAGAZINE
Health Administration, Healthcare Industry

Health Economics
986056
Editorial: The Atrium, Southern Gate, Chichester PO19 8QG **Tel:** 44 01865 778315
Email: cs-journals@wiley.com
Web site: http://onlinelibrary.wiley.com/journal/10.1002/%28ISSN%291099-1050
Freq: Monthly Not Audited
Profile: Scientific journal covering all aspects of health economics including: theoretical contributions, empirical studies and analyses of health policy from the economic perspective.
MAGAZINE
Healthcare Industry, Pharmaceuticals

Health Estate Journal
983983
Editorial: Step House, North Farm Road, Tunbridge Wells, Tunbridge Wells TN2 3DR
Tel: 44 01892 779999
Email: hej@stepcomms.com
Web site: www.healthestatejournal.com
Freq: Monthly
Circ: 5000 Not Audited
Editor: Jonathan Baillie
MAGAZINE
Health Administration, Healthcare Industry

Health Insurance Daily
980734
Editorial: Informa Business Information, Christchurch Court, 10 Newgate Street, London EC1A 7AZ **Tel:** 44 02070 174214
Email: news@hi-mag.com
Web site: www.healthinsurancedaily.com
Freq: Daily
Circ: 17902 Cision Digital Reach
Editor: David Sawers
MAGAZINE (ONLINE)
Insurance

Health Policy
996139
Editorial: Elsevier Ltd, The Boulevard, Langford Lane, Kidlington OX5 1GB
Tel: 44 01865 843000
Email: heap@elsevier.com
Web site: http://www.healthpolicyjrnl.com/current
Freq: Monthly
Circ: 35538 Not Audited
MAGAZINE
Health Administration

Health Policy and Planning
981041
Tel: 44 02076 368636
Email: hpp.editorialoffice@oup.com
Web site: www.heapol.oupjournals.org
Freq: Bi-Monthly Not Audited
MAGAZINE
Health Administration

Health Policy Insight
986883
Editorial: 105 Priory Road, Hampton, London TW12 2QB
Email: editorial@healthpolicyinsight.com
Web site: www.healthpolicyinsight.com
Freq: Daily
Circ: 13214 Cision Digital Reach
MAGAZINE (ONLINE)
Health Administration

Health Service Journal
979944
Editorial: 6-14 Underwood Street, London N1 7JQ **Tel:** 44 02074 900049
Email: hsjnews@wilmingtonhealthcare.com
Web site: www.hsj.co.uk
Freq: Weekly
Circ: 17000 Not Audited
Editor: Alastair McLellan
Profile: Magazine focusing on all aspects of health policy and management. Containing news and features, special reports and political commentary. Read by managers predominantly working in the NHS.
Ad Rate: Full Page Colour £6180.00
MAGAZINE
Government, Health Administration, Public Sector

Health, Risk & Society
998912
Editorial: 4 Park Square, Milton Park, Abingdon, Didcot OX14 4RN
Tel: 44 02070 176000
Web site: www.tandf.co.uk/journals/journal.asp?issn=1369-8575&linktype=1
Freq: Bi-Monthly Not Audited
Editor: Andy Alaszewski
MAGAZINE
Health Administration

Healthcare Business
984029
Tel: 44 07568 399995
Web site: http://healthcarebusiness.co.uk/
Freq: Monthly
Circ: 24000 Not Audited
Editor: Vivien Shepherd
Profile: Magazine covering the healthcare and care home sector.
MAGAZINE
Healthcare Industry

Healthcare Business International
995957
Editorial: 4B Thane Works, London N7 7NU
Tel: 44 02071 833779
Email: max@healthcareeuropa.com
Web site: www.healthcareeuropa.com
Freq: Monthly Not Audited
Editor: David Farbrother
MAGAZINE
Health Administration, Healthcare Industry

Healthcare Counselling and Psychotherapy Journal
999842
Editorial: Healthcare Team, BACP House, 15 St John's Business Park, Lutterworth LE17 4AB **Tel:** 44 01455 883300
Email: hcpj.editorial@bacp.co.uk
Web site: www.bacphealthcare.org.uk/journal.php
Freq: Quarterly
Circ: 1239 Not Audited
Editor: Sarah Hovington
MAGAZINE
Neurology

healthcare design & management
985943
Editorial: SBC House, Restmor Way, Wallington, London SM6 7AH
Tel: 44 02082 881080
Email: info@healthcaredm.co.uk
Web site: www.healthcaredm.co.uk
Freq: Bi-Monthly
Circ: 8295 Not Audited
Editor: Jo Makosinski
Profile: Magazine aimed at those involved in the planning, design, construction and management of healthcare buildings. It focuses on the latest new build and redevelopment schemes, highlighting the best design ideas along with news, views and in-depth analysis of healthcare funding and strategy.
Ad Rate: Full Page Colour £1875.00
MAGAZINE
Architecture & Design, Building & Construction

Healthcare Finance
988910
Editorial: 1 Temple Way, Bristol BS2 0BU
Tel: 44 01179 294789
Email: info@hfma.org.uk

Business Magazines

Web site: www.hfma.org.uk/news/healthcare-finance
Freq: Monthly
Circ: 5000 Not Audited
Editor: Steve Brown
Profile: Magazine covering healthcare finance. Aimed at members of the Healthcare Financial Management Association.
Ad Rate: Full Page Colour £3000.00
MAGAZINE
Health Administration, Healthcare Industry

Healthcare Global　996838
Editorial: Ground Floor, East Wing, 69-75 Thorpe Road, Norwich NR1 1UA
Tel: 44 01603 217530
Email: info@bizclikmedia.com
Web site: www.healthcareglobal.com
Freq: Monthly
Circ: 49869 Cision Digital Reach
MAGAZINE (ONLINE)
Healthcare Industry

Healthcare Markets　980799
Editorial: 29 Angel Gate, City Road, London EC1V 2PT **Tel:** 44 02078 339123
Email: maria@laingbuisson.co.uk
Web site: http://www.laingbuisson.co.uk/Newsletters/HMN.aspx
Freq: Monthly
Circ: 1000 Not Audited
Editor: Maria Davies
Profile: Newsletter reporting news and developments in the provision and funding of acute and primary healthcare. Includes analysis of companies in the sector, plus reports on the NHS, primary care and trends in private medical insurance.
Ad Rate: Full Page Mono £2100.00
Ad Rate: Full Page Colour £2100.00
MAGAZINE
Health Administration, Healthcare Industry

HealthInvestor Asia　998314
Editorial: Greener House, 66-68 Haymarket, London SW1Y 4RF **Tel:** 44 02071 042000
Email: adrian.murdoch@healthinvestorasia.com
Web site: www.healthinvestorasia.com
Freq: Daily
Circ: 11345 Cision Digital Reach
Editor: Adrian Murdoch
MAGAZINE (ONLINE)
Dentistry, Health Administration, Healthcare Industry, Medicine, Ophthalmology & Optometry

heart　999028
Editorial: BMJ Journals Department, BMA House, Tavistock Square, London WC1H 9JR **Tel:** 44 02073 836235
Email: info.heart@bmj.com
Web site: http://heart.bmj.com/
Freq: Bi-Weekly Not Audited
MAGAZINE
Cardiology

Heat Pumps Today　984988
Editorial: The Maltings, West Street, Bourne, Bourne PE10 9PH **Tel:** 44 01778 391000
Web site: www.heatpumps.media
Freq: Daily
Profile: Magazine covering the heat pump water heater, a new technology that is entering the domestic and light commercial sector and challenging the position of the condensing boiler as the most energy efficient solution for underfloor and sanitary hot water. Features include news of the latest products, instillation tips, guidance on legislation, case studies and updates on the industry's movers and shakers.
Ad Rate: Full Page Colour £1418.00
MAGAZINE (ONLINE)
Building & Construction, Commercial Real Estate, Interior Design, Residential Real Estate

Heathrow News　998869
Editorial: PO Box 258, Maidenhead, Maidenhead SL6 9YR **Tel:** 44 01628 482763
Email: info@airtimetv.co.uk

Web site: http://www.heathrownews.com/
Freq: Daily
Circ: 9802 Cision Digital Reach
Editor: Martin White
MAGAZINE (ONLINE)
Aviation

Heating & Plumbing Monthly　981114
Editorial: The Manor, Nepicar House, London Road, Wrotham Heath, Sevenoaks, Sevenoaks TN15 7RS **Tel:** 44 01732 748000
Web site: http://www.hpmmag.com/hpm-magazine
Freq: Monthly
Circ: 30450 Not Audited
Editor: Tim Wood
Profile: Magazine that provides up-to-date information on the latest equipment, developments, methods, product testing plus technical advice on installation and specification in heating and plumbing sector.
Ad Rate: Full Page Colour £2400.00
MAGAZINE
Building & Construction, Interior Design

Heating, Ventilating and Plumbing　981115
Editorial: 32 Vauxhall Bridge Road, London SW1V 2SS **Tel:** 44 02079 736400
Web site: www.hvpmag.co.uk
Freq: Monthly
Circ: 35283 Not Audited
MAGAZINE
Building & Construction, Interior Design

Heavy Lift & Project Forwarding International　987291
Editorial: Flint Research Institute Building, 132 Heathfield Road, Keston, London BR2 6BA **Tel:** 44 01689 857631
Email: editorial@heavyliftpfi.com
Web site: www.heavyliftpfi.com
Freq: Bi-Monthly
Circ: 15500 Not Audited
Editor: Ian Matheson
Profile: Magazine covering logistics of over-dimensional and heavy cargoes including information across the whole range of transport modes, news, interviews with prominent industry figures and topical features. Aimed at professionals involved in the business of moving heavy, out-of-gauge, and project cargo.
Ad Rate: Full Page Colour £3995.00
MAGAZINE
Shipping & Warehousing

Hedge Fund Insight　987726
Tel: 44 07977 445496
Email: simon.kerr@hedgefundinsight.org
Web site: www.hedgefundinsight.org
Freq: Daily
Circ: 3985 Cision Digital Reach
MAGAZINE (ONLINE)
Hedge Funds

The Hedge Fund Journal　981010
Editorial: 3 Gough Square, London EC4A 3DE **Tel:** 44 02079 362192
Web site: www.thehedgefundjournal.com
Freq: Monthly
Circ: 1500 Not Audited
Profile: Journal covering news, features and technical analysis relating to hedge fund investment. The publication also includes detailed profiles and interviews with news summaries, commentary, research, expert opinion and analysis and special reports. Aimed at managers of hedge funds and investors.
MAGAZINE
Hedge Funds

HedgeWeek　981507
Editorial: GFM Ltd, Floor 1, Liberation Station, St Helier, St. Helier JE2 3AS
Tel: 44 01534 719780
Email: editor@globalfundmedia.com
Web site: www.hedgeweek.com
Freq: Daily

Circ: 46356 Cision Digital Reach
MAGAZINE (ONLINE)
Hedge Funds

The HefmA Pulse　985308
Editorial: 4th Floor, Joynes House, New Road, Gravesend DA11 0AJ
Tel: 44 08455 006008
Email: editor@hefmapulse.co.uk
Web site: www.hefma.co.uk
Freq: Bi-Monthly
Circ: 5112 Not Audited
Editor: Amanda Roberts
Profile: Official magazine of HefmA. Covers the latest news in the healthcare facilities industry.
MAGAZINE
Health Administration

Helicopter International　983140
Editorial: 75 Elm Tree Road, Locking, Weston-super-Mare BS24 8EL
Tel: 44 01934 822524
Email: editorial@aviapress.co.uk
Web site: http://www.aviapress.co.uk/hi.htm
Freq: Bi-Monthly
Circ: 25000 Not Audited
Editor: Elfan ap Rees
Profile: Journal covering helicopter operations and safety, international defence, new civil sales, accidents and offshore European operations.
Ad Rate: Full Page Mono £3152.00
Ad Rate: Full Page Colour £4355.00
MAGAZINE
Aviation

Helicopter Life　983165
Editorial: 59 Great Ormond Street, London WC1N 3HZ
Email: editor@helicopterlife.com
Web site: www.helicopterlife.com
Freq: Quarterly
Circ: 5000 Not Audited
Editor: Georgina Hunter-Jones
MAGAZINE
Aviation

Hepatic Oncology　1054409
Editorial: Unitec House, 2 Albert Place, London N3 1QB **Tel:** 44 02083 716090
Email: info@future-science-group.com
Web site: http://www.futuremedicine.com/loi/hep
Freq: Quarterly
MAGAZINE
Oncology

Hertfordshire Business Directory　996054
Editorial: Suite 6B(i), Britannia House, Leagrave Road, Luton LU3 1RJ
Tel: 44 01582 488385
Email: info@mediachameleon.co.uk
Web site: www.hertsbusinessesdirectory.co.uk
Freq: Annual Not Audited
MAGAZINE
Business, Small and Medium Business

The Hertfordshire Business Independent　986455
Editorial: 2 Fountain Court, Victoria Square, St Albans, London AL1 3TF
Tel: 44 08443 585800
Email: info@businessindependent.co.uk
Web site: http://www.businessindependent.co.uk/
Freq: Monthly
Circ: 35000 Not Audited
Editor: Jenna Gould
MAGAZINE
Business

Herts Director　982907
Editorial: 14 Middletons Road, Yaxley, Peterborough PE7 3LR
Tel: 44 01733 242312
Email: info@pridepublications.co.uk
Web site: www.pridepublications.co.uk
Freq: Quarterly
Circ: 3000 Not Audited
Editor: Trevor Gehlcken

Profile: Magazine covering local news, business views and general interest features. Launched 1999, Herts Director is mailed to over 3,000 CEOs and senior partners in Hertfordshire and Luton.
Ad Rate: Full Page Mono £675.00
Ad Rate: Full Page Colour £675.00
MAGAZINE
Business

HFM Week　980854
Editorial: One London Wall, London EC2Y 5BD **Tel:** 44 02078 326500
Email: news@hfmweek.com
Web site: www.hfmweek.com
Freq: Weekly
Circ: 9453 Not Audited
Profile: Magazine providing up-to-date commentary, features and insight for the alternative investment industry. Including news on trends within the industry, fund launches, searches and senior people moves.
Ad Rate: Full Page Colour £3950.00
MAGAZINE
Fund Management, Hedge Funds

HFMCompliance　1056325
Editorial: One London Wall, London EC2Y 5BD **Tel:** 44 02078 326500
Email: customercare@pageantmedia.com
Web site: hfm.global/hfmcompliance
Freq: Monthly
MAGAZINE
Fund Management, Hedge Funds

HIV Medicine　985430
Editorial: John Wiley & Sons, 9600 Garsington Road, Oxford OX4 2DQ
Tel: 44 02084 468898
Email: hivedoffice@gmail.com
Web site: http://eu.wiley.com/WileyCDA/WileyTitle/productCd-HIV.html
Freq: Monthly
Circ: 22085 Cision Digital Reach
Editor: Brian Gazzard; **Editor:** Jens Lundgren
Profile: The official journal of the British HIV Association, Australian Society for HIV Medicine and the European AIDS Clinical Society containing international research papers in the field of HIV medicine, embracing clinical, pharmacological, epidemiological, preclinical and in vitro studies. It also focuses on evidence-based medicine as the mainstay for the successful management of HIV and AIDS.
MAGAZINE (ONLINE)
AIDS/HIV

Hoist Magazine　98349
Editorial: Progressive House, 2 Maidstone Road, Foots Cray, Sidcup, London DA14 5HZ
Web site: www.hoistmagazine.com
Freq: Monthly
Circ: 26084 Not Audited
Editor: Daniel Searle
MAGAZINE
Building & Construction, Engineering

Holography News　98531
Editorial: 4 Windmill Business Village, Brooklands Close, Sunbury-on-Thames TW16 7DY **Tel:** 44 01932 785680
Email: publications@reconnaissance-intl.com
Web site: http://www.holography-news.com/
Freq: Monthly Not Audited
Editor: Mark Deakes
Profile: Magazine covering news, analysis and commentary on the holography industry. First published in 1986, the publication has an average of 8 pages per issue. Aimed at hologram producers, suppliers, converters and users.
MAGAZINE
Industry

homelandsecurity-technology.com　99804
Editorial: John Carpenter House, John Carpenter Street, London EC4Y 0AN
Tel: 44 02079 366400

Email: onlineeditorial@kable.co.uk
Web site: www.homelandsecurity-technology.com
Freq: Daily
Circ: 1686 Cision Digital Reach
MAGAZINE (ONLINE)
Defense & National Security

Homes for Scotland   990556
Editorial: 5 New Mart Place, Edinburgh EH14 1RW **Tel:** 44 01314 558350
Email: info@homesforscotland.com
Web site: www.homesforscotland.com
Freq: Daily
Circ: 15242 Cision Digital Reach
Editor: Jennifer Kennedy
MAGAZINE (ONLINE)
Building & Construction

Horticulture   988757
Tel: 44 02476 858500
Web site: www.nfuonline.com
Freq: Quarterly
Circ: 5500 Not Audited
MAGAZINE
Animal Farming

Hospital Caterer   984051
Editorial: 11-12 School House, 2nd Avenue, Trafford Park Village, Trafford Park, Manchester M17 1DZ **Tel:** 44 01618 726667
Email: pressenquiries@hospitalcaterers.org
Web site: www.hospitalcaterers.org/publications
Freq: Bi-Monthly
Circ: 1250 Not Audited
Profile: Official journal of the Hospital Caterers Association. Aimed at ASSOL members who are key buyers in the hospital catering industry.
Ad Rate: Full Page Colour £1095.00
MAGAZINE
Health Administration

Hospital Healthcare Europe
985117
Editorial: Bastion House, 140 London Wall, London EC2Y 5DN **Tel:** 44 02072 140500
Email: hhe@cogora.com
Web site: www.hospitalhealthcare.com
Freq: Annual Not Audited
Profile: Magazine aiming to improve the communication between European hospitals and to foster efficiency and effectiveness in the organisation and operation of hospital services and the health systems within which they function. Aimed at healthcare providers.
MAGAZINE
Health Administration

Hospital Matters   990016
Editorial: Suite A, Silvester House, The Maltings, Silvester Street, Hull HU1 3HA
Tel: 44 01482 585735
Web site: www.hospital-matters.co.uk
Freq: Bi-Monthly
Circ: 6905 Not Audited
Profile: Journal focusing on nursing and clinical support services. Contains features on new products, operating theatres, infection control and sterile services. Aimed at nursing, infection control nurses and clinical and medical support teams.
Ad Rate: Full Page Colour £1650.00
MAGAZINE
Health Administration, Nursing/Nurses

hospital pharmacy europe
984571
Editorial: 140 London Wall, London EC2Y 5DN **Tel:** 44 02072 140500
Email: hpe@cogora.com
Web site: http://www.hospitalpharmacyeurope.com/
Freq: Bi-Monthly
Circ: 12000 Not Audited
Profile: Review journal covering developments in drug therapy, technology, healthcare policy and pharmacy practice. Targets professionals working in the area of hospital pharmacy, preparing drugs or dispensing. This magazine contains the following rRegular features: Clinical Review - Information on the latest clinical

trialsComment - Editorial on a topical issue Policy & Practice - Focuses on policy and practice issues of interest to hospital pharmacistsTechnology Update - Focuses on technology issues of interest to hospital pharmacists Vantage Point - Editorial focused on a european issue
Ad Rate: Full Page Mono £3500.00
Ad Rate: Full Page Colour £4450.00
MAGAZINE
Pharmaceuticals

Hospital Times   981072
Editorial: Suite A, Silvester House, The Maltings, Silvester Street, Hull HU1 3HA
Tel: 44 01482 585735
Web site: www.hospital-times.co.uk
Freq: Bi-Monthly
Circ: 6000 Not Audited
Profile: Magazine containing a wide range of articles about products and projects, plus development information. First published in 1997. Aimed at hospital estate and facilities management teams.
Ad Rate: Full Page Colour £1650.00
MAGAZINE
Health Administration

hospitalmanagement.net
980943
Editorial: John Carpenter House, John Carpenter Street, London EC4Y 0AN
Tel: 44 02079 366400
Email: onlineeditorial@kable.co.uk
Web site: www.hospitalmanagement.net
Freq: Daily
Circ: 9769 Cision Digital Reach
MAGAZINE (ONLINE)
Health Administration

Hot Dip Galvanizing Magazine
1074325
Tel: 44 01213 558838
Email: ga@hdg.org.uk
Web site: www.hdgmagazine.co.uk
Freq: Quarterly
Editor: Iqbal Johal
MAGAZINE
Manufacturing

Hotel Analyst   983214
Editorial: PO Box 1228, Cambridge CB1 0WS **Tel:** 44 02088 706388
Email: info@hotelanalyst.co.uk
Web site: www.hotelanalyst.co.uk
Freq: Bi-Monthly
Circ: 1000 Not Audited
Editor: Andrew Sangster
MAGAZINE
Hotels/Motels

Hotel Business (UK)   981230
Editorial: 21-23 Phoenix Court, Hawkins Road, Colchester, Colchester CO2 8JY
Tel: 44 01206 505900
Web site: www.hotel-magazine.co.uk
Freq: Monthly
Circ: 5781 Not Audited
Editor: Steve Holland
MAGAZINE
Hotels/Motels

Hotel Industry Magazine   986393
Email: editor@hotel-industry.co.uk
Web site: www.hotel-industry.co.uk
Freq: Quarterly
Circ: 14034 Cision Digital Reach
Editor: Lee Jamieson
MAGAZINE (ONLINE)
Hotels/Motels

Hotel Management International
981360
Editorial: John Carpenter House, John Carpenter Street, London EC4Y 0AN
Tel: 44 02079 366400
Email: editor@globaltrademedia.com
Web site: www.hmi-online.co.uk
Freq: Quarterly
Circ: 7215 Not Audited
Profile: Magazine focusing on the hospitality management industry in Europe including leading industry professionals covering the

major themes and cutting through to the key issues shaping this market. Aimed at decision-makers at the major hotel chains worldwide, four and five star hoteliers and management companies.
Ad Rate: Full Page Colour £5900.00
MAGAZINE
Hotels/Motels

Hotel Owner   986779
Editorial: 14 Rosebery Avenue, London EC1R 4TD **Tel:** 44 01206 767797
Email: newsdesk@hotelowner.co.uk
Web site: www.hotelowner.co.uk
Freq: Monthly Not Audited
Editor: Michael Northcott
Profile: Magazine covering news and features relating to the hotel sector targeted at independent hoteliers. Articles cover hotel refurbishment, technology, furniture and furnishings, hotel news and staff appointments and food and drink.
MAGAZINE
Business, Corporate Responsibility, Hotels/Motels

Hotel Spec Journal   994686
Editorial: Old School House, St Stephens Street, Tunbridge, Tonbridge TN9 2AD
Tel: 44 01732 371578
Email: info@hotelspeconline.com
Web site: www.hotelspeconline.com
Freq: Annual
Circ: 16365 Not Audited
Editor: Can Faik
MAGAZINE
Hotels/Motels

Hoteldesigns.net   984383
Editorial: Forum House, 71 Mead Lane, Hertford, Seaford SG13 7AX
Tel: 44 01992 374100
Email: office@hoteldesigns.net
Web site: www.hoteldesigns.net
Freq: Daily
Circ: 16628 Cision Digital Reach
MAGAZINE (ONLINE)
Hotels/Motels

Hotelier & Hospitality Design Magazine   988695
Editorial: The Mill, Spratling, St Manston, Manston CT12 5AN **Tel:** 44 01843 446212
Email: copy@hotelierandhospitality.com
Web site: http://hotelierandhoteldesign com/
Freq: Monthly
Circ: 73900 Not Audited
Editor: Anthony Field
Profile: Magazine covering hotel industry news and exclusive of the latest ecological-friendly green hotels and bar designs. It features the latest hotel trends in technology and innovative ideas, recent hotel renovations and openings and award-winning luxury hotels and hotel construction projects.
MAGAZINE
Architecture & Design, Graphic Design, Hotels/Motels, Interior Design, Travel Industry

Hotelmarketing.com   995969
Email: editor@hotelmarketing.com
Web site: www.hotelmarketing.com
Freq: Daily
Circ: 151533 Cision Digital Reach
Editor: Markus Busch
MAGAZINE (ONLINE)
Hotels/Motels, Marketing

Hotshoe   985192
Editorial: 29 - 31 Saffron Hill, London EC1N 8SW **Tel:** 44 02074 216009
Email: melissa@hotshoeinternational.com
Web site: http://www.hotshoemagazine.com
Freq: Quarterly
Circ: 11000 Not Audited
MAGAZINE
Photography

The House Shop   995498
Editorial: 6 Owen Street, Suite 1, London EC1V 7JX
Email: press@thehouseshop.com
Web site: www.thehouseshop.com
Freq: Daily
Circ: 127252 Cision Digital Reach
MAGAZINE (ONLINE)
Property Management & Maintenance, Residential Real Estate

Housebuilder   981087
Editorial: HBF House, 27 Broadwall, London SE1 9PL **Tel:** 44 02079 601630
Email: info@house-builder.co.uk
Web site: www.house-builder.co.uk
Freq: Monthly
Circ: 13921 Not Audited
Profile: Trade journal covering specialist services and products, financial and economic issues, design land and planning matters. Aimed at private sector house-builders and received by all NHBC registered house-builders.
Ad Rate: Full Page Mono £2400.00
Ad Rate: Full Page Colour £2400.00
MAGAZINE
Residential Real Estate

Housebuilder and Developer
981088
Editorial: Cointronic House, Station Road, Heathfield, Heathfield TN21 8DF
Tel: 44 01435 863500
Email: editorial@netmagmedia.eu
Web site: www.hbdonline.co.uk
Freq: Monthly
Circ: 15004 Not Audited
MAGAZINE
Building & Construction

Housekeeping Today UK   1060187
Editorial: Synegis House, Crockhamwell Road, Woodley, Reading RG5 3LE
Tel: 44 01189 014471
Email: info@housekeepingtoday.co.uk
Web site: http://www.housekeepingtodayuk.com/
Freq: Monthly
Circ: 3300 Not Audited
MAGAZINE
Hygiene

Housewares   981104
Editorial: 15A London Road, Maidstone, Maidstone ME16 8LY **Tel:** 44 01622 687031
Web site: www.housewareslive.net
Freq: Bi-Monthly
Circ: 4984 Not Audited
MAGAZINE
Interior Design

Housing Active   983976
Editorial: PO Box 627, Rickmansworth, London WD3 0BQ **Tel:** 44 01923 770432
Web site: http://www.housingactive.com/
Freq: Monthly
Circ: 2181 Cision Digital Reach
Editor: Jackie Simpson
MAGAZINE (ONLINE)
Building & Construction, Legal Affairs, Residential Real Estate, Sustainable Development

Housing Association   981094
Editorial: Waverley House, 11 Galena Close, Amington Industrial Estate, Tamworth B77 4AS **Tel:** 44 01827 301185
Email: press@hamag.co.uk
Web site: http://hamag.co.uk/
Freq: Monthly
Circ: 33000 Not Audited
MAGAZINE
Commercial Real Estate, Residential Real Estate, Urban Planning & Development

Housing Law Monitor   1005998
Editorial: The Ridge, South View Road, Pinner, London HA5 3YD
Tel: 44 02088 661934
Web site: http://www.singlelaw.com/housing-law-monitor

Business Magazines

Freq: Monthly Not Audited
MAGAZINE
Legal Affairs

Housing Management & Maintenance 1054595
Tel: 44 01435 863500
Email: info@netmagmedia.eu
Web site: www.housingmmonline.co.uk/
Freq: Bi-Monthly
Circ: 9295 Not Audited
MAGAZINE
Human Resources, Residential Real Estate, Urban Planning & Development

Housing Specification 986333
Editorial: Grosvenor House, Central Park, Telford TF2 9TW **Tel:** 44 01952 234000
Web site: www.housingspecification.com/hs
Freq: Bi-Monthly
Circ: 25733 Not Audited
Profile: Magazine covering product design, product performance and design and construction technology used within the house building industry.
Ad Rate: Full Page Mono £2000.00
MAGAZINE
Architecture & Design, Building & Construction, Finance, Interior Design, Legal Affairs, Residential Real Estate, Urban Planning & Development

How We Get To Next 998252
Web site: www.howwegettonext.com
Freq: Daily
Circ: 47504 Cision Digital Reach
Editor: Ian Steadman
MAGAZINE (ONLINE)
Science

HR Grapevine 980949
Editorial: Rosanne House, Parkway, Welwyn Garden City, Welwyn Garden City AL8 6HG
Tel: 44 01707 351451
Web site: www.hrgrapevine.com
Freq: Monthly
Circ: 120000 Not Audited
Profile: Magazine covering the relationship between corporate and professional recruiters. Aimed at HR directors and recruitment consultants.Previous title: The Executive Grapevine
Ad Rate: Full Page Colour £1800.00
MAGAZINE
Company News & Appointments, Education, Health & Safety, Human Resources, Recruiting

HR Magazine (UK) 979830
Editorial: St Jude's Church, Dulwich Road, London SE24 0PB **Tel:** 44 02077 385454
Email: hrnews@markallengroup.com
Web site: www.hrmagazine.co.uk
Freq: Monthly
Circ: 8050 Not Audited
MAGAZINE
Education, Health & Safety, Human Resources, Recruiting

Hr NETWORK (SCOTLAND) Magazine 984923
Tel: 44 01316 253267
Email: editor@hrnetworkscotland.co.uk
Web site: www.hrnetworkjobs.com
Freq: Bi-Monthly
Circ: 11663 Not Audited
MAGAZINE
Company News & Appointments, Education, Health & Safety, Human Resources, Recruiting

HR News 1098749
Editorial: 6A Woodridge, Bridgend CF31 4PE **Tel:** 44 01656 641085
Email: news@hrnews.co.uk
Web site: http://hrnews.co.uk/
Freq: Daily
Circ: 16829 Cision Digital Reach
Editor: Lisa Baker
MAGAZINE (ONLINE)
Company News & Appointments, Education, Health & Safety, Human Resources, Recruiting

HR Zone 982944
Editorial: 6th Floor, Bridge House, 48-52 Baldwin Street, Bristol BS1 1QB
Tel: 44 01179 158646
Email: editor@hrzone.com
Web site: http://www.hrzone.com/
Freq: Daily
Circ: 150489 Cision Digital Reach
Profile: Website focusing on HR. HR Zone is a HR community, providing advice, news and networking opportunities for HR professionals. Aimed at HR professionals, mainly managers and directors.
MAGAZINE (ONLINE)
Company News & Appointments, Education, Health & Safety, Human Resources, Recruiting

HR-inform 996969
Editorial: 151 The Broadway, London SW19 1JQ **Tel:** 44 02086 126204
Web site: http://www2.cipd.co.uk/hr-inform
Freq: Daily
Circ: 53 Cision Digital Reach
MAGAZINE (ONLINE)
Company News & Appointments, Education, Health & Safety, Human Resources, Recruiting

HRreview 984900
Editorial: 2nd Floor, 30-32 Tabard Street, London SE1 4JU **Tel:** 44 02079 932174
Email: editor@hrreview.co.uk
Web site: www.hrreview.co.uk
Freq: Daily
Circ: 16615 Cision Digital Reach
Editor: Rebecca Clarke
Profile: Website covering human resources. HRreview covers news and information on human resources in terms of strategy and practice, recruitment, health and safety, benefits, pay and reward, employment Law, diversity and quality and training.
MAGAZINE (ONLINE)
Company News & Appointments, Education, Health & Safety, Human Resources, Recruiting

HRVille 1054533
Editorial: HRVille, Unit D, Zetland House, 5-25 Scrutton Street, London EC2A 4HJ
Tel: 44 02076 087619
Email: editorial@hrville.co.uk
Web site: hrville.co.uk
Freq: Daily
Circ: 4075 Cision Digital Reach
MAGAZINE (ONLINE)
Company News & Appointments, Education, Human Resources, Recruiting

HUB 4 985759
Editorial: 27 Old Gloucester Street, London WC1N 3AX
Email: editorial@hub-4.com
Web site: www.hub-4.com
Freq: Quarterly
Circ: 6000 Not Audited
Editor: John Edwards
MAGAZINE
Building & Construction

Huddled 987944
Editorial: First Floor, Devonshire House, 36 George Street, Manchester M1 4HA
Tel: 44 08448 487000
Email: press@huddled.co.uk
Web site: www.huddled.co.uk
Freq: Daily
Circ: 13825 Cision Digital Reach
Editor: Suzanne Rose Goddard
Profile: Website covering business news. Huddled covers regional business news from the North West.
MAGAZINE (ONLINE)
Business, Small and Medium Business

Human Fertility 999012
Editorial: 4 Park Square, Milton Park, Abingdon OX14 4RN **Tel:** 44 02070 176000
Email: tf.enquiries@informa.com
Web site: http://informahealthcare.com/huf

Freq: Quarterly Not Audited
MAGAZINE
Obstetrics & Gynecology (OB/GYN)

Human Reproduction 985381
Editorial: ESHRE Journals, 5 Mill Yard, Cambridge CB23 8BA **Tel:** 44 01954 212404
Email: editorial@humanreproduction.co.uk
Web site: http://humrep.oxfordjournals.org
Freq: Monthly
Circ: 3311 Not Audited
Profile: Publication covering all aspects of human reproduction research.
Ad Rate: Full Page Mono £742.00
Ad Rate: Full Page Colour £1377.00
MAGAZINE
Diabetes, Obstetrics & Gynecology (OB/GYN)

Human Reproduction Update 985379
Editorial: Editorial Office, ESHRE Journals, 5 Mill Yard, Childerley, Cambridge CB23 8BA
Tel: 44 01954 212404
Email: editorial@humanreproduction.co.uk
Web site: http://humupd.oxfordjournals.org/
Freq: Bi-Monthly Not Audited
Profile: Journal featuring comprehensive review service of research within the field of human reproduction. Read by members of the European Society of Human Reproduction and Embryology.
Ad Rate: Full Page Mono £742.00
Ad Rate: Full Page Colour £1377.00
MAGAZINE
Diabetes, Obstetrics & Gynecology (OB/GYN), Oncology

Human Resources for Health 995534
Editorial: 236 Grays Inn Road, London WC1X 8HB
Email: info@biomedcentral.com
Web site: https://human-resources-health.biomedcentral.com/
Freq: Daily
Circ: 947605 Cision Digital Reach
MAGAZINE (ONLINE)
Healthcare Industry, Human Resources

Humanomics 995101
Editorial: Emerald Group Publishing, Howard House, Wagon Lane, Bingley BD16 1WA **Tel:** 44 01274 777700
Web site: http://www.emeraldinsight.com/loi/h
Freq: Quarterly Not Audited
MAGAZINE
Economics

HVR (Heating & Ventilating Review) 999138
Editorial: 15a London Road, Maidstone, Maidstone ME16 8LY **Tel:** 44 01622 699166
Web site: www.heatingandventilating.net
Freq: Monthly
Circ: 13730 Not Audited
Editor: Heather Ramsden
MAGAZINE
Building & Construction, Interior Design

Hydraulics & Pneumatics 981242
Editorial: 192 The High Street, Tonbridge, Tonbridge TN9 1BE **Tel:** 44 01732 370340
Email: info@dfamedia.co.uk
Web site: www.hpmag.co.uk
Freq: Bi-Monthly
Circ: 10000 Not Audited
Profile: Journal covering all aspects of fluid power equipment and systems. Aimed at machine designers, purchasers, specifiers, engineers and other decision makers.
Ad Rate: Full Page Mono £1220.00
Ad Rate: Full Page Colour £2075.00
MAGAZINE
Engineering, Industry, Manufacturing

Hydrocarbon Engineering 981137
Editorial: 15 South Street, Farnham, Farnham GU9 8Q **Tel:** 44 01252 718999
Email: enquiries@energyglobal.com

Web site: https://www.energyglobal.com/magazine/
Freq: Monthly
Circ: 10100 Not Audited
Editor: Callum O'Reilly
Profile: Hydrocarbon Engineering is the international publication covering the oil refining, gas processing and petrochemicals industry.
Ad Rate: Full Page Colour £5070.00
MAGAZINE
Engineering, Oil

hydrocarbons-technology.com 985766
Editorial: John Carpenter House, John Carpenter Street, London EC4Y 0AN
Tel: 44 02079 366400
Email: onlineeditorial@kable.co.uk
Web site: http://www.hydrocarbons-technology.com
Freq: Daily
Circ: 40535 Cision Digital Reach
Profile: Website covering hydrocarbons technology projects both in production and under development.
MAGAZINE (ONLINE)
Oil

Hydrometallurgy of China 1061451
Tel: 44 86105 1674348
Email: sfyj@bricem.com.cn
Web site: http://www.bricem.com.cn
Freq: Quarterly
Circ: 10000 Not Audited
MAGAZINE
Chemicals, Steel

Hyve News 1099269
Email: news@hyve.news
Web site: http://hyve.news/
Freq: Daily
MAGAZINE (ONLINE)
Business, Industry, Small and Medium Business

I - Global Intelligence for the CIO 999455
Editorial: 3-7 Herbal Hill, London EC1R 5EJ
Tel: 44 02077 757775
Email: editor@i-cio.com
Web site: www.i-cio.com
Freq: Daily
Circ: 20158 Cision Digital Reach
Editor: Kenny MacIver
MAGAZINE (ONLINE)
Computers, Data Management, Telecommunications/Electronic Communications

IAOPA (Europe) 994670
Editorial: AOPA UK, 50a Cambridge Street, London SW1V 4QQ **Tel:** 44 02078 345631
Email: info@aopa.co.uk
Web site: http://www.iaopa.eu/
Freq: Monthly
Circ: 3003 Cision Digital Reach
MAGAZINE (ONLINE)
Aviation

IB World 999229
Editorial: Bridge House, 69 London Road, Twickenham, London TW1 3QR
Tel: 44 02082 67501
Email: editor@ibo.org
Web site: www.ibo.org/ibworld/index.cfm
Freq: Semi-Annual
Circ: 40000 Not Audited
Editor: Sophie-Marie Odum
MAGAZINE
Schools & Institutions

IBA Global Insight 985442
Editorial: 4th Floor, 10 St Bride Street, London EC4A 4AD **Tel:** 44 02078 420090
Email: editor@int-bar.org
Web site: http://www.ibanet.org/Publications/IBA_Global_Insight.aspx
Freq: Bi-Monthly

Circ: 23000 Not Audited
MAGAZINE
Corporate Law, Criminal Law, Human Rights, Legal Services, Litigation, Tax Law

i-build
987735
Editorial: Pear Platt, Woodfalls Industrial Estate, Gravelly Way, Laddingford, Maidstone ME18 6DA **Tel:** 44 01622 873229
Web site: http://www.i-buildmagazine.com/
Freq: Monthly
Circ: 12448 Cision Digital Reach
MAGAZINE (ONLINE)
Architecture & Design, Building & Construction, Interior Design

Ice Cream Magazine
984754
Editorial: 3 Melbourne Court, Derwent Parade, Pride Park, Derby DE24 8LZ
Tel: 44 01332 203333
Email: info@ice-cream.org
Web site: http://www.ice-cream.org
Freq: Monthly Not Audited
Editor: Zelica Carr
Profile: Journal focusing on ice cream manufacturing and vending. Aimed at members of the Ice Cream Alliance and key ice cream buyers within the UK.Previous title: Ice Cream and Cafe Society A charge may be made for colour separation.
Ad Rate: Full Page Colour £462.00
MAGAZINE
Food

ICHCA Journal
998599
Editorial: Suite 5 Meridian House, 62 Station Road, London E4 7BA **Tel:** 44 02033 277560
Web site: www.ichca.com
Freq: Annual
Circ: 6961 Cision Digital Reach
Editor: Richard Brough
MAGAZINE (ONLINE)
Shipping & Warehousing

ICIS Chemical Business
979910
Editorial: The Quadrant, Sutton, London SM2 5AS **Tel:** 44 02086 523335
Email: icbeditorial@icis.com
Web site: www.icischemicalbusiness.com
Freq: Weekly
Circ: 10100 Not Audited
Profile: Magazine containing news and features concerning the chemical industry.
Ad Rate: Full Page Mono £3685.00
Ad Rate: Full Page Colour £4735.00
MAGAZINE
Chemicals

ICIS Energy
998660
Editorial: The Eye, 3rd floor, 1 Procter Street, Holborn, London WC1V 6EU
Tel: 44 02079 111920
Email: info@icisheren.com
Web site: www.icis.com/energy/
Freq: Daily
Circ: 279303 Cision Digital Reach
MAGAZINE (ONLINE)
Alternative/Renewable Energy, Carbon Emissions & Trading, Electricity, Energy, Nuclear Power, Oil, Water & Sanitation

ICIS News
983819
Editorial: The Quadrant, Sutton SM2 5AS
Tel: 44 02086 523335
Email: icisnews.europe@icis.com
Web site: www.icis.com
Freq: Daily
Circ: 474897 Cision Digital Reach
Profile: Website covering the chemical and related industries.
MAGAZINE (ONLINE)
Chemicals, Oil

ICIS Pricing
983376
Editorial: The Quadrant, Sutton, London SM2 5AS **Tel:** 44 02086 528147
Web site: http://www.icis.com/chemicals/dashboard/
Freq: Daily
Circ: 13487 Cision Digital Reach
MAGAZINE (ONLINE)
Chemicals, Commodities

IDEA Carbon
998696
Editorial: 2nd Floor, Audrey House, 16-20 Ely Place, London EC1N 6SN
Tel: 44 02076 640221
Email: editorial@ideacarbon.com
Web site: www.ideacarbon.com
Freq: Daily
Circ: 6998 Cision Digital Reach
MAGAZINE (ONLINE)
Alternative/Renewable Energy, Carbon Emissions & Trading, Electricity, Energy, Environment, Nuclear Power, Oil, Water & Sanitation

Ideas4PetRetail
1054008
Email: editorial@ideas4petretail.co.uk
Web site: www.ideas4petretail.co.uk
Freq: Daily
Circ: 10709 Cision Digital Reach
Editor: Mervyn Barnard
MAGAZINE (ONLINE)
Retail Management

IDM Infraestructura y Desarrollo en México
1060768
Email: editor@revistainfraestructura.com.mx
Web site: http://revistainfraestructura.com.mx
Freq: Bi-Monthly
Circ: 10000 Not Audited
MAGAZINE
Architecture & Design, Building & Construction

IDS Employment Law Brief
983952
Editorial: IDS Employment Law Brief - Thomson Reuters, 5th Floor, Friar's House, Blackfriars Road, London SE1 8EZ
Tel: 44 08450 772921
Email: ids.feedback@thomsonreuters.com
Web site: https://ids.thomsonreuters.com/our-services
Freq: Bi-Weekly Not Audited
Profile: The IDS Employment Law Brief provides employment law information and analysis. Written by an in-house team of specialist employment lawyers, the IDS Employment Law Brief journal covers legislation and case law, and its practical implications. It reports on the decisions of tribunals and the courts, and also covers new UK and EU laws.Aimed at personnel specialists, lawyers and trade union officials.
MAGAZINE
Employment, Human Resources

IDS HR in Practice
999108
Editorial: Finsbury Tower, 103-105 Bunhill Row, London EC1Y 8LZ
Email: ids.feedback@thomsonreuters.com
Web site: www.ids.thomsonreuters.com
Freq: Daily
Circ: 42 Cision Digital Reach
MAGAZINE (ONLINE)
Business, Corporate Responsibility

IE Today
995977
Editorial: Unit 2.4 Paintworks, Arnos Vale, Bristol BS4 3EH **Tel:** 44 01173 005526
Email: info@ie-today.co.uk
Web site: www.ie-today.co.uk
Freq: Monthly
Circ: 6500 Not Audited
MAGAZINE
Disability, Education, Higher Education, Preschool, Schools & Institutions, Students

iflr.com
987765
Editorial: 8 Bouverie Street, London EC4Y 8AX **Tel:** 44 02077 798888
Web site: www.iflr.com
Freq: Daily
Circ: 24533 Cision Digital Reach
MAGAZINE (ONLINE)
Tax Law

IFLR1000
987428
Editorial: 8 Bouverie Street, London EC4Y 8AX **Tel:** 44 02077 798888
Web site: www.iflr1000.com
Freq: Annual

i-FM
980934
Editorial: Suite 3, 12 Mulberry Place, Pinnel Road, Eltham, London SE9 6AR
Tel: 44 02088 509520
Email: newsdesk@i-fm.net
Web site: www.i-fm.net
Freq: Daily
Circ: 14794 Cision Digital Reach
Editor: Simon Iatrou
Profile: Website containing facilities management information including news, features articles, reference listings, people, technology, workplaces, FM in Europe, sustainability channels, event and training listings.
MAGAZINE (ONLINE)
Hygiene, Security & Security Systems

IFSEC Global
981265
Editorial: 240 Blackfriars Road, London SE1 9UY
Email: editors@ifsecglobal.com
Web site: http://www.ifsecglobal.com
Freq: Daily
Circ: 53373 Cision Digital Reach
MAGAZINE (ONLINE)
Engineering, Security & Security Systems

Ignites Europe
984672
Editorial: Number One, Southwark Bridge, London SE1 9HL **Tel:** 44 02078 733000
Email: editorial@igniteseurope.com
Web site: www.igniteseurope.com
Freq: Daily
Circ: 17155 Cision Digital Reach
Profile: Website covering the fund industry in Europe. Ignites Europe shares the latest news on UCITS, ETFs, product development trends, regulatory changes, fund distribution trends, fund flows, industry conferences and executive appointments.
MAGAZINE (ONLINE)
Fund Management

IHS Fairplay
980909
Editorial: Sentinel House, 163 Brighton Road, Coulsdon, London CR5 2YH
Tel: 44 02032 522216
Email: editorial@fairplay.co.uk
Web site: www.fairplay.co.uk
Freq: Weekly
Circ: 2235 Not Audited
MAGAZINE
Shipping & Warehousing

IHS Jane's C4ISR & Mission Systems
998743
Editorial: Sentinel House, 163 Brighton Road, London CR5 2YH
Tel: 44 02087 003700
Web site: http://www.janes.com/products/janes/defence/det-products/c4isr-maritime.aspx
Freq: Annual Not Audited
Editor: Malcolm Fuller
MAGAZINE
Defense & National Security

IHS McCloskey's Coal Report, Fax & Newswire
999062
Editorial: 133 Houndsditch, London EC3A 7BX **Tel:** 44 02031 593300
Email: coalemea@ihs.com
Web site: www.ihs.com/products/coal/news-analysis/global.aspx
Freq: Weekly
Circ: 145513 Cision Digital Reach
MAGAZINE (ONLINE)
Commodities

IHS Oil & Gas Risk Service
997382
Editorial: The Capitol Building, Oldbury, Bracknell, London RG12 8FZ
Tel: 44 01344 328300
Web site: www.ihs.com/products/oil-gas-risk-forecast-analysis.html
Freq: Daily

Circ: 12749 Cision Digital Reach
Editor: Sam Duke
MAGAZINE (ONLINE)
Legal Services

Circ: 113 Cision Digital Reach
MAGAZINE (ONLINE)
Oil

IHS Petrodata
999038
Editorial: The Exchange Number 1, Aberdeen Ab11 5PG **Tel:** 44 01224 597800
Web site: www.ihs.com/info/en/a/ods-petrodata/index.aspx
Freq: Daily
Circ: 113 Cision Digital Reach
MAGAZINE (ONLINE)
Oil

i-invest
1102951
Tel: 44 01283 712447
Email: info@i-investintl.com
Web site: http://www.investor-review.com
Freq: Daily
Circ: 3501 Cision Digital Reach
MAGAZINE (ONLINE)
Investment Banking

IIRSM Newsletter
998582
Editorial: Suite 7a, 77 Fulham Place Road, London W6 8JA **Tel:** 44 02087 419100
Email: info@iirsm.org
Web site: www.iirsm.org
Freq: Monthly
Circ: 14276 Cision Digital Reach
MAGAZINE (ONLINE)
Health & Safety

IM (International Mining)
981718
Editorial: 2 Claridge Court, Lower Kings Road, Berkhamsted, Berkhamsted HP4 2AF
Tel: 44 01442 870829
Email: impn@im-mining.com
Web site: www.im-mining.com
Freq: Monthly
Circ: 17500 Not Audited
Editor: Paul Moore
MAGAZINE
Mining & Quarrying

Image
985178
Editorial: Studio 9, Holborn Studios, 49-50 Eagle Wharf Road, London N1 7ED
Tel: 44 02077 396669
Email: image@aophoto.co.uk
Web site: www.the-aop.org/image
Freq: Quarterly
Circ: 22702 Not Audited
Profile: Magazine covering fashion, beauty, travel and interiors. Includes articles on the theatre, book reviews, eating out and entertainment. Aimed at affluent women aged 25 years and over.
MAGAZINE
Photography

Image Reports
981261
Editorial: 2nd Floor, 52-54 Gracechurch Street, London EC3V 0EJ
Tel: 44 02079 338999
Email: lesley.simpson@imagereportsmag.co.uk
Web site: www.imagereportsmag.co.uk
Freq: Monthly
Circ: 6554 Not Audited
Editor: Lesley Simpson
Profile: Magazine reporting on the latest products and services for the digital print industry. Read by printers, bureaux, corporate buying groups, publishers, advertising designers and the sign and screen printing industries.Alternative Title: Image Reports &Technology for Print
Ad Rate: Full Page Colour £3135.00
MAGAZINE
Publishing

Imaging & Machine Vision Europe
984892
Editorial: 4 Signet Court, Cambridge CB1 8LA **Tel:** 44 01223 221030
Email: editor.imaging@europascience.com
Web site: www.imveurope.com
Freq: Bi-Monthly
Circ: 6700 Not Audited
Editor: Greg Blackman
MAGAZINE
Computers, Data Management, Science

Business Magazines

Imaging & Therapy Practice
981194

Editorial: The Society of Radiographers, 207 Providence Square, Mill Street, London SE1 2EW **Tel:** 44 02077 407200
Email: editorial@itpmagazine.co.uk
Web site: http://www.sor.org/learning/library-publication/imaging-therapy-practice
Freq: Monthly
Circ: 21000 Not Audited
Editor: Melanie Armstrong
Profile: The latest professional and educational issues that affect the day-to-day working lives of therapy and diagnostic radiographers from The Society and College of Radiographers.
MAGAZINE
Diagnostic Imaging

The Imaging Science Journal
986391

Editorial: 2&4 Park Square, Milton Park, Abingdon, London OX14 4RN
Tel: 44 02070 176000
Email: enquiries@taylorandfrancis.com
Web site: http://www.tandfonline.com/toc/yims20/current
Freq: Bi-Monthly Not Audited
Profile: Industry/academic journal detailing research in medical photography, forensic applications and other advances in photographic technology, including chemistry and physics, imaging systems and applications. Aimed at researchers in academia and industry.
MAGAZINE
Photography, Science

Immunology
985436

Editorial: Immunology Editorial Office, The British Society for Immunology, 34 Red Lion Square, London WC1R 2SG
Tel: 44 02030 195901
Email: imm@immunology.org
Web site: www.blackwellpublishing.com/imm_enhanced/default.asp
Freq: Monthly Not Audited
MAGAZINE
Allergies

Impact
981253

Editorial: 15 Northburgh Street, London EC1V 0JR **Tel:** 44 02075 661864
Web site: https://www.mrs.org.uk/intelligence/impact
Freq: Quarterly
Circ: 10000 Not Audited
Editor: Jane Bainbridge
Profile: Website covering film. The Impact website shares the latest news on action, science fiction, thrillers and horror films.
MAGAZINE
Marketing

Implant Dentistry Today
985249

Editorial: 1 Hertford House, Farm Close, Shenley, Radlett WD7 9AB
Tel: 44 01923 851777
Email: info@fmc.co.uk
Web site: www.fmc.co.uk/publications/index.php?title=12
Freq: Quarterly
Circ: 2000 Not Audited
MAGAZINE
Dentistry

Implementation Science
995895

Editorial: c/o BioMed Central, 236 Gray's Inn Road, London WC1X 8HL
Tel: 44 02031 922009
Email: impsci@biomedcentral.com
Web site: https://implementationscience.biomedcentral.com/
Freq: Daily
Circ: 1570497 Cision Digital Reach
MAGAZINE (ONLINE)
Pharmaceuticals, Science

Improving Schools Journal
983961

Editorial: 1 Oliver's Yard, 55 City Road, London EC1Y 1SP
Web site: imp.sagepub.com

Freq: 3 Times/Year Not Audited
Editor: Terry Wrigley
MAGAZINE
Education

In Commerce
997694

Editorial: 27 City Quay, Camperdown Street, Dundee DD1 3JA
Tel: 44 01382 228545
Email: info@dundeeandanguschamber.co.uk
Web site: http://www.dundeeandanguschamber.co.uk/magazine.php
Freq: Quarterly Not Audited
MAGAZINE
Business, Small and Medium Business

In Practice
983805

Editorial: BMA House, Tavistock Square, London WC1H 9JR **Tel:** 44 02073 874409
Email: inpractice@bva-edit.co.uk
Web site: http://inpractice.bmj.com
Freq: Monthly
Circ: 5000 Not Audited
Profile: Magazine covering clinical developments and management issues relating to veterinary practice. Includes coverage of farm and companion animals, veterinary practice management and a calendar of educational meetings. Aimed at all members of the British Veterinary Association and veterinary surgeons in practice.
MAGAZINE
Veterinary Medicine

In Security
988003

Editorial: 13 Princess Street, Maidstone, Maidstone ME14 1UR **Tel:** 44 01622 201207
Email: editorial@mebmedia.co.uk
Web site: www.in-security.eu
Freq: Quarterly
Circ: 10000 Not Audited
Editor: Chris Hewett
Profile: Magazine providing features, case studies, interviews and editorials to showcase best practice when it comes to the specific intention of identifying and purchasing security solutions appropriate for turning strategy into reality. Aimed at buyers of security products across the UK and Europe.
Ad Rate: Full Page Colour £1950.00
MAGAZINE
Security & Security Systems

in.Design
983661

Editorial: The Goods Shed, Jubilee Way, Whitstable Road, Faversham ME13 8GD
Tel: 44 01795 509105
Email: editor@indesignmagazine.co.uk
Web site: www.indesignmagazine.co.uk
Freq: Monthly
Circ: 18000 Not Audited
MAGAZINE
Architecture & Design, Interior Design

inbuilding.org
986386

Editorial: The Old Forge, Little Green, Mells, Frome BA11 3QZ **Tel:** 44 02071 832511
Email: press@inbuilding.org
Web site: www.inbuilding.org
Freq: Daily
Circ: 4905 Cision Digital Reach
Profile: Website covering architect. The Inbuilding.org website is a new community for architects published by Working Communities Ltd, and we are interested in receiving any press release containing news of interest to architects and architectural consultants.
MAGAZINE (ONLINE)
Architecture & Design

inbusiness
997864

Editorial: 11 The Swan Courtyard, Charles Edward Road, Birmingham B26 1BU
Tel: 44 01217 654144
Email: inbusiness@chambermk.co.uk
Web site: http://chambermk.co.uk/profile/inbusiness
Freq: Bi-Monthly
Circ: 3000 Not Audited

Profile: Magazine focusing on news and information about local companies and initiatives and advice available to increase prosperity of county firms. Aimed at Chamber members and key businesses in Northamptonshire.
Ad Rate: Full Page Mono £1658.00
Ad Rate: Full Page Colour £1907.00
MAGAZINE
Business

InBusiness Magazine
1062730

Tel: 44 01217654144
Email: mark@goodlifepublishing.co.uk
Web site: http://www.inbusinessmag.co.uk/
Freq: Quarterly
Circ: 10000 Not Audited
Editor: Mark Roberts
MAGAZINE
Business, Small and Medium Business

Incentive and Motivation
981252

Tel: 44 01604 461546
Web site: www.incentiveandmotivation.com
Freq: Bi-Monthly
Circ: 9000 Not Audited
MAGAZINE
Education

The Independent Community Pharmacist
981217

Editorial: Linen Hall, 162-168 Regent Street, London W1B 5TB **Tel:** 44 02074 341530
Email: icp@1530.com
Web site: www.independentpharmacist.co.uk/
Freq: Monthly
Circ: 6582 Not Audited
Profile: Magazine containing pharmaceutical news relating to business, finance, merchandising, category management and marketing. Aimed at independent pharmacists.
Ad Rate: Full Page Colour £3045.00
MAGAZINE
Pharmaceuticals

Independent Investor
994646

Editorial: 11 Clonmel Road, London SW6 5BL
Email: editor@independent-investor.com
Web site: www.independent-investor.com
Freq: Daily
Circ: 2489 Cision Digital Reach
MAGAZINE (ONLINE)
Fund Management

Independent Leader Magazine
987318

Editorial: One Tetbury Place, Business Design Centre, 52 Upper Street, London N1 0QH **Tel:** 44 02072 886833
Email: info@intelligentmedia.co.uk
Web site: www.edexec.co.uk/education-executive/page/home
Freq: Monthly
Circ: 5120 Not Audited
MAGAZINE
Schools & Institutions

Independent Power Asia
985688

Editorial: Global House, 13 Market Square, Horsham, Horsham RH12 1EU
Tel: 44 01403 220750
Email: power@gmp.uk.com
Web site: http://www.gmp.uk.com/independent-power-asia/
Freq: Semi-Annual
Circ: 17120 Not Audited
Profile: Independent Power Asia (IPA) is the magazine providing news, in-depth features and keen analysis of the independent power and cogeneration markets in Asia. Includes a news section, regular country profiles, a company in power section and features.
Ad Rate: Full Page Mono £2410.00
Ad Rate: Full Page Colour £3083.00
MAGAZINE
Alternative/Renewable Energy, Building & Construction, Carbon Emissions & Trading, Electricity, Energy, Nuclear Power, Oil, Water & Sanitation

Independent School Parent
98490•

Editorial: Jubilee House, 2 Jubilee Place, London SW3 3TQ **Tel:** 44 02073 493700
Email: info@independentschoolparent.com
Web site: www.independentschoolparent.com
Freq: Bi-Monthly
Circ: 30000 Not Audited
Editor: Claudia Dudman
Profile: First Eleven is the magazine for parents of children in independent education from nursery school to university.
Ad Rate: Full Page Mono £3500.00
Ad Rate: Full Page Colour £3500.00
MAGAZINE
Education

The Independent Schools Magazine
984482

Editorial: PO Box 4136, Upper Basildon, Reading RG8 6BS **Tel:** 44 01491 671998
Email: mail@independentschoolsmagazine.co.uk
Web site: http://www.independentschoolsmagazine.co.uk/
Freq: Monthly
Circ: 4000 Not Audited
Profile: Magazine covering the latest trends and surveys, interviews, independent schools news, classroom ideas and initiatives, product and services as well as legal, financial, educational and marketing updates. Aimed at decision makers in independent schools including governors, heads, bursars and departmental managers.
Ad Rate: Full Page Colour £1300.00
MAGAZINE
Schools & Institutions

Industrial & Commercial Training
985354

Editorial: Howard House, Wagon Lane, Bingley BD16 1WA **Tel:** 44 01274 777700
Email: emerald@emeraldinsight.com
Web site: www.emeraldinsight.com/journals.htm?issn=0019-7858
Freq: Bi-Monthly Not Audited
MAGAZINE
News & Current Affairs

Industrial Analytical Instrumentation
987149

Tel: 44 01353 699456
Web site: www.industrialanalyticalinstrumentation.com
Freq: Daily Not Audited
Profile: Journal covering industrial and analytical instrumentation, research and development in all areas of science. Aimed at key executives in research, scientific and industrial laboratories. Also those involved in universities and hospitals.
Ad Rate: Full Page Mono £1000.00
Ad Rate: Full Page Colour £1250.00
MAGAZINE
Science

Industrial Compliance
984997

Editorial: 15a London Road, Maidstone, Maidstone ME16 8LY **Tel:** 44 01622 687031
Web site: www.connectingindustry.com/IndustrialCompliance/
Freq: Quarterly
Circ: 31574 Not Audited
Profile: Magazine addressing the introduction, impact and effect of all the standards, directives and legislation applicable in today's complex industrial environments. Aimed at engineers, managers, officers and directors involved in the specification, installation, maintenance and safe operation of electrical or mechanical plant equipment and machinery within hazardous areas, together with those tasked with maintaining environmental balance and the implementation of good health & safety practices.
Ad Rate: Full Page Colour £1700.00
MAGAZINE
Health & Safety

Industrial Fire Journal
981266

Editorial: 8 The Old Yarn Mills, Sherborne, Sherborne DT9 3HH **Tel:** 44 01935 816030

Web site: www.hemmingfire.com
Freq: Quarterly
Circ: 7500 Not Audited
Editor: Ann Marie Knegt
Profile: Journal reporting worldwide to industrial fire professionals within the oil, gas, chemical, power and other high risk industries in 153 countries. Read by industrial firefighters, fire protection chiefs, fire engineers, architects, surveyors, buyers and specifiers of industrial fire equipment.
Ad Rate: Full Page Colour £2199.00
MAGAZINE
Hygiene, Security & Security Systems

Industrial Law Journal   983053
Editorial: Great Clarendon Street, Oxford OX2 6DP Tel: 44 01865 353907
Web site: http://ilj.oxfordjournals.org/
Freq: Quarterly Not Audited
Profile: Journal covering analysis and information on all aspects of labour law. Includes a section on the impact of EC labour law in the UK. Aimed at lawyers, academics and lay industrial relations experts.
Ad Rate: Full Page Mono £340.00
MAGAZINE
Employment

Industrial Minerals   980136
Editorial: 8 Bouverie Street, London EC4Y 8AX Tel: 44 02077 797390
Email: edit@indmin.com
Web site: www.indmin.com
Freq: Monthly
Circ: 1351 Not Audited
Profile: Magazine covering non-fuel and non-metallic minerals. Includes business news, mineral production, processing, surveys and trade statistics. Read by companies in all sectors of the non-fuel and non-metallic business.
Ad Rate: Full Page Mono £1750.00
Ad Rate: Full Page Colour £2670.00
MAGAZINE
Alternative/Renewable Energy, Chemicals, Commodities, Mining & Quarrying

Industrial Pharmacy   996640
Editorial: Passfield Business Centre, Lynchborough Road, Passfield, Liphook, Liphook GU30 7SB Tel: 44 01428 752222
Email: publisher@euromedcommunications.com
Web site: industrialpharmacy.eu
Freq: Quarterly
Circ: 12500 Not Audited
MAGAZINE
Pharmaceuticals

Industrial Process News   987752
Editorial: 4th Floor, Maybrook House, Queensway, Halesowen B63 4AH
Tel: 44 01215 502086
Email: enquiries@businessandindustrytoday.co.uk
Web site: www.industrialprocessnews.co.uk
Freq: Monthly
Circ: 5000 Not Audited
Editor: Andre Laurent
Profile: Industrial Process News targets decision makers involved in the UK's industrial and process markets. It covers current trends and developments, new products and services launched into the marketplace.
MAGAZINE
Manufacturing

Industrial Relations Journal   995891
Editorial: The Atrium, Southern Gate, Chichester PO19 8QG Tel: 44 01865 778315
Email: cs-journals@wiley.com
Web site: http://onlinelibrary.wiley.com/journal/10.1111/(ISSN)1468-2338
Freq: Bi-Monthly
Editor: Peter Nolan
MAGAZINE
Business, Corporate Responsibility, Employment

Industrial Technology   981243
Editorial: Victoria House, 2 Mornington Road, Sale, Sale M33 2DA
Tel: 44 01613 745615
Web site: www.industrialtechnology.co.uk
Freq: Monthly
Circ: 13096 Not Audited
Editor: Mark Simms
Profile: Publication covering mechanical, electrical engineering and computer aided design. Read by product design engineers and machine builders.
Ad Rate: Full Page Mono £3120.00
Ad Rate: Full Page Colour £3120.00
MAGAZINE
Engineering

Industrial Woodworking & Panel Processing Magazine
    985569
Editorial: Flat 4929, PO Box 6945, London W1A 6US Tel: 44 01797 208059
Email: bill.willowe@gmail.com
Web site: http://industrialwoodworking.co.uk/
Freq: Monthly Not Audited
Editor: John Emslie
MAGAZINE
Manufacturing

Inex   987275
Editorial: Pear Platt, Woodfalls Industrial Estate, Gravelly Way, Maidstone ME18 6DA
Tel: 44 01622 873229
Web site: www.inex-online.com
Freq: Monthly
Circ: 10923 Cision Digital Reach
Profile: INEX online is an 'online specification portal covering interior and exterior design'.
MAGAZINE (ONLINE)
Interior Design

infant   998555
Editorial: 134 South Street, Bishop's Stortford, Bishop's Stortford CM23 3BQ
Web site: www.infantgrapevine.co.uk
Freq: Bi-Monthly
Circ: 5000 Not Audited
Editor: Lisa Leonard
Profile: Review journal containing articles with a clinical or practical bias written by experts in the field. Aimed at the multidisciplinary team caring for vulnerable, sick or premature babies in their first year of life, including neonatal nurses, neonatologists, paediatric intensive care nurses and doctors, pediatric A&E personnel and midwives.
MAGAZINE
Pediatrics

Infant Behaviour and Development   995435
Tel: 44 01865 843000
Web site: http://www.elsevier.com/wps/find/journaldescription.cws_home/620197/description#description
Freq: Quarterly Not Audited
Editor: G. Savelsbergh
MAGAZINE
Neurology, Pediatrics

Infant Observation   995857
Editorial: 120 Belsize Lane, London NW3 5BA Tel: 44 02074 357111
Web site: http://www.tandfonline.com/action/journalInformation?show=aimsScope&journalCode=riob20
Freq: 3 Times/Year
Editor: Trudy Klauber
MAGAZINE
Pediatrics

infobanknews   1061203
Tel: 44 63217 253127
Web site: http://www.infobanknews.com
Circ: 133696 Cision Digital Reach
MAGAZINE (ONLINE)
Banking

Informa   998411
Editorial: Knect House, 30-32 Mortimer Street, London W1W 7RE
Tel: 44 02070 175000
Email: headoffice@informa.com
Web site: www.informa.com
Freq: Daily
Circ: 123120 Cision Digital Reach
MAGAZINE (ONLINE)
Business

Informa Global Markets   998484
Editorial: 10-15 New Gate Street, London EC1A 7AZ Tel: 44 02070 175400
Web site: www.informagm.com
Freq: Daily
Circ: 4247 Cision Digital Reach
MAGAZINE (ONLINE)
Corporate Finance, Derivatives, Emerging Markets, Foreign Exchange Market (FOREX)

Informa's Insurance News 24   998686
Editorial: Christchurch Court, 10-15 Newgate Street, London EC1A 7AZ
Tel: 44 02070 175000
Web site: https://www.informalawlibrary.com/
Freq: Daily
Circ: 6149 Cision Digital Reach
MAGAZINE (ONLINE)
Insurance

Informed   984866
Editorial: The Investor Relations Society, 5th Floor, 30 Coleman Street, London EC2R 5AL
Tel: 44 02073 791763
Email: enquiries@irs.org.uk
Web site: http://www.irs.org.uk/news/category/informed
Freq: Quarterly
Circ: 2000 Not Audited
Profile: Magazine covering topical stories, viewpoints on latest investor relations issues and an update on the regulatory framework. Aimed at investor relation professionals.
Ad Rate: Full Page Colour £1390.00
MAGAZINE
Banking

The Informed Executive   996259
Editorial: 2 Robin Hill, Godalming GU7 2HL
Tel: 44 01483 419411
Email: davidcasey@informedexecutive.co.uk
Web site: informedexecutive.co.uk
Freq: Daily
Circ: 950 Cision Digital Reach
Editor: David Casey
MAGAZINE (ONLINE)
Business, Corporate Responsibility

Infosecurity   981593
Editorial: Gateway House, 28 The Quadrant, Richmond, London TW9 1DN
Tel: 44 02089 107893
Email: infosecurity.press@reedexpo.co.uk
Web site: www.infosecurity-magazine.com
Freq: Quarterly
Circ: 53000 Not Audited
Profile: Magazine covering news, products and issues relevant to the IT security market. It is dedicated to the strategy and technique of information security, endpoint security, delivering critical business and technical information that IT security professionals need in order to make informed purchasing decisions. Targets key decision makers responsible for purchasing IT security products and services, IT security managers, network and intranet managers, IT security architecture managers, IT security consultants and auditors
Ad Rate: Full Page Colour £3114.00
MAGAZINE
Security & Security Systems

InfraNews   980913
Editorial: 10 Queen Street Place, London EC4R 1BE Tel: 44 02037 411249
Web site: http://www.infra-news.com
Freq: Daily
Circ: 9600 Cision Digital Reach

Editor: Kate Burgess; Editor: Brendan Malkin
Profile: Website covering deal information in transport, social infrastructure and environmental, including renewable energy.
MAGAZINE (ONLINE)
Banking

Infrastructure Investor   984689
Editorial: 6th Floor, 140 London Wall, London EC2Y 5DN Tel: 44 02075 665444
Web site: www.infrastructureinvestor.com
Freq: Monthly Not Audited
Profile: Magazine providing detailed coverage of infrastructure finance and investments. Each issue looks at the people, institutions, assets and the policies shaping this new infrastructure.
MAGAZINE
Equities, Finance

Ingenia   985875
Editorial: Prince Philip House, Royal Academy of Engineering, 3 Carlton House Terrace, London SW1Y 5DG
Tel: 44 02077 660600
Email: ingenia@raeng.org.uk
Web site: www.ingenia.org.uk
Freq: Quarterly
Circ: 11000 Not Audited
Profile: Magazine featuring academy and engineering achievements.
MAGAZINE
Engineering

The In-House Lawyer   979900
Editorial: 188-190 Fleet Street, London EC4A 2AG Tel: 44 02073 969292
Web site: www.theinhouselawyer.co.uk
Freq: Quarterly
Circ: 5500 Not Audited
Profile: Magazine providing the latest in-house legal information from UK and Europe with regular features on international issues and deals. Aimed at in-house lawyers in the UK and non-lawyer executives who have been identified as key individuals in legal purchasing decisions.Previous title: The In-House Lawyer Yearbook
Ad Rate: Full Page Colour £3095.00
MAGAZINE
Corporate Law

In-House Perspective   999614
Editorial: 4th Floor, 10 St Bride Street, London EC4A 4AD Tel: 44 02078 420090
Email: editor@int bar.org
Web site: www.ibanet.org/IHP.aspx
Freq: Quarterly
Circ: 315 Cision Digital Reach
MAGAZINE (ONLINE)
Corporate Law, Legal Services

Injection World   997052
Editorial: 6 Pritchard Street, Bristol BS2 8RH Tel: 44 01179 249442
Email: editorial@injectionworld.com
Web site: www.injectionworld.com
Freq: Bi-Monthly
Circ: 2650 Cision Digital Reach
Profile: Website covering injection moulding. Injection World is a monthly digital magazine written specifically for injection moulders, mould makers and plastics product designers around the globe. It covers the latest injection moulding machinery, materials handling equipment, robots and mould technology as well as innovations in engineering and commodity plastics.
MAGAZINE (ONLINE)
Plastics

Ink Pellet   981784
Editorial: PO BOX 111, Kingsnorth, Ashford, Ashford TN23 9DX Tel: 44 01233 503055
Email: info@inkpellet.co.uk
Web site: www.inkpellet.co.uk
Freq: Bi-Monthly
Circ: 6000 Not Audited
Editor: John Hopley
Profile: Arts magazine containing information on the arts, literature, book and theatre reviews. Aimed at English and drama teachers in secondary schools. Secondary copy also sent into schools for the staffroom

Business Magazines

and teachers of other subject areas. The magazine contains the following regular features: Comment Piece - A humorous topical piece concerning current trends in teachingNoticeboard - A collection of news and information relevant to English and Drama teachers. Theatre Reviews - Reviews of plays, theatre productions and films.
Ad Rate: Full Page Mono £685.00
Ad Rate: Full Page Colour £860.00
MAGAZINE
Education

Innovate my School   987116
Editorial: Watergate Building, Crane Wharf, New Crane Street, Chester CH1 4JE
Tel: 44 01244 312720
Email: info@Innovatemyschool.com
Web site: www.innovatemyschool.com
Freq: Quarterly
Circ: 33250 Not Audited
Editor: James Cain
Profile: Magazine containing educational insights aiming to inspire and challenge schools, teachers and educators in the UK.
MAGAZINE
Education

Innovation Enterprise   1062750
Editorial: Floor 1, Linen Court, 10 East Road, London N1 6AD
Email: info@theiegroup.com
Web site: https://channels.theinnovationenterprise.com/
Freq: Daily
Circ: 276593 Cision Digital Reach
Editor: Charlie Sammonds
MAGAZINE (ONLINE)
Business, Data Management, Small and Medium Business, Supply Chain Management (SCM)

Innovation Investment Journal   999262
Editorial: 37 Evelyn Road, Dunstable, Luton LU5 4NG **Tel:** 44 01582 696911
Email: peterf@iijiij.com
Web site: www.iijiij.com
Freq: Daily
Circ: 6823 Cision Digital Reach
MAGAZINE (ONLINE)
Business, Investment Banking, Private Equity, Small and Medium Business

Innovations in Food Processing and Packaging   984998
Editorial: 17 Ashcroft Court, Burnham, Slough SL1 8JT **Tel:** 44 01628 666176
Web site: www.innovationsfood.com
Freq: Quarterly
Circ: 10800 Not Audited
Profile: Processing and packaging magazine that covers these sectors within the food technology industry.
Ad Rate: Full Page Mono £1050.00
Ad Rate: Full Page Colour £2400.00
MAGAZINE
Food, Manufacturing, Supply Chain Management (SCM)

Innovations in Food Technology   983699
Editorial: 17 Ashcroft Court, Burnham, Slough SL1 8JT
Web site: http://www.innovationsfood.com/Home1.htm
Freq: Quarterly
Circ: 10800 Not Audited
Profile: Ingredients magazine covering the latest developments and innovations taking place within the food ingredients technology industry.
Ad Rate: Full Page Mono £1700.00
Ad Rate: Full Page Colour £3900.00
MAGAZINE
Food

Innovations in Pharmaceutical Technology (IPT)   980870
Editorial: First Floor, 131 Edgware Road, London W2 2HR **Tel:** 44 02077 243456

Web site: www.iptonline.com
Freq: Quarterly
Circ: 12500 Not Audited
MAGAZINE
Medical Technology

Innovators magazine   1074317
Tel: 44 01415 700029
Email: editorial@innovatorsmag.com
Web site: http://www.innovatorsmag.com/
Freq: Monthly
Editor: Iain Robertson
MAGAZINE
Alternative/Renewable Energy, Environment

inpharmacy   995165
Editorial: Mallinson House, 38-42 St Peter's Street, St Albans, London AL1 3NP
Tel: 44 01727 858687
Email: npa@npa.co.uk
Web site: https://www.npa.co.uk/news-and-events/member-magazine/
Freq: Bi-Monthly Not Audited
MAGAZINE
Pharmaceuticals

InPublishing   983724
Editorial: Hawthorns, Station Road, Eynsford, Dartford DA4 0EJ
Tel: 44 01322 865984
Email: editorial@inpublishing.co.uk
Web site: http://www.inpublishing.co.uk/
Freq: Bi-Monthly
Circ: 5510 Not Audited
Editor: James Evelegh
Profile: Magazine covering marketing, circulation and distribution of newspapers and magazines. Aimed at corporate management and marketing, promotion, distribution and circulation directors and managers. Alternative Title: In Publishing Previous title: InCirculation
Ad Rate: Full Page Colour £1610.00
MAGAZINE
Marketing, Publishing

Inside Business (UK)   995294
Editorial: Bedford Heights Business Centre, Manton lane, Bedford, Bedford MK41 7PH
Tel: 44 03333 550150
Email: alan@touchmedia.uk.com
Web site: www.insidebusiness.co.uk
Freq: Bi-Monthly
Circ: 818 Cision Digital Reach
MAGAZINE (ONLINE)
Business, Corporate Responsibility

Inside Clean Energy   1086844
Editorial: 3rd Floor, America House, 2 America Square, London EC3N 2LU
Tel: 44 02078 710122
Email: info@solarmedia.co.uk
Web site: www.solarpowerportal.co.uk
Freq: Bi-Monthly
Circ: 5000 Not Audited
MAGAZINE
Alternative/Renewable Energy

Inside Construction   1065154
Editorial: Crest House, 19 Lewis Road, Sutton, London SM1 4BR
Tel: 44 02087 700111
Email: info@buildersconf.co.uk
Web site: www.bclive.co.uk/
Freq: Monthly
Circ: 60000 Not Audited
Editor: Mark Anthony
MAGAZINE
Building & Construction

Inside Conveyancing   008308
Editorial: Inside Conveyancing, Suite 2 Gemini Business Centre, 136-140 Old Shoreham Road, Brighton BN3 7BD
Tel: 44 01273 229333
Email: info@insideviews.co.uk
Web site: www.insideconveyancing.co.uk
Freq: Daily
Circ: 14498 Cision Digital Reach
MAGAZINE (ONLINE)
Real Estate Law

Inside Cyber   1099412
Editorial: Room 18, The Mansion, Betchley Park, Milton Keynes MK3 6EB
Tel: 44 02031 412972
Web site: https://cybersecuritychallenge.org.uk/inside-cyber/
Freq: Semi-Annual
Editor: Bryony Chinnery
MAGAZINE
Security & Security Systems

Inside FAC   984827
Editorial: 3rd Floor, 41 Eastcheap, London EC3M 1DT **Tel:** 44 02073 970615
Web site: www.insidefac.com
Freq: Monthly
Circ: 1000 Not Audited
Profile: Magazine covering the global facultative reinsurance markets.
MAGAZINE
Financial Markets, Insurance

Inside Food   987720
Editorial: John Carpenter House, John Carpenter Street, London EC4Y 0AN
Tel: 44 02079 366400
Email: onlinemags@nridigital.com
Web site: http://www.nridigital.com/inside-food-archive.html
Freq: Quarterly
Circ: 141 Cision Digital Reach
Profile: Website covering the food Industry. Inside Food is a digital publication providing in-depth information on the food processing and food service industries.
MAGAZINE (ONLINE)
Food

Inside Housing   980848
Editorial: 1 Canada Square, 21st Floor, Canary Wharf, London E14 5AP
Tel: 44 02077 728300
Email: editorial@insidehousing.co.uk
Web site: www.insidehousing.co.uk
Freq: Weekly
Circ: 16912 Not Audited
Editor: Emma Maier
Profile: Magazine covering news on all aspects of housing, including local government housing, housing association housing, private accommodation, property law, housing benefits and homelessness. Read by members and student members of the Chartered Institute of Housing, local authority housing departments, housing associations and the private sector.
Ad Rate: Full Page Colour £2969.00
MAGAZINE
Residential Real Estate

Inside ICHCA International   998371
Editorial: Suite 5 Meridian House, 62 Station Road, London E4 7BA **Tel:** 44 02033 277560
Web site: http://ichca.com
Freq: Bi-Monthly Not Audited
Editor: Richard Brough
MAGAZINE
Shipping & Warehousing

Inside Learning Technologies & Skills   994699
Editorial: 19 Hurst Park, Midhurst, Midhurst GU29 0BP **Tel:** 44 01730 817601
Email: info@learningtechnologies.co.uk
Web site: www.learningtechnologies.co.uk
Freq: Bi-Monthly
Circ: 80000 Not Audited
Editor: Don Taylor
MAGAZINE
Education, Higher Education

Inside Oil & Gas   1052808
Tel: 44 01502 566216
Email: media@insideindustry.com
Web site: www.insideoilandgas.com
Freq: Bi-Monthly
Circ: 44000 Not Audited
MAGAZINE
Oil

Inside OR   986330
Editorial: The OR Society, Seymour House, 12 Edward Street, Birmingham B1 2RX
Tel: 44 01212 339300
Email: insideor@theorsociety.com
Web site: www.theorsociety.com
Freq: Monthly
Circ: 13700 Not Audited
Editor: John Crocker
Profile: Newsletter concerned with management science including e-commerce and business topics, customer relationship management, database marketing and call centre issues. Aimed at business professionals in medium to large enterprises. Alternative Title: OR Newsletter Previous title: Operational Research Newsletter
Ad Rate: Full Page Mono £1750.00
Ad Rate: Full Page Colour £2045.00
MAGAZINE
Business, Corporate Responsibility

Inside Packaging   985693
Editorial: John Carpenter House, John Carpenter Street, London EC4Y 0AN
Tel: 44 02079 366750
Email: onlinemags@nridigital.com
Web site: http://www.nridigital.com/inside-packaging.html
Freq: Bi-Monthly
Circ: 185 Cision Digital Reach
Profile: Website covering the packaging industry. Inside Packaging is a digital magazine providing 'in-depth coverage of the latest trends and technologies in the packaging industry'.
MAGAZINE (ONLINE)
Supply Chain Management (SCM)

Inside Reference Data   994634
Editorial: Haymarket House, 28-29 Haymarket, London SW1Y 4RX
Tel: 44 02073 169000
Web site: www.waterstechnology.com/inside-reference-data
Freq: Monthly Not Audited
Profile: Magazine covering the global, financial reference data industry. Aimed at senior management involved in data management at global investment banks, institutions and financial services firms. Digital images preferred.
MAGAZINE
Banking, Data Management

InsideCXM   997869
Editorial: The Pithay, 8th floor, All Saints Street, Bristol BS1 2NB
Tel: 44 01179 274500
Web site: insidecxm.com/
Freq: Daily
Circ: 12589 Cision Digital Reach
Editor: James Ainsworth
MAGAZINE (ONLINE)
Business, Corporate Responsibility, Marketing

Insight Magazine (UK)   995447
Editorial: IRRV, 5th Floor, Northumberland House, 393-306 High Holborn, London WC1V 7JZ **Tel:** 44 02078 313505
Email: publications@irrv.org.uk
Web site: http://www.irrv.net/homenew/item.php?wid=15&iid=22104
Freq: Monthly
Circ: 3500 Not Audited
MAGAZINE
Business, Corporate Responsibility

InSite   984665
Editorial: Alban Row, 27-31 Verulam Road, St. Albans AL3 4DG **Tel:** 44 01727 893894
Web site: http://www.builders.org.uk/nfb11/industry_voice.eb
Freq: 3 Times/Year
Circ: 2100 Not Audited
Editor: Paul Bogle
Profile: Membership Magazine of the National Federation of Builders. Covers all aspects of building and construction. Read by small, medium and large building contractors and housebuilders.

Ad Rate: Full Page Colour £1495.00
MAGAZINE
Architecture & Design, Building & Construction

INSOL World
980720
Editorial: 6-7 Queen Street, London EC4N 1SP **Tel:** 44 02072 483333
Web site: www.insol.org
Freq: Quarterly
Circ: 10000 Not Audited
MAGAZINE
Accounting

Insolvency and Restructuring International
997310
Editorial: 4th Floor, 10 St Bride Street, London EC4A 4AD **Tel:** 44 02078 420090
Email: editor@int-bar.org
Web site: http://www.ibanet.org/ Publications/publications_insolvency_and_ restructuring_international.aspx
Freq: Semi-Annual
Circ: 800 Not Audited
MAGAZINE
Corporate Law

Insolvency News
1054186
Editorial: Axe & Bottle Court, 70 Newcomen Street, London SE1 1YT
Tel: 44 02079 404835
Web site: www.insolvencynews.com
Freq: Daily
Circ: 14416 Cision Digital Reach
MAGAZINE (ONLINE)
Accounting, Corporate Law

inspire
995396
Editorial: 1 Giltspur Street, London EC1A 9DD **Tel:** 44 02072 942470
Email: recruitment@cityandguilds.com
Web site: www.i-l-m.com/Insight
Freq: Daily
Circ: 7 Cision Digital Reach
Profile: Lifestyle magazine with coverage of local events and personalities including features on restaurants, wine, fashion, beauty, health, motoring, travel, interiors and gardening.
Ad Rate: Full Page Colour £895.00
MAGAZINE (ONLINE)
Business, Corporate Responsibility

Installer
981103
Editorial: Unit 7, Oakridge Office Park, Southampton Road, Salisbury SP5 3HT
Tel: 44 01722 711332
Email: editor@installermagazine.co.uk
Web site: www.installeronline.co.uk
Freq: Monthly
Circ: 40909 Not Audited
Editor: Mark McGettigan
Profile: Journal for CORGI registered gas installers, includes technical features, industry news and a training and recruitment section. Average Pages per Issue: 60. Press Day: 20th of the month. Previous title: The Gas Installer Aimed at heating, plumbing and renewable professionals.
Ad Rate: Full Page Colour £4520.00
MAGAZINE
Oil

The Installer
987174
Editorial: The Studio, 47 Hillside Avenue, Elstree & Borehamwood, London WD6 1HQ
Tel: 44 02083 815511
Email: installer@profinder.eu
Web site: www.profinder.eu
Freq: Monthly
Circ: 7000 Not Audited
Profile: Journal for CORGI registered gas installers, includes technical features, industry news and a training and recruitment section. Average Pages per Issue: 60. Press Day: 20th of the month. Previous title: The Gas Installer Aimed at heating, plumbing and renewable professionals.
Ad Rate: Full Page Colour £4520.00
MAGAZINE
Building & Construction, Interior Design

InstaPay
1095734
Editorial: 158-160 North Gower Street, London NW1 2ND **Tel:** 44 02038 249200
Web site: http://www.instapay.today/
Freq: Daily
Editor: Mark McMurtrie
MAGAZINE (ONLINE)
Banking

InstinctBusiness
1008429
Editorial: 10 Mayfield Road, Belvedere, London DA17 6DX **Tel:** 44 01322 683229
Email: info@instinctbusinessmag.com
Web site: http://instinctbusinessmag.com
Freq: Monthly Not Audited
MAGAZINE
Business

The Institute of Internal Communication
988193
Editorial: Suite G10, Gemini House, Sunrise Parkway, Linford Wood, Milton Keynes MK14 6PW **Tel:** 44 01489 861345
Email: barryrutter@mandarin-kite.com
Web site: http://ioic.org.uk/ioic-knows/ industry-news.html
Freq: Daily
Circ: 227 Cision Digital Reach
MAGAZINE (ONLINE)
Human Resources

Institute of Water Journal
984084
Editorial: 4 Carlton Court, Team Valley, Gateshead NE11 0AZ **Tel:** 44 01914 220088
Email: info@instituteofwater.org.uk
Web site: www.instituteofwater.org.uk/ journal/
Freq: Quarterly
Circ: 2000 Not Audited
Profile: Journal containing technical articles, product launches, engineering section, environmental section, IWO area news reports and water industry related news. Includes section dedicated to products and services, highlighting products, equipment and services both established and new to the water industry market. Aimed at members, senior management, engineers, key personnel and decision makers within the water and waste industries and subscribers as well as manufacturers of equipment and suppliers of services to the industry.Previous title: IWO Journal
Ad Rate: Full Page Colour £1000.00
MAGAZINE
Water & Sanitation

Instrument News
996233
Editorial: Fortuna Publishing Ltd., 87b Greswood Street, London SW16 6QW
Tel: 44 02086 777251
Web site: www.instrumentnews.co.uk
Freq: Monthly Not Audited
MAGAZINE
Science

Insurance Age
979885
Editorial: Haymarket House, 28-29 Haymarket, London SW1Y 4RX
Tel: 44 02074 849700
Web site: www.insuranceage.co.uk
Freq: Monthly
Circ: 13635 Not Audited
Profile: Magazine containing insurance-related issues in personal and commercial insurance, loss adjusting, risk and claims management. Read by general insurance brokers based within the United Kingdom.
Ad Rate: Full Page Colour £6070.00
MAGAZINE
Insurance

Insurance Asset Risk
988006
Editorial: Pentagon House, 52-54 Southwark Street, London SE1 1UN
Tel: 44 02072 519151
Web site: www.insuranceassetrisk.com
Freq: Daily
Circ: 10643 Cision Digital Reach
MAGAZINE (ONLINE)
Insurance

Insurance Business Review
1099267
Editorial: Insurance Business Review, Progressive Trade Media Ltd, 40-42 Hatton Garden, London EC1N 8EB
Email: news@industryreview.com
Web site: http://www.insurance-business-review.com/
Freq: Daily
Circ: 2626 Cision Digital Reach
MAGAZINE (ONLINE)
Insurance

Insurance Business UK
1062740
Editorial: Aldgate Tower, 2 Leman Street, London E1 8FA
Web site: http://www. insurancebusinessmag.com/uk/
Freq: Daily
Circ: 10769 Cision Digital Reach
Editor: Paul Lucas
MAGAZINE (ONLINE)
Business, Insurance, Small and Medium Business

Insurance Day
979886
Editorial: Christchurch Court, 10-15 Newgate, London EC1A 7AZ
Tel: 44 02075 519906
Email: editorial@insuranceday.com
Web site: www.insuranceday.com
Freq: Daily
Circ: 249 Not Audited
Editor: Michael Faulkner
Profile: Website covering insurance. Insurance day is an online news and research service from Informa Maritime & Professional, delivering the latest insurance news, commentary and analysis online across eight key channels, covering international insurance and risk.
Ad Rate: Full Page Mono £3500.00
Ad Rate: Full Page Colour £4375.00
MAGAZINE
Insurance

Insurance Edge
998647
Editorial: Centrix House, 26 Crow Lane, Newton-le-Willows WA12 9UH
Web site: http://insuranceedge.co.uk
Freq: Daily
Circ: 611 Cision Digital Reach
MAGAZINE (ONLINE)
Insurance

Insurance Hound
997557
Editorial: Haymarket House, 28-29 Haymarket, London SW1Y 4RX
Tel: 44 02073 169000
Email: info@insurancehound.co.uk
Web site: www.insurancehound.co.uk
Freq: Daily
Circ: 11945 Cision Digital Reach
Editor: Stephanie Denton
MAGAZINE (ONLINE)
Insurance

The Insurance Insider
980779
Editorial: 3rd Floor, 41 Eastcheap, London EC3M 1DT **Tel:** 44 02073 970615
Email: info@insuranceinsider.com
Web site: www.insuranceinsider.com
Freq: Weekly
Circ: 8123 Not Audited
Profile: Publication focusing on international insurance and reinsurance markets. The Insurance Insider provides a combination of breaking news alerts together with critical analysis of industry trends. Aimed at insurance professionals.
Ad Rate: Full Page Colour £4000.00
MAGAZINE
Insurance

Insurance Times
979887
Editorial: 120 Leman Street, London E1 8EU
Tel: 44 02076 183456
Web site: www.insurancetimes.co.uk
Freq: Bi-Weekly
Circ: 4000 Not Audited
Profile: Magazine covering news of and from the personal and commercial insurance

world. Aimed at insurance brokers and those involved in general insurance companies.
Ad Rate: Full Page Colour £7826.00
MAGAZINE
Insurance

InsuranceERM
984828
Editorial: Pentagon House, 52-54 Southwark Street, London SE1 1UN
Tel: 44 02036 517203
Web site: www.insuranceerm.com
Freq: Daily
Circ: 13665 Cision Digital Reach
Profile: Website covering insurance and risk management for businesses. InsuranceERM discusses anything from insurance policies to market risk and risk governance.
MAGAZINE (ONLINE)
Insurance

InsurancePOST
979888
Editorial: Haymarket House, 28-29 Haymarket, London SW1Y 4RX
Tel: 44 02073 169000
Email: postonline@incisivemedia.com
Web site: www.postonline.co.uk
Freq: Monthly
Circ: 24615 Not Audited
Editor: Stephanie Denton
Profile: Magazine covering UK and International insurance industry news, opinions, analysis and technical features including comprehensive and authoritative coverage of all issues of interest to the UK insurance industry through quality news and analysis, lively comment, in-depth topical features and strong technical articles and broadcasts. Read by all those involved in the insurance industry including insurance companies, brokers and intermediaries, corporate insurance buyers and service suppliers such as lawyers, IT companies and consultants.Previous title: Post Magazine & Insurance Week
Ad Rate: Full Page Colour £4608.00
MAGAZINE
Insurance

Intellectual Asset Management
980903
Editorial: New Hibernia House, Winchester Walk, London Bridge, London SE1 9AG
Tel: 44 02072 340606
Email: info@iam-magazine.com
Web site: www.iam-magazine.com
Freq: Bi-Monthly
Circ: 2500 Not Audited
Profile: Magazine covering business issues surrounding intellectual property and assets. Aimed at CEOs, finance directors, CIOs, in-house lawyers, analysts and investors.
Ad Rate: Full Page Colour £3000.00
MAGAZINE
Intellectual Property

Intellectual Property Magazine
980158
Editorial: Informa Law, Christchurch Court, 10-15 Newgate Street, London EC1A 7AZ
Tel: 44 02070 176129
Email: ipmeditorial@informa.com
Web site: www. intellectualpropertymagazine.com/
Freq: Monthly
Circ: 7500 Not Audited
Editor: Maura O'Malley
Profile: Intellectual Property Magazine delivers global Intellectual Property Intelligence to IP lawyers, CEOs, managing partners, directors and brand owners.
Ad Rate: Full Page Colour £5250.00
MAGAZINE
Intellectual Property

Intelligent Networks
999024
Editorial: Christchurch Court, 10-15 Newgate Street, London EC1A 7AZ
Tel: 44 02070 174994
Email: enquiries@ovum.com
Web site: www.ovum.com/intelligent-networks
Freq: Bi-Weekly
Circ: 44 Cision Digital Reach
MAGAZINE (ONLINE)
Mobile Communications

Business Magazines

Intelligent Sourcing 985975

Editorial: 10 Knights Way, Ilford, London IG6 2RR
Web site: http://intelligentsourcing.net/
Freq: Quarterly
Circ: 15273 Cision Digital Reach
MAGAZINE (ONLINE)
Business, Small and Medium Business

Intensive and Critical Care Nursing 981042

Editorial: Stover Court, Bampfylde Street, Exeter, Exeter EX1 2AH
Tel: 44 01392 285877
Email: iccn@elsevier.com
Web site: www.elsevier.com/wps/find/journaldescription.cws_home/623043/description
Freq: Bi-Monthly
Circ: 19000 Not Audited
Profile: Journal focusing on updates and reviews. Features articles on relevant clinical research including educational, psychological and technical aspects. Aimed at those within the nursing profession.
Ad Rate: Full Page Mono £520.00
Ad Rate: Full Page Colour £985.00
MAGAZINE
Anesthesiology, Nursing/Nurses

Intercontinental Finance & Law 985679

Editorial: The Byre, The Street, Bolney, Haywards Heath RH17 5PG
Tel: 44 01444 881004
Web site: http://intercontinental-finance.com/
Freq: Monthly
Circ: 155000 Not Audited
MAGAZINE
Banking, Investment Banking, Private Equity

Interfax Global Energy Services 999273

Editorial: 5th Floor, 19-21 Great Tower Street, London EC3R 5AQ
Tel: 44 02030 046206
Email: customer.service@interfax.co.uk
Web site: www.interfaxenergy.com
Freq: Daily
Circ: 29944 Cision Digital Reach
MAGAZINE (ONLINE)
Carbon Emissions & Trading, Commodities, Oil

Interior Design Today 983490

Editorial: 1 Accent Park, Bakewell Road, Orton Southgate, Peterborough PE2 6XS
Tel: 44 01733 385300
Email: idt@onecoms.co.uk
Web site: http://idnews.co.uk/
Freq: Bi-Monthly
Circ: 12000 Not Audited
Editor: Jade Tilley
Profile: Magazine covering products, news, applications and features regarding the interior design industry. Aimed at interior designers, architects, soft furnishings retailers, furniture retailers, department stores and mail order companies.
Ad Rate: Full Page Colour £565.00
MAGAZINE
Architecture & Design, Interior Design

Interiors Monthly 984522

Editorial: Minerva House, Bordyke, Tonbridge, Tonbridge TN9 1NR
Tel: 44 01732 441130
Email: enquiries@Interiorsmonthly.co.uk
Web site: www.interiorsmonthly.co.uk
Freq: Monthly
Circ: 7500 Not Audited
Editor: Andrew Kidd
Profile: Magazine covering furniture, flooring, interiors and retailing. Aimed at interior retailers.
Ad Rate: Full Page Colour £2400.00
MAGAZINE
Interior Design

International Accountant 980834

Editorial: Staithes 3, Watermark, Metro Riverside, Gateshead NE11 9SN
Tel: 44 01914 930281
Email: editor@aiaworldwide.com
Web site: www.aiaworldwide.com/international-accountant
Freq: Bi-Monthly
Circ: 26000 Not Audited
Editor: Rachel Rutherford
Profile: Magazine covering news of accountancy innovations, developments, economic and management issues. Contains news, features, technical information and legislative updates in the profession of accountancy. Contributions are sourced from practitioners and academics. Aimed at all those working in accountancy, auditing, finance, business, and economics.
Ad Rate: Full Page Colour £3000.00
MAGAZINE
Accounting

International Accounting Bulletin 979919

Editorial: International Accounting Bulletin, 71-73 Carter Lane, London EC4V 5EQ
Tel: 44 02079 366400
Web site: http://www.internationalaccountingbulletin.com
Freq: Monthly Not Audited
Profile: Business intelligence journal for accounting firms worldwide, coverage of medium-and smaller-sized firms. Each issue has country surveys of local accountancy industries with detailed firm-specification data. Aimed at accountants worldwide. It provides analysis and intelligence on the latest mergers and acquisitions, key appointments, firms and network strategies, alliances and staffing issues.
MAGAZINE
Accounting

International Agricultural Trade 1061481

Tel: 44 86108 7109885
Web site: http://www.agriftchina.com
Freq: Quarterly
Circ: 20005 Not Audited
MAGAZINE
Animal Farming

International Airport Review 981322

Editorial: Court Lodge, Hogtrough Hill, Brasted, Westerham TN16 1NU
Tel: 44 01959 563311
Email: airport@russellpublishing.com
Web site: www.internationalairportreview.com
Freq: Bi-Monthly
Circ: 10099 Not Audited
Editor: Craig Waters
Profile: Magazine carrying in-depth articles on technological advancements and business strategies that affect the running of commercial airports worldwide.
Ad Rate: Full Page Colour £4850.00
MAGAZINE
Aviation

International Animal Health Journal 998295

Editorial: Unit J413, The Biscuit Factory Tower Bridge Business Complex, 100 Clements Road, London SE16 4DG
Tel: 44 02072 372036
Email: info@iahjmedia.com
Web site: http://animalhealthmedia.com/
Freq: Quarterly
Circ: 17000 Not Audited
Editor: Orsolya Balogh
MAGAZINE
Veterinary Medicine

International Aquafeed 986454

Editorial: 7 St George's Terrace, St James' Square, Cheltenham, Cheltenham GL50 3PT
Tel: 44 01242 267700
Email: info@perendale.co.uk
Web site: www.aquafeed.co.uk
Freq: Bi-Monthly Not Audited

Editor: Simon Davies
Profile: Magazine covering the design, production and delivery of feed to farmed aquatic species. Aimed at fish food manufacturers.
Ad Rate: Full Page Colour £2500.00
MAGAZINE
Animal Farming, Manufacturing

International Arbitration Law Review 998677

Editorial: The Hatchery, Hill Bank Lane, Mytholmroyd HX7 5HQ
Tel: 44 02073 937000
Email: stuart.murray@thomsonreuters.com
Web site: http://www.sweetandmaxwell.co.uk/Catalogue/ProductDetails.aspx?productid=6778&recordid=375
Freq: Bi-Monthly Not Audited
MAGAZINE
Litigation

International Banker 1010714

Editorial: New House, 67-68 Hatton Garden, London EC1N 8JY **Tel:** 44 02078 872533
Email: enquiries@financepublishing.com
Web site: http://www.internationalbanker.com/
Freq: Quarterly
Circ: 62000 Not Audited
Editor: Simon Brown
MAGAZINE
Banking

International Bulk Journal 985050

Editorial: Bryn Siriol, Llangollen LL20 7BE
Tel: 44 01691 718045
Email: info@ibj-online.com
Web site: www.ibj-online.com
Freq: Bi-Monthly
Circ: 6000 Not Audited
Editor: Giles Large
Profile: Magazine providing covering the dry bulk trade, transportation and handling industry.First published in 1981. Aimed at decision makers in industry in the UK and overseas.
Ad Rate: Full Page Colour £2995.00
MAGAZINE
Commodities, Shipping & Warehousing, Supply Chain Management (SCM)

International Business Law Journal 1054400

Editorial: 100 Avenue Road, London NW3 3PF **Tel:** 44 02073 937000
Web site: www.iblj.com
Freq: Bi-Monthly Not Audited
MAGAZINE
Business, Corporate Law, Small and Medium Business

International Cement Review 980137

Editorial: Old Kings Head Court, 15 High Street, Dorking RH4 1AR
Tel: 44 01306 740363
Email: info@cemnet.com
Web site: www.cemnet.com
Freq: Monthly
Profile: Journal covering the storage, shipping and trading of cement, clinker and allied materials worldwide. Aimed at cement producers, terminal operators and distributors. Alternative Title: Revista del Cemento
Ad Rate: Full Page Mono £2000.00
Ad Rate: Full Page Colour £3000.00
MAGAZINE
Engineering, Manufacturing

International Clinical Trials 994658

Editorial: First Floor, 131 Edgware Road, London W2 2HR **Tel:** 44 02077 243456
Email: info@samedanltd.com
Web site: http://www.samedanltd.com/magazine/13
Freq: Quarterly Not Audited
Editor: Graham Hughes
MAGAZINE
Pharmaceuticals

International Construction 983054

Editorial: Southfields, Southview Road, Wadhurst, Wadhurst TN5 6TP
Tel: 44 01892 784088
Email: info@khl.com
Web site: www.khl.com/magazines/international-construction
Freq: Monthly
Circ: 26506 Not Audited
Editor: Mike Hayes
Profile: News of technological developments and techniques within the international construction industry.
Ad Rate: Full Page Colour £8200.00
MAGAZINE
Building & Construction

International Corporate Rescue 1023283

Editorial: 4 Winifred Close, Barnet, Arkley, Grays EN5 3LR
Email: submissions@chasecambria.com
Web site: www.chasecambria.com
Freq: Bi-Monthly Not Audited
MAGAZINE
Corporate Law

International Dairy Topics 983574

Editorial: PO Box 4, Driffield YO25 9DJ
Tel: 44 01377 241724
Email: info@positiveaction.co.uk
Web site: www.positiveaction.info
Freq: Bi-Monthly
Circ: 20000 Not Audited
Profile: Magazine covering health, breeding, forage production, nutrition and milking equipment for dairy cattle. Aimed at leading dairy farmers, breeders and A1 professionals, dairy veterinarians, dairy nutritionists, professional dairy advisors, statutory personnel, research and laboratory managers and dairy trainers and educators.
Ad Rate: Full Page Mono £3027.00
Ad Rate: Full Page Colour £3557.00
MAGAZINE
Animal Farming

International Dental Journal 985469

Editorial: 9600 Garsington Road, Oxford OX4 2DQ **Tel:** 44 01865 776868
Email: syoung@wiley.com
Web site: http://onlinelibrary.wiley.com/journal/10.1002/(ISSN)1875-595X
Freq: Bi-Monthly
Circ: 130 Not Audited
Profile: Scientific journal focusing on clinical dentistry. Read by dental professionals worldwide.
Ad Rate: Full Page Mono £825.00
Ad Rate: Full Page Colour £1485.00
MAGAZINE
Dentistry

International Design Engineer 984090

Editorial: Europa House, 13-17 Ironmonger Row, London EC1V 3QG
Tel: 44 02072 532545
Email: mail@setform.com
Web site: www.engineerlive.com/Design-Engineer
Freq: Monthly
Circ: 25000 Not Audited
Editor: Louise Smyth
Profile: Magazine covering the latest technological developments within Europe.
Ad Rate: Full Page Colour £5350.00
MAGAZINE
Engineering

International Development Planning Review 983950

Editorial: Dept of Civic Design, The Gordon Stephenson Building, University of Liverpool, 74 Bedford Street South, Liverpool L69 7ZT
Tel: 44 01517 943135
Email: clare.hooper@liv.ac.uk
Web site: http://online.liverpooluniversitypress.co.uk/loi/idpr

Freq: Quarterly Not Audited
MAGAZINE
Building & Construction, Urban Planning & Development

International Emergency Nursing
999429
Editorial: The Boulevard, Langford Lane, Kidlington OX5 1GB **Tel:** 44 01865 843000
Email: ienj@elsevier.com
Web site: http://www.internationalemergencynursing.com/
Freq: Quarterly Not Audited
MAGAZINE
EMS/Emergency Medical Services, Nursing/Nurses

International Energy Law Review
980895
Editorial: Thomson Reuters, Legal UK & Ireland, 5 Canada Square, Canary Wharf, London E14 5AQ **Tel:** 44 02075 426664
Web site: http://www.sweetandmaxwell.co.uk/Catalogue/ProductDetails.aspx?recordid=363
Freq: Monthly Not Audited
Profile: Journal covering legislation, court decisions and fiscal developments. For energy lawyers, tax and financial advisers and accountants.
MAGAZINE
Alternative/Renewable Energy, Carbon Emissions & Trading, Electricity, Energy, Nuclear Power, Oil, Water & Sanitation

International Financial Law Review
979927
Editorial: 8 Bouverie Street, London EC4Y 8AX **Tel:** 44 02077 798888
Web site: www.iflr.com
Freq: Monthly
Circ: 6788 Not Audited
Editor: Amélie Labbé
Profile: Magazine covering developments in financial law, banking law and capital markets, structured finance and M&A. Aimed at private practice lawyers, in-house counsel, bankers and corporate officers involved in international capital markets and banking.
Ad Rate: Full Page Mono £3595.00
Ad Rate: Full Page Colour £4495.00
MAGAZINE
Tax Law

International Fire Buyer
984985
Editorial: Goldings, Elphicks Farm, Water Lane, Hunton, Maidstone ME15 0SG
Tel: 44 01622 823920
Web site: www.firebuyer.com
Freq: Bi-Monthly
Circ: 40000 Not Audited
Profile: Magazine covering fire fighting equipment and products, industry news and a guide to relevant companies and services. Aimed at purchasers and specifiers within the fire protection industry worldwide.
Ad Rate: Full Page Colour £3950.00
MAGAZINE
Security & Security Systems

International Fire Fighter
986007
Editorial: The Abbey Manor Business Centre, Preston Road, Yeovil, Yeovil BA20 2EN **Tel:** 44 01935 426428
Email: info@mdmpublishing.com
Web site: www.iffmag.mdmpublishing.com/
Freq: Quarterly
Circ: 7000 Not Audited
Profile: Magazine that covers municipal and industrial fire training. Aimed at training officers, fire chiefs and fire training schools and colleges.
Ad Rate: Full Page Colour £1750.00
MAGAZINE
Security & Security Systems

International Fire Professional
1033438
Editorial: Ground Floor, Rayford House, School Road, Hove BN3 5HX
Tel: 44 01273 434943
Email: info@fire-magazine.co.uk
Web site: http://www.fire-magazine.com

Freq: Quarterly Not Audited
MAGAZINE
Security & Security Systems

International Fire Protection
981267
Editorial: The Abbey Manor Business Centre, Preston Road, Yeovil, Yeovil BA20 2EN **Tel:** 44 01935 426428
Email: editorial@mdmpublishing.com
Web site: www.ifpmag.mdmpublishing.com/
Freq: Quarterly
Circ: 7150 Not Audited
Profile: Magazine that provides information concerning the international fire protection industry. Aimed at specifiers, fire and safety officers, contractors, architects, building and design engineers, installers, end users and manufacturers.
Ad Rate: Full Page Colour £1750.00
MAGAZINE
Health & Safety, Security & Security Systems

International Food & Meat Topics
986033
Tel: 44 01377 241724
Email: info@positiveaction.co.uk
Web site: www.positiveaction.info
Freq: Bi-Monthly
Circ: 24000 Not Audited
Profile: Magazine covering meat and fish products including key issues on quality, processing, safety and hygiene. Aimed at those working in the meat industry, including CEOs, COOs, production and technical directors, abattoirs, QA/QC managers, production managers, supermarkets, food technologists, laboratories, technical auditors, inspectorates and suppliers.
Ad Rate: Full Page Colour £3593.00
MAGAZINE
Animal Farming

International Forest Industries (IFI)
984567
Editorial: 2 Claridge Court, Lower Kings Road, Berkhamsted, Berkhamsted HP4 2AF
Tel: 44 01442 877583
Web site: www.internationalforestindustries.com
Freq: Bi-Monthly
Circ: 13090 Not Audited
Editor: Chris Cann
MAGAZINE
Animal Farming, Environment

International Gas Report
983056
Editorial: 20 Canada Square, 12th Floor, Canary Wharf, London E14 5LH
Tel: 44 02071 767000
Email: power@platts.com
Web site: www.platts.com
Freq: Bi-Weekly Not Audited
Profile: Newsletter carrying analysis, news and market information about gas worldwide. Read by gas producers and utilities, major users, contractors and equipment manufacturers. Also suppliers, investors and analysts.
MAGAZINE
Oil

International Guide to the Coalfields
986496
Editorial: 9 Storey Avenue, Gedling, Nottingham NG4 4GN **Tel:** 44 01777 871007
Email: admin@mqworld.com
Web site: www.mqworld.com
Freq: Annual Not Audited
Editor: Trevor Barratt
Profile: Journal covering news and information on coal mining and supporting engineering services.
Ad Rate: Full Page Colour £2400.00
MAGAZINE
Mining & Quarrying

International Hatchery Practice
986031
Tel: 44 01377 241724
Email: info@positiveaction.co.uk
Web site: www.positiveaction.info
Freq: Bi-Monthly

Circ: 13000 Not Audited
Profile: Magazine covering all aspects of hatching and poultry breeding, incubating and hatching. Aimed at poultry breeder farms, hatcheries, veterinarians and nutritionists.
Ad Rate: Full Page Colour £2854.00
MAGAZINE
Animal Farming

International Hospitals & Medical Tourism Review
997308
Editorial: 19 Lower Park Row, Bristol BS1 5BN **Tel:** 44 01179 255151
Web site: www.ihmt.global
Freq: Annual
Circ: 20000 Not Audited
Editor: Sarah Watson
MAGAZINE
Healthcare Industry

International HR Adviser
982816
Editorial: P.O. Box 921, Sutton SM1 2WB
Tel: 44 02086 610186
Web site: www.internationalhradviser.co.uk
Freq: Quarterly
Circ: 6922 Not Audited
Profile: Magazine covering topics specific to the field of international human resource management including taxation, immigration, technology, employment law, compensation and benefits, relocation, health, relocation education, IHR surveys and data analysis as well as a directory and a diary dates section. Aimed at human resource professionals.
Ad Rate: Full Page Mono £2250.00
Ad Rate: Full Page Colour £2700.00
MAGAZINE
Company News & Appointments, Education, Health & Safety, Human Resources, Recruiting

International Innovation
997788
Editorial: Suite 7C Whitefriars, Bristol BS1 2NT **Tel:** 44 01173 324961
Email: info@researchmedia.com
Web site: www.internationalinnovation.com
Freq: Daily
Circ: 21874 Cision Digital Reach
MAGAZINE (ONLINE)
Environment, Government Technology, Healthcare Industry

International Insolvency Review
984535
Editorial: The Atrium, Southern Gate, Chichester PO19 8SQ **Tel:** 44 01243 779777
Email: cs-journals@wiley.co.uk
Web site: http://onlinelibrary.wiley.com/journal/10.1002/(ISSN)1099-1107
Freq: 3 Times/Year Not Audited
Editor: Ian Fletcher
Profile: Official journal of the International Association of Insolvency Practitioners (INSOL International), providing authoritative analysis and commentary on key insolvency issues across major jurisdictions in Europe and the EC, Eastern Europe, the US, the Far East, Asia and Australia. They do not wish to receive external press releases.
MAGAZINE
Accounting

International Investment
1050391
Editorial: Cairo Studios, 4 Nile Street, London N1 7RF
Email: iieditorial@odmpublishing.com
Web site: http://www.internationalinvestment.net/subscription/
Freq: Monthly
Circ: 15000 Not Audited
MAGAZINE
Financial Markets

The International Journal for Quality in Health Care
998966
Editorial: Great Clarendon Street, Oxford OX2 6DP **Tel:** 44 01865 353907
Email: ijhqc.editorialoffice@oup.com
Web site: intqhc.oxfordjournals.org/

Freq: Bi-Monthly Not Audited
MAGAZINE
Health Administration

International Journal of Cardiology
995844
Editorial: The Boulevard, Langford Lane, Kidlington OX5 1GB **Tel:** 44 01865 843000
Email: internationaljournalcardiology@gmail.com
Web site: www.elsevier.com/wps/find/journaldescription.cws_home/506041/description
Freq: Bi-Weekly Not Audited
MAGAZINE
Cardiology

International Journal of Culture and Mental Health
999131
Tel: 44 02070 176000
Web site: http://www.tandf.co.uk/journals/journal.asp?issn=1754-2863&linktype=5
Freq: Quarterly Not Audited
Editor: Kamaldeep Bhui
MAGAZINE
Neurology

International Journal of Development Issues
995390
Editorial: Emerald Group Publishing, Howard House, Wagon Lane, Bingley BD16 1WA **Tel:** 44 01274 777700
Web site: http://www.emeraldinsight.com/journal/ijdi
Freq: 3 Times/Year Not Audited
MAGAZINE
Economics

International Journal of Endocrine Oncology
1053353
Editorial: Unitec House, 2 Albert Place, London N3 1QB **Tel:** 44 02083 716090
Email: info@future-science-group.com
Web site: http://www.futuremedicine.com/loi/ije
Freq: Semi-Annual
Circ: 551 Not Audited
MAGAZINE
Diabetes, Oncology

International Journal of Experimental Pathology
996761
Editorial: IJEP Editorial Office, Division of Infection & Immunity, University College London, Cruciform Building, Gower Street, London WC1E 6BT **Tel:** 44 02031 082122
Email: b.nikolic@ucl.ac.uk
Web site: http://onlinelibrary.wiley.com/journal/10.1111/(ISSN)1365-2613
Freq: Bi-Monthly Not Audited
Editor: David R Katz
MAGAZINE
Science

International Journal of Geriatric Psychiatry
995939
Tel: 44 01865 778315
Email: orange.journal@manchester.ac.uk
Web site: http://onlinelibrary.wiley.com/journal/10.1002/(ISSN)1099-1166
Freq: Monthly Not Audited
MAGAZINE
Geriatrics, Neurology

International Journal of Gynecology & Obstetrics
997102
Editorial: FIGO House, Suite 3, Waterloo Court, 10 Theed Street, London SE1 8ST
Tel: 44 02079 281166
Email: ijgo@figo.org
Web site: www.ijgo.org
Freq: Monthly Not Audited
MAGAZINE
Obstetrics & Gynecology (OB/GYN)

International Journal of Hematologic Oncology
1054124
Editorial: Unitec House, 2 Albert Place, London N3 1QB **Tel:** 44 02083 716090
Email: info@future-science-group.com

Business Magazines

Web site: http://www.future-science-group.com/journalprofile/international-journal-of-hematologic-oncology/
Freq: Bi-Monthly
MAGAZINE
Hematology, Oncology

International Journal of Infectious Disease
998798
Editorial: IJID Editorial Office, Elsevier, The Boulevard, Langford Lane, Kidlington OX5 1GB **Tel:** 44 01865 843434
Email: ijid@elsevier.com
Web site: www.ijidonline.com
Freq: Monthly
Circ: 11185 Not Audited
MAGAZINE
Infectious Diseases

International Journal of Law & Information Technology
983377
Editorial: Great Clarendon Street, Oxford OX2 6DP **Tel:** 44 01865 353907
Web site: http://ijlit.oxfordjournals.org/
Freq: Quarterly Not Audited
MAGAZINE
Computers, Intellectual Property

International Journal of Older People Nursing
998770
Editorial: Wiley-Blackwell, 9600 Garsington Road, Oxford OX4 2DQ
Tel: 44 01865 778315
Email: opnedoffice@wiley.com
Web site: http://onlinelibrary.wiley.com/journal/10.1111/%28ISSN%291748-3743
Freq: Daily
Circ: 473 Cision Digital Reach
MAGAZINE (ONLINE)
Geriatrics, Nursing/Nurses

International Journal of Orthopaedic and Trauma Nursing
995737
Editorial: The Boulevard, Langford Lane, Kidlington OX5 1GB **Tel:** 44 01865 843000
Email: yjoon@elsevier.com
Web site: http://www.elsevier.com/wps/find/journaldescription.cws_home/722406/description
Freq: Quarterly Not Audited
MAGAZINE
Nursing/Nurses, Orthopedics

International Journal of Paediatric Dentistry
995874
Editorial: The Atrium, Southern Gate, Chichester PO19 8QG **Tel:** 44 01865 778315
Email: ijpdedoffice@wiley.com
Web site: www.blackwellpublishing.com/journal.asp?ref=0960-7439&site=1
Freq: Bi-Monthly Not Audited
MAGAZINE
Dentistry, Pediatrics

International Journal of Palliative Nursing
985141
Editorial: St Jude's Church, Dulwich Road, London SE24 0PB **Tel:** 44 02077 385454
Email: ijpn@markallengroup.com
Web site: http://www.ijpn.co.uk/
Freq: Monthly
Circ: 16000 Not Audited
Profile: Journal covering the full range of subjects encompassed in palliative care, including nursing, clinical, research, educational, ethical and professional issues. Aimed at palliative care nurses and other health professionals working in palliative care. Alternative Title: IJPN
Ad Rate: Full Page Mono £990.00
Ad Rate: Full Page Colour £1800.00
MAGAZINE
Nursing/Nurses

International Journal of Pharmaceutics
999266
Editorial: The Boulevard, Langford Lane, Kidlington, Oxford OX5 1GB
Tel: 44 01865 843000
Email: ijp@elsevier.com

Web site: http://www.journals.elsevier.com/international-journal-of-pharmaceutics/
Freq: Weekly Not Audited
MAGAZINE
Pharmaceuticals

International Journal of Pharmacokinetics
994681
Editorial: Future Science Group, Unitec House, 2 Albert Place, London N3 1QB
Tel: 44 02083 716090
Email: info@future-science.com
Web site: http://www.future-science.com/page/loi/ipk
Freq: Bi-Monthly
MAGAZINE
Healthcare Industry, Pharmaceuticals

International Journal of Pharmacy Practice
985425
Editorial: The Atrium, Southern Gate, Chichester PO19 8QG **Tel:** 44 01865 778315
Email: ijppeditorialoffice@wiley.com
Web site: http://onlinelibrary.wiley.com/journal/10.1111/(ISSN)2042-7174
Freq: Bi-Monthly Not Audited
Editor: Christine Bond
Profile: Journal covering research and review articles on all aspects of medicines management, policy, practice and education.
MAGAZINE
Pharmaceuticals

International Journal of Pressure Vessels and Piping
998766
Editorial: The Boulevard, Langford Lane, Kidlington, Kidlington OX5 1GB
Tel: 44 01865 843000
Web site: www.journals.elsevier.com/international-journal-of-pressure-vessels-and-piping
Freq: Monthly Not Audited
MAGAZINE
Engineering

International Journal of Psychiatry in Clinical Practice
999244
Editorial: 4 Park Square, Milton Park, Abingdon OX14 4RN **Tel:** 44 02070 176000
Email: ijpcp@informa.com
Web site: www.informahealthcare.com/journal/jpc
Freq: Quarterly Not Audited
MAGAZINE
Neurology

The International Journal of Psychoanalysis
987662
Editorial: The Institute of Psychoanalysis, Byron House, 112A Shirland Road, London W9 2BT
Email: ijpaoffice@wiley.com
Web site: onlinelibrary.wiley.com/journal/10.1111/%28ISSN%291745-8315
Freq: Bi-Monthly
Circ: 5000 Not Audited
Profile: Journal featuring articles on subjects including psychoanalytic theory and technique, methodology, the history of psychoanalysis, clinical communications, research and life-cycle development, education and professional issues, psychoanalytic psychotherapy and interdisciplinary studies.
Ad Rate: Full Page Mono £595.00
MAGAZINE
Neurology

The International Journal of Sales Transformation
1097890
Editorial: B1 Laser Quay, Culpeper Close, Medway City Estate, Rochester ME2 4HU
Email: editor@journalofsalestransformation.com
Web site: http://www.journalofsalestransformation.com/
Freq: Quarterly
MAGAZINE
Business, Small and Medium Business

International Journal of Science Education
999135
Email: ijscienceeducation@gmail.com
Web site: www.tandf.co.uk/journals/journal.asp?issn=0950-0693&linktype=5
Freq: Monthly
Editor: Justin Dillon; **Editor:** Jan Van Driel; **Editor:** Gail Jones; **Editor:** Rosária Justi; **Editor:** Norman G. Lederman; **Editor:** David Treagust
MAGAZINE
Science

International Journal of STD & AIDS
999134
Email: ijsaeditorial@sagepub.co.uk
Web site: http://ijsa.rsmjournals.com/
Freq: Monthly Not Audited
Editor: John White
MAGAZINE
AIDS/HIV, Sexual Health

International Journal of Therapy and Rehabilitation
985213
Editorial: St Jude's Church, Dulwich Road, London SE24 0PB **Tel:** 44 02077 385454
Email: ijtr@markallengroup.com
Web site: http://www.magonlinelibrary.com/journal/ijtr
Freq: Monthly Not Audited
Profile: Peer-reviewed clinical journal featuring original research and analysis articles on a wide range of interdisciplinary and discipline specific topics in therapy and rehabilitation. First published in 1994, the publication has an average of 56 pages per issue. Aimed at physiotherapists, occupational therapists, speech and language therapists, rehabilitation nurses, occupational therapists, dieticians and podiatrists.
Ad Rate: Full Page Mono £945.00
Ad Rate: Full Page Colour £1400.00
MAGAZINE
Occupational Therapy & Rehabilitation

International Journal of Urological Nursing
998942
Editorial: The Atrium, Southern Gate, Chichester PO19 8QG **Tel:** 44 01865 776868
Email: jt.marley@ulster.ac.uk
Web site: www.onlinelibrary.wiley.com/journal/10.1111/(ISSN)1749-771X
Freq: 3 Times/Year
Circ: 508 Not Audited
Editor: Rachel Busuttil Leaver
MAGAZINE
Nursing/Nurses, Urology

The International Journal on Hydropower & Dams
999707
Editorial: PO Box 285, Little Woodcote Estate, Wallington, London SM6 6AN
Tel: 44 02087 737240
Email: edit@hydropower-dams.com
Web site: www.hydropower-dams.com
Freq: Bi-Monthly
Circ: 3500 Not Audited
MAGAZINE
Alternative/Renewable Energy

International Labmate
983462
Editorial: Oak Court Business Centre, Sandridge Park, Porters Wood, St Albans, London AL3 6PH **Tel:** 44 01727 858840
Email: info@intlabmate.com
Web site: www.internationallabmate.com
Freq: Bi-Monthly
Circ: 30251 Not Audited
Editor: Gwyneth Astles
Profile: Magazine featuring the latest instrumentation and applications from exporters in the UK and abroad. Aimed at chemists, biochemists, biologists, lab technicians and managers.A charge may be made for the use of press release material.
Ad Rate: Full Page Colour £5995.00
MAGAZINE
Science

International Maritime & Port Security
997826
Editorial: Saville Mews, 30 Saville Rod, London W4 5HG **Tel:** 44 01753 727001
Email: info@shephardmedia.com
Web site: www.shephardmedia.com/publications/magazine/international-maritime-and-port-security/
Freq: Quarterly
Circ: 16150 Not Audited
MAGAZINE
Defense & National Security, Shipping & Warehousing

International Metal Tube
985064
Tel: 44 01732 505724
Email: imtmagazine@virginmedia.com
Web site: www.internationalmetaltube.com
Freq: Quarterly
Circ: 15219 Not Audited
MAGAZINE
Manufacturing

International Nursing Review
995940
Email: inredoffice@wiley.com
Web site: http://onlinelibrary.wiley.com/journal/10.1111/%28ISSN%291466-7657;jsessionid=284CF88F17BBB9B10C6CB3
Freq: Quarterly Not Audited
Editor: Sue Turale
MAGAZINE
Nursing/Nurses

International Oil & Gas Engineer
980894
Editorial: Europa House, 13-17 Ironmonger Row, London EC1V 3QG
Tel: 44 02072 532545
Email: editorial@setform.com
Web site: www.engineerlive.com/Oil-and-Gas-Engineer
Freq: Annual
Circ: 25000 Not Audited
Editor: Louise Smyth
Profile: Magazine covering exploration and drilling, production and processing, instrumentation, safety, environment and communications.
MAGAZINE
Engineering, Oil

International Oil Daily
999122
Editorial: 7 Down Street, 3rd Floor, London W1J 7AJ **Tel:** 44 02075 182200
Web site: www.energyintel.com/Pages/About_IOD.aspx
Freq: Daily Not Audited
Profile: Electronic newsletter providing coverage of the latest developments in the oil and gas business, including worldwide upstream and downstream developments, assessments of key market trends and prices, news on mergers and acquisitions and political changes that affect the industry.
MAGAZINE
Oil

International Paper Board Industry
984667
Editorial: 1 Salisbury Office Park, London Road, Salisbury, Salisbury SP1 3HP
Tel: 44 01722 337038
Email: publications@brunton.co.uk
Web site: www.brunton.co.uk/international-paper-board-industry/
Freq: Monthly
Circ: 7688 Not Audited
Profile: Magazine covering news, trade and developments in the corrugated packaging industry. Aimed at production managers and plant managers.
Ad Rate: Full Page Colour £2000.00
MAGAZINE
Paper

International Paramedic Practice
999496
Editorial: St Jude's Church, Dulwich Road, London SE24 0PB **Tel:** 44 02077 385454
Web site: http://www.internationaljpp.com/

Freq: Quarterly Not Audited
MAGAZINE
EMS/Emergency Medical Services

INTERNATIONAL PEST CONTROL
986009
Editorial: Grenville Court, Britwell Road, Burnham, Slough SL1 8DF
Tel: 44 01628 600499
Email: editor@international-pest-control.com
Web site: http://international-pest-control.com/
Freq: Bi-Monthly Not Audited
Profile: Journal covering the problem of pest eradication and prevention in all its aspects.
Ad Rate: Full Page Colour £995.00
MAGAZINE
Hygiene

International Pharmaceutical Industry (IPI)
998003
Editorial: Unit J413, The Biscuit Factory Tower Bridge Business Complex, 100 Clements Road, London SE16 4DG
Tel. 44 02072 372038
Email: info@ipimedia.com
Web site: www.ipimediaworld.com
Freq: Quarterly
Circ: 22300 Not Audited
Editor: Orsolya Balogh
MAGAZINE
Pharmaceuticals

International Pig Topics
986032
Tel: 44 01377 241724
Email: info@positiveaction.co.uk
Web site: www.positiveaction.info
Freq: Bi-Monthly
Circ: 17000 Not Audited
Profile: Magazine focusing on modern pig breeding and pork production. Aimed at professional pig producers, pig farmers, nutritionists, veterinarians and those in the trade.
Ad Rate: Full Page Mono £2081.00
Ad Rate: Full Page Colour £2611.00
MAGAZINE
Animal Farming, Hygiene, Security & Security Systems

International Poultry Production
986030
Tel: 44 01377 241724
Email: info@positiveaction.co.uk
Web site: www.positiveaction.info
Freq: Bi-Monthly
Circ: 18000 Not Audited
Profile: Magazine covering modern poultrymeat and egg production from the farm to the consumer. Aimed at poultrymeat and egg producers, as well as nutritionists and those in the veterinarian trade.
Ad Rate: Full Page Mono £2747.00
Ad Rate: Full Page Colour £3226.00
MAGAZINE
Animal Farming

International Process Engineer
980972
Editorial: Europa House, 13-17 Ironmonger Row, London EC1V 3QG
Tel: 44 02072 532545
Email: editorial@setform.com
Web site: www.engineerlive.com/Process-Engineer
Freq: Semi-Annual
Circ: 25000 Not Audited
Editor: Louise Smyth
Profile: Journal covering all aspects of process engineering throughout Europe.
Ad Rate: Full Page Mono £4150.00
Ad Rate: Full Page Colour £5350.00
MAGAZINE
Engineering

International Rental News
984883
Editorial: Southfields, Southview Road, Wadhurst, Wadhurst TN5 6TP
Tel: 44 01892 784088
Email: info@khl.com
Web site: www.khl.com/magazines/international-rental-news
Freq: Bi-Monthly

Circ: 13257 Not Audited
Profile: Magazine covering the International equipment rental industry, including tool hire and construction equipment rental, events and party rentals, plus specialist rental sectors such as temporary accommodation, power and temperature control equipment and aerial platforms. Aimed at managers and owners of equipment rental companies Worldwide.Previous title: European Rental News Regular features: Rental Management focuses on rental management techniques such as financing equipment purchases, maintaining a rental fleet, safety policy and rental sales.; Rental Products Round-up of new products of interest to rental companies, products that they could either add to their rental fleet or use in the course of their business.; The Rental Book Stand-alone supplement listing contact details of equipment suppliers of relevance to the rental sector as well as editorial on the global rental market.; Viewpoint An article written by someone involved in the rental industry addressing a topical issue.
Ad Rate: Full Page Colour £4930.00
MAGAZINE
Building & Construction

International Review of Sport and Exercise Psychology
996588
Editorial: 4 Park Square, Milton Park, Abingdon, Didcot OX14 4RN
Tel: 44 02070 175000
Web site: http://www.tandfonline.com/toc/rirs20/current
Freq: Annual Not Audited
MAGAZINE
Neurology, Sports Medicine

International Reviews of Immunology
995752
Editorial: Christchurch Court, 10-15 Newgate Street, London EC1A 7AZ
Tel: 44 02070 175540
Email: subscriptions@informa.com
Web site: http://informahealthcare.com/loi/iri
Freq: Monthly Not Audited
MAGAZINE
Allergies

International Sandwich & food to go news
998663
Editorial: Association House, 18c Moor Street, Chepstow NP16 5DB
Tel: 44 01291 636338
Email: editorial@papa.org.uk
Web site: www.sandwich.org.uk
Freq: Bi-Monthly
Circ: 7000 Not Audited
Editor: Simon Ambrose
MAGAZINE
Food

International School Magazine (is)
1051999
Editorial: 12 Deben Mill Business Centre, Old Maltings Approach, Melton, Woodbridge, Woodbridge IP12 1BL
Tel: 44 01394 389859
Email: editor@is-mag.co.uk
Web site: www.is-mag.co.uk
Freq: 3 Times/Year
Circ: 3000 Not Audited
MAGAZINE
Schools & Institutions

International Sheet Metal Review
1052784
Tel: 44 01707 273999
Email: ismr.magazine@trmg.co.uk
Web site: http://www.ismr.co.uk/
Freq: Monthly
Circ: 14694 Not Audited
Profile: Magazine providing insight into the technology of sheet metal processing. Contains a mix of in-depth technical articles, equipment profiles, news, views, application reports and business information.
Ad Rate: Full Page Colour £2900.00
MAGAZINE
Manufacturing, Steel

International Sugar Journal
983945
Editorial: Christchurch Court, 10-15 Newgate Street, London EC1A 7HD
Tel: 44 02070 177514
Email: editorial@world-sugar.com
Web site: www.internationalsugarjournal.com
Freq: Monthly
Circ: 4111 Not Audited
Editor: Arvind Chudasama
Profile: Journal featuring technical, analytical and research articles on beet and cane sugar production, processing and technology. Read by those involved in the International sugar industry.
Ad Rate: Full Page Mono £1170.00
Ad Rate: Full Page Colour £2200.00
MAGAZINE
Food

International Supermarket News
983674
Email: editorial@internationalsupermarketnews.com
Web site: www.internationalsupermarketnews.com
Freq: Quarterly
Circ: 15450 Not Audited
Profile: Magazine covering all aspects of the supermarket and hardware retail industry. Aimed at CEOs, MDs, key decision makers, senior buyers of supermarkets, cash and carries, hypermarkets, wholesalers, garden centres and hardware retailers via a named mailing database.
Ad Rate: Full Page Colour £2900.00
MAGAZINE
Books, Cosmetics, Fashion, Gardening, Hair, Office Supplies, Retail, Retail Management, Toys

International Tax Report
983057
Editorial: Mortimer House, 37-41 Mortimer Street, London W1T 3JH
Web site: www.internationaltaxreport.com
Freq: Monthly Not Audited
Profile: Specialist monthly newsletter that gives practical information in international tax planning. Publication reporting on tax planning opportunities worldwide. Aimed at tax specialists, lawyers and senior accountants.
MAGAZINE
Accounting

International Tax Review
980094
Editorial: 8 Bouverie Street, London EC4Y 8AX
Tel: 44 02077 798379
Web site: www.internationaltaxreview.com
Freq: Monthly Not Audited
Profile: Magazine dedicated to international tax strategy. It covers reviews of international tax law and tax structuring techniques. Aimed at tax directors within multinationals, tax lawyers and finance directors, partners of legal or accounting and academics. Published since 1990.
Ad Rate: Full Page Mono £4731.00
Ad Rate: Full Page Colour £6052.00
MAGAZINE
Tax Law

International Trade
984544
Editorial: Business Edge Network, 30 Great Guildford Street, London SE1 0HS
Tel: 44 08455 000328
Email: editor@freshbusinessthinking.com
Web site: www.internationaltrade.co.uk
Freq: Daily
Circ: 6835 Cision Digital Reach
MAGAZINE (ONLINE)
Business, Small and Medium Business

International Trade Finance
998486
Editorial: Singletons, The Ridge, South View Road, Pinner, London HA5 3YD
Tel: 44 02088 661934
Web site: http://www.singlelaw.com/international-trade-finance
Freq: Bi-Weekly Not Audited
MAGAZINE
Banking

International Trade Law & Regulation
998487
Editorial: Friars House, 160 Blackfriars Road, London SE1 8EZ
Tel: 44 02075 426664
Web site: www.sweetandmaxwell.co.uk
Freq: Quarterly Not Audited
MAGAZINE
Corporate Law

International Travel & Health Insurance Journal
983486
Editorial: 19 Lower Park Row, Bristol BS1 5BN
Tel: 44 01179 226600
Email: news@itij.com
Web site: https://www.itij.com/
Freq: Monthly
Circ: 20000 Not Audited
Editor: James Wallis; **Editor:** Sarah Watson; **Editor:** Sarah Watson
MAGAZINE
Insurance

International Water Power and Dam Construction
983989
Editorial: Progressive House, 2 Maidstone Road, Foots Cray, Sidcup, London DA14 5HZ
Tel: 44 02082 697700
Web site: www.waterpowermagazine.com
Freq: Monthly
Circ: 3941 Not Audited
Editor: Carrieann Stocks
MAGAZINE
Water & Sanitation

The Internet Advertising Bureau (IAB)
985127
Editorial: 14 Macklin Street, London WC2B 5NF
Tel: 44 02070 506969
Email: info@iabuk.net
Web site: www.iabuk.net
Freq: Daily
Circ: 478194 Cision Digital Reach
MAGAZINE (ONLINE)
Advertising Industry

intersec (The Journal of International Security)
998708
Editorial: 22 Eastworth Road, London KT16 8DN
Tel: 44 01932 566921
Email: jake@intersec.co.uk
Web site: www.intersec.co.uk
Freq: Monthly
Circ: 10500 Not Audited
Editor: Jake Charles
MAGAZINE
Defense & National Security, Security & Security Systems

Interventional Cardiology Review
999156
Editorial: 7/8 Woodlands Farm, Cookham Dean, Cookham SL6 9PN
Email: commeditor@radcliffecardiology.com
Web site: www.radcliffecardiology.com/journals/interventional-cardiology-review
Freq: 3 Times/Year
Circ: 10000 Not Audited
MAGAZINE
Cardiology

Interventional News
984397
Editorial: BIBA Medical, 526 Fulham Road, Fulham, London SW6 5NR
Tel: 44 02077 368788
Email: urmila@bibamedical.com
Web site: www.interventionalnews.com
Freq: Quarterly
Circ: 12105 Not Audited
Editor: Urmila Doraswami
Profile: Official newspaper of the Cardiovascular and Interventional Radiology Society of Europe, and the Society of Interventional Radiology.
MAGAZINE
Cardiology, Diagnostic Imaging

inTheBay
1053925
Editorial: PO Box 969, St Georges Quay, Lancaster LA1 3LD
Tel: 44 01524 848747
Web site: www.inthebay.co.uk

Business Magazines

Freq: Daily
Circ: 13504 Cision Digital Reach
MAGAZINE (ONLINE)
Business

IntraFish Aquaculture   981160
Editorial: 7th Floor, 125 Wood Street,
London EC2V 7AN **Tel:** 44 02076 452334
Email: editorial@intrafish.com
Web site: www.fishfarminginternational.com
Freq: Quarterly
Circ: 19000 Not Audited
Profile: Newspaper covering the latest news
and developments in fish and shellfish
farming worldwide. Read by decision makers
in every aspect of aquaculture.
Ad Rate: Full Page Colour £3180.00
MAGAZINE
Animal Farming

IntraFish Fisheries   980817
Editorial: IntraFish, 125 Wood Street, 7th
Floor, London EC2V 7AN
Tel: 44 02076 452334
Email: editorial@intrafish.com
Web site: www.fishingnewsinternational.
com
Freq: Monthly
Circ: 14000 Not Audited
Profile: Newspaper containing news,
features and technical reviews of the world's
commercial fishing industries. Read by the
international fishing industry.
Ad Rate: Full Page Colour £4560.00
MAGAZINE
Animal Farming

IntraFish.com   994616
Editorial: 7th Floor, 125 Wood Street,
London EC2V 7AN **Tel:** 44 02076 452334
Email: editorial@intrafish.com
Web site: www.intrafish.com
Freq: Daily
Circ: 31648 Cision Digital Reach
MAGAZINE (ONLINE)
Animal Farming

Intralogistics Magazine   988256
Editorial: 9 Dene House, Lower Stone
Street, Maidstone, Maidstone ME15 6JX
Tel: 44 08456 066765
Email: joe@ilmag.co.uk
Web site: www.intralogisticsmagazine.co.
uk/magazine.html
Freq: Monthly
Circ: 60000 Not Audited
Editor: Alan Ockelford
MAGAZINE
Shipping & Warehousing, Supply Chain
Management (SCM)

InTuition   1064622
Editorial: Anerley Business Centre, Anerley
Road, London SE20 8BD
Tel: 44 02086 765608
Email: info@createpublishing.uk.com
Web site: http://www.createpublishing.uk.
com/Our-work
Freq: Quarterly
MAGAZINE
Education, Schools & Institutions,
Students

Inverse Problems   996632
Editorial: IOP Publishing, Temple Circus,
Temple Way, Bristol BS1 6HG
Tel: 44 01179 297481
Email: ip@iop.org
Web site: http://iopscience.iop.org/0266-
5611/
Freq: Monthly Not Audited
MAGAZINE
Science

InvestHedge   980786
Editorial: 4-8 Bouverie Street, London EC4Y
8AX **Tel:** 44 02077 797330
Email: info@hedgefundintelligence.com
Web site: www.hedgefundintelligence.com/
investhedge
Freq: Monthly Not Audited
Editor: Susan Barreto

Profile: Newsletter providing breaking news
on new fund launches, mandate awards,
institutional investor profiles and
performance data for nearly 2700 funds.
Aimed at institutional investors and wealth
management advisors who want to use
multi-managers and fund of funds to access
hedge funds, multi-managers and
professional hedge fund investors who need
to know what their competitors are doing
and hedge fund managers who need to keep
abreast of developments amongst their
clients and prospective clients.
Ad Rate: Full Page Mono £5950.00
MAGAZINE
Hedge Funds

The Investigator   998986
Editorial: 13 Station Road, Stoke
Mandeville, Aylesbury HP22 5UL
Tel: 44 08446 608707
Email: editor@the-investigator.co.uk
Web site: http://www.the-investigator.co.uk/
Freq: Quarterly
Circ: 2288 Cision Digital Reach
Editor: Carol Jenkins
MAGAZINE (ONLINE)
Criminal Law

Investment & Pensions
Europe   979777
Editorial: Pentagon House, 52-54
Southwark Street, London SE1 1UN
Tel: 44 02034 659300
Email: info@ipe.com
Web site: www.ipe.com
Freq: Monthly
Circ: 9724 Not Audited
Editor: Richard Lowe
Profile: Magazine covering international
investment opportunities for European
pension funds. Aimed at institutional and
European Pension Fund investors.
Ad Rate: Full Page Colour £9950.00
MAGAZINE
Fund Management

Investment Week   979774
Editorial: Haymarket House, 28-29
Haymarket, London SW1Y 4RX
Tel: 44 02074 849700
Web site: www.investmentweek.co.uk
Freq: Weekly
Circ: 14000 Not Audited
Editor: Katrina Lloyd
Profile: Magazine covering investment and
product news. Aimed at independent
investment advisers. Investment Week and
Investmentweek.co.uk have won over 20
awards, including IMA Financial Reporting
Team of the year for three consecutive
years. Aimed at investment advisors and
wealth managers.Published since 1995.
Ad Rate: Full Page Colour £8983.00
MAGAZINE
Fund Management

InvestmentEurope   985792
Editorial: Cairo Studios, 4 Nile Street,
London N1 7RF
Web site: www.investmenteurope.net
Freq: Monthly
Circ: 4600 Not Audited
Profile: Fortnightly magazine for investors in
Europe. The publication targets retail fund
selectors operating in private banks,
commercial banks, life insurance companies,
family offices, funds of funds, independent
financial advisers and independent
distributors. It also cover wealth
management.
MAGAZINE
Fund Management

Investor Review   995351
Tel: 44 01283 712447
Email: jonathan.miles@ai-globalmedia.com
Web site: www.investor-review.com
Freq: Monthly
Circ: 3501 Cision Digital Reach
MAGAZINE (ONLINE)
Hedge Funds

Investor Today   985092
Editorial: Angels House, 5 Albemarle Road,
Beckenham, London BR3 5HZ
Tel: 44 08450 750152
Email: press@investortoday.co.uk
Web site: www.investortoday.co.uk
Freq: Daily
Circ: 17672 Cision Digital Reach
Profile: Website covering finance. The site is
aimed to empower amateur and professional
investors alike by offering the tools to take
control of their own portfolio.
MAGAZINE (ONLINE)
Investment Banking

INVESTOR'S CHAMPION   988654
Editorial: Langwood House, 63-81 High
Street, Rickmansworth, London WD3 1EQ
Tel: 44 01923 713890
Email: champion@investorschampion.com
Web site: http://www.investorschampion.
com
Freq: Daily
Circ: 11409 Cision Digital Reach
MAGAZINE (ONLINE)
Business, Small and Medium Business

iNVEZZ   988195
Editorial: Saunders House, 52-53 The Mall,
London W5 3TA
Email: editor@invezz.com
Web site: www.invezz.com
Freq: Daily
Circ: 47049 Cision Digital Reach
MAGAZINE (ONLINE)
Investment Banking

IPAWorld   995053
Editorial: Marron House, Whaddon Hall,
Milton Keynes MK17 ONA
Tel: 44 01908 521477
Web site: www.ipaworld.com
Freq: Daily
Circ: 3131 Cision Digital Reach
MAGAZINE (ONLINE)
Business, Investment Banking, Small and
Medium Business

IPD   995745
Editorial: Ten Bishops Square, London E1
6EG **Tel:** 44 02073 369200
Email: enquiries@ipd.com
Web site: https://www.msci.com/real-estate
Freq: Daily
Circ: 351469 Cision Digital Reach
MAGAZINE (ONLINE)
Office Design, Residential Real Estate,
Retail

iPMI Magazine   996352
Editorial: 20-22 Bedford Row, London
Tel: 44 02081 332227
Email: ipmi@ipmimagazine.com
Web site: www.ipmimagazine.com
Freq: Daily
MAGAZINE (ONLINE)
Insurance

IPSE Magazine   985901
Editorial: Heron House, 10 Dean Farrar
Street, London SW1H 0DX
Tel: 44 02030 530606
Email: pressoffice@ipse.co.uk
Web site: www.ipsemagazine.co.uk/
Freq: Bi-Monthly
Circ: 40000 Not Audited
MAGAZINE
Business, Small and Medium Business

IQ (Insider Quarterly)   995909
Editorial: 3rd Floor, 41 Eastcheap, London
EC3M 1DT **Tel:** 44 02073 970618
Email: info@insuranceinsider.co.uk
Web site: www.insiderquarterly.com
Freq: Quarterly
Circ: 7500 Not Audited
MAGAZINE
Insurance

IQ Business Magazine   996888
Editorial: Goodwin Business Park, Willie
Snaith Road, Newmarket, Newmarket CB8
7SQ **Tel:** 44 01638 666432
Email: info@cubiqdesign.co.uk
Web site: iqmag.co.uk
Freq: Quarterly
Circ: 3500 Not Audited
MAGAZINE
Business, Small and Medium Business

IR Magazine   980036
Editorial: 133 Whitechapel High Street,
London E1 7QA **Tel:** 44 02080 045340
Email: mail@thecrossbordergroup.com
Web site: www.irmagazine.com
Freq: Monthly
Circ: 6000 Not Audited
Editor: Tim Human
Profile: Magazine covering all matters of
interest to investor relations professionals.
Read by investor relations professionals
including IR officers, CFOs and corporate
secretaries and the relevant service
providers.
Ad Rate: Full Page Colour £4195.00
MAGAZINE
Banking

Ireland Business Insider   999270
Editorial: 8th Floor Boulton House, 17-21
Chorlton Street, Manchester M1 3HY
Tel: 44 01619 079718
Email: matthew.ord@newsco.com
Web site: http://www.insidermedia.com/
ireland
Freq: Weekly
Circ: 39703 Cision Digital Reach
MAGAZINE (ONLINE)
Business, Corporate Responsibility,
Finance, Manufacturing, Mergers &
Acquisitions, Small and Medium Business

Ireland's Dental magazine   986640
Editorial: Studio 2001, Mile End, Paisley
PA1 1JF **Tel:** 44 01415 610300
Email: info@connectcommunications.co.uk
Web site: www.irelandsdentalmag.ie
Freq: Bi-Monthly
Circ: 4000 Not Audited
Editor: Bruce Oxley
Profile: Ireland's Dental magazine reaches
registered dental professionals throughout
the Republic and Northern Ireland and is
printed on a bi-monthly basis. Featuring
news, views and clinical submissions from a
broad range of clinicians, the magazine aims
to provide the platform to promote the very
best of the profession, as well as reporting
and discussing the changing political and
economic climate.
MAGAZINE
Dentistry

Ireland's Kitchen Trade Guide   985651
Tel: 44 02891 473979
Email: editorial@iktg.ie
Web site: www.iktg.ie
Freq: Quarterly
Circ: 2200 Not Audited
Editor: Margaret Connolly
MAGAZINE
Interior Design

Irish Dentistry   983899
Editorial: 1 Hertford House, Farm Close,
Shenley, Radlett WD7 9AB
Tel: 44 01923 851777
Web site: www.irishdentist.ie
Freq: Monthly
Circ: 2800 Not Audited
MAGAZINE
Dentistry

Irish Manufacturing   981517
Editorial: 15A London Road, Maidstone,
Maidstone ME16 8LY **Tel:** 44 01622 687031
Web site: www.connectingindustry.com/
IrishManufacturing/
Freq: Quarterly
Circ: 7050 Not Audited

Profile: Magazine covering all aspects of engineering, including electrical, electronics, factory, instrumentation, design and process engineering.
Ad Rate: Full Page Colour £2885.00
MAGAZINE
Manufacturing

Irish Veterinary Journal   987182
Editorial: Floor 6, 236 Gray's Inn Road, London WC1X 8HB **Tel:** 44 02031 922009
Email: editorial@irishvetjournal.org
Web site: http://irishvetjournal.biomedcentral.com/
Freq: Daily
Circ: 163 Cision Digital Reach
MAGAZINE (ONLINE)
Animal Farming, Veterinary Medicine

Iron & Steel Today   984714
Editorial: Melting Point Media Limited, Railview Lofts, 19c Commercial Rd, Eastbourne BN21 3XE **Tel:** 44 01323 508251
Email: editor@ironandsteeltoday.com
Freq: Bi-Monthly
Circ: 5000 Not Audited
Editor: Michelle Binns
Profile: Iron & Steel Today is a fabricator trade publication that is published five times a year owned by Modern Media Communications Ltd. It features news, contracts and people, commercial and technical features, product information and a buyers guide. It was first published in 2007. Iron & Steel Today is written globally for managers involved in the purchase of plant, equipment and materials employed within an iron and steelworks or fabrication plant such as rolling mill and stock holder as well as reaching purchasers of steel.
Ad Rate: Full Page Colour £1845.00
MAGAZINE
Engineering, Manufacturing, Mining & Quarrying, Steel

Ironmaking & Steelmaking: Processes, Products and Applications   999505
Editorial: 2 & 4 Park Square, Milton Park, Abingdon OX14 4RN **Tel:** 44 02070 176000
Web site: http://www.tandfonline.com/loi/yirs20
Freq: Monthly
MAGAZINE
Steel

Is4profit.com   998667
Editorial: 6-8 Cole Street, London SE1 4YH
Tel: 44 02071 833932
Email: hello@startups.co.uk
Web site: www.is4profit.com
Freq: Daily
Circ: 33346 Cision Digital Reach
Editor: Lucy Wayment
MAGAZINE (ONLINE)
Business

ISDA   996593
Editorial: One Bishops Square, London E1 6AD **Tel:** 44 02030 883550
Email: isdaeurope@isda.org
Web site: www2.isda.org
Freq: Daily
Circ: 14319 Cision Digital Reach
MAGAZINE (ONLINE)
Derivatives

Islamic Finance Information Service   999147
Editorial: GlobalCapital, 8 Bouverie Street, London EC4Y 8AX **Tel:** 44 02077 798888
Email: news4ifis@securities.com
Web site: www.globalcapital.com/emerging-markets/islamic-finance
Freq: Daily
Circ: 120 Cision Digital Reach
MAGAZINE (ONLINE)
Banking

Island Business   984213
Tel: 44 01983 520777
Email: chamber@iwchamber.co.uk
Web site: www.iwchamber.co.uk

Freq: Monthly
Circ: 4000 Not Audited
Editor: Tom Stroud
Profile: Magazine covering national business news and reports relating to businesses in and around the Isle of Wight. Aimed at chamber members and passengers on ferries between Cowes and Southampton.
Ad Rate: Full Page Colour £795.00
MAGAZINE
Business, Small and Medium Business

ISS-mag.com   985429
Editorial: 31 -35 Kirby Street, London EC1N 8TE
Email: editor@iss-mag.com
Web site: www.iss-mag.com
Freq: Daily
Circ: 11149 Cision Digital Reach
MAGAZINE (ONLINE)
Banking, Equities, Fund Management

IT for CEOs & CFOs   998138
Editorial: 7 Greding Walk, Hutton, Brentwood CM13 2UF **Tel:** 44 01277 201554
Email: victoria.woollaston@mailonline.co.uk
Web site: http://www.creditcontrol.co.uk/
Freq: Monthly
Circ: 17867 Not Audited
MAGAZINE
Computers, Data Management, Software

IT Reseller   980959
Editorial: B2B Publishing, PO Box 3575, Barnet, Potters Bar EN5 9QD
Tel: 44 01707 664200
Email: editor@ibcpub.com
Web site: www.itrportal.com
Freq: Daily
Circ: 17049 Cision Digital Reach
Profile: Magazine dealing with issues affecting companies in the European IT Channel, including a feature section on automatic identification bar code and RFID, printing and labelling, document management, network technology for LANs and WANs, wired and wireless, including security products and UPS.
Ad Rate: Full Page Colour £3950.00
MAGAZINE (ONLINE)
Auto Aftermarket

IT Security Guru   996696
Editorial: 7 Alston Works, Alston Road, London EN5 4EL **Tel:** 44 02071 832849
Email: hello@itsecurityguru.org
Web site: www.itsecurityguru.org
Freq: Daily
Circ: 27321 Cision Digital Reach
MAGAZINE (ONLINE)
Security & Security Systems

IT Sensei   997726
Email: gary.flood@senseipublishing.co.uk
Web site: www.itsensei.co.uk
Freq: Daily
Circ: 521 Cision Digital Reach
Editor: Gary Flood
MAGAZINE (ONLINE)
Auto Aftermarket, Industry

ITP Journal   997903
Editorial: Gainsborough House, 59- 60 Thames Street, Windsor SL4 1TX
Tel: 44 01932 788861
Email: enquiries@theitp.org
Web site: www.theitp.org
Freq: Quarterly
Circ: 5000 Not Audited
MAGAZINE
News & Current Affairs

iTSHOWCASE Online   980986
Editorial: 11 Star Lane, Ringwood BH24 1AL
Tel: 44 01425 477565
Email: editorial@frameworkmedia.co.uk
Web site: www.itshowcase.co.uk
Freq: Daily
Circ: 9739 Cision Digital Reach
Editor: Alison Jones
MAGAZINE (ONLINE)
Industry, Manufacturing

iVT International   983520
Editorial: Abinger House, Church Street, Dorking, Dorking RH4 1DF
Tel: 44 01306 743744
Email: info@ukimediaevents.com
Web site: www.ivtinternational.com
Freq: Quarterly
Circ: 20000 Not Audited
Editor: Tom Stone
MAGAZINE
Shipping & Warehousing

Jane's Defence Industry   980089
Editorial: 4th floor Ropemaker Place, 25 Ropemaker Street, London EC2Y 9LY
Web site: www.ihs.com/products/janes-defence-industry-news.html
Freq: Daily Not Audited
Editor: Guy Anderson
MAGAZINE
Defense & National Security

Jane's Aero-Engines   984179
Editorial: Sentinel House, 163 Brighton Road, Coulsdon, London CR5 2YH
Tel: 44 02087 003700
Email: info@ihs.com
Web site: www.janes.com/products/janes/defence/det-products/aero-engines.aspx
Freq: Semi-Annual Not Audited
Editor: Mark Daly
Profile: Publication containing specialised information on almost every gas-turbine engine in flight. Contains profiles of engines for airliners, military aircraft, helicopters and business aircraft. Aimed at the civil air industry, defence industry, ministries of defence, transport ministries, civil operators and armed forces.Previous title: Jane's Aeroengines
Ad Rate: Full Page Mono £2370.00
Ad Rate: Full Page Colour £3955.00
MAGAZINE
Aviation, Defense & National Security

Jane's Air Traffic Control   984169
Editorial: Sentinel House, 163 Brighton Road, Coulsdon, London CR5 2YH
Tel: 44 02087 003700
Email: info@jane.com
Web site: www.ihs.com/products/janes-air-traffic-control.html
Freq: Annual
Circ: 5000 Not Audited
Editor: Jenny Beechener
Profile: Publication containing information on the very latest technology in air traffic control operations.
Ad Rate: Full Page Mono £4250.00
Ad Rate: Full Page Colour £7080.00
MAGAZINE
Aviation

Jane's Airport Review   980080
Editorial: Sentinel House, 163 Brighton Road, Coulsdon, London CR5 2YH
Tel: 44 02087 003700
Email: jar@janes.com
Web site: www.ihs.com/products/janes/transport/airport-review.aspx
Freq: Monthly
Circ: 11500 Not Audited
Editor: Ben Vogel
Profile: Magazine covering every significant event in the airports, air traffic control and ground operations market worldwide.
Ad Rate: Full Page Mono £4250.00
Ad Rate: Full Page Colour £7080.00
MAGAZINE
Aviation

Jane's Airports and Handling Agents   984178
Editorial: Sentinel House, 163 Brighton Road, Coulsdon, London CR5 2YH
Tel: 44 02087 003700
Email: press.releases@janes.com
Web site: www.ihs.com/products/janes/transport/airports-handling-agents.aspx
Freq: Annual
Profile: International series providing information on operational data for the world's airports and the handling agents and FBOs that operate at them.
Ad Rate: Full Page Colour £1455.00

Ad Rate: Full Page Colour £2255.00
MAGAZINE
Aviation

Jane's Airports, Equipment and Services   984168
Editorial: Sentinel House, 163 Brighton Road, Coulsdon, London CR5 2YH
Tel: 44 02087 003700
Web site: www.ihs.com/products/janes/transport/airports-equipment-services.aspx
Freq: Annual
Circ: 12684 Not Audited
Editor: Kylie Bull
MAGAZINE
Aviation

Jane's All the World's Aircraft   984174
Editorial: Sentinel House, 163 Brighton Road, Coulsdon, London CR5 2YH
Tel: 44 02087 003700
Web site: http://www.janes.com/
Freq: Annual Not Audited
Profile: Journal of international civil and military aircraft in production.
Ad Rate: Full Page Mono £4250.00
Ad Rate: Full Page Colour £7080.00
MAGAZINE
Aviation, Defense & National Security

Jane's Amphibious and Special Forces   999641
Editorial: Sentinel House, 163 Brighton Road, Coulsdon, London CR5 2YH
Tel: 44 02087 003700
Email: press.releases@janes.com
Web site: www.janes.com/products/janes/security/military-capabilities/amphibious-special-forces.aspx
Freq: Annual Not Audited
Editor: Ewen Southby-Tailyour
MAGAZINE
Defense & National Security

Jane's Defence Equipment and Technology Intelligence Centre   997577
Editorial: Sentinel House, 163 Brighton Road, Coulsdon, London CR5 2YH
Tel: 44 02087 003700
Email: press.releases@janes.com
Web site: https://www.ihs.com/products/janes-defence-equipment-technology.html
Freq: Daily
Circ: 7509 Cision Digital Reach
MAGAZINE (ONLINE)
Defense & National Security

Jane's Fighting Ships   984927
Editorial: Viewpoint One, Willoughby Road, Bracknell, London RG12 8FB
Tel: 44 01344 328300
Email: customer.support@ihs.com
Web site: www.ihs.com
Freq: Daily
Circ: 1556605 Cision Digital Reach
MAGAZINE (ONLINE)
Defense & National Security, Shipping & Warehousing

Jane's Intelligence Review   980919
Editorial: The Capitol Building, Oldbury, London RG12 8FZ **Tel:** 44 01344 328300
Web site: www.ihs.com/products/janes/security/news/intelligence-review.aspx
Freq: Monthly
Circ: 2170 Not Audited
Editor: Robert Munks
Profile: Magazine providing a reliable source of information and threat assessment for defence analysts and the intelligence community. Read by corporate strategic planners, law enforcement personnel, defence institutes, ministries of defence, armed forces, academic and research institutes and commercial risk assessors.
Ad Rate: Full Page Mono £1860.00
Ad Rate: Full Page Colour £2805.00
MAGAZINE
Defense & National Security, Engineering

Business Magazines

Jane's International Defence Review
980087

Editorial: Sentinel House, 163 Brighton Road, Coulsdon, London CR5 2YH
Tel: 44 02087 003700
Web site: http://www.janes.com/magazines/ihs-janes-international-defence-review
Freq: Monthly
Circ: 19954 Not Audited
Profile: Magazine featuring original, full-length articles on key strategic, tactical and defence technology subjects from around the world. Read by those in the military and defence industries as well as government departments.
Ad Rate: Full Page Mono £5055.00
Ad Rate: Full Page Colour £7630.00
MAGAZINE
Defense & National Security

Jane's Navy International
980818

Editorial: Sentinel House, 163 Brighton Road, Coulsdon, London CR5 2YH
Tel: 44 02087 003700
Email: info@ihs.com
Web site: www.janes.com
Freq: Monthly
Circ: 28764 Not Audited
Editor: Lee Willett
Profile: Jane's Navy International is a journal that covers naval affairs, defence, strategy, equipment, naval operations, ships, submarines, naval weapon systems and amphibious warfare.
Ad Rate: Full Page Mono £2320.00
Ad Rate: Full Page Colour £3505.00
MAGAZINE
Defense & National Security

Jane's Security: Country Risk
995412

Editorial: Sentinel House, 163 Brighton Road, Coulsdon, London CR5 2YH
Tel: 44 01344 328300
Email: info@ihs.com
Web site: www.ihs.com/products/janes/security/country-risk/assessments.aspx
Freq: Monthly Not Audited
Editor: Matthew Clements
MAGAZINE
Defense & National Security

Jane's Simulation and Training Systems
998880

Editorial: Sentinel House, 163 Brighton Road, Coulsdon, London CR5 2YH
Tel: 44 01344 328300
Email: info@ihs.com
Web site: www.ihs.com/products/janes-military-simulation-training.html
Freq: Annual Not Audited
MAGAZINE
Defense & National Security

Jane's Weapons: Infantry
999152

Editorial: Sentinel House, 163 Brighton Road, Coulsdon, London CR5 2YH
Tel: 44 01344 328155
Email: press.releases@janes.com
Web site: www.janes.com/products/janes/defence/det-products/infantry.aspx
Freq: Annual Not Audited
Editor: Richard Jones
MAGAZINE
Defense & National Security

Jane's World Air Forces
984861

Editorial: Sentinel House, 163 Brighton Road, Coulsdon, London CR5 2YH
Tel: 44 02087 003700
Email: info@janes.com
Web site: http://www.janes.com
Freq: Semi-Annual Not Audited
Profile: A complete analysis and order of battle breakdowns of the air forces of the world.
MAGAZINE
Aviation, Defense & National Security

Jane's World Armies
984862

Editorial: The Capitol Building, Oldbury, London RG12 8FZ **Tel:** 44 02087 003700
Email: info@janes.com
Web site: http://www.janes.com/
Freq: Semi-Annual Not Audited
Profile: Contains a complete analysis and order of battle breakdowns on the armies of the world.
MAGAZINE
Defense & National Security, Security & Security Systems

Jane's World Defence Industry
998742

Editorial: 4th floor Ropemaker Place, 25 Ropemaker Street, London EC2Y 9LY
Web site: www.ihs.com/products/janes/defence-business/industry/world-defense-industry.aspx
Freq: Semi-Annual Not Audited
Editor: Guy Anderson
MAGAZINE
Defense & National Security

Jet Fuel Intelligence
980789

Editorial: 7 Down Street, 3rd Floor, London W1J 7AJ **Tel:** 44 02075 182200
Email: energyintelligence@energyintel.com
Web site: http://www.energyintel.com/pages/about_jfi.aspx
Freq: Weekly Not Audited
Editor: Cristina Haus
MAGAZINE
Aviation

JETS
986409

Editorial: PO Box 100, Stamford PE9 1XQ
Tel: 44 01780 755131
Web site: www.jetsmag.co.uk
Freq: Bi-Monthly
MAGAZINE (ONLINE)
Aviation

Jinfo
1063272

Editorial: 4-6 Station Approach, Ashford, London TW15 2QN **Tel:** 44 01784 605000
Email: support@jinfo.com
Web site: web.jinfo.com/go/newsletter/
Freq: Bi-Weekly
Circ: 14 Cision Digital Reach
MAGAZINE (ONLINE)
Company News & Appointments, Education, Health & Safety, Human Resources, Recruiting

The Journal
998549

Editorial: 20 Aldermanbury, London EC2V 7HY **Tel:** 44 02089 898464
Web site: http://www.cii.co.uk/about/about-the-cii/the-journal/
Freq: Bi-Monthly
Circ: 80000 Not Audited
Editor: Michelle Worvell
Profile: Official publication of the Chartered Institute of Journalists. Contains news, features and reviews relevant to journalists and the journalistic profession, as well as news about the Chartered Institute of Journalists and its partner organisations. Aimed at journalists, media executives and broadcasters. Also read by PR consultants and Internet communicators.
MAGAZINE
Insurance

Journal for Clinical Studies (JCS)
988881

Editorial: Unit J413, The Biscuit Factory Tower Bridge Business Complex, 100 Clements Road, London SE16 4DG
Tel: 44 02072 372036
Email: info@pharmapubs.com
Web site: http://www.jforcs.com
Freq: Bi-Monthly
Circ: 24000 Not Audited
Editor: Orsolya Balogh
MAGAZINE
Science

Journal of Addictions Nursing
996962

Editorial: 250 Waterloo Road, London SE1 8RD **Tel:** 44 02079 810600
Web site: http://journals.lww.com/jan/pages/default.aspx
Freq: Quarterly Not Audited
MAGAZINE
Neurology, Nursing/Nurses

Journal of Advanced Nursing
985140

Editorial: 9600 Garsington Road, Oxford OX4 2DQ **Tel:** 44 01865 776868
Email: jan@wiley.com
Web site: http://www.journalofadvancednursing.com
Freq: Monthly
Circ: 2480 Not Audited
Editor: Mark Hayter; **Editor:** Jane Noyes; **Editor:** Lin Perry; **Editor:** Rita Pickler; **Editor:** Brenda Roe
Profile: International Journal containing scholarly literature on nursing, midwifery and health visiting. Papers are required to have a sound scientific, evidential, theoretical or philosophical base and to be critical, questioning and scholarly in approach. Aimed at senior nurses, midwives, health visitors and nursing students.
Ad Rate: Full Page Mono £550.00
Ad Rate: Full Page Colour £950.00
MAGAZINE
Nursing/Nurses

Journal of Aesthetic Nursing
999688

Editorial: St Jude's Church, Dulwich Road, London SE24 0PB **Tel:** 44 02077 385454
Web site: www.aestheticnursing.co.uk
Freq: Monthly Not Audited
Editor: Natasha Devan
MAGAZINE
Nursing/Nurses, Plastic/Reconstructive/Cosmetic Surgery

Journal of Anaesthesia Practice
986367

Editorial: G1-G6 East Wing, The Croft LS22 5HG, Boroughbridge Road, Kirk Deighton, Wetherby LS22 5HG
Email: jap@barkerbrooks.co.uk
Web site: www.japractice.co.uk
Freq: Bi-Monthly
Circ: 5000 Not Audited
Profile: Journal of Anaesthesia Practice is a bi monthly anaesthesia publication owned by Pelican Magazines Ltd. It is primarily devoted to new products and innovations in anaesthesia. It also includes special product features on topics of interest. First published in 2005. Journal of Anaesthesia Practice is written for medical and surgical personnel.
Ad Rate: Full Page Colour £920.00
MAGAZINE
Anesthesiology

Journal of Analytical Atomic Spectrometry
987152

Editorial: Royal Society of Chemistry, Thomas Graham House, Science Park, Milton Road, Cambridge CB4 0WF
Tel: 44 01223 432331
Email: jaas-rsc@rsc.org
Web site: www.rsc.org/publishing/journals/ja/about.asp
Freq: Monthly Not Audited
Profile: Journal covering all aspects of development and applications of analytical atomic spectrometry. Aimed at research scientists, manufacturers and users of spectrometric equipment.Alternative Title: JAAS
Ad Rate: Full Page Mono £890.00
MAGAZINE
Science

Journal of Animal Science and Veterinary Medicine
1060895

Tel: 44 86298 7092806
Web site: http://xmsyzz.periodicals.net.cn
Freq: Bi-Monthly

Circ: 10001 Not Audited
MAGAZINE
Veterinary Medicine

Journal of Antimicrobial Chemotherapy
985380

Editorial: Griffin House, 53 Regent Place, Birmingham B1 3NJ **Tel:** 44 01212 621830
Email: jac@bsac.org.uk
Web site: jac.oxfordjournals.org
Freq: Monthly Not Audited
Profile: Journal containing peer-reviewed articles on the laboratory aspects and clinical use of all antimicrobials, including antibacterial, antiviral, antifungal and antiprotozoal. Aimed at all members of British Society for Antimicrobial Chemotherapy, representatives from academia, industry and health services and those who are influential in formulary decisions.C.W.E. Drummond is the Editorial Manager to whom enquiries should be addressed.
Ad Rate: Full Page Mono £742.00
Ad Rate: Full Page Colour £1235.00
MAGAZINE
Oncology, Science

Journal of Applied Research in Intellectual Disabilities
996483

Editorial: 74 White Lund Road, Heaton with Oxcliffe, Morecambe, Morecambe LA3 3DU
Tel: 44 01865 778315
Web site: http://onlinelibrary.wiley.com/journal/10.1111/(ISSN)1468-3148
Freq: Bi-Monthly Not Audited
MAGAZINE
News & Current Affairs

Journal of Applied Toxicology
996738

Editorial: John Wiley & Sons, Ltd., The Atrium, Southern Gate, Chichester PO19 8QG **Tel:** 44 01243 779777
Email: cs-journals@wiley.com
Web site: http://onlinelibrary.wiley.com/journal/10.1002/(ISSN)1099-1263
Freq: Monthly Not Audited
MAGAZINE
Occupational Therapy & Rehabilitation

Journal of Architectural Conservation
995876

Editorial: 4 Park Square, Milton Park, Abingdon, Didcot OX14 4RN
Tel: 44 02070 176000
Web site: www.tandfonline.com/raco
Freq: 3 Times/Year
Circ: 750 Not Audited
MAGAZINE
Architecture & Design

Journal of Asset Management
983209

Editorial: 4 Crinan Street, London N1 9XW
Email: jam@palgrave.com
Web site: www.palgrave-journals.com/jam/index.html
Freq: Bi-Monthly
Circ: 300 Not Audited
Editor: Stephen Satchell
Profile: Journal covering new investment techniques, methodologies and strategies, wealth management, new products and technologies, empirical studies, regulatory and legal developments, best practice and emerging trends in the asset management industry. Read by asset managers, heads of research, CEOs, pension fund managers, risk managers, actuarial consultants, corporate treasurers, investment strategists, heads of pensions, quantitative analysts, investment consultants, chief investment officers and professors of economics.
Ad Rate: Full Page Mono £500.00
MAGAZINE
Fund Management

Journal of Asthma
999205

Editorial: Christchurch Court, 10 Newgate Street, London EC1A 7AZ
Tel: 44 02070 175000
Email: healthcare.enquiries@informa.com

Web site: informahealthcare.com/jas
Freq: Monthly Not Audited
MAGAZINE
Allergies, Respiratory Diseases

Journal of Autoimmunity 999003
Web site: www.elsevier.com/wps/find/
journaldescription.cws_home/622856/
description#description
Freq: Bi-Monthly Not Audited
MAGAZINE
Allergies

Journal of Banking Regulation 994040
Editorial: 4 Crinan Street, London N1 9XW
Tel: 44 02078 334000
Web site: www.palgrave-journals.com/jbr
Freq: Quarterly
Circ: 400 Not Audited
Editor: Dalvinder Singh
MAGAZINE
Banking

The Journal of Biochemistry 998998
Editorial: Great Clarendon Street, Oxford
OX2 6DP **Tel:** 44 01865 353907
Web site: www.jb.oxfordjournals.org
Freq: Monthly Not Audited
MAGAZINE
Science

Journal of Biological Education 986618
Editorial: Society of Biology, Charles Darwin
House, 12 Roger Street, London WC1N 2JU
Tel: 44 02076 852550
Email: jbe@societyofbiology.org
Web site: www.tandfonline.com/toc/rjbe20/
current
Freq: Quarterly Not Audited
Editor: Ian Kinchin
Profile: Journal of Biological Education (JBE)
covers policy and curriculum developments,
bringing the latest results of research into the
teaching, learning and assessment of
biology. Aimed at all workers in biology
education including both teachers and
researchers.
MAGAZINE
Science

Journal of Business Strategy 985479
Editorial: Howard House, Wagon Lane,
Bingley, Bingley BD16 1WA
Tel: 44 01274 777700
Email: emerald@emeraldinsight.com
Web site: www.emeraldgrouppublishing.
com/products/journals/journals.htm?id=jbs
Freq: Bi-Monthly Not Audited
Editor: Nanci Healy
Profile: Journal focusing on practical
applications of business theory covering
areas such as strategy, planning and
business intelligence. Also includes columns
on marketing, career development and
partnerships.
MAGAZINE
Business, Corporate Responsibility

Journal of Change Management 984458
Editorial: 2&4 Park Square, Milton Park,
Abingdon, Didcot OX14 4RN
Tel: 44 02070 176000
Web site: www.informaworld.com/rjcm
Freq: Quarterly Not Audited
Profile: Journal of Change Management is a
quarterly business publication owned by
Routledge, Taylor and Francis. It provides
insights of business in changing markets
including structure, processes, resources,
technology and culture. First published in
2000. Journal of Change Management is
written for change managers, human
resources directors, strategic planners,
CEOs, managing directors, project
managers, business development managers,
consultants, operations directors and heads
of innovation. Its readership has grown to
900.

Ad Rate: Full Page Mono £250.00
MAGAZINE
Business, Corporate Responsibility, Small
and Medium Business

Journal of Child Health Care 998943
Editorial: 1 Oliver's Yard, 55 City Road,
London EC1Y 1SP **Tel:** 44 02073 248500
Email: jchcoffice@gmail.com
Web site: http://chc.sagepub.com
Freq: Quarterly Not Audited
Editor In Chief: Bernie Carter
MAGAZINE
Nursing/Nurses, Pediatrics

The Journal of Child Psychology and Psychiatry 995886
Tel: 44 01865 778315
Email: cs-journals@wiley.com
Web site: http://onlinelibrary.wiley.com/
journal/10.1111/(ISSN)1469-7610
Freq: Monthly Not Audited
MAGAZINE
Neurology, Pediatrics

Journal of Child Psychotherapy 999192
Editorial: The Association of Child
Psychotherapists, 120 West Heath Road,
London NW3 7TU
Email: admin@childpsychotherapy.org.uk
Web site: http://www.tandf.co.uk/journals/
RJCP
Freq: 3 Times/Year Not Audited
Editor: Kate Stratton
MAGAZINE
Neurology, Pediatrics

Journal of Chinese Economic & Foreign Trade Studies 1060634
Editorial: Emerald Group Publishing,
Howard House, Wagon Lane, Bingley BD16
1WA **Tel:** 44 01274 777700
Web site: http://www.emeraldinsight.com/
journal/jcefts
Freq: 3 Times/Year Not Audited
MAGAZINE
Economics

Journal of Clinical Nursing 985158
Editorial: 9600 Garsington Road, Oxford
OX4 2DQ **Tel:** 44 01865 476212
Email: jcn@wiley.com
Web site: http://onlinelibrary.wiley.com/
journal/10.1111/%28ISSN%291365-2702
Freq: Monthly Not Audited
MAGAZINE
Nursing/Nurses

Journal of Clinical Pharmacy and Therapeutics 984508
Editorial: The Atrium, Southern Gate,
Chichester PO19 8QG
Email: jcpt@wiley.com
Web site: http://eu.wiley.com/WileyCDA/
WileyTitle/productCd-JCPT.html
Freq: Bi-Monthly
Editor: Martin J. Kendall; **Editor:** Gregory
Peterson
Profile: Journal of Clinical Pharmacy and
Therapeutics is a bi monthly pharmacy and
therapeutics publication owned by
Wiley-Blackwell Publishing. It covers
information about rational therapeutics,
evidence based practice, safety, cost
effectiveness and clinical efficacy of drugs,
drug prescribing and regulatory affairs. First
published in 1975. Journal of Clinical
Pharmacy and Therapeutics is written for
researchers, clinicians, pharmacologists and
hospital pharmacists. Its readership has
grown to 335.
MAGAZINE
Pharmaceuticals

Journal of Clinical Urology 995049
Editorial: 1 Oliver's Yard, 55 City Road,
London EC1Y 1SP

Email: authorqueries@sagepub.co.uk
Web site: http://uro.sagepub.com/
Freq: Bi-Monthly
Circ: 1520 Not Audited
MAGAZINE
Urology

Journal of Cognitive Psychology 995717
Editorial: 4 Park Square, Milton Park,
Abingdon, Didcot OX14 4RN
Tel: 44 02070 176000
Email: pecp-peerreview@tandf.co.uk
Web site: http://www.tandfonline.com/toc/
pecp21/current
Freq: Bi-Monthly Not Audited
Editor: Robert Hartsuiker
MAGAZINE
Neurology

Journal of Community Nursing 981614
Editorial: 1st Floor, Unit G, Wixford Park,
George's Elm Lane, Bidford upon Avon,
Alcester B50 4JS **Tel:** 44 01789 582000
Web site: www.jcn.co.uk
Freq: Bi-Monthly Not Audited
Editor: Jason Beckford-Ball
Profile: Journal of Community Nursing is a
monthly nursing magazine owned by PTM
Publishers Ltd. It provides original scientific
papers, review articles, case reports and
drugs news. It also includes selected articles
from community nursing literature. First
published in 1977. Journal of Community
Nursing is written for healthcare and
pharmacy professionals and hospital
management. Its readership has grown to
23,000.
Ad Rate: Full Page Mono £1110.00
Ad Rate: Full Page Colour £1730.00
MAGAZINE
Community Care (UK), Nursing/Nurses

Journal of Computer-Aided Molecular Design 996833
Web site: http://www.springer.com/
chemistry/physical+chemistry/journal/10822
Freq: Monthly Not Audited
MAGAZINE
Science

Journal of Dementia Care 985260
Editorial: Culvert House, Culvert Road,
London SW11 5DH **Tel:** 44 02077 202108
Web site: https://www.
journalofdementiacare.co.uk/
Freq: Bi-Monthly
Circ: 4000 Not Audited
Editor: Mark Ivory
Profile: Journal containing news and
features on education, care practice, training
and research as well as debate about
practical, moral and ethical issues in
dementia care.
Ad Rate: Full Page Mono £765.00
Ad Rate: Full Page Colour £1105.00
MAGAZINE
Geriatrics, Neurology

Journal of Derivatives & Hedge Funds 984263
Editorial: 4 Crinan Street, London N1 9XW
Email: jdhf@palgrave.com
Web site: http://www.palgrave-journals.
com/jdhf/index.html
Freq: Quarterly
Circ: 29646 Cision Digital Reach
Editor: Stephen Satchell
MAGAZINE (ONLINE)
Derivatives, Hedge Funds

Journal of Diabetes Nursing 985229
Editorial: A Schofield Healthcare Media
Company, 1.03 Enterprise House, 1-2
Hatfields, London SE1 9PG
Tel: 44 02076 271510
Email: jdn@sbcommunicationsgroup.com
Web site: http://www.
thejournalofdiabetesnursing.co.uk
Freq: Monthly

Circ: 7000 Not Audited
Editor: Joanne Taylor
Profile: Journal covering diabetes nursing.
Aimed at key healthcare professionals
including every diabetes specialist nurse and
practice nurse with a special interest in
diabetes health care.
Ad Rate: Full Page Colour £1339.00
MAGAZINE
Diabetes, Nursing/Nurses

Journal of Disability and Oral Health 999000
Editorial: University of Liverpool, School of
Dentistry, Pembroke Place, Liverpool L35PS
Tel: 44 01517 065215
Email: jdoheditor@liverpool.ac.uk
Web site: http://www.bsdh.org/guidelines-
and-publications/journal-home.php
Freq: Quarterly Not Audited
Editor: Shelagh Thompson
MAGAZINE
Dentistry

Journal of Economic Studies 1008681
Editorial: Emerald Group Publishing,
Howard House, Wagon Lane, Bingley BD16
1WA
Web site: www.emeraldinsight.com/journal/
jes
Freq: Bi-Monthly Not Audited
MAGAZINE
Economics

Journal of Endocrinology 996724
Editorial: 22 Apex Court, Woodlands,
Bradley Stoke, Bristol BS32 4JT
Tel: 44 01454 642220
Email: joe@endocrinology.org
Web site: http://joe.endocrinology-journals.
org/
Freq: Monthly
Circ: 550 Not Audited
MAGAZINE
Diabetes

Journal of Epidemiology and Community Health 998974
Editorial: BMA House, Tavistock Square,
London WC1H 9JR **Tel:** 44 02073 836224
Email: jech@bmj.com
Web site: http://jech.bmj.com
Freq: Monthly Not Audited
MAGAZINE
Community Care (UK), Geriatrics,
Occupational Therapy & Rehabilitation

The Journal of Family Health Care (JFHC) 995900
Editorial: Ground Floor, Rayford House,
School Road, Brighton BN3 5HX
Tel: 44 01273 434943
Email: info@jfhc.co.uk
Web site: www.jfhc.co.uk
Freq: Bi-Monthly
Circ: 6000 Not Audited
Editor: Penny Hosie
MAGAZINE
Nursing/Nurses, Obstetrics & Gynecology
(OB/GYN), Pediatrics

Journal of Feline Medicine and Surgery 985326
Editorial: International Society of Feline
Medicine, High Street, Shaftesbury SP3 6LD
Web site: http://jfm.sagepub.com/
Freq: Monthly Not Audited
Editor: Andy Sparkes
MAGAZINE
Veterinary Medicine

Journal of Financial Economic Policy 1004615
Editorial: Emerald Group Publishing,
Howard House, Wagon Lane, Bingley BD16
1WA **Tel:** 44 01274 777700
Web site: http://www.emeraldinsight.com/
journal/jfep
Freq: Quarterly Not Audited
MAGAZINE
Economics

Business Magazines

Journal of Financial Market Infrastructures 999680
Editorial: Haymarket House, 28-29 Haymarket, London SW1Y 4RX
Tel: 44 02073 169000
Email: journals@incisivemedia.com
Web site: http://www.risk.net/journal-of-financial-market-infrastructures
Freq: Quarterly Not Audited
MAGAZINE
Financial Markets

Journal of Financial Services Marketing 980161
Editorial: 4 Crinan Street, London N1 9XW
Tel: 44 02078 334000
Email: harrison@staffmail.ed.ac.uk
Web site: http://www.springer.com/finance/journal/41264
Freq: Quarterly
Circ: 300 Not Audited
Profile: Journal containing articles on recent developments, latest management thinking and best practice.
Ad Rate: Full Page Mono £500.00
Ad Rate: Full Page Colour £1000.00
MAGAZINE
Banking, Marketing

Journal of Forensic and Legal Medicine 981043
Editorial: The Boulevard, Langford Lane, Kidlington, Oxford OX5 1GB
Tel: 44 01865 843000
Email: jflm@elsevier.com
Web site: http://www.jflmjournal.org
Freq: Bi-Monthly
Circ: 740 Not Audited
Profile: The official journal of the Association of Forensic Physicians, the Australia and New Zealand Forensic Medicine Society Inc. and the British Association in Forensic Medicine.
MAGAZINE
Medical Technology, Science

Journal of Forensic Medicine 1061163
Tel: 44 86212 31852361148
Email: fyxzz@126.com
Web site: http://www.ssfjd.com
Freq: Bi-Monthly
Circ: 1801 Not Audited
MAGAZINE
Science

Journal of Forensic Practice 987003
Editorial: Howard House, Wagon Lane, Bingley BD16 1WA **Tel:** 44 01274 777700
Web site: http://www.emeraldinsight.com/loi/jfp
Freq: Quarterly Not Audited
Editor: Neil Gredecki
MAGAZINE
Neurology, Science

Journal of Health Psychology 985457
Email: editorjhp@gmail.com
Web site: http://hpq.sagepub.com
Freq: Monthly Not Audited
Editor: David F. Marks
Profile: Journal of Health Psychology is an international reviewed journal that aims to support and help shape research in health psychology from around the world. It provides a platform for traditional empirical analyses as well as more qualitative and/or critically oriented approaches. It also addresses the social contexts in which psychological and health processes are embedded. Aimed at professionals working in the area of health psychology.
Ad Rate: Full Page Mono £500.00
MAGAZINE
Neurology

Journal of Health Services Research & Policy 985647
Editorial: Department of Health Services Research & Policy, London School Hygiene and Tropical Medicine, 15-17 Tavistock

Place, London WC1H 9SH
Tel: 44 02079 272107
Web site: jhsrp.rsmjournals.com
Freq: Quarterly
Profile: Journal that provides information on health services, healthcare policy and research. It also features the latest scientific research, insightful overviews and reflections on underlying issues, and innovative, thought provoking contributions from leading academics and policy-makers. In addition, it provides ideas and hope for solving dilemmas that confront all countries. First published in 1996. Journal of Health Services Research & Policy is written for health care professionals, hospital administrators and management.
MAGAZINE
Healthcare Industry

Journal of Health Visiting 996941
Editorial: St Jude's Church, Dulwich Road, London SE24 0PB **Tel:** 44 02077 385454
Email: jhv@markallengroup.com
Web site: http://www.journalofhealthvisiting.com
Freq: Monthly
Circ: 3484 Not Audited
MAGAZINE
Community Care (UK)

Journal of Heating Ventilating and Air conditioning 1061658
Tel: 44 86108 8361727
Email: hvac@cadg.cn
Web site: http://www.hvacjournal.cn
Freq: Monthly
Circ: 25003 Not Audited
MAGAZINE
Building & Construction

Journal of Hydrologic Engineering 1061747
Tel: 44 86106 3203599
Email: j.hyd@mwr.gov.cn
Freq: Bi-Monthly
Circ: 3203 Not Audited
MAGAZINE
Alternative/Renewable Energy, Engineering, Environment

The Journal of Industry and Technology 984415
Tel: 44 01353 699456
Web site: www.thejournalofindustryandtechnology.biz/
Freq: Daily Not Audited
Profile: Journal covering news on the latest industrial developments. Includes articles on electronics, communications, total engineering and manufacturing, machine tools, automotive engineering, robots, industrial analytical instrumentation, science and research.
Ad Rate: Full Page Mono £1000.00
Ad Rate: Full Page Colour £1250.00
MAGAZINE
Industry

Journal of Innovation in Health Informatics 1054274
Editorial: First Floor, Block D, North Star House, North Star Avenue, Swindon SN2 1FA **Tel:** 44 01793 417424
Email: editoripc@gmail.com
Web site: http://hijournal.bcs.org/index.php/jhi
Freq: Quarterly
MAGAZINE
Health Administration, Healthcare Industry, Medical Technology

Journal of Intellectual Property Law & Practice 983482
Editorial: Oxford University Press, Great Clarendon Street, Oxford OX2 6DP
Tel: 44 01865 353907
Web site: jiplp.oxfordjournals.org
Freq: Monthly Not Audited
Profile: Journal dedicated to intellectual property law and practice.
MAGAZINE
Intellectual Property

Journal of International Banking and Financial Law 998562
Editorial: 30 Farringdon Street, London EC4A 4HH **Tel:** 44 02074 002500
Web site: https://store.lexisnexis.co.uk/products/butterworths-journal-of-international-banking-and-financial-
Freq: Monthly Not Audited
Editor: Amanda Cohen
MAGAZINE
Tax Law

Journal of International Pharmaceutical Research 1061238
Tel: 44 86106 6931618
Email: cuicb@sohu.com
Web site: http://www.pharmacy.ac.cn
Freq: Bi-Monthly Not Audited
MAGAZINE
Pharmaceuticals

Journal of Kidney Care 985208
Editorial: St Jude's Church, Dulwich Road, London SE24 0PB **Tel:** 44 02077 385454
Email: jrn@markallengroup.com
Web site: http://www.magonlinelibrary.com/toc/jorn/current
Freq: Bi-Monthly Not Audited
Editor: Natasha Devan
Profile: Nursing journal designed to meet the educational needs of all professionals working in renal care. The journal addresses professional and training issues and features information on the latest developments in policy, research and clinical practice. Aimed at nurses and other allied healthcare professionals specialising in renal care.
MAGAZINE
Nursing/Nurses, Urology

Journal of Management Development 982948
Editorial: Howard House, Wagon Lane, Bingley BD16 1WA **Tel:** 44 01274 777700
Web site: www.emeraldgrouppublishing.com/products/journals/journals.htm?id=jmd
Freq: Monthly Not Audited
MAGAZINE
Business, Corporate Responsibility

Journal of Medical Device Regulation 999677
Editorial: Units 317/318 Burford Business Centre, 11 Burford Road, Stratford, London E15 2ST **Tel:** 44 01305 770836
Email: editor@globalregulatorypress.com
Web site: www.globalregulatorypress.com
Freq: Quarterly Not Audited
Editor: Victoria Clark
MAGAZINE
Medical Technology

Journal of Medical Marketing 997560
Editorial: 1 Oliver's Yard, 55 City Road, London EC1Y 1SP **Tel:** 44 02073 248500
Web site: http://mmj.sagepub.com/
Freq: Quarterly
Circ: 300 Not Audited
MAGAZINE
Health Administration, Healthcare Industry

Journal of Medical Screening 986036
Editorial: 1 Wimpole Street, London W1G 0AE **Tel:** 44 02072 902921
Web site: http://msc.sagepub.com/
Freq: Quarterly Not Audited
Editor: Nicholas Wald
MAGAZINE
Diagnostic Imaging

The Journal of mHealth 997892
Email: matthew@simedics.org
Web site: www.thejournalofmhealth.com/
Freq: Bi-Monthly Not Audited

Editor: Matthew Driver
MAGAZINE
Medical Technology

Journal of Muscle Research and Cell Motility 996680
Web site: springer.com/life+sciences/cell+biology/journal/10974
Freq: Quarterly Not Audited
MAGAZINE
Biotechnology, Rheumatology

Journal of Neuropsychology 995790
Editorial: The Atrium, Southern Gate, Chichester PO19 8SG **Tel:** 44 01865 778315
Email: jnp@wiley.com
Web site: http://onlinelibrary.wiley.com/journal/10.1111/(ISSN)1748-6653
Freq: Semi-Annual Not Audited
Editor: Stephen Jackson
MAGAZINE
Neurology

Journal of Numerical Methods & Computer Applications 1061055
Tel: 44 86106 2555115
Email: gxy@icmsec.cc.ac.cn
Web site: http://www.computmath.com
Freq: Quarterly
Circ: 1705 Not Audited
MAGAZINE
Science

Journal of Nursing Management 985159
Editorial: The Atrium, Southern Gate, Chichester PO19 8SQ **Tel:** 44 01243 772007
Email: jnmedoffice@wiley.com
Web site: http://www.blackwellpublishing.com/journal.asp?ref=0966-0429
Freq: Bi-Monthly Not Audited
Profile: Journal containing case studies, training news, information and advice on new practices and staff management.
Ad Rate: Full Page Mono £550.00
Ad Rate: Full Page Colour £950.00
MAGAZINE
Nursing/Nurses

Journal of Occupational and Organizational Psychology 995838
Email: joop@wiley.com
Web site: http://onlinelibrary.wiley.com/journal/10.1111/(ISSN)2044-8325/issues
Freq: Quarterly Not Audited
MAGAZINE
Neurology

Journal of Orthodontics 985475
Editorial: 1 Carlton House Terrace, London SW1Y 5AF **Tel:** 44 02074 517300
Email: j.collinson@maneypublishing.com
Web site: http://www.tandfonline.com/toc/yjor20/current
Freq: Quarterly Not Audited
Profile: Journal containing reviews, critical commentaries, editorial and correspondence on features of orthodontic practice, teaching and research. The official journal of the British Orthodontic Society, it aims to publish original research papers that will underpin evidence-based orthodontic care.
Ad Rate: Full Page Mono £610.00
Ad Rate: Full Page Colour £1300.00
MAGAZINE
Dentistry

Journal of Paramedic Practice 999136
Editorial: St Jude's Church, Dulwich Road, London SE24 0PB **Tel:** 44 02077 385454
Email: jpp@markallengroup.com
Web site: http://www.paramedicpractice.com
Freq: Monthly
Circ: 8500 Not Audited
MAGAZINE
EMS/Emergency Medical Services

The Journal of Pathology 996651

Editorial: The Pathological Society of Great Britain & Ireland, 2 Carlton House Terrace, London SW1Y 5AF **Tel:** 44 01865 778315
Email: cs-journals@wiley.com
Web site: onlinelibrary.wiley.com/journal/10.1002/(ISSN)1096-9896
Freq: Monthly Not Audited
MAGAZINE
Biotechnology, Oncology, Science

Journal of Payments Strategy & Systems 1055940

Editorial: Russell House, 28-30 Little Russell Street, London WC1A 2HN
Tel: 44 02070 923465
Web site: www.henrystewartpublications.com/jpss
Freq: Quarterly
Circ: 1500 Not Audited
MAGAZINE
Accounting

Journal of Pediatric Urology 998958

Editorial: Health Sciences, The Boulevard, Langford Lane, Kidlington OX5 1GB
Tel: 44 01865 843672
Email: jpurol@elsevier.com
Web site: www.journals.elsevier.com/journal-of-pediatric-urology/
Freq: Bi-Monthly
Circ: 545 Not Audited
Editor: Pierre Mouriquand
MAGAZINE
Pediatrics, Urology

Journal of Petroleum Geology 988046

Editorial: Scientific Press Ltd, PO Box 21, Beaconsfield, Beaconsfield HP9 1NS
Tel: 44 01494 675139
Web site: http://onlinelibrary.wiley.com/journal/10.1111/(ISSN)1747-5457
Freq: Quarterly
Editor: Chris Tiratsoo
Profile: Journal publishing original science concerning the geology of hydrocarbons (oil and natural gas).
MAGAZINE
Oil

Journal of Pharmacy and Pharmacology 987661

Editorial: 1 Lambeth High Street, London SE1 7JN
Email: cs-journals@wiley.com
Web site: http://onlinelibrary.wiley.com/journal/10.1111/%28ISSN%292042-7158
Freq: Monthly Not Audited
Editor: David Jones
Profile: Journal covering original research papers, critical reviews and communications on the latest developments in the pharmaceutical sciences.
MAGAZINE
Pharmaceuticals

Journal of Planning & Environment Law 980882

Editorial: The Hatchery, Hall Bank Lane, Mytholmroyd, Mytholmroyd HX7 5HQ
Tel: 44 02073 937000
Web site: http://www.sweetandmaxwell.co.uk/Catalogue
Freq: Monthly Not Audited
Profile: Journal focusing on developments in planning and environmental law, compulsory purchase and related issues.
MAGAZINE
Environment, Government

Journal of Plastic Engineering 1061164

Tel: 44 86106 2912592
Email: sxgcxb@263.net
Freq: Bi-Monthly
Circ: 971 Not Audited
MAGAZINE
Plastics

The Journal of Precision Medicine 1073816

Tel: 44 01306 646449
Web site: http://www.thejournalofprecisionmedicine.com/
Freq: Bi-Monthly
Circ: 25000 Not Audited
MAGAZINE
Biotechnology, Pharmaceuticals

Journal of Psychiatric and Mental Health Nursing 985160

Editorial: 9600 Garsington Road, Oxford OX4 2DQ **Tel:** 44 01865 776868
Email: jpmhnedoffice@wiley.com
Web site: http://onlinelibrary.wiley.com/journal/10.1111/(ISSN)1365-2850/issues
Freq: Monthly Not Audited
Editor: Dawn Freshwater
Profile: Journal providing an international forum for all professionals in the field of psychiatric and mental health nursing. It publishes reviewed papers which reflect developments in knowledge, attitudes and skills and integration of these into practice. The focus is on innovations in practice that are based on development, evaluation and research. The journal is a means of communication between professionals, mainly in nursing but also attracting other mental health care workers. Read by advanced practitioners, primary carers, service users, accomplished researchers and student thesis writers.
Ad Rate: Full Page Mono £550.00
Ad Rate: Full Page Colour £950.00
MAGAZINE
Neurology, Nursing/Nurses

Journal of Public Health Policy 994976

Editorial: 4 Crinan Street, London N1 9XW
Tel: 44 02078 334000
Email: jphp@umb.edu
Web site: http://www.palgrave-journals.com/jphp/index.html
Freq: Quarterly
Circ: 500 Not Audited
Editor: Phyllis Freeman; **Editor:** Anthony Robbins
MAGAZINE
Health Administration

Journal of Public Mental Health 984898

Editorial: Howard House, Wagon Lane, Bingley BD16 1WA **Tel:** 44 01274 777700
Email: emerald@emeraldinsight.com
Web site: http://www.emeraldgrouppublishing.com/products/journals/journals.htm?id=jpmh
Freq: Quarterly Not Audited
Editor: Woody Caan
Profile: Journal covering all aspects of the mental health field. Contains news and articles written by people involved in the health and social care industry.
Ad Rate: Full Page Mono £350.00
MAGAZINE
Neurology

Journal of Radioanalytical and Nuclear Chemistry 1061440

Tel: 44 36146 48237
Email: journals@akkrt.hu
Web site: http://www.akademiai.com Not Audited
MAGAZINE
Science

Journal of Radiological Protection 995959

Editorial: Institute of Physics Publishing, Dirac House, Temple Back, Bristol BS1 6BE
Tel: 44 01179 297481
Email: jrp@iop.org
Web site: www.iopscience.org/jrp
Freq: Quarterly
Circ: 2000 Not Audited
MAGAZINE
Diagnostic Imaging, Science

Journal of Renal Care 998871

Editorial: John Wiley & Sons Inc, The Atrium, Southern Gate, Chichester PO19 8SQ **Tel:** 44 01865 778315
Email: cs-journals@wiley.com
Web site: http://onlinelibrary.wiley.com/journal/10.1111/%28ISSN%291755-6686
Freq: Quarterly
Circ: 2700 Not Audited
Editor: Nicola Thomas
MAGAZINE
Urology

Journal of Reproductive and Infant Psychology 995766

Editorial: 4 Park Square, Milton Park, Didcot OX14 4RN **Tel:** 44 02070 176000
Web site: www.tandf.co.uk/journals/CJRI
Freq: Bi-Monthly
MAGAZINE
Neurology, Obstetrics & Gynecology (OB/GYN)

Journal of Research in Nursing 998813

Editorial: 1 Oliver's Yard, 55 City Road, London EC1Y 1SP
Email: jrn@sagepub.co.uk
Web site: http://jrn.sagepub.com/
Freq: Bi-Monthly Not Audited
Editor: Ann McMahon
MAGAZINE
Nursing/Nurses

Journal of Risk Management in Financial Institutions 1012354

Editorial: 28-30 Little Russell Street, London WC1A 2HN **Tel:** 44 02070 923465
Web site: www.henrystewartpublications.com/jrm
Freq: Quarterly
Circ: 1500 Not Audited
MAGAZINE
Banking, Bonds, Hedge Funds

Journal of Securities Operations & Custody 1008430

Editorial: Russell House, 28-30 Little Russell Street, London WC1A 2HN
Tel: 44 02070 923465
Web site: www.henrystewartpublications.com/jsoc
Freq: Quarterly
Circ: 1500 Not Audited
MAGAZINE
Banking, Government, Tax Law

Journal of Sediment Research 1060873

Tel: 44 86106 8786628
Email: sedi-eng@iwhr.com
Freq: Bi-Monthly
Circ: 1001 Not Audited
MAGAZINE
Science

Journal of Small Business and Enterprise Development 987741

Editorial: Howard House, Wagon Lane, Bingley BD16 1WA **Tel:** 44 01274 777700
Email: emerald@emeraldinsight.com
Web site: http://www.emeraldgrouppublishing.com/products/journals/journals.htm?id=JSBED
Freq: Quarterly Not Audited
MAGAZINE
Business, Corporate Responsibility

Journal of Social Work Practice 995753

Editorial: 4 Park Square, Milton Park, Abingdon OX14 4RN **Tel:** 44 02070 176000
Email: revithick4gaps@btinternet.com
Web site: http://www.tandf.co.uk/journals/carfax/02650533.html
Freq: Quarterly
Editor: Juliet Koprowska
MAGAZINE
Community Care (UK)

Journal of Sports Sciences 999234

Editorial: 4 Park Square, Milton Park, Abingdon, Didcot OX14 4RN
Tel: 44 02070 176000
Web site: http://www.tandf.co.uk/journals/RJSP
Freq: Bi-Weekly Not Audited
MAGAZINE
Sports Medicine

Journal of Telemedicine and Telecare 997202

Editorial: 1 Oliver's Yard, 55 City Road, London EC1Y 1SP
Email: jtteditorial@sagepub.co.uk
Web site: jtt.sagepub.com
Freq: Bi-Monthly Not Audited
MAGAZINE
Medical Technology

The Journal of the Law Society of Scotland 984490

Editorial: Studio 2001, Mile End, Paisley PA1 1JS **Tel:** 44 01415 610300
Email: news@connectcommunications.co.uk
Web site: www.journalonline.co.uk
Freq: Monthly
Circ: 13040 Not Audited
Editor: Peter Nicholson
Profile: Official journal covering Scottish law. Aimed at Scottish solicitors; also advocates, judiciary, universities and law departments of colleges, government departments and other professionals.
Ad Rate: Full Page Colour £1931.00
MAGAZINE
Law

Journal of Tissue Viability 999025

Editorial: The Boulevard, Langford Lane, Kidlington, Oxford OX5 1GB
Tel: 44 01865 843000
Email: jtv@elsevier.com
Web site: www.journaloftissueviability.com/home
Freq: Quarterly Not Audited
MAGAZINE
Dermatology

Journal of Viral Hepatitis 996486

Editorial: Imperial College Faculty of Medicine, Department of Medicine, St Mary's Hospital Medical School, London W2 1PG **Tel:** 44 02082 207791
Email: jvhedoffice@gmail.com
Web site: http://onlinelibrary.wiley.com/journal/10.1111/(ISSN)1365-2893
Freq: Monthly Not Audited
MAGAZINE
Infectious Diseases

The Journal of Workplace Learning 981045

Editorial: Howard House, Wagon Lane, Bingley BD16 1WA **Tel:** 44 01274 777700
Web site: www.emeraldinsight.com/journal/jwl
Freq: Bi-Monthly Not Audited
Profile: Journal covering the growth of the individual within an organisation.
MAGAZINE
Human Resources

Journal of World Energy Law & Business 999571

Editorial: Great Clarendon Street, Oxford OX2 6DP **Tel:** 44 01865 353907
Web site: www.jwelb.oxfordjournals.org
Freq: Monthly Not Audited
MAGAZINE
Oil, Tax Law

The Journalist 981665

Editorial: National Union of Journalists, Headland House, 72 Acton Street, London WC1X 9NB **Tel:** 44 02072 787916
Email: journalist@nuj.org.uk
Web site: www.nuj.org.uk
Freq: Bi-Monthly
Circ: 31850 Not Audited

Business Magazines

Editor: Christine Buckley
Profile: Official journal of the NUJ. Contains coverage of all media issues from the viewpoint of working journalists.
Ad Rate: Full Page Colour £1500.00
MAGAZINE
Publishing

JSE + 1060436
Email: patrick@hsm.co.za
Freq: Quarterly
Circ: 28778 Not Audited
MAGAZINE
Banking, Business, Small and Medium Business

Junior Science 1060878
Tel: 44 86216 4704240
Email: zxkj@sste.com
Freq: Monthly
Circ: 150000 Not Audited
MAGAZINE
Science

Just For Nurses 999113
Editorial: 92 Severn Drive, Taunton TA1 2PW **Tel:** 44 01823 332275
Email: info@uk-nursing.com
Web site: www.justfornurses.co.uk
Freq: Daily
Circ: 1974 Cision Digital Reach
Editor: Nigel Freeney
MAGAZINE (ONLINE)
Nursing/Nurses

JUST-EAT BUSINESS 1061236
Tel: 44 45332 22020
Email: info@jungersted.com
Web site: http://www.jungersted.com/2009/09/just-eat-business
Freq: Quarterly
Circ: 1150 Not Audited
MAGAZINE
Business, Small and Medium Business

just-food.com 982834
Editorial: Aroq House, 17A Harris Business Park, Stoke Prior, Bromsgrove B60 4DJ
Tel: 44 01527 573600
Email: foodeditor@aroq.com
Web site: http://www.just-food.com
Freq: Daily
Circ: 67330 Cision Digital Reach
Profile: E-Zine featuring news and features covering all aspects of the food industry.
MAGAZINE (ONLINE)
Food

The K&Bzine 983974
Editorial: 155 Hook Road, Epsom, London KT19 8TU **Tel:** 44 01372 811307
Email: news@thekbzine.com
Web site: http://www.thekbzine.com/
Freq: Weekly
Circ: 706 Cision Digital Reach
Profile: Electronic newsletter including the latest news, ideas and information about the people, products and issues for the kitchen, bathroom and bedroom industry.
MAGAZINE (ONLINE)
Building & Construction, Interior Design

Kaiser Facts & News 1061464
Tel: 44 42337 72121
Email: kaiserag@kaiser.li
Web site: http://www.kaiser.li Not Audited
MAGAZINE
Building & Construction, Business, Small and Medium Business

KBBDaily 997410
Tel: 44 01206 851117
Web site: kbbdaily.com/index.php
Freq: Daily
Circ: 47 Cision Digital Reach
Editor: Ellie Pullen
Profile: Website covering retailers, manufacturers, designers and architect. kbbdaily website shares the latest information on retailers, manufacturers, designers and architect.
MAGAZINE (ONLINE)
Interior Design

kbbreview 981101
Editorial: Congress House, Lyon Road, London HA1 2EN **Tel:** 44 02085 152000
Email: info@taylistmedia.com
Web site: www.kbbreview.com
Freq: Monthly
Circ: 15000 Not Audited
Editor: Tim Wallace
Profile: Journal reviewing trends in the kitchen, bedroom and bathroom industry. Aimed at independent specialist retailers.
Ad Rate: Full Page Colour £3200.00
MAGAZINE
Interior Design, Retail Management

KB-Network 987033
Tel: 44 01787 221396
Email: grahame@kb-network.co.uk
Web site: www.kb-network.co.uk
Freq: Daily
Circ: 9800 Cision Digital Reach
Editor: Grahame Morrison
MAGAZINE (ONLINE)
Interior Design

Keeping the Balance 986016
Editorial: National Gamekeepers' Organisation, PO Box 246, Darlington DL1 9FZ **Tel:** 44 01833 660869
Email: info@nationalgamekeepers.org.uk
Web site: http://www.nationalgamekeepers.org.uk/ngo-magazine
Freq: Quarterly
Circ: 15000 Not Audited
Editor: Sophia Gallia
Profile: Magazine of the The National Gamekeepers' Organisation (NGO), the representative body for gamekeepers in England and Wales.Simed at gamekeepers across Great Britain.
MAGAZINE
Animal Farming

Kennedy's Confection 983505
Tel: 44 01732 752090
Email: editor@kennedys.co.uk
Web site: www.kennedysconfection.com
Freq: Monthly
Circ: 4973 Not Audited
Profile: Kennedy's Confection is a monthly trade confectionary publication owned by Kennedy's Publications, Ltd. It provides the needs for regular well presented information on equipment, ingredients, product development, trends, news, materials and events. First published in 1890. Kennedy's Confection is written globally for executives in the chocolate, sugar confectionary, chewing gum, ice cream and bakery manufacturing industries. Its readership has grown to 4,973.
Ad Rate: Full Page Colour £2250.00
MAGAZINE
Food

Kent Director 982905
Editorial: 14 Middletons Road, Yaxley, Peterborough PE7 3LR
Tel: 44 01733 242312
Email: info@pridepublications.co.uk
Web site: www.pridepublications.co.uk
Freq: Monthly
Circ: 9000 Not Audited
Editor: Trevor Gehlcken
Profile: Business magazine containing local news items, views and features of general interest.
Ad Rate: Full Page Mono £675.00
Ad Rate: Full Page Colour £675.00
MAGAZINE
Business

Kent Women in Business Magazine 987461
Editorial: Unit 2, Lested Farm, Plough Wents Road, Chart Sutton, Maidstone ME17 3SA
Tel: 44 01622 807930
Email: newsroom@kwib.co.uk
Web site: www.kwibmagazine.co.uk
Freq: Quarterly Not Audited
Profile: Magazine covering female business owners and career women in Kent.
MAGAZINE
Business, Corporate Responsibility

key.Aero 985556
Editorial: PO Box 100, Stamford PE9 1XQ
Tel: 44 01780 755131
Web site: http://www.key.aero/
Freq: Daily
Circ: 3811 Cision Digital Reach
MAGAZINE (ONLINE)
Aviation

Keystone Ireland 984820
Editorial: Unit C3, 6 Westbank Drive, Belfast BT3 9LA **Tel:** 44 02890 319008
Email: ksinewscopy@flagshipmedia.co.uk
Web site: http://www.flagshipmedia.co.uk/keystone.htm
Freq: Bi-Monthly
Circ: 9998 Not Audited
Editor: Coleen Dornan
Profile: Newspaper covering all aspects of the construction industry. Includes project features and new product information.
Ad Rate: Full Page Colour £2005.00
MAGAZINE
Building & Construction

Keyways 987579
Editorial: 5D Great Central Way, Woodford Halse, Daventry, Woodford NN11 3PZ
Tel: 44 01327 262255
Email: enquiries@locksmiths.co.uk
Web site: www.locksmiths.co.uk
Freq: Bi-Monthly
Circ: 1750 Not Audited
Editor: Simon Griffiths
Profile: Official Journal of the Master Locksmiths Association, covering information and news about security, locks, bolts and safes.
Ad Rate: Full Page Colour £650.00
MAGAZINE
Security & Security Systems

KITA Kiinteistö & Talotekniikka 1061908
Email: info@publico.com
Web site: http://www.kita.fi/
Freq: Quarterly Not Audited
MAGAZINE
Building & Construction

Kitchen & Bathroom Journal 984137
Editorial: Napier House, 11 Surrey Street, Lowestoft NR32 1LJ **Tel:** 44 01502 732515
Email: info@kitchenandbathroomjournal.co.uk
Web site: www.craftsmanpublishing.co.uk/kitchen-bathroom
Freq: Monthly
Circ: 9115 Not Audited
Editor: Catherine Earle
MAGAZINE
Interior Design

Kitchens & Bathrooms News 983382
Editorial: Regal House, Regal Way, Watford, London WD24 4YF **Tel:** 44 01923 237799
Web site: www.kandbnews.co.uk
Freq: Monthly
Circ: 13555 Not Audited
Editor: Philippa Turrell
Profile: Magazine covering new products, guides, case studies and specification features on kitchens and bathrooms.
Ad Rate: Full Page Colour £2400.00
MAGAZINE
Interior Design

Kitchens Review 987130
Editorial: Bolney Place, Cowfold Road, Haywards Heath RH17 5QT
Tel: 44 01444 882732
Email: editorial@kitchens-review.co.uk
Web site: www.kitchens-review.co.uk
Freq: Daily
Circ: 11176 Cision Digital Reach
Editor: Diane Lamer
MAGAZINE (ONLINE)
Interior Design

Knight Frank 995392
Editorial: 55 Baker Street, London W1U 8AN
Tel: 44 02076 298171
Web site: www.knightfrank.com
Freq: Daily
Circ: 100173 Cision Digital Reach
MAGAZINE (ONLINE)
Finance

Koring Fokus/Wheat Focus 1060629
Tel: 44 27182 930622
Email: mediacomedit1@intekom.co.za
Web site: http://www.mediacom-cc.co.za
Freq: Bi-Monthly
Circ: 6152 Not Audited
MAGAZINE
Animal Farming

Korjausrakentaminen 1061758
Email: rakennusmedia@rakennusmedia.fi
Web site: http://www.rakennusmedia.fi/News.aspx?id=10575
Freq: Quarterly
Circ: 10000 Not Audited
MAGAZINE
Architecture & Design, Building & Construction

La Revue du Droit des Affaires Internationales 998691
Editorial: Friars House, 160 Blackfriars Road, London SE1 8EZ
Tel: 44 02075 426664
Email: henrylesguillons@gmail.com
Web site: www.iblj.com
Freq: Bi-Monthly Not Audited
MAGAZINE
Corporate Law, Intellectual Property, Litigation, Real Estate Law, Tax Law

Lab Animal Europe 998573
Editorial: PO Box 24, Hull HU12 8YJ
Tel: 44 08456 445545
Web site: www.labanimaleurope.eu
Freq: Monthly
Circ: 17500 Not Audited
MAGAZINE
Animal Farming, Science

Lab Bulletin 987156
Tel: 44 01438 871968
Email: info@labbulletin.com
Web site: www.labbulletin.com
Freq: Daily
Circ: 11300 Cision Digital Reach
Editor: Sandie Purvis
Profile: Website covering laboratories. Lab Bulletin covers news, analysis and information about equipment, instruments and consumables used in laboratories. It also features a supplier directory, technical articles, application notes, video presentations, new product literature and industry events.
MAGAZINE (ONLINE)
Diagnostic Imaging, Medical Technology

Lab on a Chip 986634
Editorial: Royal Society of Chemistry, Thomas Graham House, Science Park, Milton Road, Cambridge CB4 0WF
Tel: 44 01223 420066
Email: loc-rsc@rsc.org
Web site: http://www.rsc.org/publishing/journals/lc/about.asp
Freq: Bi-Weekly Not Audited
Profile: Magazine examining miniaturisation research, technology and its applications in chemistry, biology, physics, electronics, clinical chemistry, fabrication, engineering and materials science, aiding communication and partnerships across disciplines. Aimed at scientists in these fields.
Ad Rate: Full Page Mono £890.00
MAGAZINE
Science

LabAsia 988096
Editorial: Oak Court Business Centre, Sandridge Park, Porters Wood, St.Albans, London AL3 6PH **Tel:** 44 01727 858840

Email: pr@labmate-online.com
Web site: http://www.labmate-online.com/
ejournal/labasia-buyers-guide/160
Freq: Bi-Monthly
Circ: 75114 Not Audited
Editor: Gwyneth Astles
MAGAZINE
Science

Labels & Labeling
981612
Editorial: Metro Building, 9th Floor, 1
Butterwick, London W6 8DL
Tel: 44 02088 462835
Email: editorial@labelsandlabeling.com
Web site: www.labelsandlabeling.com
Freq: Bi-Monthly
Circ: 30000 Not Audited
MAGAZINE
Publishing

Labmate UK and Ireland
981189
Editorial: Oak Court Business Centre,
Sandridge Park, Porters Wood, St Albans,
London AL3 6PH **Tel:** 44 01727 858840
Email: pr@labmate-online.com
Web site: www.labmate-online.com/
ejournal/labmate-uk-&-ireland/305/
Freq: Monthly
Circ: 16880 Not Audited
Editor: Gwyneth Astles
MAGAZINE
Science

Laboratory
1053800
Tel: 44 01923 851777
Email: info@fmc.co.uk
Web site: http://www.fmc.co.uk/shop/
private-laboratory/
Freq: Bi-Monthly
Circ: 2000 Not Audited
MAGAZINE
Dentistry

Laboratory News
981305
Editorial: 6th Floor, Davis House, 2 Robert
Street, Croydon CR0 1QQ
Tel: 44 02082 538600
Web site: www.labnews.co.uk
Freq: Monthly
Circ: 9000 Not Audited
Editor: Phil Prime
Profile: Magazine covering science. The
Laboratory News magazine covers the
current news, industry trends, latest
developments in products and their
applications, health and safety in the science
industry.
Ad Rate: Full Page Colour £2975.00
MAGAZINE
Medical Technology

LACCA News
997231
Editorial: 87 Lancaster Road, London W11
1QQ **Tel:** 44 02079 089201
Email: enquiries@laccanet.com
Web site: www.laccanet.com/news
Freq: Daily
Circ: 2796 Cision Digital Reach
MAGAZINE (ONLINE)
Corporate Law, Intellectual Property,
Legal Services, Litigation, Tax Law

Lafferty Retail Banking
Insights
1072714
Editorial: Lafferty Group, One Lyric Square,
Hammersmith, London W6 0NB
Tel: 44 02030 088415
Email: enquiries@lafferty.com
Web site: www.lafferty.com
Freq: Daily
Circ: 3416 Cision Digital Reach
MAGAZINE (ONLINE)
Banking

Lancashire Business View
983979
Editorial: East Park Lodge, East Park Lane,
Blackburn BB1 8DW **Tel:** 44 01254 297870
Email: info@lancashirebusinessview.co.uk
Web site: www.lancashirebusinessview.co.
uk
Freq: Bi-Monthly

Circ: 8000 Not Audited
Profile: Lancashire Business View is a bi
monthly local business magazine owned by
North Point Publishing. It covers major
issues and analytical business information in
Lancashire and Dolton. First published in
2005. Lancashire Business View is written
for business owners and managers. Its
readership has grown to 8,000.
Ad Rate: Full Page Colour £1475.00
MAGAZINE
Business

The Lancet Diabetes &
Endocrinology
996612
Editorial: 125 London Wall, London EC2Y
5AS **Tel:** 44 02074 244200
Email: diabetes-endocrinology@lancet.com
Web site: http://www.journals.elsevier.com/
the-lancet-diabetes-and-endocrinology/
Freq: Monthly Not Audited
Editor: Justine Davies
MAGAZINE
Diabetes

The Lancet Infectious
Diseases
984729
Editorial: 125 London Wall, London EC2Y
5AS **Tel:** 44 02074 244900
Email: ideditorial@lancet.com
Web site: http://www.journals.elsevier.com/
the-lancet-infectious-diseases/
Freq: Monthly Not Audited
Editor: John McConnell
Profile: Publication containing review
articles written by specialists, comment and
debate on hot topics in the field, interviews
with top names in infectious diseases and
news from around the world.
MAGAZINE
Infectious Diseases

The Lancet Neurology
983541
Editorial: 125 London Wall, London EC2Y
5AS **Tel:** 44 02074 244900
Email: tlneditorial@lancet.com
Web site: http://www.journals.elsevier.com/
the-lancet-neurology/
Freq: Monthly Not Audited
Editor: Elena Becker-Barroso
Profile: Journal covering neurological
research reports and comments on medical
topics. Topics covered includes
cerebrovascular disease, dementia and
alzheimer's disease, epilepsy and seizures,
genetics, headache and migraine,
neurological infections, motor neuron
disease and amyotrophic lateral sclerosis,
movement disorders, multiple sclerosis,
neuromuscular disorders, peripheral nerve
disorders, paediatric neurology, sleep
disorders, trauma and neurological tumours.
Aimed at clinical neurologists.
Ad Rate: Full Page Mono £530.00
Ad Rate: Full Page Colour £1350.00
MAGAZINE
Neurology

The Lancet Oncology
983539
Editorial: 125 London Wall, London EC2Y
5AS **Tel:** 44 02074 244922
Email: editorial@lancet.com
Web site: http://www.thelancet.com/
journals/lanonc/issue/current
Freq: Monthly Not Audited
Editor: David Collingridge
Profile: Publication which includes any
original research that advocates change in,
or illuminates, oncological clinical practice.
The journal also publishes interesting and
informative reviews, opinion pieces, news,
letters, and media reviews on any topic
connected with oncology.
Ad Rate: Full Page Mono £624.00
Ad Rate: Full Page Colour £1839.00
MAGAZINE
Oncology

The Lancet Respiratory
Medicine
999554
Editorial: 32 Jamestown Road, London
NW1 7BY **Tel:** 44 02074 244922
Email: editorial@lancet.com
Web site: http://www.thelancet.com/
journals/lanres/issue/current

Freq: Monthly Not Audited
Editor: Emma Grainger
MAGAZINE
Respiratory Diseases

Land & Business
981005
Editorial: 16 Belgrave Square, London
SW1X 8PQ **Tel:** 44 02072 350511
Email: mail@cla.org.uk
Web site: www.cla.org.uk/Members_Area/
Land_and_Business_Magazine/
Freq: Monthly
Circ: 32800 Not Audited
Profile: Official journal of the Country Land
and Business Association (CLA). Contains
advice on how members can seek their
land's full potential for food, timber
production, public access and recreation.
Read by members of the Country Land and
Business Association (CLA).Previous title:
Country Landowner
Ad Rate: Full Page Colour £2150.00
MAGAZINE
Animal Farming, Environment

Land Journal
986044
Editorial: Parliament Square, London SW1
3PD **Tel:** 44 02476 868555
Email: journals@rics.org
Web site: www.rics.org/uk/news/journals/
land-journal
Freq: Bi-Monthly
Circ: 7800 Not Audited
Editor: Mike Swain
MAGAZINE
Legal Affairs, Urban Planning &
Development

Land Mobile
981610
Editorial: St.Jude's Church, Dulwich Road,
London SE24 0PB **Tel:** 44 02077 385454
Web site: www.landmobile.co.uk
Freq: Monthly
Circ: 8500 Not Audited
Editor: Sam Fenwick
Profile: Magazine dedicated to wireless
communications for business. It spans the
whole spectrum of business radio
applications from cellular phones and
large-scale private networks through to
on-site radio, wireless LANs and low-power,
licence-free systems. Read by people
involved in the mobile communications
industry, major users and specifiers.Regular
features: Digital Focusing on GSM, Tetra and
Tetrapol mobile systems.; In Action Detailed
wireless case studies.; Looking At Focuses
on accessible technology briefs.; News
News and information covering the hottest
wireless issues.; People/Recruitment
Infomation on who is going where and who
is hunting for whom.; Products Reviews and
information on new products relating to the
wireless industry.; Switching-on Information
on the latest installed systems.
Ad Rate: Full Page Mono £1785.00
Ad Rate: Full Page Colour £2242.00
MAGAZINE
Mobile Communications

Land Warfare International
985568
Editorial: Saville Mews, 30 Saville Rod,
London W4 5HG **Tel:** 44 02031 792570
Email: info@shephardmedia.com
Web site: www.landwarfareintl.com
Freq: Bi-Monthly
Circ: 12400 Not Audited
Profile: Magazine that covers all elements of
land warfare. It covers the latest news and
technologies and features articles on military
equipment and clothing.
Ad Rate: Full Page Mono £5200.00
Ad Rate: Full Page Colour £7000.00
MAGAZINE
Defense & National Security

Landlord & Tenant Review
999109
Editorial: 100 Avenue Road, London NW3
3PF **Tel:** 44 02073 937163
Web site: www.sweetandmaxwell.co.uk/
Catalogue/ProductDetails.aspx?recordid=
352&productid=6670&searchorigin=Lan

Freq: Bi-Monthly Not Audited
MAGAZINE
Office Design, Real Estate Law,
Residential Real Estate, Retail

Landlord Focus
998868
Editorial: Hopetoun Gate, 8b McDonald
Road, Edinburgh EH7 4LZ
Tel: 44 01315 640100
Email: landlordfocus@scottishlandlords.com
Web site: www.scottishlandlords.com/
resources/landlordfocus.aspx
Freq: 3 Times/Year
Circ: 3500 Not Audited
Editor: Judith Dunn
MAGAZINE
Residential Real Estate

Landlord Today
985966
Editorial: 5 Albemarle Street, Beckenham,
London BR3 5HZ **Tel:** 44 08450 750152
Email: press@landlordtoday.co.uk
Web site: www.landlordtoday.co.uk
Freq: Daily
Circ: 92905 Cision Digital Reach
Profile: Landlord Today is a website offering
information and news from the landlord
industry.
MAGAZINE (ONLINE)
Residential Real Estate

Landscape - The Journal of
the Landscape Institute
983069
Editorial: 21 Mann Island, Liverpool L3 1BP
Tel: 44 01516 499669
Email: landscape@darkhorsedesign.co.uk
Web site: www.landscapethejournal.org/
index.php
Freq: Quarterly
Circ: 6000 Not Audited
MAGAZINE
Architecture & Design

Landscape & Urban Design
1054361
Tel: 44 01843 830249
Web site: www.landud.co.uk/
Freq: Bi-Monthly
Circ: 60000 Not Audited
Editor: Lorna Davidson
MAGAZINE
Architecture & Design, Building &
Construction, Environment, Sustainable
Development, Urban Planning &
Development

Landscape and Amenity
Product Update
981105
Editorial: Grosvenor House, Central Park,
Telford, Oakengates TF2 9TW
Tel: 44 01952 234000
Email: rebecca@tspmedia.co.uk
Web site: www.landscapeandamenity.com
Freq: Monthly
Circ: 10000 Not Audited
MAGAZINE
Building & Construction

Landscape Photography
Magazine
1052776
Tel: 44 01292 220313
Email: info@
landscapephotographymagazine.com
Web site: landscapephotographymagazine.
com
Freq: Monthly Not Audited
Editor: Dimitri Vasileiou
MAGAZINE
Photography

The Landscaper
983937
Tel: 44 02088 914850
Web site: www.landscapermagazine.com
Freq: Monthly
Circ: 22000 Not Audited
Profile: Magazine covering all aspects of
landscaping industry news, products and
machinery. Read by landscape and garden
architects and designers, senior
groundsmen and arborists.

Business Magazines

Ad Rate: Full Page Colour £1650.00
MAGAZINE
Building & Construction

The Landsman   986544
Editorial: The Granary & Sawmill, Tickenham Court, Washing Pound Lane, Nailsea BS21 6SB **Tel:** 44 01275 400778
Email: copy@thelandsman.co.uk
Web site: www.thelandsman.co.uk
Freq: Monthly
Circ: 18000 Not Audited
Editor: Rebecca Hacker
MAGAZINE
Animal Farming

LARA   980083
Editorial: 103 Mytchett Road, Mytchett, Camberley GU16 6ES **Tel:** 44 01252 545993
Email: info@hmgaerospace.com
Web site: http://www.hmgaerospace.com/lara/magazine/
Freq: Bi-Monthly
Circ: 10600 Not Audited
MAGAZINE
Aviation

Large Display Report   696547
Owner: Meko Ltd.
Tel: 44 125 283-5385
Web site: http://www.insightmedia.info
Freq: Monthly
Circ: 9454 Cision Digital Reach
MAGAZINE (ONLINE)
Displays, Displays, Graphics, & Imaging

L'Artisanat Ardèchois   998136
Tel: 44 33047 5075414
Email: contact@cma-ardeche.fr
Web site: www.cma-ardeche.fr/
Freq: Monthly
Circ: 6638 Cision Digital Reach
MAGAZINE (ONLINE)
Business, Corporate Responsibility, Public Sector

LatAm Investor   996619
Editorial: LatAm INVESTOR, Kemp House, 152-160 City Road, London EC1V 2NX
Tel: 44 02070 975121
Email: editorial@latam-investor.com
Web site: www.latam-investor.com
Freq: Quarterly
Circ: 5000 Not Audited
MAGAZINE
Investment Banking

Laterality: Asymmetries of Body, Brain and Cognition
998984
Editorial: 4 Park Square, Milton Park, Abingdon, Didcot OX14 4RN
Tel: 44 02070 176000
Email: plat-peerreview@tandf.co.uk
Web site: http://www.tandf.co.uk/journals/pp/1357650x.html
Freq: Bi-Monthly Not Audited
Editor: Chris McManus; **Editor:** Mike Nicholls; **Editor:** Giorgio Vallortigara
MAGAZINE
Neurology

Latest Homes   984215
Editorial: 14-17 Manchester Street, Brighton BN1 2TF **Tel:** 44 01273 818150
Email: editorial@thelatest.co.uk
Web site: http://www.latesthomes.co.uk/
Freq: Weekly
Circ: 100000 Not Audited
MAGAZINE
Property Management & Maintenance

Laundry & Cleaning News International
981298
Editorial: Progressive House, 2 Maidstone Road, Foots Cray, Sidcup DA14 5HZ
Tel: 44 02082 697783
Email: info@laundryandcleaningnews.com
Web site: www.laundryandcleaningnews.com
Freq: Bi-Monthly

Circ: 5280 Not Audited
MAGAZINE
News & Current Affairs

Laundry & Cleaning Today
984032
Editorial: Synegis House, Crockhamwell Road, Woodley, Reading RG5 3LE
Tel: 44 01189 690906
Email: info@laundryandcleaningtoday.co.uk
Web site: www.laundryandcleaningtoday.co.uk
Freq: Monthly
Circ: 5312 Not Audited
Profile: Newspaper covering news and articles on textile rental, all forms of textile care, laundry and dry cleaning.
Ad Rate: Full Page Colour £1911.50
MAGAZINE
Hygiene

The Lawyer   979844
Editorial: Wells Point, 79 Wells Street, London W1T 3QN **Tel:** 44 02079 704000
Email: editorial@thelawyer.com
Web site: www.thelawyer.com
Freq: Weekly
Circ: 22645 Not Audited
Editor: Catrin Griffiths
Profile: Magazine covering law. It includes features on regional and overseas legal issues, practice areas and business markets, jobs, events, views and in-depth analysis, interviews and client profiles, domestic and global news stories. Aimed at corporate lawyers, legal professionals at the top 200 UK law firms, International firms and FTSE 100 companies, high-net-worth professionals working in the UK and global legal markets.
Ad Rate: Full Page Colour £4750.00
MAGAZINE
Corporate Law

Lawyer 2B   981016
Editorial: 79 Welss Street, London W1T 3QN
Tel: 44 02079 704559
Web site: www.lawyer2b.com
Freq: Semi-Annual
Circ: 27500 Not Audited
MAGAZINE
Legal Services, Students

LC.N Weekly   998598
Editorial: New Hibernia House, Winchester Walk, London Bridge, London SE1 9AG
Tel: 44 02079 394002
Email: info@lawcareers.net
Web site: www.lawcareers.net
Freq: Daily
Circ: 50000 Not Audited
MAGAZINE
Legal Services

LCD (Leveraged Commentary & Data)
998545
Editorial: 20 Canada Sq. 8th Fl, Canary Wharf, London E14 5LH
Tel: 44 02071 763997
Web site: http://marketintelligence.spglobal.com/about-us/about-us.html#team
Freq: Daily
MAGAZINE (ONLINE)
Bonds, Corporate Management, Lending

LCGC Europe   984812
Tel: 44 01513 533500
Web site: www.lcgceurope.com
Freq: Monthly
Circ: 26252 Not Audited
MAGAZINE
Science

Leader (UK)   981540
Editorial: 130 Regent Road, Leicester LE1 7PG **Tel:** 44 01162 991122
Email: leader@ascl.org.uk
Web site: www.leadermagazine.co.uk
Freq: Bi-Monthly
Circ: 18000 Not Audited
MAGAZINE
Higher Education, Schools & Institutions

Leading Edge   982794
Editorial: Pacific House, Relay Point, Tamworth B77 5PA **Tel:** 44 01543 266886
Email: editorial@institutelm.com
Web site: https://www.institutelm.com/research-news/edge-articles.html
Freq: Bi-Monthly Not Audited
Profile: Magazine covering all aspects of calligraphy and lettering from historical and medieval manuscripts to cutting edge, contemporary calligraphy and typography.
MAGAZINE
Business, Corporate Responsibility

Leading Internet Case Law
988876
Editorial: 17 The Timber Yard, Drysdale Street, London N1 6ND
Tel: 44 02070 121380
Web site: www.e-comlaw.com/e-commerce-law-reports/index.asp Not Audited
Editor: Sophie Cameron
Profile: Journal covering e-commerce law cases including domain names and domain name disputes, intellectual property rights, copyright infringements, liability, online / behavourial advertising, distance selling regulations, privacy law, cybercrime, social networking, trademarks, telecoms and software. Aimed at lawyers and advisors to businesses involved in e-commerce.
MAGAZINE
Consumer Interest, Corporate Law, Government, Intellectual Property, Legal Services, Tax Law

The LEAF Review   985131
Editorial: John Carpenter House, John Carpenter Street, London EC4Y 0AN
Tel: 44 02079 366400
Web site: www.leading-architects.eu
Freq: Annual
Circ: 7599 Not Audited
Profile: Magazine capturing the opinions, ideas and philosophies of Europe's foremost architects, featuring articles, case studies, interviews and profiles. Aimed at architects and interior designers.
MAGAZINE
Architecture & Design

LeapRate   999683
Editorial: 16 Berkeley Street, London W1J 8DZ **Tel:** 44 02036 425828
Email: info@leaprate.com
Web site: http://www.leaprate.com
Freq: Daily
Circ: 613764 Cision Digital Reach
MAGAZINE (ONLINE)
Foreign Exchange Market (FOREX)

Learn Patch   996386
Editorial: 1 Solsbury View, Ragland Lane, Fairfield Park, Bath BA1 6HT
Email: editor@learnpatch.com
Web site: www.learnpatch.com
Freq: Daily
Circ: 8410 Cision Digital Reach
Editor: Martin Couzins
MAGAZINE (ONLINE)
Education

Leasing Life   980852
Editorial: 71-73 Carter Lane, London EC4V 5EQ **Tel:** 44 02079 366400
Email: press@timetric.co.uk
Web site: www.leasinglife.com
Freq: Monthly
Circ: 250 Not Audited
Editor: Brian Cantwell
Profile: News magazine covering the leasing and asset finance industry and related regulatory issues. Aimed at leasing professionals, dealers, manufacturers and leaseholders.
Ad Rate: Full Page Colour £2300.00
MAGAZINE
Banking

Leasing World   998944
Tel: 44 01905 621444
Email: editor@leasingworld.co.uk
Web site: http://www.leasingworld.co.uk/

Freq: Monthly
Circ: 400 Not Audited
Editor: Jan Szmigin
MAGAZINE
Banking

Leather International   981299
Editorial: Progressive House, 2 Maidstone Road, Sidcup, London DA14 5HZ
Tel: 44 02082 697700
Web site: www.leathermag.com
Freq: Monthly
Circ: 4250 Not Audited
Editor: Carl Friedmann
Profile: International magazine covering everything in the leather world, from raw materials, through scientific and technological matters, to finished leather.
Ad Rate: Full Page Mono £2950.00
Ad Rate: Full Page Colour £4053.00
MAGAZINE
Manufacturing

Legal Action   984185
Editorial: Legal Action Group, National Pro Bono Centre, 48 Chancery Lane, London WC2A 1JF **Tel:** 44 02078 332931
Email: lag@lag.org.uk
Web site: www.lag.org.uk
Freq: Monthly
Circ: 3000 Not Audited
Profile: Magazine giving practical advice on legal aid, housing law, criminal law, litigation and one's rights and civil liberties.
Ad Rate: Full Page Colour £950.00
MAGAZINE
Consumer Interest, Criminal Law, Employment, Family Law, Government, Human Rights, Legal Services, Litigation, Real Estate Law

Legal Business   979899
Editorial: 188-190 Fleet Street, London EC4A 2AG **Tel:** 44 02073 969292
Email: legalbusiness@legalease.co.uk
Web site: www.legalbusiness.co.uk
Freq: Monthly Not Audited
Profile: Magazine covering the legal industry, with an emphasis on commercial law firms in the UK. Aimed at top commercial lawyers in the UK and international firms.
Ad Rate: Full Page Colour £3995.00
MAGAZINE
Corporate Law

Legal Futures   985555
Editorial: 3-5 Bleeding Heart Yard, Farringdon, London EC1N 8SJ
Tel: 44 02035 671207
Email: contact@legalfutures.co.uk
Web site: www.legalfutures.co.uk
Freq: Daily
Circ: 93524 Cision Digital Reach
Editor: Neil Rose
MAGAZINE (ONLINE)
Legal Services

Legal Information Management
985918
Editorial: The Edinburgh Building, Shaftesbury Road, Cambridge CB2 8RU
Tel: 44 01223 326070
Web site: www.journals.cambridge.org/action/displayJournal?jid=LIM
Freq: Quarterly Not Audited
Editor: David Wills
Profile: Journal of the British and Irish Association of Law Librarians. Contains information on a wide variety of topics, including information technology of relevance to law librarians.
Ad Rate: Full Page Mono £415.00
Ad Rate: Full Page Colour £785.00
MAGAZINE
Legal Services

Legal Life   997160
Editorial: The Law Library, The Law Courts, Small Street, Bristol BS1 1DA
Tel: 44 01179 458486
Email: news@legal-life.net
Web site: http://www.bristollawsociety.com/legal-life-homepage/

Freq: Monthly
Circ: 29 Cision Digital Reach
MAGAZINE (ONLINE)
Legal Services

Legal Practice Management

988485

Editorial: 20 Mortlake High Street, Mortlake, London SW14 8JN **Tel:** 44 08701 125058
Email: lsn@legalsupportnetwork.co.uk
Web site: https://www.legalsupportnetwork.
co.uk/webform/sign-legal-practice-
management-magazine-launching-febr
Freq: Monthly
Circ: 1800 Not Audited
MAGAZINE
Legal Services

Legal Week

979845

Editorial: 7th Floor, Cheapside House, 138 Cheapside, London EC2V 6BJ
Tel: 44 02038 687552
Web site: http://www.legalweek.com/?
slreturn=20170422063907
Freq: Daily Not Audited
Editor: Georgina Stanley
Profile: Magazine dedicated to business law in private practice and commerce and industry throughout the UK. Aimed assistant solicitors, in-house lawyers, barristers, associates, top 100 UK and international firms and legal teams at the FTSE 350 companies.
Ad Rate: Full Page Colour £4523.00
MAGAZINE
Legal Services

LegalMoves

983419

Editorial: 10 Tonbridge Chambers, Pembury Road, Tonbridge TN9 2HZ
Tel: 44 01732 358861
Email: info@legalmoves.co.uk
Web site: www.legalmoves.co.uk
Freq: Bi-Weekly
Circ: 1678 Cision Digital Reach
Editor: Helen Dewar
MAGAZINE (ONLINE)
Legal Services

LegalSupportNetwork.co.uk

985417

Editorial: 20 Mortlake High Street, Mortlake, London SW14 8JN **Tel:** 44 08701 125058
Email: lsn@legalsupportnetwork.co.uk
Web site: www.legalsupportnetwork.co.uk
Freq: Daily
Circ: 13165 Cision Digital Reach
MAGAZINE (ONLINE)
Legal Services

Leicestershire Builder Magazine

984761

Editorial: PO Box 8, Markfield, Markfield LE67 9ZT **Tel:** 44 01530 244069
Email: info@buildermagazines.co.uk
Web site: www.buildermagazines.co.uk
Freq: Monthly
Circ: 3500 Not Audited
Editor: Mike Wilkinson
Profile: Magazine covering news of local building issues in Leicestershire and the East Midlands and nationwide, local developments planned, development sites and properties for sale, product news and local business news items.
Ad Rate: Full Page Mono £190.00
Ad Rate: Full Page Colour £290.00
MAGAZINE
Building & Construction, Urban Planning & Development

leisure design & build

983361

Editorial: SBC House, Restmor Way, Wallington, London SM6 7AH
Tel: 44 02082 881080
Email: info@leisuredab.co.uk
Web site: www.leisuredab.co.uk
Freq: Bi-Monthly
Circ: 2642 Cision Digital Reach
Editor: Vicky Kiernander
Profile: Magazine covering all aspects of the public and private sector leisure build market. Includes articles on the building of

hotels, pubs, leisure centres, restaurants, cinemas, universities, schools and parks. Aimed at specifiers and buyers involved in leisure build projects, architects, quantity surveyors, contractors and local authority building departments.
Ad Rate: Full Page Colour £1945.00
MAGAZINE (ONLINE)
Architecture & Design, Building & Construction, Travel Industry, Urban Planning & Development

letsrecycle.com

982836

Editorial: Elizabeth House, 39 York Road, London SE1 7NQ **Tel:** 44 02076 334500
Email: news@letsrecycle.com
Web site: www.letsrecycle.com
Freq: Daily
Circ: 42241 Cision Digital Reach
Editor: Steve Eminton
Profile: Website providing news and information including material prices for the local authority recycling business sector. Covers information about glass, metal, paper, plastics, textiles and wood recycling and transport. Also features legislation and official bodies responsible for recycling.
MAGAZINE (ONLINE)
Environment

Letting Agent Today

985965

Editorial: 5 Albemarle Street, Beckenham, London BR3 5HZ
Email: press@lettingagenttoday.co.uk
Web site: https://www.lettingagenttoday.co.
uk/
Freq: Daily
Circ: 156621 Cision Digital Reach
Profile: Website covering property. It discusses anything from news, block management and the estate industry.
MAGAZINE (ONLINE)
Finance, Legal Affairs, Residential Real Estate

Leukemia

995845

Editorial: The Macmillan Building, 4 Crinan Street, London N1 9XW
Tel: 44 02078 434530
Email: leukemia@nature.com
Web site: www.nature.com/leu/index.html
Freq: Monthly Not Audited
MAGAZINE
Hematology, Oncology

Leukemia & Lymphoma

999011

Editorial: Taylor & Francis Group, 2&4 Park Square, Milton Park, Abingdon OX14 4RN
Tel: 44 02070 176000
Email: enquiries@taylorandfrancis.com
Web site: http://www.tandfonline.com/toc/
ilal20/current
Freq: Monthly Not Audited
MAGAZINE
Hematology, Oncology

The Lex 100

995441

Editorial: 188-190 Fleet Street, London EC4A 2AG **Tel:** 44 02073 969292
Web site: www.lex100.com
Freq: Annual
Circ: 25000 Not Audited
MAGAZINE
Legal Services

Licensing Today Worldwide

984329

Editorial: 1 Churchgates, The Wilderness, Berkhamsted HP4 2UB
Tel: 44 01442 289930
Web site: www.ltwmag.com/current_issue/
october_2014.aspx
Freq: Quarterly
Circ: 12329 Not Audited
Profile: Magazine covering articles and features on new licensed products, developments, promotional and marketing tools, news and statistics worldwide. Aimed at manufacturers of consumer products, retail buyers and licensing agents.
Ad Rate: Full Page Colour £2200.00
MAGAZINE
Intellectual Property, Toys

Life Force Magazine

997154

Tel: 44 01626 680740
Web site: www.lifeforcemagazine.com
Freq: Monthly
Circ: 12852 Cision Digital Reach
Editor: Damian Bird
MAGAZINE (ONLINE)
Photography

Life Insurance International

981694

Editorial: 71-73 Carter Lane, London EC4V 5EQ **Tel:** 44 02079 366400
Email: press@timetric.com
Web site: www.lifeinsuranceinternational.
com
Freq: Weekly Not Audited
Editor: Ronan McCaughey
Ad Rate: Full Page Mono £3330.00
MAGAZINE
Insurance

Light Aviation

982890

Tel: 44 01280 846786
Email: office@laa.uk.com
Web site: http://www.
lightaircraftassociation.co.uk/
Freq: Monthly
Circ: 8500 Not Audited
Editor: Brian Hope
Profile: Publication containing features on building, restoring and operating vintage, classic and home built aircraft.
Ad Rate: Full Page Colour £1000.00
MAGAZINE
Aviation

Lighting

981135

Editorial: 3 More London Riverside, London SE1 2RE **Tel:** 44 02032 834387
Web site: www.lighting.co.uk
Freq: Monthly
Circ: 7715 Not Audited
Profile: Business publication devoted solely to all aspects of commercial, industrial, public, decorative and architectural lighting.
Ad Rate: Full Page Colour £2400.00
MAGAZINE
Building & Construction, Electricity

Lighting and Interiors

996396

Editorial: Unit 2, Business Innovation Centre, Staffordshire Technology Park, Beaconside, Stafford ST18 0AR
Email: steff@lightingandinteriorsgroup.com
Web site: www.lightingandinteriorsonline.
com
Freq: Daily
Circ: 14299 Cision Digital Reach
MAGAZINE (ONLINE)
Interior Design

Lighting Journal

984060

Editorial: Regent House, Regent Place, Rugby CV21 2PN **Tel:** 44 01788 576492
Email: lj@theilp.org.uk
Web site: www.theilp.org.uk
Freq: Monthly
Circ: 4500 Not Audited
Profile: Official journal of the Institution of Lighting Engineers. It contains information on technical developments, reports, product surveys and news on all aspects of public and commercial lighting.
Ad Rate: Full Page Colour £850.00
MAGAZINE
Architecture & Design

Lincolnshire Business

988623

Editorial: Sparkhouse, Rope Walk, Lincoln LN6 7DQ **Tel:** 44 01522 837261
Email: news@lincsbusiness.co
Web site: www.lincsbusiness.co/
Freq: Weekly
Circ: 18010 Cision Digital Reach
MAGAZINE (ONLINE)
Business, Small and Medium Business

Litigation Funding

981583

Editorial: 113 Chancery Lane, London WC2A 1PL **Tel:** 44 02078 415555
Web site: www.lawgazette.co.uk/
litigationfunding

Freq: Bi-Monthly
Editor: Rachel Rothwell
Profile: Guide to the funding and costs of litigation. Aimed at solicitors, law costs draftsmen and those involved in litigation and litigation funding.
Ad Rate: Full Page Colour £1096.00
MAGAZINE
Litigation

Litigation Futures

988814

Editorial: 3-5 Bleeding Heart Yard, Farringdon, London EC1N 8SJ
Tel: 44 02035 671207
Email: contact@litigationfutures.com
Web site: www.litigationfutures.com
Freq: Daily
Circ: 18132 Cision Digital Reach
Editor: Neil Rose
Profile: Website that covers news and information relating to new government reforms in the costs and funding of litigation, and access to justice as a result.
MAGAZINE (ONLINE)
Litigation

Little Black Book

987492

Editorial: 62 Dean Street, London W1D 4QF
Tel: 44 02074 399184
Email: newsdesk@lbbonline.com
Web site: www.lbbonline.com
Freq: Daily
Circ: 153116 Cision Digital Reach
Profile: Website covering advertising. The Little Black Book website shares the latest news and events for the advertising industry.
MAGAZINE (ONLINE)
Advertising Industry

LiveSquawk

987347

Editorial: 3 St. Helen's Place, Lower Ground Floor, London EC3A 6AB
Tel: 44 02038 663372
Email: news@livesquawk.com
Web site: http://www.livesquawk.com/
Freq: Daily
Circ: 26704 Cision Digital Reach
MAGAZINE (ONLINE)
Financial Markets

Livestock

985307

Editorial: St Jude's Church, Dulwich Road, London SE24 0PB **Tel:** 44 02077 385454
Web site: http://www.magonlinelibrary.com/
journal/live
Freq: Bi-Monthly
Circ: 3000 Not Audited
Editor: Georgina Grell
Profile: Journal covering livestock veterinary issues including farm practice. Aimed at veterinary surgeons in farm practice.
Ad Rate: Full Page Colour £1220.00
MAGAZINE
Veterinary Medicine

Lloyd's List

979894

Editorial: Christchurch Court, 10 Newgate Street, London EC1A 7AZ
Tel: 44 02070 175000
Email: editorial@lloydslist.com
Web site: www.lloydslist.com
Freq: Daily
Circ: 143478 Cision Digital Reach
Profile: Publication covering marine trade and providing expert and authoritative coverage of the global shipping markets including shipping, marine insurance, offshore energy, logistics, global trade, law and wealth management. Aimed at insurance underwriters, merchants and ship owners.
MAGAZINE (ONLINE)
Insurance, Shipping & Warehousing

The LMJ

999081

Editorial: Elizabeth House, Block 2, Part 5th Floor, 39 York Road, London SE1 7NJ
Tel: 44 02074 016033
Email: lmj@hennikgroup.com
Web site: www.leanmj.com
Freq: Monthly
Circ: 6611 Cision Digital Reach

Business Magazines

Editor: Fred Tongue
MAGAZINE (ONLINE)
Business, Corporate Responsibility, Human Resources

LNG Business Review 983352

Editorial: 10 St Bride Street, London EC4A 4AD **Tel:** 44 02073 329900
Web site: www.gasstrategies.com/publications/lng-business-review
Freq: Monthly
MAGAZINE (ONLINE)
Oil

LNG in World Markets 998236

Editorial: 101 Wigmore Street, London W1U 1QU **Tel:** 44 02037 474800
Email: lng@poten.com
Web site: www.poten.com/business-intelligence-products/lng-in-world-markets
Freq: Monthly Not Audited
MAGAZINE
News & Current Affairs

LNG Journal 980829

Editorial: 1st Floor, 30 Warner Street, London EC1R 5EX **Tel:** 44 02072 532700
Email: editor@lngjournal.com
Web site: www.lngjournal.com
Freq: Monthly
Circ: 36000 Not Audited
Editor: John McKay
Profile: Magazine containing articles on projects, trade, shipping, design and technology, safety, environmental impact, markets, pricing and new applications in the liquefied natural gas market. Readership includes key personnel in processing, shipping, construction and project management.
Ad Rate: Full Page Mono £1400.00
Ad Rate: Full Page Colour £2100.00
MAGAZINE
Oil

LNG Shipping Review 988267

Editorial: 2nd Floor, 2-5 Benjamin Street, London EC1M 5QL **Tel:** 44 02072 532700
Email: editor@lngjournal.com
Web site: http://www.lngjournal.com
Freq: Annual
Circ: 3000 Not Audited
Editor: Ian Cochran
MAGAZINE
Shipping & Warehousing

LNG Unlimited 996431

Editorial: 1st Floor, 30 Warner Street, London EC1R 4EX **Tel:** 44 02072 532700
Email: editor@lngjournal.com
Web site: http://www.lngjournal.com/index.php/unlimited
Freq: Weekly
Circ: 1000 Not Audited
Editor: Ian Cochran; **Editor:** John McKay
MAGAZINE
Oil, Supply Chain Management (SCM)

LNG World Shipping 984305

Editorial: 1st Floor, Mitre House, 66 Abbey Road, Enfield EN1 2QN
Tel: 44 02083 641551
Web site: www.lngworldshipping.com
Freq: Bi-Monthly
Circ: 4000 Not Audited
Editor: Karen Thomas
Profile: LNG World Shipping is the magazine covering the global LNG shipping industry. Contains coverage of LNG transport chain, offshore developments at the upstream end, conventional LNG carriers and terminals, small scale LNG at the consumer end.
Ad Rate: Full Page Colour £3040.00
MAGAZINE
Shipping & Warehousing

Loan Radar 999185

Editorial: 1 Bolt Court, London EC4A 3DQ
Tel: 44 02078 320823
Email: loans@loanradar.co.uk
Web site: www.loanradar.co.uk
Freq: Daily

Circ: 1438 Cision Digital Reach
MAGAZINE (ONLINE)
Bonds, Corporate Finance, Corporate Management, Credit Markets, Emerging Markets, Government, Lending, Public & Consumer Finance

Loantalk.co.uk 999667

Editorial: 71 Gloucester Place, London W1U 8JW
Web site: http://www.loantalk.co.uk/
Freq: Daily
Circ: 13556 Cision Digital Reach
Editor: Beth Fisher
MAGAZINE (ONLINE)
Lending

Local Authority Building & Maintenance 981269

Editorial: Regal House, Regal Way, Watford, London WD24 4YF **Tel:** 44 01923 237799
Email: labm@hamerville.co.uk
Web site: http://labmonline.co.uk/
Freq: Monthly
Circ: 16267 Not Audited
Editor: Claire Clutten
Profile: Journal containing news on technical issues concerning building materials and methods. Includes coverage of the Decent Homes Standard, housing refurbishment, school and hospital construction and all maintenance requirements and readers enquires. Providing news, views, product information and in-depth features on a variety of business topics relevant to the local authority building marketplace. Launched in 1985. Aimed at those in the public building sector responsible for maintaining buildings and specifying and purchasing building materials.
Ad Rate: Full Page Colour £2500.00
MAGAZINE
Building & Construction, Government, Public Sector, Residential Real Estate

Local Council Review 983231

Editorial: 109 Great Russell Street, London WC1B 3LD **Tel:** 44 02076 371865
Email: lcr@nalc.gov.uk
Web site: www.nalc.gov.uk/lcr-magazine
Freq: Quarterly
Circ: 13000 Not Audited
Editor: Marie Dill
Profile: Official journal of the National Association of Local Councils. Contains news and features about the association, events concerning local councils and new legislation.
Ad Rate: Full Page Colour £1950.00
MAGAZINE
Government

Local Government Chronicle 979787

Editorial: 3 / 4th Floor, Telephone House, 69-77 Paul Street, London EC2A 4NQ
Tel: 44 02030 332734
Email: lgcnews@emap.com
Web site: www.lgcplus.com
Freq: Weekly
Circ: 2297 Not Audited
Editor: Nick Golding
MAGAZINE
Government, Public Sector

Local Government Executive 983846

Editorial: Sith Floor, 53 Portland Street, Manchester M1 3LD **Tel:** 44 01612 362782
Web site: www.localgovernmentexecutive.co.uk
Freq: Bi-Monthly
Circ: 15000 Not Audited
Editor: Andrew Jowett
Profile: Magazine covering all aspects of news, products and services of relevance to local government including education, security, planning, technical services, facilities management, land/building management, DLO's contracting/ tendering services, commercial & operational services, IT services and HR. Aimed at chief executives and heads of department in

Central Government, Local Authorities and Health Authorities in the UK.
Ad Rate: Full Page Colour £1495.00
MAGAZINE
Government

Local Government Lawyer 985362

Editorial: Phoenix Yard, 65 King's Cross Road, London WC1X 9LW
Email: info@localgovernmentlawyer.co.uk
Web site: www.localgovernmentlawyer.co.uk
Freq: Daily
Circ: 15606 Cision Digital Reach
MAGAZINE (ONLINE)
Government

Local Government News 981270

Editorial: 32 Vauxhall Bridge Road, London SW1V 2SS **Tel:** 44 02079 736400
Web site: www.localgov.co.uk
Freq: Quarterly
Circ: 15500 Not Audited
Editor: Laura Sharman
Profile: Magazine covering all aspects of local government. Aimed at senior local government personnel in all departments.
Ad Rate: Full Page Colour £2750.00
MAGAZINE
Government

Locate In Kent 996521

Tel: 44 01732 520700
Email: enquiries@locateinkent.com
Web site: www.locateinkent.com
Freq: Daily
Circ: 10956 Cision Digital Reach
MAGAZINE (ONLINE)
Architecture & Design, Building & Construction, Commercial Real Estate, Finance, Interior Design, Legal Affairs, Office Design, Property Management & Maintenance, Residential Real Estate, Retail

Locks and Security Magazine 1065389

Email: editor@lasm.co.uk
Web site: http://www.lasm.co.uk/
Freq: Bi-Monthly
Circ: 5000 Not Audited
MAGAZINE
Security & Security Systems

The Locksmith 984972

Editorial: 2-3 Burleigh Court, South Yorkshire, Barnsley S70 1XY
Tel: 44 01226 321450
Email: me@cvgroup.co.uk
Web site: www.locksmithjournal.co.uk
Freq: Bi-Monthly
Circ: 8500 Not Audited
MAGAZINE
Engineering

The Log 1023286

Editorial: BALPA House, 5 Heathrow Boulevard, 278 Bath Road, West Drayton UB7 0DQ **Tel:** 44 02084 764000
Email: communications@balpa.org
Web site: http://www.balpa.org/about
Freq: Quarterly
Circ: 14000 Not Audited
Profile: Official journal of the British Airline Pilots' Association containing aviation-related features, industry news, interviews, letters to the editor and technical information.
Ad Rate: Full Page Colour £1500.00
MAGAZINE
Aviation

Logistics & Supply Chain 979940

Editorial: Unit 205, The Foundry, 156 Blackfriars Road, London SE1 8EN
Web site: http://www.logisticsandsupplychain.com/
Freq: Bi-Monthly
Circ: 35000 Not Audited

Editor: Malory Davies
MAGAZINE
Shipping & Warehousing, Supply Chain Management (SCM)

Logistics & Transport Focus 981327

Editorial: Earlstrees Road, Corby, Corby NN17 4AX **Tel:** 44 01536 740100
Email: focus@ciltuk.org.uk
Web site: www.ciltuk.org.uk/News/FocusJournal.aspx
Freq: Monthly
Circ: 12696 Not Audited
Profile: Containing logistics, supply-chain management and distribution management, IT, passenger and commercial transport freight articles. Aimed at management with overall responsibility in the supply chain covering purchasing, production, inventory control, warehousing and information management systems. Also, distribution, transportation, operations and general management.
Ad Rate: Full Page Colour £2500.00
MAGAZINE
Supply Chain Management (SCM)

Logistics Business 983516

Editorial: Unit D (A), Spitfire Close, Ermine Business Park, Huntington, Huntingdon PE29 6XY **Tel:** 44 01480 455660
Email: edit@logisticsbusiness.com
Web site: www.logisticsbusiness.com
Freq: Quarterly
Circ: 10000 Not Audited
Editor: Paul Hamblin
MAGAZINE
Industry, Manufacturing, Shipping & Warehousing

Logistics Handling 985048

Editorial: Latimer House, 189 High Street, Potters Bar, Potters Bar EN6 5DA
Tel: 44 01707 664200
Email: editor@ibcpub.com
Web site: www.logisticshandling.com
Freq: Daily
Circ: 15834 Cision Digital Reach
Profile: Website covering material handling and logistics news and solutions.
MAGAZINE (ONLINE)
Industry, Manufacturing

Logistics Manager 981328

Editorial: Unit 205, The Foundry, 156 Blackfriars Road, London SE1 8EN
Email: lmnewsdesk@akabomedia.co.uk
Web site: www.logisticsmanager.com
Freq: Monthly
Circ: 10458 Not Audited
Editor: Malory Davies
Profile: Magazine covering all aspects of the supply chain from sourcing raw materials through to production, materials management, transport and distribution as well as new contracts, IT, electronic commerce and warehouse and property developments. First published in 1994. Read by logistics professionals in end-user industries.
Ad Rate: Full Page Colour £2515.00
MAGAZINE
Shipping & Warehousing, Supply Chain Management (SCM)

London Accountant 982949

Editorial: ICAEW, Chartered Accountants' Hall, Moorgate Place, London EC2R 6EA
Tel: 44 02079 203504
Email: london@icaew.com
Web site: http://www.icaew.com/en/groups-and-networks/local-groups-and-societies/london-ds/london-accountant
Freq: Daily
Circ: 200650 Cision Digital Reach
MAGAZINE (ONLINE)
Accounting

London Business Matters 981359

Editorial: 33 Queen Street, London EC4R 1AP **Tel:** 44 02072 484444

Web site: https://www.excelmediasolutions.co.uk/portfolio-posts/lbm/
Freq: Monthly
Circ: 3000 Not Audited
Editor: Peter Bishop
Profile: Members' magazine of the London Chamber of Commerce and Industry. Contains local business and international news and articles on changes in legislation, seminars and new business opportunities.
Ad Rate: Full Page Colour £3400.00
MAGAZINE
Business, Small and Medium Business

London Business School Review 988822
Email: lbsr@london.edu
Web site: www.london.edu/faculty-and-research/lbsr#.WC7blbKLRpg
Freq: Quarterly
Circ: 30000 Not Audited
MAGAZINE
Business

London Capital Group 997630
Editorial: 77 Grosvenor Street, Mayfair, London W1K 3JR **Tel:** 44 02074 567681
Web site: https://www.lcg.com/uk/analysis/
Freq: Daily
Circ: 124 Cision Digital Reach
MAGAZINE (ONLINE)
Economics, Financial Markets

London Higher 998738
Editorial: London Higher, Tavistock House, Tavistock Square, London WC1H 9JB
Tel: 44 02073 830988
Email: enquiry@londonhigher.ac.uk
Web site: www.londonhigher.ac.uk
Freq: Quarterly
Circ: 11999 Cision Digital Reach
MAGAZINE (ONLINE)
Higher Education

London Photography Diary 997325
Email: editors@london-photography-diary.com
Web site: www.london-photography-diary.com
Freq: Daily
Circ: 10445 Cision Digital Reach
MAGAZINE (ONLINE)
Photography

London Property Review 998605
Editorial: 23a St James' Street, London SW1A 1HG **Tel:** 44 01536 330314
Web site: www.londonpropertyreview.co.uk
Freq: Monthly Not Audited
MAGAZINE
Property Management & Maintenance

London Property South 998116
Editorial: 23a St James' Street, London SW1A 1HG
Web site: www.londonpropertysouth.co.uk/
Freq: Monthly
Circ: 45000 Not Audited
MAGAZINE
Property Management & Maintenance

LondonLovesBusiness.com 985914
Editorial: 56 Buckingham Gate, London SW1E 6AE
Email: editor@londonlovesbusiness.com
Web site: www.londonlovesbusiness.com
Freq: Daily
Circ: 152460 Cision Digital Reach
MAGAZINE (ONLINE)
Business, Small and Medium Business

The Loop 996960
Editorial: Create Centre, Smeaton Road, Bristol BS1 6XN **Tel:** 44 01179 074107
Email: theloop@resource.uk.com
Web site: www.larac.org.uk
Freq: Quarterly
Circ: 1000 Not Audited

Editor: Libby Peake
MAGAZINE
Environment

Loss Prevention Bulletin 980958
Editorial: Davis Building, 165-189 Railway Terrace, Rugby CV21 3HQ
Tel: 44 01788 534442
Web site: http://www.icheme.org/lpb.aspx
Freq: Bi-Monthly
Circ: 450 Not Audited
Editor: Tracey Donaldson
Profile: Publication providing case studies and practical advice on specific chemical hazards. Aimed at safety professionals within the process industries.Regular features: Bulletin Briefing News items such as new work, new legislation and incidents.; Events Information regarding forthcoming events in the process safety field.; New Publications Reviews of new publications relevant to the process safety field.
MAGAZINE
Health & Safety

Low Carbon Energy Investor 997893
Editorial: PEI London, 140 London Wall, 6th Floor, London EC2Y 5DN
Tel: 44 02075 665444
Web site: www.lowcarbonenergyinvestor.com
Freq: Daily
Circ: 1198 Cision Digital Reach
MAGAZINE (ONLINE)
Alternative/Renewable Energy, Nuclear Power, Private Equity, Sustainable Development

Low Cost and Regional Airline Business 996141
Editorial: Suite E, 11 Bell Yard Mews, 175 Bermondsey Street, London SE1 3TN
Tel: 44 02077 243456
Email: info@airtransportpubs.com
Web site: www.lowcostandregional.com
Freq: Quarterly
Circ: 6000 Not Audited
MAGAZINE
Aviation

Low Temperature Architectural Technology 1061014
Tel: 44 86451 86334097
Email: lowtem@163.com
Web site: http://dwjzjs.periodicals.net.cn
Freq: Bi-Monthly
Circ: 4501 Not Audited
MAGAZINE
Architecture & Design

Lowcarboneconomy.com 984947
Tel: 44 08453 131711
Web site: www.lowcarboneconomy.com
Freq: Daily
Circ: 40714 Cision Digital Reach
MAGAZINE (ONLINE)
Environment

Low-Fare & Regional Aviation Handbook 984173
Editorial: 103 Mytchett Road, Mytchett, Camberley GU16 6ES **Tel:** 44 01252 545993
Email: bernie@hmgaerospace.com
Web site: http://www.hmgaerospace.com/lara/news/
Freq: Annual
Circ: 5500 Not Audited
Profile: Supplement of Low-Fare & Regional Airlines.
MAGAZINE
Aviation

Lowtax Network 996722
Editorial: Wolters Kluwer TAA Limited, 45 Robertson Street, Hastings, Hastings TN34 1HL
Email: editorial@lowtax.net
Web site: www.lowtax.net
Freq: Daily

Circ: 91770 Cision Digital Reach
Editor: Kitty Miv
MAGAZINE (ONLINE)
Banking, Tax Law

LP Gas (UK) 985065
Editorial: PRG, 10 Gildredge Road, Eastbourne BN21 4RL **Tel:** 44 01323 646076
Web site: www.lpgasmagazine.co.uk
Freq: Bi-Monthly
Circ: 1438 Cision Digital Reach
MAGAZINE (ONLINE)
Oil

Lube Magazine 986005
Editorial: UKLA House, 13 Chess Business Park, Moor Road, Chesham HP5 1SD
Tel: 44 01442 875922
Email: lube@ukla.org.uk
Web site: www.lube-media.com
Freq: Bi-Monthly
Circ: 7000 Not Audited
Editor: Suzy Jarman
MAGAZINE
Engineering, Industry, Manufacturing

Lung Cancer 994970
Tel: 44 01865 843434
Email: lungcancer@elsevier.com
Web site: www.elsevier.com/wps/find/journaldescription.cws_home/505953/description
Freq: Monthly Not Audited
MAGAZINE
Oncology

Lung Cancer Management 999398
Editorial: Unitec House, 2 Albert Place, London N3 1QB **Tel:** 44 02083 716090
Email: info@futuremedicine.com
Web site: http://www.futuremedicine.com/loi/lmt
Freq: Bi-Monthly Not Audited
MAGAZINE
Oncology

LUX 985957
Editorial: 3 More London Riverside, London Bridge, London SE1 2RE
Tel: 44 02032 834387
Web site: http://luxreview.com/uk/office
Freq: Monthly
Circ: 8200 Not Audited
Profile: Lifestyle magazine covering watches, cars, travel, property, interiors, gardens and personal finance.
MAGAZINE
Manufacturing

Lux Review 986841
Editorial: 3 More London Riverside, London Bridge, London SE1 2RE
Tel: 44 02032 834387
Web site: www.luxreview.com
Freq: Bi-Monthly
Circ: 50000 Not Audited
Profile: Lux Review magazine is the publication covering lighting and design.
MAGAZINE
Manufacturing

M&A Navigator 987729
Editorial: M2 Editorial, Amadeus House, 27b Floral Street, London WC2E 9DP
Tel: 44 02070 470200
Email: editorial@m2.com
Web site: www.manavigator.com
Freq: Daily
Circ: 12144 Cision Digital Reach
MAGAZINE (ONLINE)
Mergers & Acquisitions

M2 Equity Bites 1074632
Editorial: Stokewood House, Warminster Road, Limpley, Stoke-on-Trent BA2 7GB
Tel: 44 02070 470200
Email: editorial@m2.com
Web site: http://www.m2.com/m2/web/publication.php/eqb

Freq: Daily
MAGAZINE (ONLINE)
Equities

MachineBuilding.net 985058
Editorial: 38 West Street, Great Gransden, Sandy SG19 3AU
Email: editor@machinebuilding.net
Web site: www.machinebuilding.net
Freq: Daily
Circ: 5690 Cision Digital Reach
Editor: Jonathan Severn
Profile: Website covering machinery. The Machinebuilding.net website features products and systems for machinery and industrial automation, focusing on new developments and innovative applications. Offers guidance on product selection, industry issues and legislation.
MAGAZINE (ONLINE)
Engineering, Manufacturing

Machinery 980131
Editorial: Hawley Mill, Hawley Road, Dartford, Sutton at Hone DA2 7TJ
Tel: 44 01322 221144
Web site: www.machinery.co.uk
Freq: Monthly
Circ: 14794 Not Audited
Editor: Andrew Allcock
Profile: Magazine covering new technology - machine tools, tooling, work holding, CADCAM - its development and applications. Also covering manufacturing business issues and the drivers that cause manufacturers to adopt new technology or working practices. Contains blend of technology features, news and new product information keeping its readers up-to-date with production matters. Read by production engineers, production managers, production directors and managing directors in OEMS and sub-contractors engaged in metalcutting/metalforming. First published in 1912.Every month Machinery delivers technological and topical features, product developments and opinion pieces.
Ad Rate: Full Page Colour £2700.00
MAGAZINE
Engineering

Machinery Classified 980095
Editorial: Hawley Mill, Hawley Road, Dartford, Sutton at Hone DA2 7TJ
Tel: 44 01322 221144
Web site: www.machineryclassified.co.uk
Freq: Bi-Weekly
Circ: 7409 Not Audited
Editor: Andrew Allcock
Profile: Magazine covering new and used metalworking and associated machinery. Aimed at purchasers of machine tools.
Ad Rate: Full Page Colour £650.00
MAGAZINE
Engineering

Machinery Classified 980974
Editorial: Hawley Mill, Hawley Road, Dartford, Sutton at Hone DA2 7TJ
Tel: 44 01322 221144
Email: editor@machineryclassified.co.uk
Web site: www.machineryclassified.co.uk
Freq: Monthly
Circ: 7357 Not Audited
Editor: Andrew Allcock
MAGAZINE
Engineering

Machinery Market 981244
Editorial: 40 Croydon Road, West Wickham, London BR4 9HZ **Tel:** 44 02084 604224
Email: editorial@machinery-market.co.uk
Web site: http://www.machinery-market.co.uk
Freq: Weekly
Circ: 24000 Not Audited
Profile: Publication focusing on general industrial plant and machine tools. Aimed at machine tool users and other engineering equipment users.
Ad Rate: Full Page Colour £715.00
MAGAZINE
Engineering

Business Magazines

Machinery Trade International
984307

Editorial: Appleby House, Headley Road, Leatherhead, London KT22 8PT
Tel: 44 01622 859404
Email: enquiry@mtimagazine.com
Web site: http://www.mtimagazine.com/
Freq: Weekly
Circ: 4041 Not Audited
Profile: Magazine covering the latest developments in global manufacturing, featuring news and used machine tool sales. Aimed at dealers in machinery and machine tool buyers at manufacturing companies.
MAGAZINE
Manufacturing

Machinery Update
985946

Editorial: New Progress House, 34 Stafford Road, Wallington, London SM6 9AA
Tel: 44 02087 738111
Email: publishing@ppma.co.uk
Web site: http://www.machineryupdate.co.uk/
Freq: Bi-Monthly
Circ: 9500 Not Audited
Editor: Gail Hunt
Profile: Journal of the Processing and Packaging Machinery Association. Read by buyers and specifiers of processing and packaging machinery, senior engineers and design engineers and all member companies.Only accepts press releases from PPMA member companies.
Ad Rate: Full Page Mono £1070.00
Ad Rate: Full Page Colour £1520.00
MAGAZINE
Manufacturing

Machinery World
984193

Editorial: 50 Queens Road, Buckhurst Hill, London IG9 5DD **Tel:** 44 02085 041661
Email: machinery@sheenpublishing.co.uk
Web site: www.machineryworld-online.com
Freq: Monthly
Circ: 9000 Not Audited
Editor: Carol Titmuss
Profile: Magazine covering worldwide industry news, company profiles and product information. Aimed at buyers and specifiers of new and used machinery in the UK, Western Europe and major developing countries.
Ad Rate: Full Page Mono £420.00
Ad Rate: Full Page Colour £520.00
MAGAZINE
Engineering, Manufacturing

Magistrate
986004

Editorial: 28 Fitzroy Square, London W1T 6DD **Tel:** 44 02072 559007
Email: magistrate@ntlworld.com
Web site: www.magistrates-association.org.uk
Freq: Bi-Monthly
Circ: 30000 Not Audited
Editor: Jason Hughes
Profile: Official Journal of the Magistrates Association. Contents are intended to inform lay justices and others who work in the magistrates' courts in regard to law and practice.
MAGAZINE
Criminal Law, Family Law

MagNews
997774

Editorial: 57 The Philog, Cardiff CF14 1DZ
Tel: 44 02920 626643
Email: editor@ukmagsoc.org
Web site: www.ukmagsoc.org/pages/magnews
Freq: Quarterly
Circ: 900 Not Audited
MAGAZINE
Science

Mail & Express Review
988508

Editorial: 4 The Courtyard, Furlong Road, Bourne End, High Wycombe SL8 5AU
Tel: 44 01628 642910
Email: news@postandparcel.info
Web site: www.postandparcel.info
Freq: Quarterly
Circ: 5000 Not Audited
Profile: Magazine covering the mail and express industries.
Ad Rate: Full Page Colour £4150.00
MAGAZINE
Supply Chain Management (SCM)

The Main Event
983822

Editorial: 47 Church Street, Barnsley S70 2AS **Tel:** 44 01226 734639
Web site: www.themaineventmagazine.co.uk
Freq: Daily
Circ: 4838 Cision Digital Reach
Editor: Christina Eccles
Profile: Magazine focusing on all aspects of event management. Aimed at event organisers.
Ad Rate: Full Page Colour £1850.00
MAGAZINE (ONLINE)
Marketing

Maintenance & Engineering
980982

Editorial: IBE Conference Ltd, Monks Hill, Tilford, Farnham GU10 2AJ
Tel: 44 01252 783111
Email: info@maintenanceonline.co.uk
Web site: www.maintenanceonline.co.uk
Freq: Bi-Monthly
Circ: 12071 Not Audited
Editor: David Willson
MAGAZINE
Engineering

Maintenance and Equipment News for Churches and Schools
984968

Editorial: PO Box 249, Ascot, London SL5 0BZ **Tel:** 44 01189 885886
Email: enquiries@cwponline.co.uk
Web site: www.cwponline.co.uk/church-maintenance-equipment
Freq: Quarterly
Circ: 18000 Not Audited
MAGAZINE
Architecture & Design, Building & Construction, Commercial Real Estate, Finance, Interior Design, Legal Affairs, Office Design, Property Management & Maintenance, Religion, Residential Real Estate

Make It Cheaper
1105203

Editorial: 5th Floor, Lloyds Chambers, 1 Portsoken Street, London E1 8BT
Tel: 44 08001 585263
Email: media@makeitcheaper.com
Web site: www.makeitcheaper.com
Freq: Daily
Circ: 30430 Cision Digital Reach
MAGAZINE (ONLINE)
Electricity, Oil

Making Money
980917

Editorial: 49 Old Steine, Brighton BN1 1NH
Tel: 44 01273 862258
Web site: www.makingmoneymagazine.com
Freq: Monthly
Circ: 25000 Not Audited
Editor: Jeff James
Profile: Magazine covering high street franchising through to network marketing with advice on finance, taxation and the law and small business technology. Aimed at those looking to work for themselves. Magazine for business opportunities and start-ups. By addressing the whole range of opportunities, from established high street franchises through to network marketing companies, Making Money gives its readers an insight into what is available and what is required to make them successful. Additionally, it regularly covers topics such as finance, taxation and the law, alongside small business technology, communications and the internet.
Ad Rate: Full Page Mono £2595.00
Ad Rate: Full Page Colour £2595.00
MAGAZINE
Business, Corporate Responsibility

Management in Practice
984212

Editorial: Bastion House, 140 London Wall, London EC2Y 5DN **Tel:** 44 02072 140500

Email: mip@cogora.com
Web site: www.managementinpractice.com
Freq: Quarterly
Circ: 8000 Not Audited
Profile: Magazine covering news, features, reviews and views on all aspects of primary care practice management including healthcare, nursing, training, human resources, medical equipment, patient service, practice development, risk management and legislation. Aimed at primary care practice managers.
Ad Rate: Full Page Mono £2950.00
Ad Rate: Full Page Colour £2950.00
MAGAZINE
Health Administration

Management Services
982950

Editorial: 27 Castle Street, Canterbury, Canterbury CT1 2PX **Tel:** 44 01227 46060
Email: editorial@msjournal.org.uk
Web site: www.ims-productivity.com/page.cfm/content/Management-Services-Journal
Freq: Quarterly
Circ: 2000 Not Audited
Profile: Official journal of the Institute of Management Services contains features on productivity improvement.
Ad Rate: Full Page Colour £540.00
MAGAZINE
Business, Corporate Responsibility

Management Today
980130

Editorial: Bridge House, 69 London Road, Twickenham, London TW1 3SP
Tel: 44 02082 675000
Email: editorialmanagementtoday@haymarket.com
Web site: http://www.managementtoday.co.uk/
Freq: Monthly
Circ: 51022 Not Audited
Profile: Magazine covering business news stories, management advice and insight from the UK's top business leaders and entrepreneurs, it features strategy and finance stories as well as news on people and innovation. First published in 1966. Targets business decision-makers, senior and well-informed readers in business community.
Ad Rate: Full Page Colour £5900.00
MAGAZINE
Business, Corporate Responsibility

Management-Issues.com
983124

Editorial: Devonshire House, 60 Goswell Road, London EC1M 7AD
Circ: 69780 Cision Digital Reach
MAGAZINE (ONLINE)
Business, Corporate Responsibility

Managing For Success
983870

Editorial: 113 Chancery Lane, London WC2A 1PL **Tel:** 44 02073 165707
Email: lawmanagementsection@lawsociety.org.uk
Web site: communities.lawsociety.org.uk/law-management/magazine
Freq: Quarterly Not Audited
MAGAZINE
Legal Services

Managing Intellectual Property
980830

Editorial: 8 Bouverie Street, London EC4Y 8AX **Tel:** 44 02077 798888
Web site: www.managingip.com
Freq: Monthly
Circ: 10000 Not Audited
Profile: Magazine covering international patents, licensing, and trademark law as it applies to international corporations and their advisers. Aimed at lawyers working in-house for multinational companies, senior intellectual property lawyers in private practice, trademark and patent agencies, government agencies and rights administration societies.
Ad Rate: Full Page Mono £4205.00
Ad Rate: Full Page Colour £5165.00
MAGAZINE
Intellectual Property

MandateWire
983082

Editorial: Number One, Southwark Bridge, London SE1 9HL **Tel:** 44 02077 756080
Email: mandatewire@ft.com
Web site: www.mandatewire.com
Freq: Daily
Circ: 9830 Cision Digital Reach
Editor: Toby Garrod
MAGAZINE (ONLINE)
Fund Management

The Manufacturer
980039

Editorial: Elizabeth House, 39 York Road, London SE1 7NJ **Tel:** 44 02074 016033
Email: press@hennikgroup.com
Web site: www.themanufacturer.com
Freq: Monthly
Circ: 10017 Not Audited
Editor: Victoria Fitzgerald
Profile: Magazine containing national, corporate and legal manufacturing news, executive interview and coverage of manufacturing management issues in leadership and strategy, design and innovation, world class manufacturing, skills and productivity, information technology in manufacturing, logistics and supply chain and operations maintenance.
Ad Rate: Full Page Colour £3495.00
MAGAZINE
Manufacturing

Manufacturing & Logistics IT Magazine
981650

Editorial: PO Box 3575, Barnet, Potters Bar EN5 9QD **Tel:** 44 01892 536363
Email: editor@ibcpub.com
Web site: www.logisticsit.com
Freq: Quarterly
Circ: 10000 Not Audited
MAGAZINE
Auto Aftermarket, Engineering, Industry, Manufacturing

Manufacturing and Engineering Magazine
998305

Editorial: 1st Floor, Turnbridge Mills, Quay Street, Huddersfield HD1 6QT
Tel: 44 02081 233414
Email: editor@ciaranjarosz.media
Web site: http://www.memuk.org
Freq: Monthly
Circ: 15000 Not Audited
MAGAZINE
Engineering, Manufacturing

Manufacturing Automation
1061108

Tel: 44 86108 2285782
Web site: http://www.cqvip.com/QK/92337A/index.shtml
Freq: Monthly
Circ: 10000 Not Audited
MAGAZINE
Manufacturing

manufacturing chemist
981213

Editorial: Natraj Building, The Tanneries, 55 Bermondsey Street, London SE1 3XG
Tel: 44 02071 931279
Email: pharma@hpcimedia.com
Web site: www.manufacturingchemist.com
Freq: Monthly
Circ: 7885 Not Audited
Editor: Kevin Robinson
Profile: Magazine covering all aspects of the pharmaceutical industry, including development, formulation, processing and outsourcing. Aimed at manufacturers of pharmaceuticals.
Ad Rate: Full Page Colour £2275.00
MAGAZINE
Pharmaceuticals, Science

Manufacturing Global
985588

Editorial: 69-75 Thorpe Road, Norwich NR1 1UA **Tel:** 44 01603 217530
Email: info@bizclikmedia.com
Web site: http://www.manufacturingglobal.com/
Freq: Monthly
Circ: 36097 Cision Digital Reach
Editor: Nell Walker

Profile: Website covering the manufacturing industry.
MAGAZINE (ONLINE)
Manufacturing

Manufacturing Today Europe   981516
Editorial: Cringleford Business Centre, Suite 10, Intwood Road, Cringleford, Norwich NR4 6AU **Tel:** 44 01603 274130
Web site: http://www.manufacturing-today-europe.com/
Freq: Monthly Not Audited
MAGAZINE
Human Resources, Supply Chain Management (SCM)

The Maritime Advocate   1063715
Tel: 44 07887 632503
Web site: www.maritimeadvocate.com/
Freq: Daily
Circ: 6201 Cision Digital Reach
Editor: Sam Ignarski
MAGAZINE (ONLINE)
Litigation, Shipping & Warehousing

The Market Mogul   1054405
Editorial: Aldgate Tower, 6th floor, London E1 8FA
Email: editorial@themarketmogul.com
Web site: www.themarketmogul.com
Freq: Daily
Circ: 58593 Cision Digital Reach
MAGAZINE (ONLINE)
Financial Markets

Market Trade News   1053010
Editorial: A.T Graphics Limited, 4 Milnyard Square, Bakewell Road, Peterborough PE2 6GX **Tel:** 44 01733 363482
Web site: http://markettradenews.com/
Freq: Monthly
Circ: 18000 Not Audited
MAGAZINE
Automakers, Financial Markets, Insurance

Market Trader   983315
Editorial: Unit 450, Chambers Business Centre, Chapel Road, Oldham, Oldham OL8 4QQ **Tel:** 44 01616 838000
Email: info@worldsfair.co.uk
Web site: www.market-trader.co.uk
Freq: Weekly
Circ: 16000 Not Audited
Editor: Terry Ford; **Editor:** John Kirkbride
Profile: National Newspaper covering information on retail marketing and wholesaling, indoor and outdoor markets. Read by market traders and small shopkeepers.
Ad Rate: Full Page Mono £560.00
Ad Rate: Full Page Colour £725.00
MAGAZINE
Retail Management

Marketing Cheshire   999617
Editorial: Chester Railway Station, 1st Floor, West Wing, Station Road, Chester CH1 3NT
Tel: 44 01244 405600
Email: info@marketingcheshire.co.uk
Web site: www.marketingcheshire.co.uk
Freq: Daily
Circ: 10795 Cision Digital Reach
MAGAZINE (ONLINE)
Marketing

Marketing Week   979855
Editorial: Wells Point, 79 Wells Street, London W1T 3QN **Tel:** 44 02079 704000
Web site: www.marketingweek.co.uk
Freq: Weekly
Circ: 20349 Not Audited
Editor: Russell Parsons
Profile: Marketing Week is a marketing publication in the UK, read by client marketers. Each issue provides news, insight and analysis to an audience of senior decision makers. It publishes a weekly cover story featuring the latest trends and developments affecting the industry as well as interviews and profiles with key marketing professionals. First published in 1978. Aimed at senior marketing executives with

responsibility for marketing and advertising expenditure.
Ad Rate: Full Page Colour £6375.00
MAGAZINE
Marketing

MarketingTech   986394
Email: enquiries@techforge.pub
Web site: www.marketingtechnews.net
Freq: Daily
Circ: 178293 Cision Digital Reach
MAGAZINE (ONLINE)
Advertising Industry, Branding, Industry, Marketing

Master Investor   1063275
Editorial: Master Investor Ltd, Suite 88, 22 Notting Hill Gate, London W11 3JE
Tel: 44 07515 542707
Web site: https://masterinvestor.co.uk/magazine/
Freq: Monthly
Circ: 54866 Cision Digital Reach
MAGAZINE (ONLINE)
Equities, Financial Markets, Investment Banking

Materials Handling & Logistics   986792
Editorial: 15a London Road, Maidstone, Maidstone ME16 8LY **Tel:** 44 01622 687031
Web site: www.connectingindustry.com/MaterialsHandlingLogistics
Freq: Bi-Monthly
Circ: 14498 Not Audited
Editor: Jack Cheeseman
MAGAZINE
Manufacturing, Mining & Quarrying, Paper, Plastics, Shipping & Warehousing, Steel, Supply Chain Management (SCM)

Materials Handling World Magazine   984788
Editorial: 140A Huddersfield Road, Mirfield, Mirfield Wf14 8AN **Tel:** 44 01924 499639
Email: production@northlodgemedia.co.uk
Web site: www.mhwmagazine.co.uk
Freq: Monthly
Circ: 52921 Cision Digital Reach
Editor: David Ramsay
Profile: Website covering materials. The Materials Handling World Magazine covers all aspects of materials handling and logistics. The site includes articles on forklift trucks, automated storage and retrieval systems, racking systems, waste management and health and safety.
Ad Rate: Full Page Colour £625.00
MAGAZINE (ONLINE)
Manufacturing, Steel

Materials Recycling World   981143
Editorial: 3 / 4th Floor, Telephone House, 69-77 Paul Street, London EC2A 4NQ
Tel: 44 02030 332799
Email: mrw@emap.com
Web site: www.mrw.co.uk
Freq: Bi-Weekly
Circ: 2732 Not Audited
Editor: Robin Latchem
MAGAZINE
Environment, Manufacturing

Materials Today   983464
Editorial: The Boulevard, Langford Lane, Kidlington, Oxford OX5 1GB
Tel: 44 01865 843000
Email: materialstoday@elsevier.com
Web site: www.materialstoday.com
Freq: Monthly
Circ: 36000 Not Audited
Editor: Stewart Bland
Profile: Journal containing news and features alongside peer-reviewed articles. Read by academic, government and industrial researchers involved in any area of materials science.
Ad Rate: Full Page Colour £3840.00
MAGAZINE
Science

Mathematics in School   981530
Editorial: 259 London Road, Leicester LE2 3RE **Tel:** 44 01162 210013
Email: office@m-a.org.uk
Web site: http://www.m-a.org.uk/jsp/index.jsp?lnk=610
Freq: Bi-Monthly
Circ: 9000 Not Audited
Editor: Chris Pritchard
Profile: Magazine covering the latest developments in mathematics education, looking at the development of the National Curriculum in mathematics.
Ad Rate: Full Page Mono £390.00
Ad Rate: Full Page Colour £660.00
MAGAZINE
Education

Measurement & Control   984148
Editorial: 87 Gower Street, London WC1E 6AF **Tel:** 44 02073 874949
Email: publications@instmc.org
Web site: www.instmc.org.uk
Freq: Monthly
Circ: 4000 Not Audited
Profile: Journal of the Institute of Measurement and Control. Includes information, business news and features on technical advances.
Ad Rate: Full Page Mono £700.00
Ad Rate: Full Page Colour £1100.00
MAGAZINE
Engineering

Meat Management   985862
Editorial: Meat Management, PO Box 5122, Milton Keynes MK15 8ZP
Tel: 44 01908 613323
Email: editorial@meatmanagement.com
Web site: http://meatmanagement.com/
Freq: Monthly
Circ: 3712 Not Audited
Editor: Emily Ansell Elfer
Profile: Magazine covering the meat industry. Features the latest news and interviews with industry experts.
MAGAZINE
Food

Meat Trades Journal   981164
Editorial: Broadfield Park, Crawley, Crawley RH11 9RT **Tel:** 44 01293 613400
Email: mtj.news@wrbm.com
Web site: www.meatinfo.co.uk
Freq: Bi-Weekly
Circ: 5058 Not Audited
Editor: Rod Addy
Profile: Journal focusing on the meat trade in Great Britain, including poultry producers and abattoirs.
Ad Rate: Full Page Colour £2500.00
MAGAZINE
Animal Farming, Food

Media Law International   996886
Editorial: 145 -157 St. John Street, Farringdon, London EC1V 4PW
Tel: 44 07446 525299
Web site: http://medialawinternational.com
Freq: Annual Not Audited
MAGAZINE
Consumer Interest, Corporate Law, Criminal Law, Government, Intellectual Property, Legal Services

Medical & Test Journal   1061343
Tel: 44 81332 659351
Web site: http://www.jiho.co.jp/tabid/149/Default.aspx
Freq: Monthly Not Audited
MAGAZINE
Medical Technology

Medical and Veterinary Entomology   995043
Email: mve@wiley.com
Web site: http://www.blackwellpublishing.com/journal.asp?ref=0269-283X&site=1
Freq: Quarterly Not Audited
Editor: Doug Colwell
MAGAZINE
Veterinary Medicine

Medical Device Decontamination   981044
Editorial: Blackburn House, Redhouse Road, Seafield, Bathgate EH47 7AQ
Tel: 44 01506 811077
Email: info@fitwise.co.uk
Web site: http://www.idsc-uk.co.uk/publications.php
Freq: Quarterly
Circ: 600 Not Audited
Editor: Gill Ellis-Pow
Profile: Journal of the Institute of Decontamination Sciences containing features of interest to members. It covers the sterilisation of medical devices. Read by members of the Institute of Sterile Services Management, decontamination managers and technicians, sterile services managers and theatre managers.
Ad Rate: Full Page Mono £315.00
Ad Rate: Full Page Colour £760.00
MAGAZINE
Health Administration, Hygiene, Medical Technology

Medical Device Developments   988849
Editorial: Europe Atlantic Offices, John Carpenter House, John Carpenter Street, London EC4Y 0AN **Tel:** 44 02079 366400
Email: andrew.putwain@progressivedigitalmedia.com
Web site: www.medicaldevice-developments.com
Freq: Semi-Annual
Circ: 6988 Not Audited
Profile: Journal covering the development and manufacture of the technology and processes involved in the manufacture of medical devices. Aimed at Medical OEMs.
MAGAZINE
Medical Technology

Medical Imaging Technology   985325
Editorial: John Carpenter House, John Carpenter Street, London EC4Y 0AN
Tel: 44 02079 366400
Email: editor@globaltrademedia.com
Web site: http://www.hospitalmanagement.net/mediapacks/print/about-us-print.html
Freq: Semi-Annual
Circ: 4851 Not Audited
Profile: Magazine covering medical imaging. Each edition tackles the most important topics of the day, blending submissions from the industry's leading names with specific case studies showing how specific facilities have used imaging applications to improve the overall standard of patient care.
MAGAZINE
Diagnostic Imaging, Medical Technology

Medical Plastics News   985949
Editorial: Carlton House, Sandpiper Way, Chester Business Park, Chester CH4 9QE
Tel: 44 01244 680222
Email: info@rapidnews.com
Web site: www.medicalplasticsnews.com
Freq: Bi-Monthly
Circ: 6966 Not Audited
Editor: Aleksandra Jones
MAGAZINE
Medical Technology, Plastics

medicaldevice-network.com   990373
Editorial: John Carpenter House, John Carpenter Street, London EC4Y 0AN
Tel: 44 02079 366400
Email: onlineeditorial@kable.co.uk
Web site: http://www.medicaldevice-network.com
Freq: Daily
Circ: 12958 Cision Digital Reach
MAGAZINE (ONLINE)
Medical Technology

medicalphysicsweb   997121
Editorial: Temple Circus, Temple Way, Bristol BS1 6HG **Tel:** 44 01179 297481
Email: tami.freeman@iop.org
Web site: www.medicalphysicsweb.org
Freq: Daily

Business Magazines

Circ: 18011 Cision Digital Reach
Editor: Tami Freeman
MAGAZINE (ONLINE)
Biotechnology, Medical Technology, Pharmaceuticals, Science

MedNous 984884
Editorial: 39 Calabria Road, London N5 1HZ
Tel: 44 02077 041015
Email: editor@mednous.com
Web site: www.mednous.com
Freq: Monthly Not Audited
Editor: Victoria English
Profile: Journal covering medical news and reference information. It contains information on regulatory affairs, patent law, government research policy and funding.
MAGAZINE
Biotechnology, Healthcare Industry, Medical Technology, Pharmaceuticals, Science

Med-Tech Innovation magazine 986066
Editorial: Meadow Court, Faygate Lane, Faygate, Horsham RH12 4SJ
Tel: 44 01293 710041
Email: editorial@med-techinnovation.com
Web site: www.med-techinnovation.com
Freq: Bi-Monthly
Circ: 6000 Not Audited
MAGAZINE
Medical Technology

Melanoma Management 1053866
Editorial: Unitec House, 2 Albert Place, London N3 1QB **Tel:** 44 02083 716090
Email: info@futuremedicine.com
Web site: http://www.futuremedicine.com/loi/mmt
Freq: No Frequency Established Not Audited
MAGAZINE
Oncology

Menopause Matters 999435
Editorial: Skewbridge, Mouswlad, Dumfries DG1 4LY
Email: info@menopausematters.co.uk
Web site: www.menopausematters.co.uk
Freq: Daily
Circ: 198751 Cision Digital Reach
MAGAZINE (ONLINE)
Obstetrics & Gynecology (OB/GYN)

Mental Health Practice 981190
Editorial: The Heights, 59-65 Lowlands Road, Harrow on the Hill, London HA1 3AW
Tel: 44 02084 231066
Web site: https://rcni.com/mental-health-practice
Freq: Monthly
Circ: 9235 Not Audited
Editor: Colin Parish
Profile: Website covering all areas of mental health and patient care in UK. Mental Health Practice shares the latest mental health news, features, professional development articles and letters page. It's hosted by RCN Publishing Co Ltd.
MAGAZINE
Neurology

Mental Health Today 985181
Editorial: Rayford House, School Road, Hove, Brighton BN3 5HX
Tel: 44 01273 434943
Email: info@mentalhealthtoday.co.uk
Web site: http://www.mentalhealthtoday.co.uk
Freq: Bi-Monthly
Circ: 16768 Cision Digital Reach
Profile: Professional publication covering mental health services and mental health care. Includes care practice, legislation policies and professional development. Aimed at: anybody who is looking to gather information about mental health care and current news
MAGAZINE (ONLINE)
Neurology

MEPCA 986065
Editorial: The Goods Shed, Whitstable Road, Faversham, Faversham ME13 8GD
Tel: 44 01795 509105
Email: editor@mepca.com
Web site: http://mepca-engineering.com/
Freq: Monthly
Circ: 15626 Not Audited
MAGAZINE
Engineering

Mergermarket 980772
Editorial: 10 Queen Street Place, London EC4R 1BE **Tel:** 44 02037 411129
Email: pressenquiries@mergermarket.com
Web site: www.mergermarket.com
Freq: Daily
Circ: 126383 Cision Digital Reach
Editor: Kate Jenkinson
Profile: Website covering finance. mergermarket shares the latest news on mergers, deals, advice, news and real-time league tables.
MAGAZINE (ONLINE)
Mergers & Acquisitions

Metal Bulletin 981249
Editorial: 8 Bouverie Street, London EC4Y 8AX **Tel:** 44 02078 279977
Email: editorial@metalbulletin.com
Web site: www.metalbulletin.com
Freq: Monthly
Circ: 3863 Not Audited
Editor: Richard Barrett
Profile: Magazine covering industry and market news and prices on steel, metals, ores, precious metals and scrap. The publication was first published in 1913. Aimed at the steel, metals and scrap industry.
Ad Rate: Full Page Mono £2308.00
Ad Rate: Full Page Colour £3448.00
MAGAZINE
Commodities, Mining & Quarrying, Steel

Metal Powder Report 986325
Editorial: The Boulevard, Langford Lane, Kidlington, Oxford OX5 1GB
Tel: 44 01865 843638
Email: materialstoday@elsevier.com
Web site: http://www.materialstoday.com/
Freq: Bi-Monthly
Circ: 700 Not Audited
Profile: Magazine covering the powder metallurgy industry worldwide. Aimed at management executives, design engineers, business analysts and research and academic establishments worldwide with an interest in PM technology.
Ad Rate: Full Page Colour £4942.00
MAGAZINE
Steel

Metallurgical Coal Quarterly 995035
Editorial: 133 Houndsditch, London EC3A 7BX **Tel:** 44 02031 593300
Email: coalemea@ihs.com
Web site: www.ihs.com
Freq: Quarterly
Circ: 1556605 Cision Digital Reach
MAGAZINE (ONLINE)
Mining & Quarrying

Metallurgical Industry Automation 1062001
Tel: 44 86106 3841318
Email: yjzdh@tom.com
Web site: http://www.yjzdh.com
Freq: Bi-Monthly
Circ: 7001 Not Audited
MAGAZINE
Manufacturing

Metropolitan Life 986018
Editorial: No 1 Colchester Business Centre, 1 George Williams Way, Colchester, Colchester CO1 2JS **Tel:** 44 01206 369448
Email: info@police-life.co.uk
Freq: Monthly
Circ: 12000 Not Audited
Editor: Jill Bareham
Profile: Magazine covering news and lifestyle articles relevant to police service personnel working or living in London with a blend of entertainment news, articles about the job in the Met and few in depth features each month on wide ranging topics, such as Identity fraud, covert surveillance, DVD Piracy, Training alternatives, Technology and so on.
Ad Rate: Full Page Mono £1495.00
Ad Rate: Full Page Colour £1495.00
MAGAZINE
Security & Security Systems

Microlight Flying 981895
Editorial: British Microlight Aircraft Association, The Bullring, Banbury OX15 0TT
Tel: 44 01869 338888
Email: mfeditor@bmaa.org
Web site: www.microlightflying.org.uk/
Freq: Monthly
Circ: 4200 Not Audited
Editor: Geoff Hill
MAGAZINE
Aviation

MicroScope 980808
Editorial: TechTarget, 25 Christopher Street, London EC2A 2BS **Tel:** 44 02071 861400
Web site: www.microscope.co.uk
Freq: Monthly
Circ: 19000 Not Audited
Editor: Simon Quicke
Profile: Website covering technology for businesses. MicroScope is an IT channel that shares the latest news in the technology industry, also offering advice to businesses on technology services, products and IT outsourcing.
MAGAZINE
Auto Aftermarket, Computers, Industry

Microscopy & Analysis 983468
Editorial: The Atrium, Southern Gate, Chichester, Chichester PO19 8SQ
Tel: 44 01243 770443
Email: editor@microscopy-analysis.com
Web site: http://www.microscopy-analysis.com/
Freq: Bi-Monthly
Circ: 46000 Not Audited
Editor: Julian Heath
MAGAZINE
Science

Middle East and Africa Telecoms Newsletter 999073
Editorial: Mortimer House, 37-41 Mortimer Street, London W1T 3JH
Tel: 44 02070 174800
Email: keithw@cmsinfo.com
Web site: www.telecomsmarketresearch.com/research/TMAAAQHX-Middle-East-and-Africa-Wireless-Analyst.shtml
Freq: Bi-Weekly Not Audited
Editor: Mai Barakat
MAGAZINE
Telecommunications/Electronic Communications

The Middle East in Europe 996346
Editorial: 3 Shortlands, Hammersmith, London W6 8DA **Tel:** 44 02083 921122
Email: meenetinfo@eapgroup.com
Web site: http://themiddleeastineurope.net/
Freq: Bi-Monthly
Circ: 11500 Not Audited
MAGAZINE
Banking

Middle East Power 985687
Editorial: Global House, 13 Market Square, Horsham, Horsham RH12 1EU
Tel: 44 01403 220750
Email: power@gmp.uk.com
Web site: http://www.gmp.uk.com/middle-east-power/
Freq: Quarterly
Circ: 4608 Not Audited
MAGAZINE
Alternative/Renewable Energy, Carbon Emissions & Trading, Electricity, Energy, Nuclear Power, Oil, Water & Sanitation

Middle Eastern Plastics 985500
Editorial: Carlton House, Sandpiper Way, Chester Business Park, Chester CH4 9QE
Tel: 44 01244 680222
Web site: www.mideastplast.com
Freq: Daily
Circ: 14797 Cision Digital Reach
Editor: Rose Brooke
MAGAZINE (ONLINE)
Manufacturing, Plastics

Midland Farmer 988049
Editorial: Fountain Way, Reydon Business Park, Reydon, Southwold IP18 6DH
Tel: 44 01502 725800
Web site: http://midlandfarmer.co.uk/
Freq: Monthly
Circ: 5500 Not Audited
Editor: Johann Tasker
MAGAZINE
Animal Farming

Midlands Business News Online 986055
Editorial: 65 Church Street, Birmingham B3 2DP
Email: news@midlandsbusinessnews.co.uk
Web site: www.midlandsbusinessnews.co.uk
Freq: Daily
Circ: 15756 Cision Digital Reach
MAGAZINE (ONLINE)
Business, Small and Medium Business

Midlands in Business 999206
Editorial: B1 Trentham Business Quarter, Bellringer Road, Trentham Lakes, Stoke-on-Trent ST4 8GB **Tel:** 44 01782 644456
Email: info@midlandsinbusiness.com
Web site: http://www.midlandsinbusiness.com/
Freq: Bi-Monthly
Circ: 10000 Not Audited
MAGAZINE
Business

Midwives 984642
Editorial: 17-18 Britton Street, London EC1M 5TP **Tel:** 44 02078 806200
Email: editorial@midwives.co.uk
Web site: http://www.rcm.org.uk/midwives/
Freq: Quarterly
Circ: 45500 Not Audited
Editor: Emma Godfrey-Edwards
Profile: Official journal of the Royal College of Midwives. Contains research papers, review papers, news, book reviews, recruitment and letters to the editor. Aimed at midwives, medical officers, obstetricians, gynaecologists and maternity care assistants.Previous title: RCM Midwives Journal
MAGAZINE
Obstetrics & Gynecology (OB/GYN)

Military Logistics International 984574
Editorial: Saville Mews, 30 Saville Rd, London W4 5HG **Tel:** 44 01753 727001
Email: info@shephardmedia.com
Web site: www.shephardmedia.com
Freq: Quarterly
Circ: 9500 Not Audited
Profile: Magazine focusing on logistics, support, overhaul and maintenance. Aimed at defence contractors and the armed services.Regular features: Ammunition; Expeditionary Infastructure; Logistics IT; Maintainance; Power; The Logistics of Fuel; Water
Ad Rate: Full Page Colour £3000.00
MAGAZINE
Defense & National Security

Military Systems & Technology 999848
Editorial: Worth Cottage, Hele, Exeter EX5 4PS **Tel:** 44 01392 881545
Email: info@militarysystems-tech.com
Web site: www.militarysystems-tech.com
Freq: Monthly

Circ: 16000 Not Audited
MAGAZINE
Defense & National Security

Military Training & Simulation News
983645

Editorial: Saville Mews, 30 Saville Road, London W4 5HG **Tel:** 44 02031 792570
Email: info@shephardmedia.com
Web site: https://www.shephardmedia.com/news/training-simulation/
Freq: Bi-Monthly
Circ: 40000 Not Audited
Editor: Trevor Nash
Profile: Magazine covering international military organisations, the simulation and training industry, government, civil service, academic and other related industries. Aimed at senior military officers, industry managers and engineers, industry sales persons, academics and other governmental officials involved in training and simulation.
Ad Rate: Full Page Mono £2740.00
Ad Rate: Full Page Colour £3600.00
MAGAZINE
Aviation, Defense & National Security

Milling and Grain Magazine
996976

Editorial: 7 St George's Terrace, St James' Square, Cheltenham, Cheltenham GL50 3PT
Tel: 44 01242 267700
Email: info@perendale.co.uk
Web site: www.gfmt.co.uk
Freq: Monthly
Circ: 35295 Not Audited
MAGAZINE
Animal Farming, Manufacturing, Supply Chain Management (SCM)

MIMS
981191

Editorial: Bridge House, 69 London Road, Twickenham, London TW1 3RH
Tel: 44 02082 675000
Email: mims@haymarket.com
Web site: www.mims.co.uk
Freq: Monthly
Circ: 27466 Not Audited
Editor: Chloe Harman
Profile: Magazine covering prescription medicines for therapeutic use. Includes information on indications, dosage and warnings, new products reviews and licensing changes. Aimed at doctors in general practice and consultants in hospitals.
Ad Rate: Full Page Colour £4017.00
MAGAZINE
Biotechnology, Pharmaceuticals

MIMS Dermatology
996301

Editorial: Bridge House, London Road, London TW1 3RH **Tel:** 44 02082 675000
Email: mimsdermatology@haymarket.com
Web site: www.haymarket.com/mims/multi/mims_dermatology_magazine/default.aspx
Freq: Quarterly
Circ: 8000 Not Audited
MAGAZINE
Dermatology

Mindful Money
985879

Editorial: Chat About LLP, 24a St. John Street, Clerkenwell, London EC1M 4AY
Tel: 44 02075 669794
Email: editor@mindfulmoney.co.uk
Web site: www.mindfulmoney.co.uk
Freq: Daily
Circ: 9787 Cision Digital Reach
Editor: John Lappin
Profile: Website covering business and finance. The Mindful Money website discusses anything from investment and money to bank analysis and inflation.
MAGAZINE (ONLINE)
Investment Banking

MINE
1058242

Editorial: John Carpenter House, John Carpenter Street, London EC4Y 0AN
Tel: 44 02079 366400
Email: onlinemags@nridigital.com
Web site: http://www.nridigital.com/mine-magazine.html

Freq: Monthly
Circ: 75 Cision Digital Reach
MAGAZINE (ONLINE)
Mining & Quarrying

Mineral Deposits
1061663

Tel: 44 86106 8327284
Web site: http://www.kcdz.ac.cn/index.aspx
Freq: Bi-Monthly
Circ: 1000 Not Audited
MAGAZINE
Mining & Quarrying, Science

Mineral Planning
985101

Editorial: Bridge House, 69 London Road, Twickenham TW1 3QL **Tel:** 44 02082 674025
Web site: mineralplanning.co.uk
Freq: Bi-Monthly Not Audited
Editor: Alison Carter
Profile: Journal reporting on the extraction and use of minerals and the environmental effects. First published in 1979, the publication has an average of 40 pages per issue. Aimed at local authorities, government departments, environmental pressure groups, the minerals industry, educational institutions, environmental consultants and lawyers.
Ad Rate: Full Page Mono £278.00
MAGAZINE
Carbon Emissions & Trading, Oil

Mining Journal
980735

Editorial: 4th Floor, Vintners Place, 68 Upper Thames Street, London EC4V 3BJ
Tel: 44 02072 166060
Email: editorial@mining-journal.com
Web site: www.mining-journal.com
Freq: Weekly
Circ: 2926 Not Audited
Editor: Chris Cann
Profile: Journal containing news and comments on global mining issues. Includes articles on exploration, development, production equipment, research development, marketing of metals, minerals and financial activities of mining companies.
Ad Rate: Full Page Colour £2468.00
MAGAZINE
Mining & Quarrying

Mining Magazine
980736

Editorial: 4th Floor, Vintners Place, 68 Upper Thames Street, London EC4V 3BJ
Tel: 44 02072 166060
Email: info@aspermontmedia.com
Web site: www.miningmagazine.com
Freq: Monthly
Circ: 19028 Not Audited
Editor: Carly Leonida
Profile: Magazine containing product and processing updates, literature comments, mining coverage and exploration equipment reviews. Aimed at suppliers of mining equipment.
Ad Rate: Full Page Colour £3755.00
MAGAZINE
Mining & Quarrying

Mining World
984521

Tel: 44 01777 871007
Email: editor@mqworld.com
Web site: www.mqworld.com
Freq: Bi-Monthly
Circ: 12000 Not Audited
Profile: Magazine focusing on hard-rock mining and quarrying. Aimed at mining and mineral professionals.
Ad Rate: Full Page Colour £2400.00
MAGAZINE
Mining & Quarrying

mining-technology.com
987719

Editorial: John Carpenter House, John Carpenter Street, London EC4Y 0AN
Tel: 44 02079 366400
Email: onlineeditorial@kable.co.uk
Web site: www.mining-technology.com
Freq: Daily
Circ: 129371 Cision Digital Reach

Profile: Website covering mines extracting energy minerals, ferrous, base and precious metals, industrial minerals and gemstones.
MAGAZINE (ONLINE)
Mining & Quarrying

Minutehack
996590

Editorial: 8 Northumberland Avenue, London WC2N 5BY
Email: editor@minutehack.com
Web site: www.minutehack.com
Freq: Daily
Circ: 53358 Cision Digital Reach
MAGAZINE (ONLINE)
Business, Small and Medium Business

MIPIM
981354

Editorial: Procter House, 110 High Holborn, London WC1V 6DW **Tel:** 44 02079 111701
Web site: www.mipim.com
Freq: Bi-Monthly
Circ: 22000 Not Audited
Editor: Graham Parker
MAGAZINE
Commercial Real Estate, Residential Real Estate, Retail, Travel Industry

Mix Interiors
984260

Editorial: Unit 2 Abito, 85 Greengate, Manchester M3 7NA **Tel:** 44 01619 466262
Email: editorial@mixinteriors.com
Web site: www.mixinteriors.com
Freq: Monthly
Circ: 10000 Not Audited
Editor: Mick Jordan
MAGAZINE
Interior Design, Office Design

The MJ
981271

Editorial: 32 Vauxhall Bridge Road, London SW1V 2SS **Tel:** 44 02079 736400
Email: info@hgluk.com
Web site: www.themj.co.uk
Freq: Weekly
Circ: 6141 Not Audited
Editor: Heather Jameson
Profile: Magazine covering all aspects of local government, including tenders, contracts awarded and recruitment.
Ad Rate: Full Page Colour £2675.00
MAGAZINE
Government

MmIT Journal
997122

Editorial: 103 Bath Road, Willsbridge, Bristol BS30 6 ED
Web site: www.cilip.org.uk/mmit
Freq: Quarterly
Circ: 4500 Not Audited
MAGAZINE
Computers

Mobile
980184

Editorial: 4 Bloomsbury Square, London WC1A 2RP
Email: mobile@nhmedia.co.uk
Web site: www.mobiletoday.co.uk
Freq: Bi-Weekly
Circ: 6089 Not Audited
MAGAZINE
Mobile Communications, Telecommunications/Electronic Communications

Mobile Display Report
407112

Owner: Insight Media, Inc.
Tel: 44 125 283-5385
Email: news@mdreport.com
Web site: http://www.insightmedia.info
Freq: Monthly
Circ: 9454 Cision Digital Reach
MAGAZINE (ONLINE)
Displays, Graphics, & Imaging, Mobile Electronics

Mobile Europe
979960

Editorial: 2nd Floor, 52-54 Gracechurch Street, London EC3V 0EH
Tel: 44 02079 338999
Web site: www.mobileeurope.co.uk
Freq: Bi-Monthly
Circ: 4404 Not Audited

Editor: Graeme Neill
Profile: Specialist mobile communications magazine providing news, views, product information, technology developments, policy updates and in-depth market reports. Analyses the major developments in wireless technologies and markets. Offers news analysis and strong opinion, combined with specialist articles. Investigates the rapidly changing trends and patterns, informing and educating industry key decision makers. Aimed at key decision makers on mobile communications throughout Europe.
Ad Rate: Full Page Colour £4914.00
MAGAZINE
Mobile Communications, Telecommunications/Electronic Communications

Mobile Marketing
995967

Editorial: Mobile Marketing, 57-61 Charterhouse St, London EC1M 6HA
Tel: 44 02071 832920
Web site: http://mobilemarketingmagazine.com
Freq: Quarterly
Circ: 120000 Not Audited
Profile: Mobile Marketing Magazine is the online magazine dedicated to mobile marketing. Provides information about mobile marketing, including news, views, campaigns, case studies and advice. Mobile Marketing Magazine is edited by David Murphy, a journalist specializing in marketing and technology. Aimed at digital agencies, network operators and companies interested in mobile marketing.
MAGAZINE
Marketing, Telecommunications/Electronic Communications

The Mobile Network
987246

Editorial: 271a Franciscan Road, London SW17 8HE **Tel:** 44 02030 070020
Web site: www.the-mobile-network.com
Freq: Daily
Circ: 17073 Cision Digital Reach
Editor: Keith Dyer
MAGAZINE (ONLINE)
Mobile Communications, Telecommunications/Electronic Communications

Mobile News
981080

Editorial: 8-10 Godson Street, Islington, London N1 9GZ **Tel:** 44 02072 780795
Email: editor@mobilenewscwp.co.uk
Web site: www.mobilenewscwp.co.uk
Freq: Bi-Weekly
Circ: 6100 Not Audited
Profile: Mobile News is a magazine covering all aspects of the mobile communications industry including news, features, comments, analysis, profiles, reviews and markets. Topics covered include Internet of Things, M2M, mobile operators, manufacturers, mobile tech and reviews. Aimed at people working in the mobile communications and related industries.
Ad Rate: Full Page Colour £3000.00
MAGAZINE
Mobile Communications, Telecommunications/Electronic Communications

Mobile Payments World
998952

Editorial: The Stable, Hall Yard, Kelling, Holt, Holt NR25 7EW **Tel:** 44 01263 711800
Web site: www.mobilepaymentsworld.com
Freq: Bi-Weekly
Circ: 15088 Cision Digital Reach
MAGAZINE (ONLINE)
Telecommunications/Electronic Communications

Mobile World Live
986719

Editorial: Second Floor, The Walbrook Building, 25 Walbrook, London EC4N 8AF
Email: editor@mobileworldlive.com
Web site: www.mobileworldlive.com
Freq: Daily
Circ: 472958 Cision Digital Reach

Business Magazines

Profile: Website covering mobile apps, mobile devices and mobile money.
MAGAZINE (ONLINE)
Mobile Communications

MobileSquared.co.uk   985089
Editorial: Venture House, Arlington Square, Downshire Way, Bracknell RG12 1WA
Tel: 44 01344 747113
Email: info@mobilesquared.co.uk
Web site: www.mobilesquared.co.uk
Freq: Daily
Circ: 7198 Cision Digital Reach
MAGAZINE (ONLINE)
Mobile Communications, Telecommunications/Electronic Communications

Modern Builder   996944
Tel: 44 02891 451522
Email: info@modernbuilder.co.uk
Web site: www.modernbuilder.co.uk
Freq: Monthly Not Audited
Editor: Martin Boyd
MAGAZINE
Building & Construction, Sustainable Development

Modern Building Services   983892
Editorial: 5 Viewpoint, Babbage Road, Stevenage SG1 2EQ **Tel:** 44 01438 759000
Email: ksharpe@portico.uk.com
Web site: www.modbs.co.uk
Freq: Monthly
Circ: 23370 Not Audited
Editor: Ken Sharpe
Profile: Journal covering the entire supply and user chain in the building services industry. Aimed at people who work in the building services industry.
Ad Rate: Full Page Colour £2369.00
MAGAZINE
Engineering

Modern Claims Magazine   987420
Editorial: Charlton Grant Ltd, Express Building, College Business Park, Kearsley Road, Ripon, Ripon HG4 2RN
Tel: 44 01765 600909
Email: info@charltongrant.co.uk
Web site: www.modernclaimsmagazine.co.uk
Freq: Bi-Monthly
Circ: 17000 Not Audited
MAGAZINE
Insurance

Modern Japanese Economy   1061609
Tel: 44 86108 2561076
Email: info_one@sina.com
Freq: Semi-Annual
Circ: 10000 Not Audited
MAGAZINE
Economics

Modern Law   987422
Editorial: Charlton Grant Ltd, Express Building, College Business Park, Kearsley Road, Ripon HG4 2RN **Tel:** 44 01765 600909
Email: info@charltongrant.co.uk
Web site: www.modernlawmagazine.com
Freq: Bi-Monthly
Circ: 20000 Not Audited
MAGAZINE
Legal Services

Modern Methods of Construction   1005999
Editorial: PO Box 17171, Sutton Coldfield B73 9AE **Tel:** 44 01216 619484
Email: press@buildinsite.co.uk
Web site: http://buildinsite.co.uk/portfolio/mmc-magazine/
Freq: Quarterly
Circ: 9000 Not Audited
MAGAZINE
Building & Construction, Sustainable Development

Modern Power Systems   980108
Editorial: Progressive House, 2 Maidstone Road, Foots Cray, Sidcup, London DA14 5HZ **Tel:** 44 02082 697766
Web site: www.modernpowersystems.com
Freq: Monthly
Circ: 11786 Not Audited
Profile: Journal covering design, purchasing and operation of power generating, transmission and distribution systems. Target audience are those looking to purchase and/or operate power generating, transmission, and distribution systems.
Ad Rate: Full Page Mono £2730.00
Ad Rate: Full Page Colour £3655.00
MAGAZINE
Alternative/Renewable Energy, Electricity, Nuclear Power, Oil, Water & Sanitation

moderngov   981065
Editorial: 10 Buckingham Place, London SW1E 6HX **Tel:** 44 02037 706500
Email: editorial@govnet.co.uk
Web site: www.govnet.co.uk
Freq: Semi-Annual
Circ: 3500 Not Audited
Profile: Magazine covering topics affecting public sector officials including interviews with key policy makers. Aimed at public sector professionals.
Ad Rate: Full Page Colour £3595.00
MAGAZINE
Government, Public Sector

Modular Machine Tool and Automatic Manufacturing Techniques   1062087
Tel: 44 86411 86645290
Email: zhjcqk@126.com
Web site: http://www.zhjcz.com.cn
Freq: Monthly
Circ: 3002 Not Audited
MAGAZINE
Manufacturing

Modus   981110
Editorial: RICS, Parliament Square, London SW1 3PD **Tel:** 44 02078 716760
Email: editor@ricsmodus.com
Web site: www.rics.org/modus
Freq: Monthly
Circ: 83152 Not Audited
Editor: Oliver Parsons
Profile: Magazine of the Royal Institution of Chartered Surveyors. Aimed at members and non-members with an interest in the chartered surveying profession.Previous title: CSM
Ad Rate: Full Page Mono £2585.00
Ad Rate: Full Page Colour £3930.00
MAGAZINE
Architecture & Design, Building & Construction, Commercial Real Estate, Finance, Interior Design, Legal Affairs, Office Design, Property Management & Maintenance, Residential Real Estate, Retail

The Momentum Investor   981491
Editorial: PO Box 1015, Croydon CR9 5DL
Tel: 44 02086 564648
Web site: www.momentuminvestor.co.uk
Freq: Monthly Not Audited
Editor: Richard Welby
MAGAZINE
Equities

Mondo Visione   983349
Editorial: CentralPoint, 45 Beech Street, London EC2Y 8AD **Tel:** 44 02079 539797
Email: editor@mondovisione.com
Web site: www.mondovisione.com
Freq: Daily
Circ: 33438 Cision Digital Reach
MAGAZINE (ONLINE)
Financial Markets

Money Laundering Bulletin   985551
Editorial: 5 Howick Place, London SW1P 1WG **Tel:** 44 02070 175000
Email: timon.molloy@informa.com
Web site: www.moneylaunderingbulletin.com

Freq: Monthly Not Audited
Profile: It is a monthly newsletter that gives information on money laundering schemes, methods, trends and policing, terrorist financing; sanctions compliance and proliferation finance. Aimed at banks, investment trusts and houses, insurance companies, stock brokers, lawyers and accountants, money service businesses, high value dealers, money laundering reporting officers, government organisations, the police and other law enforcement agencies.
MAGAZINE
Banking

Money Makers   1075508
Tel: 44 01730 233870
Email: editor@independent-investor.com
Web site: www.money-makers.co
Freq: Daily
Circ: 10725 Cision Digital Reach
MAGAZINE (ONLINE)
Investment Banking

Moody's Investors Service   1073130
Editorial: One Canada Square, Canary Wharf, London E14 5FA
Tel: 44 02077 725454
Email: mediarelations@moodys.com
Web site: www.moodys.com
Freq: Daily
Circ: 454562 Cision Digital Reach
MAGAZINE (ONLINE)
Bonds, Corporate Finance, Corporate Management, Credit Markets, Emerging Markets, Government, Lending, Public & Consumer Finance

MotivAction   999202
Editorial: Church Farm, Ardeley, Stevenage, Stevenage SG2 7AH **Tel:** 44 01438 861821
Email: ideas@motivaction.co.uk
Web site: www.motivaction.co.uk
Freq: Daily
Circ: 7362 Cision Digital Reach
Editor: Tim Waygood
MAGAZINE (ONLINE)
Human Resources

Move Commercial   984950
Editorial: 36 Henry Street, Liverpool L1 5HS
Tel: 44 01517 093871
Email: post@movepublishing.co.uk
Web site: www.movecommercial.com
Freq: Quarterly
Circ: 20000 Not Audited
Profile: Magazine containing information on industrial, retail, offices, investment, leisure, regeneration, planning and transport and covering current events, appointments, deals, news, profiles, current trends, trading gossip, financial news and statistics. Aimed at property professionals.
MAGAZINE
Property Management & Maintenance, Residential Real Estate, Travel Industry

The Mover   999143
Editorial: 26 Swanwick Lane, Broughton, Milton Keynes MK10 9LD
Tel: 44 01908 695500
Email: editor@themover.co.uk
Web site: themover.co.uk
Freq: Monthly
Circ: 3000 Not Audited
Editor: Steve Jordan
Profile: Website covering the removals industry, including packaging materials and transportation. Aimed at those working with in the removals industry.
MAGAZINE
Property Management & Maintenance

MoveTo.co.uk   990612
Editorial: 5 Oyster Park, Chertsey Road, London KT14 7AX **Tel:** 44 02083 908980
Email: interiors@barrelfield.co.uk
Web site: www.moveto.co.uk
Freq: Daily
Circ: 20192 Cision Digital Reach
MAGAZINE (ONLINE)
Property Management & Maintenance

MRCVSonline   98767
Email: editor@mrcvs.co.uk
Web site: www.mrcvs.co.uk
Freq: Daily
Circ: 16186 Cision Digital Reach
Editor: Sarah Kidby
MAGAZINE (ONLINE)
Veterinary Medicine

MRO Management   98008
Editorial: Suite E, 175 Bell Yard Mews, 175 Bermondsey Street, London SE1 3TN
Tel: 44 02077 243456
Email: info@airtransportpubs.com
Web site: www.mromanagement.com
Freq: Quarterly
Circ: 8000 Not Audited
Editor: Ian Harbison
Profile: Magazine focusing on the aircraft maintenance, repair and overhaul sector. The magazine comprises of the maintenance, modification and aftermarket servicing of commercial aircraft, engines and components. It analyses the global trends and events in this sector and creates reports on current business strategies. Aimed at airline operators and third party service providers.
MAGAZINE
Aviation

MRO Network News   984387
Editorial: 4th Floor, Tallis House, 2 Tallis Street, London EC4Y 0AB
Tel: 44 02079 751677
Email: news@mro-network.com
Web site: http://www.mro-network.com/
Freq: Daily
Circ: 37255 Cision Digital Reach
MAGAZINE (ONLINE)
Aviation, Engineering

MRO News Focus   988621
Editorial: Suite E, 11 Bell Yard Mews, 175 Bermondsey Street, London SE1 3TN
Tel: 44 02077 243456
Email: info@airtransportpubs.com
Web site: http://www.mronewsfocus.com/
Freq: Monthly
Circ: 10000 Not Audited
Editor: Ian Harbison
MAGAZINE
Aviation

MrWeb   985459
Editorial: Studio 1.8, The Leathermarket, Western Street, London SE1 3HN
Tel: 44 02075 156040
Email: editor@mrweb.com
Web site: www.mrweb.com
Freq: Daily
Circ: 46443 Cision Digital Reach
MAGAZINE (ONLINE)
Marketing

MS&T   983962
Editorial: Sentinel House, Harvest Crescent, Ancells Business Park, Fleet GU51 2UZ
Tel: 44 01252 532000
Web site: http://halldale.com/mst
Freq: Bi-Monthly
Circ: 21198 Not Audited
MAGAZINE
Defense & National Security

mtn-i   998757
Editorial: D'Arblay House, 16 D'Arblay Street, London W1F 8EA
Tel: 44 02074 371331
Email: editorial@mtn-i.com
Web site: www.mtn-i.info
Freq: Quarterly
Circ: 3000 Not Audited
MAGAZINE
Bonds, Corporate Finance, Economics, Financial Markets, Lending

Multiple Sclerosis Journal   986046
Editorial: 1 Oliver's Yard, 55 City Road, London EC1Y 1SP **Tel:** 44 02073 248500
Email: msjournal@ucl.ac.uk
Web site: http://msj.sagepub.com

Freq: Monthly Not Audited
Profile: Journal focusing on the aetiology and pathogenesis of demyelinating and inflammatory diseases of the central nervous system and on the application of such studies to scientifically based therapy. First published in 1996, the publication has an average of 144 pages per issue. Aimed at researchers in clinical neurology, pathology, genetics, epidemiology, therapeutics, immunology, virology, psychology, rehabilitation, and clinicians involved in multiple sclerosis.
MAGAZINE
Neurology

Musculoskeletal Care
996484
Web site: www.onlinelibrary.wiley.com/journal/10.1002/(ISSN)1557-0681
Freq: Quarterly Not Audited
MAGAZINE
Occupational Therapy & Rehabilitation, Orthopedics

Museum Identity
996594
Editorial: 132 London Road, Milton Keynes MK11 1JH **Tel:** 44 01908 563511
Email: greg@museum-id.com
Web site: www.museum-id.com
Freq: Quarterly
Circ: 4000 Not Audited
MAGAZINE
Genealogy

Museum Practice
983881
Editorial: 42 Clerkenwell Close, London EC1R 0AZ **Tel:** 44 02075 667800
Email: journal@museumsassociation.org
Web site: www.museumsassociation.org/museum-practice
Freq: Daily
Circ: 198 Cision Digital Reach
Profile: Website covering the practical and technical aspects of work in museums, galleries and historic buildings. The Museum Practice website is a membership based web portal sharing the latest news and new developments and innovations on museums and galleries.
Ad Rate: Full Page Colour £1200.00
MAGAZINE (ONLINE)
Genealogy

Museums + Heritage Advisor
987920
Editorial: The Coach House, Sharman Road, Worcester WR1 3LA **Tel:** 44 01905 724734
Email: news@museumsandheritage.com
Web site: http://advisor.museumsandheritage.com/
Freq: Daily
Editor: Adrian Murphy
Profile: Covering the opening of museums with features on conservation, model making and display cases. Includes articles on conservation materials and case studies of recent restoration projects from around the United Kingdom. Aimed at conservation bodies, architects, curators, libraries and local authority conservation departments.
MAGAZINE (ONLINE)
Genealogy

Museums Journal
980828
Editorial: 42 Clerkenwell Close, London EC1R 0AZ **Tel:** 44 02075 667800
Email: journal@museumsassociation.org
Web site: www.museumsassociation.org/museums-journal
Freq: Monthly
Circ: 7992 Not Audited
Editor: Simon Stephens
Profile: Journal covering all aspects of museum and gallery administration and policy. Aimed at all museum and gallery workers.
Ad Rate: Full Page Colour £1400.00
MAGAZINE
Genealogy

My Entrepreneur Magazine
998011
Tel: 44 08447 746574
Email: businesseditor@email.com

Web site: www.myentrepreneurmagazine.com
Freq: Daily
Circ: 1728 Cision Digital Reach
Editor: Kizzi Nkwocha
MAGAZINE (ONLINE)
Business, Corporate Responsibility, Legal Services

mybusiness.co.uk
983672
Editorial: 6-8 Cole Street, London SE1 4YH
Tel: 44 02071 833932
Email: hello@startups.co.uk
Web site: www.mybusiness.co.uk
Freq: Daily
Circ: 2878 Cision Digital Reach
Editor: Lucy Wayment
MAGAZINE (ONLINE)
Business, Corporate Responsibility

MyCustomer.com
984004
Editorial: 6th Floor, Bridge House, 48-52 Baldwin Street, Bristol BS1 1QB
Tel: 44 01179 159611
Email: editor@mycustomer.com
Web site: www.mycustomer.com
Freq: Daily
Circ: 625195 Cision Digital Reach
Profile: Website containing up-to-date CRM (Customer Relationship Management) developments. Includes weekly updates on CRM related news, new products and a document library.
MAGAZINE (ONLINE)
Business, Corporate Responsibility, Human Resources, Marketing

myInvestorCircle
996190
Editorial: Horatio House, 77-85 Fulham Palace Road, Hammersmith, London W6 8JA **Tel:** 44 02030 111720
Email: infoemea@ids.thomasmurray.com
Web site: http://ids.thomasmurray.com/
Freq: Daily
Circ: 132 Cision Digital Reach
MAGAZINE (ONLINE)
Fund Management, Insurance

Nankai Business Review International
1033439
Editorial: Emerald Group Publishing Limited, Howard House, Wagon Lane, Bingley BD16 1WA
Web site: www.emeraldinsight.com/loi/nbri
Freq: Quarterly Not Audited
MAGAZINE
Business, Corporate Responsibility

Nanomedicine
997097
Editorial: Unitec House, 2 Albert Place, London N3 1QB **Tel:** 44 02083 716080
Email: info@futuremedicine.com
Web site: www.futuremedicine.com/loi/nnm
Freq: Monthly Not Audited
MAGAZINE
Biotechnology, Medical Technology, Pharmaceuticals

NATIONAL FARMER
983589
Editorial: Suite 1, 2nd Floor, 26-32 Hill Street, Poole BH15 1NV
Tel: 44 01202 666602
Email: editorial@nationalfarmer.net
Web site: www.nationalfarmer.net
Freq: Monthly
Circ: 1066 Cision Digital Reach
Profile: Magazine covering the latest agricultural independent news, product launches and special features. Aimed at arable, beef, dairy, pig and sheep farmers and decision makers within the farming community.
Ad Rate: Full Page Colour £825.00
MAGAZINE (ONLINE)
Animal Farming

National Health Executive
984046
Editorial: 2nd Floor, 82 King Street, Manchester M2 4WQ **Tel:** 44 01618 336320
Email: editorial@nationalhealthexecutive.com
Web site: www.nationalhealthexecutive.com

Freq: Bi-Monthly
Circ: 9405 Not Audited
Editor: David Stevenson
Profile: Magazine covering healthcare and national health management including infection control, wound care, cardiology, cancer therapies, mental health, quality assurance, financial planning, alternative therapies, healthy living, renal therapies, disabled access, urological therapies, respiratory drugs and security. Aimed at chief executives and senior managers of the NHS and private healthcare.
Ad Rate: Full Page Colour £1995.00
MAGAZINE
Government, Health Administration

natm
983412
Editorial: Armstrong House, First Avenue, Robin Hood Airport, Doncaster DN9 3GA
Tel: 44 01302 802055
Email: natm@fastmail.fm
Web site: http://www.natm-mag.co.uk
Freq: Monthly
Circ: 10887 Not Audited
Editor: James Durose-Rayner
Profile: Journal containing contractual information and news from within the UK civil engineering industry. Aimed at specialist contractors.
Ad Rate: Full Page Mono £510.00
Ad Rate: Full Page Colour £940.00
MAGAZINE
Engineering

Natural Stone Specialist Magazine
985043
Editorial: 7 Regent Street, Nottingham NG1 5BS **Tel:** 44 01159 411315
Email: nss@qmj.co.uk
Web site: www.naturalstonespecialist.com
Freq: Monthly
Circ: 4012 Not Audited
MAGAZINE
Mining & Quarrying

Nature
981688
Editorial: The Macmillan Building, 4 Crinan Street, London N1 9XW
Tel: 44 02078 334000
Email: nature@nature.com
Web site: www.nature.com/nature
Freq: Weekly
Circ: 53000 Not Audited
Profile: Website focusing on all aspects of science. Aimed at scientists, lecturers and doctors.
MAGAZINE
Environment, Science

Nature Cell Biology
999468
Editorial: The Macmillan Building, 4 Crinan Street, London N1 9XW
Tel: 44 02078 434924
Email: cellbio@nature.com
Web site: www.nature.com/ncb
Freq: Monthly Not Audited
MAGAZINE
Biotechnology, Science

Nature Geoscience
986638
Editorial: The Macmillan Building, 4 Crinan Street, London N1 9XW
Tel: 44 02078 334000
Email: geoscience@nature.com
Web site: www.nature.com/ngeo
Freq: Monthly Not Audited
Profile: Journal covering earth science and geosciences, encompassing field work, modelling and theoretical studies. The publication also covers, atmospheric science, biogeochemistry, climate science, geobiology, geochemistry. geoinformatics and remote sensing, geology, geomagnetism and palaeomagnetism, geomorphology, geophysics, glaciology, hydrology and limnology, mineralogy and mineral physics, oceanography, palaeontology, palaeoclimatology and palaeoceanography, petrology, planetary science, seismology, space physics, tectonics and volcanology.
MAGAZINE
Science

Nature Materials
983418
Editorial: The Macmillan Building, 4 Crinan Street, London N1 9XW
Tel: 44 02078 334000
Email: materials@nature.com
Web site: www.nature.com/nmat
Freq: Monthly Not Audited
Profile: Journal focusing on material sciences and engineering. Aimed at academics.
Ad Rate: Full Page Mono £1850.00
Ad Rate: Full Page Colour £2250.00
MAGAZINE
Engineering, Science

Nature Physics
1053658
Editorial: The Macmillan Building, 4 Crinan Street, London N1 9XW
Tel: 44 02078 334000
Email: naturephysics@nature.com
Web site: www.nature.com/nphys/index.html
Freq: Monthly
MAGAZINE
Engineering, Science

Nature Reviews Cancer
998956
Editorial: The Campus, 4 Crinan Street, London N1 9XW **Tel:** 44 02078 433620
Email: nrc@nature.com
Web site: www.nature.com/nrc/index.html
Freq: Monthly Not Audited
MAGAZINE
Oncology

Nature Reviews Cardiology
984339
Editorial: The Campus, The Macmillan Building, 4 Crinan Street, London N1 9XW
Tel: 44 02078 334000
Email: nrcardio@nature.com
Web site: www.nature.com/nrcardio
Freq: Monthly Not Audited
Profile: Journal that covers cardiology content.
MAGAZINE
Cardiology

Nature Reviews Clinical Oncology
995041
Editorial: The Macmillan Building, 4 Crinan Street, London N1 9XW
Tel: 44 02078 334000
Email: nrclinical@nature.com
Web site: www.nature.com/nrclinonc
Freq: Monthly Not Audited
MAGAZINE
Oncology

Nature Reviews Drug Discovery
984753
Editorial: The Macmillan Building, 4 Crinan Street, London N1 9XW
Tel: 44 02078 433620
Email: naturereviews@nature.com
Web site: www.nature.com/nrd/index.html
Freq: Monthly Not Audited
Profile: Journal covering articles on the drug discovery spectrum from disease mechanisms and chemistry through to clinical development. Features research highlights, progress articles, reviews, analysis and perspectives. Aimed at scientists and those working in the drug discovery and development areas.
MAGAZINE
Biotechnology, Pharmaceuticals

nature Reviews Endocrinology
997080
Editorial: The Macmillan Building, 4 Crinan Street, London N1 9XW
Tel: 44 02078 334000
Email: nrendo@nature.com
Web site: www.nature.com/nrendo/index.html
Freq: Monthly
Circ: 571 Not Audited
MAGAZINE
Diabetes

Business Magazines

Nature Reviews Gastroenterology & Hepatology
997081

Editorial: The Macmillan Building, 4 Crinan Street, London N1 9XW
Tel: 44 02078 334000
Email: nrgasthep@nature.com
Web site: www.nature.com/nrgastro/index.html
Freq: Monthly Not Audited
MAGAZINE
Gastroenterology

Nature Reviews Genetics
995758

Editorial: The Macmillan Building, 4 Crinan Street, London N1 9XW
Web site: www.nature.com/nrg
Freq: Monthly Not Audited
MAGAZINE
Science

Nature Reviews Immunology
996560

Editorial: The Macmillan Building, 4 Crinan Street, London N1 9XW
Tel: 44 02078 433620
Email: naturereviews@nature.com
Web site: www.nature.com/nri/index.html
Freq: Monthly Not Audited
Editor: Lucy Bird
MAGAZINE
Allergies

Nature Reviews Nephrology
996142

Editorial: The Macmillan Building, 4 Crinan Street, London N1 9XW
Tel: 44 02078 334000
Email: nrneph@nature.com
Web site: www.nature.com/nrneph/index.html
Freq: Monthly Not Audited
MAGAZINE
Urology

nature Reviews Neurology
985289

Editorial: The Macmillan Building, 4 Crinan Street, London N1 9XW
Tel: 44 02078 334000
Email: nrneuro@nature.com
Web site: www.nature.com/nrneurol/index.html
Freq: Monthly
Profile: Clinical review journal covering the latest updates in neurology.
MAGAZINE
Neurology

nature Reviews Rheumatology
997076

Editorial: The Macmillan Building, 4 Crinan Street, London N1 9XW
Tel: 44 02078 334000
Email: nrrheum@nature.com
Web site: www.nature.com/nrrheum/index.html
Freq: Monthly
Circ: 708 Not Audited
MAGAZINE
Rheumatology

Nature Reviews Urology
985290

Editorial: The Campus, 4 Crinan Street, London N1 9XW **Tel:** 44 02078 334000
Email: nruro@nature.com
Web site: www.nature.com/nrurol/index.html
Freq: Monthly
Circ: 311 Not Audited
Profile: Formerly known as Nature Clinical Practice Urology and launched in November 2004. Serves as a peer-reviewed journal for urologists delivering timely interpretations of key developments reported in the original research, translating the latest findings into clinical practice.
Ad Rate: Full Page Mono £1995.00
Ad Rate: Full Page Colour £2645.00
MAGAZINE
Urology

Nefte Compass
999162

Editorial: Interpark House, 7 Down Street, 3rd Floor, London W1J 7AJ
Tel: 44 02075 182200
Email: energyintelligence@energyintel.com
Web site: http://www.energyintel.com/Pages/About_NCM.aspx
Freq: Weekly Not Audited
Editor: Michael Ritchie
MAGAZINE
Oil

The Negotiator
981075

Editorial: PO Box 624, Epsom, London KT17 9JX **Tel:** 44 08447 453000
Email: mail@thenegotiator.co.uk
Web site: www.the-negotiator.co.uk
Freq: Monthly
Circ: 20000 Not Audited
Profile: Magazine covering issues relating to residential property, lettings, property management and estate agency throughout the UK and increasingly overseas. Aimed at residential sales, letting, managing and property search agents.
Ad Rate: Full Page Colour £1900.00
MAGAZINE
Residential Real Estate

Nephrology Dialysis Transplantation
996597

Editorial: Oxford University Press, Great Clarendon Street, Oxford OX2 6DP
Tel: 44 01865 353779
Email: ndt@ugent.be
Web site: http://ndt.oxfordjournals.org/
Freq: Monthly Not Audited
MAGAZINE
Urology

NetComposites
1072011

Tel: 44 01246 266244
Email: news@netcomosites.com
Web site: http://netcomposites.com/
Freq: Daily
Circ: 6140 Cision Digital Reach
Profile: NetComposites is a 'global research, consultancy and online media company, creating and using innovative technologies to advance the composites industry'. They provide a comprehensive portal with over 10,000 pages of information for composites professionals, including a guide to composites, latest industry news, calendar, glossary and industry directory.
MAGAZINE (ONLINE)
Manufacturing

Network
1069613

Tel: 44 01342 332000
Web site: http://networks.online/
Freq: Monthly
Circ: 3500 Not Audited
MAGAZINE
Electricity, Oil, Water & Sanitation

Neuro News
999484

Editorial: 526 Fulham Road, London SW6 5NR **Tel:** 44 02077 368788
Email: publishing@bibamedical.com
Web site: neuronewsinternational.com
Freq: Quarterly
Circ: 7750 Not Audited
MAGAZINE
Neurology

Neurodegenerative Disease Management
999399

Editorial: Unitec House, 2 Albert Place, London N3 1QB **Tel:** 44 02083 716090
Email: info@futuremedicine.com
Web site: http://www.futuremedicine.com/loi/nmt
Freq: Bi-Monthly Not Audited
MAGAZINE
Neurology

Neurology and Urodynamics
996650

Editorial: Room H26, H-Floor, Royal Hallamshire Hospital, Glossop Road, Sheffield S10 2JF **Tel:** 44 01142 797841
Email: neurourol@btconnect.com

Web site: http://onlinelibrary.wiley.com/journal/10.1002/(ISSN)1520-6777
Freq: Bi-Monthly
Circ: 2214 Not Audited
MAGAZINE
Urology

Neurology Central
1066393

Editorial: Unitec House, 2 Albert Place, London N3 1QB **Tel:** 44 02083 716090
Web site: http://www.neurology-central.com/
Freq: Daily
Circ: 13898 Cision Digital Reach
MAGAZINE (ONLINE)
Neurology

Neuropathology and Applied Neurobiology
996810

Editorial: Wiley-Blackwell, 9600 Garsington Road, Oxford OX4 2DQ
Tel: 44 01865 476212
Email: nan_journal@wiley.com
Web site: http://onlinelibrary.wiley.com/journal/10.1111/(ISSN)1365-2990
Freq: Bi-Monthly Not Audited
MAGAZINE
Neurology

New Business
980041

Tel: 44 02030 868400
Web site: www.newbusiness.co.uk
Freq: Quarterly Not Audited
Editor: Ian Westcott
Profile: New Business magazine is a full colour magazine providing in-depth reports and reviews on all key areas of business including finance, accounting, business planning, marketing and technology. Aimed at entrepreneurs who are looking to develop their companies.
Ad Rate: Full Page Colour £5950.00
MAGAZINE
Business, Corporate Responsibility

New Civil Engineer
980061

Editorial: 3 / 4th Floor, Telephone House, 69-77 Paul Street, London EC2A 4NQ
Tel: 44 02030 332822
Email: nceedit@emap.com
Web site: www.nce.co.uk
Freq: Weekly
Circ: 42805 Not Audited
Editor: Mark Hansford
Profile: Magazine covering UK civil engineering. It features news, analysis and technical information on civil engineering advances and problems, both in UK and abroad. The vast majority of their readers are the 55,000 members of the Institution of Civil Engineers in the UK, working on the design and construction of buildings and structures, transport planning, the management of water resources, energy supply and environmental protection. Launched in 1972 and redesigned in 2007, it targets engineering community, including consultants that design, contractors that build, and other professionals that contribute to the infrastructure.Read by qualified engineers working in all areas of the construction industry.
Ad Rate: Full Page Colour £6400.00
MAGAZINE
Building & Construction, Engineering

New Design
980060

Editorial: Pure Offices, Plato Close, Leamington Spa, Warwick CV34 6WE
Tel: 44 01926 671338
Email: info@newdesignmagazine.co.uk
Web site: www.newdesignmagazine.co.uk
Freq: Bi-Monthly
Circ: 6000 Not Audited
MAGAZINE
Graphic Design

New Energy
1061578

Tel: 44 86208 7059065
Email: editor@ms.giec.ac.cn
Web site: http://www.newenergy.org.cn
Freq: Monthly

Circ: 35001 Not Audited
MAGAZINE
Alternative/Renewable Energy, Carbon Emissions & Trading, Electricity, Energy, Nuclear Power, Oil, Water & Sanitation

New European Economy
999414

Editorial: 245 Shakespeare House, Shakespeare Road, London SW9 8RR
Tel: 44 02079 249908
Email: production@antpublishing.com
Web site: www.neweuropeaneconomy.com
Freq: Quarterly
Circ: 17500 Not Audited
Editor: Michael Ansner
MAGAZINE
Accounting, Banking, Business

New Homes Wales and The South West
982571

Editorial: Mackintosh House, 136 Newport Rd, Cardiff, Cardiff CF24 1DJ
Tel: 44 02920 303000
Email: cardiff.advertiser@virgin.net
Web site: www.cardiffandsouthwalesadvertiser.com/newhomes.htm
Freq: Monthly
Circ: 30000 Not Audited
Profile: Magazine featuring new homes in South Wales and Bristol. Covers articles on all aspects of homes and related features such as design, gardens and furniture.
Ad Rate: Full Page Colour £950.00
MAGAZINE
Property Management & Maintenance

New Houses in Northern Ireland
995809

Tel: 44 02892 652773
Email: donna@bebmedia.com
Web site: www.bebmedia.com
Freq: Quarterly
Circ: 7000 Not Audited
MAGAZINE
Property Management & Maintenance

New Law Journal
980155

Editorial: Lexis House, 30 Farringdon Street, London EC4A 4HH **Tel:** 44 02074 002500
Email: newlaw.journal@lexisnexis.co.uk
Web site: www.newlawjournal.co.uk
Freq: Weekly
Circ: 4000 Not Audited
Editor: Jan Miller
Profile: Publication containing news on topical legal matters, law reports and comprehensive parliamentary coverage. Aimed at solicitors, barristers, legal advisors, legal executives and law students.
Ad Rate: Full Page Colour £1325.00
MAGAZINE
Litigation

New London Quarterly
983711

Editorial: 26 Store Street, London WC1E 7BT **Tel:** 44 02076 364044
Email: enquiries@newlondonquarterly.com
Web site: www.newlondonquarterly.com
Freq: Quarterly
Circ: 3500 Not Audited
Editor: David Taylor
Profile: The New London Quarterly is a magazine covering the London property market. Aimed at architects, developers and property consultants.Previous title: The London Property Review
Ad Rate: Full Page Colour £1000.00
MAGAZINE
Architecture & Design, Building & Construction, Interior Design, Residential Real Estate

New Power
985138

Tel: 44 01273 814795
Email: office@newpower.info
Web site: http://www.newpower.info/
Freq: Monthly Not Audited
Editor: Janet Wood
Profile: New Power magazine is aimed at UK power station developers (CCGTS, coal, nuclear, renewables), energy and environmental regulators, energy financiers, UK power utility sector, transmission, supply

and distribution companies. Regular features: New UK power station monitor updates on all planned power stations in the UK above 10 MW
MAGAZINE
Alternative/Renewable Energy, Electricity, Oil

New Scientist   979907
Editorial: 110 Holborn, 2nd Floor, London WC1V 6EU **Tel:** 44 02086 523500
Email: news@newscientist.com
Web site: www.newscientist.com
Freq: Weekly
Circ: 126320 Not Audited
Editor: Sumit Paul-Choudhury
Profile: Magazine reporting on the latest science and technology news, stories and facts. It provides analysis opinion and jobs, enabling readers to stay up to date with the latest developments in the field. News coverage includes in depth reports and exclusives, emerging technology and editorial comment. It also includes interviews with high profile personalities, essays, book reviews, bestseller lists and political humour. First published in 1956. It targets business decision-makers and consumers from diverse backgrounds. Read by people in business, finance, government and industry.
Ad Rate: Full Page Mono £5500.00
Ad Rate: Full Page Colour £9625.00
MAGAZINE
Science

New Start   981272
Editorial: 1 George Leigh Street, Manchester M4 5DL **Tel:** 44 01625 614000
Email: editor@newstartmag.co.uk
Web site: http://newstartmag.co.uk/
Freq: Monthly
Circ: 15791 Cision Digital Reach
Editor: Clare Goff
Profile: Online magazine covering all aspects of sustainable communities and regeneration including development, community cohesion, urban design, education and housing. Aimed at people working within central government, regional development agencies, Housing associations, trusts, private consultancy, charities and voluntary organisations. Regular features: Debate A debate section on a topical issue which involves readers opinions.; Learning Curve A report on good practice.; On Location A report on a regeneration project.
MAGAZINE (ONLINE)
Public Sector

New Steel Construction   985168
Editorial: 7 Linden Close, Tunbridge Wells, Tunbridge Wells TN4 8HH
Tel: 44 01892 524455
Email: martin@newsteelconstruction.com
Web site: www.newsteelconstruction.com
Freq: Monthly
Circ: 4000 Not Audited
Editor: Nick Barrett
Profile: New Steel Construction is a magazine focusing on the use of steel in construction.
Ad Rate: Full Page Colour £1600.00
MAGAZINE
Building & Construction

News on the Block   982567
Editorial: 129 Finchley Road, London NW3 6HY **Tel:** 44 02035 388875
Email: editor@newsontheblock.com
Web site: www.newsontheblock.com
Freq: Bi-Monthly
Circ: 8292 Not Audited
Profile: Magazine covering leasehold property management and law.
Ad Rate: Full Page Colour £1500.00
MAGAZINE
Property Management & Maintenance, Residential Real Estate

News-Medical.Net   986888
Editorial: Fence House, Fence Ave, Macclesfield, Macclesfield SK10 1LT
Tel: 44 01625 615111
Email: editor@news-medical.net
Web site: http://www.news-medical.net

Freq: Daily
Circ: 1625587 Cision Digital Reach
MAGAZINE (ONLINE)
Medical Technology, Pharmaceuticals, Science

The Next Women   985492
Editorial: 10-14 Accomodation Road, London NW11 8ED
Web site: www.thenextwomen.com
Freq: Daily
Circ: 10414 Cision Digital Reach
Profile: Website covering women business. The Next Women business magazine covers new and growing businesses which are founded, run or invested in by women.
MAGAZINE (ONLINE)
Business

NFP Techno   999630
Editorial: 2 Old College Court, 29 Priory Street, Ware SG12 0DE
Tel: 44 03707 369369
Email: editor@nfptechno.org.uk
Web site: https://www.conferencehouse.co.uk/nfp-techno-news/
Freq: Bi-Weekly
MAGAZINE (ONLINE)
Business, Corporate Responsibility

NFU Online   984757
Tel: 44 02476 858500
Web site: www.nfuonline.com
Freq: Daily
Circ: 52533 Cision Digital Reach
Profile: Website of the NFU, covering all aspects of farming and agriculture including crops, dairy, horticulture, livestock, poultry, pigs, sugar and potatoes. Aimed at those within the farming and agricultural sector.
MAGAZINE (ONLINE)
Animal Farming

NFU Poultry   988047
Tel: 44 02476 858500
Web site: www.nfuonline.com
Freq: Bi-Monthly
MAGAZINE
Animal Farming

nhsManagers.net   999469
Editorial: 100 Pall Mall, St James, London SW1Y 5HP **Tel:** 44 02076 648711
Email: contact@nhsmanagers.net
Web site: www.nhsmanagers.net
Freq: Monthly
Circ: 100000 Not Audited
Editor: Roy Lilley
MAGAZINE
Health Administration, Healthcare Industry

Nikkei Construction   982926
Editorial: Barnards Inn, 86 Fetter Lane, London EC4A 1EN **Tel:** 44 02074 006700
Web site: http://www.nikkeibp.com/adinfo/printmedia/ncr.html
Freq: Bi-Weekly
Circ: 23362 Not Audited
Profile: Magazine providing coverage of overseas and domestic engineering projects in the form of direct reports. Also includes exclusive information from overseas publications. Aimed at civil engineers and related professionals in government offices, construction consultancy offices and construction companies.
Ad Rate: Full Page Mono £459000.00
Ad Rate: Full Page Colour £569000.00
MAGAZINE
Building & Construction, Engineering

Nikkei Ecology   984682
Editorial: 57-61 Charterhouse Street, London EC1M 6HA **Tel:** 44 07900 885456
Email: info@nikkeibp.co.uk
Web site: http://www.nikkeibp.com/adinfo/printmedia/eco.html
Freq: Monthly
Circ: 7355 Not Audited
Profile: Magazine reporting on the most up-to-date trends in corporate management, new product/technology development and social systems as they relate to the

environment. Aimed at managers in environment-related divisions, new product development, planning and marketing divisions as well as those within central government, public bodies and non-governmental organisations.
Ad Rate: Full Page Mono £420000.00
Ad Rate: Full Page Colour £580000.00
MAGAZINE
Environment

Nikon Pro   988897
Editorial: 85 Strand, London WC2R 0DW
Tel: 44 02075 508000
Email: nikonpro@cedarcom.co.uk
Web site: www.cedarcom.co.uk/our-work/nikon-pro.html
Freq: Quarterly
Circ: 30000 Not Audited
Profile: Magazine featuring information on Nikon products and a showcase for the work of professional photographers. Aimed at professional photographers.
MAGAZINE
Photography

Nitrogen + Syngas   984692
Editorial: Southbank House, Blackprince Road, London SE1 7SJ
Tel: 44 02077 932563
Web site: http://www.bcinsight.com/nitrogen_syngas.asp
Freq: Bi-Monthly Not Audited
MAGAZINE
Chemicals, Oil

NMBS News   987810
Tel: 44 01495 740050
Email: nmbs@constructivemedia.co.uk
Web site: www.constructivemedia.co.uk
Freq: Quarterly Not Audited
Editor: Roger Whittington
Profile: Magazine of the NMBS trade association. Includes news, products and information.
Ad Rate: Full Page Colour £850.00
MAGAZINE
Building & Construction

NMR in Biomedicine   996485
Editorial: Department of Basic Medical Sciences, St George's Hospital Medical School, University of London, Cranmer Terrace, London SW17 0RE
Web site: onlinelibrary.wiley.com/journal/10.1002/(ISSN)1099-1492
Freq: Monthly Not Audited
MAGAZINE
Biotechnology, Science

No 2 Nuclear Power   982897
Editorial: 24 Parkhead View, Edinburgh EH11 4RT **Tel:** 44 01314 441445
Web site: www.no2nuclearpower.org.uk
Freq: Daily
Circ: 13875 Cision Digital Reach
Editor: Peter Roche
MAGAZINE (ONLINE)
Nuclear Power

Noise Bulletin   985452
Editorial: The Garth, Rockshaw Road, Merstham, Redhill RH1 3DB
Tel: 44 01737 642283
Email: enquiries@empublishing.co.uk
Web site: www.empublishing.co.uk/noise/index.htm
Freq: Monthly Not Audited
Editor: Jack Pease
Profile: Noise Bulletin is a monthly newsletter covering all the latest on environmental noise, UK environmental health, nuisance and acoustics.
MAGAZINE
Environment

NOOZZ.com   983764
Editorial: 26 York Street, Mayfair, London W1U 6PZ
Email: research@noozz.com
Web site: www.noozz.com
Freq: Daily
Circ: 11370 Cision Digital Reach

Profile: Website focusing on individual emerging markets in the Middle East and providing a blend of news, commentary, analysis, research and business services.
MAGAZINE (ONLINE)
Business, Emerging Markets

North East Contact   998612
Editorial: Unit 1, Bearl Farm, Stockfield, Stocksfield NE43 7AJ **Tel:** 44 01661 844115
Email: submissions@neechamber.co.uk
Web site: http://www.necontact.co.uk/
Freq: Bi-Monthly
Circ: 7000 Not Audited
MAGAZINE
Business

North Sea Reporter   985154
Editorial: Suite 1636, Kemp House, 152 City Road, London EC1V 2NX
Web site: http://www.klenergypublishing.com/
Freq: Weekly Not Audited
Editor: Meg Leitch
Profile: Newsletter providing a comprehensive picture of upstream oil and gas activity in the North Sea, including rig market and exploration activity, engineering, fabrication, field development, production figures and company news, such as deals and acquisitions.
MAGAZINE
Oil

North Sea Rig Report   985059
Editorial: 2nd Floor, The Exchange No. 1, Market Street, Aberdeen AB11 5PJ
Tel: 44 01224 597800
Web site: www.ihs.com/products/north-sea-rig-report.html
Freq: Monthly
Circ: 150 Not Audited
Profile: Publication containing news, market analysis, and short-term supply and demand forecasts on the offshore mobile drilling rigs industry in Northwest Europe. Aimed at oil, gas exploration and production companies, drilling contractors, oil industry service companies and the financial industry.
MAGAZINE
Engineering, Oil

North West Business Insider   995965
Editorial: 8th Floor, Boulton House, 17-21 Chorlton Street, Manchester M1 3HY
Tel: 44 01619 079711
Email: insider@newsco.com
Web site: www.insidermedia.com/northwest
Freq: Monthly
Circ: 13033 Not Audited
MAGAZINE
Business, Corporate Responsibility, Finance, Mergers & Acquisitions, Small and Medium Business

Northern Builder   985859
Tel: 44 02892 612990
Email: northernbuilder@kmpltd.co.uk
Web site: www.northernbuilder.co.uk
Freq: Bi-Monthly
Circ: 5300 Not Audited
Editor: Adam Hassin
Profile: Magazine with in-depth coverage on all sections of the building industry in Northern Ireland. Read by architects, builders, quantity surveyors and specifiers.
Ad Rate: Full Page Colour £1045.00
MAGAZINE
Building & Construction

Northern Communications   1061854
Tel: 44 86242 4506712
Email: lnjtkj@163.com
Freq: Monthly Not Audited
MAGAZINE
Architecture & Design, Building & Construction, Public Sector

The Northern Farmer   988048
Editorial: Newsquest (North East) Ltd, PO Box 14, Priestgate, Darlington, Darlington DL1 1NF **Tel:** 44 01325 381313

Business Magazines

Email: mike.bridgen@nne.co.uk
Web site: www.northernfarmer.co.uk
Freq: Monthly
Circ: 15000 Not Audited
Profile: The Northern Farmer is the monthly farming news and information newspaper for the people of the North of England.
Ad Rate: Full Page Colour £1602.00
MAGAZINE
Animal Farming

Northern Ireland Veterinary Today 983177
Editorial: Penton House, 38 Heron Road, Sydenham Business Park, Belfast BT3 9LE
Tel: 44 02890 457457
Email: info@pentongroup.com
Web site: www.pentongroup.com/veterinary-today
Freq: Quarterly
Circ: 2000 Not Audited
Editor: Russell Campbell
Profile: Magazine carrying news, features and profiles on the veterinary profession. Aimed at vets, veterinary nurses and final year students in Northern Ireland.
Ad Rate: Full Page Mono £1100.00
Ad Rate: Full Page Colour £1450.00
MAGAZINE
Animal Farming

NQ Magazine 983597
Editorial: Unit 3 Block A, Kingfisher Heights, Bramwell Way, London E16 2GQ
Tel: 44 02072 166444
Web site: www.pqaccountant.com
Freq: Bi-Monthly
Circ: 13000 Not Audited
Editor: Graham Hambly
Profile: Magazine covering issues affecting newly qualified accountants.
Ad Rate: Full Page Colour £5800.00
MAGAZINE
Accounting

nubricks.com 998792
Editorial: 24 Jack's Place, Corbet Place, Spitalfields, London E1 6NN
Tel: 44 02079 527653
Email: ivan.radford@leadgalaxy.com
Web site: http://www.nubricks.com/
Freq: Daily
Circ: 6427 Cision Digital Reach
Editor: Ivan Radford
MAGAZINE (ONLINE)
Finance, Interior Design, Residential Real Estate, Urban Planning & Development

Nuclear Engineering International 981306
Editorial: 2 Maidstone Road, Foots Cray, Sidcup, London DA14 5HZ
Tel: 44 02082 697700
Web site: www.neimagazine.com
Freq: Monthly
Circ: 2371 Not Audited
Profile: Nuclear Engineering International is a monthly publication on civil nuclear power owned by Progressive Media Group Ltd. It contains research and development, world news reviews, events and feature articles. First published in 1956. Nuclear Engineering International is aimed at buyers and specifiers within the nuclear engineering industry.This magazine contains the following regular sections: Editor's viewNews CommentPower market developments SafetyNDE & inspection, diagnostics Outage managementThis magazine contains the following supplements/editions: NEI ChinaNEI Handbook
Ad Rate: Full Page Mono £2160.00
Ad Rate: Full Page Colour £2660.00
MAGAZINE
Engineering, Nuclear Power

Nuclear Future 982918
Editorial: CK International House, 1-6 Yarmouth Place, London W1J 7BU
Tel: 44 02034 754701
Email: communications@nuclearinst.com
Web site: http://www.nuclearinst.com/NuclearFuture
Freq: Bi-Monthly

Circ: 2000 Not Audited
MAGAZINE
Nuclear Power

Nurse Education in Practice 999843
Editorial: PO Box 66, Hull HU10 7XS
Tel: 44 01482 653828
Email: nep@elsevier.com
Web site: www.elsevier.com/wps/find/journaldescription.cws_home/623062/description
Freq: Bi-Monthly Not Audited
Editor: Karen Holland
MAGAZINE
Nursing/Nurses

Nurse Education Today 985185
Editorial: PO Box 66, Hull HU10 7XS
Tel: 44 01482 653828
Web site: www.elsevier.com/wps/find/journaldescription.cws_home/623061/description
Freq: Bi-Monthly Not Audited
Editor: William Lauder
Profile: International journal covering all aspects of nursing education including high quality original research and reviews, debate and discussion in nursing, midwifery and health professional education. The journal welcomes scholarly contributions which are local, national or international in scope but are of wide interest and reflect the diversity of people, health and education systems worldwide. The journal also publishes reviews of learning and teaching media and books as well as works of research, policy, theory and philosophy of health professional education. First published in 1980, the publication has an average of 124 pages per issue. Read by nurses, nurse tutors and nursing academics within the UK.
MAGAZINE
Nursing/Nurses

Nurse Prescribing 984377
Editorial: St Jude's Church, Dulwich Road, London SE24 0PB **Tel:** 44 02077 385454
Email: np@markallengroup.com
Web site: www.nurseprescribing.com
Freq: Monthly
Circ: 2500 Not Audited
Profile: Magazine covering healthcare and nursing including articles on the clinical, practical, legal, professional and policy aspects of nurse prescribing as well as covering research. Aimed at nurse prescribers, those who make clinical decisions that affect patient medication regimens and pharmacists.
Ad Rate: Full Page Colour £1900.00
MAGAZINE
Nursing/Nurses

Nurse Researcher 985218
Editorial: The Heights, 59-65 Lowlands Road, Harrow, London HA1 3AW
Tel: 44 02084 231066
Email: rcndirectjournalsteam@rcn.org.uk
Web site: rcnpublishing.com/journal/nr
Freq: Bi-Monthly
Circ: 2658 Not Audited
Editor: Liz Halcomb; **Editor:** Julie Sylvester
MAGAZINE
Nursing/Nurses

Nursing & Residential Care 984709
Editorial: St Jude's Church, Dulwich Road, London SE24 0PB **Tel:** 44 02077 385454
Email: nrc@markallengroup.com
Web site: www.nursingresidentialcare.com
Freq: Monthly Not Audited
MAGAZINE
Nursing/Nurses

Nursing Children and Young People 981207
Editorial: The Heights, 59-65 Lowlands Road, Harrow, London HA1 3AW
Tel: 44 02084 231066
Email: chris.walker@rcnpublishing.co.uk
Web site: http://rcnpublishing.com/journal/ncyp

Freq: Monthly
Circ: 9462 Not Audited
Editor: Christine Walker
Profile: Journal covering all aspects of child health and paediatric nursing with particular emphasis on clinical practice. Aimed at paediatric nurses caring for children and young people in hospitals and in the community.
Ad Rate: Full Page Colour £2250.00
MAGAZINE
Nursing/Nurses, Pediatrics

Nursing in Critical Care 985219
Editorial: 9600 Garsington Road, Oxford OX4 2DQ **Tel:** 44 08458 340370
Email: niccoffice@wiley.com
Web site: http://onlinelibrary.wiley.com/journal/10.1111/(ISSN)1478-5153
Freq: Bi-Monthly
Circ: 2063 Not Audited
Editor: John Albarran; **Editor:** Julie Scholes
Profile: Journal of the British Association of Critical Care Nurses. Contains clinical and research papers supporting critical and acute nursing. Average Pages per Issue: 56. Read by intensive and critical care nurses and nursing lecturers.
Ad Rate: Full Page Mono £550.00
Ad Rate: Full Page Colour £950.00
MAGAZINE
Anesthesiology, Nursing/Nurses

Nursing in Practice 981202
Editorial: Bastion House, 140 London Wall, London EC2Y 5DN **Tel:** 44 02072 140500
Email: nip@cogora.com
Web site: www.nursinginpractice.com
Freq: Bi-Monthly
Circ: 10038 Not Audited
Profile: Magazine providing clinical updates, news, views and features about primary care nursing. Includes features on asthma, diabetes, cardiology, wound care, neurology, clinical governance, travel medicine, vaccination, mother and baby, incontinence, allergy management and contraception. Aimed at practice, district, school and community nurses, midwives and health visitors.
Ad Rate: Full Page Mono £2950.00
Ad Rate: Full Page Colour £3950.00
MAGAZINE
Nursing/Nurses

Nursing Management (UK) 981203
Editorial: The Heights, 59-65 Lowlands Road, Harrow, London HA1 3AW
Tel: 44 02088 723166
Web site: http://journals.rcni.com
Freq: Monthly
Circ: 5951 Not Audited
MAGAZINE
Nursing/Nurses

Nursing Older People 981204
Editorial: The Heights, 59-65 Lowlands Road, Harrow, London HA1 3AW
Tel: 44 02084 231066
Web site: www.nursingolderpeople.co.uk
Freq: Monthly
Circ: 8504 Not Audited
Editor: Lisa Berry
Profile: Journal containing clinical articles, features and news on the practice of nursing for older people and is commited to inform, support and educate nurses in the pursuit of excellence in patient care. Previous called Elderly Care, the publication was first published in 1993 and has an average of 40 pages per Issue. Press Day: 1st day of the month. Aimed at nursing staff working in hospitals, intermediate and rehabilitative care, the community and care homes.
Ad Rate: Full Page Colour £2299.00
MAGAZINE
Geriatrics, Nursing/Nurses

Nursing Philosophy 995873
Email: nup@wiley.com
Web site: http://onlinelibrary.wiley.com/journal/10.1111/(ISSN)1466-769X
Freq: Quarterly Not Audited

Editor: Derek Sellman
MAGAZINE
Nursing/Nurses

Nursing Standard 981205
Editorial: The Heights, 59-65 Lowlands Road, Harrow, London HA1 3AW
Tel: 44 02084 231066
Email: news@rcni.com
Web site: http://rcnpublishing.com/journal/ns
Freq: Weekly
Circ: 37896 Not Audited
Editor: Graham Scott
Profile: Journal covering issues affecting nursing practice and career choices. Aimed at training and qualified nurses, health visitors and specialist advisors.
Ad Rate: Full Page Colour £3100.00
MAGAZINE
Nursing/Nurses

Nursing Times 981206
Editorial: 3 / 4th Floor, Telephone House, 69-77 Paul Street, London EC2A 4NQ
Tel: 44 02030 332600
Web site: www.nursingtimes.net
Freq: Weekly
Circ: 12000 Not Audited
Editor: Jenni Middleton
Profile: Publication containing news and features on management, clinical subjects and nursing education. Covers psychiatric, theatre and children's nursing, midwifery, community nursing and infection control. Read by registered and student nurses, midwives and health visitors in hospitals and the community.
Ad Rate: Full Page Colour £2625.00
MAGAZINE
Nursing/Nurses

OAG Flight Guide 999065
Editorial: 1 Capability Green, Luton, Luton LU1 3LU **Tel:** 44 01582 695050
Email: contactus@oag.com
Web site: www.oag.com
Freq: Monthly
Circ: 15514 Not Audited
MAGAZINE
Aviation

Obesity Reviews 999010
Editorial: Charles Darwin 2, 107 Gray's Inn Road, London WC1 X8TZ
Tel: 44 02076 852580
Email: obr@worldobesity.org
Web site: http://onlinelibrary.wiley.com/journal/10.1111/(ISSN)1467-789X
Freq: Monthly Not Audited
MAGAZINE
Cardiology, Diabetes, Gastroenterology

Obs Gynae & Midwifery News 986057
Editorial: 4 Greengate, Cardale Park, Harrogate HG3 1GY **Tel:** 44 08448 582890
Email: ogmn@barkerbrooks.co.uk
Web site: www.ogpnews.com
Freq: Quarterly
Circ: 7000 Not Audited
Profile: Magazine devoted to new products and innovations in obstetrics, gynaecology and midwifery. Aimed at medical and surgical personnel.
Ad Rate: Full Page Colour £900.00
MAGAZINE
Obstetrics & Gynecology (OB/GYN)

The Obstetrician & Gynaecologist (TOG) 995899
Editorial: Royal College of Obstetricians and Gynaecologists, 27 Sussex Place, Regent's Park, London NW1 4RG
Tel: 44 02077 726200
Email: tog@rcog.org.uk
Web site: www.rcog.org.uk/tog
Freq: Quarterly
Circ: 11213 Not Audited
MAGAZINE
Obstetrics & Gynecology (OB/GYN)

Obstetrics, Gynaecology and Reproductive Medicine · 995908
Editorial: The Boulevard, Langford Lane, Kidlington OX5 1GB **Tel:** 44 01865 843154
Email: journals@medicinepublishing.co.uk
Web site: http://www.obstetrics-gynaecologyandreproductivemedicine journal.co.uk
Freq: Monthly
Circ: 602 Not Audited
MAGAZINE
Obstetrics & Gynecology (OB/GYN)

Occupational and Environmental Medicine (OEM) · 980960
Editorial: BMJ Journals Department, BMA House, Tavistock Square, London WC1H 9JR **Tel:** 44 02073 836795
Email: info.oem@bmj.com
Web site: www.oem.bmj.com
Freq: Monthly
Circ: 1600 Not Audited
MAGAZINE
Health Administration

Occupational Health & Wellbeing · 980793
Editorial: Quadrant House, The Quadrant, Sutton, London SM2 5AS
Tel: 44 02086 524669
Web site: www.personneltoday.com/occupational-health-and-wellbeing/
Freq: Monthly
Circ: 1870 Not Audited
Editor: Noel O'Reilly
MAGAZINE
Health & Safety, Health Administration

Occupational Health [at work] · 985014
Editorial: Office Suite 1(i), Highstone House, 165 High Street, Barnet EN5 5SU
Tel: 44 03450 176986
Email: editorial@atworkpartnership.co.uk
Web site: www.atworkpartnership.co.uk/occupationalhealthatwork/index.php
Freq: Bi-Monthly Not Audited
Editor: John Ballard
Profile: Occupational Health [at Work] is a journal covering the science, law and practice of occupational health. Designed to bring together all the occupational health disciplines, it provides occupational health physicians, nurses, occupational hygiene and health and safety professionals with a dependable single source of expertly written legal, practical and management occupational health information. It is published six times a year by The At Work Partnership Ltd. First published in 2004. Occupational Health [at Work] is aimed at occupational health professionals including occupational health physicians, OH nurses and hygienists.
MAGAZINE
Occupational Therapy & Rehabilitation

Occupational Medicine · 985391
Editorial: c/o Society of Occupational Medicine, Hamilton House, Mabledon Place, London WC1H 9BB
Email: omjournal@som.org.uk
Web site: http://occmed.oxfordjournals.org/
Freq: Bi-Monthly Not Audited
Editor: John Hobson
Profile: Journal covering all aspects of occupational medicine. Aimed at full-time occupational physicians and GPs with a part-time appointment in industry.
Ad Rate: Full Page Mono £779.00
Ad Rate: Full Page Colour £1418.00
MAGAZINE
Occupational Therapy & Rehabilitation

Occupational Pensions · 980157
Editorial: 15 Copper Beech Close, London HP3 0DG **Tel:** 44 01442 259349
Email: op@lexisnexis.co.uk
Web site: http://www.lexisnexis.co.uk/store/uk/Occupational-Pensions/product
Freq: Monthly Not Audited
Editor: Colin Sherwood

Profile: Journal covering occupational pensions, specialising in case studies and surveys of named pension schemes and legal guidance articles. Aimed at pensions, personnel and finance managers, company secretaries, trade union officials, professional advisers and trustees.
MAGAZINE
Fund Management

Occupational Therapy News (OTnews) · 983811
Editorial: 106-114 Borough High Street, Southwark, London SE1 1LB
Tel: 44 02073 576480
Email: editorial@cot.co.uk
Web site: http://www.cot.co.uk/ot-news/otnews
Freq: Monthly
Circ: 30524 Not Audited
Editor: Tracey Samuels
MAGAZINE
Occupational Therapy & Rehabilitation

Ocular Immunology and Inflammation · 995456
Tel: 44 02070 175540
Web site: http://www.tandfonline.com/toc/ioii20/current#.VfAXfpMeqWM
Freq: Bi-Monthly Not Audited
MAGAZINE
Ophthalmology & Optometry

ODDIZZI · 999230
Tel: 44 02033 978193
Email: info@oddizzi.com
Web site: www.oddizzi.com
Freq: Daily
Circ: 34811 Cision Digital Reach
MAGAZINE (ONLINE)
Education

Office Equipment News · 994649
Editorial: Office Solutions Media Limited, Pipers Business Centre, 220 Vale Road, Tonbridge TN9 1SP **Tel:** 44 01732 441850
Web site: www.oenmagazine.com
Freq: Monthly
Circ: 10000 Not Audited
Editor: Michelle Ryder
MAGAZINE
Office Supplies

Office Products International · 983168
Editorial: Office Products International Ltd, 2nd Floor, 112 Clerkenwell Road, London EC1M 5SA **Tel:** 44 02078 412950
Email: editorial@opi.net
Web site: www.opi.net
Freq: Monthly
Circ: 11000 Not Audited
Editor: Heike Dieckmann
Profile: Guide to the international office products industry.
Ad Rate: Full Page Colour £4200.00
MAGAZINE
Office Supplies

Offshore Design & Engineering Equipment · 998007
Editorial: 192 High Street, Tonbridge, Kent, Tonbridge TN9 1BE **Tel:** 44 01732 370340
Web site: http://offshoreeuropejournal.com/
Freq: Bi-Monthly
Circ: 2306 Cision Digital Reach
Editor: Aaron Blutstein
MAGAZINE (ONLINE)
Alternative/Renewable Energy, Engineering, Oil

Offshore Red · 983460
Editorial: 19 Heathman's Road, London SW6 4TJ **Tel:** 44 02071 480188
Web site: www.os-red.com
Freq: Monthly
Circ: 2500 Not Audited
MAGAZINE
Accounting

Offshore Technology Focus · 996682
Editorial: John Carpenter House, John Carpenter Street, London EC4Y 0AN
Tel: 44 02079 366400
Email: onlinemags@nridigital.com
Web site: http://www.nridigital.com/offshore-technology-focus.html
Freq: Monthly
Circ: 8084 Cision Digital Reach
MAGAZINE (ONLINE)
Oil

Offshore Wind Engineering · 988764
Editorial: Pure Offices, Plato Close, Leamington Spa, Warwick CV34 6WE
Tel: 44 01926 671338
Email: info@energyengineering.co.uk
Web site: www.energyengineering.co.uk/OFFSHOREWINDENGINEERING.htm
Freq: Quarterly
Circ: 4500 Not Audited
MAGAZINE
Alternative/Renewable Energy

Offshore Wind Journal · 986760
Editorial: Mitre House, 66 Abbey Road, Enfield EN1 2QN **Tel:** 44 02083 641551
Email: info@rivieramm.com
Web site: http://www.owjonline.com/index.htm
Freq: Quarterly
Circ: 4250 Not Audited
Editor: David Foxwell
Profile: Magazine covering the offshore wind sector. First published in June 2012. Aimed at people interested in wind farm development, including directors and managers at all levels in companies and organisation associated with the offshore wind industry, government agencies, energy and utility companies, turbine manufacturers, marine operators, port authorities, finance and insurance companies, consultants, vessel owners, designers and builders, and companies involved in operation and maintenance.
MAGAZINE
Alternative/Renewable Energy

offshore-technology.com · 984373
Editorial: John Carpenter House, John Carpenter Street, London EC4Y 0AN
Tel: 44 02077 534200
Email: onlineeditorial@kable.co.uk
Web site: http://www.offshore-technology.com
Freq: Daily
Circ: 65458 Cision Digital Reach
Profile: Website covering offshore technology. The offshore-technology.com website focuses on current projects and information for the offshore oil and gas industry. Includes projects, products and services, exhibitions and conferences and a complete listing of relevant organisations.
MAGAZINE (ONLINE)
Oil

Oil & Gas Technology · 983656
Editorial: Cavendish Group Ltd, 5th Floor, Roman Wall House, 1-2 Crutched Friars, London EC3N 2NB **Tel:** 44 02037 944581
Email: editor@oilandgastechnology.net
Web site: www.oilandgastechnology.net
Freq: Quarterly
Circ: 10000 Not Audited
Profile: Website focusing on the key areas of the fossil fuel business. It addresses the technical challenges facing China's oil and gas sector examining the latest innovations developed in the west. Coverage includes topical developments and the latest technologies.
MAGAZINE
Oil

Oil and Energy Trends · 980897
Editorial: The Atrium, Southern Gate, Chichester, Chichester PO19 8SQ
Tel: 44 01243 770175
Web site: www.oilandenergytrends.com

Freq: Monthly Not Audited
Profile: Journal containing international energy statistics and analysis of oil exploration and production, gas production, coal production, steel production, electricity production, refinery throughput, oil demand, oil prices, international commodities trade, tanker movements and freight rates.
MAGAZINE
Oil

Oil Installer · 984738
Editorial: Caledonian House, Tatton Street, Knutsford, Knutsford WA16 6AG
Tel: 44 01565 653283
Web site: www.oilinstaller.co.uk
Circ: 11000 Not Audited
Editor: Jane Hughes
Profile: Oil Installer is a magazine providing information on training, legislation, technical topics and environmental issues to ensure that its readers are kept fully up to date with what's happening in the oil industry. Oil Installer is aimed at installers who are committed to ensuring that each and every oil installation adheres to only the very highest of standards.
Ad Rate: Full Page Colour £3500.00
MAGAZINE
Oil

Oil Market Intelligence · 900790
Editorial: Interpark House, 7 Down Street, 3rd Floor, London W1J 7AJ
Tel: 44 02075 182200
Email: energyintelligence@energyintel.com
Web site: www.energyintel.com/Pages/About_OMI.aspx
Freq: Monthly Not Audited
MAGAZINE
Oil

Oil Review Africa · 988886
Editorial: University House, 11-13 Lower Grosvenor Place, London SW1W 0EX
Tel: 44 02078 347676
Web site: www.oilreviewafrica.com
Circ: 8000 Not Audited
Profile: Oil Review Africa is a magazine published six times a year that covers oil exploration and production, as well as upstream and downstream petroleum industry across Africa. Each issue contains industry news, country reports, sector surveys, technical feature articles, exhibition and conference reviews and news of the latest industry developments and product launches. First published in 2006. Oil Review Africa is aimed at management and technical readership within national and international oil companies.
MAGAZINE
Oil

Oil Review Middle East · 981138
Editorial: University House, 11-13 Lower Grosvenor Place, London SW1W 0EX
Tel: 44 02078 347676
Email: oil@alaincharles.com
Web site: www.oilreviewmiddleeast.com
Freq: Bi-Monthly
Circ: 9057 Not Audited
Profile: Oil Review Middle East is a magazine covering the exploration and production, upstream and downstream petroleum industry from the Gulf Corporation Council states and Iran to North Africa and the Caspian. It features major projects, specific industry sector profiles, country reports, exhibition previews and product reviews. It is owned by Alain Charles Publishing Ltd and is published eight times a year. Oil Review Middle East is aimed at the regional oil, gas and petrochemicals industries and the companies supplying these industries.
Ad Rate: Full Page Mono £4070.00
Ad Rate: Full Page Colour £5990.00
MAGAZINE
Oil

Oilfield Technology · 985007
Editorial: 15 South Street, Farnham, Farnham GU9 7QU **Tel:** 44 01252 718999
Email: enquiries@oilfieldtechnology.com

Business Magazines

Web site: https://www.oilfieldtechnology.com/
Freq: Monthly
Circ: 11050 Not Audited
Editor: David Bizley
Profile: Publication that covers the latest news and developments in oilfield technology. It features industry insight via a combination of news, reviews, comments, analysis, regional reports, case studies and technical articles.
Ad Rate: Full Page Colour £4550.00
MAGAZINE
Oil

Oilprice.com 987039
Tel: 44 02032 394080
Email: admin@oilprice.com
Web site: www.oilprice.com
Freq: Weekly
Circ: 1534195 Cision Digital Reach
Editor: Heather Maher
Profile: Website covering oil, gas, alternative energy and geopolitics.
MAGAZINE (ONLINE)
Carbon Emissions & Trading, Oil

Oils & Fats International 983570
Editorial: Quartz House, 20 Clarendon Road, Redhill, Redhill RH1 1GX
Tel: 44 01737 855000
Email: oilsandfats@quartzltd.com
Web site: http://www.ofimagazine.com/
Freq: Bi-Monthly
Circ: 6500 Not Audited
Editor: Serena Lim
Profile: Oils & Fats International is a publication containing general, biotechnology, transport/logistic and oleochemicals/surfactants news as well as a market review on production and supply and demand trends affecting oils and oilseeds trade. It is published eight times a year by Quartz Business Media Ltd. First published in 1984. Oils & Fats International is aimed at buyers and specifiers of a wide range of products and services relating to the edible oils and fats industry.
Ad Rate: Full Page Mono £2871.00
Ad Rate: Full Page Colour £4293.00
MAGAZINE
Manufacturing

Oldham Property News 998476
Editorial: Basepoint Business Centre, Crab Apple Way, Vale Park, Evesham WR11 1GP
Tel: 44 01386 764911
Email: info@oldhamproperty.com
Web site: www.oldhamproperty.com
Freq: Daily
Circ: 787 Cision Digital Reach
Editor: Vernon Pethard
MAGAZINE (ONLINE)
Property Management & Maintenance

OMSIDER 1061547
Tel: 44 45893 98833
Email: info@stibozone.com
Web site: http://www.omsider.com/Default.aspx?ID=147 Not Audited
MAGAZINE
Marketing

Oncology Central 998316
Editorial: Unitec House, 2 Albert Place, London N3 1QB Tel: 44 02083 716090
Web site: www.oncology-central.com
Freq: Daily
Circ: 16827 Cision Digital Reach
Editor: Emily Brown
MAGAZINE (ONLINE)
Oncology

ONdrugDelivery 996181
Editorial: The Candlemakers, West Street, Lewes, Lewes BN7 2NZ
Tel: 44 01273 472828
Email: info@ondrugdelivery.com
Web site: www.ondrugdelivery.com
Freq: Monthly
Circ: 53523 Not Audited
MAGAZINE
Biotechnology, Pharmaceuticals

One Big Society 995331
Email: hannah.stevenson@ai-globalmedia.com
Web site: https://onebigsociety.squarespace.com/
Freq: Daily
MAGAZINE (ONLINE)
Government, Public Sector

Only Strategic 983029
Editorial: 34 West Street, Farnham, Farnham GU9 7DR Tel: 44 01252 724865
Email: mail@shillito.org.uk
Web site: www.onlystrategic.com
Freq: Daily
Circ: 6305 Cision Digital Reach
Editor: Douglas Shillito
MAGAZINE (ONLINE)
Banking, Insurance

OnOffice 983752
Editorial: Crown House, 151 High Road, Loughton, London IG10 4LF
Tel: 44 02032 255200
Email: info@onofficemagazine.com
Web site: www.onofficemagazine.com
Freq: Monthly
Circ: 15752 Not Audited
Editor: Helen Parton
Profile: onoffice is a monthly magazine focusing on all aspects of workplace and office design including technology, green issues, furniture and interior design. It is owned by Media 10 Ltd. First published in 2006. onoffice is aimed at architects, designers and facilities managers.
Ad Rate: Full Page Colour £3000.00
MAGAZINE
Architecture & Design, Interior Design, Office Design

OnRec 980953
Editorial: 9th Floor, Metro Building, 1 Butterwick, London W6 8DL
Tel: 44 02088 462700
Email: editor@onrec.com
Web site: www.onrec.com
Freq: Bi-Monthly
Circ: 96103 Cision Digital Reach
Profile: onrec is a bimonthly magazine covering all aspects of the Internet recruitment industry. It is owned by DH Publishing Ltd and includes features, opinions, information on new sites, statistics, profiles and industry analysis. First published in 2000. onrec is aimed at recruitment and HR professionals involved in Internet recruitment.
Ad Rate: Full Page Colour £2000.00
MAGAZINE (ONLINE)
Recruiting

open business council 1095584
Email: editor@openbusinesscouncil.org
Web site: http://www.openbusinesscouncil.org/
Freq: Daily
Circ: 12310 Cision Digital Reach
Editor: Fidan Aliyeva
MAGAZINE (ONLINE)
Business, Small and Medium Business

Ophthalmic and Physiological Optics 995917
Editorial: Bradford School of Optometry & Vision Science, University of Bradford, Bradford BD7 1DP Tel: 44 01274 235224
Email: opo@wiley.com
Web site: www.onlinelibrary.wiley.com/journal/10.1111/(ISSN)1475-1313
Freq: Bi-Monthly Not Audited
Editor: David B. Elliot
MAGAZINE
Ophthalmology & Optometry

Ophthalmic Epidemiology 999482
Editorial: Christchurch Court, 10 Newgate Street, London EC1A 7AZ
Tel: 44 02070 175000
Email: ophthalmic.epi@sydney.edu.au
Web site: http://informahealthcare.com/journal/ope

Freq: Bi-Monthly Not Audited
MAGAZINE
Ophthalmology & Optometry

The Ophthalmologist 997358
Editorial: Haig House, Haig Road, Knutsford, Knutsford WA16 8DX
Tel: 44 01565 745200
Email: info@texerepublishing.com
Web site: www.theophthalmologist.com
Freq: Monthly
Circ: 17934 Not Audited
Editor: Mark Hillen; Editor: Rich Whitworth
MAGAZINE
Ophthalmology & Optometry

Ophthalmology Times Europe 984506
Editorial: 4A Bridgegate House, Chester Business Park, Wrexham Road, Chester CH4 9QH
Web site: www.oteurope.com
Freq: Monthly
Circ: 21289 Not Audited
Profile: Publication featuring news and information on clinical, social and political issues, developments within the ophthalmic industry and a focus on cataract, corneal and refractive surgery, glaucoma and vitreoretinal conditions.
Ad Rate: Full Page Colour £6611.00
MAGAZINE
Ophthalmology & Optometry

Opportunity Middle East 998901
Editorial: Floor 6, 27 St James's Street, London SW1A 1HA Tel: 44 02078 392137
Email: info@the-mea.co.uk
Web site: www.the-mea.co.uk
Freq: Quarterly
Circ: 2000 Not Audited
MAGAZINE
Business, Small and Medium Business

Optical Connections Magazine 996129
Editorial: Suite 5, Building 60, Churchill Square, Kings Hill, West Malling ME19 4YU
Tel: 44 01732 752125
Email: editor@opticalconnectionsnews.com
Web site: www.opticalconnectionsnews.com
Freq: 3 Times/Year
Circ: 13000 Not Audited
Editor: Matthew Peach
MAGAZINE
Telecommunications/Electronic Communications

Optical World 984115
Editorial: 258a Fairfax Drive, Westcliff-on-Sea, Southend-on-Sea SS0 9EJ
Tel: 44 01702 345443
Email: info@optical-world.co.uk
Web site: http://www.optical-world.co.uk
Freq: Bi-Monthly
Circ: 4500 Not Audited
Profile: Magazine featuring equipment surveys, company profiles, optical exhibitions and new products section.
Ad Rate: Full Page Mono £1855.00
Ad Rate: Full Page Colour £2755.00
MAGAZINE
Ophthalmology & Optometry

Optician 981211
Editorial: St Jude's Church, Dulwich Road, London SE24 0PB
Web site: www.opticianonline.net
Freq: Weekly
Circ: 4119 Not Audited
Editor: Chris Bennett
Profile: Magazine containing news and features about all aspects of the optical industry.
Ad Rate: Full Page Colour £2648.00
MAGAZINE
Ophthalmology & Optometry

Optics.org 988762
Editorial: 2 Alexandra Gate, Fford Pengam, Cardiff CF24 2SA
Email: mike.hatcher@optics.org

Web site: http://optics.org
Freq: Daily
Circ: 63560 Cision Digital Reach
Profile: Web portal designed to serve the information needs of the worldwide photonics community.
MAGAZINE (ONLINE)
Mobile Communications

Optometry Today 981212
Editorial: 2 Woodbridge Street, London EC1R 0DG Tel: 44 02075 492076
Email: newsdesk@optometry.co.uk
Web site: www.optometry.co.uk
Freq: Bi-Weekly
Circ: 19923 Not Audited
Profile: Optometry Today is the fortnightly magazine of the Association of Optometrists. It covers news, clinical, continuing education and training, technical and practice management. It is published by Ten Alps Publishing plc. Optometry Today is aimed at optometrists and dispensing opticians.
Ad Rate: Full Page Colour £2730.00
MAGAZINE
Ophthalmology & Optometry

Oral Health 1059127
Tel: 44 01923 851777
Web site: https://www.fmc.co.uk/shop/oral-health
Freq: Bi-Monthly Not Audited
MAGAZINE
Dentistry

Oral Oncology 994969
Editorial: Stover Court, Bampfylde Street, Exeter EX1 2AH Tel: 44 01392 285800
Email: ooncology@elsevier.com
Web site: www.elsevier.com/wps/find/journaldescription.cws_home/105/description
Freq: Monthly
MAGAZINE
Oncology

Oral Surgery 995887
Editorial: 9600 Garsington Road, Oxford OX4 2DQ Tel: 44 01865 776868
Email: orsedoffice@wiley.com
Web site: http://onlinelibrary.wiley.com/journal/10.1111/(ISSN)1752-248X
Freq: Quarterly
Circ: 572 Not Audited
MAGAZINE
Dentistry

Organic Farming 983285
Editorial: South Plaza, Marlborough Street, Bristol BS1 3NX Tel: 44 01173 145000
Web site: www.soilassociation.org/farmersgrowers/magazine
Freq: Quarterly
Circ: 7000 Not Audited
Editor: Sally Morgan
Profile: Journal covering technical features and research on all aspects of organic farming.
Ad Rate: Full Page Colour £1250.00
MAGAZINE
News & Current Affairs

Organics Recycling 996564
Editorial: 25 Eccleston Place, Victoria, London SW1W 9NF Tel: 44 02079 253570
Email: organics-recycling@r-e-a.net
Web site: www.organics-recycling.org.uk
Freq: Quarterly
Circ: 1000 Not Audited
Editor: Steve Eminton
MAGAZINE
Alternative/Renewable Energy, Environment

Orthodontic Practice 1053677
Tel: 44 01923 851777
Web site: www.dentistry.co.uk
Freq: Bi-Monthly Not Audited
MAGAZINE
Dentistry

Orthopaedic Product News
984133

Editorial: G1-G6 East Wing, The Croft, Boroughbridge Road, Kirk Deighton, Harrogate LS22 5HG **Tel:** 44 01423 851150
Email: editor@opnews.com
Web site: www.opnews.com
Freq: Bi-Monthly
Circ: 7762 Not Audited
MAGAZINE
Occupational Therapy & Rehabilitation, Orthopedics

The osteopath
984282

Editorial: General Osteopathic Council, Osteopathy House, 176 Tower Bridge Road, London SE1 3LU **Tel:** 44 02073 576655
Email: editor@osteopathy.org.uk
Web site: www.osteopathy.org.uk/resources/publications/the-osteopath/
Freq: Bi-Monthly
Circ: 5000 Not Audited
Editor: Jeremy Pinel
Profile: Official journal of the General Osteopathic Council. Covers news, issues concerning healthcare regulation, professional standards and guidance, the NHS, clinical updates, research, letters, media reviews and CPD resources.
Ad Rate: Full Page Colour £330.00
MAGAZINE
Orthopedics

Osteoporosis International
985143

Editorial: 236 Gray's Inn Road, London WC1X 8HB
Web site: www.springer.com/medicine/orthopedics/journal/198
Freq: Monthly
Circ: 800 Not Audited
Profile: Journal of the International Osteoporosis Foundation and the National Osteoporosis Foundation covering the diagnosis, treatment and management of osteoporosis.
Ad Rate: Full Page Mono £520.00
Ad Rate: Full Page Colour £1397.00
MAGAZINE
Orthopedics

Osteoporosis Review
995907

Editorial: National Osteoporosis Society, Camerton, Bath BA2 0PJ
Tel: 44 01761 471771
Email: info@nos.org.uk
Web site: https://nos.org.uk/for-health-professionals/membership/osteoporosis-review/
Freq: Quarterly
Circ: 24282 Cision Digital Reach
MAGAZINE (ONLINE)
Orthopedics, Patient Support

The OT Magazine
998284

Editorial: Caledonia House, Evanton Drive, Thornliebank Industrial Estate, Glasgow G46 8JT **Tel:** 44 01414 652960
Email: enquiries@2apublishing.co.uk
Web site: www.ot-magazine.co.uk
Freq: Bi-Monthly
Circ: 13000 Not Audited
Editor: Rosalind Tulloch
MAGAZINE
Occupational Therapy & Rehabilitation

OTC bulletin
984067

Editorial: 4 Poplar Road, Dorridge, Solihull B93 8DB **Tel:** 44 01564 777550
Email: editor@otc-bulletin.com
Web site: http://www.otc-bulletin.com
Freq: Bi-Weekly
Circ: 3500 Not Audited
Editor: Matt Stewart
Profile: Business newsletter covering all aspects of Europe's consumer healthcare industry. Aimed at those with an interest in Europe's consumer healthcare industry.
Ad Rate: Full Page Mono £940.00
Ad Rate: Full Page Colour £1460.00
MAGAZINE
Healthcare Industry, Pharmaceuticals

OTC.NewDirections
996604

Editorial: 35 Alexandra Street, Southend-on-Sea, Southend-on-Sea SS1 1BW
Tel: 44 01702 220200
Email: info@nicholashall.com
Web site: http://www.otcnewdirections.nicholashall.com/welcome.asp
Freq: Weekly
Circ: 3403 Cision Digital Reach
MAGAZINE (ONLINE)
Pharmaceuticals

Outdoor Photography
982029

Editorial: Quadrant House, 4 Thomas More Square, London E1W IYW
Tel: 44 01273 477374
Email: theguild@thegmcgroup.com
Web site: www.outdoorphotographymagazine.co.uk
Freq: Monthly
Circ: 27500 Not Audited
Editor: Steven Watkins
Profile: Magazine focusing on outdoor photography. Covers landscape, wildlife, nature, architecture and outdoor events.
Ad Rate: Full Page Colour £1064.00
MAGAZINE
Photography

Outlook on Agriculture
983585

Editorial: 4th Floor, Hamilton House, Mabledon Place, Bloomsbury, London WC1H 9BB **Tel:** 44 02075 548841
Web site: www.ippublishing.com/oa.htm
Freq: Quarterly Not Audited
Editor: Jerry Knox
Profile: Outlook on Agriculture is a quarterly journal covering agricultural science, policy and strategy. It contains analysis of developments in international agricultural science and associated disciplines. Outlook on Agriculture is aimed at academics in agriculture and related disciplines.
MAGAZINE
Animal Farming, Environment, Science

Output Magazine
997233

Editorial: Camden House, Warwick Road, Kenilworth, Kenilworth CV8 1TH
Tel: 44 01926 513777
Email: mail@eua.org.uk
Web site: www.eua.org.uk
Freq: Quarterly
Circ: 1500 Not Audited
Editor: Caroline Haine
Profile: Website covering news from the print, digital, manufacturing and emerging technologies industry.
MAGAZINE
Alternative/Renewable Energy, Carbon Emissions & Trading, Electricity, Energy, Engineering, Nuclear Power, Oil, Water & Sanitation

Outsource Magazine (UK)
981626

Editorial: Central House, Ballards Lane, Finchley, London N3 1LQ
Email: jliddell@sig.org
Web site: http://outsourcemag.com/
Freq: Monthly
Circ: 16905 Cision Digital Reach
Editor: Jamie Liddell
MAGAZINE (ONLINE)
Business, Corporate Responsibility

Over The Counter
985618

Editorial: Suite A, Arun House, Office Village, River Way, Uckfield TN22 1SL
Tel: 44 01825 983105
Email: info@lewisbusinessmedia.co.uk
Web site: www.overthecounter.cc
Freq: Bi-Monthly
Circ: 4800 Not Audited
MAGAZINE
Animal Farming, Veterinary Medicine

P&HE
983975

Editorial: Warners Group Publications plc, The Maltings, West Street, Bourne PE10 9PH **Tel:** 44 01778 391128
Web site: www.ciphe.org.uk
Freq: Bi-Monthly

Circ: 10000 Not Audited
Editor: Nicky Rogers
MAGAZINE
Building & Construction, Residential Real Estate

P&T Review
998875

Editorial: 22 Leydene Avenue, Bournemouth, Bournemouth BH8 9JG
Tel: 44 01202 300033
Web site: http://www.ptreview.co.uk/
Freq: Bi-Monthly
Circ: 3000 Not Audited
Editor: Tony Letts
MAGAZINE
Engineering, Manufacturing

P1
984955

Editorial: 9 The Mill, Copley Hill Farm, Cambridge Road, Cambridge CB22 3GN
Tel: 44 01223 497060
Email: hello@p1digitalmedia.com
Web site: www.p1-mag.com
Freq: Monthly
Circ: 1544 Cision Digital Reach
Profile: Digital iPad magazine covering business aviation.
MAGAZINE (ONLINE)
Aviation

P3
983441

Editorial: Linen Hall, 162-168 Regent Street, London W1B 5TB **Tel:** 44 02074 341530
Email: p3@1530.com
Web site: www.p3pharmacy.co.uk
Freq: Monthly
Circ: 14438 Not Audited
Profile: P3 is a magazine providing business management information for the entrepreneurial pharmacist. It includes news and analysis, category management guidance, an analysis of City trends, training modules, profiles plus an examination of over the counter pharmaceutical products and retail education. It is owned by Communications International Group. P3 is aimed at pharmacists in the UK and central buying offices.
Ad Rate: Full Page Colour £3525.00
MAGAZINE
Pharmaceuticals

PA Enterprise
983973

Editorial: Terminal House, Station Approach, Shepperton, London TW17 8AS
Tel: 44 08704 104030
Email: editoruk@deskdemon.com
Web site: http://www.deskdemon.com/pages/uk/paenterprise/archive
Freq: Monthly
Circ: 85000 Not Audited
Editor: Paul Ormond
MAGAZINE
Human Resources

PA Life
983630

Editorial: Forum House, 71 Mead Lane, Hertford SG13 7AX **Tel:** 44 01992 374100
Email: editorial@palife.co.uk
Web site: www.palife.co.uk
Freq: Bi-Monthly
Circ: 12000 Not Audited
Profile: Magazine covering administrative support. Aimed at PAs, executive assistants, senior secretaries and office managers.
MAGAZINE
Human Resources

pa-assist.com
998749

Editorial: 52 High Street, Harrow-on-the-Hill, London HA1 3LL
Email: support@pa-assist.com
Web site: www.pa-assist.com
Freq: Daily
Circ: 10738 Cision Digital Reach
MAGAZINE (ONLINE)
Human Resources

Packaging & Converting Intelligence
996017

Editorial: John Carpenter House, John Carpenter Street, London EC4Y 0AN
Tel: 44 02079 366667

Web site: http://www.pci-mag.com
Freq: Semi-Annual
Circ: 7775 Not Audited
MAGAZINE
Supply Chain Management (SCM)

Packaging Gazette
983489

Editorial: 1 Accent Park, Bakewell Road, Orton Southgate, Peterborough, Peterborough PE2 6XS
Tel: 44 01733 385300
Email: pg@mediaone.co.uk
Web site: www.packaginggazette.co.uk
Freq: Bi-Monthly
Circ: 11000 Not Audited
Editor: Stephanie Cornwall
Profile: Packaging Gazette is a bimonthly magazine looking at all issues concerned with the packaging industry. It is owned by Media One Communications Ltd. Packaging Gazette is aimed at those concerned with packaging purchasing across all industries.
Ad Rate: Full Page Mono £720.00
Ad Rate: Full Page Colour £750.00
MAGAZINE
Manufacturing

Packaging News
981332

Editorial: 6th Floor, Davis House, 2 Robert Street, Croydon CR0 1QQ
Tel: 44 02082 538600
Email: packagingnews.editorial@metropolis.co.uk
Web site: www.packagingnews.co.uk
Freq: Monthly
Circ: 10100 Not Audited
Editor: Philip Chadwick
Profile: Packaging News is a monthly magazine containing information on all aspects of the packaging industry. Each issue features case studies and in-depth features on leading issues. It covers manufacturing, retail, design, logistics, updates on packaging converters, materials suppliers, designers, brand owners, news from equipment suppliers, news and reviews of the most innovative new packs and designs. It is owned by Metropolis Business Media. First published in 1947. Packaging News is aimed at executives who purchase, specify or supply packaging equipment, materials or services. It is read by packaging buyers, technologists, engineers, designers, production directors and brand managers.
Ad Rate: Full Page Colour £3583.00
MAGAZINE
Manufacturing

Packaging Scotland
981331

Editorial: The Albus, 110 Brook Street, Glasgow G40 3AP **Tel:** 44 01415 676000
Email: info@peeblesmedia.com
Web site: http://packagingscotland.com/
Freq: Quarterly
Circ: 4031 Not Audited
Editor: Gary Moug
Profile: Magazine containing news and views of the packaging industry in Scotland. Aimed at management in the packaging industry.
Ad Rate: Full Page Colour £1475.00
MAGAZINE
Supply Chain Management (SCM)

Packaging Solutions
1054607

Tel: 44 01892 522563
Email: hello@earthisland.co.uk
Web site: www.earthisland.co.uk/#!packaging-solutions/c26x
Freq: Monthly
Circ: 8500 Not Audited
MAGAZINE
Manufacturing

Packaging Technology and Science
996418

Editorial: John Wiley & Sons, PO Box 808, 1-7 Oldlands Way, Bognor Regis PO22 9SA
Web site: http://eu.wiley.com/WileyCDA/WileyTitle/productCd-PTS.html
Freq: Monthly Not Audited
Editor: David Shires
MAGAZINE
Manufacturing

Business Magazines

Packaging Today 981333
Editorial: John Carpenter House, John Carpenter Street, London EC4Y 0AN
Tel: 44 02079 366400
Web site: www.packagingtoday.co.uk
Freq: Monthly
Circ: 30000 Not Audited
Profile: Magazine containing news and features on all aspects of the packaging industry. It covers the latest corporate developments, news on the latest machinery, packaging materials and packs.
Ad Rate: Full Page Colour £3525.00
MAGAZINE
Manufacturing

Pain Management 999495
Editorial: Unitec House, 2 Albert Place, London N3 1QB **Tel:** 44 02083 716090
Email: info@futuremedicine.com
Web site: http://www.futuremedicine.com/loi/pmt
Freq: Bi-Monthly Not Audited
MAGAZINE
Pain Management

Pain News 998994
Editorial: The British Pain Society, 3rd Floor, Churchill House, 35 Red Lion Square, London WC1R 4SG **Tel:** 44 02072 697840
Email: newsletter@britishpainsociety.org
Web site: www.britishpainsociety.org/pain-news-1/
Freq: Quarterly
Circ: 1400 Not Audited
Editor: Arasu Rayen
MAGAZINE
Pain Management

Paint & Resin Times 1053637
Editorial: The Big Box Business Centre, Crowhurst Road, Hollingbury, Brighton BN1 8AF **Tel:** 44 01273 526132
Email: editorial@paintandresintimes.com
Web site: http://www.newbusinessmedia.co/brands/
Freq: Bi-Monthly
Circ: 2000 Not Audited
Profile: Paint & Resin Times is a bimonthly publication covering information on all aspects of commercial and technical production and development of paint, varnish, adhesives and printing inks. It includes industry news and reports on research developments, applications and new products, services and contracts. It is owned by Complete Circulation and Marketing Ltd. Paint & Resin Times targets key decision makers responsible for specifying, recommending, or purchasing raw materials, equipment and services for the manufacture of paint, ink, adhesives, varnishes, and sealants.
Ad Rate: Full Page Colour £620.00
MAGAZINE
Interior Design

Palliative Medicine 985145
Editorial: 1 Oliver's Yard, 55 City Road, London EC1Y 1SP **Tel:** 44 02073 248500
Web site: http://pmj.sagepub.com/
Freq: Monthly Not Audited
Profile: Journal covering all aspects of palliative care for patients with advanced diseases. Aimed at doctors, nurses, physiotherapists, psychologists, social workers, occupational therapists and the clergy.
Ad Rate: Full Page Mono £980.00
Ad Rate: Full Page Colour £1510.00
MAGAZINE
Community Care (UK)

PAM 1053757
Editorial: 5th Floor, 50 Broadway, St.James Park, London SW1H 0RG
Tel: 44 02076 740400
Email: janderson@paminsight.com
Web site: www.pamonline.com
Freq: Daily
Circ: 9585 Cision Digital Reach
MAGAZINE (ONLINE)
Fund Management

Panel & Joinery Production 985528
Editorial: 23 Uvedale Road, Enfield EN2 6HA **Tel:** 44 02083 663331
Email: ernie@p-j-production.com
Web site: http://www.p-j-production.com/
Freq: Bi-Monthly
Circ: 5870 Not Audited
Profile: Panel & Joinery Production is a bimonthly journal covering all aspects of the wood based panel industry. It includes installation stories and product pieces featuring products and manufacturers relevant to the industry. It is owned by EC Media Ltd. Panel & Joinery Production is aimed at key decision makers involved in the production and manufacture of wood based products.
Ad Rate: Full Page Colour £875.00
MAGAZINE
Manufacturing

Panel, Wood & Solid Surface 1054622
Tel: 44 01424 205428
Email: info@pawprintuk.co.uk
Web site: www.pawprintuk.co.uk
Freq: Bi-Monthly
Circ: 6000 Not Audited
Profile: Panel, Wood & Solid Surface is a magazine covering joinery, shop fitting, kitchen fitting and allied trades. It includes news and features of interest to those working in solid wood, with panel products or with any of the solid surface materials. It is owned by Pawprint Publishing Ltd. First published in 2008. Panel, Wood & Solid Surface is aimed at joiners, shop fitters, kitchen fitters and furniture manufacturers.
Ad Rate: Full Page Colour £500.00
MAGAZINE
Manufacturing

PanStadia & Arena Management 980961
Editorial: 6 Wealden Place, Bradbourne Vale Road, Sevenoaks, Sevenoaks TN13 3QQ
Tel: 44 01604 832149
Email: info@aladltd.co.uk
Web site: www.psam.uk.com
Freq: Quarterly
Circ: 24000 Not Audited
Profile: Magazine covering stadium and arena management including global news, people, diary, facility watch listing of arenas and stadiums in development and construction worldwide, and articles relating to topics of importance to commercial and operations managers in large sports and entertainment venues. First published in 1996. Aimed at facilities managers, owners, architects and engineers of stadiums and arenas.
Ad Rate: Full Page Colour £1650.00
MAGAZINE
Travel Industry

Paper Technology 985956
Editorial: Paper Technology, 5 Frecheville Court, Bury BL9 0UF **Tel:** 44 03003 020150
Email: info@pita.co.uk
Web site: www.pita.co.uk
Freq: Quarterly
Circ: 1400 Not Audited
Editor: Daven Chamberlain
Profile: Paper Technology is the official journal of The Paper Industry Technical Association. It contains information on new technology and developments in the pulp, papermaking, non-woven and converting industries. First published in 1949. Paper Technology is aimed at those associated with the paper industry.
Ad Rate: Full Page Colour £2450.00
MAGAZINE
Paper

Park Lifestyle 987238
Editorial: Cudham Tithe Barn, Berry's Hill, Cudham, London TN16 3AG
Tel: 44 01959 541444
Email: edlifestyle@kelsey.co.uk
Web site: www.parklifestyle.co.uk
Freq: Annual
Circ: 100000 Not Audited
Editor: Heather Grimes

Profile: Park Lifestyle is an annual magazine covering park, leisure and holiday homes including lifestyle and industry news. It contains features on buying and selling homes, residential property legislation, insurance and refurbishment. It is owned by Parks PR & Media. Park Lifestyle is aimed at park homes owners in England and Wales.
Ad Rate: Full Page Colour £2450.00
MAGAZINE
Property Management & Maintenance

Parking Review 984103
Editorial: Apollo House, 359 Kennington Lane, London SE11 5QY
Tel: 44 08452 707901
Email: ed.pr@landor.co.uk
Web site: www.transportxtra.com
Freq: Monthly
Circ: 2000 Not Audited
Profile: Magazine focusing on management and design of car parks and on-street enforcement worldwide. Aimed at public and private parking authorities, car park designers, builders, contractors and equipment suppliers.
Ad Rate: Full Page Colour £1900.00
MAGAZINE
Government

parliamentarybriefing.net 996608
Editorial: Davenport Close, Teddington, London TW11 9EF
Email: editor@itbriefing.net
Web site: http://www.parliamentarybriefing.net/
Freq: Daily
Circ: 521 Cision Digital Reach
MAGAZINE (ONLINE)
Government Technology, Public Sector

Partnerships Bulletin 980733
Editorial: Rockcliffe Ltd, Unit 3.23 Canterbury Court, 1-3 Brixton Road, London SW9 6DE **Tel:** 44 02086 757770
Web site: www.partnershipsbulletin.com
Freq: Monthly
Circ: 2500 Not Audited
Profile: Magazine containing updates and case studies of projects under the Private Finance Initiative together with in-depth analysis of current issues and contributions from experts in the field.
Ad Rate: Full Page Colour £995.00
MAGAZINE
Financial Markets

Party Party 984066
Editorial: Naishville, 1 Churchgates, Berkhamsted, Berkhamsted HP4 2AZ
Tel: 44 01442 289930
Web site: www.partypartymag.co.uk
Freq: Bi-Monthly
Circ: 3800 Not Audited
Profile: Party Party is a bimonthly magazine covering new products and general news concerned with the party industry. First published in 2000. Party Party is aimed at those within the party industry such as retailers, manufacturers and wholesalers of party products.
Ad Rate: Full Page Colour £1395.00
MAGAZINE
Toys

Passenger Terminal World 981345
Editorial: Abinger House, Church Street, Dorking, Dorking RH4 1DF
Tel: 44 01306 743744
Email: ptw@ukimediaevents.com
Web site: www.passengerterminaltoday.com
Freq: Quarterly
Circ: 9902 Not Audited
Editor: Hazel King
Profile: Passenger Terminal World is a quarterly magazine dealing with all aspects of projects involving airport passenger terminals. Passenger Terminal World is aimed at decision makers within terminal projects.
Ad Rate: Full Page Mono £3905.00

Ad Rate: Full Page Colour £3905.00
MAGAZINE
Aviation, Railroad

The Patent Lawyer 997951
Editorial: CTC International Media, 23 Hedgers Way, Kingsnorth, Ashford, Ashford TN23 3GN **Tel:** 44 02071 128862
Email: editor@patentlawyermagazine.com
Web site: www.patentlawyermagazine.com
Freq: Bi-Monthly
Circ: 16500 Not Audited
Editor: Jessica Lilley
MAGAZINE
Intellectual Property

The Pawnbroker 988395
Editorial: Suite 508, 107-111 Fleet Street, London EC4A 2AB **Tel:** 44 02079 369497
Web site: http://www.thenpa.com/
Freq: Quarterly
Circ: 2000 Not Audited
Editor: Peter Roper
Profile: Magazine carrying news and legislative changes affecting the pawn broking industry. Read by pawn brokers and affiliated organisations.Previous title: The Pawn Broker
Ad Rate: Full Page Colour £575.00
MAGAZINE
Business, Small and Medium Business

Pay & Benefits 980957
Editorial: Quadrant House, The Quadrant, Sutton SM2 5AS **Tel:** 44 08453 701234
Web site: www.payandbenefitsmagazine.co.uk/
Freq: Monthly
Circ: 11552 Not Audited
MAGAZINE
Human Resources

Pay Network (PPN) 996455
Tel: 44 01344 989240
Email: editor@accountspayablenews.org
Web site: http://www.p2pnetwork.org/
Freq: Daily
Circ: 10055 Cision Digital Reach
Editor: Ellen Leith
MAGAZINE (ONLINE)
Accounting

PaymentEye 987259
Editorial: 1 Broadway, Hammersmith, London W6 9DL **Tel:** 44 02080 809142
Email: editorial@paymenteye.com
Web site: www.paymenteye.com/
Freq: Daily
Circ: 52391 Cision Digital Reach
Profile: Website covering the payments sector. Payment eye discusses news and analysis from the payments sector including innovative start ups and clearing banks to merchant PoS innovators and mobile solutions companies.
MAGAZINE (ONLINE)
Banking

Payments & Fintech Lawyer 998664
Editorial: 17 The Timber Yard, Drysdale Street, London N1 6ND
Tel: 44 02070 121380
Web site: www.e-comlaw.com/e-finance-and-payments-law-and-policy/index.asp Not Audited
Editor: Sophie Cameron
MAGAZINE
Consumer Interest, Corporate Law, Government, Intellectual Property, Legal Services, Tax Law

PaymentsCompliance 998303
Editorial: Saddlers House, 44 Gutter Lane, London EC2V 6BR **Tel:** 44 02079 219996
Web site: www.paymentscompliance.com
Freq: Daily
Circ: 27261 Cision Digital Reach
MAGAZINE (ONLINE)
Banking, Economics, Financial Markets, Foreign Exchange Market (FOREX), Tax Law

Payroll World
980947

Editorial: Axe & Bottle Court, 70 Newcomen Street, London SE1 1YT
Tel: 44 02079 404801
Email: editorial@payrollworld.com
Web site: www.payrollworld.com
Freq: Monthly
Circ: 8000 Not Audited
Editor: Jerome Smail
Profile: Magazine containing the latest payroll news and articles which are relevant to a busy payroll department. In addition to publishing a monthly magazine and regular e-bulletins, Payroll World provides payroll legislation updates and support to companies such as Capita Business Services.Payroll World runs a number of in-house and open payroll training courses for both small and major UK bureaux, government departments, companies and individuals. Aimed at existing and newly appointed payroll managers.
Ad Rate: Full Page Mono £1460.00
Ad Rate: Full Page Colour £2085.00
MAGAZINE
Human Resources

PBW News
984577

Editorial: 6 The Rickyard, Clifton Reynes, Olney, Olney MK46 5LQ
Tel: 44 01234 714644
Email: editor@pbwnews.com
Web site: www.petbusinessworld.co.uk
Freq: Monthly
Circ: 7845 Not Audited
Editor: Sandra Pearce
MAGAZINE
Animal Farming

PCR
981315

Editorial: Emerson Studios, 4th Floor, 4-8 Emerson Street, London SE1 9DU
Tel: 44 02038 717377
Email: dsacco@nbmedia.com
Web site: www.pcr-online.biz
Freq: Monthly
Circ: 12766 Not Audited
Profile: PCR is a monthly magazine focusing on the computer retail industry. It includes news, analysis of industry issues, company profiles, interviews with personalities in the industry, features on consumer computer retail products and games coverage. It is also an outlet for computer hardware and software product news and provides a general guide for retail buyers. It is owned by Intent Media. PCR is aimed at managers and staff of independent and multiple computer retail stores as well as online and catalogue retailers.
Ad Rate: Full Page Colour £1155.00
MAGAZINE
Auto Aftermarket, Computers, Security & Security Systems, Software

Pediatric Allergy and Immunology
985152

Editorial: 9600 Garsington Road, Oxford OX4 2DQ **Tel:** 44 01865 776868
Email: paieditorial@charite.de
Web site: http://onlinelibrary.wiley.com/journal/10.1111/%28ISSN%291399-3038/issues
Freq: Bi-Monthly Not Audited
MAGAZINE
Allergies, Pediatrics

Pediatric Obesity
995751

Editorial: World Obesity Federation, Charles Darwin 2, 107 Gray's Inn Road, London WC1 X8TZ **Tel:** 44 01865 778315
Email: enquiries@worldobesity.org
Web site: http://onlinelibrary.wiley.com/journal/10.1111/(ISSN)2047-6310/homepage/Contact.html
Freq: Bi-Monthly Not Audited
MAGAZINE
Pediatrics

Pediatric Radiology
995829

Web site: www.springer.com/medicine/radiology/journal/247
Freq: Monthly Not Audited
MAGAZINE
Diagnostic Imaging, Pediatrics

Pensions Age
979784

Editorial: Sixth Floor, 3 London Wall Buildings, London EC2M 5PD
Tel: 44 02075 622401
Web site: www.pensionsage.com
Freq: Monthly
Circ: 15323 Not Audited
Editor: Laura Blows
Profile: Magazine covering news and information on the pensions industry. Includes articles on changes in UK and European law. Pensions Age looks to give in depth analysis and commentary on the major issues affecting the UK pensions sector. Aimed at pensions professionals.
Ad Rate: Full Page Colour £3950.00
MAGAZINE
Fund Management

Pensions Insight
985049

Editorial: 120 Leman Street, London E1 8EU
Tel: 44 02076 183456
Email: reception@nqsm.com
Web site: www.pensions-insight.co.uk
Freq: Bi-Monthly
Circ: 6997 Not Audited
Profile: Pensions Insight is a monthly magazine covering pensions-related products and services, asset management, technology, administration and consultancy. It features news digests and summaries of key developments, reports and briefings with analysis of what it means for pensions professionals. It is owned by Newsquest Specialist Media Ltd. Pensions Insight is aimed at pension managers, senior administrative staff, investment, actuarial and legal advisers.
MAGAZINE
Fund Management

Pensions Today
980162

Editorial: The Ridge, South View Road, Pinner, London HA5 3YD
Tel: 44 02088 661934
Web site: http://www.singlelaw.com/pensions-today
Freq: Monthly Not Audited
Profile: Advisory newsletter covering industry developments, legislative changes, regulations and information. Aimed at pension scheme trustees, lawyers and independent financial advisers.
MAGAZINE
Fund Management

People & Science
985009

Editorial: Wellcome Wolfson Building, 165 Queen's Gate, London SW7 5HD
Tel: 44 08707 707101
Email: press@britishscienceassociation.org
Web site: www.britishscienceassociation.org/bsa-news
Freq: Daily
Circ: 4775 Cision Digital Reach
Profile: People & Science is a quarterly magazine published by the British Science Association, focusing on public engagement in science. People & Science is aimed at decision-makers, opinion formers in government, NGOs, academics and members of the BSA.
Ad Rate: Full Page Colour £800.00
MAGAZINE (ONLINE)
Science

People Management
980027

Editorial: 151 The Broadway, London SW19 1JQ **Tel:** 44 02082 675000
Email: pmeditorial@haymarket.com
Web site: www.peoplemanagement.co.uk
Freq: Monthly
Circ: 130333 Not Audited
Editor: Robert Jeffery
Profile: Official magazine of the CIPD focusing on human resources including news, features, and all the latest thinking and advice in HR. Aimed at human resource, personnel and development professionals as well as academics and consultants.
Ad Rate: Full Page Colour £6450.00
MAGAZINE
Education, Human Resources

PERE
981570

Editorial: 140 London Wall, 6th Floor, London EC2Y 5DN **Tel:** 44 02075 665444
Web site: www.perenews.com
Freq: Monthly
Circ: 3420 Not Audited
Profile: Dedicated to the global private equity real estate markets. Launched in response to the increasing importance of private equity style investment within the real estate markets globally. Examines the theory and practice of real estate investing that goes far beyond mere property ownership.
Ad Rate: Full Page Mono £4890.00
Ad Rate: Full Page Colour £6880.00
MAGAZINE
Finance, Private Equity

PerformanceIN
986614

Editorial: 7.17/7.18 Paintworks, Bath Road, Arnos Vale, Bristol BS4 3EA
Tel: 44 01179 902900
Email: content@performancein.com
Web site: http://performancein.com/
Freq: Daily
Circ: 649605 Cision Digital Reach
MAGAZINE (ONLINE)
Marketing, Mobile Communications

Perimeter Systems
985871

Editorial: 19 Lincoln Croft, Shenstone, Lichfield, Lichfield WS14 0ND
Tel: 44 01543 480322
Email: ps@eclipse.co.uk
Web site: www.perimetersystems.co.uk
Freq: Quarterly
Circ: 6475 Not Audited
Editor: Ian Law
Profile: Magazine covering all aspects of the fencing industry and allied trades.
Ad Rate: Full Page Mono £902.00
Ad Rate: Full Page Colour £1270.00
MAGAZINE
Building & Construction

Personal Care
987151

Editorial: Step House, North Farm Road, Tunbridge Wells, Tunbridge Wells TN2 3DR
Tel: 44 01892 779999
Web site: http://www.personalcaremagazine.com
Freq: Bi-Monthly
Circ: 7919 Not Audited
Editor: Richard Scott
MAGAZINE
Chemicals

Personal Care - Asia Pacific
997253

Editorial: Step House, North Farm Road, Tunbridge Wells, Tunbridge Wells TN2 3DR
Tel: 44 01892 779999
Web site: www.personalcaremagazine.com
Freq: Bi-Monthly
Circ: 9892 Not Audited
Editor: Richard Scott
MAGAZINE
Chemicals, Science

Personal Finance Professional
1012050

Editorial: 20 Albermanbury, London EC2V 7HY **Tel:** 44 02085 300852
Web site: http://www.thepfs.org/membership/benefits-of-membership/personal-finance-professional/
Freq: Bi-Monthly
Circ: 36000 Not Audited
Editor: Michelle Worvell
MAGAZINE
Banking, Investment Banking

Personalized Medicine
998693

Editorial: Unitec House, 2 Albert Place, London N3 1QB **Tel:** 44 02083 716090
Email: info@futuremedicine.com
Web site: www.futuremedicine.com/loi/pme
Freq: Bi-Monthly Not Audited
MAGAZINE
Health Administration, Pharmaceuticals

Personnel Today
979831

Editorial: Fifth Floor, Quadrant House, The Quadrant, Sutton SM2 5AS
Tel: 44 02086 523500
Web site: www.personneltoday.com
Freq: Daily
Circ: 141119 Cision Digital Reach
Editor: Rob Moss
Profile: Website containing news and information about personnel, recruitment and training.
MAGAZINE (ONLINE)
Company News & Appointments, Education, Health & Safety, Human Resources, Recruiting

Perspective
985318

Editorial: 39 Boucher Road, Belfast BT12 6UT **Tel:** 44 02890 663311
Email: chloe.heaney@ulstertatler.com
Web site: http://www.rsua.org.uk/publications.aspx?title=Perspective+Magazine
Freq: Bi-Monthly Not Audited
Editor: Christopher Sherry
Profile: Perspective is the bimonthly journal of the Royal Society of Ulster Architects, covering architecture and the built environment in Northern Ireland, including finished projects, achievements, ideas and issues. It is published by Ulster Journals Ltd. Perspective is aimed at members of the Royal Society of Ulster Architects and architects throughout Northern Ireland.
Ad Rate: Full Page Colour £995.00
MAGAZINE
Architecture & Design

Pest
984893

Editorial: Foxhill, Stanford on Soar, Loughborough LE12 5PZ
Tel: 44 01509 233219
Email: editor@pestmagazine.co.uk
Web site: www.pestmagazine.co.uk
Freq: Bi-Monthly
Circ: 2500 Not Audited
Profile: Pest is a bimonthly magazine covering the pest management industry. It includes news, advice and technical features. It is owned by Foxhill Publishing Ltd. Pest is aimed at those working in professional pest management.
MAGAZINE
Hygiene

Pet Food Supplement
986627

Editorial: Pentlands Publishing Ltd, Plas Y Coed, Velfrey Road, Whitland SA34 0RA
Tel: 44 01994 240002
Email: mail@pentlandspublishing.com
Web site: http://www.feedcompounder.com/pfs.htm
Freq: Annual
Editor: Andrew Mounsey
Profile: Pet Food Supplement is an annual supplement of Feed Compounder magazine. It covers the pet food sector and contains articles, analysis, news, case studies, products and services. It is owned by Pentlands Publishing Ltd. Pet Food Supplement is aimed at pet food producers and their suppliers.
MAGAZINE
Food

PET GAZETTE
984936

Editorial: Wellington House, Butt Road, Colchester CO3 3DA **Tel:** 44 02035 150208
Web site: www.petgazette.biz
Freq: Monthly
Circ: 7100 Not Audited
Editor: Sara Cork
Profile: Pet Gazette is a monthly magazine for the pet trade industry featuring news, new products and features. First published in 2008. Pet Gazette is aimed at pet shops, pet supplies centres, aquarium and pond suppliers, garden centres, groomers, kennels and catteries, manufacturers, wholesalers and suppliers, saddlers and equestrian suppliers and veterinary suppliers.
Ad Rate: Full Page Colour £1425.00
MAGAZINE
Animal Farming

Business Magazines

Section 4 UK Periodicals Business

Pet Product Marketing 981165
Editorial: Media House, Lynchwood Business Park, Peterborough, Peterborough PE2 5EA **Tel:** 44 01733 468000
Web site: www.petproductmarketing.co.uk
Freq: Monthly
Circ: 5491 Not Audited
MAGAZINE
Animal Farming, Nature & Wildlife

Pet Trade World 996378
Editorial: Tivoli House, 9 Leaf Avenue, Hampton Hargate, Peterborough PE7 8EF
Tel: 44 08454 599956
Email: editor@pettradeworld.com
Web site: www.pettradeworld.com
Freq: Monthly
Circ: 1195 Cision Digital Reach
MAGAZINE (ONLINE)
Animal Farming

Peterborough Business 985002
Editorial: 94 Thorpe Park Road, Peterborough PE3 6LJ
Email: news@northlightmedia.co.uk
Web site: PeterboroughBusiness.co.uk
Freq: Daily
Circ: 521 Cision Digital Reach
Editor: Martyn Moore
Profile: Website covering news, information and advice for Peterborough's business community.
MAGAZINE (ONLINE)
Business, Small and Medium Business

Petro Industry News 984664
Editorial: Oak Court Business Centre, Sandridge Park, Porters Wood, St Albans, London AL3 6PH **Tel:** 44 01727 858840
Email: info@pin-pub.com
Web site: http://www.petro-online.com
Freq: Bi-Monthly
Circ: 30330 Not Audited
Profile: Petro Industry News is a bimonthly magazine covering scientific research and processes relating to the petroleum industry. It is published by Environmental Technology Publications Ltd. Petro Industry News is read by buyers and users of scientific instrumentation, safety control and automation products, condition monitoring and environmental compliance equipment in the oil-related industries.
Ad Rate: Full Page Colour £4850.00
MAGAZINE
Manufacturing, Oil

Petrochemical Safety and Environmental Protection Technology 1061118
Tel: 44 86108 4877006
Email: syhgaqjs@sei.com.cn
Freq: Quarterly
Circ: 11001 Not Audited
MAGAZINE
Oil

Petroleum Economist 979999
Editorial: 14 Gray's Inn Road, London WC1X 8HN
Email: editorial@petroleum-economist.com
Web site: www.petroleum-economist.com
Freq: Monthly Not Audited
Editor: Derek Brower
Profile: Petroleum Economist is a publication providing a worldwide analysis of the oil, gas, power and electricity sector. It is published ten times a year. First published in 1934. Petroleum Economist is aimed at policy and decision makers in the energy industry, financial institutions, accountancy and legal practices and governmental departments and agencies.
Ad Rate: Full Page Colour £5950.00
MAGAZINE
Oil

Petroleum Intelligence Weekly 980785
Editorial: 7 Down Street, 3rd Floor, London W1J 7AJ **Tel:** 44 02075 182200
Email: energyintelligence@energyintel.com
Web site: www.energyintel.com

Freq: Weekly
Editor: Peter Kemp
MAGAZINE
Oil

Petroleum Review 980000
Editorial: 61 New Cavendish Street, London W1G 7AR **Tel:** 44 02074 677100
Email: petrev@energyinst.org
Web site: www.energyinst.org/information-centre/ei-publications/petroleum-review
Freq: Monthly
Circ: 4500 Not Audited
Editor: Kim Jackson
Profile: Oil and gas magazine covering energy, oil, petroleum and gas news.
Ad Rate: Full Page Colour £3500.00
MAGAZINE
Oil

Petroleum Technology Quarterly 985063
Editorial: Crambeth Allen Publishing Ltd., Hopesay, Craven Arms SY7 8HD
Tel: 44 08445 888773
Email: editor@petroleumtechnology.com
Web site: www.eptq.com/default.aspx?intC1
Freq: Quarterly
Circ: 17492 Not Audited
Editor: Chris Cunningham
Profile: Petroleum Technology Quarterly is a publication covering the refining, gas, biofuels and petrochemical processing industries. It provides decision-makers with information they need on the processes, products and services necessary for them to design, build, operate and maintain their plants more efficiently and to increase margins. It is owned by Crambeth Allen Publishing. Petroleum Technology Quarterly is aimed at key personnel in every refinery, gas and petrochemical processing plant, operating company, engineering company and licensing company in the world.
Ad Rate: Full Page Mono £5635.00
Ad Rate: Full Page Colour £5635.00
MAGAZINE
Engineering, Oil

Petrospot 998117
Editorial: Petrospot House, Somerville Court, Trinity Way, Banbury OX17 3SN
Tel: 44 01295 814455
Email: news@petrospot.com
Web site: www.petrospot.com
Freq: Daily
Circ: 7338 Cision Digital Reach
Editor: Lesley Bankes-Hughes
MAGAZINE (ONLINE)
Shipping & Warehousing

PHAM News 1052375
Editorial: 1B Station Square, Flitwick, Ampthill MK45 1DP **Tel:** 44 01525 716143
Email: editor@phamnewsedit.co.uk
Web site: http://www.phamnews.co.uk/
Freq: Monthly
Circ: 29032 Not Audited
MAGAZINE
Alternative/Renewable Energy, Building & Construction, Carbon Emissions & Trading, Electricity, Energy, Nuclear Power, Oil, Residential Real Estate, Water & Sanitation

Pharma and Healthcare Insight 1052598
Editorial: 2 Broadgate Circle, London EC2M 2QS **Tel:** 44 02072 480468
Email: enquiries@bmiresearch.com
Web site: http://www.pharmaceuticalsinsight.com/
Freq: Monthly
Circ: 3365 Cision Digital Reach
MAGAZINE (ONLINE)
Healthcare Industry, Pharmaceuticals

Pharma Business International 987402
Editorial: Armstrong House, Armstrong Street, Grimsby, Grimsby DN31 2QE
Tel: 44 01472 310305
Email: pharma@blmgroup.co.uk

Web site: www.pbiforum.net
Freq: Bi-Monthly Not Audited
Profile: Publication that looks at the pharmaceutical industry.
Ad Rate: Full Page Mono £2650.00
MAGAZINE
Healthcare Industry, Pharmaceuticals

Pharma IQ 986053
Editorial: 129 Wilton Road, London SW1V
Tel: 44 02073 689300
Web site: http://www.pharma-iq.com
Freq: Daily
Circ: 9473 Cision Digital Reach
MAGAZINE (ONLINE)
Pharmaceuticals

The Pharma Letter 985266
Editorial: 39 to 43 Putney High Street, London SW15 1SP **Tel:** 44 02087 806363
Email: newsdesk@thepharmaletter.com
Web site: www.thepharmaletter.com
Freq: Daily
Circ: 62647 Cision Digital Reach
Editor: Barbara Obstoj-Cardwell
Profile: Website covering pharmaceuticals, authoritative pharma and biotechnology news.
MAGAZINE (ONLINE)
Biotechnology, Pharmaceuticals

Pharma Technology Focus 999337
Editorial: John Carpenter House, John Carpenter Street, London EC4Y 0AN
Tel: 44 02079 366400
Email: onlineeditorial@kable.co.uk
Web site: http://www.pharmaceutical-technology.com
Freq: Bi-Monthly Not Audited
Profile: Website covering pharmaceuticals. Pharma Technology Focus is a digital publication providing' in-depth coverage of the latest news, trends and developments in the pharmaceutical industry'.
MAGAZINE
Medical Technology, Pharmaceuticals

Pharmaceutical Business Review 985136
Editorial: Pharmaceutical Business Review, Progressive Trade Media Ltd., 40-42 Hatton Garden, London EC1N 8EB
Tel: 44 02079 366898
Email: news@industryreview.com
Web site: www.pharmaceutical-business-review.com
Freq: Daily
Circ: 25606 Cision Digital Reach
Profile: Website covering business in the pharmaceutical industry.
MAGAZINE (ONLINE)
Pharmaceuticals

Pharmaceutical Field 981644
Editorial: Unit 4 Clarks Courtyard, 145 Granville Street, Birmingham B1 1SB
Tel: 44 01462 476120
Email: editor@pharmafield.co.uk
Web site: www.pharmafield.co.uk
Freq: Monthly Not Audited
Editor: John Pinching
Profile: The website of Pharmaceutical Field magazine, looking at the environmental factors driving the market, from the NHS policy and reform shaping the industry's customer base to pharmaceutical innovations and corporate developments. It also looks at professional development providing insight, advice and analysis of how to progress a career in medical sales. It is owned by Health Sector Publishing Ltd. Pharmaceutical Field is aimed at field and head office based personnel within the pharmaceutical industry.
MAGAZINE
Pharmaceuticals

The Pharmaceutical Journal 980773
Editorial: 66-68 East Smithfield, London E1W 1AW **Tel:** 44 08452 572570
Email: editor@pharmj.org.uk
Web site: www.pharmaceutical-journal.com/

Freq: Monthly
Circ: 61908 Not Audited
Profile: Official journal of the Royal Pharmaceutical Society of Great Britain. Contains news coverage on all aspects of pharmacy and research and articles on pharmaceutical and related subjects. Read by pharmacists.
Ad Rate: Full Page Mono £3860.00
Ad Rate: Full Page Colour £5165.00
MAGAZINE
Pharmaceuticals

Pharmaceutical Manufacturing and Packing Sourcer (PMPS) 983601
Editorial: First Floor, 131 Edgware Road, London W2 2HR **Tel:** 44 02077 243456
Email: info@samedanltd.com
Web site: www.samedanltd.com/magazine/15
Freq: Quarterly
Circ: 10500 Not Audited
Editor: Graham Hughes
MAGAZINE
Biotechnology, Manufacturing, Medical Technology, Pharmaceuticals

Pharmaceutical Market Europe (PME) 984143
Editorial: Mansard House, Church Road, Little Bookham, London KT23 3JG
Tel: 44 01372 414200
Email: editor@pmlive.com
Web site: www.pmlive.com/pme_pharmaceutical_market_europe
Freq: Monthly
Circ: 24000 Not Audited
MAGAZINE
Healthcare Industry, Marketing, Pharmaceuticals

Pharmaceutical Medicine 999450
Editorial: 236 Gray's Inn Road, Floor 6, London WC1X 8HB **Tel:** 44 02031 922000
Web site: http://www.springer.com/adis/journal/40290
Freq: Bi-Monthly Not Audited
MAGAZINE
Pharmaceuticals

Pharmaceutical Patent Analyst 999422
Editorial: Unitec House, 2 Albert Place, London N3 1QB **Tel:** 44 02083 716090
Email: info@future-science.com
Web site: http://www.future-science.com/loi/ppa
Freq: Bi-Monthly Not Audited
MAGAZINE
Pharmaceuticals

Pharmaceutical Technology Europe 980871
Editorial: Bridegate Pavilions, 4A Chester Business Park, Wrexham Road, Chester CH4 9QH **Tel:** 44 01244 629300
Email: ptpress@advanstar.com
Web site: http://www.pharmtech.com/
Freq: Monthly
Circ: 34101 Not Audited
Profile: Publication carrying peer reviewed articles and regulatory updates on research and development, new products and manufacturing techniques for the industrial production of pharmaceuticals.
Ad Rate: Full Page Colour £6850.00
MAGAZINE
Biotechnology, Medical Technology, Pharmaceuticals

The Pharmacist 995890
Editorial: 140 London Wall, London EC2Y 5DN **Tel:** 44 02072 140500
Email: info@cogora.com
Web site: www.thepharmacist.co.uk
Freq: Quarterly
Circ: 7200 Not Audited
MAGAZINE
Pharmaceuticals

Pharmacy Business   981214

Editorial: Garavi Gujarat House, No 1, Silex Street, London SE1 0DW
Tel: 44 02079 281234
Email: editor@pharmacy.biz
Web site: www.pharmacy.biz
Freq: Monthly
Circ: 10060 Not Audited
Editor: Neil Trainis
Profile: Magazine covering clinical and business news, news analysis, features, new products, ideas for developing front of shop, management, OTC products, profiles and social events. Aimed at community pharmacists and pharmacy assistants in independent retail pharmacy outlets and pharmaceutical wholesalers.
Ad Rate: Full Page Mono £3001.00
Ad Rate: Full Page Colour £3001.00
MAGAZINE
Healthcare Industry, Pharmaceuticals

Pharmacy in Focus   984611

Editorial: 19 Ormeau Business Park, The Gas Works, Belfast BT7 2JA
Tel: 44 02890 332499
Email: editorial@profilepublishing.com
Web site: http://www.pharmacyinfocus.co.uk/
Freq: Monthly
Circ: 3500 Not Audited
Profile: Magazine covering profiles, interviews, issues and news on the pharmacy industry in Northern Ireland.
Ad Rate: Full Page Colour £1550.00
MAGAZINE
Pharmaceuticals

Pharmacy Magazine   981215

Editorial: 2nd Floor, Linen Hall, 162-168 Regent Street, London W1B 5TB
Tel: 44 02074 341530
Web site: www.pharmacymag.co.uk
Freq: Monthly
Circ: 16797 Not Audited
Editor: Richard Thomas
Profile: Magazine focusing on education, pharmacy news, product information, current affairs and features.
Ad Rate: Full Page Mono £3370.00
Ad Rate: Full Page Colour £5275.00
MAGAZINE
Pharmaceuticals

Pharmacy Online   999451

Editorial: 2 Cornflower Way, Moreton, Wirral, Birkenhead CH46 1SU
Web site: www.priory.com/pharmol.htm
Freq: Daily
Circ: 22998 Cision Digital Reach
Editor: Brian Green
MAGAZINE (ONLINE)
Pharmaceuticals

Pharmafocus   980732

Editorial: First Floor, 131 Edgware Road, London W2 2HR **Tel:** 44 02077 243456
Email: editorial@pharmafile.com
Web site: www.pharmafile.com
Freq: Monthly
Circ: 153643 Cision Digital Reach
Profile: Newspaper style publication covering the UK ethical and pharmaceutical industry and NHS. Contains features on the NHS and supply sectors.
Ad Rate: Full Page Mono £2895.00
Ad Rate: Full Page Colour £4295.00
MAGAZINE (ONLINE)
Biotechnology, Healthcare Industry, Pharmaceuticals

pharmaphorum   986811

Editorial: Rosemount House, Rosemount Avenue, West Byfleet, London KT14 6LB
Tel: 44 01932 339260
Email: editorial@pharmaphorum.com
Web site: www.pharmaphorum.com
Freq: Daily
Circ: 36076 Cision Digital Reach
Profile: Website covering pharmaceuticals. The pharmaphorum website discusses anything from healthcare industry and medicine research to pharma industry news.
MAGAZINE (ONLINE)
Biotechnology, Pharmaceuticals

Pharmaprojects   999457

Editorial: Christchurch Court, 10 Newgate Street, London EC1A 7AZ
Tel: 44 02070 175000
Email: pharmaprojects@informa.com
Web site: http://www.citeline.com/products/pharmaprojects/
Freq: Daily
Circ: 282 Cision Digital Reach
MAGAZINE (ONLINE)
Pharmaceuticals

PharmaTelevision   986885

Editorial: Fountain House, Parkway Court, John Smith Drive, Oxford OX4 2JY
Tel: 44 01865 332700
Email: enquiries@pharmatelevision.com
Web site: www.pharmatelevision.com
Freq: Daily
Circ: 5432 Cision Digital Reach
MAGAZINE (ONLINE)
Biotechnology, Pharmaceuticals

PharmaTimes   980731

Editorial: 8-10 Dryden Street, Covent Garden, London WC2E 9NA
Tel: 44 02072 406999
Email: pharma@pharmatimes.com
Web site: www.pharmatimes.com
Freq: Monthly
Circ: 22396 Not Audited
Profile: Magazine covering issues and developments in pharmaceutical management and marketing.
Ad Rate: Full Page Colour £3500.00
MAGAZINE
Pharmaceuticals

pharmiweb.com   984793

Editorial: PharmiWeb Solutions, Radius Court, 1st Floor, Eastern Road, Bracknell RG12 2UP **Tel:** 44 08455 482020
Web site: www.pharmiweb.com
Freq: Daily
Circ: 134891 Cision Digital Reach
Editor: Mike Wood
Profile: Website covering pharmaceutical. The phamiweb.com website is an portal providing news, information and recruitment solutions for the pharmaceutical sector.
MAGAZINE (ONLINE)
Pharmaceuticals

Philosophy Now   982133

Editorial: 43a Jerningham Road, London SE14 5NQ **Tel:** 44 02076 397314
Email: editors@philosophynow.org
Web site: www.philosophynow.org
Freq: Bi-Monthly
Circ: 15000 Not Audited
Editor: Rick Lewis
Profile: Magazine covering all aspects of philosophy.
Ad Rate: Full Page Mono £628.00
Ad Rate: Full Page Colour £835.00
MAGAZINE
Science

PhotoClubAlpha   1008436

Editorial: Maxwell Place, Maxwell Lane, Kelso, Kelso TD5 7BB **Tel:** 44 01573 226032
Email: iconmags@btconnect.com
Web site: www.photoclubalpha.com
Freq: Daily
Circ: 8579 Cision Digital Reach
Editor: Shirley Kilpatrick
MAGAZINE (ONLINE)
Photography

Photocritic   996934

Editorial: 34 Edinburgh Road, Newmarket, Suffolk, Newmarket CB8 0QF
Tel: 44 01638 667537
Email: hello@photocritic.org
Web site: http://www.photocritic.org/
Freq: Daily
Circ: 9418 Cision Digital Reach
MAGAZINE (ONLINE)
Photography

The Photogrammetric Record   984433

Editorial: The University of Nottingham, University Park, Nottingham NG7 2RD
Tel: 44 01159 515435
Email: rspsoc@nottingham.ac.uk
Web site: http://onlinelibrary.wiley.com/journal/10.1111/%28ISSN%291477-9730
Freq: Quarterly Not Audited
Profile: Journal of the Remote Sensing and Photogrammetry Society. Contains articles about current photogammetric practice and research around the world.
Ad Rate: Full Page Mono £420.00
MAGAZINE
Data Management, Science

The Photographer   983857

Editorial: The Coach House, The Firs, High Street, Aylesbury HP22 4SJ
Tel: 44 01296 642020
Email: editor@bipp.com
Web site: www.bipp.com
Freq: Quarterly
Circ: 2800 Not Audited
Editor: Jonathan Briggs
Profile: Magazine covering business matters, news and updates, features on issues relating to photography, interviews with working photographers and product and service reviews.
Ad Rate: Full Page Mono £1195.00
Ad Rate: Full Page Colour £1195.00
MAGAZINE
Photography

Photomonitor   999703

Editorial: 44 The Little Boltons, London SW10 9LN **Tel:** 44 07768 077062
Email: editor@photomonitor.co.uk
Web site: www.photomonitor.co.uk
Freq: Daily
Circ: 14190 Cision Digital Reach
Editor: Christiane Monarchi
MAGAZINE (ONLINE)
Photography

Photovoltaics International   988136

Editorial: Solar Media Limited, 5 Prescot Street, London E1 8PA
Tel: 44 02078 710122
Email: info@solarmedia.co.uk
Web site: www.pv-tech.org/photovoltaics-international/overview
Freq: Quarterly
Circ: 12500 Not Audited
MAGAZINE
Manufacturing

Physical & Occupational Therapy in Geriatrics   995455

Editorial: Christchurch Court, 10 Newgate Street, London EC1A 7AZ
Tel: 44 02070 175540
Web site: www.informahealthcare.com/loi/pog
Freq: Quarterly
Circ: 10000 Not Audited
MAGAZINE
Geriatrics, Occupational Therapy & Rehabilitation

Physical Education Matters   986060

Editorial: Room 117, Bredon, University of Worcester, Henwick Grove, Worcester WR2 6AJ **Tel:** 44 01905 855584
Email: editor@afpe.org.uk
Web site: www.afpe.org.uk/
Freq: Quarterly
Circ: 10000 Not Audited
Profile: Publication covering news and features relating to physical education. Aimed at teachers, lecturers, advisors and trainees.
Ad Rate: Full Page Colour £720.00
MAGAZINE
Schools & Institutions

Physical Therapy in Sport   995847

Editorial: Elsevier Publishing (Cooperate office) The Boulevard, Langford Lane, Kidlington, Oxford OX5 1GB
Tel: 44 01865 843000
Email: ptis@elsevier.com
Web site: http://www.physicaltherapyinsport.com
Freq: Quarterly
Circ: 48 Not Audited
Editor: Zoë Hudson
MAGAZINE
Sports Medicine

Physics World   981307

Editorial: Temple Circus, Temple Way, Bristol BS1 6HG **Tel:** 44 01179 297481
Email: pwld@iop.org
Web site: http://www.physicsworld.com
Freq: Monthly
Circ: 52000 Not Audited
Editor: Matin Durrani
Profile: Magazine of the Institute of Physics covering the latest physics news including features, reviews, readers' letters and regular columns. Aimed at physicists and scientists with an interest in physics.
Ad Rate: Full Page Mono £2990.00
Ad Rate: Full Page Colour £3740.00
MAGAZINE
Science

Physiotherapy   985202

Editorial: The Boulevard, Langford Lane, Kidlington, Oxford OX5 1GB
Tel: 44 01865 843672
Email: physiotherapy@elsevier.com
Web site: http://www.journals.elsevier.com/physiotherapy/
Freq: Quarterly
Circ: 224 Not Audited
Editor: Michele Harms
Profile: Publication of the Chartered Society of Physiotherapy. Contains reviews and research concerned with the scientific basis and clinical application of physiotherapy, education of practitioners and management of services. Aimed at physiotherapists.
Ad Rate: Full Page Mono £744.00
Ad Rate: Full Page Colour £1352.00
MAGAZINE
Occupational Therapy & Rehabilitation

Physiotherapy Theory and Practice   995426

Editorial: Christchurch Court, 10 Newgate Street, London EC1A 7AZ
Tel: 44 02070 175540
Web site: www.informahealthcare.com/loi/ptp
Freq: Bi-Monthly Not Audited
Editor: Scott Hasson
MAGAZINE
Occupational Therapy & Rehabilitation

The PIE (Professionals in International Education)   996428

Editorial: Unit A, Azure House, Dragonfly place, London SE4 2FP
Tel: 44 02081 335178
Email: info@thepienews.com
Web site: www.thepienews.com
Freq: Daily
Circ: 146964 Cision Digital Reach
MAGAZINE (ONLINE)
Education, Higher Education, Schools & Institutions, Students

Pieria   987277

Editorial: 1st Floor, 42 Southwark Street, London SE1 1UN
Email: info@pieria.co.uk
Web site: www.pieria.co.uk
Freq: Daily
Circ: 13109 Cision Digital Reach
MAGAZINE (ONLINE)
Banking, Economics

Pig & Poultry Marketing   986622

Editorial: Hendal Oast, Hendal Farm, Groombridge, Hartfield TN3 9NU
Tel: 44 01892 861664

Business Magazines

Email: news@farmbusiness.co.uk
Web site: www.farmbusiness.cc
Freq: Bi-Monthly
Circ: 5000 Not Audited
Profile: Magazine covering marketing within the food chain, increasing the competitiveness of UK farming, identifying future trends, anticipating customer demands and improving prices to the producer.
Ad Rate: Full Page Colour £1800.00
MAGAZINE
Animal Farming

Pig News and Information
983172
Editorial: CABI Head Office, Nosworthy Way, Wallingford, Wallingford OX10 8DE
Tel: 44 01491 832111
Web site: http://sites.cabi.org/publishing-products/online-information-resources/pig-news-and-information/
Freq: Quarterly
Circ: 100 Not Audited
Editor: Uma Sabapathy-Allen
MAGAZINE
Animal Farming

PigWorld
983173
Editorial: Suite A, Arun House, Office Village, River Way, Uckfield TN22 1SL
Tel: 44 01825 983105
Web site: www.pigworld.co.uk
Freq: Monthly
Circ: 4870 Not Audited
Editor: Alistair Driver
MAGAZINE
Animal Farming

Pilot
981897
Editorial: Evolution House, 2-6 Easthampstead Road, Wokingham, Wokingham RG40 2EG
Tel: 44 01189 742527
Email: news@pilotweb.co.uk
Web site: www.pilotweb.aero
Freq: Monthly
Circ: 10882 Not Audited
Editor: Philip Whiteman
Profile: Magazine covering all aspects of general aviation including flight testing of old and new aircraft, product tests for light aircraft, general news and book reviews. The magazine keeps pilots up to date with everything that is happening within GA. Aimed at affluent men with a passion for aviation, commercial pilots and those with a private pilot's licence.
Ad Rate: Full Page Colour £2200.00
MAGAZINE
Aviation

Pink Sheet
999288
Editorial: Christchurch Court, 10 Newgate Street, London EC1A 7AZ
Tel: 44 02070 175000
Web site: https://pink.pharmamedtechbi.com/
Freq: Daily
Circ: 24776 Cision Digital Reach
MAGAZINE (ONLINE)
Biotechnology, Healthcare Industry, Medical Technology, Pharmaceuticals

Pipe and Profile Extrusion
986020
Editorial: 6 Pritchard Street, Bristol BS2 8RH **Tel:** 44 01179 249442
Web site: www.pipeandprofile.com
Freq: Monthly
Circ: 29630 Not Audited
Editor: Lou Reade
Profile: Website covering plastic. The pipe and profile EXTRUSION website share news on plastic pips and profile extrusion.
MAGAZINE
Manufacturing, Plastics

Pipeline Coating
996140
Editorial: AMI House, 6 Pritchard Street, Bristol BS2 8RH **Tel:** 44 01179 249442
Web site: http://www.pipeline-coating.com/
Freq: Quarterly

Circ: 6087 Not Audited
MAGAZINE
Steel

Pipelines International
985069
Owner: Great Southern Press
Editorial: PO Box 21, Beaconsfield, Beaconsfield HP9 1NS
Tel: 44 01494 675139
Email: news@pipelinesinternational.com
Web site: www.pipelinesinternational.com
Freq: Quarterly
Circ: 9900 Not Audited
Profile: Magazine covering technological and operational developments in oil and gas pipeline design, construction, engineering, maintenance and servicing. Also covers news of activities, events and senior personnel.
MAGAZINE
Oil

PIR Education
1006761
Editorial: 53 Asgard Drive, Bedford MK40 3NF **Tel:** 44 01234 348878
Web site: http://www.education-magazine.co.uk/
Freq: Monthly
Circ: 7500 Not Audited
MAGAZINE
Disability, Education, Higher Education, Preschool, Schools & Institutions, Students

Pizza, Pasta & Italian Food Magazine
985074
Editorial: The Pizza, Pasta & Italian Food Association, Association House, 18c Moor Street, Chepstow NP16 5DB
Tel: 44 01291 636336
Web site: www.papa.org.uk
Freq: Bi-Monthly
Circ: 7500 Not Audited
Editor: Clare Benfield
Profile: Pizza, Pasta & Italian Food Magazine is the official journal of PAPA, the UK body representing manufacturers, suppliers and retailers. The magazine is published 6 times a year and distributed to retail buyers, caterers, restaurants, pizza takeaways & associated businesses in the industry. Publication containing news and features relating to the pizza and pasta industry and the Italian food market.
Ad Rate: Full Page Colour £1350.00
MAGAZINE
Food

PJ
981539
Editorial: 01 Maylands Business Centre, Redbourn Road, Hemel Hempstead HP2 7ES **Tel:** 44 01442 927222
Web site: www.newstech.co.uk
Freq: Monthly
Circ: 3000 Not Audited
Editor: Gary Cullum
MAGAZINE
Publishing

Place North West
984550
Editorial: Room 232, Royal Exchange, Manchester M2 7DD **Tel:** 44 07966 535262
Email: news@placenorthwest.co.uk
Web site: www.placenorthwest.co.uk
Freq: Daily
Circ: 32376 Cision Digital Reach
Editor: Paul Unger
Profile: Website covering property. The Place North West website shares the latest news and information on property in the north west.
MAGAZINE (ONLINE)
Architecture & Design, Commercial Real Estate, Finance, Legal Affairs, Office Design, Residential Real Estate, Retail, Sustainable Development, Travel Industry, Urban Planning & Development

Planet Biometrics
987675
Editorial: 25 Horseshoe Business Park, Pangbourne, Pangbourne RG8 7JW
Tel: 44 0189 844932
Web site: http://www.planetbiometrics.com/
Freq: Daily

Circ: 54856 Cision Digital Reach
Editor: Mark Lockie
Profile: Website covering science. The planet biometrics website shares information on biometric industry, promote the industry's expertise, give critical analysis, uncover breaking news, and, most importantly, provide educational information and advice for end users.
MAGAZINE (ONLINE)
Security & Security Systems

The Planner (UK)
996448
Editorial: 17 Britton Street, London EC1M 5TP **Tel:** 44 02078 807664
Email: editorial@theplanner.co.uk
Web site: www.theplanner.co.uk
Freq: Monthly
Circ: 18373 Not Audited
Editor: Martin Read
MAGAZINE
Urban Planning & Development

Planning
980878
Editorial: Bridge House, 69 London Road, Twickenham TW1 3SP **Tel:** 44 02082 674373
Email: planning@haymarket.com
Web site: www.planningresource.co.uk
Freq: Bi-Weekly Not Audited
Editor: Richard Garlick
Profile: Journal of the Royal Town Planning Institute. Carries news of transport, housing, regeneration, economic development, resource planning, environment and changes in planning law. Read by town and country planners.
Ad Rate: Full Page Colour £4085.00
MAGAZINE
Urban Planning & Development

Planning and Building Control Today
996711
Editorial: Datum House, Electra Way, Crewe Business Park, Crewe CW1 6ZF
Tel: 44 01270 502873
Web site: https://www.pbctoday.co.uk/news/
Freq: Quarterly
Circ: 19975 Cision Digital Reach
MAGAZINE (ONLINE)
Sustainable Development, Urban Planning & Development

Planning in London
984758
Editorial: Studio Petersham, Gorshott, 181 Petersham Road, London TW10 7AW
Tel: 44 02089 482387
Email: planninginlondon@mac.com
Web site: www.planninginlondon.com
Freq: Quarterly
Circ: 10000 Not Audited
Profile: Magazine focusing on the association with the London Planning Development Forum, bridging the gap between public and private sectors in planning London.
Ad Rate: Full Page Mono £660.00
Ad Rate: Full Page Colour £880.00
MAGAZINE
Urban Planning & Development

The Planning Portal
997168
Editorial: Room G08, Temple Quay House, 2 The Sqaure, Bristol BS1 6PN
Email: editorial@planningportal.gsi.gov.uk
Web site: https://www.planningportal.co.uk/
Freq: Daily
Circ: 12359 Cision Digital Reach
Editor: Paul Traynor
MAGAZINE (ONLINE)
Legal Affairs, Urban Planning & Development

Plant & Civil Engineer
984089
Tel: 44 02892 688888
Email: info@4squaremedia.net
Web site: www.plantandcivilengineer.com
Freq: Bi-Monthly
Circ: 6080 Not Audited
Profile: Magazine focusing on the plant and civil engineering industry, covering quarrying, construction and recycling waste.

Ad Rate: Full Page Colour £1200.00
MAGAZINE
Building & Construction, Engineering

Plant & Works Engineering
980975
Tel: 44 01732 370340
Email: editorial@dfamedia.co.uk
Web site: www.pwemag.co.uk
Freq: Monthly
Circ: 10037 Not Audited
Editor: Aaron Blutstein
Profile: Publication that covers works, plant and maintenance engineering. Also includes application and feature stories.
Ad Rate: Full Page Mono £1550.00
Ad Rate: Full Page Colour £1995.00
MAGAZINE
Engineering

Plant Engineer
981245
Editorial: Hawley Mill, Hawley Road, Dartford, Sutton at Hone DA2 7TJ
Tel: 44 01322 221144
Email: btinham@findlay.co.uk
Web site: www.plantengineer.org.uk/Default.aspx
Freq: Bi-Monthly
Circ: 5144 Not Audited
Profile: Magazine covering the specification, installation, operation and maintenance of all plant types for operations engineers in all industries (from manufacturing and process industries to utilities, power, transportation and the armed forces). Topics include energy efficiency, safety, education, plant equipment, plant design, inspection, process control, maintenance, repair and operations. Aimed at plant engineers, operations engineers, project managers, maintenance engineers and safety officers.
Ad Rate: Full Page Colour £1300.00
MAGAZINE
Engineering

Plastech
996398
Editorial: Stamford Ave, Springfield, Milton Keynes MK6 3LG **Tel:** 44 07525 499810
Email: info@gpublishing.com
Web site: http://www.plastechmag.com/
Freq: Quarterly
Circ: 8500 Not Audited
MAGAZINE
Manufacturing

Plastics in Packaging
984407
Editorial: Durand House, Manor Royal, Crawley, Crawley RH10 9PY
Tel: 44 01293 435100
Email: info@plasticsinpackaging.com
Web site: www.plasticsinpackaging.com
Freq: Monthly
Circ: 6000 Not Audited
Editor: Steven Pacitti
Profile: Magazine covering the flexible and rigid packaging industries. It covers news, company reports, new technology, investment, materials development and equipment reviews, together with relevant coverage of specialist areas such as recycling and bioplastics.
Ad Rate: Full Page Colour £2297.00
MAGAZINE
Plastics

Plastics News Europe
979921
Editorial: 9th Floor, Amp House, Dingwall Road, Croydon CR0 2LX
Tel: 44 02082 539600
Email: epnnews@crain.com
Web site: www.europeanplasticsnews.com
Freq: Monthly
Circ: 3218 Cision Digital Reach
Profile: Magazine covering technology, management and business issues relevant to the plastics industry in Europe.
Ad Rate: Full Page Colour £4850.00
MAGAZINE (ONLINE)
Plastics

Plating and Finishing
1061334
Tel: 44 86222 4410599
Email: ddyjs@126.com
Web site: http://www.pfoc.org.cn
Freq: Bi-Monthly

Circ: 5007 Not Audited
MAGAZINE
Engineering

Platinum Business Magazine
988647
Tel: 44 07966 244046
Email: maarten@platinumbusinessmagazine.com
Web site: www.platinumbusinessmagazine.com
Freq: Monthly
Circ: 123000 Not Audited
MAGAZINE
Business, Corporate Responsibility

PLC
979847
Editorial: Friars House Londo, 160 Blackfriars Road, Southwark, London SE1 8EZ Tel: 44 02072 021200
Email: info.practicallaw@thomsonreuters.com
Web site: http://uk.practicallaw.com/resources/uk-publications/plc-magazine
Freq: Monthly
Circ: 6000 Not Audited
Editor: Ruth Morrow
MAGAZINE
Corporate Law

PLOS Medicine
988890
Tel: 44 14156 241200
Email: plosmedicine@plos.org
Web site: http://journals.plos.org/plosmedicine/
Freq: Daily
Circ: 27048 Cision Digital Reach
MAGAZINE (ONLINE)
Biotechnology, Health Administration

Plumbheat
985924
Editorial: 4th Floor, Faulkner House, Faulkner Street, Manchester M1 4DY
Tel: 44 01619 743000
Web site: www.excelmediasolutions.co.uk/portfolio-posts/plumbheat/
Freq: Quarterly
Circ: 3500 Not Audited
Profile: Journal containing information for the Scottish and Northern Ireland Plumbing Employers Federation.
Ad Rate: Full Page Colour £975.00
MAGAZINE
Building & Construction

Plumbing and Heating Magazine
983158
Tel: 44 02892 612990
Email: phini@kmpltd.co.uk
Web site: www.plumbingmag.com
Freq: Bi-Monthly
Circ: 6500 Not Audited
Editor: Adam Hassin
MAGAZINE
Building & Construction, Residential Real Estate

The Point
995979
Editorial: 10-11 Percy Street, London W1T 1DN Tel: 44 02076 311155
Email: stories@bladonmore.com
Web site: http://www.bridgepoint.eu/en/news/the-point/
Freq: Semi-Annual
Circ: 9000 Not Audited
MAGAZINE
Private Equity

Police
984700
Editorial: Federation House, Highbury Drive, Leatherhead, London KT22 7UY
Tel: 44 01372 352000
Email: policemagazine@polfed.org
Web site: http://www.polfed.org/mag/
Freq: Monthly
Circ: 32000 Not Audited
Profile: Official magazine of the Police Federation covering all aspects of policing. Aimed at police forces throughout the UK, MPs and members of the House of Lords. Distributed nationally and internationally.
Ad Rate: Full Page Mono £1500.00

Ad Rate: Full Page Colour £1900.00
MAGAZINE
Public Sector, Security & Security Systems

POLICE Life
984701
Editorial: Unit 1 Colchester Business Centre, 1 George Williams Way, Colchester CO1 2JS Tel: 44 01206 369448
Email: info@police-life.co.uk
Web site: www.police-life.co.uk
Freq: Monthly
Circ: 42000 Not Audited
Editor: Jill Bareham
Profile: Magazine covering news relevant to police service personnel and general lifestyle including features on training, retirement, motoring, gardening, travel, overseas property, sports and leisure. Read by police service professionals.
Ad Rate: Full Page Colour £3200.00
MAGAZINE
Public Sector, Security & Security Systems

Police Oracle
986913
Editorial: 3rd Floor, Octavia House, 50 Banner House, London EC1Y 8ST
Tel: 44 02031 193303
Email: editorial@policeoracle.com
Web site: www.policeoracle.com
Freq: Daily
Circ: 60451 Cision Digital Reach
Profile: Website that covers the police and national security.
MAGAZINE (ONLINE)
Security & Security Systems

Police Product Insight
986680
Editorial: 3rd Floor, Octavia House, 50 Banner Street, London EC1Y 8ST
Tel: 44 02031 193360
Email: ppi-news@policeoracle.com
Web site: www.policeoracle.com/product-insight
Freq: Bi-Monthly
Circ: 42793 Cision Digital Reach
Profile: Magazine covering technology and services for police and national security. Aimed at those involved in the selection, assessment, procurement and implementation of police technology, equipment and services.
MAGAZINE (ONLINE)
Government Technology, Security & Security Systems

Police Professional
981670
Editorial: 7 Midshires Business House, Smeaton Close, Aylesbury HP19 8HL
Tel: 44 03333 208004
Email: editor@policeprofessional.com
Web site: www.policeprofessional.com
Freq: Weekly
Circ: 6000 Not Audited
Profile: Publication covering guidance on law and best practice, forensics, career development and training, crime analysis, technology, management and operational issues. Aimed at police officers, especially those from the rank of inspector to chief constable, heads of departments and specialists staff.
Ad Rate: Full Page Colour £2765.00
MAGAZINE
Public Sector, Security & Security Systems

Pollution Solutions
984569
Editorial: Oak Court Business Centre, Sandridge Park, Porters Wood. St Albans, London AL3 6PH Tel: 44 01727 858840
Email: pr@envirotechpubs.com
Web site: http://www.pollutionsolutions-online.com
Freq: Daily
Circ: 1447 Cision Digital Reach
Profile: Magazine covering water and waste water equipment, air clean up, consultancy services, soil remediation and waste handling. Aimed at the construction and utilities industry and governments.
Ad Rate: Full Page Mono £4150.00

Ad Rate: Full Page Colour £5145.00
MAGAZINE (ONLINE)
Alternative/Renewable Energy, Environment, Water & Sanitation

Polyester Industry
1062103
Tel: 44 86411 84793322
Email: jzgydlon@163.com
Freq: Bi-Monthly
Circ: 4000 Not Audited
MAGAZINE
Chemicals

Polymer International
984740
Editorial: The Atrium, Southern Gate, Chichester PO19 8QG Tel: 44 01865 778315
Email: polyint@wiley.com
Web site: www.interscience.wiley.com/journal/pi
Freq: Monthly Not Audited
Profile: Contains original peer-reviewed mini-reviews, research papers, rapid reports and critical analysis. Aimed at polymer and material scientists, engineers, strategists and opinion formers in academia and industry.
Ad Rate: Full Page Mono £1135.00
Ad Rate: Full Page Colour £2505.00
MAGAZINE
Science

PolymerTrack.com
996631
Editorial: 7 Centurion Business Park, Seaward Place, Glasgow G41 1HH
Tel: 44 01414 292525
Email: admin@polymertrack.com
Web site: www.polymertrack.com
Freq: Daily
Circ: 8531 Cision Digital Reach
MAGAZINE (ONLINE)
Plastics

Port Engineering Management
986324
Editorial: Office Suite 3, Enterprise House, Kings Road, Canvey Island SS8 OQY
Tel: 44 01268 511300
Email: shipaat@aol.com
Web site: portengineeringmanagement.com
Freq: Bi-Monthly
Circ: 4000 Not Audited
Editor: Alan Thorpe
MAGAZINE
Shipping & Warehousing

Post & Parcel
986014
Editorial: 4 The Courtyard, Furlong Road, Bourne End, High Wycombe SL8 5AU
Tel: 44 01628 642910
Email: news@postandparcel.info
Web site: postandparcel.info
Freq: Daily
Circ: 157152 Cision Digital Reach
Profile: Website covering the global mail and express industry. Features latest news, analysis of trends, viewpoints, top jobs and interviews with leading industry experts.
MAGAZINE (ONLINE)
Shipping & Warehousing, Supply Chain Management (SCM)

Post Reproductive Health
998844
Tel: 44 01628 890199
Email: prheditorial@sagepub.co.uk
Web site: http://mi.rsmjournals.com/
Freq: Quarterly Not Audited
MAGAZINE
Obstetrics & Gynecology (OB/GYN)

Postal Technology International
983338
Editorial: Abinger House, Church Street, Dorking, Dorking RH4 1DF
Tel: 44 01306 743744
Email: postaltech@ukipme.com
Web site: www.postaltechnologyinternational.com
Freq: Quarterly
Circ: 8000 Not Audited
Editor: Hazel King
Profile: Magazine covering all aspects of postal technology, including product profiles, reviews and news. Aimed at

directors and senior managers of postal organisations.
Ad Rate: Full Page Colour £4360.00
MAGAZINE
Industry

Postharvest News and Information
988050
Editorial: Nosworthy Way, Wallingford, Wallingford OX10 8DE Tel: 44 01491 832111
Web site: www.cabi.org/publishing-products/online-information-resources/postharvest-news-and-information
Freq: Bi-Monthly Not Audited
Profile: Journal containing abstracts, mini-reviews and conference papers on post-harvest research on grain, oilseeds, fruits, vegetables, ornamentals and other agricultural commodities.
MAGAZINE
Animal Farming

Potato Processing International
982818
Editorial: Chart House, 10 Western Road, Borough Green, Sevenoaks, Tunbridge Wells TN15 BAG Tel: 44 01883 734582
Web site: www.potatobusiness.com
Freq: Bi-Monthly
Circ: 4661 Not Audited
Editor: Aleksandar Stajcic
Profile: Magazine about the international potato processing industry including news, commentary on topical matters, new products, interviews, factory visit reports, case studies and a pre-planned, annual programme of industry-important special editorial features. Aimed at those involved in the potato industry.
Ad Rate: Full Page Colour £2750.00
MAGAZINE
Food, Manufacturing, Retail Management

Potato Review
984924
Editorial: Docwra's, Guestwick, Dereham, Dereham NR20 5AL Tel: 44 01362 684240
Email: edit@potatoreview.com
Web site: www.potatoreview.com
Freq: Bi-Monthly Not Audited
Editor: David Mossman
Profile: Journal covering in-depth review articles on market trends, technical and scientific developments and new products.
Ad Rate: Full Page Colour £2180.00
MAGAZINE
Food

Potato Storage International
986631
Editorial: Chart House, 10 Western Road, Borough Green, Sevenoaks, Tunbridge Wells TN15 BAG Tel: 44 01883 734582
Email: office@mediatrade.ro
Web site: www.potatobusiness.com
Freq: Semi-Annual
Circ: 4823 Not Audited
Editor: Aleksandar Stajcic
Profile: Magazine focusing on the global potato industry including developing trends and product innovations in the handling, packaging and storage. Aimed at storage managers and decision makers involved with the large volume storage of potatoes.
Ad Rate: Full Page Colour £2750.00
MAGAZINE
Food

Pound Sterling Live
995301
Editorial: Albany House, 14 Shute End, Wokingham, Wokingham RG40 1BJ
Tel: 44 08447 981113
Web site: www.poundsterlinglive.com
Freq: Daily
Circ: 602826 Cision Digital Reach
Editor: Gary Howes
MAGAZINE (ONLINE)
Business, Foreign Exchange Market (FOREX), Small and Medium Business

Power and Energy Solutions
998919
Editorial: PO Box 310, Bristol BS10 5WT
Tel: 44 01179 553417
Email: info@pes.eu.com

Business Magazines

Web site: www.pes.eu.com
Freq: Semi-Annual Not Audited
MAGAZINE
Alternative/Renewable Energy

The Power Engineer   980980
Editorial: Bedford Heights, Manton Lane,
Bedford MK41 7PH Tel: 44 01234 214340
Email: enquiries@idgte.org
Web site: www.idgte.org/powerengineer.
html
Freq: Quarterly
Circ: 400 Not Audited
Profile: Publication containing technical
papers and news items.
Ad Rate: Full Page Mono £380.00
Ad Rate: Full Page Colour £695.00
MAGAZINE
Engineering

Power Engineer   998491
Editorial: Europa House, 13-17 Ironmonger
Row, London EC1V 3QG
Tel: 44 02072 532545
Email: editorial@setform.com
Web site: www.engineerlive.com/Power-
Engineer
Freq: Semi-Annual
Circ: 10000 Not Audited
Editor: Louise Smyth
Profile: Publication containing technical
papers and news items.
Ad Rate: Full Page Mono £380.00
Ad Rate: Full Page Colour £695.00
MAGAZINE
Electricity

Power Engineering
International   980110
Editorial: The Water Tower, Gunpowder Mill,
Powdermill Lane, Waltham Abbey EN9 1BN
Tel: 44 01992 656600
Email: peinews@pennwell.com
Web site: www.powerengineeringint.com/
index.html
Freq: Monthly
Circ: 21900 Not Audited
Profile: Magazine covering global electric
power generation and transmission,
including news, technology, regulations and
analysis. Aimed at designers, specifiers and
planners working in power generation
companies and other allied fields.
Ad Rate: Full Page Colour £8840.00
MAGAZINE
Alternative/Renewable Energy, Electricity,
Nuclear Power, Oil, Water & Sanitation

Power Generation
Technology   998867
Editorial: 5th Floor - Roman Wall House, 1-2
Crutched Friars, London EC3N 2NB
Tel: 44 02037 944581
Email: editor@cavendishgroup.co.uk
Web site: www.powergenerationtechnology.
net
Freq: Quarterly
Circ: 10000 Not Audited
Profile: Magazine covering the latest
innovations, knowledge and expertise in the
power industry from the west to the BRIC
power bureaus, engineers and industry
professionals. It provides the emerging BRIC
power industries with comprehensive
coverage of component developments, the
latest equipment, better and more
environmentally friendly ways to deal with
power generation, power supplies and
sustainable energy. Power plant tours and
analyses of successful power campaigns
feature regularly. The magazine is mainly
distributed in China and India.
MAGAZINE
Alternative/Renewable Energy, Carbon
Emissions & Trading, Electricity, Energy,
Nuclear Power, Oil, Water & Sanitation

Power System Engineering
1061444
Tel: 44 86451 86062916
Email: dzxtgc@126.com
Web site: http://dzxtgc.periodicals.net.cn

Freq: Bi-Monthly Not Audited
MAGAZINE
Alternative/Renewable Energy, Carbon
Emissions & Trading, Electricity, Energy,
Engineering, Nuclear Power, Oil, Water &
Sanitation

power-technology.com   987715
Editorial: John Carpenter House, John
Carpenter Street, London EC4Y 0AN
Tel: 44 02079 366400
Email: onlineeditorial@kable.co.uk
Web site: www.power-technology.com
Freq: Daily
Circ: 135724 Cision Digital Reach
Profile: Website covering power
technologies. The power-technology.com
website discusses the latest global energy
industry news and projects in the renewable
energy sector.
MAGAZINE (ONLINE)
Alternative/Renewable Energy, Carbon
Emissions & Trading, Electricity, Energy,
Nuclear Power, Oil, Water & Sanitation

PPCJ   984704
Editorial: Quartz House, 20 Clarendon
Road, Redhill, Redhill RH1 1GX
Tel: 44 01737 855161
Web site: www.polymerspaintcolourjournal.
com
Freq: Monthly
Circ: 8652 Not Audited
Editor: Chris Malthouse
MAGAZINE
Plastics

PQ Magazine   983238
Editorial: Unit 3 Block A, Kingfisher Heights,
Bramwell Way, London E16 2GQ
Tel: 44 02072 166444
Web site: www.pqaccountant.com
Freq: Monthly
Circ: 32238 Not Audited
Editor: Graham Hambly
Profile: Magazine covering exam hints,
independent career advice, tips and advice.
Ad Rate: Full Page Colour £2895.00
MAGAZINE
Accounting

Practical Diabetes   985432
Editorial: John Wiley & Sons Ltd, The
Atrium, Southern Gate, Chichester PO19
8SQ Tel: 44 01243 770520
Email: cs-journals@wiley.com
Web site: http://onlinelibrary.wiley.com/
journal/10.1002/(ISSN)2047-2900
Freq: Bi-Monthly Not Audited
MAGAZINE
Diabetes

Practical Facilities
Management   981073
Editorial: 30 The Copse, St Georges,
Weston-super-Mare BS22 7SL
Tel: 44 01934 521224
Web site: www.practicalfm.co.uk
Freq: Bi-Monthly
Circ: 6000 Not Audited
Editor: Anne Donald
MAGAZINE
Building & Construction, Interior Design

Practical Farm Ideas   983581
Editorial: 11 St Mary's Street, Whitland,
Carmarthen SA34 0PY Tel: 44 01994 240978
Email: editor@farmideas.co.uk
Web site: www.farmideas.co.uk
Freq: Quarterly
Circ: 12000 Not Audited
Editor: Mike Donovan
MAGAZINE
Animal Farming

Practical Patient Care   984980
Editorial: John Carpenter House, John
Carpenter Street, London EC4Y 0AN
Tel: 44 02079 366400
Email: info@globaltrademedia.com
Web site: www.globaltrademedia.com/
products/practical-patient-care.html
Freq: Semi-Annual

Circ: 3811 Not Audited
Editor: Andrew Tunnicliffe
Profile: Journal focusing on best practice for
patient care, wound care management,
patient monitoring and safety.
Ad Rate: Full Page Colour £6900.00
MAGAZINE
Health Administration

Practical Photography   982031
Editorial: Media House, Lynch Wood,
Peterborough PE2 6EA
Tel: 44 01733 468546
Email: practical.photography@bauermedia.
co.uk
Web site: http://www.practicalphotography.
com/
Freq: Monthly
Circ: 25225 Not Audited
Profile: Magazine covering techniques,
equipment reviews and competitions. Aimed
at amateur and serious photographers.
Ad Rate: Full Page Mono £2700.00
Ad Rate: Full Page Colour £2700.00
MAGAZINE
Photography

Practical Pigs Keeping and
Rearing   995290
Editorial: PO Box 13, Westerham, London
TN16 3WT Tel: 44 01959 541444
Email: ppk.ed@kelsey.co.uk
Web site: http://www.kelsey.co.uk/brand/
specialist/practical-pigs/
Freq: Quarterly
Circ: 8000 Not Audited
Editor: Chris Graham
MAGAZINE
Animal Farming

Practical Poultry   983091
Editorial: Cudham Tithe Barn, Berry's Hill,
Cudham, London TN16 3AG
Tel: 44 01959 541444
Email: pp.ed@kelsey.co.uk
Web site: www.practicalpoultry.co.uk
Freq: Monthly
Circ: 23000 Not Audited
Profile: Magazine covering poultry advice
from incubation to housing, feeds to
breeding and showing to selling. Aimed at
domestic poultry enthusiasts.
MAGAZINE
Animal Farming

Practical Sheep, Goats &
Alpacas   987202
Editorial: Cudham Tithe Barn, Berry's Hill,
Cudham, London TN16 3AG
Tel: 44 01959 541444
Email: sga.ed@kelsey.co.uk
Web site: www.sgamagazine.co.uk
Freq: Quarterly
Circ: 20000 Not Audited
Editor: Liz Wright
Profile: Magazine covering practical
management and uses of sheep, goats and
alpacas. Aimed at livestock owners.
MAGAZINE
Animal Farming

Practice Business   983484
Editorial: One Tetbury Place, Business
Design Centre, 52 Upper Street, Islington,
London N1 0QH Tel: 44 02037 948555
Email: info@intelligentmedia.co.uk
Web site: www.practicebusiness.co.uk
Freq: Monthly
Circ: 8514 Not Audited
Profile: Magazine covering business
management information for practice
managers including industry specific news,
views and opinions.
Ad Rate: Full Page Colour £1875.00
MAGAZINE
Health Administration

Practice Management   984942
Editorial: St Jude's Church, Dulwich Road,
London SE24 0PB Tel: 44 02077 385454
Web site: www.practice-management.org.
uk
Freq: Monthly
Circ: 4500 Not Audited

Profile: An educational resource concerned
with the topic of advancing practice
management.
Ad Rate: Full Page Mono £700.00
Ad Rate: Full Page Colour £1050.00
MAGAZINE
Health Administration

Practice Nurse   981208
Tel: 44 01227 730284
Email: pnjournal@gmail.com
Web site: www.practicenurse.co.uk
Freq: Monthly Not Audited
Editor: Mandy Galloway
MAGAZINE
Nursing/Nurses

Practice Nursing   981209
Editorial: St Jude's Church, Dulwich Road,
London SE24 0PB Tel: 44 02077 385454
Web site: www.practicenursing.com
Freq: Monthly
Circ: 5481 Not Audited
Editor: Kelly Davis
Profile: Magazine containing education,
protocols, clinical and general articles.
Targets practice nurses and practice
managers.
Ad Rate: Full Page Mono £2000.00
Ad Rate: Full Page Colour £2000.00
MAGAZINE
Nursing/Nurses

Practice: Social Work in
Action   985345
Editorial: 4 Park Square, Milton Park,
Abingdon, Didcot OX14 4RN
Tel: 44 02070 176000
Email: practicejournal@bournemouth.ac.uk
Web site: http://www.tandfonline.com/toc/
cpra20/current
Freq: Quarterly Not Audited
Editor: Jane Akister; Editor: Roger Smith
Profile: Publication containing articles on
social work and social care.
MAGAZINE
Community Care (UK)

The Practising Midwife   983722
Editorial: 66 Siward Road, Bromley BR2 9JZ
Tel: 44 02083 139617
Email: laurayeates@virginmedia.com
Web site: www.thepractisingmidwife.com
Freq: Monthly Not Audited
Profile: Journal containing news, reviews,
methods, protocol and other features on
midwifery.
Ad Rate: Full Page Colour £950.00
MAGAZINE
Obstetrics & Gynecology (OB/GYN)

PRASEG   998568
Editorial: 6th Floor, 10 Dean Farrar Street,
London SW1H 0DX Tel: 44 07584 169555
Email: info@praseg.org.uk
Web site: www.praseg.org.uk
Freq: Daily
Circ: 8324 Cision Digital Reach
MAGAZINE (ONLINE)
Alternative/Renewable Energy, Electricity,
Government, Nuclear Power, Oil, Water &
Sanitation

Premier Construction   984028
Editorial: 2nd Floor, Stonebridge House, 1
Livesy Street, Rochdale, Rochdale OL16
1SS Tel: 44 01706 719972
Web site: www.romauk.net
Freq: Monthly
Circ: 40000 Not Audited
Editor: Alex Wiggan
Profile: Magazine covering news and
developments within the construction
industry.
MAGAZINE
Building & Construction

Premises & Facilities
Management   981074
Editorial: Blair House, 184/186 High Street,
Tonbridge, Tonbridge TN9 1BQ
Tel: 44 01732 359990
Email: pfm@imlgroup.co.uk

Web site: www.pfmonthenet.net
Freq: Monthly
Circ: 7168 Not Audited
Editor: Dennis Flower
MAGAZINE
Hygiene, Security & Security Systems

Pressgang.eu   998297
Editorial: 85 Tottenham Court Road, London
W1T 4TQ Tel: 44 02072 683010
Email: info@pressgang.eu
Web site: http://pressgang.eu/
Freq: Daily
Circ: 1145 Cision Digital Reach
Editor: Natalie Li
MAGAZINE (ONLINE)
Business, Small and Medium Business

Prestige Events   984814
Editorial: 108 Clydesdale Road,
Hornchurch, London RM11 1AJ
Tel: 44 01708 737393
Web site: http://www.
prestigeeventsmagazine.com/
Freq: Quarterly
Circ: 17000 Not Audited
MAGAZINE
Hotels/Motels

**Preventive Veterinary
Medicine**   997090
Editorial: The Boulevard, Langford Lane,
Kidlington, Oxford OX5 1GB
Tel: 44 01865 843000
Email: newsroom@elsevier.com
Web site: www.elsevier.com/wps/find/
journaldescription.cws_home/503315/
description#description
Freq: Bi-Weekly Not Audited
MAGAZINE
Veterinary Medicine

Preview   998753
Editorial: British Sky Broadcasting Ltd,
Grant Way, London TW7 5QD
Tel: 44 02070 323472
Web site: http://business.sky.com/sky-go-
further-range/sky-sports-preview-magazine/
Freq: Monthly Not Audited
Editor: Leaonne Hall
MAGAZINE
Business, Corporate Responsibility

**Primary Care Respiratory
Medicine**   995777
Editorial: The Macmillan Building, 4 Crinan
Street, London N1 9XW
Tel: 44 02078 334000
Email: npjpcrm@nature.com
Web site: www.nature.com/npjpcrm
Freq: Quarterly Not Audited
MAGAZINE
Respiratory Diseases

**Primary Care Women's Health
Journal**   999112
Editorial: Sherborne Gibbs Limited, 3 Arrow
Court, Adams Way, Springfield Business
Park, Alcester B49 6PU
Tel: 44 01789 766098
Email: production@pcwhj.com
Web site: http://www.womenshealthj.com/
Freq: Monthly
Circ: 1342 Cision Digital Reach
MAGAZINE (ONLINE)
Obstetrics & Gynecology (OB/GYN)

Primary Health Care   981210
Editorial: The Heights, 59-65 Lowlands
Road, Harrow, London HA1 3AW
Tel: 44 02084 231066
Web site: http://rcnpublishing.com/journal/
phc
Freq: Monthly
Circ: 6728 Not Audited
Editor: Julie Sylvester
Profile: Magazine focusing on news, views,
opinions and clinical research in health care.
Read by staff in health centres, health clinics
and major group practices in the UK.

Ad Rate: Full Page Colour £2299.00
MAGAZINE
Nursing/Nurses

**PRiME International Journal
of Aesthetic and Anti-Ageing
Medicine**   999651
Editorial: 5 Howick Place, London SW1P
1WG Tel: 44 02070 175000
Web site: www.prime-journal.com
Freq: Bi-Monthly
Circ: 10000 Not Audited
Editor: Balraj Juttla
MAGAZINE
Plastic/Reconstructive/Cosmetic Surgery

PrimeLocation   983755
Editorial: Harlequin Building, 65 Southwark
Street, London SE1 0HR
Email: editor@zoopla.co.uk
Web site: http://www.primelocation.com/
discover/property-news/
#FbpbHdI4Y3vLxoOZ.97
Freq: Daily
Circ: 13096 Cision Digital Reach
MAGAZINE (ONLINE)
Property Management & Maintenance

The Print Business   983296
Editorial: 3 Zion Cottages, Ranters Lane,
Goudhurst, Cranbrook TN17 1HR
Tel: 44 01580 236456
Email: printbusiness@me.com
Web site: http://www.
printbusinessmagazine.co.uk
Freq: Bi-Monthly
Circ: 6000 Not Audited
Profile: Magazine covering the latest market
intelligence, case studies, technology
breakthroughs and customer insights.
Ad Rate: Full Page Colour £2400.00
MAGAZINE
Publishing

Print Monthly   981262
Editorial: Unit D, Link House, Britton
Gardens, Kingswood, Bristol BS15 1TF
Tel: 44 01179 805040
Email: editor@printmonthly.co.uk
Web site: www.printmonthly.co.uk
Freq: Monthly
Circ: 10869 Not Audited
Profile: Magazine covering the latest
developments in printing. Includes articles
on 3D printing, 4D printing and digital
printing. Aimed at those working within the
printing industry.
Ad Rate: Full Page Colour £1395.00
MAGAZINE
Publishing

Print Solutions   1053418
Tel: 44 01892 522563
Email: hello@earthisland.co.uk
Web site: www.earthisland.co.uk/#!prints/
c13zq
Freq: Monthly
Circ: 12622 Not Audited
Profile: Print Solutions is a monthly title
which serves professionals working in the
print industry. Each issue contains "how to"
articles, industry leader profiles and analysis
of the latest industry news/trends. It's also
proud to contain articles on both the leading
edge technologies that will take print forward
into the future and the industry's wonderful
heritage.
MAGAZINE
Publishing

Print.IT   998328
Editorial: Amhurst House, 22 London Road,
Sevenoaks TN13 2BT Tel: 44 01732 759725
Web site: www.printitmag.co.uk
Freq: Bi-Monthly
Circ: 15000 Not Audited
Editor: James Goulding
MAGAZINE
Publishing, Software

Print.IT Reseller   988247
Editorial: Amhurst House, 22 London Road,
Sevenoaks TN13 2BT Tel: 44 01732 759725

Web site: www.printitreseller.co.uk
Freq: Monthly
Circ: 11000 Not Audited
Editor: James Goulding
Profile: Publication that looks at IT resellers.
Ad Rate: Full Page Colour £2000.00
MAGAZINE
Auto Aftermarket, Software

PrintLink   997825
Editorial: 1 Goodrington Place, Milton
Keynes, Milton Keynes MK10 9NT
Tel: 44 07525 499810
Email: info@gpublishing.com
Web site: www.printlinkmena.com/
Freq: Quarterly
Circ: 10000 Not Audited
Editor: M. Yousry Ahmed
MAGAZINE
Publishing

Printmaking Today   985597
Editorial: Cello Press Limited, Office G18
Spinners Court, 55 West End, Witney OX28
1NH Tel: 44 01993 701002
Email: cellomail@pt.cellopress.co.uk
Web site: www.cellopress.co.uk
Freq: Quarterly
Profile: Journal of the Royal Society of
Painter-Printmakers.
MAGAZINE
Publishing

PrintWeek   984684
Editorial: St Jude's Church, Dulwich Road,
Herne Hill, London SE24 0PB
Tel: 44 02077 385454
Email: printweek.newsdesk@
markallengroup.com
Web site: www.printweek.com
Freq: Bi-Weekly
Circ: 8351 Not Audited
Editor: Darryl Danielli
Profile: Magazine covering printing news,
technology and trends. Contains product
reviews and features, statistics, facts and
figures on the industry that provide in-depth
coverage of all the technical and business
issues. Includes articles on technology, 3D
printing, new contracts and a selection of
print sector jobs in its recruitment advertising
section. Aimed at printing professionals,
small and medium enterprises, and
influential printing companies in the UK.
Ad Rate: Full Page Colour £4485.00
MAGAZINE
Publishing

**Privacy & Data Protection
Journal**   995275
Editorial: Canterbury Court, Kennington
Park, London SW9 6DE
Tel: 44 02070 143399
Web site: http://www.pdpjournals.com/
overview-privacy-and-data-protection/
Freq: Bi-Monthly Not Audited
MAGAZINE
Data Management, Security & Security
Systems

Private Debt Investor   987164
Editorial: 140 London Wall, London EC2Y
5DN Tel: 44 02075 665444
Web site: www.privatedebtinvestor.com
Freq: Monthly
Circ: 4000 Not Audited
MAGAZINE
Private Equity

Private Dentistry   983901
Editorial: 1 Hertford House, Farm Close,
Shenley, Radlett WD7 9AB
Tel: 44 01923 851777
Email: info@dentistry.co.uk
Web site: http://www.dentistry.co.uk/
private-dental-news/
Freq: Monthly
Circ: 5000 Not Audited
Profile: Journal focusing on private dental
treatment and practice management.
Ad Rate: Full Page Colour £2365.00
MAGAZINE
Dentistry

Private Equity Africa   988009
Editorial: 4th Floor, 86-90 Paul Street,
London EC2A 4NE Tel: 44 02071 270402
Email: admin@peafrica.com
Web site: www.privateequityafrica.com
Freq: Quarterly Not Audited
Editor: Gail Mwamba
Profile: Private Equity Africa is published by
Rho Consult Media (Rhomedia) and covers
private equity, financial risks, derivatives,
structured products, foreign exchange
markets.
MAGAZINE
Emerging Markets, Private Equity

Private Equity Findings   999165
Tel: 44 02076 311155
Email: stories@bladonmore.com
Web site: http://www.bladonmore.com/our-
expertise/case-study/coller-institute-of-
private-equity
Freq: Semi-Annual
Circ: 20000 Not Audited
MAGAZINE
Private Equity

Private Equity International
                979788
Editorial: PEI London, 6th Floor, 140 London
Wall, London EC2Y 5DN
Tel: 44 02075 665444
Web site: http://www.
privateequityinternational.com
Freq: Monthly
Circ: 6000 Not Audited
Profile: Magazine focusing on the
fundamental issues shaping the private
equity industry. Delivers information and
insight into institutional investors and market
practitioners who have an active interest in
private equity. Articles highlight technical
issues and challenges that face the market.
Aimed at fund managers, financial
intermediaries and institutional investors.
MAGAZINE
Private Equity

Private Funds Management
                999115
Editorial: Private Funds Management, 140
London Wall, Sycamore Street, London
EC2Y 5DN Tel: 44 02075 665444
Web site: www.privatefundsmanagement.
net
Freq: Monthly Not Audited
MAGAZINE
Private Equity

Private Healthcare Investor
                996100
Editorial: 6th Floor, 140 London Wall,
London EC2Y 5DN Tel: 44 02075 665444
Web site: https://www.
privatehealthcareinvestor.com/
Freq: Daily
Circ: 864 Cision Digital Reach
MAGAZINE (ONLINE)
Healthcare Industry

Private Healthcare UK   983638
Editorial: 3 Churchgates, The Wilderness,
Berkhamsted, Berkhamsted HP4 2UB
Tel: 44 01442 817817
Email: editorial@privatehealth.co.uk
Web site: www.privatehealth.co.uk
Freq: Daily
Circ: 246430 Cision Digital Reach
Profile: Website providing information about
private healthcare services. Private
Healthcare shares the latest news on private
hospitals, doctors and specialists, private
medical insurance, cosmetic surgery,
dentistry and care for the elderly. Private
Healthcare was first published in 1996.
MAGAZINE (ONLINE)
Health Administration

Private Schools   984905
Tel: 44 01279 810080
Email: info@targetpublishing.com
Web site: www.ps-magazine.co.uk
Freq: 3 Times/Year
Circ: 20000 Not Audited

Business Magazines

Editor: Chantelle Kelly
MAGAZINE
Education

Pro Agri/Agri Trader   1060420
Tel: 44 27123 626390
Email: info@proagri.co.za
Web site: http://www.proagri.co.za
Freq: Monthly
Circ: 59353 Not Audited
MAGAZINE
Animal Farming

Pro Installer   987501
Editorial: Units 2 and 3 Burleigh Court, Burleigh Street, Barnsley, Barnsley S70 1XY
Tel: 44 01226 321450
Email: pr@clearview-uk.com
Web site: www.proinstaller.co.uk
Freq: Monthly
Circ: 35000 Not Audited
Editor: Helen Williams
MAGAZINE
Building & Construction

Pro Landscaper   987237
Editorial: 3 Churchill Court, 112 The Stree, West Sussex, Rustington BN16 3DA
Tel: 44 01903 777570
Web site: www.prolandscapermagazine.com
Freq: Monthly
Circ: 5000 Not Audited
Profile: Pro Landscaper provides researched information on landscaping, with latest products, features, interesting projects, interviews and tips. Targets industry professionals, landscape contractors, garden designers and landscape architects working across numerous industries (domestic, commercial, public and private sectors).Launched in September 2011. Regular features:News Shed – roundup of the months most relevant news Contractors news – what's going on in their worldLet's hear it fromôô. Leading industry figures speak openly to us Business tips – include industry recognised expert Sam HassallPortfolio – inspirational projects shared for us to learn from Look out forô. – up and coming leading lightsAPL/BALI news Latest Kit – what's new, what's different and specific product sector reviewsAngus Lindsay (probably the biggest buyer of kit) in-depth column Special Reports, Lawn care, Exhibition reviews, Prepare for season etc.Little Interviews – insight into our readers
Ad Rate: Full Page Colour £1400.00
MAGAZINE
Building & Construction

Proactive Investors UK   984119
Editorial: The Business Centre, Wool House, 74 Back Church Lane, London E1 1AF
Tel: 44 02079 890813
Email: uk@proactiveinvestors.com
Web site: www.proactiveinvestors.co.uk
Freq: Daily
Circ: 770717 Cision Digital Reach
Editor: Ian Lyall
MAGAZINE (ONLINE)
Equities

The Probe   981183
Editorial: The Old School House, St Stephen's Street, Tonbridge, Tonbridge TN9 2AD **Tel:** 44 01732 371570
Email: info@purplems.com
Web site: http://www.purplems.com/probe.html
Freq: Monthly
Circ: 14508 Not Audited
Editor: Anna Lambert
Profile: Journal covering practice management, clinical assessments of new techniques, previews of new materials and equipment, book reviews and dental news. Aimed at dental practitioners.
Ad Rate: Full Page Colour £2700.00
MAGAZINE
Dentistry

Process & Control   981078
Editorial: 15a London Road, Maidstone, Maidstone ME16 8LY

Web site: www.connectingindustry.com/ProcessControl/
Freq: Monthly
Circ: 11250 Not Audited
Editor: Michelle Lea
MAGAZINE
Chemicals, Manufacturing

Process and Control Today   980985
Editorial: PO Box 223, Tunbridge Wells TN2 9HU **Tel:** 44 01892 619616
Email: editorial@pandct.com
Web site: http://www.pandct.com/
Freq: Daily
Circ: 7386 Cision Digital Reach
Editor: Traci Horsley
Profile: Online publication/portal website covering the Process, Control, Automation and Manufacturing Industries. Process and Control Today publishes related news, new product, case study and white paper/opinion articles on a daily basis as they break and shares this relevant information 24/7 with its readers. Topics: Control & Instrumentation, Drives & Controls, Hazardous Area Equipment, Hydraulics & Pneumatics, Process, Solids & Materials Handling together with anything and everything that falls within these areas
MAGAZINE (ONLINE)
Engineering, Manufacturing

Process Industry Informer   984295
Editorial: 40B Passfield Business Centre, Lynchborough Road, Passfield, Liphook GU30 7SB **Tel:** 44 01428 751188
Web site: www.processindustryinformer.com
Freq: Bi-Monthly
Circ: 8500 Not Audited
Editor: Phil Black
Profile: Guide to process equipment and products. Targets managers and engineers in the process engineering, chemical engineering, process control and instrumentation, process manufacturing and process industry related disciplines.
Ad Rate: Full Page Mono £1750.00
Ad Rate: Full Page Colour £1850.00
MAGAZINE
Engineering, Manufacturing, Paper, Plastics, Steel

Procurious   998394
Editorial: 2 Eaton Gate, London SW1W 9BJ
Email: procurious@procurious.com
Web site: www.procurious.com
Freq: Daily
Circ: 50989 Cision Digital Reach
MAGAZINE (ONLINE)
Business, Small and Medium Business, Supply Chain Management (SCM)

Produce Business UK   990661
Tel: 44 20854 70129
Email: editorial@producebusinessuk.com
Web site: www.producebusinessuk.com
Freq: Daily
Circ: 18082 Cision Digital Reach
Editor: Tommy Leighton
MAGAZINE (ONLINE)
Food

Produce News   983583
Editorial: Brookes Mill, Armitage Bridge, Huddersfield HD4 7NR
Tel: 44 01484 321000
Email: rachael@planet-media.co.uk
Web site: www.foodanddrinknews.co.uk/
Freq: Monthly
Circ: 5000 Not Audited
Profile: Magazine focusing on the fresh produce and horticultural industries, including news, products and company features. Aimed at senior management and buyers, multiples, farmers, growers, wholesalers, manufacturers, processors, caterers, importers, distributors, packers, the foodservice, nurseries and garden centres.
Ad Rate: Full Page Mono £1535.00

Ad Rate: Full Page Colour £1925.00
MAGAZINE
Food

Product & Image Security   981675
Editorial: 81 Houting, Dosthill, Tamworth B77 1PB **Tel:** 44 01827 281143
Email: jeremyplimmer@aol.com
Web site: www.productandimagesecurity.org
Freq: Bi-Monthly
Circ: 350 Not Audited
Editor: Jeremy Plimmer
Profile: Journal featuring all aspects of product and image security, including anti-counterfeiting, theft and product traceability. Also covering print on packaging for the food and drink, pharmaceutical and cosmetics industries. Includes flexible packaging and product labelling, packaging origination, print processes (both narrow and wide web) and materials and folding cartons. Aimed at users and suppliers of product and image security products, victims of forgery, counterfeiting and theft and package buyers, graphic designers, technicians, technologists and people working in repro origination, package printing, industrial equipment and supply.Previous title: Product & Image Security Magazine
Ad Rate: Full Page Mono £1550.00
Ad Rate: Full Page Colour £1550.00
MAGAZINE
Security & Security Systems

Production Engineering Solutions   980085
Editorial: Featherstone House, 375 High Street, Rochester, Chatham ME1 1DA
Tel: 44 01634 830566
Email: newsdesk@pesmag.co.uk
Web site: www.pesmag.co.uk
Freq: Monthly
Circ: 15070 Not Audited
Editor: David Tudor
Profile: Magazine reporting on new machine tools and tooling, innovative CAD/CAM technology and applications in the metal working industry.
Ad Rate: Full Page Colour £2420.00
MAGAZINE
Aviation, Defense & National Security, Engineering, Manufacturing, Supply Chain Management (SCM)

Professional Builder   983381
Editorial: Regal House, Regal Way, Watford, London WD24 4YF **Tel:** 44 01923 237799
Email: pb@hamerville.co.uk
Web site: www.probuildermag.co.uk
Freq: Monthly
Circ: 119208 Not Audited
Editor: Terry Smith
Profile: Magazine covering news, products and information relating to the building industry, including information on materials, tools, techniques and deals as well as business matters, office management, tax, money and planning. Key areas covered include masonry, carpentry and joinery, plumbing, painting and decorating, roofing, flooring, tiling, and landscaping and decking. Aimed at building contractors and allied tradesmen of small and medium-sized businesses.
Ad Rate: Full Page Colour £3850.00
MAGAZINE
Building & Construction, Finance, Interior Design, Legal Affairs, Residential Real Estate, Sustainable Development, Urban Planning & Development

Professional Builders Merchant   981090
Editorial: Regal House, Regal Way, Watford, London WD24 4YF **Tel:** 44 01923 237799
Email: pbm@hamerville.co.uk
Web site: www.professionalbuildersmerchant.co.uk
Freq: Monthly
Circ: 9910 Not Audited
Editor: Paul Davies
Profile: Magazine covering merchandising, marketing, new products, legal update and news relevant to the building materials

supply trade. Aimed at key builders merchant directors, buyers, managers and personnel.Alternative Title: PBM A charge may be made for colour separation. PR by email only.
Ad Rate: Full Page Colour £2200.00
MAGAZINE
Building & Construction

Professional Engineering   979931
Editorial: Unit G4, Harbour Yard, Chelsea Harbour, London SW10 0XD
Tel: 44 02070 457500
Email: pe@caspianmedia.com
Web site: www.imeche.org/news/engineering/all
Freq: Monthly
Circ: 57406 Not Audited
Profile: Magazine covering engineering and its future. It includes topical news stories, feature articles and opinion columns. First published in 1988. Aimed at professional leading engineers, managers and directors, many of whom are members of The Institution of Mechanical Engineers.
Ad Rate: Full Page Colour £3500.00
MAGAZINE
Engineering

Professional Heating & Plumbing Installer (PHPI)   983380
Editorial: Regal House, Regal Way, Watford, London WD24 4YF **Tel:** 44 01923 237799
Email: phpi@hamerville.co.uk
Web site: http://phpionline.co.uk/
Freq: Monthly
Circ: 69263 Not Audited
Editor: Stuart Duff
MAGAZINE
Building & Construction

Professional Housebuilder & Property Developer   984622
Editorial: Regal House, Regal Way, Watford, London WD24 4YF **Tel:** 44 01923 237799
Email: phpd@hamerville.co.uk
Web site: http://phpdonline.co.uk/
Freq: Bi-Monthly
Circ: 14860 Not Audited
Editor: Jonathan Cole
Profile: Magazine covering housebuilding and developing. Each issue of PHPD includes features, news, finance, Soapbox, on-site evaluations, case studies which cover traditional and modern methods of construction, kitchens, bathrooms, showhomes, merchant news, all the latest general building and interior products plus competitions. Aimed at housebuilders and developers.
Ad Rate: Full Page Mono £2600.00
Ad Rate: Full Page Colour £2600.00
MAGAZINE
Building & Construction

Professional Imagemaker   986433
Editorial: 6 Bath Street, Rhyl LL18 3EB
Tel: 44 01745 356935
Email: info@supp.co.uk
Web site: professionalimagemaker.thesocieties.net/
Freq: Bi-Monthly
Circ: 8000 Not Audited
Editor: Mike McNamee
MAGAZINE
Photography

Professional in Payroll, Pensions and Reward   998637
Editorial: Goldfinger House, 245 Cranmore Boulevard, Shirley, Solihull B90 4ZL
Tel: 44 01217 121000
Email: info@cipp.org.uk
Web site: www.cipp.org.uk
Freq: Monthly
Circ: 13000 Not Audited
Editor: Michael Nicholas
MAGAZINE
Human Resources

Professional Investor   979783

Editorial: 4th Floor, Minster House, 42 Mincing Lane, London EC3R 7AE
Tel: 44 02076 486200
Email: info@cfauk.org
Web site: https://secure.cfauk.org/index.html
Freq: Quarterly
Circ: 11000 Not Audited
Profile: Journal of the UK Society of Investment Professionals. Covers news and investment features. Aimed at members of the society, UK and European fund managers and investment analysts.
Ad Rate: Full Page Colour £4500.00
MAGAZINE
Fund Management

Professional Manager   981062

Editorial: Capital House, 25 Chapel Street, London NW1 5DH **Tel:** 44 02037 717200
Email: professional.manager@managers.org.uk
Web site: http://www.managers.org.uk/
Freq: Quarterly
Circ: 118983 Cision Digital Reach
Profile: Journal covering developments in the management field. Read by managerial personnel.
Ad Rate: Full Page Colour £4630.00
MAGAZINE (ONLINE)
Human Resources

Professional Marketing   980922

Editorial: 422 Salisbury House, London Wall, London EC2M 5QQ **Tel:** 44 02077 869786
Email: pmmagazine@pmint.co.uk
Web site: www.pmforum.co.uk/magazine/index.aspx
Freq: Monthly
Circ: 2000 Not Audited
Profile: Journal covering news, case studies and marketing techniques for those working in the professional services.
Ad Rate: Full Page Mono £800.00
Ad Rate: Full Page Colour £1100.00
MAGAZINE
Marketing

The Professional Painter & Decorator Magazine   985096

Editorial: Stoney Lane Barn, Stoney Lane, Bovingdon, Bovingdon HP3 0LY
Tel: 44 01303 238002
Web site: www.professionalpainteranddecorator.co.uk
Freq: Quarterly
Circ: 21920 Not Audited
Editor: David Pescod
MAGAZINE
Interior Design

Professional Pensions   979782

Editorial: Haymarket House, 28-29 Haymarket, London SW1Y 4RX
Tel: 44 02073 169000
Email: profpens@incisivemedia.com
Web site: www.professionalpensions.com
Freq: Weekly
Circ: 11705 Not Audited
Profile: Magazine covering news and background on current issues in the pensions industry. delivers extensive news and features coverage for the corporate pensions and investment industry. Offering news and feature coverage of the key issues facing schemes and their sponsors, Professional Pensions hosts regular roundtable and panel debates providing in-depth analysis on a range of investment, administrative and legal topics.Aimed at pension scheme managers, trustees and pensions professionals.
Ad Rate: Full Page Colour £6595.00
MAGAZINE
Fund Management, Tax Law

Professional Photography
983712

Editorial: Quay House, The Ambury, Bath BA1 1UA **Tel:** 44 01225 442244
Web site: www.professionalphotographer.co.uk
Freq: Monthly Not Audited

Editor: Emma-Lily Pendleton
MAGAZINE
Photography

Professional Security Installer   981129

Editorial: PO BOX 332, Dartford DA1 9FF
Tel: 44 02082 958308
Email: andy.clutton@psimagazine.co.uk
Web site: www.psimagazine.co.uk
Freq: Monthly
Circ: 7000 Not Audited
Editor: Andy Clutton
MAGAZINE
Security & Security Systems

Professional Security Magazine   981668

Editorial: Westcroft House, Cannock Road, Westcroft, Wolverhampton WV10 8QW
Tel: 44 01922 415233
Email: admin@professionalsecurity.co.uk
Web site: www.professionalsecurity.co.uk
Freq: Monthly
Circ: 10000 Not Audited
MAGAZINE
Security & Security Systems

Professional Social Work 983845

Editorial: 16 Kent Street, Birmingham B5 6RD **Tel:** 44 01216 223911
Email: psw@basw.co.uk
Web site: https://www.basw.co.uk/psw/
Freq: Monthly
Circ: 20000 Not Audited
Editor: Shahid Naqvi
Profile: Journal of the British Association of Social Workers containing articles relevant to social workers and related professions also contains an employment section.
MAGAZINE
Community Care (UK)

profi international   981156

Editorial: An Daragh, Lealands, Helingy, Hailsham BN27 4DY **Tel:** 44 01323 441823
Email: editorial@profi.com
Web site: www.profi.com
Freq: Monthly
Circ: 11029 Not Audited
Profile: Magazine featuring independent tests on farm machinery plus practical ideas and tips.
Ad Rate: Full Page Mono £1712.00
Ad Rate: Full Page Colour £2396.00
MAGAZINE
Animal Farming

Profile   980519

Editorial: New Prospect House, 8 Leake Street, London SE1 7NN
Tel: 44 02079 026600
Email: profile@prospect.org.uk
Web site: www.prospect.org.uk
Freq: Quarterly
Circ: 105000 Not Audited
Profile: Magazine of Prospect Trade Union covering work-related issues for professionals, scientists, engineers and managers. Aimed at scientists, engineers and members of Prospect.
Ad Rate: Full Page Colour £4830.00
MAGAZINE
Engineering

Profit & Loss   980167

Editorial: Suite 46/48, 65 London Wall, London EC2M 5TU **Tel:** 44 02073 820331
Email: news@profit-loss.com
Web site: http://www.profit-loss.com
Freq: Monthly
Circ: 7500 Not Audited
MAGAZINE
Derivatives, Foreign Exchange Market (FOREX)

Progress in Fishery Sciences
1061312

Tel: 44 86532 85833580
Email: liusl@ysfri.ac.cn
Web site: http://www.ystri.ac.cn

Freq: Bi-Monthly Not Audited
MAGAZINE
Animal Farming

Progress in Geography   1061021

Tel: 44 86106 4889313
Email: editordlkxjz@igsnrr.ac.cn
Web site: http://www.igsnrr.ac.cn
Freq: Bi-Monthly Not Audited
MAGAZINE
Science

PROGRESS in Neurology and Psychiatry   985406

Editorial: PO Box 808, 1-7 Oldlands Way, Bognor Regis, Bognor Regis PO22 9SA
Tel: 44 01243 770362
Email: progress@wiley.com
Web site: www.progressnp.com
Freq: Bi-Monthly
Circ: 16/16 Not Audited
MAGAZINE
Neurology

Progress in Rubber, Plastics & Recycling Technology   984872

Editorial: Smithers Rapra, Shawbury, Shrewsbury, Shrewsbury SY4 4NR
Web site: www.polymerjournals.com/ProgressRubberPlastic.asp
Freq: Quarterly Not Audited
Editor: Kate Evans
Profile: Journal containing peer reviewed articles concerning rubber or plastics and recycling technology.
MAGAZINE
Plastics

Progressive Gifts & Home Worldwide   981292

Editorial: United House, North Road, London N7 9DP **Tel:** 44 02077 006740
Web site: www.progressivegifts.co.uk
Freq: Bi-Monthly
Circ: 6788 Not Audited
Editor: Sue Marks
Profile: Magazine focusing on giftware and home accessories. Aimed at giftware retailers, china and glassware outlets and department stores.
Ad Rate: Full Page Mono £995.00
Ad Rate: Full Page Colour £1395.00
MAGAZINE
Retail Management

Progressive Greetings Worldwide   983195

Editorial: United House, North Road, London N7 9DP **Tel:** 44 02077 006740
Web site: www.progressivegreetings.co.uk
Freq: Monthly
Circ: 6186 Not Audited
Profile: Magazine covering all sectors of the greeting card industry including retailing, publishing, wholesaling, artists, news, products and features. First published in 1990, the publication has an average of 80 pages per issue. Read by manufacturers, retailers, department stores, gift shops, publishers, artists and agents.
Ad Rate: Full Page Mono £1500.00
Ad Rate: Full Page Colour £1500.00
MAGAZINE
Graphic Design, Office Supplies, Publishing

Progressive Housewares 983196

Editorial: United House, North Road, London N7 9DP **Tel:** 44 02077 006740
Web site: www.progressivehousewares.co.uk
Freq: Bi-Monthly
Circ: 3500 Not Audited
Editor: Jo Howard
Profile: Magazine featuring house wares and kitchen and dining products, market reports, industry and retailer issues and news.
Ad Rate: Full Page Colour £1800.00
MAGAZINE
Food, Retail Management

Progressive Party   983197

Editorial: United House, North Road, London N7 9DP **Tel:** 44 02077 006740
Web site: www.progressiveparty.co.uk
Freq: Bi-Monthly
Circ: 7125 Not Audited
Editor: Jacqui Parr
Profile: Magazine containing news, research and specialist features with a focus on party planning.
Ad Rate: Full Page Colour £1500.00
MAGAZINE
Office Supplies, Retail Management, Toys

Project   981063

Editorial: Ibis House, Regent Park, Summerleys Road, Princes Risborough, Milton Keynes HP27 9LE
Tel: 44 01844 271640
Email: info@headlines.uk.com
Web site: www.apm.org.uk/project
Freq: Quarterly
Circ: 22037 Not Audited
MAGAZINE
Business, Corporate Responsibility

Project Accelerator   987371

Editorial: Whitehall, Worley, Nailsworth GL6 0RD **Tel:** 44 08455 192305
Email: naybour@btconnect.com
Web site: www.projectaccelerator.co.uk
Freq: Daily
Circ: 10816 Cision Digital Reach
Profile: Blog covering project management.
MAGAZINE (ONLINE)
Business, Corporate Responsibility

Project Control Professional
983696

Editorial: The Association of Cost Engineers, Administration Office, Lea House, 5 Middlewich Road, Sandbach CW11 1XL
Tel: 44 01270 764798
Email: enquiries@acoste.org.uk
Web site: www.acoste.org.uk
Freq: Bi-Monthly
Circ: 1900 Not Audited
Editor: Clive Wellings
Profile: Professional journal focusing on all aspects of the cost engineering profession. Covers project controls, planning and scheduling, resource and cost control, value engineering, estimating, quantity surveying, risk management and case studios.
Ad Rate: Full Page Mono £400.00
Ad Rate: Full Page Colour £550.00
MAGAZINE
Business, Corporate Responsibility

Project Finance International
979935

Editorial: 30 South Colonnade, Canary Wharf, London E14 5EP
Web site: www.pfie.com
Freq: Bi-Weekly
Circ: 2421 Not Audited
Editor: Rod Morrison
Profile: Publication reporting on and analysing the financing of major projects world-wide. Published every two weeks, PFI reports on the entire lifecycles of deals, from the initial rumours through to post-completion analysis, and allows you to identify every opportunity in your market while keeping a close eye on your competitors' activity too. Aimed at banks, sponsors of projects and lawyers.
Ad Rate: Full Page Mono £4000.00
Ad Rate: Full Page Colour £6000.00
MAGAZINE
Banking

Project Manager Today   981064

Editorial: Delta 1100, Delta Office Park, Welton Road, Swindon SN5 7WZ
Tel: 44 01189 326950
Web site: www.pmtoday.co.uk
Freq: Bi-Monthly
Circ: 11500 Not Audited
Editor: Amy Hatton
Profile: Magazine focusing on all aspects of project control, planning, costing and management throughout industry and commerce.

Business Magazines

Ad Rate: Full Page Mono £1860.00
Ad Rate: Full Page Colour £2495.00
MAGAZINE
Business, Corporate Responsibility

Project Plant   981107
Editorial: 11 - 12 Claremont Terrace,
Glasgow G3 7XR **Tel:** 44 01415 676000
Web site: www.projectplant.co.uk
Freq: Quarterly
Circ: 5181 Not Audited
Editor: Gary Moug
Profile: Journal covering news and features
on construction equipment.
Ad Rate: Full Page Colour £1525.00
MAGAZINE
Engineering

Project Scotland   980730
Editorial: 11-12 Claremont Terrace,
Glasgow G3 7XR **Tel:** 44 01415 676000
Web site: www.projectscot.com
Freq: Monthly
Circ: 6059 Not Audited
Editor: Gary Moug
Profile: Magazine containing articles on
construction from major civil engineering
works to housing and restoration projects,
architecture, company profiles and site
reports. Aimed at architects, surveyors,
engineers, council officers, government
departments, contractors and
sub-contractors.
Ad Rate: Full Page Colour £2600.00
MAGAZINE
Architecture & Design, Building &
Construction, Sustainable Development

Promo Marketing   982956
Editorial: 4th Floor, Holborn Hall, 193-197
High Holborn, London WC1V 7BD
Tel: 44 02038 480444
Email: news@promomarketing.info
Web site: www.promomarketing.info
Freq: Daily
Circ: 13752 Cision Digital Reach
Editor: Martin Croft
Profile: Magazine for clients, agencies and
suppliers active in sales promotion,
promotional marketing, incentives and
motivation. Read by marketing directors,
brand managers, marketing agencies,
marketing services suppliers.
Ad Rate: Full Page Colour £1690.00
MAGAZINE (ONLINE)
Marketing

Property and Development
                                    999097
Editorial: 1st Floor, Turnbridge Mills, Quay
Street, Huddersfield HD1 6QT
Tel: 44 02081 233414
Email: editor@ciaranjarosz.media
Web site: www.padmagazine.co.uk
Freq: Monthly
Circ: 14500 Not Audited
MAGAZINE
Finance, Legal Affairs, Residential Real
Estate

Property Auctions Today   990587
Editorial: Angels House, Albemarle Street,
Beckenham, London BR3 5HZ
Tel: 44 08450 750512
Email: press@propertyauctionstoday.co.uk
Web site: www.propertyauctionstoday.co.uk
Freq: Daily
Circ: 1544 Cision Digital Reach
MAGAZINE (ONLINE)
Residential Real Estate

Property in Practice   983650
Editorial: 113 Chancery Lane, London
WC2A 1PL **Tel:** 44 02073 205873
Email: propertysection@lawsociety.org.uk
Web site: http://communities.lawsociety.
org.uk/property/
Freq: Quarterly
Circ: 1600 Not Audited
MAGAZINE
Building & Construction, Legal Affairs,
Real Estate Law, Residential Real Estate

Property Industry EYE   987972
Editorial: Talbothays Farm, Winchfield,
Hook, Hartley Wintney RG27 8BZ
Tel: 44 01252 843566
Web site: www.propertyindustryeye.com
Freq: Daily
Circ: 150195 Cision Digital Reach
MAGAZINE (ONLINE)
Residential Real Estate

Property Investor News   983154
Editorial: 143 Churchill House, Stirling Way,
Borehamwood, London WD6 2HP
Tel: 44 02087 360044
Email: info@property-investor-news.com
Web site: www.property-investor-news.com
Freq: Monthly
Circ: 13000 Not Audited
Editor: Richard Bowser
Profile: Magazine covering news, analysis
and research on property and direct
investment - both residential and
commercial in the UK, Europe and overseas
markets.
Ad Rate: Full Page Colour £2575.00
MAGAZINE
Finance

Property Investor Today   1064093
Tel: 44 08450 750152
Email: press@propertyinvestortoday.co.uk
Web site: www.propertyinvestortoday.co.uk
Freq: Daily
Circ: 77252 Cision Digital Reach
Profile: Property Investor Today is a website
covering impartial property investment news
and information.
MAGAZINE (ONLINE)
Property Management & Maintenance

Property Journal   986045
Editorial: Parliament Square, London SW1
3PD **Tel:** 44 02076 951632
Email: journals@rics.org
Web site: http://www.rics.org/uk/news/
journals/property-journal
Freq: Bi-Monthly
Circ: 36000 Not Audited
Editor: Claudia Conway
MAGAZINE
Residential Real Estate

Property Law Journal   980728
Editorial: Kensington Square House, 188-
190 Fleet Street, London EC4A 2AG
Tel: 44 02073 969292
Web site: www.legalease.co.uk/Property-
Law-Journal.html
Freq: Monthly Not Audited
Profile: Journal updating UK lawyers on
developments and changes in property law
and emphasising on practical solutions to
real legal problems in everyday property
practice. Read by the legal profession and
other property professionals.
Ad Rate: Full Page Mono £995.00
MAGAZINE
Real Estate Law

Property Mall   987801
Editorial: 83-84 Long Acre, Covent Garden,
London WC2E 9NG **Tel:** 44 02078 363810
Email: press@propertymall.com
Web site: www.propertymall.com
Freq: Daily
Circ: 6720 Cision Digital Reach
Editor: Richard van Romunde
MAGAZINE (ONLINE)
Commercial Real Estate, Office Design,
Residential Real Estate, Retail, Travel
Industry, Urban Planning & Development

Property Management   980729
Editorial: Howard House, Wagon Lane,
Bingley BD16 1WA **Tel:** 44 01274 777700
Email: emerald@emeraldinsight.com
Web site: www.emeraldinsight.com/pm.htm
Freq: Bi-Monthly Not Audited
MAGAZINE
Property Management & Maintenance

Property Pages   998365
Editorial: 3 King Street, Mirfield WF14 8AW
Tel: 44 01924 493300
Web site: http://www.yorkshire-properties.
co.uk/index.php?p=1_8_Property-Pages
Freq: Monthly Not Audited
MAGAZINE
Property Management & Maintenance

Property Professional   996592
Editorial: Arbon House, 6 Tournament
Court, Edgehill Drive, Warwick CV34 6LG
Tel: 44 01926 496800
Email: ppm@propertymark.co.uk
Web site: http://www.naea.co.uk/
magazines/
Freq: Bi-Monthly
Circ: 16000 Not Audited
Profile: Magazine covering issues of interest
to members of the Institute of Auctioneers
and Valuers.
Ad Rate: Full Page Mono £1240.00
Ad Rate: Full Page Colour £1240.00
MAGAZINE
Architecture & Design, Building &
Construction, Commercial Real Estate,
Finance, Interior Design, Legal Affairs,
Office Design, Property Management &
Maintenance, Residential Real Estate,
Retail

Property Reporter   988908
Editorial: Unit 3, 81 Central, Church Street,
Blackpool FY1 1HU **Tel:** 44 01253 476319
Email: team@propertyreporter.co.uk
Web site: www.propertyreporter.co.uk
Freq: Daily
Circ: 83193 Cision Digital Reach
Editor: Warren Lewis
MAGAZINE (ONLINE)
Finance, Legal Affairs, Sustainable
Development, Urban Planning &
Development

Property Week   979897
Editorial: 6th Floor, Davis House, 2 Robert
Street, Croydon CR0 1QQ
Tel: 44 02082 538600
Email: people@propertyweek.com
Web site: www.propertyweek.com
Freq: Weekly
Circ: 12704 Not Audited
Editor: Liz Hamson
Profile: Magazine that covers the latest
news, features and commentary on the UK
and international commercial property
markets. Includes articles on law, planning,
auctions and finance. Read by property
professionals.
Ad Rate: Full Page Mono £1880.00
Ad Rate: Full Page Colour £3080.00
MAGAZINE
Architecture & Design, Building &
Construction, Finance, Interior Design,
Legal Affairs, Residential Real Estate

Property118.com   986711
Editorial: Aspiration House, Iceni Court,
Delft Way, Norwich NR6 6BB
Tel: 44 01603 489118
Email: info@property118.com
Web site: www.property118.com
Freq: Daily
Circ: 139616 Cision Digital Reach
Profile: Website covering the private rented
sector. The property118.com website
provides daily news updates including
legislation, best practice, financial
information and commentary relating to buy
to let property investment. The site also
offers due diligence calculators, a buy to let
quote engine and a property services
directory.
MAGAZINE (ONLINE)
Residential Real Estate

PROPERTYdrum   985076
Editorial: PO Box 624, Epsom, London
KT17 9JX **Tel:** 44 08447 453000
Web site: www.propertydrum.com
Freq: Daily
Circ: 6114 Cision Digital Reach
Profile: Magazine covering all property
related topics including residential sales,

lettings, auctions, commercial property,
legislation, regulation and legal issues.
Ad Rate: Full Page Colour £1700.00
MAGAZINE (ONLINE)
Residential Real Estate

Propertyexpert.tv   997084
Editorial: 40 Bowling Green Lane,
Clerkenwell, London EC1R 0NE
Tel: 44 02074 157070
Web site: www.propertyexpert.tv
Freq: Daily
Circ: 812 Cision Digital Reach
MAGAZINE (ONLINE)
Legal Affairs, Property Management &
Maintenance

propertytalk Live!   986444
Editorial: P.O. Box 468, London BR3 9FZ
Web site: http://propertytalklive.co.uk
Freq: Daily
Circ: 13912 Cision Digital Reach
MAGAZINE (ONLINE)
Property Management & Maintenance

PropertyTV   1059292
Editorial: 71-75 Shelton Street, London
WC2H 9JQ **Tel:** 44 08005 088650
Email: media@propertytelevision.tv
Web site: www.property-tv.co.uk
Freq: Daily
Circ: 2503 Cision Digital Reach
MAGAZINE (ONLINE)
Finance, Legal Affairs, Residential Real
Estate, Urban Planning & Development

PropertyWire.com   985016
Editorial: Fergusson House, 124-128 City
Road, London EC1V 2NJ
Tel: 44 02075 028220
Web site: www.propertywire.com
Freq: Daily
Circ: 97611 Cision Digital Reach
MAGAZINE (ONLINE)
Architecture & Design, Commercial Real
Estate, Residential Real Estate, Retail,
Travel Industry

Prosper   983680
Editorial: Creative Industries Centre,
University of Wolverhampton Science Park,
Glaisher Drive, Wolverhampton WV1 1ES
Tel: 44 01902 912311
Email: prosper@blackcountrychamber.co.uk
Web site: https://www.
blackcountrychamber.co.uk/chamber-
prosper-magazine
Freq: Quarterly
Circ: 3500 Not Audited
Editor: Lisa Bird
MAGAZINE
Business

Prosthetics and Orthotics
International   999839
Editorial: Wales Centre for Podiatric
Studies, Cardiff School of Health Sciences,
University of Wales Institute, Cardiff,
Western Avenue, Cardiff CF5 2YB
Tel: 44 02920 417221
Web site: http://poi.sagepub.com/
Freq: Bi-Monthly Not Audited
MAGAZINE
Occupational Therapy & Rehabilitation,
Orthopedics

PRUVODCE SORTIMENTEM
PAPÍRNICTVÍ   1060498
Tel: 44 42025 7329238
Email: drogerie-parfumerie@europrofi.cz
Web site: http://www.europrofi.cz
Freq: Annual
Circ: 2100 Not Audited
MAGAZINE
Graphic Design, Paper

PS   986896
Editorial: 113 Chancery Lane, London
WC2A 1PL **Tel:** 44 02073 205804
Email: privateclientsection@lawsociety.org.
uk

Web site: communities.lawsociety.org.uk/private-client/ps-magazine
Freq: Bi-Monthly
Circ: 3000 Not Audited
MAGAZINE
Consumer Interest, Corporate Law, Criminal Law, Employment, Family Law, Government, Human Rights, Intellectual Property, Law, Legal Services

Psychiatric Bulletin 995860
Editorial: Publications Dept, Royal College of Psychiatrists, 21 Prescot Street, London E1 8BB **Tel:** 44 02072 352351
Email: pb@rcpsych.ac.uk
Web site: pb.rcpsych.org
Freq: Bi-Monthly
Circ: 16000 Not Audited
Editor: Jonathan Pimm
MAGAZINE
Neurology

The psychologist 984454
Editorial: The British Psychological Society, St Andrews House, 48 Princess Road East, Leicester LE1 7DR **Tel:** 44 01162 549568
Email: psychologist@bps.org.uk
Web site: www.thepsychologist.org.uk
Freq: Monthly
Circ: 50000 Not Audited
Profile: Newsletter of the British Psychological Society. Contains reviews, articles, conference reports and readers letters.
Ad Rate: Full Page Colour £1050.00
MAGAZINE
Neurology

Psychology & Health 995445
Editorial: 4 Park Square, Abingdon, Didcot OX14 4RN **Tel:** 44 02070 176000
Email: enquiries@taylorandfrancis.com
Web site: http://www.tandf.co.uk/journals/GPSH
Freq: Monthly Not Audited
Editor: Mark Conner; **Editor:** Daryl O'Connor
MAGAZINE
Neurology

Psychology & Sexuality 995764
Editorial: 4 Park Square, Milton Park, Abingdon OX14 4RN **Tel:** 44 02070 176000
Web site: http://www.tandfonline.com/toc/rpse20/current
Freq: Quarterly Not Audited
Editor: Meg Barker; **Editor:** Darren Langdridge
MAGAZINE
Neurology, Sexual Health

Psychology and Psychotherapy: Theory Research and Practice 998977
Editorial: Journals Customer Services, John Wiley & Sons, Ltd., The Atrium, Chichester PO19 8SQ **Tel:** 44 01865 778315
Email: papt@wiley.com
Web site: http://onlinelibrary.wiley.com/journal/10.1111/(ISSN)2044-8341
Freq: Quarterly Not Audited
Editor: Andrew Gumley; **Editor:** Matthias Schwannauer
MAGAZINE
Neurology

Psychology of Sport and Exercise 995883
Editorial: The Boulevard, Langford Lane, Kidlington OX5 1GB **Tel:** 44 01865 843434
Web site: www.elsevier.com/wps/find/journaldescription.cws_home/620792/description
Freq: Bi-Monthly Not Audited
MAGAZINE
Sports Medicine

Psychology, Health & Medicine 995446
Editorial: 4 Park Square, Milton Park, Abingdon, Didcot OX14 4RN
Tel: 44 02070 176000
Email: ellie.gilroy@tandf.co.uk

Web site: http://www.tandf.co.uk/titles/13548506.asp
Freq: Bi-Monthly Not Audited
MAGAZINE
Neurology

Psycho-Oncology 995910
Editorial: The Atrium, Southern Gate, Chichester PO19 8QG **Tel:** 44 01865 778315
Web site: http://onlinelibrary.wiley.com/journal/10.1002/(ISSN)1099-1611
Freq: Monthly
Editor: Jimmie C. Holland; **Editor:** Maggie Watson
MAGAZINE
Neurology, Oncology

Public Finance 980182
Editorial: 17 Britton Street, London EC1M 5TP **Tel:** 44 02078 806200
Email: editorial@publicfinance.co.uk
Web site: www.publicfinance.co.uk
Freq: Monthly
Circ: 14964 Not Audited
Profile: Magazine focusing on public finance, covering central and local government, health, housing, charities and regulated utilities. Read by finance directors, treasurers, pension managers and chief executives in the wider public and relevant private sectors.
Ad Rate: Full Page Mono £2415.00
Ad Rate: Full Page Colour £3465.00
MAGAZINE
Banking, Public Sector

Public Finance International 1073642
Editorial: Public Finance International, Redactive Publishing Ltd, 17 Britton Street, London EC1M 5TP
Email: international@publicfinance.co.uk
Web site: http://www.publicfinanceinternational.org/
Freq: Daily
Circ: 20686 Cision Digital Reach
MAGAZINE (ONLINE)
Government, Public Sector

Public Health Journal 998953
Editorial: Public Health Editorial Office, Royal Society for Public Health, John Snow House, 59 Mansell Street, London E1 8AN
Tel: 44 02072 657331
Email: public.health@rsph.org.uk
Web site: http://publichealthjrnl.com/home
Freq: Monthly Not Audited
MAGAZINE
Health Administration

Public Health Today 996205
Editorial: 4 St Andrew's Place, London NW1 4LB **Tel:** 44 02036 961468
Email: news@fph.org.uk
Web site: http://www.fph.org.uk/policy%2c_publications_and_events
Freq: Quarterly
Circ: 3000 Not Audited
MAGAZINE
Community Care (UK), Health Administration

Public Law Today 998125
Editorial: Phoenix Yard, 65 King's Cross Road, London WC1X 9LW
Email: info@publiclawtoday.co.uk
Web site: http://publiclawtoday.co.uk/
Freq: Daily
Circ: 11752 Cision Digital Reach
MAGAZINE (ONLINE)
Government, Legal Services

Public Sector Build Journal 986302
Editorial: Pear Platt, Woodfalls Industrial Estate, Gravelly Way, Maidstone ME18 6DA
Tel: 44 01622 873229
Web site: www.psbj.co.uk
Freq: Monthly
Circ: 12000 Not Audited
MAGAZINE
Building & Construction, Government, Sustainable Development

Public Sector Building (PSB) 980787
Editorial: Unit 1 Sugar Brook Court, Aston Road, Bromsgrove B60 3EX
Tel: 44 01527 834444
Email: info@korumedia.co.uk
Web site: http://www.buildingtalk.com/psb-magazine-products/
Freq: Bi-Monthly
Circ: 8000 Not Audited
MAGAZINE
Building & Construction

Public Sector Building Specification 1056327
Editorial: Grosvenor House, Central Park, Telford TF2 9TW **Tel:** 44 01952 234000
Web site: http://tspmedia.co.uk/magazine/view/public-sector-building-specification
Freq: Quarterly
Circ: 12063 Not Audited
Profile: Magazine containing feature articles, case studies and a range of product information that is of relevance to specifiers and managers working in the construction industry. Aimed at specifiers and procurement officers working on construction related projects across the public sector.
MAGAZINE
Building & Construction

Public Sector Executive 983682
Editorial: 2nd Floor, 82 King Street, Manchester M2 4WQ **Tel:** 44 01618 336320
Email: newsdesk@publicsectorexecutive.com
Web site: www.publicsectorexecutive.com
Freq: Bi-Monthly
Circ: 8692 Not Audited
Editor: David Stevenson
Profile: Magazine covering issues relating to central and local government including urban management, finance, housing, recruitment, education, leisure services, e-government, conferences and exhibitions, risk and facilities management, products and services, human resource and development. Aimed at senior managers and executives in local and central government and the health services.
Ad Rate: Full Page Colour £1995.00
MAGAZINE
Government, Public Sector

Public Sector Sustainability 985921
Editorial: 42 Wymington Park, Rushden, Rushden NN10 9JP **Tel:** 44 01933 316931
Email: mail@pssmagazine.co.uk
Web site: www.pssmagazine.co.uk
Freq: Monthly
Circ: 11000 Not Audited
MAGAZINE
Environment, Government, Public Sector

Public Service Magazine 984010
Editorial: 8 Leake Street, London SE1 7NN
Tel: 44 02074 015555
Email: psm@fda.org.uk
Web site: www.fda.org.uk/Media/
Freq: Quarterly
Circ: 19000 Not Audited
Editor: Kay Hender
Profile: Magazine covering business and current affairs in or affecting the public sector.
Ad Rate: Full Page Colour £2250.00
MAGAZINE
Government, Public Sector

publictechnology.net 983753
Editorial: 21 Dartmouth Street, London SW1H 9BP **Tel:** 44 02075 935588
Email: publictechnology@dods.co.uk
Web site: www.publictechnology.net
Freq: Daily
Circ: 19388 Cision Digital Reach
MAGAZINE (ONLINE)
Government Technology, Public Sector

Pulp Paper & Logistics 986298
Editorial: Tralee, Hillcrest Road, Edenbridge, Edenbridge TN8 6JS **Tel:** 44 01732 505724
Email: news@pulp-paperworld.com
Web site: www.pulp-paperworld.com
Freq: Bi-Monthly
Circ: 26720 Not Audited
Profile: Provides information, news and articles to pulp, paper, tissue and board mills and paper merchants and industry related associations.
Ad Rate: Full Page Colour £2350.00
MAGAZINE
Paper

Pump Industry Analyst 981033
Editorial: The Boulevard, Langford Lane, Kidlington, Oxford OX5 1GB
Tel: 44 01865 843000
Web site: www.elsevier.com/journals/pump-industry-analyst/1359-6128
Freq: Monthly Not Audited
Profile: Business newsletter covering the international pump industry.
MAGAZINE
Engineering

Punchline 1053813
Editorial: The Old Fire Station, Barbican Road, Gloucester GL1 2JF
Tel: 44 01452 308781
Email: enquiries@moosepartnership.co.uk
Web site: http://www.punchline-gloucester.com
Freq: Monthly
Circ: 12000 Not Audited
Editor: Mark Owen
Profile: Business to business magazine covering business news in Gloucestershire. It contains business advice and information that is of interest to local business owners and features new launches and start-ups. It campaigns on behalf of businesses on issues such as parking and waste management. General interest, spoof articles are also featured within the magazine, providing a light-hearted look at topics from around the world. Aimed at businesses in Gloucester, Cheltenham, Stroud, Cirencester, Tewkesbury, Tetbury, the Forest of Dean and Postcodes GL1, GL2, GL3 and GL4.
Ad Rate: Full Page Mono £400.00
MAGAZINE
Business, Small and Medium Business

PV Tech Power 997322
Editorial: 3rd Floor, America House, 2 America Square, London EC3N 2LU
Tel: 44 02078 710122
Web site: www.pv-tech.org
Freq: Quarterly
Circ: 22000 Not Audited
MAGAZINE
Alternative/Renewable Energy

PV-Tech.org 987236
Editorial: Solar Media Limited, 5 Prescot Street, London E1 8PA
Tel: 44 02078 710122
Email: info@pv-tech.org
Web site: http://www.pv-tech.org
Freq: Daily
Circ: 198572 Cision Digital Reach
Profile: Website covering solar technology. PV-tech.org website discusses anything from solar news and technology to market watch.
MAGAZINE (ONLINE)
Alternative/Renewable Energy, Electricity

QA Education 981567
Editorial: Rhone House, Canal Side, Chorley, Chorley PR6 0BU
Tel: 44 01257 267677
Email: qaeducationmagazine@gmail.com
Web site: www.qaeducation.co.uk
Freq: Bi-Monthly
Circ: 10330 Not Audited
Profile: Guide containing information on cost-effective services and resources for schools.

Business Magazines

Ad Rate: Full Page Colour £1200.00
MAGAZINE
Disability, Education, Higher Education, Preschool, Schools & Institutions, Students

QB QuickBite Magazine 985923
Editorial: Unit 9, Wilkinson Court, Clywedog Road South, Wrexham LL13 9AE
Tel: 44 03330 030499
Email: editor@quickbitemagazine.co.uk
Web site: www.quickbitemagazine.co.uk
Freq: Monthly
Circ: 32000 Not Audited
Editor: Scott Rumsey
MAGAZINE
Food

Qilu Pharmaceutical Affairs
1061544
Tel: 44 86531 81216586
Email: editor@cndrug.net
Freq: Monthly Not Audited
MAGAZINE
Pharmaceuticals

QS Top Executive Guide 999069
Editorial: 1 Tranley Mews, Fleet Road, London NW3 2DG **Tel:** 44 02072 847200
Email: editorial@qs.com
Web site: https://www.topmba.com/why-mba/publications/qs-topexecutive-guide-summer-2017
Freq: Semi-Annual Not Audited
MAGAZINE
Education

Qualitative Research in Sport, Exercise and Health 995718
Editorial: Mortimer House, 37-41 Mortimer Street, London W1T 3JH
Web site: http://www.tandf.co.uk/journals/rqrs
Freq: Bi-Monthly
MAGAZINE
Sports Medicine

Quality in Primary Care 985225
Editorial: 483 Green Lanes, London N13 4BS
Email: primarycare@imedpub.com
Web site: http://primarycare.imedpub.com/
Freq: Bi-Monthly
Profile: Journal which informs those involved or interested in quality about effective methods and innovations and to stimulate discussion of topical issues. The journal is particularly concerned with clinical governance in primary care and at the interfaces between primary and secondary, and primary and social care. Aimed at leaders of clinical and organisational teams in both secondary and primary care, and also medical and healthcare libraries.
Ad Rate: Full Page Mono £400.00
MAGAZINE
Health Administration

Quality Manufacturing Today (QMT) 984518
Editorial: Eagle House, Cranleigh Cose, Sanderstead, South Croydon CR2 9LH
Email: editorial@qmtmag.com
Web site: www.qmtmag.com
Freq: Bi-Monthly
Circ: 4000 Not Audited
MAGAZINE
Manufacturing

Quality World 981066
Editorial: 2nd Floor North, Chancery Exchange, 10 Furnival Street, London EC4A 1AB **Tel:** 44 02072 456676
Email: editorial@thecqi.org
Web site: https://www.quality.org/qualityworld
Freq: Monthly
Circ: 20000 Not Audited
Editor: Robert Gibson
MAGAZINE
Business

Quantum Leap 980807
Editorial: 3 Campden House Court, 42 Gloucester Walk, London W8 4HU
Tel: 44 02079 377879
Web site: www.quantumleapnewsletter.co.uk
Freq: Monthly Not Audited
Editor: Quentin Lumsden
MAGAZINE
Financial Markets, Investment Banking

Quarry Management 981223
Editorial: 7 Regent Street, Nottingham NG1 5BS **Tel:** 44 01159 411315
Email: mail@qmj.co.uk
Web site: www.quarrymanagement.com/index.htm
Freq: Monthly
Circ: 4787 Not Audited
Editor: Stephen Adam
Profile: Monthly journal for the quarry products and associated industries. Aimed at quarry managers, executives and technologists.
Ad Rate: Full Page Mono £1000.00
Ad Rate: Full Page Colour £1775.00
MAGAZINE
Mining & Quarrying

The Quarterly Journal of Experimental Psychology
995827
Tel: 44 02070 177720
Email: qjep@telenet.be
Web site: http://www.tandfonline.com/toc/pqje20/current#.UcsKIztQH3U
Freq: Monthly Not Audited
Editor: Marc Brysbaert
MAGAZINE
Neurology

Qube Magazine 980935
Editorial: Wisteria House, Stump Cross Lane, Swineshead, Boston PE20 3JJ
Tel: 44 08453 880281
Email: editor@qubeonline.co.uk
Web site: www.qubeonline.co.uk
Freq: Monthly
MAGAZINE (ONLINE)
Building & Construction, Commercial Real Estate, Office Design

Quest 984632
Editorial: Unit B4, Beech House, Melbourn Science Park, Melbourn SG8 6HB
Tel: 44 01763 268120
Email: info@questonline.co.uk
Web site: www.questonline.co.uk
Freq: Monthly
Circ: 25000 Not Audited
Editor: Lynn Brown
Profile: Magazine providing assistance and help to members of the armed forces and their families, including education, resettlement and recruitment information.
Ad Rate: Full Page Mono £3650.00
Ad Rate: Full Page Colour £3650.00
MAGAZINE
Defense & National Security

Quick Print Pro 984281
Editorial: 36 Cheltenham Place, Brighton BN1 4AB **Tel:** 44 01273 674321
Email: editor@quickprintpro.co.uk
Web site: www.quickprintpro.co.uk
Freq: Monthly
Circ: 6600 Not Audited
Editor: Peter Foulkes
Profile: Magazine covering the digital print and 3D printing industry. It contains industry news, product information, business guidance and a suppliers index. Aimed at digital printers, copy and instant print bureaux, high street printers and in-house corporate print rooms.
Ad Rate: Full Page Mono £600.00
Ad Rate: Full Page Colour £1500.00
MAGAZINE
Publishing

Quite Fancy That magazine
1052951
Tel: 44 01243 555703
Email: studio@quitefancythat.co.uk

Web site: http://www.quitefancythat.co.uk/
Freq: Bi-Monthly
Circ: 15000 Not Audited
Editor: Dana-Jane Fisher
MAGAZINE
News & Current Affairs

Quocirca 988911
Editorial: Mountbatten House, Fairacres, Windsor, Windsor SL4 4LE
Tel: 44 01753 754838
Web site: www.quocirca.com
Freq: Daily
Circ: 14468 Cision Digital Reach
MAGAZINE (ONLINE)
Computers, Data Management, Industry, Mobile Communications, Software

R&D Focus Drug News 980774
Editorial: 210 Pentonville Road, London N1 9JY **Tel:** 44 02073 935000
Email: rdfocus@uk.imshealth.com
Web site: http://www.imshealth.com
Freq: Weekly
MAGAZINE
Biotechnology, Pharmaceuticals

R&D Management 996567
Editorial: 9600 Garsington Road, Oxford OX4 2DQ **Tel:** 44 01865 476292
Email: radmedoffice@wiley.com
Web site: http://onlinelibrary.wiley.com/journal/10.1111/(ISSN)1467-9310
Freq: Bi-Monthly Not Audited
MAGAZINE
Human Resources

RAC 981337
Editorial: Telephone House, 69-77 Paul Street, London EC2A 4NQ
Tel: 44 02030 332851
Web site: www.racplus.com
Freq: Monthly
Circ: 3472 Not Audited
Profile: Magazine covering the air conditioning and refrigeration industry including breaking-news, contract openings, new product features, troubleshooting tips and technical information. Aimed at senior decision makers and buyers in the UK and overseas. Also aimed at installers, distributors, manufacturers and end users.
Ad Rate: Full Page Colour £1780.00
MAGAZINE
Engineering

rad magazine 986329
Editorial: 11 Bardfield Centre, Great Bardfield, Braintree CM7 4SL
Tel: 44 01371 812960
Email: info@radmagazine.co.uk
Web site: www.radmagazine.co.uk
Freq: Monthly
Circ: 8500 Not Audited
Profile: Magazine covering news and features relating to medical equipment, health and hygiene, radiology, radiography, radiotherapy, nuclear medicine and ultrasonics. Aimed at radiologists, radiotherapists, medical physicists, and others working in CT, MR imaging and nuclear medicine.
Ad Rate: Full Page Mono £1860.00
Ad Rate: Full Page Colour £3660.00
MAGAZINE
Diagnostic Imaging, Medical Technology

RadcliffeCardiology.com
1105205
Email: editor@radcliffecardiology.com
Web site: www.radcliffecardiology.com
Freq: Daily
Circ: 38373 Cision Digital Reach
MAGAZINE (ONLINE)
Cardiology

Radiation Protection Dosimetry 982896
Editorial: Great Clarendon Street, Oxford OX2 6DP **Tel:** 44 01865 556767
Web site: rpd.oxfordjournals.org
Freq: Bi-Weekly Not Audited

Profile: Publication covering all aspects of personal and environmental dosimetry and monitoring, for both ionising and non-ionising radiations, including biological aspects, physical concepts, biophysical dosimetry, external and internal workplace monitoring and accident dosimetry. Aimed at radiation protection practitioners and scientists in research, industry, universities, radiation dosimetrists, regulators, radiobiologists and environmentalists.
Ad Rate: Full Page Mono £646.00
Ad Rate: Full Page Colour £1076.00
MAGAZINE
Nuclear Power

RAF News 980088
Editorial: Room 68, Lancaster Building, HQ Air Command, RAF High Wycombe, Walter's Ash HP14 4UE **Tel:** 44 01494 497412
Email: editor@rafnews.co.uk
Web site: www.tenalpspublishing.com/market-sectors/magazine/raf-news
Freq: Bi-Weekly
Circ: 40000 Not Audited
Editor: Simon Williams
Profile: Publication covering news on Royal Air Force stations, aircraft, personnel and activities. First published in 1961, the publication has an average of 28 pages per issue. Aimed at Royal Air Force personnel and former members of the service and military enthusiasts.
Ad Rate: Full Page Mono £2360.00
Ad Rate: Full Page Colour £2990.00
MAGAZINE
Defense & National Security

The Ranger 986408
Editorial: PO Box 75, Brighouse, Brighouse HD6 3SD **Tel:** 44 01484 400666
Email: keith@theranger.co.uk
Web site: www.theranger.co.uk
Freq: Monthly
Circ: 1100 Not Audited
Editor: Keith Wild
Profile: Magazine containing news and features on free range egg production including veterinary and husbandry information. Aimed at members of the British Free Range Egg Producers Association.
Ad Rate: Full Page Colour £200.00
MAGAZINE
Animal Farming

RCN Bulletin - All Editions
998620
Editorial: 20 Cavendish Square, London W1G 0RN **Tel:** 44 02084 231066
Email: bulletin@rcn.org.uk
Web site: https://www.rcn.org.uk/news-and-events/rcn-magazines
Freq: Monthly
Circ: 444369 Not Audited
MAGAZINE
Nursing/Nurses

RCPCH Focus 997568
Editorial: 5-11 Theobalds Road, London WC1X 8SH **Tel:** 44 02070 926000
Email: newsletter@rcpch.ac.uk
Web site: www.rcpch.ac.uk
Freq: Quarterly
Circ: 16000 Not Audited
MAGAZINE
Pediatrics

Re:locate Global 984440
Editorial: Spray Hill, Hastings Road, Lamberhurst, Tunbridge Wells TN3 8JB
Tel: 44 01892 891334
Email: editorial@relocatemagazine.com
Web site: www.relocatemagazine.com
Freq: Quarterly
Circ: 15000 Not Audited
MAGAZINE
Business, Company News & Appointments, Education, Employment, Health & Safety, Human Resources, Recruiting, Small and Medium Business

RE4view 996058
Editorial: Cleeve Road, Leatherhead, London KT22 7SA **Tel:** 44 01372 367345
Email: info@edifera.com

Web site: http://shop.era.co.uk/products.
asp?recnumber=26
Freq: Bi-Monthly Not Audited
MAGAZINE
Environment

Reactions 980180
Editorial: 3rd Floor, 41 Eastcheap, London
EC3M 1DT **Tel:** 44 02077 798610
Web site: www.reactionsnet.com
Freq: Monthly Not Audited
Editor: David Benyon
Profile: Magazine covering financial
intelligence including news and analysis on
insurance and reinsurance worldwide. Aimed
at executives working in the global insurance
and reinsurance markets.
Ad Rate: Full Page Mono £11032.00
Ad Rate: Full Page Colour £12225.00
MAGAZINE
Insurance

Reading:UK 996526
Editorial: South Bank House, Black Prince
Road, London SE1 7SJ
Tel: 44 02079 786840
Web site: http://www.readingukmagazine.
com/
Freq: Semi-Annual Not Audited
MAGAZINE
Business, Small and Medium Business

Real Business 979829
Editorial: Unit G4, Harbour Yard, Chelsea
Harbour, London SW10 0XD
Tel: 44 02070 457500
Email: editors@realbusiness.co.uk
Web site: www.realbusiness.co.uk
Freq: Daily
Circ: 170572 Cision Digital Reach
Editor: Hunter Ruthven
MAGAZINE (ONLINE)
Business, Small and Medium Business

Real Deals 979789
Editorial: Unit G4, Harbour Yard, Chelsea
Harbour, London SW10 0XD
Tel: 44 02070 457590
Email: editorial@realdeals.eu.com
Web site: www.realdeals.eu.com
Freq: Bi-Weekly
Circ: 5800 Not Audited
Editor: Nicholas Neveling
Profile: Magazine covering private equity
including market intelligence, deal
information and Euromarkets. First published
in 1999, the publication has an average of 48
pages per issue. Aimed at private equity
firms, lawyers, advisors, service providers
and LPs.
Ad Rate: Full Page Mono £2640.00
Ad Rate: Full Page Colour £3630.00
MAGAZINE
Private Equity

Real Estate Capital 983972
Editorial: 6th Floor, 140 London Wall,
London EC2Y 5DN **Tel:** 44 02075 665444
Web site: www.recapitalnews.com
Freq: Monthly
Circ: 9050 Not Audited
Profile: Magazine covering the key trends
and deals in commercial real estate finance.
It reports on both equity-raising and debt,
focusing on the UK capital markets and
increasingly, Germany and other large
western European markets. Subscribers
include fund managers, bankers, debt and
equity advisors, investors, property company
directors and private equity firms - senior
figures who are making complex decisions
about how to finance big-ticket commercial
property. Real Estate Capital does not cover
the residential property market, mortgages,
buy-to-let, estate agents, housebuilding,
construction, or planning issues.Subscribers
include fund managers, bankers, debt and
equity advisors, investors, property company
directors and private equity firms - senior
figures who are making complex decisions
about how to finance real estate.
Ad Rate: Full Page Mono £1500.00
Ad Rate: Full Page Colour £1500.00
MAGAZINE
Finance

Real Estate Investment Times 1101095
Editorial: Provident House 6- Beckenham,
20 Burrell Row, London BR3 5JF
Tel: 44 02037 506019
Web site: http://realestateinvestmenttimes.
com/
Freq: Daily
Circ: 15256 Cision Digital Reach
Editor: Mark Dugdale
MAGAZINE (ONLINE)
Commercial Real Estate, Finance,
Intellectual Property, Legal Affairs, Real
Estate Law, Residential Real Estate

Real Estate Law Experts 997701
Editorial: 27 Old Gloucester Street, London
WC1N 3AX **Tel:** 44 02074 195673
Web site: www.realestatelawexperts.com
Freq: Daily
Circ: 521 Cision Digital Reach
MAGAZINE (ONLINE)
Legal Affairs

Real-time Analysis & News 998839
Editorial: 22nd Floor, 110 Bishopsgate,
London EC2N 4AY **Tel:** 44 02030 174300
Email: info@ransquawk.com
Web site: www.ransquawk.com
Freq: Daily
Circ: 51195 Cision Digital Reach
MAGAZINE (ONLINE)
Bonds, Commodities, Equities, Financial
Markets, Foreign Exchange Market
(FOREX), Government, Lending, Public &
Consumer Finance

Recovered Fibre News 985328
Editorial: 1 Salisbury Office Park, London
Road, Salisbury, Salisbury SP1 3HP
Tel: 44 01722 337038
Email: publications@brunton.co.uk
Web site: http://www.brunton.co.uk/
recovered-fibre-news/
Freq: Monthly
Circ: 6500 Not Audited
Profile: Magazine covering news and prices
of waste paper and packaging waste
recovery notes in Europe. Aimed at
managers of waste-based paper mills,
printers, brokers and publishers, as well as
personnel in local government, collection
authorities and supply chains.
Ad Rate: Full Page Colour £525.00
MAGAZINE
Environment, Manufacturing

Recovery 983038
Editorial: 8th Floor, 120 Aldersgate Street,
London EC1A 4JQ **Tel:** 44 02075 664200
Email: recovery@r3.org.uk
Web site: www.r3.org.uk/recovery
Freq: Quarterly
Circ: 5000 Not Audited
Profile: Professional journal containing
industry news, views and legal updates for
the insolvency profession. Read by all those
who work with under performing businesses
including insolvency practitioners and
turnaround professionals.
Ad Rate: Full Page Colour £2230.00
MAGAZINE
Business

Recruiter 981122
Editorial: 17 Britton Street, London EC1M
5TP **Tel:** 44 02078 807606
Email: recruiter.editorial@redactive.co.uk
Web site: www.recruiter.co.uk
Freq: Monthly
Circ: 18499 Not Audited
Editor: DeeDee Doke
Profile: Magazine providing coverage of the
recruitment industry including all recruitment
offices, across all business and industry
sectors for permanent, temporary, contract
and search or selection assignments. It
covers the recruitment process and
recruitment within the finance, charity & not
for profit, construction, property, education,
health, hospitality, HR, IT, manufacturing,
energy, pharmaceutical, public sector, retail,
social care, transport & logistics and utilities

sectors. The magazine was first published in
1998 by Centaur Media and was sold to
Redactive Media Group in November 2011.
Aimed at all professionals and managers
working within the recruitment business.
Ad Rate: Full Page Colour £2478.00
MAGAZINE
Recruiting

Recruitment Agency Now 990592
Editorial: 123 King Street, Hammersmith,
London W6 9JG **Tel:** 44 02071 830117
Email: editorial@recruitmentagencynow.com
Web site: www.recruitmentagencynow.com
Freq: Daily
Circ: 13238 Cision Digital Reach
Editor: Anya Hastwell
MAGAZINE (ONLINE)
Recruiting

Recruitment Buzz 997500
Editorial: The Old Brewery Quarter, St Mary
Street, Cardiff CF10 1AD
Tel: 44 02920 232911
Email: contact@recruitmentbuzz.co.uk
Web site: www.recruitmentbuzz.co.uk
Freq: Daily
Circ: 78004 Cision Digital Reach
MAGAZINE (ONLINE)
Company News & Appointments,
Education, Health & Safety, Human
Resources, Recruiting

Recruitment Grapevine 996653
Editorial: Rosanne House, Parkway, Welwyn
Garden City, Welwyn Garden City AL8 6HG
Tel: 44 01707 351451
Web site: www.recruitmentgrapevine.com
Freq: Daily
Circ: 58291 Cision Digital Reach
MAGAZINE (ONLINE)
Recruiting

Recruitment International 980948
Editorial: 2nd Floor Lynton House, Station
Approach, Woking, London GU22 7PY
Tel: 44 01483 740874
Email: info@recruitment-international.co.uk
Web site: http://www.recruitment-
international.co.uk
Freq: Monthly
Circ: 4000 Not Audited
Profile: Magazine containing news, articles
and information on recruitment and staffing
issues. Aimed at the owners of recruitment
and staffing companies.
Ad Rate: Full Page Mono £1400.00
Ad Rate: Full Page Colour £1000.00
MAGAZINE
Recruiting

Recruitment Matters 981554
Editorial: Dorset House, First Floor, 27-45
Stamford Street, London SE1 9NT
Tel: 44 02070 092100
Email: info@rec.uk.com
Web site: www.rec.uk.com/news-and-
policy/rm-magazine
Freq: Monthly
Circ: 16800 Not Audited
Editor: Michael Oliver
Profile: Magazine of the Recruitment &
Employment Confederation covering
recruitment industry news and information.
Aimed at recruitment professionals.
Ad Rate: Full Page Colour £1980.00
MAGAZINE
Recruiting

The Recycler 984918
Editorial: Wittas House, Two Rivers, Station
Lane, Witney OX28 4BH
Tel: 44 01993 899800
Email: news@therecycler.com
Web site: http://www.therecycler.com/
Freq: Monthly Not Audited
MAGAZINE
Computers, Environment

Recycling & Waste World 983264
Editorial: Unit A, Buildings 1-5, Dinton
Business Park, Catherine Ford Road, Dinton,
Salisbury SP3 5HZ **Tel:** 44 01722 716997
Web site: www.recyclingwasteworld.co.uk
Freq: Weekly
Circ: 2448 Not Audited
Profile: Magazine covering events,
developments and news in the waste and
recycling industry including ferrous,
non-ferrous and precious metals, paper,
glass, chemicals, textiles, composting and
plastics. The journal also covers
associations, legislation, specifications and
testing, manufacturers and suppliers, also a
merchants directory.. Aimed at local
authorities, consultancies, material buyers
and sellers, all recycling and waste
management companies and energy from
waste specialists.
Ad Rate: Full Page Colour £1999.00
MAGAZINE
Environment

The Redback Reporter 1074789
Tel: 44 01736 741144
Web site: http://redbackreporter.com/
Freq: Bi-Monthly Not Audited
Editor: Charles Jago
MAGAZINE
Foreign Exchange Market (FOREX)

Refrigeration Air Conditioning & Electric Power Machinery 1061503
Tel: 44 86571 85246691
Email: lyq011@163.com
Freq: Quarterly
Circ: 7501 Not Audited
MAGAZINE
Building & Construction

Refrigeration and Air-Conditioning 1061337
Tel: 44 86106 3283510099
Email: zldt@chinajournal.net.cn
Freq: Bi-Monthly
Circ: 10003 Not Audited
MAGAZINE
Building & Construction

reFURB 984190
Editorial: 50 Queens Road, Buckhurst Hill,
London IG9 5DD **Tel:** 44 02085 041661
Email: refurb@sheenpublishing.co.uk
Web site: http://refurbprojects.com/
category/news/
Freq: Bi-Monthly
Circ: 8000 Not Audited
Editor: Peter Ashmore; **Editor:** Carol
Titmuss
Profile: Magazine covering the architectural
maintenance and UK refurbishment markets.
Read by specifiers and builders.
Ad Rate: Full Page Mono £800.00
Ad Rate: Full Page Colour £1200.00
MAGAZINE
Architecture & Design, Interior Design

Refurb & Developer Update 997378
Editorial: 4 Spratling Court Office Suites,
Spratling Street Court Office, Manston,
Manston CT12 5AN **Tel:** 44 01843 593868
Email: sam@developer-update.co.uk
Web site: http://developer-update.co.uk/
Freq: Monthly
Circ: 41000 Not Audited
Editor: Sam Andrews
MAGAZINE
Architecture & Design, Interior Design

Refurb & Renovation News 983762
Editorial: 20 Whitehall Road, Ramsgate,
Ramsgate CT12 6DF **Tel:** 44 01843 598625
Email: editorial@rrnews.co.uk
Web site: www.rrnews.co.uk
Freq: Bi-Monthly
Circ: 63775 Not Audited
Profile: Magazine covering the major UK
refurbishment projects and detailing the
latest product and designer innovations as

Business Magazines

well as updates in health and safety, conservation and the latest regulations on a broad range of building aspects. First published in 2006, the publication has an average of 48 pages per issue. Aimed at specifiers of refurbishment projects.
Ad Rate: Full Page Colour £1495.00
MAGAZINE
Architecture & Design, Building & Construction, Interior Design, Residential Real Estate

Refurb & Retrofit   983896
Editorial: PO Box 17171, Sutton Coldfield B73 9AE **Tel:** 44 01216 619484
Email: press@buildinsite.co.uk
Web site: http://buildinsite.co.uk/category/refurb-retrofit/
Freq: Bi-Monthly
Circ: 8000 Not Audited
Profile: Magazine covering building and construction including news, appointments, in-depth articles and product information as well as refurbishment and renewal within the UK building sector, both commercial and residential. Aimed at builders, developers, health and education authorities, local authorities and housing associations.
Ad Rate: Full Page Colour £1800.00
MAGAZINE
Building & Construction, Sustainable Development

Regenerative Medicine   995936
Email: info@futuremedicine.com
Web site: www.futuremedicine.com/loi/rme
Freq: Bi-Monthly Not Audited
MAGAZINE
Biotechnology, Pharmaceuticals

Regional International   987288
Editorial: Park House, 127 Guildford Road, Lightwater, Guildford GU18 5HR
Tel: 44 01276 856495
Email: corp.comms@eraa.org
Web site: http://www.eraa.org/publications/regional-international
Freq: Bi-Monthly
Circ: 3000 Not Audited
MAGAZINE
Aviation

Reinforced Plastics   985889
Editorial: Elsevier Ltd, The Boulevard, Langford Lane, Kidlington, Oxford OX5 1GB
Tel: 44 01865 843638
Email: rp@elsevier.com
Web site: http://www.materialstoday.com/reinforced-plastics/
Freq: Bi-Monthly
Circ: 16000 Not Audited
Editor: Stewart Bland
Profile: Magazine covering the latest business and technical developments in the polymer-based composites industry worldwide.
Ad Rate: Full Page Colour £5170.00
MAGAZINE
Plastics

Reinsurance   979889
Editorial: World Business Media Limited, 46 New Broad Street, London EC2M 1JH
Tel: 44 02036 515891
Web site: www.reinsurancemagazine.com
Freq: Quarterly
Circ: 7240 Not Audited
Profile: Magazine dealing with all aspects of reinsurance and providing a wide range of news, analysis, opinion, commentary and technical information for the world's insurance and reinsurance buyers, sellers and brokers covering all aspects of the global reinsurance industry. Read by reinsurance buyers, brokers and service providers.
Ad Rate: Full Page Colour £5170.00
MAGAZINE
Insurance

Removals & Storage   985518
Editorial: Tangent House, 62 Exchange Road, Watford, London WD18 0TG
Tel: 44 01923 699480
Email: info@bar.co.uk

Web site: http://www.bar.co.uk/index.php/about-bar/media/r-s-magazine/
Freq: Monthly
Circ: 4000 Not Audited
Profile: Journal of the British Association of Removers, providing information on transport, warehousing and shipping. First published in 1932, the publication has an average of 64 pages per issue. Aimed at managers in the removal and storage industry.
Ad Rate: Full Page Colour £745.00
MAGAZINE
Supply Chain Management (SCM)

Renaissance - ON HIATUS 2016   998959
Editorial: South Bank House, Black Prince Road, London SE1 7SJ
Tel: 44 02079 786840
Web site: www.renaissancenewcastle.com
Freq: Annual Not Audited
MAGAZINE
Commercial Real Estate, Sustainable Development

Renal Failure   999828
Editorial: 4 Park Square, Milton Park, Abingdon OX14 4RN **Tel:** 44 02070 176000
Email: wffinn@med.unc.edu
Web site: www.informahealthcare.com/journal/rnf
Freq: Monthly Not Audited
MAGAZINE
Urology

Renewable Energy   996473
Editorial: Elsevier Ltd, The Boulevard, Langford Lane, Kidlington, Oxford OX5 1GB
Tel: 44 01865 843000
Email: journalscustomerserviceemea@elsevier.com
Web site: http://www.journals.elsevier.com/renewable-energy/#description
Freq: Monthly
MAGAZINE
Alternative/Renewable Energy

Renewable Energy Association   998454
Editorial: 2nd Floor, 25 Eccleston Place, Victoria, London SW1W 9NF
Tel: 44 02079 253570
Email: info@r-e-a.net
Web site: www.r-e-a.net
Freq: Daily
Circ: 20193 Cision Digital Reach
MAGAZINE (ONLINE)
Alternative/Renewable Energy

Renewable Energy Focus   981497
Editorial: The Boulevard, Langford Lane, Kidlington, Oxford OX5 1GB
Tel: 44 01865 843000
Email: press_releases@renewableenergyfocus.com
Web site: www.renewableenergyfocus.com
Freq: Bi-Monthly Not Audited
Editor: David Hopwood
Profile: Magazine covering all aspects of clean power and renewable energy, including news, developments, new technology, the regulatory environment and commercialisation of renewable energy technology.
Ad Rate: Full Page Colour £4588.00
MAGAZINE
Alternative/Renewable Energy

Renewable Energy Installer   985915
Editorial: Caledonian House, Tatton Street, Knutsford, Knutsford WA16 6AG
Tel: 44 01663 714912
Email: enquiries@renewableenergyinstaller.co.uk
Web site: www.renewableenergyinstaller.co.uk
Freq: Monthly
Circ: 8000 Not Audited
Editor: Stuart Qualtrough
Profile: Magazine for microgeneration covering renewable technologies for

domestic and commercial buildings. Contains information on the latest products, legislation, training courses and case studies.
Ad Rate: Full Page Colour £1950.00
MAGAZINE
Alternative/Renewable Energy

RenewableUK Annual Review   1005479
Editorial: Greencoat House, Francis Street, London SW1P 1DH **Tel:** 44 02079 013000
Email: info@renewableuk.com
Web site: http://www.renewableuk.com/
Freq: Annual Not Audited
MAGAZINE
Alternative/Renewable Energy, Carbon Emissions & Trading, Electricity, Energy, Nuclear Power, Oil, Water & Sanitation

reNews   981500
Editorial: First Floor, St George's House, St George's Street, Winchester SO23 8BG
Tel: 44 01962 890440
Web site: www.renews.biz
Freq: Bi-Weekly
Circ: 70552 Cision Digital Reach
Profile: Website covering the renewable energy industry and market and publishes the e-newsletters; reNews Europe and reNews Americas.
MAGAZINE (ONLINE)
Alternative/Renewable Energy

The Report - Westminster and Holborn Law Society   999602
Editorial: 3tc Houese, 16 Crosby Road North, Crosby, Liverpool L22 0NY
Tel: 44 01512 364141
Web site: www.benhampublishing.com
Freq: Quarterly
Circ: 1500 Not Audited
MAGAZINE
Corporate Law, Government

Reproductive BioMedicine Online   999242
Editorial: Duck End Farm, Park Lane, Dry Drayton, Cambridge CB23 8DB
Tel: 44 01954 781812
Email: office@rbmonline.com
Web site: www.journals.elsevier.com
Freq: Monthly Not Audited
MAGAZINE
Obstetrics & Gynecology (OB/GYN)

Reproductive Health Matters   986406
Editorial: 444 Highgate Studios, 53-79 Highgate Road, London NW5 1TL
Tel: 44 02072 676567
Web site: http://www.rhm-elsevier.com
Freq: Semi-Annual Not Audited
Editor: Shirin Heidari
MAGAZINE
Obstetrics & Gynecology (OB/GYN)

Research Europe   986434
Editorial: Unit 111, Curtain House, 134-146 Curtain Road, London EC2A 3AR
Tel: 44 02072 166500
Email: news@researchresearch.com
Web site: http://info.researchprofessional.com/research-europe/
Freq: Bi-Weekly
Circ: 10000 Not Audited
Profile: Publication covering news, analysis, funding opportunities, proposals and tenders on European research policy.
MAGAZINE
Government, Public Sector, Science

Research Fortnight   983992
Editorial: Unit 111, Curtain House, 134-146 Curtain Road, London EC2A 3AR
Tel: 44 02072 166500
Email: news@researchresearch.com
Web site: www.researchresearch.com
Freq: Bi-Weekly
Circ: 10000 Not Audited
Profile: Newsletter on research and technology policy in Britain and Europe.

Ad Rate: Full Page Mono £3120.00
MAGAZINE
Higher Education, Science

Research Information   981676
Editorial: Unit 9, Clifton Court, Cambridge CB1 7BN **Tel:** 44 01223 221040
Email: editor.ri@europascience.com
Web site: www.researchinformation.info
Freq: Bi-Monthly
Circ: 8000 Not Audited
Profile: Magazine focusing on current and future developments in the provision of online information in science, technology and medicine.
Ad Rate: Full Page Colour £3500.00
MAGAZINE
Science

research-live   988732
Editorial: 15 Northburgh Street, London EC1V 0JR **Tel:** 44 02075 661864
Web site: https://www.research-live.com/
Freq: Daily
Circ: 52017 Cision Digital Reach
Editor: Jane Bainbridge
MAGAZINE (ONLINE)
Marketing

Residential Landlord   984739
Editorial: Unit C, Cliffside Court, West Hill, Dartford, London DA1 2EF
Tel: 44 01322 527007
Email: editorial@residentiallandlord.co.uk
Web site: www.residentiallandlord.co.uk
Freq: Daily
Circ: 7861 Cision Digital Reach
Profile: Website covering residential property. The Residential Landlord websites advises landlords on property news.
MAGAZINE (ONLINE)
Building & Construction, Finance, Legal Affairs, Residential Real Estate, Sustainable Development

Residential Property Investor   983631
Editorial: 1 Roebuck Lane, Manchester M33 7SY **Tel:** 44 03330 142998
Web site: www.rla.org.uk
Freq: Bi-Monthly
Circ: 21000 Not Audited
Profile: Magazine providing news, advice and information on finance, property maintenance, market trends as well as legal and tax issues. Contains articles on a wide range of topics, aimed both at novices and experienced full-time investors with large portfolios. Read by landlords in the private sector.
Ad Rate: Full Page Colour £990.00
MAGAZINE
Property Management & Maintenance, Real Estate, Residential Real Estate

Resilience Magazine   995384
Editorial: The Hawkhills, Easingwold, York YO61 3EG **Tel:** 44 01347 821972
Web site: www.the-eps.org
Freq: Quarterly
Circ: 1400 Not Audited
Editor: Bob Wade
MAGAZINE
Government, Hygiene, Public Sector, Security & Security Systems

Resilience.org   996441
Web site: www.resilience.org
Freq: Daily
Circ: 119359 Cision Digital Reach
MAGAZINE (ONLINE)
Alternative/Renewable Energy, Carbon Emissions & Trading, Electricity, Energy, Environment, Nuclear Power, Oil, Water & Sanitation

resource   983713
Editorial: Create Centre, B Bond Warehouse, Smeaton Road, Bristol BS1 6XN
Tel: 44 01179 030698
Email: info@resource.uk.com
Web site: www.resource.uk.com
Freq: Quarterly

Circ: 2500 Not Audited
Editor: Libby Peake
Profile: Magazine covering waste management including sustainability, recycling, waste and environmental issues. Aimed at the public waste industry, environmental professionals and government.
Ad Rate: Full Page Colour £1050.00
MAGAZINE
Environment

Resource Global Network
997900
Editorial: 69-79 Fulham High Street, Main Reception, Bedford House, London SW6 3JW **Tel:** 44 02071 485630
Email: editorial@resourceglobalnetwork.com
Web site: http://resourceglobalnetwork.com/
Freq: Monthly
Circ: 500000 Not Audited
MAGAZINE
Alternative/Renewable Energy, Carbon Emissions & Trading, Electricity, Energy, Nuclear Power, Oil, Water & Sanitation

Respiratory Medicine
985183
Email: respiratorymedicine@elsevier.com
Web site: www.journals.elsevier.com/respiratory-medicine
Freq: Monthly Not Audited
Profile: Journal containing information on respiratory medicine, including articles and topical reviews dealing with all aspects of respiratory diseases and therapy. Topics include paediatric and adult medicine, epidemiology, immunology and cell biology, physiology, occupational disorders and the role of allergens and pollutants. Aimed at physicians working in the field of respiratory disease.
Ad Rate: Full Page Mono £944.00
Ad Rate: Full Page Colour £1716.00
MAGAZINE
Respiratory Diseases

Responsible Investor
984359
Editorial: Response Global Media, Tower Bridge Business Centre, 46-48 East Smithfield, London E1W 1AW
Tel: 44 02077 092093
Email: info@responsible-investor.com
Web site: www.responsible-investor.com
Freq: Daily
Circ: 20099 Cision Digital Reach
Editor: Daniel Brooksbank
MAGAZINE (ONLINE)
Fund Management, Hedge Funds, Investment Banking

Retail Banker International
980014
Editorial: 71-73 Carter Lane, London EC4V 5EQ **Tel:** 44 02079 366650
Email: press@timetric.com
Web site: http://www.retailbankerinternational.com
Freq: Monthly Not Audited
Profile: Newsletter covering the global consumer financial services sector and providing regular examples of best practice in consumer financial services, news round-ups and an excellent provision for competitor analysis. Aimed at senior management in banking and finance.
Ad Rate: Full Page Colour £3300.00
MAGAZINE
Banking

The Retail Bulletin
983423
Editorial: Nicholson House, 41 Thames Street, Weybridge, London KT13 8JG
Tel: 44 01932 428376
Email: news@theretailbulletin.com
Web site: www.theretailbulletin.com
Freq: Daily
Circ: 48732 Cision Digital Reach
Editor: Angela Beevers
Profile: Website covering company news, breaking stories and summaries of media coverage of the retail sector.
MAGAZINE (ONLINE)
Retail Management

Retail Design World
988012
Editorial: 6 Morie St, Wandsworth, London SW18 1SL **Tel:** 44 02088 742728
Web site: www.retaildesignworld.com
Freq: Daily
Circ: 31947 Cision Digital Reach
MAGAZINE (ONLINE)
Graphic Design, Retail Management

The Retail Directory
981351
Editorial: Hemming Information Services, 32 Vauxhall Bridge Road, London SW1V 2SS
Tel: 44 02079 736694
Web site: http://www.theretaildirectory.co.uk
Freq: Daily
Circ: 6344 Cision Digital Reach
MAGAZINE (ONLINE)
Retail Management

Retail Express
983558
Editorial: 11 Angel Gate, City Road, London EC1V 2SD **Tel:** 44 02076 890600
Web site: http://newtrade.co.uk/our-products/print/retail-express/
Freq: Bi-Weekly
Circ: 50200 Not Audited
Editor: Louise Banham
Profile: Publication covering all trade issues for impulse and convenience retailers. Features include latest product information, launches and promotions and related articles. Aimed at management and staff in the retail business, including news retailers. Regular features: Alchohol; Crime; Launches and Promotions News on product launches and promotions.; Letters; Opinion; Product News News on fast moving consumer goods.; Profile
Ad Rate: Full Page Colour £2995.00
MAGAZINE
Retail Management

Retail Focus
985315
Tel: 44 08456 807405
Email: info@retailfocus.co
Web site: http://www.retail-focus.co.uk
Freq: Monthly
Circ: 9600 Not Audited
Editor: Lyndsey Dennis
Profile: Magazine covering the latest news and views in retail design.
MAGAZINE
Interior Design, Retail

Retail Insider
985611
Web site: www.retailinsider.com
Freq: Daily
Circ: 11905 Cision Digital Reach
Editor: Glynn Davis
MAGAZINE (ONLINE)
Retail Management

Retail Packaging
981334
Editorial: 21-23 Phoenix Court, Hawkins Road, Colchester, Colchester CO2 8JY
Tel: 44 01206 505900
Web site: www.retailpackagingmag.co.uk
Freq: Bi-Monthly
Circ: 6339 Not Audited
Profile: Magazine covering news and features on retail packaging. Aimed at directors, senior marketing, brand and sales management packaging designers, buyers, suppliers and individuals within converting and packaging equipment arenas.
Ad Rate: Full Page Colour £925.00
MAGAZINE
Marketing, Retail Management

Retail Property Analyst
999019
Editorial: ZeroTwoZero Communications Ltd, PO Box 1228, London CB1 0WS
Tel: 44 02088 706388
Email: info@retailpropertyanalyst.com
Web site: www.retailpropertyanalyst.com
Freq: Weekly
Circ: 1347 Cision Digital Reach
Profile: Magazine covering the retail property sector with a focus on the information needs of the retail property investment community.
MAGAZINE (ONLINE)
Finance, Retail

Retail Systems
980978
Editorial: Sixth Floor, 3 London Wall Buildings, London EC2M 5PD
Tel: 44 02075 622401
Web site: http://www.retail-systems.com
Freq: Daily
Circ: 47034 Cision Digital Reach
Editor: Michelle Stevens
Profile: Magazine covering developments in technology for retailing. Established in 1995, Retail Systems has become the business title for those involved in the selection process of implementing new IT. It features different aspects of technology in the retail operation, and cover new developments, trends and their implications for UK retailers and provides detailed news from the sector, broken down in to general news, EPoS, multi-channel and supply chain sections. Each issue contains a specialist supplement devoted to the most important technology and business issues. Aimed at retail IT managers, directors, senior management and those who influence technology buying.
Ad Rate: Full Page Colour £3000.00
MAGAZINE (ONLINE)
Retail Management

Retail Technology
980918
Editorial: 102 Ancton Way, Bognor Regis PO22 6JR
Email: retailtechnology@icloud.com
Web site: www.retailtechnology.co.uk
Freq: Quarterly
Circ: 7100 Not Audited
Profile: Retail Technology is the IT solutions magazine for major retailers in food, non food, hospitality, leisure, financial services and variety retailing. Focused on the business imperatives behind the deployment of technology. Provides news, products and features, new and emerging technologies within retail, reporting on cost-effective IT solutions. Writes about multichannel retailing, mobile retailing, business intelligence, back-office systems, telecoms, scanning, RFID, data capture, labelling and printing, merchandise planning, profit protection, payment systems, supply chain, customer loyalty, point of service, online retailing and instore media.Read by senior executives in medium and large UK retail organizations, marketing directors and IT managers. Aimed at IT specifiers and purchasers within medium to large UK retailers.
Ad Rate: Full Page Mono £1600.00
Ad Rate: Full Page Colour £2450.00
MAGAZINE
Computers, Retail Management

Retail Times
985907
Editorial: Retail Towers, 26 Manor House, Flockton, Wakefield WF4 4AN
Tel: 44 07973 416335
Email: fiona.briggs@retailtimes.co.uk
Web site: www.retailtimes.co.uk
Freq: Daily
Circ: 80804 Cision Digital Reach
Editor: Fiona Briggs
Profile: Website covering retail. The Retail Times website shares the latest news and information on local and global retail markets.
MAGAZINE (ONLINE)
Retail Management

The Retailer
983046
Editorial: 21 Dartmouth Street, Westminster, London SW1H 9BP **Tel:** 44 02078 548900
Email: info@brc.org.uk
Web site: www.brc.org.uk
Freq: Quarterly
Circ: 5000 Not Audited
MAGAZINE
Retail Management

Retailfraud.com
985137
Editorial: Holland Court, 2 The Close, Norwich NR1 4DY **Tel:** 44 01603 858458
Email: editor@retailfraud.com
Web site: http://news.retailrisk.com/
Freq: Daily
Circ: 4028 Cision Digital Reach

Editor: Mela Ragusa
MAGAZINE (ONLINE)
Consumer Interest, Criminal Law, Retail Management

Retailtechnologyreview.com
985399
Editorial: Latimer House, 189 High Street, Potters Bar, Potters Bar EN6 5DA
Tel: 44 01707 664200
Email: editor@ibcpub.com
Web site: www.retailtechnologyreview.com
Freq: Daily
Circ: 17414 Cision Digital Reach
MAGAZINE (ONLINE)
Engineering, Manufacturing

Rethink Wireless
988904
Tel: 44 02074 501230
Email: cgabriel@rethink-wireless.com
Web site: www.rethink-wireless.com
Freq: Daily
Circ: 14363 Cision Digital Reach
Editor: Caroline Gabriel
Profile: Website covering wireless technology.
MAGAZINE (ONLINE)
Mobile Communications

REUK.co.uk
998263
Email: neil@reuk.co.uk
Web site: www.reuk.co.uk
Freq: Daily
Circ: 207976 Cision Digital Reach
MAGAZINE (ONLINE)
Alternative/Renewable Energy

REview
1086848
Editorial: 41 Dover Street, London W1S 4NS
Tel: 44 02076 479857
Email: news@xploremarkets.com
Web site: www.xploreview.com
Freq: Daily
Circ: 10716 Cision Digital Reach
Editor: James Wallace
MAGAZINE (ONLINE)
Equities, Finance, Private Equity, Residential Real Estate, Retail

Reward
986902
Editorial: 120 Leman Street, London E1 8EU
Tel: 44 02076 183456
Web site: www.reward-guide.co.uk
Freq: Bi-Monthly
Circ: 7974 Not Audited
Editor: Helen Swire
Profile: Magazine providing a guide to workplace benefits, covering finance, HR & business.
MAGAZINE
Human Resources

Rheumatology
981641
Editorial: Bride House, 18-20 Bride Lane, London EC4Y 8EE **Tel:** 44 02078 420902
Email: editorial@rheumatology.org.uk
Web site: rheumatology.oxfordjournals.org
Freq: Monthly
Circ: 1800 Not Audited
Profile: Journal containing clinical and basic science research articles on rheumatology. Read by basic research scientists, surgeons, rheumatologists, geriatricians and other health professionals in the field of rheumatology.
Ad Rate: Full Page Mono £742.00
Ad Rate: Full Page Colour £1418.00
MAGAZINE
Rheumatology

The RIBA Journal
980187
Editorial: RIBA Journal, 66 Portland Place, London W1B 1AD **Tel:** 44 02074 968300
Email: editorial@ribaj.com
Web site: https://www.ribaj.com/
Freq: Monthly
Circ: 27905 Not Audited
Editor: Hugh Pearman
Profile: Official publication of the Royal Institute of British Architects, containing in-depth coverage of UK and international architecture, profiles of key personalities, technical and practice guidance, reviews,

Business Magazines

Web site: www.ipem.ac.uk/Publications/
SCOPE.aspx
Freq: Quarterly Not Audited
MAGAZINE
Diagnostic Imaging, Science

Scotland B2B
995518
Editorial: 14 West Vows Walk, Kirkcaldy,
Kirkcaldy KY1 1RX **Tel:** 44 01592 890528
Email: editorial@scotlandb2b-eastcoast.co.
uk
Web site: www.scotlandb2b.co.uk
Freq: Daily
Circ: 17439 Cision Digital Reach
MAGAZINE (ONLINE)
Business, Corporate Responsibility, Small
and Medium Business

Scottish Business Insider
980034
Editorial: One Central Quay, Glasgow G3
8DA
Email: editor@insider.co.uk
Web site: www.insider.co.uk
Freq: Monthly
Circ: 7585 Not Audited
Editor: Ken Symon
Profile: Magazine covering business and
politics, business start-ups, corporate
finance, IT, commercial property and
management issues in Scotland. Read by
decision makers in the business and
professional world.
Ad Rate: Full Page Colour £2600.00
MAGAZINE
Business, Small and Medium Business

Scottish Business News
Network (SBNN)
987006
Editorial: 111 Gallowgate, The Soap
Factory, Aberdeen AB25 1BU
Tel: 44 01224 619751
Email: editorial@sbnn.co.uk
Web site: http://www.sbnn.co.uk/
Freq: Daily
Circ: 18215 Cision Digital Reach
MAGAZINE (ONLINE)
Business, Corporate Responsibility

Scottish Construction Now!
988915
Editorial: Avian House, 87 Brook Street,
Dundee DD5 1DJ **Tel:** 44 01382 427037
Email: newsdesk@scottishnews.com
Web site: www.scottishconstructionnow.
com
Freq: Daily
Circ: 16158 Cision Digital Reach
Editor: Kieran Findlay
MAGAZINE (ONLINE)
Building & Construction

Scottish Dental magazine
984464
Editorial: Studio 2001, Mile End, Paisley
PA1 1JS **Tel:** 44 01415 610300
Email: scottishdental@
connectcommunications.co.uk
Web site: www.sdmag.co.uk
Freq: Bi-Monthly
Circ: 3500 Not Audited
Editor: Bruce Oxley
Profile: Magazine featuring clinical
guidelines, dental news and advice, financial
information, IT and dental industry product
reviews. Aimed at dental professionals
working in Scotland.
Ad Rate: Full Page Mono £500.00
Ad Rate: Full Page Colour £750.00
MAGAZINE
Dentistry

Scottish Energy News
987699
Editorial: Q Court, 3 Quality Street,
Livingston EH4 5BP **Tel:** 44 01314 764735
Email: editor@scottishenergynews.com
Web site: www.scottishenergynews.com
Freq: Daily
Circ: 19265 Cision Digital Reach

Editor: Mark Whittet
MAGAZINE (ONLINE)
Alternative/Renewable Energy, Carbon
Emissions & Trading, Electricity, Energy,
Nuclear Power, Oil, Water & Sanitation

Scottish Entrepreneur
1074634
Web site: https://sbnn.co.uk/scottish-
entrepreneur/
Freq: Quarterly
Circ: 493 Cision Digital Reach
Editor: Kim McAllister
MAGAZINE (ONLINE)
Business, Corporate Responsibility

The Scottish Farmer
981157
Editorial: 200 Renfield Street, Glasgow G2
3QB **Tel:** 44 01413 027700
Web site: www.thescottishfarmer.co.uk
Freq: Weekly
Circ: 15099 Not Audited
Profile: Journal covering new developments
in livestock, arable and farm machinery.
Ad Rate: Full Page Mono £2400.00
Ad Rate: Full Page Colour £2400.00
MAGAZINE
Animal Farming

Scottish Financial News
997516
Editorial: Avian House, 87 Brook Street,
Dundee DD5 1DJ **Tel:** 44 01382 427035
Email: newsdesk@scottishnews.com
Web site: http://www.scottishfinancialnews.
com/
Freq: Daily
Circ: 16162 Cision Digital Reach
MAGAZINE (ONLINE)
Business, Small and Medium Business

Scottish Housing News
981721
Editorial: Avian House, 87 Brook Street,
Dundee DD5 1DJ **Tel:** 44 01382 427037
Email: newsdesk@scottishnews.com
Web site: http://www.scottishhousingnews.
com/
Freq: Daily
Circ: 37402 Cision Digital Reach
Editor: Kieran Findlay
MAGAZINE (ONLINE)
Architecture & Design, Building &
Construction, Residential Real Estate

Scottish Pharmacist
985238
Editorial: 19 Ormeau Business Park, The
Gasworks, Belfast BT7 2JA
Tel: 44 02890 332499
Email: scottishpharmacist@
profilepublishing.com
Web site: http://www.scottishpharmacist.
co.uk/magazine/
Freq: Bi-Monthly
Circ: 5757 Not Audited
MAGAZINE
Pharmaceuticals

Scottish Pharmacy Review
981651
Editorial: 142 - 148 Albertbridge Road,
Belfast BT5 4GS **Tel:** 44 02890 999441
Web site: http://pharmacy-life.co.uk/
Freq: Quarterly
Circ: 4000 Not Audited
Editor: Sarah Nelson
Profile: Journal covering news and
developments within the pharmaceutical and
healthcare industry.\n\r\n\rAimed at
pharmacists in Scotland, decision makers in
the Department of Health and Community
Care, representatives of the industry,
wholesalers, generic manufacturers and
distributors in Scotland and England.
\n\r\n\rAlternative Title: SCR\n\r\n\rA charge
may be made for colour separation.
Ad Rate: Full Page Colour £1565.00
MAGAZINE
Pharmaceuticals

SCRIP Intelligence
980727
Editorial: Christchurch Court, 10-15
Newgate Street, London EC1A 7AZ
Tel: 44 02070 175000
Email: pr2scrip@informa.com

Web site: https://scrip.pharmamedtechbi.
com/
Freq: Daily
Circ: 24773 Cision Digital Reach
Editor: Eleanor Malone
MAGAZINE (ONLINE)
Biotechnology, Pharmaceuticals

Sea Breezes
982214
Editorial: Media House, Cronkbourne,
Douglas, Isle of Man IM4 4SB
Tel: 44 01624 696573
Email: sb.enquiries@seabreezes.co.im
Web site: www.seabreezes.co.im
Freq: Monthly
Circ: 13500 Not Audited
Profile: Publication containing marine
historical and technical data, reports on
merchant and naval ships and seamen and
the sea.
Ad Rate: Full Page Mono £295.00
Ad Rate: Full Page Colour £375.00
MAGAZINE
Shipping & Warehousing

SearchNetworking.co.uk
999393
Editorial: 1st Floor, 3-4a Little Portland
Street, London W1W 7JB
Tel: 44 02071 861400
Web site: http://searchnetworking.
techtarget.com/
Freq: Daily
Circ: 7205639 Cision Digital Reach
MAGAZINE (ONLINE)
Data Management

Seastrata Online
1053547
Editorial: 9 Prospect Hill, Redditch B97 4BS
Email: editor@online.seastrata.com
Web site: http://online.seastrata.com/
Freq: Daily
Circ: 65 Cision Digital Reach
MAGAZINE (ONLINE)
Alternative/Renewable Energy, Carbon
Emissions & Trading, Electricity, Energy,
Nuclear Power, Oil, Water & Sanitation

Seatrade Cruise Review
980827
Editorial: Seatrade House, 42 North Station
Road, Colchester CO1 1RB
Tel: 44 01206 545121
Email: seatradeeditorial@ubm.com
Web site: www.seatrade-insider.com
Freq: Quarterly
Circ: 6208 Not Audited
Editor: Mary Bond
Profile: Seatrade Cruise Review is the cruise
publication reporting on the latest
developments, innovations and
personalities. Includes industry statistics,
directories and fleet lists, new ship reviews
and the latest on refurbishments and refits.
Ad Rate: Full Page Colour £3695.00
MAGAZINE
Shipping & Warehousing

Seatrade Maritime News
980824
Editorial: Seatrade House, 42 North Station
Road, Colchester CO1 1RB
Tel: 44 01206 545121
Email: editorial@seatrade-global.com
Web site: www.seatrade-global.com
Freq: Quarterly
Circ: 6000 Not Audited
Editor: Bob Jaques
MAGAZINE
Shipping & Warehousing

SecEd
981564
Editorial: St Jude's Church, Dulwich Road,
London SE24 0PB **Tel:** 44 02075 016771
Email: editor@sec-ed.co.uk
Web site: www.sec-ed.co.uk
Freq: Weekly
Circ: 5000 Not Audited
Editor: Pete Henshaw; **Editor:** Pete
Henshaw
Profile: Newspaper covering news stories
and features relating to secondary education
and recruitment section.

Ad Rate: Full Page Colour £4950.00
MAGAZINE
Education, Schools & Institutions

SecuringIndustry
985239
Editorial: 17 Hazelton Close, Bromsgrove
B61 0JF **Tel:** 44 01527 835437
Email: newsdesk@securingindustry.com
Web site: https://www.securingindustry.
com/
Freq: Daily
Circ: 17536 Cision Digital Reach
MAGAZINE (ONLINE)
Pharmaceuticals

Securities Lending Times
986334
Editorial: 16 Bromley Road, Beckenham,
London BR3 5JE **Tel:** 44 02037 506020
Email: editor@securitieslendingtimes.com
Web site: www.securitieslendingtimes.com
Freq: Bi-Weekly
Circ: 30430 Cision Digital Reach
Editor: Mark Dugdale
MAGAZINE (ONLINE)
Derivatives

Security Buyer
984013
Editorial: Goldings, Elphicks Farm, Water
Lane, Hunton, Maidstone ME15 0SG
Tel: 44 01622 823920
Web site: www.securitybuyer.com
Freq: Monthly
Circ: 55000 Not Audited
Profile: International buyers' guide for the
security industry. Features on manufacturers
of security products and services, news,
interviews, product information and details
on exhibitions and conferences. Includes
case studies, comments and opinions, high
profile products and industry news. Aimed at
decision makers, buying authorities and
purchasing officers in the security industry.
Ad Rate: Full Page Colour £2495.00
MAGAZINE
Security & Security Systems

SECURITY INDUSTRY E-MAG
998327
Editorial: Holmes Court, 29A Bridge Street,
Kenilworth CV8 1BP **Tel:** 44 01926 853851
Email: sales@securityindustryemag.co.uk
Web site: http://www.securityindustryemag.
com
Freq: Quarterly
Circ: 36000 Not Audited
MAGAZINE
Defense & National Security, Security &
Security Systems

Security Middle East
983725
Editorial: 166 Front Lane, Upminster,
London RM14 1LN **Tel:** 44 01708 229354
Email: sme@dovetailcomms.co.uk
Web site: www.
securitymiddleeastmagazine.com
Freq: Bi-Monthly
Circ: 14000 Not Audited
Editor: Claire Mahoney
Profile: Magazine designed to provide
information and contacts for buyers and
suppliers of security products. Aimed at end
users of security products and installers in
the Middle East.
Ad Rate: Full Page Colour £3000.00
MAGAZINE
Defense & National Security, Security &
Security Systems

SecurityMiddleEast.com
988809
Editorial: Lichfield Office, Bridge House,
Station Road, Lichfield, Lichfield WS13 6HX
Tel: 44 01543 250456
Web site: securitymiddleeast.com
Freq: Daily
Circ: 42007 Cision Digital Reach
MAGAZINE (ONLINE)
Security & Security Systems

SecurityNewsDesk
987210
Editorial: Bridge House, Station Road,
Lichfield, Lichfield WS13 6HX
Tel: 44 01543 250456

Email: pr@securitynewsdesk.com
Web site: www.securitynewsdesk.com
Freq: Bi-Monthly
Circ: 6000 Not Audited
MAGAZINE
Security & Security Systems

Seizure - European Journal of Epilepsy
999283
Editorial: The Boulevard, Langford Lane, Kidlington, Oxford OX5 1GB
Tel: 44 01865 843000
Email: yseiz@elsevier.com
Web site: http://www.seizure-journal.com/
Freq: Monthly Not Audited
MAGAZINE
Neurology

SelectScience
985991
Tel: 44 01225 874666
Email: editor@selectscience.net
Web site: www.selectscience.net
Freq: Daily
Circ: 64142 Cision Digital Reach
MAGAZINE (ONLINE)
Science

Selfbuilder and Homemaker
983759
Editorial: Cointronic House, Station Road, Heathfield, Heathfield TN21 8DF
Tel: 44 01435 863500
Email: editorial@netmagmedia.eu
Web site: www.sbhonline.eu
Freq: Bi-Monthly
Circ: 10005 Not Audited
MAGAZINE
Building & Construction, Property Management & Maintenance

Serviced Apartment News
1076644
Editorial: 10 - 14 Accommodation Road, London NW11 8ED **Tel:** 44 02083 407989
Email: info@servicedapartmentnews.co.uk
Web site: www.servicedapartmentnews.com
Freq: Daily
Circ: 13553 Cision Digital Reach
Editor: George Sell
MAGAZINE (ONLINE)
Residential Real Estate

ServiceDesk360
987733
Editorial: Nile House, Nile Street, Brighton BN1 1HW **Tel:** 44 01273 645110
Email: perfectmotion_media@mac.com
Web site: http://www.servicedeskshow.com/sits-insight/
Freq: Daily
Circ: 271 Cision Digital Reach
Editor: James West
MAGAZINE (ONLINE)
Computers

Settlementagreement.co.uk
995013
Circ: 27045 Cision Digital Reach
MAGAZINE (ONLINE)
Litigation

Sexually Transmitted Infections
995846
Editorial: BMJ Journals Department, BMA House, Tavistock Square, London WC1H 9JR **Tel:** 44 02073 836879
Email: sti@bmj.com
Web site: http://sti.bmj.com/
Freq: Bi-Monthly
Editor: Jackie Cassell
MAGAZINE
AIDS/HIV, Sexual Health

Shanghai Building Materials
1061129
Tel: 44 86213 3130387
Freq: Bi-Monthly
Circ: 10003 Not Audited
MAGAZINE
Building & Construction, Manufacturing

SHD Logistics
981325
Editorial: 4th Floor, Maple House, 149 Tottenham Court Road, London W1T 7AD
Tel: 44 02070 176987
Web site: http://www.shdlogistics.com/
Freq: Monthly
Circ: 11314 Not Audited
Profile: Magazine containing the latest equipment developments, news reports and in-depth features on the fast developing world of logistics, including warehousing and distribution management.
Ad Rate: Full Page Colour £2350.00
MAGAZINE
Supply Chain Management (SCM)

Ship and Offshore Repair Journal
981711
Editorial: Office Suite 3, Enterprise House, Kings Road, Canvey Island SS8 0QY
Tel: 44 01268 511300
Email: shipaat@aol.com
Web site: http://www.shipandoffshorerepair.com/
Freq: Bi-Monthly
Circ: 5152 Not Audited
Editor: Alan Thorpe
MAGAZINE
Shipping & Warehousing

Ship Management International
984204
Editorial: Wingbury Courtyard Business Village, Upper Wingbury Farm, Wingrave, Aylesbury HP22 4LW **Tel:** 44 01296 682051
Email: editorial@elabor8.co.uk
Web site: www.shipmanagementinternational.com
Freq: Bi-Monthly
Circ: 6735 Not Audited
Profile: Magazine featuring articles and in-depth research and analysis to educate and update today's ship managers on the issuers affecting the way they manage their ships including policy and regulation, profit and loss analysis, crew, technical and commercial developments as well as financial analysis, debt management and trade route assessment. Aimed at ship owning and ship management company chief executives and managing directors.
Ad Rate: Full Page Colour £3000.00
MAGAZINE
Shipping & Warehousing

The Ship Supplier
998955
Editorial: Unit 9A, Wingbury Courtyard Business Village, Upper Wingbury Farm, Wingrave, Aylesbury HP22 4LW
Tel: 44 01296 682051
Email: issa@elabor8.co.uk
Web site: www.theshipsupplier.com
Freq: Quarterly
Circ: 5656 Not Audited
MAGAZINE
Shipping & Warehousing

Ship Technology Global
1059295
Editorial: John Carpenter House, 7 Carmelite Street, London EC4Y 0BS
Tel: 44 02079 366400
Email: onlinemags@nridigital.com
Web site: http://www.nridigital.com/ship-technology-global.html
Freq: Bi-Monthly
Circ: 141 Cision Digital Reach
MAGAZINE (ONLINE)
Shipping & Warehousing

Shipping & Transport International
980921
Editorial: Guthrum House, 145 Angel Street, Hadleigh IP7 5BY **Tel:** 44 01473 822061
Email: info@guthrumhouse.co.uk
Web site: www.stl-mag.co.uk
Freq: Quarterly Not Audited
Editor: Roger White
Profile: Magazine covering transport law, maritime law, the legal aspects of road, rail and air transport and technical features.
Ad Rate: Full Page Mono £1050.00
Ad Rate: Full Page Colour £1580.00
MAGAZINE
Shipping & Warehousing

Shop Spec Journal
998970
Editorial: The Old School House, St Stephens Street, Tonbridge, Tonbridge TN9 2AD **Tel:** 44 01732 371570
Web site: www.shopspec.com
Freq: Annual
Circ: 7182 Not Audited
Editor: Can Faik
MAGAZINE
Office Supplies

Shopping Centre
980020
Editorial: 2nd Floor, Waterloo Chambers, 19 Waterloo Street, Glasgow G2 6AY
Tel: 44 01412 222100
Web site: http://www.shopping-centre.co.uk
Freq: Monthly
Circ: 7000 Not Audited
Editor: Graham Parker
Profile: Business magazine covering news, regional property and features on shopping centre ownership and management. Readership includes centre management, estate and store operations departments, developers, architects, surveyors, facilities and project managers, sponsors, local authority planners and chief executives.
Ad Rate: Full Page Mono £2269.00
Ad Rate: Full Page Colour £2998.00
MAGAZINE
Retail Management

shots
984843
Editorial: Zetland House, 5-25 Scrutton Street, London EC2A 4HJ
Tel: 44 02030 334295
Email: spots@shots.net
Web site: www.shots.net
Freq: Bi-Monthly Not Audited
Editor: Danny Edwards
Profile: Magazine covering the latest news on international advertising and creativity. Features include comprehensive reviews of television commercials, promos, film effects and press and poster campaigns. Aimed at advertising and production professionals worldwide.
Ad Rate: Full Page Colour £2940.00
MAGAZINE
Advertising Industry

Shout99.com
983688
Editorial: 5 Broxholme Way, Maghull L31 5PL
Web site: www.shout99.com
Freq: Daily
Circ: 11201 Cision Digital Reach
Editor: Susie Hughes
Profile: Website covering freelancers . "Shout99 is one of the UK's longest established website for freelancers, providing news, information, services and products to the micro businesses in the knowledge-based economy."
MAGAZINE (ONLINE)
Business, Small and Medium Business

Show Home
985437
Editorial: Goldings, Elphicks Farm, Water Lane, Hunton, Maidstone ME15 0SG
Tel: 44 01622 823920
Email: info@yourshow-home.com
Web site: www.yourshow-home.com
Freq: Bi-Monthly
Circ: 12911 Not Audited
MAGAZINE
Architecture & Design, Building & Construction, Commercial Real Estate, Finance, Interior Design, Legal Affairs, Office Design, Property Management & Maintenance, Residential Real Estate, Retail

Show House
981092
Editorial: 5th Floor, 291-299 Borough High Street, London SE1 1JG
Tel: 44 02079 401070
Email: im@showhouse.co.uk
Web site: www.showhouse.co.uk/home-2/magazine/
Freq: Monthly
Circ: 9954 Not Audited
MAGAZINE
Residential Real Estate

Shrink That Footprint
996641
Editorial: Highfield Road, Petersfield GU32 2HN
Web site: www.shrinkthatfootprint.com
Freq: Daily
Circ: 43415 Cision Digital Reach
MAGAZINE (ONLINE)
Alternative/Renewable Energy, Environment

Sign Directions
981263
Editorial: Office 16, Minster Chambers, Church Street, Southwell, Nottingham NG25 0HD **Tel:** 44 01636 819375
Email: signdirections@btconnect.com
Web site: www.signdirectionsonline.co.uk
Freq: Monthly
Circ: 6500 Not Audited
Editor: Val Hirst
Profile: Magazine covering news and features on the sign industry.
Ad Rate: Full Page Colour £890.00
MAGAZINE
Marketing

Sign Update
984836
Editorial: 1 Allens Orchard, Chipping Warden, Banbury, Oxford OX17 1LX
Tel: 44 01784 605601
Web site: http://www.signupdate.co.uk/
Freq: Bi-Monthly
Circ: 8300 Not Audited
Editor: Kathryn Johnson
Profile: Trade magazine for Sign makers, published 7 times a year. The magazine covers all aspects of sign, engraving, POS, digital and screen printing as well as the shopfitting industry.
Ad Rate: Full Page Colour £780.00
MAGAZINE
Manufacturing

Significant Small Ships
1053882
Tel: 44 02072 354622
Email: editorial@rina.org.uk
Web site: https://www.rina.org.uk/sigsmallships.html
Freq: Daily
Circ: 3000 Not Audited
Editor: Martin Conway
MAGAZINE
Engineering

SignLink
983592
Editorial: Unit D, Link House, Britton Gardens, Kingswood, Bristol BS15 1TF
Tel: 44 01179 805040
Email: editor@signlink.co.uk
Web site: www.signlink.co.uk
Freq: Monthly
Circ: 10632 Not Audited
Profile: News and features covering the sign, screen and digital print market. Includes large-format and graphic arts sectors. Aimed at industry professionals.
Ad Rate: Full Page Colour £1295.00
MAGAZINE
Graphic Design

Simply Communicate
988124
Editorial: Impact Hub Westminster, 80 Haymarket, London SW1Y 4TE
Tel: 44 02036 646720
Email: editor@simply-communicate.com
Web site: www.simply-communicate.com
Freq: Daily
Circ: 28828 Cision Digital Reach
MAGAZINE (ONLINE)
Business, Corporate Responsibility, Human Resources, Small and Medium Business

Sin comillas
1062040
Web site: http://www.sincomillas.com
Freq: Daily
Circ: 32516 Cision Digital Reach
MAGAZINE (ONLINE)
Banking, Business, Shipping & Warehousing, Small and Medium Business, Telecommunications/Electronic Communications

Business Magazines

Sipps Professional 999604
Tel: 44 01895 676658
Email: newsdesk@portfoliopublishing.co.uk
Web site: www.sippsprofessional.co.uk
Freq: Daily
Circ: 14265 Cision Digital Reach
MAGAZINE (ONLINE)
Fund Management

Site Recorder 983044
Editorial: Equinox, 28 Commerce Road, Lynch Wood, Peterborough PE2 6LR
Tel: 44 01733 405160
Email: info@icwci.org
Web site: www.icwci.org
Freq: Monthly
Circ: 3000 Not Audited
Profile: The Journal of the Institute of Clerks of Works and Construction Inspectorate is published and distributed to its members and associates on a monthly basis. Site Recorder keeps its readers up to date with the latest developments in construction, covering news and products, health and safety topics, sustainable development, regulations and standards and member related issues and features.
Ad Rate: Full Page Colour £1045.00
MAGAZINE
Building & Construction

The Skeptic 986993
Editorial: The Anomalistic Psychology Research Unit, Department of Psychology, Goldsmiths College, New Cross, London SE14 6NW **Tel:** 44 08445 897402
Email: edit@skeptic.org.uk
Web site: www.skeptic.org.uk
Freq: Quarterly Not Audited
Editor: Deborah Hyde
Profile: UK's magazine with a sceptical look at pseudoscience and claims of the paranormal. Examines science, scepticism, secularism, critical thinking and claims of the paranormal.
MAGAZINE
Science

Skillbuilder.co.uk 1064497
Web site: http://skill-builder.uk/
Freq: Daily
Editor: Georgina Bisby
MAGAZINE (ONLINE)
Building & Construction

Skills 4 Nurses 981611
Editorial: Gibbs Yard, Auchincruive Estate, Ayr, Maybole KA6 5HN
Email: jim@gmexpos.com
Web site: www.skills4nurses.com/
Freq: Bi-Monthly
Circ: 60000 Not Audited
Editor: Shona McMahon
Profile: Magazine featuring job vacancies, recruitment opportunities and product news from both the NHS trusts and private health care providers in the UK, Ireland and overseas. Aimed at nursing professionals of all grades and disciplines.
Ad Rate: Full Page Mono £1455.00
Ad Rate: Full Page Colour £1855.00
MAGAZINE
Nursing/Nurses

Skyscrapernews.com 996138
Editorial: Independent House, 215 Bury New Road, Whitefield, Whitefield M45 8GW
Web site: www.skyscrapernews.com
Freq: Daily
Circ: 33532 Cision Digital Reach
MAGAZINE (ONLINE)
Alternative/Renewable Energy, Building & Construction, Carbon Emissions & Trading, Electricity, Energy, Engineering, Nuclear Power, Oil, Water & Sanitation

Sleep and Breathing 995741
Editorial: 236 Gray's Inn Road, Floor 6, London WC1X 8HB
Email: sleep_breath@di-ep.com
Web site: www.springer.com/medicine/internal/journal/11325

Freq: Quarterly
MAGAZINE
Neurology

Sleep Medicine Reviews 995864
Editorial: The Boulevard, Langford Lane, Kidlington OX5 1GB **Tel:** 44 01865 843000
Web site: www.elsevier.com/wps/find/journaldescription.cws_home/623074/description
Freq: Bi-Monthly
Circ: 63 Not Audited
MAGAZINE
Neurology

Sleeper Magazine 995773
Editorial: Waterloo Place, Watson Square, Stockport SK1 3AZ **Tel:** 44 0161 4 768390
Email: editorial@sleepermagazine.co.uk
Web site: www.sleepermagazine.com
Freq: Bi-Monthly
Circ: 12142 Not Audited
Editor: Catherine Martin
MAGAZINE
Hotels/Motels

The Small Company Sharewatch 981490
Editorial: PO Box 1015, Croydon CR9 5DL
Tel: 44 02086 564648
Web site: www.scsw.co.uk
Freq: Monthly Not Audited
Editor: Smit Berry
Profile: Independent monthly stockmarket newsletter that informs about opportunities amongst lesser-known growth stocks and dynamic growth shares. Provides investment advice on small and medium sized quoted companies in the UK. It is available by subscription only and is published by Equitylink Ltd. Launched in December 1993
MAGAZINE
Equities

SmallBusiness.co.uk 983684
Editorial: Vitesse Media Plc, 5th Floor, 14 Bonhill Street, London EC2A 4BX
Tel: 44 02072 507024
Web site: www.smallbusiness.co.uk
Freq: Daily
Circ: 231577 Cision Digital Reach
Editor: Ben Lobel
Profile: Website focusing on small businesses. Smallbusiness.co.uk includes information on start-ups, finance, IT, legal, sales and marketing, people and franchising.
MAGAZINE (ONLINE)
Business, Corporate Responsibility

Smart Buildings Magazine 988879
Editorial: Cardinal Point, Park Road, Rickmansworth, London WD3 1RE
Tel: 44 01923 437618
Web site: www.smartbuildingsmagazine.com
Freq: Daily
Circ: 17446 Cision Digital Reach
Editor: John Hatcher
MAGAZINE (ONLINE)
Architecture & Design, Building & Construction, Commercial Real Estate, Office Design, Retail, Sustainable Development, Urban Planning & Development

Smarta.com 984762
Editorial: No 1 Croydon, 7th Floor, 12-16 Addiscombe Road, East Croydon, London CR9 6DS
Web site: www.smarta.com
Freq: Daily
Circ: 84225 Cision Digital Reach
MAGAZINE (ONLINE)
Business, Small and Medium Business

SmartNewHomes 998287
Editorial: Harlequin Building, 65 Southwark Street, London SE1 0HR
Email: editor@zoopla.co.uk
Web site: www.smartnewhomes.com
Freq: Daily

Circ: 88954 Cision Digital Reach
MAGAZINE (ONLINE)
Property Management & Maintenance

SME Insider 998435
Editorial: Contentive, 1 Broadway, Hammersmith, London W6 9DL
Tel: 44 02080 809372
Email: editorial@smeinsider.com
Web site: www.smeinsider.com
Freq: Daily
Circ: 33151 Cision Digital Reach
MAGAZINE (ONLINE)
Business, Small and Medium Business

Smile Journal 996022
Editorial: The Old School House, St Stephens Street, Tonbridge, Tonbridge TN9 2AD **Tel:** 44 01732 371570
Web site: http://www.dentalrepublic.co.uk/smile
Freq: Bi-Monthly
Circ: 6000 Not Audited
Editor: Can Faik
MAGAZINE
Dentistry

Snacks Magazine 983429
Editorial: Rock House, Rudyard, Slough ST13 8RL **Tel:** 44 01538 306751
Email: editor@snacksmagazine.co.uk
Web site: http://thesnacksmagazine.com/
Freq: Quarterly
Circ: 3900 Not Audited
Editor: Michelle Knott
Profile: Official journal of the European Snacks Association covering the savoury snack food industry in Europe and its suppliers including new products, ingredients and equipment, market trends, production techniques and industry issues. It has an exclusive readership of Business and Associate members, representing manufacturers and suppliers worldwide, plus an international subscriber group outside of the Trade Association. Aimed at senior management and key decision makers.
Ad Rate: Full Page Mono £1090.00
Ad Rate: Full Page Colour £1370.00
MAGAZINE
Food

Social Housing 981544
Editorial: One Canada Square, 21st Floor, Canary Wharf, London E14 5AP
Tel: 44 02077 728468
Email: editor@socialhousing.co.uk
Web site: www.socialhousing.co.uk
Freq: Monthly
Circ: 2000 Not Audited
Editor: Luke Cross
Profile: Social Housing brings in-depth reporting of the latest business and finance developments, including detail of new funding initiatives and transactions, keeps abreast of the latest business and development opportunities generated by housing PFI, local authority SPVs and ALMOs, as well as established LSVT and partial stock transfer markets, examines the governance and management challenges involved in delivering Whitehall's ambitious housing agenda, highlights new legal structures and treasury management policies used by leading RSLs. Aimed at decision makers in the affordable housing sector, RSLs, ALMOs, social housing lenders, lawyers, surveyors builders, developers and government departments, housing associations, local authorities, private landlords, housebuilders, accountants, consultants.
Ad Rate: Full Page Mono £1350.00
Ad Rate: Full Page Colour £1750.00
MAGAZINE
Public Sector

Social Neuroscience 999130
Tel: 44 02070 176000
Email: authorqueries@tandf.co.uk
Web site: http://www.tandfonline.com/action/journalInformation?show=aimsScope&journalCode=psns20
Freq: Bi-Monthly Not Audited

Editor: Paul Eslinger
MAGAZINE
Neurology

Social Songbird 990684
Editorial: Stirling House, Denny End Rd, Waterbeach, Waterbeach CB25 9PB
Tel: 44 01223 969054
Email: writers@socialsongbird.com
Web site: www.socialsongbird.com
Freq: Daily
Circ: 36752 Cision Digital Reach
Editor: Sam Bonson
MAGAZINE (ONLINE)
Marketing

Social Theory and Health 998797
Editorial: Centre for Behavioural & Social Sciences in Medicine, Charles Bell House, University College London, 67-73 Riding House Street, London N1 9XW
Tel: 44 02078 334000
Email: sth@palgrave.com
Web site: http://www.palgrave-journals.com/sth
Freq: Quarterly Not Audited
Editor: Guido Giarelli; **Editor:** Ruth Graham; **Editor:** Paul Higgs; **Editor:** Richard Levinson; **Editor:** Graham Scambler
MAGAZINE
Health Administration

Social Work in Public Health 995400
Editorial: 4 Park Square, Milton Park, Abingdon, London W1T 3JH
Tel: 44 02070 176000
Email: enquiries@taylorandfrancis.com
Web site: http://www.tandfonline.com/action/aboutThisJournal?journalCode=whsp20
Freq: Bi-Monthly Not Audited
MAGAZINE
Community Care (UK)

Software World 981629
Editorial: 58 Ryecroft Way, Luton LU2 7TU
Tel: 44 01582 722219
Email: smpluton@ntlworld.com
Web site: www.softwareworldpublication.com
Freq: Bi-Monthly
Circ: 1000 Not Audited
Profile: Publication containing coverage of the software market, security issues, including sections on languages, software writing techniques, business and contract news and book reviews. Reports on software programs and packages for use in a wide range of installations. Coverage includes international software industry news, trade literature, and new product reviews. Launched in 1969.
MAGAZINE
Software

Soils and Fertilizers Sciences in China 1061800
Tel: 44 86108 2108656
Email: trfl@caas.ac.cn
Web site: http://www.iarrp.cn
Freq: Bi-Monthly Not Audited
MAGAZINE
Animal Farming, Science

Solar Power Management 987227
Editorial: Hannay House, 39 Clarendon Road, Watford, London WD17 1JA
Tel: 44 01923 690200
Web site: www.solar-international.net
Freq: Bi-Monthly
Circ: 50331 Not Audited
MAGAZINE
Alternative/Renewable Energy, Electricity

Solar Power Portal 988742
Editorial: Solar Media Limited, 3rd Floor, 2 America Square, London EC3N 2LU
Tel: 44 02078 710122
Web site: www.solarpowerportal.co.uk
Freq: Daily
Circ: 88708 Cision Digital Reach

Section 4 UK Periodicals Business

Profile: Website covering solar technology. The Solar Power Panel site discusses anything from technology and innovations to clean tech and solar panel products.
MAGAZINE (ONLINE)
Alternative/Renewable Energy

Solar UK
986823
Editorial: Hannay House, 39 Clarendon Road, Watford, London WD17 1JA
Tel: 44 01923 690200
Email: jackie.cannon@angelbc.com
Web site: www.solar-uk.net
Freq: Quarterly
Circ: 14000 Not Audited
MAGAZINE
Alternative/Renewable Energy, Electricity

Solids & Bulk Handling
981329
Editorial: 5 Howick Place, Victoria, London SW1P 1WG **Tel:** 44 02070 177105
Web site: www.solidsandbulk.co.uk
Freq: Bi-Monthly
Circ: 8062 Not Audited
Editor: Kelly Rose
MAGAZINE
Shipping & Warehousing, Supply Chain Management (SCM)

Solutions Newsletter
999581
Editorial: Croner House, Wheatfield Way, Hinckley, London LE10 1YG
Tel: 44 01455 897000
Web site: www.cronersolutions.co.uk
Freq: Monthly
Circ: 6425 Cision Digital Reach
MAGAZINE (ONLINE)
Health & Safety

Solvency II Wire
986445
Editorial: International House, 39 Great Windmill Street, London W1D 7LX
Email: info@solvencyiiwire.com
Web site: www.solvencyiiwire.com
Freq: Daily
Circ: 8948 Cision Digital Reach
MAGAZINE (ONLINE)
Insurance

The Source
1054211
Editorial: Chester House, Fulham Green 81-83, Fulham High Street, London SW6 3JA
Tel: 44 02071 938066
Email: editor@thesourcemagazine.org
Web site: www.thesourcemagazine.org
Freq: Quarterly
Circ: 15000 Not Audited
Editor: James Workman
MAGAZINE
Water & Sanitation

Source Creative
997047
Editorial: 37 Sun Street, London EC2M 2PL
Tel: 44 02072 975900
Email: sourcecreative-london@extremereach.com
Web site: https://sourcecreative.extremereach.com/cmspage/2112/home
Freq: Daily
Circ: 112 Cision Digital Reach
Editor: Jamie Madge
MAGAZINE (ONLINE)
Advertising Industry

sourcingfocus.com
984564
Editorial: 44 Wardour Street, London W1D 6QZ **Tel:** 44 02072 928691
Email: editor@sourcingfocus.com
Web site: www.sourcingfocus.com
Freq: Daily
Circ: 9787 Cision Digital Reach
Profile: Website covering sourcing information. The souringfocus.com website is a community portal featuring news, editorial comment and analysis and interviews relating to sourcing information.
MAGAZINE (ONLINE)
Business, Corporate Responsibility

South
1061829
Tel: 44 86208 7375265
Email: nfzz@21cn.net

Web site: http://www.nfyk.com
Freq: Monthly
Circ: 570000 Not Audited
MAGAZINE
Economics, Government

South East Business
980035
Tel: 44 01303 233880
Email: newsdesk@southeastbusiness.com
Web site: www.southeastbusiness.com
Freq: Bi-Monthly
Circ: 21000 Not Audited
Profile: Magazine covering business news, legal issues, finance, marketing, IT, training and executive motoring. Read by directors and senior management in the South East of England.
Ad Rate: Full Page Mono £1259.00
Ad Rate: Full Page Colour £1469.00
MAGAZINE
Business

South East Business Insider
990564
Editorial: 8th Floor, Boulton House, 17 21 Chorlton Street, Manchester M1 3HY
Tel: 44 01619 079718
Email: insider@newsco.com
Web site: http://www.insidermedia.com/southeast
Freq: Daily
Circ: 39655 Cision Digital Reach
MAGAZINE (ONLINE)
Banking, Business, Finance, Mergers & Acquisitions, Small and Medium Business

South East Farmer
981158
Editorial: South East Business, Spicer House, Lympne Business Park, Hythe CT21 4LR **Tel:** 44 01303 233880
Email: newsdesk@southeastfarmer.net
Web site: www.southeastfarmer.net
Freq: Monthly
Circ: 12598 Not Audited
Editor: John Harvey
Profile: Magazine covering news affecting all aspects of farming in the South East of England. Read by farmers and growers.
Ad Rate: Full Page Colour £1199.00
MAGAZINE
Animal Farming

South West Farmer
984691
Editorial: 3 Falmouth Business Park, Bickland Water Road, Falmouth, Falmouth TR11 4SZ **Tel:** 44 01326 213333
Email: editorial@packetseries.co.uk
Web site: www.southwestfarmer.co.uk
Freq: Monthly
Circ: 12000 Not Audited
Profile: Magazine containing news and information on farming in the South West.
MAGAZINE
Animal Farming

southwestbusiness.co.uk
985023
Editorial: Third Floor, St James' House, St James' Square, Cheltenham GL50 3PR
Tel: 44 01452 690792
Email: andrew.merrell@glosmedia.co.uk
Web site: www.southwestbusiness.co.uk
Freq: Daily
Circ: 19214 Cision Digital Reach
Profile: Southwestbusiness.co.uk is a monthly magazine featuring interviews with key figures from the region along with diary dates, reports and features. Published by Northcliffe Media and uses journalists from its titles across the South West to speak to the people making the news and shaping the region's economy. Aimed at business managers in the South West.Alternative Title: South West Business
MAGAZINE (ONLINE)
Business, Small and Medium Business

SpecFinish
985530
Editorial: Althorpe Enterprise Hub, Althorpe Street, Leamington Spa, Leamington Spa CV31 2GB **Tel:** 44 01926 420660
Email: newsdesk@campbellmarsh.com
Web site: www.specfinish.co.uk
Freq: Bi-Monthly

Circ: 6000 Not Audited
Editor: Adrian JG Marsh
Profile: SpecFinish is for specifiers and installers of drywall, ceilings, interior fit out, plastering, screeding, rendering, fibrous plasterwork, partitions, external wall insulation and steel frame systems. SpecFinish incorporates Interiors Insight magazine.The magazine readership includes: main contractors, specialist subcontractors, architects, manufacturers, distributors and merchantsoperating in the interior fit out, building finishes, facades and external wall insulation sector.
Ad Rate: Full Page Colour £1950.00
MAGAZINE
Building & Construction, Interior Design, Sustainable Development

Specialist Printing Worldwide
988898
Editorial: 1 Cantelupe Mews, Cantelupe Road, East Grinstead, East Grinstead RH19 3BG **Tel:** 44 01342 322133
Email: info@specialistprinting.com
Web site: www.specialistprinting.com
Freq: Quarterly
Circ: 15000 Not Audited
MAGAZINE
Publishing

Speciality Chemicals Magazine
985024
Editorial: Romeland House, Romeland Hill, St Albans, Redhill AL3 4ET
Tel: 44 01727 814400
Web site: www.specchemonline.com
Freq: Monthly
Circ: 50000 Not Audited
Profile: Journal covering manufacture and end-use applications of performance chemicals, including high value and low volume chemicals, fine chemicals and custom manufacture.
Ad Rate: Full Page Colour £3770.00
MAGAZINE
Chemicals

Speciality Food
981290
Editorial: 25 Phoenix Court, Hawkins Road, Colchester, Colchester CO2 8JY
Tel: 44 01206 505981
Web site: www.specialityfoodmagazine.com
Freq: Monthly
Circ: 8639 Not Audited
Editor: Holly Shackleton
Profile: Industry's food trade publication covering delicatessen, foodhall, farmshop and specialist buyers (from food halls to supermarkets, addressing key issues as they emerge through news, features, interviews, comment and analysis.
Ad Rate: Full Page Colour £2250.00
MAGAZINE
Food

Specification Magazine
983729
Editorial: Grosvenor House, Central Park, Telford TF2 9TW **Tel:** 44 01952 234000
Email: info@tspmedia.co.uk
Web site: www.specificationonline.com
Freq: Monthly
Circ: 15500 Not Audited
Profile: Magazine promoting building product services and new ideas. Aimed at those involved in the building and architecture sector.
Ad Rate: Full Page Colour £2000.00
MAGAZINE
Building & Construction

Specification Product Update Magazine
983736
Editorial: Grosvenor House, Central Park, Telford, Oakengates TF2 9TW
Tel: 44 01952 234000
Web site: www.specificationonline.co.uk
Freq: Quarterly
Circ: 15000 Not Audited
MAGAZINE
Architecture & Design, Building & Construction, Residential Real Estate

Specifier Select
985682
Editorial: Kingfisher's Retreat, The Lodges, Dunston Business Village, Stafford ST18 9AB **Tel:** 44 01785 711591
Email: kirsty@l2media.co.uk
Web site: http://www.specifierselect.co.uk/
Freq: Monthly
Circ: 10709 Cision Digital Reach
Profile: Magazine featuring the latest building products and systems.
MAGAZINE (ONLINE)
Building & Construction

Specify
981085
Editorial: Unit 34 Crescent Business Park, Lisburn BT28 2GN **Tel:** 44 02892 780108
Web site: www.specifymagazine.com
Freq: Bi-Monthly
Circ: 3630 Not Audited
Editor: Pat Burns
Profile: Launched in 1980, Specify became the magazine for the construction industry in Northern Ireland. Covering all aspects of construction, building and related trades, Specify is read by architects, engineers, builders, property developers, manufacturers and suppliers and key people in public and education establishments, offering comprehensive coverage of the entire industry.
Ad Rate: Full Page Colour £1350.00
MAGAZINE
Building & Construction

Spectroscopy Europe
983463
Tel: 44 01243 811334
Email: info@spectroscopyeurope.com
Web site: www.spectroscopyeurope.com
Freq: Bi-Monthly
Circ: 21000 Not Audited
Profile: The Journal of the Association of British Spectroscopists, covering industry news and new applications in process monitoring and quality control.
Ad Rate: Full Page Mono £3840.00
Ad Rate: Full Page Colour £5030.00
MAGAZINE
Science

Spinal News International
984399
Editorial: BIBA Medical, 526 Fulham Road, Fulham, London SW6 5NR
Tel: 44 02077 368788
Email: info@bibamedical.com
Web site: http://www.spinalnewsinternational.com/
Freq: Quarterly
Circ: 6452 Not Audited
Editor: Katherine Hignett
Profile: Professional newspaper for spine specialists.
MAGAZINE
Orthopedics

Spinal Surgery News
984132
Editorial: 9 Cardale Court, Cardale Park, Harrogate HG3 1RY
Email: ssn@barkerbrooks.co.uk
Web site: www.spinalsurgerynews.com
Freq: Quarterly
Circ: 1082 Not Audited
Editor: Kate Dance
MAGAZINE
Orthopedics

The Sports Injury Doctor
996020
Editorial: Meadow View, Tannery Lane, Bramley, Guildford GU5 0AB
Tel: 44 01483 899330
Web site: www.sportsinjurybulletin.com
Freq: Weekly Not Audited
Editor: Chris Mallac
MAGAZINE
Occupational Therapy & Rehabilitation, Sports Medicine

Sports Sponsorship Insider
997981
Editorial: SportBusiness Group, St Mark's House, Shepherdess Walk, London London N1 7BQ **Tel:** 44 02079 543514
Email: infoteam@sportbusiness.com

Business Magazines

Web site: www.sportbusiness.com/
sponsorship-insider
Freq: Daily
Circ: 34357 Cision Digital Reach
Editor: Matthew Glendinning
MAGAZINE (ONLINE)
Branding

Springboard Stories
999652
Editorial: Springboard Stories, 14 Hamilton
Terrace, Leamington Spa CV32 4LY
Tel: 44 01926 424464
Email: info@springboardstories.co.uk
Web site: www.springboardstories.co.uk
Freq: Daily
Circ: 9809 Cision Digital Reach
MAGAZINE (ONLINE)
Schools & Institutions

Stadia
983359
Editorial: Abinger House, Church Street,
Dorking, Dorking RH4 1DF
Tel: 44 01306 743744
Web site: www.stadia-magazine.com
Freq: Quarterly
Circ: 9947 Not Audited
Editor: Matt Ross
Profile: Magazine reviewing sports venue
design, operations and technology. Contains
news stories, interviews with key industry
figures, new facility profiles, operator
perspectives, technology surveys, market
studies and expert viewpoints.
Ad Rate: Full Page Colour £3650.00
MAGAZINE
Architecture & Design, Building &
Construction

Stainless Steel Focus
988025
Editorial: Morgan House, Gilbert Drive, PO
Box 238, Boston PE21 7TR
Tel: 44 01205 352273
Email: info@stainless-steel-focus.com
Web site: www.stainless-steel-focus.com
Freq: Monthly
Circ: 8500 Not Audited
Profile: Stainless Steel Focus is a source of
information for the stainless steel industry. It
has a worldwide distribution, and a specialist
readership which includes stainless steel
mills, traders, service centres and
stockholders, and users/fabricators, as well
as suppliers of raw materials. It provides
news and analysis of the markets for
stainless steel and the raw materials for
stainless steel production - nickel, chrome
and stainless steel scrap. Contents include
company news and company profiles.
market supply and demand, forecasts,
prices, processing and processors, and
applications and users.
Ad Rate: Full Page Mono £1620.00
Ad Rate: Full Page Colour £1940.00
MAGAZINE
Steel

Stand Out
983685
Editorial: The Goods Shed, Jubilee Way,
Whitstable Road, Faversham, Faversham
ME13 8GD **Tel:** 44 01795 509113
Web site: www.standoutmagazine.co.uk
Freq: Monthly
Circ: 12700 Not Audited
Editor: Caroline Clift; **Editor:** Caroline Clift
Profile: Trade magazine providing scenes
features, case studies, opinion pieces, new
product launches, trend watches, business
analysis and interviews. Targets organisers,
marketeers, agencies, local authorities and
not-for-profit organisations.
Ad Rate: Full Page Colour £2002.00
MAGAZINE
Retail Management

Start Your Business
983686
Editorial: 26 Old Brompton Road, South
Kensington, London SW7 3DL
Tel: 44 03300 270173
Email: editorial@gambitinteractive.com
Web site: www.startyourbusinessmag.com
Freq: Monthly
Circ: 28342 Not Audited
MAGAZINE
Business

The Startup Magazine
997334
Editorial: Rainmaking Loft, International
House, 1 St Katharine's Way, London E1W
1UN
Email: info@thestartupmag.com
Web site: http://thestartupmag.com/
Freq: Monthly
Circ: 52893 Cision Digital Reach
MAGAZINE (ONLINE)
Business, Corporate Responsibility, Small
and Medium Business

Startupoverseas.co.uk
997161
Editorial: Suite 6c, Whitefriars, Bristol BS1
2NT **Tel:** 44 01179 073520
Web site: www.startupoverseas.co.uk
Freq: Daily
Circ: 136635 Cision Digital Reach
MAGAZINE (ONLINE)
Business

Startups.co.uk
980847
Editorial: 6-8 Cole Street, London SE1 4YH
Tel: 44 02071 833932
Email: hello@startups.co.uk
Web site: www.startups.co.uk
Freq: Daily
Circ: 1321942 Cision Digital Reach
Editor: Lucy Wayment
Profile: Website discussing start ups,
including advice on how to start, franchising,
tech start ups and case studies.
MAGAZINE (ONLINE)
Business, Corporate Responsibility,
Industry

Stationery Magazine
999440
Editorial: Bromley Business Centre, 27
Hastings Road, London BR2 8NA
Tel: 44 02084 620721
Email: stationerymagazine@firstevents.com
Web site: www.stationeryshow.co.uk/
stationery-mag.html
Freq: Semi-Annual
Circ: 5000 Not Audited
Editor: Charlotte Kemp
MAGAZINE
Office Supplies

Steel Business Briefing
983903
Editorial: 20 Canada Square, London E14
5LH **Tel:** 44 02071 767646
Email: editors@platts.com
Web site: www.steelbb.com
Freq: Daily
Circ: 10532 Cision Digital Reach
Profile: Website covering steel industry. The
Steel Business Briefing is an electronic
newsletter containing up to date steel
market, prices and company information.
MAGAZINE (ONLINE)
Steel

Steel Markets Daily
998893
Editorial: 20 Canada Square, 12th Floor,
Canary Wharf, London E14 5LH
Tel: 44 02071 767000
Email: steel@platts.com
Web site: www.steeldaily.platts.com
Freq: Daily Not Audited
MAGAZINE
Financial Markets, Steel

Steel Times International
983745
Editorial: Quartz House, 20 Clarendon
Road, Redhill, Redhill RH1 1GX
Tel: 44 01737 855000
Email: steel@quartzltd.com
Web site: www.steeltimesint.com
Freq: Bi-Monthly
Circ: 6000 Not Audited
Editor: Matthew Moggridge
Profile: Journal containing a digest of global
news, events, statistics, and stockholding
news, as well as more detailed technical
articles, company and country profiles,
conference reports and regular regional
economic briefings. In addition to its regular
eight issues a year it publishes technical
supplements and foreign language
supplements in Chinese, Russian, Arabic

and Spanish for distribution in the
appropriate regions.
Ad Rate: Full Page Mono £2800.00
Ad Rate: Full Page Colour £3460.00
MAGAZINE
Steel

STEP Journal
981509
Editorial: Artillery House, 11-19 Artillery
Row, London SW1T 1RT
Tel: 44 02037 523700
Email: editor@step.org
Web site: http://www.step.org/
Freq: Monthly
Circ: 19757 Not Audited
Profile: Journal of the Society of Trust and
Estate Practitioners that covers the latest
developments in UK and International trust,
tax and estates. Aimed at private client
lawyers, accountants, IFAs, bankers,
barristers and trustees.
Ad Rate: Full Page Colour £3250.00
MAGAZINE
Banking

STM Publishing News
987201
Editorial: Manor View, Church Lane,
Swadlincote DE12 8DL
Tel: 44 01332 898248
Email: press@stm-publishing.com
Web site: www.stm-publishing.com
Freq: Daily
Circ: 16532 Cision Digital Reach
Profile: Blog covering news from the STM
publishing, academic and digital content
sectors. The blog has an archive dating back
to April 2011.
MAGAZINE (ONLINE)
Publishing

The Stocklists
985775
Editorial: 219 West Ella Road, West Ella,
Hull HU10 7SD **Tel:** 44 01482 659396
Web site: www.thestocklists.com
Freq: Monthly
Circ: 7000 Not Audited
MAGAZINE
Interior Design

Stockopedia
985639
Editorial: Office 224B, Macillan House,
Paddington, London W2 1FT
Tel: 44 02032 871269
Web site: http://www.stockopedia.com/
Freq: Daily
Circ: 139601 Cision Digital Reach
Editor: David Brickell
MAGAZINE (ONLINE)
Financial Markets

Stockpot Magazine
983991
Editorial: Progressive House, 2 Maidstone
Road, Sidcup DA14 5HZ
Tel: 44 02082 697900
Email: enquiries@craftguildofchefs.org
Web site: www.craftguildofchefs.org/
stockpot-magazine
Freq: Bi-Monthly
Circ: 7500 Not Audited
Editor: Diane Lane
Profile: Official quarterly publication for the
Craft Guild of Chefs providing chefs across
the UK with all the latest news and views
from the culinary world. Editorial coverage
includes: culinary competition updates,
event reviews, chef profiles, regular focus
features on ingredients, training, legislative
issues, and masterclasses.
Ad Rate: Full Page Colour £2500.00
MAGAZINE
Food

Storage & Process
1060815
Tel: 44 86222 7948711
Email: bxyjg@163.com
Freq: Bi-Monthly Not Audited
MAGAZINE
Animal Farming, Shipping & Warehousing

STORAGE Magazine
981677
Editorial: 35 Station Square, London BR5
1LZ **Tel:** 44 01689 616000
Web site: www.storagemagazine.co.uk
Freq: Bi-Monthly

Circ: 20000 Not Audited
Editor: David Tyler
MAGAZINE
Data Management, Security & Security
Systems

Strain
995996
Editorial: The Atrium, Southern Gate,
Chichester PO19 8QG **Tel:** 44 01865 778315
Email: cs-journals@wiley.com
Web site: http://onlinelibrary.wiley.com/
journal/10.1111/(ISSN)1475-1305
Freq: Bi-Monthly Not Audited
MAGAZINE
Engineering

Strategic Communication Management
981690
Editorial: 2nd Floor Apex Yard, 29 Long
Lane, London SE1 4PL
Tel: 44 02073 578888
Web site: www.melcrum.com/SCM
Freq: Bi-Monthly Not Audited
Profile: Magazine covering communication
strategy, including conference reviews, a
diary of events, Internet resources, reports,
ideas and trends in the communication field.
MAGAZINE
Marketing

Strategic Direction
984405
Editorial: Howard House, Wagon Lane,
Bingley BD16 1WA **Tel:** 44 01274 777700
Email: emerald@emeraldinsight.com
Web site: http://www.emeraldinsight.com/
loi/sd
Freq: Monthly Not Audited
Profile: Journal providing an executive
briefing of the world's best business
strategies.
MAGAZINE
Business, Corporate Responsibility

Strategic HR Review
980858
Editorial: Emerald Group, Howard House,
Waggon Lane, Bingley BD16 1WA
Tel: 44 01274 777700
Web site: http://www.emeraldinsight.com/
journals.htm?issn=1475-4398
Freq: Bi-Monthly Not Audited
Profile: Journal covering trends, techniques
and ideas in human resource strategy
through case study features and best
practice guides. The Journal does not
accept any outside press releases.
MAGAZINE
Company News & Appointments,
Education, Health & Safety, Human
Resources, Recruiting

StrategicRISK
980725
Editorial: 2nd Floor, 30 Cannon Street,
London EC4M 6YJ **Tel:** 44 02076 183456
Web site: www.strategic-risk-global.com/
Freq: Bi-Monthly
Circ: 5498 Not Audited
Profile: Magazine covering corporate
governance and risk related issues for
business as well as information on strategic,
environmental and ethical issues. Aimed at
CEOs, chief financial officers, chief risk
officers, internal auditors, treasurers, main
board directors and risk professionals. Also
those who deal with risk at strategic level
with a responsibility for corporate
governance.
Ad Rate: Full Page Colour £5461.00
MAGAZINE
Business, Corporate Responsibility,
Insurance

Strategy & Leadership
995747
Editorial: Howard House, Wagon Lane,
Bingley BD16 1WA **Tel:** 44 01274 777700
Email: emerald@emeraldinsight.com
Web site: http://www.emeraldinsight.com/
loi/sl
Freq: Bi-Monthly Not Audited
Editor: Robert Randall
MAGAZINE
Company News & Appointments,
Education, Health & Safety, Human
Resources, Recruiting

Stress and Health
999425
Editorial: The Atrium, Southern Gate, Chichester PO19 8QG **Tel:** 44 01865 778315
Email: smicdoffioc@wiley.com
Web site: http://onlinelibrary.wiley.com/journal/10.1002/(ISSN)1532-2998
Freq: Bi-Monthly Not Audited
MAGAZINE
Allergies, Cardiology, Neurology, Occupational Therapy & Rehabilitation, Sports Medicine

Stride Insurance Group
995731
Editorial: Birch House, Parklands Business Park, Forest Road, Denmead PO7 6XP
Tel: 44 02392 248790
Email: freeinfo@stride.co.uk
Web site: http://www.stride-group.co.uk
Freq: Daily
Circ: 3124 Cision Digital Reach
MAGAZINE (ONLINE)
Insurance

The Structural Engineer
981108
Editorial: 47-58 Bastwick Street, London EC1V 3PS **Tel:** 44 02072 354535
Email: tse@istructe.org
Web site: http://www.istructe.org/thestructuralengineer
Freq: Monthly
Circ: 17000 Not Audited
Editor: Robin Jones
Profile: Publication containing technical and project based articles and papers on the design and construction of buildings, bridges and similar structures worldwide. Also includes news and a products and services section.
Ad Rate: Full Page Mono £1400.00
Ad Rate: Full Page Colour £2020.00
MAGAZINE
Architecture & Design, Building & Construction, Engineering, Sustainable Development, Urban Planning & Development

Student Accountant
984002
Editorial: The Adelphi, 1-11 John Adam Street, London WC2N 6AU
Tel: 44 02070 595000
Email: info@accaglobal.com
Web site: http://www.accaglobal.com/gb/en/student/sa.html
Freq: Daily
Circ: 12913 Cision Digital Reach
Editor: Victoria Morgan
Profile: Digital only magazine published in co-operation with the Association of Chartered Certified Accountants. The magazine focuses on ACCA Qualification, Certified Accounting Technician students, and affiliates. Read by students of accountancy, finance and business. Alternative Title: Students' Newsletter Previous title: ACCA Students' Newsletter
Ad Rate: Full Page Mono £2366.00
Ad Rate: Full Page Colour £2957.00
MAGAZINE (ONLINE)
Accounting

Studio (UK)
996620
Editorial: 5th Floor Congress House, 14 Lyon Road, Harrow HA1 2EN
Email: editorial@studio-news.com
Web site: www.studio-news.com
Freq: Bi-Monthly
Circ: 10000 Not Audited
Editor: Kate Burnett
MAGAZINE
Architecture & Design, Interior Design, Residential Real Estate

Stylus
985545
Editorial: 11th Floor, Capital House, 25 Chapel Street, London NW1 5DH
Tel: 44 02038 378300
Email: editorial@stylus.com
Web site: www.stylus.com
Freq: Daily
Circ: 50035 Cision Digital Reach

Profile: Website covering consumer research. The Stylus website features news and analysis about consumer trends.
MAGAZINE (ONLINE)
Graphic Design, Interior Design, Women's Interests

sUAS News
988773
Email: gary@suasnews.com
Web site: www.suasnews.com
Freq: Daily
Circ: 150122 Cision Digital Reach
Editor: Gary Mortimer
MAGAZINE (ONLINE)
Aviation

The Subpostmaster
1053940
Editorial: Suite A, Arun House, Office Village, River Way, Uckfield TN22 1SL
Tel: 44 01825 983105
Email: thesubpostmaster@nfsp.org.uk
Web site: http://www.nfsp.org.uk/Subpostmaster-Magazine
Freq: Monthly
Circ: 5587 Not Audited
Profile: Official journal of the National Federation of SubPostmasters.
MAGAZINE
Books, Office Supplies

Subsea Engineering News
985155
Editorial: PO BOX 27, Cheltenham GL53 0YH **Tel:** 44 01242 574027
Email: sen@btinternet.com
Web site: www.subsea-news.co.uk
Freq: Bi-Weekly
Circ: 1000 Not Audited
Editor: John Sheehan
Profile: Magazine focusing on the subject of sub sea and underwater engineering, floating production systems and pipelines.
MAGAZINE
Oil

Success at School
1052542
Editorial: Success at School, 124 Chatsworth Road, London NW2 5QU
Email: editor@successatschool.org
Web site: www.successatschool.org
Freq: Daily
Circ: 22090 Cision Digital Reach
Editor: Jamie Goodland
MAGAZINE (ONLINE)
Education, Students

Sulphur
984693
Editorial: Southbank House, Blackprince Road, London SE1 7SJ
Tel: 44 02077 932567
Web site: www.bcinsight.com
Freq: Bi-Monthly Not Audited
Profile: Journal covering the sulphur and sulphuric acid related industries, with emphasis on the marketing and technology of sulphur recovery from oil, gas and coal.
Ad Rate: Full Page Mono £1250.00
Ad Rate: Full Page Colour £2000.00
MAGAZINE
Chemicals

Supplier Business
985563
Editorial: Willoughby House, 2 Broad St, Lincolnshire, Stamford PE9 1PB
Tel: 44 01733 520066
Email: info@supplierbusiness.com
Web site: http://www.ihssupplierinsight.com/
Freq: Daily
Circ: 12667 Cision Digital Reach
MAGAZINE (ONLINE)
Business, Economics, Supply Chain Management (SCM)

Supply Chain Digital
1074962
Editorial: 69-75 Thorpe Road, Norwich NR1 1UA **Tel:** 44 01603 217530
Web site: http://www.supplychaindigital.com/
Freq: Monthly
Circ: 149194 Cision Digital Reach
MAGAZINE (ONLINE)
Supply Chain Management (SCM)

Supply Chain Risk & Innovation
1054370
Editorial: 154-158 Shoreditch High Street, London E1 6HU
Email: info@innovation-forum.co.uk
Web site: http://innovation-forum.co.uk/supply-chain-risk-innovation.php
Freq: Monthly Not Audited
MAGAZINE
Supply Chain Management (SCM)

Supply Management
981018
Editorial: Bridge House, 69 London Road, Twickenham, London TW1 3SP
Tel: 44 02082 675802
Email: smeditorial@haymarket.com
Web site: https://www.cips.org/supply-management/
Freq: Monthly
Circ: 50000 Not Audited
Profile: Magazine covering news, advice and in depth features on purchasing, supply chain and logistics, from defining supply strategies to managing day-to-day procurement. Features articles dealing with e-commerce and related issues. First published in 1996, the publication has an average of 60 pages per issue. Aimed at chief executives and those involved in procurement, purchasing, operations and logistics. Also read by supply chain directors, managers and buyers at all levels.
Ad Rate: Full Page Mono £3500.00
Ad Rate: Full Page Colour £4440.00
MAGAZINE
Supply Chain Management (SCM)

Surface Coatings International
983465
Editorial: OCCA, 4th Floor, Clayton House, 59 Piccadilly, Manchester M1 2AQ
Tel: 44 01162 575488
Email: editorial@occa.org.uk
Web site: http://www.surfacecoatingsinternational.com
Freq: Bi-Monthly
Circ: 3000 Not Audited
Profile: Technological magazine covering news and articles on the paint, printing ink and allied industries.
Ad Rate: Full Page Mono £1300.00
Ad Rate: Full Page Colour £2000.00
MAGAZINE
Science

Surface Engineering
983466
Editorial: 5 Howick Place, London SW1P 1WG **Tel:** 44 02070 176000
Web site: http://www.tandfonline.com/toc/ysue20/current
Freq: Monthly
Profile: Journal covering the surface treatment and modification of engineering and functional materials, with particular emphasis on scientific and technological developments and functional applications.
Ad Rate: Full Page Mono £500.00
Ad Rate: Full Page Colour £1100.00
MAGAZINE
Engineering

Surrey Director
982906
Editorial: 14 Middletons Road, Yaxley, Peterborough PE7 3LR
Tel: 44 01733 242312
Email: info@pridepublications.co.uk
Web site: www.pridepublications.co.uk
Freq: Bi-Monthly
Circ: 3000 Not Audited
Editor: Trevor Gehlcken
Profile: Journal covering business articles, business advice and regional business news.
Ad Rate: Full Page Mono £675.00
Ad Rate: Full Page Colour £675.00
MAGAZINE
Business

Surrey Lawyer
987568
Editorial: 3tc House, 16 Crosby Road North, Crosby, Liverpool L22 0NY
Tel: 44 01512 364141
Email: admin@benhampublishing.com
Web site: www.benhampublishing.com
Freq: Quarterly
Circ: 1200 Not Audited

Editor: Sue Seakens
Profile: Official magazine of the Surrey Law Society featuring society news, members events and awards.
MAGAZINE
Corporate Law, Government, Legal Services

Sussex Business Times
980025
Editorial: Life Media Group, Unit 1, Swan Barn Business Centre, Old Swan Lane, Hailsham BN27 2BY **Tel:** 44 01323 819007
Web site: http://www.sussexbusinessgroup.co.uk
Freq: Monthly
Circ: 20000 Not Audited
MAGAZINE
Business, Small and Medium Business

Sustainable Building Matters
995772
Editorial: c/o 52 Buckingham Road, Bicester, Bicester OX26 6EF
Tel: 44 07942 885345
Web site: www.sbmsearch.com
Freq: Daily
Circ: 603 Cision Digital Reach
MAGAZINE (ONLINE)
Sustainable Development

Sustainable Business Magazine
1076408
Tel: 44 01603 516519
Email: info@sustainablebusinessmagazine.net
Web site: http://www.sustainablebusinessmagazine.net/index.html
Freq: Quarterly
MAGAZINE
Environment

Sustainable Development
980907
Editorial: The Atrium, Southern Gate, Chichester, Chichester PO19 8SQ
Tel: 44 01865 778315
Email: cs-journals@wiley.com
Web site: www.interscience.wiley.com/journal/sd
Freq: Bi-Monthly
Circ: 7500 Not Audited
Editor: Richard Welford
Profile: Journal focusing on environmental management and sustainability, including global, national and regional development issues. Aimed at policy makers in local and central government, decision makers in business, engineers, researchers and academics.
Ad Rate: Full Page Mono £2000.00
Ad Rate: Full Page Colour £4375.00
MAGAZINE
Economics, Environment, Equities

Sustainable Ireland
984153
Tel: 44 02892 688888
Email: golda@sustainableireland.co.uk
Web site: www.sustainableireland.co.uk
Freq: Quarterly
Circ: 5800 Not Audited
Profile: Magazine covering all aspects of sustainable development, including articles on energy efficiency and waste management.
Ad Rate: Full Page Colour £1100.00
MAGAZINE
Alternative/Renewable Energy, Carbon Emissions & Trading, Electricity, Environment, Sustainable Development, Water & Sanitation

Sweets & Snacks World
995801
Editorial: The Maltings, 57 Bath Street, Kent, Gravesend DA11 0DF
Tel: 44 01474 532202
Web site: http://www.sweetsandsavourysnacksworld.com/
Freq: Daily
Circ: 14524 Cision Digital Reach
Profile: Magazine covering the chocolate, confectionery, snacks and sweet bakery industry. It features expert comment and analysis with updates on the latest developments in new products, buying

Business Magazines

trends for wholesalers, retailers and independent buyers as well as distribution, branding and packaging.
MAGAZINE (ONLINE)
Food

Swindon Business News   983687
Editorial: Engine Shed, Station Approach, Temple Meads, Bristol BS1 6QH
Tel: 44 07773 040272
Email: info@swindon-business.net
Web site: www.swindon-business.net
Freq: Bi-Monthly
Circ: 8000 Not Audited
Editor: Robert Buckland
Profile: Business publication covering the expansion and growth of companies in Swindon and the South West.
Ad Rate: Full Page Mono £1524.00
Ad Rate: Full Page Colour £1828.80
MAGAZINE
Business

SwitchMyBusiness.com   990666
Editorial: Chancery Place, 50 Brown Street, Manchester M2 2JT
Web site: www.switchmybusiness.com
Freq: Daily
Circ: 26433 Cision Digital Reach
MAGAZINE (ONLINE)
Business, Small and Medium Business

Tableware International   983742
Editorial: Naishville, 1 Churchgates, The Wilderness, Berkhamsted, Berkhamsted HP4 2UB **Tel:** 44 01442 289930
Email: kate@lemapublishing.co.uk
Web site: www.tablewareinternational.com
Freq: Bi-Monthly
Circ: 15054 Not Audited
Editor: Kate Birch
Profile: Journal containing information on all aspects of the tableware, homeware and gifts business, including trade fairs.
Ad Rate: Full Page Colour £3250.00
MAGAZINE
Manufacturing

Tackle Trade World   986491
Editorial: 1 Whittle Close, Drayton Fields, Daventry, Daventry NN11 8RQ
Tel: 44 01327 315465
Web site: tackletradeworld.com
Freq: Monthly
Circ: 21000 Not Audited
Profile: Magazine covering business to business for the global fishing tackle trade.
Ad Rate: Full Page Colour £1150.00
MAGAZINE
Animal Farming

Talk Business   986388
Editorial: William Robinson Buildings, 3 Woodfield Terrace, Stansted Mountfitchet, Chelmsford CM2 8AJ **Tel:** 44 01279 818250
Web site: http://www.talk-business.co.uk/
Freq: Monthly
Circ: 18899 Cision Digital Reach
Profile: Magazine profiling business entrepreneurs and containing tips and advice for businesses. The magazine features successful entrepreneurs and discusses their past, present and future aspirations and presents ideas for start-up businesses to replicate their successes. Aimed at business managers and entrepreneurs.
MAGAZINE (ONLINE)
Business, Corporate Responsibility

TalklawGlobal   985301
Email: editor@talklawglobal.com
Web site: www.talklawglobal.com
Freq: Daily
Circ: 2771 Cision Digital Reach
MAGAZINE (ONLINE)
Corporate Law

Tank Cleaning Magazine   997794
Editorial: Marshall House, 124 Middleton Road, Morden, London SM4 6RW
Web site: globaltankcleaning.com
Freq: Quarterly
Circ: 7000 Not Audited

Editor: Liz Gyekye
MAGAZINE
Hygiene, Shipping & Warehousing, Supply Chain Management (SCM)

Tank Storage Magazine   984155
Editorial: 2nd Floor, Regal House, 70 London Road, Twickenham, London TW1 3QS **Tel:** 44 02088 438800
Email: info@tankstoragemag.com
Web site: www.tankstoragemag.com
Freq: Bi-Monthly
Circ: 2994 Not Audited
Profile: Magazine containing industry news for the tank terminal sector. Each issue contains interviews with a leading terminal operator, technical articles, updates on regulations and new products.
MAGAZINE
Chemicals, Oil

Tanker Operator   983543
Editorial: Tanker Operator Magazine, 39-41 North Road London, London N7 9DP
Tel: 44 02081 505295
Email: cochran@tankeroperator.com
Web site: www.tankeroperator.com
Freq: Bi-Monthly
Circ: 2000 Not Audited
Editor: Ian Cochran
Profile: Magazine covering news and technical issues affecting the tanker industry. Aimed at tanker operators, owners, managers, charterers, brokers and equipment manufacturers with an interest in the tanker sector.
Ad Rate: Full Page Mono £1980.00
Ad Rate: Full Page Colour £1980.00
MAGAZINE
Shipping & Warehousing

Tax Adviser   983190
Editorial: Artillery House, 11-19 Artillery Row, London SW1P 1RT
Tel: 44 02074 002500
Web site: www.taxadvisermagazine.com
Freq: Monthly
Circ: 20000 Not Audited
Profile: Magazine covering news of recent tax legislation's and topical tax issues including interviews with leading tax professionals, analysis and opinion by prominent figures, informative features on technical issues in taxation, case review, commentary on important tax cases and the latest news from the CIOT and ATT. Aimed at members of the Chartered Institute of Taxation and the Association of Taxation Technicians.
Ad Rate: Full Page Mono £3070.00
Ad Rate: Full Page Colour £3070.00
MAGAZINE
Accounting

Tax Confidential   980160
Editorial: Fergusson House, 124-128 City Road, London EC1V 2NJ
Tel: 44 02075 028231
Web site: tax-confidential.co.uk
Freq: Monthly Not Audited
MAGAZINE
Accounting

Tax Journal   980145
Editorial: Quadrant House, The Quadrant, Sutton, London SM2 5AS
Tel: 44 02033 644448
Web site: http://www.taxjournal.com/tj/
Freq: Weekly
Circ: 2000 Not Audited
Editor: Paul Stainforth
Profile: Journal containing information and news concerning taxation and in depth coverage of tax cases. the publication provides a forum for debate on topical subjects, keeps you abreast of all current and impending developments in UK direct and indirect tax, discusses all international tax developments where relevant to the UK, provides a balanced view with articles from both leading practitioners and government organisations, discusses the latest tax and VAT cases with comment on their implications, covers all VAT Tribunals, Budget, Finance Bill debates and Pre-Budget Report. It also provide reviews

of the various professional tax bodies on the latest tax proposals, back-to-basics tax articles for specialists in other fields of expertise, basic legal and accounting articles relevant to tax practitioners, discusses duty and customs developments and reviews relevant conferences and books. Aimed at tax experts in legal and accountancy firms, tax managers in public companies and finance directors in private companies. Regular features: Tax Case News News about tax cases.; Tax Cases Articles and discussion about tax cases.
Ad Rate: Full Page Mono £1240.00
Ad Rate: Full Page Colour £1715.00
MAGAZINE
Accounting

Tax Planning International Asia-Pacific Focus   983329
Editorial: 1st Floor, 38 Threadneedle Street, London EC2R 8AY **Tel:** 44 02078 475801
Email: bnaieditorial@bna.com
Web site: http://www.bna.com/
Freq: Daily
Circ: 256617 Cision Digital Reach
MAGAZINE (ONLINE)
Accounting

Tax Planning International Review   998554
Editorial: First Floor, 38 Threadneedle Street, London EC2R 8AY
Tel: 44 02078 475800
Email: bnaieditorial@bna.com
Web site: http://www.bna.com/tax/
Freq: Monthly Not Audited
MAGAZINE
Accounting

Tax Planning International: Indirect Taxes   981556
Editorial: First Floor, 38 Threadneedle Street, London EC2R 8AY
Email: bnaieditorial@bna.com
Web site: http://www.bna.com/
Freq: Monthly Not Audited
MAGAZINE
Accounting, Tax Law

Tax Shelter Report   983025
Editorial: 26th Floor, 125 Old Broad Street, London EC2N 1AR **Tel:** 44 02074 091111
Web site: www.taxshelterreport.co.uk
Freq: No Frequency Established Not Audited
Editor: Anthony Yadgaroff
Profile: Magazine covering all aspects of tax shelter investments and independent comment on UK tax efficient investments. The publication also provides reviews of all Venture Capital Trusts, Enterprise Investment Schemes, Capital Gains Tax deferral companies, Enterprise Zone Trusts and Film Partnerships. Read by advisers on tax shelter products.
MAGAZINE
Accounting

Taxation   980146
Editorial: Quadrant House, The Quadrant, Brighton Road, Sutton SM2 5AS
Email: taxation@lexisnexis.co.uk
Web site: www.taxation.co.uk
Freq: Weekly
Circ: 4841 Not Audited
Editor: Richard Curtis
Profile: Journal written by tax practitioners for tax practitioners containing practical solutions to problems, lively debate, commentary, announcements, news and book reviews. Covers changes in legislation affecting tax practice, tax software and technical issues. Primarily aimed at United Kingdom tax practitioners.
Ad Rate: Full Page Colour £2785.00
MAGAZINE
Accounting

taxgrotto.com   983679
Editorial: Ridding House, Durham DL13 2TQ
Tel: 44 07961 315145
Web site: www.taxgrotto.com
Freq: Daily

Circ: 8392 Cision Digital Reach
MAGAZINE (ONLINE)
Accounting, Recruiting

TCT Magazine   984308
Editorial: Carlton House, Sandpiper Way, Chester Business Park, Chester CH4 9QE
Tel: 44 01244 680222
Web site: www.tctmagazine.com
Freq: Bi-Monthly
Circ: 9473 Not Audited
Profile: Magazine for the additive manufacturing and professional 3D printing industry covering time compression engineering, design engineering and rapid product development including 3D CAD/CAM/CAE, software analysis (FEA/CFD, virtual prototyping), rapid prototyping and rapid tooling, production tooling, reverse engineering metrology, inspection and materials. Read by design engineers and senior management involved with the implementation of new technologies to reduce product development time and cost.
Ad Rate: Full Page Mono £2000.00
Ad Rate: Full Page Colour £2000.00
MAGAZINE
Manufacturing

Teach Accounting   996297
Editorial: The Adelphi, 1-11 John Adam Street, London WC2N 6AU
Tel: 44 02070 595000
Email: teach.accounting@accaglobal.com
Web site: http://www.accaglobal.com/gb/en.html
Freq: Monthly
Circ: 6000 Not Audited
Editor: Victoria Morgan
MAGAZINE
Accounting

Teach Primary   985296
Editorial: 25 Phoenix Court, Hawkins Road, Colchester CO2 8JY **Tel:** 44 01206 505925
Web site: http://www.teachprimary.com/
Freq: Monthly
Circ: 22000 Not Audited
Editor: Elaine Bennett
MAGAZINE
Schools & Institutions

Teach Secondary   987378
Editorial: 25 Phoenix Court, Hawkins Rd, Colchester, Colchester CO2 8JY
Tel: 44 01206 505900
Email: editor@teachsecondary.com
Web site: http://www.teachsecondary.com/
Freq: Bi-Monthly
Circ: 20000 Not Audited
Editor: Helen Mulley
MAGAZINE
Schools & Institutions

Teaching Drama   983641
Editorial: Rhinegold House, 20 Rugby Street, London WC1N 3QZ
Tel: 44 07785 613149
Email: teaching.drama@rhinegold.co.uk
Web site: http://www.rhinegold.co.uk/rhinegold-publishing/magazines/teaching-drama/
Freq: Bi-Monthly
Circ: 4000 Not Audited
Profile: Magazine providing product reviews, new ideas and lesson plans on drama and performing arts education. Magazine is published twice termly and offers a dynamic mixture of news, features, schemes of work and in-depth reviews.
Ad Rate: Full Page Mono £1220.00
Ad Rate: Full Page Colour £1480.00
MAGAZINE
Schools & Institutions

Tech Tank News   1101205
Editorial: Kemp House, 152 City Road, London EC1V 2NX **Tel:** 44 02076 865431
Email: info@technative.io
Web site: https://www.technative.io/
Freq: Daily

Circ: 18271 Cision Digital Reach
MAGAZINE (ONLINE)
Computers, Data Management, Industry, Software

Technavio 998059
Tel: 44 02081 231770
Web site: www.technavio.com
Freq: Daily
Circ: 616669 Cision Digital Reach
MAGAZINE (ONLINE)
Marketing

The Technical Analyst 980855
Editorial: 10 Quarry Street, London GU1 3UY **Tel:** 44 01483 573150
Email: editor@technicalanalyst.co.uk
Web site: www.technicalanalyst.co.uk
Freq: Daily
Circ: 13443 Cision Digital Reach
Editor: Matthew Clements
Profile: Magazine covering trading strategies for the financial markets and bringing technical trading ideas to the global markets supported by regular events and training courses. The publication provides news, features and commentary from key players around the world. Aimed at fund managers, traders and information and software providers.
Ad Rate: Full Page Colour £1900.00
MAGAZINE (ONLINE)
Equities, Fund Management, Hedge Funds

Technical Review Middle East 981067
Editorial: University House, 11-13 Lower Grosvenor Place, London SW1W 0EX
Tel: 44 02078 347676
Email: trme@alaincharles.com
Web site: www.technicalreviewmiddleeast.com
Freq: Bi-Monthly
Circ: 11911 Not Audited
Profile: Magazine covering trade, information technology, water, aviation, travel, manufacturing, industry, telecommunications, transport, logistics, power, oil and gas in the Middle East and North Africa. Read by senior executives in Middle Eastern businesses and government departments throughout the Middle East and North Africa.
Ad Rate: Full Page Mono £2950.00
Ad Rate: Full Page Colour £4350.00
MAGAZINE
Building & Construction, Business, Corporate Responsibility, Electricity, Manufacturing, Oil, Water & Sanitation

Technology Networks 987158
Editorial: Woodview, Bull Lane Industrial Estate, Sudbury CO10 0FD
Tel: 44 01787 319234
Web site: https://www.technologynetworks.com/
Freq: Daily
Circ: 34230 Cision Digital Reach
Editor: Ashley Board
Profile: Website covering technology. The Technology Networks website shares the latest life science & drug discovery providing the latest scientific, business and product news.
MAGAZINE (ONLINE)
Biotechnology, Science

TeleCareNewsonline.co.uk 995177
Editorial: 5 Argent Way, Sittingbourne, Sittingbourne ME10 5AR
Tel: 44 01795 435913
Email: news@telecarenewsonline.co.uk
Web site: www.telecarenewsonline.co.uk
Freq: Weekly
Circ: 521 Cision Digital Reach
Editor: Karen Lott
MAGAZINE (ONLINE)
Geriatrics, Medical Technology

TelecomFinance 979895
Editorial: 292 Vauxhall Bridge Road, London SW1V 1AE

Email: info@telecomfinance.com
Web site: www.telecomfinance.com
Freq: Monthly
Circ: 1500 Not Audited
MAGAZINE
Telecommunications/Electronic Communications

telecoms.com 983289
Editorial: 5 Howick Place, London SW1P 1WG **Tel:** 44 02070 174800
Web site: http://telecoms.com/
Freq: Daily
Circ: 155697 Cision Digital Reach
Profile: Website covering news, analysis and insight on the global telecommunications industry, technological advancements and market trends, including M2M (machine to machine communications), internet of things (IoT), collaboration and network security.
MAGAZINE (ONLINE)
Telecommunications/Electronic Communications

TelecomsTech 987314
Email: editorial@techforge.pub
Web site: www.telecomstechnews.com
Freq: Daily
Circ: 50778 Cision Digital Reach
MAGAZINE (ONLINE)
Telecommunications/Electronic Communications

TelecomTV 983331
Editorial: 86-90 Paul Street, London EC2A 4NE **Tel:** 44 02074 481070
Email: info@telecomtv.com
Web site: www.telecomtv.com
Freq: Daily
Circ: 58900 Cision Digital Reach
Profile: Website covering daily news and analysis for the global telecommunications industry.
MAGAZINE (ONLINE)
Telecommunications/Electronic Communications

Temperature Controlled Storage and Distribution 999338
Editorial: PO Box 88, Edenbridge, Edenbridge TN8 6ZW **Tel:** 44 01732 868288
Email: publisher@tcsandd.com
Web site: www.tcsandd.com
Freq: Bi-Monthly
Circ: 4500 Not Audited
MAGAZINE
Food, Manufacturing, Supply Chain Management (SCM)

Ten26 983591
Editorial: National Federation of Young Farmers' Clubs, YFC Centre, 10th Street, Stoneleigh Park, Kenilworth CV8 2LG
Tel: 44 02476 857200
Email: magazine@nfyfc.org.uk
Web site: www.nfyfc.org.uk
Freq: 3 Times/Year
Circ: 25000 Not Audited
MAGAZINE
Animal Farming

TEST Magazine 987439
Editorial: 41-42 Daisy Business Park, 19-35 Sylvan Grove, London SE15 1PD
Tel: 44 08708 636930
Email: info@testingmagazine.com
Web site: www.testingmagazine.com/
Freq: Bi-Monthly
Circ: 10760 Not Audited
Editor: Cecilia Rehn
Profile: Magazine covering all aspects of electronic product testing.
Ad Rate: Full Page Colour £1395.00
MAGAZINE
Industry, Software

TETRA Today 987496
Editorial: St. Jude's Church, Dulwich Road, London SE24 0PB **Tel:** 44 01722 716997
Web site: www.tetratoday.com
Freq: Bi-Monthly
Circ: 6500 Not Audited

Editor: Sam Fenwick
MAGAZINE
Mobile Communications

TheBusinessDesk.com 984540
Editorial: Manchester One, 53 Portland Street, Manchester M1 3LF
Web site: www.TheBusinessDesk.com
Freq: Daily
Circ: 153959 Cision Digital Reach
Editor: Joanne Birtwistle; **Editor:** Sam Metcalf; **Editor:** Alex Turner
MAGAZINE (ONLINE)
Business, Corporate Responsibility

thecattlesite.com 987186
Editorial: 8 Smithy Wood Drive, Sheffield S35 1QN **Tel:** 44 01865 790880
Email: newsdesk@5mpublishing.com
Web site: www.thecattlesite.com
Freq: Daily
Circ: 55320 Cision Digital Reach
MAGAZINE (ONLINE)
Animal Farming

theCsuite.co.uk 988214
Editorial: 40 Bowling Green Lane, London EC1R 0NE **Tel:** 44 02079 705690
Email: max@spartapublishing.co.uk
Web site: www.thecsuite.co.uk
Freq: Daily
Circ: 30000 Not Audited
Profile: Website covering news on corporate titles, finance, corporate finance, corporate treasury, global trade, banking, accounting, human resources, technological innovation.
MAGAZINE (ONLINE)
Business, Corporate Responsibility

theEWord 1065602
Editorial: Swan Square, 79 Tib Street, Salford M4 1LS **Tel:** 44 08000 149884
Email: contact@theeword.co.uk
Web site: www.theeword.co.uk
Freq: Daily
Circ: 77669 Cision Digital Reach
MAGAZINE (ONLINE)
Marketing

thefishsite.com 985691
Editorial: 5M Enterprises Ltd, Unit 10, Southall Business Park, Chipping Norton OX7 3EW **Tel:** 44 01865 790880
Email: newsdesk@5mpublishing.com
Web site: www.thefishsite.com
Freq: Daily
Circ: 63384 Cision Digital Reach
MAGAZINE (ONLINE)
Animal Farming

theHRDIRECTOR 981717
Tel: 44 01454 292063
Email: editor@thehrdirector.com
Web site: www.thehrdirector.com
Freq: Monthly
Circ: 10500 Not Audited
Editor: Jason Spiller
Profile: Website featuring in-depth hr analysis and proven hr strategies to enable HR directors to keep on top of this fast-paced industry.
MAGAZINE
Company News & Appointments, Education, Health & Safety, Human Resources, Recruiting

TheMoveChannel.com 984258
Editorial: 24 Jack's Place, Shoreditch, London E1 6NN **Tel:** 44 02079 527653
Email: info@themovechannel.com
Web site: www.themovechannel.com
Freq: Daily
Circ: 158042 Cision Digital Reach
Editor: Ivan Radford
Profile: Website covering property news. TheMoveChannel.com shares the latest news, information or reviews on property news and prices. The outlet offers RSS (Really Simple Syndication)
MAGAZINE (ONLINE)
Residential Real Estate

thepigsite.com 987681
Editorial: Benchmark House, 8 Smithy Wood Drive, Sheffield S35 1QN
Tel: 44 01234 818180
Email: newsdesk@5mpublishing.com
Web site: www.thepigsite.com
Freq: Daily
Circ: 154956 Cision Digital Reach
MAGAZINE (ONLINE)
Animal Farming

thepoultrysite.com 985125
Editorial: Benchmark House, 3 Smithywood Drive, Sheffield S35 1QN
Tel: 44 01234 818180
Email: you2us@5mpublishing.com
Web site: www.thepoultrysite.com
Freq: Daily
Circ: 155412 Cision Digital Reach
MAGAZINE (ONLINE)
Animal Farming

Therapeutic Advances in Cardiovascular Disease 000400
Editorial: 1 Oliver's Yard, 55 City Road, London EC1Y 1SP **Tel:** 44 02073 248500
Email: tpp@sagepub.co.uk
Web site: http://tak.sagepub.com/
Freq: Bi-Monthly Not Audited
MAGAZINE
Cardiology

Therapeutic Advances in Endocrinology and Metabolism 999480
Editorial: 1 Oliver's Yard, 55 City Road, London EC1Y 1SP **Tel:** 44 02073 248500
Web site: http://tae.sagepub.com/
Freq: Bi-Monthly Not Audited
MAGAZINE
Diabetes

Therapeutic Advances in Medical Oncology 996240
Editorial: 1 Oliver's Yard, 55 City Road, London EC1Y 1SP **Tel:** 44 02073 248500
Web site: http://tam.sagepub.com/
Freq: Bi-Monthly Not Audited
MAGAZINE
Oncology

TheRedZone 1060723
Tel: 44 27118 032040
Email: jeremy@thefuture.co.za
Web site: http://www.theredzone.co.za
Circ: 6421 Cision Digital Reach
MAGAZINE (ONLINE)
Advertising Industry, Economics, Marketing

thewealthnet.com 983048
Editorial: 107 Cheapside, London EC2V 6DN **Tel:** 44 02078 698043
Email: news@thewealthnet.com
Web site: www.thewealthnet.com
Freq: Daily
Circ: 8732 Cision Digital Reach
MAGAZINE (ONLINE)
Banking

This Is Africa 984847
Editorial: Number One, Southwark Bridge, London SE1 9HL **Tel:** 44 02078 733000
Email: thisisafrica@ft.com
Web site: www.thisisafricaonline.com
Freq: Daily
Circ: 41975 Cision Digital Reach
Editor: Adrienne Klasa
MAGAZINE (ONLINE)
Business, Small and Medium Business

Thomson Reuters GRC 980965
Editorial: 30 South Colonnade, Canary Wharf, London E14 5EP
Tel: 44 02072 501122
Web site: https://risk.thomsonreuters.com/
Freq: Daily
Circ: 286256 Cision Digital Reach
MAGAZINE (ONLINE)
Banking

Business Magazines

Thorax
999690
Editorial: BMA House, Tavistock Square, London WC1H 9JR **Tel:** 44 02073 836318
Email: thorax@bmjgroup.com
Web site: http://thorax.bmj.com
Freq: Monthly Not Audited
Editor: Gisli Jenkins; **Editor:** Alan Smyth
MAGAZINE
Allergies, Respiratory Diseases

Tile and Stone Journal (TSJ)
984832
Editorial: Garden Cottage, The Chesnuts, Main Street, Beckley, Tunbridge Wells TN3 6RS **Tel:** 44 01892 752400
Email: tandsjournal@aol.com
Web site: www.tileandstonejournal.com
Freq: Monthly
Circ: 6514 Not Audited
Editor: Joe Simpson
MAGAZINE
Building & Construction

Tilezine
985499
Editorial: The Tile Association, Forum Court, 83 Copers Cope Road, London BR3 1NR
Tel: 44 03003 658453
Email: news@tilezine.co.uk
Web site: www.tilezine.co.uk
Freq: Daily
Circ: 10480 Cision Digital Reach
Profile: Website covering the tiling industry. Tilezine is an online magazine covering the latest news and information from the tiling industry.
MAGAZINE (ONLINE)
Building & Construction

Timber Trades Journal (TTJ)
983183
Editorial: Progressive House, 2 Maidstone Road, Foots Cray, Sidcup, London DA14 5HZ **Tel:** 44 02082 697700
Web site: www.ttjonline.com
Freq: Monthly
Circ: 6000 Not Audited
MAGAZINE
Manufacturing

Times Higher Education (THE)
981524
Editorial: TES Global, 26 Red Lion Square, London WC1R 4HQ **Tel:** 44 02031 943000
Web site: www.timeshighereducation.co.uk
Freq: Weekly
Circ: 15579 Not Audited
Editor: John Gill
MAGAZINE
Education, Higher Education

Tips & Advice Company Director
980987
Editorial: Calgarth House, 39-41 Bank Street, Ashford, Ashford TN23 1DQ
Tel: 44 01233 653500
Web site: http://lite.indicator.co.uk/companydirector/home.php
Freq: Bi-Weekly
Editor: Tony Court
Profile: Newsletter covering personnel and employment issues, with legal, financial and tax advice.
MAGAZINE
Business

Tips & Advice Health & Safety
996001
Editorial: Calgarth House, 39-41 Bank Street, Kent, Ashford TN23 1DQ
Tel: 44 01233 653500
Email: editorial@indicator.co.uk
Web site: http://lite.indicator.co.uk/healthandsafety/home.php
Freq: Bi-Weekly Not Audited
Editor: Simon Wakeham
MAGAZINE
Health & Safety

Tips & Advice Personnel
980950
Editorial: Calgarth House, 39-41 Bank Street, Kent, Ashford TN23 1DQ
Tel: 44 01233 653500

[Tips & Advice Personnel continued]
Email: editorial@indicator.co.uk
Web site: http://lite.indicator.co.uk/personnel/home.php
Freq: Bi-Weekly Not Audited
Profile: Newsletter containing practical advice and tips on personnel and employment law issues.
MAGAZINE
News & Current Affairs

Tips & Advice Tax
982957
Editorial: Calgarth House, 39-41 Bank Street, Ashford, Ashford TN23 1DQ
Tel: 44 01233 653500
Web site: http://lite.indicator.co.uk/tax/home.php
Freq: Bi-Weekly
Editor: Tony Court
Profile: Newsletter covering practical and feasible tips for deducting business expenses, recovering VAT, capital allowances, cutting costs, extracting profit from a business and recent legislation. Includes practical tips for saving tax and keeping abreast of the tax changes. Aimed at small business owners, entrepreneurs, company directors, advisors, accountants, financial managers.
MAGAZINE
Banking

Tobacco Science & Technology
1060854
Tel: 44 86371 67672637
Email: tst@tobaccoinfo.com.cn
Web site: http://www.tobaccoinfo.com.cn
Freq: Monthly
Circ: 10000 Not Audited
MAGAZINE
Tobacco

Today's Conveyancer
987137
Web site: www.todaysconveyancer.co.uk
Freq: Daily
Circ: 16038 Cision Digital Reach
MAGAZINE (ONLINE)
Real Estate Law

Tom-Brown.com
995882
Editorial: Mediaclash, Circus Mews House, Circus Mews, Bath BA1 2PW
Tel: 44 01225 475800
Email: editor@tom-brown.com
Web site: http://www.tom-brown.com
Freq: Daily
Circ: 6855 Cision Digital Reach
Editor: Gail Dixon
MAGAZINE (ONLINE)
Education

Tomorrow's Care
987776
Editorial: Zurich House, Hulley Road, Macclesfield, Macclesfield SK10 2SF
Tel: 44 01625 426054
Web site: www.tomorrowscare.co.uk
Freq: Bi-Monthly
Circ: 10024 Cision Digital Reach
Editor: Alison Carter
MAGAZINE (ONLINE)
Health Administration

Tomorrow's FM
985655
Editorial: Zurich House, Hulley Road, Macclesfield, Macclesfield SK10 2SF
Tel: 44 01625 426054
Web site: www.tomorrowsfm.com
Freq: Monthly
Circ: 62000 Not Audited
Editor: Rebekah Thompson
Profile: Website covering facilities management. The Tomorrow's FM is an online magazine covering facilities management. The website provides coverage on the very latest news, issues and advancements, communication software and safety campaigns.
Ad Rate: Full Page Colour £850.00
MAGAZINE
Finance, Health & Safety, Hygiene, Interior Design, Legal Affairs, Sustainable Development

Tomorrow's Tile & Stone
1102301
Tel: 44 01625 426054
Email: info@opusbusinessmedia.co.uk
Web site: www.tomorrowstileandstone.co.uk
Freq: Daily
Circ: 59000 Not Audited
Editor: Rebekah Thompson
MAGAZINE
Architecture & Design, Building & Construction, Interior Design

Tomorrow's Cleaning
985514
Editorial: Zurich House, Hulley Road, Macclesfield, Macclesfield SK10 2SF
Tel: 44 01625 426054
Email: info@opusbusinessmedia.co.uk
Web site: www.tomorrowscleaning.com
Freq: Monthly
Circ: 57163 Not Audited
Profile: Website covering cleaning industry, including the latest news, advice and products available.
MAGAZINE
Hygiene

Tomorrow's Cleaning Ireland
999544
Editorial: Zurich House, Hulley Road, Macclesfield, Macclesfield SK10 2SF
Tel: 44 01625 426054
Email: martin@opusbm.co.uk
Web site: www.tomorrowscleaning.com/tc-ireland-issues–800.html
Freq: Quarterly
Circ: 58000 Not Audited
MAGAZINE
Hygiene

Tomorrow's Contract Floors
985515
Editorial: Zurich House, Hulley Road, Macclesfield, Macclesfield SK10 2SF
Tel: 44 01625 426054
Web site: www.tomorrowsflooring.com
Freq: Monthly
Circ: 73101 Not Audited
Editor: Sarah Robinson
MAGAZINE
Interior Design

Tomorrow's Energy Management
1053085
Tel: 44 01625 426054
Email: info@opusbusinessmedia.co.uk
Web site: http://www.tomorrowsem.com/
Freq: Quarterly
Circ: 44000 Not Audited
Editor: Rebekah Thompson
MAGAZINE
Alternative/Renewable Energy, Carbon Emissions & Trading, Electricity, Energy, Nuclear Power, Oil, Water & Sanitation

Tomorrow's Health & Safety
986437
Editorial: Zurich House, Hulley Road, Macclesfield, Macclesfield SK10 2SF
Tel: 44 01625 426054
Email: info@opusbusinessmedia.co.uk
Web site: www.tomorrowshs.com
Freq: Bi-Monthly
Circ: 42000 Not Audited
Editor: Alison Carter
Profile: Website covering all the latest on health and safety compliance and news.
MAGAZINE
Health & Safety, Security & Security Systems

Tomorrow's Retail Floors
1053632
Tel: 44 01625 426054
Email: info@opusbusinessmedia.co.uk
Web site: www.tomorrowsretailfloors.com
Freq: Quarterly
Circ: 30124 Not Audited
MAGAZINE
Interior Design

Tool Business + Hire
984623
Editorial: Wiston, Coppice Way, Haywards Heath, Haywards Heath RH16 4NN
Tel: 44 01444 440188
Email: info@airstream.co.uk
Web site: www.toolbusiness.co.uk
Freq: Monthly
Circ: 5250 Not Audited
Editor: Anne Hall
Profile: Magazine covering news, products and features on portable tools.
Ad Rate: Full Page Colour £1285.00
MAGAZINE
Building & Construction

Top Consultants News Letter
998949
Editorial: Longdeane House, Hedgehog Lane, Haslemere, London GU27 2PH
Tel: 44 02076 676880
Web site: http://www.top-consultant.com/UK/Career/Appointments.asp
Freq: Weekly
Circ: 32000 Not Audited
MAGAZINE
Business, Corporate Responsibility

Top Sales World Magazine
997439
Web site: www.topsalesworld.com
Freq: Monthly
Circ: 250000 Not Audited
Editor: Jonathan Farrington
MAGAZINE
Business

TopicUK
1072204
Tel: 44 07711 539047
Email: editor@topicuk.co.uk
Web site: http://topicuk.co.uk/
Freq: Bi-Monthly
Circ: 30000 Not Audited
MAGAZINE
Business, Small and Medium Business

Torque Magazine
988878
Editorial: 18 Alban Park, Hatfield Road, Hertfordshire, St. Albans AL4 0JJ
Tel: 44 01727 739160
Web site: http://torque-expo.com/
Freq: Bi-Monthly
Circ: 6000 Not Audited
Editor: Jonathon Harker
Profile: Magazine covering the distribution industry and features topics including hand and power tools, hardware and ironmongery, DIY products, fasteners, fixings and adhesives, locks and security, trade displays and shopfittings, abrasives and lubricants, clothing, safety and janitorial and consumables. Aimed at key decision-makers including managing directors, owners and senior buyersin stockist, distribution and wholesale businesses throughout the UK and Ireland.
MAGAZINE
Manufacturing

Total Brand Licensing
1053237
Tel: 44 01892 782220
Email: enquiries@totallicensing.com
Web site: www.totallicensing.com
Freq: Quarterly
Circ: 84000 Not Audited
Profile: Magazine covering the corporate, trademark and brand sectors. It looks at standalone brands and a brands lifecycle as well as best practices, innovative programs, new retail and merchandising opportunities and creates a forum for brand licensors to promote and enhance their brands. Aimed at senior executives involved in brand licensing, brand building and brand extension.
MAGAZINE
Intellectual Property

Total Franchise
987217
Editorial: Unit 2a, Abbey Enterprise Centre, Premier Way, Romsey, Romsey SO51 9DF
Tel: 44 08458 693855
Email: info@totalfranchise.co.uk
Web site: www.totalfranchise.co.uk
Freq: Daily

Circ: 14270 Cision Digital Reach
Profile: Website covering franchise. The total franchise website shares the latest news and information on franchise in the UK.
MAGAZINE (ONLINE)
Business, Corporate Responsibility, Retail Management, Small and Medium Business

Total Grooming Magazine
1074318
Web site: http://totalgroomingmagazine.co.uk/
Freq: Monthly
Circ: 10431 Not Audited
MAGAZINE
Business, Corporate Responsibility

Total Licensing UK
984621
Editorial: 4 Wadhurst Business Park, Faircrouch Lane, Wadhurst TN5 6PT
Tel: 44 01892 782220
Email: enquiries@totallicensing.com
Web site: www.totallicensing.com
Freq: Quarterly
Circ: 82000 Not Audited
MAGAZINE
Publishing

Total Telecom
990358
Editorial: Wren House, 43 Hatton Garden, London EC1N 8EL **Tel:** 44 02076 087030
Email: newsdesk@totaltele.com
Web site: www.totaltele.com
Freq: Daily
Circ: 57173 Cision Digital Reach
Profile: Website covering telecommunications. Totaltele provides information and research on the global communications industry, from breaking news to expert analysis, research reports and archives. Topic coverage includes network, services, technology including M2M and industry news.
MAGAZINE (ONLINE)
Telecommunications/Electronic Communications

Total Telecom +
988209
Editorial: Wren House, 43 Hatton Garden, London EC1N 8EL **Tel:** 44 02076 087030
Email: newsdesk@totaltele.com
Web site: www.totaltele.com
Freq: Bi-Monthly
Circ: 57173 Cision Digital Reach
MAGAZINE (ONLINE)
Telecommunications/Electronic Communications

touchENDOCRINOLOGY.com
995422
Editorial: The White House, Mill Road, Goring RG8 9DD **Tel:** 44 02071 933009
Email: info@touchmedicalmedia.com
Web site: www.touchendocrinology.com
Freq: Daily
Circ: 11529 Cision Digital Reach
MAGAZINE (ONLINE)
Diabetes

touchNEUROLOGY.com
995763
Editorial: 4 Reading Road, Pangbourne, Reading RG8 7LY **Tel:** 44 02071 936093
Email: info@touchmedicalmedia.com
Web site: www.touchneurology.com
Freq: Daily
Circ: 13718 Cision Digital Reach
MAGAZINE (ONLINE)
Neurology

touchONCOLOGY.com
995762
Editorial: The White House, Mill Road, Goring RG8 9DD **Tel:** 44 02071 933009
Email: editor@touchmedicalmedia.com
Web site: www.touchoncology.com
Freq: Daily
Circ: 9606 Cision Digital Reach
MAGAZINE (ONLINE)
Oncology

touchOPHTHALMOLOGY.com
996914
Editorial: The White House, Mill Road, Goring RG8 9DD **Tel:** 44 02071 933186
Email: editor@touchmedicalmedia.com
Web site: www.touchophthalmology.com
Freq: Daily
Circ: 12476 Cision Digital Reach
MAGAZINE (ONLINE)
Ophthalmology & Optometry

Town & Country Planning
980908
Editorial: 17 Carlton House Terrace, London SW1Y 5AS **Tel:** 44 02079 308903
Email: nick.matthews@tcpa.org.uk
Web site: http://www.tcpa.org.uk/pages/our-journal.html
Freq: Monthly
Circ: 1000 Not Audited
Editor: Nick Matthews
Profile: Magazine containing land use planning, regional planning, housing and town development, transport and environmental issues.
Ad Rate: Full Page Mono £325.00
Ad Rate: Full Page Colour £425.00
MAGAZINE
Sustainable Development, Urban Planning & Development

Town Planning Review
983949
Editorial: Department of Civic Design, The University of Liverpool, 74 Bedford Street South, Liverpool L69 7ZQ
Tel: 44 01517 943135
Web site: http://online.liverpooluniversitypress.co.uk/loi/tpr
Freq: Bi-Monthly
Circ: 1000 Not Audited
MAGAZINE
Urban Planning & Development

Toy & Game Inventors Bulletin
996122
Tel: 44 01992 535646
Web site: www.toynews-online.biz
Freq: Weekly
Circ: 5711 Not Audited
Editor: Billy Langsworthy
MAGAZINE
Toys

Toy World Magazine
999293
Editorial: Symbio Place, Whiteleaf Road, Hemel Hempstead, London HP3 9PH
Tel: 44 01442 502408
Web site: www.toyworldmag.co.uk
Freq: Monthly
Circ: 5100 Not Audited
MAGAZINE
Toys

ToyNews
981303
Editorial: Saxon House, 6a St Andrew Street, Hertford, Hertford SG14 1JA
Tel: 44 01992 535646
Web site: www.toynews-online.biz
Freq: Monthly
Circ: 5419 Not Audited
Editor: Billy Langsworthy
Profile: Magazine covering all aspects of the toy trade. Read by members of the British Association of Toy Retailers, other independent toy retailers, wholesalers, multiple retailers and chains.
Ad Rate: Full Page Colour £1155.00
MAGAZINE
Toys

Toyology.co.uk
983756
Editorial: 29 St Joseph Vale, Blackheath, London SE3 0XF
Web site: www.toyology.co.uk
Freq: Daily
Circ: 10142 Cision Digital Reach
MAGAZINE (ONLINE)
Toys

Toys N Playthings
981304
Editorial: 1 Churchgates, The Wilderness, Berkhamsted, Berkhamsted HP4 2UB
Tel: 44 01442 289930

Web site: www.toysnplaythings.co.uk
Freq: Monthly
Circ: 5121 Not Audited
MAGAZINE
Toys

Tractor and Farming Heritage Magazine
999668
Editorial: Cudham Tithe Barn, Berry's Hill, Cudham, London TN16 3AG
Tel: 44 01959 541444
Email: tfh.ed@kelsey.co.uk
Web site: www.tractormagazine.co.uk
Freq: Monthly
Circ: 52640 Not Audited
Editor: Tony Hoyland
MAGAZINE
Animal Farming

The TRADE
980862
Editorial: Asset International, Upper Ground Floor South, 200 Aldersgate Street, London EC1A 4HD **Tel:** 44 02073 973817
Web site: www.thetradenews.com
Freq: Quarterly
Circ: 7000 Not Audited
Editor: Joe Parsons
Profile: A quarterly publication focused on the business of institutional global securities trading. Covers broad spectrum of activities that buy side firms undertake to implement their investment decisions end-to-end in order to reduce market impact costs and maximise portfolio returns.
MAGAZINE
Commodities, Equities, Financial Markets

Trade & Forfaiting Review
980966
Editorial: 6-14 Underwood Street, London N1 7JQ **Tel:** 44 02074 900049
Email: editor@tfreview.com
Web site: www.tfreview.com
Freq: Monthly Not Audited
Editor: Binyamin Ali
Profile: Magazine reporting and analysing developments within the global trade, commodity and export finance market.
Ad Rate: Full Page Mono £3300.00
Ad Rate: Full Page Colour £3790.00
MAGAZINE
Banking, Supply Chain Management (SCM)

Trade Finance
980111
Editorial: 6-8 Bouverie Street, London EC4Y 8AX **Tel:** 44 02077 798610
Web site: https://tradefinanceanalytics.com/
Freq: Bi-Monthly
Circ: 3000 Not Audited
Profile: Magazine reporting on international trade, commodity financing, trade services and supply chain, emerging and export finance markets. Covers new financial services and products, major deals and changes in market conditions. The publication also provides market intelligence, articles, potential leads and other resource information as well as intelligence vital to exporters/importers, financiers, insurers, and other service providers. Aimed at corporate exporters, heads of trade and commodity, finance, supply chain finance, trade services and logistics providers, finance workers in banks, export credit agencies, as well as other service providers such as lawyers, insurers, risk managers and trade officials.
Ad Rate: Full Page Mono £7000.00
Ad Rate: Full Page Colour £8200.00
MAGAZINE
Banking

Trade International Digest
985055
Editorial: 145 London Road, Kingston Upon Thames, London KT2 6SR
Tel: 44 02085 473333
Email: enquiries@croner.co.uk
Web site: http://cronersolutions.co.uk/
Freq: Monthly
Circ: 28500 Not Audited
MAGAZINE
Shipping & Warehousing, Supply Chain Management (SCM)

TradePoint Magazine
998386
Editorial: Caledonia House, Evanton Drive, Thornliebank Ind Est, Glasgow G46 8JT
Tel: 44 01414 652960
Email: enquiries@2apublishing.co.uk
Web site: tradepointmagazine.co.uk
Freq: Bi-Monthly
Circ: 5500 Not Audited
Editor: Rosalind Tulloch
MAGAZINE
Business, Disability

The Trading Mesh
990580
Tel: 44 02032 868629
Email: enquiries@thetradingmesh.com
Web site: http://www.thetradingmesh.com/
Freq: Daily
Circ: 12158 Cision Digital Reach
MAGAZINE (ONLINE)
Computers, Data Management, Financial Markets

Trading Risk
984616
Editorial: 3rd Floor, 41 Eastcheap, London EC3M 1DT **Tel:** 44 02073 970615
Web site: www.trading-risk.com
Freq: Monthly
Circ: 7422 Not Audited
Editor: Fiona Robertson
Profile: Publication providing insight and intelligence on all aspects of the trading of insurance-related risk, regularly including news and analysis on the latest cat bond transactions and other insurance linked securities (ILS), tracking in-storm derivative trading, industry loss warranties, a comprehensive deal directory and other essential market data, together with other forms of alternative trading, such as weather and emissions. Aimed at (re)insurance buyers, professional advisers, banks, (re)insurers and brokers.
MAGAZINE
Corporate Finance, Insurance

Training & Management Development Methods
981026
Editorial: Howard House, Wagon Lane, Bingley BD16 1WA **Tel:** 44 01274 777700
Email: emerald@emeraldinsight.com
Web site: www.emeraldgrouppublishing.com
Freq: Bi-Monthly Not Audited
Editor: David Pollitt
Profile: Journal giving practical guidelines on key training and development methods in management. Includes new and interesting ideas and guidance on their use. Read by training and management development personnel.
MAGAZINE
Human Resources

Training Journal
981025
Editorial: 11th Floor, The Shard, 32 London Bridge Street, London SE1 9SG
Tel: 44 02075 935759
Email: contact@trainingjournal.com
Web site: www.trainingjournal.com
Freq: Monthly
Circ: 4990 Not Audited
MAGAZINE
Education

Training Matters
984007
Editorial: 207 Linen Hall, 162-168 Regent Street, London W1B 5TB
Tel: 44 02074 341530
Email: tm@1530.com
Web site: www.tmmagazine.co.uk
Freq: Monthly
Circ: 16300 Not Audited
Editor: Gemma O'Sullivan
MAGAZINE
Pharmaceuticals

TrainingZone
983916
Editorial: 6th Floor, Bridge House, 48-52 Baldwin Street, Bristol BS1 1QB
Tel: 44 01179 153344
Email: editor@trainingzone.co.uk
Web site: www.trainingzone.co.uk
Freq: Daily
Circ: 231678 Cision Digital Reach

Business Magazines

Profile: Website covering human resources and business. The trainingzone website contains news on features, comment, resources and information on training, learning and development.
MAGAZINE (ONLINE)
Education, Recruiting

Transactions of the IMF 996144
Editorial: 2&4 Park Square, Milton Park, Abingdon OX14 4RN **Tel:** 44 02070 176000
Email: david@materialsfinishing.org
Web site: http://www.tandfonline.com/toc/ytim20/current
Freq: Bi-Monthly Not Audited
MAGAZINE
Manufacturing, Mining & Quarrying, Steel

Transfer Pricing Report 981557
Editorial: 38 Threadneedle Street, London EC2R 8AY **Tel:** 44 02078 475801
Email: marketing@bna.com
Web site: http://www.bna.com/transfer-pricing-report-p17179911958/
Freq: Monthly Not Audited
MAGAZINE
Accounting

Transform 988242
Editorial: 26-32 Voltaire Road, London SW4 6DH **Tel:** 44 02074 987008
Web site: www.transformmagazine.net
Freq: Bi-Monthly Not Audited
Editor: Brittany Golob
Profile: Publication that focuses on rebranding and brand redevelopment and how companies develop their brands over time and how brand impacts corporate reputation and public awareness.
MAGAZINE
Branding

Transfusion Medicine 998137
Email: transmed.edit@gmail.com
Web site: http://onlinelibrary.wiley.com/journal/10.1111/%28ISSN%291365-3148
Freq: Bi-Monthly Not Audited
MAGAZINE
Hematology

Transport Engineer 981348
Editorial: Hawley Mill, Hawley Road, Dartford DA2 7TJ **Tel:** 44 01322 221144
Web site: www.transportengineer.org.uk
Freq: Monthly
Circ: 14672 Not Audited
Profile: Magazine covering all aspects of commercial vehicle engineering, transport engineering, fleet management and workshop engineering, including news, products, training and technology. Aimed at those who specify, maintain and manage fleets of trucks, tippers, trailers, rigids, specialist vehicles, vans, buses and coaches.
MAGAZINE
Engineering

Transport Monthly 987464
Editorial: Unit 3.6 Holmfield Mills, Holdsworth Road, Holmfield, Halifax HX3 6SN **Tel:** 44 01422 249162
Email: info@monthlymedia.co.uk
Web site: http://transportmonthly.co.uk
Freq: Monthly
Circ: 81000 Not Audited
Profile: Magazine covering all aspects of the transport industry.
MAGAZINE
Shipping & Warehousing, Supply Chain Management (SCM)

Trauma 985439
Editorial: 1 Oliver's Yard, 55 City Road, London EC1Y 1SP **Tel:** 44 02073 248500
Email: traumajournaluk@gmail.com
Web site: www.uk.sagepub.com/journals/Journal201832
Freq: Quarterly
Circ: 330 Not Audited
Editor: Ian Greaves; **Editor:** Keith M Porter
Profile: Journal reviewing all aspects of trauma care, from prevention through to rehabilitation.

Ad Rate: Full Page Mono £500.00
MAGAZINE
Anesthesiology, EMS/Emergency Medical Services, Neurology, Occupational Therapy & Rehabilitation

Travel Weekly 979866
Editorial: 52 Grosvenor Gardens, London SW1W 0AU **Tel:** 44 02078 814800
Email: editorial@travelweekly.co.uk
Web site: www.travelweekly.co.uk
Freq: Weekly
Circ: 14515 Not Audited
MAGAZINE
Travel

The Treasurer 979957
Editorial: 68 King William Street, London EC4N 7DZ **Tel:** 44 02078 472540
Email: enquiries@treasurers.org
Web site: http://www.treasurers.org/thetreasurer
Freq: Monthly
Circ: 10500 Not Audited
Editor: Liz Loxton
Profile: Official journal of the Association of Corporate Treasurers.
Ad Rate: Full Page Mono £3660.00
Ad Rate: Full Page Colour £8000.00
MAGAZINE
Banking

Treasury Management International 979785
Editorial: 3 Wesley Gate, Queen's Road, Reading, Reading RG1 4AP
Tel: 44 01189 478057
Email: tmi@treasury-management.com
Web site: http://www.treasury-management.com
Freq: Monthly
Circ: 8000 Not Audited
Editor: Helen Sanders
Profile: Magazine containing treasury information and topics such as the globalisation of business, the rising importance of the European, wealth management, NSBP, Asian and emerging markets, and news of international treasury associations. The publication showcases topical, pragmatic solutions and strategic insights on the issues which are affecting today's treasury and financial professionals, together with treasury and finance news, education and opinion. Read by corporate treasurers, finance directors and advisers.
Ad Rate: Full Page Colour £7300.00
MAGAZINE
Banking

Treasury Perspectives 985619
Editorial: Floor 5, 20 Cabot Square, Canary Wharf, London E14 4QA
Tel: 44 02075 768555
Email: editor@eurofinance.com
Web site: http://www.eurofinance.com/publications/treasury-perspectives
Freq: Annual
Circ: 40000 Not Audited
MAGAZINE
Banking

Treasury Today 979786
Editorial: Courtyard Offices, Harnet Street, Sandwich, Sandwich CT13 9ES
Tel: 44 01304 629000
Email: editorial@treasurytoday.com
Web site: www.treasurytoday.com
Freq: Monthly Not Audited
MAGAZINE
Banking

Trend Watch 998808
Editorial: FREEPOST ANG9505, Redbourn AL3 4BR **Tel:** 44 01727 762629
Email: editor@trendwatch.co.uk
Web site: http://www.trend-watch.co.uk
Freq: Monthly
Circ: 300 Not Audited
MAGAZINE
Financial Markets

Trends in Urology & Men's Health 984128
Editorial: The Atrium, Southern Gate, Chichester PO19 8SQ **Tel:** 44 01865 778315
Email: trends@wiley.com
Web site: www.trendsinurology.com
Freq: Bi-Monthly
Circ: 11433 Not Audited
Editor: Roger Kirby
Profile: Journal containing articles on current opinion and practice in urology, gynaecology and sexual health.
MAGAZINE
Sexual Health, Urology

TRFNews 983824
Editorial: 3 Cobden Court, Wimpole Close, London BR2 9JF **Tel:** 44 02084 666987
Email: info@bcrpub.co.uk
Web site: www.trfnews.com
Freq: Daily
Circ: 10953 Cision Digital Reach
MAGAZINE (ONLINE)
Manufacturing

Trillion Fund 996380
Editorial: Knyvett House, The Causeway, London TW18 3BA **Tel:** 44 02077 179708
Email: contact@trillionfund.com
Web site: www.trillionfund.com
Freq: Daily
Circ: 6695 Cision Digital Reach
MAGAZINE (ONLINE)
Alternative/Renewable Energy

Tropical Doctor 985454
Editorial: SAGE Publications, 1 Oliver's Yard, 55 City Road, London EC1Y 1SP
Tel: 44 02073 248500
Web site: http://tdo.sagepub.com
Freq: Quarterly Not Audited
MAGAZINE
Infectious Diseases

Tropical Medicine & International Health 985164
Editorial: London School of Hygiene and Tropical Medicine, Department of Infectious Disease Epidemiology, Room G15a Keppel Street, London WC1E 7HT
Web site: www.onlinelibrary.wiley.com/journal/10.1111/%28ISSN%291365-3156
Freq: Monthly
Circ: 7000 Not Audited
Editor: Henri Van Asten; **Editor:** Patrick Van Der Stuyft
Profile: Journal containing information on the field of tropical medicine and international health, including infectious and non-infectious diseases, parasitology, clinical sciences, tropical medicine, epidemiological theory and fieldwork, tropical medical microbiology, medical entomology and community medicine.
Ad Rate: Full Page Mono £582.00
Ad Rate: Full Page Colour £1461.00
MAGAZINE
Infectious Diseases

Truck and Track 986558
Editorial: The Arches, Adderley Street, Digbeth, Birmingham B9 4EE
Tel: 44 01564 702035
Web site: www.truckandtrackmagazine.com
Freq: Quarterly
Circ: 25000 Not Audited
Editor: Oliver Haines
Profile: Magazine covering transportation including road haulage and logistics. Aimed at transportation professionals.
Ad Rate: Full Page Colour £1700.00
MAGAZINE
Shipping & Warehousing, Supply Chain Management (SCM)

Trusts & Estates (UK) 982941
Editorial: Informa House, 30-32 Mortimer St, London W1W 7RE **Tel:** 44 02070 175000
Web site: www.trusts-estates.co.uk
Freq: Monthly Not Audited
MAGAZINE
Family Law

Trusts & Trustees 985635
Editorial: Oxford University Press, Great Clarendon Street, Oxford OX2 6DP
Tel: 44 01865 353907
Email: jnls.cust.serv@oup.com
Web site: www.tandt.oxfordjournals.org
Freq: Monthly
Circ: 320 Not Audited
Profile: Journal containing articles and reports on the law and practice of international trusts and foundations particularly in the UK, USA and offshore countries. Aimed at trustees and bankers, trust and estate lawyers, accountants and tax advisors and international investment advisors.
Ad Rate: Full Page Mono £1200.00
Ad Rate: Full Page Colour £1500.00
MAGAZINE
Family Law

Trusts and Estates Law & Tax Journal 998494
Editorial: 188 Fleet Street, London EC4A 2AG **Tel:** 44 02073 969292
Web site: www.legalease.co.uk/Trusts-Estates-Law-Tax-Journal.html
Freq: Monthly Not Audited
Editor: Katharine Freeland
MAGAZINE
Family Law, Legal Services, Tax Law

TU-Automotive 985052
Editorial: 7-9 Fashion Street, London E1 6PX **Tel:** 44 02073 757576
Web site: http://analysis.tu-auto.com/
Freq: Daily
Circ: 16047 Cision Digital Reach
MAGAZINE (ONLINE)
Mobile Communications, Telecommunications/Electronic Communications

Tube and Pipe Technology 983701
Editorial: 46 Holly Walk, Leamington Spa, Leamington Spa CV32 4HY
Tel: 44 01926 334137
Email: tpt@intras.co.uk
Web site: www.read-tpt.com
Freq: Bi-Monthly
Circ: 24000 Not Audited
Editor: Rory McBride
MAGAZINE
Engineering, Industry, Manufacturing

Tube Products INTERNATIONAL 984749
Editorial: 46 Holly Walk, Leamington Spa, Leamington Spa CV32 4HY
Tel: 44 01926 334137
Email: tpi@intras.co.uk
Web site: www.read-tpi.com
Freq: Bi-Monthly
Circ: 26000 Not Audited
Editor: Rory McBride
MAGAZINE
Engineering, Industry, Manufacturing

TUCO 985932
Editorial: 4th Floor, Joynes House, New Road, Gravesend DA11 0AJ
Tel: 44 08455 006008
Web site: www.tuco.org
Freq: Monthly
Circ: 6455 Not Audited
Editor: Morag Wilson
Profile: TUCO magazine is the official title for The University Caterers Organisation. Targets UK universities of colleges where they provide an in-house catering service and bars, including all 160 TUCO members.
MAGAZINE
Food, Higher Education

Tunnels & Tunnelling International 983987
Editorial: John Carpenter House, 7 Carmelite Street, London EC4Y 0BS
Tel: 44 02079 366400
Email: editor@tunnelsandtunnelling.com
Web site: www.tunnelsonline.info
Freq: Monthly

Circ: 6715 Not Audited
Editor: Alex Conacher
Profile: The official magazine of the British Tunnelling Society covering all areas of underground construction from large bore tunnels to micro tunnelling. Includes international news, developments, contracts, project coverage, technology and techniques. First published in 1969, the publication has an average of 60 pages per issue. Aimed at engineers working in all sectors of the world tunnelling market.
Ad Rate: Full Page Mono £2443.00
Ad Rate: Full Page Colour £2988.00
MAGAZINE
Engineering

TXF News
996714
Editorial: 1- 3 Brixton Road, London SW9 6DE **Tel:** 44 02037 355180
Email: team@txfmedia.com
Web site: www.txfnews.com
Freq: Daily
Circ: 12363 Cision Digital Reach
MAGAZINE (ONLINE)
Banking, Supply Chain Management (SCM)

UK Construction Excellence
980885
Editorial: Stirling House, Ackhurst Business Park, Foxhole Road, Chorley, Chorley PR7 1NY **Tel:** 44 01257 231900
Email: edit@ukconstructionmedia.co.uk
Web site: http://www.ukconstructionmedia.co.uk/
Freq: Monthly
Circ: 110000 Not Audited
Profile: Magazine covering nationwide construction projects, legislation changes, EU edicts and new products and services. Aimed at quantity surveyors, architects, contractors, construction companies, suppliers, local authorities and housing associations.
Ad Rate: Full Page Colour £1950.00
MAGAZINE
Building & Construction

UK Landlord
984572
Editorial: 22-26 Albert Embankment, London SE1 7TJ **Tel:** 44 02032 351800
Email: uklandlord@analyticamedia.com
Web site: www.landlords.org.uk/support-advice/uk-landlord-magazine
Freq: Bi-Monthly
Circ: 29000 Not Audited
Profile: Newsletter of the National Landlords' Association containing recent news and announcements relating to the private rented sector of housing, as well as features on various aspects of being a landlord and making buy-to-let investments.
Ad Rate: Full Page Colour £1450.00
MAGAZINE
Residential Real Estate

UK Power News
986630
Editorial: Global House, 13 Market Square, Horsham, Horsham RH12 1EU
Tel: 44 01403 220750
Email: power@gmp.uk.com
Web site: http://www.gmp.uk.com/uk-power-news/
Freq: Quarterly
Circ: 47500 Not Audited
Profile: Magazine covering the products, processes, innovation, technology and management focusing, covering and affecting all aspects of on?site, critical, emergency power and CHP cogeneration and renewables within the UK stand?by and independent power markets. Aimed at consultants, consulting engineers, electrical engineers, consulting managers, managing directors, chairmen, project managers, energy and environmental managers, energy consultants, architectural engineers, technical directors, purchasing and procurement managers, specifiers and facilities managers.
Ad Rate: Full Page Colour £2300.00
MAGAZINE
Alternative/Renewable Energy, Carbon Emissions & Trading, Electricity, Energy, Nuclear Power, Oil, Water & Sanitation

UKAuthority.com
982854
Editorial: PO Box 2087, Shoreham-by-Sea, Shoreham-by-Sea BN43 5RH
Tel: 44 01273 273941
Email: editorial@ukauthority.co.uk
Web site: www.ukauthority.com
Freq: Daily
Circ: 15897 Cision Digital Reach
Profile: Website covering technology in the public sector. The UKAuthority.com website shares the latest news and information on technology in the public sector.
MAGAZINE (ONLINE)
Government Technology

UKEdMagazine
997429
Tel: 44 03303 304673
Email: editor@ukedchat.com
Web site: ukedchat.com
Freq: Monthly Not Audited
Editor: Martin Burrett
MAGAZINE
Schools & Institutions

Ulster Business
981068
Editorial: Belfast Telegraph House, Clarendon Dock, Belfast BT1 3BG
Tel: 44 02890 264263
Email: d.elliott@independentmagazinesni.co.uk
Web site: www.ulsterbusiness.com
Freq: Monthly
Circ: 5989 Not Audited
Editor: David Elliott
Profile: Business magazine for Northern Ireland, that covers news, profiles, appointments and comment.
Ad Rate: Full Page Mono £1350.00
Ad Rate: Full Page Colour £1995.00
MAGAZINE
Business

Ulster Grocer
981296
Editorial: Belfast Telegraph House, 33 Clarendon Road, Belfast, Antrim BT1 3BG
Tel: 44 02890 264000
Web site: www.ulstergrocer.com
Freq: Monthly
Circ: 4366 Not Audited
Editor: Alyson Magee
Profile: Magazine covering news and views of the independent grocery trade including product news, category features, personnel, company profiles, industry issues and business advice. Read by retailers, wholesalers, agents and distributors, food manufacturers and associated businesses in the grocer, convenience and CTN market in Northern Ireland.
Ad Rate: Full Page Colour £1785.00
MAGAZINE
Food, Retail Management

Unified Communications Insight
1075818
Tel: 44 02038 418500
Email: ucinsighteditor@imagotechmedia.com
Web site: http://www.ucinsight.com/
Freq: Daily
Circ: 11268 Cision Digital Reach
MAGAZINE (ONLINE)
Data Management, Industry, Telecommunications/Electronic Communications

University Business (UK)
997175
Editorial: Unit 2.4 Paintworks, Arnos Vale, Bristol BS4 3EH **Tel:** 44 01173 005526
Email: info@universitybusiness.co.uk
Web site: www.universitybusiness.co.uk
Freq: Monthly
Circ: 5500 Not Audited
MAGAZINE
Higher Education

Unmanned Vehicles
983644
Editorial: Saville Mews, 30 Saville Road, London W4 5HG **Tel:** 44 02031 792570
Email: info@shephardmedia.com
Web site: www.uvonline.com
Freq: Bi-Monthly
Circ: 6400 Not Audited

Profile: B2B publication covering all aspects of the unmanned systems industry. Aimed at ministries of defence, armies, navies, governments, air forces and military/civil venture including manufacturers and associated organisations.
Ad Rate: Full Page Colour £7000.00
MAGAZINE
Defense & National Security

unquote"
979976
Editorial: 10 Queen Street Place, London EC4R 1BE **Tel:** 44 02037 411000
Email: editorial@unquote.com
Web site: http://www.unquote.com/
Freq: Daily
Circ: 37160 Cision Digital Reach
Profile: Publication covering the latest news on UK private equity and the venture capital industry including daily breaking news stories, thought-provoking features and analysis pieces and comprehensive job opportunities within the industry. Read by lawyers, debt providers and those involved in the UK venture capital industry.
Ad Rate: Full Page Mono £1650.00
Ad Rate: Full Page Colour £3300.00
MAGAZINE (ONLINE)
Private Equity

Upholsterer & Soft Furnisher
997120
Editorial: Unit 11, Riverside Business Centre, Riverside House, Riverlawn Road, Tonbridge TN9 1EP **Tel:** 44 01756 795374
Email: editorial@upholsterers.co.uk
Web site: http://www.upholsterers.co.uk/industry/
Freq: Quarterly
Circ: 1100 Not Audited
Editor: Jan Turner
MAGAZINE
Interior Design

Urban Design
998846
Editorial: 70 Cowcross Street, London EC1M 6EJ **Tel:** 44 02072 500892
Email: administration@udg.org.uk
Web site: www.udg.org.uk
Freq: Quarterly
Circ: 1500 Not Audited
Editor: Louise Thomas
MAGAZINE
Architecture & Design, Urban Planning & Development

Urban Realm
983446
Editorial: 2G Garnet Court, Glasgow G4 9NT
Tel: 44 01413 565333
Web site: www.urbanrealm.co.uk
Freq: Quarterly
Circ: 4000 Not Audited
Profile: Magazine covering architecture and urban development in Scotland, North of England and abroad including current major projects in Scotland, interiors and design. Aimed at all architects and other building professionals, planners, surveyors and engineers.
Ad Rate: Full Page Colour £1400.00
MAGAZINE
Architecture & Design

Urban Studies
983946
Editorial: University of Glasgow, Adam Smith Building, Glasgow G12 8RT
Web site: http://usj.sagepub.com
Freq: Monthly Not Audited
Profile: Journal containing articles and book reviews on the subject of urban and regional planning, politics and economics. Aimed at academics and professionals in planning and housing.
MAGAZINE
Urban Planning & Development

Urban Water Journal
984078
Editorial: Centre for Water Systems, University of Exeter, Harrison Building, North Park Road, Exeter EX4 4QF
Tel: 44 01392 264064
Web site: http://www.tandfonline.com/loi/nurw20
Freq: Bi-Monthly Not Audited

Profile: Journal covering all aspects of urban water engineering. Aimed at professionals working in universities, research organisations, software houses, consulting companies, water utilities and governmental bodies.
MAGAZINE
Water & Sanitation

Urethanes Technology International
983660
Editorial: 9th Floor, Amp House, Dingwall Road, Croydon CR0 2LX
Tel: 44 02082 539600
Web site: http://www.urethanes-technology-international.com
Freq: Bi-Monthly
Circ: 6302 Not Audited
Editor: Simon Robinson
Profile: Magazine covering commercial and technical developments within the global polyurethanes industry. Aimed at polyurethane based product manufacturers and the suppliers of raw materials, additives and processing equipment.Previous title: Urethanes Technology Regular features: Survey of Polyurethane Processing Machinery Manufacturers Details of all involved companies; Statistics on sales/turnover, PU equipment, staffing levels, size and location of activities, types of equipment supplied, markets served sorted by application and geographic location.; Survey of Automotive Developments Examination of the latest trends in the automotive sector, highlighting the most recent advances in the use of polyurethane-based products in this key innovative sector.
Ad Rate: Full Page Colour £2350.00
MAGAZINE
Chemicals

Urology News
984538
Tel: 44 01315 574184
Web site: www.urologynews.uk.com
Freq: Bi-Monthly
Circ: 4000 Not Audited
Profile: Magazine with features of relevance to urology, journal, book and web reviews, reports on international urology conferences, events calendar and information on new products.
Ad Rate: Full Page Mono £1086.00
Ad Rate: Full Page Colour £1516.00
MAGAZINE
Urology

useful social media
995553
Editorial: 7-9 Fashion Street, London E1 6PX **Tel:** 44 02073 757222
Email: info@usefulsocialmedia.com
Web site: http://www.incite-group.com/
Freq: Daily
Circ: 49065 Cision Digital Reach
MAGAZINE (ONLINE)
Marketing

Utilities Law Review
985075
Editorial: Office G18, Spinners Court, 55 West End, Witney OX28 1NH
Tel: 44 01993 706183
Email: ltp@lawtext.com
Web site: www.lawtext.com/lawtextweb/default.jsp?PageID=2
Freq: Bi-Monthly Not Audited
Profile: Journal containing information on international utilities law, including legal cases, legislative and policy changes, recent surveys and analytical articles.
MAGAZINE
Corporate Law

Utility Week
979884
Editorial: Windsor Court, Wood Street, East Grinstead, East Grinstead RH19 1UZ
Tel: 44 01342 332000
Email: utility.week@fav-house.com
Web site: www.utilityweek.co.uk
Freq: Weekly
Circ: 3580 Not Audited
Profile: Magazine that covers news, analysis and comment on Britain's major electricity, water and gas utilities.
Ad Rate: Full Page Mono £2546.00

Business Magazines

Ad Rate: Full Page Colour £3571.00
MAGAZINE
Alternative/Renewable Energy, Carbon Emissions & Trading, Electricity, Energy, Nuclear Power, Oil, Telecommunications/ Electronic Communications, Water & Sanitation

Valuer Magazine
995448
Editorial: IRRV, 5th Floor, Northumberland House, 393-306 High Holborn, London WC1V 7JZ **Tel:** 44 02078 313505
Email: publications@irrv.org.uk
Web site: http://irrv.net/homenew/item.php?iid=22099&wid=15&did=3
Freq: Quarterly
Circ: 1500 Not Audited
MAGAZINE
Accounting, Business, Corporate Responsibility

Valve User
984666
Editorial: 1A Banbury Business Village, Noral Way, Banbury OX16 2SB
Tel: 44 01295 221270
Email: enquiry@bvaa.org.uk
Web site: www.valveuser.com
Freq: Quarterly Not Audited
Editor: Rob Bartlett
Profile: Magazine of the BVAA, providing association news, industry news, updates on product developments, application stories and training articles.
MAGAZINE
Manufacturing

Varoom!
988940
Editorial: Somerset House, Strand, London WC2R 1LA **Tel:** 44 02077 591013
Email: info@varoom-mag.com
Web site: http://theaoi.com/varoom-mag/
Freq: Quarterly Not Audited
Editor: John O'Reilly
MAGAZINE
Graphic Design

Vascular News
984400
Editorial: 526 Fulham Road, London SW6 5NR **Tel:** 44 02077 368788
Email: publishing@bibamedical.com
Web site: www.vascularnews.com
Freq: Quarterly
Circ: 19700 Not Audited
Profile: Vascular News, a quarterly newspaper dedicated to providing news and features for vascular specialists. The publication comes out four times per year to an audience of 15,000 vascular professionals. Aimed at vascular professionals in Europe and North America.
MAGAZINE
Cardiology

The Vegetable Farmer
983853
Editorial: Lion House, 21 Church Street, Maidstone, Maidstone ME14 1EN
Tel: 44 01622 695656
Email: veg@actpub.co.uk
Web site: vegetablefarmer.co.uk
Freq: Monthly
Circ: 3016 Not Audited
Editor: Joseph Champneys
Profile: Magazine covering all aspects of vegetable, potato and outdoor salad growing.
Ad Rate: Full Page Mono £1090.00
Ad Rate: Full Page Colour £1680.00
MAGAZINE
Animal Farming

Vending International
983691
Editorial: 15A London Road, Maidstone, Maidstone ME16 8LY **Tel:** 44 01622 687031
Email: vending@datateam.co.uk
Web site: www.vendinginternational-online.com
Freq: Monthly
Circ: 17000 Not Audited
Editor: Bryony Andrews
Profile: Magazine covering news and information concerning the automatic merchandising business. Aimed at end-users, operators, manufacturers and suppliers within the industry.

Ad Rate: Full Page Colour £1575.00
MAGAZINE
Retail Management

Verdict News
1008431
Editorial: John Carpenter House, John Carpenter Street, London EC4Y 0AN
Tel: 44 02075 519750
Email: enquiries@verdict.com
Web site: http://www.globaldata.com/retail/
Freq: Daily
Circ: 25395 Cision Digital Reach
MAGAZINE (ONLINE)
Retail Management

Veterinary Anaesthesia and Analgesia
997087
Editorial: The Atrium, Southern Gate, Chichester PO19 8QG **Tel:** 44 01865 778315
Email: cs-journals@wiley.com
Web site: http://onlinelibrary.wiley.com/journal/10.1111/(ISSN)1467-2995
Freq: Bi-Monthly Not Audited
Editor: Shannon Axiak; **Editor:** Cynthia M. Trim
MAGAZINE
Veterinary Medicine

Veterinary and Comparative Oncology
995896
Web site: http://onlinelibrary.wiley.com/journal/10.1111/(ISSN)1476-5829
Freq: Quarterly Not Audited
MAGAZINE
Veterinary Medicine

The Veterinary Business Journal
985313
Editorial: Olympus House, Werrington Centre, Peterborough PE4 6NA
Tel: 44 01733 325522
Web site: http://www.vetsonline.com
Freq: Monthly
Circ: 19640 Not Audited
Editor: James Westgate
Profile: Magazine covering management and financial issues, services and equipment for veterinary practices.
Ad Rate: Full Page Colour £1700.00
MAGAZINE
Veterinary Medicine

Veterinary Clinical Pathology
995914
Editorial: John Wiley & Sons, Ltd., The Atrium, Southern Gate, Chichester PO19 8SQ **Tel:** 44 01865 778315
Email: cs-journals@wiley.com
Web site: http://onlinelibrary.wiley.com/journal/10.1111/(ISSN)1939-165X
Freq: Quarterly
Circ: 1000 Not Audited
MAGAZINE
Veterinary Medicine

Veterinary Dermatology
995915
Editorial: 9600 Garsington Road, Oxford OX4 2DQ **Tel:** 44 01865 776868
Email: vdeedoffice@wiley.com
Web site: http://onlinelibrary.wiley.com/journal/10.1111/(ISSN)1365-3164
Freq: Bi-Monthly Not Audited
MAGAZINE
Veterinary Medicine

The Veterinary Journal
998936
Editorial: The Boulevard, Langford Lane, Oxford OX5 1GB **Tel:** 44 01865 843577
Email: tvj@aht.org.uk
Web site: www.elsevier.com/locate/tvjl
Freq: Monthly Not Audited
MAGAZINE
Veterinary Medicine

The Veterinary Nurse
985761
Editorial: St Jude's Church, Dulwich Road, London SE24 0PB **Tel:** 44 02077 385454
Web site: www.theveterinarynurse.com
Freq: Monthly Not Audited
Editor: Georgina Grell
MAGAZINE
Nursing/Nurses, Veterinary Medicine

Veterinary Nursing Journal
984340
Email: vnjeditorinchief@bvna.co.uk
Web site: http://www.bvna.org.uk/publications/veterinary-nursing-journal
Freq: Monthly
Circ: 5500 Not Audited
MAGAZINE
Nursing/Nurses, Veterinary Medicine

Veterinary Practice
985825
Editorial: 15 Chaseside Gardens, Chertsey KT16 6JP **Tel:** 44 01932 563595
Email: editor@veterinary-practice.com
Web site: http://www.veterinary-practice.com
Freq: Monthly
Circ: 15000 Not Audited
Editor: David Ritchie
Profile: Magazine covering the issues facing veterinary practices in the 21st century.
Ad Rate: Full Page Colour £1200.00
MAGAZINE
Veterinary Medicine

Veterinary Practice Today
987680
Email: editor@mrcvs.co.uk
Web site: www.veterinarypracticetoday.com/vpt-en/
Freq: Quarterly Not Audited
Profile: Publication that covers veterinary practice.
MAGAZINE
Veterinary Medicine

Veterinary Record
981167
Editorial: BMA House, Tavistock Square, London W1G 9NQ **Tel:** 44 02073 874409
Email: editorial@bva-edit.co.uk
Web site: http://veterinaryrecord.bmj.com/
Freq: Weekly
Circ: 12118 Not Audited
Profile: Journal of the British Veterinary Association. Contains professional news, comment, letters and clinical research papers.
MAGAZINE
Veterinary Medicine

Veterinary Times
981169
Editorial: Olympus House, Werrington Centre, Werrington, Peterborough PE4 6NA
Tel: 44 01733 383559
Web site: https://www.vettimes.co.uk/
Freq: Weekly
Circ: 19640 Not Audited
Editor: Paul Imrie; **Editor:** James Westgate
Profile: Magazine covering veterinary medical topics, products, equipment, referral practice, industry news and meeting reports.
Ad Rate: Full Page Colour £2390.00
MAGAZINE
Veterinary Medicine

VetNurse.co.uk
984444
Editorial: The Old Forge, Little Green, Mells, Frome BA11 3QZ **Tel:** 44 02071 832511
Web site: www.vetnurse.co.uk
Freq: Daily
Circ: 53711 Cision Digital Reach
Profile: Website covering clinical articles, diary events, training materials and job opportunities of interest to the veterinary profession.
MAGAZINE (ONLINE)
Veterinary Medicine

VetSurgeon.org
984445
Editorial: The Old Forge, Little Green, Mells, Frome BA11 3QZ **Tel:** 44 02071 832511
Web site: www.vetsurgeon.org
Freq: Daily
Circ: 13558 Cision Digital Reach
Profile: Website covering all aspects of veterinary medicine and practice featuring a newsfeed, veterinary forums, products and services, jobs and a CPD and events diary. Aimed at veterinary surgeons and practice managers.
MAGAZINE (ONLINE)
Veterinary Medicine

Vicinitee
995821
Editorial: 12 Exchange Square, London EC2A 2BQ **Tel:** 44 02075 054100
Web site: http://www.vicinitee.london/
Freq: Daily
Editor: Carol Shields
MAGAZINE (ONLINE)
Residential Real Estate

Victoria
1069073
Editorial: Victoria, 3 Princes Street, London W1B 2LD
Web site: http://www.pubbiz.com/section/content/10
Freq: Semi-Annual
Circ: 20000 Not Audited
Editor: Jonathan Whiley
MAGAZINE
Equities, Hedge Funds

VIGEO EIRIS
996562
Editorial: EIRIS (Ethical Investment Research), 8th Floor The Tower Building, 11 York Road, London SE1 7NX
Tel: 44 02078 405716
Email: news@eiris.org
Web site: http://www.vigeo-eiris.com/en/
Freq: Daily
Circ: 12879 Cision Digital Reach
MAGAZINE (ONLINE)
Banking, Business, Corporate Responsibility

Virus Bulletin
988842
Editorial: The Pentagon, Abingdon Science Park, Abingdon OX14 3YP
Tel: 44 01235 555139
Email: editorial@virusbtn.com
Web site: https://www.virusbulletin.com/
Freq: Daily
Circ: 20261 Cision Digital Reach
Editor: Martijn Grooten
Profile: Website covering computer viruses. The Virus Bulletin features reports and analysis of malicious computer programs, monitors new developments in virus and spam prevention and removal.
MAGAZINE (ONLINE)
Computers, Government Technology

Vision Now
984251
Editorial: Clermont House, Cranbrook, Kent, Cranbrook TN17 3DN **Tel:** 44 01580 713698
Email: enquiries@nationaleyecare.co.uk
Web site: www.nationaleyecare.co.uk
Freq: Monthly
Circ: 1500 Not Audited
Profile: Magazine for members of the National Eyecare Group. Provides product and services news as well as finance and marketing articles.
MAGAZINE
Ophthalmology & Optometry

Visual Cognition
999458
Editorial: 27 Church Road, Hove, Brighton BN3 2FA **Tel:** 44 02070 177720
Email: pvis-peerreview@tandf.co.uk
Web site: http://www.tandfonline.com/toc/pvis20/current#.UihIUNLBOMI
Freq: Monthly Not Audited
MAGAZINE
Ophthalmology & Optometry

VITAL
996772
Editorial: Chartered Accountants' Hall, Moorgate Place, London EC2 6EA
Tel: 44 01908 248250
Email: vital@icaew.com
Web site: http://www.icaew.com/en/qualifications-and-programmes/aca-evolved/aca-student-groups-and-support/vit
Freq: Quarterly
Editor: Marie Lake
MAGAZINE
Accounting

VN Times
981170
Editorial: Olympus House, Werrington Centre, Werrington, Peterborough PE4 6NA
Tel: 44 01733 325522
Email: editor@vettimes.co.uk
Web site: https://www.vettimes.co.uk/

Freq: Monthly
Circ: 14371 Not Audited
Editor: Rebecca Hubbard
Profile: Magazine covering all aspects of veterinary nursing, including information on products and developments and articles from nurses about veterinary experiences. Aimed at qualified, final year and second year student veterinary nurses.
Ad Rate: Full Page Colour £1610.00
MAGAZINE
Veterinary Medicine

VNonline 987679
Email: editor@vnonline.co.uk
Web site: www.vnonline.co.uk
Freq: Daily
Circ: 12371 Cision Digital Reach
MAGAZINE (ONLINE)
Veterinary Medicine

VR Tech 1076161
Web site: http://www.virtualreality-news.net/
Freq: Daily
Circ: 18861 Cision Digital Reach
MAGAZINE (ONLINE)
Data Management, Industry

VRFocus 995147
Editorial: Trident House, 38-44 Victoria Road, Farnborough, Farnborough GU14 7PG
Email: keva@vrfocus.com
Web site: http://vrfocus.com/
Freq: Daily
Circ: 632204 Cision Digital Reach
MAGAZINE (ONLINE)
Software

Wales Business Insider 983243
Editorial: Motorpoint Arena Cardiff, Mary Ann Street, Cardiff CF10 2EQ
Tel: 44 02920 574751
Email: insider@newsco.com
Web site: http://www.insidermedia.com/wales
Freq: Monthly
Circ: 7000 Not Audited
Editor: Douglas Friedli
MAGAZINE
Business, Corporate Responsibility, Finance, Mergers & Acquisitions, Small and Medium Business

Warehouse 985521
Editorial: 11 Gower Street, London WC1E 6HB **Tel:** 44 02076 368856
Email: editor@ukwa.org.uk
Web site: www.ukwa.org.uk
Freq: Monthly
Circ: 1500 Not Audited
Editor: Lloyd Akrill
Profile: The official organ of UKWA - United Kingdom Warehousing Association covering news, materials handling and logistics-related equipment and services including warehouse management systems.
MAGAZINE
Supply Chain Management (SCM)

Warehouse & Logistics News 981003
Editorial: 12 Kings Park, Primrose Hill, Kings Langley, London WD4 8ST
Tel: 44 01923 272960
Email: james@warehousenews.co.uk
Web site: www.warehousenews.co.uk
Freq: Bi-Weekly
Circ: 7526 Not Audited
Editor: James Surridge
Profile: Magazine focusing on the warehouse equipment and services sector, including property news and logistics. Aimed at warehouse operatives, managers, e-commerce, logistics and IT managers.
Ad Rate: Full Page Colour £1690.00
MAGAZINE
Supply Chain Management (SCM)

Waste Planning 995865
Editorial: Bridge House, 69 London Road, Twickenham TW1 3QL **Tel:** 44 02082 674025
Web site: wasteplanning.co.uk
Freq: Bi-Monthly Not Audited

Editor: Alison Carter
Profile: Publication focusing on the environmental and practical planning aspects of waste, particularly in the fields of legislation and policy, in theory and practice. Aimed at local authorities, government departments, environmental pressure groups, the waste industry, educational institutions, environmental consultants and lawyers.
Ad Rate: Full Page Mono £278.00
MAGAZINE
Environment

Water & Sewerage Journal 983714
Editorial: Kings House, Royal Court, Brook Street, Macclesfield SK11 7AE
Tel: 44 01625 667535
Web site: www.waterjournal.co.uk
Freq: Quarterly
Circ: 25000 Not Audited
Editor: Marie Roberts
Profile: Journal covering all aspects of water engineering and sewage treatment. Aimed at privatised water utilities and all those who work in and service the water and service utilities.
Ad Rate: Full Page Mono £1560.00
Ad Rate: Full Page Colour £1950.00
MAGAZINE
Water & Sanitation

Water & Wastewater Treatment 981140
Editorial: Windsor Court, Wood Street, East Grinstead, East Grinstead RH19 1XA
Tel: 44 01342 332000
Web site: www.edie.net/wwt
Freq: Monthly
Circ: 8680 Not Audited
Editor: James Brockett
Profile: Magazine covering all aspects of the treatment and supply of potable water, the treatment and transport of sewage and sludge and the treatment of industrial effluent.
Ad Rate: Full Page Mono £1620.00
Ad Rate: Full Page Colour £1920.00
MAGAZINE
Hygiene, Water & Sanitation

Water Active 983260
Editorial: Unit 2, 57 Bushey Grove Road, Bushey, Watford, London WD23 2JW
Tel: 44 01923 235050
Email: info@wateractive.co.uk
Web site: www.wateractive.co.uk
Freq: Monthly
Circ: 21463 Not Audited
Profile: Magazine covering water treatment, distribution, sewage and effluent treatment, instrumentation, papers, pumps, valves, tanks, filtration, trench less technology and pollution control. Aimed at management and engineering professionals within the water industry.
Ad Rate: Full Page Colour £1650.00
MAGAZINE
Water & Sanitation

Water and Environment Journal 987536
Editorial: 106-109 Saffron Hill, London EC1N 8QS **Tel:** 44 02078 313110
Email: cs-journals@wiley.com
Web site: www.ciwem.org/information-and-resources/publications/water-and-environment-journal.aspx
Freq: Quarterly Not Audited
Profile: Journal covering a wide range of issues within the environment sector.
Ad Rate: Full Page Mono £1175.00
Ad Rate: Full Page Colour £1795.00
MAGAZINE
Environment

Water Asset Management International 984069
Editorial: Alliance House, 12 Caxton Street, London SW1H 0QS **Tel:** 44 02076 545500
Web site: http://www.iwaponline.com/wami/default.htm
Freq: Quarterly Not Audited

Profile: Newsletter focusing on asset management in water and wastewater utilities.
MAGAZINE
Water & Sanitation

Water Briefing 984071
Editorial: Royal London Buildings, Baldwin Street, Bristol BS1 1PN
Email: waterbriefing@imsbis.org
Web site: www.waterbriefing.org
Freq: Daily
Circ: 12619 Cision Digital Reach
MAGAZINE (ONLINE)
Water & Sanitation

The Water Report 997443
Email: karma@thewaterreport.co.uk
Web site: www.thewaterreport.co.uk
Freq: Monthly Not Audited
Editor: Karma Ockenden
MAGAZINE
Water & Sanitation

Water Resources Planning & Design 1061137
Tel: 44 86108 2026259
Email: shuiliguihua@giwp.org.cn
Web site: http://www.giwp.org.cn
Freq: Monthly Not Audited
MAGAZINE
Environment

Water Reuse & Desalination 996223
Editorial: 46 Lexington, 40 City Road, London EC1Y 2AN **Tel:** 44 02072 518778
Web site: http://www.wef.org/resources/publications/all-magazines/WW-WRD/
Freq: Quarterly
Circ: 24081 Not Audited
MAGAZINE
Alternative/Renewable Energy, Chemicals, Environment, Science, Water & Sanitation

Water. desalination + reuse 998717
Editorial: Windsor Court, Wood Street, East Grinstead, East Grinstead RH19 1XA
Tel: 44 01342 332000
Email: desalination@fav-house.com
Web site: www.desalination.biz
Freq: Quarterly
Circ: 4000 Not Audited
MAGAZINE
Engineering, Environment

water-technology.net 984072
Editorial: John Carpenter House, John Carpenter Street, London EC4Y 0AN
Tel: 44 02079 366400
Email: onlineeditorial@kable.co.uk
Web site: http://www.water-technology.net
Freq: Daily
Circ: 57614 Cision Digital Reach
Profile: Website covering water technology projects both in production and under development as well as products and services, conferences, exhibitions and events.
MAGAZINE (ONLINE)
Water & Sanitation

WealthBriefing.com 981604
Editorial: 19 Heathman's Road, London SW6 4TJ **Tel:** 44 02071 480188
Web site: www.wealthbriefing.com
Freq: Daily
Circ: 2979 Cision Digital Reach
MAGAZINE (ONLINE)
Banking, Fund Management

Wealthmonitor 999222
Editorial: 10 Queen Street Place, London EC4R 1BE **Tel:** 44 02070 106245
Email: info@mergermarket.com
Web site: www.wealthmonitor.com
Freq: Daily
Circ: 5892 Cision Digital Reach
MAGAZINE (ONLINE)
Mergers & Acquisitions

Welding World Magazine 987978
Editorial: AWD, Secure Hold Business Centre, Studley Road, Redditch B98 7LG
Tel: 44 01952 290036
Email: editor@welding.weld.com
Web site: www.welding-world.com
Freq: Bi-Monthly Not Audited
Profile: Magazine focusing on welding products. Contains market information, company profiles, product reviews, interviews, safety and legal updates.
Ad Rate: Full Page Colour £1210.00
MAGAZINE
Manufacturing, Steel

Well Connected 987376
Editorial: 1 Old Hall Street, Liverpool L3 9HG **Tel:** 44 01512 271234
Email: editorial@liverpoolchamber.org.uk
Web site: www.excelpublishing.co.uk/services/magazines/well-connected
Freq: Quarterly
Circ: 10000 Not Audited
Editor: Kathryn Ashman
MAGAZINE
Business, Corporate Responsibility

Welsh Farmer 981159
Tel: 44 01970 820820
Web site: www.welshfarmer.com
Freq: Monthly
Circ: 7000 Not Audited
MAGAZINE
Animal Farming

Welsh Pharmacy Review 984610
Editorial: 142-148 Albert Bridge Road, Belfast BT5 4GS **Tel:** 44 02890 999441
Web site: http://pharmacy-life.co.uk/
Freq: Quarterly
Circ: 1200 Not Audited
Editor: Sarah Nelson
Profile: Magazine covering the pharmaceuticals industry. Also contains general news, views, business issues and articles on clinical and educational matters, human interest, finance, lifestyle, new products and current trials. Aimed at GPs, consultants, pharmacists, hospital doctors and health-care professionals.
MAGAZINE
Pharmaceuticals

West Midlands Business Information Portal 996426
Editorial: Birmingham Science Park Aston, Faraday Wharf, Holt Street, Birmingham B7 4BB
Web site: www.thebiponline.co.uk/bip/
Freq: Daily
Circ: 12384 Cision Digital Reach
MAGAZINE (ONLINE)
Business

WET News 981141
Editorial: Windsor Court, Wood Street, East Grinstead, East Grinstead RH19 1XA
Tel: 44 01342 332000
Email: newsdesk@fav-house.com
Web site: wwtonline.edie.net/info/wetnews
Freq: Monthly
Circ: 6110 Not Audited
Profile: Newspaper for the water and effluent treatment industries.
Ad Rate: Full Page Mono £1750.00
Ad Rate: Full Page Colour £2150.00
MAGAZINE
Hygiene, Water & Sanitation

What Franchise Magazine 985403
Editorial: 49 Old Steine, Brighton BN1 1NH
Tel: 44 01273 862258
Email: jeff@partridgeltd.co.uk
Web site: http://www.what-franchise.com/
Freq: Bi-Monthly
Circ: 13422 Not Audited
Editor: Jeff James
MAGAZINE
Business

Business Magazines

WhichInvestmentTrust.com
996384

Editorial: 9th Floor, London City Point Tower, 1 Ropemaker Street, London EC2Y 9HT **Tel:** 44 02071 532251
Email: enquiries@whichinvestmenttrust.com
Web site: www.whichinvestmenttrust.com
Freq: Daily
Circ: 10271 Cision Digital Reach
MAGAZINE (ONLINE)
Fund Management

Whole Hog Brief
995028

Tel: 44 01733 253006
Email: editor@porkinfo.com
Web site: http://www.porkinfo.com
Freq: Monthly
Circ: 1469 Cision Digital Reach
MAGAZINE (ONLINE)
Animal Farming

Wind Energy
980899

Editorial: The Atrium, Southern Gate, Chichester PO19 8SQ **Tel:** 44 01243 779777
Web site: http://onlinelibrary.wiley.com/journal/10.1002/%28ISSN%291099-1824
Freq: Monthly Not Audited
Profile: Journal reporting on the advances and technology available for harnessing clean energy from the wind.
Ad Rate: Full Page Mono £1175.00
Ad Rate: Full Page Colour £2575.00
MAGAZINE
Alternative/Renewable Energy

Wind Energy Network
985981

Editorial: The Oaks, Oakwood Park Business Centre, Bishop Thornton, Harrogate, Ripon HG3 3BF
Tel: 44 01765 644224
Web site: www.windenergynetwork.co.uk
Freq: Bi-Monthly
Circ: 10700 Not Audited
Editor: Duncan McGilvray
MAGAZINE
Alternative/Renewable Energy, Electricity

Wind Energy Update
985360

Editorial: 7-9 Fashion St, London E1 6PX
Tel: 44 02073 757500
Email: info@windenergyupdate.com
Web site: www.analysis.windenergyupdate.com/
Freq: Daily
Circ: 11711 Cision Digital Reach
Profile: Website covering wind energy. Wind Energy Update is a reference point for senior executives working in the wind power generation industry. The website covers news, information and developments in the wind power industry.
MAGAZINE (ONLINE)
Alternative/Renewable Energy

Wind Power Technology
1101939

Editorial: Commonwealth House, 1-19 New Oxford Street, London WC1A 1NU
Tel: 44 02037 944581
Email: enquiries@renewable-energy-technology.net
Web site: http://www.renewable-energy-technology.net/
Freq: Quarterly
Circ: 10000 Not Audited
MAGAZINE
Alternative/Renewable Energy

Windows Active
984712

Editorial: Windows Active, PO Box 627, Rickmansworth, London WD3 0BQ
Tel: 44 01923 770432
Email: john.cowie@windowsactive.co.uk
Web site: www.windowsactive.com
Freq: Monthly
Circ: 26000 Not Audited
Editor: Jackie Simpson
Profile: Magazine covering specification, fabrication and installation of windows, doors and conservatories. Contains informative articles, news and product information. Includes general business related features on topics such as human resources, business management and economic trends. Targets fabricators and installers of windows, doors and conservatories in the UK. Regular features: Business; Director of the Month; Fabricator Focus; Promotional Campaign
Ad Rate: Full Page Colour £1170.00
MAGAZINE
Building & Construction

Windpower Monthly
981501

Editorial: Bridge House, 69 London Road, Twickenham TW1 3SP **Tel:** 44 02082 674011
Email: wpm.editorial@haymarket.com
Web site: www.windpowermonthly.com
Freq: Monthly
Circ: 15000 Not Audited
Profile: Windpower Monthly magazine covers the wind power industry and provides news and discussion on the environmental, technical and business developments from the sector. The magazine is a 'concise yet detailed overview of the essential political, industrial, environmental and technical developments in the global wind energy arena'.
MAGAZINE
Alternative/Renewable Energy

Windpower Offshore
999519

Editorial: 174 Hammersmith Road, London W6 7JP **Tel:** 44 02082 675000
Email: editorial@windpoweroffshore.com
Web site: www.windpoweroffshore.com
Freq: Daily
Circ: 16496 Cision Digital Reach
MAGAZINE (ONLINE)
Alternative/Renewable Energy, Environment

Winning Edge
982958

Editorial: 19 Eastbourne Terrace, Paddington Station, Platform 1, London W2 6LG **Tel:** 44 02038 704949
Email: magazine@ismm.co.uk
Web site: https://www.ismprofessional.com/
Freq: Bi-Monthly
Circ: 7000 Not Audited
Editor: Marc Beishon
Profile: Official magazine of the Institute of Sales and Marketing Management. Covers market intelligence, sales techniques and marketing strategy. Read by members of the Institute.
Ad Rate: Full Page Colour £1540.00
MAGAZINE
Business, Marketing

Wire & Cable Asia
985961

Editorial: 46 Holly Walk, Leamington Spa CV32 4HY **Tel:** 44 01926 334137
Email: wca@intras.co.uk
Web site: www.read-wca.com
Freq: Bi-Monthly
Circ: 16500 Not Audited
Editor: David Bell
Profile: Journal covering the latest developments in production. Includes articles on supply and processing machinery plus, cable and wire industry news.
Ad Rate: Full Page Mono £1204.00
Ad Rate: Full Page Colour £1701.00
MAGAZINE
Industry, Mobile Communications

WiRELESS
985963

Editorial: Noble House Media Ltd, 4 Bloomsbury Square, London WC1A 2RP
Tel: 44 07896 727433
Email: wireless@nhmedia.co.uk
Web site: www.wireless-mag.com
Freq: Bi-Monthly
Circ: 23100 Not Audited
MAGAZINE
Mobile Communications

Wireline
997645

Editorial: 6th Floor East, Portland House, Bressenden Place, London SW1E 5BH
Email: editorial@oilandgasuk.co.uk
Web site: http://oilandgasuk.co.uk/
Freq: Quarterly
Circ: 7000 Not Audited
MAGAZINE
Oil

Wolverhampton West
999829

Editorial: 1 Lytham Road, Perton, Wolverhampton WV6 7YY
Tel: 44 01902 744217
Email: info@wolverhamptonwestmag.co.uk
Web site: www.wolverhamptonwestmag.co.uk
Freq: Bi-Monthly
Circ: 24500 Not Audited
Editor: Geoff Hall
MAGAZINE
Business, Small and Medium Business

The Woman Engineer (UK)
980981

Editorial: Michael Faraday House, Six Hills Way, Stevenage, Stevenage SG1 2AY
Tel: 44 01438 765506
Email: editor@wes.org.uk
Web site: www.wes.org.uk
Freq: Quarterly
Circ: 1000 Not Audited
MAGAZINE
Engineering

Womanthology
998302

Web site: www.womanthology.co.uk
Freq: Daily
Circ: 16527 Cision Digital Reach
MAGAZINE (ONLINE)
Business, Corporate Responsibility

Women's Health
997567

Editorial: 1 Oliver's Yard, London EC1Y 1SP
Tel: 44 20732 48500
Email: market@sagepub.co.uk
Web site: https://us.sagepub.com/en-us/nam/womens-health/journal202572#description
Freq: Bi-Monthly Not Audited
Profile: Magazine covering women's health including lifestyle, slimming, dieting, sex, love, beauty, fashion, celebrity, fitness and nutrition. Aimed at women of all ages.
Ad Rate: Full Page Colour £6900.00
MAGAZINE
Obstetrics & Gynecology (OB/GYN)

The Woodland Heritage Journal
986635

Editorial: Woodland Heritage, PO Box 168, Haslemere GU27 1XQ **Tel:** 44 01428 652159
Email: enquiries@woodlandheritage.org
Web site: http://www.woodlandheritage.org/library/journal-downloads/item/92-journal-downloads
Freq: Annual
Circ: 3000 Not Audited
Editor: Peter Goodwin
Profile: Official Journal of Woodland Heritage, containing information on the management of trees and woodlands, publication of reports of study tours and projects funded by Woodland Heritage.
MAGAZINE
Environment

Woodworking News
985527

Editorial: The Old Sun, Crete Hall Road, Northfleet, London DA11 9AA
Tel: 44 01474 536535
Email: nhs@nelton.co.uk
Web site: www.woodworkingnews.co.uk
Freq: Monthly
Circ: 9860 Not Audited
Editor: Neil Herbert-Smith
Profile: Newspaper combining a mixture of industry news, new products and technical articles.
Ad Rate: Full Page Colour £2139.00
MAGAZINE
Manufacturing

Work Your Way
997196

Editorial: Unit 1G, 24 Malyons Road, London SE13 7XG **Tel:** 44 08450 568828
Email: enquiries@workyourway.co.uk
Web site: www.workyourway.co.uk
Circ: 1655 Cision Digital Reach
Editor: Mary Cummings
MAGAZINE (ONLINE)
Recruiting, Women's Interests

Work.
988639

Editorial: Bridge House, 69 London Road, Twickenham TW1 3SP **Tel:** 44 02082 675013
Email: info@haymarketnetwork.com
Web site: http://www.haymarketnetwork.com/clients/cipd
Freq: Quarterly Not Audited
Editor: Claire Warren
MAGAZINE
Human Resources

working mums
985592

Editorial: PO Box 53228, London N3 1YR
Tel: 44 02084 326094
Web site: www.workingmums.co.uk
Freq: Daily
Circ: 153118 Cision Digital Reach
MAGAZINE (ONLINE)
Recruiting

Workplace Insight
1072214

Tel: 44 02032 393418
Web site: workplaceinsight.net
Freq: Daily
Circ: 97675 Cision Digital Reach
MAGAZINE (ONLINE)
Architecture & Design, Health & Safety, Human Resources, Interior Design, Office Design

Works Management
981247

Editorial: Hawley Mill, Hawley Road, Dartford, Sutton at Hone DA2 7TJ
Tel: 44 01322 221144
Email: enquiries@findlay.co.uk
Web site: http://www.worksmanagement.co.uk/manufacturing-magazine/
Freq: Monthly
Circ: 17000 Not Audited
MAGAZINE
Manufacturing

World Allergy Organization Journal
1102294

Editorial: c/o BioMed Central, 236 Gray's Inn Road, London WC1X 8HB
Email: waoj@worldallergy.org
Web site: http://waojournal.biomedcentral.com
Freq: Daily
Circ: 342272 Cision Digital Reach
MAGAZINE (ONLINE)
Allergies

World Architecture News
984198

Editorial: Suite 104, 15-17 Middle Street, Brighton BN1 1AL **Tel:** 44 01273 201120
Email: newsdesk@worldarchitecturenews.com
Web site: www.worldarchitecturenews.com
Freq: Daily
Circ: 182462 Cision Digital Reach
Profile: Website covering world news. World Architecture News website discusses the latest news in the world.
MAGAZINE (ONLINE)
Architecture & Design

World Coal
981224

Editorial: 15 South Street, Farnham, Farnham GU9 7QU **Tel:** 44 01252 718999
Email: editorial@worldcoal.com
Web site: http://www.worldcoal.com/magazines/latestissue/world-coal.aspx
Freq: Monthly
Circ: 4610 Not Audited
Profile: Magazine covering the international coal industry, from mining to end-use. Includes coal news, monthly international reports, trade forecasts, technical case-studies, mine reports and product news.
Ad Rate: Full Page Colour £3500.00
MAGAZINE
Carbon Emissions & Trading, Mining & Quarrying

World Commerce Review
985738

Editorial: Phoenix Multimedia, 5 The Old Grammar, Old Grammar Lane, Bungay NR35 1PU **Tel:** 44 01986 892028
Email: info@worldcommercereview.com
Web site: www.worldcommercereview.com

Freq: Quarterly Not Audited
MAGAZINE
Banking, Corporate Law, Law

World Construction Network
1066389
Editorial: 40-42 Hatton Garden, London
EC1N 8EB **Tel:** 44 02079 366400
Web site: http://www.
worldconstructionnetwork.com/
Freq: Daily
Circ: 11681 Cision Digital Reach
MAGAZINE (ONLINE)
Building & Construction

World Data Protection Report
999181
Editorial: 1st Floor, 38 Threadneedle Street,
London EC2R 8AY **Tel:** 44 02078 475801
Web site: http://www.bna.com/world-data-
protection-p6718/
Freq: Monthly Not Audited
MAGAZINE
Data Management

World Economic Yearbook
1060888
Tel: 44 86108 5195760
Email: iwep_sjnj@cass.org.cn
Web site: http://www.inep.org.cn
Freq: Annual Not Audited
MAGAZINE
Economics

World Energy Council
1074212
Email: info@worldenergyfocus.org
Web site: https://www.worldenergy.org/
Freq: Daily
Circ: 50511 Cision Digital Reach
MAGAZINE (ONLINE)
Alternative/Renewable Energy, Carbon
Emissions & Trading, Electricity, Energy,
Nuclear Power, Oil, Water & Sanitation

World Energy Focus
1074210
Email: info@worldenergyfocus.org
Web site: https://www.worldenergy.org/
focus/
Freq: Monthly
Circ: 1 Cision Digital Reach
MAGAZINE (ONLINE)
Alternative/Renewable Energy, Carbon
Emissions & Trading, Electricity, Energy,
Nuclear Power, Oil, Water & Sanitation

World Expro
994610
Editorial: John Carpenter House, John
Carpenter Street, London EC4Y 0AN
Tel: 44 02079 366400
Web site: www.worldexpro.com
Freq: Semi-Annual
Circ: 7893 Not Audited
Editor: Andrew Tunnicliffe
MAGAZINE
Oil

World Finance
983815
Editorial: 37-42 Compton Street, London
EC1V 0BD **Tel:** 44 02072 535100
Email: enquiries@worldfinance.com
Web site: www.worldfinance.com
Freq: Bi-Monthly
Circ: 120000 Not Audited
Profile: Magazine covering current news and
features on the financial markets and report
reporting on capital markets, risk
management, trading, technology, corporate
governance issues and regional markets
including Asia, Latin America and EMEA.
Aimed at directors and senior decision
makers.Regular features: Corporate
Governance; Executive Education; Global
Roundup; Private Wealth Management;
Transfer Pricing
Ad Rate: Full Page Colour £18140.00
MAGAZINE
Banking

World Gas Intelligence
980791
Editorial: Interpark House, 7 Down Street,
3rd Floor, London W1J 7AJ
Tel: 44 02075 182200

Email: energyintelligence@energyintel.com
Web site: http://www.energyintel.com/
Pages/About_WGI.aspx
Freq: Weekly Not Audited
Editor: Peter Kemp
MAGAZINE
Oil

World Highways
981680
Editorial: Waterbridge Court, 50 Spital
Street, Dartford, Swanley DA1 2DT
Tel: 44 01322 612055
Email: media@ropl.com
Web site: www.worldhighways.com
Freq: Monthly
Circ: 17536 Not Audited
Editor: Dan Gilkes; **Editor:** Mike Woof
MAGAZINE
Engineering

World Intellectual Property
Report
998611
Editorial: 38 Threadneedle Street, London
EC2R 8AY **Tel:** 44 02078 475800
Email: lpeditorial@bna.com
Web site: http://www.bna.com/world-
intellectual-property-report-p6798/
Freq: Monthly Not Audited
MAGAZINE
Intellectual Property

World Manufacturing
Engineering & Market
1062147
Tel: 44 86106 3345695
Email: wmem@cmtba.org.cn
Web site: http://www.cimtshow.com/wmem
Freq: Bi-Monthly
Circ: 30001 Not Audited
MAGAZINE
Manufacturing

World Mining Frontiers
1066705
Editorial: 40-42 Hatton Garden, London
EC1N 8EB **Tel:** 44 02079 366400
Email: info@globaltrademedia.com
Web site: www.world-mining-frontiers.com
Freq: Semi-Annual
Circ: 2883 Not Audited
Editor: Andrew Tunnicliffe
MAGAZINE
Mining & Quarrying

World Nuclear News
984728
Editorial: Tower House, 10 Southampton
Street, London WC2E 7HA
Tel: 44 02074 511520
Email: editor@world-nuclear-news.org
Web site: www.world-nuclear-news.org
Freq: Daily
Circ: 78869 Cision Digital Reach
Editor: Claire-Louise Isted
MAGAZINE (ONLINE)
Nuclear Power

World of Renewables
985947
Editorial: Phoenix House, Westgate Terrace,
London SW10 9BT **Tel:** 44 01268 574400
Email: editorial@worldofrenewables.com
Web site: http://worldofrenewables.net/
Freq: Daily
Circ: 45704 Cision Digital Reach
MAGAZINE (ONLINE)
Alternative/Renewable Energy

World Oil Tanker Trends
999184
Editorial: Lloyds Chambers, 1 Portsoken
Street, London E1 8PH
Tel: 44 02079 777400
Email: research@ssy.co.uk
Web site: www.ssyonline.com
Freq: Semi-Annual Not Audited
MAGAZINE
Oil

World Pharmaceutical
Frontiers
981218
Editorial: John Carpenter House, John
Carpenter Street, London EC4Y 0AN
Tel: 44 02079 366661
Email: info@globaltrademedia.com
Web site: www.worldpharmaceuticals.net

Freq: Semi-Annual
Circ: 7300 Not Audited
Profile: World Pharmaceutical Frontiers
provides information for the world's leading
pharmaceutical companies with intelligence
on emerging trends and technologies to help
them make business decisions. Focusing on
all areas of the pharmaceutical industry, its
perspectives, requirements and
developments. Aimed at senior executives in
charge of purchasing, R&D and
manufacturing.
Ad Rate: Full Page Mono £5100.00
Ad Rate: Full Page Colour £5900.00
MAGAZINE
Biotechnology, Pharmaceuticals

World Pipelines
981139
Editorial: 15 South Street, Farnham,
Farnham GU9 7QU **Tel:** 44 01252 718999
Web site: https://www.energyglobal.com/
magazine/world-pipelines/
Freq: Monthly
Circ: 10030 Not Audited
Editor: Elizabeth Corner
Profile: Magazine addressing all aspects of
the international oil and gas pipeline
industry, including global industry news,
reports and developments with information
on new contracts and tenders, regional
overviews and economic and technical
features.
Ad Rate: Full Page Colour £5300.00
MAGAZINE
Oil

World Pumps
981034
Editorial: The Boulevard, Langford Lane,
Kidlington OX5 1GB **Tel:** 44 01865 843000
Web site: www.worldpumps.com
Freq: Monthly
Circ: 21000 Not Audited
Editor: Alan Burrows
Profile: Magazine focusing on pumps and
pumping system technology worldwide.
Ad Rate: Full Page Colour £5180.00
MAGAZINE
Engineering

World risk insight
1053937
Editorial: ALS Media Ltd., 33 Creechurch
Lane, London EC3A 5EB
Tel: 44 07713 873237
Web site: www.wrinsight.com
Freq: Weekly
Circ: 5800 Not Audited
MAGAZINE
Insurance

World Trademark Review 984627
Editorial: New Hibernia House, Winchester
Walk, London Bridge, London SE1 9AG
Tel: 44 02072 340606
Web site: www.worldtrademarkreview.com
Freq: Bi-Monthly
Circ: 2500 Not Audited
Editor: Trevor Little
Profile: Bi-monthly publication targeting
trademark professionals. Each issue
provides coverage of emerging national and
regional trends, analysis of important
markets, examples of industry best practice
and interviews with high-profile trademark
personalities, columns on trademark
management, online issues and
counterfeiting.
MAGAZINE
Advertising Industry, Branding, Marketing

World Water
998610
Editorial: 6 Brewery Square, St. John Street,
London EC1V 4LE **Tel:** 44 02072 518778
Web site: www.wefworldwater.com
Freq: Bi-Monthly
Circ: 23245 Not Audited
MAGAZINE
Water & Sanitation

World Water: Stormwater
Management
997204
Editorial: 46 Lexington, 40 City Road,
London EC1Y 2AN **Tel:** 44 02072 518778

Web site: http://www.wef/resources/
publications/all-magazines/world-water-
stormwater/
Freq: Bi Monthly
Circ: 24435 Not Audited
MAGAZINE
Water & Sanitation

World Wind Technology
987518
Editorial: John Carpenter House, John
Carpenter Street, London EC4Y 0AN
Tel: 44 02079 366400
Email: editor@globaltrademedia.com
Web site: www.windpower-international.
com
Freq: Semi-Annual
Circ: 7211 Not Audited
MAGAZINE
Alternative/Renewable Energy

WorldCargo News
981324
Editorial: The Coach House, 24 Bridge
Street, Leatherhead, London KT22 8BX
Tel: 44 01372 375511
Web site: www.worldcargonews.com
Freq: Monthly
Circ: 7210 Not Audited
Profile: Magazine covering most kinds of
cargo handling, containerisation,
intermodalism and port development.
Ad Rate: Full Page Mono £4065.00
Ad Rate: Full Page Colour £5285.00
MAGAZINE
Shipping & Warehousing, Supply Chain
Management (SCM)

WorldECR
1049246
Editorial: 20-22 Wenlock Road, London N1
7GU
Email: info@worldecr.com
Web site: www.worldecr.com
Freq: Monthly
MAGAZINE
Corporate Law, Shipping & Warehousing

Worldwide Business
Research
996295
Editorial: Third Floor, 129 Wilton Road,
London SW1V 1JZ **Tel:** 44 02073 689465
Web site: www.wbresearch.com
Freq: Daily
Circ: 660661 Cision Digital Reach
MAGAZINE (ONLINE)
Business, Small and Medium Business

Worldwide Independent
Power
980112
Editorial: Global House, 13 Market Square,
Horsham, Horsham RH12 1EU
Tel: 44 01403 220750
Email: powereditorial@gmp.uk.com
Web site: http://www.gmp.uk.com/
worldwide-independent-power/
Freq: Monthly
Circ: 10489 Not Audited
Profile: Publication containing company
profiles, regular coverage on Gen-Sets,
CHP, engines and applications, renewables,
turbines, fuels and in-depth news analysis.
Includes updates and association news,
Internet reviews, market analysis and
utilities.
Ad Rate: Full Page Mono £2840.00
Ad Rate: Full Page Colour £3512.00
MAGAZINE
Alternative/Renewable Energy, Electricity,
Nuclear Power, Oil, Water & Sanitation

XpertHR (UK)
983988
Editorial: Quadrant House, The Quadrant,
Sutton, London SM2 5AS
Tel: 44 02086 523500
Email: editorial@xperthr.co.uk
Web site: www.xperthr.co.uk
Freq: Daily
Circ: 80319 Cision Digital Reach
MAGAZINE (ONLINE)
Company News & Appointments,
Education, Health & Safety, Human
Resources, Recruiting

Business Magazines

Yorkshire Business Daily 987222
Email: news@yorkshirebusinessdaily.co.uk
Web site: www.yorkshirebusinessdaily.co.uk
Freq: Daily
Circ: 16225 Cision Digital Reach
Editor: Steve Everett
MAGAZINE (ONLINE)
Business, Small and Medium Business

Yorkshire Business Insider
979961
Editorial: Suite D5, Joseph's Well, Hanover Walk, Leeds LS3 1AB **Tel:** 44 01132 204410
Web site: http://www.insidermedia.com/yorkshire
Freq: Monthly
Circ: 9083 Not Audited
MAGAZINE
Business, Corporate Responsibility, Finance, Mergers & Acquisitions

Yorkshire Property Guide
998507
Editorial: 3 King Street, Mirfield WF14 8AW
Tel: 44 01924 493300
Email: enquiries@yorkshire-properties.co.uk
Web site: http://www.yorkshire-properties.co.uk
Freq: Monthly
Circ: 12000 Not Audited
MAGAZINE
Property Management & Maintenance

Young Company Finance 980154
Editorial: 8 Oxford Terrace, Edinburgh EH4 1PX **Tel:** 44 01313 154443
Email: jonathan@ycf.co.uk
Web site: http://www.ycfscotland.co.uk/
Freq: Monthly Not Audited
Editor: Jonathan Harris

Profile: Newsletter providing a source of information about early stage high growth ventures and the commercialisation environment in which they operate, with special reference to how they are financed. Aimed at investors and business support organisations.
MAGAZINE
Banking

Your Build Magazine 985967
Editorial: The Manor Nepicar House, London Road, Wrotham Heath, Sevenoaks, Sevenoaks TN15 7RS **Tel:** 44 01732 748000
Web site: www.your-build.co.uk
Freq: Quarterly
Circ: 6000 Not Audited
Editor: Matthew Downs
MAGAZINE
Building & Construction

Your Business (UK) 998804
Editorial: The Mezzanine, Glasgow Prestwick Airport, Prestwick KA9 2PL
Tel: 44 01292 678666
Email: enquiries@ayrshire-chamber.org
Web site: https://www.ayrshire-chamber.org/member-benefits-services/business-magazine
Freq: Quarterly
Circ: 2000 Not Audited
MAGAZINE
Business, Small and Medium Business

Your Leicester 982505
Editorial: Leicester City Council, City Hall, 115 Charles Street, Leicester LE1 1FZ
Tel: 44 01164 544160
Email: newsletter@leicester.gov.uk
Web site: http://www.leicester.gov.uk/your-council/media-and-communications/your-leicester-newsletters/

Freq: Quarterly
Circ: 90230 Cision Digital Reach
Profile: Civic magazine covering news of the City Council's policies and services in Leicester. Aimed at householders in the city of Leicester.
MAGAZINE (ONLINE)
Government

Your Oil & Gas News 985645
Editorial: INTERKAB House, Grandholm Mill, Grandholm Village, Aberdeen AB22 8BB
Tel: 44 01224 392828
Email: info@yourindustrynews.com
Web site: www.youroilandgasnews.com
Freq: Daily
Circ: 45215 Cision Digital Reach
MAGAZINE (ONLINE)
Oil

Your Property Network 986575
Editorial: Scotland Farm, Scotland Lane, Rudge, Frome BA11 2QG
Tel: 44 08000 966088
Email: editor@yourpropertynetwork.co.uk
Web site: www.yourpropertynetwork.co.uk
Freq: Monthly
Circ: 10000 Not Audited
Profile: Magazine covering all aspects of property investment from buy-to-let, refurbisments and renovation, buy-to-sell and development. Aimed at people with an interest in property markets and those looking to invest.Twitter handle: YPNMagazine.
MAGAZINE
Finance

YourGuide's Construction Industry Buyers Guide 996094
Tel: 44 01706 828280
Email: info@yourguides.net

Web site: http://www.yourguides.net/construction
Freq: Quarterly
Circ: 27000 Not Audited
MAGAZINE
Building & Construction

youTalkinsurance 998300
Email: enquiries@youtalk-insurance.com
Web site: www.youtalk-insurance.com
Freq: Daily
Circ: 15627 Cision Digital Reach
MAGAZINE (ONLINE)
Insurance

Zephyr 995179
Editorial: Zephus Ltd, 4th Floor, Free Trade Exchange Building, 37 Peter Street, Manchester M2 5GB **Tel:** 44 01618 389555
Email: info@bvdinfo.com
Web site: https://zephyr.bvdinfo.com/version-2016718/home.serv?product=zephyrneo
Freq: Daily
MAGAZINE (ONLINE)
Mergers & Acquisitions

Zoonoses and Public Health
999407
Editorial: 9600 Garsington Road, Oxford OX4 2DQ **Tel:** 44 01865 776868
Email: zph@wiley.com
Web site: http://onlinelibrary.wiley.com/journal/10.1111/(ISSN)1863-2378
Freq: Bi-Monthly Not Audited
MAGAZINE
Infectious Diseases, Veterinary Medicine

Consumer Magazines

#OMY Magazine
996115
Email: info@ourmyyour.com
Web site: www.ourmyyour.com
Freq: Semi-Annual
Circ: 10676 Cision Digital Reach
MAGAZINE (ONLINE)
Art, Country, Folk, Bluegrass, Dance Music, Entertainment, Fashion, Jazz & Blues, Literature, Local Entertainment Guides, Movies & Video, Pop Music

#studentfarmer
997146
Tel: 44 02476 858671
Email: studentfarmer@nfu.org.uk
Web site: https://www.nfuonline.com/membership/your-nfu-publications/new-student-farmer-out-now/
Freq: 3 Times/Year
Circ: 10000 Not Audited
MAGAZINE
Animal Farming, Careers

.Cent
983477
Editorial: 20A, 2nd Floor, Block B, Tower Workshops, 58 Riley Road, London SE1 3DG Tel: 44 02072 371030
Email: jo@centmagazine.co.uk
Web site: www.centmagazine.co.uk
Freq: Quarterly
Circ: 10000 Not Audited
MAGAZINE
Fashion, Men's Interests, Women's Interests

[smiths]
999051
Editorial: Goldsmiths College Student Union, GCSU Dixon Road, London SE14 6NW
Email: smiths.gsu@gmail.com
Web site: www.smithsmagazine.co.uk
Freq: Quarterly Not Audited
MAGAZINE
Student Lifestyle

10 Magazine
983528
Editorial: 3 Lower John Street, London W1F 9DX Tel: 44 02074 340042
Email: info@10magazine.com
Web site: www.10magazine.com
Freq: Semi-Annual
Circ: 40000 Not Audited
Profile: Magazine focusing on fashion, contemporary art and beauty and offering an environment for photographers and stylists to showcase their work. Aimed at fashion focused men and women.
MAGAZINE
Fashion, Men's Interests, Women's Interests

100% Biker
983322
Editorial: The Old School, Higher Kinnerton, Flint CH4 9AJ Tel: 44 01244 663400
Email: editor@100-biker.com
Web site: www.100-biker.com
Freq: Monthly
Circ: 22720 Not Audited
Editor: Blue Miller
MAGAZINE
Motorcycles

100% MINT Magazine
1052819
Editorial: 83 Victoria St, Westminster, London SW1H 0HW Tel: 44 02035 854021
Email: letters@themintmag.co.uk
Web site: http://skyjackpublishing.co.uk/
Freq: Monthly
MAGAZINE
Elementary School, Teen/Young Adult

101 Holidays
986068
Editorial: PO Box 7136, Beaminster, Bridport DT6 9DD
Email: catherine@101holidays.co.uk

Web site: www.101holidays.co.uk
Freq: Daily
Circ: 126653 Cision Digital Reach
Editor: Mark Frary
MAGAZINE (ONLINE)
Airline Inflight, Railroad, Travel

110% Gaming
988473
Editorial: 80 Kingsway East, Dundee DD4 8SL Tel: 44 01382 575637
Web site: www.110gaming.com
Freq: Monthly
Circ: 24185 Not Audited
Editor: Lucy Galloway
MAGAZINE
Computer & Video Games, Teen/Young Adult

1843
984386
Editorial: 25 St James Street, London SW1A 1HG Tel: 44 02078 307000
Email: 1843magazine@economist.com
Web site: www.1843magazine.com
Freq: Bi-Monthly
Circ: 460000 Not Audited
Editor: Emma Duncan
MAGAZINE
Men's Interests, Women's Interests

1883 Magazine
985783
Editorial: 121 Spicer Close, London SW9 7UE
Email: info@1883magazine.com
Web site: www.1883magazine.com
Freq: Daily
Circ: 11425 Cision Digital Reach
MAGAZINE (ONLINE)
Beauty & Grooming, Cosmetics, Fashion, Hair

2 Forks
998175
Web site: www.2forks.co.uk
Freq: Daily
Circ: 907 Cision Digital Reach
MAGAZINE (ONLINE)
Bars, Clubs & Pubs, Cooking & Baking, Food, Restaurant Reviews

220 Triathlon
982188
Editorial: 9th Floor, Tower House, Fairfax Street, Bristol BS1 3BN
Tel: 44 01179 279009
Email: 220triathlon@immediate.co.uk
Web site: www.220triathlon.com
Freq: Monthly
Circ: 22109 Not Audited
Editor: Helen Webster
Profile: Magazine that covers triathlon including swimming, running and cycling training programmes as well as information on nutrition, international and national events, product reviews and injury prevention and cure. Aimed at all triathlon, adventure sports and run-bike enthusiasts.
Ad Rate: Full Page Colour £1650.00
MAGAZINE
Sports

247 Magazine
983740
Editorial: Hebron House, Sion Road, Bedminster, Bristol BS3 3BD
Tel: 44 01179 536363
Email: 247@outofhand.co.uk
Web site: www.247magazine.co.uk
Freq: Monthly
Editor: Nigel Muntz
MAGAZINE (ONLINE)
Bars, Clubs & Pubs, Comedy, Dance Music, Entertainment, Local Entertainment Guides, Movies & Video, Pop Music, Regional General Interest, Rock Music

24Games
1060382
MAGAZINE (ONLINE)
Games, Competitions & Events

25 Beautiful Homes
981837
Editorial: The Blue Fin Building, 110 Southwark Street, London SE1 0SU
Tel: 44 02031 485000
Email: 25beautifulhomes@timeinc.com

Web site: http://www.idealhome.co.uk/25-beautiful-homes
Freq: Monthly
Circ: 72389 Not Audited
Profile: Magazine featuring the style, colour schemes, and furnishings of 25 different homes. Aimed at people with an interest in home decorating.
Ad Rate: Full Page Colour £6790.00
MAGAZINE
Do-It-Yourself (DIY)

2dartist
997870
Editorial: 29 Foregate Street, Worcester, Worcester WR1 1DS
Email: news@3dtotal.com
Web site: 2dartistmag.com
Freq: Monthly
Circ: 2000 Not Audited
MAGAZINE
Visual Arts

2-in-1 Wordsearch
996059
Editorial: Academic House, 24-28 Oval Road, London NW1 7DT
Tel: 44 02072 418000
Email: eclipsepuzzles@bauer.co.uk
Web site: www.puzzlemagazines.co.uk
Freq: Monthly Not Audited
Editor: Christine Scott
MAGAZINE
Games, Competitions & Events

360 Fashion
1061847
Web site: http://www.360fashion.net
Freq: Daily
Circ: 6094 Cision Digital Reach
MAGAZINE (ONLINE)
Fashion

360 magazine
1104810
Editorial: 71-73 Carter Lane, London EC4V 5EQ Tel: 44 02030 962668
Email: chris.evans@progressivecontent.com
Web site: www.progressivecontent.com
Freq: Semi-Annual
Circ: 22000 Not Audited
Editor: Michael Jones
MAGAZINE
Bars, Clubs & Pubs, Comedy, Cosmetics, Entertainment, Fashion, Local Entertainment Guides, Luxury Goods, Movies & Video, Retail Management

3D Artist
985130
Editorial: Richmond House, 33 Richmond Hill, Bournemouth, Bournemouth BH2 6EZ
Tel: 44 01202 586200
Email: 3dartist@imagine-publishing.co.uk
Web site: www.3dartistonline.com
Freq: Monthly
Circ: 11000 Not Audited
Profile: Magazine showcasing 3D images and features interviews with people in the 3D industry and looks at development and technologies that shape what is seen on TV and in film, in advertising and architecture and in art. Anyone with an interest in 3D art.
MAGAZINE
Visual Arts

3D Print HQ
996042
Email: info@3dprinthq.com
Web site: http://3dprinthq.com/
Freq: Daily
Circ: 27713 Cision Digital Reach
MAGAZINE (ONLINE)
News & Current Affairs

3D World
981726
Editorial: Quay House, The Ambury, Bath BA1 1UA Tel: 44 01225 442244
Web site: www.3dworldmag.com
Freq: Monthly
Circ: 8769 Not Audited
Profile: Design magazine focusing on the creation of 3D graphics for use in TV and film, computer games, advertising and product design and visualization. Contains news, inspiration and practical advice about 3D graphics. 3D World comes out every four weeks, and copies go on sale throughout the world.

Ad Rate: Full Page Colour £2289.00
MAGAZINE
Apple, Personal Computers, Visual Arts

3DTotal
985124
Editorial: 29 Foregate Street, Worcester, Worcester WR1 1DS
Email: news@3dtotal.com
Web site: www.3dtotal.com
Freq: Daily
Circ: 467995 Cision Digital Reach
MAGAZINE (ONLINE)
Visual Arts

3g
987983
Editorial: 16 Gold Tops, Newport NP20 4PH
Web site: http://www.3g.co.uk/
Freq: Daily
Circ: 124238 Cision Digital Reach
Editor: Kevin Thomas
MAGAZINE (ONLINE)
Mobile Electronics

The 405
990572
Email: hi@thefourohfive.com
Web site: www.thefourohfive.com
Freq: Daily
Circ: 151575 Cision Digital Reach
Profile: Website covering music, film and art. The 405 provides the latest arts and entertainment news, reviews and features. It was launched spring 2008.
MAGAZINE (ONLINE)
Broadcasting, Classical/Choral/Band Music, Country, Folk, Bluegrass, Dance Music, Jazz & Blues, Local Entertainment Guides, Movies & Video, Music, Pop Music, R&B, Urban, World

4barsrest.com
996657
Email: general@4barsrest.com
Web site: www.4barsrest.com
Freq: Daily
Circ: 45092 Cision Digital Reach
MAGAZINE (ONLINE)
Classical/Choral/Band Music, Jazz & Blues

4rfv.co.uk
988402
Editorial: Unit C3, 6 Westbank Drive, Belfast BT3 9LA Tel: 44 02890 319008
Email: bfvnewscopy@flagshipmedia.co.uk
Web site: www.4rfv.co.uk
Freq: Daily
Circ: 49548 Cision Digital Reach
Editor: Jacqueline Purse
Profile: Website covering film and television industry news. 4rfv.co.uk features industry news and a directory of film and TV industry professionals.
MAGAZINE (ONLINE)
Broadcasting

4thWay
1099501
Email: editorial@4thway.co.uk
Web site: http://www.4thway.co.uk/
Freq: Daily
Circ: 9495 Cision Digital Reach
MAGAZINE (ONLINE)
Personal Finance

4x4 Magazine
982595
Editorial: PO Box 978, Peterborough PE1 9FL Tel: 44 01733 347559
Email: 4x4.ed@kelsey.co.uk
Web site: www.4x4i.com
Freq: Monthly
Circ: 12000 Not Audited
Profile: Magazine containing articles on 4-wheel drive motors, road tests, foreign travel, technical aspects, accessories and competitions. It covers the latest models, hot news from around the world, essential buying, practical information and provides the readers with information about the joys of off-roading. Read by 4-wheel drive owners and enthusiasts.
MAGAZINE
Off-road & 4-Wheel Drive Vehicles

Consumer Magazines

5 STYLE - Your destination for minimal luxury
1059291
Email: hello@5style.com
Web site: https://5style.com/
Freq: Daily
Circ: 10475 Cision Digital Reach
MAGAZINE (ONLINE)
Fashion, Luxury Goods, Travel

50 Plus magazine
985476
Editorial: 6th Floor, 120 Bark Street, Manchester Road, Bolton BL1 2AX
Tel: 44 01204 860194
Email: artwork@mcgrathmedia.co.uk
Web site: http://www.50plusmagazine.co.uk/
Freq: Quarterly Not Audited
Profile: Publication for older people featuring mature lifestyle topics for people who are over 50 or who have retired.
MAGAZINE
Retirement Savings

50Connect.co.uk
983271
Editorial: 2nd Floor, 25 Nutford Place, London W1H 5YQ Tel: 44 02070 341900
Email: editor@olderiswiser.com
Web site: www.50Connect.co.uk
Freq: Daily
Circ: 13159 Cision Digital Reach
MAGAZINE (ONLINE)
Retirement Savings

52 Insights Magazine
1054565
Tel: 44 07729 405889
Email: editorial@52-insights.com
Web site: http://www.52-insights.com/
Freq: Daily
Circ: 17245 Cision Digital Reach
Editor: Michael Simon; Editor: Ari Stein
MAGAZINE (ONLINE)
Classical/Choral/Band Music, Cooking & Baking, Country, Folk, Bluegrass, Dance Music, Fashion, Food, Grocery Stores, Jazz & Blues, Men's Interests, Movies & Video

55PAGES
995291
Editorial: 86 Florence Road, Finsbury Park, London N4 4DP Tel: 44 07956 932679
Email: info@55factory.net
Web site: www.55factory.net
Freq: Semi-Annual
Circ: 21000 Not Audited
MAGAZINE
Art, Classical/Choral/Band Music, Country, Folk, Bluegrass, Dance Music, Fashion, Jazz & Blues, Literature, Music, Photography, Pop Music

5pm.co.uk
1069072
Email: customercare@5pm.co.uk
Web site: http://www.5pm.co.uk/
Freq: Daily
Circ: 146104 Cision Digital Reach
MAGAZINE (ONLINE)
Cooking & Baking, Organic Food, Restaurant Reviews, Vegetarianism & Veganism

5StarWeddingDirectory.com
985598
Editorial: 3 Fallowfield, Stevenage, Stevenage SG2 9PJ Tel: 44 02032 399804
Email: pr@5starweddingdirectory.com
Web site: www.5starweddingdirectory.com
Freq: Daily
Circ: 126344 Cision Digital Reach
Editor: Yasmine Torab
MAGAZINE (ONLINE)
Weddings

60secondreviews.com
999487
Editorial: 145-157 St John St, London EC1 4PW
Web site: http://www.60secondreviews.com
Freq: Daily
Circ: 2678 Cision Digital Reach
MAGAZINE (ONLINE)
Literature, Movies & Video, Restaurant Reviews, Wine/Winemaking

7
988613
Editorial: Prospect House, Rouen Road, Norwich, Norwich NR1 1RE
Tel: 44 01603 664242
Email: seven.jeep@archant.co.uk
Web site: ownersgroup.jeep.com/uk/en
Freq: Semi-Annual
Circ: 55000 Not Audited
MAGAZINE
Automakers

91 Magazine
1075489
Email: info@91magazine.co.uk
Web site: www.91magazine.co.uk/#themagazine
Freq: Semi-Annual Not Audited
MAGAZINE
Crafts, Do-It-Yourself (DIY), Shopping

911 & Porsche World
982599
Editorial: 1 The Alma Building, Brewer Street, Bletchingley, London RH1 4QP
Tel: 44 01883 731150
Email: porscheworld@chpltd.com
Web site: www.911porscheworld.com
Freq: Monthly
Circ: 38500 Not Audited
Editor: Steve Bennett
Profile: Independent magazine focusing on all models of Porsche past and present. Aimed at Porsche owners and enthusiasts.
Ad Rate: Full Page Mono £1150.00
Ad Rate: Full Page Colour £1420.00
MAGAZINE
Antique & Collectible Cars, Automakers, Automotive, Motorsports

9Fi5th (UK)
1098750
Email: olivia.palamountain@9fi5th.com
Web site: http://www.9fi5th.com/
Freq: Quarterly
Circ: 25000 Not Audited
MAGAZINE
Art, Do-It-Yourself (DIY), Luxury Goods, Property Management & Maintenance, Real Estate, Travel

A HOTEL LIFE
1052533
Email: hello@ahotellife.com
Web site: www.ahotellife.com
Freq: Daily
Circ: 12102 Cision Digital Reach
MAGAZINE (ONLINE)
Airline Inflight, Railroad, Travel

A Kentish Ceremony
998685
Editorial: 28 Teville Road, Worthing, Worthing BN11 1UG Tel: 44 07803 613628
Email: kentish.ceremony@kent.gov.uk
Web site: www.akentishceremony.com
Freq: Quarterly
Circ: 10000 Not Audited
Editor: Kirsty Baker
MAGAZINE
Regional General Interest, Weddings

A Little Bird
986659
Email: contact@a-littlebird.com
Web site: www.a-littlebird.com
Freq: Daily
Circ: 13885 Cision Digital Reach
Editor: Clare Coulson
MAGAZINE (ONLINE)
Regional General Interest, Women's Interests

A Place in the Sun
982808
Editorial: 3rd Floor, Thames House, 18 Park Street, London SE1 9EL
Tel: 44 02032 072920
Web site: www.aplaceinthesun.com
Freq: Quarterly
Circ: 35000 Not Audited
Profile: Magazine covering international property news and features, inspirational homes and case studies as well as property related advice.
Ad Rate: Full Page Colour £3995.00
MAGAZINE
Real Estate

A Spokesman Said
1074307
Web site: https://www.aspokesmansaid.com/
Freq: Daily
Circ: 41159 Cision Digital Reach
MAGAZINE (ONLINE)
Consumer Affairs, Personal Finance

A Younger Theatre
988198
Email: features@ayoungertheatre.com
Web site: www.ayoungertheatre.com/
Freq: Daily
Circ: 15314 Cision Digital Reach
MAGAZINE (ONLINE)
Literature, Theater & Performing Arts

AA MOBILITY MAGAZINE
1060372
Email: aasa@aasa.co.za Not Audited
MAGAZINE
Antique & Collectible Cars, Automakers, Automotive, Driving, Motorcycles, Off-road & 4-Wheel Drive Vehicles, Trucks & SUVs

The AA Pub Guide
999031
Editorial: Fanum House, Basing View, Basingstoke RG21 4EA
Tel: 44 01256 491577
Email: lifestyleguides@theaa.com
Web site: http://www.theaa.com/pubs
Freq: Annual
Circ: 16500 Not Audited
MAGAZINE
Restaurant Reviews

The AA Restaurant Guide
999032
Editorial: Fanum House, Basingstoke RG21 4EA
Email: restaurants@theaa.com
Web site: www.theaa.com
Freq: Annual
Circ: 8000 Not Audited
MAGAZINE
Restaurant Reviews

AAA Music
986979
Editorial: 7 Hereford House, Rushcroft Road, Brixton, London SW2 1LQ
Web site: www.aaamusic.co.uk
Freq: Daily
Circ: 9668 Cision Digital Reach
MAGAZINE (ONLINE)
Classical/Choral/Band Music, Country, Folk, Bluegrass, Dance Music, Jazz & Blues, Music, Pop Music, R&B, Urban, World, Rap & Hip Hop, Rock Music

ABC Magazine (Surrey)
982392
Editorial: PO Box 2780, Brighton, Brighton BN1 5QR Tel: 44 01273 542257
Email: surrey@abcmag.co.uk
Web site: http://abcmag.co.uk/digital-editions/
Freq: 3 Times/Year
Circ: 25000 Not Audited
Editor: Rachel Boyle
MAGAZINE
Family & Parenting

ABC Magazine (Sussex)
158628
Owner: Diario ABC, S.L.
Editorial: PO Box 2780, Brighton, Brighton BN1 5QR Tel: 44 01273 542257
Email: sussex@abcmag.co.uk
Web site: http://abcmag.co.uk/digital-editions/
Freq: 3 Times/Year
Circ: 35000 Not Audited
MAGAZINE
Family & Parenting

ABC Magazine (Sussex)
982391
Editorial: PO Box 2780, Brighton, Brighton BN1 5QR Tel: 44 01273 542257
Email: sussex@abcmag.co.uk
Web site: www.abcmag.co.uk
Freq: 3 Times/Year
Circ: 35000 Not Audited
Editor: Rachel Boyle
MAGAZINE
Family & Parenting

ability
985273
Editorial: Pellingbrook, Lewes Road, Scaynes Hill, Haywards Heath RH17 7NG
Tel: 44 01444 831226
Email: john.lamb@abilitymagazine.org.uk
Web site: www.abilitymagazine.org.uk
Freq: Quarterly
Circ: 4500 Not Audited
Editor: John Lamb
Profile: Magazine providing insight into the products, techniques and skills required to deliver systems for users who find it difficult to use IT. Aimed at those who make decisions about IT for disabled people. Regular features: Events; Interview; Resources; Work Study. The site also covers recreational activities for disabled people including disability sports.
Ad Rate: Full Page Mono £850.00
Ad Rate: Full Page Colour £850.00
MAGAZINE
Computers, Disability

Ability Needs
985711
Editorial: 7 Montgomerie Terrace, Ayr KA7 1JL Tel: 44 01292 287574
Email: info@abilityneeds.co.uk
Web site: www.abilityneeds.co.uk
Freq: Quarterly Not Audited
Editor: Karen McNaught
MAGAZINE
Disability

Ability NI / Klassability
984808
Editorial: 7B Lower Ballinderry Road, Upper Ballinderry, Lisburn BT28 2JB
Tel: 44 02892 652773
Email: info@bebmedia.com
Web site: www.bebmedia.com/?P=Ability
Freq: Bi-Monthly
Circ: 6000 Not Audited
MAGAZINE
Disability

able magazine
981819
Editorial: Pentagon Centre, 36-38 Washington Street, Glasgow G3 8AZ
Tel: 44 01412 854000
Email: editor@ablemagazine.co.uk
Web site: www.ablemagazine.co.uk
Freq: Bi-Monthly
Circ: 35000 Not Audited
Editor: Tom Jamison
MAGAZINE
Disability

Abode2
996207
Editorial: Abode House, Aylesbury Road, Aylesbury, Aylesbury HP22 5DW
Tel: 44 01296 381041
Email: editor@abode2.com
Web site: www.abode2.com
Freq: 3 Times/Year
Circ: 50000 Not Audited
MAGAZINE
Real Estate

About Guildford
995787
Editorial: Millmead House, Millmead, London GU2 4BB Tel: 44 01483 505050
Web site: http://www.guildford.gov.uk/aboutguildford
Freq: Quarterly
Circ: 59800 Not Audited
Editor: Angela Lovell
MAGAZINE
Regional General Interest

About Manchester
1101285
Email: nigelbarlow@aboutmanchester.co.uk
Web site: http://aboutmanchester.co.uk/
Freq: Daily
Circ: 17955 Cision Digital Reach
MAGAZINE (ONLINE)
Regional General Interest

About The House
981999
Editorial: Tower House, Fairfax Street, Bristol BS1 3BN
Web site: www.roh.org.uk
Freq: Quarterly

Circ: 30000 Not Audited
MAGAZINE
News & Current Affairs

About Thetford
1065606
Tel: 44 07742 157967
Web site: www.aboutthetfordmagazine.co.uk/
Freq: Monthly
Circ: 12000 Not Audited
Editor: Terry Jermy
MAGAZINE
Regional

About Time. Magazine
987722
Editorial: 3rd Floor, Circus House, 21 Great Titchfield Street, London W1W 8BA
Web site: www.abouttimemagazine.co.uk/
Freq: Daily
Circ: 91491 Cision Digital Reach
MAGAZINE (ONLINE)
Regional General Interest, Restaurant Reviews

AboutMyGeneration.com
983813
Editorial: Kingfisher House, 21-23 Elmfield Road, Bromley BR1 1LT
Tel: 44 02086 507661
Email: editor@aboutmygeneration.com
Web site: www.aboutmygeneration.com
Freq: Daily
Circ: 15958 Cision Digital Reach
Editor: Christine Hurley
MAGAZINE (ONLINE)
Men's Interests, Retirement Savings, Travel, Women's Interests

ABP
987707
Editorial: PO Box 8338, Kirby Muxloe, Leicester LE9 2WW Tel: 44 01162 390519
Web site: www.abpclub.co.uk
Freq: Daily
Circ: 12947 Cision Digital Reach
Profile: Website covering automobile. The ABP website hosts auto body professional guides and advice to its members.
MAGAZINE (ONLINE)
Automotive

Absolute
982536
Editorial: Tower Point MWB, 44 North Road, Brighton, Brighton BN1 1YR
Email: editor@absolutemagazine.co.uk
Web site: www.absolutemagazine.co.uk
Freq: Monthly
Circ: 60000 Not Audited
Profile: Magazine featuring news and features on destinations, locations, events, objects, gadgets, garments and lifestyle.
MAGAZINE
Regional General Interest

Absolute Bridal
986022
Editorial: No 3 Old Park Farm Business Centre, Ford End, Great Waltham CM3 1LN
Tel: 44 01245 895470
Email: editorial@mainweddingsandevents.co.uk
Web site: www.mainweddingsandevents.co.uk
Freq: 3 Times/Year
Circ: 11100 Not Audited
Editor: Anne McFarlane
Profile: Wedding magazine for Essex, Hertfordshire and Suffolk.
MAGAZINE
Weddings

Absolute Gadget
984277
Editorial: 78 Queens Road, Buckhurst Hill, London IG9 5BS
Email: newsdesk@absolutegadget.com
Web site: www.absolutegadget.com
Freq: Daily
Circ: 1518 Cision Digital Reach
Editor: Rene Millman
Profile: Website covering Gadgets. Absolute Gadgets covers the latest UKs gadget news and reviews. It reviews about home cinemas

to entertainment and from camcorders to phones.
MAGAZINE (ONLINE)
Audio Video Trade, Cameras, Consumer Electronics, Electronics, Mobile Electronics, Movies & Video

absolute Herefordshire
1096033
Tel: 44 07943 741827
Email: editor@absoluteherefordshire.co.uk
Web site: http://www.absoluteherefordshire.co.uk/index.html
Freq: Monthly
Circ: 8700 Not Audited
Editor: Bob Calver
MAGAZINE
Regional General Interest

Absolute Horse
983320
Editorial: Home Barn, Grove Hill, Ipswich IP8 3LS Tel: 44 01473 731220
Email: info@ahmagazine.com
Web site: http://www.absolutehorsemagazine.com/
Freq: Monthly
Circ: 8000 Not Audited
Profile: Magazine covering equestrian disciplines with informative articles, local news, results and full show dates listings. Aimed at horse owners and riders aged between 6 and 60 years old.
Ad Rate: Full Page Colour £580.00
MAGAZINE
Equestrian Sports

Absolutely Magazines
997552
Editorial: 1st Floor, 197 City Road, London EC1V 1JN Tel: 44 02077 040588
Email: editorial@zest-media.com
Web site: zest.london
Freq: Monthly
Circ: 311000 Not Audited
MAGAZINE
Luxury Goods, Regional General Interest

ABTA Golf
985258
Editorial: Unit 310, Highgate Studios, 53-79 Highgate Road, London NW5 1TL
Tel: 44 02072 539906
Email: editorial@aplmedia.co.uk
Web site: www.countrybycountry.com/ezines/abta-golf
Freq: Annual
Circ: 55000 Not Audited
Profile: Publication promoting golf clubs, resorts, destinations and hotels, which cater for golfers and their families to the travel trade. First Published in 1997. Read by ABTA travel agents and tour operators as well as those attending the International Golf Travel Market.
Ad Rate: Full Page Colour £8750.00
MAGAZINE
Golf, Travel

ABTA Magazine
981236
Editorial: Unit 310, Highgate Studios, 53-79 Highgate Road, London NW5 1TL
Tel: 44 02072 539906
Email: editorial@abtamagazine.co.uk
Web site: www.countrybycountry.com/ezines/abta-magazine
Freq: Quarterly
Circ: 55000 Not Audited
Profile: Travel trade magazine featuring membership news and travel features. Aimed at members of ABTA, travel agents, tour operators and corporate travel planners.
Ad Rate: Full Page Colour £5950.00
MAGAZINE
Travel

ACCESS-FASHION.COM
999626
Email: info@access-fashion.com
Web site: http://access-fashion.com
Freq: Daily
Circ: 8814 Cision Digital Reach
MAGAZINE (ONLINE)
Classical/Choral/Band Music, Country, Folk, Bluegrass, Dance Music, Fashion, Jazz & Blues, Music, Pop Music, R&B, Urban, World, Rap & Hip Hop, Rock Music

Accounting, Auditing & Accountability Journal
981724
Editorial: Howard House, Wagon Lane, Bingley BD16 1WA Tel: 44 01274 777700
Web site: www.emeraldinsight.com/loi/aaaj
Freq: Bi-Monthly Not Audited
Profile: Journal exploring the philosophies and traditions that underpin the accounting profession. Contains analysis and assessment of practices, new policy alternatives and the impact of accountancy on the socio-economic and political environment. The publication was first published in 1988 and has on average 120 pages per issue. Read by accounting and management researchers, undergraduate and postgraduate students, accounting and auditing policy makers.
MAGAZINE
News & Current Affairs

ACHICA Living
1060249
Editorial: Achica Ltd., ACHICA, Worldstores Company, Brettenham House, 5 Lancaster Place, London WC2E 7EN
Web site: www.achicaliving.com
Freq: Quarterly
Circ: 120000 Not Audited
MAGAZINE
Do-It-Yourself (DIY)

Achieve Magazine
987820
Editorial: 2nd Floor Offices, 17 Mandervell Road, Oadby, Leicester LE2 5LR
Tel: 44 01162 712573
Email: editorial@crossproductions.co.uk
Web site: http://www.achieve-magazine.co.uk/
Freq: Quarterly
Circ: 70000 Not Audited
MAGAZINE
Alumni, Careers, Education, Student Lifestyle, Teachers

Achievers Mindset
1052734
Editorial: 100 Old Hall Street, Bruntwood Plaza, Liverpool L3 9QJ
Email: info@achievers-mindset.com
Web site: www.achievers-mindset.com/
Freq: Monthly
Circ: 521 Cision Digital Reach
MAGAZINE (ONLINE)
Fitness & Exercise, Nutrition

Acoustic
983389
Editorial: Quay House, The Ambury, Bath BA1 1UA Tel: 44 01225 442244
Web site: www.acousticmagazine.com
Freq: Monthly
Circ: 22000 Not Audited
MAGAZINE
Classical/Choral/Band Music, Country, Folk, Bluegrass, Music, Rock Music

AcousticBulletin
997351
Email: acousticbulletin@ecophon.se
Web site: http://www.acousticbulletin.com
Freq: Daily
Circ: 15643 Cision Digital Reach
MAGAZINE (ONLINE)
Music

The Acquirer
985100
Web site: www.livingstonepartners.co.uk
Freq: 3 Times/Year
Circ: 40000 Not Audited
Profile: Corporate finance magazine from Livingstone Partners, covering acquisitions and mergers. Aimed at small to medium businesses.
MAGAZINE
News & Current Affairs

Action On Hearing Loss
981822
Editorial: 19-23 Featherstone Street, London EC1Y 8SL Tel: 44 02072 968000
Web site: www.actiononhearingloss.org.uk
Freq: Quarterly
Circ: 25000 Not Audited
Editor: Dawn Dimond
Profile: Action on Hearing Loss membership magazine covering reviews, news, celebrity interviews and advice on tinnitus and hearing

loss and tinnitus. (The site also covers recreational activities and disability sport) Includes campaigns information, features on new products and the latest on hearing aids.
MAGAZINE
Charitable Foundations, Patient Support

Active Magazine
994965
Editorial: The Grey House, 3 Broad Street, Stamford, Stamford PE9 1PG
Tel: 44 01780 480789
Email: info@theactivemag.com
Web site: www.theactivemag.com
Freq: Monthly
Circ: 11000 Not Audited
MAGAZINE
Fitness & Exercise

Active Traveller
982320
Editorial: 39 Castle Street, Cirencester, Cirencester GL7 1QD Tel: 44 01285 644181
Email: editor@doubleamedia.com
Web site: active-traveller.com
Freq: Annual
Circ: 28000 Not Audited
MAGAZINE
Bicycles, Outdoor Recreation, Travel, Winter Sports

Activityvillage.co.uk
996963
Editorial: Unit 323, Wolsey House, 46 High Street, London KT10 9RB
Web site: www.activityvillage.co.uk
Freq: Daily
Circ: 1962610 Cision Digital Reach
Editor: Lindsay Small
MAGAZINE (ONLINE)
Family & Parenting

Addictive Behaviors
995048
Editorial: The Boulevard, Langford Lane, Kidlington OX5 1GB Tel: 44 01865 843000
Email: millerpm@musc.edu
Web site: www.elsevier.com/wps/find/journaldescription.cws_home/471/description
Freq: Monthly Not Audited
Editor: Peter Miller
MAGAZINE
Community Care (UK), Medicine

Adjacent Open Access
087553
Editorial: Datum House, Electra Way, Crewe Business Park, Crewe, Crewe CW1 6ZF
Tel: 44 08435 044560
Web site: http://www.adjacentopenaccess.org/
Freq: Daily
Circ: 4456 Cision Digital Reach
Editor: Laura Evans
MAGAZINE (ONLINE)
Alternative/Renewable Energy, Automotive, Aviation, Banking, Education, Environment, Government, Government Technology, Public Sector, Railroad

Adoption & Fostering
985351
Editorial: 1 Oliver's Yard, 55 City Road, London EC1Y 1SP Tel: 44 02074 212600
Email: mail@baaf.org.uk
Web site: http://intl-aaf.sagepub.com/
Freq: Quarterly Not Audited
Profile: International journal containing features written by scholars and practitioners in the child care field. Also includes articles on legislation, medical research and book reviews. First published in 1953. Aimed at local authority and voluntary adoption agencies, medical and child care professionals and university social work departments.
Ad Rate: Full Page Mono £440.00
MAGAZINE
Family & Parenting

Adoption Today
998904
Editorial: Units 11 and 12, Vantage Business Park, Bloxham Road, Banbury OX16 9UX
Tel: 44 01295 752240
Email: editor@adoptionuk.org.uk
Web site: www.adoptionuk.org
Freq: Bi-Monthly

Section 4 UK Periodicals Consumer

Consumer Magazines

Circ: 8000 Not Audited
MAGAZINE
Family & Parenting

Adorn Insight
995327
Editorial: Mulberry House, 53 Church Street, Weybridge, London KT13 8DJ
Email: info@adorninsight.com
Web site: www.adorn-london.com
Freq: Daily
Circ: 10650 Cision Digital Reach
MAGAZINE (ONLINE)
Fashion

Advance Production News
987159
Editorial: 54 Dartmouth Court, London SE10 8AT **Tel:** 44 02082 935015
Email: enquiries@crimsonuk.com
Web site: www.crimsonuk.com
Freq: Monthly Not Audited
Editor: Alan Williams
Profile: Magazine giving advance information on television programmes and films about to be made in the UK. Also includes media diary and reviews.
MAGAZINE
Broadcasting, Movies & Video

Advanced Carp Fishing
982169
Editorial: 1 Whittle Close, Daventry, Daventry NN11 8RQ **Tel:** 44 01327 311999
Email: info@dhpub.co.uk
Web site: www.advancedcarpfishing.com
Freq: Monthly
Circ: 16912 Not Audited
Profile: Magazine that focuses on tactical carp angling including articles on equipment, tactics, tips and techniques. Aimed at the more advanced carp angler.
Ad Rate: Full Page Colour £720.00
MAGAZINE
Fishing

Advanced Photographer
985769
Editorial: Bright House, 82 High Street, Sawston, Sawston CB22 3HJ
Tel: 44 01223 499450
Email: vip@absolutephoto.com
Web site: http://www.absolutephoto.com/index.php/magazines/advanced-photographer
Freq: Monthly
Circ: 18000 Not Audited
Editor: William Cheung
Profile: Advanced Photographer informs about latest creative photography trends through pictures, technique advice and product reviews.
Ad Rate: Full Page Colour £1900.00
MAGAZINE
Cameras, Photography

Advanced Photoshop
983369
Editorial: Richmond House, 33 Richmond Hill, Bournemouth BH2 6EZ
Tel: 44 01202 586200
Email: advancedphotoshop@futurenet.com
Web site: www.advancedphotoshop.co.uk
Freq: Monthly
Circ: 14000 Not Audited
Profile: Magazine covering all elements of photoshop with tutorials, interviews, product reviews and artist portfolios.
Ad Rate: Full Page Colour £2300.00
MAGAZINE
Apple, Personal Computers, Visual Arts

Advanced-Television.com
981621
Editorial: Unit N202, Westminster Business Square, 1-45 Durham Street, London SE11 5JH **Tel:** 44 02035 671444
Web site: www.advanced-television.com
Freq: Daily
Circ: 151305 Cision Digital Reach
Profile: Website covering developments in media with a focus on TV, business and technology. Aimed at those involved in the broadcasting industry.
MAGAZINE (ONLINE)
Broadcasting

Adventure Bike Rider
988345
Editorial: 1a/1b Atherstone Barn, Atherstone on Stour, Stratford upon Avon, Stratford-upon-Avon CV37 8NE **Tel:** 44 01789 450000
Web site: adventurebikerider.com
Freq: Bi-Monthly
Circ: 30000 Not Audited
Editor: Bryn Davies
Profile: Magazine covering motorcycles and motorcycle travel. It focuses on the adventure motorcycle and touring motorcycle sectors with a secondary focus on sports tourers and enduro bikes. It includes first person travel stories along with 'where to go' and 'how to do it' style features, indepth bike reviews, accessories, motorcycle clothing and travel and outdoor gear. Articles are generally geared at European and longer haul trips. Aimed at affluent ABC1 males, aged 40+ with a passion for motorcycles.
Ad Rate: Full Page Colour £1595.00
MAGAZINE
Motorcycles

Adventure Cornwall
990375
Editorial: St Joseph's, St Mawgan, Newquay TR8 4ES **Tel:** 44 01209 706315
Email: info@adventure-cornwall.co.uk
Web site: www.adventure-cornwall.co.uk
Freq: Daily
Circ: 1326 Cision Digital Reach
Editor: Elliot Walker
MAGAZINE (ONLINE)
Field Sports

Adventure Travel
982321
Editorial: 1a/1b Atherstone Barns, Atherstone on Stour, Stratford-upon-Avon CV37 8NE **Tel:** 44 01789 450000
Web site: www.atmagazine.co.uk
Freq: Bi-Monthly
Circ: 45000 Not Audited
Profile: Magazine covering worldwide and UK adventure and outdoor travel, specialising in trekking and mountaineering with destination features and information.
Ad Rate: Full Page Colour £2400.00
MAGAZINE
Outdoor Recreation, Travel

The Advertiser
997185
Editorial: 3 Octavian Way, Team Valley Trading Estate, Gateshead NE11 OHZ
Tel: 44 01914 871834
Email: info@teamvalleypublications.co.uk
Web site: www.teamvalleypublications.co.uk/the-advertiser
Freq: Weekly
Circ: 42000 Not Audited
Profile: Website covering news of Buckingham. The website covers local news, property, jobs, business, sport, dating, events and exhibitions.
MAGAZINE
Regional General Interest

Adviser
983965
Editorial: Citizens Advice Specialist Support, Lockside, 5 Scotland Street, Birmingham B1 2RR **Tel:** 44 03000 231231
Web site: www.citizensadvice.org.uk/index/adviser_resources/adviser_magazine.htm
Freq: Bi-Monthly Not Audited
Editor: Martin Coates
Profile: Publication containing a guide to housing, social security, employment, consumer and money advice. Also has Abstracts section which contains summaries of cases including the most important decisions of the Social Security and Child Support Commissions. Aimed at advisors, practitioners and others working in the field of social welfare.
Ad Rate: Full Page Mono £650.00
MAGAZINE
Charitable Foundations

Adviser Business Review
997787
Editorial: 17 Burgess Road, Basingstoke, Basingstoke RG21 5NP
Tel: 44 01444 831620
Email: news@kgrms.co.uk
Web site: http://adviserbusinessreview.com/
Freq: Bi-Monthly Not Audited

Aeon
987004
Editorial: 2402/31 Spring Street, Melbourne VIC Australia 3000, London
Web site: https://aeon.co/
Freq: Daily
Circ: 850716 Cision Digital Reach
Editor: Pamela Weintraub
MAGAZINE (ONLINE)
News & Current Affairs

Aerostat
981891
Editorial: Flat 2, 34-35 High Street, Lewes, Derby BN7 2LU
Web site: bbac.org
Freq: Bi-Monthly
Circ: 2000 Not Audited
Profile: Official journal of the British Balloon and Airship Club containing news and updates from around the world including equipment reviews, adventures, competitions, photographs, items for sale and listings. The publication is published bi-monthly and has 52 glossy full colour pages. Read by balloonists.
Ad Rate: Full Page Colour £640.00
MAGAZINE
News & Current Affairs

Aesthetica
985300
Editorial: PO Box 371, York YO23 1WL
Tel: 44 01904 629137
Email: pr@aestheticamagazine.com
Web site: www.aestheticamagazine.com
Freq: Bi-Monthly
Circ: 60000 Not Audited
Profile: Magazine with current and up-to-date information on British arts and culture including literature, visual arts, music, film and theatre.
Ad Rate: Full Page Colour £975.00
MAGAZINE
Art, Literature, Photography, Theater & Performing Arts, Visual Arts

Affinity Finance International
995968
Editorial: The Office Farringdon, 24 Greville Street, London EC1N 8SS
Tel: 44 02031 782556
Web site: www.finaccord.com
Freq: Daily
Circ: 6741 Cision Digital Reach
Editor: Alan Leach
MAGAZINE (ONLINE)
News & Current Affairs

Affinity Magazine
997142
Editorial: 10 Francis Groves Close, Brickhill, Bedford MK41 7DH **Tel:** 44 01234 962106
Email: affinitymagjanef@gmail.com
Web site: www.affinitymag.co.uk
Freq: Monthly
Circ: 13000 Not Audited
MAGAZINE
Luxury Goods, Regional General Interest

Affinity Weddings
996851
Editorial: 10 Francis Groves Close, Brickhill, Bedford MK41 7DH **Tel:** 44 01234 962106
Email: affinityweddingmag@gmail.com
Web site: http://affinityweddingsmagazine.co.uk/
Freq: Quarterly
Circ: 10000 Not Audited
MAGAZINE
Weddings

Africa Confidential
983422
Editorial: 73 Farringdon Road, London EC1M 3JQ **Tel:** 44 02078 313511
Email: editorial@africa-confidential.com
Web site: www.africa-confidential.com
Freq: Bi-Weekly Not Audited
Editor: Patrick Smith
Profile: Newsletter providing reports, comment and analysis covering the entire African continent. Also reports on international issues affecting the social, political and economic future of Africa. Read

by politicians, officials, business people, military personnel and academics.
MAGAZINE
Africa, International News

Africa Nursing Practice Review
1060561
Tel: 44 27124 812193
Email: elizabethm@foundation.co.za
Freq: Quarterly Not Audited
MAGAZINE
Health & Medicine, Nursing/Nurses

Africa Oil and Gas
985081
Editorial: Fraser Publications Ltd, PO Box 503, Winchester SO23 3DG
Tel: 44 01962 711756
Email: ed@africaoilandgas.com
Web site: www.africaoilandgas.com
Freq: Bi-Weekly Not Audited
Editor: Mark Dixon
Profile: Newsletter covering oil and gas developments and political and economic risks in Africa. Aimed at business development executives in the oil and gas industry.Previous title: Hart Africa Oil and Gas
MAGAZINE
Africa, Oil

Africa Outlook
984747
Editorial: Outlook Publishing, 2nd Floor, Woburn House, 84 St Benedicts Street, Norwich NR2 4AB **Tel:** 44 01603 959655
Web site: www.africaoutlookmag.com
Freq: Monthly
Circ: 165000 Not Audited
MAGAZINE
Airline Inflight, Business, Railroad, Travel

Africa Today
984765
Editorial: Suite 6, Third Floor, AMC House, 12 Cumberland Avenue, London NW10 7QL
Tel: 44 02088 385900
Email: publisher@africatoday.com
Web site: www.africatoday.com
Freq: Bi-Monthly
Circ: 35000 Not Audited
Profile: Magazine concerned with news and business features. Aimed at professionals, decision makers, industrialists, government officials including ministers, civil servants and diplomats, travelling foreign investors in African markets, managers and CEOs.
Ad Rate: Full Page Mono £4700.00
Ad Rate: Full Page Colour £6290.00
MAGAZINE
Africa, International News

AfricaFashion.co.uk
1054536
Email: updateus@africafashion.co.uk
Web site: www.africafashion.co.uk
Freq: Daily
Circ: 867 Cision Digital Reach
Editor: Loreen Brown
MAGAZINE (ONLINE)
Fashion

African Business
984136
Editorial: 7 Coldbath Square, London EC1R 4LQ **Tel:** 44 02078 413210
Email: editorial@icpublications.com
Web site: www.africanbusinessmagazine.com
Freq: Monthly
Circ: 26472 Not Audited
Editor: Lanre Akinola
Profile: Journal specialising in African economic, financial business and development issues.
Ad Rate: Full Page Colour £5800.00
MAGAZINE
Africa, Business, Emerging Markets

African Journal of Economics and Management Studies
997498
Editorial: Emerald Group Publishing, Howard House, Wagon Lane, Bingley BD16 1WA **Tel:** 44 01274 777700
Web site: http://www.emeraldinsight.com/journal/ajems

Freq: Bi-Monthly Not Audited
MAGAZINE
News & Current Affairs

African Wireless Communications Yearbook
996704
Editorial: Brassey House, New Zealand Avenue, London KT12 1QD
Tel: 44 01932 886537
Web site: www.kadiumpublishing.com/yearbook.html
Freq: Annual
Circ: 7000 Not Audited
MAGAZINE
Internet, Mobile Communications

Afridiziak Theatre News
996083
Email: info@afridiziak.com
Web site: www.afridiziak.com
Freq: Daily
Circ: 1211 Cision Digital Reach
Editor: Sophia Jackson
MAGAZINE (ONLINE)
Africa, Theater & Performing Arts

AFRONOIRE
997329
Email: editor@afronoire.com
Web site: www.afronoire.com
Freq: Daily
Circ: 1048 Cision Digital Reach
Editor: Deborah Marie
MAGAZINE (ONLINE)
Beauty & Grooming, Cosmetics, Fashion, Hair

Afropean
997652
Editorial: 6 Woodburn Drive, Belfast BT15 5FR
Email: info@afropean.com
Web site: www.afropean.com
Freq: Daily
Circ: 8185 Cision Digital Reach
Editor: Nat Illumine
MAGAZINE (ONLINE)
Africa

After Nyne Magazine
995536
Editorial: Elm Barn, Manor Farm Barns, Faringdon, Worcester SN7 8ED
Email: features@afternyne.com
Web site: http://afternyne.com/
Freq: Bi-Monthly
Circ: 250000 Not Audited
MAGAZINE
Art, Fashion, Literature, Photography, Visual Arts

Aftermarket
981254
Editorial: 192 High Street, Tonbridge, Gillingham TN9 1BE **Tel:** 44 01732 370340
Email: enquiries@aftermarket.co.uk
Web site: www.aftermarketonline.net
Freq: Monthly
Circ: 23577 Not Audited
Profile: Magazine containing regular technical and training updates, a new product and equipment guide and a free reader enquiry service. First published in 1992, the publication has an average of 60 pages per issue. Press Day: 2 weeks prior to publication. Aimed at wholesalers, franchised dealers, independent garages, fast-fits, body shops and MOT stations primarily for passenger cars and light commercial vehicles.
Ad Rate: Full Page Colour £3517.00
MAGAZINE
Automotive

Age & Ageing
985205
Editorial: 31 St John's Square, London EC1M 4DN
Web site: ageing.oxfordjournals.org
Freq: Bi-Monthly Not Audited
MAGAZINE
News & Current Affairs

The Agility Voice
984833
Editorial: 21 Maes Glas, Coed-Y-Cwm, Pontypridd, Glyncoch CF37 3EJ
Email: editor@agilityclub.org
Web site: www.agilityclub.org

Freq: Monthly
Circ: 2000 Not Audited
Profile: Magazine of the Agility Club covering shows and events in the agility calendar. It contains show news, a show diary, the latest news from the Kennel Club, training articles, show reports and product reviews. Aimed at people competing in dog agility trials. The magazine only accepts press materials relating to dogs.
Ad Rate: Full Page Colour £150.00
MAGAZINE
Nature & Wildlife

Agri Investor
987847
Editorial: 140 London Wall, 6th Floor, London EC2Y 5DN **Tel:** 44 02075 665444
Web site: www.agriinvestor.com
Freq: Daily
Circ: 11758 Cision Digital Reach
MAGAZINE (ONLINE)
News & Current Affairs

aidsmap
998914
Editorial: Acorn House, 314-320 Gray's Inn Road, London WC1X 8DP
Tel: 44 02078 376988
Email: info@nam.org.uk
Web site: www.aidsmap.com
Freq: Daily
Circ: 138305 Cision Digital Reach
MAGAZINE (ONLINE)
AIDS/HIV, Patient Support

Air Cadet Magazine
983160
Tel: 44 01400 261201
Email: editoraircadet@hotmail.com
Web site: www.aircadets.org
Freq: Quarterly
Circ: 30000 Not Audited
Editor: Carol McCombe
MAGAZINE
Armed Forces, Aviation

Air Gun World
982277
Editorial: Air Gun World, Evolution House, 2-6 Easthampstead Road, Wokingham RG40 2EG **Tel:** 44 01189 742500
Web site: www.airgunshooting.org
Freq: Monthly
Circ: 14500 Not Audited
MAGAZINE
Shooting/Guns

Air Gunner
982278
Editorial: Air Gunner / Airgun World, Evolution House, 2-6 Easthampsted Road, Wokingham RG40 2EG
Tel: 44 01189 742500
Web site: www.airgunshooting.org
Freq: Monthly
Circ: 11725 Not Audited
Editor: Phill Price
Profile: Magazine containing gun and kit reviews, features on target shooting, airgun hunting and technical aspects. Aimed at airgun enthusiasts of all ages.
Ad Rate: Full Page Colour £900.00
MAGAZINE
Shooting/Guns

AIR MAIL
981970
Editorial: Unit 3, 5 Sybron Way, Milbrook Industrial Estate, Crowborough, Crowborough TN6 3DZ
Tel: 44 01892 600192
Web site: www.rafatrad.co.uk
Freq: Quarterly
Circ: 52240 Not Audited
Editor: Colin Pullen
Profile: Journal of the Royal Air Force Association, containing articles about the RAF past and present. Read by serving and ex-RAF members.
Ad Rate: Full Page Mono £1082.00
Ad Rate: Full Page Colour £1483.00
MAGAZINE
Armed Forces, Aviation

Aircraft Engineering and Aerospace Technology
980076
Editorial: Howard House, Wagon Lane, Bingley BD16 1WA **Tel:** 44 01274 777700

Web site: www.emeraldinsight.com/journals.htm?issn=0002-2667
Freq: Bi-Monthly Not Audited
Editor: Askin Isikveren
MAGAZINE
News & Current Affairs

airrail NEWS
985220
Editorial: Link House, 140 Tolworth Broadway, Surbiton KT6 7HT
Tel: 44 02083 396124
Email: info@globalairrail.com
Web site: https://www.globalairrail.com/
Freq: Daily
Circ: 7830 Cision Digital Reach
Profile: Website covering airrail NEWS, the first of its kind, a key source of information for all those seeking up-to-date industry news. We believe that railways, airports and airlines should join forces to create an excellent journey experience.
MAGAZINE (ONLINE)
Aviation, Railroad

Airsoft International
983540
Editorial: The Court Yard, Chopdike Drove, Gosberton Clough, Spalding PE11 4JP
Tel: 44 01529 488100
Email: editorial@ai-mag.com
Web site: http://www.ai-mag.com
Freq: Monthly
Circ: 20000 Not Audited
Editor: Ben Webb
Profile: Magazine covering war games with reviews, previews, commentary and discussion of the global world of Airsoft.
Ad Rate: Full Page Colour £750.00
MAGAZINE
Armed Forces

Ala CHAMP Magazine
998135
Editorial: CHAMP STUDIO London, 77 Mildmay Road, London N1 4PU
Email: yo@champ-magazine.com
Web site: champ-magazine.com
Freq: Semi-Annual Not Audited
MAGAZINE
Art, Fashion, Literature, Photography, Visual Arts

Albert
1052695
Tel: 44 01206 863211
Email: su@essex.ac.uk
Web site: www.essexstudent.com
Freq: 3 Times/Year
MAGAZINE
Student Lifestyle

Alice Reviews
998258
Editorial: Flat 14, Kings Court Mansion, 729 Fulham Road, London SW6 5PB
Tel: 44 07880 499432
Email: alice@alice.reviews
Web site: www.alice.reviews
Freq: Daily
Circ: 3802 Cision Digital Reach
Editor: Alice Kahrmann
MAGAZINE (ONLINE)
Art, Beauty & Grooming, Cosmetics, Fashion, Hair, Literature

Alison at Home
996461
Editorial: 3rd Floor, Crown House, 143-147 Regent Street, Westminster, London W1B 4JB
Web site: https://www.alisonathome.com/shop/
Freq: Daily
Circ: 313 Cision Digital Reach
MAGAZINE (ONLINE)
News & Current Affairs

A-LISTED Magazine
987671
Editorial: 24 Elgwood, Northwood HA6 3QS
Email: info@a-listed.co.uk
Web site: www.a-listed.co.uk
Freq: Daily
Circ: 9097 Cision Digital Reach
Editor: Saima Saeed
MAGAZINE (ONLINE)
Beauty & Grooming, Cosmetics, Fashion, Hair, Women's Interests

Alive
983390
Editorial: 142 Fleminghouse Lane, Almondbury, Huddersfield HD5 8UD
Tel: 44 01484 451730
Email: mail@alive.co.uk
Web site: www.alive.co.uk
Freq: Monthly
Circ: 42000 Not Audited
MAGAZINE
Bars, Clubs & Pubs, Comedy, Dance Music, Entertainment, Local Entertainment Guides, Movies & Video, Pop Music, Rap & Hip Hop, Rock Music

All About Family
1074797
Editorial: All About Family, Shakespeare House, 37-39 Shakespeare Street, Southport PR8 5AB **Tel:** 44 01704 531888
Email: info@allabout-family.co.uk
Web site: http://allabout-family.co.uk/
Freq: Quarterly
Circ: 78000 Not Audited
MAGAZINE
Elementary School, Family & Parenting, Teen/Young Adult

All About History
987841
Editorial: Richmond House, 33 Richmond Hill, Bournemouth, Bournemouth BH2 6EZ
Tel: 44 01202 586200
Web site: www.historyanswers.co.uk
Freq: Monthly
Circ: 80347 Not Audited
Editor: Jack Parsons
Profile: Magazine that looks at all aspects of world history, from ancient civilisation to the cold war.
MAGAZINE
History

All About Space
986884
Editorial: Richmond House, 33 Richmond Hill, Bournemouth, Bournemouth BH2 6EZ
Tel: 44 01202 586200
Email: allaboutspace@futurenet.com
Web site: www.spaceanswers.com
Freq: Monthly
Circ: 182075 Not Audited
Editor: Gemma Lavender
Profile: Magazine covering space exploration, astronomy and the universe.
MAGAZINE
Astronomy

All About Symbian
987737
Editorial: Greenbank, Shepherds Hill, Uckfield, Buxted TN22 4PX
Email: rafe@allaboutsymbian.com
Web site: www.allaboutsymbian.com/
Freq: Daily
Circ: 122729 Cision Digital Reach
MAGAZINE (ONLINE)
Mobile Electronics

All About Windows Phone
995548
Editorial: Greenbank, Shepherds Hill, Uckfield, Buxted TN22 4PX
Email: info@allaboutwindowsphone.com
Web site: www.allaboutwindowsphone.com/
Freq: Daily
Circ: 156268 Cision Digital Reach
MAGAZINE (ONLINE)
Mobile Communications, Mobile Electronics

All At Sea (UK)
982203
Editorial: The Binnacle, 33 Victoria Avenue, Hayling Island, Hayling Island PO11 9AJ
Email: editor@allatsea.co.uk
Web site: www.allatsea.co.uk
Freq: Monthly
Circ: 25000 Not Audited
Editor: Jane Hyde
MAGAZINE
Boating & Yachting, Marine & Boat Trade

All Horse
995266
Editorial: Unit 2 Devizes Trade Centre, Hopton Park, Devizes, Devizes SN10 2EH
Tel: 44 01380 730888
Email: sales@redpin.com

Consumer Magazines

Web site: http://www.all-horse.co.uk/
Freq: Monthly
Circ: 7350 Not Audited
Profile: Magazine covering all-round equestrian interests and disciplines. It features articles, product reviews and events. Aimed at riders in the West Midlands.
MAGAZINE
Equestrian Sports

All Ireland Kitchen Guide   981839
Editorial: PO Box 42, Bangor BT19 7AD
Tel: 44 02891 473979
Email: editorial@ihil.net
Web site: www.ihil.net
Freq: Semi-Annual
Circ: 2395 Not Audited
Editor: Margaret Connolly
Profile: Specialist kitchen magazine featuring readers kitchens as well as the latest in kitchen design, appliances and accessories. Aimed at women interested in new ideas for the kitchen.
Ad Rate: Full Page Colour £1600.00
MAGAZINE
Do-It-Yourself (DIY)

All Out Cricket   984476
Editorial: All Out Cricket, TriNorth Ltd, Fourth Floor, Bedster Stand, Kia Oval, Kennington, London SE11 5SS
Tel: 44 02036 965740
Email: comments@alloutcricket.com
Web site: http://www.alloutcricket.com/cricket//
Freq: Monthly
Circ: 25000 Not Audited
Editor: Phil Walker
Profile: Magazine focused on the international and domestic cricket scene, aiming to bring in-depth discussion and insight on the game. The magazine is a 116 page monthly publication with 'a vibrant and enthusiastic celebration of our great summer pastime'. Aimed at followers of cricket aged from 15 years old.
Ad Rate: Full Page Colour £1595.00
MAGAZINE
Cricket

All Things Local   997565
Editorial: 74 Woodhouse Road, Kilburn, Belper, Kilburn DE56 0NA
Tel: 44 01332 882882
Web site: www.allthingslocal.co.uk
Freq: Bi-Monthly
Circ: 27000 Not Audited
MAGAZINE
Regional General Interest

All Together NOW!   982573
Editorial: The Bradbury Centre, Youens Way, Liverpool L14 2EP
Tel: 44 01512 300307
Email: news@alltogethernow.org.uk
Web site: http://www.alltogethernow.org.uk/
Freq: Bi-Monthly
Circ: 110000 Not Audited
Editor: Tom Dowling
Profile: Magazine providing news and information for people whose lives are affected by disability and, or, age. The magazine covers disability issues including those with wide ranging health problems, the elderly and their carers. Sections on employment, education, training, housing, welfare benefits, holidays, transport, motoring, aids and equipment, the arts, leisure and recreation, and sport.First published in 2005, the publication has an average of 32 pages per issue. Aimed at disabled people, the elderly, their families, carers and professionals.
Ad Rate: Full Page Mono £1800.00
Ad Rate: Full Page Colour £3000.00
MAGAZINE
Disability

All4Brass   1064099
Email: news@all4brass.com
Web site: http://www.all4brass.com/
Freq: Daily

Circ: 10646 Cision Digital Reach
MAGAZINE (ONLINE)
Music

AllAboutCareers.com   985504
Editorial: 170 Shepherdess Walk, Angel Wharf, Angel, London N1 7JL
Tel: 44 02036 514919
Email: billy.sexton@allaboutgroup.org
Web site: www.allaboutcareers.com
Freq: Daily
Circ: 137048 Cision Digital Reach
Editor: Jay Collins
MAGAZINE (ONLINE)
Careers

allaboutfinancecareers.com
    988173
Editorial: 170 Shepherdess Walk, Angel Wharf, Angel, London N1 7JL
Tel: 44 02036 514919
Email: hello@allaboutgroup.org
Web site: http://www.allaboutfinancecareers.co.uk/
Freq: Daily
Circ: 2043 Cision Digital Reach
Editor: Jay Collins
MAGAZINE (ONLINE)
Careers

allaboutlaw.co.uk   998900
Editorial: 170 Shepherdess Walk, Angel Wharf, Angel, London N1 7JL
Tel: 44 02036 514919
Email: hello@allaboutgroup.org
Web site: www.allaboutlaw.co.uk
Freq: Daily
Circ: 80526 Cision Digital Reach
Editor: Jay Collins
MAGAZINE (ONLINE)
Careers, Legal Services

allaboutschoolleavers.co.uk
    987875
Editorial: 170 Shepherdess Walk, Angel Wharf, Angel, London N1 7JL
Tel: 44 02036 514919
Email: hello@allaboutgroup.org
Web site: www.allaboutschoolleavers.co.uk
Freq: Daily
Circ: 15764 Cision Digital Reach
Editor: Jay Collins
MAGAZINE (ONLINE)
Careers

Allaboutshipping.co.uk   988866
Email: info@allaboutshipping.co.uk
Web site: http://www.allaboutshipping.co.uk
Freq: Daily
Circ: 11705 Cision Digital Reach
MAGAZINE (ONLINE)
Marine & Boat Trade, Shipping & Warehousing

Allergy Newsletter   983705
Editorial: PO Box 278, Twickenham TW1 4QQ **Tel:** 44 02088 924949
Email: help@actionagainstallergy.org
Web site: https://actionagainstallergy.org/
Freq: 3 Times/Year
Circ: 1500 Not Audited
Editor: Patricia Holt Schooling
Profile: Newsletter containing news, views and tips for AAA members, plus conference reports and articles by allergists. Covers the whole spectrum of medical research, diagnostic practice and treatment of allergies and allergy-related illness. Regular feature on products and services to help the allergy sufferer. Aimed at allergy sufferers and health professionals dealing with allergic illness.
Ad Rate: Full Page Colour £350.00
MAGAZINE
Allergies, Patient Support

Allergy UK   986613
Web site: www.allergyuk.org
Freq: Daily
Circ: 110663 Cision Digital Reach

Profile: Website covering medical conditions. The allergy.co.uk website shares the latest news and information on allergies.
MAGAZINE (ONLINE)
News & Current Affairs

allgigs.co.uk   995898
Editorial: 3 Silverdale Drive, London SE9 4DH
Email: enquiries@allgigs.co.uk
Web site: www.allgigs.co.uk
Freq: Daily
Circ: 113580 Cision Digital Reach
Editor: Daniel O'Connell
MAGAZINE (ONLINE)
Classical/Choral/Band Music, Country, Folk, Bluegrass, Dance Music, Entertainment, Jazz & Blues, Local Entertainment Guides, Pop Music, R&B, Urban, World, Rap & Hip Hop, Rock Music

Alliance   983653
Editorial: 1st Floor, 15 Prescott Place, London SW4 6BS **Tel:** 44 02070 628920
Email: alliance@alliancemagazine.org
Web site: www.alliancemagazine.org
Freq: Quarterly
Circ: 10000 Not Audited
MAGAZINE
Charitable Foundations

AllinLondon.co.uk   985462
Tel: 44 08444 774789
Email: contact@allinlondon.co.uk
Web site: www.allinlondon.co.uk
Freq: Daily
Circ: 753655 Cision Digital Reach
Editor: Paul Carter
MAGAZINE (ONLINE)
Bars, Clubs & Pubs, Comedy, Entertainment, Local Entertainment Guides, Movies & Video, Regional General Interest, Travel

allmediascotland.com   990367
Editorial: Third Floor, 44 Hanover Street, Edinburgh EH2 2DR **Tel:** 44 01316 249854
Email: info@allmediascotland.com
Web site: www.allmediascotland.com
Freq: Daily
Circ: 20088 Cision Digital Reach
MAGAZINE (ONLINE)
Advertising Industry, Branding, Broadcasting, Graphic Design, Marketing, Media & Communications, Photography, Publishing

allmygoodness.com   996951
Email: devoogdpublishing@gmail.com
Web site: www.allmygoodness.com
Freq: Daily
Circ: 647 Cision Digital Reach
Editor: Charlotte de la Rambelje-de Voogd
MAGAZINE (ONLINE)
Airline Inflight, Alcohol & Spirits, Bars, Clubs & Pubs, Beer, Beverages, Cooking & Baking, Ethical/Moral Issues, Family & Parenting, Fashion, Food

Allotment & Leisure Gardener
    981953
Editorial: 1 Rothwell Grange Court, Rothwell Road, Kettering, Rothwell NN16 8XF
Tel: 44 01536 266576
Email: natsoc@nsalg.org.uk
Web site: www.nsalg.org.uk
Freq: Quarterly
Circ: 14000 Not Audited
Editor: Karen Maher
Profile: Magazine of the National Society for Allotment and Leisure Gardeners containing news, letters and topical articles. Read by leisure and allotment gardeners.
Ad Rate: Full Page Mono £550.00
Ad Rate: Full Page Colour £700.00
MAGAZINE
Gardening

AllWaysTraveller   999016
Editorial: Hampton House, 77 The Ridgeway, North Chingford, London E4 6QW
Web site: www.allwaystraveller.co.uk
Freq: Daily

Circ: 521 Cision Digital Reach
MAGAZINE (ONLINE)
Travel

Aloud.com   998439
Editorial: Unit 1, Castle Quay, Castlefield, Manchester M15 4PR **Tel:** 44 02072 955000
Web site: www.aloud.com
Freq: Daily
Circ: 11398 Cision Digital Reach
MAGAZINE (ONLINE)
Bars, Clubs & Pubs, Dance Music, Entertainment, Local Entertainment Guides, Rap & Hip Hop, Rock Music

Alpha Man   995267
Email: editorial@alphamanmag.com
Web site: http://alphamanmag.com/
Freq: Monthly
Circ: 1735 Cision Digital Reach
MAGAZINE (ONLINE)
Fitness & Exercise, Men's Interests

AlphaGalileo   986072
Editorial: AlphaGalileo Foundation, Coppergate House, Suite 112, 16 Brune Street, London E1 7NJ
Web site: www.alphagalileo.org
Freq: Daily
Circ: 160998 Cision Digital Reach
MAGAZINE (ONLINE)
Art, Business, Science

alphr   988929
Editorial: Alphr, 31 - 32 Alfred Place, London WC1E 7DP **Tel:** 44 02079 076000
Web site: http://www.alphr.com/
Freq: Daily
Circ: 1190358 Cision Digital Reach
MAGAZINE (ONLINE)
Computers, Data Management, Electronics, Industry, Internet, Mobile Communications, Software

Alter The Press   985608
Email: news@alterthepress.com
Web site: www.alterthepress.com
Freq: Daily
Circ: 8885 Cision Digital Reach
MAGAZINE (ONLINE)
Rock Music

The Alternative Guide   982865
Editorial: 18 Magdalen Road, Hastings TN37 6EP **Tel:** 44 01424 465543
Email: david@altguide.com
Web site: www.altguide.com
Freq: Quarterly
Circ: 120000 Not Audited
Editor: David Baird
Profile: Guide to alternative and complementary medicine, spirituality and self development. Contains a comprehensive listing of local events, plus information on a variety of therapies and details of the therapists who provide them. First published in 1994. Aimed at health store consumers and those with an interest in complementary medicine and self development. Distributed throughout natural health and whole food stores, hospitals and libraries.Regular features: Events Events listings in London, Kent, Sussex and The New Forest.
MAGAZINE
Alternative Medicine

Alternative Vision   998821
Editorial: 60 Hampton Street, Tetbury, Tetbury GL8 8LE **Tel:** 44 07758 236264
Email: trigger@alternativevision.co.uk
Web site: www.alternativevision.co.uk
Freq: Daily
Circ: 752 Cision Digital Reach
Editor: Trigger AV
MAGAZINE (ONLINE)
Rock Music

ALT-MU   997245
Email: editor@altmumagazine.co.uk
Web site: www.altmumagazine.co.uk
Freq: Quarterly
Circ: 8000 Not Audited

Editor: Jennifer Le Roux
MAGAZINE
News & Current Affairs

Altrincham Today   1055149
Web site: altrincham.today
Freq: Daily
Circ: 14880 Cision Digital Reach
Editor: David Prior
MAGAZINE (ONLINE)
Regional

AltSounds   998961
Editorial: PO BOX 10003, East Leake, Loughborough LE11 9GT
Tel: 44 07894 240751
Web site: http://watch.altsounds.com/
Freq: Daily
Circ: 71 Cision Digital Reach
MAGAZINE (ONLINE)
Rock Music

ALVAR   995170
Email: hello@alvarmagazine.com
Web site: www.alvarmagazine.com
Freq: Semi-Annual Not Audited
MAGAZINE
Fashion

AM   981255
Editorial: Media House, Lynchwood, Peterborough PE2 6EA
Tel: 44 01733 468000
Email: am@bauermedia.co.uk
Web site: www.am-online.com
Freq: Monthly
Circ: 10331 Not Audited
Profile: Journal covering business information for the UK automotive industry. First published in 1990. Read by senior personnel of franchised dealers, vehicle manufacturers, independent car dealers, independent service and repair garages and motor parts distributors.
Ad Rate: Full Page Colour £5120.00
MAGAZINE
Automotive

AM Magazine   1075515
Tel: 44 01865 400400
Email: hqstaff@amoc.org
Web site: http://www.amoc.org/
Freq: Quarterly
Circ: 5900 Not Audited
Editor: David Lewington
MAGAZINE
Antique & Collectible Cars, Automakers

AM The Aston Martin Magazine   984417
Editorial: 46-48 East Smithfield, London E1W 1AW **Tel:** 44 02074 261010
Email: hello@iln.co.uk
Web site: www.astonmartin.com/en/live/magazine
Freq: Quarterly
Circ: 44000 Not Audited
Profile: Customer magazine covering Aston Martins. It contains interviews, interesting drives, style, gastronomy, travel and sporting pursuits. First published in 2006.
MAGAZINE
Automakers, Luxury Goods, Men's Interests

AM2   997687
Editorial: Portmill House, Portmill Lane, Hitchin, Hitchin SG5 1DJ
Tel: 44 01462 431385
Email: newsdesk@leisuremedia.com
Web site: http://am2.jobs/
Freq: Weekly Not Audited
MAGAZINE
Bars, Clubs & Pubs, Fitness & Exercise, Hotels/Motels, Travel

Amanda Magazine   1052689
Email: letters@amandamagazine.com
Web site: www.amandamagazine.com/
Freq: Quarterly

Editor: Amanda Amanda
MAGAZINE
Alternative Medicine, Cooking & Baking, Do It Yourself (DIY), Fashion, Nutrition, Organic Food, Restaurant Reviews, Travel, Women's Interests

Amanecer   1061887
Tel: 44 52668 8180814
Email: revistaamanecer@hotmail.com
Web site: http://www.amanecersinaloa.com
Freq: Daily Not Audited
MAGAZINE
International News, National News

Amateur Gardening   981954
Editorial: Time Inc. UK, Westover House, West Quay Road, Poole BH15 1JG
Tel: 44 01202 440840
Email: amateurgardening@timeinc.com
Web site: www.amateurgardening.com
Freq: Weekly
Circ: 30060 Not Audited
Editor: Tim Rumball
Profile: Magazine containing practical gardening tips, celebrity garden experts, news, letters, advice on gardening problems, a kitchen garden section, making growing fruit and vegetables straightforward, and a tea break puzzles page. Read by those interested in plants and gardening.
Ad Rate: Full Page Mono £2160.00
Ad Rate: Full Page Colour £2825.00
MAGAZINE
Gardening

Amateur Photographer (Online)   989634
Tel: 44 01252 555000
Web site: http://www.amateurphotographer.co.uk
Circ: 584734 Cision Digital Reach
MAGAZINE (ONLINE)
News & Current Affairs

Ambit   981871
Email: contact@ambitmagazine.co.uk
Web site: www.ambitmagazine.co.uk
Freq: Quarterly
Circ: 3000 Not Audited
Profile: Literary and artwork quarterly magazine covering poems, short stories, reviews and art. First published in 1959, the publication has an average of 96 pages per issue. Read by art and literature enthusiasts.
Ad Rate: Full Page Colour £280.00
MAGAZINE
Art, Literature

Amelia's magazine   984068
Editorial: 44 Goldman Close, London E2 6EF
Web site: www.ameliasmagazine.com
Freq: Daily
Circ: 10690 Cision Digital Reach
MAGAZINE (ONLINE)
Art, Fashion, Photography, Visual Arts

The American (UK)   998760
Editorial: Old Byre House, East Knoyle, Salisbury, Salisbury SP3 6AW
Tel: 44 01747 830520
Email: editor@theamerican.co.uk
Web site: www.theamerican.co.uk
Freq: Bi-Monthly
Circ: 25000 Not Audited
MAGAZINE
Americas

American in Britain   982593
Editorial: PO Box 921, London SM1 2WB
Tel: 44 02086 610186
Email: helen@theamericanhour.com
Web site: www.americaninbritain.co.uk
Freq: Quarterly
Circ: 20000 Not Audited
Profile: Magazine covering news, features and places to visit in the UK. Includes articles on finance, education, property, theatre and women's clubs news. First published in 1983, the publication has an average of 40 pages per issue. Aimed at Americans living in Britain.
Ad Rate: Full Page Mono £2200.00

MAGAZINE
Americas, Expatriates

Amor Magazine   996820
Editorial: Amor Magazine Ltd, Unit 3A, Juno Way, London SE14 5RW
Tel: 44 02086 918191
Email: info@amormagazine.co.uk
Web site: www.amormagazine.co.uk
Freq: Quarterly
Circ: 10000 Not Audited
Editor: Ruby Moore
MAGAZINE
Women's Interests

An Essex Wedding   984161
Editorial: Pantile House, Newland Drive, Witham, Witham CM8 2AP
Tel: 44 01376 611000
Email: editor@anessex.wedding
Web site: anessexwedding.co.uk
Freq: Bi-Monthly
Circ: 10000 Not Audited
Profile: Magazine covering all aspects of weddings including venues, fashion, real weddings, honeymoons, grooms, cakes, catering, news, events, give-aways, letters, questions and answer. Aimed at brides and grooms in the Essex area and surrounds.
Ad Rate: Full Page Colour £900.00
MAGAZINE
Weddings

AN Magazine   990377
Editorial: S19, Toffee Factory, Lower Steenbergs Yard, Newcastle NE1 2DF
Tel: 44 03003 300706
Email: edit@a-n.co.uk
Web site: http://www.a-n.co.uk
Freq: Daily
Circ: 82378 Cision Digital Reach
Profile: Magazine containing features on visual arts practice, reviews of artist-led events, jobs and opportunities for artists, directory of art services suppliers, and extensive exhibition listings. Aimed at visual and applied artists, photographers and arts professionals.
Ad Rate: Full Page Colour £1555.00
MAGAZINE (ONLINE)
Art, Literature, Photography, Theater & Performing Arts, Visual Arts

Andover & Villages   1104809
Editorial: Suite 450 Andover House, George Yard, Andover SP10 1PB
Tel: 44 01264 738066
Email: editor@andoverandvillages.co.uk
Web site: www.andoverandvillages.co.uk
Freq: Daily
Circ: 69751 Cision Digital Reach
Editor: Anna Hall
MAGAZINE (ONLINE)
Regional, Regional General Interest

Andy's Amazing Adventures   1059128
Editorial: Vineyard House, 44 Brook Green, London W6 7BT **Tel:** 44 02071 505000
Web site: www.bbc.co.uk/cbeebies/shows/andys-wild-adventures
Freq: Monthly
Circ: 41821 Not Audited
Editor: Ruth Cassidy
MAGAZINE
Crafts, Nature & Wildlife

Angelina Ballerina   995798
Editorial: Unit 16 Greenway Farm, Bath Road, Wick, Bristol BS30 5RL
Tel: 44 01179 373003
Email: info@kennedypublishing.co.uk
Web site: http://www.kennedypublishing.co.uk/magazines/angelina-ballerina-magazine
Freq: Monthly
Circ: 40000 Not Audited
MAGAZINE
Teen/Young Adult, Trading Cards & Comics

angels & urchins   984139
Editorial: A47 The Ugli Campus, 56 Wood Lane, London W12 7SB
Tel: 44 02087 411035
Web site: www.angelsandurchins.co.uk
Freq: Quarterly
Circ: 50000 Not Audited
Editor: Annie Reid
Profile: Magazine covering day trips, shopping, restaurant reviews, nannies, children's party ideas, parenting resources and pregnancy advice as well as travel ideas with and without children, homeopathic remedies, book and film and an extensive kids' London section including drama, sports, music and movement classes. Aimed at parents of children aged under 10 years old in London.
Ad Rate: Full Page Colour £1500.00
MAGAZINE
Family & Parenting, Local Entertainment Guides

Angler's Mail   982170
Editorial: Pinehurst 2, Pinehurst Road, Farnborough Business Park, Farnborough, London GU14 7BF **Tel:** 44 01252 555000
Email: anglersmail@timeinc.com
Web site: www.anglersmail.co.uk
Freq: Weekly
Circ: 19306 Not Audited
Editor: Tim Knight
Profile: Magazine focusing on coarse and sea fishing events, performances and tackle. First published in 1964 with and average of 72 pages per issue, the magazine comes out every Tuesday. Every issue contains the week's must-read news coverage, including the biggest fish caught and where to catch them. The magazine also contains instruction features full of top tips, where to fish advice, reviews of the latest tackle, match fishing results and the best advice for the carp and pike specialist as well as features and true stories! Aimed at coarse anglers and some sea anglers.
Ad Rate: Full Page Colour £1500.00
MAGAZINE
Fishing

Angling International   1069071
Editorial: Angling International, 4 Milnyard Square, Peterborough PE2 6GX
Tel: 44 01733 392970
Email: enquiries@angling-international.com
Web site: www.angling-international.com
Freq: Monthly
Circ: 10000 Not Audited
Editor: Anthony Hawkswell
Profile: Magazine for the global fishing tackle industry and global angling trade.
MAGAZINE
Fishing

Angling Times   982171
Editorial: Media House, Peterborough Business Park, Peterborough PE2 6EA
Tel: 44 01733 468000
Email: newsdesk@anglingtimes.co.uk
Web site: www.gofishing.co.uk
Freq: Weekly
Circ: 25878 Not Audited
Editor: Steve Fitzpatrick
Profile: Publication covering angling news and features on coarse and sea fishing. Includes the latest match results and product reviews. First published in 1953, the publication has an average of 56 pages per issue. Press Day on Tuesday. Aimed at those with a general interest in fishing.
Ad Rate: Full Page Colour £2500.00
MAGAZINE
Fishing

AniMagic   996758
Editorial: Marlborough House, Headley Road, Grayshott, Hindhead GU26 6LG
Tel: 44 01428 601020
Email: animagic@djmurphy.co.uk
Web site: djmurphy.co.uk/publications/magazines/animagic-magazine/
Freq: Monthly Not Audited
Editor: Penny Rendall
MAGAZINE
Preschool, Teen/Young Adult

Section 4 UK Periodicals Consumer

Consumer Magazines

Animal Action
982461

Editorial: Wilberforce Way, Southwater, Horsham, Southwater RH13 9RS
Tel: 44 03001 230392
Email: animalaction@rspca.org.uk
Web site: www.rspca.org.uk
Freq: Bi-Monthly
Circ: 13784 Not Audited
Profile: Official magazine of the RSPCA. Contains news stories relating to animal welfare, environmental issues and topical campaigns. Also includes celebrity interviews, competitions and a creature feature page.
Ad Rate: Full Page Colour £1850.00
MAGAZINE
Charitable Foundations, Nature & Wildlife

Animals and You
982449

Editorial: 80 Kingsway East, Glasgow DD4 8SL **Tel:** 44 01382 223131
Email: animalsandyou@dcthomson.co.uk
Web site: www.animalsandyou.co.uk
Freq: Monthly
Circ: 33236 Not Audited
MAGAZINE
Nature & Wildlife, Teen/Young Adult

Animals Matter
982007

Editorial: King's Bush Farm, London Road, Godmanchester, Godmanchester PE29 2NH
Tel: 44 08442 488181
Email: info@woodgreen.org.uk
Web site: www.woodgreen.org.uk
Freq: No Frequency Established
Circ: 32000 Not Audited
Profile: Magazine about the work of the Wood Green Animal Shelters and issues concerned with animal welfare.
Ad Rate: Full Page Colour £1200.00
MAGAZINE
Nature & Wildlife

Animated
999459

Editorial: LCB Depot, 31 Rutland Street, Leicester LE1 1RE **Tel:** 44 01162 533453
Email: info@communitydance.org.uk
Web site: www.communitydance.org.uk/animated-magazine.html
Freq: 3 Times/Year
Circ: 2000 Not Audited
MAGAZINE
Theater & Performing Arts

annabelkarmel.com
996762

Editorial: 18A Pindock Mews, London W9 2PY **Tel:** 44 02072 893808
Email: sarah.hartland@annabelkarmel.com
Web site: www.annabelkarmel.com
Freq: Daily
Circ: 124401 Cision Digital Reach
MAGAZINE (ONLINE)
Family & Parenting, Nutrition

Anorak magazine
983596

Editorial: Unit L/M - Reliance Wharf, 2-10 Hertford Road, London N1 5EW
Tel: 44 07967 174954
Email: anorakmagazine@gmail.com
Web site: www.anorakmagazine.com
Freq: Quarterly
Circ: 20000 Not Audited
MAGAZINE
Elementary School

AnOther Mag
995810

Editorial: 3rd Floor, 2 Arundel Street, London WC2R 3DA **Tel:** 44 02073 360766
Web site: http://www.anothermag.com/
Freq: Semi-Annual
Circ: 134000 Not Audited
MAGAZINE
Fashion, Women's Interests

Another Man
983068

Editorial: 3rd Floor, 2 Arundel Street, London WC2R 3DA **Tel:** 44 02073 360766
Email: info@dazedmedia.com
Web site: www.anothermag.com
Freq: Semi-Annual
Circ: 88517 Not Audited
Profile: In 2005 AnOther Man was launched to cater to an expanding menswear market

and resurgence of creativity in men's fashion. Aimed at modern thinking, culture savvy and stylish men.
Ad Rate: Full Page Mono £14932.00
Ad Rate: Full Page Colour £14932.00
MAGAZINE
Fashion, Men's Interests

Anthropology & Medicine
995765

Editorial: UCL Division of Psychiatry, 67 - 73 Riding House Street, 2nd Floor, Charles Bell House, Oxford W1W 7EJ
Tel: 44 02070 176000
Email: anthmed@ucl.ac.uk
Web site: www.tandf.co.uk/journals/titles/13648470.asp
Freq: 3 Times/Year Not Audited
MAGAZINE
Medicine

Antiquarian Horology
987214

Editorial: New House, High Street, Ticehurst, Wadhurst TN5 7AL
Tel: 44 01580 200155
Email: secretary@ahsoc.org
Web site: www.ahsoc.org
Freq: Quarterly Not Audited
Profile: Journal containing information concerning antique clocks, watches and other time telling instruments, plus the proceedings of the Antiquarian Horological Society.
Ad Rate: Full Page Mono £156.00
MAGAZINE
Antiques/Collectibles

Antique Collecting
981867

Editorial: Sandy Lane, Old Martlesham, Woodbridge, Woodbridge IP12 4SD
Tel: 44 01394 389950
Email: magazine@antique-acc.com
Web site: www.antique-collecting.co.uk
Freq: Monthly
Circ: 5000 Not Audited
Editor: Georgina Wroe
Profile: Magazine containing articles and features on antiques with an emphasis on practical information. Aimed at those with a serious interest in antiques.Regular features: Auction Calendar; Fairs Calendar; News and Views Contains details of forthcoming antiques-related exhibitions and events.
Ad Rate: Full Page Mono £400.00
Ad Rate: Full Page Colour £650.00
MAGAZINE
Antiques/Collectibles

Antiques are Green
997130

Tel: 44 01494 673277
Email: info@antiquesaregreen.org
Web site: www.antiquesaregreen.org
Freq: Daily
Circ: 4618 Cision Digital Reach
MAGAZINE (ONLINE)
Antiques/Collectibles

Antiques Diary
981868

Editorial: PO Box 6271, Christchurch, Christchurch BH23 9BF
Tel: 44 01425 279304
Email: info@antiquesdiary.com
Web site: www.antiquesdiary.com
Freq: Bi-Monthly
Circ: 5000 Not Audited
Editor: Peter Allwright
Profile: Regional guide to antique fairs, markets and auctions. Aimed at collectors, organisers and participants in fairs, markets and auctions in the UK.
Ad Rate: Full Page Mono £170.00
Ad Rate: Full Page Colour £212.50
MAGAZINE
Antiques/Collectibles

Antiques News and Fairs
982823

Tel: 44 01666 504651
Email: mail@antiquesnewsandfairs.co.uk
Web site: http://www.antiquesnews.co.uk/news.php
Freq: Daily
Circ: 10415 Cision Digital Reach
Profile: Website reporting on the news and views of the British antiques trade.
MAGAZINE (ONLINE)
Antiques/Collectibles

Antiques, Collectables, Memorabilia
997778

Editorial: Suite 6B(i), Britannia House, Leagrave Road, Luton LU3 1RJ
Tel: 44 01582 488385
Email: info@mediachameleon.com
Web site: www.antiqueswebsite.co.uk
Freq: Annual
Circ: 19000 Not Audited
MAGAZINE
Antiques/Collectibles

Antiquity
985835

Editorial: Department of Archaeology, Durham University, South Road, Durham DH1 3LE **Tel:** 44 01913 341125
Email: editor@antiquity.ac.uk
Web site: www.antiquity.ac.uk
Freq: Quarterly
Circ: 2000 Not Audited
Editor: Chris Scarre
Profile: International archaeological journal containing in-depth reports, news, projects, book reviews and heritage issues. Includes articles on new methods and technologies, new research and archaeological debate. Aimed at students, academics, researchers, amateurs and those involved or interested in archaeology.
Ad Rate: Full Page Mono £365.00
MAGAZINE
Antiques/Collectibles, History

Antiviral Therapy
998950

Editorial: Admiral House, 76-78 Old Street, London EC1V 9AZ **Tel:** 44 02073 980700
Web site: www.intmedpress.com/index.cfm?pid=12
Freq: Bi-Monthly Not Audited
MAGAZINE
Medicine

AOL
986468

Editorial: Shropshire House, 11-20 Capper Street, London WC1E 6JA
Tel: 44 02074 921000
Web site: aol.co.uk
Freq: Daily
Circ: 9749808 Cision Digital Reach
MAGAZINE (ONLINE)
International News, National News, Regional

Apollo
981872

Editorial: 22 Old Queen Street, London SW1H 9HP **Tel:** 44 02079 610150
Web site: www.apollo-magazine.com
Freq: Monthly
Circ: 10000 Not Audited
Editor: Thomas Marks
Profile: Magazine covering everything from antiquities to contemporary work containing articles on fine art, sculpture, renaissance sculpture, design and antiques as well as exclusive new photographic portraits and Galleries reviews. Aimed at those interested in art and antiques, art galleries and museums.Regular features: Around the Galleries A quick round-up of the interesting commercial exhibitions that are about to open.; Collectors Focus An in-depth feature on a particular area of the art market.; Ten to Catch The top ten events of interest taking place over the next month.; The Art Market An overview of what is up and coming on the art market and a look at recent significant sales and commercial exhibitions.
Ad Rate: Full Page Colour £1840.00
MAGAZINE
Art

The Apprenticeship Guide
997110

Editorial: 9 Cardale Court, Cardale Park, Harrogate HG3 1RY **Tel:** 44 01423 851150
Email: editor@apprenticeshipguide.co.uk
Web site: http://www.apprenticeshipguide.co.uk/
Freq: Annual
Circ: 9000 Not Audited
Editor: Sophie Dilley
MAGAZINE
Careers

AppSpy
1053998

Editorial: The House, Kelston Park, Bath BA1 9AE
Email: news@appspy.com
Web site: www.appspy.com
Freq: Daily
Circ: 91729 Cision Digital Reach
MAGAZINE (ONLINE)
Computer & Video Games

AQUILA
982462

Editorial: Studio 2, Willowfield Studios, 67a Willowfield Road, Eastbourne, Eastbourne BN22 8AP **Tel:** 44 01323 431313
Email: aquila.editor@btconnect.com
Web site: aquila.co.uk
Freq: Monthly
Circ: 12500 Not Audited
MAGAZINE
Elementary School

The Arab Horse News
998450

Editorial: Agriculture House, Charnham Lane, Hungerford RG17 0EY
Tel: 44 01672 521411
Web site: www.arabhorsesociety.org
Freq: Semi-Annual
Circ: 2200 Not Audited
MAGAZINE
Equestrian Sports

The Arab Weekly
1054228

Editorial: Al Arab Publishing Centre Headquarter (London), Kensington Centre, 66 Hammersmith Road, London W14 8UD
Tel: 44 02076 023999
Email: editor@thearabweekly.com
Web site: www.thearabweekly.com
Freq: Weekly
Circ: 15613 Cision Digital Reach
MAGAZINE (ONLINE)
International News

Arabisk
1073409

Editorial: Arabisk London, 47 – 49 Park Royal Road, London NW10 7LQ
Tel: 44 02080 900464
Email: info@arabisklondon.com
Web site: http://www.arabisklondon.com/
Freq: Monthly
Circ: 4000 Not Audited
MAGAZINE
Asia, Business, Small and Medium Business

Arabs Today
995720

Editorial: 11-12 Southcombe Street, West Kensington, London W14 0RA
Web site: www.arabstoday.net
Freq: Daily
Circ: 751864 Cision Digital Reach
MAGAZINE (ONLINE)
International News

The Arbuturian
985060

Editorial: 1A Cleveland Square, London W2 6DH
Email: info@arbuturian.com
Web site: www.arbuturian.com
Freq: Daily
Circ: 14789 Cision Digital Reach
Editor: Rebecca Lipkin
Profile: Website covering lifestyle. THE ARBUTURIAN website shares the latest news and information on food, style, culture, fashion, travel and lifestyle.
MAGAZINE (ONLINE)
Alcohol & Spirits, Antiques/Collectibles, Art, Bars, Clubs & Pubs, Beer, Beverages, Cooking & Baking, Fashion, Literature, Luxury Goods

Area
996120

Editorial: The Penthouse, 10 Evelaw House, 43 Worcester Street, Stourbridge DY8 1AT
Tel: 44 01384 837362
Web site: www.areamagazine.wordpress.com
Freq: Monthly Not Audited
Profile: Free magazine covering culture, lifestyle and events in West Midlands and Birmingham.

Ad Rate: Full Page Colour £220.00
MAGAZINE
Regional General Interest

Armenian Voice
982592

Editorial: Hayashen, 105a Mill Hill Road, Acton, London W3 8JF
Tel: 44 02089 924621
Email: info@caia.org.uk
Web site: www.caia.org.uk
Freq: Semi-Annual
Circ: 3000 Not Audited
Editor: Misak Ohanian
MAGAZINE
Africa, Americas, Asia, Australia, Ethnic & Multicultural, Europe, Expatriates, Politics, Social Issues

The Armourer
998865

Editorial: The Maltings, West Street, Bourne, Bourne PE10 9PH **Tel:** 44 01778 392077
Email: armourer@warnersgroup.co.uk
Web site: www.armourer.co.uk
Freq: Bi-Monthly Not Audited
MAGAZINE
Armed Forces

Army & You
984035

Editorial: Army Families Federation, IDL 414, Floor 1, Zone 6, Ramillies Building, Marlborough Lines, Monxton Road, Andover SP11 8HJ **Tel:** 44 01264 382315
Email: editor@aff.org.uk
Web site: www.armyandyou.co.uk
Freq: Quarterly
Circ: 45000 Not Audited
Editor: Charlotte Eadie
MAGAZINE
Charitable Foundations, Defense & National Security

Aromatherapy Times
999436

Editorial: 146 South Ealing Road, Ealing, London W5 4QJ **Tel:** 44 02085 672243
Email: office@ifaroma.org
Web site: www.ifaroma.org/us/home
Freq: Quarterly
Circ: 5000 Not Audited
Editor: Lauren Allen
MAGAZINE
Alternative Medicine

Around Arena
985364

Editorial: 70 Copthorne Avenue, Bromley, London BR2 8NN
Web site: www.arena.org.uk
Freq: Quarterly Not Audited
Profile: Newsletter containing industry and business news for the hospitality sector. Aimed at members of Arena, including operators, wholesalers, distributors, manufacturers and service providers.
MAGAZINE
News & Current Affairs

Around Town (UK)
987753

Editorial: Graphic House, Radford Way, Billericay, Billericay CM12 0DX
Tel: 44 01277 658444
Email: sales@aroundtownmagazines.co.uk
Web site: www.aroundtownmagazines.co.uk
Freq: Monthly
Circ: 50000 Not Audited
MAGAZINE
News & Current Affairs

Arrowwords
998937

Editorial: Academic House, 24-28 Oval Road, London NW1 7DT
Tel: 44 02072 418000
Email: arrowwords@bauermedia.co.uk
Web site: http://www.puzzlemagazines.co.uk/arrowwords
Freq: Monthly
Circ: 121000 Not Audited
MAGAZINE
Games, Competitions & Events

Ars Technica UK
998008

Editorial: 13 Hanover Square, London W1S 1HN
Web site: http://arstechnica.co.uk/

Freq: Daily
Circ: 1333000 Cision Digital Reach
MAGAZINE (ONLINE)
Computers, Data Management, Electronics, Government Technology, Industry, Internet, Mobile Communications, Mobile Electronics, Security & Security Systems, Software

Arsenal Magazine
982252

Editorial: Highbury House, 75 Drayton Park, London N5 1BU **Tel:** 44 02077 044130
Email: magazine@arsenal.co.uk
Web site: www.arsenal.com/magazine
Freq: Monthly
Circ: 20000 Not Audited
Editor: Andy Exley
MAGAZINE
Soccer

Art + Framing Today
984262

Editorial: 2 Wyo House, 6 Enterprise Way, London SW18 1FZ **Tel:** 44 02073 816616
Email: info@fineart.co.uk
Web site: www.fineart.co.uk
Freq: Bi-Monthly
Circ: 2000 Not Audited
Editor: Lynn Jones
Profile: Publication containing features relevant to the art trade, such as gallery design, picture selling and framing methods. Read by gallery owners, framers, artists, publishers, fine art printers, frame manufacturers, designers and trade suppliers.
Ad Rate: Full Page Colour £1820.00
MAGAZINE
Art

Art Buyer
987664

Editorial: Naishville, 1 Churchgates, The Wilderness, Berkhamstead, Berkhamsted HP4 2UB **Tel:** 44 01442 289930
Email: tracey@lemapublishing.co.uk
Web site: www.artbuyermag.com
Freq: 3 Times/Year
Circ: 11500 Not Audited
Editor: Tracey Bearton
Profile: Magazine devoted to art, design and image licensing. Includes company profiles and information from licensors and agents involved in marketing all types of art-based properties around the world. Aimed at decision makers in the art licensing industry. Regular features: Featured Artist; Your Opinion
Ad Rate: Full Page Colour £1300.00
MAGAZINE
Art, Retail Management

Art Mag
986647

Editorial: Suite 603/603A, St. Margaret's House, 151 London Road, Edinburgh EH7 6AE **Tel:** 44 01316 610765
Email: editor@artmag.co.uk
Web site: www.artmag.co.uk
Freq: Bi-Monthly
Circ: 30200 Not Audited
Editor: Ian Sclater
MAGAZINE
Art, Crafts

Art Monthly
981873

Editorial: 4th Floor, 28 Charing Cross Road, London WC2H 0DB **Tel:** 44 02072 400389
Email: info@artmonthly.co.uk
Web site: www.artmonthly.co.uk
Freq: Monthly
Circ: 5000 Not Audited
Editor: Patricia Bickers
Profile: Magazine covering modern and contemporary visual arts, interviews with leading artists, profiles, art law, news, reports from salesrooms and book reviews. Read by artists, critics, curators, art historians, students, dealers, art administrators and those interested in the arts.
Ad Rate: Full Page Mono £1330.00
MAGAZINE
Art

The Art Newspaper
981886

Editorial: 70 South Lambeth Road, London SW8 1RL **Tel:** 44 02034 169000

Email: theartnewspaper@dsbnet.co.uk
Web site: www.theartnewspaper.com
Freq: Monthly
Circ: 23000 Not Audited
Editor: Javier Pes
Profile: Newspaper covering art news and visual culture worldwide. Reviews and previews of exhibitions, books, archaeology, sculpture, renaissance sculpture and conservation, plus in-depth discussion of the art market, dealers and galleries from around the world. Founded in 1990, The Art Newspaper is a monthly publication based in London and New York. Read by artists, private collectors, art dealers, auctioneers, art historians, museum curators, trustees and directors.
Ad Rate: Full Page Colour £5200.00
MAGAZINE
Art

Art Nouveau Greece
1062039

Email: douka.artnouveau@gmail.com
Web site: http://www.artnouveau.com.gr
Freq: Daily
Circ: 4112 Cision Digital Reach
MAGAZINE (ONLINE)
Antiques/Collectibles, Art, Arts, Interior Design, Literature, Photography, Theater & Performing Arts, Visual Arts

The Art of Beauty & Well-being
1053287

Tel: 44 01843 830249
Email: info@theartofbeautyandwellbeing.co.uk
Web site: www.theartofbeautyandwellbeing.co.uk/
Freq: Bi-Monthly
Circ: 90000 Not Audited
Editor: Suki Henderson
MAGAZINE
Beauty & Grooming, Cosmetics, Hair

The Art of Bespoke
999608

Web site: theartofbespoke.com
Freq: Daily
Circ: 8277 Cision Digital Reach
MAGAZINE (ONLINE)
Do-It-Yourself (DIY), Luxury Goods, Property Management & Maintenance

Art Quarterly
981874

Editorial: 2 Granary Square, King's Cross, London N1C 4BH **Tel:** 44 02072 254856
Email: artquarterly@artfund.org
Web site: www.artfund.org
Freq: Quarterly
Circ: 85000 Not Audited
Profile: General interest visual arts magazine covering art, design, sculpture, renaissance sculpture and photography. Read by members of the National Art Collections Fund, interested public and art world institutions and research students.
Ad Rate: Full Page Colour £2595.00
MAGAZINE
Antiques/Collectibles, Art, Arts, Literature, Photography, Theater & Performing Arts, Visual Arts

Arthritis Today (UK)
981818

Editorial: Copeman House, St Mary's Court, St Mary's Gate, Chesterfield, Chesterfield S41 7TD **Tel:** 44 03007 900400
Email: enquiries@arthritisresearchuk.org
Web site: www.arthritisresearchuk.org
Freq: Quarterly
Circ: 100000 Not Audited
Editor: Jane Tadman
MAGAZINE
Health & Medicine, Rheumatology

Arthur's Place
987766

Email: editor@arthursplace.co.uk
Web site: http://arthursplace.co.uk/
Freq: Daily
Circ: 11979 Cision Digital Reach
Editor: Sarah Woodhead
MAGAZINE (ONLINE)
Men's Interests, Rheumatology, Women's Interests

The Artist
1101517

Tel: 44 01580 763315
Email: info@tapc.co.uk
Web site: www.painters-online.co.uk
Freq: Monthly
Circ: 29000 Not Audited
Editor: Sally Bulgin
MAGAZINE
Art

Artists & Illustrators
982797

Editorial: Jubilee House, 2 Jubilee Place, London SW3 3TQ **Tel:** 44 02073 493700
Email: info@artistsandillustrators.co.uk
Web site: www.artistsandillustrators.co.uk
Freq: Monthly Not Audited
MAGAZINE
Crafts

Artlyst
1100169

Editorial: 10 - 12 New College Parade, Finchley Road, London NW3 5EP
Tel: 44 02074 490695
Email: press@artlyst.com
Web site: www.artlyst.com
Freq: Daily
Circ: 145521 Cision Digital Reach
Editor: Paul Carter-Robinson
MAGAZINE (ONLINE)
Art, Visual Arts

ArtNewsLetter
998678

Editorial: The Red House, Portsmouth Road, Milford, Godalming GU8 5HJ
Tel: 44 01483 422602
Email: david.coombs@artnewsletter.com
Web site: www.artnewsletter.com
Freq: Bi-Monthly
Circ: 1251 Cision Digital Reach
Editor: David Coombs
MAGAZINE (ONLINE)
Art

artrepublic.com
997735

Editorial: Unit 12, St Joseph's Business Park, Hove BN3 7HG **Tel:** 44 03456 461234
Email: support@artrepublic.com
Web site: artrepublic.com
Freq: Daily
Circ: 56816 Cision Digital Reach
MAGAZINE (ONLINE)
Art

ArtReview
981875

Editorial: ArtReview Ltd., 1 Honduras Street, London EC1Y 0TH **Tel:** 44 02074 908138
Web site: www.artreview.com
Freq: Bi-Monthly
Circ: 50000 Not Audited
Editor: Mark Rappolt
Profile: Magazine covering all aspects of the British and international, modern and contemporary, visual art scene including 20th and 21st century arts news and information, with features every month. Aimed at gallery visitors, art buyers and collectors as well as those interested in art for business and pleasure.Alternative Title: Art Review Regular features: Consumed Article covering good buys in the modern and contemporary visual art world.; News Feature covering new events in the art world.
Ad Rate: Full Page Colour £2500.00
MAGAZINE
News & Current Affairs

Artrocker
998679

Editorial: 43 Chute House, Stockwell Park Road, Brixton, London SW9 0DW
Email: info@artrockermagazine.com
Web site: www.artrockermagazine.com
Freq: Daily
Circ: 75000 Not Audited
Editor: Tom Fawcett
MAGAZINE
Dance Music, Pop Music, Rap & Hip Hop, Rock Music

Arts & Collections
984138

Editorial: Suite 2, 143 Caledonian Road, King's Cross, London N1 0SL
Tel: 44 02078 709000
Email: editorial@damsonmedia.com

Consumer Magazines

Web site: www.artsandcollections.com
Freq: Quarterly
Circ: 35000 Not Audited
MAGAZINE
Antiques/Collectibles, Art

Arts Award Voice   1054278
Editorial: Trinity College London, AMP House, Dingwall Road, London CR0 2LX
Tel: 44 02078 206178
Email: hello@artsawardvoice.com
Web site: http://www.artsawardvoice.com/
Freq: Daily
Circ: 13512 Cision Digital Reach
MAGAZINE (ONLINE)
Antiques/Collectibles, Art, Arts, Literature, Photography, Theater & Performing Arts, Visual Arts

Arts Co   995494
Editorial: 3 Campden Hill Square, London W8 7LB
Email: info@arts-co.com
Web site: http://arts-co.com
Freq: Daily
Circ: 1012'Cision Digital Reach
MAGAZINE (ONLINE)
Antiques/Collectibles, Art, Arts, Literature, Photography, Theater & Performing Arts, Visual Arts

Arts Culture   997009
Editorial: 19 Gloucester Road, Newton Abbot, Newton Abbot TQ12 1AY
Tel: 44 01626 202202
Email: info@newsandmediarepublic.org
Web site: artsculture.newsandmediarepublic.org
Freq: Daily
Circ: 69 Cision Digital Reach
Editor: Lee Morgan
MAGAZINE (ONLINE)
Antiques/Collectibles, Art, Arts, Literature, Photography, Theater & Performing Arts, Visual Arts

Arts Industry   1013040
Editorial: Reydon Business Park, Fountain Way, Reydon, Southwold IP18 6DH
Tel: 44 01502 725862
Email: editors@artsindustry.com
Web site: www.artsindustry.co.uk
Freq: Monthly
Circ: 1000 Not Audited
MAGAZINE
Art, Literature, Photography, Theater & Performing Arts, Visual Arts

The Arts Shelf   996621
Email: info@theartsshelf.com
Web site: www.theartsshelf.com
Freq: Daily
Circ: 14606 Cision Digital Reach
Editor: Adam Gonet
MAGAZINE (ONLINE)
Art, Entertainment, Literature, Movies & Video, Theater & Performing Arts, Visual Arts

Artsbeat   995375
Editorial: 19 Nottingham Road, Belper, Belper DE56 1JG
Email: editor@arts-beat.co.uk
Web site: www.artsbeatblog.com
Freq: Monthly
Circ: 7000 Not Audited
Editor: Amanda Penman
MAGAZINE
Antiques/Collectibles, Art, Arts, Literature, Photography, Regional, Regional General Interest, Theater & Performing Arts, Visual Arts

ArtsProfessional   984087
Editorial: PO Box 1010, Histon, Cambridge CB24 9WH Tel: 44 01223 200200
Email: editors@artsprofessional.co.uk
Web site: www.artsprofessional.co.uk
Freq: Daily
Circ: 19093 Cision Digital Reach
Editor: Liz Hill
Profile: Magazine containing news and features relating to the management,

administration, funding and development of the arts sector across all art forms and types of organisation. Read by managers, administrators and officers at all levels in arts and related organisations.
Ad Rate: Full Page Mono £1290.00
Ad Rate: Full Page Colour £1350.00
MAGAZINE (ONLINE)
Antiques/Collectibles, Art, Arts, Literature, Photography, Theater & Performing Arts, Visual Arts

Artwork   983918
Editorial: P.O Box 3, Ellon AB41 9EA
Tel: 44 01651 842429
Email: artwork@famedram.com
Web site: www.artwork.co.uk
Freq: Quarterly
Circ: 100000 Not Audited
Editor: Bill Williams
Profile: Publication providing a guide to the arts including interviews, reviews and opinions plus a comprehensive listing of arts event throughout the North of Britain. Read by those interested in arts policy exhibitions and events in Scotland and the North of England.
MAGAZINE
Art

artymagazines.com   998268
Editorial: 12 Kemp Street, Brighton BN1 4EF
Tel: 44 01273 670426
Email: info@artymagazines.com
Web site: www.artymagazines.businesscatalyst.com
Freq: Daily
Circ: 13600 Cision Digital Reach
MAGAZINE (ONLINE)
Art

ASBO Magazine   1095949
Web site: www.asbomagazine.com
Freq: Daily
Circ: 11259 Cision Digital Reach
MAGAZINE (ONLINE)
Beauty & Grooming, Cosmetics, Dance Music, Fashion, Hair, Jazz & Blues, Men's Interests, Pop Music, Rap & Hip Hop, Rock Music

Ashdown Forest Living   995306
Tel: 44 01342 300152
Email: info@ashdownforestliving.co.uk
Web site: http://www.ashdownforestliving.co.uk/
Freq: Monthly
Circ: 18500 Not Audited
Editor: Tally Bhangu
MAGAZINE
Regional

Asia Attractions   995020
Editorial: 137 Newshaw Lane, Hadfield, Glossop SK13 2AT Tel: 44 01457 865500
Web site: www.asiaattractions.net
Freq: Monthly
Circ: 3000 Not Audited
MAGAZINE
Travel

Asian Art Newspaper   981876
Editorial: PO Box 22521, London W8 4GT
Tel: 44 02072 296040
Email: info@asianartnewspaper.com
Web site: www.asianartnewspaper.com
Freq: Monthly
Circ: 10000 Not Audited
Editor: Sarah Callaghan
Profile: Magazine covering Asian and Islamic art and culture worldwide.
Ad Rate: Full Page Mono £1145.00
Ad Rate: Full Page Colour £2195.00
MAGAZINE
Art

Asian Bride   982417
Editorial: Santon House, 53-55 Uxbridge Road, London W5 5SA
Tel: 44 08445 855508
Email: editorial@prama.co.uk
Web site: http://www.asianbride.me/
Freq: Bi-Monthly
Circ: 23819 Not Audited

Profile: Magazine featuring bridal and wedding ideas including a directory of services and products for planning your ideal wedding. Aimed at women in the Asian community.
Ad Rate: Full Page Colour £3600.00
MAGAZINE
Asia, Weddings

Asian Correspondent   986837
Editorial: Hybrid News Limited, Colston Tower Level 9, Colston Street, Bristol BS1 4UX Tel: 44 01172 443750
Email: fbm@hybridnewsgroup.com
Web site: http://asiancorrespondent.com
Freq: Daily
Circ: 714936 Cision Digital Reach
MAGAZINE (ONLINE)
Asia, International News, National News

Asian Culture Vulture   997364
Email: editor@asianculturevulture.com
Web site: http://asianculturevulture.com/
Freq: Daily
Circ: 13511 Cision Digital Reach
Editor: Sailesh Ram
MAGAZINE (ONLINE)
Antiques/Collectibles, Art, Arts, Asia, Literature, Photography, Theater & Performing Arts, Visual Arts

Asian Environmental Technology   987698
Editorial: Oak Court Business Centre, Sandridge Park, Porters Wood, St Albans, London AL3 6PH Tel: 44 01727 858840
Email: info@aet-pub.com
Web site: http://www.envirotech-online.com/ejournal/asian-environmental-technology/249
Freq: Quarterly
Circ: 20012 Not Audited
Profile: Asian Environmental Technology is a subscription only magazine, contacting news and features on the latest developments in pollution monitoring, water and waste management, air analysis and gas detection. The publication was first published in 1996 and has on average 60 pages per issue. Aimed at environmental scientists and decision makers throughout Asia and Australasia.
Ad Rate: Full Page Colour £4550.00
MAGAZINE
Electronics, Environment

Asian Express (National)   988105
Editorial: St Andrews House, St Andrew's Street, Leeds LS3 1LS Tel: 44 08703 608606
Email: editor@asianexpress.co.uk
Web site: www.asianexpress.co.uk
Freq: Weekly
Circ: 250000 Not Audited
MAGAZINE
Asia

Asian Express (Yorkshire)   996494
Editorial: St Andrews House, St Andrew's Street, Leeds LS3 1LS Tel: 44 08703 608606
Email: editor@asianexpress.co.uk
Web site: www.asianexpress.co.uk
Freq: Weekly
Circ: 42000 Not Audited
MAGAZINE
Asia

The Asian Post   995982
Editorial: 779 High Road, Leytonstone, London E11 4QS Tel: 44 02085 392434
Email: editor@theasianpost.co.uk
Web site: www.theasianpost.co.uk
Freq: Weekly
Circ: 45000 Not Audited
Profile: Newspaper covering news on British Asians of South Asian origins with a focus on entertainment followed by British Asian News. Aimed at Asian communities in the UK.
Ad Rate: Full Page Mono £2800.00
Ad Rate: Full Page Colour £3600.00
MAGAZINE
Asia

Asian Wealth Magazine   995344
Tel: 44 02084 068992
Email: info@media-36.com
Web site: www.asianwealthmag.co.uk
Freq: Quarterly
MAGAZINE
Business, Corporate Responsibility, Luxury Goods, Small and Medium Business

Asiana Wedding   982418
Editorial: Asiana House, 8 Quebec Wharf, 14 Thomas Road, London E14 7AF
Tel: 44 02075 379618
Email: info@asiana.tv
Web site: http://www.asianamag.com/
Freq: Quarterly
Circ: 61800 Not Audited
Editor: Anisha Vasani
Profile: Magazine covering wedding fashion, tradition, bridal beauty, planning and advice and the big day. Aimed at Asian brides to be.
Ad Rate: Full Page Colour £4000.00
MAGAZINE
Asia, Weddings, Women's Interests

Asiana.TV   982365
Editorial: Unit 8, Quebec Wharf, 14 Thomas Road, London E14 7AF
Tel: 44 02075 379618
Email: anisha@asiana.tv
Web site: www.asiana.tv/
Freq: Daily
Circ: 8311 Cision Digital Reach
Editor: Anisha Vasani
MAGAZINE (ONLINE)
Asia, Women's Interests

AsiansUK   995546
Editorial: Suite 2, The Wellington, 78 High Street, Uttoxeter ST14 7JD
Tel: 44 08454 671994
Email: admin@asiansuk.com
Web site: http://www.asiansuk.com
Freq: Quarterly
Circ: 20000 Not Audited
MAGAZINE
Asia

ASOS.com   983760
Editorial: Greater London House, Hampstead Road, London NW1 7FB
Tel: 44 02077 561000
Email: press@asos.com
Web site: http://www.asos.com/
Freq: Quarterly
Circ: 453300 Not Audited
MAGAZINE
Fashion

Aspect County   982535
Editorial: 6 Old Ladies Court, High Street, Battle, Battle TN33 0AH
Tel: 44 01424 777444
Email: mail@aspect-county.co.uk
Web site: www.aspect-county.co.uk
Freq: Monthly
Circ: 26000 Not Audited
Editor: Cindy-Lou Dale
Profile: Magazine covering motoring, property, travel, music, fashion & beauty, wining & dining, antiques, homes & gardens, history and rural issues.The publication was first published in 1989 and has on average 32 pages per issue, with a variable press day. Aimed at 28 to 60 year olds in West Kent and East Sussex.
Ad Rate: Full Page Colour £650.00
MAGAZINE
Regional General Interest

Aspirational   985477
Editorial: Barrington House, Leake Road, Costock, Loughborough LE12 6XA
Tel: 44 01509 852927
Web site: aspirational.uk.com
Freq: Semi-Annual
Circ: 20000 Not Audited
Editor: Matthew Hayes
MAGAZINE
Luxury Goods, Regional, Regional General Interest

Aspire
985950

Editorial: 52 Grosvenor Gardens, London SW1W 0AU **Tel:** 44 02078 814853
Email: aspire@travelweekly.co.uk
Web site: http://www.aspiretravelclub.co.uk
Freq: Quarterly
Circ: 6000 Not Audited
Profile: Magazine covering property, products and people involved in the hospitality industry.
Ad Rate: Full Page Colour £2500.00
MAGAZINE
Luxury Goods, Travel

Assembly Automation
996348

Editorial: Howard House, Wagon Lane, Bingley BD16 1WA **Tel:** 44 01274 777700
Web site: www.emeraldinsight.com/loi/aa
Freq: Quarterly Not Audited
MAGAZINE
News & Current Affairs

Asset Intelligence - CEASED
997465

Editorial: Upper Ground Floor South, 200 Aldersgate Street, London EC1A 4HD
Web site: http://www.assetinternational.com/
Freq: Weekly Not Audited
MAGAZINE
Equities, Financial Markets

The Assignment Report
998031

Editorial: 11 Main Street, Caldecote, Cambridge CB23 7NU **Tel:** 44 01223 263880
Email: subs@theassignmentreport.com
Web site: www.theassignmentreport.com
Freq: Monthly Not Audited
Editor: Ed Tranham
MAGAZINE
Disability, Education, Higher Education, Preschool, Schools & Institutions, Students

ASTA network
995468

Editorial: Unit 310, Highgate Studios, 53-79 Highgate Road, London NW5 1TL
Tel: 44 02072 539906
Email: editorial@aplmedia.co.uk
Web site: aplmedia.co.uk/portfolio/astanetwork/
Freq: Quarterly
Circ: 22000 Not Audited
Editor: Zane Henry
MAGAZINE
Travel

Asthma magazine
985170

Editorial: Asthma UK, 18 Mansell Street, London E1 8AA **Tel:** 44 02077 864900
Email: editor@asthma.org.uk
Web site: www.asthma.org.uk
Freq: 3 Times/Year
Profile: Magazine with the latest news on asthma care and developments in research. Also includes handy hints on coping and living with asthma and news on the charity's campaigning and other activities. The publication was first published in 1993 and has on average 36 pages per issue. Aimed at members of Asthma UK and people with an interest in asthma.
Ad Rate: Full Page Colour £1150.00
MAGAZINE
Charitable Foundations, Respiratory Diseases

Astonishing Spider-Man
1094457

Editorial: Brockbourne House, 77 Mount Ephraim, Tunbridge Wells, Tunbridge Wells TN4 8BS **Tel:** 44 01892 500100
Email: astonspid@panini.co.uk
Web site: http://www.paninicomics.co.uk/web/guest/catalogues/collection_detail?id=42259
Freq: Bi-Weekly
Circ: 6800 Not Audited
Editor: Brady Webb
MAGAZINE
Cartoons, Trading Cards & Comics

Astronomy Now
981889

Editorial: PO Box 175, Tonbridge, Tonbridge TN10 4ZY **Tel:** 44 01732 446111
Email: admin10018@astronomynow.com
Web site: www.astronomynow.com
Freq: Monthly Not Audited
Editor: Keith Cooper
Profile: Magazine covering astronomy. It contains a news section, book reviews, beginners' guide and features on observing, cosmology, the history of astronomy and space science. Read by professional and amateur astronomers, students and star gazers.
Ad Rate: Full Page Colour £950.00
MAGAZINE
Astronomy

astrostyle.com
1054114

Email: astrotwins@astrostyle.com
Web site: http://astrostyle.com/
Freq: Daily
Circ: 482459 Cision Digital Reach
MAGAZINE (ONLINE)
Astrology & Parapsychology

at home
983697

Editorial: Central House, 1 Ballards Lane, Finchley Central, London N3 1LQ
Tel: 44 02084 443401
Web site: www.athomemagazine.co.uk
Freq: Monthly
Circ: 250000 Not Audited
Editor: Rashmi Madan
Profile: Magazine covering travel, interiors, property at home and abroad, cookery, gardening, DIY, parenting and relationships as well as advice each month, from a leading celebrity on their field of expertise. Aimed at women aged 25 to 55 years old.
MAGAZINE
Beauty & Grooming, Celebrities, Cooking & Baking, Cosmetics, Do-It-Yourself (DIY), Family & Parenting, Fashion, Fitness & Exercise, Food, Gardening

At The Table
996093

Web site: www.atthetable.co.uk
Freq: Daily
Circ: 12101 Cision Digital Reach
MAGAZINE (ONLINE)
News & Current Affairs

Athletics Weekly
982189

Editorial: 22 Long Acre, Covent Garden, London WC2E 9LY
Email: officemanager@athleticsweekly.com
Web site: www.athleticsweekly.com/
Freq: Weekly
Circ: 15000 Not Audited
Editor: Jason Henderson
Profile: Magazine covering track and field events, fell racing, race walking, road running, cross-country and Olympic news. The publication was first published in 1945 and has, on average, 52 pages per issue. Aimed at athletes, coaches, fans and administrators.
Ad Rate: Full Page Colour £1500.00
MAGAZINE
Sports

Atlas
1074793

Email: info@theatlasmagazine.com
Web site: www.theatlasmagazine.com
Freq: Semi-Annual
Profile: Magazine focusing on artists work containing prints and drawings. Aimed at those interested in art.
MAGAZINE
Art, Fashion, Movies & Video

ATPWorldTour.com
997586

Editorial: 79 High Street, Thames Ditton, London KT7 0SF
Email: info@atpmedia.tv
Web site: www.atpworldtour.com
Freq: Daily
Circ: 8792195 Cision Digital Reach
MAGAZINE (ONLINE)
Racquet Sports

Attire Accessories
984442

Editorial: Pantile House, Newland Drive, Witham, Witham CM8 2AP
Tel: 44 01376 514000
Email: info@attireaccessories.com
Web site: www.attireaccessories.com
Freq: Bi-Monthly
Circ: 6500 Not Audited
Profile: Magazine providing product and market analysis and the latest trends with information on trade shows, financial and legal matters and reviews on new and innovative products. Aimed at buyers in independent fashion shops, jewellers, boutiques, shoe shops, bag shops, accessory shops and buyers in national fashion chains and department stores.
Ad Rate: Full Page Colour £1475.00
MAGAZINE
Fashion

ATTIRE Bridal
984584

Editorial: Pantile House, Newlands Drive, Witham, Witham CM8 2AP
Tel: 44 01376 514000
Email: editor@attirebridal.com
Web site: www.attirebridal.com
Freq: Bi-Monthly
Circ: 3050 Not Audited
Profile: Magazine covering fashion, visual merchandising, trader show previews and industry news. Aimed at bridal retailers.
Ad Rate: Full Page Colour £1475.00
MAGAZINE
Weddings

Attitude
983449

Editorial: 33 Pear Tree Street, London EC1V 3AG
Email: attitude@attitude.co.uk
Web site: www.attitude.co.uk
Freq: Monthly
Circ: 60000 Not Audited
Profile: Lifestyle magazine covering movies, fashion, music and book reviews. It includes grooming, technology, music, clubbing, health, fitness, travel, advice, celebrities and entertainment features. Aimed primarily, but not exclusively, at gay men.
Ad Rate: Full Page Colour £3500.00
MAGAZINE
LGBT

Attractions Management
981046

Editorial: Portmill House, Portmill Lane, Hitchin SG5 1DJ **Tel:** 44 01462 431385
Email: newsdesk@leisuremedia.com
Web site: www.attractionsmanagement.com
Freq: Quarterly
Circ: 70176 Not Audited
Profile: Publication covering business issues in the theme parks, science centres, zoos and aquariums, visitor attractions, museums and heritage, galleries and waterpark markets. First published in 1995, the publication has an average of 100 pages per issue. Aimed at owners, operators, investors, designers and consultants in the theme parks, science centres, zoos and aquariums, visitor attractions, museums and heritage, galleries and water park markets.
Ad Rate: Full Page Colour £1790.00
MAGAZINE
Travel

ATV Today
999049

Editorial: Block 50, Number 4, Ryal Walk, Kenton, Newcastle upon Tyne NE3 3YF
Tel: 44 08448 848792
Email: team@atvtoday.co.uk
Web site: www.atvtoday.co.uk
Freq: Daily
Circ: 31753 Cision Digital Reach
Editor: Doug Lambert
MAGAZINE (ONLINE)
Broadcasting

Audi Driver
983306

Editorial: Campion House, 1 Greenfield Road, Westoning, Flitwick MK45 5JD
Tel: 44 01525 750500
Email: mail@autometrix.co.uk
Web site: www.audidrivermag.co.uk
Freq: Monthly
Circ: 4000 Not Audited

Editor: Neil Birkitt
Profile: Publication containing road tests of new Audi models, owner profiles, technical developments and car prices. Includes information on performance tuning, equipment, accessories and motor sport coverage. Aimed predominantly at males aged 25 and upwards who are owners of new and company Audi cars.
Ad Rate: Full Page Colour £650.00
MAGAZINE
Automakers

Audi Magazine
983325

Editorial: Northstar, Northdown House, 11-21 Northdown Street, London N1 9BN
Tel: 44 02078 337410
Email: editor@magazine.audi.co.uk
Web site: www.thisisnorthstar.com/portfolio/project-1
Freq: Quarterly
Circ: 340000 Not Audited
Profile: Magazine containing a mix of Audi lifestyle features, news and in-depth stories, stories about people and products in the world of Audi. Read by owners and prospective owners of Audi cars and those interested in the marque.
MAGAZINE
Automakers, Driving

Audiation Magazine
1053956

Email: info@audiationmagazine.com
Web site: www.audiationmagazine.com
Freq: Monthly
Circ: 8633 Cision Digital Reach
MAGAZINE (ONLINE)
Art, Classical/Choral/Band Music, Country, Folk, Bluegrass, Dance Music, Jazz & Blues, Literature, Music, Photography, Pop Music, R&B, Urban, World

Audience
983391

Editorial: 26 Dorset Street, London W1U 8AP **Tel:** 44 02074 867007
Email: info@audience.uk.com
Web site: www.audience.uk.com
Freq: Monthly
Circ: 3700 Not Audited
Editor: Mike Gartside
Profile: Magazine focusing on the international contemporary live music industry. Aimed at concert promoters, venues, booking agents, record and publishing company executives, equipment and transport companies, festivals, lawyers and accountants.Regular features: City Focus Brief profile of a city where international contemporary music acts perform and the venues used.; Market Focus Feature on a country and its live music infrastructure including promoters, festivals and venues for contemporary international artistes.
MAGAZINE
Music

Audio Media International
981693

Editorial: Emerson Studio, 4th Floor, 4-8 Emerson Street, London SE1 9DU
Tel: 44 02073 546002
Web site: www.audiomediainternational.com
Freq: Monthly
Circ: 18000 Not Audited
Editor: Adam Savage
Profile: Website covering the audio industry featuring live sound, commercial audio, recording, post production and broadcast audio. It is aimed at present and future audio professionals. This outlet offers RSS (Really Simple Syndication)
MAGAZINE
Audio Video Trade, Electronics, Music

AudiTuner
995464

Web site: audituner.com
Freq: Monthly Not Audited
Editor: Davy Lewis
MAGAZINE
Automakers, Automotive, Driving

Consumer Magazines

Audrey Milkshakes
998105
Tel: 44 02082 154468
Email: info@audreymilkshakes.com
Web site: www.audreymilkshakes.com
Freq: Daily
Circ: 1983 Cision Digital Reach
MAGAZINE (ONLINE)
Fashion, Women's Interests

Australian Times
982792
Editorial: Australian Times, Riverbank House, 1 Putney Bridge Approach, London SW6 3BC
Email: info@australiantimes.co.uk
Web site: www.australiantimes.co.uk
Freq: Daily
Circ: 73511 Cision Digital Reach
Profile: Magazine covering Australian news as well as London news including lifestyle, entertainment, events, property, recruitment and sport. The magazine is aimed at Australians living in London.THIS OUTLET DOES NOT ACCEPT EDITORIAL MATERIAL. NO PRESS RELEASES SHOULD BE SUBMITTED.
Ad Rate: Full Page Colour £500.00
MAGAZINE (ONLINE)
News & Current Affairs

Autism Eye
999150
Editorial: 25A Hillbury Road, London SW17 8JT **Tel:** 44 02086 738496
Email: autismeye@gmail.com
Web site: www.autismeye.com
Freq: Quarterly
Circ: 13000 Not Audited
Editor: Gillian Loughran
MAGAZINE
Disability, Family & Parenting, Health & Medicine, Nutrition

Auto Dealer: Zululand
1060483
Tel: 44 27357 990500
Email: zulobs@iafrica.com
Freq: Weekly Not Audited
MAGAZINE
Antique & Collectible Cars, Automakers, Automotive, Driving, Motorcycles, Off-road & 4-Wheel Drive Vehicles, Trucks & SUVs

Auto Express
982624
Editorial: 31-32 Alfred Place, London WC1E 7DP **Tel:** 44 02079 076000
Web site: www.autoexpress.co.uk
Freq: Weekly
Circ: 43468 Not Audited
Profile: Magazine covering car news. It features motoring news stories, pictures, new cars, road tests, first drives, readers' letters and feedback, product tests, long-term tests, used cars, motorsport and comment columns. It covers such topics as future car models and changes in the motoring law. First published in 1989. Aimed at men aged between 25 and 54 years old who are interested in the motoring industry.
Ad Rate: Full Page Colour £7150.00
MAGAZINE
Antique & Collectible Cars, Automakers, Automotive, Driving, Motorcycles, Off-road & 4-Wheel Drive Vehicles, Sales & Marketing, Trucks & SUVs

Auto Italia (UK)
982625
Editorial: 1 High Avenue, Letchworth, Letchworth Garden City SG6 3RL
Tel: 44 01462 811115
Email: claire@gingerbeerpromotions.com
Web site: http://www.auto-italia.co.uk
Freq: Monthly Not Audited
MAGAZINE
News & Current Affairs

Auto Retail Agenda
996975
Editorial: 21 Midland Court, Station Approach, Oakham LE15 6RA
Tel: 44 01572 724687
Web site: http://www.auto-retail.co.uk/agenda
Freq: Weekly
Circ: 788 Cision Digital Reach
Profile: Auto Retail Agenda is a weekly newsletter distributed on Sunday night. It covers auto retail industry.
MAGAZINE (ONLINE)
Automotive

Auto Retail Bulletin
983971
Editorial: 21 Midland Court, Station Approach, Oakham, Oakham LE15 6RA
Tel: 44 01572 724687
Web site: www.auto-retail.co.uk/bulletin
Freq: Monthly
Circ: 1200 Not Audited
Editor: Mark Simms
Profile: Publication covering all aspects of the automotive retail industry including the latest news and analysis. Aimed at senior directors within the automotive retail industry.
MAGAZINE
Automotive, Retail Management

Auto Retail Profit
986479
Editorial: 21 Midland Court, Station Approach, Oakham LE15 6RA
Tel: 44 01572 336600
Web site: www.auto-retail.com
Freq: Monthly
Circ: 1000 Not Audited
MAGAZINE
Automotive

Auto Trader
983142
Editorial: Auto Trader, 3rd Floor, 2 Pancras Square, London N1C 4AG
Tel: 44 02037 477100
Email: editorial@autotrader.co.uk
Web site: www.autotrader.co.uk
Freq: Daily
Circ: 7140054 Cision Digital Reach
MAGAZINE (ONLINE)
Antique & Collectible Cars, Automakers, Automotive, Driving, Motorcycles, Off-road & 4-Wheel Drive Vehicles, Sales & Marketing, Trucks & SUVs

Autocar
982626
Editorial: Bridge House, 69 London Road, Twickenham TW1 3SP **Tel:** 44 02082 675000
Email: autocar@haymarket.com
Web site: www.autocar.co.uk
Freq: Weekly
Circ: 33521 Not Audited
Profile: Magazine containing car news and reviews including new model, industry, consumer and used car, road tests, profiles, Grand Prix coverage and a variety of automotive features. Aimed at new car buyers seeking advice.
Ad Rate: Full Page Colour £2800.00
MAGAZINE
Antique & Collectible Cars, Automakers, Automotive, Driving, Motorcycles, Off-road & 4-Wheel Drive Vehicles, Trucks & SUVs

AUTOiNFORM
996261
Web site: http://www.autoinform.co.uk
Freq: Daily
Circ: 2090 Cision Digital Reach
MAGAZINE (ONLINE)
News & Current Affairs

The Automobile
982618
Editorial: King's Farm, Dorking Road, Kingsfold, Horsham RH12 3SA
Tel: 44 01306 628339
Email: enquiries@theautomobile.co.uk
Web site: www.theautomobile.co.uk
Freq: Monthly
Circ: 30000 Not Audited
Editor: Jonathan Rishton
Profile: International magazine devoted exclusively to pre-1960 cars and commercial vehicles. Read by those interested in buying, selling and restoring old vehicles.
Ad Rate: Full Page Colour £900.00
MAGAZINE
Antique & Collectible Cars

Automotive Industry Data Newsletter
988019
Editorial: 31 Cape Road, Warwick CV34 4JP
Tel: 44 01926 410040

Email: info@eagleaid.com
Web site: http://www.eagleaid.com
Freq: Bi-Weekly Not Audited
Editor: Peter Schmidt
MAGAZINE
Automotive

Automotive Logistics
980996
Editorial: Ultima Media Ltd, 401 King Street, London W6 9NJ **Tel:** 44 02089 870900
Web site: www.automotivelogisticsmagazine.com
Freq: Quarterly
Circ: 9000 Not Audited
Editor: Christopher Ludwig
Profile: Magazine covering all aspects of logistics in the automotive industry. Contains interviews, company profiles, news roundup, major suppliers and regional focus. First published in 1998. Read by senior management of logistics companies, vehicle makers, automotive industry suppliers and logistic service providers.
Ad Rate: Full Page Colour £5250.00
MAGAZINE
Automotive, Supply Chain Management (SCM)

Automotive Manufacturing Solutions
980968
Editorial: Ultima Media Ltd, 401 King Street, London W6 9NJ **Tel:** 44 02089 870900
Web site: www.automotivemanufacturingsolutions.com
Freq: Bi-Monthly
Circ: 61800 Not Audited
Editor: Nick Holt
Profile: Magazine offering an insight into the latest manufacturing technologies being employed by leading auto manufacturers and suppliers. Contains a highly focused manufacturing news section and several news analysis features. Interviews from heads of manufacturing, supplier profiles and strategies, regional reports, case studies and factory visits. Aimed at specifiers and purchasers of machinery and equipment at automaker and supplier plants.Alternative Title: AMS
Ad Rate: Full Page Colour £6950.00
MAGAZINE
Automotive, Manufacturing

Automotive Megatrends
997223
Editorial: 1 - 3 The Washington Building, Stanwell Road, Penarth CF64 2AD
Tel: 44 02920 707021
Email: hello@automotiveworld.com
Web site: http://www.automotiveworld.com/
Freq: Quarterly
Circ: 20000 Not Audited
Editor: Martin Kahl
MAGAZINE
Automotive

Automotive Purchasing and Supply Chain
997496
Editorial: 286 Chase Road, London N14 6HF **Tel:** 44 44012 76534640
Web site: www.automotivepurchasing.com
Freq: Weekly
Circ: 10000 Not Audited
MAGAZINE
Automotive

Automotive Testing Technology International
984785
Editorial: Abinger House, Church Street, Dorking, Dorking RH4 1DF
Tel: 44 01306 743744
Email: testing@ukipme.com
Web site: www.automotivetestingtechnologyinternational.com
Freq: Quarterly
Circ: 14257 Not Audited
Editor: John Thornton
Profile: Magazine covering the latest research and developments within the area of automotive test and evaluation. Includes breaking stories in the fields of vehicle reliability, durability, safety, quality, NVH,

and dynamics testing and evaluation. Aimed at automotive engineers worldwide.
Ad Rate: Full Page Colour £3750.00
MAGAZINE
Automotive

Autosport
982669
Editorial: Bridge House, 69 London Road, Twickenham, London TW1 3QR
Tel: 44 02082 675998
Email: autosport@haymarket.com
Web site: www.autosport.com
Freq: Weekly
Circ: 20833 Not Audited
Editor: Kevin Turner
Profile: Autosport magazine is a weekly publication providing comprehensive coverage of the motorsports world from Formula 1 and championship cars to touring cars including news, analysis and race reports. Aimed at motor sport enthusiasts and those working in the industry.
Ad Rate: Full Page Colour £3832.00
MAGAZINE
Motorsports

AutoTrade News
988518
Editorial: 5 Marlbrook Gardens, Catshill, Bromsgrove B61 0HN **Tel:** 44 02037 477100
Email: mark@impressioncommunications.co.uk
Web site: www.autotradenews.co.uk
Freq: Daily
Circ: 1040 Cision Digital Reach
MAGAZINE (ONLINE)
Automotive

AV Magazine
979994
Editorial: 6th Floor, Davis House, 2nd Robert Street, Croydon CR0 1QQ
Tel: 44 02082 534600
Email: avnewsdesk@metropolis.co.uk
Web site: www.avinteractive.com
Freq: Bi-Monthly
Circ: 33073 Not Audited
Editor: Clive Couldwell
Profile: Magazine focusing on audio-visual applications in business and education.
Ad Rate: Full Page Colour £3240.00
MAGAZINE
Electronics

AV News
982962
Editorial: PO Box 356, Deal, Deal CT14 6WH **Tel:** 44 08453 700470
Email: editorial@avnews.co.uk
Web site: www.avnews.co.uk
Freq: Monthly
Circ: 7400 Not Audited
Profile: Trade magazine for dealers, resellers and retailers of audio-visual equipment and services in business-to-business and consumer markets. Read by resellers, dealers and retailers specialist, independent and multiples in AV, IT, office equipment, home cinema and specified vertical markets as well as manufacturers and distributors.
Ad Rate: Full Page Colour £2680.00
MAGAZINE
Auto Aftermarket, Electronics

Avaunt
997283
Editorial: Unit 6 Albion Riverside Building, 8 Hester Road, London SW11 4AX
Tel: 44 02031 193077
Web site: www.avauntmagazine.com
Freq: Semi-Annual
Circ: 66700 Not Audited
MAGAZINE
Art, Fashion, Men's Interests, Outdoor Recreation, Women's Interests

AVCC (Antiviral Chemistry & Chemotherapy)
998989
Editorial: Admiral House, 76-78 Old Street, London EC1V 9AZ **Tel:** 44 02073 248500
Web site: http://journals.sagepub.com/home/avc
Freq: Daily
Circ: 10 Cision Digital Reach
MAGAZINE (ONLINE)
Medicine, Science

Ave Noctum
997522

Editorial: 6 Kingston House, 232-234 Imperial Drive, Harrow, London HA2 7HJ
Email: pete@avenoctum.com
Web site: http://www.avenoctum.com/
Freq: Daily
Circ: 12220 Cision Digital Reach
Editor: Pete Woods
MAGAZINE (ONLINE)
Rock Music

Avenir Magazine (UK)
997662

Email: info@avenirmagazine.com
Web site: http://avenirmagazine.com/
Freq: Quarterly Not Audited
MAGAZINE
Art, Fashion, Literature, Photography, Visual Arts

Avenue
981751

Editorial: University of Glasgow, Development & Alumni Office, 2 The Square, Glasgow G12 8QQ **Tel:** 44 01413 304951
Email: avenue@glasgow.ac.uk
Web site: www.gla.ac.uk/avenue
Freq: Semi-Annual
Circ: 114000 Not Audited
MAGAZINE
Alumni

Average Janes
999675

Email: havefun@averagejanesblog.com
Web site: http://www.averagejanes.co.uk/
Freq: Daily
Circ: 11283 Cision Digital Reach
MAGAZINE (ONLINE)
Beauty & Grooming, Cosmetics, Fashion, Hair, Women's Interests

AVForums.com
985978

Editorial: 21a Plymouth Road, Barnt Green, Birmingham B45 8JF
Email: news@avforums.com
Web site: www.avforums.com
Freq: Daily
Circ: 3791507 Cision Digital Reach
Editor: Phil Hinton
MAGAZINE (ONLINE)
Audio Video Trade, Electronics, Movies & Video

AW Monthly
998894

Editorial: 2nd Floor Offices, 1-3 Washington Buildings, Stanwell Road, Penarth CF64 2AD
Tel: 44 02920 707021
Email: editorial@automotiveworld.com
Web site: www.automotiveworld.com
Freq: Monthly
Circ: 20000 Not Audited
Editor: Martin Kahl
MAGAZINE
Automotive

axis magazine
985118

Editorial: Tooke House, 20 Bull Plain, Hertford SG14 1DT **Tel:** 44 01992 500198
Email: news@axispublications.co.uk
Web site: www.axismagazine.co.uk
Freq: Monthly
Circ: 10000 Not Audited
Editor: Aaron Gransby
Profile: Magazine covering useful, informative, relevant local news, features, what's on and dining out information, shopping news, gardening news, health, beauty and well-being pages, education, business, finance, legal and property news and features along with motoring and advertising. This outlet covers areas within Enfield Borough.
Ad Rate: Full Page Colour £500.00
MAGAZINE
Regional General Interest

A-Z ELEKTRO
1060168

Freq: Bi-Weekly Not Audited
MAGAZINE
Defense & National Security, Electronics, Engineering, Industry, Manufacturing, Marine & Boat Trade, Mining & Quarrying, Paper, Plastics, Steel

A-Z ELEKTRO
1060703

Freq: Bi-Weekly Not Audited
MAGAZINE
Defense & National Security, Electronics, Engineering, Industry, Manufacturing, Marine & Boat Trade, Mining & Quarrying, Paper, Plastics, Steel

AZoNano
988107

Editorial: Fence House, Fence Ave, Macclesfield, Macclesfield SK10 1LT
Tel: 44 01625 615111
Email: editorial@azonano.com
Web site: www.azonano.com/
Freq: Daily
Circ: 56127 Cision Digital Reach
MAGAZINE (ONLINE)
Electronics, Science

Azzarenko
996131

Editorial: 47 Abdale Road, London W12 7ER
Email: info@azzarenko.com
Web site: http://www.azzarenko.com/
Freq: Semi-Annual
Circ: 40000 Not Audited
MAGAZINE
Fashion, Men's Interests

B Baby Magazine
988294

Editorial: 19 Cecile Park, London N8 9AX
Tel: 44 02083 402212
Email: info@bbabymagazine.co.uk
Web site: www.bbabymagazine.co.uk
Freq: Quarterly
Circ: 40000 Not Audited
MAGAZINE
Family & Parenting

b inspired
995087

Editorial: Blackburn house, Blackburn Road, London NW6 1RZ **Tel:** 44 02076 250700
Email: jane.wright@ink-global.com
Web site: http://ink-live.com/emagazines/binspired#
Freq: Monthly
MAGAZINE
Airline Inflight, Travel

B&I Catering
995831

Editorial: 4th Floor, Joynes House, New Road, Gravesend DA11 0AJ
Tel: 44 08455 006008
Email: henry@h2opublishing.co.uk
Web site: http://www.bandicatering.co.uk/
Freq: Monthly
Circ: 5139 Not Audited
Editor: Henry Norman
Profile: Magazine providing crucial market intelligence on the £4bn contract catering industry. Features include interviews with industry professionals, breaking news stories and topical features. Aimed at buying and operation departments for B and I, retail, healthcare, education and public services.
Ad Rate: Full Page Colour £2500.00
MAGAZINE
Alcohol & Spirits, Bars, Clubs & Pubs, Food

BAA Magazine
995721

Editorial: Blackburn House, Redhouse Road, Seafield, Whitburn EH47 7AQ
Tel: 44 01625 290046
Email: magazine@baaudiology.org
Web site: www.baaudiology.org
Freq: Quarterly
Circ: 2000 Not Audited
MAGAZINE
Medical Technology, Medicine

BabMag
1066391

Editorial: Boxxed, 104-108 Floodgate Street, Birmingham B5 5SR
Email: contact@babmag.co.uk
Web site: www.babmag.co.uk
Freq: Quarterly
Circ: 5000 Not Audited
MAGAZINE
Art, Classical/Choral/Band Music, Country, Folk, Bluegrass, Dance Music, Fashion, Jazz & Blues, Music, Pop Music, R&B, Urban, World, Rap & Hip Hop

Baby & You
984526

Editorial: 3 Upper Street, 3rd Floor, Islington, London N1 0PQ
Tel: 44 02076 651111
Email: media@babyandyou.co.uk
Web site: www.babyandyou.co.uk
Freq: Semi-Annual
Circ: 700000 Not Audited
Profile: Magazine covering pregnancy and baby issue up to a year old. Aimed at pregnant women in their second trimester through their midwife.
MAGAZINE
Family & Parenting

The Baby Directory
983405

Editorial: Studio 7, Eurolink Business Centre, Effra Road, Brixton, London SW2 1BZ **Tel:** 44 02077 330088
Email: info@babydirectory.com
Web site: www.babydirectory.com
Freq: Daily
Circ: 354 Cision Digital Reach
Editor: Clare Flawn-Thomas
Profile: Listings magazine with reviews and features on education, health, travel, days out, food, books, videos, music, clothes, toys, baby goods and fashion. Aimed at pregnant women, and mothers with babies and children under 5 years old in London.
MAGAZINE (ONLINE)
Family & Parenting

Baby Hampshire
985578

Editorial: Jubilee House, 2 Jubilee Place, London SW3 3TQ **Tel:** 44 02073 493700
Email: editorial@littlemedia.co.uk
Web site: www.babyhampshire.co.uk
Freq: Bi-Monthly Not Audited
Profile: The magazine contains baby care, baby fashion, beauty, new products and interviews. The editorial team does not want to receive any external PR materials.
MAGAZINE
Family & Parenting

Baby London
985458

Editorial: Jubilee House, 2 Jubilee Place, London SW3 3QW **Tel:** 44 02073 493700
Email: editorial@littlemedia.co.uk
Web site: www.babylondon.co.uk
Freq: Bi-Monthly
Circ: 95000 Not Audited
Profile: The magazine contains baby care, baby fashion, beauty, new products and interviews.
MAGAZINE
Family & Parenting

Baby Surrey
985534

Editorial: Jubilee House, 2 Jubilee Place, London SW3 3TQ **Tel:** 44 02073 493700
Email: editorial@babysurrey.co.uk
Web site: www.babysurrey.co.uk
Freq: Bi-Monthly
Circ: 40000 Not Audited
Profile: The magazine contains baby care, baby fashion, beauty, new products and interviews. The editorial team does not want to receive any external PR materials.
MAGAZINE
Family & Parenting

Baby2Body
996125

Editorial: Commercial Unit 2, Aurora Building, 124 East Road, London N1 6FD
Email: team@baby2body.com
Web site: www.baby2body.com
Freq: Daily
Circ: 5184 Cision Digital Reach
MAGAZINE (ONLINE)
Beauty & Grooming, Cosmetics, Family & Parenting, Fitness & Exercise, Hair, Nutrition, Women's Interests

BabyCentre
983277

Editorial: Rouen House, 3rd Floor North, Rouen Road, Norwich NR1 1RB
Tel: 44 01603 692290
Email: sasha.miller@babycentre.co.uk
Web site: www.babycentre.co.uk
Freq: Daily
Circ: 3713975 Cision Digital Reach
Profile: Website covering parenting and pregnancy. The babycentre website discusses the latest and news about medical information about pre-pregnancy, birth, child development, family life including travel, buying for baby and baby equipment.
MAGAZINE (ONLINE)
Family & Parenting

Baby-Friendly Boltholes
996587

Editorial: 123 Eustace Building, 372 Queenstown Rd, London SW8 4PP
Tel: 44 02036 031160
Email: info@babyfriendlyboltholes.co.uk
Web site: www.babyfriendlyboltholes.co.uk
Freq: Daily
Circ: 66734 Cision Digital Reach
MAGAZINE (ONLINE)
Airline Inflight, Family & Parenting, Railroad, Travel

babygoes2.com
983253

Editorial: 50 Hampstead Road, Brighton BN1 5NG **Tel:** 44 01273 230669
Email: contactus@babygoes2.com
Web site: www.babygoes2.com
Freq: Daily
Circ: 5000 Cision Digital Reach
Editor: Debi Green
MAGAZINE (ONLINE)
Airline Inflight, Family & Parenting, Railroad, Travel

Bachtrack
999491

Editorial: Unit 5, The Courtyard, 50 Lynton Road, London N8 8SL **Tel:** 44 02083 484027
Email: press@bachtrack.com
Web site: www.bachtrack.com
Freq: Daily
Circ: 97432 Cision Digital Reach
MAGAZINE (ONLINE)
Classical/Choral/Band Music, Theater & Performing Arts, Travel

Back Street Heroes
982649

Editorial: Media Centre, Morton Way, Horncastle, London LN9 6JR
Tel: 44 01507 529529
Web site: www.backstreetheroes.com
Freq: Monthly
Circ: 35000 Not Audited
Editor: Nik Samson
Profile: Magazine focusing on customised bikes and the ethos and lifestyle behind the machinery. Read by biker enthusiasts.
Ad Rate: Full Page Colour £1260.00
MAGAZINE
Motorcycles

Backpax Magazine
999068

Editorial: Unit 19, The Coach House, 2 Upper York Street, Bristol BS2 8QN
Tel: 44 07767 112964
Email: enquiries@backpaxtravel.com
Web site: www.backpaxtravel.com
Freq: 3 Times/Year Not Audited
Editor: Sharon Henshall
MAGAZINE
Travel

Backwards Compatible
995466

Email: info@backwardscompatible.co.uk
Web site: www.backwardscompatible.co.uk
Freq: Daily
Circ: 10622 Cision Digital Reach
MAGAZINE (ONLINE)
Audio Video Trade, Cameras, Computer & Video Games, Consumer Electronics, Mobile Electronics, Movies & Video

The Badger
995944

Editorial: Media Office, Students' Union, Falmer House, University of Sussex, Falmer, Brighton BN2 9WF **Tel:** 44 01273 678875
Email: badger@sussexstudent.com
Web site: http://thebadgeronline.com/
Freq: Weekly
Circ: 3500 Not Audited
Profile: Publication containing student-related features including music, film, arts, TV, radio and games reviews and sports. Also includes university and local news, plus local entertainment listings and a

Consumer Magazines

spoof section. Aimed at students of the University of Sussex.
Ad Rate: Full Page Mono £450.00
Ad Rate: Full Page Colour £595.00
MAGAZINE
Student Lifestyle

The Bailgate Independent
987868
Editorial: 173 Burton Road, Lincoln LN1 3LW **Tel:** 44 01522 531717
Web site: www.bailgateindependent.co.uk
Freq: Monthly
Circ: 10000 Not Audited
Profile: Magazine featuring new and existing businesses within the Lincoln area. It also contains articles on arts events, charities and stories of interest.
MAGAZINE
News & Current Affairs

Baily's Hunting Directory 998814
Editorial: Baily's Office, Ivy Lodge, Main Road, Boston PE22 9AT
Tel: 44 07738 079647
Email: info@bailyshuntingdirectory.com
Web site: www.bailyshuntingdirectory.com
Freq: Daily
Circ: 7227 Cision Digital Reach
Editor: Peter Brook
MAGAZINE (ONLINE)
Field Sports

Baku
987581
Editorial: 13 Hanover Square, London W1S 1HN **Tel:** 44 02074 999080
Web site: www.baku-magazine.com
Freq: Quarterly
Circ: 25000 Not Audited
Profile: A quarterly magazine covering lifestyle, fashion, art, and Azeri culture.
MAGAZINE
Art, Fashion, Literature, Men's Interests, Visual Arts, Women's Interests

balance (Diabetes UK) 1004620
Editorial: Wells Lawrence House, 126 Back Church Lane, London E1 1FH
Tel: 44 02074 241000
Email: balance@diabetes.org.uk
Web site: www.diabetes.org.uk/How_we_help/Magazines/Balance/
Freq: Bi-Monthly
Circ: 210000 Not Audited
MAGAZINE
Charitable Foundations, Diabetes, Patient Support

The Balance Plan 998350
Tel: 44 01959 543609
Email: editor@balanceplan.co.uk
Web site: balanceplan.co.uk
Freq: Daily
Circ: 904 Cision Digital Reach
MAGAZINE (ONLINE)
Alternative Medicine

Balancing Act 1060494
Tel: 44 44207 5825220
Email: info@balancingact-africa.com
Web site: http://www.balancingact-africa.com
Circ: 49810 Cision Digital Reach
MAGAZINE (ONLINE)
Advertising Industry, Branding, Broadcasting, Business, Graphic Design, Industry, Internet, Marketing, Media & Communications, Photography

Ballad Of 996580
Editorial: 4 Spectrum Place, London SE17 2GP
Email: ballad@balladof.co.uk
Web site: www.balladof.co.uk
Freq: Semi-Annual
Circ: 4000 Not Audited
MAGAZINE
Art, Literature, Photography, Theater & Performing Arts, Visual Arts

Ballast Water Treatment Technology 997872
Editorial: Mitre House, 66 Abbey Road, Enfield EN1 2QN **Tel:** 44 02083 641551
Email: paul.gunton@rivieramm.com
Web site: www.ballastwatermanagement.co.uk
Freq: Annual
Circ: 5000 Not Audited
MAGAZINE
Marine & Boat Trade

BAM Magazine 1075480
Email: bammagni@gmail.com
Web site: http://bamni.co.uk/
Freq: Daily
Circ: 13402 Cision Digital Reach
MAGAZINE (ONLINE)
Bars, Clubs & Pubs, Comedy, Entertainment, Local Entertainment Guides, Movies & Video, Regional General Interest

Banking Automation Bulletin
981710
Editorial: 393 Richmond Road, London TW1 2EF **Tel:** 44 02088 317300
Email: bulletin@rbrlondon.com
Web site: www.rbrlondon.com/newsletters
Freq: Monthly
Circ: 3000 Not Audited
Editor: Dominic Hirsch
Profile: Newsletter focusing on developments in automated banking and payment systems in Europe and worldwide. Includes global news and analysis of key issues in self-service banking, cards and payments. First published in 1979, the publication has an average of 28 pages per issue. Previous title: BABE Banking Automation Bulletin for Europe Aimed at key decision makers across the financial services industry, banks, card schemes, CIT companies, network processors, suppliers and central banks worldwide.
Ad Rate: Full Page Colour £3750.00
MAGAZINE
Banking, Data Management, Electronics

Banzai Japanese Cars 998646
Editorial: Becket House, Vestry Road, Sevenoaks, Sevenoaks TN14 5EJ
Tel: 44 01732 748000
Web site: www.banzaimagazine.com
Freq: Monthly
Circ: 33104 Not Audited
Editor: Andy Basoo
MAGAZINE
Automotive

BAPOmag 996768
Editorial: BAPO Secretariat, Unit 64 Sir James Clark Building, Abbeymill Business Centre, Paisley PA1 1TJ
Tel: 44 01415 617217
Email: bapomag@bapo.com
Web site: www.bapo.com
Freq: 3 Times/Year Not Audited
MAGAZINE
Patient Support

The BAPTIST TIMES 982143
Editorial: PO Box 54, 129 Broadway, Didcot, Didcot OX11 8XB
Tel: 44 01235 517709
Email: editor@baptisttimes.co.uk
Web site: http://www.baptist.org.uk/Groups/220248/Latest_News.aspx?redirected=1
Freq: Daily
Circ: 146 Cision Digital Reach
Editor: Paul Hobson
Profile: Website containing news and views regarding the Baptist denomination and coverage of wider Christian issues including Christian reflection on world and national news. Read by members of Baptist churches.
MAGAZINE (ONLINE)
Religion

Bar 983562
Editorial: The Goods Shed, Jubilee Way, Whitstable Road, Faversham ME13 8GD
Tel: 44 01795 509109
Email: bar@cimltd.co.uk
Web site: www.barmagazine.co.uk
Freq: Monthly
Circ: 12500 Not Audited
Editor: Mark Ludmon
MAGAZINE
Alcohol & Spirits, Bars, Clubs & Pubs

BarberNV 995156
Tel: 44 01412 125525
Email: contact@salonnv.co.uk
Web site: www.salonnv.co.uk
Freq: Bi-Monthly
Circ: 20000 Not Audited
MAGAZINE
Beauty & Grooming, Cosmetics, Hair

Barbican Life 985418
Editorial: 5 Brandon Mews, Barbican, London EC2Y 8BE **Tel:** 44 02033 559088
Email: barbicanlife@gmail.com
Web site: www.barbicanlife.com
Freq: Quarterly
Circ: 2800 Not Audited
MAGAZINE
Regional General Interest

Barbie 982450
Editorial: 1st Floor, The Yellow Building, 1 Nicholas Road, London W11 4AN
Tel: 44 02032 200400
Email: info@euk.egmont.com
Web site: www.egmont.co.uk
Freq: Monthly
Circ: 29412 Not Audited
MAGAZINE
Teen/Young Adult

Bare Fiction 996496
Editorial: 177 Copthorne Road, Shrewsbury, Shrewsbury SY3 8NA
Web site: www.barefictionmagazine.co.uk/
Freq: Quarterly Not Audited
MAGAZINE
News & Current Affairs

Barefaced 995305
Editorial: 6B Dalmeny Road, Tufnell Park, London N70HH
Email: info@barefacedmag.com
Web site: barefacedmag.co.uk
Freq: Daily
Circ: 801 Cision Digital Reach
MAGAZINE (ONLINE)
Regional General Interest, Women's Interests

Barney 995722
Editorial: Unit 16 Greenway Farm, Bath Road, Wick, Bristol BS30 5RL
Tel: 44 01179 373003
Email: info@kennedypublishing.co.uk
Web site: www.kennedypublishing.co.uk/magazines/barney-magazine
Freq: Bi-Monthly
Circ: 20000 Not Audited
MAGAZINE
Preschool, Teen/Young Adult

BASC Shooting and Conservation magazine 999302
Editorial: Marford Mill, Rossett, Wrexham LL12 0HL **Tel:** 44 01244 573000
Email: enq@basc.org.uk
Web site: www.basc.org.uk
Freq: Bi-Monthly
Circ: 132825 Not Audited
Editor: Steve Moore
MAGAZINE
Shooting/Guns

Bass Guitar Magazine 982084
Editorial: Lawrence House, Morrell Street, Leamington Spa, Leamington Spa CV32 5SZ
Tel: 44 01926 339808
Web site: www.bassguitarmagazine.com
Freq: Monthly
Circ: 20000 Not Audited

Editor: Joel McIver
Profile: Magazine covering all aspects of bass playing, including gear and equipment reviews, interviews, transcriptions and tutorials. Aimed at anyone interested or involved in bass guitars.
Ad Rate: Full Page Colour £795.00
MAGAZINE
Music

Bath Impact 1011120
Editorial: Students Union University of Bath, Norwood House, Claverton Down, Bath BA2 7AY **Tel:** 44 01225 386151
Email: impact-editor@bath.ac.uk
Web site: www.bathimpact.co.uk
Freq: Bi-Weekly Not Audited
Profile: Newspaper covering articles on student lifestyle, events that affect the student population, music, travel, books, fashion, jobs, computer games and sport.
Ad Rate: Full Page Mono £360.00
Ad Rate: Full Page Colour £675.00
MAGAZINE
Student Lifestyle

Bath Life 984006
Editorial: Circus Mews House, Circus Mews, Bath BA1 2PW **Tel:** 44 01225 475800
Email: info@mediaclash.co.uk
Web site: www.mediaclash.co.uk/magazines/local-magazines/bath-life/
Freq: Bi-Weekly
Circ: 10000 Not Audited
Editor: Lisa Evans
Profile: Property and lifestyle magazine for Bath with features on wine, food, arts and out and about. Aimed at affluent home owners in Bath.
Ad Rate: Full Page Colour £750.00
MAGAZINE
Regional General Interest

The Bath Magazine 982525
Editorial: 2 Princes Building, George Street, Bath BA1 2ED **Tel:** 44 01225 424499
Email: info@thebathmagazine.co.uk
Web site: www.thebathmag.co.uk
Freq: Monthly
Circ: 20100 Not Audited
Editor: Georgette McCready
Profile: Magazine covering lifestyle, leisure, local issues, arts, events, culture, property, antiques, gardening, food, commercial activities, architecture and regional news.
Ad Rate: Full Page Colour £1075.00
MAGAZINE
Regional General Interest

Bath Mums 997230
Editorial: The Breaks Company (UK) Ltd, 33a James Street West, Bath BA1 2BT
Tel: 44 01225 430369
Email: editor@bathmums.co.uk
Web site: www.bathmums.co.uk
Freq: Daily
Circ: 2141 Cision Digital Reach
Editor: Lisa Speigal
MAGAZINE (ONLINE)
Family & Parenting

Batman: Arkham 997038
Editorial: Titan House, 144 Southwark Street, London SE1 0UP
Tel: 44 02076 200200
Email: arkhamcomicuk@titanemail.com
Web site: http://titanmagazines.com/t/batman-arkham
Freq: Monthly Not Audited
MAGAZINE
Trading Cards & Comics

Batteries & Energy Storage Technology 984429
Editorial: 70 Goring Road, Goring by Sea, Worthing, Worthing BN12 4AB
Tel: 44 08451 947338
Web site: www.bestmag.co.uk
Freq: Quarterly
Circ: 10000 Not Audited
Editor: Gerry Woolf
MAGAZINE
Electricity, Electronics

Batteries International
981703
Tel: 44 01243 782275
Email: editor@batteriesinternational.com
Web site: www.batteriesinternational.com
Freq: Quarterly
Circ: 20000 Not Audited
Editor: Mike Halls
Profile: Magazine covering all types of battery manufacturing, battery chemistry, energy storage and battery applications, including electric vehicles.
Ad Rate: Full Page Mono £2250.00
Ad Rate: Full Page Colour £2250.00
MAGAZINE
News & Current Affairs

Battlespace News
983334
Editorial: 8 Sinclair Gardens, London W14 0AT **Tel:** 44 02076 105520
Web site: www.battle-technology.com
Freq: Bi-Monthly
Circ: 10108 Not Audited
Editor: Julian Nettlefold
Profile: International newspaper focusing on news and information about new defence systems and defence electronics.
Ad Rate: Full Page Mono £2155.00
Ad Rate: Full Page Colour £2940.00
MAGAZINE
Defense & National Security, Electronics

BBC Focus (UK)
999847
Editorial: 2nd Floor, Tower House, Fairfax Street, Bristol BS1 3BN
Tel: 44 01173 147388
Email: editorialenquiries@sciencefocus.com
Web site: www.sciencefocus.com
Freq: Monthly
Circ: 63214 Not Audited
MAGAZINE
Audio Video Trade, Cameras, Consumer Electronics, Electronics, Mobile Electronics, Movies & Video, Science

BBC Good Food
983033
Editorial: Vineyard House, 44 Brook Green, Hammersmith, London W6 7BT
Tel: 44 02084 333983
Email: enquiries@bbcgoodfoodmagazine.com
Web site: www.bbcgoodfood.com
Freq: Monthly
Circ: 186667 Not Audited
Profile: Magazine covering home-cooked food, from easy midweek suppers to smart entertaining and sophisticated dishes. Each issue is packed with over 100 recipes for everyday meals, easy entertaining and dishes from celebrity chefs. Every recipe is tested by the Good Food cookery team, and the team's tips will help you every step of the way. Plus, each month the TV section includes recipes from popular cookery programmes. First published in 1989, the publication has an average of 146 pages per issue. Press Day: First/Second week of the month. Aimed at everyone who loves cooking and eating.
Ad Rate: Full Page Colour £11000.00
MAGAZINE
Cooking & Baking

BBC History Magazine (UK)
981974
Editorial: Tower House, Fairfax Street, Bristol BS1 3BN **Tel:** 44 01179 279009
Email: historymagazine@historyextra.com
Web site: www.historyextra.com
Freq: Monthly
Circ: 97550 Not Audited
Editor: Rob Attar; **Editor:** Rob Attar; **Editor:** Rob Attar
MAGAZINE
History

BBC Home Cooking Series
995778
Editorial: BBC Worldwide, 101 Wood Lane, London W12 7FA **Tel:** 44 02071 505000
Web site: www.bbcgoodfood.com
Freq: Bi-Monthly
Circ: 25408 Not Audited
MAGAZINE
Cooking & Baking

BBC Knowledge & Learning
994968
Editorial: MediaCityUK, Quay House, Salford M50 2QH **Tel:** 44 01613 356000
Web site: www.bbc.co.uk/blogs/internet/entries/76239bbb-6f6f-3c51-a81b-85c76d8cd4cb
Freq: Daily
Circ: 30 Cision Digital Reach
MAGAZINE (ONLINE)
News & Current Affairs

BBC Music
982068
Editorial: BBC Music, Tower House, Fairfax Street, Bristol BS1 3BN
Tel: 44 01179 279009
Email: music@classical-music.com
Web site: www.classical-music.com
Freq: Monthly
Circ: 36338 Not Audited
Editor: Olivor Condy
MAGAZINE
Classical/Choral/Band Music

BBC News Online
980750
Editorial: BBC Broadcasting House, Room B1, Portland Place, London W1A 1AA
Tel: 44 02087 438000
Email: newsonline.ukdesk@bbc.co.uk
Web site: www.bbc.co.uk/news
Freq: Daily
Circ: 16327854 Cision Digital Reach
MAGAZINE (ONLINE)
National News

BBC News Online - BBC Travel
1001257
Tel: 02087 438000
Email: uknewsplan@bbc.co.uk
Web site: http://www.bbc.com/travel
Circ: 49796 Cision Digital Reach
MAGAZINE (ONLINE)
News & Current Affairs

BBC Online & Red Button
995800
Editorial: 4th Floor, BBC Quay House, MediaCityUK, Salford M50 2QH
Tel: 44 01613 356000
Web site: www.bbc.co.uk/aboutthebbc/insidethebbc/whatwedo/redbutton/
Freq: Daily
Circ: 178 Cision Digital Reach
MAGAZINE (ONLINE)
News & Current Affairs

BBC Sky at Night
982692
Editorial: Immediate Media Company Bristol Ltd, Tower House, Fairfax Street, Bristol BS1 3BN **Tel:** 44 01179 279009
Email: skyatnight@bbcmagazines.com
Web site: www.skyatnightmagazine.com
Freq: Monthly
Circ: 23453 Not Audited
Editor: Chris Bramley
MAGAZINE
Astronomy

BBC Three
983255
Editorial: New Broadcasting House, Portland Place, London W1A 1AA
Tel: 44 02087 438000
Web site: www.bbc.co.uk/bbcthree
Freq: Daily
Circ: 96505 Cision Digital Reach
MAGAZINE (ONLINE)
News & Current Affairs

BBC Top Gear Magazine
982627
Editorial: 2nd Floor A, Energy Centre, Media Village, 201 Wood Lane, London W12 7TQ
Tel: 44 02071 505558
Email: editor@topgear.com
Web site: www.topgear.com
Freq: Monthly
Circ: 114973 Not Audited
Editor: Sam Philip
Profile: Magazine covering motoring, complementing the BBC TV programme. It features a car buyer's guide, a range of features and motoring experience. First published in October 1993. Aimed at all motoring enthusiasts and those with an interest in the BBC programme.

Ad Rate: Full Page Colour £3500.00
MAGAZINE
Antique & Collectible Cars, Automakers, Automotive Driving, Motorcycles, Off-road & 4-Wheel Drive Vehicles, Trucks & SUVs

BBC Wildlife Magazine
981990
Editorial: 9th Floor, Tower House, Fairfax Street, Bristol BS1 3BN
Tel: 44 01173 147366
Email: wildlifemagazine@immediate.co.uk
Web site: http://www.discoverwildlife.com/
Freq: Monthly
Circ: 34947 Not Audited
Editor: Sheena Harvey
Profile: Magazine covering wildlife, conservation and the environment. It contains images and features on a broad range of animals and habitats, as well as advice, tips and ideas for days out. First published in 1963. Aimed at those wishing to understand more about natural history, conservation and the environment.
Ad Rate: Full Page Colour £3558.00
MAGAZINE
Energy & Environment, Nature & Wildlife, Travel

BBeyond Magazine
995293
Editorial: 40 Craven St, London WC2N 5NG
Tel: 44 02077 514198
Email: editor@bbeyondmagazine.com
Web site: www.bbeyondmagazine.com
Freq: Quarterly
Circ: 7500 Not Audited
Editor: Caroline Brand
MAGAZINE
Art, Banking, Ethical/Moral Issues

BC-GB
1075817
Email: adamstevens+bcgb@gmail.com
Web site: http://bc-gb.com/
Freq: Daily
Circ: 29211 Cision Digital Reach
MAGAZINE (ONLINE)
Computer & Video Games

BDS
1060678
Tel: 44 48224 273651
Email: editors@bsdmag.org
Web site: http://bsdmag.org
Freq: Monthly
Circ: 34123 Cision Digital Reach
MAGAZINE (ONLINE)
Auto Aftermarket, Computers, Data Management, Electronics, Government Technology, Industry, Internet, Mobile Communications, Security & Security Systems, Software

Be Healthy
1059461
Tel: 44 01413 750504
Email: john@thinkpublishing.co.uk
Web site: www.benenden.co.uk/health/cover/healthcare/behealthy
Freq: Quarterly
Circ: 380000 Not Audited
MAGAZINE
Health & Medicine

Beachtomato.com
985856
Editorial: No 40-42, 1st Floor, Scrutton Street, London EC2A 4PP
Tel: 44 02074 269928
Email: enquiry@beachtomato.com
Web site: www.beachtomato.com
Freq: Daily
Circ: 4838 Cision Digital Reach
Editor: Hannah Underwood
MAGAZINE (ONLINE)
Travel

Beacon
985927
Tel: 44 01983 522123
Email: editor@iwbeacon.com
Web site: iwbeacon.com
Freq: Monthly
Circ: 46000 Not Audited
MAGAZINE
Regional General Interest

Bead & Jewellery
1052746
Tel: 44 01903 884988
Email: editor@beadmagazine.co.uk
Web site: www.beadmagazine.co.uk/
Freq: Monthly Not Audited
Editor: Katie Dean
MAGAZINE
Crafts

Bearded
995893
Email: info@beardedmagazine.com
Web site: www.beardedmagazine.co.uk
Freq: Daily
Circ: 1582 Cision Digital Reach
MAGAZINE (ONLINE)
Classical/Choral/Band Music, Country, Folk, Bluegrass, Dance Music, Jazz & Blues, Music, Pop Music, R&B, Urban, World, Rap & Hip Hop, Rock Music

The Beat Magazine
983920
Editorial: Kingsley House Publising, Home Close, Teffont, Salisbury SP3 5QY
Tel: 44 01722 716268
Email: david@yourvalleynews.co.uk
Web site: http://www.beat-magazine.co.uk
Freq: Monthly
Circ: 1800 Not Audited
Profile: Quarterly magazine covering pop culture, pop music, entertainment and fashion.
MAGAZINE
Country, Folk, Bluegrass, Jazz & Blues, Pop Music, Rock Music

BEAT Magazine
998385
Editorial: BEAT, Print House, Ashwin Street, London E8 3DL
Email: info@thebeatjuice.com
Web site: www.thebeatjuice.com
Freq: Quarterly
Circ: 67000 Not Audited
Profile: Quarterly magazine covering pop culture, pop music, entertainment and fashion.
MAGAZINE
Classical/Choral/Band Music, Country, Folk, Bluegrass, Dance Music, Jazz & Blues, Music, Pop Music, R&B, Urban, World, Rap & Hip Hop, Rock Music

Beating Bowel Cancer News
985190
Editorial: Harlequin House, 7 High Street, Teddington, London TW11 8EE
Tel: 44 02086 143855
Email: press@beatingbowelcancer.org
Web site: www.beatingbowelcancer.org/news
Freq: 3 Times/Year
Circ: 10500 Not Audited
MAGAZINE
Gastroenterology, Patient Support

Beau Travel
996666
Editorial: 3 Hagley Court North, The Waterfront, Brierley Hill DY5 1XF
Tel: 44 01214 456985
Web site: www.beautravelmagazine.com
Freq: Quarterly
Circ: 47060 Not Audited
Profile: Publication that covers travel from long haul destinations to short haul weekend city breaks.
MAGAZINE
Airline Inflight, Railroad, Travel

Beautiful Gardens
1006081
Editorial: Bridge House, 69 London Road, Twickenham, London TW1 3QR
Tel: 44 02082 675000
Web site: http://haymarketnetwork.com/
Freq: Annual
Circ: 4000000 Not Audited
MAGAZINE
Gardening

Beautiful South
1096361
Tel: 44 01730 260746
Email: editor@beautiful-south.co.uk
Web site: http://www.beautiful-south.co.uk/
Freq: Bi-Monthly
Circ: 20000 Not Audited

Consumer Magazines

Editor: Henry Ascoli
MAGAZINE
Luxury Goods, Regional General Interest

Beauty And Style Edit   998107
Email: info@beautyandstyleedit.com
Web site: beautyandstyleedit.com
Freq: Daily
Circ: 10511 Cision Digital Reach
MAGAZINE (ONLINE)
Beauty & Grooming, Cosmetics, Fashion,
Hair

Beauty And The Dirt   986083
Editorial: 85a Great Portland Street, London
W1W 7JR **Tel:** 44 02076 370303
Web site: www.beautyandthedirt.com
Freq: Daily
Circ: 41589 Cision Digital Reach
MAGAZINE (ONLINE)
Bars, Clubs & Pubs, Beauty & Grooming,
Celebrities, Comedy, Cooking & Baking,
Cosmetics, Entertainment, Hair, Local
Entertainment Guides, Movies & Video

Beauty Bay   1053672
Editorial: 21 Davrom House, Lyons Rd.,
Trafford Park, Manchester M17 1RN
Tel: 44 01618 484799
Web site: http://www.beautybay.com/
Freq: Daily
Circ: 896625 Cision Digital Reach
MAGAZINE (ONLINE)
Beauty & Grooming, Cosmetics, Hair,
Women's Interests

Beauty Magazine   981177
Editorial: 207 Linen Hall, 162-168 Regent
Street, London W1B 5TB
Tel: 44 02074 341530
Web site: www.beauty-magazine.co.uk
Freq: Monthly
Circ: 15336 Not Audited
Editor: Emily Hunter
Profile: Magazine covering the latest news
from the cosmetics industry, focusing on
new services and techniques. Every issue
covers beauty news, product innovations,
editorial features and gossip from the
industry. It provides a strong emphasis on
product launch and development within the
industry. It also features regular expert
columnists, including CTPA column and
Beauty Bible authoress Josephine Fairley as
well as training and education supplements.
Ad Rate: Full Page Colour £3300.00
MAGAZINE
Cosmetics

Beauty Papers   997323
Editorial: Beauty Papers, 7A Paper Mill
Building City Garden Row, London N1 8DW
Tel: 44 02077 347775
Email: maxine@beautypapers.com
Web site: http://www.beautypapers.com/
Freq: Semi-Annual
Circ: 15000 Not Audited
MAGAZINE
Beauty & Grooming, Cosmetics, Fashion,
Hair

Beauty Unboxed   997372
Editorial: 1-2 Castle Lane, London SW1E
6DR **Tel:** 44 02035 981587
Web site: http://www.glossybox.co.uk/
magazine/
Freq: Daily
Circ: 50 Cision Digital Reach
MAGAZINE (ONLINE)
Beauty & Grooming, Cosmetics, Hair

BeautyMART   997428
Editorial: 106 Regent House, 1 Thane Villas,
Regents Studios, London N7 7PH
Tel: 44 08000 281118
Email: press@thisisbeautymart.com
Web site: https://thisisbeautymart.com/
category/features/
Freq: Daily
Circ: 27103 Cision Digital Reach
MAGAZINE (ONLINE)
Beauty & Grooming, Cosmetics, Hair

BeautyServe.com   1064287
Editorial: Macmillan Building, Parcel
Terrace, Derby DE1 1LY
Tel: 44 01332 227690
Email: info@beautyserve.net
Web site: www.beautyserve.com
Freq: Daily
Circ: 12144 Cision Digital Reach
MAGAZINE (ONLINE)
Cosmetics, Fitness & Exercise

because   985287
Editorial: 91-93 Great Portland Street,
London W1W 7NX **Tel:** 44 02076 370303
Email: info@becausemagazine.com
Web site: http://becauselondon.com/
Freq: Daily
Circ: 11384 Cision Digital Reach
Profile: Website covering fashion. Because
is a online fashion magazine created by the
team at Tank. They provide the latest trends
in fashion and accessories, beauty, jewellery
and culture. The website has an archive
dating back to May 2007. Twitter handle:
http://twitter.com/tankmagazineThe outlet
offers RSS (Really Simple Syndication).
MAGAZINE (ONLINE)
Beauty & Grooming, Cosmetics, Fashion,
Hair

The Beckett Online   998479
Editorial: Leeds Beckett Students Union,
Civic Quarter, Calverley Street, Leeds LS1
3HE
Email: bemedia.leedsbeckett@gmail.com
Web site: www.bemedia.org.uk
Freq: Daily
Circ: 521 Cision Digital Reach
MAGAZINE (ONLINE)
Student Lifestyle

Bedfordshire & Milton Keynes
Focus   1008678
Editorial: Suite 6B(i), Britannia House,
Leagrave Road, Luton LU3 1RJ
Tel: 44 01582 488385
Email: info@mediachameleon.co.uk
Web site: www.bedfordshire-focus.co.uk
Freq: Annual
Circ: 30000 Not Audited
MAGAZINE
Antique & Collectible Cars, Antiques/
Collectibles, Armed Forces, Astrology &
Parapsychology, Astronomy, Automakers,
Automotive, Aviation, Basketball, Bicycles

Bedfordshire County Life
Magazine   982469
Editorial: PO Box 32, Biggleswade,
Biggleswade SG18 8TE
Tel: 44 01462 819496
Email: editor@countylifemagazines.co.uk
Web site: http://countylifemagazines.co.uk/
Freq: Quarterly
Circ: 12000 Not Audited
Profile: Magazine containing historical
profiles on local villages and towns. Covers
gardening, homes, eating out, recipes,
motoring, industrial heritage, local history
and events. Read by residents, ex-residents
and visitors to Bedfordshire.
Ad Rate: Full Page Mono £820.00
Ad Rate: Full Page Colour £1050.00
MAGAZINE
Regional General Interest

Bee Craft   985173
Editorial: Stoneycroft, Back Lane, Little
Addington, Kettering NN14 4AX
Email: editor@bee-craft.com
Web site: www.bee-craft.com
Freq: Monthly
Circ: 7200 Not Audited
Editor: Claire Waring
Profile: Official journal of the British
Beekeepers' Association, with news and
articles on bees, beekeeping techniques and
related subjects, also includes the 'B' Kids.
Read by those interested in the countryside
and in keeping bees.
Ad Rate: Full Page Mono £261.00
Ad Rate: Full Page Colour £382.00
MAGAZINE
Animal Farming

BEER   984887
Editorial: 230 Hatfield Road, St Albans,
London AL1 4LW **Tel:** 44 01727 867201
Email: editor@camra.org.uk
Web site: www.camra.org.uk
Freq: Quarterly
Circ: 125774 Not Audited
Editor: Tom Stainer
Profile: Magazine containing information
about real ales, ciders and pubs. Aimed at
real ale enthusiasts.
MAGAZINE
Alcohol & Spirits, Bars, Clubs & Pubs,
Beer

Beer Insider   997281
Email: glynn@busicomm.co.uk
Web site: www.beerinsider.com/
Freq: Daily
Circ: 11607 Cision Digital Reach
Editor: Glynn Davis
MAGAZINE (ONLINE)
Alcohol & Spirits

Beer Today   986982
Editorial: 3 Curnows Road, Hayle, Hayle
TR27 4RZ **Tel:** 44 07867 585395
Email: darren@beertoday.co.uk
Web site: www.beertoday.co.uk
Freq: Daily
Circ: 14742 Cision Digital Reach
Profile: Website covering real ale news
mainly from around the UK, with brewery
and ale listings and news of events and beer
festivals. Also highlights the best places for
good pints and a specialist interest in
matching beer with food. Aimed at beer
drinkers in general but particularly real ale
enthusiasts.
MAGAZINE (ONLINE)
Beer

BeginnersTech   1054945
Email: ryan@beginnerstech.co.uk
Web site: www.beginnerstech.co.uk
Freq: Daily
Circ: 1005 Cision Digital Reach
MAGAZINE (ONLINE)
Audio Video Trade, Cameras, Computer &
Video Games, Consumer Electronics,
Mobile Electronics, Movies & Video

Behind the Couch   999349
Web site:
watchinghorrorfilmsfrombehindthecouch.
blogspot.com/
Freq: Daily
Circ: 6899 Cision Digital Reach
Editor: James Gracey
MAGAZINE (ONLINE)
Entertainment, Movies & Video

Behind The Spin   983941
Editorial: 4 Brame Hall Farm, Norwood,
London HG3 1SB
Email: editor@behindthespin.com
Web site: www.behindthespin.com
Freq: Daily
Circ: 13235 Cision Digital Reach
Editor: Richard Bailey
Profile: Website covering public relations.
The BEHIND THE SPIN website shares the
latest news and information on fashion and
entertainment PR to charity.
MAGAZINE (ONLINE)
Marketing, Student Lifestyle

The Belfast Gazette   987154
Editorial: 19a Weavers Court, Weavers
Court Business Park, Linfield Road, Belfast
BT12 5GH **Tel:** 44 02890 895135
Email: belfast@thegazette.co.uk
Web site: www.thegazette.co.uk
Freq: Weekly Not Audited
Profile: Publication containing official,
statutory, legal, bankruptcy and liquidation
notices relating to Northern Ireland.
MAGAZINE
News & Current Affairs

Belfast Live   988829
Editorial: Belfast Live, 415 Holywood Road,
Belfast BT4 2GU **Tel:** 44 02890 568000
Email: news@belfastlive.co.uk

Web site: http://www.belfastlive.co.uk/
Freq: Daily
Circ: 169401 Cision Digital Reach
Editor: Chris Sherrard
MAGAZINE (ONLINE)
News & Current Affairs

Belgravia   982510
Editorial: 3 Princes Street, London W1B 2LD
Tel: 44 02072 591050
Web site: www.pubbiz.com
Freq: Bi-Monthly
Circ: 8000 Not Audited
Editor: Jonathan Whiley
Profile: Magazine containing news and
features on life and work in the Belgravia
area of London. Aimed at residents and
businesses within the area of Belgravia.
Ad Rate: Full Page Mono £2029.00
Ad Rate: Full Page Colour £2329.00
MAGAZINE
Regional General Interest

Belgravia Residents' Journal
    1053602
Editorial: 6th Floor, One Canada Square,
Canary Wharf, London E14 5AX
Tel: 44 02079 874320
Email: belgravia@residentsjournal.co.uk
Web site: rwmg.co.uk
Freq: Monthly
Circ: 10000 Not Audited
MAGAZINE
Luxury Goods, Regional General Interest

Bella   982431
Editorial: Academic House, 24 - 28 Oval
Road, London NW1 7DT
Tel: 44 02072 418000
Web site: www.bellamagazine.co.uk
Freq: Weekly
Circ: 161647 Not Audited
Profile: Magazine covering celebrity
features, gossip and style tips. It features
real-life stories and articles on fashion,
beauty, health, food and travel. First
published in 1987. Aimed at female
consumers aged between 25 and 44 years
old.
Ad Rate: Full Page Colour £4600.00
MAGAZINE
Women's Interests

Belle About Town   995431
Email: editor@belleabouttown.com
Web site: www.belleabouttown.com
Freq: Daily
Circ: 16155 Cision Digital Reach
MAGAZINE (ONLINE)
Women's Interests

Belowtheriver   996970
Editorial: Interchange Atrium, Stables
Market, Chalk Farm Road, London NW1 8AB
Email: info@belowtheriver.co.uk
Web site: www.belowtheriver.co.uk/
Freq: Daily
Circ: 11612 Cision Digital Reach
MAGAZINE (ONLINE)
Regional General Interest

benchpeg   997898
Editorial: benchpeg ltd, 18 Market Place,
Romsey, Romsey SO51 8NA
Email: info@benchpeg.com
Web site: benchpeg.com
Freq: Daily
Circ: 11920 Cision Digital Reach
MAGAZINE (ONLINE)
Crafts, Education, Fashion, Graphic
Design, Luxury Goods, Manufacturing

benhealth   985595
Editorial: Holgate Park Drive, London YO26
4GG **Tel:** 44 08004 148286
Email: benhealth@caspianmedia.com
Web site: benenden.co.uk/social
Freq: Quarterly
Circ: 351831 Not Audited
MAGAZINE
Health & Medicine, Lifestyle, Men's
Interests, Regional General Interest,
Women's Interests

Bent
982058

Editorial: 1 Commercial Court, Briggate, Leeds LS1 6ER
Email: editor@bent.com
Web site: http://mag.bent.com/
Freq: Monthly
Circ: 60000 Not Audited
Editor: Gordon Hopps
Profile: Magazine containing news, celebrity interviews, events coverage, what's on section, music, games, book reviews and competitions. Aimed primarily at the gay market.Previous title: NOW UK Regular features: Beauty The latest beauty news, tips and new products.; Books Feature covering reviews of the latest book releases.; Culture Reviews of the latest art exhibitions, music releases and dance shows.; Fashion The latest fashion for men and women.; Film Feature covering reviews of the latest film and DVD releases.; Gadgets Reviews of the latest gadgets.; Gay Club Scene A listing of events that are on in the gay club scene.; Gay News The latest news from the Gay community.; Health Feature covering fitness information.; Music; Sauna Guide; Theatre Reviews of current theatre shows.
Ad Rate: Full Page Colour £995.00
MAGAZINE
LGBT

Bentley Magazine
984382

Tel: 44 01270 255155
Email: communications@bentley.co.uk
Web site: www.bentleymedia.com
Freq: Quarterly
Circ: 66000 Not Audited
Editor: Julia Marozzi
Profile: Magazine covering lifestyle & motoring issues and articles on new and old Bentleys and forthcoming Bentley products, travel, leisure, homes, luxury goods and owner profiles. First published in 2002, the publication has an average of 80 pages per issue. Aimed at Bentley owners.
Ad Rate: Full Page Colour £7950.00
MAGAZINE
Antique & Collectible Cars, Driving, Luxury Goods, Men's Interests

Berkeley Magazine
1095183

Web site: http://www.berkeleygroup.co.uk/property-developers/berkeley/berkeley-magazine
Freq: Annual
Circ: 30000 Not Audited
MAGAZINE
Luxury Goods

Berkhamsted Living
982497

Editorial: 27b The Old Silk Mill, Tring, Tring HP23 5EF **Tel:** 44 01442 824300
Email: info@livingmags.info
Web site: www.livingmags.info
Freq: Quarterly
Circ: 12000 Not Audited
Profile: Publication that covers regional general interest and community news.
MAGAZINE
Regional General Interest

Berkshire Life
982470

Editorial: 28 Teville Road, Worthing, Worthing BN11 1UG
Web site: berksandbucks.greatbritishlife.co.uk/home
Freq: Monthly
Circ: 1000 Not Audited
Editor: Janice Raycroft
MAGAZINE
Regional General Interest

Bermuda Parent
1060625

Tel: 44 14415 042937
Email: info@bermudaparent.bm
Web site: http://www.bermudaparent.bm
Freq: Quarterly Not Audited
MAGAZINE
Alternative Medicine, Disability, Elementary School, Family & Parenting, Fitness & Exercise, Health & Medicine, Lifestyle, Local Entertainment Guides, Media Relations, Medicine

Bermuda: Re + ILS
986594

Editorial: Kingfisher House, 21-23 Elmfield Road, London BR1 1LT
Freq: Bi-Monthly
Circ: 3710 Not Audited
MAGAZINE
News & Current Affairs

Bernoulli
983350

Editorial: 841 High Road, London N12 8PT
Tel: 44 02084 462100
Email: info@kimberleymediagroup.com
Web site: http://www.racetechmag.com
Freq: Annual
Circ: 15000 Not Audited
Profile: Magazine covering the theory and practice of road and race car aerodynamics. Aimed at those involved in optimising the performance of road and race cars, from design right through to the actual competitive events. Also read by wind tunnel developers and suppliers of rolling roads, instrumentation and flow visualisation technology.
Ad Rate: Full Page Mono £2500.00
Ad Rate: Full Page Colour £3000.00
MAGAZINE
Antique & Collectible Cars, Automakers, Automotive, Driving, Engineering, Motorcycles, Off-road & 4-Wheel Drive Vehicles, Trucks & SUVs

Beside Magazine
1056567

Email: contact@besidemag.co.uk
Web site: http://besidemag.co.uk/
Freq: Monthly
Circ: 559 Not Audited
MAGAZINE
Europe, Lifestyle, Men's Interests, Regional General Interest, Women's Interests

The Bespoke Black Book
997131

Email: info@thebespokeblackbook.com
Web site: www.thebespokeblackbook.com
Freq: Daily
Circ: 13385 Cision Digital Reach
MAGAZINE (ONLINE)
Luxury Goods, Men's Interests, Women's Interests

Bespoke Mag
998071

Editorial: 106 Chapman Road, London CR0 3NW
Email: info@bespokemag.co.uk
Web site: www.bespokemag.co.uk
Freq: Daily
Circ: 14823 Cision Digital Reach
Editor: Sidney Korboe
MAGAZINE (ONLINE)
Art, Basketball, Dance Music, Fashion, Literature, Men's Interests, Motorsports, Rap & Hip Hop, Relationships, Soccer

best
980752

Editorial: 33 Broadwick Street, London W1F 9EP **Tel:** 44 02074 395000
Email: best@hearst.co.uk
Web site: www.hearst.co.uk/brands/best
Freq: Weekly
Circ: 139635 Not Audited
Profile: Magazine featuring celebrity news and real life stories. Each issue features celebrity columnists, fashion, beauty, diet and cookery. First published in 1987. Aimed at the BC1C2 woman aged between 40 and 50.
Ad Rate: Full Page Colour £20555.00
MAGAZINE
Women's Interests

Best Baby and Toddler Gear Magazine
1101097

Tel: 44 01205 751649
Web site: https://www.mumii.co.uk/award
Freq: Annual Not Audited
MAGAZINE
Family & Parenting

Best Buggy
1103633

Web site: www.bestbuggy.co.uk
Freq: Daily

Circ: 59238 Cision Digital Reach
MAGAZINE (ONLINE)
Family & Parenting

Best Health - CEASED
986449

Editorial: BMJ Evidence Centre, BMA House, Tavistock Square, London WC1H 9JR
Email: support@bmj.com
Web site: www.bmj.com/company/products-services/#service15
Freq: Daily
Circ: 5153 Cision Digital Reach
MAGAZINE (ONLINE)
Health & Medicine

Best of British
983249

Editorial: Unit 101, The Perfume Factory, 140 Wales Farm Road, London W3 6UG
Tel: 44 02087 528181
Email: info@bestofbritishmag.co.uk
Web site: www.bestofbritishmag.co.uk/
Freq: Monthly
Circ: 36000 Not Audited
Editor: Simon Stabler
Profile: Magazine focusing on nostalgia from the 1940s, 1950s and 1960s together with the best of British life today. Aimed at people aged 45 years old and over and all those interested in history, heritage and nostalgia.
Ad Rate: Full Page Colour £900.00
MAGAZINE
History

The Best of Health
998030

Email: hello@thebestofhealth.co.uk
Web site: www.thebestofhealth.co.uk
Freq: Daily
Circ: 10452 Cision Digital Reach
MAGAZINE (ONLINE)
Health & Medicine, Retirement Savings

The Best of Irish Kitchens
999220

Tel: 44 02891 478703
Email: enquiries@bayviewpublishing.net
Web site: www.bayviewpublishing.net/irish-kitchens.html
Freq: Bi-Monthly
Circ: 8000 Not Audited
Editor: Claire Craig
MAGAZINE
Do-It-Yourself (DIY)

Best Value Wordsearch
996106

Editorial: Academic House, 24-28 Oval Road, London NW1 7DT
Tel: 44 02072 418000
Email: eclipsepuzzles@bauer.co.uk
Web site: www.puzzlemagazines.co.uk
Freq: Monthly Not Audited
Editor: Christine Scott
MAGAZINE
Games, Competitions & Events

The Best You
999654

Editorial: 3rd Floor, 5 Percy Street, London W1T 1DG **Tel:** 44 02079 276500
Email: info@thebestyou.co
Web site: www.thebestyoumagazine.co
Freq: Monthly
Circ: 35695 Cision Digital Reach
Editor: Bernardo Moya
MAGAZINE (ONLINE)
Careers, Family & Parenting, Health & Medicine, Personal Finance, Relationships

BESTFIT
1053256

Editorial: Crown House, 94 Armley Road, Leeds LS12 2EJ **Tel:** 44 01133 224400
Email: info@bestfitmagazine.co.uk
Web site: www.bestfitmagazine.co.uk
Freq: Monthly
Circ: 90000 Not Audited
MAGAZINE
Bodybuilding, Fitness & Exercise, Nutrition

BeTheRedCarpet.co.uk
1055934

Editorial: 151-153 Lector Court, Farringdon Road, London EC1R 3AF
Tel: 44 07814 957727

Web site: www.betheredcarpet.co.uk
Freq: Daily
Circ: 521 Cision Digital Reach
MAGAZINE (ONLINE)
Entertainment, Local Entertainment Guides, Movies & Video, Theater & Performing Arts

Better Retailing
1053707

Tel: 44 01223 894200
Email: info@jfnproductions.co.uk
Web site: www.betterretailingmagazine.co.uk
Freq: Quarterly
Circ: 4000 Not Audited
Editor: Alistair Forrest
Profile: Publication that covers retail business issues and expert business advice.
MAGAZINE
Health & Medicine, Nutrition

Better Society
1053860

Editorial: Sixth Floor, 3 London Wall Buildings, London EC2M 5PD
Tel: 44 02075 622400
Web site: www.bettersociety.net
Freq: Daily
Circ: 15806 Cision Digital Reach
Editor: Matt Ritchie
MAGAZINE (ONLINE)
Business, Charitable Foundations, Corporate Responsibility, Environment, Government, Social Issues, Sustainable Development

Better Society Network
1052764

Editorial: Sixth Floor, 3 London Wall Buildings, London EC2M 5PD
Email: info@bettersociety.net
Web site: http://bettersociety.net/
Freq: Daily
Circ: 15806 Cision Digital Reach
MAGAZINE (ONLINE)
Business, Charitable Foundations, Corporate Responsibility, Environment, Public Sector, Social Issues

Bettercaring.com
999478

Editorial: Suite 4, The Hub, 3 Drove Road, Newhaven BN9 0AD **Tel:** 44 01273 757313
Email: bettercaring@valuingcarefm.com
Web site: www.bettercaring.com
Freq: Daily
Circ: 6189 Cision Digital Reach
MAGAZINE (ONLINE)
Retirement Savings

Betting Business Interactive
981617

Editorial: Oak House, 1st Floor, 4 Highstreet, Chorley PR7 1DW
Tel: 44 01257 277400
Email: info@gbmedia.eu
Web site: http://www.betting-business.co/
Freq: Monthly
Circ: 4030 Not Audited
Editor: Imogen Goodman
Profile: Magazine covering the latest business developments within the betting industry. Aimed at betting office managers and online betting operators.
Ad Rate: Full Page Mono £960.00
Ad Rate: Full Page Colour £1200.00
MAGAZINE
Computer & Video Games

Betty magazine
996156

Email: info@bettymagazine.co.uk
Web site: www.bettymagazine.co.uk
Freq: Annual Not Audited
Editor: Charlotte Jacklin
MAGAZINE
Beauty & Grooming, Cosmetics, Fashion, Hair, Women's Interests

Beyond Bespoke
1053195

Editorial: Mayfair, London
Tel: 44 02033 274006
Email: enquires@beyond-bespoke.com
Web site: https://beyond-bespoke.com
Freq: Daily

Consumer Magazines

Freq: Daily
Circ: 9111 Cision Digital Reach
MAGAZINE (ONLINE)
Entertainment, Movies & Video

Blood Sweat and Fashion 997059
Email: info@bloodsweatandfashion.com
Web site: www.bloodsweatandfashion.com
Freq: Daily
Circ: 1538 Cision Digital Reach
MAGAZINE (ONLINE)
Airline Inflight, Beauty & Grooming, Cosmetics, Fashion, Hair, Railroad, Travel

Blooloop.com 999001
Editorial: Cuckoo Farm, West Anstey, South Molton, South Molton EX36 3PN
Tel: 44 02081 239777
Email: info@blooloop.com
Web site: www.blooloop.com
Freq: Daily
Circ: 30029 Cision Digital Reach
Editor: Owen Ralph
MAGAZINE (ONLINE)
Travel

The Blue and White Fanzine
999665
Editorial: Amcrol Ltd, Unit 1, Rowleys Park, Shotton, Deeside, Shotton CH5 1QJ
Email: info@theblueandwhitefanzine.co.uk
Web site: http://theblueandwhitefanzine.co.uk
Freq: 3 Times/Year
Circ: 400 Not Audited
MAGAZINE
Soccer

Bluemoon 996409
Editorial: University of Hertfordshire SU, College Lane, Hatfield Al10 9AB
Tel: 44 01707 285005
Email: printeditor@tridentmedia.org
Web site: http://tridentmedia.org/category/bluemoon/
Freq: Bi-Monthly Not Audited
MAGAZINE
Student Lifestyle

Blueprint Guide 997302
Editorial: Suite 1, Sabrina Hous, Sabrina Court, Longden Coleham, Shrewsbury SY3 7BF **Tel:** 44 01743 231135
Email: news@blueprintmedia.org.uk
Web site: www.blueprintguide.co.uk
Freq: Daily
Circ: 11071 Cision Digital Reach
Editor: Nick Bevan
MAGAZINE (ONLINE)
Travel

Blues & Rhythm 982686
Tel: 44 01234 826158
Email: enquiries@bluesandrhythm.co.uk
Web site: www.bluesandrhythm.co.uk
Freq: Monthly
Circ: 1000 Not Audited
Editor: Tony Burke
MAGAZINE
Jazz & Blues

Blues & Soul 982086
Editorial: PO Box 1976, Croydon CR90 9FX
Tel: 44 02031 748020
Email: editorial@bluesandsoul.com
Web site: www.bluesandsoul.com
Freq: Bi-Monthly
Circ: 55000 Not Audited
Editor: Lee Tyler
Profile: Comprehensive review of urban music, Hip-Hop, Soul, Jazz, Dance and R&B. Focuses on clubs, charts, record reviews, and includes reports from the USA and celebrity interviews. Read by males between 16 and 50 years and females between 16 and 38 years.
MAGAZINE
Jazz & Blues

Blues in Britain 982087
Editorial: Blues In Britain, 11 Langdon Avenue, Aylesbury HP21 9UL
Tel: 44 01296 393877

Web site: www.bluesinbritain.org
Freq: Monthly
Circ: 4500 Not Audited
Profile: Magazine covering the contemporary British blues scene with news, interviews and profiles, live, events, CD and DVD reviews and a national Gig Guide to blues events. Aimed at those interested in the live British blues scene and blues music in general.Previous title: Blueprint - The Magazine of the British Blues Connection Regular features: Blues News Details on forthcoming festivals, tours, events and band news relating to the blues music scene.; CDs To date these have been compilations of original material written and played by current UK artists.; Demo Box Usually 1 page featuring reviews of demo CD's and tapes.; E-Letters Articles written by artists in the first person, usually 700-800 words plus a photograph.; Festivals Reviews of Blues festivals in the UK, Europe and USA, occasionally other parts of the world.; Gig Guide Featuring 4 pages of forthcoming live gigs, mostly in the UK but also Ireland and Europe. Plus page for contact phone numbers or email addresses for venues and clubs.; Interviews Interviews with blues artists either resident in the UK or playing live in the UK.; Live and Blue Featuring 6 pages of reviews of live blues gigs.; New & Blue Featuring 8 pages of CD reviews, DVD's and books etc.
MAGAZINE
Jazz & Blues

Blues Matters! 1102953
Editorial: PO Box 18, Bridgend CF33 6YW
Tel: 44 01656 745628
Email: editor@bluesmatters.com
Web site: www.bluesmatters.com
Freq: Bi-Monthly
Circ: 9000 Not Audited
MAGAZINE
Jazz & Blues

Bluesci 983288
Email: news@bluesci.co.uk
Web site: www.bluesci.org
Freq: 3 Times/Year
Circ: 4500 Not Audited
Profile: Magazine offering a forum for students from all disciplines interested in topical science debate. Aimed at graduates and undergraduates of Cambridge University.
Ad Rate: Full Page Colour £500.00
MAGAZINE
Science, Student Lifestyle

BLUFF Europe 983421
Editorial: Temple Chambers, Temple Avenue, London EC4Y OHP
Web site: www.bluffeurope.com
Freq: Monthly
Circ: 49000 Not Audited
MAGAZINE
Casinos & Gaming

Bluffers.com 996882
Editorial: Hammersley House, 5-8 Warwick Street, London W1B 5LX
Tel: 44 02071 835015
Web site: http://bluffers.com/
Freq: Daily
Circ: 7067 Cision Digital Reach
MAGAZINE (ONLINE)
Men's Interests, Women's Interests

BMA News 980800
Editorial: BMA House, Tavistock Square, London WC1H 9JP **Tel:** 44 02073 874499
Email: bmanews@bma.org.uk
Web site: http://www.bma.org.uk/
Freq: Weekly
Circ: 100000 Not Audited
Profile: Magazine containing news about the British Medical Association, NHS news, medical politics, features and analysis. The magazine offers a mix of news, comment and analysis — with BMA exclusives, opinion and insight from the leaders of the profession and the grassroots BMA members — and provides a forum for debate of the key issues affecting doctors in their day-to-day practice and the wider NHS

Read by members of the British Medical Association.
Ad Rate: Full Page Mono £3045.00
Ad Rate: Full Page Colour £4860.00
MAGAZINE
Medicine

BMFA News 981980
Editorial: Chacksfield House, 31 St Andrews Road, Leicester LE2 8RE
Tel: 44 0162 440028
Email: admin@bmfa.org
Web site: www.bmfa.org
Freq: Bi-Monthly
Circ: 33000 Not Audited
Editor: Pete Dodds
Profile: Journal covering all aspects of model flying and building. Aimed at enthusiasts and members of the association.
Ad Rate: Full Page Colour £840.00
MAGAZINE
Crafts, Hobbies, & Collecting

The BMJ 981184
Editorial: BMA House, Tavistock Square, London WC1H 9JP **Tel:** 44 02073 874410
Email: editor@bmj.com
Web site: www.bmj.com/thebmj
Freq: Weekly Not Audited
Editor: Kamran Abbasi
Profile: International medical journal with the mission to lead the debate on health and to engage, inform, and stimulate doctors, researchers, and other health professionals in ways that will improve outcomes for patients. It provides the latest research, education, news, and comment articles. Read by general practitioners and hospital doctors.
Ad Rate: Full Page Colour £5500.00
MAGAZINE
Medicine

The BMJ - bmj.com (U.S.)
1001424
Web site: www.bmj.com/about-bmj/editorial-staff/bmj-united-states
Freq: Daily
Circ: 53 Cision Digital Reach
MAGAZINE (ONLINE)
News & Current Affairs

BMJ Quality & Safety 985868
Editorial: BMA House, Tavistock Square, London WC1H 9JR **Tel:** 44 02073 836373
Email: info.bmjqs@bmj.com
Web site: http://qualitysafety.bmj.com/
Freq: Monthly
Circ: 100000 Not Audited
Profile: BMJ Quality & Safety (formerly QSHC) is a international peer review journal providing information to improve patient safety and quality of care.
MAGAZINE
Health Administration, Medicine

BMW Car 982633
Editorial: The Manor Nepicar House, London Road, Wrotham Healt, Sevenoaks TN15 7RS **Tel:** 44 01732 748000
Email: bmwcar@unity-media.com
Web site: www.bmwcarmagazine.com
Freq: Monthly
Circ: 30000 Not Audited
Editor: Bob Harper
Profile: Magazine containing news and information on the BMW car. Includes products and articles on BMW tuned vehicles.
Ad Rate: Full Page Colour £1650.00
MAGAZINE
Automakers

BMW Magazine 982634
Editorial: Talbert House, 52A Borough High Street, London SEI 1XN
Email: crmcommunications@bmw.co.uk
Web site: www.bmwmagazine.com
Freq: Semi-Annual
Circ: 372588 Not Audited
MAGAZINE
Automakers

BN1 Magazine 987478
Editorial: Above Emporium, 88 London Road, Brighton, London BN1 4JF
Tel: 44 01273 911919
Email: info@bn1magazine.co.uk
Web site: www.bn1magazine.co.uk
Freq: Monthly
Circ: 12500 Not Audited
Editor: Chris Sadler
MAGAZINE
Regional General Interest

BoardroomMum 987498
Editorial: c/o UHY Peacheys, Lanyon House, Mission Court, Newport NP20 2DW
Email: media@boardroommum.com
Web site: www.boardroommum.com
Freq: Daily
Circ: 5014 Cision Digital Reach
MAGAZINE (ONLINE)
Careers

Boat International 982204
Editorial: First Floor, 41-47 Hartfield Road, Wimbledon, London SW19 3RQ
Tel: 44 02085 459330
Email: info@boatinternationalmedia.com
Web site: www.boatinternational.com
Freq: Monthly
Circ: 35000 Not Audited
Editor: Stewart Campbell
Profile: Magazine covering all aspects of luxury yachting including news, legal column, technology, international show previews, design focus, review and on board features of yachts from around the world, charter and brokerage, charter features and market intelligence. Includes latest builds, projects and designs. First published in 1983, the publication has an average of 320 pages per issue. Aimed at affluent boat owners and industry professionals.
Ad Rate: Full Page Colour £5219.00
MAGAZINE
Boating & Yachting

Boat Trader 983575
Editorial: Boatshop 24 Ltd, London Road, Sayers Common, Hassocks BN6 9HS
Tel: 44 01243 533394
Email: sales@boatshop24.co.uk
Web site: http://www.boatsandoutboards.co.uk/Boat-Trader
Freq: Monthly
Circ: 31500 Not Audited
Profile: Publication that focuses on boating and yachting listing boats for sale. The magazine is split into clearly defined price ranges; boats under £10k, £20k, £30k, £40k and boats £40k and over. Additionally, Boat Trader constantly reviews the pricing guide for used boats, contains a buyer's and seller's guide, an events guide and has Boat Jumble pages. Aimed at those looking to purchase a boat.The publication is mostly an advertising magazine.
Ad Rate: Full Page Colour £465.00
MAGAZINE
Boating & Yachting

Boating & Watersports 997946
Editorial: Suite 6ci and 6cii, Britannia House, Leagrave Road, Luton LU3 1RJ
Tel: 44 01582 488385
Email: info@mediachameleon.co.uk
Web site: boatsandwatersportswebsite.co.uk
Freq: Annual
Circ: 121700 Not Audited
MAGAZINE
Boating & Yachting, Swimming/Watersports

Boating Business 984242
Editorial: The Old Mill, Lower Quay, Fareham, Fareham PO16 0RA
Tel: 44 01329 825335
Email: editor@boatingbusiness.com
Web site: www.boatingbusiness.com
Freq: Monthly
Circ: 4220 Not Audited
Profile: Magazine covering news, features, new products, personnel movements and developments within the British leisure

marine industry. Read by the boating and yachting trade.
Ad Rate: Full Page Mono £1775.00
Ad Rate: Full Page Colour £2345.00
MAGAZINE
Boating & Yachting, Marine & Boat Trade

Bodyshop Magazine
981250
Tel: 44 01296 642800
Email: info@bodyshopmag.com
Web site: www.bodyshopmag.com
Freq: Monthly
Circ: 7725 Not Audited
Editor: Mark Hadaway
Profile: Magazine covering both the car and commercial vehicle refinishing and crash repair market. Read by proprietors, key personnel of body shops, factors and distributors, specialist bodybuilders, coachbuilders, product manufacturers, vehicle manufacturers and insurance companies
Ad Rate: Full Page Colour £1575.00
MAGAZINE
Automotive

Bolder
997919
Tel: 44 07890 560315
Email: info@be-bolder.com
Web site: http://be-bolder.com/
Freq: Daily
Circ: 8623 Cision Digital Reach
MAGAZINE (ONLINE)
Retirement Savings

Bolide
1102570
Editorial: 19A Buckingham Street, Brighton BN1 3LT **Tel:** 44 07976 299636
Email: cars@bolide.co.uk
Web site: www.bolide.co.uk
Freq: Daily
Circ: 2631 Cision Digital Reach
Editor: Nicholas Froome
MAGAZINE (ONLINE)
Antique & Collectible Cars

Bomb Petite
1104001
Editorial: 21 Finchley House, 176 Finchley Road, London NW3 6BT
Email: editor@bombpetite.com
Web site: http://bombpetite.com/
Freq: Daily
Circ: 8917 Cision Digital Reach
Editor: Yuliya Petryk
MAGAZINE (ONLINE)
Fashion

Bon
994614
Editorial: 3-7 Herbal Hill, London EC1R 5EJ
Tel: 44 01924 700100
Email: magazine.editor@bonmarche.co.uk
Web site: www.bonmarche.co.uk
Freq: Quarterly
Circ: 100000 Not Audited
MAGAZINE
Fashion, Women's Interests

Bonafide
998608
Editorial: Swan Wharf, 60 Dace Road, London E3 2NQ
Email: mailbox@bonafidemag.com
Web site: http://www.bonafidemag.com/
Freq: Semi-Annual
Circ: 10000 Not Audited
MAGAZINE
Rap & Hip Hop

Bonhams Magazine
998899
Editorial: 101 New Bond Street, London W1S 1SR **Tel:** 44 02074 688394
Email: magazine@bonhams.com
Web site: https://www.bonhams.com/publications/bonhams_magazine/
Freq: Quarterly
Circ: 35000 Not Audited
Editor: Lucinda Bredin
MAGAZINE
Antiques/Collectibles, Art

Bonnes Vacances
994973
Editorial: 2 Seven Dials, Bath BA1 1EN
Tel: 44 01225 463752
Email: editor@frenchentree.com

Web site: www.frenchentree.com
Freq: Monthly
Circ: 132760 Cision Digital Reach
MAGAZINE (ONLINE)
Travel

The Book Collector
984039
Editorial: 22 Clarendon Road, London W11 3AB **Tel:** 44 02076 020502
Email: editor@thebookcollector.co.uk
Web site: www.thebookcollector.co.uk
Freq: Quarterly Not Audited
Profile: Journal containing articles of interest to book collectors, booksellers and librarians, including sales, catalogues, exhibitions, publications, book reviews and current events. First published in 1952. Aimed at book collectors, bibliographers and university and public libraries in the UK and USA.
Ad Rate: Full Page Mono £220.00
MAGAZINE
Antiques/Collectibles, Literature

Bookanista
996625
Email: editors@bookanista.com
Web site: bookanista.com
Freq: Daily
Circ: 12843 Cision Digital Reach
Editor: Mark Reynolds
MAGAZINE (ONLINE)
Literature

BookBrunch
984890
Tel: 44 07949 594093
Email: editor@bookbrunch.co.uk
Web site: www.bookbrunch.co.uk
Freq: Daily
Circ: 16866 Cision Digital Reach
Profile: Website covering literature. The BookBrunch shares the latest news and information relating to literature.
MAGAZINE (ONLINE)
Literature, Publishing

Books for Keeps
990685
Editorial: Unit 1, Brampton Park Road, Wood Green, London N22 6BG
Tel: 44 07762 003464
Email: enquiries@booksforkeeps.co.uk
Web site: www.booksforkeeps.co.uk
Freq: Bi-Monthly
Circ: 14527 Cision Digital Reach
Profile: Website with an overview of children's book publishing. Aimed at teachers, professionals and parents interested in children's books.Richard Hill is the Managing Director to whom press releases should be addressed.
Ad Rate: Full Page Mono £700.00
Ad Rate: Full Page Colour £700.00
MAGAZINE (ONLINE)
Elementary School, Literature, Teen/Young Adult

books monthly
987878
Email: editor@booksmonthly.co.uk
Web site: www.booksmonthly.co.uk
Freq: Daily
Circ: 5699 Cision Digital Reach
Editor: Paul Norman
Profile: Website covering books reviews, features articles, original stories and competitions. Aimed at anyone who likes books.Previous title: gatewaymonthly.co.uk
MAGAZINE (ONLINE)
Literature

Bookshelf Boyfriend
998726
Editorial: 2nd Floor, Tavistock Enterprise Hub, Elbow Lane, Tavistock PL19 0BN
Tel: 44 08456 805917
Email: press@bookshelfboyfriend.com
Web site: http://www.bookshelfboyfriend.com/
Freq: Daily
Circ: 2173 Cision Digital Reach
MAGAZINE (ONLINE)
Women's Interests

boom
985894
Email: hello@boomuk.net
Web site: www.boomuk.net
Freq: Daily

Circ: 845 Cision Digital Reach
Editor: Richard Fallon
MAGAZINE (ONLINE)
Classical/Choral/Band Music, Country, Folk, Bluegrass, Dance Music, Entertainment, Jazz & Blues, Movies & Video, Music, Pop Music, R&B, Urban, World, Rap & Hip Hop

Boots Health & Beauty
982366
Editorial: Sea Containers, 18 Upper Ground, London SE1 9RQ **Tel:** 44 02037 877000
Web site: http://www.boots.com/en/Welcome-to-the-home-of-Health-Beauty-magazine_1191135/
Freq: Bi-Monthly
Circ: 3500000 Not Audited
Editor: Helen Daly
Profile: Magazine focusing on health and beauty issues. Contains articles on hair, skincare and medical problems. Aimed at Boots' Advantage Card holders, primarily women aged between 25 and 45 years old.
Ad Rate: Full Page Colour £24150.00
MAGAZINE
Beauty & Grooming, Cosmetics, Hair, Health & Medicine

Boots Parenting Club
984556
Editorial: 18 Upper Ground, Sea Containers House, London SE1 9RQ
Tel: 44 02037 877000
Email: info@redwoodgroup.net
Web site: http://www.boots.com/en/Mother-Baby/Parenting-Club/
Freq: Monthly
Circ: 1000000 Not Audited
Editor: Vicky Carlisle
MAGAZINE
Family & Parenting

Boots.com
997113
Editorial: Boots.com Digital Marketing, Boots Head Office, Thane Road, Nottingham NG90 1BS **Tel:** 44 01159 506111
Web site: http://www.boots.com/
Freq: Daily
Circ: 8831309 Cision Digital Reach
MAGAZINE (ONLINE)
Beauty & Grooming, Cosmetics, Hair, Health & Medicine

BordersRugby.net
999474
Editorial: Hotdisc Studios, 21 Redpath Crescent, Galashiels, Selkirk TD1 2QD
Tel: 44 01750 20014
Email: bordersrugby@hotmail.com
Web site: http://www.bordersrugby.net/
Freq: Daily
Circ: 11904 Cision Digital Reach
Editor: Stuart Cameron
MAGAZINE (ONLINE)
Rugby

Borough Insight
999072
Editorial: Town Hall, The Parade, Epsom, London KT18 5BY **Tel:** 44 01372 732000
Email: boroughinsight@epsom-ewell.gov.uk
Web site: http://insight.epsom-ewell.gov.uk/issue-31-september-2016/this-issue/welcome-to-this-months-e-boroug
Freq: 3 Times/Year
Circ: 36000 Not Audited
MAGAZINE
News & Current Affairs

Bossa Brazil Magazine
1072716
Tel: 44 02076 177284
Web site: www.bbmag.co.uk
Freq: Quarterly
Circ: 10000 Not Audited
MAGAZINE
Regional General Interest

The Boundary Magazine
996155
Tel: 44 01454 774061
Email: theboundaryonline@gmail.com
Web site: http://www.theboundary-online.co.uk
Freq: Monthly
Circ: 9500 Not Audited
MAGAZINE
Regional General Interest

Boundless
995928
Editorial: Britannia House, 21 Station Road, Brighton BN1 4DE **Tel:** 44 08006 69944
Email: hello@boundlessmag.co.uk
Web site: www.boundless.co.uk
Freq: Bi-Weekly
Circ: 241987 Not Audited
MAGAZINE
Automotive, Driving

Bounty
984498
Editorial: 29 Broadwater Road, Welwyn Garden City, Welwyn Garden City AL7 3BQ
Tel: 44 01707 294000
Email: editor@bounty.com
Web site: www.bounty.com
Freq: Daily
Circ: 458486 Cision Digital Reach
Profile: Website covering family, childcare, pregnancy, beauty, fashion, health and relationships.
MAGAZINE (ONLINE)
Family & Parenting

Bounty Baby Product Guide
999144
Editorial: 29 Broadwater Road, Welwyn Garden City, Welwyn Garden City AL7 3BQ
Tel: 44 01707 294000
Email: bountymedia@bounty.com
Web site: www.bounty.com/bmedia
Freq: Semi-Annual
Circ: 260000 Not Audited
Editor: Emily Barun
MAGAZINE
Family & Parenting

Bournemouth News & Info
1052820
Tel: 44 07784 148419
Email: news@bournemouthnews.info
Web site: bournemouthnews.info
Freq: Daily
Circ: 12116 Cision Digital Reach
MAGAZINE (ONLINE)
Bars, Clubs & Pubs, Entertainment, Local Entertainment Guides, Regional General Interest

Bournemouth Town
997464
Editorial: 376 Ringwood Road, Poole, Poole BH12 3LT **Tel:** 44 01202 580200
Email: info@bournemouthtown.co.uk
Web site: bournemouthtown.co.uk
Freq: Daily
Circ: 521 Cision Digital Reach
MAGAZINE (ONLINE)
Regional General Interest

Bournville News
996575
Email: info@bournvillevillage.com
Web site: http://bournvillevillage.com/
Freq: Daily
Circ: 13034 Cision Digital Reach
Editor: Dave Harte
MAGAZINE (ONLINE)
Regional General Interest

Boutique.
985709
Editorial: The Goods Shed, Jubilee Way, Whistable Road, Faversham, Faversham ME13 8GD **Tel:** 44 01795 509106
Web site: www.boutique-magazine.com
Freq: Monthly
Circ: 5000 Not Audited
Editor: Gemma Ward
Profile: Website covering independent womenswear retailers. Its covers the latest fashion industry news, buying essentials and business advice. Aimed at independent retailers.
MAGAZINE
Fashion

Bow International
985095
Editorial: Lawrence House, Morrell Street, Leamington Spa, Leamington Spa CV32 5SZ
Email: fieldsports@futurenet.com
Web site: www.bow-international.com
Freq: Bi-Monthly Not Audited
Profile: Magazine covering archery including stories, product reviews, news and information from Great Britain and across

the world. Aimed at traditional and modern archers.
MAGAZINE
Field Sports

Bowls International   982226
Editorial: Key Publishing Ltd, PO Box 100, Peterborough PE9 1XQ
Tel: 44 01780 755131
Email: bowls@keypublishing.com
Web site: www.bowlsinternational.com
Freq: Monthly
Circ: 5000 Not Audited
Editor: Sian Honnor
Profile: Magazine containing news and coaching tips. Covers sport's biggest names and personalities, provides tip-top instruction and advice aimed at improving the readers game, coupled with expert opinion, debate and words of wisdom on all aspects of the sport. Read by bowls players and enthusiasts.
Ad Rate: Full Page Mono £1136.00
Ad Rate: Full Page Colour £1340.00
MAGAZINE
Bowling

Boxing Monthly   982227
Editorial: 40 Morpeth Road, London E9 7LD
Tel: 44 02089 864141
Email: mail@boxing-monthly.co.uk
Web site: www.boxing-monthly.co.uk
Freq: Monthly
Circ: 15000 Not Audited
Profile: Magazine covering all aspects of boxing. Features fight previews, ringside reports, book and video reviews and interviews. Aimed predominantly at men under the age of 45 as well as boxers, promoters, trainers and others involved at every level of the sport.
Ad Rate: Full Page Mono £800.00
Ad Rate: Full Page Colour £900.00
MAGAZINE
Boxing

Boxing News   982228
Editorial: 30 Cannon Street, London EC4M 6YJ **Tel:** 44 02076 183072
Email: info@newsquestspecialistmedia.com
Web site: www.boxingnewsonline.net
Freq: Weekly
Circ: 7117 Not Audited
Editor: Matt Christie
Profile: Magazine covering the latest previews, reviews and boxing information from around the world. Aimed at 18 to 45 year old men with an interest in boxing.
Ad Rate: Full Page Colour £1315.00
MAGAZINE
Boxing

The Boys' Brigade Gazette
982441
Editorial: The Boys' Brigade UK Headquarters, Felden Lodge, Felden, London HP3 0BL **Tel:** 44 01442 231681
Email: gazette@boys-brigade.org.uk
Web site: boys-brigade.org.uk/media/about-the-gazette
Freq: Quarterly
Circ: 9000 Not Audited
MAGAZINE
Teen/Young Adult

Boys By Girls   1053366
Web site: http://www.boysbygirls.co.uk
Freq: Semi-Annual
MAGAZINE
Fashion, Men's Interests

Boyz   982059
Editorial: 18 Brewer Street, London W1F 0SH **Tel:** 44 02070 256100
Email: listings@boyz.co.uk
Web site: www.boyz.co.uk
Freq: Weekly
Circ: 50000 Not Audited
Editor: Luke Till
Profile: Magazine containing features, celebrity interviews, club scene news and arts reviews. Aimed at gay men.
Ad Rate: Full Page Colour £850.00
MAGAZINE
LGBT

Brass Band World   982065
Editorial: PO Box 53, Penarth CF64 5XY
Tel: 44 02920 704325
Email: editor@brassbandworld.net
Web site: www.brassbandworld.co.uk
Freq: Monthly
Circ: 3000 Not Audited
Editor: David Childs
Profile: Magazine containing independent international information on brass band playing and concert news. Aimed at those who enjoy listening to, or playing in brass bands in Britain and overseas.Regular features: Bands People Profile Featuring a profile on a prominent brass band personality.; Brass Tips Featuring readers letters and questions relating to brass bands.; CD Reviews Reviews of brass band related CD's.; Funding Advice A feature offering funding advice to brass bands.; Staccato A question and answer feature relating to brass bands.
Ad Rate: Full Page Colour £650.00
MAGAZINE
Classical/Choral/Band Music, Jazz & Blues

The Brass Herald   982803
Editorial: 2 The Coppice, Impington, Cambridge CB24 9YR **Tel:** 44 01223 234090
Email: editor@thebrassherald.com
Web site: www.thebrassherald.com
Freq: Bi-Monthly
Circ: 7000 Not Audited
Editor: Philip Biggs
Profile: Magazine covering the full range of brass music from brass bands to orchestral brass, Salvation Army bands to big bands and Military bands to jazz. Aimed at players of all types of brass instrument.
MAGAZINE
Classical/Choral/Band Music, Jazz & Blues, Music

Breakaway Reviewers   1063927
Editorial: Flat 10, View Point Lodge, 614 Ashley Road, Poole BH14 0AW
Tel: 44 01202 733879
Email: rony.breakawayreviewers@outlook.com
Web site: www.breakawayreviewers.co.uk
Freq: Daily
Circ: 9866 Cision Digital Reach
MAGAZINE (ONLINE)
Literature

BREAKING travel news   982819
Editorial: Momentum House, Lower Road, London SE1 8SJ **Tel:** 44 02034 324351
Email: editor@breakingtravelnews.com
Web site: www.breakingtravelnews.com
Freq: Daily
Circ: 159732 Cision Digital Reach
Editor: Chris O'Toole
Profile: Website covering travel news. BREAKING Travel News shares the latest news and insights into the travel and tourism sector.
MAGAZINE (ONLINE)
Travel

Breast Cancer Care   984663
Editorial: 5-13 Great Suffolk Street, London SE1 0NS **Tel:** 44 08450 920800
Email: info@breastcancercare.org.uk
Web site: www.breastcancercare.org.uk
Freq: Daily
Circ: 142552 Cision Digital Reach
Profile: Blog covering news updates on breast care health and treatments to cancer support groups.
MAGAZINE (ONLINE)
Charitable Foundations, Patient Support

The Brent Magazine   983060
Editorial: Brent Civic Centre, Engineer's Way, Wembley HA9 0FJ
Tel: 44 02089 371062
Email: tbm@brent.gov.uk
Web site: http://www.brent.gov.uk/council-news/the-brent-magazine/
Freq: Quarterly
Circ: 103000 Not Audited
Profile: Magazine of Brent County Council, covering local residents, council news,

things to do in Brent. This outlet covers areas within the Borough of Brent.
MAGAZINE
Regional General Interest

Brentwood Live   981708
Editorial: 91 Orsett Road, Grays, Grays RM17 5EX **Tel:** 44 01268 522792
Email: bwnnews@newsquest.co.uk
Web site: http://www.brentwoodlive.co.uk/
Freq: Weekly
Circ: 13836 Cision Digital Reach
Editor: Gary Pearson
Profile: The Brentwood Weekly News is a weekly, local newspaper covering all the latest news, sport and leisure for the surrounding area.
MAGAZINE (ONLINE)

The Brewer and Distiller International   980815
Editorial: 44A Curlew Street, Butler's Wharf, London SE1 2ND **Tel:** 44 02074 998144
Email: editor@ibd.org.uk
Web site: www.ibd.org.uk
Freq: Monthly
Circ: 5000 Not Audited
MAGAZINE
Alcohol & Spirits, Bars, Clubs & Pubs, Manufacturing

Brewers' Guardian   980812
Editorial: Suite 4A, Alma House, Alma Road, Reigate RH2 0AX **Tel:** 44 01737 221232
Freq: Daily
Circ: 6631 Cision Digital Reach
Profile: International journal featuring technological developments and market trends, giving an overview of the brewing industry. Each issue contains news and opinion pieces together with in-depth features for an objective overview of the industry today. Read by brewery industry executives worldwide.Regular features: Contests; Guest Columnist; Innovations; Marketing; Now and Then Diary dates and pages looked at in previous issues.
Ad Rate: Full Page Colour £1200.00
MAGAZINE (ONLINE)
Alcohol & Spirits, Bars, Clubs & Pubs

The Brewery Manual   996147
Editorial: 3rd Floor, Alma House, Alma Road, Reigate, Reigate RH2 0AX
Tel: 44 01737 221232
Freq: Annual
Circ: 12050 Not Audited
MAGAZINE
Alcohol & Spirits, Bars, Clubs & Pubs

brewerymanual.com   997795
Editorial: 3rd Floor, Alma House, Alma Road, Reigate, Reigate RH2 0AX
Tel: 44 01737 221232
Email: info@advantagepublishing.co.uk
Web site: www.brewerymanual.com
Freq: Daily
Circ: 9682 Cision Digital Reach
MAGAZINE (ONLINE)
Alcohol & Spirits, Bars, Clubs & Pubs

Bricks Magazine   1094858
Email: submissions@bricksmagazine.co.uk
Web site: www.bricksmagazine.co.uk
Freq: Quarterly
MAGAZINE
Art, Fashion, Photography

Bridal Buyer   984092
Editorial: 1 Canada Square, Canary Wharf, London E14 5AP **Tel:** 44 02071 938300
Web site: www.bridalbuyer.com
Freq: Bi-Monthly
Circ: 17000 Not Audited
Profile: Magazine focused on the UK bridalwear market, the bridal business and related exhibitions. Also contains merchandise information and solid business advice to retailers, including legal, financial and marketing. Aimed at bridal retailers, suppliers and manufacturers.
Ad Rate: Full Page Colour £2240.00
MAGAZINE
Fashion, Weddings

Bridalbeautyeditor.com   1053614
Web site: www.bridalbeautyeditor.com/
Freq: Daily
Circ: 521 Cision Digital Reach
MAGAZINE (ONLINE)
Weddings

Bride   999040
Editorial: Cumberland House, Oriel Road, Cheltenham GL50 1BB
Tel: 44 01242 216050
Email: info@weddingsite.co.uk
Web site: http://www.bridemagazine.co.uk/magazines/
Freq: Annual
Circ: 320000 Not Audited
Editor: Amanda Griffiths
MAGAZINE
Weddings

Brides Abroad   985675
Editorial: Kilndene Studios, Kirk, Deighton, Wetherby LS22 4EA **Tel:** 44 08002 118255
Email: terri@bridesabroad.tv
Web site: www.bridesabroad.tv
Freq: Bi-Monthly
Circ: 30000 Not Audited
Editor: Terri Cody-Owen
Profile: Magazine featuring information and advice when planning a wedding abroad. Features destinations, honeymoon ideas and real wedding stories.
MAGAZINE
Airline Inflight, Travel, Weddings

Bridge   981898
Editorial: Ryden Grange, Knaphill, London GU21 2TH **Tel:** 44 01483 489961
Email: bridge@mrbridge.co.uk
Web site: www.mrbridge.co.uk
Freq: Monthly
Circ: 50000 Not Audited
Editor: John Magee
Profile: Church of England newspaper covering news, listings and book reviews relevant to churchgoers. Also contains articles featuring community issues of relevance. Aimed at churchgoers within the Diocese of Southwark.This outlet covers areas within Bexley Borough, Bromley Borough, Greenwich Borough, Croydon Borough, Kingston upon Thames Borough, Lambeth Borough, Lewisham Borough, Merton Borough, Richmond upon Thames Borough, Southwark Borough, Sutton Borough and Wandsworth Borough.
MAGAZINE
Games

Bridge For Design   984863
Editorial: Unit 16, Millbrook Trading Estate, Sybron Way, Jarvis Book, Crowborough TN6 3DZ **Tel:** 44 01892 667600
Web site: http://www.bridgefordesign.com/
Freq: Quarterly
Circ: 25000 Not Audited
Profile: Interior design magazine. Aimed at interior designers, hotel specifiers and architects.
Ad Rate: Full Page Colour £1750.00
MAGAZINE
Do-It-Yourself (DIY), Luxury Goods

Bridge Magazine   981899
Editorial: 44 Baker Street, London W1U 7RT
Tel: 44 02074 867015
Email: info@bridgeshop.com
Web site: http://shop.chess.co.uk/BRIDGE-Magazine-Online-s/1824.htm
Freq: Daily
Circ: 11263 Cision Digital Reach
Editor: Mark Horton
MAGAZINE (ONLINE)
Games

Brig   983816
Editorial: Stirling Univ. Students Association, The Robbins Centre, University of Stirling, Stirling FK9 4LA
Tel: 44 01786 467176
Email: editor@brignewspaper.com
Web site: http://brignews.com/
Freq: Monthly
Circ: 1500 Not Audited

Profile: Student publication covering news, politics and sport with a features and entertainment supplement. Aimed at students at the University of Stirling.
MAGAZINE
Student Lifestyle

Bright Shiny News
986548

Editorial: Bright Shiny News, First Floor, 102 Albion Road, London N16 9PD
Tel: 44 07900 917545
Email: editorial@brightshinynews.com
Web site: www.brightshinynews.com
Freq: Daily
Circ: 1251 Cision Digital Reach
MAGAZINE (ONLINE)
Celebrities, Women's Interests

Brighton and Hove News
995335

Web site: www.brightonandhovenews.org
Freq: Daily
Circ: 113049 Cision Digital Reach
MAGAZINE (ONLINE)
News & Current Affairs

Brighton Magazine
998595

Editorial: 9-12 Middle Street, Brighton, Brighton BN1 1AL
Web site: http://magazine.brighton.co.uk/
Freq: Daily
Circ: 49194 Cision Digital Reach
MAGAZINE (ONLINE)
Regional General Interest, Travel

Brighton Source
985468

Web site: http://brightonsource.co.uk/
Freq: Daily
Circ: 14929 Cision Digital Reach
Editor: James Kendall
Profile: Online guide to what's on in Brighton including clubbing, eating out, theatre, concerts, fashion and shopping. Aimed at Brighton residents and visitors between 18 to 35 year old.
MAGAZINE (ONLINE)
Regional General Interest

Brighton Style Magazine
997015

Web site: www.brightonstylemag.com
Freq: Daily Not Audited
MAGAZINE
News & Current Affairs

Brighton Visitor
985180

Tel: 44 01273 770044
Email: editorial@brightonvisitor.com
Web site: www.brightonvisitor.com
Freq: 3 Times/Year
Circ: 50000 Not Audited
Editor: Nick Mosley
MAGAZINE
Regional General Interest

Brighton.co.uk
982857

Editorial: The Media Centre, 9-12 Middle Street, Brighton BN1 1AL
Tel: 44 01273 381100
Email: editor@brighton.co.uk
Web site: www.brighton.co.uk
Freq: Daily
Circ: 70098 Cision Digital Reach
Editor: Mike Cobley
Profile: Website covering lifestyle. The brighton.co.uk website provides information on local facilities and entertainment in the Brighton and Hove area.
MAGAZINE (ONLINE)
Local Entertainment Guides, Travel

Bring The Noise UK
985161

Editorial: 191 West Green Road, Tottenham, London N15 5EA
Web site: www.bringthenoiseuk.com
Freq: Daily
Circ: 13397 Cision Digital Reach
Editor: Hannah Gillicker
MAGAZINE (ONLINE)
Audio Video Trade, Cameras, Consumer Electronics, Country, Folk, Bluegrass, Dance Music, Electronics, Fashion, Jazz & Blues, Mobile Electronics, Movies & Video

Bristol 24/7
985254

Editorial: Unit 2.4 Paintworks, Arnos Vale, Bristol BS4 3EH **Tel:** 44 01172 309247
Email: editor@bristol247.com
Web site: www.bristol247.com
Freq: Monthly
Circ: 20000 Not Audited
MAGAZINE
Classical/Choral/Band Music, Country, Folk, Bluegrass, Dance Music, Jazz & Blues, Music, Pop Music, R&B, Urban, World, Rap & Hip Hop, Regional, Regional General Interest

Bristol Life
983448

Editorial: Circus Mews House, Circus Mews, Bath BA1 2PW **Tel:** 44 01225 475800
Email: info@mediaclash.co.uk
Web site: www.mediaclash.co.uk
Freq: Monthly
Circ: 10000 Not Audited
MAGAZINE
Regional General Interest

The Bristol Magazine
983447

Editorial: 2 Princes Building, George Street, Bath BA1 2AD **Tel:** 44 01179 742800
Email: editor@thebristolmagazine.co.uk
Web site: www.thebristolmagazine.co.uk
Freq: Monthly
Circ: 20000 Not Audited
Editor: Amanda Nicholls
Profile: Magazine covering lifestyle, leisure, local issues, events, culture, property, antiques, gardening, food, commercial activities, architecture and regional news. Aimed at owners of property in Bristol and the surrounding areas that have a value in excess of £200,000.
Ad Rate: Full Page Colour £1075.00
MAGAZINE
Regional General Interest

The Brit Crowd
1066386

Email: emily@britcrowd.com
Web site: http://britcrowd.com/
Freq: Daily
Circ: 13667 Cision Digital Reach
Editor: Emily Vilares
MAGAZINE (ONLINE)
Travel

BRITAIN
982338

Editorial: Jubilee House, 2 Jubilee Place, London SW3 3TQ **Tel:** 44 02073 493700
Email: editor@britain-magazine.co.uk
Web site: http://www.britain-magazine.com
Freq: Bi-Monthly
Circ: 80000 Not Audited
Profile: Magazine published on behalf of Visit Britain and telling the story of Britain, from ancient times through to the present day and including features on all aspects of travel in Britain. Aimed at visitors to Britain.
Ad Rate: Full Page Colour £3200.00
MAGAZINE
Travel

Britain at War
985062

Editorial: PO BOX 100, Peterborough PE9 1XQ **Tel:** 44 01780 755131
Email: contact@britainatwar.com
Web site: www.britainatwar.com
Freq: Monthly
Circ: 10843 Not Audited
Editor: Andy Saunders
MAGAZINE
History

BritEvents
1052831

Email: info@britevents.com
Web site: http://www.britevents.com/
Freq: Daily
Circ: 6412 Cision Digital Reach
MAGAZINE (ONLINE)
Bars, Clubs & Pubs, Comedy, Entertainment, Local Entertainment Guides, Movies & Video

British Airways High Life Shop
982802

Editorial: 85 Strand, London WC2R 0DW
Tel: 44 02075 508000

Web site: www.cedarcom.co.uk/our-work/highlife-shop.html
Freq: Quarterly
Circ: 230000 Not Audited
MAGAZINE
Airline Inflight

British Archaeology
1074635

Editorial: Beatrice de Cardi House, 66 Bootham, York YO30 7BZ
Tel: 44 01904 671417
Email: editor@archaeologyuk.org
Web site: http://www.britisharchaeology.org/
Freq: Bi-Monthly
Circ: 16000 Not Audited
Editor: Mike Pitts
MAGAZINE
History

British Army Review
995730

Editorial: War Development, Land Warfare Centre, Warminster BA12 0DJ
Tel: 44 01985 223050
Email: armyreview@armymail.mod.uk
Freq: Quarterly Not Audited
Editor: Graham Thomas
MAGAZINE
Armed Forces

The British Art Journal
983886

Editorial: 46 Grove Lane, London SE5 8ST
Email: editor@britishartjournal.co.uk
Web site: www.britishartjournal.co.uk/
Freq: 3 Times/Year Not Audited
Editor: Robin Simon
Profile: Journal covering all periods of the history of British art including painting, sculpture, architecture, photography and decorative arts.
Ad Rate: Full Page Mono £1500.00
Ad Rate: Full Page Colour £2500.00
MAGAZINE
Art

British Association of Teachers of the Deaf Magazine
998616

Editorial: 21 Keating Close, Rochester ME1 1EQ **Tel:** 44 08456 435181
Email: magazine@batod.org.uk
Web site: www.batod.org.uk
Freq: Bi-Monthly
Circ: 1500 Not Audited
Editor: Paul Simpson
MAGAZINE
Disability, Education

The British Automobile Racing Club Magazine
982680

Tel: 44 01264 882200
Email: info@barc.net
Web site: www.barc.net
Freq: Quarterly
Circ: 5000 Not Audited
MAGAZINE
Motorsports

The British Bandsman
982066

Editorial: 68 Westgate, Mid Calder, Livingston EH53 0SP **Tel:** 44 01506 882985
Email: news@britishbandsman.com
Web site: www.britishbandsman.com
Freq: Weekly
Circ: 5500 Not Audited
Profile: Magazine containing contest results, news items, concerts and technical articles on brass playing and music. Aimed at those interested in brass bands and their music.
Ad Rate: Full Page Mono £419.00
Ad Rate: Full Page Colour £625.00
MAGAZINE
Classical/Choral/Band Music

British Chess Magazine
981911

Editorial: The Lodge, 51 Prospect Road, Farnbrough, Farnborough GU14 8NT
Email: editor@britishchessmagazine.com
Web site: http://www.britishchessmagazine.co.uk/
Freq: Monthly
Circ: 1200 Not Audited

Profile: Worldwide coverage of chess, practical play, literature, book reviews, history, player profiles and computer chess. Read by UK and overseas chess enthusiasts.
Ad Rate: Full Page Mono £150.00
Ad Rate: Full Page Colour £150.00
MAGAZINE
Chess

British Comedy Guide
990549

Editorial: 58 London Road, Liphook, Liphook GU30 7TA
Email: contact@comedy.co.uk
Web site: www.comedy.co.uk
Freq: Daily
Circ: 234657 Cision Digital Reach
MAGAZINE (ONLINE)
Comedy

British Deaf News
981823

Editorial: 3rd Floor, 356 Holloway Road, London N7 6PA **Tel:** 44 02076 974140
Web site: www.bda.org.uk
Freq: Monthly
Circ: 5000 Not Audited
Profile: Magazine containing news, events, reviews, topical articles, personal opinions and features on every subject that affects deaf people and their families, including lifestyle, entertainment, sports and disability sports. Read by deaf and hard of hearing people and their families, British Sign Language students, teachers for the deaf, librarians, educationalists, interpreters, international social activists, social services and the charity sector in the UK and overseas.
Ad Rate: Full Page Mono £1000.00
Ad Rate: Full Page Colour £1100.00
MAGAZINE
Disability, Patient Support

British Dealer News
984249

Editorial: 10 Daddon Court, Clovelly Road Ind Est, Bideford EX39 3FH
Tel: 44 01237 422660
Email: editorial@dealernews.co.uk
Web site: www.britishdealernews.co.uk
Freq: Monthly
Circ: 8661 Not Audited
Editor: Paul Smith
Profile: Magazine focusing on the British motorcycle and scooter industry. Aimed at dealers, importers, distributors, wholesalers, parts and accessory manufacturers.
Ad Rate: Full Page Colour £1360.00
MAGAZINE
Automotive, Supply Chain Management (SCM)

British Dressage
982232

Tel: 44 02476 698830
Email: whitepebblemedia@btinternet.com
Web site: http://www.britishdressage.co.uk/
Freq: Bi-Monthly
Circ: 15000 Not Audited
Editor: Barbara Young
Profile: Official magazine of British Dressage covering horse dressage including complete listings of scheduled events throughout the country, reports on training, dressage, international events, junior level reports and committee news. Aimed at members of British Dressage.
Ad Rate: Full Page Colour £2000.00
MAGAZINE
Equestrian Sports

The British Equestrian Directory
982243

Editorial: Stockeld Park, Wetherby, Spofforth LS22 4AW **Tel:** 44 01937 582111
Email: directories@beta-int.com
Web site: www.britishequestriandirectory.com/
Freq: Daily
Circ: 3449 Cision Digital Reach
MAGAZINE (ONLINE)
News & Current Affairs

British Eventing Life Magazine
998853

Tel: 44 02476 698856
Email: info@britisheventing.com

Consumer Magazines

Web site: www.britisheventing.com
Freq: Bi-Monthly
Circ: 12500 Not Audited
Editor: Nina Lloyd-Jones
MAGAZINE
Equestrian Sports

The British Fantasy Society
995171
Web site: http://www.britishfantasysociety.
org/
Freq: Daily
Circ: 10450 Cision Digital Reach
MAGAZINE (ONLINE)
Entertainment, Literature, Movies &
Video, Science Fiction

British Food Journal
983577
Editorial: Howard House, Wagon Lane,
Bingley BD16 1WA **Tel:** 44 01274 777700
Web site: http://www.
emeraldgrouppublishing.com/products/
journals/journals.htm?id=BFJ
Freq: Monthly Not Audited
Profile: Journal containing news on food
quality, processing and manufacturing.
Aimed at academic researchers in the food
area.
MAGAZINE
News & Current Affairs

British Guild of Beer Writers
998098
Editorial: Woodcote, 2 Jury Road,
Dulverton, Dulverton TA22 9DU
Tel: 44 01398 324314
Web site: www.beerguild.co.uk
Freq: Daily
Circ: 13535 Cision Digital Reach
MAGAZINE (ONLINE)
Beer

British Heritage
997419
Email: info@britishheritage.com
Web site: britishheritage.com
Freq: Bi-Monthly
Circ: 20000 Not Audited
MAGAZINE
Travel

British Homing World
982270
Editorial: Severn Farm Industrial Estate,
Severn Road, Welshpool, Welshpool SY21
7DF **Tel:** 44 01938 552360
Email: editor@britishhomingworld.co.uk
Web site: www.rpra.org/british-homing-
world
Freq: Weekly
Circ: 20000 Not Audited
Editor: Steven Richards
Profile: Pigeon racing and showing
magazine. Includes race and show results,
features on winning birds and performances
and articles on the management and
conditioning of pigeons for racing. Read by
pigeon racers and breeders.
Ad Rate: Full Page Mono £164.85
Ad Rate: Full Page Colour £216.32
MAGAZINE
Games, Competitions & Events

British Horse
982233
Editorial: The British Horse Society, Abbey
Park, Stareton, Kenilworth CV8 2XZ
Tel: 44 02476 840463
Email: communications@bhs.org.uk
Web site: www.bhs.org.uk
Freq: Bi-Monthly
Circ: 78677 Not Audited
Editor: David Prince
Profile: Magazine covering the involvement
of The British Horse Society in equestrian
welfare, safety, education and access to the
countryside. First published in 1985. Aimed
at members of the British Horse Society.
Ad Rate: Full Page Colour £2750.00
MAGAZINE
Equestrian Sports

British Journal of Aesthetics
985377
Editorial: Oxford University Press, Great
Clarendon Street, Oxford OX2 6DP
Tel: 44 01865 353907
Email: bja@sheffield.ac.uk
Web site: https://academic.oup.com/
bjaesthetics
Freq: Quarterly
Circ: 23854 Cision Digital Reach
Editor: Elisabeth Schellekens
MAGAZINE (ONLINE)
Plastic/Reconstructive/Cosmetic Surgery

British Journal of Hospital Medicine
981620
Editorial: St Jude's Church, Dulwich Road,
London SE24 0PB **Tel:** 44 02077 385454
Email: bjhm@markallengroup.com
Web site: http://www.magonlinelibrary.com/
toc/hmed/current
Freq: Monthly
Circ: 2500 Not Audited
Profile: Journal containing clinical reviews of
new developments in hospital medicine. First
published in 1996. Read by doctors,
surgeons and nurses.
MAGAZINE
Medicine

British Journal of Nutrition
999060
Editorial: 10 Cambridge Court, 210
Shepherds Bush Road, London W6 7NJ
Tel: 44 02076 020228
Email: bjn.edoffice@cambridge.org
Web site: www.nutritionsociety.org/
publications/nutrition-society-journals/
british-journal-of-nutrition
Freq: Bi-Weekly Not Audited
MAGAZINE
Nutrition

British Journal of Surgery
985346
Editorial: 151 West George Street, Glasgow
G2 2JJ
Email: bjs@wiley.com
Web site: www.bjs.co.uk
Freq: Monthly Not Audited
Profile: Journal focusing on developments in
surgical practice, with articles on clinical and
laboratory based research on all aspects of
general surgery and related topics. Aimed at
general and vascular surgeons.
Ad Rate: Full Page Mono £625.00
MAGAZINE
Medicine

British Medical Bulletin
985378
Editorial: Oxford University Press, Great
Clarendon Street, Oxford OX2 6DP
Tel: 44 01865 556767
Email: bmb.editorialoffice@oup.com
Web site: bmb.oxfordjournals.org
Freq: Quarterly Not Audited
MAGAZINE
Medicine

The British Museum Magazine
981877
Editorial: Great Russell Street, London
WC1B 3DG **Tel:** 44 02073 238000
Email: information@britishmuseum.org
Web site: www.britishmuseum.org
Freq: 3 Times/Year
Circ: 30000 Not Audited
Editor: Mira Hudson
Profile: Magazine containing articles on
news, exhibitions, research and new
acquisitions at British Museum; also
archaeological work and outside research.
Read by members of the British Museum
Friends and those with an interest in the
British Museum.
Ad Rate: Full Page Mono £1200.00
Ad Rate: Full Page Colour £1800.00
MAGAZINE
Art, History

British Patchwork & Quilting
981948
Editorial: Traplet House, Willow End Park,
Blackmore Park Road, Malvern WR13 6NN
Tel: 44 01684 588500
Email: pq@traplet.com
Web site: inspiredtomake.com/zone/
patchwork-quilting/home
Freq: Monthly Not Audited
Editor: Joanna Kent
MAGAZINE
Crafts

British Philatelic Bulletin
984532
Editorial: Tallents House, 21 South Gyle
Crescent, Edinburgh EH12 9PB
Email: bulletinenquiries@royalmail.com
Freq: Monthly
Circ: 20000 Not Audited
Editor: William Doherty
Profile: Journal covering news and features
on British stamps and stamp collecting.
Aimed at philatelists and postal historians.
MAGAZINE
Antiques/Collectibles

British Railway Modelling
981981
Editorial: The Maltings, West Street, Bourne,
Bourne PE10 9PH **Tel:** 44 01778 391116
Web site: https://www.world-of-railways.co.
uk/
Freq: Monthly
Circ: 28000 Not Audited
Profile: Magazine reflecting the various
aspects of railway modelling as a creative
hobby. First published in 1993. Aimed at
those who enjoy railway modelling as a
hobby.
Ad Rate: Full Page Mono £380.00
Ad Rate: Full Page Colour £609.00
MAGAZINE
Crafts, Hobbies, & Collecting

British Showjumping
982683
Tel: 44 02476 698806
Email: press@britishshowjumping.co.uk
Web site: http://www.britishshowjumping.
co.uk/
Freq: Bi-Monthly
Circ: 45000 Not Audited
Editor: Maria Clayton
Profile: Magazine covering showjumping.
MAGAZINE
Equestrian Sports

British Theatre Guide
1053092
Email: editor@britishtheatreguide.info
Web site: www.britishtheatreguide.info/
Freq: Daily
Circ: 19481 Cision Digital Reach
Editor: David Chadderton
Profile: Website covering theatre. The
British Theatre Guide website shares the
latest theatre news, reviews, book reviews,
interviews and feature articles. Aimed at
industry professionals and keen
theatregoers.
MAGAZINE (ONLINE)
Classical/Choral/Band Music,
Entertainment, Literature, Local
Entertainment Guides, Theater &
Performing Arts

British Wildlife
981995
Editorial: 1-6 The Stables, Ford Road,
Totnes, Oxford TQ9 5LE
Tel: 44 01865 811316
Email: enquiries@britishwildlife.com
Web site: www.britishwildlife.com
Freq: Bi-Monthly
Circ: 7800 Not Audited
Editor: Malcolm Tait
MAGAZINE
Nature & Wildlife

BritishTheatre.com
987541
Editorial: 3rd Floor, 207 Regent Street,
London W1B 3HH
Email: news@britishtheatre.com
Web site: www.britishtheatre.com
Freq: Daily
Circ: 17365 Cision Digital Reach

Editor: Douglas Mayo
MAGAZINE (ONLINE)
Theater & Performing Arts

Britpopnews
988354
Email: jamie@britpopnews.com
Web site: http://britpopnews.com/
Circ: 26627 Cision Digital Reach
MAGAZINE (ONLINE)
Classical/Choral/Band Music, Country,
Folk, Bluegrass, Dance Music, Jazz &
Blues, Music, Pop Music, R&B, Urban,
World, Rap & Hip Hop, Rock Music

Britten's Info
985659
Editorial: Maple Cottage, Stody, Melton
Constable NR24 2ED **Tel:** 44 01263 862093
Web site: www.brittensinfo.com
Freq: Daily
Circ: 10709 Cision Digital Reach
Editor: Keith Britten
MAGAZINE (ONLINE)
Bars, Clubs & Pubs, Hotels/Motels

Broadband Journal
984961
Editorial: Communications House, 41a
Market Street, Watford, London WD18 0PN
Tel: 44 01923 815500
Email: office@thescte.eu
Web site: www.thescte.eu
Freq: Quarterly
Circ: 7000 Not Audited
Profile: Magazine covering cable
telecommunication engineering and featuring
reviews on new products. Read by members
of the Society of Cable Telecommunication
Engineers and other qualified persons.
MAGAZINE
Industry, Internet

Broadband TV News
984607
Editorial: PO Box 499, Cambridge CB1 0AH
Tel: 44 01223 464359
Email: news@broadbandtvnews.com
Web site: www.broadbandtvnews.com
Freq: Daily
Circ: 138194 Cision Digital Reach
Profile: Website covering business of
multiscreen television with news from cable
TV, satellite TV, IPTV, Mobile TV, DTT and
HDTV.
MAGAZINE (ONLINE)
Broadcasting

broadbandchoices.co.uk
985139
Editorial: First Floor, High Holborn House,
52-54 High Holborn, London WC1V 6RL
Tel: 44 02074 006200
Email: pr@broadbandchoices.co.uk
Web site: www.broadbandchoices.co.uk
Freq: Daily
Circ: 563485 Cision Digital Reach
MAGAZINE (ONLINE)
Audio Video Trade, Cameras, Consumer
Electronics, Electronics, Internet, Mobile
Electronics, Movies & Video,
Telecommunications/Electronic
Communications

Broadcast
979856
Editorial: Zetland House, 5-25 Scrutton
Street, London EC2A 4HJ
Tel: 44 02081 020900
Web site: www.broadcastnow.co.uk
Freq: Weekly
Circ: 6383 Not Audited
Editor: Chris Curtis
Profile: Magazine of the television and radio
industry covering all aspects of television,
radio, cable and satellite. Provides news,
analysis and commentary on latest events,
business and the broadcast industry.
Includes interviews with the biggest industry
names, latest TV ratings and in-depth
features on production, finance and digital.
Aimed at decision makers in the
broadcasting industry.
Ad Rate: Full Page Colour £3800.00
MAGAZINE
Broadcasting

Broadcast Film & Video 984962
Editorial: Unit C3, 6 Westbank Drive, Belfast BT3 9LA **Tel:** 44 02890 319008
Email: bfvnewscopy@flagshipmedia.co.uk
Web site: www.bftv.co.uk
Freq: Monthly
Circ: 9259 Not Audited
Editor: Jacqueline Purse
MAGAZINE
Broadcasting

Broadway Baby 1052658
Web site: www.broadwaybaby.com
Freq: Daily
Circ: 13406 Cision Digital Reach
MAGAZINE (ONLINE)
Theater & Performing Arts

Broccoli & Brains 1054324
Editorial: Cavendish House, Harlow Business Park, Parkway, Harlow CM19 5QF
Email: editor@broccoliandbrains.co.uk
Web site: www.broccoliandbrains.co.uk
Freq: Semi-Annual
MAGAZINE
Fitness & Exercise, Health & Medicine, Nutrition

Broderie Créative 998096
Tel: 44 33047 8729254
Freq: Bi-Monthly Not Audited
MAGAZINE
Do-It-Yourself (DIY)

brownbeautytalk 988137
Email: hello@brownbeautytalk.com
Web site: www.brownbeautytalk.com
Freq: Daily
Circ: 8797 Cision Digital Reach
MAGAZINE (ONLINE)
Beauty & Grooming, Cosmetics, Hair

Brummell 987356
Editorial: Ground Floor, 1-2 Ravey Street, London EC2A 4QP **Tel:** 44 02032 220101
Email: info@showmedialondon.com
Web site: http://brummellmagazine.co.uk/
Freq: Bi-Monthly
Circ: 20000 Not Audited
Profile: Lifestyle magazine covering information on elegant living including interiors, travel, property, style, art and motoring. Aimed at people working in the financial services.
Ad Rate: Full Page Colour £6000.00
MAGAZINE
Luxury Goods

BSBI News 995985
Editorial: Botanical Society of Britain and Ireland, 57 Walton Road, Shirehampton, Bristol BS11 9TA **Tel:** 44 07971 972529
Email: louise.marsh@bsbi.org
Web site: www.bsbi.org.uk
Freq: 3 Times/Year
Circ: 2850 Not Audited
Editor: Trevor James
MAGAZINE
Gardening

BSHAA News 995372
Editorial: C/O EBS Ltd, City Wharf, Davidson Road, Lichfield WS14 9DZ
Tel: 44 01543 442155
Email: editor@bshaa.com
Web site: www.bshaa.com
Freq: Bi-Monthly Not Audited
Editor: Trevor Andrews
MAGAZINE
Medicine

BT.com 987323
Editorial: 292 Vauxhall Bridge Road, London SW1V 1AE **Tel:** 44 02079 637000
Web site: http://home.bt.com
Freq: Daily
Circ: 21252 Cision Digital Reach
MAGAZINE (ONLINE)
News & Current Affairs

Btekt 987706
Web site: https://www.youtube.com/user/btekt/
Freq: Daily
Circ: 1804 Cision Digital Reach
Editor: Basil Kronfli
Profile: Website covering technology. Btekt shares the latest news and information on phones, tablets and general technology news.
MAGAZINE (ONLINE)
Mobile Electronics

BTF News 995360
Editorial: 2nd Floor, 3 Devonshire Place, Harrogate HG1 4AA **Tel:** 44 01423 810093
Email: editor@btf-thyroid.org
Web site: http://www.btf-thyroid.org/
Freq: 3 Times/Year
Circ: 4000 Not Audited
MAGAZINE
Diabetes, Patient Support

BTO News 981996
Editorial: The Nunnery, Thetford IP24 2PU
Tel: 44 01842 750050
Email: info@bto.org
Web site: www.bto.org
Freq: Bi-Monthly
Circ: 14000 Not Audited
Editor: Jeff Baker
Profile: Magazine of the British Trust for Ornithology. Details results of bird survey work and related articles. Aimed at birdwatchers.
MAGAZINE
Nature & Wildlife

Buckinghamshire & Berkshire Focus 1008680
Editorial: Suite 6B(i), Britannia House, Leagrave Road, Luton LU3 1RJ
Tel: 44 01582 488385
Email: info@mediachameleon.co.uk
Web site: www.buckinghamshire-focus.co.uk
Freq: Annual Not Audited
MAGAZINE
Antique & Collectible Cars, Automakers, Automotive, Basketball, Bicycles, Billiards, Boating & Yachting, Bodybuilding, Bowling, Boxing

Buckinghamshire Life 1098314
Web site: berksandbucks.greatbritishlife.co.uk
Freq: Monthly
Circ: 2000 Not Audited
Editor: Janice Raycroft
MAGAZINE
Regional General Interest

Bucks TV 999175
Editorial: Suite F 1st Floor, Elsinore House, Buckingham Street, Aylesbury HP20 2NQ
Tel: 44 01494 568883
Email: info@buckstv.co.uk
Web site: www.buckstv.co.uk
Freq: Daily
Circ: 13643 Cision Digital Reach
MAGAZINE (ONLINE)
Regional

Buddypower.net 984951
Editorial: 40 Bowling Green Lane, Clerkenwell, London EC1R 0NE
Tel: 44 02074 157070
Web site: www.buddypower.net
Freq: Daily
Circ: 1420 Cision Digital Reach
Profile: Website containing a range of national and international news on obesity and obesity related health stories with members helping one another share tips and support to lose and manage their weight. Aimed at members of Anne Diamond's Weight Management site.Previous title: FatHappens.com
MAGAZINE (ONLINE)
Nutrition

The Budgerigar 982021
Editorial: 6 Toutie Street, Alyth, Blairgowrie, Forfar PH11 8BP **Tel:** 44 01828 633030
Email: budgerigarsocietypa@live.co.uk
Web site: www.budgerigarsociety.com
Freq: Bi-Monthly
Circ: 2500 Not Audited
Profile: Magazine about keeping, breeding and exhibiting budgerigars.
MAGAZINE
Nature & Wildlife

Build It 981835
Editorial: 7 Kings Street Cloisters, Clifton Walk, London W6 0GY
Tel: 44 02036 273240
Email: buildit@castlemedia.co.uk
Web site: http://www.self-build.co.uk/
Freq: Monthly
Circ: 10477 Not Audited
Editor: Chris Bates
Profile: Magazine with case studies and product information on house building. Aimed at people organising the building and conversion of their own home.
Ad Rate: Full Page Colour £1935.00
MAGAZINE
Architecture & Design, Do-It-Yourself (DIY), Property Management & Maintenance

Building & Facilities Management 980931
Editorial: 17 Whitley Close, Irthlingborough, Irthlingborough NN9 5GN
Tel: 44 01933 800294
Email: bfm@abbeypublishing.co.uk
Web site: www.bfmmagazine.co.uk
Freq: Monthly
Circ: 8500 Not Audited
MAGAZINE
Charitable Foundations, Commercial Real Estate, Government, Interior Design, Legal Affairs, Office Design, Public Sector, Sustainable Development, Urban Planning & Development

Bulletin 985952
Editorial: Royal College of Speech and Language Therapists, 2 White Hart Yard, London SE1 1NX **Tel:** 44 02073 783012
Email: bulletin@rcslt.org
Web site: www.rcslt.org/about/publications/overview
Freq: Monthly
Circ: 14700 Not Audited
Editor: Steven Harulow
Profile: Publication containing news and views from The British Ecological Society and informative features on ecological issues.
Ad Rate: Full Page Mono £450.00
Ad Rate: Full Page Colour £900.00
MAGAZINE
Medicine

The Bulletin 998768
Editorial: The Hunt House, Paulerspury, Towcester NN12 7NA **Tel:** 44 01327 811788
Email: admin@rrec.org.uk
Web site: www.rrec.org.uk
Freq: Bi-Monthly
Circ: 10000 Not Audited
Profile: Publication containing news and views from The British Ecological Society and informative features on ecological issues.
Ad Rate: Full Page Mono £450.00
Ad Rate: Full Page Colour £900.00
MAGAZINE
Automakers

The Bulletin of The Vintage Sports-Car Club 982619
Editorial: The Old Post Office, West Street, Chipping Norton, Chipping Norton OX7 5EL
Tel: 44 01608 644777
Email: johnstaveley@ic24.net
Web site: www.vscc.co.uk
Freq: Quarterly
Circ: 7300 Not Audited
Editor: John Staveley
MAGAZINE
Antique & Collectible Cars

Bulletin the News 1054649
Freq: Semi-Annual
MAGAZINE
Africa, Fashion, Literature, Photography, Visual Arts

Bullring.co.uk 999235
Editorial: Bullring Shopping Centre, Birmingham B5 4BU **Tel:** 44 01216 321526
Email: marketing@bullring.co.uk
Web site: www.bullring.co.uk
Freq: Daily
Circ: 83516 Cision Digital Reach
Editor: Emma Roberts
MAGAZINE (ONLINE)
Beauty & Grooming, Cosmetics, Fashion, Hair

Bumps, Babies and Beyond 1094456
Tel: 44 01604 706023
Web site: bumpsbabiesandbeyond.info
Freq: Bi-Monthly
Circ: 20000 Not Audited
MAGAZINE
Family & Parenting

bunkered 982256
Tel: 44 01413 532222
Email: editorial@bunkered.co.uk
Web site: www.bunkered.co.uk
Freq: Bi-Monthly
Circ: 21504 Not Audited
Editor: Bryce Ritchie
Profile: Magazine covering all aspects of golf including interviews, player profiles, product reviews and golf instruction as well as competitions and offers. First published in 1996, the publication has an average of 174 pages per issue. Aimed at all levels of golfers, club secretaries and greenkeepers.
Ad Rate: Full Page Colour £1595.00
MAGAZINE
Golf

Bunkerworld 998698
Editorial: Regency House, First Floor, 4 Clarence Road, Windsor, Windsor SL4 5AD
Tel: 44 01753 410940
Email: unni@bunkerworld.com
Web site: www.bunkerworld.com
Freq: Daily
Circ: 122514 Cision Digital Reach
MAGAZINE (ONLINE)
Marine & Boat Trade, Shipping & Warehousing

BunnieBuzz - SUSPENDED JUNE 2016 997342
Web site: http://bunniebuzz.com/about-bunnie-buzz/
Freq: Daily
Circ: 92 Cision Digital Reach
MAGAZINE (ONLINE)
Family & Parenting

Burda Media Polska 1060529
Tel: 44 48224 488000
Email: kontakt@burdamedia.pl
Web site: http://www.burdamedia.pl Not Audited
MAGAZINE
Advertising Industry, Branding, Broadcasting, Graphic Design, Marketing, Media & Communications, Photography, Publishing

The Bureau of Investigative Journalism 985857
Tel: 44 07969 466285
Email: info@thebureauinvestigates.com
Web site: www.thebureauinvestigates.com
Freq: Daily
Circ: 52499 Cision Digital Reach
Profile: Website covering investigative journalism. The Bureau of Investigative Journalism covers the latest news from print and broadcast media.
MAGAZINE (ONLINE)
Broadcasting, National News, Publishing

Consumer Magazines

The Burlington Magazine 984036
Editorial: 14–16 Duke's Road, London
WC1H 9SZ Tel: 44 02073 881228
Email: burlington@burlington.org.uk
Web site: www.burlington.org.uk
Freq: Monthly Not Audited
Profile: Magazine covering fine and
decorative arts with articles on exhibitions,
reviews and books and a world wide
calendar of events. Read by art collectors
and fine art enthusiasts.
Ad Rate: Full Page Mono £1065.00
Ad Rate: Full Page Colour £1535.00
MAGAZINE
Art

Burnham-On-Sea.com 983690
Editorial: 36 Palmers Close, Burnham-On-
Sea, Burnham-on-sea TA8 2SS
Email: feedback@burnham-on-sea.com
Web site: www.burnham-on-sea.com
Freq: Daily
Circ: 149982 Cision Digital Reach
MAGAZINE (ONLINE)
Regional

Bury & West Suffolk Magazine
1074323
Tel: 44 01284 729117
Email: theburymag@bbpmagazines.com
Web site: www.bbpmagazines.com/
magazines
Freq: Monthly Not Audited
MAGAZINE
Regional

Bus & Coach Buyer 983928
Editorial: 4 Milnyard Square, Bakewell
Road, Orton Southgate, Peterborough PE2
6GX Tel: 44 01733 362300
Web site: www.busandcoachbuyer.com
Freq: Weekly
Circ: 5708 Not Audited
Editor: Stuart Jones
Profile: Magazine covering all aspects of
buying and selling buses, coaches,
mini-buses and related items. Aimed at
coach, minibus and bus company operators,
manufacturers and dealers.
Ad Rate: Full Page Colour £660.00
MAGAZINE
Automotive

Bus & Coach Preservation
983926
Editorial: 12 Redland Close, Aldermans
Green Industrial Estate, Coventry CV2 2NP
Tel: 44 02476 616930
Email: busandcoachpreservation@gmail.
com
Web site: http://www.presbuspublishing.
com/bcp.php
Freq: Monthly
Circ: 10000 Not Audited
Editor: Philip Lamb
Profile: Magazine containing news, features
and technical advice on older buses and
coaches.
Ad Rate: Full Page Mono £120.00
Ad Rate: Full Page Colour £120.00
MAGAZINE
Automakers, Automotive

Bus and Coach Professional
983924
Editorial: Unit 4, Marshbrook Business Park,
Church Stretton, Telford SY6 6QE
Tel: 44 01694 731510
Email: editor@busandcoach.com
Web site: www.busandcoach.com
Freq: Monthly
Circ: 5000 Not Audited
Profile: Magazine containing news briefings,
analysis, media reviews, professional
profiles, technology, government policies
and articles covering topical issues relating
to the bus and coach industry.
Ad Rate: Full Page Colour £990.00
MAGAZINE
Automotive

Bus User 998722
Editorial: Terminal House, Shepperton W17
8AS

Web site: www.bususers.org
Freq: Quarterly
Circ: 1800 Not Audited
MAGAZINE
Automotive, Environment, Travel

Buses 983927
Editorial: PO Box 14644, Leven KY9 1WX
Tel: 44 01780 755131
Email: buseseditor@btconnect.com
Web site: www.busesmag.com
Freq: Monthly
Circ: 12511 Not Audited
Editor: Alan Millar
Profile: Magazine containing information
and news on bus fleets, operators and
manufacturers. The magazine was published
by Ian Allen Publishing until 2012, when Key
Publishing aquired the title. Read by bus
industry professionals and enthusiasts
worldwide.
Ad Rate: Full Page Colour £630.00
MAGAZINE
Automotive

Business Car Manager 984098
Editorial: unit K, Reliance Wharf, Hertford
Road, London N1 5EW
Tel: 44 02037 736133
Email: editor@businesscarmanager.co.uk
Web site: www.businesscarmanager.co.uk
Freq: Daily
Circ: 19483 Cision Digital Reach
Profile: Online business motoring magazine.
Features include new car news, new
legislation, special reports on running
business vehicles, road tests, tax and
legislation advice.
MAGAZINE (ONLINE)
Automotive

Business Cloud 1065392
Editorial: UKFast Campus, Birley Fields,
Manchester M15 5QJ Tel: 44 02080 454945
Email: news@businesscloud.co.uk
Web site: http://www.businesscloud.co.uk/
Freq: Bi-Monthly
Circ: 20000 Not Audited
Editor: Chris Maguire
MAGAZINE
Auto Aftermarket, Business, Computers,
Data Management, Electronics,
Government Technology, Industry,
Internet, Mobile Communications,
Security & Security Systems

Business Destinations 983300
Editorial: 40 Compton Street, London EC1V
0AP Tel: 44 02070 140330
Email: enquiries@businessdestinations.com
Web site: www.businessdestinations.co.uk
Freq: Quarterly
Circ: 98766 Not Audited
Profile: Magazine combining up-to-date
country and city guides, interviews and
industry comment. Aimed at business
travellers.
Ad Rate: Full Page Colour £16960.00
MAGAZINE
Travel

Business Info 981057
Editorial: Amhurst House, 22 London Road,
Sevenoaks, Sevenoaks TN13 2BT
Tel: 44 01732 759725
Web site: www.binfo.co.uk
Freq: Bi-Monthly
Circ: 70000 Not Audited
Editor: James Goulding
MAGAZINE
Computers, Data Management,
Electronics, Internet, Office Supplies

**Business Life (British
Airways)** 979929
Editorial: 6th Floor, 85 Strand, London
WC2R ODW Tel: 44 02075 508000
Email: businesslife@cedarcom.co.uk
Web site: https://www.britishairways.com/
en-gb/business-travel/articles
Freq: Monthly
Circ: 92770 Not Audited

Editor: Tim Hulse
MAGAZINE
Airline Inflight, Business, Small and
Medium Business

Business Moneyfacts 980150
Editorial: Moneyfacts House, 66-70 Thorpe
Road, Norwich NR1 1BJ
Tel: 44 01603 476476
Email: enquiries@moneyfacts.co.uk
Web site: www.moneyfactsgroup.co.uk
Freq: Monthly
Circ: 2477 Not Audited
Editor: Lee Tillcock
Profile: Guide to business finance. Covers
buy to let mortgages, investment accounts,
business current account tariffs, commercial
business charge and credit cards, venture
capital and factoring. Also covers all aspects
of wealth management. First published in
1994, the publication has an average of 100
pages per issue. Aimed at accountants,
financial advisors, solicitors and any other
business finance intermediary.
Ad Rate: Full Page Mono £1300.00
Ad Rate: Full Page Colour £1500.00
MAGAZINE

Business Networx 999841
Editorial: 3 Octavian Way, Team Valley,
Trading Estate, Gateshead NE11 OHZ
Tel: 44 01914 871834
Email: info@teamvalleypublications.co.uk
Web site: http://teamvalleypublications.co.
uk/business-networx/
Freq: Bi-Monthly
Circ: 1500 Not Audited
MAGAZINE
Branding, Education, Environment, Health
& Safety, Legal Services, Marketing,
Travel

The Business of Everything
997678
Editorial: No 10, 143 George Street, London
W1H 5LB
Email: info@boemagazine.com
Web site: http://www.boemagazine.com/
Freq: Daily
Circ: 31037 Cision Digital Reach
MAGAZINE (ONLINE)
Bars, Clubs & Pubs, Luxury Goods,
Restaurant Reviews, Travel, Women's
Interests

Business Of Fashion 986097
Editorial: 6th Floor, Moray House, 23-31
Great Titchfield Street, London W1W 7PA
Email: info@businessoffashion.com
Web site: http://www.businessoffashion.
com/
Freq: Daily
Circ: 1352570 Cision Digital Reach
Profile: Website covering the fashion
industry. The Business of Fashion website
shares the latest on business in the fashion
industry, 'delivering fashion business
intelligence on emerging designers,
disruptive technologies and global brands'.
The daily newsletter has 80,000+
subscribers.
MAGAZINE (ONLINE)
Fashion

**Business Of Fashion -
Business Of Fashion (China)
Bureau** 1003756
Email: info@businessoffashion.com
Web site: http://cn.businessoffashion.com
Circ: 46183 Cision Digital Reach
MAGAZINE (ONLINE)
News & Current Affairs

**Business Process
Management Journal** 982936
Editorial: Howard House, Wagon Lane,
Bingley BD16 1WA
Web site: http://www.emeraldinsight.com/
loi/bpmj
Freq: Bi-Monthly Not Audited
Editor: Majed Al-Mashari
MAGAZINE
News & Current Affairs

**Business Review USA &
Canada** 1074963
Tel: 44 01603 217530
Web site: http://www.businessreviewusa.
com/
Freq: Monthly
MAGAZINE
News & Current Affairs

Business Travel IQ 988840
Editorial: Wells Point, 79 Wells Street,
London W1T 3QN Tel: 44 02079 704302
Web site: http://www.businesstravel-iq.com
Freq: Daily
Circ: 16479 Cision Digital Reach
Editor: Mark Frary
MAGAZINE (ONLINE)
Travel

**The Business Travel
Magazine** 983704
Editorial: Suffolk House, George Street,
Croydon CR9 1SR Tel: 44 02086 497233
Email: editorial@bmipublishing.co.uk
Web site: www.thebusinesstravelmag.com
Freq: Bi-Monthly
Circ: 18566 Not Audited
Profile: Publication covering a mix of news,
views and in-depth analysis of the most
relevant business travel topics. Content
ranges from back-to-basics guides to
reports and topical debate. Aimed at
business travel and meetings arrangers,
PAs, secretaries, finance managers,
purchase organisers and business travel
agents.
Ad Rate: Full Page Colour £3750.00
MAGAZINE
Travel

Business Travel News 985071
Editorial: PO Box 758, Edgware, London
HA8 4QF
Web site: http://www.businesstravelnews.
com/
Freq: Weekly
Circ: 99223 Cision Digital Reach
Profile: Website covering travel. The
Business Travel News website shares the
latest travel business news.
MAGAZINE (ONLINE)
Travel

Business Traveller 980133
Editorial: 41-43 Maddox Street, London
W1S 2PD Tel: 44 02078 212700
Email: editorial@businesstraveller.com
Web site: www.businesstraveller.com
Freq: Monthly
Circ: 65858 Not Audited
Profile: Magazine containing news and
features on international business travel.
Aimed at business and frequent travellers.
Ad Rate: Full Page Colour £6500.00
MAGAZINE
Travel

The Business Value Exchange
995491
Editorial: Staines One, Station Approach,
London TW18 4LY
Web site: businessvalueexchange.com
Freq: Daily
Circ: 49112 Cision Digital Reach
MAGAZINE (ONLINE)
Business, Computers, Corporate
Responsibility, Data Management,
Government Technology, Human
Resources, Industry, Internet, Mobile
Communications, Security & Security
Systems

Business Vans 984735
Editorial: Unit K, Reliance Wharf, Hertford
Road, London N1 5EW
Tel: 44 02037 736138
Email: editor@businesscarmanager.co.uk
Web site: www.businessvans.co.uk
Freq: Daily
Circ: 16637 Cision Digital Reach
MAGAZINE (ONLINE)
Automotive

Business Women Scotland
985277

Editorial: 11 Lymurloch Crescent, Glasgow G3 6EQ Tel: 44 01413 328801
Email: edit@bwsltd.co.uk
Web site: www.bws.co.uk
Freq: Bi-Monthly
Circ: 10000 Not Audited
Profile: Magazine featuring businesses from different working sectors in Scotland. Includes independent business advice as well as fashion and top tips on haircare, food and recipies.
MAGAZINE
Beauty & Grooming, Business, Cosmetics, Fashion, Hair, Small and Medium Business, Women's Interests

BusinessCar
981343

Editorial: Progressive House, 2 Maidstone Road, Foots Cray, London DA14 5HZ
Tel: 44 02082 697945
Email: editorial@businesscar.co.uk
Web site: www.businesscar.co.uk
Freq: Bi-Weekly
Circ: 16030 Not Audited
Profile: Magazine covering current news and trends affecting business cars including business car leasing, fleet management, hire purchase, contract hire and personal leasing, finance, insurance, business taxation, company car tax, car safety, risk management, test drives, fuel and fuel prices. Aimed at fleet managers and other senior management involved in running company cars.
Ad Rate: Full Page Mono £3330.00
Ad Rate: Full Page Colour £3330.00
MAGAZINE
Automotive

BusinessMole.com
1057956

Editorial: Hope Mill, 113 Pollard Street, Manchester M4 7JB
Email: editorial@businessmole.com
Web site: www.businessmole.com
Freq: Daily
Circ: 11843 Cision Digital Reach
Editor: Beth Haven
MAGAZINE (ONLINE)
Business, International News

Busy Woman
985516

Editorial: 14 Eastwood Road, London N10 1NL
Web site: www.busywoman.co.uk
Freq: Daily
Circ: 548 Cision Digital Reach
Editor: Melanie Carson
MAGAZINE (ONLINE)
Beauty & Grooming, Cosmetics, Fashion, Hair, Restaurant Reviews, Women's Interests

Buying Business Travel
982806

Editorial: 41-43 Maddox Street, Mayfair, London W1S 2PD Tel: 44 02078 212700
Email: editor@buyingbusinesstravel.com
Web site: www.buyingbusinesstravel.com
Freq: Bi-Monthly
Circ: 18000 Not Audited
Editor: Mark Frary; Editor: Paul Revel
Profile: Magazine covering the latest news, product information and updates within the corporate travel industry.
Ad Rate: Full Page Colour £4500.00
MAGAZINE
Travel

Buzz
984948

Editorial: 220c Cowbridge Road East, Canton, Cardiff CF5 1GY
Tel: 44 02920 226767
Email: editorial@buzzmag.co.uk
Web site: www.buzzmag.co.uk
Freq: Monthly
Circ: 100000 Not Audited
Profile: Buzz is a magazine featuring a what's on guide to Cardiff and South Wales including cinema, culture, theatre, nightlife, visual arts, food, gigs, fashion, beauty, music, sport and lifestyle as well as local events and current affairs. Aimed at those visiting and residing in South Wales.The magazine contains the following regular

features: Art - News from the art world and reviews of art related exhibitions and events. Clube - Feature about club events in South Wales.Fashion - The latest looks and themes for the season.Film - Reviews of ten of the latest film releases. Food and Drink - News and reviews of restaurants, cafes, bars and clubs.News - Feature covering news in South Wales. Previews - Previews of stage shows and other live performances.Reviews - Features reviews of CDs, DVDs, books, games and live events. Sport - Sports news and events.Travel - Reviews of travel destinations.
Ad Rate: Full Page Mono £720.00
Ad Rate: Full Page Colour £900.00
MAGAZINE
Regional General Interest

BVRLA News
984343

Editorial: River Lodge, Badminton Court, Amersham, Amersham HP7 0DD
Tel: 44 01494 434747
Email: info@bvrla.co.uk
Web site: www.bvrla.co.uk
Freq: Bi-Monthly
Circ: 4000 Not Audited
Profile: Official publication of the British Vehicle, Rental and Leasing Association. Covers motoring and transport issues, used-car market, vehicle security, topical news, environment-related issues, safety, insurance and current legislation and e-commerce. Read by senior executives in member companies, as well as government departments, MPs and MEPs.
Ad Rate: Full Page Colour £2100.00
MAGAZINE
Automotive

Byrdie UK
1053481

Email: contact@cliquemediainc.com
Web site: www.byrdie.co.uk
Freq: Daily
Circ: 904098 Cision Digital Reach
MAGAZINE (ONLINE)
Beauty & Grooming, Cosmetics, Fashion, Hair

C&IT
979993

Editorial: Bridge House, 69 London Road, Twickenham, London TW1 3QR
Tel: 44 02082 674285
Email: cit@haymarket.com
Web site: www.citmagazine.com
Freq: Monthly
Circ: 18500 Not Audited
MAGAZINE
Marketing, Travel

C21Media.net
980976

Editorial: 2nd Floor, 148 Curtain Road, London EC2A 3AT Tel: 44 02077 297460
Email: press@c21media.net
Web site: www.c21media.net
Freq: Daily
Circ: 106053 Cision Digital Reach
Editor: Jonathan Webdale
MAGAZINE (ONLINE)
Broadcasting

CA Today
995118

MAGAZINE (ONLINE)
Accounting, Banking, Business, Charitable Foundations, Company News & Appointments, Computers, Corporate Responsibility, Economics, Education, Government

Cable & Satellite International
980141

Editorial: Sixth Floor, 3 London Wall Buildings, London EC2M 5PD
Tel: 44 02075 622416
Web site: www.csimagazine.com
Freq: Bi-Monthly
Circ: 7000 Not Audited
Editor: Goran Nastic
MAGAZINE
Electronics

Cable.co.uk
988580

Editorial: Existent Ltd, 53 Wade Street, Lichfield WS13 6HL Tel: 44 01543 416762

Email: news@cable.co.uk
Web site: www.cable.co.uk
Freq: Daily
Circ: 181577 Cision Digital Reach
MAGAZINE (ONLINE)
Electronics, Mobile Electronics, Movies & Video

CABLEtalk
984080

Editorial: Studio 2001, Mile End Mill, 12 Seedhill Road, Paisley PA1 1JS
Tel: 44 01415 6103000
Web site: http://www.cabletalkmagazine.com/
Freq: Bi-Monthly
Circ: 2000 Not Audited
Profile: Official journal of Electrical Contractors Association of Scotland containing product features, international and association news and articles on health and safety. Also covers new products, training, business news and environmental issues. CABLEtalk is produced monthly.
Ad Rate: Full Page Mono £2050.00
Ad Rate: Full Page Colour £2650.00
MAGAZINE
Electronics

Cack Blabbath
997399

Web site: www.cackblabbath.com
Freq: Daily
Circ: 13898 Cision Digital Reach
Editor: Iain Hawkins
MAGAZINE (ONLINE)
Rock Music

Caduceus
985678

Editorial: 9 Nine Acres, Midhurst, Midhurst GU29 9EP
Web site: www.caduceus.info
Freq: Quarterly
Circ: 10000 Not Audited
Editor: Simon Best; Editor: Simon Best
Profile: Journal focusing on healing, health and holistic therapies and spiritual, personal, psychological and emotional development, as well as ecological/environmental healing.
Ad Rate: Full Page Mono £790.00
Ad Rate: Full Page Colour £1160.00
MAGAZINE
Alternative Medicine

CaerphillyObserver.co.uk
986362

Editorial: Britannia House, Caerphilly Business Park, Van Road, Caerphilly CF83 3GG Tel: 44 02921 250855
Email: news@caerphillyobserver.co.uk
Web site: www.caerphillyobserver.co.uk
Freq: Daily
Circ: 15908 Cision Digital Reach
MAGAZINE (ONLINE)
Regional

Cafe Culture Magazine
983627

Editorial: The Cafe Society, The Association, 18c Moore Street, Chepstow NP16 5DB
Tel: 44 01291 636336
Web site: http://www.thecafelife.co.uk/index.php/magazines/titles/cafe-culture-magazine
Freq: Bi-Monthly
Circ: 7000 Not Audited
Editor: Clare Benfield
MAGAZINE
Alcohol & Spirits, Bars, Clubs & Pubs

Caffeine Magazine
996972

Web site: https://caffeinemag.com/
Freq: Bi-Monthly
Circ: 17000 Not Audited
MAGAZINE
Restaurant Reviews

Cage & Aviary Birds
982008

Editorial: Cudham Tithe Barn, Berry's Hill, Cudham, London TN16 3AG
Tel: 44 01959 541444
Email: birds.general@kelsey.co.uk
Web site: cageandaviarybirds.co.uk
Freq: Weekly
Circ: 21500 Not Audited

Profile: Newspaper containing information about keeping, breeding and showing birds of all kinds. Aimed at birdkeepers and those interested in birds.Blog: http://cageandaviarybirds.blogspot.com; Twitter http://twitter.com/CageAviaryBirds.
Ad Rate: Full Page Mono £790.00
Ad Rate: Full Page Colour £1100.00
MAGAZINE
Nature & Wildlife

Cake Decoration & Sugarcraft
981937

Editorial: The Maltings, West Street, Bourne, Nuneaton PE10 9PH Tel: 44 01778 392427
Web site: http://www.cake-craft.com
Freq: Monthly Not Audited
Editor: Leeanne Cooper
MAGAZINE
Cooking & Baking, Crafts

Cake Masters magazine
997665

Tel: 44 02084 326051
Email: editor@cakemasters.co.uk
Web site: cakemasters.co.uk
Freq: Monthly Not Audited
Editor: Rosie Mazumder
MAGAZINE
Cooking & Baking

CALIBRE
987953

Editorial: 71-75 Shelton Street, Covent Garden, London WC2H 9JQ
Tel: 44 02070 783210
Email: enquires@international-media.com
Web site: http://calibrequarterly.com/
Freq: Quarterly
Circ: 60000 Not Audited
Profile: Magazine covering watches.
MAGAZINE
Alcohol & Spirits, Audio Video Trade, Banking, Cameras, Consumer Electronics, Cooking & Baking, Men's Interests, Mobile Electronics, Movies & Video, Restaurant Reviews

Call Sign
984925

Editorial: Owner Drivers Radio Taxi Service Ltd, Dial-a-Cab House, 39-47 East Road, London N1 6AH Tel: 44 02072 510581
Email: callsignmag@aol.com
Web site: www.dac-callsign.com
Freq: Monthly
Circ: 12500 Not Audited
Editor: Alan Fisher
Profile: Magazine covering products and services for London's licensed taxi trade, coming events, letters and general news. Also contains by-lined articles. Read by taxi drivers and related staff.
Ad Rate: Full Page Colour £300.00
MAGAZINE
Automotive

CAM
981752

Tel: 44 01223 332288
Email: cameditor@alumni.cam.ac.uk
Web site: www.alumni.cam.ac.uk/magazine
Freq: 3 Times/Year
Circ: 215000 Not Audited
Profile: Magazine covering the latest news, research and political developments in complementary and alternative medicine including nutrition, diet, herbal medicine, naturopathy, bodywork, homeopathy, acupuncture and the therapeutic application of mind-body research. Aimed at practitioners.
Ad Rate: Full Page Colour £2909.00
MAGAZINE
Alumni

CAM Magazine (Complementary and Alternative Medicine)
994693

Tel: 44 01279 810080
Email: info@targetpublishing.com
Web site: www.cam-mag.com
Freq: Monthly
Circ: 6500 Not Audited
Editor: Simon Martin
MAGAZINE
Alternative Medicine, Nutrition

Consumer Magazines

Cambridge Edition 987165
Editorial: Bright House, 82 High Street, Sawston, Sawston CB22 3HJ
Tel: 44 01223 499450
Email: hello@bright-publishing.com
Web site: www.cambsedition.co.uk
Freq: Monthly
Circ: 35000 Not Audited
Editor: Nicola Foley
Profile: Cambridge Edition is a lifestyle publication for Cambridgeshire. Published monthly, the magazine is freely distributed directly to Cambridge households.
Ad Rate: Full Page Colour £1400.00
MAGAZINE
Regional General Interest

Cambridge Magazine 987573
Editorial: Winship Road, Milton, Cambridge CB24 6BQ Tel: 44 01223 434434
Email: newsdesk@cambridge-news.co.uk
Web site: www.cambridge-magazines.co.uk/Cambridge-Magazine
Freq: Monthly
Circ: 20000 Not Audited
Profile: Magazine covering regional lifestyle in the Cambridge area. It features articles on homes and gardens, property, people and places, arts and culture, fashion and shopping, health, fitness and beauty, education and family, food and drink, travel, motoring and technology. Aimed at Cambridge residents.
Ad Rate: Full Page Colour £1095.00
MAGAZINE
Regional General Interest

Cambridge Network 985349
Editorial: The Entrepreneurship Centre, The Hauser Forum, 3 Charles Babbage Road, Cambridge CB3 0GT Tel: 44 01223 760109
Email: editor@cambridgenetwork.co.uk
Web site: www.cambridgenetwork.co.uk
Freq: Daily
Circ: 97886 Cision Digital Reach
MAGAZINE (ONLINE)
Regional

The Cambridge Student 1023284
Editorial: The Cambridge Student Newspaper, University Of Cambridge, Old Examination Hall, Free School Lane, Cambridge CB2 3RF Tel: 44 01223 333313
Email: editor@tcs.cam.ac.uk
Web site: www.tcs.cam.ac.uk
Freq: Weekly
Circ: 10000 Not Audited
MAGAZINE
Student Lifestyle

Cambridgeshire County Life Magazine 982472
Editorial: PO Box 32, Biggleswade, Biggleswade SG18 8TE
Tel: 44 01462 819496
Email: editor@countylifemagazines.co.uk
Web site: www.countylifemagazines.co.uk
Freq: Quarterly
Circ: 7000 Not Audited
Profile: Magazine containing historical profiles on local villages and towns. Covers gardening, homes, eating out, recipes, motoring, industrial heritage, local history and events. Read by residents, ex-residents and visitors to Cambridgeshire.
Ad Rate: Full Page Mono £820.00
Ad Rate: Full Page Colour £1050.00
MAGAZINE
Regional General Interest

Cambridgeshire Pride 982473
Editorial: 14 Middletons Road, Yaxley, Peterborough PE7 3LR
Tel: 44 01733 242312
Email: news@pridepublications.co.uk
Web site: www.pridepublications.co.uk
Freq: Monthly
Circ: 10000 Not Audited
Profile: Magazine covering county news, book reviews, motoring, finance, property, education, music, books, gardening, fashion, travel, fishing, lifestyle, wine, food, restaurants and features on schools. Aimed at residents of Cambridgeshire and Stamford with a high disposable income.

Ad Rate: Full Page Colour £675.00
MAGAZINE
Regional General Interest

Camden 995937
Editorial: Communications team, Camden Town Hall, Judd Street, London WC1H 9JE
Tel: 44 02079 745717
Email: camdenmagazine@camden.gov.uk
Web site: http://www.camden.gov.uk/theme/fc-sw2/ccm/navigation/council-and-democracy/publications-and-finances
Freq: Monthly
Circ: 190000 Not Audited
MAGAZINE
Regional General Interest

Camera Labs 985171
Web site: www.cameralabs.com
Freq: Daily
Circ: 446341 Cision Digital Reach
Editor: Gordon Laing
MAGAZINE (ONLINE)
Cameras

Camouflage 999076
Editorial: Army Recruiting and Training Division (Ops), Building 370, Trenchard Lines, Pewsey SN9 6BE
Tel: 44 08456 008080
Web site: http://www.army.mod.uk/camouflage/
Freq: Daily
Circ: 9845 Cision Digital Reach
MAGAZINE (ONLINE)
Armed Forces, Careers, Teen/Young Adult

Camping 999070
Editorial: The Maltings, West Street, Bourne, Bourne PE10 9PH Tel: 44 01778 391000
Email: editorial@campingmagazine.co.uk
Web site: http://www.outandaboutlive.co.uk/Camping/Camping-Magazine/_ch3_mg6
Freq: Monthly
Circ: 25000 Not Audited
Editor: Iain Duff
MAGAZINE
Camping and RV Travel, Outdoor Recreation

Camping & Caravanning 982309
Editorial: Greenfields House, Westwood Way, Coventry CV4 8JH
Tel: 44 02476 475274
Email: magazine@thefriendlyclub.co.uk
Web site: www.campingandcaravanningclub.co.uk/magazine
Freq: Monthly
Circ: 274027 Not Audited
Profile: Magazine containing articles on touring, road tests, holiday ideas, tips and equipment information. Read by members of The Camping and Caravanning Club.Regular features: Gear Guide Featuring a regular round-up of specific products relating to camping and caravanning.; Stuff Featuring new product news and give-aways relating to camping and caravanning.
Ad Rate: Full Page Colour £3730.00
MAGAZINE
Camping and RV Travel

Camping, Caravan & Motorhome 997938
Editorial: Suite 6ci and 6cii, Britannia House, Leagrave Road, Luton LU3 1RJ
Tel: 44 01582 488385
Email: info@mediachameleon.co.uk
Web site: www.outdoorholiday.co.uk
Freq: Annual Not Audited
MAGAZINE
Camping and RV Travel

Campus Estate Management 986768
Editorial: MEB Media, 13 Princes Street, Maidstone, Maidstone ME14 1UR
Tel: 44 01622 201207
Email: editorial@mebmedia.co.uk
Web site: www.campusestate.co.uk
Freq: Quarterly
Circ: 10000 Not Audited

Editor: Chris Hewett
MAGAZINE
Architecture & Design, Building & Construction, Commercial Real Estate, Disability, Higher Education, Schools & Institutions, Students, Sustainable Development, Urban Planning & Development

Camvista.com 994662
Editorial: Wemyss House, Frances Industrial Park, Dysart, Kirkcaldy KY1 2XZ
Tel: 44 08452 416040
Web site: www.camvista.com
Freq: Daily
Circ: 113392 Cision Digital Reach
Editor: Alex Kilgour
MAGAZINE (ONLINE)
Travel

Canal Boat 982205
Editorial: 3 The Courtyard, Denmark Street, Wokingham RG40 2AZ
Tel: 44 01189 742512
Email: editor@canalboat.co.uk
Web site: http://www.canalboat.co.uk/home
Freq: Monthly
Circ: 10000 Not Audited
Editor: Nick Wall
Profile: Magazine containing technical features and cruise articles on all aspects of boating on rivers, canals and lakes. Read by boat-owners, hirers and waterway enthusiasts.
Ad Rate: Full Page Mono £700.00
Ad Rate: Full Page Colour £755.00
MAGAZINE
Marine & Boat Trade

Canary Wharf magazine 987930
Editorial: Level 6, One Canada Square, Canary Wharf, London E14 5AB
Tel: 44 02079 874320
Web site: www.luxurylondon.co.uk
Freq: Monthly
Circ: 75000 Not Audited
Profile: Magazine covering fashion, beauty, art, entertainment, motoring, lifestyle, property, food and drink and shopping. Aimed at high earners in London E14.
Ad Rate: Full Page Colour £5995.00
MAGAZINE
Luxury Goods, Regional General Interest

Candid Magazine 988278
Editorial: Suite 1, 22 St. James's Square, London SW1Y 4JH Tel: 44 02078 395059
Email: candid@farblackpublishing.com
Web site: http://www.candidmagazine.com/
Freq: Quarterly
Circ: 10000 Not Audited
Editor: Courtney Blackman
MAGAZINE
Art, Fashion, Men's Interests

Candid Money 996581
Email: press@candidmoney.com
Web site: www.candidmoney.com
Freq: Daily
Circ: 1586 Cision Digital Reach
MAGAZINE (ONLINE)

Candis 982367
Editorial: New Hall Lane, Hoylake, Wirral CH47 4BQ Tel: 44 01516 327649
Email: hello@newhallpublishing.com
Web site: www.candis.co.uk
Freq: Monthly
Circ: 95894 Not Audited
Profile: Magazine featuring general features, health and relationship advice. Includes recipes, knitting, gardening, competitions and reports on charities.Aimed at women with families.
Ad Rate: Full Page Colour £6995.00
MAGAZINE
Women's Interests

Cannock Mercury 995949
Tel: 44 01827 848486
Email: cannock.editorial@cintamworth.co.uk
Web site: www.cannockmercury.co.uk
Freq: Daily

Circ: 47313 Cision Digital Reach
MAGAZINE (ONLINE)
News & Current Affairs

Canoe Focus 982297
Editorial: 49 Greenfields, St Ives, Huntingdon PE27 5HB Tel: 44 01480 465081
Email: canoeingnews@bcu.org.uk
Web site: https://www.britishcanoeing.org.uk/
Freq: Daily
Circ: 45156 Cision Digital Reach
Profile: Magazine of the British Canoe Union. It covers news, events, features and competitions. The magazine was first published in 1976. Read by members and those interested in canoeing.
Ad Rate: Full Page Colour £725.00
MAGAZINE (ONLINE)
Swimming/Watersports

Canoeing South Africa 1060569
Tel: 44 27824 626850
Email: secretary@canoesa.org.za
Web site: http://www.canoesa.org.za
Circ: 6951 Cision Digital Reach
MAGAZINE (ONLINE)
Basketball, Bicycles, Billiards, Boating & Yachting, Bodybuilding, Bowling, Boxing, Cricket, Equestrian Sports, Extreme/Adventure Sports

Capacity 981622
Editorial: 6-8 Bouverie Street, London EC4Y 8AX Tel: 44 02077 797227
Web site: www.capacitymagazine.com
Freq: Bi-Monthly
Circ: 4265 Not Audited
Editor: Alan Burkitt-Gray
MAGAZINE
Data Management, Electronics, Industry, Internet, Mobile Communications, Software, Telecommunications/Electronic Communications

Captive International 988490
Editorial: Kingfisher House, 21-23 Elmfield Road, London BR1 1LT
Freq: Daily
Circ: 7325 Cision Digital Reach
MAGAZINE (ONLINE)
News & Current Affairs

CapX 1058246
Editorial: 57 Tufton Street, London SW1P 3QL Tel: 44 02072 224488
Web site: http://capx.co/
Freq: Daily
Circ: 131032 Cision Digital Reach
MAGAZINE (ONLINE)
Financial Markets, Government, Investment Banking

CAR 982628
Editorial: Media House, Lynchwood, Peterborough, Peterborough PE2 6EA
Tel: 44 01733 468485
Email: car@bauermedia.co.uk
Web site: www.carmagazine.co.uk
Freq: Monthly
Circ: 43654 Not Audited
Editor: Phil McNamara
Profile: Magazine containing news, features and reviews of cars. First published in 1962. Read by motoring enthusiasts and people involved in the motoring industry.
Ad Rate: Full Page Colour £2000.00
MAGAZINE
Automakers, Automotive, Driving, Motorcycles, Motorsports, Off-road & 4-Wheel Drive Vehicles

Car Dealer 984654
Editorial: Blackball Media, Haslar Marine Technology Park, Haslar Road, Gosport PO12 2AG Tel: 44 02392 522434
Email: editorial@blackballmedia.co.uk
Web site: www.cardealermagazine.co.uk
Freq: Monthly
Circ: 12000 Not Audited
Profile: Magazine featuring industry news, car reviews, products, features on the motor trade and expert comment from industry leaders.

Ad Rate: Full Page Colour £1495.00
MAGAZINE
Automotive

Car Design News
988952
Editorial: Ultima Media Ltd, 401 King Street, London W6 9NJ **Tel:** 44 20898 70900
Email: editorial@cardesignnews.com
Web site: www.cardesignnews.com
Freq: Daily
Circ: 48110 Cision Digital Reach
Profile: Online magazine giving a global overview of automotive design news, coverage of major autoshows and student design exhibitions, design reviews and feature articles on design processes.
MAGAZINE (ONLINE)
Automotive, Manufacturing

Car Mechanics
982629
Editorial: Media House, Lynchwood, Peterborough PE2 0EA
Tel: 44 01733 468000
Email: carmechanics@bauermedia.co.uk
Web site: www.carmechanicsmag.co.uk
Freq: Monthly
Circ: 30000 Not Audited
Editor: Martyn Knowles
Profile: Magazine covering everything from servicing to repairing major accident damage. Includes the latest news and views from the motor trade. Read by the motor trade and enthusiastic DIY mechanics.
Ad Rate: Full Page Colour £1200.00
MAGAZINE
Antique & Collectible Cars, Automakers, Automotive, Driving, Motorcycles, Off-road & 4-Wheel Drive Vehicles, Trucks & SUVs

Caravan
982310
Editorial: The Maltings, West Street, Bourne, Bourne PE10 9PH **Tel:** 44 01778 391000
Email: caravan@warnersgroup.co.uk
Web site: www.caravanmagazine.co.uk
Freq: Monthly
Circ: 9765 Not Audited
Profile: Magazine featuring touring caravans and car testing as well as park reports and reviews of a full range of accessories. Aimed at caravan enthusiasts and owners.
Ad Rate: Full Page Mono £1191.00
Ad Rate: Full Page Colour £2028.00
MAGAZINE
Camping and RV Travel

The Caravan Channel
995892
Editorial: c/o Information TV, 64 Newman Streeet, London W1T 3EF
Tel: 44 02037 640572
Email: editorial@caravanchannel.co.uk
Web site: www.caravanchannel.co.uk
Freq: Daily
Circ: 1787 Cision Digital Reach
MAGAZINE (ONLINE)
Automotive

The Caravan Club Magazine
982316
Editorial: The Caravan Club, East Grinstead House, East Grinstead, East Grinstead RH19 1UA **Tel:** 44 01342 326944
Email: magazine@caravanclub.co.uk
Web site: www.caravanclub.co.uk
Freq: Monthly
Circ: 352046 Not Audited
Editor: Gary Martin
Profile: Magazine containing caravan, motor caravan and car reviews with information on touring in the UK and Europe, book reviews, CD-ROMs and products of interest, as well as technical matters and legislation affecting the touring caravanner in the UK and abroad. Aimed at those who own a caravan, motor caravan or trailer tent and stay on Club sites and those thinking of purchasing a caravan. Regular features: Book Review Featuring reviews of camping and caravanning books.; Caravan Club News Featuring Caravan Club news and events.; Competitions Featuring competitions and quizzes.; Letters; New Products Featuring details of new products for caravanning enthusiasts.; Product Reviews; Test Reports Featuring reports of tests on caravans, motor caravans and tow cars.; Touring Report Featuring reviews of

camp sites and destinations in the UK and mainland Europe.
Ad Rate: Full Page Colour £6624.00
MAGAZINE
Camping and RV Travel

Caravan Industry and Park Operator
987787
Editorial: PO Box 618, Norwich NR7 0QT
Tel: 44 01257 267677
Web site: http://
caravanindustryandparkoperator.co.uk/
Freq: Monthly
Circ: 6000 Not Audited
Editor: Chris Cattrall
MAGAZINE
Travel

Caravan Magazine
999325
Editorial: The Maltings, West Street, Bourne, Bourne PE10 9PH **Tel:** 44 01778 391000
Web site: caravanmagazine.co.uk
Freq: Annual
Circ: 8951 Not Audited
Editor: Claire Tupholme
MAGAZINE
Camping and RV Travel

Caravan Times
995283
Editorial: 501 Metropolitan Wharf Buildings, 70 Wapping Wall, London E1W 3SS
Tel: 44 02071 672664
Email: news@caravantimes.co.uk
Web site: www.caravantimes.co.uk
Freq: Daily
Circ: 48777 Cision Digital Reach
MAGAZINE (ONLINE)
Camping and RV Travel

Carbon Commentary
984483
Web site: www.carboncommentary.com
Freq: Daily
Circ: 14858 Cision Digital Reach
MAGAZINE (ONLINE)
News & Current Affairs

Carbuyer.co.uk
985814
Editorial: 31-32 Alfred Place, London WC1E 7DP **Tel:** 44 02079 076000
Email: reception@dennis.co.uk
Web site: www.carbuyer.co.uk
Freq: Daily
Circ: 1098256 Cision Digital Reach
Editor: Stuart Milne
MAGAZINE (ONLINE)
Automotive

Card & Payments World
982937
Editorial: 3A Market Place, Uppingham, Oakham LE15 9QH **Tel:** 44 01572 820088
Web site: www.cardworldonline.com
Freq: Monthly
Circ: 60000 Not Audited
Profile: Newsletter which focuses on the international market for plastic cards for all uses, including financial, access, identity, transit and loyalty prepaid, mobile payments, contactless schemes. Also includes information about the associated technology. Read by those working in financial services, banking, the credit card industry, retail, transit, government and major corporations.
MAGAZINE
Banking, Electronics, Industry

Cardiff Life
984527
Editorial: Circus Mews House, Circus Mews, Bath BA1 2PW **Tel:** 44 01225 475800
Email: info@mediaclash.co.uk
Web site: www.mediaclash.co.uk
Freq: Monthly
Circ: 10000 Not Audited
Editor: Velimir Ilic
Profile: Magazine covering life and living in Cardiff, Cowbridge and Penarth including property, interiors, food, arts and out and about.
Ad Rate: Full Page Colour £787.00
MAGAZINE
Regional General Interest

Cardiff Times
987244
Editorial: 313 Albany Road, Roath, Cardiff CF24 3NY **Tel:** 44 02920 463028
Email: info@cardiff-times.co.uk
Web site: www.cardiff-times.co.uk
Freq: Monthly
Circ: 17000 Not Audited
Editor: Louise Denning
MAGAZINE
Regional General Interest

Cardmaking & Papercraft
984021
Editorial: Tower House, Fairfax Street, Bristol BS1 3BN **Tel:** 44 01179 338081
Web site: www.cardmakingandpapercraft.com
Freq: Monthly
Circ: 37000 Not Audited
Editor: Sienna Parulis-Cook
Profile: Magazine covering card and papercraft designs with clear step by step instructions, expert advice, free gifts, best buys, give aways, competitions and events listings.
Ad Rate: Full Page Colour £1050.00
MAGAZINE
Crafts

Cards International
981350
Editorial: 71-73 Carter Lane, London EC4V 5EQ **Tel:** 44 02079 366400
Email: press@timetric.com
Web site: www.cardsinternational.com
Freq: Monthly Not Audited
Profile: Publication covering wealth management, card operations in banks and retail outlets and providing market intelligence, interviews, research and analysis news. Average Pages per Issue: 28 Aimed at senior executives in banks and retailing organisations, technology suppliers, card processors and personnel within payment systems companies.
MAGAZINE
Personal Finance

Care on the Road
982622
Editorial: 28 Calthorpe Road, Edgbaston, Birmingham 1RP **Tel:** 44 01212 482000
Email: acoleman@rospa.com
Web site: www.rospa.com
Freq: Bi-Monthly
Circ: 11000 Not Audited
Editor: Andrew Coleman
Profile: Magazine covering vehicle and product design, all aspects of road safety, driver training, new legislation and road safety statistics.
Ad Rate: Full Page Mono £895.00
MAGAZINE
Driving

Career Development International
980951
Editorial: Howard House, Wagon Lane, Bingley BD16 1WA
Web site: www.emeraldinsight.com/journals.htm?issn=1362-0436
Freq: Bi-Monthly Not Audited
Editor: Professor Jim Jawahar
Profile: Scholarly journal publishing international research on Careers and Development.
MAGAZINE
News & Current Affairs

Career Matters
987431
Editorial: Ground Floor, Copthall House, 1 New Road, Stourbridge, Stourbridge DY8 1PH **Tel:** 44 01384 376464
Email: editor@thecdi.net
Web site: www.thecdi.net/Career-Matters
Freq: Quarterly
Circ: 3500 Not Audited
Editor: Alison Dixon
Profile: Journal featuring news, information, research and discussion concerning careers guidance issues. Aimed at career guidance professionals, schools careers teachers and IAG workers.
Ad Rate: Full Page Colour £2320.00
MAGAZINE
Careers

The Careers Service Guides
998888
Editorial: The Fountain Building, Howbery Park, Benson Lane, Wallingford, Wallingford OX10 8BA **Tel:** 44 01491 828939
Email: info@groupgti.com
Web site: www.groupgti.com
Freq: Annual Not Audited
MAGAZINE
Careers

Careway
985481
Editorial: 19 Ormeau Business Park, The Gasworks, Belfast BT7 2JA
Tel: 44 02890 332499
Email: editorial@profilepublishing.com
Web site: http://careway.co.uk/in-this-issue/
Freq: Quarterly
Circ: 227500 Not Audited
MAGAZINE
Alternative Medicine, Health & Medicine, Nutrition

Caribbean Intelligence
997133
Tel: 44 02070 784152
Email: caribbeanintelligence@gmail.com
Web site: www.caribbeanintelligence.com
Freq: Daily
Circ: 13456 Cision Digital Reach
Editor: Debbie Ransome
MAGAZINE (ONLINE)
International News

The Caribbean Property Investor
998921
Editorial: 63 Noko, 3-6 Banister Road, London W10 4AR **Tel:** 44 02089 601010
Email: info@7thheavenproperties.com
Web site: www.7thheavenproperties.com/register-caribbean-property-investor-magazine.html
Freq: Annual
Circ: 30000 Not Audited
MAGAZINE
Residential Real Estate, Travel

CarKeys.co.uk
982826
Editorial: Floor 13, 20 Chapel Street, Liverpool L3 9AG **Tel:** 44 08444 457863
Email: editorial@carkeys.co.uk
Web site: www.carkeys.co.uk
Freq: Daily
Circ: 167247 Cision Digital Reach
Profile: Website containing news and information on road tests, car launches, features, columns and motorsports. Aimed at those interested in new car launches and cars in general.Regular features: Books; Classic/Historic; Daily News Update; Everything Else Including 'Big In America'.; Industry News on what is happening in the industry.; New Model Launches; People; Product Products section.; Road Tests; Sport Formula 1, Motor Rallies.; Technical
MAGAZINE (ONLINE)
Antique & Collectible Cars, Automakers, Automotive, Driving, Motorcycles, Motorsports, Off-road & 4-Wheel Drive Vehicles, Trucks & SUVs

Carlisle Living
984894
Editorial: The White House, Dalston Road, Carlisle CA2 5UA **Tel:** 44 01228 612333
Email: carlisleliving@cnmedia.co.uk
Web site: www.carlisleliving.co.uk
Freq: Monthly
Circ: 7000 Not Audited
Editor: Richard Eccles
Profile: Lifestyle magazine covering local news and celebrities with profiles and interviews, interiors, fashion, beauty, motoring, property, arts and Q&As. Aimed at residents in Carlisle and the surrounding area predominantly aged 30 to 45 years old.
MAGAZINE
Lifestyle, Men's Interests, Regional General Interest, Women's Interests

Carousel
985763
Editorial: Unit 1, West Court, Saxon Business Park, Birmingham B60 4AD
Tel: 44 07413 980203
Email: office@carouselguide.co.uk
Web site: www.carouselguide.co.uk

Consumer Magazines

Freq: 3 Times/Year
Circ: 10000 Not Audited
Editor: Dave Chant; Editor: Elaine Chant
MAGAZINE
Literature

Carousel 988446
Editorial: Community Base, 113 Queens Road, Brighton BN1 3XG
Tel: 44 01273 234734
Email: enquiries@carousel.org.uk
Web site: www.carousel.org.uk
Freq: Daily
Circ: 11592 Cision Digital Reach
MAGAZINE (ONLINE)
Disability

Carp-Talk 982173
Editorial: Sandholme Grange, Newport, Brough HU15 2QG Tel: 44 01430 440624
Email: newsdesk@carptalk-online.co.uk
Web site: http://www.carptalk-online.co.uk
Freq: Weekly
Circ: 15000 Not Audited
MAGAZINE
Fishing

Carpworld 982180
Editorial: Regent House, 101 Broadfield Road, Sheffield S8 OXH
Tel: 44 01142 580812
Email: info@anglingpublications.co.uk
Web site: http://www.carpworldmagazine.com
Freq: Monthly
Circ: 20000 Not Audited
Editor: Steve Broad
Profile: Magazine covering articles and advice on all aspects of carp fishing, including bait and tactics.
Ad Rate: Full Page Colour £500.00
MAGAZINE
Fishing

Carriage Driving 982234
Tel: 44 01722 716996
Email: edit@carriage-driving.com
Web site: http://www.carriage-driving.com
Freq: Monthly
Circ: 8000 Not Audited
Editor: Stephanie Kill; Editor: Stephanie Kill; Editor: Stephanie Kill
Profile: Magazine dedicated to all forms of carriage driving.
Ad Rate: Full Page Colour £900.00
MAGAZINE
Equestrian Sports

CarSport 982670
Editorial: Unit 34 Crescent Business Park, Lisburn BT28 2GN Tel: 44 02892 780108
Email: info@greerpublications.com
Web site: http://www.carsportmagazine.com
Freq: Annual
Circ: 7500 Not Audited
Editor: Pat Burns
Profile: Magazine with an emphasis on motor sport, but also covering the new car market, including new car design, technology and test drives. Aimed at motoring and motor sports enthusiasts.
MAGAZINE
Motorsports

The Cartographic Journal 998985
Editorial: 2&4 Park Square, Milton Park, Abingdon, Leeds OX14 4RN
Web site: www.editorialmanager.com/caj
Freq: Quarterly Not Audited
MAGAZINE
Science

Carve Surfing 982298
Editorial: Berry Road Studios, Newquay, Cornwall, Newquay TR7 1AT
Tel: 44 01637 878074
Email: info@carvemag.com
Web site: www.carvemag.com
Freq: Bi-Monthly
Circ: 60000 Not Audited

Editor: Roger Sharp
MAGAZINE
Swimming/Watersports

carwitter 996071
Email: contact@carwitter.com
Web site: http://carwitter.com
Freq: Daily
Circ: 12270 Cision Digital Reach
MAGAZINE (ONLINE)
Antique & Collectible Cars, Automakers, Automotive, Driving, Motorcycles, Motorsports, Off-road & 4-Wheel Drive Vehicles, Trucks & SUVs

Casebook 998522
Editorial: Medical Protection Society, Victoria House, Leeds LS11 5AE
Tel: 44 01132 410707
Email: casebook@medicalprotection.org
Web site: http://www.medicalprotection.org/uk/casebook
Freq: Semi-Annual
Circ: 180000 Not Audited
MAGAZINE
Health Administration, Medicine, Nursing/Nurses

CASEnotes 984486
Editorial: 11 Wilderton Road, London N16 5QY Tel: 44 07743 503920
Email: casemail@campaignforstateeducation.org.uk
Web site: www.campaignforstateeducation.org.uk
Freq: Quarterly Not Audited
MAGAZINE
Disability, Education, Government, Higher Education, Preschool, Schools & Institutions, Students

Cash & Carry Management 981634
Editorial: PO Box 366, East Grinstead RH19 4ZE Tel: 44 01342 712100
Email: mail.winlove@btconnect.com
Web site: www.cashandcarrymanagement.co.uk
Freq: Monthly
Circ: 4572 Not Audited
MAGAZINE
Alcohol & Spirits, Food, Retail Management

Casino International 983723
Editorial: 15A London Road, Maidstone, Maidstone ME16 8LY Tel: 44 01622 687031
Email: casino@datateam.co.uk
Web site: www.casinointernational-online.com
Freq: Monthly
Circ: 4500 Not Audited
Profile: Magazine covering news, products and issues in the gaming industry.
Ad Rate: Full Page Colour £2100.00
MAGAZINE
Computer & Video Games

Casino Life 985097
Editorial: 4 Carriers Place, Blackham, Tunbridge Wells TN3 9UQ
Tel: 44 01892 740869
Email: info@ace123.com
Web site: www.casinolifemagazine.com
Freq: Monthly
Circ: 9085 Not Audited
Editor: Glyn Thomas
Profile: Magazine covering all aspects of running a casino. Also features articles of interest to casino managers including personal development, lifestyle, travel and entertainment.
Ad Rate: Full Page Colour £2000.00
MAGAZINE
Casinos & Gaming, Computer & Video Games

Cask and Still 988861
Editorial: 496 Ferry Road, Forth EH5 2DL
Tel: 44 01315 511000
Email: rbath@scottishfield.co.uk
Web site: www.caskandstillmagazine.co.uk
Freq: Semi-Annual

Circ: 10000 Not Audited
MAGAZINE
Alcohol & Spirits

Casual Dining Magazine 987815
Editorial: 4th Floor, Joynes House, New Road, Gravesend DA11 0AJ
Tel: 44 03455 006008
Email: editor@casualdiningmagazine.co.uk
Web site: www.casualdiningmagazine.co.uk
Freq: Monthly
Circ: 10028 Not Audited
MAGAZINE
Bars, Clubs & Pubs, Restaurant Reviews

The Cat 995354
Web site: www.cats.org.uk/get-involved/support-us/cat-magazine-menu
Freq: Quarterly
Circ: 30000 Not Audited
Editor: Francesca Watson
MAGAZINE
News & Current Affairs

CAT (Car & Accessory Trader) 981257
Editorial: Bridge House, 69 London Road, Twickenham, London TW1 3QR
Tel: 44 02082 675000
Web site: www.catmag.co.uk
Freq: Monthly
Circ: 15992 Not Audited
Editor: Greg Whitaker
Profile: Magazine dedicated to the distribution of components and accessories. Contains news, views, features and product category features. First published in 1979, the publication has an average of 60 pages per issue. Press Day: around the 13th, 14th and 15th. Aimed at motor factors, retailers, franchised dealer parts departments and cash and carry outlets.
Ad Rate: Full Page Colour £1735.00
MAGAZINE
Automotive

Cat Planet 990568
Tel: 44 01264 738066
Email: webmaster@catplanet.co.uk
Web site: www.catplanet.co.uk
Freq: Daily
Circ: 6763 Cision Digital Reach
Editor: Anna Hall
MAGAZINE (ONLINE)
Nature & Wildlife

The Caterer 979915
Editorial: 52 Grosvenor Gardens, London SW1W 0AU Tel: 44 02078 814808
Email: info@thecaterer.com
Web site: www.thecaterer-magazine.co.uk/
Freq: Weekly
Circ: 7657 Not Audited
Editor: Amanda Afiya
Profile: Magazine focusing on all aspects of the hospitality industry and featuring catering news, letters to the editor, news from the industry and forthcoming events. Aimed at people in all sectors of the catering industry, particularly staff in hotels, restaurants, pubs and the contract catering sector.
Ad Rate: Full Page Colour £3975.00
MAGAZINE
Alcohol & Spirits, Bars, Clubs & Pubs, Food, Hotels/Motels

The Caterer, Licensee and Hotelier 984056
Editorial: Roddis House, Old Christchurch Road, Bournemouth, Bournemouth BH1 1LJ
Tel: 44 01202 552333
Email: edit@catererlicensee.com
Web site: www.catererlicensee.com
Freq: Monthly
Circ: 20000 Not Audited
MAGAZINE
Alcohol & Spirits, Food

Catering Scotland 983715
Editorial: 2 Douglas Gardens, Edinburgh EH4 3DA Tel: 44 08001 303731
Web site: http://www.cateringscotland.com/
Freq: Daily

Circ: 9350 Cision Digital Reach
Editor: Alex Buchanan
MAGAZINE (ONLINE)
Alcohol & Spirits, Bars, Clubs & Pubs, Food, Hotels/Motels

The Catholic Herald 982158
Editorial: Herald House, 15 Lamb's Passage, Bunhill Row, London EC1Y 8TQ
Tel: 44 02074 483603
Email: editorial@catholicherald.co.uk
Web site: www.catholicherald.co.uk
Freq: Weekly
Circ: 20000 Not Audited
Editor: Luke Coppen
Profile: Newspaper includes news from home and abroad. Includes analysis of secular stories from a church viewpoint.
Ad Rate: Full Page Mono £2700.00
Ad Rate: Full Page Colour £2700.00
MAGAZINE
Religion

The Catholic People 998623
Editorial: Archbishops House, 43 Cathedral Road, Cardiff CF11 9HD
Tel: 44 02920 220411
Email: publications@rcadc.org
Web site: www.rcadc.org
Freq: Monthly
Circ: 10000 Not Audited
Editor: James Campbell
MAGAZINE
Religion

Catholic Pictorial 982145
Editorial: 36 Henry Street, Liverpool L1 5BS
Tel: 44 01517 097567
Email: catholicpictorial@rcaol.co.uk
Web site: www.catholicpic.co.uk
Freq: Monthly
Circ: 10000 Not Audited
Editor: Peter Henegham
Profile: Newspaper of the Roman Catholic Archdiocese of Liverpool, covering religious issues.
Ad Rate: Full Page Colour £915.00
MAGAZINE
Religion

The Catholic Times 983407
Editorial: Guardian Print Centre, Longbridge Road, Trafford Park, Manchester M17 1SN
Tel: 44 01612 141200
Web site: www.thecatholicuniverse.com
Freq: Weekly
Circ: 14000 Not Audited
Editor: Kevin Flaherty
Profile: Newspaper covering issues of relevance to Catholicism.
Ad Rate: Full Page Mono £3280.00
Ad Rate: Full Page Colour £4100.00
MAGAZINE
Religion

The Catholic Voice Group 998583
Editorial: 99 Commonside, Ansdell, Lytham, Preston PR1 3TY Tel: 44 01253 736630
Email: voicenews@hotmail.co.uk
Web site: http://www.catholicvoiceoflancaster.co.uk/
Freq: Monthly
Circ: 12000 Not Audited
Editor: Edwina Gillett
MAGAZINE
Religion

Catworld 982009
Editorial: Unit 5e Park Farm, Chichester Road, Arundel, Arundel BN18 0AG
Tel: 44 01903 884088
Web site: www.catworld.co.uk
Freq: Monthly
Circ: 21225 Not Audited
Editor: Jill Mundy
MAGAZINE
Nature & Wildlife

CAV 1060488
Tel: 44 56239 38000
Web site: http://www.lacav.cl

Freq: Monthly Not Audited
MAGAZINE
Wine/Winemaking

Cayman Captive 996920
Editorial: Kingfisher House, 21-23 Elmfield Road, London BR1 1LT
Web site: http://www.captiveinternational.com/channel/cayman-islands
Freq: Annual Not Audited
MAGAZINE
News & Current Affairs

Cayman Funds 988342
Editorial: Kingfisher House, 21-23 Elmfield Road, London BR1 1LT
Web site: http://www.caymanfundsmagazine.com/
Freq: Annual
Circ: 5000 Not Audited
Profile: Publication for the funds industry in Cayman. Covering best practice in the industry as well as promoting Cayman as a domicile.
Ad Rate: Full Page Colour £4650.00
MAGAZINE
News & Current Affairs

Cayman Funds Newsletter
988489
Editorial: Kingfisher House, 21-23 Elmfield Road, London BR1 1LT
Freq: Monthly
MAGAZINE (ONLINE)
News & Current Affairs

cazenove+loyd 1053741
Tel: 44 02073 842332
Email: info@cazloyd.com
Web site: www.cazloyd.com/en-gb
Freq: Daily
Circ: 141 Cision Digital Reach
MAGAZINE (ONLINE)
Luxury Goods, Travel

CBeebies Art 984878
Editorial: Vineyard House, 44 Brook Green, London W6 7BT **Tel:** 44 02071 505000
Email: hello@cbeebiesmagazine.com
Web site: http://www.immediate.co.uk/brands/cbeebies-art/
Freq: Monthly
Circ: 52649 Not Audited
MAGAZINE
Preschool

CBeebies Magazine 995994
Editorial: Vineyard House, 44 Brook Green, London W6 7BT **Tel:** 44 02071 505000
Email: hello@cbeebiesmagazine.com
Freq: Bi-Weekly
Circ: 53569 Not Audited
MAGAZINE
Elementary School

Cbeebies Special 994978
Editorial: Vineyard House, 44 Brook Green, London W6 7BT **Tel:** 44 02071 505000
Web site: www.bbc.co.uk/cbeebies/shows/something-special
Freq: Monthly
Circ: 45474 Not Audited
Editor: Andrea Turton
MAGAZINE
Preschool

CBRNe World 998848
Editorial: Suite 26 Basepoint, 1 Winnall Valley Road, Winchester SO23 0LD
Tel: 44 01962 832534
Web site: www.cbrneworld.com
Freq: Bi-Monthly
Circ: 12184 Not Audited
MAGAZINE
Defense & National Security

CDC News 987499
Editorial: Unit 4, Minerva Business Park, Lynch Wood, Peterborough PE2 6FT
Tel: 44 01733 405730
Email: editor@coachdriversclub.com
Web site: www.coachdriversclub.com

Freq: Monthly
Circ: 5000 Not Audited
Editor: Jessamy Chapman
Profile: Magazine covering coaches and coach tours, including planning guidance for group visits.
Ad Rate: Full Page Colour £525.00
MAGAZINE
Automotive, Travel

Celebrity Angels 988704
Editorial: 143 Caledonian Rd, London N1 0SL **Tel:** 44 02078 711000
Email: info@damsonmedia.com
Web site: www.celebrityangels.co.uk
Freq: Daily
Circ: 12298 Cision Digital Reach
MAGAZINE (ONLINE)
Beauty & Grooming, Celebrities, Cooking & Baking, Cosmetics, Fashion, Hair, Health & Medicine, Travel, Women's Interests

Celebrity Intelligence 995972
Editorial: Centaur Marketing, 4th Floor, 79 Wells Street, London W1T 3QN
Tel: 44 02079 704299
Email: uk@celebrityintelligence.com
Web site: http://celebrityintelligence.com/
Freq: Daily
Circ: 51028 Cision Digital Reach
Profile: Arts and entertainments agency carrying advance details of celebrities and events.
MAGAZINE (ONLINE)
Celebrities

CelebrityRadio.biz 995027
Web site: www.celebrityradio.biz
Freq: Daily
Circ: 12606 Cision Digital Reach
MAGAZINE (ONLINE)
Celebrities, Theater & Performing Arts, Travel

CellarVie Wines 999558
Editorial: Regal House - 5th Floor, 70 London Road, London TW1 3QS
Tel: 44 02088 923042
Email: help@cellarviewines.com
Web site: www.cellarviewines.com
Freq: Daily
Circ: 26302 Cision Digital Reach
MAGAZINE (ONLINE)
Wine/Winemaking

CELLOPHANELAND* 996742
Email: editorial@cellophaneland.com
Web site: www.cellophaneland.com
Freq: Daily
Circ: 13618 Cision Digital Reach
Editor: Julie Eagleton
MAGAZINE (ONLINE)
Airline Inflight, Antiques/Collectibles, Art, Arts, Beauty & Grooming, Cooking & Baking, Cosmetics, Fashion, Food, Grocery Stores

Celtic View 982248
Editorial: The Celtic Football Club, Celtic Park, Glasgow G40 3RE
Tel: 44 01415 514264
Email: celticview@celticfc.co.uk
Web site: http://www.celticfc.net/pages/celticview
Freq: Weekly Not Audited
Editor: Paul Cuddihy
Profile: The Celtic View is the official weekly magazine of Celtic Football Club launched in August 1965. Magazine containing articles and features on Celtic Football Club. Aimed at Celtic Football Club fans.
Ad Rate: Full Page Colour £900.00
MAGAZINE
Soccer

Central Horse News What's On 986572
Editorial: Unit 8, Glebe Business Park, Horley, Horley OX15 6BN
Tel: 44 01295 404077
Web site: www.centralhorsenews.co.uk
Freq: Monthly

Circ: 6000 Not Audited
MAGAZINE
Field Sports, Nature & Wildlife

Centrefold magazine 1095578
Editorial: Flat 2F(1) 71-73 Hackney Road, Shoreditch, London E2 8ET
Email: info@centrofoldmagazine.com
Web site: www.centrefoldmagazine.co.uk
Freq: Semi-Annual
Circ: 5000 Not Audited
MAGAZINE
Art, Fashion, Men's Interests, Photography, Women's Interests

CENTURION 998493
Editorial: Flat 11, 8-9 Cleveland Square, London W2 6DH **Tel:** 44 02077 061069
Email: heydari@journal-international.com
Web site: http://www.centurion-magazine.com
Freq: Quarterly
Circ: 228600 Not Audited
MAGAZINE
Art, Fashion, Luxury Goods, Travel

Ceramic Review 984048
Editorial: 63 Great Russell Street, Bloomsbury, London WC1B 3BF
Tel: 44 02071 835583
Email: editorial@ccramicreview.com
Web site: www.ceramicreview.com
Freq: Bi-Monthly
Circ: 40000 Not Audited
Profile: Magazine providing articles on ceramic production, history and exhibitions. Contains mix of practical and critical features on contemporary ceramic art and craft from around the world. Read by professional and amateur potters, collectors and suppliers and those based within art colleges, schools, galleries and art centres.
Ad Rate: Full Page Colour £1010.00
MAGAZINE
Art

Cereal 987129
Editorial: Bristol & Exeter House, Unit S8, Lower Station Approach, Bristol BS1 6QS
Email: editorial@readcereal.com
Web site: www.readcereal.com
Freq: Quarterly
Circ: 30000 Not Audited
Editor: Rosa Park
Profile: Magazine covering travel and food.
MAGAZINE
Cooking & Baking, Food, Grocery Stores, Organic Food, Restaurant Reviews, Travel, Vegetarianism & Veganism

Ceril Campbell 984699
Editorial: Suite 101, 405 Kings Road, London SW10 0BB
Email: ceril@cerilstyle.com
Web site: www.cerilcampbell.com
Freq: Daily
Circ: 9053 Cision Digital Reach
MAGAZINE (ONLINE)
Beauty & Grooming, Cosmetics, Do-It-Yourself (DIY), Fashion, Hair, Women's Interests

CFOWorld Swedish Edition
1003578
Tel: 44 46084 536000
Web site: www.cfoworld.idg.se Not Audited
MAGAZINE
News & Current Affairs

Chaat! 985929
Editorial: 6 Bute Street, Cardiff Bay, Cardiff CF10 5AN **Tel:** 44 02920 496725
Email: info@britishcurryclub.co.uk
Web site: https://www.chaatmagazine.co.uk/
Freq: Quarterly
Circ: 25000 Not Audited
Profile: Magazine published by the British Curry Club. It covers curries and spices as well as health and advice.
MAGAZINE
Cooking & Baking, Food, Grocery Stores, Organic Food, Restaurant Reviews, Vegetarianism & Veganism

Champions Matchday 1009161
Editorial: Bridge House, 69 London Road, Twickenham, London TW1 3QR
Tel: 44 02082 675000
Email: champions@haymarket.com
Web site: www.uefa.com/uefachampionsleague/championsmagazine
Freq: Monthly
Circ: 20000 Not Audited
Editor: Paul Simpson
MAGAZINE
Soccer

Changing Careers 1095576
Editorial: Baltic Business Centre, Saltmeadows Road, Gateshead, Gateshead NE8 3DA **Tel:** 44 01914 424009
Email: changingcareers@balticpublications.co.uk
Web site: http://www.balticpublications.com/
Freq: Monthly
Circ: 20000 Not Audited
MAGAZINE
Careers

The Channel 996230
Editorial: PO Box 141, Cranbrook TN17 9AJ
Tel: 44 02079 932557
Web site: http://aib.org.uk/the-channel/
Freq: Daily
Circ: 6600 Not Audited
Profile: Magazine covering cross-border broadcasting news, strategy, programming, technology, engineering and appointments with technology reports and listings of shows and conferences. Read by senior executives in the media and related industries - broadcasting companies, equipment manufacturers and distribution companies, service providers and consultants involved in cross-border broadcasting.
Ad Rate: Full Page Mono £750.00
Ad Rate: Full Page Colour £1225.00
MAGAZINE
Broadcasting

Channel4.com 984509
Editorial: 124 Horseferry Road, London SW1P 2TX **Tel:** 44 02073 964444
Web site: www.channel4.com
Freq: Daily
Circ: 11514108 Cision Digital Reach
MAGAZINE (ONLINE)
News & Current Affairs

ChannelBiz 986743
Editorial: 7 Carlisle Street, London W1D 3BW
Web site: www.channelbiz.co.uk
Freq: Daily
Circ: 55100 Cision Digital Reach
Profile: Website covering technology. The ChannelBiz website is hosted by NetMediaEurope. The website shares the latest news and information on technology news and software to security and personal computers.
MAGAZINE (ONLINE)
Computers, Data Management, Electronics, Industry, Internet, Security & Security Systems, Software

Channelflip.com 998917
Editorial: ChannelFlip Media, The Shepherds Building, Charecroft Way, London W14 0EE **Tel:** 44 02082 224656
Email: enquiries@channelflip.com
Web site: www.channelflip.com
Freq: Daily
Circ: 10054 Cision Digital Reach
MAGAZINE (ONLINE)
Audio Video Trade, Cameras, Computer & Video Games, Consumer Electronics, Mobile Electronics, Movies & Video

Channelnomics Europe 1052546
Editorial: Haymarket House, 28-29 Haymarket, London SW1Y 4RX
Tel: 44 02073 169000
Web site: www.channelnomics.eu
Freq: Daily

Consumer Magazines

Circ: 56359 Cision Digital Reach
MAGAZINE (ONLINE)
Auto Aftermarket, Computers, Data
Management, Industry, Internet, Security
& Security Systems, Software

ChannelPro　　　　　985044
Editorial: 30 Cleveland Street, London W1T
4JD **Tel:** 44 02079 076658
Email: christine_horton@dennis.co.uk
Web site: www.channelpro.co.uk
Freq: Daily
Circ: 93988 Cision Digital Reach
Editor: Will Garside
MAGAZINE (ONLINE)
Auto Aftermarket, Computers, Data
Management, Electronics, Government
Technology, Industry, Internet, Mobile
Communications, Security & Security
Systems, Software

The Chap　　　　　998838
Editorial: The Maltings, Castle Precincts,
Lewes, Lewes BN7 1YH
Tel: 44 01778 392022
Email: chap@thechap.co.uk
Web site: http://thechap.co.uk/
Freq: Bi-Monthly
Circ: 10000 Not Audited
Editor: Gustav Temple
Profile: Journal covering culture, sartorial,
men's fashion, style, etiquette and grooming.
MAGAZINE
Men's Interests

Charee Magazine　　　　　1049241
Editorial: 20 Albyn Road, London SE8 4EF
Email: admin@chareemag.com
Web site: chareemag.com
Freq: Daily
Circ: 8517 Cision Digital Reach
Editor: Jeanette Davies
MAGAZINE (ONLINE)
Fashion

Charities Management　　　　　980887
Editorial: PO Box 29, South Petherton TA13
5WE **Tel:** 44 01460 241106
Email: news@charitiesmanagement.com
Web site: www.charitiesmanagement.com
Freq: Bi-Monthly Not Audited
Profile: Journal covering news, issues and
management features including banking,
investment, insurance, fundraising, direct
and digital marketing, contact centres, data
management, risk management, wealth
management, pensions and leadership.
Aimed at chief executives, finance directors,
fundraising managers, administrators and
solicitors.
Ad Rate: Full Page Colour £1700.00
MAGAZINE
Charitable Foundations

Charity Choice　　　　　986397
Editorial: 6-14 Underwood Street, London
N1 7JQ **Tel:** 44 02075 492542
Email: enquiries@charitychoice.co.uk
Web site: http://www.charitychoice.co.uk/
Freq: Daily
Circ: 98501 Cision Digital Reach
MAGAZINE (ONLINE)
Charitable Foundations

Charity Digital News　　　　　987351
Editorial: 1 Broadway, Hammersmith,
London W6 9DL
Email: info@charitydigitalnews.co.uk
Web site: www.charitydigitalnews.co.uk
Freq: Daily
Circ: 60798 Cision Digital Reach
MAGAZINE (ONLINE)
Charitable Foundations, Government
Technology

Charity Finance　　　　　979996
Editorial: 15 Prescott Place, London SW4
6BS **Tel:** 44 02078 191200
Email: newsdesk@civilsociety.co.uk
Web site: www.civilsociety.co.uk/
magazines/charity_finance/
Freq: Monthly
Circ: 5000 Not Audited
Editor: Gareth Jones

Profile: Publication covering all aspects of
accounting, tax, investment, banking,
property, IT and law. Shows those involved
in charities how to manage them in the
proper way. Aimed at finance managers and
chief executives of UK charities.
Ad Rate: Full Page Colour £2725.00
MAGAZINE
Charitable Foundations

Charity Times　　　　　979882
Editorial: Sixth Floor, 3 London Wall
Buildings, London EC2M 5PD
Tel: 44 02075 622401
Web site: www.charitytimes.com
Freq: Bi-Monthly
Circ: 8500 Not Audited
Editor: Matt Ritchie
Profile: Magazine covering all areas of
financial, business and fundraising
management as well as wealth management
for charities. Read by decision-makers in
voluntary groups, managers and directors of
charities, trustees and fundraisers.
Ad Rate: Full Page Colour £3041.00
MAGAZINE
Charitable Foundations

Charity Today　　　　　997454
Tel: 44 01733 343464
Email: support@charitytoday.co.uk
Web site: www.charitytoday.co.uk
Freq: Daily
Circ: 17824 Cision Digital Reach
MAGAZINE (ONLINE)
Charitable Foundations

Charlie & Lola　　　　　996154
Editorial: Unit 16 Greenway Farm, Bath
Road, Wick, Bristol BS30 5RL
Tel: 44 01179 373003
Email: info@kennedypublishing.co.uk
Web site: http://www.kennedypublishing.co.
uk/magazines/charlie-lola-magazine
Freq: Monthly
Circ: 38000 Not Audited
MAGAZINE
Crafts, Elementary School, Preschool

Chart & Compass　　　　　984246
Editorial: Seafarer House, 74 St Annes
Road, Southampton SO19 9FF
Tel: 44 02380 515950
Email: press@sailors-society.org
Web site: http://www.sailors-society.org/
Freq: Quarterly
Circ: 40000 Not Audited
Editor: Stuart Rivers
Profile: Magazine of the British &
International Sailors' Society, a charity for
seafarers, including news, articles on the
year's events and marine industry
information.
Ad Rate: Full Page Mono £445.00
Ad Rate: Full Page Colour £595.00
MAGAZINE
Boating & Yachting

Chartwell Journal　　　　　986757
Editorial: 17 Queen Street, Mayfair, London
W1J 5PH **Tel:** 44 02074 090545
Email: enquiries@chartwell-group.com
Web site: http://www.chartwell-media.com
Freq: Quarterly
Circ: 15000 Not Audited
MAGAZINE
Luxury Goods, Property Management &
Maintenance, Real Estate

Chasseur Magazine　　　　　996987
Editorial: 68 Wooler Street, London SE17
2EF
Email: info@chasseurmagazine.com
Web site: http://chasseurmagazine.com/
Freq: Quarterly Not Audited
MAGAZINE
Art, Fashion, Visual Arts

Chat　　　　　980753
Editorial: 161 Marsh Wall, London E14 9AP
Tel: 44 02031 485000
Email: chat_magazine@timeinc.com
Web site: http://www.lifedeathprizes.com/
Freq: Weekly

Circ: 225436 Not Audited
Editor: Gilly Sinclair
Profile: Magazine containing true life stories,
puzzles, fashion and travel articles. Aimed at
women between 20 and 50 years old.
Ad Rate: Full Page Colour £5000.00
MAGAZINE
Careers, Celebrities, Crime & Violence,
Family & Parenting, Health & Medicine,
Lifestyle, Personal Finance,
Relationships, Women's Interests

Chat it's fate　　　　　983259
Editorial: 161 Marsh Wall, London E14 9AP
Tel: 44 02031 485000
Email: itsfate@timeinc.com
Web site: http://www.lifedeathprizes.com/
uncategorized/chat-its-fate-magazine-14871
Freq: Monthly
Circ: 469407 Not Audited
MAGAZINE
Astrology & Parapsychology,
Relationships

cheapflights　　　　　984126
Editorial: One Alfred Place, London WC1E
7EB **Tel:** 44 02032 197553
Email: pr.enquiries@cheapflights.com
Web site: www.cheapflights.co.uk
Freq: Daily
Circ: 1754664 Cision Digital Reach
MAGAZINE (ONLINE)
Airline Inflight, Travel

The Cheese Grater　　　　　998882
Editorial: UCL Union, 25 Gordon Street,
London WC1H 0AY
Email: editor@cheesegratermagazine.org
Web site: www.cheesegratermagazine.org
Freq: Bi-Monthly Not Audited
MAGAZINE
Student Lifestyle

Chef Magazine (UK)　　　　　984291
Editorial: 28 Ball Moor, Celtic Court,
Buckingham MK18 1RQ
Tel: 44 02070 971396
Web site: www.chefpublishing.com
Freq: Bi-Monthly
Circ: 3000 Not Audited
MAGAZINE
Food

The Chef's Directory　　　　　999599
Web site: www.thechefsdirectory.com
Freq: Daily
Circ: 1373 Cision Digital Reach
MAGAZINE (ONLINE)
Bars, Clubs & Pubs, Food

Chelsea Magazine　　　　　982253
Editorial: One Canada Square, Canary
Wharf, London E14 5AP
Tel: 44 01514 722322
Web site: www.chelseafc.com
Freq: Monthly
Circ: 1347998 Cision Digital Reach
Editor: David Antill
Profile: Magazine covering fixtures, match
reports, previews, player interviews and
football news. Aimed at Chelsea Football
Club season ticket holders and general fans.
Ad Rate: Full Page Colour £4950.00
MAGAZINE (ONLINE)
Soccer

Chelsea Monthly　　　　　986373
Editorial: 40 Bloomsbury Way, Unit 2 Lower
Ground floor, London WC1A 2SE
Tel: 44 02033 027160
Web site: www.chelseamonthly.com
Freq: Monthly
Circ: 150000 Not Audited
MAGAZINE
Luxury Goods, Regional General Interest,
Shopping

The Cheltonian　　　　　986001
Editorial: Suite 104 Eagle Tower, Montpellier
Drive, Cheltenham, Cheltenham GL50 1TA
Tel: 44 01242 220239
Email: info@thecheltonian.com
Web site: www.thecheltonian.com

Freq: Monthly
Circ: 8000 Not Audited
Editor: Carley Jones
Profile: Magazine containing features,
reviews, what's on and a directory of local
information. Aimed at residents of
Montpellier, Tivoli, Pittville, Charlton Kings
and Leckhampton.
Ad Rate: Full Page Colour £310.00
MAGAZINE
Regional General Interest

Cherwell　　　　　981756
Tel: 44 01865 722780
Email: editor@cherwell.org
Web site: www.cherwell.org
Freq: Weekly
Circ: 15000 Not Audited
Profile: Newspaper covering news, sport,
the arts, features, opinion and debate. Read
by students at Oxford University.
Ad Rate: Full Page Colour £1080.00
MAGAZINE
Student Lifestyle

Cheshire Life　　　　　982478
Editorial: United Business Centres Ltd,
Cinnabar Court, 5300 Daresbury Park,
Warrington WA4 4GE **Tel:** 44 01928 240668
Web site: www.cheshirelife.co.uk
Freq: Monthly
Circ: 13320 Not Audited
Editor: Kate Houghton; **Editor:** Paul
Mackenzie; **Editor:** Louise Taylor
Profile: Magazine covering food, cookery,
dining out, fashion, gardening and property.
Also features motoring, antiques, socialising,
weddings and the heritage and agricultural
interest in Cheshire.
Ad Rate: Full Page Colour £2090.00
MAGAZINE
Regional General Interest

The Cheshire Magazine　　　　　987558
Editorial: Level 6, One Canada Square,
Canary Wharf, London E14 5AB
Tel: 44 02079 874320
Email: info@rwmg.co.uk
Web site: http://www.rwmg.co.uk
Freq: Monthly
Circ: 20500 Not Audited
Editor: Louisa Castle
Profile: Publication for the residents of
Cheshire it covers luxury lifestyle items and
regional general interest.
MAGAZINE
Luxury Goods, Regional General Interest

Cheshire Magazines　　　　　1076745
Editorial: 186 Ashley Road, side door, Hale
Altrincham, Altrincham WA15 9SF
Email: cheshiremags@gmail.com
Freq: Monthly
Circ: 25000 Not Audited
Editor: Francois Garcia
MAGAZINE
Regional General Interest

Chess　　　　　981912
Editorial: 44 Baker Street, London W1U 7RT
Tel: 44 02074 867015
Email: info@chess.co.uk
Web site: www.chess.co.uk
Freq: Monthly
Circ: 12400 Not Audited
Editor: Richard Palliser
MAGAZINE
Chess

The Chesterfield Post　　　　　986377
Editorial: 3 Camerory Way, New Whitington,
Chesterfield S43 2QF **Tel:** 44 07745 872333
Email: info@chesterfieldpost.co.uk
Web site: www.chesterfieldpost.co.uk
Freq: Daily
Circ: 12542 Cision Digital Reach
Editor: Karen Johnson
Profile: Website covering local news. The
Chesterfield Post website shares the latest
news and information on local news, sports
and features.
MAGAZINE (ONLINE)
News & Current Affairs

Chic Chat - CEASED 984831
Editorial: 1 Warwick Road, Beaconsfield, Beaconsfield HP9 2PE
Freq: Daily
Circ: 493 Cision Digital Reach
MAGAZINE (ONLINE)
Regional General Interest, Women's Interests

The Chic Geek 986802
Editorial: 32 Aldwick Road, Beddington, London CR0 4PL
Email: askthegeek@thechicgeek.co.uk
Web site: www.thechicgeek.co.uk
Freq: Daily
Circ: 14861 Cision Digital Reach
MAGAZINE (ONLINE)
Beauty & Grooming, Cosmetics, Fashion, Hair, Men's Interests

Chic Londres 995457
Editorial: 32 Rainham Road, London NW10 5DJ
Web site: www.chiclondres.com
Freq: Daily
Circ: 521 Cision Digital Reach
MAGAZINE (ONLINE)
Bars, Clubs & Pubs, Beauty & Grooming, Celebrities, Cosmetics, Entertainment, Fashion, Hair, Restaurant Reviews, Travel

Chichester & Arundel Lifestyle Magazine 1053985
Tel: 44 01225 343710
Web site: www.chichesterlifestyle.co.uk
Freq: Bi-Monthly
Circ: 7500 Not Audited
MAGAZINE
Regional General Interest

Child Development 995475
Editorial: John Wiley & Sons, Ltd., The Atrium, Southern Gate, Chichester PO19 8SQ **Tel:** 44 01865 778315
Email: cs-journals@wiley.com
Web site: http://onlinelibrary.wiley.com/journal/10.1111/(ISSN)1467-8624
Freq: Bi-Monthly
Circ: 10400 Not Audited
Editor: Cynthia Garcia Coll
MAGAZINE
Medicine, Pediatrics

Child Language Teaching & Therapy 985955
Editorial: 1 Oliver's Yard, 55 City Road, London EC1Y 1SP **Tel:** 44 02073 248500
Web site: http://clt.sagepub.com/
Freq: 3 Times/Year Not Audited
MAGAZINE
Medicine, Pediatrics

Childalert.co.uk 998516
Editorial: 64 Ellerby Street, London SW6 6EZ **Tel:** 44 07973 215407
Web site: www.childalert.co.uk
Freq: Daily
Circ: 7273 Cision Digital Reach
Editor: Clare Scott Dryden
MAGAZINE (ONLINE)
Family & Parenting

Children & Young People Now 981277
Editorial: St Jude's Church, Dulwich Road, London SE24 0PB **Tel:** 44 02077 385454
Web site: www.cypnow.co.uk
Freq: Bi-Weekly
Circ: 18000 Not Audited
Editor: Derren Hayes
Profile: Magazine produced in partnership with the National Youth Agency and the NCB. Covers articles on youth work, young people and those working with young people, features on the public sector, voluntary sector and private sector and children's organisations. Aimed at professionals that work with children and young people, including youth workers, youth justice workers, policymakers, teachers and those involved in personal and social education and the voluntary sector,

workers in children's services from education and health to social work.
Ad Rate: Full Page Mono £2340.00
Ad Rate: Full Page Colour £2660.00
MAGAZINE
Charitable Foundations, Education, Preschool

Childrenswork 986921
Editorial: Premier, PO Box 17911, London SW1P 4YX **Tel:** 44 02073 161300
Web site: http://www.premierchildrenswork.com/
Freq: Bi-Monthly
Circ: 6000 Not Audited
Profile: Magazine containing ideas, resources and guidance for Christian children's leaders. The magazine can be contacted via the contact us page on the website.
Ad Rate: Full Page Colour £620.00
MAGAZINE
Religion

Chiltern & Thames Rider 995084
Editorial: Media House, 21 Kingsway, Bedford MK42 9BJ **Tel:** 44 01234 224995
Web site: www.chilternrider.com/
Freq: Bi-Monthly
Circ: 6000 Not Audited
MAGAZINE
Equestrian Sports

Chiltern News 982471
Editorial: Chiltern Society, White Hill Centre, Chesham HP5 1AG
Web site: www.chilternsociety.org.uk
Freq: Quarterly Not Audited
Editor: Richard Bradbury
MAGAZINE
Charitable Foundations, Regional General Interest

Chiltern Traveller 995002
Tel: 44 02075 698676
Email: newsdesk@chilterntraveller.co.uk
Web site: www.chilterntraveller.co.uk
Freq: Monthly
Circ: 250000 Not Audited
Editor: Avril O'Connor
MAGAZINE
Lifestyle, Men's Interests, Regional General Interest, Women's Interests

China Agricultural Economic Review 997143
Editorial: Emerald Group Publishing, Howard House, Wagon Lane, Bingley BD16 1WA **Tel:** 44 01274 777700
Web site: http://www.emeraldinsight.com/loi/CAER
Freq: Quarterly Not Audited
MAGAZINE
News & Current Affairs

China Gems 1062153
Tel: 44 86108 4274810
Email: fayi@vip.qq.com
Web site: http://www.chinagemsmag.com
Freq: Quarterly
Circ: 30001 Not Audited
MAGAZINE
News & Current Affairs

China-Britain Business FOCUS 981692
Editorial: 3rd Floor, Portland House, Bressenden Place, London SW1E 5EH
Tel: 44 02078 022000
Email: enquiries@cbbc.org
Web site: www.cbbc.org
Freq: Monthly
Circ: 20000 Not Audited
MAGAZINE
Asia, Business

chinadialogue.net 999137
Editorial: Suite 306 Grayston Centre, 28 Charles Square, London N1 6HT
Tel: 44 02073 244767
Email: ideas@chinadialogue.net
Web site: www.chinadialogue.net
Freq: Daily

Circ: 64106 Cision Digital Reach
Editor: Isabel Hilton
MAGAZINE (ONLINE)
Energy & Environment, Environment

Chinese Journal of Liquid Crystals and Displays 1061062
Tel: 44 86431 86176059
Email: yjxs@ciomp.ac.cn
Freq: Bi-Monthly
Circ: 10000 Not Audited
MAGAZINE
Electronics

Chinese Journal of Pharmaceutical Analysis 1062133
Tel: 44 86106 7058427
Email: ywfx@nicpbp.org.cn
Web site: http://www.ywfxzz.cn
Freq: Monthly
Circ: 8002 Not Audited
MAGAZINE
Healthcare Industry, Medicine, Pharmaceuticals

The Chinese Weekly 1074206
Editorial: The Chinese Weekly, 99 Gower Street, London WC1E 6AA
Email: editor@thechineseweekly.com
Web site: www.ihuawen.com
Freq: Weekly
MAGAZINE
National News

Chip Online 1061848
Tel: 44 86106 5157887
Web site: http://www.chip.cn
Freq: Daily
Circ: 2516 Cision Digital Reach
MAGAZINE (ONLINE)
Auto Aftermarket, Computers, Data Management, Electronics, Government Technology, Industry, Internet, Mobile Communications, Security & Security Systems, Software

Chippy Chat & Fast Food Magazine 996421
Editorial: Oak Lane, Littleport, Ely, Littleport CB6 1RS **Tel:** 44 01353 865966
Email: info@chippychat.co.uk
Web site: www.chippychat.co.uk
Freq: Monthly
Circ: 7800 Not Audited
MAGAZINE
Bars, Clubs & Pubs

Choice 983193
Editorial: First Floor, 2 King Street, Peterborough PE1 1LT
Tel: 44 01733 555123
Email: editorial@choicemag.co.uk
Web site: www.choicemag.co.uk
Freq: Monthly
Circ: 65000 Not Audited
Editor: Norman Wright
Profile: Full glossy monthly magazine published by Choice Publishing. Providing information on new technology, computers, health, travel, hobbies, gardening, motoring, food and drink, finance and pensions. Gives practical advice and ideas for people over 50 on fitness, nutrition, relationships and new medicine.
Ad Rate: Full Page Colour £4955.00
MAGAZINE
Health & Medicine, Men's Interests, Personal Finance, Women's Interests

Choir & Organ 982071
Editorial: Rhinegold House, 20 Rugby Street, London WC1N 3QZ
Tel: 44 02073 331729
Email: choirandorgan@rhinegold.co.uk
Web site: www.choirandorgan.com
Freq: Bi-Monthly
Circ: 12000 Not Audited
Editor: Maggie Hamilton
Profile: Magazine covers all aspects of secular and sacred choral music, organs and organ music.

Ad Rate: Full Page Colour £1150.00
MAGAZINE
Classical/Choral/Band Music

Cholesterol News 998672
Editorial: 7 North Road, Maidenhead, Maidenhead SL6 1PE **Tel:** 44 01628 777046
Email: ask@heartuk.org.uk
Web site: heartuk.org.uk
Freq: 3 Times/Year
Circ: 2500 Not Audited
Editor: Michael Crozier
MAGAZINE
Cardiology, Charitable Foundations

Chopsy Baby 984921
Editorial: Chopsy Baby, 6 Wade Court, Wade Street, Bristol BS2 9AF
Tel: 44 01173 003620
Email: editorial@chopsybaby.com
Web site: www.chopsybaby.com
Freq: Daily
Circ: 10008 Cision Digital Reach
Editor: Jen Smith
Profile: Website covering parenting. The CHOPSY BABY website shares the latest news and information on parenting reviews and advice to competitions.
MAGAZINE (ONLINE)
Family & Parenting

Chortle 984588
Editorial: 112 Norman Road, London E11 4RL **Tel:** 44 02082 815204
Email: feedback@chortle.co.uk
Web site: www.chortle.co.uk
Freq: Daily
Circ: 167608 Cision Digital Reach
Editor: Steve Bennett
Profile: Website covering comedy. Chortle shares the latest news on British comedy, comedians, shows, comedy book releases and reviews.
MAGAZINE (ONLINE)
Comedy, Local Entertainment Guides

chozadigital.com 1060685
Email: contacto@chozadigital.com
Web site: http://www.chozadigital.com
Freq: 3 Times/Week
Circ: 25684 Cision Digital Reach
MAGAZINE (ONLINE)
Auto Aftermarket, Computer & Video Games, Computers, Data Management, Electronics, Government Technology, Industry, Internet, Mobile Communications, Security & Security Systems

Christian Aid News - CEASED DECEMBER 2015 987703
Email: info@christian-aid.org
Web site: www.christianaid.org.uk/aboutus/who/ca-news/
Freq: Monthly
Circ: 52118 Cision Digital Reach
Profile: Magazine containing news and features about overseas projects supported by Christian Aid, plus fundraising and campaigning activities in the UK.
MAGAZINE (ONLINE)
Charitable Foundations

Christian Today 988331
Editorial: Church on the Corner, First Floor Unit, 64 Barnsbury Road, London N1 0ES
Tel: 44 02037 951686
Web site: www.christiantoday.com
Freq: Daily
Circ: 1538333 Cision Digital Reach
Profile: Website covering religion. The Christian Today website shares the latest news and information on the general christian public.
MAGAZINE (ONLINE)
Religion

Christianity Magazine 998467
Editorial: 22 Chapter Street, London SW1P 4NP **Tel:** 44 02073 161450
Email: ccp@premier.org.uk
Web site: www.christianitymagazine.co.uk
Freq: Monthly

Consumer Magazines

Circ: 18000 Not Audited
MAGAZINE
Religion

Christie's International Real Estate Magazine 987758
Editorial: 82 Baker Street, London W1 6AE
Tel: 44 02077 493300
Email: kitty.finstad@augustmedia.com
Web site: www.christiesrealestate.com/eng/real-estate-magazine
Freq: Quarterly
Circ: 71250 Not Audited
MAGAZINE
Property Management & Maintenance, Real Estate

Christie's Magazine 981878
Editorial: Jubilee House, 213 Oxford Street, London W1D 2LG **Tel:** 44 02073 892032
Email: info@christies.com
Web site: www.christies.com
Freq: Monthly Not Audited
MAGAZINE
Art

Christmas 1052380
Web site: www.gardenersworld.com
MAGAZINE
News & Current Affairs

The Christmas Magazine 984520
Editorial: Cudham Tithe Barn, Berry's Hill, Cudham, London TN16 3AG
Tel: 44 01959 541444
Email: editors@thechristmasmagazine.com
Web site: www.thechristmasmag.com
Freq: Annual
Circ: 113973 Not Audited
Profile: A women's interest Christmas magazine.
MAGAZINE
Do-It-Yourself (DIY)

Church Music Quarterly 982072
Editorial: 19 The Close, Salisbury SP1 2EB
Tel: 44 01722 424848
Email: cmq@rscm.com
Web site: www.rscm.com/publications/cmq.php
Freq: Quarterly
Circ: 12000 Not Audited
Profile: Publication containing articles on church music and related topics. Includes news of courses and other activities, also carries book, music and record reviews.
Ad Rate: Full Page Mono £775.00
Ad Rate: Full Page Colour £1125.00
MAGAZINE
Classical/Choral/Band Music

The Church of England Newspaper 982159
Editorial: Religious Intelligence Ltd, 14 Great College Street, Westminster, London SW1P 3RX **Tel:** 44 02072 228700
Email: cen@churchnewspaper.com
Web site: www.churchnewspaper.com
Freq: Weekly
Circ: 6000 Not Audited
Editor: Colin Blakely
Profile: The Church of England Newspaper is the church newspaper launched in 1828. Publication containing news and features on the Church nationally and internationally, plus articles on how faith affects the everyday life of Christians.
Ad Rate: Full Page Mono £925.00
Ad Rate: Full Page Colour £1025.00
MAGAZINE
Religion

Church of Ireland Gazette
982147
Tel: 44 02892 675743
Email: gazette@ireland.anglican.org
Web site: www.gazette.ireland.anglican.org
Freq: Weekly
Circ: 2000 Not Audited
Profile: Periodical covering religion and theology.
Ad Rate: Full Page Mono £480.00

Ad Rate: Full Page Colour £480.00
MAGAZINE
Religion

Church Times 982148
Editorial: 3rd Floor, Invicta House, 108-114 Golden Lane, London EC1Y 0TG
Tel: 44 02077 761060
Email: news@churchtimes.co.uk
Web site: www.churchtimes.co.uk
Freq: Weekly
Circ: 20500 Not Audited
Profile: The Church Times, founded in 1863, is the Anglican weekly newspaper. Covering news and comments about current affairs and church events.
Ad Rate: Full Page Mono £2335.00
Ad Rate: Full Page Colour £2455.00
MAGAZINE
Religion

Cine Outsider 1104000
Email: mail@cineoutsider.com
Web site: www.cineoutsider.com
Freq: Daily
Circ: 13280 Cision Digital Reach
Editor: Julian Wheeler
MAGAZINE (ONLINE)
Entertainment, Movies & Video

Cinema Technology 986041
Tel: 44 01980 610544
Web site: www.cinematechnologymagazine.com
Freq: Quarterly
Circ: 30000 Not Audited
MAGAZINE
Auto Aftermarket, Computers, Data Management, Electronics, Government Technology, Industry, Internet, Mobile Communications, Security & Security Systems, Software

Cinemas Online 987452
Email: theeditor@cinemas-online.co.uk
Web site: www.cinemas-online.co.uk
Freq: Daily
Circ: 44668 Cision Digital Reach
Editor: Dave Lancaster
MAGAZINE (ONLINE)
Entertainment, Local Entertainment Guides, Movies & Video

Cine-Vue 986427
Editorial: 23 Gleneldon Road, Streatham, London SW16 2AX
Email: editor@cine-vue.com
Web site: www.cine-vue.com
Freq: Daily
Circ: 44733 Cision Digital Reach
MAGAZINE (ONLINE)
Local Entertainment Guides, Movies & Video

CIO Connect 981624
Editorial: 56 Church Street, Weybridge KT13 8DP **Tel:** 44 02078 427999
Email: info@cio-connect.com
Web site: http://www.cio-connect.co.uk/?region-change=3662
Freq: Quarterly
Circ: 10709 Cision Digital Reach
Editor: Jamie Kirkland
Profile: Magazine providing support for the key leadership role of CIOs in bringing together the requirements of business and technology. Delivers support, guidance and services aimed at senior technologists and their teams. Launched in 2003, the publication is published quarterly by Connect Publishing. Aimed at senior IT executives.
Ad Rate: Full Page Colour £4025.00
MAGAZINE (ONLINE)
Auto Aftermarket, Computers, Data Management, Electronics, Government Technology, Industry, Internet, Mobile Communications, Security & Security Systems, Software

cipr.co.uk 981667
Editorial: CIPR, 52-53 Russell Square, London WC1B 4HP **Tel:** 44 02076 316918
Email: info@cipr.co.uk

Web site: www.cipr.co.uk
Freq: Daily
Circ: 225272 Cision Digital Reach
MAGAZINE (ONLINE)
Advertising Industry, Branding, Broadcasting, Graphic Design, Marketing, Media & Communications, Photography, Publishing

Circle Update 998658
Email: editor@circleofwinewriters.org
Web site: http://www.circleofwinewriters.org/circleupdate/
Freq: Bi-Monthly
Circ: 5000 Not Audited
MAGAZINE
Wine/Winemaking

Circuit World 984413
Editorial: Howard House, Wagon Lane, Bingley BD16 1WA **Tel:** 44 01274 777700
Web site: www.emeraldinsight.com
Freq: Quarterly Not Audited
Profile: Journal covering electronics including standards, design, analysis, materials, process, reliability and manufacturing. Also provides a central, international and independent forum for all those with a research or application interest in the development of the various technologies, processes and procedures associated with printed circuit board design and manufacture. Aimed at researchers, senior technical staff and practising engineers within industry manufacturers and component users and all academic branches of engineering and science together with their information providers; namely academic, institutional, technical and corporate libraries.
MAGAZINE
Electronics

cirencester.co.uk 995450
Editorial: Oakley House, Tetbury Road, Cirencester, Cirencester GL7 1US
Email: info@cirencester.co.uk
Web site: www.cirencester.co.uk
Freq: Daily
Circ: 7131 Cision Digital Reach
MAGAZINE (ONLINE)
News & Current Affairs

Citizen Femme 1102298
Email: sheena@citizen-femme.com
Web site: http://citizen-femme.com
Freq: Daily
Circ: 15421 Cision Digital Reach
MAGAZINE (ONLINE)
Travel

City Kids Magazine 1060193
Editorial: 22 Swanscombe Road, London W4 2HQ
Email: editor@citykidsmagazine.co.uk
Web site: www.citykidsmagazine.co.uk
Freq: Quarterly
Circ: 20000 Not Audited
MAGAZINE
Cooking & Baking, Education, Elementary School, Family & Parenting, Fashion, Men's Interests, Shopping, Teen/Young Adult, Women's Interests

City Life (Cardiff) 995823
Editorial: Cardiff House, Cardiff Road, Barry, Barry CF63 2AW **Tel:** 44 08451 306452
Email: jennifer@goodlifepublishing.co.uk
Web site: www.citylifecardiff.co.uk
Freq: Quarterly
Circ: 10000 Not Audited
MAGAZINE
Regional General Interest

The City Magazine 983445
Editorial: Level 6, One Canada Square, Canary Wharf, London E14 5AB
Tel: 44 02079 874320
Email: info@rwmg.co.uk
Web site: www.runwildmedia.com
Freq: Monthly
Circ: 74000 Not Audited
Editor: Richard Brown

Profile: Magazine covering topics such as fashion, beauty, entertainment, motoring, lifestyle, property, food, drink, shopping and events. First published in 2007, the publication has an average of 140 pages per issue. Aimed at high earners in The City, N1, E1 and WC1 areas of London.
Ad Rate: Full Page Colour £5995.00
MAGAZINE
Lifestyle, Luxury Goods, Men's Interests, Regional General Interest, Women's Interests

City Mayors 999410
Editorial: City Mayors, 15 Whitehall, London SW1A 2DD **Tel:** 44 02076 300615
Email: info@citymayors.com
Web site: www.citymayors.com
Freq: Daily
Circ: 119636 Cision Digital Reach
MAGAZINE (ONLINE)
Politics

City of London & Dockland Times 994635
Editorial: 10 College East, Gunthorpe Street, London E1 7RL **Tel:** 44 02072 472524
Email: cldt@btinternet.com
Freq: Bi-Weekly Not Audited
Editor: Dennis Delderfield
Profile: The City of London & Dockland Times is a weekly local newspaper covering all the latest on local news in London and Docklands.
Ad Rate: Full Page Mono £912.00
MAGAZINE
News & Current Affairs

The City Planter 994997
Tel: 44 02074 245835
Email: news@cityplanter.co.uk
Web site: www.cityplanter.co.uk/
Freq: Daily
Circ: 2664 Cision Digital Reach
Editor: Rhiannon James
MAGAZINE (ONLINE)
Gardening

City Scene Magazine 997020
Editorial: Eventus, Sunderland Road, Market Deeping, Market Deeping PE6 8FD
Tel: 44 01778 382762
Email: info@scenepublishing.co.uk
Web site: www.thescenemagazine.co.uk
Freq: Monthly
Circ: 15000 Not Audited
MAGAZINE
Regional General Interest

The City Talking 997499
Editorial: Duke Studios, Munro House, Leeds LS9 8AG
Email: news@thecitytalking.com
Web site: www.thecitytalking.com
Freq: Monthly
Circ: 15903 Cision Digital Reach
MAGAZINE (ONLINE)
Regional General Interest

Citylife 980552
Editorial: Room 161, Civic Centre, Newcastle upon Tyne NE99 2BN
Email: citylife@newcastle.gov.uk
Web site: https://www.newcastle.gov.uk/your-council-and-democracy/consultations-and-community-engagement/cityl
Freq: 3 Times/Year
Circ: 120000 Not Audited
Profile: Magazine covering news and information from Newcastle City Council.
Ad Rate: Full Page Colour £2000.00
MAGAZINE
Regional General Interest

CityMetric 996857
Editorial: 71-3 Carter Lane, London EC4V 5EQ **Tel:** 44 02079 366400
Web site: www.citymetric.com
Freq: Daily
Circ: 155891 Cision Digital Reach

Editor: Jonn Elledge
MAGAZINE (ONLINE)
Business, Consumer Affairs, Politics, Small and Medium Business

Citywealth 983153
Editorial: 11a Montagu Mews North, Marylebone, London W1H 2JZ
Tel: 44 02074 875858
Web site: https://www.citywealthmag.com/
Freq: Monthly
Circ: 15800 Cision Digital Reach
Profile: Electronically delivered newsletter covering features on banks, trust companies, accountants and lawyers working in the area of wealth management around the world, including events, people, pictures, interviews, lifestyle, travel restaurants and spas.
MAGAZINE (ONLINE)
Banking, Personal Finance

Civil Society News 984731
Editorial: 15 Prescott Place, London SW4 6BS Tel: 44 02078 191200
Email: newsdesk@civilsociety.co.uk
Web site: www.civilsociety.co.uk
Freq: Daily
Circ: 97450 Cision Digital Reach
Editor: Gareth Jones
MAGAZINE (ONLINE)
Charitable Foundations, Public Sector

Civilian 996247
Editorial: Civilian Publishing, Unit 38, Red Square, London N16 9AW
Email: editorial@civilianglobal.com
Web site: www.civilianglobal.com
Freq: Daily
Circ: 12193 Cision Digital Reach
Editor: Stephen Unwin
MAGAZINE (ONLINE)
Luxury Goods, Travel

Clapham, Battersea & Fulham Time & Leisure 983478
Editorial: 14 Apprentice Shop, Merton Abbey Mills, London SW19 2RD
Tel: 44 02085 456777
Web site: www.timeandleisure.co.uk
Freq: Monthly
Circ: 115000 Not Audited
MAGAZINE
Regional General Interest

Clarinet & Saxophone 982119
Editorial: Clarinet and Saxophone Society of Great Britain, 48 Henniker Point, Leytonstone Road, London E15 1LQ
Tel: 44 08456 440187
Email: info@cassgb.org
Web site: www.cassgb.org
Freq: Quarterly
Circ: 2000 Not Audited
Profile: Magazine featuring new music, records, concerts and new instruments. Also includes general articles on players.
Ad Rate: Full Page Mono £320.00
Ad Rate: Full Page Colour £390.00
MAGAZINE
Music

Clarity News 998193
Email: editor@claritynews.co.uk
Web site: claritynews.co.uk
Freq: Daily
Circ: 521 Cision Digital Reach
Editor: Ben Mackay
MAGAZINE (ONLINE)
Consumer Affairs, Politics, Social Issues

CLASH 982102
Editorial: Studio 86, Hackney Downs Studios, Amhurst Terrace, London E8 2BT
Email: press@clashmusic.com
Web site: www.clashmusic.com
Freq: Bi-Monthly
Circ: 70500 Not Audited
Profile: Magazine covering music, fashion and lifestyle, DVDs and live reviews. Clash Magazine is distributed through WHSmiths, HMV, Virgin, Borders and newsagents worldwide, and is published 12 times per

year. Aimed at 18 to 35 year old music savvy, culture conscious people.
Ad Rate: Full Page Colour £2800.00
MAGAZINE
Rock Music

Classic & Sports Car 982601
Editorial: Bridge House, 69 London Road, Twickenham, London TW1 3QR
Tel: 44 02082 675399
Email: letters.classicandsportscar@haymarket.com
Web site: www.classicandsportscar.com
Freq: Monthly
Circ: 67356 Not Audited
Profile: Magazine focussing on classic cars and containing features on buying, maintaining and restoring cars. It features the finest cars from across the globe, combining unrivalled editorial, the finest photography and beautiful design, as well as providing the ideal medium for buying and selling classic and sports cars because thousands are advertised every month. Aimed at classic and sportscar enthusiasts.
Ad Rate: Full Page Colour £4064.00
MAGAZINE
Antique & Collectible Cars

Classic & Vintage Commercials 986383
Editorial: Cudham Tithe Barn, Berry's Hill, Cudham, London TN16 3AG
Tel: 44 01959 541444
Email: cvc.ed@kelseypb.co.uk
Web site: www.cvcmag.co.uk
Freq: Monthly
Circ: 18456 Not Audited
Profile: Classic & Vintage Commercials is a magazine dedicated to heavy commercial vehicles. Focusing on the truck manufacturers from the heyday of road haulage over the past eight decades, Classic & Vintage Commercials features examples of all the popular makes.
Ad Rate: Full Page Mono £500.00
Ad Rate: Full Page Colour £800.00
MAGAZINE
Antique & Collectible Cars

Classic American 982602
Editorial: Media Centre, Morton Way, Horncastle, Horncastle LN9 6JR
Tel: 44 01507 524004
Email: info@classic-american.com
Web site: www.classic-american.com
Freq: Monthly
Circ: 23000 Not Audited
Editor: Ben Klemenzson
Profile: Magazine dedicated to the pleasure of owning and driving an American automobile, from pre-war classics to current hi-tech models.
Ad Rate: Full Page Colour £670.00
MAGAZINE
Antique & Collectible Cars

Classic Angling 982174
Editorial: The Old Anchor, Church Street, Hemmingford Grey, Huntingdon PE28 9DF
Tel: 44 01480 494142
Email: angling@classictitles.com
Web site: www.classictitles.com
Freq: Bi-Monthly
Circ: 2900 Not Audited
Editor: Keith Elliott
Profile: International magazine covering vintage and collectable fishing tackle, art, books and the history of angling.
Ad Rate: Full Page Colour £800.00
MAGAZINE
Fishing

Classic Bike 982603
Editorial: Media House, Lynchwood, Peterborough PE2 6EA
Tel: 44 01733 468000
Email: classic.bike@bauermedia.co.uk
Web site: www.classicbike.co.uk
Freq: Monthly
Circ: 37135 Not Audited
Editor: Gary Pinchin
Profile: Magazine covering classic and thoroughbred motorcycles from the 1950s to the 1980s, including Japanese machines.

Launched in 1978. Aimed at classic motorcycle enthusiasts.
Ad Rate: Full Page Colour £1919.00
MAGAZINE
Antique & Collectible Cars, Motorcycles

Classic Bike Guide 982604
Editorial: Media Centre, Morton Way, Horncastle, Horncastle LN9 6JR
Tel: 44 01507 529529
Email: editor@classicbikeguide.com
Web site: www.classicbikeguide.com
Freq: Monthly
Circ: 55000 Not Audited
Editor: Frank Westworth
Profile: Guide to owning and riding mainly British, with some European, American and an occasional Japanese classic motorcycle. Includes specification guides and articles on restoration, servicing and maintenance. Read by classic motorcycle enthusiasts.
Ad Rate: Full Page Colour £1250.00
MAGAZINE
Antique & Collectible Cars, Motorcycles

Classic Boat 982206
Editorial: Jubilee House, 2 Jubilee House, London SW3 3TQ Tel: 44 02073 493700
Web site: www.classicboat.co.uk
Freq: Monthly
Circ: 50000 Not Audited
Editor: Rob Peake
Profile: Magazine covering vintage craft and traditionally styled new boats, power and sail, large and small. Also contains technical articles, boat tests and product reviews. Aimed at the classic boat enthusiasts.
Ad Rate: Full Page Colour £2285.00
MAGAZINE
Boating & Yachting

Classic Car Buyer 986392
Editorial: Kelsey Publishing, Cudham Tithe Barn, Berrys Hill, Cudham TN16 3AG
Tel: 44 01959 543747
Email: ccb.ed@kelseypb.co.uk
Web site: www.classic-car-buyer.co.uk
Freq: Weekly
Circ: 18000 Not Audited
Profile: Magazine covering news, auction reports and events relating to classic cars.
MAGAZINE
Antique & Collectible Cars

Classic Car Mart 982814
Editorial: PO Box 978, Peterborough PE1 9FL Tel: 44 01733 347559
Email: ccm.ed@kelsey.co.uk
Web site: www.classic-car-mart.co.uk
Freq: Monthly
Circ: 15000 Not Audited
Editor: Paul Wager
Profile: Magazine with features on classic cars. Includes information on spare parts and servicing.
MAGAZINE
Antique & Collectible Cars, Sales & Marketing

Classic Car Weekly 982605
Editorial: Media House, Lynch Wood, Peterborough Business Park, Peterborough PE2 6EA Tel: 44 01733 468000
Email: editorial@classiccarweekly.co.uk
Web site: www.classiccarweekly.co.uk
Freq: Weekly
Circ: 23856 Not Audited
Profile: Newspaper containing news and features on the buying and selling of classic cars, plus other features of interest to classic car owners. Aimed at classic car enthusiasts.
Ad Rate: Full Page Colour £900.00
MAGAZINE
Antique & Collectible Cars

Classic Cars 982606
Editorial: Media House, Lynchwood, Peterborough Business Park, Peterborough PE2 6EA Tel: 44 01733 468000
Email: classic.cars@bauermedia.co.uk
Web site: www.classiccarsmagazine.co.uk
Freq: Monthly
Circ: 37426 Not Audited
Editor: Phil Bell

Profile: Magazine containing news, practical, historical and driving features, also details of classic car runs and events. Classic Cars is known as Thoroughbred & Classic Cars in overseas markets. Aimed at classic car enthusiasts between 15 and 55 years old with Triumphs and MG's the most popular makes.
Ad Rate: Full Page Colour £3578.00
MAGAZINE
Antique & Collectible Cars

Classic Ford 982607
Editorial: Cudham Tithe Barn, Berry's Hill, Cudham, London TN16 3AG
Tel: 44 01959 541444
Email: classicford.ed@kelsey.co.uk
Web site: http://shop.kelsey.co.uk/subscription/CFD
Freq: Monthly
Circ: 17642 Not Audited
Profile: Magazine covering Ford cars dating from the 1960s to the early 1980s including modified and standard cars. First published in 1997, the publication has an average of 162 pages per issue. Press Day: 3rd Friday of the month. Read mainly by 18 to 65 year old men.
Ad Rate: Full Page Colour £875.00
MAGAZINE
Antique & Collectible Cars, Automakers

Classic Land Rover 987317
Editorial: PO Box 100, Peterborough PE9 1XQ Tel: 44 01780 755131
Web site: www.classiclandrover.com
Freq: Monthly
Circ: 12000 Not Audited
Editor: John Carroll
Profile: Magazine covering Series and classic Land Rovers. Including pre-nineties Land Rovers and Range Rover classics.
Ad Rate: Full Page Colour £800.00
MAGAZINE
Antique & Collectible Cars, Off-road & 4-Wheel Drive Vehicles

Classic Massey & Ferguson Enthusiast 986413
Editorial: PO Box 13, Westerham, London TN16 3AG Tel: 44 01959 541444
Web site: tractormagazine.co.uk/classic-massey-ferguson
Freq: Bi-Monthly
Circ: 19000 Not Audited
Profile: Magazine covering Massey Ferguson tractors.
MAGAZINE
Antique & Collectible Cars

Classic Mercedes Magazine 996998
Editorial: Sundial House, 17 Wickham Road, Beckenham, London BR3 5JS
Tel: 44 02086 394400
Email: info@classicmercedesmagazine.com
Web site: www.classicmercedesmagazine.com/
Freq: Quarterly Not Audited
Editor: David Sutherland
MAGAZINE
Antique & Collectible Cars, Automakers

Classic Military Vehicle 981977
Editorial: PO Box 100, Peterborough PE9 1XQ Tel: 44 01780 755131
Web site: www.cmvmag.co.uk
Freq: Monthly
Circ: 18500 Not Audited
Editor: Ian Cushway
Profile: Magazine covering all aspects of the military vehicle scene. Includes news, events, vehicle and manufacturer profiles. Contains coverage of all kinds of military hardware that featured in conflicts around the world.
Ad Rate: Full Page Mono £485.00
Ad Rate: Full Page Colour £485.00
MAGAZINE
Antique & Collectible Cars, Armed Forces

Classic Motor Monthly 982608
Editorial: Classic Motor Monthly, PO Box 129, Bolton, Bolton BL3 4YQ
Tel: 44 01204 657212

Consumer Magazines

Email: editor@classicmotor.co.uk
Web site: www.classicmotor.co.uk
Freq: Monthly
Circ: 33000 Not Audited
Editor: John Hodson
Profile: Magazine covering the general classic car scene. Includes shows, runs, auctions, club meetings, autojumbles and hints and tips. Aimed at classic car enthusiasts.
Ad Rate: Full Page Colour £1700.00
MAGAZINE
Antique & Collectible Cars

The Classic Motorcycle   982620
Editorial: Media Centre, Morton Way, Horncastle, Horncastle LN9 6JR
Tel: 44 01507 529529
Email: info@classicmotorcycle.co.uk
Web site: www.classicmotorcycle.co.uk
Freq: Monthly
Circ: 78993 Not Audited
Editor: James Robinson
Profile: Magazine covering vintage and classic motorcycles and their riders, with special emphasis on historical research. Aimed at two wheel enthusiasts.
Ad Rate: Full Page Colour £1250.00
MAGAZINE
Antique & Collectible Cars

Classic Motorcycle Mechanics   982600
Editorial: Media Centre, Morton Way, Horncastle LN9 6JR **Tel:** 44 01507 523456
Email: editor@classicmechanics.com
Web site: www.classicmechanics.com
Freq: Monthly Not Audited
Editor: Bertie Simmonds
Profile: Magazine containing information on motorcycle restoration projects and tests. Also includes practical advice. Aimed at restorers and collectors of pre-1990 motorcycles.
Ad Rate: Full Page Colour £765.00
MAGAZINE
Antique & Collectible Cars, Motorcycles

Classic Motoring   987276
Editorial: 21-23 Phoenix Court, Hawkins Road, Colchester CO2 8JY
Tel: 44 01206 506250
Email: classiccarsforsale@mspublications.co.uk
Web site: http://www.classiccars4sale.net/
Freq: Monthly
Circ: 32000 Not Audited
Editor: Alan Anderson
MAGAZINE
Antique & Collectible Cars

Classic Pop   995417
Editorial: Suite 6, Piccadilly House, London Road, Bath BA1 6PL **Tel:** 44 01225 489984
Web site: www.classicpopmag.com
Freq: Bi-Monthly
Circ: 27000 Not Audited
Editor: Steve Harnell
MAGAZINE
Pop Music

Classic Racer   982609
Editorial: Classic Racer, PO Box 99, Horncastle, Horncastle LN9 6LZ
Tel: 44 01507 529529
Email: editor@classicracer.com
Web site: www.classicracer.com
Freq: Bi-Monthly Not Audited
Editor: Malcolm Wheeler
Profile: Magazine covering road racing from the turn of the century to present day with a focus on the current classic scene. Aimed at classic racing enthusiasts.
Ad Rate: Full Page Colour £742.00
MAGAZINE
Antique & Collectible Cars, Motorcycles

Classic Sailor   1073488
Tel: 44 01273 420730
Email: editor@classicsailor.com
Web site: http://classicsailor.com/
Freq: Monthly
Circ: 5500 Not Audited

Editor: Dan Houston
MAGAZINE
Boating & Yachting

Classic Speedway   987763
Editorial: 103 Douglas Road, Hornchurch, London RM11 1AW **Tel:** 44 01708 734502
Email: editorial@retro-speedway.com
Web site: www.retro-speedway.com
Freq: Quarterly
Circ: 3000 Not Audited
Editor: Tony McDonald
Profile: Magazine covering speedway predominantly from to 1950s and 60s.
MAGAZINE
Motorsports

Classic Tractor   986935
Editorial: Sundial House, 17 Wickham Road, Beckenham, London BR3 5JS
Tel: 44 02086 394400
Email: editor@classictractormagazine.co.uk
Web site: http://www.classictractormagazine.co.uk
Freq: Monthly
Circ: 37000 Not Audited
Editor: Rory Day
Profile: Magazine covering all makes of tractors and farm machinery built over the last 40 years.
Ad Rate: Full Page Mono £495.00
Ad Rate: Full Page Colour £750.00
MAGAZINE
Animal Farming, Antique & Collectible Cars

Classic Van & Pick Up   982610
Editorial: Cudham Tithe Barn, Berry's Hill, Cudham, London TN16 3AG
Tel: 44 01959 541444
Email: van.ed@kelsey.co.uk
Web site: www.classicvan.co.uk
Freq: Monthly
Circ: 8100 Not Audited
Editor: Ted Connolly
MAGAZINE
Antique & Collectible Cars

Classic Veteran & Vintage Cars   997780
Editorial: Suite 6B(i), Britannia House, Leagrave Road, Luton LU3 1RJ
Tel: 44 01582 488385
Email: info@mediachamelion.co.uk
Web site: www.classiccarwebsite.com
Freq: Annual Not Audited
MAGAZINE
Antique & Collectible Cars

Classical Music   982069
Editorial: Rhinegold House, 20 Rugby Street, London WC1N 3QZ
Tel: 44 02073 331731
Email: classical.music@rhinegold.co.uk
Web site: http://www.rhinegold.co.uk/rhinegold-publishing/magazines/classical-music/
Freq: Monthly
Circ: 25000 Not Audited
Editor: Owen Mortimer
Profile: News magazine covering all aspects of the classical music industry in Britain. Aimed at anyone involved in the performance, promotion and management of classical music in Britain.
Ad Rate: Full Page Mono £1220.00
Ad Rate: Full Page Colour £1600.00
MAGAZINE
Classical/Choral/Band Music, Music

Classicalsource.com   984590
Editorial: 26 Great Queen Street, London WC2B 5BB **Tel:** 44 02083 037089
Email: info@classicalsource.com
Web site: http://www.classicalsource.com/
Freq: Daily
Circ: 12596 Cision Digital Reach
Editor: Colin Anderson
MAGAZINE (ONLINE)
Classical/Choral/Band Music

ClassicDriver.com   982827
Editorial: Fountain Court, 2 Victoria Square, St.Albans, London AL1 3TF
Email: editor@classicdriver.com
Web site: www.classicdriver.com
Freq: Daily
Circ: 727552 Cision Digital Reach
MAGAZINE (ONLINE)
Antique & Collectible Cars

Clay Shooter   995781
Tel: 44 01189 742508
Email: editor@clayshooter.co.uk
Web site: http://www.sportingshooter.co.uk/magazines/clay-shooter-magazine
Freq: Bi-Monthly
Circ: 30000 Not Audited
MAGAZINE
Shooting/Guns

Clay Shooting   982279
Editorial: Lawrence House, Morrell Street, Leamington Spa, Leamington Spa CV32 5SZ
Tel: 44 01926 339808
Web site: www.clay-shooting.com
Freq: Monthly
Circ: 28000 Not Audited
Profile: Magazine covering clay target shooting including coming events, results, championship reports, shooting tips, advice from the world's best shooters and a weekly bulletin providing the latest shooting information. Read by clay pigeon shooting enthusiasts.
Ad Rate: Full Page Mono £600.00
Ad Rate: Full Page Colour £600.00
MAGAZINE
Shooting/Guns

Clean Energy Pipeline   998806
Editorial: 2nd Floor, 79 Wells Street, London W1T 3QN **Tel:** 44 02072 518000
Email: press@vbresearch.com
Web site: http://www.cleanenergypipeline.com/Home.aspx
Freq: Daily
Circ: 432 Cision Digital Reach
MAGAZINE (ONLINE)
Alternative/Renewable Energy, Carbon Emissions & Trading, Electricity, Energy, Energy & Environment, Environment, Nuclear Power, Oil, Water & Sanitation

The Clerkenwell Post   987477
Editorial: Crown House, 151 High Street, London IG10 4LF **Tel:** 44 02032 255200
Email: info@media-ten.com
Web site: www.theclerkenwellpost.com
Freq: Bi-Monthly
Circ: 10500 Not Audited
Editor: Melissa Crowther
Profile: Magazine covering local lifestyle issues for the Clerkenwell area of London. Features include the design, heritage, craft and restaurants in the area. Aimed at residents in the EC1 area of London.
MAGAZINE
Regional General Interest

Clic Digital   1072711
Email: info@clic-digital.com
Web site: http://www.clic-digital.com/
Freq: Daily
Circ: 12153 Cision Digital Reach
MAGAZINE (ONLINE)
News & Current Affairs

Click Liverpool   985280
Editorial: c/o Nine Trees Media, 3 Covent Garden, Liverpool L2 8UA
Email: editorial@clickliverpool.com
Web site: www.clickliverpool.com
Freq: Daily
Circ: 36809 Cision Digital Reach
Profile: Website covering news in Liverpool. Click Liverpool is hosted by Click Creative. The website shares the latest news on sport, culture, lifestyle, entertainment and business in Liverpool.
MAGAZINE (ONLINE)
Regional

Clicks ClubCard Magazine   1060440
Tel: 44 27214 601937
Email: ccms@newclicks.com
Freq: Bi-Monthly
Circ: 552930 Not Audited
MAGAZINE
Beauty & Grooming, Books, Cosmetics, Fashion, Gardening, Grocery Stores, Hair, Office Supplies, Retail, Retail Management

Client   1073132
Web site: www.clientmagazine.co.uk/about/
Freq: Quarterly Not Audited
Profile: Magazine covering menswear and male grooming features.
MAGAZINE
Fashion, Men's Interests, Photography, Visual Arts

Climate Bonds Initiative   998326
Editorial: 2 Bath Place, Rivington Street, London EC2A 3DR
Web site: http://www.climatebonds.net/
Freq: Daily
Circ: 20664 Cision Digital Reach
MAGAZINE (ONLINE)
News & Current Affairs

Climate Home   986616
Editorial: 8th Floor, Elizabeth House, 39 York Road, London SE1 7NQ
Tel: 44 02073 402865
Email: info@rtcc.org
Web site: http://www.climatechangenews.com/
Freq: Daily
Circ: 63221 Cision Digital Reach
MAGAZINE (ONLINE)
Alternative/Renewable Energy, Energy & Environment, Environment

Climate News Network   988919
Email: info@climatenewsnetwork.net
Web site: www.climatenewsnetwork.net
Freq: Daily
Circ: 19919 Cision Digital Reach
MAGAZINE (ONLINE)
Alternative/Renewable Energy, Energy & Environment, Environment

Climb   982788
Editorial: 160-164 Barkby Road, Leicester LE16 8FZ **Tel:** 44 01162 022728
Email: climbmagazine@gmail.com
Web site: https://www.climbmagazine.com/
Freq: Bi-Monthly
Circ: 11000 Not Audited
Profile: Magazine covering rock climbing, hill climbing and mountaineering. Aimed at active rock climbers and mountaineers.
Ad Rate: Full Page Colour £1500.00
MAGAZINE
Outdoor Recreation

Climber   981901
Editorial: 19 Robinson Road, Sheffield, Sheffield S2 5QW
Web site: www.climber.co.uk
Freq: Bi-Monthly
Circ: 18000 Not Audited
Profile: Magazine covering rock climbing. Dedicated to all aspects of rock climbing and mountaineering, trad climbing, sport climbing, bouldering, alpine climbing, winter and ice climbing and expeditions.
Ad Rate: Full Page Colour £1530.00
MAGAZINE
Outdoor Recreation

Clinical Medicine   984501
Editorial: 11 St Andrews Place, Regent's Park, London NW1 4LE
Web site: www.rcplondon.ac.uk/resources/clinical-medicine-journal
Freq: Bi-Monthly
Circ: 20000 Not Audited
Editor: Humphrey Hodgson
Profile: Journal covering peer reviewed articles relevant to science and the practice of international medicine.
Ad Rate: Full Page Mono £944.00

Ad Rate: Full Page Colour £1584.00
MAGAZINE
Medicine

Clocks 981870
Editorial: 141b Lower Granton Road, Edinburgh EH5 1EX **Tel:** 44 01313 313200
Email: clocksmagazine@googlemail.com
Web site: www.clocksmagazine.com
Freq: Monthly
Circ: 3000 Not Audited
Editor: John Hunter
Profile: Magazine covering collecting, restoring and repairing of clocks from around the world.
Ad Rate: Full Page Mono £275.00
Ad Rate: Full Page Colour £400.00
MAGAZINE
Antiques/Collectibles

Close Up (business) 998523
Editorial: John Smith Stadium, Stadium Way, Huddersfield HD1 GPG
Tel: 44 01484 483660
Web site: http://www.mycci.co.uk/close-up-magazine
Freq: Quarterly
Circ: 40000 Not Audited
MAGAZINE
News & Current Affairs

Closer 982360
Editorial: Academic House, 24-28 Oval Road, Camden, London NW1 7DT
Tel: 44 02072 418000
Email: closer@closermag.co.uk
Web site: http://lifestyle.one/closer/
Freq: Weekly
Circ: 196126 Not Audited
Editor: Lisa Burrow
Profile: Magazine combining news, gossip, glamour and celebrity news, along with real-life content. Contains a lifestyle section with topical fashion and beauty, diet, health and TV listings. First published in 2002. Aimed at women aged between 25 and 40 years old.
Ad Rate: Full Page Colour £18618.00
MAGAZINE
Celebrities, Women's Interests

The Closet 1075502
Tel: 44 07403 121919
Email: info@hitthefloor.com
Web site: http://thecloset.hitthefloor.com/
Freq: Daily
Circ: 7406 Cision Digital Reach
MAGAZINE (ONLINE)
Beauty & Grooming, Cosmetics, Fashion, Hair, Regional General Interest, Women's Interests

Close-Up Film 988823
Email: jeanl@close-upfilm.com
Web site: http://www.close-upfilm.com
Freq: Daily
Circ: 9505 Cision Digital Reach
Editor: Jean Lynch
Profile: Website covering films from the latest blockbuster release to independent art house releases with film reviews, interviews, practical advice on film making and events. Aimed at active film lovers.
MAGAZINE (ONLINE)
Entertainment, Movies & Video

The Clothes Maiden 998399
Editorial: The Clothes Maiden Studio, 22 Blackbrook Court, Durham Road, Corby LE115UA
Email: press@theclothesmaiden.com
Web site: http://www.theclothesmaiden.com/
Freq: Daily
Circ: 37902 Cision Digital Reach
MAGAZINE (ONLINE)
Art, Beauty & Grooming, Classical/Choral/Band Music, Cosmetics, Country, Folk, Bluegrass, Dance Music, Fashion, Hair, Jazz & Blues, Music

Cloud Computing World 996685
Editorial: E Space Business Centre, 181 Wisbech Road, Littleport, Ely CB7 4EX
Tel: 44 01353 771460
Web site: www.cloudcomputingworld.co.uk
Freq: Daily
Circ: 18000 Not Audited
Editor: Nick Wells
MAGAZINE
Internet, Security & Security Systems

Cloud Hosting 996854
Editorial: 35 Station Square, London BR5 1LZ **Tel:** 44 01689 616000
Web site: www.cloudhostingmagazine.co.uk
Freq: Bi-Monthly
Circ: 17500 Not Audited
Editor: David Tyler
MAGAZINE
Data Management, Industry, Internet, Mobile Communications

Cloud Services World 987416
Editorial: Hannay House, 39 Clarendon Road, London WD17 1JA
Tel: 44 01923 690200
Email: cloudservices-world@angelbc.com
Web site: https://digitalisationworld.com/
Freq: Daily
Circ: 15827 Cision Digital Reach
MAGAZINE (ONLINE)
Computers, Internet, Mobile Communications

CloudTech 987251
Email: editorial@techforge.pub
Web site: www.cloudcomputing-news.net
Freq: Daily
Circ: 117431 Cision Digital Reach
MAGAZINE (ONLINE)
Internet

The Club (British Airways) 996654
Editorial: 85 Strand, London WC2R 0DW
Tel: 44 02075 508000
Web site: theclub.ba.com
Freq: Monthly
Circ: 3300000 Not Audited
MAGAZINE
Airline Inflight, Lifestyle, Men's Interests, Railroad, Regional General Interest, Travel, Women's Interests

Club House Europe 988232
Editorial: Gainsborough House, 59-60 Thames Street, Windsor, Windsor SL4 1TS
Tel: 44 01753 272022
Email: editor@cmaeurope.plus.com
Web site: www.clubhouseeurope.com
Freq: Quarterly Not Audited
MAGAZINE
Bars, Clubs & Pubs, Business, Corporate Responsibility, Golf

Club Journal 998518
Editorial: 59/60 Thames Street, Berkshire, Windsor SL4 1TS **Tel:** 44 01753 272022
Email: justin@clubjournal.co.uk
Web site: http://www.wmciu.org.uk/Club_Journal.html
Freq: Monthly
Circ: 26254 Not Audited
Editor: Justin O'Regan
MAGAZINE
Bars, Clubs & Pubs

Club Mirror 983749
Editorial: Gainsborough House, 59- 60 Thames Street, Windsor SL4 1TX
Tel: 44 01753 272022
Email: info@clubmirror.com
Web site: www.clubmirror.com
Freq: Monthly
Circ: 12986 Not Audited
Profile: Magazine covering legal and financial matters, equipment, live entertainment, catering, sports and fitness and the licensed leisure industry.
Ad Rate: Full Page Colour £3295.00
MAGAZINE
Alcohol & Spirits, Bars, Clubs & Pubs

CMUSE 998140
Email: contact@cmuse.org
Web site: www.cmuse.org
Freq: Daily
Circ: 112724 Cision Digital Reach
MAGAZINE (ONLINE)
Classical/Choral/Band Music, Jazz & Blues, Pop Music, Rock Music

CN Focus 985423
Editorial: Studio 2, Mill Studio Business Centre, Crane Mead, Ware SG12 9PY
Tel: 44 01920 444060
Email: info@cm-2.co.uk
Web site: www.nutrition2me.com/publications/cn-focus
Freq: 3 Times/Year
Circ: 11800 Not Audited
Editor: Lynne Garton
Profile: Magazine covering all areas of primary care nutrition, including articles on the latest news, products and research.
Ad Rate: Full Page Colour £1450.00
MAGAZINE
Nutrition

CNET (London Office) 985172
Editorial: The Warehouse, The Bower, 207-211 Old Street, London EC1V 9NR
Tel: 44 02070 211000
Email: edit@cnet.co.uk
Web site: www.cnet.com/uk/
Freq: Daily
Circ: 3063509 Cision Digital Reach
MAGAZINE (ONLINE)
Audio Video Trade, Cameras, Consumer Electronics, Mobile Electronics, Movies & Video

Coach (UK) 1053090
Editorial: 31-32 Alfred Place, London WC1E 7DP
Web site: www.coachmag.co.uk
Freq: Weekly
Circ: 159736 Cision Digital Reach
MAGAZINE (ONLINE)
Fitness & Exercise, Health & Medicine

Coach and Bus Week 981341
Editorial: 3 The Office Village, Cygnet Park, Forder Way, Peterborough, Hampton PE7 8FD **Tel:** 44 01733 293240
Web site: https://cbwmagazine.com/
Freq: Weekly
Circ: 5000 Not Audited
Editor: Gareth Evans
MAGAZINE
Automotive

Coach Tours UK 983930
Editorial: 4 Milnyard Square, Bakewell Road, Orton Southgate, Peterborough PE2 6GX **Tel:** 44 01733 362300
Web site: http://www.coachtoursuk.com/
Freq: Monthly
Circ: 5736 Not Audited
Editor: Karen Wright
Profile: Magazine containing features on potential tour and entertainment venues in the UK and Europe.
Ad Rate: Full Page Mono £1314.00
Ad Rate: Full Page Colour £1852.00
MAGAZINE
Travel

Coarse Fishing Answers 1076636
Editorial: 1 Whittle Close, Drayton Fields, Daventry NN11 8RQ **Tel:** 44 01327 311999
Email: editor@total-fishing.com
Web site: http://www.coarsefishinganswers.com/
Freq: Monthly
Circ: 20000 Not Audited
Editor: Rob Smith
MAGAZINE
Fishing

Coast 982807
Editorial: Cudham Tithe Barn, Berry's Hill, Cudham, London TN16 3AG
Tel: 44 01959 541444
Email: coast.enquiries@kelsey.co.uk
Web site: www.coastmagazine.co.uk

Freq: Monthly
Circ: 31793 Not Audited
Editor: Alex Fisher
Profile: Magazine covering life by the sea including houses, hotels, restaurants, B&Bs, decorating and design ideas, cooking seasonal food, complementary health and beauty, fashion, profiles of people who live or work by the sea and photographs of seascapes and coastal landscapes. Aimed at active, discerning women aged 35 to 50 years old with a high household income, like to visit or live on the coast and are health, fitness, fashion and beauty conscious.
Ad Rate: Full Page Colour £3333.00
MAGAZINE
Property Management & Maintenance, Regional General Interest, Travel

Coca-Cola.co.uk 995792
Editorial: Western Transit Shed, 12-13 Stable Street, London N1C 1AB
Tel: 44 02036 978600
Email: hello@thisiszone.com
Web site: http://www.coca-cola.co.uk
Freq: Daily
Circ: 164311 Cision Digital Reach
Editor: Victoria Noble
MAGAZINE (ONLINE)
Alcohol & Spirits, Bars, Clubs & Pubs, Beer, Beverages, Wine/Winemaking

The COCKTAIL LOVERS 999365
Editorial: 13 Tavistock Chambers, 40 Bloomsbury Way, London WC1A 2SE
Tel: 44 02072 422546
Email: mail@thecocktaillovers.com
Web site: www.thecocktaillovers.com
Freq: Quarterly
Circ: 15000 Not Audited
Editor: Sandrae Lawrence; **Editor:** Gary Sharpen
MAGAZINE
Alcohol & Spirits, Bars, Clubs & Pubs

The Cocoa Diaries 1098997
Email: thecocoadiaries@gmail.com
Web site: http://cocoadiaries.com/
Freq: Daily
Circ: 26851 Cision Digital Reach
Editor: Keysha Davis
MAGAZINE (ONLINE)
Africa, Broadcasting, Cooking & Baking, Jazz & Blues, Literature, Rap & Hip Hop, Theater & Performing Arts

Cocotraie 999533
Editorial: Belvedere Road, Crystal Palace, London SE19 2HY **Tel:** 44 08451 162758
Email: info-media@cocotraie.com
Web site: www.cocotraie.com
Freq: Quarterly
Circ: 65000 Not Audited
Editor: Sebastian Isaacs
MAGAZINE
Do-It-Yourself (DIY), Real Estate, Travel

Codebreakers 998938
Editorial: Academic House, 24-28 Oval Road, London NW1 7DT
Tel: 44 02072 418000
Email: codebreakers@bauer.co.uk
Web site: http://www.puzzlemagazines.co.uk/code-breakers
Freq: Monthly
Circ: 61000 Not Audited
MAGAZINE
Games, Competitions & Events

Codebreakers Collection 998701
Editorial: Academic House, 24-28 Oval Road, London NW1 7DT
Tel: 44 02072 418000
Email: codebreakers@bauer.co.uk
Web site: www.puzzlemagazines.co.uk/codebreakers-collection
Freq: Monthly
Circ: 32000 Not Audited
MAGAZINE
Games, Competitions & Events

Consumer Magazines

Coffee & Cocoa International
981281
Editorial: Office 8, Unit 1-2, Wyvern Estate, Beverley Way, New Malden KT3 4PH
Tel: 44 02089 490088
Email: coffeemagazine@yahoo.co.uk
Web site: www.coffeeandcocoa.net
Freq: Bi-Monthly
Circ: 7510 Not Audited
Editor: David Foxwell
MAGAZINE
Alcohol & Spirits, Food

Coggles
996344
Editorial: Meridian House, Gadbrook Park, Rudheath, Northwich CW9 7RA
Tel: 44 01618 131497
Email: contact@coggles.com
Web site: www.coggles.com
Freq: Daily
Circ: 704099 Cision Digital Reach
MAGAZINE (ONLINE)
Antiques/Collectibles, Art, Arts, Fashion, Literature, Photography, Theater & Performing Arts, Visual Arts

Coin News
985142
Editorial: Orchard House, Duchy Road, Heathpark, Honiton EX14 1YD
Tel: 44 01404 46972
Email: info@tokenpublishing.com
Web site: www.tokenpublishing.com/coins.asp
Freq: Monthly Not Audited
MAGAZINE
Antiques/Collectibles

Coinslot
998639
Editorial: 20 New Road, Brighton BN1 1UF
Freq: Weekly
Circ: 4500 Not Audited
MAGAZINE
News & Current Affairs

Coinslot International
988162
Editorial: 20 New Road, Brighton BN1 1UF
Tel: 44 01273 699900
Email: ks@sjc.co.uk
Freq: Weekly
Circ: 14000 Not Audited
Profile: Journal focusing on coin-operated machines for amusement arcades, pubs and clubs. Also covers theme parks, bingo halls, casinos, licensed betting, Internet gaming and visitor attractions.
Ad Rate: Full Page Colour £1460.00
MAGAZINE
Computer & Video Games

Collectively
1074792
Editorial: 5th Floor, 6 St. Andrew Street, London EC4A 3AE
Email: editorial@collectively.org
Web site: https://collectively.org/
Freq: Daily
Circ: 35901 Cision Digital Reach
MAGAZINE (ONLINE)
Energy & Environment, Health & Medicine, Organic Food, Relationships

Collectors Gazette
981914
Editorial: The Maltings, West Street, Bourne, Bourne PE10 9PH Tel: 44 01778 391000
Web site: www.collectorsgazette.com
Freq: Monthly
Circ: 12000 Not Audited
Editor: Rob Burman
Profile: Magazine containing articles on old toys, trains and toy soldiers, dolls and teddies, Meccano, tinplate, TV and film-related models, toy fairs and auction news.
Ad Rate: Full Page Colour £750.00
MAGAZINE
Antiques/Collectibles

ColourGirl
1076409
Tel: 44 01743 364433
Email: info@redan.com
Web site: www.redan.co.uk/Colour%20Girl.html
Freq: Bi-Monthly
Circ: 40000 Not Audited

Editor: Caroline Jenkins
MAGAZINE
Elementary School, Teen/Young Adult

Colouring Heaven
1063926
Editorial: Suite 6, Piccadilly House, London Road, Bath BA1 6PL Tel: 44 01225 489984
Email: enquiries@anthem-publishing.com
Web site: www.anthem-publishing.com/colouring-heaven
Freq: Monthly Not Audited
MAGAZINE
Crafts

Column
984455
Editorial: National Back Exchange, Linden Barns, Greens Norton Road, Towcester, Towcester NN12 8AW Tel: 44 01327 358855
Email: admin@nationalbackexchange.org
Web site: www.nationalbackexchange.org
Freq: Quarterly
Circ: 1000 Not Audited
Editor: Carol Johnson
Profile: Magazine covering back care issues and advice for the prevention of work related, musculoskeletal problems.
MAGAZINE
Patient Support

Combat & Survival
981978
Editorial: 1st Floor, Turnbridge Mills, Quay Street, Huddersfield HD1 6QT
Tel: 44 02081 233414
Email: editor@ciaranjarosz.media
Web site: www.combatandsurvival.com
Freq: Monthly
Circ: 30000 Not Audited
Editor: Bob Morrison
MAGAZINE
Armed Forces

Combat Aircraft Monthly
980082
Editorial: Foundry Road, Stamford, Stamford PE9 2PP Tel: 44 01780 484630
Web site: www.combataircraft.net
Freq: Monthly
Circ: 15820 Not Audited
Editor: Jamie Hunter
MAGAZINE
Armed Forces, Aviation

Come Into Land
996512
Email: travis@comeinto.land
Web site: comeintoland.com
Freq: Daily
Circ: 6565 Cision Digital Reach
Editor: Travis Lee Street
MAGAZINE (ONLINE)
Art, Fashion

Comic Book and Movie Reviews
1069609
Email: cbamr@talktalk.net
Web site: http://www.comicbookandmoviereviews.com/
Freq: Daily
Circ: 40490 Cision Digital Reach
Editor: David Lee Andrews
MAGAZINE (ONLINE)
Cartoons, Entertainment, Movies & Video, Trading Cards & Comics

Comic Heroes
995557
Editorial: Quay House, The Ambury, Bath BA1 1UA Tel: 44 02070 424000
Freq: Quarterly Not Audited
Profile: Magazine covering the latest superhero movies, videogames and comic books with news, previews, reviews and features.
MAGAZINE
Literature, Visual Arts

Commando
998946
Editorial: 185 Fleet Street, London EC4A 2HS Tel: 44 01382 223131
Email: editor@commandocomics.com
Web site: www.commandocomics.com
Freq: Bi-Weekly
Circ: 17231 Not Audited
MAGAZINE
Armed Forces

The Commentator
986579
Email: submissions@thecommentator.com
Web site: www.thecommentator.com
Freq: Daily
Circ: 62297 Cision Digital Reach
MAGAZINE (ONLINE)
International News, National News, Politics

Commercial Fleet
998152
Editorial: Media House, Lynchwood, Peterborough PE2 6EA
Tel: 44 01733 468306
Web site: www.commercialfleet.org
Freq: Monthly
Circ: 17416 Not Audited
Profile: Publication that provides insight, analysis and best practice solutions to commercial vehicle operators to help companies run more effective and efficient van fleets.
Ad Rate: Full Page Colour £2827.00
MAGAZINE
Automotive

The Commercial Greenhouse Grower
983854
Editorial: 21 Church St, Maidstone, Maidstone ME14 1EN Tel: 44 01622 695656
Email: green@actpub.co.uk
Web site: http://greenhousegrower.co.uk/
Freq: Monthly
Circ: 4400 Not Audited
Editor: John Downey
Profile: Magazine covering news, products, ideas and advice on flowers, plants and salads.
Ad Rate: Full Page Mono £1148.00
Ad Rate: Full Page Colour £1840.00
MAGAZINE
Animal Farming

Commercial Motor
979917
Editorial: 6th Floor, Chancery House, St Nicholas Way, Sutton SM1 1JB
Tel: 44 02089 122170
Email: webteam@roadtransport.com
Web site: www.commercialmotor.com
Freq: Weekly
Circ: 9788 Not Audited
Editor: Will Shiers
Profile: Magazine covering all aspects of the road transport industry with an emphasis on product reporting and regular vehicle road tests. Aimed at commercial vehicle purchasing decision makers across all fleet sites who operate vehicles of 3.5 tonnes and above.
Ad Rate: Full Page Colour £3500.00
MAGAZINE
Automotive

Commercial Vehicle Dealer
985053
Editorial: Focus Publishing, 100 Bridge Street, Peterborough PE1 1DY
Tel: 44 01733 566933
Email: info@cvdealer.co.uk
Web site: www.cvdealer.co.uk
Freq: Monthly
Circ: 10000 Not Audited
Editor: Jason Hodge
Profile: Magazine covering product news, people moves and industry news for the commercial vehicle sector.
Ad Rate: Full Page Colour £1150.00
MAGAZINE
Automotive

Commercial Vehicle Engineer
986358
Tel: 44 01428 605605
Email: info@aztecxpress.com
Web site: www.cvengineer.com
Freq: Monthly
Circ: 5605 Not Audited
Profile: Website covering commercial vehicles. The COMMERCIAL VEHICLE ENGINEER website shares the latest news on the commercial vehicle market and after-market, transport engineering, technology, events, jobs and training.

Ad Rate: Full Page Mono £495.00
MAGAZINE
Automotive, Shipping & Warehousing

Commercial Vehicle Workshop
984488
Editorial: Regal House, Regal Way, Watford, London WD24 4YF Tel: 44 01923 237799
Email: cvw@hamerville.co.uk
Web site: www.cvwmagazine.co.uk
Freq: Monthly
Circ: 9156 Not Audited
Profile: Magazine covering the commercial vehicle aftermarket. Includes articles on safety, product tests and training. Aimed at independent repair workshops and in-house fleet workshops.Regular features: Health and Safety; Legislation; News; Product Tests; Trade Media; Workshop Management
Ad Rate: Full Page Colour £1990.00
MAGAZINE
Automotive, Shipping & Warehousing

commercialvehicleinsight.com
1064625
Web site: http://www.commercialvehicleinsight.com/
Freq: Daily
Circ: 1461 Cision Digital Reach
Editor: Georgina Bisby
MAGAZINE (ONLINE)
Automotive

Communication Matters Journal
996955
Editorial: Leeds Innovation Centre, 103 Clarendon Road, Leeds LS2 9DF
Tel: 44 08454 568211
Email: admin@communicationmatters.org.uk
Web site: www.communicationmatters.org.uk/page/cm-journal
Freq: 3 Times/Year Not Audited
Editor: Sally Millar
MAGAZINE
Medicine

Communications Consumer Panel
999669
Editorial: Riverside House, 2a Southwark Bridge Road, London SE1 9HA
Tel: 44 02077 834078
Email: media@communicationsconsumerpanel.org.uk
Web site: http://www.communicationsconsumerpanel.org.uk/news-current-year/current-year-1
Circ: 2535 Cision Digital Reach
MAGAZINE (ONLINE)
Business, Small and Medium Business

Communications Law
980142
Editorial: Maxwelton House, 41-43 Boltro Road, Haywards Heath, Haywards Heath RH16 1BJ Tel: 44 01444 416119
Email: customerservice@bloomsburyprofessional.com
Web site: www.bloomsburyprofessional.com
Freq: Quarterly Not Audited
MAGAZINE
News & Current Affairs

Communicator
987882
Editorial: Airport House, Purley Way, London CR0 0XZ Tel: 44 02082 534506
Email: istc@istc.org.uk
Web site: www.istc.org.uk/our-publications/communicator
Freq: Quarterly Not Audited
Profile: Journal of the Institute of Scientific and Technical Communicators (ISTC). Contains news and features of interest to authors, managers, consultants, educators, editors, illustrators and translators, involved in publishing technical and scientific information in all media.
Ad Rate: Full Page Colour £725.00
MAGAZINE
Computers, Data Management, Internet

Community
996002
Freq: Quarterly Not Audited
MAGAZINE
News & Current Affairs

Community Living
997166
Editorial: 2 St. Georges Close, Dunster, Dunster TA24 6SS **Tel:** 44 01643 822513
Web site: www.cl-initiatives.co.uk
Freq: Quarterly
Circ: 11883 Cision Digital Reach
MAGAZINE (ONLINE)
Disability

The Commuter
997884
Editorial: Suite D0115, 265-269 Kingston Road, Wimbledon, London SW19 3NW
Tel: 44 01795 880039
Email: commutermagazines@gmail.com
Web site: www.commutermagazines.co.uk/1.html
Freq: Monthly Not Audited
MAGAZINE
Lifestyle, Men's Interests, Regional General Interest, Women's Interests

Companions
982010
Editorial: Whitechapel Way, Priorslee, Telford TF2 9PQ **Tel:** 44 08009 172509
Email: pr@pdsa.org.uk
Web site: http://www.pdsa.org.uk
Freq: Quarterly
Circ: 56586 Not Audited
MAGAZINE
Nature & Wildlife

Company Car & Van
996712
Editorial: 12 Oakwood Lane, Bowdon, Altrincham WA14 3DL **Tel:** 44 0161 9 414296
Web site: www.companycarandvan.co.uk
Freq: Bi-Monthly
Circ: 2100 Not Audited
MAGAZINE
News & Current Affairs

Compare the Cloud
1053356
Editorial: Office 318, 117 Waterloo Road, London SE1 8UL
Circ: 39910 Cision Digital Reach
MAGAZINE (ONLINE)
Data Management, Internet, Security & Security Systems

Compass
985984
Editorial: 6th Floor, 30 Millbank, London SW1P 4EE **Tel:** 44 02078 085694
Email: info@coxandkings.co.uk
Web site: http://www.coxandkings.co.uk/
Freq: 3 Times/Year
Circ: 45000 Not Audited
Editor: Jennifer Cox
MAGAZINE
Travel

Compass Sport
981902
Editorial: 6 Glenmore Park, Tunbridge Wells TN2 5NZ **Tel:** 44 07720 952241
Email: nick@compasssport.co.uk
Web site: http://www.compasssport.co.uk
Freq: Bi-Monthly
Circ: 1500 Not Audited
Editor: Nick Barrable
Profile: Magazine covering mountain marathons and all forms of orienteering, including mountain bike orienteering, ski-orienteering and trail orienteering.
Ad Rate: Full Page Colour £395.00
MAGAZINE
Outdoor Recreation

Compellier
987730
Email: enquiries@compellier.com
Web site: www.compellier.com
Freq: Daily
Circ: 14000 Not Audited
Editor: Lauren Knowles
MAGAZINE
Antiques/Collectibles, Art, Arts, Beauty & Grooming, Cosmetics, Fashion, Hair, Lifestyle, Literature, Luxury Goods

Competitions Galore
1073819
Tel: 44 01865 664970
Email: info@theoxfordpuzzlecompany.com
Web site: www.theoxfordpuzzlecompany.com
Freq: Bi-Monthly
Circ: 50000 Not Audited
Profile: Magazine with puzzles and competitions. Each issue of Prizes Galore Magazine contains over thirty easy to enter exclusive competitions to win prizes.
MAGAZINE
Games, Competitions & Events

Complete Kit Car
986371
Editorial: Unit 3, Site 4, Alma Park Road, Grantham, Worthing NG31 9SE
Tel: 44 01823 617908
Web site: www.completekitcar.co.uk
Freq: Monthly
Circ: 12000 Not Audited
MAGAZINE
Automakers

Complete Nutrition (CN)
983831
Editorial: CM2, Studio 002, Mill Studio Business Centre, Crane Mead, Ware, Ware SG12 9PY **Tel:** 44 01920 444060
Email: info@cm-2.co.uk
Web site: www.nutrition2me.com/publications/complete-nutrition
Freq: Bi-Monthly
Circ: 13000 Not Audited
Editor: Lynne Garton
MAGAZINE
Nutrition

The Complete University Guide
999563
Editorial: First Floor, Bedford House, 69-79 Fulham High Street, London SW6 3JW
Tel: 44 02072 689700
Email: editorial@thecompleteuniversityguide.co.uk
Web site: www.thecompleteuniversityguide.co.uk
Freq: Daily
Circ: 1701916 Cision Digital Reach
MAGAZINE (ONLINE)
Alumni, Education, Higher Education

Completion
995836
Editorial: 3 Upper Street, 3rd Floor, Islington, London N1 0PQ
Tel: 44 03333 441350
Email: editorial@cwpg.com
Web site: www.completiononline.co.uk
Freq: Semi-Annual
Circ: 200000 Not Audited
MAGAZINE
Do-It-Yourself (DIY), Interior Design, Property Management & Maintenance, Residential Real Estate

Complex UK
1070075
Editorial: 15-20 The Oval, London E2 9DX
Email: editorial@w00t.complex.com
Web site: uk.complex.com
Freq: Daily
Circ: 257852 Cision Digital Reach
MAGAZINE (ONLINE)
Men's Interests

Compliance & Risk Journal
997720
Editorial: Canterbury Court, Kennington Park, London SW9 6DE
Tel: 44 02070 143399
Email: uk_office@pdpwebsite.com
Web site: www.pdpjournals.com/overview-compliance-and-risk-journal
Freq: Bi-Monthly Not Audited
MAGAZINE
News & Current Affairs

Compliance Matters
999589
Editorial: 19 Heathman's Road, London SW6 4TJ **Tel:** 44 02071 480188
Web site: www.comp-matters.com
Freq: Monthly
Circ: 11116 Cision Digital Reach

Editor: Chris Hamblin
MAGAZINE (ONLINE)
Banking, Fund Management, Personal Finance

Compliance Monitor
981573
Editorial: Christchurch Court, 10 Newgate Street, London EC1A 7AZ
Tel: 44 02070 176323
Email: lawmarketing@informa.com
Web site: http://www.compliancemonitor.com/
Freq: Monthly Not Audited
Editor: Esther Martin
Profile: Newsletter containing news and practitioner analysis of UK financial services regulation and compliance as well as wealth management. Provides UK financial services' analysis and comments, latest initiatives, practical advice for implementation of new and existing rules. Aimed at compliance officers and others who specialise in UK financial services compliance and regulation.
MAGAZINE
Economics

Compliance Resource Network
994697
Editorial: 5th Floor, 120 Alderstage Street, London EC1 A JQ **Tel:** 44 02075 396500
Email: uksupport@wolterskluwer.com
Web site: www.complianceresourcenetwork.com
Freq: Daily
Circ: 1910 Cision Digital Reach
MAGAZINE (ONLINE)
News & Current Affairs

Components in Electronics
981316
Editorial: 15A London Road, Maidstone, London ME16 8LY **Tel:** 44 01622 699199
Email: editorial@cieonline.co.uk
Web site: www.cieonline.co.uk
Freq: Monthly
Circ: 12585 Not Audited
Editor: Amy Wallington
MAGAZINE
Electronics, Industry

Composites in Manufacturing
987220
Editorial: Featherstone House, 375 High Street, Rochester, Chatham ME1 1DA
Tel: 44 01634 830566
Web site: www.composites-manufacturing.com
Freq: Bi-Monthly
Circ: 10037 Not Audited
Editor: Mike Richardson
MAGAZINE
Defense & National Security, Engineering, Industry, Manufacturing, Marine & Boat Trade, Mining & Quarrying, Paper, Plastics, Steel

Compound Semiconductor
984973
Editorial: Hannay House, 39 Clarendon Road, Watford, London WD17 1JA
Tel: 44 01923 690200
Email: richard.stevenson@angelbc.com
Web site: www.compoundsemiconductor.net
Freq: Monthly
Circ: 60103 Not Audited
Profile: Magazine focusing on current developments within the global compound semiconductor industry.
Ad Rate: Full Page Colour £3480.00
MAGAZINE
Computers, Internet, Mobile Communications

The Compton Chronicle
999548
Editorial: c/o Contone House, Bridge Street, Fenny Compton, Banbury CV47 2XY
Tel: 44 01295 690191
Email: comptonchronicle@yahoo.co.uk
Web site: www.fennycompton-pc.gov.uk/fennycompton-2105.cfm
Freq: Monthly
Circ: 700 Not Audited

Editor: Amy Aylward
MAGAZINE
Regional General Interest

Compute Scotland
987142
Editorial: Flat 6, 21 Hillside Crescent, Edinburgh EH7 5EB **Tel:** 44 01315 564610
Email: gpurvis@gmail.com
Web site: www.computescotland.com/
Freq: Daily
Circ: 9394 Cision Digital Reach
Editor: Gail Purvis
Profile: Website covering technology. The Compute Scotland is a technology and computer portal that shares the latest local and global information on new technology innovations and developments.
MAGAZINE (ONLINE)
Auto Aftermarket, Computers, Data Management, Electronics, Government Technology, Industry, Internet, Mobile Communications, Security & Security Systems, Software

Computer Business Review
979934
Editorial: John Carpenter House, John Carpenter Street, London EC4Y 0AN
Tel: 44 02079 366400
Email: news@industryreview.com
Web site: www.cbronline.com
Freq: Monthly
Profile: Magazine providing business orientated analysis of events, trends and companies in the IT industry. Features news on M2M (machine to machine communications), internet of things (IoT), collaboration, data storage and network security. Computer Business Review magazine was launched in 1993 with the aim of bridging the gap between the traditional technical IT press and the business press sectors.Published by Progressive Media Group.
Ad Rate: Full Page Colour £4850.00
MAGAZINE
Computers, Internet, Mobile Communications, Security & Security Systems, Software

Computer Music
981727
Editorial: Quay House, The Ambury, Bath BA1 1UA **Tel:** 44 01225 442244
Email: computermusic@futurenet.com
Web site: www.musicradar.com/computermusic
Freq: Monthly
Circ: 12920 Not Audited
Editor: Joe Rossitter
Profile: Magazine covering all aspects of how to make music with a computer. Covers news, reviews and tutorials.
Ad Rate: Full Page Colour £1075.00
MAGAZINE
Music

Computer Shopper (UK)
981735
Editorial: 31 - 32 Alfred Place, London WC1E 7DP **Tel:** 44 02079 076000
Web site: www.expertreviews.co.uk/computershopper
Freq: Monthly
Circ: 16776 Not Audited
Editor: Madeline Bennett
MAGAZINE
Apple, Personal Computers

Computer Weekly
979858
Editorial: TechTarget, 25 Christopher Street, London EC2A 2BS **Tel:** 44 02071 861400
Email: cw-news@computerweekly.com
Web site: www.computerweekly.com
Freq: Weekly
Circ: 1690930 Cision Digital Reach
Editor: Simon Quicke
MAGAZINE (ONLINE)
Auto Aftermarket, Computers, Internet, Security & Security Systems, Software

Computeractive
980893
Editorial: 31-32 Alfred Place, London WC1E 7DP **Tel:** 44 02079 076000
Email: editor@computeractive.co.uk
Web site: www.computeractive.co.uk
Freq: Bi-Weekly

Section 4 UK Periodicals Consumer

Consumer Magazines

Circ: 87565 Not Audited
Profile: Technology magazine published fortnightly. Contains guides, PC problem-solving advice, hints, tips and practical buying advice. Each issue includes news covering technology developments, features and tools in popular applications, and new products that have been tested and rated. First published in 1998, the publication has an average of 100 pages per issue. Press Day: 2nd and 4th Wednesday of every month.
Ad Rate: Full Page Colour £5640.00
MAGAZINE
Internet, Personal Computers

Computing
979859
Editorial: Haymarket House, 32-34 Broadwick Street, London W1A 2HG
Tel: 44 02073 169000
Web site: www.computing.co.uk
Freq: Monthly
Circ: 85000 Not Audited
Profile: Business IT magazine featuring IT news, analysis, opinion and technology developments. It covers the latest trends and issues that will inform readers decisions on how to use technology for the benefit of their organisations. Topics discussed Internet of Things, network security, hardware, software and communications. First published in 1973. Aimed at senior IT decision-makers, IT managers, IT-related directors and managers, chief executive officers, chief operations officers and IT consultants.This magazine publishes the following supplements: Computing Business.
Ad Rate: Full Page Colour £7500.00
MAGAZINE
Auto Aftermarket, Computers, Data Management, Internet, Security & Security Systems, Software

Computing SA
1060404
Tel: 44 27112 805833
Email: bachers@avusa.co.za
Web site: http://www.computingsa.co.za
Circ: 2518 Cision Digital Reach
MAGAZINE (ONLINE)
Auto Aftermarket, Computers, Data Management, Electronics, Government Technology, Industry, Internet, Mobile Communications, National News, Security & Security Systems

Concourse
981757
Email: editor@concourseonline.com
Web site: www.concourseonline.com
Freq: Monthly Not Audited
Profile: Magazine featuring news, events, music, films and art.
Ad Rate: Full Page Mono £200.00
Ad Rate: Full Page Colour £280.00
MAGAZINE
Student Lifestyle

Condé Nast Brides
982420
Editorial: Vogue House, Hanover Square, London W1S 1JU **Tel:** 44 02074 999080
Email: bridesfeatures@condenast.com
Web site: www.bridesmagazine.co.uk
Freq: Bi-Monthly
Circ: 42784 Not Audited
Editor: Jade Beer
Profile: Magazine containing features on bridal wear, dresses and accessories including wedding receptions and catering, beauty tips and products, travel and honeymoon, home furnishings and decoration. Previously called Conde Nast Brides, the publication was first published in 1955 in the USA and has an average of 330 pages per issue. Aimed at women intending to marry in the near future.
Ad Rate: Full Page Colour £9539.00
MAGAZINE
Weddings

Condé Nast Johansens
984419
Editorial: 13 Hanover Square, London W1S 1HN **Tel:** 44 02071 523563
Email: info@johansens.com
Web site: www.johansens.com
Freq: Annual

Circ: 166550 Not Audited
MAGAZINE
Hotels/Motels, Luxury Goods, Travel

Condé Nast Traveller (UK)
982330
Editorial: Conde Nast Traveller, Vogue House, Hanover Square, London W1S 1JU
Tel: 44 02074 999080
Email: cntraveller.assistant@condenast.co.uk
Web site: www.cntraveller.com
Freq: Monthly
Circ: 78091 Not Audited
Editor: Melinda Stevens
MAGAZINE
Luxury Goods, Railroad, Travel

Confetti
982860
Editorial: Ace Mill, Gorse Street, Chadderton, Oldham OL9 9RJ
Tel: 44 08448 489797
Email: pr@confetti.co.uk
Web site: www.confetti.co.uk
Freq: Daily
Circ: 244972 Cision Digital Reach
Profile: Magazine covering all aspects of wedding planning, including articles on venues, dresses, beauty, health and honeymoons.
Ad Rate: Full Page Colour £2200.00
MAGAZINE (ONLINE)
Beauty & Grooming, Cosmetics, Hair, Weddings

Confused.com
985251
Editorial: 3rd Floor, Greyfriars House, Greyfriars Road, Cardiff CF10 3AL
Tel: 44 02920 434342
Web site: www.confused.com
Freq: Daily
Circ: 1230554 Cision Digital Reach
Profile: Insurance price comparison website that makes it easy for you to find the right deals on car insurance, home insurance, utilities and much more.
MAGAZINE (ONLINE)
Personal Finance

connect (CWT UK)
1008682
Editorial: Maple House, High Street, Potters Bar, Potters Bar EN6 5RF
Tel: 44 02033 530000
Email: connect@carlsonwagonlit.co.uk
Web site: www.carlsonwagonlit.co.uk/en/countries/uk
Freq: Quarterly Not Audited
MAGAZINE
Travel

Connected (University of Reading Alumni)
996826
Editorial: London Road Campus, 4 Redlands Road, Reading RG1 5EX
Tel: 44 01183 788006
Email: alumni@reading.ac.uk
Web site: www.extra.rdg.ac.uk/alumni
Freq: Annual
Circ: 100000 Not Audited
MAGAZINE
Alumni

The Connection
999591
Tel: 44 01744 416383
Web site: www.connectionmagazine.co.uk
Freq: Monthly
Circ: 6250 Not Audited
MAGAZINE
Sales & Marketing

Connections Magazine (U.K.)
984989
Editorial: 17 Britton Street, Clerkenwell, London EC1M 5TP **Tel:** 44 02078 806200
Email: info@redactive.com
Web site: www.niceic.com
Freq: Quarterly
Circ: 36000 Not Audited
MAGAZINE
Building & Construction, Electricity, Electronics, Manufacturing

Connect-World
999141
Editorial: 1 & 2 Riverside Offices, 17 Towcester Road, London E3 3ND
Tel: 44 02075 379255
Email: editor@connect-world.com
Web site: www.connect-world.com
Freq: Monthly Not Audited
Profile: Website covering ICT. The Connect-World website shares the latest news on ICT and telecommunications.
MAGAZINE
Internet, Telecommunications/Electronic Communications

Conrad Magazine
1070231
Editorial: Suite 9, Beaufort Court, Admirals Way, Canary Wharf, London E14 9XL
Tel: 44 02037 724850
Email: enquiries@fms.co.uk
Web site: conradhotels3.hilton.com/en/explore/conrad-magazine/index.html
Freq: Annual
MAGAZINE
Luxury Goods

The Conservative Woman
996265
Email: info@conservativewoman.co.uk
Web site: www.conservativewoman.co.uk
Freq: Daily
Circ: 84488 Cision Digital Reach
MAGAZINE (ONLINE)
Politics, Social Issues

Consumer Credit Magazine
995738
Editorial: Airedale House, Aire Valley Business Park, Dowley Gap Lane, Bingley BD16 1WA **Tel:** 44 01274 714959
Email: info@ccta.co.uk
Web site: www.ccta.co.uk
Freq: Quarterly
Circ: 1000 Not Audited
MAGAZINE
Personal Finance

The Consumer Voice
996158
Editorial: Little Potheridge Farm, Merton, Okehampton EX20 3DW
Tel: 44 01805 603430
Email: editor@theconsumervoice.co.uk
Web site: http://www.theconsumervoice.co.uk/
Freq: Daily
Circ: 919 Cision Digital Reach
MAGAZINE (ONLINE)
Audio Video Trade, Beauty & Grooming, Cameras, Consumer Electronics, Cosmetics, Do-It-Yourself (DIY), Electronics, Fashion, Gardening, Hair

ContactMusic.com
982868
Editorial: Ploverfield, Ben Rhydding Drive, Ilkley LS29 8BA **Tel:** 44 1943 865111
Email: hello@contactmusic.com
Web site: www.contactmusic.com
Freq: Daily
Circ: 2542428 Cision Digital Reach
Editor: Jo Harrison
MAGAZINE (ONLINE)
Country, Folk, Bluegrass, Dance Music, Movies & Video, Music, Pop Music, Rap & Hip Hop, Rock Music

Contagious Magazine
996825
Editorial: Contagious Head Office, 3rd Floor, Dunstan House, 14a St Cross Street, London EC1N 8XA **Tel:** 44 02032 069250
Email: submit@contagious.com
Web site: www.contagious.com
Freq: Quarterly
Circ: 2500 Not Audited
MAGAZINE
Advertising Industry, Branding, Broadcasting, Graphic Design, Marketing, Media & Communications, Photography, Publishing

Continental Modeller
988661
Tel: 44 01297 20580
Email: cm-editor@btconnect.com
Web site: http://www.pecopublications.co.uk/continental-modeller.html

Freq: Monthly Not Audited
Editor: Andrew Burnham
Profile: Magazine covering information on model railways from all over the world. Read by anyone interested in model railways from around the world.
Ad Rate: Full Page Colour £255.00
MAGAZINE
Crafts, Hobbies, & Collecting

Continuity Central
984658
Editorial: PO Box 1393, Huddersfield, Huddersfield HD1 9TN **Tel:** 44 08456 441110
Email: editor@continuitycentral.com
Web site: www.continuitycentral.com
Freq: Daily
Circ: 30265 Cision Digital Reach
Editor: David Honour
MAGAZINE (ONLINE)
Internet, Software

ContractHireAndLeasing.com
986380
Editorial: Domain House, 4 Watchgate, Newby Road, Stockport SK7 5DB
Tel: 44 01614 827650
Email: news@reallygooddomains.com
Web site: http://www.contracthireandleasing.com/
Freq: Daily
Circ: 84390 Cision Digital Reach
MAGAZINE (ONLINE)
Automotive

ContractRecruit
995512
Editorial: The Old Court House, 15 - 17 Prince's Street, Brighton, Brighton BN1 2WE
Tel: 44 02033 300711
Email: enquiries@contractrecruit.co.uk
Web site: www.contractrecruit.co.uk
Freq: Daily
Circ: 9035 Cision Digital Reach
MAGAZINE (ONLINE)
News & Current Affairs

Control Engineering Europe
983072
Editorial: Blair House, 184/186 High Street, Tonbridge, Tonbridge TN9 1BQ
Tel: 44 01732 359990
Web site: www.controlengeurope.com
Freq: Bi-Monthly
Circ: 22289 Not Audited
Editor: Suzanne Gill
Profile: Magazine designed to help engineers increase the performance in manufacturing and processing plants across all industries. Aimed at research and development, engineering and production professionals working in process manufacturing and original equipment manufacturing industries.
Ad Rate: Full Page Colour £4690.00
MAGAZINE
Electronics, Industry

Control Risks
997602
Editorial: Cottons Centre, Cottons Lane, London SE1 2QG **Tel:** 44 02079 702100
Web site: https://www.controlrisks.com/
Freq: Daily
Circ: 128670 Cision Digital Reach
MAGAZINE (ONLINE)
News & Current Affairs

Controls, Drives & Automation
986533
Editorial: 2nd Floor - North Suite, Kings House, 13-21 Cantelupe Road, East Grinstead, East Grinstead RH19 3BE
Tel: 44 01342 314300
Email: cda@western-bp.co.uk
Web site: http://www.controlsdrivesautomation.com/Home
Freq: Bi-Monthly
Circ: 19000 Not Audited
Editor: Charlotte Stonestreet
Profile: Bi-monthly publication read by UK decision makers, buyers and specifiers involved in motion engineering, power transmission and automation. Each issue includes five regular product and technology sections: Power transmission, Drives &

Motors, Controls, Automation and Machine Building & Engineering.
Ad Rate: Full Page Colour £2500.00
MAGAZINE
Automotive, Engineering, Manufacturing

Convenience Store   980018
Editorial: Broadfield Park, Crawley, Crawley RH11 9RT **Tel:** 44 01293 613400
Web site: www.conveniencestore.co.uk
Freq: Bi-Weekly
Circ: 40455 Not Audited
Editor: David Rees
Profile: Magazine covering groceries, off-licensed trade, confectionery, tobacco, newsagents, petrol, lottery and all convenience store goods. Each issue contains a mix of industry news, business news and advice, in-depth features and retailer profiles, backed up by news and special focus features on the 35-plus product categories sold through convenience stores including confectionery, alcohol, snacks, soft drinks, chilled products and freshly made food-to-go.
Ad Rate: Full Page Colour £3535.00
MAGAZINE
Alcohol & Spirits, Food, Retail Management

The Conversation UK   995102
Editorial: 7th Floor University Building, Northampton Square, London EC1V 0HB
Tel: 44 02070 400043
Email: uk-editorial@theconversation.com
Web site: www.theconversation.com/uk
Freq: Daily
Circ: 573107 Cision Digital Reach
Editor: Stephen Khan
MAGAZINE (ONLINE)
National News

Converter   981715
Editorial: 15a London Road, Maidstone, Maidstone ME16 8LY **Tel:** 44 01622 687031
Web site: www.convertermag.co.uk
Freq: Monthly
Circ: 3807 Not Audited
Profile: Magazine covering converting, packaging, printing and associated industries. This includes flexible packaging, foil, flexographic and offset printing, nonwovens, cartons, labels and labelling, paper and board and ancillary converting processes such as static elimination, components, drives and controls. adhesives, drying and curing and many others. Aimed at key decision makers, purchasers and buyers within the industry.
Ad Rate: Full Page Mono £1235.00
Ad Rate: Full Page Colour £1756.00
MAGAZINE
Electronics, Industry, Manufacturing

The Conway Bulletin   999622
Editorial: 1 St Colme Street, Edinburgh EH3 6AA
Email: editor@theconwaybulletin.com
Web site: http://theconwaybulletin.com
Freq: Weekly Not Audited
Editor: James Kilner
MAGAZINE
Asia, International News

Cooked.com   997837
Editorial: 50 Bedford Square, London WC1B 3DP
Email: info@cooked.co.uk
Web site: cooked.com
Freq: Daily
Circ: 50386 Cision Digital Reach
MAGAZINE (ONLINE)
Alcohol & Spirits, Bars, Clubs & Pubs, Beer, Beverages, Cooking & Baking, Wine/Winemaking

Cool As Leicester   996036
Email: info@coolasleicester.co.uk
Web site: www.coolasleicester.co.uk
Freq: Daily
Circ: 11101 Cision Digital Reach
Editor: Gabrielle Miller
MAGAZINE (ONLINE)
Men's Interests, Women's Interests

Coolcamping.co.uk   999284
Editorial: 81 Rivington Street, London EC2A 3AY **Tel:** 44 02078 209333
Email: enquiries@coolcamping.co.uk
Web site: www.coolcamping.co.uk
Freq: Daily
Circ: 122976 Cision Digital Reach
MAGAZINE (ONLINE)
Camping and RV Travel, Travel

Cooler   982687
Editorial: 2 Tun Yard, Peardon Street, London SW8 3HT **Tel:** 44 02073 329700
Email: info@factorymedia.com
Web site: https://coolerlifestyle.com
Freq: Daily
Circ: 44915 Cision Digital Reach
Profile: Magazine covering women's action sports in Europe including snowboarding, skiing, surfing, skating, mountain biking, fixed gear cycling and with features on lifestyle, travel, culture and fashion. First published in 2005. Aimed at 16 to 25 year old women who live, or aspire to, the board and free sports culture.
Ad Rate: Full Page Colour £4700.00
MAGAZINE (ONLINE)
Extreme/Adventure Sports, Swimming/ Watersports, Winter Sports, Women's Interests

Cooler Plus   983256
Editorial: 7 Kingsmead Square, Bath BA1 2AB **Tel:** 44 01225 327890
Email: ci@foodbev.com
Web site: www.foodbev.com
Freq: Bi-Monthly
Circ: 7161 Not Audited
Profile: Magazine featuring news, views and analysis of both the bottled water cooler and point of use water cooler sectors.
Ad Rate: Full Page Colour £1500.00
MAGAZINE
Alcohol & Spirits

Cooltura   984437
Editorial: Unit 8, Odeon Parade, 480 London Road, Isleworth TW7 4RL
Tel: 44 02088 463615
Email: redakcja@cooltura.co.uk
Web site: www.cooltura.co.uk
Freq: Weekly
Circ: 60000 Not Audited
Editor: Kordian Klaczyski
Profile: Polish weekly magazine covering news, fashion, culture, technology, sport, jobs and national and local events.
Ad Rate: Full Page Colour £1450.00
MAGAZINE
Europe, International News

The Coolture   997491
Web site: http://www.thecoolture.com/
Freq: Daily
Circ: 2416 Cision Digital Reach
MAGAZINE (ONLINE)
Art, Fashion, Photography, Visual Arts

The Co-Operative News   985898
Editorial: Holyoake House, Hanover Street, Manchester M60 0AS **Tel:** 44 01612 140870
Email: editorial@thenews.coop
Web site: http://www.thenews.coop/
Freq: Bi-Weekly
Circ: 30000 Not Audited
Profile: Retail trade newspaper covering news and features on the Co-operative movement. Launched in 1871.
Ad Rate: Full Page Colour £1695.00
MAGAZINE
Consumer Affairs, Crime & Violence, Defense & National Security, Energy & Environment, Ethical/Moral Issues, International News, Law, National News, News & Current Affairs, Northern Ireland

Corinthia Hotel London magazine   1102299
Web site: www.corinthia.com
Freq: Semi-Annual
Circ: 20000 Not Audited
MAGAZINE
Luxury Goods, Men's Interests, Women's Interests

Cornish Brides   987931
Tel: 44 07855 835186
Email: Info@cornishbrides.co.uk
Web site: www.cornishbrides.co.uk
Freq: Quarterly Not Audited
Profile: Directory covering all aspects of wedding planning including information on florists, jewellers, weddings gowns and how to get married. Aimed at brides to be.
Ad Rate: Full Page Colour £660.00
MAGAZINE
Weddings

Cornucopia   1076638
Editorial: PO Box 13311, Hawick TD9 7YF
Tel: 44 01450 379933
Email: editor@cornucopia.net
Web site: cornucopia.net
Freq: Semi-Annual
Circ: 20000 Not Audited
MAGAZINE
Travel

Cornwall Life   983810
Editorial: Cornwall Life, Penstraze Business Centre, Penstraze, Truro TR4 8PN
Tel: 44 01803 860910
Email: cornwalllife@archant.co.uk
Web site: www.cornwalllife.co.uk
Freq: Monthly
Circ: 8000 Not Audited
Editor: Carol Burns
Profile: Magazine containing features on the Cornwall area. Published nationally, it is aimed at residents of, and visitors to, Cornwall.
Ad Rate: Full Page Colour £880.00
MAGAZINE
Regional General Interest

Cornwall Living   986796
Tel: 44 01326 726015
Email: contact@cornwall-living.co.uk
Web site: http://www.cornwall-living.co.uk
Freq: Monthly
Circ: 181000 Not Audited
Editor: Mandy Milano
Profile: Magazine covering Cornish lifestyle. It features Cornish restaurants, seaside getaways and properties for sale. Aimed at people looking to move to Cornwall.
MAGAZINE
Regional General Interest

Cornwall Today   982480
Editorial: High Water House, City Wharf, Malpas Road, Truro, Truro TR1 1QH
Tel: 44 01872 247458
Web site: www.cornwalltoday.co.uk
Freq: Monthly
Circ: 10000 Not Audited
Editor: Kirstie Newton
Profile: Lifestyle magazine focusing on issues of interest to those living in and around Cornwall.
Ad Rate: Full Page Colour £600.00
MAGAZINE
Regional General Interest, Travel

Corporate Adviser   983485
Editorial: Wells Point, 79 Wells Street, London W1T 3QN **Tel:** 44 02079 438000
Web site: www.corporate-adviser.co.uk
Freq: Monthly
Circ: 521 Cision Digital Reach
Editor: John Greenwood
Profile: Magazine covering pensions, investments and employee benefits.
Ad Rate: Full Page Colour £2650.00
MAGAZINE (ONLINE)

Corporate INTL   981699
Editorial: JRS Corporate Ltd, Charles House, 148/149 Great Charles Street, Birmingham B3 3HT
Web site: www.corp-intl.com
Freq: Monthly
Circ: 70000 Not Audited
MAGAZINE
News & Current Affairs

Corporate LiveWire   986474
Web site: www.corporatelivewire.com
Freq: Daily

Circ: 128768 Cision Digital Reach
MAGAZINE (ONLINE)
News & Current Affairs

Corridor8   997766
Editorial: 97 Vantage Quay, 5 Brewer Street, Manchester M1 2ER **Tel:** 44 01612 365885
Email: info@corridor8.co.uk
Web site: www.corridor8.co.uk
Freq: Daily
Circ: 12607 Cision Digital Reach
MAGAZINE (ONLINE)
Literature, Visual Arts

Cosmetics Business   984328
Editorial: Natraj Building, The Tanneries, 55 Bermondsey Street, London SE1 3XG
Tel: 44 02071 931279
Email: cosmetics@hpcimedia.com
Web site: www.cosmeticsbusiness.com
Freq: Daily
Circ: 148132 Cision Digital Reach
Editor: Lucy Copp
Profile: Website covering different news of all cosmetics spheres.
MAGAZINE (ONLINE)
Cosmetics

Cosmetics Business Markets   983868
Editorial: Natraj Building, The Tanneries, 55 Bermondsey St, London SE1 3XG
Tel: 44 02071 931279
Email: cosmetics@hpcimedia.com
Web site: http://www.cosmeticsbusiness. com/Category/Cosmetics_Business_ Markets
Freq: Monthly
Circ: 2000 Not Audited
Editor: Jo Allen; **Editor:** Lucy Copp
MAGAZINE
Cosmetics

Cosmetics Business News   988767
Editorial: Natraj Building The Tanneries, 55 Bermondsey St, 17 Mill Street, London SE1 3XG **Tel:** 44 02071 931279
Email: cosmetics@hpcimedia.com
Web site: http://www.cosmeticsbusiness. com/Category/Cosmetics_Business_News
Freq: Weekly
Circ: 23000 Not Audited
Editor: Lucy Copp
MAGAZINE
Cosmetics

COSMOPOLITAN   980755
Editorial: 33 Broadwick Street, London W1F 0DQ **Tel:** 44 02073 123083
Email: info@cosmopolitan.co.uk
Web site: www.cosmopolitan.co.uk
Freq: Monthly
Circ: 403887 Not Audited
Editor: Nandini Bhalla; **Editor:** Farrah Storr
Profile: Magazine covering relationships, sex, health, careers, self-improvement, celebrities, fashion and beauty. The magazine was first published in the USA in 1886 and launched in the United Kingdom in 1971. Aimed at young professional women.
Ad Rate: Full Page Colour £17010.00
MAGAZINE
Women's Interests

Cost Sector Catering   981144
Editorial: Progressive House, 2 Maidstone Road, Sidcup DA14 5HZ
Tel: 44 08450 002500
Email: costsector@dewberryredpoint.co.uk
Web site: www.costsectorcatering.co.uk
Freq: Monthly
Circ: 8831 Not Audited
Profile: Magazine providing information on all aspects of catering, including contracts, appointments and equipment for restaurants, schools, hospitals, prisons and airlines.
Ad Rate: Full Page Colour £3995.00
MAGAZINE
Alcohol & Spirits, Bars, Clubs & Pubs, Food

Consumer Magazines

Cotswold Life
982492

Editorial: Archant House, Oriel Road, Cheltenham GL50 1BB
Tel: 44 01242 216050
Email: info@cotswoldlife.co.uk
Web site: www.cotswoldlife.co.uk
Freq: Monthly
Circ: 101975 Not Audited
Profile: Lifestyle magazine covering property, fashion, dining, interiors, beauty, celebrity interviews, town features, rural issues, heritage, arts, antiques, business, gardens and events.
Ad Rate: Full Page Colour £1300.00
MAGAZINE
Regional General Interest

Cotswold Preview
985217

Tel: 44 01993 833239
Email: eleanor@guidemedia.co.uk
Web site: www.guidemedia.co.uk
Freq: Monthly
Circ: 12000 Not Audited
Profile: Magazine covering regional lifestyle in the Cotswolds, with a focus on luxury products. It features articles on home interiors, gardening, health & beauty, fashion, travel, property, food & drink, schools, local highlights, books, movies, local events and interviews. Aimed at Cotswold residents.
MAGAZINE
Regional General Interest

Cotswold Style
985000

Editorial: Suite 104 Eagle Tower, Montpellier Drive, Cheltenham GL50 1TA
Tel: 44 01242 220239
Email: editor@stylemagazines.co.uk
Web site: www.cotswoldstyle.co.uk
Freq: Monthly
Circ: 8000 Not Audited
Editor: Emma Logan
Profile: Magazine covering fashion, beauty, food, health, home and entertainment news in the Cotswolds. Aimed at residents of, and visitors to, the Cotswolds.
MAGAZINE
Fashion, Regional General Interest

Cotswolds Country Gardener
999053

Editorial: Country Gardener Magazines, Mount House, Halse, Taunton TA4 3AD
Email: editorial@countrygardener.co.uk
Web site: www.countrygardener.co.uk
Freq: Monthly
Circ: 21000 Not Audited
MAGAZINE
Gardening

The Cottage Gardener
998925

Editorial: 12 Chatsworth Avenue, Haslemere, Haslemere GU27 1BA
Email: cgs.ed@btinternet.com
Web site: http://thecottagegardensociety.org.uk/Magazine/The-Cottage-Gardener
Freq: Quarterly
Circ: 4000 Not Audited
Editor: Julia Boulton
MAGAZINE
Gardening

Counsel
983774

Editorial: LexisNexis, Lexis House, 30 Farringdon Street, London EC4A 4HH
Tel: 44 02074 002500
Web site: http://www.counselmagazine.co.uk
Freq: Monthly
Circ: 24000 Not Audited
Editor: Sarah Grainger
Profile: The Journal of the Bar of England and Wales.
Ad Rate: Full Page Colour £2250.00
MAGAZINE
Bankruptcy, Company News & Appointments, Consumer Interest, Corporate Law, Criminal Law, Employment, Estate Planning, Family Law, Federal Courts, Food & Drug Administration

Counsel & Heal
987876

Email: info@counselheal.com
Web site: www.counselheal.com
Freq: Daily
Circ: 150770 Cision Digital Reach
MAGAZINE (ONLINE)
Health & Medicine

Country & Town House
984152

Editorial: Studio 2, Chelsea Gate Studios, 115 Harwood Road, London SW6 4QL
Tel: 44 02073 849011
Email: editorial@countryandtownhouse.co.uk
Web site: www.countryandtownhouse.co.uk
Freq: Monthly
Circ: 60000 Not Audited
Editor: Lucy Cleland
Profile: Country & Town House is a lifestyle magazine covering fashion, style, interiors, gardens, travel, food and property. Aimed at Londoners wanting to invest in rural property.
Ad Rate: Full Page Colour £1875.00
MAGAZINE
Property Management & Maintenance, Regional General Interest

Country Child
986062

Editorial: 32A Salisbury Street, Shaftesbury, Shaftesbury SP7 8EJ **Tel:** 44 07794 447105
Email: info@countrychild.co.uk
Web site: www.countrychild.co.uk
Freq: Quarterly
Circ: 10000 Not Audited
MAGAZINE
Regional General Interest

Country Doctor
983535

Editorial: 5 Manor Farm Close, Gate Lane, Broughton, Kettering NN14 1ND
Web site: www.countrydoctor.co.uk
Freq: Daily
Circ: 1599 Cision Digital Reach
Editor: David Roberts
MAGAZINE (ONLINE)
Medicine

Country Homes & Interiors
981862

Editorial: 161 Marsh Wall, London E14 9AP
Tel: 44 02031 485000
Email: countryhomes@timeinc.com
Web site: http://www.idealhome.co.uk/country-homes-and-interiors
Freq: Monthly
Circ: 70478 Not Audited
Editor: Rhoda Parry
Profile: Magazine covering all aspects of country homes and interior design including accessories, fabrics and furnishings. Also carries features on food, travel and lifestyle ideas. Aimed predominantly at women between 35 and 55 years old.
Ad Rate: Full Page Colour £6590.00
MAGAZINE
Do-It-Yourself (DIY)

Country Illustrated
995901

Editorial: 11 Princes Street, Mayfair, London W1B 2LJ **Tel:** 44 02073 992960
Email: memberservices@countryclubuk.com
Web site: www.countryclubuk.com/countryillustrated.htm
Freq: Annual
Circ: 40000 Not Audited
Profile: Magazine covering all aspects of life in the country, including environmental matters, hunting, fishing, shooting and conservation. Aimed at those who live in or are interested in the countryside.
Ad Rate: Full Page Mono £2275.00
Ad Rate: Full Page Colour £3075.00
MAGAZINE
Field Sports

Country Images Magazine
994705

Editorial: Unit 5, Keys Road, Alfreton, Alfreton DE55 7FQ **Tel:** 44 01773 830344
Email: info@imagespublishing.co.uk
Web site: www.countryimagesmagazine.co.uk
Freq: Monthly

Circ: 30000 Not Audited
MAGAZINE
Field Sports, Regional General Interest

Country Life
981000

Editorial: Pinehurst 2, Pinehurst Road, Farnborough Business Park, London GU14 7BF **Tel:** 44 01252 555000
Web site: www.countrylife.co.uk
Freq: Weekly
Circ: 40047 Not Audited
Profile: Magazine featuring country-related editorial and property advertising. Each issue contains articles on architecture, the arts, gardens and gardening, the countryside, field-sports and wildlife. It features interviews with experts, houses and gardens of distinction and opinions on countryside issues. Targeting high-earning, stylish and discerning readers, the magazine is aimed at those who live in, or are interested in the countryside.
Ad Rate: Full Page Colour £3700.00
MAGAZINE
Field Sports, Men's Interests, Property Management & Maintenance, Women's Interests

Country Living
981863

Editorial: 33 Broadwick Street, London W1F 9EP **Tel:** 44 02074 395000
Email: country.living@hearst.co.uk
Web site: http://www.countryliving.co.uk/
Freq: Monthly
Circ: 187394 Not Audited
Profile: Magazine providing inspiration and practical advice on homes and decorating, gardening, seasonal food and craft. It offers information on health, rural affairs, nature and the environment. Each issue contains recipes for cooking seasonal food, stories about real rural people and their lives, health and beauty tips, information on farming and rural affairs. First published in 1985. Targeting readers interested in rural affairs and life in the countryside, the magazine is aimed at homeowners aged 35 years old and over who either live or aspire to living in the country.
Ad Rate: Full Page Colour £3700.00
MAGAZINE
Do-It-Yourself (DIY), Gardening, Women's Interests

Country Music People
982075

Editorial: 24 Darley Close, Wittering, Peterborough PE8 6EQ
Tel: 44 01780 783689
Email: countrymusicpeople@gmail.com
Web site: www.cmpcountry.com
Freq: Monthly
Circ: 18000 Not Audited
Editor: Duncan Warrick
Profile: Country music magazine carrying UK and import record reviews, charts, star features and news.
Ad Rate: Full Page Mono £695.00
Ad Rate: Full Page Colour £895.00
MAGAZINE
Country, Folk, Bluegrass

Country Smallholding
981924

Editorial: Unit 3, Old Station Road, Barnstable, Barnstaple EX32 8PB
Tel: 44 01271 341652
Email: editorial.csh@archant.co.uk
Web site: www.countrysmallholding.com
Freq: Monthly
Circ: 23000 Not Audited
Editor: Simon McEwan
Profile: Magazine containing information on smallholding, hobby farming, poultry, smallholding animals, organic gardening, alternative lifestyle and organic living.
Ad Rate: Full Page Mono £635.00
Ad Rate: Full Page Colour £635.00
MAGAZINE
Animal Farming, Field Sports

Country Style - LAUNCHING
981851

Editorial: Cudham Tithe Barn, Berrys Hill, Cudham, London TN16 3AG
Tel: 44 01959 541444
Freq: Monthly
Circ: 23500 Not Audited

Editor: Zoe Balding

Profile: Period Homes & Interiors is a monthly magazine covering period homes and interiors, including features and new ideas for homes with character. It also includes information on every aspect of old house restoration and home decoration, expert gardening advice and a cookery section. The publication was formerly called Period House magazine. It is owned by Kelsey Publishing Ltd. Period Homes & Interiors is aimed at owners of period properties, designers and period house enthusiasts.
Ad Rate: Full Page Colour £2995.00
MAGAZINE
Do-It-Yourself (DIY)

Country Walking
981903

Editorial: Media House, Lynchwood, Peterborough Business Park, Peterborough PE2 6EA **Tel:** 44 01733 468000
Email: country.walking@bauermedia.co.uk
Web site: www.livefortheoutdoors.com/Our-outdoor-magazines/Country-Walking
Freq: Monthly
Circ: 25074 Not Audited
Editor: Guy Procter
Profile: Magazine offering advice and information on places, routes and equipment for walking. Aimed at 30 to 65 year olds interested in walking and the countryside.
Ad Rate: Full Page Colour £3150.00
MAGAZINE
Field Sports, Outdoor Recreation

countrybycountry.com
999639

Editorial: Unit 310, Highgate Studios, 53-79 Highgate Road, London NW5 1TL
Tel: 44 02072 539906
Email: editorial@aplmedia.co.uk
Web site: www.countrybycountry.com
Freq: Daily
Circ: 16223 Cision Digital Reach
MAGAZINE (ONLINE)
Travel

CountryClubuk
981925

Editorial: 11 Princes Street, Mayfair, London W1B 2LJ **Tel:** 44 02073 992960
Email: editorial@countryclubuk.com
Web site: www.countryclubuk.com
Freq: Quarterly
Circ: 40000 Not Audited
Profile: Magazine covering country pursuits, rural politics, farming, conservation, events and country sports including hunting, shooting and fishing. Includes fashion, luxury travel, food and wine section.
Ad Rate: Full Page Mono £2500.00
Ad Rate: Full Page Colour £3300.00
MAGAZINE
Do-It-Yourself (DIY), Field Sports, Gardening, Travel, Wine/Winemaking

Countryfile Magazine
984202

Editorial: 14th Floor, Tower House, Fairfax Street, Bristol BS1 3BN
Tel: 44 01179 279009
Email: editor@countryfile.com
Web site: www.countryfile.com
Freq: Monthly
Circ: 43879 Not Audited
Editor: Fergus Collins
MAGAZINE
Field Sports

The Countryman
981932

Editorial: The Watermill, Broughton Hall, Skipton, Broughton BD23 3AG
Tel: 44 01756 701381
Email: editorial@thecountryman.co.uk
Web site: www.countrymanmagazine.co.uk
Freq: Monthly
Circ: 8047 Not Audited
Editor: Mark Whitley
Profile: Magazine containing countryside, wildlife, country people, traditions, crafts and rural issues.
Ad Rate: Full Page Colour £1050.00
MAGAZINE
Field Sports

The Countryman's Weekly 981004

Editorial: PO Box 258, Plymouth PL5 9AE
Tel. 44 01752 762000
Email: editorial@countrymansweekly.com
Web site: www.countrymansweekly.com
Freq: Weekly
Circ: 22000 Not Audited
Profile: The Countryman's Weekly covers interests relating to outdoor pursuits and country living including gundogs, lurchers, terriers, ferrets, falconry, hunting, game fishing, game shooting, rough shooting, wildfowling, game and coarse fishing, stalking, country shows, gamekeeping, pest control, sporting art, gun trade news and auctions, sporting history and country recipes.
Ad Rate: Full Page Mono £400.00
Ad Rate: Full Page Colour £560.00
MAGAZINE
Field Sports

Country-Side 998809

Editorial: P.O.Box BM8120 BNA, London WC1N 3XX **Tel:** 44 08448 921817
Email: info@bna-naturalists.org
Web site: www.bna-naturalists.org
Freq: Semi-Annual
Circ: 1500 Not Audited
MAGAZINE
Nature & Wildlife

Countryside Alliance 1095950

Editorial: 1 Spring Mews, Tinworth Street, London SE11 5AN
Email: info@countrysidealliance.org
Web site: http://www.countryside-alliance.org/category/membership/membership-news/
Freq: Quarterly
Editor: Jill Grieve
Profile: Website covering the countryside and rural life. Countryside Alliance shares the latest news on rural business, general political and campaigning news relevant to the countryside and rural people as hunting, shooting and fishing.
MAGAZINE
Field Sports, Nature & Wildlife

Countryside Jobs Service Daily 1065603

Editorial: The Moorlands, Goathland, Whitby, Whitby YO22 5LZ
Tel: 44 01947 896007
Email: newsdesk@countryside-jobs.com
Web site: www.countryside-jobs.com
Freq: Daily
Circ: 29126 Cision Digital Reach
MAGAZINE (ONLINE)
Careers

Countryside Jobs Service Focus 998997

Editorial: The Moorlands, Goathland, Whitby YO22 5LZ **Tel:** 44 01947 896007
Email: ranger@countryside-jobs.com
Web site: http://www.countryside-jobs.com/Focus/Information.htm
Freq: Quarterly
Circ: 100000 Not Audited
MAGAZINE
Careers, Environment

Countryside Jobs Service Professional 998455

Editorial: The Moorlands, Goathland, Whitby, Whitby YO22 5LZ
Tel: 44 01947 896007
Email: newsdesk@countryside-jobs.com
Web site: www.countryside-jobs.com
Freq: Monthly
Circ: 29126 Cision Digital Reach
MAGAZINE (ONLINE)
Careers

Countryside Jobs Service Weekly 998456

Editorial: The Moorlands, Goathland, Whitby, Whitby YO22 5LZ
Tel: 44 01947 896007
Email: newsdesk@countryside-jobs.com

Web site: www.countryside-jobs.com
Freq: Weekly
Circ: 8500 Not Audited
MAGAZINE
Careers

Countryside La Vie 982566

Editorial: 53a Arlington Mews, Overton Road, Leicester LE5 0JB
Tel: 44 08443 247132
Web site: www.countryside-lavie.com
Freq: Bi-Monthly
Circ: 10000 Not Audited
Editor: Sue Brindley
Profile: Lifestyle magazine covering prestige country homes, homes and gardens, interiors, motoring, fashions, health, beauty and eating out.
Ad Rate: Full Page Colour £1000.00
MAGAZINE
Property Management & Maintenance, Regional General Interest

Countryside Magazine 980989

Tel: 44 02476 858500
Web site: www.countrysideonline.co.uk
Freq: Monthly
Circ: 33412 Not Audited
Editor: Martin Stanhope
Profile: Magazine covering countryside issues and lifestyle, with practical advice on land management, smallholding, animal husbandry, veterinary matters, horses, dogs, gardening, environment, wildlife, conservation, travel, rural skills, campaigns and product reviews.
Ad Rate: Full Page Colour £3500.00
MAGAZINE
Field Sports

County Concierge 995054

Editorial: 18 Station Approach, Virginia Water, London GU25 4DW
Tel: 44 01344 644523
Email: sue@countyconcierge.co.uk
Web site: www.countyconcierge.co.uk
Freq: Quarterly
Circ: 5000 Not Audited
Editor: Sue Seakens
MAGAZINE
Business, Luxury Goods, Small and Medium Business

The Courier (Newcastle University) 998557

Editorial: The University of Newcastle Student, Union Society, Kings Walk, Newcastle upon Tyne NE1 8QB
Tel: 44 01912 393940
Email: editor.union@ncl.ac.uk
Web site: www.thecourieronline.co.uk
Freq: Weekly
Circ: 4000 Not Audited
MAGAZINE
Student Lifestyle

The Courier (UW Aberystwyth University) 1006441

Editorial: Aberystwyth University Student Union, Penglais, Aberystwyth, Aberystwyth SY23 3DX **Tel:** 44 01970 621709
Email: asm@aberstudentmedia.com
Web site: http://aberstudentmedia.com
Freq: Bi-Monthly
Circ: 2000 Not Audited
MAGAZINE
Student Lifestyle

Court News UK 987799

Editorial: Sterling House, Hatchlands Road, Redhill, Reigate RH1 6RW
Email: sales@courtnewsuk.co.uk
Web site: www.courtnewsuk.co.uk
Freq: Daily
Circ: 84035 Cision Digital Reach
MAGAZINE (ONLINE)
Crime & Violence, Law, National News

Courtside 1100939

Editorial: National Badminton Centre, Bradwell Road, Loughton Lodge, Milton Keynes MK8 9LA **Tel:** 44 01908 268400
Email: enquiries@badmintonengland.co.uk

Web site: www.badmintonengland.co.uk
Freq: Quarterly
Circ: 33000 Not Audited
MAGAZINE
Racquet Sports

Cover Magazine 983738

Editorial: 8 Ability Plaza, Arbutus Street, London E8 4DT **Tel:** 44 02037 274940
Web site: www.cover-magazine.com
Freq: Quarterly Not Audited
Editor: Lucy Upward
MAGAZINE
Fashion

COVERED mag 996208

Web site: www.gocompare.com/covered
Freq: Daily
Circ: 264 Cision Digital Reach
Editor: Kristian Dando
MAGAZINE (ONLINE)
Driving, Personal Finance

CR6 Magazine 996040

Editorial: 1 Marcuse Road, Hambledon Park, Caterham, London CR3 5FP
Tel: 44 01883 343001
Email: info@cr6.biz
Web site: www.cr6.biz
Freq: Monthly
Circ: 5200 Not Audited
MAGAZINE
Regional General Interest

CRACK 985780

Editorial: Office No 12, Studio 31, Berkeley Square, Bristol BS8 1HP
Email: crack@crackmagazine.net
Web site: www.crackmagazine.net
Freq: Monthly
Circ: 35000 Not Audited
Profile: Magazine covering events and entertainment in and around the North East including music, arts, fashion, news and views. Aimed at 18-35 year olds living and visiting the area.
Ad Rate: Full Page Colour £1800.00
MAGAZINE
Art, Theater & Performing Arts

The Crack 999248

Editorial: Unit 1, Woods Pottery, Stepeney Bank, Newcastle upon Tyne NE1 2NP
Tel: 44 01912 303038
Email: info@thecrackmagazine.com
Web site: www.thecrackmagazine.com
Freq: Monthly
Circ: 21800 Not Audited
Editor: Robert Meddes
Profile: Magazine covering events and entertainment in and around the North East including music, arts, fashion, news and views. Aimed at 18-35 year olds living and visiting the area.
Ad Rate: Full Page Colour £1800.00
MAGAZINE
Art, Cooking & Baking, Country, Folk, Bluegrass, Dance Music, Fashion, Jazz & Blues, Literature, Local Entertainment Guides, Movies & Video, Pop Music

Craft & Design 984031

Tel: 44 01377 255213
Email: info@craftanddesign.net
Web site: www.craftanddesign.net
Freq: Bi-Monthly
Circ: 5000 Not Audited
Editor: Angie Boyer
MAGAZINE
Crafts

Craft Beer Rising 997475

Editorial: First Floor, 9 Gowlett Road, London SE15 4HX **Tel:** 44 02076 395556
Web site: craftbeerrising.co.uk
Freq: Quarterly Not Audited
MAGAZINE
Beer

Craft Beer World UK 997873

Editorial: 1a Pages Orchard, Sonning Common, Sonning Common RG4 9LW
Tel: 44 01183 485029

Email: press@craftbeerworld.co.uk
Web site: www.craftbeerworld.co.uk
Freq: Daily
Circ: 59221 Cision Digital Reach
MAGAZINE (ONLINE)
Alcohol & Spirits

Craft Business 983639

Editorial: 25 Phoenix Court, Hawkins Road, Colchester, Colchester CO2 8JY
Tel: 44 01206 505983
Web site: www.craftbusiness.com
Freq: Bi-Monthly
Circ: 7004 Not Audited
Profile: Magazine covering current news, features, profiles and product showcase from within the craft industry. Aimed at wholesalers, retailers and designers.
Ad Rate: Full Page Colour £1450.00
MAGAZINE
Fashion

Craft Focus 984583

Editorial: Pantile House, Newlands Drive, Witham, Witham CM8 2AP
Tel: 44 01376 514000
Email: info@craftfocus.com
Web site: www.craftfocus.com
Freq: Bi-Monthly
Circ: 6086 Not Audited
Editor: Julie Bonnar
MAGAZINE
Fashion, Retail Management

The Craft Network 1097885

Editorial: Blue Fin Building, 110 Southwark Street, London SE1 0SU
Tel: 44 02031 485000
Email: thecraftnetwork@timeinc.com
Web site: www.craftnetwork.net
Freq: Monthly Not Audited
MAGAZINE
Crafts

Craft Stamper 984807

Editorial: Traplet House, Willow End Park, Blackmore Park Road, Malvern WR13 6NN
Tel: 44 01684 588500
Email: cs@traplet.com
Web site: http://inspiredtomake.com/zone/craft-stamper/home
Freq: Monthly Not Audited
Editor: Trish Latimer
Profile: Magazine covering all aspects of stamping. Includes techniques, inspirational projects, best buys, ideas, embossing, ink sponging, braying and paper-making. Also quilling, tea bag folding, parchment craft and step by step projects from cards to entire rooms.
Ad Rate: Full Page Colour £695.00
MAGAZINE
Antiques/Collectibles, Crafts

Crafts 981938

Editorial: 44a Pentonville Road, Islington, London N1 9BY **Tel:** 44 02078 062539
Email: editorial@craftscouncil.org.uk
Web site: www.craftscouncil.org.uk/crafts-magazine/
Freq: Bi-Monthly
Circ: 13000 Not Audited
Editor: Grant Gibson
Profile: Journal of the applied and decorative arts. Features expert coverage of all crafts media including studio work, modern experimental work and traditional and historic designs.
MAGAZINE
Crafts

Crafts Beautiful 983508

Editorial: 1 Phoenix Court, Hawkins Road, Colchester, Colchester CO2 8JY
Tel: 44 01206 505974
Email: lynn.martin@aceville.co.uk
Web site: www.crafts-beautiful.com
Freq: Monthly
Circ: 85000 Not Audited
Editor: Sarah Crosland
Profile: Magazine covering traditional and modern crafts and celebrity interviews, as well as simple projects, step-by-step

instructions and photographs of the finished products.
Ad Rate: Full Page Mono £726.00
Ad Rate: Full Page Colour £935.00
MAGAZINE
Crafts

Crafts Scotland
998725
Editorial: 15 Coburg Street, Leith, Edinburgh EH6 6ET **Tel:** 44 01314 663870
Email: hello@craftsscotland.org
Web site: www.craftsscotland.org
Freq: Daily
Circ: 20575 Cision Digital Reach
Editor: Julia Ossenbruegge
MAGAZINE (ONLINE)
Crafts

Crafty Carper
982176
Editorial: Angling Publications, Regent House, 101 Broadfield Road, Sheffield S8 0XH
Email: info@anglingpublications.co.uk
Web site: http://www.craftycarper.co/
Freq: Monthly
Circ: 18000 Not Audited
Editor: James Turner
Profile: Magazine containing information, articles and advice on all aspects of carp fishing, including bait, tackle and tactics.
Ad Rate: Full Page Colour £600.00
MAGAZINE
Fishing

CRAMGAMING
995484
Email: rob@cramgaming.com
Web site: www.cramgaming.com
Freq: Daily
Circ: 42159 Cision Digital Reach
MAGAZINE (ONLINE)
Computer & Video Games

Crane.tv
985776
Editorial: 9 Great Newport Street, London WC2H 7JA **Tel:** 44 02034 329420
Email: info@crane.tv
Web site: www.crane.tv
Freq: Daily
Circ: 16601 Cision Digital Reach
MAGAZINE (ONLINE)
Fashion, Men's Interests, Visual Arts, Women's Interests

Cranes Today
980970
Editorial: 40-42 Hatton Garden, London EC1N 3EB **Tel:** 44 02079 366400
Web site: www.cranestodaymagazine.com
Freq: Monthly
Circ: 16660 Not Audited
Profile: Magazine covering events within the international lifting industry. Provides information on all types of cranes used in a wide variety of industries.
Ad Rate: Full Page Mono £2480.00
Ad Rate: Full Page Colour £3405.00
MAGAZINE
Automotive, Aviation, Railroad, Shipping & Warehousing, Supply Chain Management (SCM), Transportation

Crash Test Technology International
985027
Editorial: Abinger House, Church Street, Dorking, Dorking RH4 1DF
Tel: 44 01306 743744
Email: testing@ukipme.com
Web site: www.ukipme.com/pub-automotive.php?mag=4
Freq: Annual
Editor: John Thornton
MAGAZINE
Automotive

Crash.net
982873
Editorial: Crash Media Group, Crash.net, 78-80 St John Street, Farringdon, London EC1M 4EH **Tel:** 44 02075 492945
Email: press@crash.net
Web site: www.crash.net
Freq: Daily
Circ: 825304 Cision Digital Reach
Profile: Global motor sport portal covering all forms of motor sport, including F1, WRC, MOTO GP, NASCAR, WSBK, BSB, BTCC

and world super bikes. Aimed at motor sport enthusiasts, motor sport professionals and those in the motor sports industry.6 Expert Journalists, 50 News Stories added per day, 21 Leading Championships Covered, 1000's of pictures uploaded live from events worldwide.
MAGAZINE (ONLINE)
Motorsports

Crave Online UK
994987
Editorial: 16-17 Wardour Mews, London W1F 8AT **Tel:** 44 02030 581743
Email: uk.editor@craveonline.com
Web site: http://www.craveonline.co.uk/
Freq: Daily
Circ: 66970 Cision Digital Reach
MAGAZINE (ONLINE)
Computer & Video Games, Electronics, Men's Interests, Movies & Video

Create Victoria
1053911
Editorial: Victoria St, London SW1
Web site: www.createvictoria.com
Freq: Daily
Circ: 9560 Cision Digital Reach
MAGAZINE (ONLINE)
News & Current Affairs

Creative Artists Foundation Magazine
1052957
Editorial: 3rd Floor, 125 Charing Cross Road, London WC2H 0EW
Tel: 44 02032 860884
Email: info@creativeartistsfoundation.org
Web site: http://caffoundation.org/
Freq: Daily
Circ: 1737 Cision Digital Reach
MAGAZINE (ONLINE)
Art, Fashion, Photography, Theater & Performing Arts, Travel, Visual Arts

Creative HEAD
983425
Editorial: 21 Timber Yard, Drysdale Street, London N1 6ND **Tel:** 44 02073 247540
Email: enquiries@alfol.co.uk
Web site: www.creativeheadmag.com
Freq: Monthly
Circ: 8021 Not Audited
Editor In Chief: Amanda Nottage
Profile: Magazine containing hairdressing including products, news, fashion collections, features and comments on the hairdressing industry in the UK. Aimed at hairdressing salon owners and managers, creative directors and senior stylists.
Ad Rate: Full Page Colour £2750.00
MAGAZINE
Hair

Creative Review
979862
Editorial: 79 Wells Street, London W1T 3QN
Tel: 44 02079 704000
Web site: www.creativereview.co.uk
Freq: Monthly
Circ: 12000 Not Audited
Editor: Patrick Burgoyne
Profile: Magazine focusing on graphic design including new media, digital media, illustration, photography, video, film, computer animation, packaging, advertising, typography and features on computer technology relating to design. Launched in 1980 the publication has now subscribers in over 80 countries and readers online in over 120. Aimed at those working in communications art.
Ad Rate: Full Page Colour £4125.00
MAGAZINE
Advertising Industry, Branding, Broadcasting, Graphic Design, Marketing, Media & Communications, Photography, Publishing

Creative Steps
998827
Editorial: PO Box 111, Kingsnorth, Ashford, Ashford TN23 9DX **Tel:** 44 01233 503055
Email: info@creativesteps.co.uk
Web site: www.creativesteps.co.uk
Freq: Quarterly
Circ: 3000 Not Audited
Editor: John Hopley
MAGAZINE
Elementary School, Preschool

Creative Tourist
986446
Email: info@creativetourist.com
Web site: www.creativetourist.com
Freq: Daily
Circ: 43788 Cision Digital Reach
MAGAZINE (ONLINE)
Art, Literature, Photography, Regional General Interest, Theater & Performing Arts, Visual Arts

The Creators Project - The Creators Project (Italy)
1004174
Web site: https://creators.vice.com/it
Circ: 33430 Cision Digital Reach
MAGAZINE (ONLINE)
News & Current Affairs

The Creators Project - The Creators Project (Netherlands)
1004176
Email: editor@thecreatorsproject.com
Web site: https://creators.vice.com/nl
Circ: 38542 Cision Digital Reach
Editor: Leander Roet
MAGAZINE (ONLINE)
News & Current Affairs

The Creators Project - The Creators Project (Spain)
1004175
Web site: https://creators.vice.com/es
Circ: 7285 Cision Digital Reach
MAGAZINE (ONLINE)
News & Current Affairs

Credit Control Journal
983600
Editorial: 7 Greding Walk, Hutton, Brentwood CM13 2UF **Tel:** 44 01277 201554
Web site: www.creditcontrol.co.uk
Freq: Monthly
Circ: 17625 Not Audited
Profile: Journal of academic research dedicated to the advancement of asset and risk management, wealth management and credit management knowledge. It incorporates practical illustrations as well as theoretical analysis and empirical studies which address the key issues facing multinational corporations. Launched in 1979. Read by chief executive officers, chief financial officers, finance directors, credit analysts, credit managers, controllers, analysts, accountants and academics.
Ad Rate: Full Page Mono £650.00
Ad Rate: Full Page Colour £1620.00
MAGAZINE

Creme de la Bride
998198
Email: info@cremedelabride.co.uk
Web site: http://www.cremedelabride.com/
Freq: Daily
MAGAZINE
Weddings

The Crew Report
985524
Editorial: Lansdowne House, 3 - 7 Northcote Road, London SW11 1NG
Tel: 44 02079 244004
Email: info@thesuperyachtgroup.com
Web site: www.thecrewreport.com
Freq: Quarterly
Circ: 7500 Not Audited
Editor: Lulu Trask
MAGAZINE
Boating & Yachting, Shipping & Warehousing

The Cricket Paper
999499
Editorial: Lower Ground Floor, Tuition House, St Georges Road, London SW19 4EU **Tel:** 44 02089 714333
Email: newsdesk@thecricketpaper.com
Web site: www.thecricketpaper.com
Freq: Weekly
Circ: 10000 Not Audited
MAGAZINE
Cricket

Cricket World
982229
Editorial: 24-26 London Road, Grantham NG31 6EJ **Tel:** 44 01476 565569
Email: info@cricketworld.com
Web site: www.cricketworld.com

Freq: Daily
Circ: 487722 Cision Digital Reach
Profile: Magazine covering test and international cricket, recreational cricket, player profiles, school, youth and women's league, club news and features.
Ad Rate: Full Page Colour £3750.00
MAGAZINE (ONLINE)
Cricket

The Cricketer
982230
Editorial: 120 New Cavendish Street, London W1W 6XX **Tel:** 44 02031 981356
Email: magazine@thecricketer.com
Web site: www.thecricketer.com
Freq: Monthly
Circ: 20903 Not Audited
Profile: Magazine covering international and first class cricket throughout the world. Includes comment, interviews, up-to-date test match analysis, book reviews, statistics, TV and radio cricket listings. First published in 2003, the publication has an average of 100 pages per issue. Read by cricket lovers of all ages.
Ad Rate: Full Page Colour £2500.00
MAGAZINE
Cricket

Crime Confidential
999064
Editorial: 33 Broadwick Street, London W1F 0DQ **Tel:** 44 02073 394656
Email: features@realpeoplemag.co.uk
Web site: www.realpeoplemag.co.uk/crime-confidential
Freq: Quarterly Not Audited
MAGAZINE
Crime & Violence

Crime Review
999585
Editorial: 38 Delvin Road, Westbury on Trym, Bristol BS10 5EJ
Email: lindawilson@crimereview.co.uk
Web site: www.crimereview.co.uk
Freq: Daily
Circ: 13738 Cision Digital Reach
Editor: Sharon Wheeler; **Editor:** Linda Wilson
MAGAZINE (ONLINE)
Literature

Crime Time
985804
Editorial: Oldcastle Books, P.O. Box 394, Harpenden AL5 1XJ **Tel:** 44 02072 495940
Web site: www.crimetime.co.uk
Freq: Daily
Circ: 15813 Cision Digital Reach
Profile: Website covering all aspects of fictional crime including books and the cinema. The CRIMETIME website shares the latest news and information on books, movies and TV covering fictional crime. The site also contains features and advice from crime writers.
Ad Rate: Full Page Mono £100.00
MAGAZINE (ONLINE)
Literature

Crimesquad.com
984591
Editorial: 213 The Hide, Netherfield, Milton Keynes, Milton Keynes MK6 4HR
Email: chrissimmons@crimesquad.com
Web site: www.crimesquad.com
Freq: Daily
Circ: 10255 Cision Digital Reach
Profile: Website covering crime fiction. crimesquad.com shares the latest news on reviews, authors, new crime fiction writers and events.
MAGAZINE (ONLINE)
Literature

Crimestoppers
1105209
Editorial: PO Box 324, Wallington SM6 6BG
Tel: 44 02088 353726
Email: digital@crimestoppers-uk.org
Web site: https://crimestoppers-uk.org/
Freq: Daily
Circ: 50758 Cision Digital Reach
MAGAZINE (ONLINE)
News & Current Affairs

Crimewave 987682
Editorial: 5 Martins Lane, Witcham, Ely, Ely CB6 2LB
Web site: www.ttapress.com/crimewave
Freq: Semi-Annual Not Audited
MAGAZINE
News & Current Affairs

Criss Cross Collection 998727
Editorial: Academic House, 24-28 Oval Road, London NW1 7DT
Tel: 44 02072 418000
Email: crisscross@bauer.co.uk
Web site: www.puzzlemagazines.co.uk
Freq: Monthly
Circ: 51800 Not Audited
MAGAZINE
Games, Competitions & Events

Crochet Now 1070073
Editorial: St Christopher House, 217 Wellington Road South, Stockport SK2 6NG
Tel: 44 01615 611202
Web site: www.crochetnow.co.uk
Freq: Monthly
MAGAZINE
Crafts

Crohns & Colitis News 995407
Editorial: 45 Grosvenor Road, St Albans, London AL1 3AW Tel: 44 01727 830038
Email: info@crohnsandcolitis.org.uk
Web site: www.crohnsandcolitis.org.uk
Freq: Quarterly
Circ: 31000 Not Audited
Editor: Alex Johnson
MAGAZINE
Patient Support

Croner 983634
Editorial: 145 London Road, London KT2 6SR Tel: 44 08006 341700
Email: cronerinfo@wolterskluwer.co.uk
Web site: www.croner.co.uk
Freq: Daily
Circ: 50750 Cision Digital Reach
MAGAZINE (ONLINE)
Computers, Employment, Internet

Cross Stitch Card Shop 982800
Editorial: 9th Floor, Tower House, Fairfax Street, Bristol BS1 3BN
Tel: 44 01179 279009
Email: csc@immediate.co.uk
Web site: http://www.cross-stitching.com
Freq: Bi-Monthly
Circ: 33000 Not Audited
Editor: Ruth Southorn
MAGAZINE
Crafts

Cross Stitch Collection 988102
Editorial: Tower House, Fairfax Street, Bath BS1 3BN
Email: csc@dennis.co.uk
Web site: http://crossstitchcollection.com/
Freq: Monthly Not Audited
Editor: Susan Penny
Profile: Magazine containing designs, projects, news, kit reviews, technique advice and letters relating to cross stitching.
Ad Rate: Full Page Colour £688.00
MAGAZINE
Crafts

Cross Stitch Crazy 981939
Editorial: 11th Floor, Tower House, Fairfax Street, Bristol BS1 3BN
Tel: 44 01179 338023
Web site: www.cross-stitching.com/magazines/cross-stitch-crazy
Freq: Monthly
Circ: 16960 Not Audited
Editor: Rachel Beckwith
Profile: Magazine containing cross stitch designs and technical information, including stories, puzzles and news.
Ad Rate: Full Page Colour £1050.00
MAGAZINE
Crafts

Cross Stitch Gold 982801
Editorial: 9th Floor, Tower House, Fairfax Street, Bristol BS1 3BN
Tel: 44 01179 279009
Web site: http://www.cross-stitching.com
Freq: Bi-Monthly
Circ: 20000 Not Audited
Profile: Magazine covering large cross stitch designs from around the world.
Ad Rate: Full Page Colour £1030.00
MAGAZINE
Crafts

crossed grain 983834
Editorial: 3rd Floor, Apollo Centre, Desborough Road, High Wycombe HP11 2QW Tel: 44 01494 437278
Email: crossedgrain@coeliac.org.uk
Web site: www.coeliac.org.uk/gluten-free-diet-and-lifestyle/crossed-grain-magazine/
Freq: 3 Times/Year
Circ: 70000 Not Audited
Editor: Holly Knowles
Profile: Magazine covering everything about gluten free living, lifestyle, keeping fit, general health, travel, holidays, research on coeliac disease and new products.
Ad Rate: Full Page Colour £3750.00
MAGAZINE
Nutrition, Patient Support

CrossStitcher 981940
Editorial: Tower House, Fairfax Street, Bath BS1 3BN
Email: crossstitcher@dennis.co.uk
Web site: http://crossstitchermag.com/
Freq: Monthly
Circ: 20714 Not Audited
Editor: Susan Penny
Profile: Magazine for every cross stitcher. Contains a mix of large and small projects, free gifts and design information.
Ad Rate: Full Page Colour £1875.00
MAGAZINE
Crafts

Crowdedbrain 990690
Email: contact@crowdedbrain.co.uk
Web site: www.crowdedbrain.co.uk
Freq: Daily
Circ: 46096 Cision Digital Reach
Editor: Brett James
MAGAZINE (ONLINE)
Audio Video Trade, Cameras, Computers, Consumer Electronics, Data Management, Electronics, Industry, Internet, Mobile Communications, Mobile Electronics

CrowdFundBeat 996784
Editorial: 10/11 Charterhouse Square, London EC1M 6EH Tel: 44 02033 564922
Email: news@crowdfundbeat.co.uk
Web site: http://crowdfundbeat.com
Freq: Daily
Circ: 46023 Cision Digital Reach
MAGAZINE (ONLINE)
News & Current Affairs

The Croydon Citizen 987346
Editorial: Sussex Innovation Croydon, 11th Floor, No.1 Croydon, 12-16 Addiscombe Road, Croydon CR0 0XT
Email: editors@thecroydoncitizen.com
Web site: www.thecroydoncitizen.com
Freq: Monthly
Circ: 15000 Not Audited
Editor: James Naylor
Profile: Publication that covers news, culture, politics, campaigns and sport from around Croydon and the surrounding area.
MAGAZINE
Regional

Cruise Adviser 988601
Editorial: Collective Temperance Hospital, 110 Hampstead Road, London NW1 2LS
Email: info@cruise-adviser.com
Web site: www.cruise-adviser.com
Freq: Bi-Monthly
Circ: 7000 Not Audited
MAGAZINE
Boating & Yachting, Travel

Cruise International 985623
Editorial: The Chelsea Magazine Company, Jubilee House, 2 Jubilee Place, London SW3 0TQ Tel: 44 02073 493700
Email: editorial@cruiseinternational.com
Web site: cruise-international.com
Freq: Bi-Monthly
Circ: 80000 Not Audited
Editor: Liz Jarvis
Profile: Magazine containing features and photographs of exotic destinations, romantic ports and secret hideaways. Includes information about life on board and advice on which ship to choose and the best time to travel. Aimed at anyone who has ever dreamed of a holiday at sea.
MAGAZINE
Travel

Cruise Trade News 988889
Editorial: 115 Sydney Road, London N10 2ND
Web site: http://www.cruisetradenews.com/
Freq: Bi-Monthly Not Audited
Profile: Magazine containing cruise and ferry news and features. Read by travel agents and executives in the cruise and ferry industry.
Ad Rate: Full Page Colour £2200.00
MAGAZINE
Travel

Cruise Trade News' Destinations 1053613
Tel: 44 02084 442554
Web site: www.cpandd.co.uk
Freq: Quarterly
Circ: 6000 Not Audited
MAGAZINE
Travel

cruisecritic.co.uk 986809
Editorial: 7 Soho Square, London WC1D 3QB Tel: 44 02033 203241
Email: editor@cruisecritic.co.uk
Web site: www.cruisecritic.co.uk/
Freq: Daily
Circ: 1029940 Cision Digital Reach
Editor: Kerry Spencer
MAGAZINE (ONLINE)
Travel

Cruising 982207
Editorial: CA House, 1 Northey Street, Limehouse Basin, London E14 8BT
Tel: 44 02075 372828
Email: editor@theca.org.uk
Web site: www.theca.org.uk/public/cruising
Freq: Quarterly
Circ: 4000 Not Audited
Editor: Camilla Herrmann
MAGAZINE
Boating & Yachting

Crumbs 986904
Editorial: Circus Mews House, Circus Mews, Bath BA1 2PW Tel: 44 01225 475800
Web site: www.crumbsmag.com
Freq: Monthly
Circ: 36000 Not Audited
Editor: Matt Bielby; Editor: Jessica Carter
Profile: Publication that covers the bars, cafes, restaurants and gastropubs from around the cities of Bath and Bristol. It also features news on chefs and venues as well as recipes and ingredients.
Ad Rate: Full Page Colour £878.00
MAGAZINE
Cooking & Baking, Food, Grocery Stores, Organic Food, Restaurant Reviews, Vegetarianism & Veganism

Crumbs Devon 997982
Editorial: Circus Mews House, Circus Mews, Bath BA1 2PW
Freq: Monthly
Circ: 12000 Not Audited
MAGAZINE
Alcohol & Spirits, Bars, Clubs & Pubs, Beer, Beverages, Cooking & Baking, Organic Food, Restaurant Reviews, Vegetarianism & Veganism, Wine/Winemaking

CTMfile 1064997
Freq: Daily
Circ: 15642 Cision Digital Reach
MAGAZINE (ONLINE)
Banking

Cuba Si 982577
Editorial: C/o Unite, 33-37 Moreland Street, London EC1V 8BB Tel: 44 02074 905715
Email: communications@cuba-solidarity.org.uk
Web site: www.cuba-solidarity.org
Freq: Quarterly
Circ: 5000 Not Audited
Editor: Natasha Hickman
MAGAZINE
Americas, International News, Politics

Cubed3 988442
Editorial: 14A Bonnersfield Lane, Harrow, London HA1 2JH
Email: jb@cubed3.com
Web site: www.cubed3.com/
Freq: Daily
Circ: 51298 Cision Digital Reach
Profile: Website covering computer games. CUBED 3 is a worldwide, multi-format videogame and entertainment website which started in January 2003.
MAGAZINE (ONLINE)
Computer & Video Games, Movies & Video

Cuckfield Life 996896
Editorial: The Barn, Hurstwood Grange, Hurstwood Lane, Haywards Heath RH17 7QX Tel: 44 01444 884115
Email: editor@cuckfieldlife.co.uk
Web site: www.cuckfieldlife.co.uk
Freq: Monthly
Circ: 3800 Not Audited
Editor: David Tingley
MAGAZINE
Regional

Cuddles 1054335
Editorial: Unit 16 Greenway Farm, Bath Road, Wick, Bristol BS30 5RL
Tel: 44 01179 373003
Email: info@kennedypublishing.co.uk
Web site: http://www.kennedypublishing.co.uk/magazines/cuddles-magazine
Freq: Monthly Not Audited
MAGAZINE
Preschool, Teen/Young Adult

Cue Entertainment 983049
Editorial: Hoadsbrook, Mockbeggar Lane, East End, Beneden, Cranbrook TN17 4BG
Tel: 44 01580 243441
Email: info@cueentertainment.com
Web site: www.cueentertainment.com
Freq: Quarterly
Circ: 2500 Not Audited
Profile: Magazine covering home entertainment including, DVD players, games, TV and video on demand.
Ad Rate: Full Page Colour £1500.00
MAGAZINE
Computers, Electronics

Culinary News 995260
Editorial: British Culinary Federation, PO Box 10532, Alcester B50 4ZY
Email: chefjimeaves@yahoo.co.uk
Web site: www.britishculinaryfederation.co.uk
Freq: Quarterly Not Audited
Editor: Jim Eaves
MAGAZINE
Bars, Clubs & Pubs, Food

Cult Beauty 984338
Editorial: 38-39 St Johns Lane, London EC1M 4BJ Tel: 44 08001 088822
Email: info@cultbeauty.co.uk
Web site: www.cultbeauty.co.uk
Freq: Daily
Circ: 592356 Cision Digital Reach
MAGAZINE (ONLINE)
Beauty & Grooming, Cosmetics, Hair

Consumer Magazines

Cult Hub
1101749
Email: info@culthub.com
Web site: www.culthub.com
Freq: Daily
Circ: 1806 Cision Digital Reach
Editor: Genevieve Sibayan
MAGAZINE (ONLINE)
Lifestyle, Men's Interests, Regional
General Interest, Women's Interests

CultBox
986436
Web site: www.cultbox.co.uk
Freq: Daily
Circ: 888222 Cision Digital Reach
MAGAZINE (ONLINE)
Broadcasting

The Cultural Voyager
987872
Editorial: 6 Oakwood Avenue, Beckenham,
London BR3 6PJ Tel: 44 02082 894545
Email: admin@theculturalvoyager.com
Web site: www.theculturalvoyager.com
Freq: Daily
Circ: 14285 Cision Digital Reach
MAGAZINE (ONLINE)
Antiques/Collectibles, Art, Arts,
Literature, Photography, Theater &
Performing Arts, Visual Arts

Culture & Life
995365
Editorial: 80 Cheshire Street, London E2
6EH Tel: 44 02074 409826
Web site: http://cultureandlife.co.uk
Freq: Daily
Circ: 10805 Cision Digital Reach
Editor: Andrew Soar
MAGAZINE (ONLINE)
Country, Folk, Bluegrass, Dance Music,
Fashion, Jazz & Blues, Literature, Music,
Pop Music, Rap & Hip Hop, Regional
General Interest, Rock Music

Culture Trip
988672
Editorial: 16-25 Bastwick Street,
Clerkenwell, London EC1V 3PS
Tel: 44 02077 171580
Email: info@theculturetrip.com
Web site: www.theculturetrip.com
Freq: Daily
Circ: 1230373 Cision Digital Reach
MAGAZINE (ONLINE)
Art, Cooking & Baking, Dance Music, Jazz
& Blues, Literature, Movies & Video,
Photography, Pop Music, R&B, Urban,
World, Rap & Hip Hop

Culture Whisper
988622
Editorial: 9 Great Newport Street, London
WC2 H7JA Tel: 44 02071 831147
Web site: http://www.culturewhisper.com
Freq: Daily
Circ: 51602 Cision Digital Reach
MAGAZINE (ONLINE)
Local Entertainment Guides

Culture24
982822
Editorial: Office 4, 28 Kensington Street,
Brighton BN1 4AJ Tel: 44 01273 623266
Email: newsdesk@culture24.org.uk
Web site: www.culture24.org.uk
Freq: Daily
Circ: 79041 Cision Digital Reach
Editor: Richard Moss
MAGAZINE (ONLINE)
History

CultureorTrash
996090
Web site: www.cultureortrash.com
Freq: Daily
Circ: 11383 Cision Digital Reach
MAGAZINE (ONLINE)
Dance Music, Entertainment, Pop Music,
Rock Music, Theater & Performing Arts

Cumbria Crack
996464
Editorial: 9a Duke Street, Penrith, Penrith
CA11 7LY Tel: 44 01768 868051
Email: admin@cumbriacrack.com
Web site: www.cumbriacrack.com
Freq: Daily
Circ: 66518 Cision Digital Reach

Editor: Carl Fallowfield
MAGAZINE (ONLINE)
News & Current Affairs

Cumbria Life
982481
Editorial: The White House, Dalston Road,
Carlisle CA2 5UA Tel: 44 01228 612334
Web site: www.cumbrialife.co.uk
Freq: Monthly
Circ: 10552 Not Audited
Editor: Richard Eccles
Profile: Magazine containing features and
information on Cumbria.
Ad Rate: Full Page Colour £1450.00
MAGAZINE
Regional General Interest

Cumbria Live
990674
Editorial: Newspaper House, Dalston Road,
Carlisle CA2 5UA Tel: 44 01228 612600
Email: nick.turner@cnmedia.co.uk
Web site: www.cumbrialive.co.uk
Freq: Daily
Circ: 19399 Cision Digital Reach
MAGAZINE (ONLINE)
Regional

Cumbria Magazine
1075514
Editorial: The Water Mill, Broughton Hall,
Skipton, Broughton BD23 3AG
Tel: 44 01756 701381
Web site: www.cumbriamagazine.co.uk
Freq: Monthly
Circ: 10196 Not Audited
Editor: John Manning
MAGAZINE
Regional General Interest

Curly Hair Magazine
995500
Email: info@hellochm.com
Web site: http://www.hellochm.com/
Freq: Semi-Annual Not Audited
Editor: Sandra Lewis
MAGAZINE
Hair

Currency News
985312
Web site: www.currencynews.co.uk
Freq: Daily
Circ: 66507 Cision Digital Reach
Profile: Newsletter covering all aspects of
currency. Covers news, analysis, events,
standards, companies, people and
technologies shaping the developments of
banknotes and coins around the world.
MAGAZINE (ONLINE)
News & Current Affairs

Current Archaeology
985874
Editorial: Thames Works, Church Street,
London W4 2PD Tel: 44 02088 195580
Email: subs@currentpublishing.com
Web site: www.archaeology.co.uk
Freq: Bi-Monthly
Circ: 70000 Not Audited
Profile: Magazine containing the latest
archaeological news in Britain.
MAGAZINE
History

Current Awareness Service
996030
Editorial: BILD, Birmingham Research Park,
97 Vincent Drive, Edgbaston, Birmingham
B15 2SQ Tel: 44 01214 156960
Email: enquiries@bild.org.uk
Web site: http://www.bild.org.uk/our-
services/journals/cas/
Freq: Monthly
Circ: 900 Not Audited
Editor: Kate Brackley
MAGAZINE
Disability

Current Opinion in Clinical Nutrition and Metabolic Care
999022
Editorial: 250 Waterloo Road, London SE1
8RD Tel: 44 02079 810600
Web site: journals.lww.com/co-
clinicalnutrition/pages/default.aspx
Freq: Bi-Monthly Not Audited

Editor: Yvon A. Carpentier; Editor: Luc A
Cynober
MAGAZINE
Diabetes, Gastroenterology, Nutrition

Curva
988086
Email: info@curvamag.com
Web site: www.curvamag.com
Freq: Monthly Not Audited
Profile: Magazine covering fashion and style
for plus size women.
MAGAZINE
Fashion, Women's Interests

The Cusp
1097899
Web site: http://thecuspmagazine.com/
Freq: Daily
Circ: 12661 Cision Digital Reach
MAGAZINE (ONLINE)
Art, Classical/Choral/Band Music, Theater
& Performing Arts, Visual Arts

Custom Car
982630
Editorial: Kelsey Publishing, Cudham Tithe
Barn, Berrys Hill, Peterborough TN16 3AG
Tel: 44 01733 347559
Email: cc.ed@kelsey.co.uk
Web site: www.customcarmag.co.uk
Freq: Monthly
Circ: 12400 Not Audited
Editor: Dave Biggadyke
Profile: Magazine covering news and
features on custom cars, hot rods, drag
racing, street machines, custom car action
from around the world and related products
as well as technical advice and drag racing
news. Launched in 1970.
Ad Rate: Full Page Colour £900.00
MAGAZINE
Antique & Collectible Cars, Automakers,
Automotive, Driving, Motorcycles,
Motorsports, Off-road & 4-Wheel Drive
Vehicles, Trucks & SUVs

Custom PC
981728
Editorial: 30 Cleveland Street, London W1T
4JD Tel: 44 02079 076000
Web site: www.subscribe.custompc.co.uk
Freq: Monthly
Circ: 7925 Not Audited
Editor: Ben Hardwidge
Profile: Magazine covering performance
hardware and customization. Includes
features on high-end IT and articles on the
latest technology. Each issue includes
coverage of PC hardware, technology and
games as well as the latest tech news,
unique features, interactive reader
challenges and reviews of cutting-edge
hardware. Aimed predominantly at male
hardware fanatics between 18 and 35 years
old, who are passionate about PC
technology and hardware.
Ad Rate: Full Page Colour £2167.00
MAGAZINE
Computers, Personal Computers

Cute
995806
Editorial: Unit 16 Greenway Farm, Bath
Road, Wick, Bristol BS30 5RL
Tel: 44 01179 373003
Email: info@kennedypublishing.co.uk
Web site: http://www.kennedypublishing.co.
uk/magazines/cute-magazine
Freq: Monthly
Circ: 35000 Not Audited
MAGAZINE
Teen/Young Adult, Trading Cards &
Comics

CWB
983207
Editorial: RAS Publishing, The Old Town
Hall, Lewisham Road, Slaithwaite,
Huddersfield HD7 5AL Tel: 44 01484 846069
Email: laura@ras-publishing.com
Web site: http://www.cwb-online.co.uk/
Freq: Bi-Monthly
Circ: 3500 Not Audited
MAGAZINE
Fashion

CWL News
982146
Editorial: PO Box 1227, Cheltenham GL50
9XH Tel: 44 01242 584940

Email: natsec@cwlhq.org.uk
Web site: www.catholicwomensleague.org
Freq: 3 Times/Year
Circ: 5000 Not Audited
MAGAZINE
Religion

The Cyber Investigator
997292
Editorial: 13 Station Road, Stoke
Mandeville, Aylesbury HP22 5UL
Tel: 44 08446 608707
Email: editor@the-investigator.co.uk
Web site: www.the-investigator.co.uk
Freq: Quarterly Not Audited
Editor: Carol Jenkins
MAGAZINE
News & Current Affairs

Cycle
982193
Editorial: PO Box 313, Scarborough YO12
6WZ
Email: editor@ctc.org.uk
Web site: www.ctc.org.uk
Freq: Bi-Monthly
Circ: 53000 Not Audited
Editor: Dan Joyce
Profile: Cycle is the magazine of the
Cyclists' Touring Club which campaigns for
the rights and safety of all cyclists and
promotes leisure and utility cycling and
cycling travel.
Ad Rate: Full Page Mono £1390.00
Ad Rate: Full Page Colour £1740.00
MAGAZINE
Bicycles

Cycle Commuter Magazine
995144
Editorial: Unit 7b, Green Park Station, Bath
BA1 1JB
Web site: http://www.cyclescheme.co.uk/
cycle-commuter-magazine
Freq: Semi-Annual
Circ: 600000 Not Audited
MAGAZINE
Bicycles

Cycle Traveller
1101290
Tel: 44 01285 644181
Email: editor@doubleamedia.com
Web site: active-traveller.com
Freq: Annual
Circ: 34000 Not Audited
MAGAZINE
Bicycles

CycleTechReview.com
1063719
Web site: http://cycletechreview.com/
Freq: Daily
Circ: 12097 Cision Digital Reach
MAGAZINE (ONLINE)
Bicycles

Cycling Fitness
985884
Editorial: Leon House, 233 Highstreet,
Croydon, London CR9 1HZ
Tel: 44 02087 268453
Email: cycling@timeinc.com
Web site: www.timeincuk.com/brands/
cycling-fitness
Freq: Quarterly
Circ: 15000 Not Audited
MAGAZINE
Bicycles

Cycling Plus
982195
Editorial: Tower House, Fairfax Street,
Bristol BS1 3BN Tel: 44 01179 279009
Email: cyclingplus@immediate.co.uk
Web site: www.bikeradar.com
Freq: Monthly
Circ: 43746 Not Audited
Editor: Rob Spedding
Profile: Magazine covering all forms of
performance, leisure and utility cycling.
Includes equipment tests, fitness and touring
advice. Read by experienced cyclists,
cycling enthusiasts and complete beginners
aged between 25 and 40 years old.
Ad Rate: Full Page Colour £1720.00
MAGAZINE
Bicycles

Cycling UK
982875
Editorial: Parklands, Railton Road, Guildford, London GU2 9JX
Tel: 44 01483 238337
Email: cycling@cyclinguk.org
Web site: http://www.cyclinguk.org/
Freq: Daily
Circ: 20640 Cision Digital Reach
Editor: Dan Joyce
MAGAZINE (ONLINE)
Bicycles

Cycling Weekly
982196
Editorial: Leon House, 233 Highstreet, Croydon, London CR9 1HZ
Email: cycling@timeinc.com
Web site: www.cyclingweekly.co.uk
Freq: Weekly
Circ: 24448 Not Audited
Editor: Luke Evans; **Editor:** Simon Richardson
Profile: Magazine containing a comprehensive guide to the cycling scene and covering all aspects of cycling including road racing, time trialling, mountain biking and touring as well as equipment and material. First published in 1891, the publication has an average of 88 pages per issue. Aimed at cyclists, triathletes, road racers and mountain bikers.
Ad Rate: Full Page Colour £1638.00
MAGAZINE
Bicycles

Cycling World
982197
Editorial: Myrtle Oast, Kemsdale Road, Faversham, Faversham ME13 9JL
Tel: 44 01227 750153
Email: editorial@cyclingworld.eu
Web site: www.cyclingworldmag.co.uk
Freq: Monthly
Circ: 40000 Not Audited
Profile: Magazine covering touring and recreational cycling.
Ad Rate: Full Page Colour £2795.00
MAGAZINE
Bicycles

Cycling.TV
998475
Editorial: NeuLion London, 21/22 Warwick Street, London W1B 5NF
Email: team@cycling.tv
Web site: www.cycling.tv
Freq: Daily
Circ: 18752 Cision Digital Reach
MAGAZINE (ONLINE)
Bicycles

Cyclingnews.com
984783
Editorial: Tower House, Fairfax Street, Bristol BS1 3BN **Tel:** 44 01179 279009
Email: cyclingnews@cyclingnews.com
Web site: www.cyclingnews.com
Freq: Daily
Circ: 3478357 Cision Digital Reach
MAGAZINE (ONLINE)
Bicycles

Cyclist
986933
Editorial: 31-32 Alfred Place, London WC1E 7DP **Tel:** 44 02079 076000
Email: cyclist@dennis.co.uk
Web site: www.cyclistmag.co.uk
Freq: Monthly
Circ: 24891 Not Audited
Editor: Peter Muir
Profile: Monthly title that covers road cycling. It is aimed at road cycling enthusiasts who like to travel as well as covering ride performance and style.
MAGAZINE
Bicycles

DAD.info
988356
Editorial: Moggerhanger Park, Park Road, Moggerhanger, Bedford MK44 3RW
Tel: 44 01767 641002
Web site: www.dad.info
Freq: Daily
Circ: 60715 Cision Digital Reach
Editor: Dean Beamont
MAGAZINE (ONLINE)
Family & Parenting, Men's Interests

Daily Business
988658
Editorial: 1/11 Burnbrae Park, East Craigs, Edinburgh EH12 8AN **Tel:** 44 07971 686038
Email: newsdesk@dailybusinessgroup.co.uk
Web site: http://dailybusinessgroup.co.uk
Freq: Daily
Circ: 18167 Cision Digital Reach
Editor: Terry Murden
MAGAZINE (ONLINE)
Business, National News, Personal Finance, Politics, Small and Medium Business

The Daily Cloth
1075479
Editorial: 2nd Floor, Gensurco House, 3 5 Spafield Street, London EC1R 4QB
Email: mph@thedailycloth.com
Web site: www.thedailycloth.com/
Freq: Daily
Circ: 548 Cision Digital Reach
MAGAZINE (ONLINE)
Basketball, Bicycles, Billiards, Boating & Yachting, Bodybuilding, Bowling, Boxing, Classical/Choral/Band Music, Country, Folk, Bluegrass, Cricket

The Daily Muse - Fenwick Magazine
996062
Editorial: 63 New Bond Street, London W1A 3BS **Tel:** 44 02076 299161
Web site: www.fenwick.co.uk/daily-muse
Freq: Daily
Circ: 24 Cision Digital Reach
MAGAZINE (ONLINE)
Beauty & Grooming, Celebrities, Cosmetics, Do-It-Yourself (DIY), Fashion, Hair

The Daily Sail
986780
Editorial: 10 Melina Road, London W12 9HZ
Email: news@thedailysail.com
Web site: www.thedailysail.com
Freq: Daily
Circ: 3118 Cision Digital Reach
Editor: James Boyd
Profile: Website covering sailing. The Daily Sail website shares the latest news, features and photographs about performance yacht and dinghy racing in the UK and abroad.
MAGAZINE (ONLINE)
Boating & Yachting

Dairy-Free Delicious
997926
Web site: www.dairyfreedelicious.com
Freq: Daily
Circ: 4054 Cision Digital Reach
MAGAZINE (ONLINE)
Cooking & Baking

Dales Life
982912
Editorial: 90 Tadcaster Road, York YO24 1LT **Tel:** 44 01904 629295
Web site: www.daleslife.com
Freq: Bi-Monthly
Circ: 20000 Not Audited
Editor: Sue Gillman
Profile: Local interest magazine delivered to homes and businesses throughout North Yorkshire.
Ad Rate: Full Page Colour £575.00
MAGAZINE
Regional General Interest

Dalesman
982544
Editorial: The Water Mill, Broughton Hall, Skipton, Broughton BD23 3AG
Tel: 44 01756 701381
Email: editorial@dalesman.co.uk
Web site: http://www.dalesman.co.uk
Freq: Monthly
Circ: 23285 Not Audited
Editor: Adrian Braddy
Profile: Magazine covering articles specifically on the Yorkshire countryside, people, customs and traditions.
Ad Rate: Full Page Colour £1700.00
MAGAZINE
Regional General Interest

Dance Europe
982000
Editorial: P.O.Box 12661, London E5 9TZ
Web site: www.danceeurope.net
Freq: Monthly

Circ: 50000 Not Audited
Editor: Emma Manning Kauldhar
Profile: Magazine covering ballet and classical dancing including reviews, dance companies across Europe, leading figures in the dance world and a comprehensive performance diary. Launched in 1995. Aimed at professional students and dancers and their audiences.
Ad Rate: Full Page Mono £595.00
Ad Rate: Full Page Colour £845.00
MAGAZINE
News & Current Affairs

Dance Gazette
982001
Editorial: 36 Battersea Square, London SW11 3RA **Tel:** 44 02073 268000
Email: gazette@rad.org.uk
Web site: http://www.rad.org.uk/more/dance-gazette
Freq: 3 Times/Year
Circ: 14000 Not Audited
Editor: David Jays
Profile: Magazine of the Royal Academy of Dance covering articles on dancers, dance companies, training and teaching, choreography, ballet and related features. Read by dance teachers, students, examiners and those interested in dance.
Ad Rate: Full Page Mono £550.00
Ad Rate: Full Page Colour £750.00
MAGAZINE
Theater & Performing Arts

Dance Today
982002
Editorial: 36 Battersea Square, London SW11 3RA **Tel:** 44 02072 503006
Email: dt@dancing-times.co.uk
Web site: www.dance-today.co.uk
Freq: Monthly
Circ: 3000 Not Audited
Editor: Jonathan Gray
Profile: Magazine focusing on ballroom and Latin dance as well as other social dance forms, containing news, features, advice on technique, health and nutrition articles, interviews and competition reports.
Ad Rate: Full Page Mono £146.00
Ad Rate: Full Page Colour £268.00
MAGAZINE
Theater & Performing Arts

DanceSport.UK.com
998668
Editorial: 11 Odeon Parade, 480 London Road, Isleworth, London TW7 4RL
Tel: 44 02085 680083
Email: webmaster@zem.co.uk
Web site: www.dancesport.uk.com
Freq: Daily
Circ: 51473 Cision Digital Reach
MAGAZINE (ONLINE)
Theater & Performing Arts

DanceTabs
1101754
Email: info@dancetabs.com
Web site: http://dancetabs.com/
Freq: Daily
Circ: 16080 Cision Digital Reach
MAGAZINE (ONLINE)
Theater & Performing Arts

Dancing Astronaut
998255
Email: contact@dancingastronaut.com
Web site: www.dancingastronaut.com
Freq: Daily
Circ: 481096 Cision Digital Reach
MAGAZINE (ONLINE)
Dance Music, Theater & Performing Arts

Dancing Times
982003
Editorial: 36 Battersea Square, London SW11 3RA **Tel:** 44 02072 503006
Email: dt@dancing-times.co.uk
Web site: www.dancing-times.co.uk
Freq: Monthly
Circ: 8000 Not Audited
Editor: Jonathan Gray
Profile: Magazine covering all types of stage dancing but mainly focusing on ballet, contemporary dance and musical theatre.
Ad Rate: Full Page Mono £612.00
Ad Rate: Full Page Colour £855.00
MAGAZINE
Theater & Performing Arts

The Dandy Annual
996541
Editorial: DC Thomson, 80, Kingsway East, Dundee DD4 8SL
Web site: www.dandy.com
Freq: Annual Not Audited
MAGAZINE
News & Current Affairs

DANTEmag
986376
Editorial: 12 Charing Cross Mansion, 26 Charing Cross Road, London WC2H 0DG
Email: info@dantemag.com
Web site: http://www.dantemag.com/
Freq: Bi-Monthly Not Audited
Editor In Chief: Massimo Gava
MAGAZINE
History, Politics

DARE Magazine
984129
Editorial: Garden Floor, 16 Connaught Place, London W2 2ES
Tel: 44 02074 206535
Web site: dare.superdrug.com
Freq: Bi-Monthly
Circ: 600000 Not Audited
MAGAZINE
Beauty & Grooming, Cosmetics, Fashion, Hair, Health & Medicine, Women's Interests

The Dark Side
982040
Editorial: 29 Cheyham Way, South Cheam, London SM2 7HX **Tel:** 44 02086 610065
Email: editor@thedarksidemagazine.com
Web site: www.thedarksidemagazine.com
Freq: Bi-Monthly
Circ: 31000 Not Audited
Editor: Allan Bryce
Profile: Magazine focusing on horror and fantasy. Covers books, videos, memorabilia, computer games and comics.
Ad Rate: Full Page Mono £550.00
Ad Rate: Full Page Colour £830.00
MAGAZINE
Entertainment, Literature, Movies & Video

Dark World Gaming
995474
Email: info@darkworldgaming.com
Web site: www.darkworldgaming.com
Freq: Daily
Circ: 13215 Cision Digital Reach
MAGAZINE (ONLINE)
Computer & Video Games

Darling
1075723
Editorial: 211 Coombe Lane, West Wimbledon, London SW20 0RG
Email: info@darlingmagazine.co.uk
Web site: www.darlingmagazine.co.uk
Freq: Bi-Monthly
Circ: 7500 Not Audited
MAGAZINE
Regional General Interest, Women's Interests

Darlington Today
983933
Editorial: 45 Atkinson Gardens, Aycliffe Village, Newton Aycliffe DL5 6LH
Tel: 44 01325 304360
Freq: Bi-Monthly
Circ: 45000 Not Audited
MAGAZINE
Regional, Regional General Interest

Dartford Living
997920
Editorial: PO Box 283, Dartford, Kent, London DA1 9BW **Tel:** 44 01322 507817
Email: editor@dartfordliving.com
Web site: www.dartfordliving.net/
Freq: Monthly
Circ: 25000 Not Audited
Editor: Vijay Jain
MAGAZINE
Regional General Interest

Dartmoor Magazine
985892
Editorial: 2 Steward Cottages, Moretonhampstead, Newton TQ13 8SD
Tel: 44 01647 441174
Email: editor@dartmoormagazine.co.uk
Web site: www.dartmoormagazine.co.uk
Freq: Quarterly

Consumer Magazines

Circ: 12000 Not Audited
Editor: Sue Viccars
Profile: Magazine containing local information, national park news, towns and villages, walks, personalities, local history, outdoor equipment, book reviews, events, wine and dine.
Ad Rate: Full Page Mono £375.00
Ad Rate: Full Page Colour £425.00
MAGAZINE
Regional General Interest

Darts World
982231
Tel: 44 01233 733558
Email: info@darts.world
Web site: dartsworld.com
Freq: Monthly
Circ: 18000 Not Audited
Editor: Michael Beeken
Profile: Magazine covering all aspects of marketing at all levels within the darts world. Features match reports and sports news. Read by darts enthusiasts and sport officials.
Ad Rate: Full Page Mono £538.00
Ad Rate: Full Page Colour £735.00
MAGAZINE
Games, Competitions & Events

Data Centre News
999706
Editorial: Alexander House, 38 Forehill, Ely, Ely CB7 4AF **Tel:** 44 01353 616100
Web site: www.datacentrenews.co.uk
Freq: Monthly
Circ: 15514 Cision Digital Reach
MAGAZINE (ONLINE)
Auto Aftermarket, Computers, Data Management, Electronics, Internet, Mobile Communications, Security & Security Systems, Software

Data Transmission
999424
Editorial: 83 Great Titchfield Street, London W1W 6RH
Web site: https://datatransmission.co/
Freq: Daily
Circ: 15536 Cision Digital Reach
MAGAZINE (ONLINE)
Dance Music

Database & Network Journal
981628
Editorial: 58 Ryecroft Way, Luton LU2 7TU
Tel: 44 01582 722219
Email: smpluton@ntlworld.com
Web site: www.softwareworldpublication.com
Freq: Bi-Monthly
Circ: 1000 Not Audited
MAGAZINE
Data Management, Internet

DATACENTRE.ME
988913
Web site: www.datacentre.me
Freq: Daily
Circ: 15183 Cision Digital Reach
MAGAZINE (ONLINE)
News & Current Affairs

Datamonitor
1068249
Editorial: Informa Group PLC, 5 Howick Place, London SW1P 1WG
Tel: 44 02070 176970
Email: euroinfo@datamonitor.com
Web site: www.datamonitor.com
Freq: Daily
Circ: 42873 Cision Digital Reach
MAGAZINE (ONLINE)
News & Current Affairs

The Day
998905
Editorial: Pennine House, 28 Leman Street, London E1 8EW
Freq: Daily
Circ: 90953 Cision Digital Reach
MAGAZINE (ONLINE)
Education, International News

Days Out
982336
Editorial: 6 Greatford Gardens, Greatford, Stamford PE9 4PX **Tel:** 44 01778 561767
Email: elisabeth@daysout.co.uk
Web site: www.daysout.co.uk

Freq: Annual Not Audited
Editor: Elisabeth Beckett
Profile: Magazine covering a whole range of family attractions throughout Great Britain. Aimed at families planning days out.
Ad Rate: Full Page Colour £3850.00
MAGAZINE
Local Entertainment Guides, Travel

Dazed
981793
Editorial: 3rd Floor, 2 Arundel Street, London WC2R 3DA **Tel:** 44 02073 360766
Web site: www.dazeddigital.com
Freq: Bi-Monthly
Circ: 89600 Not Audited
Profile: Magazine covering urban lifestyle and entertainment including fashion, beauty, arts, culture, photography, illustration, video, film and music. Aimed at club going, fashion conscious young people.
Ad Rate: Full Page Colour £6382.00
MAGAZINE
Men's Interests

DC Universe Presents: Justice League Trinity
995744
Editorial: Titan House, 144 Southwark Street, London SE1 0UP
Tel: 44 02076 200200
Email: dcuniversepresents@titanemail.com
Web site: titanmagazines.com/t/dc-universe/
Freq: Bi-Monthly Not Audited
MAGAZINE
Teen/Young Adult, Trading Cards & Comics

Deadpress.co.uk
999697
Email: contact@deadpress.co.uk
Web site: www.deadpress.co.uk
Freq: Daily
Circ: 15028 Cision Digital Reach
MAGAZINE (ONLINE)
Rock Music

Deafness and Education International
981520
Editorial: 297 Euston Road, London NW1 3AD **Tel:** 44 02074 517300
Email: dei.ed@maneypublishing.com
Web site: http://www.tandfonline.com/toc/ydei20/current
Freq: Quarterly
Circ: 2200 Not Audited
Editor: Linda Watson
MAGAZINE
Disability

Dear Doctor (UK)
999089
Editorial: Suite 2, 143 Caledonian Road, London N1 0SL **Tel:** 44 02078 711000
Email: info@damsonmedia.com
Web site: http://www.celebrityangels.co.uk
Freq: Semi-Annual Not Audited
MAGAZINE
Health & Medicine

Dearly Departures
996698
Web site: http://dearlydepartures.com/
Freq: Daily
Circ: 754 Cision Digital Reach
MAGAZINE (ONLINE)
Travel, Vegetarianism & Veganism

The Debrief
987685
Editorial: Endeavour House, 189 Shaftesbury Avenue, London WC2H 8JG
Tel: 44 02072 955574
Email: theteam@thedebrief.co.uk
Web site: www.thedebrief.co.uk
Freq: Daily
Circ: 172427 Cision Digital Reach
Profile: The Debrief is a website covering women's interests, including celebrity, life, fashion, sex and things to do. The website is aimed at the twenty-something woman.
MAGAZINE (ONLINE)
Beauty & Grooming, Cosmetics, Fashion, Hair, Relationships, Women's Interests

Debt Management Today
985533
Editorial: 71 Gloucester Place, London W1U 8JW

Web site: http://www.debtmanagementtoday.co.uk/
Freq: Daily
Circ: 1787 Cision Digital Reach
Editor: Beth Fisher
MAGAZINE (ONLINE)
Personal Finance

Decanter
981749
Editorial: The Blue Fin Building, 110 Southwark Street, London SE1 0SU
Tel: 44 02031 485000
Email: editor@decanter.com
Web site: www.decanter.com
Freq: Monthly
Circ: 43000 Not Audited
Profile: Magazine containing features on wines and spirits including wine tasting and wine regions worldwide. First published in 1976, the publication has an average of 120 pages per issue. Aimed at wine enthusiasts, connoisseurs and wine trade professionals.
Ad Rate: Full Page Mono £1740.00
Ad Rate: Full Page Colour £3515.00
MAGAZINE
Alcohol & Spirits, Wine/Winemaking

Deck Magazine
1061273
Email: info@deck.co.zw
Web site: http://www.deck-magazine.com
Freq: Daily
Circ: 611 Cision Digital Reach
MAGAZINE (ONLINE)
Bars, Clubs & Pubs, Comedy, Entertainment, Fashion, Lifestyle, Local Entertainment Guides, Men's Interests, Movies & Video, Regional General Interest, Women's Interests

Decomag.co.uk
986997
Email: info@decomag.co.uk
Web site: www.decomag.co.uk
Freq: Daily
Circ: 11615 Cision Digital Reach
Editor: Abby Trow
MAGAZINE (ONLINE)
Do-It-Yourself (DIY), Energy & Environment, Ethical/Moral Issues

Decor Kitchens and Interiors
996073
Editorial: 2nd Floor, Conway Mill, Conway Street, Belfast BT13 2DE
Tel: 44 02895 215610
Email: info@decor-living.com
Web site: www.decor-living.com
Freq: Bi-Monthly Not Audited
Editor: Judith Robinson-Lyttle
MAGAZINE
Do-It-Yourself (DIY)

The Defiant
995108
Email: team@defiantmagazine.com
Web site: www.thedefiantzine.com
Freq: Semi-Annual
Circ: 521 Cision Digital Reach
MAGAZINE (ONLINE)
Antiques/Collectibles, Architecture & Design, Art, Arts, Fashion, Literature, Movies & Video, Photography, Theater & Performing Arts, Visual Arts

Definition Magazine
995950
Editorial: The Studio 64, Old Station Road, Newmarket CB8 8AA **Tel:** 44 01223 492246
Web site: www.definitionmagazine.com
Freq: Monthly
Circ: 7154 Not Audited
MAGAZINE
Broadcasting, Photography

Defy Age
1104808
Editorial: Suite 7, 40 Craven Street, London WC2N 5NG **Tel:** 44 02077 514198
Email: info@defy-age.org
Web site: http://www.defy-age.org/
Freq: Daily
Circ: 521 Cision Digital Reach
MAGAZINE (ONLINE)
Health & Medicine, Plastic/Reconstructive/Cosmetic Surgery

DeHavilland Online News
98010
Editorial: c/o Top Right Group Limited, The Prow, 1 Wilder Walk, London W1B 5AP
Tel: 44 02030 333870
Email: newsdesk@dehavilland.co.uk
Web site: https://www1.dehavilland.co.uk/
Freq: Daily
Circ: 11238 Cision Digital Reach
MAGAZINE (ONLINE)
Politics

delicious.magazine
981804
Editorial: Axe & Bottle Court, 3rd floor, 70 Newcomen Street, London SE1 1YT
Tel: 44 02078 034100
Email: readers@deliciousmagazine.co.uk
Web site: www.deliciousmagazine.co.uk
Freq: Monthly
Circ: 60574 Not Audited
Editor: Karen Barnes
Profile: Magazine covering food recipes and gastronomy including features on the food industry, the people behind food business and chefs as well as topical food issues. First Published: 2003. Aimed at all food lovers but predominantly those aged between 25 and 45 years old.
Ad Rate: Full Page Colour £5000.00
MAGAZINE
Cooking & Baking

Dementia UK (newsletter)
997078
Editorial: Dementia UK, Second Floor, Resource for London, 356 Holloway Road, London N7 6PA **Tel:** 44 02076 974160
Email: info@dementiauk.org
Web site: www.dementiauk.org
Freq: Bi-Monthly Not Audited
MAGAZINE
Geriatrics, Neurology, Patient Support

Demerara Waves News
1061144
Tel: 44 59222 53990
Web site: http://www.caribnewsdesk.com/
Circ: 1084 Cision Digital Reach
MAGAZINE (ONLINE)
National News

Den of Geek
984560
Editorial: 31-32 Alfred Place, London WC1E 7DP
Email: geekcontent@gmail.com
Web site: http://www.denofgeek.com/uk
Freq: Daily
Circ: 197089 Cision Digital Reach
Editor: Simon Brew
MAGAZINE (ONLINE)
Computer & Video Games, Movies & Video, Science Fiction, Trading Cards & Comics

Dennis and Gnasher Epic Magazine
996745
Editorial: 80 Kingsway East, Glasgow DD4 8SL **Tel:** 44 01382 223131
Email: beano@dcthomson.co.uk
Web site: www.dennisandgnasher.com
Freq: Monthly
Circ: 17170 Not Audited
MAGAZINE
Trading Cards & Comics

DEPARTURES International
999566
Editorial: Flat 11, 8-9 Cleveland Square, London W2 6DH **Tel:** 44 02077 061069
Web site: http://www.departures-international.com
Freq: Quarterly
Circ: 259500 Not Audited
MAGAZINE
Luxury Goods

Derbyshire Life and Countryside
982483
Editorial: 61 Friar Gate, Derby DE1 1DJ
Tel: 44 01332 227850
Email: editorial@derbyshirelife.co.uk
Web site: http://www.derbyshirelife.co.uk
Freq: Monthly
Circ: 18106 Not Audited

Editor: Joy Hales
MAGAZINE
Regional General Interest

Des Pardes Weekly 982581
Editorial: 8 The Crescent, Southall, London UB1 1BE **Tel:** 44 02085 711127
Email: despardesuk@btconnect.com
Web site: www.despardesweekly.co.uk
Freq: Weekly
Circ: 34000 Not Audited
Editor: G.S Virk
MAGAZINE
Asia

Descent - The Magazine of Underground Exploration
981904
Editorial: PO Box 100, Abergavenny NP7 9WY **Tel:** 44 01873 737707
Email: descent@wildplaces.co.uk
Web site: http://www.wildplaces.co.uk
Freq: Bi-Monthly Not Audited
Editor: Chris Howes
Profile: Magazine that covers the sport of cave and mine exploration. Includes equipment and book reviews, news, competitions and articles on underground structures.
Ad Rate: Full Page Mono £605.00
Ad Rate: Full Page Colour £1045.00
MAGAZINE
Outdoor Recreation

The Descrier 998235
Editorial: 284a Battersea Park Road, London SW11 3BT **Tel:** 44 02032 396243
Email: editor@descrier.co.uk
Web site: www.descrier.co.uk
Freq: Daily
Circ: 14592 Cision Digital Reach
Editor: Tim Dickinson
MAGAZINE (ONLINE)
Consumer Affairs, International News, Politics

DesiBlitz 998139
Editorial: iCentrium, 6 Holt Street, Birmingham B7 4PB **Tel:** 44 01212 855288
Email: editor@desiblitz.com
Web site: http://www.desiblitz.com/
Freq: Daily
Circ: 160834 Cision Digital Reach
MAGAZINE (ONLINE)
Asia

Design Et Al 984422
Editorial: Watergate House, Watergate Street, Chester CH1 2LF
Email: editorial@design-et-al.co.uk
Web site: http://www.design-et-al.co.uk
Freq: Monthly
Circ: 40000 Not Audited
Editor: Joanne Beedles
Profile: Magazine covering all aspects of interior design including the latest looks, trends and forecasts from around the world. Aimed at interior designers, architects and high end, discerning consumers who want to gain real inspiration and direction.Digital images preferred.
Ad Rate: Full Page Colour £2300.00
MAGAZINE
Do-It-Yourself (DIY)

Design Talks 985706
Editorial: 2 Aldridge Road Villas, London W11 1BP
Web site: http://www.d-talks.com/
Freq: Daily
Circ: 7818 Cision Digital Reach
MAGAZINE (ONLINE)
Architecture & Design, Automotive, Engineering, Graphic Design

Designing 981521
Editorial: 16 Wellesbourne House, Walton Road, Wellesbourne, Warwick CV35 9JB
Tel: 44 01789 470007
Email: info@data.org.uk
Web site: www.data.org.uk
Freq: 3 Times/Year Not Audited

Profile: Publication covering all areas of design technology education at primary, secondary undergraduate and postgraduate levels.
Ad Rate: Full Page Colour £1100.00
MAGAZINE
Education, Preschool, Schools & Institutions, Students

Designmynight.com 986457
Editorial: Ground Floor PG03, 23-28 Penn Street, London N1 5DL
Email: marketing@designmynight.com
Web site: www.designmynight.com
Freq: Daily
Circ: 644017 Cision Digital Reach
MAGAZINE (ONLINE)
Bars, Clubs & Pubs, Comedy, Entertainment, Local Entertainment Guides, Movies & Video, Restaurant Reviews

Despoke 900240
Editorial: Media 10 Limited, Crown House, 151 High Road, London IG10 4LF
Email: editor@despoke.com
Web site: www.despoke.com
Freq: Daily
Circ: 4630 Cision Digital Reach
MAGAZINE (ONLINE)
Architecture & Design, Do-It-Yourself (DIY), Gardening, Home, Property Management & Maintenance, Real Estate

Destination Cowes 984229
Tel: 44 01983 521555
Email: info@visitwight.org
Web site: https://www.visitisleofwight.co.uk/cowes
Freq: Daily
Circ: 6744 Cision Digital Reach
MAGAZINE (ONLINE)
Boating & Yachting

Destination UK 983866
Editorial: 47 Church Street, Barnsley, Barnsley S70 2AS **Tel:** 44 01226 734639
Email: ce@scriptmedia.co.uk
Web site: www.destination.uk.com
Freq: Quarterly
Circ: 10000 Not Audited
Editor: Christina Eccles
Profile: Magazine promoting the UK travel and tourism industry covering the latest news and information, attractions across England, Wales and Scotland, in-depth features exploring special areas of interest, market trends and growth opportunities. Aimed at travel trade professionals in Britain and abroad including group travel organisers, corporate travel specialists, independent travel agents, tour agents, coach tour companies, Internet travel companies and organisers of domestic travel and tourism.
Ad Rate: Full Page Colour £1850.00
MAGAZINE
Travel

Destination Weddings & Honeymoons Abroad 988488
Editorial: Warwick House, 65/66 Queen Street, London EC4R 1EB
Tel: 44 02072 362515
Email: info@dwha.co.uk
Web site: www.dwha.co.uk
Freq: Bi-Monthly Not Audited
MAGAZINE
Travel, Weddings

Destinos 1062061
Tel: 44 59133 419790
Email: revista@sugrey.com
Web site: http://www.destinos.com.bo
Freq: Monthly Not Audited
MAGAZINE
Airline Inflight, Alternative Medicine, Antiques/Collectibles, Art, Arts, Auto Aftermarket, Computers, Cooking & Baking, Data Management, Disability

Development and Learning in Organizations 980990
Editorial: Howard House, Wagon Lane, Bingley BD16 1WA **Tel:** 44 01274 777700
Web site: www.emeraldinsight.com/journal/dlo
Freq: Bi-Monthly Not Audited
Profile: Independent journal covering news and views on development and learning.
MAGAZINE
News & Current Affairs

Development News 995814
Editorial: 38 Heddon Court Avenue, Cockfosters, London EN4 9NE
Tel: 44 02087 332613
Email: info@amateur-fa.com
Web site: www.amateur-fa.com
Freq: Quarterly
Circ: 8231 Cision Digital Reach
Editor: Jeff Salmon
MAGAZINE (ONLINE)
Soccer

Device Management Forum 1101206
Tel: 44 02037 147023
Email: news@devicemanagement.org
Web site: http://www.devicemanagement.org/
Freq: Daily
Circ: 6237 Cision Digital Reach
MAGAZINE (ONLINE)
Computers, Electronics, Mobile Communications, Software

Devizes Messenger 995812
Editorial: Town Hall, St Johns Street, Devizes, Devizes SN10 1BN
Tel: 44 01380 722160
Email: enquiry@devizes-tc.gov.uk
Web site: http://www.devizes-tc.gov.uk
Freq: Quarterly
Circ: 5500 Not Audited
Editor: Elanor Oddy
MAGAZINE
Regional General Interest

Devon Life 982486
Editorial: Newberry House, Fair Oak Close, Exeter Airport Business Park, Clyst Honiton, Exeter EX5 2UL **Tel:** 44 01392 888413
Email: devonlife@archant.co.uk
Web site: www.devonlife.co.uk
Freq: Monthly
Circ: 18000 Not Audited
Editor: Carol Burns
Profile: Magazine containing features on the Devon area. Contains coverage of regional places, people, history and culture. Includes restaurant reviews, social scene, picture pages on parties and events.
Ad Rate: Full Page Colour £1368.00
MAGAZINE
Regional General Interest

The Devon week 999224
Editorial: 19 Gloucester Road, Newton Abbot, Newton Abbot TQ12 1AY
Tel: 44 01626 202202
Email: info@newsandmediarepublic.org
Web site: http://thedevonweek.newsandmediarepublic.org/
Freq: Daily
Circ: 38 Cision Digital Reach
Editor: Lee Morgan
MAGAZINE (ONLINE)
Regional

Devonshire Magazine 998304
Editorial: Beech Royd, 6 Bennetts Hill, Sidmouth EX10 9XH **Tel:** 44 01395 513383
Email: letterbox@devonshiremagazine.co.uk
Web site: www.devonshiremagazine.co.uk
Freq: Bi-Monthly
Circ: 20200 Not Audited
Editor: Nigel Jones
MAGAZINE
Regional General Interest

Dexerto 995082
Web site: www.dexerto.com
Freq: Daily

Circ: 158742 Cision Digital Reach
MAGAZINE (ONLINE)
Computer & Video Games

Diabetes Wellness News 985188
Editorial: Diabetes Research & Wellness Foundation, The Roundhouse, Northney Marina, Hayling Island, Hayling Island PO11 0NH **Tel:** 44 02392 637808
Email: newsletter@drwf.org.uk
Web site: www.drwf.org.uk
Freq: Monthly
Circ: 11000 Not Audited
Profile: Newsletter of the Diabetes Wellness Network containing news of recent advancements in treatment, personal stories and practical advice on all aspects of life with diabetes, encouraging good self-management and helping readers improve their blood glucose control. Sent to members of the Network and diabetes clinics across the country.
MAGAZINE
Diabetes, Patient Support

Diabetes.co.uk 1097882
Editorial: Technology House, Sir William Lyons Road, University of Warwick Science Park, Coventry CV4 7EZ
Tel: 44 02476 712201
Email: info@diabetes.co.uk
Web site: http://www.diabetes.co.uk/
Freq: Daily
Circ: 996945 Cision Digital Reach
Profile: Website covering medical health. Diabetes.co.uk discusses anything from information on diabetes and exercise to health education. As well as providing a wealth of diabetes information, Diabetes.co.uk's primary goal is to reduce suffering in the diabetes community.
MAGAZINE (ONLINE)
Diabetes, Health & Medicine

Diagnostic Engineering CEASED 981032
Editorial: Project Building, 581A Leeds Road, Outwood, Wakefield, Wakefield WF1 2JL
Web site: www.diagnosticengineers.org
Freq: Quarterly
Circ: 1300 Not Audited
Profile: Journal covering problem solving and fault finding within the engineering world.
Ad Rate: Full Page Mono £250.00
Ad Rate: Full Page Colour £335.00
MAGAZINE
Engineering

Diagnostic Histopathology 995880
Editorial: The Boulevard, Langford Lane, Kidlington OX5 1GB **Tel:** 44 01865 843154
Email: journals@medicinepublishing.co.uk
Web site: www.diagnostichistopathology.co.uk
Freq: Monthly
Circ: 1394 Not Audited
MAGAZINE
Diagnostic Imaging, Medicine

DIARY directory 983567
Editorial: 79A York Street, Marylebone, London W1H 1QQ **Tel:** 44 02077 247770
Email: di@diaryd.com
Web site: www.diarydirectory.com
Freq: Daily
Circ: 152476 Cision Digital Reach
Editor: Holly Buckley
Profile: Website covering all PR and media moves within the fashion, beauty, homes and interiors industries. Aimed at PR companies and the press.
MAGAZINE (ONLINE)
Advertising Industry, Branding, Broadcasting, Cosmetics, Fashion, Graphic Design, Hair, Marketing, Media & Communications, Photography

DICE 1104002
Editorial: The Brew 203, 116 Commercial St, London E1 6NF
Email: press@dice.fm
Web site: http://blog.dice.fm

Consumer Magazines

Freq: Daily
Circ: 35811 Cision Digital Reach
MAGAZINE (ONLINE)
Country, Folk, Bluegrass, Dance Music,
Jazz & Blues, Pop Music, Rap & Hip Hop,
Rock Music

Didsbury Magazine   989984
Editorial: The Old Bank, 99 Palatine Road,
Didsbury, Manchester M20 3JQ
Tel: 44 01614 452883
Email: info@salutions.co.uk
Web site: http://www.didsburymagazine.
com/
Freq: Bi-Monthly
Circ: 20000 Not Audited
Profile: Magazine covering local news and
events as well as lifestyle, fashion, motors,
health, property, gardening, food and drink,
travel, family and education. Aimed at
residents and businesses in Didsbury.
Ad Rate: Full Page Colour £1495.00
MAGAZINE
Regional General Interest

Didsbury Magazine   1075487
Editorial: 5 The Stable, Manchester M20
5PG **Tel:** 44 01614 452883
Email: info@salutions.co.uk
Web site: http://www.didsburymagazine.
com/
Freq: Bi-Monthly
Circ: 6000 Not Audited
Profile: Magazine covering local news and
events as well as lifestyle, fashion, motors,
health, property, gardening, food and drink,
travel, family and education. Aimed at
residents and businesses in Didsbury.
Ad Rate: Full Page Colour £1495.00
MAGAZINE
Regional General Interest

Diecast Collector   981915
Editorial: The Maltings, West Street, Bourne,
Bourne PE10 9PH **Tel:** 44 01778 391000
Email: diecastletters@warnersgroup.co.uk
Web site: www.collectors-club-of-great-
britain.co.uk/Diecast-Collecting/_ch26
Freq: Monthly
Circ: 16500 Not Audited
Editor: Tim Morgan
Profile: Magazine featuring collectors and
their diecast models and vehicle collections.
Ad Rate: Full Page Mono £380.00
Ad Rate: Full Page Colour £580.00
MAGAZINE
Antiques/Collectibles

DieselCar   983298
Editorial: 40 Nevendon Road, Basildon,
Basildon SS13 1AW **Tel:** 44 01268 288515
Email: editorial@dieselcar.com
Web site: www.dieselcarmagazine.co.uk
Freq: Monthly
Circ: 43194 Not Audited
Profile: Magazine covering information
about diesel and alternative vehicles. Aimed
at people interested in cars.
MAGAZINE
Antique & Collectible Cars, Automakers,
Automotive, Driving, Motorcycles, Off-
road & 4-Wheel Drive Vehicles, Trucks &
SUVs

Dietetics Today   998815
Editorial: 5th Floor, Charles House, 148/9
Great Charles Street Queensway,
Birmingham B3 3HT **Tel:** 44 01212 008080
Email: editor@bda.uk.com
Web site: https://www.bda.uk.com/dt/home
Freq: Monthly
Circ: 8000 Not Audited
MAGAZINE
Diabetes, Nutrition

diffordsguide.com   998541
Editorial: 1 Futura House, 169 Grange Road,
London SE1 3BN **Tel:** 44 02072 312550
Email: info@diffordsguide.com
Web site: www.diffordsguide.com
Freq: Daily
Circ: 138230 Cision Digital Reach
MAGAZINE (ONLINE)
Alcohol & Spirits, Bars, Clubs & Pubs

Dig BMX Magazine   982198
Email: info@digbmx.com
Web site: http://digbmx.com/
Freq: Daily
Circ: 42604 Cision Digital Reach
Profile: Magazine featuring new products,
interviews with BMX riders, BMX lifestyle
and coverage of events worldwide.
MAGAZINE (ONLINE)
Bicycles

digest   987002
Email: digest@digestmag.com
Web site: http://digestmag.com/
Freq: Monthly
Circ: 686 Cision Digital Reach
MAGAZINE (ONLINE)
Cooking & Baking, Food, Grocery Stores,
Organic Food, Restaurant Reviews,
Vegetarianism & Veganism

digiguide.tv   994677
Editorial: EBS, 16B Whitehorse Street,
Baldock, Baldock SG7 6QN
Tel: 44 01462 492227
Email: press@digiguide.tv
Web site: https://digiguide.tv/
Freq: Daily
Circ: 136241 Cision Digital Reach
Editor: Barry Swain
MAGAZINE (ONLINE)
Broadcasting, Entertainment, Local
Entertainment Guides

diginomica   987734
Web site: www.diginomica.com
Freq: Daily
Circ: 162370 Cision Digital Reach
Profile: Blog covering digital enterprise.
diginomica blog discusses anything from
analysis of the digital landscape and digital
enterprise transformation to case studies of
digital enterprise in various organisations.
The blog has an archive dating back to
March 2013. The outlet offers RSS (Really
Simple Syndication).
MAGAZINE (ONLINE)
News & Current Affairs

Digital Arts   981310
Editorial: 7th Floor, Clifton House, 101
Euston Road, London NW1 2RA
Tel: 44 02077 562800
Email: digitalartsnews@idg.co.uk
Web site: www.digitalartsonline.co.uk
Freq: Daily
Circ: 1843447 Cision Digital Reach
Editor: Neil Bennett
Profile: Online magazine covering the latest
technologies and techniques in graphic arts,
design and page layout. Includes features on
multimedia, CD-ROM, digital video, 3D
modelling, animation and image editing.
Every issue comes with a CD with the latest
software and downloads, demos, stock
photos and fonts.
MAGAZINE (ONLINE)
Apple, Art, Cameras, Graphic Design,
Movies & Video, Software, Visual Arts

Digital Camera   982026
Editorial: Quay House, The Ambury, Bath
BA1 1UA **Tel:** 44 01225 442244
Email: digitalcamera@futurenet.com
Web site: www.digitalcameraworld.com
Freq: Monthly
Circ: 31867 Not Audited
Editor: Ben Brain
MAGAZINE
Cameras, Photography

Digital FilmMaker   985973
Editorial: Select Publisher Services Ltd, PO
Box 6337, Bournemouth, Bournemouth BH1
9EH **Tel:** 44 01202 586848
Email: robclymo@digpe.com
Web site: dfmmag.com
Freq: Monthly
Circ: 10442 Cision Digital Reach
Editor: Rob Clymo
MAGAZINE (ONLINE)
Cameras, Movies & Video, Photography

The Digital Fix   987455
Editorial: 11 Ffordd Glas Y Dorlan, Llantwit
Fardre, Pontypridd, Church Village CF38
2BZ
Email: info@thedigitalfix.com
Web site: www.thedigitalfix.com
Freq: Daily
Circ: 120921 Cision Digital Reach
Editor: Douglas Baptie
Profile: Website covering entertainment.
thedigitalfix website shares the latest news
and information within the entertainment
industry. The site discusses anything from
music and home cinema to TV and gaming.
MAGAZINE (ONLINE)
Comedy, Computer & Video Games,
Entertainment, Local Entertainment
Guides, Movies & Video, Music

Digital Investigation   998526
Editorial: 125 London Wall, London EC2Y
5AS **Tel:** 44 02074 244200
Email: editorialdi@elsevier.com
Web site: www.elsevier.com/wps/find/
journaldescription.cws_home/702130/
description#description
Freq: Quarterly Not Audited
MAGAZINE
Electronics

Digital Marketing Magazine
988599
Tel: 44 08455 000327
Email: editor@digitalmarketingmagazine.co.
uk
Web site: http://digitalmarketingmagazine.
co.uk
Freq: Daily
Circ: 166932 Cision Digital Reach
Editor: Jonathan Davies
MAGAZINE (ONLINE)
Auto Aftermarket, Computers, Data
Management, Electronics, Government
Technology, Industry, Internet, Mobile
Communications, Security & Security
Systems, Software

Digital Media Newsletter   998680
Editorial: Informa Business Intelligence,
Christchurch Court, 10-15 Newgate Street,
London EC1A 7AZ **Tel:** 44 02070 174994
Email: enquiries@ovum.com
Web site: www.ovum.com
Freq: Bi-Weekly
Circ: 50728 Cision Digital Reach
MAGAZINE (ONLINE)
Computers, Internet

Digital Photographer   982027
Editorial: Richmond House, 33 Richmond
Hill, Bournemouth BH2 6EQ
Tel: 44 01202 586200
Email: team@dphotographer.co.uk
Web site: www.dphotographer.co.uk
Freq: Monthly
Circ: 14511 Not Audited
Profile: Magazine containing information on
contemporary photography, buyers guide,
tips and advice on digital imaging
techniques.
Ad Rate: Full Page Colour £2094.00
MAGAZINE
Cameras, Photography

Digital Photography Now   981630
Editorial: Apsley Mills Cottage, London
Road, London HP3 9RL
Tel: 44 01442 242960
Email: news@dpnow.com
Web site: www.dpnow.com
Freq: Daily
Circ: 8754 Cision Digital Reach
Profile: Website covering all aspects of
digital photography including cameras,
printers, scanners, software and
accessories.
MAGAZINE (ONLINE)
Cameras, Photography

Digital Quadrant   997691
Editorial: 22 Hill St, St Helier, St. Helier JE2
4UA
Email: editor@dqmagazine.com
Web site: www.dqmagazine.com

Freq: Daily
Circ: 1620 Cision Digital Reach
Editor: Kirsten Morel
MAGAZINE (ONLINE)
Computers, Data Management,
Electronics, Government Technology,
Industry, Internet, Mobile
Communications, Software

Digital Ship   981339
Editorial: 2nd Floor, 2- 5 Benjamin Street,
London EC1M 5QL **Tel:** 44 02072 532700
Web site: www.thedigitalship.com
Freq: Bi-Monthly
Circ: 2800 Not Audited
Profile: Digital Ship magazine provides the
latest information about maritime satellite
communications technology, software
systems, navigation technology, computer
networks, data management and TMSA.
Ad Rate: Full Page Colour £4450.00
MAGAZINE
Marine & Boat Trade

Digital SLR Photography   983856
Editorial: Digital SLR Photography, PO BOX
1327, Stamford PE9 2PT
Tel: 44 02079 076000
Email: enquiries@dslrphotomag.co.uk
Web site: www.digitalslrphoto.com
Freq: Monthly
Circ: 11776 Not Audited
Editor: Daniel Lezano
Profile: Magazine with tests and reviews of
digital SLR equipment, technique guides,
expert advice and interviews with top-end,
professional photographers. Each issue aims
to inform, entertain and educate readers,
through a blend of technique articles,
inspirational images, news and authoritative
reviews of DSLRs and accessories. It's the
magazine written for photographers, by
photographers, with an expert advice, share
techniques from a community of readers all
passionate about improving their SLR skills.
The outlet offers RSS feed: http://www.
digitalslrphoto.com/index.rss.Aimed at high
end enthusiast, semi-pro and professional
photographers.
Ad Rate: Full Page Mono £2750.00
Ad Rate: Full Page Colour £2500.00
MAGAZINE
Cameras, Photography

Digital Spy   986123
Editorial: 72 Broadwick Street, London W1F
0DQ **Tel:** 44 02073 123800
Email: newsdesk@digitalspy.co.uk
Web site: http://www.digitalspy.com/
Freq: Daily
Circ: 3148930 Cision Digital Reach
Profile: Website covering digital news.
Digital Spy discusses anything from news
and features in entertainment areas such as
showbiz, movies, music and television.
MAGAZINE (ONLINE)
Apple, Audio Video Trade, Broadcasting,
Cameras, Celebrities, Comedy, Computer
& Video Games, Computers, Consumer
Electronics, Dance Music

Digital Textile   983555
Editorial: West One, 114 Wellington Street,
Leeds LS1 1BA **Tel:** 44 01133 884882
Email: info@wtin.com
Web site: http://www.wtin.com/e-store/
digital-textile/
Freq: Bi-Monthly
Circ: 6873 Not Audited
Profile: Magazine dedicated wholly to textile
applications in the rapidly developing field of
digital printing.
Ad Rate: Full Page Colour £2700.00
MAGAZINE
Fashion

Digital TV Europe   981619
Editorial: Maple House, 149 Tottenham
Court Road, London W1T 7AD
Tel: 44 02070 175000
Email: dtve@informa.com
Web site: www.digitaltveurope.net
Freq: Bi-Monthly Not Audited
Editor: Stuart Thomson
Profile: Magazine covering the international
business of multi-channel television

distribution. Aimed at TV operators, equipment manufacturers, distributors, network providers, consultants, agencies and the government. All press materials should be sent to the editor. The magazine was first published in 1983. Previous title: Cable & Satellite Europe; Satellite Europe Average Pages per Issue: 60PR Accepted in: English
Ad Rate: Full Page Colour £2675.00
MAGAZINE
Electronics, Internet

Digital Warble
998259
Editorial: PO BOX 10003, Loughborough LE11 9GT
Email: info@digitalwarble.com
Web site: digitalwarble.com
Freq: Daily
Circ: 25678 Cision Digital Reach
MAGAZINE (ONLINE)
Audio Video Trade, Broadcasting, Cameras, Computer & Video Games, Consumer Electronics, Dance Music, Electronics, Fashion, Fitness & Exercise, Men's Interests

digiupdates
1061774
Web site: http://digiupdates.com
Freq: Daily
Circ: 2309 Cision Digital Reach
MAGAZINE (ONLINE)
Auto Aftermarket, Computers, Data Management, Electronics, Government Technology, Industry, Internet, Mobile Communications, Security & Security Systems, Software

Dine Birmingham
1054045
Editorial: Moseley Exchange, 149 - 153 Alcester Road, Birmingham B13 8JP
Email: hello@dinebirmingham.co.uk
Web site: www.dinebirmingham.co.uk/
Freq: Daily
Circ: 11802 Cision Digital Reach
Editor: Ahmed Ahmed
MAGAZINE (ONLINE)
Restaurant Reviews

dinky guide
1105386
Tel: 44 08447 722214
Email: info@codexinternational.com
Web site: http://www.dinkyguide.com/
Freq: Daily
Circ: 10710 Cision Digital Reach
MAGAZINE (ONLINE)
Airline Inflight, Railroad, Travel

Diplomat
982128
Editorial: PO Box 71273, London SW11 9GX
Tel: 44 02076 521420
Email: info@diplomatmagazine.com
Web site: http://www.diplomatmagazine.com/
Freq: Monthly
Circ: 8000 Not Audited
Editor: Venetia Van Kuffeler
Profile: Magazine covering international current affairs, consumer issues, property, motoring, education, books, eating out, art, retail and other social activities.
Ad Rate: Full Page Colour £3000.00
MAGAZINE
International News, Politics, Social Issues

Direct Commerce
981623
Editorial: 31 Belmont Road, Ilfracombe, Ilfracombe EX34 8DR **Tel:** 44 01271 866112
Web site: www.directcommerce.biz
Freq: Bi-Monthly
Circ: 5000 Not Audited
Profile: Merchandising publication for offline and online cataloguers and multichannel retailers in the U.K.
Ad Rate: Full Page Colour £1950.00
MAGAZINE
Books, Cosmetics, Fashion, Food, Gardening, Hair, Internet, Office Supplies, Retail, Retail Management

director-e
995916
Editorial: South House 3A, Suite 4, Bond Estate, Bond Avenue, Bletchley, Milton Keynes MK1 1SW **Tel:** 44 01908 658890

Email: info@director-e.com
Web site: www.director-e.com
Freq: Bi-Monthly
Circ: 8000 Not Audited
MAGAZINE
Fashion

Dirt Bike Rider
982651
Editorial: 41 Northgate, White Lund Industrial Estate, Morecambe, Morecambe LA3 3PA **Tel:** 44 01524 385950
Web site: www.dirtbikerider.com
Freq: Monthly
Circ: 19000 Not Audited
Editor: Anthony Sutton
Profile: Website of Dirt Bike Rider magazine giving an overview of the off-road bike scene. Provides latest news and stories on motocross, supercross and the rest of the off-road motorcycle world. Includes interviews with people of the off-road world and authoritative tests of the latest machines. Does not disclose circulation figures. Aimed at motorcyclists and fans of off-road motorcycling.
MAGAZINE
Motorcycles

Dirt Mountainbike Magazine
982199
Editorial: Wyastone Business Park, Monmouth, Monmouth NP25 3SR
Web site: www.dirtmag.co.uk
Freq: Monthly
Circ: 38000 Not Audited
Editor: Mike Rose
Profile: Magazine covering downhill mountain bike racing, BSX, trails, free riding and off road biking including bike tests, accessories, news and reports of the sport. Aimed at those interested in mountain biking, dual slalom racing, trials riding, dirt bike riding, motocross and BMX.
Ad Rate: Full Page Colour £2000.00
MAGAZINE
Bicycles

Disability Arts Online
996847
Editorial: 9 Jew Street, Brighton BN1 1UT
Tel: 44 07411 824458
Email: editor@disabilityartsonline.org.uk
Web site: www.disabilityartsonline.org.uk/
Freq: Daily
Circ: 6254 Cision Digital Reach
Editor: Colin Hambrook
MAGAZINE (ONLINE)
Disability, Patient Support

Disability Horizons
988382
Email: editor@disabilityhorizons.com
Web site: http://disabilityhorizons.com/
Freq: Daily
Circ: 14767 Cision Digital Reach
Profile: Website offering 'a 21st century view of disability' and covering disabled lifestyle and resources on how to make a disabled lifestyle more active. The website covers anything from entertainment, news, politics, relationships, sport, tech, travel and work.
MAGAZINE (ONLINE)
Disability

Disability News Service
985951
Tel: 44 01926 930519
Email: info@disabilitynewsservice.com
Web site: www.disabilitynewsservice.com
Freq: Daily
Circ: 19638 Cision Digital Reach
Profile: Website covering health news. The Disability News Service site discusses disability news and posts all news content every 3 months. This is an subscription based services and has over 10 subscribers.
MAGAZINE (ONLINE)
Disability

Disability Review Magazine
995719
Editorial: 184 Main Road, Biggin Hill, Westerham, London TN16 3BB
Tel: 44 01959 543650
Web site: http://www.disabilityreviewmag.com

Freq: Semi-Annual
Circ: 150000 Not Audited
MAGAZINE
Disability

Discerning Gent
1053495
Email: amit@discerninggent.com
Web site: www.discerninggent.com
Freq: Daily
Circ: 10535 Cision Digital Reach
MAGAZINE (ONLINE)
Fashion, Luxury Goods, Men's Interests

Discover
998173
Editorial: Quay House, The Ambury, Bath BA1 1UA **Tel:** 44 01225 442244
Web site: www.travelsphere.co.uk
Freq: 3 Times/Year
Circ: 175000 Not Audited
MAGAZINE
Travel

Discover & Escape
987383
Editorial: 5, 17 Sinclair Road, Kensington, London W14 0NS
Email: hello@discoverandescape.com
Web site: www.discoverandescape.com
Freq: Daily
Circ: 521 Cision Digital Reach
Profile: Website covering luxury lifestyle. DISCOVER & ESCAPE covers luxury travel, fashion, style, beauty, restaurants and bars.
MAGAZINE (ONLINE)
Cosmetics, Fashion, Hair, Luxury Goods, Travel

Discover Animals
997857
Editorial: 6 Wellington Square, Hastings TN34 1PB **Tel:** 44 01424 572081
Email: abbe@discoveranimals.co.uk
Web site: www.discoveranimals.co.uk
Freq: Daily
Circ: 13215 Cision Digital Reach
MAGAZINE (ONLINE)
Nature & Wildlife, Travel

Discover Benelux
1060204
Editorial: 15B Bell Yard Mews, Bermondsey Street, London SE1 3TY
Tel: 44 08709 330423
Email: info@discoverbenelux.com
Web site: www.discoverbenelux.com
Freq: Monthly
Circ: 15430 Not Audited
Editor: Anna Villeleger
MAGAZINE
Europe, Travel

Discover Britain
981928
Editorial: Jubilee House, 2 Jubilee Place, London SW3 3TQ **Tel:** 44 02073 493700
Email: editorial@discoverbritainmag.com
Web site: www.discoverbritainmag.com
Circ: 50000 Not Audited
Profile: Magazine that contains illustrated features about British life, history, places to visit and the countryside. Aimed at those over 30 years old.
Ad Rate: Full Page Colour £2800.00
MAGAZINE
History, Travel

Discover Germany, Switzerland & Austria
996159
Editorial: 15B Bell Yard Mews, Bermondsey Street, London SE1 3TY
Tel: 44 08709 330423
Email: info@discovergermany.com
Web site: www.discovergermany.com
Freq: Bi-Monthly Not Audited
Editor: Nane Steinhoff
MAGAZINE
Europe

Discover Your Ancestors
1070232
Email: editor@discoveryourancestors.co.uk
Web site: www.discoveryourancestors.co.uk/
Freq: Annual

Editor: Andrew Chapman
MAGAZINE
News & Current Affairs

Discovering March
995062
Editorial: Discovering Magazines, Benwick Road Industrial Estate, Benwick Road, Whittlesey PE7 2I ID **Tel:** 44 01778 421427
Email: editor.march@discoveringmagazines.co.uk
Web site: http://www.discoveringmagazines.co.uk/march/index.html
Freq: Monthly
Circ: 9500 Not Audited
Editor: Jack Harris
MAGAZINE
Regional General Interest

Disegno
986595
Editorial: 7 Ability Plaza, Arbutus Street, London E8 4DT **Tel:** 44 02072 491155
Email: editorial@disegnomagazine.com
Web site: www.disegnodaily.com
Freq: Semi-Annual
Circ: 30000 Not Audited
MAGAZINE
Architecture & Design, Fashion, Graphic Design

Disney and Me - CEASED 2017
982451
Editorial: 1st Floor, The Yellow Building, 1 Nicholas Road, London W8 6SA
Web site: https://www.egmont.co.uk/magazines/disney/
Freq: Monthly
Circ: 16536 Not Audited
MAGAZINE
Elementary School, Preschool, Teen/ Young Adult

Disney Frozen
996113
Editorial: 1st Floor, The Yellow Building, 1 Nicholas Road, London W11 4AN
Tel: 44 02032 200400
Email: info@egmont.co.uk
Web site: http://www.egmont.co.uk/magazines/disney-frozen/
Freq: Monthly
Circ: 82010 Not Audited
MAGAZINE
Teen/Young Adult, Trading Cards & Comics

Disney Presents
997604
Editorial: Brockbourne House, 77 Mount Ephraim, Tunbridge Wells, Tunbridge Wells TN4 8BS **Tel:** 44 01892 500100
Web site: http://www.paninicomics.co.uk/web/guest/catalogues/collection_detail?id=42358
Freq: Monthly
Circ: 55000 Not Audited
MAGAZINE
Trading Cards & Comics

Disney Princess Palace Pets
1059417
Editorial: 1st Floor, The Yellow Building, 1 Nicholas Road, London W8 6SA
Tel: 44 02032 200400
Email: info@euk.egmont.co.uk
Web site: http://www.egmont.co.uk/magazines/disney-palace-pets/
Freq: Bi-Weekly
Circ: 19009 Not Audited
MAGAZINE
Nature & Wildlife, Teen/Young Adult

Disney Stars (UK)
987817
Editorial: 1st Floor, The Yellow Building, 1 Nicholas Road, London
Tel: 44 02032 200400
Web site: www.egmont.co.uk/magazines/disney-stars/
Freq: Weekly
Circ: 31535 Not Audited
Editor: Laura Quinn
MAGAZINE
Trading Cards & Comics

Consumer Magazines

DISORDER UK 995786
Editorial: WeWork London, 1 Primrose Street, London EC2A 2EX
Web site: www.disordermagazine.com
Freq: Bi-Monthly
Circ: 65000 Not Audited
MAGAZINE
Men's Interests, Women's Interests

DISRUPTIVE magazine 1052536
Web site: www.disruptivemagazine.com
Freq: Monthly
MAGAZINE
News & Current Affairs

DIVA 982390
Editorial: Unit 32, Spectrum House, 32-34 Gordon House Road, London NW5 1LP
Tel: 44 02072 679602
Web site: www.divamag.co.uk
Freq: Monthly
Circ: 55640 Not Audited
Profile: Magazine focussing on lesbians and bisexual women's interest including features on lifestyle, fashion, current affairs, entertainment, travel, music, cinema, video, books, club culture, health, fitness, beauty, activism, home and motoring. First published in 1994, the publication has an average of 116 pages per issue. Aimed at lesbians and bisexual women.
Ad Rate: Full Page Colour £1700.00
MAGAZINE
LGBT

DivaScribe Magazine 997005
Editorial: Suite 107, 23 Fernshaw Road, Chelsea, London SW10 0TG
Email: editorialsandenquiries@divascribe.com
Web site: www.divascribe.com
Freq: Quarterly
Circ: 40000 Not Audited
MAGAZINE
Women's Interests

Dive 982299
Editorial: 3.2, Q West, Great West Road, London TW8 0GP Tel: 44 02083 328410
Email: info@dive.uk.com
Web site: www.divemagazine.co.uk
Freq: Daily
Circ: 25443 Cision Digital Reach
Editor: Marion Kutter
MAGAZINE (ONLINE)
Nature & Wildlife, Swimming/Watersports

Diver 982300
Editorial: Suite B, 74 Oldfield Road, London TW12 2HR Tel: 44 02089 418152
Email: enquiries@divermag.co.uk
Web site: www.divernet.com
Freq: Monthly
Circ: 25000 Not Audited
Editor: Steve Weinman
Profile: Magazine covering all aspects of leisure diving. Includes destinations, reefs and wrecks, equipment reviews, marine biology, archaeology, boats, technical diving, conservation, training and safety. Read by sport diving enthusiasts and professionals, marine biologists, underwater archaeologists, conservationists and holiday divers.
Ad Rate: Full Page Colour £1860.00
MAGAZINE
Swimming/Watersports

DIY 987265
Editorial: 2nd Floor, Unit 23, Tileyard Studios, Tileyard Road, London N7 9AH
Email: info@diymag.com
Web site: www.diymag.com/magazine
Freq: Monthly
Circ: 36801 Not Audited
Profile: Magazine covering music and lifestyle.
MAGAZINE
Dance Music, Pop Music, Rap & Hip Hop, Rock Music

DJ Mag 998532
Editorial: 3A Chapel Market, London N19EZ
Tel: 44 02030 588855

Web site: www.djmag.com
Freq: Monthly
Circ: 35000 Not Audited
Editor: Carl Loben
MAGAZINE
Dance Music

DK Travel 1057337
Editorial: The Travel DK Team - DK Limited, 80 Strand, London WC2R 0RL
Tel: 44 02070 103000
Email: editor@traveldk.com
Web site: http://www.traveldk.com/
Freq: Daily
Circ: 33351 Cision Digital Reach
MAGAZINE (ONLINE)
Travel

dluxe BIRMINGHAM & SOLIHULL 986063
Editorial: A210 LCB Depot, 31 Rutland Street, Leicester LE1 1RE
Tel: 44 01162 533445
Email: info@sixtynine-ltd.co.uk
Web site: http://www.dluxe-magazine.co.uk
Freq: Quarterly
Circ: 10000 Not Audited
Profile: Regional lifestyle publication for Birmingham and Solihull. Covers local events, home, food & drink, motoring, shopping and travel.
MAGAZINE
Airline Inflight, Antique & Collectible Cars, Automakers, Beauty & Grooming, Celebrities, Cooking & Baking, Cosmetics, Do-It-Yourself (DIY), Fashion, Hair

dluxe LEICESTERSHIRE & RUTLAND 985700
Editorial: A210 LCB Depot, 31 Rutland Street, Leicester LE11RE
Tel: 44 01162 533445
Email: info@sixtynine-ltd.co.uk
Web site: http://www.dluxe-magazine.co.uk
Freq: Quarterly
Circ: 10000 Not Audited
MAGAZINE
Airline Inflight, Antique & Collectible Cars, Automakers, Beauty & Grooming, Celebrities, Cooking & Baking, Cosmetics, Do-It-Yourself (DIY), Fashion, Hair

DM Magazine 981632
Editorial: 35 Station Square, London BR5 1LZ Tel: 44 01689 616000
Web site: www.document-manager.com
Freq: Bi-Monthly
Circ: 13000 Not Audited
Editor: David Tyler
MAGAZINE
Data Management, Internet, Security & Security Systems

DMC World Magazine 998533
Editorial: PO Box 89, Slough, Burnham SL1 8NA Tel: 44 01628 667124
Email: info@dmcworld.com
Web site: www.dmcworld.net
Freq: Daily Not Audited
Editor: Dan Prince
MAGAZINE
Dance Music

do more 999416
Editorial: Venator House, 9 St. Stephen's Court, 15-17 St. Stephen's Road, Bournemouth BH2 6LA
Email: alice@domoremag.com
Web site: www.domoremag.com
Freq: Daily
Circ: 6839 Cision Digital Reach
MAGAZINE (ONLINE)
Bars, Clubs & Pubs, Comedy, Entertainment, Local Entertainment Guides, Movies & Video, Regional General Interest

Doc McStuffins (UK) 995525
Editorial: Brockbourne House, 77 Mount Ephraim, Tunbridge Wells, Tunbridge Wells TN4 8GN Tel: 44 01892 500100

Web site: http://www.paninicomics.com/
Freq: Monthly
Circ: 20641 Not Audited
MAGAZINE
Preschool, Teen/Young Adult, Trading Cards & Comics

Docrafts Creativity 984606
Tel: 44 01202 811000
Web site: www.docrafts.com
Freq: Monthly
Circ: 45000 Not Audited
Editor: Tina Piper
MAGAZINE
Crafts

Doctor Who Magazine 982464
Editorial: Brockbourne House, 77 Mount Ephraim, Tunbridge Wells, Tunbridge Wells TN4 8BS Tel: 44 01892 500100
Email: dwm@panini.co.uk
Web site: www.paninicomics.co.uk
Freq: Monthly
Circ: 21913 Not Audited
MAGAZINE
Elementary School, Preschool, Teen/Young Adult, Trading Cards & Comics

Doctors.net.uk 981652
Editorial: 20 Western Avenue, Milton Park, Abingdon, Didcot OX14 4SH
Tel: 44 01235 828400
Email: info@mess.doctors.org.uk
Web site: www.doctors.net.uk
Freq: Daily
Circ: 181265 Cision Digital Reach
Profile: Website covering health. The Doctors.net.uk discusses anything from internal medicine to Pharmaceutical and medical devices.
MAGAZINE (ONLINE)
Medicine

Dodo 1052699
Email: hello@dodomagazine.com
Web site: http://www.dodomagazine.com/
Freq: Semi-Annual Not Audited
MAGAZINE
Science, Science Fiction

Dods Monitoring UK 996655
Editorial: 21 Dartmouth Street, Westminster, London SW1H 9BP Tel: 44 02075 935500
Email: pressreleases@dods.co.uk
Web site: www.dodsinformation.com/product/uk-monitoring
Freq: Daily
Circ: 11893 Cision Digital Reach
Editor: Daisy Drury
MAGAZINE (ONLINE)
Politics

DOG 1101204
Web site: www.readdogmag.com
Freq: Semi-Annual Not Audited
MAGAZINE
Nature & Wildlife

Dog Friendly 999353
Editorial: Dog Friendly Ltd., PO Box 1202, Cambridge CB23 3WR
Tel: 44 01733 270089
Web site: www.dogfriendly.co.uk/dogfriendly-magazine/
Freq: Bi-Monthly
Circ: 7000 Not Audited
Editor: Gareth Salter
MAGAZINE
Nature & Wildlife

Dogs Monthly 982012
Editorial: The Old Print House, 62 The High Street, Surrey, London GU24 8AA
Tel: 44 01276 858880
Web site: http://www.dogsmonthly.co.uk
Freq: Monthly
Circ: 20000 Not Audited
Editor: Gill Shaw
Profile: Magazine aimed at dog owners, featuring articles on physical and mental canine health care, training, equipment, products, ownership, training, lifestyles,

general care, activities, breeding and feeding.
Ad Rate: Full Page Colour £1020.00
MAGAZINE
Nature & Wildlife

Dogs Today 982013
Editorial: The Old Print House, 62 The High Street, Chobham, London GU24 8AA
Tel: 44 01276 858880
Email: editorial@dogstodaymagazine.co.uk
Web site: www.dogstodaymagazine.co.uk
Freq: Monthly
Circ: 35000 Not Audited
Editor: Beverley Cuddy
Profile: Magazine containing information, news, features and advice on choosing the correct breed of dog. Aimed at dog lovers.
Ad Rate: Full Page Colour £1925.00
MAGAZINE
Nature & Wildlife

Doily Days Loves Weddings 1075507
Web site: http://www.doilydays.co.uk/
Freq: Semi-Annual Not Audited
Editor: Helen Ruff
MAGAZINE
Crafts, Weddings

Dolls House & Miniature Scene 981941
Editorial: The Maltings, West Street, Bourne PE10 9PH Tel: 44 01778 393313
Email: dhmscomments@warnersgroup.co.uk
Web site: www.dollshousemag.co.uk
Freq: Monthly
Circ: 8000 Not Audited
Editor: Carl Golder
MAGAZINE
Antiques/Collectibles, Crafts

The Doll's House Magazine 987924
Editorial: 166 High Street, Lewes, Lewes BN7 1XU Tel: 44 01273 477374
Web site: www.craftsinstitute.com/dolls-house
Freq: Monthly
Circ: 7000 Not Audited
MAGAZINE
Crafts

Dolls House World 981942
Editorial: Unit 5e Park Farm, Chichester Road, Arundel, Arundel BN18 0AG
Tel: 44 01903 884988
Web site: www.dollshouseworld.com
Freq: Monthly
Circ: 14000 Not Audited
Profile: Magazine covering all aspects of doll's houses and miniatures.
Ad Rate: Full Page Mono £550.00
Ad Rate: Full Page Colour £850.00
MAGAZINE
Crafts

Don't Panic 983397
Editorial: 8 Elder Street, London E1 6BT
Tel: 44 02077 376556
Email: panic@dontpaniconline.com
Web site: www.dontpaniconline.com
Freq: Daily
Circ: 49456 Cision Digital Reach
Editor: Fin Murphy
Profile: Website covering entertainment. The Don't Panic website covers the latest news and information on art, music, style, film, technology, and current events.
MAGAZINE (ONLINE)
Bars, Clubs & Pubs, Comedy, Dance Music, Entertainment, Local Entertainment Guides, Movies & Video, Pop Music, Rap & Hip Hop, Rock Music

The Door 982160
Editorial: Church House Oxford, Longford Locks, Kidlington OX5 1GF
Tel: 44 01865 208227
Email: jo.duckles@oxford.anglican.org
Web site: www.oxford.anglican.org
Freq: Monthly

Circ: 34500 Not Audited
Editor: Jo Duckles
Profile: Newspaper of The Diocese of Oxford covering all issues on Christianity. Includes reports and comments on Christian news, views and articles of interest.
MAGAZINE
Religion

Dork Adore   985309
Email: mail@dorkadore.com
Web site: www.dorkadore.com
Freq: Daily
Circ: 6499 Cision Digital Reach
MAGAZINE (ONLINE)
Apple, Audio Video Trade, Cameras, Computer & Video Games, Computers, Consumer Electronics, Internet, Mobile Electronics, Movies & Video, Personal Computers

Dorset Country Gardener
981957
Editorial: Country Gardener Magazines, Mount House, Halse, Taunton TA4 3AD
Email: editorial@countrygardener.co.uk
Web site: www.countrygardener.co.uk
Freq: Monthly
Circ: 22000 Not Audited
Profile: Magazine covering gardening and Outdoor activities. The edition is a part of the Country Gardener and covers the Dorset region.
MAGAZINE
Gardening

Dorset Life   982488
Editorial: 7 The Leanne, Wareham, Wareham BH20 4DY **Tel:** 44 01929 551264
Email: editor@dorsetlife.co.uk
Web site: www.dorsetlife.co.uk
Freq: Monthly
Circ: 10000 Not Audited
Editor: Joël Lacey
MAGAZINE
Regional General Interest

Dorset Magazine   982487
Editorial: Archant House, Babbage Road, Totnes TQ9 5JA **Tel:** 44 01903 703754
Email: helen.stiles@archant.co.uk
Web site: www.dorsetmagazine.co.uk
Freq: Monthly
Circ: 10000 Not Audited
Editor: Carol Burns; **Editor:** Helen Stiles
MAGAZINE
Regional General Interest

Dorset Society   984649
Editorial: Richmond Hill, Bournemouth BH2 6HH **Tel:** 44 01202 411302
Web site: www.dorsetsociety.co.uk
Freq: Monthly
Circ: 20000 Not Audited
Profile: Lifestyle magazine covering luxury property, food and drink, beauty, fashion, interiors, gardens, celebrity interviews and a society events diary. Aimed at affluent 30 to 55 year olds living in Dorset.
Ad Rate: Full Page Colour £769.00
MAGAZINE
Regional General Interest

The Double Negative   987377
Editorial: Static Gallery, 23 Roscoe Lane, Liverpool L1 9JD
Email: hello@thedoublenegative.co.uk
Web site: www.thedoublenegative.co.uk
Freq: Daily
Circ: 18358 Cision Digital Reach
MAGAZINE (ONLINE)
Art, Photography, Theater & Performing Arts, Visual Arts

Down Your Way   982545
Editorial: The Water Mill, Broughton Hall, Skipton, Broughton BD23 3AG
Tel: 44 01756 701381
Email: editorial@downyourway.co.uk
Web site: www.downyourway.co.uk
Freq: Monthly
Circ: 16000 Not Audited
Editor: Lindsey Moore

Profile: Magazine covering all aspects of Yorkshire heritage including local and family history, artists, recipes and readers' letters. Also includes features on restoration and preservation.
Ad Rate: Full Page Colour £475.00
MAGAZINE
History, Regional General Interest

Download   995112
Editorial: 1st Floor, The Yellow Building, 1 Nicholas Road, London W11 4AN
Tel: 44 02032 200400
Email: sward@euk.egmont.com
Freq: No Frequency Established
Circ: 55000 Not Audited
Editor: Simon Ward
MAGAZINE
Computer & Video Games, Elementary School

Dr Foster   984557
Editorial: 3 Dorset Rise, London EC4Y 8EN
Tel: 44 02073 328800
Email: info@drfoster.com
Web site: http://www.drfoster.com/
Freq: Daily
Circ: 6201 Cision Digital Reach
MAGAZINE (ONLINE)
Health & Medicine, Medicine

Dr Lauretta Ihonor   995350
Email: lauretta@drlaurettaihonor.com
Web site: http://drlaurettaihonor.com/
Freq: Daily
Circ: 8850 Cision Digital Reach
MAGAZINE (ONLINE)
Fitness & Exercise, Nutrition

DR P1 Stedsans   1061310
Email: stedsans@dr.dk
Web site: http://www.dr.dk/P1/Stedsans/20071217160314.htm
Freq: Weekly Not Audited
MAGAZINE
Antiques/Collectibles, Art, Arts, Literature, Photography, Theater & Performing Arts, Visual Arts

DR P3 Formiddagen   1061149
Web site: http://www.dr.dk/P3/Formiddagen/forside.htm
Freq: Daily
Circ: 240000 Not Audited
MAGAZINE
Consumer Affairs, Crime & Violence, Defense & National Security, Energy & Environment, Ethical/Moral Issues, International News, Law, National News, News & Current Affairs, Northern Ireland

DR P3 Go'Morgen P3   1061071
Email: p3nyheder@dr.dk
Web site: http://www.dr.dk/P3/gomorgen/forside.htm
Freq: Daily
Circ: 278000 Not Audited
MAGAZINE
Consumer Affairs, Crime & Violence, Defense & National Security, Energy & Environment, Ethical/Moral Issues, International News, Law, National News, News & Current Affairs, Northern Ireland

DRAM   983220
Editorial: Upper Floor, Finnieston House, 1 The Stables Yard, 1103 Argyle Street, Glasgow G3 8ND **Tel:** 44 01412 216965
Email: news@mediaworldltd.com
Web site: www.dramscotland.co.uk
Freq: Monthly
Circ: 8500 Not Audited
MAGAZINE
Alcohol & Spirits, Bars, Clubs & Pubs

Drama   982005
Email: publications@nationaldrama.org.uk
Web site: www.dramamagazine.co.uk
Freq: Semi-Annual
Circ: 1000 Not Audited
Profile: Journal of National Drama covering theory and practice, key issues, research and analysis. Aimed at members of National

Drama, teachers and advisers for drama and English and theatre workers.
MAGAZINE
Theater & Performing Arts

DRAMA Magazine   984250
Editorial: Flat 4 Residential, Sheldon Building, 1 Baltic Place, London N1 5AQ
Email: editorial@dramamag.com
Web site: http://www.drama-magazine.com
Freq: Annual Not Audited
MAGAZINE
Fashion

Drama Quarterly   998050
Editorial: C21Media, Second Floor, 148 Curtain Road, London EC2A3AT
Tel: 44 02077 297460
Email: dq@c21media.net
Web site: http://dramaquarterly.com/
Freq: Quarterly
Circ: 4805 Not Audited
Editor: Michael Pickard
MAGAZINE
Theater & Performing Arts, Visual Arts

Drapers   979793
Editorial: Telephone House, 69-77 Paul Street, London EC2A 4NQ
Tel: 44 02030 332600
Email: drapers@emap.com
Web site: www.drapersonline.com
Freq: Weekly
Circ: 7100 Not Audited
Editor: Keely Stocker
Profile: Publication covering all aspects of the fashion industry including breaking news, industry analysis and product information, brands, leading retailers and the independent retail market. Aimed at retailers of womenswear, childrenswear, menswear and footwear and their suppliers.
Ad Rate: Full Page Colour £6168.00
MAGAZINE
Fashion

Drinks Business Review   986996
Editorial: 40-42 Hatton Garden, London EC1N 8EB **Tel:** 44 02079 366898
Email: news@industryreview.com
Web site: http://www.drinks-business-review.com/
Freq: Daily
Circ: 1827 Cision Digital Reach
Profile: Website covering the beverage industry. Drink Business Review provides the latest news, comment and industry information from the beverage industry.
MAGAZINE (ONLINE)
Alcohol & Spirits

Drinks International   980813
Editorial: Drinks International, Agile Media, Longley House, International Drive, Southgate Avenue, Crawley RH10 6AQ
Tel: 44 01293 590040
Web site: www.drinksint.com
Freq: Monthly
Circ: 10000 Not Audited
Editor: Christian Davis
Profile: Magazine covering international alcoholic drink products, marketing and trends.
Ad Rate: Full Page Colour £3290.00
MAGAZINE
Alcohol & Spirits

Drinks Maven   1066706
Editorial: Drinks Maven, The Hideout, 19 Queen's Gardens, North Laine, Brighton BN1 4AR
Email: jessica@drinksmaven.com
Web site: http://drinksmaven.com/
Freq: Daily
Circ: 13633 Cision Digital Reach
MAGAZINE (ONLINE)
Alcohol & Spirits, Bars, Clubs & Pubs, Beer, Beverages, Wine/Winemaking

The Drinks Report   985108
Tel: 44 01603 633808
Email: editor@thedrinksreport.com
Web site: www.thedrinksreport.com
Freq: Daily

Circ: 15826 Cision Digital Reach
Editor: Felicity Murray
Profile: Website covering the drink industry. The Drinks Report is an online business magazine focusing on the global marketing and packaging of wines, spirits and other alcoholic beverages.
MAGAZINE (ONLINE)
Alcohol & Spirits

Drinks Retailing News   980021
Editorial: Longley House, International Drive, Crawley, Crawley RH10 6AQ
Tel: 44 01293 590056
Email: getintouch@drinksretailingnews.co.uk
Web site: www.drinksretailingnews.co.uk
Freq: Bi-Weekly
Circ: 9010 Not Audited
Editor: Martin Green
Profile: The website of OLN Off Licence News, covering news from within major off licence outlets, including supermarkets, cash and carry stores and the wider drinks industry. It is owned by Agile Media Ltd. OLN Off Licence News is read by managers and decision makers within major off licence outlets and head offices of drinks suppliers and producers.
MAGAZINE
Alcohol & Spirits, Retail Management, Tobacco

The Drinks Wholesaler   1101752
Freq: Monthly
Editor: Andrew Catchpole
MAGAZINE
Alcohol & Spirits

drinks-insight-network.com
988615
Editorial: John Carpenter House, John Carpenter Street, London EC4Y 0AN
Tel: 44 02079 366400
Email: onlineeditorial@kable.co.uk
Web site: www.drinks-insight-network.com
Freq: Daily
Circ: 10778 Cision Digital Reach
MAGAZINE (ONLINE)
Alcohol & Spirits

DrinkUp.london   1054134
Email: press@drinkup.london
Web site: https://drinkup.london/
Freq: Daily
Circ: 34991 Cision Digital Reach
MAGAZINE (ONLINE)
Alcohol & Spirits, Bars, Clubs & Pubs, Beer, Beverages, Wine/Winemaking

Drives & Controls   980971
Editorial: 192 High Street, Tunbridge, Tonbridge TN9 1BE **Tel:** 44 01732 465367
Web site: http://www.drivesncontrols.com/
Freq: Monthly
Circ: 20041 Not Audited
Editor: Tony Sacks
Profile: Magazine covering power transmission, drives, automation and motion control equipment. Also includes electronics, electrical, hydraulic, pneumatic and mechanical drive equipment.
Ad Rate: Full Page Colour £2887.00
MAGAZINE
Automotive, Engineering, Manufacturing

Driving Business   997344
Editorial: Media House, Lynchwood, Peterborough PE2 6EA
Tel: 44 01733 468306
Web site: www.fleetnews.co.uk/driving-business
Freq: Quarterly Not Audited
MAGAZINE
Automotive

Driving Instructor   998784
Editorial: Leon House, 233 High Street, Croydon, London CR0 9XT
Tel: 44 02086 868010
Email: amy@driving.org
Web site: www.driving.org
Freq: Monthly

Consumer Magazines

Circ: 12000 Not Audited
MAGAZINE
Automotive

Driving Magazine 982623
Editorial: Leon House, 233 High Street,
Croydon, London CR0 9XT
Tel: 44 02086 868010
Web site: www.driving.org
Freq: Quarterly
Circ: 18000 Not Audited
MAGAZINE
Automotive, Driving

DRONE Magazine 1074316
Web site: www.dronemagazine.uk
Freq: Monthly Not Audited
MAGAZINE
News & Current Affairs

DronePunks 1054611
Tel: 44 07729 405889
Email: dronepunks@gmail.com
Web site: http://dronepunks.com/
Freq: Daily
Circ: 10618 Cision Digital Reach
Editor: Michael Simon
MAGAZINE (ONLINE)
Cameras, Electronics, Photography

Drowned in Sound 983326
Editorial: Room 6, 93 Lee Road, London
SE3 9EN
Email: press.releases@drownedinsound.
com
Web site: www.drownedinsound.com
Freq: Daily
Circ: 156995 Cision Digital Reach
Editor: Sean Adams; Editor: Robert
Leedham
Profile: Website covering music. Drowned in
Sound shares the latest news on new,
independent, innovative and groundbreaking
music, as well as the best from established
artists and international talents.
MAGAZINE (ONLINE)
Dance Music, Pop Music, Rap & Hip Hop,
Rock Music

Drug and Therapeutics
Bulletin 980769
Editorial: BMA House, Tavistock Square,
London WC1H 9JR
Email: dtb@bmjgroup.com
Web site: www.dtb.bmj.com
Freq: Monthly Not Audited
Editor: David Phizackerley
MAGAZINE
Medicine, Pharmaceuticals

The Drum (UK) 981638
Editorial: 4th Floor, The Mercat Building, 26
Gallowgate, Glasgow G1 5AB
Tel: 44 01415 525858
Email: editorial@thedrum.com
Web site: www.thedrum.com
Freq: Bi-Weekly
Circ: 15000 Not Audited
Editor: Stephen Lepitak
MAGAZINE
Advertising Industry, Branding,
Broadcasting, Graphic Design, Marketing,
Media & Communications, Photography,
Publishing

DrunkenWerewolf 988839
Email: tiffany@drunkenwerewolf.com
Web site: www.drunkenwerewolf.com
Freq: Daily
Circ: 42615 Cision Digital Reach
Editor: Tiffany Daniels
MAGAZINE (ONLINE)
Rock Music

Drydock Magazine 984290
Editorial: Peel House, Upper South View,
Farnham, Farnham GU9 7JN
Tel: 44 01252 732220
Email: info@drydockmagazine.com
Web site: www.mpigroup.co.uk/publishing/
drydock-magazine
Freq: Quarterly
Circ: 8000 Not Audited

Editor: Mark Langdon
Profile: International journal covering ship
repair, maintenance and conversion.
Ad Rate: Full Page Mono £1500.00
Ad Rate: Full Page Colour £2250.00
MAGAZINE
Marine & Boat Trade, Shipping &
Warehousing

Dumfries & Galloway Life 984713
Editorial: The White House, Dalston Road,
Carlisle CA2 5UA Tel: 44 01228 612333
Email: magazines@cnmedia.co.uk
Web site: http://www.
dumfriesandgallowaylife.co.uk
Freq: Monthly
Circ: 5250 Not Audited
Editor: Richard Eccles
MAGAZINE
Regional General Interest

Dummy 983371
Editorial: Unit 14, Hiltongrove Business
Centre, Southgate Road, London N1 3LY
Email: editorial@dummymag.com
Web site: www.dummymag.com
Freq: Daily
Circ: 139947 Cision Digital Reach
Profile: Website covering pop music, new
music, reviews, mixes and pop culture.
MAGAZINE (ONLINE)
Dance Music, Jazz & Blues, Rap & Hip
Hop, Rock Music

DUPE 1073820
Email: dupemag@gmail.com
Web site: www.dupemag.com
Freq: Monthly Not Audited
MAGAZINE
News & Current Affairs

Duty Free News International
  983230
Editorial: 140 Wales Farm Road, London W3
6UG Tel: 44 02082 538615
Email: editorial@dfnionline.com
Web site: www.dfnionline.com
Freq: Monthly
Circ: 2000 Not Audited
Editor: Kapila Gohel
Profile: Magazine covering the duty free
market worldwide.
Ad Rate: Full Page Colour £3720.00
MAGAZINE
Alcohol & Spirits, Consumer Goods &
Products, Fashion, Food, Retail
Management, Tobacco

Duuro 995023
Web site: www.duuro.net
Freq: Daily
Circ: 12462 Cision Digital Reach
MAGAZINE (ONLINE)
Art

DVD Active 986597
Editorial: 2 Bantock Close, Inns Court,
Bristol BS4 1XD
Email: press@dvdactive.com
Web site: www.dvdactive.com
Freq: Daily
Circ: 66027 Cision Digital Reach
MAGAZINE (ONLINE)
Entertainment, Movies & Video

DVD-and-beyond.com 988901
Editorial: 26 Windridge Close, London AL3
4JP Tel: 44 01727 764556
Email: info@dvd-and-beyond.com
Web site: http://www.dvd-and-beyond.com/
Freq: Annual
Circ: 10000 Not Audited
MAGAZINE
Electronics

E&T Magazine 983622
Editorial: The IET, Michael Faraday House,
Six Hills Way, Stevenage SG1 2AY
Tel: 44 01438 313311
Email: engtechmag@theiet.org
Web site: www.theiet.org/
Freq: Monthly

Circ: 141980 Not Audited
MAGAZINE
Auto Aftermarket, Computers, Data
Management, Electronics, Engineering,
Government Technology, Industry,
Internet, Mobile Communications,
Security & Security Systems

e.learning age 981633
Editorial: George House, Coventry Business
Park, Herald Avenue, Coventry CV5 6UB
Tel: 44 01183 800350
Web site: http://www.learningtechnologies.
co.uk/Content/elearning-age/52/
Freq: Bi-Monthly
Circ: 40000 Not Audited
Editor: Peter Williams
Profile: Magazine covering all aspects of
e-learning including news, training,
development and management. Aimed at
chief learning officers and training managers
in e-learning, information technology, and
human resources who organise and
implement training courses.
Ad Rate: Full Page Colour £2650.00
MAGAZINE
Auto Aftermarket, Computers, Data
Management, Disability, Education,
Electronics, Government Technology,
Higher Education, Industry, Internet

E1 Life 1059124
Tel: 44 02030 111194
Email: editorial@e1ife.co.uk
Web site: http://e1ife.com/
Freq: Bi-Monthly
Circ: 30000 Not Audited
MAGAZINE
Lifestyle, Men's Interests, Regional
General Interest, Women's Interests

Ealing Times 985279
Editorial: Observer House, Caxton Way,
Watford, London WD18 8RJ
Tel: 44 08704 450155
Email: newsdesk@newsassociates.co.uk
Web site: www.ealingtimes.co.uk
Freq: Daily
Circ: 12916 Cision Digital Reach
Profile: Website covering what's on in
Ealing, with events, cinema listings for today
and upcoming days and weeks.
MAGAZINE (ONLINE)
Regional

The Early Hour 1053365
Email: info@theearlyhour.com
Web site: theearlyhour.com
Freq: Daily
Circ: 12319 Cision Digital Reach
MAGAZINE (ONLINE)
Family & Parenting

Early Music 985367
Editorial: Oxford University Press, Great
Clarendon Street, Oxford OX2 6DP
Tel: 44 01865 353907
Email: earlymusic@oup.com
Web site: http://em.oxfordjournals.org/
Freq: Quarterly
Circ: 1060 Not Audited
Profile: Journal covering medieval,
renaissance, baroque and pre-classical
music. Read by amateurs, students and
performers.
Ad Rate: Full Page Mono £460.00
Ad Rate: Full Page Colour £875.00
MAGAZINE
Classical/Choral/Band Music, Country,
Folk, Bluegrass

Early Music Performer 982689
Editorial: Early Music Performer, Scout
Bottom Farm, Mytholmroyd HX7 5JS
Tel: 44 01422 882751
Email: sales@recordermail.co.uk
Web site: http://www.earlymusic.info/
Performer.php
Freq: Semi-Annual
Circ: 500 Not Audited
Profile: Magazine covering news and
features on medieval, baroque, renaissance
and pre-classical music.

Ad Rate: Full Page Mono £125.00
MAGAZINE
Advertising Industry, Classical/Choral/
Band Music, Music

Early Music Today 982077
Editorial: Rhinegold House, 20 Rugby
Street, London WC1N 3QZ
Tel: 44 02073 331729
Email: emt@rhinegold.co.uk
Web site: www.earlymusictoday.com
Freq: Quarterly
Circ: 30000 Not Audited
Editor: Adrian Horsewood
Profile: Magazine containing news and
features on the early music scene. It spans
all aspects of the subject, with features on
today's top performers, issues of
performance practice and innovative early
music projects and festivals taking place all
over the world.
Ad Rate: Full Page Mono £975.00
Ad Rate: Full Page Colour £1575.00
MAGAZINE
Classical/Choral/Band Music

The Earth Times 986538
Editorial: 9 Teasel Close, Devizes, Devizes
SN10 3AQ Tel: 44 01380 730939
Web site: www.earthtimes.org
Freq: Daily
Circ: 63979 Cision Digital Reach
Profile: Website covering environmental
issues. Earth Times website shares the latest
news and information on environmental
news and business to nature and pollution.
MAGAZINE (ONLINE)
Energy & Environment

Earthmatters 982125
Editorial: 1st Floor, The Printworks, 139
Clapham Road, London SW9 0HP
Tel: 44 02074 901555
Email: info@foe.co.uk
Web site: https://www.foe.co.uk/resource/
38881
Freq: Semi-Annual
Circ: 75000 Not Audited
Editor: Dominic Murphy
Profile: Magazine covering the activities of
the Friends of The Earth. Includes articles on
climate change, food, waste, transport,
resource use and corporate accountability.
Aimed at members of Friends of The Earth.
Ad Rate: Full Page Colour £1850.00
MAGAZINE
Energy & Environment

Easier.com 984774
Editorial: 11 Queen Street, Wellington,
Telford Shropshire, TF1 1EH
Email: news@easier.com
Web site: www.easier.com
Freq: Daily
Circ: 32921 Cision Digital Reach
MAGAZINE (ONLINE)
Antique & Collectible Cars, Audio Video
Trade, Automakers, Automotive,
Cameras, Consumer Electronics, Driving,
Mobile Electronics, Motorcycles, Movies
& Video

East Anglia Rider 995343
Editorial: Unit 2 Devizes Trade Centre,
Hopton Park, Devizes, Devizes SN10 2EH
Tel: 44 01380 730888
Email: sales@redpin.co.uk
Web site: http://www.eastangliarider.co.uk
Freq: Monthly
Profile: Magazine covering horse riding in
East Anglia including dressage, show
jumping, veterinary, equipment and events.
Aimed at horse riding amateurs and
professional in the area.
MAGAZINE
Equestrian Sports

East Grinstead Living 996077
Tel: 44 01342 300152
Email: info@egliving.co.uk
Web site: www.egliving.co.uk
Freq: Monthly
Circ: 18500 Not Audited

Editor: Tally Bhangu
MAGAZINE
Regional

East Kent Lifestyle 987178

Editorial: Barley House, Sopers Road, Cuffley, Cuffley FN6 4RY
Tel: 44 01707 878026
Email: sales@psapublishing.co.uk
Web site: www.psapublishing.co.uk/publications/east-kent-lifestyle/
Freq: Quarterly
Circ: 10000 Not Audited
Profile: Magazine covering regional lifestyle. It covers the areas of Canterbury, Folkestone, Hythe, Ashford, Thanet, Tenterden, Faversham, Whitstable, Dover, and Deal. Aimed at ABC1 individuals living in East Kent.
MAGAZINE
Regional General Interest

East London Lines 985353

Editorial: East London Lines, Goldsmiths College, Lewisham Way, London SE14 6NW
Email: news@eastlondonlines.co.uk
Web site: www.eastlondonlines.co.uk
Freq: Daily
Circ: 16794 Cision Digital Reach
MAGAZINE (ONLINE)
Regional

East Lothian Life 982556

Editorial: 1 Beveridge Row, Belhaven, Dunbar, Dunbar EH42 1TP
Tel: 44 01368 863593
Email: info@eastlothianlife.co.uk
Web site: www.eastlothianlife.co.uk
Freq: Quarterly
Circ: 3500 Not Audited
Editor: Pauline Jaffray
Profile: County magazine that contains features on property, fashion, books, food, sports, health and beauty, gardening and the arts.
Ad Rate: Full Page Mono £550.00
Ad Rate: Full Page Colour £795.00
MAGAZINE
Regional General Interest

East Week 984432

Editorial: 1st Floor, Unit 3, The Technology Park, Colindeep Lane, Colindale, London NW9 6BX **Tel:** 44 02087 327622
Email: editor@singtao.co.uk
Web site: www.singtao.co.uk
Freq: Weekly
Circ: 30000 Not Audited
Profile: Newspaper covering health and food, entertainment, law and finance with feature stories relating to Chinese communities in Europe.
Ad Rate: Full Page Colour £660.00
MAGAZINE
Bars, Clubs & Pubs, Comedy, Entertainment, International News, Local Entertainment Guides, Movies & Video

Eastbourne Buzz 1073827

Email: office@eastbournebuzz.co.uk
Web site: www.eastbournebuzz.co.uk
Freq: Daily
Circ: 16784 Cision Digital Reach
MAGAZINE (ONLINE)
Regional

Eastern Airways Inflight Magazine 998636

Editorial: Arch Workspace, Abbey Road, Pity Me, Durham DH1 5JZ
Tel: 44 01913 832838
Email: e-magazine@gravity-consulting.com
Web site: www.easternairways.com/magazine
Freq: Quarterly Not Audited
MAGAZINE
Airline Inflight

Eastern Art Report 981879

Editorial: Eastern Art Report/Eastern Art Report Online, EAPGROUP, 3 Shortlands, Hammersmith', London W6 8DA
Tel: 44 02083 921122
Email: ear@eapgroup.com

Web site: www.eapgroup.com
Freq: Quarterly
Circ: 14600 Not Audited
Profile: Magazine covering the traditional and contemporary arts of Asia, Africa, Oceania and the multi-cultural scene in Europe and North America. Aimed at private and institutional collectors, dealers, auction houses, museums, art schools and galleries.
Ad Rate: Full Page Mono £1450.00
Ad Rate: Full Page Colour £2450.00
MAGAZINE
Art

Eastern Eye 982582

Editorial: 1 Silex Street, London SE1 0DW
Tel: 44 02079 281234
Email: trader@gujarat.co.uk
Web site: www.easterneye.eu
Freq: Weekly
Circ: 22000 Not Audited
Profile: Newspaper covering general news and features including Bollywood, entertainment listings, TV listings, fashion and music. Aimed at second and third generation Asians living in the UK aged between 16 and 40 years old.
Ad Rate: Full Page Mono £4556.00
Ad Rate: Full Page Colour £5467.20
MAGAZINE
Asia, International News, National News

EastleighNews.co.uk 999201

Editorial: 7 Northlands Road, Eastleigh SO50 9AW **Tel:** 44 02380 345305
Email: news@eastleighnews.co.uk
Web site: www.eastleighnews.co.uk
Freq: Daily
Circ: 12313 Cision Digital Reach
Editor: Stephen Slominski
MAGAZINE (ONLINE)
Regional

eastlife 986991

Editorial: Unit 4, Avenue Business Park, Elsworth, Cambridge CB23 4HY
Tel: 44 01954 267904
Email: enquiries@eastlife.co.uk
Web site: www.eastlife.co.uk
Freq: Monthly
Circ: 25000 Not Audited
Editor: Emma Kemsley
Profile: A monthly glossy magazine and covering the whole of the East Anglia region - Bedfordshire, Cambridgeshire, Essex, Hertfordshire, Norfolk, Northamptonshire & Suffolk. Eastlife is the region's essential guide to 'What's On' throughout East Anglia and covers events, places to visit, eating and drinking.
MAGAZINE
Regional General Interest

Eastside 982546

Editorial: 6 Broadfield Court, Broadfield Business Park, Sheffield S8 0XF
Tel: 44 01142 506300
Email: eastside@rmcmedia.co.uk
Web site: http://www.rmcmedia.co.uk/magazines/eastside/
Freq: Monthly
Circ: 20000 Not Audited
MAGAZINE
Regional General Interest

Easy Cook 982795

Editorial: BBC Worldwide, 101 Wood Lane, London W12 7FA **Tel:** 44 02071 505000
Email: easycook@bbc.com
Web site: www.bbcgoodfood.com/magazines/bbc-easy-cook
Freq: Monthly
Circ: 29181 Not Audited
MAGAZINE
Cooking & Baking

easyJet Traveller 982317

Editorial: Blackburn House, Blackburn Road, West Hampstead, London NW6 1RZ
Email: info@ink-global.com
Web site: traveller.easyjet.com
Freq: Monthly
Circ: 4500000 Not Audited
Editor: Jonny Ensall

Profile: In-flight magazine containing celebrity interviews, music, fashion, humour, lifestyle, health and beauty, property and business. First published in 1997, the publication has an average of 196 pages per issue. Read by easyJet passengers.
Ad Rate: Full Page Colour £12046.00
MAGAZINE
Airline Inflight

Eat Out 981597

Editorial: 2 Maidstone Road, Sidcup DA14 5HZ **Tel:** 44 08450 002500
Web site: www.eatoutmagazine.co.uk
Freq: Monthly
Circ: 120000 Not Audited
Profile: Magazine covering news, case studies, analysis and in-depth articles for the modern day restaurateur.
Ad Rate: Full Page Colour £3995.00
MAGAZINE
Bars, Clubs & Pubs

Eat Travel Live 987300

Editorial: 41 Ennerdale Road, Richmond, London TW9 2DN
Email: info@email.eattravellive.com
Web site: www.eattravellive.com
Freq: Daily
Circ: 1741 Cision Digital Reach
Editor: John Gregory-Smith
MAGAZINE (ONLINE)
Alcohol & Spirits, Bars, Clubs & Pubs, Beauty & Grooming, Beer, Beverages, Cooking & Baking, Cosmetics, Fashion, Food, Grocery Stores

Eat.Drink.Sleep 997699

Editorial: Suite 1 and 2, Spratling Court Offices, Spratling Street, Manston, Manston CT12 5AN **Tel:** 44 01843 591523
Email: matthew@eat-drink-sleep.com
Web site: www.eat-drink-sleep.com
Freq: Monthly
Circ: 81089 Not Audited
Editor: Jeremy Tring
MAGAZINE
Alcohol & Spirits, Bars, Clubs & Pubs, Fitness & Exercise, Food, Hotels/Motels

EatNorth 1054131

Email: editor@eatnorth.co.uk
Web site: eatnorth.co.uk
Freq: Daily
Circ: 11168 Cision Digital Reach
MAGAZINE (ONLINE)
Alcohol & Spirits, Bars, Clubs & Pubs, Beer, Beverages, Cooking & Baking, Food, Grocery Stores, Organic Food, Restaurant Reviews, Vegetarianism & Veganism

eBritain 998843

Editorial: Avicenna House, 252-262 Romford Road, London E7 9HZ
Tel: 44 02085 523071
Email: probinson@bite.ac.uk
Web site: www.bite.ac.uk
Freq: Quarterly
Circ: 15000 Not Audited
Editor: Peter Robinson
MAGAZINE
Audio Video Trade, Cameras, Consumer Electronics, Industry, Mobile Electronics, Movies & Video

Echoes 982116

Editorial: Echoes, 3 Elsinore Road, Forrest Hill, London SE23 2SH
Tel: 44 01763 245235
Email: editor@echoesmagazine.co.uk
Web site: www.echoesmagazine.co.uk/
Freq: Monthly
Circ: 20000 Not Audited
Editor: Chris Wells
Profile: Magazine focusing on soul, r'n'b, jazz, reggae and hip hop music. Contains album reviews and interviews.
Ad Rate: Full Page Colour £1200.00
MAGAZINE
Dance Music, Rap & Hip Hop

Echoes and Dust 996885

Email: editor@echoesanddust.com
Web site: www.echoesanddust.com
Freq: Daily
Circ: 14554 Cision Digital Reach
Editor: Dan Salter
MAGAZINE (ONLINE)
Rock Music

Eco Kids Planet 1053748

Tel: 44 08006 891365
Email: hello@ecokidsplanet.co.uk
Web site: http://www.ecokidsplanet.co.uk
Freq: Monthly
Circ: 5500 Not Audited
Editor: Anya Dimelow
MAGAZINE
Elementary School, Energy & Environment, Nature & Wildlife

The Ecologist 988933

Editorial: Ford House, Hartland, Bideford, Bideford EX39 6EE
Email: editorial@theecologist.org
Web site: www.theecologist.org
Freq: Daily
Circ: 152487 Cision Digital Reach
Editor: Oliver Tickell
Profile: Website containing environmental. The ECOLOGIST website share the latest news and information on the environment industry. It covers general environment news, science, pollution control, animals, ecology, conservation and earth science.
MAGAZINE (ONLINE)
Energy & Environment, Environment

The Economic Voice 985996

Editorial: c/o J & S Chartered Accountants Ltd, 6 Northlands Road, Southampton, Southampton SO15 2LF
Tel: 44 01722 770043
Email: editor@economicvoice.com
Web site: www.economicvoice.com
Freq: Daily
Circ: 57675 Cision Digital Reach
Editor: Richard Henley Davis; **Editor:** Jeff Taylor
MAGAZINE (ONLINE)
Economics, Politics

Econsultancy 985292

Editorial: Wells Point, 79 Wells Street, London W1T 3QN **Tel:** 44 02031 998474
Web site: www.econsultancy.com
Freq: Daily
Circ: 1560304 Cision Digital Reach
MAGAZINE (ONLINE)
Advertising Industry, Branding, Broadcasting, Graphic Design, Marketing, Media & Communications, Photography, Publishing

Ecophiles 1053799

Email: team@ecophiles.com
Web site: https://ecophiles.com/
Freq: Daily
Circ: 16248 Cision Digital Reach
MAGAZINE (ONLINE)
Energy & Environment, Travel

Ecotextile News 984365

Editorial: Hallcroft House, Castleford Road, Pontefract, Normanton WF6 2DW
Tel: 44 01977 708488
Email: info@ecotextile.com
Web site: www.ecotextile.com
Freq: Bi-Monthly
Circ: 30024 Not Audited
Profile: Magazine covering sustainable textiles and clothing including recycled fabrics, organics and industry news. Aimed at retailers and brands including fabric specifiers and textile mills.
Ad Rate: Full Page Colour £1815.00
MAGAZINE
Environment, Fashion

Edenbridge Chronicle 987145

Editorial: Winterton House, High Street, Westerham, Westerham TN16 1AT
Tel: 44 01959 564766
Email: editorial.chronicle@tindlenews.co.uk

Consumer Magazines

Web site: www.tandridge-chronicle.co.uk
Freq: Monthly
Circ: 48000 Not Audited
Editor: Siggy Sherrell
Profile: Website for local paper the Edenbridge Chronicle covering the latest local news and events from Edenbridge and the surrounding area.
MAGAZINE
Regional, Regional General Interest

EDGE
983032
Editorial: Quay House, The Ambury, Bath BA1 1UA Tel: 44 01225 442244
Email: edge@futurenet.com
Web site: www.gamesradar.com/edge
Freq: Monthly
Circ: 18082 Not Audited
Profile: Magazine covering all aspects of calligraphy and lettering from historical and medieval manuscripts to cutting edge, contemporary calligraphy and typography.
MAGAZINE
Computer & Video Games

The Edinburgh Gazette
987153
Editorial: The Edinburgh Gazette, PO Box 3584, Norwich NR7 7WD
Tel: 44 01316 597032
Email: edinburgh@thegazette.co.uk
Web site: www.thegazette.co.uk
Freq: Weekly Not Audited
Profile: Publication covering statutory, legal, bankruptcy and liquidation notices relating to Scotland.
MAGAZINE
News & Current Affairs

Edinburgh Life
986943
Editorial: PO Box 28948, Gorebridge EH22 9BD Tel: 44 07850 938407
Email: editorial@edinburghlifemagazine.com
Web site: www.edinburghlifemagazine.com
Freq: Bi-Monthly
Circ: 10000 Not Audited
Editor: Peter Bourhill
MAGAZINE
Regional General Interest

The Edinburgh Reporter
990544
Editorial: 32A Abercromby Place, Edinburgh EH3 6QE Tel: 44 07791 406498
Email: editor@theedinburghreporter.co.uk
Web site: www.theedinburghreporter.co.uk
Freq: Daily
Circ: 18225 Cision Digital Reach
Editor: Phyllis Stephen
MAGAZINE (ONLINE)
Regional

The Edit
999084
Editorial: 70 Cowcaddens Rd, Lanarkshire, Glasgow G4 0BA Tel: 44 01413 313886
Email: editor@theeditgcu.com
Web site: www.theeditgcu.com
Freq: Bi-Monthly
Circ: 108000 Not Audited
MAGAZINE
Student Lifestyle

Edition Online
984600
Editorial: 28 Coronation Close, Happisburgh, Norwich NR12 0RL
Tel: 44 01692 650837
Email: office@edition-mag.co.uk
Web site: www.edition-mag.co.uk
Freq: Daily
Circ: 1306 Cision Digital Reach
Editor: Phil Stewart
MAGAZINE (ONLINE)
Movies & Video, Regional, Regional General Interest

EDN Magazine Europe
998502
Email: edn-editor@eetimes.be
Web site: www.edn-europe.com
Freq: Monthly
Circ: 45372 Not Audited
MAGAZINE
Electronics, Engineering, Industry, Manufacturing

EDNIndia.com
1061356
Web site: http://www.ednindia.com/
Freq: Daily
Circ: 787 Cision Digital Reach
MAGAZINE (ONLINE)
Electronics

eDogAdvisor
996097
Email: hello@edogadvisor.co.uk
Web site: http://www.edogadvisor.co.uk/
Freq: Daily
Circ: 11413 Cision Digital Reach
MAGAZINE (ONLINE)
Nature & Wildlife

EDP Norfolk
982518
Editorial: Tower House, Sovereign Park, Lathkill Street, Norwich LE16 9EF
Tel: 44 08448 484211
Web site: http://www.norfolkmag.co.uk/home
Freq: Monthly
Circ: 12841 Not Audited
Editor: Angela Kennedy
MAGAZINE
Regional General Interest

Educate
996776
Editorial: 36 Henry Street, Liverpool L1 5BS
Tel: 44 01517 097567
Email: post@merseymirror.com
Web site: www.educatemagazine.com
Freq: 3 Times/Year
Circ: 30000 Not Audited
Editor: Alan Birkett
MAGAZINE
Careers, Education

Education Business
981036
Editorial: 226 High Road, Loughton IG10 1ET Tel: 44 02085 320055
Email: editorial@psigroupltd.co.uk
Web site: www.educationbusinessuk.net
Freq: Monthly
Circ: 6483 Not Audited
Editor: Angela Pisanu
Profile: Magazine that covering the business end of state and private education requirements. Aimed at head teachers and bursars.
Ad Rate: Full Page Colour £2495.00
MAGAZINE
Disability, Education, Higher Education, Preschool, Schools & Institutions, Students

Education Direct
996172
Web site: www.ambientcreative.co.uk/education-branding-collateral/education-direct-magazine Not Audited
MAGAZINE
News & Current Affairs

Education Executive
984452
Editorial: One Tetbury Place, Business Design Centre, 52 Upper Street, London N1 0QH Tel: 44 02072 886833
Email: info@intelligentmedia.co.uk
Web site: www.edexec.co.uk
Freq: Monthly
Circ: 15800 Not Audited
Profile: Monthly Business Management publication for schools and colleges. Aimed at those dealing with business and financial management in schools.
Ad Rate: Full Page Colour £1875.00
MAGAZINE
Disability, Education, Higher Education, Preschool, Schools & Institutions, Students

Education for Everybody
981566
Editorial: Rhone House, Canalside, Chorley PR6 0BU Tel: 44 01257 267677
Email: editorial@euromedia-al.com
Web site: www.educationforeverybody.co.uk
Freq: Quarterly
Circ: 7000 Not Audited
Profile: Magazine covering education news and regular features on autism, visual impairment (including RNI), hearing

impairment (including RND), dyslexia, ICT, sport and music.
Ad Rate: Full Page Colour £1500.00
MAGAZINE
Disability

Education for the Military
988075
Tel: 44 07803 729958
Email: joanne@educationforthemilitaryfamily.org.uk
Web site: www.educationforthemilitaryfamily.org.uk
Freq: Quarterly
Circ: 30000 Not Audited
Editor: Joanne Nattress
Profile: Magazine for the Military Family looking at all aspects of Education.
MAGAZINE
Defense & National Security, Disability, Education, Higher Education, Preschool, Schools & Institutions, Students

Education in Science
981541
Editorial: College Lane, Hatfield, Hatfield AL10 9AA Tel: 44 01707 283000
Email: info@ase.org.uk
Web site: https://www.ase.org.uk/journals/education-in-science/
Freq: Quarterly
Circ: 8000 Not Audited
Profile: Magazine of the Association for Science Education, covering issues relating to science education and the activities of the ASE.
Ad Rate: Full Page Mono £580.00
Ad Rate: Full Page Colour £580.00
MAGAZINE
Disability, Education, Higher Education, Preschool, Schools & Institutions, Science, Students

Education Investor
985033
Editorial: Investor Publishing, Greener House, 66-68 Haymarket, London SW1Y 4RF Tel: 44 02071 042000
Email: info@educationinvestor.co.uk
Web site: www.educationinvestor.co.uk
Freq: Monthly
Circ: 7000 Not Audited
MAGAZINE
Disability, Education, Higher Education, Preschool, Schools & Institutions, Students

Education Journal
981523
Editorial: Devonia House, 4 Union Terrace, Crediton, Crediton EX17 3DY
Tel: 44 01363 774455
Email: info@educationpublishing.com
Web site: www.educationpublishing.com
Freq: Weekly
Circ: 5000 Not Audited
Profile: Journal containing policy, management, research, opinions, leadership features, new documents digest, reviews and coverage of Parliament including answers to Parliamentary questions.
Ad Rate: Full Page Mono £650.00
Ad Rate: Full Page Colour £950.00
MAGAZINE
Education, Higher Education, Preschool, Schools & Institutions, Students

Education Law Monitor
988165
Editorial: The Ridge, South View Road, Pinner, London HA5 3YD
Tel: 44 02088 661934
Web site: http://www.singlelaw.com/education-law-monitor
Freq: Monthly Not Audited
Profile: Newsletter reviewing the latest developments in law.
MAGAZINE
Disability, Higher Education, Schools & Institutions

Education Today (UK)
981037
Editorial: 15a London Road, Maidstone ME16 8LY Tel: 44 01622 687031
Email: education@datateam.co.uk
Web site: http://www.education-today.co.uk
Freq: Monthly

Circ: 45000 Not Audited
MAGAZINE
Disability, Education, Higher Education, Preschool, Schools & Institutions, Students

Educational Psychology
995759
Editorial: 4 Park Square, Milton Park, Abingdon, Didcot OX14 4RN
Tel: 44 02070 176000
Email: edpsych@ied.edu.hk
Web site: www.tandf.co.uk/journals/journal.asp?issn=0144-3410&linktype=5
Freq: Bi-Monthly Not Audited
Editor: Magdalena Mo Ching Mok
MAGAZINE
Disability, Education, Higher Education, Neurology, Preschool, Schools & Institutions, Students

The Educator Magazine
996319
Email: director@the-educator.org
Web site: http://www.the-educator.org/
Freq: 3 Times/Year
Circ: 37500 Not Audited
MAGAZINE
Preschool, Schools & Institutions

ee.co.uk
997451
Editorial: 37 North Wharf Road, London W2 1AG
Web site: www.ee.co.uk
Freq: Daily
Circ: 7725863 Cision Digital Reach
MAGAZINE (ONLINE)
News & Current Affairs

efestivals.co.uk
985102
Editorial: PO Box 3127, Bristol BS5 5FR
Tel: 44 05602 055329
Email: newsroom@efestivals.co.uk
Web site: www.efestivals.co.uk
Freq: Daily
Circ: 246349 Cision Digital Reach
Editor: Scott Williams
MAGAZINE (ONLINE)
Country, Folk, Bluegrass, Dance Music, Jazz & Blues, Pop Music, R&B, Urban, World, Rock Music

EGR Intel
1053753
Editorial: One London Wall, London EC2Y 5EA Tel: 44 02078 326500
Email: support@egr.global
Web site: http://www.egrmobileintelligence.com/
Freq: Monthly Not Audited
MAGAZINE
Mobile Communications

EGR North America
1053867
Editorial: One London Wall, London EC2Y 5EA Tel: 44 02078 326561
Web site: http://www.egrnorthamerica.com/
Freq: Monthly Not Audited
MAGAZINE
Computer & Video Games

EGR Technology
981513
Editorial: One London Wall, London EC2Y 5EA Tel: 44 02078 326500
Web site: www.egrmagazine.com
Freq: Monthly Not Audited
Profile: Magazine covering all aspects of the online gaming and gambling industry. Includes articles on payment processing, legal issues, marketing strategies, regulation and technology. Aimed at decision makers within the gambling industry.
Ad Rate: Full Page Colour £4500.00
MAGAZINE
Computer & Video Games, Internet

The Eighty-Eight
1054121
Email: ac@the88journal.com
Web site: www.the88journal.com
Freq: No Frequency Established
MAGAZINE
News & Current Affairs

Eikoku News Digest
998504
Editorial: 6 Southampton Place, Holborn, London WC1A 2DB Tel: 44 02076 110166

Email: info@news-digest.co.uk
Web site: www.news-digest.co.uk
Freq: Bi-Weekly
Circ: 20000 Not Audited
MAGAZINE
Asia

Elaph
986451
Editorial: Gainsbrough House, 2 Sheen Road, London TW9 1AE
Email: editor@elaph.com
Web site: www.elaph.com
Freq: Daily
Circ: 1828319 Cision Digital Reach
MAGAZINE (ONLINE)
Africa, Asia, Expatriates, National News

E-Learning Update
981561
Editorial: 309 Scott House, The Custard Factory, Gibb Street, Digbeth, Birmingham B9 4AA **Tel:** 44 01212 247578
Web site: www.teachingtimes.com/publications/e-learningupdate.htm
Freq: Monthly
Circ: 10 Cision Digital Reach
Editor: Raspal Chima
Profile: Website covering e-learning. The e-learning Update shares the latest information on online education news and programs.
MAGAZINE (ONLINE)
Computers, Disability, Education, Higher Education, Preschool, Schools & Institutions, Students

e-lec.org
988916
Editorial: 1 Hogan Way, Stafford ST16 3YN
Tel: 44 01785 607385
Email: news@e-lec.org
Web site: www.e-lec.org
Freq: Daily
Circ: 1366 Cision Digital Reach
Editor: Jeffrey Bennett
MAGAZINE (ONLINE)
Electronics

Electric & Hybrid Marine Technology International
1062731
Editorial: Abinger House, Church Street, Dorking RH4 1DF **Tel:** 44 01306 743744
Email: electricandhybridmarine@ukipme.com
Web site: http://www.ukimediaevents.com/pub-marine.php?mag=1
Freq: Semi-Annual
Circ: 18000 Not Audited
Editor: John Thornton
MAGAZINE
Marine & Boat Trade

Electric & Hybrid Vehicle Technology International
984390
Editorial: Abinger House, Church Street, Dorking, Dorking RH4 1DF
Tel: 44 01306 743744
Web site: www.ukipme.com/mag_electric.htm
Freq: Semi-Annual
Circ: 30000 Not Audited
Editor: Matt Ross
Profile: Magazine providing technical international information about vehicle design including technology and innovation in electric, hybrid and fuel-cell vehicle development and manufacture. Aimed at automotive engineers and decision-makers throughout the global automotive industry.
Ad Rate: Full Page Colour £3650.00
MAGAZINE
Automotive

Electric Banana
1054120
Web site: http://www.electric-banana.co.uk
Freq: Daily
Circ: 8229 Cision Digital Reach
Editor: Andy Parker
Profile: Website covering indie music. The electric banana website shares the latest

music news, single and album reviews and tour news.
MAGAZINE (ONLINE)
Rock Music

Electric Sheep
986599
Email: thepuppetmaster@electricsheepmagazine.com
Web site: www.electricsheepmagazine.com
Freq: Daily
Circ: 2038 Cision Digital Reach
Editor: Virginie Sélavy
MAGAZINE (ONLINE)
Entertainment, Movies & Video

Electrical Contracting News
981701
Editorial: Alexander House, 38 Forehill, Ely, Ely CB7 4ZA **Tel:** 44 01353 616100
Web site: www.electricalcontractingnews.co.uk
Freq: Monthly
Circ: 10016 Not Audited
MAGAZINE
Electronics, Internet, Telecommunications/Electronic Communications

Electrical Engineering
981130
Editorial: 15a London Road, Maidstone, Maidstone ME16 8LY **Tel:** 44 01622 699153
Web site: www.connectingindustry.com/ElectricalEngineering/
Freq: Monthly
Circ: 11245 Not Audited
Editor: Lisa Peake
Profile: Journal containing news, features and information on electrical components and equipment for industrial and commercial electrical contractors, and electrical engineers. Read by electrical engineers, designers, maintenance engineers and contractors.
Ad Rate: Full Page Colour £2200.00
MAGAZINE
Electronics, Industry

Electrical Review
981131
Editorial: SJP Business Media Ltd, 2nd Floor, 52-54 Gracechurch Street, London EC3V 0EJ **Tel:** 44 02079 338999
Email: elinorem@electricalreview.co.uk
Web site: www.electricalreview.co.uk
Freq: Monthly
Circ: 8000 Not Audited
Editor: Elinore Mackay
Profile: Magazine covering features, news, analysis, comment and products concerning all aspects of the electrotechnical industry in the UK. Read by electrical engineers and consultants.
Ad Rate: Full Page Colour £3071.00
MAGAZINE
Electronics

Electrical Times
980092
Editorial: The Old School House, St Stephen's Street, Tonbridge, Tonbridge TN9 2AD **Tel:** 44 01732 371570
Email: rodney.jack@purplems.com
Web site: www.electricaltimes.co.uk
Freq: Monthly
Circ: 10555 Not Audited
Editor: Rodney Jack
Profile: Magazine covering the electrical installation industry including technological and business developments. Aimed at contractors, project engineers and wholesalers andeveryone in the construction industry's specifying chain.
Ad Rate: Full Page Colour £3282.00
MAGAZINE
Electronics

Electrical Trade Magazine
995554
Editorial: Rhone House, Canal Side, Chorley, Chorley PR6 0BU
Tel: 44 01257 267677
Web site: http://www.electricaltrademagazine.co.uk/
Freq: Bi-Monthly

Circ: 9617 Not Audited
MAGAZINE
Electronics

Electrical Wholesaler
981132
Editorial: 15a London Road, Maidstone, Kent, Maidstone ME16 8LY
Tel: 44 01622 687031
Web site: www.ewnews.co.uk
Freq: Monthly
Circ: 3266 Not Audited
Profile: Magazine covering wholesale product news and features. Aimed at executives working in the electrical wholesaling and bulk buying industry. Previous title: Electrical Wholesaler & Buyer A charge may be made for colour separation.
Ad Rate: Full Page Colour £1720.00
MAGAZINE
Electronics

Electronic Payments International
981636
Editorial: 71-73 Carter Lane, London EC4V 5EQ **Tel:** 44 02079 366400
Email: briefings@verdict.co.uk
Web site: www.electronicpaymentsinternational.com
Freq: Monthly Not Audited
Editor: Anna Milne
Profile: Electronic Payments International provides industry news, analysis and features, key trends in the global market.
MAGAZINE
Banking, Data Management, Internet, Security & Security Systems

Electronic Product Design & Test
981317
Editorial: Blair House, 184 High Street, Tonbridge, Tonbridge TN9 1BQ
Tel: 44 01732 359990
Email: emt@imlgroup.co.uk
Web site: www.epdtonthenet.net
Freq: Monthly
Circ: 9921 Not Audited
Profile: A technical journal covering all aspects of electronics design and test for every industry area including automotive, military/hi-rel and other applications. Regular supplements include Distribution, Test and Measurement and Electronics Outsourcing. Aimed at senior design engineers.
MAGAZINE
Electronics, Industry, Manufacturing

Electronic Sound
997690
Editorial: Electronic Sound, Studio 18 Capitol House, 2-4 Heigham Street, Norwich NR2 4TE
Email: neil@electronicsound.co.uk
Web site: electronicsound.co.uk
Freq: Monthly
Circ: 15935 Cision Digital Reach
Editor: Push .
MAGAZINE (ONLINE)
Dance Music, Music

Electronic Specifier Design
999017
Editorial: Comice Place, Woodfalls Farm, Gravelly Ways, Maidstone ME18 6DA
Tel: 44 01622 871944
Email: editor@electronicspecifier.com
Web site: www.electronicspecifier.com
Freq: Monthly
Circ: 66792 Not Audited
Editor: Joe Bush
Profile: ElectronicSpecifier Design provides in-depth technical analysis on all aspects of electronics design, including: Aerospace & Defence, Alternative Energy, Analog, Automotive, Connection, Displays, Embedded, MCUs, Medical Electronics, Optoelectronics, Passives, Power, Programmable Logic, Sensors, Test and Measurement, Wireless.
MAGAZINE
Auto Aftermarket, Computers, Data Management, Electronics, Government Technology, Industry, Internet, Mobile Communications, Retail Management, Security & Security Systems

Electronic Specifier Product
999254
Editorial: Comice Place, Woodfalls Farm, Gravelly Ways, Maidstone ME18 6DA
Tel: 44 01622 871944
Email: editor@electronicspecifier.com
Web site: www.electronicspecifier.com
Freq: Monthly
Circ: 66792 Not Audited
Profile: Electronic pan European newsletter delivering new products and technology to over 66,000 design engineers.
MAGAZINE
Auto Aftermarket, Computers, Data Management, Electronics, Government Technology, Industry, Internet, Mobile Communications, Retail Management, Security & Security Systems

Electronics
995854
Editorial: 15a London Road, Maidstone, Maidstone ME16 8LY **Tel:** 44 01622 687031
Web site: www.connectingindustry.com/Electronics
Freq: Monthly
Circ: 12594 Not Audited
Editor: Michelle Lea; **Editor:** Michelle Winny
MAGAZINE
Electronics

Electronics Optics and Control
1060963
Tel: 44 86379 63327293
Email: dgykz@vip.163.com
Freq: Bi-Monthly Not Audited
MAGAZINE
Auto Aftermarket, Aviation, Computers, Data Management, Electronics, Government Technology, Industry, Internet, Mobile Communications, Security & Security Systems

Electronics Sourcing Europe
1012620
Editorial: Suite 2, 1-3 Warren Court, Park Road, Crowborough, Crowborough TN6 2QX
Tel: 44 01892 613400
Web site: www.electronics-sourcing.com/europe
Freq: Bi-Monthly
Circ: 33000 Not Audited
MAGAZINE
Auto Aftermarket, Electronics

Electronics Sourcing UK & Ireland
981584
Editorial: Suite 2, 1-3 Warren Court, Park Road, Crowborough, Crowborough TN6 2QX
Tel: 44 01892 613400
Web site: www.electronics-sourcing.com/uk
Freq: Monthly
Circ: 8495 Not Audited
MAGAZINE
Auto Aftermarket, Electronics

Electronics Weekly
979911
Editorial: 6th Floor Davis House, 2 Robert Street, Croydon, Croydon CR0 1QQ
Tel: 44 02082 538600
Email: tech@electronicsweekly.com
Web site: www.electronicsweekly.com
Freq: Weekly
Circ: 12123 Not Audited
Profile: Magazine covering electronics. The Electronics Weekly magazine contains technical and business news of the electronics manufacturing and using industries. Targets electronics professionals, offering analysis, feature and business stories. Aimed at technical directors and other senior directors, engineers and engineering management and buyers working in the UK electronics industry.A charge may be made for colour separation.
Ad Rate: Full Page Colour £3275.00
MAGAZINE
Electronics, Industry

Electronics World
981318
Editorial: 2nd Floor, 52-54 Gracechurch Street, London EC3V 0EH
Tel: 44 02079 338999
Email: electronicsworld@circdata.com
Web site: www.electronicsworld.co.uk

Consumer Magazines

Freq: Monthly
Circ: 6606 Not Audited
Editor: Svetlana Josifovska
Profile: Magazine covering all areas of electronics design, presenting innovation, news, research methodologies and techniques. Contains specialist coverage of new technology emergence and the tracking of innovative applications, design, technology, research and software. Special sections are: Radio Frequency, Test and Measurement, Computing, Semiconductors and Power.Read by electronics professionals and technology-transfer enthusiasts. Previous title: Electronics World + Wireless World
Ad Rate: Full Page Colour £1995.00
MAGAZINE
Electronics, Industry, Mobile Communications, Software

Electropages 981613
Editorial: 4 Axium Centre, Lytchettminster, Poole BH16 6FE **Tel:** 44 02031 264955
Email: info@electropages.com
Web site: www.electropages.com
Freq: Daily
Circ: 14808 Cision Digital Reach
Editor: Brian Butler
MAGAZINE (ONLINE)
Auto Aftermarket, Electronics

Eleven 988885
Editorial: 10 Broomhill Road, Orpington, London BR6 0EW
Email: info@elevenmagazine.co.uk
Web site: www.elevenmagazine.co.uk
Freq: Daily
Circ: 2631 Cision Digital Reach
Editor: Jonathan Wilson
MAGAZINE (ONLINE)
Soccer

Elite GB Magazine 995479
Editorial: 114 Ridge Road, London N21 3EN
Tel: 44 02083 603823
Web site: http://elitegb.co.uk/
Freq: Quarterly
Circ: 50000 Not Audited
MAGAZINE
Fashion, Railroad, Shopping, Travel, Women's Interests

Elite Life 985657
Editorial: 45 Wolverhampton Road, Stafford ST17 4DF
Email: editor@eliteluxuryworld.com
Web site: www.eliteluxuryworld.com/ elitemagazine.html
Freq: Monthly
Circ: 15000 Not Audited
MAGAZINE
Luxury Goods, Travel

Elite Living Africa 1052878
Editorial: University House, 11-13 Lower Grosvenor Place, London SW1W 0EX
Tel: 44 02078 347676
Web site: www.elitelivingafrica.com
Freq: Bi-Monthly
Circ: 20625 Not Audited
MAGAZINE
Africa, Luxury Goods

ELIXIR 983750
Editorial: 7 Monroe House, Lorne Close, London NW8 7JN **Tel:** 44 02075 698676
Email: editor@elixirnews.com
Web site: www.elixirnews.com
Freq: Quarterly
Circ: 39394 Cision Digital Reach
Editor: Avril O'Connor
Profile: Magazine covering everything anti-aging including aesthetics, cosmetics, cosmetic surgery, cosmetic dentistry, lifestyle, nutrition, exercise, complimentary medicine, spas, holidays, leisure, gadgets and pets. Aimed at men and women aged over 30 years old with the ability to spend on anti-ageing products and services and lifestyle.

Ad Rate: Full Page Colour £9950.00
MAGAZINE (ONLINE)
Cosmetics, Health & Medicine, Retirement Savings

ELLE 982368
Editorial: 72 Broadwick Street, London W1F 9EP **Tel:** 44 02074 395000
Email: editorial@elleuk.com
Web site: www.elleuk.com
Freq: Monthly
Circ: 172193 Not Audited
Editor: Muireann Carey-Campbell
Profile: Magazine covering fashion designers, celebrities, models, photographers and stylists. It is focused on fashion, shopping and celebrity style news and reports from the latest international collections. It also features beauty news, celebrity style secrets, spa guides, diets, hair and beauty trends from the catwalk, celebrity trends, what to buy in designer stores and on the high street. Launched in 1985. Aimed at women between 18 and 26 years of age with high disposable incomes and a passion for shopping.
Ad Rate: Full Page Colour £9000.00
MAGAZINE
Women's Interests

ELLE DECORATION 983234
Editorial: 72 Broadwick Street, London W1F 9EP **Tel:** 44 02074 395000
Email: elledecoration@hearst.co.uk
Web site: elledecoration.co.uk
Freq: Monthly
Circ: 71794 Not Audited
Profile: Magazine covering interior design. It offers expert interior advice, creative ideas and shoots from all over the world. Each issue features the latest information and products along with tools to help decorate, renovate, and entertain. First published in 1989. Aimed at a design conscious, cosmopolitan, audience of trend setters and opinion formers.
Ad Rate: Full Page Colour £5500.00
MAGAZINE
Do-It-Yourself (DIY)

The Elmbridge Lifestyle Magazine 982531
Editorial: Kingsway Business Park, Oldfield Road, Hampton, London TW12 2HD
Tel: 44 02089 395601
Email: editelm@sheengate.co.uk
Web site: www.sheengate.co.uk
Freq: Monthly
Circ: 43700 Not Audited
Editor: Fiona Adams; **Editor:** Rosanna Greenstreet
Profile: Magazine containing mainly lifestyle and local interest articles and interviews, including features on history, fashion, theatre, art, health, education, shopping and property. This outlet covers areas within Kingston upon Thames Borough.
Ad Rate: Full Page Colour £1155.00
MAGAZINE
Property Management & Maintenance, Regional General Interest

Elysium Magazine 986439
Email: editorial@elysium-uk.com
Web site: www.elysium-uk.com
Freq: Daily
Circ: 11000 Cision Digital Reach
Profile: Website covering men's lifestyle. Elysium Magazine shares the latest news on technology & gadgets, entertainment, developing your business or career, travel, food & drink, sports.
MAGAZINE (ONLINE)
Alcohol & Spirits, Audio Video Trade, Bars, Clubs & Pubs, Beer, Beverages, Cameras, Comedy, Consumer Electronics, Electronics, Entertainment

EMEA Captive 985781
Editorial: Kingfisher House, 21-23 Elmfield Road, London BR1 1LT
Web site: http://www.captiveinternational. com/channel/emea
Freq: Annual

Circ: 5000 Not Audited
MAGAZINE
News & Current Affairs

Emerald Rugby 984858
Tel: 44 02838 344333
Email: editor@emeraldrugby.com
Web site: www.emeraldrugby.com
Freq: Monthly
Circ: 19000 Not Audited
Editor: Manus Lappin
Profile: Magazine covering all aspects of Irish rugby. Featuring news, reviews and interviews with leading rugby figures from Ireland and abroad and a training and coaching section with training tips and techniques. Aimed at fans, players and administrators of Irish rugby.
Ad Rate: Full Page Mono £1200.00
Ad Rate: Full Page Colour £1700.00
MAGAZINE
Rugby

Emerald Street 987510
Editorial: 1-5 Portpool Lane, London EC1N 7UU **Tel:** 44 02076 119700
Email: info@emeraldstreet.com
Web site: www.emeraldstreet.com
Freq: Daily
Circ: 142396 Cision Digital Reach
Profile: Email publication with supporting website that covers fashion, beauty and things to do in your city. Emerald Street shares the latest news on interior design, fashion, beauty, bars & restaurants and careers. It was launched on April 18, 2011 and is provided by Stylist Magazine. Emerald Street provides a daily email put together by the Stylist team.
MAGAZINE (ONLINE)
Women's Interests

Emerging Themes in Epidemiology 996633
Editorial: 236 Gray's Inn Road, London WC1X 8HB **Tel:** 44 02031 922009
Email: etejournal@biomedcentral.com
Web site: http://www.ete-online.com/
Freq: Monthly Not Audited
MAGAZINE
Infectious Diseases, Medicine

Emma's Diary 984306
Editorial: Temple House, Regatta Place, Marlow Road, Bourne End, High Wycombe SL8 5TD **Tel:** 44 01628 522776
Email: editor@emmasdiary.co.uk
Web site: www.emmasdiary.co.uk
Freq: Semi-Annual
Circ: 400895 Not Audited
Profile: Pregnancy guide published on behalf of the RCGP, given out to women on confirmation of their pregnancy. Read by expectant mothers.
Ad Rate: Full Page Colour £13566.00
MAGAZINE
Family & Parenting

EMPIRE 981790
Editorial: 24-28 Oval Road, Camden, London NW1 7DT **Tel:** 44 02072 418000
Email: empire@bauermedia.co.uk
Web site: www.empireonline.com
Freq: Monthly
Circ: 123004 Not Audited
Profile: Magazine covering the latest cinema and DVD releases including breaking movie news, film and DVD reviews, interviews and unique regular features. First published in 1989, the publication has an average of 200 pages per issue. Press Day: Middle of the month. Aimed at film lovers and DVD fans.
Ad Rate: Full Page Colour £8476.00
MAGAZINE
Entertainment, Movies & Video, Music

EMSNow 986552
Editorial: A411, The Jam Factory, London SE1 4TT
Email: editors@emsnow.com
Web site: www.emsnow.com
Freq: Daily
Circ: 6202 Cision Digital Reach
MAGAZINE (ONLINE)
Electronics, Manufacturing

En 3 Casa 1061367
Tel: 44 52161 41262567
Email: contacto@en3casa.com
Web site: http://www.en3casa.com
Freq: Weekly
Circ: 685 Cision Digital Reach
MAGAZINE (ONLINE)
National News

EN magazine 999126
Editorial: 63 High Street, Potters Bar, Potters Bar EN6 5AS **Tel:** 44 02083 639444
Email: editorial@enmagazine.co.uk
Web site: www.enmagazine.co.uk
Freq: Monthly
Circ: 30000 Not Audited
MAGAZINE
Regional General Interest

enable 986441
Editorial: DC Publishing Ltd, 200 Bath Street, Glasgow G2 4HG
Tel: 44 08442 499007
Web site: www.enablemagazine.co.uk
Freq: Bi-Monthly
Circ: 30000 Not Audited
Profile: Bi-monthly magazine covering disability lifestyle including disabled product news, holiday destinations, art reviews, disability sports, employment advice and education.
MAGAZINE
Disability, Health & Medicine

End of Life Journal 998781
Editorial: BMA House, Tavistock Square, London WC1H 9JR **Tel:** 44 02073 836909
Email: info.eolj@bmj.com
Web site: eolj.bmj.com
Freq: Daily
Circ: 108 Cision Digital Reach
Editor: Helen Scott
MAGAZINE (ONLINE)
Community Care (UK), Medicine, Nursing/ Nurses

Endource.com 997331
Web site: www.endource.com
Freq: Daily
Circ: 45285 Cision Digital Reach
MAGAZINE (ONLINE)
Fashion

Endurance GB Magazine 982681
Tel: 44 01708 688075
Email: magazineeditor@endurancegb.co.uk
Web site: https://endurancegb.co.uk/main
Freq: Bi-Monthly
Circ: 3400 Not Audited
Editor: Cindy Russell
MAGAZINE
Equestrian Sports

energy focus 980891
Editorial: 6th Floor, Manchester One, 53 Portland Street, Manchester M1 3LD
Tel: 44 01612 362182
Email: info@eic.co.uk
Web site: www.excelpublishing.co.uk/ services/magazines/energy-focus
Freq: Quarterly Not Audited
MAGAZINE
Defense & National Security, Electricity, Engineering, Industry, Manufacturing, Marine & Boat Trade, Mining & Quarrying, Oil, Paper, Plastics

Enforcd 1097881
Email: info@enforcd.com
Web site: www.enforcd.com
Freq: Daily
Circ: 685 Cision Digital Reach
MAGAZINE (ONLINE)
Corporate Finance, Corporate Management, Emerging Markets, Fund Management, Personal Finance, Tax Law

Engine Technology International 985026
Editorial: Abinger House, Church Street, Dorking, Dorking RH4 1DF
Tel: 44 01306 743744
Email: info@ukimediaevents.com

Web site: www.
enginetechnologyinternational.com
Freq: Quarterly
Circ: 10332 Not Audited
Editor: John O'Brien
Profile: Magazine dealing with the future of power transmission and latest developments in automotive and truck engine components including OE engine and powertrain design, manufacture, technologies and services. The publication was first published in 1997. Read by people working in the international engine technology industry.
Ad Rate: Full Page Colour £3950.00
MAGAZINE
Automotive

Engineering Designer   998490
Editorial: Hawley Mill, Hawley Road, Dartford, Sutton at Hone DA2 7TJ
Tel: 44 01322 221144
Email: editorial@engineeringdesigner.co.uk
Web site: www.engineeringdesigner.co.uk
Freq: Bi-Monthly
Circ: 4000 Not Audited
Profile: Journal containing features on engineering and product design, related technology and other relevant subjects.
Ad Rate: Full Page Mono £750.00
Ad Rate: Full Page Colour £875.00
MAGAZINE
News & Current Affairs

Engineering in Miniature   981982
Editorial: The Fosse, Fosse Way, Leamington Spa, Leamington Spa CV31 1XN
Tel: 44 01778 391000
Email: editor@engineeringinminiature.co.uk
Web site: www.engineeringinminiature.co.uk
Freq: Monthly
Circ: 10000 Not Audited
Profile: Magazine containing information on how to build steam locomotives and stationary engines on a miniature scale. Also features club and association rally reports, new product reviews and historical articles.
Ad Rate: Full Page Mono £360.00
Ad Rate: Full Page Colour £500.00
MAGAZINE
Crafts, Hobbies, & Collecting

England Rugby   982273
Tel: 44 08712 222120
Email: media@therfu.com
Web site: http://www.englandrugby.com/
Freq: Daily
Circ: 158056 Cision Digital Reach
Editor: Howard Johnson
Profile: Official magazine of the England RFU and England Rugby Supporters Club. Covering all levels of rugby featuring player's interviews, tactics and fitness advice.
Ad Rate: Full Page Colour £5500.00
MAGAZINE (ONLINE)
Rugby

English Bridge   981900
Editorial: Broadfields, Bicester Road, Aylesbury, Aylesbury HP19 8AZ
Tel: 44 01296 317200
Web site: www.ebu.co.uk
Freq: Bi-Monthly
Circ: 45000 Not Audited
Editor: Louise Hobhouse
MAGAZINE
Games

English Club Golfer   984644
Tel: 44 01413 532222
Email: info@psp.uk.net
Web site: www.englishclubgolfer.com
Freq: Bi-Monthly
Circ: 50356 Not Audited
Profile: Magazine covering amateur golf in England including fixtures, results, player profiles and interviews and equipment reviews. Aimed at amateur golfers in England.
Ad Rate: Full Page Colour £1795.00
MAGAZINE
Golf

The English Garden   981964
Editorial: The Chelsea Magazine Company, Jubilee House, 2 Jubilee Place, London SW3 3TQ **Tel:** 44 02073 483700
Email: theenglishgarden@chelseamagazines.com
Web site: www.theenglishgarden.co.uk
Freq: Monthly
Circ: 28838 Not Audited
Editor: Clare Foggett
Profile: Magazine covering all aspects of the British garden particularly features on design and planting.
Ad Rate: Full Page Colour £3600.00
MAGAZINE
Gardening

English Heritage Members' Magazine   981929
Editorial: Brook Green, Hammersmith, London W6 7BT **Tel:** 44 02071 505000
Email: hello@iln.co.uk
Web site: www.english-heritage.org.uk/members-area/members-magazine
Freq: Quarterly
Circ: 368931 Not Audited
Profile: Magazine containing news and features relating to historic English buildings, architecture and monuments of national importance.
Ad Rate: Full Page Colour £6000.00
MAGAZINE
History

The English Home   981855
Editorial: Third Floor Offices, Cumberland House, Oriel Road, Cheltenham GL50 1BB
Tel: 44 03330 143215
Email: theenglishhome@chelseamagazines.com
Web site: www.theenglishhome.co.uk
Freq: Monthly
Circ: 71138 Not Audited
Editor: Kerryn Harper-Cuss
Profile: Magazine covering properties and home furnishings. Each issues includes articles on interior design, home decoration, furnitures and home textiles. First published in 2000. Aimed at female readers aged over 35.
Ad Rate: Full Page Colour £3750.00
MAGAZINE
Do-It-Yourself (DIY), Gardening, Property Management & Maintenance

English in Education   901526
Editorial: Unit 410, Aizlewood Business Centre, Aizlewood's Mill Nursery Street, Sheffield S3 8GG **Tel:** 44 01142 823545
Email: info@nate.org.uk
Web site: www.nate.org.uk/index.php?page=64
Freq: 3 Times/Year Not Audited
Editor: John Hodgson
MAGAZINE
Disability, Education, Higher Education, Preschool, Schools & Institutions, Students

English Today   999154
Editorial: University Printing House, Shaftesbury Road, Cambridge CB2 8RU
Tel: 44 01223 326070
Email: englishtoday@cambridge.org
Web site: www.cambridge.org/core/journals/english-today
Freq: Quarterly
Circ: 1850 Not Audited
Editor: Kingsley Bolton
MAGAZINE
Literature

EnglishLuxury.com   996553
Editorial: 30 Bloomsbury St, London WC1B 3QJ **Tel:** 44 02079 320802
Email: editorial@englishluxury.com
Web site: englishluxury.com
Freq: Daily
Circ: 10709 Cision Digital Reach
MAGAZINE (ONLINE)
Audio Video Trade, Beauty & Grooming, Cameras, Consumer Electronics, Cosmetics, Electronics, Fashion, Hair, Lifestyle, Luxury Goods

EniGma Magazine   998699
Editorial: 211 Piccadilly, London W1J 9HF
Tel: 44 02079 179445
Email: enigma@enigma-mag.com
Web site: www.enigma-mag.com
Freq: Monthly
Circ: 45000 Not Audited
MAGAZINE
Asia, Men's Interests, Women's Interests

Enjoy Jersey   982337
Editorial: PO Box 243, St Helier, Jersey
Web site: www.enjoyjersey.co.uk
Freq: Annual
Circ: 50000 Not Audited
Editor: Liz Jones
Profile: Glossy magazine with top hotel distribution around Jersey, available in hotel rooms/suites. Editorial sections include sightseeing, retail attractions, diary of events, shopping, weddings, business, travel around the Island and to neighbouring islands, leisure and sport, eating out, night life - plus special features which vary each year. Aimed at business and holiday visitors.
Ad Rate: Full Page Colour £3250.00
MAGAZINE
Travel

Enjoy the South   998500
Editorial: 15 Whitecliff Road, Poole, Poole BH14 8DU **Tel:** 44 01202 746900
Email: info@enjoythesouth.co.uk
Web site: www.enjoythesouth.co.uk
Freq: Annual Not Audited
Editor: Zoe Wilson
MAGAZINE
Travel

Enjoying MG   982612
Editorial: MG Owners Club, Octagon House, 1 Over Road, Longstanton CB24 4QZ
Tel: 44 01954 231125
Email: mgmagazine@mgownersclub.co.uk
Web site: www.mgownersclub.co.uk
Freq: Monthly
Circ: 30000 Not Audited
Editor: Richard Ladds
Profile: Magazine containing articles relating to modern MG Rover and classic MG sports cars. In the context of historical, mechanical, technical, as well as motorsport, rally and travel information.
Ad Rate: Full Page Mono £1020.00
Ad Rate: Full Page Colour £1492.00
MAGAZINE
Automakers

Ensemble Magazine   1066025
Tel: 44 01926 512005
Email: media@mma-online.org.uk
Web site: http://www.mma-online.org.uk/publications/ensemble/
Freq: 3 Times/Year
Circ: 7000 Not Audited
Editor: Keith Ayling
MAGAZINE
News & Current Affairs

ENT & Audiology news   986422
Editorial: 9 Gayfield Square, Edinburgh EH1 3NT **Tel:** 44 01315 574184
Email: editorial@pinpoint-scotland.com
Web site: www.entandaudiologynews.com
Freq: Monthly Not Audited
Profile: Journal covering news and the latest developments in the field of ear, nose and throat, audiology and oral and maxillo-facial medicine. Read by otolaryngologists, audiologists, hospital managers, nurses and doctors, and plastic surgeons.
Ad Rate: Full Page Colour £1428.00
MAGAZINE
Medicine

enterprise apps tech   987315
Email: james@techforge.pub
Web site: www.appstechnews.com
Freq: Daily
Circ: 59586 Cision Digital Reach
MAGAZINE (ONLINE)
Mobile Communications, Mobile Electronics

Enterprise Magazine   979760
Web site: http://magazine.enterprise.co.uk
Freq: Daily
Circ: 7134 Cision Digital Reach
MAGAZINE (ONLINE)
Driving, Travel

Enterprise Management 360   996387
Editorial: 105-107 Farringdon Road, London EC1R 3BU **Tel:** 44 02071 484444
Web site: www.enterprisemanagement360.com
Freq: Quarterly
Circ: 27410 Cision Digital Reach
Editor: Sylvia Entwistle
Profile: Magazine covering management. The ENTERPRISE MANAGEMENT 360 website shares the latest information on business management, information management and security management.
MAGAZINE (ONLINE)
Auto Aftermarket, Computers, Data Management, Electronics, Government Technology, Industry, Internet, Mobile Communications, Security & Security Systems, Software

Enterprise Times   997724
Editorial: 15 Ravens Close, Knaphill, London GU21 2LD **Tel:** 44 01483 888378
Web site: www.enterprisetimes.co.uk
Freq: Daily
Circ: 81365 Cision Digital Reach
Editor: Ian Murphy
MAGAZINE (ONLINE)
Computers, Data Management, Electronics, Mobile Communications, Security & Security Systems, Software

Enterprising Scotland   984182
Editorial: 5 Station Road, Grangemouth, Falkirk FK3 8DG **Tel:** 44 01324 332034
Web site: http://www.enterprisingscotland.com/
Freq: Monthly
Circ: 20000 Not Audited
Profile: Magazine covering all aspects of business and economic developments in Scotland. Read by managing directors and senior decision makers.
Ad Rate: Full Page Mono £1495.00
Ad Rate: Full Page Colour £1970.00
MAGAZINE
Engineering, Manufacturing, Marine & Boat Trade, Mining & Quarrying, Paper, Plastics, Steel

Entertainment Focus   987454
Email: info@entertainment-focus.com
Web site: www.entertainment-focus.com
Freq: Daily
Circ: 66506 Cision Digital Reach
Editor: Pip Ellwood-Hughes
MAGAZINE (ONLINE)
Audio Video Trade, Broadcasting, Cameras, Classical/Choral/Band Music, Computer & Video Games, Consumer Electronics, Country, Folk, Bluegrass, Dance Music, Jazz & Blues, Literature

Entertainment Prizes Galore   1073821
Tel: 44 01865 664970
Email: info@theoxfordpuzzlecompany.com
Web site: www.theoxfordpuzzlecompany.com
Freq: Bi-Monthly
Circ: 50000 Not Audited
MAGAZINE
Games, Competitions & Events, Men's Interests, Women's Interests

Entertainment Technology   984882
Editorial: The Studio, High Green, Great Shelford, Cambridge CB22 5EG
Tel: 44 01223 550805
Email: editor@etnow.com
Web site: www.etnow.com/etmag/
Freq: Monthly
Circ: 4100 Not Audited
Editor: John Offord

Consumer Magazines

Section 4 UK Periodicals Consumer

Profile: Magazine covering news from within the entertainment technology industry including special features and reports, job listings and profiles of prominent professionals within the industry. Published monthly by Entertainment Technology Press and launched in 2001, the magazine is free to members of organizations trading in the entertainment and presentation technology sectors within the UK and Europe. Aimed at those working in the entertainment and presentation technology sectors within the UK.
Ad Rate: Full Page Colour £1295.00
MAGAZINE
Auto Aftermarket, Computers, Data Management, Electronics, Government Technology, Industry, Internet, Mobile Communications, Security & Security Systems, Software

Entertainmentdaily.co.uk
1054521
Tel: 44 01225 430091
Email: hello@entertainmentdaily.co.uk
Web site: www.entertainmentdaily.co.uk
Freq: Daily
Circ: 1288176 Cision Digital Reach
MAGAZINE (ONLINE)
Celebrities

Entertainmentwise.com
984804
Editorial: 10-16 Scrutton Street, London EC2A 4RU **Tel:** 44 02073 779914
Web site: www.entertainmentwise.com
Freq: Daily
Circ: 183137 Cision Digital Reach
MAGAZINE (ONLINE)
Bars, Clubs & Pubs, Celebrities, Comedy, Entertainment, Local Entertainment Guides, Movies & Video

entouraaj
988081
Editorial: 14 Bonhill Street, 6th Floor, London EC2A 4BX **Tel:** 44 02035 145409
Email: info@entouraaj.com
Web site: www.entouraaj.com
Freq: Daily
Circ: 848 Cision Digital Reach
Editor: Gary Singh
Profile: Website covering men's lifestyle. Entouraaj is a website for the Asian men in the UK providing news and advice on style, health, entertainment, technology, sport, opinion and wedding planning.
MAGAZINE (ONLINE)
Asia, Beauty & Grooming, Cosmetics, Fashion, Hair, Men's Interests

Entrepreneur & Investor Magazine
1054950
Email: editorial@entrepreneurandinvestor.com
Web site: www.entrepreneurandinvestor.com
Freq: Bi-Monthly
Circ: 20000 Not Audited
MAGAZINE
Alcohol & Spirits, Antique & Collectible Cars, Automakers, Automotive, Bars, Clubs & Pubs, Beauty & Grooming, Beer, Beverages, Business, Comedy

EntsWeb.co.uk
994663
Editorial: Orchard Cottage, Main Street, Driffield YO25 3DS
Email: newsdesk@entsweb.co.uk
Web site: https://www.entsweb.co.uk/
Freq: Daily
Circ: 46572 Cision Digital Reach
Editor: Alan Best
MAGAZINE (ONLINE)
Bars, Clubs & Pubs, Classical/Choral/Band Music, Comedy, Country, Folk, Bluegrass, Dance Music, Jazz & Blues, Music, Pop Music, R&B, Urban, World, Rap & Hip Hop

EOS Magazine
982028
Editorial: The Old Barn, Ball Lane, Tackley, Kidlington, Kidlington OX5 3AG
Tel: 44 01869 331741
Email: editorial@eos-magazine.com
Web site: www.eos-magazine.com
Freq: Quarterly

Circ: 21854 Not Audited
Profile: Magazine about Canon EOS cameras and photographic techniques.
Ad Rate: Full Page Colour £1100.00
MAGAZINE
Cameras, Photography

EP Europace
998920
Editorial: Oxford University Press, Great Clarendon Street, Oxford OX2 6DP
Tel: 44 01865 353907
Email: europace.editorialoffice@oup.com
Web site: www.europace.oxfordjournals.org
Freq: Monthly
Circ: 3200 Not Audited
MAGAZINE
Cardiology, Medicine

EPICUREAN LIFE
981806
Editorial: 790 Fulham Road, London SW6 5SL **Tel:** 44 02077 317747
Email: azzy@epicureanlife.co.uk
Web site: www.epicureanlife.co.uk
Freq: Quarterly
Circ: 150000 Not Audited
Editor: Christina Raptis
Profile: Luxury lifestyle magazine covering restaurants, travel, fashion, motoring, lifestyle and society. Aimed at those aged 25 to 55 years old with a high disposable income.
MAGAZINE
Luxury Goods

Epigram
981759
Editorial: University of Bristol Students' Union, Queens Rd, Clifton, Bristol BS8 1LN
Tel: 44 01173 313531
Email: editor@epigram.org.uk
Web site: www.epigram.org.uk
Freq: Bi-Weekly
Circ: 20000 Not Audited
Profile: Bristol University's independent student newspaper covering Bristol and student news, music, the arts, travel and sport.
Ad Rate: Full Page Mono £840.00
Ad Rate: Full Page Colour £840.00
MAGAZINE
Student Lifestyle

Epsom and Ewell Talking Newspaper
1069611
Tel: 44 01372 721519
Web site: eetn.org.uk
Freq: Daily
Circ: 1667 Cision Digital Reach
MAGAZINE (ONLINE)
Disability, National News, Regional

Equal Opportunities Review
980954
Editorial: PO Box 61064, London SE1P 5BQ
Tel: 44 02079 538796
Web site: www.equalitypublishing.co.uk/?page_id=99
Freq: Monthly
Circ: 2000 Not Audited
Editor: Sue Johnstone
Profile: Magazine focusing on equal opportunities law and employment practice.
MAGAZINE
News & Current Affairs

Equestrian Plus
995174
Editorial: Unit 2 Devizes Trade Centre, Hopton Park, Devizes, Devizes SN10 2EH
Tel: 44 01380 730888
Email: sales@redpin.co.uk
Web site: www.equestrianplus.co.uk
Freq: Monthly Not Audited
Profile: Magazine covering all-round equestrian interests and disciplines, feature articles, product reviews and events.
MAGAZINE
Equestrian Sports

Equestrian Trade News
984312
Editorial: Stockeld Park, Wetherby, Spofforth LS22 4AW **Tel:** 44 01937 582111
Email: editor@equestriantradenews.com
Web site: www.equestriantradenews.com
Freq: Monthly

Circ: 5250 Not Audited
Editor: Liz Benwell
Profile: Magazine covering saddlery, harness, riding and outdoor clothing, equipment, feedstuffs and horse care products. Founded in 1979, Equestrian Trade News (ETN) remains the leading monthly trade journal for the equestrian industry.ETN is read by equestrian retailers, manufacturers and distributors.
Ad Rate: Full Page Colour £1320.00
MAGAZINE
Animal Farming, Equestrian Sports

Equi-Ads
982235
Editorial: 126 Derby Road, Long Eaton, Nottingham, Long Eaton NG10 4LS
Tel: 44 01159 461146
Email: news@equi-ads.com
Web site: www.equiads.net
Freq: Monthly
Circ: 49000 Not Audited
Editor: Bob Griffiths
Profile: Magazine covering equestrian news and products. The magazine is distributed in nationally in tack shops, feed merchants, country chain stores and equestrian centres.
MAGAZINE
Equestrian Sports

Equine-world.co.uk
982876
Editorial: 18 Shepherds Close, Grove, Wantage OX12 0NX **Tel:** 44 01235 224633
Email: acorn.internet@equine-world.co.uk
Web site: http://www.equineworld.co.uk/
Freq: Daily
Circ: 2399 Cision Digital Reach
Editor: Lorraine Hill
MAGAZINE (ONLINE)
Equestrian Sports

Equity
997519
Editorial: Guild House, Upper St Martins Lane, London WC2H 9EG
Tel: 44 02073 796000
Email: editorial@equity.org.uk
Web site: www.equity.org.uk/news-and-events/equity-magazine
Freq: Quarterly
Circ: 56000 Not Audited
MAGAZINE
Theater & Performing Arts

EQY
995117
Editorial: 496 Ferry Road, Edinburgh, Forth EH5 2DL **Tel:** 44 01315 511000
Email: editor@scottishequestrianyear.co.uk
Web site: www.eqymagazine.co.uk
Freq: Annual
Circ: 10000 Not Audited
MAGAZINE
Equestrian Sports

ER magazine
998022
Editorial: 8 Market Street, Whittlesey, Peterborough, Whittlesey PE7 1BA
Tel: 44 01733 205938
Email: james@easyresettlement.co.uk
Web site: http://www.easyresettlement.com
Freq: Quarterly
Circ: 11000 Not Audited
Editor: Martin Newman
MAGAZINE
Careers, Company News & Appointments, Defense & National Security, Education, Recruiting

Erisea Magazine
988190
Editorial: 20 Eton Street, Halifax, Evesham HX1 4LQ
Email: info.eriseamag@gmail.com
Web site: http://erisea-mag.com/
Freq: Daily
Circ: 11237 Cision Digital Reach
Profile: Website covering lifestyle, beauty, entertainment, fashion, food, home, garden, parenting and travel.
MAGAZINE (ONLINE)
Beauty & Grooming, Cooking & Baking, Cosmetics, Do-It-Yourself (DIY), Family & Parenting, Fashion, Hair, Horse Racing, Racquet Sports, Soccer

Ernest Journal
997211
Email: admin@ernestjournal.co.uk
Web site: www.ernestjournal.co.uk
Freq: Semi-Annual Not Audited
MAGAZINE
Crafts, Men's Interests, Women's Interests

Erotic Review
981785
Editorial: 120 New Kings Road, Fulham, London SW6 4LZ
Email: editorial@ermagazine.co.uk
Web site: www.eroticreviewmagazine.com
Freq: Daily
Circ: 22806 Cision Digital Reach
Editor: Ian Dunt
Profile: Website covering sexual behavior. The Erotic review website covers all aspects of erotica and sexual behavior including the historical, medical, scientific, psychological and socio-political aspects.
Ad Rate: Full Page Colour £600.00
MAGAZINE (ONLINE)
Sexual/Adult Products

Erotic Trade Only
981786
Editorial: Suite 2, Lakeside Court, Llantarnam Park Way, Cwmbran NP44 3GA
Tel: 44 01633 480751
Email: editorial@erotictradeonly.com
Web site: www.erotictradeonly.com
Freq: Monthly
Circ: 4500 Not Audited
Editor: Dale Bradford
Profile: Magazine covering all aspects of the commercial adult industry.
Ad Rate: Full Page Mono £1200.00
Ad Rate: Full Page Colour £1200.00
MAGAZINE
Business, Sexual/Adult Products

ERT
981133
Editorial: 5th Floor, Congress House, Lyon Road, Harrow, London HA1 2EW
Tel: 44 02085 152000
Web site: www.ertonline.co.uk
Freq: Monthly
Circ: 5754 Not Audited
Editor: Sean Hannam
Profile: Magazine containing the latest news on the electrical retailing industry including market analysis and in-depth features. First published in 1890, the publication has an average of 36 pages per issue. Aimed at electrical retailers, manufacturers, importers and wholesalers.
Ad Rate: Full Page Colour £3444.00
MAGAZINE
Auto Aftermarket, Electronics

ERT Ireland
988612
Editorial: 5th Floor, Congress House, Lyon Road, Harrow, London HA1 2EW
Tel: 44 02085 152000
Email: info@taylistmedia.com
Web site: www.ertonline.co.uk
Freq: Bi-Monthly
Circ: 3000 Not Audited
Editor: Sean Hannam
Profile: Magazine focusing on electrical retailing in Ireland. Includes industry news, analysis and product reviews with product-related supplements. Aimed at electrical retailers, manufacturers, importers, distributors and wholesalers.
Ad Rate: Full Page Colour £1200.00
MAGAZINE
Electronics, Retail Management

escape
982799
Editorial: Capital House, 25 Chapel Street, London NW1 5DH **Tel:** 44 01413 750504
Email: escapeeditor@thinkpublishing.co.uk
Web site: http://www.thinkpublishing.co.uk/
Freq: Quarterly
Circ: 75000 Not Audited
Profile: Magazine covering forthcoming films, reviews, behind the scene news, features and competitions. Aimed at customers of Empire cinemas.
MAGAZINE
Railroad, Travel

Escape
986646
Editorial: Victoria Court, 8 Dormer Place, Leamington Spa, Leamington Spa CV32 5AE
Tel: 44 01926 319923
Email: escape@summersault.co.uk
Freq: Bi-Monthly
Circ: 600000 Not Audited
Editor: Jim Staton
Profile: Magazine covering forthcoming films, reviews, behind the scene news, features and competitions. Aimed at customers of Empire cinemas.
MAGAZINE
Entertainment, Movies & Video

Escape
1052964
Web site: https://www.travelbag.co.uk/brochures
Freq: Semi-Annual
Circ: 40000 Not Audited
Profile: Magazine covering forthcoming films, reviews, behind the scene news, features and competitions. Aimed at customers of Empire cinemas.
MAGAZINE
Airline Inflight, Railroad, Travel

Escapement
1053487
Email: info@escapement.uk.com
Web site: www.escapementmagazine.com
Freq: Daily
Circ: 38210 Cision Digital Reach
Profile: Escapement is a website covering watches and luxury goods. Aimed 'at individuals with a passion for watch collecting, who appreciate "the finer things in life" '.
MAGAZINE (ONLINE)
Luxury Goods

Escapism
987282
Editorial: 5 Tun Yard, Peardon St, London SW8 3HT **Tel:** 44 02078 199999
Email: editorial@squareupmedia.com
Web site: www.escapismmagazine.com/
Freq: Monthly
Circ: 101700 Not Audited
Profile: Magazine covering travel.
Ad Rate: Full Page Colour £7500.00
MAGAZINE
Travel

eSeller
996834
Editorial: 2nd Floor, 52-54 Gracechurch Street, London EC3V 0EH
Tel: 44 02079 338999
Email: press@eseller.net
Web site: http://eseller.net/
Freq: Daily
Circ: 53579 Cision Digital Reach
MAGAZINE (ONLINE)
Business, Internet, Small and Medium Business

ESG Magazine
1074799
Tel: 44 02077 092036
Web site: www.esg-magazine.com
Freq: Quarterly
Circ: 15000 Not Audited
MAGAZINE
Investment Banking, Personal Finance

esp Magazine
984064
Editorial: 11 Peterborough Road, Castor, Peterborough PE5 7AX
Tel: 44 01733 381266
Email: office@espmag.co.uk
Web site: www.espmag.co.uk
Freq: Monthly
Circ: 21000 Not Audited
Editor: Sharon McAllister
Profile: Entertainment and lifestyle guide for the Greater Peterborough area. Covers live music, sport, cinema, theatre, arts, events, pubs, clubs, eating out, news, fitness, travel, motoring, reviews, competitions and features on celebrities and health and beauty. Aimed at predominantly 18 to 40 year old residents of the Greater Peterborough area.
Ad Rate: Full Page Mono £580.00

Ad Rate: Full Page Colour £580.00
MAGAZINE
Antique & Collectible Cars, Automakers, Automotive, Driving, Fashion, Motorcycles, Off-road & 4-Wheel Drive Vehicles, Regional General Interest, Trucks & SUVs

ESPNCricinfo.com
982874
Editorial: 3 Queen Caroline Street, Hammersmith, London W6 9PE
Email: editorial@cricinfo.com
Web site: http://www.espncricinfo.com/
Freq: Daily
Circ: 8135570 Cision Digital Reach
Editor: Kamran Abbasi
MAGAZINE (ONLINE)
Cricket

Esprit Magazine
983211
Editorial: 87 Roundwood Way, Banstead, London SM7 1EJ **Tel:** 44 01737 373099
Email: esprit@esprit-magazine.co.uk
Web site: http://www.esprit-magazine.co.uk
Freq: Monthly
Circ: 5000 Not Audited
MAGAZINE
Cosmetics, Hair

Esquire
980756
Editorial: 72 Broadwick Street, London W1F 9EP **Tel:** 44 02074 395000
Web site: www.esquire.co.uk
Freq: Monthly
Circ: 62051 Not Audited
Profile: Men's interest magazine covering men's fashion, style and grooming, culture, women, entertainment, food, drinks, design, technology, arts, music and lifestyle. First published in 1991, Esquire has an average of 260 pages per issue. Read by men between 20 and 40 years old.
Ad Rate: Full Page Colour £14371.00
MAGAZINE
Men's Interests

essence
985505
Editorial: Howard House, 70 Baker Street, Weybridge, London KT13 8AL
Tel: 44 01932 988677
Email: editor@essence-magazine.co.uk
Web site: www.essence-magazine.co.uk
Freq: Monthly
Circ: 1068214 Not Audited
MAGAZINE
Regional General Interest

The Essential Business Magazine
997404
Editorial: 145-157 St John Street, London EC1V 4PW **Tel:** 44 02032 902980
Email: production@essentialbusinessmag.com
Web site: www.essentialbusinessmag.com
Freq: Monthly
Circ: 500000 Not Audited
MAGAZINE
Business

Essential Install
985626
Editorial: Suite 4, 6-8 Revenge Road, Lordswood, Chatham, Chatham ME5 8UD
Tel: 44 01634 673163
Web site: www.essentialinstall.com
Freq: Monthly
Circ: 5398 Not Audited
MAGAZINE
Electronics, Mobile Communications

Essential Kitchen Bathroom Bedroom Magazine
981840
Editorial: The Tower, Phoenix Square, Colchester CO4 9HU **Tel:** 44 01206 851117
Web site: www.ekbb.co.uk
Freq: Monthly
Circ: 31000 Not Audited
Editor: Ciara Elliott
MAGAZINE
Do-It-Yourself (DIY)

Essentially America
982322
Editorial: 55 Hereford Road, London W2 5BB **Tel:** 44 02072 436954

Web site: www.essentiallyamerica.com
Freq: 3 Times/Year
Circ: 50000 Not Audited
Editor: Mary Moore Mason
Profile: Magazine covering travel and lifestyle to and within the USA, Canada and Mexico.
Ad Rate: Full Page Colour £7794.00
MAGAZINE
Travel

Essentially Catering Magazine
984573
Editorial: Albion House, Wathen Road, Dorking, Dorking RH4 1JU
Tel: 44 01306 868250
Email: us@thecreativeteam.co.uk
Web site: www.essentiallycatering.co.uk
Freq: Monthly
Circ: 10267 Cision Digital Reach
Editor: Nicola Belfrage
MAGAZINE (ONLINE)
Alcohol & Spirits, Bars, Clubs & Pubs, Food

Essex Baby
997262
Tel: 44 07939 991621
Email: info@essexbaby.co.uk
Web site: www.essexbaby.co.uk
Freq: Daily
Circ: 10486 Cision Digital Reach
Editor: Tamsin Malone
MAGAZINE (ONLINE)
Family & Parenting

Essex Focus
998343
Editorial: Suite 6B(i), Britannia House, Leagrave Road, Luton LU3 1RJ
Tel: 44 01582 488385
Email: info@mediachameleon.co.uk
Web site: www.essex-focus.co.uk
Freq: Annual Not Audited
MAGAZINE
Antiques/Collectibles, Cooking & Baking, Family & Parenting, Field Sports, Gardening, Restaurant Reviews

Essex Life
982491
Editorial: Portman House, 120 Princes Street, Ipswich IP4 1RS
Email: julian.read@archant.co.uk
Web site: www.essexlifemag.co.uk/home
Freq: Monthly
Circ: 15000 Not Audited
Profile: Magazine focusing on Essex featuring places, people, antiques, gardening, food and drink, property and coming events.
Ad Rate: Full Page Colour £1800.00
MAGAZINE
Regional General Interest

Etc North East
1075961
Editorial: Echo House, Pennywell, Sunderland SR4 9ER **Tel:** 44 01915 017191
Web site: N/A
Freq: Monthly
Circ: 12000 Not Audited
MAGAZINE
Regional General Interest

eTeknix
986662
Editorial: 1 Laurence Hamilton Lane, Repton Park, Ashford, Ashford TN23 3FH
Email: press@eteknix.com
Web site: www.eteknix.com
Freq: Daily
Circ: 720487 Cision Digital Reach
Editor: Peter Donnell
MAGAZINE (ONLINE)
Apple, Computer & Video Games, Computers, Data Management, Electronics, Internet, Mobile Communications, Personal Computers, Software

ethical consumer
983076
Editorial: Unit 21, 41 Old Birley Street, Manchester M15 5RF **Tel:** 44 01612 262929
Email: news@ethicalconsumer.org
Web site: www.ethicalconsumer.org
Freq: Bi-Monthly
Circ: 6500 Not Audited

Editor: Rob Harrison
Profile: Magazine which considers the social, ethical and environmental policies of the companies behind the brand name.
Ad Rate: Full Page Colour £875.00
MAGAZINE
Ethical/Moral Issues

The Ethical-Hedonist
987368
Editorial: The Lions, 154 High St, Ventnor, Ventnor PO38 1NA
Email: ethicalhedonistmagazine@gmail.com
Web site: www.ethical-hedonist.com
Freq: Daily
Circ: 17454 Cision Digital Reach
Profile: Luxury sustainability e-magazine covering local, organic, artisan and sustainable ways of living, culture, fashion, food, green travel, celebrity interviews, health and beauty.
MAGAZINE (ONLINE)
Banking, Beauty & Grooming, Bonds, Commodities, Corporate Finance, Corporate Management, Cosmetics, Derivatives, Economics, Emerging Markets

Ethnic Now
995811
Editorial: 4 Park Royal Metro Centre, Britannia Way, London NW10 7PA
Tel: 44 02088 192548
Email: press@ethnicnow.com
Web site: http://www.ethnicnow.com/
Freq: Daily
Circ: 11652 Cision Digital Reach
MAGAZINE (ONLINE)
Africa, Americas, Asia, Australia, Ethnic & Multicultural, Europe, Expatriates

EU Food Policy
997512
Editorial: 5 Kerrison Road, London W5 5NW
Web site: www.eufoodpolicy.com
Freq: Daily
Circ: 9305 Cision Digital Reach
MAGAZINE (ONLINE)
News & Current Affairs

Euan's Guide
996076
Editorial: 10 Constitution Street, Edinburgh EH6 7BT **Tel:** 44 01315 105106
Email: hello@euansguide.com
Web site: https://www.euansguide.com/
Freq: Daily
Circ: 18360 Cision Digital Reach
Editor: Euan MacDonald
MAGAZINE (ONLINE)
Bars, Clubs & Pubs, Disability

Euro Crime
985797
Web site: www.eurocrime.co.uk
Freq: Daily
Circ: 19707 Cision Digital Reach
MAGAZINE (ONLINE)
Literature

EUROGAMER.net
986132
Editorial: 1 Grand Parade, Brighton BN2 9QB **Tel:** 44 01273 746864
Email: news@eurogamer.net
Web site: www.eurogamer.net
Freq: Daily
Circ: 3373993 Cision Digital Reach
Editor: Oli Welsh
MAGAZINE (ONLINE)
Computer & Video Games

Euromedia Magazine
980795
Editorial: Unit N202, Westminster Business Square, 1-45 Durham Street, London SE11 5JH **Tel:** 44 02035 671444
Web site: www.advanced-television.com
Freq: Bi-Monthly
Circ: 5500 Not Audited
MAGAZINE
Broadcasting

European Business Review
984497
Editorial: Howard House, Wagon Lane, Bingley BD16 1WA **Tel:** 44 01274 777700
Web site: http://www.emeraldinsight.com/loi/ebr
Freq: Bi-Monthly Not Audited

Consumer Magazines

Editor: Göran Svensson
Profile: Journal featuring all aspects of European review legislative and management covering EC markets, legislation and corporate taxation.
MAGAZINE
News & Current Affairs

European Electronic Markets Forecast (EEMF)   983498
Editorial: Harvard House, Grove Technology Park, Wantage OX12 9FF
Tel: 44 01235 227310
Web site: http://www.rer.co.uk/
Freq: Monthly Not Audited
Editor: Andrew Fletcher
MAGAZINE
Electronics

European Journal of Clinical Nutrition   999418
Editorial: The Macmillan Building, 4 Crinan Street, London N1 9XW
Tel: 44 02078 334000
Email: ejcn@nature.com
Web site: www.nature.com/ejcn/index.html
Freq: Monthly Not Audited
MAGAZINE
Nutrition

European Journal of Marketing   995768
Editorial: Howard House, Wagon Lane, Bingley BD16 1WA
Web site: http://www.emeraldinsight.com/loi/ejm
Freq: Monthly Not Audited
Editor: Nick Lee
MAGAZINE
News & Current Affairs

European Journal of Nutrition
996931
Editorial: Floor 6, 236 Gray's Inn Road, London WC1X 8HB
Email: eurjnutr@gmail.com
Web site: http://www.springer.com/food+science/journal/394
Freq: Bi-Monthly Not Audited
MAGAZINE
Nutrition

European Journal of Vascular and Endovascular Surgery
995427
Editorial: The Boulevard, Langford Lane, Kidlington OX5 1GB **Tel:** 44 01865 843000
Email: ejves@elsevier.com
Web site: www.ejves.com
Freq: Monthly
Circ: 2146 Not Audited
MAGAZINE
Cardiology, Medicine

European Railway Review
981335
Editorial: Court Lodge, Hogtrough Hill, Brasted, Westerham TN16 1NU
Tel: 44 01959 563311
Email: info@russellpublishing.com
Web site: www.europeanrailwayreview.com
Freq: Bi-Monthly
Circ: 7499 Not Audited
Editor: Craig Waters
Profile: Magazine focusing on the railway industry, providing European coverage and comment, with a business bias on technological advances, new products and design developments. First published in 1994. Aimed at railway industry purchasing personnel throughout Europe.
Ad Rate: Full Page Colour £4081.00
MAGAZINE
Railroad

European Spa   984421
Editorial: Halifax House, Halifax Place, Nottingham NG1 1QN **Tel:** 44 01159 504748
Email: sarah.camilleri@spapublishing.com
Web site: www.europeanspamagazine.com
Freq: Bi-Monthly
Circ: 5000 Not Audited

Profile: Magazine focusing on spa industry news, interviews, spa reviews, new treatments and products, treatments and products, expert views and advice, trends and spa design.
MAGAZINE
Fitness & Exercise

The European Times   999176
Email: info@european-times.com
Web site: http://www.european-times.com
Freq: Bi-Monthly Not Audited
Editor: Vicky Kox
MAGAZINE
Business, Travel

The European Tour   1103013
Tel: 44 01344 840400
Web site: http://www.europeantour.com/
Freq: Daily
Circ: 1348400 Cision Digital Reach
MAGAZINE (ONLINE)
Golf

Eurotransport   983287
Editorial: Court Lodge, Hogtrough Hill, Brasted, Westerham TN16 1NU
Tel: 44 01959 563311
Email: info@russellpublishing.com
Web site: www.eurotransportmagazine.com
Freq: Bi-Monthly
Circ: 9800 Not Audited
Editor: Craig Waters
Profile: Magazine covering European integrated transport, including articles on new technologies and developments within the transport industry.
Ad Rate: Full Page Colour £497.00
MAGAZINE
Railroad

EuroTravel   995382
Editorial: 4 Imperial Place, Maxwell Road, Borehamwood WD6 1JN
Tel: 44 02082 133078
Email: editorial.tem@aglpublications.com
Web site: http://eurotravelmag.com
Freq: Monthly
Circ: 1399 Cision Digital Reach
MAGAZINE (ONLINE)
Travel

EuroWire   985962
Editorial: 46 Holly Walk, Leamington Spa CV32 4HY **Tel:** 44 01926 334137
Email: eurowire@intras.co.uk
Web site: www.read-eurowire.com
Freq: Bi-Monthly
Circ: 20000 Not Audited
Editor: David Bell
Profile: International trade magazine covering the wire and cable manufacturing industries.
Ad Rate: Full Page Mono £1612.00
Ad Rate: Full Page Colour £2163.00
MAGAZINE
Electronics, Industry, Mobile Communications

Evangelical Times   982149
Editorial: 3 Trinity Court, Faverdale North, Darlington DL3 0PH **Tel:** 44 01325 380232
Email: office@evangelical-times.org
Web site: www.evangelical-times.org
Freq: Monthly
Circ: 5000 Not Audited
Editor: Roger Fay
Profile: Newspaper providing news and articles for today's Christian church. It contains relevant and readable articles and analyses on topics as varied as church history, biography, science and ethics, Bible doctrine and exposition, ministry, and trends in evangelicalism.
Ad Rate: Full Page Mono £895.00
MAGAZINE
Religion

Evergreen   998810
Editorial: The Lypiatts, Lansdown Road, Cheltenham, Cheltenham GL50 2JA
Tel: 44 01242 225780
Email: editor@evergreenmagazine.co.uk
Web site: www.thisengland.co.uk

Freq: Quarterly
Circ: 75000 Not Audited
Editor: Stephen Garnett
MAGAZINE
History

Every Child Journal   998390
Editorial: 309 Scott House, The Custard Factory, Gibb Street, Birmingham B9 4DT
Tel: 44 01212 247599
Email: enquiries@imaginativeminds.co.uk
Web site: http://www.teachingtimes.com/zone/every-child.htm
Freq: Bi-Monthly
Circ: 57 Cision Digital Reach
MAGAZINE (ONLINE)
Disability, Preschool, Schools & Institutions, Students

Every Model Magazine   985330
Editorial: First Floor, Tailby House, Bath Road, Kettering NN16 8NL
Tel: 44 07980 733241
Email: editor@everymodelgroup.com
Web site: http://www.everymodelmagazine.co.uk/
Freq: Quarterly
Circ: 1000 Not Audited
Editor: Ruth Deane
Profile: Publication that the covers the latest news and information with regards fashion models and the modelling industry.
MAGAZINE
Beauty & Grooming, Cosmetics, Fashion, Hair

Everyday Diabetes   1053460
Email: everydaydiabetes365@gmail.com
Web site: www.everydaydiabetes.com/
Freq: Daily
Circ: 13480 Cision Digital Reach
MAGAZINE (ONLINE)
Cooking & Baking, Diabetes, Health & Medicine, Nutrition

Everyday Practical Electronics   985977
Editorial: 113 Lynwood Drive, Wimborne, Oakley BH21 1UU **Tel:** 44 01202 880299
Email: editorial@wimborne.co.uk
Web site: www.epemag3.com
Freq: Monthly
Circ: 20000 Not Audited
Editor: Matthew Pulzer
Profile: Magazine featuring projects and news on electronics. Also including information on building techniques, circuits and components. Aimed at students, trainers and those interested in electronics.Previous title: Everyday Practical Electronics with ETI Regular features: Circuit Sugery Readers' queries are answered.; Interface Feature covering information about interfacing computers.; Network Feature about various aspects of the internet.; Pic 'n' Mix Feature covering microprocessor programming.; Projects; TechnoTalk The latest electronics industry news.
Ad Rate: Full Page Colour £500.00
MAGAZINE
Computers, Electronics

EverythingEppingForest.co.uk   985762
Email: everythingeppingforest@googlemail.com
Web site: www.everythingeppingforest.co.uk
Freq: Daily
Circ: 8506 Cision Digital Reach
Editor: David Jackman
MAGAZINE (ONLINE)
Regional, Regional General Interest

EverythingHarlow.co.uk   1105201
Email: everythingharlow@googlemail.com
Web site: www.everythingharlow.co.uk
Freq: Daily
Circ: 10760 Cision Digital Reach
Editor: David Jackman
MAGAZINE (ONLINE)
Regional General Interest

Eve's Watch   999673
Tel: 44 08452 990200
Email: editorial@eveswatch.com
Web site: www.eveswatch.com/
Freq: Daily
Circ: 8880 Cision Digital Reach
MAGAZINE (ONLINE)
Fashion, Luxury Goods

evo   982631
Editorial: Unit 5 Tower Court, Irchester Road, Wollaston, Wellingborough NN29 7PJ
Tel: 44 02079 07600
Email: eds@evo.co.uk
Web site: www.evo.co.uk
Freq: Monthly
Circ: 40215 Not Audited
Profile: Magazine focusing on the latest performance cars. Contains road test articles, car reviews and news on motor sport and the motor industry. First published in 1998. Aimed at car enthusiasts between 25 and 50 years old.
Ad Rate: Full Page Colour £4563.00
MAGAZINE
Automotive, Driving

Evolve   997478
Editorial: evolve, Cromwell Road, London SW7 5BD **Tel:** 44 02079 425899
Email: evolve@nhm.ac.uk
Web site: www.nhm.ac.uk/visit-us/become-a-member/magazines/evolve/index.html
Freq: Quarterly
Circ: 6700 Not Audited
MAGAZINE
History

EVOLVE   998907
Email: sarahp@evolve-magazine.com
Web site: www.evolve-magazine.com
Freq: Bi-Monthly
Circ: 1823 Cision Digital Reach
MAGAZINE (ONLINE)
Fashion, Women's Interests

Evolver   984040
Editorial: 8 Buckland Road, Pen Mill Trading Estate, Yeovil, Yeovil BA21 5EA
Tel: 44 01935 474947
Email: info@evolver.org.uk
Web site: http://www.evolver.org.uk/
Freq: Bi-Monthly
Circ: 8000 Not Audited
Editor: Simon Barber
Profile: Magazine covering the arts in Wessex with listings and news about arts events including theatre shows, art exhibitions and music events.
MAGAZINE
Art, Literature, Photography, Theater & Performing Arts, Visual Arts

exceed   997297
Editorial: Sheridan House, Bridge Industrial Estate, Speke Hall Rd, Liverpool L24 9HB
Tel: 44 01512 395050
Email: news@exceed-magazine.com
Web site: www.exceed-magazine.com
Freq: Quarterly
Circ: 4000 Not Audited
Editor: Lucy Mason
MAGAZINE
Fitness & Exercise

Excelente   998044
Editorial: 6th Floor, 85 Strand, London WC2R 0DW **Tel:** 44 02075 508000
Freq: Monthly
Circ: 35000 Not Audited
MAGAZINE
Airline Inflight, Luxury Goods

Excelle Magazine   998492
Editorial: New Barn House, Hall Mews, Boston Spa LS23 6DT **Tel:** 44 01937 581400
Email: info@excellemagazine.co.uk
Web site: www.excellemagazine.co.uk
Freq: Bi-Monthly
Circ: 40000 Not Audited
MAGAZINE
Regional General Interest

Exclusive
983114
Editorial: St George Street, Leicester LE1 9FQ **Tel:** 44 01162 224173
Web site: http://exclusivemagazine.online/
Freq: Monthly Not Audited
Editor: Jennie Findley
MAGAZINE
Regional General Interest

Exclusive (Berkshire)
995128
Editorial: 9 Chiltern Court, Asheridge Road, Chesham, Chesham HP5 2PX
Tel: 44 01494 771144
Email: info@exclusivemagazines.co.uk
Web site: http://www.exclusivemagazines.co.uk/
Freq: Monthly Not Audited
Editor: Rosalind Sack
MAGAZINE
Luxury Goods

Exclusive (Buckinghamshire)
995099
Editorial: 9 Chiltern Court, Asheridge Road, Chesham, Chesham HP5 2PX
Tel: 44 01494 771144
Email: info@exclusivemagazines.co.uk
Web site: http://www.exclusivemagazines.co.uk/
Freq: Monthly Not Audited
Editor: Rosalind Sack
MAGAZINE
Luxury Goods

Exclusive (Hertfordshire)
988790
Editorial: 9 Chiltern Court, Asheridge Road, Chesham, Chesham HP5 2PX
Tel: 44 01494 771144
Email: info@exclusivemagazines.co.uk
Web site: http://www.exclusivemagazines.co.uk/
Freq: Monthly Not Audited
Editor: Rosalind Sack
MAGAZINE
Luxury Goods

Exclusive (London)
985919
Editorial: 9 Chiltern Court, Asheridge Road, Chesham, Chesham HP5 2PX
Tel: 44 01494 771144
Email: info@exclusivemagazines.co.uk
Web site: www.exclusivemagazines.co.uk
Freq: Monthly Not Audited
Editor: Rosalind Sack
MAGAZINE
Luxury Goods

Exclusive (Surrey)
995150
Editorial: 9 Chiltern Court, Asheridge Road, Chesham, Chesham HP5 2PX
Tel: 44 01494 771144
Email: info@exclusivemagazines.co.uk
Web site: http://www.exclusivemagazines.co.uk/
Freq: Monthly Not Audited
Editor: Rosalind Sack
MAGAZINE
Luxury Goods

Exclusively British Magazine
996117
Editorial: Mitchell House, Brook Avenue, Warsash, Hampshire, Southampton SO31 9HP **Tel:** 44 01489 660680
Email: editorial@exclusivelybritishmagazine.co.uk
Web site: exclusivelybritishmagazine.co.uk
Freq: Bi-Monthly
Circ: 40000 Not Audited
Editor: Samantha Rutherford
MAGAZINE
Luxury Goods, Men's Interests, Travel, Women's Interests

Excursions Magazine
996305
Editorial: 25 Cheriton, Queens Crescent, London NW5 4EZ **Tel:** 44 02078 130677
Email: info@excursionsuk.com
Web site: www.excursionsuk.com
Freq: Bi-Monthly

Circ: 200000 Not Audited
MAGAZINE
Antiques/Collectibles, Art, Arts, Bars, Clubs & Pubs, Comedy, Computer & Video Games, Entertainment, Fitness & Exercise, Genealogy, Hotels/Motels

Executive Compensation Briefing
983642
Editorial: 19 Heathmans Road, London SW6 4TJ **Tel:** 44 02071 480188
Email: info@clearviewpublishing.com
Web site: www.executive-compensation-briefing.com
Freq: Monthly
Circ: 1079 Cision Digital Reach
Editor: Nick Parmee
Profile: Newsletter containing expert advice on executive rewards and corporate governance.
Ad Rate: Full Page Colour £1000000.00
MAGAZINE (ONLINE)
Company News & Appointments, Corporate Law, Education, Employment, Health & Safety, Human Resources, Human Rights, Personal Finance, Recruiting

Executive Traveller
983297
Editorial: Editorial Department, 33 Donkin House, Galleywall Road, London SE16 3PQ
Tel: 44 07984 021973
Web site: http://executivetraveller.net/index.html
Freq: Daily
Circ: 171 Cision Digital Reach
Profile: Website covering travel. Executive Traveller shares the latest news on the travel industry, including tourist and exclusive destinations, with detailed travel features from around the world, tried and tested gadgets as well as food and drink reviews.
MAGAZINE (ONLINE)
Genealogy, Travel

Exposé
981760
Editorial: Exeter University Guild of Students, Devonshire House, Exeter EX4 4QR **Tel:** 44 01392 263513
Email: editors@exepose.com
Web site: exepose.com
Freq: Bi-Weekly Not Audited
Profile: Publication of Exeter University Guild of Students containing news, sport, entertainment listings and a culture section.
Ad Rate: Full Page Colour £600.00
MAGAZINE
Student Lifestyle

EXETER
999085
Editorial: Northcote House, The Queens Drive, Exeter EX4 4QJ **Tel:** 44 01392 723360
Web site: www.exeter.ac.uk/alumnisupporters/news/onlinemagazine/
Freq: Annual
Circ: 55000 Not Audited
MAGAZINE
Alumni

The Exeter Daily
987025
Editorial: 6 Northernhay Place, Exeter EX4 3QJ **Tel:** 44 01392 270291
Email: ted@thedailyuk.com
Web site: www.theexeterdaily.co.uk
Freq: Daily
Circ: 53011 Cision Digital Reach
Editor: Mary Youlden
MAGAZINE (ONLINE)
Regional

Exeter Living
984009
Editorial: Circus Mews House, Circus Mews, Bath BA1 2PW **Tel:** 44 01225 475800
Email: info@mediaclash.co.uk
Web site: http://www.mediaclash.co.uk/magazines/local-magazines/exeter-living/
Freq: Monthly
Circ: 10000 Not Audited
Editor: Anna Britten
Profile: Property and lifestyle magazine covering food, arts, out and about and gardening. The magazine only covers stories with a focus on Devon. Published every three weeks.

Ad Rate: Full Page Colour £650.00
MAGAZINE
Regional General Interest

Exeunt Magazine
1052571
Email: info@exeuntmagazine.com
Web site: http://exeuntmagazine.com/
Freq: Daily
Circ: 19289 Cision Digital Reach
MAGAZINE (ONLINE)
Theater & Performing Arts

Exit Magazine
983420
Editorial: Suite 146, 77 Beak Street, Soho, London W1F 9DB
Email: info@exitmagazine.co.uk
Web site: www.exitmagazine.co.uk
Freq: Semi-Annual
Circ: 47000 Not Audited
MAGAZINE
Art, Fashion, Photography, Visual Arts

Exmoor Magazine
984049
Editorial: PO Box 281, Parracombe, Barnstaple EX31 4WW
Web site: www.exmoormagazine.co.uk
Freq: Quarterly Not Audited
Editor: Naomi Cudmore
MAGAZINE
Regional General Interest

Expat Living
998359
Editorial: 25 west Gate, Plumpton, Lewes BN7 3BQ **Tel:** 44 01273 891262
Email: expat@expatnetwork.com
Web site: www.worldofexpats.com
Freq: Quarterly Not Audited
MAGAZINE
Expatriates

Expat Network
998027
Email: expats@expatnetwork.com
Web site: www.expatnetwork.com
Freq: Daily
Circ: 26989 Cision Digital Reach
MAGAZINE (ONLINE)
Expatriates

The Expatriate's Guide to Living in the UK
995960
Editorial: P.O. Box 921, Sutton SM1 2WB
Tel: 44 02086 610186
Web site: http://www.expatsguidetotheuk.com/
Freq: Annual
Circ: 25000 Not Audited
MAGAZINE
Africa, Americas, Asia, Australia, Company News & Appointments, Education, Ethnic & Multicultural, Europe, Expatriates, Health & Safety

Expedia Postcard
1094738
Web site: https://www.expedia.co.uk/postcard
Freq: Daily
Circ: 9315 Cision Digital Reach
MAGAZINE (ONLINE)
Airline Inflight, Travel

Expert Review of Vaccines
995284
Editorial: Christchurch Court, 10-15 Newgate Street, London EC1A 7AZ
Tel: 44 02070 175000
Web site: http://www.tandfonline.com/toc/ierv20/current
Freq: Monthly Not Audited
MAGAZINE
Medicine

Expert Reviews
987218
Editorial: 31 - 32 Alfred Place, London WC1E 7DP **Tel:** 44 02079 076000
Email: editor@expertreviews.co.uk
Web site: www.expertreviews.co.uk
Freq: Daily
Circ: 895453 Cision Digital Reach
Editor: David Court
MAGAZINE (ONLINE)
Apple, Audio Video Trade, Cameras, Computer & Video Games, Computers,

Consumer Electronics, Electronics, Internet, Mobile Electronics, Movies & Video

Express North
994995
Web site: http://expressnorth.co.uk/
Freq: Daily
Circ: 11308 Cision Digital Reach
Editor: Lucy Richardson
MAGAZINE (ONLINE)
Women's Interests

Exquisite Essex
987537
Editorial: Suite 2, 284 Warley Hill, Brentwood, Brentwood CM13 3AB
Tel: 44 01277 888721
Email: teresa@refined-media.co.uk
Web site: www.refined-media.co.uk
Freq: Quarterly
Circ: 30000 Not Audited
Profile: Magazine covering regional interest news in Essex. It features restaurant and bar reviews, up and coming events, ideas for days out, fashion, interior design, real life weddings and a black book style directory of the best services in Essex.
MAGAZINE
Lifestyle, Luxury Goods, Men's Interests, Regional General Interest, Women's Interests

Extorted
1075491
Email: extortedmag@gmail.com
Web site: http://www.extorted.com/
Freq: Daily
Circ: 10498 Cision Digital Reach
MAGAZINE (ONLINE)
Celebrities, Fashion, Movies & Video, Pop Music, Rap & Hip Hop, Rock Music

EYE
983869
Editorial: St Jude's Church, Dulwich Road, London SE24 0PB **Tel:** 44 02075 016763
Web site: www.magonlinelibrary.com/toc/eyed/current
Freq: Monthly
Circ: 12500 Not Audited
Profile: Magazine featuring a range of professional and practical articles. Topics include training, research, professional development, outdoor learning, in-depth analysis, focus on early years, foundation stage and reception year.
Ad Rate: Full Page Mono £995.00
Ad Rate: Full Page Colour £995.00
MAGAZINE
Education, Preschool

Eye for Film
986602
Editorial: 2FR, 1 Seaport St, Edinburgh EH6 6SJ **Tel:** 44 01315 553822
Email: eyeforfilm@yahoo.com
Web site: www.eyeforfilm.co.uk
Freq: Daily
Circ: 65875 Cision Digital Reach
MAGAZINE (ONLINE)
Entertainment, Movies & Video

Eye For Transport
998602
Editorial: 7/9 Fashion Street, London E1 6PX **Tel:** 44 02073 757500
Email: info@eyefortransport.com
Web site: http://www.eft.com/
Freq: Daily
Circ: 13875 Cision Digital Reach
MAGAZINE (ONLINE)
Automotive, Aviation, Railroad, Shipping & Warehousing, Supply Chain Management (SCM), Transportation

Eye for travel
982943
Editorial: 7-9 Fashion Street, London E1 6PX **Tel:** 44 02073 757500
Email: nikhil@eyefortravel.com
Web site: www.eyefortravel.com
Freq: Daily
Circ: 145492 Cision Digital Reach
Editor: Pamela Whitby
MAGAZINE (ONLINE)
Travel

Consumer Magazines

Eye Spy Intelligence Magazine
983267

Editorial: PO Box 10, Skipton, Skipton BD23 5US **Tel:** 44 01756 770199
Email: eyespy@eyespymag.com
Web site: www.eyespymag.com
Freq: Bi-Monthly
Circ: 40000 Not Audited
Profile: Magazine covering UK/USA and global aspects of intelligence, espionage, security, special forces, terrorism, counter-intelligence, specialist equipment for the intelligence trade, analysis and comment.
Ad Rate: Full Page Colour £600.00
MAGAZINE
Armed Forces, Defense & National Security

Eyestylist
1062756

Web site: http://www.eyestylist.com/
Freq: Daily
Circ: 9066 Cision Digital Reach
MAGAZINE (ONLINE)
Luxury Goods

The F Word
986000

Email: media@thefword.org.uk
Web site: www.thefword.org.uk
Freq: Daily
Circ: 78033 Cision Digital Reach
MAGAZINE (ONLINE)
Human Rights, Social Issues

F.C. Business
985414

Editorial: Baltic Publications Ltd, Gear House, Saltmeadows Road, Gateshead, Gateshead NE8 3AH **Tel:** 44 01914 414008
Web site: www.fcbusiness.co.uk
Freq: Bi-Monthly
Circ: 45000 Not Audited
Editor: Aaron Gourley
Profile: Magazine focusing on good practices in all areas involved in running a football club. Aimed at chairmen of football clubs and business people involved in football.
Ad Rate: Full Page Colour £1569.00
MAGAZINE
Fitness & Exercise

F.O. Licht's International Coffee Report
984041

Editorial: Christchurch Court, 10-15 Newgate Street, London EC1A 7AZ
Tel: 44 02070 177500
Web site: www.agra-net.com/portal2/home.jsp?template=productpage&pubid=ag049
Freq: Bi-Monthly
Circ: 462 Cision Digital Reach
Profile: Newsletter containing a complete overview of the world coffee market with international reports and detailed production, consumption and trade statistics.
MAGAZINE (ONLINE)
Alcohol & Spirits

F.TAPE
984874

Editorial: 12 Benyon Wharf, 295 Kingsland Road, London E8 4DQ **Tel:** 44 02075 036004
Email: info@ftape.com
Web site: www.ftape.com
Freq: Daily
Circ: 47419 Cision Digital Reach
MAGAZINE (ONLINE)
Fashion

F1 Racing (UK)
982671

Editorial: Bridge House, 69 London Road, Twickenham, London TW1 3QR
Tel: 44 02082 675806
Email: f1racingcontact@haymarket.com
Web site: www.f1racing.co.uk
Freq: Monthly
Circ: 44610 Not Audited
Editor: Anthony Rowlinson
MAGAZINE
Motorsports

Fab Radio International
998266

Editorial: 23 Nicholas Street, Manchester m1 4qt **Tel:** 44 01612 389050
Email: studio@fabradiointernational.com

Web site: www.fabradiointernational.com/
Freq: Daily
Circ: 14114 Cision Digital Reach
MAGAZINE (ONLINE)
Celebrities, Classical/Choral/Band Music, Country, Folk, Bluegrass, Dance Music, Jazz & Blues, LGBT, Lifestyle, Men's Interests, Music, Pop Music

Fabian Review
984780

Editorial: 61 Petty France, Westminster, London SW1H 9EU **Tel:** 44 02072 274900
Email: review@fabian-society.org.uk
Web site: www.fabians.org.uk
Freq: Quarterly
Profile: Magazine containing detailed information on political issues. Forum for debate on public policy and politics, it features articles by leading political figures and commentators. First published in 1884. Read by Fabian members, policy makers, MPs, journalists and academics.
Ad Rate: Full Page Colour £900.00
MAGAZINE
Government, Politics

Fabric
981841

Editorial: The Griffin Building, 83 Clerkenwell Road, London EC1R 5AR
Tel: 44 02077 342303
Email: fabric.magazine@forwardww.com
Web site: www.fabricmagazine.co.uk
Freq: Monthly
Circ: 70000 Not Audited
MAGAZINE
Do-It-Yourself (DIY), Property Management & Maintenance

Fabrications, Quilting for You
997580

Editorial: Traplet House, Willow End Park, Blackmore Park Road, Malvern WR13 6NN
Tel: 44 01684 588500
Web site: http://gb.trapletshop.com/fabrications-quilting-for-you-julyaugust-2016
Freq: Bi-Monthly
Circ: 19800 Not Audited
MAGAZINE
Crafts

Facets
998277

Editorial: 4 Cavendish Square, London W1G 0PG **Tel:** 44 02075 533250
Web site: www.facetspr.com
Freq: Quarterly
Circ: 1200 Not Audited
MAGAZINE
Fashion

Facilities
980939

Editorial: Howard House, Wagon Lane, Bingley BD16 1WA
Web site: http://www.emeraldinsight.com/journals.htm?issn=0263-2772
Freq: Bi-Monthly Not Audited
Profile: International journal covering research, news, information and comment on key issues regarding maximising building space resources.
MAGAZINE
News & Current Affairs

Façonner Editorial
996456

Tel: 44 02037 314131
Email: faconner@faconner.co.uk
Web site: http://www.faconner.co.uk/
Freq: Quarterly
Circ: 3000 Not Audited
MAGAZINE
Do-It-Yourself (DIY), Fashion, Women's Interests

FACT
983333

Editorial: 16-18 Marshall Street, London W1F 7BE **Tel:** 44 02070 251385
Email: editors@factmag.com
Web site: www.factmag.com
Freq: Daily
Circ: 1194707 Cision Digital Reach
Profile: Website covering dance music. FACT is an online magazine providing the latest news on anything from album releases to events. It provides features, reviews,

interviews and music downloads. Fact was launched in October 2005.
MAGAZINE (ONLINE)
Country, Folk, Bluegrass, Dance Music, Jazz & Blues, Pop Music, Rap & Hip Hop, Rock Music

Factor
988200

Editorial: John Carpenter House, John Carpenter Street, London EC4Y 0AN
Tel: 44 02078 323590
Web site: www.factor-tech.com
Freq: Monthly
Circ: 30000 Not Audited
Editor: Lucy Ingham
MAGAZINE
Auto Aftermarket, Computers, Data Management, Electronics, Government Technology, Industry, Internet, Mobile Communications, Security & Security Systems, Software

FACTS
984436

Editorial: 34 Bernard Street, Edinburgh EH6 6PR **Tel:** 44 01315 541129
Web site: www.factsmagazine.co.uk
Freq: Monthly
Circ: 7000 Not Audited
Profile: Magazine focusing on fleet, agriculture and commercial transport in Scotland.
Ad Rate: Full Page Colour £1755.00
MAGAZINE
Automotive, Shipping & Warehousing

Fairer Finance
994988

Editorial: 10 Finsbury Square, London EC2A 1AF **Tel:** 44 02030 268541
Email: media@fairerfinance.com
Web site: www.fairerfinance.com
Circ: 10423 Cision Digital Reach
MAGAZINE (ONLINE)
Personal Finance

Fairies
987473

Editorial: The Stables, Peper Harow Park, Nr Godalming, Godalming GU8 6BQ
Tel: 44 01483 779500
Web site: http://www.signaturepl.co.uk/portfolio/Fairies.html
Freq: Bi-Monthly
Circ: 28000 Not Audited
MAGAZINE
Teen/Young Adult

The Fairway Golfing News
982265

Editorial: Fairway Golfing News, Pinewood, 193 Aberthaw Road, Newport NP19 9PW
Tel: 44 01633 666700
Email: enquiries@fairway.org.uk
Web site: www.fairway.org.uk
Freq: Bi-Monthly
Circ: 30000 Not Audited
Editor: John Doherty
Profile: Newspaper covering events and items of interest from the world of golf. Aimed at golfers of all ages both amateur and professional.
Ad Rate: Full Page Mono £1000.00
Ad Rate: Full Page Colour £1700.00
MAGAZINE
Golf

Falcata Times
997931

Web site: http://falcatatimes.blogspot.com
Freq: Daily
Circ: 10255 Cision Digital Reach
Editor: Gareth Wilson
MAGAZINE (ONLINE)
Literature, Science Fiction

The Falconers & Raptor Conservation Magazine
981933

Editorial: Tayfield House, 38 Poole Road, Westbourne, Bournemouth BH4 9DW
Tel: 44 01202 751611
Email: newsdesk@pwpublishing.ltd.com
Web site: pwpublishing.ltd.uk/falconers
Freq: Quarterly
Circ: 1200 Not Audited
Editor: Peter Eldrett

Profile: Magazine featuring articles and news on falcons and falconry both in the UK and abroad.
Ad Rate: Full Page Mono £300.00
Ad Rate: Full Page Colour £490.00
MAGAZINE
Field Sports, Nature & Wildlife

Fall-Line
982286

Editorial: 4 Milnyard Square, Bakewell Road, Orton Southgate, Peterborough PE2 6GX **Tel:** 44 01733 293250
Web site: www.fall-line.co.uk
Freq: Monthly
Circ: 13000 Not Audited
Editor: Nicola Iseard
Profile: Magazine covering all aspects of alpine sports including skiing, snowboarding, destination information, tips on what to do before you go and when you get there, products, reviews and news. First published in 1991, the publication has an average of 132 pages per issue. Aimed at ski and snowboarding enthusiasts.
Ad Rate: Full Page Colour £1100.00
MAGAZINE
Winter Sports

The False Nine
1053210

Email: thefalsenine@yahoo.co.uk
Web site: http://www.thefalsenine.co.uk/
Freq: Daily
Circ: 10448 Cision Digital Reach
MAGAZINE (ONLINE)
Soccer

Families
1064281

Editorial: Manchester Business Park, 3000 Aviator Way, Wilmslow M22 5TG
Tel: 44 01628 535499
Email: headoffice@mumsintheknow.co.uk
Web site: www.familiesonline.co.uk
Freq: Daily
Circ: 134298 Cision Digital Reach
Editor: Gaynor Jackson
MAGAZINE (ONLINE)
Family & Parenting

Families Bedfordshire
986857

Editorial: Remenham House, Regatta Place, Marlow Road, Bourne End, London SL8 5TD
Tel: 44 01727 373929
Email: editor@familiesbedfordshire.co.uk
Web site: https://www.familiesonline.co.uk/locations/bedfordshire
Freq: Bi-Monthly
Circ: 14000 Not Audited
Editor: Judith Dow
MAGAZINE
Family & Parenting

Families Birmingham
986879

Editorial: 17 Riggindale Road, London SW16 1QL **Tel:** 44 07807 352087
Email: editor@familiesbirmingham.co.uk
Web site: https://www.familiesonline.co.uk/locations/birmingham
Freq: Bi-Monthly
Circ: 20600 Not Audited
Editor: Suzanne Brown
MAGAZINE
Family & Parenting

Families Cambridgeshire
1076639

Tel: 44 01945 861336
Email: editor@familiescambridgeshire.co.uk
Web site: https://www.familiesonline.co.uk/locations/cambridgeshire
Freq: Bi-Monthly
Circ: 20000 Not Audited
Editor: Sarah Carr; **Editor:** Lisa Exell
MAGAZINE
Family & Parenting

Families Central Scotland
999523

Editorial: 17 Riggindale Road, London SW16 1QL **Tel:** 44 07930 264979
Email: editor@familiescentralscotland.co.uk
Web site: https://www.familiesonline.co.uk/locations/central-scotland
Freq: Bi-Monthly

Circ: 12000 Not Audited
Editor: Louise Boyle
MAGAZINE
Family & Parenting

Families Cheshire   1076635

Editorial: PO Box 581, Macclesfield SK10 9FN Tel: 44 01625 801801
Email: editor@familiescheshire.co.uk
Web site: https://www.familiesonline.co.uk/locations/cheshire
Freq: Bi-Monthly
Circ: 25000 Not Audited
Editor: Jayne Keep
MAGAZINE
Family & Parenting

Families Chiltern   982394

Editorial: PO Box 1037, Beaconsfield, Beaconsfield HP9 1ZF Tel: 44 01206 686686
Email: editor@familieschiltern.co.uk
Web site: https://www.familiesonline.co.uk/families-magazines/families-chiltern-magazine
Freq: Bi-Monthly
Circ: 20000 Not Audited
Editor: Chrissie Wilson
Profile: Magazine with local news and information as well as articles on child care, health, education, travel and events.
Ad Rate: Full Page Colour £1220.00
MAGAZINE
Family & Parenting

Families Edinburgh   982396

Editorial: PO Box 23802, Edinburgh EH7 4XL Tel: 44 0316 220405
Email: editor@familiesedinburgh.co.uk
Web site: www.familiesonline.co.uk/locations/edinburgh
Freq: Bi-Monthly
Circ: 20000 Not Audited
Editor: Sarah Adair
Profile: Magazine providing information on local clubs, classes, shows, events and local features on parenting.
Ad Rate: Full Page Colour £1220.00
MAGAZINE
Family & Parenting

Families Fife, Perth & Kinross
                              999448
Tel: 44 01383 841686
Email: editor@familiesfife.co.uk
Web site: http://www.familiesonline.co.uk/locations/fife-perth-kinross
Freq: Bi-Monthly
Circ: 12000 Not Audited
MAGAZINE
Family & Parenting

Families First   982406

Editorial: The Mothers' Union Office, Mary Sumner House, 24 Tufton Street, London SW1P 3RB Tel: 44 02072 225533
Email: familiesfirst@mothersunion.org
Web site: www.familiesfirstmagazine.com
Freq: Bi-Monthly
Circ: 18010 Not Audited
Editor: Tola Fisher
Profile: Lifestyle magazine containing practical featues about making marriages loving and lasting, good parenting, plus Christian faith in action.
Ad Rate: Full Page Colour £1200.00
MAGAZINE
Family & Parenting

Families Glasgow   986873

Editorial: 4 Craigbank Grove, Eaglesham, Glasgow G76 0DY
Email: editor@familiesglasgow.co.uk
Web site: www.familiesonline.co.uk/locations/glasgow
Freq: Bi-Monthly
Circ: 20000 Not Audited
Profile: Magazine covering activities, news, education, book reviews, health and information.
Ad Rate: Full Page Colour £1220.00
MAGAZINE
Family & Parenting

Families Gloucestershire   986874

Editorial: PO Box 94, Dursley, Dursley GL11 9AQ Tel: 44 01453 544658
Email: editor@familiesgloucestershire.co.uk
Web site: www.familiesonline.co.uk/locations/gloucestershire
Freq: Bi-Monthly
Circ: 18500 Not Audited
Editor: Diane Clifford
Profile: Magazine covering activities, news, education, book reviews, health and information.
MAGAZINE
Family & Parenting

Families Hampshire North
                              1008432
Editorial: 7 Hatch Warren Lane, Basingstoke, Basingstoke RG22 4DB
Tel: 44 07789 882467
Email: editor@familieshampshirenorth.co.uk
Web site: www.familiesonline.co.uk/locations/hampshire-north
Freq: Bi-Monthly
Circ: 15000 Not Audited
Editor: Rebecca Carr
MAGAZINE
Family & Parenting

Families Hampshire West
                              986881
Tel: 44 07789 882467
Web site: https://www.familiesonline.co.uk/locations/hampshire-west
Freq: Bi-Monthly
Circ: 21000 Not Audited
Editor: Rebecca Carr
MAGAZINE
Family & Parenting

Families Hereford & Worcestershire   1076747

Tel: 44 01684 770566
Email: editor@familiesherefordandworcs.co.uk
Web site: www.familiesonline.co.uk/locations/hereford-and-worcester
Freq: Bi-Monthly
Circ: 22000 Not Audited
Editor: Diane Clifford
MAGAZINE
Family & Parenting

Families Herts   982398

Editorial: PO Box 434, Pinner HA5 9AH
Tel: 44 02084 286384
Email: editor@familiesherts.co.uk
Web site: www.familiesonline.co.uk/locations/herts
Freq: Bi-Monthly
Circ: 23000 Not Audited
Editor: Shelley Cooper
Profile: Magazine covering family activities, news, education, book reviews, health and information for parents. Aimed at parents and nannies with young children living in Chorleywood, Hemel Hempstead, St Albans, Harpenden, Welwyn Garden City, Stevenage, Hitchin and the surrounding areas.
Ad Rate: Full Page Colour £1220.00
MAGAZINE
Family & Parenting

Families Leeds   986872

Editorial: PO Box 403, Leeds LS17 1EP
Tel: 44 07799 667041
Email: editor@familiesleeds.co.uk
Web site: www.familiesonline.co.uk/locations/leeds
Freq: Bi-Monthly
Circ: 20000 Not Audited
Editor: Claire Bottomley
Profile: Magazine covering parenting, activities, news, education, book reviews, health and information.
Ad Rate: Full Page Colour £1220.00
MAGAZINE
Family & Parenting

Families London - Kent Borders   999149

Editorial: PO Box 1088, Bromley BR1 9RD
Tel: 44 0792 000040
Email: editor@familieslondonkent.co.uk
Web site: https://www.familiesonline.co.uk/families-magazines/families-london-kent-borders-magazine
Freq: Bi-Monthly
Circ: 16500 Not Audited
Editor: Mima Walia
MAGAZINE
Family & Parenting

Families London - Surrey Borders   982397

Editorial: 34 Marchmont Road, Wallington, London SM6 9NU Tel: 44 01923 775680
Email: editor@families-lsb.co.uk
Web site: www.familiesonline.co.uk/locations/london-surrey-borders
Freq: Bi-Monthly
Circ: 21000 Not Audited
Editor: Tamar Pearson
MAGAZINE
Family & Parenting

Families Manchester   986870

Editorial: PO Box 581, Macclesfield SK10 9FN Tel: 44 01625 801801
Email: editor@familiesmanchester.co.uk
Web site: www.familiesonline.co.uk/locations/manchester
Freq: Bi-Monthly
Circ: 25000 Not Audited
Editor: Jayne Keep
Profile: Magazine covering activities, news, education, book reviews, health and information.
MAGAZINE
Family & Parenting

Families Need Fathers   998745

Editorial: 134 Curtain Road, London EC2A 3AR Tel: 44 02076 135060
Email: media@fnf.org.uk
Web site: www.fnf.org.uk
Freq: Daily
Circ: 11900 Cision Digital Reach
MAGAZINE (ONLINE)
Charitable Foundations, Family & Parenting

Families North & East London
                              982395
Editorial: 120 Brent Street, Hendon, London NW4 2DT Tel: 44 02082 022034
Email: editor@familiesnwlondon.co.uk
Web site: https://www.familiesonline.co.uk/locations/london-east
Freq: Bi-Monthly
Circ: 28000 Not Audited
MAGAZINE
Family & Parenting

Families North West London
                              982399
Editorial: PO Box 2378, Watford WD18 1RF
Tel: 44 01923 237004
Email: editor@familiesnwlondon.co.uk
Web site: www.familiesonline.co.uk/locations/london-north-west
Freq: Bi-Monthly
Circ: 29000 Not Audited
MAGAZINE
Family & Parenting

Families Online   988407

Editorial: Remenham House, Regatta Place, Marlow Road, Bourne End, London SL8 5TD
Tel: 44 01628 535499
Email: ho.editorial@familiesonline.co.uk
Web site: http://www.familiesonline.co.uk/
Freq: Daily
Circ: 134288 Cision Digital Reach
Editor: Emma Flanagan
MAGAZINE (ONLINE)
Family & Parenting

Families Oxfordshire   982400

Editorial: PO Box 167, Wantage OX12 8ZJ
Tel: 44 01993 815966

Email: editor@familiesoxfordshire.co.uk
Web site: www.familiesonline.co.uk/locations/oxfordshire
Freq: Bi-Monthly
Circ: 40000 Not Audited
Editor: Ema Murphy
MAGAZINE
Family & Parenting

Families Pennines   999447

Tel: 44 07580 612800
Email: editor@familiespennines.co.uk
Web site: https://www.familiesonline.co.uk/families-magazines/families-pennines-east-lancs-west-yorks-magazine
Freq: Bi-Monthly
Circ: 20000 Not Audited
Editor: Emily Raleigh
MAGAZINE
Family & Parenting

Families SE London   998751

Editorial: PO Box 11591, London SE26 6WB
Tel: 44 02086 997240
Email: editor@familiesse.co.uk
Web site: www.familiesonline.co.uk/locations/london-south-east
Freq: Bi-Monthly
Circ: 17000 Not Audited
Editor: Robina Cowan
MAGAZINE
Family & Parenting

Families Solent East   986880

Editorial: 42 Ringwood Road, Southsea, Portsmouth PO4 9JL Tel: 44 02393 117561
Email: editor@familiessolenteast.co.uk
Web site: https://www.familiesonline.co.uk/families-magazines/families-solent-east-magazine
Freq: Bi-Monthly
Circ: 22000 Not Audited
Profile: Magazine covering activities, news, education, book reviews, health and information.
MAGAZINE
Family & Parenting

Families Suffolk   1076744

Tel: 44 07951 946736
Email: editor@familiessuffolk.co.uk
Web site: www.familiesonline.co.uk/locations/suffolk
Freq: Bi-Monthly
Circ: 17000 Not Audited
Editor: Stacey Phillips
MAGAZINE
Family & Parenting

Families Surrey East   986878

Editorial: 37 Springcopse Road, Reigate, London RH2 7HH Tel: 44 07769 222347
Email: editor@familiessurreyeast.co.uk
Web site: https://www.familiesonline.co.uk/locations/surrey-east
Freq: Bi-Monthly
Circ: 23000 Not Audited
Editor: Hannah Grogan
Profile: Magazine covering activities, news, education, book reviews, health and information.
MAGAZINE
Family & Parenting

Families Surrey West   986877

Editorial: PO Box 2910, Coulsden, London CR5 3WP Tel: 44 01737 558898
Email: editor@familiessurreywest.co.uk
Web site: https://www.familiesonline.co.uk/families-magazines/families-surrey-west-magazine
Freq: Bi-Monthly
Circ: 24000 Not Audited
Editor: Sarah Hatch
Profile: Magazine covering activities, news, education, book reviews, health and information.
Ad Rate: Full Page Colour £1220.00
MAGAZINE
Family & Parenting

Families Sussex Coast   986876

Tel: 44 02393 117561
Email: editor@familiessussexcoast.co.uk

Web site: https://www.familiesonline.co.uk/families-magazines/families-sussex-coast-magazine
Freq: Bi-Monthly
Circ: 18500 Not Audited
Editor: Mandy Earle
Profile: Magazine covering activities, news, education, book reviews, health and information.
MAGAZINE
Family & Parenting

Families SW London   982393
Editorial: 17 Riggindale Road, London SW16 1QL
Web site: www.familiessouthwest.co.uk
Freq: Monthly
Circ: 30000 Not Audited
Editor: Pascale Gravell
Profile: Magazine covering activities, news, education, book reviews, health and information. This outlet covers areas within Westminster Borough, Hammersmith & Fulham Borough, Kensington & Chelsea Borough, Kingston upon Thames Borough, Lambeth Borough, Merton Borough, Newham Borough, Richmond upon Thames Borough and Wandsworth Borough.
Ad Rate: Full Page Mono £940.00
Ad Rate: Full Page Colour £1220.00
MAGAZINE
Family & Parenting

Families Thames Valley East
982401
Editorial: PO Box 3902, Maidenhead SL60 1AD **Tel:** 44 01628 627586
Email: editor@familiestveast.co.uk
Web site: https://www.familiesonline.co.uk/families-magazines/families-thames-valley-east-magazine
Freq: Bi-Monthly
Circ: 20000 Not Audited
Editor: Claire Winter
Profile: Magazine with local news and information, competitions, features on education, child care, health, leisure, travel, school holiday activities and an in-depth What's On section.
Ad Rate: Full Page Mono £940.00
Ad Rate: Full Page Colour £1220.00
MAGAZINE
Family & Parenting

Families Thames Valley West
982402
Editorial: PO Box 2955, Caversham, Reading RG1 9PH **Tel:** 44 01189 546893
Email: editor@familiestvw.co.uk
Web site: https://www.familiesonline.co.uk/families-magazines/families-thames-valley-west-magazine
Freq: Bi-Monthly
Circ: 19000 Not Audited
MAGAZINE
Family & Parenting

Families Upon Thames   982403
Editorial: Hersham Road, London KT12 5PZ
Tel: 44 02082 410423
Email: editor@familiesuponthames.co.uk
Web site: www.familiesuponthames.co.uk
Freq: Bi-Monthly
Circ: 30000 Not Audited
Editor: Linda Stone
Profile: Magazine with local news and information including education, childcare, health, travel and events. This outlet covers areas within Hounslow Borough and Kingston upon Thames Borough.
Ad Rate: Full Page Mono £890.00
Ad Rate: Full Page Colour £1157.00
MAGAZINE
Family & Parenting

Families Vale of York   982404
Editorial: PO Box 201, Goole DN14 9ZW
Tel: 44 01405 860831
Email: editor@familiesvoy.co.uk
Web site: www.familiesonline.co.uk/locations/vale-of-york
Freq: Bi-Monthly
Circ: 18000 Not Audited

Editor: Belinda Maunsell
MAGAZINE
Family & Parenting

Families Warwickshire   986875
Tel: 44 01926 335004
Email: editor@familieswarwickshire.co.uk
Web site: https://www.familiesonline.co.uk/families-magazines/families-warwickshire-magazine
Freq: Bi-Monthly
Circ: 21000 Not Audited
Editor: Claire Jones
Profile: Magazine with local news and information as well as articles on child care, health, education, travel and events. Aimed at parents in Warwickshire.
MAGAZINE
Family & Parenting

Families West London   982405
Editorial: PO Box 32231, London W5 1JR
Tel: 44 02089 304707
Email: familieswest@yahoo.com
Web site: https://www.familiesonline.co.uk/families-magazines/families-london-west-magazine
Freq: Bi-Monthly
Circ: 17000 Not Audited
Editor: Roma Mahbubani Reeves
MAGAZINE
Family & Parenting

Family   996565
Editorial: Garth House, Leon Avenue, Cardiff CF15 7RG
Email: mail@cff.org.uk
Web site: www.careforthefamily.org.uk
Freq: Quarterly Not Audited
MAGAZINE
Charitable Foundations

Family Focus Scotland   988736
Editorial: 200 Renfield Street, Glasgow G2 3QB **Tel:** 44 01413 027000
Email: joan@familyfocus.scot
Web site: www.familyfocus.scot/
Freq: Quarterly
Circ: 75000 Not Audited
Editor: Joan McFadden
MAGAZINE
Family & Parenting

Family Go Live   987133
Editorial: The Old Bank, 382 Aigburth Road, Liverpool L18 3QD **Tel:** 44 01514 325651
Email: info@familygolive.com
Web site: www.familygolive.com
Freq: Bi-Monthly
Circ: 54000 Not Audited
Profile: Publication aimed at busy parents and their families in and around Liverpool.
MAGAZINE
Family & Parenting, Local Entertainment Guides

Family Grapevine   988918
Editorial: 53 Lethbridge Road, Wells, Somerset, Wells BA5 2FW
Tel: 44 01372 209200
Email: group@thefamilygrapevine.co.uk
Web site: http://thefamilygrapevine.co.uk/
Freq: 3 Times/Year Not Audited
Profile: Free local telephone directory for families covering places to go, things to do, education, helplines, support services and leisure.
MAGAZINE
Family & Parenting

Family Practice   985324
Editorial: Great Clarendon Street, Oxford OX2 6DP **Tel:** 44 01865 556767
Email: fampra.editorialoffice@oup.com
Web site: www.fampra.oxfordjournals.org
Freq: Bi-Monthly
Circ: 150 Not Audited
Editor: Victoria Neale
Profile: Journal which intends to serve as a means of broadening the International base of family medicine in general practice. It covers healthcare delivery, epidemiology, public health and medical sociology.
Ad Rate: Full Page Mono £646.00

Ad Rate: Full Page Colour £1235.00
MAGAZINE
Community Care (UK), Medicine

Family Traveller   987247
Editorial: 5 Langley Street, Covent Garden, London WC2H 9JA **Tel:** 44 02078 126369
Email: info@familytraveller.com
Web site: www.familytraveller.com
Freq: Bi-Monthly
Circ: 50000 Not Audited
Profile: Magazine covering family travelling. It covers holiday destinations in the UK and abroad, luxury travel, driving holidays, activity holidays, beach-side breaks, as well as beauty tips for holidaying in the sun and practical advice on travelling with children. Each issue contains city guides, food and drink stories, fashion, health and beauty, technology, motoring and finance features. Aimed at families travelling with babies, children and teenagers.
MAGAZINE
Family & Parenting, Travel

Family Tree   985274
Email: editorial@family-tree.co.uk
Web site: www.family-tree.co.uk
Freq: Monthly
Circ: 18000 Not Audited
Editor: Helen Tovey
Profile: Magazine focusing on family history and genealogy including a computer section, news, views and name lists. Aimed at those with an interest in family history and genealogy.
Ad Rate: Full Page Colour £550.00
MAGAZINE
Family & Parenting, History

Family Wealth Report   984956
Editorial: 19 Heathman's Road, London SW6 4TJ **Tel:** 44 02071 480188
Web site: www.familywealthreport.com
Freq: Daily
Circ: 1993 Cision Digital Reach
MAGAZINE (ONLINE)
Fund Management, Personal Finance

FAN   997426
Editorial: St Michael Paternoster Royal, College Hill, London EC4R 2RL
Tel: 44 02072 485202
Email: ben.alcraft@missiontoseafarers.org
Web site: www.missiontoseafarers.org/media-centre/publications/flying-angel-news
Freq: Quarterly Not Audited
Editor: Ben Alcraft
MAGAZINE
Marine & Boat Trade, Shipping & Warehousing

The Fan Carpet   987449
Editorial: 14 Sunny Nook Gardens, South Croydon CR2 6PX **Tel:** 44 07877 348196
Email: contact@thefancarpet.com
Web site: www.thefancarpet.com
Freq: Daily
Circ: 14306 Cision Digital Reach
MAGAZINE (ONLINE)
Movies & Video

FAN THE FIRE   988699
Web site: http://fanthefiremagazine.com/
Freq: Daily
Circ: 5219 Cision Digital Reach
Profile: Website covering culture. The FAN THE FIRE magazine is an on-line publication that shares the latest news and events on youth culture.
MAGAZINE (ONLINE)
News & Current Affairs

Fantastic Funworld   995922
Editorial: Old Dairy, Peper Harow Park, Nr Godalming, Godalming GU8 6BQ
Tel: 44 01483 779487
Web site: www.signaturepl.co.uk/portfolio/fantastic.html
Freq: Monthly
Circ: 30000 Not Audited
MAGAZINE
Preschool

Far Out Magazine   998325
Web site: http://faroutmagazine.co.uk/
Freq: Daily
Circ: 15282 Cision Digital Reach
MAGAZINE (ONLINE)
Classical/Choral/Band Music, Country, Folk, Bluegrass, Dance Music, Jazz & Blues, Music, Pop Music, R&B, Urban, World, Rap & Hip Hop, Rock Music

Farm Contractor and Large Scale Farmer   981154
Editorial: Offices 2 & 3, Brixfield Farm, Kineton, Banbury CV35 0ED
Web site: http://www.farmcontractor-uk.com
Freq: Monthly
Circ: 9960 Not Audited
MAGAZINE
Animal Farming

Farm North East - CEASED
984650
Editorial: 11 Sunnyside Gardens, Drumoak, by Banchory, Stonehaven AB31 5EZ
Freq: Bi-Monthly
Circ: 5000 Not Audited
Profile: Magazine covering news and technical/business developments within the agri-food industry in North and North-East Scotland.
Ad Rate: Full Page Mono £550.00
Ad Rate: Full Page Colour £750.00
MAGAZINE
Animal Farming

The Farnham Magazine   985993
Editorial: Kingsway Business Park, Oldfield Road, Hampton, London TW12 2HD
Tel: 44 02089 395601
Email: editguild@sheengate.co.uk
Web site: www.sheengate.co.uk
Freq: Monthly
Circ: 40100 Not Audited
Editor: Nikki Ackerley
Profile: Lifestyle magazine containing local interest articles and interviews as well as features on fashion, theatre, health, education, shopping and property. Distributed to households and businesses in the boroughs of Guildford, Woking and Waverley, covering the towns and villages of Guildford, Godalming, Wonersh, Bramley, Shalford, Woking, Ripley, Send, Clandon, West Byfleet, The Horsleys, Effingham, Shere, Peaslake, Cranleigh, Ewhurst, Farnham and Haslemere.
MAGAZINE
Property Management & Maintenance, Regional General Interest

Fashercise   1053627
Tel: 44 02034 419779
Email: info@fashercise.com
Web site: http://www.fashercise.com/
Freq: Daily
Circ: 38126 Cision Digital Reach
Editor: Alexandra Vanthournout
Profile: Website covering fitness and exercise. The FASHERCISE blog discusses anything from sportswear and fashion to music and food.
MAGAZINE (ONLINE)
Fashion, Fitness & Exercise

Fashion and Beauty Monitor
984315
Editorial: Wells Point, 79 Wells Street, London W1T 3QN
Web site: http://www.fashionmonitor.com/#/
Freq: Daily
Circ: 151645 Cision Digital Reach
MAGAZINE (ONLINE)
News & Current Affairs

Fashion Forensics   998253
Tel: 44 07899 962525
Email: info@fashionforensics.com
Web site: www.fashionforensics.com
Freq: Daily
Circ: 17000 Not Audited

Editor: Kiri Bloore
MAGAZINE
Airline Inflight, Cooking & Baking, Fashion, Food, Grocery Stores, Organic Food, Railroad, Restaurant Reviews, Travel, Vegetarianism & Veganism

Fashion Forte UK
988775
Email: editorial@fashionforte.co.uk
Web site: http://www.fashionforte.co.uk/
Freq: Daily
Circ: 11861 Cision Digital Reach
MAGAZINE (ONLINE)
Fashion

Fashion Grads
997332
Web site: http://www.fashiongrads.co.uk
Freq: Daily
Circ: 716 Cision Digital Reach
MAGAZINE (ONLINE)
Careers, Education, Fashion, Student Lifestyle, Students

Fashion London
986665
Editorial: 18 Berkeley Crescent, Barnet, London EN4 8BP **Tel:** 44 02036 033169
Email: editor@fashionlondon.co
Web site: www.fashionlondon.co
Freq: Bi-Monthly
Circ: 50000 Not Audited
Profile: Magazine covering men and women's fashion. It features the latest fashion items and must haves, such as clothes, shoes, bags, ties, cologne, perfume, make up, belts and hair accessories and covers the top designers as well as high street chains and specifically covers fashion trends within London. The content comprises regular features, reports on new events, designers and the latest looks.
Ad Rate: Full Page Colour £2320.00
MAGAZINE
Fashion

Fashion VS Sport
1054416
Email: info@fashionvssport.com
Web site: http://fashionvssport.com
Freq: Daily
Circ: 2019 Cision Digital Reach
Profile: Website covering fashion and sports. The FASHION VS SPORT website shares the latest news and information on fashion, design, culture and sports.
MAGAZINE (ONLINE)
Fashion, Fitness & Exercise, Women's Interests

FashionBeans
986137
Web site: www.fashionbeans.com
Freq: Daily
Circ: 915041 Cision Digital Reach
MAGAZINE (ONLINE)
Fashion, Men's Interests

FashionBite
985281
Email: eseares@fashionbite.co.uk
Web site: www.fashionbite.co.uk
Freq: Daily
Circ: 3088 Cision Digital Reach
MAGAZINE (ONLINE)
Art, Beauty & Grooming, Cooking & Baking, Cosmetics, Fashion, Hair, Health & Medicine, Literature, Photography, Theater & Performing Arts

Fashioncapital.co.uk
983488
Editorial: Unit 14, Crusader Industrial Estate, 167 Hermitage Road, London N4 1LZ
Tel: 44 02088 093311
Email: info@fashioncapital.co.uk
Web site: http://www.fashioncapital.co.uk/
Freq: Daily
Circ: 75693 Cision Digital Reach
Editor: JoJo Iles
MAGAZINE (ONLINE)
Fashion

Fast Bikes
982817
Editorial: Media Centre, Morton Way, Horncastle LN9 6JR **Tel:** 44 01507 523456
Web site: www.fastbikesmag.com
Freq: Monthly
Circ: 15257 Not Audited

Profile: Magazine covering all aspects of sports bike riding. Includes news, equipment, road tests and personality profiles.
Ad Rate: Full Page Colour £1978.00
MAGAZINE
Motorcycles, Motorsports

Fast Car
982663
Editorial: Quay House, The Ambury, Bath BA1 1UA **Tel:** 44 01959 541444
Web site: www.fastcar.co.uk
Freq: Monthly
Circ: 27000 Not Audited
Editor: Jules Truss
MAGAZINE
Automotive

Fast Food Professional Magazine
981283
Editorial: Unit 30, Acton Business Park, Shrewsbury Avenue, Peterborough PE2 7BX
Tel: 44 07725 434173
Email: athol@fastfoodpro.com
Web site: www.fastfoodpro.com
Freq: Bi-Monthly
Circ: 12500 Not Audited
MAGAZINE
Alcohol & Spirits, Food

Fast Ford
982664
Editorial: Cudham Tithe Barn, Berry's Hill, Cudham TN16 3AG **Tel:** 44 01959 541444
Email: fastford.ed@kelsey.co.uk
Web site: www.fastfordmag.co.uk
Freq: Monthly
Circ: 18000 Not Audited
Profile: Magazine covering independent advice on tuning and modifying all Ford models, plus road tests on new launches. Includes features on reader's cars and informed industry and sport comments. Read by Ford enthusiasts between 17 and 35 years old.Regular features: Buying GuideCompany Profile Dymo Shoot OutModifying Guide New ProductsReaders Cars -Reader contributions concerning their cars Tooled Up - 'How To' guides.
MAGAZINE
Automakers, Automotive

FAULT Magazine
984605
Editorial: Suite 7, 40 Craven Street, London WC2N 5NG
Email: info@fault-magazine.com
Web site: www.fault-magazine.com
Freq: Quarterly
Circ: 47015 Not Audited
Editor: Miles Holder
MAGAZINE
Art, Dance Music, Fashion, Jazz & Blues, Movies & Video, Music, Photography, Pop Music, R&B, Urban, World, Rap & Hip Hop

Faultline
983817
Editorial: Unit G-5, Lower Station Approach, Temple Meads, Romsey BS1 6QS
Tel: 44 01794 521411
Email: info@rethinkresearch.biz
Web site: www.rethinkresearch.biz/product/faultline
Freq: Weekly
Circ: 235 Cision Digital Reach
MAGAZINE (ONLINE)
Computers, Internet, Mobile Communications

FDPP
1100934
Tel: 44 01843 830249
Web site: http://fdpp.co.uk/
Freq: Monthly
Circ: 10709 Cision Digital Reach
Editor: Amanda Buckingham
MAGAZINE (ONLINE)
Alcohol & Spirits, Food

FEAST Magazine
999014
Editorial: 1st Floor, Turnbridge Mills, Quay Street, Huddersfield HD1 6QT
Tel: 44 02081 233414
Email: editor@ciaranjarosz.media
Web site: www.feastmagazine.org
Freq: Monthly

Circ: 100000 Not Audited
MAGAZINE
Audio Video Trade, Bars, Clubs & Pubs, Cameras, Comedy, Consumer Electronics, Electronics, Entertainment, Food, Local Entertainment Guides, Mobile Electronics

Feast Norfolk
1053191
Web site: http://www.feastnorfolkmagazine.co.uk/
Freq: Monthly Not Audited
Editor: Sarah Hardy
MAGAZINE
Cooking & Baking, Food, Grocery Stores, Organic Food, Restaurant Reviews, Vegetarianism & Veganism

Feel Good You
986419
Editorial: The Blue Fin Building, 110 Southwark Street, London SE1 0SU
Tel: 44 02031 485000
Email: wandhmail@ipcmedia.com
Web site: www.womanandhome.com
Freq: Quarterly
MAGAZINE
Health & Medicine, Nutrition, Women's Interests

feelunique.com
986785
Editorial: 4th Floor, Berkshire House, 168-173 High Holborn, London WC1V 7AA
Tel: 44 02072 572580
Email: pr@feelunique.com
Web site: http://www.feelunique.com
Freq: Daily
Circ: 385766 Cision Digital Reach
MAGAZINE (ONLINE)
Beauty & Grooming, Cosmetics, Hair

Female Arts
998270
Email: editor@femalearts.com
Web site: www.femalearts.com
Freq: Daily
Circ: 9991 Cision Digital Reach
MAGAZINE (ONLINE)
Art, Literature, Photography, Theater & Performing Arts, Visual Arts

Female First
983621
Editorial: 70 Gerard Street, Ashton-in-Makerfield, Ashton-in-Makerfield WN4 9AE
Tel: 44 01942 712000
Web site: www.femalefirst.co.uk
Freq: Daily
Circ: 1373346 Cision Digital Reach
Profile: Website covering lifestyle. FEMALE FIRST shares the latest news on love & sex, fashion, beauty, entertainment, shopping, celebrities, relationships and travel.
MAGAZINE (ONLINE)
Celebrities, Women's Interests

The Female Lead
996095
Editorial: 2 Riding House Street, London W1W 7FA **Tel:** 44 02037 707555
Email: eve@whatiseeproject.com
Web site: http://www.thefemalead.com/
Freq: Daily
Circ: 16217 Cision Digital Reach
Editor: Bea Appleby
MAGAZINE (ONLINE)
Careers, Consumer Affairs, Politics, Women's Interests

Fest Magazine
1052821
Tel: 44 01314 674630
Email: hello@festmag.co.uk
Web site: www.festmag.co.uk/
Freq: Annual
Circ: 125000 Not Audited
MAGAZINE
Comedy, Theater & Performing Arts

FF Magazine Scotland
995274
Tel: 44 01315 16700
Email: info@ffmagsscotland.uk
Web site: http://www.ffmagscotland.uk/
Freq: Daily
Circ: 1002 Cision Digital Reach

Editor: Yemi King
MAGAZINE (ONLINE)
Art, Fashion, Literature, Photography, Theater & Performing Arts, Visual Arts

Fidelity
987934
Web site: https://www.fidelity.co.uk/investor/default.page
Freq: Daily
Circ: 1054518 Cision Digital Reach
MAGAZINE (ONLINE)
Investment Banking, Personal Finance

The Field
981934
Editorial: Pinehurst 2, Pinehurst Road, Farnborough Business Park, London GU14 7BF **Tel:** 44 01252 555000
Email: field_secretary@timeinc.com
Web site: www.thefield.co.uk
Freq: Monthly
Circ: 23827 Not Audited
Editor: Jonathan Young
Profile: Magazine covering hunting, shooting, dogs, guns, accessories, property, country living, food & drinks, fine arts and antiques. Founded in 1853 for those who loved shooting, fishing, hunting. Aimed at country residents and hunting enthusiasts.
Ad Rate: Full Page Colour £3318.00
MAGAZINE
Field Sports

Field Marketing & Brand Experience
985830
Editorial: Field Marketing and Brand Experience, Frank Publishing Ltd, PO Box 5069, Chippenham SN15 9HX
Tel: 44 01249 465521
Email: fm@fieldmarketing.com
Web site: www.fieldmarketing.com
Freq: Quarterly
Circ: 12500 Not Audited
Editor: Frank Wainwright
MAGAZINE
Advertising Industry, Branding, Broadcasting, Graphic Design, Marketing, Media & Communications, Photography, Publishing

Fieldsports
983969
Editorial: 1-6 Buckminster Yard, Main Street, Buckminster, Grantham, Grantham NG33 5SB **Tel:** 44 01476 859840
Web site: www.fieldsportsmagazine.com
Freq: Bi-Monthly
Circ: 44000 Not Audited
Editor: Marcus Janssen
Profile: Magazine that covers field sports including shooting and fishing. Aimed at men and women who are passionate about field sports.
Ad Rate: Full Page Colour £2880.00
MAGAZINE
Field Sports

FieldsportsChannel.tv
999417
Editorial: The Old Coach House, Wellisford, Wellington, Taunton TA21 0SB
Web site: www.fieldsportschannel.tv
Freq: Daily
Circ: 7032 Cision Digital Reach
MAGAZINE (ONLINE)
Fishing, Shooting/Guns

Fife Reporter
1054423
Email: fifereporter@gmail.com
Web site: http://www.fifereporter.com/
Freq: Daily
Circ: 10638 Cision Digital Reach
MAGAZINE (ONLINE)
News & Current Affairs

Fight Through
995153
Tel: 44 07803 729958
Email: joanne@educationforthemilitaryfamily.org.uk
Web site: www.educationforthemilitaryfamily.org.uk
Freq: Quarterly
Circ: 20000 Not Audited
Editor: Joanne Nattress
MAGAZINE
Defense & National Security, Disability

Consumer Magazines

Fighters Only
985653

Editorial: Unit 2, Bankside, The Watermark, Gateshead, Gateshead NE11 9SY
Tel: 44 01912 332225
Email: fomeditor@gmail.com
Web site: www.fightersonlymag.com
Freq: Monthly Not Audited
Profile: Magazine covering mixed martial arts including training, events and equipment. Aimed martial arts enthusiasts.
MAGAZINE
Bodybuilding, Boxing, Martial Arts, MMA & Self-Defense

Fighting Spirit Magazine
983433

Editorial: 3 East Avenue, Bournemouth, Bournemouth BH3 7BW
Tel: 44 01202 586035
Email: fsmuncooked@gmail.com
Web site: www.fightingspiritmagazine.co.uk
Freq: Monthly
Circ: 30000 Not Audited
Editor: Brian Elliot
Profile: Magazine covering pro-wrestling, mixed martial arts, features, interviews and events. First published in 2006, the publication has an average of 82 pages per issue. Aimed at fight enthusiasts.
Ad Rate: Full Page Colour £2350.00
MAGAZINE
Martial Arts, MMA & Self-Defense

The Filling Business
984294

Editorial: Durand House, Manor Royal, Crawley, Crawley RH10 9PY
Tel: 44 01293 435100
Email: info@sayers-publishing.com
Web site: www.thefillingbusiness.com
Freq: Daily
Circ: 3109 Cision Digital Reach
MAGAZINE (ONLINE)
Manufacturing, Plastics

Film & Video Maker
985123

Editorial: McCracken Park, Great North Road, Gosforth, Newcastle upon Tyne NE3 2DT **Tel:** 44 01913 038960
Email: magazine@theiac.org.uk
Web site: www.fvi.org.uk/iac/fvm/fvm.htm
Freq: Bi-Monthly
Circ: 1750 Not Audited
Editor: Garth Hope
MAGAZINE
Cameras, Movies & Video

Filmaluation
987124

Web site: www.filmaluation.com
Freq: Daily
Circ: 8451 Cision Digital Reach
Editor: Hemanth Kissoon
MAGAZINE (ONLINE)
Broadcasting, Movies & Video, Theater & Performing Arts

FilmiFIN
1060876

Email: tolmitus@filmifin.com
Web site: http://www.filmifin.com
Freq: Daily
Circ: 1205 Cision Digital Reach
MAGAZINE (ONLINE)
Movies & Video

FilmJuice
1004618

Editorial: 7 Churchfield Mansions, 321- 345 New Kings Road, London SW6 4RA
Web site: www.filmjuice.com
Freq: Daily
Circ: 6371 Cision Digital Reach
Editor: Alex Moss
MAGAZINE (ONLINE)
Movies & Video

Film-News.co.uk
999387

Editorial: 27 Lothair Road, London N4 1EN
Tel: 44 02083 479279
Web site: www.film-news.co.uk
Freq: Daily
Circ: 128860 Cision Digital Reach
Editor: Marco Gandolfi
MAGAZINE (ONLINE)
Movies & Video

Financial Adviser
979771

Editorial: Number One, Southwark Bridge, London SE1 9HL **Tel:** 44 02078 733000
Email: fa.newsdesk@ft.com
Web site: www.ftadviser.com/FinancialAdviser
Freq: Weekly
Circ: 20600 Not Audited
Editor: Emma Ann Hughes
Profile: Magazine covering the financial services sector. It was launched in 1988 after the Financial Services Act 1986 defined the role of the independent financial adviser. Aimed at professional financial advisers.
Ad Rate: Full Page Colour £7064.00
MAGAZINE
Fund Management, Personal Finance

Financial IT
985615

Editorial: 27 London Road, Bromley, London BR1 1DG **Tel:** 44 02088 193253
Email: news@financialit.net
Web site: www.financialit.net
Freq: Quarterly
Circ: 2000 Not Audited
Profile: Magazine covering financial technology. It features the latest trends and issues in payments and cash management, securities services and trade & supply chain finance, as well as the technology and business solutions and market infrastructures that underpin those businesses.
MAGAZINE
Auto Aftermarket, Computers, Data Management, Electronics, Government Technology, Industry, Internet, Mobile Communications, Security & Security Systems, Software

Financial News
979839

Editorial: The News Building, 1 London Bridge Street, London SE1 9GF
Tel: 44 02034 261314
Email: news@efinancialnews.com
Web site: https://www.fnlondon.com/
Freq: Weekly
Circ: 309642 Not Audited
Editor: Jessica Mills-Davies
Profile: Magazine covering the investment banking and securities industry. It provides comprehensive coverage across asset management, investment banking, private equity, trading, wealth management and technology, news, analysis and comments on the European investment banking, securities and the fund management industry, with a series of highly focused and effective marketing solutions. It includes coverage of M&A, debt and equity capital markets, fund management, information technology and recruitment. First published in 1996, the magazine targets senior practitioners and their clients, senior executives and decision-makers across the UK and international securities industry. Aimed at those involved in the securities and investment banking sector.
Ad Rate: Full Page Colour £12180.00
MAGAZINE
Auto Aftermarket, Banking, Bonds, Commodities, Computers, Corporate Finance, Corporate Management, Data Management, Derivatives, Electronics

Financial Planning Today
1103014

Tel: 44 01895 678629
Email: newsdesk@portfoliopublishing.co.uk
Web site: https://www.financialplanningtoday.co.uk/fp-today-magazine
Freq: Bi-Monthly
Circ: 15000 Not Audited
MAGAZINE
News & Current Affairs

Financial Services Research
983011

Editorial: PO Box 612, Northampton NN1 9AU
Web site: www.fsresearch.co.uk
Freq: 3 Times/Year Not Audited
MAGAZINE
News & Current Affairs

financialreporter
986382

Editorial: Unit 3, 81 Church Street, Blackpool, Blackpool FY1 1HU
Tel: 44 01253 476319
Email: rozi@barcadiamedia.co.uk
Web site: www.financialreporter.co.uk
Freq: Daily
Circ: 55780 Cision Digital Reach
Editor: Rozi Jones
Profile: Website covering finance. The financialreporter website shares the latest news and information on financial services, including mortgages, loans, debt & insolvency, insurance, bridging & commercial, business, economy, regulation, technology, equity release & pensions, investments, and conveyancing and surveying news.
MAGAZINE (ONLINE)
Personal Finance

Fine Sussex & Surrey
987511

Editorial: 26 North Street, Horsham, Horsham RH12 1RQ **Tel:** 44 01243 717578
Email: content@finemagazine.co.uk
Web site: www.finesussex.co.uk
Freq: Bi-Monthly
Circ: 20000 Not Audited
MAGAZINE
Luxury Goods, Regional General Interest

Finextra.com
981689

Editorial: 101 St Martin's Lane, London WC2N 4AZ **Tel:** 44 02031 003670
Email: news@finextra.com
Web site: www.finextra.com
Freq: Daily
Circ: 713529 Cision Digital Reach
MAGAZINE (ONLINE)
Auto Aftermarket, Banking, Computers, Data Management, Electronics, Government Technology, Industry, Internet, Mobile Communications, Security & Security Systems

Finimize
1053684

Email: hello@finimize.com
Web site: http://www.finimize.com/
Freq: Daily
Circ: 34545 Cision Digital Reach
MAGAZINE (ONLINE)

Finished Vehicle Logistics
985916

Editorial: Ultima Media Ltd, 401 King Street, London W6 9NJ **Tel:** 44 02089 870900
Web site: http://automotivelogistics.media/magazines/finished-vehicle-logistics
Freq: Quarterly
Circ: 9000 Not Audited
Editor: Christopher Ludwig
Profile: Magazine that covers all aspects of the finished vehicle outbound supply chain. It includes the latest developments and business strategies employed in vehicle logistics. Includes the news and views of the world's leading vehicle makers and service providers.
Ad Rate: Full Page Colour £5250.00
MAGAZINE
Automotive, Supply Chain Management (SCM)

Fireman Sam
983757

Editorial: 1st Floor, The Yellow Building, 1 Nicholas Road, London W8 6SA
Tel: 44 02032 200400
Email: info@egmont.co.uk
Web site: http://www.egmont.co.uk/magazines.asp?pane=underseven&mag=firemansam
Freq: Monthly
Circ: 28037 Not Audited
MAGAZINE
Preschool, Teen/Young Adult

First
982318

Editorial: 85 Strand, London WC2R 0DW
Tel: 44 02075 508000
Email: info@cedarcom.co.uk
Freq: Bi-Monthly
Circ: 19000 Not Audited
Editor: Tim Hulse

Profile: Magazine covering luxury travel, gadgets, fashion, restaurants, hotels and spas worldwide. Aimed at passengers in first class cabins on British Airways flights.
Ad Rate: Full Page Colour £4218.00
MAGAZINE
Airline Inflight

FIRST
984902

Editorial: Victory House, 99-101 Regent Street, London W1B 4EZ
Tel: 44 02074 403500
Email: publisher@firstmagazine.com
Web site: www.firstmagazine.com
Freq: Quarterly
Circ: 27000 Not Audited
Profile: Magazine covering world politics and government policies affecting business. Aimed at business, financial and political leaders.
Ad Rate: Full Page Mono £12500.00
Ad Rate: Full Page Colour £15200.00
MAGAZINE
Business, Politics

First Car
995465

Editorial: 1st floor Crossweys House, 28-30 High Street, Guildford GU1 3EL
Tel: 44 08454 747035
Web site: http://www.firstcar.co.uk
Freq: Annual
Circ: 200000 Not Audited
MAGAZINE
Driving

First Ear
1054133

Web site: http://firstearmusic.com/
Freq: Daily
Circ: 521 Cision Digital Reach
MAGAZINE (ONLINE)
Dance Music, Rap & Hip Hop

Firstchoice.co.uk
997186

Web site: www.firstchoice.co.uk
Freq: Daily
Circ: 1607919 Cision Digital Reach
MAGAZINE (ONLINE)
Airline Inflight, Travel

Fish On Friday
998271

Email: info@fishonfriday.org.uk
Web site: www.fishonfriday.org.uk
Freq: Daily
Circ: 14285 Cision Digital Reach
MAGAZINE (ONLINE)
Cooking & Baking

fish2fork
1064100

Editorial: 3rd Floor South Building Somerset House, Strand, London WC2R 1LA
Tel: 44 02078 455852
Email: info@fish2fork.com
Web site: www.fish2fork.com
Freq: Daily
Circ: 4894 Cision Digital Reach
MAGAZINE (ONLINE)
Cooking & Baking, Food, Restaurant Reviews

FishingMagic.com
982877

Editorial: Brewhouse, Old Hollow, Worth, Crawley RH10 4TA **Tel:** 44 01293 888828
Email: info@fishandfly.com
Web site: www.fishingmagic.com
Freq: Daily
Circ: 408 Cision Digital Reach
Editor: Ian Welch
MAGAZINE (ONLINE)
Fishing

Fishipedia.com
1101941

Editorial: 1 Wingrave Road, London W6 9HF
Web site: www.fishipedia.com
Freq: Daily
Circ: 2815 Cision Digital Reach
Editor: Rory Batho
MAGAZINE (ONLINE)
Fishing

Fit & Well
988777

Editorial: The Blue Fin Building, 110 Southwark Street, London SE1 0SU
Tel: 44 02031 485000
Web site: http://www.womanmagazine.co.uk/fit-well-magazine
Freq: Monthly Not Audited
Profile: Magazine covering health and fitness. It contains diet plans and recipes.
MAGAZINE
Cooking & Baking, Fitness & Exercise, Nutrition, Women's Interests

Fit Indeed
998373

Email: hello@fit-indeed.co.uk
Web site: fit-indeed.co.uk
Freq: Daily
Circ: 8221 Cision Digital Reach
MAGAZINE (ONLINE)
Fitness & Exercise, Nutrition

Fitness & Beauty Professional
1053048

Tel: 44 01843 570944
Web site: www.fitnessnbeauty.co.uk
Freq: Daily
Circ: 73571 Not Audited
Editor: Andrew Harper
MAGAZINE
Beauty & Grooming, Cosmetics, Fitness & Exercise, Hair

Fitpro
985193

Editorial: Kalbarri House, 107 - 113 London Road, London E13 0DA
Tel: 44 02085 860101
Email: publish@fitpro.com
Web site: www.fitpro.com
Freq: Quarterly
Circ: 10000 Not Audited
Profile: Magazine covering the latest industry research and trends within the fitness industry. Aimed at group exercise instructors and personal trainers.
Ad Rate: Full Page Colour £1700.00
MAGAZINE
Fitness & Exercise

Five Star Magazine
988926

Editorial: Office 410, 98 Woodlands Road, Glasgow G36HB **Tel:** 44 08451 248548
Email: info@fivestarmagazine.co.uk
Web site: www.fivestarmagazine.co.uk
Freq: Daily
Circ: 8465 Cision Digital Reach
Editor: Renata Parolari
Profile: Magazine covering outstanding luxury hotels and resorts, their services and symbiotic companies. It also features articles on luxury lifestyle.
MAGAZINE (ONLINE)
Luxury Goods, Men's Interests, Travel, Women's Interests

Flavourmag
984484

Editorial: 66 Gloucester Drive, London N4 2LN
Email: hello@flavourmag.co.uk
Web site: www.flavourmag.co.uk
Freq: Daily
Circ: 101000 Not Audited
Profile: Urban lifestyle magazine covering new talent in the world of music, sport, entertainment, art and fashion as well as technology, events and book reviews. Aimed at multicultural men and women aged 18 to 30 years old in London and within the M25.
Ad Rate: Full Page Colour £750.00
MAGAZINE
Beauty & Grooming, Cosmetics, Fashion, Hair, Photography, Rap & Hip Hop, Teen/Young Adult

Flecking Records
1105207

Email: contact@fleckingrecords.co.uk
Web site: www.fleckingrecords.co.uk
Freq: Daily
Circ: 12705 Cision Digital Reach
MAGAZINE (ONLINE)
Celebrities

Fleet Manager
987417

Editorial: Bank House Studios, Warwick Street, Prestwich, Manchester M25 3HN
Tel: 44 01617 923223
Email: admin@jdmpub.co.uk
Web site: http://www.fleetmanageronline.co.uk/magazines.html
Freq: Bi-Monthly Not Audited
Editor: Sue Hurst
MAGAZINE
Automotive, Charitable Foundations, Government, Public Sector

Fleet News
979925

Editorial: Media House, Lynchwood, Peterborough PE2 6EA
Tel: 44 01733 468306
Web site: www.fleetnews.co.uk
Freq: Bi-Weekly
Circ: 19089 Not Audited
Profile: Magazine covering developments in the company car and van markets, including new vehicle reviews, vehicle finance, accident management and running cost tables for 1500 new cars.
Ad Rate: Full Page Mono £6563.00
Ad Rate: Full Page Colour £6563.00
MAGAZINE
Automotive

Fleet World
981029

Editorial: 18 Alban Park, Hatfield Road, London AL4 0JJ **Tel:** 44 01727 739160
Email: info@fleetworldgroup.co.uk
Web site: http://fleetworld.co.uk/
Freq: Monthly
Circ: 18052 Not Audited
Editor: Alex Grant
Profile: Magazine containing management style features on cars and light commercial vehicles, plus features on fleet management decision makers.
Ad Rate: Full Page Colour £4670.00
MAGAZINE
Automotive

FleetPoint
987456

Editorial: 26 Eaton Avenue, Matrix Park, Leyland PR7 7NA **Tel:** 44 01772 585111
Email: editor@fleetpoint.org
Web site: www.fleetpoint.org
Freq: Daily
Circ: 16369 Cision Digital Reach
Profile: Website covering fleet news. FLEETPOINT shares the latest news, information or reviews fleet management and news. The outlet offers RSS (Really Simple Syndication).
MAGAZINE (ONLINE)
Automotive, Supply Chain Management (SCM)

FLEX
982224

Editorial: 10 Windsor Court, Clarence Drive, Harrogate HG1 2PE
Email: editorial@weideruk.com
Web site: www.flexonline.co.uk
Freq: Monthly
Circ: 29000 Not Audited
Profile: Magazine covering weight training and bodybuilding including training and nutrition. Aimed at hardcore bodybuilding enthusiasts.
Ad Rate: Full Page Colour £1463.00
MAGAZINE
Bodybuilding

Flexible Boss - SUSPENDED Spring 2016
999464

Editorial: c/o Distilled, 4th Floor, Chapter House, 18-20 Crucifix Lane, London SE1 3JW **Tel:** 44 07717 456339
Web site: www.flexibleboss.com
Freq: Quarterly
Circ: 37000 Not Audited
MAGAZINE
Human Resources

Flight Time
988244

Editorial: The Cowshed, Ladycross Farm, Hollow Lane, Dormansland, East Grinstead RH7 6PB **Tel:** 44 01342 872020
Email: flybemag@streampublishing.net

Web site: http://www.flybe.com/flight-time-magazine/
Freq: Monthly
Circ: 50000 Not Audited
Editor: Emily Gravenor
MAGAZINE
Airline Inflight

FlipTime
998120

Editorial: 9 Riverview Avenue, North Ferriby HU14 3DY
Email: editorial@msonemedia.co.uk
Web site: www.fliptime.co.uk
Freq: Daily
Circ: 2036 Cision Digital Reach
MAGAZINE (ONLINE)
Men's Interests, Women's Interests

Flora International
981958

Editorial: Wimborne Publishing Ltd, 113 Lynwood Drive, Merley, Wimborne BH21 1UU **Tel:** 44 01202 880299
Email: enquiries@flora-magazine.co.uk
Web site: http://www.flora-magazine.co.uk
Freq: Quarterly
Circ: 24000 Not Audited
Editor: Nina Tucknott
Profile: Magazine covering flower arranging and floristry with floral crafts, new plants and flower arrangers' gardens.
Ad Rate: Full Page Mono £650.00
Ad Rate: Full Page Colour £650.00
MAGAZINE
Gardening

The Florist
981282

Editorial: Riverside Studios, 65 Aspenlea Road, Hammersmith, London W6 8LH
Tel: 44 02082 371108
Email: hello@purplespotted.com
Web site: theflorist.co.uk
Freq: Daily
Circ: 11714 Cision Digital Reach
Editor: Caroline Marshall-Foster
MAGAZINE (ONLINE)
Gardening

Flourish
982150

Editorial: 196 Clyde Street, Glasgow G1 4JY
Tel: 44 01412 265898
Email: flourish@rcag.org.uk
Web site: http://www.flourishnewspaper.co.uk/
Freq: Monthly
Circ: 50000 Not Audited
Editor: Vincent Toal
Profile: Official journal of the Archdiocese of Glasgow (RC) containing news and comment.
Ad Rate: Full Page Colour £750.00
MAGAZINE
Religion

The Flower Arranger
981965

Tel: 44 02072 475567
Email: flowers@nafas.org.uk
Web site: www.nafas.org.uk
Freq: Quarterly
Circ: 45000 Not Audited
Profile: Journal of the National Association of Flower Arrangement Societies. Includes news, events, tips and trends in flower arrangements.
Ad Rate: Full Page Colour £1600.00
MAGAZINE
Crafts, Gardening

Fluid Handling Magazine
988894

Editorial: Marshall House, 124 Middleton Road, Surrey, London SM4 6RW
Tel: 44 02086 874126
Web site: http://fluidhandlingmag.com
Freq: Bi-Monthly Not Audited
MAGAZINE
Bars, Clubs & Pubs, Chemicals, Shipping & Warehousing

FLUSH Magazine
986983

Editorial: 33 Townhouse Road, Norwich, Norwich NR8 5BS **Tel:** 44 01603 387120
Email: pete@flushmagazine.co.uk
Web site: www.flushmagazine.co.uk
Freq: Bi-Monthly

Circ: 1247 Cision Digital Reach
Editor: Pete Graham
MAGAZINE (ONLINE)
Airline Inflight, Antique & Collectible Cars, Antiques/Collectibles, Art, Arts, Audio Video Trade, Automakers, Automotive, Cameras, Classical/Choral/Band Music

FLUX
981794

Editorial: 2nd Floor, 42 Edge Street, Manchester M4 1HN **Tel:** 44 01706 839550
Email: editorial@fluxmagazine.com
Web site: www.fluxmagazine.com
Freq: Daily
Circ: 144473 Cision Digital Reach
Profile: Culture and fashion magazine containing profiles on international arts and fashion figures and influential individuals shaping the future, plus features on music, culture, nightlife, entertainment, fashion, films, art, travel and clubs. Includes interviews with bands and artists, and ideas from thinkers and creatives.
Ad Rate: Full Page Colour £3500.00
MAGAZINE (ONLINE)
Antiques/Collectibles, Art, Arts, Classical/Choral/Band Music, Country, Folk, Bluegrass, Dance Music, Fashion, Jazz & Blues, Literature, Music

Fly Fishing & Fly-Tying
982177

Tel: 44 01887 829868
Email: rollingriver@mac.com
Web site: http://www.flyfishing-and-flytying.co.uk
Freq: Monthly
Circ: 8952 Not Audited
Editor: Mark Bowler
MAGAZINE
Fishing

Fly2Let
986341

Editorial: Old Mill Cottage, High Street, Bexley, London DA5 1LG
Tel: 44 01322 556622
Email: editorial@fly2let.co.uk
Web site: https://fly2let.co.uk/
Freq: Daily
Circ: 10709 Cision Digital Reach
MAGAZINE (ONLINE)
Finance, Legal Affairs, Real Estate, Residential Real Estate

The Flyer Newspaper
999075

Editorial: 17b Carlingford Road, London N15 3ED **Tel:** 44 02088 815761
Email: eventsinprint@yahoo.co.uk
Web site: www.flyernewspaper.com
Freq: Monthly
Circ: 14000 Not Audited
Editor: Matthew Hinchcliffe
MAGAZINE
Africa, Americas, Asia, Regional General Interest

Flying Scale Models
983164

Editorial: Doolittle Mill, Doolittle Lane, Totternhoe, Eaton Bray LU6 1QX
Tel: 44 01525 222573
Web site: www.flyingscalemodels.com
Freq: Monthly
Circ: 11000 Not Audited
Editor: Tony Dowdeswell
Profile: Magazine covering all aspects of flying and building scale-model aircraft.
Ad Rate: Full Page Mono £400.00
Ad Rate: Full Page Colour £425.00
MAGAZINE
Aviation, Crafts, Hobbies, & Collecting

FMCG
984057

Editorial: The Old Church, 17 Old Leeds Road, Huddersfield, Huddersfield HD1 1SG
Tel: 44 01484 441400
Email: editorial@codebluegroup.co.uk
Web site: fmcgmagazine.co.uk
Freq: Monthly
Circ: 14500 Not Audited
Editor: Nigel Martin
Profile: Magazine containing UK and world news affecting the FMCG (Fast Moving Consumable Goods) industry. Focuses on the food and drink sector, chilled and frozen industry, manufacturing and grocery and

Consumer Magazines

produce sector.Read by manufacturers, suppliers and those within the wholesale and retail trades.
Ad Rate: Full Page Mono £1395.00
Ad Rate: Full Page Colour £1965.00
MAGAZINE
Alcohol & Spirits, Food

FMCG News
983495
Editorial: 1 Accent Park, Bakewell Road, Orton Southgate, Peterborough PE2 6XS
Tel: 44 01733 385300
Email: fmcg@mediaone.co.uk
Web site: http://www.fmcgnews.co.uk/
Freq: Bi-Monthly
Circ: 13500 Not Audited
Editor: Stephanie Cornwall
Profile: Magazine covering fast moving consumer goods. Featuring news and information, analysis, product information and editorial on manufacturing, packaging, storage and handling, distribution and logistics. Aimed at executives and decision makers in the fast moving consumer goods sector. Alternative Title: Fast Moving Consumer Goods News.
Ad Rate: Full Page Colour £565.00
MAGAZINE
Alcohol & Spirits, Food

FMS Magazine
998971
Editorial: 132 The Shaftesburys, Barking IG11 7JA
Email: info@fms-mag.com
Web site: www.fms-mag.com
Freq: Daily
Circ: 14346 Cision Digital Reach
Editor: Sarah Hardy
MAGAZINE (ONLINE)
Antiques/Collectibles, Art, Arts, Classical/Choral/Band Music, Country, Folk, Bluegrass, Dance Music, Fashion, Jazz & Blues, Literature, Music

FMV Magazine
988680
Email: leon@fmvmagazine.com
Web site: http://www.fmvmagazine.com/
Freq: Daily
Circ: 2151 Cision Digital Reach
Editor: Leon Nicholson
MAGAZINE (ONLINE)
Classical/Choral/Band Music, Computer & Video Games, Country, Folk, Bluegrass, Dance Music, Entertainment, Jazz & Blues, Movies & Video, Music, Pop Music, R&B, Urban, World

Focus
987649
Editorial: 6 The Crescent, Kexby, York YO41 5LE
Email: focusmag@mangozine.com
Web site: www.bsfa.co.uk/bsfa-publications/focus
Freq: Semi-Annual Not Audited
Profile: Magazine containing articles on property, interiors, gardening, independent education, travel, art, antiques, health and fitness and eating out.
Ad Rate: Full Page Colour £1213.00
MAGAZINE
Science Fiction

FOCUS Magazine
999039
Editorial: 12 The Drive, Loughton, London IG10 1HB **Tel:** 44 02089 236068
Email: focus@iov.co.uk
Web site: www.iov.co.uk/focus
Freq: Bi-Monthly
Circ: 2500 Not Audited
Editor: Tony Manning
MAGAZINE
Movies & Video

Focus Magazine (UK)
999106
Editorial: 9th floor, Tower House, Fairfax Street, Bristol BS1 3BN
Tel: 44 01173 147388
Email: editorialenquiries@sciencefocus.com
Web site: www.sciencefocus.com/
Freq: Monthly Not Audited
MAGAZINE
Regional General Interest

Focus on Alternative and Complementary Therapies
985426
Editorial: 9600 Garsington Road, Oxford OX4 2DQ **Tel:** 44 01865 476361
Web site: http://onlinelibrary.wiley.com/journal/10.1111/(ISSN)2042-7166
Freq: Quarterly Not Audited
Profile: Journal presenting the evidence on complementary and alternative medicine in an analytical and impartial manner.
MAGAZINE
Alternative Medicine

Folk North West
982078
Editorial: 5 May Avenue, Wallasey, Wirral, Wallasey CH44 9EP **Tel:** 44 01516 394285
Web site: www.folknorthwest.co.uk
Freq: Quarterly
Circ: 1000 Not Audited
Editor: Steve Hughes
Profile: Magazine covering traditional and contemporary folk music in the North West. Contains club dates, features, CD articles, interviews and live reviews.
Ad Rate: Full Page Mono £84.00
Ad Rate: Full Page Colour £84.00
MAGAZINE
Country, Folk, Bluegrass

Food
986643
Editorial: Garden Floor, 16 Connaught Place, London W2 2ES
Tel: 44 02074 207000
Email: co-operativefoodmag@therivergroup.co.uk
Web site: http://www.co-operativefood.co.uk/food-magazine/
Freq: Bi-Monthly
Circ: 1000000 Not Audited
Profile: Magazine that promotes the best local eating, shopping, accommodation and activities. Features celebrity chefs, local producers, recipes, products, accommodation and restaurant guide and details on when, where and how to buy the best food. Aimed predominantly at affluent, 30 to 65 year old women.
Ad Rate: Full Page Colour £930.00
MAGAZINE
Grocery Stores

The Food & Drink Innovation Network
985077
Email: newsdesk@fdin.org.uk
Web site: www.fdin.org.uk
Freq: Daily
Circ: 14561 Cision Digital Reach
MAGAZINE (ONLINE)
Alcohol & Spirits, Food

Food & Drink International
980778
Editorial: Armstrong House, Armstrong Street, Grimsby, Grimsby DN31 2QE
Tel: 44 01472 310305
Email: fdi@blmgroup.co.uk
Web site: www.fdiforum.net
Freq: Monthly
Circ: 60000 Not Audited
Profile: Magazine covering new products and services plus current legislation and issues facing food and drink. Aimed at senior decision makers and buyers.
Ad Rate: Full Page Colour £1770.00
MAGAZINE
Alcohol & Spirits, Bars, Clubs & Pubs, Food

Food & Drink Law Monthly
988167
Editorial: The Ridge, South View Road, Pinner, London HA5 3YD
Tel: 44 02088 661934
Web site: http://www.singlelaw.com/food-and-drink-law-monthly
Freq: Monthly Not Audited
Profile: Newsletter providing coverage of legislative developments in the UK food and drink industries.
MAGAZINE
Alcohol & Spirits, Food

Food & Drink Matters
984816
Editorial: 4th Floor, Maybrook House, Queensway, Halesowen B63 4AH
Tel: 44 01562 756960
Email: info@foodanddrinkmatters.co.uk
Web site: http://www.foodanddrinkmatters.co.uk
Freq: Monthly
Circ: 5000 Not Audited
Profile: Publication that looks at all aspects of the food and drinks industry.
MAGAZINE
Alcohol & Spirits, Food

Food & Drink Technology
983347
Editorial: The Maltings, 57 Bath Street, Gravesend, London DA11 0DF
Tel: 44 01474 532202
Email: info@bellpublishing.com
Web site: www.foodanddrinktechnology.com
Freq: Monthly
Circ: 5880 Not Audited
Editor: Carly Wood
Profile: Magazine covering ingredients, processing and packaging in the food and beverage industries. It features technical and business news, analysis, comment, plant profiles, interviews and product developments. It also has regular geographic and industry sector reviews, giving a comprehensive view of the European food industry. Covers industry developments, exhibitions, conferences and industry events. Includes legislation issues, hygiene and food safety, research, EU news, ingredients and raw materials, packaging developments, processing machinery and equipment. Aimed at major specifiers within the food industry.
Ad Rate: Full Page Colour £2165.00
MAGAZINE
Alcohol & Spirits, Food

FOOD AND DRINK NETWORK UK
985969
Editorial: 46 Heneage Road, Grimsby DN32 9ES
Web site: https://foodanddrinknetwork-uk.co.uk/
Freq: Monthly
Circ: 14000 Not Audited
Profile: Publication containing up-to-date news on the food and drink industry as well as information on the latest in technology, company profiles, product reviews, exhibitions and forthcoming events.
Ad Rate: Full Page Mono £1426.00
Ad Rate: Full Page Colour £1745.00
MAGAZINE
Alcohol & Spirits, Food

Food and Travel
981807
Editorial: Suite 51, The Business Centre, Ingate Place, London SW8 3NS
Tel: 44 02075 010511
Email: info@foodandtravel.com
Web site: www.foodandtravel.com
Freq: Monthly
Circ: 30000 Not Audited
Editor: Mark Sansom
Profile: Magazine featuring short and long haul travel, weekend breaks, food and drink ideas, restaurant reviews and entertaining. Aimed at people who are passionate about the best in food, wine and travel.Regular features: Gormet travellers 10 page feature focusing on the food of a region/city
Ad Rate: Full Page Colour £4500.00
MAGAZINE
Cooking & Baking, Food, Grocery Stores, Organic Food, Railroad, Restaurant Reviews, Travel, Vegetarianism & Veganism, Wine/Winemaking

Food Chain
983045
Editorial: 10 Cringleford Business Centre, Suite 10, Intwood Road, Norwich NR4 6AU
Tel: 44 01603 274130
Web site: www.foodchainmagazine.com
Freq: Monthly Not Audited
MAGAZINE
Alcohol & Spirits, Food

Food Edited.
988627
Email: hello@foodedited.com
Web site: foodedited.com
Freq: Daily
Circ: 867 Cision Digital Reach
MAGAZINE (ONLINE)
Cooking & Baking, Restaurant Reviews

Food et al
1054081
Tel: 44 01954 261066
Email: info@foodetal.com
Web site: http://www.foodetal.com/
Freq: Quarterly Not Audited
Editor: Fiona Thomson Marshall
MAGAZINE
Cooking & Baking, Organic Food

food magazine
983678
Editorial: 5 Cross Street, Barnstaple, Barnstaple EX31 1BA
Freq: Monthly
Circ: 55000 Not Audited
Editor: Jo Rees
MAGAZINE
News & Current Affairs

Food Network UK
990565
Editorial: 111 Buckingham Palace Road, London SW1W 0SR **Tel:** 44 02075 789700
Email: contactus@foodnetwork.co.uk
Web site: www.foodnetwork.co.uk
Freq: Daily
Circ: 761091 Cision Digital Reach
Editor: Sanjana Modha-Patel
MAGAZINE (ONLINE)
Cooking & Baking, Food, Grocery Stores, Organic Food, Restaurant Reviews, Vegetarianism & Veganism

Food To Love
985041
Editorial: Academic House, 24-28 Oval Road, London NW1 7DT
Tel: 44 02072 418000
Email: cookeryed@eatinmagazine.co.uk
Web site: https://www.foodtolovemagazine.co.uk/
Freq: Monthly
Circ: 17833 Not Audited
Profile: Magazine offering food lovers inspiration on creating dishes, using quality, affordable and easily accessible ingredients. Aimed at anyone and everyone who loves to cook.
Ad Rate: Full Page Colour £3000.00
MAGAZINE
Cooking & Baking

FoodBev.com
986938
Editorial: 7 Kingsmead Square, Bath BA1 2AB **Tel:** 44 01225 327890
Email: info@foodbev.com
Web site: http://www.foodbev.com
Freq: Daily
Circ: 66561 Cision Digital Reach
Profile: Website with latest global food and drink industry news, analysis, comment and opinion from the leading international publisher, Zenith International.
MAGAZINE (ONLINE)
Alcohol & Spirits, Food

Foodepedia
984909
Editorial: 22 Carnaby Street, London W1F 7DB
Web site: www.foodepedia.co.uk
Freq: Daily
Circ: 15394 Cision Digital Reach
Profile: Website covering food, restaurants, bars, recipes and cookery books.
MAGAZINE (ONLINE)
Cooking & Baking, Restaurant Reviews

The Foodie Report
999600
Editorial: Unit M3, The Old Pumping Station, Pump Alley, Brentford TW8 0AP
Tel: 44 02082 318880
Web site: https://www.moodiedavittreport.com/foodie-newsletter-archive/
Freq: Monthly Not Audited
MAGAZINE
Alcohol & Spirits, Food, Travel

Foodies
1005290

Editorial: 26a St Andrews Square, Edinburgh EH2 1AF **Tel:** 44 01312 267766
Email: editorial.mediacompany@gmail.com
Web site: http://www.foodies-magazine.co.uk/
Freq: Monthly
Circ: 50000 Not Audited
Profile: Website for the agazine featuring recipes, interviews with celebrity and local chefs, in-season food, hotel restaurant, bar and club reviews, food and travel as well as monthly competitions. Aimed at an ABC1 audience, with an interest in quality food and drink products, who enjoy eating out and entertaining at home.
MAGAZINE
Cooking & Baking, Food, Organic Food

Foodism (UK)
987693

Editorial: 4 Tun Yard, Peardon St, London SW8 3HT **Tel:** 44 02078 199999
Email: info@squareupmedia.com
Web site: www.foodism.co.uk
Freq: Weekly
Circ: 50624 Cision Digital Reach
Editor: Suresh Doss
MAGAZINE (ONLINE)
Alcohol & Spirits, Bars, Clubs & Pubs, Beer, Beverages, Cooking & Baking, Restaurant Reviews, Wine/Winemaking

FoodNoise
1052574

Email: info@foodnoise.co.uk
Web site: www.foodnoise.co.uk
Freq: Daily
Circ: 11834 Cision Digital Reach
MAGAZINE (ONLINE)
News & Current Affairs

Foods Matter
983273

Editorial: 5 Lawn Road, London NW3 2XS
Tel: 44 02077 222866
Email: info@foodsmatter.com
Web site: www.foodsmatter.com
Freq: Daily
Circ: 36719 Cision Digital Reach
Profile: Website covering all aspects of allergy, food allergies and restricted diets. Foods Matter website discusses anything from food tolerance information and recipes to food supplements.
Ad Rate: Full Page Colour £635.00
MAGAZINE (ONLINE)
Allergies, Cooking & Baking, Nutrition

Foodtripper.com
985107

Editorial: 1 Castle Yard, Richmond, London TW10 6TF
Email: editorial@foodtripper.com
Web site: www.foodtripper.com
Freq: Daily
Circ: 7109 Cision Digital Reach
MAGAZINE (ONLINE)
Airline Inflight, Cooking & Baking, Food, Grocery Stores, Organic Food, Railroad, Restaurant Reviews, Travel, Vegetarianism & Veganism

The Foody Traveller
986342

Email: hello@foodytraveller.com
Web site: www.foodytraveller.com
Freq: Daily
Circ: 9463 Cision Digital Reach
Profile: The Foody Traveller is an online travel magazine covering 'worldwide travel destinations with the added bonus of learning more about the local food/ingredients, local producers and suppliers, and the stories that lie behind them'.
MAGAZINE (ONLINE)
Cooking & Baking, Food, Grocery Stores, Organic Food, Restaurant Reviews, Vegetarianism & Veganism

Football and Stadium Management
981071

Editorial: Chambers Business Centre, Chapel Road, Oldham OL8 4QQ
Tel: 44 01616 838000
Email: fsm-editorial@worldsfair.co.uk
Web site: http://www.fsm-online.co.uk
Freq: Bi-Monthly
Circ: 4500 Not Audited
Editor: Terry Ford
Profile: Magazine covering football and stadium management including indoor and outdoor sports venues throughout the UK and Ireland. Aimed at decision makers with buying authority in professional and semi-professional clubs, in football, both codes of rugby, athletics, cricket and tennis.
Ad Rate: Full Page Colour £1550.00
MAGAZINE
Soccer, Travel Industry

The Football League Paper
1056557

Editorial: Tuition House, St George's Road, Wimbledon SW19 4EU
Tel: 44 02089 714333
Email: newsdesk@theleaguepaper.com
Web site: www.theleaguepaper.com
Freq: Weekly
Circ: 16000 Not Audited
MAGAZINE
Soccer

Football.co.uk
985611

Editorial: Augustus Mews, 109 High Street, Braintree, Braintree CM7 1JS
Tel: 44 01376 809000
Web site: www.football.co.uk
Freq: Daily
Circ: 255277 Cision Digital Reach
MAGAZINE (ONLINE)
Soccer

Football365.com
983113

Editorial: 1 City Square, Leeds LS1 2ES
Tel: 44 01133 663167
Email: theeditor@football365.com
Web site: www.football365.com
Freq: Daily
Circ: 3266724 Cision Digital Reach
Editor: Sarah Winterburn
Profile: Website covering up-to-the-minute football news, team specific daily news, match reports and live scores.
MAGAZINE (ONLINE)
Soccer

FootballVita
997972

Editorial: 40 Hillfield Park Mews, Muswell Hill, London N10 3RT
Email: prontolimited@gmail.com
Web site: www.footballvita.com
Freq: Daily
Circ: 10305 Cision Digital Reach
MAGAZINE (ONLINE)
Soccer

Footprint
984727

Editorial: 29 Throgmorton Street, London EC2N 2AT
Web site: www.foodservicefootprint.com
Freq: Bi-Monthly
Circ: 8326 Not Audited
MAGAZINE
Alcohol & Spirits, Bars, Clubs & Pubs, Environment, Food

Footprint Handbooks
995057

Editorial: 5 Riverside Court, Lower Bristol Road, Bath BA2 3DZ **Tel:** 44 01225 469141
Email: flaughton@footprinttravelguides.com
Web site: www.footprinttravelguides.com
Freq: No Frequency Established Not Audited
MAGAZINE
Travel

Footprints
997112

Editorial: BRA Administration Office, Monks Orchard, Whitbourne, Worcester WR6 5RB
Tel: 44 01886 821207
Email: bra@britreflex.com
Web site: http://www.britreflex.co.uk/content/bra-newsletter
Freq: Quarterly Not Audited
Editor: Diane Morgan
MAGAZINE
Alternative Medicine

Footwear Today
984811

Editorial: 15a London Road, Maidstone, Maidstone ME16 8LY **Tel:** 44 01622 687031
Email: footwear@datateam.co.uk
Web site: www.footweartoday.co.uk
Freq: Monthly
Editor: Bryony Andrews
Profile: Magazine covering news, products, events, services and footwear industry information. Aimed at footwear, leather goods and fashion retailers. Also mail order companies, manufacturers, distributors and those involved in associated services.
Ad Rate: Full Page Colour £1350.00
MAGAZINE
Fashion

For Folk's Sake
1102567

Web site: www.forfolkssake.com
Freq: Daily
Circ: 10434 Cision Digital Reach
Editor: Ian Parker
MAGAZINE (ONLINE)
Country, Folk, Bluegrass

Fore & Aft
998940

Editorial: Marine House, Thorpe Lea Road, Egham, London TW20 8BF
Tel: 44 01784 223817
Email: lgordon@britishmarine.co.uk
Web site: www.tyha.co.uk
Freq: Quarterly
Circ: 2500 Not Audited
Editor: Libby Gordon
MAGAZINE
Boating & Yachting

Forge Magazine
1053222

Email: hello@forgemag.co.uk
Web site: http://forgemag.co.uk/
Freq: Daily
Circ: 521 Cision Digital Reach
MAGAZINE (ONLINE)
Art, Dance Music, Literature, Pop Music, Rap & Hip Hop, Regional, Visual Arts

Forge Press
983772

Editorial: Western Bank, Sheffield S10 2TG
Tel: 44 01142 228646
Email: editor@forgetoday.com
Web site: www.forgetoday.com
Freq: Bi-Weekly
Circ: 15000 Not Audited
Profile: Newspaper and magazine covering student issues, local Sheffield news, sport, entertainment, music, clubs and bars, food and drink, film and arts.
Ad Rate: Full Page Mono £840.00
Ad Rate: Full Page Colour £995.00
MAGAZINE
Student Lifestyle

Formula Money
985906

Editorial: Eighth Floor, 6 New Street Square, New Fetter Lane, London EC4A 3AQ
Email: info@formulamoney.com
Web site: www.formulamoney.com
Freq: Annual Not Audited
MAGAZINE
Automotive

Fortean Times
982046

Editorial: 31-32 Alfred Place, London WC1E 7DP **Tel:** 44 02079 076235
Web site: www.forteantimes.com
Freq: Monthly
Circ: 13904 Not Audited
Editor: David Sutton
Profile: Magazine which documents strange phenomena from around the world. Includes news, reviews and research on strange phenomena and experiences, curiosities, prodigies and portents.
Ad Rate: Full Page Colour £2500.00
MAGAZINE
Science Fiction

Fortitude Magazine
987187

Editorial: Flat 3, Adam Lodge, 2 Buchanan Close, London N21 1SG
Email: info@fortitudemagazine.co.uk
Web site: www.fortitudemagazine.co.uk
Freq: Daily
Circ: 66754 Cision Digital Reach
MAGAZINE (ONLINE)
News & Current Affairs

Forum Publications
1053469

Tel: 44 01962 735137
Email: editor@forumpublications.co.uk
Web site: http://forumpublications.co.uk/
Freq: Monthly
Circ: 20000 Not Audited
Editor: Mark Tubb
MAGAZINE
Alcohol & Spirits, Art, Bars, Clubs & Pubs, Beer, Beverages, Books, Business, Comedy, Cooking & Baking, Cosmetics

Foster Care
985352

Editorial: 87 Blackfriars Road, London SE1 8HA **Tel:** 44 02076 206400
Email: info@fostering.net
Web site: www.fostering.net
Freq: Quarterly
Circ: 35000 Not Audited
Editor: Daniel Sinclair
MAGAZINE
Family & Parenting

Foto8 Magazine
997099

Editorial: 1 Honduras Street, London EC1Y 0TH **Tel:** 44 02072 538801
Email: info@foto8.com
Web site: www.foto8.com
Freq: Daily
Circ: 12029 Cision Digital Reach
MAGAZINE (ONLINE)
Photography, Visual Arts

The Founder
997523

Editorial: Orchard Building, Royal Holloway, University of London, Egham, London TW20 0EX
Email: editor@thefounder.co.uk
Freq: Bi-Weekly
Circ: 3000 Not Audited
MAGAZINE
Student Lifestyle

FOUR
986644

Editorial: 2nd Floor, 239 Kensington High Street, London W8 6SN
Tel: 44 02034 055840
Email: editorial@four-magazine.com
Web site: www.four-magazine.com
Freq: Quarterly
Circ: 85000 Not Audited
Profile: Publication that covers the best chefs and restaurants, as well as featuring news and information on luxury lifestyle, arts, high-end travel destinations, cookery techniques and trends.
MAGAZINE
Cooking & Baking

The Four Shires
982468

Editorial: Borough House, Marlborough Road, Banbury OX16 5TH
Tel: 44 01295 273138
Email: copy@fourshires.co.uk
Web site: www.fourshires.co.uk
Freq: Monthly
Circ: 5000 Not Audited
Profile: Website covering all aspects of life in the four shires - countryside, wining and dining, going out and about, food fairs, property, social pages, health, pictures from the past, all that celebrates the area and all that's good about the area.
MAGAZINE
Regional General Interest

FourFourTwo
982249

Editorial: Bridge House, 69 London Road, Twickenham, London TW1 3QL
Tel: 44 02082 675337
Email: contact@fourfourtwo.com
Web site: www.fourfourtwo.com
Freq: Monthly
Circ: 60227 Not Audited
Editor: Hitesh Ratna
Profile: Magazine covering football and featuring player profiles, interviews, features and readers letters. First published in 1994, the publication has an average of 150 pages per issue. Press Day: Third week of the month. Aimed at football fans aged 16 years old and over.

Consumer Magazines

Ad Rate: Full Page Colour £5875.00
MAGAZINE
Soccer

Fourth Source 986359
Editorial: Fulham Green, Chester House, 81-83 Fulham High Street, London SW6 3JA
Email: editor@fourthsource.com
Web site: http://www.fourthsource.com/
Freq: Daily
Circ: 150905 Cision Digital Reach
Profile: Website covering digital media and marketing. The FOURTH SOURCE website shares the latest news in the digital marketing and media industry.
MAGAZINE (ONLINE)
Advertising Industry, Branding, Broadcasting, Graphic Design, Marketing, Media & Communications, Photography, Publishing

FOXES 1101753
Email: info@foxesmagazine.com
Web site: www.foxesmagazine.com
Freq: Monthly Not Audited
MAGAZINE
Country, Folk, Bluegrass, Fashion, Jazz & Blues, Pop Music, Rock Music

The Foxley Docket 1074630
Tel: 44 08443 356635
Email: editorial@thefoxleydocket.com
Web site: www.thefoxleydocket.com
Freq: Quarterly
MAGAZINE
Crafts, Luxury Goods

FQ 982063
Editorial: 35 Hanover Road, London NW10 3DJ
Web site: www.fqmagazine.co.uk
Freq: Quarterly
Circ: 9637 Cision Digital Reach
Editor: Natalie Brown
MAGAZINE (ONLINE)
Family & Parenting, Men's Interests

Fractional Life 999494
Editorial: 10-14 Accomodation Road, Golders Green, London NW11 8ED
Tel: 44 02083 407989
Email: info@fractionallife.com
Web site: www.fractionallife.com
Freq: Daily
Circ: 6707 Cision Digital Reach
MAGAZINE (ONLINE)
Luxury Goods

Frame Rated 997792
Email: editor@framerated.co.uk
Web site: www.framerated.co.uk
Freq: Daily
Circ: 14093 Cision Digital Reach
MAGAZINE (ONLINE)
Broadcasting, Movies & Video

FRANCE (UK) 982331
Editorial: Cumberland House, Oriel Road, Cheltenham GL50 1BB
Tel: 44 01242 216050
Email: editorial@francemag.com
Web site: www.completefrance.com
Freq: Monthly
Circ: 14655 Not Audited
MAGAZINE
Travel

France Today 987372
Editorial: 2 Seven Dials, Bath BA1 1EN
Tel: 44 01225 463752
Email: info@francetoday.com
Web site: http://www.francetoday.com/
Freq: Bi-Monthly
Circ: 210000 Not Audited
Profile: Magazine covering French travel and culture. Includes features on social trends, French artists, business and politics, guides for travellers to France, French learning methods and information on French products and services available in the United States. Aimed at travellers and those interested in France.
Ad Rate: Full Page Mono £1500.00

Ad Rate: Full Page Colour £2000.00
MAGAZINE
Travel

Freak Deluxe 985506
Editorial: 20A Jasmine Street, London SE20 8JW **Tel:** 44 07904 956299
Email: info@freakdeluxe.co.uk
Web site: www.freakdeluxe.co.uk
Freq: Daily
Circ: 6895 Cision Digital Reach
Editor: Cyrena Arnold
Profile: Website covering lifestyle. The Freak Deluxe website shares the latest news and information on fashion, beauty, culture, music, technology, and events.
MAGAZINE (ONLINE)
Audio Video Trade, Beauty & Grooming, Cameras, Consumer Electronics, Cosmetics, Dance Music, Electronics, Fashion, Hair, Jazz & Blues

FREDAG 1062110
Email: toimitus@fredagmagazine.com
Web site: http://www.fredagmagazine.com/
Freq: 2 Times/Week
Circ: 493 Cision Digital Reach
MAGAZINE (ONLINE)
Airline Inflight, Beauty & Grooming, Broadcasting, Cosmetics, Hair, Movies & Video, Railroad, Travel, Women's Interests

Free From Heaven 995523
Editorial: Suite 6, Piccadilly House, London Road, Bath BA1 6PL **Tel:** 44 01225 489984
Web site: http://www.freefromheaven.com
Freq: Bi-Monthly
Editor: Nick Gregory
MAGAZINE
Cooking & Baking

The Free Life Magazine 1053245
Email: timefor@thefreelifemag.com
Web site: http://www.thefreelifemag.com
Freq: Semi-Annual
MAGAZINE
Field Sports, Fitness & Exercise, Women's Interests

Freeform Dynamics 996337
Editorial: 11 The Willows, New Milton, Christchurch BH25 7BE
Tel: 44 01425 626501
Email: info@freeformdynamics.com
Web site: www.freeformdynamics.com
Freq: Daily
Circ: 14549 Cision Digital Reach
MAGAZINE (ONLINE)
Auto Aftermarket, Computers, Data Management, Electronics, Government Technology, Industry, Internet, Mobile Communications, Security & Security Systems, Software

Freemasonry Today 986581
Editorial: Freemasons' Hall, Great Queen Street, London WC2B 5AZ
Tel: 44 02078 319811
Email: editor@ugle.org.uk
Web site: www.freemasonrytoday.com
Freq: Quarterly Not Audited
Profile: Magazine covering the history, present and future of freemasonry. Contains news, entertainment pages and articles of interest.
Ad Rate: Full Page Colour £3760.00
MAGAZINE
Religion

French Property News 981864
Editorial: Cumberland House, Oriel Road, Cheltenham GL50 1BB
Tel: 44 01242 216050
Web site: www.french-property-news.com
Freq: Monthly
Circ: 22000 Not Audited
Profile: Magazine covering the issues involved in buying property and living in France. Aimed at those interested in purchasing French property.
Ad Rate: Full Page Colour £1750.00
MAGAZINE
Real Estate

French Radio London 999343
Editorial: 50 Lisson Street, London NW1 5DF
Email: info@frenchradiolondon.com
Web site: http://www.frenchradiolondon.com/
Freq: Daily
Circ: 7217 Cision Digital Reach
MAGAZINE (ONLINE)
News & Current Affairs

Fresh Produce Journal 983180
Editorial: 132 Wandsworth Road, London SW8 2LB **Tel:** 44 02075 010300
Email: editorial@fpj.co.uk
Web site: http://www.fruitnet.com/fpj
Freq: Bi-Weekly
Circ: 3500 Not Audited
Editor: Michael Barker
Profile: Journal covering all aspects of the fresh produce trade including associated service industries such as transport, packaging and machinery. Read by the fresh produce supply chain, from seed breeders through to in-store produce managers at major retailers.
Ad Rate: Full Page Colour £1400.00
MAGAZINE
Alcohol & Spirits, Food

The Friend 982161
Editorial: 173 Euston Road, London NW1 2BJ **Tel:** 44 02076 631010
Email: editorial@thefriend.org
Web site: www.thefriend.org
Freq: Weekly
Circ: 3000 Not Audited
Editor: Ian Kirk-Smith
Profile: Magazine featuring interviews with celebrities who support green issues as well as fashion, art, sport and politics.
MAGAZINE
Religion

Frieze 981880
Editorial: 1 Montclare Street, London E2 7EU **Tel:** 44 02033 726111
Email: editors@frieze.com
Web site: www.frieze.com
Freq: Bi-Monthly
Circ: 36436 Not Audited
Profile: Magazine about contemporary art and culture. Read by higher income earners between 18 and 34 years old with an interest in visual arts and contemporary culture.
Ad Rate: Full Page Mono £2850.00
Ad Rate: Full Page Colour £3350.00
MAGAZINE
Art

FrightFest 1006320
Editorial: 10 Wiltshire Gardens, Twickenham, London TW2 6ND
Tel: 44 02082 960555
Email: frightfest@mac.com
Web site: www.frightfest.co.uk
Freq: Daily
Circ: 50077 Cision Digital Reach
Editor: Ian Rattray
MAGAZINE (ONLINE)
Entertainment

Fringe Opera 1052552
Tel: 44 07892 979459
Email: francescawickers@fringeopera.com
Web site: http://www.fringeopera.com
Freq: Daily
Circ: 3345 Cision Digital Reach
MAGAZINE (ONLINE)
Classical/Choral/Band Music, Entertainment

FringeReview 1104815
Email: gubbins@fringereview.co.uk
Web site: http://fringereview.co.uk/
Freq: Daily
Circ: 10829 Cision Digital Reach
Editor: Paul Levy
MAGAZINE (ONLINE)
Theater & Performing Arts

Frodsham Life 982899
Editorial: New Media Centre, Old Road, Warrington, Warrington WA4 1AT
Tel: 44 01925 623631
Email: info@frodshamlife.co.uk
Web site: http://www.warrington-worldwide.co.uk/category/frodsham-life/
Freq: Monthly
Circ: 4200 Not Audited
MAGAZINE
Regional General Interest

FRONT 982054
Editorial: Hoxton Mix 86-90, London EC2A 4NE
Email: front@frontarmy.co.uk
Web site: www.frontarmy.com
Freq: Monthly Not Audited
MAGAZINE
Men's Interests

Front Row Reviews 999678
Editorial: K103, The Biscuit Factory, Bermondsey, London SE16 4DG
Tel: 44 02036 325134
Web site: www.frontrowreviews.co.uk
Freq: Daily
Circ: 98390 Cision Digital Reach
MAGAZINE (ONLINE)
Entertainment, Local Entertainment Guides, Movies & Video

Frontier 983814
Editorial: 6th Floor, Davis House, 2 Robert Street, Croydon, London CR0 1QQ
Tel: 44 02082 538394
Web site: www.frontiermagazine.co.uk
Freq: Monthly
Circ: 3500 Not Audited
Editor: Colette Doyle
Profile: Magazine covering all aspects of travel retail including news, products, industry interviews, regional reports and analysis of regions worldwide. Aimed at international management of travel retail including directors, marketing and purchasing personnel and brand managers.
Ad Rate: Full Page Colour £2800.00
MAGAZINE
Travel

fRoots 982079
Editorial: PO Box 3072, Bristol BS8 9GF
Tel: 44 01173 179020
Email: editorial@frootsmag.com
Web site: www.frootsmag.com
Freq: Monthly
Circ: 13000 Not Audited
Editor: Ian Anderson
Profile: Magazine about folk, roots and world music with news, reviews, interviews and features on the UK and international scene. Covers modern and traditional music with roots from around the globe.
Ad Rate: Full Page Mono £725.00
Ad Rate: Full Page Colour £930.00
MAGAZINE
Country, Folk, Bluegrass

Frost Magazine 995432
Editorial: No 6, 50 Burr Road, London SW18 4SS
Email: frostmagazine@gmail.com
Web site: www.frostmagazine.com
Freq: Daily
Circ: 29079 Cision Digital Reach
MAGAZINE (ONLINE)
Celebrities, Literature, Men's Interests, Movies & Video, Women's Interests

Fruitnet.com 1101936
Editorial: 132 Wandsworth Road, London SW8 2LB
Profile: Website covering global fresh produce portal.
MAGAZINE (ONLINE)
News & Current Affairs

FRUK magazine 1052672
Email: info@frukmagazine.com
Web site: www.frukmagazine.com
Freq: Daily Not Audited

Editor: Elizabeth Ajomale
MAGAZINE
Beauty & Grooming, Cosmetics, Dance
Music, Fashion, Hair, Jazz & Blues, Pop
Music, Rap & Hip Hop

FStech 980059
Editorial: Sixth Floor, 3 London Wall
Buildings, London EC2M 5PD
Tel: 44 02075 622413
Web site: www.fstech.co.uk
Freq: Bi-Monthly
Circ: 8500 Not Audited
Editor: Michelle Stevens
Profile: Financial Sector Technology (FST) is
one of the business titles for IT decision
makers in the UK and European financial
services sector. Targets IT decision makers
within banks, building societies, insurers,
trading houses, exchanges and other
financial institutions. FST publish 6 issues
per year, providing the latest news and
developments within the sector. Covers
wealth management.Aimed at finance IT
managers, CIOs, CTOs and other key IT
decision makers.
Ad Rate: Full Page Colour £3909.00
MAGAZINE
Banking, Data Management, Electronics,
Security & Security Systems

FTAdviser.com 981508
Editorial: Number One, Southwark Bridge,
London SE1 9HL **Tel:** 44 02078 733000
Email: ftadviser.enquiries@ft.com
Web site: www.ftadviser.com
Freq: Daily
Circ: 87819 Cision Digital Reach
Editor: Emma Ann Hughes
Profile: News website offering the latest
breaking news and industry analysis for the
UK intermediary market. The website
combines content from FTAdviser along with
that of the magazines Financial Adviser,
Investment Adviser, Mortgage Adviser and
Money Management. Read by independent
financial advisors, intermediaries, brokers
and product providers in retail finance.
MAGAZINE (ONLINE)
Fund Management, Personal Finance

FUBAR Radio 996408
Editorial: FUBAR Radio, The Busworks,
United House, North Road, London N7 9DP
Tel: 44 03302 230200
Web site: www.fubarradio.com
Freq: Daily
Circ: 15653 Cision Digital Reach
MAGAZINE (ONLINE)
Bars, Clubs & Pubs, Comedy, Country,
Folk, Bluegrass, Dance Music,
Entertainment, Jazz & Blues, Local
Entertainment Guides, Movies & Video,
Music, National News

Független Civil Fórum 1061771
Tel: 44 36623 11111
Email: goldpress@invitel.hu
MAGAZINE (ONLINE)
Advertising Industry, Branding,
Broadcasting, Graphic Design, Marketing,
Media & Communications, Photography,
Publishing

Fulham Residents' Journal
1052537
Editorial: 6th Floor, One Canada Square,
Canary Wharf, London E14 5AX
Tel: 44 02079 874320
Email: info@rwmg.co.uk
Web site: https://issuu.com/runwildmedia/
docs/issuu_fulham_feb
Freq: Monthly
Circ: 12750 Not Audited
MAGAZINE
Regional General Interest

Fuller's Finest 996047
Editorial: 5th Floor, Drury House, 34-43
Russell Street, London WC2B 5HA
Tel: 44 02070 100999
Freq: Monthly
Circ: 5000 Not Audited

Editor: Lauren Dowey
MAGAZINE
Bars, Clubs & Pubs

Fultime 999439
Editorial: 959-961 Fulham Road, London
SW6 5HY **Tel:** 44 08432 081222
Web site: www.fulhamfc.com
Freq: Daily
Circ: 136317 Cision Digital Reach
MAGAZINE (ONLINE)
Soccer

Fun To Learn - Friends 982458
Editorial: Suites 3 & 4 Canon Court East,
Abbey Lawn, Shrewsbury, Shrewsbury SY2
5DE **Tel:** 44 01743 364433
Email: info@redan.com
Web site: www.redan.co.uk/Friends.html
Freq: Bi-Weekly
Circ: 49644 Not Audited
Editor: Anita Cash
MAGAZINE
Preschool

Fun to Learn - Peppa Pig 983994
Editorial: Suites 3 & 4 Canon Court East,
Abbey Lawn, Shrewsbury SY2 5DE
Tel: 44 01743 364433
Email: info@redan.com
Web site: http://www.redan.co.uk/Peppa%
20Pig.html
Freq: Bi-Weekly
Circ: 64108 Not Audited
Editor: Debra Harrison
MAGAZINE
Preschool, Teen/Young Adult

Functional Sports Nutrition
988604
Tel: 44 01279 810080
Web site: www.fsnmag.com
Freq: Bi-Monthly Not Audited
MAGAZINE
Fitness & Exercise, Nutrition

Fundraising 981020
Editorial: 15 Prescott Place, London SW4
6BS **Tel:** 44 02078 191200
Email: newsdesk@civilsociety.co.uk
Web site: https://www.civilsociety.co.uk/
fundraising.html
Freq: Monthly
Circ: 5000 Not Audited
Editor: Gareth Jones
Profile: Magazine covering latest news,
issues and debates in the fundraising sector.
Ad Rate: Full Page Colour £1995.00
MAGAZINE
Charitable Foundations

Funny Women 996796
Editorial: St. David's House, 15 Worple
Way, London TW10 6DG
Tel: 44 02089 484444
Email: editor@funnywomen.com
Web site: www.funnywomen.com
Freq: Daily
Circ: 14764 Cision Digital Reach
Editor: Kate Stone
MAGAZINE (ONLINE)
Comedy, Women's Interests

Fur & Feather 984829
Tel: 44 01473 652789
Email: info@furandfeather.co.uk
Web site: www.furandfeather.co.uk
Freq: Monthly Not Audited
Editor: Patt Gaskin
MAGAZINE
Nature & Wildlife

Furniture & Cabinet Making
982050
Editorial: 166 High Street, Lewes, Lewes
BN7 1XU **Tel:** 44 01273 477374
Email: pubs@thegmcgroup.com
Web site: http://www.thegmcgroup.com/pc/
viewCategories.asp?idCategory=701
Freq: Monthly
Circ: 17000 Not Audited

Editor: Derek Jones
MAGAZINE
Woodworking

Fuse FM 1006080
Editorial: University of Manchester Student
Union, Oxford Road, Manchester M13 9PR
Tel: 44 01612 757071
Email: info@fusefm.co.uk
Web site: fusefmmanchester.wordpress.
com
Freq: Daily
Circ: 7 Cision Digital Reach
MAGAZINE (ONLINE)
Regional

Fused 982540
Editorial: The Penthouse, 10 Evelaw House,
43 Worcester Street, Stourbridge DY8 1AT
Tel: 44 01384 837362
Web site: www.fusedmagazine.com
Freq: Quarterly
Circ: 20000 Not Audited
Profile: Cutting-edge youth culture
magazine covering music, art and fashion.
Ad Rate: Full Page Colour £800.00
MAGAZINE
Airline Inflight, Antiques/Collectibles, Art,
Arts, Bars, Clubs & Pubs, Classical/
Choral/Band Music, Country, Folk,
Bluegrass, Dance Music, Entertainment,
Fashion

Fusion Flowers 985819
Editorial: Fusion Flowers Magazine, Hillcroft,
Fore Road, Aberdeen FK8 3DT
Web site: www.fusionflowers.com
Freq: Bi-Monthly
Circ: 12500 Not Audited
MAGAZINE
Do-It-Yourself (DIY), Gardening

**Fusion Flowers Weddings
Magazine** 1095577
Editorial: Hillcroft, Fore Road, Aberdeen
FK8 3DT
Web site: www.fusionflowers.com/section.
php/3/1/weddings
Freq: Annual
Circ: 13000 Not Audited
MAGAZINE
Beauty & Grooming, Cosmetics, Hair,
Weddings

Future Intelligence 987011
Tel: 44 02071 001389
Email: futureintelligence@outlook.com
Web site: www.futureintelligence.co.uk
Freq: Daily
Circ: 3155 Cision Digital Reach
Profile: Material accepted: Technology and
science news especially stories on all
aspects of cyber crime. Serves: All British
media including national and regional
newspapers, TV, Radio and the Internet.
MAGAZINE (ONLINE)
Auto Aftermarket, Computers, Data
Management, Electronics, Government
Technology, Industry, Internet, Mobile
Communications, Security & Security
Systems, Software

Future Microbiology 998874
Editorial: Unitec House, 2 Albert Place,
London N3 1QB **Tel:** 44 02083 716090
Email: info@futuremedicine.com
Web site: www.futuremedicine.com/loi/fmb
Freq: Monthly Not Audited
MAGAZINE
Medicine, Science

Future Music 982098
Editorial: Quay House, The Ambury, Bath
BA1 1UA **Tel:** 44 01225 442244
Email: news@futuremusic.com
Web site: www.futuremusic.co.uk
Freq: Monthly
Circ: 11181 Not Audited
Editor: Si Truss
Profile: Magazine containing a guide to the
equipment required to create, play and
record music using the latest technology.

Ad Rate: Full Page Colour £1600.00
MAGAZINE
Music

Future Rail 1058690
Editorial: John Carpenter House, John
Carpenter Street, London EC4Y 0AN
Tel: 44 02077 534200
Web site: http://www.nridigital.com/future-
rail.html
Freq: Monthly
Circ: 3705 Not Audited
MAGAZINE
Railroad

Future Textiles 983556
Editorial: West One, 114 Wellington Street,
Leeds LS1 1BA **Tel:** 44 01138 198155
Email: info@wtin.com
Web site: http://www.wtin.com/e-store-
products/future-materials/
Freq: Bi-Monthly
Circ: 5819 Not Audited
Profile: Future Materials is a magazine
covering industrial and technical materials
including technical textiles, nonwovens,
paper and resin. Read by European
manufacturers and converters working in
technical textiles, nonwovens, glass, films,
composites and laminates.
Ad Rate: Full Page Mono £1227.00
Ad Rate: Full Page Colour £2500.00
MAGAZINE
Fashion

Future Virology 997082
Editorial: Unitec House, 2 Albert Place,
London N3 1QB **Tel:** 44 02083 716080
Email: info@futuremedicine.com
Web site: www.futuremedicine.com/loi/fvl
Freq: Monthly Not Audited
MAGAZINE
Medicine

Futurewise 998980
Editorial: 1st Floor, St George's House,
Knoll Road, Camberley, Camberley GU15
3SY **Tel:** 44 01491 820382
Email: helpline@inspiringfutures.org.uk
Web site: www.myfuturewise.org.uk
Freq: Daily
Circ: 5649 Cision Digital Reach
MAGAZINE (ONLINE)
Alumni, Careers, Education, Student
Lifestyle, Teachers

Fyne Times 984063
Editorial: 4 Ram Court, Wicklesham Farm,
Oxfordshire, Faringdon SN7 7PN
Tel: 44 01235 856300
Email: news@fyne.co.uk
Web site: www.fyne.co.uk
Freq: 3 Times/Year
Circ: 10000 Not Audited
Editor: Natalie Thorne
Profile: Lifestyle magazine containing
features on local news, travel, motors,
health, general articles, gossip, chat,
property and recruitment.
MAGAZINE
LGBT, Sexuality

G3 Magazine 985302
Editorial: Samson House, 457 Manchester
Road, Walkden M29 7BR
Tel: 44 01942 879291
Web site: http://www.g3newswire.com/
Freq: Monthly
Circ: 4500 Not Audited
Editor: Lewis Pek
Profile: Magazine covering lesbian
community, arts and culture, community,
sports, Internet, music, bars and clubs.
Aimed at gay, urban women.
Ad Rate: Full Page Colour £2500.00
MAGAZINE
Computer & Video Games

GAB Consultancy 996789
Editorial: The Press Rooms, 23 New Mount
Street, Manchester M4 4DE
Tel: 44 01612 121017
Web site: gabconsultancy.co.uk
Freq: Daily

Consumer Magazines

Circ: 787 Cision Digital Reach
MAGAZINE (ONLINE)
Bars, Clubs & Pubs, Fitness & Exercise, Hotels/Motels, Lifestyle, Men's Interests, Music, Regional General Interest, Travel, Women's Interests

GadgetHead Magazine 1054113
Editorial: Littlegate Publishing Ltd, Suite 10, Thorpe House, 79 Thorpe Road, Norwich NR1 1UA **Tel:** 44 01603 296100
Web site: www.gadgetheadmag.com
Freq: Monthly
Circ: 521 Cision Digital Reach
MAGAZINE (ONLINE)
Mobile Communications

GadgetsBoy 986804
Editorial: 31 Union Road, Stockwell, London EC2A 4LU
Email: gadgets@gadgetsboy.co.uk
Web site: www.gadgetsboy.co.uk
Freq: Daily
Circ: 9703 Cision Digital Reach
MAGAZINE (ONLINE)
Audio Video Trade, Cameras, Consumer Electronics, Electronics, Mobile Electronics, Movies & Video

GadgetSpeak.com 984553
Editorial: 163 Heronswood Road, Welwyn Garden City, Welwyn Garden City AL7 3EJ
Tel: 44 01707 891840
Email: editor@gadgetspeak.com
Web site: www.gadgetspeak.com
Freq: Daily
Circ: 28076 Cision Digital Reach
Editor: Peter Wilson
MAGAZINE (ONLINE)
Audio Video Trade, Cameras, Consumer Electronics, Mobile Electronics, Movies & Video

Gadgette 996079
Editorial: Gadgette, PO Box 68636, London E15 9EU
Email: editorial@gadgette.com
Web site: www.gadgette.com
Freq: Daily
Circ: 134984 Cision Digital Reach
MAGAZINE (ONLINE)
Apple, Audio Video Trade, Cameras, Computer & Video Games, Computers, Consumer Electronics, Electronics, Internet, Mobile Electronics, Movies & Video

gal-dem.com 1054529
Email: info@gal-dem.com
Web site: www.gal-dem.com
Freq: Daily
Circ: 18256 Cision Digital Reach
MAGAZINE (ONLINE)
Art, Beauty & Grooming, Cosmetics, Fashion, Hair, International News, Photography, Politics, Social Issues, Theater & Performing Arts

Galleries 984042
Editorial: Riverside Studios, 65 Aspenlea Road, London W6 8LH
Tel: 44 02082 371180
Email: features@galleries.co.uk
Web site: www.galleries.co.uk
Freq: Monthly
Circ: 20000 Not Audited
Profile: Listings guide of art galleries containing news, previews, Internet guide and maps.
Ad Rate: Full Page Mono £550.00
Ad Rate: Full Page Colour £940.00
MAGAZINE
Photography, Visual Arts

GalleriesNow.net 997802
Editorial: 52-53 Margaret St, London W1W 8SW **Tel:** 44 02075 807227
Email: team@galleriesnow.net
Web site: http://www.galleriesnow.net/
Freq: Daily
Circ: 14409 Cision Digital Reach

Editor: Liene Pulture
MAGAZINE (ONLINE)
Antiques/Collectibles, Art, Arts, Literature, Photography, Theater & Performing Arts, Visual Arts

Gallery (Isle of Man) 997463
Editorial: Quay House, South Quay, Douglas, Douglas IM1 5AR
Tel: 44 01624 619540
Email: editorial@gallery.co.im
Web site: gallery.co.im
Freq: Monthly
Circ: 8000 Not Audited
MAGAZINE
Lifestyle, Men's Interests, Regional General Interest, Women's Interests

Gallery (Jersey) 985293
Editorial: Mindon Base, 10 Mindon Street, St. Helier, St. Helier JE2 4WR
Tel: 44 01534 811100
Email: editorial@gallery.je
Web site: http://www.gallery.je/
Freq: Monthly
Circ: 10000 Not Audited
Editor: Ben Davies
MAGAZINE
Lifestyle, Men's Interests, Regional General Interest, Women's Interests

The Gallivanter's Guide 988804
Email: mail@gallivantersguide.com
Web site: www.gallivantersguide.com
Freq: Monthly Not Audited
Profile: Newsletter with the aim of unearthing idyllic places for the dedicated traveller. Covers every aspect of each hotel visited, from rooms and suite descriptions and service standards, to restaurant menus sampled.
MAGAZINE
Travel

Galore 1053480
Web site: www.galoremag.com
Freq: Quarterly
MAGAZINE
Beauty & Grooming, Celebrities, Cosmetics, Fashion, Hair, Health & Medicine, Relationships, Women's Interests

GambleGeek 995159
Email: hello@gamblegeek.com
Web site: http://gamblegeek.com/
Freq: Daily
Circ: 10808 Cision Digital Reach
MAGAZINE (ONLINE)
Casinos & Gaming, Computer & Video Games, Soccer

Gambling Compliance 983963
Editorial: House, 4th Floor, 44 Kemp Little Llp Saddlers House, Gutter Lane, London EC2V 6BR **Tel:** 44 02079 219980
Email: info@gamblingcompliance.com
Web site: www.gamblingcompliance.com
Freq: Daily
Circ: 39974 Cision Digital Reach
MAGAZINE (ONLINE)
Computer & Video Games

Gambling Insider 986310
Editorial: 7 Chapel Place, Rivington Street, London EC2A 3DQ **Tel:** 44 02077 396999
Web site: www.gamblinginsider.com
Freq: Bi-Monthly Not Audited
Profile: Publication that covers the latest news and information with regards the online gambling industry.
MAGAZINE
Computer & Video Games

Gambling.com 1093865
Editorial: Temple Chambers, Temple Avenue, London EC4Y OHP
Email: info@lyceummedia.com
Web site: https://www.gambling.com/news
Freq: Daily
Circ: 6 Cision Digital Reach
Profile: Website covering casino games and sports including card games, slots, video

poker and bingo as well as a gaming specific search engine.
MAGAZINE (ONLINE)
Computer & Video Games

Game Smack 995109
Email: game-smack@hotmail.com
Web site: game-smack.net
Freq: Daily
Circ: 10709 Cision Digital Reach
MAGAZINE (ONLINE)
Computer & Video Games

Gamefisher 983178
Editorial: Fishmonger's Hall, London Bridge, London EC4R 9EL **Tel:** 44 02072 835838
Email: hq@salmon-trout.org
Web site: http://www.salmon-trout.org
Freq: Semi-Annual Not Audited
MAGAZINE
Fishing

GameGrin 988457
Email: press@gamegrin.com
Web site: www.gamegrin.com
Freq: Daily
Circ: 159370 Cision Digital Reach
Editor: Emsey Walker
Profile: Website covering computer games.
MAGAZINE (ONLINE)
Computer & Video Games

Gamer Network 997904
Editorial: 3rd Floor, 1 Grand Parade, Brighton BN2 9QB **Tel:** 44 01273 746864
Web site: www.gamer-network.net
Freq: Daily
Circ: 89806 Cision Digital Reach
Editor: Oli Welsh
MAGAZINE (ONLINE)
Computer & Video Games

The Games Shed 995175
Email: info@thegamesshed.com
Web site: www.thegamesshed.com
Freq: Daily
Circ: 10685 Cision Digital Reach
MAGAZINE (ONLINE)
Computer & Video Games

games xtreme 982830
Editorial: 49 Petworth Gardens, Southampton SO16 8EF
Tel: 44 07855 496798
Email: pr.emails@gamesxtreme.com
Web site: http://www.gamesxtreme.com/
Freq: Daily
Circ: 64102 Cision Digital Reach
Editor: Benjamin Jones
Profile: Website covering computer games. Games xtreme features the latest gaming news, reviews, interviews, previews, screenshots and videos. It covering all major consoles, such as Xbox 360, PlayStation 3, Wii, PlayStation 2, PC and many more. Games xtreme is also a social network for gamers.
MAGAZINE (ONLINE)
Computer & Video Games

GamesIndustry.biz 983043
Editorial: 3rd Floor, 1-6 Grand Parade, Brighton BN2 9QB
Email: news@gamesindustry.biz
Web site: www.gamesindustry.biz
Freq: Daily
Circ: 592696 Cision Digital Reach
Profile: Website covering 'the global videogames industry, covering all aspects of the interactive entertainment value chain.'
MAGAZINE (ONLINE)
Computer & Video Games, Computers, Industry, Software

GamesMaster 981733
Editorial: Quay House, The Ambury, Bath BA1 1UA **Tel:** 44 01225 442244
Email: gamesmaster@futurenet.com
Web site: http://www.gamesradar.com/
Freq: Monthly
Circ: 12849 Not Audited
Profile: GamesMaster is a monthly multi-format computer and video game

magazine published by Future Publishing. Official magazine of the 'GamesMaster' TV show. Provides reviews and previews of the latest video games to rent or buy on every gaming format: Xbox 360, PS3, Wii, PS2, PSP, Xbox, Gamecube, GBA, DS and PC. The magazine was launched in January 1993. Read by gamers and owners of electronic games machines.
Ad Rate: Full Page Colour £3500.00
MAGAZINE
Computer & Video Games

gamesTM 981729
Editorial: Richmond House, 33 Richmond Hill, Bournemouth BH2 6EZ
Tel: 44 01202 586200
Email: gamestm@imagine-publishing.co.uk
Web site: www.gamestm.co.uk
Freq: Monthly
Circ: 30000 Not Audited
Editor: Jonathan Gordon
Profile: Magazine covering past, present and future videogames. Contains 180 pages with dedicated sections for market news, recruitment, previews, news and reviews for every gaming format, covering PS2, PS3, Xbox 360, Nintendo Wii, DS, PC and online. Features a dedicated section to retro content every issue, plus interviews and opinions about all the console and handheld formats and their titles.Aimed at aspirational videogamers aged 25 years old plus and people who take gaming seriously.
Ad Rate: Full Page Colour £3200.00
MAGAZINE
Computer & Video Games

Gamesweasel 987673
Email: show@gamesweasel.tv
Web site: http://www.gamesweasel.tv/
Freq: Daily
Circ: 1005 Cision Digital Reach
MAGAZINE (ONLINE)
Computer & Video Games

Gamewise 981926
Editorial: BurgateManor, Fordingbridge, Fordingbridge SP6 1EF
Tel: 44 01425 652381
Email: editor@gwct.org.uk
Web site: www.gwct.org.uk
Freq: 3 Times/Year
Circ: 18000 Not Audited
Editor: Louise Shervington
MAGAZINE
Field Sports

The Gaming Review 995482
Editorial: 17 Lancaster Avenue, Aldridge, Aldridge WS9 8RE
Email: tgrpress@thegamingreview.com
Web site: www.thegamingreview.com
Freq: Daily
Circ: 14300 Cision Digital Reach
Editor: Iain Garland
MAGAZINE (ONLINE)
Computer & Video Games

Gamingfloor.com 985151
Editorial: 14 Hanover Street, Mayfair, London W1S 1YH **Tel:** 44 08700 113020
Email: editorial@gamingfloor.com
Web site: www.gamingfloor.com
Freq: Daily
Circ: 10052 Cision Digital Reach
MAGAZINE (ONLINE)
Computer & Video Games

GamingIntelligence.com 985699
Editorial: Studio 15, Riverside Building, 55 Trinity Buoy Wharf, London E14 0FP
Tel: 44 08450 523816
Email: support@gamingintelligence.com
Web site: www.gamingintelligence.com
Circ: 94424 Cision Digital Reach
Editor: Steve Hoare
MAGAZINE (ONLINE)
Computer & Video Games

GamingLives 997970
Web site: www.gaminglives.com
Freq: Daily
Circ: 34712 Cision Digital Reach

Editor: Mark Reid
MAGAZINE (ONLINE)
Computer & Video Games

gapyear.com
986882
Editorial: 9th Floor CI Tower, St George's Square, High Street, New Malden, London KT3 4TE **Tel:** 44 08453 447666
Email: editor@gapyear.com
Web site: www.gapyear.com
Freq: Daily
Circ: 486573 Cision Digital Reach
Editor: Will Jones
Profile: Website covering travel and backpacking. gapyear.com shares the latest news on budget travel, gap year, countries, volunteering and advice.
MAGAZINE (ONLINE)
Travel

GARAGE
986709
Owner: Vice Media
Editorial: New North Place, London EC2A 4JA **Tel:** 44 02077 497990
Email: assistant@garagemag.com
Web site: http://garagemag.com
Freq: Semi-Annual Not Audited
Profile: Magazine covering the worlds of fashion and art. It is sold in WHSmith, Barnes and Noble bookstores, first class lounges, private airports and helipads, art galleries, museums, and boutiques, art galleries and museums. Targets women aged between 16 and 40.
Ad Rate: Full Page Colour £10918.00
MAGAZINE
News & Current Affairs

Garage and MOT Professional
984719
Editorial: 2 Crown Street, Wellington, Telford, Telford TF1 1LP
Tel: 44 01952 415334
Web site: http://garageexpo.co.uk/
Freq: Monthly
Circ: 18500 Not Audited
MAGAZINE
Automotive

Garage Trader
984289
Editorial: 34 Crescent Business Park, Lisburn BT27 2GN **Tel:** 44 02892 780099
Web site: http://www.garagetrader.co.uk/
Freq: Quarterly
Circ: 6500 Not Audited
Editor: Pat Burns
Profile: Magazine covering garage trade news for the Republic of Ireland and Northern Ireland.
Ad Rate: Full Page Mono £880.00
Ad Rate: Full Page Colour £980.00
MAGAZINE
Automotive

Garage Wire
988870
Editorial: 111 Hagley Road, Edgbaston, Birmingham B16 8LB **Tel:** 44 03305 550170
Email: info@garagewire.co.uk
Web site: http://garagewire.co.uk/
Freq: Daily
Circ: 15722 Cision Digital Reach
MAGAZINE (ONLINE)
Automotive

Garageland
983321
Editorial: Unit 25A, Regent Studios, 8 Andrews Road, London E8 4QN
Tel: 44 02072 544202
Email: info@transitiongallery.co.uk
Web site: www.transitiongallery.co.uk/garageland.htm
Freq: Semi-Annual
Circ: 3000 Not Audited
Editor: Cathy Lomax
Profile: Magazine covering art, ideas and culture with features about emerging art, artists and art movements.
MAGAZINE
Art, Literature, Photography, Theater & Performing Arts, Visual Arts

Garavi Gujarat
982583
Editorial: Garavi Gujarat House, No 1 Silex Street, London SE1 0DW
Tel: 44 02079 281234
Web site: www.gg2.net
Freq: Weekly
Circ: 43000 Not Audited
Profile: Journal containing Asian news from the British Asian viewpoint.
Ad Rate: Full Page Colour £3201.00
MAGAZINE
Asia, International News

The Garden
981966
Editorial: 4th Floor, Churchgate, New Road, Spalding, Peterborough PE1 1TT
Tel: 44 01733 294630
Email: thegarden@rhs.org.uk
Web site: www.rhs.org.uk
Freq: Monthly
Circ: 425115 Not Audited
Editor: Chris Young
Profile: Journal of the Royal Horticultural Society, containing news and information with a focus on practical gardening.
Ad Rate: Full Page Colour £10000.00
MAGAZINE
Gardening

Garden & Hardware News
983565
Editorial: 1 Accent Park, Bakewell Road, Orton Southgate, Peterborough PE2 6XS
Tel: 44 01733 385300
Email: ghn@mediaone.co.uk
Web site: www.diyretailer.co.uk
Freq: Bi-Monthly
Circ: 4500 Not Audited
Profile: Magazine covering garden and hardware industry news including tools, security, planting and new product information. Aimed at purchasers, garden centres, equipment dealers and wholesalers.
Ad Rate: Full Page Mono £750.00
Ad Rate: Full Page Colour £750.00
MAGAZINE
Gardening, Retail Management

Garden Answers
981609
Editorial: Media House, Lynchwood, Peterborough PE2 6EA
Tel: 44 01733 468000
Email: gardenanswers@bauermedia.co.uk
Web site: www.gardenanswersmagazine.co.uk
Freq: Monthly
Circ: 33521 Not Audited
Editor: Liz Potter
Profile: Magazine covering practical advice and inspirational gardening ideas. Read by those with a passion for gardening.
Ad Rate: Full Page Colour £600.00
MAGAZINE
Gardening

Garden Centre & Farm Shop Catering
1054172
Editorial: 4th Floor, Joynes House, New Road, Gravesend DA11 0AJ
Tel: 44 08455 006008
Web site: http://www.h2opublishing.co.uk/publications/garden-centres-farm-shops/
Freq: Quarterly
Circ: 3000 Not Audited
Profile: Magazine covering catering within garden centres and farm shops.
MAGAZINE
Alcohol & Spirits, Food

Garden Centre Buyer
984189
Editorial: Media House, Hallidays Yard, Stamford PE9 1ED **Tel:** 44 01780 765960
Email: sales@giftwarereview.net
Web site: http://www.giftwarereview.net/2-uncategorised/11-garden-centre-buyer
Freq: Bi-Monthly
Circ: 4000 Not Audited
Editor: Charlotte Cowell
Profile: Publication that covers news about garden centres and garden related trade shows.
MAGAZINE
Gardening

Garden Centre Retail
988860
Editorial: 3 Churchill Court, 112 The Street, West Sussex, Rustington BN16 3DA
Tel: 44 01903 777570
Email: gcreditor@eljays44.com
Web site: http://gardencentreretail.com/
Freq: Monthly
Circ: 3500 Not Audited
MAGAZINE
Gardening

Garden Centre Update
983939
Editorial: 15A London Road, Maidstone, Maidstone ME16 8LY **Tel:** 44 01622 687031
Web site: www.gardencentreupdate.com
Freq: Monthly
Circ: 4000 Not Audited
Editor: Fiona Garcia; **Editor:** Gregor Muir
MAGAZINE
Gardening

Garden Design Journal
983938
Editorial: 90 Walcot St, Bath BA1 5BG
Web site: www.gardendesignjournal.com
Freq: Monthly
Circ: 3000 Not Audited
Profile: Journal containing inspiration and practical information for the professional garden designer.
Ad Rate: Full Page Colour £1000.00
MAGAZINE
Building & Construction, Gardening

Garden News
981959
Editorial: Media House, Lynchwood, Peterborough PE2 6EA
Tel: 44 01733 468000
Email: gn.letters@bauermedia.co.uk
Web site: www.gardennewsmagazine.co.uk
Freq: Weekly
Circ: 38614 Not Audited
Profile: Magazine containing helpful gardening hints and tips, including articles on creative ideas, people and their gardens, product information and regular news from gardening experts.
Ad Rate: Full Page Colour £1900.00
MAGAZINE
Gardening

Garden Rail
981983
Editorial: The Maltings, West Street, Bourne, Saltash PL10 9PH **Tel:** 44 01778 391000
Web site: www.world-of-railways.co.uk/garden-rail
Freq: Monthly
Circ: 5600 Not Audited
Editor: David Williams
Profile: Magazine covering all aspects of outdoor railway modelling.
Ad Rate: Full Page Mono £250.00
Ad Rate: Full Page Colour £279.00
MAGAZINE
Crafts, Hobbies, & Collecting

Garden Trade News
983787
Editorial: The Old School, 4 Crowland Road, Eye, Peterborough PE6 7TN
Tel: 44 01733 775700
Email: gardentradenews@tgcmc.co.uk
Web site: www.gardentradenews.co.uk
Freq: Monthly
Circ: 5500 Not Audited
Editor: Neil Pope
Profile: Journal providing news, features and business advice relating to the UK retail garden trade.
Ad Rate: Full Page Colour £1785.00
MAGAZINE
Gardening

Garden Trade Specialist
987548
Editorial: 53 High Street, Arundel, Arundel BN18 9AJ **Tel:** 44 01903 889531
Email: editor@gardentradespecialist.com
Web site: http://www.gardentradespecialist.com/
Freq: Bi-Monthly
Circ: 6000 Not Audited
Editor: Peddy Balfour
MAGAZINE
Gardening

Gardeners' World (magazine)
981955
Editorial: Vineyard House, 44 Brook Green, London W6 7BT **Tel:** 44 02071 506700
Email: magazine@gardenersworld.com
Web site: www.gardenersworld.com
Freq: Monthly
Circ: 208262 Not Audited
Editor: Lucy Hall
MAGAZINE
Gardening

Gardenforum.co.uk
983523
Email: info@gardenforum.co.uk
Web site: www.gardenforum.co.uk
Freq: Daily
Circ: 12696 Cision Digital Reach
Editor: George Bulivant
Profile: Website covering the UK retail garden industry.
MAGAZINE (ONLINE)
Gardening

Gardens Illustrated
981960
Editorial: Tower House, Fairfax Street, Bristol BS1 3BN **Tel:** 44 01173 147440
Email: gardens@gardensillustrated.com
Web site: www.gardensillustrated.com
Freq: Monthly
Circ: 38471 Not Audited
Profile: Magazine about plants, gardens and gardeners. Includes articles on travel and landscape design. Aimed at discerning gardeners between 30 and 54 years old.
Ad Rate: Full Page Mono £2970.00
Ad Rate: Full Page Colour £2970.00
MAGAZINE
Gardening

Gardens to visit
995930
Editorial: Hatchlands Park, East Clandon, Guildford GU4 7RT **Tel:** 44 01483 211535
Email: ngs@ngs.org.uk
Web site: www.ngs.org.uk
Freq: Annual
Circ: 40000 Not Audited
MAGAZINE
Gardening

Gasholder
997965
Editorial: Interchange Atrium, Stables Market, Chalk Farm Road, London NW1 8AB
Email: info@gasholder.london
Web site: www.gasholder.london/
Freq: Monthly
Circ: 10000 Not Audited
MAGAZINE
Regional General Interest

The Gateway
998975
Tel: 44 02078 714429
Email: editor@thegatewayonline.com
Web site: www.thegatewayonline.com
Freq: Daily
Circ: 26325 Cision Digital Reach
MAGAZINE (ONLINE)
Business, Small and Medium Business, Student Lifestyle

The Gaudie
981763
Editorial: Butchart Centre, University Road, Old Aberdeen, Aberdeen AB24 3UT
Tel: 44 01224 272980
Email: editor@thegaudie.co.uk
Web site: www.thegaudie.co.uk
Freq: Bi-Weekly
Circ: 2000 Not Audited
Profile: University of Aberdeen Student newspaper containing all aspects of student life including staff information.
Ad Rate: Full Page Mono £430.00
Ad Rate: Full Page Colour £660.00
MAGAZINE
Student Lifestyle

Gay Star News
986561
Editorial: 15 Page's Walk, SE1 4SB, London
Tel: 44 02072 377834
Email: news@gaystarnews.com
Web site: www.gaystarnews.com
Freq: Daily

Consumer Magazines

Circ: 1230836 Cision Digital Reach
MAGAZINE (ONLINE)
LGBT

Gay Times
982060
Editorial: Unit 10, Stratford Office Village,
14-30 Romford Road, London E15 4EA
Tel: 44 02074 247400
Email: edit@gaytimes.co.uk
Web site: www.gaytimes.co.uk
Freq: Monthly
Circ: 65000 Not Audited
Editor: Darren Scott
Profile: GT Magazine is a monthly UK
magazine writing about gay men's lifestyle
and current affairs. It covers, news and
reviews, arts, politics, travel, health, film and
theatre. Gay Times grew from a marriage of
Him magazine and Gay News and was
founded in 1984. GT magazine is one of the
longest established gay magazine in the
world.
Ad Rate: Full Page Colour £2200.00
MAGAZINE
LGBT

Gay to Z Directory
982061
Editorial: 35 Talacre Road, London NW5
3PJ Tel: 44 07770 265660
Email: info@gaytoz.com
Web site: www.gaytoz.com
Freq: Daily
Circ: 6863 Cision Digital Reach
Profile: Web-based directory covering
everything gay in the UK including LGBT
business and community directory, what's
on, hotels, bars, clubs and gay research.
MAGAZINE (ONLINE)
LGBT

GAYist
985945
Web site: https://gayist.co/
Freq: Daily
Circ: 3511 Cision Digital Reach
MAGAZINE (ONLINE)
LGBT, Sexuality

GB Mag
985986
Tel: 44 02077 592040
Web site: www.greatbritishmag.co.uk
Freq: Daily
Circ: 11321 Cision Digital Reach
Editor: David Swift
Profile: Lifestyle magazine for oversees
students living in the UK. Each issue
contains student tips as well as music, food,
sport and entertainment.
MAGAZINE (ONLINE)
Student Lifestyle

GDC Interiors Journal
997294
Tel: 44 08456 474310
Email: press@gdcinteriors.com
Web site: www.gdcinteriors.com
Freq: Weekly
Circ: 3805 Cision Digital Reach
MAGAZINE (ONLINE)
Architecture & Design, Do-It-Yourself
(DIY)

Gear Wheels
985944
Email: editor@gearwheelsmag.com
Web site: http://www.gearwheelsmag.co.
uk/
Freq: Daily
Circ: 739 Cision Digital Reach
Editor: David Simpson
Profile: Website covering motoring. The
Gear Wheels website shares the latest news,
developments, events, road tests, clubs,
classics and advice in the motor industry.
MAGAZINE (ONLINE)
Antique & Collectible Cars, Automakers,
Automotive, Driving, Motorcycles, Off-
road & 4-Wheel Drive Vehicles, Trucks &
SUVs

GearUp
995743
Editorial: Cardiff House, Cardiff Road, Barry,
Barry CF63 2AW Tel: 44 08451 808182
Email: mark@goodlifepublishing.co.uk
Web site: www.gearupmag.co.uk
Freq: Quarterly
Circ: 10000 Not Audited

Editor: Mark Roberts
MAGAZINE
Motorcycles

Geekanoids
985448
Editorial: Basepoint Folkestone, Shearway
Road, Shearway Business Park, Folkestone
CT19 4RH Tel: 44 07538 882000
Email: geekanoids@gmail.com
Web site: www.geekanoids.co.uk
Freq: Daily
Circ: 7281 Cision Digital Reach
Profile: Website covering technology.
GEEKANOIDS website shares the latest
news and information on Macintosh
technology and gadgets as well as reviews
of computer software, hardware and
peripherals.
MAGAZINE (ONLINE)
Apple, Audio Video Trade, Cameras,
Computer & Video Games, Computers,
Consumer Electronics, Internet, Mobile
Electronics, Movies & Video, Personal
Computers

GEEKchocolate
996819
Web site: www.geekchocolate.co.uk
Freq: Daily
Circ: 14326 Cision Digital Reach
MAGAZINE (ONLINE)
Broadcasting, Entertainment, Literature,
Movies & Video, Science, Trading Cards &
Comics

Geeky Monkey
1052665
Tel: 44 08453 306540
Web site: www.geekymonkey.tv
Freq: Monthly
MAGAZINE
Computer & Video Games, Movies &
Video

Genealogists Magazine
984426
Editorial: 14 Charterhouse Buildings,
Goswell Road, London EC1M 7BA
Tel: 44 02072 518799
Email: publishing@sog.org.uk
Web site: www.sog.org.uk
Freq: Quarterly
Circ: 11000 Not Audited
Editor: Michael Gandy
MAGAZINE
Family & Parenting, History

Generation.Buzz
998012
Email: buzz@worryandpeace.com
Web site: http://worryandpeace.com/buzz/
Freq: Daily
Circ: 12 Cision Digital Reach
MAGAZINE (ONLINE)
Cameras, Computer & Video Games,
Mobile Electronics

Gentleman's Journal
987177
Editorial: Phoenix Brewery, 5th Floor, 13
Bramley Road, London W10 6SZ
Tel: 44 02035 981190
Email: contact@thegentlemansjournal.com
Web site: www.thegentlemansjournal.co.uk
Freq: Quarterly
Circ: 50000 Not Audited
Profile: Website covering lifestyle. The
Gentleman's Journal website covering style,
grooming, food, drink, lifestyle, culture, travel
and technology.
MAGAZINE
Airline Inflight, Alcohol & Spirits, Antique
& Collectible Cars, Automotive, Bars,
Clubs & Pubs, Beer, Beverages, Cooking
& Baking, Driving, Fashion

The Gentlewoman
985523
Editorial: 73-75 Kenton Street, 2nd Floor,
London WC1N 1NN Tel: 44 02086 165433
Email: office@thegentlewoman.com
Web site: www.thegentlewoman.com
Freq: Semi-Annual Not Audited
Profile: The Gentlewoman is a biannual style
magazine, featuring inspirational,
international women, it pairs journalism with
a sartorial and intelligent perspective on
fashion that is focused on personal style, the
way women actually look, think and dress.

Aimed at women with an interest in personal
style, business and fashion.
Ad Rate: Full Page Mono £8500.00
MAGAZINE
Fashion

GEOConnexion International
985176
Editorial: PO Box 594, Cambridge CB1 0FY
Tel: 44 01223 279151
Email: editor-geo@geoconnexion.com
Web site: www.geoconnexion.com
Freq: Monthly
Circ: 10000 Not Audited
Profile: Geographical technology magazine
covering the uses of GIS, GPS, remote
sensing, photogrammetry, surveying,
cartography, image processing, telematics
and Location Based Services.
Ad Rate: Full Page Mono £1305.00
Ad Rate: Full Page Colour £1980.00
MAGAZINE
Data Management, Electronics, Internet,
Mobile Communications

GEOConnexion UK
988026
Editorial: PO Box 594, Cambridge CB1 0FY
Tel: 44 01223 279151
Email: info@geoconnexion.com
Web site: www.geoconnexion.com
Freq: Monthly
Circ: 10000 Not Audited
Editor: Peter FitzGibbon
MAGAZINE
Data Management, Electronics,
Government Technology, Industry,
Internet, Mobile Communications,
Security & Security Systems, Software

Geoforum
998674
Editorial: 32 Jamestown Road, London
NW1 7BY Tel: 44 01865 843434
Web site: www.journals.elsevier.com/
geoforum/
Freq: Bi-Monthly Not Audited
MAGAZINE
News & Current Affairs

Geographical
982324
Editorial: Suite 3.20, QWest, Great West
Road, Brentford, London TW8 0GP
Tel: 44 02083 328434
Email: magazine@geographical.co.uk
Web site: www.geographical.co.uk
Freq: Monthly
Circ: 21217 Not Audited
Editor: Paul Presley
Profile: Magazine of the Royal Geographical
Society focusing on current geopolitical,
cultural and environmental issues. Also
covers expeditions, exploration and
scientific developments and adventure
travel. First published in 1935. Aimed at
society members, professional geographers,
frequent holidaymakers, alternative travellers
of all ages and those interested in the world
around them.
Ad Rate: Full Page Colour £2250.00
MAGAZINE
Travel

Geomatics World
984439
Editorial: 2B North Road, Stevenage,
Stevenage SG1 4AT
Web site: www.pvpubs.com
Freq: Bi-Monthly
Circ: 4500 Not Audited
Profile: Magazine focusing on land,
engineering and hydrographic surveying.
Ad Rate: Full Page Colour £1995.00
MAGAZINE
News & Current Affairs

Get Busy
005301
Editorial: Unit 16 Greenway Farm, Bath
Road, Wick, Bristol BS30 5RL
Tel: 44 01179 373003
Email: info@kennedypublishing.co.uk
Web site: http://www.kennedypublishing.co.
uk/magazines/get-busy-magazine
Freq: Bi-Monthly
Circ: 20000 Not Audited
MAGAZINE
Elementary School, Preschool

Get Connected
998826
Tel: 44 01420 544587
Web site: www.gcmagazine.co.uk
Freq: Monthly
Circ: 5980 Not Audited
Profile: Website focusing on domestic
electrical appliances.
MAGAZINE
Electronics, Retail Management

Get Surrey
988810
Editorial: Stoke Mill, Woking Road,
Guildford GU1 1QA Tel: 44 01483 508700
Email: tms-digitalmedia@trinitymirror.com
Web site: http://www.getsurrey.co.uk/
Freq: Daily
Circ: 420679 Cision Digital Reach
MAGAZINE (ONLINE)
News & Current Affairs

Get the Gloss
987125
Editorial: Ground Floor, 2 Kensington
Square, London W8 5EP
Email: enquiries@getthegloss.com
Web site: www.getthegloss.com
Freq: Daily
Circ: 149347 Cision Digital Reach
Profile: Get the Gloss is an online expert
health and beauty magazine, 'founded on
the principle that you can have brains and
beauty'. The website covers beauty tips and
products, skincare, hair, anti-aging and
personal health. The website was founded in
October 2012.
MAGAZINE (ONLINE)
Beauty & Grooming, Cosmetics, Hair,
Health & Medicine

Get West London
988060
Editorial: Stoke Mill, Woking Road,
Guildford, London GU1 1QA
Tel: 44 01483 508700
Web site: www.getwestlondon.co.uk
Freq: Daily
Circ: 905151 Cision Digital Reach
MAGAZINE (ONLINE)
Regional

Gethin's Inflight News
996161
Tel: 44 02078 282397
Email: publisher@gethinsinflight.com
Web site: www.gethinsinflight.com
Freq: Weekly
Circ: 11538 Cision Digital Reach
MAGAZINE (ONLINE)
Airline Inflight

Getreading
988776
Editorial: Abbeyhouse, 1650 Arlington
Business Park, Theale, Reading RG7 4SA
Tel: 44 01189 298501
Email: getreading@trinitymirror.com
Web site: www.getreading.co.uk/
Freq: Daily
Circ: 594513 Cision Digital Reach
Profile: Online version of Get Reading
newspaper covering local news and sports.
MAGAZINE (ONLINE)
News & Current Affairs

Getting Married In Northern
Ireland
982422
Tel: 44 02887 722788
Email: info@reddotpublications.co.uk
Web site: www.gettingmarried-ni.co.uk
Freq: Quarterly
Circ: 9000 Not Audited
Editor: Alexandra Mckee
Profile: Magazine covering all aspects of
getting married and setting-up home in
Northern Ireland. Aimed at those who need
help and information on how to plan for the
big day.
Ad Rate: Full Page Colour £950.00
MAGAZINE
Weddings

Gibbons Stamp Monthly
981916
Editorial: 7 Parkside, Christchurch Road,
Hampshire, Ringwood BH24 3SH
Tel: 44 01425 472363
Email: gsm@stanleygibbons.com
Web site: www.gibbonsstampmonthly.com

Freq: Monthly
Circ: 16000 Not Audited
Editor: Dean Shepherd
Profile: Journal providing articles on philatelic topics. Includes news, tips, book reviews and new stamp issues.
Ad Rate: Full Page Mono £950.00
Ad Rate: Full Page Colour £950.00
MAGAZINE
Antiques/Collectibles

giddylimits 986064
Editorial: 12 Priory Avenue, Totnes, Totnes TQ9 5HR
Web site: www.giddylimits.co.uk
Freq: Daily
Circ: 6157 Cision Digital Reach
Editor: Joan Cassie
Profile: Website covering mature lifestyle. The giddylimit website shares the latest news, advice and information for men and women over the age of 50. The site covers anything from business advice and retirement options to food and health.
MAGAZINE (ONLINE)
News & Current Affairs

Gift Focus 983201
Editorial: Pantile House, Newland Drive, Witham, Witham CM8 2AP
Tel: 44 01376 514000
Email: info@giftfocus.com
Web site: www.giftfocus.com
Freq: Bi-Monthly
Circ: 7072 Not Audited
Editor: Rachel Westall
Profile: Magazine covering every aspect of the giftware industry including news, reviews and reports on trade fairs. Aimed at buyers and retailers in the giftware industry.
Ad Rate: Full Page Mono £1300.00
Ad Rate: Full Page Colour £1300.00
MAGAZINE
Books, Cosmetics, Fashion, Gardening, Hair, Retail Management, Toys

Gifts Today 981291
Editorial: Naishville, 1 Churchgates, The Wilderness, Berkhamstead, Berkhamsted HP4 2AZ **Tel:** 44 01442 289930
Email: info@lemapublishing.co.uk
Web site: http://www.gifts-today.co.uk
Freq: Bi-Monthly
Circ: 7093 Not Audited
Profile: Magazine containing information on gift products. Aimed at all those involved in gift retailing and manufacturing. A charge may be made for colour separation. Regular features: In Conversation With Editor speaks to someone in the industry.
Ad Rate: Full Page Colour £1595.00
MAGAZINE
Books, Cosmetics, Fashion, Gardening, Hair, Office Supplies, Toys

Giftware Review 983206
Editorial: Media House, Hallidays Yard, Radcliffe Road, Stamford PE9 1ED
Tel: 44 01780 765960
Web site: www.giftwarereview.net
Freq: Bi-Monthly
Circ: 8660 Not Audited
Editor: Charlotte Cowell
Profile: Magazine focusing on new product news within the giftware industry. Aimed at retailers.
Ad Rate: Full Page Colour £1395.00
MAGAZINE
Books, Cosmetics, Fashion, Gardening, Hair, Office Supplies, Retail, Retail Management, Toys

Gigging NI 1095733
Email: reviews@giggingni.com
Web site: www.giggingni.com
Freq: Daily
Circ: 16521 Cision Digital Reach
Editor: Mark Dunn
MAGAZINE (ONLINE)
Comedy, Country, Folk, Bluegrass, Dance Music, Entertainment, Jazz & Blues, Local Entertainment Guides, Pop Music, Rock Music, Theater & Performing Arts

Gigslutz 998075
Web site: www.gigslutz.co.uk
Freq: Daily
Circ: 56171 Cision Digital Reach
Editor: Steve Aston
MAGAZINE (ONLINE)
Country, Folk, Bluegrass, Dance Music, Pop Music, Rap & Hip Hop, Rock Music

GIGsoup 1053299
Editorial: 2 Walerand Road, London SE13 7PG **Tel:** 44 07545 393474
Email: contact@gigsoup.co.uk
Web site: www.gigsoup.co.uk
Freq: Daily
Circ: 6647 Cision Digital Reach
MAGAZINE (ONLINE)
Country, Folk, Bluegrass, Dance Music, Jazz & Blues, Music, Pop Music, Rap & Hip Hop, Rock Music

Gigwise 984587
Editorial: 10-16 Scrutton St, London EC2A 4RU **Tel:** 44 02073 779914
Web site: www.gigwise.com
Freq: Daily
Circ: 477390 Cision Digital Reach
Profile: Website covering new music, music news, interviews, videos, reviews and photos.
MAGAZINE (ONLINE)
Broadcasting, Computer & Video Games, Pop Music, Rap & Hip Hop, Rock Music

Gin Foundry 1073647
Web site: www.ginfoundry.com
Freq: Daily
Circ: 40995 Cision Digital Reach
MAGAZINE (ONLINE)
Alcohol & Spirits, Bars, Clubs & Pubs

GINNED! 1062732
Email: katy@craftginclub.co.uk
Web site: http://www.craftginclub.co.uk/ginnedmagazine/
Freq: Monthly Not Audited
MAGAZINE
Alcohol & Spirits

Gintime.com 1102950
Editorial: 17a St Bernards Crescent, Edinburgh EH4 1NR **Tel:** 44 07967 979170
Email: info@gintime.com
Web site: www.gintime.com
Freq: Daily
Circ: 8630 Cision Digital Reach
MAGAZINE (ONLINE)
Alcohol & Spirits, Bars, Clubs & Pubs

GIQ 996596
Editorial: Studio 15, Riverside Building, 55 Trinity Buoy Wharf, London E14 0FP
Tel: 44 08450 523816
Email: support@gamingintelligence.com
Web site: www.gamingintelligence.com/giq-magazine
Freq: Quarterly Not Audited
Editor: Steve Hoare
MAGAZINE
Computer & Video Games

Girl 985543
Editorial: LCD PUBLISHING, VICI HOUSE, 2 MALLARD ROAD, Exeter EX2 7LD
Tel: 44 01392 664141
Freq: Monthly
Circ: 60000 Not Audited
Editor: Joanne Trump
Profile: Magazine covering young fashion and pop music, with quizzes and stories.
MAGAZINE
Teen/Young Adult

Girl about the Globe 996482
Editorial: 78 Skipper Way, Lee-on-the-Solent PO13 9EZ **Tel:** 44 07823 886807
Email: info@girlabouttheglobe.com
Web site: www.girlabouttheglobe.com
Freq: Daily
Circ: 36216 Cision Digital Reach
MAGAZINE (ONLINE)
Airline Inflight, Railroad, Travel

Girl Gamers UK 996143
Email: editor@girlgamersuk.com
Web site: www.girlgamersuk.com
Freq: Daily
Circ: 8547 Cision Digital Reach
Editor: Diane Hutchinson
MAGAZINE (ONLINE)
Computer & Video Games

Girl Talk 982453
Editorial: Vineyard House, 44 Brook Green, London W6 7BT **Tel:** 44 02071 505000
Email: hello@girltalkmagazine.com
Web site: www.girltalkmagazine.com
Freq: Bi-Weekly
Circ: 40302 Not Audited
Profile: Children's magazine containing comic strips, interactive games and quizzes, as well as features on pop bands, fashion, craft and pets.
Ad Rate: Full Page Colour £3025.00
MAGAZINE
Teen/Young Adult

Girl Talk Art 986940
Editorial: Vineyard House, 44 Brook Green, London W6 7BT **Tel:** 44 02071 505000
Email: girltalkart@immediate.co.uk
Web site: http://www.immediate.co.uk/brands/girl-talk-art/
Freq: Monthly
Circ: 28144 Not Audited
Profile: Magazine about arts and crafts. It is aimed at pre-teen girls who love drawing, painting, craft and learning new skills.
MAGAZINE
Teen/Young Adult

Girlie Gossip 984967
Editorial: 3 Ham Lane, Burnham on Sea, Burnham-on-Sea TA8 1QA
Email: kez@girliegossip.com
Web site: http://girliegossip.com/
Freq: Daily
Circ: 13512 Cision Digital Reach
Editor: Kez Richards
MAGAZINE (ONLINE)
Beauty & Grooming, Celebrities, Cosmetics, Fashion, Hair, Travel, Women's Interests

Girls Love 986889
Editorial: Old Dairy, Peper Harow Park, Nr Godalming, Godalming GU8 6BQ
Tel: 44 01483 779500
Web site: www.signaturepl.co.uk/portfolio/GirlsLove.html
Freq: Bi-Monthly
Circ: 30000 Not Audited
MAGAZINE
Teen/Young Adult

GIS Professional 984558
Editorial: 2B North Road, Stevenage, Stevenage SG1 4AT
Web site: http://www.pvpubs.com/GISProfessional/Home
Freq: Bi-Monthly
Circ: 4500 Not Audited
Profile: Magazine covering case studies; reviews and impressions; peer-reviewed material; industry news; new products, systems and services.
Ad Rate: Full Page Mono £995.00
Ad Rate: Full Page Colour £1595.00
MAGAZINE
News & Current Affairs

Giving Nation 998690
Editorial: First Floor, 50 Featherstone Street, London EC1Y 8RT **Tel:** 44 02075 664141
Email: info@citizenshipfoundation.org.uk
Web site: www.g-nation.org.uk
Freq: Daily
Circ: 6724 Cision Digital Reach
MAGAZINE (ONLINE)
Charitable Foundations, Education, Teen/Young Adult

Gizmodo UK 984641
Editorial: 1-10 Praed Mews, Paddington, London W2 1QY
Email: tips@gizmodo.com

Web site: www.gizmodo.co.uk
Freq: Daily
Circ: 1586462 Cision Digital Reach
Profile: Website covering technology, gadgets, consumer electronics, 3D printing and televisions to camera's and home entertainment.
MAGAZINE (ONLINE)
Audio Video Trade, Cameras, Consumer Electronics, Mobile Electronics, Movies & Video

GL magazine 998058
Editorial: Floor 3 St James' House, St James' Square, Cheltenham GL50 3PR
Tel: 44 01242 278000
Web site: www.glmagazine.co.uk/
Freq: Monthly
Circ: 62000 Not Audited
MAGAZINE
News & Current Affairs

GLAM AFRICA 1053582
Email: editor@glamafrica.com
Web site: www.glamafrica.com
Freq: Quarterly
MAGAZINE
Beauty & Grooming, Cosmetics, Fashion, Hair

GLAMOUR 980759
Editorial: 13 Hanover Square, London W1S 1HN **Tel:** 44 02074 999080
Email: glamoureditorial@condenast.co.uk
Web site: www.glamour.com
Freq: Monthly
Circ: 275536 Not Audited
Editor: Jo Elvin
Profile: Magazine covering fashion, beauty, celebrities and real-life stories, in depth features as well as entertainment, health, fitness, food and travel articles. Aimed at fashion and beauty conscious women aged between 18 and 34 years old.
Ad Rate: Full Page Colour £25414.00
MAGAZINE
Women's Interests

GLAMOUR - Russia Bureau
1001293
Editorial: Condé Nast International, 5th Floor, 25-29 Maddox Street, London W1S 2QN **Tel:** /495/ 455565
Email: info@glamour.ru
Web site: http://www.glamour.ru/ Not Audited
MAGAZINE
News & Current Affairs

The Glare - CEASED APRIL 2015 995289
Editorial: 18 Castletown Road, London W14 9HQ
Web site: www.the-glare.com
Freq: Daily
Circ: 3178 Cision Digital Reach
MAGAZINE (ONLINE)
Beauty & Grooming, Cosmetics, Fashion, Hair, Men's Interests, Travel, Women's Interests

Glasgow Eyes 1052958
Tel: 44 07549 442528
Email: glasgoweyes1@gmail.com
Web site: http://www.glasgoweyes.com/
Freq: Monthly
Circ: 10000 Not Audited
MAGAZINE
News & Current Affairs

The Glasgow Guardian 981764
Editorial: Glasgow University Students Representative Council, John McIntyre Building, University Ave, Glasgow G12 8QQ
Tel: 44 01413 416215
Email: news@glasgowguardian.co.uk
Web site: www.glasgowguardian.co.uk
Freq: Monthly
Circ: 10000 Not Audited
MAGAZINE
Student Lifestyle

Consumer Magazines

Freq: Daily
Circ: 1798869 Cision Digital Reach
MAGAZINE (ONLINE)
Women's Interests

Gooner　　　　　　　　　　996959
Editorial: BCM Box 7499, London WC1N 3XX
Email: gooner.ed@gmail.com
Web site: www.onlinegooner.com
Freq: Monthly
Circ: 5000 Not Audited
Editor: Kevin Whitcher
MAGAZINE
Soccer

Gorkana Alerts (U.K.)　　　998851
Editorial: 6 Mitre Passage, London SE10 0ER
Email: newsandmoves@gorkana.com
Web site: http://www.gorkana.com/journalist-services/
Freq: Daily
Circ: 153023 Cision Digital Reach
MAGAZINE (ONLINE)
Broadcasting, Publishing

GOSH　　　　　　　　　　983280
Editorial: Great Ormond Street Hospital, Great Ormond, London WC1N 3JH
Tel: 44 02074 059200
Web site: www.gosh.nhs.uk
Freq: Daily
Circ: 71365 Cision Digital Reach
MAGAZINE (ONLINE)
Charitable Foundations, Health & Medicine

Goss.ie　　　　　　　　　1101938
Email: news@goss.ie
Web site: goss.ie
Freq: Daily
Circ: 152601 Cision Digital Reach
MAGAZINE (ONLINE)
Beauty & Grooming, Celebrities, Cosmetics, Fashion, Hair, Northern Ireland

GoThinkBig.co.uk　　　　987080
Editorial: Think Big hub, 16 Hoxton Square, London N1 6NT **Tel:** 44 02072 418000
Email: info@gothinkbig.co.uk
Web site: www.gothinkbig.co.uk
Freq: Daily
Circ: 85130 Cision Digital Reach
Profile: Website covering employment for youths. The GOTHINKBIG.co.uk website shares the latest news and information for youths trying to find employment.
MAGAZINE (ONLINE)
Careers

The Gourmand　　　　　997762
Editorial: The Gourmand, Ground Floor, 2–16 Bayford Street, London E8 3SE
Email: info@thegourmand.co.uk
Web site: thegourmand.co.uk
Freq: Semi-Annual Not Audited
MAGAZINE
Alcohol & Spirits, Bars, Clubs & Pubs, Beer, Beverages, Cooking & Baking, Wine/Winemaking

Governance & Leadership
　　　　　　　　　　　　　　984849
Editorial: 15 Prescott Place, London SW4 6BS **Tel:** 44 02078 191200
Email: news@civilsociety.co.uk
Web site: www.civilsociety.co.uk
Freq: Bi-Monthly Not Audited
Editor: Gareth Jones
Profile: Magazine covering all aspects of charity governance including model documents, legal, financial and charity commission updates, legal and financial matters and practical advice.
MAGAZINE
Charitable Foundations

Government　　　　　　997413
Editorial: Network House, 17 John Bradshaw Court, Alexandria Way, Congleton CW12 1LB **Tel:** 44 01260 273802

Email: editor@paneuropeannetworks.com
Web site: http://www.paneuropeannetworks.com/government-publications/government-publication/
Freq: Quarterly
Circ: 238000 Not Audited
MAGAZINE
Government, Health & Medicine, Healthcare Industry, Public Sector

Government & Public Sector Journal　　　　　　　　984336
Editorial: 18 -19 Salmon Fields Business Village, Royton, Royton OL2 6HT
Tel: 44 08453 455222
Email: editor@gpsj.co.uk
Web site: www.gpsj.co.uk
Freq: Quarterly
Circ: 16000 Not Audited
Profile: Journal covering news, latest developments, legislation, investment, PFI, PPP and building and engineering projects carried out in these sectors.
Ad Rate: Full Page Colour　...........£3500.00
MAGAZINE
Charitable Foundations, Government, Public Sector

Government Computing　987229
Editorial: John Carpenter House, 7 Carmelite Street, London EC4Y 0AN
Tel: 44 02079 366400
Web site: www.governmentcomputing.com
Freq: Daily
Circ: 20556 Cision Digital Reach
Editor: David Bicknell
Profile: Magazine covering the use of information management in public services. It features news, analysis and comment on information management in the public sector and tracks the thinking of key ICT decision-makers within local authorities and NHS trusts.
MAGAZINE (ONLINE)
Charitable Foundations, Computers, Government, Government Technology, Public Sector

The Gown　　　　　　　998640
Editorial: Queens University Belfast Students Union, University Road, Belfast BT7 1NF **Tel:** 44 02890 971057
Email: editor@thegown.net
Web site: https://thegownatqub.wordpress.com/
Freq: Monthly Not Audited
MAGAZINE
Student Lifestyle

GP　　　　　　　　　　981186
Editorial: Bridge House, 69 London Road, Twickenham, London TW1 3QR
Tel: 44 02082 675000
Email: gponline@haymarket.com
Web site: www.gponline.com
Freq: Daily
Circ: 59500 Cision Digital Reach
Editor: Emma Bower
MAGAZINE (ONLINE)
Medicine

GQ (UK)　　　　　　　　982055
Editorial: Vogue House, Hanover Square, London W1S 1JU **Tel:** 44 02074 999080
Web site: www.gq-magazine.co.uk
Freq: Monthly
Circ: 114035 Not Audited
Editor: Dylan Jones; **Editor:** Lou Stoppard
MAGAZINE
Beauty & Grooming, Cosmetics, Fashion, Hair, Luxury Goods, Men's Interests

GQ Style　　　　　　　983212
Editorial: Vogue House, 1 Hanover Square, London W1S 1JU **Tel:** 44 02074 999080
Email: gqstyleassistant@condenast.co.uk
Web site: www.gq-magazine.co.uk/style/gq-style-magazine
Freq: Semi-Annual
Circ: 100000 Not Audited
Editor: Dylan Jones
Profile: Magazine published twice a year as a stand alone publication related to GQ magazine covering men's fashion and style.

Aimed at men aged between 20 and 45 years old.
Ad Rate: Full Page Colour　...........£8873.00
MAGAZINE
Fashion, Men's Interests

GradJobs　　　　　　　995816
Editorial: 2-4 St Georges Road, Wimbledon, London SW19 4DP **Tel:** 44 02083 945200
Email: editor@gradjobs.co.uk
Web site: www.gradjobs.co.uk
Freq: Annual
Circ: 175000 Not Audited
MAGAZINE
Careers

Graduate Fog　　　　　985566
Editorial: Artist House, First Floor, 35 Little Russell Street, London WC1A 2HH
Web site: www.graduatefog.co.uk
Freq: Daily
Circ: 13524 Cision Digital Reach
MAGAZINE (ONLINE)
Careers

Grafik　　　　　　　　　981642
Editorial: 31 New Inn Yard, London EC2A 3EY
Web site: www.grafik.net/
Freq: Daily
Circ: 87547 Cision Digital Reach
MAGAZINE (ONLINE)
Graphic Design, Visual Arts

Grammy.com　　　　　999251
Web site: www.grammy.com
Freq: Daily
Circ: 583047 Cision Digital Reach
MAGAZINE (ONLINE)
Classical/Choral/Band Music, Country, Folk, Bluegrass, Dance Music, Jazz & Blues, Music, Pop Music, R&B, Urban, World, Rap & Hip Hop, Rock Music

Gramophone　　　　　982067
Editorial: St. Jude's Church, Dulwich Road, London SE24 0PB **Tel:** 44 02077 385454
Email: gramophone@markallengroup.com
Web site: www.gramophone.co.uk
Freq: Monthly
Circ: 23162 Not Audited
Profile: Magazine covering reviews of classical CDs, videos and audio equipment.
Ad Rate: Full Page Mono　............£2063.00
Ad Rate: Full Page Colour　...........£3806.00
MAGAZINE
Classical/Choral/Band Music

Grand Designs Magazine　995803
Editorial: Crown House, 151 High Road, Loughton IG10 4LF **Tel:** 44 02032 255200
Email: info@granddesignsmagazine.com
Web site: www.granddesignsmagazine.com
Freq: Monthly
Circ: 27265 Not Audited
MAGAZINE
Architecture & Design, Do-It-Yourself (DIY), Property Management & Maintenance

Granta　　　　　　　　984261
Editorial: 12 Addison Avenue, London W11 4QR **Tel:** 44 02076 051360
Email: editorial@granta.com
Web site: granta.com
Freq: Quarterly
Circ: 20000 Not Audited
Profile: Magazine covering literature and new writing including fiction, memoir, poetry and photography from the brightest emerging talents and finest authors on the planet. First published in 1979, the publication has an average of 256 pages per issue. Read by avid book buyers.
Ad Rate: Full Page Mono　............£1400.00
Ad Rate: Full Page Colour　...........£2200.00
MAGAZINE
Literature, Photography

The Grapevine　　　　　988410
Editorial: 4 Belfry Road, Droitwich WR9 7QX
Tel: 44 07951 813636
Email: editor@atthegrapevine.com

Web site: atthegrapevine.com
Freq: Daily
Circ: 521 Cision Digital Reach
MAGAZINE (ONLINE)
Audio Video Trade, Cameras, Comedy, Consumer Electronics, Entertainment, Mobile Electronics, Movies & Video, Politics

GRAZIA　　　　　　　　982369
Editorial: 24-28 Oval Road, Camden, London NW1 7DT **Tel:** 44 02072 418000
Email: graziadaily@graziamagazine.co.uk
Web site: www.graziadaily.co.uk
Freq: Weekly
Circ: 110031 Not Audited
Editor: Natasha Pearlman
Profile: Magazine containing news and fashion content, published weekly. Each issue features designer fashion, shopping, celebrity news and articles on how to lead a stylish life. The magazine was launched in 2005 and was voted PPA Magazine of the Year in 2008. Targets upmarket women in their 30s, who are affluent, high spenders on fashion and beauty.
Ad Rate: Full Page Colour　...........£6500.00
MAGAZINE
Women's Interests

Great British Chefs　　　990699
Editorial: Unit 4, Pride Court, 80-82 White Lion Street, London N1 9PF
Tel: 44 02078 375925
Email: pr@greatbrtishchefs.com
Web site: www.greatbritishchefs.com
Freq: Daily
Circ: 620910 Cision Digital Reach
MAGAZINE (ONLINE)
Cooking & Baking

Great British Food　　　984990
Editorial: 21-23 Phoenix Court, Hawkins Road, Colchester, Colchester CO2 8JY
Tel: 44 01206 505900
Email: natasha@aceville.co.uk
Web site: www.greatbritishfoodmagazine.com
Freq: Monthly
Circ: 44700 Not Audited
Editor: Natasha Lovell-Smith
Profile: Magazine covering British food. Includes features on food producers, recipes, interviews with top chefs, showcases of the latest food in the shops.
MAGAZINE
Cooking & Baking, Food, Grocery Stores, Organic Food, Restaurant Reviews, Vegetarianism & Veganism

GREAT BRITISH LIFE.co.uk
　　　　　　　　　　　　　　985732
Editorial: Prospect House, Rouen Road, Norwich NR1 1 RE **Tel:** 44 01603 772772
Email: shop@greatbritishlife.co.uk
Web site: www.greatbritishlife.co.uk
Freq: Daily
Circ: 27477 Cision Digital Reach
Editor: Laura Nunn
MAGAZINE (ONLINE)
Regional General Interest

Great Food Mag　　　　999055
Editorial: 40 Craven Street, Melton Mowbray LE13 0QU **Tel:** 44 01664 500070
Web site: http://www.greatfoodclub.co.uk/
Freq: Daily
Circ: 14609 Cision Digital Reach
MAGAZINE (ONLINE)
Alcohol & Spirits, Bars, Clubs & Pubs, Beer, Beverages, Cooking & Baking, Food, Grocery Stores, Organic Food, Regional General Interest, Restaurant Reviews

Great for Groups magazine
　　　　　　　　　　　　　　982343
Editorial: 6th Floor, Davis House, 2 Robert Street, London CR0 1QQ
Tel: 44 02082 538632
Email: editor@greatforgroups.co.uk
Web site: http://www.the-pass.co.uk
Freq: Bi-Monthly
Circ: 11000 Not Audited

Profile: Magazine avaliable by subscription to group travel organisers only. It features the latest group travel news and events. Their aim is to provide readers with the right attractions for large groups to ideas on how to plan a day's trip or holiday. Includes features and editorial covering UK attractions to explore, news of discounts, a regional focus, offers and competitions. Aimed at group travel organisers.
Ad Rate: Full Page Colour £1750.00
MAGAZINE
Travel

Great Golf Magazine 986925
Editorial: 30 Eridge Road, Tunbridge Wells, Tunbridge Wells TN4 8HR
Tel: 44 01892 544872
Email: info@greatgolfmagazine.co.uk
Web site: www.greatgolfmagazine.co.uk
Freq: Bi-Monthly
Circ: 27000 Not Audited
Editor: Nils Bjornes
Profile: Magazine covering luxury lifestyle of interest to golfers. It features travel destinations, luxury products and services for high net worth individuals. Aimed at golfers who enjoy luxury living. It is distributed at luxury golf resorts including Gleneagles, Turnberry, St Andrews and Bovey Castle. It is also available in the Business Class Lounges of British Airways and Virgin Atlantic.
Ad Rate: Full Page Mono £1600.00
MAGAZINE
Golf

The Great Outdoors 981908
Editorial: Cudham Tithe Barn, Berry's Hill, Cudham, London TN16 3AG
Tel: 44 01959 541444
Email: tgo.ed@kelsey.co.uk
Web site: www.tgomagazine.co.uk
Freq: Monthly
Circ: 7762 Not Audited
Editor: Emily Rodway
Profile: Journal containing in-depth features on hill walking and backpacking in the UK and overseas.
Ad Rate: Full Page Mono £1161.00
Ad Rate: Full Page Colour £1889.00
MAGAZINE
Outdoor Recreation

Green Fleet Magazine 996933
Editorial: 226 High Road, Loughton, London IG10 1ET **Tel:** 44 02085 320055
Email: editorial@psigroupltd.co.uk
Web site: www.greenfleet.net
Freq: Monthly
Circ: 5575 Not Audited
Editor: Angela Pisanu
MAGAZINE
Automotive, Environment

Green Guide 985702
Editorial: 31 Regal Road, Weasenham Lane Industrial Estate, Wisbech, Wisbech PE13 2RQ
Email: editor@greenguide.co.uk
Web site: www.greenguide.co.uk
Freq: Daily
Circ: 7539 Cision Digital Reach
Editor: Gavin Markham
Profile: Website covering news and a consumer and business directory for environment, sustainability, CSR, conservation, climate and ethics.
MAGAZINE (ONLINE)
Alternative/Renewable Energy, Animal Farming, Beauty & Grooming, Business, Corporate Responsibility, Cosmetics, Education, Energy & Environment, Environment, Fashion

The Green Parent 983708
Editorial: PO Box 104, East Hoathly, Lewes, Lewes BN7 9AX
Email: pr@thegreenparent.co.uk
Web site: www.thegreenparent.co.uk
Freq: Bi-Monthly
Circ: 25000 Not Audited
Editor: Melissa Corkhill
Profile: Magazine covering parenting and green issues including house and garden,

pregnancy and birth, nutrition, education, health and beauty.
Ad Rate: Full Page Colour £1990.00
MAGAZINE
Energy & Environment, Ethical/Moral Issues, Family & Parenting

Green Soccer Journal 1053390
Editorial: Unit 8 Waterside, 44—48 Wharf Road, London N1 7UX **Tel:** 44 02072 759294
Email: info@thegreensoccerjournal.com
Web site: http://thegreensoccerjournal.com/
Freq: Quarterly Not Audited
MAGAZINE
Soccer

Green Star Media 998927
Editorial: Meadow View, Tannery Lane, Bramley, London GU5 0AB
Tel: 44 01483 892894
Email: info@greenstarmedia.net
Web site: www.greenstarmedia.net
Freq: Daily
Circ: 6647 Cision Digital Reach
MAGAZINE (ONLINE)
Rugby, Soccer

Green World 984350
Editorial: Development House, 56-64 Lennard Street, London BC2A 4LT
Tel: 44 02036 919400
Email: editor@greenworld.org.uk
Web site: www.greenworld.org.uk
Freq: Quarterly
Circ: 60000 Not Audited
Editor: Libby Peake
Profile: Magazine covering Green Party news, UK green politics, environmental and social issues.
Ad Rate: Full Page Mono £450.00
Ad Rate: Full Page Colour £450.00
MAGAZINE
Charitable Foundations, Government

GreenCarGuide.co.uk 984915
Editorial: 14 High Elm Road, Hale Barns, Altrincham WA15 0HS **Tel:** 44 01619 806436
Email: info@green-car-guide.co.uk
Web site: http://www.greencarguide.co.uk/
Freq: Daily
Circ: 12924 Cision Digital Reach
MAGAZINE (ONLINE)
Antique & Collectible Cars, Automakers, Automotive, Driving, Environment, Motorcycles, Off-road & 4-Wheel Drive Vehicles, Trucks & SUVs

Greenforallseasons.com 988036
Editorial: Foley House, 24 Clifford Road, New Barnet, London EN5 5PG
Email: stories@greenforallseasons.com
Web site: www.greenforallseasons.com
Freq: Daily
Circ: 691 Cision Digital Reach
MAGAZINE (ONLINE)
Alternative Medicine, Beauty & Grooming, Cosmetics, Fitness & Exercise, Hair, Nutrition, Travel

GreenMotor.co.uk 1095732
Email: feedback@greenmotor.co.uk
Web site: http://www.greenmotor.co.uk/
Freq: Daily
Circ: 8255 Cision Digital Reach
Editor: Lem Bingley
MAGAZINE (ONLINE)
Automotive, Driving

Greentraveller.co.uk 1104365
Tel: 44 01225 326888
Email: info@greentraveller.co.uk
Web site: www.greentraveller.co.uk
Freq: Daily
Circ: 50665 Cision Digital Reach
MAGAZINE (ONLINE)
Airline Inflight, Ethical/Moral Issues, Railroad, Travel

Greyhound Star 982033
Editorial: Kiln House, Tea Green, Luton LU2 8PU **Tel:** 44 01582 483749
Email: admin@greyhoundstar.co.uk
Web site: http://greyhoundstar.co.uk/

Freq: Monthly
Circ: 11306 Cision Digital Reach
Editor: Floyd Amphlett
Profile: Magazine providing coverage of every major greyhound race. Includes articles on breeding and veterinary advice. Read by owners, trainers, track operators and breeders.
Ad Rate: Full Page Mono £675.00
Ad Rate: Full Page Colour £775.00
MAGAZINE (ONLINE)
Casinos & Gaming, Games, Competitions & Events

Groby & Field Head Spotlight 984597
Editorial: PO Box 8, Markfield, Markfield LE67 9ZT **Tel:** 44 01530 244069
Email: info@grobyspotlight.co.uk
Web site: www.grobyspotlight.co.uk
Freq: Monthly
Circ: 7000 Not Audited
Editor: Mike Wilkinson
Profile: Magazine covering local news articles from the Groby & Field Head area of Leicestershire, events, book and DVD reviews, profiles of local clubs and societies, competitions, jokes and quotes.
Ad Rate: Full Page Mono £140.00
Ad Rate: Full Page Colour £190.00
MAGAZINE
Regional, Regional General Interest

The Grocer 979791
Editorial: Broadfield Park, Crawley RH11 9RT **Tel:** 44 01293 613400
Web site: www.thegrocer.co.uk
Freq: Weekly
Circ: 30252 Not Audited
Editor: Adam Leyland
Profile: The Grocer is a weekly magazine to serve the food and drink retail sector. It covers news on latest products, promotions and pricing information for meat and fish, dairy, fresh food, and all other food and drink. The magazine was first published in 1862. Aimed at retailers, manufacturers, suppliers and distributors in the food industry. It targets directors of the large multiples, independent retailers, sales and marketing professionals.
Ad Rate: Full Page Mono £1440.00
Ad Rate: Full Page Colour £3730.00
MAGAZINE
Food

GroomedandGlossy.com 986532
Email: editor@groomedandglossy.com
Web site: www.groomedandglossy.com
Freq: Daily
Circ: 10249 Cision Digital Reach
MAGAZINE (ONLINE)
Beauty & Grooming, Cosmetics, Hair, Weddings, Women's Interests

The Grooming Guide 995358
Email: contact@thegroomingguide.com
Web site: http://thegroomingguide.com
Freq: Daily
Circ: 11155 Cision Digital Reach
MAGAZINE (ONLINE)
Beauty & Grooming, Cosmetics, Hair, Men's Interests

Ground Improvement 980883
Editorial: 1 Great George Street, London SW1P 3AA **Tel:** 44 02076 652453
Web site: www.icevirtuallibrary.com/content/serial/grim
Freq: Quarterly
Circ: 1500 Not Audited
MAGAZINE
News & Current Affairs

The Groundsman 983693
Editorial: 28 Stratford Office Village, Walker Avenue, Wolverton Mill East, Milton Keynes MK12 5TW **Tel:** 44 01908 312511
Email: editor@iog.org
Web site: www.iog.org
Freq: Monthly
Circ: 3300 Not Audited
Profile: Magazine covering grounds management, maintenance and care of

leisure facilities, major stadiums and pitches in football, cricket and rugby, plus general landscaping, drainage and management of golf courses, bowling greens, horseracing circuits, polo pitches and artificial surfaces. Also covers management of school, college and university sports and horticultural facilities.
Ad Rate: Full Page Colour £1135.00
MAGAZINE
Gardening

Group Leisure 983301
Editorial: PO Box 5122, Milton Keynes, Milton Keynes MK15 8ZP
Tel: 44 01908 613323
Email: editorial@groupleisure.com
Web site: www.groupleisure.com
Freq: Monthly
Circ: 4500 Not Audited
Profile: Magazine with news, information and features of interest to group travel organisers from clubs, societies and associations. The aim of the magazine is to provide ideas, contacts and advice for people organising day trips, short breaks and holidays of all types for leisure groups from retired groups to parties of friends, sports & social clubs, or any form of special interest group. The publication was first launched in March 1995. Aimed at decision makers and organisers in the group leisure and travel industry
Ad Rate: Full Page Colour £1800.00
MAGAZINE
Travel

Group Tourism & Travel Magazine 983414
Editorial: Unit 4 - Minerva Business Park, Lynch Wood, Peterborough PE2 6FT
Tel: 44 01733 405730
Email: news@grouptourismtravel.com
Web site: http://www.grouptourismtravel.com/
Freq: Monthly
Circ: 3500 Not Audited
Editor: Jessamy Chapman
Profile: Magazine covering news and features on coach tourism, attractions and destinations at home and abroad. Aimed at coach tour operators, planners, managers and drivers.Previous title: Route One On Tour Only press material relating to coach tourism and coach holidays will be accepted.
Ad Rate: Full Page Colour £1275.00
MAGAZINE
Automotive

Group Travel Organiser 981237
Editorial: 6 Wellington Square, Hastings TN34 1PB **Tel:** 44 01424 572080
Email: editorial@grouptravelorganiser.com
Web site: www.grouptravelorganiser.com
Freq: Bi-Monthly
Circ: 8993 Not Audited
Profile: Magazine covering organisation and commissioning of travel arrangements on behalf of groups of 20 or more people. First published in 1988, the publication has an average of 60 pages per issue. Aimed at group travel organisers.
Ad Rate: Full Page Colour £1150.00
MAGAZINE
Travel

Group Travel Today 984188
Tel: 44 01214 456961
Email: beaubusinessmedia@gmail.com
Web site: www.grouptravel-today.com
Freq: Bi-Monthly
Circ: 7000 Not Audited
MAGAZINE
Travel

Group Travel World 987132
Editorial: 3 Cygnet Park, Forder Way, Hampton PE7 8GX **Tel:** 44 01733 293249
Web site: http://grouptravelworld.com/
Freq: Monthly
Circ: 23000 Not Audited
Profile: Group Travel World is a monthly magazine containing news, features and information about the group travel industry in the UK and Europe. It is owned by Rouncy

Consumer Magazines

Media Ltd. Group Travel World is aimed at organisers of group travel in Europe.
MAGAZINE
Travel

Grow Your Own
981927
Editorial: 25 Phoenix Court, Hawkins Road, Colchester, Colchester CO2 8JY
Tel: 44 01206 505979
Web site: www.growfruitandveg.co.uk
Freq: Monthly
Circ: 65000 Not Audited
Profile: Magazine with tips on how to live the good life including how to grow your own fruit and vegetables and recipes using garden fresh produce as well as keeping your own bees and chickens. Aimed at those in their 30s and 40s whether they have a small back garden, a substantial plot or an allotment.
Ad Rate: Full Page Mono £835.00
Ad Rate: Full Page Colour £1075.00
MAGAZINE
Gardening

Grub4Life.org.uk
984954
Editorial: 40 Bowling Green Lane, Clerkenwell, London EC1R 0NE
Tel: 44 02074 157070
Web site: www.grub4life.org.uk
Freq: Daily
Circ: 1892 Cision Digital Reach
Profile: Online community covering nutrition for pre-school children. Aimed at parents, teachers and carers of pre-school children.
MAGAZINE (ONLINE)
Cooking & Baking, Nutrition

The Gryffe Advertizer
996707
Editorial: 1st Floor, Neva Place, High Street, Bishopton PA11 3PN **Tel:** 44 01505 613340
Email: info@advertizer.co.uk
Web site: www.gryffeadvertizer.wix.com/gryffeadvertizer2013
Freq: Monthly
Circ: 14000 Not Audited
MAGAZINE
Regional General Interest

The Gryphon
995966
Editorial: Leeds Student Office, Leeds University Union, Lifton Place, Leeds LS2 9JZ **Tel:** 44 01133 801413
Email: editor@thegryphon.co.uk
Web site: www.thegryphon.co.uk/
Freq: Weekly
Circ: 3000 Not Audited
MAGAZINE
Student Lifestyle

GS Magazine
983958
Editorial: 19 Wharfdale Road, London N1 9SB **Tel:** 44 02078 333772
Email: editor@gsmagazine.co.uk
Web site: www.gsmagazine.co.uk
Freq: Quarterly
Circ: 8500 Not Audited
Editor: Stirling Johnstone
Profile: Independent magazine for the hospitality industry containing product reviews and design related articles. Aimed at restaurateurs, hoteliers, theme bars, pub chains, hotel and leisure groups, designers and architects.
Ad Rate: Full Page Colour £2950.00
MAGAZINE
Bars, Clubs & Pubs, Hotels/Motels

GSCENE
985728
Editorial: 74-82 Portland Road, Hove BN3 5DL **Tel:** 44 01273 749947
Email: info@gscene.com
Web site: www.gscene.com
Freq: Monthly
Circ: 48000 Not Audited
Editor: James Ledward
Profile: Community news and listings magazine.
Ad Rate: Full Page Colour £500.00
MAGAZINE
LGBT, Sexuality

GSMArena.com
999598
Email: info@gsmarena.com
Web site: www.gsmarena.com
Freq: Daily
Circ: 11259846 Cision Digital Reach
MAGAZINE (ONLINE)
Mobile Electronics

Guardian Professional Networks
1073818
Editorial: Kings Place, 90 York Way, London N1 9GU **Tel:** 44 02033 532000
Web site: www.theguardian.com/guardian-professional
Freq: Daily
Circ: 195243 Cision Digital Reach
MAGAZINE (ONLINE)
Charitable Foundations, Government, Health Administration, Higher Education, Public Sector

The Guards Magazine
988851
Editorial: Horse Guards, Whitehall, London SW1A 2AX
Email: editor@guardsmagazine.co.uk
Web site: www.guardsmagazine.com
Freq: 3 Times/Year
Circ: 15000 Not Audited
Editor: Simon Doughty
MAGAZINE
Defense & National Security

Guernsey Now
995867
Editorial: PO Box 57, Braye Road, Vale, Guernsey GY1 3BW **Tel:** 44 01481 240240
Email: newsroom@guernseypress.com
Web site: www.guernseypress.com
Freq: Quarterly
Circ: 17000 Not Audited
Editor: Helen Hubert
Profile: Guernsey Now is a quarterly supplement distributed with the Guernsey Press and Star. It covers a wide range of lifestyle subjects including homes, gardening, fashion, motoring, the arts, entertainment, food, drink, travel, sport and consumer products.
Ad Rate: Full Page Colour £850.00
MAGAZINE
Regional General Interest

Guestlist
995832
Editorial: 170 Cannon Street Road, Whitechapel, London E1 2LH
Tel: 44 02035 817676
Email: enquiries@guestlist.net
Web site: www.guestlist.net
Freq: Monthly
Circ: 100000 Not Audited
Editor: Cristina Trujillo
MAGAZINE
Classical/Choral/Band Music, Country, Folk, Bluegrass, Dance Music, Jazz & Blues, Music, Pop Music, R&B, Urban, World, Rap & Hip Hop, Regional General Interest, Rock Music

The Guide Magazines
1062742
Editorial: Phoenix Enterprise Centre, Jacktrees Road, Cleator Moor CA25 5BD
Tel: 44 01946 816716
Email: info@theguidemediagroup.com
Web site: www.theguidemags.com
Freq: Bi-Monthly
Circ: 30000 Not Audited
MAGAZINE
Regional General Interest, Travel

Guidelines in Practice
984500
Editorial: MGP Ltd, MGP House, East Street, Chesham HP5 1DG
Tel: 44 01442 876100
Email: ginp@mgp.co.uk
Web site: www.guidelinesinpractice.co.uk
Freq: Monthly
Editor: Julia Morris
MAGAZINE
Health Administration, Medicine

Guides.Global
995495
Editorial: 23 Bridewell Lane, Bury St Edmunds, Bury St. Edmunds IP33 1RE
Tel: 44 01284 719964

Email: news@guides.global
Web site: www.guides.global/index.php
Freq: Daily
MAGAZINE (ONLINE)
Corporate Law, Employment, Expatriates, Real Estate Law, Tax Law

Guiding Magazine
983417
Editorial: Girl Guiding UK, 17-19 Buckingham Palace Road, London SW1W 0PT **Tel:** 44 02078 346242
Email: yourvoice@girlguiding.org.uk
Web site: www.girlguiding.org.uk
Freq: Quarterly
Circ: 90000 Not Audited
MAGAZINE
Charitable Foundations, Teen/Young Adult

Guild Gazette
985671
Editorial: Guild House, 320 Burton Road, Derby DE23 6AF **Tel:** 44 08452 177383
Email: info@beautyguild.com
Web site: www.beautyguild.com
Freq: Bi-Monthly
Circ: 22560 Not Audited
MAGAZINE
Beauty & Grooming, Cosmetics, Hair

Guild News
981171
Editorial: Macmillan Building, Parcel Terrace, Derby DE1 1LY
Tel: 44 01332 227690
Email: info@beautyserve.net
Web site: http://www.beautyserve.com/guild-news.jsp
Freq: Monthly
Circ: 18019 Not Audited
Profile: Beauty trade magazine covering beauty, nails, tanning and holistic therapies. Also includes coverage of new product and equipment launches, industry news, training courses, business and marketing advice and information on health and safety. Aimed at the Beauty, Nail and Spa Market and read by the salon and spa owners, salon and spa managers, qualified beauty therapists and nail technicians, mobile and home-based therapists, holistic therapists, college lecturers and final year students. Launched in 1995.
Ad Rate: Full Page Colour £1895.00
MAGAZINE
Cosmetics

Guild News (Guild of Master Craftsmen)
995363
Editorial: 166 High Street, Lewes BN7 1XU
Tel: 44 01273 478449
Email: guildnews@thegmcgroup.com
Web site: www.guildmc.com
Freq: Quarterly
Circ: 1500 Not Audited
MAGAZINE
News & Current Affairs

The Guild Property Magazine
995804
Editorial: 121 Park Lane, London W1K 7AG
Tel: 44 02076 294141
Email: admin@property-platform.com
Web site: www.guildproperty.co.uk/index.php
Freq: Monthly
Circ: 750000 Not Audited
MAGAZINE
Residential Real Estate

The Guildford Magazine
982533
Editorial: Kingsway Business Park, Oldfield Road, Hampton, London TW12 2HD
Tel: 44 02089 395601
Email: editguild@sheengate.co.uk
Web site: www.sheengate.co.uk
Freq: Monthly
Circ: 40100 Not Audited
Profile: Lifestyle magazine containing local interest articles and interviews as well as features on fashion, theatre, health, education, shopping and property.
Ad Rate: Full Page Colour £1155.00
MAGAZINE
Property Management & Maintenance, Regional General Interest

Guitar & Bass
982082
Editorial: Suite 6, Piccadilly House, London Road, Bath BA1 6PL **Tel:** 44 01225 489984
Email: guitarandbass@anthem-publishing.com
Web site: www.guitar-bass.net
Freq: Monthly
Circ: 9000 Not Audited
Editor: Chris Vinnicombe
Profile: Magazine featuring equipment reviews, personality interviews, printed music and technical articles. Includes reviews of latest guitars, amps, effects and basses, tips on buying second hand and vintage gear. Read by practising guitarists.
Ad Rate: Full Page Colour £895.00
MAGAZINE
Music

Guitar Techniques
982081
Editorial: Quay House, The Ambury, Bath BA1 1UA **Tel:** 44 01225 442244
Email: guitartechniques@futurenet.com
Web site: www.musicradar.com/guitartechniques
Freq: Monthly
Circ: 19000 Not Audited
Editor: Neville Marten
Profile: Guitar Techniques is a magazine focusing on guitar learning techniques, featuring master classes from expert tutors and step-by-step guides to playing the guitar. Includes CD and album reviews and long transcriptions. The magazine is published in 13 installments throughout the year.
Ad Rate: Full Page Colour £1095.00
MAGAZINE
Music

Guitarist
982083
Editorial: Quay House, The Ambury, Bath BA1 1UA **Tel:** 44 01225 442244
Email: guitarist@futurenet.com
Web site: www.musicradar.com/guitarist
Freq: Monthly
Circ: 25047 Not Audited
Editor: Jamie Dickson
Profile: Magazine covering all aspects of acoustic, bass and electric guitars. Includes product news, reviews, interviews and techniques.
Ad Rate: Full Page Colour £1690.00
MAGAZINE
Music

Guitarist Presents Acoustic
997704
Editorial: Quay House, The Ambury, Bath BA1 1UA **Tel:** 44 01225 442244
Email: guitarist@futurenet.com
Web site: www.musicradar.com/acoustic
Freq: Quarterly Not Audited
MAGAZINE
Music

Gujarat Samachar
982584
Editorial: 12 Hoxton Market, London N1 6HW **Tel:** 44 02077 494080
Email: support@abplgroup.com
Web site: www.abplgroup.com
Freq: Weekly
Circ: 33000 Not Audited
Editor: Chandrakant Patel
Profile: Publication covering news from India for members of the Gujarat community. Includes features on cooking, beauty, health, finance and property. Read by students, teachers, professionals and those who are involved in charitable and community organisations.
MAGAZINE
Asia

Gulf States News
986443
Editorial: 4 Bank Buildings, Station Road, Hastings, Hastings TN34 1NG
Tel: 44 01424 721667
Email: admin@cbi-research.com
Web site: www.gsn-online.com
Freq: Daily
Circ: 2894 Cision Digital Reach
MAGAZINE (ONLINE)
International News

Gun Trade World
987677

Editorial: 1 Whittle Close, Drayton Fields, Daventry, Daventry NN11 8RQ
Tel: 44 01327 315412
Web site: www.guntradeworld.com
Freq: Monthly
Circ: 10234 Not Audited
Profile: Magazine covering the shooting trade. Its major role is to put manufacturers in one part of the world in direct contact with wholesalers, distributors and key retailers in other parts. first published in 2010.
Ad Rate: Full Page Colour £995.00
MAGAZINE
Shooting/Guns

Gunmart
982280

Editorial: 21-23 Phoenix Court, Hawkins Road, Colchester, Colchester CO2 8JY
Tel: 44 01206 506247
Email: gunmart@aceville.co.uk
Web site: www.gunmart.net
Freq: Monthly
Circ: 30000 Not Audited
Editor: Graham Allen
MAGAZINE
Shooting/Guns

gurgle
990448

Editorial: Media 10 Ltd, Crown House, 151 High Road, Loughton IG10 4LF
Tel: 44 02032 255200
Email: editorial@gurgle.com
Web site: www.gurgle.com
Freq: Daily
Circ: 36616 Cision Digital Reach
Editor: Scarlett Brady
Profile: Parenting magazine for modern mums of babies and toddler up to 4 years of age. It features fashion must-haves and celebrity news.
MAGAZINE (ONLINE)
Family & Parenting

Gutter
998915

Editorial: 49-53 Virginia Street, Glasgow G1 1TS **Tel:** 44 01415 525303
Email: info@guttermag.co.uk
Web site: www.guttermag.co.uk
Freq: Semi-Annual
Circ: 1000 Not Audited
MAGAZINE
Literature

GuysLikeU.com
1054596

Email: christian@guyslikeu.com
Web site: http://www.guyslikeu.com/
Freq: Daily
Circ: 15751 Cision Digital Reach
MAGAZINE (ONLINE)
LGBT

Gx
997420

Editorial: 3rd floor, Colechurch House, 1 London Bridge Walk, London SE1 2SX
Tel: 44 02073 789890
Web site: http://www.yourgx.com
Freq: Daily
Circ: 3597 Cision Digital Reach
MAGAZINE (ONLINE)
Financial Markets, Personal Finance

Gym Owner Monthly
1072712

Editorial: Stangrove Lodge, Manor House Gardens, Edenbridge TN8 5EG
Email: enquiries@pw-media.co.uk
Web site: www.gymownermonthly.co.uk
Freq: Monthly
Circ: 13495 Cision Digital Reach
MAGAZINE (ONLINE)
Fitness & Exercise

The Gymnast
982268

Editorial: 1 Deer Park Road, London SW19 3TL
Web site: www.british-gymnastics.org
Freq: Quarterly
Editor: Mark Young
MAGAZINE
Gymnastics

H Edition
1060553

Editorial: 24th Floor, The Shard, London SE1 9SG **Tel:** 44 02036 950020
Email: info@hamblemediacomms.com
Web site: https://www.facebook.com/heditionmagazine/
Freq: Quarterly
Circ: 10747 Cision Digital Reach
MAGAZINE (ONLINE)
Business, Luxury Goods, Small and Medium Business

H&E Naturist
986636

Editorial: PO Box 545, Hull HU9 9JF
Tel: 44 01482 342000
Email: editor@henaturist.net
Web site: www.henaturist.net
Freq: Monthly
Circ: 10000 Not Audited
Editor: Sam Hawcroft
Profile: Magazine covering naturist travel, arts, naturist resorts, news, clubs and swimming.
Ad Rate: Full Page Colour £500.00
MAGAZINE
News & Current Affairs

H&N Magazine
1074633

Editorial: H&N Magazine, 2 The Covet, Apperley Bridge, Bradford BD10 9TH
Tel: 44 01274 420091
Email: hello@madpublications.co.uk
Web site: www.hnmagazine.co.uk
Freq: Bi-Monthly
Circ: 40000 Not Audited
Editor: Angela Riches
MAGAZINE
Beauty & Grooming, Cooking & Baking, Cosmetics, Fashion, Fitness & Exercise, Food, Grocery Stores, Hair, Health & Medicine, Men's Interests

H2B Magazine
986867

Editorial: H2B Magazine, The Old Paint Works, 120 Burley Road, Horsforth LS3 1JP
Tel: 44 01132 580752
Web site: http://www.h2bmagazine.co.uk/
Freq: Quarterly
Circ: 200000 Not Audited
MAGAZINE
Regional General Interest

Hack Circus
988024

Editorial: Hack Circus, c/o Dot Forge, Digital Campus, Sheffield S1 2BJ
Web site: hackcircus.com
Freq: Quarterly Not Audited
Editor: Leila Johnston
Profile: Magazine covering the entertaining and engaging side of inventive thought. Each issue is based upon a theme.
MAGAZINE
Art

Hair
982387

Editorial: Freebournes House, Freebournes Road, Witham, Witham CM8 3US
Tel: 44 01376 534500
Email: info@hairmags.co.uk
Web site: www.hairmagazine.co.uk
Freq: Monthly
Circ: 30000 Not Audited
Profile: Magazine covering hair and beauty advice. Aimed at women between 18 and 30 years old.
Ad Rate: Full Page Colour £5377.00
MAGAZINE
Hair

Hairdressers Journal International
981172

Editorial: 1. 17 The Plaza, 535 Kings Road, London SW10 0SZ **Tel:** 44 02073 510536
Web site: www.hji.co.uk
Freq: Monthly
Circ: 12810 Not Audited
Profile: Journal containing industry related news, profiles and business advice, plus latest hair shots, techniques and products. Aimed at hair salon partners, managers, stylists, juniors, trainees and students, it covers the latest hair fashion, products and techniques and contains industry related news as well as predictions of future trends.

Ad Rate: Full Page Colour £2212.00
MAGAZINE
Cosmetics, Hair

Hairstyles Only
982389

Editorial: Freebournes House, Freebournes Road, Witham, Witham CM8 3US
Tel: 44 01376 534525
Email: info@hairstylesonly.co.uk
Web site: itunes.apple.com/gb/app/hairstyles-only-magazine/id582958293?mt=8/
Freq: Weekly
Circ: 35012 Not Audited
Profile: Magazine containing articles and photographs of modern hairstyles.
Ad Rate: Full Page Colour £1500.00
MAGAZINE
Hair

HalalFocus.com
996218

Tel: 44 01799 542852
Email: info@halalfocus.com
Web site: halalfocus.net
Freq: Daily
Circ: 12866 Cision Digital Reach
MAGAZINE (ONLINE)
Cooking & Baking, Food, Grocery Stores, Organic Food, Regional General Interest, Religion, Restaurant Reviews, Vegetarianism & Veganism

HALCYON
996359

Editorial: 16 Connect Business Village, Tate Suite 9, 24 Derby Road, Liverpool L5 9PR
Tel: 44 01512 077744
Email: contact@halcyonmag.com
Web site: www.halcyonmag.com
Freq: Bi-Monthly
Circ: 10000 Not Audited
Editor: Jonathan Turton
MAGAZINE
Boxing, Country, Folk, Bluegrass, Dance Music, Fashion, Fitness & Exercise, Men's Interests, Movies & Video, Regional General Interest, Rock Music, Soccer

Halcyon
999392

Tel: 44 02032 393069
Web site: http://www.inkwell-services.co.uk/section.php/4/1/halcyon
Freq: 3 Times/Year Not Audited
Editor: Dan Hayes
MAGAZINE
Airline Inflight, Luxury Goods

Hale & Bowdon Magazine
983388

Editorial: 5 The Stables, Manchester M20 5PG **Tel:** 44 01614 452883
Email: info@salutions.co.uk
Web site: http://www.salutions.co.uk/
Freq: Bi-Monthly
Circ: 6000 Not Audited
Profile: A glossy lifestyle magazine for the style concious citizens of Hale & Bowden and South Manchester. It covers local news and events as well as lifestyle, fashion, health and beauty, men's and women's fashion, property, education, business, motors and food and drink. Aimed at both affluent families and single professionals, the magazine is distrubuted to homes in Hale, Hale Barns and Bowdon.
Ad Rate: Full Page Colour £1495.00
MAGAZINE
Regional General Interest

Hampshire Life
982494

Editorial: 28 Teville Road, Worthing, Worthing BN11 1UG **Tel:** 44 01903 703730
Email: enquiries@hampshire-life.co.uk
Web site: www.hampshire-life.co.uk/home
Freq: Monthly
Circ: 10000 Not Audited
Editor: Elizabeth Kirby
Profile: Magazine covering lifestyle, food, fashion, local issues, property, interiors, entertainment and events. Focussing on local people, local businesses and local life, Hampshire Life is aimed at those living throughout the county.
MAGAZINE
Regional General Interest

Hampshire Society
983496

Editorial: Newspaper House, Test Lane, Redbridge, Southampton SO16 9JX
Tel: 44 02380 424490
Email: hampshire.society@dailyecho.co.uk
Web site: www.hampshiresociety.co.uk
Freq: Monthly
Circ: 20000 Not Audited
Profile: Lifestyle magazine covering travel, fashion, home and garden, eating out, property and local events. Aimed at affluent people aged between 35 and 60 years old living in Hampshire.
Ad Rate: Full Page Colour £600.00
MAGAZINE
Regional General Interest

Hampshire Sporting Shooter
1074067

Web site: http://www.hampshiresportingshooter.co.uk/
Freq: Daily
Circ: 1088 Cision Digital Reach
MAGAZINE (ONLINE)
Shooting/Guns

Hampton Gazette
996212

Editorial: 153 County Road, Hampton Vale, Peterborough PE7 8ET
Circ: 5500 Not Audited
MAGAZINE
News & Current Affairs

The Handbook
986354

Editorial: 523 Old York Road, Wandsworth, London SW18 1TG **Tel:** 44 02030 210898
Email: editorial@thehandbook.com
Web site: www.thehandbook.com
Freq: Daily
Circ: 31099 Cision Digital Reach
Editor: Emily Gray
MAGAZINE (ONLINE)
Bars, Clubs & Pubs, Branding, Restaurant Reviews

Haqiqah
997406

Tel: 44 07710 918351
Email: press@imamsonline.com
Web site: www.imamsonline.com/blog/haqiqah-what-is-the-truth-behind-isis/
Freq: Monthly Not Audited
MAGAZINE
News & Current Affairs

Harbour Club
1053194

Editorial: 790 Fulham Road, London SW6 5SL **Tel:** 44 02077 317747
Email: info@epicureanlife.co.uk
Web site: www.thealexandergroup.co.uk
Freq: Quarterly
Circ: 20000 Not Audited
Editor: Christina Raptis
MAGAZINE
Fitness & Exercise

Harden's Guide
990531

Editorial: The Brew, Victoria House, Paul Street, London EC2A 4NA
Tel: 44 02078 394763
Email: editorial@hardens.com
Web site: www.hardens.com
Freq: Daily
Circ: 48252 Cision Digital Reach
MAGAZINE (ONLINE)
Restaurant Reviews

Hardware Heaven
985708

Editorial: Unit 9, The Incubator Building, Alconbury Weald, Huntingdon PE28 4WX
Tel: 44 01480 420820
Email: news@hardwareheaven.com
Web site: www.hardwareheaven.com
Freq: Daily
Circ: 138160 Cision Digital Reach
MAGAZINE (ONLINE)
Apple, Computer & Video Games, Computers, Internet, Personal Computers

Haringey People
984075

Editorial: Communications Unit, River Park House, 225 High Road, London N22 8HQ
Tel: 44 02084 894584
Email: pressdesk@haringey.gov.uk

Consumer Magazines

Web site: www.haringey.gov.uk/index/
news_and_events/haringeypeople.htm
Freq: Bi-Monthly Not Audited
Editor: Sally Lowe
Profile: Magazine covering features on
major issues affecting the Borough. Also
includes articles on entertainment, events
and lifestyle. This outlet covers areas within
the Borough of Haringey.
Ad Rate: Full Page Colour £2500.00
MAGAZINE
Regional General Interest

Harper's Bazaar   982370
Editorial: 72 Broadwick Street, London W1F
9EP Tel: 44 02074 395000
Email: info@harpersbazaar.co.uk
Web site: www.harpersbazaar.co.uk
Freq: Monthly
Circ: 111424 Not Audited
Profile: Magazine covering the latest fashion
and beauty news and trends. It features
fashion stories, arts coverage, beauty pages
and travel features. First published in 1970
as Harpers & Queen. Aimed at upmarket,
discerning adults.
Ad Rate: Full Page Colour £15781.00
MAGAZINE
Beauty & Grooming, Cosmetics, Fashion,
Hair, Luxury Goods, Women's Interests

Harpers Wine and Spirit   983155
Editorial: Longley House, International Drive,
Southgate Avenue, Crawley RH10 6AQ
Tel: 44 01293 590040
Web site: www.harpers.co.uk
Freq: Monthly
Circ: 5868 Not Audited
Editor: Andrew Catchpole
Profile: Publication containing news and
information about the wine and spirit trade.
Aimed at multiple and specialist retailers,
sommeliers, restaurateurs, hoteliers and
those involved in the wine and spirit trade.
Previous title: Harpers The Wine and Spirit
Weekly
Ad Rate: Full Page Colour £2482.00
MAGAZINE
Alcohol & Spirits

Harpsichord & Fortepiano
982091
Editorial: 1 Leamington Road, Broadway,
Broadway WR12 7EF
Email: editor@hfmagazine.info
Web site: www.hfmagazine.info
Freq: Semi-Annual Not Audited
Editor: Dr Micaela Schmitz
Profile: Magazine featuring scholarly and
informal articles on early keyboard
instruments.
Ad Rate: Full Page Mono £250.00
MAGAZINE
Classical/Choral/Band Music, Music

Harrods Home and Property
1054418
Editorial: 87-135 Brompton Rd,
Knightsbridge, London SW1X 7XL
Tel: 44 02077 301234
Email: magazine@harrods.com
Web site: http://www.harrodsestates.com/
mag/home_and_property_2015
Freq: Quarterly
Circ: 65000 Not Audited
Editor: Jan Masters
MAGAZINE
Architecture & Design, Do-It-Yourself
(DIY), Gardening, Home, Property
Management & Maintenance, Real Estate

Harrods Magazine   984459
Editorial: 68 Hammersmith Road, London
W14 8YW Tel: 44 02077 301234
Email: magazine@harrods.com
Web site: www.harrods.com/content/about-
us/publications
Freq: Monthly
Circ: 124218 Not Audited
Editor: Jan Masters
Profile: Magazine containing features on
lifestyle including interiors, food, fashion and
beauty.

Ad Rate: Full Page Colour £6500.00
MAGAZINE
Luxury Goods, Shopping

Harrods Travel   1012048
Editorial: 87-135 Brompton Road,
Knightsbridge, Camberwell SE1X 7XL
Tel: 44 02077 301234
Email: magazine@harrods.com
Web site: www.harrods.com/content/about-
us/publications
Freq: Semi-Annual
Circ: 65000 Not Audited
Editor: Jan Masters
MAGAZINE
Airline Inflight, Railroad, Travel

Harrogate Informer   986414
Email: news@harrogate-news.co.uk
Web site: www.harrogate-news.co.uk
Freq: Daily
Circ: 15767 Cision Digital Reach
MAGAZINE (ONLINE)
Regional

Harrow People   984054
Editorial: Harrow Council, Civic Centre PO
Box 21, Station Road, Harrow HA1 2XF
Tel: 44 02088 635611
Email: communications@harrow.gov.uk
Web site: www.harrow.gov.uk
Freq: Bi-Monthly
Circ: 100000 Not Audited
MAGAZINE
Regional, Regional General Interest

harveynichols.com   985332
Editorial: 361-365 Chiswick High Road,
Chiswick, London W4 4HS
Tel: 44 02072 355000
Web site: www.harveynichols.com
Freq: Daily
Circ: 256672 Cision Digital Reach
MAGAZINE (ONLINE)
Fashion, Luxury Goods, Shopping

Hashtag Life   1073279
Email: editor@hashtaglife.co.uk
Web site: http://hashtaglife.co.uk/
Freq: Daily
Circ: 629 Cision Digital Reach
Editor: Joanna Malek
MAGAZINE (ONLINE)
Airline Inflight, Cooking & Baking, Health
& Medicine, Luxury Goods, Men's
Interests, Restaurant Reviews, Travel,
Women's Interests

The HAT Magazine   985431
Editorial: Unit 3, 7 – 15 Greatorex Street,
London E1 5NF Tel: 44 02072 471120
Email: info@thehatmagazine.com
Web site: www.thehatmagazine.com
Freq: Quarterly
Circ: 2000 Not Audited
Editor: Nigel Denford
Profile: Independent journal for the Hat
Trade Aimed at those working within the hat
manufacturing industry and readers include
department store buyers, independent retail
buyers, hire shop buyers, designers,
manufacturers, wholesalers, independent
milliners and fashion college students.
MAGAZINE
Fashion

Haunted   998987
Editorial: 6 Peveril Drive, Sutton in Ashfield,
Sutton-in-Ashfield NG17 2GT
Email: paul@deadgoodpublishing.com
Web site: http://www.
haunteddigitalmagazine.com/
Freq: Daily
Circ: 8098 Cision Digital Reach
Editor: Paul Stevenson
MAGAZINE (ONLINE)
Science Fiction

HC Magazine   995379
Editorial: 7 Nuffield Way, Abingdon,
Abingdon OX14 1RL Tel: 44 01235 856300
Web site: www.oxhc.co.uk
Freq: Bi-Monthly

Circ: 10094 Not Audited
MAGAZINE
Luxury Goods, Regional General Interest

HDTVtest   987015
Editorial: 28 Romana Square, Altrincham
WA14 5QB
Email: news@hdtvtest.co.uk
Web site: www.hdtvtest.co.uk
Freq: Daily
Circ: 598659 Cision Digital Reach
Profile: Website covering reviews of high
definition television.
MAGAZINE (ONLINE)
Movies & Video

headlinemoney   983151
Editorial: 79 Wells street, London W1T 3QN
Tel: 44 02079 704690
Email: news@headlinemoney.co.uk
Web site: www.headlinemoney.co.uk
Freq: Daily
Circ: 47704 Cision Digital Reach
MAGAZINE (ONLINE)

Headteacher Update   981560
Editorial: St Jude's Church, Dulwich Road,
Herne Hill, London SE24 0PB
Tel: 44 02077 385454
Web site: www.headteacher-update.com
Freq: Bi-Monthly
Circ: 25000 Not Audited
Editor: Pete Henshaw; Editor: Pete
Henshaw
Profile: Magazine containing management
and leadership issues including information
on products and resources. Headteacher
Update is delivered directly to every primary
school headteacher in the UK.
Ad Rate: Full Page Colour £2550.00
MAGAZINE
Disability, Education, Higher Education,
Preschool, Schools & Institutions,
Students

Health & Fitness   981829
Editorial: 31-32 Alfred Place, London WC1E
7DP Tel: 44 02035 150144
Email: healthandfitness@servicehelpline.co.
uk
Web site: www.healthandfitnessonline.co.uk
Freq: Monthly
Circ: 12183 Not Audited
Editor: Mary Comber
Profile: Health & Fitness Magazine is a
monthly UK magazine for health conscious
women. It covers exercise, beauty, sport,
fashion, nutrition, health and fitness news
and competitions. It contains features on
beauty products, books reviews, events
related to health and fitness, fashion trends
in sports clothing, fitness news, food
recipes, health, body and mind and travel.
The Workout Handbook section provides
workout plans and guidance to help readers
get the most from their exercise sessions.
First published in 1983. Aimed at health
conscious women who are passionate about
staying fit and healthy.
Ad Rate: Full Page Colour £2200.00
MAGAZINE
Fitness & Exercise, Nutrition

Health & Happiness 4 You -
CEASED   997347
Freq: Quarterly Not Audited
MAGAZINE
Health & Medicine

Health and Enigmatic   1061231
Not Audited
MAGAZINE
Consumer Affairs, Crime & Violence,
Defense & National Security, Energy &
Environment, Ethical/Moral Issues,
International News, Law, National News,
News & Current Affairs, Northern Ireland

Health and Homeopathy   981816
Editorial: Hahnemann House, 29 Park Street
West, Luton LU1 3BE Tel: 44 01582 408675
Email: info@britishhomeopathic.org
Web site: www.britishhomeopathic.org/
Freq: 3 Times/Year

Circ: 2500 Not Audited
Editor: John Burry
MAGAZINE
Alternative Medicine, Charitable
Foundations

Health Club Management
981027
Editorial: Portmill House, Portmill Lane,
Hitchin SG5 1DJ Tel: 44 01462 431385
Email: newsdesk@leisuremedia.com
Web site: http://www.
healthclubmanagement.co.uk/
Freq: Monthly
Circ: 6000 Not Audited
Profile: Magazine covering all aspects of
health and fitness affecting the owner,
operator, developer or manager of a private
or public facility. Aimed at middle and senior
management and professionals in health and
fitness throughout the UK and Europe.
Ad Rate: Full Page Colour £1680.00
MAGAZINE
Fitness & Exercise

Health Education   980993
Editorial: Howard House, Wagon Lane,
Bingley BD16 1WA Tel: 44 01274 777700
Email: collections@emeraldinsight.com
Web site: www.emeraldinsight.com/
journals.htm?issn=0965-4283
Freq: Bi-Monthly Not Audited
Editor: Katherine Weare
Profile: Journal focusing on all aspects of
health awareness and education.
MAGAZINE
Disability, Education, Health
Administration, Higher Education,
Preschool, Schools & Institutions,
Students

Health Food Business   983133
Tel: 44 01279 810080
Email: rachel.symonds@targetpublishing.
com
Web site: www.healthfoodbusiness.co.uk
Freq: Monthly
Editor: Rachel Symonds
Profile: UK trade magazine for the
independent natural health market providing
information and advice on matters relating to
alternative and complimentary health
markets, such as legislation, new products,
market analysis, training & education and
retailing for natural health food products.
Ad Rate: Full Page Colour £2570.00
MAGAZINE
Alternative Medicine, Food, Nutrition

The Health Store Magazine
981828
Editorial: Unit 10, Blenheim Park Road,
Nottingham NG6 8YP Tel: 44 01159 767200
Email: info@thehealthstore.co.uk
Web site: www.thehealthstore.co.uk
Freq: Bi-Monthly
Circ: 150000 Not Audited
Editor: Jane Garton
Profile: Consumer magazine distributed to
members of the National Association of
Health Stores. Covers diet, nutritional
information and natural remedies.
Ad Rate: Full Page Colour £2350.00
MAGAZINE
Food, Nutrition

Health Today   1061235
Web site: http://www.healthtoday.net
Freq: Annual Not Audited
MAGAZINE
Alternative Medicine, Disability, Fitness &
Exercise, Health & Medicine, Media
Relations, Medicine, Nutrition, Patient
Support, Personal Health & Wellness,
Psychology

health triangle   995418
Editorial: 27 Old Gloucester Street, London
WC1N 3AX Tel: 44 02032 394423
Web site: ukhealthradio.com/magazine
Freq: Monthly Not Audited
MAGAZINE
Alternative Medicine, Cardiology, Fitness
& Exercise, Geriatrics, Health & Medicine,

Neurology, Nutrition, Oncology, Sexual Health

Healthcare Leader
995458

Editorial: Bastion House, 140 London Wall, London EC2Y 5DN Tel: 44 02072 140500
Web site: http://healthcareleadernews.com/
Freq: Quarterly
Circ: 10500 Not Audited
MAGAZINE
Disability, Health & Medicine, Health Administration, Medicine, Nutrition

Healthcare Risk Management Review
997871

Editorial: Kingfisher House, 21-23 Elmfield Road, Grantham NG33 5NR
Freq: Monthly
Circ: 6000 Not Audited
MAGAZINE
News & Current Affairs

HealthGauge
988268

Tel: 44 01225 464179
Email: Info@healthgauge.com
Web site: www.healthgauge.com
Freq: Daily
Circ: 12444 Cision Digital Reach
Editor: Andrew Wildey
MAGAZINE (ONLINE)
Fitness & Exercise, Nutrition

HealthInvestor
981709

Editorial: Greener House, 66-68 Haymarket, London SW1Y 4RF Tel: 44 02071 042000
Email: editorial@healthinvestor.co.uk
Web site: www.healthinvestor.co.uk
Freq: Monthly
Circ: 7000 Not Audited
Editor: Ploy Radford
Profile: Magazine covering the commercial implications of recent developments in primary care, property, dentistry, pharmacy, foundation hospitals, PFI, mergers and acquisitions and private equity. Also includes company and fund profiles, European news and company results.
Ad Rate: Full Page Colour £1500.00
MAGAZINE
Dentistry, Health Administration, Healthcare Industry, Medicine, Ophthalmology & Optometry

HEALTHISTA.
987415

Editorial: 85 Frampton Street London, London NW8 8NQ Tel: 44 02085 030091
Email: editor@healthista.com
Web site: www.healthista.com
Freq: Daily
Circ: 148633 Cision Digital Reach
Profile: HEALTHISTA. is a website aimed at women and gives information and advice on the body, beauty, fertility, mind, nutrition, personal health, sex, sport, surgery and wellbeing. Regular features include the Glow Girl column which discusses being beautiful on the inside and out, and the 5-minute Therapist section which involves a reader in a therapy session with a psychotherapist.
MAGAZINE (ONLINE)
Fitness & Exercise, Health & Medicine, Nutrition, Women's Interests

Healthizmo
1052541

Editorial: Warnford Court 29, Throgmorton Street, London EC2N 2AT
Tel: 44 02079 479640
Email: news@healthizmo.com
Web site: www.healthizmo.com
Freq: Daily
Circ: 13879 Cision Digital Reach
Editor: Chloe Nichols
MAGAZINE (ONLINE)
Biotechnology, Fitness & Exercise, Health & Medicine, Health Administration, Nutrition

Healthmatters
984468

Web site: www.healthmatters.org.uk
Freq: Daily
Circ: 9216 Cision Digital Reach
MAGAZINE (ONLINE)
Health Administration, Healthcare Industry, Medicine, Nursing/Nurses

Healthoo.com
1062037

Tel: 44 86106 8012929
Web site: http://www.healthoo.com
Freq: Daily
Circ: 23050 Cision Digital Reach
MAGAZINE (ONLINE)
Health & Medicine

Healthoo.com - Pharmaceutical Ingredients Channel
1061119

Tel: 44 86106 8032463
Email: bianch@healthoo.com
Web site: http://www.healthoo.com/B3/
Circ: 12673 Cision Digital Reach
MAGAZINE (ONLINE)
Medicine, Pharmaceuticals

healthtalk.org
995746

Editorial: DIPEx, PO Box 428, Witney, Witney OX28 9EU Tel: 44 01865 280320
Email: info@healthtalkonline.org
Web site: www.healthtalk.org
Freq: Daily
Circ: 113098 Cision Digital Reach
MAGAZINE (ONLINE)
News & Current Affairs

Healthy
980994

Editorial: Garden Floor, 16 Connaught Place, London W2 2ES
Tel: 44 02073 060304
Email: healthy@riverltd.co.uk
Web site: www.healthy-magazine.co.uk
Freq: Bi-Monthly
Circ: 90055 Not Audited
Profile: Focuses on maintaining a healthy lifestyle including articles on vegetarianism, new products and information on alternative therapies and supplements. Aimed at men and women interested in health, fitness and natural lifestyle.
Ad Rate: Full Page Colour £6500.00
MAGAZINE
Fitness & Exercise, Health & Medicine, Nutrition, Women's Interests

Healthy Food Guide
985872

Editorial: Axe & Bottle Court, 3rd floor, 70 Newcomen Street, London SE1 1YT
Tel: 44 02078 034100
Email: info@healthyfood.co.uk
Web site: http://healthyfood.co.uk/
Freq: Monthly
Circ: 31055 Not Audited
Editor: Andrea Duvall
MAGAZINE
Cooking & Baking, Food, Grocery Stores, Organic Food, Restaurant Reviews, Vegetarianism & Veganism

Healthy For Men
983676

Editorial: Garden Floor, 16 Connaught Place, London W2 2ES
Tel: 44 02074 207000
Email: hfm@therivergroup.co.uk
Web site: http://www.healthyformen.com/
Freq: Bi-Monthly
Circ: 26196 Not Audited
Profile: Health and fitness magazine covering sports nutrition, celebrity sports interviews and work out plans. Each issue contains news and features and expert advice for a healthy lifestyle. First published in 1999, the publication has an average of 64 pages per issue. Aimed at those with a serious interest in fitness.
Ad Rate: Full Page Colour £3750.00
MAGAZINE
Health & Medicine, Men's Interests

Healthy Soul
985908

Tel: 44 01737 555322
Email: feedback@healthysoul.co.uk
Web site: www.healthysoul.co.uk
Freq: Daily
Circ: 9664 Cision Digital Reach
Profile: Website covering health and wellbeing. Healthy Soul UK discusses news and features covering personal health, wellbeing, nutrition and medicine.
MAGAZINE (ONLINE)
Alternative Medicine, Nutrition

Hearing Times
985040

Editorial: Unit 212, Lansbury Business Estate, 102 Lower Guildford Road, Woking, London GU21 2EP Tel: 44 08452 930688
Email: editorial@hearingtimes.co.uk
Web site: www.hearingtimes.co.uk
Freq: Quarterly
Circ: 16000 Not Audited
Editor: Helen Dewey
MAGAZINE
Disability, Medicine

Hearst Empowering Women
996119

Tel: 44 02074 395000
Web site: http://empowering.hearst.co.uk/
Freq: Daily
Circ: 76544 Cision Digital Reach
MAGAZINE (ONLINE)
Social Issues

heart matters
986015

Editorial: BHF, Greater London House, 180 Hampstead Road, London NW1 7AW
Tel: 44 02075 540000
Email: hmeditor@bhf.org.uk
Web site: www.bhf.org.uk/heartmattersmag
Freq: Bi-Monthly
Circ: 450000 Not Audited
Editor: Sarah Brealey
Profile: British Heart Foundation magazine covering all issues surrounding heart care including the latest treatment and medication, insurance and patient services as well as healthy living tips, recipes and readers offers. Aimed at those with heart conditions and their carers. Previous title: Heart Health
MAGAZINE
Cardiology, Patient Support

Heart Streatham Magazine
998028

Editorial: 31 Hambro Rd, London SW16 6JD
Tel: 44 02081 334629
Email: info@heartstreatham.co.uk
Web site: http://www.heartstreatham.co.uk/
Freq: Monthly
Circ: 17000 Not Audited
MAGAZINE
Regional General Interest

heat
982361

Editorial: 24-28 Oval Road, Camden, London NW1 7DT Tel: 44 02072 418000
Email: heat@bauermedia.co.uk
Web site: http://lifestyle.one/heat/
Freq: Weekly
Circ: 120175 Not Audited
Profile: Magazine covering celebrities, lifestyle, gossip and entertainment. It features movie and music reviews, TV listings and major celebrity interviews. Aimed at women aged between 18 and 40.
Ad Rate: Full Page Colour £22822.00
MAGAZINE
Celebrities, Women's Interests

Heaver
995733

Editorial: 255 Balham High Road, Heaver Estate, London SW17 7BE
Tel: 44 02087 677079
Email: hello@pagepop.co.uk
Web site: www.heavermagazine.co.uk
Freq: No Frequency Established Not Audited
MAGAZINE
Do-It-Yourself (DIY), Property Management & Maintenance, Regional General Interest

Heavy Horse World
982237

Editorial: Linford Cottage, Church Lane, Cocking, Midhurst, Midhurst GU29 0HW
Tel: 44 01730 812419
Email: editor@heavyhorseworld.co.uk
Web site: www.heavyhorseworld.co.uk
Freq: Quarterly
Circ: 3500 Not Audited
Editor: Diana Zeuner
Profile: Magazine devoted to news, features and events involving heavy horse breeds.
Ad Rate: Full Page Mono £230.00

Ad Rate: Full Page Colour £300.00
MAGAZINE
Equestrian Sports

hecklerspray
985938

Editorial: 4th Floor, The Corner, 91-93 Farringdon Road, London EC1M 3LN
Email: hecklerspray@gmail.com
Web site: www.hecklerspray.com
Freq: Daily
Circ: 1531541 Cision Digital Reach
MAGAZINE (ONLINE)
News & Current Affairs

heDD
999375

Editorial: Unit 17 Quayside House, 302 Kensal Road, London W10 5BF
Tel: 44 07949 901691
Email: info@heddmagazine.co
Web site: www.heddmagazine.co/
Freq: Daily
Circ: 11259 Cision Digital Reach
Editor: Jonathan Devo
MAGAZINE (ONLINE)
Automotive, Computer & Video Games, Dance Music, Electronics, Entertainment, Fashion, Fitness & Exercise, Health & Medicine, Local Entertainment Guides, Men's Interests

Hedge
984548

Editorial: 4 Tun Yard, Peardon Street, London SW8 3HT Tel: 44 02078 199999
Email: hedge.editorial@hedgemagazine.co.uk
Web site: https://www.hedgemagazine.co.uk/
Freq: Quarterly
Circ: 6800 Not Audited
MAGAZINE
Hedge Funds, Luxury Goods

HedgeThink
1095580

Email: info@hedgethink.com
Web site: hedgethink.com
Freq: Daily
Circ: 49200 Cision Digital Reach
Editor: Fidan Aliyeva
MAGAZINE (ONLINE)
Banking, Bonds, Commodities, Corporate Finance, Corporate Management, Credit Markets, Derivatives, Economics, Emerging Markets, Equities

Hellion Magazine
005349

Email: editor@hellionmag.com
Web site: http://www.hellionmag.com/
Freq: Daily
Circ: 12091 Cision Digital Reach
MAGAZINE (ONLINE)
Dance Music, Fashion, Jazz & Blues, Rap & Hip Hop, Theater & Performing Arts, Visual Arts

HELLO!
982432

Editorial: Wellington House, 69-71 Upper Ground, London SE1 9PQ
Tel: 44 02076 678700
Web site: www.hellomagazine.com
Freq: Weekly
Circ: 230940 Not Audited
Profile: Magazine featuring celebrity news and gossip. Each issue contains interviews, practical features and topical photo-coverage of high society events such as cocktail parties, receptions, gallery openings and charity dinners. The magazine also features a weekly round-up of news and celebrities from the entertainment industry, advice for a healthy lifestyle, recipes and nutritional guidance. The magazine includes a 32 page fashion and beauty section, which contains haute couture fashion, shopping pages, accessories and new ranges. The magazine was first published in 1988. Aimed at ABC1 women aged 25 to 44 years old.
Ad Rate: Full Page Colour £18664.00
MAGAZINE
Celebrities, Fashion, Women's Interests

HELLO! Fashion Monthly
988496

Editorial: Wellington House, 69-71 Upper Ground, London SE1 9PQ
Tel: 44 02078 860936

Consumer Magazines

Web site: http://fashion.hellomagazine.com/
Freq: Monthly
Circ: 74543 Not Audited
MAGAZINE
Fashion

Hemel Hempstead Living 996272
Editorial: 27 The Old Silk Mill, Tring, Tring
HP23 5EF **Tel:** 44 01442 824300
Email: info@livingmags.info
Web site: www.livingmags.info
Freq: Quarterly
Circ: 21665 Not Audited
MAGAZINE
Regional

Henley Life 986924
Editorial: Caxton House, 1 Station Road,
Henley-on-Thames, Henley-on-Thames RG9
1AD **Tel:** 44 01491 419449
Web site: www.henleylife.co.uk
Freq: Monthly
Circ: 11000 Not Audited
Editor: Simon Bradshaw
Profile: Magazine featuring local people and
their businesses, food and drink, leisure,
restaurants, competitions and special offers.
MAGAZINE
Regional General Interest

The Herald (Southampton)
982496
Editorial: 6 High Street, Hythe, Hythe SO45
6AH **Tel:** 44 02380 845700
Email: editor@herald-publishing.co.uk
Web site: http://www.herald-publishing.co.uk
Freq: Monthly
Circ: 10500 Not Audited
Editor: Louise Martin
MAGAZINE
Regional General Interest

herbs 985782
Editorial: PO Box 196, Liverpool L18 1XE
Email: info@herbsociety.org.uk
Web site: www.herbsociety.org.uk
Freq: Quarterly
Circ: 1300 Not Audited
Editor: Barbara Segall
Profile: Journal of The Herb Society. Covers
all aspects of the cultivation and uses of
herbs.
Ad Rate: Full Page Mono £110.00
Ad Rate: Full Page Colour £220.00
MAGAZINE
Gardening

Here Is The City 983951
Editorial: 28 Ormiston Grove, London W12
0JT **Tel:** 44 02084 830090
Email: mail@hereisthecity.com
Web site: www.hitc.com
Freq: Daily
Circ: 9825408 Cision Digital Reach
MAGAZINE (ONLINE)
Banking, Business, Computer & Video
Games, Cricket, Golf, Mobile Electronics,
Rugby, Small and Medium Business,
Soccer

Herefordshire Society 983399
Editorial: Holmer Road, Hereford HR4 9UJ
Tel: 44 01432 274413
Email: hsociety@midlands.newsquest.co.uk
Web site: www.thisishereford.co.uk
Freq: Quarterly
Circ: 10000 Not Audited
Profile: Lifestyle magazine covering profiles
of county personalities, events, fashion,
beauty, society pages and food all with a
Hereford slant.
Ad Rate: Full Page Mono £515.00
Ad Rate: Full Page Colour £515.00
MAGAZINE
Regional General Interest

HerFamily.ie 1053636
Editorial: Her.ie, The Distillery Building,
Fumbally Court, Fumbally Lane, Dublin 8
Tel: 44 01669 6900
Email: hello@herfamily.ie
Web site: http://www.herfamily.ie/

Freq: Daily
Circ: 61255 Cision Digital Reach
Editor: Sive O'Brien
MAGAZINE (ONLINE)
Family & Parenting

Heritage Railway 982040
Editorial: Media Centre, Morton Way,
Horncastle, Horncastle LN9 6JR
Tel: 44 01507 529529
Email: info@heritagerailway.co.uk
Web site: www.heritagerailway.co.uk
Freq: Monthly
Circ: 29000 Not Audited
Editor: Robin Jones
Profile: Magazine dedicated to preserving
heritage railways including steam, diesel and
electric locomotive engines. Aimed at railway
enthusiasts.
Ad Rate: Full Page Colour £710.00
MAGAZINE
Railroad

HERO 986673
Editorial: Third Floor, 8 Charterhouse
Buildings, London EC1M 7AN
Email: hero@hero-magazine.com
Web site: www.hero-magazine.com
Freq: Semi-Annual
Circ: 84000 Not Audited
Profile: Magazine covering men's fashion.
Contains fashion news, stories and
interviews.
MAGAZINE
Art, Dance Music, Fashion, Movies &
Video, Pop Music, Rap & Hip Hop, Rock
Music

Hero & Leander 1073280
Web site: www.hero-and-leander.com
Freq: Daily
Circ: 14507 Cision Digital Reach
MAGAZINE (ONLINE)
Alcohol & Spirits, Bars, Clubs & Pubs,
Beer, Beverages, Cooking & Baking,
Men's Interests, Restaurant Reviews,
Travel, Wine/Winemaking, Women's
Interests

HEROINE 1052667
Editorial: Third Floor, 8 Charterhouse
Buildings, London EC1M 7AN
Email: hero@hero-magazine.com
Web site: http://theheroinemagazine.com/
Freq: Semi-Annual
Circ: 123000 Not Audited
MAGAZINE
Antiques/Collectibles, Art, Arts, Bars,
Clubs & Pubs, Comedy, Dance Music,
Entertainment, Fashion, Literature, Local
Entertainment Guides

Hertfordshire County Life
Magazine 1053352
Tel: 44 01462 819496
Email: editor@countylifemagazines.co.uk
Web site: www.countylifemagazines.co.uk
Freq: Quarterly
Circ: 9000 Not Audited
MAGAZINE
Regional General Interest

Hertfordshire Focus 998358
Editorial: Suite 6B(i), Britannia House,
Leagrave Road, Luton LU3 1RJ
Tel: 44 01582 488385
Email: info@mediachameleon.co.uk
Web site: www.hertfordshire-focus.co.uk
Freq: Annual
Circ: 30000 Not Audited
MAGAZINE
Regional General Interest

Hertfordshire Life 982498
Editorial: Bank House, Primett Road,
Stevenage SG1 3EE **Tel:** 44 07918 721644
Email: news@hertfordshirelife.co.uk
Web site: www.hertfordshirelife.co.uk
Freq: Monthly
Circ: 10000 Not Audited
Editor: Richard Young
Profile: County magazine containing
features on interiors, events, people, places,

sights and sounds, restaurants, food and
wine. Also includes homes and gardens,
antiques, competitions and a county events
guide.
Ad Rate: Full Page Colour £1600.00
MAGAZINE
Regional General Interest

HEST ONLINE hestonline.dk
1061173
Email: lisberg@dlmedier.dk
Web site: http://www.hest-online.dk Not
Audited
MAGAZINE
Equestrian Sports, Nature & Wildlife

Heswall Magazine 998983
Editorial: Whitfield Buildings, 188-200
Pensby Road, Heswall CH60 7RJ
Tel: 44 07796 945745
Email: editor@heswallmagazine.co.uk
Web site: www.heswallmagazine.co.uk
Freq: Bi-Monthly
Circ: 16000 Not Audited
Editor: John Bion
MAGAZINE
Regional General Interest

HEXUS.net 984552
Editorial: 5 Elstree Way, London WD6 1SF
Email: pr@hexus.net
Web site: www.hexus.net
Freq: Daily
Circ: 1367909 Cision Digital Reach
Editor: Tarinder Sandhu
MAGAZINE (ONLINE)
Audio Video Trade, Auto Aftermarket,
Cameras, Computers, Consumer
Electronics, Data Management,
Electronics, Government Technology,
Industry, Internet

Hey Duggee Magazine 1053652
Editorial: Vineyard House, 44 Brook Green,
Hammersmith, London W6 7BT
Tel: 44 02071 505020
Email: heyduggeemagazine@immediate.co.uk
Freq: Monthly
Circ: 20675 Not Audited
Editor: Andrea Turton
MAGAZINE
Preschool

Hg2: A Hedonist's Guide To...
1006437
Editorial: 6th Floor, Newcombe House, 45
Notting Hill Gate, London SW3 4BA
Email: news@hg2.com
Web site: www.hg2.com
Freq: Daily
Circ: 25790 Cision Digital Reach
Editor: Katie Manning
MAGAZINE (ONLINE)
Bars, Clubs & Pubs, History, Restaurant
Reviews, Travel

Hidden Wires 984613
Editorial: Blair House, High Street,
Tonbridge, Tonbridge TN9 1BQ
Tel: 44 01732 359990
Email: info@hiddenwires.co.uk
Web site: www.hiddenwires.co.uk
Freq: Daily
Circ: 18023 Cision Digital Reach
MAGAZINE (ONLINE)
Audio Video Trade, Cameras, Consumer
Electronics, Electronics, Mobile
Electronics, Movies & Video

Hide 'n' Seek Wordsearch
998702
Editorial: Academic House, 24-28 Oval
Road, London NW1 7DT
Tel: 44 02072 418000
Email: hide.nseek@bauer.co.uk
Web site: http://www.puzzlemagazines.co.uk/hide-n-seek
Freq: Monthly
Circ: 48000 Not Audited
Editor: Christine Scott
MAGAZINE
Games, Competitions & Events

Hi-Fi Choice 981740
Editorial: My Time Media, Enterprise House,
Enterprise Way, Edenbridge TN8 6HF
Tel: 44 01689 869909
Web site: www.hifichoice.co.uk
Freq: Monthly
Circ: 6532 Not Audited
Editor: Lee Dunkley
Profile: Magazine containing information on
buying a hi-fi. Includes product tests, news
and general articles. Covers products from
vinyl and valves, to multi-channel digital
audio and high-fidelity video. The outlet
offers RSS feed: http://www.hifichoice.co.uk/rss/hifichoice.Aimed at hi-fi enthusiasts
and prospective purchasers of home audio
equipment. Regular features: Buyer's guide;
Interviews; Letters; Music Reviews; News
News section.; Product Reviews Tests on
equipment.; Reviews Reviews section.
Ad Rate: Full Page Colour £1600.00
MAGAZINE
Audio Video Trade

Hi-Fi News & Record Review
996023
Editorial: Hadlow House, 9 High Street,
Green Street Green, London BR6 6BG
Tel: 44 01689 869909
Web site: www.hifinews.co.uk
Freq: Monthly
Circ: 10500 Not Audited
MAGAZINE
Audio Video Trade

Hi-Fi World 981741
Editorial: Studio 204, Buspace Studio,
Conlan Street, Notting Hill, London W10 5AP
Tel: 44 08446 933033
Email: editorial@hi-fiworld.co.uk
Web site: www.hi-fiworld.co.uk
Freq: Monthly
Circ: 13500 Not Audited
Profile: Magazine covering hi-fi, audio visual
equipment, computers and music, both
classical and popular. Each issue contains
articles on the latest audio news and
equipment whilst paying our respect to the
classics of yesteryear.
Ad Rate: Full Page Colour £1800.00
MAGAZINE
Audio Video Trade

Hi-Fi+ 981742
Editorial: Unit 3, Sandleheath Industrial
Estate, Sandleheath, Fordingbridge SP6 1PA
Tel: 44 01425 655255
Email: editor@hifiplus.com
Web site: www.hifiplus.com
Freq: Monthly
Circ: 14000 Not Audited
Editor: Alan Sircom
MAGAZINE
Audio Video Trade

High Content 1063451
Email: mj@high-content.com
Web site: http://high-content.com/
Freq: Daily
Circ: 10308 Cision Digital Reach
Editor: Mary-Jane Gotidoc
MAGAZINE (ONLINE)
Cosmetics, Fashion, Women's Interests

High Flyer 997103
Editorial: 200 Renfield Street, Glasgow G2
3QB **Tel:** 44 01417 731801
Freq: 3 Times/Year
Circ: 80000 Not Audited
Editor: Karen Peattie
MAGAZINE
Airline Inflight

High Life 979928
Editorial: 85 Strand, London WC2R 0DW
Tel: 44 02075 508000
Email: highlife@cedarcom.co.uk
Web site: http://highlife.ba.com
Freq: Monthly
Circ: 121664 Not Audited
Editor: Kerry Smith
Profile: In flight magazine of British Airways
featuring travel and lifestyle including
celebrity profiles, fashion, beauty features as

well as hotels, spas, destinations and shopping. Aimed at passengers on British Airways scheduled flights.
Ad Rate: Full Page Colour £13670.00
MAGAZINE
Airline Inflight

High50
987109
Editorial: Circus House, 2nd Floor, 21 Great Titchfield Street, London W1W 8BA
Tel: 44 02072 997450
Email: support@high50.com
Web site: www.high50.com
Freq: Daily
Circ: 117684 Cision Digital Reach
Profile: Website covering lifestyle for over-fifties. The High 50 website shares the latest news for the over fifties discussing anything from shopping and money to food and health.
MAGAZINE (ONLINE)
Lifestyle, Men's Interests, Regional General Interest, Women's Interests

Highland Life
985649
Editorial: New Century House, Stadium Road, Inverness IV1 1FG
Tel: 44 01463 732222
Email: editor@highland-life.co.uk
Web site: http://www.highland-life.co.uk
Freq: Monthly
Circ: 50000 Not Audited
MAGAZINE
Beauty & Grooming, Cooking & Baking, Cosmetics, Food, Grocery Stores, Hair, Organic Food, Regional General Interest, Restaurant Reviews, Vegetarianism & Veganism

Highways
981106
Editorial: 6 Wealden Place, Bradbourne Vale Road, Sevenoaks, Sevenoaks TN13 3QQ
Tel: 44 01732 459683
Email: info@aladltd.co.uk
Web site: www.highways-mag.co.uk
Freq: Monthly
Circ: 7005 Not Audited
Profile: Magazine focusing on the road building, maintenance, traffic control, street management and utility works industries. Aimed at county, borough and district councils, civil engineering and highways contractors, consulting engineers and personnel within government departments.
Ad Rate: Full Page Mono £1417.00
Ad Rate: Full Page Colour £2110.00
MAGAZINE
Automotive, Engineering, Shipping & Warehousing

Hillingdon People
984052
Editorial: 3E/07 Civic Centre, High Street, Uxbridge, London UB8 1UW
Tel: 44 01895 250828
Email: hillingdonpeople@hillingdon.gov.uk
Web site: http://www.hillingdon.gov.uk/hillingdonpeople
Freq: Bi-Monthly
Circ: 250000 Not Audited
Editor: Emma Gilbertson
Profile: Council magazine covering news and information on council services, events and local issues.
Ad Rate: Full Page Colour £1400.00
MAGAZINE
Regional General Interest

Hip & Healthy
986303
Editorial: Goodwin House, 5 Union Court, Richmond, London TW9 1AA
Email: info@hipandhealthy.com
Web site: http://hipandhealthy.com/
Freq: Daily
Circ: 38011 Cision Digital Reach
Profile: Website covering healthy lifestyle. The Hip and Healthy website discusses the latest news on health, fitness, well being, recipes, beauty, style and travel with a healthy twist.
MAGAZINE (ONLINE)
Beauty & Grooming, Cosmetics, Fitness & Exercise, Hair, Health & Medicine, Nutrition, Travel

HIP Magazine
984018
Editorial: Vienna House, International Square, Birmingham International Park, Solihull B37 7GN **Tel:** 44 08707 743049
Email: editor@sng-publishing.co.uk
Web site: www.hip-magazine.co.uk
Freq: Quarterly
Circ: 12500 Not Audited
Editor: Becky Martin
MAGAZINE
News & Current Affairs

HIPE Magazine
1053086
Tel: 44 07837 324139
Email: hipemagazine@yahoo.co.uk
Web site: www.hipemagazine.co.uk
Freq: Daily
Circ: 819 Cision Digital Reach
MAGAZINE (ONLINE)
Art, Entertainment, Fashion, Local Entertainment Guides, Travel, Visual Arts

His & Hers Magazine
986998
Editorial: Second Floor, Liverpool
Web site: http://www.hisandhersmag.co.uk/
Freq: Monthly
Circ: 10000 Not Audited
Profile: A glossy magazine for style-conscious men and women. Covers the best the North West has to offer in terms of style, fashion, entertainment, fine dining and travel.
Ad Rate: Full Page Colour £500.00
MAGAZINE
Fashion, Men's Interests, Women's Interests

The Historian
988365
Editorial: 59a Kennington Park Road, London SE11 4JH **Tel:** 44 03001 000223
Email: enquiries@history.org.uk
Web site: www.history.org.uk/publications/categories/the-historian
Freq: Quarterly
Circ: 3000 Not Audited
MAGAZINE
History

Historic Gardens Review
986922
Editorial: 34 River Court, Upper Ground, London SE1 9PE **Tel:** 44 02076 339165
Email: office@historicgardens.org
Web site: http://www.historicgardens.org
Freq: Semi-Annual Not Audited
Editor: Gillian Mawrey
Profile: Magazine of the Historic Gardens Foundation containing articles on historic gardens worldwide and their conservation. The Review aims to raise the profile of parks and gardens everywhere. Aimed at amateurs and professionals concerned with the preservation, restoration and management of historic gardens.
MAGAZINE
History

Historic House
982126
Editorial: The Historic Houses Association, Publishing Department, 2 Chester Street, London SW1X 7BB **Tel:** 44 02072 595688
Email: info@hha.org.uk
Web site: www.hha.org.uk
Freq: Quarterly
Circ: 20000 Not Audited
Profile: Journal of the Historic Houses Association, covering country houses, gardens and parks, conservation, tourism, technical problems, taxation and fine arts.
Ad Rate: Full Page Mono £624.00
Ad Rate: Full Page Colour £753.00
MAGAZINE
Energy & Environment

Historic Racing Technology
988067
Editorial: 841 High Road, Finchley, London N12 8PT **Tel:** 44 02084 462100
Email: info@kimberleymediagroup.com
Web site: http://www.historicracingtechnology.com
Freq: Quarterly
Circ: 6000 Not Audited
Editor: William Kimberley

Profile: Magazine dedicated to vintage cars, motorsports and the engineering and technology of historic motorsport.
MAGAZINE
Antique & Collectible Cars

Historic Scotland
982557
Editorial: Suite 2.3, Red Tree Business Suites, 33 Dalmarnock Road, Glasgow G40 4LA **Tel:** 44 01413 750504
Web site: http://www.historic-scotland.gov.uk
Freq: Quarterly
Circ: 60000 Not Audited
Editor: Kathleen Morgan
MAGAZINE
History

Historical Honey
996665
Email: annabelle@historicalhoney.com
Web site: www.historicalhoney.com
Freq: Daily
Circ: 12284 Cision Digital Reach
MAGAZINE (ONLINE)
History

History of Photography Journal
986399
Editorial: Mortimer House, 37-41 Mortimer Street, London W1T 3JH
Web site: www.tandf.co.uk/journals/tf/03087298.html
Freq: Quarterly Not Audited
Editor: Luke Gartlan
MAGAZINE
News & Current Affairs

History of Royal Women
1097895
Web site: www.historyofroyalwomen.com
Freq: Daily
Circ: 11483 Cision Digital Reach
Editor: Moniek Bloks
MAGAZINE (ONLINE)
History, Royalty

History of Royals
1073281
Editorial: Richmond House, 33 Richmond Hill, Bournemouth BH2 6EQ
Tel: 44 01202 586200
Email: historyofroyals@futurenet.com
Web site: www.historyanswers.co.uk
Freq: Monthly
Circ: 50447 Not Audited
MAGAZINE
History

History of War
987805
Editorial: Richmond House, 33 Richmond Hill, Bournemouth, Bournemouth BH2 6EZ
Tel: 44 01202 586261
Web site: www.historyanswers.co.uk/category/history-of-war
Freq: Monthly
Circ: 35000 Not Audited
Editor: Tim Williamson
MAGAZINE
History

History Revealed
987786
Editorial: Tower House, Fairfax Street, Bristol BS1 3BN **Tel:** 44 01179 279009
Email: editor@historyrevealed.com
Web site: www.historyrevealed.com
Freq: Monthly Not Audited
Editor: Paul McGuinness
Profile: Publication that looks at major historical events through the ages.
MAGAZINE
History

History Scotland
987013
Editorial: 5th Floor, 31-32 Park Row, Leeds LS1 5JD **Tel:** 44 01132 002929
Email: editorial@historyscotland.com
Web site: www.celebrate-scotland.co.uk/store/subscriptions/history-scotland
Freq: Bi-Monthly
Circ: 7000 Not Audited
Editor: Alasdair Ross
Profile: Magazine covering archaeology and history of Scotland and the Scots. Aimed at

those interested in Scotland and Scottish history.
Ad Rate: Full Page Mono £800.00
Ad Rate: Full Page Colour £1000.00
MAGAZINE
History, Scotland

History Today
982129
Editorial: 2nd Floor, 9 Staple Inn, London WC1V 7QH **Tel:** 44 02032 197810
Email: admin@historytoday.com
Web site: www.historytoday.com
Freq: Monthly
Circ: 17522 Not Audited
Editor: Paul Lay
Profile: Magazine focusing on current issues from a historical perspective. Includes news items of relevance to historical research. Aimed at those who have a specialist or general interest in history, heritage and current affairs.This magazine contains the following regular sections: History NewsPoint of Departure ReviewsThis Month In History
Ad Rate: Full Page Colour £1850.00
MAGAZINE
History

Hit the Floor
988078
Editorial: 12 Willicombe Road, Paignton, Paignton TQ3 3RU **Tel:** 44 07403 121919
Email: info@hitthefloor.com
Web site: www.hitthefloor.com
Freq: Daily
Circ: 42494 Cision Digital Reach
MAGAZINE (ONLINE)
Broadcasting, Dance Music, Fashion, Men's Interests, Movies & Video, Pop Music, Rap & Hip Hop, Rock Music, Women's Interests

hitched.co.uk
985802
Editorial: Hitched Limited, Unit 7 Stanhope Gate, Stanhope Road, Camberley GU15 3DW **Tel:** 44 08448 800011
Web site: www.hitched.co.uk
Freq: Daily
Circ: 1003135 Cision Digital Reach
Profile: Website covering weddings. The Hitched.co.uk website shares the latest news and information on weddings including venues, fashion, gifts, honeymoons and stag and hen nights.
MAGAZINE (ONLINE)
Relationships, Weddings

HM
1054543
Tel: 44 01512 395050
Email: info@masonmedia.co.uk
Freq: 3 Times/Year
Editor: Lucy Mason
MAGAZINE
Alcohol & Spirits, Automotive, Bars, Clubs & Pubs, Beer, Beverages, Comedy, Cooking & Baking, Driving, Entertainment, Fashion

HMV.com
987656
Editorial: Mermaid House, Puddle Dock, Blackfriars, London EC4V 3DB
Tel: 44 02076 366324
Web site: www.hmv.com
Freq: Daily
Circ: 463812 Cision Digital Reach
MAGAZINE (ONLINE)
Classical/Choral/Band Music, Computer & Video Games, Country, Folk, Bluegrass, Dance Music, Jazz & Blues, Movies & Video, Music, Pop Music, R&B, Urban, World, Rap & Hip Hop

The Holborn
988789
Web site: theholbornmag.com
Freq: Quarterly Not Audited
Profile: Magazine covering covering food, drink, crafts and fashion.
MAGAZINE
Alcohol & Spirits, Antiques/Collectibles, Art, Bars, Clubs & Pubs, Beer, Beverages, Cooking & Baking, Fashion, Literature, Luxury Goods

HoldtheFrontPage.co.uk
985685
Editorial: Laurie House, Colyear Street, Derby DE1 1JY **Tel:** 44 01332 895972

Email: editor@htfp.co.uk
Web site: www.holdthefrontpage.co.uk
Freq: Daily
Circ: 163643 Cision Digital Reach
Profile: Website containing news and job adverts for and about people in the regional newspaper industry. Aimed at regional UK print and online journalists, newspaper photographers, sub-editors and editors, freelance writers and students interested in journalism as a career.Paul Linford is the Publisher to whom press releases should be addressed.
MAGAZINE (ONLINE)
Company News & Appointments, Publishing

hole & corner   987663
Email: info@holeandcornermagazine.com
Web site: holeandcornermagazine.com/
Freq: Semi-Annual Not Audited
MAGAZINE
Regional General Interest

Holiday Living   1072718
Tel: 44 01959 541444
Web site: http://shop.kelsey.co.uk/subscription/HLI
Freq: Bi-Monthly
Circ: 25000 Not Audited
Editor: Bella Brodie
MAGAZINE
Camping and RV Travel

Holiday Magazine   996091
Tel: 44 02089 930475
Email: mike.pickup@live.co.uk
Web site: holidaymag.co.uk
Freq: Daily
Circ: 12196 Cision Digital Reach
MAGAZINE (ONLINE)
Travel

Holiday Park Scene   1064096
Editorial: Waterland House, The Warren, Witchford, Ely CB6 2HN
Tel: 44 01353 666663
Email: info@holidayparkscene.com
Web site: www.holidayparkscene.com
Freq: Bi-Monthly
Circ: 5000 Not Audited
MAGAZINE
Hotels/Motels

Holistic Therapist Magazine
                                      988874
Editorial: Holistic Therapist magazine, 30 Kent Avenue, Sittingbourne, Rochester ME101HA **Tel:** 44 01795 479957
Web site: http://www.holistictherapistmagazine.com/
Freq: Quarterly
Circ: 15000 Not Audited
Profile: Publication that covers business and industry features of holistic health professionals.
Ad Rate: Full Page Colour £2200.00
MAGAZINE
Alternative Medicine

The Hollywood News   986559
Web site: www.thehollywoodnews.com
Freq: Daily
Circ: 149874 Cision Digital Reach
Profile: Website covering showbiz. The Hollywood News websites shares the latest news on film reviews, celebrities and Hollywood.
MAGAZINE (ONLINE)
Entertainment, Movies & Video

Holyrood   982130
Tel: 44 01312 851605
Email: editor@holyrood.com
Web site: www.holyrood.com
Freq: Bi-Weekly
Circ: 5000 Not Audited
MAGAZINE
Politics, Scotland

Home & Garden   997671
Editorial: Britannia House, Leagrave Road, Luton, Luton LU3 1RJ **Tel:** 44 01582 488385

Email: info@mediachameleon.co.uk
Web site: www.homeandgardenwebsite.co.uk
Freq: Daily
Circ: 8408 Cision Digital Reach
MAGAZINE (ONLINE)
Do-It-Yourself (DIY), Gardening, Property Management & Maintenance

Home Childcarer   988850
Editorial: Alhambra House, 9 St Michaels Road, Croydon, London CR9 3DD
Tel: 44 08452 570900
Web site: www.homechildcarer.co.uk
Freq: Bi-Monthly Not Audited
Editor: Tommy Leighton
MAGAZINE
Family & Parenting

Home Cinema Choice   981746
Editorial: AVTech Media, Suite 25, Eden House, Enterprise Way, Edenbridge TN8 6HF **Tel:** 44 01689 869899
Email: letters@homecinemachoice.com
Web site: www.homecinemachoice.com
Freq: Monthly
Circ: 10867 Not Audited
Editor: Mark Craven
Profile: Magazine focusing on home cinema and home entertainment equipment. Covers large screen televisions, amplifiers, speakers, projectors, plus video and audio-related gadgetry. Includes reviews on flatscreen TVs and Blu-ray players, surround sound systems and PVRs . Aimed at those interested in home cinema technology and home entertainment technology.
Ad Rate: Full Page Colour £2380.00
MAGAZINE
Movies & Video

Home Farmer   984800
Editorial: PO Box 536, Preston PR2 9ZY
Tel: 44 01772 633444
Web site: www.homefarmer.co.uk
Freq: Monthly
Circ: 10000 Not Audited
Editor: Paul Melnyczuk
Profile: Magazine covering all aspects of self sufficiency, small holdings, food production, renewable energy, recycling, composting and the environment. Aimed at those interested in the good life whether in the country or in towns.
Ad Rate: Full Page Colour £550.00
MAGAZINE
Gardening, Organic Food

Home House   994982
Editorial: 790 Fulham Road, London SW6 5SL **Tel:** 44 02076 702000
Email: info@epicureanlife.co.uk
Web site: https://homehouse.co.uk/homehouselondon/
Freq: Semi-Annual
Circ: 100000 Not Audited
Editor: Christina Raptis
MAGAZINE
Antique & Collectible Cars, Automotive, Cooking & Baking, Driving, Luxury Goods, Men's Interests, Off-road & 4-Wheel Drive Vehicles, Restaurant Reviews, Travel, Women's Interests

Home Magazine   997031
Editorial: 5 Coningsby Close, Maidenhead, Berkshire, Maidenhead SL6 3YU
Tel: 44 07834 233346
Email: info@lifestyle-magazines.co.uk
Web site: www.homemag.co.uk
Freq: Quarterly
Circ: 16000 Not Audited
Editor: Caroline Seekings
MAGAZINE
Celebrities, Property Management & Maintenance, Regional General Interest

Home UK Magazine   997583
Email: editor@homeukmagazine.co.uk
Web site: www.homeukmagazine.co.uk
Freq: Bi-Monthly
Circ: 521 Cision Digital Reach

Editor: Marie Carter
MAGAZINE (ONLINE)
Do-It-Yourself (DIY)

Homebuilding & Renovating
                                      980850
Editorial: 2 Sugar Brook Court, Aston Road, Bromsgrove B60 3EX **Tel:** 44 01527 834400
Email: homebuilding@centaurmedia.com
Web site: www.homebuilding.co.uk
Freq: Monthly
Circ: 25390 Not Audited
Editor: Claire Lloyd
Profile: Magazine that covers advice and features on building, renovating, converting and extensions. Aimed at active self-builders, architects, designers and home owners.
Ad Rate: Full Page Colour £2277.00
MAGAZINE
Building & Construction, Do-It-Yourself (DIY), Interior Design

Home-Designer & Architect Magazine   997719
Editorial: Suite 1 and 2, Spratling Court Offices, Spratling Street, Manston, Manston CT12 5AN **Tel:** 44 01843 580862
Web site: www.homedesignerandarchitect.co.uk
Freq: Monthly
Circ: 40000 Not Audited
Editor: Jenna Burridge
MAGAZINE
Architecture & Design, Building & Construction, Do-It-Yourself (DIY), Interior Design

homefocus   984752
Editorial: Kent House, Romney Place, Maidstone ME15 6LH **Tel:** 44 01622 772407
Web site: www.homefocusmagazine.co.uk
Freq: Bi-Monthly
Circ: 50000 Not Audited
Editor: Alex Randell
Profile: Homefocus is a free magazine dedicated to helping first time buyers get on the housing ladder through affordable home ownership schemes. Homefocus magazine is available from housing associations and other housing providers, as well as in local supermarkets.
Ad Rate: Full Page Colour £3250.00
MAGAZINE
Do-It-Yourself (DIY), Gardening, Property Management & Maintenance

Homeopathy   985447
Editorial: The Boulevard, Langford Lane, Kidlington, Oxford OX5 1GB
Tel: 44 01865 843672
Email: journal@trusthomeopathy.org
Web site: www.elsevier.com/wps/find/journaldescription.cws_home/623042/description
Freq: Quarterly Not Audited
Editor: Peter Fisher
Profile: International journal dedicated to improving the understanding of homeopathy and clinical practice of homeopathy. Includes peer-reviewed articles on clinical and basic research and evidence based practice homeopathy. Also covers literature, meetings, debate and reviews. Aimed at health professionals practicing homeopathy and at doctors, veterinarians, dentists, pharmacists and scientists using traditional medicine.Previous title: British Homeopathic Journal
Ad Rate: Full Page Mono £579.00
Ad Rate: Full Page Colour £1053.00
MAGAZINE
Alternative Medicine

Homeport   985029
Editorial: Building 25, HMS Excellent, Whale Island, Portsmouth PO2 8ER
Tel: 44 02392 654374
Email: editor@nff.org.uk
Web site: www.nff.org.uk
Freq: Quarterly
Circ: 32000 Not Audited

Editor: Sarah Woods
MAGAZINE
Armed Forces, Defense & National Security

Homes & Antiques   981861
Editorial: 9th Floor, Tower House, Fairfax Street, Bristol BS1 3BN
Tel: 44 01173 147444
Email: homesandantiques@immediate.co.uk
Web site: www.homesandantiques.com
Freq: Monthly
Circ: 46463 Not Audited
Editor: Samantha Scott-Jeffries
Profile: Magazine combining a blend of home, antiques and heritage related features. It includes coverage of antiques and collectables, expert opinion by the Roadshow specialists and features inspiring real interiors, and style and decorating ideas. Aimed at antiques enthusiasts.
Ad Rate: Full Page Colour £6870.00
MAGAZINE
Antiques/Collectibles, Do-It-Yourself (DIY)

Homes & Gardens   981842
Editorial: 161 Marsh Wall, London E14 9AP
Tel: 44 02031 485000
Email: homesandgardens@timeinc
Web site: http://www.idealhome.co.uk/homes-and-gardens
Freq: Monthly
Circ: 102199 Not Audited
Profile: Magazine covering homes, furnishing, cookery, gardening and travel. Aimed at those aged 30 years old and over who are interested in creating a beautiful home.
Ad Rate: Full Page Colour £12535.00
MAGAZINE
Do-It-Yourself (DIY), Gardening

Homes & Interiors Scotland
                                      981843
Editorial: 11/12 Claremont Terrace, Glasgow G3 7XR **Tel:** 44 01415 676000
Web site: www.homesandinteriorsscotland.com
Freq: Bi-Monthly
Circ: 10045 Not Audited
Editor: Beth Forsyth; **Editor:** Gillian Welsh
Profile: Magazine offering advice and ideas on home improvement and decorating. Aimed at adults aged 25 years old and over seeking to invest in the quality of their living environment.
Ad Rate: Full Page Colour £2400.00
MAGAZINE
Architecture & Design, Do-It-Yourself (DIY), Property Management & Maintenance

Homes & Travel   995459
Tel: 44 02077 365552
Web site: http://homesandtravel.co.uk/
Freq: Daily
Circ: 122486 Cision Digital Reach
Editor: Stewart Andersen
MAGAZINE (ONLINE)
Property Management & Maintenance, Real Estate

HomeStyle   988896
Editorial: The Tower, Phoenix Square, Colchester CO4 9HU **Tel:** 44 01206 851117
Email: homestyle@burdamagazines.co.uk
Web site: www.homestylemag.co.uk
Freq: Bi-Monthly
Circ: 52789 Not Audited
Editor: Lorraine Luximon
MAGAZINE
Do-It-Yourself (DIY)

Homoculture   1054472
Editorial: First Floor, 16-22 Pritchards Road, London E2 9AP **Tel:** 44 02032 863580
Email: theboys@outtheremagazine.com
Web site: www.homoculturemag.com
Freq: Annual
Circ: 1000 Not Audited
MAGAZINE
LGBT

The Hoot
1086846
Tel: 44 01454 312125
Web site: http://hoot.cluttoncox.co.uk/
Freq: Monthly
Circ: 34 Cision Digital Reach
MAGAZINE (ONLINE)
Cooking & Baking, Residential Real
Estate, Travel

Hop & Barley
1064090
Web site: www.hopandbarley.co.uk
Freq: Quarterly Not Audited
MAGAZINE
Beer

HOPE not hate
996176
Editorial: PO Box 1084, London HA9 1HT
Tel: 44 02079 521181
Email: media@hopenothate.org.uk
Web site: http://www.hopenothate.org.uk
Freq: Bi-Monthly Not Audited
MAGAZINE
Charitable Foundations, Politics, Social
Issues

HOPE ST
987890
Editorial: HOPE ST Publishing Marketing
Office, Suite 308, 4th Floor, Central
Chambers, 93 Hope Street, London G2 6LD
Tel: 44 01412 211362
Email: editor@hopestreetmag.com
Web site: www.hopestreetmag.com
Freq: Semi-Annual
Circ: 55000 Not Audited
Editor: Sara Hill
Profile: Publication that looks at the world of
fashion, luxury brands and fashion
designers. Aimed at people in the fashion
industry and people with an interest in
luxury, who want the latest thing and to keep
on trend.
MAGAZINE
Beauty & Grooming, Cosmetics, Fashion,
Hair

Hornby Magazine
984108
Editorial: Units 1-4 Gwash Way Industrial
Estate, Ryhall Road, Stamford, Stamford
PE9 1XP **Tel:** 44 01780 484630
Email: hornbymagazine@keypublishing.com
Web site: www.hornbymagazine.com/
Freq: Monthly
Circ: 30846 Not Audited
Editor: Mike Wild
Profile: Magazine covering 1950s and 1960s
railways in model form with features to assist
readers starting to build their own model
railways. The magazine was published by Ian
Allen Publishing until 2012, when Key
Publishing aquired the title. Aimed at model
railway enthusiasts.
MAGAZINE
Crafts, Hobbies, & Collecting, Railroad

The Horological Journal
983506
Tel: 44 01636 813795
Email: hj@bhi.co.uk
Web site: www.bhi.co.uk
Freq: Monthly
Circ: 2400 Not Audited
Editor: Eve Makepeace
Profile: Journal covering all aspects of
horology, containing technical articles about
watches and clocks with trade news and
adverts.
Ad Rate: Full Page Mono £435.00
Ad Rate: Full Page Colour £652.50
MAGAZINE
Antiques/Collectibles, Luxury Goods,
Manufacturing

Horrible Histories
987035
Editorial: Vineyard House, 44 Brook Green,
Hammersmith, London W6 7BT
Tel: 44 02071 505000
Email: shout@hhmag.co.uk
Web site: www.hhmag.co.uk
Freq: Monthly
Circ: 20813 Not Audited
Profile: Publication that make history
accessible for children by using jokes,
cartoons, posters, competitions and games.
MAGAZINE
Elementary School, History, Preschool,
Teen/Young Adult, Trading Cards &
Comics

Horror Asylum
987475
Editorial: 46 Ravenbank Road, Luton, Luton
LU2 8EJ
Email: info@horror-asylum.com
Web site: www.horror-asylum.com
Freq: Daily
Circ: 43250 Cision Digital Reach
Editor: Steven Davies
MAGAZINE (ONLINE)
Entertainment, Movies & Video

Horse
982241
Editorial: Enterprise House, Enterprise Way,
Edenbridge, Edenbridge TN8 6HF
Tel: 44 01689 869840
Web site: www.horsemagazine.co.uk
Freq: Monthly
Circ: 13164 Not Audited
Editor: Joanna Browne
Profile: Magazine focusing on some of the
best riders and biggest names in the
equestrian world. Featuring real rider's
experiences and all things equestrian with
features, news, gossip, vet articles,
behind-the-scenes content, training tips and
shopping pages. Aimed at riders of all levels,
especially those competing in both affiliated
and unaffiliated events, leisure riders and
those looking to improve their veterinary and
horse care knowledge.
Ad Rate: Full Page Mono £1800.00
Ad Rate: Full Page Colour £2400.00
MAGAZINE
Equestrian Sports

Horse & Countryside
982798
Editorial: 1st Floor, Turnbridge Mills, Quay
Street, Huddersfield HD1 6QT
Tel: 44 02081 233414
Email: editor@ciaranjarosz.media
Web site: www.horseandcountryside.com
Freq: Bi-Monthly
Circ: 30000 Not Audited
Profile: Magazine that covers equestrianism
as well as feature interviews, tips and advice
about horse and dog care, travel and
accommodation, equestrian property,
country shows and events, AGA cookery
features and hen-keeping.
Ad Rate: Full Page Colour £1320.00
MAGAZINE
Equestrian Sports, Field Sports

Horse & Hound
982238
Editorial: Pinehurst 2, Pinehurst Road,
Farnborough Business Park, Farnborough,
London GU14 7BF **Tel:** 44 01252 555000
Web site: www.horseandhound.co.uk
Freq: Weekly
Circ: 32894 Not Audited
Profile: Magazine covering all aspects of
equestrianism. Includes news, reports,
training and advice on horse care. First
published in 1884, the publication has an
average of 150 pages per issue. Press Day:
Monday Aimed at horse enthusiasts.
Ad Rate: Full Page Mono £2286.00
Ad Rate: Full Page Colour £4085.00
MAGAZINE
Equestrian Sports, Field Sports

Horse and Rider
982240
Editorial: Marlborough House, Headley
Road, Grayshott, Hindhead GU26 6LG
Tel: 44 01428 601020
Email: editor@djmurphy.co.uk
Web site: www.horseandrideruk.com
Freq: Monthly
Circ: 26351 Not Audited
MAGAZINE
Equestrian Sports

Horsemanship Journal
995158
Editorial: 219 Creek Road, March, March
PE15 8RY
Email: info@horsemanship-journal.com

Web site: http://www.horsemanship-journal.
com/
Freq: Bi-Monthly
Circ: £000 Not Audited
MAGAZINE
Equestrian Sports

Horticulture Week
981163
Editorial: Bridge House, 69 London Road,
Twickenham, London TW1 3SP
Tel: 44 02082 674277
Email: hortweek@haymarket.com
Web site: www.horticultureweek.co.uk
Freq: Weekly
Circ: 7000 Not Audited
Editor: Kate Lowe
Profile: Magazine featuring horticultural
news with business advice and technical
features. First published in 1841. Aimed at
commercial and retail nurseries, garden
centres and landscapers, colleges,
arboriculturists, the turf market and local
authority parks managers.
Ad Rate: Full Page Mono £1995.00
Ad Rate: Full Page Colour £2950.00
MAGAZINE
Gardening

The Horticulturist
985010
Editorial: Chartered Institute of Horticulture,
Horticulture House, Chilton, Didcot OX11
0RN **Tel:** 44 01992 707025
Email: cih@horticulture.org.uk
Web site: horticulture.org.uk
Freq: Quarterly
Circ: 1500 Not Audited
Editor: Barbara Segall
Profile: Journal containing articles on all
aspects of professional horticulture including
book reviews.
Ad Rate: Full Page Colour £1000.00
MAGAZINE
Gardening

HORTUS
986919
Editorial: Bryan's Ground, Stapleton, Bristol
LD8 2LP **Tel:** 44 01544 260001
Email: all@hortus.co.uk
Web site: http://www.hortus.co.uk
Freq: Quarterly
Circ: 1500 Not Audited
Editor: David Wheeler
Profile: Journal providing articles on
gardens, plants, people, books, history,
design and ornament. Aimed at private
gardeners, botanic gardens, horticultural
colleges and libraries.
Ad Rate: Full Page Mono £175.00
MAGAZINE
Gardening

Hospital Dr
995748
Editorial: Orchard House, Wicklewood
Green, Kimberley NR18 9PX
Web site: www.hospitaldr.co.uk/index.php
Freq: Daily
Circ: 190 Cision Digital Reach
MAGAZINE (ONLINE)
Medicine

Hospital Food & Service
1074794
Tel: 44 03455 006008
Email: editor@hospitalfoodandservice.co.uk
Web site: www.hospitalfoodandservice.co.
uk
Freq: Bi-Monthly
Circ: 3418 Not Audited
Editor: Amanda Roberts
MAGAZINE
Food, Nutrition

Hospitality & Events North
985182
Editorial: Ground Floor, Stockdale House, 8
Victoria Road, Headingley Business Park,
Leeds LS6 1PF **Tel:** 44 08450 522911
Email: info@nutsforprint.co.uk
Web site: www.hospitalityandeventsnorth.
com
Freq: Bi-Monthly
Circ: 15000 Not Audited
Profile: Magazine covering conferences,
meetings, events, exhibitions and team
building events. First published in 2007, the

publication has an average of 44 pages per
issue. Aimed at managing directors,
commercial directors, HR managers, PAs
and organisers looking to purchase
hospitality events.
Ad Rate: Full Page Colour £1250.00
MAGAZINE
Bars, Clubs & Pubs, Hotels/Motels

Hospitality and Catering News
987014
Editorial: BEcause HQ, Berkshire House,
39-51 Ascot High Street, London SL5 7HY
Tel: 44 01344 637912
Web site: www.hospitalityandcateringnews.
com
Freq: Daily
Circ: 47554 Cision Digital Reach
MAGAZINE (ONLINE)
Bars, Clubs & Pubs, Hotels/Motels

Hospitality Interiors
984284
Editorial: 4 Red Barn Mews, High Street,
Battle, Battle TN33 0AG
Tel: 44 01424 774982
Web site: http://www.hospitality-interiors.
net/
Freq: Bi-Monthly
Circ: 7000 Not Audited
Profile: Magazine covering interior
furnishings for the contract sector. A charge
may be added for the use of press release
material. Aimed at architects, designers and
specifiers in the hotel, restaurant, bar, pub
and leisure industries. Also for buyers,
specifiers, owners, managers and
decision-makers throughout the hospitality
interiors marketplace.
Ad Rate: Full Page Colour £1795.00
MAGAZINE
Bars, Clubs & Pubs, Hotels/Motels

Hospitality Quarterly
980944
Editorial: 4th Floor, Joynes House, New
Road, Gravesend DA11 0AJ
Tel: 44 03455 006008
Email: info@h2opublishing.co.uk
Web site: www.instituteofhospitality.org/
Publications/Hospitality-Magazine/hospitality
Freq: Quarterly
Circ: 8000 Not Audited
Editor: Ben Walker
Profile: Magazine for hospitality, leisure and
tourism management professionals. Leading
features incorporate exclusive interviews
with inspirational entrepreneurs, workable
examples of successful management
practice, legislative advice and challenging
roundtable debates on topics including
technology, education, CSR and
recruitment. These run alongside quarterly
news round-ups, events listings and
announcements. Produced for members of
the Hotel and Catering International
Management Association and independent
subscribers.
Ad Rate: Full Page Colour £2250.00
MAGAZINE
Bars, Clubs & Pubs, Hotels/Motels

Hospitality Review NI
981054
Editorial: Belfast Telegraph House, 33
Clarendon Road, Belfast BT1 3BG
Tel: 44 02890 264000
Web site: http://hospitalityreviewni.com/
Freq: Monthly
Circ: 4258 Not Audited
Editor: Alyson Magee
Profile: Official publication of the Federation
of The Retail Licensed Trade Northern
Ireland, the Northern Ireland Hotels
Federation and the Northern Ireland
Association of Chefs and Cooks. Covers
hospitality and hotel industry including news
and comment. First published in 1977, the
publication has an average of 76 pages per
issue. Press Day: Tuesday Aimed at all
sectors of the hospitality industry and
licensed trade.
Ad Rate: Full Page Colour £1860.00
MAGAZINE
Alcohol & Spirits, Bars, Clubs & Pubs,
Food

Consumer Magazines

Hospitality Today
999119

Editorial: Belfry House, Batts Field, Bruton BA10 0DX **Tel:** 44 01749 814908
Email: news@hospitalitytoday.com
Web site: www.hospitalitytoday.com
Freq: Bi-Monthly
Circ: 5413 Cision Digital Reach
Editor: David Weston
Profile: Magazine covering the UK's hospitality sector. First published in 2011.
MAGAZINE (ONLINE)
Bars, Clubs & Pubs, Hotels/Motels

Host City
983332

Editorial: Cavendish Group Ltd, 2nd Floor Front, 116-118 Chancery Lane, London WC2A 1PP **Tel:** 44 02036 759530
Email: queries@hostcity.com
Web site: www.hostcity.net
Freq: Quarterly
Circ: 10000 Not Audited
Profile: Magazine featuring reviews on organisations and infrastructure behind the successful hosting of sporting events. The magazine examines the hosting experiences of many countries, including Athens and Sydney. It acts as a guide to those currently in the process of organising large-scale events. Aimed at event owners, bidding countries and cities as well as key suppliers and support services.
Ad Rate: Full Page Colour £4250.00
MAGAZINE
Olympic Sports

Host Online
985581

Editorial: 7 Brampton Bank, Five Oak Green Road, Tudeley, Tonbridge, Capel TN11 0PN
Tel: 44 01732 358823
Email: hello@thehostonline.co.uk
Web site: thehostonline.co.uk
Freq: Daily
Circ: 1447 Cision Digital Reach
Editor: Chris Callander
MAGAZINE (ONLINE)
Bars, Clubs & Pubs

Hot Brands Cool Places
996728

Tel: 44 01392 876988
Email: editorial@hotbrandscoolplaces.co.uk
Web site: www.hotbrandscoolplaces.com
Freq: Daily
Circ: 60000 Not Audited
MAGAZINE
Luxury Goods

Hot Dinners
985204

Editorial: Hot Dinners, Flat G, 1 Stable Place, London N4 2JB **Tel:** 44 07979 234837
Email: news@hot-dinners.com
Web site: http://www.hot-dinners.com
Freq: Daily
Circ: 147098 Cision Digital Reach
MAGAZINE (ONLINE)
Restaurant Reviews

Hot Rum Cow
986461

Editorial: 54 Timberbush, Edinburgh EH6 6QH **Tel:** 44 01315 556494
Email: info@hotrumcow.co.uk
Web site: www.hotrumcow.co.uk
Freq: Quarterly Not Audited
Profile: Magazine covering the drinks industry, beers, wines & spirits.
MAGAZINE
Alcohol & Spirits, Bars, Clubs & Pubs, Beer, Beverages, Wine/Winemaking

Hot Tub Retailer
996879

Editorial: 23 Doncaster Road, Bawtry, Doncaster DN106NQ **Tel:** 44 01302 714257
Email: nick@whatspa.com
Web site: www.hottubretailer.co.uk
Freq: Annual
Circ: 1500 Not Audited
Editor: Andrew Slater
MAGAZINE
Fitness & Exercise

Hotcourses
998972

Editorial: 1st Floor, Bedford House, Fulham Green, 69-79 Fulham High Street, London SW6 3JW **Tel:** 44 02073 846000

Web site: www.hotcourses.com
Freq: Semi-Annual Not Audited
Profile: Hotcourses provides a searchable directory of course listings at school, college, undergraduate and postgraduate level, as well as courses for those not in education. They also produce a newspaper distributed outside London train stations.
MAGAZINE
Careers

Hotel Analyst Distribution and Technology
990660

Editorial: PO Box 1228, Cambridge CB1 0WS
Email: info@hotelanalyst.co.uk
Web site: ha-dt.com
Freq: Weekly
Circ: 521 Cision Digital Reach
Profile: Website covering hospitality technology. The Hotel Analyst Distribution and Technology shares the latest technologies, news and business in the hospitality industry.
MAGAZINE (ONLINE)
Electronics, Hotels/Motels, Software

The Hotel Culture
996755

Editorial: Hunter Street, London WC1N
Email: editor@thehotelculture.com
Web site: www.thehotelculture.com
Freq: Daily
Circ: 12251 Cision Digital Reach
Editor: Imran Hussain
MAGAZINE (ONLINE)
Airline Inflight, Railroad, Travel

Hotel F&B Magazine (UK)
995535

Editorial: 4th Floor, Joynes House, New Road, Gravesend DA11 0AJ
Tel: 44 08455 006008
Email: editor@hotelfandb.co.uk
Web site: www.hotelfandb.co.uk
Freq: Monthly
Circ: 24273 Not Audited
MAGAZINE
Alcohol & Spirits, Food, Hotels/Motels

The Hotel Guru
985073

Editorial: Woodyett, Aberdeen FK8 3AF
Tel: 44 02031 370694
Email: info@thehotelguru.com
Web site: www.thehotelguru.com
Freq: Daily
Circ: 41204 Cision Digital Reach
Editor: James Dunford Wood
MAGAZINE (ONLINE)
Travel

HotelsThatWereNot.com
995819

Web site: www.hotelsthatwerenot.com
Freq: Daily
Circ: 2229 Cision Digital Reach
MAGAZINE (ONLINE)
Travel

Hounds
982239

Editorial: Rose Cottage, Hughley, Shrewsbury, Much Wenlock SY5 6NX
Tel: 44 01746 785637
Email: linda.sagar2@gmail.com
Web site: houndsmagazineonline.co.uk
Freq: Bi-Monthly
Circ: 18000 Not Audited
Editor: Michael Sagar
Profile: Magazine containing information on keeping and breeding hounds and articles on hunting. Aimed at hunt masters, hound owners and those interested in field sports.
Ad Rate: Full Page Mono £400.00
Ad Rate: Full Page Colour £400.00
MAGAZINE
Field Sports

Hounslow Matters
982511

Editorial: Civic Centre, Lampton Road, Hounslow, London TW3 4DN
Tel: 44 02085 832000
Email: hm@hounslow.gov.uk
Web site: www.hounslow.gov.uk
Freq: Quarterly
Circ: 100000 Not Audited

Editor: Alexandra Cochrane
MAGAZINE
Regional General Interest

The Hour - Suspended
1059463

Editorial: Floor 3 10-16, Scrutton Street, London EC2A 4RU
Email: inquiry@thehourmagazine.com
Web site: www.thehourmagazine.com
Freq: Bi-Monthly Not Audited
MAGAZINE
Art, Fashion, Luxury Goods, Men's Interests, Photography, Shopping, Visual Arts

The House
995785

Editorial: Floor 11, The Shard, 32 London Bridge Street, London SE1 9SG
Tel: 44 02075 935775
Email: editorial.housemag@dods.co.uk
Web site: https://www.politicshome.com/articles/magazine/house
Freq: Weekly
Circ: 2701 Not Audited
Editor: Gisela Stuart
Profile: Magazine covering homes in Dorset. Each issue contains House magazine covers property in Dorset, Hampshire, Poole, Bournemouth, Christchurch, Sandbanks, Wimborne, Ringwood, Ferndown, Creekmoor, Boscombe, Canford Cliffs, Westbourne and Branksome. It also covers articles on motoring, health, fitness, wellbeing, beauty, sports, eating out, clubs and nights out, fashion, shopping, interiors, furniture, gardening and local events. Aimed at people living in Dorset.
MAGAZINE
Politics

House & Garden
981844

Editorial: Vogue House, Hanover Square, London W1S 1JU **Tel:** 44 02074 999080
Email: houseandgarden@condenast.co.uk
Web site: www.houseandgarden.co.uk
Freq: Monthly
Circ: 111017 Not Audited
Profile: Magazine covering all areas of home and garden design and decoration. Each issue covers interior design, home decoration as well as unique homes and outdoor features, ranging from town houses, converted barns and apartments to island retreats. It also contains articles on travel, wine, food, lifestyle and shopping. Aimed at women aged between 25 and 54 years old within the AB social bracket.
Ad Rate: Full Page Colour £24329.00
MAGAZINE
Do-It-Yourself (DIY), Gardening, Property Management & Maintenance

House Beautiful
980761

Editorial: 33 Broadwick Street, London W1F 9EP **Tel:** 44 02074 395000
Email: houseb.mail@natmags.co.uk
Web site: www.housebeautiful.co.uk
Freq: Monthly
Circ: 109970 Not Audited
Profile: Magazine offering ideas and inspiration on home improvements, decor and lifestyle features. Read mainly by homeowners between 25 and 44 years old.
Ad Rate: Full Page Colour £10567.00
MAGAZINE
Do-It-Yourself (DIY)

HOUSE FOUR
995178

Editorial: Soho House, 72-74 Dean Street, London W1D 3SG **Tel:** 44 02078 512300
Email: housefour@sohohouse.com
Web site: http://housefour.com/
Freq: Daily
Circ: 578 Cision Digital Reach
MAGAZINE (ONLINE)
Alcohol & Spirits, Bars, Clubs & Pubs, Beer, Beverages, Consumer Affairs, Cooking & Baking, Food, Grocery Stores, International News, Lifestyle

House of Coco
996124

Tel: 44 02030 957366
Email: laura@houseofcoco.net
Web site: http://www.houseofcoco.net/
Freq: Daily

Circ: 92395 Cision Digital Reach
MAGAZINE (ONLINE)
Fashion, Luxury Goods, Travel

The House of Peroni
998083

Editorial: 36 Golden Square, London W1F 9EE **Tel:** 44 02075 443600
Web site: www.thehouseofperoni.com
Freq: Daily
Circ: 10318 Cision Digital Reach
MAGAZINE (ONLINE)
Art, Bars, Clubs & Pubs, Cooking & Baking, Europe, Fashion, Lifestyle, Men's Interests, Movies & Video, R&B, Urban, World, Regional General Interest

HOUSE SEVEN
995322

Editorial: Soho House, 72-74 Dean Street, London W1D 3SG **Tel:** 44 02078 512300
Web site: http://houseseven.com
Freq: Daily
Circ: 136761 Cision Digital Reach
MAGAZINE (ONLINE)
Alcohol & Spirits, Art, Bars, Clubs & Pubs, Beer, Beverages, Comedy, Cooking & Baking, Dance Music, Entertainment, Fashion

House Sitting
1074064

Web site: www.housesittingmagazine.com
Freq: Monthly
Circ: 10296 Cision Digital Reach
MAGAZINE (ONLINE)
Mobile Electronics, Nutrition, Travel

House Style
998092

Editorial: 5 Coningsby Close, Maidenhead, Maidenhead SL6 3YU **Tel:** 44 07834 233346
Email: info@lifestyle-magazines.co.uk
Web site: http://www.lifestyle-magazines.co.uk/housestyle.html
Freq: Quarterly
Circ: 521 Cision Digital Reach
Editor: Caroline Seekings
MAGAZINE (ONLINE)
Do-It-Yourself (DIY), Property Management & Maintenance

Housing Technology
984565

Editorial: Hoppingwood Farm, Robin Hood Way, London SW20 0AB
Tel: 44 02083 362293
Email: news@housing-technology.com
Web site: www.housing-technology.com
Freq: Bi-Monthly
Circ: 12500 Not Audited
Editor: Alastair Tweedie
Profile: Magazine providing IT, technology and telco news and information to those responsible for technology strategy and business decision-making in the UK social housing sector, housing associations and local government. Aimed at those responsible for technology strategy and business decision making in housing associations, the UK housing sector and local government.
MAGAZINE
Electronics, Industry, Internet, Mobile Communications, Residential Real Estate, Software, Telecommunications/Electronic Communications

How It Works
985288

Editorial: Richmond House, 33 Richmond Hill, Bournemouth BH2 6EZ
Tel: 44 01202 586200
Email: howitworks@futurenet.com
Web site: www.howitworksdaily.com
Freq: Monthly
Circ: 81571 Cision Digital Reach
Profile: Magazine covering science, technology, space, history and the environment. Aimed at a male ABC1 demographic between the ages of 25 and 44.
MAGAZINE (ONLINE)
Audio Video Trade, Cameras, Consumer Electronics, Energy & Environment, History, Mobile Electronics, Movies & Video, Science

huck
983855
Editorial: 71a Leonard Street, London EC2A 4QS **Tel:** 44 02077 293675
Email: hello@tcolondon.com
Web site: www.huckmagazine.com
Freq: Bi-Monthly
Circ: 50000 Not Audited
Profile: Magazine covering surfing, skating, snowboarding. It takes inspiration from the radical heritage of action sports to look under the skin of cultural developments, social movements, emerging scenes and new thoughts and ideas. First published in 2006, the publication has an average of 140 pages per issue. Aimed at sports enthusiasts aged between 18 and 35 years old.
MAGAZINE
Extreme/Adventure Sports, Men's Interests, Women's Interests

HuffPost (UK)
986040
Editorial: Shropshire House, 11-20 Cappor Street, London WC1E 6JA
Tel: 44 02074 921000
Email: huffpostuk@huffingtonpost.com
Web site: huffingtonpost.co.uk
Freq: Daily
Circ: 6796365 Cision Digital Reach
MAGAZINE (ONLINE)
Consumer Affairs, International News, National News, Politics

The HullFire
1023285
Editorial: Hull University Students' Union, University House, Cottingham Road, Hull HU6 7RX **Tel:** 44 01482 445361
Email: editor@hullfire.com
Web site: www.thehullfire.com
Freq: Monthly Not Audited
MAGAZINE
Student Lifestyle

The Humanion
1053181
Email: editor@thehumanion.com
Web site: http://www.thehumanion.com/
Freq: Daily
Circ: 521 Cision Digital Reach
MAGAZINE (ONLINE)
Consumer Affairs, International News, National News, Politics, Religion, Science, Social Issues

HUNGER
086531
Editorial: 110 - 114 Grafton Road, Kentish Town, London NW5 4BA
Tel: 44 02072 847320
Email: editorial@hungertv.com
Web site: www.hungertv.com
Freq: Semi-Annual Not Audited
Editor: Holly Fraser
MAGAZINE
Art, Beauty & Grooming, Celebrities, Cosmetics, Entertainment, Fashion, Hair, Literature, Movies & Video, Photography

Hungry Eye
986306
Editorial: Life Media Group House, 19 The Avenue, Eastbourne, Eastbourne BN21 3YD
Email: feedback@hungryeyemagazine.com
Web site: hungryeyemagazine.com
Freq: Quarterly
Circ: 12500 Not Audited
Profile: Magazine covering film making and photography, featuring creative and technological developments in the industry.
MAGAZINE
Photography, Visual Arts

Hurlingham
985750
Editorial: Ground Floor, 1-2 Ravey Street, London EC2A 4QP **Tel:** 44 02032 220101
Email: info@showmedialondon.com
Web site: http://hurlinghampolo.com/
Freq: 3 Times/Year
Circ: 10000 Not Audited
Profile: Magazine of the Hurlingham Polo Association covering the latest news and information about polo in the UK and around the world. Also has profiles of players as well as features on lifestyle, travel, food, drink and adventure. Aimed at polo players, riders and fans members of the Hurlingham Polo Association.

Ad Rate: Full Page Colour £4000.00
MAGAZINE
Equestrian Sports

Hybrid Wake
1076746
Web site: www.hybridwakemag.com/
Freq: Bi-Monthly
Circ: 5000 Not Audited
MAGAZINE
Swimming/Watersports

Hyponik
1054273
Editorial: 16 Waterson St, London E2 8HL
Tel: 44 02076 130144
Email: info@hyponik.com
Web site: hyponik.com
Freq: Daily
Circ: 28496 Cision Digital Reach
Editor: Hugo Laing
MAGAZINE (ONLINE)
Dance Music, Rap & Hip Hop

I CHOOSE Birmingham
996718
Tel: 44 01212 727072
Web site: ichoosebirmingham.com
Freq: Weekly
Circ: 14796 Cision Digital Reach
Editor: Tom Cullen
MAGAZINE (ONLINE)
Bars, Clubs & Pubs, Comedy, Cooking & Baking, Entertainment, Food, Grocery Stores, Local Entertainment Guides, Men's Interests, Movies & Video, Organic Food

I Like Music
985717
Editorial: St John's Studios, 6-8 Church Road, London TW9 2QA
Freq: Daily
Circ: 29392 Cision Digital Reach
MAGAZINE (ONLINE)
Country, Folk, Bluegrass, Dance Music, Jazz & Blues, Music, Pop Music, Rap & Hip Hop, Rock Music

I Love MCR
1075497
Editorial: 447-449 Royal Exchange, St Ann's Square, Manchester M2 7EP
Tel: 44 01617 102665
Email: editor@ilovemanchester.com
Web site: www.ilovemanchester.com
Freq: Daily
Circ: 50505 Cision Digital Reach
Editor: Stephen Lewis
MAGAZINE (ONLINE)
Alcohol & Spirits, Art, Bars, Clubs & Pubs, Basketball, Beer, Beverages, Bicycles, Business, Cooking & Baking, Cricket

I Programmer
985696
Email: newsdesk@i-programmer.info
Web site: http://www.i-programmer.info
Freq: Daily
Circ: 514046 Cision Digital Reach
Editor: Mike James
Profile: Website covering programming and software development. It provides news articles covering technology and electronics as well as eBook reviews. I Programmer states that "The legends of the computing industry made huge technological advances often against the odds. Some names you will know from current news - Bill Gates, Steve Jobs, Alan Sugar - but computer history started much earlier and there are many pioneers you should know about". They present an informal history of the most revolutionary time in technology.
MAGAZINE (ONLINE)
Auto Aftermarket, Computers, Data Management, Electronics, Government Technology, Industry, Internet, Mobile Communications, Security & Security Systems, Software

I, Science
999686
Editorial: Imperial College Union, Beit Quad, Prince Consort Road, London SW7 2BB
Email: i.science@imperial.ac.uk
Web site: www.isciencemag.co.uk
Freq: Daily
Circ: 8980 Cision Digital Reach
MAGAZINE (ONLINE)
Science, Student Lifestyle

IBS Journal
995795
Editorial: Kings Cross Lenta Business Centre, Suite 109, 180-186 Kings Cross Road, London WC1X 9DE
Tel: 44 02075 202630
Web site: www.ibsintelligence.com
Freq: Monthly
Circ: 2000 Not Audited
MAGAZINE
Banking

Iceni Magazine
997409
Tel: 44 01603 510856
Email: submissions@icenimagazine.co.uk
Web site: http://www.icenimagazine.co.uk/
Freq: Monthly
Circ: 12500 Not Audited
MAGAZINE
Lifestyle, Men's Interests, Regional General Interest, Women's Interests

iChild.co.uk
983552
Editorial: Unit 433, Highgate Studios, 53-79 Highgate Road, London NW5 1TL
Email: editor@ichild.co.uk
Web site: www.ichild.co.uk
Freq: Daily
Circ: 65251 Cision Digital Reach
Editor: Sara Maslin
Profile: Online magazine featuring developmental and educational activities and covers parenting, child development, news, features and health. Aimed at working mums of children aged 0 to 5 years old. Previous title: iChild.tv
MAGAZINE (ONLINE)
Family & Parenting

Ici Londres
988813
Editorial: 10-12 Exhibition Road, London SW7 2HF **Tel:** 44 02075 811588
Email: editorial@ici-londres.com
Web site: www.ici-londres.com/en
Freq: Monthly
Circ: 30000 Not Audited
MAGAZINE
Art, Expatriates, Railroad, Theater & Performing Arts, Travel, Visual Arts

ICNM Journal
985116
Editorial: Can-Mezzanine, 32-36 Loman Street, London SE1 0EH
Tel: 44 02079 227980
Email: info@icnm.org.uk
Web site: http://icnm.org.uk/journal
Freq: Quarterly
Circ: 1000 Not Audited
Editor: Jo-Anne Flack
Profile: Journal covering complementary and natural medicine. Aimed at complementary practitioners.This magazine contains the following regular features: Book reviewsCompetitions EventsFocus on a particular complimentary therapy NewsReader giveaways Seasonal Topics
Ad Rate: Full Page Colour £315.00
MAGAZINE
Alternative Medicine

ICON (UK)
980062
Editorial: Crown House, 151 High Road, Loughton, London IG10 4LF
Tel: 44 02032 255200
Web site: www.iconeye.com
Freq: Monthly
Circ: 27256 Not Audited
Editor: James McLachlan
MAGAZINE
Architecture & Design, Do-It-Yourself (DIY)

Iconic Gifts
985411
Web site: http://www.iconicgifts.com/
Freq: Daily
Circ: 11380 Cision Digital Reach
MAGAZINE (ONLINE)
Shopping

iCreate
981730
Editorial: 1-10 Praed Mews, Paddington, London W2 1QY **Tel:** 44 01202 586200
Email: icreate@futurenet.com
Web site: https://www.gadgetdaily.xyz/

Freq: Monthly Not Audited
Profile: Magazine with reviews and tutorials for software for Macs also has a cover mounted CD. Offering creative guides, exciting features and in-depth analytical articles for Mac and iPod users. Covers iMovie, iPhoto, iDVD, iWeb, GarageBand and iTunes as well as the Apple Pro Apps and Mac OS X. Contains 50 pages of tutorials each month, dedicated iPod and iPhone content as well as help and advice for common system problems. Aimed at users of Macs.
Ad Rate: Full Page Colour £2300.00
MAGAZINE
Apple

ICT for Education
981559
Editorial: 14A Queens Road, Ryde, Ryde PO33 3BG **Tel:** 44 01983 812305
Email: info@ictmedialtd.com
Web site: www.ictforeducation.co.uk
Freq: Daily
Circ: 12845 Cision Digital Reach
Profile: Magazine covering information and communication technology including hardware, software and equipment reviews to help teachers. Aimed at ICT co-ordinators and heads of ICT responsible for purchasing technology for schools.
Ad Rate: Full Page Colour £800.00
MAGAZINE (ONLINE)
Disability, Education, Higher Education, Preschool, Schools & Institutions, Students

ICT in Education
985890
Editorial: Priestley House, Priestley Gardens, Chadwell Heath, London RM6 4SN
Tel: 44 01916 451046
Web site: www.ictineducation.org
Freq: Daily
Circ: 21001 Cision Digital Reach
Editor: Terry Freedman
MAGAZINE (ONLINE)
Computers, Disability, Education, Higher Education, Preschool, Schools & Institutions, Students

ICXM
1103634
Email: inbox@icxm.net
Web site: http://www.icxm.net/x/
Freq: Daily
Circ: 100134 Cision Digital Reach
MAGAZINE (ONLINE)
Computer & Video Games

i-D
981795
Editorial: New North Place, London EC2A 4JA **Tel:** 44 02077 497999
Email: editorial@i-d.co
Web site: i-d.vice.com/en_gb
Freq: Bi-Monthly
Circ: 103000 Not Audited
Profile: Website of i-D Magazine, covering fashion, youth culture and music. Aimed at men and women between 16 and 30 years old.
MAGAZINE
Fashion, Men's Interests, Women's Interests

IDC UK
988912
Editorial: IDC UK, 5th Floor, Ealing Cross, 85 Uxbridge Road, London W5 5TH
Tel: 44 02089 877100
Web site: www.uk.idc.com
Freq: Daily
Circ: 354 Cision Digital Reach
MAGAZINE (ONLINE)
Computers, Data Management, Electronics, Industry, Mobile Communications, Software, Telecommunications/Electronic Communications

IDEAL (UK)
990588
Web site: www.idealmagazine.co.uk
Freq: Daily
Circ: 49781 Cision Digital Reach
MAGAZINE (ONLINE)
Women's Interests

Consumer Magazines

Ideal Home
980762

Editorial: 161 Marsh Wall, London E14 9AP
Tel: 44 02031 485000
Email: ideal_home@timeinc.com
Web site: www.idealhomemagazine.co.uk
Freq: Monthly
Circ: 162110 Not Audited
Profile: Interiors magazine covering contemporary living. It features transformed houses, kitchens and bathrooms and showcases the latest trends and inspirational decorating stories. Each issue includes the latest home looks from top retailers and designers. First published in 1920. Aimed predominantly at females aged between 25 and 45 years old who are interested in home improvements.
Ad Rate: Full Page Colour £13600.00
MAGAZINE

Do-It-Yourself (DIY)

Idealhome.co.uk
984309

Editorial: The Blue Fin Building, 110 Southwark Street, London SE1 0SU
Tel: 44 02031 485000
Email: housetohome@timeinc.com
Web site: http://www.idealhome.co.uk/
Freq: Daily
Circ: 18936 Cision Digital Reach
MAGAZINE (ONLINE)
Do-It-Yourself (DIY)

IDG Connect (UK)
987221

Editorial: Friendship House, 49/51 Gresham Road, Staines, London TW18 2BF
Tel: 44 01784 210210
Web site: http://www.idgconnect.com/
Freq: Daily
Circ: 150309 Cision Digital Reach
Editor: Kathryn Cave
MAGAZINE (ONLINE)

Auto Aftermarket, Computers, Data Management, Electronics, Government Technology, Industry, Internet, Mobile Communications, Security & Security Systems, Software

The Idle Man
1101937

Editorial: Unit 102W, 88-94 Wentworth Street, London E1 7SA
Tel: 44 02079 935369
Email: info@theidleman.com
Web site: theidleman.com/manual
Freq: Daily
Circ: 12651 Cision Digital Reach
MAGAZINE (ONLINE)
Fashion, Men's Interests

The Idler
990540

Editorial: 81 Westbourne Park Road, London W2 5QH **Tel:** 44 02072 215908
Email: mail@idler.co.uk
Web site: www.idler.co.uk
Freq: Quarterly
Editor: Tom Hodgkinson
Profile: Magazine offering alternative views on life and society.
MAGAZINE
Literature

IDOL magazine
998322

Web site: www.idolmag.co.uk
Freq: Semi-Annual
Circ: 16000 Not Audited
Profile: Website covering fashion. The IDOL MAGAZINE website shares the latest news and information on fashion events and fashion industry.
MAGAZINE
Art, Country, Folk, Bluegrass, Dance Music, Fashion, Jazz & Blues, Men's Interests, Pop Music, Rap & Hip Hop, Rock Music, Women's Interests

IDS Executive Compensation Review
983982

Editorial: Friars House, 160 Blackfriars Road, London SE1 8EZ
Web site: http://www.incomesdata.co.uk/ online-services/executive-compensation/
Freq: Monthly Not Audited
Profile: Magazine providing essential information on salaries, benefits and the labour market for managers and professionals. Aimed at compensation and benefit specialists, HR staff involved in remuneration, consultancies and recruitment firms.Previous title: IDS Management Pay Review Adam Elston is the Principal Researcher to whom enquiries should be addressed.Regular features: Case Studies Featuring case studies of human resources professionals.; Job Market Update Featuring news in the job market.; Speaker's Corner Featuring the views of guest commentators on topical reward issues.; Survey Review Featuring a review of surveys relating to employment issues.
MAGAZINE
Human Resources

IET Science, Measurement & Technology
998918

Editorial: Michael Faraday House, Six Hills Way, Stevenage SG1 2AY
Tel: 44 01438 767603
Email: iet_smt@theiet.org
Web site: http://digital-library.theiet.org/ content/journals/iet-smt
Freq: Bi-Monthly Not Audited
MAGAZINE
Auto Aftermarket, Computers, Data Management, Electronics, Government Technology, Industry, Internet, Mobile Communications, Science, Security & Security Systems

IFA Magazine
985911

Editorial: Loft 3, The Tobacco Factory, Raleigh Road, Bristol BS3 1TF
Tel: 44 01179 089686
Email: editor@ifamagazine.com
Web site: www.ifamagazine.com
Freq: Monthly
Circ: 6600 Not Audited
Editor in Chief: Michael Wilson
Profile: IFA Magazine contains news review, comment and analysis, columnists insight, features, product news, company profiles. Targets policy makers, financial planners, directors and key decision makers in top IFA businesses.
Ad Rate: Full Page Colour £3750.00
MAGAZINE

IFM (Independent Forecourt Magazine)
999485

Editorial: 22 Hook Farm Road, Bridgnorth, Bridgnorth WV16 4RA **Tel:** 44 01746 218290
Email: mark@garagewatch.org
Web site: www.garagewatch.org
Freq: Bi-Monthly
Circ: 6500 Not Audited
Editor: Mark Bradshaw
MAGAZINE
Automotive

iGaming Business
984716

Editorial: Bedford House, 69-79 Fulham High Street, London SW6 3JW
Tel: 44 02073 848269
Email: news@igamingbusiness.com
Web site: www.igamingbusiness.com
Freq: Bi-Monthly
Circ: 7250 Not Audited
Profile: Magazine covering the online gambling industry. Provides news, insights and analysis for the online gambling market.
Ad Rate: Full Page Colour £3275.00
MAGAZINE
Computer & Video Games

iGaming Business North America
999534

Editorial: Fulham Green, Bedford House, 69-79 Fulham High Street, London SW6 3JW
Tel: 44 02079 543500
Email: editorial@igamingbusiness.com
Web site: http://igamingnorthamerica.com/
Freq: Bi-Monthly Not Audited
MAGAZINE
Computer & Video Games

IGD
985051

Editorial: Grange Lane, Letchmore Heath, Watford, Aldenham WD25 8GD
Tel: 44 01923 857141
Email: press@igd.com
Web site: www.igd.com

Freq: Daily
Circ: 49341 Cision Digital Reach
MAGAZINE (ONLINE)
Alcohol & Spirits, Food, Retail Management

IHS Dredging and Port Construction
995923

Editorial: 163 Brighton Road, Coulsdon, London CR5 2YH **Tel:** 44 02087 003700
Web site: www.dpcmagazine.com
Freq: Monthly
Circ: 1117 Not Audited
MAGAZINE
Marine & Boat Trade

IHS Ports & Harbors
997165

Editorial: 4th Floor Ropemaker Place, 25 Ropemaker Street, London EC2Y 9LY
Tel: 44 02072 602000
Email: editorialexternal@ihs.com
Web site: https://www.ihs.com/products/ ports-and-harbors-magazine.html
Freq: Bi-Monthly
Circ: 2345 Not Audited
MAGAZINE
Marine & Boat Trade, Shipping & Warehousing

IHS Safety at Sea
995133

Editorial: Sentinel House, 163 Brighton Road, Coulsdon, London CR5 2YH
Tel: 44 02087 003700
Web site: www.ihsmaritime360.com/
Freq: Monthly
Circ: 6033 Not Audited
MAGAZINE
Health & Safety, Marine & Boat Trade, Shipping & Warehousing

IJGlobal
996769

Editorial: 6-8 Bouverie Street, London EC4Y 8AX **Tel:** 44 02077 798870
Web site: http://www.ijonline.com/
Freq: Bi-Monthly Not Audited
Editor: Jon Whiteaker
Profile: Website covering infrastructure. IJGlobal shares the latest news on data and analysis for the global infrastructure finance marketplace. The website covers the sectors of power, oil and gas, transport, telecommunications, water, renewables as well as policy and legal advice. Aimed at government ministers and officials, developers, investors, financiers, lawyers and consultants.
MAGAZINE
Alternative/Renewable Energy, Automotive, Aviation, Carbon Emissions & Trading, Electricity, Energy, Nuclear Power, Oil, Railroad, Shipping & Warehousing

IKEA FAMILY MAGAZINE
981845

Editorial: 82 Baker Street, London W1 6AE
Tel: 44 02079 357744
Email: hello@augustmedia.com
Web site: http://www. ikeafamilylivemagazine.com/gb/en
Freq: Quarterly
Circ: 135000 Not Audited
MAGAZINE
Do-It-Yourself (DIY)

Ikonz
998728

Tel: 44 01215 231057
Web site: http://www.ikonzmag.co.uk/
Freq: Daily
Circ: 10532 Cision Digital Reach
Editor: Reena Combo
MAGAZINE (ONLINE)
Asia, Celebrities

IKSURFMAG
998979

Editorial: 26 Tudor Road, Cantebury, Canterbury CT1 3SY
Email: pressrelease@iksurfmag.com
Web site: www.iksurfmag.com
Freq: Bi-Monthly
Circ: 41825 Cision Digital Reach
MAGAZINE (ONLINE)
Swimming/Watersports

iLoveMyGrub.com
984551

Editorial: 6 Winters Road, Thames Ditton, London KT7 0XW **Tel:** 44 02081 338417
Web site: www.ilovemygrub.com
Freq: Daily
Circ: 3188 Cision Digital Reach
Profile: Website covering food. The ILoveMyGrub.com website shares the latest news on food. The website discusses anything from food events and food recipes to reviews.
MAGAZINE (ONLINE)
Cooking & Baking, Food, Grocery Stores, Organic Food, Restaurant Reviews, Vegetarianism & Veganism

iLoveVideo.tv
995286

Editorial: 1 Heddon Street, Mayfair, London W1B 4BD
Email: helloeurope@ilovevideo.tv
Web site: http://gb.ilovevideo.tv/
Freq: Daily
Circ: 297 Cision Digital Reach
MAGAZINE (ONLINE)
Broadcasting

i-MAGAZINE
994679

Editorial: Liberty House, 222 Regent Street, London W1B 5TR **Tel:** 44 02037 553644
Email: theeditor@imagazine.gb.com
Web site: www.imagazine.gb.com
Freq: Semi-Annual
Circ: 18500 Not Audited
MAGAZINE
Business, Luxury Goods, Men's Interests, Politics, Small and Medium Business, Women's Interests

Image
983184

Editorial: Unit 6, Broadfield Business Park, Sheffield S8 0XF **Tel:** 44 01142 506300
Email: chris.wilson@rmcmedia.co.uk
Web site: www.rmcmedia.co.uk/magazines/ image/
Freq: Monthly
Circ: 18000 Not Audited
Profile: Lifestyle magazine covering regional general interest including fashion, beauty, competitions, society, local business, travel, motoring, entertainment, restaurants, food and drink. Aimed at households in Sheffield, Eckington, Killamarsh, Mosborough and Beighton.
Ad Rate: Full Page Colour £944.00
MAGAZINE
Fashion, Regional General Interest

Images
984595

Editorial: Lioncare House, 58a Livingstone Road, Hove BN3 3WL **Tel:** 44 01273 748482
Email: editorial@images-magazine.com
Web site: www.images-magazine.com
Freq: Monthly
Circ: 5000 Not Audited
Profile: Journal covering textile screen printing, embroidery and garment decoration. Aimed at textile printers, embroiderers, promotion companies, suppliers, manufacturers and designers.
MAGAZINE
Fashion

ImagineFX
983312

Editorial: Quay House, The Ambury, Bath BA1 1UA **Tel:** 44 01225 442244
Email: mail@imaginefx.com
Web site: www.creativebloq.com/imaginefx
Freq: Monthly
Circ: 18000 Not Audited
Profile: Magazine with community news, reviews, interviews, workshops and tips. Aimed at fantasy and sci-fi enthusiasts.
Ad Rate: Full Page Colour £2068.00
MAGAZINE
Computer & Video Games, Graphic Design, Science Fiction, Software

IMarEST News
106412

Editorial: Unit G4, Harbour Yard, Chelsea Harbour, London SW10 0XD
Tel: 44 02070 457534
Email: marine@caspianmedia.com
Web site: www.imarest.org
Freq: Daily

Consumer Magazines

Circ: 23075 Cision Digital Reach
MAGAZINE (ONLINE)
Engineering, Marine & Boat Trade,
Science

Imbibe 987756
Editorial: Gateway House, 28 The Quadrant,
Richmond, London TW9 1DN
Tel: 44 02089 107071
Email: imbibe@imbibe.com
Web site: www.imbibe.com
Freq: Bi-Monthly
Circ: 15293 Not Audited
Editor: Chris Losh
MAGAZINE
Alcohol & Spirits, Bars, Clubs & Pubs

IMI Magazine 999099
Editorial: Fanshaws, Brickendon, Hertford
SG13 8PQ Tel: 44 01992 511521
Web site: http://magazine.theimi.org.uk/
magazine
Freq: Monthly
Circ: 12631 Not Audited
Editor: Tim Kiek
MAGAZINE
Automotive

The IMIA Report 997562
Editorial: 17 Tetbury Drive, Witney, Witney
OX28 5GF Tel: 44 02085 815151
Email: info@imiamaps.org
Web site: www.imiamaps.org
Freq: Monthly
Circ: 500 Not Audited
MAGAZINE
Environment

Impact (UK) 983171
Editorial: 1st Floor, Turnbridge Mills, Quay
Street, Huddersfield HD1 6QT
Tel: 44 03717 054656
Email: info@hitmedialtd.com
Web site: www.impactonline.co
Freq: Daily
Circ: 14405 Cision Digital Reach
MAGAZINE (ONLINE)
Computer & Video Games, Local
Entertainment Guides, Movies & Video

Impact Magazine 983775
Editorial: Nottingham Univ. Students' Union,
Portland Building, University Park,
Nottingham NG7 2RD
Email: editorinchief@impactnottingham.com
Web site: www.impactnottingham.com
Freq: Monthly Not Audited
MAGAZINE
Student Lifestyle

Imperial Engineer 995796
Editorial: Faculty Building - Level 2, South
Kensington Campus, Imperial College
London, London SW7 2AZ
Web site: https://www.imperial.ac.uk/
engineering/alumni/imperial-engineer/
Freq: Semi-Annual Not Audited
MAGAZINE
News & Current Affairs

Impolite Conversation 995033
Email: info@impoliteconversation.co.uk
Web site: www.impoliteconversation.co.uk/
Freq: Daily
Circ: 10511 Cision Digital Reach
MAGAZINE (ONLINE)
Alternative Medicine, Antiques/
Collectibles, Books, Cartoons, Consumer
Affairs, Energy & Environment, Ethical/
Moral Issues, Health & Medicine,
International News, LGBT

Improve Your Coarse Fishing
982179
Editorial: Media House, Lynchwood,
Peterborough Business Park, Peterborough
PE2 6EA Tel: 44 01733 468000
Web site: www.gofishing.co.uk/Angling-
Times/Section/Coarse-Magazines/Improve-
Your-Coarse-Fishing-Magazine
Freq: Monthly
Circ: 25400 Not Audited

Profile: Magazine covering coarse fishing
including advice and features on tackle. Also
includes information on where to fish. Aimed
at anglers who want to improve their skills.
Ad Rate: Full Page Colour £2500.00
MAGAZINE
Fishing

In and Around Covent Garden
981799
Editorial: 59 St. Martin's Lane, Covent
Garden, London WC2N 4JS
Tel: 44 02072 409731
Email: info@coventgarden.uk.com
Web site: www.coventgarden.uk.com
Freq: Monthly
Circ: 40000 Not Audited
Profile: Magazine covering entertainment,
theatre, shopping, wining and dining, history,
property and reviews as well as issues in
and around Covent Garden. Aimed at
households, businesses and visitors to
London WC2, Covent Garden, Central
London and the West End.
Ad Rate: Full Page Colour £2575.00
MAGAZINE
Local Entertainment Guides, Regional
General Interest

IN London 984688
Editorial: 2nd Floor, Samuel House, St
Alban's St, London SW1Y 4SQ
Tel: 44 02072 425222
Web site: www.mvplondon.net/in-london
Freq: Quarterly
Circ: 74249 Not Audited
Profile: Magazine containing news and
reviews on London. Includes features on art,
theatre, fairs, business, property, shopping
and restaurants for affluent visitors to
London.
Ad Rate: Full Page Colour £7320.00
MAGAZINE
Luxury Goods, Travel

In The Snow 985980
Tel: 44 01494 862423
Email: info@inthesnow.com
Web site: www.inthesnow.com
Freq: Monthly
Circ: 55000 Not Audited
Editor: Patrick Thorne
Profile: Magazine covering news and
features on skiing, snowboarding and
mountain lifestyle. Aimed at those interested
in skiing and snowboarding.
MAGAZINE
Travel, Winter Sports

In Touch Magazine 998248
Editorial: Ashdown House, Charlwoods
Road, East Grinstead, East Grinstead RH19
2HJ Tel: 44 01342 312570
Web site: http://in-touchmagazine.co.uk/
Freq: Bi-Monthly Not Audited
MAGAZINE
Regional General Interest

in2town 984639
Editorial: 9 Ariston Street, Grimsby DN32
8HQ
Email: editor@in2town.co.uk
Web site: www.in2town.co.uk
Freq: Daily
Circ: 12290 Cision Digital Reach
Editor: Tim Ellis
MAGAZINE (ONLINE)
Celebrities, Local Entertainment Guides,
Regional General Interest

Inapub 986432
Editorial: Inapub, 9 Britannia Court, The
Green, West Drayton UB7 7PN
Tel: 44 08452 301986
Email: editorial@inapub.co.uk
Web site: http://trade.inapub.co.uk/
Freq: Monthly
Circ: 20000 Not Audited
Editor: Matt Eley
Profile: Website covering pubs. The Inapub
website covering the latest news and
information on pub trading. The website
shares reviews on bars, drinks and food.
MAGAZINE
Alcohol & Spirits, Bars, Clubs & Pubs

InAVate 983152
Editorial: Blair House, 184/186 High Street,
Tonbridge, Tonbridge TN9 1BQ
Tel: 44 01732 359990
Email: inavate@imlgroup.co.uk
Web site: www.inavateonthenet.net
Freq: Monthly
Circ: 11000 Not Audited
Editor: Paul Milligan
Profile: Magazine covering the latest news,
views, product reviews and market analysis
on audio visual technology.
Ad Rate: Full Page Colour £2500.00
MAGAZINE
Electronics, Industry

InBath 1095956
Tel: 44 01225 958105
Web site: http://www.inbath.net/
Freq: Bi-Monthly
Editor: Craig Maplesden
MAGAZINE
Regional General Interest

InBroadcast 987540
Tel: 44 02890 610420
Email: inbroadcast@inbroadcast.com
Web site: www.inbroadcast.com
Freq: Monthly
Circ: 10360 Cision Digital Reach
Editor: Steven Preston
MAGAZINE (ONLINE)
Broadcasting, Computers, Software

INCheshire Magazine 988872
Editorial: Suite 2, 9-11 Princess Street,
Knutsford, Knutsford WA16 6BY
Tel: 44 01565 633336
Email: editor@incheshiremagazine.co.uk
Web site: http://incheshiremagazine.co.uk/
Freq: Monthly Not Audited
MAGAZINE
Regional General Interest

Incisor magazine 997172
Editorial: Hampshire Gate, Langley, Rake,
Petersfield GU33 7JR Tel: 44 01730 895614
Web site: www.incisor.tv
Freq: Monthly
Circ: 30000 Not Audited
Editor: Vince Holton
MAGAZINE
Auto Aftermarket, Computers, Data
Management, Electronics, Government
Technology, Industry, Internet, Mobile
Communications, Security & Security
Systems, Software

inCOMPLIANCE 995782
Editorial: Wrens Court, 52-54 Victoria Road,
Sutton Coldfield, Birmingham B72 1SX
Tel: 44 01213 627747
Email: jthomas284@btinternet.com
Web site: http://www.int-comp.org
Freq: Quarterly
Circ: 4500 Not Audited
Editor: James Thomas
MAGAZINE
News & Current Affairs

in-cumbria 996187
Editorial: Newspaper House, Dalston Road,
Carlisle CA2 5UA Tel: 44 01228 612600
Email: nick.turner@cnmedia.co.uk
Web site: www.in-cumbria.com
Freq: Quarterly
Circ: 5482 Not Audited
Editor: Richard Eccles
MAGAZINE
Regional

IND13 Magazine 1054265
Email: editorial@ind13.com
Web site: http://ind13.com/
Freq: Quarterly
Circ: 13937 Cision Digital Reach
MAGAZINE (ONLINE)
Computer & Video Games, Entertainment

Independent Living 996702
Editorial: 127 Marina, Hastings TN38 0BN
Tel: 44 02081 330628

Email: editor@independentliving.co.uk
Web site: www.independentliving.co.uk
Freq: Daily
Circ: 26042 Cision Digital Reach
Editor: Frances Leckie
MAGAZINE (ONLINE)
Community Care (UK), Disability, Health &
Medicine

**Independent Practitioner
Today** 984846
Editorial: PO Box 198, Cranleigh GU6 9BB
Web site: http://www.independent-
practitioner-today.co.uk
Freq: Monthly
Circ: 11330 Not Audited
Profile: Magazine featuring news, reports on
the latest developments in private health
care and views and opinions of the key
figures in the industry. Aimed at doctors with
a private practice.
MAGAZINE
Health Administration, Healthcare
Industry, Medicine

Independent Retail News 980058
Editorial: 6th Floor, Davis House, 2 Robert
Street, Croydon CR0 1QQ
Email: irn@metropolis.co.uk
Web site: www.talkingretail.com/
independent-retail-news-magazine
Freq: Bi-Weekly
Circ: 40000 Not Audited
Editor: David Shrimpton
Profile: Journal providing retail news and
product information. Aimed at independent
retailers.
MAGAZINE
Alcohol & Spirits, Consumer Goods &
Products, Food, Retail Management,
Tobacco

Independent School Sport
1103795
Editorial: Unit 2.4 Paintworks, Arnos Vale,
Bristol BS4 3EH Tel: 44 01173 005526
Web site: http://ie-today.co.uk/iSS-
Magazine
Freq: Bi-Monthly
Circ: 6500 Not Audited
MAGAZINE
Education, Fitness & Exercise

independent.co.uk 1066898
Editorial: 2 Derry Street, London W8 5HF
Tel: 44 02070 052000
Email: newsdesk@independent.co.uk
Web site: www.independent.co.uk
Freq: Daily
Circ: 17477622 Cision Digital Reach
Editor: Christian Broughton
MAGAZINE (ONLINE)
Consumer Affairs, Crime & Violence,
Defense & National Security, Energy &
Environment, Ethical/Moral Issues,
International News, Law, National News,
News & Current Affairs, Northern Ireland

The Index Magazine 983089
Editorial: Publications House, 39 Little
Mount Sion, Tunbridge Wells, Tunbridge
Wells TN1 1YS
Web site: www.indexdigital.co.uk
Freq: Monthly
Circ: 50000 Not Audited
Profile: Lifestyle magazine covering health,
fitness, travel, education, fashion, motoring,
interviews, property, gardens and
entertainment.
Ad Rate: Full Page Colour £890.00
MAGAZINE
Men's Interests, Women's Interests

Index on Censorship 988528
Editorial: 292 Vauxhall Bridge Road, London
SW1V 1AE Tel: 44 02079 637262
Email: info@indexoncensorship.org
Web site: www.indexoncensorship.org
Freq: Quarterly
Circ: 41500 Not Audited
Editor: Rachael Jolley

Consumer Magazines

Profile: Publication covering all aspects of free expression.
MAGAZINE
Law, Politics, Social Issues

India Link International   982585
Editorial: 42 Farm Ave, London HA2 7LR
Tel: 44 02088 668421
Email: indialink@hotmail.com
Web site: www.indialink-online.com
Freq: Bi-Monthly
Circ: 10000 Not Audited
Profile: Magazine covering politics, business and international news as well as lifestyle, travel, health and sport. Aimed at Indians living in the UK, USA and South Africa.
Ad Rate: Full Page Colour £600.00
MAGAZINE
Asia, National News

Indian Growth and Development Review   1004614
Editorial: Emerald Group Publishing, Howard House, Wagon Lane, Bingley BD16 1WA **Tel:** 44 01274 777700
Web site: www.emeraldinsight.com/loi/igdr
Freq: Semi-Annual Not Audited
MAGAZINE
News & Current Affairs

Indoor Play   999015
Editorial: Alhambra House, 9 St Michaels Road, Croydon, London CR9 3DD
Tel: 44 02086 030946
Web site: www.indoorplaymagazine.co.uk
Freq: Bi-Monthly
Circ: 6700 Not Audited
Editor: Tommy Leighton
MAGAZINE
Computer & Video Games, Schools & Institutions

Industrial Management & Data Systems   984409
Editorial: Howard House, Wagon Lane, Bingley BD16 1WA
Web site: www.emeraldinsight.com/imds.htm
Freq: Bi-Monthly Not Audited
Profile: Magazine covering management information and data systems. Also contains industry surveys, news stories and features on industrial management. Aimed at managers who wish to gain an understanding of key issues in technology and application.
MAGAZINE
News & Current Affairs

Industrial Measurement   1062119
Tel: 44 86106 3810195
Email: gj@gyjl.com.cn
Web site: http://www.gyjl.com.cn
Freq: Bi-Monthly
Circ: 20000 Not Audited
MAGAZINE
Auto Aftermarket, Computers, Data Management, Electronics, Government Technology, Industry, Internet, Mobile Communications, Security & Security Systems, Software

Industrial Plant & Equipment   981221
Editorial: 2nd Floor, North Suite, Kings House, 13-21 Cantelupe Road, East Grinstead RH19 3BE **Tel:** 44 01342 314300
Web site: www.ipesearch.com
Freq: Bi-Monthly
Circ: 18000 Not Audited
Editor: Val Kealey
MAGAZINE
Engineering, Manufacturing, Marine & Boat Trade, Mining & Quarrying, Paper, Plastics, Steel

Industrial Plant & Equipment Ireland   997648
Editorial: 2nd Floor - North Suite, Kings House, 13-21 Cantelupe Road, East Grinstead, East Grinstead RH19 3BE
Tel: 44 01342 314300
Web site: www.ipesearch.co.uk/Ireland

Freq: Quarterly Not Audited
Editor: Val Kealey
MAGAZINE
Defense & National Security, Engineering, Industry, Manufacturing, Marine & Boat Trade, Mining & Quarrying, Paper, Plastics, Steel

Industrial Robot: An International Journal   996481
Editorial: Howard House, Wagon Lane, Bingley BD16 1WA **Tel:** 44 01274 777700
Email: emerald@emeraldinsight.com
Web site: www.emeraldinsight.com/journals.htm?issn=0143-991X
Freq: Bi-Monthly Not Audited
MAGAZINE
News & Current Affairs

Industry Europe   981222
Editorial: Alkmaar House, Alkmaar Way, Norwich, Norwich NR6 6BF
Tel: 44 01603 414444
Email: editor@industryeurope.net
Web site: www.industryeurope.net
Freq: Monthly Not Audited
Editor: Peter Mercer
Profile: Magazine reporting on European manufacturing. It focuses increasingly on industrial developments in Central and Eastern Europe as well as in Russia, Ukraine and Turkey. Aimed at senior managers across Europe.
Ad Rate: Full Page Colour £4480.00
MAGAZINE
Engineering, Manufacturing, Marine & Boat Trade, Mining & Quarrying, Paper, Plastics, Steel

infinityhousemagazine.com   995116
Web site: http://infinityhousemagazine.com/
Freq: Daily
Circ: 9784 Cision Digital Reach
MAGAZINE (ONLINE)
Alternative Medicine, Cooking & Baking, Health & Medicine, Luxury Goods, Nutrition, Organic Food, Relationships, Religion, Restaurant Reviews, Vegetarianism & Veganism

Inflight   984167
Editorial: 103 Mytchett Road, Mytchett, Camberley GU16 6ES **Tel:** 44 01252 545993
Email: info@hmgaerospace.com
Web site: www.hmgaerospace.com/inflight/inflight-magazine/
Freq: Bi-Monthly
Circ: 18000 Not Audited
Editor: Alexander Preston
Profile: Magazine covering the in-flight passenger entertainment and passenger communications industry. Aimed at aviation and telecoms authorities, equipment manufacturers, service providers and technical and marketing personnel in airlines and operators.Accepts digital images only.
MAGAZINE
Airline Inflight, Aviation

INFO   988726
Editorial: French Chamber of Commerce in Great Britain, Lincoln House, 4th Floor, 300 High Holborn, London WC1V 7JH
Tel: 44 02070 926600
Email: mail@ccfgb.co.uk
Web site: http://www.ccfgb.co.uk
Freq: Bi-Monthly
Circ: 3000 Not Audited
Profile: Journal covering policy, regulation and strategy for telecommunications, information services and the media. Aimed at those concerned with corporate strategy and planning including regulatory bodies and government departments.
MAGAZINE
Business, Europe, Government

Infologue.com   988887
Tel: 44 08451 304008
Email: news@infologue.com
Web site: http://www.infologue.com/
Freq: Daily

Circ: 10219 Cision Digital Reach
MAGAZINE (ONLINE)
News & Current Affairs

Information Age   979860
Editorial: Vitesse Media Plc, 5th Floor, 14 Bonhill Street, London EC2A 4BX
Tel: 44 02072 507010
Web site: www.information-age.com
Freq: Monthly
Circ: 30000 Not Audited
Profile: Information Age, since its launch in 1995, has focused on the strategies and technologies involved in maximizing business performance through effective information and technology management. Creates environments to connect business with providers of information technology products and services. Information Age discusses IT management, Internet of Things, cloud, applications, information management, network security, software and hardware. Aimed at executives involved in the application of technology for strategic, competitive advantage and improved efficiency.
Ad Rate: Full Page Colour £5050.00
MAGAZINE
Computers, Data Management, Electronics, Internet, Mobile Communications, Security & Security Systems, Software

The Information Daily   984134
Editorial: Walker Building, 58 Oxford Street, Birmingham B5 5NR **Tel:** 44 08456 012247
Web site: www.theinformationdaily.com
Freq: Daily
Circ: 14048 Cision Digital Reach
Profile: Website covering government policy. The INFORMATION DAILY website is a roundup of key developments concerning electronic government and the public sector ICT marketplace, as well as the communication and technology markets. Aimed at senior executives in government and the IT industry, ministers, MPs, consultants and analysts.
MAGAZINE (ONLINE)
Charitable Foundations, Government, Public Sector

Information Network   1061545
Tel: 44 86105 8552261
Web site: http://www.ctbri.com.cn/publish/qkjj.jsp
Freq: Monthly
Circ: 30000 Not Audited
MAGAZINE
Auto Aftermarket, Computers, Data Management, Electronics, Government Technology, Industry, Internet, Mobile Communications, Security & Security Systems, Software

Information Research   1062085
Tel: 44 86591 87883359
Email: qbts@mail.si.net.cn
Web site: http://www.qbts.org
Freq: Monthly
Circ: 10000 Not Audited
MAGAZINE
Auto Aftermarket, Computers, Data Management, Electronics, Government Technology, Industry, Internet, Mobile Communications, Security & Security Systems, Software

Informed Cities Edinburgh   999379
Editorial: 6b Forres Street, Edinburgh EH3 6BJ **Tel:** 44 01312 252323
Web site: http://www.informededinburgh.co.uk/
Freq: Daily
Circ: 6644 Cision Digital Reach
MAGAZINE (ONLINE)
Local Entertainment Guides, Regional General Interest

ingénu/e magazine   988930
Email: pressdesk@ingenuemagazine.co.uk
Web site: www.ingenuemagazine.co.uk
Freq: Quarterly
Circ: 15000 Not Audited

Editor: Gill Kaye
MAGAZINE
Art, Classical/Choral/Band Music, Country, Folk, Bluegrass, Dance Music, Jazz & Blues, Literature, Music, Photography, Pop Music, R&B, Urban, World

Ingredients Global   1072015
Editorial: Kemp House, 152 - 160 City Road, London EC1V 2NX **Tel:** 44 02031 953828
Email: contact@ingredientsglobal.com
Web site: http://www.ingredientsglobal.com/
Freq: Daily
Circ: 521 Cision Digital Reach
MAGAZINE (ONLINE)
Alcohol & Spirits, Food

Inharness Magazine   1053752
Tel: 44 01380 730888
Email: inharness@redpin.co.uk
Web site: http://www.inharness.co.uk
Freq: Bi-Monthly
MAGAZINE
Equestrian Sports

inhouseflash   1060845
Tel: 44 42323 51122
Email: inhouseflash@lgt.com
Web site: http://www.lgt.com
Freq: Quarterly
Circ: 2450 Not Audited
MAGAZINE
News & Current Affairs

Ink Sweat and Tears   996209
Web site: www.inksweatandtears.co.uk
Freq: Daily
Circ: 12117 Cision Digital Reach
Editor: Helen Ivory
MAGAZINE (ONLINE)
Literature

Innerplace.co.uk   985121
Editorial: 73 Great Titchfield Street, London W1W 6RD **Tel:** 44 02076 364385
Email: info@innerplace.co.uk
Web site: www.innerplace.co.uk
Freq: Daily
Circ: 7282 Cision Digital Reach
Editor: Nick Savage
MAGAZINE (ONLINE)
Bars, Clubs & Pubs, Luxury Goods, Restaurant Reviews

Innovative Electrical Retailing   981134
Editorial: 15A London Road, Maidstone, Maidstone ME16 8LY **Tel:** 44 01622 687031
Web site: www.innovativeelectricalretailing.co.uk/
Freq: Monthly
Circ: 6083 Not Audited
Editor: Gregor Muir
Profile: Magazine covering all processes involved in the retail and manufacture of electrical appliances including business, market and product information across the three main sectors of the electrical trade: consumer electronics; major domestic appliances; small appliances. Aimed at senior management in user and vendor organisations and independent electrical retailers in the UK.
Ad Rate: Full Page Colour £3200.00
MAGAZINE
Electronics, Retail Management

inQuire   981765
Editorial: Kent Union, Mandela Building, University of Kent, Canterbury CT2 7NW
Tel: 44 01227 824200
Email: editor@inquiremedia.co.uk
Web site: www.inquirelive.co.uk
Freq: Bi-Weekly
Circ: 14500 Not Audited
Profile: inQuire is a free fortnightly newspaper produced entirely by University of Kent students covering campus news, sport, art and music reviews.
Ad Rate: Full Page Colour £350.00
MAGAZINE
Student Lifestyle

The INQUIRER
981679

Editorial: Haymarket House, 28-29 Haymarket, London SW1Y 4RX
Tel: 11 00070 100000
Web site: www.theinquirer.net
Freq: Daily
Circ: 1626988 Cision Digital Reach
Profile: Magazine covering aspects of Unitarianism, including book reviews, letters, meditations and international religious news. Aimed at people interested in liberal religion and Unitarians.Regular features: Book Reviews; Letters
MAGAZINE (ONLINE)
Apple, Auto Aftermarket, Computers, Data Management, Electronics, Internet, Mobile Communications, Personal Computers, Security & Security Systems, Software

INRIX
1055929

Editorial: 91 Charterhouse Street, London EC1M 6HR Tel: 44 02070 123500
Email: mediainfo@inrix.com
Web site: http://inrix.com/default.asp
Freq: Daily
Circ: 346 Cision Digital Reach
MAGAZINE (ONLINE)
Automotive, Aviation, Railroad, Shipping & Warehousing, Supply Chain Management (SCM), Transportation

Inside CI
987880

Editorial: First Floor, Element House, Clarendon Business Centres, 42-43 Upper Berkley Street, London W1H 5PW
Tel: 44 07860 328192
Email: info@insideci.co.uk
Web site: www.insideci.co.uk/
Freq: Daily
Circ: 18400 Cision Digital Reach
MAGAZINE (ONLINE)
Electronics

Inside Commissioning
997248

Editorial: Bridge House, 69 London Road, Twickenham, London TW1 3QR
Tel: 44 02082 675000
Web site: www.gponline.com/about/inside-commissioning
Freq: Daily
Circ: 877 Cision Digital Reach
MAGAZINE (ONLINE)
Medicine, Pharmaceuticals

Inside Drinks
1058241

Editorial: John Carpenter House, John Carpenter Street, London EC4Y 0AN
Tel: 44 02079 366400
Email: onlinemags@nridigital.com
Web site: http://www.nridigital.com/inside-drinks.html
Freq: Quarterly
Circ: 24 Cision Digital Reach
MAGAZINE (ONLINE)
Alcohol & Spirits

Inside Marine
988865

Editorial: Baltic Chambers, 2 Waveney Road, Lowestoft, Lowestoft NR32 1BN
Tel: 44 01502 576953
Email: media@insidemarine.com
Web site: www.insidemarine.com
Freq: Bi-Monthly
Circ: 41000 Not Audited
MAGAZINE
Marine & Boat Trade

Inside Networks
990528

Editorial: PO Box 3504, Norwich NR7 7QL
Tel: 44 07708 972170
Email: rob@chalkhillmedia.com
Web site: www.insidenetworks.co.uk
Freq: Monthly
Circ: 10181 Cision Digital Reach
Editor: Rob Shepherd
MAGAZINE (ONLINE)
Internet

Inside Satellite TV
999125

Tel: 44 02089 488561
Web site: www.insidesatellite.com
Freq: Bi-Weekly Not Audited

Profile: Website covering the communications satellite business. The website discusses broadcasting, internet, telecommunications and satellite technology.
MAGAZINE
Broadcasting

Inside Snooker
997397

Email: contact@inside-snooker.com
Web site: http://www.inside-snooker.com/
Freq: Daily
Circ: 1582 Cision Digital Reach
MAGAZINE (ONLINE)
Billiards

Inside Soap
982350

Editorial: 33 Broadwick Street, London W1F 0DQ Tel: 44 02073 394588
Email: editor@insidesoap.co.uk
Web site: www.insidesoap.co.uk
Freq: Weekly
Circ: 98226 Not Audited
Editor: Steven Murphy
Profile: Magazine covering news and stories on television soap operas and those who star in them. Aimed at soap opera enthusiasts.
Ad Rate: Full Page Colour £4000.00
MAGAZINE
Broadcasting

Inside the Games (UK)
985488

Editorial: MK TWO Business Centres, Bletchley, 1-9 Barton Road, Milton Keynes MK3 3HU
Web site: www.insidethegames.biz
Freq: Daily
Circ: 612550 Cision Digital Reach
MAGAZINE (ONLINE)
Basketball, Bicycles, Billiards, Boating & Yachting, Bodybuilding, Bowling, Boxing, Cricket, Equestrian Sports, Extreme/Adventure Sports

Inside Track
984724

Editorial: 2nd Floor, Shropshire House, 179 Tottenham Court Road, London W1T 7NZ
Email: inside.track@homeoffice.gsi.gov.uk
Freq: Bi-Monthly
Circ: 6000 Not Audited
Editor: Helena Markovic
Profile: Newspaper providing a round-up of news about Home Office staff and events.
MAGAZINE
Politics

Inside United
998734

Editorial: Sir Matt Busby Way, Old Trafford, Salford M16 0RA Tel: 44 01618 688000
Email: insideunited@manutd.co.uk
Web site: www.manutd.com/en/Fanzone.aspx
Freq: Monthly
Circ: 26817 Not Audited
Editor: Ben Ashby
MAGAZINE
Soccer

Inside Vue
995056

Editorial: 136-142 Bramley Road, London W10 6SR Tel: 44 02078 303979
Freq: Monthly
Circ: 150000 Not Audited
MAGAZINE
Movies & Video

insideKENT
985652

Editorial: The Panorama, Park Street, Ashford TN24 8EZ Tel: 44 01233 226240
Email: insidekent@sidewaysmedia.co.uk
Web site: www.insidekentmagazine.co.uk
Freq: Monthly
Circ: 25000 Not Audited
Profile: Magazine covering regional lifestyle news in Kent. It features events, fashion, dining, accommodation, businesses, travel, days out, entertainment, celebrities and interviews. Aimed at residents in Kent.
MAGAZINE
Alcohol & Spirits, Antiques/Collectibles, Art, Bars, Clubs & Pubs, Beer, Careers, Do-It-Yourself (DIY), Education, Fitness & Exercise, Gardening

Insider Media
979978

Editorial: Livery Place, 35 Livery St, Birmingham B3 2PB
Web site: https://www.insidermedia.com/
Freq: Monthly
Circ: 158728 Cision Digital Reach
MAGAZINE (ONLINE)
Business, Corporate Responsibility, Finance, Mergers & Acquisitions

insideSussex
988825

Editorial: 3rd Floor Queensberry House, 106 Queens Road, Brighton BN1 3XF
Tel: 44 01273 915110
Email: insidesussex@sidewaysmedia.co.uk
Web site: http://www.insidesussexmagazine.co.uk/
Freq: Monthly
Circ: 85000 Not Audited
Editor: Polly Humphris
Profile: Publication that covers best-of-the-best in Sussex, across fashion, local food and dining, entertainment and events, days out, business, art, travel, getaways and technology.
Ad Rate: Full Page Colour £995.00
MAGAZINE
Regional General Interest

insidetime
985676

Editorial: Botley Mills, Botley, Southampton SO30 2GB Tel: 44 01489 795945
Email: enquiries@insidetime.org
Web site: www.insidetime.org
Freq: Monthly
Circ: 60000 Not Audited
Editor In Chief: Erwin James
MAGAZINE
National News

Insight DIY
1063924

Editorial: Regents Place, 338 Euston Road, London NW1 3BT
Email: news@insightdiy.co.uk
Web site: www.insightdiy.co.uk
Freq: Daily
Circ: 48053 Cision Digital Reach
Editor: Steve Collinge
MAGAZINE (ONLINE)
Beauty & Grooming, Books, Cosmetics, Fashion, Gardening, Hair, Office Supplies, Retail, Retail Management, Toys

Insight Online (RNIB)
983217

Editorial: 105 Judd Street, London WC1H 9NE Tel: 44 02073 881266
Email: insightonline@rnib.org.uk
Web site: http://www.rnib.org.uk/insight-online
Freq: Bi-Monthly
Circ: 44564 Cision Digital Reach
MAGAZINE (ONLINE)
Disability, Ophthalmology & Optometry

Insights
995163

Editorial: Prostate Cancer UK, The Counting House, 53 Tooley Street, London SE1 2QN
Tel: 44 02033 107000
Email: editor@prostatecanceruk.org
Web site: http://prostatecanceruk.org/about-us/who-we-are/our-magazine
Freq: Semi-Annual Not Audited
Profile: Magazine featuring general interest articles, short stories and crosswords.
MAGAZINE
Patient Support

Insignia Lifestyle Boutique
1105193

Editorial: 7th floor, Portland House, Bressenden Place, London SW1E 5RS
Tel: 44 02075 350300
Email: editorial@insignia-lb.com
Web site: www.insignia-lb.com
Freq: Daily
Circ: 10435 Cision Digital Reach
MAGAZINE (ONLINE)
Expatriates, Luxury Goods

Insolvency Intelligence
980719

Editorial: Sweet & Maxwell, 160 Blackfriars Road, London SE1 8EZ
Tel: 44 02075 426867

Web site: http://www.sweetandmaxwell.co.uk/catalogue/productdetails.aspx?recordid=426&productid=6958
Freq: Bi-Monthly Not Audited
Profile: Journal covering news and views on all aspects of insolvency law.
MAGAZINE
Accounting, Corporate Law

Insomniac
996105

Email: editorial@insomniac.com
Web site: www.insomniac.com
Freq: Daily
Circ: 97813 Cision Digital Reach
MAGAZINE (ONLINE)
Dance Music, Theater & Performing Arts

inspiratia
985810

Editorial: The Plaza, 535 Kings Road, London SW10 0SZ Tel: 44 02073 519451
Email: news@inspiratia.com
Web site: www.inspiratia.com
Freq: Daily
Circ: 10465 Cision Digital Reach
Profile: Website covering the infrastructure finance landscape. It discusses anything from social infrastructure, transport, renewable energy and nuclear. The outlet offers RSS (Really Simple Syndication).
MAGAZINE (ONLINE)
Alternative/Renewable Energy, Automotive, Aviation, Railroad, Security & Security Systems, Shipping & Warehousing

Inspirational Birmingham
987026

Editorial: Barrington House, Leake Rd, Costock, Loughborough LE12 6XA
Tel: 44 08453 313031
Email: info@championsukplc.com
Web site: www.inspirational.uk.com
Freq: Semi-Annual
Circ: 20000 Not Audited
Editor: Matthew Hayes
Profile: Bi-annual magazine covering luxury living in Birmingham.
Ad Rate: Full Page Colour £1500.00
MAGAZINE
Luxury Goods, Regional, Regional General Interest

Inspire
983245

Editorial: CPO, Garcia Estate, Canterbury Road, Worthing BN13 1BW
Tel: 44 01903 604331
Email: editor@inspiremagazine.org.uk
Web site: www.inspiremagazine.org.uk
Freq: Monthly
Circ: 50000 Not Audited
Editor: Russ Bravo
Profile: Lifestyle magazine with coverage of local events and personalities including features on restaurants, wine, fashion, beauty, health, motoring, travel, interiors and gardening.
Ad Rate: Full Page Colour £895.00
MAGAZINE
Religion

Inspire
995780

Editorial: 275 Newmarket Road, Cambridge CB5 8JE Tel: 44 01223 378026
Email: inspire@arthritiscare.org.uk
Web site: www.inspirearthritiscare.org.uk
Freq: Quarterly
Circ: 50000 Not Audited
Profile: Lifestyle magazine with coverage of local events and personalities including features on restaurants, wine, fashion, beauty, health, motoring, travel, interiors and gardening.
Ad Rate: Full Page Colour £895.00
MAGAZINE
Charitable Foundations, Patient Support

Inspire Weddings
996617

Editorial: 2nd Floor, Conway Mill, 5 -7 Conway Street, Belfast BT13 2DE
Tel: 44 02895 215610
Email: editorial@inspire-weddings.com
Web site: www.inspire-weddings.com
Freq: Quarterly Not Audited

Consumer Magazines

Editor: Louise Corrigan
MAGAZINE
Weddings

Inspired Travel Magazine
1101207
Web site: http://inspiredtravelmag.com/
Freq: Bi-Monthly
MAGAZINE
Travel

Installation
983615
Editorial: 4th floor, The Emerson Building, 4-8 Emerson Street, London SE1 9DU
Tel: 44 02073 546002
Email: ukpressreleases@nbmedia.com
Web site: www.installation-international.com
Freq: Monthly
Circ: 12000 Not Audited
Editor: Paddy Baker
Profile: Magazine covering design and integration within the audio, video and lighting industries. Includes business and product news and features on management. Aimed at systems integrators, installers, architects and project consultants.
Ad Rate: Full Page Colour £2440.00
MAGAZINE
Electronics

Institute for War & Peace Reporting
990381
Editorial: 48 Gray's Inn Road, London WC1X 8LT **Tel:** 44 02078 311030
Web site: www.iwpr.net
Freq: Daily
Circ: 24108 Cision Digital Reach
MAGAZINE (ONLINE)
International News, Politics

Instrumentation
981319
Editorial: 15a London Road, Maidstone, Maidstone ME16 8LY **Tel:** 44 01622 687031
Web site: www.connectingindustry.com/Instrumentation/
Freq: Monthly
Circ: 10994 Not Audited
Profile: Publication covering control instruments, tests and measurements. First published in 1968, the publication has an average of 52 pages per issue. Aimed at buyers and specifiers.
Ad Rate: Full Page Colour £2100.00
MAGAZINE
Electronics

InStyle
982372
Editorial: 161 Marsh Wall, London E14 9AP
Tel: 44 02031 485000
Web site: www.instyle.co.uk
Freq: Monthly
Circ: 598922 Cision Digital Reach
Editor In Chief: Charlotte Moore
Profile: Magazine covering fashion, beauty, homes and entertainment. It looks at the lives and style of international celebrities. First published in 2001. Aimed at women aged between 25 and 35 years old.
Ad Rate: Full Page Colour £5000.00
MAGAZINE (ONLINE)
Beauty & Grooming, Celebrities, Cosmetics, Fashion, Hair, Women's Interests

Insurance Daily
984609
Freq: Daily
Circ: 16412 Cision Digital Reach
MAGAZINE (ONLINE)
News & Current Affairs

Integrated Wiring Products Buyers' Guide
1061091
Tel: 44 86106 8008610
Email: zxf80910@163.com
Freq: Annual Not Audited
MAGAZINE
Electronics, Manufacturing

Intelligent Cat Care
1052631
Editorial: International Cat Care, High Street, Shaftesbury SP3 6LD
Tel: 44 01747 871872
Email: magazine@icatcare.org

Web site: www.icatcare.org
Freq: Monthly
Circ: 11000 Not Audited
Editor: Cat Jordan
MAGAZINE
Charitable Foundations, Nature & Wildlife, Veterinary Medicine

Intelligent CatCare Magazine
998669
Editorial: High Street, Shaftesbury SP3 6LD
Tel: 44 01747 871872
Email: info@icatcare.org
Web site: https://icatcare.org
Freq: Quarterly
Circ: 113483 Cision Digital Reach
MAGAZINE (ONLINE)
Nature & Wildlife

Intelligent Insurer
985512
Editorial: Newton Media Ltd, Kingfisher House, 21-23 Elmfield Road, Bromley BR1 1LT
Freq: Quarterly
Circ: 10570 Not Audited
Profile: Magazine focusing on banking and insurance including finance, reinsurance, regulatory issues and industry news.
MAGAZINE
News & Current Affairs

Interactive Investor
983077
Editorial: First Floor, Standon House, 21 Mansell Street, London EC1 8AA
Tel: 44 02076 803600
Web site: www.iii.co.uk
Freq: Daily
Circ: 1667608 Cision Digital Reach
Profile: Website covering personal finance. The website discusses anything from news and features on investments to analysis and gives financial advice.
MAGAZINE (ONLINE)
Personal Finance

Interestment.co.uk
996403
Email: info@interestment.co.uk
Web site: www.interestment.co.uk
Freq: Daily
Circ: 12999 Cision Digital Reach
MAGAZINE (ONLINE)
Airline Inflight, Classical/Choral/Band Music, Country, Folk, Bluegrass, Dance Music, Fashion, Jazz & Blues, Lifestyle, Men's Interests, Music, Pop Music

InterGame
984815
Editorial: Office Block 1, Southlink Business Park, Hamilton Street, Oldham OL4 1DE
Tel: 44 01616 330100
Email: info@intergame.ltd.uk
Web site: www.intergameonline.com
Freq: Monthly
Circ: 12000 Not Audited
Profile: International magazine containing news from the coin-operated games and leisure industries. Aimed at personnel within family entertainment centres and people involved in the coin-operated games and casino industries.This magazine contains the following regular features: Products - The latests products to hit the market.
Ad Rate: Full Page Colour £1995.00
MAGAZINE
Casinos & Gaming, Computer & Video Games

InterGaming
981231
Editorial: Unit 1, Southlink Business Park, Hamilton Street, Oldham OL4 1DE
Tel: 44 01616 330100
Email: editorial@intergame.ltd.uk
Web site: www.intergameonline.com
Freq: Monthly
Circ: 10000 Not Audited
Profile: Magazine containing international casino industry news, including new casino projects, changes in legislation, new products, supplier activity and in-depth features on industry trends, technology and legal issues.

Ad Rate: Full Page Colour £1995.00
MAGAZINE
Casinos & Gaming, Computer & Video Games

Interior Motives
983362
Editorial: 401 King Street, London W6 9NJ
Tel: 44 02089 870900
Email: info@ultimamedia.com
Web site: www.interiormotivesmagazine.com
Freq: Quarterly
Circ: 5100 Not Audited
Editor: Farah Alkhalisi
Profile: Magazine covering automotive interior, design, material and purchasing. Read by designers, buyers, product planners, vehicle line executives and high tier suppliers.
Ad Rate: Full Page Colour £3000.00
MAGAZINE
Automotive, Supply Chain Management (SCM)

Interior Scene
1105184
Email: accounts@interiorscene.co.uk
Web site: http://interiorscene.co.uk/
Freq: Daily
Circ: 521 Cision Digital Reach
MAGAZINE (ONLINE)
Do-It-Yourself (DIY)

Interiors Focus
984773
Editorial: Olton Bridge - Unit 4, 245 Warwick Road, Solihull, Solihull B92 7AH
Tel: 44 01217 070077
Email: info@thefis.org
Web site: www.thefis.org
Freq: Semi-Annual
Circ: 12000 Not Audited
Editor: Jane Cook
Profile: Official publication of the Association of Interior Specialists. Content is predominantly concerned with interior fit-outs and refurbishment in the retail, commercial and public sectors, including partitioning, suspended ceilings, access floors, operable walls, drylining, wall and floor coverings, glass and glazing.
Ad Rate: Full Page Colour £2098.00
MAGAZINE
Architecture & Design, Do-It-Yourself (DIY), Property Management & Maintenance

intern
1101757
Editorial: 211 Islington Mill, James Street, Salford, Manchester M3 5HW
Web site: www.intern-mag.com
Freq: Semi-Annual Not Audited
Profile: Magazine focussing on interns and internships in the creative industries. It provides a showcase for the talent currently working in these fields as interns or otherwise unpaid. It debates the current state of the intern culture and its potential implications.
MAGAZINE
Careers

Intern Magazine
988234
Editorial: 211 Islington Mill, James Street, Salford, Salford M3 5HW
Web site: www.intern-mag.com/
Freq: Semi-Annual Not Audited
MAGAZINE
Art, Literature

International Adviser
983250
Editorial: Fleet House, 1st Floor, 59-61 Clerkenwell Road, London EC1M 5LA
Tel: 44 02073 825970
Email: iam@lastwordmedia.com
Web site: www.international-adviser.com
Freq: Monthly
Circ: 9684 Not Audited
Editor: Mark Battersby
Profile: News magazine covering the latest on changes to tax, new investment trends, regulatory developments and portfolio strategy advice as they affect investors in offshore products. Aimed at those who distribute international and offshore fund, life and banking products to high net worth individuals, families and trusts.

Ad Rate: Full Page Colour £1995.00
MAGAZINE
Banking, Fund Management, Personal Finance

International Affairs
984908
Editorial: Chatham House, 10 St James's Square, London SW1Y 4LE
Tel: 44 02079 575728
Email: contact@chathamhouse.org
Web site: www.onlinelibrary.wiley.com
Freq: Bi-Monthly Not Audited
Profile: Journal covering international relations.
MAGAZINE
International News, Politics

International Arts Manager
982576
Editorial: Studio 514, Hope Mill, 113 Pollard Street, Ancoats, Manchester M4 7JA
Tel: 44 01825 983105
Email: info@lewisbusinessmedia.co.uk
Web site: http://www.internationalartsmanager.com/
Freq: Monthly
Circ: 15000 Not Audited
Editor: Maria Roberts
Profile: Magazine covering news, recruitment, artist management, recording services, financial matters, policy and legal developments for the international performing arts industry, with a primary focus on classical music and opera. Aimed at senior executives in the performing arts industry.
Ad Rate: Full Page Colour £2495.00
MAGAZINE
Classical/Choral/Band Music, Music, Theater & Performing Arts

International Badminton Magazine
982294
Tel: 44 08448 797949
Email: info@isportgroup.com
Web site: isportgroup.com/iSPORTmedia/Badminton-Magazine
Freq: Quarterly
Circ: 40000 Not Audited
Profile: Magazine featuring club players information, national and international event reports, features on players, general badminton news and sports product news. News from the governing body and how it affects the club player. Aimed at enthusiasts, club players and those with a keen interest in badminton.
Ad Rate: Full Page Colour £2500.00
MAGAZINE
Racquet Sports

International Boat Industry
984227
Editorial: 6 Tiberius Square, Kings park, St. Albans AL3 4GE
Email: info@ibiplus.co.uk
Web site: www.ibinews.com
Freq: Bi-Monthly
Circ: 12000 Not Audited
Editor: Ed Slack
MAGAZINE
Marine & Boat Trade

International Bottler and Packer
985408
Editorial: 53 Basepoint, Caxton Close, East Portway Industrial Estate, Andover SP10 3FG **Tel:** 44 01264 326480
Email: editorial@binstedgroup.com
Web site: www.binstedgroup.com/pubs/ibp.html
Freq: Monthly
Circ: 5237 Not Audited
Editor: Ed Binsted
MAGAZINE
Alcohol & Spirits, Manufacturing, Supply Chain Management (SCM)

International Comparative Legal Guide Series
995925
Editorial: 59 Tanner Street, London SE1 3PL
Web site: https://iclg.com/
Freq: Annual

Circ: 120000 Not Audited

MAGAZINE

News & Current Affairs

International Cranes and Specialized Transport
980973

Editorial: Southfields, Southview Road, Wadhurst, Wadhurst TN5 6TP

Tel: 44 01892 784088

Web site: http://www.khl.com/magazines/international-cranes-and-specialized-transport/

Freq: Monthly

Circ: 17409 Not Audited

Editor: Alex Dahm

MAGAZINE

Automotive

International Cruise & Ferry Review
983777

Editorial: Tudor Rose, 6 Friar Lane, Leicester LE1 5RA Tel: 44 01162 229900

Email: news@cruiseandferry.net

Web site: www.cruiseandferry.net

Freq: Semi-Annual

Circ: 3527 Not Audited

Editor: Michele Witthaus

Profile: Professional magazine covering cruise and ferry business, building and refurbishment, marine operations, onboard experience, ports and destinations.

Ad Rate: Full Page Colour £5000.00

MAGAZINE

Travel

International Dealer News
985363

Editorial: 5 Rendlesham Mews, Rendlesham, Woodbridge, Woodbridge IP12 2SZ Tel: 44 01892 511516

Web site: www.dealer-world.com

Freq: Bi-Monthly Not Audited

Profile: Motorcycle trade journal providing an international link between parts and accessories dealers and the industry that serves them all.

Ad Rate: Full Page Colour £1895.00

MAGAZINE

Automotive

International Dyer
983557

Editorial: West One, 114 Wellington Street, Leeds LS1 1BA Tel: 44 01138 198155

Email: info@wtin.com

Web site: http://www.wtin.com/e-store/international-dyer/

Freq: Monthly

Circ: 7940 Not Audited

Profile: International Dyer is a magazine containing specialised information on all areas of textile dyeing, finishing, printing and coating. Aimed at the textile dyeing, finishing and printing industry world-wide. Regular features: Diary of Events Information on relevant forthcoming exhibitions and conferences around the world.; Dyes & Chemicals New dyeing and chemical products.; Machinery & Services New products and services.; World News Company and industry news for dyers, finishers and printers.

Ad Rate: Full Page Mono £1240.00

Ad Rate: Full Page Colour £2700.00

MAGAZINE

Fashion

International Environmental Technology
980902

Editorial: Oak Court Business Centre, Sandridge Park, Porters Wood, St Albans, London AL3 6PH Tel: 44 01727 858840

Email: editor@envirotechpubs.com

Web site: www.envirotech-online.com

Freq: Bi-Monthly

Circ: 34151 Not Audited

Profile: Journal detailing the latest equipment, instruments and services available for environmental monitoring, pollution control and safety.

Ad Rate: Full Page Colour £5595.00

MAGAZINE

Electronics, Environment

International Finance Magazine
996182

Editorial: 843 Finchley Road, London NW11 8NO Tel: 44 02091 320436

Email: press@ifinancemag.com

Web site: www.internationalfinancemagazine.com

Freq: Daily

Circ: 128760 Cision Digital Reach

Editor: Dhiraj Shetty

MAGAZINE (ONLINE)

Banking, Emerging Markets, Financial Markets, Personal Finance

International Fleet World
983716

Editorial: 18 Alban Park, Hatfield Road, St Albans, London AL4 0JJ

Tel: 44 01727 739160

Email: info@fleetworldgroup.co.uk

Web site: http://internationalfleetworld.co.uk

Freq: Monthly

Circ: 13875 Not Audited

Editor: Alex Grant; Editor: John Kendall

Profile: Magazine covering strategic fleet purchasing and policy issues. Includes articles on human resources, market information and finance.

Ad Rate: Full Page Colour £6810.00

MAGAZINE

Automotive

International In-house Counsel Journal
999479

Editorial: Salisbury House, Station Road, Cambridge CB1 2LA Tel: 44 01223 750755

Web site: www.iicj.net

Freq: Quarterly Not Audited

Editor: Michael Bond

MAGAZINE

News & Current Affairs

The International Journal of Antimicrobial Agents
985282

Editorial: The Boulevard, Langford Lane, Kidlington OX5 1GB Tel: 44 01865 843434

Email: ijaa@elsevier.com

Web site: www.elsevier.com/wps/find/journaldescription.cws_home/505521/description

Freq: Monthly Not Audited

Editor In Chief: J.M. Rolain

MAGAZINE

Medicine

The International Journal of Behavioral Nutrition and Physical Activity
997932

Editorial: Floor 6, 236 Gray's Inn Road, London WC1X 8HB Tel: 44 02031 922009

Email: info@biomedcentral.com

Web site: http://ijbnpa.biomedcentral.com/

Freq: Daily

Circ: 751356 Cision Digital Reach

MAGAZINE (ONLINE)

Nutrition, Sports Medicine

The International Journal of Clinical Practice
985440

Editorial: 9600 Garsington Road, Oxford OX4 2DQ Tel: 44 01865 476488

Email: ijcp_editorial@wiley.com

Web site: http://onlinelibrary.wiley.com/journal/10.1111/(ISSN)1742-1241

Freq: Monthly Not Audited

Profile: Journal containing review articles, editorials, original papers, preliminary communications, discussion papers, papers on the history of medicine, case reports, meeting reports, lectures, student studies, letters and book reviews. Read by doctors involved in research worldwide and scientists in the worldwide pharma industry.

MAGAZINE

Medicine, Pharmaceuticals

International Journal of Epidemiology
985382

Editorial: School of Social and Community Medicine, University of Bristol, Oakfield House, Oakfield Grove, Bristol BS8 2BN

Tel: 44 01173 310052

Email: ije-editorial@bristol.ac.uk

Web site: ije.oxfordjournals.org

Freq: Bi-Monthly Not Audited

Profile: Journal of epidemiology covering infectious and non-infectious diseases. Aimed at those working in social and preventive medicine.

Ad Rate: Full Page Colour £1418.00

MAGAZINE

Medicine

International Journal of Food Microbiology
999008

Editorial: The Boulevard, Langford Lane, Kidlington OX5 1GB Tel: 44 01865 843434

Web site: www.elsevier.com/wps/find/journaldescription.cws_home/505514/description

Freq: Bi-Weekly Not Audited

MAGAZINE

Nutrition

International Journal of Health Governance
985232

Editorial: Howard House, Wagon Lane, Bingley BD16 1WA Tel: 44 01274 777700

Web site: http://www.emeraldinsight.com/journal/cgij

Freq: Quarterly

Profile: Journal covering multi-professional healthcare auditing, evidence-based practice, fund monitoring and clinical effectiveness.

MAGAZINE

Medicine

International Journal of Language & Communication Disorders
985953

Editorial: The Atrium, Southern Gate, Chichester, Chichester PO19 8SQ

Tel: 44 01243 779777

Web site: http://onlinelibrary.wiley.com/journal/10.1111/(ISSN)1460-6984

Freq: Bi-Monthly Not Audited

MAGAZINE

Medicine

International Journal of Manpower
980977

Editorial: Howard House, Wagon Lane, Bingley BD16 1WA Tel: 44 01274 777700

Web site: http://www.emeraldinsight.com/journal/ijm

Freq: Bi-Monthly Not Audited

Profile: Publication covering issues in manpower resources management and labour economics at all levels of corporate local, national and international perspective.

MAGAZINE

News & Current Affairs

International Journal of Nonprofit and Voluntary Sector Marketing
995813

Web site: www.onlinelibrary.wiley.com/journal/10.1002/(ISSN)1479-103X;jsessionid=0DCEACE9D1AED35B9BAC9A363B45A

Freq: Quarterly Not Audited

MAGAZINE

News & Current Affairs

International Journal of Retail & Distribution Management
980783

Editorial: Howard House, Wagon Lane, Bingley BD16 1WA Tel: 44 01274 777700

Web site: http://www.emeraldgrouppublishing.com/products/journals/journals.htm?id=ijrdm

Freq: Monthly

Circ: 2000 Not Audited

Profile: Journal covering case studies and industry reports, information and reviews and research institute papers.

MAGAZINE

News & Current Affairs

International Journal of Social Economics
1004617

Editorial: Emerald Group Publishing, Howard House, Wagon Lane, Bingley BD16 1WA Tel: 44 01274 777700

Web site: http://www.emeraldinsight.com/journal/ijse

Freq: Monthly Not Audited

MAGAZINE

News & Current Affairs

International Journal of Sport Nutrition and Exercise Metabolism
999009

Web site: http://journals.humankinetics.com/IJSNEM

Freq: Bi-Monthly Not Audited

MAGAZINE

Nutrition, Sports Medicine

International Law Office
983176

Editorial: New Hibernia House, Winchester Walk, London Bridge, London SE1 9AG

Tel: 44 02072 340606

Email: press@internationallawoffice.com

Web site: www.internationallawoffice.com

Freq: Daily

Circ: 48651 Cision Digital Reach

Profile: Website covering legal developments, a directory of firms and partners. The website discusses a database of the world's major deals and the legal advisers involved with a global news round-up.

MAGAZINE (ONLINE)

News & Current Affairs

International Leather Maker
996162

Editorial: The Leathermarket, LF3.04, 11-13 Weston Street, London SE1 3ER

Tel: 44 02037 356538

Web site: http://www.internationalleathermaker.com/

Freq: Bi-Monthly

Circ: 3000 Not Audited

MAGAZINE

Fashion

The International Map Collector's Society Journal
996961

Tel: 44 01799 540765

Web site: http://www.imcos.org/imcos-journal

Freq: Quarterly Not Audited

Editor: Ljiljana Ortolja-Baird

MAGAZINE

Antiques/Collectibles

International Marketing Review
982946

Editorial: Howard House, Wagon Lane, Bingley BD16 1WA Tel: 44 01274 777700

Web site: http://emeraldgrouppublishing.com/products/journals/journals.htm?id=imr

Freq: Bi-Monthly Not Audited

MAGAZINE

News & Current Affairs

International Medical Travel Journal
984102

Editorial: 3 Churchgates, Wilderness, Berkhamsted, Berkhamsted HP4 2UB

Tel: 44 01442 817817

Email: editorial@imtj.com

Web site: https://www.imtj.com/

Freq: Daily

Circ: 129273 Cision Digital Reach

Profile: Website covering the medical travel sector.

MAGAZINE (ONLINE)

Healthcare Industry, Travel

International Meetings Review
1005240

Web site: http://www.internationalmeetingsreview.com/

Freq: Daily

Circ: 15254 Cision Digital Reach

MAGAZINE (ONLINE)

News & Current Affairs

International Ocean Systems
984241

Editorial: 8 Mount Mews, Hampton, London TW12 2SH **Tel:** 44 02089 418152
Web site: www.intoceansys.co.uk
Freq: Bi-Monthly
Circ: 10003 Not Audited
Editor: Daniel Johnson
Profile: Magazine covering ocean data gathering, underwater surveying and instrumentation worldwide. Aimed at people working in the commercial oceanology market.Previous title: International Ocean Systems Design Regular features: Events A guide to forthcoming events.; It's New Information on new products.; Ocean News Features the latest news and developments regarding ocean data gathering.; We've sold Details of contracts awarded.
Ad Rate: Full Page Mono £1545.00
Ad Rate: Full Page Colour £2075.00
MAGAZINE
Environment, Marine & Boat Trade

International Piano
982092

Editorial: Rhinegold House, 20 Rugby Street, London WC1N 3QZ
Tel: 44 02073 331733
Email: international.piano@rhinegold.co.uk
Web site: www.international-piano.com
Freq: Bi-Monthly
Circ: 30000 Not Audited
Editor: Owen Mortimer
Profile: Magazine covering the piano world including concert reviews, interviews with pianists, articles on historical pianists, sheet music reviews and features on technique and repertoire. Aimed at piano enthusiasts, record collectors and pianists.Regular features: News, reviews section reviews of concerts, CD's, DVD's, books and sheet music, rising stars young pianists, tutorials.
Ad Rate: Full Page Colour £1270.00
MAGAZINE
Classical/Choral/Band Music, Music

International Press Foundation
1054267

Email: hello@the-ipf.com
Web site: http://the-ipf.com
Freq: Daily
Circ: 15587 Cision Digital Reach
Editor: Rebecca Shearer
MAGAZINE (ONLINE)
Politics

International Prime Properties
1094459

Freq: Quarterly
Circ: 40000 Not Audited
MAGAZINE
News & Current Affairs

International Project Finance Association
983415

Editorial: 2nd Floor, 150 Fleet Street, London EC4A 2DQ **Tel:** 44 02074 270900
Email: info@ipfa.org
Web site: www.ipfa.org
Freq: Daily
Circ: 13923 Cision Digital Reach
MAGAZINE (ONLINE)
Banking, Personal Finance

International Property & Travel
981866

Editorial: The Mill House, Bishop Hall Lane, Chelmsford, Chelmsford CM1 1LG
Tel: 44 01245 250981
Email: info@ipropertymedia.com
Web site: http://ipropertymedia.com/
Freq: Bi-Monthly
Circ: 30000 Not Audited
Editor: Jill Keene
Profile: Luxury lifestyle magazine covering luxury real estate, luxury goods and cars, as well as high end resorts and hotels. First published in 1990. Aimed at international travellers, home buyers and sellers.
Ad Rate: Full Page Colour £4300.00
MAGAZINE
Real Estate, Travel

International Railway Journal
983080

Editorial: 46 Killigrew Street, Falmouth, Falmouth TR11 3PP **Tel:** 44 01326 313945
Email: irj@railjournal.com
Web site: www.railjournal.com
Freq: Monthly
Circ: 10611 Not Audited
Profile: Journal focusing on railway and transit systems worldwide, including managerial, technical and engineering articles.
Ad Rate: Full Page Mono £2600.00
Ad Rate: Full Page Colour £3600.00
MAGAZINE
Railroad

International Squash Magazine
984253

Tel: 44 08448 797949
Email: info@isportgroup.com
Web site: www.isportgroup.com/iSPORTmedia/Squash-Magazine
Freq: Quarterly
Circ: 60000 Not Audited
Profile: Magazine reviews of the squash world tour events within each quarter as well as player profiles. Aimed at squash players of all levels.
Ad Rate: Full Page Colour £2500.00
MAGAZINE
Racquet Sports

International Therapist
981175

Editorial: 18 Shakespeare Business Centre, Hathaway Close, Eastleigh SO50 4SR
Tel: 44 02380 624350
Email: info@fht.org.uk
Web site: http://www.fht.org.uk/international-therapist
Freq: Quarterly
Circ: 15169 Not Audited
Editor: Karen Young
Profile: Journal covering beauty, complementary and sport therapies including aromatherapy, reflexology and remedial massage.
Ad Rate: Full Page Mono £1365.00
Ad Rate: Full Page Colour £1575.00
MAGAZINE
Alternative Medicine, Occupational Therapy & Rehabilitation

The International Travel Writers Alliance
998783

Editorial: Hampton House, 77 The Ridgeway, North Chingford, London E4 6QW
Tel: 44 07764 198286
Email: ashley@itwalliance.com
Web site: www.internationaltravelwritersalliance.com
Freq: Daily
Circ: 10399 Cision Digital Reach
MAGAZINE (ONLINE)
Travel

International Tug & OSV
980826

Editorial: ABR House, Prospect Place, Trowbridge, Trowbridge BA14 8UA
Tel: 44 01225 868821
Email: info@tugandosv.com
Web site: www.tugandsalvage.com
Freq: Bi-Monthly
Circ: 9430 Not Audited
Editor: John McCready
MAGAZINE
Marine & Boat Trade

Internet of Business
1053830

Editorial: Tagwright House 35-41 Westland Place, 2 Bath Place, Rivington Street, London N1 7LP **Tel:** 44 02038 418333
Web site: https://internetofbusiness.com
Freq: Daily
Circ: 17940 Cision Digital Reach
MAGAZINE (ONLINE)
Auto Aftermarket, Computers, Data Management, Electronics, Government Technology, Industry, Internet, Mobile Communications, Security & Security Systems, Software

Internet Retailing
983874

Editorial: 52-54 Gracechurch Street, London EC3V 0EH **Tel:** 44 02079 338999
Email: press@internetretailing.net
Web site: http://internetretailing.net/
Freq: Bi-Monthly
Circ: 7084 Not Audited
Profile: Magazine and web portal providing insight and analysis into retailing in the UK from the focus point of the online business. It provides a source of ideas, competitive intelligence and briefing for both internet only and multi-channel retailers. Every aspect of the business is covered from strategy and marketing to IT, delivery and internet of things (IoT). Aimed at managing directors and heads of departments of internet and multi-channel retailers.Digital images preferred.
Ad Rate: Full Page Colour £3576.00
MAGAZINE
Internet, Retail Management

InterPark Magazine
998683

Editorial: 137 Newshaw Lane, Hadfield, Glossop, Glossop SK13 2AT
Tel: 44 01457 865500
Email: lily@interpark.co.uk
Web site: www.interpark.co.uk
Freq: Bi-Monthly
Circ: 5000 Not Audited
Editor: Andrew Mellor
MAGAZINE
Genealogy, Travel

intervene
983848

Editorial: Addiction Recovery Foundation, 193 Victoria Street, London SW1E 5NE
Tel: 44 02072 335333
Email: info@addictiontoday.org
Web site: http://www.intervene.org.uk/
Freq: Monthly
Circ: 4000 Not Audited
Editor: Melissa Gordon
Profile: Magazine containing articles on practical education for all professionals involved in addiction recovery. Aimed at treatment providers, purchasers and policy makers throughout the UK.
Ad Rate: Full Page Colour £1115.00
MAGAZINE
Charitable Foundations, Neurology

Interzone
984629

Editorial: 5 Martins Lane, Witcham, Ely, Ely CB6 2LB
Web site: www.ttapress.com/interzone
Freq: Bi-Monthly Not Audited
MAGAZINE
News & Current Affairs

Into Film
1010715

Editorial: 31 Islington Green, London N1 8DU **Tel:** 44 02072 884520
Email: support@filmclub.org
Web site: www.filmclub.org
Freq: Daily
Circ: 31208 Cision Digital Reach
MAGAZINE (ONLINE)
Movies & Video

INTO IT
1054271

Tel: 44 07930 358326
Email: sayhi@intoit.london
Web site: www.intoit.london
Freq: Daily
Circ: 17090 Cision Digital Reach
MAGAZINE (ONLINE)
Beauty & Grooming, Cosmetics, Fashion, Hair, Women's Interests

Into_View Magazine
1053187

Email: contact@theinterview-london.com
Web site: www.theinterview-london.com
Freq: Daily
Circ: 11000 Cision Digital Reach
MAGAZINE (ONLINE)
Business, Cooking & Baking, Fashion, Hotels/Motels, Regional General Interest, Small and Medium Business

The Intolerant Gourmand
996072

Tel: 44 07760 277987
Email: info@intolerantgourmand.com
Web site: http://www.intolerantgourmand.com/
Freq: Daily
Circ: 11172 Cision Digital Reach
MAGAZINE (ONLINE)
Allergies, Health & Medicine

Introducer Today
984361

Editorial: Angels House, 5 Albemarle Road, Beckenham BR3 5HZ **Tel:** 44 08450 750152
Email: press@introducertoday.co.uk
Web site: www.introducertoday.co.uk
Freq: Daily
Circ: 13155 Cision Digital Reach
Profile: Website covering mortgages. Introducer Today shares the latest news on advertising and marketing solutions. It was set up to develop websites and offer clients within the mortgage intermediary market an on-line solution to advertising and marketing through the web.
MAGAZINE (ONLINE)
Personal Finance

Inversor LATAM
1061712

Tel: 44 54113 5262690
Email: redaccion@inversorlatam.com
Web site: http://www.inversorlatam.com
Freq: Daily
Circ: 12627 Cision Digital Reach
MAGAZINE (ONLINE)
Banking, Business, International News, Small and Medium Business

Investment Life & Pensions Moneyfacts
983027

Editorial: Moneyfacts House, 66-70 Thorpe Road, Norwich NR1 1BJ
Tel: 44 01603 476476
Email: enquiries@moneyfacts.co.uk
Web site: www.moneyfactsgroup.co.uk
Freq: Monthly
Circ: 3139 Not Audited
Editor: Richard Eagling
Profile: Publication providing editorial and data on life assurance, pensions, annuities, unit trusts, investment trusts and ISAs. Includes information on premium rates, plan details, fund performance and commission. Read by financial advisors and financial institutions including IFAs, banks, building societies, accountants, solicitors, life companies and investment houses. Alternative Title: Life & Pensions Money£acts Previous title: Life & Pensions Moneyfacts
Ad Rate: Full Page Colour £1500.00
MAGAZINE

Investment Sense
986701

Editorial: Lace Market House, 54-56 High Pavement, Lace Market, Nottingham NG1 1HW **Tel:** 44 01159 338433
Email: info@investmentsense.co.uk
Web site: www.investmentsense.co.uk
Freq: Daily
Circ: 11622 Cision Digital Reach
MAGAZINE (ONLINE)
Personal Finance

Investment Trust Newsletter
983706

Editorial: St Brandon's House, 29 Great George Street, Bristol BS1 5QT
Tel: 44 01179 200070
Email: enquiries@mchattie.co.uk
Web site: www.tipsheets.co.uk
Freq: Monthly Not Audited
Editor: Andrew McHattie
Profile: Published since 1996, Investment Trust Newsletter provides private investors with independent advice on how to buy the right trusts at the right time and offers insight into the trusts on offer.
MAGAZINE
Fund Management

Investors Chronicle
979827

Editorial: Number One, Southwark Bridge, London SE1 9HL **Tel:** 44 02078 733000
Email: john.hughman@ft.com

Web site: www.investorschronicle.co.uk
Freq: Weekly
Circ: 30324 Not Audited
Editor: John Hughman
Profile: Magazine covering direct stock market investment offering news, advice and analysis. Includes features on areas of personal finance.
Ad Rate: Full Page Colour £4000.00
MAGAZINE
Personal Finance

Invision Game Community
997973
Email: admin@invisioncommunity.co.uk
Web site: www.invisioncommunity.co.uk
Freq: Daily
Circ: 83264 Cision Digital Reach
MAGAZINE (ONLINE)
Computer & Video Games

I-on
983084
Editorial: Suite 9, 2 Commercial Street, Edinburgh EH6 6JA **Tel:** 44 01315 554126
Email: info@ionmagazine.co.uk
Web site: http://www.ionmagazine.co.uk/
Freq: Monthly
Circ: 44389 Not Audited
Editor: Nicky Howden
MAGAZINE
Local Entertainment Guides, Regional General Interest

IOT Insights
1052664
Tel: 44 02037 147023
Email: news@iotinsights.com
Web site: www.iotinsights.com
Freq: Daily
Circ: 11661 Cision Digital Reach
MAGAZINE (ONLINE)
Internet

IoT Now
985854
Tel: 44 01732 807411
Web site: www.iot-now.com
Freq: Bi-Monthly
Circ: 29800 Not Audited
Editor: George Malim
MAGAZINE
Auto Aftermarket, Computers, Electronics, Government Technology, Industry, Internet, Security & Security Systems, Software, Telecommunications/Electronic Communications

IoT World (UK)
1054117
Editorial: 20-22 Wenlock Road, London N1 7GU **Tel:** 44 02089 383258
Email: info@iotworldmagazine.com
Web site: http://iotworldmagazine.com/
Freq: Daily
Circ: 10560 Cision Digital Reach
MAGAZINE (ONLINE)
Auto Aftermarket, Computers, Data Management, Electronics, Government Technology, Industry, Internet, Mobile Communications, Security & Security Systems, Software

IPPro The Internet
997151
Editorial: 16 Bromley Road, Beckenham, London BR3 5JE **Tel:** 44 02037 506028
Email: editor@ipprotheinternet.com
Web site: www.ipprotheinternet.com
Freq: Bi-Weekly Not Audited
Editor: Mark Dugdale
MAGAZINE
Internet

Ipswich 24
986013
Editorial: Ipswich24, Suite 9, 85 Dales Road, Ipswich IP1 4JR **Tel:** 44 01473 351270
Email: info@ipswich24.co.uk
Web site: www.ipswich24.co.uk
Freq: Monthly
Circ: 18000 Not Audited
Editor: Mark Keeble
MAGAZINE
Bars, Clubs & Pubs, Comedy, Entertainment, Lifestyle, Local Entertainment Guides, Men's Interests, Movies & Video, Regional General Interest, Women's Interests

IQ Magazine
986632
Editorial: Unit 31, Tileyard Road, Kings Cross, London N7 9AH
Tel: 44 02037 430303
Email: gordon@iq-mag.net
Web site: http://www.iq-mag.net/
Freq: Monthly
Circ: 4000 Not Audited
Editor: Gordon Masson
MAGAZINE
Music

Ireland's Forecourt and Convenience Retailer
983252
Editorial: Penton House, 38 Heron Road, Sydenham Business Park, Belfast BT3 9LE
Tel: 44 02890 457457
Email: info@pentongroup.com
Web site: http://forecourtretailer.com/
Freq: Bi-Monthly
Circ: 4127 Not Audited
Editor: Russell Campbell; **Editor:** Damien Whinnery
Profile: Magazine covering all aspects of forecourt retailing, including interviews and news.
Ad Rate: Full Page Colour £1895.00
MAGAZINE
Alcohol & Spirits, Consumer Goods & Products, Food, Retail Management, Tobacco

Ireland's Homes Interiors & Living
981847
Tel: 44 02891 473979
Email: editorial@ihil.net
Web site: www.ihil.net
Freq: Monthly
Circ: 6483 Not Audited
Editor: Margaret Connolly
MAGAZINE
Do-It-Yourself (DIY)

Ireland's Wedding Journal
982428
Editorial: Penton House, 38 Heron Road, Sydenham Business Park, Belfast BT3 9LE
Tel: 44 02890 457457
Email: info@weddingjournalonline.com
Web site: www.weddingjournalonline.com
Freq: Quarterly
Circ: 14064 Not Audited
Editor: Tara Craig
Profile: Magazine covering all aspects of weddings. Articles include choosing the dress, organising the wedding list, booking the reception, honeymoon features and setting up home. Launched in 1995. Aimed at brides-to-be, grooms, mothers of future brides and bridesmaids.
Ad Rate: Full Page Colour £1450.00
MAGAZINE
Weddings

Irish Beauty
984086
Editorial: The Courtyard Wixford Park, Georges Elm Lane, Bidford-on-avon, Alcester B50 4JS **Tel:** 44 01789 773434
Web site: http://www.irishbeauty.ie/magazine.jsp
Freq: Monthly
Circ: 8000 Not Audited
Profile: Magazine covering all aspects of the Irish beauty, nails and spa industry, including news, product reviews and competitions.
Ad Rate: Full Page Colour £845.00
MAGAZINE
Cosmetics, Fitness & Exercise

IronLife
997587
Email: editorial@ironlifemag.com
Web site: www.ironlifemag.com
Freq: Monthly
Circ: 13734 Cision Digital Reach
MAGAZINE (ONLINE)
Fitness & Exercise

IS Opportunities
981311
Editorial: Chambers Business Centre, Chapel Road, Oldham, Oldham OL8 4QQ
Tel: 44 01616 838034
Email: isopps-editorial@worldsfair.co.uk
Web site: www.worldsfair.co.uk/index.php
Freq: Monthly

Circ: 12000 Not Audited
Editor: Terry Ford
Profile: Magazine providing the latest industry news, surveys, problem solving pieces and "how to" features for IT salespeople and marketing professionals.
Ad Rate: Full Page Colour £1650.00
MAGAZINE
Auto Aftermarket, Computers, Data Management, Electronics, Government Technology, Industry, Internet, Mobile Communications, Security & Security Systems, Software

ISA Journal
995314
Editorial: Gainsborough House, 59- 60 Thames Street, Windsor SL4 1TX
Tel: 44 01753 272022
Web site: www.isaschools.org.uk
Freq: 3 Times/Year Not Audited
MAGAZINE
Disability, Education, Higher Education, Preschool, Schools & Institutions, Students

iScot
1075815
Tel: 44 01436 678158
Web site: http://iscot.scot
Freq: Monthly
MAGAZINE
Regional General Interest, Scotland

iSellMobile
1054554
Editorial: 4 Bloomsbury Square, London WC1A 2RP **Tel:** 44 02074 403872
Email: info@isellmobile.co.uk
Web site: http://www.isellmobile.co.uk/
Freq: Daily
Circ: 61465 Cision Digital Reach
MAGAZINE (ONLINE)
Mobile Communications, Mobile Electronics, Telecommunications/Electronic Communications

iShoot
1066899
Tel: 44 01225 687426
Email: fieldsports@futurenet.com
Web site: www.ishootmag.com
Freq: Monthly
Circ: 14000 Not Audited
Editor: Peter Carr
MAGAZINE
Shooting/Guns

The Isis Magazine
994621
Editorial: 7 St Aldates, Oxford OX1 1BS
Tel: 44 01865 246461
Email: editor@isismagazine.org.uk
Web site: www.isismagazine.org.uk
Freq: Quarterly Not Audited
MAGAZINE
Student Lifestyle

Island Echo
988774
Tel: 44 01983 898288
Email: editor@islandecho.co.uk
Web site: www.islandecho.co.uk
Freq: Daily
Circ: 158196 Cision Digital Reach
MAGAZINE (ONLINE)
Regional

Island Life
984922
Tel: 44 01983 216111
Email: islandlife@me.com
Web site: http://www.visitilife.com
Freq: Bi-Monthly
Circ: 30000 Not Audited
Editor: Tanya Potter
MAGAZINE
Regional General Interest

Island Visitor
983400
Editorial: 46-48 East Smithfield Street, London E1W 1AW **Tel:** 44 02074 261010
Web site: www.iln.co.uk
Freq: Annual
Circ: 350000 Not Audited
MAGAZINE
Travel

Isle magazine
985680
Editorial: 39 Grange Road, Broadstairs, Broadstairs CT10 3ER **Tel:** 44 01843 866082
Email: info@islemagazine.co.uk
Web site: http://www.islemagazine.co.uk/
Freq: Semi-Annual
Circ: 35000 Not Audited
Editor: Kiki Case
MAGAZINE
Regional General Interest

IsleofMan.com
982867
Editorial: Manx Telecom Ltd, Isle of Man Business Park, Cooil Road, Isle of Man IM99 1HX **Tel:** 44 01624 641555
Email: newsroom@isleofman.com
Web site: www.isleofman.com
Freq: Daily
Circ: 56707 Cision Digital Reach
MAGAZINE (ONLINE)
Regional General Interest

Ispectrum Magazine
997935
Tel: 44 07938 707164
Email: admin@ispectrummagazine.com
Web site: http://ispectrummagazine.com/wp/
Freq: Bi-Monthly Not Audited
MAGAZINE
Astrology & Parapsychology, Energy & Environment, Health & Medicine, History, Neurology, Science

iSportConnect
987761
Editorial: 6 Glenthorne Mews, 115A Glenthorne Road, Hammersmith, London W6 0LJ **Tel:** 44 02032 395400
Email: news@isportconnect.com
Web site: www.isportconnect.com
Freq: Daily
Circ: 28977 Cision Digital Reach
Profile: Website covering sports. The isportconnect website shares the latest news and information on the sports industry.
MAGAZINE (ONLINE)
Basketball, Bicycles, Billiards, Boating & Yachting, Bodybuilding, Bowling, Boxing, Business, Cricket, Equestrian Sports

ISPreview
981648
Email: send2news@ispreview.co.uk
Web site: www.ispreview.co.uk
Freq: Daily
Circ: 161100 Cision Digital Reach
MAGAZINE (ONLINE)
Internet, Telecommunications/Electronic Communications

IT @ MONOist
1061895
Email: monoist@atmarkit.co.jp
Freq: Daily
MAGAZINE (ONLINE)
Antique & Collectible Cars, Automakers, Automotive, Driving, Manufacturing, Motorcycles, Off-road & 4-Wheel Drive Vehicles, Software, Trucks & SUVs

IT Contractor
997534
Email: info@craicon.com
Web site: www.itcontractor.com
Freq: Daily
Circ: 6819 Cision Digital Reach
MAGAZINE (ONLINE)
Accounting, Business, Corporate Responsibility

IT Europa
981553
Editorial: 3rd Floor, Armstrong House, 38 Market Square, London UB8 1TG
Tel: 44 01895 454458
Web site: www.iteuropa.com
Freq: Daily
Circ: 17130 Cision Digital Reach
Editor: John Garratt
Profile: IT Europa is a bi-weekly newsletter owned by BPL Business Media Ltd. It provides Pan-European information and analysis on Europe's IT and consumer electronics channels including enterprise, SME and consumer sectors in Europe. It also includes features on ISVs assemblers, distributors retailers, system integrators, VARs, outsourcing firms and IT service companies. First published in 1991. IT

Consumer Magazines

Europa is written for senior managers and directors within the IT industry responsible for European sales and marketing. Readership has grown to 5,000.
MAGAZINE (ONLINE)
Auto Aftermarket, Computers, Data Management, Electronics, Government Technology, Industry, Internet, Mobile Communications, Security & Security Systems, Software

The IT Factor   997210
Editorial: 9 Seagrave Road, London SW6 1RP
Web site: http://theitfactormag.com/
Freq: Bi-Monthly
Circ: 9985 Cision Digital Reach
MAGAZINE (ONLINE)
Lifestyle, Men's Interests, Regional General Interest, Women's Interests

IT Law Today   980904
Editorial: Singletons, The Ridge, South View Road, Pinner, London HA5 3YD
Tel: 44 02088 661934
Web site: http://www.singlelaw.com/it-law-today
Freq: Monthly Not Audited
MAGAZINE
Computers, Corporate Law, Data Management, Intellectual Property, Internet, Security & Security Systems, Telecommunications/Electronic Communications

IT Pro   983493
Editorial: 31-32 Alfred Place, London WC1E 7DP **Tel:** 44 02079 076000
Email: jerina_hardy@dennis.co.uk
Web site: www.itpro.co.uk
Freq: Daily
Circ: 1557776 Cision Digital Reach
Profile: Website covering all aspects of business IT technology with news, features and reviews. Offers IT solutions for real IT projects, in-depth reviews and group tests of the latest business hardware and software, breaking news, analysis and insight written for UK IT professionals, interviews with key commentators on major technology trends and directions, practical advice including step-by-step guides to solving technical problems. Aimed at business and IT managers, IT PRO's users across small, medium and large enterprises.Alternative Title: ITPro.co.uk Digital images preferred.
MAGAZINE (ONLINE)
Computers, Electronics, Industry, Software

It's Nice That   990538
Editorial: 21 Downham Road, London N1 5AA **Tel:** 44 02077 395222
Web site: www.itsnicethat.com
Freq: Daily
Circ: 582631 Cision Digital Reach
Editor: Owen Pritchard
MAGAZINE (ONLINE)
Art, Graphic Design

Italia!   982691
Editorial: Suite 6, Piccadilly House, London Road, Bath BA1 6PL **Tel:** 44 01225 489984
Email: italia@anthem-publishing.com
Web site: http://www.italia-magazine.com
Freq: Monthly
Circ: 30000 Not Audited
Profile: Italia! is a monthly news and society magazine owned by Anthem Publishing Ltd. It covers Italian culture, food and wine, holidays and property. First issue published in 2004. The Italia! is written for people who holiday or are interested in buying a property in Italy.Associated Blogs: Italia! Magazine Blog (http://www.italia-magazine.com/blog)
Ad Rate: Full Page Colour £950.00
MAGAZINE
Europe, Real Estate

The ITAM Review   1105188
Editorial: Basepoint Business Centre, Rivermead Drive, Westlea, Swindon SN5 7EX **Tel:** 44 08451 303166
Web site: http://www.itassetmanagement.net/

Freq: Daily
Circ: 77918 Cision Digital Reach
MAGAZINE (ONLINE)
News & Current Affairs

ITCM   983302
Tel: 44 01225 705555
Email: itcm@incentivetravel.co.uk
Web site: www.incentivetravel.co.uk
Freq: Daily
Circ: 54935 Cision Digital Reach
MAGAZINE (ONLINE)
Genealogy, Travel

itm   985450
Editorial: Goldings, Elphicks Farm, Water Lane, Hunton, Maidstone ME15 0SG
Tel: 44 01622 823920
Web site: http://www.intrademagazine.com
Freq: Monthly
Circ: 16000 Not Audited
Profile: Magazine covering international trade.
MAGAZINE
Automotive, Aviation, Railroad, Shipping & Warehousing, Supply Chain Management (SCM), Transportation

ITNOW   981595
Editorial: 1st Floor Block D, North Star House, North Star Avenue, Swindon SN2 1FA **Tel:** 44 01793 417417
Email: editor@bcs.org
Web site: www.bcs.org/category/17705
Freq: Quarterly
Circ: 75000 Not Audited
Profile: Bi-monthly magazine covering professional issues, IT innovations and technological developments. Formerly known as The Computer Bulletin, is read by both members of BCS and the wider IT community. ITNOW is a member of UPENET (UPGRADE European Network), the network of CEPIS societies' publications.Targets key decision makers in the IT industry. First published in 1957.Aimed at IT professionals, heads of IT, directors, software systems engineering, IT consultants, university researchers, programmers and designers.
Ad Rate: Full Page Colour £2513.00
MAGAZINE
Auto Aftermarket, Computers, Data Management, Electronics, Government Technology, Industry, Internet, Mobile Communications, Security & Security Systems, Software

ITProPortal   983954
Editorial: 1-10 Praed Mews, London W2 1QY
Email: pr@itproportal.com
Web site: www.itproportal.com
Freq: Daily
Circ: 439220 Cision Digital Reach
Editor: Désiré Athow
Profile: Website covering technology commentary and analysis, including enterprise, cloud, software, hardware, security, public sector, mobile, start ups, web and networks.
MAGAZINE (ONLINE)
Computers, Internet

It's a Boy Thing   999618
Email: itsaboything.net@gmail.com
Web site: www.itsaboything.net
Freq: Daily
Circ: 1268 Cision Digital Reach
Editor: Naomi MacKay
MAGAZINE (ONLINE)
Family & Parenting

ITS International   984109
Editorial: Waterbridge Court, 50, Spital St, Dartford, London DA1 2DT
Tel: 44 01322 612055
Email: itseditor@ropl.com
Web site: www.itsinternational.com
Freq: Bi-Monthly
Circ: 22523 Not Audited
Editor: Colin Sowman
Profile: ITS International (Intelligent Transport Systems International) is an A4-sized business-to-business magazine covering intelligent transport systems since

1995. Published every other month, ITS international concentrates on the deployment of technology as well as on the technology itself and tries to examine the effectiveness of solutions and assess how systems perform in real-time. The publication covers the full range of land-based transport systems including mass transit, traffic management, electronic payment, enforcement, light rail, and deployment of satellite positioning systems. Part of the magazine's mission is to illustrate the benefits of multi-modal transport systems in urban environments. The magazine is read by public transport officials, road owners, rail and bus operators, transport consultants, traffic engineers, system integrators, vehicle and material producers and suppliers, parking companies, and students. A majority of the readership, according to the editor, is in the United States and Canada. ITS International has been selected as the exclusive official publication for several major industry trade shows including Intertraffic, ITS America Annual Meeting, and ITS World Congress. Regular features include the TranSmart report on all aspects of transit and a product highlight. Other columns include Tough Talking, where an industry member is encouraged to "sound off" about a trend or event in the industry and Last Word, a slightly less opinionated, page-long opinion column written by an industry leader. Articles are always independently researched and written. The lead time for features is six weeks. The deadlines are not set in stone, but things begin to get wrapped up about four weeks before publication. Published every other month around the end of odd-numbered months, the publication schedule is not set, but rather fitted around the dates of major industry trade shows. In addition to the contributing editor, who works on-site, the publication has an off-site news editor, and an off-site technology editor. The contributing editor will forward appropriate press releases. The publication's reader service is Web-based and has moved away from "old fashioned bingo cards." The editors honor non-disclosure agreements.
Ad Rate: Full Page Colour £4005.00
MAGAZINE
Automotive, Aviation, Railroad, Shipping & Warehousing, Supply Chain Management (SCM), Transportation

It's Rude To Stare   985873
Editorial: 17 Shelton Street, London WC2H 9JN
Email: editor@itsrudetostare.com
Web site: www.itsrudetostare.com
Freq: Daily
Circ: 9325 Cision Digital Reach
MAGAZINE (ONLINE)
Alcohol & Spirits, Bars, Clubs & Pubs, Beer, Beverages, Classical/Choral/Band Music, Cooking & Baking, Dance Music, Health & Medicine, Jazz & Blues, Lifestyle

ITV.com   984141
Editorial: London Televison Centre, 58-72 Upper ground, London SE1 9LT
Tel: 44 02071 573000
Email: itvcommercial@itv.com
Web site: www.itv.com
Freq: Daily
Circ: 11510571 Cision Digital Reach
MAGAZINE (ONLINE)
News & Current Affairs

iVisit London   1053771
Editorial: Belgrove Street, Kings Cross, London WC1H 8AA **Tel:** 44 01446 776950
Email: hello@ivisitlondon.co.uk
Web site: www.ivisitlondon.org
Freq: Daily
MAGAZINE
Regional General Interest

IVORY   997254
Email: info@ivorymagazine.com
Web site: ivorymagazine.com
Freq: Daily
Circ: 11429 Cision Digital Reach

Editor: Gemma Rowbotham
MAGAZINE (ONLINE)
Alternative Medicine

iwitness24   986598
Editorial: Prospect House, Rouen Road, Norwich NR1 1RE **Tel:** 44 01603 628311
Web site: www.iwitness24.co.uk
Freq: Daily
Circ: 3143 Cision Digital Reach
MAGAZINE (ONLINE)
News & Current Affairs

IWSR Magazine   984280
Editorial: 39 Moreland Street, London EC1V 8BB **Tel:** 44 02076 896841
Email: info@iwsr.co.uk
Web site: http://www.iwsrmagazine.com/
Freq: Monthly
Circ: 15000 Not Audited
Editor: Alex Smith
MAGAZINE
Alcohol & Spirits, Wine/Winemaking

IX Magazine   996773
Editorial: Bearpark, Abbotswood, Guildford, London GU1 1UX **Tel:** 44 02032 899779
Email: editorial@internationalexcellence.co.uk
Web site: internationalexcellence.co.uk
Freq: Quarterly
Circ: 60000 Not Audited
MAGAZINE
Airline Inflight, Antique & Collectible Cars, Antiques/Collectibles, Art, Arts, Automotive, Lifestyle, Literature, Luxury Goods, Men's Interests

Ja Ja Ja   997257
Email: editorial@jajajamusic.com
Web site: jajajamusic.com
Freq: Daily
Circ: 13492 Cision Digital Reach
Editor: Francine Gorman
MAGAZINE (ONLINE)
Dance Music, Rap & Hip Hop, Rock Music

The Jackdaw   985255
Editorial: 93 Clissold Crescent, London N16 9AS **Tel:** 44 02072 544027
Email: info@thejackdaw.co.uk
Web site: www.thejackdaw.co.uk
Freq: Bi-Monthly
Circ: 1000 Not Audited
Editor: David Lee
Profile: Magazine taking an alternative look at visual arts and visual arts news.
Ad Rate: Full Page Mono £100.00
MAGAZINE
Art, Literature, Photography, Theater & Performing Arts, Visual Arts

Jaguar Driver   982636
Editorial: Jaguar House, 18 Stuart Street, Luton, Luton LU1 2SL **Tel:** 44 01582 419332
Email: enquiries@jdclub.co.uk
Web site: www.jaguardriver.co.uk
Freq: Monthly
Circ: 10000 Not Audited
Editor: Steve Fermor
Profile: Official journal of the Jaguar Drivers Club. Includes developments of new models, technical innovations and the competition scene.
Ad Rate: Full Page Mono £330.00
Ad Rate: Full Page Colour £600.00
MAGAZINE
Automakers

Jaguar Enthusiast   982637
Editorial: 3 The Hollows, School Lane, Doncaster DN9 3LB **Tel:** 44 01302 771818
Email: nigel.thorley@jec.org.uk
Web site: www.jec.org.uk
Freq: Monthly Not Audited
Editor: Nigel Thorley
Profile: Magazine featuring new and classic Jaguars, information, spares and tools.
Ad Rate: Full Page Colour £1000.00
MAGAZINE
Automakers

Jaguar World 982638
Editorial: PO Box 978, Peterborough PE1 9FL **Tel:** 44 01733 347559
Email: jwm.ed@kelsey.co.uk
Web site: www.jaguar-world.com
Freq: Monthly
Circ: 18000 Not Audited
Editor: Paul Walton
MAGAZINE
Automakers

Jail Mail 997749
Editorial: PO Box 10419, Nottingham NG2 9QF **Tel:** 44 08452 262841
Email: admin@jailmail.co.uk
Web site: www.jailmail.co.uk
Freq: Monthly Not Audited
MAGAZINE
Law, National News

Jake 999173
Email: hello@jaketm.com
Web site: www.jaketm.com
Freq: Daily
Circ: 2664 Cision Digital Reach
Editor: Stephen Unwin
MAGAZINE (ONLINE)
LGBT

Jamie Magazine 984919
Editorial: 33 Broadwick Street, London W1F 9EP **Tel:** 44 02033 755000
Email: contact@jamiemagazine.com
Web site: www.jamieolivermagazine.com
Freq: Monthly
Circ: 47021 Not Audited
Profile: Magazine from Jamie Oliver. Each issue is packed with new recipes created in Jamie's home kitchen, plus there are recipes from Jamie's friends and colleagues.
MAGAZINE
Cooking & Baking

Jane's Defence Weekly 979914
Editorial: Sentinel House, 163 Brighton Road, Coulsdon, London CR5 2YH
Tel: 44 02087 003700
Email: jdw@ihs.com
Web site: http://www.janes.com/magazines/ihs-janes-defence-weekly
Freq: Weekly
Circ: 28100 Not Audited
Editor: Peter Felstead
MAGAZINE
Defense & National Security, Engineering, Marine & Boat Trade

Jane's World Navies 998889
Editorial: Sentinel House, 163 Brighton Road, Coulsdon, London CR5 2YH
Tel: 44 02032 532221
Email: info@ihs.com
Web site: http://www.janes.com/products/janes/security/military-capabilities/world-navies.aspx
Freq: Semi-Annual Not Audited
MAGAZINE
Defense & National Security, Marine & Boat Trade

Janomot Bengali Newsweekly 982586
Editorial: Unit 2, 20B Spelman Street, Spitalfields & Bangla Town, London E1 5LQ
Tel: 44 02073 776032
Email: janomot@btconnect.com
Web site: http://www.janomot.com
Freq: Weekly
Circ: 11000 Not Audited
Editor: Nobab Uddin
Profile: Newspaper containing news from Bangladesh and from Bangladeshi emigrants living around the world.
Ad Rate: Full Page Mono £1800.00
Ad Rate: Full Page Colour £2000.00
MAGAZINE
Asia

Järva Teataja 1060896
Tel: 44 37238 49200
Email: toimetus@jt.ee
Web site: http://www.jt.ee
Freq: Daily

Circ: 47667 Cision Digital Reach
MAGAZINE (ONLINE)
Consumer Affairs, Crime & Violence, Defense & National Security, Energy & Environment, Ethical/Moral Issues, International News, Law, National News, News & Current Affairs, Northern Ireland

Jazz Journal 982088
Editorial: Lower Queens Road, Ashford, Ashford TN24 8HH **Tel:** 44 01233 648895
Email: admin@jazzjournal.co.uk
Web site: www.jazzjournal.co.uk
Freq: Monthly
Circ: 7500 Not Audited
Editor: Mark Gilbert
Profile: Magazine covering record, book, cinema and video reviews. Includes features on jazz history and interviews with musicians. Aimed primarily at jazz record collectors.Regular features: Obituaries Obituaries within the jazz scene.; Readers' Letters; Reviews Featuring over 20 pages of jazz record reviews.; Who's Where Featuring details of jazz gigs and events.
MAGAZINE
Jazz & Blues

The Jazz Rag 982090
Editorial: PO Box 944, Edgbaston, Birmingham B16 8UT **Tel:** 44 01214 647020
Email: jazzrag@bigbearmusic.com
Web site: www.bigbearmusic.com/category/the-jazz-rag
Freq: Bi-Monthly
Circ: 4500 Not Audited
Profile: Magazine covering all aspects of the British and international jazz scene. Aimed at jazz enthusiasts between 25 and 75 years old.Regular features: Reviews Reviews of jazz CD's, DVD's and books.
Ad Rate: Full Page Mono £510.00
Ad Rate: Full Page Colour £995.00
MAGAZINE
Jazz & Blues

Jazz Standard 1064936
Editorial: 16 Elbrough Street, London SW18 5DW
Email: tina@thisisjazzstandard.com
Web site: http://thisisjazzstandard.com/
Freq: Daily
Circ: 15714 Cision Digital Reach
MAGAZINE (ONLINE)
Jazz & Blues

Jazzwise 982089
Editorial: St Jude's Church, Dulwich Road, Herne Hill, London SE24 0PB
Tel: 44 02086 770012
Web site: www.jazzwisemagazine.com
Freq: Monthly
Circ: 5000 Not Audited
Editor: Mike Flynn
Profile: Magazine covering contemporary jazz, jazz-dance and world jazz with news features and reviews. Aimed at record collectors, musicians and jazz fans.
Ad Rate: Full Page Mono £1250.00
Ad Rate: Full Page Colour £1500.00
MAGAZINE
Jazz & Blues, R&B, Urban, World

JD Group Club A Magazine 1060567
Tel: 44 27217 010064
Email: info@quantumpublishers.co.za
Freq: Monthly
Circ: 485000 Not Audited
MAGAZINE
Antiques/Collectibles, Armed Forces, Astrology & Parapsychology, Astronomy, Aviation, Beauty & Grooming, Boating & Yachting, Books, Camping and RV Travel, Cartoons

JD Group Club B Magazine 1060352
Tel: 44 27217 010064
Email: info@quantumpublishers.co.za
Freq: Monthly

Circ: 185000 Not Audited
MAGAZINE
Antiques/Collectibles, Armed Forces, Astrology & Parapsychology, Astronomy, Aviation, Beauty & Grooming, Boating & Yachting, Books, Camping and RV Travel, Cartoons

The Jellied Eel 999157
Editorial: Sustain, Development House, 56-64 Leonard Street, London EC2A 4LT
Tel: 44 02070 650902
Email: thejelliedeel@sustainweb.org
Web site: http://www.sustainweb.org/jelliedeel
Freq: 3 Times/Year
Circ: 15000 Not Audited
Editor: Chris Young
MAGAZINE
Cooking & Baking, Food, Grocery Stores, Organic Food, Restaurant Reviews, Vegetarianism & Veganism

The Jersey Life 995726
Editorial: Chamber House, 25 Pier Road, St Helier, Jersey JE1 4HF
Tel: 44 01481 727884
Web site: http://www.thelifemagazines.com
Freq: Monthly Not Audited
MAGAZINE
Regional General Interest

The Jeweller 984062
Editorial: 45 Britton Street, London EC1M 5NA **Tel:** 44 02076 134445
Web site: www.naj.co.uk/en/Industry-news/the-jeweller-magazine.cfm
Freq: Bi-Monthly
Circ: 6000 Not Audited
Editor: Belinda Morris
Profile: Magazine covering all aspects of the jewellery, watch and giftware industry. Covers news, features and new products. Aimed at jewellery, watch and gift retailers and members of the jewellery industry and British Jewellers Association.A charge may be made for colour separation.
Ad Rate: Full Page Colour £950.00
MAGAZINE
Fashion

The Jewellery Editor 987490
Email: info@thejewelleryeditor.com
Web site: www.thejewelleryeditor.com
Freq: Daily
Circ: 97025 Cision Digital Reach
Profile: Website covering luxury jewellery and watches.
MAGAZINE (ONLINE)
Luxury Goods

Jewellery Focus 984127
Editorial: 14 Rosebery Avenue, London EC1R 4TD **Tel:** 44 02075 207066
Email: newsdesk@jewelleryfocus.co.uk
Web site: www.jewelleryfocus.co.uk
Freq: Monthly
Circ: 9100 Not Audited
Profile: Magazine focusing on the jewellery trade including industry news, interviews and product reviews. Aimed at retailers in the jewellery trade.
Ad Rate: Full Page Colour £2110.00
MAGAZINE
Fashion

Jewish Quarterly 985815
Editorial: 28 St. Albans Lane, London NW11 7QE
Email: editor@jewishquarterly.org
Web site: www.jewishquarterly.org
Freq: Quarterly
Circ: 5000 Not Audited
Editor: Nicola Christie
Profile: The magazine contains all aspect of Jewish life, from contemporary writing with articles of political interest, history, philosophy, arts, films, music, poetry and literary reviews.
Ad Rate: Full Page Mono £400.00
Ad Rate: Full Page Colour £500.00
MAGAZINE
Religion

Jewish Renaissance 987899
Editorial: 353-359 Finchley Road, London NW3 6ET
Email: editor@jewishrenaissance.org.uk
Web site: www.jewishrenaissance.org.uk
Freq: Quarterly Not Audited
Profile: The Magazine covers Jewish arts, music, literature, history, community, ideas and events.
MAGAZINE
Religion

The Jewish Vegetarian 1075484
Editorial: 855 Finchley Road, Golders Green, London NW11 8LX
Tel: 44 02084 550692
Email: editor@jvs.org.uk
Web site: http://www.jvs.org.uk/
Freq: Quarterly
Circ: 2000 Not Audited
Profile: Official journal of the Jewish Vegetarian and Natural Health Society. Contains features on ethics, health, diet, alternative medicine, recipes, beauty, travel, books and animal rights.
Ad Rate: Full Page Mono £150.00
Ad Rate: Full Page Colour £225.00
MAGAZINE
Vegetarianism & Veganism

Jewpro 995387
Editorial: 314 Regents Park Road, Finchley, London N3 2JX **Tel:** 44 02071 935429
Email: editor@jewpro.co.uk
Web site: http://www.jewpro.co.uk/
Freq: Daily
Circ: 1813 Cision Digital Reach
Editor: Spencer Shaw
MAGAZINE (ONLINE)
Regional General Interest, Religion

JFW Magazine 984871
Editorial: JFW Magazine, 13 Dorset Square, London NW1 6QB **Tel:** 44 02033 185205
Web site: http://www.jfwmagazine.com/index.php
Freq: Quarterly
Circ: 113000 Not Audited
MAGAZINE
Fashion

Jisc 988794
Editorial: Brettenham House, 5 Lancaster Place, London WC2E 7EN
Tel: 44 02030 066099
Email: info@jisc.ac.uk
Web site: www.jisc.ac.uk
Freq: Daily
Circ: 166155 Cision Digital Reach
MAGAZINE (ONLINE)
Careers, Education, Higher Education

JLife 985583
Editorial: Beech House, Sycamore Lodge, 7a Woodhouse Cliff, Leeds LS6 2HF
Tel: 44 08450 522911
Email: info@nutsforprint.co.uk
Web site: www.jlifemagazine.co.uk
Freq: Monthly
Circ: 15000 Not Audited
Editor: Elliot Landy
MAGAZINE
Religion

JMU Journalism Liverpool Life 1060231
Web site: http://jmu-journalism.org.uk/
Freq: Daily
Circ: 11959 Cision Digital Reach
MAGAZINE (ONLINE)
Student Lifestyle

Jobs and Careers 996821
Editorial: Central House, 1 Ballards Lane, London N3 1LQ **Tel:** 44 02084 443401
Email: editorial@empgroup.co.uk
Web site: www.jobsandcareersmag.com
Freq: Monthly Not Audited
Editor: Rashmi Madan
MAGAZINE
Alumni, Careers, Education, Student Lifestyle, Teachers

Consumer Magazines

Editor: Kieran White
MAGAZINE (ONLINE)
Dance Music, Pop Music, Rap & Hip Hop, Rock Music

Just Music Daily
1059602
Editorial: 33 Glebe Street, Castleford, Castleford WF10 4AJ
Email: just.music@gmail.com
Web site: www.paper.li/jmyorks/1385854511
Freq: Daily
Editor: Dave Butterfield
MAGAZINE (ONLINE)
Audio Video Trade, Cameras, Consumer Electronics, Mobile Electronics, Movies & Video, Pop Music, Rock Music, Soccer

Just Opened London
987017
Email: editor@justopenedlondon.com
Web site: www.justopenedlondon.com
Freq: Daily
Circ: 48974 Cision Digital Reach
Profile: Website covering London lifestyle, culture, restaurants, bars, fashion, hotels and wellness.
MAGAZINE (ONLINE)
Regional General Interest

Just Weddings
985638
Web site: http://www.justweddingsmag.co.uk/
Freq: Semi-Annual
Circ: 30000 Not Audited
MAGAZINE
Weddings

just-auto.com
982833
Editorial: Aroq House, 17A Harris Business Park, Bromsgrove, Bromsgrove B60 4DJ
Tel: 44 01527 573723
Email: autoeditor@aroq.com
Web site: www.just-auto.com
Freq: Daily
Circ: 65075 Cision Digital Reach
Profile: Website covering automotive business. The just-auto website shares the latest business news and features covering all aspects of the automotive industry.
MAGAZINE (ONLINE)
Automotive

just-drinks.com
980814
Editorial: Aroq House, 17A Harris Business Park, Stoke Prior, Bromsgrove B60 4DJ
Tel: 44 01527 573600
Email: news@just-drinks.com
Web site: http://www.just-drinks.com
Freq: Daily
Circ: 142837 Cision Digital Reach
Editor: Olly Wehring
MAGAZINE (ONLINE)
Alcohol & Spirits

just-style.com
982835
Tel: 44 01527 573728
Email: newsdesk@just-style.com
Web site: http://www.just-style.com
Freq: Daily
Circ: 97509 Cision Digital Reach
MAGAZINE (ONLINE)
Fashion

K9 Magazine
982014
Tel: 44 08451 631238
Email: admin@k9magazine.com
Web site: www.k9magazine.com
Freq: Monthly
Circ: 105000 Not Audited
Profile: Magazine covering dogs. It features health, product reviews, hints and tips from the Animal Advisory Panel, reviews of pet friendly cars, celebrity interviews, home and garden features and holiday features.
Ad Rate: Full Page Colour £1265.00
MAGAZINE
Nature & Wildlife

Kalendar
998048
Web site: www.cheltenham.co.uk/assets/kalendar/spring/files/assets/basic-html/page1.html
Freq: Semi-Annual

Circ: 10000 Not Audited
Editor: Jessica Phillipson
MAGAZINE
Equestrian Sports, Horse Racing

KamCity
988466
Editorial: Venture House, 2 Arlington Square, Downshire Way, Bracknell RG12 1WA **Tel:** 44 08456 434481
Web site: www.kamcity.com/
Freq: Daily
Circ: 9774 Cision Digital Reach
Editor: Mark Craft
Profile: Website covering Kamcity a website that provides news, tools and information for Key/National Account Managers (KAMs/NAMs), and related departments working in the FMCG retail / manufacturing industry.
MAGAZINE (ONLINE)
Alcohol & Spirits, Education, Food, Retail Management

Kantar Media
998649
Editorial: 1 Broadgate, London EC2M 2QS
Freq: Daily
Circ: 3300 Cision Digital Reach
MAGAZINE (ONLINE)
Banking, Business, Small and Medium Business

Kariéra
1062008
Freq: Weekly Not Audited
MAGAZINE
Advertising Industry, Branding, Broadcasting, Business, Careers, Company News & Appointments, Education, Graphic Design, Health & Safety, Human Resources

Karting Magazine
982672
Editorial: 15 Moorfield Road, Orpington, Bromley BR6 OXD
Email: news@kartingmagazine.com
Web site: www.kartingmagazine.com
Freq: Daily
Circ: 22109 Cision Digital Reach
Profile: Karting magazine is a monthly kart racing publication owned by Lodgemark Press. It includes information for newcomers and old hands alike such as technical developments, race reports, track and club news. It was the first magazine to cover kart racing. First published in 1959. Karting magazine is written for karting enthusiasts in 70 countries worldwide of ages between 8-50+, teams and karting manufacturers. Its readership has grown to 12,800.
Ad Rate: Full Page Mono £600.00
Ad Rate: Full Page Colour £800.00
MAGAZINE (ONLINE)
Motorsports

Kasmo Online
998885
Editorial: 6b Chevening Road, London NW6 6DD **Tel:** 44 02035 568723
Email: info@kasmonewspaper.com
Web site: www.kasmonewspaper.com
Freq: Daily
Circ: 1036 Cision Digital Reach
Editor: Abdulkadir Farah
MAGAZINE (ONLINE)
Africa

Kasterborous
998299
Email: brian@kasterborous.com
Web site: http://www.kasterborous.com/
Freq: Daily
Circ: 121131 Cision Digital Reach
MAGAZINE (ONLINE)
Broadcasting, Science Fiction

KaterinaPerez.com
1070424
Email: info@katerinaperez.com
Web site: http://www.katerinaperez.com/
Freq: Daily
Circ: 25167 Cision Digital Reach
MAGAZINE (ONLINE)
Luxury Goods

Katolikus Kalendárium
1061455
Tel: 44 36464 12911 Not Audited
MAGAZINE
Religion

Katzenworld
995545
Editorial: Flat 20 Barnstaple House, 51 Taunton Road, London SE12 8PL
Tel: 44 07969 738331
Email: info@katzenworld.co.uk
Web site: www.katzenworld.co.uk
Freq: Daily
Circ: 78264 Cision Digital Reach
Editor: Charlotte Ehrukainen
MAGAZINE (ONLINE)
Cameras, Nature & Wildlife, Pets & Pet Products, Veterinary Medicine

Katzenworld - Katzenworld DE
1004110
Email: ann-kristin.unger@katzenworld.co.uk
Web site: http://de.katzenworld.uk/
Freq: Daily
Circ: 629 Cision Digital Reach
MAGAZINE (ONLINE)
News & Current Affairs

Kawa
1060402
Tel: 44 48223 538542
Web site: http://www.ekawa.net
Freq: Bi-Monthly
Circ: 10000 Not Audited
MAGAZINE
Antiques/Collectibles, Art, Arts, Celebrities, Lifestyle, Literature, Men's Interests, Photography, Regional General Interest, Theater & Performing Arts

The Keep
1067887
Tel: 44 01497 820167
Email: contact@hayandwye.com
Web site: http://www.thekeepmagazine.com/
Freq: Semi-Annual Not Audited
MAGAZINE
Literature, Photography

Keep the Faith
984195
Editorial: Suite 48, 88-90 Hatton Garde, London EC1N 8PN **Tel:** 44 08451 934433
Email: editorial@keepthefaith.co.uk
Web site: www.keepthefaith.co.uk
Freq: Monthly
Circ: 50000 Not Audited
MAGAZINE
Social Issues

Kennel Gazette
998960
Editorial: 1-5 Clarges Street, Piccadilly, London W1J 8AB **Tel:** 44 02075 181016
Email: kennel.gazette@thekennelclub.org.uk
Web site: http://www.thekennelclub.org.uk/our-resources/publications/the-kennel-gazette/
Freq: Monthly Not Audited
MAGAZINE
Nature & Wildlife

Kensington & Chelsea Magazine
987009
Editorial: Level 6, One Canada Square, Canary Wharf, London E14 5AX
Tel: 44 02079 874320
Email: info@rwmg.co.uk
Web site: www.runwildmedia.com
Freq: Monthly
Circ: 31500 Not Audited
Profile: Magazine covering news concerning local residents and events happening in and around the Royal Borough, as well as features on property, places, products and services of relevance to its audience. Interviews with prominent people from different luxury industries in the local area also feature monthly. Aimed at residents within Kensington and Chelsea. This outlet covers areas within Kensington & Chelsea Borough.
MAGAZINE
Regional General Interest

Kensington & Chelsea Review
985456
Editorial: 3 Ravensworth Road, London NW10 5NP **Tel:** 44 02030 867373
Email: info@kensingtonandchelseareview.com
Web site: www.kensingtonreview.co.uk

Freq: Monthly
Circ: 23000 Not Audited
Profile: Magazine covering art, auction, culture and luxury lifestyle in the Kensington & Chelsea area. This outlet covers areas within Kensington & Chelsea Borough.
Ad Rate: Full Page Colour £3000.00
MAGAZINE
Regional General Interest

The Kensington Magazine
985607
Editorial: Pavilion Business Centre, 96 Kensington High Street, London W8 4SG
Freq: Monthly
Circ: 11500 Not Audited
Profile: Magazine promoting local business news and events to the residents of Kensington. This outlet covers areas within Kensington & Chelsea Borough.
MAGAZINE
News & Current Affairs

Kent Focus
998357
Editorial: Suite 6B(i), Britannia House, Leagrave Road, Luton LU3 1RJ
Tel: 44 01582 488385
Email: info@mediachameleon.co.uk
Web site: www.kent-focus.co.uk
Freq: Annual Not Audited
MAGAZINE
Antiques/Collectibles, Beauty & Grooming, Cosmetics, Do-It-Yourself (DIY), Family & Parenting, Field Sports, Gardening, Hair, Health & Medicine, Nature & Wildlife

Kent Life
982501
Editorial: 81 Station Road, Hythe Road, Smeeth, Ashford, Ashford TN23 1PP
Tel: 44 01233 653460
Email: sarah.sturt@archant.co.uk
Web site: http://www.kent-life.co.uk/home
Freq: Monthly
Circ: 6442 Not Audited
Editor: Sarah Sturt
Profile: Magazine covering all aspects of county life. Includes personalities, nostalgia, crafts and contemporary events. Also covers property, food and drink, arts, antiques, fashion, interiors, books, gardening and sport.
Ad Rate: Full Page Colour £1610.00
MAGAZINE
Regional General Interest

Kent Profile
982502
Editorial: PO Box 761, Haywards Heath RH16 9FZ **Tel:** 44 01444 831512
Web site: www.kentprofile.co.uk
Freq: Bi-Monthly
Circ: 20000 Not Audited
Profile: County lifestyle magazine containing topics like regeneration, 'green' issues, sustainable living, higher education, property development, business matters, tourism, local produce, features, financial advice, gardening, major features on sectors and sections of Kent and a 60 day county-wide entertainment guide.
Ad Rate: Full Page Colour £1040.00
MAGAZINE
Regional General Interest

Kentishtowner
985816
Editorial: Interchange Atrium, Stables Market, Chalk Farm Road, London NW1 8AB
Email: info@kentishtowner.co.uk
Web site: www.kentishtowner.co.uk
Freq: Monthly
Circ: 20000 Not Audited
Profile: Publication that is dedicated to cultural affairs – art, food, pubs, culture, community, history, architecture and music around the borough of Camden as well as the wider London area.
MAGAZINE
Regional General Interest

kentnews.co.uk
984473
Editorial: Kent House, 81 Station Road, Ashford TN23 1PP **Tel:** 44 01233 653475
Email: editorial@kosmedia.co.uk
Web site: www.kentnews.co.uk
Freq: Daily

Circ: 87154 Cision Digital Reach
Profile: Website covering local news, sports and business for the surrounding area.
MAGAZINE (ONLINE)
News & Current Affairs

Kerrang! 982105
Editorial: 90-92 Pentonville Road, London N1 9HS **Tel:** 44 02070 788430
Email: feedback@kerrang.com
Web site: www.kerrang.com
Freq: Weekly
Circ: 18462 Not Audited
Editor: James McMahon
Profile: Magazine containing news, features gig guides and reviews of metal, rock and punk music. Aimed at metal, rock and punk music fans.
Ad Rate: Full Page Colour £3025.00
MAGAZINE
Rock Music

Kettle Mag 990569
Editorial: 273-287 Regent Street, London W1B 2HA **Tel:** 44 02075 500594
Email: info@kettlemag.co.uk
Web site: www.kettlemag.co.uk
Freq: Daily
Circ: 12325 Cision Digital Reach
MAGAZINE (ONLINE)
Men's Interests, Women's Interests

Kew 981961
Editorial: Herbarium Wing E, RBG Kew, Richmond, London TW9 3AB
Tel: 44 02083 325000
Email: magazine@kew.org
Web site: http://www.kew.org/kew-magazine
Freq: Quarterly
Circ: 51959 Not Audited
Editor: Christina Harrison
MAGAZINE
Gardening

Khush Wedding 987257
Editorial: 12 Cody Road, London E16 4SR
Tel: 44 02033 025250
Email: editorial@khushmag.com
Web site: www.khushmag.com
Freq: Quarterly
Circ: 70000 Not Audited
MAGAZINE
Weddings

Kicca 997800
Email: u2us@kicca.com
Web site: www.kicca.com
Freq: Daily
Circ: 44744 Cision Digital Reach
MAGAZINE (ONLINE)
Basketball, Bicycles, Billiards, Boating & Yachting, Bodybuilding, Bowling, Boxing, Cricket, Equestrian Sports, Extreme/ Adventure Sports

Kick Back Times 996089
Tel: 44 02920 694695
Web site: http://www.kickbacktimes.co.uk/
Freq: Daily
Circ: 11271 Cision Digital Reach
MAGAZINE (ONLINE)
Cooking & Baking, Entertainment, Railroad, Travel

Kick Off 1060559
Tel: 44 27214 083800
Email: neil.greig@touchline.co.za
Web site: http://www.kickoff.com
Freq: Weekly
Circ: 49821 Not Audited
MAGAZINE
Africa, Americas, Asia, Australia, Basketball, Bicycles, Billiards, Boating & Yachting, Bodybuilding, Bowling

KiCK! 983373
Editorial: Unit 16, Greenway Farm, Bath Road, Wick, Bristol BS30 5RL
Tel: 44 01179 373003
Email: info@kennedypublishing.co.uk
Web site: www.kickmag.co.uk
Freq: Monthly

Circ: 100000 Not Audited
MAGAZINE
Elementary School, Soccer, Teen/Young Adult

KiCK! Extra! 1053868
Editorial: Unit 16 Greenway Farm, Bath Road, Wick, Bristol BS30 5RL
Tel: 44 01179 373003
Email: info@kennedypublishing.co.uk
Web site: http://www.kennedypublishing.co.uk/magazines/kick-extra-magazine
Freq: Monthly
Circ: 30000 Not Audited
MAGAZINE
Elementary School, Soccer, Teen/Young Adult

KidAround (UK) 983279
Tel: 44 01245 206577
Email: info@kidaround.biz
Web site: www.kidaround.biz
Freq: Quarterly
Circ: 126000 Not Audited
MAGAZINE
Family & Parenting

KIDS About Town 995273
Email: info@kidsabouttown.com
Web site: www.kidsabouttown.com/
Freq: Daily
Circ: 1394 Cision Digital Reach
MAGAZINE (ONLINE)
Family & Parenting, Regional General Interest

Kids Alive! 985215
Tel: 44 02073 674911
Email: kidsalive@salvationarmy.org.uk
Web site: http://www.salvationarmy.org.uk/kidsalive
Freq: Weekly
Circ: 14000 Not Audited
Editor: Justin Reeves
Profile: Children's magazine containing entertaining, educational and evangelical articles. Aimed at children between 7 and 12 years old.Regular features: Bible Story; Competitions; Joke & Puzzles; KA World Promoting a healthy lifestyle and how to stay drug, smoke and alcohol free.
MAGAZINE
Elementary School, Preschool, Teen/ Young Adult, Trading Cards & Comics

Kids in Museums 997698
Editorial: CAN Mezzanine, 7-14 Great Dover Street, Borough, London SE1 4YR
Email: getintouch@kidsinmuseums.org.uk
Web site: http://kidsinmuseums.org.uk
Freq: Daily
Circ: 15175 Cision Digital Reach
MAGAZINE (ONLINE)
Antiques/Collectibles, Art, Charitable Foundations, Literature, Photography, Theater & Performing Arts, Visual Arts

Kids Nutrition Report 985893
Editorial: Crown House, 72 Hammersmith Road, London W14 8TH
Tel: 44 02076 177032
Email: enquiries@new-nutrition.com
Web site: http://www.new-nutrition.com/kidsnutrition
Freq: Quarterly Not Audited
Editor: Julian Mellentin
Profile: Kids Nutrition Report (KNR) is the international journal focused on worldwide kids' nutritional marketplace. Includes news analysis, category insights and case studies on kids' nutrition, ingredients and technologies.
MAGAZINE
Nutrition

kidzcoolit.com 996945
Editorial: 8 Firmin Rd, Dartford, London DA1 3AR **Tel:** 44 01322 402680
Web site: http://www.kidzcoolit.com
Freq: Daily
Circ: 14606 Cision Digital Reach

Editor: Nick Gibbs-McNeil
MAGAZINE (ONLINE)
Broadcasting, Computer & Video Games, Elementary School, Entertainment, Movies & Video, Preschool, Teen/Young Adult, Toys

KidzCruises 1053084
Tel: 44 01462 732777
Web site: https://www.packthepjs.com/
Freq: Daily
Circ: 11292 Cision Digital Reach
MAGAZINE (ONLINE)
Family & Parenting, Travel

Kiloklubi.fi 1061958
Email: info@kiloklubi.fi
Web site: http://kiloklubi.fi/
Freq: Daily
Circ: 41499 Cision Digital Reach
MAGAZINE (ONLINE)
Nutrition

kin 995278
Editorial: 13.2.1 The Leathermarket, Weston Street, London SE1 3ER
Tel: 44 02074 017297
Email: mark@lscpublishing.com
Web site: www.lscpublishing.com/magazines/
Freq: Quarterly
Circ: 48620 Not Audited
Editor: Mark Riddaway
MAGAZINE
Family & Parenting

Kindred Spirit 981817
Editorial: 19 Cecil Court, London WC2N 4EZ
Tel: 44 02078 594893
Email: editor.kindred@gmail.com
Web site: kindredspirit.co.uk
Freq: Bi-Monthly
Circ: 31800 Not Audited
Editor: Claire Gillman
Profile: Kindred Spirit is a bi monthly holistic journal published by Diamond Publishing. It covers spiritual and personal development, health, healing, medicine and natural products, environmental issues and travel. First published in 1987. Kindred Spirit is written for women actively seeking to improve and maintain their health, well being and spirituality.
Ad Rate: Full Page Colour £1400.00
MAGAZINE
Alternative Medicine

KING&why 997896
Email: kingandwhy@gmail.com
Web site: kingandwhy.com
Freq: Daily
Circ: 11562 Cision Digital Reach
MAGAZINE (ONLINE)
Business, Fashion, Small and Medium Business, Software

KingLoaf.com 1013041
Editorial: PO BOX 10003, East Leake, Loughborough LE11 9GT
Tel: 44 07894 240751
Email: info@kingloaf.com
Web site: www.kingloaf.com
Freq: Daily
Circ: 854 Cision Digital Reach
MAGAZINE (ONLINE)
Broadcasting, Men's Interests, Movies & Video

Kingpin 981913
Editorial: 1 West Smithfield, London EC1A 9JU **Tel:** 44 02073 329700
Web site: https://kingpinmag.com
Freq: Daily
Circ: 42642 Cision Digital Reach
Editor: Jan Kliewer
Profile: Magazine covering interviews, tournament reports and leading masters' advice. Also covers tips on improving one's game, book reviews and satire.
MAGAZINE (ONLINE)
Extreme/Adventure Sports

Kingston Courier 997042
Freq: Daily
Circ: 9586 Cision Digital Reach
MAGAZINE (ONLINE)
News & Current Affairs

The Kingston Magazine 985593
Editorial: Kingsway Business Park, Oldfield Road, Hampton, London TW12 2HD
Tel: 44 02089 395600
Email: editelm@sheengate.co.uk
Web site: www.sheengate.co.uk
Freq: Monthly
Circ: 37000 Not Audited
Editor: Rosanna Greenstreet
Profile: Magazine with lifestyle and local interest articles including fashion, beauty, art, history, motoring, property and interviews. This outlet covers areas within Kingston upon Thames Borough.
Ad Rate: Full Page Mono £1155.00
Ad Rate: Full Page Colour £1155.00
MAGAZINE
Property Management & Maintenance, Regional General Interest

Kingston Time & Leisure 999079
Editorial: 14 Apprentice Shop, Merton Abbey Mills, London SW19 2RD
Tel: 44 02085 456777
Web site: www.timeandleisure.co.uk
Freq: Monthly Not Audited
MAGAZINE
Regional General Interest

Kiosk Solutions 1094164
Tel: 44 01353 771460
Email: info@lgnmedia.co.uk
Web site: http://www.kiosksolutionsmagazine.com/
Freq: Bi-Monthly
Circ: 15000 Not Audited
Editor: James Abbott
MAGAZINE
Electronics, Industry, Manufacturing

Kiran 1061833
Tel: 44 92213 2721777
Email: khawateendigest@hotmail.com
Web site: http://pkdigest.com
Freq: Monthly
Circ: 75003 Not Audited
MAGAZINE
Women's Interests

Kit Guru 986661
Email: zardon@kitguru.net
Web site: www.kitguru.net
Freq: Daily
Circ: 943024 Cision Digital Reach
MAGAZINE (ONLINE)
Apple, Electronics, Industry, Internet, Mobile Electronics, Personal Computers, Software

Kit Magazine 998127
Email: heygirl@kit-magazine.com
Web site: kit-magazine.com
Freq: Monthly
Circ: 897 Cision Digital Reach
MAGAZINE (ONLINE)
Beauty & Grooming, Cosmetics, Fashion, Hair, Restaurant Reviews, Women's Interests

Kitchen Garden 981962
Editorial: Media Centre, Morton Way, Horncastle, Horncastle LN9 6JR
Tel: 44 01507 529396
Web site: www.kitchengarden.co.uk
Freq: Monthly
Circ: 70000 Not Audited
Editor: Steve Ott
Profile: Magazine about growing fruit, vegetables and herbs used in the home kitchen.
Ad Rate: Full Page Colour £930.00
MAGAZINE
Gardening

Consumer Magazines

Kitchens, Bedrooms & Bathrooms
981849

Editorial: Congress House, Lyon Road, Middlesex, Harrow HA1 2EN
Tel: 44 02085 152000
Web site: www.kbbmagazine.com
Freq: Monthly
Circ: 27854 Not Audited
Editor: Ruth Bell
MAGAZINE
Do-It-Yourself (DIY)

Kiteworld
982301

Editorial: 25 Lintot Square, Southwater, Horsham, Brighton RH13 9LA
Tel: 44 01273 808601
Email: admin@kiteworldmag.com
Web site: www.kiteworldmag.com
Freq: Bi-Monthly
Circ: 30000 Not Audited
Editor: Jim Gaunt
Profile: Kiteworld is a bi monthly kite surfing magazine owned by 328 Media. It provides information on kite-surfing and snow-kiting with equipment reviews, interviews, news and stories. First published in 2002. Kiteworld is written for predominantly at men aged between 20 and 50 years old who are involved in the sport. Its readership has grown to 32,000.
Ad Rate: Full Page Colour £1385.00
MAGAZINE
Swimming/Watersports

kitplus
984983

Editorial: PO BOX 6090, Newbury RG14 9BB **Tel:** 44 01635 237237
Email: info@kitplus.com
Web site: https://www.kitplus.com
Freq: Monthly
Circ: 5500 Not Audited
MAGAZINE
Broadcasting, Movies & Video

Kixtv.co.uk
988236

Editorial: PO Box 782425, Golden Square, 25 Golden Square, London W1R 9LU
Email: info@kixtv.co.uk
Web site: www.kixtv.co.uk
Freq: Daily
Circ: 58685 Cision Digital Reach
MAGAZINE (ONLINE)
Teen/Young Adult

Knit Now
987110

Editorial: St Christopher House, 217 Wellington Road South, Stockport SK2 6NG
Tel: 44 08445 611202
Email: info@practicalpublishing.co.uk
Web site: http://www.knitnowmag.co.uk/
Freq: Monthly
Circ: 38000 Not Audited
Editor: Kate Heppell
Profile: Knit Now magazine contains designs for the modern knitter. It covers a wide variety of techniques with step-by-step instructions and expert hints and tips.
MAGAZINE
Crafts

The Knitter
984899

Editorial: Units 1 & 2, Cotterell Court, Monmouth Place, Bath BA1 2NP
Tel: 44 01179 279009
Email: theknitter@immediate.co.uk
Web site: theknitter.co.uk
Freq: Monthly
Circ: 22229 Not Audited
Profile: Magazine covering knitting, fashions and trends, lifestyle, home, crafts and gadgets. Aimed at experienced knitters.
MAGAZINE
Crafts

Knitting
981943

Editorial: Guild of Master Craftsman Publications Ltd, Quadrant House 4, Thomas More Square, London E1W 1YW
Tel: 44 01273 477374
Web site: www.knittinginstitute.co.uk
Freq: Monthly
Circ: 30000 Not Audited
Editor: Christine Boggis

Profile: Consumer magazine for hand knitters featuring patterns, news, products, reviews and events. Also includes feature articles on yarns, sources, techniques and designers and some crochet patterns.
Ad Rate: Full Page Colour £800.00
MAGAZINE
Crafts

Knitting International
983554

Editorial: WestOne, 114 Wellington Street, Leeds LS1 1BA **Tel:** 44 01133 884882
Email: info@wtin.com
Web site: http://www.wtin.com/e-store/knitting-international/
Freq: Monthly
Circ: 8237 Not Audited
Editor: Jonathan Dyson
Profile: Magazine that covers the latest trends and technological developments in all areas of knitting and hosiery. Read by professionals in the textiles, knitting and hosiery industries.
Ad Rate: Full Page Mono £1359.00
Ad Rate: Full Page Colour £2500.00
MAGAZINE
Fashion, Interior Design

knoten
1060930

Tel: 44 42323 26320
Email: knoten@scout.li
Web site: http://www.scout.li
Freq: Quarterly
Circ: 450 Not Audited
MAGAZINE
Elementary School, Preschool, Teen/Young Adult, Trading Cards & Comics

Know Your Mobile
984385

Editorial: 30 Cleveland Street, London W1T 4JD
Web site: www.knowyourmobile.com
Freq: Daily
Circ: 1760002 Cision Digital Reach
Editor: Richard Goodwin
Profile: Website covering mobile phones. The website discusses mobile phone news, reviews, themes, downloads, user guides, technical specifications, prices, mobile phone apps, brands and games.
MAGAZINE (ONLINE)
Mobile Electronics

The Knowledge
987188

Editorial: Zetland House, 5-25 Scrutton Street, London EC2A 4HJ
Tel: 44 02081 020900
Web site: http://www.theknowledgeonline.com/
Freq: Daily
Circ: 27720 Cision Digital Reach
Profile: Directory of production contacts and industry knowledge. The directory does not accept any outside press materials and should only be contacted with advertising queries.
MAGAZINE (ONLINE)
Broadcasting

The Koalition
988435

Web site: www.thekoalition.com
Freq: Daily
Circ: 157567 Cision Digital Reach
MAGAZINE (ONLINE)
Computer & Video Games

kodomo.com
987290

Editorial: The Flat, Shell Bay Marine, Ferry Road, Studland, Swanage BH19 3BA
Email: cass@kodomo.com
Web site: www.kodomo.com
Freq: Daily
Circ: 10763 Cision Digital Reach
MAGAZINE (ONLINE)
Family & Parenting, Luxury Goods, Travel

Koi Carp
982015

Editorial: Alexander House, Ling Road, Tower Park, Poole BH12 4NZ
Tel: 44 01929 459288
Email: wendy@koi.co.uk
Web site: http://www.koimag.co.uk/

Freq: Monthly Not Audited
MAGAZINE
Nature & Wildlife

Kotaku UK
988066

Editorial: 1 - 10 Praed Mews, Paddington, London W2 1QY **Tel:** 44 02070 424000
Email: newstips@kotaku.co.uk
Web site: www.kotaku.co.uk/
Freq: Daily
Circ: 894543 Cision Digital Reach
Editor: Keza MacDonald
Profile: KOTAKU UK covers gaming including Xbox, playstation games, Nintendo and PC games. The blog has an archive dating back to April 2014
MAGAZINE (ONLINE)
Computer & Video Games

Kraze!
983374

Editorial: Unit 16, Greenway Farm, Bath Road, Wick, Bristol BS30 5RL
Tel: 44 01179 373003
Email: info@kennedypublishing.co.uk
Web site: http://kennedymagazines.co.uk/?gallery=futura-specials-2
Freq: Monthly
Circ: 30000 Not Audited
MAGAZINE
Elementary School, Teen/Young Adult

KrisWorld
1076637

Editorial: 83 Clerkenwell Road, London EC1R 5AR **Tel:** 44 02077 342303
Email: london@bookmarkcontent.com
Web site: http://bookmarkcontent.com/
Freq: Monthly
Circ: 65000 Not Audited
MAGAZINE
Airline Inflight

Krystal
1104596

Email: info@krystalmag.co.uk
Web site: www.krystalmag.co.uk
Freq: Daily
Circ: 521 Cision Digital Reach
Editor: Melissa Allison-Forbes
MAGAZINE (ONLINE)
Women's Interests

KUBE Radio
982740

Email: controller@kuberadio.com
Web site: www.kuberadio.com
Freq: Daily
Circ: 1594 Cision Digital Reach
MAGAZINE (ONLINE)
Student Lifestyle

Kudos
997934

Tel: 44 01892 300321
Email: editorial@badbettymedia.co.uk
Web site: www.kudoskent.co.uk
Freq: Bi-Monthly
Circ: 20000 Not Audited
MAGAZINE
Antiques/Collectibles, Art, Arts, Bars, Clubs & Pubs, Classical/Choral/Band Music, Comedy, Country, Folk, Bluegrass, Dance Music, Entertainment, Jazz & Blues

The Kurios
1055298

Email: info@thekuriosmagazine.com
Web site: http://thekurios.com/
Freq: Quarterly
Circ: 758 Cision Digital Reach
MAGAZINE (ONLINE)
Africa, Americas, Antiques/Collectibles, Art, Arts, Asia, Literature, Photography, Theater & Performing Arts, Visual Arts

Kychan Teen
997791

Editorial: 114 Nightingale Grove, 114 Nightingale Grove, London SE13 6DZ
Email: kychanteen@kychan.co.uk
Web site: www.kychan.co.uk
Freq: Monthly
Circ: 3500 Not Audited
MAGAZINE
Teen/Young Adult

La Di Da
987549

Editorial: Clavering House, Clavering Place, Newcastle upon Tyne NE1 3NG
Tel: 44 01914 661028
Email: yourmaj@ladida.co.uk
Web site: www.ladida.co.uk
Freq: Quarterly
Circ: 10000 Not Audited
Editor: Linda Jane Westphal
Profile: Magazine covering affluent lifestyle. It contains fashion, beauty, food and drink, society and travel.
MAGAZINE
Luxury Goods, Regional General Interest

La Opinion BA
1062098

Web site: http://laopinionba.com
Circ: 521 Cision Digital Reach
MAGAZINE (ONLINE)
Airline Inflight, Railroad, Travel

La Tundra
998018

Tel: 44 07968 915627
Email: info@latundra.com
Web site: www.latundra.com
Freq: Quarterly Not Audited
Editor: Silvia Demetilla
MAGAZINE
Antiques/Collectibles, Art, Arts, Literature, Photography, Theater & Performing Arts, Visual Arts

Laboratorytalk
981686

Editorial: Castle House, 89 High Street, Berkhamsted HP4 2DF
Circ: 16373 Cision Digital Reach
Profile: Website covering laboratory services. The Laboratorytalk website shares the latest news and information on laboratory science and services.
MAGAZINE (ONLINE)
Electronics, Engineering

The LAD Bible
990602

Editorial: 20 Dale Street, Manchester M1 1EZ **Tel:** 44 01612 287637
Email: enquiries@theladbible.com
Web site: http://www.ladbible.com/
Freq: Daily
Circ: 15445 Cision Digital Reach
MAGAZINE (ONLINE)
Men's Interests

Lads Holiday Guide
1052660

Email: contact@ladsholidayguide.com
Web site: ladsholidayguide.com
Freq: Daily
Circ: 933 Cision Digital Reach
MAGAZINE (ONLINE)
Cooking & Baking, Men's Interests, Travel

The Lady
982438

Editorial: 39-40 Bedford Street, Strand, London WC2E 9ER **Tel:** 44 02073 794717
Email: editors@lady.co.uk
Web site: www.lady.co.uk
Freq: Weekly
Circ: 26469 Not Audited
Editor: Sam Taylor
Profile: Magazine covering women's interest including celebrities, entertainment, food, travel, beauty, fashion, lifestyle, home, gardening, history, culture, exhibitions, the arts and human interest. Includes articles documenting social news, housekeeping and cookery. The Lady was founded in 1885 by Thomas Gibson Bowles. Aimed at women aged 40 years and over.
Ad Rate: Full Page Colour £2750.00
MAGAZINE
Women's Interests

Lady Golfer
982262

Editorial: 2 Arena Park, Tarn Lane, Scarcroft, Leeds LS17 9BF
Tel: 44 01132 893979
Email: info@sportspub.co.uk
Web site: ladygolferonline.com
Freq: Monthly
Circ: 13435 Not Audited
Profile: Lady Golfer is a monthly womens' golf magazine owned by Sports Publications Ltd. It provides information on women's golf featuring celebrity interviews, news, tips,

advice, travel, fashion and competitions. Lady Golfer is written for female golfers. Its readership has grown to 20,000 readers.
Ad Rate: Full Page Colour £1139.40
MAGAZINE
Golf

LadyCity
1061432
Tel: 44 74952 024650
Email: admin@ladycity.ru
Web site: http://ladycity.ru
Circ: 530466 Cision Digital Reach
MAGAZINE (ONLINE)
Antiques/Collectibles, Armed Forces, Astrology & Parapsychology, Astronomy, Aviation, Boating & Yachting, Camping and RV Travel, Careers, Cartoons, Casinos & Gaming

Lakeland Walker
981905
Editorial: The Water Mill, Broughton Hall, Skipton, Broughton BD23 3AG
Tel: 44 01756 701381
Web site: http://www.lakeland-walker.com
Freq: Bi-Monthly
Circ: 12000 Not Audited
Editor: John Manning
Profile: Magazine containing Lake District news, countryside features, where to stay, walks and gear features. Aimed at walkers and backpackers in the Lake District.
Ad Rate: Full Page Colour £500.00
MAGAZINE
Outdoor Recreation

The Lamp and Owl
996628
Editorial: The News Room, Birkbeck University, 43 Gordon Square, London WC1H 0PD
Email: editor@lampandowl.co.uk
Web site: www.lampandowl.co.uk
Freq: Bi-Monthly Not Audited
MAGAZINE
Student Lifestyle

The Lanark Website
1070429
Email: andy@lanark.co.uk
Web site: www.lanark.co.uk
Freq: Daily
Circ: 10030 Cision Digital Reach
MAGAZINE (ONLINE)
Regional General Interest

The Lancashire & Yorkshire Railway Society Magazine
099044
Editorial: 563 Woodgrange Drive, Thorpe Bay, Southend-on-Sea SS1 3EJ
Tel: 44 01702 585708
Email: editor@lyrs.org.uk
Web site: www.lyrs.org.uk
Freq: Quarterly
Circ: 900 Not Audited
Editor: Roger Mellor
MAGAZINE
Railroad

Lancashire Life
982503
Editorial: United Business Centres Ltd, Cinnabar Court, 5300 Daresbury Park, Warrington WA4 4GE Tel: 44 01928 240668
Web site: www.lancashirelife.co.uk
Freq: Monthly
Circ: 19475 Not Audited
Editor: Paul Mackenzie
Profile: Magazine containing coverage of towns, villages, the county's history and heritage, features, about life in the county, property, antiques, fashion, interior design, gardening, food and wine and motoring.
Ad Rate: Full Page Mono £1840.00
Ad Rate: Full Page Colour £2105.00
MAGAZINE
Regional General Interest

The Lancashire Magazine
982504
Editorial: Blackpool Football Club, Seasiders Way, Blackpool, Blackpool FY1 6NZ Tel: 44 01253 336588
Email: info@lancashiremagazine.co.uk
Web site: www.thelancashiremagazine.co.uk
Freq: Monthly

Circ: 35279 Not Audited
Profile: Magazine covering features about Lancashire, property, home, interiors, contry living, arts, local history, regional tourism, antiques, health and beauty, restaurants, gardening and the great outdoors. Aimed at Lancashire residents and Lancastrians overseas.
Ad Rate: Full Page Colour £1500.00
MAGAZINE
Regional General Interest

The Lancet
981543
Editorial: 125 London Wall, London EC2Y 5AS Tel: 44 02074 244922
Email: editorial@lancet.com
Web site: http://www.journals.elsevier.com/the-lancet
Freq: Weekly
Circ: 5880 Not Audited
Editor: Richard Horton
Profile: Journal covering medical news, original research and reviews on all aspects of clinical medicine and International Health. It is published weekly along with six monthly speciality journals covering global health, diabetes and endocrinology, oncology, neurology, respiratory medicine, and infectious diseases. First published 5th October 1823. Aimed at hospital-based clinicians and research academics.
Ad Rate: Full Page Colour £1350.00
MAGAZINE
Pharmaceuticals

Land Rover Monthly
982596
Editorial: Tower Court, Irchester Road, Wollaston, Wellingborough NN29 7PJ
Tel: 44 02079 076878
Email: editorial@lrm.co.uk
Web site: www.landroveraddict.com
Freq: Monthly
Circ: 22075 Not Audited
Editor: Dave Phillips
MAGAZINE
Driving, Off-road & 4-Wheel Drive Vehicles

Land Rover OneLife
983307
Editorial: Bankside 3, 90 Southwark Street, London SE1 0SW Tel: 44 02037 877000
Email: info@redwoodgroup.net
Web site: http://onelife.landrover.com/#!onelife
Freq: Semi-Annual
Circ: 400000 Not Audited
Profile: Magazine covering travel and adventure with details on new Land Rover product developments and services.
MAGAZINE
Automakers

Land Rover Owner International
982597
Editorial: Media House, Lynchwood, Peterborough PE2 6EA
Tel: 44 01733 468000
Email: landrover.owner@bauermedia.co.uk
Web site: www.lro.com
Freq: Monthly
Circ: 32375 Not Audited
Editor: Mike Goodbun
MAGAZINE
Off-road & 4-Wheel Drive Vehicles

LandLove
986751
Editorial: The Tower, Phoenix Square, Wyncolls Road, Colchester CO4 9HU
Tel: 44 01206 851117
Email: landlove@burdamagazines.co.uk
Web site: http://www.landlove.com/
Freq: Bi-Monthly
Circ: 50000 Not Audited
Profile: Magazine looking at the British traditional way of life and the beauty of the countryside. It offers recipe ideas using seasonal British produce from the market, the garden and the hedgerows and explores the most interesting places in the British Isles, the local customs and traditions. Each issue includes practical advice and inspiration for those who garden and enjoy crafting.
MAGAZINE
Field Sports, Gardening

Landlust (UK)
1054037
Tel: 44 49025 018016161
Email: contact@landlust.co.uk
Web site: www.landlust.co.uk/
Freq: Bi-Monthly
Circ: 30000 Not Audited
MAGAZINE
Do-It-Yourself (DIY), Gardening, Regional General Interest, Women's Interests

LandScape
986750
Editorial: Media House, Peterborough Business Park, Peterborough PE2 6EA
Tel: 44 01733 468000
Email: landscapemagazine@bauermedia.co.uk
Web site: www.landscapemagazine.co.uk
Freq: Bi-Monthly
Circ: 39161 Not Audited
Editor: Hilary Scott
Profile: Magazine covering gardens, simple seasonal kitchen food, traditional British crafts, nature and the countryside.
MAGAZINE
Cooking & Baking, Crafts, Gardening, History

Landworker
983587
Editorial: 128 Theobald's Road, London WC1X 8TN Tel: 44 02033 712065
Web site: www.unitetheunion.org/
Freq: Bi-Monthly
Circ: 20000 Not Audited
Editor: Amanda Campbell
Profile: Newspaper covering food safety, the environment and the protection of working conditions.
Ad Rate: Full Page Colour £900.00
MAGAZINE
News & Current Affairs

LAPF Investments
985236
Editorial: Temple Chambers, 3-7 Temple Avenue, London EC4Y 0HP
Tel: 44 02073 539134
Email: info@dgpublishing.com
Web site: www.lapfinvestments.com
Freq: Bi-Monthly
Circ: 6000 Not Audited
Editor: Brian Gielty
MAGAZINE
Personal Finance

LAPV - Local Authority Plant & Vehicle
981268
Editorial: 8 The Old Yarn Mills, Sherborne, Sherborne DT9 3HH Tel: 44 01935 374001
Web site: www.lapv.co.uk
Freq: Quarterly
Circ: 4500 Not Audited
Editor: Ann-Marie Knegt
MAGAZINE
Automotive, Public Sector

Large Display Monitor
981631
Editorial: 134 Upper Chobham Road, Camberley, Camberley GU15 1EJ
Tel: 44 01252 835385
Email: news@meko.co.uk
Web site: www.meko.co.uk/index.php/display-monitor/47-displaymonitor
Freq: Weekly Not Audited
MAGAZINE
Advertising Industry, Electronics, Marketing

Laser Systems Europe
986435
Editorial: 4 Signet Court, Cambridge CB1 8LA Tel: 44 01223 221030
Email: editor.lasersystems@europascience.com
Web site: www.lasersystemseurope.com
Freq: Quarterly
Circ: 12000 Not Audited
Editor: Greg Blackman
MAGAZINE
News & Current Affairs

Last Minute Theatre Tickets
1102295
Editorial: 27 Old Gloucester Street, London WC1N 3AX Tel: 44 02074 921602
Email: admin@uklondontheatretickets.com

Web site: www.lastminutetheatretickets.com
Freq: Daily
Circ: 6315 Cision Digital Reach
MAGAZINE (ONLINE)
Local Entertainment Guides

LatAm Insurance Review - CEASED
986335
Editorial: Thavies Inn House, 3-4 Holborn Circus, London EC1N 2HA
Web site: www.insurancelatam.com
Freq: Monthly
Circ: 5500 Not Audited
Profile: Magazine that covers the corporate insurance industry in Latin America. It looks at areas including construction, marine and property, and a wide variety of topics including regulation, microinsurance and emerging risks.
MAGAZINE
Insurance

Late Tackle
999471
Editorial: Lower Ground Floor, Tuition House, St Georges Road, London SW19 4EU Tel: 44 02089 714333
Email: latetackle@hotmail.co.uk
Web site: http://www.latetacklemagazine.com/
Freq: Bi-Monthly
Circ: 2000 Not Audited
MAGAZINE
Soccer

Laterlife.com
984355
Editorial: Hillside Court, Bowling Hill, Yate BS37 6JX
Email: news@laterlife.com
Web site: www.laterlife.com
Freq: Daily
Circ: 447 Cision Digital Reach
MAGAZINE (ONLINE)
Men's Interests, Retirement Savings, Women's Interests

Latest 7
985374
Editorial: Unit 1, Level 5 North, New England House, New England Street, Brighton BN1 4GH Tel: 44 01273 818150
Email: editorial@thelatest.co.uk
Web site: www.thelatest.co.uk
Freq: Weekly
Circ: 100000 Not Audited
Profile: Latest 7 is a weekly entertainment and news magazine owned by Latest Homes Ltd. It covers entertainment, listings, fashion and beauty, food & drink, music, sport, theatre, film and celebrity news. It also contains the 8 page TV guide and comes with Latest Homes, the weekly property sales and lettings magazine. First published in 2001. Latest 7 is written for those 18-40 age range and are residents of Brighton and Sussex. Its readership has grown to 100,000.
Ad Rate: Full Page Colour £500.00
MAGAZINE
Regional General Interest

Latin American Weekly Report
985964
Editorial: 61 Old Street, London EC1V 9HW
Tel: 44 02036 952790
Web site: www.latinnews.com/latin-american-weekly-report.html
Freq: Weekly Not Audited
Editor: Jonathan Farmer
Profile: Newsletter providing analysis of news as it breaks in Latin America, covering the economic and political scene, long-term trends and the effects for business organisations. Directed at businesses with interests in Latin America including bankers, businessmen, corporate planners, diplomats, politicians and academics.
Alternative Title: Latin American Special Reports
MAGAZINE
Economics, International News, Politics

Latin Correspondent UK
998317
Editorial: Colston Tower Level 9, Colston Street, Bristol BS1 4UX
Tel: 44 01172 443750

Consumer Magazines

Email: editor@hybridnewsgroup.com
Web site: http://latincorrespondent.com/
Freq: Daily
Circ: 39908 Cision Digital Reach
MAGAZINE (ONLINE)
News & Current Affairs

Latin Lawyer 983629

Editorial: 87 Lancaster Road, London W11
1QQ Tel: 44 02079 089941
Email: briefing@latinlawyer.com
Web site: www.latinlawyer.com
Freq: Monthly
Circ: 9500 Not Audited
Editor: Rosie Cresswell
Profile: Latin Lawyer is a monthly Business
Law magazine for Latin America owned by
Law Business Research Ltd. It provides
information on economic, legal regulatory
and political issues affecting the practice of
law in the region. It also covers news, cases,
deals analysis and policy developments. A
email briefing published twice weekly is also
available. First published in 2001. Latin
Lawyer is written for providers and users of
legal services in Latin America. Its
readership has grown to 9,500.
Ad Rate: Full Page Colour £3200.00
MAGAZINE
Consumer Interest, Corporate Law,
Criminal Law, Employment, Family Law,
Government, Human Rights, Intellectual
Property, Law, Legal Services

Latino Life 995843

Email: info@latinolife.co.uk
Web site: www.latinolife.co.uk
Freq: Quarterly
Circ: 20000 Not Audited
MAGAZINE
Americas

The Law Society Gazette 979846

Editorial: 113 Chancery Lane, London
WC2A 1PL Tel: 44 02072 421222
Web site: www.lawgazette.co.uk
Freq: Weekly
Circ: 102175 Not Audited
Profile: Official publication of the Law
Society of Ireland.
Ad Rate: Full Page Mono £2525.00
Ad Rate: Full Page Colour £3050.00
MAGAZINE
Bankruptcy, Company News &
Appointments, Consumer Interest,
Corporate Law, Criminal Law,
Employment, Estate Planning, Family
Law, Federal Courts, Food & Drug
Administration

LawCareers.Net 983662

Editorial: New Hibernia House, Winchester
Walk, London Bridge, London SE1 9AG
Tel: 44 02072 340606
Email: editorial@lawcareers.net
Web site: www.lawcareers.net
Freq: Daily
Circ: 104049 Cision Digital Reach
MAGAZINE (ONLINE)
Careers, Legal Services

Lawyer Monthly 985648

Editorial: 2 Parkside Court, Greenhough Rd,
Lichfield, Lichfield WS13 7FE
Tel: 44 01543 255537
Email: editor@lawyer-monthly.com
Web site: www.lawyer-monthly.com
Freq: Monthly
Circ: 77063 Not Audited
Profile: Lawyer Monthly is a monthly
business law magazine owned by Parity
Media. It provides information on corporate
legal news, expert law guides, top legal firm
features and global deal transaction
reporting in both the legal and the corporate
world. Lawyer Monthly is written for business
leaders, in-house counsel, the banking
fraternity, investment professionals,
accountants, public and private equity and
high net-worth individuals. Its readership has
grown to 51,185.
Ad Rate: Full Page Colour £1949.00
MAGAZINE
Consumer Interest, Corporate Law,
Criminal Law, Employment, Family Law,

Government, Human Rights, Intellectual
Property, Law, Legal Services

Layered 987928

Tel: 44 02071 838275
Email: editor@layeredonline.com
Web site: www.layeredonline.com
Freq: Daily
Circ: 10552 Cision Digital Reach
MAGAZINE (ONLINE)
Hair

LDNCard.com 1066538

Editorial: Unit 4 Oliver Business Park, Oliver
Road, London NW10 7JB
Tel: 44 02036 646602
Email: info@ldncard.com
Web site: www.ldncard.com
Freq: Daily
Circ: 4799 Cision Digital Reach
MAGAZINE (ONLINE)
News & Current Affairs

Le Cool London 1093866

Web site: http://london.lecool.com/
Freq: Weekly
Circ: 50000 Not Audited
Profile: Website covering weekly cultural
events and leisure activities going on around
the London region, including art, film, music,
club nights, bars and restaurants.
MAGAZINE
Alcohol & Spirits, Antiques/Collectibles,
Art, Arts, Bars, Clubs & Pubs, Beer,
Beverages, Broadcasting, Classical/
Choral/Band Music, Comedy

Le Nurb 998544

Editorial: Brunel University Students Union,
Brunel University, London UB8 3PH
Tel: 44 01895 269269
Email: 1309586@my.brunel.ac.uk
Web site: http://lenurb.co.uk/
Freq: Monthly
Circ: 16000 Not Audited
MAGAZINE
Student Lifestyle

Leadership & Organization Development Journal 998855

Editorial: Howard House, Wagon Lane,
Bingley BD16 1WA Tel: 44 01274 777700
Web site: http://www.
emeraldgrouppublishing.com/products/
journals/editorial_team.htm?id=lodj
Freq: Bi-Monthly Not Audited
Editor: Marie McHugh
MAGAZINE
News & Current Affairs

Leadership Focus 981529

Editorial: 1 Heath Square, Boltro Road,
Haywards Heath, Haywards Heath RH16
1BL Tel: 44 01444 472873
Email: info@naht.org.uk
Web site: www.naht.org.uk
Freq: Bi-Monthly
Circ: 30151 Not Audited
Profile: Magazine providing a forum for the
exchange of educational ideas.
MAGAZINE
Disability, Education, Higher Education,
Preschool, Schools & Institutions,
Students

Leading Culture Destinations 996038

Editorial: 23B Westbourne Park, London W2
5PX Tel: 44 07795 036525
Email: office@leadingculturedestinations.
com
Web site: www.leadingculturedestinations.
com
Freq: Daily
Circ: 611 Cision Digital Reach
MAGAZINE (ONLINE)
Architecture & Design, Art

League Express 982275

Editorial: Wellington House, Briggate,
Brighouse HD6 1DN Tel: 44 01484 401895
Email: news@totalrl.com
Web site: www.totalrl.com

Freq: Weekly
Circ: 48000 Not Audited
MAGAZINE
Rugby

Learning Disability Practice 981201

Editorial: The Heights, 59-65 Lowlands
Road, Harrow, Harrow HA1 31W
Tel: 44 02084 231066
Email: nursing.standard@rcni.com
Web site: https://rcni.com/learning-
disability-practice
Freq: Monthly
Circ: 3341 Not Audited
Editor: Christine Walker
Profile: Publication focusing on recent
fundamental changes in the field of learning
disabilities. Covers the areas of practice,
policy, research and education, as well as
carrying profiles of prominent people within
the field. Read by members of the Royal
College of Nursing and people working in the
learning disability field.
Ad Rate: Full Page Colour £1880.00
MAGAZINE
Community Care (UK), Disability,
Medicine, Nursing/Nurses

Learning Disability Today 984451

Editorial: Rayford House, School Road,
Hove, Brighton BN3 5HX
Tel: 44 01273 434943
Email: info@learningdisabilitytoday.co.uk
Web site: www.learningdisabilitytoday.co.
uk/ldt-home
Freq: Daily
MAGAZINE (ONLINE)
Disability

Learning Magazine 998909

Editorial: 2-4 St Georges Road, Wimbledon,
London SW19 4DP Tel: 44 02083 945100
Email: editorial@vmgl.com
Web site: www.learnevents.com
Freq: Annual
Circ: 8000 Not Audited
MAGAZINE
Disability, Education, Higher Education,
Preschool, Schools & Institutions,
Students

L'ECHO Magazine 998005

Editorial: 35 Cromwell Road, London SW7
2DG
Email: redaction@lechomagazine.uk
Web site: lecho.org.uk
Freq: Bi-Monthly Not Audited
MAGAZINE
Education, Expatriates, Family &
Parenting, Health & Medicine

Leeds & Yorkshire Lawyer 984317

Editorial: 9 Cardale Court, Cardale Park,
Beckwith Head Road, Harrogate HG3 1RY
Tel: 44 01423 851150
Web site: http://www.leedslawsociety.org.
uk/leeds+and+yorkshire+lawyer
Freq: Bi-Monthly
Circ: 8000 Not Audited
Editor: Marek Handzel
Profile: Journal of the Leeds Law Society
containing news and features relating to the
legal profession and the law both nationally
and in the Yorkshire region.
Ad Rate: Full Page Colour £1600.00
MAGAZINE
News & Current Affairs

Leeds-List.com 988607

Editorial: 64 Wellington Street, Leeds, Leeds
LS1 2EE Tel: 44 01133 200710
Email: editor@leeds-list.com
Web site: leeds-list.com
Freq: Daily
Circ: 49890 Cision Digital Reach
Profile: Website covering Leeds lifestyle.
The LEEDS-LISTED.COM website shares the
latest news and information on style, culture,

music, attractions, food, drinks and events in
Leeds.
MAGAZINE (ONLINE)
Art, Bars, Clubs & Pubs, Comedy,
Entertainment, Literature, Local
Entertainment Guides, Movies & Video,
Photography, Restaurant Reviews,
Shopping

Leeds-Manchester.pl 995997

Editorial: 7 Lord Austin Drive, Malbrook,
Bromsgrove, Leeds B60 1RB
Tel: 44 01315 619825
Email: office@leeds-manchester.pl
Web site: http://www.leeds-manchester.pl
Freq: Daily
Circ: 35258 Cision Digital Reach
MAGAZINE (ONLINE)
Europe

LeftLion 1102297

Editorial: 8 Stoney Street, The Lace Market,
Nottingham NG1 1LH
Web site: www.leftlion.co.uk
Freq: Monthly
Circ: 12000 Not Audited
Editor: Ali Emm
MAGAZINE
Regional General Interest

The Legal 996215

Editorial: 8 Campo Lane, Sheffield S1 2EF
Tel: 44 01142 723655
Email: editorial@sheffieldlawsociety.co.uk
Web site: http://www.sheffieldlawsociety.co.
uk/magazine/the-legal/
Freq: Quarterly
Circ: 2500 Not Audited
Profile: A unique bi-monthly publication for
Sheffield & District Law Society members
and leading commercial professionals in
South Yorkshire. Please note that the
magazine will only cover topics and subjects
directly relevant to businesses and law firms
within the Sheffield City and Barnsley
regions.
Ad Rate: Full Page Mono £1000.00
MAGAZINE
Consumer Interest, Corporate Law,
Criminal Law, Employment, Family Law,
Government, Human Rights, Intellectual
Property, Law, Legal Services

Legal and Criminological Psychology 995755

Editorial: The Atrium Southern Gate,
Chichester PO19 8QG Tel: 44 01865 778315
Email: cs-journals@wiley.com
Web site: onlinelibrary.wiley.com/journal/10.
1111/%28ISSN%292044-8333
Freq: Semi-Annual Not Audited
Editor: Paul Taylor
MAGAZINE
News & Current Affairs

Legal Cheek 988175

Editorial: Unit 3, Excel Building, 6-16
Arbutus Street, London E8 4DT
Tel: 44 02072 547283
Email: tips@legalcheek.com
Web site: www.legalcheek.com
Freq: Daily
Circ: 56606 Cision Digital Reach
MAGAZINE (ONLINE)
Bankruptcy, Company News &
Appointments, Consumer Interest,
Corporate Law, Criminal Law,
Employment, Estate Planning, Family
Law, Federal Courts, Food & Drug
Administration

Legal Compliance Association 1075725

Editorial: 6-14 Underwood Street, London
N1 7JQ Tel: 44 02074 900049
Email: lca@wilmington.com
Web site: http://www.
legalcomplianceassociation.co.uk/
Freq: Daily
Circ: 985 Cision Digital Reach
MAGAZINE (ONLINE)
Bankruptcy, Company News &
Appointments, Consumer Interest,
Corporate Law, Criminal Law,

Employment, Estate Planning, Family Law, Federal Courts, Food & Drug Administration

Legal IT Insider
981707

Editorial: Oak Lodge, Darrow Green Road, Denton IP20 0AY **Tel:** 44 01986 788666
Email: news@legaltechnology.com
Web site: www.legaltechnology.com
Freq: Monthly
Circ: 52000 Not Audited
Profile: Newsletter containing information and guidance on law office computer systems.
Ad Rate: Full Page Colour £350.00
MAGAZINE
Computers, Data Management, Internet, Legal Services, Software

Legalbrief
1060373

Email: cserv@juta.co.za
Web site: http://www.legalbrief.co.za
Circ: 14845 Cision Digital Reach
MAGAZINE (ONLINE)
Bankruptcy, Company News & Appointments, Consumer Interest, Corporate Law, Criminal Law, Employment, Estate Planning, Family Law, Federal Courts, Food & Drug Administration

Legion
999110

Editorial: 8 Baldwin Sreet, London EC1V 9NU **Tel:** 44 0075 653000
Email: editorial@legion-magazine.co.uk
Web site: www.britishlegion.org.uk/membership/members-information/legion-magazine
Freq: Quarterly
Circ: 224387 Not Audited
MAGAZINE
Armed Forces

Legion Scotland Today
998361

Editorial: Suite 2.3, Red Tree Business Suites, 33 Dalmarnock Road, Glasgow G40 4LA **Tel:** 44 01315 501549
Web site: legionscotland.org.uk/news-events/magazine
Freq: Quarterly
Circ: 20000 Not Audited
MAGAZINE
Armed Forces, Defense & National Security

LEGO NEXO KNIGHTS
1100570

Editorial: Vineyard House, 44 Brook Green, London W6 7BT **Tel:** 44 02071 505000
Freq: Monthly
Circ: 51005 Not Audited
MAGAZINE
Teen/Young Adult, Trading Cards & Comics

LEGO NINJAGO
1057076

Editorial: Vineyard House, 44 Brook Green, London W6 7BT **Tel:** 44 02071 505000
Web site: www.lego.com/en-gb/ninjago
Freq: Quarterly
Circ: 74887 Not Audited
MAGAZINE
Teen/Young Adult

Leicester City Football Club
982250

Editorial: Walkers Stadium, Filbert Way, Leicester LE2 7FL **Tel:** 44 01162 294923
Email: media@lcfc.co.uk
Web site: www.lcfc.com
Freq: No Frequency Established
Circ: 152812 Cision Digital Reach
MAGAZINE (ONLINE)
Soccer

Leisure Kicks
984646

Editorial: Floor 2, 47 Woodberry Avenue, London N21 3LE **Tel:** 44 02088 821943
Email: lifestyle@leisurekicks.com
Web site: leisurekicks.com
Freq: Annual
Circ: 325000 Not Audited
Editor: Andy Turner

Profile: Sport & leisure guide with three main sections consisting of lifestyle features, a sport section edited by the major national governing bodies and finally a gym and sports centre finder. The lifestyle section covers issues relating to sport, health & fitness ranging from body, mind, technology, food, drink, active travel, outdoors through to beauty, health and kids fun. Aimed at sports and leisure centres, high street retails outlets, multiples, education sector (schools, FE Colleges and universities). Also targets families, the education sector plus segmentation specific for 25+ working people, elderly, diverse ethnic backgrounds and the disabled.
Ad Rate: Full Page Colour £5450.00
MAGAZINE
Basketball, Bicycles, Billiards, Boating & Yachting, Bodybuilding, Bowling, Boxing, Cricket, Equestrian Sports, Extreme/Adventure Sports

Leisure Management
980744

Editorial: Portmill House, Portmill Lane, Hitchin SG5 1DJ **Tel:** 44 01462 431385
Email: newsdesk@leisuremedia.com
Web site: http://www.leisuremanagement.co.uk/
Freq: Annual
Circ: 8657 Cision Digital Reach
Profile: Magazine catering for the information needs of leisure industry professionals. Readership includes owners, operators, managers, policy makers, investors, consultants and architects in the International leisure industry.
Ad Rate: Full Page Colour £1500.00
MAGAZINE (ONLINE)
Bars, Clubs & Pubs, Computer & Video Games, Fitness & Exercise, Genealogy, Hotels/Motels, Leisure Activities, Music, Travel

Leisure Opportunities
981234

Editorial: Portmill House, Portmill Lane, Hitchin SG5 1DJ **Tel:** 44 01462 431385
Email: newsdesk@leisuremedia.com
Web site: http://www.leisureopportunities.co.uk/
Freq: Bi-Weekly
Circ: 16300 Not Audited
Profile: Magazine containing news and recruitment information on current developments in the leisure sector.
MAGAZINE
Bars, Clubs & Pubs, Computer & Video Games, Fitness & Exercise, Genealogy, Hotels/Motels, Leisure Activities, Music, Travel

Leisure Painter
984065

Editorial: Caxton House, 63-65 High Street, Tenterden, Tenterden TN30 6BD
Tel: 44 01580 763315
Email: info@tapc.co.uk
Web site: www.painters-online.co.uk
Freq: Monthly Not Audited
Editor: Ingrid Lyon
Profile: Magazine providing guidance and inspiration with step-by-step instruction. Includes set projects, working methods, helpful tips and ideas. Read by amateur painters of all ages, particularly beginners. Regular features: Art Club Challenge A critique of work sent in by art club members on a theme set by Tony Paul.; Books Reviews of the latest art related books.; Dates A listing of forthcoming events on at the art club.; Exhibitions A listing of exhibitions that are on or that are beginning in the forthcoming month.; Let's Start with Art A monthly step by step beginners series.; Marketlink Feature covering product test reports, new materials and other product news.; News News from the art club.; Painting Project Critique A look at readers work from the painting project.; Painting Projects The monthly project is introduced with a photograph. Readers can work on their painting of the photograph throughout the month and then compare their work with that of the contributing artist in the following issue.; Personal Tutorials A look at some of the readers work.; Readers' Letters
Ad Rate: Full Page Colour £1295.00
MAGAZINE
Art, Visual Arts

The Leisure Review
997695

Editorial: 1 New Cross Road, Oxford OX3 8LP
Email: news@theleisurereview.co.uk
Web site: www.theleisurereview.co.uk
Freq: Monthly
Circ: 1250 Not Audited
Editor: Jonathan Ives
Profile: The Leisure Review is a magazine offering an independent view of the leisure industry for leisure professionals working in the management, development and promotion of all aspects of leisure, culture and sport.
MAGAZINE
Antiques/Collectibles, Armed Forces, Astrology & Parapsychology, Astronomy, Aviation, Basketball, Bicycles, Billiards, Boating & Yachting, Bodybuilding

Leisure-Kit.net
983931

Editorial: Portmill House, Portmill Lane, Hitchin SG5 1DJ **Tel:** 44 01462 431385
Email: newsdesk@leisuremedia.com
Web site: www.leisure-kit.net
Freq: Daily
Circ: 7593 Cision Digital Reach
Profile: Website covering leisure products and management. The leisure-kit.net website features product listings, news and job opportunities.
MAGAZINE (ONLINE)
Fitness & Exercise

leisureweek.com
984999

Editorial: Portmill House, Portmill Lane, Hitchin SG5 1DJ **Tel:** 44 01462 431385
Email: newsdesk@leisuremedia.com
Web site: www.leisureweek.com
Freq: Daily
Circ: 685 Cision Digital Reach
MAGAZINE (ONLINE)
Bars, Clubs & Pubs, Computer & Video Games, Fitness & Exercise, Genealogy, Hotels/Motels, Leisure Activities, Music, Travel

The Leither
996981

Editorial: 136b Constitution Street, Edinburgh EH6 6AJ
Web site: www.leithermagazine.com
Freq: Monthly
Circ: 9000 Not Audited
Editor: Billy Gould
MAGAZINE
Classical/Choral/Band Music, Country, Folk, Bluegrass, Dance Music, Jazz & Blues, Music, Pop Music, R&B, Urban, World, Rap & Hip Hop, Regional General Interest, Rock Music

LEN (European Aquatics Highlights)
1062108

Tel: 44 36125 10690
Email: lenmagazine@lenmagazine.com
Web site: http://www.lenmagazine.com
Freq: Quarterly Not Audited
MAGAZINE
Antiques/Collectibles, Armed Forces, Astrology & Parapsychology, Astronomy, Aviation, Basketball, Bicycles, Billiards, Boating & Yachting, Bodybuilding

Leopard Magazine
982558

Editorial: University of Aberdeen, King's College, Aberdeen AB24 3FX
Tel: 44 01224 313723
Email: editor@leopardmag.co.uk
Web site: www.leopardmag.co.uk
Freq: Monthly
Circ: 3000 Not Audited
Editor: Judy Mackie
Profile: Magazine covering all aspects of Scottish culture. Includes articles on archaeology, local history, place names, environment, the arts, gardens, sport, crosswords, diary, book reviews and family history. Read by residents, ex-patriots and visitors to Scotland.Regular features: Book Reviews; Fiction; Gardening; History and Culture; Humour; Restaurants; Writing in Scots
Ad Rate: Full Page Mono £285.00

Ad Rate: Full Page Colour £400.00
MAGAZINE
History, Regional General Interest

Leros
997357

Editorial: PO Box 7769, London W1A 1LU
Tel: 44 07939 973100
Email: leros@leros.co.uk
Web site: www.leros.co.uk
Freq: Monthly Not Audited
Editor: Vicente Lou
MAGAZINE
Americas, Expatriates

Let's Get Crafting
984581

Editorial: Units 21-22, 1 Phoenix Court, Hawkins Road, Colchester, Colchester CO2 8JY **Tel:** 44 01206 505900
Email: patternqueries@letsgetcrafting.com
Web site: www.letsgetcrafting.com
Freq: Monthly
Circ: 40000 Not Audited
Editor: Rosie Savage
MAGAZINE
Crafts

Let's Get Weddy
990696

Editorial: 2nd Floor, Regus, Highbridge Industrial Estate, Oxford Road, Uxbridge, London UB8 1HR **Tel:** 44 01895 876607
Email: hello@letsgetweddy.com
Web site: https://letsgetweddy.co.uk/
Freq: Daily
Circ: 68480 Cision Digital Reach
MAGAZINE (ONLINE)
Weddings

Let's Go With The Children
985567

Editorial: Manor House, Manor Park, Aldershot, Aldershot GU12 4JU
Tel: 44 01252 368325
Email: info@boomerangfamily.co.uk
Web site: https://letsgowiththechildren.co.uk/
Freq: Daily
Circ: 10944 Cision Digital Reach
Editor: Penelope Smith
MAGAZINE (ONLINE)
Travel

Let's Knit
984582

Editorial: 1 Phoenix Court, Hawkins Road, Colchester, Colchester CO2 8JY
Tel: 44 01206 505900
Web site: www.letsknit.co.uk
Freq: Monthly
Circ: 62000 Not Audited
Editor: Sarah Neal
Profile: Magazine including fashionable and fun to knit patterns, features, shopping, practical advice and a strong community element.
Ad Rate: Full Page Colour £950.00
MAGAZINE
Crafts

Let's Talk
981971

Editorial: Prospect House, Rouen Road, Norwich NR1 1RE **Tel:** 44 01603 628311
Email: letstalk@archant.co.uk
Web site: www.letstalk24.co.uk
Freq: Monthly
Circ: 11575 Not Audited
Profile: Website covering local and international news and current affairs. This online magazine provides a platform for its' visitors to interact with each other. It also covers regular features on i.e. travel and eating out.
MAGAZINE
Regional General Interest, Retirement Savings

Let's Talk Tech
987736

Email: fabio@letstalk-tech.com
Web site: letstalk-tech.com
Freq: Daily
Circ: 45209 Cision Digital Reach
Editor: Fabio Virgi
Profile: Website covering consumer electronics. Let's Talk Tech covers

Consumer Magazines

smartphones, apps, tablets, computing, gadgets and audio.
MAGAZINE (ONLINE)
Audio Video Trade, Cameras, Consumer Electronics, Electronics, Mobile Electronics, Movies & Video

lets-do-diy.com 984891
Editorial: 30 Gay Street, Bath BA1 1 PA
Email: editor@lets-do-diy.com
Web site: http://www.lets-do-diy.com
Freq: Daily
Circ: 25767 Cision Digital Reach
MAGAZINE (ONLINE)
Do-It-Yourself (DIY)

LetsSaveMoney.com 999543
Editorial: unit1b, Thames Court, High Street, Goring, Goring RG8 9AQ
Web site: https://www.letssavemoney.com/
Freq: Daily
Circ: 23805 Cision Digital Reach
MAGAZINE (ONLINE)
Personal Finance

Lewisham Life 984696
Editorial: Town Hall, Catford, London SE6 4RU **Tel:** 44 02083 147027
Email: lewishamlife@lewisham.gov.uk
Web site: www.lewisham.gov.uk/
NewsAndEvents/LewishamLife/
Freq: Quarterly
Circ: 116000 Not Audited
Editor: Ben Hoare
MAGAZINE
Regional General Interest

LexLatin 1075490
Tel: 44 02077 200754
Email: editor@lexlatin.com
Web site: http://lexlatin.com/
Freq: Daily
Circ: 15149 Cision Digital Reach
MAGAZINE (ONLINE)
Americas, Company News & Appointments, Corporate Law, International News, Legal Services, Mergers & Acquisitions

Leytonstoner 988831
Editorial: Interchange Atrium, Stables Market, Chalk Farm Road, London NW1 8AB
Tel: 44 03301 330331
Email: info@leytonstoner.london
Web site: www.leytonstoner.london
Freq: Daily
Circ: 9760 Cision Digital Reach
MAGAZINE (ONLINE)
Regional General Interest

Liaoning Journal of Traditional Chinese Medicine 1061773
Tel: 44 86243 1207233
Email: lnzy@vip.163.com
Web site: http://lnzyzz.periodicals.net.cn
Freq: Monthly Not Audited
MAGAZINE
Alternative Medicine

Liberti Magazine 999269
Editorial: PO Box 3070, Littlehampton, Littlehampton BN17 6WX
Tel: 44 01903 732190
Web site: www.libertimagazine.com
Freq: Quarterly
Circ: 5000 Not Audited
Editor: Bekah Legg
MAGAZINE
Religion, Women's Interests

Libertine 987296
Editorial: 62 Harwood Road, London SW6 4PZ
Email: info@interestedwomen.com
Web site: http://liberti.ne/
Freq: Quarterly
Circ: 4500 Not Audited
Editor: Debbi Evans
MAGAZINE
Women's Interests

Liberty Belle 1073824
Email: editor.libertybellemag@gmail.com
Web site: http://libertybellemag.com/
Freq: Daily
Circ: 10741 Cision Digital Reach
Editor: Sophie Cockett
MAGAZINE (ONLINE)
Student Lifestyle

Licensed & Catering News 981146
Editorial: Penton House, 38 Heron Road, Sydenham Business Park, Belfast BT3 9LE
Tel: 44 02890 457457
Email: info@pentongroup.com
Web site: http://licensedandcateringnews.com/
Freq: Monthly
Circ: 4691 Not Audited
Editor: Russell Campbell
MAGAZINE
Alcohol & Spirits, Bars, Clubs & Pubs, Food, Retail Management

Licensing Source Book Europe 984620
Editorial: United House, North Road, London N7 9DP **Tel:** 44 02077 006740
Email: ianh@max-publishing.co.uk
Web site: www.thelicensingsourcebook.co.uk
Freq: Semi-Annual
Circ: 20000 Not Audited
Editor: Jacqui Parr
MAGAZINE
Books, Cosmetics, Fashion, Gardening, Hair, Office Supplies, Retail, Retail Management, Toys

Licensing.biz 985484
Editorial: Saxon House, 6a St Andrew Street, Hertford, Hertford SG14 1JA
Tel: 44 01992 535646
Web site: www.licensing.biz
Freq: Daily
Circ: 45917 Cision Digital Reach
Editor: Billy Langsworthy
Profile: Website covering business. The Licensing.biz discusses anything from business news and brand profiles to trade information and the global licensing industry.
MAGAZINE (ONLINE)
Beauty & Grooming, Books, Cosmetics, Fashion, Gardening, Hair, Office Supplies, Retail, Retail Management, Toys

Lichfield Live 996586
Editorial: 7 Dyott Close, Lichfield WS13 8LG
Tel: 44 08450 758535
Email: editor@lichfieldlive.co.uk
Web site: http://lichfieldlive.co.uk
Freq: Daily
Circ: 14929 Cision Digital Reach
MAGAZINE (ONLINE)
Regional

Liechtenstein journal 1061701
Email: redaktion@liechtenstein-journal.li
Web site: http://www.liechtenstein-journal.li
Freq: Quarterly
Circ: 1000 Not Audited
MAGAZINE
Banking, Bankruptcy, Business, Company News & Appointments, Consumer Interest, Corporate Law, Criminal Law, Economics, Employment, Estate Planning

Life & Living 995386
Editorial: Garden Floor, 16 Connaught Place, London W2 2ES
Tel: 44 02074 207000
Email: info@therivergroup.co.uk
Web site: http://www.mccarthyandstone.co.uk/life-and-living/
Freq: 3 Times/Year
Circ: 150000 Not Audited
MAGAZINE
Retirement Savings

Life & Soul 996744
Email: soul@lifeandsoulmagazine.com
Web site: http://www.lifeandsoulmagazine.com/

Freq: Daily
Circ: 11903 Cision Digital Reach
Editor: Huria Choudhari
MAGAZINE (ONLINE)
Airline Inflight, Classical/Choral/Band Music, Country, Folk, Bluegrass, Dance Music, Fashion, Jazz & Blues, Lifestyle, Men's Interests, Music, Pop Music

Life & Work 982153
Tel: 44 01312 255722
Email: magazine@lifeandwork.org
Web site: www.churchofscotland.org.uk/news_and_events/life_and_work
Freq: Monthly
Circ: 18475 Not Audited
Editor: Lynne McNeil
MAGAZINE
Religion

Life Magazine 1060671
Tel: 44 27214 243517
Email: snewham@tppsa.co.za
Web site: http://www.tppsa.co.za
Freq: Quarterly
Circ: 97500 Not Audited
MAGAZINE
Antiques/Collectibles, Armed Forces, Astrology & Parapsychology, Astronomy, Aviation, Boating & Yachting, Camping and RV Travel, Cartoons, Casinos & Gaming, Chess

Life Magazines 995120
Editorial: Life Magazines Ltd, Tindle House, High Street, Bordon GU35 0AY
Tel: 44 01420 477272
Email: info@lifemags.co.uk
Web site: newlifemagazines.tumblr.com
Freq: Bi-Monthly
Circ: 10000 Not Audited
MAGAZINE
Regional General Interest

Life Magazines (Buckinghamshire & Chilterns) 999562
Editorial: The Ridings, Woodfield Lane, Essendon, Hatfield AL9 6JJ
Tel: 44 08448 008439
Web site: http://www.life-mags.com/
Freq: Monthly Not Audited
Editor: Faye Manning
MAGAZINE
Regional General Interest

Life Magazines (Essex) 999682
Editorial: The Ridings, Woodfield Lane, Essendon, Hatfield AL9 6JJ
Tel: 44 08448 008439
Web site: http://www.thelifemagazines.com/
Freq: Monthly Not Audited
Editor: Faye Manning
MAGAZINE
Regional General Interest

Life Magazines (Hertfordshire) 999561
Editorial: The Ridings, Woodfield Lane, Essendon, Hatfield AL9 6JJ
Tel: 44 08448 008439
Web site: http://www.thelifemagazines.com/
Freq: Monthly Not Audited
Editor: Faye Manning
MAGAZINE
Regional General Interest

Life Magazines (Kent) 999556
Editorial: The Ridings, Woodfield Lane, Essendon, Hatfield AL9 6JJ
Tel: 44 08448 008439
Web site: http://www.thelifemagazines.com/
Freq: Monthly Not Audited
Editor: Faye Manning
MAGAZINE
Regional General Interest

Life Magazines (London North) 996194
Editorial: The Ridings, Woodfield Lane, Essendon, Hatfield AL9 6JJ
Tel: 44 08448 008439

Web site: http://www.life-mags.com/
Freq: Monthly Not Audited
Editor: Faye Manning
MAGAZINE
Regional General Interest

Life Magazines (London South) 999560
Editorial: The Ridings, Woodfield Lane, Essendon, Hatfield AL9 6JJ
Tel: 44 08448 008439
Web site: http://www.life-mags.com/
Freq: Monthly Not Audited
Editor: Faye Manning
MAGAZINE
Regional General Interest

Life Magazines (Surrey & Berkshire) 999557
Editorial: The Ridings, Woodfield Lane, Essendon, Hatfield AL9 6JJ
Tel: 44 08448 008439
Web site: http://www.thelifemagazines.com/
Freq: Monthly Not Audited
Editor: Faye Manning
MAGAZINE
Regional General Interest

Life Sciences Intellectual Property Review 997243
Editorial: Kingfisher House, 21-23 Elmfield Road, London BR1 1LT
Web site: http://www.lifesciencesipreview.com/
Freq: Quarterly
Circ: 5000 Not Audited
MAGAZINE
News & Current Affairs

Life Sciences Intellectual Property Review Newsletter 997914
Editorial: Kingfisher House, 21-23 Elmfield Road, London BR1 1LT
Web site: http://www.lifesciencesipreview.com/
Freq: Monthly
Circ: 18483 Cision Digital Reach
MAGAZINE (ONLINE)
News & Current Affairs

Life With Pets 987529
Email: editor@lifewithpetsmagazine.com
Web site: http://www.lifewithpetsmagazine.com/
Freq: Quarterly
Circ: 800 Not Audited
MAGAZINE
Nature & Wildlife

Life! Death! Prizes! 1053557
Editorial: The Blue Fin Building, 110 Southwark Street, London SE1 0SU
Tel: 44 02031 486150
Email: lifedeathprizes@timeinc.com
Web site: www.lifedeathprizes.com
Freq: Daily
Circ: 47828 Cision Digital Reach
Editor: Gilly Sinclair
MAGAZINE (ONLINE)
Careers, Crime & Violence, Family & Parenting, Health & Medicine, Lifestyle, Personal Finance, Relationships

Life&Style 999642
Editorial: 11- 12 Centre Court, Vine Lane, Halesowen B63 3EB **Tel:** 44 01582 393700
Email: lifeandstyle@firstport.co.uk
Web site: http://www.firstport.co.uk/lifeandstyle
Freq: Semi-Annual
Circ: 70000 Not Audited
MAGAZINE
Retirement Savings

The Lifeboat 987010
Editorial: West Quay Road, Poole BH15 1HZ **Tel:** 44 08451 226999
Email: info@rnli.org.uk
Web site: http://rnli.org
Freq: Quarterly

Circ: 270000 Not Audited
Editor: Rory Stamp
Profile: Magazine focusing on the Royal National Lifeboat Institution, including news of people and places within the institution and accounts of noteworthy rescues. Read by RNLI members, supporters and people working at lifeboat stations and fundraising branches.
Ad Rate: Full Page Colour £5000.00
MAGAZINE
Charitable Foundations, EMS/Emergency Medical Services

Lifehacker UK   988087
Editorial: 1-10 Praed Mews, London W2 1QY **Tel:** 44 02070 424000
Email: mail@lifehacker.co.uk
Web site: www.lifehacker.co.uk
Freq: Daily
Circ: 910292 Cision Digital Reach
Profile: Blog covering tips for living in the digital age. Lifehacker UK discusses anything from life and work hacks to food and money, health and DIY tips. The blog has an archive dating back to February 2014.
MAGAZINE (ONLINE)
Apple, Cameras, Computer & Video Games, Computers, Data Management, Electronics, Government Technology, Internet, Mobile Communications, Mobile Electronics

Lifestyle   986762
Editorial: 2 Barnhill Road, Liverpool L15 5BE
Email: editor@lifestylemonthly.co.uk
Web site: www.lifestylemonthly.co.uk
Freq: Monthly
Circ: 25000 Not Audited
Editor: Joy Lewis
Profile: Lifestyle magazine covering news of the Motability Scheme and disability related features. Aimed at those with disabilities. Previous title: Motability Lifestyle Regular features: Disability Wise Topical news stories affecting disabled people.
Ad Rate: Full Page Colour £11150.00
MAGAZINE
Regional General Interest

Lifestyle (Motability)   994648
Editorial: 22 Stephenson Way, London NW1 2HD **Tel:** 44 02073 808580
Email: lifestyle@bigpublishing.com
Web site: www.motabilitylifestyle.co.uk
Freq: Quarterly
Circ: 610000 Not Audited
MAGAZINE
Disability

The Lifestyle Edit   997928
Email: hello@thelifestyleedit.com
Web site: www.thelifestyleedit.com
Freq: Daily
Circ: 11845 Cision Digital Reach
Editor: Naomi Mdudu
MAGAZINE (ONLINE)
Women's Interests

The Lifestyle Library   1052553
Email: press@thelifestylelibrary.com
Web site: www.thelifestylelibrary.com
Freq: Daily
Circ: 87000 Not Audited
MAGAZINE
Beauty & Grooming, Cosmetics, Fitness & Exercise, Hair, Health & Medicine, Women's Interests

LifeStyle Linked   1059601
Editorial: 3 Ham Lane, Burnham-on-Sea, Burnham-on-Sea TA8 1QA
Web site: http://lifestylelinked.com/
Freq: Daily
Circ: 13791 Cision Digital Reach
MAGAZINE (ONLINE)
Alcohol & Spirits, Bars, Clubs & Pubs, Beauty & Grooming, Beer, Beverages, Comedy, Cooking & Baking, Cosmetics, Do-It-Yourself (DIY), Entertainment

Lifestyle lowdown   997062
Editorial: Member Communications, Ten, Fitzroy House, 355 Euston Road, London NW1 3AL **Tel:** 44 02030 564919
Email: articles@tengroup.com
Web site: https://www.tenlifestyle.com/
Freq: Daily
Circ: 2059 Cision Digital Reach
MAGAZINE (ONLINE)
Luxury Goods

Lifestyle Tails   1098312
Email: tails@lifestyletails.com
Web site: http://www.lifestyletails.com/
Freq: Daily
Circ: 13854 Cision Digital Reach
MAGAZINE (ONLINE)
Nature & Wildlife

Lift Off   1052617
Email: info@legology.co.uk
Web site: www.legology.co.uk
Freq: Bi-Weekly Not Audited
MAGAZINE
Fitness & Exercise, Health & Medicine, Men's Interests, Nutrition, Women's Interests

ligature magazine   996166
Editorial: 11 Copperfield House, Wolsely Street, London SE1 2BN
Freq: Semi-Annual Not Audited
MAGAZINE
Art, Beauty & Grooming, Cosmetics, Fashion, Hair, Literature, Photography, Theater & Performing Arts, Visual Arts

Light & Lighting   1061920
Tel: 44 86236 5126335
Freq: Quarterly
Circ: 3003 Not Audited
MAGAZINE
Electronics

Light & Sound International (LSi)   981228
Editorial: Redoubt House, 1 Edward Road, Eastbourne BN23 8AS **Tel:** 44 01323 524120
Web site: www.lsionline.co.uk
Freq: Monthly
Circ: 7799 Not Audited
Profile: Magazine covering the broad range of the professional lighting, audio, staging and audio-visual industry. Including the use of such equipment and services relating to professional entertainment, presentation, display, communication and architectural installation. Aimed at designers, installers, specifers and venue managers working in entertainment, corporate presentation, leisure, architectural installation and communications markets.
Ad Rate: Full Page Mono £1860.00
Ad Rate: Full Page Colour £1860.00
MAGAZINE
Computers, Electronics, Industry, Software

Light Lunch   996200
Editorial: Tavis House, 1-6 Tavistock Square, London WC1H 9NA
Tel: 44 02072 483538
Web site: http://www.clinks.org/resources-ebulletins/light-lunch
Freq: Weekly
Circ: 10000 Not Audited
Editor: Ben Watson
MAGAZINE
Charitable Foundations

LighterLife   983219
Editorial: Cavendish House, Parkway, Harlow Business Park, Harlow CM19 5QF
Tel: 44 01279 636998
Email: inform@lighterlife.com
Web site: www.lighterlife.com
Freq: Bi-Monthly
Circ: 38765 Cision Digital Reach
MAGAZINE (ONLINE)
Nutrition

lighting digest   997408
Editorial: 1 Hogan Way, Stafford ST16 3YN
Email: news@lightingdigest.co.uk
Web site: www.lightingdigest.co.uk/index.php
Freq: Daily
Circ: 11962 Cision Digital Reach
Editor: Jeffrey Bennett
MAGAZINE (ONLINE)
Electronics

Lime   995877
Editorial: LimeMagazine, Got Media Ltd, 13 West Hill, London SW18 1RB
Tel: 44 02074 765716
Email: web@thisislime.net
Web site: www.thisislime.net
Freq: Daily
Circ: 7029 Cision Digital Reach
MAGAZINE (ONLINE)
Regional General Interest

The Lincolnite   986648
Editorial: Sparkhouse, Ropewalk, Lincoln, Lincoln LN6 7DQ **Tel:** 44 01522 837217
Email: contact@thelincolnite.co.uk
Web site: www.thelincolnite.co.uk
Freq: Daily
Circ: 164084 Cision Digital Reach
Profile: Website covering news and events in Lincoln.
MAGAZINE (ONLINE)
Regional

Lincolnshire in Focus   982506
Editorial: 46 Heneage Road, Grimsby DN32 9ES **Tel:** 44 01472 359036
Web site: www.lincolnshireinfocus.co.uk
Freq: Bi-Monthly
Circ: 56000 Not Audited
Profile: Magazine covering county news, fashion, places of interest, leisure, local events, designer outlets and property. Aimed at those with an average to high disposable income within the Lincolnshire region.
Ad Rate: Full Page Mono £942.00
Ad Rate: Full Page Colour £1149.00
MAGAZINE
Regional General Interest

Lincolnshire Life   982507
Editorial: County House, 9 Checkpoint Court, Sadler Road, Lincoln LN6 3PW
Tel: 44 01522 527127
Email: editorial@lincolnshirelife.co.uk
Web site: www.lincolnshirelife.co.uk
Freq: Monthly
Circ: 10000 Not Audited
Editor: Caroline Bingham
Profile: County magazine containing features on county life past and present, people, places, culture and heritage.
Ad Rate: Full Page Mono £655.00
Ad Rate: Full Page Colour £820.00
MAGAZINE
Regional General Interest

Lincolnshire Pride   982508
Editorial: Elm Grange Studios, East Heckington, Boston, Sleaford PE20 3QF
Tel: 44 01529 469977
Email: editor@lincolnshirepride.co.uk
Web site: www.lincolnshirepride.co.uk
Freq: Monthly
Circ: 11500 Not Audited
Editor: Rob Davis
MAGAZINE
Regional General Interest

Lincolnshire Reporter   1100777
Editorial: Sparkhouse, Rope Walk, Lincoln LN6 7DQ **Tel:** 44 01522 837267
Email: news@lincolnshirereporter.co.uk
Web site: http://lincolnshirereporter.co.uk/
Freq: Daily
Circ: 17560 Cision Digital Reach
MAGAZINE (ONLINE)
News & Current Affairs

Lincolnshire Today   982509
Editorial: Armstrong House, Armstrong Street, Grimsby, Grimsby DN31 2QE
Tel: 44 01472 310302
Web site: www.lincolnshiretoday.net
Freq: Monthly

Circ: 45000 Not Audited
Profile: Magazine containing articles on hair and beauty, towns, travel, hotels and restaurants, motoring, leisure, heritage, antiques, outdoor pursuits, health and fitness, holidays, fashion and celebrities. Aimed at those living in Lincolnshire and Yorkshire.
Ad Rate: Full Page Mono £835.00
Ad Rate: Full Page Colour £1150.00
MAGAZINE
Regional General Interest

Lindfield Life   996451
Editorial: The Barn, Hurstwood Grange, Hurstwood Lane, Haywards Heath RH17 7QX **Tel:** 44 01444 884115
Email: editor@lindfieldlife.co.uk
Web site: www.lindfieldlife.co.uk
Freq: Monthly
Circ: 4600 Not Audited
Editor: David Tingley
MAGAZINE
Regional

The Line Of Best Fit   986426
Editorial: 30 Lansdowne Wood Close, London SE27 0BY
Email: hello@thelineofbestfit.com
Web site: www.thelineofbestfit.com
Freq: Daily
Circ: 103277 Cision Digital Reach
Editor: Paul Bridgewater
Profile: Website covering music. The Line of Best Fit provides the "best in new and alternative sounds". They feature new content daily from music writers and photographers globally, provides reviews and interviews as well as showcasing bands and talents from Europe, America and beyond.
MAGAZINE (ONLINE)
Dance Music, Pop Music, Rock Music

Linedancer Magazine   998531
Editorial: Clare House, 166 Lord Street, Southport PR9 0QA **Tel:** 44 01704 392300
Email: editor@linedancermagazine.com
Web site: www.linedancermagazine.com
Freq: Monthly
Circ: 20000 Not Audited
Editor: Laurent Saletto
MAGAZINE
Country, Folk, Bluegrass

Line-Up   999609
Editorial: 19-21 Hatton Garden, London EC1N 8BA
Email: info@lineupnow.com
Web site: https://lineupnow.com/
Freq: Daily
Circ: 12799 Cision Digital Reach
MAGAZINE (ONLINE)
Entertainment, Local Entertainment Guides

Lingerie Insight   985752
Editorial: ITP Promedia, 16-25 Bastwick Street, London EC1V 3PS
Tel: 44 02031 764228
Web site: www.lingerieinsight.com
Freq: Monthly
Circ: 4100 Not Audited
Editor: Sarah Clarke
Profile: Magazine covering the lingerie industry. Features news, comment, trading intelligence and buying inspiration, serving the multi-billion pound British lingerie and swimwear industry. The monthly magazine and website provide the latest global trends, expert business advice from retailers, wholesalers and designers; facts and figures on the state of the industry.
Ad Rate: Full Page Colour £1884.00
MAGAZINE
Fashion

The Linguist   986061
Editorial: The Chartered Institute of Linguists, Dunstan House (4th floor), 14a St Cross Street, London EC1N 8XA
Tel: 44 02079 403100
Email: linguist.editor@ciol.org.uk
Web site: www.ciol.org.uk/
Freq: Bi-Monthly

Consumer Magazines

Circ: 6500 Not Audited
Editor: Miranda Moore
Profile: Official journal of the Institute of Linguists. Contains articles for a more specialised readership, together with items of current and more popular interest in the field of language and culture.
Ad Rate: Full Page Mono £750.00
Ad Rate: Full Page Colour £900.00
MAGAZINE
Africa, Americas, Asia, Australia, Charitable Foundations, Ethnic & Multicultural, Europe, Expatriates, Literature

Link 2 Media
1060369
Tel: 44 27117 821600
Email: stephanie@sapa.org.za
Web site: http://www.link2media.co.za
Circ: 611 Cision Digital Reach
MAGAZINE (ONLINE)
Advertising Industry, Branding, Broadcasting, Graphic Design, Marketing, Media & Communications, Photography, Publishing

Linux Format
981602
Editorial: Beauford Court, 30 Monmouth Street, Bath BA1 2BW **Tel:** 44 01225 442244
Email: lxf.letters@futurenet.com
Web site: www.linuxformat.co.uk
Freq: Monthly
Circ: 18001 Not Audited
Profile: Magazine covering all aspects of Linux operating system including news, developments, tutorials, products, technical advice, software and reviews. Published monthly UK Linux magazine highlights the latest developments in the world of open source, examines new software and book releases. Aimed at Linux users of all levels from business professionals to enthusiasts.
Ad Rate: Full Page Colour £2500.00
MAGAZINE
Personal Computers

Linux User & Developer
981731
Editorial: Quay House, The Ambury, Bath BA1 1UA **Tel:** 44 01225 442244
Email: linuxuser@futurenet.com
Freq: Monthly
Circ: 165097 Not Audited
Profile: Linux User and Developer is a magazine aimed at Linux professionals and IT decision makers. Magazine covering Linux-related news, opinion, features and reviews from a professional perspective. Every month it provides tutorials, hardware reviews, information and inspiration to help GNU/Linux professionals expand their knowledge base and perform more effectively in the workplace. The magazine also features informative interviews with leading figures from the GNU/Linux scene and high-profile companies that have built their businesses using OpenSource software.
MAGAZINE
Computers, Personal Computers, Software

Linux Voice
996299
Editorial: 8 Edreds Court, Calne SN11 8BA
Email: info@linuxvoice.com
Web site: www.linuxvoice.com
Freq: Monthly Not Audited
Editor: Graham Morrison
MAGAZINE
Personal Computers

The Lion
996876
Editorial: The HSU, Heythrop College, Kensington Square, London W8 5HN
Email: thelion@heythrop.ac.uk
Web site: http://www.heythroplion.co.uk
Freq: Monthly
Circ: 1000 Not Audited
Profile: Magazine of The Lions of Great Britain and Ireland, covering events, club news and information on the latest projects.
Ad Rate: Full Page Mono £475.00
Ad Rate: Full Page Colour £600.00
MAGAZINE
Student Lifestyle

Lipstick Media
1068845
Editorial: Kemp House, 152-160 City Road, London EC1V 2DW
Web site: www.lipstick-media.com/
Freq: Quarterly
Circ: 4000 Not Audited
MAGAZINE
Women's Interests

Liputan6
1061985
Tel: 44 62217 229681
Email: redaksi@liputan6.com
Web site: http://www.liputan6.com
Freq: Daily
Circ: 24365052 Cision Digital Reach
MAGAZINE (ONLINE)
Consumer Affairs, Crime & Violence, Defense & National Security, Energy & Environment, Ethical/Moral Issues, International News, Law, National News, News & Current Affairs, Northern Ireland

Liquor-Making Science & Technology
1061599
Tel: 44 86851 5796163
Email: njkj@263.net
Freq: Monthly
Circ: 17000 Not Audited
MAGAZINE
Alcohol & Spirits, Auto Aftermarket, Computers, Data Management, Defense & National Security, Electronics, Engineering, Government Technology, Industry, Internet

The List
999095
Editorial: 14 High Street, Edinburgh EH1 1TE **Tel:** 44 01315 503050
Email: editor@list.co.uk
Web site: www.list.co.uk
Freq: Bi-Monthly
Circ: 24670 Not Audited
Editor: Yasmin Sulaiman
Profile: Entertainment and lifestyle guide for Glasgow and Edinburgh. Covers film, music, travel, theatre, clubs, books, food and contemporary issues. Aimed at 18 to 35 year olds.
Ad Rate: Full Page Mono £660.00
Ad Rate: Full Page Colour £930.00
MAGAZINE
Entertainment, Local Entertainment Guides

The List Eating & Drinking Guide to Edinburgh & Glasgow
999033
Editorial: 14 High Street, Edinburgh EH1 1TE **Tel:** 44 01315 503050
Email: eat@list.co.uk
Web site: www.list.co.uk
Freq: Annual
Circ: 30000 Not Audited
MAGAZINE
Bars, Clubs & Pubs, Restaurant Reviews

L'Italo Europeo
988827
Email: director@italoeuropeo.co.uk
Web site: http://www.italoeuropeo.com/
Freq: Daily
Circ: 12560 Cision Digital Reach
Editor: Philip Baglini
MAGAZINE (ONLINE)
News & Current Affairs

Literary Review
983804
Editorial: 44 Lexington Street, London W1F 0LW **Tel:** 44 02074 379392
Email: editorial@literaryreview.co.uk
Web site: www.literaryreview.co.uk
Freq: Monthly
Circ: 45000 Not Audited
Editor: Nancy Sladek
Profile: Magazine covering literary book reviews, short stories, poetry and cartoons. Read by those interested in literature.
Ad Rate: Full Page Mono £1800.00
Ad Rate: Full Page Colour £1995.00
MAGAZINE
Literature

The Literateur
990575
Email: editor@literateur.com
Web site: literateur.com
Freq: Daily
Circ: 12220 Cision Digital Reach
Editor: Eleanor Careless; **Editor:** Adam Crothers; **Editor:** James Marriott
MAGAZINE (ONLINE)
Literature

Litopia
997573
Editorial: 186 Bickenhall Mansions, Bickenhall St, London W1U 6BX
Web site: http://litopia.com/
Freq: Daily
Circ: 7674 Cision Digital Reach
MAGAZINE (ONLINE)
Literature, Publishing

Litro
996165
Editorial: 1-15 Cremer Street, Studio 213, London E2 8HD **Tel:** 44 02033 719971
Email: editor@litro.co.uk
Web site: www.litro.co.uk
Freq: Monthly
Circ: 50000 Not Audited
MAGAZINE
Literature

Little London
988229
Editorial: Jubilee House, 2 Jubilee Place, London SW3 3TQ **Tel:** 44 02073 493700
Email: editor@littlelondonmagazine.co.uk
Web site: www.littlelondonmagazine.co.uk
Freq: Bi-Monthly Not Audited
MAGAZINE
Family & Parenting

Little Look
1053505
Email: hello@little-look.com
Web site: www.little-look.com
Freq: Daily
Circ: 685 Cision Digital Reach
Editor: Rose Brookes
MAGAZINE (ONLINE)
Fashion, Literature

Little Performer
1062043
Tel: 44 86106 5286313
Email: 67602829@163.com
Freq: Monthly Not Audited
MAGAZINE
Classical/Choral/Band Music, Country, Folk, Bluegrass, Dance Music, Jazz & Blues, Music, Pop Music, R&B, Urban, World, Rap & Hip Hop, Rock Music

The Little Ship
985525
Editorial: Bell Wharf Lane, Upper Thames Street, London EC4R 3TB
Tel: 44 02072 367729
Email: office@littleshipclub.co.uk
Web site: www.littleshipclub.co.uk
Freq: Daily
Circ: 10145 Cision Digital Reach
Profile: Magazine covering news on sail and engine-driven yachts. Read by members of The Little Ship Club and by boating and yachting enthusiasts.
MAGAZINE (ONLINE)
Boating & Yachting, Swimming/ Watersports

The Little Style Book
985777
Editorial: 41 Lexham gardens, Flat 2, London W8 5JR
Email: hello@thelittlestylebook.com
Web site: www.thelittlestylebook.com
Freq: Daily
Circ: 1066 Cision Digital Reach
Editor: Daniela Gubitz
MAGAZINE (ONLINE)
Family & Parenting

Little White Lies
983605
Editorial: 71a Leonard Street, London EC2A 4QS **Tel:** 44 02077 293675
Email: editorial@tcolondon.com
Web site: http://lwlies.com/
Freq: Bi-Monthly
Circ: 16000 Not Audited

Editor: David Jenkins
MAGAZINE
Entertainment, Movies & Video

Littlest Pet Shop
995030
Editorial: Old Dairy, Peper Harow Park, Nr Godalming, Godalming GU8 6BQ
Tel: 44 01483 779500
Web site: www.signaturepl.co.uk/portfolio/ LittlestPetShop.html
Freq: Bi-Monthly
Circ: 30000 Not Audited
MAGAZINE
Teen/Young Adult, Trading Cards & Comics

Live 24-Seven
985887
Editorial: PO Box 5258, Coventry CV4 0GA
Email: themd@live24-seven.com
Web site: www.live24-seven.com
Freq: Bi-Monthly
Circ: 40000 Not Audited
Profile: Magazine covering fashion, beauty, entertainment, leisure, style, interiors, property, restaurants and health. Aimed at those living in Birmingham.
Ad Rate: Full Page Colour £1400.00
MAGAZINE
Regional General Interest, Women's Interests

Live Mendips
1070072
Email: news@livemendips.co.uk
Web site: livemendips.co.uk/
Freq: Daily
Circ: 521 Cision Digital Reach
Editor: Sophia Beyer
MAGAZINE (ONLINE)
Regional General Interest

Live Preston & Fylde
985539
Editorial: Longridge Business Centre, Stonebridge Mill, Kestor Lane, Longridge PR3 3AD **Tel:** 44 08455 198815
Email: info@live-magazines.co.uk
Web site: www.live-magazines.co.uk
Freq: Monthly
Circ: 18000 Not Audited
Editor: Tracy Hargreaves
MAGAZINE
Regional General Interest

Live Ribble Valley
985538
Editorial: Longridge Business Centre, Stonebridge Mill, Kestor Lane, Longridge PR3 3AD **Tel:** 44 08455 198815
Email: info@live-magazines.co.uk
Web site: www.live-magazines.co.uk
Freq: Monthly
Circ: 18000 Not Audited
Editor: Jan Woolley
MAGAZINE
Luxury Goods, Regional General Interest

Live Share Travel
1096362
Email: info@livesharetravel.com
Web site: http://livesharetravel.com/
Freq: Daily
Circ: 45156 Cision Digital Reach
Editor: Sarah Lee
MAGAZINE (ONLINE)
Travel

LIVE UK
987881
Editorial: 26 Dorset Street, London W1U 8AP **Tel:** 44 02074 867007
Email: info@liveuk.com
Web site: www.liveuk.com
Freq: Monthly
Circ: 2500 Not Audited
Editor: Mike Gartside
Profile: Magazine covering the UK's contemporary live music industry providing news, features and tour information and examining the people, venues and services involved. Aimed at the country's music promoters, festival organisers, venues, artist managers, booking agents of other live music-related sectors.
Ad Rate: Full Page Colour £1365.00
MAGAZINE
Music

Live4ever
998015

Email: news@live4ever.uk.com
Web site: live4ever.uk.com
Freq: Daily
Circ: 37668 Cision Digital Reach
Editor: David Smith
MAGAZINE (ONLINE)
Country, Folk, Bluegrass, Music, Pop
Music, Rock Music

Livelife
1100040

Editorial: Unit 4, Avenue Business Park,
Elsworth, Cambridge CB23 4EY
Tel: 44 01954 268129
Web site: www.livelifemag.co.uk
Freq: Semi-Annual Not Audited
Editor: Emma Kemsley
MAGAZINE
Lifestyle, Men's Interests, Regional,
Regional General Interest, Retirement
Savings, Women's Interests

Liverpool FC Magazine
995839

Tel: 44 01512 272000
Web site: http://www.sportmediashop.com/
products/details/liverpool_subscriptions/
liverpoolfc_magazine_subscrip
Freq: Monthly
Editor: David Cottrell
MAGAZINE
Soccer

Live-Smart
1069614

Editorial: Blue Fin Building, 10 Southwark
Street, London SE1 0SU
Tel: 44 02031 485000
Email: live-smart@timeinc.com
Web site: http://www.live-smart.co/
Freq: Daily
Circ: 6234 Cision Digital Reach
Editor: Nick Merritt
MAGAZINE (ONLINE)
Audio Video Trade, Cameras, Consumer
Electronics, Electronics, Mobile
Electronics, Movies & Video

Livin Cool
986054

Email: info@livincool.com
Web site: www.livincool.com
Freq: Daily
Circ: 7561 Cision Digital Reach
MAGAZINE (ONLINE)
Art, Classical/Choral/Band Music,
Country, Folk, Bluegrass, Dance Music,
Fashion, Jazz & Blues, Movies & Video,
Music, Pop Music, R&B, Urban, World

Living Along the Thames
996829

Editorial: Living Along the Thames, Studio
108, 5 High Street, Maidenhead SL6 1JN
Tel: 44 01628 627488
Email: office@alongthethames.co.uk
Web site: http://vividtitles.co.uk/
Freq: Bi-Monthly
Circ: 12500 Not Audited
Profile: Magazine covering regional lifestyle
news and contains articles on fashion,
beauty, hair, motoring, health, gardening,
food and dining. First published in 2006.
Aimed at residents in Marlow, Maidenhead,
Henley, Cookham and Bourne End.
MAGAZINE
Regional General Interest

Living Earth - The Soil Association Magazine
998458

Editorial: South Plaza, Marlborough Street,
Bristol BS1 3NX **Tel:** 44 01173 145000
Web site: www.soilassociation.org
Freq: 3 Times/Year Not Audited
MAGAZINE
Organic Food

Living Edge
982479

Editorial: Warrington Regus, Cinnamon
House, Cinnamon Park, Crab Lane,
Warrington WA2 0XP **Tel:** 44 01925 661904
Email: livingedge@btinternet.com
Web site: http://www.livingedge.co.uk/home
Freq: Monthly
Circ: 15000 Not Audited
Editor: Kate Houghton

Profile: Lifestyle magazine covering local
news with features on food, fashion,
motoring and interiors. Aimed at affluent
professionals in Cheshire and Manchester.
Ad Rate: Full Page Mono £970.00
Ad Rate: Full Page Colour £970.00
MAGAZINE
Regional General Interest

Living France
982332

Tel: 44 01242 216050
Email: editorial@livingfrance.com
Web site: www.livingfrance.com
Freq: Monthly
Circ: 16000 Not Audited
Profile: Guide to France and French
property, including regional information,
advice on taxation, readers' experiences and
other matters relevant to living in France.
Also contains articles on French food, wine
and travel. The magazine was first published
in October 1989 under the title of French
Living. It was purchased in 2002 by Archant
and was the second title to be added to the
Archant Life France portfolio. Read by
people who are interested in purchasing
property in and travellers to France.
Ad Rate: Full Page Colour £1350.00
MAGAZINE
Real Estate

Living in Havering
997524

Editorial: Town Hall, Main Road, Romford
RM1 3BD **Tel:** 44 01708 434771
Email: living@havering.gov.uk
Web site: https://www.havering.gov.uk/
Pages/Services/Living-in-Havering.aspx
Freq: Quarterly
Circ: 106000 Not Audited
MAGAZINE
Charitable Foundations, Regional General
Interest

Living North
982519

Editorial: Studio 2, St Nicholas Chare,
Newcastle NE1 1RJ **Tel:** 44 01912 618944
Email: info@livingnorth.com
Web site: www.livingnorth.com
Freq: Monthly
Circ: 15500 Not Audited
Profile: Regional intrest and lifestyle monthly
magazine celebrating what is excellent about
the North of England. It also publishes a
number of supplements (directories) which
highlight the best of various subject areas in
the region. It contains a What's On section
and covers Fashion, Weddings, Health, Food
& Drink, Art, Travel, Gardening, Property and
Motoring. Aimed at those aged 25 years old
and over who live in the North East of
England.
Ad Rate: Full Page Colour £775.00
MAGAZINE
Regional General Interest

Living North East
997181

Editorial: Priestgate, Darlington DL1 1NF
Tel: 44 01325 381313
Web site: http://www.livingnortheast.co.uk
Freq: Monthly
Circ: 15000 Not Audited
Editor: Francine Clee
MAGAZINE
Regional General Interest

Living Plus Bristol
999340

Tel: 44 07833 208953
Email: livingplusuk@gmail.com
Web site: https://livingplusuk.wordpress.
com/
Freq: Monthly
Circ: 5000 Not Audited
MAGAZINE
Regional General Interest

Livingetc
981850

Editorial: 161 Marsh Wall, London E14 9AP
Tel: 44 02031 485000
Email: livingetc@timeinc.com
Web site: www.livingetc.co.uk
Freq: Monthly
Circ: 76630 Not Audited
Editor: Suzanne Imre
Profile: Magazine covering the latest
decorating trends and design stories,

providing ideas, inspiration and practical
advice. Each issue includes pages on
shopping and trends, as well as articles on
inspiring homes and decorating projects.
First published in 1998. Aimed at affluent
adults, aged between 25 and 44, with an
interest in interior design.
Ad Rate: Full Page Colour £7700.00
MAGAZINE
Do-It-Yourself (DIY)

Liz Earle Wellbeing magazine
1053346

Editorial: 3-4 Albert Studios, Albert Bridge
Road, Battersea, London SW11 4QD
Tel: 44 02077 389378
Email: pr@lizearlewellbeing.com
Web site: www.lizearlewellbeing.com/
Freq: Quarterly
Circ: 11414 Cision Digital Reach
Editor: Polly Beard
MAGAZINE (ONLINE)
Beauty & Grooming, Cooking & Baking,
Cosmetics, Hair, Nutrition, Women's
Interests

Lloyd's Loading List
981323

Editorial: Mortimer House, 37-41 Mortimer
Street, London W1T 3JH
Tel: 44 02070 175000
Email: lloydsloadinglist@informa.com
Web site: www.lloydsloadinglist.com
Freq: Daily
Circ: 15527 Cision Digital Reach
Profile: Magazine containing a directory of
export services by sea, road, rail and air,
from the UK to worldwide destinations, plus
weekly news reviews, features and special
reports. Also includes in-depth analysis of
deep-sea liner trades. Read by major
manufacturing companies, freight
forwarders, shipping lines, international road
hauliers and airlines.
Ad Rate: Full Page Mono £290.00
Ad Rate: Full Page Colour £1600.00
MAGAZINE (ONLINE)
Shipping & Warehousing, Supply Chain
Management (SCM)

LNG Industry
983580

Editorial: 15 South Street, Farnham,
Farnham GU9 7QU **Tel:** 44 01252 718999
Email: enquiries@energyglobal.com
Web site: https://www.energyglobal.com/
Freq: Monthly
Circ: 6250 Not Audited
Profile: LNG Industry magazine covers LNG
news and solutions, FLNG, shipping costs,
storage and coating solutions. Includes
regional reports from Europe, North and
South America, Africa, Asia and the Middle
East.
Ad Rate: Full Page Colour £4660.00
MAGAZINE
Engineering, Manufacturing, Marine &
Boat Trade, Mining & Quarrying, Oil,
Paper, Plastics, Steel

LO:PA Magazine
997789

Editorial: 66 Highgate Road, London NW5
1PA **Tel:** 44 07962 266898
Email: editor@lo-pa.com
Web site: www.lo-pa.com
Freq: Daily
Circ: 521 Cision Digital Reach
MAGAZINE (ONLINE)
Regional General Interest

loaded
1058240

Editorial: 114 The Strand, London WC2R
0AG **Tel:** 44 02089 004590
Email: editorial@loaded.co.uk
Web site: http://loaded.co.uk/
Freq: Daily
Circ: 155052 Cision Digital Reach
MAGAZINE (ONLINE)
Men's Interests

The Loadout: Tech for Tomorrow's Professional
996087

Editorial: Room 11, Norwood House, 3
Brighton Grove, Manchester M14 5JT
Tel: 44 01618 500460
Email: the_loadout@bookofthefuture.co.uk

Web site: www.the-loadout.com
Freq: Daily
Circ: 10282 Cision Digital Reach
MAGAZINE (ONLINE)
Audio Video Trade, Cameras, Computers,
Consumer Electronics, Electronics,
Mobile Electronics, Movies & Video,
Software

The Loadstar
986739

Editorial: 3 Morocco Street, London SE1
3HB **Tel:** 44 02074 032005
Email: editor@theloadstar.co.uk
Web site: www.theloadstar.co.uk
Freq: Daily
Circ: 86466 Cision Digital Reach
MAGAZINE (ONLINE)
Automotive, Aviation, Railroad, Shipping
& Warehousing, Supply Chain
Management (SCM), Transportation

Lobster
985373

Editorial: 214 Westbourne Avenue, Hull HU5
3JB **Tel:** 44 01482 447558
Web site: http://www.lobster-magazine.co.
uk
Freq: Semi-Annual
Circ: 26450 Cision Digital Reach
Profile: Website covering politics,
parapolitics and contemporary history.
LOBSTER discusses topics on economics,
economic politics and conspiracy theories.
MAGAZINE (ONLINE)
Politics

Local Living
995808

Editorial: PO Box 208, Stamford,
Peterborough PE9 9FY
Tel: 44 01780 765571
Email: nicholas@bestlocalliving.co.uk
Web site: www.bestlocalliving.co.uk
Freq: Monthly
Circ: 45000 Not Audited
MAGAZINE
Regional General Interest

Local Transport Today
983431

Editorial: Apollo House, 359 Kennington
Lane, London SE11 5QY
Tel: 44 02070 917875
Email: ed.ltt@landor.co.uk
Web site: www.transportxtra.com
Freq: Bi-Weekly
Circ: 1000 Not Audited
Editor: Andrew Forster
Profile: Publication focusing on urban and
regional transport issues, with analysis of
transport policies, plans and finance. Aimed
at professionals, students and technicians in
all areas of transport.
Ad Rate: Full Page Mono £4170.00
Ad Rate: Full Page Colour £4670.00
MAGAZINE
Automotive, Aviation, Railroad, Shipping
& Warehousing, Supply Chain
Management (SCM), Transportation

localmummy.com
995061

Email: marketing@localmummy.com
Web site: http://www.localmummy.com/
Freq: Weekly
Circ: 687 Cision Digital Reach
MAGAZINE (ONLINE)
Family & Parenting

Localrider Magazine
995356

Editorial: 2 Littleworth Cottages,
SpeldhurstSpeldhurst, Speldhurst,
Tunbridge Wells TN3 0TP
Tel: 44 01892 863062
Email: info@localrider.co.uk
Web site: http://www.localrider.co.uk
Freq: Monthly
Editor: Fiona Rafferty
Profile: Localrider Magazine is a paid
magazine dedicated to equestrianism in the
South East, with a mix of reported regional
and national show reports, educational
features, reader and rider profiles, news,
pictures and results. Localrider is the
sponsor the Grassroots sections of the
South East Eventers League and also the
BSJA Southern and South East Regional
Amateur Championships.Aimed at amateur
competition, pony club, riding club and

Consumer Magazines

professional riders. Previous title: Local Rider MagazineRegular features: People Reviews; Reader of the Month; Roundup; Spot Light; Tried and Tested
Ad Rate: Full Page Colour £650.00
MAGAZINE
Equestrian Sports

The Locals   996184
Editorial: 31 Camden Passage, London N1 8EA
Email: contact@the-locals.net
Web site: http://www.the-locals.net
Freq: Daily
Circ: 11937 Cision Digital Reach
MAGAZINE (ONLINE)
Antiques/Collectibles, Art, Arts, Bars, Clubs & Pubs, Comedy, Cooking & Baking, Entertainment, Fitness & Exercise, Food, Grocery Stores

Locavore   988795
Editorial: 110 Bertram Road, Enfield, London EN1 1LS
Email: editor@locavoremagazine.co
Web site: locavoremagazine.co
Freq: Quarterly Not Audited
Editor: Gavin Markham
Profile: Publication that covers sustainable food, food producers and seasonal food.
MAGAZINE
Cooking & Baking, Energy & Environment, Organic Food, Restaurant Reviews, Vegetarianism & Veganism

Locomotives International
982041
Editorial: 3 Broadleaze, Upper Seagry, Chippenham SN15 5EY
Tel: 44 01275 845012
Web site: www.locomotivesinternational.co.uk
Freq: Bi-Monthly
Circ: 1500 Not Audited
Editor: Iain McCall
MAGAZINE
Railroad

Lofo   1061474
Email: lofo@lofo.ee
Web site: http://www.lofo.ee/ Not Audited
MAGAZINE
Consumer Affairs, Crime & Violence, Defense & National Security, Energy & Environment, Ethical/Moral Issues, International News, Law, National News, News & Current Affairs, Northern Ireland

Logistics Business IT   986387
Editorial: Unit D(A) Spitfire Close, Ermine Business Park, Huntingdon, Huntingdon PE29 6XY **Tel:** 44 01480 455660
Email: edit@logisticsbusinessit.com
Web site: www.logisticsbusinessit.com
Freq: Bi-Monthly
Circ: 8500 Not Audited
Profile: Magazine covering all aspects of technology and services spanning the entire supply chain. Focusing on business software as used throughout the supply chain, including manufacturing, warehousing and transportation software solutions, automotive data capture, industrial mobile computing, and voice directed systems for warehouse operations such as picking. First published in 2007. Logistics Business IT is read at senior level across the entire supply chain including supply chain and logistics managers and directors, CEO's, MD's, warehouse managers, IT and operational management and systems integrators.Aimed at high-level logistics IT decision makers in major end-user companies, third party logistics specialists and providers as well as purchases, systems integrators, specifiers and practitioners in the supply chain and management IT fields.
MAGAZINE
Industry, Internet, Mobile Communications, Software, Supply Chain Management (SCM)

London Archaeologist   985012
Editorial: 44 Tantallon Road, London SW12 8DG
Web site: www.londonarchaeologist.org.uk

Freq: Quarterly Not Audited
Profile: Magazine containing reports on current aspects of archaeology and allied history within the London region.
Ad Rate: Full Page Mono £150.00
Ad Rate: Full Page Colour £150.00
MAGAZINE
History

London Bangla   995872
Editorial: Montefiore Centre, Hanbury Street, London E1 5HZ
Tel: 44 02072 473006
Email: info@londonbangla.com
Web site: http://londonbangla.com/
Freq: Weekly
Circ: 150000 Not Audited
Editor: K M Abu Taher Choudhury
MAGAZINE
Asia, Expatriates

London Cocktail Week   997043
Editorial: Elixir House, Park Royal, London NW10 7SF **Tel:** 44 02088 389455
Email: press@drinkup.london
Web site: www.drinkup.london/cocktailweek
Freq: Monthly
Circ: 107898 Cision Digital Reach
MAGAZINE (ONLINE)
Alcohol & Spirits, Bars, Clubs & Pubs, Men's Interests, Restaurant Reviews, Women's Interests

London Cyclist   982200
Editorial: 2 Newhams Row, London SE1 3UZ **Tel:** 44 02072 349310
Email: editorlondoncyclist@yahoo.com
Web site: http://lcc.org.uk/pages/free-london-cyclist-magazine
Freq: Bi-Monthly
Circ: 12000 Not Audited
Editor: John Kitchiner
Profile: Magazine of the London Cycling Campaign. Includes articles on cycling, politics, safety, bikes, accessories, clothing, books, routes, health and fitness.
Ad Rate: Full Page Colour £1250.00
MAGAZINE
Bicycles

The London Economic   987514
Email: jack@thelondoneconomic.com
Web site: http://www.thelondoneconomic.com/
Freq: Daily
Circ: 62770 Cision Digital Reach
Editor: Jack Peat
MAGAZINE (ONLINE)
Art, Bars, Clubs & Pubs, Classical/Choral/Band Music, Cooking & Baking, Country, Folk, Bluegrass, Dance Music, Driving, Economics, Jazz & Blues, Lifestyle

The London Gazette   995975
Editorial: PO Box 3584, Norwich NR7 7WD
Tel: 44 08706 003322
Email: london@thegazette.co.uk
Web site: www.thegazette.co.uk
Freq: Daily Not Audited
Profile: Publication covering statutory, legal, bankruptcy and liquidation notices relating to England.
MAGAZINE
News & Current Affairs

London Glossy   985895
Editorial: 71 Queens Gate, London SW7 5JT
Tel: 44 08456 005507
Email: info@londonglossy.com
Web site: londonglossy.com
Freq: Monthly
Circ: 100000 Not Audited
Profile: Magazine covering local & global news, fashion and style, beauty, health and wealth. Aimed at people interseted in local & Global news and fashion.
Ad Rate: Full Page Colour £3000.00
MAGAZINE
Lifestyle, Men's Interests, Regional General Interest, Women's Interests

London in Stereo   987299
Editorial: 5 Finn House, Bevenden Street, London N1 6BN
Web site: www.londoninstereo.com
Freq: Monthly
Circ: 15000 Not Audited
Editor: Jess Partridge
Profile: Magazine covering live music in London. In contains recommended gigs, full listings and live music reviews. Aimed at music lovers.
MAGAZINE
Classical/Choral/Band Music, Country, Folk, Bluegrass, Dance Music, Jazz & Blues, Local Entertainment Guides, Music, Pop Music, R&B, Urban, World, Rap & Hip Hop, Rock Music

London Love Wine   997304
Web site: www.londonlovewine.com
Freq: Daily
Circ: 1463 Cision Digital Reach
MAGAZINE (ONLINE)
Cooking & Baking, Wine/Winemaking

London Macadam   985336
Editorial: Suite 239, 2 Old Brompton Road, London SW7 3DQ **Tel:** 44 02076 032773
Email: londonmacadam@googlemail.com
Web site: www.londonmacadam.com
Freq: Weekly
Circ: 20000 Not Audited
Profile: Lifestyle magazine covering fashion, beauty, people and shopping. Aimed at the French community in London.
Ad Rate: Full Page Colour £1200.00
MAGAZINE
Europe

The London Magazine   981856
Editorial: 85 Strand, London WC2R 0DW
Tel: 44 02075 508000
Email: anne.cuthbertson@cedarcom.co.uk
Web site: www.thelondonmagazine.co.uk
Freq: Monthly
Circ: 68849 Not Audited
Profile: Magazine covering a review of literature and the arts.
Ad Rate: Full Page Mono £150.00
Ad Rate: Full Page Colour £200.00
MAGAZINE
Property Management & Maintenance, Regional General Interest

London Magazine   985928
Editorial: 11 Queen's Gate, London SW7 5EL **Tel:** 44 02075 845977
Email: admin@thelondonmagazine.org
Web site: thelondonmagazine.org
Freq: Bi-Monthly
Circ: 5000 Not Audited
Editor: Steven O'Brien
Profile: Magazine covering a review of literature and the arts.
Ad Rate: Full Page Mono £150.00
Ad Rate: Full Page Colour £200.00
MAGAZINE
Literature

London Mums   985195
Email: info@londonmumsmagazine.com
Web site: www.londonmumsmagazine.com
Freq: Daily
Circ: 30000 Not Audited
MAGAZINE
Family & Parenting

London Planner   982340
Editorial: 2nd Floor, Samuel House, St Alban's St, London SW1Y 4SQ
Tel: 44 02072 425222
Email: london.planner@morriseurope.com
Web site: http://www.mvplondon.uk/london-planner-magazine
Freq: Monthly
Circ: 100000 Not Audited
Profile: Listings magazine covering theatre, dance and music, sightseeing, museums and galleries, shopping, eating out and travel accommodation. Published monthly, London Planner is Visit London's and Visit Britain's official monthly visitor guide to England's capital. Over 125,000 free copies are strategically distributed in 30 countries

worldwide, through Tourist Information Centres across the UK and in selected London outlets. London Planner is a pocket-sized guide to the city and serves as an invaluable pre-destination and on-arrival tool for the visitor planning their trip in the capital. Aimed at tourists visiting London.
Ad Rate: Full Page Colour £2020.00
MAGAZINE
Regional General Interest, Travel

London Property: Central & South   985509
Editorial: 23 Stanley Close, North Hinksey, Botley, Oxford OX2 0LB
Web site: www.londonpropertymagazines.com
Freq: Monthly
Circ: 400000 Not Audited
MAGAZINE
Do-It-Yourself (DIY), Property Management & Maintenance

London Property: Islington, City & Docklands   985510
Editorial: 23 Stanley Close, North Hinksey, Botley, Oxford OX2 0LB
Web site: www.londonpropertymagazines.com
Freq: Monthly
Circ: 65000 Not Audited
MAGAZINE
Do-It-Yourself (DIY), Property Management & Maintenance

London Property: North West & Central   985508
Editorial: Regional office, 23 Stanley Close, North Hinksey, Botley, Oxford OX2 0LB
Web site: www.londonpropertymagazines.com
Freq: Monthly
Circ: 400000 Not Audited
MAGAZINE
Do-It-Yourself (DIY), Property Management & Maintenance

London Review of Books   981975
Editorial: 28 Little Russell Street, London WC1A 2HN **Tel:** 44 02072 091101
Email: edit@lrb.co.uk
Web site: www.lrb.co.uk
Freq: Bi-Weekly
Circ: 67529 Not Audited
Editor: Mary-Kay Wilmers
Profile: Magazine covering the tradition of the literary and intellectual essay in English. Each issue contains up to 15 long reviews and essays by academics, writers and journalists. There are also shorter art and film reviews, as well as poems and a letters page. Aimed at intellectuals, writers, broadcasters, academics and philosophers. Books for consideration should be sent for the attention of Adam Shatz, 20 Jay Street, Suite 1010, New York 11201-8346.
Ad Rate: Full Page Colour £4760.00
MAGAZINE
Literature

London Select Traveller   996578
Editorial: Publishing House, 3 Bridgebank Industrial Estate, Taylor Street, Horwich, Bolton BL6 7PD **Tel:** 44 01204 478817
Web site: http://www.selecttravelmedia.com/magazines/london/
Freq: Quarterly
Circ: 30000 Not Audited
Editor: Jayne Meadowcroft
MAGAZINE
Airline Inflight

London Show Tickets   1073822
Editorial: 1st Floor, Turnbridge Mills, Quay Street, Huddersfield HD1 6QT
Tel: 44 02081 233414
Email: editor@ciaranjarosz.media
Web site: www.londonshowtickets.co.uk
Freq: Daily
Circ: 1234 Cision Digital Reach
MAGAZINE (ONLINE)
Classical/Choral/Band Music, Theater & Performing Arts

London Visitors
983458

Editorial: The Penthouse, Bank Chambers, 185 Wardour Street, London W1F 8WU
Tel: 44 02074 340421
Email: londonvisitors@kibointernational.co.uk
Web site: www.thelondonvisitors.co.uk
Freq: Monthly
Circ: 200000 Not Audited
Editor: Vicky Huntley
MAGAZINE
Regional General Interest, Travel

London West End
985276

Editorial: 5 Wootton Street, Waterloo, London SE1 8TG **Tel:** 44 02079 027600
Email: info@westendlondon.com
Web site: www.leicestersquare.london
Freq: Daily
Circ: 36062 Cision Digital Reach
MAGAZINE (ONLINE)
Bars, Clubs & Pubs, Comedy, Entertainment, Local Entertainment Guides, Theater & Performing Arts

London Wine Week
997040

Editorial: Elixir House, Park Royal, London NW10 7SF **Tel:** 44 02088 389455
Email: press@drinkup.london
Web site: https://drinkup.london/wineweek
Freq: Monthly
Circ: 107872 Cision Digital Reach
MAGAZINE (ONLINE)
Bars, Clubs & Pubs, Comedy, Entertainment, Local Entertainment Guides, Men's Interests, Movies & Video, Restaurant Reviews, Wine/Winemaking, Women's Interests

London X
988747

Editorial: 130 Shaftesbury Avenue, 2nd Floor, London W1D 5EU
Tel: 44 02035 407748
Email: info@londonx.co.uk
Web site: www.londonx.co.uk
Freq: Bi-Weekly Not Audited
Editor: James Bendien
MAGAZINE
Entertainment, Local Entertainment Guides, Regional General Interest

LondonCalling.com
988755

Editorial: 14a Ardleigh Road, London N1 4HP **Tel:** 44 02072 757225
Email: press@londoncalling.com
Web site: www.londoncalling.com
Freq: Daily
Circ: 27607 Cision Digital Reach
MAGAZINE (ONLINE)
Art, Bars, Clubs & Pubs, Comedy, Entertainment, Literature, Local Entertainment Guides, Movies & Video, Photography, Theater & Performing Arts, Visual Arts

LondonCityGirl
999696

Email: editorial@londoncitygirl.com
Web site: www.londoncitygirl.co.uk
Freq: Daily
Circ: 578 Cision Digital Reach
Editor: Simantha Mahmud
MAGAZINE (ONLINE)
Women's Interests

londondance.com
1101758

Email: editor@londondance.com
Web site: www.londondance.com
Freq: Daily
Circ: 32391 Cision Digital Reach
Editor: Carmel Smith
Profile: Website covering all aspects of dance in London. Which includes performance listings, reviews, classes and workshops, video clips, directory of venues, companies, rehearsal spaces and dance organisations, job watch page and notice boards. Aimed at those interested in dance both audiences and professionals.
MAGAZINE (ONLINE)
Theater & Performing Arts

Londonisfunny.com
999476

Email: info@londonisfunny.com
Web site: www.londonisfunny.com

Freq: Daily
Circ: 5863 Cision Digital Reach
Editor: Paul Fleckney
MAGAZINE (ONLINE)
Comedy, Local Entertainment Guides

Londonist
986191

Editorial: 3rd Floor, 72-74 Paul Street, London EC2A 4NA **Tel:** 44 02071 937022
Email: hello@londonist.com
Web site: www.londonist.com
Freq: Daily
Circ: 466913 Cision Digital Reach
Profile: Website covering London lifestyle, tourism, things to do and events including restaurants, bars, theatre and the arts.
MAGAZINE (ONLINE)
Airline Inflight, Bars, Clubs & Pubs, Comedy, Cooking & Baking, Entertainment, Food, Grocery Stores, Local Entertainment Guides, Movies & Video, Organic Food

London-se1.co.uk Community Website
982837

Editorial: 27 Blackfriars Road, London SE1 8NY **Tel:** 44 02076 330766
Email: james.hatts@banksidepress.com
Web site: www.london-se1.co.uk
Freq: Daily
Circ: 128491 Cision Digital Reach
Editor: James Hatts
MAGAZINE (ONLINE)
Regional General Interest

LondonTown.com
982869

Editorial: 90 Long Acre, Covent Garden, London WC2E 9RZ **Tel:** 44 02074 374370
Email: content@londontown.com
Web site: www.londontown.com
Freq: Daily
Circ: 424645 Cision Digital Reach
MAGAZINE (ONLINE)
Regional General Interest

Londra Gazete
995986

Editorial: 177 Green Lanes, London N13 4UR **Tel:** 44 02088 895025
Email: news@londragazete.com
Web site: http://www.londragazete.com/
Freq: Weekly
Circ: 25000 Not Audited
Profile: Newspaper covering news, features, photos and sport concerning Turkish-speaking people in London and UK and summary of London, UK, Turkey and Cyprus news. Aimed at the Turkish-speaking communities in Britain and other interested organizations and statutory bodies.
MAGAZINE
Asia, Europe

Lonely Planet
997321

Editorial: 6th Floor, 240 Blackfriars Road, London SE1 8NW **Tel:** 44 02037 715100
Web site: www.lonelyplanet.com
Freq: Annual Not Audited
Profile: Web site with practical info about a destination then build on that with insider knowledge, thorough reviews, little-known facts and authoritative recommendations. Aimed predominantly at frequent travellers with the time and means to indulge their passion.
MAGAZINE
Travel

Lonely Planet Traveller
984823

Editorial: 240 Blackfriars Road, London SE1 9UF **Tel:** 44 02037 715100
Web site: www.lonelyplanet.com/magazine
Freq: Monthly
Circ: 41599 Not Audited
Editor: Peter Grunert
MAGAZINE
Travel

The Long Room
998703

Editorial: 90 Chancery Lane, London WC2A 1EU **Tel:** 44 02070 250000
Email: contact@lordstaverners.org
Web site: http://www.lordstaverners.org/
Freq: 3 Times/Year

Circ: 5500 Not Audited
MAGAZINE
Charitable Foundations, Cricket

LOOK
983906

Editorial: 161 Marsh Wall, London E14 9AP
Tel: 44 02031 485000
Email: lookys@timeinc.com
Web site: www.look.co.uk
Freq: Weekly
Circ: 59390 Not Audited
Editor: Gilly Ferguson; **Editor:** Emily Wadsworth
Profile: Magazine covering high street fashion and celebrity news. It contains articles on affordable fashion, high street shopping advice, celebrity style and real life stories. First published in 2007. Targets women aged between 18 and 30.
Ad Rate: Full Page Colour £14000.00
MAGAZINE
Women's Interests

LookLocal Esher
985031

Editorial: 5 Hazel Way, Fetcham, Leatherhead, London KT22 9QF
Tel: 44 01372 200000
Web site: www.looklocalmagazine.co.uk/Our-Magaines.html
Freq: Monthly
Circ: 7000 Not Audited
Editor: Rosalind Thomas
MAGAZINE
Regional General Interest

Loot recruit
998569

Editorial: Suite 1A, 1 Lindsey Street, London EC1A 9HP **Tel:** 44 02089 004500
Email: recruit@loot.com
Web site: www.lootrecruit.com
Freq: Weekly
Circ: 83940 Not Audited
MAGAZINE
News & Current Affairs

Lost in London
996397

Web site: http://cargocollective.com/lostinlondon
Freq: Quarterly
Circ: 500 Not Audited
MAGAZINE
Regional General Interest

Lothian Life
982559

Editorial: 4/8 Downfield Place, Edinburgh EH11 2EW **Tel:** 44 07905 614402
Web site: www.lothianlife.co.uk
Freq: Daily
Circ: 6521 Cision Digital Reach
Editor: Anne Hamilton
MAGAZINE (ONLINE)
Art, Do-It-Yourself (DIY), Entertainment, Gardening, Movies & Video, Regional General Interest, Restaurant Reviews, Wine/Winemaking

Loud
983999

Editorial: 14 Greville Street, London EC1N 8SB **Tel:** 44 02076 094254
Email: contact@studentandgraduate.com
Web site: www.loudmag.co.uk
Freq: Bi-Monthly
Circ: 200000 Not Audited
Editor: Jude Schofield
MAGAZINE
Careers, Education, Teen/Young Adult

Loud And Quiet
986714

Editorial: PO Box 67915, London NW1W 8TH
Email: info@loudandquiet.com
Web site: www.loudandquiet.com
Freq: Monthly Not Audited
Editor: Stuart Stubbs
Profile: Magazine covering alternative and new music.
MAGAZINE
Dance Music, Rock Music

LOVE
984867

Editorial: 2nd Floor, Jamieson House, 146-148 Clerkenwell Road, London EC1R 5DG
Tel: 44 02074 999080

Email: loveedit01@condenast.co.uk
Web site: www.thelovemagazine.co.uk
Freq: Semi-Annual
Circ: 100000 Not Audited
Profile: Magazine featuring fashion news, reviews and luxury fashion. The magazine aims to explain why a particular fashion collection looks the way it looks, why it is what it is, where it came from and where it will be heading next season. It looks at the developments within creative industries such as music and art and the impact these have to the fashion industry. First published in 2009. Aimed at designers, artists and people with a love of fashion and design.
Ad Rate: Full Page Colour £10500.00
MAGAZINE
Fashion

Love A Happy Ending
997840

Web site: www.loveahappyending.com
Freq: Daily
Circ: 12480 Cision Digital Reach
MAGAZINE (ONLINE)
Men's Interests, Women's Interests

Love Food Love Drink
984764

Editorial: GOF House, 42-44 Thomas Road, London E14 7BJ
Web site: http://www.worldofzing.com/love-food-love-drink-magazine/
Freq: Daily
Circ: 93 Cision Digital Reach
Editor: Pritesh Mody
Profile: Website covering food and drinks. Love Food Love Drink is a weekly lifestyle e-magazine providing a fun and friendly look at the world of food and drink, with around 12,000 mainly London based registered subscribers.
MAGAZINE (ONLINE)
Alcohol & Spirits, Bars, Clubs & Pubs, Beer, Beverages, Cooking & Baking, Food, Grocery Stores, Organic Food, Restaurant Reviews, Vegetarianism & Veganism

Love From
1053096

Editorial: Unit 16, Greenway Farm, Bath Road, Wick, Bristol BS30 5RL
Tel: 44 01179 373003
Web site: http://www.kennedypublishing.co.uk/magazines/love-magazine
Freq: Monthly
Circ: 30000 Not Audited
MAGAZINE
Elementary School, Preschool, Teen/Young Adult

Love it!
983268

Editorial: Floor 3, Maclaren House, Lancastrian Office Centre, Manchester M32 0FP **Tel:** 44 01613 810161
Email: editor@loveitmagazine.co.uk
Web site: http://www.loveitmagazine.co.uk/
Freq: Weekly
Circ: 82830 Not Audited
Profile: Magazine covering real-life stories and celebrity news and features. Each issue contains celebrity gossip, recipes, fashion, beauty, travel and interviews. Aimed at women aged between 18 and 35 years old.
Ad Rate: Full Page Colour £4000.00
MAGAZINE
Careers, Crime & Violence, Family & Parenting, Health & Medicine, Lifestyle, Personal Finance, Relationships, Women's Interests

Love Knitting for Baby
997278

Editorial: 2nd Floor, Tower House, Fairfax Street, Bristol BS1 3BN
Tel: 44 01173 148799
Web site: www.immediate.co.uk/brands/love-knitting-for-baby
Freq: Bi-Monthly
Circ: 8000 Not Audited
Editor: Lucy Whyld
MAGAZINE
Crafts

Love Letters
995090

Editorial: Ground Floor Office/Studio Suite, The Old Mill, 45 London Road, East

Consumer Magazines

Grinstead, East Grinstead RH19 1AW
Tel: 44 01342 325558
Email: info@loveletterspublishing.co.uk
Web site: www.loveletterspublishing.co.uk
Freq: Daily
Circ: 894 Cision Digital Reach
MAGAZINE (ONLINE)
Banking, Bonds, Commodities, Corporate
Finance, Corporate Management,
Derivatives, Economics, Emerging
Markets, Equities, Financial Markets

Love London   985519
Email: hello@love-london.co.uk
Web site: www.love-london.co.uk/
Freq: Daily
Circ: 13041 Cision Digital Reach
MAGAZINE (ONLINE)
Regional General Interest, Restaurant
Reviews, Women's Interests

Love London Love Culture
1053220
Web site: lovelondonloveculture.com
Freq: Daily
Circ: 11498 Cision Digital Reach
MAGAZINE (ONLINE)
Theater & Performing Arts, Visual Arts

Love Our Wedding   1074310
Editorial: 68a Oldham Road, Manchester
M4 5EE **Tel:** 44 0161 2 366712
Web site: http://www.loveourweddingmag.
com/
Freq: Monthly
Circ: 20000 Not Audited
Editor: Jade Pepperell
MAGAZINE
Weddings

Love Patchwork & Quilting
987646
Editorial: 9th Floor Tower House, Fairfax
Stree, Bristol BS1 3BN
Tel: 44 01179 279009
Email: lovequilting@immediate.co.uk
Web site: http://www.
lovepatchworkandquilting.com
Freq: Monthly Not Audited
Profile: Publication that looks at quilting and
patchwork.
MAGAZINE
Crafts

Love Sewing   996067
Editorial: St Christopher House, 217
Wellington Road South, Stockport,
Manchester SK2 6TZ **Tel:** 44 08445 611202
Web site: www.lovesewingmag.co.uk
Freq: Bi-Weekly
Circ: 30000 Not Audited
Editor: Amy Thomas
MAGAZINE
Crafts

Love The Mountains   1053248
Tel: 44 01494 862423
Email: info@inthesnow.com
Web site: http://www.lovethemountains.co.
uk/
Freq: Semi-Annual
Circ: 55000 Not Audited
Editor: Patrick Thorne
MAGAZINE
Fashion, Winter Sports

Love to Knit & Crochet   1086849
Tel: 44 02031 485000
Email: thecraftnetwork@timeinc.com
Web site: www.theknittingnetwork.co.uk
Freq: Monthly
MAGAZINE
Crafts

love: mini   997494
Editorial: 1 Winewall Lane, Colne, Colne
BB8 8BX
Email: editor@love-mini.co.uk
Web site: www.love-mini.co.uk
Freq: Daily
Circ: 6126 Cision Digital Reach

Editor: Craig Mcbeth
MAGAZINE (ONLINE)
Automakers

Lovedbyparents.com   985222
Email: info@lovedbyparents.com
Web site: www.lovedbyparents.com
Freq: Daily
Circ: 12069 Cision Digital Reach
MAGAZINE (ONLINE)
Family & Parenting

loveFOOD   985845
Editorial: 2nd Floor, 112-116 Old Street,
London EC1V 9BG
Email: uknews@lovefood.com
Web site: www.lovefood.com
Freq: Daily
Circ: 38924 Cision Digital Reach
Profile: Website covering food and recipes.
MAGAZINE (ONLINE)
Cooking & Baking

lovehome.co.uk   984670
Editorial: UKTV, 10 Hammersmith Grove,
London W6 7AP **Tel:** 44 02072 996200
Email: viewers@uktv.co.uk
Web site: network.uktv.co.uk/article/home-
channel
Freq: Daily
Circ: 187937 Cision Digital Reach
MAGAZINE (ONLINE)
Architecture & Design, Do-It-Yourself
(DIY), Fashion, Gardening, Home,
Property Management & Maintenance,
Real Estate, Women's Interests

LoveINCORPORATED   1056318
Editorial: 2nd Floor, 112-116 Old Street,
London EC1V 9BG
Email: support@love.zendesk.com
Web site: www.loveincorporated.com
Freq: Daily
Circ: 611 Cision Digital Reach
Editor: Damian Clarkson
MAGAZINE (ONLINE)
Beauty & Grooming, Celebrities,
Consumer Affairs, Cooking & Baking,
Cosmetics, Do-It-Yourself (DIY), Hair,
Men's Interests, Movies & Video, Property
Management & Maintenance

loveMONEY   985045
Editorial: 2nd Floor, 112-116 Old Street,
London EC1V 9BG
Email: uknews@lovemoney.com
Web site: www.lovemoney.com
Freq: Daily
Circ: 261333 Cision Digital Reach
Editor: Damian Clarkson
MAGAZINE (ONLINE)
Personal Finance

LovePork.co.uk   995373
Tel: 44 02476 478809
Email: loveporkenquiries@ahdb.org.uk
Web site: www.lovepork.co.uk
Freq: Daily
Circ: 10545 Cision Digital Reach
MAGAZINE (ONLINE)
News & Current Affairs

Loverboy   996330
Tel: 44 07540 737685
Web site: www.loverboymagazine.com
Freq: Semi-Annual
Circ: 1000 Not Audited
MAGAZINE
Bars, Clubs & Pubs, Comedy,
Entertainment, Fashion, LGBT, Lifestyle,
Local Entertainment Guides, Men's
Interests, Movies & Video, Regional
General Interest

lovereading.co.uk   986331
Editorial: 59 High Street, East Grinstead,
East Grinstead RH19 3DD
Tel: 44 03443 351126
Email: contact@lovereading.co.uk
Web site: www.lovereading.co.uk
Freq: Daily
Circ: 85786 Cision Digital Reach
Editor: Louise Weir

Profile: Website covering books.
MAGAZINE (ONLINE)
Literature

Loving the Cotswolds   997284
Editorial: 12 Cornfield Way, Ashton under
Hill, Evesham, Worcester WR11 7TA
Tel: 44 01386 881402
Email: david@lovingthecotswolds.com
Web site: www.lovingthecotswolds.com
Freq: Daily
Circ: 12285 Cision Digital Reach
Editor: David Wood
MAGAZINE (ONLINE)
Regional General Interest

The Low Down   996751
Editorial: Suite 8, 3rd Floor, Parr Street
Studios, 33-45 Parr Street, Liverpool L1 4JN
Email: info@thelowdownmagazine.com
Web site: http://www.thelowdownmagazine.
com
Freq: Weekly Not Audited
MAGAZINE
Art, Bars, Clubs & Pubs, Comedy,
Entertainment, Literature, Local
Entertainment Guides, Movies & Video,
Photography, Regional General Interest,
Theater & Performing Arts

Loyalty Magazine   1054926
Editorial: 3A Market Place, Uppingham,
Oakham LE15 9QH **Tel:** 44 01572 820088
Web site: www.loyaltymagazine.com
Freq: 3 Times/Year Not Audited
Profile: Website covering customer
retention. The Loyalty website covers the
latest news and issues on customer
retention, loyalty schemes and customer
relationship management (CRM) including
business to business, net based
programmes, e-commerce and employee
loyalty.
MAGAZINE
Branding, Business, Corporate
Responsibility, Marketing, Retail
Management

LS:N Global   985718
Editorial: 26 Elder Street, London E1 6BT
Tel: 44 02077 912020
Email: reception@thefuturelaboratory.com
Web site: www.lsnglobal.com
Freq: Daily
Circ: 28978 Cision Digital Reach
Editor: Jonathan Openshaw
MAGAZINE (ONLINE)
Advertising Industry, Beauty & Grooming,
Books, Branding, Broadcasting,
Cosmetics, Fashion, Gardening, Graphic
Design, Hair

LSE Connect   999078
Editorial: Editor, LSE Connect, Houghton
Sreet, London WC2A 2AE
Tel: 44 02079 557057
Email: lsemagazine@lse.ac.uk
Web site: www.lse.ac.uk/resources/
LSEMagazine/
Freq: Semi-Annual
Circ: 100000 Not Audited
Editor: Jess Winterstein
MAGAZINE
Alumni

Lucky Break   1073826
Tel: 44 01865 664970
Email: info@theoxfordpuzzlecompany.com
Web site: www.theoxfordpuzzlecompany.
com
Freq: Bi-Monthly
Circ: 50000 Not Audited
Profile: Magazine covering crosswords and
puzzles as well as entertainment reviews and
gadgets. Lucky Break is a bi-monthly
magazine with exclusive competitions with
prizes going to subscribers of the magazine.
Aimed at puzzle enthusiasts aged 25 years
old plus.
MAGAZINE
Games, Competitions & Events

Lula   984687
Editorial: 28 Charlotte Street, London W1F
2NF **Tel:** 44 02076 375697
Email: me@lulamag.com
Web site: www.lulamag.com
Freq: Semi-Annual
Circ: 72000 Not Audited
Profile: Magazine covering fashion.
MAGAZINE
Beauty & Grooming, Cosmetics, Fashion,
Hair, Women's Interests

Lumipallo   1060987
Email: info@lumipallo.fi
Web site: http://www.lumipallo.fi
Circ: 2483 Cision Digital Reach
MAGAZINE (ONLINE)
Airline Inflight, Extreme/Adventure
Sports, Railroad, Travel, Winter Sports

Lunch Magazine   994967
Email: info@lunchmag.com
Web site: www.lunchmag.com
Freq: Daily
Circ: 1084 Cision Digital Reach
MAGAZINE (ONLINE)
Luxury Goods, Regional General Interest,
Restaurant Reviews, Travel

lunchboxworld.co.uk   985295
Editorial: 9 Russett, Chalfont St Peter,
Gerrards Cross, Gerrards Cross SL9 8JY
Email: hello@lunchboxworld.co.uk
Web site: http://lunchboxworld.co.uk/
Freq: Daily
Circ: 10039 Cision Digital Reach
Editor: Caroline Job
MAGAZINE (ONLINE)
Cooking & Baking

Lure Magazine   1076650
Web site: http://www.lure-mag.com/
Freq: Daily
Circ: 1160 Cision Digital Reach
MAGAZINE (ONLINE)
Fishing

Lusso   983560
Editorial: 64-65 Cowcross Street, London
EC1M 6EG
Email: editorial@lus.so
Web site: http://lus.so/
Freq: Bi-Monthly
Circ: 38000 Not Audited
Editor: Rob Clayman
Profile: Lifestyle magazine covering all
aspects of the men's luxury lifestyle market,
from luxury property, travel, luxury goods to
leisure activities. Aimed at 25 to 55 year old
high earners, frequent travellers with an
interest in expensive hobbies.
Ad Rate: Full Page Colour £5100.00
MAGAZINE
Luxury Goods

LUX   997461
Editorial: Unit 10, Barton Marina, Barton
Turn, Barton under Needwood, Burton on
Trent, Barton-under-Needwood DE13 8AS
Tel: 44 02037 256842
Web site: http://lux.acquisition-intl.com/
Freq: Monthly
Circ: 238000 Not Audited
Profile: Lifestyle magazine covering
watches, cars, travel, property, interiors,
gardens and personal finance.
MAGAZINE
Luxury Goods

Lux Worldwide   987032
Editorial: 1 Lyric Square, London W6 0NB
Tel: 44 03330 110808
Email: enquiries@luxios.com
Web site: www.luxworldwide.com
Freq: Daily
Circ: 26230 Cision Digital Reach
Profile: Website covering luxury lifestyle.
The LUX WORLDWIDE website shares the
latest news and information on luxury
services and products worldwide.
MAGAZINE (ONLINE)
Luxury Goods

Luxe Magazine
985570
Tel: 44 01914 266300
Web site: http://www.luxe-magazine.co.uk
Freq: Bi-Monthly
Circ: 20000 Not Audited
Editor: Kathryn Armstrong
MAGAZINE
Regional General Interest

Luxepitality
1076649
Web site: www.luxepitality.com
Freq: Daily
Circ: 548 Cision Digital Reach
Editor: Nicola El-Mouelhy
MAGAZINE (ONLINE)
Airline Inflight, Audio Video Trade, Cameras, Consumer Electronics, Electronics, Hotels/Motels, Luxury Goods, Men's Interests, Mobile Electronics, Movies & Video

Luxure
984555
Editorial: 26 Dover Street, London W1S 4LY
Tel: 44 02074 119059
Email: info@luxuremagazine.com
Web site: www.luxuremagazine.com
Freq: Semi-Annual
Circ: 25000 Not Audited
Editor: Shivani Lal
Profile: Magazine covering luxury lifestyle and brands.
MAGAZINE
Fashion, Luxury Goods

Luxuria Lifestyle
987163
Editorial: 110 Butterfield Park, Great Marlings, Stopsley, Luton LU2 8DL
Tel: 44 07887 811550
Email: editor@luxurialifestyle.com
Web site: www.luxurialifestyle.com
Freq: Daily
Circ: 13137 Cision Digital Reach
Profile: Website covering luxury lifestyle. Luxuria Lifestyle is 'an all-encompassing guide to the affluent lifestyle', with information on luxury products, technology and brands.
MAGAZINE (ONLINE)
Luxury Goods

Luxurious Magazine
987206
Editorial: 5 St Johns Lane, London EC1M 4BH Tel: 44 02071 938380
Email: editorial@luxrs.com
Web site: www.luxuriousmagazine.com
Freq: Quarterly
Circ: 12500 Not Audited
Editor: Jon McKnight
Profile: Online magazine covering luxury property, fine dining, arts, fashion, style, luxury goods and luxury travel.
MAGAZINE
Lifestyle, Luxury Goods, Men's Interests, Regional General Interest, Women's Interests

Luxury Briefing
983284
Editorial: Suite 9, Beaufort Court, Admirals Way, Canary Wharf, London E14 9XL
Tel: 44 02037 724850
Email: information@luxury-briefing.com
Web site: www.luxury-briefing.com
Freq: Monthly
Circ: 12000 Not Audited
Profile: Magazine focusing on the luxury industry as a whole, as defined by the customer base, rather than the merchandise. It provides a monthly coverage of all sectors: fashion, accessories, beauty, jewellery, watches, hotels, restaurants, design and media.Read by luxury brands and those in surrounding industries including finance, property, marketing, advertising and PR. Associated Blogs: Luxury Briefing
MAGAZINE
Business, Luxury Goods, Small and Medium Business

The Luxury Channel
984781
Editorial: Studio 21, 2nd Floor, Hurlingham Studios, Ranelagh Gardens, London SW6 3PA Tel: 44 02077 316191
Email: info@theluxurychannel.com
Web site: www.theluxurychannel.com

Freq: Daily
Circ: 9680 Cision Digital Reach
Editor: Antonia Peck
Profile: Website covering luxury lifestyle THE LUXURY CHANNEL website shares the latest news and information on travel, lifestyle, culture, fashion and ethics.
MAGAZINE (ONLINE)
Luxury Goods

Luxury Lifestyle Magazine
1053947
Email: info@luxurylifestylemag.co.uk
Web site: http://www.luxurylifestylemag.co.uk/
Freq: Daily
Circ: 15234 Cision Digital Reach
Editor: Nick Gilmartin
MAGAZINE (ONLINE)
Luxury Goods

Luxury London
1053497
Editorial: Level 6, One Canada Square, Canary Wharf, London E14 5AX
Tel: 44 02079 874320
Email: editorial@luxurylondon.co.uk
Web site: www.luxurylondon.co.uk
Freq: Daily
Circ: 16862 Cision Digital Reach
MAGAZINE (ONLINE)
Luxury Goods

The Luxury Report
1097889
Editorial: 28 Beaufort Court, Admirals Way, Canary Wharf, London E14 9XL
Tel: 44 02070 933748
Email: enquiries@the-luxuryreport.com
Web site: www.the-luxuryreport.com
Freq: 3 Times/Year
Circ: 45000 Not Audited
MAGAZINE
News & Current Affairs

Lyst.com
998006
Editorial: 48 Hoxton Square, London N1 6PB
Email: press@lyst.com
Web site: www.lyst.com/
Freq: Daily
Circ: 5258365 Cision Digital Reach
MAGAZINE (ONLINE)
Fashion

M Magazine
1059126
Editorial: 2 Pancras Square, London N1C 4AG Tel: 44 02075 805544
Email: magazine@prsformusic.com
Web site: http://www.m-magazine.co.uk/
Freq: Daily
Circ: 124000 Not Audited
Profile: Magazine covering music, featuring songwriter and composer profiles and interviews, music business news and issues. Read by PRS for music members, songwriters, composers and music publishers.
MAGAZINE
Classical/Choral/Band Music, Country, Folk, Bluegrass, Dance Music, Entertainment, Jazz & Blues, Local Entertainment Guides, Music, Pop Music, R&B, Urban, World, Rap & Hip Hop

M Magazine (London)
983384
Editorial: M Magazine, 2 Pancras Square, London N1C 4AG Tel: 44 02075 805544
Email: magazine@prsformusic.com
Web site: www.m-magazine.co.uk
Freq: Quarterly
Circ: 50000 Not Audited
Editor: Paul Nichols
MAGAZINE
Classical/Choral/Band Music, Country, Folk, Bluegrass, Dance Music, Jazz & Blues, Music, Pop Music, R&B, Urban, World, Rap & Hip Hop, Rock Music

M&M Global
979924
Editorial: 115 Southwark Bridge Road, 1st Floor, London SE1 0AX
Tel: 44 02073 676990
Email: editor@mandmglobal.com
Web site: www.mandmglobal.com

Freq: Daily
Circ: 54606 Cision Digital Reach
Profile: Website covering global media and advertising. The M&M Global website shares news and information relating to the world of global media and advertising. Aimed at global advertisers.
MAGAZINE (ONLINE)
Advertising Industry, Branding, Broadcasting, Graphic Design, Marketing, Media & Communications, Photography, Publishing

MacFormat
981725
Editorial: Quay House, The Ambury, Bath BA1 1UA Tel: 44 01225 442244
Web site: macformat.techradar.com
Freq: Monthly
Circ: 22457 Not Audited
Profile: Magazine covering all aspects of Apple produce, including the Mac, iPod and iPhone. Provides news, reviews, product guides and other information relating to the industry. Every issue brings reviews of the latest Mac kit, help and advice on Apple applications, and a disc contains full programs and the latest demos. Read by users of Apple Mac computers and those with an interest in computer hardware and software.
Ad Rate: Full Page Colour £1825.00
MAGAZINE
Apple

Machine 2 Machine
987531
Editorial: 20-22 Wenlock Road, London N1 7GU Tel: 44 02089 383258
Email: info@m2mmagazine.co.uk
Web site: www.machinetomachinemagazine.com
Freq: Monthly Not Audited
MAGAZINE
Electronics, Healthcare Industry, Industry, Manufacturing

Machine Knitting Monthly
981944
Editorial: P.O.Box 1479, Maidenhead, Maidenhead SL6 8YX Tel: 44 01628 783080
Email: mail@machineknittingmonthly.net
Web site: www.machineknittingmonthly.net
Freq: Monthly Not Audited
Editor: Anne Smith
Profile: Magazine covering all aspects of machine knitting. Includes patterns and product reviews. Aimed at machine knitters of all ages.
Ad Rate: Full Page Mono £464.00
Ad Rate: Full Page Colour £512.00
MAGAZINE
Crafts

Macho Zapp
1054306
Editorial: Unit 5125, PO Box 4336, Manchester M61 0BW
Email: hello@machozapp.com
Web site: http://www.machozapp.com/features
Freq: Daily
Circ: 377 Cision Digital Reach
Editor: Dan Leach
MAGAZINE (ONLINE)
Classical/Choral/Band Music, Country, Folk, Bluegrass, Dance Music, Jazz & Blues, Music, R&B, Urban, World, Rock Music

Macworld (UK)
981312
Editorial: 7th Floor, Clifton House, 101 Euston Road, London NW1 2RA
Tel: 44 02077 562800
Email: news@macworld.co.uk
Web site: www.macworld.co.uk
Freq: Monthly
Circ: 5000 Not Audited
Editor: Neil Bennett
MAGAZINE
Apple, Electronics

Mad Cornish Projectionist
1064289
Tel: 44 07747 193447
Email: webmaster@madcornishprojectionist.co.uk

Web site: www.madcornishprojectionist.co.uk
Freq: Daily
Circ: 8748 Cision Digital Reach
MAGAZINE (ONLINE)
Movies & Video

MadDogSki.com
990570
Editorial: MadDogSki, 3rd Floor, 86-90 Paul Street, London EC2A 4NE
Tel: 44 08450 542906
Email: info@maddogski.com
Web site: www.maddogski.com
Freq: Daily
Circ: 7718 Cision Digital Reach
MAGAZINE (ONLINE)
Winter Sports

MADE (Mums and Dads Edinburgh)
999351
Editorial: PO Box 28825, Edinburgh EH14 9BA Tel: 44 07738 068022
Email: mademag@live.co.uk
Web site: www.mademagazine.co.uk
Freq: Bi-Monthly
Circ: 30000 Not Audited
Editor: Louise Wilson
MAGAZINE
Family & Parenting

Made in Shoreditch Magazine
987495
Editorial: 35 Kingsland Road, London E2 8AA
Email: info@madeinshoreditch.co.uk
Web site: www.madeinshoreditch.co.uk
Freq: Daily
Circ: 44919 Cision Digital Reach
MAGAZINE (ONLINE)
Regional General Interest

MadeForMums
985157
Editorial: Vineyard House, 44 Brook Green, Hammersmith, London W6 7BT
Tel: 44 02071 505000
Email: editor@madeformums.com
Web site: www.madeformums.com
Freq: Daily
Circ: 700385 Cision Digital Reach
MAGAZINE (ONLINE)
Family & Parenting

The Mag
000610
Editorial: Toffee Factory, Lower Steenbergs Yard, Quayside, Newcastle upon Tyne NE1 2DF Tel: 44 01914 324409
Email: enquiries@themag.co.uk
Web site: www.themag.co.uk
Freq: Daily
Circ: 163820 Cision Digital Reach
Editor: Mark Jensen
MAGAZINE (ONLINE)
Soccer

The Magdalen
983829
Editorial: Dundee University Students Assoc., Airlie Place, Dundee DD1 4HP
Tel: 44 01382 386060
Email: themagdalen@dusa.co.uk
Web site: https://dusamedia.com/the-magdalen/
Freq: Monthly
Circ: 4500 Not Audited
Profile: Magazine covering news around the campus, arts and culture, sport, music and general interest.
Ad Rate: Full Page Colour £400.00
MAGAZINE
Alumni, Student Lifestyle

MaggieSemple.com
999164
Editorial: 4 Goodwin's Court, Off St Martins Lane, London WC2N 4LL
Tel: 44 02078 366001
Email: jenna@maggiesemple.com
Web site: www.maggiesemple.com
Freq: Daily
Circ: 14570 Cision Digital Reach
MAGAZINE (ONLINE)
Fashion

Consumer Magazines

Magicseaweed 1097883
Editorial: Magicseaweed Unit 7, Station Yard Industrial Estate, Kingsbridge TQ7 1ES
Tel: 44 01548 854660
Email: press@magicseaweed.com
Web site: http://magicseaweed.com/
Freq: Daily
Circ: 1436436 Cision Digital Reach
Editor: Ed Temperley
MAGAZINE (ONLINE)
Swimming/Watersports

Magnet 982537
Editorial: 70 New Town, Uckfield, Uckfield TN22 5DE **Tel:** 44 08458 722885
Email: magnet@magnetpublications.co.uk
Web site: www.magnetpublications.co.uk
Freq: Monthly
Circ: 25000 Not Audited
Editor: Adele Trathan
Profile: Local interest magazine featuring events listings, lifestyle articles and news.
Ad Rate: Full Page Colour £850.00
MAGAZINE
Regional General Interest

MAGNIFY 988662
Email: info@hellomagnify.com
Web site: http://hellomagnify.com/
Freq: Semi-Annual
Circ: 8000 Not Audited
MAGAZINE
Fashion, Religion, Women's Interests

Maiden Voyage 1104361
Editorial: maiden-voyage.com Ltd, 1st Floor, Elizabeth House, 13-19 Queen Street, Leeds LS1 2TW **Tel:** 44 01133 149000
Email: press@maiden-voyage.org
Web site: http://www.maiden-voyage.com
Freq: Daily
Circ: 10103 Cision Digital Reach
MAGAZINE (ONLINE)
Airline Inflight, Railroad, Travel

Maidstone and Medway News 997365
Editorial: Westcliffe House, West Cliff Gardens, Folkestone, Folkestone CT20 1SZ
Tel: 44 01303 851658
Email: newsdesk.maidstone@krnmedia.co.uk
Web site: http://www.kentlive.news/medway
Freq: Daily Cision Digital Reach
MAGAZINE (ONLINE)
Regional

Majesty 986502
Editorial: 29 Lincoln's Inn Fields, London WC2A 3EG **Tel:** 44 02074 364006
Email: mail@majestymagazine.com
Web site: www.majestymagazine.com
Freq: Monthly
Circ: 80000 Not Audited
Profile: Magazine containing articles about the personalities and lifestyles of the British and worldwide royal families. Aimed at those interested in the monarchy in Britain and worldwide.
Ad Rate: Full Page Colour £2000.00
MAGAZINE
Royalty

Make It Today 997431
Editorial: 1 Phoenix Court, Hawkins Road, Colchester CO2 8JY **Tel:** 44 01206 505494
Email: jane.goulding@aceville.co.uk
Web site: www.makeittoday.co.uk
Freq: Monthly
Circ: 25000 Not Audited
MAGAZINE
Crafts

Making Cards 981945
Editorial: The Maltings, West Street, Bourne, Bourne PE10 9PH **Tel:** 44 01778 391000
Web site: www.makingcardsmagazine.com
Freq: Monthly
Circ: 21000 Not Audited
Profile: Publication that covers the latest techniques, projects, ideas and inspiration

from the world of card making and paper crafts.
MAGAZINE
Crafts

Making Jewellery 985078
Editorial: 86 High Street, Lewes, Lewes BN7 1XN **Tel:** 44 01273 477374
Email: makingjewellery@thegmcgroup.com
Web site: www.makingjewellery.com
Freq: Monthly
Circ: 25000 Not Audited
Editor: Sian Hamilton
Profile: Magazine featuring projects, techniques, inspiration and expert guidance to make jewellery. Aimed at anybody with an interest in jewellery making.
MAGAZINE
Crafts

MaleXtra 983620
Editorial: 69-71 Gerard Street, Ashton-in-Makerfield, Wigan WN4 9AG
Tel: 44 01942 712000
Web site: www.malextra.com
Freq: Daily
Circ: 37770 Cision Digital Reach
Profile: Website covering men's lifestyle. The website discusses the latest news and information on men's interest such as sports, motoring, entertainment, celebrity and fashion.
MAGAZINE (ONLINE)
Celebrities, Men's Interests

mallowstreet 999540
Editorial: 125 Old Broad Street, 26th Floor, London EC2N 1AR **Tel:** 44 02034 638098
Email: hello@mallowstreet.com
Web site: http://www.mallowstreet.com/
Freq: Daily
Circ: 2303 Cision Digital Reach
MAGAZINE (ONLINE)
Fund Management

Mama Style 1054017
Email: editor@mama-style.co.uk
Web site: www.mama-style.co.uk
Freq: Daily
Circ: 15585 Cision Digital Reach
Editor: Danielle Carstairs
MAGAZINE (ONLINE)
Family & Parenting

Man About Town 984794
Editorial: Studio F, Rochelle School, Arnold Circus, London E2 7ES
Tel: 44 02072 439966
Web site: www.manabouttown.tv
Freq: Semi-Annual
Circ: 160000 Not Audited
Profile: Magazine covering fashion, style, art, film and design. Aimed at men with a high disposable income.
Ad Rate: Full Page Mono £7000.00
Ad Rate: Full Page Colour £7000.00
MAGAZINE
Fashion, Men's Interests

MAN London 1104595
Email: reception@man.london
Web site: www.man.london/
Freq: Quarterly Not Audited
MAGAZINE
Luxury Goods, Men's Interests

Man Made Lifestyle 1061516
Email: toimitus@manmadelifestyle.com
Web site: http://www.manmadelifestyle.com/
Freq: Daily
Circ: 3549 Cision Digital Reach
MAGAZINE (ONLINE)
Alcohol & Spirits, Antiques/Collectibles, Art, Arts, Consumer Goods & Products, Food, Literature, Men's Interests, Photography, Theater & Performing Arts

MAN v FAT 996823
Tel: 44 08000 209535
Email: hello@manvfat.com
Web site: manvfat.com
Freq: Daily

Circ: 22685 Cision Digital Reach
Editor: Andrew Shanahan
MAGAZINE (ONLINE)
Men's Interests, Nutrition

Management Decision 998856
Editorial: Howard House, Wagon Lane, Bingley BD16 1WA **Tel:** 44 01274 777700
Web site: http://www.emeraldgrouppublishing.com/products/journals/journals.htm?id=md
Freq: Monthly Not Audited
MAGAZINE
News & Current Affairs

The Manager 999837
Tel: 44 01283 576350
Email: lma@lmasecure.com
Web site: www.leaguemanagers.com
Freq: Quarterly
Circ: 10000 Not Audited
MAGAZINE
Fitness & Exercise, Soccer

Managing Leisure 998517
Editorial: 4 Park Square, Milton Park, Didcot OX14 4RN **Tel:** 44 02070 176000
Web site: http://www.tandfonline.com/toc/rmle20/current#.VSuB7NzF_hd
Freq: Bi-Monthly Not Audited
MAGAZINE
Bars, Clubs & Pubs, Computer & Video Games, Fitness & Exercise, Genealogy, Hotels/Motels, Leisure Activities, Music, Travel

Manchester Confidential 999101
Editorial: Second Floor, Castlefield House, Liverpool Road, Manchester M3 4SB
Tel: 44 01618 322880
Email: editorial1@confidentials.com
Web site: http://confidentials.com/manchester/
Freq: Daily
MAGAZINE (ONLINE)
Regional General Interest

Manchester Gossip 999624
Editorial: Express Networks, 1 George Leigh Street, Manchester M4 5DL
Email: editor@manchestergossip.com
Web site: www.manchestergossip.com
Freq: Daily
Circ: 846 Cision Digital Reach
Editor: Craig Nelson
MAGAZINE (ONLINE)
Celebrities, Regional

Manchester Select Traveller 996577
Editorial: 3 Bridgebank Industrial Estate, Taylor Street, Horwich, Horwich BL6 7PD
Tel: 44 01204 478817
Web site: http://www.selecttravelmedia.com/magazines/manchester/
Freq: Quarterly
Circ: 10000 Not Audited
Editor: Jayne Meadowcroft
MAGAZINE
Airline Inflight

Mancunian Matters 987120
Editorial: Barclay House, 35 Whitworth Street West, Manchester M1 5NG
Tel: 44 01619 717768
Email: newsdesk@mancunianmatters.co.uk
Web site: www.mancunianmatters.co.uk
Freq: Daily
Circ: 76277 Cision Digital Reach
MAGAZINE (ONLINE)
Regional, Regional General Interest

The Mancunion 981775
Editorial: The Mancunion, University of Manchester Students' Union, Oxford Road, Manchester M13 9PR **Tel:** 44 01612 752943
Email: editor@mancunion.com
Web site: www.mancunion.com
Freq: Weekly Not Audited
Profile: Official student newspaper of Greater Manchester. The magazine covers news, features, lifestyle, travel, sport, music

and art. Also includes clubbing, film and television, culture and the Internet.
Ad Rate: Full Page Mono £1139.00
Ad Rate: Full Page Colour £1500.00
MAGAZINE
Student Lifestyle

MANOR 997296
Editorial: MANOR Publishing Ltd, Broadmeadow, Drewsteignton, Exeter EX6 6QW
Email: info@manormagazine.co.uk
Web site: http://www.manormagazine.co.uk/
Freq: Quarterly
Circ: 20000 Not Audited
MAGAZINE
Beauty & Grooming, Cosmetics, Do-It-Yourself (DIY), Fashion, Hair, Lifestyle, Men's Interests, Regional General Interest, Women's Interests

Mantality Magazine 1076160
Email: hello@mantalitymagazine.com
Web site: www.mantalitymagazine.com
Freq: Weekly
Circ: 28479 Not Audited
MAGAZINE
Fitness & Exercise, Men's Interests

MAP 981881
Editorial: 350 Sauchiehall Street, Glasgow G2 3JD
Email: info@mapmagazine.co.uk
Web site: www.mapmagazine.co.uk
Freq: Daily
Circ: 11337 Cision Digital Reach
MAGAZINE (ONLINE)
Art

Marfa Journal 997345
Email: contact@marfajournal.com
Web site: www.marfajournal.com
Freq: Semi-Annual Not Audited
MAGAZINE
Art, Fashion, Photography

marie claire 982374
Editorial: 161 Marsh Wall, London E14 9AP
Tel: 44 02031 485000
Email: inbox@marieclaire.co.uk
Web site: www.marieclaire.co.uk
Freq: Monthly
Circ: 155723 Not Audited
Profile: Fashion magazine covering style. It features fashion and beauty articles, with everything from catwalk to high street. It also covers broader women's interest topics, from careers to celebrity interviews. First published in 1988. Aimed at professional women aged 25-34, with an inclination to spend on clothes and cosmetics.
Ad Rate: Full Page Colour £16500.00
MAGAZINE
Women's Interests

marie claire RUNWAY 986418
Editorial: Blue Fin Building, 110 Southwark Street, London SE1 0SU
Tel: 44 02031 485000
Web site: www.marieclaire.co.uk
Freq: Semi-Annual
Circ: 48000 Not Audited
MAGAZINE
Fashion

Marina 988587
Editorial: 130 Old Street, London EC1V 9BD
Tel: 44 01823 974308
Email: info@marinamag.com
Web site: http://www.marinamag.com/
Freq: Monthly Not Audited
MAGAZINE
Boating & Yachting

Marina World 981338
Editorial: School Farm, School Road, Terrington, St John, Reigate PE14 7SJ
Tel: 44 01945 881018
Web site: www.marinaworld.co.uk
Freq: Bi-Monthly
Circ: 6882 Not Audited

Profile: Magazine featuring news led coverage on new marina developments, emerging marina markets and marinas around the world. Aimed at marina planners, owners, managers and developers; equipment suppliers; key industry associations; municipal authorities developing waterfronts worldwide; and marinaservice providers.
Ad Rate: Full Page Colour £2020.00
MAGAZINE
Marine & Boat Trade

Marine & Energy Risk   996362
Editorial: World Business Media Limited, 46 New Broad Street, London EC2M 1JH
Email: reinsuranceasia@wbmediagroup.com
Freq: Quarterly
Circ: 4000 Not Audited
MAGAZINE
Insurance, Marine & Boat Trade

Marine & Offshore Technology   999546
Editorial: 2nd Floor Front, 116-118 Chancery Lane, London WC2A 1PP
Tel: 44 02037 944581
Email: editor@marineoffshoretechnology.net
Web site: www.marineoffshoretechnology.net
Freq: Quarterly
Circ: 35000 Not Audited
MAGAZINE
Marine & Boat Trade

Marine Catering Technology International   1062745
Tel: 44 01306 743744
Web site: http://www.ukipme.com/pub-marine.php?mag=2
Freq: Semi-Annual
Circ: 10000 Not Audited
MAGAZINE
Marine & Boat Trade

Marine Conservation   984542
Editorial: Overross House, Ross Park, Ross-on-Wye, Ross-on-Wye HR9 7US
Tel: 44 01989 566017
Email: info@mcsuk.org
Web site: www.mcsuk.org
Freq: Quarterly
Circ: 6000 Not Audited
Editor: Richard Harrington
Profile: Official magazine of the Marine Conservation Society, featuring articles on habitat and species conservation, education and project news.
Ad Rate: Full Page Colour £760.00
MAGAZINE
Energy & Environment

Marine Electronics & Communications   984534
Editorial: Mitre House, 66 Abbey Road, Enfield EN1 2QN **Tel:** 44 02083 641551
Web site: www.marinemec.com
Freq: Bi-Monthly
Circ: 10337 Not Audited
Editor: Martyn Wingrove
MAGAZINE
Marine & Boat Trade

Marine Maintenance Technology International   1062739
Editorial: Abinger House, Church Street, Dorking RH4 1DF **Tel:** 44 01306 743744
Web site: http://www.ukipme.com/pub-marine.php?mag=3
Freq: Semi-Annual
Circ: 10000 Not Audited
MAGAZINE
Marine & Boat Trade

Marine Modelling International   988837
Editorial: Traplet House, Willow End Park, Blackmore Park Road, Malvern WR13 6NN
Tel: 44 01684 588500
Email: mmi@traplet.com
Web site: http://gb.trapletshop.com/mmi-magazine

Freq: Monthly Not Audited
Editor: Barrie Stevens
Profile: Magazine containing an overall view of marine modelling.
Ad Rate: Full Page Mono £336.00
Ad Rate: Full Page Colour £653.00
MAGAZINE
Crafts, Hobbies, & Collecting

The Marine Professional   988645
Editorial: Unit G4, Harbour Yard, Chelsea Harbour, London SW10 0XD
Tel: 44 02070 457530
Email: marine@caspianmedia.com
Web site: www.imarest.org/themarineprofessional
Freq: Monthly
Circ: 17214 Not Audited
MAGAZINE
Marine & Boat Trade

Marine Propulsion & Auxiliary Machinery   980911
Editorial: Mitre House, 66 Abbey Road, Enfield, London EN1 2QN
Tel: 44 02083 641551
Web site: http://www.rivieramm.com/publications/marine-propulsion-and-auxiliary-machinery-6
Freq: Bi-Monthly
Circ: 15250 Not Audited
Editor: Paul Fanning
Profile: Magazine covering the latest developments in marine propulsion systems and auxiliary shipboard machinery. Aimed at maritime engineers, ship operators, naval architects and consultants.
Ad Rate: Full Page Colour £2485.00
MAGAZINE
Engineering, Marine & Boat Trade

Marine Trader   984813
Editorial: East Bridge House, East Street Colchester, Colchester CO1 2TX
Tel: 44 01206 798907
Web site: impa.net/marine-trader
Freq: Monthly
Circ: 2500 Not Audited
Editor: Tom Holmes
Profile: Journal of the International Marine Purchasing Association. Covers many aspects of the marine industry but with an emphasis on marine purchasing. Read by members of the International Marine Purchasing Association.
Ad Rate: Full Page Colour £1780.00
MAGAZINE
Marine & Boat Trade

Maritime Journal   980825
Tel: 44 01329 825335
Email: editor@maritimejournal.com
Web site: www.maritimejournal.com
Freq: Monthly
Circ: 6197 Not Audited
Editor: Jake Frith
Profile: Magazine dedicated to the European, in-shore, off-shore coastal zone and short sea commercial maritime business.
Ad Rate: Full Page Colour £2765.00
MAGAZINE
Marine & Boat Trade

Marjonsu.co.uk   995820
Editorial: Marjon Student Union, Derriford Road, Plymouth, Plymouth PL6 8BH
Tel: 44 01752 636771
Web site: www.marjonsu.com
Freq: Daily
Circ: 7869 Cision Digital Reach
MAGAZINE (ONLINE)
Student Lifestyle

Market Leader   982951
Editorial: 85 Newman Street, London W1T 3EY **Tel:** 44 02074 678100
Email: market_leader@warc.com
Web site: www.warc.com/MarketLeader
Freq: Quarterly
Circ: 4000 Not Audited

Editor: Judie Lannon
MAGAZINE
Advertising Industry, Branding, Broadcasting, Graphic Design, Marketing, Media & Communications, Photography, Publishing

The Marketing Site   1060651
Email: winn@themarketingsite.com
Web site: http://www.themarketingsite.com
Circ: 37356 Cision Digital Reach
MAGAZINE (ONLINE)
Business, Marketing, National News, Small and Medium Business

MarketingWorld   1055941
Editorial: 10 Mayfield Road, Belvedere, London DA17 6DX **Tel:** 44 01322 683229
Web site: www.marketingworldmag.com
Freq: Monthly
Circ: 2000 Not Audited
MAGAZINE
Advertising Industry, Branding, Broadcasting, Marketing, Publishing

marksandspencer.com   988494
Editorial: Level 7, 5 Merchant Square, London W2 1AS
Web site: www.marksandspencer.com/c/style-and-living
Freq: Daily
Circ: 7017 Cision Digital Reach
Editor: Rachel Sullivan
MAGAZINE (ONLINE)
Shopping

Marksman Style   988589
Email: mark@marksmanstyle.com
Web site: www.marksmanstyle.com/
Freq: Daily
Circ: 3079 Cision Digital Reach
MAGAZINE (ONLINE)
Fashion, Men's Interests

The Marshwood Vale Magazine   984840
Editorial: Lower Atrim, Bridport, Bridport DT6 5PX **Tel:** 44 01308 423031
Web site: www.marshwoodvale.com
Freq: Monthly
Circ: 25000 Not Audited
Editor: Fergus Byrne
Profile: Magazine for the community covering local events, arts and entertainment, food, dining, house, gardens, health and environment.
Ad Rate: Full Page Mono £310.00
Ad Rate: Full Page Colour £310.00
MAGAZINE
Regional General Interest

Martial Arts Illustrated   982269
Editorial: 1st Floor, Turnbridge Mills, Quay Street, Huddersfield HD1 6QT
Tel: 44 02081 233414
Email: editor@ciaranjarosz.media
Web site: www.maionline.co.uk
Freq: Monthly
Circ: 30000 Not Audited
Editor: Bob Sykes; **Editor:** Bob Sykes
Profile: Magazine covering articles on techniques, tournament results and martial arts profiles.
Ad Rate: Full Page Colour £400.00
MAGAZINE
Martial Arts, MMA & Self-Defense

Marvel Play Time   1075510
Tel: 44 01892 500100
Email: ehammond@panini.co.uk
Web site: http://www.paninicomics.co.uk/web/guest/catalogues/collection_detail?id=88904
Freq: Monthly
Circ: 55000 Not Audited
Editor: Ed Hammond
MAGAZINE
Cartoons, Elementary School, Teen/Young Adult, Trading Cards & Comics

Marvel Super Heroes   1098311
Tel: 44 01892 500100
Email: collectorsed@panini.co.uk

Web site: http://www.paninicomics.co.uk/web/guest/catalogues/collection_detail?id=42329
Freq: Monthly
Circ: 35000 Not Audited
MAGAZINE
Trading Cards & Comics

The Marylebone & Fitzrovia Magazine   1097886
Tel: 44 02079 874320
Email: Info@rwmg.co.uk
Web site: rwmg.co.uk/website/advertising_montly_titles.php
Freq: Monthly
Circ: 50000 Not Audited
MAGAZINE
Luxury Goods, Regional General Interest

The Marylebone Journal   984686
Editorial: Unit 13.2.1 The Leather Market, Weston Street, London SE1 3ER
Tel: 44 02074 017297
Web site: www.marylebonejournal.com
Freq: Bi-Monthly
Circ: 25000 Not Audited
Editor: Mark Riddaway
Profile: Journal featuring articles covering the culture, history, food, architecture, property and shops of Marylebone. Aimed at those living in or around Marylebone and those who shop and relax there.
Ad Rate: Full Page Colour £1100.00
MAGAZINE
Regional General Interest

Mass Movement   995871
Email: info@massmovement.co.uk
Web site: www.massmovement.co.uk
Freq: Quarterly
Circ: 20000 Not Audited
Editor: Tim Cundle
MAGAZINE
Rock Music

Master Detective   988132
Editorial: PO Box 735, London SE26 5NQ
Tel: 44 02087 780514
Email: enquiries@truecrimelibrary.com
Web site: http://www.truecrimelibrary.com/
Freq: Monthly Not Audited
Profile: Magazine covering all aspects of criminology. Aimed at those interested in criminology.
MAGAZINE
Crime & Violence

Masterchefs   984106
Editorial: Woodmans, Brithem Bottom, Cullompton, Tiverton EX15 1NB
Tel: 44 07887 984849
Email: masterchefs@msn.com
Web site: www.masterchefs.co.uk
Freq: Annual
Circ: 3000 Not Audited
Editor: Susan McGeever
MAGAZINE
Bars, Clubs & Pubs, Cooking & Baking, Hotels/Motels

Match Day   1060672
Tel: 44 27214 160141
Email: gary@hsm.co.za Not Audited
MAGAZINE
Basketball, Bicycles, Billiards, Boating & Yachting, Bodybuilding, Bowling, Boxing, Cricket, Equestrian Sports, Extreme/Adventure Sports

Match Fishing Magazine   982181
Editorial: 1 Whittle Close, Drayton Fields, Daventry NN11 8RQ **Tel:** 44 01327 311999
Email: match-scene@dhpub.co.uk
Web site: www.matchfishingmagazine.com
Freq: Monthly
Circ: 20400 Not Audited
Profile: Magazine containing technical advice, match fishing news and new product reviews.
MAGAZINE
Fishing

Consumer Magazines

Match of the Day Magazine
984653

Editorial: Vineyard House, 44 Brook Green, London W6 7BT **Tel:** 44 02071 505000
Email: shout@motdmag.com
Web site: www.motdmag.com
Freq: Weekly
Circ: 43016 Not Audited
Editor: Ian Foster
Profile: Magazine covering football skills, features on players, news and gossip as well as competitions, posters and quizzes. Aimed at girls and boys aged 8 to 14 years old.
MAGAZINE
Soccer

MATCH!
982251

Editorial: Media House, Lynchwood, Peterborough Business Park, Peterborough PE2 6EA **Tel:** 44 01733 468008
Email: match.magazine@bauermedia.co.uk
Web site: matchmag.co.uk
Freq: Weekly
Circ: 18803 Not Audited
Editor: James Bandy
MAGAZINE
Soccer

Materials World
981028

Editorial: 297 Euston Road, London NW1 3AQ **Tel:** 44 02074 517300
Email: materials.world@iom3.org
Web site: www.iom3.org/materialsworld
Freq: Monthly
Circ: 13150 Not Audited
Profile: Official magazine of the Institute of Materials, Minerals and Mining. Covering the latest developments in engineering materials worldwide. Includes advanced materials; metals, composites, ceramics, plastics and rubber. Also covers the primary extraction industries, minerals and mining industries and related technologies such as composite engineering. Read by members of the Institute as well as materials scientists, technologists and engineers in industry, research and education.
Ad Rate: Full Page Mono £1470.00
Ad Rate: Full Page Colour £2120.00
MAGAZINE
Engineering, Manufacturing, Marine & Boat Trade, Mining & Quarrying, Paper, Plastics, Science, Steel

Maternal and Child Nutrition
998775

Editorial: Maternal and Child Nutrition Editorial Office, Maternal and Infant Nutrition and Nurture Unit (MAINN), Brook Building, University of Central Lancashire, Preston PR1 2HE **Tel:** 44 01772 893830
Email: mcnjournal@uclan.ac.uk
Web site: http://onlinelibrary.wiley.com/journal/10.1111/(ISSN)1740-8709
Freq: Quarterly Not Audited
MAGAZINE
Nutrition, Pediatrics

Maternity Buyer
997438

Editorial: Saunders House, 52-53 The Mall, London W5 3TA **Tel:** 44 02087 350855
Email: liz@maternitybuyer.com
Web site: http://www.maternitybuyer.co.uk/
Freq: Daily
Circ: 8830 Cision Digital Reach
Editor: Liz Pilgrim
MAGAZINE (ONLINE)
Fashion

MaternityCover.com
999620

Tel: 44 02070 991800
Email: info@maternitycover.com
Web site: www.maternitycover.com
Freq: Daily
Circ: 1660 Cision Digital Reach
MAGAZINE (ONLINE)
Careers, Recruiting

Mathematics Teaching
981531

Editorial: Unit 7, Prime Industrial Park, Shaftesbury Street, Derby DE23 8YB
Tel: 44 01332 346599
Email: journaleditor@atm.org.uk

Web site: http://www.atm.org.uk/Mathematics-Teaching-Journal-Archive/Mathematics-Teaching-Journal-Archive
Freq: Bi-Monthly
Circ: 3000 Not Audited
MAGAZINE
Disability, Education, Higher Education, Preschool, Schools & Institutions, Students

matthewjukes.com
1075813

Editorial: 86 Eaton Terrace, London SW1W 8UG **Tel:** 44 02077 300201
Web site: www.matthewjukes.com
Freq: Daily
Circ: 18064 Cision Digital Reach
MAGAZINE (ONLINE)
Wine/Winemaking

Mature Times
983681

Editorial: Unit 6, Railway Wharf, Station Road, Wrington, Bristol BS40 5LL
Tel: 44 01934 864410
Email: editorial@maturetimes.co.uk
Web site: www.maturetimes.co.uk
Freq: Monthly
Circ: 200000 Not Audited
Profile: Magazine covering campaigns on issues such as ageism, council tax, pensions and healthcare as well as sections dedicated to lifestyle issues of genuine interest to mature readers including finance, health and beauty, property, motoring, holidays and leisure, the home, mobility, pets, crosswords, puzzles and competitions. Aimed at the over 50s.
Ad Rate: Full Page Colour £5250.00
MAGAZINE
Retirement Savings

Maverick
982076

Tel: 44 01622 823920
Email: info@maverick-country.com
Web site: www.maverick-country.com
Freq: Monthly
Circ: 20000 Not Audited
Profile: Magazine covering American country and roots music news including album reviews, tour dates, gig reports and artist profiles.
MAGAZINE
Country, Folk, Bluegrass

Maximum Pop!
999354

Editorial: Laura Fulton, 2 Springfort Lodge, Dollingstown, Craigavon BT66 7BE
Web site: www.maximumpop.co.uk
Freq: Daily
Circ: 164597 Cision Digital Reach
MAGAZINE (ONLINE)
Elementary School, Fashion, Literature, Movies & Video, Pop Music, Preschool, Teen/Young Adult, Trading Cards & Comics

The Mayfair Magazine
986459

Editorial: Level 6, One Canada Square, Canary Wharf, London E14 5AB
Tel: 44 02079 874320
Email: info@rwmg.co.uk
Web site: www.rwmg.co.uk
Freq: Monthly
Circ: 50000 Not Audited
Profile: Regional lifestyle publiation covering fashion, food and drink and motoring news.
MAGAZINE
Luxury Goods, Regional General Interest

Mayfair Times
980414

Editorial: 3 Princes Street, London W1B 2LD
Tel: 44 02072 591050
Email: mayfair.times@pubbiz.com
Web site: http://www.mayfairtimes.co.uk/
Freq: Monthly
Circ: 21218 Not Audited
Editor: Selma Day
Profile: Lifestyle magazine containing news, celebrity interviews, fashion, health and beauty, food and drink, art and antiques, events, theatre and business in and around the West End of London.
Ad Rate: Full Page Colour £1550.00
MAGAZINE
Regional General Interest

The Mayhew
982006

Editorial: Trenmar Gardens, London NW10 6BJ **Tel:** 44 02089 628000
Email: info@mayhewanimalhome.org
Web site: www.mayhewanimalhome.org
Freq: 3 Times/Year
Circ: 9000 Not Audited
Profile: Magazine of the Mayhew Animal Home, containing features about animal welfare and events.
Ad Rate: Full Page Colour £1500.00
MAGAZINE
Charitable Foundations, Nature & Wildlife

MCA
980748

Editorial: Broadfield Park, Crawley, Crawley RH11 9RT **Tel:** 44 01293 613400
Web site: www.mca-insight.com
Freq: Monthly
Circ: 15896 Cision Digital Reach
Editor: Mark Wingett
MAGAZINE (ONLINE)
Bars, Clubs & Pubs, Retail Management

MCM BUZZ
997947

Web site: http://www.mymbuzz.com/
Freq: Daily
Circ: 17256 Cision Digital Reach
Editor: Stuart Claw
MAGAZINE (ONLINE)
Movies & Video, Trading Cards & Comics

MCN
982653

Editorial: Media House, Lynchwood, Peterborough Business Park, Peterborough PE2 6EA **Tel:** 44 01733 468000
Email: mcn@motorcyclenews.com
Web site: www.motorcyclenews.com
Freq: Weekly
Circ: 74503 Not Audited
Editor: Michael Guy
MAGAZINE
Motorcycles

MCV
981313

Editorial: The Emerson Building, 4th Floor, 4-8 Emerson Street, London SE1 9DU
Tel: 44 02038 717388
Email: mcv@nbmedia.com
Web site: www.mcvuk.com
Freq: Weekly
Circ: 14000 Not Audited
Profile: Website covering all latest news from games industry.
MAGAZINE
Computer & Video Games, Computers, Electronics, Software

Meade
988650

Email: fossy@meadeonline.com
Web site: http://meadeonline.com/
Freq: Daily Not Audited
MAGAZINE
Fashion, Men's Interests, Women's Interests

Medal News
985723

Editorial: Orchard House, Duchy Road, Heathpark, Honiton EX14 1YD
Tel: 44 01404 46972
Email: info@tokenpublishing.com
Web site: www.tokenpublishing.com/medals.asp
Freq: Monthly Not Audited
Profile: Magazine containing information on the market scene, profiles on medals and those they were awarded to, a badges section and a medal tracker service that allows readers to locate lost medals. Aimed at medallists, military historians, collectors and dealers.This magazine contains the following regular features: Stop thief - Section for recently stolen medals which helps police and owners reclaim their property.
Ad Rate: Full Page Mono £315.00
Ad Rate: Full Page Colour £640.00
MAGAZINE
Antiques/Collectibles

Media and Technology Digest
996151

Editorial: Ropemaker Place, 25 Ropemaker Street, London EC2Y 9LY
Tel: 44 02072 602000
Web site: technology.ihs.com/424257/media-technology-digest-pdf-only
Freq: Monthly Not Audited
MAGAZINE
Industry, Internet, Mobile Communications

Media Diversified
1053357

Email: mediadiversityuk@gmail.com
Web site: www.mediadiversified.org
Freq: Daily
Circ: 41857 Cision Digital Reach
MAGAZINE (ONLINE)
Africa, Asia

Media Lawyer
983239

Editorial: 292 Vauxhall Bridge Road, London SW1V 1AE **Tel:** 44 02079 637000
Email: medialawyer@pressassociation.com
Web site: www.medialawyer.press.net
Freq: Bi-Monthly
Circ: 450 Not Audited
Editor: Mike Dodd
Profile: Newsletter covering libel, contempt of court, reporting restrictions, data protection, privacy and other media law topics. The printed newsletter provides notes and reports on media law developments and cases in the UK in a two month period. The same material is uploaded on to the website as it happens. Aimed at media lawyers, editors, journalists, journalism trainers and media academics.
Ad Rate: Full Page Mono £1950.00
MAGAZINE
News & Current Affairs

Media Medics
995956

Editorial: Claybrooke, Haywards Pound Hill, Crawley, Crawley RH10 3TR
Tel: 44 01293 889100
Email: info@media-medics.co.uk
Web site: www.media-medics.co.uk
Freq: Daily
Circ: 1623 Cision Digital Reach
MAGAZINE (ONLINE)
Media Relations, Medicine, Nutrition, Psychology

Media+Networks
984507

Editorial: 37-41 Mortimer House, Mortimer Street, London W1T 3JH
Tel: 44 02070 175130
Email: editor@iptv-news.com
Web site: https://knect365.com/media-networks/
Freq: Daily
Circ: 70 Cision Digital Reach
Editor: Thomas Campbell
Profile: Website covering the Internet Protocol Television (IPTV) industry.
MAGAZINE (ONLINE)
Auto Aftermarket, Computers, Data Management, Electronics, Government Technology, Industry, Internet, Mobile Communications, Security & Security Systems, Software

MediaMagazine
983836

Editorial: The English and Media Centre, 18 Compton Terrace, London N1 2UN
Tel: 44 02073 598080
Email: web@englishandmedia.co.uk
Web site: www.mediamagazine.org.uk
Freq: Quarterly Not Audited
Editor: Jenny Grahame
MAGAZINE
Student Lifestyle, Teen/Young Adult

Medical News Today
984449

Editorial: 130 Queens Road, First Floor, Brighton BN1 3WB **Tel:** 44 08454 680075
Email: editors@medicalnewstoday.com
Web site: www.medicalnewstoday.com
Freq: Daily
Circ: 3159420 Cision Digital Reach
Profile: Website covering medical news. The Medical News Today website is an Independent health and medical news

website updated with more than 150 articles on weekdays and 40 articles at the weekend.
MAGAZINE (ONL INF)
AIDS/HIV, Allergies, Alternative Medicine, Anesthesiology, Biotechnology, Cardiology, Community Care (UK), Dentistry, Dermatology, Diabetes

Medicine
981038
Editorial: The Boulevard, Langford Lane, Kidlington OX5 1GB **Tel:** 44 01865 843000
Email: medicine@medicinepublishing.co.uk
Web site: https://www.elsevier.com/journals/medicine/1357-3039
Freq: Monthly
Circ: 2380 Not Audited
Profile: International journal of up-to-date medical information.
Ad Rate: Full Page Mono £863.00
Ad Rate: Full Page Colour £1568.00
MAGAZINE
Medicine

MedTech Engine
1055155
Editorial: The Metal Box Factory, 30 Great Guildford Street, London SE1 0HS
Tel: 44 02037 358915
Web site: https://medtechengine.com
Freq: Daily
Circ: 16540 Cision Digital Reach
MAGAZINE (ONLINE)
News & Current Affairs

Meetings and Incentive Travel
981147
Editorial: Fairway House, Portland Road, East Grinstead, East Grinstead RH19 4ET
Tel: 44 01342 306700
Email: editorial@cat-publications.com
Web site: http://www.meetpie.com/Modules/PublicationModule/MIT/MainPage.aspx
Freq: Bi-Monthly
Circ: 23949 Not Audited
MAGAZINE
Travel

me-me-me.tv
984130
Editorial: 12 Moor Street, London W1D 5NG
Email: info@me-me-me.tv
Web site: www.me-me-me.tv
Freq: Daily
Circ: 19230 Cision Digital Reach
Editor: Stephen Unwin
MAGAZINE (ONLINE)
LGBT

The Memo
996127
Editorial: The Memo, Wayra, 20 Air Street, London W1B 5AN
Email: editorial@thememo.com
Web site: www.thememo.com
Freq: Daily
Circ: 159021 Cision Digital Reach
MAGAZINE (ONLINE)
Auto Aftermarket, Business, Computers, Data Management, Electronics, Government Technology, Industry, Internet, Mobile Communications, Security & Security Systems

Mendip Times
984638
Editorial: Coombe Lodge, Blagdon, Bristol BS40 7RG **Tel:** 44 01761 463888
Email: editor@mendiptimes.co.uk
Web site: www.mendiptimes.co.uk
Freq: Monthly
Circ: 22500 Not Audited
Profile: Free monthly glossy magazine celebrating life on the Mendips and surrounding areas covering local news and people, local history, events and lifestyle.
MAGAZINE
Regional General Interest

Mens Fashion Magazine
988624
Editorial: 74 The Chase, Benfleet, Rayleigh SS7 3BY **Tel:** 44 02081 445850
Email: contributions@mensfashionmagazine.co.uk
Web site: www.mensfashionmagazine.com
Freq: Daily

Circ: 39492 Cision Digital Reach
MAGAZINE (ONLINE)
Fashion, Men's Interests

Men's Fitness
981830
Editorial: 30 Cleveland Street, London W1T 4JD
Web site: http://subscribe.mensfitness.co.uk/
Freq: Monthly
Circ: 30998 Not Audited
Profile: Magazine covering men's physical, mental, emotional and sexual fitness. Contains product reviews and features on sport, travelling, training and healthy eating.
Ad Rate: Full Page Colour £3500.00
MAGAZINE
Fitness & Exercise, Men's Interests

Men's Health
981831
Editorial: 33 Broadwick Street, London W1F 0DQ **Tel:** 44 02074 395000
Email: contact@menshealth.co.uk
Web site: www.menshealth.co.uk
Freq: Monthly
Circ: 174672 Not Audited
Editor: Toby Wiseman
Profile: Magazine providing tips on male fitness, health, sex, career, weight loss and muscle building. Launched in 1995. Targeting active, successful, intelligent men who want to make the most of their physical, professional and emotional lives, the magazine is read by men aged between 25 and 45 years old.
Ad Rate: Full Page Mono £10572.00
Ad Rate: Full Page Colour £5000.00
MAGAZINE
Fitness & Exercise, Men's Interests, Nutrition

Men's Health Forum
985297
Editorial: The Men's Health Forum, 32-36 Loman Street, Southwark, London SE1 0EH
Tel: 44 02079 227908
Web site: http://www.menshealthforum.org.uk
Freq: Daily
Circ: 40273 Cision Digital Reach
Profile: Website covering male health problems.
MAGAZINE (ONLINE)
Patient Support

Men's Running (UK)
985719
Editorial: 1st Floor, Gable House, 18-24 Turnham Green Terrace, Chiswick W4 1QP
Tel: 44 02089 965089
Email: editorial@mensrunninguk.co.uk
Web site: www.mensrunninguk.co.uk
Freq: Monthly
Circ: 9271 Not Audited
MAGAZINE
Fitness & Exercise, Men's Interests, Nutrition

MenStyleFashion
988818
Editorial: 100 Marine Crescent, Worthing, Worthing BN12 4JH **Tel:** 44 01273 915079
Email: contact@menstylefashion.com
Web site: www.menstylefashion.com
Freq: Daily
Circ: 157382 Cision Digital Reach
Editor: Arthur Van De Laak
MAGAZINE (ONLINE)
Fashion, Men's Interests

Mental Gamers
997449
Email: aceman@mentalgamers.com
Web site: www.mentalgamers.com
Freq: Daily
Circ: 1203 Cision Digital Reach
Editor: Darren Harris
MAGAZINE (ONLINE)
Computer & Video Games

Mental Health Review Journal
985230
Editorial: Howard House, Wagon Lane, Bingley BD16 1WA
Web site: http://www.emeraldinsight.com/journal/mhrj
Freq: Quarterly

Editor: Mark Freestone
Profile: Journal featuring case studies, communications updates, news and key developments in mental health policy. Aimed at purchasers, policy analysts, provider managers, senior practitioners, social services and the independent sector.
MAGAZINE
Community Care (UK), Medicine, Neurology, Nursing/Nurses

Menu Magazine Dorset
998340
Editorial: Egdon Hall, Lynch Lane, Weymouth, Weymouth DT4 9DN
Tel: 44 01305 897172
Email: info@menu-dorset.co.uk
Web site: http://www.menu-dorset.co.uk/
Freq: Monthly Not Audited
MAGAZINE
Cooking & Baking, Food, Grocery Stores, Organic Food, Restaurant Reviews, Vegetarianism & Veganism

Mercedes Benz Retail
999306
Editorial: Starline House, 130 Mowbray Drive, Blackpool, Blackpool FY3 7UN
Tel: 44 01253 319882
Email: sales@mmcmedia.com
Web site: www.mmcmedia.com
Freq: Annual
Circ: 20000 Not Audited
MAGAZINE
Automakers, Luxury Goods

Mercedes Enthusiast
982639
Editorial: Sundial House, 17 Wickham Road, Beckenham, London BR3 5JS
Tel: 44 02086 394400
Email: info@mercedesenthusiast.co.uk
Web site: www.mercedesenthusiast.co.uk
Freq: Monthly
Circ: 30000 Not Audited
Editor: Kyle Molyneux
Profile: Magazine covering Mercedes-Benz cars, including related products, events, motorsports and buying information. Aimed at owners, enthusiasts and buyers of classic and contemporary Mercedes cars.
Ad Rate: Full Page Colour £1095.00
MAGAZINE
Automakers

Mercedes Owner
982640
Editorial: Langton Road, Langton Green, Tunbridge Wells, Tunbridge Wells TN3 0EG
Tel: 44 01892 710570
Email: info@mercedesclub.org.uk
Web site: www.mercedesclub.org.uk/magazine.html
Freq: Monthly
Circ: 75000 Not Audited
Editor: Ian Campbell
Profile: Magazine covering news and events in the world of Mercedes-Benz including historical pieces, technical information and reviews. Also features a non-motoring section covering show previews, restaurants and holiday guide. Aimed at owners and potential owners of Mercedes cars.A charge may be made for colour separation. Regular features: Arnie Answer's Technical advice section for readers.; Buying used Advice on buying used Mercedes.; Classic Focus; Model Launches; Newsline News section.; Road Test; Torque Back Readers letters.
Ad Rate: Full Page Colour £745.00
MAGAZINE
Automakers

Mergermarket - Lithuania Bureau
1001328
Circ: 126383 Cision Digital Reach
MAGAZINE (ONLINE)
News & Current Affairs

Meridian Magazine
982512
Editorial: 8 The Village, Charlton, London SE7 8UD **Tel:** 44 02083 190555
Email: editor@meridian-magazine.co.uk
Web site: http://www.meridian-magazine.co.uk
Freq: Monthly
Circ: 50000 Not Audited
Editor: Valerie Breese

Profile: Local interest magazine covering news features in and around Greenwich, Blackheath and Docklands. Provides comprehensive listings and events guide, news and competitions, independent restaurant reviews, regular business, education, health and beauty, fashion, retail and property columns. Aimed at residents of Greenwich, Blackheath and Docklands.This outlet covers areas within Bromley Borough and Tower Hamlets Borough.
Ad Rate: Full Page Colour £1450.00
MAGAZINE
Regional General Interest

Metal-Pages
983905
Editorial: Metal Pages - Argus House, 175 St. John Street, Clerkenwell, London EC1V 4LW **Tel:** 44 02077 804200
Email: editor@metal-pages.com
Web site: www.metal-pages.com
Freq: Daily
Circ: 46648 Cision Digital Reach
Editor: Andi Spicer
MAGAZINE (ONLINE)
Commodities, Engineering, Manufacturing, Marine & Boat Trade, Mining & Quarrying, Paper, Plastics, Steel

Metalreviews.com
995760
Email: contact@metalreviews.com
Web site: www.metalreviews.com
Freq: Daily
Circ: 44749 Cision Digital Reach
MAGAZINE (ONLINE)
Rock Music

MetalSucks
999226
Email: news@metalsucks.net
Web site: www.metalsucks.net
Freq: Daily
Circ: 958244 Cision Digital Reach
MAGAZINE (ONLINE)
Rock Music

Methodist Recorder
985314
Editorial: 3-5 Lambeth Road, London SE1 7DE **Tel:** 44 02077 930033
Email: editorial@methodistrecorder.co.uk
Web site: www.methodistrecorder.co.uk
Freq: Weekly
Circ: 22000 Not Audited
Profile: Newspaper featuring home and worldwide news, articles, reviews and resources for the Methodist church.
MAGAZINE
Religion

Methods Unsound
1054600
Email: contact@methodsunsound.com
Web site: http://www.methodsunsound.com/
Freq: Daily
Circ: 13918 Cision Digital Reach
Editor: Christopher Ratcliff
MAGAZINE (ONLINE)
Entertainment, Movies & Video, Rock Music

Metro Report International
987157
Editorial: 7th Floor, Chancery House, St Nicholas Way, Sutton, London SM1 1JB
Tel: 44 02086 525200
Email: editor@railwaygazette.com
Web site: www.railwaygazette.com/
Freq: Quarterly
Circ: 6000 Not Audited
Editor: Karol Zemek
Profile: Quarterly publication which showcases best practice in light rail, metros, automated peoplemovers and commuter rail.
MAGAZINE
Railroad

Metro.co.uk
997266
Editorial: 3rd Floor Northcliffe House, 2 Derry Street, London W8 5TT
Tel: 44 02079 386000
Web site: metro.co.uk
Freq: Daily
Circ: 13562683 Cision Digital Reach
MAGAZINE (ONLINE)
News & Current Affairs

Consumer Magazines

Metropolitan
985564

Editorial: 6th Floor, 85 Strand, London WC2R 0DW **Tel:** 44 02075 508000
Web site: https://www.cedarcom.co.uk/
Freq: Monthly
Circ: 165000 Not Audited
Editor: Marie-Noelle Bauer
Profile: Magazine distributed on Eurostar covering celebrities and people, ideas, culture, society, fashion, food and travel in London, Paris and Brussels, offering a mix of features and profiles. First published in 2010, the publication has an average of 132 pages per issue. Aimed at passengers on Eurostar train visiting London, Paris and Brussels.
Ad Rate: Full Page Colour £11750.00
MAGAZINE
Railroad, Regional General Interest, Travel

MG Enthusiast
982613

Editorial: Cudham Tithe Barn, Berry's Hill, Cudham TN16 3AG **Tel:** 44 01733 353381
Email: mg.ed@kelseypb.co.uk
Web site: www.mgenthusiast.com
Freq: Monthly
Circ: 15000 Not Audited
Editor: Simon Goldsworthy
Profile: Website providing news and information for the MG car owner or enthusiast. Aimed at people who drive or would like to own an MG car.
MAGAZINE
Antique & Collectible Cars, Automakers

Mgcars.org.uk
998591

Email: mxp@mg-cars.org.uk
Web site: http://www.mg-cars.org.uk/
Freq: Daily
Circ: 125402 Cision Digital Reach
Editor: Mike Plumstead
MAGAZINE (ONLINE)
Antique & Collectible Cars

MI Business Mag
997423

Web site: www.mibusinessmag.com
Freq: Daily
Circ: 14809 Cision Digital Reach
MAGAZINE (ONLINE)
Business, Careers, Men's Interests, Small and Medium Business, Women's Interests

MI Magazine
996500

Editorial: 13 Bayley Street, London WC1B 3HD
Email: marta.j@mimagazine.net
Web site: https://mimagazine.es/
Freq: Daily
Circ: 10501 Cision Digital Reach
MAGAZINE (ONLINE)
Celebrities, Cooking & Baking, Fashion, Fitness & Exercise, Health & Medicine, Travel

MI Pro
981232

Editorial: Saxon House, 6a St Andrews Street, Hertford SG14 1JA
Tel: 44 02038 717374
Web site: http://www.mi-pro.co.uk
Freq: Daily
Circ: 20581 Cision Digital Reach
Editor: Laura Barnes
Profile: Magazine covering news, analysis and opinion on the latest music instrument industry and pro audio issues as well as an overview of stock not yet in the market place. Aimed at those within the professional music instrument and professional audio businesses.
Ad Rate: Full Page Colour £1155.00
MAGAZINE (ONLINE)
Music

Mid Kent Living
986900

Editorial: 2 Forge House, Bearsted Green Business Park, Bearsted, Maidstone ME14 4DT **Tel:** 44 01622 630330
Email: info@downsmail.co.uk
Web site: http://www.downsmail.co.uk/publications/Mid_Kent_Living/
Freq: Quarterly
Circ: 20000 Not Audited

Editor: Simon Finlay
MAGAZINE
Regional General Interest

The Middle East
983741

Editorial: 46 Cleveland Road, London E18 2AL **Tel:** 44 02089 899551
Email: info@themiddleeastmagazine.com
Web site: www.themiddleeastmagazine.com
Freq: Monthly
Circ: 22141 Not Audited
Profile: Magazine reporting on current affairs, business and finance issues, country reports, industry surveys and book reviews from the Middle East region and the Arab world.
Ad Rate: Full Page Colour £5700.00
MAGAZINE
International News, Politics

Middle East Eye
995111

Web site: www.middleeasteye.net
Freq: Daily
Circ: 472297 Cision Digital Reach
MAGAZINE (ONLINE)
International News

The Midlands Rocks
1105208

Email: editorinchief@themidlandsrocks.com
Web site: www.themidlandsrocks.com
Freq: Daily
Circ: 10772 Cision Digital Reach
MAGAZINE (ONLINE)
Rock Music

Midlands What's On
987643

Editorial: 13 - 14 Abbey Foregate, Shrewsbury SY2 6AE **Tel:** 44 01743 281777
Email: info@whatsonlive.co.uk
Web site: www.whatsonlive.co.uk/
Freq: Monthly
Circ: 220000 Not Audited
MAGAZINE
Regional General Interest

Midlands Zone
983313

Editorial: 13-14 Abbey Foregate, Shrewsbury, Shrewsbury SY2 6AE
Tel: 44 01743 281777
Email: info@midlandszone.co.uk
Web site: www.midlandszone.co.uk
Freq: Monthly
Circ: 20000 Not Audited
Editor: Ryan Humphreys
Profile: What's on magazine covering news, film, theatre, music, videos, travel, events and holidays. Aimed at the gay, lesbian and bisexual community in the Midlands.
Ad Rate: Full Page Mono £1030.50
Ad Rate: Full Page Colour £1145.00
MAGAZINE
LGBT, Regional General Interest

The Midult
1097880

Web site: http://themidult.com/
Freq: Daily
Circ: 14321 Cision Digital Reach
MAGAZINE (ONLINE)
Women's Interests

midwivesonline.com
985388

Editorial: DC Thomson & Co. Ltd., 80 Kingsway East, Glasgow DD4 8SL
Email: info@midwivesonline.com
Web site: www.midwivesonline.com
Freq: Daily
Circ: 2177 Cision Digital Reach
Profile: Website covering pregnancy. The midwivesonline.com provides information about starting a family and being on the pregnancy journey. Midwivesonline.com is a midwifery led website for midwives, health care professionals and expectant and new parents. It's hosted by Bright Solid.
MAGAZINE (ONLINE)
Family & Parenting

Mighty World of Marvel
1096555

Editorial: Brockbourne House, 77 Mount Ephraim, Tunbridge Wells, Tunbridge Wells TN4 8BS **Tel:** 44 01892 500100
Email: paninicomics@panini.co.uk

Web site: www.paninicomics.co.uk/web/guest/catalogues/collection_detail?id=42330
Freq: Monthly
Circ: 5430 Not Audited
Editor: Scott Gray
MAGAZINE
Cartoons, Trading Cards & Comics

Mike the Knight
986970

Editorial: Vineyard House, 44 Brook Green, London W6 7BT **Tel:** 44 02071 505000
Web site: http://www.miketheknight.com
Freq: Monthly
Circ: 20000 Not Audited
Editor: Andrea Turton
Profile: Educational children's title aimed at 3-5 year olds based on the CBeebies TV programme of the same name. It covers the medieval world including sticker pages, competitions and medieval historical facts.
MAGAZINE
Preschool

Military History Monthly
985698

Editorial: Thames Works, Church Street, London W4 2PD **Tel:** 44 02088 195580
Email: editorial@military-history.org
Web site: http://www.military-history.org
Freq: Monthly
Circ: 24000 Not Audited
Editor: Neil Faulkner
Profile: Military History Monthly covers the history of war. Aimed at those with an interest in military history.
Ad Rate: Full Page Colour £1200.00
MAGAZINE
Armed Forces

Military Modelling
985467

Editorial: PO Box 718, Orpington, London BR6 1AP **Tel:** 44 01689 869840
Web site: www.militarymodelling.com
Freq: Monthly
Circ: 15000 Not Audited
Profile: Modelling magazine covering miniature military vehicles and model soldiers. Aimed at enthusiasts of military models.
Ad Rate: Full Page Colour £695.00
MAGAZINE
Crafts, Hobbies, & Collecting

Milkround
997191

Editorial: The News Building, News UK, 1 London Bridge Street, London SE1 9GF
Tel: 44 02030 034000
Email: info@milkround.com
Web site: www.milkround.com
Freq: Daily
Circ: 93977 Cision Digital Reach
MAGAZINE (ONLINE)
Alumni, Careers, Education, Student Lifestyle, Teachers

Milkshake! magazine
996450

Editorial: Old Dairy, Peper Harow Park, Nr Godalming, Godalming GU8 6BQ
Tel: 44 01483 779500
Email: milkshake@milkshake.tv
Web site: www.milkshake.tv/content/milkshake-magazine
Freq: Monthly
Circ: 55000 Not Audited
MAGAZINE
Elementary School

MIMS Learning
1052715

Editorial: Bridge House, London Road, Twickenham TW1 3RH
Web site: mimslearning.co.uk
Freq: Monthly
Circ: 35000 Not Audited
Editor: Pat Anderson
MAGAZINE
Health Administration, Medicine, Nursing/Nurses

MINE Magazine
1055142

Editorial: 38 Chiltern Street, London W1U 7QL **Tel:** 44 02074 867870
Email: info@minemagazinelondon.com
Web site: http://www.minemagazinelondon.com/

Freq: Quarterly
Editor: Astrid Joss
Profile: Website covering mining. Mine Magazine is a digital magazine providing the latest information and news on the latest trends and technologies in the mining industry
MAGAZINE
News & Current Affairs

Minecraft Mayhem
1101289

Web site: http://www.futureplc.com/
Freq: Monthly Not Audited
MAGAZINE
Computer & Video Games

Minecraft World
997341

Tel: 44 02079 076000
Web site: www.minecraftworldmagazine.co.uk/
Freq: Monthly
Circ: 45000 Not Audited
Editor: Simon Brew
MAGAZINE
Computer & Video Games

Mineria Camimex
1061510

Tel: 44 52555 5406788
Email: camimex@prodigy.net.mx
Web site: http://www.camimex.org.mx
Freq: Quarterly
Circ: 2500 Not Audited
MAGAZINE
International News, Mining & Quarrying

Minerva
986384

Editorial: 20 Orange Street, London WC2H 7EF **Tel:** 44 02073 890808
Email: editorial@minervamagazine.com
Web site: www.minervamagazine.co.uk
Freq: Bi-Monthly
Circ: 10000 Not Audited
Editor: Lindsay Fulcher
Profile: Magazine containing museum and gallery exhibitions, auction previews and reviews, numismatic reviews, ancient art, book reviews, excavation announcements and archaeological tours. Aimed at practising archaeologists, the general public and those interested in ancient art, archaeology, antiquities and museums.
Ad Rate: Full Page Colour £1000.00
MAGAZINE
History

Mini Magazine (UK)
982641

Editorial: Cudham Tithe Barn, Berry's Hill, Cudham, London TN16 3AG
Tel: 44 01959 541444
Email: minimag.ed@kelsey.co.uk
Freq: Monthly
Circ: 12000 Not Audited
Editor: Jeff Ruggles
MAGAZINE
Automakers

Mini World
982642

Editorial: PO Box 13, Westerham, London TN16 3WT **Tel:** 44 01959 541444
Email: miniworldmagazine@gmail.com
Web site: www.miniworld.co.uk
Freq: Monthly
Circ: 25132 Not Audited
Editor: Karen Drury
MAGAZINE
Automakers

Minimalissimo
1053836

Web site: www.minimalissimo.com/
Freq: Quarterly
MAGAZINE
Architecture & Design, Art, Do-It-Yourself (DIY), Fashion, Graphic Design, Photography

miniPLUS
995388

Editorial: Unit 4, Minerva Business Park, Lynch Wood, Peterborough PE2 6FT
Tel: 44 01733 405730
Email: editor@miniplus.co.uk
Web site: http://miniplus.co.uk
Freq: Quarterly

Circ: 26000 Not Audited
MAGAZINE
Automotive

Minor Matters
1097741
Editorial: P.O.Box 1098, Derby DE23 8ZX
Tel: 44 01332 291675
Email: minormatters@mmoc.org.uk
Web site: www.mmoc.org.uk
Freq: Bi-Monthly
Circ: 12000 Not Audited
Editor: Nicola Parkins
MAGAZINE
Antique & Collectible Cars, Automakers

Mirage Magazine
1095586
Email: hello@miragemag.com
Web site: www.miragemag.com
Freq: Annual
Circ: 28000 Not Audited
MAGAZINE
Fashion

Miss Jones
994981
Editorial: Miss Jones PA, 1B Kensington Park Mews, London W11 2EY
Tel: 44 02077 923310
Email: enquiries@missjonespa.com
Web site: www.missjonespa.com
Freq: Daily
Circ: 9054 Cision Digital Reach
MAGAZINE (ONLINE)
Bars, Clubs & Pubs, Beauty & Grooming, Business, Cosmetics, Fashion, Hair, Hotels/Motels, Luxury Goods, Mobile Electronics

Mister Maker
1059464
Editorial: Vineyard House, 44 Brook Green, London W6 7BT **Tel:** 44 02071 505000
Web site: www.mistermaker.com
Freq: Monthly
Circ: 24570 Not Audited
MAGAZINE
Crafts, Preschool

Mix
987762
Editorial: Unit 2, 10b Branch Place, London N1 5PH **Tel:** 44 02036 272388
Email: marketing@colourhive.com
Web site: https://shop.colourhive.com/collections/mix-magazine
Freq: Quarterly
Circ: 24000 Not Audited
MAGAZINE
Art, Graphic Design, Marketing, Photography

The Mix
1053121
Editorial: 50 Featherstone Street, London EC1Y 8RT **Tel:** 44 02072 505716
Email: media@youthnet.org
Web site: http://www.themix.org.uk/
Freq: Daily
Circ: 20638 Cision Digital Reach
Profile: Website covering support and guidance for young adults aged 16-25. THESITE is hosted by YouthNet UK. The website shares information and advice on sex, relationships, health and wellbeing, drink, drugs, law, money, education, study and travel. YouthNet is a registered charity.
MAGAZINE (ONLINE)
Charitable Foundations, Teen/Young Adult

Mixmag
982095
Editorial: 90-92 Pentonville Road, London N1 9HS **Tel:** 44 02070 788400
Web site: www.mixmag.net
Freq: Monthly
Circ: 14602 Not Audited
Editor: Duncan Dick
Profile: Dance music magazine with fashion, record reviews and lifestyle features. Includes clubbing, electronica, house and urban styles. Aimed at dance music fans and clubgoers.
Ad Rate: Full Page Colour £4005.00
MAGAZINE
Dance Music

MMA Uncaged
996178
Editorial: 1st Floor, Turnbridge Mills, Quay Street, Huddersfield HD1 6QT
Tel: 44 02081 233414
Email: editor@ciaranjarosz.media
Web site: www.mmauncagedmag.com
Freq: Bi-Monthly
Circ: 30000 Not Audited
MAGAZINE
Martial Arts, MMA & Self-Defense

MMAPLUS
995098
Email: info@mmaplus.co.uk
Web site: www.mmaplus.co.uk
Freq: Daily
Circ: 14773 Cision Digital Reach
MAGAZINE (ONLINE)
Martial Arts, MMA & Self-Defense

MMM
998238
Editorial: GHL House, 12-14 Albion Place, First Floor, Maidstone, Maidstone ME14 5DZ
Tel: 44 01622 299035
Email: editorial@mmm-media.com
Web site: www.mmm-media.com
Freq: Monthly
Circ: 24000 Not Audited
Editor: Tom White
MAGAZINE
Lifestyle, Men's Interests, Regional General Interest, Women's Interests

MMO Games
1101940
Email: contact@mmogames.com
Web site: www.mmogames.com
Freq: Daily
Circ: 616546 Cision Digital Reach
MAGAZINE (ONLINE)
Computer & Video Games

MO (Mandarin Oriental)
982328
Editorial: 6th floor, 85 Strand, London WC2R 0DW **Tel:** 44 02074 999080
Web site: http://www.mandarinoriental.com/destination-mo/
Freq: Semi-Annual
Circ: 33500 Not Audited
MAGAZINE
Cooking & Baking, Food, Grocery Stores, Luxury Goods, Organic Food, Restaurant Reviews, Travel, Vegetarianism & Veganism

Mobile Choice
981744
Editorial: 1-10 Praed Mews, Paddington, London W2 1QY **Tel:** 44 07896 727735
Web site: www.mobilechoiceuk.com
Freq: Quarterly
Circ: 24000 Not Audited
Profile: Magazine covering all aspects of mobile phones and mobile phone networks. Includes latest news in mobile technology, reviews and previews of new smartphones and tablets. Aimed at general consumers and professionals choosing a mobile phone.
Ad Rate: Full Page Colour £3096.00
MAGAZINE
Mobile Electronics

Mobile Innovations
1070074
Tel: 44 01572 820088
Email: publisher@cm-media.net
Web site: http://www.mobileinnovationsmagazine.com/
Freq: Quarterly
MAGAZINE
Electronics, Industry, Mobile Communications, Software

Mobile Security Brief
998802
Editorial: Gratwicke House, 10 East Street, Littlehampton, Littlehampton BN17 6AW
Tel: 44 01903 734677
Email: info@smartcard.co.uk
Web site: www.smartcard.co.uk
Freq: Monthly
Circ: 2000 Not Audited
Editor: Lesley Dann
MAGAZINE
Electronics, Mobile Communications, Security & Security Systems

MobileDista
1060643
Email: contact@mobiledista.com
Web site: http://mobiledista.com
Circ: 11227 Cision Digital Reach
MAGAZINE (ONLINE)
Audio Video Trade, Cameras, Consumer Electronics, Electronics, Mobile Communications, Mobile Electronics, Movies & Video

mobileworld
997745
Editorial: 10 Mayfield Road, Belvedere, London DA17 6DX
Email: info@mobileworldmag.com
Web site: www.mobileworldmag.com
Freq: Monthly
Circ: 5000 Not Audited
MAGAZINE
Internet, Mobile Communications, Telecommunications/Electronic Communications

MoDaCo
987438
Editorial: 7 Frenze Road, Diss, Diss IP22 4PA **Tel:** 44 01379 888101
Email: paul@modaco.com
Web site: www.modaco.com
Freq: Daily
Circ: 443851 Cision Digital Reach
MAGAZINE (ONLINE)
Mobile Electronics

MODE Magazine
996389
Editorial: MODE HQ, Woodfield Business Centre, Carr Hill, Doncaster DN4 8DE
Tel: 44 01302 515125
Email: info@mode.mg
Web site: www.whatmodeareyouin.co.uk/
Freq: Monthly
Circ: 20000 Not Audited
Editor: Coral Keers
MAGAZINE
Regional General Interest

Model Aircraft
981896
Editorial: Media House, 21 Kingsway, Bedford, Bedford MK42 9BJ
Tel: 44 01234 211245
Email: mail@sampublications.com
Web site: http://www.sampublications.com/
Freq: Monthly
Circ: 33745 Not Audited
Profile: Magazine providing reference material including scale plans and information on a variety of aviation subjects. Aimed at people working within the aviation industry.
Ad Rate: Full Page Mono £800.00
Ad Rate: Full Page Colour £980.00
MAGAZINE
Aviation, Crafts, Hobbies, & Collecting

Model Boats
981984
Editorial: PO Box 9890, Brentwood, Chelmsford CM13 9EF
Email: editor@modelboats.co.uk
Web site: www.modelboats.co.uk
Freq: Monthly
Circ: 16000 Not Audited
Editor: Paul Freshney
Profile: Magazine covering all aspects of model boating from radio controlled warships to stately galleons, as well as projects, news of the latest developments and new products, free plans and plan features and kit reviews. Also includes coverage of model boat shows and exhibitions in the UK and abroad. Aimed at model boat and yachting enthusiasts around the world.
Ad Rate: Full Page Colour £550.00
MAGAZINE
Crafts, Hobbies, & Collecting

Model Collector
981917
Editorial: Enterprise House, Enterprise Way, Edenbridge, Edenbridge TN8 6HF
Tel: 44 01689 869840
Web site: www.modelcollector.co.uk
Freq: Monthly
Circ: 7613 Not Audited
Editor: Lindsey Amrani
Profile: Magazine containing articles predominantly on die cast and tin plate

transport models, plus price guides and updates on new releases. Aimed at die cast and tin plate model collectors.
Ad Rate: Full Page Mono £619.00
Ad Rate: Full Page Colour £1062.00
MAGAZINE
Crafts, Hobbies, & Collecting

Model Engineer
985465
Editorial: Enterprise House, Enterprise Way, Edenbridge, Edenbridge TN8 6HF
Tel: 44 01689 869840
Web site: www.model-engineer.co.uk
Freq: Bi-Weekly
Circ: 16000 Not Audited
Editor: Diane Carney
Profile: Magazine covering all aspects of model engineering with articles on workshop equipment, tools and processes, internal combustion engines, rally and exhibition reports, clock-making, steam engine and locomotive construction, traction engines and related topics. Aimed at model engineers.
Ad Rate: Full Page Mono £620.00
Ad Rate: Full Page Colour £850.00
MAGAZINE
Crafts, Hobbies, & Collecting

Model Engineers' Workshop
985466
Editorial: Enterprise House, Enterprise Way, Edenbridge, Edenbridge TN8 6HF
Tel: 44 01689 869840
Web site: www.model-engineer.co.uk
Freq: Monthly
Circ: 21000 Not Audited
Editor: Neil Wyatt
Profile: Magazine providing workshop activities from selecting the right machines and tools to producing finished model engineering items. Aimed at amateur workshop operators and model engineers of all levels of experience.
Ad Rate: Full Page Mono £620.00
Ad Rate: Full Page Colour £820.00
MAGAZINE
Crafts, Hobbies, & Collecting

Model Farmer
996224
Editorial: 3 Orchard Close, Saracen's Head, Holbeach, Spalding PE12 8AR
Tel: 44 01406 424681
Email: info@igp-ltd.com
Freq: Bi-Monthly Not Audited
MAGAZINE
Crafts, Hobbies, & Collecting

Model Military International
998866
Editorial: Doolittle Mill, Doolittle Lane, Totternhoe, Eaton Bray LU6 1QX
Tel: 44 01525 222573
Email: editor@modelmilitary.com
Web site: www.modelmilitary.com
Freq: Monthly
Circ: 31000 Not Audited
Editor: Brett Green
MAGAZINE
Crafts, Hobbies, & Collecting

Model Rail
981985
Editorial: Media House, Lynchwood, Peterborough Business Park, Peterborough PE2 6EA **Tel:** 44 01733 468000
Email: modelrail@bauermedia.co.uk
Web site: http://www.model-rail.co.uk
Freq: Monthly
Circ: 25363 Not Audited
Editor: Richard Foster
Profile: Magazine covering railway layout and construction, including reports on what's new in model railways. Read by those with an interest in modelling.
Ad Rate: Full Page Colour £835.00
MAGAZINE
Crafts, Hobbies, & Collecting

Modern Advertising
1060942
Tel: 44 86106 3317498
Email: ad6898@vip.sina.com
Web site: http://www.maad.com.cn
Freq: Monthly

Consumer Magazines

Circ: 60003 Not Audited
MAGAZINE
Advertising Industry, Branding, Broadcasting, Graphic Design, Marketing, Media & Communications, Photography, Publishing

Modern Barber
998087
Editorial: Three Acre Barn, Thorpe Road, Upper Wardington, Banbury OX17 1SP
Tel: 44 01295 533755
Web site: www.modernbarber.co.uk
Freq: Quarterly Not Audited
MAGAZINE
Hair

Modern Gardens
1065605
Tel: 44 01733 468000
Web site: www.moderngardensmagazine.co.uk/
Freq: Monthly
MAGAZINE
Do-It-Yourself (DIY), Gardening

Modern Guide to Fashion Etiquette
1073644
Editorial: Tu Tu Much Media UK, 27 Old Gloucester Street, London WC1N 3AX
Tel: 44 02032 896235
Email: j.osei-tutu@tutumuchmedia.com
Web site: www.mgfe.co.uk
Freq: Daily
Circ: 521 Cision Digital Reach
MAGAZINE (ONLINE)
Fashion, Men's Interests

Modern Instruments
1062081
Tel: 44 86106 5132649
Email: info@csimc.com.cn
Web site: http://www.moderninstrs.org.cn
Freq: Bi-Monthly
Circ: 8001 Not Audited
MAGAZINE
Auto Aftermarket, Computers, Data Management, Electronics, Government Technology, Industry, Internet, Mobile Communications, Security & Security Systems, Software

Modern Investor
996109
Editorial: Citywire, 1st Floor, 87 Vauxhall Walk, London SE11 5HJ
Tel: 44 02078 402250
Email: moderninvestorchannel@citywire.co.uk
Web site: www.moderninvestor.com
Freq: Monthly Not Audited
MAGAZINE
Fund Management

Modern Matter
997070
Editorial: Second Floor, 6 Baker's Yard, London EC1R 3DD **Tel:** 44 02072 787462
Email: office@kilimag.com
Web site: amodernmatter.com
Freq: Semi-Annual Not Audited
MAGAZINE
Art, Audio Video Trade, Cameras, Consumer Electronics, Fashion, Literature, Mobile Electronics, Movies & Video, Photography, Theater & Performing Arts

Modern Mini
984636
Editorial: PO Box 978, Peterborough PE1 9FL **Tel:** 44 01733 347559
Email: mm.ed@kelseypb.co.uk
Web site: www.modernmini.co.uk
Freq: Bi-Monthly
Circ: 7000 Not Audited
Profile: Magazine dedicated to the new BMW Mini with news, reviews, road tests and profiles of modifications. Target audiences are current and prospective owners of BMW Minis.
Ad Rate: Full Page Colour £900.00
MAGAZINE
Automakers

Modern Mum
983265
Editorial: 19 Ormeau Business Park, The Gasworks, Belfast BT7 2JA
Tel: 44 02890 332499
Freq: Quarterly

Circ: 25000 Not Audited
Profile: Magazine covering health, beauty, fashion, child development and family lifestyle. Aimed at parents of children aged between 0 and 8 years old as well as women aged 20 to 50 years old.
Ad Rate: Full Page Mono £950.00
Ad Rate: Full Page Colour £1200.00
MAGAZINE
Family & Parenting

Modern Railways
979942
Editorial: Foundry Road, Stamford, Stamford PE9 2PP **Tel:** 44 01892 863358
Email: modern.railways@googlemail.com
Web site: http://www.modern-railways.com
Freq: Monthly
Circ: 16287 Not Audited
Editor: James Abbott
Profile: Journal covering British and European railways, including business marketing and technical trends. Aimed at people who work in the British and European railway industries.
Ad Rate: Full Page Mono £915.00
Ad Rate: Full Page Colour £1310.00
MAGAZINE
Railroad

Modular Magazine
1054404
Email: info@modularmag.com
Web site: http://modularmag.com/
Freq: Daily
Circ: 1292 Cision Digital Reach
MAGAZINE (ONLINE)
Dance Music, Rap & Hip Hop

MOJO
982107
Editorial: Endeavour House, 189 Shaftesbury Avenue, London WC2H 8JG
Tel: 44 02074 379011
Email: mojo@bauermedia.co.uk
Web site: www.mojo4music.com
Freq: Monthly
Circ: 70445 Not Audited
Profile: Magazine covering popular music both past and present. Covers music from rock to soul, jazz to folk, dubstep to grindcore. Aimed at fans of music.
Ad Rate: Full Page Colour £6867.00
MAGAZINE
Pop Music, Rock Music

Mojomums
987008
Editorial: Scotsbridge House, Scots Hill, Croxley Green, Rickmansworth, London WD3 3BB **Tel:** 44 08455 192836
Email: info@mojomums.co.uk
Web site: www.mojomums.co.uk
Freq: Daily
Circ: 16761 Cision Digital Reach
MAGAZINE (ONLINE)
Careers, Family & Parenting, Women's Interests

Moldova Azi
1061582
Tel: 44 37322 213652
Email: editor@ijc.md
Web site: http://www.azi.md
Freq: Daily
Circ: 1695 Cision Digital Reach
MAGAZINE (ONLINE)
Consumer Affairs, Crime & Violence, Defense & National Security, Energy & Environment, Ethical/Moral Issues, International News, Law, National News, News & Current Affairs, Northern Ireland

Mollie Makes
985931
Editorial: Tower House, Fairfax Street, Bristol BS1 3BN **Tel:** 44 01179 279009
Email: molliemakes@immediate.co.uk
Web site: www.molliemakes.com
Freq: Monthly
Circ: 36962 Not Audited
Editor: Cath Dean
Profile: Magazine covering lifestyle and crafts. Aimed at women interested in crafts
MAGAZINE
Crafts

The Moment Magazine
996379
Editorial: 4 Milnyard Square, Bakewell Road, Orton Southgate, Peterborough PE2 6GX **Tel:** 44 01733 810902
Email: editor@themomentmagazine.com
Web site: www.themomentmagazine.com/
Freq: Bi-Monthly
Circ: 23000 Not Audited
Editor: Toby Venables
MAGAZINE
Regional General Interest

Momente
999687
Editorial: Belgrave Road, Bristol BS8 2XN
Freq: Daily
Circ: 1002 Cision Digital Reach
MAGAZINE (ONLINE)
Cooking & Baking, Retirement Savings, Travel

Mondaq
980865
Editorial: 16 West Barnes Lane, West Wimbledon, London SW20 0BU
Web site: www.mondaq.com
Freq: Daily
Circ: 259948 Cision Digital Reach
Profile: Website covering finance. The mondaq website shares information on international trade and investment from the professional financial advisors' perspective.
MAGAZINE (ONLINE)
Business

mondo*arc
983768
Editorial: Waterloo Place, Watson Square, Stockport SK1 3AZ **Tel:** 44 01614 768350
Email: mondo@mondiale.co.uk
Web site: www.mondoarc.com
Freq: Bi-Monthly
Circ: 12000 Not Audited
Editor: Paul James
Profile: Magazine covering all aspects of architectural lighting. Targets lighting specification market, retail and commercial lighting specialists.
Ad Rate: Full Page Colour £2400.00
MAGAZINE
Electronics

mondo*dr
984651
Editorial: Waterloo Place, Watson Square, Stockport SK1 3AZ **Tel:** 44 01614 765580
Web site: www.mondodr.com
Freq: Bi-Monthly
Circ: 14000 Not Audited
Editor: Rachael Rogerson
Profile: Magazine providing worldwide coverage of developments in the entertainment technology equipment market. Contains international coverage of venues, companies, industry shows and products. Targets distributors, dealers and installers of lighting, sound and video equipment across all aspects of entertainment installation market.
Ad Rate: Full Page Colour £2300.00
MAGAZINE
Electronics, Music

The Money Advice Service
986992
Editorial: Holborn Centre, 120 Holborn, London EC1N 2TD **Tel:** 44 02079 430593
Email: melanie.dowding@moneyadviceservice.org.uk
Web site: www.moneyadviceservice.org.uk
Freq: Daily
Circ: 669510 Cision Digital Reach
MAGAZINE (ONLINE)
Personal Finance

Money Management (UK)
979821
Editorial: Number One, Southwark Bridge, London SE1 9HL **Tel:** 44 02078 733000
Web site: www.ftadviser.com/moneymanagement
Freq: Monthly
Circ: 7999 Not Audited
Editor: Dan Jones
MAGAZINE

Money Marketing
979775
Editorial: 79 Wells Street, London W1T 3QN
Tel: 44 02079 438000
Web site: www.moneymarketing.co.uk
Freq: Weekly
Circ: 25255 Not Audited
Profile: Magazine covering independent financial advisers, life assurance, news, pensions, mortgages, investments, products and information related to the financial services industry. Aimed at professional intermediaries.
Ad Rate: Full Page Mono £5093.00
Ad Rate: Full Page Colour £7200.00
MAGAZINE
Personal Finance

Money Observer
979820
Editorial: First Floor, Standon House, 21 Mansell Street, London E1 8AA
Tel: 44 02076 803555
Web site: www.moneyobserver.com
Freq: Monthly
Circ: 11922 Not Audited
Editor: Faith Glasgow
Profile: Magazine focusing on all aspects of investment, personal finance and money matters. Aimed at discerning private investors who want to maximise the return on their investments.
Ad Rate: Full Page Colour £4100.00
MAGAZINE
Personal Finance

money.co.uk
988201
Editorial: The Castle, Cecily Hill, Cirencester, Cirencester GL7 2EF
Tel: 44 01285 730100
Email: press@money.co.uk
Web site: www.money.co.uk
Freq: Daily
Circ: 1165312 Cision Digital Reach
MAGAZINE (ONLINE)
Personal Finance

MoneyAgonyAunt.com
999098
Editorial: 40 Bowling Green Lane, Clerkenwell, London EC1R 0NE
Tel: 44 02074 157070
Web site: moneyagonyaunt.com
Freq: Daily
Circ: 800 Cision Digital Reach
MAGAZINE (ONLINE)
Personal Finance

MoneyExpert
988771
Editorial: Huxley House, Weyside Park, Catteshall Lane, Godalming GU7 1XE
Tel: 44 01942 710910
Email: marketing@moneyexpert.com
Web site: http://www.moneyexpert.com
Freq: Daily
Circ: 23939 Cision Digital Reach
MAGAZINE (ONLINE)
Personal Finance

Moneyextra.com
980738
Editorial: Moneyextra.com Ltd, 52 Princess Street, Manchester M1 6JX
Web site: www.moneyextra.com
Freq: Daily
Circ: 24401 Cision Digital Reach
MAGAZINE (ONLINE)

Moneyfacts
980745
Editorial: Moneyfacts House, 66-70 Thorpe Road, Norwich NR1 1BJ
Tel: 44 01603 476476
Email: press@moneyfactsgroup.co.uk
Web site: www.moneyfactsgroup.co.uk
Freq: Monthly
Circ: 10390 Not Audited
Editor: Richard Eagling; **Editor:** Lee Tillcock
Profile: Guide to UK savings, credit card, personal loan, current account and mortgage rates. Aimed at IFAs, banks, building societies, solicitors, accountants and those interested in personal finance.
Ad Rate: Full Page Colour £2800.00
MAGAZINE

MoneyHighStreet.com
985294

Editorial: 162-164 High Street, Rayleigh, Essex, Rayleigh SS6 7BS
Tel: 44 01822 613567
Web site: www.moneyhighstreet.com
Freq: Daily
Circ: 13631 Cision Digital Reach
Editor: Diane Ray
Profile: Website covering personal finance.
MAGAZINE (ONLINE)
Personal Finance

Moneymagpie.com
984230

Editorial: Suite 5, 22 Pembridge Gardens, London W2 4DX
Email: editorial@moneymagpie.com
Web site: http://www.moneymagpie.com
Freq: Daily
Circ: 155593 Cision Digital Reach
Editor: Jasmine Birtles
MAGAZINE (ONLINE)
Personal Finance

Moneynet
980746

Editorial: 19 Spring Gardens, Manchester M2 1FB
Email: info@moneynet.co.uk
Web site: www.moneynet.co.uk
Freq: Daily
Circ: 7273 Cision Digital Reach
Profile: Website covering finance. The site Includes comparison tools and online application facilities for mortgages, credit cards, loans, savings and current accounts and insurance products.
MAGAZINE (ONLINE)
Personal Finance

MoneySavingExpert.com
980841

Editorial: 19-22 Rathbone Place, London W1T 1HY **Tel:** 44 02073 489104
Email: editorial@moneysavingexpert.com
Web site: www.moneysavingexpert.com
Freq: Daily
Circ: 11536826 Cision Digital Reach
Profile: Website covering finance. The MoneySavingExpert.com website contains research led articles and tips on the best buys and the top products across consumer finance.
MAGAZINE (ONLINE)
Personal Finance

moneysupermarket.com
984335

Editorial: Moneysupermarket House, St David's Park, Ewloe, Shotton CH5 3UZ
Tel: 44 08453 455708
Email: editorial@moneysupermarket.com
Web site: www.moneysupermarket.com
Freq: Daily
Circ: 3255796 Cision Digital Reach
Profile: Website covering finance. Moneysupermarket.com is a finance and travel price comparison website, where the reader can compare cheap loans, mortgages and credit cards as well as home and car insurance quotes.
MAGAZINE (ONLINE)
Personal Finance

MoneyWeek
979834

Editorial: 31-32 Alfred Place, London WC1E 7DP **Tel:** 44 02076 333651
Web site: www.moneyweek.com
Freq: Weekly
Circ: 45207 Not Audited
Profile: MoneyWeek is a weekly investment magazine that covers financial and economic news and provides commentary and analysis across UK and global markets. MoneyWeek is edited in London and published every Friday. It is aimed at private investors and financial professionals.
Ad Rate: Full Page Colour £5000.00
MAGAZINE
Personal Finance

Moneywise
979823

Editorial: 1st floor, Standon House, 21 Mansell Street, London E1 8AA
Tel: 44 02076 803658
Email: editorial@moneywise.co.uk
Web site: www.moneywise.co.uk

Freq: Monthly
Circ: 10157 Not Audited
Editor: Moira O'Neill
Profile: Magazine covering all aspects of personal finance in the UK. Includes features on the stock market, pensions, insurance, investments, banking, borrowing and tax. Aimed at people with an interest in personal finance.
Ad Rate: Full Page Colour £4850.00
MAGAZINE
Personal Finance

monitor.ba
1062073

Tel: 44 38736 333055
Web site: http://www.monitor.ba
Circ: 2288 Cision Digital Reach
MAGAZINE (ONLINE)
Basketball, Bicycles, Billiards, Boating & Yachting, Bodybuilding, Bowling, Boxing, Business, Consumer Affairs, Cricket

Monmouthshire Living
986666

Editorial: Cardiff Road, Maesglas, Newport, Newport NP20 3QN **Tel:** 44 01633 777240
Email: jo.barnes@gwent-wales.co.uk
Web site: www.monmouthshirecountylife.co.uk
Freq: Bi-Monthly
Circ: 10000 Not Audited
Profile: Magazine covering fashion, food and drink, gardens, health and beauty, motors, antiques, property, restaurants, entertainment and travel. Aimed at those living in and/or interested in visiting Monmouthshire County.
Ad Rate: Full Page Colour £800.00
MAGAZINE
Regional General Interest

Monochrome Watches
1054412

Web site: www.monochrome-watches.com
Freq: Daily
Circ: 151309 Cision Digital Reach
MAGAZINE (ONLINE)
News & Current Affairs

Monocle
983839

Editorial: Midori House, 1 Dorset Street, London W1U 4EG **Tel:** 44 02077 254388
Email: info@monocle.com
Web site: www.monocle.com
Freq: Monthly
Circ: 81504 Not Audited
Profile: Magazine focusing on geopolitical affairs, business, culture and design. Aimed at affluent, well travelled, well informed readers that work across a range of industries - in particular finance, media, IT, manufacturing, retail and hospitality. Aged between 25 and 55 years old.
Ad Rate: Full Page Mono £10750.00
Ad Rate: Full Page Colour £10750.00
MAGAZINE
International News, National News

Monster Machines
995505

Editorial: LCD PUBLISHING, VICI HOUSE, 2 MALLARD ROAD, Exeter EX2 7LD
Tel: 44 01392 664141
Freq: Monthly Not Audited
Editor: Joanne Trump
MAGAZINE
Teen/Young Adult

monstersandcritics.de
988235

Editorial: 2/2 42 Tassie Street, Glasgow G41 3QF **Tel:** 44 07711 349933
Email: james.wray@monstersandcritics.com
Web site: http://www.monstersandcritics.de/
Freq: Daily
Circ: 9887 Cision Digital Reach
MAGAZINE (ONLINE)
Dance Music, Jazz & Blues, Literature, Movies & Video, Music, Pop Music, R&B, Urban, World, Rap & Hip Hop, Rock Music

Mood Food / Menu Magazine
990467

Editorial: PO Box 416, Surbiton, London KT1 9BJ **Tel:** 44 0283 994831
Email: editor@moodfoodmag.com
Web site: www.moodfoodmag.com

Freq: Daily
Circ: 3470 Cision Digital Reach
Editor: Peter J. Grove
MAGAZINE (ONLINE)
Cooking & Baking, Restaurant Reviews

The Moodie Davitt Report
983966

Editorial: Moodie International, 69 Boston Manor Road, Brentford, London TW8 9JJ
Tel: 44 02082 317201
Web site: www.moodiedavittreport.com
Freq: Daily
Circ: 18055 Cision Digital Reach
Profile: Newsletter covering the global travel retail sector. Aimed at those working within the travel industry.
MAGAZINE (ONLINE)
Alcohol & Spirits, Consumer Goods & Products, Food, Tobacco, Travel

More About Advertising
987615

Editorial: 46 Claremont Road, London N6 5BY **Tel:** 44 02031 264948
Email: editor@moreaboutadvertising.com
Web site: www.moreaboutadvertising.com
Freq: Daily
Circ: 54128 Cision Digital Reach
Editor: Stephen Foster
Profile: Website covering the media and advertising industry. The More About Advertising website shares the latest news in the media, advertising and marketing industry.
MAGAZINE (ONLINE)
Advertising Industry, Branding, Broadcasting, Graphic Design, Marketing, Media & Communications, Photography, Publishing

More Than The Music
995538

Email: lisa@morethanthemusic.co.uk
Web site: www.morethanthemusic.co.uk
Freq: Daily
Circ: 10707 Cision Digital Reach
MAGAZINE (ONLINE)
Pop Music, Rap & Hip Hop, Rock Music

The Morning Advertiser
980022

Editorial: Broadfield Park, Crawley RH11 9RT **Tel:** 44 01293 613400
Email: ma.editorial@wrbm.com
Web site: www.morningadvertiser.co.uk
Freq: Bi-Weekly
Circ: 30000 Not Audited
Editor: Ed Bedington
MAGAZINE
Alcohol & Spirits, Food

Mortgage Finance Gazette
979770

Editorial: 6th Floor, Davis House, 2 Robert Street, Croydon CR0 1QQ
Tel: 44 02082 538618
Web site: www.mortgagefinancegazette.com
Freq: Monthly
Circ: 3645 Not Audited
Profile: Magazine covering issues in the mortgage market, including insurance, technology, lenders and legal matters. First published in 1869. Aimed at banks, building societies, insurance companies, management consultancies, systems providers and solicitors.
Ad Rate: Full Page Colour £3249.00
MAGAZINE

Mortgage Introducer
979769

Editorial: Fergusson House, 124-128 City Road, London EC1V 2NJ
Tel: 44 02075 028220
Web site: http://www.mortgageintroducer.com/
Freq: Monthly
Circ: 5000 Not Audited
Profile: Magazine providing mortgage product information, industry news and developments, Commercial mortgages and finance as well for the combined title Commercial Finance Introducer. Also protection news - products, developments etc in that industry. Aimed at pre-qualified IFAs, mortgage brokers, accountants,

solicitors, estate agents, tied agents and all types of mortgage advisers.
Ad Rate: Full Page Colour £2000.00
MAGAZINE
Personal Finance

Mortgage Strategy
979768

Editorial: 79 Wells Street, London W1T 3QN
Tel: 44 02079 438000
Web site: www.mortgagestrategy.co.uk
Freq: Weekly
Circ: 5500 Not Audited
Profile: Magazine covering all aspects of mortgages. Includes news, in-depth analysis and trends. Aimed at mortgage brokers and independent financial advisers. It is the only financial trade website dedicated to the mortgage intermediary.
Ad Rate: Full Page Colour £3347.00
MAGAZINE

Mosaic
1074213

Editorial: Wellcome Trust, Gibbs Building, 215 Euston Road, London NW1 2BE
Tel: 44 02076 118888
Email: mosaic@wellcome.ac.uk
Web site: http://mosaicscience.com
Freq: Weekly
Circ: 151039 Cision Digital Reach
MAGAZINE (ONLINE)
Community Care (UK), Health & Medicine, Science

MOSH
1075496

Tel: 44 07403 121919
Email: info@hitthefloor.com
Web site: http://mosh.hitthefloor.com/
Freq: Daily
Circ: 19930 Cision Digital Reach
MAGAZINE (ONLINE)
Rock Music

Moshi Monsters
995403

Editorial: 83 Victoria Street, London SW1H 0HW **Tel:** 44 02035 854021
Email: moshimag@skyjackpublishing.co.uk
Web site: www.moshimag.com
Freq: Monthly
Circ: 208535 Not Audited
MAGAZINE
Preschool, Teen/Young Adult

Mostly Food & Travel Journal
985369

Email: mostlyfood@yahoo.com
Web site: www.mostlyfood.co.uk
Freq: Daily
Circ: 10113 Cision Digital Reach
Profile: Website covering food and travel. The Mostly Food & Travel Journal website shares the latest cook book reviews, restaurant reviews and travel guides.
MAGAZINE (ONLINE)
Cooking & Baking, Food, Grocery Stores, Organic Food, Restaurant Reviews, Vegetarianism & Veganism

MOT Workshop
997041

Editorial: 12 Princes Gardens, London W5 1SD **Tel:** 44 01753 646591
Email: editor@motester.co.uk
Web site: www.motester.co.uk
Freq: Quarterly
Circ: 18713 Not Audited
Editor: Jim Punter
MAGAZINE
Automotive

Mother & Baby
980763

Editorial: Media House, Lynchwood, Peterborough PE2 6EA
Tel: 44 01733 468000
Email: ask@motherandbaby.co.uk
Web site: http://www.motherandbaby.co.uk/
Freq: Bi-Monthly
Circ: 20203 Not Audited
Profile: Magazine covering pregnancy, birth, baby care and the early years of a child's life, with features on health and consumer issues. Contains news stories and features on pregnancy as well as practical tips on baby and toddler-care, health pieces, real-life stories, fashion, celebrities and

Consumer Magazines

shopping pages in the business. Aimed at expectant mothers and those with children between 0 and 3 years old.
Ad Rate: Full Page Colour £5821.00
MAGAZINE
Family & Parenting

Mothers Who Work   984981
Editorial: 105 Roundable Road, Bromley BR1 5LF
Email: features@motherswhowork.co.uk
Web site: www.motherswhowork.co.uk
Freq: Daily
Circ: 12355 Cision Digital Reach
Editor: Joycellyn Akuffo
Profile: Website covering news and trends affecting working mothers.
MAGAZINE (ONLINE)
Women's Interests

Mothership   1101755
Email: hello@mothershipmag.co.uk
Freq: Daily
MAGAZINE (ONLINE)
Classical/Choral/Band Music, Country, Folk, Bluegrass, Dance Music, Fashion, Jazz & Blues, Music, Pop Music, R&B, Urban, World, Rap & Hip Hop, Rock Music

The Motley Fool (UK)   980747
Editorial: 60 Charlotte Street, 5th Floor, London W1T 2NU Tel: 44 02074 624300
Email: uknews@fool.co.uk
Web site: www.fool.co.uk
Freq: Daily
Circ: 999747 Cision Digital Reach
MAGAZINE (ONLINE)
Equities, Investment Banking, Personal Finance

Moto Magazine (UK)   982652
Editorial: 78-80 St John Street, Farringdon, London EC1M 4EH Tel: 44 02075 492945
Web site: www.motomagazine.co.uk
Freq: Monthly
Circ: 1716 Cision Digital Reach
MAGAZINE (ONLINE)
Motorcycles

Motor Boat & Yachting   982209
Editorial: Pinehurst 2, Pinehurst Road, Farnborough Business Park, Farnborough, London GU14 7BF Tel: 44 01252 555000
Email: mby@timeinc.com
Web site: www.mby.com
Freq: Monthly
Circ: 13263 Not Audited
Editor: Hugo Andreae
Profile: Magazine containing boat reports, equipment tests, advice on navigation and cruise accounts. Its core focus is on boats up to 80ft, while six times a year the magazine also carries Custom Yachting, a special focus on 80ft plus boats. First published in 1904, the publication has an average of 176 pages per issue. Aimed at those aged 35 years old and over with an interest in motor boats.
Ad Rate: Full Page Mono £1767.00
Ad Rate: Full Page Colour £3723.00
MAGAZINE
Boating & Yachting

Motor Caravanner   983316
Editorial: Reydon Business Park, Fountain Way, Reydon, Southwold IP18 6DH
Tel: 44 01502 725862
Email: danny.lewis@micropress.co.uk
Web site: www.motorcaravanners.eu
Freq: Monthly
Circ: 7500 Not Audited
Profile: Publication for members of the Motor Caravanners Association who are all owners of motor caravans containing articles and correspondence of interest to Motor Caravanners with road tests, travel reports, technical and news items as well as trade announcements and adverts.First published in 1960, the publication has an average of 40 pages per issue. Press Day: 1st of the month preceding. Aimed at the motor caravanning enthusiast.
Ad Rate: Full Page Colour £450.00
MAGAZINE
Camping and RV Travel

Motor Cycle Monthly   988352
Editorial: Media Centre, Morton Way, Horncastle, Horncastle LN9 6BR
Tel: 44 01507 529529
Email: editorial@motorcyclemonthly.co.uk
Web site: motorcyclemonthly.co.uk
Freq: Monthly
Circ: 67717 Not Audited
Editor: Tony Carter
Profile: Publication featuring real stories about real bikers, a what, where, when section, BSB and WSB racing, manufacturers news and information on the latest riding laws and ride out details. Aimed at motorcyclists.
Ad Rate: Full Page Colour £1795.00
MAGAZINE
Motorcycles

Motor Finance   980853
Editorial: International Accounting Bulletin, 71-73 Carter Lane, London EC4V 5EQ
Tel: 44 02079 366400
Web site: www.motorfinanceonline.com
Freq: Monthly
Circ: 18000 Not Audited
Editor: Jonathan Minter
Profile: Magazine focusing on UK and European credit finance news. Also covers personnel movements, corporate news, legal issues, commercial issues, wealth management and new products. Aimed at providers of consumer and motor finance including those which provide services to the industry.
Ad Rate: Full Page Colour £1500.00
MAGAZINE
Automotive

Motor Sport   982673
Editorial: 18-20 Rosemont Road, London NW3 6NE Tel: 44 02073 498484
Email: editorial@motorsportmagazine.co.uk
Web site: www.motorsportmagazine.co.uk
Freq: Monthly
Circ: 34494 Not Audited
Profile: Magazine covering international motor sport, featuring material on Formula 1, sports car racing, the vintage racing scene and speed record attempts. Aimed at motor sport enthusiasts.
Ad Rate: Full Page Colour £2475.00
MAGAZINE
Automotive, Driving, Motorsports

Motor TradeBook   999493
Editorial: Oakleigh, Woodwell Road, Bristol BS11 9UG Tel: 44 07412 594253
Web site: http://www.motortradebook.com/
Freq: Daily
Circ: 34477 Cision Digital Reach
MAGAZINE (ONLINE)
Automotive

Motor Trader   981258
Editorial: 6th Floor, Davis House, 2 Robert Street, Croydon CR0 1QQ
Tel: 44 02082 538716
Web site: www.motortrader.com
Freq: Monthly
Circ: 10142 Not Audited
Editor: Curtis Hutchinson
Profile: Journal focusing on the automotive industry. Includes news and information on the latest developments within the industry. Read by senior management in franchised dealerships, car manufacturers, importers and service and repair garages.
Ad Rate: Full Page Colour £4095.00
MAGAZINE
Antique & Collectible Cars, Automakers, Automotive, Driving, Motorcycles, Off-road & 4-Wheel Drive Vehicles, Trucks & SUVs

Motor Transport   979908
Editorial: 6th Floor, Chancery House, St Nicholas Way, Sutton SM1 1JB
Tel: 44 02089 122170
Web site: www.motortransport.co.uk
Freq: Bi-Weekly
Circ: 12521 Not Audited
Editor: Steve Hobson
Profile: Newspaper for the haulage and logistics industry, covering news of hauliers

and supply chain companies, truck and technical news and management issues including communications, computers in haulage companies and distribution property. Read by truck purchasers in transport operations running 11 or more commercial vehicles over 3.5 tonnes.
Ad Rate: Full Page Colour £3500.00
MAGAZINE
Automotive, Shipping & Warehousing, Supply Chain Management (SCM)

motorbar.co.uk   984647
Editorial: Suite 2030, KentSpace, 6 - 8 Revenge Road, Lordswood, Chatham ME5 8UD
Email: motorbarcom@gmail.com
Web site: www.motorbar.co.uk
Freq: Daily
Circ: 1151 Cision Digital Reach
Editor: Leonard Fraser-Scott
MAGAZINE (ONLINE)
Antique & Collectible Cars, Automakers, Automotive, Bars, Clubs & Pubs, Comedy, Driving, Entertainment, Local Entertainment Guides, Motorcycles, Movies & Video

MotorbikeTimes   995337
Editorial: 501 Metropolitan Wharf Buildings, 70 Wapping Wall, London E1W 3SS
Tel: 44 02071 672667
Email: news@motorbiketimes.com
Web site: http://www.motorbiketimes.com/
Freq: Daily
Circ: 12160 Cision Digital Reach
MAGAZINE (ONLINE)
Motorcycles

Motorboat Owner   1097884
Tel: 44 01268 922991
Email: editorial@motorboatowner.co.uk
Web site: http://www.motorboatowner.co.uk
Freq: Monthly
Circ: 8029 Cision Digital Reach
Editor: Neale Byart
MAGAZINE (ONLINE)
Boating & Yachting

Motorcar Directory   997781
Editorial: Suite 6B(i), Britannia House, Leagrave Road, Luton LU3 1RJ
Tel: 44 01582 488385
Email: info@mediachameleon.co.uk
Web site: www.motorcardirectory.co.uk
Freq: Annual
Circ: 14000 Not Audited
MAGAZINE
Antique & Collectible Cars, Automotive, Driving, Off-road & 4-Wheel Drive Vehicles

Motorcaravan Motorhome Monthly   982311
Editorial: The Maltings, West Street, Bourne, Bourne PE10 9PH Tel: 44 01778 391000
Email: mmm@warnersgroup.co.uk
Web site: www.mmmonline.co.uk
Freq: Monthly
Circ: 29530 Not Audited
MAGAZINE
Camping and RV Travel

Motorcycle Racer   986694
Editorial: 484 Didsbury Road, Stockport SK4 3BS Tel: 44 01614 431000
Web site: https://www.motorcycleracer.com/
Freq: Monthly
Circ: 10000 Not Audited
Profile: Magazine covering British and American road racing and world superbikes. Includes news and features on race results, new products, developments and profiles of racing stars. Aimed at motorcycle racing enthusiasts.
Ad Rate: Full Page Colour £1000.00
MAGAZINE
Motorsports

The Motorcycle Reference Directory   998035
Editorial: Suite 6ci and 6cii, Britannia House, Leagrave Road, Luton LU3 1RJ
Tel: 44 01582 488385
Email: info@mediachameleon.co.uk
Web site: www.motorcyclewebsite.com
Freq: Annual
Circ: 17000 Not Audited
MAGAZINE
Motorcycles

Motorcycle Rider   983323
Editorial: 3 Oswin Road, Brailsford Industrial Estate, Braunstone, Norwich LE3 1HR
Tel: 44 01603 664242
Email: rider@bmf.co.uk
Web site: http://www.ridermagazine.co.uk/
Freq: Quarterly
Circ: 14000 Not Audited
Profile: Journal of the British Motorcyclists Federation. Includes political, regional, commercial and leisure information. Aimed at BMF members and those with an interest in the future of motorcycling.
MAGAZINE
Motorcycles

Motorcycle Sport & Leisure   982654
Editorial: Media Centre, Morton Way, Horncastle LN9 6JR Tel: 44 01507 529529
Web site: www.mslmagazine.co.uk
Freq: Monthly
Circ: 46035 Not Audited
Editor: John Milbank
MAGAZINE
Motorcycles

Motorcycle Trader   983067
Editorial: Stud Farm, Seaford Road, Newhaven, Newhaven BN9 0EF
Tel: 44 01273 616040
Email: news@motorcycletrader.net
Web site: www.motorcycletrader.net
Freq: Monthly
Circ: 7200 Not Audited
Profile: Magazine containing information about the motorcycle trade and industry covering issues of pricing, legality, new products and trade news. Aimed at all those involved in the motorcycle trade and industry.
Ad Rate: Full Page Colour £600.00
MAGAZINE
Automotive

Motoring Insight   996715
Editorial: Swiss House, Beckingham Streer, Tolleshunt Major, Tiptree CM9 8LZ
Tel: 44 02031 516410
Email: danny.hewitt@motortradesinsight.co.uk
Web site: http://www.mtin.co.uk/
Freq: Daily
Circ: 521 Cision Digital Reach
Editor: Danny Hewitt
MAGAZINE (ONLINE)
Automotive

MotorPunk   995361
Web site: http://motorpunk.co.uk/
Freq: Daily
Circ: 9916 Cision Digital Reach
MAGAZINE (ONLINE)
Antique & Collectible Cars, Automakers, Automotive, Driving, Motorcycles, Off-road & 4-Wheel Drive Vehicles, Trucks & SUVs

motors.co.uk   997119
Editorial: Unit 1 - 4, West Central 127, Milton Park, Abingdon, Oxford OX14 4SA
Tel: 44 08452 656000
Email: marketing@motors.co.uk
Web site: www.motors.co.uk
Freq: Daily
Circ: 1684213 Cision Digital Reach
MAGAZINE (ONLINE)
Antique & Collectible Cars, Automakers, Automotive, Driving, Motorcycles, Off-road & 4-Wheel Drive Vehicles, Trucks & SUVs

The MotorShip
980819

Editorial: Spinnaker House, Waterside Gardens, Fareham, Fareham PO16 8SD
Tel: 44 01329 825335
Email: editor@motorship.com
Web site: www.motorship.com
Freq: Monthly
Circ: 7309 Not Audited
Editor: Gavin Lipsith
Profile: Motorship is a journal covering worldwide developments in marine technology.
Ad Rate: Full Page Colour £2795.00
MAGAZINE
Marine & Boat Trade, Shipping & Warehousing

Motorsport News
982674

Editorial: Bridge House, 69 London Road, Twickenham, London TW1 3QL
Tel: 44 02082 675385
Email: mn.letters@haymarket.com
Web site: www.motorsport-news.co.uk
Freq: Weekly
Circ: 8219 Not Audited
Editor: Matt James
Profile: Motorsport News is a magazine covering British motorsport. The weekly magazine is available on news stands and delivers up to date, entertaining and reliable, reports and results. Aimed at British motorsport enthusiasts.
Ad Rate: Full Page Mono £2436.00
Ad Rate: Full Page Colour £3696.00
MAGAZINE
Motorsports

Motorsport South Africa
1060432

Tel: 44 27114 662440
Email: assistpr@motorsport.co.za
Web site: http://www.motorsport.co.za
Circ: 54102 Cision Digital Reach
MAGAZINE (ONLINE)
Motorsports

MotorStars
997642

Editorial: 15 Match Court, 5 Blondin Street, London E3 2UU
Email: editor@motor-stars.com
Web site: www.motor-stars.com
Freq: Monthly
Circ: 15000 Not Audited
Editor: Raj Hunjan
MAGAZINE
Antique & Collectible Cars, Automotive, Driving, Off-road & 4-Wheel Drive Vehicles

MotorTradeNews.com
986798

Editorial: 145 - 157 St. John Street, London EC1V 4PY **Tel:** 44 01832 710635
Email: editorial@motortradenews.com
Web site: www.motortradenews.com
Freq: Daily
Circ: 14815 Cision Digital Reach
Profile: Website covering motoring and automotive. Motor Trade News shares the latest business news on the automotive industry and also provides details of automotive jobs, events and exhibitions.
MAGAZINE (ONLINE)
Automotive

motortransport.co.uk
999120

Editorial: 6th Floor, Chancery House, St Nicholas Way, London SM1 1JB
Tel: 44 02089 122170
Web site: www.motortransport.co.uk
Freq: Daily
Circ: 16570 Cision Digital Reach
Editor: Steve Hobson
MAGAZINE (ONLINE)
Automotive, Shipping & Warehousing, Supply Chain Management (SCM)

Mountain Bike Rider (MBR)
998948

Editorial: Bluefin Building, 110 Southwark Street, London SE1 0SU
Tel: 44 02525 55000
Web site: www.mbr.co.uk
Freq: Monthly
Circ: 15112 Not Audited

Editor: Danny Milner
MAGAZINE
News & Current Affairs

Mountain Biking UK
982201

Editorial: Tower House, Fairfax Street, Bristol BS1 3BN **Tel:** 44 01179 279009
Email: mbuk@immediate.co.uk
Web site: magazine.bikeradar.com/category/mountain-biking-uk
Freq: Monthly
Circ: 28992 Not Audited
Profile: Magazine covering all aspects of mountain biking as a sport in the UK. Aimed at mountain bike enthusiasts.
Ad Rate: Full Page Colour £1925.00
MAGAZINE
Bicycles

Mousebreaker
997095

Editorial: The Blue Fin Building, 110 Southwark Street, London SE1 0SU
Tel: 44 02031 485000
Web site: www.mousebreaker.com
Freq: Daily
Circ: 1232663 Cision Digital Reach
MAGAZINE (ONLINE)
News & Current Affairs

MouthLondon
999301

Editorial: Castle Court, 41 London Road, Reigate RH2 9RJ
Email: feedme@mouthlondon.com
Web site: www.mouthlondon.com
Freq: Daily
Circ: 5175 Cision Digital Reach
Editor: David Holloway
MAGAZINE (ONLINE)
Student Lifestyle

Movie Muser
999271

Editorial: The Senate, Southernhay Gardens, Exeter EX1 1UG
Tel: 44 01392 434831
Email: timisaac@moviemuser.co.uk
Web site: www.moviemuser.co.uk
Freq: Daily
Circ: 12407 Cision Digital Reach
MAGAZINE (ONLINE)
Entertainment, Movies & Video

Movies Games and Tech
999574

Email: andrew@moviesgamesandtech.com
Web site: http://moviesgamesandtech.com/
Freq: Daily
Circ: 20869 Cision Digital Reach
Editor: Andrew Edney
MAGAZINE (ONLINE)
Audio Video Trade, Cameras, Computer & Video Games, Consumer Electronics, Electronics, Mobile Electronics, Movies & Video

MOVIES4KIDS
996836

Email: movies4kidsuk@gmail.com
Web site: www.movies4kids.co.uk
Freq: Daily
Circ: 10511 Cision Digital Reach
Editor: Jo Berry
MAGAZINE (ONLINE)
Broadcasting, Entertainment, Movies & Video

movieScope
984852

Editorial: 105 Bridge House, 3 Mills Studios, Three Mill Lane, London E3 3DU
Tel: 44 08450 946263
Email: editor@moviescopemag.com
Web site: www.moviescopemag.com
Freq: Daily
Circ: 6368 Cision Digital Reach
Editor: Matt Gallagher
MAGAZINE (ONLINE)
Broadcasting, Marketing, Movies & Video

MoziPlussz.hu
1061096

Tel: 44 36203 278219
Email: szerkesztoseg@moziplussz.hu

Web site: http://www.moziplussz.hu Not Audited
MAGAZINE
Antiques/Collectibles, Art, Arts, Literature, Movies & Video, Photography, Theater & Performing Arts, Visual Arts

MPORA
988844

Editorial: 2 Tun Yard, Peardon Street, London SW8 3HT **Tel:** 44 02073 329700
Email: contact@mpora.com
Web site: www.mpora.com
Freq: Daily
Circ: 442162 Cision Digital Reach
MAGAZINE (ONLINE)
Bicycles, Extreme/Adventure Sports, Swimming/Watersports, Winter Sports

Mr & Mrs Smith
983934

Editorial: The Shepherds Building, Rockley Road, London W14 0DA
Tel: 44 02037 522904
Email: enquries@mrandmrssmith.com
Web site: https://www.mrandmrssmith.com/
Freq: Daily
Circ: 185418 Cision Digital Reach
Profile: Website covering luxury travel. The Mr & Mrs Smith website shares the latest information on boutique hotels and spa destinations with features and travel news.
MAGAZINE (ONLINE)
Luxury Goods, Travel

Mr Hyde
987512

Editorial: 26-34 Emerald Street, London WC1N 3QA **Tel:** 44 02076 119700
Email: editorial@shortlist.com
Web site: www.mrhyde.com
Freq: Daily
Circ: 43434 Cision Digital Reach
MAGAZINE (ONLINE)
Men's Interests

Mr Men Little Miss
995367

Editorial: Unit 16 Greenway Farm, Bath Road, Wick, Bristol BS30 5RL
Tel: 44 01179 373003
Email: info@kennedypublishing.co.uk
Web site: http://www.kennedypublishing.co.uk/magazines/mr-men-little-miss-magazine
Freq: Monthly
Circ: 40000 Not Audited
MAGAZINE
Elementary School, Preschool

Mr.H
996118

Email: contact@misterhagan.com
Web site: www.misterhagan.com
Freq: Quarterly
MAGAZINE
Art, Fashion, Luxury Goods, Men's Interests, Travel

MS Matters
981821

Editorial: MS National Centre, 372 Edgware Road, London NW2 6ND
Tel: 44 02084 380700
Email: msmatters@mssociety.org.uk
Web site: www.mssociety.org.uk
Freq: Quarterly
Circ: 38000 Not Audited
Editor: Frances Whinder
Profile: Magazine covering research and articles of interest to those with multiple sclerosis. Aimed at people with MS, their families and carers, as well as health professionals.
Ad Rate: Full Page Colour £2758.00
MAGAZINE
Charitable Foundations, Patient Support

MSA
982675

Tel: 44 01753 765000
Email: media@msauk.org
Web site: www.msauk.org
Freq: Quarterly
Circ: 43000 Not Audited
Profile: Magazine containing actual and proposed regulation changes, general news and competitor information. Read by motorsport competition licence holders, club members, officials, team members and manufacturers.

Ad Rate: Full Page Colour £2500.00
MAGAZINE
Motorsports

MSA Newslink
983330

Editorial: 101 Wellington Road North, Stockport, Stockport SK4 2LP
Tel: 44 01614 299669
Email: mail@msagb.co.uk
Web site: www.msagb.co.uk
Freq: Monthly
Circ: 7000 Not Audited
Editor: John Lepine
Profile: Journal of the Motor Schools Association of Great Britain covering the driving, training and testing industry throughout Europe. Includes regulations, testing, events and research news. Aimed at Britain's driving instructors, driving test centres, the Department for Transport and those interested in road or transport safety.
Ad Rate: Full Page Colour £1800.00
MAGAZINE
Automotive

msafiri
986420

Editorial: GECKO PUBLISHING LTD, 13 Kelly's Road, Wheatley, Oxford OX33 1NT
Tel: 44 01844 278883
Email: msafiri@geckomags.com
Web site: msafirimag.com
Freq: Monthly Not Audited
Editor: William Gray
Profile: In-flight magazine of Kenya Airways containing news, travel and fashion features, sport, entertainment and business. First published in 1971, the publication has an average of 192 pages per issue. Press Day: 6 weeks prior to publication. Aimed at national and international government officials, business and leisure travellers to Africa, Europe, the Middle East, Asia and the Far East.
Ad Rate: Full Page Mono £3222.00
Ad Rate: Full Page Colour £3580.00
MAGAZINE
Airline Inflight

Mslexia
983351

Editorial: PO Box 656, Newcastle upon Tyne NE99 1PZ **Tel:** 44 01912 048860
Email: postbag@mslexia.co.uk
Web site: www.mslexia.co.uk
Freq: Quarterly
Circ: 9000 Not Audited
Profile: Magazine containing features, interviews, reviews and news on writing, poetry and prose. Also covers literature events, jobs, publications, courses and venues around the country. Aimed predominantly at self-improving women who write, want to write, teach creative writing or have a special interest in women's literature.
Ad Rate: Full Page Mono £875.00
Ad Rate: Full Page Colour £1050.00
MAGAZINE
Literature

MSN UK
982839

Editorial: 2 Kingdom Street, Paddington, London W2 6BD
Web site: http://www.msn.com/en-gb
Freq: Daily
Circ: 88715 Cision Digital Reach
Editor: Rob Clymo
Profile: MSN UK website shares the latest news and information on sports, entertainment, money, cares, health and technology.
MAGAZINE (ONLINE)
International News, Men's Interests, Women's Interests

Multiple Matters
982415

Editorial: Manor House, Church Hill, Aldershot, London GU12 4JU
Tel: 44 01252 332344
Email: multiplematters@hotmail.co.uk
Web site: www.tamba.org.uk
Freq: Quarterly
Circ: 18000 Not Audited
Editor: Rachael Claye
Profile: Magazine covering details on personal experiences and human-interest features of those with twins, triplets and more. Also contains advice on childcare and

Consumer Magazines

parenting issues, travel guide for families and a product testing page. Read by members of the Twins and Multiple Births Association. Also aimed at twin club members, parents of twins or more and health education professionals.
Ad Rate: Full Page Colour £450.00
MAGAZINE
News & Current Affairs

Mumfidential
998308
Email: info@mumfidential.com
Web site: http://www.mumfidential.com/
Freq: Daily
Circ: 13379 Cision Digital Reach
MAGAZINE (ONLINE)
Family & Parenting

Mumii
997447
Editorial: Teach House, Gilbert Drive, Boston, Boston PE21 7TQ
Tel: 44 01205 751649
Email: editor@native-media.co.uk
Web site: www.mumii.co.uk
Freq: Daily
Circ: 11123 Cision Digital Reach
MAGAZINE (ONLINE)
Family & Parenting

MumKnowsBest.com
985194
Editorial: Tyburn House, 5 Hangmans Lane, Hinckley, Hinckley LE10 1SU
Tel: 44 01455 459523
Email: pr@mumknowsbest.com
Web site: www.mumknowsbest.com
Freq: Daily
Circ: 10421 Cision Digital Reach
Editor: Sue Williams
MAGAZINE (ONLINE)
Family & Parenting

Mummy and Me
996358
Editorial: 114 Stamfordham Drive, Allerton, Liverpool L19 4XF **Tel:** 44 01514 270124
Email: info@mummyandmemagazine.co.uk
Web site: www.mummyandmemagazine.co.uk
Freq: Monthly Not Audited
MAGAZINE
Family & Parenting

Mummy Money Matters
996183
Editorial: Studio 28, 8 Hornsey Street, London N7 8EG **Tel:** 44 07717 858414
Email: kalpana@mummymoneymatters.com
Web site: www.mummymoneymatters.com
Freq: Daily
Circ: 8868 Cision Digital Reach
MAGAZINE (ONLINE)
Personal Finance

MummyPages
995345
Tel: 44 03333 444686
Email: hello@mummypages.com
Web site: http://www.mummypages.co.uk/
Freq: Daily
Circ: 905303 Cision Digital Reach
MAGAZINE (ONLINE)
Family & Parenting

Mums Magazine
996679
Editorial: 5 Coningsby Close, Maidenhead, Maidenhead SL6 3YU **Tel:** 44 07834 233346
Email: info@lifestyle-magazines.co.uk
Web site: http://www.mums-magazine.co.uk/
Freq: Quarterly
Circ: 8000 Not Audited
Editor: Caroline Seekings
MAGAZINE
Family & Parenting

Mumsnet
983254
Editorial: Deane House Studios (Studios 13-16), Greenwood Place, Highgate Road, London NW5 1LB **Tel:** 44 02030 510167
Email: contactus@mumsnet.com
Web site: www.mumsnet.com
Freq: Daily
Circ: 3812465 Cision Digital Reach
Editor: Kate Williams
Profile: Parenting website run by parents, for parents. Containing product reviews,

local listings, social networking, competitions, parenting and childcare, forums for advice and support by other parents. Aimed at parents of children from 0 to 18 years old.Alternative Title: mumsnet. com Justine Roberts is the Managing Director to whom press releases should be addressed.
MAGAZINE (ONLINE)
Family & Parenting

Mundial
997437
Email: orders@mundialstudio.com
Web site: www.mundialmag.com
Freq: Quarterly Not Audited
MAGAZINE
News & Current Affairs

Mung Beans and Champagne
996439
Email: hello@mungbeansandchampagne.com
Web site: www.mungbeansandchampagne.com
Freq: Daily
Circ: 493 Cision Digital Reach
MAGAZINE (ONLINE)
Beauty & Grooming, Cooking & Baking, Cosmetics, Hair, Health & Medicine, Lifestyle, Men's Interests, Regional General Interest, Women's Interests

Municipal Vehicle Operator
987001
Editorial: 9 Saxon Court, St Peter's Gardens, Marefair, Northampton NN1 1SX
Tel: 44 01604 620426
Email: ciwm@ciwm.co.uk
Web site: www.ciwm-journal.co.uk/mvo
Freq: Quarterly
Circ: 7000 Not Audited
Editor: Ben Wood
MAGAZINE
Automotive, Engineering, Manufacturing

Murder Most Foul
997001
Editorial: PO Box 735, London SE26 5NQ
Tel: 44 02087 780514
Email: enquiries@truecrimelibrary.com
Web site: www.truecrimelibrary.com/
Freq: Quarterly Not Audited
MAGAZINE
Crime & Violence

Muscle & Fitness (UK)
981832
Editorial: 10 Windsor Court, Clarence Drive, Harrogate, Harrogate HG1 2PE
Email: editorial@weideruk.com
Web site: http://www.muscle-fitness.co.uk/
Freq: Monthly
Circ: 49000 Not Audited
MAGAZINE
Bodybuilding, Fitness & Exercise, Nutrition

Musclemag International
982225
Editorial: Unit 38, Minworth Industrial Estate, Sutton Coldfield, Sutton Coldfield B76 1AH
Email: editors@muscleandperformancemag.com
Web site: www.musclemag.com
Freq: Monthly
Circ: 22500 Not Audited
MAGAZINE
Bodybuilding

Music & Copyright
981606
Editorial: Informa Business Information, Christchurch Court, 10-15 Newgate Street, London EC1A 7AZ Not Audited
Editor: Simon Dyson
Profile: Journal containing news and information on the music and copyright business worldwide. Provides international music and publishing industry news with business research and analysis, collaborations, deals and alliances, sector profiles, trends and developments.Aimed at senior executives in the record and music publishing industry and related areas.
MAGAZINE
Music

Music Ally
983652
Editorial: Studio 11, Holborn Studios, 49-50 Eagle Wharf Rd, London N1 7ED
Tel: 44 02072 503637
Email: mail@musically.com
Web site: www.musically.com
Freq: Daily
Circ: 98534 Cision Digital Reach
Profile: Website covering digital music industry news, digital music, music video downloads, digital right management, Bluetooth, recommended engines, and marketing. Music Ally as a company has been providing publications, consulting, research, events and training to the music and technology industries since 2001. Their website has an archive dating back to January 2003. Aimed at digital music lovers. Contactable via online comments form.
MAGAZINE (ONLINE)
Music

Music and Vision
983406
Editorial: Flat D, 25 Oxford Road, Ealing, London W5 3SP **Tel:** 44 02088 401564
Web site: www.mvdaily.com
Freq: Daily
Circ: 11734 Cision Digital Reach
Editor: Basil Ramsay
MAGAZINE (ONLINE)
Classical/Choral/Band Music

Music Business Worldwide
998065
Editorial: 27 Old Gloucester Street, London WC1N 3AX
Email: email@musicbizworldwide.com
Web site: www.musicbusinessworldwide.com
Freq: Daily
Circ: 157606 Cision Digital Reach
MAGAZINE (ONLINE)
Music

Music Education UK
1033437
Editorial: 86-90 Paul Street, London EC2A 4NE **Tel:** 44 02082 424236
Email: meuk@1hub.co
Web site: http://www.musiceducationuk.com
Freq: Daily
Circ: 37450 Cision Digital Reach
MAGAZINE (ONLINE)
Music

Music Existence
1074062
Web site: www.musicexistence.com
Freq: Daily
Circ: 42839 Cision Digital Reach
MAGAZINE (ONLINE)
News & Current Affairs

Music Eyz
997599
Email: musiceyz@gmail.com
Web site: http://musiceyz.co.uk/
Freq: Daily
Circ: 521 Cision Digital Reach
MAGAZINE (ONLINE)
Classical/Choral/Band Music, Country, Folk, Bluegrass, Dance Music, Jazz & Blues, Music, Pop Music, R&B, Urban, World, Rap & Hip Hop, Rock Music

Music for the Masses
1104177
Web site: www.musicforthemasses.co.uk
Freq: Daily
Circ: 521 Cision Digital Reach
Editor: Thom Burgess
MAGAZINE (ONLINE)
Classical/Choral/Band Music, Country, Folk, Bluegrass, Dance Music, Jazz & Blues, Music, Pop Music, R&B, Urban, World, Rap & Hip Hop, Rock Music

Music Teacher
983035
Editorial: Rhinegold House, 20 Rugby Street, London WC1N 3QZ
Email: music.teacher@rhinegold.co.uk
Web site: www.rhinegold.co.uk/rhinegold-publishing/magazines/music-teacher
Freq: Monthly
Circ: 20000 Not Audited
Editor: Alex Stevens

Profile: Magazine covering all aspects of the teaching of music. Aimed at all those involved in music education particularly peripatetic teachers and those in private practice.
Ad Rate: Full Page Colour £1890.00
MAGAZINE
Higher Education, Music, Preschool, Schools & Institutions

Music Week
981233
Editorial: The Emerson Building, 4-8 Emerson Street, London SE1 9DU
Tel: 44 02072 267246
Email: musicweek@abacusemedia.com
Web site: www.musicweek.com
Freq: Weekly
Circ: 5241 Not Audited
Editor: Mark Sutherland
Profile: Magazine covering all aspects of the music industry. Aimed at those in the music industry, record companies and distributors.
Ad Rate: Full Page Colour £3250.00
MAGAZINE
Music

Musical Opinion
982070
Editorial: Musical Opinion, 1 Exford Road, London SE12 9HD
Email: musicalopinion@hotmail.co.uk
Web site: www.musicalopinion.com
Freq: Quarterly
Circ: 8000 Not Audited
Editor: Robert Matthew-Walker
Profile: Magazine covering concerts, festivals, opera and dance featuring articles on new music, anniversaries and personalities. Aimed at music lovers, professionals, students, performers and members of orchestral and choral societies.
Ad Rate: Full Page Colour £950.00
MAGAZINE
Classical/Choral/Band Music

Musical Theatre Review
988328
Email: lisa@musicaltheatrereview.com
Web site: musicaltheatrereview.com
Freq: Daily
Circ: 14937 Cision Digital Reach
MAGAZINE (ONLINE)
Theater & Performing Arts

The Musical Times
998928
Editorial: The Musical Times, Unit 8 The Old Silk Mill, Brook Street, Tring, Tring HP23 5EF
Tel: 44 01442 820580
Email: mted@gotadsl.co.uk
Web site: http://themusicaltimes.blogspot.com
Freq: Quarterly Not Audited
Editor: Anthony Bye
MAGAZINE
Classical/Choral/Band Music

Musical Traditions Internet Magazine - mustrad.org.uk
998772
Editorial: 1 Castle Street, Stroud, Stroud GL5 2HP
Web site: www.mustrad.org.uk
Freq: Daily
Circ: 6505 Cision Digital Reach
Editor: Rod Stradling
MAGAZINE (ONLINE)
News & Current Affairs

Musician magazine
998499
Editorial: 60-62 Clapham Road, London SW9 0JJ **Tel:** 44 02075 825566
Email: info@themu.org
Web site: www.musiciansunion.org.uk
Circ: 33000 Not Audited
Editor: Keith Ames
MAGAZINE
Music

Music-News.com
984741
Editorial: 27 Lothair Road, London N4 1EN
Tel: 44 02083 479279
Web site: www.music-news.com
Freq: Daily
Circ: 152581 Cision Digital Reach

Consumer Magazines

Editor: Marco Gandolfi; **Editor:** Marco Gandolfi
Profile: Website covering music. Music News.com provides daily updates on anything from features news, reviews and interviews to competitions, the latest releases and "all the gossip from the current music scene". Music-News.com was launched in October 2003.
MAGAZINE (ONLINE)
Classical/Choral/Band Music, Country, Folk, Bluegrass, Dance Music, Jazz & Blues, Music, Pop Music, R&B, Urban, World, Rap & Hip Hop, Rock Music

musicOMH 984275
Web site: http://www.musicomh.com/
Freq: Daily
Circ: 44383 Cision Digital Reach
Editor: Michael Hubbard
Profile: London-based independent music publication focusing on new music, reviews and features, including reviews of albums, gigs, festivals, classical music and opera. Features include interviews, Q&As, spotlights, previews and occasional podcasts. Also features photo galleries, new music posts (videos) and a weekly London gigs diary selection.Aimed at fans of all types of music in the UK and beyond.
MAGAZINE (ONLINE)
Classical/Choral/Band Music, Country, Folk, Bluegrass, Dance Music, Jazz & Blues, Music, Pop Music, R&B, Urban, World, Rap & Hip Hop, Rock Music

musicradar.com 984539
Editorial: Quay House, The Ambury, Bath BA1 1UA **Tel:** 44 01225 442244
Web site: www.musicradar.com
Freq: Daily
Circ: 1482503 Cision Digital Reach
MAGAZINE (ONLINE)
Music

MusicTech 982099
Editorial: Suite 6 / Piccadilly House, London Road, Bath BA1 6PL **Tel:** 44 01225 489984
Email: editorial@anthem-publishing.com
Web site: www.musictech.net
Freq: Monthly
Circ: 18124 Not Audited
MAGAZINE
Music

MusicVita 997907
Editorial: 40 Hillfield Park Mews, Muswell Hill, London N10 3RT
Email: prontolimited@gmail.com
Web site: http://musicvita.com/
Freq: Daily
Circ: 10597 Cision Digital Reach
MAGAZINE (ONLINE)
Country, Folk, Bluegrass, Dance Music, Jazz & Blues, Pop Music, Rap & Hip Hop, Rock Music

Muso's Guide 998614
Editorial: Flat 6, 4 West Pilton Green, Edinburgh EH4 4HT
Email: mail.musosguide@gmail.com
Web site: www.musosguide.org.uk
Freq: Daily
Circ: 11171 Cision Digital Reach
MAGAZINE (ONLINE)
Pop Music, Rock Music

Mute 996935
Tel: 44 02032 879005
Email: collective@metamute.org
Web site: www.metamute.org
Freq: Semi-Annual
Circ: 4000 Not Audited
Editor: Josephine Berry Slater
MAGAZINE
Antiques/Collectibles, Art, Arts, Literature, Photography, Politics, Theater & Performing Arts, Visual Arts

The Mutton Club 1053233
Editorial: Unit 2, 22 Packenham Street, London WC1X 0LB
Email: info@themuttonclub.com
Web site: http://www.themuttonclub.com/

Freq: Daily
Circ: 12573 Cision Digital Reach
MAGAZINE (ONLINE)
Entertainment, Health & Medicine, Personal Finance, Travel, Women's Interests

MVP 999035
Editorial: 369B High Road, Leyton, London E10 5NA **Tel:** 44 07710 509728
Email: mark@britsball.com
Web site: www.mvp247.com
Freq: Bi-Monthly
Circ: 10521 Cision Digital Reach
MAGAZINE (ONLINE)
Basketball

MWB 983571
Editorial: The Old Town Hall, Lewisham Road, Slaithwaite HD7 5AL
Tel: 44 01484 846069
Email: victoria@ras-publishing.com
Web site: www.mwb-online.co.uk
Freq: Monthly
Circ: 5900 Not Audited
MAGAZINE
Fashion

My Baba 1053065
Email: info@mybaba.com
Web site: http://mybaba.com/
Freq: Daily
Circ: 15359 Cision Digital Reach
MAGAZINE (ONLINE)
Cooking & Baking, Family & Parenting, Women's Interests

My Gaming 1060379
Tel: 44 27116 875159
Email: james@mygaming.co.za
Web site: http://www.mygaming.co.za
Circ: 502478 Cision Digital Reach
MAGAZINE (ONLINE)
Auto Aftermarket, Computers, Data Management, Electronics, Games, Competitions & Events, Government Technology, Industry, Internet, Mobile Communications, Security & Security Systems

My Glory Ride 997024
Tel: 44 02081 336375
Web site: www.mygloryride.com
Freq: Daily
Circ: 521 Cision Digital Reach
Editor: Paula Wynne
MAGAZINE (ONLINE)
News & Current Affairs

My Little Pony 983428
Tel: 44 01483 779500
Email: info@signaturepl.co.uk
Web site: www.signaturepl.co.uk/portfolio/My_Little_Pony.html
Freq: Monthly
Circ: 60000 Not Audited
MAGAZINE
Elementary School, Preschool, Teen/Young Adult

My Little Pony Equestria Girls 996110
Editorial: Old Dairy, Peper Harow Park, Nr Godalming, Godalming GU8 6BQ
Tel: 44 01483 779500
Email: info@signaturepl.co.uk
Web site: http://www.signaturepl.co.uk/portfolio/EquestriaGirls.html
Freq: Bi-Monthly
Circ: 30000 Not Audited
MAGAZINE
Preschool, Teen/Young Adult

My Merton 984074
Editorial: London Borough of Merton, 8th Floor, Civic Centre, London SM4 5DX
Tel: 44 02085 453783
Email: communications@merton.gov.uk
Web site: www.merton.gov.uk/mymerton
Freq: Quarterly
Circ: 86000 Not Audited
Editor: Bronwen Pickering

Profile: Community magazine covering news, views and issues across the Borough of Merton. Includes a comprehensive what's on listings guide. Aimed at those who live, work and learn in the London Borough of Merton. This outlet covers areas within Merton Borough.
Ad Rate: Full Page Colour £1600.00
MAGAZINE
Charitable Foundations

My Pet Online 996814
Editorial: Walton Manor, Walton, Milton Keynes, Milton Keynes MK7 7AJ
Email: editor@mypetonlinc.co.uk
Web site: www.mypetonline.co.uk
Freq: Daily
Circ: 10663 Cision Digital Reach
Editor: Elizabeth Peplow
MAGAZINE (ONLINE)
Nature & Wildlife

My Renovation Magazine 996134
Tel: 44 08447 746574
Email: editor@myrenovationmagazine.com
Web site: www.myrenovationmagazine.com
Freq: Daily
Circ: 1140 Cision Digital Reach
Editor: Melanie Jarvis-Vaughan
MAGAZINE (ONLINE)
Architecture & Design, Do-It-Yourself (DIY), Gardening, Home, Property Management & Maintenance, Real Estate

My Unique Home 999676
Email: info@myuniquehome.co.uk
Web site: www.myuniquehome.co.uk
Freq: Quarterly
Circ: 7918 Cision Digital Reach
Profile: Digital magazine covering interior design. My Unique Home features design ideas and interviews with interior design professionals.
MAGAZINE (ONLINE)
Do-It-Yourself (DIY)

My VIP 994963
Editorial: 136-142 Bramley Road, London W10 6SR **Tel:** 44 01928 732261
Web site: www.petsathome.com/
Freq: Quarterly
Circ: 645035 Not Audited
Editor: Kate Cornish
MAGAZINE
Nature & Wildlife

My Weekly 980764
Editorial: 80 Kingsway East, Dundee DD4 8SL **Tel:** 44 01382 223131
Email: myweekly@dcthomson.co.uk
Web site: www.myweekly.co.uk
Freq: Weekly
Circ: 94814 Not Audited
Profile: My Weekly is the magazine for contemporary mature women who enjoy good reading. Each week it provides relaxing fiction, great food and cookery, travel inspiration, useful financial advice, inspirational real life articles, stylish fashion, beauty and shopping news and tips. Aimed at women aged 50 years and over.
Ad Rate: Full Page Mono £4060.00
Ad Rate: Full Page Colour £6100.00
MAGAZINE
Women's Interests

myageingparent.com 997492
Email: info@myageingparent.com
Web site: www.myageingparent.com
Freq: Daily
Circ: 40777 Cision Digital Reach
Editor: Deborah Stone
MAGAZINE (ONLINE)
Retirement Savings

myCornwall 983602
Editorial: Krowji, West Park, Redruth TR15 3AJ **Tel:** 44 01209 314147
Email: news@mycornwall.tv
Web site: www.thatsmycornwall.com
Freq: Bi-Monthly Not Audited
Profile: Magazine covering Cornish heritage, history and news. Aimed at those originating from, or interested in Cornwall.

Ad Rate: Full Page Colour £450.00
MAGAZINE
Regional General Interest

Myeloma Matters 995905
Editorial: Myeloma UK, 22 Logie Mill, Beaverbank Business Park, Edinburgh EH7 4HG **Tel:** 44 01315 573332
Email: myelomauk@myeloma.org.uk
Web site: www.myeloma.org.uk/information/myeloma-matters
Freq: Quarterly
Circ: 2000 Not Audited
Editor: Kirsty Tomassi
MAGAZINE
Hematology, Patient Support

MyFamilyClub 986551
Editorial: MyFamilyClub, London
Email: marketing@myfamilyclub.co.uk
Web site: www.myfamilyclub.co.uk
Freq: Daily
Circ: 76346 Cision Digital Reach
MAGAZINE (ONLINE)
Family & Parenting, Personal Finance

myfootballwriter.com 998632
Web site: http://norwichcity.myfootballwriter.com/
Freq: Daily
Circ: 2065 Cision Digital Reach
Editor: Rick Waghorn
MAGAZINE (ONLINE)
Soccer

MyGreenPod 997209
Editorial: Suite 2, 5th Floor, Vantage Point, New England Road, Brighton BN1 4GW
Tel: 44 02030 020990
Email: katie@mygreenpod.com
Web site: www.mygreenpod.com/
Freq: Daily
Circ: 15738 Cision Digital Reach
Editor: Katie Hill
MAGAZINE (ONLINE)
Energy & Environment

MyLittleStyleFile 988486
Web site: www.mylittlestylefile.com
Freq: Daily
Circ: 842 Cision Digital Reach
Profile: My Little Style File is a website covering design for family living, including books, media, interiors, products, toys and travel for children.
MAGAZINE (ONLINE)
Fashion, Preschool

MyM Magazine 988103
Editorial: 10 Bowen Square, Daventry NN11 4DR
Web site: www.mymags.net
Freq: Monthly Not Audited
MAGAZINE
Broadcasting, Computer & Video Games, Movies & Video, Science Fiction

MyOutdoors 1054346
Editorial: 19 Suffolk Close, Macclesfield SK10 3HD **Tel:** 44 01625 668841
Email: editorial@myoutdoors.co.uk
Web site: http://www.myoutdoors.co.uk/
Freq: Daily
Circ: 17052 Cision Digital Reach
MAGAZINE (ONLINE)
Bicycles, Outdoor Recreation, Winter Sports

myReviewer 984694
Editorial: 99 Falmouth Avenue, Highams Park, London EC4 9QR
Email: dvd@myreviewer.com
Web site: www.myreviewer.com
Freq: Daily
Circ: 10350 Cision Digital Reach
Editor: Robert Shepherd
Profile: Website covering entertainment reviews. The website discusses reviews of the latest movies, DVD releases, blu-ray, computer games, books, music and anime.
MAGAZINE (ONLINE)
Entertainment, Movies & Video

Consumer Magazines

MyScience 1061881
Web site: http://www.myscience.fi
Freq: Daily
Circ: 6980 Cision Digital Reach
MAGAZINE (ONLINE)
Advertising Industry, Branding,
Broadcasting, Graphic Design, Internet,
Marketing, Media & Communications,
Photography, Publishing, Science

mywelshpool.co.uk 985926
Editorial: 41 Croft Road, Welshpool,
Welshpool SY21 7QD
Email: editor@mywelshpool.co.uk
Web site: www.mywelshpool.co.uk
Freq: Daily
Circ: 10984 Cision Digital Reach
Editor: David Williams
MAGAZINE (ONLINE)
Wales

n by Norwegian 987665
Editorial: Blackburn House, Blackburn
Road, West Hampstead, London NW6 1RZ
Tel: 44 02076 138777
Email: info@ink-global.com
Web site: www.ink-live.com/emagazines/
norwegian-magazine
Freq: Monthly Not Audited
Editor: Sarah Warwick
Profile: Airline Norwegian's in-flight
magazine covers everything from
Scandinavian culture to Norwegian's own
destination cities and travel.
MAGAZINE
Airline Inflight, Men's Interests, Travel,
Women's Interests

n.paradoxa 1052909
Editorial: 38 Bellot Street, London SE10
0AQ
Email: katy@ktpress.co.uk
Web site: www.ktpress.co.uk
Freq: Semi-Annual Not Audited
Editor: Katy Deepwell
Profile: Journal on international feminist art
(visual arts), containing thematic issues with
articles, interviews and features by women
about the relationship between feminist
theory and contemporary women's art
practices worldwide. Aimed at academics,
curators, artists and museums of
contemporary and modern art.
Ad Rate: Full Page Mono £800.00
MAGAZINE
Antiques/Collectibles, Art, Arts,
Charitable Foundations, History,
Literature, Photography, Theater &
Performing Arts, Visual Arts

NADFAS Review 981883
Editorial: NADFAS House, 8 Guilford Street,
London WC1N 1DA Tel: 44 02074 300730
Email: enquiries@nadfas.org.uk
Web site: www.nadfas.org.uk
Freq: Quarterly
Circ: 79111 Not Audited
Editor: Susanna Clarke
Profile: Magazine of the National
Association of Decorative and Fine Arts
Societies. Published quarterly and
showcases the work of the charity at both
Society and national level. Includes
information on art courses and Study Days,
listings on current events, articles on the arts
from some of the country's leading arts
writers. Aimed at members and those
interested in fine arts.
Ad Rate: Full Page Colour £2130.00
MAGAZINE
Art, Theater & Performing Arts, Visual Arts

Namnews 985079
Editorial: Venture House, 2 Arlington
Square, Downshire Way, Bracknell RG12
1WA Tel: 44 08456 434481
Email: mailbox@namnews.com
Web site: http://www.kamcity.com/
namnews/asp/latestnews.asp
Freq: Monthly
Circ: 5000 Not Audited
Editor: Mark Craft
Profile: EC newsletter covering import and
export news, marketing, management and

features on FMCG brands. Read by national
account managers.
MAGAZINE
Alcohol & Spirits, Food, Retail
Management

NappyValleyNet 1101622
Email: nappyvalleynet@btinternet.com
Web site: www.nappyvalleynet.com
Freq: Daily
Circ: 39899 Cision Digital Reach
MAGAZINE (ONLINE)
Family & Parenting

NARC. 985565
Editorial: John Buddle Work Village, Buddle
Road, Newcastle upon Tyne NE4 8AW
Tel: 44 01912 267980
Email: info@narcmedia.com
Web site: http://narcmagazine.com/
Freq: Monthly
Circ: 6000 Not Audited
Editor: Claire Dupree
MAGAZINE
Classical/Choral/Band Music, Country,
Folk, Bluegrass, Dance Music,
Entertainment, Jazz & Blues, Local
Entertainment Guides, Music, Pop Music,
R&B, Urban, World, Rap & Hip Hop

National Club Golfer 982263
Editorial: 2 Arena Park, Tarn Lane,
Scarcroft, Leeds LS17 9BF
Tel: 44 01132 893979
Email: info@sportspub.co.uk
Web site: nationalclubgolfer.com
Freq: Monthly
Circ: 58136 Not Audited
Profile: Magazine focusing on golf clubs,
courses and players. Includes news,
instruction, reviews, travel and celebrity
interviews. Magazine for an amateur golfer
with the comments on all aspects of the
world of golf. Aimed at members of golf
clubs and driving ranges.
Ad Rate: Full Page Colour £2253.96
MAGAZINE
Golf

**National Geographic
Traveller - Family** 987023
Editorial: Unit 310, Highgate Studios, 53-79
Highgate Road, London NW5 1TL
Tel: 44 02072 539906
Email: editorial@natgeotraveller.co.uk
Web site: www.natgeotraveller.co.uk
Freq: Monthly
Circ: 58242 Not Audited
Profile: Magazine covering family travel.
MAGAZINE
Family & Parenting, Travel

**National Geographic
Traveller (UK)** 985743
Editorial: Unit 310, Highgate Studios, 53-79
Highgate Road, London NW5 1TL
Tel: 44 02072 539909
Email: editorial@natgeotraveller.co.uk
Web site: http://www.natgeotraveller.co.uk/
Freq: Bi-Monthly
Circ: 42936 Not Audited
Editor: Pat Riddell
MAGAZINE
Travel

**National Rifle Association
Journal** 982281
Editorial: Lawrence House, Morrell Street,
Leamington Spa, Leamington Spa CV32 5SZ
Tel: 44 01225 687426
Web site: www.nra.org.uk
Freq: Quarterly
Circ: 6500 Not Audited
Profile: Journal covering all aspects of rifle
and pistol target shooting, book and product
reviews, features, event meetings and
profiles.
Ad Rate: Full Page Mono £290.00
Ad Rate: Full Page Colour £480.00
MAGAZINE
Shooting/Guns

The National Student 985622
Tel: 44 02078 402960
Email: info@bigchoicegroup.com
Web site: www.thenationalstudent.com
Freq: Daily
Circ: 48285 Cision Digital Reach
Editor: Lucy Miller
Profile: Website covering student lifestyle.
The National Student website shares the
latest news on entertainment and sport to
college and university advice and
technology.
MAGAZINE (ONLINE)
Student Lifestyle

National Trust Magazine 981935
Editorial: National Trust Central Office,
Heelis, Kemble Drive, Swindon SN2 2NA
Tel: 44 01793 817400
Email: magazine@nationaltrust.org.uk
Web site: www.nationaltrustmagazine.co.uk
Freq: 3 Times/Year
Circ: 2310299 Not Audited
Editor: Sally Palmer
Profile: Magazine covering the conservation
of buildings, countryside and coastal areas
in the care of the National Trust. Aimed at
National Trust members.
Ad Rate: Full Page Colour £21167.00
MAGAZINE
Field Sports, History

National Weddings magazine
987233
Editorial: Ground Floor Offices, Hill House,
Stoney Hollow, Lutterworth LE17 4BJ
Tel: 44 01455 556957
Email: editor@nationalweddingsmagazine.
co.uk
Web site: www.nationalweddingsmagazine.
co.uk
Freq: Quarterly
Circ: 40000 Not Audited
Editor: Denise Russell
Profile: Magazine covering wedding
services and providers from all over the
country. It includes articles on wedding
dresses and wedding venues as well as
real-life wedding stories. Aimed at people
planning a wedding.
MAGAZINE
Weddings

Native Monster 990606
Editorial: 51-53 Queen Street,
Wolverhampton WV1 1ES
Tel: 44 01902 319368
Email: info@nativemonster.com
Web site: www.nativemonster.com
Freq: Daily
Circ: 36258 Cision Digital Reach
MAGAZINE (ONLINE)
Bars, Clubs & Pubs, Comedy,
Entertainment, Local Entertainment
Guides, Regional General Interest

The Native Pony Magazine
1053855
Tel: 44 01380 734374
Email: nativepony@redpin.co.uk
Web site: http://www.thenativepony.com
Freq: Bi-Monthly
MAGAZINE
Equestrian Sports

Natives.co.uk 990458
Editorial: 263 Putney Bridge Road, London
SW15 2PU Tel: 44 01772 639046
Web site: www.natives.co.uk
Freq: Daily
Circ: 6964 Cision Digital Reach
MAGAZINE (ONLINE)
Careers, Winter Sports

Natural Health (UK) 981826
Editorial: 21-23 Phoenix Court, Hawkins
Road, Colchester, Colchester CO2 8JY
Tel: 44 01206 505900
Email: news@naturalhealthmagazine.co.uk
Web site: www.naturalhealthmagazine.co.uk
Freq: Monthly
Circ: 60000 Not Audited

Editor: Claire Munnings
MAGAZINE
Alternative Medicine, Health & Medicine,
Nutrition

**The Natural Health Website
for Women** 996584
Editorial: 14 St Johns Road, Tunbridge
Wells TN4 9NP Tel: 44 08705 329244
Email: health@marilynglenville.com
Web site: www.marilynglenville.com/
Freq: Daily
Circ: 39981 Cision Digital Reach
Editor: Marilyn Glenville
MAGAZINE (ONLINE)
Alternative Medicine, Health & Medicine,
Obstetrics & Gynecology (OB/GYN)

Natural Lifestyle 981827
Tel: 44 01279 810080
Email: info@targetpublishing.com
Web site: www.mynaturallifestyle.co.uk
Freq: Monthly
Circ: 50000 Not Audited
Editor: Rachel Symonds
MAGAZINE
Alternative Medicine

Natural Pharmacy Business
987445
Tel: 44 01279 810080
Email: info@targetpublishing.com
Web site: www.naturalpharmacybusiness.
com
Freq: Quarterly Not Audited
Editor: James Harrison
MAGAZINE
Alternative Medicine, Pharmaceuticals

Natural Products 983677
Editorial: Nile House, Nile Street, Brighton
BN1 1HW Tel: 44 01273 645110
Web site: www.naturalproductsonline.co.uk
Freq: Monthly
Circ: 5354 Not Audited
Editor: Jim Manson
Profile: Magazine covering news, views and
trends from the health food industry. Aimed
at health store retailers and manufacturers.
Ad Rate: Full Page Colour £2412.00
MAGAZINE
Alcohol & Spirits, Food

NaturalBlender.com 1057339
Editorial: 4th Floor, 76 Oxford Street,
London W1D 1BS Tel: 44 02038 236668
Email: hello@naturalblender.com
Web site: https://naturalblender.com/
Freq: Daily
Circ: 2268 Cision Digital Reach
MAGAZINE (ONLINE)
Bars, Clubs & Pubs

Nature Climate Change 997370
Editorial: Nature Publishing Group, The
Macmillan Building, 4 Crinan Street, London
N1 9XW
Email: nclimate@nature.com
Web site: www.nature.com/nclimate/index.
html
Freq: Monthly
Circ: 797 Not Audited
MAGAZINE
News & Current Affairs

Nature's Home 981993
Editorial: The Lodge, Potton Road, Sandy,
Sandy SG19 2DL Tel: 44 01767 680551
Email: mark.ward@rspb.org.uk
Web site: www.rspb.org.uk
Freq: Quarterly
Circ: 610968 Not Audited
MAGAZINE
Charitable Foundations, Nature & Wildlife

**Nautilus International
Telegraph** 984245
Editorial: 1&2 The Shrubberies, George
Lane, South Woodford, London E18 1BD
Tel: 44 02089 896677
Email: telegraph@nautilusint.org
Web site: www.nautilusint.org

Freq: Monthly
Circ: 34471 Not Audited
Editor: Andrew Linington
Profile: Journal of Nautilus International the union of maritime professionals. Covers international shipping industry and trade union news. Aimed at the shipping industry and professional staff.
Ad Rate: Full Page Mono £3975.00
Ad Rate: Full Page Colour £3975.00
MAGAZINE
Marine & Boat Trade

The Naval Architect
980821
Editorial: 8-9 Northumberland Street, London WC2N 5DA **Tel:** 44 02072 354622
Email: editorial@rina.org.uk
Web site: http://www.rina.org.uk/tna.html
Freq: Monthly
Circ: 9711 Not Audited
Profile: International journal of the Royal Institution of Naval Architects. Aimed at naval architects, marine superintendents, marine consultants, surveyors and other marine personnel worldwide.
Ad Rate: Full Page Colour £2980.00
MAGAZINE
Engineering, Marine & Boat Trade, Shipping & Warehousing

naval-technology.com
983162
Editorial: John Carpenter House, John Carpenter Street, London EC4Y 0AN
Tel: 44 02079 366400
Email: onlineeditorial@kable.co.uk
Web site: http://www.naval-technology.com
Freq: Daily
Circ: 59154 Cision Digital Reach
Profile: Website covering the naval technology. "Naval-technology.com brings you up-to-date international news and features on technology in the defence industry, covering projects, trends, products, services and more in the naval sector."
MAGAZINE (ONLINE)
Defense & National Security, Marine & Boat Trade

Navigation News
984926
Editorial: 1 Kensington Gore, London SW7 2AT **Tel:** 44 02075 913134
Email: editor@rin.org.uk
Web site: www.rin.org.uk/general/Navigation-News
Freq: Bi-Monthly
Circ: 2900 Not Audited
Editor: Tony Fyler
Profile: Magazine focusing on all forms of navigation: in space, in the air, on land and at sea. Aimed at members of the Royal Institute of Navigation and anyone interested in navigation, from mariners and aviators to orienteers and rally drivers.
Ad Rate: Full Page Colour £1150.00
MAGAZINE
Automotive, Aviation, Shipping & Warehousing

Navy News
983051
Editorial: MP 1.4 Navy Command, Leach Building, HMS Excellent, Portsmouth PO2 8BY **Tel:** 44 02392 625255
Email: edit@navynews.co.uk
Web site: www.navynews.co.uk
Freq: Monthly
Circ: 35000 Not Audited
Editor: Mike Gray
Profile: Newspaper for the Royal Navy, Sea Cadets and the Royal Naval Association containing features. Aimed at the Royal Navy and the general public.
Ad Rate: Full Page Colour £2870.00
MAGAZINE
Armed Forces

NB Online
983218
Editorial: 105 Judd Street, London WC1H 9NE **Tel:** 44 02073 881266
Email: nbonline@rnib.org.uk
Web site: www.rnib.org.uk/nb-online
Freq: Bi-Monthly
Circ: 11 Cision Digital Reach
Profile: Magazine covering the latest developments in eye health, social care and policy. News, features by leading experts, case histories and personal views, advice,

letters, products, conferences, training and job adverts in the field of sight loss and eye health. Aimed at all sight loss and eye health professionals.
MAGAZINE (ONLINE)
Charitable Foundations, Ophthalmology & Optometry, Patient Support

Nee Hao
997675
Email: hello@neehao.co.uk
Web site: www.neehao.co.uk
Freq: Daily
Circ: 47794 Cision Digital Reach
MAGAZINE (ONLINE)
Art, Asia, Expatriates, Fashion, Literature, Local Entertainment Guides, Photography, Theater & Performing Arts, Travel, Visual Arts

Neighbour Net Ltd
999279
Editorial: The Courtyard, 4 Evelyn Road, Chiswick, London W4 5JL
Tel: 44 02089 947888
Email: info@neighbournet.com
Web site: www.neighbournet.com
Freq: Daily
Circ: 10560 Cision Digital Reach
MAGAZINE (ONLINE)
Regional General Interest

NEO
985502
Editorial: 3 East Ave, Bournemouth, Bournemouth BH3 7BW
Email: mail@neomag.co.uk
Web site: www.neomag.co.uk
Freq: Monthly Not Audited
Editor: Gemma Cox
Profile: Magazine covering new wave action entertainment features, news and reviews of the latest anime, manga, film and games releases. Aimed at 15 to 30 year old fans of action entertainment.
Ad Rate: Full Page Colour £2495.00
MAGAZINE
Asia, Cartoons, Entertainment, Movies & Video

Neon
999420
Email: info@neonmagazine.co.uk
Web site: www.neonmagazine.co.uk
Freq: Quarterly
Circ: 10392 Cision Digital Reach
Editor: Krishan Coupland
MAGAZINE (ONLINE)
Literature

Neon Filler
1105196
Email: info@neonfiller.com
Web site: www.neonfiller.com
Freq: Daily
Circ: 14911 Cision Digital Reach
MAGAZINE (ONLINE)
Rock Music

The Nerd Recites
1100499
Editorial: 16 Phorpres House, 189 London Road, Peterborough PE2 9DS
Email: info@thenerdrecites.com
Web site: http://thenerdrecites.com/
Freq: Daily
Circ: 13805 Cision Digital Reach
MAGAZINE (ONLINE)
Computer & Video Games, Movies & Video

Nerve
981767
Editorial: Bournemouth University Students' Union, Talbot Campus, Fern Barrow, Poole BH12 5BB **Tel:** 44 01202 965774
Email: editor@nervemedia.org.uk
Web site: www.nervemedia.org.uk
Freq: Bi-Monthly
Circ: 1000 Not Audited
Profile: Magazine promoting grass roots art and culture, artists' profiles, visual arts, film, theatre and poetry as well as political and social issues in Merseyside, major political issues, international affairs and public issues such as ID cards and homelessness. Aimed at discerning readers looking for something a bit different.
Ad Rate: Full Page Colour £400.00
MAGAZINE
Student Lifestyle

Nerve (Merseyside)
999462
Editorial: 1st Floor, 96 Bold Street, Liverpool L1 4HY **Tel:** 44 01517 099948
Email: nervemagazine@gmail.com
Web site: www.catalystmedia.org.uk
Freq: Daily
Circ: 15000 Not Audited
MAGAZINE
Regional

Nescot
998863
Tel: 44 02083 941731
Email: info@nescot.ac.uk
Web site: www.nescot.ac.uk
Freq: Daily
Circ: 9609 Cision Digital Reach
MAGAZINE (ONLINE)
Careers, Education, Higher Education, Student Lifestyle, Students

NEST Magazine
997307
Editorial: 23 Church Street, Willingham, Cambridgeshire, Willingham CB24 5HS
Tel: 44 01954 260940
Email: nest@hockeys.co.uk
Web site: www.hockeys.co.uk/
Freq: Monthly
Circ: 10350 Not Audited
Editor: Amy Grace
MAGAZINE
Alcohol & Spirits, Architecture & Design, Bars, Clubs & Pubs, Beauty & Grooming, Beer, Beverages, Celebrities, Cooking & Baking, Cosmetics, Do-It-Yourself (DIY)

net
981496
Editorial: Quay House, The Ambury, Bath BA1 1UA **Tel:** 44 01225 442244
Email: netmag@futurenet.com
Web site: www.creativebloq.com/net-magazine
Freq: Monthly
Circ: 10632 Not Audited
Profile: Magazine covering all aspects of the Internet. Includes news, technical tips, software and features on how to build websites. Contains tutorials from leading agencies, interviews with the web's biggest names, agenda-setting features, marketing issues, usability and accessibility, information architecture, issues of security and copywriting.Covers topics such as CSS, PHP, Flash, JavaScript, web graphics. Designed for web designers and developers. Aimed at expert internet users and website designers and developers.Alternative Title: Web Builder
Ad Rate: Full Page Colour £2850.00
MAGAZINE
Internet

NET-A-PORTER.COM
984019
Editorial: 1 The Village Offices, Westfield London Shopping Centre, Ariel Way, London W12 7GF **Tel:** 44 02034 714500
Email: editors@net-a-porter.com
Web site: www.NET-A-PORTER.com
Freq: Daily
Circ: 11521802 Cision Digital Reach
Editor: Jenny Dickinson
MAGAZINE (ONLINE)
Fashion, Luxury Goods

Netball
982192
Editorial: Netball House, 1-12 Old Park Road, Hitchin SG5 2JR
Tel: 44 01462 442344
Email: editor@englandnetball.co.uk
Web site: www.englandnetball.co.uk
Freq: Quarterly
Circ: 60000 Not Audited
MAGAZINE
Basketball

NetDoctor
983274
Editorial: 72 Broadwick Street, London W1F 9EP **Tel:** 44 02073 123941
Email: pressreleases@netdoctor.co.uk
Web site: www.netdoctor.co.uk
Freq: Daily
Circ: 2906330 Cision Digital Reach
Profile: Website covering medical information. The NetDoctor.co.uk shares the latest news, information and advice on

men's, women's and children's health, and includes articles on travel medicine, sexual health, wellbeing, pharmaceuticals and symptoms.
MAGAZINE (ONLINE)
Health & Medicine

Netimperative
980794
Editorial: The Digital Hub, 8 Macklin Street, London WC2B 5NF **Tel:** 44 02072 449661
Web site: www.netimperative.com
Freq: Daily
Circ: 50267 Cision Digital Reach
Editor: Robin Langford
Profile: Website covering the digital marketing and business. netimperative shares the latest news on services for businesses, consumers, observers and commentators interested in all aspects of digital business, including commentary, opinion, features, case studies, profiles, research, statistics, published reports and events concerning key digital sectors and industry issues.
MAGAZINE (ONLINE)
Internet

Netmission
1061110
Email: info@netmission.fi
Web site: http://www.netmission.fi/
Freq: Daily
Circ: 6983 Cision Digital Reach
MAGAZINE (ONLINE)
Religion

netmums.com
983269
Editorial: Henry Wood House, 2 Riding House Street, London W1W 7FA
Email: pressrelease@netmums.com
Web site: www.netmums.com
Freq: Daily
Circ: 3813115 Cision Digital Reach
Editor: Simantha Mahmud
MAGAZINE (ONLINE)
Family & Parenting

Network Communications News
981657
Editorial: Alexander House, 38 Forehill, Ely, Ely CB7 4ZA **Tel:** 44 01353 616117
Web site: www.networkcommunicationsnews.co.uk
Freq: Monthly
Circ: 22000 Not Audited
MAGAZINE
Internet

Network Computing (UK)
980955
Editorial: 35 Station Square, Petts Wood, Orpington BR5 1LZ **Tel:** 44 01689 616000
Web site: www.networkcomputing.co.uk
Freq: Bi-Monthly
Circ: 17000 Not Audited
Editor: Ray Smyth
MAGAZINE
Computers, Internet

Network Wales
981019
Editorial: Baltic House, Mount Stuart Square, Cardiff CF10 5FH
Tel: 44 08002 888329
Email: help@wcva.org.uk
Web site: www.wcva.org.uk
Freq: Bi-Weekly
Circ: 1200 Not Audited
Editor: Lynne Reynolds
Profile: Magazine covering updates for Wales Council for Voluntary Action. Includes news and funding information. Aimed at WCVA membership national and regional charities, voluntary groups and agencies, local community groups, local authorities, members of parliament and assembly members.
MAGAZINE
Charitable Foundations

Networking+
981674
Editorial: Brassey House, New Zealand Avenue, Walton-on-Thames, London KT12 1QD **Tel:** 44 01932 481728
Web site: www.networkingplus.co.uk
Freq: Monthly

Consumer Magazines

Noble Rot Magazine 1074960
Editorial: 51 Lamb's Conduit Street, London
WC1N 3NB **Tel:** 44 02072 428963
Email: hello@noblerot.co.uk
Web site: http://noblerot.co.uk/
Freq: 3 Times/Year
Circ: 2500 Not Audited
Editor: Mark Andrew; **Editor:** Dan Keeling
MAGAZINE
Cooking & Baking, Food, Grocery Stores,
Organic Food, Restaurant Reviews,
Vegetarianism & Veganism, Wine/
Winemaking

Noctis 996554
Editorial: 14 Pepys House, Kirkwall Place,
Bethnal Green, London E2 0NB
Email: info@noctismag.com
Web site: www.noctismag.com
Freq: Quarterly Not Audited
Editor: Leoni Blue Fleming
Profile: Digital magazine covering art, music,
fashion and culture. First published in 2011.
MAGAZINE
Art, Fashion

The Non-League Paper 984186
Editorial: Lower Ground Floor, Tuition
House, St Georges Road, London SW19
4EU **Tel:** 44 02089 714333
Email: nlp@greenwayspublishing.co.uk
Web site: www.thenonleaguefootballpaper.
com
Freq: Weekly
Circ: 32000 Not Audited
Profile: Newspaper covering non-league
football from the conference down to
regional and local based leagues. Covers
match reports, features, news, statistics,
player profiles and guest columns. Aimed at
football fans, chairmen, managers, players
and coaches.
Ad Rate: Full Page Colour £1995.00
MAGAZINE
Soccer

**Nonwovens Report
International** 983559
Editorial: West One, 114 Wellington Street,
Leeds LS1 1BA **Tel:** 44 01138 198155
Email: info@wtin.com
Web site: http://www.wtin.com/magazine/
nonwovens-report-international/
Freq: Bi-Monthly
Circ: 10470 Not Audited
Profile: Publication covering the products,
processes, equipment and commercial
activities of the world's nonwovens
industries. Aimed at the nonwovens industry
and its suppliers.
Ad Rate: Full Page Mono £1205.00
Ad Rate: Full Page Colour £2600.00
MAGAZINE
Fashion

Nordic Intelligence 1095579
Email: editor@nordicintelligence.com
Web site: http://nordicintelligence.com/
Freq: Daily
Circ: 744 Cislon Digital Reach
MAGAZINE (ONLINE)
Airline Inflight, Architecture & Design,
Business, Fashion, Industry, Small and
Medium Business

Norfolk On My Mind 986456
Editorial: Queens House, Queens Square,
Attleborough, Brundall NR17 2AE
Tel: 44 01953 456789
Web site: www.norfolkonmymind.co.uk
Freq: Bi-Monthly
Circ: 10000 Not Audited
Editor: Anna Wignall
Profile: Magazine covering news and events
in Norfolk. Each issue includes interviews,
food, fashion, interiors, motoring, health,
legal affairs, entertainment and gardening
features.
MAGAZINE
Regional General Interest

Norfolk Voice 998969
Editorial: Milburn House, Dean Street,
Newcastle upon Tyne NE1 1LF

Freq: Bi-Monthly
Circ: 4000 Not Audited
MAGAZINE
Business

North East Connected 1098313
Editorial: Portrack Grange Road, Stockton-
on-Tees TS18 2PF **Tel:** 44 01642 633765
Email: newsdesk@neconnected.co.uk
Web site: www.neconnected.co.uk
Freq: Monthly
Circ: 2000 Not Audited
MAGAZINE
Regional General Interest

North East Lifestyle 999628
Editorial: 415 Chillingham Road, Heaton,
Newcastle upon Tyne NE6 5QU
Tel: 44 01912 666390
Email: northeastpublishing@hotmail.com
Web site: http://www.nelifestyle.co.uk/
Freq: Monthly
Circ: 20000 Not Audited
Editor: Sally Proud
Profile: Blog covering lifestyle. North East
Lifestyle blog discusses anything from
lifestyle and travel to fashion and beauty.
The blog has an archive dating back to
November 2010.
MAGAZINE
Regional General Interest

North East Times 982539
Tel: 44 01912 460212
Email: enquiries@netimesmagazine.co.uk
Web site: www.netimesmagazine.co.uk
Freq: Monthly
Editor: Alison Cowie
MAGAZINE
Automakers, Business, Fashion, Regional,
Residential Real Estate, Retail, Social
Issues, Travel Industry

North Somerset Life 986788
Editorial: Life Editor, North Somerset
Council, First Floor Town Hall, Weston-
super-Mare BS23 1UJ **Tel:** 44 01275 884139
Email: editor@n-somerset.gov.uk
Web site: https://northsomersetlife.
wordpress.com/
Freq: Bi-Monthly
Circ: 92000 Not Audited
Editor: Nicola Clarke
MAGAZINE
Regional General Interest

Northampton Life 997510
Editorial: Portfolio Innovation Centre, St
Georges Avenue, Northampton NN2 6FB
Tel: 44 01604 633796
Email: press@northantslife.co.uk
Web site: www.northantslife.co.uk
Freq: Monthly
Circ: 25000 Not Audited
MAGAZINE
Regional General Interest

The Northbank 996538
Editorial: West Wing, Somerset House,
Strand, London WC2R 1LA
Tel: 44 02036 979270
Email: info@thenorthbank.london
Web site: www.thenorthbank.org/the-
northbank-magazine
Freq: 3 Times/Year
Circ: 20000 Not Audited
Editor: Jonathan Whiley
MAGAZINE
Regional General Interest

**Northern African Wireless
Communications** 984673
Editorial: Brassey House, New Zealand
Avenue, Walton-on-Thames, London KT12
1QD **Tel:** 44 01932 886537
Web site: www.kadiumpublishing.com/
nawc.html
Freq: Bi-Monthly
Circ: 7000 Not Audited
Profile: Publication dedicated to wireless
communications throughout northern
equatorial Africa and providing direct contact
with key wireless communications buyers

and specifies throughout the region. Aimed
at companies and organisations that use
mobile and wireless communications as part
of their business.
Ad Rate: Full Page Colour £3695.00
MAGAZINE
Industry, Internet, Mobile
Communications, Telecommunications/
Electronic Communications

Northern Correspondent 996880
Email: editor@jesmondlocal.com
Web site: www.northerncorrespondent.com
Freq: Monthly
Circ: 1000 Not Audited
MAGAZINE
Regional, Regional General Interest

Northern Engineer 1100938
Web site: www.northernengineer.co.uk
Freq: Daily
Circ: 11146 Cision Digital Reach
Editor: Chris Rowell
MAGAZINE (ONLINE)
Alternative/Renewable Energy,
Electronics, Engineering, Manufacturing,
Oil

Northern Horse Magazine 995059
Email: info@northernhorsemagazine.co.uk
Web site: www.northernhorsemagazine.co.
uk
Freq: Bi-Monthly Not Audited
MAGAZINE
Equestrian Sports

**Northern Ireland Healthcare
Review** 981192
Editorial: Pharmacy Life, 142 - 148
Albertbridge Road, Belfast BT5 4GS
Tel: 44 02890 999441
Email: editor@nimedical.info
Web site: http://nihealthcare.com/
Freq: Quarterly
Circ: 3750 Not Audited
Editor: Sarah Nelson
Profile: Magazine covering the politics and
current affairs of GPs and hospital doctors.
Also contains general news, views, business
issues and articles on clinical and
educational matters, human interest,
finance, lifestyle, new products and current
trials. Aimed at GPs, consultants, hospital
doctors and health-care professionals in
Northern Ireland.
Ad Rate: Full Page Mono £1595.00
Ad Rate: Full Page Colour £1595.00
MAGAZINE
Medicine

**Northern Ireland Homes &
Lifestyle** 984652
Editorial: PO Box 355, Co Down, Bangor
BT20 9ER **Tel:** 44 02891 478703
Email: enquiries@bayviewpublishing.net
Web site: www.bayviewpublishing.net/
northern-ireland-homes.html
Freq: Bi-Monthly
Circ: 8000 Not Audited
Editor: Claire Craig
Profile: Magazine covering homes, interiors
and lifestyle including arts and crafts, people
and places, food and wine, travel, motoring
and local homes.
Ad Rate: Full Page Colour £1350.00
MAGAZINE
Do-It-Yourself (DIY)

**Northern Ireland Travel and
Leisure News** 995775
Editorial: Unit 1, Windsor Business Park, 16-
18 Lower Windsor Avenue, Belfast BT9 7DW
Tel: 44 02890 666151
Email: info@nitravelnews.com
Web site: www.nitravelnews.com
Freq: Monthly
Circ: 23000 Not Audited
Editor: Brian Ogle
MAGAZINE
Travel

**Northern Ireland Visitors
Journal** 982341
Editorial: 38 Heron Road, Sydenham
Business Park, Belfast BT3 9LE
Tel: 44 02890 457457
Email: info@pentongroup.com
Web site: http://www.pentongroup.com/
northern-irelands-visitors-journal/
Freq: Semi-Annual
Circ: 18000 Not Audited
Editor: Tara Craig
Profile: Comprehensive reference guide to
Northern Ireland's leisure, entertainment and
holiday facilities. First published in 1997, the
publication has an average of 150 pages per
issue. Aimed at those visiting Northern
Ireland, and the home tourist.
Ad Rate: Full Page Colour £1850.00
MAGAZINE
Travel

**Northern Ireland's
Neighbourhood Retailer** 995983
Editorial: Penton House, 38 Heron Road,
Sydenham Business Park, Belfast BT3 9LE
Tel: 44 02890 457457
Email: info@neighbourhoodretailer.com
Web site: www.neighbourhoodretailer.com
Freq: Monthly
Circ: 4521 Not Audited
Editor: Russell Campbell; **Editor:** Damien
Whinnery
MAGAZINE
Alcohol & Spirits, Food, Retail
Management

Northern Life Magazine 983919
Editorial: Loop Publishing Ltd, 2 Sun Street,
Colne, Colne BB8 0JJ **Tel:** 44 01282 861982
Email: info@looppublishing.co.uk
Web site: http://www.northernlifemagazine.
co.uk/
Freq: Bi-Monthly
Circ: 27000 Not Audited
Editor: Karen Shaw
Profile: Magazine providing local information
concerning life in the north including a
what's on guide to theatre, arts and places
to visit in the area.
Ad Rate: Full Page Colour £1250.00
MAGAZINE
Regional General Interest

Northern Soul 997515
Web site: www.northernsoul.me.uk
Freq: Daily
Circ: 14980 Cision Digital Reach
MAGAZINE (ONLINE)
Regional General Interest

Northern Woman (Ireland) 982555
Editorial: 33 Clarendon Road, Clarendon
Dock, Belfast BT1 3BG
Tel: 44 02890 264264
Web site: www.northernwoman.co.uk
Freq: Bi-Monthly
Circ: 7934 Not Audited
MAGAZINE
Fashion, Women's Interests

Northside 982547
Editorial: RMC House, 6 Broadfield Court,
Broadfield Business Park, Sheffield S8 0XF
Tel: 44 01142 506300
Email: northside@rmcmedia.co.uk
Web site: http://www.rmcmedia.co.uk/
magazines/northside/
Freq: Monthly
Circ: 20000 Not Audited
MAGAZINE
Regional General Interest

The Northumbrian 982913
Editorial: Unit 17, St Peter's Wharf,
Newcastle upon Tyne NE6 1TZ
Tel: 44 01661 845020
Email: editor@thenorthumbrian.co.uk
Web site: www.thenorthumbrian.co.uk
Freq: Bi-Monthly
Circ: 44000 Not Audited
Editor: Stewart Bonney

Profile: Local interest magazine covering people, places and events and gardening. Aimed at residents and ex-pats of Northumbria who enjoy the countryside.
Ad Rate: Full Page Mono £740.00
Ad Rate: Full Page Colour £900.00
MAGAZINE
Regional General Interest

Northwest Aviation 1060783
Tel: 44 86298 8481309
Web site: http://2146937.atobo.com.cn/CN/WebSite/2146937.html
Freq: Monthly
Circ: 15003 Not Audited
MAGAZINE
Airline Inflight, Antiques/Collectibles, Art, Arts, Bars, Clubs & Pubs, Comedy, Entertainment, Lifestyle, Literature, Local Entertainment Guides

Norwich Resident 987471
Editorial: Prospect House, Rouen Road, Norwich NR1 1RE
Web site: www.norwichresident.co.uk
Freq: Monthly
Circ: 8500 Not Audited
Profile: Luxury lifestyle magazine for Norwich and the surrounding area. It features fashion, interiors, technology and gadgets, food and drink, beauty, health, weekend leisure and interviews with well-known people in Norwich, plus everything you need to know to live your life in style.
MAGAZINE
Luxury Goods, Regional General Interest

NOTED 986981
Web site: http://www.noted-magazine.com/
Freq: Daily
Circ: 521 Cision Digital Reach
Editor: Kate Lam
Profile: Website covering lifestyle. NOTED website shares the latest news on lifestyle magazine covering art, culture, beauty, design, fashion, food, drink, lifestyle and travel.
MAGAZINE (ONLINE)
Women's Interests

Noted 998331
Email: info@notedtech.net
Web site: http://www.notedtech.net/
Freq: Daily
Circ: 883 Cision Digital Reach
Profile: Website covering lifestyle. NOTED website shares the latest news on lifestyle magazine covering art, culture, beauty, design, fashion, food, drink, lifestyle and travel.
MAGAZINE (ONLINE)
Audio Video Trade, Cameras, Consumer Electronics, Electronics, Mobile Electronics, Movies & Video

NOTION 982096
Editorial: NOTION Magazine, Unit PG02, 23-28 Penn Street, London N1 5DL
Web site: www.notionmagazine.com
Freq: Quarterly
Circ: 35000 Not Audited
Editor: Phie McKenzie
MAGAZINE
Dance Music, Fashion, Rap & Hip Hop, Rock Music

Notting Hill & Holland Park Magazine 988140
Editorial: 6th Floor, One Canada Square, Canary Wharf, London E14 5AB
Tel: 44 02079 874320
Email: info@rwmg.co.uk
Web site: http://rwmg.co.uk/website/advertising__description.php?id_advertising=349
Freq: Monthly
Circ: 25000 Not Audited
MAGAZINE
Luxury Goods, Regional General Interest

Nouse 981768
Editorial: York University Students Union, Grimston House, Vanbrugh House, York YO10 5DD **Tel:** 44 01904 323724
Email: editor@nouse.co.uk
Web site: www.nouse.co.uk
Freq: Bi-Monthly
Circ: 4000 Not Audited
MAGAZINE
Student Lifestyle

Novelicious 995526
Web site: www.novelicious.com
Freq: Daily
Circ: 13188 Cision Digital Reach
MAGAZINE (ONLINE)
Literature

Now 982362
Editorial: 161 Marsh Wall, London E14 9AP
Tel: 44 02031 485000
Email: nowmagletters@timeinc.com
Web site: www.celebsnow.co.uk
Freq: Weekly
Circ: 86838 Not Audited
Profile: Magazine covering celebrity lifestyle. It features celebrity news and gossip as well as articles on fashion and beauty. Aimed at young, independent female urbanites aged between 16 and 35 years old.
Ad Rate: Full Page Colour £18000.00
MAGAZINE
Celebrities, Women's Interests

NowGamer 985004
Editorial: Richmond House, 33 Richmond Hill, Bournemouth, Bournemouth BH2 6EZ
Tel: 44 01202 586200
Web site: www.nowgamer.com
Freq: Daily
Circ: 119075 Cision Digital Reach
MAGAZINE (ONLINE)
Computer & Video Games

NOWNESS 985489
Editorial: 115 Golden Lane, London EC1Y 0TJ **Tel:** 44 02036 405810
Email: editorial@nowness.com
Web site: www.nowness.com
Freq: Daily
Circ: 431086 Cision Digital Reach
MAGAZINE (ONLINE)
Antiques/Collectibles, Art, Arts, Fashion, Literature, Luxury Goods, Photography, Theater & Performing Arts, Visual Arts

Nowy Czas 999438
Editorial: 63 King's Grove, London SE15 2NA **Tel:** 44 02076 398507
Email: editor@nowyczas.co.uk
Web site: http://www.nowyczas.co.uk/
Freq: Monthly
Circ: 10000 Not Audited
Editor: Greg Malkiewioz
MAGAZINE
Europe, National News

N-Photo 986458
Editorial: Quay House, The Ambury, Bath BA1 1UA **Tel:** 44 01225 442244
Email: mail@nphotomag.com
Web site: www.nphotomag.com
Freq: Monthly
Circ: 26486 Not Audited
Editor: Paul Grogan
MAGAZINE
Cameras, Photography

NSU/LIFE 998478
Editorial: Northumbria Students' Union, 2 Sandyford Road, Newcastle upon Tyne NE1 8SB **Tel:** 44 01912 274757
Email: nsulifeteam@gmail.com
Web site: http://nsu-media.com/
Freq: Monthly
Circ: 20000 Not Audited
MAGAZINE
Student Lifestyle

The Nudge 999372
Editorial: 4th Floor Runway East, Monmouth House, 58-64 City Road, London EC1Y 2AL
Email: editor@thenudge.com
Web site: www.thenudge.com
Freq: Daily
Circ: 138728 Cision Digital Reach
MAGAZINE (ONLINE)
Bars, Clubs & Pubs, Comedy, Cooking & Baking, Local Entertainment Guides, Movies & Video, Restaurant Reviews

NUIT Magazine 998273
Editorial: 23 Arsenal Way, Flat 3, Woolwich, London SE18 6TE
Email: press@nuitmagazine.com
Web site: www.nuitmagazine.com
Freq: Daily
Circ: 12487 Cision Digital Reach
MAGAZINE (ONLINE)
Beauty & Grooming, Cosmetics, Fashion, Hair, Men's Interests, Travel, Women's Interests

Numb 997876
Web site: www.numb-uk.com
Freq: Daily
Circ: 872 Cision Digital Reach
MAGAZINE (ONLINE)
Broadcasting, Classical/Choral/Band Music, Computer & Video Games, Country, Folk, Bluegrass, Dance Music, Fashion, Jazz & Blues, Movies & Video, Music, Photography

Nursery Management Today 984755
Editorial: Culvert House, 2nd Floor, London SW11 5DH **Tel:** 44 01626 852030
Web site: http://www.nmt-magazine.co.uk
Freq: Bi-Monthly
Circ: 8000 Not Audited
Editor: Sue Churchill
Profile: Magazine covering nursery business, property and management issues.
Ad Rate: Full Page Colour £1185.00
MAGAZINE
Preschool

Nursery Today 983719
Editorial: Naishville, 1 Churchgates, The Wilderness, Berkamsted, Berkhamsted HP4 2UB **Tel:** 44 01442 289930
Web site: www.nursery-today.co.uk
Freq: Monthly
Circ: 4443 Not Audited
Editor: Penny Franks
Profile: Nursery Today is a magazine providing news, details of exhibitions, new product information and articles about the retail nursery trade. It is published nine times a year by Lema Publishing. First published in 1997. Nursery Today is aimed at buyers, retailers, suppliers and manufacturers of nursery products.
Ad Rate: Full Page Colour £1350.00
MAGAZINE
Preschool

Nursery World 981121
Editorial: MA Education, St Jude's Church, Dulwich Road, London SE24 0PB
Tel: 44 02075 016695
Email: news.nw@markallengroup.com
Web site: www.nurseryworld.co.uk
Freq: Bi-Weekly
Circ: 10333 Not Audited
Editor: Liz Roberts
Profile: Nursery World is a fortnightly magazine covering all aspects of baby and child care, education and training. First published in 1925. Nursery World is aimed at early years professionals, nursery managers, teachers, nursery nurses, nannies and child minders.
Ad Rate: Full Page Mono £1690.00
Ad Rate: Full Page Colour £2670.00
MAGAZINE
Preschool

Nursery-online.com 984746
Tel: 44 01512 036301
Email: cathy@nursery-online.com
Web site: www.nursery-online.com
Freq: Daily
Circ: 10709 Cision Digital Reach
Editor: Cathy Bryan
MAGAZINE (ONLINE)
Preschool

Nutraceutical Business Review 996746
Editorial: Natraj Building The Tanneries, 55 Bermondsey Street, London SE1 3XG
Tel: 44 02071 931279
Email: info@hpcimedia.com
Web site: www.nutraceuticalbusinessreview.com
Freq: Quarterly Not Audited
MAGAZINE
Nutrition, Retail Management

Nutraceuticals Now 988246
Editorial: 6 Victoria Terrace, Inverness IV2 3QA **Tel:** 44 01463 718993
Email: info@nutraceuticalsnow.com
Web site: www.nutraceuticalsnow.com
Freq: Quarterly Not Audited
Editor: Charles Faulkner
Profile: Magazine providing the latest information on functional products and ingredients which are defined as having a disease preventing and/or health promoting benefit in addition to their nutritional value.
MAGAZINE
Nutrition

Nutrition & Food Science 985389
Editorial: Howard House, Wagon Lane, Bingley BD16 1WA **Tel:** 44 01274 777700
Web site: www.emeraldinsight.com/loi/nfs
Freq: Bi-Monthly Not Audited
Profile: Educational journal concerned with all aspects of nutrition and food science. Also deals with home economics areas such as consumer issues, money matters and family health and welfare. The journal aims to reflect contemporary thinking so that professionals in the food and nutrition field can keep pace with developments and look at current preoccupations from industry, health, and public perspectives. First published in 1970, the publication has an average of 48 pages per issue. Read by academics and researchers in the field including dieticians, food company managers, food research institutes, health care professionals and nutritionists.
MAGAZINE
News & Current Affairs

Nutrition & Metabolism 985428
Editorial: c/o BioMed Central, 236 Gray's Inn Road, London WC1X 8HB
Tel: 44 02031 922009
Email: nutritionandmetabolism@biomedcentral.com
Web site: https://nutritionandmetabolism.biomedcentral.com/
Freq: Daily
Circ: 718435 Cision Digital Reach
MAGAZINE (ONLINE)
Nutrition

Nutrition and Food Sciences 996167
Editorial: Nosworthy Way, Wallingford, Wallingford OX10 8DE **Tel:** 44 01491 829408
Email: nutrition@cabi.org
Web site: www.cabi.org/nutrition
Freq: Daily
Circ: 113 Cision Digital Reach
MAGAZINE (ONLINE)
Nutrition

Nutrition Bulletin 985163
Editorial: British Nutrition Foundation, Imperial House 6th Floor, 15-19 Kingsway, London WC2B 6UN **Tel:** 44 02072 400696
Email: nbu@wiley.com
Web site: http://onlinelibrary.wiley.com/journal/10.1111/(ISSN)1467-3010
Freq: Quarterly
Editor: Lucy Chambers; **Editor:** Sara Stanner
Profile: Official publication of the British Nutrition Foundation. Contains scientific reviews on aspects of nutrition and news of issues in the field of human nutrition including biochemichemistry and physiology, discussion of observational (epidemiological)

Consumer Magazines

associations between diet/nutrients and aspects of health, application of nutrition to disease prevention or the particular needs of population sub-groups as well as the impact of methods of food production and processing on the composition of food, and general aspects of nutrition policy and its communication. Aimed at researchers and nutritionists working in universities and research institutes, public health nutritionists, dieticians and other health professionals, nutritionists, technologists and others in the food industry and teachers and journalists with an interest in nutrition.
Ad Rate: Full Page Mono £550.00
Ad Rate: Full Page Colour £950.00
MAGAZINE
Nutrition

Nutrition Journal
995833
Editorial: c/o BioMed Central, 236 Gray's Inn Road, London WC1X 8HL
Tel: 44 02031 922001
Email: nutrition@biomedcentral.com
Web site: http://nutritionj.biomedcentral.com/
Freq: Daily
Circ: 392081 Cision Digital Reach
MAGAZINE (ONLINE)
Nutrition

Nutrition Rocks
999086
Editorial: Fifth Floor, Harrods, Knightsbridge, London SW1X 7XL
Email: info@nutrition-rocks.co.uk
Web site: http://www.nutrition-rocks.co.uk
Freq: Daily
Circ: 11827 Cision Digital Reach
MAGAZINE (ONLINE)
Beauty & Grooming, Cosmetics, Fashion, Hair, Health & Medicine, Nutrition

Nyhedsbrev for Bestyrelser
1060862
Tel: 44 45702 34010
Email: redaktion@bestyrelsen.dk
Web site: http://bestyrelsen.dk/ Not Audited
MAGAZINE
Banking, Defense & National Security, Engineering, Industry, Manufacturing, Marine & Boat Trade, Mining & Quarrying, Paper, Plastics, Steel

Obstacle Race Magazine
996523
Editorial: 370 Wheelwright Lane, Ash Green, Coventry CV7 9HL
Web site: www.obstacleracemagazine.com
Freq: Bi-Monthly
Circ: 7000 Not Audited
Editor: Carl Wibberley
MAGAZINE
Sports

OC Movie Reviews
1053396
Email: mark@ocmoviereviews.com
Web site: http://ocmoviereviews.com
Freq: Daily
Circ: 10709 Cision Digital Reach
Editor: Mark OC
MAGAZINE (ONLINE)
Entertainment, Movies & Video

ocadolife
985035
Editorial: 82 Baker Street, London W1 6AE
Tel: 44 02079 357744
Email: ocadolife@ocado.com
Web site: www.augustmedia.com/our-work/ocadolife-magazine
Freq: Bi-Monthly
Circ: 150000 Not Audited
MAGAZINE
Cooking & Baking, Grocery Stores

OCC Outdoor
984939
Editorial: 3 Morton Street, Leamington Spa CV32 5SY **Tel:** 44 01926 339808
Web site: www.occoutdoor.co.uk
Freq: Monthly
Circ: 607 Not Audited
Profile: OCC Outdoor is a magazine owned by Alibi Publishing Ltd that focuses on the outdoor industry, including clothing, accessories, footwear and equipment. It contains news, advice, opinions and ideas.

First published in 1994. OCC Outdoor is aimed at suppliers, retailers and distributors in the outdoor trade.
Ad Rate: Full Page Colour £1265.00
MAGAZINE
Travel

oceanbuzz
999605
Editorial: The Pike House, George Street, Nailsworth, Stroud, Nailsworth GL6 0AG
Tel: 44 01453 836363
Email: oceanbuzz@divcom.co.uk
Web site: www.oceanbusiness.com/en/oceanbuzz
Freq: Weekly
Circ: 12000 Not Audited
Editor: Sarah Jackson
MAGAZINE
Marine & Boat Trade

The Ocelot
995714
Editorial: The Ocelot, Arclite House, Century Road, Marlborough SN5 5YN
Tel: 44 01793 781986
Web site: www.theocelot.co.uk
Freq: Monthly
Circ: 10000 Not Audited
Editor: Jamie Hill
MAGAZINE
Regional General Interest

Octane
982614
Editorial: Bedford Technology Park, Thurleigh, Bedford MK44 2YA
Tel: 44 02079 076585
Email: info@octane-magazine.com
Web site: http://subscribe.octane-magazine.com/
Freq: Monthly
Circ: 39371 Not Audited
Profile: Magazine covering the world's greatest cars and the people involved with them as well as accessories, art and automobilia, auctions, events and rallies, books and literature, car insurance and specialist services. Aimed at enthusiasts of classic cars and modern supercars.
Ad Rate: Full Page Colour £2150.00
MAGAZINE
Antique & Collectible Cars, Automotive

ODDITY
1054547
Editorial: Unit 12, Waterside Complex, 44-48 Wharf Road, London N1 7UX
Email: info@odditymag.com
Web site: www.odditymag.com
Freq: Daily
Circ: 521 Cision Digital Reach
MAGAZINE (ONLINE)
Art, Dance Music, Fashion, Luxury Goods, Men's Interests, Theater & Performing Arts, Travel, Women's Interests

ODEON Magazine
984516
Editorial: Quay House, The Ambury, Bath BA1 1UA **Tel:** 44 01225 442244
Web site: www.odeon.co.uk/odeon-magazine
Freq: Monthly
Circ: 183360 Not Audited
Editor: Paul Fitzpatrick
Profile: Magazine covering current film releases. Features film news, previews, reviews and interviews with film stars. Aimed at customers of Odeon cinemas.
Ad Rate: Full Page Colour £4000.00
MAGAZINE
Movies & Video

OFF BLACK
1054447
Editorial: Unit 8, 203-213 Mare Street, London E8 3EQ
Email: info@offblackmagazine.com
Web site: http://www.offblackmagazine.com/
Freq: Semi-Annual Not Audited
MAGAZINE
Art, Beauty & Grooming, Cosmetics, Fashion, Hair, Literature, Photography, Visual Arts

Off the Post News
1075624
Web site: http://www.offthepostnews.co.uk/
Freq: Daily

Circ: 10680 Cision Digital Reach
MAGAZINE (ONLINE)
Soccer

Off-Grid.Net
984932
Editorial: 17 Scawfell Street, London E2 8NG **Tel:** 44 07971 543703
Email: news@off-grid.net
Web site: www.off-grid.net
Freq: Daily
Circ: 56067 Cision Digital Reach
MAGAZINE (ONLINE)
Energy & Environment

The Official Ferrari magazine
987916
Editorial: 13 Hanover Square, London W1S 1HN **Tel:** 44 02071 523800
Email: tofm@ferrari.com
Web site: www.magazine.ferrari.com/
Freq: Quarterly Not Audited
MAGAZINE
Automakers

The Official Jacqueline Wilson Mag
995307
Editorial: 80 Kingsway East, Glasgow DD4 8SL **Tel:** 44 01382 223131
Email: jwmag@dcthomson.co.uk
Web site: www.jw-mag.com
Freq: Monthly
Circ: 38780 Not Audited
MAGAZINE
Teen/Young Adult

The Official London Theatre Guide
1072715
Editorial: 32 Rose Street, London WC2E 9ET **Tel:** 44 02075 576700
Email: news@soltukt.co.uk
Web site: http://www.officiallondontheatre.co.uk/
Freq: Bi-Weekly
Circ: 145000 Not Audited
MAGAZINE
Theater & Performing Arts

Official PlayStation Magazine (UK)
983830
Editorial: Quay House, The Ambury, Bath BA1 1UA **Tel:** 44 01225 442244
Email: opm@futurenet.com
Web site: www.gamesradar.com/opm
Freq: Monthly
Circ: 31774 Not Audited
Editor: Ian Dean
MAGAZINE
Computer & Video Games

Officialcharts.com
997221
Editorial: 2nd Floor, Riverside Building County Hall, Westminster Bridge Road, London SE1 7JA **Tel:** 44 02076 207450
Web site: www.officialcharts.com
Freq: Daily
Circ: 1201477 Cision Digital Reach
Editor: Rob Copsey
MAGAZINE (ONLINE)
Classical/Choral/Band Music, Country, Folk, Bluegrass, Dance Music, Jazz & Blues, Music, Pop Music, R&B, Urban, World, Rap & Hip Hop, Rock Music

Offshore Investment
983864
Editorial: Cairo Studios, 4th Floor, 4 Nile Street, London N1 7RF
Tel: 44 02037 279925
Email: editorial@offshoreinvestment.com
Web site: www.offshoreinvestment.com
Freq: Monthly
Circ: 18500 Not Audited
Profile: Journal covering all aspects of the offshore financial world. Includes trusts, private banking, managed funds, tax and estate planning, offshore leasing and other associated topics. Aimed at professionals in the offshore world and their clients.
Ad Rate: Full Page Mono £4200.00
Ad Rate: Full Page Colour £5300.00
MAGAZINE
Banking

Offshore Marine Monthly
984347
Editorial: 2nd Floor, The Exchange No. 1, Market Street, Aberdeen AB11 5PJ
Tel: 44 01224 597800
Web site: http://www.ihs.com/products/oil-gas/news-analysis/offshore-marine-monthly.aspx
Freq: Monthly Not Audited
Profile: Magazine covering marine activity for offshore markets. Includes latest newbuilds, market trends and fixtures of supply vessels and other support vessels. Also covers market information and analysis as well as issues facing supply vessel owners, such as crewing and equipment shortages.
MAGAZINE
Marine & Boat Trade, Shipping & Warehousing

Offshore Marine Technology
997847
Tel: 44 02072 354622
Email: editorial@rina.org.uk
Web site: http://www.rina.org.uk/omt.html
Freq: Quarterly
Circ: 16685 Not Audited
Editor: Martin Conway
MAGAZINE
Marine & Boat Trade, Shipping & Warehousing

Offshore Support Journal
980820
Editorial: Mitre House, 66 Abbey Road, Enfield EN1 2QN **Tel:** 44 02083 641551
Web site: www.osjonline.com
Freq: Monthly
Circ: 27000 Not Audited
Editor: David Foxwell
Profile: Magazine covering the technology used in the offshore support vessel industry. It looks at the vessels that support the offshore oil, gas and renewables industries, including their design, technology, equipment and operation.
Ad Rate: Full Page Mono £2515.00
MAGAZINE
Engineering, Marine & Boat Trade

Oh Comely
1005289
Editorial: Unit M6, The Finsbury Business Centre, 40 Bowling Green Lane, London EC1R 0NE **Tel:** 44 02078 318645
Email: ohcomely@icebergpress.co.uk
Web site: www.ohcomely.co.uk
Freq: Bi-Monthly
Circ: 15000 Not Audited
Editor: Alice Charlotte Snape
MAGAZINE
Art, Cooking & Baking, Food, Grocery Stores, Literature, Organic Food, Restaurant Reviews, Vegetarianism & Veganism

Oh My Quad
988808
Web site: www.omqfitnessmagazine.co.uk/
Freq: Daily
Circ: 46274 Cision Digital Reach
MAGAZINE (ONLINE)
Fitness & Exercise, Nutrition

Oil & Gas News
980896
Editorial: Crescent Court, 102 Victor Road, Teddington, London TW11 8SS
Web site: www.oilandgasnewsworldwide.com
Freq: Weekly
Circ: 8539 Not Audited
Editor: Sree Kumar
MAGAZINE
News & Current Affairs

Oink
984608
Editorial: 28 Rosslyn Hill, London NW3 1NH
Tel: 44 02089 940272
Email: mail@piggybank.co.uk
Web site: www.piggybank.co.uk
Freq: Monthly
Circ: 1674 Cision Digital Reach
Editor: Ernest Henry
MAGAZINE (ONLINE)
Elementary School

OK
1061688

Freq: Monthly Not Audited
MAGAZINE
Bars, Clubs & Pubs, Celebrities, Comedy, Entertainment, Lifestyle, Local Entertainment Guides, Men's Interests, Movies & Video, Regional General Interest, Women's Interests

OK!
982434

Editorial: Northern & Shell Building, 10 Lower Thames Street, London EC3R 6EN
Tel: 44 02086 127000
Web site: www.ok.co.uk
Freq: Weekly
Circ: 170231 Not Audited
Editor: Kirsty Tyler
Profile: Magazine containing stories, photographs, celebrity news from the world of showbiz and entertainment. It provides the inside scoop about celebrities as well as movies, music, TV, celebrity weddings, babies, fashion, relationship news. First published in 1996. Aimed at women of all ages.
Ad Rate: Full Page Colour £10000.00
MAGAZINE
Celebrities, Women's Interests

OKgrl
1056765

Email: hello@okgrl.com
Web site: http://www.okgrl.com/
Freq: Monthly
Circ: 2234 Cision Digital Reach
MAGAZINE (ONLINE)
Fashion, Teen/Young Adult

Old Bike Mart
982615

Editorial: Media Centre, Morton Way, Horncastle, Horncastle LN9 6JR
Tel: 44 01507 523456
Email: obmeditor@mortons.co.uk
Web site: www.oldbikemart.co.uk
Freq: Monthly
Circ: 32500 Not Audited
Editor: Pete Kelly
Profile: Magazine focusing on classic motorcycles. Aimed at middle to retirement aged riders, collectors and enthusiasts of classic motorcycles.
MAGAZINE
Antique & Collectible Cars, Motorcycles

Old Tat Magazine
997888

Email: oldtatmagazine@gmail.com
Web site: www.oldtatmag.com
Freq: Semi-Annual Not Audited
MAGAZINE
Antiques/Collectibles, Art, Do-It-Yourself (DIY), Fashion, Visual Arts

Olderiswiser.com
1102952

Tel: 44 02070 341900
Email: editor@olderiswiser.com
Web site: www.olderiswiser.com
Freq: Daily
Circ: 133540 Cision Digital Reach
MAGAZINE (ONLINE)
Retirement Savings

The Oldie
982138

Editorial: 23/31 Great Titchfield Street, London W1W 7PA **Tel:** 44 02074 368801
Email: editorial@theoldie.co.uk
Web site: www.theoldie.co.uk
Freq: Monthly
Circ: 45296 Not Audited
Profile: Magazine covering humour, satire, current interest articles, books, film and theatre. Includes articles on music, radio and television reviews and cartoons.
Ad Rate: Full Page Colour £1590.00
MAGAZINE
National News, Politics, Retirement Savings, Social Issues

olive
981808

Editorial: Vineyard House, 44 Brook Green, London W6 7BT **Tel:** 44 02071 505000
Email: oliveweb@immediate.co.uk
Web site: www.olivemagazine.com
Freq: Monthly
Circ: 32496 Not Audited
Editor: Laura Rowe
Profile: Magazine covering food including great-value restaurants, bargain travel ideas and recipes from around the world. First published in 2003. Aimed at food lover Women aged between 25 and 44 years old who enjoy cooking, eating out and foodie travel.
Ad Rate: Full Page Colour £4950.00
MAGAZINE
Cooking & Baking

Olor a Mi Tierra
1062088

Tel: 44 52951 5178645
Email: oloramitierra@yahoo.com.mx
Web site: http://www.oloramitierra.com.mx
Circ: 4452 Cision Digital Reach
MAGAZINE (ONLINE)
National News

om yoga & lifestyle
985316

Editorial: Park House, The Business Centre, Earls Tolne Business Park, Colchester CO6 2NS **Tel:** 44 01787 224040
Email: news@ommagazine.com
Web site: http://www.ommagazine.com/
Freq: Monthly
Circ: 70000 Not Audited
Editor: Martin D. Clark
Profile: OM Yoga & Lifestyle is a magazine covering yoga and the associated lifestyle. It is published ten times a year by Prime Impact Events & Media Ltd. Designed to inspire and to energise, OM magazine wants to help you enjoy a more active and rewarding life, drawing on the physical and mental disciplines of yoga, an ancient practice just as popular today as it was thousands of years ago. The publication aims to nourish body, mind and spirit, and to challenge how readers feel about the world around them and the people and things in it. First published in 2009. OM Yoga & Lifestyle is aimed at yoga amateurs and professionals.
Ad Rate: Full Page Colour £1300.00
MAGAZINE
Alternative Medicine, Fitness & Exercise

Ombudsman News
990586

Editorial: The Financial Ombudsman Service, Exchange Tower, London E14 9SR
Tel: 44 0207/9 641000
Email: complaint.info@financial-ombudsman.org.uk
Web site: www.financial-ombudsman.org.uk
Freq: Bi-Monthly
Circ: 115229 Cision Digital Reach
MAGAZINE (ONLINE)
Legal Services, Personal Finance

OME Information
1061261

Tel: 44 86431 86176853
Email: xxfw@ciomp.ac.cn
Web site: http://mall.cnki.net/magazine/magalist/GJDX.htm
Freq: Monthly
Circ: 5001 Not Audited
MAGAZINE
Auto Aftermarket, Computers, Data Management, Electronics, Government Technology, Industry, Internet, Mobile Communications, Security & Security Systems, Software

OMG - One Media Group
998861

Editorial: Staffordshire Student Union, College Road, Stoke-on-Trent, Stoke-on-Trent ST4 2DE **Tel:** 44 01782 294890
Email: omg@staffs.ac.uk
Web site: www.omgstaffs.com
Freq: Daily
Circ: 10969 Cision Digital Reach
MAGAZINE (ONLINE)
Student Lifestyle

OMOTG
986763

Editorial: 21 Dorset Square, Marylebone, London NW1 6QG **Tel:** 44 01892 537295
Email: admin@omotg.com
Web site: www.omotg.com
Freq: Daily
Circ: 13161 Cision Digital Reach
MAGAZINE (ONLINE)
Travel

On Business
985790

Editorial: Prospect House, Rouen Road, Norwich NR1 1RE **Tel:** 44 01603 664242
Email: info@archantdialogue.co.uk
Web site: http://www.archantdialogue.co.uk/
Freq: 3 Times/Year
Circ: 12000 Not Audited
Profile: Magazine covering business travel including news and features on topical issues facing the international business travel organiser. Aimed at corporate travel decision-makers, organisers, senior managers, directors and senior secretaries/PA.
Ad Rate: Full Page Colour £3500.00
MAGAZINE
Travel

On In London
998076

Email: enquiries@oninonline.com
Web site: onin.london
Freq: Daily
Circ: 4872 Cision Digital Reach
MAGAZINE (ONLINE)
Regional General Interest

On The Hill
997924

Email: onthehillinfo@phca.cc
Web site: http://onthehill.info/
Freq: Monthly
Circ: 7500 Not Audited
MAGAZINE
Regional General Interest

On The Horizon
996245

Editorial: Howard House, Wagon Lane, Bingley BD16 1WA **Tel:** 44 01274 777700
Email: emerald@emeraldinsight.com
Web site: www.emeraldinsight.com/journals.htm?issn=1074-8121
Freq: Quarterly Not Audited
Editor: Tom Abeles
MAGAZINE
News & Current Affairs

On the Rocks
988733

Editorial: 52b Whitmore Road, London N1 5QG **Tel:** 44 02034 325117
Email: magazine@o-t-r.co
Web site: www.o-t-r.co
Freq: Semi-Annual Not Audited
MAGAZINE
Fashion

On/Off
999840

Editorial: 1 Hardwick Street, London EC1R 4RB **Tel:** 44 02078 417061
Email: info@thedoll.org
Web site: www.onoff.tv
Freq: Daily
Circ: 6380 Cision Digital Reach
MAGAZINE (ONLINE)
Fashion

On: Yorkshire Magazine
984720

Editorial: 19 Broadlands Gardens, Pudsey, West Yorkshire, Pudsey LS28 9GD
Email: editor@on-magazine.co.uk
Web site: http://www.on-magazine.co.uk
Freq: Quarterly
Circ: 25000 Not Audited
Editor: Matthew Callard
MAGAZINE
Regional General Interest

Onboard Hospitality
984022

Editorial: Suffolk House, George Street, Croydon CR9 1SR **Tel:** 44 02086 497233
Email: enquiries@bmipublishing.co.uk
Web site: www.onboardhospitality.com
Freq: Quarterly
Circ: 14400 Not Audited
Profile: OnBoard Hospitality is the official publication of the International Travel Catering Association, reporting on association news and events and all aspects of the industry worldwide including on board services industries for cruise, rail, airlines and ferries. It also covers extensive topics from on-board food supply to technology, innovations, conference reviews, sustainable issues, events and the movers and shakers within the travel hospitality industry. OnBoard Hospitality is aimed at decision-makers within the travel hospitality industry throughout the world.
Ad Rate: Full Page Colour £2990.00
MAGAZINE
Alcohol & Spirits, Food

One Africa, One Voice
1060367

Email: patrick@hsm.co.za
Freq: Annual
Circ: 20000 Not Audited
MAGAZINE
International News, Politics

One News Page
985601

Email: enquiries@onenewspage.com
Web site: http://www.onenewspage.co.uk
Freq: Daily
Circ: 112215 Cision Digital Reach
MAGAZINE (ONLINE)
Consumer Affairs, Crime & Violence, Defense & National Security, Energy & Environment, Ethical/Moral Issues, International News, Law, National News, News & Current Affairs, Northern Ireland

One on One
1072205

Email: danny@oneononemusic.co.uk
Web site: www.oneononemusic.co.uk
Freq: Daily
Circ: 10995 Cision Digital Reach
MAGAZINE (ONLINE)
Country, Folk, Bluegrass, Dance Music, Jazz & Blues, Pop Music, Rap & Hip Hop, Rock Music

One World International
999170

Editorial: 1st Floor, CAN Mezzanine, 32-36 Loman Street, London SE1 0EH
Tel: 44 02079 227844
Email: hello@oneworld.org
Web site: http://oneworld.org/
Freq: Daily
Circ: 21603 Cision Digital Reach
Editor: Daniel Nelson
MAGAZINE (ONLINE)
International News

One&Other
986546

Editorial: One&Other CIC, 11 Fairfax St, York YO1 6EB
Email: vicky@oneandother.com
Web site: www.oneandother.com
Freq: Daily
Circ: 28497 Cision Digital Reach
MAGAZINE (ONLINE)
Regional General Interest

One&Other Magazine
988080

Editorial: 11 Fairfax St, York YO1 6EB
Email: creative@oneandother.com
Web site: www.oneandother.com
Freq: Quarterly
Circ: 20000 Not Audited
MAGAZINE
Regional General Interest

one4review
1052673

Web site: www.one4review.co.uk/
Freq: Daily
Circ: 6305 Cision Digital Reach
MAGAZINE (ONLINE)
Bars, Clubs & Pubs, Comedy, Country, Folk, Bluegrass, Dance Music, Entertainment, Jazz & Blues, Local Entertainment Guides, Rock Music, Theater & Performing Arts

OneMetal
1075482

Editorial: 29 Westfield Road, Acocks Green, Birmingham, Darlaston B27 7TN
Web site: www.onemetal.com
Freq: Daily
Circ: 356 Cision Digital Reach
Editor: Phil Whitehouse
MAGAZINE (ONLINE)
Men's Interests, Rock Music

Consumer Magazines

Section 4 UK Periodicals Consumer

Oz Clarke Wine A-Z
996000
Tel: 44 02074 621500
Email: info@pavilionbooks.com
Web site: www.ozclarke.com
Freq: Annual Not Audited
MAGAZINE
Wine/Winemaking

Pacenotes Rally Magazine
999063
Editorial: Unit 45, Banbridge Enteprise Centre, Scarva Road Industrial Estate, Banbridge BT32 4QD **Tel:** 44 02840 660390
Email: editor@pacenotes.net
Web site: www.pacenotes.net
Freq: Monthly
Circ: 7000 Not Audited
MAGAZINE
Motorsports

Packaging Europe
984395
Editorial: Alkmaar House, Alkmaar Way, Norwich, Norwich NR6 6BF
Tel: 44 01603 414444
Email: editor@packagingeurope.com
Web site: www.packagingeurope.com
Freq: Bi-Monthly
Circ: 30000 Not Audited
MAGAZINE
Business, Cosmetics, Food, Manufacturing, Paper, Plastics, Publishing, Steel, Sustainable Development

packaging-gateway.com
988617
Editorial: John Carpenter House, John Carpenter Street, London EC4Y 0AN
Tel: 44 02079 366400
Email: onlineeditorial@kable.co.uk
Web site: www.packaging-gateway.com/
Freq: Daily
Circ: 25517 Cision Digital Reach
Profile: Website covering packaging. PACKAGING-GATEWAY.COM features news, analysis and white papers relating to packaging and the packaging industry.
MAGAZINE (ONLINE)
News & Current Affairs

Paddington Now - CEASED
988570
Editorial: 3 Princes Street, London W1B 2LD
Freq: Quarterly
Circ: 20000 Not Audited
MAGAZINE
Regional General Interest

paintinganddecoratingnews.co.uk
996202
Editorial: 5 Mosslea Road, Whyteleafe, London CR3 0DR **Tel:** 44 02086 452433
Email: enquiries@paintinganddecoratingnews.co.uk
Web site: http://www.paintinganddecoratingnews.co.uk/
Freq: Daily
Circ: 9412 Cision Digital Reach
Editor: Paul Murray
MAGAZINE (ONLINE)
Do-It-Yourself (DIY), Interior Design

Panel Building and Systems Integration
998603
Editorial: Blair House, 184/186 High Street, Tonbridge, Tonbridge TN9 1BQ
Tel: 44 01732 359990
Email: pbsi@imlgroup.co.uk
Web site: www.psbonthenet.net
Freq: Monthly
Circ: 24000 Not Audited
MAGAZINE
Electronics, Industry, Manufacturing

Panjab Times
982589
Editorial: Bridle Gate Lane, Derby DE24 0QW **Tel:** 44 01332 372851
Email: panjabtimes@gmail.com
Web site: www.panjabtimes.co.uk
Freq: Weekly
Circ: 38200 Not Audited

Editor: Maninder S Purewal
MAGAZINE
Asia, International News

Papercraft Essentials
987207
Editorial: Suite G2 St Christopher House, 217 Wellington Road South, Stockport SK2 6NG **Tel:** 44 08445 611202
Email: info@practicalpublishing.co.uk
Web site: www.practicalpublishing.co.uk
Freq: Monthly
Circ: 35000 Not Audited
Profile: Papercraft Essentials is a magazine covering predominantly papercraft as well as general craft with hints, tips, ideas, money saving suggestions and step by step instructions. It is published every four weeks by Practical Publishing International Ltd. Papercraft Essentials is aimed at anyone with an interest in papercraft.
Ad Rate: Full Page Colour £900.00
MAGAZINE
News & Current Affairs

PaperCraft Inspirations
984370
Editorial: 2nd Floor Tower House, Fairfax Street, Bristol BS1 3BN
Tel: 44 01179 279009
Email: papercraft@immediate.co.uk
Web site: www.papercraftinspirationsmagazine.co.uk
Freq: Monthly
Circ: 23334 Not Audited
Editor: Hannah Bellis
Profile: Papercraft Inspirations is a monthly magazine covering cards, papercrafts and scrapbooking. Papercraft Inspirations is aimed at women aged between 35 and 55 years old with an interest in papercraft.
Ad Rate: Full Page Mono £1290.00
Ad Rate: Full Page Colour £1290.00
MAGAZINE
Crafts

PaperCrafter
987256
Editorial: 1 Phoenix Court, Hawkins Road, Colchester, Colchester CO2 8JY
Tel: 44 01206 505900
Web site: www.papercraftermagazine.co.uk
Freq: Monthly
Circ: 34000 Not Audited
Editor: Rosie Savage
Profile: Magazine containing card designs and ideas as well as features on how to improve card making, card designers, the latest products, practical advice and step by step techniques. Aimed at card makers at all skill levels.
Ad Rate: Full Page Colour £1100.00
MAGAZINE
Crafts

Paradigm Shift
995716
Editorial: 13 Willow Drive, Guildford, London GU3 2EJ **Tel:** 44 01483 813641
Email: info@paradigmshiftmagazine.com
Web site: www.paradigmshiftmagazine.com/
Freq: Quarterly Not Audited
MAGAZINE
News & Current Affairs

Para-Radio
1061938
Tel: 44 36209 618413
Email: info@pararadio.hu
Web site: http://www.para-radio.hu
Circ: 1154 Cision Digital Reach
MAGAZINE (ONLINE)
Bars, Clubs & Pubs, Comedy, Consumer Affairs, Crime & Violence, Defense & National Security, Energy & Environment, Entertainment, Ethical/Moral Issues, International News, Law

Parchment Craft
981947
Editorial: The Maltings, West Street, Bourne, Bourne PE10 9PH **Tel:** 44 01778 391000
Web site: www.parchmentcraftmagazine.com
Freq: Monthly
Circ: 9000 Not Audited
Editor: Carl Golder

Profile: Publication with latest techniques, projects, ideas and inspiration from the world of Parchment Craft.
MAGAZINE
Crafts

Parent Talk
982409
Editorial: Newtons, Churchstanton, Taunton, Taunton TA3 7QF **Tel:** 44 01458 250461
Email: editor@parenttalk.org.uk
Web site: www.parenttalk.org.uk
Freq: Monthly
Circ: 31000 Not Audited
Editor: Tamsin Humphreys
Profile: Parent Talk is a magazine containing information, competitions and features on education, health, the home, fashion and events. It is published eleven times a year. Parent Talk is aimed at parents of pre-teen children in Somerset.
Ad Rate: Full Page Colour £750.00
MAGAZINE
Family & Parenting

Parent Zone
1056568
Editorial: Unit 2, Pride Court, 80-82 White Lion St, London N1 9PF
Tel: 44 02076 867225
Email: content@parentzone.org.uk
Web site: www.parentzone.org.uk
Freq: Daily
Circ: 17813 Cision Digital Reach
MAGAZINE (ONLINE)
Internet

Parent24
1060679
MAGAZINE (ONLINE)
Preschool

Parenting Solo
995009
Tel: 44 07546 507397
Email: editor@parentingsolo.co.uk
Web site: http://parentingsolo.co.uk/
Freq: Daily
Circ: 947 Cision Digital Reach
Editor: Kelly Rose Bradford
MAGAZINE (ONLINE)
Family & Parenting

Parenting UK
1052995
Tel: 44 02075 533080
Email: info@familylives.org.uk
Web site: http://www.parentinguk.org/
Freq: Daily
Circ: 10391 Cision Digital Reach
MAGAZINE (ONLINE)
Family & Parenting

Parenting Without Tears
984492
Editorial: 6 Darrell Road, London SE22 9NL
Tel: 44 02086 937482
Web site: www.parentingwithouttears.com
Freq: Daily
Circ: 11383 Cision Digital Reach
Editor: Anne Coates
Profile: Website covering family lifestyle. The Parenting Without Tears website shares the latest news and information on family parenting health tips, travel idea, days out, cinema reviews, books reviews and fitness.
MAGAZINE (ONLINE)
Family & Parenting

Parents News (London South, East Surrey & West Kent)
982411
Editorial: 10 The Manor Drive, Worcester Park, London KT4 7LG
Tel: 44 02083 376337
Web site: www.parents-news.co.uk
Freq: Monthly
Circ: 54000 Not Audited
MAGAZINE
Family & Parenting

Park & Holiday Home Inspiration
1060246
Tel: 44 01778 391000
Email: phhi@warnersgroup.co.uk
Web site: https://www.outandaboutlive.co.uk/lodges

Freq: Quarterly
MAGAZINE
Do-It-Yourself (DIY), Luxury Goods, Property Management & Maintenance, Real Estate Law

Park Home & Holiday Caravan
982313
Editorial: PO Box 13, Westerham, London TN16 3WT **Tel:** 44 01959 541444
Email: phhc.ed@kelsey.co.uk
Web site: www.parkhomemagazine.co.uk
Freq: Monthly
Circ: 10500 Not Audited
Editor: Alex Melvin
Profile: Magazine focusing on new and established sites for park homes and caravan holiday homes. Also includes reviews of new models and equipment. Aimed at residents and owners of park homes, caravan holiday homes and prospective purchasers.
Ad Rate: Full Page Colour £1945.00
MAGAZINE
Camping and RV Travel

Park World
984930
Editorial: 15a London Road, Maidstone, Maidstone ME16 8LY **Tel:** 44 01622 687031
Email: parkworld@btopenworld.com
Web site: http://www.parkworld-online.com
Freq: Monthly
Circ: 3500 Not Audited
Profile: Park World is a magazine covering the theme and amusement park and family entertainment centre industry including new products, concepts, licensing and global trends. It is published 11 times a year by Datateam Business Media Ltd. Park World is read by operators, developers, project managers and decision makers within the industry.
Ad Rate: Full Page Colour £1470.00
MAGAZINE
Travel

Parkers
982840
Editorial: Bauer Media, Lynchwood, Peterborough PE2 6EA
Tel: 44 01733 468000
Web site: www.parkers.co.uk
Freq: Daily
Circ: 1713414 Cision Digital Reach
Editor: Keith Adams
MAGAZINE (ONLINE)
Antique & Collectible Cars, Automakers, Automotive, Driving, Motorcycles, Off-road & 4-Wheel Drive Vehicles, Sales & Marketing, Trucks & SUVs

Parking News
984101
Editorial: British Parking Association, Stuart House, 41-43 Perrymount Road, Cambridge RH16 3BN **Tel:** 44 01444 447300
Email: editor@britishparking.co.uk
Web site: http://www.britishparking.co.uk/Parking-News
Freq: Monthly
Circ: 1243 Not Audited
Editor: Rob Coston
Profile: Parking News is a monthly magazine covering all aspects of vehicle parking in the UK and abroad with feature articles, news, products and the latest technology. The publication was first published in 1969 and has on average 52 pages per issue. Parking News is read by members of the British Parking Association, including officials in local authorities, central government, hospitals and educational establishments who organise vehicle parking.
Ad Rate: Full Page Mono £798.00
Ad Rate: Full Page Colour £1128.00
MAGAZINE
Automotive

The Parkinson
996246
Editorial: 215 Vauxhall Bridge Road, London SW1V 1EJ **Tel:** 44 02079 318080
Email: hello@parkinsons.org.uk
Web site: www.parkinsons.org.uk/content/parkinson-magazine
Freq: Quarterly
Circ: 30000 Not Audited

Editor: Vicky Hancock
MAGAZINE
Patient Support

Parrots
982017
Editorial: The Old Cart House, Applesham Farm, Coombes, Lancing BN15 0RP
Tel: 44 01273 464777
Email: editorial@imaxweb.co.uk
Web site: www.parrotmag.com
Freq: Monthly
Circ: 5000 Not Audited
Editor: John Catchpole
Profile: Parrots is a monthly magazine covering all aspects of the keeping of parrots. It includes articles on breeding, general care, veterinarian advice, conservation issues and readers' stories. It is owned by Imax Visual Ltd. First published in 1995. Parrots is aimed at parrot keepers and breeders worldwide and those involved with conservation.
Ad Rate: Full Page Mono £850.00
Ad Rate: Full Page Colour £875.00
MAGAZINE
Nature & Wildlife

Partners
982495
Editorial: East Hampshire District Council, Penns Place, Petersfield GU31 4EX **Tel:** 44 01730 266551
Email: info@easthants.gov.uk
Web site: www.easthants.gov.uk
Freq: Semi-Annual
Circ: 53000 Not Audited
Editor: Will Parsons
MAGAZINE
Charitable Foundations

Passenger Ship Technology
980816
Editorial: Mitre House, 66 Abbey Road, Enfield EN1 2QN **Tel:** 44 02083 641551
Web site: www.passengership.info
Freq: Quarterly
Circ: 4000 Not Audited
Editor: Rebecca Moore
Profile: Journal covering all aspects of the worldwide ferry industry including construction, design, operation, safety, propulsion and including articles on future technology. First published in 1995. Aimed at ferry and fast ferry operators, shipbuilders, naval architects, equipment suppliers and naval architects and consultants.
Ad Rate: Full Page Colour £2365.00
MAGAZINE
Marine & Boat Trade, Shipping & Warehousing

Passenger Transport (UK)
985896
Editorial: Adelaide Wharf, 21 Whiston Road, London E2 8EX **Tel:** 44 02077 496909
Email: editorial@passengertransport.co.uk
Web site: www.passengertransport.co.uk
Freq: Bi-Weekly
Circ: 1200 Not Audited
MAGAZINE
Automotive, Aviation, Railroad, Shipping & Warehousing, Supply Chain Management (SCM), Transportation

passionforfreshideas.com
998805
Email: news@passionfortheplanet.com
Web site: passionforfreshideas.com
Freq: Daily
Circ: 11839 Cision Digital Reach
MAGAZINE (ONLINE)
Energy & Environment, Health & Medicine

Passport
986995
Editorial: Garden Floor, 16 Connaught Place, London W2 2ES
Tel: 44 02074 207000
Web site: www.monarch.co.uk/offers/flights/monarch-passport
Freq: Quarterly
Circ: 1800000 Not Audited
MAGAZINE
Airline Inflight

Passportstamps.uk
1054463
Email: helen@passportstamps.uk
Web site: http://passportstamps.uk/
Freq: Daily
Circ: 3802 Cision Digital Reach
MAGAZINE (ONLINE)
Travel

The Pastoral Review
982155
Editorial: St Mary's University College, Waldgrave Road, Strawberry Hill, Twickenham TW1 4SX **Tel:** 44 02082 404019
Web site: www.thepastoralreview.org
Freq: Bi-Monthly
Circ: 4000 Not Audited
Editor: Michael A Hayes
Profile: Magazine covering catholic Christian religion news and issues including pastoral theology and practical advice. Aimed at priests and laypeople within parish communities.
Ad Rate: Full Page Mono £290.00
Ad Rate: Full Page Colour £350.00
MAGAZINE
Religion

Pat Chapman's Curry Club
999704
Editorial: 50 West Street, Haslemere, Haslemere GU27 2AP **Tel:** 44 01428 658327
Email: pat@patchapman.co.uk
Web site: www.patchapman.co.uk
Freq: Daily
Circ: 6345 Cision Digital Reach
Editor: Pat Chapman
MAGAZINE (ONLINE)
Cooking & Baking, Restaurant Reviews

Pathfinder Magazine
980952
Editorial: Baltic Business Centre, Saltmeadows Road, Gateshead NE8 3DA
Tel: 44 01914 420197
Email: pathfinder@balticpublications.co.uk
Web site: www.pathfinderinternational.co.uk
Freq: Monthly
Circ: 25000 Not Audited
MAGAZINE
Careers, Education, Recruiting

Patient
985400
Editorial: Rawdon House, Green Lane, Yeadon, Leeds LS19 7BY
Web site: http://patient.info/
Freq: Daily
Circ: 6652227 Cision Digital Reach
Profile: Website covering healthcare. The Patient.co.uk website provides news and information on all aspects of health, disease and healthcare.
MAGAZINE (ONLINE)
Health & Medicine

Patient Education and Counseling
997111
Editorial: The Boulevard, Langford Lane, Kidlington OX5 1GB **Tel:** 44 01865 843434
Email: pec@elsevier.com
Web site: www.elsevier.com/wps/find/journaldescription.cws_home/505955/description
Freq: Monthly Not Audited
MAGAZINE
Health Administration, Medicine, Nursing/Nurses

Patmos radio
1061554
Email: patmos@patmos.fi
Web site: http://www.patmos.fi/
Freq: Daily
Circ: 2924 Cision Digital Reach
MAGAZINE (ONLINE)
Religion

PAUSE
987527
Editorial: 37 Camden High St, London NW1 7JE
Email: info@pausemag.co.uk
Web site: www.pausemag.co.uk
Freq: Daily
Circ: 500000 Not Audited

Profile: Magazine covering male fashion. Aimed at young males.
MAGAZINE
Fashion, Men's Interests, Photography

The Pavement
982684
Web site: http://www.thepavement.org.uk/
Freq: Monthly
Circ: 3500 Not Audited
Profile: Magazine covering homelessness and housing with news, health and legal advice, issues such as ASBOs and the Vagrancy Law. Aimed at the homeless in Central London and Glasgow and Edinburgh
MAGAZINE
News & Current Affairs

Paw Patrol Magazine
1068963
Editorial: 1st Floor, The Yellow Building, 1 Nicholas Road, London W11 4AN
Tel: 44 02032 200400
Email: info@euk.egmont.com
Web site: https://www.egmont.co.uk/magazines/paw-patrol/
Freq: Monthly
Circ: 49024 Not Audited
MAGAZINE
Preschool

Pawprint
1053488
Editorial: Blue Cross, 7 Hugh Street, London SW1V 1QG **Tel:** 44 02079 324060
Email: press@bluecross.org.uk
Web site: https://www.bluecross.org.uk/publications
Freq: Semi-Annual
Circ: 140000 Not Audited
Editor: Rachael Millar
MAGAZINE
Charitable Foundations, Nature & Wildlife

Paws
982018
Editorial: Battersea Dogs & Cats Home, 4 Battersea Park Road, London SW8 4AA
Tel: 44 02076 279294
Web site: https://www.battersea.org.uk/about-us/publications
Freq: 3 Times/Year Not Audited
Editor: Caroline Stringer
Profile: Paws is the magazine of Battersea Dogs & Cats Home and is published four times a year. It features informative mix of articles, advice, news from the Home and updates from canine and feline ex-residents. First published in 1999. Paws is aimed at those who have given a home to a Battersea dog or cat, as well as patrons and supporters of the Battersea Dogs & Cats Home.
Ad Rate: Full Page Colour £1500.00
MAGAZINE
Charitable Foundations, Nature & Wildlife

Payments Cards & Mobile
981637
Editorial: The Stable, Hall Yard, Kelling, Holt, Holt NR25 7EW **Tel:** 44 01263 711800
Web site: www.paymentscardsandmobile.com
Freq: Bi-Monthly
Circ: 11000 Not Audited
Editor: Denise Gee
Profile: Payments Cards & Mobile is a pan-European magazine covering all aspects of the European payment card industry, including smart cards, credit card programmes, loyalty cards, technology innovations and related management issues. Payments Cards & Mobile covers card processing, NFC and contactless systems, POS terminals, mobile payments, internet payments and innovations in payment technology. It provides editorial coverage in its area of the publishing business, blending news with in-depth analysis and features contributed by a range of outside experts. First published in November 1994. Payments Cards & Mobile is aimed at bankers, credit card managers, manufacturers and private label card programme managers.
Ad Rate: Full Page Mono £1750.00
Ad Rate: Full Page Colour £2350.00
MAGAZINE
Data Management, Electronics

PC Gamer (UK)
981736
Editorial: Quay House, The Ambury, Bath BA1 1UA **Tel:** 44 01225 442244
Email: pcgamer@futurenet.com
Web site: www.pcgamer.com/uk/
Freq: Monthly
Circ: 17624 Not Audited
MAGAZINE
Computer & Video Games

PC Invasion
982866
Editorial: Office 7B, Unit 3, East Key, Bridgwater TA6 4DB
Email: editor@pcinvasion.com
Web site: www.pcinvasion.com
Freq: Daily
Circ: 149049 Cision Digital Reach
Profile: Website covering video games. The website discusses the latest news and reviews on video games.
MAGAZINE (ONLINE)
Computer & Video Games

PC Mag UK
988833
Editorial: Third Floor, 18 Mansell Street, London E1 8AA **Tel:** 44 02037 015700
Web site: uk.pcmag.com
Freq: Daily
Circ: 195703 Cision Digital Reach
MAGAZINE (ONLINE)
Apple, Cameras, Computers, Data Management, Internet, Mobile Electronics, Personal Computers, Security & Security Systems, Software

PC Pilot
985449
Editorial: PO Box 100, Peterborough PE9 1XQ **Tel:** 44 01780 755131
Email: mail@pcpilot.net
Web site: www.pcpilot.net
Freq: Bi-Monthly
Circ: 12321 Not Audited
Editor: Derek Davis
Profile: Magazine containing news, advice and views on all aspects of flight simulation. Includes regular reviews and features on Microsoft's Flight Simulator X and associated third-party add-ons, tutorial on Mission Building in FSX, reviews on airliners, GA and military aircraft, as well as scenery packages. Also contains tutorials on air combat, GA flying, airliner flying and regular flight tutorials from Flight Simulator, interviews with publishers and developers within the industry and a hardware section, covering everything from graphics cards to motion platforms. PC Pilot is professionally produced by flight simmers for flight simmers, the readers are predominantly male, with the majority being in the 26 to 55 year age bracket. Published bi-monthly. Founded in 1999.
Ad Rate: Full Page Colour £1575.00
MAGAZINE
Computer & Video Games

PC Pro
983036
Editorial: 31-32 Alfred Place, London WC1E 7DP **Tel:** 44 02079 076000
Email: news@pcpro.co.uk
Web site: http://www.alphr.com/
Freq: Monthly
Circ: 27413 Not Audited
Profile: Magazine covering information technology including labs-based reviews, product testing, business hardware and software, features, endpoint security, technology trends and practical advice from experts and consultants. First published in 1994, the publication has an average of 300 pages per issue. Aimed at professional PC users and and early technology adopters involved in buying computer equipment and PC enthusiasts.
Ad Rate: Full Page Colour £4425.00
MAGAZINE
Internet, Mobile Electronics, Personal Computers

PCE International
985922
Editorial: Peel House, Upper South View, Farnham, Farnham GU9 7JN
Tel: 44 01252 732220
Email: info@protectivecoatingseurope.com
Web site: www.mpigroup.co.uk/publishing/pce-international/

Consumer Magazines

Freq: Quarterly
Circ: 8000 Not Audited
Editor: Mark Langdon
Profile: Magazine covering practical aspects of protective coatings in heavy duty and marine industries.
Ad Rate: Full Page Colour £2200.00
MAGAZINE
Chemicals, Marine & Boat Trade

PCGamesN   988406
Editorial: Circus Mews House, Circus Mews, Bath BA1 2PW
Email: editor@pcgamesn.com
Web site: www.pcgamesn.com
Freq: Daily
Circ: 1236778 Cision Digital Reach
Profile: Website covering video games. The PCGamesN website shares the latest news and information on computer video games.
MAGAZINE (ONLINE)
Computer & Video Games

pcGameware.co.uk   996735
Email: info@pcgameware.co.uk
Web site: www.pcgameware.co.uk
Freq: Daily
Circ: 129681 Cision Digital Reach
MAGAZINE (ONLINE)
Personal Computers

PDAMania.hu   1061669
Tel: 44 36143 71100
Email: contact@pdamania.hu
Web site: http://www.pdamania.hu
Circ: 3449 Cision Digital Reach
MAGAZINE (ONLINE)
Advertising Industry, Branding, Broadcasting, Computers, Data Management, Graphic Design, Marketing, Media & Communications, Photography, Publishing

Peach Report   986908
Editorial: CGA Peach, Waterloo Place, Watson Square, Stockport SK1 3AZ
Tel: 44 01614 769140
Email: hello@cgapeach.co.uk
Web site: www.peach-report.com
Freq: Bi-Monthly
Circ: 5000 Not Audited
Profile: Magazine covering the changing emphasis of the out-of-home food and drink market. Focuses on the market-shaping trends, latest data and insight, hot concepts and top operators both in the UK and globally.
MAGAZINE
Bars, Clubs & Pubs

pearlanddean.com   1105185
Editorial: Corinthian House, 279 Tottenham Court Road, London W1T 7RJ
Tel: 44 02071 992400
Email: comments@pearlanddean.com
Web site: http://www.pearlanddean.com/
Freq: Daily
Circ: 21501 Cision Digital Reach
MAGAZINE (ONLINE)
Movies & Video

Pegasus   986676
Editorial: RHQ PARA, Merville Barracks, Colchester, London CO2 7UT
Tel: 44 01206 817088
Email: lisa@pegasusjournal.org
Web site: www.pegasusjournal.org
Freq: 3 Times/Year
Circ: 9000 Not Audited
Editor: Robert Kemp
Profile: Pegasus is a monthly horse magazine featuring articles on livery and training, fencing, paddock maintenance, health, feeds, tack and show results. First published in 1993. Pegasus is aimed at the equestrian market.
Ad Rate: Full Page Mono £361.00
Ad Rate: Full Page Colour £450.00
MAGAZINE
Charitable Foundations, Defense & National Security

Pell Mell and Woodcote   981930
Editorial: Pall Mall Clubhouse, 89 Pall Mall, London SW1Y 5HS
Email: pellmell@royalautomobileclub.co.uk
Web site: www.royalautomobileclub.co.uk
Freq: Quarterly
Circ: 20000 Not Audited
Editor: Holly Dawson
MAGAZINE
Driving

Pen 2 Paper   1053156
Tel: 44 01732 759725
Web site: www.p2pmag.co.uk
Freq: Quarterly
Editor: James Goulding
Profile: Pen 2 Paper is a bimonthly magazine focusing on office stationery and business machines. It includes news, reviews and company profiles. First published in 2002. Pen 2 Paper is aimed at directors of SMEs employing 15 to 350 office based staff.
Ad Rate: Full Page Colour £2200.00
MAGAZINE
News & Current Affairs

Pennant   984117
Editorial: 68 South Lambeth Road, London SW8 1RL **Tel:** 44 02075 820469
Web site: www.forcespensionsociety.org/our-magazine
Freq: Semi-Annual
Circ: 33000 Not Audited
Profile: Pennant is the biannual magazine of the Forces Pension Society. It includes pension information and rates, activities, events and articles of a military theme. Pennant is read by serving and retired forces personnel of all ranks and their families. This magazine contains the following regular features: News - The latest news related to armed forces pensions.
Ad Rate: Full Page Mono £725.00
Ad Rate: Full Page Colour £825.00
MAGAZINE
Armed Forces, Retirement Savings

Pension Funds Online   999118
Editorial: 6-14 Underwood Street, London N1 7JQ **Tel:** 44 02075 668252
Web site: www.pensionfundsonline.co.uk
Freq: Daily
Circ: 12232 Cision Digital Reach
Editor: Neil Blain
Profile: Website covering finance. The Pension Funds Online website shares information on pensions funds and investment.
MAGAZINE (ONLINE)
Fund Management, Personal Finance

The Pensioner   984453
Editorial: Square7 Media, 3 More London, London SE1 2RE **Tel:** 44 02032 834055
Email: editor@cspa.co.uk
Web site: www.cspa.co.uk
Freq: Quarterly
Circ: 50000 Not Audited
Editor: Ralph Groves
MAGAZINE
Charitable Foundations, Retirement Savings

Pensions Expert   979780
Editorial: Number One Southwark Bridge, London SE1 9HL **Tel:** 44 02078 733000
Web site: www.pensions-expert.com
Freq: Daily
Circ: 8014 Not Audited
Editor: Sandra Wolf
Profile: Pensions Expert is a weekly publication covering all aspects of the pensions industry. It includes company news, information, features on pension schemes and business and market reports. It is owned by the FT Group. First published in 1998. Pensions Expert is aimed at professionals running and advising on occupational pension schemes.
Ad Rate: Full Page Colour £4200.00
MAGAZINE
Fund Management, Personal Finance

People Tree Magazine   1102292
Editorial: People Tree Ltd, 5 Huguenot Place, 17a Heneage Street, London E1 5LN
Tel: 44 08454 504595
Email: people@peopletree.co.uk
Web site: http://www.peopletree.co.uk/
Freq: Daily
Circ: 92019 Cision Digital Reach
MAGAZINE (ONLINE)
Ethical/Moral Issues, Fashion

The People's Friend   982435
Editorial: 80 Kingsway East, Dundee DD4 8SL **Tel:** 44 01382 223131
Email: peoplesfriend@dcthomson.co.uk
Web site: www.thepeoplesfriend.co.uk
Freq: Weekly
Circ: 186817 Not Audited
Editor: Angela Gilchrist
Profile: Fiction-based magazine established in 1869 and incorporating serials, short stories and poetry along with interesting features that reflect readers' interests such as craft, knitting, travel and cookery. Aimed at women, with 78% of their readers being over 60.
Ad Rate: Full Page Colour £6500.00
MAGAZINE
Literature, Retirement Savings, Women's Interests

People's Republic of South Devon   985393
Editorial: 19 Gloucester Road, Newton Abbot, Newton Abbot TQ12 1AY
Tel: 44 01626 202202
Email: info@theprsd.co.uk
Web site: http://www.theprsd.co.uk/
Freq: Daily
Circ: 13919 Cision Digital Reach
Editor: Lee Morgan
MAGAZINE (ONLINE)
Regional

Peppa Pig Bag-o-Fun   995368
Editorial: Suites 3 & 4 Canon Court East, Abbey Lawn, Shrewsbury SY2 5DE
Tel: 44 01743 364433
Email: peppapig@redan.com
Web site: http://www.redan.co.uk/Peppa%20Pig%20Bag-O-Fun.html
Freq: Monthly
Circ: 77037 Not Audited
MAGAZINE
Preschool

Perfect Wedding   983986
Editorial: 2nd Floor Tower House, Fairfax Street, Bristol BS1 3BN
Tel: 44 01179 279009
Web site: www.planyourperfectwedding.com
Freq: Monthly
Circ: 19288 Not Audited
Profile: Perfect Wedding is a monthly magazine covering all aspects of weddings including fashion, hair, beauty, venues, planning and real life weddings. It is owned by Immediate Media. Perfect Wedding is aimed at brides to be.
Ad Rate: Full Page Mono £2000.00
Ad Rate: Full Page Colour £2000.00
MAGAZINE
Fashion, Weddings

Perform   985913
Editorial: 5th Floor, 8 Park Row, Leeds LS1 5HD **Tel:** 44 02033 720600
Email: dl-uk-editorial@performgroup.com
Web site: http://www.performgroup.com/
Freq: Daily
Circ: 1331832 Cision Digital Reach
MAGAZINE (ONLINE)
Broadcasting, Internet, Movies & Video

Performance Bikes   982655
Editorial: Media House, Lynchwood, Peterborough PE2 6EA
Tel: 44 01733 468000
Email: perf.bikes@bauermedia.co.uk
Web site: www.performancebikes.co.uk
Freq: Monthly
Circ: 16864 Not Audited
Editor: Matt Wildee

Profile: Magazine covering road tests on high performance bikes. Includes reports on motorcycle sport and articles on modified motorcycles owned and built by readers.
Ad Rate: Full Page Colour £3276.00
MAGAZINE
Automotive, Motorcycles

Performance BMW   982665
Editorial: Unity Media, The Manor, Nepicar House, London Road, Sevenoaks TN15 7RS
Tel: 44 01732 748000
Web site: www.performancebmwmag.com
Freq: Monthly
Circ: 38000 Not Audited
Editor: Elizabeth de Latour
Profile: Performance BMW is a monthly magazine focusing on modified performance BMW cars. It covers performance tuning and aftermarket car accessories including wheels, suspension, body styling and in-car hi-fi systems. It is owned by Unity Media plc. First published in 1998. Performance BMW is aimed at BMW owners and enthusiasts aged 17 to 35 years old. This magazine contains the following regular features: News Feature - Covering any new products for the BMW tuning and general car tuning scene. Our Cars - Article regarding BMWs owned by the writers on the magazine being fitted with aftermarket products such as suspension, wheels, brakes, interior, exterior, engine and paintwork. Suppliers can provide products and the writers test and review them on their own BMWs.
Ad Rate: Full Page Mono £950.00
Ad Rate: Full Page Colour £950.00
MAGAZINE
Automakers, Automotive

Performance French Cars   982667
Editorial: Old Community Centre, Midfield Terrace, Steelend, Dunfermline KY12 9NB
Tel: 44 01383 852100
Email: features@performancefrenchcars.co.uk
Web site: http://www.performancefrenchcars.co.uk/
Freq: Bi-Monthly
Circ: 28000 Not Audited
Editor: Simon Comins
Profile: Performance French Cars is a bimonthly magazine covering modified French cars, tuning and accessories. Performance French Cars is aimed at French performance car owners and enthusiasts.
Ad Rate: Full Page Colour £950.00
MAGAZINE
Antique & Collectible Cars, Automotive, Driving, Off-road & 4-Wheel Drive Vehicles

Performance Reviewed   997505
Editorial: 40 Craven Street, Suite 7, London WC2N 5NG
Email: info@performancereviewed.com
Web site: performancereviewed.com
Freq: Daily
Circ: 661 Cision Digital Reach
Editor: Vanessa Conway
MAGAZINE (ONLINE)
Theater & Performing Arts, Visual Arts

Performance Vauxhall   983977
Editorial: Cudham Tithe Barn, Berry's Hill, Cudham, London TN16 3AG
Tel: 44 01959 541444
Web site: www.performancevauxhallshow.co.uk
Freq: Bi-Monthly
Circ: 11196 Not Audited
Editor: Dan Furr
MAGAZINE
Automakers

Performance VW   982668
Editorial: Becket House, Vestry Road, Sevenoaks, Sevenoaks TN14 5EJ
Tel: 44 01732 748000
Email: pvw@unity-media.com
Web site: www.performancevwmag.com
Freq: Monthly
Circ: 30000 Not Audited

Consumer Magazines

Profile: Performance VW is a monthly magazine containing information and features on Volkswagen cars, including engine tuning, body kits, ICE, wheels, suspension and car security. It is owned by Unity Media plc. Performance VW is aimed at VW owners, drivers and enthusiasts.
Ad Rate: Full Page Colour £950.00
MAGAZINE
Automakers, Automotive

The Perfume Society 997405
Editorial: 6th Floor, Liberty House, 222 Regent Street, London W1B 5TR
Tel: 44 02072 972022
Email: info@perfumesociety.org
Web site: www.perfumesociety.org
Freq: Daily
Circ: 15523 Cision Digital Reach
MAGAZINE (ONLINE)
Cosmetics

Period Ideas 981852
Editorial: 25 Phoenix Court, Hawkins Road, Colchester CO2 8JY **Tel:** 44 01206 505976
Web site: www.periodideas.com
Freq: Monthly
Circ: 38500 Not Audited
Editor: Susan Dickerson
Profile: Magazine containing inspiration and practical advice on decorating and renovating period homes. Includes sections on property and gardening as well as monthly special features devoted to specific areas of the home such as the kitchen and bathroom.
Ad Rate: Full Page Colour £1645.00
MAGAZINE
Do-It-Yourself (DIY)

Period Living 981853
Editorial: 2 Sugar Brook Court, Aston Road, Bromsgrove B60 3EX **Tel:** 44 01527 834435
Email: periodliving@centaur.co.uk
Web site: www.periodliving.co.uk
Freq: Monthly
Circ: 26755 Not Audited
Editor: Melanie Griffiths
Profile: Magazine covering traditional homes and furnishings. Each issue includes practical help and advice on all aspects of traditional homes, including interiors, gardens, antiques & renovation. It also features decorating schemes, tips on how to create the look, as well as buyer's guides. First published in 1990.
Ad Rate: Full Page Colour £3800.00
MAGAZINE
Do-It-Yourself (DIY)

Permaculture Magazine 999595
Editorial: The Sustainability Centre, Droxford Road, East Meon, Petersfield GU32 1HR **Tel:** 44 01730 823311
Email: info@permaculture.co.uk
Web site: www.permaculture.co.uk
Freq: Quarterly
Circ: 20000 Not Audited
Editor: Maddy Harland
MAGAZINE
Energy & Environment, Ethical/Moral Issues

Personnel Review 981124
Editorial: Howard House, Wagon Lane, Bingley BD16 1WA **Tel:** 44 01274 777700
Web site: www.emeraldinsight.com/loi/PR
Freq: Bi-Monthly Not Audited
MAGAZINE
News & Current Affairs

Pet Focus 984818
Editorial: PetFocus Magazine, Elmtree Business Park, Bury St. Edmunds IP30 9HR
Tel: 44 01359 243400
Email: editorial@petfocus.com
Web site: www.petfocus.com
Freq: Quarterly
Circ: 3000 Not Audited
Editor: Sarah Kidby
MAGAZINE
Nature & Wildlife

Pet News Today 1054021
Email: woof@petnewstoday.com
Web site: https://petnewstoday.com/
Freq: Daily
Circ: 521 Cision Digital Reach
Editor: Polly Stewart
MAGAZINE (ONLINE)
Nature & Wildlife

Pet People 982019
Editorial: 207 Union Street, London SE1 0LN **Tel:** 44 02078 716760
Web site: www.petplan.co.uk/my-petplan/ petpeople_magazine.asp
Freq: Semi-Annual
Circ: 568903 Not Audited
Editor: Jessie Lear
MAGAZINE
Nature & Wildlife

Pet Trade Xtra 997411
Web site: http://pettradextra.newsweaver. com/Newsletter/q5xlxsxlmbn
Freq: Weekly
Editor: Neil Pope
MAGAZINE (ONLINE)
News & Current Affairs

Peter Rabbit magazine 996145
Editorial: Vineyard House, 44 Brook Green, London W6 7BT **Tel:** 44 02071 505000
Email: hello@peterrabbitmag.co.uk
Web site: www.immediate.co.uk
Freq: Monthly
Circ: 25845 Not Audited
Editor: Ruth Cassidy
MAGAZINE
Preschool

The Pets & Animals Directory 997939
Editorial: Suite 6ci and 6cii, Britannia House, Leagrave Road, Luton LU3 1RJ
Tel: 44 01582 488385
Email: info@mediachameleon.co.uk
Web site: www.petsandanimals.co.uk
Freq: Annual
Circ: 486000 Not Audited
MAGAZINE
Nature & Wildlife

Pets Magazine 999477
Email: editor@petsmag.co.uk
Web site: https://www.petsmag.co.uk/
Freq: Monthly
Circ: 12007 Cision Digital Reach
MAGAZINE (ONLINE)
Nature & Wildlife

PGA European Tour 985721
Editorial: European Tour Building, Wentworth Drive, Virginia Water, London GU25 4LX **Tel:** 44 01344 840400
Email: website.feedback@europeantour. com
Web site: www.europeantour.com
Freq: Daily
Circ: 1348177 Cision Digital Reach
MAGAZINE (ONLINE)
Golf

The PGA Professional 982264
Editorial: Centenary House, The Belfry, Wishaw B76 9PT **Tel:** 44 01675 470333
Email: editor@pga.org.uk
Web site: www.pga.info
Freq: Monthly
Circ: 7775 Not Audited
Editor: Adrian Milledge
Profile: Official magazine of The Professional Golfers' Association covering news, features and tournament. Read by members of the association.
Ad Rate: Full Page Mono £1034.00
Ad Rate: Full Page Colour £1335.00
MAGAZINE
Golf

Phaidon.com 985749
Editorial: Phaidon Press Limited, Regent's Wharf, All Saints Street, London N1 9PA
Tel: 44 02078 431000

Email: enquiries@phaidon.com
Web site: www.phaidon.com
Freq: Daily
Circ: 00030 Cision Digital Reach
Editor: Eve O'Sullivan; **Editor:** Mat Smith
MAGAZINE (ONLINE)
Architecture & Design, Art, Cooking & Baking, Photography, Restaurant Reviews

The Phantom 1053149
Editorial: University of Derby Students' Union, Kedleston Road, Derby DE22 1GB
Tel: 44 01332 591507
Email: newspapereditor@phantom-media. co.uk
Web site: www.phantom-media.co.uk
Freq: Bi-Monthly
Circ: 4000 Not Audited
MAGAZINE
Student Lifestyle

PHASE9 987451
Tel: 44 02032 863444
Email: nigelm@phase9.tv
Web site: www.phase9.tv
Freq: Daily
Circ: 11604 Cision Digital Reach
MAGAZINE (ONLINE)
Entertainment, Movies & Video

Philanthropy Impact Magazine 995162
Editorial: CAN Mezzanine, 7 - 14 Great Dover Street, London SE1 4YR
Tel: 44 02074 077879
Email: editor@philanthropy-impact.org
Web site: www.philanthropy-impact.org
Freq: Quarterly
Circ: 16732 Cision Digital Reach
MAGAZINE (ONLINE)
Charitable Foundations

philmarriott.net 995081
Email: phil.marriott@hotmail.co.uk
Web site: http://www.philmarriott.net/
Freq: Daily
Circ: 17103 Cision Digital Reach
MAGAZINE (ONLINE)
Dance Music, Movies & Video, Pop Music, Rock Music

The Philosopher's Magazine 984787
Editorial: C/O Webscribe Ltd, The Philosophers Magazine Unit 8 The Old Silk Mill, Brook Street, Tring HP23 5EF
Email: editor@philosophersmag.com
Web site: www.philosophersmag.com
Freq: Quarterly
Circ: 4000 Not Audited
Editor: James Garvey
MAGAZINE
Religion

PHOENIX 985643
Editorial: 61 Queen Anne Street, London W1G 9HH **Tel:** 44 020/4 864288
Email: info@phoenixmag.co.uk
Web site: www.phoenixmag.co.uk
Freq: Semi-Annual
Circ: 10000 Not Audited
Profile: Magazine covering current affairs and business news, with political satire and gossip.
Ad Rate: Full Page Colour £4300.00
MAGAZINE
Fashion

The Phoenix 996014
Editorial: 44 & 45 Great Russell Street, London WC1B 3JL **Tel:** 44 02076 361188
Email: info@coincraft.com
Web site: www.coincraft.com/the-phoenix-our-free-publication
Freq: Monthly Not Audited
Editor: Richard Lobel
Profile: Magazine covering current affairs and business news, with political satire and gossip.
Ad Rate: Full Page Colour £4300.00
MAGAZINE
Antiques/Collectibles

Photographica World 999042
Web site: www.pccgb.com
Freq: 3 Times/Year Not Audited
Editor: John Marriage
MAGAZINE
Photography

Photography News 1053610
Tel: 44 01223 499450
Web site: www.absolutephoto.com/index. php/magazines/photography-news
Freq: Monthly
Circ: 47500 Not Audited
Editor: William Cheung
MAGAZINE
Cameras, Photography

Photography Week 997991
Editorial: Quay House, The Ambury, Bath BA1 1UA **Tel:** 44 01225 442244
Freq: Weekly
MAGAZINE (ONLINE)
Cameras, Photography

PhotoPlus: The Canon Magazine 998211
Editorial: Quay House, The Ambury, Bath BA1 1UA **Tel:** 44 01225 442244
Web site: http://www.techradar.com/ digitalcameraworld
Freq: Monthly
Circ: 22453 Not Audited
Editor: Peter Travers
MAGAZINE
Cameras, Photography

Photoshop Creative 983530
Editorial: Richmond House, 33 Richmond Hill, Bournemouth BH2 6EZ
Tel: 44 01202 586200
Email: photoshopcreative@ imagine-publishing.co.uk
Web site: www.photoshopcreative.co.uk
Freq: Monthly
Circ: 10835 Not Audited
Editor: Sarah Bankes
Profile: Magazine with step by step tutorial for using Adobe Photoshop.
Ad Rate: Full Page Colour £2300.00
MAGAZINE
Photography, Visual Arts

Phys.org 987115
Editorial: Middlesex House, 34-42 Cleveland Street, London W1T 4LB
Email: feedback@physorg.com
Web site: http://phys.org/
Freq: Daily
Circ: 6322684 Cision Digital Reach
Profile: Website covering science and technology. Discusses anything from physics, earth science, medicine, nanotechnology, electronics, space, biology, chemistry, computer sciences, engineering, mathematics and other sciences and technologies.
MAGAZINE (ONLINE)
Astrology & Parapsychology, Astronomy, Biotechnology, Computers, Diagnostic Imaging, Electronics, Engineering, Healthcare Industry, Medical Technology, Pharmaceuticals

Phys.org - MedicalXpress. com 1003963
Email: feedback@physorg.com
Web site: medicalxpress.com
Freq: Daily
Circ: 1547613 Cision Digital Reach
MAGAZINE (ONLINE)
News & Current Affairs

Physical Activity Facilities 1093869
Tel: 44 02082 881080
Email: info@stable-media.co.uk
Web site: http://www.pactfacilities.co.uk/
Freq: Quarterly
Circ: 5000 Not Audited
Editor: Vicky Kiernander
MAGAZINE
Fitness & Exercise

Consumer Magazines

PI Magazine
996136

Editorial: PI Media, c/o PKWA, Off Manor Way, Batley WF17 7BX
Tel: 44 07506 466385
Email: info@pi-media.co.uk
Web site: www.passionislam.com
Freq: Monthly
Circ: 40000 Not Audited
Editor: Shakir Ahmed
MAGAZINE
Religion

Pianist
982093

Editorial: 5th Floor, 31-32 Park Row, Leeds LS1 5JD **Tel:** 44 01132 002929
Email: editor@pianistmagazine.com
Web site: www.pianistmagazine.com
Freq: Bi-Monthly
Circ: 18000 Not Audited
Editor: Erica Worth
Profile: Magazine covering music news, reviews, music scores, playing tips and techniques as well as features on famous piano performers. Read by those who enjoy playing the piano from beginners to advanced players.
MAGAZINE
Classical/Choral/Band Music

Pick (West Oxfordshire)
1099270

Tel: 44 01235 856300
Email: natalie@fyne.co.uk
Web site: www.pickwestoxfordshire.co.uk
Freq: Monthly
Editor: Natalie Thorne
MAGAZINE
News & Current Affairs

Pick Me Up!
982436

Editorial: 161 Marsh Wall, London E14 9AP
Tel: 44 02031 485000
Email: pickmeup@timeinc.com
Web site: http://www.lifedeathprizes.com
Freq: Weekly
Circ: 121503 Not Audited
Editor: Gilly Sinclair
MAGAZINE
Careers, Crime & Violence, Family & Parenting, Health & Medicine, Lifestyle, Personal Finance, Relationships, Women's Interests

Picture Postcard Monthly
981918

Editorial: 6 Carmarthen Avenue, Drayton, Portsmouth PO6 2AQ **Tel:** 44 02092 423527
Email: info@picturepostcardmagazine.co.uk
Web site: http://www.picturepostcardmagazine.co.uk/
Freq: Monthly
Circ: 4000 Not Audited
Profile: Magazine with a focus on picture postcards. Contains features, artist profiles, auctions and prices, also club news, views and a diary.
Ad Rate: Full Page Mono £175.00
Ad Rate: Full Page Colour £210.00
MAGAZINE
Antiques/Collectibles

The PIE Review
996153

Editorial: Unit A, Azure House, Dragonfly Place, London SE4 2FP
Tel: 44 02035 350873
Email: info@thepienews.com
Web site: www.thepiereview.com
Freq: Quarterly
Circ: 5000 Not Audited
MAGAZINE
Disability, Education, Higher Education, Preschool, Schools & Institutions, Students

The Pig Guide
997369

Editorial: Create Centre, B Bond Warehouse, Smeaton Road, Bristol BS1 6XN
Tel: 44 01179 224376
Email: info@thepigguide.com
Web site: www.thepigguide.com
Freq: Daily
Circ: 12147 Cision Digital Reach
Editor: Melissa Blease
MAGAZINE (ONLINE)
Restaurant Reviews

Pigeons & Peacocks
996803

Web site: www.pigeonsandpeacocks.com
Freq: Annual Not Audited
MAGAZINE
Antiques/Collectibles, Art, Arts, Fashion, Literature, Photography, Theater & Performing Arts, Visual Arts

Pike & Predators
982182

Editorial: Sandholme Grange, Newport, Brough HU15 2QG **Tel:** 44 01430 440624
Email: editorial@pikeandpredators.co.uk
Web site: www.pikeandpredators.co.uk
Freq: Monthly
Circ: 7500 Not Audited
Editor: Neville Fickling
Profile: Magazine focusing on predatory fishing in the UK. Contains articles on all aspects of pike, catfish, zander and eel fishing. The magazine features articles on all aspects of pike and pike fishing from dead baits and live baits to fishing from boats and from the bank. Aimed at anglers who enjoy predatory fishing.
Ad Rate: Full Page Mono £260.00
Ad Rate: Full Page Colour £370.00
MAGAZINE
Fishing

Pillow
995442

Editorial: C/O Zone Ltd, 12-13 Stable Street, London N1C 4AB
Tel: 44 07879 570967
Email: angharad@pillowmagazine.com
Web site: http://pillowmagazine.com/
Freq: Daily
Circ: 1813 Cision Digital Reach
Profile: Blog covering fashion, beauty and lifestyle.
MAGAZINE (ONLINE)
Airline Inflight, Antiques/Collectibles, Art, Arts, Beauty & Grooming, Cosmetics, Hair, Literature, Men's Interests, Photography

pilotguides.com
986771

Editorial: The Old Studio, 18 Middle Row, London W10 5AT **Tel:** 44 02089 602771
Email: editor@pilot.co.uk
Web site: www.pilotguides.com
Freq: Daily
Circ: 41369 Cision Digital Reach
MAGAZINE (ONLINE)
Travel

PINCH
986604

Editorial: 1st Floor, 40-42 Scrutton Street, London EC2A 4PP **Tel:** 44 02074 269888
Email: hellopinch@blacktomato.com
Web site: www.pinch-magazine.com
Freq: Daily
Circ: 5436 Cision Digital Reach
Editor: Hannah Underwood
Profile: Website covering culture. PINCH discusses travel, design, arts, style, food and culture.
MAGAZINE (ONLINE)
Regional General Interest, Travel

PING!
996673

Editorial: Suite 8, Daisy Business Park, 19-35 Sylvan Grove, London SE15 1PD
Tel: 44 07411 480372
Email: contact@pingmagazine.tv
Web site: http://www.pingmagazine.tv/
Freq: Daily
Circ: 1260 Cision Digital Reach
Editor: Buchi Henry Mbagwu
MAGAZINE (ONLINE)
Audio Video Trade, Cameras, Consumer Electronics, Electronics, Mobile Electronics, Movies & Video

Pink
995903

Editorial: Unit 16 Greenway Farm, Bath Road, Wick, Bristol BS30 5RL
Tel: 44 01179 373003
Email: info@kennedypublishing.co.uk
Web site: http://www.kennedypublishing.co.uk/magazines/pink-magazine
Freq: Monthly

Circ: 90000 Not Audited
MAGAZINE
Teen/Young Adult, Trading Cards & Comics

Pink Local Directory
982476

Editorial: St Augustine House, South Wootton, Kings Lynn, King's Lynn PE30 3TE
Tel: 44 01553 675885
Email: enquiry@pinklocaldirectory.co.uk
Web site: www.pinklocaldirectory.co.uk
Freq: Annual
Circ: 23500 Not Audited
MAGAZINE
Business, Regional

Pink Ribbon
982375

Editorial: 63 Norfolk Street, Wigan WN6 7BH **Tel:** 44 07900 267988
Email: info@pinkribbon.co.uk
Web site: www.pinkribbon.co
Freq: Daily
Circ: 1785 Cision Digital Reach
Profile: Lifestyle magazine covering issues on breast cancer awareness and the Awareness Month in a positive and upbeat style.
MAGAZINE (ONLINE)
Women's Interests

The Pink 'Un Magazine
1074309

Editorial: The Pink 'Un magazine, Prospect House, Rouen Road, Norwich NR1 1RE
Email: norfolksport@archant.co.uk
Web site: www.pinkun.com
MAGAZINE
Basketball, Bicycles, Bowling, Boxing, Cricket, Equestrian Sports, Games, Competitions & Events, Golf, Gymnastics, Hockey

PinkNews
988792

Editorial: PinkNews, PO BOX 74009, London EC1P 1TX **Tel:** 44 02032 900505
Email: news@pinknews.co.uk
Web site: www.pinknews.co.uk
Freq: Daily
Circ: 4504472 Cision Digital Reach
Profile: Website covering gay news. The Pink News website shares the latest news for the LGBT. It covers anything from politics and law to finance and entertainment.
MAGAZINE (ONLINE)
International News, LGBT, National News

Pioneers Post
981273

Editorial: Unit 6, Textile Building, Belsham Street, London E9 6NG
Tel: 44 02038 613350
Email: news@pioneerspost.com
Web site: www.pioneerspost.com
Freq: Quarterly Not Audited
Profile: Pioneers Post is an informative and useful resource for business people who are passionate about changing lives, building communities and nurturing the environment. Presents stories, the news that matters, controversial opinions, digs into issues, leading debate and setting agendas.
Ad Rate: Full Page Colour £1498.00
MAGAZINE
Charitable Foundations, Public Sector

PistonHeads.com
982841

Editorial: Teddington Studios, Broom Road, Teddington, London TW11 8BE
Tel: 44 02082 675000
Email: news@pistonheads.com
Web site: www.pistonheads.com
Freq: Daily
Circ: 3790739 Cision Digital Reach
Profile: Website covering motoring. The PistonHeads covers cars and includes car reviews, resource information on car insurance and finance and motorsports.
MAGAZINE (ONLINE)
Automotive, Motorsports

Pitchcare
984285

Editorial: Units 2/3, Allscott, Wellington TF6 5DY **Tel:** 44 01902 440270
Email: mail@pitchcare.com
Web site: www.pitchcare.com
Freq: Bi-Monthly

Circ: 7000 Not Audited
Editor: Kerry Haywood
Profile: Magazine covering all aspects of the sports turf industry including news, products, education, training, health and safety and venues. Aimed at groundsmen, greenkeepers, parks local authority managers, contractors, manufacturers, service providers and education colleges.
Ad Rate: Full Page Colour £1200.00
MAGAZINE
Gardening

Pitchup.com
986550

Editorial: The Barley Mow Centre, 10 Barley Mow Passage, London W4 4PH
Web site: www.pitchup.com
Freq: Daily
Circ: 119395 Cision Digital Reach
MAGAZINE (ONLINE)
News & Current Affairs

Pixel
984450

Editorial: 1 Swan Business Centre, Swan Barn Road, Hailsham, Hailsham BN27 2BY
Tel: 44 01323 819007
Web site: http://lifemediagroup.co.uk/
Freq: Monthly
Circ: 9000 Not Audited
Profile: Magazine proving news and views of the photography and video trade, sale, manufacture and marketing of imaging products, accessories and services.
Ad Rate: Full Page Colour £1270.00
MAGAZINE
Advertising Industry, Branding, Broadcasting, Graphic Design, Marketing, Media & Communications, Photography, Publishing

Pixel Dynamo
990665

Tel: 44 02032 390355
Email: contact@pixeldynamo.com
Web site: http://www.pixeldynamo.com/
Freq: Daily
Circ: 140517 Cision Digital Reach
MAGAZINE (ONLINE)
Computer & Video Games, Mobile Electronics

Pixel Judge
996860

Email: pixeljudge@gmail.com
Web site: pixeljudge.com
Freq: Daily
Circ: 11674 Cision Digital Reach
MAGAZINE (ONLINE)
Computer & Video Games

Places&Faces
986937

Editorial: Beacon Innovation Centre, Beacon Park, Gorleston, Great Yarmouth, Gorleston NR31 7RA **Tel:** 44 01493 742091
Web site: www.placesandfaces.co.uk/
Freq: Monthly
Circ: 13600 Not Audited
Editor: Carolyn Atkins
MAGAZINE
Luxury Goods, Regional General Interest

The Plain Truth
982162

Editorial: PO Box 4421, Worthing BN14 8WQ **Tel:** 44 01638 741549
Email: editor@plaintruth.co.uk
Web site: www.plain-truth.org.uk
Freq: 3 Times/Year
Circ: 7000 Not Audited
Editor: Mary Hammond
Profile: Magazine covering contemporary Christian and charity issues.
Ad Rate: Full Page Mono £995.00
Ad Rate: Full Page Colour £1095.00
MAGAZINE
Religion

Planet Ivy - CEASED
999679

Editorial: York House, 207-221 Pentonville Rd, London N1 9UZ
Freq: Daily
Circ: 105121 Cision Digital Reach
MAGAZINE (ONLINE)
Antiques/Collectibles, Art, Arts, International News, Literature, National News, Photography, Theater & Performing Arts, Visual Arts

Planet Retail
985474

Editorial: 2nd Floor, AirW1, 20 Air Street, London W1B 5AN **Tel:** 44 08081 687088
Email: info@planetretail.net
Web site: www1.planetretail.net
Freq: Daily
Circ: 9786 Cision Digital Reach
MAGAZINE (ONLINE)
News & Current Affairs

Planet Whiskies
987121

Editorial: Flat 5, 14 Station Road, Dumbarton G82 1SA
Email: contact@planetwhiskies.com
Web site: http://www.planetwhiskies.com/
Freq: Daily
Circ: 368 Cision Digital Reach
MAGAZINE (ONLINE)
Alcohol & Spirits

PlaneTalking
999204

Editorial: The Hangar, Kingskerswell, Kingskerswell TQ12 5JR
Tel: 44 01803 898369
Email: contact@planetalking.com
Web site: http://www.planetalking.co.uk/
Freq: Daily
Circ: 10312 Cision Digital Reach
MAGAZINE (ONLINE)
Airline Inflight, Railroad, Travel

Plant & Machinery Model World
996720

Tel: 44 01406 424681
Email: info@igp-ltd.com
Web site: www.themodelhobbyshop.com/product-p/pmmw001.htm
Freq: Bi-Monthly
Circ: 7000 Not Audited
Editor: Steven Downes
MAGAZINE
Crafts, Hobbies, & Collecting

The Plantsman
983943

Editorial: Churchgate, New Road, Peterborough PE1 1TT
Tel: 44 01733 294636
Email: theplantsman@rhs.org.uk
Web site: www.rhs.org.uk/plantsman
Freq: Quarterly
Circ: 3500 Not Audited
Editor: Mike Grant
Profile: Magazine dedicated to a deeper understanding and appreciation of garden plants. Covers plant groups and genera in detail, new plants entering cultivation, plant breeding, new cultivation and propagation techniques, developments in plant taxonomy, conservation of wild and cultivated plants, RHS science and plant trials, forthcoming events and book reviews.
MAGAZINE
Gardening

Platform Magazine
983793

Editorial: Nottingham Trent Students Union, Byron House (NTU Student Shop), Shakespeare Street, Nottingham NG1 4GH
Tel: 44 01158 486200
Email: platformonlinenotts@gmail.com
Web site: www.platform-online.net
Freq: Quarterly Not Audited
MAGAZINE
Student Lifestyle

Play
981739

Editorial: Richmond House, 33 Richmond Hill, Bournemouth BH2 6EZ
Tel: 44 01202 586200
Email: play@imagine-publishing.co.uk
Web site: www.play-mag.co.uk
Freq: Monthly
Circ: 54258 Not Audited
Editor: Luke Albiges
Profile: Launched in 1995, Play was the UK's first independent PlayStation magazine. Delivers forthright reviews and cover-exclusives. Every issue of Play comes with a DVD with the latest PlayStation game footage, trailers and features, as well as game saves, wallpapers and free software to help you get the most out of your PlayStation consoles. Aimed at the serious games

player, predominantly male between 14 and 26 years old.
Ad Rate: Full Page Colour £3500.00
MAGAZINE
Computer & Video Games

Play3r.net
987545

Editorial: 7 Penwarden Way, Bosham, Chichester, Bosham PO18 8LG
Email: press@play3r.net
Web site: www.play3r.net
Freq: Daily
Circ: 103671 Cision Digital Reach
MAGAZINE (ONLINE)
Audio Video Trade, Cameras, Consumer Electronics, Electronics, Mobile Electronics, Movies & Video

The Player
984789

Editorial: Broughton House, 6-8 Sackville Street, London W1S 3DG
Email: theplayermagazine@gmail.com
Web site: www.theplayer.co.uk
Freq: Quarterly
Circ: 17256 Not Audited
Editor: Melissa Cole
Profile: Bookazine produced for members of The Player Club featuring luxury products and services. Aimed at wealthy men.
MAGAZINE
Luxury Goods

The Playground
985104

Editorial: Unit 12, 5 Fountayne Rd, Seven Sisters, London N15 4QL
Tel: 44 02088 089829
Email: editors@theplayground.co.uk
Web site: www.theplayground.co.uk
Freq: Daily
Circ: 131849 Cision Digital Reach
MAGAZINE (ONLINE)
Art, Dance Music, Fashion, Pop Music, Rap & Hip Hop, Rock Music, Theater & Performing Arts

Plays International
981800

Editorial: 33a Lurline Gardens, London SW11 4DD **Tel:** 44 02077 201950
Email: info@playsinternational.org.uk
Web site: www.playsinternational.org.uk
Freq: Bi-Monthly Not Audited
Profile: Plays International is a London-based theatre magazine published bi-monthly. It reports on London's West End stage, presents illustrated reviews and comprehensive listings. It also has lively in-depth interviews with dramatists, directors and actors involved in upcoming productions.
MAGAZINE
Theater & Performing Arts

PlayStation Trophies
997916

Email: tips@ps3t.org
Web site: www.playstationtrophies.org
Freq: Daily
Circ: 789027 Cision Digital Reach
MAGAZINE (ONLINE)
Computer & Video Games

PlaystoSee.com
997222

Email: editorial@playstosee.com
Web site: playstosee.com
Freq: Daily
Circ: 13083 Cision Digital Reach
MAGAZINE (ONLINE)
Entertainment, Theater & Performing Arts

Plaza Interiör Online
1060189

Email: louisa@plazainterior.se
Web site: http://www.plazainterior.se/
Circ: 6002 Cision Digital Reach
MAGAZINE (ONLINE)
Do-It-Yourself (DIY), Interior Design

Plaza Interiör Online
1060708

Email: louisa@plazainterior.se
Web site: http://www.plazainterior.se/
Circ: 6002 Cision Digital Reach
MAGAZINE (ONLINE)
Do-It-Yourself (DIY), Interior Design

Plectrum - The Cultural Pick
999522

Email: guysangsteradams@gmail.com
Web site: www.theculturalpick.com
Freq: Daily
Circ: 1471 Cision Digital Reach
Editor: Guy Sangster Adams
MAGAZINE (ONLINE)
Art, Classical/Choral/Band Music, Country, Folk, Bluegrass, Dance Music, Do-It-Yourself (DIY), Entertainment, Jazz & Blues, Literature, Movies & Video, Music

Plug London
998032

Editorial: 28 Roxwell Road, Shepherd's Bush, London W12 9QF
Tel: 44 07715 571485
Email: elliot@plug.london
Web site: www.plug.london
Freq: Daily
MAGAZINE (ONLINE)
Men's Interests

The Plus Paper
997768

Email: contact@thepluspaper.com
Web site: www.thepluspaper.com
Freq: Daily
Circ: 12607 Cision Digital Reach
MAGAZINE (ONLINE)
Art, Fashion, Graphic Design, Music, Photography, Visual Arts

The Plymouth Daily
987228

Editorial: 6 Northernhay Place, Exeter EX4 3QJ **Tel:** 44 01752 423427
Email: ted@thedailyuk.com
Web site: www.theplymouthdaily.co.uk
Freq: Daily
Circ: 13648 Cision Digital Reach
Editor: Mary Youlden
MAGAZINE (ONLINE)
Regional

The Plymouth Magazine
984434

Editorial: 28 Old Park Road, Peverell, Plymouth PL3 4PY **Tel:** 44 01752 225623
Email: info@cornerstonevision.com
Web site: http://www.cornerstonevision.com/plymouth-publications/the-plymouth-magazine/
Freq: Monthly
Circ: 47000 Not Audited
Editor: Chris Girdler
Profile: Magazine covering lifestyle including interior design, property, personal finance, events guide, eating out, health and welfare.
Ad Rate: Full Page Colour £525.00
MAGAZINE
Regional General Interest

PMI News
980152

Editorial: PMI House, 4-10 Artillery Lane, London E1 7LS **Tel:** 44 02072 471452
Web site: http://www.pensions-pmi.org.uk
Freq: Monthly
Circ: 6500 Not Audited
Profile: Journal covering notification of the PMIs conferences, wealth management and seminars. Includes news of pension legislation, student information and regional group news. Read by the members of The Pensions Management Institute.
Ad Rate: Full Page Colour £1750.00
MAGAZINE

PN Review
999470

Editorial: 4th Floor, Alliance House, 30 Cross Street, Manchester M2 7AQ
Tel: 44 01618 348730
Email: info@carcanet.co.uk
Web site: www.pnreview.co.uk
Freq: Bi-Monthly
Circ: 1500 Not Audited
Editor: Michael Schmidt
MAGAZINE
Literature

Pocket Gamer
984659

Editorial: The House, Kelston Park, Bath BA1 9AE
Email: feedback@pocketgamer.co.uk
Web site: www.pocketgamer.co.uk

Freq: Daily
Circ: 980739 Cision Digital Reach
Profile: Website covering mobile and handheld console games. POCKET GAMER shares the latest news, reviews and features on mobile, iPhone, PSP, DS, Android and other handheld games.
MAGAZINE (ONLINE)
Computer & Video Games

Pocket Manchester
1054002

Editorial: 493-495 Chester Road, Stretford, Manchester M16 9HF **Tel:** 44 01617 060004
Email: digital@msmuk.com
Web site: http://www.pocketmanchester.com/
Freq: Daily
Circ: 15848 Cision Digital Reach
MAGAZINE (ONLINE)
Local Entertainment Guides, Regional, Restaurant Reviews, Rugby, Soccer, Sports

Pocket Tactics
996846

Tel: 44 07879 640305
Email: joer@pockettactics.com
Web site: www.pockettactics.com
Freq: Daily
Circ: 140272 Cision Digital Reach
MAGAZINE (ONLINE)
Computer & Video Games, Mobile Electronics

PocketGPSWorld
984759

Email: team@pocketgpsworld.com
Web site: www.pocketgpsworld.com
Freq: Daily
Circ: 114172 Cision Digital Reach
MAGAZINE (ONLINE)

Pocket-Lint.com
986219

Editorial: PO Box 4770, Ascot SL5 5DP
Web site: www.pocket-lint.com
Freq: Daily
Circ: 3476125 Cision Digital Reach
Editor: Chris Hall
Profile: Website covering technology and consumer electronics. Pocket-lint covers news, reviews and features on consumer electronics and technology including smart phones, tablets, cameras, apps and computer and video games.
MAGAZINE (ONLINE)
Audio Video Trade, Cameras, Consumer Electronics, Men's Interests, Mobile Electronics, Movies & Video

Podiatry Now
985998

Editorial: 1 Fellmongers Path, Tower Bridge Road, London SE1 3LY
Tel: 44 02072 348620
Email: td@scpod.org
Web site: http://www.scpod.org/publications-to-download/podiatry-now-subscription
Freq: Monthly
Circ: 11000 Not Audited
Editor: Clare Richards
Profile: Journal of the Society of Chiropodists and Podiatrists. Contains news, political comment, legislative issues and continuing professional development. Read by society members.
Ad Rate: Full Page Mono £1055.00
Ad Rate: Full Page Colour £1430.00
MAGAZINE
Medicine

Podium Magazine
1100032

Editorial: 24 Double Hedges Park, Edinburgh EH16 6YL **Tel:** 44 07941 205360
Email: sport@podiummagazine.co.uk
Web site: www.podiummagazine.co.uk
Freq: Quarterly
Circ: 5000 Not Audited
MAGAZINE
Bicycles, Fitness & Exercise, Gymnastics, Olympic Sports, Outdoor Recreation, Sports

Poetry Review
981976

Editorial: 22 Betterton Street, London WC2H 9BX **Tel:** 44 02074 209880
Email: info@poetrysociety.org.uk

Consumer Magazines

Web site: www.poetrysociety.org.uk
Freq: Quarterly
Circ: 15000 Not Audited
Editor: Maurice Riordan
Profile: Magazine containing poems, reviews and features on all aspects of poetry and the work of poets. Aimed at poets, teachers, students and general readers of poetry.
Ad Rate: Full Page Mono £370.00
MAGAZINE
Literature

The Poetry Society 990366
Editorial: 22 Betterton Street, London WC2H 9BX **Tel:** 44 02074 209880
Email: info@poetrysociety.org.uk
Web site: www.poetrysociety.org.uk
Freq: Daily
Circ: 46217 Cision Digital Reach
MAGAZINE (ONLINE)
Literature

Point Blank Plus 996219
Editorial: 23-28 Penn Street, London N1 5DL **Tel:** 44 02077 294884
Email: enquiries@pointblanklondon.com
Web site: http://plus.pointblankmusicschool.com/
Freq: Daily
Circ: 3041 Cision Digital Reach
MAGAZINE (ONLINE)
Dance Music

Poker Industry Pro 997644
Web site: https://pokerindustrypro.com/
Freq: Daily
Circ: 8409 Cision Digital Reach
MAGAZINE (ONLINE)
Computer & Video Games

Poker Player 982821
Editorial: 2nd Floor, 105 Farringdon Road, London EC1R 3BU
Email: pokerplayer@plyp.co.uk
Web site: www.pokerplayer365.com
Freq: Monthly
Circ: 17240 Not Audited
Profile: Magazine with tips, strategies, opinions and features as well as chances to play with the top Poker professionals. Aimed at poker players at all levels of skill.Regular features: Player & Celebrity Profiles; Readers Playing the Pros; Strategy
Ad Rate: Full Page Colour £6454.00
MAGAZINE
Casinos & Gaming, Poker

PokerNews.com 987504
Editorial: 4th Floor Exchange House, 54-58 Athol Street, Douglas, Isle of Man IM1 1JD
Email: info@pokernews.com
Web site: http://uk.pokernews.com/
Freq: Daily
Circ: 24682 Cision Digital Reach
MAGAZINE (ONLINE)
Poker

Polaroids and Polar Bears 996173
Web site: polaroidsandpolarbears.co.uk
Freq: Daily
Circ: 1499 Cision Digital Reach
Editor: Chris Brown
MAGAZINE (ONLINE)
Antiques/Collectibles, Art, Arts, Classical/Choral/Band Music, Country, Folk, Bluegrass, Dance Music, Jazz & Blues, Literature, Music, Photography

Pole Fishing Magazine 999104
Editorial: 1 Whittle Close, Drayton Fields, Daventry NN11 8RQ **Tel:** 44 01327 311999
Email: polefishing@dhpub.co.uk
Web site: www.polefishingmagazine.com
Freq: Monthly
Circ: 17500 Not Audited
Editor: Alex Bones
MAGAZINE
Fishing

policyreview.eu 987728
Editorial: PO Box 67084, London SW2 9JU
Tel: 44 02037 514138
Email: editor@policyreview.eu
Web site: www.policyreview.eu
Freq: Daily
Circ: 14016 Cision Digital Reach
Editor: Tim McNamara
MAGAZINE (ONLINE)
Government, Politics, Public Sector

Political Studies Review 986037
Editorial: Sage Publications, 1 Oliver's Yard, 55 City Road, London EC1Y 1SP
Tel: 44 02073 248701
Email: market@sagepub.co.uk
Web site: http://psw.sagepub.com/
Freq: 3 Times/Year
Circ: 700 Not Audited
Profile: Journal provides unrivalled review coverage of new books and literature on political science and international relations.
MAGAZINE
Careers, Education, Politics

Politics First 986621
Editorial: c/o Government Knowledge, Suite 4 Metropolitan House, 38-40 High Street, Croydon CR0 1YB
Email: editor@firstpublishing.org
Web site: www.politicsfirst.org.uk
Freq: Bi-Monthly
Circ: 1110 Not Audited
MAGAZINE
Politics

PoliticsHome 985422
Editorial: Dods Parliamentary Communications Ltd, 11th Floor The Shard, 32 London Bridge Street, London SE1 9SG
Tel: 44 02075 935500
Email: news@politicshome.com
Web site: www.politicshome.com
Freq: Daily
Circ: 62163 Cision Digital Reach
Editor: Kevin Schofield
Profile: Website covering politics. The PoliticsHome website shares the latest news on the London government.
MAGAZINE (ONLINE)
Politics

Polity 1060631
Email: newsdesk@polity.org.za
Web site: http://www.polity.org.za
Circ: 51004 Cision Digital Reach
MAGAZINE (ONLINE)
National News, Politics

PollstarPro.com 998981
Editorial: Suite 4M, Leroy House, 436 Essex Road, London N1 3QP **Tel:** 44 02073 591110
Email: editorial@pollstar.com
Web site: www.pollstarpro.com
Freq: Daily
Circ: 131515 Cision Digital Reach
MAGAZINE (ONLINE)
Pop Music, Rock Music

The Polo Magazine 985409
Editorial: Hill Farm Studios, Wainlodes Lane, Bishop's Norton, Norton GL2 9LN
Tel: 44 01452 730770
Email: info@thepolomagazine.com
Web site: www.thepolomagazine.com
Freq: Quarterly
Circ: 10000 Not Audited
Profile: Magazine covering the polo scene including interviews, features, polo reports and spotlights on luxury lifestyle articles as well as coverage of the best polo parties of the season. Aimed at polo amateurs and affluent people.
MAGAZINE
Equestrian Sports

Polo Quarterly 998452
Editorial: The Old Stables, South Wonston Farm, Hampshire, Winchester SO21 3HL
Tel: 44 01962 888569
Web site: www.pqinternational.com

Freq: Quarterly Not Audited
MAGAZINE
Equestrian Sports, Luxury Goods

Polo Times 982245
Editorial: Hill Harm Studios, Wainlodes Lane, Norton GL2 9LN **Tel:** 44 01452 730770
Email: info@polotimes.co.uk
Web site: www.polotimes.co.uk
Freq: Monthly
Circ: 2000 Not Audited
Profile: Magazine covering polo around the world. Includes information from clubs and associations, tournament and team news, polo reports, social news, polo destination features and player profiles. Aimed at both polo spectators and players.
Ad Rate: Full Page Colour £1200.00
MAGAZINE
Equestrian Sports

Polyester Magazine 1100577
Email: hello@polyesterzine.com
Web site: www.polyesterzine.com/ Not Audited
MAGAZINE
Fashion, Photography

Pom Pom Quarterly 1052717
Email: contact@pompommag.com
Web site: www.pompommag.com
Freq: Quarterly
Circ: 28000 Not Audited
MAGAZINE
Art, Classical/Choral/Band Music, Cooking & Baking, Country, Folk, Bluegrass, Crafts, Dance Music, Fashion, Jazz & Blues, Music, Photography

PONY Magazine 982242
Editorial: Marlborough House, Headley Road, Grayshott, Hindhead GU26 6LG
Tel: 44 01428 601020
Email: pony@djmurphy.co.uk
Web site: ponymag.com
Freq: Monthly
Circ: 26697 Not Audited
Profile: Magazine containing features to help improve readers' riding and horse care knowledge, including tips from famous riders and trainers. Aimed at children and teenage riding enthusiasts.
Ad Rate: Full Page Colour £2400.00
MAGAZINE
Equestrian Sports, Teen/Young Adult

The Pool 996133
Editorial: 1st Floor, Epatra House, 58-60 Berners Street, London W1T 3NQ
Tel: 44 02073 393084
Email: hello@thepoolltd.com
Web site: www.the-pool.com
Freq: Daily
Circ: 160026 Cision Digital Reach
MAGAZINE (ONLINE)
Women's Interests

POP 981884
Editorial: Emigre Studios, 3rd Floor, 274 Richmond Road, London E8 3QW
Email: office@thepop.com
Web site: thepop.com
Freq: Semi-Annual
Circ: 60000 Not Audited
Profile: Magazine predominantly covering contemporary art and fashion. Includes news and music features.
Ad Rate: Full Page Colour £8400.00
MAGAZINE
Fashion

Pop Scoop! 996965
Editorial: Sackville Place, 44-48 Magdalen Stree, Norwich NR3 1JU
Tel: 44 05603 687211
Email: info@popscoop.org
Web site: www.popscoop.org
Freq: Daily
Circ: 11128 Cision Digital Reach
MAGAZINE (ONLINE)
Celebrities, Dance Music, Pop Music, Rap & Hip Hop, Rock Music

Popbitch 984237
Email: hello@popbitch.com
Web site: www.popbitch.com
Freq: Weekly
Circ: 49218 Cision Digital Reach
MAGAZINE (ONLINE)
Celebrities, Pop Music

PopBucket 997137
Editorial: Flat 9 Kearton Place, 169-171 Croydon Road, Caterham, London CR3 6PU
Tel: 44 07515 538333
Email: pr@popbucket.co.uk
Web site: www.popbucket.co.uk
Freq: Daily
Circ: 8374 Cision Digital Reach
MAGAZINE (ONLINE)
Broadcasting, Computer & Video Games, Movies & Video

PopBuzz 1053888
Editorial: 30 Leicester Square, London WC2H 7LA **Tel:** 44 02077 666000
Email: info@pop-buzz.com
Web site: http://www.popbuzz.co.uk/
Freq: Daily
Circ: 17454 Cision Digital Reach
MAGAZINE (ONLINE)
Pop Music

Popjustice.com 985112
Email: press.releases@popjustice.com
Web site: www.popjustice.com
Freq: Daily
Circ: 156504 Cision Digital Reach
Editor: Peter Robinson
MAGAZINE (ONLINE)
Pop Music

Poppet 998037
Editorial: 83 Victoria Street, London SW1H OHW
Email: hello@moshimonsters.com
Web site: http://www.poppet.com/
Freq: Monthly Not Audited
MAGAZINE
News & Current Affairs

Popular Patchwork 981949
Editorial: Enterprise House, Enterprise Way, Edenbridge, Edenbridge TN8 6HF
Tel: 44 01332 912989
Web site: www.popularpatchwork.com
Freq: Monthly
Circ: 17000 Not Audited
Editor: Elizabeth Betts
Profile: Magazine covering articles on traditional and contemporary quilts and information on quilt makers. Includes designs and ideas for patchwork, quilting and appliqué, exhibition reviews and competitions. Read by people interested in patchwork, quilting and appliqué as well as educators and students.
Ad Rate: Full Page Colour £600.00
MAGAZINE
Crafts

Population & Economics 1061691
Tel: 44 86106 5976473
Email: rks@cueb.edu.cn
Web site: http://www.cueb.edu.cn
Freq: Bi-Monthly
Circ: 10001 Not Audited
MAGAZINE
Social Issues

Porsche Post 982643
Editorial: Cornbury House, Cotswold Business Village, Moreton in Marsh, Moreton-in-Marsh GL56 0JQ
Tel: 44 01608 652911
Email: editor@porscheclubgb.com
Web site: www.porscheclubgb.com
Freq: Monthly
Circ: 12000 Not Audited
Profile: Publication containing Porsche-related articles, news and features from the Porsche Club of Great Britain. Aimed at members and Porsche enthusiasts.
Ad Rate: Full Page Colour £925.00
MAGAZINE
Automakers

PORT
985846

Editorial: Port Publishing Ltd, Unit 6 Albion Riverside Building, 8 Hester Road, London SW11 4AX **Tel:** 44 02031 193077
Email: info@port-magazine.com
Web site: www.port-magazine.com
Freq: Semi-Annual
Circ: 92650 Not Audited
Profile: Covers lifestyle, men's fashion, travel, design and living, architecture, literature, entertainment.
MAGAZINE
Fashion, Men's Interests

Port Finance International
988867

Editorial: 1st Floor, 30 Warner Street, London EC1R 5EX **Tel:** 44 02072 532700
Web site: http://portfinanceinternational. com
Freq: Daily
Circ: 8428 Cision Digital Reach
Profile: Website covering the global port industry. Port Finance International provides global news and developments from the port industry, coverage of international port finance, investment and operations news including features and interviews
MAGAZINE (ONLINE)
Marine & Boat Trade

Port Strategy
984243

Editorial: The Old Mill, Lower Quay, Fareham, Fareham PO16 0RA
Tel: 44 01329 825335
Email: editor@portstrategy.com
Web site: www.portstrategy.com
Freq: Monthly
Circ: 5510 Not Audited
Editor: Carly Fields
Profile: Magazine that covers news and features on the key changes and opportunities within the international marine port industry. Includes regional surveys and articles on investment pricing, cargo handling, port engineering and management, vessel training, logistics, insurance and loss prevention. Aimed at government strategists, port executives, maritime terminal operators and key port users.
Ad Rate: Full Page Colour £3985.00
MAGAZINE
Marine & Boat Trade, Shipping & Warehousing

Port Technology International
984244

Editorial: 3rd Floor, Two America Square, London EC3N 2LU **Tel:** 44 02078 710123
Email: info@porttechnology.org
Web site: www.porttechnology.org
Freq: Quarterly
Circ: 20000 Not Audited
Profile: Preview and review of advanced technologies for ports, harbours and terminals worldwide. Aimed at harbour masters, port authorities, terminal operators, industry associations and professionals.
Ad Rate: Full Page Colour £4200.00
MAGAZINE
Marine & Boat Trade, Shipping & Warehousing

PORTER magazine
987802

Editorial: 1 The Village Offices, Westfield London, Ariel Way, London W12 7GF
Tel: 44 02034 714500
Email: editors@net-a-porter.com
Web site: http://www.net-a-porter.com/
Freq: Bi-Monthly
Circ: 152000 Not Audited
MAGAZINE
Fashion

PORTFOLIO
998237

Tel: 44 07931 537588
Email: lynne@portfoliopublications.co.uk
Web site: www.portfoliopublications.co.uk
Freq: Monthly
Circ: 8000 Not Audited
Profile: Newspaper with news and features on future developments, human interest stories, sports, personal finance, business, property, travel, motoring, IT and lifestyle. Aimed at local and business readers in

Dublin both men and women aged between 24 and 34 years old.
Ad Rate: Full Page Colour £1500.00
MAGAZINE
Bars, Clubs & Pubs, Do-It-Yourself (DIY), Interior Design, Property Management & Maintenance, Residential Real Estate, Urban Planning & Development

Portfolio Adviser
983703

Editorial: Fleet House, 1st Floor, 59-61 Clerkenwell Road, London EC1M 5LA
Tel: 44 02076 386354
Email: pam@lastwordmedia.com
Web site: http://www.portfolio-adviser.com
Freq: Monthly
Circ: 4975 Not Audited
Profile: Publication covering wealth management, investment strategies for professional advisers to help with clients' portfolio construction and asset allocation decisions. Aimed at intermediaries and discretionary advisers who make investment decisions on behalf of their clients.
Ad Rate: Full Page Colour £5550.00
MAGAZINE
Banking, Fund Management, Personal Finance

portfolio institutional
985736

Editorial: Office 5.05 – Fifth Floor, Fleet House, 8-12 New Bridge Street, London EC4V 6AL **Tel:** 44 02078 228522
Email: london@portfolio-verlag.com
Web site: www.portfolio-institutional.co.uk
Freq: Monthly
Circ: 7500 Not Audited
Profile: The magazine focuses exclusively on requirements of institutional investors. Provides in-depth analysis on the available asset allocation options for UK institutional investors. It also cover wealth management.
Ad Rate: Full Page Colour £6500.00
MAGAZINE
Fund Management, Hedge Funds, Investment Banking, Personal Finance

pos'ability
987566

Editorial: Caledonia House, Evanton Drive, Thornliebank Ind Est, Glasgow G46 8JT
Tel: 44 01414 652960
Email: enquiries@2apublishing.co.uk
Web site: http://posabilitymagazine.co.uk/
Freq: Bi-Monthly
Circ: 31000 Not Audited
Editor: Rosalind Tulloch
MAGAZINE
Disability

Posh Tea and Cake
998142

Email: poshteaandcake@gmail.com
Web site: www.poshteaandcake.com
Freq: Daily
Circ: 936 Cision Digital Reach
MAGAZINE (ONLINE)
Airline Inflight, Alcohol & Spirits, Bars, Clubs & Pubs, Beer, Beverages, Cooking & Baking, Food, Grocery Stores, Luxury Goods, Organic Food

Positive News
983721

Editorial: 24 Greencoat Place, London SW1P 1RD **Tel:** 44 02077 986006
Email: editorial@positive.news
Web site: http://www.positive.news/
Freq: Quarterly
Circ: 40000 Not Audited
Profile: Newspaper covering positive environmental news from around the world. Includes news on health, education, organic food, economics and business, new products, alternative transport and the environment. Aimed at environmentalists, educationalists and those interested in alternative health issues, organic, safe foods and world issues.
Ad Rate: Full Page Mono £900.00
Ad Rate: Full Page Colour £1025.00
MAGAZINE
Ethical/Moral Issues, International News, National News

Positive Parkinson's
999369

Editorial: 11 Viking Way, Christchurch BH23 4AQ
Email: pax@peace.co.uk

Web site: www.positiveparkinsons.com
Freq: Daily
Circ: 1040 Cision Digital Reach
MAGAZINE (ONLINE)
Neurology, Patient Support

Positive Pressure
998922

Editorial: Wolfson Institute of Preventative Medicine, Charterhouse Medicine, London EC1M 6BQ **Tel:** 44 02078 826255
Email: info@bloodpressureuk.org
Web site: www.bloodpressureuk.org/ HelpingUs/Joinus/Magazine
Freq: Semi-Annual
Circ: 3500 Not Audited
MAGAZINE
Charitable Foundations, Patient Support

Postcards
985434

Editorial: Unit 310, Highgate Studios, 53-79 Highgate Road, London NW5 1TL
Tel: 44 02072 539906
Email: editorial@aplmedia.co.uk
Web site: aplmedia.co.uk/portfolio/ destination-vacation/
Freq: Quarterly
Circ: 30000 Not Audited
MAGAZINE
Luxury Goods, Railroad, Travel

Postgrad Magazine
995298

Editorial: Prospect House, Booth Street East, Manchester M13 9EP
Tel: 44 01612 775200
Email: editorial@prospects.ac.uk
Web site: www.prospects.ac.uk
Freq: 3 Times/Year
Circ: 540000 Not Audited
MAGAZINE
Careers

Postgraduate Medical Journal
985882

Editorial: BMA House, Tavistock Square, London WC1H 9JR **Tel:** 44 02073 836622
Email: pmj@bmj.com
Web site: pmj.bmj.com/
Freq: Monthly Not Audited
Editor: Penny Fitzharris; **Editor:** Ana Grenfell; **Editor:** Bob Klaber; **Editor:** Kathryn McPherson
Profile: Journal focusing on medical education and covers a range of topics relevant to the practising clinician and teacher. Aimed at postgraduate tutors, clinical trainers and trainees, clinicians in any specialty and postgraduate nurses who wish to further their medical education.
Ad Rate: Full Page Mono £910.00
Ad Rate: Full Page Colour £1610.00
MAGAZINE
Medicine

POSTmatter
997138

Editorial: 124 Aldersgate Street, London EC1A 4JQ **Tel:** 44 02077 807250
Email: info@postmatter.com
Web site: www.postmatter.com
Freq: Daily
Circ: 25972 Cision Digital Reach
MAGAZINE (ONLINE)
Art, Fashion, Literature, Men's Interests, Photography, Science, Visual Arts, Women's Interests

Pow Mag
997782

Editorial: MDX House, The Burroughs, London NW4 4BT **Tel:** 44 02084 116450
Email: editor@mdxsu.com
Web site: www.mdxsu.com
Freq: Monthly Not Audited
MAGAZINE
Regional General Interest, Student Lifestyle

Powder
1058245

Editorial: 161 Marsh Wall, London E14 9AP
Tel: 44 02031 485000
Email: hello@thisispowder.co.uk
Web site: https://www.thisispowder.co.uk/
Freq: Daily

Circ: 49665 Cision Digital Reach
MAGAZINE (ONLINE)
Beauty & Grooming, Cosmetics, Hair

Power Electronics Europe
986035

Editorial: 192 High Street, Tonbridge TN9 1BE **Tel:** 44 01732 370340
Web site: www.power-mag.com
Freq: Bi-Monthly
Circ: 16000 Not Audited
Editor: Achim Scharf
Profile: Magazine covering all aspects of electronics including emerging technologies and the application of advanced components, sub-assemblies, systems and solutions. Aimed at engineers specialising in automotive, industrial and consumer electronics.
Ad Rate: Full Page Colour £2675.00
MAGAZINE
Electricity, Electronics

Power Electronics World
996457

Editorial: Hannay House, 39 Clarendon Road, Watford, Watford WD17 1JA
Tel: 44 01923 690200
Email: jackie.cannon@angelbc.com
Web site: www. powerelectronicsworld.net/
Freq: Quarterly
Circ: 53430 Not Audited
Profile: Website covering electronics. The POWER ELECTRONICS WORLD website shares the latest information on electronics industry.
MAGAZINE
Electronics

Powerboat & RIB Magazine
982211

Editorial: The Old Coach House, Kentisbeare, Horley EX15 2DY
Tel: 44 01884 266100
Email: hms@powerboatandrib.com
Web site: powerboatandrib.com
Freq: Bi-Monthly
Circ: 15000 Not Audited
Editor: Hugo Montgomery-Swan
Profile: Magazine that covers all aspects of the rigid inflatable boats including RIBs, RHIBS or Rigid Inflatable Boats being used as as lifeboats, patrol craft, standby vessels, FOCs, expeditionary craft, cruising vessels, adventure craft, race boats, family leisure craft. Features include RIB tests, safety procedures, environmental concerns, record breaking attempts and expeditions. Aimed at those with an interest in rigid inflatable boats and their worldwide market.
Ad Rate: Full Page Colour £1350.00
MAGAZINE
Boating & Yachting

powerboatp1.com
995050

Editorial: Queen Anne Mansions, 86-87 Wimpole Street, London W1G 9RL
Tel: 44 02079 354977
Email: info@powerboatp1.com
Web site: www.powerboatp1.com
Freq: Daily
Circ: 4600 Cision Digital Reach
MAGAZINE (ONLINE)
Marine & Boat Trade

PR Moment
985285

Editorial: 1 Redlands Lane, Redlands Cottage, Winchester PO10 7SN
Web site: www.prmoment.com
Freq: Daily
Circ: 46832 Cision Digital Reach
Editor: Daney Parker
MAGAZINE (ONLINE)
Advertising Industry, Branding, Broadcasting, Graphic Design, Marketing, Media & Communications, Photography, Publishing

Practical Boat Owner
982210

Editorial: Time Inc. UK, Westover House, West Quay Road, Poole BH15 1JG
Tel: 44 01202 440820
Email: pbo@timeinc.com
Web site: www.pbo.co.uk

Consumer Magazines

Freq: Monthly
Circ: 24087 Not Audited
Editor: David Pugh
Profile: Magazine covering boating including in-depth, hands-on information about boats and gear, maintenance, pilotage and seamanship. Includes major tests of the latest electronics and life-saving gear and lots of buyer's advice, with a special Motorboat section in every issue. First published in 1967, the publication has an average of 180 pages per issue. Aimed at boating enthusiasts.
MAGAZINE
Boating & Yachting

Practical Caravan   982314
Editorial: Bridge House, 69 London Road, Twickenham, London TW1 3SP
Email: practical.caravan@haymarket.com
Web site: www.practicalcaravan.com
Freq: Monthly
Circ: 22896 Not Audited
Profile: Magazine covering caravan and product tests, touring features, towcars and real-life caravanning experiences. Average Pages per Issue: 180. Aimed at touring caravanners.
Ad Rate: Full Page Colour £3586.00
MAGAZINE
Camping and RV Travel

Practical Classics   982616
Editorial: Media House, Lynchwood, Peterborough Business Park, Peterborough PE2 6EA **Tel:** 44 01733 468582
Email: practical.classics@bauermedia.co.uk
Web site: www.practicalclassics.co.uk
Freq: Monthly
Circ: 45401 Not Audited
Editor: Danny Hopkins
Profile: Magazine covering all aspects of classic cars including product tests and accessories. First published in 1980, the publication has an average of 180 pages per issue. Aimed at owners who are interested in restoring, maintaining and running cars made in the 1930s to the 1980s.
Ad Rate: Full Page Mono £1161.00
Ad Rate: Full Page Colour £1890.00
MAGAZINE
Antique & Collectible Cars

Practical Fishkeeping   982020
Editorial: Media House, Lynchwood Business Park, Cambridgeshire, Peterborough PE2 6EA
Tel: 44 01733 468000
Email: editorial@practicalfishkeeping.co.uk
Web site: www.practicalfishkeeping.co.uk
Freq: Monthly
Circ: 12247 Not Audited
Editor: Karen Youngs
Profile: Magazine providing guidance on aquariums, ponds and their inhabitants. First published in 1981, the publication has an average of 124 pages per issue. Aimed at fish keepers of all levels of experience.
Ad Rate: Full Page Colour £2700.00
MAGAZINE
Nature & Wildlife

Practical Lawyer   985179
Editorial: Kensington Square House, 12-14 Ansdell Street, London W8 5BN
Tel: 44 02073 969313
Web site: www.practicallawyer.co.uk
Freq: Monthly Not Audited
Profile: Digest of latest developments in the law, containing selected articles from a wide variety of magazines and journals.
MAGAZINE
Law

Practical Motorhome   982315
Editorial: Teddington Studios, Broom Road, Teddington, London TW11 9BE
Tel: 44 02082 675629
Email: practical.motorhome@haymarket. com
Web site: www.practicalmotorhome.com
Freq: Monthly
Circ: 12621 Not Audited
Editor: Niall Hampton
Profile: Magazine covering all aspects of motorhomes including travel sites, technical

matters, improvements, new models and buying information. Provides travel features, product reviews, advice and columns to bring essential information to experienced motorhome owners and potential buyers. Aimed at motorhome owners and those considering buying.
Ad Rate: Full Page Colour £1797.00
MAGAZINE
Camping and RV Travel

Practical Performance Car
987869
Tel: 44 01536 771874
Web site: www.ppcmag.co.uk
Freq: Monthly
Circ: 17000 Not Audited
Editor: Will Holman
Profile: Magazine covering affordable performance cars, driving adventures and technical features. First published in 2004, the publication has an average of 156 pages per issue. Aimed at car enthusiasts.
Ad Rate: Full Page Colour £1100.00
MAGAZINE
Automotive

Practical Pre-School   985198
Editorial: St Jude's Church, Dulwich Road, London SE24 0PB **Tel:** 44 02077 385454
Web site: www.magonlinelibrary.com/toc/prps/current
Freq: Monthly
Circ: 6000 Not Audited
Editor: Karen Faux
Profile: Magazine providing news, reviews of books and equipment, features, competitions and practical help and guidance. Aimed at reception teachers, nursery teachers, managers, playgroups and pre-schools.
Ad Rate: Full Page Colour £995.00
MAGAZINE
Preschool

Practical Reptile Keeping
986407
Editorial: Cudham Tithe Barn, Berry's Hill, Cudham, London TN16 3AG
Tel: 44 01959 541444
Email: prk.ed@kelsey.co.uk
Web site: www.practicalreptilekeeping.co.uk
Freq: Monthly
Circ: 9000 Not Audited
Editor: David Alderton
Profile: Magazine covering all aspects of reptiles care including news, places to visit and health advice.
MAGAZINE
Nature & Wildlife

Practical Sportsbikes   985491
Editorial: Media House, Lynchwood, Peterborough Business Park, Peterborough PE2 6EA **Tel:** 44 01733 468081
Web site: www.practicalsportsbikesmag.co.uk
Freq: Monthly
Circ: 19862 Not Audited
Editor: Jim Moore
Profile: Magazine covering buying, restoring and riding the motorbikes. Each issue covers restoration stories, workshop tips, advice, buyers' guides, road tests and restoration knowledge.
MAGAZINE
Motorcycles

Practical Wireless   984256
Editorial: Tayfield House, 38 Poole Road, Westbourne, Bournemouth BH4 9DW
Tel: 44 01202 751611
Web site: www.pwpublishing.ltd.uk
Freq: Monthly
Circ: 10000 Not Audited
Editor: Don Field
Profile: Magazine containing new product and technology news, articles on techniques, construction and operation.
Ad Rate: Full Page Mono £775.00
Ad Rate: Full Page Colour £880.00
MAGAZINE
Electronics

The Practitioner   981196
Editorial: 10 Fernthorpe Road, London SW16 6DR **Tel:** 44 02086 773508
Email: editor@thepractitioner.co.uk
Web site: www.thepractitioner.co.uk
Freq: Monthly
Circ: 15000 Not Audited
Editor: Corinne Short
MAGAZINE
Medicine

preciousonline.co.uk   982842
Editorial: c/o Foluke Akinlose MBE, 71-75 Shelton Street, Covent Garden, London WC2H 9JQ
Email: editorial@preciousonline.co.uk
Web site: http://preciousonline.co.uk/
Freq: Daily
Circ: 13083 Cision Digital Reach
MAGAZINE (ONLINE)
Africa, Americas, Business, Corporate Responsibility, Women's Interests

Preferred Travel   1053629
Editorial: Capital House, 25 Chapel Street, London NW1 5DH **Tel:** 44 02037 717200
Email: preferredtravel@thinkpublishing.co.uk
Web site: www.thinkpublishing.co.uk
Freq: 3 Times/Year
Circ: 120000 Not Audited
MAGAZINE
Travel

Pregnancy and Parenting
1062049
Tel: 44 86108 4041150
Web site: http://www.mzjk.com
Freq: Monthly
Circ: 430000 Not Audited
Profile: Magazine covering all aspects of parenting including health, nutrition, early education and development as well as product news.
Ad Rate: Full Page Colour £2400.00
MAGAZINE
Family & Parenting, Pediatrics

Premier Hospitality   1053150
Tel: 44 01706 719972
Email: admin@romauk.net
Web site: www.premierconstructionnews.com/category/premier-hospitality
Freq: Monthly Not Audited
Editor: Alex Wiggan
Profile: Magazine focusing on the latest developments in the leisure and hospitality industry. Each issue highlights projects currently taking shape throughout the UK and overseas, covering everything from restaurants and bars through to hotels and spas.
MAGAZINE
Bars, Clubs & Pubs, Hotels/Motels, Travel Industry

Premier Living   985747
Editorial: 90A George Street, Edinburgh EH2 3DF **Tel:** 44 01316 248000
Email: premierliving@espc.com
Web site: www.espc.com/premierliving
Freq: Semi-Annual
Circ: 25000 Not Audited
Editor: Caroline Young
Profile: Magazine covering high end properties for sale in Edinburgh. It features town-houses and country homes as well as design advice, gadgets, furniture and property advice and local market knowledge.
MAGAZINE
Do-It-Yourself (DIY), Luxury Goods, Property Management & Maintenance

Premier Magazine   987555
Editorial: ISS House, 2 Williams Court, Little Mead Ind. Estate, Cranleigh GU6 8NE
Tel: 44 01483 272072
Email: info@right-impression.com
Web site: www.gupremier.co.uk
Freq: Quarterly
Circ: 22000 Not Audited
Editor: Tim Price
MAGAZINE
Beauty & Grooming, Cosmetics, Do-It-Yourself (DIY), Fashion, Hair, Health &

Medicine, Property Management & Maintenance, Railroad, Travel

The Presbyterian Herald   982163
Editorial: Assembly Buildings, Fisherwick Place, Belfast BT1 6DW
Tel: 44 02890 322284
Email: herald@presbyterianireland.org
Web site: http://www.presbyterianireland. org/herald
Freq: Monthly
Circ: 13000 Not Audited
Editor: Sarah Harding
Profile: Magazine of the Presbyterian Church in Ireland. Includes news, events and views.
Ad Rate: Full Page Mono £450.00
Ad Rate: Full Page Colour £450.00
MAGAZINE
Religion

Prescriber   983538
Editorial: The Atrium, Southern Gate, Chichester, Chichester PO19 8SQ
Email: prescriber@wiley.com
Web site: www.prescriber.co.uk
Freq: Bi-Monthly
Circ: 24106 Not Audited
Profile: Journal containing commissioned articles about rational prescribing. Focuses on prescribing and medicines management. Features articles on all areas of therapeutics and prescribing policy.
Ad Rate: Full Page Mono £1380.00
Ad Rate: Full Page Colour £1840.00
MAGAZINE
Health Administration, Medicine

The Presenter Magazine   997989
Email: mail@thepresenter.net
Web site: www.thepresenter.net
Freq: Daily
Circ: 521 Cision Digital Reach
Editor: Richie Litchfield
MAGAZINE (ONLINE)
Broadcasting

Press Gazette   979863
Editorial: 40 Hatton Garden, London EC1N 8EB **Tel:** 44 02079 366433
Email: pged@pressgazette.co.uk
Web site: www.pressgazette.co.uk
Freq: Daily
Circ: 263438 Cision Digital Reach
Editor: Dominic Ponsford
Profile: Website that covering a review of UK journalism. It provides insight, analysis, tips, tools, gossip and in-depth features.
MAGAZINE (ONLINE)
News & Current Affairs

Prestbury Living   984929
Editorial: Suite 2, 9-11 Princess Street, Knutsford, Knutsford WA16 6BY
Tel: 44 01565 633336
Email: editor@prestburyliving.co.uk
Web site: http://incheshiremagazine.co.uk/reader-offers/
Freq: Monthly
Circ: 4000 Not Audited
MAGAZINE
Regional General Interest

Pretty Ugly   987572
Editorial: York Court, Cowper Road, Berkhamsted, Berkhamsted HP4 3FW
Email: contact@prettyugly.co.uk
Web site: www.prettyugly.co.uk
Freq: Daily
Circ: 9876 Cision Digital Reach
Profile: Blog covering beauty products, cosmetics and make up tutorials. The outlet also offers a vlog.
MAGAZINE (ONLINE)
Beauty & Grooming, Cosmetics, Fitness & Exercise, Hair, Health & Medicine

Pretty52   1066394
Editorial: 20 Dale Street, Manchester M1 1EZ
Email: social@pretty52.com
Web site: http://www.pretty52.com/
Freq: Daily

Circ: 14474524 Cision Digital Reach
MAGAZINE (ONLINE)
Women's Interests

PRIDE
982384
Editorial: 1 Garratt Lane, London SW18 4AQ
Tel: 44 02088 714443
Email: info@pridemagazine.com
Web site: www.pridemagazine.com
Freq: Monthly
Circ: 19000 Not Audited
MAGAZINE
Women's Interests

Pride & Family
999389
Editorial: 2 Mount Sion, Royal Tunbridge Wells, Tunbridge Wells TN1 1UE
Email: info@prideandlife.com
Web site: www.prideandlife.com
Freq: Bi-Monthly Not Audited
Editor: Giorgio Severi
MAGAZINE
Family & Parenting, LGBT

PRIDE LIFE
985415
Editorial: 2nd floor, 52 Tottenham Court Road, London W1T 2QE
Email: info@pridelife.com
Web site: http://pridelife.com/
Freq: Quarterly
Circ: 100000 Not Audited
Editor in Chief: Nigel Robinson
Profile: Magazine covering the LGBT community, with gay news stories and features on all aspects of LGBT life including gay travel, careers and diversity issues, and legal and financial advice. Aimed at the LGBT community.
MAGAZINE
LGBT

Prima
982376
Editorial: 33 Broadwick Street, London W1F 9EP **Tel:** 44 02074 395000
Email: prima@hearst.co.uk
Web site: prima.co.uk
Freq: Monthly
Circ: 240924 Not Audited
Profile: Magazine providing guidance, inspiration and ideas to simplify reader's lives. Each issue contains articles on style, beauty, money, recipes, homes and gardens. First published in 1986. Aimed at young and active highly affluent women aged between 16 and 32 years old.
Ad Rate: Full Page Colour £19465.00
MAGAZINE
Women's Interests

Primary Science
985270
Editorial: The Association for Science Education, College Lane, Hatfield, Hatfield AI 10 9AA **Tel:** 44 01707 283000
Email: janehanrott@ase.org.uk
Web site: www.ase.org.uk/journals/primary-science/2013/09/129/?
Freq: Bi-Monthly
Circ: 3000 Not Audited
Profile: Refereed professional journal about science in primary education.
Ad Rate: Full Page Mono £400.00
Ad Rate: Full Page Colour £400.00
MAGAZINE
Schools & Institutions, Science

Primary Teacher Update
981558
Editorial: St Jude's Church, Dulwich Road, London SE24 0PB **Tel:** 44 02077 385454
Web site: http://www.magonlinelibrary.com/toc/prtu/current
Freq: Monthly
Circ: 7000 Not Audited
Editor: Karen Faux
Profile: Publication covering all aspects primary teaching including the latest pedagogy and thinking from the classroom, practical suggestions to apply this in the primary school environment. The magazine also publishes essential guidance on preparing for Ofsted and tackling discipline in the classroom, as well as the latest news and policy debate. Aimed at professionals working in primary education, including headteachers, classroom teachers,

higher-level teaching assistants, SENCOs and local authority advisors.
Ad Rate: Full Page Mono £995.00
Ad Rate: Full Page Colour £995.00
MAGAZINE
Disability, Education, Preschool, Schools & Institutions, Students

Primary Times (Group)
995852
Editorial: St James's House, 118 Greys Road, Henley-On-Thames, Henley-on-Thames RG9 1QW **Tel:** 44 01491 411848
Web site: www.primarytimes.net
Freq: Bi-Monthly
Circ: 2500000 Not Audited
Editor: Mike Gartside; **Editor:** Mandy Mellor
MAGAZINE
Education, Elementary School, Family & Parenting, Local Entertainment Guides

PrimeResi Quarterly
996254
Editorial: Level One, Devonshire House, One Mayfair Place, London W1J 8AJ
Tel: 44 03332 079004
Email: editor@primeresi.com
Web site: https://www.primeresi.com/quarterly/
Freq: Quarterly
Circ: 5000 Not Audited
MAGAZINE
Luxury Goods, Property Management & Maintenance

Printed Electronics World
988906
Editorial: Station Road, Swaffham Bulbeck, Cambridge CB25 0NB **Tel:** 44 01223 812300
Web site: http://www.printedelectronicsworld.com/
Freq: Daily
Circ: 26072 Cision Digital Reach
Editor: Teresa Henry
Profile: Website covering the printed electronics technologies and markets, with commentary, analysis and industry developments.
MAGAZINE (ONLINE)
Electronics

Printwear & Promotion
984043
Editorial: 15a London Road, Maidstone, Maidstone ME16 8LY **Tel:** 44 01622 687031
Web site: www.printwearandpromotion.co.uk
Freq: Monthly
Circ: 6550 Not Audited
Editor: Melanie Attlesey
Profile: Magazine concentrating on garment decoration, screen-printing, heat transfers, digital printing and decorative embroidery for leisure and sportswear, school wear, workwear, industrial work wear textiles and t-shirts. Also covers marketing, promotions and incentives. Aimed at garment decorators in the leisurewear and promotional industry.
Ad Rate: Full Page Colour £1549.00
MAGAZINE
Fashion, Marketing

Privacy Laws & Business
981548
Editorial: 2nd Floor, Monument House, 215 Marsh Road, Pinner, London HA5 5NE
Web site: www.privacylaws.com
Freq: Bi-Monthly Not Audited
Editor: Stewart Dresner
Profile: Newsletter on data protection laws and their impact on business operations.
MAGAZINE
News & Current Affairs

PrivatAir
982690
Editorial: Blackburn House, Blackburn Road, West Hampstead, London NW6 1RZ
Tel: 44 02076 138777
Email: privatair.ed@ink-global.com
Web site: www.ink-live.com/emagazines/privatair-magazine
Freq: Quarterly
Circ: 11000 Not Audited
MAGAZINE
Airline Inflight, Luxury Goods

Private Art Investor
988582
Editorial: Hartland House, 45 Church Street, Reigate, Reigate RH2 0AD
Tel: 44 01737 844383
Web site: www.privateartinvestor.com
Freq: Daily
Circ: 1685 Cision Digital Reach
MAGAZINE (ONLINE)
Art, Graphic Design, Photography, Visual Arts

Private Banker International
980065
Editorial: 71-73 Carter Lane, London EC4V 5EQ **Tel:** 44 02079 366650
Web site: www.privatebankerinternational.com
Freq: Monthly
Circ: 34015 Not Audited
Editor: Ronan McCaughey
Profile: Newsletter covering new private banking products and services, international marketing strategies, regulatory updates and industry trends. Aimed at those with an interest in wealth management.
MAGAZINE
Banking, Personal Finance

Private Client Business Journal
996585
Editorial: Sweet & Maxwell, 100 Avenue Road, London NW3 3PF
Tel: 44 01422 888000
Web site: www.sweetandmaxwell.co.uk/Catalogue/ProductDetails.aspx?recordid=484&productid=7159#aDesc
Freq: Bi-Monthly Not Audited
MAGAZINE
Banking, Family Law, Private Equity, Tax Law

Private Eye
982134
Editorial: 6 Carlisle Street, London W1D 3BN
Web site: www.private-eye.co.uk
Freq: Bi-Weekly
Circ: 249927 Not Audited
Editor: Ian Hislop
Profile: Magazine focusing on news and current affairs and offering a unique blend of humor, social and political observations and investigative journalism. Founded in 1961, the magazine is published fortnightly. Aimed at those with an interest in news.
Ad Rate: Full Page Colour £5500.00
MAGAZINE
Consumer Affairs, Crime & Violence, Defense & National Security, Energy & Environment, Ethical/Moral Issues, International News, Law, National News, News & Current Affairs, Northern Ireland

Private Hire and Courier
999521
Editorial: 119 Chiltern Drive, Surbiton, London KT5 8LS **Tel:** 44 02083 994678
Email: editorial@phcmag.com
Web site: www.phcmag.com
Freq: Monthly
Circ: 12000 Not Audited
Editor: John Sanderson
MAGAZINE
Automotive

Private Practice
997152
Editorial: BACP House, 15 St. John's Business Park, Lutterworth, Lutterworth LE17 4HB **Tel:** 44 01455 883300
Email: privatepractice.editorial@bacp.co.uk
Web site: bacppp.org.uk/journal
Freq: Quarterly
Circ: 3292 Not Audited
Editor: John Daniel
MAGAZINE
Medicine, Neurology

PrivatSea
984598
Editorial: 9 Little St. James's Street, London SW1A 1DP **Tel:** 44 02073 965464
Email: info@privatsea.com
Web site: www.privatsea.com
Freq: Annual

Circ: 8000 Not Audited
MAGAZINE
Boating & Yachting, Luxury Goods

Prize Quest
1073823
Tel: 44 01865 664970
Web site: www.theoxfordpuzzlecompany.com
Freq: Bi-Monthly
Circ: 50000 Not Audited
Profile: Magazine with crosswords and puzzles as well as entertainment reviews, gadgets and travel. Aimed at puzzle enthusiasts aged 25 years old plus.
MAGAZINE
Games, Competitions & Events, Men's Interests, Women's Interests

Prizes & Puzzles Special
1073814
Tel: 44 01865 664970
Email: info@theoxfordpuzzlecompany.com
Web site: www.theoxfordpuzzlecompany.com
Freq: Bi-Monthly
Circ: 50000 Not Audited
Profile: Magazine containing crosswords, puzzles and promotional competitions.
MAGAZINE
Games, Competitions & Events, Men's Interests, Women's Interests

Prizes Galore
983912
Editorial: Cranbrook House, 287-291 Banbury Road, Oxford OX2 7JF
Tel: 44 01865 664970
Email: info@theoxfordpuzzlecompany.com
Web site: www.theoxfordpuzzlecompany.com
Freq: Bi-Monthly
Circ: 50000 Not Audited
Profile: Competition magazine, covering home, leisure, holidays, travel, money, health and beauty.
Ad Rate: Full Page Colour £3000.00
MAGAZINE
Games, Competitions & Events, Men's Interests, Women's Interests

PRK Promotions
997710
Web site: prkpromotions.com
Freq: Daily
Circ: 521 Cision Digital Reach
MAGAZINE (ONLINE)
Asia, Local Entertainment Guides, R&B, Urban, World, Theater & Performing Arts

PRN Magazine
997666
Email: hello@prnmagazine.com
Web site: www.prnmagazine.com
Freq: Daily
Circ: 2147 Cision Digital Reach
Editor: Anna Magnowska
MAGAZINE (ONLINE)
Health & Medicine, Health Administration, Healthcare Industry, Nursing/Nurses

Pro Audio Asia
986027
Editorial: 17 Upper Grosvenor Road, Tunbridge Wells TN1 2DU
Tel: 44 01892 676280
Web site: http://www.proaudio-central.com/latest-magazines
Freq: Bi-Monthly
Circ: 10000 Not Audited
Profile: Magazine focusing on the live, installation, broadcast, post production and recording market throughout Asia.
Ad Rate: Full Page Colour £2100.00
MAGAZINE
Audio Video Trade, Movies & Video

Pro Audio MEA
986936
Editorial: 17 Upper Grosvenor Road, Tunbridge Wells TN1 2DU
Tel: 44 01892 676280
Web site: http://www.proaudio-central.com/latest-magazines
Freq: Bi-Monthly
Circ: 5000 Not Audited
MAGAZINE
Audio Video Trade, Movies & Video

Consumer Magazines

PRO Hair & Beauty 987167
Editorial: Ground Floor, 16 Connaught Place, London W2 2ES
Web site: http://www.sallyexpress.com/pro-hair-beauty-magazine-article/
Freq: Bi-Monthly
Circ: 20812 Not Audited
Profile: Magazine covering hair and beauty. Discusses hair trends, the latest innovations in beauty and creative nail techniques. Aimed at customers of Sally Salon Services.
MAGAZINE
Cosmetics, Hair

Pro Moviemaker 1053474
Tel: 44 01223 499450
Email: hello@promoviemaker.net
Web site: www.promoviemaker.net
Freq: Monthly Not Audited
Editor: Terry Hope
MAGAZINE
Movies & Video

Pro Shop Europe 985094
Tel: 44 01322 221144
Web site: www.proshopeurope.co.uk
Freq: Monthly
Circ: 3842 Not Audited
Editor: Laura Cork
Profile: Magazine covering news and information on the golf retail trade. It includes interviews with industry leaders, the latest golfing products, new technology and the latest company news. Each issue provides business advice to improve revenues, delivered by industry experts. Aimed at key decision makers and buyers in the European golf trade including golf professionals, retailers, golf course members, manufacturers, distributors and other industry members.
Ad Rate: Full Page Colour £1700.00
MAGAZINE
Fitness & Exercise

Pro Traveller Magazine 997169
Editorial: 2 Fremantle Road, Folkestone CT20 3PY **Tel:** 44 01303 850801
Email: editor@protraveller.co.uk
Web site: www.protraveller.co.uk
Freq: Bi-Monthly
Circ: 74000 Not Audited
Editor: Trevor Claringbold
MAGAZINE
Travel

Process Engineering 979906
Editorial: Castle House, 89 High Street, Berkhamsted HP4 2DF
Tel: 44 01442 200650
Email: penews@synthesismedia.co.uk
Web site: www.processengineering.co.uk
Freq: Monthly
Circ: 10010 Not Audited
Profile: Magazine covering practical applications of process plant, systems, equipment and management techniques. Aimed at senior process and chemical engineers employed in UK process industries.
Ad Rate: Full Page Colour £2495.00
MAGAZINE
Alcohol & Spirits, Chemicals, Engineering, Environment, Food, Manufacturing, Nuclear Power, Oil, Water & Sanitation

Procurement Leaders 984293
Editorial: Prospero House, 241 Borough High Street, London SE1 1GA
Tel: 44 02075 010530
Email: editor@procurementleaders.com
Web site: www.procurementleaders.com
Freq: Bi-Monthly
Circ: 17500 Not Audited
MAGAZINE
Business, Data Management, Internet, Small and Medium Business

Procycling 982202
Editorial: Tower House, Fairfax Street, Bristol BS1 3BN **Tel:** 44 01179 279009
Email: procycling@immediate.co.uk
Web site: www.cyclingnews.com
Freq: Monthly

Circ: 57000 Not Audited
Editor: Edward Pickering
Profile: Magazine that covers all aspects of international cycling including news, features, interviews, equipment, gear, nutrition and bike tests. Aimed at people with an interest in the professional race scene, from the active cyclist to the armchair fan.
Ad Rate: Full Page Colour £1760.00
MAGAZINE
Bicycles

Professional Adviser 979776
Editorial: Haymarket House, 28-29 Haymarket, London SW1Y 4RX
Tel: 44 02073 169000
Web site: www.professionaladviser.com
Freq: Daily
Circ: 156631 Cision Digital Reach
Editor: Julian Marr
Profile: Website covering finance. IFAonline website provides information on mortgages, investments, pensions, and insurance. IFAonline's aim is to deliver the essential news and information financial intermediaries need to conduct their business, as it happens.
MAGAZINE (ONLINE)
Fund Management, Investment Banking, Personal Finance

Professional Beauty 981173
Editorial: 1.17 The Plaza, 535 Kings Road, London SW10 0SZ **Tel:** 44 02073 510536
Email: info@professionalbeauty.co.uk
Web site: www.professionalbeauty.co.uk
Freq: Monthly
Circ: 17253 Not Audited
Profile: Magazine covering all aspects of health and beauty treatment and therapy, including spas, beauty and nail salons. Aimed at beauty/nail salon and spa managers and owners, beauty therapists, nail technicians and students.Alternative Title: Professional Beauty Incorporating Spa and Nails
Ad Rate: Full Page Colour £2750.00
MAGAZINE
Cosmetics, Retail Management

Professional Development Today 981532
Editorial: 309 Scott House, Gibb Street, Birmingham B9 4DT **Tel:** 44 01212 247599
Email: enquiries@imaginativeminds.co.uk
Web site: www.teachingtimes.com/publications/professional-development-today.htm
Freq: Quarterly
Circ: 24 Cision Digital Reach
Profile: Journal covering professional development in the field of education.
MAGAZINE (ONLINE)
Disability, Education, Higher Education, Preschool, Schools & Institutions, Students

Professional Electrician & Installer 981714
Editorial: Regal House, Regal Way, Watford, London WD24 4YF **Tel:** 44 01923 237799
Email: pe@hamerville.co.uk
Web site: www.professional-electrician.com
Freq: Monthly
Circ: 70988 Not Audited
MAGAZINE
Electronics, Industry

Professional Hairdresser 983378
Editorial: Regal House, Regal Way, Watford, London WD24 4YF **Tel:** 44 01923 237799
Email: office@hamerville.co.uk
Web site: www.professionalhairdresser.co.uk
Freq: Monthly
Circ: 14421 Not Audited
Editor: Nicola Shannon
Profile: Magazine covering the hairdressing industry. Includes articles on fashion, new products, education and training. Contains new techniques and essential business advice for the industry's key professionals. Every issue features the latest products and news, step by steps and technical advice

plus business and training as well as interviews with top stylists, and dedicated sections for extensions and 'Gents'. Aimed at salon owners and stylists.
Ad Rate: Full Page Mono £1995.00
Ad Rate: Full Page Colour £1995.00
MAGAZINE
Hair

Professional Jeweller 985490
Editorial: 16-25 Bastwick Street, London EC1V 3PS **Tel:** 44 02031 764228
Email: info@professionaljeweller.com
Web site: www.professionaljeweller.com
Freq: Monthly
Circ: 5560 Not Audited
Profile: Magazine serving the British jewellery and watch industry, featuring breaking news, comment, trading insight and buying inspiration. Aimed at anybody with an interest in profiting from the sale of jewellery and watches.
Ad Rate: Full Page Colour £1750.00
MAGAZINE
Fashion

Professional Motor Factor 983348
Editorial: Regal House, Regal Way, Watford, London WD24 4YF **Tel:** 44 01923 237799
Email: pmf@hamerville.co.uk
Web site: www.pmfmag.co.uk
Freq: Monthly
Circ: 3694 Not Audited
Profile: Magazine providing coverage of key issues affecting factor business. Featuring information on all aspects of business, editorial coverage of product developments, new markets and industry news. Aimed at key buyers and decision makers at branch level.
Ad Rate: Full Page Colour £1650.00
MAGAZINE
Automotive

Professional Motor Mechanic 983379
Editorial: Regal House, Regal Way, Watford, London WD24 4YF **Tel:** 44 01923 237799
Email: pmm@hamerville.co.uk
Web site: http://pmmonline.co.uk/
Freq: Monthly
Circ: 68000 Not Audited
Profile: Magazine containing news, business and technical advice, product information and mechanic profiles. Every issue features the latest products and equipment, plus business and training information, details of events which are relevant to the independent service and repair business. Aimed at those involved in the automotive services and body repair professionals.Regular features: Literature and Electronic Media; News; Product Round-ups; Products and Ideas; Tools and Equipment
Ad Rate: Full Page Colour £2750.00
MAGAZINE
Automotive

Professional Motorsport Circuit 997101
Editorial: Abinger House, Church Street, Dorking, Dorking RH4 1DF
Tel: 44 01306 743744
Email: motorsport@ukpime.com
Web site: www.pmw-magazine.com/latest_issue.php
Freq: Annual
Circ: 10000 Not Audited
Editor: John O'Brien
MAGAZINE
Automotive

Professional Motorsport World 985025
Editorial: Abinger House, Church Street, Dorking RH4 1DF **Tel:** 44 01306 743744
Web site: www.pmw-magazine.com
Freq: Quarterly
Circ: 25000 Not Audited
Editor: Adam Gavine; **Editor:** John O'Brien
Profile: Magazine covering the latest developments within the world of professional motor sport with news, interviews and articles covering technology,

components, testing, transportation, marketing, politics, strategies and business operation. Aimed at all people associated with professional motor sport including teams, drivers, promoters and support crews.
Ad Rate: Full Page Colour £3400.00
MAGAZINE
Automotive, Motorsports

Professional Paraplanner 1054003
Editorial: 80 Coleman Street, London EC2R 5BJ **Tel:** 44 02071 042235
Email: editorial@researchinfinance.co.uk
Web site: www.professionalparaplanner.co.uk
Freq: Monthly Not Audited
Editor: Robert Kingsbury
MAGAZINE
Banking, Commodities, Derivatives, Economics, Equities, Financial Markets, Foreign Exchange Market (FOREX), Fund Management, Hedge Funds, Investment Banking

Professional Photo 984668
Editorial: Bright House, 82 High Street, Sawston, Sawston CB2 4HJ
Tel: 44 01223 499450
Web site: www.absolutephoto.com
Freq: Monthly
Circ: 19000 Not Audited
Editor: Terry Hope
MAGAZINE
Cameras, Photography

Professional Recovery 983383
Editorial: Bridge Road, Wellington, Telford, Telford TF1 1RY **Tel:** 44 01952 415334
Web site: www.profrecovery.co.uk
Freq: Monthly
Circ: 9000 Not Audited
Editor: James Baylis
Profile: Journal containing news and features for the vehicle recovery industry.
Ad Rate: Full Page Mono £700.00
Ad Rate: Full Page Colour £1200.00
MAGAZINE
Automotive

Professional Wealth Management 979781
Editorial: Number One, Southwark Bridge, London SE1 9HL **Tel:** 44 02078 733000
Email: pwm@ft.com
Web site: www.pwmnet.com
Freq: Monthly
Circ: 12142 Not Audited
Profile: Magazine covering the mechanics, application and benefits of product development including investment strategies and techniques, management styles and the benefits of using a variety of products. Also gives an insight into wealth management market trends. Aimed at private banks, wealth management, institutions, fund management houses, investment banks, family offices, consultants, brokers, IFAs, retail banks and other distributors of wealth investment products to wealthy individuals.
Ad Rate: Full Page Colour £9250.00
MAGAZINE
Banking, Fund Management, Personal Finance, Private Equity

Professionaladviser.com 980835
Editorial: Haymarket House, 28-29 Haymarket, London SW1Y 4RX
Tel: 44 01858 438800
Web site: http://www.professionaladviser.com/
Freq: Daily
Circ: 155616 Cision Digital Reach
MAGAZINE (ONLINE)
Fund Management, Investment Banking

Progress 986607
Editorial: Third Floor, 11 Tufton Street, London SW1P 3QB **Tel:** 44 02034 359854
Email: office@progressonline.org.uk
Web site: www.progressonline.org.uk/magazines/

Freq: Monthly
Circ: 6000 Not Audited
Editor: Richard Angell
Profile: Magazine featuring general interest articles, short stories and crosswords.
MAGAZINE
Politics

Progressive Preschool 987034
Editorial: United House, North Road, London N7 9DP **Tel:** 44 02077 006740
Web site: www.progressive-preschool.com
Freq: Bi-Monthly
Circ: 10849 Not Audited
Editor: Jacqui Parr
Profile: Magazine aimed at the baby to toddler to child market (0-5 years). It covers a range of products for this age group including pushchairs, apparel, toys, furnishings and feeding.
MAGAZINE
Preschool

Project Ada 997856
Email: news@projectada.co.uk
Web site: www.projectada.co.uk
Freq: Daily
Circ: 10514 Cision Digital Reach
MAGAZINE (ONLINE)
Social Issues

Project Baby 997354
Tel: 44 07957 294061
Email: natasha@project-baby.co.uk
Web site: www.project-baby.co.uk
Freq: Bi-Monthly
Circ: 80000 Not Audited
MAGAZINE
Family & Parenting

Project M 996092
Circ: 155772 Cision Digital Reach
MAGAZINE (ONLINE)
Personal Finance

project-news.com 997176
Tel: 44 01432 379250
Email: mail@project-news.com
Web site: http://www.pncentral.co.uk/
Freq: Daily
Circ: 720 Cision Digital Reach
MAGAZINE (ONLINE)
News & Current Affairs

Prolific North 987239
Editorial: Prolific North, 16 Fairfax Ave, Manchester M20 6AJ **Tel:** 44 07788 417660
Email: news@prolificnorth.co.uk
Web site: http://www.prolificnorth.co.uk
Freq: Daily
Circ: 165071 Cision Digital Reach
Editor: David Prior
Profile: Website covering media. The PROLIFIC NORTH website shares the latest news, informed opinion and features about the media industry and companies.
MAGAZINE (ONLINE)
Advertising Industry, Branding, Broadcasting, Graphic Design, Marketing, Media & Communications, Photography, Publishing

Propel 987028
Editorial: The Goose House, Brighton Road, Lower Beeding, Horsham RH13 6NQ
Tel: 44 01444 810306
Web site: www.propelinfonews.com
Freq: Daily
Circ: 8314 Cision Digital Reach
MAGAZINE (ONLINE)
Bars, Clubs & Pubs, Hotels/Motels

proper 988008
Web site: www.propermag.com
Freq: Semi-Annual Not Audited
MAGAZINE
Fashion

Property Overseas Today 987019
Editorial: Angela House, 5 Albemarle Road, Beckenham, London BR3 5HZ
Tel: 44 08450 750512
Web site: http://www.propertyoverseastoday.com/
Freq: Daily
Circ: 8957 Cision Digital Reach
Profile: Property Oversees Today is a website covering overseas property news and information.
MAGAZINE (ONLINE)
Real Estate

Prospect 980163
Editorial: 2 Queen Anne's Gate, London SW1H 9AA **Tel:** 44 02072 551344
Email: editorial@prospect-magazine.co.uk
Web site: http://www.prospect-magazine.co.uk
Freq: Monthly
Circ: 44545 Not Audited
Editor: Tom Clark
Profile: Magazine covering politics, international affairs, social and cultural issues and the arts. Read by company directors, politicians, journalists and academics.
Ad Rate: Full Page Colour £2600.00
MAGAZINE
National News

Prospects 995299
Editorial: Prospect House, Booth Street East, Manchester M13 9EP
Tel: 44 01612 775200
Email: editorial@prospects.ac.uk
Web site: www.prospects.ac.uk
Freq: Annual
Circ: 1933482 Cision Digital Reach
MAGAZINE (ONLINE)
Careers

Prospects Law 996031
Editorial: Prospect House, Booth Street East, Manchester M13 9EP
Tel: 44 01612 775200
Email: editorial@prospects.ac.uk
Web site: www.prospects.ac.uk
Freq: Annual
MAGAZINE
Careers

Prostate Matters 995164
Editorial: Kemp House, 152 City Road, London EC1V 2NX **Tel:** 44 07977 144020
Email: press@tackleprostate.org
Web site: www.tackleprostate.org/newsletter-signup.php
Freq: Quarterly Not Audited
Editor: Hugh Gunn
MAGAZINE
Patient Support

The Protagonist Magazine 995089
Editorial: 73c Southampton Row, Bloomsbury, London WC1B 4ET
Email: contact@theprotagonistmagazine.com
Web site: http://www.theprotagonistmagazine.com/
Freq: Semi-Annual
Circ: 100000 Not Audited
Editor: Daen Palma Huse
MAGAZINE
Fashion, Movies & Video, Photography, Theater & Performing Arts, Visual Arts

Province 1060610
Tel: 44 27214 160141
Email: gary@hsm.co.za
Freq: Monthly Not Audited
MAGAZINE
Basketball, Bicycles, Billiards, Boating & Yachting, Bodybuilding, Bowling, Boxing, Cricket, Equestrian Sports, Extreme/Adventure Sports

PRUVODCE SORTIMENTEM PAPÍRNICTVÍ 1060196
Tel: 44 42025 7329238
Email: drogerie-parfumerie@europrofi.cz
Web site: http://www.europrofi.cz
Freq: Annual
Circ: 2100 Not Audited
MAGAZINE
Graphic Design, Paper

PRWeek (UK) 979881
Editorial: Teddington Studios, Broom Road, Teddington, London TW11 9BE
Tel: 44 02082 675000
Email: prweek@haymarket.com
Web site: www.prweek.com
Freq: Monthly Not Audited
MAGAZINE
Advertising Industry, Branding, Broadcasting, Graphic Design, Marketing, Media & Communications, Photography, Publishing

PS Vita Hub 995328
Email: admin@psvitahub.com
Web site: www.psvitahub.com
Freq: Daily
Circ: 5475 Cision Digital Reach
Editor: Mohammed Husnain
MAGAZINE (ONLINE)
Computer & Video Games

PSMG Magazine 983275
Editorial: 55 Charlotte Road, Ashford EC2A 3QF **Tel:** 44 02070 339150
Web site: www.psmg.co.uk
Freq: Bi-Monthly
Circ: 5000 Not Audited
Profile: Magazine covering all aspects of marketing and business development in the global professional services sector.
MAGAZINE
Advertising Industry, Branding, Broadcasting, Marketing, Photography, Publishing

PSN Europe 983282
Editorial: 1st Floor, Suncourt House, 18-26 Essex Road, London N1 8LN
Tel: 44 02073 546002
Web site: www.psneurope.com
Freq: Monthly
Circ: 6014 Not Audited
Editor: David Robinson
MAGAZINE
Electronics, Software

PSYCHOLOGIES 982811
Editorial: Cudham Tithe Barn, Berry's Hill, Cudham, London TN16 3AG
Tel: 44 01959 541444
Web site: www.psychologies.co.uk
Freq: Monthly
Circ: 67898 Not Audited
Editor: Suzy Greaves
Profile: Magazine covering psychology and positive living for a mainstream consumer audience. It contains articles on how readers think, feel, connect and communicate, along with features on beauty, travel, food, wine and home. First published in 2005.
Ad Rate: Full Page Colour £6000.00
MAGAZINE
Alternative Medicine, Women's Interests

PT Magazine 987148
Editorial: 93-95 Fore Street, Ipswich, Ipswich IP4 1JZ
Web site: www.ptmagazine.co.uk
Freq: Monthly Not Audited
MAGAZINE
Fitness & Exercise

PTA+ Magazine 998850
Editorial: Community Inspired Ltd, Unit 2, Bulrushes Farm, Coombe Hill Road, East Grinstead, East Grinstead RH19 4LZ
Tel: 44 01342 718679
Email: editorial@pta.co.uk
Web site: www.pta.co.uk
Freq: Quarterly
Circ: 20000 Not Audited

Editor: Nikki Burch
MAGAZINE
Charitable Foundations, Disability, Education, Higher Education, Preschool, Schools & Institutions, Students

Pub & Bar 986365
Editorial: 4th Floor, Joynes House, New Road, Gravesend DA11 0AJ
Tel: 44 08455 006008
Email: editor@pubandbar.com
Web site: www.pubandbaronline.co.uk
Freq: Bi-Weekly
Circ: 29600 Not Audited
Profile: Magazine covering the premium and contemporary pub and bar industry.
Ad Rate: Full Page Colour £3500.00
MAGAZINE
Alcohol & Spirits, Bars, Clubs & Pubs

Public Affairs News 984162
Editorial: Floor 11, The Shard, 32 London Bridge Street, London SE1 9SG
Tel: 44 02075 935769
Email: pan@dods.co.uk
Web site: www.publicaffairsnews.com
Freq: Weekly
Circ: 18091 Cision Digital Reach
Profile: Magazine focusing on lobbying in Westminster and Brussels.
MAGAZINE (ONLINE)
News & Current Affairs

Public Health Nutrition 995805
Editorial: The Edinburgh Building, Shaftesbury Road, Cambridge CB2 8RU
Tel: 44 01223 312393
Email: journals@cambridge.org
Web site: journals.cambridge.org/action/displayJournal?jid=PHN
Freq: Monthly Not Audited
MAGAZINE
Nutrition

Public Procurement Law Review 999027
Editorial: Sweet & Maxwell, Friars House, 160 Blackfriars Road, London SE1 8EZ
Web site: http://www.sweetandmaxwell.co.uk/catalogue
Freq: Bi-Monthly Not Audited
MAGAZINE
Government

PublicNet 983921
Editorial: PO Box 7003, Southend-on-Sea SS0 0TH **Tel:** 44 07903 185077
Web site: www.publicnet.co.uk
Freq: Daily
Circ: 6623 Cision Digital Reach
Editor: Don Morley
Profile: Website concerned with the modernisation of the entire public sector. Provides news and features relating to the governance and management of public services.
MAGAZINE (ONLINE)
Charitable Foundations, Government, Public Sector

Pueblo Juarez 1061111
Tel: 44 52614 4106006
Email: comentarios@elpueblo.com
Web site: http://www.elpueblo.com/juarez
Freq: Daily
Circ: 10438 Cision Digital Reach
MAGAZINE (ONLINE)
National News

Pullbuoy 1076220
Web site: http://www.pullbuoy.co.uk/
Freq: Daily
Circ: 9663 Cision Digital Reach
Editor: Steve Buckley
MAGAZINE (ONLINE)
Olympic Sports, Sports, Swimming/Watersports

Pulse 981193
Editorial: 140 London Wall, London EC2Y 5DN **Tel:** 44 02072 140500
Email: editor@pulsetoday.co.uk
Web site: www.pulsetoday.co.uk

Consumer Magazines

Freq: Monthly
Circ: 35422 Not Audited
Editor: Nigel Praities
Profile: Magazine covering all aspects of air traffic services and management.
MAGAZINE
Medicine

Pulse 997632
Editorial: c/o The Carnival Centre, 3 St.Mary's Road, Luton LU1 3JA
Email: info@pulseconnects.com
Web site: www.pulseconnects.com
Freq: Quarterly Not Audited
Profile: Magazine covering all aspects of air traffic services and management.
MAGAZINE
R&B, Urban, World, Theater & Performing Arts

Pulse 1054933
Editorial: RMC House, 6 Broadfield Court, Broadfield Business Park, Sheffield S8 0XF
Tel: 44 01142 506300
Email: phoebe.seymour@rmcmedia.co.uk
Web site: www.rmcmedia.co.uk/magazines/pulse/
Freq: Monthly
Circ: 10000 Not Audited
Profile: Magazine covering all aspects of air traffic services and management.
MAGAZINE
Regional General Interest

Pulse Magazine 1074790
Editorial: Incon House, 10 Stilebrook Rd, Olney, Milton Keynes MK46 5EA
Tel: 44 01908 465488
Email: editor@pulsemagazine.co.uk
Web site: www.pulsemagazine.co.uk
Freq: Monthly
Circ: 52000 Not Audited
Editor: Kerry Lewis-Stevenson
MAGAZINE
Beauty & Grooming, Cosmetics, Do-It-Yourself (DIY), Fashion, Gardening, Hair, Property Management & Maintenance, Regional, Regional General Interest

Punjab2000.com 995295
Tel: 44 07773 650721
Email: info@punjab2000.com
Web site: http://punjab2000.com/
Freq: Daily
Circ: 14992 Cision Digital Reach
MAGAZINE (ONLINE)
Asia, Expatriates

Punto en Linea 1062052
Tel: 44 52555 6226205
Email: puntoenlinea@gmail.com
Web site: http://www.puntoenlinea.unam.mx
Circ: 4574665 Cision Digital Reach
MAGAZINE (ONLINE)
Antiques/Collectibles, Art, Arts, International News, Literature, Photography, Theater & Performing Arts, Visual Arts

Punto Hispano 1062164
Email: phespacio@gmail.com
Web site: http://puntoh.ning.com
Circ: 1105 Cision Digital Reach
MAGAZINE (ONLINE)
Internet

The Purbeck Gazette 987024
Editorial: 17b Commercial Road, Swanage, Swanage BH19 1DF **Tel:** 44 01929 424239
Email: ed@purbeckgazette.co.uk
Web site: www.purbeckgazette.co.uk
Freq: Monthly
Circ: 20000 Not Audited
Editor: Nico Johnson
Profile: Magazine covering local business, arts, people and events from The World Heritage Jurassic Coast Area.
MAGAZINE
Regional

Pure Beauty 981178
Tel: 44 02071 931279
Email: cosmetics@hpcimedia.com

Web site: http://www.cosmeticsbusiness.com/Category/Pure_Beauty
Freq: Monthly
Circ: 11081 Not Audited
Editor: Laura Husband
Profile: Blog covering beauty products and cosmetics. The blog has an archive dating back to October 2010.
MAGAZINE
Cosmetics, Hair

Pure Movies 985169
Editorial: 12 Grosvenor Way, Clapton, London E5 9ND
Email: info@puremovies.co.uk
Web site: www.puremovies.co.uk
Freq: Daily
Circ: 12314 Cision Digital Reach
MAGAZINE (ONLINE)
Entertainment, Movies & Video

Pure Wander Magazine 962938
Editorial: 190 Cedars Road Flat 7, London SW4 0PP
Web site: http://www.purewander.com
Freq: Daily
Circ: 42296 Cision Digital Reach
MAGAZINE (ONLINE)
Children & Youth, Cruises, Family Travel, Food, Honeymoon Travel, Hotels/Motels, Travel, Wine/Winemaking

PureBuxton 984910
Editorial: PO Box 140, Buxton SK17 1AU
Email: editor@purebuxton.co.uk
Web site: www.purebuxton.co.uk
Freq: Bi-Monthly
Circ: 10000 Not Audited
Editor: Steve Caddy
MAGAZINE
Regional General Interest

Purerawk.com 999227
Email: news@purerawk.com
Web site: www.purerawk.com
Freq: Daily
Circ: 14262 Cision Digital Reach
MAGAZINE (ONLINE)
Rock Music

PuristSPro 1053080
Email: newscentral@puristspro.com
Web site: www.watchprosite.com
Freq: Daily
Circ: 95707 Cision Digital Reach
MAGAZINE (ONLINE)
Luxury Goods

Push & Pull 982042
Editorial: Haworth Station, Keighley, Haworth BD22 8NJ **Tel:** 44 01535 645214
Email: admin@kwvr.co.uk
Web site: www.kwvr.co.uk
Freq: Quarterly
Circ: 5000 Not Audited
MAGAZINE
Railroad

PUSH IT 985252
Editorial: Studio D, 22 Fairlop Road, London E11 1BL
Email: editorial@pushitmagazine.com
Web site: pushitmagazine.com
Freq: Quarterly
Circ: 30000 Not Audited
Editor: Gabriel Opoku
Profile: PUSH IT is the international fashion magazine covering fashion, music, art and style. Launched in in December 2008.
MAGAZINE
Fashion

Pushchair Expert 996609
Editorial: Teach House, Gilbert Drive, Boston, Boston PE21 7TQ
Tel: 44 01205 751649
Email: info@pushchairexpert.com
Web site: www.pushchairexpert.com
Freq: Daily
Circ: 34395 Cision Digital Reach
MAGAZINE (ONLINE)
Family & Parenting

PUSS PUSS Magazine 998318
Editorial: 4-17 Frederick Terrace, London E8 4EW
Email: info@pusspussmagazine.com
Web site: http://www.pusspussmagazine.com/
Freq: Semi-Annual Not Audited
MAGAZINE
Classical/Choral/Band Music, Country, Folk, Bluegrass, Dance Music, Fashion, Jazz & Blues, Men's Interests, Music, Nature & Wildlife, Photography, Pop Music

The Puzzler Collection 999167
Editorial: Stonecroft, 69 Station Road, Redhill, Redhill RH1 1EY
Tel: 44 01737 378700
Email: info@puzzler.com
Web site: www.puzzler.com
Freq: Monthly
Circ: 109998 Not Audited
MAGAZINE
Games, Competitions & Events

PYLOT 1101514
Email: contact@pylotmagazine.com
Web site: http://www.pylotmagazine.com/
Freq: Semi-Annual
MAGAZINE
Fashion, Photography

Q 982109
Editorial: Academic House, 24-28 Oval Road, Camden, London NW1 7DT
Tel: 44 02072 955000
Email: qmag@qthemusic.com
Web site: www.qthemusic.com
Freq: Monthly
Circ: 40003 Not Audited
Profile: Magazine covering modern music. It features a reviews of new music releases, reissues and compilations, as well as film, radio, television and live concert reviews. First published in October 1986. Aimed at people aged between 18 and 35 years old.
Ad Rate: Full Page Colour £3500.00
MAGAZINE
Country, Folk, Bluegrass, Dance Music, Entertainment, Local Entertainment Guides, Music, Pop Music, Rap & Hip Hop, Rock Music

QA-Financial.com 1065390
Editorial: 6-8 Cole Street, London SE1 4YH
Tel: 44 02032 860280
Email: info@qa-financial.com
Web site: http://qa-financial.com/
Freq: Daily
Circ: 15075 Cision Digital Reach
MAGAZINE (ONLINE)
Data Management, Industry, Internet, Mobile Communications, Security & Security Systems

QJM 985392
Editorial: Oxford University Press, Great Clarendon Street, Oxford OX2 6DP
Tel: 44 01865 353907
Email: qjm.editorialoffice@oup.com
Web site: http://qjmed.oxfordjournals.org/
Freq: Monthly Not Audited
MAGAZINE
Medicine, Pharmaceuticals, Science

QLI 999311
Email: felix.hirsch@qliweb.com
Web site: http://www.qlitravel.com/
Freq: Daily
Circ: 3768 Cision Digital Reach
MAGAZINE (ONLINE)
Restaurant Reviews, Travel, Wine/Winemaking

Qosy 997823
Editorial: The Manor House, Howbery Park, Benson Lane, Wallingford, Wallingford OX10 8FD
Email: info@qosy.co
Web site: http://qosy.co
Freq: Daily

Circ: 35508 Cision Digital Reach
MAGAZINE (ONLINE)
Automotive, Luxury Goods, Railroad, Travel

QP Magazine 984345
Editorial: QP Magazine, 111 Buckingham Palace Rd, London SW1W 0WQ
Tel: 44 02079 313988
Email: edit@qpmagazine.com
Web site: www.qpmagazine.com
Freq: Quarterly
Circ: 23000 Not Audited
Editor: James Buttery
MAGAZINE
Luxury Goods

Quad Online 984996
Editorial: Stud Farm, Seaford Road, Newhaven, Newhaven BN9 0EF
Tel: 44 01273 616040
Email: edit@quad-online.co.uk
Web site: http://www.quad-online.co.uk/
Freq: Daily
Circ: 5670 Cision Digital Reach
MAGAZINE (ONLINE)
Motorcycles

Quality in Ageing and Older Adults 985940
Editorial: Emerald Group Publishing Limited, Howard House, Wagon Lane, Bingley BD16 1WA
Web site: http://emeraldgrouppublishing.com/products/journals/journals.htm?id=qaoa
Freq: Quarterly Not Audited
Editor: Fiona Poland
Profile: Journal with a focus on real issues affecting older people and those who work with them, including quality of life and support services.
Ad Rate: Full Page Mono £350.00
MAGAZINE
Community Care (UK), Geriatrics

Quaysnews.net 995443
Email: editor@quaysnews.net
Web site: http://quaysnews.net
Freq: Daily
Circ: 17403 Cision Digital Reach
MAGAZINE (ONLINE)
Regional General Interest, Student Lifestyle

QueensofVintage.com 984959
Web site: www.queensofvintage.com
Freq: Daily
Circ: 38947 Cision Digital Reach
MAGAZINE (ONLINE)
Fashion

Quel Homme 998097
Editorial: 304a Holloway Road, London N7 6NJ
Email: editor@quelhomme.com
Web site: http://www.quelhomme.com/
Freq: Daily
Circ: 5000 Not Audited
Editor: Calum Donoghue
MAGAZINE
Alcohol & Spirits, Bars, Clubs & Pubs, Beauty & Grooming, Beer, Beverages, Cooking & Baking, Cosmetics, Fashion, Food, Grocery Stores

Quib.ly 999656
Editorial: Standbrook House, 2-5 Old Bond Street, London W1S 4PD
Web site: http://quib.ly/
Freq: Daily
Circ: 111887 Cision Digital Reach
MAGAZINE (ONLINE)
News & Current Affairs

Quick Cards Made Easy 985451
Editorial: Tower House, Fairfax Street, Bristol BS1 3BN **Tel:** 44 01179 279009
Web site: www.cardmakingandpapercraft.com
Freq: Monthly
Circ: 18331 Not Audited

Profile: Magazine covering cards that are quick and easy to make with easy paper craft card designs, great ideas, tips and tricks.
Ad Rate: Full Page Colour £1050.00
MAGAZINE
Crafts

Quiet   995419
Editorial: The British Tinnitus Association, Ground Floor, Unit 5, Acorn Business Park, Woodseats Close, Sheffield S8 0TB
Tel: 44 01142 509933
Web site: www.tinnitus.org.uk
Freq: Quarterly
Editor: Nic Wray
MAGAZINE
News & Current Affairs

The Quietus   985666
Editorial: The Lexington, 96-98 Pentonville Rd, London N1 9JB
Email: info@thequietus.com
Web site: www.thequietus.com
Freq: Daily
Circ: 470063 Cision Digital Reach
Profile: Website covering music. The QUIETUS website provides the latest news on indie music and bands covering anything from dubstep, death metal and post punk to hip hop, pop and spacerock. The site gives in-depth features, reviews and "opinion pieces from the best new writers and established greats". They also cover film, books, TV and comics, old and new.
MAGAZINE (ONLINE)
Country, Folk, Bluegrass, Dance Music, Jazz & Blues, R&B, Urban, World, Rap & Hip Hop, Rock Music

Quintessentially   982574
Editorial: Suite 9, Beaufort Court, Admirals Way, Canary Wharf, London E14 9XL
Tel: 44 02037 724850
Email: editorial@quintessentially.com
Web site: www.quintessentiallymagazine.com
Freq: Quarterly
Circ: 25000 Not Audited
MAGAZINE
Luxury Goods

Quiz Factor   999597
Web site: http://www.quizfactor.com/
Freq: Daily
Circ: 115244 Cision Digital Reach
Editor: Rick Eastman
MAGAZINE (ONLINE)
Games, Competitions & Events

QX Magazine   982062
Editorial: Firststar Ltd, New House, 67-68 Hatton Garden, London EC1N 8JY
Tel: 44 02073 797887
Email: editorial@qxmagazine.com
Web site: www.qxmagazine.com
Freq: Weekly
Circ: 25000 Not Audited
Profile: Magazine covering the gay lifestyle scene including articles on music, travel, politics, arts, bars, and club reviews. Aimed at socially active gay men aged between 18 and 65 years old.
Ad Rate: Full Page Colour £550.00
MAGAZINE
LGBT

R2 (Rock 'N' Reel)   982110
Editorial: PO Box 38, Cleator Moor CA25 5WA
Web site: www.rock-n-reel.co.uk
Freq: Bi-Monthly
Circ: 25000 Not Audited
Editor: Sean McGhee
MAGAZINE
Rock Music

RA Magazine   980170
Editorial: Burlington House, Piccadilly, London W1J 0BD **Tel:** 44 02073 008000
Email: ramagazine@royalacademy.org.uk
Web site: https://www.royalacademy.org.uk/ra-magazine
Freq: Quarterly

Circ: 105000 Not Audited
Editor: Sam Phillips
Profile: Magazine of the Royal Academy of Arts covering arts including articles on the exhibitions of the Royal Academy, Royal Academicians and schools as well as more general arts features, fine arts, sculpture and renaissance sculpture features. First published in 1983, the publication has an average of 100 pages per issue. Read by friends and sponsors of the Royal Academy.
Ad Rate: Full Page Mono £3100.00
Ad Rate: Full Page Colour £3800.00
MAGAZINE
Antiques/Collectibles, Art, Literature, Photography, Theater & Performing Arts, Visual Arts

Rabbiting On   987725
Email: hq@rabbitwelfare.co.uk
Web site: www.rabbitwelfare.co.uk/resources/?section=ro.html
Freq: Quarterly
Circ: 3500 Not Audited
Editor: Claire Speight
Profile: Magazine about pet rabbits, including features on care, behaviour and health advice. Aimed at pet rabbit owners, veterinary professionals and members of the Rabbit Welfare Association.
MAGAZINE
Nature & Wildlife

Rabona Magazine   996670
Editorial: 28 Biggin Hill, London SE19 3HY
Email: hello@rabonamag.com
Web site: www.rabonamag.com
Freq: No Frequency Established Not Audited
MAGAZINE
Soccer

RAC Club Magazine   999616
Editorial: Fourth Floor, Embassy House, Queens Avenue, Bristol BS8 1SB
Tel: 44 01454 664123
Email: press.enquiries@rac.co.uk
Web site: https://www.rac.co.uk/drive/
Freq: Quarterly
Circ: 181310 Cision Digital Reach
MAGAZINE (ONLINE)
Driving

Race Engine Technology   982676
Editorial: Whitfield House, Cheddar Road, Wedmore, Wedmore BS28 4EJ
Tel: 44 01934 713957
Email: info@highpowermedia.com
Web site: www.highpowermedia.com
Freq: Bi-Monthly
Circ: 6000 Not Audited
Profile: Magazine covering all aspects of contemporary racing powertrain technology. Aimed at design and development engineers, competition engine builders and enthusiastic amateurs.
MAGAZINE
Automotive, Motorsports

Race Tech   982677
Editorial: 841 High Road, Finchley, London N12 8PT **Tel:** 44 02084 462100
Email: info@kimberleymediagroup.com
Web site: www.racetechmag.com
Freq: Monthly
Circ: 30000 Not Audited
Editor: William Kimberley
Profile: Magazine that covers the techniques and technology of amateur and professional motorsport. Contains in-depth coverage of car design and development, driving skills and new products for racers. Aimed at engineers, designers, drivers, teams, team managers, suppliers, race circuit owners and the informed enthusiast.
Ad Rate: Full Page Colour £1800.00
MAGAZINE
Automotive, Motorsports

raceboat international   996239
Editorial: 37 Border Road, Poole, Poole BH16 5EE **Tel:** 44 01202 625048
Email: editor@raceboatinternational.com
Web site: www.raceboatinternational.com
Freq: Quarterly
Circ: 40000 Not Audited

Editor: David Sewell
MAGAZINE
Swimming/Watersports

Racecar engineering   982678
Editorial: Jubilee House, 2 Jubilee Place, London SW3 3TQ
Email: editor@racecar-engineering.com
Web site: http://www.racecar-engineering.com
Freq: Monthly
Circ: 35000 Not Audited
Editor: Andrew Cotton
Profile: Magazine covering all types of motor sports technology including four-wheeled competition vehicles such as Formula 1 cars, rally cars and touring cars. Read by motor sport professionals, race car engineers, drivers, mechanics and the motor sports industry.
Ad Rate: Full Page Colour £1500.00
MAGAZINE
Motorsports

Racer Ready   985473
Editorial: 27 The Brambles, Crowthorne, Crowthorne RG45 6EF
Web site: racer-ready.co.uk
Freq: Quarterly
Circ: 1200 Not Audited
Profile: Magazine covering winter sports including ski racing, snowboarding, freestyle, jumping and ski bike racing. First published in 2001. Aimed at competitive winter sports enthusiasts.
Ad Rate: Full Page Mono £350.00
Ad Rate: Full Page Colour £450.00
MAGAZINE
Winter Sports

Racing & Football Outlook   982035
Editorial: 1 Canada Square, Canary Wharf, London E14 5AP **Tel:** 44 02082 630100
Email: rfo@rfoutlook.com
Web site: racingpost.com
Freq: Weekly Not Audited
Editor: Dylan Hill
Profile: Magazine covering horse racing and football poole including greyhounds and other betting sports such as golf. Aimed at those interested in betting on sports.
Ad Rate: Full Page Mono £1836.00
Ad Rate: Full Page Colour £2295.00
MAGAZINE
Casinos & Gaming, Horse Racing, Soccer

Racing Ahead   984513
Editorial: 27-37 St George's Road, Wimbledon SW19 4EU
Tel: 44 02089 714339
Email: info@racingahead.net
Web site: www.racingahead.net
Freq: Monthly
Circ: 5000 Not Audited
Editor: Stephen Mullen
Profile: Magazine covering horse racing including interviews with trainers, horses to follow, statistics and betting tips. Aimed at people who bet on horse racing.
Ad Rate: Full Page Colour £1000.00
MAGAZINE
Horse Racing

The Racing Calendar   998575
Editorial: Sanders Road, Wellingborough, Wellingborough NN8 4BX
Tel: 44 01933 440077
Web site: www.weatherbys.co.uk
Freq: Weekly
Circ: 2000 Not Audited
Editor: Christine Frankland
Profile: Official journal of British Cycling Federation covering cycling news, equipment testing and competitions. Aimed at members of the British Cycling Federation and racing cyclists.
MAGAZINE
Casinos & Gaming

The Racing Pigeon   982272
Editorial: Unit G5, Seedbed Centre, Wyncolls Rd, Colchester, Colchester CO4 9HT **Tel:** 44 01206 843456
Email: rpeditor@btconnect.com

Web site: www.racingpigeon.co.uk
Freq: Weekly
Circ: 10000 Not Audited
Editor: Lee Fribbins
MAGAZINE
Games, Competitions & Events

Racing Pigeon Pictorial International   982271
Editorial: Unit G5, Seedbed Centre, Wyncolls Road, Colchester, Colchester CO4 9HT **Tel:** 44 01206 843456
Email: rpeditor@btconnect.com
Web site: www.racingpigeon.co.uk
Freq: Monthly Not Audited
Editor: Lee Fribbins
MAGAZINE
Games, Competitions & Events

Racing Post   982036
Editorial: 1 Canada Square, Canary Wharf, London E14 5AP **Tel:** 44 02082 630100
Email: copy@racingpost.com
Web site: www.racingpost.com
Freq: Daily Not Audited
Editor: Bruce Millington
Profile: Newspaper containing horse and greyhound racing news and betting information in Britain and Ireland focusing on statistics and results. Includes features from racing journalists, news from the training centres and comprehensive previews, reviews and results section for point to point in the UK and Ireland. First published in 1986, the publication has an average of 80 pages per issue. Read by those within the betting industry and racing enthusiasts.
Ad Rate: Full Page Mono £6120.00
Ad Rate: Full Page Colour £10200.00
MAGAZINE
Casinos & Gaming, Horse Racing

Racing Post Weekender   982037
Editorial: 1 Canada Square, Canary Wharf, London E14 5AP **Tel:** 44 02072 932001
Email: weekender@racingpost.com
Web site: www.racingpost.co.uk
Freq: Weekly Not Audited
Editor: Dylan Hill
Profile: Newspaper covering weekend racing in Britain and Ireland focusing on statistics and results. Includes features from racing journalists, news from the training centres and comprehensive previews, reviews and results section for point to point in the UK and Ireland. Aimed at those in the betting industry and racing enthusiasts.
Ad Rate: Full Page Colour £1900.00
MAGAZINE
Casinos & Gaming, Horse Racing

Radiant Magazine   1060348
Email: nicole@radiantmag.co.za
Web site: http://radiantmagazine.wordpress.com
Freq: Monthly
MAGAZINE (ONLINE)
Fashion, Health & Medicine, Preschool, Religion, Women's Interests

The Radio Academy Newsletter   1070426
Editorial: 3rd Floor, 55 New Oxford Street, London WC1A 1BS **Tel:** 44 02031 741180
Email: info@radioacademy.org
Web site: www.radioacademy.org
Freq: Weekly
Circ: 9362 Cision Digital Reach
MAGAZINE (ONLINE)
Broadcasting

Radio Control Jet International   981988
Editorial: Traplet House, Willow End Park, Blackmore Park Road, Worcester WR13 6NN **Tel:** 44 01684 588500
Email: rcji@traplet.com
Web site: www.rcjetinternational.com
Freq: Bi-Monthly
Circ: 20000 Not Audited
Editor: Tony van Geffen
Profile: Magazine dedicated to radio control model jet aircraft. Aimed at radio control enthusiasts.

Consumer Magazines

Ad Rate: Full Page Mono £505.00
Ad Rate: Full Page Colour £760.00
MAGAZINE
Crafts, Hobbies, & Collecting

Radio Engineering of China
1060785

Tel: 44 86311 86924962
Email: gch@mail.cti.ac.cn
Freq: Monthly
Circ: 20000 Not Audited
MAGAZINE
Broadcasting, Electronics, Engineering

Radio Guyana
1061917
Web site: http://www.radioguyana.net
Circ: 521 Cision Digital Reach
MAGAZINE (ONLINE)
Africa, Americas, Asia, Australia, Ethnic & Multicultural, Europe, Expatriates

Rádió Mi
1060991
Tel: 44 36304 681719
Email: rmiszeged@gmail.com
Web site: http://www.radiomi.hu
Circ: 2516 Cision Digital Reach
MAGAZINE (ONLINE)
Bars, Clubs & Pubs, Comedy, Consumer Affairs, Crime & Violence, Defense & National Security, Energy & Environment, Entertainment, Ethical/Moral Issues, International News, Law

Radio Times
982351
Editorial: Vineyard House, 44 Brook Green, Hammersmith, London W6 7BT
Tel: 44 02071 505800
Email: feedback@radiotimes.com
Web site: www.radiotimes.com
Freq: Weekly
Circ: 622773 Not Audited
Profile: Magazine with TV and radio listings and guide for all national and local channels, plus film reviews and critics' recommendations. The publication provides a guide to BBC television, BBC radio, ITV, Channel 4, Channel 5, Satellite, Cable and Digital Television. First Published in 1923. Aimed at people interested in TV and radio.
Ad Rate: Full Page Colour £7800.00
MAGAZINE
Broadcasting

Radio Today
983507
Editorial: 68 The Greenhouse, MediaCityUK, Salford Quays, Salford M50 2EQ
Tel: 44 01612 621004
Web site: www.radiotoday.co.uk
Freq: Daily
Circ: 96615 Cision Digital Reach
MAGAZINE (ONLINE)
Broadcasting

Radio-Electronics
987826
Web site: http://www.radio-electronics.com/rec-information/about-us.php
Freq: Daily
Circ: 261 Cision Digital Reach
MAGAZINE (ONLINE)
Electronics

RadioUser
984257
Editorial: Tayfield House, 38 Poole Road, Westbourne, Bournemouth BH4 9DW
Tel: 44 01202 751611
Email: ru@pwpublishing.ltd.uk
Web site: www.radiouser.co.uk
Freq: Monthly
Circ: 9500 Not Audited
Profile: Magazine covering hobby radio communication. Includes equipment reviews, CB news, short-wave listening, amateur, scanning, DAB digital radio and air band listening. Aimed at radio enthusiasts.
Ad Rate: Full Page Mono £583.00
Ad Rate: Full Page Colour £583.00
MAGAZINE
Electronics

Raider
987390
Editorial: The Court Yard, Chopdike Drove, Gosberton Clough, Spalding, Spalding PE11 4JP **Tel:** 44 01529 488100
Web site: www.raider-mag.com

Freq: Monthly
Circ: 8000 Not Audited
Editor: Connor Monaf
Profile: Magazine covering military technology, military equipment and clothing, history, unit profiles and employment with an interest in elite forces and special operations from WWII to the present day. Aimed at elite forces and special operations British soldiers serving in Iraq and Afghanistan.
Ad Rate: Full Page Colour £750.00
MAGAZINE
Armed Forces

Rail
979941
Editorial: Media House, Lynchwood, Peterborough Business Park, Peterborough PE2 6EA **Tel:** 44 01733 468000
Email: rail@bauermedia.co.uk
Web site: www.railmagazine.com/
Freq: Bi-Weekly
Circ: 20063 Not Audited
Profile: Magazine covering railways including information, features and news of the full spectrum of activity, from Government policy and involvement, to operations, maintenance and services provided by Network Rail, train operators and the wider industry. Aimed at railway professionals and enthusiasts.
Ad Rate: Full Page Colour £1950.00
MAGAZINE
Railroad

Rail Business Intelligence
983513
Editorial: 7th Floor, Chancery House, St Nicholas Way, Sutton, London SM1 1JB
Tel: 44 02086 525200
Email: editor@railwaygazette.com
Web site: www.railwaygazette.com
Freq: Bi-Weekly Not Audited
Editor: Robert Preston
Profile: Newsletter identifying new contracts and providing details of bids and bidders, plus analysis of the UK railway industry. Aimed at professionals in the railway industry, including the financial, legal and regulatory sectors as well as manufacturers and operators.
MAGAZINE
Railroad

The Rail Engineer
983367
Editorial: Rail Media House, Samson Road, Coalville, Coalville LE67 3FP
Tel: 44 01530 816444
Email: news@rail-media.com
Web site: www.therailengineer.com
Freq: Monthly
Circ: 14500 Not Audited
Profile: Magazine focusing on all aspects of UK and European rail infrastructure, including railway lines, stations, signalling systems, level crossings, bridges, tunnels and other physical structures. Aimed at senior management and engineers within the rail industry.
Ad Rate: Full Page Colour £1695.00
MAGAZINE
Engineering, Railroad

Rail Express
983511
Editorial: Morton Way, Horncastle LN9 6JR
Tel: 44 01507 529529
Email: info@railexpress.co.uk
Web site: www.railexpress.co.uk
Freq: Monthly
Circ: 15000 Not Audited
Editor: Paul Bickerdyke
Profile: Magazine covering British railway news. Read by those with general railway interest plus railway industry professionals and enthusiasts.
Ad Rate: Full Page Colour £750.00
MAGAZINE
Crafts, Hobbies, & Collecting, Railroad

Rail Infrastructure
983549
Editorial: 26 Priory Gardens, Langstone, Newport NP18 2JG **Tel:** 44 01633 411949
Web site: www.railinfrastructure.com
Freq: Bi-Monthly Not Audited

Profile: Magazine covering the rail infrastructure industry.
MAGAZINE
Railroad

Rail Network
1059412
Editorial: 31-33 Lottage road, Aldbourne, Marlborough, Marlborough SN8 2EB
Email: fiona@railnetwork.info
Web site: www.railnetwork.info
Freq: Daily
Circ: 611 Cision Digital Reach
Editor: Fiona Greaves
MAGAZINE (ONLINE)
Railroad

Rail Professional
983366
Tel: 44 01268 711811
Email: admin@railpro.co.uk
Web site: www.railpro.co.uk
Freq: Monthly
Circ: 7894 Not Audited
Editor: Lorna Slade
Profile: Magazine covering information and support to all professionals working in the UK rail industry. First published in 1996. Read by rail business managers and directors and rail industry stake holders.
Ad Rate: Full Page Colour £1800.00
MAGAZINE
Railroad

Rail Technology Magazine
983512
Editorial: 2nd Floor, 82 King Street, Manchester M2 4WQ **Tel:** 44 01618 336320
Email: editorial@railtechnologymagazine.com
Web site: www.railtechnologymagazine.com
Freq: Bi-Monthly
Circ: 8891 Not Audited
Editor: David Stevenson
Profile: Magazine covering commercial and political developments, latest technology, major projects and purchasing strategies within the rail industry. Aimed at senior executives, directors, managers and engineers within the rail industry as well as government officials.
Ad Rate: Full Page Colour £1995.00
MAGAZINE
Railroad

Railnews
983393
Editorial: PO Box 7779, Wellingborough NN8 9HU **Tel:** 44 01438 281200
Email: news@railnews.co.uk
Web site: www.railnews.co.uk
Freq: Monthly
Circ: 100000 Not Audited
Profile: Magazine covering railway industry developments, changes of rail company policy and staff news. Aimed at those working in the rail industry throughout the UK.
Ad Rate: Full Page Mono £1945.00
Ad Rate: Full Page Colour £2245.00
MAGAZINE
Railroad

RailStaff
983514
Editorial: Rail Media House, Samson Road, Coalville, Ashby-de-la-Zouch LE67 3FP
Tel: 44 01530 816444
Email: news@rail-media.com
Web site: www.railstaff.co.uk
Freq: Monthly
Circ: 44940 Not Audited
Editor: Andy Milne
Profile: Magazine covering current news and issues affecting the UK rail industry including news, in-depth reports and interviews of key industry personnel. Aimed at railway staff.
Ad Rate: Full Page Colour £2295.00
MAGAZINE
Engineering, Railroad

The Railway Centre
998561
Editorial: 1 Burns Court, Marine Parade, Dawlish, Dawlish EX7 9DL
Tel: 44 07525 619118
Email: modernlocomotivesillustrated@gmail.com
Web site: www.railway-centre.com
Freq: Daily

Circ: 2225 Cision Digital Reach
Editor: Colin Marsden
MAGAZINE (ONLINE)
Railroad

Railway Directory
996037
Editorial: 7th Floor, Chancery House, St Nicholas Way, Sutton, London SM1 1JB
Tel: 44 02086 528608
Email: editor@railwaygazette.com
Web site: www.railwaydirectory.net
Freq: Annual Not Audited
Editor: Andy Hellawell
MAGAZINE
Railroad

Railway Gazette International
979833
Editorial: 7th Floor, Chancery House, St Nicholas Way, Sutton, London SM1 1JB
Tel: 44 02086 525200
Email: editor@railwaygazette.com
Web site: www.railwaygazette.com
Freq: Monthly
Circ: 11150 Not Audited
Editor: Robert Preston
Profile: Magazine featuring technical and operational articles and news about the international railway industry. Aimed at railway management, railway operators and suppliers.
Ad Rate: Full Page Mono £3460.00
Ad Rate: Full Page Colour £5080.00
MAGAZINE
Railroad

Railway Herald
983561
Editorial: PO Box 252, Scunthorpe, Scunthorpe DN17 2WY
Tel: 44 01904 500175
Email: editor@railwayherald.com
Web site: www.railwayherald.co.uk
Freq: Weekly
Circ: 1724 Cision Digital Reach
Editor: Richard Tuplin
Profile: Website covering railways. The Railway Herald online magazine features news stories from the rail industry worldwide.
MAGAZINE (ONLINE)
Railroad

Railway Interiors International
983494
Editorial: Abinger House, Church Street, Dorking, Dorking RH4 1DF
Tel: 44 01306 743744
Email: info@ukipme.com
Web site: www.ukipme.com/mag_railway.htm
Freq: Annual
Circ: 10401 Not Audited
Profile: Magazine covering the latest trends and developments in the design, furnishing, equipment and management of passenger railway carriage interiors. Aimed at rail operators and manufacturers.
Ad Rate: Full Page Colour £3720.00
MAGAZINE
Railroad

Railway Magazine
979943
Editorial: Media Centre, Morton Way, Horncastle LN9 6JR **Tel:** 44 01507 529529
Web site: www.railwaymagazine.co.uk
Freq: Monthly
Circ: 37250 Not Audited
Editor: Chris Milner
Profile: Magazine focusing on rail practice and performance, with photo and feature articles on locomotives, train operating companies, underground systems, steam, heritage and preservation. Aimed at those with an interest in railway performance.
Ad Rate: Full Page Mono £551.00
Ad Rate: Full Page Colour £948.00
MAGAZINE
Railroad

Railway Modeller
981986
Tel: 44 01297 21542
Email: info@pecobeer.co.uk
Web site: www.pecopublications.co.uk/railway-modeller.html

Freq: Monthly
Circ: 33828 Not Audited
Editor: Steve Flint
Profile: Magazine covering the construction and operation of railway models in the smaller scales. Includes scale-drawings, trade reports, planning and historical articles. Aimed at railway enthusiasts of all ages.
Ad Rate: Full Page Colour £690.00
MAGAZINE
Crafts, Hobbies, & Collecting

Railway News
995381
Editorial: 11 -15 Dix's Field, Exeter EX1 1QA
Tel: 44 01392 580002
Email: info@railway-news.com
Web site: http://www.railway-news.com
Freq: Daily
Circ: 13703 Cision Digital Reach
MAGAZINE (ONLINE)
Railroad

Railway Pro
1104003
Tel: 44 01316 189828
Email: office@railwaypro.com
Web site: http://www.railwaypro.com/wp/
Freq: Monthly
MAGAZINE
Railroad

Railway Strategies
981336
Editorial: Suite 10, Cringleford Business Centre, Intwood Road, Norwich NR6 6AU
Tel: 44 01603 274130
Email: pmonument@schofieldpublishing.co.uk
Web site: http://www.railway-strategies.com/
Freq: Monthly
Circ: 5557 Not Audited
Editor: Gay Sutton
Profile: Magazine providing in-depth news and information on all aspects of railway management, reports on finance, contracts, franchise issues, safety, security, rolling stock, station developments, integrated transport, freight, appointments and trade exhibitions. Aimed at directors and senior management within companies operating railway franchises, Government departments, official agencies, Network Rail and specialists with an interest in the development of railway systems.
Ad Rate: Full Page Colour £1800.00
MAGAZINE
Railroad

Railways Illustrated
983547
Editorial: PO BOX 100, Stamford, Peterborough PE9 1XQ
Tel: 44 01780 484630
Web site: www.railwaysillustrated.com
Freq: Monthly Not Audited
Profile: Magazine covering railway companies, train operators and infrastructure functions as well as main line steam operations, private railway heritage sites and the National Railway Museum. Aimed at railway enthusiasts.
Ad Rate: Full Page Colour £650.00
MAGAZINE
Railroad

railway-technology.com
987716
Editorial: John Carpenter House, John Carpenter Street, London EC4Y 0AN
Tel: 44 02079 366400
Email: onlineeditorial@kable.co.uk
Web site: www.railway-technology.com
Freq: Daily
Circ: 96431 Cision Digital Reach
Profile: Website covering news, information and related projects for the railway technology industry, including project news, products and services, industry events, a complete listing of railway industry organisations and a free regular e-bulletin.
MAGAZINE (ONLINE)
Railroad

Rainbow Fun
1054076
Tel: 44 01483 779500
Web site: www.signaturepl.co.uk/portfolio/easypeazy.html

Freq: Monthly
Circ: 30000 Not Audited
MAGAZINE
Teen/Young Adult

Raise
985395
Editorial: Mynster House, Harrow Road East, Dorking, Dorking RH4 2AU
Tel: 44 01306 509147
Email: raise@fundraisingmedia.co.uk
Web site: www.raisemagazine.co.uk
Freq: Monthly
Circ: 8500 Not Audited
Profile: Magazine featuring news and ideas on fundraising, legacies, volunteering, the environment and organic living.
MAGAZINE
Bicycles, Charitable Foundations

The Rake
995824
Editorial: 36 Upper Brook Street, Mayfair, London W1K 7QJ **Tel:** 44 02037 528880
Email: info@therakemagazine.com
Web site: http://therake.com/
Freq: Bi-Monthly
Circ: 105000 Not Audited
Editor: Tom Chamberlin
MAGAZINE
Fashion, Men's Interests

RAMzine
1075498
Email: info@ramzine.co.uk
Web site: www.ramzine.co.uk
Freq: Semi-Annual Not Audited
Editor: Victoria Purcell
Profile: Website covering rock and metal music. RAMzine covers features, interviews, reviews and news on the latest rock and metal music.
MAGAZINE
Rock Music

The Ransom Note
996285
Editorial: 24 Holywell Row, London EC2A 4JB
Email: editorial@theransomnote.co.uk
Web site: http://www.theransomnote.co.uk/
Freq: Weekly
Circ: 60817 Cision Digital Reach
MAGAZINE (ONLINE)
Art, Dance Music

Rapid Prototyping Journal
984406
Editorial: Howard House, Wagon Lane, Bingley BD16 1WA **Tel:** 44 01274 777700
Web site: www.emeraldinsight.com/journal/rpj
Freq: Bi-Monthly Not Audited
Profile: International journal covering developments and applications in additive manufacturing (AM) and related technologies. Read by industrialists and academics.
MAGAZINE
News & Current Affairs

Rapid TV News
984970
Tel: 44 07887 535288
Email: graham.pitman@eurotvguild.com
Web site: www.rapidtvnews.com
Freq: Daily
Circ: 138324 Cision Digital Reach
Profile: Website covering broadcast media and the television industry.
MAGAZINE (ONLINE)
Broadcasting

Rapport (Peugeot)
983616
Editorial: Fourth Floor, Embassy House, Queens Avenue, Clifton, Bristol BS8 1SB
Tel: 44 01179 251696
Email: info@specialistuk.com
Web site: www.specialistuk.com
Freq: Semi-Annual
Circ: 150000 Not Audited
MAGAZINE
Automakers

Rapture Magazine
996677
Email: info@rapturemagazine.com
Web site: http://rapturemagazine.com/
Freq: Daily

Circ: 10628 Cision Digital Reach
Editor: Anna Ridley
MAGAZINE (ONLINE)
Classical/Choral/Band Music, Country, Folk, Bluegrass, Dance Music, Jazz & Blues, Music, Pop Music, R&B, Urban, World, Rap & Hip Hop, Rock Music

Raring2go!
985435
Tel: 44 01273 447101
Email: info@raring2go.co.uk
Web site: www.raring2go.co.uk
Freq: Quarterly
Circ: 650000 Not Audited
Editor: Sophie Belcher
Profile: Guide of what to do and where to go for parents and children aged between 0 and 11 years old.
MAGAZINE
Elementary School, Preschool

Rascals of London
996690
Email: info@rascalsoflondon.co.uk
Web site: www.rascalsoflondon.co.uk
Freq: Quarterly
Circ: 40000 Not Audited
MAGAZINE
Family & Parenting, Local Entertainment Guides

Rashtra Dharma
1061705
Tel: 44 91922 95693685
Email: rastradharma@rastradharma.com
Web site: http://www.rastradharma.com
Freq: Monthly
Circ: 10001 Not Audited
MAGAZINE
Religion

Raskas Kalusto
1061737
Tel: 44 35862 810170
Email: iikka.kekko@raskaskalusto.fi
Web site: http://www.raskaskalusto.fi
Freq: Bi-Monthly
Circ: 30000 Not Audited
MAGAZINE
Animal Farming, Automakers, Manufacturing

RasPi
995300
Editorial: Richmond House, 33 Richmond Hill, Bournemouth BH2 6EZ
Tel: 44 01202 586200
Email: raspi@futurenet.com
Web site: http://www.futureplc.com/
Freq: Monthly Not Audited
Editor: April Madden
Profile: Digital publication that looks at Raspberry Pi software.
MAGAZINE
Computers, Personal Computers

Raw Meat
996149
Editorial: 56b Grand Parade, Harringay Green Lanes, London N4 1AF
Email: info@wearerawmeat.com
Web site: www.wearerawmeat.com
Freq: Daily
Circ: 11156 Cision Digital Reach
MAGAZINE (ONLINE)
Classical/Choral/Band Music, Country, Folk, Bluegrass, Dance Music, Jazz & Blues, Music, Pop Music, R&B, Urban, World, Rap & Hip Hop, Rock Music

Raw Vision
984073
Editorial: PO Box 44, Watford, London WD25 8LN **Tel:** 44 01923 853175
Email: info@rawvision.com
Web site: www.rawvision.com
Freq: Quarterly
Circ: 5500 Not Audited
Editor: John Maizels
Profile: Magazine covering a variety of styles of art, particularly outsider art and contemporary folk art. Aimed at those interested in art.
Ad Rate: Full Page Colour £1155.00
MAGAZINE
Antiques/Collectibles, Art, Literature, Photography, Theater & Performing Arts, Visual Arts

RAZMAG™
1053145
Email: razorianfly@gmail.com
Web site: http://www.razmag.com/
Freq: Daily
Circ: 17038 Cision Digital Reach
MAGAZINE (ONLINE)
Apple, Computers, Electronics, Mobile Electronics, Personal Computers

RC Model World
988836
Editorial: Traplet House, Willow End Park, Blackmore Park Road, Malvern WR13 6NN
Tel: 44 01684 588500
Email: rcmw@traplet.com
Web site: www.rcmodelworld.com
Freq: Monthly
Circ: 32000 Not Audited
Editor: Kevin Crozier
MAGAZINE
Crafts, Hobbies, & Collecting

RCI Ventures
985268
Editorial: Kettering Parkway, Kettering, Kettering NN15 6EY **Tel:** 44 01536 310101
Email: helen.foster@rci.com
Web site: www.rciventures.com
Freq: Semi-Annual
Circ: 5000 Not Audited
Profile: Magazine covering news and concerns of hotel and timeshared holiday ownership industry including showcase of ideas from the hospitality industry at large. Aimed at hotel, time-share and high-end shared holiday ownership resort developers, managers, marketers and those associated with the industry, including hotel partners.
Ad Rate: Full Page Colour £2300.00
MAGAZINE
Airline Inflight, Railroad, Travel

RCM&E
982838
Editorial: Hadlow House, 9 High Street, Green Street Green, London BR6 6BG
Tel: 44 01689 869840
Web site: www.modelflying.co.uk
Freq: Monthly
Circ: 38000 Not Audited
MAGAZINE
Crafts, Hobbies, & Collecting

RCSLT Bulletin
999172
Editorial: RCSLT, 2 White Hart Yard, London SE1 1NX **Tel:** 44 02073 781200
Email: bulletin@rcslt.org
Web site: www.rcslt.org/about/publications/overview
Freq: Monthly
Circ: 14700 Not Audited
Editor: Steven Harulow
MAGAZINE
Medicine

RE Today
982156
Editorial: Imperial Court, Sovereign Road, Birmingham B30 3FH **Tel:** 44 01214 583313
Email: admin@retoday.org.uk
Web site: www.retoday.org.uk
Freq: 3 Times/Year
Circ: 4000 Not Audited
Editor: Lat Blaylock
MAGAZINE
Education, Religion

Reach
996493
Editorial: Unit N2 Blois Meadow Business Centre, Steeple Bumpstead, Haverhill, Haverhill CB9 7BN **Tel:** 44 02071 126710
Email: info@cathcom.org
Web site: www.CathComReach.com
Freq: Quarterly
Circ: 45000 Not Audited
Editor: Nick Layton
MAGAZINE
Education, Family & Parenting

Reaction
1097897
Email: editors@thereaction.life
Web site: http://reaction.life/
Freq: Daily
Editor: Iain Martin
MAGAZINE (ONLINE)
Politics

Consumer Magazines

Reader's Digest
980169

Editorial: 57 Margaret Street, London W1W 8SJ
Email: theeditor@readersdigest.co.uk
Web site: www.readersdigest.co.uk
Freq: Monthly
Circ: 102221 Not Audited
Profile: General-interest family magazine featuring inspiring stories, famous people, money-saving and home decorating tips, with advice and ideas on how to simplify and enrich your life. Launched in UK in 1938, the title has 48 editions in 19 different languages published around the world. Aimed at men and women of all ages.
Ad Rate: Full Page Colour £5210.00
MAGAZINE
Literature

ReadySteadyBook
988644

Editorial: 7 Quernmore Road, Lancaster LA1 3EB
Web site: www.readysteadybook.com
Freq: Daily
Circ: 10857 Cision Digital Reach
MAGAZINE (ONLINE)
Literature

ReadySteadyBook
998793

Editorial: 7 Quernmore Road, Lancaster LA1 3EB
Web site: www.readysteadybook.com
Freq: Daily
Circ: 10857 Cision Digital Reach
MAGAZINE (ONLINE)
Literature

Real Crime
997985

Tel: 44 01202 586200
Web site: www.realcrimedaily.com
Freq: Monthly
Circ: 35706 Not Audited
Editor: Ben Biggs
MAGAZINE
Crime & Violence

Real Homes
981857

Editorial: 2 Sugar Brook Court, Aston Road, Bromsgrove, Bromsgrove B60 3EX
Tel: 44 01527 834400
Email: realhomes@futurenet.com
Web site: www.realhomesmagazine.co.uk
Freq: Monthly
Circ: 24289 Not Audited
Profile: Magazine covering home improvement. It features news, project advice, decorating inspiration and information for homeowners looking to make the most of their living space. Each issue features articles on home improvement, room decoraction, garden design ideas, DIY and product reviews. First published in 1998. Aimed at people interested in home and interior design.
Ad Rate: Full Page Colour £4000.00
MAGAZINE
Do-It-Yourself (DIY)

Real People
983263

Tel: 44 02074 395000
Email: features@realpeoplemag.co.uk
Web site: www.realpeoplemag.co.uk
Freq: Weekly
Circ: 124859 Not Audited
Profile: Women's interest magazine covering real life stories, fashion, health and beauty tips, pets, puzzles, discounted deals and special offers. First published in 2006. Aimed at women of all ages who enjoy real life stories.
Ad Rate: Full Page Colour £8900.00
MAGAZINE
Careers, Crime & Violence, Family & Parenting, Health & Medicine, Lifestyle, Personal Finance, Relationships, Women's Interests

realbrighton.com
984276

Editorial: 36 Kensington Place, Brighton BN1 4EJ **Tel:** 44 01273 252250
Web site: www.realbrighton.com
Freq: Daily
Circ: 5083 Cision Digital Reach

Editor: Sam Milford
MAGAZINE (ONLINE)
LGBT, Regional General Interest

realbuzz.com
995739

Editorial: 12 Nicholas Street, Chester, Chester CH1 2NX **Tel:** 44 01244 311111
Email: info@therealbuzzgroup.com
Web site: www.realbuzz.com
Freq: Daily
Circ: 133593 Cision Digital Reach
MAGAZINE (ONLINE)
Alternative Medicine, Fitness & Exercise, Nutrition

RecipesPlus
998025

Editorial: Media House, Lynchwood, Peterborough Business Park, Peterborough PE2 6EA
Email: support@recipes-plus.co.uk
Web site: www.recipes-plus.co.uk
Freq: Daily
Circ: 72303 Cision Digital Reach
Editor: Kortney Gruenwald
MAGAZINE (ONLINE)
Cooking & Baking

Reckless Gardener
983955

Email: recklessgardener@btinternet.com
Web site: http://reckless-gardener.co.uk/
Freq: Daily
Circ: 16071 Cision Digital Reach
Editor: Emma Felton
Profile: Website covering gardening. The Reckless Gardner website provides basic help and advice with garden features, design ideas and designer profiles, jobs this month, garden visits, book reviews and show information and coverage (including major RHS shows). Including section on bed and breakfast for gardeners and online shop.
MAGAZINE (ONLINE)
Gardening

Reclaim
1076407

Web site: www.reclaimmagazine.uk
Freq: Monthly
MAGAZINE
Do-It-Yourself (DIY)

Recombu.com
985083

Editorial: Recombu, 7 Henrietta Street, Covent Garden, London WC2E 8PS
Email: edit@recombu.com
Web site: https://recombu.com/
Freq: Daily
Circ: 641270 Cision Digital Reach
MAGAZINE (ONLINE)
Audio Video Trade, Cameras, Consumer Electronics, Electronics, Internet, Mobile Electronics, Movies & Video

Record Collector
983394

Editorial: Unit 101, 140 Wales Farm Road, London W3 6UG **Tel:** 44 02087 528172
Web site: www.recordcollectormag.com
Freq: Monthly
Circ: 35000 Not Audited
Profile: Magazine celebrating the history of popular music from 1950s to the present day, includes news, reviews, interviews, discographies and record values. Aimed at record collectors and general music fans.
Ad Rate: Full Page Mono £885.00
Ad Rate: Full Page Colour £1085.00
MAGAZINE
Classical/Choral/Band Music, Country, Folk, Bluegrass, Jazz & Blues, R&B, Urban, World, Rock Music

Record of the Day
984602

Editorial: PO Box 49554, London E17 9WB
Tel: 44 02082 231224
Email: info@recordoftheday.com
Web site: www.recordoftheday.com
Freq: Daily
Circ: 27598 Cision Digital Reach
Profile: Website covering music. The RECORD of the DAY website provides access to a daily music industry newsletter and weekly electronic magazine. Includes

information on media news, audio clips, statistics, business news and new artists.
MAGAZINE (ONLINE)
Music, Rock Music

The Recorder Magazine
982120

Editorial: Scout Bottom Farm, Mytholmroyd, Mytholmroyd HX7 5JS **Tel:** 44 01422 882751
Email: info@recordermail.co.uk
Web site: www.recordermail.co.uk
Freq: Quarterly
Circ: 2500 Not Audited
Editor: Laura Justice
Profile: Magazine containing articles, reports and reviews on all aspects of the recorder and its music. Includes tips on improving technique, as well as features on the history of the recorder, interviews with players and makers, and concert and book reviews.
MAGAZINE
Music

Recovery Operator Magazine
984279

Editorial: Avro House, 1 Bath Street, Rugby CV21 3JF **Tel:** 44 01694 781283
Web site: www.avrouk.com
Freq: Bi-Monthly
Circ: 4000 Not Audited
MAGAZINE
Automotive

Recycle
998420

Freq: Quarterly
Circ: 10000 Not Audited
MAGAZINE
Hotels/Motels

Red
980765

Editorial: 72 Broadwick Street, London W1F 9EP **Tel:** 44 02074 395548
Email: red@redmagazine.co.uk
Web site: www.redonline.co.uk
Freq: Monthly
Circ: 166340 Not Audited
Profile: Magazine covering fashion, beauty and lifestyle. Each issue contains the latest fashion styles, hair and beauty tips, celebrity interviews, interior design ideas and product reviews. The magazine also features topical issues, ranging from health conditions to international current affairs. Launched in 1998. Aimed at women aged 30 years and over with an interest in fashion.
Ad Rate: Full Page Colour £18841.00
MAGAZINE
Women's Interests

The Red Bulletin (UK)
998601

Editorial: 155 - 171 Tooley Street, London SE1 2JP
Email: contact@at.redbulletin.com
Web site: www.redbulletin.com
Freq: Monthly
Circ: 180000 Not Audited
Editor: Ruth Morgan
MAGAZINE
Motorsports

Red Carpet
997114

Email: info@redcarpetmagazine.co.uk
Web site: redcarpetmagazine.co.uk
Freq: Daily
Circ: 10245 Cision Digital Reach
Editor: Sat Bal
MAGAZINE (ONLINE)
Bars, Clubs & Pubs, Comedy, Entertainment, Local Entertainment Guides, Luxury Goods, Movies & Video

Red Life
995272

Email: redlife@bravenewworld.co
Web site: http://www.redvalentino.com/experience/en/red-life/
Freq: Daily
Circ: 16 Cision Digital Reach
Editor: Charlotte Hogarth-Jones
MAGAZINE (ONLINE)
Classical/Choral/Band Music, Cooking & Baking, Country, Folk, Bluegrass, Dance Music, Fashion, Jazz & Blues, Movies & Video, Music, Pop Music, R&B, Urban, World

Red Pepper
98213

Editorial: 44-48 Shepherdess Walk, London N1 7JP **Tel:** 44 02073 245068
Email: office@redpepper.org.uk
Web site: www.redpepper.org.uk
Freq: Bi-Monthly
Circ: 4000 Not Audited
Profile: Magazine covering domestic and international issues including left politics and culture, feminist, green and libertarian politics as well as articles on the arts, book reviews and leisure. Aimed at politically aware individuals.
MAGAZINE
Politics

Redbrick
981770

Editorial: Birmingham University Guild of Students, Edgbaston Park Road, Birmingham B15 2TT **Tel:** 44 01212 512462
Email: news@redbrickonline.co.uk
Web site: www.redbrick.me
Freq: Bi-Weekly
Circ: 1500 Not Audited
Profile: Publication covering student news, the arts and sport at local and national level. Aimed at students and staff at Birmingham university.
Ad Rate: Full Page Mono £635.00
Ad Rate: Full Page Colour £895.00
MAGAZINE
Student Lifestyle

Redhanded
984114

Editorial: The Coach House, 40 Partridge Road, Cardiff CF24 3QX
Tel: 44 02920 190224
Email: redhanded@conroymedia.co.uk
Web site: www.redhandedmagazine.co.uk
Freq: Quarterly
Circ: 17279 Not Audited
Editor: Jeremy Head
MAGAZINE
Men's Interests, Regional General Interest

Redhill Reigate Horley Life
980544

Editorial: Argus House, Crowhurst Road, Hollingbury, Brighton BN1 8AR
Tel: 44 01273 544544
Email: news@theargus.co.uk
Web site: www.redhillandreigatelife.co.uk
Freq: Daily
Circ: 4600 Cision Digital Reach
MAGAZINE (ONLINE)
News & Current Affairs

RedHotCurry.com
982843

Editorial: Unit 28, I/O Centre, Hearle Way, Hatfield Business Park, Hatfield AL10 9EW
Tel: 44 01707 269666
Web site: www.redhotcurry.com
Freq: Daily
Circ: 5150 Cision Digital Reach
Profile: Website covering Asian lifestyle and shares news and information on fashion, beauty, food, drink, entertainment, health, sport and travel.
MAGAZINE (ONLINE)
Asia, Restaurant Reviews

Reflections
982513

Editorial: 118 Saltergate, Chesterfield, Chesterfield S40 1NG **Tel:** 44 01246 550488
Email: mail@reflections-magazine.com
Web site: http://www.reflections-magazine.com/
Freq: Monthly
Circ: 19000 Not Audited
Editor: Barrie Farnsworth
Profile: Magazine covering local history, current events and features of local interest. Aimed at residents and tourists to North Derbyshire.
Ad Rate: Full Page Colour £625.00
MAGAZINE
Regional General Interest

Reform
982157

Editorial: 86 Tavistock Place, London WC1H 9RT **Tel:** 44 02079 168630
Email: reform@urc.org.uk
Web site: www.reform-magazine.co.uk
Freq: Monthly

Circ: 7000 Not Audited

Profile: Magazine of the United Reformed Church covering religious news, events and views. Aimed at people with an interest in and members of the United Reformed Church.

Ad Rate: Full Page Colour £750.00

MAGAZINE

Religion

Regent Street Online   983849

Editorial: 5 Wootton Street, Waterloo, London SE1 8TG

Email: editor@regentstreetonline.com

Web site: www.regentstreetonline.com

Freq: Daily

Circ: 21403 Cision Digital Reach

MAGAZINE (ONLINE)

Shopping

The Register   981601

Editorial: First Floor, The Lightwell, 12-16 Laystall Street, London EC1R 4PF

Tel: 44 02037 703147

Email: news@theregister.co.uk

Web site: www.theregister.co.uk

Freq: Daily

Circ: 4516598 Cision Digital Reach

Profile: Website covering technology and science news including software, networks, security, business, hardware and Internet of Things.

MAGAZINE (ONLINE)

Auto Aftermarket, Computers, Electronics, Internet

Registered Gas Engineer   985068

Editorial: 30 Park Street, London SE1 9EQ

Tel: 44 02078 423000

Email: editorial@registeredgasengineer.co.uk

Web site: www.registeredgasengineer.co.uk

Freq: Monthly

Circ: 72503 Not Audited

Editor: Nicki Shearer

Profile: Magazine focusing on the in-depth knowledge of gas engineers, the issues that affect them, as well as the latest news and product tests. Aimed at all Gas Safe registered engineers.

Ad Rate: Full Page Colour £4250.00

MAGAZINE

News & Current Affairs

Relaa.com   1061593

Email: info@ulko.fi

Web site: http://relaa.com/

Freq: Weekly

Circ: 36838 Cision Digital Reach

MAGAZINE (ONLINE)

Outdoor Recreation

Reloved   999586

Editorial: P.O. Box 6337, Bournemouth BH1 9EH **Tel:** 44 01202 586848

Email: contact@tailormadepublishing.co.uk

Web site: www.relovedmag.co.uk

Freq: Monthly Not Audited

MAGAZINE

Crafts

Remote Employment   997611

Tel: 44 02081 336375

Web site: www.remoteemployment.com

Freq: Daily

Circ: 6558 Cision Digital Reach

Editor: Paula Wynne

MAGAZINE (ONLINE)

News & Current Affairs

Renewable Energy Technology   985586

Editorial: Cavendish Group Ltd, 5th Floor, Roman Wall House, 1-2 Crutched Friars, London EC3N 2NB **Tel:** 44 02037 944581

Email: info@cavendishgroup.co.uk

Web site: www.renewable-energy-technology.net

Freq: Quarterly

Circ: 10000 Not Audited

Profile: Renewable Energy Technology is a quarterly magazine covering the latest technologies and innovations from the renewable energy industries in Brazil,

Russia, India and China (BRIC). The magazine covers wind and solar energy, marine and bioenergy as well as energy storage.

Ad Rate: Full Page Colour £5650.00

MAGAZINE

Alternative/Renewable Energy, Auto Aftermarket, Computers, Data Management, Electronics, Environment, Government Technology, Industry, Internet, Mobile Communications

Renowned for Sound   996942

Web site: www.renownedforsound.com

Freq: Daily

Circ: 28492 Cision Digital Reach

Editor: Brendon Veevers

MAGAZINE (ONLINE)

Classical/Choral/Band Music, Country, Folk, Bluegrass, Dance Music, Jazz & Blues, Music, Pop Music, R&B, Urban, World, Rap & Hip Hop, Rock Music

Report   981533

Editorial: 7 Northumberland Street, London WC2N 5RD **Tel:** 44 02079 306441

Email: report@atl.org.uk

Web site: www.atl.org.uk/report

Freq: Monthly

Circ: 170000 Not Audited

Profile: Magazine covering key education issues and news which affect teachers, lecturers and educational support staff. Aimed at members of the Association of Teachers and Lecturers.

Ad Rate: Full Page Colour £2730.00

MAGAZINE

Disability, Education, Higher Education, Preschool, Schools & Institutions, Students

Rescue & Animal Care   998121

Tel: 44 01787 228027

Email: rescue@jspmedia.co.uk

Web site: www.rescueapet.co.uk

Freq: Monthly

Circ: 35000 Not Audited

Editor: Jennifer Prowse

MAGAZINE

Nature & Wildlife

The Resident   985863

Editorial: Archant London, Charles House, 108-110 Finchley Road, Hampstead NW3 5JJ **Tel:** 44 02076 052200

Web site: www.theresident.co.uk

Freq: Monthly

Circ: 54000 Not Audited

Profile: Magazine covering all aspects of London life, especially Kensington and Chelsea's premier locations. It incorporates local news and events, profiles, property, high-end luxury travel features, restaurant and food reviews section. Other comprehensive sections include health and beauty, interiors, fashion, shopping and book reviews. Aimed at residents in the Kensington, Chelsea and Central London areas.Geographical Coverage: The Resident is delivered each month to homes in Chelsea, Knightsbridge, Kensington, Notting Hill, Holland Park, South Kensington, Belgravia, Pimlico and Fulham. It is also available at local newsagents. This outlet covers areas within Kensington & Chelsea Borough.

Ad Rate: Full Page Colour £1667.00

MAGAZINE

Regional General Interest

Resolution   984618

Tel: 44 01444 410675

Web site: www.resolutionmag.com

Freq: Bi-Monthly Not Audited

Profile: Magazine focusing on audio production includes information on recording, post production, audio for broadcast, multimedia and mastering.

Ad Rate: Full Page Colour £1997.00

MAGAZINE

News & Current Affairs

Resort - Cornwall   998633

Editorial: St Nicholas House, 3 St Nicholas Street, Weymouth, Weymouth DT4 8AD

Tel: 44 01305 770111

Email: info@resortmarketing.uk

Web site: http://www.resortsouthwest.com/

Freq: Annual

Circ: 150000 Not Audited

MAGAZINE

Travel

Resort - Dorset   996012

Editorial: St Nicholas House, 3 St Nicholas Street, Weymouth, Weymouth DT4 8AD

Tel: 44 01305 770111

Email: info@resortmarketing.uk

Web site: www.resortmarketing.co.uk

Freq: Annual

Circ: 200000 Not Audited

MAGAZINE

Travel

Resort - South Hants & West Sussex   999058

Editorial: St Nicholas House, 3 St Nicholas Street, Weymouth, Weymouth DT4 8AD

Tel: 44 01305 770111

Email: info@resortmarketing.uk

Web site: www.resortmarketing.co.uk

Freq: Annual

Circ: 75000 Not Audited

MAGAZINE

Travel

Resort - Southern Devon   998926

Editorial: St Nicholas House, 3 St Nicholas St, Weymouth, Weymouth DT4 8AD

Tel: 44 01305 770111

Email: info@resortmarketing.uk

Web site: www.resortmarketing.co.uk

Freq: Annual

Circ: 150000 Not Audited

MAGAZINE

Travel

Resources Science   1061621

Tel: 44 86106 4889446

Email: zykx@igsnrr.ac.cn

Web site: http://www.resci.cn

Freq: Monthly

Circ: 1203 Not Audited

MAGAZINE

Alternative/Renewable Energy, Carbon Emissions & Trading, Electricity, Energy, Energy & Environment, Environment, Nuclear Power, Oil, Science, Water & Sanitation

The Restaurant Club   1101288

Editorial: The Studio, 50 Flower Lane, Mill Hill, London NW7 2JL

Web site: https://therestaurantclub.com/

Freq: Daily

Circ: 12685 Cision Digital Reach

MAGAZINE (ONLINE)

Restaurant Reviews, Travel, Wine/ Winemaking

restaurant magazine   980743

Editorial: Broadfield Park, Crawley RH11 9RT **Tel:** 44 01293 613400

Web site: http://www.bighospitality.co.uk/ Info/Restaurant

Freq: Monthly

Circ: 16642 Not Audited

Profile: Magazine covering the restaurant industry including management, supplies, products, service and catering as well as industry news and developments with recruitment advertising. First published in 2001, the publication has an average of 68 pages per issue. Aimed at restaurateurs, food critics, industry employees and consumers.

Ad Rate: Full Page Colour £2495.00

MAGAZINE

Bars, Clubs & Pubs

Resurgence & Ecologist magazine   982127

Editorial: Ford House, Hartland, Bideford, Bideford EX39 6EE **Tel:** 44 01237 441293

Email: info@resurgence.org

Web site: www.resurgence.org

Freq: Bi-Monthly

Circ: 14000 Not Audited

Editor: Greg Neale

MAGAZINE

Energy & Environment, Environment

Retail & Leisure International   983098

Editorial: Suite 15 Hardmans Business Centre, New Hall Hey Road, Rawtenstall, Rossendale BB4 6HH **Tel:** 44 01706 212200

Email: info@rli.uk.com

Web site: www.rli.uk.com

Freq: Monthly

Circ: 20000 Not Audited

Profile: Magazine covering the retail and leisure markets including global news, specialist features, profiles and regular sections on property, legal, design investment and technology. Aimed at key decision makers, each of whom play a key role in the development of the retail and leisure sectors.

Ad Rate: Full Page Colour £2250.00

MAGAZINE

Bars, Clubs & Pubs, Computer & Video Games, Hotels/Motels, Retail, Retail Management, Travel Industry

Retail Gazette   985746

Editorial: 1 Great Cumberland Place, Marble Arch, London W1H 7LW

Tel: 44 02082 220503

Email: editorial@retailgazette.com

Web site: www.retailgazette.co.uk

Freq: Daily

Circ: 94918 Cision Digital Reach

Editor: Elias Jahshan

Profile: Website covering retail news. The Retail Gazette website covers retail sector industries news on employment trends, surveys, property, technology and supply chain.

MAGAZINE (ONLINE)

Books, Cosmetics, Fashion, Hair, Office Supplies, Retail Management, Toys

Retail Jeweller   981297

Editorial: Telephone House, 69-77 Paul Street, London EC2A 4NQ

Tel: 44 02073 914520

Email: retail.jeweller@emap.com

Web site: http://www.retail-jeweller.com/

Freq: Monthly

Circ: 2000 Not Audited

Editor: Ruth Faulkner

Profile: Magazine covering up-to-date business news, trends and new products in the jewellery, watch and objects market.

Ad Rate: Full Page Colour £2500.00

MAGAZINE

Fashion

Retail Week   979790

Editorial: 33 Kingsway, London WC2B 69F

Tel: 44 02077 156566

Web site: www.retail-week.com

Freq: Weekly

Circ: 7785 Not Audited

Profile: Business magazine covering news and information on all aspects of the UK retailing industry. Each issue provides industry news, analysis, key data, and job listings from across the entire retail sector. It also features in-depth interviews and features, columnists and analysis of the issues that matter to retailers. First published in 1988, the publication has an average of 36 pages per issue. Press Day on Wednesday. Aimed at executives of large retail chains.

Ad Rate: Full Page Colour £6224.00

MAGAZINE

Alcohol & Spirits, Books, Consumer Goods & Products, Cosmetics, Fashion, Food, Hair, Retail Management, Tobacco

Retirement Planner   1053818

Editorial: Haymarket House, 32-34 Broadwick Street, London W1A 2HG

Tel: 44 02073 169000

Web site: http://www.retirement-planner.co.uk

Freq: Monthly

Circ: 10855 Not Audited

Profile: Magazine covering retirement planning issues including fund management, tax planning, savings, wealth management

Consumer Magazines

and investment management. Aimed at independent financial advisers.
Ad Rate: Full Page Colour £7054.00
MAGAZINE
Banking, Fund Management

Retirement Today 998694
Editorial: The Old Lavender Mill, 46A Brook Street, Aston Clinton, Aston Clinton HP22 5ES **Tel:** 44 01296 632700
Email: editor@retirement-today.co.uk
Web site: http://www.retirement-today.co.uk
Freq: Bi-Monthly
Circ: 98000 Not Audited
Editor: Sarah James
MAGAZINE
Retirement Savings

retiremove.co.uk 997107
Web site: www.retiremove.co.uk
Freq: Daily
Circ: 11835 Cision Digital Reach
Editor: Jane Slade
MAGAZINE (ONLINE)
Property Management & Maintenance, Retirement Savings

retiresavvy.co.uk 998195
Email: info@retiresavvy.co.uk
Web site: https://retiresavvy.skipton.co.uk/
Freq: Daily
Circ: 34161 Cision Digital Reach
MAGAZINE (ONLINE)
Personal Finance, Retirement Savings

re-title.com 996309
Editorial: BM Box 5163, London WC1N 3XX
Tel: 44 08709 220438
Email: info@re-title.com
Web site: www.re-title.com
Freq: Daily
Circ: 32414 Cision Digital Reach
MAGAZINE (ONLINE)
Antiques/Collectibles, Art, Photography, Theater & Performing Arts, Visual Arts

Retreading Business 988023
Editorial: PO Box 320, Crewe, Cheshire, Crewe CW2 6WY **Tel:** 44 01270 668718
Email: retreadingbusiness@btconnect.com
Web site: www.retreadingbusiness.com
Freq: Quarterly
Circ: 4300 Not Audited
Editor: Ewan Scott
Profile: Magazine covering the tyre retreading industry. Aimed at tyre retreading companies, casing dealers and suppliers of retreading materials and equipment.
MAGAZINE
Automotive

Retro Cars 982617
Editorial: Retro Cars Magazine, Cudham Tithe Barn, Berry's Hill, Cudham TN16 3AG
Tel: 44 01959 541444
Email: retrocars.ed@kelsey.co.uk
Web site: www.retrocarsmag.com
Freq: Monthly
Circ: 30000 Not Audited
Profile: Magazine covering different information about retro cars.
MAGAZINE
Antique & Collectible Cars

Retro Ford 983430
Editorial: 14 Victoria Road, Sutton, Surrey, London SM1 4RT **Tel:** 44 07841 412199
Web site: www.retrofordmagazine.co.uk
Freq: Monthly Not Audited
Editor: Ben Morley
Profile: Magazine covering modified street and track, pre 1980s Ford cars. Aimed at enthusiasts of classic Fords.Regular features: Poduct Tests; Race Cars; Show Reports; Street Cars; Technical Features
Ad Rate: Full Page Colour £950.00
MAGAZINE
Automakers

Retro Gamer 981737
Editorial: Richmond House, 33 Richmond Hill, Bournemouth, Bournemouth BH2 6EZ
Tel: 44 01202 586200
Email: retrogamer@imagine-publishing.co.uk
Web site: www.retrogamer.net
Freq: Monthly
Circ: 96149 Not Audited
Editor: Darran Jones
Profile: Magazine covering classic games, computers and consoles. It features interviews with classic developers, reviews on the latest retro-themed games and an in-depth buyer's guide for those wanting to add to their existing collections.
Ad Rate: Full Page Colour £3200.00
MAGAZINE
Computer & Video Games

Reuters - Panama, Panama City Bureau 1000265
Circ: 43469539 Cision Digital Reach
MAGAZINE (ONLINE)
News & Current Affairs

Reveal 982364
Editorial: 33 Broadwick Street, London W1F 0DQ **Tel:** 44 02074 395000
Web site: http://www.reveal.co.uk
Freq: Weekly
Circ: 100685 Not Audited
Profile: Magazine covering celebrities and gossip, real life stories, fashion and beauty tips, dieting advice, relationship stories as well as puzzles and a TV guide. The publication was first published in 2004. Aimed at women aged between 20 and 40 years old.
Ad Rate: Full Page Colour £15570.00
MAGAZINE
Celebrities, Women's Interests

The Review 1005095
Editorial: 1st Floor, Prudential Buildings, 11-19 Wine Street, Bristol BS1 2PH
Tel: 44 01173 252822
Web site: www.thereviewmag.co.uk
Freq: Quarterly
Circ: 103000 Not Audited
MAGAZINE
Airline Inflight, Alcohol & Spirits, Antique & Collectible Cars, Antiques/Collectibles, Art, Audio Video Trade, Automotive, Bars, Clubs & Pubs, Beauty & Grooming, Beer

Review 31 998202
Email: editor@review31.co.uk
Web site: www.review31.co.uk
Freq: Daily
Circ: 11084 Cision Digital Reach
MAGAZINE (ONLINE)
Literature

Review Graveyard 999298
Editorial: The Granary, Roundhouse, Buckland in the Moor, Newton Abbot TQ13 7HN **Tel:** 44 01364 653445
Web site: www.reviewgraveyard.com
Freq: Daily
Circ: 10624 Cision Digital Reach
Editor: Darren Rea
MAGAZINE (ONLINE)
Broadcasting, Entertainment, Movies & Video, Music

The Reviews Hub 988554
Editorial: 27 Davey Close, Ipswich IP3 0EF
Email: info@thereviewshub.com
Web site: www.thereviewshub.com
Freq: Daily
Circ: 19835 Cision Digital Reach
MAGAZINE (ONLINE)
Art, Classical/Choral/Band Music, Comedy, Country, Folk, Bluegrass, Dance Music, Entertainment, Jazz & Blues, Music, Pop Music, R&B, Urban, World

Revista Asi 1060932
Tel: 44 52662 2165929
Email: portalreviasi@gmail.com
Web site: http://www.revistaasi.com.mx/

Circ: 18000 Not Audited
MAGAZINE
National News, Regional

Revista Panoramas 1060551
Tel: 44 56258 14547
Web site: http://www.revistapanoramas.cl
Circ: 15911 Cision Digital Reach
MAGAZINE (ONLINE)
Airline Inflight, Food, Railroad, Restaurant Reviews, Travel, Wine/Winemaking

REVL 1059125
Email: jenh@revl.world
Web site: www.revl.world
Freq: Daily
Circ: 2796 Cision Digital Reach
MAGAZINE (ONLINE)
Entertainment, Lifestyle, Men's Interests, Regional, Regional General Interest, Women's Interests

Revolution UK 987968
Editorial: 36 Upper Brook Street, London W1K 7QJ **Tel:** 44 02037 528884
Web site: https://www.revolution.watch/magazine/
Freq: Quarterly Not Audited
Profile: Magazine covering watches. It contains watch product reviews, in-depth articles on watch culture, technical features and interviews with industry professionals. First published in 2014.
MAGAZINE
Luxury Goods

RH Uncovered 1075478
Tel: 44 01342 718348
Email: info@mantramagazines.co.uk
Web site: www.rhuncovered.co.uk
Freq: Monthly
Circ: 28000 Not Audited
MAGAZINE
Regional General Interest

Rhythm 982100
Editorial: Quay House, The Ambury, Bath BA1 1UA **Tel:** 44 01225 442244
Email: rhythm@futurenet.com
Web site: http://www.musicradar.com/rhythm
Freq: Monthly
Circ: 7295 Not Audited
Editor: Chris Burke
Profile: Drum and percussion magazine containing comprehensive features, technique articles, gear reviews and interviews with famous and up and coming drummers. Comes complete with tuitional Rhythm CD.
Ad Rate: Full Page Colour £1235.00
MAGAZINE
Music

Rhythm Passport 996041
Email: press-release@rhythmpassport.com
Web site: www.rhythmpassport.com
Freq: Daily
Circ: 12423 Cision Digital Reach
Editor: Kia Coates
MAGAZINE (ONLINE)
R&B, Urban, World

Ri5 985979
Editorial: Melbury House, Southborough Road, Bickley, London BR1 2EB
Tel: 44 02032 371044
Email: editorial@ri5.co.uk
Web site: www.ri5.co.uk
Freq: Daily
Circ: 14698 Cision Digital Reach
MAGAZINE (ONLINE)
Advertising Industry, Careers, Marketing, Recruiting

The Richmond Magazine (UK) 982534
Editorial: Unit 4A, Kingsway Business Park, Oldfield Road, Hampton, London TW12 2HD
Tel: 44 02089 395601
Web site: www.richmondmagazine.co.uk
Freq: Monthly
Circ: 37000 Not Audited

Editor: Fiona Adams
MAGAZINE
Property Management & Maintenance, Regional General Interest

Riddle 997769
Email: contact@riddlemagazine.com
Web site: http://riddlemagazine.com/
Freq: Daily Not Audited
MAGAZINE
Luxury Goods

RiDE 982656
Editorial: Media House, Lynchwood, Peterborough Business Park, Peterborough PE2 6EA **Tel:** 44 01733 468000
Email: ride@ride.co.uk
Web site: www.ride.co.uk
Freq: Monthly
Circ: 33685 Not Audited
Editor: Colin Overland
Profile: Magazine with features on new and used motorcycles and product tests. Provides information on how to get the best value out of a motorcycle.
Ad Rate: Full Page Colour £3024.00
MAGAZINE
Motorcycles

RIDE Cycling Review 998060
Editorial: Pro Sport Publishing Limited, Eight Bells House, 14 Church Street, Tetbury, Tetbury GL8 8JG **Tel:** 44 01666 500089
Email: info@ridemag.co.uk
Web site: www.ridecyclingreview.co.uk
Freq: Daily
Circ: 521 Cision Digital Reach
MAGAZINE (ONLINE)
Bicycles

RideLondon 995313
Tel: 44 02079 020212
Email: helpdesk@ridelondon.co.uk
Web site: www.prudentialridelondon.co.uk
Freq: Daily
Circ: 54650 Cision Digital Reach
MAGAZINE (ONLINE)
Bicycles

RIDER 1059462
Tel: 44 02476 840518
Email: rachael.hollely@bhs.org.uk
Web site: www.bhs.org.uk
Freq: Quarterly
Circ: 30926 Not Audited
Editor: Rachael Hollely
MAGAZINE
Equestrian Sports

The Rider's Digest 982659
Editorial: PO Box 240, Huddersfield HD9 9DQ **Tel:** 44 02087 070655
Email: editor@theridersdigest.co.uk
Web site: www.theridersdigest.co.uk
Freq: Bi-Monthly
Circ: 5006 Cision Digital Reach
Editor: Dave Gurman
Profile: Magazine containing motorcycle news and transport, technical vehicle information and general motorcycling writing.
Ad Rate: Full Page Colour £400.00
MAGAZINE (ONLINE)
Motorcycles

Riders.dk 1061816
Tel: 44 45331 36300
Email: info@riders.dk
Web site: http://www.riders.dk
Freq: Daily
Circ: 12695 Cision Digital Reach
MAGAZINE (ONLINE)
Basketball, Bicycles, Billiards, Boating & Yachting, Bodybuilding, Bowling, Boxing, Cricket, Equestrian Sports, Extreme/Adventure Sports

Ridgeway Rider 995086
Editorial: Unit 2 Devizes Trade Centre, Hopton Park, Devizes, Devizes SN10 2EH
Tel: 44 01380 730888
Email: sales@redpin.co.uk
Web site: http://www.ridgewayrider.co.uk

Freq: Monthly
Profile: Magazine covering all-round equestrian interests and disciplines, feature articles, product reviews and events.
MAGAZINE
Equestrian Sports

Rifle Shooter
1054531
Tel: 44 01189 742508
Email: editor@sportingshooter.co.uk
Web site: http://www.sportingshooter.co.uk/rifle-shooter
Freq: Monthly Not Audited
MAGAZINE
Shooting/Guns

Right Start
982414
Editorial: PO Box 481, Fleet, Fleet GU51 9FA
Email: info@rightstartmagazine.co.uk
Web site: www.rightstartmagazine.co.uk
Freq: Bi-Monthly
Circ: 52000 Not Audited
Editor: Lynette Lowthian
Profile: Magazine covering advice on health, behaviour, child development and learning at home and school. The guide to parenting, children's education, family matters, food concerns, child health issues, play and activity ideas. Aimed at parents with children aged 6 months to 7 years.Regular features: Child Behaviour Feature looking at some aspect of child behaviour.; Education Feature looking at education issues for pre-school children through to children at key stage 1 (year 2).; Fashion Feature looking at the latest trends for children.; Giveaways; Health Feature looking at topical health issues for children.; Healthy Eating Current information about healthy eating for children.; Letters; News The latest news relevant to parent's and children.; Travel Feature looking at family holiday destinations.
MAGAZINE
Family & Parenting

Rightboat.com
990688
Tel: 44 03333 222628
Email: info@rightboat.com
Web site: www.rightboat.com
Freq: Daily
Circ: 9238 Cision Digital Reach
MAGAZINE (ONLINE)
Boating & Yachting

The River
998996
Editorial: Kingston University, Penrhyn Road, Kingston upon Thames, London KT1 2EE
Email: editors.river@gmail.com
Web site: www.riveronline.co.uk
Freq: Bi-Weekly Not Audited
MAGAZINE
Student Lifestyle

The River (Lambeth & Southwark)
1094737
Editorial: 14, The Maples, Banstead, London SM7 3QZ **Tel:** 44 08000 211484
Email: info@therivermagazine.co.uk
Web site: www.therivermagazine.co.uk
Freq: Quarterly
Circ: 10000 Not Audited
Editor: Angela Webb
MAGAZINE
Alcohol & Spirits, Art, Bars, Clubs & Pubs, Beer, Beverages, Cooking & Baking, Fashion, Literature, Local Entertainment Guides, Photography

River Thames News
986038
Tel: 44 07976 792130
Email: editor@riverthamesnews.com
Web site: www.riverthamesnews.com
Freq: Daily
Circ: 9166 Cision Digital Reach
Editor: Paul Erlam
MAGAZINE (ONLINE)
Boating & Yachting, Outdoor Recreation, Travel

The Riverside Journals
997874
Editorial: Palladia, St. Mary's Court, Amersham, Amersham HP7 0UT
Tel: 44 01494 784920
Email: editorial@redbrookmedia.com
Web site: http://theriversidejournals.com/
Freq: Bi-Monthly
Circ: 4000 Not Audited
MAGAZINE
Art, Entertainment, Lifestyle, Local Entertainment Guides, Luxury Goods, Men's Interests, Regional General Interest, Restaurant Reviews, Theater & Performing Arts, Women's Interests

RMI Gazette
1060716
Email: gazette@ntamar.net
Freq: Monthly
Circ: 1000 Not Audited
MAGAZINE
Government, International News, Politics, Regional

RMT News
984247
Editorial: Unity House, 39 Chalton Street, London NW1 1JD **Tel:** 44 02073 874771
Email: info@rmt.org.uk
Web site: www.rmt.org.uk
Freq: Monthly Not Audited
Profile: Official journal of The National Union of Rail, Maritime and Transport Workers. Covers news, events and information on members. RMT's 64,000 members work in railways, London Underground and marine transport. The magazine provides important information about the workplace and their changing industry. Read by members of the shipping section of the RMT and London Underground workers.
Ad Rate: Full Page Colour £2100.00
MAGAZINE
Automotive, Aviation, Railroad, Shipping & Warehousing, Supply Chain Management (SCM), Transportation

Road
985099
Tel: 44 07946 610193
Web site: www.roadmagazine.co.uk
Freq: Monthly
Circ: 9121 Cision Digital Reach
MAGAZINE (ONLINE)
Antique & Collectible Cars, Automakers, Automotive, Driving, Motorcycles, Off-road & 4-Wheel Drive Vehicles, Trucks & SUVs

The Road
997460
Editorial: Central Office, P.O. Box 750, Warwick CV34 9FU **Tel:** 44 01926 844064
Email: theroad@mag-uk.org
Web site: www.mag-uk.org/en/index/a6296
Freq: Bi-Monthly Not Audited
Editor: Ian Mutch
MAGAZINE
Motorcycles

Road CC
997635
Editorial: Unit 7b, Green Park Station, Bath BA1 1JB **Tel:** 44 01225 588855
Email: info@road.cc
Web site: www.road.cc
Freq: Daily
Circ: 879581 Cision Digital Reach
Editor: Tony Farrelly
MAGAZINE (ONLINE)
Bicycles

Road Smart
985552
Editorial: 8th Floor, Capital House, 25 Chapel Street, London NW1 5DH
Tel: 44 02037 717200
Email: advanceddriving@iam.org.uk
Web site: https://www.iamroadsmart.com/
Freq: 3 Times/Year
Circ: 100000 Not Audited
Profile: Magazine covering driving, traffic and road safety news, plus reports on new cars and foreign touring. Read by members of the Institute of Advanced Motorists.
Ad Rate: Full Page Colour £1991.00
MAGAZINE
Driving

Road To Rio 2016
1060434
Tel: 44 27214 160141
Email: gary@hsm.co.za
Freq: Quarterly
Circ: 16653 Not Audited
MAGAZINE
Basketball, Bicycles, Billiards, Boating & Yachting, Bodybuilding, Bowling, Boxing, Cricket, Equestrian Sports, Extreme/Adventure Sports

RoadTestReports.co.uk
986379
Editorial: Domain House, 4 Watchgate, Newby Road, Hazel Grove, Stockport SK7 5DB **Tel:** 44 01614 827650
Email: info@reallygooddomains.com
Web site: www.roadtestreports.co.uk
Freq: Daily
Circ: 69346 Cision Digital Reach
MAGAZINE (ONLINE)
Automotive

roadtraffic-technology.com
984953
Editorial: John Carpenter House, John Carpenter Street, London EC4Y 0AN
Tel: 44 02079 366400
Email: onlineeditorial@kable.co.uk
Web site: http://www.roadtraffic-technology.com
Freq: Daily
Circ: 34535 Cision Digital Reach
Profile: Website covering global road traffic industry. The roadtraffictechnology.com website shares the latest news on the global road traffic industry.
MAGAZINE (ONLINE)
Automotive

Roadway
984096
Editorial: The Old Forge, South Road, Weybridge KT13 9DZ **Tel:** 44 01932 838919
Email: roadway@rha.uk.net
Web site: https://www.rha.uk.net/membership/member-benefits/roadway-magazine
Freq: Monthly
Circ: 7000 Not Audited
Profile: Trade magazine published by the Road Haulage Association. Covers industry's news, views and developments. Incorporates fastFORWARD section of the former magazine for training and careers in the logistics and road transport industry.
Ad Rate: Full Page Mono £1346.00
Ad Rate: Full Page Colour £2007.00
MAGAZINE
Automotive

Roary the Racing Car
987171
Editorial: Unit 16 Greenway Farm, Bath Road, Wick, Bristol BS30 5RL
Tel: 44 01179 373003
Email: info@kennedypublishing.co.uk
Web site: www.kennedymagazines.co.uk/?gallery=roary-the-racing-car-2
Freq: Bi-Monthly
Circ: 27000 Not Audited
MAGAZINE
Teen/Young Adult

Robert Gordon University Student Guide
998441
Editorial: RGU Students' Union, University Street, RGU Garthdee Campus, Garthdee Road, Aberdeen AB10 7GE
Tel: 44 01224 262266
Email: hello@rguunion.co.uk
Web site: www.rguunion.co.uk/about/guide/
Freq: Annual Not Audited
MAGAZINE
Student Lifestyle

Robin's Reviews
996361
Editorial: 24 All Saints Crescent, Farnborough, Farnborough GU14 9DE
Web site: www.robinsreviews.info
Freq: Daily
Circ: 521 Cision Digital Reach
Editor: Robin Vyrnwy-Pierce
MAGAZINE (ONLINE)
Literature

Robinsons Mercedes-Benz Magazine
997910
Editorial: Goodwin Business Park, Willie Snaith Road, Newmarket CB8 7SQ
Tel: 44 01638 666432
Email: info@cubiqdesign.co.uk
Web site: http://www.cubiqdesign.co.uk/
Freq: Semi-Annual Not Audited
MAGAZINE
Automakers

Rochdale Online
984920
Editorial: 122 Yorkshire Street, Rochdale OL16 1LA **Tel:** 44 01706 523583
Email: news@rochdaleonline.co.uk
Web site: www.rochdaleonline.co.uk
Freq: Daily
Circ: 134784 Cision Digital Reach
MAGAZINE (ONLINE)
Regional

Rock is a Hard Place
996116
Email: editor@rockisahardplace.com
Web site: www.rockisahardplace.com
Freq: Daily
Circ: 521 Cision Digital Reach
Editor: Scout Beck
MAGAZINE (ONLINE)
Country, Folk, Bluegrass, Rock Music

Rock n Roll Bride Magazine
987274
Email: magazine@rocknrollbride.com
Web site: http://www.rocknrollbride.com
Freq: Bi-Monthly
Circ: 10000 Not Audited
MAGAZINE
Fashion, Weddings

Rock Sound
982111
Editorial: Unit 2.38 Whitechapel Technology Centre, 75 Whitechapel Road, London E1 1DU **Tel:** 44 02078 778770
Email: rsvp@rocksound.tv
Web site: www.rocksound.tv
Freq: Monthly
Circ: 14057 Not Audited
Editor: David McLaughlin
Profile: Magazine concentrating on rock, metal, indie and alternative music. Includes the latest news and features, album, single, live reviews and fashion related items.
Ad Rate: Full Page Colour £1815.00
MAGAZINE
Rock Music

Rock-A-Rolla
984795
Editorial: PO Box 60318, London WC1X 9WL
Email: info@rock-a-rolla.com
Web site: www.rock-a-rolla.com
Freq: Bi-Monthly Not Audited
MAGAZINE
Rock Music

rockfeedback
1057079
Email: info@rockfeedback.com
Web site: http://www.rockfeedback.com/magazine
Freq: Daily
Circ: 23 Cision Digital Reach
MAGAZINE (ONLINE)
News & Current Affairs

Rock's Backpages
999278
Editorial: 94-95 South Worple Way, London SW14 8ND **Tel:** 44 02079 980695
Email: info@rocksbackpages.com
Web site: www.rocksbackpages.com
Freq: Daily
Circ: 52847 Cision Digital Reach
MAGAZINE (ONLINE)
Classical/Choral/Band Music, Country, Folk, Bluegrass, Dance Music, Jazz & Blues, Music, Pop Music, R&B, Urban, World, Rap & Hip Hop, Rock Music

Rockshot
996948
Web site: www.rockshot.co.uk
Freq: Daily

Consumer Magazines

Circ: 16643 Cision Digital Reach
MAGAZINE (ONLINE)
Rock Music

rocksins.com 995858
Editorial: 46 Northside, The Cardinals,
Tongham, Farnham GU10 1ED
Web site: www.rocksins.com
Freq: Daily
Circ: 12485 Cision Digital Reach
Editor: Neil Skoglund
MAGAZINE (ONLINE)
Rock Music

Roco Magazine 988702
Email: info@rocomag.com
Web site: http://www.rocomag.com/
Freq: Daily
Circ: 7003 Cision Digital Reach
MAGAZINE (ONLINE)
Do-It-Yourself (DIY)

Rollacoaster 985701
Editorial: 133 Notting Hill Gate, London W11
3LB Tel: 44 02072 439966
Email: info@rollacoaster.tv
Web site: www.rollacoaster.tv
Freq: Semi-Annual
Circ: 25000 Not Audited
Profile: Magazine covering music, fashion
and culture.
MAGAZINE
Fashion, Men's Interests, Women's
Interests

RollonFriday.com 983064
Editorial: Hamilton House, 1 Temple
Avenue, London EC4Y 0HA
Web site: www.rollonfriday.com
Freq: Daily
Circ: 46217 Cision Digital Reach
MAGAZINE (ONLINE)
News & Current Affairs

Ronda 998462
Editorial: 6th floor, 85 Strand, London
WC2R 0DW Tel: 44 02075 508000
Freq: Monthly
Circ: 35000 Not Audited
MAGAZINE
Airline Inflight

Room Thirteen 984601
Email: editorial@roomthirteen.com
Web site: www.roomthirteen.com
Freq: Daily
Circ: 11562 Cision Digital Reach
MAGAZINE (ONLINE)
Rock Music

The Rose 981968
Editorial: Articulate Studio, First Floor, 12A,
Emsworth, Emsworth PO10 7DQ
Tel: 44 08458 334344
Email: mail@rnrs.org.uk
Web site: www.rnrs.org.uk
Freq: 3 Times/Year
Circ: 3000 Not Audited
Profile: Publication featuring general interest
articles on roses, plus show reports, book
reviews and competitions.
MAGAZINE
Gardening

Rotary 984398
Editorial: RIBI, Kinwarton Road, Alcester,
Alcester B49 6PB Tel: 44 01789 765411
Email: editor@ribi.org
Web site: www.ribi.org
Freq: Bi-Monthly
Circ: 60000 Not Audited
MAGAZINE
Charitable Foundations

Rough Guides 985754
Editorial: 80 Strand, London WC2R 0RL
Email: mail@roughguides.com
Web site: www.roughguides.com
Freq: Daily
Circ: 902855 Cision Digital Reach
MAGAZINE (ONLINE)
Travel

Rough Trade 1069279
Editorial: Old Truman Brewery, 91 Brick
Lane, London E1 6QL
Email: press@roughtrade.com
Web site: http://www.roughtrade.com/
Freq: Monthly
MAGAZINE
Country, Folk, Bluegrass, Dance Music,
Jazz & Blues, Music, Pop Music, R&B,
Urban, World, Rap & Hip Hop, Rock Music

Rouleur 986319
Editorial: Stage House, 47 Bermondsey
Street, London SE1 3XF
Tel: 44 02071 993817
Email: editorial@rouleur.cc
Web site: www.rouleur.cc
Freq: Bi-Monthly
Circ: 16000 Not Audited
MAGAZINE
Bicycles

Round & About 982521
Editorial: Windrush Innovation Centre,
Howbery Park, Crowmarsh Gifford,
Wallingford, Wallingford OX10 8BA
Tel: 44 01491 837621
Email: editor@roundandabout.co.uk
Web site: www.roundandabout.co.uk
Freq: Monthly
Circ: 452000 Not Audited
Editor: Richard Tilley
MAGAZINE
Regional General Interest

RoundReviews 995501
Email: admin@roundreviews.co.uk
Web site: www.roundreviews.co.uk
Freq: Daily
Circ: 11909 Cision Digital Reach
MAGAZINE (ONLINE)
Audio Video Trade, Cameras, Computers,
Consumer Electronics, Data
Management, Electronics, Industry,
Internet, Mobile Communications, Mobile
Electronics

routeONE 983432
Editorial: Unit 4, Minerva Business Park,
Lynch Wood, Peterborough PE2 6FT
Tel: 44 01733 405747
Email: editorial@route-one.net
Web site: http://www.route-one.net/
Freq: Weekly
Circ: 5114 Not Audited
Editor: Jessamy Chapman; Editor: Mel
Holley
MAGAZINE
Automotive

Rowing & Regatta 982302
Editorial: 6 Lower Mall, London W6 9DJ
Tel: 44 02082 376701
Email: magazine@britishrowing.org
Web site: www.britishrowing.org
Freq: Bi-Monthly
Circ: 26902 Not Audited
Editor: Wendy Kewley
Profile: Magazine covering news and
reviews about rowing in the UK and around
the world. Read by members and those with
an interest in rowing.Previous title: Regatta
Ad Rate: Full Page Colour £1550.00
MAGAZINE
Rowing

The Royal Coast Resident
987609
Editorial: Prospect House, Routen Road,
Norwich NR1 1RE Tel: 44 01603 772380
Web site: www.royalresident.co.uk
Freq: Quarterly
Circ: 8500 Not Audited
MAGAZINE
Fashion, Royalty

Royal Life 987658
Editorial: Prestige House, Valleybridge
Road, Clacton On Sea, Clacton-on-Sea
CO15 4AD Tel: 44 08449 971680
Email: info@legacymagazines.co.uk
Web site: royalbritainmagazine.co.uk
Freq: Bi-Monthly

Circ: 19880 Not Audited
MAGAZINE
Royalty

**The Royal London Financial
Planner** 996476
Editorial: 7th Floor, Reading Bridge House,
Kings Meadow Road, Reading, Reading
RG1 8LS
Web site: www.royallondon.com
Freq: Daily
Circ: 140032 Cision Digital Reach
MAGAZINE (ONLINE)
Personal Finance

Royal Wings 985511
Editorial: The Pumphouse, 13-16 Jacobs
Well Mews, London W1U 3DY
Tel: 44 02079 062001
Web site: http://www.rj.com/en/magazines/
royal_wings/_/473
Freq: Bi-Monthly
Circ: 30000 Not Audited
Profile: Royal Jordanian In-flight magazine
covering travel news, lifestyle and
entertainment features. Includes topical
international features, articles on Jordan's
sites and culture, people profiles, and a
guide to the airline's routes and facilities.
Aimed at passengers travelling with Royal
Jordanian Airlines.
Ad Rate: Full Page Colour £3050.00
MAGAZINE
Airline Inflight

RSA Journal 983061
Editorial: 5th Floor, Drury House, 34-43
Russell Street, London WC2B 5HA
Tel: 44 02070 100999
Email: editor@rsa.org.uk
Web site: www.theRSA.org
Freq: Quarterly
Circ: 27000 Not Audited
Profile: Magazine of the Royal Society for
the encouragement of Arts, Manufactures
and Commerce. Covers RSA project work
and lectures in the fields of art, design,
education, environment, manufactures and
commerce.
MAGAZINE
Art, Visual Arts

Rude Health 1054201
Tel: 44 01223 894200
Email: info@rudehealthmagazine.ie
Web site: www.rudehealthmagazine.ie
Freq: Bi-Monthly
Circ: 25000 Not Audited
Editor: Lucy Taylor
MAGAZINE
Health & Medicine, Nutrition

Rugby League World 982274
Editorial: Wellington House, Briggate,
Brighouse, Brighouse HD6 1DN
Tel: 44 01484 401895
Email: news@totalrl.com
Web site: www.totalrl.com
Freq: Monthly
Circ: 11000 Not Audited
Profile: Magazine providing worldwide
coverage of the rugby game and rugby
league with a particular emphasis on the
game in Great Britain.
Ad Rate: Full Page Colour £1800.00
MAGAZINE
Rugby

The Rugby Paper 986808
Editorial: Lower Ground Floor, Tuition
House, 27-37 St Georges Road, London
SW19 4EU Tel: 44 02089 714333
Email: newsdesk@therugbypaper.co.uk
Web site: www.therugbypaper.co.uk
Freq: Weekly
Circ: 17000 Not Audited
Profile: Newspaper covering rugby match
reports, round-ups and news from England,
Scotland, Ireland and Wales.
Ad Rate: Full Page Colour £1596.00
MAGAZINE
Rugby

Rugby Unplugged 996197
Editorial: The Loft, 72 Gordon Ave, St
Margarets, Twickenham TW1 1NQ
Email: info@rugbyunplugged.com
Web site: www.rugbyunplugged.com/
Freq: Daily
Circ: 9140 Cision Digital Reach
MAGAZINE (ONLINE)
Rugby

Rugby World 982276
Editorial: 7th Floor, Blue Fin Building, 110
Southwark Street, London SE1 0SU
Tel: 44 01252 555000
Email: rugbyworldletters@timeinc.com
Web site: www.rugbyworld.com
Freq: Monthly
Circ: 22780 Not Audited
Editor: Owain Jones
Profile: Magazine offering a comprehensive
round-up of rugby action, results and
fixtures.
Ad Rate: Full Page Colour £2995.00
MAGAZINE
Rugby

Run - Riot 984986
Editorial: Platform 1, Village Underground,
54 Holywell Lane, London EC2A 3PQ
Email: editor@run-riot.com
Web site: http://www.run-riot.com/
Freq: Daily
Circ: 13345 Cision Digital Reach
MAGAZINE (ONLINE)
Local Entertainment Guides

Run247.com 987783
Editorial: 23 Manor Road North, Hinchley
Wood, Esher, London KT10 0AA
Web site: www.run247.com/
Freq: Daily
Circ: 12582 Cision Digital Reach
Editor: Britta Sendlhofer
MAGAZINE (ONLINE)
Sports

runABC Midlands 998052
Editorial: Suite 5a, 23 Eagle Street, Craighall
Business Park, Glasgow G4 9XA
Tel: 44 01413 328643
Email: freetime@tfti.demon.co.uk
Web site: www.midlandsrunningguide.com
Freq: Quarterly
Circ: 35000 Not Audited
MAGAZINE
Fitness & Exercise, Sports

runABC North 999087
Editorial: Suite 5a, 23 Eagle Street, Craighall
Business Park, Glasgow G4 9XA
Tel: 44 01413 328643
Email: freetime@tfti.demon.co.uk
Web site: www.northernrunningguide.com
Freq: Quarterly
Circ: 35000 Not Audited
MAGAZINE
Fitness & Exercise, Sports

runABC Scotland 1101762
Editorial: Suite 5a 23, Eagle Street, Craighall
Business Park, Glasgow G4 9XA
Tel: 44 01413 328643
Email: freetime@tfti.demon.co.uk
Web site: www.scottishrunningguide.com
Freq: Quarterly
Circ: 35000 Not Audited
MAGAZINE
Fitness & Exercise, Sports

runABC South 1101748
Editorial: 5 Craighall House, 58a High
Craighall Road, Glasgow G4 9UD
Tel: 44 01413 328643
Email: freetime@tfti.demon.co.uk
Web site: www.southernrunningguide.com
Freq: Quarterly
Circ: 35000 Not Audited
MAGAZINE
Fitness & Exercise, Sports

Runner's World (UK)
982190

Editorial: Runner's World, 33 Broadwick Street, London W1F 0DQ
Tel: 44 02074 395000
Email: editor@runnersworld.co.uk
Web site: www.runnersworld.co.uk
Freq: Monthly
Circ: 78496 Not Audited
Editor: Andy Dixon
MAGAZINE
Sports

Running
982191

Editorial: Cudham Tithe Barn, Berry's Hill, Cudham, Peterborough TN16 3AG
Tel: 44 01959 541444
Email: rf.ed@kelsey.co.uk
Web site: http://www.runnersradar.com/
Freq: Monthly
Circ: 21000 Not Audited
MAGAZINE
Sports

Running in Heels
985028

Editorial: 33 Clements Road, Bermondsey, London SE16 4DW
Email: editor@runninginheels.co.uk
Web site: runninginheels.com
Freq: Daily
Circ: 14107 Cision Digital Reach
Profile: Website covering women's interest. The Running In Heels website shares the latest news and reviews on like fashion, shoes, politics, culture, travel and beauty.
MAGAZINE (ONLINE)
Fashion, Women's Interests

The Rural Voice
1054178

Editorial: Bourne House, Ashford TN26 3SZ
Email: editor@theruralvoice.uk
Web site: http://theruralvoice.uk/
Freq: Daily
MAGAZINE (ONLINE)
Energy & Environment, Regional, Regional General Interest

Russian Gap
1103797

Email: katia@russiangap.com
Web site: http://www.russiangap.com/
Freq: Quarterly
Circ: 7000 Not Audited
MAGAZINE
Art, Bars, Clubs & Pubs, Business, Movies & Video, Personal Finance, Small and Medium Business, Theater & Performing Arts

RussianUK
986567

Editorial: Pushkin House, 5A Bloomsbury Square, London WC1A 2TA
Tel: 44 02084 456465
Email: lc@russianuk.com
Web site: www.russianuk.com
Freq: Quarterly
Circ: 12000 Not Audited
Editor: Larisa Grodskaya
Profile: Lifestyle glossy A4 magazine devoted entirely to the life of the Russian community in the UK. Covers property, fashion, interior design, shopping, travel, leisure, eating out, health and beauty, investment opportunities.
Ad Rate: Full Page Colour £1900.00
MAGAZINE
Expatriates

The Rusty Wire Service
999066

Email: o_loonasa@hotmail.com
Web site: www.therustywireservice.blogspot.com
Freq: Daily
Circ: 1347 Cision Digital Reach
MAGAZINE (ONLINE)
Basketball, Bicycles, Billiards, Boating & Yachting, Bodybuilding, Bowling, Boxing, Cricket, Equestrian Sports, Extreme/Adventure Sports

RWD
982115

Editorial: 4th Floor, 60-62 Commercial Street, London E1 6LT **Tel:** 44 02031 764299
Web site: www.rwdmag.com
Freq: Quarterly

Circ: 98806 Not Audited
Editor: Tego Sigel
Profile: Magazine covering urban music including UK garage, hip hop, R&B, drum n bass and US house as well as fashion, artist interviews, reviews of new artists and competitions. Covers latest in gadgets, games and phone technology, funny editorial blends news, style and sport with columns, film, TV, reviews and current affairs.
Ad Rate: Full Page Colour £2650.00
MAGAZINE
Men's Interests, Rap & Hip Hop, Teen/Young Adult

RYA Magazine
982212

Editorial: RYA House, Ensign Way, Hamble, Southampton SO31 4YA
Tel: 44 02380 604100
Email: pressoffice@rya.org.uk
Web site: www.rya.org.uk
Freq: Quarterly
Circ: 89796 Not Audited
Editor: Deborah Cornick
Profile: Magazine of the Royal Yachting Association. Includes news, government regulations affecting boaters, plus cruising, training and racing articles. Read by RYA members, clubs and boat owners. Regular features: Book Reviews Featuring reviews of publications covering yachting.; Competitions; Members' Letters Featuring letters from RYA members.; RYA News Featuring news from the cruising, racing and training areas of the Royal Yachting Association.
MAGAZINE
Boating & Yachting

Rye News
997702

Email: info@ryenews.org.uk
Web site: www.ryenews.org.uk
Freq: Daily
Circ: 9396 Cision Digital Reach
MAGAZINE (ONLINE)
Regional, Regional General Interest

S&PA Professional
987113

Editorial: 17-18 Britton Street, London EC1M 5TP **Tel:** 44 02078 806200
Email: sandpa@redactive.co.uk
Web site: www.cimspa.co.uk/en/information/spaprofessional-magazine/
Freq: Quarterly Not Audited
MAGAZINE
Fitness & Exercise

SA Music
1060704

Email: editor@samusic.co.za
Web site: http://www.samusic.co.za
Circ: 5592 Cision Digital Reach
MAGAZINE (ONLINE)
Celebrities, Classical/Choral/Band Music, Country, Folk, Bluegrass, Dance Music, Jazz & Blues, Music, Pop Music, R&B, Urban, World, Rap & Hip Hop, Rock Music

SA Typographical Jnl
1060696

Tel: 44 27114 763702
Email: mediacomedit3@interkom.co.za
Freq: Monthly
Circ: 8000 Not Audited
MAGAZINE
Business, Defense & National Security, Engineering, Graphic Design, Industry, Manufacturing, Marine & Boat Trade, Mining & Quarrying, Paper, Plastics

Saab Driver
982644

Editorial: Festoon Rooms, Sunny Bank Mills, Farsley, Leeds, Pudsey LS28 5UJ
Tel: 44 01132 577180
Email: editor@saabclub.co.uk
Web site: www.saabclub.co.uk
Freq: Bi-Monthly
Circ: 2700 Not Audited
Editor: Os Reid
Profile: Official magazine of the Saab Owners Club of Great Britain. Contains news, views, technical information and letters.
Ad Rate: Full Page Mono £415.00
Ad Rate: Full Page Colour £528.00
MAGAZINE
Automakers

SABLE LitMag
1103794

Email: info@sablelitmag.org
Web site: www.sablelitmag.org
Freq: 3 Times/Year
MAGAZINE
Visual Arts

Sabotage Times
985646

Email: sabotage@sabotagetimes.com
Web site: www.sabotagetimes.com
Freq: Daily
Circ: 164238 Cision Digital Reach
Editor: Tom Armstrong
Profile: Website covering general lifestyle news. The Sabotage Times website discusses anything from football, fashion and sport to opinion, relationships, drink and film.
MAGAZINE (ONLINE)
Men's Interests, Movies & Video, Travel, Women's Interests

SABRININA KOUZLA
1060214

Freq: Bi-Weekly Not Audited
MAGAZINE
Elementary School, Lifestyle, Men's Interests, Preschool, Regional General Interest, Teen/Young Adult, Trading Cards & Comics, Women's Interests

Safety Fast!
983308

Editorial: PO Box 251, Kimber House, Abingdon OX14 1FF **Tel:** 44 01235 555552
Email: mgcc@mgcc.co.uk
Web site: www.mgcc.co.uk
Freq: Monthly
Circ: 11500 Not Audited
Editor: Andy Knott
Profile: Magazine covering all aspects of MG cars.
MAGAZINE
Automakers

Saffron
1097888

Tel: 44 97147 025341122
Email: info@saffronme.com
Web site: http://www.saffroninsider.com/
Freq: Bi-Weekly
MAGAZINE
Art, Bars, Clubs & Pubs, Celebrities, Comedy, Entertainment, Lifestyle, Literature, Local Entertainment Guides, Men's Interests, Movies & Video

Saga Magazine
981972

Editorial: The Saga Pavilion, Enbrook Park, Folkestone, Folkestone CT20 3SE
Tel: 44 01303 771523
Email: editor@saga.co.uk
Web site: http://www.saga.co.uk/magazine
Freq: Monthly
Circ: 286525 Not Audited
Editor: Katy Bravery
Profile: Magazine covering mature lifestyle. It contains a range of general interest articles, including home, health, gardening, hobbies, money, technology, culture and celebrity. The magazine includes profiles of different countries with popular destinations for holidays, the latest on the changing property market and a section on all things relevant to the home including interiors, recipe ideas, wine reviews and cookery tips. It also features an entertainment section with arts, music, film and books. First published in 1984. Aimed at those over 50 years old.
Ad Rate: Full Page Colour £11950.00
MAGAZINE
Men's Interests, Retirement Savings, Women's Interests

Sail Racing Magazine
990576

Web site: http://www.sailracingmagazine.com/
Freq: Monthly
Circ: 433 Cision Digital Reach
Editor: Justin Chisholm
MAGAZINE (ONLINE)
Boating & Yachting

Sailing Today
982213

Editorial: Jubilee House, 2 Jubilee Place, London SW3 3TQ **Tel:** 44 02073 493752
Email: editor@sailingtoday.co.uk

Web site: www.sailingtoday.co.uk
Freq: Monthly
Circ: 21500 Not Audited
Profile: Magazine covering boating and sailing including features on new and used boat testing, equipment tests, sailing skills, boat improvements and chartering. First published in 1997, the publication has an average of 186 pages per issue. Aimed at sailing enthusiasts interested in the boating industry.
Ad Rate: Full Page Colour £2433.00
MAGAZINE
Boating & Yachting

Sainsbury's magazine
981811

Editorial: 3-7 Herbal Hill, London EC1R 5EJ
Tel: 44 02077 757775
Email: editor@seven.co.uk
Web site: www.sainsburysmagazine.co.uk
Freq: Monthly
Circ: 166158 Not Audited
Profile: Magazine covering food. Each issue contains recipes, wine, cooking, baking and chef profiles as well as health, beauty, home, gardens, travel and celebrity interviews. Aimed at customers of Sainsbury's supermarkets.
Ad Rate: Full Page Colour £13835.00
MAGAZINE
Grocery Stores, Nutrition

The Saint
999096

Editorial: St Andrews Students' Association, St Mary's Place, St Andrews, St. Andrews KY16 9UZ
Email: news@thesaint-online.com
Web site: www.thesaint-online.com
Freq: Bi-Weekly
Circ: 2000 Not Audited
Profile: Newspaper with local news, features, society events, sport and arts coverage from across Scotland and the UK.
MAGAZINE
Student Lifestyle

SAKURA
1060973

Email: info@sakuramama.jp
Web site: http://sakuramama.jp
Freq: Quarterly
Circ: 100000 Not Audited
MAGAZINE
Family & Parenting, Lifestyle, Men's Interests, Regional General Interest, Women's Interests

Salford Star
984784

Editorial: Office 6C, Antz Junction, Unit 10, Junction Eco Park, Rake Lane, Swinton, Salford M27 9LR **Tel:** 44 01617 287611
Email: info@salfordstar.com
Web site: www.salfordstar.com
Freq: Quarterly
Circ: 20000 Not Audited
Editor: Stephen Kingston
Profile: Publication that investigates news stories from around Salford.
MAGAZINE
Regional

The Salfordian
999021

Editorial: University House, The Crescent, Salford, Manchester M5 4WT
Tel: 44 01613 515400
Email: newsdesk@thesalfordian.co.uk
Web site: www.salfordstudents.com
Freq: Weekly
Circ: 15000 Not Audited
MAGAZINE
Student Lifestyle

Sali Hughes Beauty
987258

Editorial: 4 Walpole Road, Brighton BN2 0EA
Email: info@salihughesbeauty.com
Web site: http://www.salihughesbeauty.com
Freq: Daily
Circ: 44608 Cision Digital Reach
MAGAZINE (ONLINE)
Beauty & Grooming, Cosmetics, Hair

Salisbury Life
984008

Editorial: Circus Mews House, Circus Mews, Bath BA1 2PW **Tel:** 44 01225 475800

Consumer Magazines

Email: info@mediaclash.co.uk
Web site: http://www.mediaclash.co.uk/city/
Freq: Monthly
Circ: 10000 Not Audited
Profile: Property and lifestyle magazine covering food, arts, out and about, fashion, beauty and gardening. Aimed at affluent home owners in Salisbury and surrounding villages.
MAGAZINE
Regional General Interest

Salon Business 984211
Editorial: Office 104, 176 South Street, Romford RM1 1BW
Email: info@salonbusiness.co.uk
Web site: www.salonbusiness.co.uk
Freq: Monthly
Circ: 10028 Not Audited
Profile: Magazine covering product news, special offers and investigative features. Aimed specifically at salon owners.
Ad Rate: Full Page Colour £2195.00
MAGAZINE
Hair

The Salon Magazine 984302
Editorial: The Goods Shed, Jubilee Way, Whistable Road, Faversham, Faversham ME13 8GD **Tel:** 44 01795 509112
Web site: www.thesalonmagazine.co.uk
Freq: Monthly
Circ: 12000 Not Audited
Editor: Gemma Ward
Profile: Publication covering all aspects of the hair, beauty, nails and tanning industry. Aimed at salon owners, stylists and therapists.
Ad Rate: Full Page Colour £1200.00
MAGAZINE
Cosmetics, Hair

SalonFocus 985733
Editorial: One Abbey Court, Fraser Road, Priory Business Park, Bedford, Bedford MK44 3WH **Tel:** 44 01234 831965
Email: sfenquiries@salonfocus.co.uk
Web site: https://www.nhf.info/advice-and-resources/salonfocus/
Freq: Bi-Monthly
Circ: 14000 Not Audited
Profile: Newsletter of the National Hairdressers' Federation. Contains news and details on new legislation, new products and services.
Ad Rate: Full Page Colour £1295.00
MAGAZINE
Hair

SalonNV 995093
Editorial: 132 West Regent Street, Glasgow G2 2RQ **Tel:** 44 01412 125525
Email: contact@salonnv.co.uk
Web site: http://www.salonnv.co.uk
Freq: Monthly
MAGAZINE
News & Current Affairs

Salt 1105387
Editorial: 13 Hanover Square, London W1S 1HN
Web site: www.condenastinternational.com
Freq: Semi-Annual
Circ: 25000 Not Audited
Editor: Harriet Quick
Profile: Magazine containing compassionate business thinking. It looks at ways to reduce the social and environmental damage being caused by businesses.
MAGAZINE
Fashion, Luxury Goods

Salvage World 997289
Editorial: Holland House, 1-4 Bury Street, London EC3A 5AW **Tel:** 44 02072 206597
Web site: www.marine-salvage.com
Freq: Quarterly Not Audited
MAGAZINE
News & Current Affairs

Salvationist 998788
Editorial: The Salvation Army, 101 Newington Causeway, London SE1 6BN
Tel: 44 02073 674890

Email: salvationist@salvationarmy.org.uk
Web site: www.salvationarmy.org.uk/salvationist
Freq: Weekly
Circ: 19000 Not Audited
MAGAZINE
Religion

SAMSON Magazine - CEASED 996622
Web site: www.samson-magazine.com
Freq: 3 Times/Year Not Audited
MAGAZINE
Basketball, Bicycles, Billiards, Boating & Yachting, Bodybuilding, Bowling, Boxing, Cricket, Equestrian Sports, Extreme/Adventure Sports

Sanmarinonotizie.com 1060752
Tel: 44 37805 49909041
Email: redazione@sanmarinonotizie.com
Web site: http://www.sanmarinonotizie.com
Circ: 3666 Cision Digital Reach
MAGAZINE (ONLINE)
Basketball, Bicycles, Billiards, Boating & Yachting, Bodybuilding, Bowling, Boxing, Consumer Affairs, Cricket, Crime & Violence

The Sapper 983141
Editorial: RHQ RE, Brompton Barracks, Chatham, Gillingham ME4 4UG
Tel: 44 01634 822121
Email: sappermag@royalengineers.com
Web site: http://www.army.mod.uk/royalengineers/34455.aspx
Freq: Bi-Monthly
Circ: 7500 Not Audited
Editor: Lt Col Charles Holman
Profile: Magazine covering the activities of the serving and territorial Royal Engineers, branches of the Royal Engineers Association, notices, calling old comrades, births, marriages, anniversaries and deaths.
Ad Rate: Full Page Mono £600.00
Ad Rate: Full Page Colour £850.00
MAGAZINE
Armed Forces

Sardines Magazine 998878
Editorial: 22 Rutland Way, Orpington, London BR5 4DZ **Tel:** 44 01689 853980
Email: editorial@sardinesmagazine.co.uk
Web site: sardinesmagazine.co.uk
Freq: Quarterly
Circ: 13000 Not Audited
Editor: Paul Johnson
MAGAZINE
Theater & Performing Arts

The Sassy Bird 988688
Editorial: Scouse Bird Problems HQ, The Secret Warehouse (The Old Foundry), Syren Street, Liverpool L20 8HN
Tel: 44 01512 815178
Email: sb@thesassybird.com
Web site: http://thesassybird.com/
Freq: Daily
Circ: 10754 Cision Digital Reach
MAGAZINE (ONLINE)
Beauty & Grooming, Cosmetics, Fashion, Hair, Restaurant Reviews, Travel, Women's Interests

Save the Student! 997384
Tel: 44 01618 830224
Email: mail@savethestudent.org
Web site: www.savethestudent.org
Circ: 62169 Cision Digital Reach
MAGAZINE (ONLINE)
Students

Savile Row Style Magazine 998650
Editorial: Elizabeth House, 54-58 High St, Edgware HA8 7EJ **Tel:** 44 02082 385000
Email: editor@savilerow-style.com
Web site: http://savilerow-style.com
Freq: 3 Times/Year Not Audited
MAGAZINE
Fashion, Luxury Goods, Men's Interests

SavvyWoman.co.uk 985299
Editorial: Dalton House, 60 Windsor Avenue, London SW19 2RR
Email: info@savvywoman.co.uk
Web site: www.savvywoman.co.uk
Freq: Daily
Circ: 50368 Cision Digital Reach
MAGAZINE (ONLINE)
Personal Finance

Sawf News 1061501
Web site: http://www.news.sawf.org
MAGAZINE (ONLINE)
Bars, Clubs & Pubs, Comedy, Entertainment, Fashion, Lifestyle, Local Entertainment Guides, Men's Interests, Movies & Video, National News, Regional General Interest

SBTV.co.uk 997265
Editorial: Second Floor, 1 Cavendish Place, London W1G 0QF
Email: info@sbtv.co.uk
Web site: sbtv.co.uk
Freq: Daily
Circ: 96281 Cision Digital Reach
MAGAZINE (ONLINE)
Audio Video Trade, Broadcasting, Cameras, Dance Music, Movies & Video, Pop Music, Rap & Hip Hop, Visual Arts

Scale Aviation Modeller International 981987
Editorial: Media House, 21 Kingsway, Bedford MK42 9BJ
Email: mail@sampublications.com
Web site: www.sampublications.com
Freq: Monthly
Circ: 40000 Not Audited
Editor: David Francis
Profile: Magazine focusing on all forms of static scale aviation model making.
Ad Rate: Full Page Colour £995.00
MAGAZINE
Crafts, Hobbies, & Collecting

Scale Military Modeller International 998536
Editorial: Media House, 21 Kingsway, Bedford MK42 9BJ **Tel:** 44 01902 750939
Email: mail@sampublications.com
Web site: www.sampublications.com
Freq: Monthly
Circ: 30000 Not Audited
MAGAZINE
Crafts, Hobbies, & Collecting

Scan 984992
Editorial: Slaidburn House, Lancaster University, Bailrigg, Lancaster LA1 4YA
Tel: 44 01524 592613
Email: scan.news@lusu.co.uk
Web site: http://scan.lusu.co.uk/
Freq: Bi-Weekly
Circ: 8000 Not Audited
Profile: Student newspaper of Lancaster University containing news and features from the University, Lancaster area and national student sources. Covers a wide range of arts, sport, music and comment.
Ad Rate: Full Page Mono £400.00
Ad Rate: Full Page Colour £550.00
MAGAZINE
Student Lifestyle

Scan Magazine 981771
Editorial: 15B Bell Yard Mews, Bermondsey Street, London SE1 3TY
Tel: 44 08709 330423
Email: info@scanmagazine.co.uk
Web site: www.scanmagazine.co.uk
Freq: Monthly
Circ: 20000 Not Audited
MAGAZINE
Europe

Scents 988772
Editorial: Garden Floor, 16 Connaught Place, London W2 2ES
Tel: 44 02074 207000
Email: info@therivergroup.com
Web site: http://blog.theperfumeshop.com/
Freq: Quarterly Not Audited

Editor: Lauren Carbran
MAGAZINE
Cosmetics

schlaubi.de 997135
Editorial: First Floor, High Holborn House, 52-54 High Holborn, London WC1V 6RL
Tel: 44 02074 006200
Email: kontakt@schlaubi.de
Web site: www.schlaubi.de
Freq: Daily
Circ: 55675 Cision Digital Reach
MAGAZINE (ONLINE)
Internet, Movies & Video, Telecommunications/Electronic Communications

Scholastic Resource Bank: Early Years 1069753
Web site: http://education.scholastic.co.uk/resourcebank/earlyyears
Freq: Daily
MAGAZINE (ONLINE)
Family & Parenting, Preschool

Scholastic Resource Bank: Primary 1069754
Web site: http://education.scholastic.co.uk/resourcebank/primary
Freq: Daily
Circ: 94353 Cision Digital Reach
MAGAZINE (ONLINE)
Elementary School

Schön! 999094
Editorial: 123 Cornell Square, London SW8 2ES **Tel:** 44 02035 651890
Email: submissions@schonmagazine.com
Web site: www.schonmagazine.com
Freq: Semi-Annual
Circ: 40000 Not Audited
MAGAZINE
Fashion

School Sport Magazine 998782
Editorial: 76 Loxwood Road, Lovedean, Horndean PO8 9TY **Tel:** 44 02392 594536
Email: info@schoolsportmag.co.uk
Web site: www.schoolsportmag.co.uk
Freq: Bi-Monthly
Circ: 10000 Not Audited
Editor: Phil Tusler
MAGAZINE
News & Current Affairs

School Travel Today 999430
Editorial: Publishing House, Windrush, Ash Lane, Birmingham B48 7TS
Tel: 44 01214 456961
Email: beaubusinessmedia@gmail.com
Web site: www.beaubusiness-media.com/#!school-travel-today
Freq: Quarterly
Circ: 28000 Not Audited
MAGAZINE
Schools & Institutions, Travel

Schools Equipment News Direct 981536
Editorial: PO Box 249, Ascot, London SL5 0BZ **Tel:** 44 01189 885886
Email: crownwood@btconnect.com
Web site: www.cwponline.co.uk
Freq: Quarterly
Circ: 11500 Not Audited
Profile: Magazine covering schools equipment and furniture, details of exhibitions, travel and security, PA/sound systems, IT and anything to do with the upkeep of the building, contents and grounds.
Ad Rate: Full Page Colour £765.00
MAGAZINE
Disability, Education, Higher Education, Preschool, Schools & Institutions, Students

SCHOTTLAND 995408
Editorial: Schottland Media Ltd., 9 South East Circus Place, Edinburgh EH36TJ
Tel: 44 01312 257330
Email: redaktion@schottland.co
Web site: www.schottland.co

Freq: Semi-Annual
Circ: 10000 Not Audited
MAGAZINE
Travel

Science & Technology Management Research   1061038
Tel: 44 86208 3163517
Email: kjgl@chinajournal.net.cn
Web site: http://kjgl.chinajournal.net.cn
Freq: Monthly
Circ: 3000 Not Audited
MAGAZINE
Auto Aftermarket, Computers, Data Management, Electronics, Government Technology, Industry, Internet, Mobile Communications, Science, Security & Security Systems

Science in Parliament   982136
Editorial: 3 Birdcage Walk, Wesminster, London SW1H 9JJ **Tel:** 44 02072 227085
Email: office@scienceinparliament.org.uk
Web site: www.scienceinparliament.org.uk
Freq: Quarterly
Circ: 1200 Not Audited
Profile: Journal providing the scientific community with an insight into the information and briefings supplied to members of Parliament on scientific subjects. Topics covered include policy issues and activities, legislation and selected debates.
Ad Rate: Full Page Mono £500.00
MAGAZINE
Politics, Science

Sci-Fi Bulletin   996429
Email: scifibulletin@gmail.com
Web site: http://scifibulletin.com
Freq: Daily
Circ: 14235 Cision Digital Reach
MAGAZINE (ONLINE)
Broadcasting, Literature, Movies & Video, Science Fiction

Sci-Fi London   986590
Editorial: c/o FestivalBiz, 2nd Floor, 145-157 St John Street, London EC1V 4PY
Email: info@sci-fi-london.com
Web site: http://www.sci-fi-london.com
Freq: Daily
Circ: 13542 Cision Digital Reach
MAGAZINE (ONLINE)
Entertainment, Literature, Movies & Video, Science Fiction

SciFiNow   984420
Editorial: Richmond House, 33 Richmond Hill, Bournemouth BH2 6EZ
Tel: 44 01959 541444
Web site: www.scifinow.co.uk
Freq: Monthly
Circ: 18000 Not Audited
Profile: Magazine covering scifi fantasy, horror and cult TV. Aimed at fans of the genre predominantly men between 25 and 45 years of age.
Ad Rate: Full Page Colour £1850.00
MAGAZINE
Science Fiction

sci-fi-online.com   999698
Editorial: The Granary, Roundhouse, Buckland in the Moor, Newton Abbot TQ13 7HN
Email: darren@reviewgraveyard.com
Web site: http://www.sci-fi-online.com
Freq: Daily
Circ: 405 Cision Digital Reach
Editor: Darren Rea
MAGAZINE (ONLINE)
Science Fiction

SCMA's Childminding Magazine   1057068
Editorial: 7 Melville Terrace, Stirling FK8 2ND **Tel:** 44 01786 445377
Email: information@childminding.org
Web site: www.childminding.org
Freq: Quarterly
Circ: 5000 Not Audited

Editor: Leigh Irvine
MAGAZINE
Charitable Foundations, Family & Parenting

S-cool.co.uk   998750
Web site: www.s-cool.co.uk
Freq: Daily
Circ: 127810 Cision Digital Reach
MAGAZINE (ONLINE)
News & Current Affairs

Scooter Trade & Industry   984228
Editorial: 1 Warwick Avenue, Whickham, Whickham NE16 5QR **Tel:** 44 01914 881947
Email: reliables@tradeandindustry.net
Web site: www.tradeandindustry.net
Freq: Quarterly
Circ: 3200 Not Audited
MAGAZINE
Automotive

Scootering   982657
Editorial: Scootering, PO Box 99, Horncastle LN9 6LZ **Tel:** 44 01507 525771
Email: editorial@scootering.com
Web site: www.scootering.com
Freq: Monthly
Circ: 79954 Not Audited
Profile: Magazine covering all aspects of scooters and scootering.
Ad Rate: Full Page Colour £810.00
MAGAZINE
Motorcycles

Scot-Buzz   997528
Tel: 44 01567 830258
Email: bill@scot-buzz.co.uk
Web site: www.scot-buzz.co.uk
Freq: Daily
Circ: 10019 Cision Digital Reach
MAGAZINE (ONLINE)
Business, Politics, Scotland, Small and Medium Business

scotchwhisky.com   995271
Editorial: Elixir House, Whitby Avenue, Park Royal, London NW10 7SF
Tel: 44 02088 389368
Email: becky@scotchwhisky.com
Web site: www.scotchwhisky.com
Freq: Daily
Circ: 51440 Cision Digital Reach
Editor: Becky Paskin
MAGAZINE (ONLINE)
Alcohol & Spirits

Scotland In Trust   981931
Editorial: Suite 2.3, Red Tree Business Suites, 33 Dalmarnock Road, Glasgow G40 4LA **Tel:** 44 01413 750504
Email: sit@thinkpublishing.co.uk
Web site: http://www.nts.org.uk/magazine
Freq: 3 Times/Year
Circ: 202614 Not Audited
Editor: Clare Harris
Profile: Magazine covering the works of the National Trust Scotland with features on its properties and conservation work in the built heritage, gardens and open countryside. It also promotes the products and services, provided by the Trust for its members, through news and features about holidays and retail and provides background information to new appeals launched by the charity.
Ad Rate: Full Page Colour £3195.00
MAGAZINE
Field Sports

Scotland IS   988830
Editorial: Oracle Campus, Blackness Road, Springfield, Linlithgow EH49 7LR
Tel: 44 01506 472200
Email: info@scotlandis.com
Web site: www.scotlandis.com
Freq: Daily
Circ: 16000 Cision Digital Reach
Profile: Website of ScotlandIS, the trade body for the information and communications technologies (ICT) industry, which represents software, telecomms, IT

and creative technologies businesses throughout Scotland.
MAGAZINE (ONLINE)
Computers, Data Management, Electronics, Industry, Internet, Mobile Communications, Software

Scotland Magazine   982560
Editorial: King Street House, 15 Upper King Street, Norwich NR3 1RB
Tel: 44 01603 633808
Email: editor@scotlandmag.com
Web site: www.scotlandmag.com
Freq: Bi-Monthly
Circ: 32650 Not Audited
Profile: Magazine covering all things Scottish including local news, entertainment, travel, famous personalities, style, culture and a leisure directory.
Ad Rate: Full Page Colour £2760.00
MAGAZINE
Regional General Interest

Scotland Outdoors   984876
Tel: 44 01313 000295
Email: editor@scotoutdoors.com
Web site: www.scotoutdoors.com
Freq: Bi-Monthly
Circ: 7000 Not Audited
Editor: David McMurray
Profile: Magazine covering all aspects of the Scottish outdoors, including adventure travel, wildlife, ecology, conservation and outdoor activities such as walking, climbing, mountain biking, paddle sports more. Each issue features articles on outdoor clothing, accommodation, local food and drink, adventure and specialist travel. Aimed at visitors and residents of Scotland, who enjoy undertaking outdoor pursuits.
MAGAZINE
Field Sports, Nature & Wildlife, Outdoor Recreation

Scotland Select Traveller   1075513
Editorial: Publishing House, 3 Bridgebank Industrial Estate, Taylor Street, Horwich, Bolton BL6 7PD **Tel:** 44 01204 478817
Email: info@selecttravelmedia.com
Web site: www.selecttravelmedia.com
Freq: Quarterly
Circ: 20000 Not Audited
Editor: Jayne Meadowcroft
MAGAZINE
Airline Inflight

Scots Auto Scene   984287
Editorial: 34 Bernard Street, Edinburgh EH6 6PR **Tel:** 44 01315 541129
Email: webmaster@belljohnstone.co.uk
Web site: www.autosceneuk.co.uk
Freq: Monthly
Circ: 8000 Not Audited
Editor: Rory Mackenzie
Profile: Magazine focusing on the automotive industry including sales, parts, manufacture and repair market.
Ad Rate: Full Page Colour £1855.00
MAGAZINE
Automotive

Scots Heritage Magazine   999576
Editorial: 496 Ferry Road, Edinburgh EH5 2DL **Tel:** 44 01315 511000
Email: editor@scotsheritagemagazine.com
Web site: www.scotsheritagemagazine.com
Freq: Quarterly
Circ: 25000 Not Audited
MAGAZINE
Regional General Interest

The Scots Magazine   982563
Editorial: 80 Kingsway East, Dundee DD4 8SL **Tel:** 44 01382 223131
Email: editor@scotsmagazine.com
Web site: www.scotsmagazine.com
Freq: Monthly
Circ: 24349 Not Audited
Editor: Robert Wight
Profile: Magazine focusing on Scottish culture and heritage that covers walking and climbing, history and traditions, wildlife, environmental issues, books and music.

Ad Rate: Full Page Mono £856.00
Ad Rate: Full Page Colour £1244.00
MAGAZINE
Regional General Interest

ScotsGay   984091
Editorial: PO Box 666, Edinburgh EH7 5YW
Tel: 44 01315 390666
Email: editorial@scotsgay.co.uk
Web site: www.scotsgay.co.uk
Freq: Monthly
Circ: 10000 Not Audited
Profile: Magazine containing news, views, gossip, reviews and features on the media, travel and holidays.
Ad Rate: Full Page Colour £460.00
MAGAZINE
LGBT, Sexuality

Scotsman Food and Drink   1052633
Tel: 44 01316 0507618
Email: foodanddrink@scotsman.com
Web site: http://foodanddrink.scotsman.com/
Freq: Daily
Circ: 952 Cision Digital Reach
MAGAZINE (ONLINE)
Alcohol & Spirits, Bars, Clubs & Pubs, Beer, Beverages, Cooking & Baking, Food, Grocery Stores, Organic Food, Restaurant Reviews, Vegetarianism & Veganism

Scottish Catholic Observer   984790
Editorial: 19 Waterloo Street, Glasgow G2 6BT **Tel:** 44 01412 214956
Email: info@sconews.co.uk
Web site: www.sconews.co.uk
Freq: Weekly
Circ: 50000 Not Audited
Editor: Ian Dunn
Profile: National Catholic newspaper of Scotland.
Ad Rate: Full Page Mono £1132.20
Ad Rate: Full Page Colour £1415.25
MAGAZINE
Religion

Scottish Club Golfer   984643
Editorial: 50 High Craighall Road, Glasgow G4 9UD **Tel:** 44 01413 532222
Web site: www.scottishclubgolfer.com
Freq: Bi-Monthly Not Audited
Editor: Bryce Ritchie
Profile: Magazine covering amateur golf in Scotland including fixtures, results, player profiles and interviews and equipment reviews.
Ad Rate: Full Page Colour £1800.00
MAGAZINE
Golf

Scottish Cycling   987525
Editorial: 200 Renfield Street, Glasgow G2 3QB **Tel:** 44 01413 027700
Web site: www.scottishcyclingmag.co.uk
Freq: Quarterly
Circ: 80000 Not Audited
Profile: Magazine that looks looks at cycling in Scotland featuring route ideas as well as looking at the cycling kit and equipment.
MAGAZINE
Bicycles

Scottish Diver   985549
Editorial: 23 Eagle Street, Glasgow G4 9XA
Tel: 44 01413 323933
Email: editor@scotsac.com
Web site: http://www.scotsac.com/join-now
Freq: Bi-Monthly Not Audited
Editor: Jack Morrison
Profile: Magazine of the Scottish Sub-Aqua Club containing news updates and features on local clubs, diving abroad, equipment, techniques, new products and diving destinations in Scotland.
Ad Rate: Full Page Colour £340.00
MAGAZINE
Swimming/Watersports

Consumer Magazines

Scottish Educational Journal
984478

Editorial: 46 Moray Place, Edinburgh EH3 6BH **Tel:** 44 01312 256244
Email: sej@eis.org.uk
Web site: www.eis.org.uk
Freq: Bi-Monthly
Circ: 60000 Not Audited
Profile: Magazine covering issues from nursery, primary, secondary and special schools through to further and higher education.
Ad Rate: Full Page Colour £1917.00
MAGAZINE
Disability, Education, Higher Education, Preschool, Schools & Institutions, Students

Scottish Environment News
984683

Editorial: Polldoran, Clachan Seil, Oban, Argyll PA34 4TJ
Web site: www.scenes.org.uk
Freq: Monthly Not Audited
MAGAZINE
News & Current Affairs

Scottish Farming Leader
1058693

Tel: 44 01314 724000
Web site: http://www.nfus.org.uk/
Freq: Monthly
Circ: 8500 Not Audited
Editor: Ruth McClean
Profile: Magazine of the National Farmer's Union within Scotland. Aimed at farmers.
Ad Rate: Full Page Mono £660.00
Ad Rate: Full Page Colour £825.00
MAGAZINE
News & Current Affairs

Scottish Field
982561

Editorial: Scottish Field Magazine, Fettes Park, 496 Ferry Road, Edinburgh EH5 2DL
Tel: 44 01315 511000
Email: editor@scottishfield.co.uk
Web site: www.scottishfield.co.uk
Freq: Monthly
Circ: 17105 Not Audited
Profile: Magazine covering Scottish contemporary life, including people, style, culture, landscape, natural history and attractions, plus history and heritage. Aimed at people with a high disposable income who are interested in Scottish lifestyle.
Ad Rate: Full Page Colour £2175.00
MAGAZINE
Regional General Interest

Scottish Grocer & Convenience Retailer
981295

Editorial: Peebles Media Group, The Albus, 110 Brook Street, Glasgow G40 3AP
Tel: 44 01415 676000
Web site: www.scottishgrocer.co.uk
Freq: Monthly
Circ: 8017 Not Audited
MAGAZINE
Alcohol & Spirits, Food, Retail Management

Scottish Hosteller
998473

Editorial: SYHA National Office, 7 Glebe Crescent, Stirling FK8 2JA
Tel: 44 01786 891400
Email: hosteller@syha.org.uk
Web site: www.syha.org.uk
Freq: Annual Not Audited
Editor: Jane Mackie
MAGAZINE
Outdoor Recreation, Travel

Scottish Islands Explorer
982342

Tel: 44 01379 890270
Email: info@scottishislandsexplorer.com
Web site: www.scottishislandsexplorer.com
Freq: Bi-Monthly
Circ: 4000 Not Audited
Editor: John Humphries
Profile: Magazine with articles about the Scottish Islands including wildlife, culture, environment, archaeology, lifestyle, history,

travel and current affairs. Aimed at those interested in the Scottish Islands.
Ad Rate: Full Page Colour £520.00
MAGAZINE
Travel

Scottish Legal News
995879

Editorial: Avian House, 87 Brook Street, Dundee DD5 1DJ **Tel:** 44 01382 427038
Email: newsdesk@scottishnews.com
Web site: www.scottishlegal.com
Freq: Daily
Circ: 32951 Cision Digital Reach
Profile: Website covering legal news. The Scottish Legal News is a a free daily email newsletter covering the latest legal news in Scotland.
MAGAZINE (ONLINE)
Consumer Interest, Corporate Law, Criminal Law, Employment, Family Law, Government, Human Rights, Intellectual Property, Law, Legal Services

Scottish Licensed Trade News
981055

Editorial: 11-12 Claremount Terrace, Glasgow G3 7XR **Tel:** 44 01415 676000
Email: info@peeblesmedia.com
Web site: www.sltn.co.uk
Circ: 15164 Not Audited
Editor: Gillian McKenzie
Profile: Newspaper for the drinks retailing, hospitality and licensed leisure industries in Scotland. Containing news articles and features on licensing and other laws, licensed business issues, licensed trade representative groups, industry initiatives, products and promotions. First published in 1964.
Ad Rate: Full Page Colour £2620.00
MAGAZINE
Alcohol & Spirits, Bars, Clubs & Pubs

Scottish Medical Journal 984778

Editorial: 1 Wimpole Street, London W1G 0AE **Tel:** 44 02073 248500
Web site: http://scm.sagepub.com/
Freq: Quarterly Not Audited
Editor: Robert Carachi
Profile: Journal containing original articles, case reports and historical reports related to medicine.
MAGAZINE
Health Administration, Medicine, Nursing/Nurses, Pharmaceuticals

Scottish Rider
995355

Editorial: Unit 2 Devizes Trade Centre, Hopton Park, Devizes, Devizes SN10 2EH
Tel: 44 01380 730888
Email: sales@redpin.co.uk
Web site: www.scottish-rider.co.uk
Freq: Monthly Not Audited
MAGAZINE
Equestrian Sports

Scottish Slimmers
983272

Editorial: 47 St Mary's Court, Huntly Street, Aberdeen AB10 1TH **Tel:** 44 01224 256118
Email: editorial@scottishslimmers.com
Web site: scottishslimmers.com
Freq: 3 Times/Year
Circ: 15000 Not Audited
MAGAZINE
Beauty & Grooming, Cosmetics, Hair, Nutrition, Women's Interests

Scottish Sporting Gazette
982282

Editorial: 1-6 Buckminster Yard, Main Street, Buckminster, Grantham, Grantham NG33 5SB **Tel:** 44 01476 859849
Email: info@scottishsportinggazette.co.uk
Web site: www.scottishsportinggazette.co.uk
Freq: Semi-Annual
Circ: 12000 Not Audited
Editor: Marcus Janssen
MAGAZINE
Field Sports

Scottish Travel Agents News Magazine
983858

Editorial: 190-194 Main Street, Glasgow G78 1SL **Tel:** 44 01418 804305
Email: susan@stannews.co.uk
Web site: www.stanselections.co.uk
Freq: Weekly
Circ: 1300 Not Audited
MAGAZINE
Travel

Scottish Walks
1094736

Tel: 44 01413 027722
Email: mandy.mcharg@scottishwalks.com
Web site: www.scottishwalks.com
Freq: Quarterly
Circ: 50000 Not Audited
MAGAZINE
Outdoor Recreation

Scottish Wedding Directory
982425

Editorial: 80 Kingsway East, Glasgow DD4 8SL **Tel:** 44 01382 575908
Email: info@scottishweddingdirectory.co.uk
Web site: www.scottishweddingdirectory.co.uk
Freq: Quarterly
Circ: 25000 Not Audited
Editor: Natasha Radmehr
Profile: Magazine includes features on bridal wear, wedding receptions, beauty, travel, furnishing and decor.
Ad Rate: Full Page Mono £1140.00
Ad Rate: Full Page Colour £1140.00
MAGAZINE
Weddings

Scottish Woman
982377

Editorial: Scotia House, 4 Beechwood Park, Livingston EH54 8SN **Tel:** 44 01506 200890
Email: editorial@scottishwomanmagazine.com
Web site: http://www.scottishwomanmagazine.com/
Freq: Bi-Monthly
Circ: 28000 Not Audited
Profile: Magazine covering hair, health, beauty and fashion. Aimed at women in Scotland.
Ad Rate: Full Page Colour £1600.00
MAGAZINE
Beauty & Grooming, Cosmetics, Fashion, Hair, Women's Interests

Scouting Magazine
996027

Editorial: Scout Information Centre, Gilwell Park, Chingford, London E4 7QW
Tel: 44 02084 337100
Email: scouting.magazine@scouts.org.uk
Web site: https://members.scouts.org.uk/supportresources/search?cat=810
Freq: Quarterly
Circ: 99917 Not Audited
MAGAZINE
Charitable Foundations

Scratch
981174

Editorial: 1 The Courtyard, Market Square, Westerham, Westerham TN16 1AZ
Tel: 44 01959 547000
Email: editorial@scratchmagazine.co.uk
Web site: www.scratchmagazine.co.uk
Freq: Monthly
Circ: 14296 Not Audited
Editor: Helena Biggs
Profile: Magazine covering nail industry innovations, news, products, techniques and services, treatments for hand, nail and foot grooming. First published in 2003, the publication has an average of 96 pages per issue. Aimed at nail professionals and beauty therapists.
Ad Rate: Full Page Colour £1875.00
MAGAZINE
Cosmetics

SCREAM
986553

Email: office@screamhorrormag.com
Web site: http://www.screamhorrormag.com/
Freq: Bi-Monthly
Circ: 26000 Not Audited

Editor: Richard Cooper
MAGAZINE
Movies & Video

Screen International
981052

Editorial: 1st Floor Unit F2/G, Zetland House, 5-25 Scrutton Street, London EC2A 4HJ **Tel:** 44 02081 020900
Web site: www.screendaily.com
Freq: Monthly
Circ: 9609 Not Audited
Editor: Matt Mueller
Profile: Magazine containing news, statistics and analysis of the issues shaping the international film business. Read by senior personnel within the entertainment business.
Ad Rate: Full Page Colour £8331.00
MAGAZINE
Broadcasting, Movies & Video

Screen Shot Magazine
1103792

Email: info@screenshot-magazine.com
Web site: screenshot-magazine.com
Freq: Semi-Annual
MAGAZINE
Politics, Social Issues, Visual Arts

screenjabber.com
985223

Tel: 44 07906 097744
Email: stuart@screenjabber.com
Web site: https://screenjabber.com/
Freq: Daily
Circ: 7216 Cision Digital Reach
MAGAZINE (ONLINE)
Movies & Video

Screenmedia
982963

Editorial: Event Live Media, 6th Floor, 111 Cannon Street, London EC4N 5AR
Tel: 44 01843 866607
Email: screenmedia@circdata.com
Web site: www.screenmediamag.com
Freq: Bi-Monthly
Circ: 6000 Not Audited
Profile: Magazine covering digital signage. Aimed at the retail sector, leisure and hospitality industry, transport and public sector, agencies, network owners and integrators.
MAGAZINE
Advertising Industry, Electronics, Graphic Design, Industry, Marketing, Software

Screentrade
985022

Editorial: PO Box 144, Orpington, London BR6 6LZ **Tel:** 44 01689 833117
Email: editorial@screentrademagazine.com
Web site: www.screentrademagazine.com
Freq: Quarterly
Circ: 4700 Not Audited
MAGAZINE
Movies & Video

SCRIP Intelligence - SCRIP Asia team Bureau
1101763

Web site: https://scrip.pharmamedtechbi.com/
Freq: Daily
Circ: 24773 Cision Digital Reach
MAGAZINE (ONLINE)
News & Current Affairs

SCRIP Intelligence - SCRIP US team Bureau
1072466

Web site: https://scrip.pharmamedtechbi.com/
Freq: Daily
Circ: 24773 Cision Digital Reach
MAGAZINE (ONLINE)
News & Current Affairs

SCRUM
995802

Editorial: 34 Bernard Street, Edinburgh EH6 6PR **Tel:** 44 01315 541129
Email: info@scrummagazine.com
Web site: www.scrummagazine.com
Freq: Monthly
Circ: 54000 Not Audited
Editor: Stuart MacLennan

Profile: Magazine covering rugby union with news, club features, kit reviews, interviews with players and lifestyle articles.
MAGAZINE
Rugby

ScrumQueens.com 999415
Editorial: 17-21 Old Street, London EC1V 9HF
Web site: www.scrumqueens.com
Freq: Daily
Circ: 14175 Cision Digital Reach
MAGAZINE (ONLINE)
Rugby

SE Magazines 995531
Web site: http://semagazines.co.uk/
Freq: Monthly
MAGAZINE
News & Current Affairs

Sea & I 984703
Editorial: 15 Sackville Street, London W1S 3DJ **Tel:** 44 02070 091950
Email: info@lon.cnyachts.com
Web site: www.camperandnicholsons.com/about/sea-i-magazine.htm
Freq: Quarterly
Circ: 48000 Not Audited
Profile: Magazine covering luxury travel. It celebrates the exceptional, the extraordinary, the priceless, the indulgent, the esteemed and the ultimate that the world can offer.
MAGAZINE
Boating & Yachting, Luxury Goods

Sea Angler 982183
Editorial: Media House, Lynchwood, Peterborough PE2 6EA
Tel: 44 01733 468000
Web site: www.seaangler.co.uk
Freq: Monthly
Circ: 20334 Not Audited
Editor: Cliff Brown
Profile: Magazine covering all aspects of the sea fishing scene, with equipment reviews and location reports as well sea fishing news, tackle, tactics and marks to fish. Aimed at sea anglers.
Ad Rate: Full Page Colour £18000.00
MAGAZINE
Fishing

Seahorse International Sailing 982215
Editorial: 5 Brittania Place, Station Street, Lymington, Lymington SO41 3BA
Tel: 44 01590 671898
Email: info@seahorse.co.uk
Web site: http://www.seahorsemagazine.com/
Freq: Monthly
Circ: 22000 Not Audited
Editor: Andrew Hurst
Profile: Official magazine of the Royal Ocean Racing Club, covering international sailing news and races. Includes articles on various technical sailing topics.
Ad Rate: Full Page Colour £3546.00
MAGAZINE
Boating & Yachting

The Searcher 985038
Editorial: 17 Down Road, Merrow, Guildford GU1 2PX **Tel:** 44 01483 830133
Email: info@thesearcher.co.uk
Web site: www.thesearcher.co.uk
Freq: Monthly Not Audited
Profile: Magazine covering metal detection. It covers identification, news and views, collections, detailed articles about finds, field tests and book reviews.
MAGAZINE
History

Searchlight Magazine 998932
Editorial: PO Box 1576, Ilford IG5 0NG
Tel: 44 02085 501805
Email: searchlightmag@gmail.com
Web site: www.searchlightmagazine.com
Freq: Quarterly Not Audited
MAGAZINE
Politics

Seasoned By Chefs 997029
Tel: 44 01945 871585
Email: sbcmag@rmedia-communications.co.uk
Web site: www.seasonedbychefs.co.uk
Freq: Bi-Monthly
Circ: 7000 Not Audited
MAGAZINE
Cooking & Baking

Seatplans.com 984851
Editorial: 5th Floor, Warwick House, 25 Buckingham Palace Road, London SW1W 0PP **Tel:** 44 02078 212700
Email: enquiries@seatplans.com
Web site: www.seatplans.com
Freq: Daily
Circ: 91389 Cision Digital Reach
MAGAZINE (ONLINE)
Airline Inflight, Aviation

SeaView 988815
Editorial: Little Gaddesden, Berkhamsted HP4 1PN **Tel:** 44 01442 843050
Email: editorial@seaview.co.uk
Web site: http://www.seaview.co.uk/
Freq: Daily
Circ: 6289 Cision Digital Reach
Editor: David Simpson
Profile: Website covering cruise and ferry travel. seaview website shares the latest news on cruise lines, cruise ships, cruise information, ferry operators, ferries, ferry information and hotels.
MAGAZINE (ONLINE)
Marine & Boat Trade, Shipping & Warehousing, Travel

Seaways 984349
Tel: 44 02079 281351
Email: member@nautinst.org
Web site: http://www.nautinst.org/en/Publications/seaways/index.cfm
Freq: Monthly
Circ: 7500 Not Audited
Editor: Lucy Budd
Profile: The Journal of the Nautical Institute; covering maritime subjects, marine equipment and professional issues.
Ad Rate: Full Page Mono £1378.00
Ad Rate: Full Page Colour £1678.00
MAGAZINE
Marine & Boat Trade, Shipping & Warehousing

Secondaries Investor 996591
Editorial: 140 London Wall, 6th Floor, London EC2Y 5DN **Tel:** 44 02075 665444
Web site: www.secondariesinvestor.com
Freq: Daily
Circ: 12367 Cision Digital Reach
MAGAZINE (ONLINE)
Corporate Finance, Fund Management, Personal Finance, Private Equity

SecondsOut.com 995999
Editorial: Accounts House, 16 Dalling Road, Hammersmith, London W6 0JB
Email: boxingeditorial@secondsout.com
Web site: www.secondsout.com
Freq: Daily
Circ: 30074 Cision Digital Reach
MAGAZINE (ONLINE)
Boxing

SECRET EARTH 1105190
Email: content@secretearth.com
Web site: www.secretearth.com
Freq: Daily
Circ: 1776 Cision Digital Reach
MAGAZINE (ONLINE)
Travel

Secret World Retreats 997610
Tel: 44 02081 336375
Web site: www.secretworldretreat.com
Freq: Daily
Circ: 1512 Cision Digital Reach
Editor: Paula Wynne
MAGAZINE (ONLINE)
News & Current Affairs

Securities & Investment Review 980923
Editorial: 5th Floor, Drury House, 34-43 Russell Street, London WC2B 5HA
Tel: 44 02070 100999
Web site: www.cisi.org/cisiweb2/cisi-news/s-i-review
Freq: Quarterly
Circ: 20499 Not Audited
Profile: Magazine covering news, technology, strategies and members profiles. Read by members of the Securities & Investment Institute.
Ad Rate: Full Page Colour £4345.00
MAGAZINE
Bonds, Derivatives, Economics, Equities, Financial Markets, Personal Finance

Security Document World 987354
Editorial: Science Media Partners Ltd, 25 Horseshoe Business Park, Pangbourne, Pangbourne RG8 7JW
Web site: http://securitydocumentworld.com
Freq: Daily
Circ: 35097 Cision Digital Reach
Editor: Mark Lockie
Profile: Website covering government security. The Security Document World covers government security news.
MAGAZINE (ONLINE)
News & Current Affairs

Seen in the City 987848
Tel: 44 02033 882222
Email: info@seeninthecity.co.uk
Web site: www.seeninthecity.co.uk
Freq: Daily
Circ: 17602 Cision Digital Reach
MAGAZINE (ONLINE)
Airline Inflight, Bars, Clubs & Pubs, Beauty & Grooming, Cooking & Baking, Cosmetics, Fashion, Food, Grocery Stores, Hair, Lifestyle

Seen Liverpool 999239
Editorial: Suite 605, Cotton Exchange Building, Old Hall Street, Liverpool L3 9LQ
Web site: www.seenliverpool.com
Freq: Bi-Monthly
Circ: 5000 Not Audited
Editor: Rebecca Keegan
MAGAZINE
LGBT, Sexuality

seenit.co.uk 984630
Editorial: 20-22 Wenlock Road, London N1 7GU
Email: feedback@seenit.co.uk
Web site: www.seenit.co.uk
Freq: Daily
Circ: 28798 Cision Digital Reach
Editor: Martin Hoscik
MAGAZINE (ONLINE)
Broadcasting, Entertainment, Movies & Video

Self Build Homes 987500
Editorial: Myrtle Oast, Kemsdale Road, Fostall, Faversham ME13 9JL
Tel: 44 01227 750153
Email: info@selfbuildhomesmag.com
Web site: www.sbhmag.co.uk/
Freq: Monthly
Circ: 60000 Not Audited
Profile: Magazine covering self-build homes.
MAGAZINE
Architecture & Design, Do-It-Yourself (DIY)

The Self Builder 984879
Editorial: Crown House, 151 High Road, Loughton IG10 4LF **Tel:** 44 02032 255200
Web site: www.theselfbuilder.com
Freq: Bi-Monthly
Circ: 10005 Not Audited
MAGAZINE
Do-It-Yourself (DIY)

SelfBuild & Design 981836
Tel: 44 01283 742950
Web site: www.selfbuildanddesign.com

Freq: Monthly
Circ: 10138 Not Audited
Editor: Ross Stokes
Profile: Website covering building news, advice, beginners guide. The SelfBuild & Design is an online version of the magazine featuring the complexities of home construction. Provides practical information, covering the options available and their cost implications.
MAGAZINE
Architecture & Design, Do-It-Yourself (DIY), Property Management & Maintenance

Selfbuild & Improve Your Home 984575
Tel: 44 02897 510570
Email: info@selfbuild.ie
Web site: www.selfbuild.ie
Freq: Quarterly
Circ: 11574 Not Audited
MAGAZINE
Architecture & Design, Do-It-Yourself (DIY), Property Management & Maintenance

SelfCare 998911
Editorial: Regency House, 2 Wood Street, Bath BA1 2JQ **Tel:** 44 07717 496180
Email: editor@selfcarejournal.com
Web site: www.selfcarejournal.com
Freq: Bi-Monthly Not Audited
MAGAZINE
Health & Medicine, Medicine, Pharmaceuticals

Selling Canada 995509
Editorial: Suffolk House, George Street, Croydon CR9 1SR **Tel:** 44 02086 497233
Email: editorial@bmipublishing.co.uk
Web site: www.sellingtravel.co.uk
Freq: 3 Times/Year
Circ: 14925 Not Audited
MAGAZINE
Travel

Selling Travel 982805
Editorial: Suffolk House, George Street, Croydon CR9 1SR **Tel:** 44 02086 497233
Email: editorial@sellingtravel.co.uk
Web site: www.sellingtravel.co.uk
Freq: Monthly
Circ: 15000 Not Audited
Profile: Journal covering information for travel agents. Also includes a training guide.
Ad Rate: Full Page Colour £3750.00
MAGAZINE
Travel

Selvedge 984376
Editorial: Editorial Office, 162 Archway Road, London N6 5BB **Tel:** 44 02083 419721
Email: editorial@selvedge.org
Web site: www.selvedge.org
Freq: Bi-Monthly
Circ: 25000 Not Audited
Profile: Magazine covering textile art, design and craft with features on contemporary textile art, internationally renowned makers and ethnographic textiles as well as travel, shopping, future trends and the history and social history of textiles. Also includes book reviews, exhibitions and listings.
Ad Rate: Full Page Colour £1500.00
MAGAZINE
Crafts

Semi China 1061665
Tel: 44 86105 1906086
Email: semichina@semi.org
Web site: http://www.semi.org.cn
Freq: Daily
Circ: 23086 Cision Digital Reach
MAGAZINE (ONLINE)
Electronics

Semiconductor Manufacturing Magazine 1060823
Tel: 44 86105 1906086
Email: semichina@semi.org
Web site: http://www.semi.org.cn
Freq: Monthly

Consumer Magazines

Circ: 9601 Not Audited
MAGAZINE
Electronics

Semiconductor Today   985982
Editorial: Suite No. 133, 20 Winchcombe
Street, Cheltenham GL52 2LY
Tel: 44 01869 811577
Web site: www.semiconductor-today.com
Freq: Monthly
Circ: 27580 Cision Digital Reach
Editor: Mark Telford
Profile: Digital magazine for the compound
semiconductor and advanced silicon
industries covering applications including
wireless communications, fiber-optic
communications, LEDs and solar cells.
MAGAZINE (ONLINE)
Electronics, Software

SEN   981565
Editorial: 5 Chapel House, Shawbridge
Street, Clitheroe, Clitheroe BB7 1LY
Tel: 44 01200 409800
Email: editor@senmagazine.co.uk
Web site: www.senmagazine.co.uk
Freq: Bi-Monthly
Circ: 9000 Not Audited
Editor: Peter Sutcliffe
MAGAZINE
Disability, Education

SEN Leader Magazine   998345
Editorial: Forum Business Media Ltd, 3rd
Floor Regal House, 70 London Road,
Twickenham TW1 3QS
Tel: 44 02082 438704
Web site: www.senmagonline.co.uk
Freq: Quarterly Not Audited
MAGAZINE
Disability

Senior Moments   1099503
Editorial: Hova House, 1 Hova Villas, Hove
BN3 3DH Tel: 44 01273 257037
Email: info@titlemedia.co.uk
Web site: www.titlemedia.co.uk/senior-
moments
Freq: Monthly
Circ: 10000 Not Audited
MAGAZINE
Retirement Savings

Sensor Review   984077
Editorial: Howard House, Wagon Lane,
Bingley BD16 1WA Tel: 44 01274 777700
Web site: http://www.emeraldinsight.com/
loi/sr
Freq: Quarterly Not Audited
Profile: Publication featuring articles and
reviews of sensor technology in
manufacturing processes. Aimed at
industrial management development, design
and production engineers in a wide range of
user industries such as domestic appliance,
food and pharmaceuticals and mechanical,
electrical and electronic engineering.
MAGAZINE
News & Current Affairs

sepaview.com   996595
Editorial: Strathallan House, The Castle
Business Park, Newcastle upon Tyne FK9
4TZ Tel: 44 01786 452546
Email: communications@sepa.org.uk
Web site: www.sepaview.com
Freq: Daily
Circ: 12507 Cision Digital Reach
MAGAZINE (ONLINE)
Energy & Environment, Environment,
Regional

Seroword   998296
Tel: 44 07961 619558
Email: info@seroword.com
Web site: www.seroword.com
Freq: Daily
Circ: 521 Cision Digital Reach
MAGAZINE (ONLINE)
Art, Comedy, Country, Folk, Bluegrass,
Dance Music, Entertainment, Literature,
Movies & Video, Music, Photography, Pop
Music

Service Dealer   1075625
Tel: 44 01491 837117
Web site: www.servicedealer.co.uk
Freq: Bi-Monthly
Circ: 3300 Not Audited
Editor: Steve Gibbs
Profile: Magazine containing news, views
and comment on the agricultural, garden and
turf care machinery and equipment market.
Ad Rate: Full Page Colour £1250.00
MAGAZINE
Gardening

Service Talk   983492
Editorial: 150 Wharfedale Road, Winnersh
Triangle, Wokingham RG415RB
Tel: 44 01189 186500
Email: service-talk@itsmf.co.uk
Web site: www.itsmf.co.uk
Freq: Quarterly
Circ: 12000 Not Audited
Editor: Mark Lillycrop
MAGAZINE
Internet

The Set Pieces   1069280
Email: hello@thesetpieces.com
Web site: www.thesetpieces.com
Freq: Daily
Circ: 57412 Cision Digital Reach
Editor: Matthew Stanger
MAGAZINE (ONLINE)
Soccer

Seven Shades of Black   997772
Web site: http://www.7sobm.co.uk
Freq: Daily
Circ: 752 Cision Digital Reach
MAGAZINE (ONLINE)
Art, Classical/Choral/Band Music,
Country, Folk, Bluegrass, Dance Music,
Jazz & Blues, Music, Pop Music, R&B,
Urban, World, Rap & Hip Hop, Rock Music

SevenStreets   995776
Editorial: SevenStreets, Studio E, Baltic
Creative Campus, Liverpool L1 0AH
Tel: 44 07748 308308
Email: info@sevenstreets.com
Web site: www.sevenstreets.com
Freq: Daily
Circ: 6626 Cision Digital Reach
MAGAZINE (ONLINE)
Art, Bars, Clubs & Pubs, Cooking &
Baking, Regional General Interest,
Restaurant Reviews, Travel

Seventh Man   985177
Editorial: 1-14 Colville Square, Notting Hill,
London W11 2BQ
Email: info@7thmanmagazine.com
Web site: www.7thmanmagazine.com
Freq: Semi-Annual Not Audited
MAGAZINE
Beauty & Grooming, Cosmetics, Fashion,
Hair, Luxury Goods, Men's Interests,
Shopping

Seventhsister   1057619
Editorial: Interchange Atrium, Stables
Market, Chalk Farm Road, London NW1 8AB
Tel: 44 03301 330331
Email: info@seventhsister.london
Web site: www.seventhsister.london
Freq: Daily
Circ: 5706 Cision Digital Reach
MAGAZINE (ONLINE)
Regional General Interest

Seventy2   1096359
Email: info@seventy2magazine.co.uk
Web site: www.seventy2magazine.co.uk
Freq: Monthly
Circ: 21000 Not Audited
Editor: Joe Campbell
MAGAZINE
Soccer

Sew   985098
Editorial: 1 Phoenix Court, Hawkins Road,
Colchester, Colchester CO2 8JY
Tel: 44 01206 505900
Web site: www.sewmag.co.uk

Freq: Monthly
Circ: 35000 Not Audited
Profile: Magazine covering hint and tips,
features and stories relating to sewing.
MAGAZINE
Crafts

Sew Today   982793
Editorial: New Lane, Havant, Havant PO9
2ND Tel: 44 01243 374523
Web site: www.sewtoday.co.uk/
Freq: Monthly Not Audited
Profile: Magazine containing sewing
patterns reflecting looks from the fashion
runway, fabric forecasts, Editor's picks,
what's new section, book reviews, diary
dates, advice from experts and readers
offers.
Ad Rate: Full Page Colour £1595.00
MAGAZINE
Crafts

Sewing World   984875
Editorial: Traplet House, Willow End Park,
Blackmore Park Road, Worcester WR13
6NN Tel: 44 01689 869840
Email: sw@mytimemedia.com
Web site: www.inspiredtomake.com/zone/
sewing-world
Freq: Monthly
Circ: 31500 Not Audited
Editor: Emma Horrocks
Profile: Magazine covering machine sewing
skills, dressmaking, projects and techniques.
Ad Rate: Full Page Mono £655.00
Ad Rate: Full Page Colour £835.00
MAGAZINE
Crafts

Seyexclusive   996877
Editorial: 47 Hall Lane, Branston, Branston
LN4 1PY Tel: 44 08448 009722
Email: enquiries@seyexclusive.com
Web site: www.seyexclusive.com
Freq: Daily
Circ: 1362 Cision Digital Reach
MAGAZINE (ONLINE)
Travel

SF Edinburgh   995167
Editorial: Fettes Park, 496 Ferry Road, Forth
EH5 2DL Tel: 44 01315 511000
Email: editor@scottishfield.co.uk
Web site: www.sfedinburgh.co.uk
Freq: Bi-Monthly
Circ: 20000 Not Audited
MAGAZINE
Regional General Interest

SF Glasgow   1076406
Editorial: Scottish Field Magazine, Fettes
Park, 496 Ferry Road, Edinburgh EH5 2DL
Tel: 44 01315 511000
Email: editor@scottishfield.co.uk
Web site: www.scottishfield.co.uk
Freq: Quarterly
Circ: 20000 Not Audited
MAGAZINE
News & Current Affairs

SFX   982047
Editorial: Quay House, The Ambury, Bath
BA1 1UA Tel: 44 01225 442244
Email: sfx@futurenet.com
Web site: http://www.gamesradar.com/sfx/
Freq: Monthly
Circ: 20230 Not Audited
Editor: Richard Edwards
Profile: Science fiction and fantasy
magazine covering films, TV, books, video,
comics and games. Aimed at enthusiasts of
science fiction and fantasy.Regular features:
Interviews Regular actor, author or other
creative people profiles.; Letters; News
Science fiction news.; Reviews TV, movies,
games, books and comics reviewed and
rated.
Ad Rate: Full Page Colour £1995.00
MAGAZINE
Movies & Video, Science Fiction

SGB (Sporting Goods
Business)   996422
Editorial: 15a London Road, Maidstone,
Maidstone ME16 8LY
Web site: www.sgb-sports.com
Freq: Monthly
Circ: 7753 Not Audited
MAGAZINE
Fitness & Exercise

SGB Golf   985880
Editorial: 15a London Road, Maidstone,
Maidstone ME16 8LY Tel: 44 02037 522263
Web site: www.sgbgolf.co.uk
Freq: Monthly
Circ: 4500 Not Audited
Profile: Magazine covering the latest golf
industry news, product information and
market intelligence including golfing
equipment reviews, interviews, clothing and
accessories, buying groups, PGA of Europe
and directory of manufacturers.
Ad Rate: Full Page Colour £1575.00
MAGAZINE
Fitness & Exercise

SGB Outdoor   999231
Editorial: 15a London Road, Maidstone,
Maidstone ME16 8LY Tel: 44 01622 687031
Web site: www.sgboutdoor.co.uk
Freq: Quarterly
Circ: 4500 Not Audited
Editor: Heather Ramsden
Profile: Magazine covering the outdoor retail
sector. Contains industry updates, company
profiles, exhibitions, equipment, footwear,
clothing and product reviews. Includes
international news, trade shows, marketing
influences and in-depth talk from top names.
Sports Active sections covers the action and
lifestyle sectors for those involved in skate,
surf, snow or bikes, through to active
lifestyle interests such as pilates, yoga and
wellness. Aimed at outdoor retailers and mail
order houses.Previous title: SGB Outdoor
Ad Rate: Full Page Colour £1320.00
MAGAZINE
Fitness & Exercise

Shadowlocked   996490
Email: shadowlockedmail@gmail.com
Web site: http://www.shadowlocked.com/
index.php
Freq: Daily
Circ: 11703 Cision Digital Reach
MAGAZINE (ONLINE)
Entertainment, Local Entertainment
Guides, Movies & Video, Science Fiction

Shadows On The Wall   985243
Email: shadows@wall.net
Web site: www.shadowsonthewall.co.uk
Freq: Daily
Circ: 15049 Cision Digital Reach
Editor: Rich Cline
Profile: Website covering film reviews, news
and interviews. Aimed at film lovers.
MAGAZINE (ONLINE)
Entertainment, Movies & Video

Shakespeare Magazine   994983
Editorial: 67 Sylvia Avenue, Bristol BS3 5BU
Email: shakespearemag@outlook.com
Web site: http://www.
shakespearemagazine.com/
Freq: Monthly
Circ: 10000 Not Audited
Editor: Pat Reid
MAGAZINE
Literature, Theater & Performing Arts

Sharenet   1060578
Tel: 44 27217 004800
Email: support@sharenet.co.za
Web site: http://www.sharenet.co.za
Circ: 473205 Cision Digital Reach
MAGAZINE (ONLINE)
Consumer Affairs, Crime & Violence,
Defense & National Security, Energy &
Environment, Ethical/Moral Issues,
International News, Law, National News,
News & Current Affairs, Northern Ireland

SHARES 979824
Editorial: 49 Southwark Bridge Road, London SE1 9HH **Tel:** 44 02073 784124
Email: editorial@shares.msm.co.uk
Web site: www.sharesmagazine.com
Freq: Weekly
Circ: 1082 Cision Digital Reach
Editor: Daniel Coatsworth
Profile: Magazine containing share market tables, company reviews and features on share market sectors, managed funds as well as commodities such as precious metals and oil, foreign exchange and derivative equity instruments. First published in 1999. Aimed at all share market investors, professional and private.
Ad Rate: Full Page Mono £3190.00
Ad Rate: Full Page Colour £4180.00
MAGAZINE (ONLINE)
Equities, Personal Finance

She Kicks 984481
Editorial: Gear House, Saltmeadows Road, Gateshead NE8 3DA **Tel:** 44 01914 424001
Email: info@shekicks.net
Web site: www.shekicks.net
Freq: Bi-Monthly Not Audited
Editor: Jen O'Neill
MAGAZINE
Soccer

SheerLuxe.com 984140
Editorial: 4-6 Morie Street, London SW18 1SL **Tel:** 44 02073 687848
Email: info@sheerluxe.com
Web site: www.sheerluxe.com
Freq: Daily
Circ: 147539 Cision Digital Reach
Profile: Website covering lifestyle. SheerLuxe.com features fashion and beauty news and tips, recipes, culture, diet and fitness pages and a directory of 1,500 retailers.
MAGAZINE (ONLINE)
Beauty & Grooming, Cosmetics, Fashion, Hair, Luxury Goods, Shopping, Women's Interests

SheInspires 996721
Editorial: 37b York Grove, London SE15 2NY **Tel:** 44 02034 026138
Email: info@sheinspires.co.uk
Web site: www.sheinspires.co.uk
Freq: Bi-Monthly
Circ: 10000 Not Audited
MAGAZINE
Women's Interests

Shema - teenagers' supplement 1000944
Not Audited
MAGAZINE
Consumer Affairs, Crime & Violence, Defense & National Security, Energy & Environment, Ethical/Moral Issues, International News, Law, National News, News & Current Affairs, Northern Ireland

Shetland Life 983034
Editorial: The Shetland Times Ltd, Gremista, Lerwick, Shetland ZE1 0PX
Tel: 44 01595 693622
Email: shetlandlife@shetlandtimes.co.uk
Web site: www.shetlandtimes.co.uk/
Freq: Monthly
Circ: 1500 Not Audited
Editor: Adam Civico
Profile: Local interest magazine for the Shetland Islands.
Ad Rate: Full Page Colour £320.00
MAGAZINE
Regional General Interest

Shetland News 980708
Editorial: The Knowes, Lunning, Vidlin, Shetland ZE2 9QB **Tel:** 44 01806 577332
Email: news@shetnews.co.uk
Web site: www.shetnews.co.uk
Freq: Daily
Circ: 86385 Cision Digital Reach
Editor: Hans Marter
MAGAZINE (ONLINE)
Regional

Shindig! Magazine 997317
Editorial: 64 North View Road, London N8 7LL
Web site: http://www.shindig-magazine.com/
Freq: Bi-Monthly
Circ: 20000 Not Audited
MAGAZINE
Country, Folk, Bluegrass, Jazz & Blues, Music, Pop Music, Rock Music

Shine! magazine 995119
Email: editor@shinemagazine.co.uk
Web site: http://shinemagazine.co.uk/
Freq: Daily
Circ: 521 Cision Digital Reach
MAGAZINE (ONLINE)
Health & Medicine, Relationships, Travel, Women's Interests

Ship & Boat International 980823
Editorial: 8-9 Northumberland Street, London WC2N 5DA **Tel:** 44 02072 354622
Email: editorial@rina.org.uk
Web site: http://www.rina.org.uk/sbi.html
Freq: Bi-Monthly
Circ: 5672 Not Audited
Editor: Martin Conway
Profile: Publication containing news on the latest technical developments and technical descriptions of new vessels, building techniques and equipment.
Ad Rate: Full Page Colour £1915.00
MAGAZINE
Marine & Boat Trade, Shipping & Warehousing

Shipping & Marine 986793
Editorial: 10 Cringleford Business Centre, Suite 10, Intwood Road, Norwich NR4 6AU
Tel: 44 01603 274130
Web site: www.shipping-and-marine.com
Freq: Monthly Not Audited
MAGAZINE
Marine & Boat Trade, Shipping & Warehousing

Shipping: Today & Yesterday 982216
Editorial: HPC Publishing, 7-8 Edison Road, Eastbourne, Hastings BN23 6PT
Tel: 44 01323 514435
Email: editor@shippingtandy.com
Web site: www.shippingtandy.com
Freq: Monthly
Circ: 16000 Not Audited
Editor: Nigel Lawrence
MAGAZINE
Marine & Boat Trade

Shiprepair & Maintenance 981340
Editorial: 8-9 Northumberland Street, London WC2N 5DA **Tel:** 44 02072 354622
Email: editorial@rina.org.uk
Web site: https://www.rina.org.uk/shiprepair-maintenance
Freq: Quarterly
Circ: 5494 Not Audited
MAGAZINE
Engineering, Marine & Boat Trade, Shipping & Warehousing

Ships Monthly 982217
Editorial: Cudham Tithe Barn, Berry's Hill, Cudham, London TN16 3AG
Tel: 44 01959 541444
Email: sm.ed@kelsey.co.uk
Web site: www.shipsmonthly.com
Freq: Monthly
Circ: 18000 Not Audited
Editor: Nicholas Leach
Profile: Magazine containing news and articles on all types of deep sea shipping including new cruise ships, ferries, naval vessels and cargo ships. Includes articles on tugs, new ships and preserved vessels as well as personal recollections and voyages reports plus interviews with ship's captains, chief engineers, department heads and a historical look back at shipping companies and their ships.
Ad Rate: Full Page Mono £430.00

Ad Rate: Full Page Colour £650.00
MAGAZINE
Marine & Boat Trade

ship-technology.com 986858
Editorial: John Carpenter House, John Carpenter Street, London EC4Y 0AN
Tel: 44 02079 366400
Email: onlineeditorial@kable.co.uk
Web site: http://www.ship-technology.com/
Circ: 56516 Cision Digital Reach
Profile: Website covering tankers, gas carriers, floating offshore facilities, cruise liners, dry cargo vessels, ferries and support vessels as well as marine equipment, products and services, and marine industry exhibitions, conferences and events.
MAGAZINE (ONLINE)
Marine & Boat Trade

Shooting Gazette 980964
Editorial: Pinehurst 2, Pinehurst Road, Farnborough Business Park, Stamford GU14 7BF **Tel:** 44 01252 555000
Web site: www.shootinguk.co.uk/shooting-gazette-home
Freq: Monthly
Circ: 9103 Not Audited
Editor: William Hetherington
Profile: Magazine covering British gun sport. It features driven game, gun dogs, deer stalking wildfowling and pigeon shooting, as well as article relating to gun ownership and licensing. Aimed at shooting enthusiasts with high disposable incomes.
Ad Rate: Full Page Mono £2325.00
Ad Rate: Full Page Colour £3115.00
MAGAZINE
Shooting/Guns

Shooting Sports 982283
Editorial: 21-23 Phoenix Court, Hawkins Road, Colchester, Colchester CO2 8JY
Tel: 44 01206 525697
Email: peter.moore403@ntlworld.com
Web site: http://www.gunmart.net/
Freq: Monthly
Circ: 25000 Not Audited
Editor: Peter Moore
Profile: Magazine containing articles on all aspects of shooting, including product reviews and accessories. Aimed at gun enthusiasts.
Ad Rate: Full Page Colour £550.00
MAGAZINE
Shooting/Guns

Shooting Times & Country Magazine 981002
Editorial: Pinehurst 2, Pinehurst Road, Farnborough Business Park, Farnborough, London GU14 7BF **Tel:** 44 01252 555213
Email: steditorial@timeinc.com
Web site: www.shootingtimes.co.uk
Freq: Weekly
Circ: 15749 Not Audited
Profile: Magazine covering all disciplines of shooting including game, rough and stalking. Includes coverage on issues of conservation and land management. Each issue contains shooting news, sport and countryside action. The magazine was first published under the title of Wildfowler's Shooting Times and Kennel News with the first edition printed in September 1882. Aimed at shooting sportsmen.
Ad Rate: Full Page Mono £1875.00
Ad Rate: Full Page Colour £2500.00
MAGAZINE
Shooting/Guns

Shooting UK 984379
Editorial: Pinehurst 2, Pinehurst Road, Farnborough Business Park, Farnborough, London GU14 7BF **Tel:** 44 01252 555000
Email: shootinguk@timeinc.com
Web site: www.shootinguk.co.uk
Freq: Daily
Circ: 141279 Cision Digital Reach
MAGAZINE (ONLINE)
Field Sports

SHOP (UK) 985166
Editorial: 90-92 Pentonville Road, London N1 9HS **Tel:** 44 02078 123475
Web site: http://www.global-blue.com
Freq: Semi-Annual
Circ: 75000 Not Audited
MAGAZINE
Shopping

Shop Chelsea 997682
Email: info@shopchelsea.co.uk
Web site: www.shopchelsea.co.uk
Freq: Daily
Circ: 10453 Cision Digital Reach
MAGAZINE (ONLINE)
Art, Beauty & Grooming, Cosmetics, Do-It-Yourself (DIY), Fashion, Hair, Local Entertainment Guides, Luxury Goods, Restaurant Reviews, Shopping

Shop Insider 1054602
Editorial: 40 Broadway, London SW1H 0BT
Email: press@intudigital.co.uk
Web site: http://intu.co.uk/inspire-me
Freq: Daily
Circ: 25030 Cision Digital Reach
MAGAZINE (ONLINE)
Beauty & Grooming, Cooking & Baking, Cosmetics, Do-It-Yourself (DIY), Fashion, Food, Grocery Stores, Hair, Health & Medicine, Organic Food

Shopping 1002018
Editorial: 30 Cleveland Street, London, London W1T 4JD **Tel:** 44 02079 076000
Web site: www.mensfitness.co.uk
MAGAZINE
News & Current Affairs

Shopto 994989
Editorial: Unit 2 Western Centre(Western Road), Bracknell, London RG12 1RW
Tel: 44 08443 181328
Email: online-presence@shopto.net
Web site: www.shopto.net
Freq: Daily
Circ: 486587 Cision Digital Reach
MAGAZINE (ONLINE)
Computer & Video Games

ShortList 984371
Editorial: 26-34 Emerald Street, London WC1N 3QA **Tel:** 44 02076 119700
Email: editorial@shortlist.com
Web site: www.shortlist.com
Freq: Weekly
Circ: 503089 Not Audited
Profile: The ShortList is a database of thousands of products and materials from all of the leading suppliers, with section dedicated to specifications for each type of equipment.
MAGAZINE
Men's Interests

Shout 982466
Editorial: 2 Albert Square, Dundee DD1 9QJ
Tel: 44 01382 223131
Email: shout@dcthomson.co.uk
Web site: www.shoutmag.co.uk
Freq: Monthly
Circ: 37128 Not Audited
MAGAZINE
Beauty & Grooming, Cosmetics, Fashion, Hair, Teen/Young Adult

The Showbiz Lion 1102300
Web site: http://www.theshowbizlion.com/
Freq: Daily
Circ: 10878 Cision Digital Reach
MAGAZINE (ONLINE)
Celebrities

Shropshire Magazine 982522
Editorial: Shropshire Newspapers Ltd, Ketley, Telford, Telford TF1 5HU
Tel: 44 01952 241455
Web site: shropshiremagazine.com
Freq: Monthly
Circ: 15000 Not Audited
Editor: Neil Thomas

Consumer Magazines

Profile: Magazine containing articles on personalities, book reviews, wining and dining, antiques, education, festivals and family histories. Also features local culture, a social diary, extensive live entertainment listings for the area and a regular horse racing diary.
MAGAZINE
Regional General Interest

The Shropshire Review   982523
Editorial: Building 9, Stanmore Industrial Estate, Bridgnorth, Stanmore WV15 5HR
Tel: 44 01746 766848
Web site: www.shropshirereview.co.uk
Freq: Monthly
Circ: 30000 Not Audited
Editor: Alison Ashmore
Profile: Magazine containing local news, events, fashion, lifestyle, health, beauty, history, motoring, property, sport, travel and features on the county of Shropshire. Aimed at every home and business within south-east Shropshire and home buyers within the Shropshire county.
Ad Rate: Full Page Colour £975.00
MAGAZINE
Regional General Interest

Shropshirelive.com   985424
Editorial: PO Box 4764, Shrewsbury SY1 9EJ **Tel:** 44 01743 818095
Email: news@shropshirelive.com
Web site: www.shropshirelive.com
Freq: Daily
Circ: 26561 Cision Digital Reach
Profile: Website covering Shropshire lifestyle. The shropshirelive.com website shares the latest news, events, entertainment and information in Shropshire.
MAGAZINE (ONLINE)
Regional

Shut Up & Sit Down   995168
Email: susd@pretend-money.com
Web site: http://www.shutupandsitdown. com/
Freq: Daily
Circ: 650098 Cision Digital Reach
MAGAZINE (ONLINE)
Chess, Computer & Video Games, Entertainment

SID Magazine   988290
Email: info@sid-magazine.com
Web site: www.sid-magazine.com
Freq: Semi-Annual Not Audited
Profile: Magazine covering menswear.
MAGAZINE
Fashion, Luxury Goods

SideStory   1094461
Tel: 44 02034 328187
Email: info@sidestory.co
Web site: www.sidestory.co
Freq: Daily
Circ: 9020 Cision Digital Reach
MAGAZINE (ONLINE)
Alcohol & Spirits, Architecture & Design, Art, Bars, Clubs & Pubs, Beer, Beverages, Cooking & Baking, Fashion, Photography, Restaurant Reviews

Sidewalk   982246
Editorial: 2 Tun Yard, London SW8 3HT
Tel: 44 02073 329700
Web site: www.sidewalkmag.com
Freq: Monthly
Circ: 27000 Not Audited
Editor: Ben Powell
MAGAZINE
Extreme/Adventure Sports

Sight & Sound   983037
Editorial: 21 Stephen Street, London W1T 1LN **Tel:** 44 02072 551444
Email: s&s@bfi.org.uk
Web site: www.bfi.org.uk/sightandsound
Freq: Monthly
Circ: 16644 Not Audited
Editor: Nick James
Profile: Magazine contains features, comment and news on films, both new and classic, by leading writers.

Ad Rate: Full Page Mono £1575.00
Ad Rate: Full Page Colour £2250.00
MAGAZINE
Movies & Video

Sightline   987030
Editorial: The Studio, High Green, Great Shelford, Cambridge CB22 5EG
Tel: 44 01223 550805
Email: editor@etnow.com
Web site: www.etnow.com/sightline
Freq: Quarterly Not Audited
Editor: Paul Connolly
Profile: Magazine providing technical information on matters of theatrical technology.
Ad Rate: Full Page Colour £695.00
MAGAZINE
Auto Aftermarket, Computers, Data Management, Electronics, Government Technology, Industry, Internet, Mobile Communications, Security & Security Systems, Software

Significance   998799
Editorial: 12 Errol Street, London EC1Y 8LX
Tel: 44 02076 388998
Email: significance@rss.org.uk
Web site: https://www. significancemagazine.com/
Freq: Bi-Monthly
Circ: 26000 Not Audited
Editor: Brian Tarran
MAGAZINE
Economics, Politics, Science

The Sikh Courier   984715
Editorial: 33 Wargrave Road, Harrow HA2 8LL **Tel:** 44 02088 649228
Email: bablibharara@hotmail.com
Web site: www.sikhcourierintl.org
Freq: Semi-Annual
Circ: 1000 Not Audited
MAGAZINE
Religion

Silent Voices   997508
Email: editor@silentvoicesmagazine.com
Web site: http://www.silentvoices.org.uk
Freq: Quarterly Not Audited
MAGAZINE
Astrology & Parapsychology

Silhouette   983317
Editorial: 32 Friars Walk, Southgate, London N14 5LP **Tel:** 44 02083 612942
Email: camerapixuk@btinternet.com
Web site: www.airseychelles.com
Freq: 3 Times/Year
Circ: 30000 Not Audited
Editor: Roger Barnard
Profile: In-flight magazine of Air Seychelles, with travel articles and general features. Read by customers of Air Seychelles.
Ad Rate: Full Page Mono £2810.00
Ad Rate: Full Page Colour £3640.00
MAGAZINE
Airline Inflight

Silicon Roundabout   999648
Editorial: 18b Charles St, London W1J 5DU
Tel: 44 02076 676813
Email: info@kushnerproperty.com
Web site: http://www.siliconroundabout.org. uk/
Freq: Daily
Circ: 15126 Cision Digital Reach
MAGAZINE (ONLINE)
Auto Aftermarket, Business, Computers, Data Management, Electronics, Government Technology, Industry, Internet, Mobile Communications, Security & Security Systems

Silicon Semiconductor   981672
Editorial: Hannay House, 39 Clarendon Road, Watford WD17 1JA
Tel: 44 01923 690200
Email: jackie.cannon@angelbc.com
Web site: www.siliconsemiconductor.net
Freq: Quarterly
Circ: 37482 Not Audited
Profile: Magazine covering equipment and materials used in the design and

manufacture of semiconductor devices. Also includes related European and Asian news and politics.
Ad Rate: Full Page Colour £3460.00
MAGAZINE
Electronics, Industry

Silicon UK   985003
Editorial: 48 Charlotte Street, London W1T 2NS
Email: uk-editorial@netmediaeurope.com
Web site: www.silicon.co.uk
Freq: Daily
Circ: 21561 Cision Digital Reach
Editor: Steve McCaskill
MAGAZINE (ONLINE)
Computers, Electronics, Internet, Mobile Communications, Security & Security Systems

Silver Travel Advisor   1058244
Email: news@silvertravel.co.uk
Web site: www.silvertraveladvisor.com
Freq: Daily
Circ: 45512 Cision Digital Reach
MAGAZINE (ONLINE)
Travel

Silversurfers   995383
Editorial: Albury Mill, Mill Lane, Chilworth, Guildford GU4 8RU
Email: silverhairs@hotmail.co.uk
Web site: www.silversurfers.com
Freq: Daily
Circ: 45340 Cision Digital Reach
Editor: Martin Lock
MAGAZINE (ONLINE)
Retirement Savings

Sim Racer   998072
Editorial: The Court Yard, Chopdike Drove, Gosberton Clough, Spalding, Spalding PE11 4JP **Tel:** 44 01775 750005
Web site: www.simracer-mag.com
Freq: Bi-Monthly
Circ: 30000 Not Audited
Editor: Connor Monaf
MAGAZINE
Automotive, Computer & Video Games, Driving

The Simple Things   986966
Editorial: Unit M6, The Finsbury Business Centre, 40 Bowling Green Lane, London EC1R 0NE **Tel:** 44 02074 157238
Email: thesimplethings@icebergpress.co.uk
Web site: www.thesimplethings.com
Freq: Monthly
Circ: 65000 Not Audited
Profile: Magazine covering the simple things in life, looking at homemade values and simple living. It covers topics ranging from urban gardening to thrift store shopping, simple cooking and relaxed entertaining. It features articles on interiors, gardening, cookery, lifestyle and craft. First published in September 2012.
MAGAZINE
Women's Interests

Simply Baby Names   1070427
Tel: 44 08445 930239
Email: hello@simplybabynames.com
Web site: www.simplybabynames.com
Freq: Daily
Circ: 720 Cision Digital Reach
Editor: Sim Mistry
MAGAZINE (ONLINE)
Asia, Family & Parenting, Preschool

Simply Cards & Papercraft   984372
Editorial: Suite G2, St. Christopher House, 217 Wellington Road South, Stockport SK2 6NG **Tel:** 44 08445 611202
Email: info@practicalpublishing.co.uk
Web site: www.papercraftmagazines.com/ the-magazines/simply-cards-papercraft
Freq: Monthly
Circ: 40000 Not Audited
Editor: Amy Gray
Profile: Magazine covering cards and papercraft. The magazine is distributed

through major UK newstrade outlets as well as supermarkets and specialist craft stores. Each issue comes with a high-quality covermount gift. Aimed predominantly at intermediate and advance paper crafters, with 98% female readership, and the majority of readers being aged between 30and 60.
Ad Rate: Full Page Colour £900.00
MAGAZINE
Crafts

Simply Colour   1053375
Editorial: Unit 16 Greenway Farm, Bath Road, Wick, Bristol BS30 5RL
Tel: 44 01179 373003
Email: info@kennedypublishing.co.uk
Web site: http://www.kennedypublishing.co. uk/magazines/simply-colour-magazine
Freq: Bi-Monthly
MAGAZINE
Crafts

Simply Crochet   987193
Editorial: Quay House, The Ambury, Bath BA1 1UA **Tel:** 44 01179 279009
Email: simplycrochet@immediate.co.uk
Web site: www.simplycrochetmag.co.uk
Freq: Monthly
Circ: 35000 Not Audited
Profile: Magazine for people that like to crochet. Includes designs, instructions and tips on how to make fashion accessories, clothing and gift ideas.
MAGAZINE
Crafts

Simply HE   987020
Editorial: PO Box 7741, Ringwood BH24 9FA **Tel:** 44 08448 482000
Email: info@simplyhe.com
Web site: https://www.simplyhe.com/blogs/ news
Freq: Daily
Editor: Dan Hunter
MAGAZINE (ONLINE)
Entertainment, Movies & Video

Simply Homemade   985933
Editorial: St Christopher House, 217 Wellington Road South, Stockport SK2 6NG
Tel: 44 08445 611202
Email: info@practicalpublishing.co.uk
Web site: www.simplyhomemademag.com/
Freq: Monthly
Circ: 25000 Not Audited
Editor: Diane Grimshaw
MAGAZINE
Cooking & Baking, Crafts

Simply Knitting   983978
Editorial: Quay House, The Ambury, Bath BA1 1UA **Tel:** 44 01179 279009
Email: simplyknitting@immediate.co.uk
Web site: www.simplyknitting.co.uk
Freq: Monthly
Circ: 39220 Not Audited
Profile: Magazine covering knitting and crochet, practical fashion for all the family, toys and home furnishings.
Ad Rate: Full Page Colour £1170.00
MAGAZINE
Crafts

Simply Prizes   998910
Editorial: The Malthouse, William Street, Leamington Spa CV32 4HJ
Tel: 44 01926 298986
Email: info@oxonpress.co.uk
Web site: www.simplyprizes.com
Freq: Monthly
Circ: 10000 Not Audited
Editor: Sammy Fairman
MAGAZINE
Games, Competitions & Events

Simply Sewing   988826
Editorial: Vineyard House, 44 Brook Green, London W6 7BT.
Email: simplysewing@immediate.co.uk
Web site: www.simplysewingmag.com
Freq: Monthly Not Audited
Editor: Charlie Moorby

Profile: Magazine dedicated to the art of sewing. Aimed at sewing enthusiasts as well as novices and those learning to sew.
MAGAZINE
Crafts

SimplyDV 984946
Editorial: Milton Keynes Business Centre, Foxhunter Drive, Linford Wood, Milton Keynes MK14 6GD **Tel:** 44 01908 698938
Email: info@simplydv.co.uk
Web site: http://simplydv.biz/
Freq: Daily
Circ: 6402 Cision Digital Reach
MAGAZINE (ONLINE)
Audio Video Trade, Cameras

Simpsons Comics 999077
Editorial: Titan House, 144 Southwark Street, London SE1 0UP
Tel: 44 02076 200200
Email: simpsonscomics@titanemail.com
Web site: http://titanmagazines.com/t/simpsons-comics/
Freq: Monthly
Circ: 22771 Not Audited
MAGAZINE
Cartoons, Trading Cards & Comics

Sindy Loves Vintage 986416
Editorial: 24 Kempton Road, London E6 2LD
Email: sindy@sindylovesvintage.co.uk
Web site: www.sindylovesvintage.co.uk
Freq: Daily
Circ: 10439 Cision Digital Reach
MAGAZINE (ONLINE)
Women's Interests

Sinfini 999411
Editorial: Beaumont House, Avonmore Road, Kensington Village, Kensington W14 8TS **Tel:** 44 02071 491122
Email: info@sinfinimusic.com
Web site: www.deutschegrammophon.com/en/album/sinfinimusic.html
Freq: Daily
Circ: 45695 Cision Digital Reach
MAGAZINE (ONLINE)
Classical/Choral/Band Music

Sing Up 998916
Tel: 44 02079 085148
Email: magazine@singup.org
Web site: www.singup.org
Freq: 3 Times/Year
Circ: 50000 Not Audited
MAGAZINE
Education, Elementary School

Singletrack 983883
Editorial: Lockside Mill, Dale Street, Todmorden, Todmorden OL14 5PX
Tel: 44 01706 813344
Email: newsdesk@singletrackworld.com
Web site: www.singletrackworld.com
Freq: Bi-Monthly
Circ: 10000 Not Audited
Editor: Chipps Chippendale
Profile: Magazine covering all aspects of mountain biking including photography from around the world, travel features, bike reviews and route guides. Aimed at serious mountain bikers between 25 and 40 years old.
Ad Rate: Full Page Colour £1391.50
MAGAZINE
Bicycles

Sixer 982549
Editorial: RMC House, Broadfield Court, Broadfield Business Park, Sheffield S8 0XF
Tel: 44 01142 506300
Email: chris.wilson@rmcmedia.co.uk
Web site: www.rmcmedia.co.uk/magazines/sixer/
Freq: Monthly
Circ: 20000 Not Audited
Profile: Magazine covering lifestyle and leisure, local issues, local people, fashion, motoring and travel. Aimed at residents of Sheffield.

Ad Rate: Full Page Colour £1000.00
MAGAZINE
Regional General Interest

SIXTYNINE DEGREES 983116
Editorial: A210 LCB Depot, 31 Rutland Street, Leicester LE1 1RE
Tel: 44 01162 533445
Email: info@sixtynine-ltd.co.uk
Web site: http://69-degrees.co.uk/
Freq: Quarterly
Circ: 30000 Not Audited
MAGAZINE
Fashion, Lifestyle, Men's Interests, Regional General Interest, Women's Interests

Sixtyplusurfers.co.uk 983251
Editorial: 3 Central Avenue, Pinners, London HA5 5BT **Tel:** 44 02088 663686
Web site: www.sixtyplusurfers.co.uk
Freq: Monthly
Circ: 9290 Cision Digital Reach
Editor: Jenny Itzcovitz
MAGAZINE (ONLINE)
Bars, Clubs & Pubs, Beauty & Grooming, Classical/Choral/Band Music, Comedy, Cosmetics, Country, Folk, Bluegrass, Crafts, Dance Music, Entertainment, Fashion

Ski & Snowboard 982285
Editorial: 111 Buckingham Palace Road, London SW1W 0DT **Tel:** 44 02079 313950
Email: skimag@telegraph.co.uk
Web site: www.telegraph.co.uk/travel/snowandski/
Freq: Monthly
Circ: 30000 Not Audited
Editor: Henry Druce
Profile: Magazine offering essential information on all aspects of skiing and snowboarding. Aimed at winter sports enthusiasts.
Ad Rate: Full Page Colour £3000.00
MAGAZINE
Winter Sports

Ski + Board 982288
Editorial: The White House, 57-63 Church Road, Wimbledon, London SW19 5SB
Tel: 44 02084 102010
Email: harriet.johnston@skiclub.co.uk
Web site: www.skiclub.co.uk
Freq: Bi-Monthly
Circ: 19907 Not Audited
Editor: Colin Nicholson
MAGAZINE
Winter Sports

SKIDDLE.COM 985858
Editorial: Ashley Hall Farm, Inglewhite Road, Goosnargh, Goosnargh PR3 2EB
Tel: 44 08432 893333
Email: editorial@skiddle.com
Web site: www.skiddle.com
Freq: Daily
Circ: 3258299 Cision Digital Reach
Profile: Website covering guides. The Skiddle.com website shares that latest news and information on nights outs and festivals.
MAGAZINE (ONLINE)
Antiques/Collectibles, Art, Arts, Bars, Clubs & Pubs, Classical/Choral/Band Music, Comedy, Country, Folk, Bluegrass, Dance Music, Entertainment, Jazz & Blues

Skier & Snowboarder 982290
Editorial: The Lodge, Ashgrove Road, Sevenoaks, Sevenoaks TN13 1ST
Tel: 44 07768 670158
Web site: www.skierandsnowboarder.co.uk
Freq: Quarterly
Circ: 30000 Not Audited
MAGAZINE
Winter Sports

Skin Deep 985577
Web site: www.skindeep.co.uk
Freq: Monthly
Circ: 31014 Not Audited
Profile: The magazine gives the reader a source of reference and practical advice

about the art of tattooing and the low-down on all the important health and safety issues. Provides information on colorful tattoos from Great Britain to the far corners of the world, book reviews and monthly supplements featuring the cross over between tattooing and other cultures.
Ad Rate: Full Page Colour £830.00
MAGAZINE
News & Current Affairs

The Skinny 984320
Editorial: 1.9 Techcube, Summerhall, 1 Summerhall Place, Edinburgh EH9 1PL
Tel: 44 01314 674630
Email: hello@theskinny.co.uk
Web site: www.theskinny.co.uk
Freq: Monthly
Circ: 27332 Not Audited
Profile: The Skinny is a monthly magazine covering music, arts, books, film, theatre, fashion, food, comedy, news, travel and listings for Scotland. The magazine is aimed at anybody living in Scotland with an interest in cultural events.
MAGAZINE
Art, Bars, Clubs & Pubs, Comedy, Country, Folk, Bluegrass, Dance Music, Entertainment, Jazz & Blues, Literature, Local Entertainment Guides, Movies & Video

SkinsMatter 985558
Editorial: 5 Lawn Road, London NW3 2XS
Tel: 44 02077 222866
Email: info@skinsmatter.com
Web site: www.skinsmatter.com
Freq: Daily
Circ: 11698 Cision Digital Reach
MAGAZINE (ONLINE)
Allergies, Dermatology, Health & Medicine

SKINT LONDON 997002
Email: editorial@skintlondon.com
Web site: www.skintlondon.com
Freq: Daily
Circ: 16986 Cision Digital Reach
MAGAZINE (ONLINE)
News & Current Affairs

Skool Girl Online 996264
Email: talisha@skoolgirlonline.co.uk
Web site: www.skoolgirlonline.co.uk
Freq: Daily
Circ: 10161 Cision Digital Reach
MAGAZINE (ONLINE)
Teen/Young Adult

Skwigly 1099268
Email: press@skwigly.co.uk
Web site: http://www.skwigly.co.uk
Freq: Daily
Circ: 50000 Not Audited
Editor: Steve Henderson
MAGAZINE
Computer & Video Games

Sky TV 982352
Editorial: NHC5, Grant Way, Isleworth, London TW7 5QD **Tel:** 44 03331 000333
Email: skypress@sky.uk
Web site: my.sky.com/mysky/latestnews/article/my-sky-updates/my-sky-week/
Freq: Weekly
Circ: 1 Cision Digital Reach
MAGAZINE (ONLINE)
Broadcasting

Sky.com 985057
Editorial: Westcross House, No1 West Cross Way, Brentford TW8 9DE
Email: dl-skycom@bskyb.com
Web site: www.sky.com
Freq: Daily
Circ: 19413948 Cision Digital Reach
MAGAZINE (ONLINE)
News & Current Affairs

Skydive 982247
Editorial: Prospect House, Rouen Road, Norwich NR1 1RE **Tel:** 44 01603 664242
Email: editor@skydivethemag.com
Web site: www.skydivethemag.com

Freq: Bi-Monthly
Circ: 6000 Not Audited
Editor: Liz Ashley
MAGAZINE
Extreme/Adventure Sports

Skylanders Universe Magazine 995160
Editorial: Vineyard House, 44 Brook Green, Hammersmith, London W6 7BT
Tel: 44 02071 505000
Web site: www.uk.skylandersmag.com
Freq: Bi-Monthly
Circ: 13686 Not Audited
MAGAZINE
Elementary School, Teen/Young Adult

Skyscanner 1098999
Web site: https://www.skyscanner.net/
Freq: Daily
Circ: 8758015 Cision Digital Reach
MAGAZINE (ONLINE)
Travel

Skywings 982889
Editorial: 8 Merus Court, Meridian Business Park, Harleston LE19 1RJ
Tel: 44 01379 855021
Email: skywings@bhpa.co.uk
Web site: www.bhpa.co.uk
Freq: Monthly
Circ: 8000 Not Audited
Editor: Joe Schofield
Profile: Skywings magazine publishes up-to-date national and international news from the world of free-flying, features on related sports equipment, new product reviews, aircraft tests, competition reports, interviews with personalities within the sport, safety advice, pilot's discussion forum. All editorial material is from voluntary contributors.
Ad Rate: Full Page Colour £627.00
MAGAZINE
Extreme/Adventure Sports

The Sleep Matters Club 998077
Editorial: 10 St John Street, Chester CH1 1DA **Tel:** 44 01244 564500
Web site: http://www.dreams.co.uk/sleep-matters-club/
Freq: Daily
Circ: 110963 Cision Digital Reach
MAGAZINE (ONLINE)
Health & Medicine

Slick Mummy 1053436
Email: hello@slickmummy.com
Web site: www.slickmummy.com
Freq: Quarterly
Circ: 5000 Not Audited
Editor: Sarah Benn
MAGAZINE
Family & Parenting

Slightly Foxed 997086
Editorial: 53 Hoxton Square, London N1 6PB **Tel:** 44 02070 330258
Email: all@foxedquarterly.com
Web site: www.foxedquarterly.com
Freq: Quarterly Not Audited
MAGAZINE
Literature

Slimming World magazine 981833
Editorial: PO Box 55, Alfreton, South Normanton DE55 4SW
Email: editorial@slimmingworld.co.uk
Web site: https://www.slimmingworld.co.uk/magazine/latest-issue.aspx
Freq: Bi-Monthly
Circ: 640012 Not Audited
Editor: Sara Ward
MAGAZINE
Fitness & Exercise, Nutrition

SLiNK 985970
Editorial: 93 Princes Park Avenue, London NW11 0JS
Email: slinkmagazine@live.co.uk
Web site: www.slinkmagazine.com

Consumer Magazines

Freq: Bi-Monthly
Circ: 10000 Not Audited
Profile: Magazine covering fashion, beauty and lifestyle news.
MAGAZINE
Women's Interests

SLOAN! 995277
Editorial: 276 Hill House, London SW15 6NP
Email: editorial@sloanmagazine.com
Web site: http://www.sloanmagazine.com/
Freq: Bi-Monthly
Circ: 40000 Not Audited
MAGAZINE
Alternative Medicine, Antique & Collectible Cars, Bars, Clubs & Pubs, Driving, Fashion, Fitness & Exercise, Men's Interests, Nutrition, Off-road & 4-Wheel Drive Vehicles, Restaurant Reviews

Sloane Square 982514
Editorial: 3 Princes Street, London W1B 2LD
Tel: 44 02072 591050
Email: lorna@pubbiz.com
Web site: http://www.pubbiz.com/publications/sloane-square/
Freq: Bi-Monthly
Circ: 30000 Not Audited
Profile: Lifestyle magazine covering local news as well as food, drink, fashion, property and the arts.
Ad Rate: Full Page Colour £2200.00
MAGAZINE
Regional General Interest

The Sloaney 986608
Email: editor@thesloaney.com
Web site: www.thesloaney.com
Freq: Daily
Circ: 10411 Cision Digital Reach
Editor: Laura Toogood
Profile: Website covering luxury lifestyle including luxury goods, fashion, beauty, luxury travel, lifestyle news, home and garden.
MAGAZINE (ONLINE)
Luxury Goods

Slot Magazine 997424
Editorial: Doolittle Mill, Doolittle Lane, Totternhoe, Eaton Bray LU6 1QX
Tel: 44 01525 222573
Email: editor@slotmagazine.co.uk
Web site: www.slotmagazine.co.uk
Freq: Bi-Monthly
Circ: 12000 Not Audited
Editor: Gary Cannell
MAGAZINE
Crafts, Hobbies, & Collecting

Small Furry Pets 986438
Editorial: Cudham Tithe Barn, Berrys Hill, Cudham, Cudham TN16 3AG
Tel: 44 01959 541444
Email: sfp.ed@kelsey.co.uk
Web site: shop.kelsey.co.uk/subscription/SFU
Freq: Bi-Monthly
Circ: 12500 Not Audited
Editor: David Alderton
MAGAZINE
Nature & Wildlife

Small Ships & Workboats 988864
Editorial: Victoria House, 2 Mornington Road, Cheshire, Sale M33 2DA
Tel: 44 01613 745615
Email: editorial@smallships.co.uk
Web site: http://www.smallships.co.uk/d/index.php?pageId=0
Freq: Daily
Editor: George Bennett
MAGAZINE (ONLINE)
Engineering, Marine & Boat Trade

Smallholder 985358
Editorial: 3 Falmouth Business Park, Bickland Water Road, Falmouth, Falmouth TR11 4SZ **Tel:** 44 01326 213338
Email: editorial@smallholder.co.uk
Web site: www.smallholder.co.uk
Freq: Monthly
Circ: 10000 Not Audited

Editor: Paul Armstrong
Profile: Publication covering a range of topics relating to the country and producing food in an ecological and welfare-orientated way. Includes poultry, crop growing, animal husbandry, bee-keeping and financial issues.
Ad Rate: Full Page Mono £456.00
Ad Rate: Full Page Colour £578.00
MAGAZINE
Animal Farming, Field Sports

Smallish 986663
Editorial: 9 Chiltern Court, Asheridge Road, Chesham, Chesham HP5 2PX
Email: info@smallishmagazine.com
Web site: www.smallishmagazine.com
Freq: Monthly
Circ: 50000 Not Audited
Profile: Magazine providing a guide to parenting.
MAGAZINE
Family & Parenting, Luxury Goods

Smart Chimps 986700
Email: heather@mclean-media.com
Web site: http://www.smartchimps.com/
Freq: Daily
Circ: 15517 Cision Digital Reach
MAGAZINE (ONLINE)
Mobile Communications, Mobile Electronics

Smarter Living Magazine 1098968
Editorial: British Photovoltaic Association, 2nd Floor Berkeley Square House, Berkeley Square, London W1J 6BD
Tel: 44 02082 675000
Email: smarterliving@haymarket.com
Web site: www.themagazineshop.com/bookazines/smarter-living/
Editor: Stephanie Wilkinson
MAGAZINE
News & Current Affairs

SmartRail World 1068250
Editorial: 3rd Floor, Petersham House, 57a Hatton Garden, London EC1N 8JG
Tel: 44 02070 450900
Email: editor@globaltransportforum.com
Web site: www.smartrailworld.com
Freq: Daily
Circ: 18966 Cision Digital Reach
Editor: Luke Upton
MAGAZINE (ONLINE)
Railroad

SME South Africa 1060491
Tel: 44 27110 266658
Email: info@smesouthafrica.co.za
Web site: http://www.smesouthafric.co.za
Circ: 521 Cision Digital Reach
MAGAZINE (ONLINE)
Banking, Business, Consumer Affairs, Crime & Violence, Defense & National Security, Economics, Emerging Markets, Energy & Environment, Ethical/Moral Issues, International News

smittlish 995708
Editorial: 3 Upper Street, Islington, London N5 1ST **Tel:** 44 03333 441370
Web site: www.smittlish.co.uk
Freq: Daily
Circ: 3124 Cision Digital Reach
MAGAZINE (ONLINE)
Accounting, Architecture & Design, Auto Aftermarket, Banking, Bankruptcy, Building & Construction, Business, Commercial Real Estate, Company News & Appointments, Computers

Smoke Magazine 983825
Editorial: 74a Great Portland Street, London W1W **Tel:** 44 02079 115000
Email: smokemagazine@su.westminster.ac.uk
Web site: http://uwsu.com/mag/
Freq: 3 Times/Year Not Audited
MAGAZINE
Student Lifestyle

Snakebite Reviews 995113
Email: snakebitehorror@live.co.uk
Web site: www.snakebitehorror.co.uk
Freq: Daily
Circ: 1547 Cision Digital Reach
Editor: Mark Goddard
MAGAZINE (ONLINE)
Entertainment, Movies & Video

Snooker Scene 982292
Editorial: Hayley Green Court, 130 Hagley Road, Hayley Green, Halesowen B63 1DY
Tel: 44 0121 5 859188
Email: info@snookerscene.co.uk
Web site: www.snookerscene.co.uk
Freq: Monthly
Circ: 8000 Not Audited
Editor: Clive Everton
Profile: Publication containing news and features on snooker and other cue sports.
Ad Rate: Full Page Mono £650.00
Ad Rate: Full Page Colour £925.00
MAGAZINE
Billiards

Snow 982289
Editorial: 39 Castle Street, Cirencester, London GL7 1QD **Tel:** 44 02088 789758
Email: admin@doubleamedia.com
Web site: www.snowmagazine.com
Freq: Annual
Circ: 32000 Not Audited
Profile: Magazine with news and features on skiing, snowboarding and mountain lifestyle.
Ad Rate: Full Page Colour £2200.00
MAGAZINE
Winter Sports

Snowangel.co.uk 1059600
Email: editorial@snowangel.co.uk
Web site: http://snowangel.co.uk/
Freq: Daily
Circ: 495 Cision Digital Reach
MAGAZINE (ONLINE)
Bars, Clubs & Pubs, Winter Sports

Snowboard Club 985365
Editorial: 3 Chandos House, 26 North Street, Brighton, Brighton BN1 1EB
Email: info@actionsports.club
Web site: www.snowboardclub.co.uk
Freq: Daily
Circ: 46148 Cision Digital Reach
Editor: Duncan Worrell
MAGAZINE (ONLINE)
Extreme/Adventure Sports, Winter Sports

So Darling! 985443
Email: hello@sodarling.co.uk
Web site: www.sodarling.co.uk
Freq: Daily
Circ: 11117 Cision Digital Reach
Editor: Surita Jhumat
Profile: Website covering fashion, beauty and lifestyle. The So Darling! website shares the latest news, view and reviews on fashion, beauty and lifestyle.
MAGAZINE (ONLINE)
Beauty & Grooming, Cosmetics, Fashion, Hair, Women's Interests

So It Goes 1053188
Email: info@soitgoescreative.com
Web site: http://soitgoesmag.com/
Freq: Semi-Annual
Profile: Magazine featuring the entertainment industry and the influential voices within the industry. It features seven chapters; The Actors, The Directors, The Artists, The Collection, The Musicians, The Places and The Writers.
MAGAZINE
Movies & Video, Photography

SO magazines 984877
Editorial: 16 Lonsdale Gardens, Tunbridge Wells, Tunbridge Wells TN1 1NU
Tel: 44 01892 779650
Email: info@onemediauk.com
Web site: www.somagazine.co.uk
Freq: Monthly
Circ: 20000 Not Audited

Editor: Charlie Bond
MAGAZINE
Regional General Interest

So Sensational 997156
Editorial: 6 Coolgardie Avenue, Chigwell, London IG7 5AU **Tel:** 44 02085 005916
Email: janshure@sosensational.co.uk
Web site: www.sosensational.co.uk
Freq: Daily
Circ: 75731 Cision Digital Reach
MAGAZINE (ONLINE)
Beauty & Grooming, Cosmetics, Fashion, Hair

SO YOU 997646
Tel: 44 01443 209739
Email: info@keelinpublications.co.uk
Web site: www.soyoumagazine.co.uk
Freq: Semi-Annual
Circ: 15000 Not Audited
MAGAZINE
Beauty & Grooming, Cosmetics, Do-It-Yourself (DIY), Family & Parenting, Fashion, Hair, Health & Medicine, Restaurant Reviews, Women's Interests

Soaplife 982353
Editorial: 161 Marsh Wall, London E14 9AP
Tel: 44 02031 485000
Email: soaplife@timeinc.com
Web site: http://www.timeincuk.com/brands/soaplife/
Freq: Bi-Weekly
Circ: 44761 Not Audited
Editor: Paul Brooks
Profile: Magazine covering soap stories and plots, pictures from the soaps, celebrity news and gossip, celebrity fashion and real-life celebrity interviews. It includes TV listings which include day-by-day soap previews and story-lines. First published in 1999. Read by women who are interested in soaps.
Ad Rate: Full Page Colour £3700.00
MAGAZINE
Broadcasting, Celebrities

Soar 1105194
Editorial: LCB Depot, 31 Rutland Street, Leicester LE1 1RE
Web site: http://www.soarmedia.co.uk/
Freq: Daily
Circ: 8316 Cision Digital Reach
MAGAZINE (ONLINE)
Basketball, Bicycles, Billiards, Boating & Yachting, Bodybuilding, Bowling, Boxing, Cricket, Equestrian Sports, Extreme/Adventure Sports

SoBristol 1064935
Tel: 44 01242 210330
Email: info@sopublishing.com
Web site: www.sobristol.com
Freq: Daily
Circ: 809 Cision Digital Reach
MAGAZINE (ONLINE)
Regional General Interest

Soccer Coach Weekly 999048
Editorial: Meadow View, Tannery Lane, Bramley, Guildford GU5 OAB
Web site: http://www.soccercoachingclub.co.uk/
Freq: Weekly
Circ: 5388 Not Audited
Editor: David Clarke
MAGAZINE
Soccer

Soccer Laduma 1060516
Tel: 44 27214 251200
Email: editor@soccerladuma.co.za
Web site: http://www.soccerladuma.co.za
Freq: Weekly
Circ: 245704 Not Audited
MAGAZINE
Basketball, Bicycles, Billiards, Boating & Yachting, Bodybuilding, Bowling, Boxing, Cricket, Equestrian Sports, Extreme/Adventure Sports

Consumer Magazines

SoccerBible
1097898
Email: u2us@soccerbible.com
Web site: http://www.soccerbible.com/
Freq: Daily
Circ: 139779 Cision Digital Reach
MAGAZINE (ONLINE)
Soccer

Social Care Worker - CEASED
995129
Editorial: 4th Floor, 86-90 Paul Street, London EC2A 4NE
Freq: Daily
Circ: 5865 Cision Digital Reach
MAGAZINE (ONLINE)
Community Care (UK)

Social Concierge
1053924
Editorial: The Hatch, 37 Heneage Street, London E1 5LJ **Tel:** 44 07467 949495
Web site: http://socialconcierge.co.uk/
Freq: Daily
Circ: 8785 Cision Digital Reach
MAGAZINE (ONLINE)
Relationships, Restaurant Reviews

Socialism Today
998362
Editorial: PO Box 24697, London E11 1YD
Tel: 44 02089 888777
Email: socialismtoday@socialistparty.org.uk
Web site: http://www.socialismtoday.org
Freq: Monthly
Circ: 2000 Not Audited
MAGAZINE
National News, Politics, Social Issues

Socialist Review
985860
Editorial: PO Box 71327, London SE11 9BW
Tel: 44 02078 405630
Email: editor@socialistreview.org.uk
Web site: www.socialistreview.org.uk
Freq: Monthly
Circ: 4200 Not Audited
Editor: Sally Campbell
Profile: Magazine covering socialism, anti-capitalism and anti-imperialism today including news, various articles, theatre, film and book reviews. Read by members of the Socialist Workers Party and anti-war and anti-capitalist activists.
MAGAZINE
Politics, Social Issues

Socialist Worker
985744
Editorial: PO Box 71327, London SE11 9BW
Tel: 44 02078 405656
Email: reports@socialistworker.co.uk
Web site: www.socialistworker.co.uk
Freq: Weekly Not Audited
Editor: Charlie Kimber
Profile: Newspaper covering news on workers from a socialist perspective.
MAGAZINE
Politics

Society of Independent Brewers
997353
Tel: 44 08453 379158
Web site: siba.co.uk
Freq: Daily
Circ: 48446 Cision Digital Reach
MAGAZINE (ONLINE)
Beer

Sofeminine
984461
Editorial: Henry Wood House, 2 Riding House Street, London W1W 7FA
Email: team@sofeminine.co.uk
Web site: www.sofeminine.co.uk
Freq: Daily
Circ: 1819990 Cision Digital Reach
Editor: Lareese Craig
Profile: Website covering women's interests. So feminine shares the latest news on fashion, beauty, Luxury, celebrities, relationship, parenting, personal finance, health, fitness and food. It was established in 1999.
MAGAZINE (ONLINE)
Beauty & Grooming, Celebrities, Cosmetics, Entertainment, Fashion, Fitness & Exercise, Hair, Movies & Video, Relationships, Shopping

Sofia The First
995161
Editorial: Brockbourne House, 77 Mount Ephraim, Tunbridge Wells, Tunbridge Wells TN4 8AR **Tel:** 44 01892 500100
Web site: www.paninicomics.co.uk/web/guest/catalogues/collection_detail?id=82490
Freq: Monthly
Circ: 25516 Not Audited
MAGAZINE
Elementary School, Teen/Young Adult

Soft Drinks International
983700
Editorial: PO BOX 9187, Wimborne BH21 9HU **Tel:** 44 01202 842222
Email: editorial@softdrinksinternational.com
Web site: www.softdrinksinternational.com
Freq: Monthly
Circ: 5000 Not Audited
Editor: Phil Tappenden
Profile: Read in over 100 countries with correspondents in all continents, Soft Drinks International is the English language magazine published in Europe and devoted exclusively to the manufacture, distribution and marketing of all soft drinks, fruit juices and bottled waters. Includes the latest, most comprehensive news and editorial features from correspondents in Europe, North and South America, Middle East, India, Asia, Pacific Rim and Africa.
Ad Rate: Full Page Colour £2750.00
MAGAZINE
Alcohol & Spirits

SoGlos
984362
Editorial: 9 Imperial Square, Cheltenham, Cheltenham GL50 1QB
Tel: 44 01242 210330
Email: info@sopublishing.com
Web site: www.soglos.com
Freq: Daily
Circ: 18540 Cision Digital Reach
MAGAZINE (ONLINE)
Regional General Interest

SoGlos Weddings
988786
Editorial: 9 Imperial Square, Gloucestershire, Cheltenham GL50 1QB
Tel: 44 01242 210330
Email: info@sopublishing.com
Web site: www.soglosweddings.com
Freq: Daily
Circ: 14632 Cision Digital Reach
MAGAZINE (ONLINE)
Weddings

Soldering & Surface Mount Technology
984414
Editorial: Howard House, Wagon Lane, Bingley BD16 1WA
Web site: www.emeraldinsight.com/loi/ssmt
Freq: Quarterly
Profile: International and multi-disciplinary periodical for those with a research and application interest in all branches of soldering and surface mount technologies. The journal covers all aspects of SMT from alloys, pastes and fluxes, to reliability and environmental effects, and is currently providing an important dissemination route for new knowledge on lead-free solders and processes. The journal provides state of the art, technical papers and editorials by leading industry experts, complemented by reports, international industry trends, society news, new products and international diary of events.
MAGAZINE
News & Current Affairs

Soldier
983136
Editorial: Ordnance Barracks, Government Road, Aldershot, Aldershot GU11 2DU
Tel: 44 01252 787096
Email: news@soldiermagazine.co.uk
Web site: www.soldiermagazine.co.uk
Freq: Monthly
Circ: 250000 Not Audited
Editor: Sarah Goldthorpe
MAGAZINE
Armed Forces

Solicitors Journal
980866
Editorial: 6-14 Underwood Street, London N1 7JQ **Tel:** 44 02074 900049
Email: editorial@solicitorsjournal.co.uk
Web site: www.solicitorsjournal.com
Freq: Weekly
Circ: 20000 Not Audited
MAGAZINE
News & Current Affairs

Solomon Mines
1094165
Editorial: Berkeley Square House, Mayfair, London W1J 6BD **Tel:** 44 02071 128286
Email: info@solomonmines.com
Web site: http://www.solomonmines.com/
Freq: Quarterly
Circ: 40000 Not Audited
MAGAZINE
Art, Audio Video Trade, Beauty & Grooming, Broadcasting, Building & Construction, Business, Cameras, Commercial Real Estate, Consumer Electronics, Cosmetics

Somerset Country Gardener
981963
Editorial: Country Gardener Magazines, Mount House, Halse, Taunton TA4 3AD
Email: editorial@countrygardener.co.uk
Web site: www.countrygardener.co.uk
Freq: Monthly
Circ: 22000 Not Audited
Profile: Somerset free A4 publication printed in traditional black and white, with some full colour. Published 8 times a year to compliment the gardening season, March to July monthly, September October and a Winter issue. Country Gardener provides information on local gardening. Each edition contains a mix of practical and informative editorial, all written by seasoned experts.
MAGAZINE
Gardening

Somerset Life
982524
Editorial: Somerset Life, Archant House, Baggaage Road, Weston-super-Mare TQ9 5JA **Tel:** 44 01803 860910
Email: charlotte.skidmore@archant.co.uk
Web site: www.somerset-life.co.uk
Freq: Monthly
Circ: 8000 Not Audited
Editor: Carol Burns; **Editor:** Charlotte Skidmore
Profile: Magazine covering regional general interest including features and news on the Somerset area, towns, villages, the county's history and heritage, food and drink, property, antiques, fashion, interior design, gardens, motoring, arts and Somerset's social scene. Aimed at those living and visiting Somerset.
Ad Rate: Full Page Colour £962.00
MAGAZINE
Regional General Interest

Somerset Live
1098751
Tel: 44 01935 709700
Email: newsdesk@westgaz.co.uk
Web site: www.somersetlive.co.uk
Freq: Daily
Circ: 18421 Cision Digital Reach
MAGAZINE (ONLINE)
Art, Bars, Clubs & Pubs, Comedy, Entertainment, Literature, Local Entertainment Guides, Movies & Video, Photography, Theater & Performing Arts, Visual Arts

Somerset Society
1094742
Tel: 44 01823 365151
Email: newsdesk@countygazette.co.uk
Web site: www.limitededitionsomerset.co.uk
Freq: Monthly Not Audited
MAGAZINE
News & Current Affairs

Something Different on Their Shoulders
1076410
Email: support@somethingdifferentontheirshoulders.com
Web site: http://magazine.somethingdots.com/

Freq: Daily
MAGAZINE (ONLINE)
Social Issues

Something Sweet
996270
Editorial: Battersea Studios 2, 82 Silverthorne Road, Battersea, London SW8 3HE
Web site: www.somethingsweetcollection.co.uk/
Freq: Weekly Not Audited
MAGAZINE
Cooking & Baking

SomethingAboutMagazine
998256
Email: info@somethingaboutmagazine.com
Web site: http://somethingaboutmagazine.com/
Freq: Daily
Circ: 14547 Cision Digital Reach
MAGAZINE (ONLINE)
Art, Fashion, Literature, Photography, Visual Arts

Songlines
982122
Editorial: Mark Allen Group, St Jude's Church, Dulwich Road, London SE24 0PB
Tel: 44 02077 385454
Email: info@songlines.co.uk
Web site: www.songlines.co.uk
Freq: Bi-Monthly
Circ: 20000 Not Audited
Editor: Jo Frost
Profile: Magazine covering music from traditional and popular to contemporary and fusion with CD reviews, artist interviews, guides to world music traditions, concert listings and travel stories.
Ad Rate: Full Page Mono £1152.00
Ad Rate: Full Page Colour £1524.00
MAGAZINE
R&B, Urban, World

SongLink
999236
Editorial: 23 Belsize Crescent, London NW3 5QY **Tel:** 44 02077 942540
Web site: www.songlink.com
Freq: Daily
Circ: 8694 Cision Digital Reach
MAGAZINE (ONLINE)
Music

Songwriting & Composing Magazine
998521
Tel: 44 01207 500825
Email: gisc@btconnect.com
Web site: http://www.songwriters-guild.co.uk/magazine.htm
Freq: Quarterly Not Audited
MAGAZINE
Music

Sonic Shocks
996376
Editorial: Flat 4, 28 Hornsey Park Road, London N8 0JP **Tel:** 44 02088 884134
Email: info@sonicshocks.com
Web site: www.sonicshocks.com
Freq: Daily
Circ: 1730 Cision Digital Reach
MAGAZINE (ONLINE)
Bars, Clubs & Pubs, Classical/Choral/Band Music, Comedy, Country, Folk, Bluegrass, Dance Music, Entertainment, Jazz & Blues, Local Entertainment Guides, Movies & Video, Music

Sorted
984769
Editorial: PO Box 3070, Littlehampton, Littlehampton BN17 6WX
Tel: 44 01903 732190
Web site: http://www.sorted-magazine.com
Freq: Bi-Monthly
Circ: 25000 Not Audited
Profile: Men's lifestyle magazine covering motoring, gadgets, finance, films, finance, fitness, faith, sport and features.
Ad Rate: Full Page Mono £1700.00
Ad Rate: Full Page Colour £1700.00
MAGAZINE
Men's Interests, Religion

Consumer Magazines

Sortedfood.com
988501
Email: hello@sortedfood.com
Web site: www.sortedfood.com
Freq: Daily
Circ: 138500 Cision Digital Reach
MAGAZINE (ONLINE)
Cooking & Baking

Sortim BCN
1076165
Tel: 44 34932 384550
Email: sortimbcn@aspb.cat
Web site: http://www.sortimbcn.cat/
Freq: Daily
Circ: 9256 Cision Digital Reach
MAGAZINE (ONLINE)
Fitness & Exercise, Health & Medicine, Local Entertainment Guides, Movies & Video, Nutrition, Photography, Pop Music, Psychology, Regional General Interest, Relationships

Sotheby's
995793
Editorial: 34-35 New Bond Street, London W1A 2AA **Tel:** 44 02072 935000
Email: preview@sothebys.com
Web site: www.sothebys.com
Freq: Bi-Monthly
Circ: 35000 Not Audited
Editor: Paul Johnston
MAGAZINE
Art

Soul & Spirit
984576
Editorial: 25 Phoenix Court, Hawkins Road, Colchester CO2 8JY **Tel:** 44 01206 508628
Web site: www.soulandspiritmagazine.com
Freq: Monthly
Circ: 50000 Not Audited
Editor: Emily Louise Haddington
Profile: Magazine covering astrology, energy therapies, divination, life coaching, psychology, meditation, personality quizzes and wellbeing. Aimed at women aged between 25 and 60 years old.
Ad Rate: Full Page Colour £1395.00
MAGAZINE
Women's Interests

Sound on Sound
982101
Editorial: Media House, Trafalgar Way, Bar Hill, Cambridge CB23 8SQ
Tel: 44 01954 789888
Email: sos@soundonsound.com
Web site: www.soundonsound.com
Freq: Monthly
Circ: 24077 Not Audited
Profile: Magazine covering all aspects of hi-tech music and recording technology.
Ad Rate: Full Page Colour £2000.00
MAGAZINE
Music

Soundblab
995096
Editorial: Soundblab Ltd, PO Box 1213, Warrington WA4 9PH
Web site: www.soundblab.com
Freq: Daily
Circ: 7453 Cision Digital Reach
MAGAZINE (ONLINE)
Classical/Choral/Band Music, Country, Folk, Bluegrass, Dance Music, Jazz & Blues, Music, Pop Music, R&B, Urban, World, Rap & Hip Hop, Rock Music

Soundscape Magazine
995006
Editorial: 12 Lawrence Road, Romford, London RM2 5SS
Email: info@soundscapemagazine.com
Web site: www.soundscapemagazine.com
Freq: Daily
Circ: 12325 Cision Digital Reach
Editor: Natalie Humphries
MAGAZINE (ONLINE)
Music, R&B, Urban, World, Rock Music

Soundsphere
999409
Editorial: The Phoenix Centre, York St John University, York YO31 7QZ
Email: editor@soundspheremag.com
Web site: www.soundspheremag.co.uk
Freq: 3 Times/Year

Circ: 4000 Not Audited
MAGAZINE
Dance Music, Rock Music

The Source
1052966
Editorial: 10 Cabot Square, Canary Wharf, London E14 5AB **Tel:** 44 02073 453000
Email: scott.manson@ogilvy.com
Web site: http://www.britishgas.co.uk/the-source
Freq: Daily
Circ: 329 Cision Digital Reach
MAGAZINE (ONLINE)
Careers, Environment, Mobile Electronics, Oil

The Source (Coventry)
998859
Editorial: 1st Floor, The Hub, Coventry, Coventry CV1 5QT **Tel:** 44 02477 655200
Email: editor.source@gmail.com
Web site: www.cusu.org
Freq: Monthly
Circ: 4000 Not Audited
MAGAZINE
Student Lifestyle

Sous Chef
1105183
Editorial: Access Storage Building, 15 Tottenham Lane, London N8 9DJ
Tel: 44 02079 985066
Email: hello@souschef.co.uk
Web site: www.souschef.co.uk
Freq: Daily
Circ: 135769 Cision Digital Reach
MAGAZINE (ONLINE)
Cooking & Baking

South African Good News
1060654
Email: steuart@sagoodnews.co.za
Web site: http://www.sagoodnews.co.za
Circ: 62829 Cision Digital Reach
MAGAZINE (ONLINE)
Consumer Affairs, Crime & Violence, Defense & National Security, Energy & Environment, Ethical/Moral Issues, International News, Law, National News, News & Current Affairs, Northern Ireland

South Asian Wireless Communications
985849
Editorial: Brassey House, New Zealand Avenue, Walton-on-Thames, London KT12 1QD **Tel:** 44 01932 886537
Web site: www.kadiumpublishing.com/sasian.html
Freq: Quarterly
Circ: 7000 Not Audited
Profile: Publication dedicated to wireless communications throughout south Asia and providing direct contact with key wireless communications buyers and specifies throughout the region. Aimed at companies and organisations that use mobile and wireless communications as part of their business.
MAGAZINE
Industry, Internet, Mobile Communications, Telecommunications/Electronic Communications

South Belfast Life
984224
Editorial: 39 Boucher Road, Belfast BT12 6UT **Tel:** 44 02890 663311
Email: southbelfastlife@ulstertatler.com
Web site: www.ulstertatler.com/publications
Freq: Semi-Annual
Circ: 15000 Not Audited
Editor: Christopher Sherry
Profile: Magazine covering women's and men's fashion, local events profiles of local people and businesses, interiors, art, property, health and beauty.
Ad Rate: Full Page Colour £900.00
MAGAZINE
Regional General Interest

South Cambs
982474
Editorial: South Cambs District Council, South Cambridge Hall, Cambourne Business Park, Cambridge CB23 6EA
Tel: 44 03450 450500
Email: south.cambsmagazine@scambs.gov.uk

Web site: www.scambs.gov.uk
Freq: Quarterly
Circ: 65000 Not Audited
MAGAZINE
Regional General Interest

South East London Journal
997770
Freq: Bi-Monthly
Circ: 41000 Not Audited
MAGAZINE
News & Current Affairs

South East Rider
995060
Editorial: Unit 2 Devizes Trade Centre, Hopton Park, Devizes, Devizes SN10 2EH
Tel: 44 01380 730888
Email: sales@redpin.co.uk
Web site: http://www.southeastrider.co.uk
Freq: Monthly
Profile: Magazine covering horse riding in the South East.
MAGAZINE
Equestrian Sports

South East Walker
981907
Editorial: 8 Faircroft, 37 St Andrew's Grove, London N16 5NJ **Tel:** 44 02073 398500
Email: southeastwalker@gmail.com
Web site: www.surreyramblers.org.uk
Freq: Quarterly
Circ: 23000 Not Audited
Editor: Les Douglas
Profile: Regional newsletter reporting on Ramblers' Association activities.
MAGAZINE
Outdoor Recreation

South Yorkshire Times
983018
Editorial: 39 Printing Office Street, Doncaster DN1 1TN **Tel:** 44 01302 819111
Email: editorial@dearnetoday.co.uk
Web site: www.southyorkshiretimes.co.uk
Freq: Weekly
Circ: 47449 Cision Digital Reach
Profile: Online version of the South Yorkshire Times newspaper covering local news and sports for the surrounding area.
MAGAZINE (ONLINE)

Southam District Advertiser
995155
Editorial: 14 Market Hill, Southam, Southam CV47 0HF **Tel:** 44 01926 811911
Web site: www.districtadvertisers.co.uk
Freq: Monthly
Circ: 22500 Not Audited
MAGAZINE
News & Current Affairs

Southend Rising
997664
Editorial: 345 Westbourne Grove, Southend-on-Sea, Westcliff-on-Sea, Southend-on-Sea SS0 0PU **Tel:** 44 07921 361856
Email: info@southendrising.com
Web site: www.southendrising.com
Freq: Daily
Circ: 10618 Cision Digital Reach
MAGAZINE (ONLINE)
Business, Regional General Interest, Small and Medium Business

Southern African Wireless Communications
984674
Editorial: Brassey House, New Zealand Avenue, Walton-on-Thames, London KT12 1QD **Tel:** 44 01932 886537
Web site: www.kadiumpublishing.com/sawc.html
Freq: Bi-Monthly
Circ: 7000 Not Audited
Profile: Publication dedicated to wireless communications throughout east, west and south Africa and providing direct contact with key wireless communications buyers and specifies throughout the region. Aimed at companies and organisations that use mobile and wireless communications as part of their business.

Ad Rate: Full Page Colour £4550.00
MAGAZINE
Industry, Internet, Mobile Communications, Telecommunications/Electronic Communications

Southport Reporter
982930
Editorial: 4a Post Office Avenue, Southport, Southport PR9 0US **Tel:** 44 01704 513569
Email: news24@southportreporter.com
Web site: www.southportreporter.co.uk
Freq: Weekly
Circ: 1410 Cision Digital Reach
Editor: Patrick Trollope
Profile: The Southport Reporter is an online only newspaper and covers local news and sports for the surrounding area.
MAGAZINE (ONLINE)
Regional

Southside
987749
Editorial: 6 Broadfield Court, Broadfield Business Park, Sheffield S8 0XF
Tel: 44 01142 506300
Email: info@rmcmedia.co.uk
Web site: www.regionalmagazine.co.uk/RMC_Extra/article.asp?cl=25
Freq: Monthly
Circ: 20000 Not Audited
MAGAZINE
Regional General Interest

Southwark Life
984524
Editorial: 160 Tooley Street, London SE1 2QH **Tel:** 44 02075 257052
Email: southwark.life@southwark.gov.uk
Web site: www.southwark.gov.uk/southwarklife
Freq: Quarterly
Circ: 125000 Not Audited
MAGAZINE
Regional General Interest

Spa Business
981048
Editorial: Portmill House, Portmill Lane, Hitchin SG5 1DJ **Tel:** 44 01462 431385
Email: newsdesk@leisuremedia.com
Web site: www.spabusiness.com
Freq: Quarterly
Circ: 27928 Not Audited
Profile: Spa Business magazine was launched in 2003 and is written for spa market investors and developers, operators and buyers, designers and suppliers. Provides latest news, jobs, features and interviews from the industry.
Ad Rate: Full Page Colour £2280.00
MAGAZINE
Fitness & Exercise

Spa Opportunities
983984
Editorial: Portmill House, Portmill Lane, Hitchin, Hitchin SG5 1DJ
Tel: 44 01462 431385
Email: newsdesk@leisuremedia.com
Web site: www.spaopportunities.com
Freq: Bi-Weekly
Circ: 50000 Not Audited
Profile: Magazine containing news about the international spa industry. Carries latest jobs in spas and resorts worldwide plus details of training courses and institutions as well as featuring up-to-the minute news about the spa industry.
Ad Rate: Full Page Colour £1550.00
MAGAZINE
Fitness & Exercise

The Spa Spy
1072211
Email: spy@the-spa-spy.com
Web site: https://www.theluxuryspaedit.com/
Freq: Daily
Circ: 11301 Cision Digital Reach
MAGAZINE (ONLINE)
Airline Inflight, Travel

Spa Wellbeing
1060245
Tel: 44 01932 400800
Web site: http://spawellbeing.com
Freq: Daily
Circ: 521 Cision Digital Reach
MAGAZINE (ONLINE)
Luxury Goods, Travel

The Space
997879

Editorial: Studio 30, Fazeley Studios, 191 Fazeley Street, Birmingham B5 5SE
Tel: 44 01216 631488
Email: contactus@thespace.org
Web site: http://www.thespace.org/
Freq: Daily
Circ: 10929 Cision Digital Reach
MAGAZINE (ONLINE)
Art

Spaceflight
985214

Editorial: 27-29 South Lambeth Road, London SW8 1SZ **Tel:** 44 02077 353160
Email: mail@bis-space.com
Web site: www.bis-space.com
Freq: Monthly
Circ: 5000 Not Audited
Editor: David Baker
Profile: Spaceflight is the international magazine of space launched in 1956. Regular features, often written by those directly involved in a particular technology or project, cover all aspects of space technology and exploration, astronomy, satellites, commercial space, political activities, educational programmes and detailed space mission reports.
Ad Rate: Full Page Mono £750.00
Ad Rate: Full Page Colour £1000.00
MAGAZINE
Astronomy

The Spaces
988877

Email: info@thespaces.com
Web site: thespaces.com
Freq: Daily
Circ: 47943 Cision Digital Reach
MAGAZINE (ONLINE)
Architecture & Design, Art, Property Management & Maintenance

The Spark
981773

Tel: 44 01183 784156
Email: editor.spark@reading.ac.uk
Web site: www.sparknewspaper.co.uk
Freq: Monthly
Circ: 2000 Not Audited
MAGAZINE
Student Lifestyle

Spark magazine
986901

Editorial: The David Puttnam Media Centre, St Peters Campus, Sunderland SR6 0DD
Tel: 44 01915 153875
Email: news@sparksunderland.com
Web site: www.sparksunderland.com
Freq: Quarterly
Circ: 6000 Not Audited
Profile: Publication that covers music, entertainment, lifestyle and sports content as well as listings for events in the Sunderland and wider North East region.
MAGAZINE
Regional General Interest

Sparkle World
982455

Editorial: Suites 3 & 4 Canon Court East, Abbey Lawn, Shrewsbury SY2 5DE
Tel: 44 01743 364433
Email: mysparkleworld@redan.com
Web site: http://www.mysparkleworld.com/
Freq: Monthly
Circ: 47304 Not Audited
Editor: Helen Rushton
Profile: Children's magazine with fun stories and activities based around popular children's characters including Polly Pocket, My Little Pony, Rainbow Magic and Strawberry Shortcake. Every issue comes with a 24-page pull-out workbook, 4-page cut-out activities or poster, competitions and a free gift. Aimed at girls aged 3 to 7 years old.
Ad Rate: Full Page Colour £1800.00
MAGAZINE
Teen/Young Adult

SparkSpread
998930

Tel: 44 02071 928662
Email: info@sparkspread.com
Web site: www.sparkspread.com
Freq: Daily

Circ: 9297 Cision Digital Reach
MAGAZINE (ONLINE)
Alternative/Renewable Energy, Electricity, Nuclear Power, Oil, Water & Sanitation

SPC
984265

Editorial: Natraj Building, The Tanneries, 55 Bermondsey Street, London SE1 3XG
Tel: 44 02071 931279
Email: spc@hpcimedia.com
Web site: www.cosmeticsbusiness.com/Category/SPC
Freq: Monthly
Circ: 6000 Not Audited
Editor: Julia Wray
MAGAZINE
Cosmetics

Spear's
983261

Editorial: John Carpenter House, John Carpenter Street, London EC4Y 0AN
Tel: 44 02079 366445
Web site: www.spearswms.com
Freq: Bi-Monthly
Circ: 27000 Not Audited
Profile: Magazine covering all aspects of wealth management including hedge funds and pension funds as well as lifestyle, wine, arts, luxury travel and jewellery. Aimed at the most wealthy, successful and influential individuals around the world.Premium subscription by invitation only. Alternative Title: WMS
Ad Rate: Full Page Colour £7250.00
MAGAZINE
Banking, Luxury Goods

Special Children
981535

Editorial: Optimus Education Ltd, 6th Floor, Elizabeth House, 39 York Road, London SE1 7NQ
Email: specialchildren@optimus-education.com
Web site: http://my.optimus-education.com/special-children-magazine-issue-234-jan-feb-2017
Freq: Bi-Monthly
Circ: 5055 Not Audited
Ad Rate: Full Page Colour £1100.00
MAGAZINE
Disability, Education

Specialist Finance Introducer
1097891

Editorial: Fergusson House, 124-128 City Road, London EC1V 2NJ
Tel: 44 02075 028220
Web site: http://specialistfinanceintroducer.co.uk/
Freq: Daily
Circ: 13341 Cision Digital Reach
MAGAZINE (ONLINE)
Banking, Lending, Personal Finance

Specsavers Magazine
995978

Editorial: Embassy House, Queens Avenue, Clifton, Bristol BS8 1SB
Tel: 44 01179 251696
Email: uk.pressoffice@specsavers.com
Web site: https://www.specsavers.co.uk/loveglasses
Freq: Semi-Annual
Circ: 106508 Not Audited
MAGAZINE
Health & Medicine, Ophthalmology & Optometry

The Spectator
980802

Editorial: 22 Old Queen Street, London SW1H 9HP **Tel:** 44 02079 610200
Email: editor@spectator.co.uk
Web site: www.spectator.co.uk
Freq: Weekly
Circ: 85429 Not Audited
Editor: Fraser Nelson
Profile: Magazine covering politics including news and current affairs, arts, culture, books, business, investments, food, drinks and events. First published in 1828. Aimed at those interested in politics, the art world, theatre and culture.
Ad Rate: Full Page Colour £5078.00
MAGAZINE
Politics

The Spectator - The Spectator Australia
1001340

Email: editor@spectator.co.uk
Web site: www.spectator.co.uk/australia
Freq: Weekly
Circ: 8341 Not Audited
MAGAZINE
News & Current Affairs

Speedscene
982679

Editorial: The Laurels, Acton Turville, Badminton GL9 1HH **Tel:** 44 01454 218550
Email: editor@hillclimbandsprint.co.uk
Web site: www.speedscene.co.uk
Freq: Bi-Monthly
Circ: 600 Not Audited
Editor: Chris Bennett
Profile: Magazine dedicated to sprinting and hillclimbing is published five or six times a year. Subscription is free to HSA members. Contains reports, articles, photographs and features covering all aspects of sprinting and speed hillclimbing.
Ad Rate: Full Page Mono £150.00
Ad Rate: Full Page Colour £225.00
MAGAZINE
Motorsports

SPELL
985103

Editorial: 6 Jubilee Way, London SW19 3XD
Tel: 44 02082 543600
Email: editorial@spellmagazine.com
Web site: www.spellmagazine.com
Freq: Monthly
Circ: 7000 Not Audited
Profile: Magazine covering the latest hair and beauty news and specifically looks at products and styles that suit women with black or Asian skin. Aimed at women from an ethnic background.
MAGAZINE
Beauty & Grooming, Cosmetics, Hair

Sphere
982326

Editorial: 46-48 East Smithfield, London E1W 1AW **Tel:** 44 02074 261010
Email: sphere@iln.co.uk
Web site: www.spherelife.com
Freq: Quarterly
Circ: 63853 Not Audited
Editor: Jemima Sissons
Profile: Magazine containing features on arts, fashion, cuisine and shopping with profiles of those in the international spotlight. Also includes a guide to events around each Orient-Express hotel, train or cruise ship. Read by travellers on the Venice Simplon-Orient-Express and in Orient-Express Hotels worldwide.Previous title: Orient-Express Magazine Laura Richardson is the Editor to whom press releases should be addressed.
Ad Rate: Full Page Colour £6150.00
MAGAZINE
Luxury Goods, Railroad, Travel

Sphere Asia
989670

Editorial: 46-48 East Smithfield, London E1W 1AW **Tel:** 44 02074 261010
Email: iln@iln.co.uk
Web site: www.orient-expressmagazine.com
Profile: Magazine covering travel, fashion, art, celebrities, theatre and entertainment.
Ad Rate: Full Page Mono £4000.00
Ad Rate: Full Page Colour £4000.00
MAGAZINE
Luxury Goods, Travel

spiked
982844

Editorial: 27 Holywell Row, London EC2A 4JB **Tel:** 44 02074 040470
Email: general-enquiries@spiked-online.com
Web site: www.spiked-online.com
Freq: Daily
Circ: 693704 Cision Digital Reach
Editor: Brendan O'Neill
Profile: Website providing a combination of comment, news and in-depth documentary on a range of topics. Subjects include Politics, IT, science, liberties and culture. Aimed at those not satisfied by the mainstream press and those who enjoy enlightened thinking and freedom of expression in journalism.Nathalie Rothschild

is the Commissioning Editor to whom press releases should be addressed.
MAGAZINE (ONLINE)
National News

SPIKES
984839

Editorial: Bridge House, 69 London Road, Twickenham, London TW1 3QR
Email: editor@spikesmag.com
Web site: https://spikes.iaaf.org/
Freq: Daily
Circ: 36050 Cision Digital Reach
Editor: Michelle Sammet
MAGAZINE (ONLINE)
Sports

The Spin Alley
997124

Email: news@thespinalley.co.uk
Web site: www.thespinalley.co.uk
Freq: Daily
Circ: 5659 Cision Digital Reach
MAGAZINE (ONLINE)
News & Current Affairs

Spindle
986583

Editorial: Heartspace Studio 31, Hackney Downs Studios, Amhurst Terrace, London E8 2BT **Tel:** 44 07707 125235
Email: info@spindlemagazine.com
Web site: www.spindlemagazine.com
Freq: Semi-Annual Not Audited
Profile: Spindle is a quarterly free magazine covering fashion, music, art and design.
Ad Rate: Full Page Colour £1000.00
MAGAZINE
Art, Classical/Choral/Band Music, Country, Folk, Bluegrass, Dance Music, Fashion, Jazz & Blues, Literature, Music, Photography, Pop Music

Spirit & Destiny
983663

Editorial: Academic House, 24-28 Oval Road, London NW1 7DT
Tel: 44 02072 418395
Email: spirit.destiny@bauer.co.uk
Web site: www.spiritanddestiny.co.uk
Freq: Monthly
Circ: 31802 Not Audited
Editor: Sue Ricketts
Profile: Magazine covering astrology, alternative therapies, self discovery and spiritual self improvement. Includes features on psychic matters and enlightening ideas on holistic therapies and alternative lifestyles. launched in 2002. Aimed at women aged between 25 and 50 years old.
Ad Rate: Full Page Mono £4150.00
Ad Rate: Full Page Colour £8300.00
MAGAZINE
Alternative Medicine, Astrology & Parapsychology, Women's Interests

The Spirits Business
984512

Editorial: Units 122-124, 30 Great Guildford Street, London SE1 0HS
Tel: 44 02078 032420
Email: info@thespiritsbusiness.com
Web site: www.thespiritsbusiness.com
Freq: Monthly
Circ: 13000 Not Audited
Profile: Magazine dedicated to what is going on globally in the world of spirits including vodka, whisky, gin, cognac, brandy, liqueurs and cocktails.
Ad Rate: Full Page Colour £4150.00
MAGAZINE
Alcohol & Spirits

SPLAT!
997486

Editorial: 2 Lindal Road, London SE4 1EJ
Email: vincent@soupermedia.com
Freq: Bi-Monthly
Circ: 4185 Cision Digital Reach
Editor: Vincent Vincent
MAGAZINE (ONLINE)
Teen/Young Adult

SPN
983344

Editorial: Priory Lodge, Halse, Taunton, Taunton TA4 3AE **Tel:** 44 02083 068150
Email: info@swimmingpoolnews.co.uk
Web site: www.swimmingpoolnews.co.uk
Freq: Bi-Monthly

Consumer Magazines

Circ: 7000 Not Audited
MAGAZINE
Fitness & Exercise

SPOnG.com
988425
Editorial: New Media Centre, West Parade, Wakefield WF1 1LT Tel: 44 08458 621603
Web site: spong.com
Freq: Daily
Circ: 37235 Cision Digital Reach
MAGAZINE (ONLINE)
Computer & Video Games

Sport Industry Group
983851
Editorial: First Floor, Flitcroft House, 114-116 Charing Cross Roa, London WC2H 0JR
Tel: 44 02072 407700
Email: news@sportindustry.biz
Web site: www.sportindustry.biz
Freq: Daily
Circ: 45703 Cision Digital Reach
Profile: Website covering the sports industry. SPORT INDUSTRY GROUP features news, analysis and information on business issues within sport including sponsorship, TV rights, governance and commerce.
MAGAZINE (ONLINE)
Fitness & Exercise

The Sport Review
985520
Editorial: 16 Beaufort Court, Admirals Way, London E14 9XL
Email: newsdesk@thesportreview.com
Web site: www.thesportreview.com
Freq: Daily
Circ: 261543 Cision Digital Reach
Profile: Website covering sport news. The Sport Review shares the latest news on football, tennis, rugby and Formula 1.
MAGAZINE (ONLINE)
Boxing, Cricket, Golf, Motorsports, Olympic Sports, Racquet Sports, Rugby, Soccer, Sports, Winter Sports

Sport.co.uk
984718
Editorial: Augustus Mews, 109 High Street, Braintree, Braintree CM7 1JS
Tel: 44 01376 809000
Web site: www.sport.co.uk
Freq: Daily
Circ: 101736 Cision Digital Reach
MAGAZINE (ONLINE)
Basketball, Bicycles, Billiards, Boating & Yachting, Bodybuilding, Bowling, Boxing, Cricket, Equestrian Sports, Extreme/ Adventure Sports

SportBusiness International
982820
Editorial: 7th Floor, 133 Whitechapel High Street, London E1 7QA
Tel: 44 02072 654100
Email: infoteam@sportbusiness.com
Web site: www.sportbusiness.com/ sportbusiness-international
Freq: Monthly
Circ: 20000 Not Audited
Editor: Ben Cronin
MAGAZINE
Fitness & Exercise

Sporting Gun
982284
Editorial: Pinehurst 2, Pinehurst Road, Farnborough Business Park, Farnborough, London GU14 7BF Tel: 44 01252 555000
Email: sportinggun@timeinc.com
Web site: www.sportinggun.co.uk
Freq: Monthly
Circ: 19645 Not Audited
Editor: Matt Clark
Profile: Magazine containing shooting instruction, gun-care and maintenance. Includes game shoots, antique guns, pigeon and clay shooting, wildfowling, gun dog training, shooting fixtures, news and results.
Ad Rate: Full Page Mono £2275.00
Ad Rate: Full Page Colour £3045.00
MAGAZINE
Shooting/Guns

Sporting Rifle
985941
Editorial: 2nd Floor, Lawrence House, Morrell Street, Leamington Spa, Leamington Spa CV32 5SZ Tel: 44 01225 687426
Email: fieldsports@futurenet.com
Web site: www.sporting-rifle.com
Freq: Monthly
Circ: 18500 Not Audited
Editor: Peter Carr
Profile: Magazine covering all aspects of live quarry shooting, rabbits, foxes, deer and overseas big game as well as reviews of kits, guns, clothing and gadgets. Aimed at sports rifle shooting enthusiasts.
MAGAZINE
Shooting/Guns

Sporting Shooter
980963
Tel: 44 01189 742508
Email: editor@sportingshooter.co.uk
Web site: http://www.sportingshooter.co.uk/ home
Freq: Monthly
Circ: 11868 Not Audited
Profile: Magazine covering shooting sports especially game shooting, pigeons, gun dogs, gun trade, clay pigeons and game keeping as well as associated activities such as beating, 4x4s, game cookery, etc. Aimed at those interested in shooting.
Ad Rate: Full Page Colour £850.00
MAGAZINE
Shooting/Guns

sportingintelligence.com
986668
Editorial: PO Box 26676, Helensburgh, Helensburgh G84 4DT Tel: 44 07444 463430
Web site: www.sportingintelligence.com
Freq: Daily
Circ: 41276 Cision Digital Reach
MAGAZINE (ONLINE)
Basketball, Bicycles, Billiards, Boating & Yachting, Bodybuilding, Bowling, Boxing, Cricket, Equestrian Sports, Extreme/ Adventure Sports

SportingLife.com
982883
Tel: 44 01133 895823
Email: editorial@sportinglife.com
Web site: http://www.sportinglife.com/
Freq: Daily
Circ: 3807295 Cision Digital Reach
Editor: Dave Ord
MAGAZINE (ONLINE)
Basketball, Bicycles, Billiards, Boating & Yachting, Bodybuilding, Bowling, Boxing, Casinos & Gaming, Cricket, Equestrian Sports

Sports & Leisure Catering
988858
Editorial: 4th Floor, Joynes House, New Road, Gravesend DA11 0AJ
Tel: 44 08455 006008
Web site: http://www.h2opublishing.co.uk/ publications/sports-leisure
Freq: Quarterly
Circ: 3437 Not Audited
Profile: Publication dedicated to catering at the UK's top sports venues and tourist attractions.
Ad Rate: Full Page Colour £1500.00
MAGAZINE
Fitness & Exercise

Sports Betting Community
995034
Editorial: 103-105 Brighton Road, Coulsden, London CR5 2NG
Web site: www.sbcnews.co.uk
Freq: Daily
Circ: 159342 Cision Digital Reach
MAGAZINE (ONLINE)
Casinos & Gaming, Computer & Video Games

SPORTS CLUB (Foschini)
1060684
Email: gary@hsm.co.za
Freq: Monthly

Circ: 239320 Not Audited
MAGAZINE
Basketball, Bicycles, Billiards, Boating & Yachting, Bodybuilding, Bowling, Boxing, Cricket, Equestrian Sports, Extreme/ Adventure Sports

Sports Club Magazine
1101935
Web site: www.sportsclubmag.co.uk
Freq: Weekly
MAGAZINE
Fitness & Exercise

Sports Gazette
995377
Tel: 44 02082 404111
Email: journalism@stmarys.ac.uk
Web site: www.sportsgazette.co.uk
Freq: Daily
Circ: 12787 Cision Digital Reach
MAGAZINE (ONLINE)
Basketball, Bicycles, Billiards, Boating & Yachting, Bodybuilding, Bowling, Boxing, Cricket, Equestrian Sports, Extreme/ Adventure Sports

Sports Industry Group
999105
Editorial: First Floor, Flitcroft House, 114-116 Charing Cross Road, London WC2H 0JR Tel: 44 02072 407702
Email: news@sportindustry.biz
Web site: www.sportindustry.biz
Freq: Daily
Circ: 45703 Cision Digital Reach
MAGAZINE (ONLINE)
Basketball, Bicycles, Billiards, Boating & Yachting, Bodybuilding, Bowling, Boxing, Cricket, Equestrian Sports, Extreme/ Adventure Sports

Sports Insight
983744
Editorial: 21-23 Phoenix Court, Hawkins Road, Colchester CO2 8JY
Tel: 44 01273 505900
Web site: http://www.sports-insight.co.uk
Freq: Monthly
Circ: 5352 Not Audited
Profile: Magazine covering the UK sports trade including retail management, sports good, equipment, footwear, clothing, marketing and branding. First published in 2004, the publication has an average of 68 pages per issue. Aimed at retailer, manufacturer, wholesaler, distributor and sports buyer in the industry.
Ad Rate: Full Page Colour £1500.00
MAGAZINE
Fitness & Exercise

Sports Liberated
996982
Email: sportsliberated@gmail.com
Web site: www.sportsliberated.com
Freq: Daily
Circ: 9544 Cision Digital Reach
MAGAZINE (ONLINE)
Basketball, Bicycles, Billiards, Boating & Yachting, Bodybuilding, Bowling, Boxing, Cricket, Equestrian Sports, Extreme/ Adventure Sports

Sports Management
981047
Editorial: Portmill House, Portmill Lane, Hitchin, Hitchin SG5 1DJ
Tel: 44 01462 431385
Email: newsdesk@leisuremedia.com
Web site: www.sportsmanagement.co.uk
Freq: Quarterly
Circ: 40805 Not Audited
Profile: Magazine featuring sports news, jobs, training, features, products, tenders, property and diary dates for the leisure industry. It is the official magazine of the Sports and Play Contractors Association (SAPCA). First published in 1997. Read by members of SAPCA as well as managers of sports clubs, stadia and sports governing bodies.
Ad Rate: Full Page Colour £1169.00
MAGAZINE
Fitness & Exercise

Sports Mole
986985
Editorial: Unit 2a, The Chandlery, London SE1 7QY Tel: 44 02079 935703
Email: contact@sportsmole.com
Web site: www.sportsmole.co.uk

Freq: Daily
Circ: 811524 Cision Digital Reach
Editor: Neil Wilkes
MAGAZINE (ONLINE)
Basketball, Bicycles, Billiards, Boating & Yachting, Bodybuilding, Bowling, Boxing, Cricket, Equestrian Sports, Extreme/ Adventure Sports

Sports Post
1060522
Email: info@sportpost.com
Web site: http://www.sportpost.com
Circ: 8985 Cision Digital Reach
MAGAZINE (ONLINE)
Basketball, Bicycles, Billiards, Boating & Yachting, Bodybuilding, Bowling, Boxing, Cricket, Equestrian Sports, Extreme/ Adventure Sports

The Sports, Health & Leisure Directory
997761
Editorial: Britannia House, Leagrave Road, Luton LU3 1RJ Tel: 44 01582 488385
Email: info@mediachameleon.co.uk
Web site: www.sportswebsite.co.uk
Freq: Annual
Circ: 121700 Not Audited
MAGAZINE
Basketball, Bicycles, Billiards, Boating & Yachting, Bodybuilding, Bowling, Boxing, Cricket, Equestrian Sports, Extreme/ Adventure Sports

Sports4Bars
995336
Editorial: Gainsborough House, 59-60 Thames Street, Windsor SL4 1TX
Tel: 44 01753 272022
Web site: www.sports4bars.com
Freq: Daily
Circ: 11636 Cision Digital Reach
Editor: Justin O'Regan
MAGAZINE (ONLINE)
Bars, Clubs & Pubs, Basketball, Bicycles, Billiards, Boating & Yachting, Bowling, Boxing, Equestrian Sports, Extreme/ Adventure Sports, Football (American)

Sportsister
984975
Editorial: Unit 3.40 Canterbury Court, Kennington Business Park Centre, 1-3 Brixton Road, London SW9 6DE
Email: editorial@sportsister.com
Web site: www.sportsister.com
Freq: Daily
Circ: 12963 Cision Digital Reach
Editor: Danielle Sellwood
Profile: Website covering women's sports. Sportsister covers everything from sports news and anaylsis to training advice and equipment reviews.
MAGAZINE (ONLINE)
Basketball, Bicycles, Billiards, Boating & Yachting, Bodybuilding, Bowling, Boxing, Cricket, Equestrian Sports, Extreme/ Adventure Sports

SportsPro
984838
Editorial: 3rd Floor, America House, 2 America Square, London EC3 2LU
Tel: 44 02075 493250
Email: editor@sportspromedia.com
Web site: www.sportspromedia.com
Freq: Daily
Circ: 20000 Not Audited
Editor: Eoin Connolly
Profile: International monthly publication for the sports industry. It offers feature stories, industry analysis and places a focus on the overall sponsorship and financing of the sports industry, as well as marketing and management.
Ad Rate: Full Page Colour £5995.00
MAGAZINE
News & Current Affairs

SportStyleFashion
998118
Editorial: 100 Marine Crescent, Worthing, Worthing BN12 4JH Tel: 44 01273 915079
Web site: www.sportstylefashion.com
Freq: Daily
Circ: 949 Cision Digital Reach

Editor: Arthur Van De Laak
MAGAZINE (ONLINE)
Basketball, Bicycles, Fashion, Motorsports, Soccer, Swimming/Watersports, Winter Sports

Sportsvibe
985046
Editorial: The Basement, 33 Union Street, London SE1 1SD **Tel:** 44 02079 406252
Email: info@sportsvibe.co.uk
Web site: www.sportsvibe.co.uk
Freq: Daily
Circ: 68235 Cision Digital Reach
Editor: Steven Green
MAGAZINE (ONLINE)
Basketball, Bicycles, Billiards, Boating & Yachting, Bodybuilding, Bowling, Boxing, Cricket, Equestrian Sports, Extreme/Adventure Sports

Sportswoman
1096363
Tel: 44 08007 720669
Email: newsdesk@sportswomanmag.co.uk
Web site: http://sportswomanmag.co.uk/
Freq: Monthly
Circ: 20000 Not Audited
MAGAZINE
Bicycles, Olympic Sports, Racquet Sports, Rowing, Soccer, Sports

The Spurs Web
1102293
Editorial: PO BOX 10, London SA129UR
Email: neil@totally360.com
Web site: http://www.spurs-web.com
Freq: Daily
Circ: 42280 Cision Digital Reach
Editor: Neil Vaughan
MAGAZINE (ONLINE)
Soccer

SpyCycle
1062755
Editorial: 32 Bull Road, Ipswich IP3 8GP
Email: newsdesk@spycycle.uk
Web site: http://www.spycycle.uk/
Freq: Daily
Circ: 7738 Cision Digital Reach
Editor: Richard Atkins
MAGAZINE (ONLINE)
Bicycles

Square Mile
983062
Editorial: 5 Tun Yard, 8 Peardon Street, London SW8 3HT **Tel:** 44 02078 199999
Email: editorial@squareupmedia.com
Web site: www.squaremile.com
Freq: Monthly
Circ: 59422 Not Audited
Profile: Magazine covering men's interest and affluent lifestyle including travel, events, luxury goods, fashion, food, wine, motors, sports, property, interiors and health and fitness. Aimed at professional men in the square mile of London with a high disposable income.
Ad Rate: Full Page Colour £5995.00
MAGAZINE
Lifestyle, Luxury Goods, Men's Interests, Regional General Interest, Women's Interests

Squash Player
982293
Editorial: Longhouse, 460 Bath Road, Longford, London UB7 0EB
Tel: 44 01753 775511
Email: editor@squashplayer.co.uk
Web site: www.squashplayer.co.uk
Freq: Bi-Monthly
Circ: 14000 Not Audited
Profile: Magazine covering news, reports, tournament coverage and results, articles and stories from the world of squash.
Ad Rate: Full Page Colour £300.00
MAGAZINE
Racquet Sports

SquidBeak
996435
Editorial: 5 Summerhouse Mews, York YO30 7ED **Tel:** 44 01904 611360
Email: info@squidbeak.co.uk
Web site: www.squidbeak.co.uk
Freq: Daily

Circ: 8091 Cision Digital Reach
MAGAZINE (ONLINE)
Restaurant Reviews

SSAW Magazine
1061007
Email: hello@ssawmagazine.com
Web site: www.ssawmagazine.com/
Freq: Semi-Annual Not Audited
MAGAZINE
Antiques/Collectibles, Art, Arts, Fashion, Literature, Photography, Theater & Performing Arts, Visual Arts

St David's Notebook
998294
Editorial: The Content Emporium, Studio 2, 300 North Street, Bristol BS3 1JU
Tel: 44 07799 537532
Web site: www.thecontentemporium.co.uk
Freq: Semi-Annual Not Audited
MAGAZINE
Beauty & Grooming, Cosmetics, Fashion, Hair, Restaurant Reviews, Shopping

St Helens Reporter
980441
Editorial: Martland Mill, Martland Mill Lane, Wigan WN5 0LX **Tel:** 44 01942 228000
Email: sthelens.reporter@lancspublications.co.uk
Web site: www.sthelensreporter.co.uk
Freq: Daily
Circ: 11269 Cision Digital Reach
Profile: The St Helens Reporter is a weekly, local newspaper covering local news, sport and lifestyle for the St Helens and Prescot areas. The newspaper is published on a Wednesday.
Ad Rate: Full Page Mono £3231.36
MAGAZINE (ONLINE)
News & Current Affairs

The St John's Wood Magazine
1097887
Tel: 44 02079 874320
Email: info@rwmg.co.uk
Web site: rwmg.co.uk/website/advertising__montly_titles.php
Freq: Monthly
Circ: 50000 Not Audited
MAGAZINE
Luxury Goods, Regional General Interest

St. George Magazine
1070237
Editorial: Suite 9, Beaufort Court, Admirals Way, Canary Wharf, London E14 9XL
Web site: www.berkeleygroup.co.uk/property-developers/st-george/st-george-magazine
Freq: Annual
MAGAZINE
Luxury Goods

Stadiavision
983028
Editorial: 12 Kings Park, Primrose Hill, London WD4 8ST **Tel:** 44 01923 272900
Email: info@grandflame.co.uk
Web site: www.stadiavision.co.uk
Freq: Quarterly
Circ: 10535 Not Audited
Editor: James Surridge
Profile: Magazine covering major UK and European sports venues with features, news reviews and topics relating to the day to day management within the football and sports arena markets. Includes industry news, retail news stadium development, security, pitch management and hospitality. Aimed at directors and senior managers/department heads who are charged with the day to day running of the various departments within the football and sports arenas throughout the UK.
Ad Rate: Full Page Colour £2950.00
MAGAZINE
Fitness & Exercise

The Staff Canteen
999603
Editorial: Unit B10, Arena Business Centre, Holyrood Close, Poole, Poole BH17 7FL
Tel: 44 01202 612123
Email: admin@thestaffcanteen.com
Web site: www.thestaffcanteen.com
Freq: Daily
Circ: 30555 Cision Digital Reach

Editor: Cara Houchen
MAGAZINE (ONLINE)
Bars, Clubs & Pubs

Staffordshire Life
982527
Editorial: Sentinel House, Bethesda Street, Hanley, Stoke-on-Trent ST1 3GN
Tel: 44 01782 864100
Web site: www.staffordshirelife.co.uk
Freq: Monthly
Circ: 7000 Not Audited
Profile: County magazine containing news and features on local people, places and events. Covers fashion and beauty, homes and gardens, travel and entertainment.
Ad Rate: Full Page Mono £925.00
Ad Rate: Full Page Colour £1270.00
MAGAZINE
Regional General Interest

Staffordshire Living
983515
Editorial: B1 Trentham Business Quarter, Bellringer Road, Trentham Lakes, Stoke-on-Trent ST4 8GB **Tel:** 44 01782 644456
Email: features@staffsmedia.com
Web site: www.staffordshireliving.co.uk
Freq: Bi-Monthly
Circ: 25000 Not Audited
Profile: Magazine covering home, leisure, events, health, fitness, travel, fashion, property, motoring and finance. Aimed at residents of Staffordshire.
Ad Rate: Full Page Colour £1095.00
MAGAZINE
Regional General Interest

Staffs Live
995389
Editorial: Staffs Live, University of Staffordshire, College Road, Stoke-on-Trent ST4 2DE **Tel:** 44 01782 294000
Email: news@staffslive.co.uk
Web site: www.staffslive.co.uk
Freq: Daily
Circ: 13069 Cision Digital Reach
MAGAZINE (ONLINE)
News & Current Affairs

The Stag
998543
Editorial: Univ. of Surrey Students' Union, Union House, Guildford, London GU2 7XH
Tel: 44 01483 689223
Email: editor@thestagsurrey.co.uk
Web site: http://thestagsurrey.co.uk
Freq: Bi-Weekly Not Audited
MAGAZINE
Student Lifestyle

The Stage
981229
Editorial: Stage House, 47 Bermondsey Street, London SE1 3XT
Tel: 44 02074 031818
Email: newsdesk@thestage.co.uk
Web site: www.thestage.co.uk
Freq: Weekly
Circ: 13000 Not Audited
MAGAZINE
Entertainment, Local Entertainment Guides, Theater & Performing Arts

Stage Review
995342
Editorial: 153A Heath Road, Leighton Buzzard, Leighton Buzzard LU7 3AD
Web site: www.stagereview.co.uk
Freq: Daily
Circ: 14439 Cision Digital Reach
Editor: Anne Cox
MAGAZINE (ONLINE)
Theater & Performing Arts

Stagedoor FM
996734
Web site: stagedoor.fm
Freq: Daily
Circ: 17396 Cision Digital Reach
MAGAZINE (ONLINE)
Dance Music, Jazz & Blues, Music, Pop Music, Rap & Hip Hop, Rock Music

Staggered
985199
Editorial: 41a Maltby Street, London SE1 3PA **Tel:** 44 02072 991831
Email: info@iamstaggered.com
Web site: http://www.chillisauce.co.uk/staggered/

Freq: Daily
Circ: 5501 Cision Digital Reach
Profile: Website covering wedding inspiration for men. staggered discusses the latest news on proposals, wedding planning, stag-do, style, speeches, being best man and honeymoon.
MAGAZINE (ONLINE)
Men's Interests, Weddings

Stamp & Coin Mart
982815
Editorial: 5th Floor, 31-32 Park Row, Leeds LS1 5JD **Tel:** 44 01132 002929
Web site: www.stampandcoin.co.uk
Freq: Monthly
Circ: 10000 Not Audited
Editor: Matt Hill
Profile: Magazine containing informative, topical articles on stamps and coins as well as a New Issues section and buy and sell section.
Ad Rate: Full Page Colour £532.40
MAGAZINE
Antiques/Collectibles

Stamp Lover
981919
Editorial: Harvard House, 621 London Road, Isleworth, London TW7 4ER
Tel: 44 02085 682433
Email: stamplover@ukphilately.org.uk
Web site: www.ukphilately.org.uk/nps/lover/lover.htm
Freq: Bi-Monthly
Circ: 800 Not Audited
Editor: Michael L Goodman
Profile: Stamp Lover is the official journal of the National Philatelic Society. The magazine has appeared regularly without a break for over 90 years. It is available issued free to members of the National PS as part of their annual subscription.
Ad Rate: Full Page Colour £130.00
MAGAZINE
Antiques/Collectibles

Stamp Magazine
981920
Editorial: Enterprise House, Enterprise Way, Edenbridge, Edenbridge TN8 6HF
Tel: 44 08444 122262
Web site: www.stampmagazine.co.uk
Freq: Monthly
Circ: 10000 Not Audited
Editor: Guy Thomas
Profile: Magazine focusing on philately. Covers auctions, exhibitions and thematic collecting.
Ad Rate: Full Page Mono £715.00
Ad Rate: Full Page Colour £980.00
MAGAZINE
Antiques/Collectibles

Standard Issue
998339
Email: advertising@standardissuemagazine.com
Web site: standardissuemagazine.com/
Freq: Daily
Circ: 59348 Cision Digital Reach
MAGAZINE (ONLINE)
News & Current Affairs

Standpoint
984721
Editorial: 10 Greenwich Quay, London SE8 3EY **Tel:** 44 02075 639840
Email: editor@standpointmag.co.uk
Web site: www.standpointmag.co.uk
Freq: Monthly
Circ: 14000 Not Audited
Editor: Daniel Johnson
Profile: Magazine covering culture, politics, arts and books.
Ad Rate: Full Page Colour £2990.00
MAGAZINE
Government, Politics, Religion, Science

Star
982363
Editorial: Northern & Shell Tower, 10 Lower Thames Street, London EC3R 6EN
Tel: 44 02086 127000
Email: starmagazine@express.co.uk
Web site: www.star-magazine.co.uk
Freq: Weekly
Circ: 107840 Not Audited
Profile: Magazine covering celebrity news, gossip, fashion, beauty, travel, TV listings

and reviews. Includes week's events, exclusive pictures of the stars, fashion and beauty tips, celebrity diets, health and lifestyle advice.Aimed at 18-35 year old female readers. .
Ad Rate: Full Page Colour £12100.00
MAGAZINE
Celebrities

Star Girl
982456
Editorial: LCD PUBLISHING, VICI HOUSE, 2 MALLARD ROAD, Exeter EX2 7LD
Tel: 44 01392 664141
Freq: Monthly Not Audited
Editor: Joanne Trump
MAGAZINE
Teen/Young Adult

Star Wars Adventures
1060211
Editorial: First Floor, The Yellow Building, 1 Nicholas Road, London W11 4AN
Tel: 44 02032 200400
Web site: www.egmont.co.uk/magazines/star-wars-adventures
Freq: Monthly
Circ: 38014 Not Audited
Editor: Ned Hartley
MAGAZINE
Elementary School

Star Wars Insider
982348
Editorial: Titan House, 144 Southwark Street, London SE1 0UP
Tel: 44 02078 031831
Email: starwars@titanemail.com
Web site: http://titanmagazines.com/t/star-wars-insider/
Freq: Bi-Monthly
Circ: 133170 Not Audited
Editor: Jonathan Wilkins
MAGAZINE
Movies & Video, Science Fiction

Star Wars Lego
1060242
Editorial: 1st Floor, The Yellow Building, 1 Nicholas Road, London W8 6SA
Web site: www.egmont.co.uk/magazines/lego-star-wars
Freq: Monthly
Circ: 80012 Not Audited
Editor: Ned Hartley
MAGAZINE
Teen/Young Adult

Star Wars Rebels
1060224
Editorial: First Floor, The Yellow Building, 1 Nicholas Road, London W11 4AN
Tel: 44 02032 200400
Web site: http://www.egmont.co.uk/magazines/star-wars-rebels/
Freq: Monthly
Circ: 18003 Not Audited
Editor: Ned Hartley
MAGAZINE
Teen/Young Adult, Trading Cards & Comics

Starburst
994620
Editorial: PO Box 4508, Manchester M61 0GY
Email: press@starburstmagazine.com
Web site: www.starburstmagazine.com
Freq: Monthly
Circ: 10000 Not Audited
Editor: Jordan Royce
MAGAZINE
Entertainment, Movies & Video, Science Fiction

StartReplay
995353
Email: contact@startreplay.com
Web site: www.startreplay.com
Freq: Daily
Circ: 11720 Cision Digital Reach
MAGAZINE (ONLINE)
Computer & Video Games

STATE Magazine
988797
Editorial: The Vellum Building, 183-185 Bermondsey Street, London SE1 3UW
Tel: 44 02034 4158585152
Email: admin@state-media.com
Web site: http://www.state-media.com/

Freq: Bi-Monthly
Circ: 48500 Not Audited
MAGAZINE
Art

Stationary Engine
986410
Editorial: PO Box 13, Westerham, London TN16 3WT **Tel:** 44 01959 541444
Email: se.ed@kelsey.co.uk
Web site: http://shop.kelsey.co.uk/subscription/SEN
Freq: Monthly
Circ: 9400 Not Audited
Editor: Patrick Knight
Profile: Magazine covering restoration, buying and selling and the history of stationary (internal combustion) engines.
Ad Rate: Full Page Colour £485.00
MAGAZINE
History

stayandshopinlondon.com
999508
Editorial: 45 The Drive, London E4 7AJ
Tel: 44 02085 056743
Email: info@stayandshopinlondon.com
Web site: www.stayandshopinlondon.com
Freq: Daily
Circ: 1787 Cision Digital Reach
Editor: Catherine Dekker
MAGAZINE (ONLINE)
Regional General Interest

Steam Railway
982044
Editorial: Media House, Lynchwood, Peterborough Business Park, Peterborough PE2 6EA **Tel:** 44 01733 468000
Email: steam.railway@bauermedia.co.uk
Web site: http://www.steamrailway.co.uk/
Freq: Monthly
Circ: 30541 Not Audited
Profile: Magazine covering steam engines, preserved railways and the history of steam. It contains articles on the present day steam scene, historical and archive material as well as details on forthcoming steam events, galas and main line rail tours. It also features reviews of the latest railway books and visual media. Aimed at those interested in steam traction.
Ad Rate: Full Page Colour £1050.00
MAGAZINE
Railroad

Steam World
982045
Editorial: 1st Floor, 2 King Street, Peterborough PE1 1LT
Tel: 44 01733 555123
Email: steamworld@choicemag.co.uk
Web site: http://steamworldmag.co.uk/
Freq: Monthly
Circ: 25000 Not Audited
Editor: Andy Roden
Profile: Magazine covering steam on Britain's railways pre-1968. Read by those interested in UK railway history, largely post-war.
Ad Rate: Full Page Mono £620.00
Ad Rate: Full Page Colour £870.00
MAGAZINE
Railroad

StephanieMatti.com
1056324
Freq: Daily
Circ: 11039 Cision Digital Reach
MAGAZINE (ONLINE)
News & Current Affairs

stilorama.com
984949
Editorial: 46 Lindfield Road, London W5 1QR **Tel:** 44 02087 282299
Email: magazine@stilorama.com
Web site: www.stilorama.com
Freq: Daily
Circ: 30674 Cision Digital Reach
Profile: Website covering lifestyle. Silorama.com discusses anything from fashion to beauty and boutiques to shopping.
MAGAZINE (ONLINE)
Beauty & Grooming, Cosmetics, Fashion, Hair, Luxury Goods, Travel

Stir it Up
986366
Editorial: 4 & 5 Jupiter House, Mercury Rise, Altham Business Park, Accrington BB5 5BY
Tel: 44 08452 093777
Email: editor@stiritupmagazine.co.uk
Web site: www.stiritupmagazine.co.uk
Freq: Monthly
Circ: 50000 Not Audited
Editor: Janine Nelson
MAGAZINE
Bars, Clubs & Pubs, Food

Stitch
987441
Editorial: 1 Kings Road, Walton on Thames, London KT12 2RA **Tel:** 44 01932 260738
Email: stitcheditor@embroiderersguild.com
Web site: http://www.embroiderersguild.com/index.php?page_no=210&page_menu=stitch-magazine
Freq: Bi-Monthly
Circ: 25000 Not Audited
Editor: Kate Chappell
Profile: Magazine containing designs and ideas for creative needlework projects. Includes features on contemporary and traditional embroidery, designers, products, community needlework projects, competitions and book reviews.
Ad Rate: Full Page Colour £1100.00
MAGAZINE
Crafts

Stockportal
1053385
Editorial: Pepper House, 1 Pepper Road, Hazel Grove, Stockport SK7 5DP
Tel: 44 01614 510770
Web site: http://www.marketingstockport.co.uk/
Freq: Quarterly Not Audited
MAGAZINE
Business, Corporate Responsibility, Regional

Stockton News
982917
Editorial: PO Box 11, Stockton Borough Council, Municipal Building, Stockton-on-Tees TS18 1LD **Tel:** 44 01642 393939
Email: communications@stockton.gov.uk
Web site: https://www.stockton.gov.uk/stockton-council/
Freq: Quarterly
Circ: 80600 Not Audited
Profile: Magazine containing community news and information of local interest.
Ad Rate: Full Page Mono £995.00
Ad Rate: Full Page Colour £995.00
MAGAZINE
Regional, Regional General Interest

STOKE PARK
995508
Editorial: 790 Fulham Road, London SW6 5SL **Tel:** 44 02077 317747
Email: info@epicureanlife.co.uk
Web site: https://www.thealexandergroup.co.uk/stoke-park
Freq: Semi-Annual
Circ: 30000 Not Audited
Editor: Christina Raptis
MAGAZINE
Antique & Collectible Cars, Cooking & Baking, Driving, Golf, Lifestyle, Luxury Goods, Men's Interests, Motorcycles, Regional General Interest, Travel

Storm Force
1063713
Editorial: West Quay Road, Poole BH15 1HZ
Web site: http://rnli.org/shorething/joinin/otherwaystojoinin/Pages/Join-Storm-Force.aspx
Freq: Quarterly
Circ: 15000 Not Audited
Editor: Jon Jones
MAGAZINE
Teen/Young Adult

Storytime
998079
Editorial: Storytime, Studio 2B18, Technopark, 90 London Road, London SE1 6LN **Tel:** 44 01795 414913
Email: hello@storytimemagazine.com
Web site: www.storytimemagazine.com

Freq: Monthly Not Audited
MAGAZINE
Elementary School, Preschool

Stour-on-Avon Magazine
998530
Tel: 44 01963 365100
Email: mbarber@bvmedia.co.uk
Web site: http://www.blackmorevale.co.uk/stourandavonnews
Freq: Weekly
Circ: 31500 Not Audited
MAGAZINE
Regional General Interest

The Strad
982114
Editorial: 120 Leman Street, London E1 8EU
Tel: 44 02076 183095
Email: thestrad@thestrad.com
Web site: www.thestrad.com
Freq: Monthly
Circ: 5804 Not Audited
Profile: Magazine covering bowed string instruments. Includes concert and CD reviews and profiles of famous string artists. Aimed at musicians, instrument makers and lovers of string music.
Ad Rate: Full Page Mono £1990.00
Ad Rate: Full Page Colour £1990.00
MAGAZINE
Classical/Choral/Band Music

Straight Up London
1076753
Web site: http://straightuplondon.com
Freq: Daily
Circ: 11219 Cision Digital Reach
MAGAZINE (ONLINE)
Alcohol & Spirits, Bars, Clubs & Pubs, Beer, Beverages, Restaurant Reviews, Wine/Winemaking

Strange Hill High
997714
Editorial: Marlborough House, Headley Road, Grayshott, Hindhead GU26 6LG
Tel: 44 01428 601020
Email: djm@djmurphy.co.uk
Web site: www.bbc.co.uk/cbbc/shows/strange-hill-high
Freq: Monthly Not Audited
Editor: Penny Rendall
MAGAZINE
Elementary School

Strange Horizons
999050
Editorial: 22 Emperor Court, 19 Brookbank Close, Cheltenham, Cheltenham GL50 3NL
Email: editor@strangehorizons.com
Web site: www.strangehorizons.com
Freq: Daily Not Audited
MAGAZINE
Science Fiction

Strangers and Candy
105254
Email: info@strangersandcandy.com
Web site: http://strangersandcandy.com/
Freq: Daily
Circ: 521 Cision Digital Reach
MAGAZINE (ONLINE)
Antiques/Collectibles, Art, Arts, Literature, Photography, Theater & Performing Arts, Visual Arts

Strategic Comments
99550
Web site: www.iiss.org/en/publications/strategic-s-comments
Freq: Weekly
Circ: 374 Cision Digital Reach
Editor: Jonathan Stevenson
MAGAZINE (ONLINE)
News & Current Affairs

Strathclyde Telegraph
9817
Editorial: Univ of Strathclyde Students' Assoc, The Media Centre, 90 John Street, Glasgow G1 1JH **Tel:** 44 01415 675000
Email: editor@strathclydetelegraph.com
Web site: www.strathclydetelegraph.com
Freq: Monthly
Circ: 2000 Not Audited
Profile: Student newspaper covering student issues, university news and sport, general arts and music.
MAGAZINE
Student Lifestyle

Streets
988846

Editorial: 92 Richmond Road, Dalston, London E8 3HW
Email: info@streetsmagazine.com
Web site: streetsmagazine.com
Freq: Semi-Annual Not Audited
Profile: Magazine focusing on high-end luxury fashion.
MAGAZINE
Fashion

Strike! Magazine
995304

Email: editor@strikemag.org
Web site: http://www.strikemag.org
Freq: Bi-Monthly Not Audited
MAGAZINE
Art, Literature, Politics, Social Issues, Visual Arts

Strike-it!
987818

Editorial: Level 2, Brockbourne House, Mount Ephraim, Tunbridge Wells
Tel: 44 01892 500100
Email: strike-it@panini.co.uk
Web site: www.paninicomics.co.uk/web/guest/catalogues/collection_detail?id=83664
Freq: Monthly
Circ: 15217 Not Audited
Editor: Patrick Bishop
MAGAZINE
Soccer

STROKE news
984447

Editorial: Stroke House, 240 City Road, London EC1V 2PR **Tel:** 44 02075 660300
Email: strokenews@stroke.org.uk
Web site: www.stroke.org.uk
Freq: Quarterly Not Audited
Profile: Magazine from The Stroke Association.
Ad Rate: Full Page Colour £2920.00
MAGAZINE
Neurology, Patient Support

Strong Young Thing
1069617

Email: info@sytmagazine.com
Web site: www.sytmagazine.com/
Freq: Daily
Circ: 12706 Cision Digital Reach
MAGAZINE (ONLINE)
Beauty & Grooming, Celebrities, Cosmetics, Fashion, Hair, Social Issues, Women's Interests

Stroud Life
998729

Editorial: 14 Union Street, Stroud GL5 2HE
Tel: 44 01453 755955
Email: stroudlife@glosmedia.co.uk
Web site: www.gloucestershirelive.co.uk
Freq: Weekly
Circ: 9091 Not Audited
Editor: Ben Falconer
Profile: This is the online version of the Stroud Life, a weekly local newspaper covering local news and leisure in the surrounding area.
MAGAZINE
Regional General Interest

The Student (Edinburgh)
998559

Editorial: 60 Pleasance, Edinburgh EH8 9TJ
Tel: 44 01316 509189
Email: news@studentnewspaper.org
Web site: www.studentnewspaper.org
Freq: Weekly
Circ: 4000 Not Audited
MAGAZINE
Student Lifestyle

student bmj
986934

Editorial: BMA House, Tavistock Square, London WC1H 9JP
Email: studenteditor@bmj.com
Web site: http://student.bmj.com/student/student-bmj.html
Freq: Quarterly
Circ: 20000 Not Audited
Editor: Matthew Billingsley
Profile: Magazine covering medical education and student life, with socio-political and medical news.
Ad Rate: Full Page Mono £685.00

Ad Rate: Full Page Colour £1390.00
MAGAZINE
Education, Medicine, Students

Student Career Guide
995797

Editorial: Prospect House, Booth Street East, Manchester M13 9EP
Tel: 44 01612 775200
Email: prospects@prospects.ac.uk
Web site: www.prospects.ac.uk
Freq: Annual
Circ: 80000 Not Audited
MAGAZINE
Careers

Student Money Saver
988730

Editorial: Student Money Saver, 9-10 Charterhouse Buildings, London EC1M 7AN
Tel: 44 02071 834671
Email: info@studentmoneysaver.co.uk
Web site: www.studentmoneysaver.co.uk
Freq: Daily
Circ: 142941 Cision Digital Reach
MAGAZINE (ONLINE)
Student Lifestyle

The Student Moneymanual
996193

Editorial: 15 Prescott Place, London SW4 6BS **Tel:** 44 02070 628933
Email: hello@themoneycharity.org.uk
Web site: themoneycharity.org.uk/student-moneymanual/
Freq: Annual
Circ: 15000 Not Audited
MAGAZINE
Personal Finance, Students

The Student Pocket Guide
997225

Editorial: The Student Pocket Guide Ltd, EPIC Studios, 112-114 Magdalen Street, Norwich NR3 1JD **Tel:** 44 01603 727768
Email: info@thestudentpocketguide.com
Web site: www.thestudentpocketguide.com
Freq: Daily
Circ: 28891 Cision Digital Reach
MAGAZINE (ONLINE)
Student Lifestyle

Student Times
984479

Editorial: 1, The Prill, Nesscliffe, Shrewsbury, Sevenoaks SY4 1DD
Tel: 44 02036 593499
Email: editor@studenttimes.org
Web site: www.studenttimes.org
Freq: Daily
Circ: 12050 Cision Digital Reach
Profile: Independent national student newspaper, written by students for students. Covering national and global issues affecting students as well as entertainment and sport. Provides the best coverage of entertainment and lifestyle aimed at the 16-25. Aimed at students aged between 16 and 25 years old.
Ad Rate: Full Page Mono £3000.00
Ad Rate: Full Page Colour £3000.00
MAGAZINE (ONLINE)
Student Lifestyle

studento.com
999404

Editorial: Technology House, Sir William Lyons Road, University of Warwick, Science Park, Coventry CV4 7EZ
Tel: 44 02476 712201
Email: arj@studento.com
Web site: www.studento.com
Freq: Daily
Circ: 1625 Cision Digital Reach
Editor: Arjun Panesar
MAGAZINE (ONLINE)
Student Lifestyle

StudioTech
995502

Web site: http://www.studiotech.tv/
Freq: Daily
Circ: 6096 Cision Digital Reach
Editor: Mark Johnson
MAGAZINE (ONLINE)
Audio Video Trade, Internet

Study International
995269

Editorial: Colston Tower Level 9, Colston Street, Bristol BS1 4UX
Tel. 44 01172 440750
Email: info@studyinternational.com
Web site: http://www.studyinternational.com/
Freq: Daily
Circ: 59898 Cision Digital Reach
MAGAZINE (ONLINE)
Careers, Higher Education, Student Lifestyle, Students

Study Travel Magazine
986043

Editorial: 11-15 Emerald Street, London WC1N 3QL **Tel:** 44 02074 404020
Web site: www.hothousemedia.com/etm/index.htm
Freq: Monthly
Circ: 29400 Not Audited
Editor: Nicola Hancox
MAGAZINE
Careers, Disability, Education, Higher Education, Preschool, Schools & Institutions, Students

Study UK
987539

Editorial: Bridgewater House, 58–60 Whitworth Street, Manchester M1 6BB
Web site: https://study-uk.britishcouncil.org/
Freq: Daily
Circ: 245748 Cision Digital Reach
MAGAZINE (ONLINE)
News & Current Affairs

Stuff
982056

Editorial: Bridge House, 69 London Road, Twickenham, London TW1 3SP
Tel: 44 02082 675036
Email: stuff@haymarket.com
Web site: www.stuff.tv
Freq: Monthly
Circ: 56183 Not Audited
Editor: Robert Leedham
Profile: Magazine covering men's lifestyle and consumer electronics including music players, Hi-Fi, home cinema, mobile phones, digital cameras, computers, laptops, application and software, 3D printing, tablets, gaming, sat-nav, blue ray, TVs and gadgets as well as general technology latest news, innovation and reviews. Aimed at men between 25 and 34 years of age.
Ad Rate: Full Page Colour £4200.00
MAGAZINE
Audio Video Trade, Cameras, Consumer Electronics, Electronics, Men's Interests, Mobile Electronics, Movies & Video

Style Altitude
987622

Editorial: 1 Anscombe Road, Worthing, Worthing BN11 5EN
Email: style@stylealtitude.com
Web site: stylealtitude.com
Freq: Daily
Circ: 1387 Cision Digital Reach
Editor: Elaine Deed
Profile: Online magazine covering ski and snowboarding. It focuses on fashion and style.
MAGAZINE (ONLINE)
Winter Sports

Style and life
1060830

Not Audited
MAGAZINE
Consumer Affairs, Crime & Violence, Defense & National Security, Energy & Environment, Ethical/Moral Issues, International News, Law, National News, News & Current Affairs, Northern Ireland

Style at Home
985833

Editorial: The Blue Fin Building, 110 Southwark Street, London SE1 0SU
Tel: 44 02031 485000
Email: styleathome@timeinc.com
Web site: http://www.idealhome.co.uk/style-at-home
Freq: Monthly
Circ: 77518 Not Audited

Profile: Magazine covering affordable shopping and decorating ideas, stunning real homes and easy to make ideas.
Ad Rate: Full Page Colour £4635.00
MAGAZINE
Do-It-Yourself (DIY)

Style Birmingham
983826

Editorial: 606B, The Big Peg, 120 Vyse Street, Birmingham B18 6NF
Tel: 44 01217 692808
Email: editorial@stylebham.com
Web site: http://stylebham.com/
Freq: Bi-Monthly
Circ: 25000 Not Audited
MAGAZINE
Beauty & Grooming, Cosmetics, Fashion, Hair, Lifestyle, Men's Interests, Regional General Interest, Restaurant Reviews, Shopping, Women's Interests

STYLE COMPARE
999304

Editorial: TechHub London, 4-5 Bonhill Street, London EC2A 4BX
Email: press@stylecompare.co.uk
Web site: www.stylecompare.co.uk
Freq: Daily
Circ: 119015 Cision Digital Reach
MAGAZINE (ONLINE)
Fashion

The Style Lane
986852

Editorial: The Old Post Office, Church Street, Limington, Yeovil BA22 8EQ
Web site: www.thestylelane.com
Freq: Daily
Circ: 11688 Cision Digital Reach
Editor: Penny Lane
Profile: The Style Lane provides a guide to the latest fashion trends, news, beauty heroes, timeless classics and product launches, cocktail haunts, luxury bars and travel spots, plus beautiful home style, with easy updates and tips.
MAGAZINE (ONLINE)
Women's Interests

Style Reins
1052705

Web site: www.stylereins.com
Circ: 13962 Cision Digital Reach
MAGAZINE (ONLINE)
News & Current Affairs

StyleAble
985799

Email: info@styleable.co.uk
Web site: www.styleable.co.uk
Freq: Daily
Circ: 9274 Cision Digital Reach
Editor: Kiesha Meikle
MAGAZINE (ONLINE)
Beauty & Grooming, Cosmetics, Fashion, Hair

Stylebible.com
984337

Email: hello@stylebible.com
Web site: www.stylebible.com
Freq: Daily
Circ: 3971 Cision Digital Reach
Editor: Amanda Zuydervelt
MAGAZINE (ONLINE)
Beauty & Grooming, Cosmetics, Fashion, Hair, Travel

STYLEetc
987333

Email: styleetceditor@gmail.com
Web site: http://style-etc.co.uk/
Freq: Quarterly
Circ: 12263 Cision Digital Reach
MAGAZINE (ONLINE)
Fashion, Regional General Interest, Women's Interests

StyleNest
986308

Editorial: 54 Macready House, 75 Crawford Street, London W1H 5LP
Tel: 44 02032 898990
Email: charlie@stylenest.co.uk
Web site: www.stylenest.co.uk
Freq: Daily
Circ: 69906 Cision Digital Reach
Profile: Website covering women's lifestyle. StyleNest discusses the latest news on

Consumer Magazines

fashion, beauty, children, food, life and travel.
MAGAZINE (ONLINE)
Beauty & Grooming, Cosmetics, Fashion, Hair, Women's Interests

StylePilot
1053209
Editorial: Suite 1.01, Linton House, 164-168 Union St, London SE1 0LH
Tel: 44 02037 948651
Web site: http://www.stylepilot.com/
Freq: Daily
Circ: 7874 Cision Digital Reach
MAGAZINE (ONLINE)
Beauty & Grooming, Cosmetics, Fashion, Hair, Health & Medicine, Men's Interests, Nutrition

StyleTails
999657
Editorial: 4th Floor, 86-90 Paul Street, London EC2A 4NE
Email: press@styletails.com
Web site: www.styletails.com
Freq: Daily
Circ: 40720 Cision Digital Reach
MAGAZINE (ONLINE)
Nature & Wildlife

STYLIST
985175
Editorial: 26-34 Emerald Street, London WC1N 3QA **Tel:** 44 02076 119700
Email: editor@stylist.co.uk
Web site: www.stylist.co.uk
Freq: Weekly
Circ: 400942 Not Audited
Profile: Magazine covering women's interest fashion and style including design, accessories, clothing, fashion shows, beauty, skin care, hair, careers, celebrity, life, entertainment, arts, books, travel, food and going out features. Aimed at smart, successful and sophisticated women aged between 20 and 40 years old.
Ad Rate: Full Page Colour £19035.00
MAGAZINE
Fashion, Women's Interests

Styloko
986611
Editorial: 16 Bowling Green Lane, London EC1R 0BD
Email: press@styloko.com
Web site: www.styloko.com
Freq: Daily
Circ: 113143 Cision Digital Reach
MAGAZINE (ONLINE)
Fashion

SUBBA-CULTCHA
984782
Web site: http://www.subba-cultcha.com/
Freq: Daily
Circ: 10951 Cision Digital Reach
MAGAZINE (ONLINE)
Rock Music

Subcity Radio
998576
Editorial: John McIntyre Building, University Avenue, Glasgow G12 8QQ
Tel: 44 01413 305438
Email: programmes@subcity.org
Web site: www.subcity.org
Freq: Daily
Circ: 11511 Cision Digital Reach
MAGAZINE (ONLINE)
Student Lifestyle

Sublime
983499
Editorial: 167 Southwood Lane, Highgate, London N6 5TA **Tel:** 44 02083 747695
Email: editorial@sublimemagazine.com
Web site: www.sublimemagazine.com
Freq: Daily
Circ: 11776 Cision Digital Reach
Editor: Laura Santamaria
Profile: Lifestyle magazine covering culture, music, architecture, fashion, food, travel, environment, soul and sustainable living. Launched in March 2004. Aimed at men and women aged between 20 and 45 years old.
Ad Rate: Full Page Colour £7000.00
MAGAZINE (ONLINE)
Ethical/Moral Issues, Men's Interests, Women's Interests

Subsea UK News
997851
Editorial: 30 Abercrombie Court, Arnhall Business Park, Prospect Road, Westhill, Aberdeen AB32 6FE **Tel:** 44 08455 053535
Email: magazine@subseauk.com
Web site: www.subseauk.com/1405/magazines
Freq: Quarterly
Circ: 2000 Not Audited
MAGAZINE
Marine & Boat Trade, Oil, Water & Sanitation

Suffolk Norfolk Life
982528
Editorial: The Publishing House, Station Road, Framlingham, Woodbridge IP13 9EE
Tel: 44 01728 622030
Email: info@suffolknorfolklife.com
Web site: www.suffolknorfolklife.com
Freq: Monthly
Circ: 30000 Not Audited
Editor: Kevin Davis
Profile: Magazine containing local news and features on food, wine, property, motoring, health, finance, travel and county events.
Ad Rate: Full Page Colour £800.00
MAGAZINE
Regional, Regional General Interest

Suffolk Wildlife
1097068
Editorial: Brooke House, The Street, Ashbocking, Ipswich IP6 9JY
Tel: 44 01473 890089
Email: info@suffolkwildlifetrust.org
Web site: www.suffolkwildlifetrust.org
Freq: 3 Times/Year
Circ: 12000 Not Audited
MAGAZINE
Nature & Wildlife

SUITCASE
986818
Editorial: Sophisticated House, 1-3 Mount Street, London W1K 3NB
Email: hello@suitcasemag.com
Web site: http://suitcasemag.com/
Freq: Quarterly
Circ: 77000 Not Audited
Profile: Magazine covering culture, fashion, beauty, travel and food. First published in 2012.
MAGAZINE
Fashion, Travel

Summit
984505
Editorial: 177-179 Burton Road, Manchester M20 2BB **Tel:** 44 01614 456111
Email: summit@thebmc.co.uk
Web site: www.thebmc.co.uk/cats/all/summit_magazine
Freq: Quarterly
Circ: 46000 Not Audited
Editor: Alex Messenger
Profile: Official magazine of the British Mountaineering Council covering climbing, hiking, rock climbing, outdoor recreation, mountaineering and travel. The magazine features articles relating to access improvements, cliff and mountain conservation as well as good practice, facilities, training and equipment.
Ad Rate: Full Page Mono £1050.00
Ad Rate: Full Page Colour £1600.00
MAGAZINE
Outdoor Recreation, Winter Sports

Sunday Girl Magazine
1052967
Email: hello.sundaygirlmag@outlook.com
Web site: www.sundaygirlmagazine.bigcartel.com
Freq: Quarterly
MAGAZINE
Dance Music, Entertainment, Fashion, Pop Music, Rap & Hip Hop, Women's Interests

The Sunday Times Travel Magazine
982333
Editorial: 1 London Bridge Street, London SE1 9GF **Tel:** 44 02077 825681
Email: travelmag@sundaytimes.co.uk
Web site: www.sundaytimes.co.uk
Freq: Monthly
Circ: 67934 Not Audited
Editor: Ed Grenby

Profile: The Sunday Times Travel Magazine is a supplement of The Sunday Times and covers travel, tourism, holidays, food, drink and luxury travel. The supplement is published on a monthly basis.
Ad Rate: Full Page Colour £6950.00
MAGAZINE
Railroad, Travel

Sunday Woman
994984
Email: editor@sundaywoman.com
Web site: http://www.sundaywoman.com/
Freq: Daily
Circ: 8319 Cision Digital Reach
MAGAZINE (ONLINE)
Careers, Family & Parenting, Relationships, Women's Interests

Sunseeker
984412
Editorial: Suite 9, Beaufort Court, Admirals Way, Canary Wharf, London E14 9XL
Tel: 44 02037 724850
Web site: https://www.sunseeker.com/
Freq: Quarterly
Circ: 20000 Not Audited
Profile: Luxury lifestyle magazine covering travel, motoring, fashion, watches, jewellery, gastronomy and sport.
Ad Rate: Full Page Colour £6950.00
MAGAZINE
Boating & Yachting, Luxury Goods

super/collider
997179
Editorial: 200 Cambridge Heath Road, London E2 9PA
Email: hello@super-collider.com
Web site: http://www.super-collider.com
Freq: Daily
Circ: 5300 Cision Digital Reach
MAGAZINE (ONLINE)
Astronomy, Science, Visual Arts

SuperBike
982658
Email: john@superbike.co.uk
Web site: www.superbike.co.uk
Freq: Daily
Circ: 1100000 Not Audited
Editor: John Hogan
Profile: Magazine featuring tests, racing coverage and features on Motorcycle Racing.
Ad Rate: Full Page Colour £3060.00
MAGAZINE
Motorcycles

SuperDeluxeEdition
998216
Editorial: PO Box 68477, London N16 1EN
Web site: http://www.superdeluxeedition.com/
Freq: Daily
Circ: 653379 Cision Digital Reach
MAGAZINE (ONLINE)
Classical/Choral/Band Music, Country, Folk, Bluegrass, Dance Music, Jazz & Blues, Music, Pop Music, R&B, Urban, World, Rap & Hip Hop, Rock Music

Superfood
1097894
Tel: 44 01273 477374
Web site: www.superfoodmagazine.com
Freq: Bi-Monthly
Editor: Sian Hamilton
MAGAZINE
Cooking & Baking

Superyacht Business
984775
Editorial: Pinehurst 2, Pinehurst Road, Farnborough Business Park, Farnborough, London GU14 7BF **Tel:** 44 01252 555000
Email: juliet.benning@timeinc.com
Web site: www.superyachtbusiness.net
Freq: Bi-Monthly
Circ: 9250 Not Audited
Editor: Ed Slack
Profile: Magazine covering news and developments from designers, stylists, boat builders, project managers, surveyors, equipment manufactures and service providers. Also featuring analysis on what's going on in the yacht broker, yacht charter and yacht management areas, new product reviews, applications and techniques. Aimed at the yachting industry including those involved with the design, building,

maintenance and operation of professional crewed yachts.
Ad Rate: Full Page Colour £2565.00
MAGAZINE
Marine & Boat Trade

Superyacht Investor
995320
Editorial: Hartland House, 45 Church Street, Reigate, Reigate RH2 0AD
Tel: 44 01737 245151
Email: louisa@superyachtinvestor.com
Web site: www.superyachtinvestor.com
Freq: Daily
Circ: 13635 Cision Digital Reach
MAGAZINE (ONLINE)
Boating & Yachting, Shipping & Warehousing

The Superyacht Owner
986453
Editorial: Landsdowne house, 3-7 Northcote Road, London SW11 1NG
Tel: 44 02079 244004
Email: info@thesuperyachtowner.com
Web site: www.thesuperyachtowner.com
Freq: Quarterly
Circ: 10000 Not Audited
MAGAZINE
Boating & Yachting

The Superyacht Report
998634
Editorial: Landsdowne house, 3-7 Northcote Road, London SW11 1NG
Tel: 44 02079 244004
Email: info@thesuperyachtgroup.com
Web site: www.thesuperyachtreport.com/
Freq: Monthly
Circ: 17000 Not Audited
Editor: William Mathieson
Profile: Magazine providing news and advice on the construction, management and operation of large yachts.
Ad Rate: Full Page Colour £2835.00
MAGAZINE
Boating & Yachting, Shipping & Warehousing

SuperYacht World
984675
Editorial: Pinehurst 2, Pinehurst Road, Farnborough Business Park, Farnborough, London GU14 7BF **Tel:** 44 01252 555000
Email: superyachtworld@timeinc.com
Web site: www.superyachtworld.com
Freq: Bi-Monthly
Circ: 22000 Not Audited
Editor: Paul Ashton
MAGAZINE
Boating & Yachting

SuperyachtNews.com
985669
Editorial: Landsdowne House, 3-7 Northcote Road, London SW11 1NG
Tel: 44 02079 244004
Email: newsdesk@thesuperyachtgroup.com
Web site: www.superyachtnews.com
Freq: Daily
Circ: 26350 Cision Digital Reach
MAGAZINE (ONLINE)
Boating & Yachting

superyachts.com
985670
Editorial: Unit 1, Flower Lane, Mill Hill Industrial Estate, London NW7 2HV
Tel: 44 02089 066047
Email: press@superyachts.com
Web site: www.superyachts.com
Freq: Daily
Circ: 154038 Cision Digital Reach
MAGAZINE (ONLINE)
Boating & Yachting

SUPPER
1075485
Editorial: Strawberry Studios, Stockport SK1 3AZ **Tel:** 44 01614 765580
Web site: www.suppermagazine.co.uk
Freq: Quarterly
Circ: 28042 Not Audited
Editor: Harry McKinley
MAGAZINE
Bars, Clubs & Pubs, Hotels/Motels

Supplement Magazine
1053988
Editorial: 53a Brewer Street, London W1F 9UH

Web site: www.supplementmagazine.co.uk
Freq: Quarterly
MAGAZINE
Art, Literature, Photography, Visual Arts

Support for Learning   983865
Editorial: School of Education, University
College, Park Campus, Boughton Green
Road, Northampton NN2 7AL
Web site: http://onlinelibrary.wiley.com/
journal/10.1111/(ISSN)1467-9604
Freq: Quarterly Not Audited
Profile: The articles in Support for Learning
examine the practical and theoretical issues
surrounding the education of pupils with
special educational needs in mainstream
schools. Support for Learning aims to act as
a bridge between academics and
practitioners. All aspects of curriculum
delivery, classroom management and the
use of support services are covered.
Strategies to eliminate underachievement
and promote best practice are especially
featured. Most, but not all, issues of Support
for Learning, focus on a topical theme.
Ad Rate: Full Page Mono £520.00
MAGAZINE
News & Current Affairs

Surf Europe   982304
Editorial: 2 Tun Yard, London SW8 3HT
Tel: 44 02073 329700
Email: info@factorymedia.com
Web site: https://surfeuropemag.com/
Freq: Daily
Circ: 41195 Cision Digital Reach
MAGAZINE (ONLINE)
Swimming/Watersports

Surface World   983467
Editorial: Marash House, 2-5 Brook Street,
Tring, Tring HP23 5ED Tel: 44 01442 826826
Email: sworlded@aol.com
Web site: www.surfaceworldshow.com
Freq: Monthly
Circ: 10000 Not Audited
Profile: Journal covering all forms of surface
engineering, surface treatment, surface
coating and product finishing technology
and associated products, processes and
equipment.
Ad Rate: Full Page Mono £950.00
Ad Rate: Full Page Colour £1400.00
MAGAZINE
Defense & National Security, Engineering,
Industry, Manufacturing, Marine & Boat
Trade, Mining & Quarrying, Paper,
Plastics, Steel

Surfers Against Sewage (SAS)
998791
Editorial: Unit 2, Wheal Kitty Workshops, St
Agnes, St. Agnes TR5 0RD
Tel: 44 01872 555951
Email: info@sas.org.uk
Web site: http://www.sas.org.uk/
Freq: Daily
Circ: 19933 Cision Digital Reach
MAGAZINE (ONLINE)
Energy & Environment, Environment,
Swimming/Watersports

SurfGirl Magazine   999046
Editorial: Berry Road Studios, Berry Road,
Newquay, Newquay TR7 1AT
Tel: 44 01637 878074
Email: info@surfgirlmag.com
Web site: www.surfgirlmag.com
Freq: Quarterly
Circ: 15000 Not Audited
Editor: Louise Searle
MAGAZINE
Swimming/Watersports

Surgery   985162
Editorial: Medicine Publishing, The
Boulevard Langford Lane, Kidlington OX5
1GB
Web site: www.surgeryjournal.co.uk
Freq: Monthly Not Audited
Profile: Journal forming a continuously
updated postgraduate textbook of surgery.
Aimed at senior house officers in all
specialities preparing for MRCS, but also

relevant to consultants who are involved in
surgical training.
Ad Rate: Full Page Mono £713.00
Ad Rate: Full Page Colour £1298.00
MAGAZINE
Medicine

Surgerydoor.co.uk   981653
Editorial: 3 Churchgates, The Wilderness,
Berkhamsted, Berkhamsted HP4 2UB
Tel: 44 08707 770401
Email: editorial@privatehouse.co.uk
Web site: www.surgerydoor.co.uk
Freq: Daily
Circ: 6831 Cision Digital Reach
MAGAZINE (ONLINE)
Health & Medicine

Surrey Downs Magazine   984935
Editorial: Unit A4, Kingsway Business Park,
Oldfield Road, Hampton, London TW12 2HD
Tel: 44 02089 395601
Email: editsd@sheengate.co.uk
Web site: www.sheengate.co.uk
Freq: Monthly
Circ: 34000 Not Audited
Editor: Emily Horton
Profile: Magazine covering local news and a
full colour property section for estate agents
and developers. This outlet covers areas
within Southwark Borough and Sutton
Borough.
Ad Rate: Full Page Colour £1155.00
MAGAZINE
Property Management & Maintenance,
Regional General Interest

Surrey Life   982530
Editorial: PO Box 412, Reigate, Reigate RH2
2DJ Tel: 44 01903 703730
Email: editor@surreylife.co.uk
Web site: www.surreylife.co.uk
Freq: Monthly
Circ: 11875 Not Audited
Profile: Magazine covering art, antiques,
food & drink, eating out, farmers' markets,
local produce, pubs, places to go, local
history, the environment, fashion, interiors,
health and beauty, gardening, property and
what's on.
Ad Rate: Full Page Colour £1800.00
MAGAZINE
Regional General Interest

Surrey Magazine   1064618
Tel: 44 01483 479533
Email: info@excellencegroup.co.uk
Web site: www.surreymagazineonline.co.uk
Circ: 15000 Not Audited
MAGAZINE
Regional General Interest

Surrey Matters   997201
Editorial: County Hall, Penrhyn Road,
London KT1 2DW Tel: 44 03456 009009
Email: surreymatters@surreycc.gov.uk
Web site: www.surreycc.gov.uk/
surreymatters
Freq: 3 Times/Year
Circ: 500000 Not Audited
MAGAZINE
Regional, Regional General Interest

Surrey Nature   981997
Editorial: School Lane, Pirbright, Woking,
London GU24 0JN Tel: 44 01483 795440
Web site: www.surreywildlifetrust.org
Freq: 3 Times/Year
Circ: 16500 Not Audited
Profile: Magazine produced by Surrey
Wildlife Trust. Contains news, articles and
information about Trust activities and the
activities of kindred organisations in Surrey,
management and general information about
Surrey Wildlife Trust reserves, details of
conservation work and general
environmental and wildlife issues.
Ad Rate: Full Page Mono £590.00
Ad Rate: Full Page Colour £650.00
MAGAZINE
Nature & Wildlife

Surrey Occasions Magazine
982529
Editorial: Briarwood, Weston Green Road,
Thames Ditton KT7 0JN
Email: editor@surreyoccasions.co.uk
Web site: www.surreyoccasions.co.uk
Freq: Quarterly
Circ: 12500 Not Audited
Editor: Claire Mahoney
MAGAZINE
Regional General Interest

Surrey Time & Leisure   987135
Editorial: 14 Apprentice Shop, Merton
Abbey Mills, London SW19 2RD
Tel: 44 02085 456777
Web site: www.timeandleisure.co.uk
Freq: Monthly Not Audited
MAGAZINE
Regional General Interest

Surveyor - MERGED WITH
HIGHWAYS 2016   981274
Editorial: 32 Vauxhall Bridge Road, London
SW1V 2SS
Web site: http://www.transport-network.co.
uk/
Freq: Monthly
Circ: 5427 Not Audited
Profile: Magazine covering all aspects of
local authority technical services including
highway maintenance, parking, traffic control
and transport policy and articles on waste
management, contaminated land, coastal
protection and drainage. Aimed at
professionals in the areas of highways and
transportation, waste management and
environmental protection within local
government technical services and their
contractors.
Ad Rate: Full Page Colour £1900.00
MAGAZINE
Engineering, Government, Public Sector

Sussex Focus   998356
Editorial: Suite 6B(i), Britannia House,
Leagrave Road, Luton LU3 1RJ
Tel: 44 01582 488385
Email: info@mediachameleon.co.uk
Web site: www.sussex-focus.co.uk
Freq: Annual Not Audited
MAGAZINE
Antiques/Collectibles, Beauty &
Grooming, Cosmetics, Do-It-Yourself
(DIY), Family & Parenting, Gardening, Hair,
Health & Medicine, Nature & Wildlife, Pop
Music

Sussex Life   982538
Editorial: 28 Teville Road, Worthing,
Worthing BN11 1UG Tel: 44 01903 703730
Web site: www.sussexlife.co.uk
Freq: Monthly
Circ: 16500 Not Audited
Editor: Jenny Mark-Bell
Profile: Magazine containing features on
property, fashion, books, food, antiques,
gardening, interiors, wildlife, environment,
health and beauty, finance and the arts.
Ad Rate: Full Page Colour £2118.00
MAGAZINE
Regional General Interest

Sussex Living   987513
Tel: 44 01273 835355
Email: editorial@sussexliving.com
Web site: www.sussexliving.com
Freq: Monthly
Circ: 17000 Not Audited
Profile: Magazine including articles of local
interest with upcoming events across the
villages with history and local heritage. All
editorial locally derived and directed. Aimed
at residents of Sussex.
Ad Rate: Full Page Colour £750.00
MAGAZINE
Regional General Interest

Sussex Local   1057955
Web site: http://www.sussexlocal.net/
welcome.html
Freq: Monthly
Circ: 23500 Not Audited

Editor: Kristina Thomas
MAGAZINE
Regional, Regional General Interest

The Sussex Newspaper   995761
Editorial: PO Box 1128, Crawley RH11 0BP
Tel: 44 08447 746574
Email: editorial@thesussexnewspaper.com
Web site: www.thesussexnewspaper.com
Freq: Daily
Circ: 12367 Cision Digital Reach
Editor: Kizzi Nkwocha
MAGAZINE (ONLINE)
Regional, Regional General Interest

Sussex Style   986929
Editorial: 2nd Floor, Afon House, Worthing
Road, Horsham RH12 1TL
Tel: 44 01403 801800
Web site: www.sussexstyle.co.uk
Freq: Monthly
Circ: 25000 Not Audited
Profile: Magazine covering fashion, beauty
and entertainment in Sussex. It also features
articles on local property, interiors, business,
farming, motoring, food and drink.
MAGAZINE
Luxury Goods, Regional General Interest,
Women's Interests

suttoncoldfieldlocal.co.uk
995480
Editorial: Our Place Community Hub, 1-2
Farthing Lane, Sutton Coldfield, Sutton
Coldfield B72 1NR
Web site: www.suttoncoldfieldlocal.co.uk
Freq: Daily
Circ: 15236 Cision Digital Reach
Editor: Najm Clayton
MAGAZINE (ONLINE)
Regional

SVI - Sound Vision Install   995279
Editorial: 21-23 Phoenix Court, Hawkins
Road, Colchester, Colchester CO2 8JY
Tel: 44 01206 505900
Email: editorial@svimag.com
Web site: www.svimag.com
Freq: Monthly
Circ: 4331 Not Audited
MAGAZINE
Electronics

SW Londoner   986623
Editorial: 247 The Broadway, London SW19
1SD Tel: 44 02085 451662
Email: newsdesk@swlondoner.co.uk
Web site: www.swlondoner.co.uk
Freq: Daily
Circ: 52385 Cision Digital Reach
MAGAZINE (ONLINE)
Regional General Interest

Swansea Life   984580
Editorial: Urban Village, 220 High Street,
Swansea SA1 1NW Tel: 44 01792 545530
Email: peter.slee@swwmedia.co.uk
Web site: http://www.southwales-
eveningpost.co.uk/swansealifemagazine
Freq: Monthly
Circ: 5500 Not Audited
Profile: Lifestyle magazine covering fashion,
interior design, culture, arts, food and drink.
Ad Rate: Full Page Colour £500.00
MAGAZINE
Regional General Interest

Swashbuckle   996128
Email: ahoy@swashbucklemagazine.com
Freq: Monthly
Circ: 33551 Not Audited
MAGAZINE
Preschool, Teen/Young Adult, Trading
Cards & Comics

SweetCrude Nigeria   1061449
Web site: http://sweetcrudereports.com
Freq: Daily
Circ: 625892 Cision Digital Reach
MAGAZINE (ONLINE)
Alternative/Renewable Energy, Carbon
Emissions & Trading, Electricity, Energy,

Consumer Magazines

Energy & Environment, International News, Nuclear Power, Oil, Water & Sanitation

sweetretailing.co.uk 986517
Tel: 44 08455 196518
Email: mail@sweetretailing.co.uk
Web site: www.sweetretailing.co.uk
Freq: Daily
Circ: 2306 Cision Digital Reach
Editor: Anna Metcalfe
MAGAZINE (ONLINE)
News & Current Affairs

Swimming Pool Scene Magazine 985416
Editorial: Waterland House, The Warren, Ely CB6 2HN Tel: 44 01353 666663
Email: editorial@poolandspascene.com
Web site: www.poolandspascene.com
Freq: Bi-Monthly
Circ: 10000 Not Audited
Profile: Magazine covering design and construction technology for domestic and commercial pools, saunas and spas. Aimed at swimming pool builders, pool and spa retailers, architects, specifiers, local authorities, hotel chains and wet leisure facility operators.
Ad Rate: Full Page Colour £1050.00
MAGAZINE
Fitness & Exercise

Swimming Times 982305
Editorial: Pavillion 3, Sport Park, 3 Oakwood Drive, Loughborough LE11 3QF
Tel: 44 01509 640230
Email: swimmingtimes@swimming.org
Web site: www.swimming.org/asa/clubs-and-members/swimming-times-magazine1479
Freq: Monthly
Circ: 20000 Not Audited
Editor: Peter Hassall
MAGAZINE
Swimming/Watersports

Swindon Link 982542
Editorial: 37 Basepoint, Rivermead Drive, Swindon SN5 7EX Tel: 44 01793 744677
Email: publisher@swindonlink.com
Web site: www.swindonlink.com
Freq: Monthly
Circ: 27000 Not Audited
Profile: Website covering local news, events, views and information.
MAGAZINE
Regional General Interest

SwindonWeb 984777
Editorial: The Pembroke Centre, Swindon SN2 2PQ Tel: 44 01793 862020
Email: admin@swindonweb.com
Web site: www.swindonweb.com
Freq: Daily
Circ: 40917 Cision Digital Reach
Editor: Phil Poulton
MAGAZINE (ONLINE)
News & Current Affairs

SWIPE 1093867
Editorial: B54, 1 Ugli Campus, 56 Wood Lane, London W12 7SB
Web site: http://www.swipemag.co.uk/
Freq: Bi-Weekly
Circ: 20000 Not Audited
Editor: Barney Guiton
MAGAZINE
Consumer Affairs, Energy & Environment, International News, National News, Politics, Science, Social Issues

SWISSMAG 1060173
Email: inzerce@snow.cz
Web site: http://www.snow.cz
Freq: Semi-Annual
Circ: 5000 Not Audited
MAGAZINE
Airline Inflight, Railroad, Travel

SWISSMAG 1060359
Email: inzerce@snow.cz
Web site: http://www.snow.cz

Freq: Semi-Annual
Circ: 5000 Not Audited
MAGAZINE
Airline Inflight, Railroad, Travel

The Sword 987297
Editorial: 1 Baron's Gate, 33 Rothschild Rd, London W4 5HT Tel: 44 02087 423032
Web site: http://www.britishfencing.com/news/thesword/
Freq: Quarterly Not Audited
Editor: Edward Rogers
Profile: Magazine that contains news and features about fencing at home and abroad.
Ad Rate: Full Page Colour £400.00
MAGAZINE
Olympic Sports

The Sybarite 1101623
Editorial: 250 York Road, Battersea, London SW11 3SJ Tel: 44 02033 718331
Email: info@thesybarite.org
Web site: https://experienceluxury.co/
Freq: Daily
Circ: 14907 Cision Digital Reach
MAGAZINE (ONLINE)
Alcohol & Spirits, Art, Bars, Clubs & Pubs, Beer, Beverages, Cooking & Baking, Investment Banking, Lifestyle, Luxury Goods, Men's Interests

Synsygus 1061407
Email: synsygus@suol.fi
Web site: http://www.suol.fi/index.php/synsygus Not Audited
MAGAZINE
Religion

t! magazine 1101096
Editorial: 2 Chelsea Embankment, London SW3 4LG Tel: 44 02077 515750
Email: office@tmagazine.co.uk
Web site: http://www.tmagazine.co.uk/
Freq: Daily
Circ: 1825 Cision Digital Reach
Editor: Eileen Cole
MAGAZINE (ONLINE)
Art, Beauty & Grooming, Cosmetics, Fashion, Fitness & Exercise, Hair, Health & Medicine, Literature, Theater & Performing Arts, Women's Interests

T21 1061487
Tel: 44 52555 6827079
Web site: http://www.t21.com.mx/
Freq: Monthly
Circ: 7000 Not Audited
MAGAZINE
Antique & Collectible Cars, Automakers, Automotive, Aviation, Driving, Motorcycles, Off-road & 4-Wheel Drive Vehicles, Railroad, Shipping & Warehousing, Supply Chain Management (SCM)

T3 982057
Editorial: Quay House, The Ambury, Bath BA1 1UA Tel: 44 01225 442244
Email: inbox@t3.com
Web site: www.t3.com
Freq: Monthly
Circ: 43125 Not Audited
MAGAZINE
Audio Video Trade, Cameras, Consumer Electronics, Electronics, Men's Interests, Mobile Electronics, Movies & Video

The Tab 985888
Editorial: 2-4 Great Eastern Street, London EC2A 3NW Tel: 44 02037 514540
Email: info@thetab.com
Web site: www.thetab.com
Freq: Daily
Circ: 627624 Cision Digital Reach
Editor: Dan Baggott
MAGAZINE (ONLINE)
Student Lifestyle

TablePouncer.com 995414
Editorial: Venator House, Unit 9 St Stephens Court, 15-17 St Stephens Roa, Bournemouth BH2 6LA
Web site: www.tablepouncer.com

Freq: Daily
Circ: 24211 Cision Digital Reach
MAGAZINE (ONLINE)
News & Current Affairs

The Tablet 982164
Editorial: 1 King Street Cloisters, Clifton Walk, London W6 0QZ Tel: 44 02087 488484
Email: thetablet@thetablet.co.uk
Web site: www.thetablet.co.uk
Freq: Weekly
Circ: 18200 Not Audited
Profile: Catholic publication covering religion, politics, society, ethical issues, books and the arts. Also includes news concerning the work of the church at home and abroad. First published in 1842, the publication has an average of 44 pages per issue. Aimed at Catholics and the wider church.
Ad Rate: Full Page Mono £890.00
Ad Rate: Full Page Colour £1090.00
MAGAZINE
Religion

Tackle & Guns 1074315
Tel: 44 07967 507996
Email: nickmarlow72@gmail.com
Web site: http://www.tandgmagazine.com/
Freq: Monthly
Circ: 5500 Not Audited
Profile: The monthly trade magazine for the fishing and shooting industry. Magazine contains news, product reviews and business to business information.
Ad Rate: Full Page Mono £950.00
Ad Rate: Full Page Colour £834.00
MAGAZINE
Fishing, Shooting/Guns

Tai Chi & Alternative Health 996765
Editorial: Tai Chi Worldwide Limited, Limehouse Basin, Block B5, 5 Branch Road, London E14 7JU
Web site: https://www.taichialternativehealth.com/
Freq: Quarterly Not Audited
MAGAZINE
Alternative Medicine, Martial Arts, MMA & Self-Defense

Take a Break 982437
Editorial: Academic House, 24-28 Oval Road, London NW1 7DT
Tel: 44 02072 418000
Email: tab.features@bauer.co.uk
Web site: takeabreak.co.uk
Freq: Weekly
Circ: 515019 Not Audited
Editor: Rebecca Fleming
Profile: Woman's weekly magazine with puzzles and competitions offering cash prizes, cars and holidays as well as pages on health and relationships, fashion and beauty and household tips. Contains real life stories and useful features, cookery and health tips. The publication was first published in 1990 and has an average of 70 pages per issue. Aimed mainly at women aged between 25 and 55 with children.
Ad Rate: Full Page Colour £10600.00
MAGAZINE
Careers, Crime & Violence, Family & Parenting, Health & Medicine, Lifestyle, Personal Finance, Relationships, Women's Interests

Take a Break's Puzzle Selection 005152
Editorial: Academic House, 24-28 Oval Road, London NW1 7DT
Tel: 44 02072 418000
Email: puzzle.selection@bauer.co.uk
Web site: www.puzzlemagazines.co.uk/puzzle-selection
Freq: Monthly
Circ: 139000 Not Audited
Editor: Kaylie Mackenzie
MAGAZINE
Games, Competitions & Events

Take a Break's Fate & Fortune 1049242
Editorial: Academic House, 24-28 Oval Road, London NW1 7DT
Tel: 44 02072 418000
Email: fateandfortunefeedback@bauer.co.uk
Web site: http://www.fateandfortunemagazine.co.uk/
Freq: Monthly Not Audited
Editor: Sue Ricketts
MAGAZINE
Astrology & Parapsychology, Women's Interests

Take a Break's My Favourite Recipes 997063
Editorial: Academic House, 24-28 Oval Road, London NW1 7DT
Tel: 44 02072 418000
Email: myfavouriterecipes@bauer.co.uk
Web site: www.myfavouriterecipes.net
Freq: Monthly
Circ: 147572 Not Audited
Editor: Sheena Horton
MAGAZINE
Cooking & Baking

Take a Break's Season Puzzle Collection 997833
Email: puzzle.collection@bauer.co.uk
Web site: http://www.puzzlemagazines.co.uk/summer-puzzle-collection
Freq: Bi-Monthly
Circ: 158658 Not Audited
Editor: Kaylie Mackenzie
MAGAZINE
News & Current Affairs

Take A Crossword 999168
Editorial: Academic House, 24-28 Oval Road, London NW1 7DT
Tel: 44 02072 418000
Email: take.crossword@bauer.co.uk
Web site: www.bauer.co.uk/magazines/take-crossword
Freq: Monthly
Circ: 191000 Not Audited
Editor: Michael Baker
MAGAZINE
Games, Competitions & Events

Take a Puzzle 999169
Editorial: Academic House, 24-28 Oval Road, London NW1 7DT
Tel: 44 02072 418000
Email: take.puzzle@bauer.co.uk
Web site: www.puzzlemagazines.co.uk/takeapuzzle
Freq: Monthly
Circ: 180000 Not Audited
Editor: Babetta Mann
MAGAZINE
Games, Competitions & Events

Take Stock 986822
Editorial: Ground Floor, Nesfield House, Broughton Hall Business Park, Skipton BD23 3AE Tel: 44 01756 636777
Email: hello@takestockmagazine.com
Web site: http://www.takestockmagazine.com
Freq: Bi-Monthly
Circ: 22000 Not Audited
Editor: Tracy Johnson
Profile: Magazine covering the foodservice trade including catering and industry news. Aimed at Fairway's client base of independent caterers, primarily in the profit sector.
Ad Rate: Full Page Colour £3995.00
MAGAZINE
Alcohol & Spirits, Bars, Clubs & Pubs, Food, Hotels/Motels

takethefamily.com 999501
Web site: https://www.takethefamily.com/
Freq: Daily
Circ: 36503 Cision Digital Reach
MAGAZINE (ONLINE)
Family & Parenting, Travel

Talented Ladies Club   1105186
Email: info@talentedladiesclub.com
Web site: http://www.talentedladiesclub.com/
Freq: Daily
Circ: 58435 Cision Digital Reach
MAGAZINE (ONLINE)
Family & Parenting, Women's Interests

Talk Retail   997476
Editorial: William Robinson Buildings, 3 Woodfield Terrace, Stansted Mountfitchet, Stansted Mountfitchet CM24 8AJ
Tel: 44 02036 174680
Web site: www.talk-retail.co.uk
Freq: Daily
Circ: 1387 Cision Digital Reach
MAGAZINE (ONLINE)
Beauty & Grooming, Books, Cosmetics, Fashion, Gardening, Hair, Office Supplies, Retail, Retail Management, Toys

Talk Stuff   1054951
Web site: https://www.talkstuff.net/index.php/index.html
Freq: Daily
Circ: 10569 Cision Digital Reach
MAGAZINE (ONLINE)
News & Current Affairs

Talk Talk   983823
Editorial: 11 Evesham Street, London W11 4AR **Tel:** 44 02034 171000
Email: press.office@talktalkplc.com
Web site: https://sales.talktalk.co.uk/
Freq: Daily
Circ: 3723341 Cision Digital Reach
MAGAZINE (ONLINE)
Shopping

talkhealth   986957
Editorial: Winchfield Lodge, Old Potbridge Road, Hartley Wintney RG27 8BT
Tel: 44 01256 962250
Email: info@talkhealthpartnership.com
Web site: www.talkhealthpartnership.com
Freq: Daily
Circ: 43140 Cision Digital Reach
MAGAZINE (ONLINE)
Health & Medicine, Patient Support

Talking Baws   1063148
Tel: 44 07825 333070
Email: editor@talkingbaws.com
Web site: www.talkingbaws.com
Freq: Daily
Circ: 161041 Cision Digital Reach
MAGAZINE (ONLINE)
Basketball, Boxing, Cricket, Football (American), Golf, Racquet Sports, Rugby, Soccer

Talking Pictures   982845
Editorial: 1 Orchard Cottages, Colebrook, Plymouth PL7 4AJ **Tel:** 44 01752 347200
Web site: www.talkingpix.co.uk
Freq: Daily
Circ: 13107 Cision Digital Reach
Editor: Nigel Watson
Profile: Website covering entertainment. TALKING PICTURES website provides news and information on films, television, video, computer games and the media.
MAGAZINE (ONLINE)
Computer & Video Games, Movies & Video

talkingretail.com   984266
Editorial: 6th Floor, Davis House, 2 Robert Street, Croydon CR0 1QQ
Tel: 44 02082 534617
Email: editor@talkingretail.com
Web site: www.talkingretail.com
Freq: Daily
Circ: 45358 Cision Digital Reach
Editor: David Shrimpton
Profile: Website providing information about grocery retail in the UK and overseas.
MAGAZINE (ONLINE)
Alcohol & Spirits, Food, Retail Management

TameBay   987460
Web site: http://tamebay.com/
Freq: Daily
Circ: 139300 Cision Digital Reach
MAGAZINE (ONLINE)
News & Current Affairs

Tandoori Magazine   983276
Editorial: South Park Studio, 88 Peterborough Road, London SW6 3HH
Tel: 44 02073 487997
Email: info@tandoorimagazine.com
Web site: www.tandoorimagazine.com
Freq: Bi-Monthly
Circ: 7000 Not Audited
Editor: Humayun Hussain
Profile: Magazine reporting on upcoming trends in the Indian food and drink industry. Features new products, book and website reviews, recipe ideas, restaurant interiors, hotels, travel, drinks, information on basic hygiene, equipment and kitchen design issues. Aimed at the Indian restaurant market and consumers interested in Indian food and drink including key decision-makers, owners, managers, chefs, journalists and other members of the industry.
Ad Rate: Full Page Colour £2500.00
MAGAZINE
Bars, Clubs & Pubs, Food

Tangled Web   1105187
Web site: www.twbooks.co.uk
Freq: Daily
Circ: 6858 Cision Digital Reach
Editor: Amanda Caven
MAGAZINE (ONLINE)
Literature

TANK   983137
Editorial: 91-93 Great Portland Street, London W1W 7NX **Tel:** 44 02076 370303
Web site: www.tankmagazine.com
Freq: Semi-Annual
Circ: 60000 Not Audited
Profile: Magazine containing fashion and photography features, art, architecture and short stories. Aimed at design orientated professional men and women between 18 and 40 years old.
Ad Rate: Full Page Colour £4000.00
MAGAZINE
Fashion, Men's Interests, Women's Interests

Tanker Shipping & Trade   984297
Editorial: Mitre House, 66 Abbey Road, Enfield EN1 2QN **Tel:** 44 02083 641551
Web site: www.tankershipping.com
Freq: Bi-Monthly
Circ: 4000 Not Audited
Profile: Publication looking at the elements that contribute to successful tanker management both commercial and technical covering all types and sizes of oil and chemical tankers. Topics covered include news from around the world, safety, operational and technical issues, design, propulsion and developments.
Ad Rate: Full Page Colour £2365.00
MAGAZINE
Marine & Boat Trade, Shipping & Warehousing

TantrumXYZ   1063714
Editorial: 31 New Inn Yard, London EC2A 3EY
Email: info@tantrum.xyz
Web site: https://tantrum.xyz/
Freq: Daily Cision Digital Reach
Editor: Lisa Williams
MAGAZINE (ONLINE)
Elementary School, Family & Parenting, Preschool

TaP-room.com   1053859
Email: info@tap-room.co.uk
Web site: www.tap-room.com
Freq: Monthly
Circ: 3500 Not Audited
MAGAZINE
Bars, Clubs & Pubs, Beer

TapSmart.com   997440
Editorial: St. Brandon's House, 29 Great George Street, Bristol BS1 5QT
Email: andy@intelligentl.com
Web site: www.tapsmart.com
Freq: Daily
Circ: 45761 Cision Digital Reach
Editor: Andy Price
MAGAZINE (ONLINE)
Mobile Electronics

Target MD   981824
Editorial: 61A Great Suffolk Street, London SE1 0BU **Tel:** 44 02078 034800
Email: targetmd@musculardystrophyuk.org
Web site: www.musculardystrophyuk.org
Freq: Quarterly
Circ: 10000 Not Audited
Editor: Ruth Martin
Profile: Publication containing articles on muscular dystrophy and related disorders, medical research news, medical management issues and disability issues. Read by people with, or affected by muscular dystrophy, medical professionals and researchers.
MAGAZINE
Disability, Patient Support

taste buds   999503
Editorial: Roe Valley Barn, 2 Rocombe Court, Lower Rocombe, Stokeinteignhead, Newton Abbot TQ12 4QL
Tel: 44 01626 871161
Email: editorial@tastebudsmagazine.co.uk
Web site: www.tastebudsmagazine.co.uk
Freq: Bi-Monthly
Circ: 16000 Not Audited
MAGAZINE
Cooking & Baking, Food, Grocery Stores, Organic Food, Restaurant Reviews, Vegetarianism & Veganism

The Tastemaker   1104807
Editorial: Suite 7, 40 Craven Street, Charing Cross, London WC2N 5NG
Tel: 44 02077 514198
Email: info@thetastemaker.org
Web site: thetastemaker.org
Freq: Daily
Circ: 702 Cision Digital Reach
MAGAZINE (ONLINE)
Bars, Clubs & Pubs, Luxury Goods, Restaurant Reviews, Travel

Tasteofmanchester.com   984678
Editorial: Office 57, 4th Floor, 24 Lever Street, Manchester M1 1DZ
Tel: 44 01612 280315
Email: hello@foodanddrinkfestival.com
Web site: www.tasteofmanchester.com
Freq: Daily
Circ: 13384 Cision Digital Reach
MAGAZINE (ONLINE)
Alcohol & Spirits, Bars, Clubs & Pubs, Beer, Beverages, Cooking & Baking, Food, Grocery Stores, Organic Food, Restaurant Reviews, Vegetarianism & Veganism

The Taster   1054544
Tel: 44 01446 771731
Email: thetastermagazine@gmail.com
Web site: www.thetastermagazine.com
Freq: Quarterly
Circ: 20000 Not Audited
Editor: Catrin Thomas-Price
MAGAZINE
Alcohol & Spirits, Bars, Clubs & Pubs, Beer, Beverages, Cooking & Baking, Food, Grocery Stores, Organic Food, Restaurant Reviews, Vegetarianism & Veganism

Tasting Britain   987578
Web site: www.tastingbritain.co.uk/
Freq: Daily
Circ: 14475 Cision Digital Reach
Editor: Bryony Chinnery

Profile: Website covering food. TB website covers food, drink, healthy eating, recipes and restaurant reviews.
MAGAZINE (ONLINE)
Cooking & Baking, Food, Grocery Stores, Organic Food, Restaurant Reviews, Vegetarianism & Veganism

tastyfanzine.org.uk   998779
Email: info@tastyfanzine.org.uk
Web site: tastyfanzine.org.uk
Freq: Daily
Circ: 702 Cision Digital Reach
Editor: Shane Blanchard
MAGAZINE (ONLINE)
Rock Music

TATE ETC   981885
Editorial: 20 John Islip Street, Millbank, London SW1P 4RG **Tel:** 44 02078 878724
Email: tateetc@tate.org.uk
Web site: www.tate.org.uk/tateetc
Freq: 3 Times/Year
Circ: 105000 Not Audited
Editor: Simon Grant
Profile: International art magazine offering a fresh perspective on historic, modern and contemporary art from outstanding writers and artists.
Ad Rate: Full Page Colour £3750.00
MAGAZINE
Art

Tatler   982378
Editorial: Vogue House, Hanover Square, London W1S 1JU **Tel:** 44 02074 999080
Web site: www.tatler.com
Freq: Monthly
Circ: 80035 Not Audited
Editor: Kate Reardon
Profile: Magazine covering women's interest and affluent lifestyle including fashion, beauty, jewellery, luxury goods, travel, property, restaurants, motoring, shopping and celebrity interviews. Covers a broad range of topics, but its primary focus is on social trends of the upper class. Parties and society events are portrayed throughout, but most prevalently in the Bystander column, towards the back of the magazine. First published in 1707. Read by affluent socialites.
Ad Rate: Full Page Colour £12200.00
MAGAZINE
Celebrities, Fashion, Luxury Goods, Women's Interests

Tattoo Master   999444
Tel: 44 01244 663400
Email: editor@tattoomaster.com
Web site: www.tattoomaster.com
Freq: Quarterly
Circ: 7000 Not Audited
Editor: Trent Aitken-Smith
MAGAZINE
Fashion

Tax Planning International European Tax Service   981555
Editorial: 38 Threadneedle Street, London EC2R 8AY **Tel:** 44 02078 475800
Web site: http://www.bnai.com/
Freq: Monthly Not Audited
Profile: Magazine with news and analysis of European tax issues and their application in Member States. Aimed at International tax specialists.Alternative Title: European Union Focus Previous title: Tax Planning International European Union Focus
MAGAZINE
News & Current Affairs

TaxationWeb.co.uk   983450
Editorial: 6 Coleby Avenue, Peel Hall, Manchester M22 5HH
Web site: www.taxationweb.co.uk
Freq: Daily
Circ: 100175 Cision Digital Reach
MAGAZINE (ONLINE)
Accounting, Tax Law

TAXI Newspaper   1053492
Tel: 44 02072 861046
Email: taxinewspaper@ltda.co.uk

Consumer Magazines

Web site: www.taxinewspaper.co.uk
Freq: Bi-Weekly
Circ: 15000 Not Audited
Profile: Publication of the Licensed Taxi Drivers' Association. Contains news and articles on the taxi industry, law, finance, leisure, motoring and taxation.
Ad Rate: Full Page Mono £931.00
Ad Rate: Full Page Colour £1269.00
MAGAZINE
Automotive

Taylor 1064098
Web site: http://taylormagazine.com/
Freq: Daily
Circ: 12576 Cision Digital Reach
MAGAZINE (ONLINE)
Bars, Clubs & Pubs, Celebrities, Relationships, Women's Interests

TBseen 1100166
Web site: https://tbseen.com/
Freq: Daily
Circ: 53616 Cision Digital Reach
MAGAZINE (ONLINE)
News & Current Affairs

T-C News 998600
Editorial: 12a Gourlay's Wynd, Duns TD11 3AZ **Tel:** 44 01361 315003
Web site: http://www.t-cnews.com
Freq: Quarterly Not Audited
Editor: Jeff Abbott
MAGAZINE
News & Current Affairs

TEA - women's supplement
1061951
Not Audited
MAGAZINE
Consumer Affairs, Crime & Violence, Defense & National Security, Energy & Environment, Ethical/Moral Issues, International News, Law, National News, News & Current Affairs, Northern Ireland

Teach Early Years 987379
Editorial: 25 Phoenix Court, Hawkins Rd, Colchester, Colchester CO2 8JY
Tel: 44 01206 505900
Web site: http://www.teachwire.net/
Circ: 18000 Not Audited
Editor: Jacob Stow
MAGAZINE
Preschool

The Teacher 981589
Web site: www.teachers.org.uk/teacher-online/
Freq: Bi-Monthly
Circ: 330000 Not Audited
Profile: Magazine of the National Union of Teachers. Contains news and features on education in England and Wales. Also includes information about NUT policy. Aimed at NUT members, student members and education departments of colleges and universities.Submitting digital photos, please ensure that they are high resolution – i.e. at least 300 dpi at standard print size (10cm x 15cm). Photos can be emailed to teacher@nut.org.uk, but check the file size before you send. If an image is less that 150k it is likely to be too low quality to use in print. If the total size of all attachments can't exceed 6MB, as being rejected.
Ad Rate: Full Page Colour £7326.00
MAGAZINE
News & Current Affairs

Teaching English 998250
Editorial: Unit 410, Aizlewood Business Centre, Aizlewood's Mill Nursery Street, Sheffield S3 8GG **Tel:** 44 01142 823545
Email: gary@gabrielsnapper.co.uk
Web site: www.nate.org.uk/index.php?page=79
Freq: 3 Times/Year Not Audited
Editor: Gary Snapper
MAGAZINE
Disability, Education, Higher Education, Preschool, Schools & Institutions, Students

Teaching Instruments and Experiments 1061940
Tel: 44 86106 2514749
Email: bjb4749@sina.com
Freq: Monthly
Circ: 20000 Not Audited
MAGAZINE
Disability, Education, Higher Education, Preschool, Schools & Institutions, Students

Teaching Scotland 985021
Editorial: Clerwood House, 96 Clermiston Road, Edinburgh EH12 6UT
Tel: 44 01313 146000
Email: teachingscotland@gtcs.org.uk
Web site: www.gtcs.org.uk
Freq: Bi-Monthly
Circ: 70000 Not Audited
Profile: Teaching Scotland is a magazine for teachers. Issued three times a year, it covers a range of issues relevant for the profession as well as regularly updating teachers on GTC support and responsibilities. It has a balance of features, resources, contacts and information for teachers and educational partners in Scotland as well as news about the Councils activities and key aims.
Ad Rate: Full Page Colour £4125.00
MAGAZINE
Disability, Education, Higher Education, Preschool, Schools & Institutions, Students

Teaching Today 983843
Editorial: Hillscourt Education Centre, Rose Hill, Rednal, Birmingham B45 8RS
Tel: 44 01214 536150
Email: nasuwt@mail.nasuwt.org.uk
Web site: https://www.nasuwt.org.uk/news/teaching-today.html
Freq: Bi-Monthly
Circ: 300000 Not Audited
Profile: Magazine providing information, news, updates and features on issues relevant to education and trade union sectors. Read by members of NASUWT in primary, secondary and further education and student members, also anybody with an interest or involvement in education and schools. Distributed to the homes of NASUWT members.
Ad Rate: Full Page Colour £3502.00
MAGAZINE
Disability, Education, Higher Education, Preschool, Schools & Institutions, Students

Teachingtimes.com 984480
Editorial: 309 Scott House, The Custard Factory, Gibb Street, Birmingham B9 4DT
Tel: 44 01212 247576
Web site: http://www.teachingtimes.com/
Freq: Daily
Circ: 7381 Cision Digital Reach
Editor: Raspal Chima
MAGAZINE (ONLINE)
Disability, Education, Higher Education, Preschool, Schools & Institutions, Students

Team Locals 987647
Editorial: 44 Castle Road, Southsea, Portsmouth PO5 3DE **Tel:** 44 02392 823477
Email: info@teamlocals.co.uk
Web site: www.teamlocals.co.uk
Freq: Daily
Circ: 16705 Cision Digital Reach
MAGAZINE (ONLINE)
Local Entertainment Guides, Regional, Regional General Interest

Teamtalk.com 982846
Editorial: Grant Way, Isleworth, London TW7 5QD
Email: editor@teamtalk.com
Web site: www.teamtalk.com
Freq: Daily
Circ: 1757699 Cision Digital Reach
MAGAZINE (ONLINE)
Soccer

TEC (Traffic Engineering & Control) 984104
Editorial: 32 Vauxhall Bridge Road, London SW1V 2SS **Tel:** 44 02079 736401
Web site: www.tecmagazine.com
Freq: Quarterly
Circ: 4500 Not Audited
MAGAZINE
Automotive

Tech City 1074957
Editorial: Runway East, 10 Finsbury Square, London EC2A 1AF
Email: pressoffice@techcityuk.com
Web site: http://www.techcityuk.com/
Freq: Daily
Circ: 51961 Cision Digital Reach
MAGAZINE (ONLINE)
Auto Aftermarket, Computers, Data Management, Electronics, Government Technology, Industry, Internet, Mobile Communications, Security & Security Systems, Software

Tech City Insider 987701
Editorial: Second Floor, 148 Curtain Road, London EC2A 3AT **Tel:** 44 02077 297460
Email: press@c21media.net
Web site: http://www.techcityinsider.net/
Freq: Daily
Circ: 2326 Cision Digital Reach
MAGAZINE (ONLINE)
Computers, Data Management, Electronics, Internet, Mobile Communications

Tech Dragons 997850
Tel: 44 07582 179251
Web site: http://techdragons.wales/
Freq: Daily
Circ: 6165 Cision Digital Reach
MAGAZINE (ONLINE)
Computers, Data Management, Electronics, Government Technology, Industry, Internet, Mobile Communications

Tech on the Go 985734
Email: info@techonthego.co.uk
Web site: www.techonthego.co.uk
Freq: Daily
Circ: 12336 Cision Digital Reach
Editor: Rob Gordon; **Editor:** John Scudd
MAGAZINE (ONLINE)
Apple, Audio Video Trade, Cameras, Computers, Consumer Electronics, Electronics, Government Technology, Internet, Mobile Communications, Mobile Electronics

Tech Oven 1051156
Email: info@techoven.com
Web site: www.techoven.com
Freq: Daily
Circ: 685 Cision Digital Reach
Editor: Rob Gordon
MAGAZINE (ONLINE)
Audio Video Trade, Cameras, Consumer Electronics, Mobile Electronics, Movies & Video

Tech Reviews 986051
Editorial: 67 High Street, Halberton, Tiverton, Tiverton EX16 7AG
Email: news@tech-reviews.co.uk
Web site: www.tech-reviews.co.uk
Freq: Daily
Circ: 41924 Cision Digital Reach
MAGAZINE (ONLINE)
Apple, Audio Video Trade, Cameras, Computer & Video Games, Computers, Consumer Electronics, Electronics, Internet, Mobile Electronics, Movies & Video

TechBritannia 995513
Tel: 44 02082 552345
Email: hello@techbritannia.co.uk
Web site: www.techbritannia.co.uk
Freq: Daily

Circ: 723 Cision Digital Reach
MAGAZINE (ONLINE)
Biotechnology, Computers, Data Management, Electronics, Government Technology, Internet, Mobile Communications, Security & Security Systems, Software

TechEye.net 998164
Email: news@techeye.net
Web site: www.techeye.net
Freq: Daily
Circ: 58358 Cision Digital Reach
Editor: Mike Magee
MAGAZINE (ONLINE)
Auto Aftermarket, Computers, Data Management, Electronics, Government Technology, Industry, Internet, Mobile Communications, Security & Security Systems, Software

TechFruit 988752
Editorial: 284A Battersea Park Road, London SW11 3BT
Email: info@techfruit.com
Web site: www.techfruit.com
Freq: Daily
Circ: 35319 Cision Digital Reach
Editor: Tim Dickinson
MAGAZINE (ONLINE)
Audio Video Trade, Cameras, Consumer Electronics, Electronics, Law, Mobile Electronics, Movies & Video, Music

Techicize 1053633
Web site: www.techicize.com
Freq: Daily
Circ: 11717 Cision Digital Reach
MAGAZINE (ONLINE)
Computers, Personal Computers

Techinvest 981695
Editorial: St Brandon's House, 29 Great George Street, Bristol BS1 5QT
Tel: 44 01179 200070
Email: techinvest@mchattie.co.uk
Web site: www.techinvest.ie
Freq: Monthly Not Audited
Editor: Andrew McHattie
MAGAZINE
Auto Aftermarket, Computers, Data Management, Electronics, Fund Management, Government Technology, Industry, Internet, Mobile Communications, Security & Security Systems

TechMarketView 987085
Tel: 44 01252 781545
Email: sales@techmarketview.com
Web site: www.techmarketview.com
Freq: Daily
Circ: 29337 Cision Digital Reach
MAGAZINE (ONLINE)
Auto Aftermarket, Computers, Data Management, Electronics, Government Technology, Industry, Internet, Mobile Communications, Security & Security Systems, Software

Technical Textiles International 986300
Editorial: 44 Friar Street, Droitwich, Droitwich WR9 8ED **Tel:** 44 08701 657210
Email: editorial@intnews.com
Web site: www.technical-textiles.net
Freq: Bi-Monthly
Circ: 17000 Not Audited
Editor: Nick Butler
Profile: Magazine covering advanced textiles and fibres used in technical applications.
Ad Rate: Full Page Mono £1477.00
Ad Rate: Full Page Colour £2287.00
MAGAZINE
Crafts, Manufacturing

TechNuovo 988089
Editorial: 2 Brunswick Quay, London SE16 7PY
Email: social@technuovo.com
Web site: technuovo.com
Freq: Daily

Circ: 13572 Cision Digital Reach
MAGAZINE (ONLINE)
Audio Video Trade, Cameras, Consumer Electronics, Electronics, Mobile Electronics, Movies & Video

TechRadar
983522
Editorial: 1-10 Praed Mews, Paddington, London W2 1QY **Tel:** 44 02070 424000
Email: news@techradar.com
Web site: www.techradar.com
Freq: Daily
Circ: 11503588 Cision Digital Reach
Editor: James Abbott; **Editor:** Désiré Athow; **Editor:** Basil Kronfli; **Editor:** Gerald Lynch; **Editor:** Paul Taylor
Profile: Website covering consumer technology. The techradar website covers the latest technology news, reviews and information on smart phones, TVs, cameras, laptops, tablets and car tech.
MAGAZINE (ONLINE)
Apple, Audio Video Trade, Cameras, Computer & Video Games, Computers, Consumer Electronics, Electronics, Internet, Mobile Electronics, Movies & Video

Techsparx
1097893
Email: news@techsparxuk.co.uk
Web site: www.techsparx.co.uk
Freq: Daily
Circ: 10814 Cision Digital Reach
Editor: Ranbir Sahota
MAGAZINE (ONLINE)
Auto Aftermarket, Computers, Data Management, Electronics, Government Technology, Industry, Internet, Mobile Communications, Security & Security Systems, Software

Techworld
981594
Editorial: 7th Floor, Clifton House, 101 Euston Road, London NW1 2RA
Tel: 44 02077 562800
Web site: www.techworld.com
Freq: Daily
Circ: 472084 Cision Digital Reach
Editor: Rohan Pearce
Profile: Website covering 'news and views on tech innovation, startups, disruptive technology and their impact on UK business and society'. It also contains in-depth and expert information on topics such as security, data control, operating systems, personal technology, 3D printing, networking, mobile & wireless, application development, Tech City and Internet of Things.
MAGAZINE (ONLINE)
Internet

Teckish.com
1054658
Editorial: 29 Branscombe Street, London SE13 7AY
Web site: http://www.teckish.com
Freq: Daily
Circ: 1120 Cision Digital Reach
MAGAZINE (ONLINE)
Computer & Video Games

Teddy Bear Times
981921
Editorial: Unit 5e Park Farm, Chichester Road, Arundel, Arundel BN18 0AG
Tel: 44 01903 884988
Web site: www.teddybeartimes.com
Freq: Bi-Monthly
Circ: 14000 Not Audited
Editor: Jill Mundy
Profile: Publication that looks at toy collecting and Teddy Bears.
MAGAZINE
Antiques/Collectibles

Teeth Magazine
995476
Email: info@teethmag.net
Web site: http://www.teethmag.net
Freq: Semi-Annual
MAGAZINE
Art, Dance Music, Fashion, Jazz & Blues, Photography, Pop Music, Rap & Hip Hop, Rock Music

Telemedia Magazine
981017
Editorial: Virginia Cottage, Nash Lane, Scaynes Hill, Haywards Heath RH17 7NJ
Tel: 44 01444 831909
Web site: www.telemediamagazine.com
Freq: Bi-Monthly
Circ: 2000 Not Audited
MAGAZINE
Broadcasting, Internet

Television
984870
Editorial: 3 Dorset Rise, London EC4Y 8EN
Tel: 44 02078 222810
Email: info@rts.org.uk
Web site: www.rts.org.uk
Freq: Monthly
Editor: Steve Clarke
Profile: Journal of The Royal Television Society. Contains details of RTS events and television news.
MAGAZINE
Broadcasting

Television Business International
981696
Editorial: Maple House, 149 Tottenham Court Road, London W1T 7AD
Tel: 44 02070 175000
Email: tbi@knect365.com
Web site: www.tbivision.com
Freq: Bi-Monthly
Circ: 8000 Not Audited
MAGAZINE
Broadcasting

Televisual
979857
Editorial: 48 Charlotte Street, London W1T 2NS **Tel:** 44 02030 085750
Web site: www.televisual.com
Freq: Monthly
Circ: 4693 Not Audited
Editor: Tim Dams
Profile: Magazine containing news from the broadcasting, production, corporate communication and facilities services sectors. Aimed at independent producers, broadcasters, commissioners, editors and directors in the TV industry.
Ad Rate: Full Page Colour £2195.00
MAGAZINE
Broadcasting

TellyCafe.com
1061535
Web site: http://tellycafe.com
Freq: Daily
Circ: 493 Cision Digital Reach
MAGAZINE (ONLINE)
Broadcasting

Tempo (UK)
982123
Editorial: PO Box 171, Herne Bay, Herne Bay CT6 6WD **Tel:** 44 01223 358331
Email: tempoeditor@cambridge.org
Web site: http://journals.cambridge.org/action/displayJournal?jid=TEM
Freq: Quarterly
Circ: 3000 Not Audited
Editor: Christopher Fox
MAGAZINE
Classical/Choral/Band Music, Country, Folk, Bluegrass, Dance Music, Jazz & Blues, Local Entertainment Guides, Pop Music, R&B, Urban, World, Rap & Hip Hop, Rock Music

Tempus
986612
Editorial: 3-5 Wardour Street, London W1D 6PB **Tel:** 44 02079 934183
Email: info@curvecontent.com
Web site: tempusmagazine.co.uk
Freq: Monthly
Circ: 16000 Not Audited
Profile: Tempus magazine is a publication focusing on watches and luxury living. It also includes coverage of cars, yachts, fashion, luxury travel and fine dining. Tempus magazine is distributed by Frost of London, five star hotels in London and airlines, targeting private jet and first and business class passengers.
MAGAZINE
Luxury Goods

Tenants Extra
1054123
Editorial: The Griffin Brewery, Chiswick Lane South, London W4 2QB
Freq: Monthly
Circ: 300 Not Audited
MAGAZINE
Beer

TenEighty
1064619
Email: contact@teneightymagazine.com
Web site: www.teneightymagazine.com
Freq: Daily
Circ: 36958 Cision Digital Reach
MAGAZINE (ONLINE)
Internet

Tennis Today
988785
Editorial: Suite Y0011, 262-269 Kingston Road, Wimbledon, London SW19 3NW
Tel: 44 02034 245022
Email: newsdesk@tennis-today.net
Web site: http://www.tennis-today.net/
Freq: Daily
Circ: 2105 Cision Digital Reach
Editor: Henry Wancke
Profile: Magazine about tennis at International club and regional level, including regular features for club administrators.
Ad Rate: Full Page Colour £693.00
MAGAZINE (ONLINE)
Racquet Sports

tennishead
984957
Editorial: Suite 142, 61 Victoria Road, Surbiton, London KT6 4JX
Tel: 44 44020 84087148
Email: info@tennishead.net
Web site: www.tennishead.net
Freq: Bi-Monthly
Circ: 20000 Not Audited
Profile: Magazine featuring international tennis news, expert comment and opinion, coaching and fitness drills and lots of insight into what's happening on the circuit. Aimed at tennis enthusiasts.
MAGAZINE
Racquet Sports

Terror-Byte Gaming
995332
Email: terrorbytegaming@gmail.com
Web site: www.terrorbytegaming.co.uk
Freq: Daily
Circ: 916 Cision Digital Reach
Editor: Stephen Whittaker
MAGAZINE (ONLINE)
Computer & Video Games

Terrorizer
982934
Editorial: 48 Leigh Road, Essex, Southend-on-Sea SS9 1LF **Tel:** 44 02077 297666
Email: editorial@darkartsltd.com
Web site: www.terrorizer.com
Freq: Monthly
Circ: 9217 Not Audited
Profile: Music magazine covering metal, hardcore and industrial music. Aimed at metal, hardcore and industrial music fans.
Ad Rate: Full Page Colour £2000.00
MAGAZINE
Men's Interests, Rock Music

TES
981525
Editorial: 26 Red Lion Square, London WC1R 4HQ **Tel:** 44 02031 943000
Email: newsdesk@tes.com
Web site: www.tes.co.uk
Freq: Weekly
Circ: 378000 Not Audited
MAGAZINE
Disability, Education, Higher Education, Preschool, Schools & Institutions, Students

Tesco Loves Baby Club
995818
Tel: 44 02077 342303
Email: editor@tesco-baby.co.uk
Web site: www.tesco.com/babyclub
Freq: Daily Not Audited
MAGAZINE
Family & Parenting

Tesco magazine
981812
Editorial: 85 Strand, London WC2R 0DW
Tel: 44 02075 508000
Email: tesco@tescomagazine.co.uk
Web site: www.tescoliving.com
Freq: Monthly
Circ: 1962965 Not Audited
Editor: Aviva Attias
Profile: Website of Tesco magazine covering food, fashion, health, beauty, travel, gardening, the home, product reviews, book, CD, computer games and DVD reviews. Aimed at women aged between 25 and 45 years old who lead busy lives.
MAGAZINE
Grocery Stores, Nutrition

The TEST PIT
988941
Email: info@thetestpit.com
Web site: http://www.thetestpit.com/
Freq: Daily
Circ: 17561 Cision Digital Reach
MAGAZINE (ONLINE)
Audio Video Trade, Cameras, Electronics, Mobile Electronics

Test01 Outlet
1053218
MAGAZINE (ONLINE)
News & Current Affairs

Tewkesbury ADMAG
1064937
Tel: 44 01905 748200
Email: news@worcesternews.co.uk
Web site: http://www.tewkesburyadmag.co.uk/
Freq: Daily
Circ: 12446 Cision Digital Reach
MAGAZINE (ONLINE)
News & Current Affairs

Textile Evolution
1064932
Tel: 44 01977 708488
Web site: www.tevonews.com
Freq: Bi-Monthly Not Audited
MAGAZINE
Fashion

Textile Month International
984456
Editorial: WestOne, 114 Wellington Street, Leeds LS1 1BA **Tel:** 44 01133 884882
Email: info@wtin.com
Web site: www.wtin.com/e-store-products/textile-month-international/
Freq: Bi-Monthly
Circ: 10077 Not Audited
Profile: Journal covering the machinery and processes involved in the manufacture of textiles, from fibre through to finished product.
Ad Rate: Full Page Colour £3300.00
MAGAZINE
Fashion

Textiles
983754
Editorial: First Floor, St James's Buildings, 79 Oxford Street, Manchester M1 6FQ
Tel: 44 01612 371188
Email: tiihq@textileinst.org.uk
Web site: www.texi.org/PublicationsMags.asp
Freq: Quarterly
Circ: 4000 Not Audited
Editor: Vanessa Knowles
Profile: textiles is the international membership publication of The Textile Institute providing informative articles on all aspects of the textile chain from fibre production to retailing, including clothing and footwear.
Ad Rate: Full Page Mono £2200.00
Ad Rate: Full Page Colour £3500.00
MAGAZINE
Fashion

TFM Insights
998321
Editorial: 240 Blackfriars Road, London SE1 9UY **Tel:** 44 02079 553714
Web site: tfminsights.com
Freq: Daily

Consumer Magazines

Circ: 55229 Cision Digital Reach
MAGAZINE (ONLINE)
Advertising Industry, Auto Aftermarket, Business, Computers, Data Management, Electronics, Government Technology, Industry, Internet, Marketing

Thames Guardian magazine
980001
Editorial: 151 Station Street, Burton-on-Trent DE14 1BG
Web site: www.riverthamessociety.org.uk/magazine.aspx
Freq: Quarterly
Circ: 6000 Not Audited
Editor: Sarah Henshaw
MAGAZINE
Regional General Interest

that's life!
980737
Editorial: Academic House, 24-28 Oval Road, London NW1 7DT
Tel: 44 02072 418000
Email: stories@thatslife.co.uk
Web site: www.thatslife.co.uk
Freq: Weekly
Circ: 204065 Not Audited
Editor: Sophie Hearsey
MAGAZINE
Careers, Crime & Violence, Family & Parenting, Health & Medicine, Lifestyle, Personal Finance, Relationships

Thatsoyoo
999318
Editorial: 19 Catherine Place, London SW1E 6DX **Tel:** 44 02078 211111
Email: info@thatsoyoo.com
Web site: www.thatsoyoo.com
Freq: Daily
Circ: 1500 Cision Digital Reach
MAGAZINE (ONLINE)
Fashion, Shopping

Theatre & Performance
986737
Email: info@theatreperform.com
Web site: www.theatreperform.com
Freq: Quarterly Not Audited
Editor: Michael Darton
MAGAZINE
Movies & Video, Theater & Performing Arts

Theatre Record
981801
Editorial: 131 Sherringham Avenue, London N17 9RU **Tel:** 44 01305 775990
Email: editor@theatrerecord.com
Web site: www.theatrerecord.com
Freq: Bi-Weekly
Circ: 1000 Not Audited
Profile: Magazine containing a running archive of the English stage. Reprints all the reviews of the national newspaper drama critics with photographs and cast lists. Also lists forthcoming premieres.
Ad Rate: Full Page Mono £250.00
MAGAZINE
Theater & Performing Arts

Theatrefullstop
997471
Email: theatrefullstop@gmail.com
Web site: http://theatrefullstop.com/
Freq: Daily
Circ: 12187 Cision Digital Reach
MAGAZINE (ONLINE)
Theater & Performing Arts

theatreVOICE
988517
Email: contact@theatrevoice.com
Web site: http://www.theatrevoice.com/
Freq: Daily
Circ: 11096 Cision Digital Reach
MAGAZINE (ONLINE)
Theater & Performing Arts

TheBabyWebsite.com
990473
Editorial: Sophia House, 28 Cathedral Road, Cardiff CF11 9LJ **Tel:** 44 02920 843786
Email: contact@thebabywebsite.com
Web site: www.thebabywebsite.com
Freq: Daily
Circ: 35481 Cision Digital Reach

Editor: Kathryn Crawford
MAGAZINE (ONLINE)
Family & Parenting

thebfa.org
996206
Editorial: 85f Park Drive, Milton Park, Didcot OX14 4RY
Freq: Daily
Circ: 39101 Cision Digital Reach
MAGAZINE (ONLINE)
News & Current Affairs

The-Buyer.net
1073945
Email: editorial@the-buyer.com
Web site: http://www.the-buyer.net/
Freq: Daily
Circ: 17738 Cision Digital Reach
MAGAZINE (ONLINE)
Alcohol & Spirits, Bars, Clubs & Pubs, Hotels/Motels

TheFuss.co.uk
988816
Editorial: Unit 4 Sinclair Way, Prescot Business Park, Liverpool L34 1QL
Tel: 44 01514 260317
Web site: www.thefuss.co.uk
Freq: Daily
Circ: 52721 Cision Digital Reach
MAGAZINE (ONLINE)
Women's Interests

TheGayUK
990590
Editorial: 3rd Floor, 727A Green Lanes, London N21 3RX **Tel:** 44 02083 513173
Email: newsdesk@thegayuk.com
Web site: www.thegayuk.com
Freq: Daily
Circ: 149958 Cision Digital Reach
MAGAZINE (ONLINE)
LGBT, Local Entertainment Guides

thegirlsare
999209
Editorial: Studio 3, 32 Indigo Mews, Carysfort Road, Stoke Newington, London N16 9AE
Email: info@thegirlsare.com
Web site: www.thegirlsare.com
Freq: Daily
Circ: 15000 Not Audited
MAGAZINE
Classical/Choral/Band Music, Country, Folk, Bluegrass, Dance Music, Ethical/Moral Issues, Jazz & Blues, Music, Pop Music, R&B, Urban, World, Rap & Hip Hop, Rock Music

TheGuide2Surrey
1063456
Editorial: Unit 6 Cobbett Park, 22-28 Moorfield Road, Slyfield Industrial Estate, Guildford GU1 1RU **Tel:** 44 01483 456001
Email: admin@tgmediagroup.co.uk
Web site: http://www.theguide2surrey.com/
Freq: Daily
Circ: 14555 Cision Digital Reach
MAGAZINE (ONLINE)
Regional General Interest

thehospitalclub.com
997092
Editorial: 24 Endell Street, Covent Garden, London WC2H 9HQ **Tel:** 44 02071 709100
Web site: www.thehospitalclub.com
Freq: Daily
Circ: 40203 Cision Digital Reach
MAGAZINE (ONLINE)
Advertising Industry, Branding, Broadcasting, Graphic Design, Marketing, Media & Communications, Photography, Publishing

thekiteshow.tv
996841
Editorial: 25 Lintot Square, Southwater, Horsham, Brighton RH13 9LA
Tel: 44 01273 808601
Email: info@thekiteshow.tv
Web site: www.thekiteshow.tv
Freq: Daily
Circ: 4240 Cision Digital Reach
Editor: Jim Gaunt
MAGAZINE (ONLINE)
Extreme/Adventure Sports, Swimming/Watersports

TheMedGuru
1061620
Web site: http://www.themedguru.com
Freq: Daily
Circ: 9312 Cision Digital Reach
MAGAZINE (ONLINE)
Alternative Medicine, Disability, Fitness & Exercise, Health & Medicine, Media Relations, Medicine, Nutrition, Patient Support, Personal Health & Wellness, Psychology

Themoneypages.com
979826
Editorial: Themoneypages.com, 6th Floor, Davis House, 2 Robert Street, Croydon CR0 1QQ **Tel:** 44 02082 538608
Web site: www.themoneypages.com
Freq: Daily
Circ: 15841 Cision Digital Reach
Profile: Website covering all areas of personal finance. Includes savings and investments, mortgages, insurance, pensions, borrowing and alternative investments. Also covers stocks and shares, unit trusts, portfolio management and tax.
MAGAZINE (ONLINE)
Personal Finance

the-news.co
997887
Email: editor@the-news.co
Web site: http://www.the-news.co/
Freq: Daily
Circ: 10069 Cision Digital Reach
Editor: William Mills
MAGAZINE (ONLINE)
Regional

TheOnlineRule
1100935
Tel: 44 07860 945404
Email: scott@theonlinerule.com
Web site: http://theonlinerule.com
Freq: Daily
Circ: 10439 Cision Digital Reach
Editor: Scott Goodacre
MAGAZINE (ONLINE)
Basketball, Bicycles, Billiards, Boating & Yachting, Bodybuilding, Bowling, Boxing, Cricket, Equestrian Sports, Extreme/Adventure Sports

Therapeutic Advances in Chronic Disease
996220
Editorial: 1 Oliver's Yard, 55 City Road, London EC1Y 1SP **Tel:** 44 02073 248500
Web site: http://taj.sagepub.com/
Freq: Bi-Monthly Not Audited
MAGAZINE
AIDS/HIV, Allergies, Cardiology, Dermatology, Diabetes, Gastroenterology, Hematology, Infectious Diseases, Medicine, Neurology

The Therapeutic Care Journal
983262
Editorial: The MBS, Abingdon Road, Standlake, Oxford OX29 7RW
Email: editor@childrenwebmag.com
Web site: http://www.thetcj.org/
Freq: Daily
Circ: 6861 Cision Digital Reach
Editor: John Diamond
Profile: Website covering information about care of children and young people. Aimed at those who work with children and young people across the world.Alternative Title: Children and Young People
MAGAZINE (ONLINE)
Family & Parenting

Therapy Today
985186
Editorial: BACP House, 15 St. John's Business Park, Lutterworth, Lutterworth LE17 4HB **Tel:** 44 01455 883361
Email: therapytoday@bacp.co.uk
Web site: www.therapytoday.net
Freq: Monthly
Circ: 43903 Not Audited
Profile: Journal of the British Association for Counselling and Psychotherapy covering news, features, theory, developments, book reviews, practice management and world perspectives.
Ad Rate: Full Page Mono £830.00

Ad Rate: Full Page Colour £1400.00
MAGAZINE
Alternative Medicine, Neurology

theROOMedit.com
988903
Tel: 44 02031 485000
Web site: www.theroomedit.com
Freq: Daily
Circ: 114923 Cision Digital Reach
MAGAZINE (ONLINE)
Do-It-Yourself (DIY), Shopping

TheSchoolRun.com
982796
Editorial: PO Box 120, Bexley DA5 9DJ
Email: enquiries@theschoolrun.com
Web site: www.theschoolrun.com
Freq: Daily
Circ: 129478 Cision Digital Reach
MAGAZINE (ONLINE)
Family & Parenting

TheShiznit.co.uk
995405
Email: ali@theshiznit.co.uk
Web site: http://www.theshiznit.co.uk/
Freq: Daily
Circ: 212706 Cision Digital Reach
Editor: Ali Gray
MAGAZINE (ONLINE)
Movies & Video

thesoapshow.com
995051
Editorial: 27 Old Gloucester Street, London WC1N 3AX **Tel:** 44 01442 862628
Email: info@thesoapshow.com
Web site: www.thesoapshow.com
Freq: Daily
Circ: 6395 Cision Digital Reach
Editor: Ian Skillicorn
MAGAZINE (ONLINE)
Broadcasting

thesportfeed.com
996390
Editorial: 1 Stanley Grove, Heaton Moor, Stockport SK4 4HP
Email: info@thesportfeed.com
Web site: http://www.thesportfeed.com/
Freq: Daily
Circ: 13383 Cision Digital Reach
Editor: Hugh O'Brien
MAGAZINE (ONLINE)
Basketball, Bicycles, Billiards, Boating & Yachting, Bodybuilding, Bowling, Boxing, Cricket, Equestrian Sports, Extreme/Adventure Sports

TheSprout.co.uk
998908
Editorial: Unit 12, Royal Stuart Workshops, Adelaide Place, Cardiff CF10 5BR
Tel: 44 02920 462222
Web site: www.thesprout.co.uk
Freq: Daily
Circ: 13732 Cision Digital Reach
Editor: Sam Easterbrook
MAGAZINE (ONLINE)
Teen/Young Adult

TheStack.com
997803
Editorial: CloserStill Media, Unit 17, Exhibition House, Addison Bridge Place, London W14 8XP
Email: content@thestack.com
Web site: http://thestack.com
Freq: Daily
Circ: 162229 Cision Digital Reach
Editor: Martin Anderson
MAGAZINE (ONLINE)
Auto Aftermarket, Computers, Data Management, Electronics, Government Technology, Industry, Internet, Mobile Communications, Security & Security Systems, Software

theweddinggirl.co.uk
985120
Editorial: 7 Alexander House, Royal Quarter, Seven Kings Way, London KT2 5BY
Web site: www.theweddinggirl.co.uk
Freq: Daily
Circ: 13259 Cision Digital Reach
Editor: Danielle Coplans
MAGAZINE (ONLINE)
Weddings

thewinegang.com
998709
Editorial: The Wine Gang, 6 Kirklee Road, Glasgow G12 0TP **Tel:** 44 01415 764958
Email: info@thewinegang.com
Web site: www.thewinegang.com
Freq: Daily
Circ: 10653 Cision Digital Reach
MAGAZINE (ONLINE)
Wine/Winemaking

Thiis.co.uk
988069
Editorial: The Stables, 16c High Street, Kettering NN14 1RQ **Tel:** 44 01536 710050
Email: info@thiis.co.uk
Web site: www.thiis.co.uk
Freq: Monthly
Circ: 15740 Cision Digital Reach
MAGAZINE (ONLINE)
News & Current Affairs

The Thin Air
996102
Email: info@thethinair.net
Web site: www.thethinair.net
Freq: Monthly Not Audited
MAGAZINE
Country, Folk, Bluegrass, Dance Music, Jazz & Blues, Pop Music, Rap & Hip Hop, Rock Music

Things and Ink
996060
Email: hello@thingsandink.com
Web site: http://www.th-ink.co.uk/
Freq: Quarterly Not Audited
MAGAZINE
News & Current Affairs

thinkbroadband.com
988907
Email: team@thinkbroadband.com
Web site: www.thinkbroadband.com
Freq: Daily
Circ: 683684 Cision Digital Reach
MAGAZINE (ONLINE)
News & Current Affairs

Thinking Cities
997395
Editorial: H3B Media, 15 Onslow Gardens, Wallington SM6 9QL **Tel:** 44 02034 639482
Email: info@h3bm.com
Web site: thinkingcities.com/latest-issues
Freq: 3 Times/Year
Circ: 24000 Not Audited
MAGAZINE
Automotive, Aviation, Railroad, Shipping & Warehousing, Supply Chain Management (SCM), Transportation

Thinking Highways
986806
Editorial: H3B Media, 15 Onslow Gardens, Wallington SM6 9QL **Tel:** 44 02034 639482
Email: kevin@h3bm.com
Web site: http://thinkinghighways.com/
Freq: Quarterly
Circ: 18656 Not Audited
MAGAZINE
Automotive, Aviation, Shipping & Warehousing, Supply Chain Management (SCM)

Thinking in Practice
987328
Editorial: Balmond Studio, Unit 9, 190a New North Road, London N1 7BJ
Tel: 44 02070 430651
Web site: http://tip.balmondstudio.com/tip/
Freq: Daily
Circ: 4 Cision Digital Reach
MAGAZINE (ONLINE)
Architecture & Design, Art, Photography, Science, Visual Arts

ThinkingDrinkers.com
995140
Web site: http://www.thinkingdrinkers.com/
Freq: Daily
Circ: 7080 Cision Digital Reach
Editor: Tom Sandham
MAGAZINE (ONLINE)
Alcohol & Spirits, Bars, Clubs & Pubs, Beer, Beverages, Wine/Winemaking

Third Force News
981021
Editorial: SCVO, Mansfield Traquair Centre, 15 Mansfield Place, Edinburgh EH3 6BB
Tel: 44 01314 748000

Email: tfn@scvo.org.uk
Web site: www.thirdforcenews.org.uk
Freq: Weekly
Circ: 4750 Not Audited
Editor: Susan Smith; **Editor:** Susan Smith
Profile: Newspaper of the Scottish Council for Voluntary Organisations. Covers Scottish voluntary sector news, features, comment and debate.
Ad Rate: Full Page Mono £1200.00
Ad Rate: Full Page Colour £1500.00
MAGAZINE
Charitable Foundations

Third Sector
980181
Editorial: Bridge House, 69 London Road, Twickenham, London TW1 3SP
Tel: 44 02082 674694
Email: thirdsector@haymarket.com
Web site: www.thirdsector.co.uk
Freq: Monthly
Circ: 6245 Not Audited
Editor: Andy Hillier
Profile: Magazine covering news, fundraising features, analysis and issues. Read by those involved in charities, fundraising and voluntary organisations.
Ad Rate: Full Page Colour £3280.00
MAGAZINE
Charitable Foundations

This England
981936
Editorial: The Lypiatts, Lansdown Road, Cheltenham, Cheltenham GL50 2JA
Tel: 44 01242 225780
Email: editor@thisengland.co.uk
Web site: www.thisengland.co.uk
Freq: Quarterly
Circ: 55000 Not Audited
Editor: Stephen Garnett
Profile: Patriotic magazine covering the the best things about England and the English way of life. It features articles on historic towns and picturesque villages, the countryside, English customs, curiosities and traditions as well as history and heritage.
MAGAZINE
Field Sports

This Festival Feeling
999500
Editorial: Roxburgh House, 273-287 Regent Street, London W1B 2HA
Email: info@thisfestivalfeeling.com
Web site: www.thisfestivalfeeling.com/
Freq: Daily
Circ: 725 Cision Digital Reach
MAGAZINE (ONLINE)
Pop Music, Rock Music

This Is Anfield
986266
Email: thisisanfield@thisisanfield.com
Web site: www.thisisanfield.com
Circ: 1255332 Cision Digital Reach
Profile: Official matchday programme of Liverpool Football Club with features based on the days match as well as interviews with past and present players.
Ad Rate: Full Page Colour £3950.00
MAGAZINE (ONLINE)
Soccer

This is Local London
982848
Editorial: Floors 9 & 10, Quadrant House, The Quadrant, Sutton SM2 5AS
Email: newsdesk@london.newsquest.co.uk
Web site: www.thisislocallondon.co.uk
Freq: Daily
Circ: 255036 Cision Digital Reach
MAGAZINE (ONLINE)
News & Current Affairs

This Is London
982344
Editorial: Stour Space, 7 Roach Road, Fish Island, London E3 2PA
Tel: 44 02074 341281
Email: editorial@til.com
Web site: www.til.com
Freq: Weekly
Circ: 10000 Not Audited
Profile: Magazine featuring arts, entertainment and restaurant information.
Ad Rate: Full Page Mono £695.00

Ad Rate: Full Page Colour £795.00
MAGAZINE
Travel

This Is Our Town
997343
Editorial: The Factory, 2 Acre Road, London KT2 6EF **Tel:** 44 02082 471855
Email: hello@thisisourtown.co.uk
Web site: http://www.thisisourtown.co.uk/richmond/
Freq: Daily
Circ: 13125 Cision Digital Reach
MAGAZINE (ONLINE)
Regional General Interest

This is Wales
982335
Editorial: QED Centre, Main Avenue, Treforest Industrial Estate, Pontypridd CF37 5YR **Tel:** 44 03000 615512
Email: info@visitwales.co.uk
Web site: http://www.visitwales.com/brochures
Freq: Annual
Circ: 200000 Not Audited
MAGAZINE
Travel

This is Your Kingdom
1075621
Email: thoughts@thisisyourkingdom.co.uk
Web site: www.thisisyourkingdom.co.uk
Freq: Daily
Circ: 48094 Cision Digital Reach
MAGAZINE (ONLINE)
Camping and RV Travel, Field Sports, Lifestyle, Men's Interests, Regional General Interest, Restaurant Reviews, Travel, Women's Interests

ThisisCheshire.co.uk
983085
Editorial: Guardian & World Series Newspapers, The Academy, Bridge Street, Warrington WA1 2RU
Web site: http://www.thisischeshire.co.uk/news/
Freq: Daily
Circ: 55 Cision Digital Reach
Editor: Hayley Smith
MAGAZINE (ONLINE)
Regional

ThisisLancashire.co.uk
983086
Editorial: 1 High Street, Blackburn BB1 1HT
Tel: 44 01254 678678
Email: lt_editorial@nqnw.co.uk
Web site: www.ThisisLancashire.co.uk
Freq: Daily
Circ: 62192 Cision Digital Reach
MAGAZINE (ONLINE)
Regional

thisisthewestcountry.co.uk
1053355
Email: newsdesk@countygazette.co.uk
Web site: www.thisisthewestcountry.co.uk
Freq: Daily
Circ: 67003 Cision Digital Reach
MAGAZINE (ONLINE)
News & Current Affairs

thisistomorrow.info
995092
Editorial: 74 Blackfriars Road, London SE1 8HA
Email: james@thisistomorrow.info
Web site: http://thisistomorrow.info/
Freq: Daily
Circ: 35983 Cision Digital Reach
MAGAZINE (ONLINE)
Art, Photography, Theater & Performing Arts, Visual Arts

thisisxbox.com
990698
Email: info@thisisxbox.com
Web site: www.thisisxbox.com
Freq: Daily
Circ: 54446 Cision Digital Reach
MAGAZINE (ONLINE)
Computer & Video Games

ThisWeek London
1098315
Editorial: Kemp House, 152 City Road, London EC1V 2NX **Tel:** 44 02070 999050
Email: twlondon@unlimitedmedia.co.uk

Web site: http://thisweeklondon.com/
Freq: Daily
Circ: 13371 Cision Digital Reach
MAGAZINE (ONLINE)
Antiques/Collectibles, Art, Arts, Bars, Clubs & Pubs, Classical/Choral/Band Music, Comedy, Country, Folk, Bluegrass, Dance Music, Entertainment, Jazz & Blues

Thomas and Friends
982460
Editorial: 1st Floor, The Yellow Building, 1 Nicholas Road, London W8 6SA
Tel: 44 02032 200400
Email: info@egmont.co.uk
Web site: http://www.egmont.co.uk/magazines/thomas-friends/
Freq: Monthly
Circ: 35013 Not Audited
MAGAZINE
Preschool

Thomas Cook Travel Magazine
984698
Editorial: Blackburn House, Blackburn Road, West Hampstead, London NW6 1RZ
Tel: 44 02076 250700
Email: thomascook.ed@ink-global.com
Web site: http://thomascooktravelmagazine.com/
Freq: Quarterly
Circ: 250000 Not Audited
Profile: Customer magazine of Thomas Cook Airlines covering travel, lifestyle, food, gadgets, fashion, beauty and sport. The editorial content is topical, travel-related and aimed at holiday goers. It incorporates destination specific content alongside lifestyle features. The magazine also features the duty free products and menu available onboard. The readers are holidaymakers, with core ages between 25 and 54. Aimed at travellers on Thomas Cook Airlines. Previous title: Thomas Cook Air
Ad Rate: Full Page Colour £9995.00
MAGAZINE
Airline Inflight

Thomson Reuters Foundation
1098514
Editorial: 5th Floor, South Colonnade, Canary Wharf, London E14 5EP
Tel: 44 02075 423344
Email: news.foundation@thomsonreuters.com
Web site: www.trust.org
Freq: Daily
Circ: 276978 Cision Digital Reach
MAGAZINE (ONLINE)
News & Current Affairs

Thomson.co.uk
997688
Web site: www.thomson.co.uk
Freq: Daily
Circ: 4416775 Cision Digital Reach
MAGAZINE (ONLINE)
Airline Inflight, Travel

Thoroughbred Owner & Breeder Incorporating Pacemaker
996016
Editorial: 1st Floor, 75 High Holborn, London WC1V 6LS **Tel:** 44 02071 520209
Email: editor@ownerbreeder.co.uk
Web site: www.ownerbreeder.co.uk
Freq: Monthly
Circ: 9500 Not Audited
Editor: Edward Rosenthal
MAGAZINE
Equestrian Sports, Horse Racing

The Thread
998558
Editorial: Univ. of Wolverhampton Students' Union, Wulfruna Street, Wolverhampton WV1 1LY
Email: contact@the-thread.co.uk
Web site: http://the-thread.wixsite.com/thethread
Freq: Bi-Monthly Not Audited
MAGAZINE
Student Lifestyle

Consumer Magazines

three and in 1105200
Email: editor@threeandin.com
Web site: http://threeandin.com/
Freq: Daily
Circ: 41318 Cision Digital Reach
MAGAZINE (ONLINE)
Soccer

ThreeWeeks Edinburgh 1053099
Editorial: 3CM Enterprises Lyd, Kemp House, 152 City Road, London EC1V 2NX
Circ: 5000000 Not Audited
MAGAZINE
Entertainment, Local Entertainment Guides, Theater & Performing Arts

Thrive 1097900
Email: hello@thrivepublishing.co.uk
Web site: www.thrive-magazine.co.uk
Freq: Quarterly
Circ: 10000 Not Audited
MAGAZINE
Cooking & Baking, Nutrition, Organic Food

T'HUD Magazine 998858
Editorial: Huddersfield Students' Union, Floor 5, Queensgate, Huddersfield HD1 3DH
Tel: 44 01484 473555
Email: editor@t-hud.co.uk
Web site: www.t-hud.co.uk
Freq: Monthly
Circ: 5000 Not Audited
MAGAZINE
Student Lifestyle

Thump 996104
Email: thump@vice.com
Web site: thump.vice.com/en_uk
Freq: Daily
Circ: 110724 Cision Digital Reach
MAGAZINE (ONLINE)
Dance Music, Theater & Performing Arts

TIARA 982426
Tel: 44 01443 209739
Email: info@keelinpublications.co.uk
Web site: www.tiaramagazine.co.uk
Freq: 3 Times/Year
Circ: 10000 Not Audited
Profile: Bridal magazine covering fashion, beauty, venues, photography, flowers, cakes and cards.
Ad Rate: Full Page Colour £875.00
MAGAZINE
Weddings

TIBS News 1052713
Email: tibsnews2016@gmail.com
Web site: www.tibsnews.com
Freq: Daily
Circ: 10362 Cision Digital Reach
MAGAZINE (ONLINE)
Bicycles, Billiards, Boxing, Cricket, Fitness & Exercise, Games, Competitions & Events, Golf, Motorsports, Racquet Sports, Rugby

Tie the Knot Scotland 982424
Editorial: 11-12 Claremont Terrace, Glasgow G3 7XR Tel: 44 01415 676000
Web site: www.tietheknot.scot
Freq: Bi-Monthly
Circ: 20000 Not Audited
Editor: Beth Forsyth
MAGAZINE
Weddings

Timberweb.com 985529
Web site: www.timberweb.com
Freq: Daily
Circ: 2229 Cision Digital Reach
Editor: Keith Richmond
MAGAZINE (ONLINE)
News & Current Affairs

Time Out London 981789
Editorial: 4th Floor, 125 Shaftesbury Ave, London WC2H 8AD Tel: 44 02078 133000
Email: hello@timeout.com
Web site: www.timeout.com/london
Freq: Weekly

Circ: 309030 Not Audited
Profile: Magazine providing entertainment and event listings for London. It contains news, features and a guide to London's entertainment scene. Includes reviews of gigs, events, bars, restaurants and club nights, film releases and shopping spots. First published in 1968. Aimed at those who are visiting or live in London.
Ad Rate: Full Page Colour £8400.00
MAGAZINE
Bars, Clubs & Pubs, Comedy, Entertainment, Local Entertainment Guides, Movies & Video, Regional General Interest, Restaurant Reviews, Theater & Performing Arts, Travel

Timeless Travels 998276
Tel: 44 01747 870017
Email: editorial@timeless-travels.co.uk
Web site: http://www.timeless-travels.co.uk/
Freq: Quarterly Not Audited
MAGAZINE
Art, History, Travel

timeoutdoors 1096367
Tel: 44 03335 778200
Email: social@timeoutdoors.com
Web site: https://www.timeoutdoors.com
Freq: Daily
Circ: 40703 Cision Digital Reach
MAGAZINE (ONLINE)
Bicycles, Field Sports, Outdoor Recreation

The Times Literary Supplement 981571
Editorial: 1 London Bridge Street, London SE1 9GF Tel: 44 02077 825000
Email: editor@the-tls.co.uk
Web site: www.the-tls.co.uk
Freq: Weekly
Circ: 32166 Not Audited
Profile: Supplement covering forty to fifty book reviews every week. Read by the general and academic reader.
Ad Rate: Full Page Mono £2910.40
Ad Rate: Full Page Colour £2992.00
MAGAZINE
Literature

TimeZone 1053624
Web site: http://www.timezone.com
Freq: Daily
Circ: 426353 Cision Digital Reach
MAGAZINE (ONLINE)
Luxury Goods

tiny pop 988237
Editorial: PO Box 34992, London SW6 4XB
Email: info@tinypop.com
Web site: www.tinypop.com
Freq: Daily
Circ: 47362 Cision Digital Reach
MAGAZINE (ONLINE)
Teen/Young Adult

Tips & Advice Internet 981691
Editorial: Calgarth House, 39-41 Bank Street, Ashford TN23 1DQ
Tel: 44 01233 653500
Email: editorial@indicator.co.uk
Web site: http://lite.indicator.co.uk/internet/home.php
Freq: Bi-Weekly Not Audited
Profile: Newsletter covering information on new sites, Internet software and tips on how to make the most of your time surfing the Internet. Each issue contain topics: useful new UK websites, search engines, e-mail, software, user tips, news groups, website authoring, tools, trends, news, entertainment. Published fortnightly, delivers tips about specialized search engines, e-mail, 'must-have' software and useful tools. Launched in 1998.
MAGAZINE
Internet

TIPS Ltd 996932
Editorial: PO Box 8583, 12 Church Street, Troon KA10 7WT Tel: 44 01292 312410
Email: info@tipslimited.com
Web site: www.tipslimited.co.uk
Freq: Daily

Circ: 8127 Cision Digital Reach
Editor: Sharon Trotter
MAGAZINE (ONLINE)
Family & Parenting

TIRADE Magazine 997312
Email: info@tirademagazine.com
Web site: www.tirademagazine.com/
Freq: Monthly Not Audited
MAGAZINE
Photography, Visual Arts

Tire Technology International 981346
Editorial: Abinger House, Church Street, Dorking, Dorking RH4 1DF
Tel: 44 01306 743744
Email: tire@ukipme.com
Web site: www.tiretechnologyinternational.com
Freq: Quarterly
Circ: 5402 Not Audited
Profile: Magazine covering the technology and systems used in the production, research and future development of tyres, including articles on the chemistry, testing, inspection and basic engineering of tyres. Aimed at tyre manufacturers and supplier companies.
Ad Rate: Full Page Mono £5500.00
Ad Rate: Full Page Colour £5500.00
MAGAZINE
Automotive, Engineering

Title Sussex Magazine 988852
Tel: 44 01273 257037
Email: info@titlemedia.co.uk
Web site: titlesussex.co.uk
Freq: Monthly
Circ: 10000 Not Audited
MAGAZINE
Regional General Interest

TKC Mag 982884
Editorial: 52 Sunnybank, Warlingham, London CR6 9SS Tel: 44 01883 372085
Web site: www.tkcmag.co.uk
Freq: Bi-Monthly Not Audited
Editor: Steve Hole
Profile: Magazine covering news, viewpoints, road tests, what's on and old kit cars.
Ad Rate: Full Page Colour £500.00
MAGAZINE
Automakers, Automotive

tmrw 987528
Email: joe@tmrwmagazine.com
Web site: www.tmrwmagazine.com
Freq: Semi-Annual
Circ: 20000 Not Audited
MAGAZINE
Art, Broadcasting, Country, Folk, Bluegrass, Entertainment, Fashion, Movies & Video, Photography, Pop Music, Restaurant Reviews, Rock Music

TMT Finance 987795
Editorial: Tulip House, 70 Borough High Street, London SE1 1XF
Tel: 44 02037 474603
Email: editor@tmtfinance.com
Web site: www.tmtfinance.com
Freq: Daily
Circ: 12751 Cision Digital Reach
Profile: Website covering finance. The TMT Finance website shares the latest news and information on telecom investments, mergers and acquisitions, financing and strategy globally.
MAGAZINE (ONLINE)
Auto Aftermarket, Computers, Data Management, Electronics, Government Technology, Industry, Internet, Mergers & Acquisitions, Mobile Communications, Security & Security Systems

TMT News 1057947
Tel: 44 02037 256842
Email: hannah.stevenson@ai-globalmedia.com
Web site: http://tmt-news.com/
Freq: Monthly

Circ: 10779 Cision Digital Reach
MAGAZINE (ONLINE)
Branding, Broadcasting, Government Technology, Industry, Marketing, Telecommunications/Electronic Communications

TMX News 998460
Editorial: 41 Northgate, Whitelund Industrial Estate, Morecambe LA3 3PA
Tel: 44 01524 385901
Email: reports@tmxnews.co.uk
Web site: www.tmxnews.co.uk
Freq: Weekly
Circ: 28500 Not Audited
Editor: Anthony Sutton
MAGAZINE
Motorcycles

TN Uncovered 1075495
Tel: 44 01342 718348
Email: info@mantramagazines.co.uk
Web site: www.tnuncovered.co.uk
Freq: Monthly
Circ: 23000 Not Audited
MAGAZINE
Regional

Tnooz 999195
Email: info@tnooz.com
Web site: www.tnooz.com
Freq: Daily
Circ: 895624 Cision Digital Reach
MAGAZINE (ONLINE)
Aviation, Data Management, Travel

TNT Magazine (UK) 982345
Editorial: 3rd Floor, St. Vedast House, St. Vedast Street, Norwich NR1 1BT
Tel: 44 02080 504546
Email: webmaster@tntmagazine.com
Web site: www.tntmagazine.com
Freq: Monthly
Circ: 80000 Not Audited
MAGAZINE
Airline Inflight, Railroad, Regional General Interest, Travel

To Do List 987269
Editorial: 44c Shardeloes Road, London SE14 6SL
Email: info@todolist.org.uk
Web site: https://todolist.org.uk/
Freq: Daily
Circ: 10935 Cision Digital Reach
Editor: Rupert Dannreuther
Profile: Blog covering things to do in London. to do list discusses anything from free events and cheap activities to London area guides. The blog has an archive dating back to August 2010 and shares a short blogroll.
MAGAZINE (ONLINE)
Bars, Clubs & Pubs, Comedy, Entertainment, Local Entertainment Guides, Movies & Video, Regional General Interest

TOAST.LIFE 1059599
Editorial: Kemp House, 152 -160 City Road, London EC1V 2NX
Email: info@toast.life
Web site: http://toast.life/theedit
Freq: Daily
Profile: Magazine covering music. It features local music news, gossip, interviews, media and entertainment reviews, property, fashion and music listings guide for the month ahead. Aimed at 18-40 year old music lovers in Sheffield.
MAGAZINE (ONLINE)
Regional General Interest

Today's Golfer 982266
Editorial: Media House, Peterborough PE2 6EA Tel: 44 01733 468243
Email: editorial@todaysgolfer.co.uk
Web site: www.todaysgolfer.co.uk
Freq: Monthly
Circ: 45688 Not Audited
Editor: Chris Jones
Profile: Magazine covering golf. It contains tips on improving your game, courses to play, equipment reviews and interviews. First

published in 1988. Aimed at amateur and professional golfers.
Ad Rate: Full Page Colour £4300.00
MAGAZINE
Golf

Today's Quilter
1053864
Tel: 44 01179 279009
Web site: http://www.todaysquilter.com
Freq: Monthly Not Audited
MAGAZINE
Crafts

Today's Railways Europe
999233
Editorial: 52 Broadfield Road, Sheffield S8
0XJ Tel: 44 01142 552625
Email: editorial@platform5.com
Web site: http://www.platform5.com
Freq: Monthly
Circ: 7500 Not Audited
Editor: David Haydock
MAGAZINE
Railroad

Today's Railways UK
983509
Editorial: Platform 5 Publishing Ltd, 52
Broadfield Road, Sheffield S8 0XJ
Tel: 44 01142 552625
Email: editorial@platform5.com
Web site: www.platform5.com/
Freq: Monthly
Circ: 11000 Not Audited
Editor: Jonathan Webb
Profile: Magazine covering railways and LRT
systems throughout the UK. Read by
consumers, enthusiasts and industry
members.
MAGAZINE
Railroad

Toddle About
997106
Editorial: Unit 3, Yorks Farm Business
Centre, Watling Street, Towcester NN12 8EU
Tel: 44 01327 830171
Email: media@toddleabout.co.uk
Web site: www.toddleabout.co.uk
Freq: Quarterly
Circ: 46000 Not Audited
Editor: Tim Freed
MAGAZINE
Family & Parenting, Preschool

Together
984094
Editorial: Aeroworks, 5 Adair Street,
Manchester M1 2NQ Tel: 44 02890 941661
Email: info@ctauk.org
Web site: www.ctauk.org
Freq: Quarterly
Circ: 2000 Not Audited
Profile: Journal of the Community Transport
Association covering community transport
with essential news, reviews and features
Aimed at community transport and other
voluntary operators and local authority
officers and academics working in this field.
Ad Rate: Full Page Colour £850.00
MAGAZINE
Automotive, Aviation, Charitable
Foundations, Railroad, Shipping &
Warehousing, Transportation

Tolling Review
997396
Editorial: H3B Media, 15 Onslow Gardens,
London SM6 9QL Tel: 44 02034 639482
Email: kevin@h3bm.com
Web site: thinkingcities.com/latest-issues
Freq: Annual
Circ: 13000 Not Audited
MAGAZINE
Automotive

Tomorrow's Guides
1059458
Editorial: Unit 4, Station Yard, Station Road,
Hungerford RG17 0DY Tel: 44 01488 684321
Email: info@tomorrows.co.uk
Web site: www.tomorrows.co.uk
Freq: Daily
Circ: 4643 Cision Digital Reach
MAGAZINE (ONLINE)
Community Care (UK), Disability, Family &
Parenting, Geriatrics, Preschool,
Retirement Savings, Travel

Toni & Guy
982804
Editorial: 58-60 Stamford Street, London
3E1 9LX Tel: 44 02070 210000
Email: media@toniandguy.co.uk
Web site: http://magazine.toniandguy.com/
Freq: 3 Times/Year
Circ: 100000 Not Audited
MAGAZINE
Hair

Top 100 Golf Courses
1105206
Email: info@top100golfcourses.co.uk
Web site: www.top100golfcourses.co.uk
Freq: Daily
Circ: 106811 Cision Digital Reach
Editor: Keith Baxter
MAGAZINE (ONLINE)
Golf

Top of the Pops
982467
Editorial: Vineyard House, 44 Brook Green,
London W6 7BT Tel: 44 02071 505000
Email: totpmag@totpmag.com
Web site: www.totpmag.com
Freq: Monthly
Circ: 45036 Not Audited
Editor: Peter Hart
Profile: Magazine focusing on pop music.
Contains interviews with pop stars, album
reviews, concert dates and competitions.
Each issue contains star gossip, fashion and
beauty advice, a personality quiz,
horoscopes and song lyrics. Aimed at 10 to
16 year old pop music fans.
Ad Rate: Full Page Colour £3025.00
MAGAZINE
Celebrities, Pop Music, Teen/Young Adult

Top Santé
981825
Editorial: 14 Priestgate, Peterborough PE1
1JA Tel: 44 01959 541444
Email: talkback@topsante.co.uk
Web site: www.topsante.co.uk
Freq: Monthly
Circ: 40032 Not Audited
Editor: Katy Louise Sunnassee
Profile: Magazine covering all aspects of
healthy lifestyle including health, beauty,
recipes and nutrition as well as news,
emotional wellbeing, anti-ageing secrets and
diet and weight-loss. First published in 1993,
the publication has an average of 132 pages
per issue. Aimed at women of all ages.
Ad Rate: Full Page Colour £3000.00
MAGAZINE
Beauty & Grooming, Cosmetics, Fitness &
Exercise, Hair, Health & Medicine,
Nutrition, Women's Interests

Top10Films.co.uk
988403
Email: editor@top10films.co.uk
Web site: www.Top10Films.co.uk
Freq: Daily
Circ: 81977 Cision Digital Reach
MAGAZINE (ONLINE)
Movies & Video

Topshop Magazine
998228
Web site: http://www.topshop.com/en/tsuk/
category/topshop-magazine-2663381/home
Freq: Bi-Monthly
Circ: 16 Cision Digital Reach
MAGAZINE (ONLINE)
Fashion

Total 911
982572
Editorial: Richmond House, 33 Richmond
Hill, Bournemouth, Bournemouth BH2 6EZ
Tel: 44 01202 586200
Email: total911@futurenet.com
Web site: www.total911.com
Freq: Monthly Not Audited
Editor: Lee Sibley
Profile: Magazine covering all aspects and
all models of the Porsche 911.
Ad Rate: Full Page Colour £1250.00
MAGAZINE
Automakers

Total Carp
982789
Editorial: 1 Whittle Close, Drayton Fields,
Daventry NN11 8RQ Tel: 44 01327 311999
Web site: www.totalcarpmagazine.com

Freq: Monthly
Circ: 21369 Not Audited
Editor: Marc Coulson
Profile: Magazine covering all aspects of
carp fishing.
MAGAZINE
Fishing

Total Cat Magazine
999127
Tel: 44 08451 631238
Email: admin@petbuzz.it
Web site: www.totalcat.co.uk
Freq: Quarterly
Circ: 35000 Not Audited
MAGAZINE
Nature & Wildlife

Total Dog Magazine
999128
Tel: 44 08451 631238
Web site: www.totaldog.co.uk
Freq: Daily
Circ: 26936 Cision Digital Reach
MAGAZINE (ONLINE)
Nature & Wildlife

Total Film
981791
Editorial: 1-10 Praed Mews, London W2
1QY Tel: 44 02070 424000
Email: totalfilm@futurenet.com
Web site: http://gamesradar.com/totalfilm/
Freq: Monthly
Circ: 45410 Not Audited
Profile: Total Film is a magazine featuring
news, reviews and articles on all current and
future video, film, book, soundtrack and
multimedia releases relating to film and the
film industry. Aimed at male and female
readers aged between 15 and 35 years old.
Ad Rate: Full Page Colour £4620.00
MAGAZINE
Movies & Video, Music

Total FlyFisher
982184
Editorial: 1 Whittle Close, Drayton Fields,
Daventry NN11 8RQ Tel: 44 01327 311999
Email: totalflyfisher@dhpub.co.uk
Web site: www.totalflyfisher.com
Freq: Monthly
Circ: 18000 Not Audited
Editor: Andy Taylor
Profile: Instructional magazine covering all
aspects of fly fishing. Includes advice,
tackle, fishing destinations and problem
solving solutions.
Ad Rate: Full Page Colour £650.00
MAGAZINE
Fishing

Total Guitar
082086
Editorial: Total Guitar, Quay House, The
Ambury, Bath BA1 2BW
Tel: 44 01225 442244
Email: totalguitar@futurenet.com
Web site: musicradar.com/totalguitar
Freq: Monthly
Circ: 19262 Not Audited
Editor: Neville Marten; Editor: Stuart
Williams
Profile: Magazine covering all aspects of
guitars and guitar playing.
Ad Rate: Full Page Colour £1640.00
MAGAZINE
Music

Total Investor
985937
Editorial: Minster House, 42 Mincing Lane,
London EC3R 7AE
Email: editor@totalinvestor.co.uk
Web site: www.totalinvestor.co.uk
Freq: Daily
Circ: 689 Cision Digital Reach
Editor: Stewart Andersen; Editor: Steven
Weiss
MAGAZINE (ONLINE)
Fund Management, Personal Finance

Total MK
988340
Editorial: 88F Polruan Place, Fishermead,
Milton Keynes MK6 2EA
Email: info@totalmk.co.uk
Web site: www.totalmk.co.uk
Freq: Daily

Circ: 16732 Cision Digital Reach
MAGAZINE (ONLINE)
Antiques/Collectibles, Art, Arts, Classical/
Choral/Band Music, Cooking & Baking,
Country, Folk, Bluegrass, Dance Music,
Jazz & Blues, Literature, Movies & Video

Total Off Road
982598
Editorial: Repton House, G11 Bretby
Business Media, Swadlincote DE15 0YZ
Tel: 44 01283 553243
Email: tor@assignment-media.co.uk
Web site: www.toronline.co.uk
Freq: Monthly
Circ: 16000 Not Audited
Editor: Alan Kidd
MAGAZINE
Off-road & 4-Wheel Drive Vehicles

Total Politics
984568
Editorial: Total Politics, Floor 11, The Shard,
32 London Bridge St, London SE1 9SG
Tel: 44 02075 935500
Email: tp@dods.co.uk
Web site: www.totalpolitics.com
Freq: Daily
Circ: 48360 Cision Digital Reach
Profile: Website covering cross party
politics including campaigning, interviews,
features, cartoons and humour. Aimed at
elected politicians in Britain and those with
an interest in politics.
MAGAZINE (ONLINE)
Politics

Total Production
International
981588
Editorial: Waterloo Place, Watson Square,
Stockport SK1 3AZ Tel: 44 01614 768360
Web site: www.tpimagazine.com
Freq: Monthly
Circ: 9000 Not Audited
Editor: Kelly Murray
Profile: Magazine containing news and
reviews on all aspects of live performance
production, including sound, lighting, set
design and video.
Ad Rate: Full Page Colour £1900.00
MAGAZINE
Marketing, Music

Total Rock
982776
Editorial: 10 Oakwood Road, London NW11
6QX Tel: 44 02084 553108
Email: info@totalrock.com
Web site: www.totalrock.com
Freq: Daily
Circ: 7012 Cision Digital Reach
Editor: Jim Beerman
Profile: Station broadcasting rock and heavy
metal with news, interviews and live
concerts. Aimed at fans of rock music.
MAGAZINE (ONLINE)
Rock Music

Total Sea Fishing
982185
Editorial: 1 Whittle Close, Drayton Fields,
Daventry NN11 8RQ Tel: 44 01327 311999
Email: info@dhpub.co.uk
Web site: www.totalseamagazine.com
Freq: Monthly
Circ: 10984 Not Audited
Editor: Paul Dennis
Profile: Instructional magazine covering all
aspects of sea fishing including beach, pier,
match and boat fishing.
Ad Rate: Full Page Colour £575.00
MAGAZINE
Fishing

Total TV Guide
982354
Editorial: Academic House, 24-28 Oval
Road, London NW1 7DT
Tel: 44 02072 418000
Web site: www.tvchoicemagazine.co.uk
Freq: Weekly
Circ: 92211 Not Audited
Profile: TV guide with digital and satellite
listings as well as features, celebrity
interviews and entertainment documentaries.
It covers more than 90 channels every week,
including terrestrial, sport, movies, drama,
entertainment, factual, lifestyle and kids
programmes. Launched in September 2003.

Consumer Magazines

Aimed at users of multi-channel TV with a core readership of men and women aged 25 to 44.
Ad Rate: Full Page Colour £7000.00
MAGAZINE
Broadcasting

Total Women's Cycling   987141
Editorial: 2 Tun Yard, London SW8 3HT
Tel: 44 02073 329700
Email: editor@totalwomenscycling.com
Web site: www.totalwomenscycling.com
Freq: Daily
Circ: 145924 Cision Digital Reach
MAGAZINE (ONLINE)
Bicycles

Totally Aesthetic Magazine
1064934
Tel: 44 07871 823572
Email: editor@totallyaesthetic.com
Web site: www.totallyaesthetic.com
Freq: Quarterly Not Audited
Editor: Lisajane Davies
MAGAZINE
Beauty & Grooming, Cosmetics, Dentistry, Fitness & Exercise, Hair, Health & Medicine, Plastic/Reconstructive/Cosmetic Surgery

Totally Jewish Travel   994971
Email: admin@totallyjewishtravel.com
Web site: www.totallyjewishtravel.com
Freq: Daily
Circ: 9685 Cision Digital Reach
MAGAZINE (ONLINE)
Airline Inflight, Railroad, Travel

Totally Money   986850
Editorial: Churchill House, 142-146 Old Street, London EC1V 9BW
Tel: 44 02078 413438
Email: press@totallymoney.com
Web site: www.totallymoney.com
Freq: Daily
Circ: 129712 Cision Digital Reach
MAGAZINE (ONLINE)
Personal Finance

Tots100   987000
Web site: www.tots100.co.uk
Freq: Daily
Circ: 154772 Cision Digital Reach
MAGAZINE (ONLINE)
Family & Parenting

Toun Cryer - East Lothian   995176
Editorial: PO Box 13625, Melrose TD6 6AD
Tel: 44 01835 824847
Email: lynn@touncryer.co.uk
Web site: www.touncryer.co.uk
Freq: Bi-Monthly
Circ: 20000 Not Audited
Editor: Lynn Stewart
MAGAZINE
Regional General Interest

TouringandTenting.com   998776
Editorial: 178 South Avenue, Southend-on-sea, Southend-on-Sea SS2 4HU
Tel: 44 01702 611208
Email: admin@touringandtenting.com
Web site: www.touringandtenting.com
Freq: Daily
Circ: 8224 Cision Digital Reach
Editor: Mark Fusher; **Editor:** Sonja Fusher
MAGAZINE (ONLINE)
Camping and RV Travel

Tourism   983895
Editorial: Queens House, 55-56 Lincoln's Inn Fields, London WC2A 3BH
Tel: 44 02072 699693
Email: admin@tourismsociety.org
Web site: www.tourismsociety.org
Freq: Quarterly
Circ: 1700 Not Audited
Profile: Journal of the Tourism Society carrying news, articles and book reviews concerning the tourism industry.
Ad Rate: Full Page Colour £610.00
MAGAZINE
Travel

Tower Hamlets Mums   996740
Email: info@towerhamletsmums.com
Web site: www.towerhamletsmums.com
Freq: Daily
Circ: 12106 Cision Digital Reach
MAGAZINE (ONLINE)
Family & Parenting, Local Entertainment Guides

Town & City   1053611
Tel: 44 02392 294408
Email: daniel@town-city.co.uk
Web site: http://www.town-city.co.uk/
Freq: Quarterly
Editor: Daniel Tidbury
MAGAZINE
Regional General Interest

Town & Country (UK)   987784
Editorial: 72 Broadwick Street, London W1F 9EP **Tel:** 44 02074 395000
Web site: http://www.townandcountrymag.co.uk
Freq: Quarterly
Circ: 60000 Not Audited
MAGAZINE
Luxury Goods

Town & Village Life Magazine
997723
Editorial: 1 Lytham Road, Perton, Wolverhampton WV6 7YY
Tel: 44 01902 744217
Email: info@townandvillagelifemag.co.uk
Web site: www.townandvillagelifemag.co.uk/
Freq: Bi-Monthly
Circ: 16000 Not Audited
Editor: Geoff Hall
MAGAZINE
Regional

Town Crier   997501
Web site: www.twtowncrier.co.uk
Freq: Monthly
Circ: 28100 Not Audited
MAGAZINE
News & Current Affairs

Town Daily   986859
Editorial: 6 Derby Street, London W1J 7AD
Tel: 44 02074 371298
Email: contact@townmagazine.co.uk
Web site: www.townmagazine.co.uk
Freq: Daily
Circ: 5915 Cision Digital Reach
MAGAZINE (ONLINE)
Regional General Interest

Townswoman   983776
Editorial: Capital House, 25 Chapel Street, London NW1 5DH **Tel:** 44 02037 717247
Email: contact@the-tg.com
Web site: http://www.the-tg.com/townswoman-magazine.aspx
Freq: Quarterly
Circ: 34000 Not Audited
Profile: Official magazine of the Townswomen's Guilds. Includes arts, cookery, health, crafts, fashion, lifestyle and political and social issues. Also covers individual Guild news and national Townswomen's Guilds news.
Ad Rate: Full Page Colour £2200.00
MAGAZINE
Ethical/Moral Issues, Women's Interests

TownTalk   986761
Editorial: 63 Wostenholme Road, Sheffield S7 1LE **Tel:** 44 08456 865855
Email: info@towntalk.co.uk
Web site: www.towntalk.co.uk
Freq: Daily
Circ: 71075 Cision Digital Reach
MAGAZINE (ONLINE)
Regional

TownTalk   997290
Editorial: 63 Wostenholm Road, Sheffield S7 1LE **Tel:** 44 08456 865855
Email: info@towntalk.co.uk
Web site: www.towntalk.co.uk

Freq: Daily
Circ: 71075 Cision Digital Reach
MAGAZINE (ONLINE)
News & Current Affairs

Towpath Talk   983454
Editorial: Media Centre, Morton Way, Horncastle LN9 6JR **Tel:** 44 01507 529529
Email: editorial@towpathtalk.co.uk
Web site: www.towpathtalk.co.uk
Freq: Monthly
Circ: 35000 Not Audited
Editor: Janet Richardson
Profile: Newspaper covering life and leisure around Britain's canals with insights into life on the canals and places to explore from English pubs to quaint villages and historic pubs.
Ad Rate: Full Page Colour £621.00
MAGAZINE
Boating & Yachting

Toxic Magazine   982443
Editorial: 1st Floor, The Yellow Building, 1 Nicholas Road, London W11 4AN
Tel: 44 02032 200400
Email: toxic@euk.egmont.com
Web site: www.toxicmag.co.uk
Freq: Weekly
Circ: 40523 Not Audited
Editor: Simon Ward
MAGAZINE
Elementary School, Teen/Young Adult

Toy Soldier & Model Figure
1054348
Tel: 44 01903 884988
Email: support@ashdown.co.uk
Web site: www.toy-soldier.com
Freq: Monthly
Circ: 6000 Not Audited
MAGAZINE
Antiques/Collectibles, Armed Forces, Crafts

TQS Magazine   987648
Web site: www.tqsmagazine.co.uk/
Freq: Daily
Circ: 61027 Cision Digital Reach
Editor: Jamie McHale
MAGAZINE (ONLINE)
Bars, Clubs & Pubs, Comedy, Dance Music, Entertainment, Literature, Local Entertainment Guides, Movies & Video, Pop Music, Rap & Hip Hop, Rock Music

Track Car Performance   1076162
Editorial: 841 High Road, London N12 8PT
Tel: 44 02084 462100
Email: info@kimberleymediagroup.com
Web site: www.trackcarperformance.com
Freq: Monthly
Circ: 30000 Not Audited
Editor: William Kimberley
MAGAZINE
Automotive, Motorsports

TRACTION   985361
Editorial: The Maltings, West Street, Bourne PE10 9PH
Web site: https://www.world-of-railways.co.uk/traction/
Freq: Bi-Monthly
Circ: 6000 Not Audited
Editor: Stephen Rabone
Profile: Magazine covering classic diesels and electrics railway trains past and present. Contains news, nostalgia features, railway work insight, heritage scene, reviews of books, models and videos. Includes reviews of the latest books, models, videos and CD-ROMs that are related to railway classic diesels and electric locomotives and units. Aimed at rail enthusiasts.
Ad Rate: Full Page Mono £270.00
Ad Rate: Full Page Colour £350.00
MAGAZINE
Railroad

Tractor & Machinery   981922
Editorial: Cudham Tithe Barn, Berry's Hill, Cudham, London TN16 3AG
Tel: 44 01959 541444

Email: tm.ed@kelsey.co.uk
Web site: www.tractor-and-machinery.co.uk
Freq: Monthly
Circ: 60000 Not Audited
Profile: Magazine covering antique and classic tractors and machinery around the world. Includes features on history and restoration projects, vintage news, sales, models, toys, for sales section and monthly price guide. Also looks at the modern scene. Read by farmers, vintage and classic collectors and tractor enthusiasts throughout the world.
Ad Rate: Full Page Colour £900.00
MAGAZINE
Antique & Collectible Cars

Trade and Industry   984940
Editorial: 1 Warwick Avenue, Whickham, Whickham NE16 5QR **Tel:** 44 01914 881947
Email: office@tradeandindustry.net
Web site: www.tradeandindustry.net
Freq: Monthly
Circ: 4000 Not Audited
Profile: Outdoor Trade and Industry is a monthly publication covering the outdoor trade, including camping, caravanning, hiking, backpacking, the world of ice, climbing and skiing. It is owned by the KSA Partnership. Outdoor Trade and Industry is aimed at retailers, manufacturers, distributors, exhibitors and suppliers of outdoor goods and equipment.
MAGAZINE
Fitness & Exercise, Outdoor Recreation, Winter Sports

Trademarks & Brands Online
997616
Editorial: Kingfisher House, 21-23 Elmfield Road, London BR1 1LT
Freq: Quarterly
Circ: 5000 Not Audited
MAGAZINE
News & Current Affairs

Trademarks & Brands Online Newsletter   997841
Editorial: Kingfisher House, 21-23 Elmfield Road, London BR1 1LT
Web site: http://www.trademarksandbrandsonline.com/
Freq: Monthly
Circ: 16756 Cision Digital Reach
MAGAZINE (ONLINE)
News & Current Affairs

tradersdna.com   1095582
Email: editor@tradersdna.com
Web site: http://www.tradersdna.com/
Freq: Daily
Circ: 45075 Cision Digital Reach
Editor: Fidan Aliyeva
MAGAZINE (ONLINE)
Banking, Bonds, Commodities, Corporate Finance, Corporate Management, Credit Markets, Derivatives, Economics, Emerging Markets, Equities

Traffic Technology International   981347
Editorial: Abinger House, Church Street, Dorking RH4 1DF **Tel:** 44 01306 743744
Email: traffic@ukipme.com
Web site: www.traffictechnologytoday.com
Freq: Bi-Monthly
Circ: 17412 Not Audited
Editor: Tom Stone
Profile: Magazine focusing on advanced traffic management and control, ITS and traffic technologies around the world.
Ad Rate: Full Page Colour £4350.00
MAGAZINE
Automotive

Trail   981909
Editorial: Media House, Lynchwood, Peterborough PE2 6EA
Tel: 44 01733 468000
Email: trail@bauermedia.co.uk
Web site: www.livefortheoutdoors.com
Freq: Monthly
Circ: 19600 Not Audited
Editor: Simon Ingram

Profile: Magazine covering routes for walking, climbing, scrambling, mountain biking and trail running. Also contains outdoor clothing and equipment tests, personality profiles and advice on fitness, diet and health.
Ad Rate: Full Page Colour £2950.00
MAGAZINE
Field Sports, Outdoor Recreation

Trail Running
985603
Editorial: Media House, Lynchwood, Peterborough PE2 6EA
Tel: 44 01733 468205
Email: trailrunning@bauermedia.co.uk
Web site: http://www.trailrunningmag.co.uk
Freq: Bi-Monthly
Circ: 12000 Not Audited
Profile: Publication dedicated to the pursuit of outdoor and off-road running.
MAGAZINE
Field Sports, Sports

Trailbike and Enduro Magazine
982660
Editorial: 191 Uxbridge Road, London W13 9AA **Tel:** 44 02088 404760
Web site: www.trailbikemag.com
Freq: Monthly
Circ: 15000 Not Audited
Profile: Magazine covering on and off road motorcycling. Includes news, reviews, features and maintenance tips.
Ad Rate: Full Page Colour £850.00
MAGAZINE
Motorcycles, Motorsports

Trailfinder Magazine
982791
Editorial: 23 Abingdon Road, London W8 6AH
Web site: www.trailfinders.com
Freq: 3 Times/Year
Circ: 1500000 Not Audited
Editor: Lee Holden
MAGAZINE
Travel

TRAIN Magazine
987700
Editorial: Unit 2, Bankside, The Watermark, Gateshead NE11 9SY **Tel:** 44 01912 332225
Email: info@train-mag.com
Web site: www.train-mag.com
Freq: Monthly Not Audited
Editor: Ray Klerck
MAGAZINE
Fitness & Exercise

Trainer
998512
Editorial: 14 Berwick Courtyard, Berwick St Leonard, Salisbury SP3 5UA
Tel: 44 01380 816777
Email: info@trainermagazine.com
Web site: www.trainermagazine.com
Freq: Quarterly
Circ: 4000 Not Audited
MAGAZINE
Horse Racing

TrainTravelEat
995487
Email: editorial@traintraveleat.com
Web site: www.traintraveleat.com
Freq: Daily
Circ: 521 Cision Digital Reach
MAGAZINE (ONLINE)
Cooking & Baking, Fitness & Exercise, Health & Medicine, Men's Interests, Nutrition, Restaurant Reviews, Travel, Women's Interests

Tramways & Urban Transit
984099
Editorial: No 13, Orton Enterprise Centre, Bakewell Road, Orton Southgate, Peterborough PE2 6XU
Tel: 44 01733 367601
Email: editor@lrta.org
Web site: www.tramnews.net
Freq: Monthly
Circ: 8000 Not Audited
Editor: Simon Johnston
Profile: Magazine of the Light Rail Transit Association, containing news and information about urban rail transport

worldwide. Aimed at urban transit manufacturers and decision makers in transport planning offices and supply industries. Also read by transport enthusiasts.
Ad Rate: Full Page Colour £1500.00
MAGAZINE
Railroad

Transmission Technology International
995000
Editorial: Abinger House, Church Street, Dorking, Dorking RH4 1DF
Tel: 44 01306 743744
Web site: http://www.ukipme.com/pub-automotive.php?mag=13
Freq: Annual
Circ: 12000 Not Audited
MAGAZINE
Automotive

Transport & Construction
1060558
Tel: 44 27443 821606
Email: stuart@lloydsgroup.net
Freq: Monthly
Circ: 14000 Not Audited
MAGAZINE
Automotive, Aviation, Railroad, Shipping & Warehousing, Supply Chain Management (SCM), Transportation

Transport & Logistics
986340
Editorial: 1st Floor, Turnbridge Mills, Quay Street, Huddersfield HD1 6QT
Tel: 44 02081 233414
Email: editor@ciaranjarosz.media
Web site: www.tandlonline.com
Freq: Monthly
Circ: 12916 Not Audited
Profile: Magazine covering the transport and logistics industry. It features issues such as environmental impact of transport, investments into efficiency, to new projects in the UK.
MAGAZINE
Automotive, Aviation, Railroad, Shipping & Warehousing, Supply Chain Management (SCM), Transportation

Transport Briefing
985187
Editorial: 20 Havelock Road, Hastings, Frome TN34 1BP
Email: editor@transportbriefing.co.uk
Web site: www.transportbriefing.co.uk
Freq: Daily
Circ: 11333 Cision Digital Reach
Editor: Daniel Harvey
MAGAZINE (ONLINE)
Automotive, Aviation, Railroad, Shipping & Warehousing, Supply Chain Management (SCM), Transportation

Transport Management
983998
Editorial: The Old Studio, 25 Greenfield Road, Westoning, Flitwick MK45 5JD
Tel: 44 01525 634940
Email: director@iota.org.uk
Web site: www.iota.org.uk
Freq: Annual
Circ: 2500 Not Audited
Profile: Official newsletter of the Institute of Transport Administration. Contains information on activities within the institute and features on general transport issues.
Ad Rate: Full Page Mono £250.00
Ad Rate: Full Page Colour £290.00
MAGAZINE
Automotive, Aviation, Railroad, Shipping & Warehousing, Supply Chain Management (SCM), Transportation

Transport News
984000
Editorial: Wheatsheaf House, Montgomery Street, The Village, West Kilbride G74 4JS
Tel: 44 01355 279077
Email: info@transportnews.co.uk
Web site: www.transportnews.co.uk
Freq: Monthly
Circ: 9500 Not Audited
Editor: Alistair Vallance
Profile: Magazine covering all aspects of the road haulage industry and commercial vehicles. First published in 1978, the

publication has an average of 64 pages per issue. Read by owner operators, drivers and commercial vehicle buyers in road haulage firms and the major Scottish and North of England companies.
Ad Rate: Full Page Mono £675.00
Ad Rate: Full Page Colour £990.00
MAGAZINE
Automotive

Transport Operator
985881
Editorial: Station House, Aigburth Station, Liverpool L17 6AG **Tel:** 44 01514 271950
Web site: www.transportoperator.co.uk
Freq: Bi-Monthly
Circ: 12000 Not Audited
Editor: Will Cooper
Profile: Magazine covering the latest information relating to the commercial vehicle fleet industry. Each issue provides industry news, new legislation and the latest product information.
MAGAZINE
Automotive, Shipping & Warehousing

Transport Times
983075
Editorial: 27 Beaufort Court, Admirals Way, London E14 9XL **Tel:** 44 02078 283804
Email: enquiries@transporttimes.co.uk
Web site: www.transporttimes.co.uk
Freq: Monthly
Circ: 1400 Not Audited
Profile: Magazine covering surface public transport, focusing on policy, strategy and sustainable transport. Published monthly and provides news, information, analysis and comment on surface transport in the UK. Aimed at industry professionals, politicians, academics and civil servants in the public transport world and those involved in making decisions on the future of passenger and freight service provision.Press materials, news, features and letters should be emailed to editorial@transporttimes.co.uk. Regular features: Consultant Profile Key facts about consulting engineering firms and their expertise in the field of transport.; Day in the Life Day in the life of a transport industry professional.; Interview An interview with a leading transport professional.; Opinion Guest columnists comments and opinion on the surface transport industry.
Ad Rate: Full Page Colour £3500.00
MAGAZINE
Automotive, Aviation, Railroad, Shipping & Warehousing, Supply Chain Management (SCM), Transportation

Transportation Professional
981109
Editorial: 7 Linden Close, Tunbridge Wells TN4 8HH **Tel:** 44 01892 524455
Email: info@transportation-mag.com
Web site: www.ciht.org.uk/en/publications/transportation-professional/index.cfm
Freq: Monthly
Circ: 9409 Not Audited
Editor: Mike Walter
Profile: Journal of the Institution of Highways and Transportation containing features, news, product and services update and a classified section. Aimed at highway engineers and planners, railway engineers, public transport planners, consultants, county surveyors, central government, safety officers, local authorities and maintenance contractors.
Ad Rate: Full Page Mono £1600.00
Ad Rate: Full Page Colour £1600.00
MAGAZINE
Automotive, Aviation, Railroad, Shipping & Warehousing

Trap Magazine
985885
Editorial: Studio 22, 5-9 Amhurst Terrace, Hackney Downs Studios, London E8 2BT
Email: editorial@trapmagazine.co.uk
Web site: www.trapmagazine.co.uk
Freq: Bi-Monthly
Circ: 10000 Not Audited
MAGAZINE
Music

Travel & Tourism News Middle East
996152
Editorial: Crescent Court, 102 Victor Road, Teddington, London TW11 8SS
Tel: 44 02089 433630
Email: post@hilal.com
Web site: www.ttnworldwide.com
Freq: Monthly
Circ: 57884 Not Audited
MAGAZINE
Airline Inflight, Travel

Travel Africa Magazine
983310
Editorial: The Dovecote, Little Baldon, Oxford OX44 9PU **Tel:** 44 01844 278883
Email: editor@travelafricamag.com
Web site: www.travelafricamag.com
Freq: Quarterly
Circ: 25000 Not Audited
Editor: Laura Griffith-Jones
Profile: Magazine featuring African travel destinations, wildlife and culture. Includes coverage of national parks, cities and tribes.
Ad Rate: Full Page Colour £1685.00
MAGAZINE
Travel

Travel Bulletin
980623
Editorial: University House, 11 - 13 Lower Grosvenor Place, London SW1W 0EX
Tel: 44 02078 346661
Email: post@travelbulletin.co.uk
Web site: www.travelbulletin.co.uk
Freq: Weekly
Circ: 6502 Not Audited
Editor: Lauretta Wright
Profile: Travel Bulletin is the weekly magazine for UK travel agents. Launched in 1975, Travel Bulletin covers all the latest news from every sector of the travel industry delivered by tour operators, airlines, cruise companies, hotels, tourist offices, ferry and rail operators, car hire companies or theme parks. Includes training updates, worldwide destination features, comment from leading travel industry experts, competitions and puzzles, weekly travel agent columns and regular glossy destination supplements. Aimed at travel agents.Regular features: Business Travel Focuses on all aspects of business travel.; Hotel News The latest news and information regarding hotels.; Product News Information on new products relevant to the travel industry.
Ad Rate: Full Page Mono £2080.00
Ad Rate: Full Page Colour £2900.00
MAGAZINE
Genealogy, Travel

Travel Mag
982850
Editorial: 1 Long Drove, Burbage, Nr Marlborough, Hinckley SN8 3AH
Tel: 44 01672 810202
Email: ed@travelmag.co.uk
Web site: www.travelmag.co.uk
Freq: Daily
Circ: 11418 Cision Digital Reach
MAGAZINE (ONLINE)
Airline Inflight, Railroad, Travel

The Travel Magazine
982346
Editorial: 1 East Lodge, Holly Park Gardens, London N3 3NH
Web site: http://www.thetravelmagazine.net/
Freq: Daily
Circ: 111852 Cision Digital Reach
Profile: Magazine covering features, articles, news, previews of new hotels, reviews of destinations and events worldwide.
Ad Rate: Full Page Colour £1300.00
MAGAZINE (ONLINE)
Railroad, Travel

Travel Retail Business
983968
Editorial: 157 Francis Close, Epsom, London KT19 0JT **Tel:** 44 01732 850142
Web site: www.trbusiness.com
Freq: Monthly
Circ: 5000 Not Audited
Profile: Magazine providing regional and national news and analytical commentary on the duty free and travel retail industry. Aimed

Consumer Magazines

at leaders and decision makers in the duty and tax free industry.
MAGAZINE
Retail Management, Travel

Travel Retailer International   984011
Editorial: 140 Wales Farm Road, London W3 6UG **Tel:** 44 02082 538615
Email: editorial@dfnionline.com
Web site: www.dfnionline.com/about-us/
Freq: 3 Times/Year
Circ: 4175 Not Audited
Editor: Kapila Gohel
MAGAZINE
Books, Cosmetics, Fashion, Gardening, Hair, Office Supplies, Retail, Retail Management, Toys, Travel

travelGBI   981238
Editorial: Travel Weekly Group, 52 Grosvenor Gardens, Victoria, London SW1W 0AU **Tel:** 44 02078 814838
Email: editorial@travelgbi.com
Web site: www.travelgbi.com
Freq: Monthly
Circ: 12934 Not Audited
Editor: George Clode
MAGAZINE
Travel

Traveller   994691
Editorial: Dorset House, 3rd Floor, 27-45 Stamford Street, London SE1 9PY
Tel: 44 02075 900610
Email: traveller@fifthfloorpublishing.com
Web site: www.wexas.com/traveller-magazine
Freq: 3 Times/Year
Circ: 18500 Not Audited
Editor: Amy Sohanpaul
Profile: Travel destination portal that is part of easyjet.com. Contains reportage and lifestyle, travel, sports and business.
MAGAZINE
Railroad, Travel

Travel-Lists   983293
Editorial: 25 Exchange House, Crouch End Hill, London N8 8DF **Tel:** 44 02083 412866
Email: newsdesk@travel-lists.co.uk
Web site: http://www.travel-lists.co.uk/
Freq: Daily
Circ: 67816 Cision Digital Reach
Editor: Alastair McKenzie
Profile: Website covering travel. Travel Lists is an Independent expert directory for British holiday-makers and travellers who want to browse a simple and comprehensive list of only the best and most relevant travel providers. Alternative Title: Travel-Lists.co.uk
MAGAZINE (ONLINE)
Travel

TravelMag.com   1052756
Web site: http://www.travelmag.com
Freq: Daily
Circ: 10005 Cision Digital Reach
MAGAZINE (ONLINE)
Airline Inflight, Railroad, Travel

Travelplus   980132
Editorial: Office 11, Studio 8 Dana Trading Estate, Transfeasa Road, Tonbridge, Tynemouth TN12 6UT **Tel:** 44 01892 837934
Email: editorial@travelplus.co.uk
Web site: http://travelplus.co.uk/
Freq: Daily
Circ: 3705 Cision Digital Reach
Profile: Website covering travel. Travelplus website covers travel, tourism and the world it inhabits.
MAGAZINE (ONLINE)
Travel

TravelTech World   1052818
Editorial: 18 Alban Park, Hatfield Road, Hertfordshire, St. Albans AL4 0JJ
Tel: 44 01727 739160
Web site: www.fleetworld.co.uk
Freq: Bi-Monthly

Circ: 18000 Not Audited
MAGAZINE
Computers, Electronics, Industry, Internet, Mobile Communications

Travelzoo.co.uk   995906
Editorial: 151 Shaftesbury Avenue, London WC2H 8AL **Tel:** 44 02074 200400
Web site: https://www.travelzoo.com/uk/
Freq: Daily
Circ: 799098 Cision Digital Reach
MAGAZINE (ONLINE)
Airline Inflight, Railroad, Travel

Travolution   983205
Editorial: 52 Grosvenor Gardens, London SW1W 0AU **Tel:** 44 02078 814800
Web site: http://www.travolution.com/
Freq: Daily
Circ: 49913 Cision Digital Reach
Profile: Magazine covering all aspects of the online travel industry. Each issue covers the traditional travel market along with the new online players. Travolution provides information, commentary, market intelligence and analysis for anyone in, or running an online travel business. Launched in November 2005. Aimed at mid to senior management in the travel industry.
Ad Rate: Full Page Colour £2500.00
MAGAZINE (ONLINE)
Genealogy, Travel

Treasure Hunting   985011
Editorial: 119 Newland Street, Witham, Witham CM8 1WF **Tel:** 44 01376 521900
Email: info@treasurehunting.co.uk
Web site: www.treasurehunting.co.uk
Freq: Monthly
Circ: 15000 Not Audited
Editor: Greg Payne
Profile: Magazine carrying metal detector and ancillary equipment tests, historical articles and site guides. Aimed at the detecting enthusiast.
Ad Rate: Full Page Mono £550.00
Ad Rate: Full Page Colour £745.00
MAGAZINE
Antiques/Collectibles

Treatwell   984792
Editorial: c/o Calder & Co, 16 Charles II Street, London SW1Y 4NW
Tel: 44 03301 003515
Email: press@treatwell.co.uk
Web site: www.treatwell.co.uk
Freq: Daily
Circ: 137474 Cision Digital Reach
MAGAZINE (ONLINE)
Alternative Medicine, Cosmetics, Health & Medicine

Tree Fu Tom   996530
Editorial: Vineyard House, 44 Brook Green, London W6 7BT **Tel:** 44 02071 505000
Email: hello@treefutommagazine.com
Web site: www.immediate.co.uk/brands/tree-fu-tom/
Freq: Monthly
Circ: 15451 Not Audited
MAGAZINE
Preschool

Trek & Mountain   985494
Editorial: Rangefield Court, Farnham Trading Estate, Farnham, Farnham GU9 9NP
Tel: 44 01172 306085
Email: info@trekandmountain.com
Web site: www.trekandmountain.com
Freq: Monthly
Circ: 21000 Not Audited
Editor: Chris Kempster
Profile: Magazine launched in November 2009 and covering worldwide trekking and mountaineering including hillwalking and rock climbing in the UK and around the world. Aimed at mountaineering and trekking enthusiasts.
MAGAZINE
Outdoor Recreation

Trend   984475
Editorial: 192 Holburn Street, Aberdeen, Aberdeen AB10 6DA **Tel:** 44 01224 596223

Email: info@trendmagazine.co.uk
Web site: www.trendmagazine.co.uk
Freq: Bi-Monthly
Circ: 20000 Not Audited
Editor: Alison Daniels
Profile: Lifestyle magazine covering restaurants, delis, wine, fashion, beauty, property, motoring and interviews with local personalities.
Ad Rate: Full Page Mono £1500.00
Ad Rate: Full Page Colour £1500.00
MAGAZINE
Beauty & Grooming, Cosmetics, Fashion, Hair, Health & Medicine, Regional General Interest

TrendLife Magazine   995398
Editorial: 960 Capability Green, Luton LU1 3PE **Tel:** 44 07494 196205
Email: editorial@trendlifemagazine.com
Web site: www.trendlifemagazine.com
Freq: Monthly
Circ: 10000 Not Audited
Editor: Lee Hall
MAGAZINE
Regional General Interest

Trendstop.com   984514
Editorial: 32-39 The Quadrant, 135 Salisbury Road, London NW6 6RJ
Tel: 44 08707 886888
Email: press@trendstop.com
Web site: www.trendstop.com
Freq: Daily
Circ: 39854 Cision Digital Reach
MAGAZINE (ONLINE)
Fashion

Trendzoom   998581
Editorial: Gainsborough House, 81 Oxford Street, London W1D 2EU
Email: info@fashioninformation.com
Web site: http://trendzoom.com/
Freq: Daily
Circ: 9312 Cision Digital Reach
MAGAZINE (ONLINE)
Fashion

Tri247.com   987782
Web site: http://www.tri247.com/
Freq: Daily
Circ: 29927 Cision Digital Reach
MAGAZINE (ONLINE)
Bicycles, Sports, Swimming/Watersports

Triathlon Plus - CEASED July 2017   985005
Editorial: Cudham Tithe Barn, Berry's Hill, Cudham, London TN16 3AG
Web site: http://www.triradar.com/
Freq: Monthly Not Audited
Profile: Magazine focusing on the triathlon sports of running, cycling and swimming. Includes tutorials, features and reviews of events and equipment. Provides kit reviews, training tips, training routes, buyer's guide, interviews, features, nutrition, coaching, race listings. Aimed at triathlon enthusiasts at all levels.
MAGAZINE
Bicycles, Olympic Sports, Sports, Swimming/Watersports

Tribune   980165
Editorial: Transport House, 46-48 New Road, Dagenham RM9 5AN
Email: mail@tribunemagazine.co.uk
Web site: www.tribunemagazine.co.uk
Freq: Bi-Weekly
Circ: 8250 Not Audited
Editor: Chris McLaughlin
Profile: Newspaper of the Labour Party covering policy debates, issues and campaigns.
Ad Rate: Full Page Mono £980.00
Ad Rate: Full Page Colour £1100.00
MAGAZINE
Politics

Tribu-te (UK)   986429
Editorial: 20 Mortlake High Street, London SW14 8JN **Tel:** 44 02082 411058
Email: info@tribu-te.co.uk
Web site: www.tribu-te.co.uk

Freq: Quarterly
Circ: 7500 Not Audited
MAGAZINE
Hair

Tring Living   997083
Editorial: 27b The Old Silk Mill, Tring, Tring HP23 5EF **Tel:** 44 01442 824300
Email: info@livingmags.info
Web site: www.livingmags.info/tring-living
Freq: Quarterly
Circ: 10331 Not Audited
MAGAZINE
Regional General Interest

TripReporter   995471
Editorial: 14 Riddell Lodge, 27 Bycullah Road, Enfield EN2 8EP
Tel: 44 07956 313808
Email: editor@tripreporter.co.uk
Web site: www.tripreporter.co.uk
Freq: Daily
Circ: 15985 Cision Digital Reach
MAGAZINE (ONLINE)
Travel

Triumph World   982645
Editorial: Cudham Tithe Barn, Berry's Hill, Cudham, London TN16 3AG
Tel: 44 01959 541444
Email: tw.ed@kelsey.co.uk
Web site: www.classicsworld.co.uk
Freq: Bi-Monthly
Circ: 26500 Not Audited
Editor: Simon Goldsworthy
Profile: Motoring magazine devoted to Triumph and Standard cars and Triumph-based specials with features on all aspects of the cars from restoring to maintaining, historical articles, interviews with ex-factory personnel, owners reports and listings of triumph clubs and events around the world.
Ad Rate: Full Page Mono £880.00
Ad Rate: Full Page Colour £980.00
MAGAZINE
Automakers

Trout & Salmon   982186
Editorial: Media House, Lynchwood, Peterborough PE2 6EA
Tel: 44 01733 468000
Email: troutandsalmon@bauermedia.co.uk
Web site: www.gofishing.co.uk/trout-and-salmon/
Freq: Monthly
Circ: 20736 Not Audited
Editor: Andrew Flitcroft
MAGAZINE
Fishing

Trout Fisherman   982187
Editorial: Media House, Lynchwood, Peterborough Business Park, Peterborough PE2 6EA **Tel:** 44 01733 468000
Web site: www.gofishing.co.uk
Freq: Monthly
Circ: 13173 Not Audited
Editor: Russell Hill
Profile: Magazine covering all aspects of stillwater fly-fishing. Includes features on fishing tackle, advice on tactics and trout articles. Aimed predominantly at stillwater trout fishermen as well as novice and experienced fly anglers.
Ad Rate: Full Page Colour £1800.00
MAGAZINE
Fishing

Truck & Bus Builder   984095
Editorial: PO Box 15, Williton, Taunton, Taunton TA4 4YP **Tel:** 44 01984 618707
Email: info@truckandbusbuilder.com
Web site: www.truckandbusbuilder.com
Freq: Monthly
Circ: 7000 Not Audited
Editor: Jim Gibbins
Profile: Newsletter containing news and information on commercial vehicle manufacturing developments.
MAGAZINE
Automotive, Manufacturing

Truck & Driver
979918

Editorial: 6th Floor, Chancery House, St Nicholas Way, London SM1 1JB
Tel: 44 02089 122170
Web site: www.truckanddriver.co.uk
Freq: Monthly
Circ: 17812 Not Audited
Editor: Dan Parton
MAGAZINE
Automotive

Truck Model World
985724

Tel: 44 01406 424681
Email: info@igp-ltd.com
Web site: www.truckmodelworld.com
Freq: Monthly
Circ: 8500 Not Audited
Editor: Steven Downes
Profile: Magazine dedicated to building and collecting truck models. Includes reviews of new models, kits and accessories plus news of people and events.
Ad Rate: Full Page Mono £205.00
Ad Rate: Full Page Colour £338.00
MAGAZINE
Crafts, Hobbies, & Collecting

Trucking
981349

Editorial: Cudham Tithe Barn, Berry's Hill, Cudham, London TN16 3AG
Tel: 44 01733 347559
Email: trucking.ed@kelsey.co.uk
Web site: www.truckingmag.co.uk
Freq: Monthly
Circ: 21000 Not Audited
Editor: Andrew Stewart
Profile: Magazine featuring operators profiles, road tests, legal advice and exclusive news on the trucking industry.
Ad Rate: Full Page Colour £1453.00
MAGAZINE
Automotive, Shipping & Warehousing, Supply Chain Management (SCM)

Truckstop News
985128

Editorial: KELSEY Publishing Group, Cudham Tithe Barn, Berry's Hill, Peterborough TN16 3AG
Tel: 44 01733 347559
Email: trucking.ed@kelsey.co.uk
Web site: www.truckingmag.co.uk/truckstopnews
Freq: Monthly Not Audited
Editor: Andrew Stewart
Profile: Newspaper covering truck manufacturing, components, ancillary equipment, truck racing and general information on the haulage business.
Ad Rate: Full Page Colour £3424.00
MAGAZINE
Automotive

True Crime
988133

Editorial: PO Box 735, London SE26 5NQ
Tel: 44 02087 780514
Email: enquiries@truecrimelibrary.com
Web site: www.truecrimelibrary.com/
Freq: Monthly Not Audited
Profile: Magazine covering the area of true life crime and criminology.
MAGAZINE
Crime & Violence

True Detective Magazine
997017

Editorial: PO Box 735, London SE26 5NQ
Tel: 44 02087 780514
Email: enquiries@truecrimelibrary.com
Web site: www.truecrimelibrary.com/
Freq: Monthly Not Audited
MAGAZINE
Crime & Violence

True Health
1053891

Tel: 44 01279 810080
Email: info@targetpublishing.com
Web site: www.truehealthmag.co.uk
Freq: Monthly
Circ: 12000 Not Audited
Editor: Chantelle Kelly
MAGAZINE
Health & Medicine, Nutrition

The Trumpet
982142

Editorial: 44a Selby Road, Leytonstone, London E11 3LT
Email: info@the-trumpet.com
Web site: http://trumpetmediagroup.com/the-trumpet
Freq: Bi-Weekly
Circ: 25000 Not Audited
Editor: Femi Okutubo
Profile: Newspaper covering articles of interest to the African community including general news, sport, arts, features and finance.
Ad Rate: Full Page Mono £3040.00
Ad Rate: Full Page Colour £3648.00
MAGAZINE
International News

Trust
998823

Editorial: Calton Square, 1 Greenside Row, Edinburgh EH1 3AN **Tel:** 44 01312 752000
Email: trustenquiries@bailliegifford.com
Web site: www.trustmagazine.co.uk
Freq: 3 Times/Year
Circ: 70000 Not Audited
Profile: Magazine covering investment, examining and reporting on the world of investment trusts including OEICS, ISAs, PEPs, children's savings plans, share plans, wealth management and self invested personal pensions. Aimed at customers of the investment house Baillie Gifford.
MAGAZINE
Personal Finance

TrustedReviews
982852

Editorial: Pinehurst 2, Pinehurst Road, Farnborough Business Park, Farnborough GU14 7BF **Tel:** 44 01252 555000
Web site: www.trustedreviews.com
Freq: Daily
Circ: 11550751 Cision Digital Reach
Editor: Evan Kypreos
MAGAZINE (ONLINE)
Apple, Audio Video Trade, Cameras, Computer & Video Games, Computers, Consumer Electronics, Electronics, Internet, Mobile Electronics, Movies & Video

TRVL
996061

Email: hello@trvl.com
Web site: www.trvl.com
Freq: Weekly
Circ: 12695 Cision Digital Reach
MAGAZINE (ONLINE)
Travel

Try This For
997417

Editorial: 34 Acton House, Haggerston, London E8 4HQ
Email: info@trythisfor.com
Web site: www.trythisfor.com
Freq: Daily
Circ: 1232 Cision Digital Reach
MAGAZINE (ONLINE)
Cooking & Baking, Restaurant Reviews

TSSA Journal
985278

Editorial: Walkden House, 10 Melton Street, London NW1 2EJ **Tel:** 44 02073 872101
Email: enquiries@tssa.org.uk
Web site: www.tssa.org.uk
Freq: Annual
Circ: 20000 Not Audited
Profile: Magazine of the Transport Salaried Staffs' Association containing industry news, members' features and employment issues.
MAGAZINE
Railroad

TTG
979867

Editorial: 8th Floor, Friar's House, 160 Blackfriars Road, London SE1 8EZ
Tel: 44 02037 144108
Web site: www.ttgdigital.com
Freq: Weekly
Circ: 17153 Not Audited
Profile: Magazine covering professional travel including news, hospitality, resorts, cruises, holidays, luxury and business travel, destination reviews and market reports as well as features, careers advice, jobs, analysis and competitions. First published in

1954. Aimed at retail travel agents, tour operators, hotels, airlines, cruise lines, car hire companies, travel technology companies, travel insurance companies, airports, ferry lines and rail companies.
Ad Rate: Full Page Colour £5880.00
MAGAZINE
Travel

TTG Luxury
984463

Editorial: Friars House, 160 Blackfriars Road, London SE1 8EZ
Web site: https://www.ttgmedia.com/
Freq: Quarterly
Circ: 12000 Not Audited
Editor: April Hutchinson
Profile: Magazine covering the luxury travel market with destination focused features and tips on how to sell destination products more effectively. Featuring reviews of products and services available in the market, luxury leisure travel, business travel and meetings and events products. Aimed at premium travel professionals, agents and suppliers working within the luxury travel industry.
Ad Rate: Full Page Colour £4800.00
MAGAZINE
Travel

Tug Technology & Business
1057336

Web site: www.tugtechnologyandbusiness.com
Freq: Quarterly
Circ: 9887 Not Audited
Editor: Martyn Wingrove
MAGAZINE
Marine & Boat Trade, Shipping & Warehousing

Turf Business
984194

Editorial: Green Hedges, Melfort Road, Crowborough, Crowborough TN6 1QT
Tel: 44 01892 664555
Email: editorial@turfbusiness.co.uk
Web site: turfbusiness.co.uk
Freq: Monthly
Circ: 29000 Not Audited
Editor: Mervyn Barnard
Profile: Magazine covering all aspects of professional turf care. Aimed at groundsmen, green keepers and local authority personnel.
Ad Rate: Full Page Colour £1200.00
MAGAZINE
Gardening

Turnstyle.co.uk
988441

Editorial: Contented Group, 2nd Floor, 1 Cavendish Place, London W1G 0QF
Tel: 44 02072 916120
Web site: www.turnstyle.co.uk
Freq: Daily
Circ: 58529 Cision Digital Reach
MAGAZINE (ONLINE)
Men's Interests

TV & Satellite Week
982355

Editorial: 161 Marsh Wall, London E14 9AP
Tel: 44 02031 485000
Web site: www.timeincuk.com/brands/tv-satellite-week/
Freq: Weekly
Circ: 111232 Not Audited
Editor: Ian Abbott
Profile: Magazine providing a comprehensive guide to TV and satellite listings. Includes all the week's sport, day-by-day highlights of the best films and evening at-a-glance guide to what not to miss. First published in 1993. Aimed at those aged 30 to 45.
Ad Rate: Full Page Colour £5715.00
MAGAZINE
Broadcasting

TV Everywhere International
995971

Editorial: Unit N202, Vox Studios, 1-45 Durham Street, London SE11 5JH
Tel: 44 02035 671444
Web site: www.advanced-television.com
Freq: Quarterly

Circ: 5364 Not Audited
MAGAZINE
Broadcasting

TV Guide UK
990681

Editorial: TVGuide.co.uk, 104 Oxford Street, London W1D 1LP
Email: contact@tvguide.co.uk
Web site: www.tvguide.co.uk
Freq: Daily
Circ: 4398192 Cision Digital Reach
MAGAZINE (ONLINE)
Broadcasting

TV Sports Markets
983475

Editorial: 133 Whitechapel High Street, London EC1 7QA **Tel:** 44 02072 654100
Email: tvsm@tvsportsmarkets.com
Web site: www.TVSportsMarkets.com
Freq: Monthly Not Audited
Profile: Industry newsletter covering the business of television sport.
MAGAZINE
Broadcasting

TV Times
982358

Editorial: 161 Marsh Wall, London E14 9AP
Tel: 44 02031 485000
Email: tvtimes@timeinc.com
Web site: www.whatsontv.co.uk
Freq: Weekly
Circ: 176929 Not Audited
Editor: Ian Abbott
Profile: Magazine containing previews of TV, satellite and radio programmes. Includes TV news, gossip and behind-the-scenes features. Also includes film reviews, video and cinema releases and celebrity interviews. First published in 1955. Aimed at those interested in TV and radio programmes.
Ad Rate: Full Page Colour £16450.00
MAGAZINE
Broadcasting, Local Entertainment Guides

TVBEurope
983801

Editorial: Emerson Studios, 4th Floor, 4-8 Emerson Street, London SE1 9DU
Tel: 44 02073 546002
Email: contact@tvbeurope.com
Web site: www.tvbeurope.com
Freq: Monthly
Circ: 8500 Not Audited
Profile: Magazine containing features and information from the television broadcasting industry, including new broadcasting innovations and technology. Aimed at TV operations chiefs, chief engineers, decision makers and management within the broadcasting industry.
Ad Rate: Full Page Colour £3550.00
MAGAZINE
Broadcasting

TVBomb
1053083

Freq: Daily
Circ: 24667 Cision Digital Reach
Profile: Website covering entertainment. The TVBOMB website shares the latest news and information on theater, music and film.
MAGAZINE (ONLINE)
News & Current Affairs

TVChoice
982356

Editorial: Academic House, 24-28 Oval Road, London NW1 7DT
Tel: 44 02072 418000
Email: tvchoice@bauer.co.uk
Web site: www.tvchoicemagazine.co.uk
Freq: Weekly
Circ: 1200487 Not Audited
Profile: Magazine containing TV listings, focusing on the terrestrial TV channels, including a film guide, horoscopes and show-biz news. Aimed at those who have an interest in show-biz news.Readership figures: National Readership Survey (NRS) Readership Estimates - General Weekly MagazinesAIR - Latest 12 Months: April 2012 - March 2013 Est.Population 15+: 50828(000)Total Adult AIR: 1841(000)= 3.6% Total Men AIR: 596(000)= 2.4%Total Women AIR: 1245(000)= 4.8% Total 15-34 AIR: 529(000)= 3.2%Total 35+ AIR: 1312(000)= 3.

Consumer Magazines

8% Total ABC1 AIR: 697(000)= 2.5%Total
C2DE AIR: 1144(000)= 4.9%
Ad Rate: Full Page Colour £17000.00
MAGAZINE
Broadcasting

TVWise
986774
Email: info@tvwise.co.uk
Web site: www.tvwise.co.uk
Freq: Daily
Circ: 90704 Cision Digital Reach
MAGAZINE (ONLINE)
Broadcasting, Local Entertainment
Guides

Twenty Something London
995413
Email: info@twentysomethinglondon.com
Web site: http://twentysomething.com/
Freq: Daily
Circ: 5802 Cision Digital Reach
MAGAZINE (ONLINE)
Regional General Interest

Twenty6
985930
Editorial: 1st Floor, 20 Great Portland
Street, London W1W 8QR
Tel: 44 02035 833436
Email: editorial@twenty6magazine.com
Web site: www.twenty-6.co.uk
Freq: Semi-Annual
Circ: 1733 Cision Digital Reach
MAGAZINE (ONLINE)
Art, Beauty & Grooming, Cosmetics,
Fashion, Hair, Lifestyle, Men's Interests,
Regional General Interest, Women's
Interests

Twin
985789
Email: info@twinfactory.co.uk
Web site: www.twinfactory.co.uk
Freq: Semi-Annual Not Audited
Profile: Magazine covering art, fashion and
culture.
MAGAZINE
Fashion, Photography

Twist
998627
Editorial: WestOne, 114 Wellington Street,
Leeds LS1 1BA **Tel:** 44 01138 198155
Email: info@wtin.com
Web site: http://www.wtin.com/e-store-
products/twist/
Freq: Monthly
Circ: 10080 Not Audited
Editor: Jonathan Dyson
Profile: News and events occurring in
Chesterfield.
Ad Rate: Full Page Colour £2190.00
MAGAZINE
Fashion

Twist & Go
982661
Editorial: PO Box 99, Horncastle LN9 6JR
Tel: 44 01507 529408
Email: mau@twistngo.com
Web site: http://www.twistngo.com/
Freq: Bi-Monthly
Circ: 35000 Not Audited
Editor: Mau Spencer
Profile: Magazine covering commuter and
automatic scooters. Includes road tests,
product reviews, price guides and articles on
tuning and workshops along with quads and
learner legal motorcycles.
Ad Rate: Full Page Mono £525.00
Ad Rate: Full Page Colour £650.00
MAGAZINE
Motorcycles

TwitCelebGossip
1054116
Email: hello@twitcelebgossip.com
Web site: http://www.twitcelebgossip.com
Freq: Daily
Circ: 29930 Cision Digital Reach
MAGAZINE (ONLINE)
Celebrities

Two Point Four
997288
Editorial: 48 Brindley Close, Stoney Stanton,
Stoney Stanton LE9 4GL
Tel: 44 01455 273281

Email: editorial@twopointfourmagazine.co.
uk
Web site: www.twopointfourmagazine.co.uk
Freq: Bi-Monthly Not Audited
MAGAZINE
Education, Family & Parenting, Fitness &
Exercise, Health & Medicine, Lifestyle,
Men's Interests, Regional General
Interest, Women's Interests

Two Travellers
1053354
Email: lucas@thetwotravellers.com
Web site: http://www.thetwotravellers.com/
Freq: Daily
Circ: 2734 Cision Digital Reach
MAGAZINE (ONLINE)
Hotels/Motels, Luxury Goods, Travel

Tyre Trade News
983996
Editorial: 5 Dymock Court, Quainton,
Aylesbury HP22 4DF **Tel:** 44 01296 655833
Email: tyres@tyretradenews.co.uk
Web site: www.tyretradenews.co.uk
Freq: Monthly
Circ: 6000 Not Audited
Profile: Magazine covering the tyre industry
including news, products and information.
Aimed at people working in the tyre and
after-market industry.
Ad Rate: Full Page Colour £1190.00
MAGAZINE
News & Current Affairs

Tyres & Accessories
981259
Editorial: Federation House, Stoke-on-Trent
ST4 2SA **Tel:** 44 01782 214224
Email: theeditor@tyrepress.com
Web site: http://www.tyrepress.com/
magazine/epaper/
Freq: Monthly
Circ: 6000 Not Audited
Editor: Christopher Anthony
Profile: Journal covering retail, fitting, repair,
manufacture and re-treading of tyres and
vehicle accessories. Aimed at all those
involved in the tyre, wheel and automotive
trade.Regular features: Career Tracks
Appointments and promotions etc.;
Company News Corporate news from the
most relevant companies.; International Tyre
Market News and features focussing on
influential and emerging overseas markets.;
Leader; News in Brief; Product News Details
of new product releases.; UK Tyre Market
News and features focussing on the UK tyre
market.
Ad Rate: Full Page Colour £1465.00
MAGAZINE
Automotive

U Self Publish
997244
Tel: 44 02081 336375
Web site: uselfpublish.com
Freq: Daily
Circ: 1225 Cision Digital Reach
Editor: Paula Wynne
MAGAZINE (ONLINE)
News & Current Affairs

ucan2 magazine
981820
Editorial: Rhone House, Canal Side,
Chorley, Chorley PR6 0BU
Tel: 44 01257 267677
Web site: http://www.ucan2magazine.co.uk/
Freq: Quarterly
Circ: 14000 Not Audited
MAGAZINE
Disability

UFFSite
997767
Email: staff@rpgsite.net
Web site: www.rpgsite.net
Freq: Daily
Circ: 335276 Cision Digital Reach
MAGAZINE (ONLINE)
Computer & Video Games

UK Carp
986488
Editorial: Media House, Lynchwood,
Peterborough Business Park, Peterborough
PE2 6EA **Tel:** 44 01733 468000
Web site: www.gofishing.co.uk
Freq: Monthly
Circ: 30015 Not Audited

Profile: Magazine covering all aspects of
carp fishing including product reviews and
fishing lifestyle. Includes latest carp tactics
from the country's anglers and in-depth
reviews on carp products. Aimed at carp
fishing enthusiasts.
Ad Rate: Full Page Colour £750.00
MAGAZINE
Fishing

UK Haulier
988787
Tel: 44 08444 098188
Email: info@ukhaulier.co.uk
Web site: http://www.ukhaulier.co.uk
Freq: Daily
Circ: 17379 Cision Digital Reach
MAGAZINE (ONLINE)
Automotive, Shipping & Warehousing

UK Retail Briefing
983956
Editorial: 11 Pilgrim Street, London EC4V
6RN **Tel:** 44 02076 064533
Email: info@mintel.com
Web site: www.mintel.com
Freq: Monthly Not Audited
MAGAZINE
News & Current Affairs

UK Screen Alliance
998870
Editorial: 2nd Floor, 18 Soho Square, Soho,
London W1D 3QL **Tel:** 44 02077 346060
Web site: www.ukscreenassociation.co.uk
Freq: Daily
Circ: 12222 Cision Digital Reach
MAGAZINE (ONLINE)
Broadcasting

UK Times London
995855
Editorial: Trident Business Centre, 89
Bickersteth Road, London SW17 9SH
Tel: 44 02083 553484
Email: info@uktl.co.uk
Web site: www.uktimelondon.com
Freq: Daily
Circ: 35000 Not Audited
MAGAZINE
Asia, International News

UK Women Magazine
995461
Editorial: NFC Publishing, LLP 9 Mulberry
Court, Stour Road Christchurch,
Christchurch BH23 1PS
Email: magazines@nfcpublishing.co.uk
Web site: www.womenuk.co.uk/
Freq: Quarterly
Circ: 30000 Not Audited
MAGAZINE
Women's Interests

UKBD News
998773
Editorial: 108 Whitechapel Road, London E1
1JD
Email: news@ukbdnews.com
Web site: www.ukbdnews.com
Freq: Daily
Circ: 38170 Cision Digital Reach
Editor: Shoeb Uddin Kabir
MAGAZINE (ONLINE)
Asia

UKHairdressers.com
982855
Editorial: The Sands, Shore Road, Ainsdale,
Southport, Southport PR8 2QD
Tel: 44 01704 577111
Email: admin@ukhairdressers.com
Web site: www.ukhairdressers.com
Freq: Daily
Circ: 179939 Cision Digital Reach
MAGAZINE (ONLINE)
Hair

UKMums.tv
987170
Editorial: 18 Cottesbrooke Park, Heartlands,
Daventry, Daventry NN11 8YL
Tel: 44 01327 227010
Web site: www.ukmums.tv
Freq: Daily
Circ: 93416 Cision Digital Reach
Profile: Website covering motherhood. The
UKMUMS.TV websites shares the latest

news and information on parenting tips,
news, fashion, gossip for mums.
MAGAZINE (ONLINE)
Family & Parenting

UKPets.co.uk
982853
Editorial: Lynnwood BDC, Lynnwood
Terrace, Newcastle upon Tyne NE4 6UL
Tel: 44 01912 844131
Email: magazine@ukpets.co.uk
Web site: www.ukpets.co.uk
Freq: Daily
Circ: 6669 Cision Digital Reach
Editor: Steve O'Malley
MAGAZINE (ONLINE)
Nature & Wildlife

UKTN
987128
Editorial: Fergusson House, 124-128 City
Road, London EC1V 2NJ
Tel: 44 02075 028222
Email: editorial@uktech.news
Web site: https://www.uktech.news
Freq: Daily
Circ: 159145 Cision Digital Reach
Editor: Emily Spaven
Profile: Magazine covering technology. Tech
City News shares the latest news,
information and reviews on technology and
businesses.
MAGAZINE (ONLINE)
Auto Aftermarket, Computers, Data
Management, Electronics, Government
Technology, Industry, Internet, Mobile
Communications, Security & Security
Systems, Software

ukvine
999633
Editorial: North Block, Redhill Aerodrome,
Kingsmill Lane, Redhill, London RH1 5JY
Tel: 44 02037 711950
Email: info@ukvine.com
Web site: www.ukvine.com
Freq: Bi-Monthly
MAGAZINE
Alcohol & Spirits, Wine/Winemaking

UKVMA
988085
Editorial: 4 North Street, Rothersthorpe,
Northampton NN7 3JB
Tel: 44 01604 832149
Email: mark-webb@msn.com
Web site: http://www.ukvma.org/
Freq: Weekly
Circ: 1500 Cision Digital Reach
MAGAZINE (ONLINE)
Fitness & Exercise, Travel Industry

The Ulster Graduate
981754
Editorial: Alumni Relations Office, University
of Ulster, Co Antrim, Newtownabbey BT37
0QB **Tel:** 44 02870 123456
Email: alumni@ulster.ac.uk
Web site: www.ulster.ac.uk/alumni
Freq: Annual
Circ: 108623 Not Audited
MAGAZINE
Alumni

Ulster Tatler
982379
Editorial: 39 Boucher Road, Belfast BT12
6UT **Tel:** 44 02890 663311
Email: edit@ulstertatler.com
Web site: www.ulstertatler.com
Freq: Monthly
Circ: 10996 Not Audited
Editor: Christopher Sherry
Profile: Magazine containing features on
social coverage, sport and leisure, food &
drink, property, health, fashion and holidays.
Ad Rate: Full Page Colour £1370.00
MAGAZINE
Fashion, Women's Interests

Ulster Tatler Bride
982416
Editorial: 39 Boucher Road, Belfast BT12
6UT **Tel:** 44 02890 663311
Email: edit@ulstertatler.com
Web site: https://www.ulstertatler.com/
publications/
Freq: Quarterly
Circ: 44000 Not Audited
Editor: Christopher Sherry

Profile: Magazine covering all aspects of weddings including fashion, beauty, honeymoons, photography, hotels, receptions, transport, men's wear, entertainment, mother of the bride and interiors.
Ad Rate: Full Page Colour £1240.00
MAGAZINE
Weddings

Ulster Tatler Interiors 984226
Editorial: 39 Boucher Road, Belfast BT12 6HR **Tel:** 44 02890 663311
Email: edit@ulstertatler.com
Web site: www.ulstertatlerinteriors.com
Freq: Quarterly Not Audited
Editor: Christopher Sherry
Profile: Publication featuring interior design for the home.
Ad Rate: Full Page Colour £850.00
MAGAZINE
Do-It-Yourself (DIY)

Ultimate Spider-Man 995326
Editorial: Level 2 - Brockbourne House, 77 Mount Ephraim, Tunbridge Wells, Tunbridge Wells TN4 8BS **Tel:** 44 01892 500100
Email: ehammond@panini.co.uk
Web site: http://www.paninicomics.co.uk/web/guest/catalogues/collection_detail?id=36665
Freq: Monthly
Circ: 23308 Not Audited
Editor: Ed Hammond
MAGAZINE
Teen/Young Adult, Trading Cards & Comics

Ultimate Wedding Magazine 999386
Editorial: 11 Larks Rise, Chesham, Chesham HP5 1RG **Tel:** 44 01442 780808
Email: hello@ultimateweddingmagazine.co.uk
Web site: www.ultimateweddingmagazine.co.uk
Freq: Bi-Monthly
Circ: 13060 Cision Digital Reach
Editor: Tina Reading
MAGAZINE (ONLINE)
Weddings

Ultra VW 982646
Editorial: 21 Benjamin Road, Maidenbower, Crawley, Crawley RH10 7QY
Tel: 44 01293 270720
Web site: www.ultravw.com
Freq: Monthly Not Audited
Editor: Paul Knight
Profile: Magazine covering air-cooled VWs, water cooled new Beetles and the new Transporters as well as classic and vintage Porsches.
Ad Rate: Full Page Mono £880.00
Ad Rate: Full Page Colour £980.00
MAGAZINE
Automakers

Umbrella 985674
Editorial: 121 Buckler Court, Eden Grove, London N7 8GQ
Email: info@umbrellamagazine.co.uk
Web site: www.umbrellamagazine.co.uk
Freq: Quarterly Not Audited
Editor: Anthony Teasdale
MAGAZINE
Men's Interests

UNA-UK 988141
Editorial: UNA-UK, 3 Whitehall Court, London SW1A 2EL **Tel:** 44 02077 663454
Email: info@una.org.uk
Web site: http://www.una.org.uk/magazine
Freq: Quarterly
Circ: 25000 Not Audited
MAGAZINE
Africa, Americas, Asia, Australia, Ethnic & Multicultural, Europe, Expatriates, International News, Politics

Unbound - CEASED MARCH 2016 988799
Freq: Daily
Circ: 40636 Cision Digital Reach
MAGAZINE (ONLINE)
Fitness & Exercise

Uncut 982113
Editorial: 9th Floor, The Blue Fin Building, 110 Southwark Street, London SE1 0SU
Tel: 44 02031 485000
Web site: www.uncut.co.uk
Freq: Monthly
Circ: 43235 Not Audited
Editor: John Mulvey
Profile: Magazine providing in-depth coverage of the latest developments in the world of music and film including interviews, reviews, special features, concerts, tours, tickets and artist news. First published in 1997. Aimed at men between 25 and 45 years old.
Ad Rate: Full Page Colour £4190.00
MAGAZINE
Movies & Video, Rock Music

Under 5 985582
Editorial: Pre-school Learning Alliance National Centre, The Fitzpatrick Building, 188 York Way, London N7 9AD
Tel: 44 02076 972504
Email: editor.u5@pre-school.org.uk
Web site: www.pre-school.org.uk/under-5-magazine
Freq: Monthly
Circ: 60000 Not Audited
Profile: Journal covering practical advice on the care and education of babies and young children in nursery, toddler, playgroup and pre-school settings.
Ad Rate: Full Page Colour £1885.00
MAGAZINE
Preschool

Under the Influence 988472
Editorial: Studio F, 21-27 Millers Terrace, London E8 2DJ
Email: contact@undertheinfluencemagazine.com
Web site: www.undertheinfluencemagazine.com
Freq: Semi-Annual
Circ: 20500 Not Audited
Profile: Magazine covering fashion, photography, design, writing, art and music.
MAGAZINE
Art, Classical/Choral/Band Music, Country, Folk, Bluegrass, Dance Music, Fashion, Jazz & Blues, Music, Pop Music, R&B, Urban, World, Rap & Hip Hop

Under the Scope 986854
Editorial: 19 Woodbury Avenue, Petersfield, Petersfield GU32 2ED **Tel:** 44 01730 300836
Email: victoria@underthescope.co.uk
Web site: www.underthescope.co.uk
Freq: Daily
Circ: 1885 Cision Digital Reach
Editor: Victoria Lambert
Profile: Website covering health. The Under the Scope website shares the latest news and information on 'matters of health, family, education and life-in-general'.
MAGAZINE (ONLINE)
Education, Family & Parenting, Health & Medicine

Undercurrent News 987611
Editorial: E1 Business Centre, Unit 204, 7 Whitechapel Road, London E1 1DU
Tel: 44 02076 525258
Email: editorial@undercurrentnews.com
Web site: www.undercurrentnews.com
Freq: Daily
Circ: 148763 Cision Digital Reach
Editor: Tom Seaman
Profile: Website covering seafood business. The undercurrent news website shares the latest business news on the seafood industry.
MAGAZINE (ONLINE)
Animal Farming, Marine & Boat Trade

Underlines 984457
Editorial: Suite 102, Curtain House, 134-146 Curtain Road, London EC2A 3AR
Tel: 44 02035 834697
Email: newsunderlines@aol.com
Web site: www.underlinesmagazine.com
Freq: Bi-Monthly
Circ: 6000 Not Audited
Profile: Magazine containing articles about the lingerie, hosiery and swimwear industry. Read by manufacturers, retailers and buyers within the clothing industry.
Ad Rate: Full Page Mono £1900.00
Ad Rate: Full Page Colour £2750.00
MAGAZINE
Fashion

UnderTheChristmasTree 996916
Editorial: The Schoolhouse, Mouswald, Dumfries DG1 4LT **Tel:** 44 01387 830606
Email: underxmastree@btinternet.com
Web site: www.underthechristmastree.co.uk
Freq: Daily
Circ: 10742 Cision Digital Reach
MAGAZINE (ONLINE)
Do-It-Yourself (DIY), Shopping, Travel

Unfiltered Magazine 1070071
Editorial: The Vaults, 87 Giles Street, Edinburgh EH6 6BZ **Tel:** 44 01315 552929
Email: unfiltered@smws.com
Web site: https://www.smws.com/unfiltered-magazine
Freq: Quarterly Not Audited
MAGAZINE
Alcohol & Spirits

UNIfied 998624
Editorial: Christ Church Students' Union, St George's Centre, 41 St George's Place, Canterbury CT1 1UT **Tel:** 44 01227 782817
Email: unified@ccsu.co.uk
Web site: http://unified.ccsu.co.uk/
Freq: Monthly Not Audited
MAGAZINE
Student Lifestyle

UNILAD 1052961
Editorial: 83 Ducie Street, Manchester M1 2JQ
Email: contact@unilad.co.uk
Web site: http://www.unilad.co.uk
Freq: Daily
Circ: 6778244 Cision Digital Reach
MAGAZINE (ONLINE)
Men's Interests

UniServity 994661
Editorial: 2nd Floor, 12 Friar Street, Reading RG1 1DB **Tel:** 44 08708 555751
Email: info@uniservity.com
Web site: www.uniservity.com
Freq: Daily
Circ: 6185 Cision Digital Reach
MAGAZINE (ONLINE)
Disability, Education, Higher Education, Preschool, Schools & Institutions, Students

Unite Works 1052963
Editorial: 128 Theobald's Road, London WC1X 8TN **Tel:** 44 02033 712065
Email: uniteworks@unitetheunion.org
Web site: www.unitetheunion.org
Freq: Quarterly
Editor: Amanda Campbell
MAGAZINE
News & Current Affairs

UNITY Magazine 995323
Tel: 44 03300 553763
Email: press@unity-magazine.com
Web site: unity-magazine.com
Freq: Daily
Circ: 521 Cision Digital Reach
Editor: Debra-Derieux Matos
MAGAZINE (ONLINE)
Luxury Goods

UniVerse 998626
Editorial: University of Hertfordshire SU, College Lane, Hatfield AL10 9AB
Tel: 44 01707 285001
Email: vp.comms@hertfordshire.su
Web site: http://tridentmedia.org/
Freq: Monthly
Circ: 1000 Not Audited
Profile: Founded in 1860, The Universe is a Catholic newspaper for the UK and Ireland. Its regular columnists include Lord Alton of Liverpool, Nobel-nominated human rights campaigner Father Shay Cullen, leading Labour MP and government advisor John Battle, and theologian Father Michael Buckley. Regular weekly news direct from Rome is supplied by Vatican Correspondent Gerry O'Connell.
MAGAZINE
Student Lifestyle

UNIverse 1054322
Editorial: University Of Gloucestershire, The Park, Cheltenham GL50 2RH
Tel: 44 01242 714360
Email: universeuog@gmail.com
Web site: www.yourstudentsunion.com/universe
Freq: Daily
Circ: 4550 Cision Digital Reach
Profile: Founded in 1860, The Universe is a Catholic newspaper for the UK and Ireland. Its regular columnists include Lord Alton of Liverpool, Nobel-nominated human rights campaigner Father Shay Cullen, leading Labour MP and government advisor John Battle, and theologian Father Michael Buckley. Regular weekly news direct from Rome is supplied by Vatican Correspondent Gerry O'Connell.
MAGAZINE (ONLINE)
Student Lifestyle

The University Paper 996069
Editorial: Third Floor, 23 – 24 Margaret Street, London W1W 8RU
Tel: 44 02075 806419
Email: editor@unipaper.co.uk
Web site: www.unipaper.co.uk
Freq: Monthly
Circ: 600000 Not Audited
MAGAZINE
Student Lifestyle

Unmissable.com 995268
Editorial: Unit 12, Deane House Studios, Greenwood Place, London NW5 1LB
Email: hello@unmissable.com
Web site: www.unmissable.com
Freq: Daily
Circ: 10399 Cision Digital Reach
MAGAZINE (ONLINE)
Bars, Clubs & Pubs, Cooking & Baking, Lifestyle, Men's Interests, Regional General Interest, Restaurant Reviews, Travel, Women's Interests

Unwrapp.co.uk 1052662
Email: editor@unwrapp.co.uk
Web site: www.unwrapp.co.uk
Freq: Daily
Circ: 47854 Cision Digital Reach
MAGAZINE (ONLINE)
Audio Video Trade, Cameras, Consumer Electronics, Do-It-Yourself (DIY), Fashion, Fitness & Exercise, Mobile Electronics, Movies & Video

Up All Hours 997182
Email: hello@upallhours.com
Web site: www.upallhours.com
Freq: Daily
Circ: 8496 Cision Digital Reach
Editor: Sam Sims
MAGAZINE (ONLINE)
Family & Parenting

Up Country 998840
Editorial: PO Box 4257, Sheffield S25 9DA
Tel: 44 01909 561003
Email: puddleduck1@btconnect.com
Web site: www.upcountrymagazine.co.uk
Freq: Monthly Not Audited

Consumer Magazines

Editor: Rob Davis
MAGAZINE
Country, Folk, Bluegrass

Up to Speed
985620
Editorial: 85 Strand, London WC2R ODW
Tel: 44 02075 508000
Web site: www.tenalpspublishing.com/services/consumer/up-to-speed
Freq: Monthly
Circ: 41000 Not Audited
Profile: Monthly magazine for British Airways employees, focusing on the people who make the airline. Contains latest news, insight into the airline's strategy, insight from inside and outside the company, travel tips.
MAGAZINE
Airline Inflight, Aviation, Travel

The Upcoming
986927
Editorial: 114 Mansfield Road, London NW3 2JB
Email: info@theupcoming.co.uk
Web site: www.theupcoming.co.uk
Freq: Daily
Circ: 90285 Cision Digital Reach
MAGAZINE (ONLINE)
Regional General Interest

Upminster & Cranham Residents' Association
999071
Editorial: 28 Derham Gardens, Cranham, London RM14 3HA **Tel:** 44 01708 501238
Email: bulletinra@yahoo.co.uk
Web site: http://www.ucra.co.uk/
Freq: Monthly
Circ: 19000 Not Audited
Editor: Ron Ower
MAGAZINE
Charitable Foundations, Regional General Interest

Upset
1055161
Web site: www.upsetmagazine.com/
Freq: Monthly
MAGAZINE
Rock Music

ur7s.com
997094
Editorial: Global Rugby Sevens, 53 Gloucester Road, London SW7 4QN
Email: press@ur7s.com
Web site: www.ur7s.com
Freq: Daily
Circ: 6452 Cision Digital Reach
MAGAZINE (ONLINE)
Rugby

Urban Fox
1058247
Web site: www.theurban-fox.co.uk
Freq: Monthly
Circ: 15000 Not Audited
Profile: Regional lifestyle magazine for Leicestershire and Rutland. It contains articles on fashion, beauty, celebrity, business, properties and entertainment. Aimed at residents in Leicestershire and Rutland and distributed to Stoneygate, Knighton, Clarendon Park, Oadby, Evington Village, South-East Leicester, as well Stoughton, GreatGlen, Kibworth, The Langtons and Horninghold.
Ad Rate: Full Page Colour £399.00
MAGAZINE
Beauty & Grooming, Cosmetics, Entertainment, Fashion, Hair, Interior Design, Local Entertainment Guides, Luxury Goods, Women's Interests

Urban Junkies
983517
Editorial: 34a Marshall Street, Third Floor, London W1F 7EU **Tel:** 44 02072 874772
Email: info@urbanjunkies.com
Web site: www.urbanjunkies.com
Freq: Daily
Circ: 11247 Cision Digital Reach
Editor: Taryn Ross
Profile: Website covering things to do in London including bar launches, events, travel tips, sample sales and fashion trends.
MAGAZINE (ONLINE)
Men's Interests, Women's Interests

Urban Life
983149
Editorial: 10 Greycoat Place, London SW1P 1SB **Tel:** 44 08719 898206
Email: info@urbanlife-magazine.com
Web site: http://www.urbanlife-magazine.com
Freq: Quarterly
Circ: 35000 Not Audited
MAGAZINE
Men's Interests, Women's Interests

US Captive
996921
Editorial: Kingfisher House, 21-23 Elmfield Road, London BR1 1LT
Freq: Annual Not Audited
MAGAZINE
News & Current Affairs

US Magazine (UUSU)
1008765
Editorial: University of Ulster Students' Union, Jordanstown Campus, Newtownabbey BT37 0QB
Tel: 44 02890 366050
Email: info@uusu.org
Web site: www.uusu.org
Freq: Quarterly Not Audited
MAGAZINE
Student Lifestyle

UT2
986361
Editorial: Society for Underwater Technology, 1 Fetter Lane, London EC4A 1BR **Tel:** 44 01480 370007
Web site: www.sut.org/publications/ut2-ut3-magazines
Freq: Bi-Monthly
Circ: 3800 Not Audited
Editor: John Howes
Profile: Magazine covering sub-sea sectors including offshore, survey and sub-sea engineering. Aimed at members of the SUT - Society For Underwater Technology and qualified non-members and available at SUT training courses and trade exhibitions.
Ad Rate: Full Page Colour £2140.00
MAGAZINE
Marine & Boat Trade, Shipping & Warehousing

Utilities Policy
998449
Editorial: The Boulevard, Langford Lane, Oxford OX5 1GB **Tel:** 44 01865 843000
Web site: www.sciencedirect.com/science/journal/09571787
Freq: Quarterly Not Audited
MAGAZINE
News & Current Affairs

Utility Fleet
987418
Editorial: Bank House Studios, Warwick Street, Prestwich, Manchester M25 3HN
Web site: http://www.fleetmanageronline.co.uk/magazines.html
Freq: Bi-Monthly Not Audited
Editor: Sue Hurst
MAGAZINE
Automotive, Electricity, Oil, Water & Sanitation

Utopia Kitchen & Bathroom
984150
Tel: 44 01787 221396
Email: kbeye.editorial@propub.co.uk
Web site: www.utopiamag.co.uk
Freq: Monthly
Circ: 27000 Not Audited
Profile: Magazine covering interior designs and home decorating including products and design trends with particular focus on high end, luxury kitchens and bathrooms. Aimed at homeowners with a high disposable income, independent professional women, ladies that lunch, interior designers and architects.
Ad Rate: Full Page Colour £3350.00
MAGAZINE
Do-It-Yourself (DIY)

V&A Magazine
981887
Editorial: 27B Tradescant Road, London SW8 1XD **Tel:** 44 02077 352631
Web site: www.vam.ac.uk/info/va-magazine
Freq: 3 Times/Year

Circ: 50000 Not Audited
Profile: V&A Magazine is a magazine covering everything to do with the Victoria & Albert Museum in London. Published three times a year, the magazine writes on all aspects of the visual arts -architecture, design, craft, photography, fashion and fine art - taking the V&A's exhibition and display programme as its starting point. V&A Magazine aims to be as accessible, intelligent, entertaining and visually appealing as the museum itself.
Ad Rate: Full Page Colour £4000.00
MAGAZINE
Art

V3
981627
Editorial: Haymarket House, 28-29 Haymarket, London SW1Y 4RX
Tel: 44 02073 169000
Web site: www.v3.co.uk
Freq: Daily
Circ: 973630 Cision Digital Reach
MAGAZINE (ONLINE)
Auto Aftermarket, Computers, Data Management, Electronics, Government Technology, Industry, Internet, Mobile Communications, Security & Security Systems, Software

Vada Magazine
987508
Editorial: c/o Dog Horn Publishing, 8 Cedric Street, Salford M5 5JY **Tel:** 44 01619 436088
Email: adamlowe@vadamagazine.com
Web site: www.vadamagazine.com
Freq: Daily
Circ: 15875 Cision Digital Reach
Profile: Website covering gay lifestyle and opinion. VADA magazine covers arts, entertainment, events, film, fashion, gadgets and music.
MAGAZINE (ONLINE)
Airline Inflight, Antiques/Collectibles, Art, Arts, Bars, Clubs & Pubs, Comedy, Entertainment, Fashion, LGBT, Literature

Vale Life
984082
Editorial: The Business Centre, Cardiff House, Cardiff Road, Barry CF63 2AW
Tel: 44 08451 306452
Email: jennifer@goodlifepublishing.co.uk
Web site: www.valelife.co.uk
Freq: Quarterly
Circ: 10000 Not Audited
Profile: A magazine about Wales covering all aspects of life in Wales from fashion, to food and drink, what's on listings and features, with a focus on local businesses.
MAGAZINE
Business, Lifestyle, Men's Interests, Regional General Interest, Small and Medium Business, Women's Interests

Vale Life Magazine
995430
Editorial: 23 Glenham Road, Thame, Thame OX9 3WD **Tel:** 44 07702 006218
Email: editor@vale-life.co.uk
Web site: www.vale-life.co.uk
Freq: Bi-Monthly
Circ: 11500 Not Audited
Editor: Charlie Trott
MAGAZINE
Regional, Regional General Interest

Valley News
988289
Editorial: 19 Crow Lane, Wilton, Salisbury SP2 OHB **Tel:** 44 01722 716268
Email: editorial@yourvalleynews.co.uk
Web site: www.yourvalleynews.co.uk
Freq: Monthly
Circ: 30000 Not Audited
Profile: Magazine covering community news including business, sports, travel, education, property, eating out, entertainment, events, health, beauty, gardening and classified adds. Aimed at households in Wiltshire villages.
Ad Rate: Full Page Colour £300.00
MAGAZINE
Regional

Valleys Life
986364
Editorial: Cardiff House, Cardiff Road, Barry, Barry CF63 2AW **Tel:** 44 08451 801234
Email: jennifer@goodlifepublishing.co.uk

Web site: www.valleyslife.co.uk
Freq: Quarterly
Circ: 10000 Not Audited
Profile: Magazine covering regional lifestyle news for the Valleys area in Wales. It features advice and tips on where to shop, food reviews featuring the best restaurants and most talented chefs, a what's on section which includes the 'out of valleys' feature with suggestions for a great day out, mini break or holiday outside the area. It also includes articles on homes, interiors, sports, leisure and a regular charity feature. Aimed at people living in the Valleys.
MAGAZINE
Regional General Interest

Van Advisor
997740
Editorial: 2nd Floor, 9 Sutton Court Road, London SM1 4SZ **Tel:** 44 02089 122156
Web site: www.vanadvisor.com
Freq: Monthly
Circ: 10259 Cision Digital Reach
MAGAZINE (ONLINE)
Automotive

Van Fleet World
981342
Editorial: 18 Alban Park, Hatfield Road, St Albans, London AL4 0JJ
Tel: 44 01727 739160
Email: dan@fleetworldgroup.co.uk
Web site: http://vanfleetworld.co.uk/
Freq: Monthly
Circ: 18052 Not Audited
Editor: Dan Gilkes
Profile: Magazine providing high quality advice and guidance for senior LCV fleet decision-makers. It contains articles on finance, taxation and legislation, which are specifically written for director-level readers, as well as road tests, group tests, industry news and operator profiles.
Ad Rate: Full Page Colour £4670.00
MAGAZINE
Automotive

Van User
984239
Editorial: Fountain Way, Reydon, Southwold IP18 6DH **Tel:** 44 01502 725800
Web site: www.vanuser.co.uk
Freq: Monthly
Circ: 10000 Not Audited
Editor: Dan Gilkes
Profile: Publication providing articles on new light commercial vehicles and products, including leasing, major manufacturers and users.
Ad Rate: Full Page Colour £1500.00
MAGAZINE
Automotive

VANDEROHE BEAUTY
996693
Web site: http://www.vanderohe.com/
Freq: Daily
Circ: 733 Cision Digital Reach
MAGAZINE (ONLINE)
Beauty & Grooming, Cosmetics, Hair

Vanilla Magazine
998529
Editorial: Vanilla Magazine, East Coast Publishing Limited, The Street, Belper IP9 2QS **Tel:** 44 01473 327592
Email: editorial@vanilla-magazine.co.uk
Web site: http://vanilla-magazine.co.uk/
Freq: Bi-Monthly
Circ: 16000 Not Audited
Editor: Laura Hall
MAGAZINE
Regional General Interest

VanillaPlus
981682
Tel: 44 01732 844017
Email: editorial@vanillaplus.com
Web site: www.vanillaplus.com
Freq: Bi-Monthly Not Audited
Editor: George Malim
MAGAZINE
Computers, Data Management, Electronics

Vanity Fair
982381
Editorial: Vogue House, Hanover Square, London W1S 1JU **Tel:** 44 02074 999080
Email: vanityfaireditorial@condenast.co.uk

Web site: www.vanityfair.co.uk
Freq: Monthly
Circ: 72012 Not Audited
Editor: Annabel Davidson
MAGAZINE
Luxury Goods, Women's Interests

VantagePoint Magazine 997416
Editorial: Vantage Publishing Limited, 2 Chestnut Suite, Guardian House, Borough Road, Godalming GU7 2AE
Tel: 44 01483 421601
Web site: vantagepointmag.co.uk
Freq: Monthly
Circ: 118300 Not Audited
Editor: Stefan Reynolds
MAGAZINE
Regional General Interest

Varsity 981781
Editorial: 16 Mill Lane, Cambridge CB2 1RX
Tel: 44 01223 337575
Email: editor@varsity.co.uk
Web site: www.varsity.co.uk
Freq: Weekly
Circ: 10000 Not Audited
Profile: Publication providing news and sports coverage, plus features on a range of arts.
Ad Rate: Full Page Colour £1320.00
MAGAZINE
Student Lifestyle

Vauxhall Magazine 1073491
Editorial: Stream Publishing Ltd The Cowshed, Ladycross Farm Hollow Lane, Dormansland, Luton RH7 6PB
Tel: 44 01582 721122
Email: vmeditor@vauxhall.co.uk
Web site: http://vauxhallmagazine.com/
Freq: Semi-Annual
Circ: 450000 Not Audited
Editor: Emily Gravenor
MAGAZINE
Automakers

Vavista Life 996170
Editorial: Lysander House, Cribbs Causeway, Bristol BS10 7TQ
Tel: 44 08449 027278
Email: support@vavistalife.com
Web site: https://www.vavistalife.com/
Freq: Daily
Circ: 7096 Cision Digital Reach
MAGAZINE (ONLINE)
Nutrition, Women's Interests

Vector (UK) 996759
Editorial: 14 Antony House, Pembury Place, London E5 8GZ
Email: vector.editors@gmail.com
Web site: www.bsfa.co.uk
Freq: Annual Not Audited
MAGAZINE
Science, Science Fiction

The Vegan 981814
Editorial: Donald Watson House, 21 Hylton Street, Birmingham B18 6HJ
Tel: 44 01215 231730
Email: editor@vegansociety.com
Web site: www.vegansociety.com
Freq: Quarterly
Circ: 7000 Not Audited
Editor: Elena Orde
Profile: Magazine focusing on vegan issues, from animal rights to ecology, with food news and recipes from the national society.
Ad Rate: Full Page Mono £305.00
Ad Rate: Full Page Colour £425.00
MAGAZINE
Energy & Environment, Vegetarianism & Veganism

Vegan Life Magazine 996873
Editorial: Park House, The Business Centre, Earls Colne Business Park, Earls Colne, Colchester CO6 2NS **Tel:** 44 01787 224040
Email: claire@primeimpact.co.uk
Web site: www.veganlifemag.co.uk
Freq: Monthly

Circ: 40000 Not Audited
MAGAZINE
Vegetarianism & Veganism

The Vegetarian 981815
Editorial: Parkdale, Dunham Road, Altrincham WA14 4QG **Tel:** 44 01619 252000
Email: editor@vegsoc.org
Web site: www.vegsoc.org
Freq: Quarterly
Circ: 10000 Not Audited
Editor: John Soonaye
Profile: In-house magazine of the Vegetarian Society. Covers cookery, nutrition, animal welfare, the environment, lifestyle and philosophy.
Ad Rate: Full Page Colour £1150.00
MAGAZINE
Vegetarianism & Veganism

Vegetarian Living 985864
Editorial: P.O Box 6337, Bournemouth BH1 9EH **Tel:** 44 01202 586848
Email: editorial@vegmag.co.uk
Web site: www.vegetarianliving.co.uk
Freq: Monthly
Circ: 55000 Not Audited
Editor: Lindsey Harrad
Profile: The magazine covering vegetarian lifestyle – whether you are vegetarian, vegan or simply want to cut down your meat intake.
Ad Rate: Full Page Colour £1395.00
MAGAZINE
Vegetarianism & Veganism

Veggie 997100
Editorial: 25 Phoenix Court, Hawkins Road, Colchester, Colchester CO2 8JY
Tel: 44 01206 505491
Web site: www.vegetarianrecipesmag.com
Freq: Monthly
Circ: 50000 Not Audited
Editor: Fae Gilfillan
MAGAZINE
Cooking & Baking, Nutrition, Vegetarianism & Veganism

VeggieVision TV 983890
Editorial: MAD Promotions, Independent House, Radford Business Centre, Radford Way, Billericay CM12 0BZ
Tel: 44 07970 732668
Email: info@veggievision.co.uk
Web site: www.veggievision.tv
Freq: Daily
Circ: 13250 Cision Digital Reach
Profile: Website covering vegetarian food. The veggievision website shares the latest news and information on vegetarian food.
MAGAZINE (ONLINE)
Vegetarianism & Veganism

Vehicle Dynamics International 983471
Editorial: Abinger House, Church Street, Dorking, Dorking RH4 1DF
Tel: 44 01306 743744
Email: vehicledynamics@ukipme.com
Web site: www.vehicledynamicsinternational.com
Freq: Semi-Annual
Circ: 6914 Not Audited
Editor: John O'Brien
Profile: Magazine covering news, technologies and developments relating to suspension, chassis, engineering, stability and traction controls, steering, braking, ride, handling and corner module engineering.
Ad Rate: Full Page Colour £3750.00
MAGAZINE
Automotive

Vehicle Electronics 998539
Editorial: 72 Westwood Road, Nottingham NG2 4FS **Tel:** 44 01582 722460
Email: editor@vehicle-electronics.biz
Web site: http://vehicle-electronics.biz
Freq: Monthly
Circ: 7400 Not Audited
Profile: This is a website for the Vehicle Electronics free, monthly magazine covering

all the latest news for automotive electronics engineers.
MAGAZINE
Automotive, Electronics

Vehicle Salvage Professional 984358
Editorial: Unit 4, Marshbrook Business Park, Church Stretton, Telford SY6 6QE
Tel: 44 01694 731510
Web site: http://www.plumpublishing.co.uk/publications.html
Freq: Quarterly
Circ: 1500 Not Audited
Profile: Magazine covering all aspects of the vehicle salvage industry.
Ad Rate: Full Page Colour £1240.00
MAGAZINE
Automotive

Velo Vision 985990
Editorial: Freshfields, Main Street, Gayton le Marsh, York LN13 0NS
Tel: 44 07948 271763
Email: info@velovision.com
Web site: www.velovision.com
Freq: 3 Times/Year
Circ: 2100 Not Audited
MAGAZINE
Bicycles

Velocity 982319
Editorial: The Courtyard, Ladycross Farm, Hollow Lane, East Grinstead RH7 6PB
Tel: 44 01342 872020
Email: adam.duxbury@streampublishing.net
Web site: www.cityjetmagazine.com
Freq: Monthly Not Audited
Editor: Emily Gravenor
MAGAZINE
Airline Inflight

Velocity 984817
Editorial: 26 Chapter Street, London SW1P 4NP **Tel:** 44 02088 492323
Email: velocity@cimaglobal.com
Web site: www.cimaglobal.com/velocity
Freq: Bi-Monthly
Circ: 61813 Cision Digital Reach
MAGAZINE (ONLINE)
Student Lifestyle

Velvet Magazine 985795
Editorial: Winship Road, Milton, Cambridge CD24 6PP **Tel:** 44 01204 757057
Email: info@velvetmag.co.uk
Web site: www.velvetmag.co.uk
Freq: Monthly
Circ: 15000 Not Audited
MAGAZINE
Bars, Clubs & Pubs, Beauty & Grooming, Cosmetics, Hair, Lifestyle, Men's Interests, Regional General Interest, Restaurant Reviews, Women's Interests

Venue Magazine 995807
Tel: 44 01223 882200
Email: features@venuemagazine.co.uk
Web site: http://www.venuemagazine.co.uk/
Freq: Quarterly
Circ: 15000 Not Audited
Editor: Frances Goss
MAGAZINE
Art, Theater & Performing Arts, Visual Arts

VERGE 985851
Editorial: The Shard, 24th floor, 32 London Bridge Street, London SE1 9SG
Tel: 44 02036 129547
Email: info@vergemagazine.co.uk
Web site: www.vergemagazine.co.uk
Freq: Daily
Circ: 800000 Not Audited
MAGAZINE
Men's Interests, Student Lifestyle, Women's Interests

Verve 983783
Editorial: TMG-75 Tower Building, 166-220 Holloway Road, London N7 8DB
Tel: 44 02071 334171
Email: vervemagazine@londonmet.ac.uk

Web site: https://www.londonmetsu.org.uk/verve/magazine/
Freq: Monthly Not Audited
Profile: Women's lifestyle publication featuring fashion, beauty, food, homes and garden news and features.
MAGAZINE
Student Lifestyle

Verve Magazine 983872
Tel: 44 01622 687874
Email: info@verve-magazine.co.uk
Web site: www.verve-magazine.co.uk/
Freq: Monthly
Circ: 25000 Not Audited
Editor: Elizabeth Norton
Profile: Student publication of the London Metropolitan University. It features news on student issues, lifestyle, features, sports and entertainment.
MAGAZINE
Regional General Interest

Very 987621
Tel: 44 02086 127000
Web site: www.very.co.uk
Freq: Monthly
Circ: 300000 Not Audited
Profile: Magazine from the online fashion retailer featuring fashion and lifestyle news.
MAGAZINE
Beauty & Grooming, Cosmetics, Fashion, Hair, Shopping

VERY 997848
Editorial: 67B Queen's Gardens, London W2 3AH **Tel:** 44 02072 620612
Web site: www.verymagazine.org
Freq: Semi-Annual
Circ: 918 Cision Digital Reach
Profile: Magazine from the online fashion retailer featuring fashion and lifestyle news.
MAGAZINE (ONLINE)
Art, Environment, Fashion, Movies & Video, Photography, Visual Arts

Very Nearly Almost 988126
Editorial: 36 Bear Lane, London SE1 0UH
Email: info@verynearlyalmost.com
Web site: www.verynearlyalmost.com
Freq: Quarterly
Circ: 10000 Not Audited
Editor: George Macdonald
MAGAZINE
Art, Photography, Visual Arts

VeryExclusive.co.uk 997748
Web site: http://www.veryexclusive.co.uk/
Freq: Daily
Circ: 150284 Cision Digital Reach
MAGAZINE (ONLINE)
Fashion

VeryFirstTo 1102296
Tel: 44 02074 286394
Email: press@veryfirstto.com
Web site: www.VeryFirstTo.com
Freq: Daily
Circ: 10969 Cision Digital Reach
MAGAZINE (ONLINE)
Lifestyle, Luxury Goods, Men's Interests, Regional General Interest, Women's Interests

VeryVery 1076158
Editorial: 40 Langham Street, London W1W 7AS **Tel:** 44 02032 050042
Email: editor@vv-media.com
Web site: www.vvmag.com
Freq: Quarterly
Circ: 35000 Not Audited
MAGAZINE
Luxury Goods

VG24/7 986279
Web site: www.vg247.com
Freq: Daily
Circ: 3272767 Cision Digital Reach
Editor: Matt Martin
MAGAZINE (ONLINE)
Apple, Computer & Video Games, Computers, Internet, Personal Computers

Consumer Magazines

VGChartz 999663
Editorial: VGChartz Limited, 10 Lea Park Rise, Bromsgrove B61 0AU
Email: contact@vgchartz.com
Web site: www.vgchartz.com
Freq: Daily
Circ: 2016502 Cision Digital Reach
MAGAZINE (ONLINE)
Computer & Video Games

VICE (UK) 981797
Editorial: New North Place, London EC2A 4JA **Tel:** 44 02077 497810
Web site: http://www.vice.com/en_uk
Freq: Daily
Circ: 2218267 Cision Digital Reach
Editor: Joe Zadeh
MAGAZINE (ONLINE)
Fashion, Men's Interests, Women's Interests

VICE NEWS (UK) 997327
Editorial: New North Place, London EC2A 4JA **Tel:** 44 02077 497810
Email: ukpressoffice@vice.com
Web site: https://www.vice.com/en_uk/topic/news
Freq: Daily
Circ: 27184 Cision Digital Reach
MAGAZINE (ONLINE)
International News, National News

Victoria 1055162
Tel: 44 01932 896000
Web site: www.victoria.co.uk
Freq: Daily
Circ: 11630 Cision Digital Reach
MAGAZINE (ONLINE)
Women's Interests

Victoria London Starts Here
998320
Editorial: 3 Princes Street, London W1B 2LD
Tel: 44 02072 591050
Email: day@pubbiz.com
Web site: www.pubbiz.com/section/content/10
Freq: Quarterly Not Audited
MAGAZINE
Regional General Interest

victoriahealth 1055156
Tel: 44 02089 514144
Web site: www.victoriahealth.com/brand/Procter-and-Gamble/545
Freq: Daily
MAGAZINE (ONLINE)
Health & Medicine

VideoCardz.com 995091
Email: news+contact@videocardz.com
Web site: www.videocardz.com
Freq: Daily
Circ: 150554 Cision Digital Reach
MAGAZINE (ONLINE)
News & Current Affairs

VideoGamer.com 984617
Editorial: Ugli Campus, Unit 45A, 56 Wood Lane, London W12 7SB
Email: contact@videogamer.com
Web site: www.videogamer.com
Freq: Daily
Circ: 1574493 Cision Digital Reach
Profile: Website covering video games. Video Gamer shares the latest news, reviews, previews, features and competitions on the latest and greatest games.
MAGAZINE (ONLINE)
Computer & Video Games

videonet 985571
Editorial: Burleigh House, 357 Strand, London WC2R 0HS **Tel:** 44 01206 752594
Email: justin@mediatelevents.com
Web site: www.v-net.tv
Freq: Daily
Circ: 39769 Cision Digital Reach
Editor: John Moulding; **Editor:** John Moulding

Profile: Website covering video technology. The videonet website shares the latest news, analysis and strategic insight about video television.
MAGAZINE (ONLINE)
Broadcasting

View London 982856
Editorial: The Workshop, 32-40 Tontine Street, Folkestone CT20 1JU
Tel: 44 01303 764222
Email: socialmedia@view.co.uk
Web site: http://www.view.co.uk/london
Freq: Daily
Circ: 41902 Cision Digital Reach
MAGAZINE (ONLINE)
Local Entertainment Guides, Regional General Interest

View Magazines 995992
Editorial: View House, 10 The Ventry, Salisbury, Salisbury SP1 3ES
Tel: 44 01722 502464
Email: info@viewmagazines.co.uk
Web site: www.viewmagazines.co.uk
Freq: Monthly
Circ: 30000 Not Audited
MAGAZINE
Regional General Interest

Viewfinder 984001
Editorial: 77 Wells Street, London W1T 3QJ
Tel: 44 02073 931500
Email: ask@bufvc.ac.uk
Web site: http://bufvc.ac.uk/viewfinder
Freq: Quarterly
Circ: 4500 Not Audited
Profile: Magazine of the British Universities Film and Video Council, containing articles on the production, study and use of film, television and related media for higher education and research.
Ad Rate: Full Page Colour £350.00
MAGAZINE
Careers, Education, Movies & Video

Viewpoint 984125
Email: info@view-publications.com
Web site: http://www.view-publications.com/
Freq: Semi-Annual Not Audited
MAGAZINE
Luxury Goods

Vilda 997655
Tel: 44 07938 012358
Email: sascha@vildamagazine.com
Web site: www.vildamagazine.com
Freq: Daily Not Audited
MAGAZINE
Beauty & Grooming, Cosmetics, Fashion, Hair, Men's Interests, Travel, Women's Interests

The Village 982517
Editorial: 16 The Square, Alvechurch, Alvechurch B48 7LA **Tel:** 44 01214 456757
Email: editor@villageonline.co.uk
Web site: www.villageonline.co.uk
Freq: Monthly
Circ: 10000 Not Audited
Profile: Local news magazine covering health, beauty, fashion, motoring, travel, lifestyle, entertainment, restaurants and property.
Ad Rate: Full Page Colour £550.00
MAGAZINE
Regional General Interest

Village Directory 1076641
Tel: 44 01282 619389
Web site: N/A
Freq: Monthly
Circ: 6000 Not Audited
MAGAZINE
Regional General Interest

Vinco Sport 1052555
Email: info@vincosport.com
Web site: http://www.runjumpthrow.com/
Freq: Daily
Circ: 13032 Cision Digital Reach
MAGAZINE (ONLINE)
Sports

Vintage Life 986766
Editorial: Dane Mill Business Centre, Broadhurst Lane, Congleton, Congleton CW12 1LA **Tel:** 44 01260 291536
Email: submissions@vintagelifemagazine.com
Web site: www.vintagelifemagazine.com
Freq: Monthly
Circ: 24000 Not Audited
Editor: Rachel Egglestone-Evans
Profile: Magazine covering vintage style. It features articles on fashion, hair, beauty, house and home, music and film from the 1920s through to the 1970s. Aimed at people with a love of vintage style.
MAGAZINE
Fashion, Women's Interests

Vintage Rock 1063930
Editorial: Piccadilly House, London Road, Bath BA1 6PL
Web site: www.vintagerockmag.com
Freq: Quarterly
Circ: 24000 Not Audited
Profile: Magazine covering rock music from the 1950s and 1960s. Features concert reviews, interviews and latest news.
MAGAZINE
Rock Music

Violet 997882
Email: info@violetbook.co.uk
Web site: violetbook.co.uk
Freq: Semi-Annual Not Audited
MAGAZINE
Fashion, Women's Interests

VIPER 996334
Email: info@vipermag.com
Web site: www.vipermag.com
Freq: Semi-Annual Not Audited
MAGAZINE
Fashion, Rap & Hip Hop

Virgin Media Presents 984448
Editorial: Bankside 3, 90 Southwark Street, London SE1 0SW **Tel:** 44 02037 877000
Web site: www.virginmediapresents.com
Freq: Weekly
Circ: 41145 Cision Digital Reach
Profile: Newsletter covering all the latest Virgin Media news and entertainment. Aimed at Virgin Media customers.
MAGAZINE (ONLINE)
Basketball, Bicycles, Billiards, Boating & Yachting, Bodybuilding, Bowling, Boxing, Broadcasting, Classical/Choral/Band Music, Country, Folk, Bluegrass

Virgin Retail Therapy 996201
Editorial: 3rd Floor, 34 Ship Street, Brighton BN1 1AD **Tel:** 44 01273 715915
Email: contact@identity.uk.com
Web site: http://identity.uk.com/clients/virgin-atlantic/#
Freq: Quarterly
Circ: 100000 Not Audited
MAGAZINE
Airline Inflight

Virgin.com 985829
Editorial: The School House, 50 Brook Green, London W6 7RR
Web site: www.virgin.com
Freq: Daily
Circ: 2121009 Cision Digital Reach
MAGAZINE (ONLINE)
Airline Inflight, Audio Video Trade, Cameras, Classical/Choral/Band Music, Consumer Electronics, Country, Folk, Bluegrass, Dance Music, Jazz & Blues, Lifestyle, Men's Interests

Virtual Shropshire 985642
Editorial: 6c Stretton Road, Much Wenlock TF13 6AS
Email: info@virtual-shropshire.co.uk
Web site: http://www.virtual-shropshire.co.uk
Freq: Daily
Circ: 11190 Cision Digital Reach
Profile: Website covering tourism. Virtual Shropshire shares the latest news on

tourism, accommodation, attractions and events in Shropshire.
MAGAZINE (ONLINE)
Travel

Vision Zero International 988828
Editorial: Abinger House, Church Street, Dorking, Dorking RH4 1DF
Tel: 44 01306 743744
Email: visionzero@ukipme.com
Web site: http://www.ukipme.com/pub-its.php?mag=4
Freq: Semi-Annual Not Audited
Editor: Izzy Kington
Profile: Magazine looking at the development of next-generation active and passive vehicle safety technologies to help reduce road deaths serious injuries globally. The magazine's primary focus is on collision avoidance, with technical articles covering ADAS such as automatic emergency braking, stability control, 360° object detection, visible light communications, driver distraction solutions, impaired driving countermeasures, pedestrian-sensing, eye gaze, lane assist, V2X communications and HMIs. Integrated passive safety systems including advanced airbags and restraints are also investigated, in addition to ADAS testing and vehicle integrity, materials and crashworthiness. The magazine also features interviews with high-profile professionals from government, safety bodies, vehicle-makers and Tier 1 suppliers. Aimed at road safety engineers and professionals within the world's automotive, truck and motorcycle manufacturers and their suppliers, highways authorities and transportation departments, road safety organizations and government legislation departments worldwide.
Ad Rate: Full Page Colour £4350.00
MAGAZINE
Automotive

Visit Gay London 988681
Email: news@visitgay.london
Web site: www.visitgay.london
Freq: Daily
Circ: 2628 Cision Digital Reach
MAGAZINE (ONLINE)
Art, Bars, Clubs & Pubs, Beauty & Grooming, Cosmetics, Dance Music, Fashion, Hair, LGBT, Literature, Local Entertainment Guides

Visit Scotland 995058
Editorial: Ocean Point One, 94 Ocean Drive, Edinburgh EH6 6JH **Tel:** 44 01316 258625
Email: info@visitscotland.com
Web site: www.visitscotland.com
Freq: Daily
Circ: 459007 Cision Digital Reach
MAGAZINE (ONLINE)
Travel

Visit USA Travel Planner 998654
Editorial: Suffolk House, George Street, Croydon CR9 1SR **Tel:** 44 02086 497233
Email: visitusa@bmipublishing.co.uk
Web site: http://www.visitusa.org.uk
Freq: Annual
Circ: 50000 Not Audited
MAGAZINE
Travel

VisitBirmingham.com 998732
Editorial: Baskerville House, Centenary Square, Broad Street, Birmingham B1 2ND
Tel: 44 01212 025115
Email: press@marketingbirmingham.com
Web site: www.visitbirmingham.com
Freq: Daily
Circ: 60745 Cision Digital Reach
MAGAZINE (ONLINE)
Regional General Interest, Travel

VisitBrighton.com 998594
Tel: 44 01273 290337
Email: media@visitbrighton.com
Web site: www.visitbrighton.com
Freq: Daily
Circ: 45592 Cision Digital Reach
MAGAZINE (ONLINE)
Travel

VisitBritain 983959
Editorial: Sanctuary Buildings, 20 Great Smith Street, London SW1P 3BT
Tel: 44 02075 781000
Web site: www.visitbritain.com
Freq: Daily
Circ: 685468 Cision Digital Reach
MAGAZINE (ONLINE)
Travel

VisitLondon.com 982858
Editorial: 6th Floor, 2 More London Riverside, London SE1 2RR
Tel: 44 02072 345800
Email: editorial@londonandpartners.com
Web site: www.visitlondon.com
Freq: Daily
Circ: 1512729 Cision Digital Reach
Editor: Jenny Owen
MAGAZINE (ONLINE)
Regional General Interest, Travel

The Visitor 982526
Editorial: PO Box 1, Castle Cary, Castle Cary BA7 7BG **Tel:** 44 01963 351256
Email: info@thevisitormagazine.co.uk
Web site: www.thevisitormagazine.co.uk
Freq: Monthly
Circ: 27000 Not Audited
Editor: Helen Dunion
Profile: Magazine of general interest covering current events, history, house and home, gardening and leisure.
Ad Rate: Full Page Mono £360.00
MAGAZINE
Regional General Interest

Visordown.com 982662
Editorial: Vineyard House, 44 Brook Green, Hammersmith, London W6 7BT
Web site: www.visordown.com
Freq: Daily
Circ: 444461 Cision Digital Reach
Editor: Steve Farrell
Profile: Online motorcycle community with daily motorcycle news, reviews, features and forums, product reviews and accessories. Aimed at UK motorcyclists and anyone with an interest in motorcycles.Ben Cope is the Managing Editor to whom press releases should be addressed.
MAGAZINE (ONLINE)
Motorcycles

Vitality 1074208
Editorial: 3-7 Herbal Hill, London EC1R 5EJ
Tel: 44 02077 757775
Web site: www.vitality.co.uk
Freq: Daily
Circ: 863971 Cision Digital Reach
Profile: Journal of BABTAC. Includes news and information on the beauty industry both in the UK and overseas.
Ad Rate: Full Page Colour £1245.00
MAGAZINE (ONLINE)
Cooking & Baking, Fitness & Exercise, Health & Medicine, Nutrition, Vegetarianism & Veganism

Viva Brighton 987480
Editorial: Brighton Junction, 1a Isetta Square, Brighton, Brighton BN1 4GQ
Tel: 44 01273 810259
Email: hello@vivabrighton.com
Web site: www.vivabrighton.com
Freq: Monthly
Circ: 15000 Not Audited
Profile: Magazine about what on in Brighton and Hove. Includes editorial, interviews and articles looking at the characters, business community and contemporary culture in Brighton and Hove.
Ad Rate: Full Page Colour £495.00
MAGAZINE
Art, Classical/Choral/Band Music, Country, Folk, Bluegrass, Dance Music, Jazz & Blues, Literature, Music, Photography, Pop Music, R&B, Urban, World

Viva Lewes 1053625
Tel: 44 01273 488882
Email: alex@vivamagazines.com
Web site: http://www.vivalewes.com/

Freq: Monthly
Circ: 11500 Not Audited
Profile: Magazine covering events in Lewes, includes music, film and art events.
MAGAZINE
Art, Classical/Choral/Band Music, Country, Folk, Bluegrass, Dance Music, Jazz & Blues, Literature, Music, Photography, Pop Music, R&B, Urban, World

Viva Magazine 985453
Editorial: Fourway House, Part Second Floor, 57 Hilton Street, Manchester M1 2EJ
Tel: 44 01614 646284
Email: info@vivalifestyle.co.uk
Web site: www.vivamanchester.co.uk
Freq: Quarterly
Circ: 20000 Not Audited
MAGAZINE
Bars, Clubs & Pubs, Beauty & Grooming, Cosmetics, Fashion, Hair, Lifestyle, Men's Interests, Regional General Interest, Restaurant Reviews, Women's Interests

Viva! life 999178
Editorial: 8 York Court, Wilder Street, Bristol BS2 8QH **Tel:** 44 01179 441000
Email: info@viva.org.uk
Web site: www.viva.org.uk
Freq: 3 Times/Year Not Audited
Editor: Tony Wardle
MAGAZINE
Ethical/Moral Issues, Vegetarianism & Veganism

Vive Le Rock 999036
Editorial: Studio G12, Regent House, 1 Thane Villas, London N7 7PH
Tel: 44 02072 818880
Email: info@vivelerock.net
Web site: www.vivelerock.net
Freq: Bi-Monthly
Circ: 13000 Not Audited
MAGAZINE
Rock Music

Vivo 984850
Editorial: 72 New Bond Street, London W1S 1RR **Tel:** 44 08451 631238
Email: mail@vivomedia.co.uk
Web site: www.vivomagazine.co.uk
Freq: Daily
Circ: 1011 Cision Digital Reach
MAGAZINE (ONLINE)
Luxury Goods, Men's Interests, Women's Interests

VOD Professional 986450
Editorial: 10-14 Accommodation Road, London NW11 8ED
Web site: www.vodprofessional.com
Freq: Daily
Circ: 5066 Cision Digital Reach
Editor: Kauser Kanji
MAGAZINE (ONLINE)
Broadcasting

VODzilla.co 997594
Email: info@vodzilla.co
Web site: http://vodzilla.co/
Freq: Daily Not Audited
Editor: Ivan Radford
MAGAZINE
Entertainment, Movies & Video

VOGUE 982383
Editorial: Vogue House, Hanover Square, London W1S 1JU **Tel:** 44 02074 999080
Web site: www.vogue.co.uk
Freq: Monthly
Circ: 190021 Not Audited
Profile: Fashion magazine covering beauty, style, glamour, design, fashion and contemporary culture. It contains interviews with leading designers, runway reviews, practical style tips and must-have buys. First printed in the UK in 1916. Read by professional women aged between 20 and 44 years old.
Ad Rate: Full Page Colour £27200.00
MAGAZINE
Fashion, Luxury Goods, Women's Interests

The Voice (Worcester University) 999139
Editorial: Worcester Students' Union, Henwick Grove, Worcester WR2 6AJ
Tel: 44 01905 543210
Web site: https://thevoiceworcester. wordpress.com/
Freq: Bi-Monthly
Circ: 2000 Not Audited
MAGAZINE
Student Lifestyle

Voice For Arran 998596
Editorial: Burnfoot, Whiting Bay, Isle of Arran KA27 8QL **Tel:** 44 01770 700574
Email: info@voiceforarran.com
Web site: www.voiceforarran.com
Freq: Monthly
Circ: 2117 Cision Digital Reach
MAGAZINE (ONLINE)
Regional

Voice of the ROK 1061741
Freq: Semi-Annual Not Audited
MAGAZINE
Armed Forces

The Void 984321
Editorial: 53 Raymond Avenue, Canterbury, Canterbury CT1 3JY **Tel:** 44 07779 004643
Email: mike@the-void.co.uk
Web site: http://www.the-void.co.uk
Freq: Daily
Circ: 9564 Cision Digital Reach
Editor: Mike Shaw
Profile: Blog covering the welfare and benefit system. The blog has an archive dating back to July 2004.
MAGAZINE (ONLINE)
Broadcasting, Comedy, Computer & Video Games, Entertainment, Martial Arts, MMA & Self-Defense, Movies & Video, Theater & Performing Arts

Voir Fashion 1073133
Tel: 44 07801 992287
Email: editorial@voirfashion.co.uk
Web site: http://www.voirfashion.co.uk/
Freq: Quarterly
Circ: 225000 Not Audited
MAGAZINE
Fashion

Volkswagen Driver 982647
Editorial: Campion House, 1 Greenfield Road, Westoning, Flitwick MK45 5JD
Tel: 44 01525 750500
Email: mail@autometrix.co.uk
Web site: www.autometrix.co.uk
Freq: Monthly
Circ: 17000 Not Audited
Editor: Neil Birkitt
Profile: Publication containing road tests of new Volkswagen models, owner profiles, technical developments and car prices. Includes information on performance tuning, equipment, accessories and motor sport coverage. Aimed at owners and enthusiasts of Volkswagen cars.
Ad Rate: Full Page Colour £650.00
MAGAZINE
Automakers

Volksworld 982648
Editorial: Leon House, 233 High Street, Croydon, London CR9 1HZ
Tel: 44 01959 541444
Web site: www.volksworld.com
Freq: Monthly
Circ: 32500 Not Audited
Profile: Magazine containing news, events, products and features.
Ad Rate: Full Page Mono £715.00
Ad Rate: Full Page Colour £1200.00
MAGAZINE
Automakers

Volt 985333
Editorial: Ground Floor, 1-2 Ravey St, London EC2A 4QP **Tel:** 44 02072 269898
Email: info@volt-mag.com
Web site: www.voltcafe.com
Freq: Semi-Annual

Circ: 60000 Not Audited
Editor: Rui Faria
Profile: Magazine covering fashion. The magazine features original (specifically commissioned) work from international fashion talents.
MAGAZINE
Art, Country, Folk, Bluegrass, Dance Music, Fashion, Pop Music, Rap & Hip Hop, Rock Music, Theater & Performing Arts

Voltimum 984081
Editorial: Lincoln House, 137-143 Hammersmith Road, London W14 0QL
Tel: 44 02077 513900
Email: enquiries@voltimum.co.uk
Web site: www.voltimum.co.uk
Freq: Daily
Circ: 78155 Cision Digital Reach
MAGAZINE (ONLINE)
Electronics

Volume - CEASED 995991
Editorial: 22 Marmora Road, London
Web site: http://volumemagazine.tumblr. com/
Freq: Daily
Circ: 68292 Cision Digital Reach
MAGAZINE (ONLINE)
Art, Country, Folk, Bluegrass, Dance Music, Fashion, Literature, Photography, R&B, Urban, World, Rap & Hip Hop, Rock Music, Theater & Performing Arts

Vortez 990675
Web site: www.vortez.net
Freq: Daily
Circ: 114393 Cision Digital Reach
MAGAZINE (ONLINE)
Computer & Video Games, Personal Computers

VOW 999384
Email: contact@thevoiceofawoman.com
Web site: www.thevoiceofawoman.com
Freq: Daily
Circ: 6884 Cision Digital Reach
MAGAZINE (ONLINE)
Charitable Foundations, International News, National News, Women's Interests

VOW Magazine 997963
Editorial: MediaClash, Circus Mews House, Circus Mews, Bath BA1 2PW
Tel: 44 01225 475800
Web site: http://www.mediaclash.co.uk/ magazines/wedding/vow/
Freq: Quarterly
Circ: 6000 Not Audited
Editor: Matt Bielby
MAGAZINE
Weddings

Vulture Hound Magazine 997293
Email: editor@vulturehound.com
Web site: vulturehound.co.uk
Freq: Monthly Not Audited
MAGAZINE
Movies & Video, Pop Music, Rock Music

VW Camper & Bus 996355
Editorial: Leon House, 233 Highstreet, Croydon, London CR9 1HZ
Tel: 44 01959 541444
Email: camperandbus@timeinc.com
Web site: www.vwcamperandbus.com
Freq: Monthly Not Audited
MAGAZINE
Automakers

W1 Magazine 983827
Tel: 44 02077 887547
Email: enquiries@w1magazine.co.uk
Web site: http://westlondonmagazine.co.uk/
Freq: Monthly Not Audited
Editor: Jaz Walia
Profile: Magazine covering movies, restaurants, theatre, fashion, gadgets, health, beauty, property. travel, shopping and events.

Consumer Magazines

Ad Rate: Full Page Colour £1250.00
MAGAZINE
Art, Theater & Performing Arts

Waffle Mag
997994
Web site: www.wafflemag.com
Freq: Daily
Circ: 1486 Cision Digital Reach
Editor: Andy Wells
MAGAZINE (ONLINE)
Regional General Interest

Wag!
985421
Editorial: 17 Wakley Street, London EC1V 7RQ **Tel:** 44 02078 370006
Email: wag@dogstrust.org.uk
Web site: https://www.dogstrust.org.uk/about-us/publications/
Freq: 3 Times/Year
Circ: 710000 Not Audited
Editor: Deana Selby
MAGAZINE
Charitable Foundations, Nature & Wildlife

Waitrose Food
981813
Editorial: 8 Baldwin St, London EC1V 9NU
Tel: 44 02075 653000
Email: waitrosefood@waitrose.co.uk
Web site: http://www.waitrose.com/content/waitrose/en/home/mywaitrose/waitrose-food-magazine.html
Freq: Monthly
Circ: 690058 Not Audited
Editor: William Sitwell
MAGAZINE
Grocery Stores

Waitrose Garden Magazine
1102015
Tel: 44 02078 034100
Email: waitrosegarden@waitrose.co.uk
Web site: www.waitrosegarden.com/magazine
Freq: Quarterly
MAGAZINE
Gardening

Waitrose Weekend
985900
Editorial: Doncastle Road, Southern Industrial Area, Bracknell, London RG12 8YA
Tel: 44 01344 424680
Web site: www.waitrose.com/home/inspiration/waitrose_weekend.html#.UzVKcqh_uvg
Freq: Weekly
Circ: 340000 Not Audited
Editor: David Roshier
Profile: Magazine containing recipes for the weekend including news and comment, health and beauty, home and garden, DVD and book reviews. Aimed at customers of Waitrose supermarkets and people with an interest in cooking.
MAGAZINE
Cooking & Baking, Grocery Stores

The Waldorf Astoria Magazine
1070235
Editorial: Suite 9, Beaufort Court, Admirals Way, Canary Wharf, London E14 9XL
Email: enquiries@fms.co.uk
Web site: waldorfastoria3.hilton.com/en/wa-magazine/index.html
Freq: Semi-Annual
MAGAZINE
Luxury Goods

Wales World Wide
999662
Editorial: Raglan House, Cardiff Gate Business Park, Cardiff CF23 8BA
Tel: 44 02920 545381
Email: ask@walesworldwide.org
Web site: www.walesworldwide.org
Freq: Daily
Circ: 2837 Cision Digital Reach
MAGAZINE (ONLINE)
Business, International News, Regional, Small and Medium Business, Wales

Walk
981910
Editorial: 2nd Floor, Camelford House, 89 Albert Embankment, London SE1 7TW
Tel: 44 02073 398500

Email: walkmag@ramblers.org.uk
Web site: www.ramblers.org.uk/walkmag
Freq: Quarterly
Circ: 88590 Not Audited
Editor: Matthew Jones
Profile: Magazine covering reports and features on walking and countryside issues including walking, hiking, outdoors, environment, health issues and travel. First published in 2003, the publication has an average of 100 pages per issue. Press Day: 2 weeks prior to publication. Aimed at Ramblers' Association members, potential members, walkers, hikers and the outdoor industry.
Ad Rate: Full Page Colour £6500.00
MAGAZINE
Outdoor Recreation

Wallpaper*
981798
Editorial: 161 Marsh Wall, London E14 9AP
Tel: 44 02031 485000
Email: contact@wallpaper.com
Web site: http://www.wallpaper.com/
Freq: Monthly
Circ: 100008 Not Audited
Profile: Magazine focusing on what to do and where to go in various cities.
MAGAZINE
Do-It-Yourself (DIY)

The Waltham Cat
1104811
Email: editor@walthamcat.com
Web site: http://walthamcat.com/
Freq: Daily
Circ: 521 Cision Digital Reach
Editor: Rebecca Shahoud
MAGAZINE (ONLINE)
Regional, Regional General Interest

Waltham Forest News
995995
Editorial: Room 014, Waltham Forest Town Hall, Forest Road, London E17 4JF
Tel: 44 02084 963000
Web site: www.walthamforest.gov.uk
Freq: Bi-Weekly
Circ: 97161 Not Audited
Editor: Jenny Singh
MAGAZINE
News & Current Affairs

Wanderlust
982334
Editorial: 1 Leworth Place, Mellor Walk, Windsor SL4 1EB **Tel:** 44 01753 620426
Email: editorial@wanderlust.co.uk
Web site: www.wanderlust.co.uk
Freq: Monthly
Circ: 37500 Not Audited
Editor: Phoebe Smith
Profile: Magazine covering worldwide destinations and travel related topics, including health and eco-tourism. Aimed at affluent and avid travel consumers seeking soft-adventure or cultural experiences other than the conventional package holiday.
Ad Rate: Full Page Colour £2900.00
MAGAZINE
Railroad, Travel

The Wandsworth Magazine
1075509
Tel: 44 02089 395601
Email: samlaurie@sheengate.co.uk
Web site: www.sheengate.co.uk
Freq: Monthly
Circ: 38000 Not Audited
Editor: Samantha Laurie
MAGAZINE
Property Management & Maintenance, Regional General Interest

The War Cry
982166
Editorial: War Cry, The Salvation Army, 101 Newington Causeway, London SE1 6BN
Tel: 44 02073 674900
Email: warcry@salvationarmy.org.uk
Web site: www.salvationarmy.org.uk/warcry
Freq: Weekly
Circ: 40000 Not Audited
Editor: Major Nigel Bovey

Profile: Newspaper of the Salvation Army providing Christian comment on topical issues. Aimed at the general public.
MAGAZINE
Religion

WARC.com
990455
Editorial: 85 Newman Street, London W1T 3EX **Tel:** 44 02074 678100
Email: enquiries@warc.com
Web site: www.warc.com
Freq: Daily
Circ: 695333 Cision Digital Reach
Editor: Brian Carruthers
MAGAZINE (ONLINE)
Advertising Industry, Branding, Broadcasting, Graphic Design, Marketing, Media & Communications, Photography, Publishing

Wardrobe Icons
997366
Email: info@wardrobeicons.com
Web site: http://wardrobeicons.com/
Freq: Daily
Circ: 23988 Cision Digital Reach
MAGAZINE (ONLINE)
Fashion

Wareable
988231
Editorial: Creative 229, 225 Shoreditch High Street, London E1 6PG
Email: editors@wareable.com
Web site: www.wareable.com
Freq: Daily
Circ: 5227818 Cision Digital Reach
Editor: Michael Sawh
MAGAZINE (ONLINE)
Electronics, Mobile Electronics

Warehouse Home
1095731
Email: hello@mywarehousehome.com
Web site: mywarehousehome.com
Freq: Annual
Editor: Sophie Bush
MAGAZINE
Do-It-Yourself (DIY)

Wargamer
1104594
Tel: 44 07879 640305
Email: joer@wargamer.com
Web site: http://www.wargamer.com/
Freq: Daily
Circ: 145225 Cision Digital Reach
MAGAZINE (ONLINE)
Computer & Video Games

Warpaint
998537
Editorial: 21 Burstow Road, London SW20 8ST **Tel:** 44 02085 401177
Email: info@warpaintmakeup.co.uk
Web site: www.warpaintmag.com
Freq: Weekly
Circ: 13552 Cision Digital Reach
Editor: Alison Milner Ineson
MAGAZINE (ONLINE)
Cosmetics

Warren Miller
1095575
Editorial: 15 Bedford Street, Covent Garden, London WC2E 9HE **Tel:** 44 02072 404071
Email: info@blackdiamond.co.uk
Web site: www.warrenmiller.co.uk
Freq: Annual
Circ: 16500 Not Audited
MAGAZINE
Winter Sports

Warrington Worldwide
982859
Editorial: The New Media Centre, Old Road, Warrington, Warrington WA4 1AT
Tel: 44 01925 623631
Email: info@warrington-worldwide.co.uk
Web site: www.warrington-worldwide.co.uk
Freq: Monthly
Circ: 20000 Not Audited
MAGAZINE
Regional General Interest

Warship Technology
988924
Editorial: 8-9 Northumberland Street, London WC2N 5DA **Tel:** 44 02072 354622
Email: editorial@rina.org.uk

Web site: http://www.rina.org.uk/wt.html
Freq: Bi-Monthly
Circ: 16685 Not Audited
Editor: David Foxwell
Profile: Journal covering the latest advances in the construction, design and outfitting of naval vessels. Includes news and reports on ship technology.
Ad Rate: Full Page Colour £2980.00
MAGAZINE
Defense & National Security, Marine & Boat Trade

Warship World
981979
Editorial: Unit 6B, Heathlands Road, Liskeard PL14 4DH **Tel:** 44 01579 343663
Email: warshipworld@navybooks.com
Web site: https://www.navybooks.com/warship-world-magazine-products.html
Freq: Bi-Monthly
Circ: 4000 Not Audited
Editor: Steve Bush
Profile: Magazine covering all aspects of the old and new Royal Navy, including ship preservation, disposals, news on the RFA and RMAS and an overseas section.
MAGAZINE
Armed Forces

Warships International Fleet Review
982812
Editorial: Drury Lane, St. Leonards-on-Sea TN38 9BJ **Tel:** 44 01424 723167
Email: editor@warshipsifr.com
Web site: www.warshipsifr.com
Freq: Monthly
Circ: 16000 Not Audited
Editor: Iain Ballantyne
Profile: Magazine containing information on the latest developments in the world's navies, topics include news, news analysis, fleet profiles, type/class profiles of warships, commentaries on geo-political events involving navies, naval heritage/history and books covered, Amphibious forces and their missions, maritime aviation and defence industry news topics relating to naval forces.
Ad Rate: Full Page Colour £500.00
MAGAZINE
Armed Forces, Marine & Boat Trade

The Warwick Boar
998656
Editorial: SUHQ, Floor Two, University of Warwick, University Road, Coventry CV4 7AL **Tel:** 44 02476 572777
Email: editor@theboar.org
Web site: www.theboar.org
Freq: Bi-Weekly
Circ: 3000 Not Audited
MAGAZINE
Student Lifestyle

Warwickshire Life
982541
Editorial: Archant House, Oriel Road, Cheltenham, Cheltenham GL50 1BB
Tel: 44 01242 216050
Email: editorial@warwickshirelifemagazine.co.uk
Web site: www.warwickshirelife.co.uk
Freq: Daily
Circ: 49531 Cision Digital Reach
MAGAZINE (ONLINE)
Regional General Interest

Waste Management World
983593
Editorial: The Water Tower, Gunpowder Mill, Powdermill Lane, London EN9 1BN
Tel: 44 01992 656600
Web site: http://www.waste-management-world.com
Freq: Bi-Monthly
Circ: 20000 Not Audited
Profile: Magazine focusing on sustainable waste management including news, articles and forthcoming events.
Ad Rate: Full Page Mono £2400.00
Ad Rate: Full Page Colour £3180.00
MAGAZINE
Hygiene

Watch Agora
1054535
Tel: 44 02002 224044
Web site: www.watch-agora.com

Freq: Daily
Circ: 25201 Cision Digital Reach
MAGAZINE (ONLINE)
Luxury Goods

WatchPro
986821
Editorial: ITP Promedia, 16-25 Bastwick Street, London EC1V 3PS
Tel: 44 02031 764228
Email: info@watchpro.com
Web site: www.watchpro.com
Freq: Monthly
Circ: 5500 Not Audited
Profile: WatchPro is a free subscription magazine containing watch news, features and products.
MAGAZINE
Fashion

Water Craft
986781
Editorial: Bridge Shop, Gweek, Helston, Helston TR12 6UD **Tel:** 44 01326 221424
Email: ed@watercraft-magazine.com
Web site: http://watercraft-magazine.com
Freq: Bi-Monthly
Circ: 9000 Not Audited
MAGAZINE
Boating & Yachting, Marine & Boat Trade

Waterfront
984570
Editorial: Beaconsfield House, 1 Beaconsfield Road, Farnworth, Widnes WA8 9LB **Tel:** 44 03339 003000
Web site: www.waterfrontmagazines.co.uk
Freq: Monthly
Circ: 30000 Not Audited
Profile: Luxury lifestyle magazine covering fashion, motors, travel, homes, events and happenings.
Ad Rate: Full Page Colour £1950.00
MAGAZINE
Luxury Goods, Regional General Interest

Waterfront (Swansea)
998546
Editorial: Swansea University Student Union, Union House, Singleton Park, Swansea SA2 8PP **Tel:** 44 01792 295466
Email: waterfronteditor@ swanseastudentmedia.com
Web site: www.waterfrontonline.co.uk
Freq: Bi-Weekly Not Audited
MAGAZINE
Student Lifestyle

Waterlines
984070
Editorial: The Schumacher Centre, Bourton on Dunsmore, Rugby, Rugby CV23 9QZ
Tel: 44 01926 634400
Email: news@practicalaction.org.uk
Web site: www.practicalaction.org/ waterlines
Freq: Quarterly
Circ: 700 Not Audited
Profile: Journal covering all aspects of water supply and sanitation in developing countries. First published in 1979, the publication has an average of 80 pages per issue. Aimed at water and sanitation engineers within international development agencies.
Ad Rate: Full Page Mono £500.00
Ad Rate: Full Page Colour £900.00
MAGAZINE
Charitable Foundations, Water & Sanitation

Waterski & Wakeboard
982307
Editorial: The Forum, Hanworth Lane, Chertsey, London KT16 9JX
Tel: 44 01932 560007
Email: editor@bwsf.co.uk
Web site: www.britishwaterski.org.uk
Freq: Quarterly
Circ: 10500 Not Audited
Editor: Nikki Patefield
MAGAZINE
Swimming/Watersports

Waterways
982218
Editorial: Island House, Moor Road, Chesham HP5 1WA **Tel:** 44 01494 783453
Email: iwa@waterways.org.uk
Web site: www.waterways.org.uk
Freq: Quarterly

Circ: 13000 Not Audited
Editor: Sarah Henshaw
MAGAZINE
Boating & Yachting

Waterways World
982219
Tel: 44 01283 742950
Email: editorial@waterwaysworld.com
Web site: www.waterwaysworld.com
Freq: Monthly
Circ: 8803 Not Audited
Editor: Bobby Cowling
Profile: Magazine covering inland waterways at home and abroad. Includes cruising, boats and boating and history. Read by people owning or interested in narrowboats and river cruisers.
Ad Rate: Full Page Colour £709.00
MAGAZINE
Boating & Yachting

Watkins: Mind Body Spirit
997164
Editorial: 4a Woodside Road, Southbourne, Bournemouth, Bournemouth BH5 2AZ
Tel: 44 01202 424695
Web site: www.watkinsbooks.com/mbs
Freq: Quarterly
Circ: 31000 Not Audited
Editor: Stephen Gawtry
MAGAZINE
Literature

Wattle Publishing
997073
Editorial: Third Floor, 207 Regent Street, London W1B 3HH
Email: enquiries@wattlepublishing.com
Web site: www.wattlepublishing.com
Freq: Daily
Circ: 1988 Cision Digital Reach
MAGAZINE (ONLINE)
Literature, Luxury Goods

Waveguide
984717
Editorial: 42 Windsor Court, Sunbury-on-Thames TW16 7RA
Web site: www.waveguide.co.uk
Freq: Daily
Circ: 6028 Cision Digital Reach
Editor: John Cull
MAGAZINE (ONLINE)
Broadcasting

Wavelength
983123
Editorial: 49 Trebarwith Crescent, Newquay, Newquay TR7 1BZ **Tel:** 44 01637 222580
Email: hello@wlmedia.co.uk
Web site: wavelengthmag.co.uk
Freq: Monthly
Circ: 45000 Not Audited
Editor: Steve Bough
Profile: Surfing magazine covering all aspects of the British and international surf scene.
Ad Rate: Full Page Colour £960.00
MAGAZINE
Swimming/Watersports

WDPJ
998033
Editorial: 2 High Street, Stockbridge, Stockbridge SO20 6EY
Web site: www.wdpj.co.uk
Circ: 3203 Cision Digital Reach
MAGAZINE (ONLINE)
News & Current Affairs

We Are Family
987173
Tel: 44 01173 003614
Web site: http://www.wearefamilymagazine. co.uk
Freq: Quarterly
Circ: 5000 Not Audited
Profile: A subscription based lifestyle magazine aimed at the LGBTQ community, that celebrates and supports lesbian, gay, bisexual and transgender families. It features content of interest to LGBTQ parents and grandparents, straight parents with LGBTQ children, as well as young people coming to terms with their sexuality.
MAGAZINE
Family & Parenting, LGBT, Sexuality

We Got Served
995401
Editorial: 7 The Woodlands, Towcester NN12 8TS **Tel:** 44 01327 856908
Web site: www.wegotserved.com
Freq: Daily
Circ: 259490 Cision Digital Reach
Editor: Terry Walsh
MAGAZINE (ONLINE)
Audio Video Trade, Cameras, Consumer Electronics, Mobile Electronics, Movies & Video

We Heart Living
988206
Editorial: We Heart Living, Unit 011 Netil House, 1 Westgate Street, Hackney E8 3RL
Web site: http://weheartliving.com/
Freq: Daily
Circ: 15960 Cision Digital Reach
Profile: Website covering fitness, exercise, healthy eating, wellbeing, style and beauty.
MAGAZINE (ONLINE)
Beauty & Grooming, Cooking & Baking, Cosmetics, Fashion, Fitness & Exercise, Hair, Health & Medicine, Nutrition

We Love Pop
986309
Editorial: 1st Floor, The Yellow Building, 1 Nicholas Road, London W11 4AN
Tel: 44 02032 200400
Web site: www.welovepopmag.co.uk
Freq: Monthly
Circ: 26615 Not Audited
Editor: Malcolm MacKenzie
Profile: Magazine covering pop music including interviews with pop music artists. Aimed at teenage girls aged between 13 and 15 years old.
MAGAZINE
Pop Music, Teen/Young Adult

Wealden Times
984154
Editorial: Kettle Chambers, 21 Stone Street, Cranbrook, Cranbrook TN17 3HF
Tel: 44 01580 714705
Email: info@wealdentimes.co.uk
Web site: www.wealdentimes.co.uk
Freq: Monthly
Circ: 20500 Not Audited
Editor: Lucy Fleming
Profile: Magazine covering homes, gardens, education, health and beauty, locally grown food and drink and a monthly French feature.
Ad Rate: Full Page Colour £915.00
MAGAZINE
Regional General Interest

Wealth & Finance International
997620
Editorial: 1st Floor, Suite F, The Maltsters, 1-2 Wetmore Road, Barton-under-Needwood DE14 1LS **Tel:** 44 02037 256842
Email: editor@wealthandfinance-intl.com
Web site: wealthandfinance-intl.com
Freq: Monthly
Circ: 130000 Not Audited
Editor: Kanchan Thapa
MAGAZINE
Banking, Bonds, Commodities, Economics, Financial Markets, Investment Banking, Personal Finance

The Wealth Scene
988782
Email: admin@thewealthscene.com
Web site: www.thewealthscene.com
Freq: Daily
Circ: 12908 Cision Digital Reach
MAGAZINE (ONLINE)
Luxury Goods

Wear & Where
987559
Email: info@wearandwhere.co.uk
Web site: www.wearandwhere.co.uk
Freq: Daily
Circ: 8657 Cision Digital Reach
MAGAZINE (ONLINE)
Airline Inflight, Beauty & Grooming, Cooking & Baking, Cosmetics, Family & Parenting, Fashion, Hair, Health & Medicine, Railroad, Relationships

WeAr Magazine
996074
Editorial: 67 Elgin Crescent, Unit 4, London W11 2JE **Tel:** 44 02074 604655

Email: sv@wear-magazine.com
Web site: www.wear-magazine.com
Freq: Quarterly Not Audited
MAGAZINE
Fashion

wearable tech
997672
Web site: http://www.wearabletechnology-news.com
Freq: Daily
Circ: 26822 Cision Digital Reach
Editor: Ryan Daws
MAGAZINE (ONLINE)
Electronics

Web Designer
981024
Editorial: Richmond House, 33 Richmond Hill, Bournemouth, Bournemouth BH2 6EZ
Tel: 44 01202 586200
Email: hello@gadgetdaily.xyz
Web site: www.webdesignermag.co.uk
Freq: Monthly
Circ: 224272 Not Audited
Editor: Steve Jenkins
Profile: Magazine providing advice and practical information on all aspects of Internet web design. Web Designer targets online creatives and industry professionals. The monthly title offers practical projects spanning XHTML, CSS, Flash and WordPress as well as features and interviews with the web community's most influential people. Each issue contains Industry section covering news and views from the trade and a free CD of useful resources.
Ad Rate: Full Page Colour £2300.00
MAGAZINE
Internet, Personal Computers

Web Newswire
1061229
Email: editor@webnewswire.com
Web site: http://www.webnewswire.com
Freq: Daily
Circ: 127458 Cision Digital Reach
MAGAZINE (ONLINE)
Alternative Medicine, Antique & Collectible Cars, Antiques/Collectibles, Art, Arts, Auto Aftermarket, Automakers, Automotive, Banking, Bars, Clubs & Pubs

Web User
981515
Editorial: 31 - 32 Alfred Place, London WC1E 7DP **Tel:** 44 02079 076000
Email: webuser@dennis.co.uk
Web site: www.webuser.co.uk
Freq: Bi-Weekly
Circ: 28298 Not Audited
Profile: Magazine offering advice and tips on how to make the most of your time on the Internet. Covers features, news and product/ software reviews. Aimed at web users of all ages and levels of ability.
Ad Rate: Full Page Colour £1945.00
MAGAZINE
Internet

Website
989666
Editorial: 216 Christchurch Road, Newport, Newport NP19 8BJ
Web site: www.fairway.org.uk
Circ: 548 Cision Digital Reach
MAGAZINE (ONLINE)
News & Current Affairs

Wed magazine - Cornwall
996727
Editorial: 28 Reens Crescent, Heamoor, Penzance, Penzance TR18 3HW
Tel: 44 01736 331456
Email: wed@wedmagazine.co.uk
Web site: www.wedmagazine.co.uk
Freq: Quarterly
Circ: 16000 Not Audited
Editor: Rebecca Matthews
MAGAZINE
Weddings

Wed magazine - Devon
988238
Editorial: 28 Reens Crescent, Heamoor, Penzance, Penzance TR18 3HW
Tel: 44 01736 331456
Email: wed@wedmagazine.co.uk
Web site: www.wedmagazine.co.uk
Freq: Quarterly

Consumer Magazines

Circ: 16000 Not Audited
Editor: Rebecca Matthews
MAGAZINE
Weddings

WEDDING   982427

Editorial: The Tower, Phoenix Square,
Wyncolls Road, Colchester CO4 9HU
Tel: 44 01206 851117
Email: online@weddingmagazine.co.uk
Web site: http://www.
weddingandweddingflowers.co.uk/
Freq: Monthly
Circ: 91864 Cision Digital Reach
Profile: Supplement of Image magazine.
MAGAZINE (ONLINE)
Weddings

Wedding Finder   997818

Editorial: Media Chameleon Ltd, Suite 6B(i),
Britannia House, Leagrave Road, Luton LU3
1RJ Tel: 44 01582 488385
Email: info@mediachameleon.co.uk
Web site: www.theweddingfinder.co.uk
Freq: Annual
Circ: 121700 Not Audited
MAGAZINE
Weddings

Wedding Flowers   982429

Editorial: The Tower, Phoenix Square,
Wyncolls Road, Colchester CO4 9HU
Tel: 44 01206 851117
Email: online@weddingmagazine.co.uk
Web site: http://www.
weddingandweddingflowers.co.uk/
Freq: Bi-Monthly
Circ: 90222 Cision Digital Reach
Editor: Laura Atri
Profile: Magazine covering all aspects of
planning wedding flowers including the
bride's bouquet, reception flowers and
fashion. Aimed at brides-to-be.
Ad Rate: Full Page Colour £5050.00
MAGAZINE (ONLINE)
Weddings

Wedding Ideas   983318

Editorial: Creech Castle, Taunton TA1 2DX
Tel: 44 01823 288344
Email: hello@weddingideasmag.com
Web site: www.weddingideasmagazine.co.
uk
Freq: Monthly
Circ: 23355 Not Audited
Profile: Magazine covering all aspects of
getting married including dresses, caterers,
venues, honeymoons, flowers, hair and
beauty.
Ad Rate: Full Page Colour £2000.00
MAGAZINE
Weddings

The Wedding Planner   998864

Editorial: Clyde House, Sand Lane, Northill,
Biggleswade SG18 9AE
Tel: 44 01767 626111
Email: info@the-weddingplanner.com
Web site: http://www.the-weddingplanner.
com
Freq: Semi-Annual
Circ: 120000 Not Audited
Editor: Claire Cook
MAGAZINE
Weddings

Wedding Venues and Services

998617
Editorial: Shire House, Shire Lane,
Chorleywood, London WD3 5NR
Tel: 44 01923 283443
Email: info@weddingvenues.co.uk
Web site: www.weddingvenues.co.uk
Freq: Quarterly
Circ: 30000 Not Audited
Editor: Abigael Sullivan
MAGAZINE
Weddings

The Week   982139

Editorial: 31 - 32 Alfred Place, London
WC1E 7DP Tel: 44 02079 076180
Email: editorialadmin@theweek.co.uk

Web site: www.theweek.co.uk
Freq: Weekly
Circ: 201932 Not Audited
Profile: Magazine containing a digest of the
best items from the British and foreign
media, including news, opinion, business,
arts, lifestyle, celebrities, sports as well as
the forthcoming events and exhibitions in the
industry. First published in 1995. Aimed at
professional adults working and living in and
around London.
Ad Rate: Full Page Colour £5748.00
MAGAZINE
International News, National News

The Week Junior   1053007

Tel: 44 02079 076000
Web site: www.theweekjunior.co.uk
Freq: Weekly
Circ: 32000 Not Audited
Editor: Anna Bassi
MAGAZINE
International News, National News

Weekender Life   995378

Editorial: Unit A302, Tower Bridge Business
Complex, Clements Road, London SE16
4DG Tel: 44 02072 315258
Email: news@weekender.co.uk
Web site: www.myweekender.co.uk/
Freq: Bi-Weekly
Circ: 70000 Not Audited
MAGAZINE
Regional General Interest

The Weekly Gleaner   982579

Editorial: Unit 236, Elephant & Castle
Shopping Centre, London SE1 6TE
Tel: 44 02075 100340
Email: george.ruddock@gleaneruk.com
Web site: www.jamaica-gleaner.com
Freq: Weekly
Circ: 18000 Not Audited
Profile: Publication containing current
affairs, news and an entertainment guide of
interest to the Jamaica and Caribbean
communities in the UK.
Ad Rate: Full Page Mono £2040.00
Ad Rate: Full Page Colour £2652.00
MAGAZINE
Americas, International News

The Weekly News   996029

Editorial: The Weekly News, 107 Fleet
Street, London EC4A 2HS
Tel: 44 01382 223131
Email: weeklynews@dcthomson.co.uk
Web site: www.twns.co.uk
Freq: Weekly
Circ: 15145 Not Audited
Editor: Richard Prest
Profile: The Weekly News is a publication
which bridges the gap between local
newspapers, Sunday tabloids and women's
weeklies. Includes the following sections:
Soap Gossip and Celebrity Interviews,
Human Interest Stories, Film and DVD
Releases, Sport Articles and TV and Satellite
Viewing. Read by adults primarily 35 years
old and over.
Ad Rate: Full Page Mono £5232.00
Ad Rate: Full Page Colour £6278.00
MAGAZINE
Broadcasting, Celebrities, Gardening,
Movies & Video

Weekly Potrika   985070

Editorial: O'Leary Square, 218 Jubilee
Street, London E1 3BS
Tel: 44 02074 239270
Email: info@potrika.com
Web site: http://potrika.com/
Freq: Weekly
Circ: 50000 Not Audited
Editor: Mohammed Chowdhury
MAGAZINE
Asia, Expatriates

Weight Watchers Magazine

981834
Editorial: 3-7 Herbal Hill, London EC1R 5EJ
Tel: 44 02077 757775
Email: pressoffice@weight-watchers.co.uk
Web site: https://www.weightwatchers.com/
uk/what-we-offer/magazine

Freq: Monthly
Circ: 100297 Not Audited
Profile: Magazine covering diet and nutrition
including celebrity profiles, general women's
interest features and low fat recipes. Read
by members of Weight Watchers and those
interested in slimming.
Ad Rate: Full Page Colour £5500.00
MAGAZINE
Fitness & Exercise, Health & Medicine,
Nutrition

Wellbeing Magazine   990468

Editorial: 2 The Hall, Turners Green Road,
Wadhurst, Wadhurst TN5 6TR
Web site: http://wellbeingmagazine.com/
Freq: Bi-Monthly
Circ: 12397 Cision Digital Reach
Profile: Magazine looking at the food we eat,
how to look after our bodies and minds as
well as our home and working environment.
Editorial features are centred around
women's and men's health, mental health,
fitness, weightloss, posture, beauty, eco
products and wellness travel features. Also
includes tried and tested products and
treatments and information on illnesses such
as diabetes, asthma, heart conditions and
cancer and readers offers, competitions and
book reviews.Aimed at those interested in
taking responsibility for their own health and
wellbeing as well as for their families.
Ad Rate: Full Page Colour £2450.00
MAGAZINE (ONLINE)
Alternative Medicine, Cooking & Baking,
Fitness & Exercise, Food, Grocery Stores,
Nutrition, Organic Food, Regional General
Interest, Restaurant Reviews,
Vegetarianism & Veganism

Wellbeloved   996864

Editorial: Fourth Floor, Embassy House,
Queens Avenue, Bristol BS8 1SB
Tel: 44 01179 251696
Email: reception@specialistuk.com
Web site: www.wellbeloved.com
Freq: 3 Times/Year Not Audited
Editor: Anna Harris
MAGAZINE
Nature & Wildlife

Welldoing.org   996660

Editorial: 4 Dunmore Road, London NW6
6TR Tel: 44 02089 308906
Email: mailwelldoing@gmail.com
Web site: www.welldoing.org
Freq: Daily
Circ: 18183 Cision Digital Reach
MAGAZINE (ONLINE)
Alternative Medicine, Health & Medicine,
LGBT, Neurology, Relationships, Sexuality

Welltodo   997359

Editorial: 14 Bedford Square, London WC1B
3JA
Email: hello@welltodolondon.com
Web site: http://www.welltodolondon.com/
Freq: Daily
Circ: 30189 Cision Digital Reach
MAGAZINE (ONLINE)
Alcohol & Spirits, Audio Video Trade,
Bars, Clubs & Pubs, Beauty & Grooming,
Beer, Beverages, Business, Cameras,
Consumer Electronics, Cooking & Baking

WeLove2Ski   985405

Editorial: 5 Earlsdown, Winchester,
Winchester SO23 0JW Tel: 44 01962 868677
Email: editor@welove2ski.com
Web site: www.welove2ski.com
Freq: Daily
Circ: 39076 Cision Digital Reach
Editor: Felice Hardy
Profile: Website covering skiing. The
Welove2ski discusses skiing, sharing advice
and tips on 'how to ski', snow reports, ski
resorts and information for ski enthusiasts.
MAGAZINE (ONLINE)
Winter Sports

WeLoveDates   987434

Tel: 44 08000 334053
Email: contact@welovedates.com
Web site: www.welovedates.com
Freq: Daily

Circ: 33805 Cision Digital Reach
MAGAZINE (ONLINE)
Relationships

Welsh Border Life   984304

Tel: 44 01691 662709
Email: editorial@borderpublishing.com
Web site: www.borderpublishing.com
Freq: Monthly
Circ: 10000 Not Audited
Editor: Charlotte Van Praagh
MAGAZINE
Regional General Interest

Welsh Coastal Life   986355

Tel: 44 01691 662709
Email: editorial@borderpublishing.com
Web site: www.borderpublishing.com
Freq: Monthly
Circ: 43000 Not Audited
Editor: Charlotte Van Praagh
Profile: Magazine covering property, homes,
interiors, art, crafts, product page, literature,
poetry, walking, hostels, wildlife, history,
education, food and drink, fashion,
gardening, motoring, finance and what's on.
Aimed at residents and visitors to Wales.
MAGAZINE
Regional General Interest

Welsh Country   984901

Editorial: Welsh Country, Aberbanc,
Llandysul, Newcastle Emlyn SA44 5NP
Tel: 44 01559 372010
Email: info@welshcountry.co.uk
Web site: www.welshcountry.co.uk
Freq: Bi-Monthly
Circ: 9984 Not Audited
Editor: Kath Rhodes
Profile: Magazine covering areas of interest
to Welsh people and those living and visiting
Wales. Features covered include wildlife,
property, Welsh food as well as recipes,
farmers markets, farm shops, food festivals,
eating out, fishing, places to stay, interviews,
gardening, rural and country matters, book
reviews, CD review, wine, motoring, diary
dates, green issues, conservation and
horoscopes.
Ad Rate: Full Page Colour £1150.00
MAGAZINE
Regional General Interest

Welsh Football Magazine

1053782
Email: info@welsh-football.net
Web site: www.welsh-football.net
Freq: Bi-Monthly
MAGAZINE
News & Current Affairs

Welsh Rider   995017

Editorial: Unit 2 Devizes Trade Centre,
Hopton Park, Devizes, Devizes SN10 2EH
Tel: 44 01380 730888
Email: sales@redpin.co.uk
Web site: www.welshrider.co.uk
Freq: Monthly Not Audited
Profile: Magazine covering all-round
equestrian interests and disciplines, feature
articles, product reviews and events.
MAGAZINE
Equestrian Sports

We're News (News
International's in-house
newspaper)   998769

Editorial: 1 London Bridge Street, London
SE1 9GF Tel: 44 02077 826311
Web site: http://www.news.co.uk/
Freq: Quarterly
Circ: 6000 Not Audited
Editor: Neal Harrington
MAGAZINE
News & Current Affairs

Wessex Scene   981782

Editorial: Southampton University Students
Uni, University Rd, Highfield, Southampton
SO17 1BJ Tel: 44 02380 595200
Email: news@wessexscene.co.uk
Web site: www.wessexscene.co.uk

Freq: Monthly Not Audited
MAGAZINE
Student Lifestyle

West Bridgford Wire　997824
Editorial: Bridgford Business Centre, Bridgford Road, West Bridgford, Nottingham NG2 6AU **Tel:** 44 01159 775445
Email: westbridgfordwire@gmail.com
Web site: westbridgfordwire.com
Freq: Daily
Circ: 16941 Cision Digital Reach
Editor: Pat Gamble
MAGAZINE (ONLINE)
Regional General Interest

West Essex Life　985794
Editorial: 35a Marsh Hill, Homerton, London E9 5QA **Tel:** 44 01473 230023
Email: editor.westessex@archant.co.uk
Web site: www.westessexlife.co.uk/home
Freq: Monthly
Circ: 25000 Not Audited
Profile: Magazine covering leisure, lifestyle, motoring, property, interiors, men's and women's fashion, food and drink, events and exhibitions.
Ad Rate: Full Page Colour £1439.00
MAGAZINE
Regional General Interest

West Hampstead Life　988264
Web site: http://www.westhampsteadlife.com/
Freq: Daily
Circ: 14728 Cision Digital Reach
MAGAZINE (ONLINE)
Regional General Interest

West Highland News Plus
998794
Editorial: Ardsheal, Orchy Gardens, Oban PA34 4JR **Tel:** 44 01631 562915
Email: westhighlandline@btinternet.com
Web site: www.westhighlandline.org.uk
Freq: 3 Times/Year
Circ: 700 Not Audited
Editor: Doug Carmichael
MAGAZINE
Railroad

West Kirby Today　1055145
Web site: westkirby.today
Freq: Daily
Circ: 4550 Cision Digital Reach
Editor: Mark Thomas
MAGAZINE (ONLINE)
Regional, Regional General Interest

West London Living　985111
Editorial: flat 1, 39 Norland Square, London W11 4PZ
Email: lucy.land@westlondonliving.co.uk
Web site: www.westlondonliving.co.uk
Freq: Daily
Circ: 9631 Cision Digital Reach
Editor: Olivia Allwood-Mollon
Profile: Website covering lifestyle. The West London LIVING discusses the latest news on local life, culture, fashion, restaurants, bars, pubs, sport, health and beauty.
MAGAZINE (ONLINE)
Regional General Interest

West Wales Chronicle　1054455
Editorial: Units 1-4, Llanelli Enterprise Workshops, 100 Lower Trostre Road, Llanelli SA15 9EB **Tel:** 44 01554 772056
Email: editor@westwaleschronicle.co.uk
Web site: www.westwaleschronicle.co.uk
Freq: Daily
Circ: 12486 Cision Digital Reach
MAGAZINE (ONLINE)
Regional

West Weddings　982419
Editorial: 4th Floor, 1 Temple Way, Bristol BS2 0BY **Tel:** 44 01179 343000
Email: westweddings@b-nm.co.uk
Web site: http://www.west-weddings.co.uk
Freq: Quarterly
Circ: 10000 Not Audited

Profile: Blog covering bridal fashion and weddings.
MAGAZINE
Weddings

West World　998401
Editorial: UWESU, 5th Floor, F Block, Frenchay Campus, Coldharbour Lane, Bristol BS1 1QY **Tel:** 44 01173 282842
Email: westworld@westerneye.net
Web site: www.westerneye.net
Freq: Bi-Monthly Not Audited
MAGAZINE
Student Lifestyle

Westcountry FOODLOVER
986679
Tel: 44 01458 224555
Email: editor@foodlovermagazine.com
Web site: http://www.foodlovermagazine.com/
Freq: Monthly
Circ: 29000 Not Audited
Editor: Emily Knight
MAGAZINE
Cooking & Baking, Restaurant Reviews

Westender Magazine　995946
Editorial: 5 Ormiston Avenue, Scotstoun, Glasgow G14 9DT
Web site: http://www.westendermagazine.com
Freq: Bi-Monthly Not Audited
MAGAZINE
News & Current Affairs

Western Eye　994650
Editorial: UWESU, 5th Floor, F Block, Frenchay Campus, Coldharbour Lane, Bristol BS1 1QY **Tel:** 44 01173 282842
Email: editor@westerneye.net
Web site: www.westerneye.net
Freq: Bi-Monthly
Circ: 6000 Not Audited
MAGAZINE
Student Lifestyle

Western Horse UK　984559
Editorial: 219 Creek Road, March, March PE15 8RY
Email: info@westernhorseuk.com
Web site: www.westernhorseuk.com
Freq: Bi-Monthly
Circ: 2000 Not Audited
Profile: Magazine that covers western riding and American horses, featuring all breeds from the American paint horse, appaloosa, quarter horse, morgan, saddlebred and paso fino and covering all disciplines and activities.
Ad Rate: Full Page Colour £395.00
MAGAZINE
Equestrian Sports

Westside　982550
Editorial: 6 Broadfield Court, Broadfield Business Park, Sheffield S8 0XF
Tel: 44 01142 506300
Email: westside@rmcmedia.co.uk
Web site: http://www.rmcmedia.co.uk/magazines/westside/?cI=21
Freq: Monthly
Circ: 20000 Not Audited
MAGAZINE
Regional General Interest

WGSN　983710
Editorial: AirW1, 2nd Floor, 20 Air Street, London W1B 5AN **Tel:** 44 02077 156200
Email: news@wgsn.com
Web site: www.wgsn.com/en
Freq: Daily
Circ: 187143 Cision Digital Reach
Editor: Sarah Owen
Profile: Website covering B2B trends, research and news for the fashion industry. Contains store reports and photos, lifestyle and street reports, catwalk show reports, also technical and production news.
MAGAZINE (ONLINE)
Fashion

Whale & Dolphin　997839
Editorial: Brookfield House, 38 St Paul Street, Chippenham, Glasgow QN16 1LJ
Tel: 44 01249 449500
Email: info@whales.org
Web site: uk.whales.org
Freq: Quarterly
Circ: 20000 Not Audited
MAGAZINE
Energy & Environment

What Car?　982632
Editorial: Teddington Studios, Teddington, London TW11 9BE **Tel:** 44 02082 675000
Email: editorial@whatcar.com
Web site: http://www.whatcar.com/
Freq: Monthly
Circ: 56177 Not Audited
Editor: Steve Huntingford
Profile: Magazine with news and specifications on the latest cars, plus advice on purchasing secondhand and new cars. Features include road tests, safety and security tips and information on used cars. First published in 1973. Aimed at prospective car buyers.
Ad Rate: Full Page Colour £13410.00
MAGAZINE
Automotive, Driving

What Doctors Don't Tell You
984563
Editorial: Unit 9, Woodman Works, 204 Durnsford Road, London SW19 8DR
Tel: 44 02089 449555
Web site: www.wddty.com
Freq: Monthly
Circ: 20000 Not Audited
Editor: Bryan Hubbard; **Editor:** Lynne McTaggart
Profile: Newsletter covering alternative approaches to orthodox medicine.
Ad Rate: Full Page Colour £1500.00
MAGAZINE
Alternative Medicine, Fitness & Exercise, Health & Medicine, Nutrition

What Hi-Fi?　981743
Editorial: Teddington Studios, Broom Road, Teddington, London TW11 9BE
Tel: 44 02082 675000
Email: whathifi@haymarket.com
Web site: www.whathifi.com
Freq: Monthly
Circ: 28935 Not Audited
Profile: Magazine containing technical features and reviews of the latest hi-fi and home cinema equipment including news on consumer electronics, television, MP3 players, tests and advice sections with step-by-step information, music and movies. First published in 1976. Aimed at people aged 16 years and upwards interested in the latest hi-fi and home cinema.
Ad Rate: Full Page Colour £5800.00
MAGAZINE
Audio Video Trade, Movies & Video

What House?　900057
Editorial: 5th Floor, 291 - 299 Borough High Street, London SE1 1JG
Tel: 44 02079 401070
Web site: www.whathouse.com
Freq: Daily
Circ: 44802 Cision Digital Reach
Editor: Keith Osborne
Profile: Website covering property. The What House? website shares the latest news and information on new and resale houses, mortgages, developing a property and interiors. Includes listings of 1000s of brand new homes for sale.
MAGAZINE (ONLINE)
Property Management & Maintenance, Real Estate, Residential Real Estate

What Investment　979825
Editorial: Vitesse Media Plc, 5th Floor, 14 Bonhill Street, London EC2A 4BX
Tel: 44 02072 507010
Web site: www.whatinvestment.co.uk
Freq: Monthly
Circ: 7240 Not Audited
Profile: Magazine focusing on all aspects of personal finance and investment including

wealth managament, in-depth news and feature coverage of all investment issues. Aimed at the individual investor.
Ad Rate: Full Page Colour £3500.00
MAGAZINE
Banking, Bonds, Corporate Finance, Corporate Management, Emerging Markets, Equities, Financial Markets, Foreign Exchange Market (FOREX), Fund Management, Government

What Mobile　981745
Editorial: 8-10 Godson Street, London N1 9GZ **Tel:** 44 02031 220870
Email: editorial@whatmobile.net
Web site: www.whatmobile.net
Freq: Daily
Circ: 57700 Cision Digital Reach
Profile: Consumer buyers' guide to mobile phones and portable gadgets.
Ad Rate: Full Page Colour £2100.00
MAGAZINE (ONLINE)
Mobile Electronics

What Mortgage　979828
Editorial: 6th Floor, Davis House, 2 Robert Street, Croydon CR0 1QQ
Tel: 44 02082 538600
Web site: www.whatmortgage.co.uk
Freq: Monthly
Circ: 14000 Not Audited
Profile: Magazine providing information on mortgages and home buying related products. Includes mortgage comparison tables with detailed information on the best mortgage deals currently available. Aimed at first-time buyers and those buying as an investment, re-mortgaging or for any other aspect of the purchasing chain.
Ad Rate: Full Page Colour £2780.00
MAGAZINE
Finance

What Motorhome　983052
Editorial: The Maltings, West Street, Bourne, Bourne PE10 9PH **Tel:** 44 01778 391000
Web site: www.outandaboutlive.co.uk/motorhomes/store/subscriptions/what-motorhome/
Freq: Monthly
Circ: 5701 Not Audited
Editor: Peter Vaughan
MAGAZINE
Camping and RV Travel

What Mountain Bike　982675
Editorial: Tower House, Fairfax Street, Bristol BS1 3BN **Tel:** 44 01179 279009
Email: wmb@immediate.co.uk
Web site: www.bikeradar.com/magazine/what-mountain-bike
Freq: Monthly
Circ: 11131 Not Audited
Profile: Product led mountain bike magazine containing guides, bike tests, news, reviews and features. First published in 2000, the publication has an average of 186 pages per issue. Aimed at mountain bike enthusiasts.
Ad Rate: Full Page Colour £1300.00
MAGAZINE
Bicycles

What Pool & Hot Tub　984964
Editorial: Priory Lodge, Halse, Taunton, Taunton TA4 3AE **Tel:** 44 02083 068150
Web site: www.whatpoolandhottubmag.co.uk
Freq: Annual
Circ: 12000 Not Audited
Profile: Magazine covering home, swimming and outdoor living including, swimming pools, spas, hot tubs, saunas and related products.
Ad Rate: Full Page Colour £1250.00
MAGAZINE
Fitness & Exercise

What Uni　1052823
Editorial: 1st Floor, Bedford House, Fulham Green, 69-79 Fulham High St, London SW6 3JW **Tel:** 44 02073 846000
Email: editor@whatuni.com
Web site: www.whatuni.com
Freq: Daily

Consumer Magazines

Circ: 135938 Cision Digital Reach
MAGAZINE (ONLINE)
Alumni, Careers, Education, Student
Lifestyle, Teachers

What Van? 981022
Editorial: Progressive House, 2 Maidstone
Road, London DA14 5HZ
Tel: 44 02082 697741
Email: editorial@whatvan.co.uk
Web site: www.whatvan.co.uk
Freq: Monthly
Circ: 8724 Not Audited
Profile: Guide to buying new vans. Includes
prices, reviews and accessories.
Ad Rate: Full Page Colour £2030.00
MAGAZINE
Automotive

What's Good To Do 986535
Editorial: 69 Ashcroft Road, Luton, Luton
LU2 9AX Tel: 44 07826 524782
Email: info@whatsgoodtodo.com
Web site: http://www.whatsgoodtodo.com/
Freq: Daily
Circ: 1932 Cision Digital Reach
MAGAZINE (ONLINE)
Bars, Clubs & Pubs, Comedy,
Entertainment, Local Entertainment
Guides, Movies & Video, Regional General
Interest, Travel

WhatCulture 986211
Editorial: What Culture LTD 7th Floor, Baltic
Place South Shore Road, Gateshead Quays,
Newcastle NE8 3AE Tel: 44 01914 066484
Email: editor@whatculture.com
Web site: whatculture.com
Freq: Daily
Circ: 10095557 Cision Digital Reach
MAGAZINE (ONLINE)
Broadcasting, Computer & Video Games,
Movies & Video, Music, Pop Music, Rap &
Hip Hop, Soccer

What's Brewing 981748
Editorial: 230 Hatfield Road, St. Albans AL1
4LW Tel: 44 01727 867201
Email: wb.editor@camra.org.uk
Web site: www.camra.org.uk
Freq: Monthly
Circ: 105000 Not Audited
Editor: Tom Stainer
Profile: Newspaper containing brewing
reports, beer (real ale) and cider news.
Includes articles on traditional draught beer
and regular features on microbrewers, pub
preservation, home brewing, bottles beers,
cooking with beer, pubs, pub awards and
campaigns. Aimed at members of CAMRA.
Regular features: Mild Month promotion of
'mild' - a style of beer during the month of
May
Ad Rate: Full Page Mono £1925.00
Ad Rate: Full Page Colour £2950.00
MAGAZINE
Alcohol & Spirits, Beer

What's On (KM Group) 983240
Editorial: Medway House, Ginsbury Close,
Sir Thomas Longley Road, Medway City Est,
Strood, Rochester ME2 4DU
Tel: 44 01622 717880
Email: whatsoneditor@thekmgroup.co.uk
Web site: www.kentonline.co.uk
Freq: Weekly
Circ: 80752 Not Audited
MAGAZINE
Bars, Clubs & Pubs, Comedy,
Entertainment, Local Entertainment
Guides, Movies & Video

Whats on Bristol 996869
Editorial: 62 North Street, Bedminster,
Bristol BS3 1HJ Tel: 44 01179 632263
Web site: http://www.whatsonbristol.co.uk/
Student%20Guide
Freq: Daily
Circ: 365 Cision Digital Reach
Editor: Nikki Cook
MAGAZINE (ONLINE)
Regional General Interest

What's on London 997251
Editorial: Reach Media Limited, 35-37
Blackstock Road, London N4 2JF
Email: info@whats-on-london.co.uk
Web site: http://whatson.london/
Freq: Daily
Circ: 29460 Cision Digital Reach
Editor: Chris Evans
MAGAZINE (ONLINE)
Entertainment, Local Entertainment
Guides, Regional General Interest

What's On Somerset 984562
Editorial: 56/58 Station Road, Taunton,
Taunton TA1 1NS Tel: 44 01823 279008
Email: whatsonsomerset@btinternet.com
Web site: www.whatsonsomerset.com
Freq: Quarterly
Circ: 18000 Not Audited
Profile: Magazine covering a wide variety of
entertainment listings and features about
interesting people and activities in Somerset.
Ad Rate: Full Page Colour £998.00
MAGAZINE
Regional General Interest

What's on TV 982359
Editorial: 161 Marsh Wall, London E14 9AP
Tel: 44 02031 485000
Email: wotv_enquiries@timeinc.com
Web site: www.whatsontv.co.uk
Freq: Weekly
Circ: 885595 Not Audited
Profile: Magazine covering TV listings, TV
features, celebrity gossip and reviews.
Includes latest soap news and gossip,
puzzles and competitions. First published in
1991. Aimed at those interested in TV and
radio programmes.
Ad Rate: Full Page Colour £20160.00
MAGAZINE
Broadcasting, Local Entertainment
Guides

What's on UK 988635
Editorial: P.O Box 6160, Birmingham,
Birmingham B16 8XA Tel: 44 01216 360830
Email: editorial@whatson.uk.com
Web site: uk.whatson.uk.com
Freq: Daily Not Audited
MAGAZINE
Local Entertainment Guides

What's On-Scotland 983871
Editorial: 208-210 Great Junction Street,
Edinburgh, Midlothian, Edinburgh EH6 5LW
Tel: 44 07731 862190
Email: events@whatsonscotland.com
Web site: http://www.whatsonscotland.com
Freq: Monthly
Circ: 8443 Cision Digital Reach
Editor: Tom Hogarth
MAGAZINE (ONLINE)
Regional General Interest

WhatsonBath.co.uk 998681
Editorial: 62 North Street, Bedminster,
Bristol BS3 1HJ Tel: 44 01179 632263
Web site: www.whatsonbath.co.uk
Freq: Daily
Circ: 1919 Cision Digital Reach
Editor: Nikki Cook
MAGAZINE (ONLINE)
Regional General Interest

WhatsonBristol.co.uk 996405
Editorial: 62 North Street, Bedminster,
Bristol BS3 1HJ Tel: 44 01179 632263
Web site: www.whatsonbristol.co.uk
Freq: Daily
Circ: 10637 Cision Digital Reach
Editor: Nikki Cook
MAGAZINE (ONLINE)
Regional General Interest

WhatsonCardiff.co.uk 1104174
Editorial: 62 North Street, Bedminster,
Bristol BS3 1HJ Tel: 44 01179 632263
Web site: www.whatsoncardiff.co.uk
Freq: Daily
Circ: 2377 Cision Digital Reach

Editor: Nikki Cook
MAGAZINE (ONLINE)
Regional General Interest

WhatsOnStage.com 981802
Editorial: 16 Carlisle St, London W1D 3BT
Tel: 44 02073 179100
Email: editorial@whatsonstage.com
Web site: www.whatsonstage.com
Freq: Daily
Circ: 138118 Cision Digital Reach
MAGAZINE (ONLINE)
Theater & Performing Arts

WhatsonWestonsupermare. co.uk 998682
Editorial: 62 North Street, Bedminster,
Bristol BS3 1HJ Tel: 44 01179 632263
Web site: www.whatsonwestonsupermare.
co.uk
Freq: Daily
Circ: 1857 Cision Digital Reach
Editor: Nikki Cook
MAGAZINE (ONLINE)
Regional General Interest

whattodowiththekids.co.uk 987126
Editorial: 92 Whitby Avenue, Guisborough,
Guisborough TS14 7BA
Tel: 44 07812 108372
Email: hello@whattodowiththekids.co.uk
Web site: www.whattodowiththekids.co.uk
Freq: Daily
Circ: 10386 Cision Digital Reach
MAGAZINE (ONLINE)
Family & Parenting

Wheels Within Wales 998964
Email: info@wheelswithinwales.uk
Web site: http://www.wheelswithinwales.uk/
Freq: Daily
Circ: 11901 Cision Digital Reach
Editor: Robin Roberts
MAGAZINE (ONLINE)
Antique & Collectible Cars, Automakers,
Automotive, Driving, Motorcycles,
Motorsports, Off-road & 4-Wheel Drive
Vehicles, Trucks & SUVs

WheelWorldReviews.co.uk 999158
Editorial: 3 Odine Court, Grimsby, Grimsby
DN33 3RH
Email: editor@wheelworldreviews.co.uk
Freq: Daily
Editor: David Hooper
MAGAZINE (ONLINE)
Antique & Collectible Cars, Automakers,
Automotive, Camping and RV Travel,
Driving, Motorcycles, Off-road & 4-Wheel
Drive Vehicles

When Saturday Comes 982254
Editorial: E1 Business Centre, Studio 202, 7
Whitechapel Road, London E1 1DU
Tel: 44 02037 357580
Email: editorial@wsc.co.uk
Web site: www.wsc.co.uk
Freq: Monthly
Circ: 15716 Not Audited
Editor: Andy Lyons
Profile: Magazine containing articles on
football culture from the supporters'
viewpoint. Launched in 1986. Aimed at men
aged between 18 and 34 years old.
Ad Rate: Full Page Colour £2100.00
MAGAZINE
Soccer

Where London 983434
Editorial: 2nd Floor, Samuel House, St
Alban's St, London SW1Y 4SQ
Tel: 44 02072 425222
Web site: mvplondon.net/where-london
Freq: Monthly
Circ: 75542 Not Audited
Profile: Magazine covering London dining,
shopping, entertainment and information.
Contains useful articles, comprehensive
listings and complete guide to the city's top
restaurants, shops, shows, exhibits and

tours. Aimed at travellers that are planning to
visit London.
Ad Rate: Full Page Colour £3920.00
MAGAZINE
Regional General Interest, Travel

Where to Ski and Snowboard 999443
Editorial: Beech House, The Spinney, Hall
Street, Sudbury CO10 9JS
Tel: 44 08449 911123
Email: news@wtss.co.uk
Web site: www.wheretoskiandsnowboard.
com
Freq: Daily
Circ: 8621 Cision Digital Reach
MAGAZINE (ONLINE)
Extreme/Adventure Sports, Winter Sports

WhereCanWeGo.com 984344
Editorial: PO Box 4136, Upper Basildon,
Reading RG8 6BS Tel: 44 01491 671998
Email: info@wherecanwego.com
Web site: www.wherecanwego.com
Freq: Daily
Circ: 55060 Cision Digital Reach
MAGAZINE (ONLINE)
Local Entertainment Guides

Which? 980726
Editorial: 2 Marylebone Road, London NW1
4DF
Email: editor@which.co.uk
Web site: www.which.co.uk
Freq: Monthly
Circ: 519300 Not Audited
Editor: Richard Headland
Profile: Magazine containing product tests
and campaigns for improvements in goods
and services. Includes reports on everything
that affects the quality of life, from everyday
purchases to one-off investments. Aimed at
consumers who want the best products and
services.
MAGAZINE
Antique & Collectible Cars, Architecture &
Design, Audio Video Trade, Automakers,
Automotive, Cameras, Consumer
Electronics, Do-It-Yourself (DIY), Driving,
Electronics

Which? Computing 981625
Editorial: 2 Marylebone Road, London NW1
4DF Tel: 44 02077 707000
Email: computing@which.co.uk
Web site: www.which.co.uk/publications/
magazines/which-computing/
Freq: Bi-Monthly
Circ: 211000 Not Audited
Editor: Richard Parris
Profile: Magazine covering computing and
includes articles on Internet Service
Providers, wireless technology, DVD burners
as well as the latest sports software, from
laptops, printers and broadband to
scanners, shredders and webcams. Also
provides information on what to buy for your
home computer to have it upgraded.
Launched in 2001. Aimed at home computer
owners.Advertising is not accepted.
MAGAZINE
Apple, Personal Computers

Which? Conversation 985614
Editorial: 2 Marylebone Road, London NW1
4DF Tel: 44 02077 707000
Web site: https://conversation.which.co.uk/
Freq: Daily
Circ: 335339 Cision Digital Reach
Editor: Patrick Steen
MAGAZINE (ONLINE)
Alcohol & Spirits, Beauty & Grooming,
Books, Consumer Goods & Products,
Cosmetics, Fashion, Food, Gardening,
Hair, Office Supplies

Which? Gardening 983751
Editorial: 2 Marylebone Road, London NW1
4DF Tel: 44 02077 707000
Email: gardening@which.co.uk
Web site: www.which.co.uk
Freq: Monthly
Circ: 72000 Not Audited
Editor: Ceri Thomas

Profile: Magazine providing advice and new product information for gardeners.
MAGAZINE
Gardening

Which? Money 984038

Editorial: 2 Marylebone Road, London NW1 4DF **Tel:** 44 02077 707000
Web site: www.which.com/money
Freq: Monthly
Circ: 86000 Not Audited
Editor: Harry Rose
Profile: Magazine providing an independent source of information on personal finance. The publication tests household products like washing machines and digital cameras, confronts important consumer issues, tackles from mis-selling to hospital food and commits to providing unbiased advice to consumers. Aimed at consumers.
MAGAZINE
Personal Finance

Which? Travel 982329

Editorial: 2 Marylebone Road, London NW1 4DF **Tel:** 44 02077 707000
Email: travel@which.co.uk
Web site: www.which.co.uk/publications/magazines/which-travel/
Freq: Bi-Monthly
Circ: 55000 Not Audited
Profile: Magazine covering travel and holiday related consumer issues including destinaltions, tour operators, airlines, customer service, and best ways to find value-for-money holidays. Also provides practical travel advice, recommendations, and inspirational ideas. Aimed at consumers who want the best travel products and services.
MAGAZINE
Travel

whichfranchise.com 984423

Editorial: whichfranchise.com, Suite 4/4, 75 Bothwell Street, Glasgow G2 6TS
Tel: 44 01412 040050
Email: enquiry@whichfranchise.com
Web site: www.whichfranchise.com
Freq: Daily
Circ: 37285 Cision Digital Reach
Profile: Website covering franchise information, advice and opportunities.
MAGAZINE (ONLINE)
News & Current Affairs

Whisky Drinker 996244

Editorial: 6 Logie Mill, Edinburgh EH7 4HG
Email: magnus@whisky-drinker.com
Web site: www.whisky-drinker.com
Freq: Daily
Circ: 652 Cision Digital Reach
MAGAZINE (ONLINE)
Alcohol & Spirits

The Whisky Exchange 988394

Editorial: Whitby Ave, London NW10 7SF
Tel: 44 02088 389388
Email: sales@specialitydrinks.com
Web site: www.thewhiskyexchange.com
Freq: Daily
Circ: 1587055 Cision Digital Reach
MAGAZINE (ONLINE)
Alcohol & Spirits

Whisky Magazine 981750

Editorial: St Faiths House, Mountergate, Norwich NR1 1PY **Tel:** 44 01603 633808
Email: editorial@whiskymag.com
Web site: www.whiskymag.com
Freq: Bi-Monthly
Circ: 19300 Not Audited
Profile: Magazine covering news, products, celebrity interviews, whisky tasting plus events and features from around the world.
Ad Rate: Full Page Colour £4845.00
MAGAZINE
Alcohol & Spirits

The White Review 986025

Editorial: 243 Knightsbridge, London SW7 1DN
Email: editors@thewhitereview.org
Web site: www.thewhitereview.org

Freq: Quarterly
Circ: 1500 Not Audited
Profile: Journal covering arts, culture and politics. It features review articles, features and interviews.
MAGAZINE
Art, Literature, Photography, Theater & Performing Arts, Visual Arts

Whitelines Snowboarding 982291

Editorial: 2 Tun Yard, Peardon Street, London SW8 3HT **Tel:** 44 02073 329700
Web site: www.whitelines.com
Freq: Daily
Circ: 609199 Cision Digital Reach
Editor: Ed Blomfield
MAGAZINE (ONLINE)
Winter Sports

Whizz Pop Bang 1104176

Tel: 44 03302 233790
Email: hello@whizzpopbang.com
Web site: whizzpopbang.com
Freq: Monthly
MAGAZINE
Elementary School, Science

Who Cares? 986019

Editorial: 15-18 White Lion Street, London N1 9PG **Tel:** 44 02072 513117
Email: magazine@thewhocarestrust.org.uk
Web site: www.thewhocarestrust.org.uk
Freq: Quarterly
Circ: 15000 Not Audited
Editor: Emma Price
Profile: Magazine covering teenage interest including celebrities, photostories, interviews, letters, poems and reviews of films, games and music Read by 10 to 18 year olds in public care throughout the UK.
MAGAZINE
Charitable Foundations, Teen/Young Adult

Who Cares?Junior 999286

Editorial: 15-18 White Lion Street, London N1 9PG **Tel:** 44 02072 513117
Email: mailbox@thewhocarestrust.org.uk
Web site: www.thewhocarestrust.org.uk
Freq: Quarterly
Circ: 9000 Not Audited
Editor: Emma Price
MAGAZINE
Charitable Foundations, Teen/Young Adult

Who Do You Think You Are? 984554

Editorial: Tower House, Fairfax Street, Bristol BS1 3BN **Tel:** 44 01173 147400
Email: editorial@bbcwhodoyouthinkyouare.com
Web site: http://www.immediate.co.uk/brands/who-do-you-think-you-are/
Freq: Monthly
Circ: 17513 Not Audited
Editor: Sarah Williams
MAGAZINE
Family & Parenting, History

Wholesale Manager 985335

Editorial: 12 Kings Park, Primrose Hill, Kings Langley, London WD4 8ST
Tel: 44 01923 272960
Email: mail@wholesalemanager.co.uk
Web site: www.wholesalemanager.co.uk
Freq: Bi-Monthly
Circ: 5126 Not Audited
Profile: Magazine delivering a mix of industry news, product reviews, interviews and features on a wide spectrum of industry topics. Aimed at senior buyers, directors, managers and other decision makers within the UK wholesale and cash and carry industry.
Ad Rate: Full Page Colour £1690.00
MAGAZINE
Alcohol & Spirits, Food, Retail Management

Wholesale News 981294

Editorial: Suite A, Arun House, Office Village, River Way, Uckfield TN22 1SL
Tel: 44 01825 983105
Email: info@lewisbusinessmedia.co.uk
Web site: www.wholesalenews.co.uk
Freq: Monthly
Circ: 4648 Not Audited
Editor: Kevin Whitlock
Profile: Magazine covering all aspects of the grocery, alcohol and tobacco wholesale trade in both retail and catering. Aimed at grocery wholesalers, both cash and carry, delivered and major suppliers.
Ad Rate: Full Page Colour £1520.00
MAGAZINE
Alcohol & Spirits, Consumer Goods & Products, Food, Retail Management, Tobacco

Who's Jack 984325

Editorial: 93 Barker Drive, Camden, London NW1 0JG
Email: lu@wjlondon.com
Web site: www.wjlondon.com
Freq: Monthly
Circ: 35000 Not Audited
Editor: Louise Orcheston-Findlay
Profile: Magazine covering new grassroots upwards music, fashion, art, the London scene and opinion. Louise Orcheston-Findlay is the editor of the magazine and main editorial contact.
Ad Rate: Full Page Colour £600.00
MAGAZINE
Lifestyle, Men's Interests, Regional General Interest, Restaurant Reviews, Women's Interests

WI Life 980988

Editorial: NFWI, 104 New Kings Road, London SW6 4LY **Tel:** 44 02073 719300
Email: wilife@nfwi.org.uk
Web site: www.thewi.org.uk
Freq: Bi-Monthly
Circ: 221554 Not Audited
Profile: Magazine covering national and county WI news and members and their activities as well as cookery, gardening, books, health and crafts. Published eight times a year, WI Life is delivered directly to more than 205,000 WI members. Aimed at members of the WI in England and Wales.
Ad Rate: Full Page Colour £15000.00
MAGAZINE
Women's Interests

WIB Agency 1105192

Editorial: Unit A3, West 12 Studios, 2A Askew Crescent, London W12 9DP
Tel: 44 02077 049111
Email: info.london@wibagency.com
Web site: www.wibagency.com
Freq: Daily
Circ: 1806 Cision Digital Reach
MAGAZINE (ONLINE)
Fashion

Wideopenmag 986021

Email: hello@wideopenmag.co.uk
Web site: www.wideopenmag.co.uk
Freq: Daily
Circ: 4473 Cision Digital Reach
Editor: Jamie Edwards
MAGAZINE (ONLINE)
Bicycles

Wightlife 995799

Editorial: Suite 7, 30 Quay Street, Newport, London PO30 5BA **Tel:** 44 01983 556844
Email: info@solent.co
Web site: www.wightlife.com
Freq: Semi-Annual
Circ: 300000 Not Audited
MAGAZINE
Regional General Interest, Travel

Wild World 996035

Editorial: Cromwell Road, London SW7 5BD
Tel: 44 02079 425000
Email: wildworld@nhm.ac.uk
Web site: http://www.nhmshop.co.uk/buy-evolve-wildworld-magazines-subscription

Freq: Quarterly Not Audited
MAGAZINE
Elementary School, History

Wildabout 1094163

Email: contact@wildaboutmagazine.com
Web site: http://www.wildaboutmagazine.com/
Freq: Daily
Circ: 12600 Cision Digital Reach
MAGAZINE (ONLINE)
Art, Dance Music, Fashion, Jazz & Blues, Photography, Pop Music, Rap & Hip Hop, Rock Music, Visual Arts

Wildlife Durham 997352

Editorial: Durham Wildlife Trust, Rainton Meadows Nature Reserve, Chilton Moor, Houghton le Spring DH4 6PU
Tel: 44 01915 843112
Email: mail@durhamwt.co.uk
Web site: www.durhamwt.co.uk
Freq: 3 Times/Year
Circ: 5000 Not Audited
MAGAZINE
Charitable Foundations, Nature & Wildlife

Will & Aimee's Wordsearch 996107

Editorial: Academic House, 24-28 Oval Road, London NW1 7DT
Tel: 44 02072 418000
Email: eclipsepuzzles@bauer.co.uk
Web site: www.puzzlemagazines.co.uk
Freq: Monthly Not Audited
Editor: Christine Scott
MAGAZINE
News & Current Affairs

Wiltshire Life 982543

Tel: 44 01722 716996
Email: wl@markallengroup.co.uk
Web site: www.wiltshirelife.co.uk
Freq: Monthly Not Audited
Editor: Claire Waring
Profile: Regional magazine with features on village life, walking, local history, food and drink, local issues, gardening and arts and crafts. Each month it focuses on different towns and villages throughout Wiltshire. It contain special features include subjects such as independent schools, weddings, interiors, restaurants, days out, motoring and healthy living. First published in 1946, the publication has an average of 84 pages per issue. Read by Wiltshire residents and those living on the borders and ex-pats.
Ad Rate: Full Page Colour £835.00
MAGAZINE
Regional General Interest

Wiltshire Society 983532

Editorial: 8-12 Rollestone Street, Salisbury SP1 1DY **Tel:** 44 01722 426500
Email: newsdesk@salisburyjournal.co.uk
Web site: http://www.salisburyjournal.co.uk/wiltsoc/
Freq: Monthly
Circ: 8000 Not Audited
Editor: Karen Bate
Profile: Monthly magazine covering local issues and including features on fashion, beauty, travel, shopping, entertainment and places of local interest in the Salisbury, South Wiltshire & West Hampshire areas.
Ad Rate: Full Page Colour £475.00
MAGAZINE
Regional General Interest

Wimbledon Time & Leisure 996228

Editorial: 14 Apprentice Shop, Merton Abbey Mills, London SW19 2RD
Tel: 44 02085 456777
Web site: www.timeandleisure.co.uk
Freq: Monthly Not Audited
MAGAZINE
Regional General Interest

Winchester Lifestyle 1053336

Tel: 44 01225 343710
Web site: http://www.winchesterlifestyle.co.uk/
Freq: Bi-Monthly

Consumer Magazines

Circ: 7500 Not Audited
MAGAZINE
Alcohol & Spirits, Cooking & Baking, Do-It-Yourself (DIY), Gardening, Lifestyle, Men's Interests, Regional General Interest, Travel, Wine/Winemaking, Women's Interests

Winchester Magazine   998073
Editorial: Winchester Magazine, Old Rectory Cottage, Park Lane, Winchester SO21 1DT
Tel: 44 07930 324623
Email: liz@winchestermag.com
Web site: www.winchestermag.com
Freq: Quarterly
Circ: 10000 Not Audited
Editor: Liz Kavanagh
Profile: Regional lifestyle magazine covering local people's interests and discussion points as well as reviews of the city's best restaurants and coverage of music and arts events, homes and interiors, shopping and hints and tips from local specialists. Aimed at an AB1 audience based in Winchester.
MAGAZINE
Regional General Interest

Winchester News Online
                                          1052374
Email: winolnews@gmail.com
Web site: http://www.winol.co.uk/
Freq: Daily
Circ: 9017 Cision Digital Reach
MAGAZINE (ONLINE)
Regional

Windows 7 Help & Advice   996229
Editorial: Beauford Court, 30 Monmouth Street, Bath BA1 2BW Tel: 44 01225 442244
Freq: Monthly Not Audited
MAGAZINE
Personal Computers

Winds   982121
Editorial: Fron, Llansadwrn, Menai Bridge, Beaumaris LL59 5SL
Email: winds@basbwe.net
Web site: www.basbwe.net
Freq: Quarterly Not Audited
Editor: Bruce Hicks
Profile: Journal of the British Association of Symphonic Bands and Wind Ensembles. Includes music and book reviews, composer interviews, band profiles and articles on teaching and conducting.
Ad Rate: Full Page Mono £360.00
Ad Rate: Full Page Colour £500.00
MAGAZINE
Music

Windsor & Ascot Magazine
                                          1054623
Tel: 44 02089 395601
Email: editwa@sheengate.co.uk
Web site: www.sheengate.co.uk
Freq: Monthly
Circ: 32000 Not Audited
Editor: Emily Horton
MAGAZINE
Property Management & Maintenance, Regional General Interest

Windsurf Magazine   982308
Editorial: PO Box 386, Kidlington OX5 1LG
Email: editor@windsurf.co.uk
Web site: www.windsurf.co.uk
Freq: Monthly
Circ: 16000 Not Audited
Editor: Finn Mullen
Profile: Magazine that covers all aspects of windsurfing, including new products, equipment and techniques.
Ad Rate: Full Page Colour £1165.00
MAGAZINE
Swimming/Watersports

The Wine Merchant   1068846
Tel: 44 01323 871836
Email: winemerchantteam@gmail.com
Web site: www.winemerchantmag.com
Freq: Monthly
Circ: 1000 Not Audited

Profile: Magazine covering key issues facing the independent wine sector. It includes retailer profiles, business building features, product reviews and country profiles. Aimed at independent wine retailers.
MAGAZINE
Alcohol & Spirits

WineChap   988145
Editorial: The Bon Marché Centre, 241 Ferndale Road, London SW9 8BJ
Tel: 44 02036 031646
Email: marie@honestgrapes.co.uk
Web site: http://winechap.com/
Freq: Daily
Circ: 5355 Cision Digital Reach
Editor: Tom Harrow
MAGAZINE (ONLINE)
Wine/Winemaking

wine-pages.com   982861
Editorial: 6 Kirklee Road, Glasgow G12 0TP
Tel: 44 01415 764958
Email: info@wine-pages.com
Web site: www.wine-pages.com
Freq: Daily
Circ: 9764 Cision Digital Reach
MAGAZINE (ONLINE)
Wine/Winemaking

WINGS   985757
Editorial: Blackburn House, Blackburn Road, West Hampstead, London NW6 1RZ
Tel: 44 02076 250700
Web site: www.ink-live.com/emagazines/wings-magazine#6pakePLtTsyHsYrj.97
Freq: Bi-Monthly
Circ: 650000 Not Audited
Editor: Lydia Polzer
MAGAZINE
Airline Inflight, Antiques/Collectibles, Armed Forces, Astrology & Parapsychology, Astronomy, Aviation, Boating & Yachting, Camping and RV Travel, Cartoons, Casinos & Gaming

Winq   995488
Editorial: 33 Pear Tree Street, London EC1V 3AG Tel: 44 02076 086305
Web site: www.winq.com
Freq: Bi-Monthly
Circ: 22662 Not Audited
MAGAZINE
LGBT

Winter Sports Technology International   985917
Editorial: Abinger House, Church Street, Dorking RH4 1DF Tel: 44 01306 743744
Web site: www.ukipme.com/pub-listing-full.php?mag=39
Freq: Semi-Annual
Circ: 8000 Not Audited
Editor: Matt Ross
Profile: Magazine covering ski resort and snowdome design, operation and technology. It covers access control, ski lifts, safety systems, and timing technologies as well as architecture, maintenance technologies, snow grooming and snowmaking systems. The magazine features interviews with the industry's key figures, plus in-depth case studies on the latest venues and technologies. Aimed at those working within the winter sport technology industry.
Ad Rate: Full Page Colour £3850.00
MAGAZINE
Fitness & Exercise, Winter Sports

The Wire   982112
Editorial: Unit 5, The Textile Bulding, 2a Belsham Street, London E9 6NG
Tel: 44 02074 225010
Email: listings@thewire.co.uk
Web site: www.thewire.co.uk
Freq: Monthly
Circ: 25000 Not Audited
Editor: Derek Walmsley
Profile: Independent music magazine covering the more leftfield areas of rock, electronic, jazz, improvised, modern classical and global music. Aimed at music

fans of all kinds of specialist music from the ages of 20 to 70 years old.
Ad Rate: Full Page Mono £995.00
Ad Rate: Full Page Colour £1450.00
MAGAZINE
Country, Folk, Bluegrass, Dance Music, Jazz & Blues, Pop Music, R&B, Urban, World, Rap & Hip Hop, Rock Music

Wire   983281
Editorial: Peter Benenson, 1 Easton Street, London WC1X 0DW Tel: 44 02074 135500
Email: thewire@amnesty.org
Web site: www.amnesty.org/en/wire-magazine/
Freq: Quarterly Not Audited
Profile: Magazine with news and features on human rights issues around the world. Also carries key campaign news and occasional book, music and theatre reviews. Aimed at Amnesty International members.
Ad Rate: Full Page Colour £3500.00
MAGAZINE
Charitable Foundations

The Wired World in...   986999
Editorial: Conde Nast Publication Ltd, 13 Hanover Square, London W1S 1JU
Tel: 44 02074 999080
Web site: www.wired.co.uk
Freq: Annual
MAGAZINE
Audio Video Trade, Business, Cameras, Consumer Electronics, Electronics, Energy & Environment, Healthcare Industry, Men's Interests, Mobile Electronics, Movies & Video

WireIN   981683
Editorial: 1 Clydeford Drive, Uddingston, Glasgow G71 7DH Tel: 44 01698 816014
Email: wi@enwi.co.uk
Web site: www.wirein.co.uk
Freq: Bi-Monthly
Circ: 10000 Not Audited
Profile: Magazine focusing on the electrical industry in Scotland and Ireland. Includes the latest leads, tenders, opportunities, unbiased industry news, technical features, new products, all legislation and developments affecting the industry. Aimed at electrical contractors, installers, builders, councils, specifiers, wholesalers and end users.
Ad Rate: Full Page Colour £2750.00
MAGAZINE
Electronics, Industry

Wireless Watch   983818
Editorial: Unit G-5, Lower Station Approach, Temple Meads, Romsey BS1 6QS
Tel: 44 01794 521411
Email: info@rethinkresearch.biz
Web site: www.rethinkresearch.biz/product/wireless-watch
Freq: Weekly
Circ: 21 Cision Digital Reach
Editor: Caroline Gabriel
Profile: Research service covering wireless broadband, ultra wideband, mobile telephony, enterprise wireless, mobility, PDAs, smart antenna and smartphones.
MAGAZINE (ONLINE)
Computers, Internet, Mobile Communications

Wisden Cricketers' Almanack
                                          985866
Editorial: 50, Bedford Sqaure, London WC1B 3DP Tel: 44 02076 315600
Web site: www.wisden.com
Freq: Annual Not Audited
Profile: Publication giving a comprehensive coverage of cricket worldwide.
MAGAZINE
Cricket

WithGuitars   1068966
Web site: www.withguitars.com
Freq: Daily
Circ: 12812 Cision Digital Reach
Editor: Steve Janes
MAGAZINE (ONLINE)
Entertainment, Rock Music

WIZZ   983074
Editorial: Blackburn House, Blackburn Road, London NW6 1RZ
Tel: 44 02076 138777
Email: wizzair.magazine@ink-global.com
Web site: www.wizzmagazine.com
Freq: Bi-Monthly
Circ: 300000 Not Audited
Profile: Magazine with city guides for all Wizz Air's destinations plus news and features linked to cities to which Wizz flies. Topics include food and drink, people, sights, culture, nightlife, business, property and sport. Aimed at passengers of Wizz Air.
Ad Rate: Full Page Colour £8900.00
MAGAZINE
Airline Inflight

WM   983479
Editorial: Wales Online, 6 Park Street, Cardiff CF10 1XR Tel: 44 02920 243602
Email: newsdesk@walesonline.co.uk
Web site: http://www.walesonline.co.uk/lifestyle/
Freq: Quarterly
Circ: 21176 Not Audited
Profile: Journal covering all aspects of manufacturing management. Aimed at decision makers in manufacturing establishments with over 50 employees.
Ad Rate: Full Page Colour £2900.00
MAGAZINE
Regional General Interest, Women's Interests

The Woking Lifestyle Magazine   985992
Editorial: Kingsway Business Park, Oldfield Road, Hampton, London TW12 2HD
Tel: 44 02089 395600
Email: editguild@sheengate.co.uk
Web site: www.sheengate.co.uk
Freq: Monthly
Circ: 40100 Not Audited
Profile: Lifestyle magazine covering local interest articles and interviews as well as features on fashion, theatre, education, shopping and property.
Ad Rate: Full Page Colour £1155.00
MAGAZINE
Property Management & Maintenance, Regional General Interest

Wolverhampton Magazine
                                          988873
Editorial: 51-53 Queen Street, Wolverhampton WV1 1ES
Tel: 44 01902 319415
Web site: www.wolverhamptonmagazine.com/
Freq: Monthly
Circ: 14500 Not Audited
Editor: Karen Knowles
Profile: Magazine covering general regional interest including lifestyle, country living and events. Aimed at residents and visitor of the area.
MAGAZINE
Regional General Interest, Women's Interests

Woman   982439
Editorial: 161 Marsh Wall, London E14 9AP
Tel: 44 02031 485000
Email: editor@timeinc.com
Web site: www.womanmagazine.co.uk
Freq: Weekly
Circ: 183872 Not Audited
Editor: Karen Livermore
Profile: Weekly magazine covering women's interest and celebrity news including TV insider gossip, real-life stories, health and diet recommendations, shopping advice, wearable fashion, beauty, homes and interiors, food and lifestyle tips. Founded in 1937, the publication has 84 pages on average per issue. Press Days are Thursdays and Fridays. Aimed at 30 and 40-something, modern family woman.
Ad Rate: Full Page Colour £19050.00
MAGAZINE
Women's Interests

Woman Alive
982167
Editorial: Garcia Estate, Canterbury Road, Worthing BN13 1BW **Tel:** 44 01903 604352
Email: womanalive@cpo.org.uk
Web site: www.womanalive.co.uk
Freq: Monthly
Circ: 30000 Not Audited
Editor: Jackie Harris
Profile: Magazine with articles which inspire, encourage and resource women in their faith, alongside general health and lifestyle articles. Aimed at Christian women.Regular features: Contemporary Issues; Health; Interviews; Personal Stories; Whats On
Ad Rate: Full Page Mono £550.00
Ad Rate: Full Page Colour £665.00
MAGAZINE
Religion

Woman Diet Special
986797
Editorial: 5th floor, 110 Southwark Street, London SE1 0SU **Tel:** 44 02031 485000
Email: woman@timeinc.com
Web site: www.womanmagazine.co.uk
Freq: Monthly Not Audited
Profile: Bi-Monthly supplement of the magazine Women covering women's nutrition and diet. Aimed at 30 and 40-something, modern family woman.
MAGAZINE
Nutrition

Woman Fashion
988525
Editorial: Blue Fin Building, 110 Southwark Street, London SE1 0SU
Tel: 44 02031 485000
Email: editor@timeinc.com
Freq: Semi-Annual Not Audited
MAGAZINE
Fashion, Women's Interests

woman&home
980768
Editorial: 161 Marsh Wall, London E14 9AP
Tel: 44 02031 485000
Email: womanandhome@timeinc.com
Web site: www.womanandhome.com
Freq: Monthly
Circ: 302600 Not Audited
Editor: Kath Brown
Profile: Magazine covering women's lifestyle features including fashion and beauty tips, fitness, exercise, travel, arts, real life stories, homes, careers, recipes, food and diets. First published in 1926, the publication has an average of 242 pages per issue. Aimed at women aged 35 years old and over.
Ad Rate: Full Page Colour £13928.00
MAGAZINE
Women's Interests

woman&home Fashion
988575
Editorial: The Blue Fin Building, 110 Southwark Street, London SE1 0SU
Tel: 44 02031 485000
Email: wandhmail@ipcmedia.com
Web site: www.womanandhome.com
Freq: Semi-Annual Not Audited
MAGAZINE
Fashion

woman&home Feel Good Food
987122
Editorial: 161 Marsh Wall, London E14 9AP
Tel: 44 02031 485000
Web site: www.womanandhome.com/recipes/534618/feel-good-food-mag
Freq: Quarterly
Circ: 51654 Not Audited
MAGAZINE
Cooking & Baking

Woman's Own
980767
Editorial: 161 Marsh Wall, London E14 9AP
Tel: 44 02031 485000
Email: womansown@timeinc.com
Web site: www.womansown.co.uk
Freq: Weekly
Circ: 170385 Not Audited
Editor: Karen Livermore
Profile: Magazine delivering a weekly mix of news, views, celebrity gossip and real-life stories. Contains advice on raising children, healthy recipes, relationships, health advice and diet plans. First published in 1932, the

publication has an average of 68 pages per issue and press day is at the end of the week. Aimed at women over 35 years old who know how to enjoy life, are fun-loving and confident.
Ad Rate: Full Page Colour £23650.00
MAGAZINE
Women's Interests

Woman's Weekly
980766
Editorial: The Blue Fin Building, 110 Southwark Street, London SE1 0SU
Tel: 44 02031 485000
Email: womansweeklypostbag@timeinc.com
Web site: www.womansweekly.co.uk
Freq: Weekly
Circ: 267081 Not Audited
Editor: Diane Kenwood
Profile: Woman's Weekly celebrates the home, family and lives of mature women, providing them with practical help, advice and inspiration. Contains recipes and baking tips, health advice, exercise tips and relationship advice. Founded in 1932. Aimed at women over 40 years old.
Ad Rate: Full Page Colour £1000.00
MAGAZINE
Women's Interests

Women & Golf
982267
Editorial: 12 Shore Point, 46 High Road, Buckhurst Hill, London IG9 5JE
Tel: 44 02084 980428
Web site: http://womenandgolf.com/
Freq: Bi-Monthly
Circ: 12000 Not Audited
Editor: Alison Root
Profile: Magazine containing articles about golf, including instructions, fashion and travel. First published in 1991, the publication has an average of 84 pages per issue. Aimed at female golf players.
Ad Rate: Full Page Colour £1600.00
MAGAZINE
Golf

Women in Prison
995154
Editorial: Unit 10, The Ivories, 6 Northampton Street, London N1 2HY
Tel: 44 02073 596674
Email: info@womeninprison.org.uk
Web site: www.womeninprison.org.uk
Freq: Quarterly
Circ: 5000 Not Audited
MAGAZINE
Crime & Violence, Social Issues

Women Together
981854
Editorial: 19 Victoria Street, Aberdeen AB10 1UU **Tel:** 44 01224 646491
Email: magazine@theswi.org.uk
Web site: http://www.theswi.org.uk
Freq: Monthly
Circ: 4700 Not Audited
MAGAZINE
Women's Interests

Women24 Online
1060541
MAGAZINE (ONLINE)
Women's Interests

Women's Fitness
983765
Editorial: Unit 011, Netil House, 1 Westgate street, London E8 3RL
Web site: www.womensfitness.co.uk
Freq: Monthly
Circ: 10070 Not Audited
Profile: Magazine covering fitness including working out at home and in the gym. Includes information on diet, nutrition, weight-loss, with an emphasis on combining healthy living with a busy lifestyle.
Ad Rate: Full Page Colour £2600.00
MAGAZINE
Fitness & Exercise, Nutrition, Women's Interests

Women's Health
986493
Editorial: 33 Broadwick Street, London W1F 0DQ **Tel:** 44 02074 395000
Email: womenshealth@womenshealthmag.co.uk
Web site: www.womenshealthmag.co.uk
Freq: Monthly

Circ: 131960 Not Audited
Profile: Magazine covering women's health including lifestyle, slimming, dieting, sex, love, beauty, fashion, celebrity, fitness and nutrition. Aimed at women of all ages.
Ad Rate: Full Page Colour £6900.00
MAGAZINE
Alternative Medicine, Beauty & Grooming, Celebrities, Cosmetics, Fashion, Fitness & Exercise, Hair, Health & Medicine, Nutrition, Relationships

The Women's Institute
999670
Editorial: 104 New Kings Road, London SW6 4LY **Tel:** 44 02073 719300
Web site: www.thewi.org.uk
Freq: Daily
Circ: 40994 Cision Digital Reach
MAGAZINE (ONLINE)
Charitable Foundations, Government, Public Sector, Women's Interests

Women's Running (UK)
985305
Editorial: 1st Floor, Gable House, 18-24 Turnham Green Terrace, Chiswick W4 1QP
Tel: 44 02089 965135
Email: womensrunning@wildbunchmedia.co.uk
Web site: www.womensrunninguk.co.uk
Freq: Monthly
Circ: 20253 Not Audited
Editor: Elizabeth Hufton
MAGAZINE
Fitness & Exercise, Sports

Women's Thoughts
999472
Editorial: Gate House Farm, Bowling Bank, Wrexham, Wrexham LL13 9 RL
Web site: www.womensthoughts.co.uk
Freq: Daily
Circ: 12756 Cision Digital Reach
MAGAZINE (ONLINE)
Do-It-Yourself (DIY), Women's Interests

The Wonderful World of Dance
997220
Web site: thewonderfulworldofdance.com
Freq: Daily
Circ: 11861 Cision Digital Reach
MAGAZINE (ONLINE)
Theater & Performing Arts

Wonderland
982914
Editorial: 133 Notting Hill Gate, London W11 3LB **Tel:** 44 02072 439966
Email: info@wonderlandmagazine.com
Web site: www.wonderlandmagazine.com
Freq: Quarterly
Circ: 140000 Not Audited
Profile: Magazine covering fashion, luxury goods, visual culture, beauty, people, celebrities, art, film and music. Aimed at affluent men and women aged between 18 and 40 with a high disposable income.
Ad Rate: Full Page Colour £7000.00
MAGAZINE
Luxury Goods, Men's Interests, Women's Interests

Wonderpedia
986810
Editorial: Academic House, 24-28 Oval Road, London NW1 7DT
Tel: 44 02072 418000
Email: editorial@wonderpediamagazine.co.uk
Web site: www.wonderpediamagazine.co.uk
Freq: Monthly
Circ: 19000 Not Audited
Profile: Magazine that covers areas of science, nature, technology, world events, the human body and history.
MAGAZINE
History, Science

Wonkhe
988753
Editorial: PO Box 72961, London N7 1DY
Email: team@wonkhe.com
Web site: http://wonkhe.com/
Freq: Quarterly
Circ: 17479 Cision Digital Reach
Profile: OnWindows.com covers new product and service launches, customer successes, the latest thought-leadership and

market insights released every day by Microsoft partners.
MAGAZINE (ONLINE)
Computers, Data Management, Electronics, Industry, Internet, Software

Wood Based Panels International
981112
Editorial: John Carpenter House, 7 Carmelite Street, London EC4Y 0BS
Tel: 44 02079 366848
Web site: www.wbpionline.com
Freq: Bi-Monthly
Circ: 4774 Not Audited
Profile: Journal covering all aspects of wood based panels and agricultural fibre based panels.
Ad Rate: Full Page Mono £5500.00
Ad Rate: Full Page Colour £7425.00
MAGAZINE
News & Current Affairs

Woodnote
1086845
Web site: http://www.certainlywood.co.uk/magazine/
Freq: Monthly
Circ: 242 Cision Digital Reach
MAGAZINE (ONLINE)
Cooking & Baking, Do-It-Yourself (DIY), Gardening

Woodturning
984402
Editorial: The Guild of Master Craftsmen, 166 High Street, Lewes, Lewes BN7 1XU
Tel: 44 01273 477374
Email: helenchrystie@thegmcgroup.com
Web site: http://www.woodworkersinstitute.com/page.asp?p=4
Freq: Monthly
Circ: 17000 Not Audited
Editor: Mark Baker
Profile: Journal of The Guild of Master Craftsmen. Covers new tools, specialist equipment and machinery, with articles on technique and project ideas.
Ad Rate: Full Page Mono £825.00
Ad Rate: Full Page Colour £825.00
MAGAZINE
Woodworking

The Woodworker
982052
Editorial: Enterprise House, Enterprise Way, Edenbridge, Edenbridge TN8 6HF
Tel: 44 08444 122262
Email: editor@getwoodworking.com
Web site: http://www.getwoodworking.com/
Freq: Monthly
Circ: 12732 Not Audited
Editor: Mark Cass
Profile: Magazine featuring woodworking projects, techniques and equipment news.
Ad Rate: Full Page Colour £800.00
MAGAZINE
Woodworking

Woodworking Plans & Projects
985153
Editorial: 166 High Street, Lewes BN7 1XU
Web site: https://www.thegmcgroup.com/pc/viewCategories.asp?idCategory=707
Freq: Monthly Not Audited
Profile: Woodworking magazine containing project ideas, technical tips, product tests and industry contacts.
Ad Rate: Full Page Mono £850.00
Ad Rate: Full Page Colour £1150.00
MAGAZINE
Woodworking

Worcestershire Now
996760
Editorial: 2nd Floor, Richardson House, 24 New Street, Worcester WR1 2DP
Tel: 44 01905 723011
Email: enquiries@pw-media.co.uk
Web site: www.worcestershirenow.co.uk/listings.php
Freq: Monthly
Circ: 15500 Not Audited
Editor: Dawn Pardoe
MAGAZINE
Regional General Interest

Wordplay 995729
Editorial: Wordplay Studios, 20 Green Hills Road, Norwich NR3 3ET
Email: flicks@wordplaymagazine.com
Web site: www.wordplaymagazine.com
Freq: Quarterly
Circ: 10000 Not Audited
Editor: Matt Neville
MAGAZINE
Art, Rap & Hip Hop

Wordsearch 998724
Editorial: Academic House, 24-28 Oval Road, London NW1 7DT
Tel: 44 02072 418000
Web site: http://www.puzzlemagazines.co.uk/word-searches
Freq: Monthly
Circ: 158658 Not Audited
MAGAZINE
Games, Competitions & Events

WORDSEARCHES COLLECTION 1086852
Editorial: Academic House, 24-28 Oval Road, London NW1 7DT
Tel: 44 02072 418000
Web site: www.bauer.co.uk
Freq: Monthly
Circ: 48000 Not Audited
MAGAZINE
Games, Competitions & Events

Work Out 983343
Editorial: 47 Church Street, Barnsley S70 2AS **Tel:** 44 01226 734694
Email: ce@scriptmedia.co.uk
Web site: http://www.workout-uk.co.uk
Freq: Monthly
Circ: 8052 Not Audited
Editor: Christina Eccles
Profile: Magazine covering all aspects of the UK fitness industry. Read by proprietors of fitness clubs and fitness managers.
MAGAZINE
Fitness & Exercise

Working Capital 997547
Editorial: Capital City Partnership, The Canon Mill, 1-3 Canon Street, Edinburgh EH3 5HE **Tel:** 44 01312 706030
Email: joinedupforjobs@capitalcitypartnership.org
Web site: www.joinedupforjobs.org.uk/working-capital-magazine.html
Freq: Quarterly Not Audited
Editor: Katie Weavers
MAGAZINE
Careers

Working Together 986767
Editorial: 22 Green Court, The Green, Southwick, Southwick BN42 4GS
Tel: 44 08712 440747
Email: admin@tti.org
Web site: www.tti.org
Freq: Quarterly Not Audited
Editor: Liz Rylance
Profile: Newsletter covering issues affecting people in West Wiltshire from community and housing issues to consumer products. Aimed at social housing tenants in West Wiltshire.
MAGAZINE
Automotive, Aviation, Railroad, Shipping & Warehousing, Supply Chain Management (SCM), Transportation

Working with Older People 984707
Editorial: Emerald Group Publishing Limited, Howard House, Wagon Lane, Bingley BD16 1WA **Tel:** 44 01274 777700
Web site: http://www.emeraldinsight.com/journals.htm?issn=1366-3666&show=latest
Freq: Quarterly Not Audited
Profile: Journal covering policy and practice developments related to the elderly care sector.
Ad Rate: Full Page Mono £350.00
MAGAZINE
News & Current Affairs

Workshop Magazine 1057616
Tel: 44 02392 522434
Email: editorial@blackballmedia.co.uk
Web site: www.workshopmagazine.co.uk
Freq: Monthly
Circ: 10000 Not Audited
MAGAZINE
Automotive

World Accounting Report 995856
Editorial: Christchurch Court, 10-15 Newgate Street, London EC1A 7AZ
Tel: 44 02070 175000
Email: worldaccounting@gmx.com
Web site: www.worldaccountingreport.com
Freq: Monthly Not Audited
Editor: Peter Walton
MAGAZINE
News & Current Affairs

World Bunkering 986029
Editorial: Suite 19 Hurlingham Studios, Ranelagh Gardens, London SW6 3PA
Tel: 44 02073 866100
Email: editor@mar-media.com
Web site: www.worldbunkering.com
Freq: Quarterly
Circ: 8000 Not Audited
Profile: Magazine covering all aspects of the supply and purchase of fuel for world shipping.
Ad Rate: Full Page Colour £3950.00
MAGAZINE
Marine & Boat Trade, Shipping & Warehousing

The World Bus and Coach Manufacturing Industry 984100
Editorial: PO Box 15, Williton, Taunton TA4 4YP **Tel:** 44 01984 618707
Email: info@truckandbusbuilder.com
Web site: www.truckandbusbuilder.com
Freq: Annual Not Audited
Editor: Jim Gibbins
Profile: Report giving an overview of the global bus industry with market reviews and forecasts for markets from all regions.
Ad Rate: Full Page Colour £2250.00
MAGAZINE
Automotive, Manufacturing

World Cement 981093
Editorial: 15 South Street, Farnham, Farnham GU9 7QU **Tel:** 44 01252 718999
Email: enquiries@worldcement.com
Web site: www.worldcement.com
Freq: Monthly
Circ: 5752 Not Audited
Editor: Jonathan Rowland
Profile: Periodical covering all business and technical aspects of cement and lime manufacture from quarrying of raw materials to the distribution of the finished product. Read by executives within the cement and lime industries, cement and lime plant managers and associated personnel.
Ad Rate: Full Page Colour £2400.00
MAGAZINE
News & Current Affairs

World Cruise Industry Review 981227
Editorial: John Carpenter House, John Carpenter Street, London EC4Y 0AN
Tel: 44 02079 366400
Web site: www.worldcruiseindustryreview.com
Freq: Annual
Circ: 4473 Not Audited
Profile: Magazine covering all aspects of the world cruise industry. Aimed at presidents, CEOs, vice-presidents, operations directors, cruise directors, chief concessionaires, naval architects, itinerary planners, ship superintendents, port and harbour authorities, shipping agencies and travel agencies throughout the world.Regular features: Environmental Issues; Gaming and Entertainment; Interior Design; Onboard Services; Operations Management; Ports and Destinations; Safety at Sea; Shipbuilding, Maintenance and Repair
MAGAZINE
Travel

The World Financial Review 996811
Tel: 44 02086 788991
Email: info@worldfinancialreview.com
Web site: www.worldfinancialreview.com
Freq: Bi-Monthly Not Audited
MAGAZINE
Business, Politics

World Fishing & Aquaculture 981162
Editorial: The Old Mill, Lower Quay, Fareham, Fareham PO16 0RA
Tel: 44 01329 825335
Email: editor@worldfishing.net
Web site: www.worldfishing.net
Freq: Monthly
Circ: 3306 Not Audited
Profile: Magazine containing news on commercial fishing, processing, gear and equipment, vessels and shipyards worldwide.
Ad Rate: Full Page Colour £2365.00
MAGAZINE
Animal Farming, Marine & Boat Trade

World Footwear 983761
Editorial: 36 Crosby Road North, Liverpool L22 0QN **Tel:** 44 01519 289288
Web site: www.footwearbiz.com
Freq: Bi-Monthly
Circ: 6600 Not Audited
Editor: Stephen Tierney
Profile: Magazine covering all aspects of the footwear industry, including business management, technology, materials, design and news. The magazine aims to provide updated news service for the footwear market for 20 years and offers the latest in-depth technical features, along with a collection of articles on footwear and related materials.
Ad Rate: Full Page Mono £3276.00
Ad Rate: Full Page Colour £5040.00
MAGAZINE
Fashion

World Horse Welfare News 1075968
Editorial: Anne Colvin House, Snetterton, Norwich NR16 2LR **Tel:** 44 01953 498682
Email: info@worldhorsewelfare.org
Web site: www.worldhorsewelfare.org
Freq: 3 Times/Year Not Audited
MAGAZINE
Charitable Foundations, Nature & Wildlife

World Intellectual Property Review 986769
Editorial: Kingfisher House, 21-23 Elmfield Road, London BR1 1LT
Freq: Bi-Monthly
Circ: 4942 Not Audited
Profile: The World IP Review's bi-monthly edition is dedicated to the needs of professionals involved in the management and protection of IP assets. It informs and educates IP owners and their international legal counsel and consultants of the latest strategies for managing, protecting and profiting from their increasingly valuable intellectual property. Each issue of the World IP Review's bi-monthly edition contains interviews with some of the most prominent IP owners and in-house counsel. It uses a combination of articles and case studies to showcase business strategies. In addition, it reviews case law and IP legislation worldwide. Aimed at professionals involved in the management and protection of IP assets.Alternative Title: WIPR World IP Review
MAGAZINE
News & Current Affairs

World Leather 981300
Editorial: 36 Crosby Road North, Liverpool L22 0QN **Tel:** 44 01519 289288
Web site: www.leatherbiz.com
Freq: Bi-Monthly
Circ: 4400 Not Audited
Editor: Stephen Tierney
Profile: Magazine covering news, features and new product information for the leather industry worldwide.

Ad Rate: Full Page Mono £3276.00
Ad Rate: Full Page Colour £5040.00
MAGAZINE
Fashion

World of Cars 995558
Editorial: 1st Floor, The Yellow Building, 1 Nicholas Road, London W11 4AN
Tel: 44 02032 200400
Email: info@euk.egmont.com
Web site: www.egmont.co.uk
Freq: Monthly
Circ: 20047 Not Audited
MAGAZINE
Cartoons, Trading Cards & Comics

The World of Cross Stitching 981950
Editorial: 9th Floor, Tower House, Fairfax Street, Bristol BS1 3BN
Tel: 44 01173 148755
Web site: www.cross-stitching.com
Freq: Monthly
Circ: 34726 Not Audited
Editor: Ruth Southorn
Profile: Magazine covering cross stitch, designs and practical information.
Ad Rate: Full Page Colour £1050.00
MAGAZINE
Crafts

World of Cruising 983408
Tel: 44 02084 442554
Web site: www.worldofcruisingmagazine.com
Freq: Bi-Monthly
Circ: 21661 Not Audited
Editor: Louise Robinson
Profile: Magazine with up to date news and articles on leading cruise lines as well as top hotel and spas.
Ad Rate: Full Page Colour £3250.00
MAGAZINE
Luxury Goods, Travel

World of Expats 998026
Email: info@worldofexpats.com
Web site: www.worldofexpats.com
Freq: Daily
Circ: 26194 Cision Digital Reach
MAGAZINE (ONLINE)
Expatriates

The World of Fine Wine 983169
Editorial: John Carpenter House, 7 Carmelite Street, London EC4Y 0BS
Tel: 44 02079 366400
Email: neil.beckett@worldoffinewine.com
Web site: www.finewinemag.com
Freq: Quarterly
Circ: 8800 Not Audited
Editor: Neil Beckett
Profile: Magazine covering fine wine including book reviews and cultural and historical articles with an emphasis on fine wine. Aimed at lovers of fine wine internationally.
Ad Rate: Full Page Colour £2250.00
MAGAZINE
Wine/Winemaking

The World of Hospitality 988902
Editorial: St Augustines Business Centre, 125 Canterbury Road, Westgate On Sea, Margate CT8 8NL
Web site: http://www.theworldofhospitality.com
Freq: Bi-Monthly
Circ: 154386 Not Audited
Editor: Simone Couture
Profile: Magazine covering breaking news on the topics that are shaping the modern Hospitality sector, providing both guidance and contacts. Each issue features articles from the world's leading luxury hotels, fine-dining restaurants, bars and casinos.
Ad Rate: Full Page Colour £2100.00
MAGAZINE
Bars, Clubs & Pubs, Hotels/Motels, Travel Industry

The World of Interiors 981858
Editorial: Vogue House, 6 Hanover Square, London W1S 1JU **Tel:** 44 02074 999080

Web site: worldofinteriors.co.uk
Freq: Monthly
Circ: 55059 Not Audited
Profile: Magazine highlighting elaborate home and garden designs and art events. Aimed at men and women who have an interest in all kinds of design.
Ad Rate: Full Page Colour £11500.00
MAGAZINE
Do-It-Yourself (DIY)

World Port Development   983904
Web site: www.worldportdevelopment.com
Freq: Monthly Not Audited
MAGAZINE
News & Current Affairs

World Snowboard Guide   986734
Editorial: Regency House, 2 Wood Street, Bath BA1 2JQ
Email: info@worldsnowboardguide.com
Web site: www.worldsnowboardguide.com
Freq: Daily
Circ: 31119 Cision Digital Reach
Profile: The online version of the guide appeared in 2000 with plenty more to make sure the World Snowboard Guide remains the best source of knowledge when planning your next snowboarding trip.
MAGAZINE (ONLINE)
Winter Sports

World Soccer   982255
Editorial: 7th Floor, Blue Fin Building, 110 Southwark Street, London SE1 0SU
Tel: 44 01252 555000
Web site: www.worldsoccer.com
Freq: Monthly
Circ: 25132 Not Audited
Editor: Gavin Hamilton
Profile: Magazine containing world football news, results and fixtures on the world cup, champion league, UEFA Cup, African nations and Copa America. Aimed at people interested in football.
Ad Rate: Full Page Colour £1500.00
MAGAZINE
Soccer

World Spa & Wellness   997918
Editorial: 1.17 The Plaza, 535 Kings Road, London SW10 0SZ **Tel:** 44 02073 510536
Email: info@worldspawellness.com
Web site: http://worldspawellness.com/site/Home
Freq: Bi-Monthly
Circ: 6000 Not Audited
Editor: Nora Elias
MAGAZINE
Fitness & Exercise

World Sports Advocate   997093
Editorial: World Sports Law Report, 17 The Timber Yard, Drysdale Street, London N1 6ND **Tel:** 44 02070 121380
Web site: www.e-comlaw.com/world-sports-law-report Not Audited
Editor: Sophie Cameron
MAGAZINE
News & Current Affairs

The World Today   982140
Editorial: Chatham House, 10 St James's Square, London SW1Y 4LE
Tel: 44 02079 575700
Email: contact@chathamhouse.org
Web site: www.chathamhouse.org/publications/twt
Freq: Bi-Monthly
Circ: 9000 Not Audited
Editor: Alan Philps
Profile: Magazine with analysis of international issues. Presents views and comments on a variety of current topics.
Ad Rate: Full Page Colour £1000.00
MAGAZINE
International News

World Transport Policy & Practice   984107
Editorial: 41 Church Street, Church Stretton SY6 6DQ **Tel:** 44 01694 722365
Web site: http://worldtransportjournal.com/
Freq: Quarterly

Circ: 1875 Cision Digital Reach
Editor: John Whitelegg
Profile: Website covering transport, public policy, the environment and infrastructure. World Transport Policy & Practice is a "a quarterly journal which provides a high quality medium for original and creative work in world transport."
MAGAZINE (ONLINE)
Automotive

World Travel Guide   983305
Editorial: J207 The Biscuit Factory, 100 Clements Road, London SE16 4DG
Tel: 44 02037 403240
Email: travel.editorial@columbustravelmedia.com
Web site: www.worldtravelguide.net
Freq: Daily
Circ: 376237 Cision Digital Reach
Profile: Website focusing on world travel and tourism. The website discusses the latest news and information on travel and tourism, and also features destination guides.
MAGAZINE (ONLINE)
Travel

World Watch Monitor   996322
Email: news@worldwatchmonitor.org
Web site: www.worldwatchmonitor.org
Freq: Daily
Circ: 16855 Cision Digital Reach
MAGAZINE (ONLINE)
Consumer Affairs, Crime & Violence, Defense & National Security, Energy & Environment, Ethical/Moral Issues, International News, Law, National News, News & Current Affairs, Northern Ireland

The World Weekly   999666
Editorial: Westbourne Studios, 242 Acklam Road, London W10 5JJ
Tel: 44 02037 355347
Email: editorial@theworldweekly.com
Web site: www.theworldweekly.com
Freq: Weekly
Circ: 54894 Cision Digital Reach
MAGAZINE (ONLINE)
International News, Politics

Worldleisurejobs.com   1104180
Tel: 44 01462 431385
Email: theteam@leisuremedia.com
Web site: www.worldleisurejobs.com
Freq: Daily
Circ: 7745 Cision Digital Reach
MAGAZINE (ONLINE)
Bars, Clubs & Pubs, Fitness & Exercise, Hotels/Motels, Travel

WorldRemit   990682
Editorial: 62 Buckingham Gate, London SW1E 6AJ **Tel:** 44 0207/1 485800
Web site: www.worldremit.com
Freq: Daily
Circ: 629097 Cision Digital Reach
MAGAZINE (ONLINE)
News & Current Affairs

Worldwide Food and Drink News   997171
Editorial: 12-14 Hainton Avenue, Grimsby DN32 9BB **Tel:** 44 01472 359036
Web site: www.worldwidefoodanddrinkonline.com
Freq: Monthly
Circ: 521 Cision Digital Reach
MAGAZINE (ONLINE)
Alcohol & Spirits, Food

Worship AVL   988805
Editorial: 17 Upper Grosvenor Road, Tunbridge Wells TN1 2DU
Tel: 44 01892 676280
Email: fwells@worshipavl.com
Web site: http://www.proaudio-central.com/latest-magazines
Freq: Quarterly
Circ: 5500 Not Audited
Editor: Frank Wells
MAGAZINE
Electronics

Wounds International   995712
Editorial: 1.01 Cargo Works, 1-2 Hatfields, London SE1 9PG **Tel:** 44 02076 271510
Email: info@woundsinternational.com
Web site: www.woundsinternational.com
Freq: Quarterly
Circ: 21651 Cision Digital Reach
Editor: Adam Bushby
MAGAZINE (ONLINE)
Medicine, Nursing/Nurses

WOW247   987161
Tel: 44 01313 117311
Email: enquiries@wow247.co.uk
Web site: www.wow247.co.uk
Freq: Daily
Circ: 880961 Cision Digital Reach
Profile: Website covering events. The WOW247 website is an events guide to what's happening near you.
MAGAZINE (ONLINE)
Local Entertainment Guides

wrexham.com   996513
Editorial: 67 Regent Street, Wrexham LL11 1PF **Tel:** 44 01978 288288
Email: news@wrexham.com
Web site: www.wrexham.com
Freq: Daily
Circ: 52502 Cision Digital Reach
MAGAZINE (ONLINE)
Regional, Regional General Interest

Write Out Loud   998042
Email: news@writeoutloud.net
Web site: www.writeoutloud.net
Freq: Daily
Circ: 15346 Cision Digital Reach
MAGAZINE (ONLINE)
Literature

Writers' Forum   985861
Editorial: Writers' Forum, P.O. Box 6337, Bournemouth BH1 9EH
Tel: 44 01202 586848
Email: news@writers-forum.com
Web site: www.writers-forum.com
Freq: Monthly
Circ: 18000 Not Audited
Editor: Carl Styants
Profile: Magazine covering all aspects of the craft and business of writing including short fiction, novels, non-fiction books, freelance journalism and poetry. Contains market news, reviews, advice on writing techniques and features on writers, editors and publishers.
Ad Rate: Full Page Colour £1350.00
MAGAZINE
Literature

WriteYou   1095184
Email: community@writeyou.london
Web site: www.writeyou.co.uk
Freq: Daily
Circ: 17604 Cision Digital Reach
MAGAZINE (ONLINE)
Airline Inflight, Alcohol & Spirits, Antiques/Collectibles, Art, Arts, Audio Video Trade, Bars, Clubs & Pubs, Basketball, Beer, Beverages

Writing Magazine   984886
Editorial: 5th Floor, 31-32 Park Row, Leeds LS1 5JD **Tel:** 44 01132 002929
Web site: www.writers-online.co.uk
Freq: Monthly
Circ: 66000 Not Audited
Editor: Jonathan Telfer
Profile: Magazine containing news and articles on writing and techniques.
Ad Rate: Full Page Mono £1100.00
Ad Rate: Full Page Colour £1320.00
MAGAZINE
Literature

WSA   981235
Editorial: 36 Crosby Road North, Liverpool L22 0QN **Tel:** 44 01519 289288
Email: clare@worldtrades.co.uk
Web site: http://sportstextiles.com/
Freq: Bi-Monthly
Circ: 6500 Not Audited

Editor: Stephen Tierney
Profile: Magazine that covers the performance and technology of fibres, textiles and components. Has previously been recognised internationally as the World's leading publication for material development in the activewear market.
Ad Rate: Full Page Mono £4400.00
Ad Rate: Full Page Colour £5500.00
MAGAZINE
Fashion

WT VOX   998219
Editorial: 2nd Floor, Regus Building, 239 Kensington High Street, Kensington W8 3SN
Tel: 44 02031 376633
Email: contact@wtvox.com
Web site: www.wtvox.com
Freq: Daily
Circ: 157710 Cision Digital Reach
MAGAZINE (ONLINE)
Biotechnology, Computers, Data Management, Electronics, Government Technology, Internet, Mobile Electronics

WTiN   998074
Editorial: West One, 114 Wellington Street, Leeds LS1 1BA **Tel:** 44 01138 198155
Email: info@wtin.com
Web site: www.wtin.com
Freq: Daily
Circ: 14024 Cision Digital Reach
MAGAZINE (ONLINE)
Environment, Fashion

WUWO Media   999413
Editorial: Temple Court, 5 High Street, Woking, London GU21 6BH
Tel: 44 01483 808560
Email: info@wuwomedia.com
Web site: http://www.wuwomedia.com/
Freq: Daily
Circ: 2548 Cision Digital Reach
MAGAZINE (ONLINE)
Art, Audio Video Trade, Bars, Clubs & Pubs, Broadcasting, Cameras, Comedy, Computer & Video Games, Consumer Electronics, Cooking & Baking, Electronics

WWB   983572
Editorial: The Old Town Hall, Lewisham Road, Slaithwaite, Huddersfield HD7 5AL
Tel: 44 01484 846069
Email: isabella@ras-publishing.com
Web site: www.wwb-online.co.uk
Freq: Monthly
Circ: 7300 Not Audited
MAGAZINE
Fashion

WWE Kids   999452
Editorial: 80 Kingsway East, Glasgow DD4 8SL **Tel:** 44 01382 575637
Web site: www.dcthomson.co.uk/brands/wwe-kids-magazine
Freq: Monthly
Circ: 27384 Not Audited
Editor: Lucy Galloway
MAGAZINE
Trading Cards & Comics

WWF Action   984645
Editorial: The Living Planet Centre, Rufford House, Brewery Road, Woking GU21 4LL
Tel: 44 01483 412383
Email: press@wwf.org.uk
Web site: www.wwf.org.uk
Freq: 3 Times/Year
Circ: 100000 Not Audited
Profile: Magazine covering environmental and wildlife issues.
MAGAZINE
Charitable Foundations, Energy & Environment

WWT Waterlife   981998
Editorial: Wildfowl & Wetlands Trust, Slimbridge, Gloucester GL2 7BT
Tel: 44 01453 891900
Email: waterlife@wwt.org.uk
Web site: http://www.wwt.org.uk/waterlife/waterlife/
Freq: Quarterly

Consumer Magazines

Circ: 93824 Not Audited
Profile: Magazine of the Wildfowl & Wetlands Trust with news of conservation work, research and educational activities relating to ducks, geese, swans and other water-birds and freshwater wetlands. Read by members of WWT, visitors to WWT's nine wetlands centres around the UK, and those with an interest in wildfowl, wetlands or conservation.
Ad Rate: Full Page Colour £4500.00
MAGAZINE
Nature & Wildlife

www.aycliffetoday.co.uk
999527
Editorial: Enterprise House, The HUB, Welbury Way, Newton Aycliffe DL5 6ZE
Tel: 44 01325 728024
Web site: www.aycliffetoday.co.uk
Freq: Daily
Circ: 14559 Cision Digital Reach
MAGAZINE (ONLINE)
Regional

www.comparaiso.es
997144
Editorial: Consumerchoices.co.uk, Third Floor, High Holborn House, London WC1V 6RL London **Tel:** 44 34911 980482
Email: contacto@comparaiso.es
Web site: www.comparaiso.es
Freq: Daily Not Audited
MAGAZINE
Internet, Telecommunications/Electronic Communications

www.fabafterfifty.co.uk
986345
Tel: 44 08456 210350
Email: editor@fabafterfifty.com
Web site: www.fabafterfifty.co.uk
Freq: Daily
Circ: 48911 Cision Digital Reach
MAGAZINE (ONLINE)
Retirement Savings, Women's Interests

www.mortgagesolutions.co.uk
980073
Editorial: 7th Floor, Lincoln House, 296-302 High Holborn, London WC1V 7JH
Tel: 44 02038 153670
Web site: www.mortgagesolutions.co.uk
Freq: Daily
Circ: 79297 Cision Digital Reach
Profile: Website covering credit crunch and breaking mortgage industry news including financial news and products, equity release, commercial mortgages. Mortgage Solutions also produces a number of essential online supplements for its readers. These enable us to cover hot issues in-depth. The range includes buy-to-let, equity release, first-time buyers, self-employed borrowers, sales and advice technique, regulation & compliance, conveyancing, commercial mortgages and fraud. Aimed at mortgage intermediaries.
MAGAZINE (ONLINE)
Personal Finance

www.rsvipnetwork.co.uk
999395
Editorial: Lace Market House, 54-56 High Pavement, The Lace Market, Nottingham NG1 1HW **Tel:** 44 01159 417548
Email: info@rsvipnetwork.co.uk
Web site: www.rsvipnetwork.co.uk
Freq: Daily
Circ: 11321 Cision Digital Reach
MAGAZINE (ONLINE)
Business, Small and Medium Business, Women's Interests

www.teqnewsonline.com - Technology News, Online
995352
Email: info@teqnewsonline.com
Web site: www.teqnewsonline.com
Freq: Daily
Circ: 12811 Cision Digital Reach
Editor: Magesh Panchanathan
MAGAZINE (ONLINE)
Auto Aftermarket, Computers, Data Management, Electronics, Government Technology, Industry, Internet, Mobile

Communications, Security & Security Systems, Software

www.the-rhapsody.com
996034
Email: info@the-rhapsody.com
Web site: www.the-rhapsody.com
Freq: Daily
Circ: 10511 Cision Digital Reach
MAGAZINE (ONLINE)
Classical/Choral/Band Music, Country, Folk, Bluegrass, Dance Music, Jazz & Blues, Music, Pop Music, R&B, Urban, World, Rap & Hip Hop, Rock Music

Wylde
987487
Editorial: Studio 305 Curtain House, 134-146 Curtain Road, London EC2A 3AR
Email: editor@wyldemag.com
Web site: www.wyldemag.co.uk
Freq: Semi-Annual
Circ: 50000 Not Audited
Editor: David Newton
Profile: Magazine covering fashion, beauty, travel, lifestyle and culture.
MAGAZINE
Fashion

Xbox Achievements
997773
Email: tips@x360a.org
Web site: www.xboxachievements.com
Freq: Daily
Circ: 560331 Cision Digital Reach
MAGAZINE (ONLINE)
Computer & Video Games

Xbox One UK
1104591
Web site: http://www.xboxoneuk.com/
Freq: Daily
Circ: 155420 Cision Digital Reach
Editor: Chris Turk
MAGAZINE (ONLINE)
Computer & Video Games

Xbox: The Official Magazine (U.K.)
983063
Editorial: Quay House, The Ambury, Bath BA1 1UA **Tel:** 44 01225 442244
Email: oxm@futurenet.com
Web site: www.gamesradar.com/oxm
Freq: Monthly
Circ: 24958 Not Audited
Editor: Daniella Lucas; **Editor:** Paul Taylor
MAGAZINE
Computer & Video Games

XK Gazette
983309
Editorial: PO Box 2, Tenbury Wells, Tenbury Wells WR15 8XX **Tel:** 44 01584 781588
Email: info@xkclub.com
Web site: www.xkclub.com
Freq: Monthly
Circ: 1400 Not Audited
Editor: Malcolm McKay; **Editor:** Malcolm McKay
Profile: Magazine focusing on XK Jaguar cars. Contains features, events, practical and technical advice, historical articles, interviews, profiles and reports from around the world.
MAGAZINE
Automakers

Xn
1095193
Editorial: Crown House, 231 Kings Road, Reading RG1 4LS **Tel:** 44 01183 272662
Email: editor@xnmedia.co.uk
Web site: www.xnmedia.co.uk
Freq: Monthly
Circ: 15000 Not Audited
MAGAZINE
Regional General Interest

xsnoize
1062752
Email: mark@xsnoize.com
Web site: www.xsnoize.com
Freq: Daily
Circ: 15171 Cision Digital Reach
Editor: Mark Millar
MAGAZINE (ONLINE)
Country, Folk, Bluegrass, Dance Music, Jazz & Blues, Music, Rap & Hip Hop, Rock Music

XtraTime
1053861
Editorial: Suite 171, Edgar Buildings, George Street, Bath BA1 2FJ
Tel: 44 01174 032747
Web site: http://www.xtratimewest.co.uk/
Freq: Monthly
Circ: 30000 Not Audited
MAGAZINE
Basketball, Cricket, Golf, Olympic Sports, Racquet Sports, Rowing, Rugby, Soccer, Sports, Swimming/Watersports

Xtreme Gaming
995460
Editorial: 63 High Street, Colchester, Colchester CO1 1DN **Tel:** 44 01206 561535
Email: enquiries@xtremegaming.co.uk
Web site: http://www.xtremegaminguk.co.uk/
Freq: Daily
Circ: 3958 Cision Digital Reach
MAGAZINE (ONLINE)
Computer & Video Games

Xtreme Radio
982785
Editorial: 3rd Floor Union House, University of Wales Swansea, Singleton Park, Swansea SA2 8PP **Tel:** 44 01792 295466
Email: radio@swansea-societies.co.uk
Web site: www.swanseastudentmedia.com/
Freq: Daily
Circ: 10276 Cision Digital Reach
MAGAZINE (ONLINE)
Student Lifestyle

XtremeGo.com
997960
Email: info@xtremego.com
Web site: xtremego.com
Freq: Daily
Circ: 10626 Cision Digital Reach
Editor: Sophie Madsen
MAGAZINE (ONLINE)
Extreme/Adventure Sports, Travel

Y Wawr
997170
Editorial: Canolfan Genedlaethol Merched y Wawr, Stryd yr Efail, Aberystwyth, Aberystwyth SY23 1JH
Tel: 44 01970 611661
Email: swyddfa@merchedywawr.cymru
Web site: http://merchedywawr.cymru/magazine/y-wawr-rhif-195-haf-2017/
Freq: Quarterly
Circ: 6000 Not Audited
MAGAZINE
Charitable Foundations, Government, Public Sector, Women's Interests

Yacht Investor
1054378
Editorial: 20 Orange Street, London WC2H 7EF
Email: servanne@yachtinvestor.com
Web site: http://www.yachtinvestor.com/
Freq: Bi-Monthly
Circ: 30000 Not Audited
MAGAZINE
Boating & Yachting, Luxury Goods

Yachting and Boating World (YBW.com)
985344
Editorial: Pinehurst 2, Pinehurst Road, Farnborough Business Park, Farnborough, Camberwell GU14 7BF
Tel: 44 02031 484299
Web site: www.ybw.com
Freq: Daily
Circ: 442639 Cision Digital Reach
MAGAZINE (ONLINE)
Boating & Yachting

Yachting Life
982220
Editorial: Wheatsheaf House, Montgomery Street, The Village, West Kilbride G74 4JS
Tel: 44 01355 279077
Email: info@yachtinglife.co.uk
Web site: www.yachtinglife.co.uk
Freq: Bi-Monthly
Circ: 9500 Not Audited
Editor: Alistair Vallance
Profile: Magazine dealing with local issues at yacht club level as well as reporting on local heroes on the race circuit, with an emphasis on Scotland, the North of England and Northern Ireland. Aimed at yachting

skippers and crews.Regular features: 'Spot The Pic' Featuring photographs from yachting events.; All Classes Dinghy News Featuring news for all classes of dinghy owners.; Regional Reports Featuring boating reports from Scotland, Northern Ireland and Northern England.
Ad Rate: Full Page Mono £675.00
Ad Rate: Full Page Colour £990.00
MAGAZINE
Boating & Yachting

Yachting Matters
985531
Editorial: 14A Upper Olland Street, Bungay, Bungay NR35 1BG **Tel:** 44 01986 894333
Email: colinsquire@yachtingmatters.com
Web site: www.YachtingMatters.com
Freq: Semi-Annual
Circ: 10000 Not Audited
Profile: Magazine covering superyachts. It features travel routes, yachting events and a section of boats for sale. Aimed at owners of luxury yachts and superyachts.
MAGAZINE
Boating & Yachting, Luxury Goods

Yachting Monthly
982221
Editorial: Pinehurst 2, Pinehurst Road, Farnborough Business Park, Farnborough, London GU14 7BF **Tel:** 44 02031 485000
Email: yachting_monthly@timeinc.com
Web site: www.yachtingmonthly.com
Freq: Monthly
Circ: 22199 Not Audited
Editor: Kieran Flatt
Profile: Magazine featuring all aspects of cruising under sail, including reviews, seamanship and boat handling. Includes reports on yachting equipment, new technology and new and second-hand boats.
Ad Rate: Full Page Colour £3910.00
MAGAZINE
Boating & Yachting

Yachting World
982222
Editorial: The Blue Fin Building, 110 Southwark Street, London SE1 0SU
Tel: 44 01252 555000
Email: yachting.world@timeinc.com
Web site: www.yachtingworld.com
Freq: Monthly
Circ: 16154 Not Audited
Editor: Elaine Bunting
Profile: Magazine containing information on events, cruising, techniques and equipment. Published monthly from the UK it is distributed in over 100 countries. It carries the latest news stories and features and presents high quality pictures. Coverage includes blue water cruising, global sailing epics, international yacht racing, superyachting, international events and charter. Aimed at the international yachtsman.Previous title: Yachting World International
Ad Rate: Full Page Colour £3800.00
MAGAZINE
Boating & Yachting

Yachts & Yachting
982223
Editorial: Jubilee House, 2 Jubilee Place, London SW3 3TQ
Email: club@yachtsandyachting.com
Web site: www.yachtsandyachting.com
Freq: Monthly
Circ: 24000 Not Audited
Editor: Georgie Corlett-Pitt
Profile: Publication covering UK and international sailing as well as performance tips, personality profiles and gossip. Aimed at sailing enthusiasts.
Ad Rate: Full Page Colour £3029.00
MAGAZINE
Boating & Yachting

yachtworld.com
998941
Editorial: Cams Hall, Cams Hill, Fareham, Fareham PO16 8AB **Tel:** 44 01329 222300
Web site: www.yachtworld.co.uk/boat-content/features
Freq: Daily
Circ: 6514 Cision Digital Reach
MAGAZINE (ONLINE)
Boating & Yachting, Travel

Yahoo UK
984363

Editorial: 11-20 Capper Street, Shropshire House, London WC1E 6JA
Tel: 44 02071 311000
Web site: https://uk.yahoo.com/
Freq: Daily
Circ: 107189 Cision Digital Reach
Editor: Andy Wells
MAGAZINE (ONLINE)
National News

Yeovil Express
980513

Editorial: 44 St James Street, Taunton TA1 1JR **Tel:** 44 01823 365000
Email: newsdesk@chardandilminsternews.co.uk
Web site: www.yeovilexpress.co.uk
Freq: Daily
Circ: 61584 Cision Digital Reach
Profile: Website covering local news from Yeovil and the surrounding areas.
MAGAZINE (ONLINE)
News & Current Affairs

Yet another review site
990689

Email: reviews@yetanotherreviewsite.co.uk
Web site: www.yetanotherreviewsite.co.uk
Freq: Daily
Circ: 9026 Cision Digital Reach
Profile: Website covering computer games. YET ANOTHER REVIEW SITE provides reviews on computer games and consoles.
MAGAZINE (ONLINE)
Computer & Video Games

YOGA Magazine
985228

Editorial: 233 Bethnal Green Road, London E2 6AB **Tel:** 44 02077 295454
Email: info@yogamagazine.com
Web site: www.yogamagazine.com
Freq: Monthly
Circ: 90000 Not Audited
Editor: Yogi Malik
Profile: Magazine that covers all aspects of yoga as well as articles on mind, body and spirit issues fashion, travel, reviews, advice and shopping. Provides yoga features and celebrity interviews. Aimed predominantly at women between 20 and 55 years old of all yoga levels.
Ad Rate: Full Page Colour £1117.00
MAGAZINE
Fitness & Exercise

York Vision
994651

Editorial: University of York Students Union, Grimston House, Vanbrugh College, University of York, York YO10 5DD
Email: vision@yusu.org
Web site: www.yorkvision.co.uk
Freq: Bi Monthly
Circ: 3000 Not Audited
MAGAZINE
Student Lifestyle

York What's On
982911

Editorial: Oaktree Farm, The Moor, Haxby, York YO1 6WR
Web site: http://www.yourlocallink.co.uk/index2.php
Freq: Monthly
Circ: 20000 Not Audited
Profile: Guide for visitors and residents to exhibitions and entertainment in the local area. Aimed at residents and visitors of York.
Ad Rate: Full Page Colour £300.00
MAGAZINE
News & Current Affairs

YorkMix
987812

Editorial: 5-6 Kings Court, Shambles, York YO1 7LD **Tel:** 44 01904 848766
Email: info@yorkmix.com
Web site: www.yorkmix.com
Freq: Daily
Circ: 54986 Cision Digital Reach
Editor: Chris Titley
MAGAZINE (ONLINE)
Regional

YorkPress.co.uk - Merged with The Press (York)
983088

Editorial: PO Box 29, 84-86 Walmgate, York YO1 9YN
Web site: http://www.yorkpress.co.uk/
Circ: 1001909 Cision Digital Reach
MAGAZINE (ONLINE)
News & Current Affairs

Yorkshire Advertiser
982919

Editorial: Kirkdale Road, Kirkbymoorside, Kirkbymoorside YO62 6YB
Tel: 44 01439 408096
Freq: Monthly
Circ: 6000 Not Audited
MAGAZINE
News & Current Affairs

Yorkshire Golfer
996971

Editorial: 31 Branch Road, Batley, Batley WF17 5SB **Tel:** 44 01924 470296
Email: news@yorkshire-golfer.com
Freq: Monthly
Circ: 100000 Not Audited
MAGAZINE
Golf

Yorkshire Life
982551

Editorial: United Business Centres Ltd, Cinnabar Court, 5300 Daresbury Park, Warrington WA4 4GE **Tel:** 44 01928 240668
Web site: www.yorkshirelife.co.uk/home
Freq: Monthly
Circ: 16326 Not Audited
Editor: Esther Leach; **Editor:** Paul Mackenzie
Profile: Magazine covering regional general interest including features on personalities, food and drink, gardening, property, the arts and town and village profiles. Aimed at residents of Yorkshire and those who enjoy the finer things in life.
Ad Rate: Full Page Colour £2005.00
MAGAZINE
Regional General Interest

Yorkshire Living
1053635

Editorial: Living Yorkshire, PO Box 29, 84-86 Walmgate, York YO1 9YN
Tel: 44 01904 653051
Web site: http://www.yorkshire-living.co.uk/
Freq: Monthly
Circ: 15000 Not Audited
Editor: Francine Clee
Profile: High quality monthly free magazine targeting AB customers in York and North Yorkshire. Covers property, leisure, luxury, fashion, health and lifestyle. Distribution of 15,000 copies to AB homes and outlets in York, Malton, Helmsley, Pickering, Easingwold, Harrogate and surrounding village
Ad Rate: Full Page Colour £1000.00
MAGAZINE
Regional General Interest

The Yorkshire Times
986570

Editorial: British School, Otley Street, Skipton BD23 1EW **Tel:** 44 01756 668125
Email: editor@yorkshiretimes.co.uk
Web site: www.yorkshiretimes.co.uk
Freq: Daily
Circ: 17795 Cision Digital Reach
Editor: Angela Boddy
Profile: The Yorkshire Times is a website covering business, events, news, sport, arts and lifestyle in Yorkshire.
MAGAZINE (ONLINE)
Regional

Yorkshire Women's Life
983657

Editorial: PO Box 113, Leeds LS8 2WX
Tel: 44 01132 621409
Email: ywlmagenquiries@btinternet.com
Web site: www.yorkshirewomenslife.co.uk
Freq: 3 Times/Year
Circ: 32000 Not Audited
Editor: Dawn-Maria France; **Editor:** Dawn-Maria France
MAGAZINE
Regional General Interest, Women's Interests

You & Your Growing Family
995137

Editorial: 29 Broadwater Road, Welwyn Garden City, Welwyn Garden City AL7 3BQ
Tel: 44 01707 294000
Email: editor@bounty.com
Web site: www.bounty.com
Freq: Semi-Annual
Circ: 150000 Not Audited
MAGAZINE
Family & Parenting

You & Your Newborn
995136

Editorial: 29 Broadwater Road, Welwyn Garden City, Welwyn Garden City AL7 3BQ
Tel: 44 03458 300200
Email: mediabounty@bounty.com
Web site: www.bounty.com
Freq: Semi-Annual
Circ: 410000 Not Audited
MAGAZINE
Family & Parenting

You & Your Pregnancy
998723

Editorial: 29 Broadwater Road, Welwyn Garden City, Welwyn Garden City AL7 3BQ
Tel: 44 01707 294000
Email: editor@bounty.com
Web site: www.bounty.com
Freq: Semi-Annual
Circ: 430000 Not Audited
MAGAZINE
Family & Parenting

You & Your Wedding
982430

Editorial: Vineyard House, 44 Brook Green, London W6 7BT **Tel:** 44 02071 505000
Web site: www.youandyourwedding.co.uk
Freq: Bi-Monthly
Circ: 26438 Not Audited
Profile: Magazine containing everything for the modern young bride, from wedding outfits to honeymoon destinations and setting up home. Aimed at brides-to-be between 25 and 34 years old.
Ad Rate: Full Page Colour £12105.00
MAGAZINE
Weddings

Young Academic
999133

Editorial: 11 Parkgate Road, Chester, Chester CH1 4AD **Tel:** 44 01244 889943
Email: editor@youngacademic.co.uk
Web site: www.youngacademic.co.uk
Freq: Quarterly Not Audited
MAGAZINE
Student Lifestyle

Young Performer
985905

Editorial: Commonwealth House, One New Oxford Street, London WC1A 1NU
Tel: 44 02078 782300
Web site: http://www.stagecoach.co.uk/young-performer-magazine.html
Freq: Bi-Monthly
Circ: 22000 Not Audited
Editor: Liz Granlrer
Profile: Magazine with features about TV, film, the stage, singing, music and dance, as well as competitions, interviews and news of what's happening in the world of performing arts. Published for Stagecoach Theatre Arts. Aimed at young people for whom acting, singing and dancing is a passion.
MAGAZINE
Education, Music, Pop Music

Young Scot
986641

Editorial: Rosebery House, 9 Haymarket Terrace, Edinburgh EH12 5EZ
Tel: 44 08088 010338
Email: info@youngscot.org
Web site: www.youngscot.org
Freq: Daily
Circ: 6657 Cision Digital Reach
Profile: Magazine of Young Scot the national youth information and discount charity covering information and ideas for young people in Scotland including film, book, and computer game reviews as well as news, features and interviews. Published quarterly inside the Sunday Mail newspaper. First published in 2001, the publication has an average of 16 pages per issue. Read by 11 to 26 year olds in Scotland.
MAGAZINE (ONLINE)
Teen/Young Adult

YoungMinds
984313

Editorial: Suite 11, Baden Place, Crosby Row, London SE1 1YW
Tel: 44 02070 895050
Web site: www.youngminds.org.uk
Freq: Monthly
Circ: 80358 Cision Digital Reach
MAGAZINE (ONLINE)
Charitable Foundations

Your Autism Magazine
985259

Editorial: 393 City Road, London EC1V 1NG
Tel: 44 02078 332299
Email: nas@nas.org.uk
Web site: http://www.autism.org.uk/get-involved/membership/magazine.aspx
Freq: Quarterly
Circ: 25000 Not Audited
MAGAZINE
Neurology, Patient Support

Your Berks, Bucks & Oxon Wedding
985020

Editorial: Pantile House, Newland Drive, Witham, Witham CM8 2AP
Tel: 44 01376 514000
Email: editor@yourberksbuckswedding.com
Web site: www.yourberksbuckswedding.co.uk
Freq: Bi-Monthly
Circ: 10000 Not Audited
Profile: Magazine covering all aspects of weddings including venues, fashion, real weddings, honeymoons, grooms, cakes, catering, news, events, give-aways, letters and questions and answers. Aimed at brides and grooms in Berkshire, Buckinghamshire and Oxfordshire.
Ad Rate: Full Page Colour £900.00
MAGAZINE
Weddings

Your Bristol & Somerset Wedding
984619

Editorial: Pantile House, Newland Drive, Witham, Witham CM8 2AP
Tel: 44 01376 535611
Email: editor@yourbristolsomersetwedding.co.uk
Web site: www.yourbristolsomersetwedding.co.uk
Freq: Bi-Monthly
Profile: Magazine covering all aspects of weddings including venues, fashion, real weddings, honeymoons, grooms, cakes, catering, news, events, give-aways, letters and questions and answers. Aimed at brides and grooms in the Bristol and Somerset area.
Ad Rate: Full Page Mono £900.00
MAGAZINE
Weddings

Your Cat
982023

Editorial: 1-6 Buckminster Yard, Main Street, Buckminster, Grantham, Grantham NG33 5SB **Tel:** 44 01476 859820
Email: editorial@yourcat.co.uk
Web site: www.yourcat.co.uk
Freq: Monthly
Circ: 140000 Not Audited
Editor In Chief: Sarah Wright
Profile: Magazine containing practical information on behaviour, grooming and all aspects of healthcare. Includes lifestyle features, interviews, cat shopping, fashion and celebrities and a buyers' guide to practical products. Aimed at all cat lovers.
Ad Rate: Full Page Colour £1935.00
MAGAZINE
Nature & Wildlife

Your Cheshire & Merseyside Wedding
986564

Editorial: Pantile House, Newlands Drive, Witham, Witham CM8 2AP
Tel: 44 01376 514000
Email: editor@yourmerseysidewedding.com
Web site: www.yourmerseysidewedding.com

Consumer Magazines

Freq: Bi-Monthly
Circ: 10000 Not Audited
Profile: Magazine covering all aspects of weddings including venues, fashion, real weddings, honeymoons, grooms, cakes, catering, news, events, give-aways, letters and questions and answers. Aimed at brides and grooms in the Merseyside area.
MAGAZINE
Weddings

Your Coffee Break   986752
Editorial: 124 Landor Road, Stockwell, London SW99JB
Email: inquiries@yourcoffeebreak.co.uk
Web site: http://yourcoffeebreak.co.uk
Freq: Daily
Circ: 50912 Cision Digital Reach
Profile: Website covering women's lifestyle. Your COFFEE BREAK website shares the latest news and information on fashion, career management, health, dating and relationships, celeb spotlight, beauty and travel.
MAGAZINE (ONLINE)
Beauty & Grooming, Cosmetics, Fashion, Hair, Travel, Women's Interests

Your Comic Heroes   1101287
Editorial: Quay House, The Ambury, Bath BA1 1UA
Web site: http://www.futureplc.com/
Freq: Monthly Not Audited
MAGAZINE
Trading Cards & Comics

Your Community Scene   996148
Editorial: Unit 12, Eventus, Sunderland Road, Market Deeping, Market Deeping PE6 8FD **Tel:** 44 01778 382762
Email: info@scenepublishing.co.uk
Web site: www.thescenemagazine.co.uk
Freq: Monthly
Circ: 10000 Not Audited
MAGAZINE
Regional General Interest

Your Devon & Cornwall Wedding   1059418
Tel: 44 01376 514000
Email: editor@yourdevoncornwallwedding.com
Web site: www.yourdevoncornwallwedding.com
Freq: Bi-Monthly
Circ: 4000 Not Audited
Editor: Claire Ridley
MAGAZINE
Weddings

your Docklands & City   985548
Editorial: Cascades Tower, 2 Westferry Road, London E14 8JN
Tel: 44 02075 151339
Email: info@yourmedialondon.com
Web site: www.yourmedialondon.com/
Freq: Monthly
Circ: 20000 Not Audited
Editor: Emma Tompkins
Profile: Lifestyle magazine covering the Docklands and City areas of London. Aimed at the ABC1 population living and working within the two financial districts of Docklands and the City of London.This outlet covers areas within Tower Hamlets Borough.
MAGAZINE
Regional General Interest

Your Dog   982024
Editorial: 1-6 Buckminster Yard, Main Street, Buckminster, Grantham, Grantham NG33 5SB **Tel:** 44 01476 859830
Email: editorial@yourdog.co.uk
Web site: www.yourdog.co.uk
Freq: Monthly
Circ: 90000 Not Audited
Editor In Chief: Sarah Wright
Profile: Magazine focusing on the latest news on dogs, breeds, canine health and show results.
Ad Rate: Full Page Mono £2068.00
Ad Rate: Full Page Colour £2068.00
MAGAZINE
Nature & Wildlife

Your East Anglian Wedding   987191
Editorial: Pantile House, Newlands Drive, Witham, Witham CM8 2AP
Tel: 44 01376 514000
Email: editor@youreastanglianwedding.com
Web site: www.youreastanglianwedding.com
Freq: Bi-Monthly
Circ: 5000 Not Audited
Editor: Sarah Reeve
Profile: Magazine covering all areas of weddings including wedding planning, bridal fashion and beauty and honeymoons.
MAGAZINE
Weddings

Your East Midlands Wedding   988610
Editorial: Pantile House, Newland Drive, Witham, Witham CM8 2AP
Tel: 44 01376 514000
Email: editor@youreastmidlandsweddingmagazine.com
Web site: youreastmidlandsweddingmagazine.com
Freq: Bi-Monthly
Circ: 10000 Not Audited
MAGAZINE
Weddings

Your East Riding   998635
Editorial: Communications, Room GG53, Beverley HU17 9BA **Tel:** 44 01482 887700
Email: youreastriding@eastriding.gov.uk
Web site: www2.eastriding.gov.uk/council/press-office/printed-publications/your-eastriding/
Freq: Quarterly
Circ: 148664 Not Audited
Editor: Nick Procter
MAGAZINE
Regional

Your Family Tree   981969
Editorial: Dennis Publishing Ltd., 31-32 Alfred Place, London WC1E 7DP
Tel: 44 01865 922923
Email: yft@historymags.co.uk
Web site: www.yourfamilytreemag.co.uk
Freq: Monthly
Circ: 8376 Not Audited
Editor: Andrew Chapman; **Editor:** Nell Darby
Profile: Magazine with advice on how to trace your family history, tips from genealogy experts, guidance on using historical sources, case studies and the latest news for family historians. First published in 2004, the publication has an average of 100 pages per issue. Aimed at amateur genealogists and family historians.There is a size limit of 2MB on the main email address.
Ad Rate: Full Page Colour £900.00
MAGAZINE
Family & Parenting, History

Your Fitness   985554
Editorial: 25 Phoenix Court, Hawkins Road, Colchester, Colchester CO2 8JY
Tel: 44 01206 505900
Web site: http://www.yourfitnesstoday.com/
Freq: Monthly
Circ: 40000 Not Audited
Editor: Claire Munnings
Profile: Magazine containing workouts, training tips, nutrition plans and motivational coaching, all specifically targeted at improving performance. Focused on women's sport and fitness with recipes and nutrition plans devised for optimum health and performance, not just weight loss. The fitness magazine for motivated, goal-driven women who love to exercise.
Ad Rate: Full Page Colour £1395.00
MAGAZINE
Fitness & Exercise, Nutrition, Women's Interests

Your Gaming Heroes   1101286
Editorial: Quay House, The Ambury, Bath BA1 1UA
Web site: http://www.futureplc.com/

Freq: Monthly Not Audited
MAGAZINE
Computer & Video Games

Your Guide to Amusement and Gaming   995954
Tel: 44 01706 828280
Email: info@yourguides.net
Web site: http://www.yourguides.net/amusement-gaming
Freq: Quarterly
Circ: 27000 Not Audited
MAGAZINE
Computer & Video Games

Your Hampshire & Dorset Wedding   984146
Editorial: Pantile House, Newland Drive, Witham, Witham CM8 2AP
Tel: 44 01376 514000
Email: editor@yourhampshirewedding.co.uk
Web site: www.yourhampshirewedding.co.uk
Freq: Bi-Monthly
Editor: Sarah Reeve
Profile: Magazine covering all aspects of weddings including venues, fashion, real weddings, honeymoons, grooms, cakes, catering, news, events, give-aways, letters and questions and answers. Aimed at brides and grooms in the Hampshire and Dorset area.
Ad Rate: Full Page Colour £900.00
MAGAZINE
Weddings

Your Healthy Living   986916
Editorial: Unit 2, Three Hills Farm, Ashdon Road, Bartlow, Cambridge CB21 4EN
Tel: 44 01223 894200
Email: info@yourhealthyliving.co.uk
Web site: www.yourhealthyliving.co.uk
Freq: Monthly
Circ: 100000 Not Audited
Editor: Liz Parry
Profile: Your Healthy Living magazine is aimed at health conscious consumers. It contains information about the latest products and foods available to improve and balance your health naturally across all areas of your life including mind, body and well being.
MAGAZINE
Alternative Medicine, Cooking & Baking, Health & Medicine, Nutrition, Organic Food, Women's Interests

Your Herts & Beds Wedding   984157
Editorial: Pantile House, Newland Drive, Witham, Witham CM8 2AP
Tel: 44 01376 535611
Email: editor@yourhertsbedswedding.co.uk
Web site: yourhertsbedswedding.co.uk
Freq: Bi-Monthly Not Audited
Profile: Magazine covering all aspects of weddings including venues, fashion, real weddings, honeymoons, grooms, cakes, catering, news, events, give-aways and questions and answers. Aimed at brides and grooms in Hertfordshire and Bedfordshire.
Ad Rate: Full Page Colour £900.00
MAGAZINE
Weddings

Your Home   981859
Editorial: The Tower, Phoenix Square, Colchester CO4 9HU **Tel:** 44 01206 851117
Email: yourhome@burdamagazines.co.uk
Web site: www.yourhomemagazine.co.uk
Freq: Monthly
Circ: 109727 Not Audited
Profile: Magazine providing information on home decorating and home improvements for all rooms in the house. Contains a selection of quick and simple projects, complete room makeovers, home improvement advice and space-saving solutions. First published in 1997. Aimed at homeowners aged between 25 and 45 years old who are interested in giving their homes a fresh new look.
Ad Rate: Full Page Colour £5840.00
MAGAZINE
Do-It-Yourself (DIY)

Your Horse   982244
Editorial: Media House, Peterborough Business Park, Lynch Wood, Peterborough PE2 6EA **Tel:** 44 01733 468000
Email: getinvolved@yourhorse.co.uk
Web site: www.yourhorse.co.uk
Freq: Monthly
Circ: 17522 Not Audited
Editor: Imogen Johnson
Profile: Magazine containing ideas, techniques and inspiration for horse owners and riders. Aimed at horse owners and riders.
Ad Rate: Full Page Colour £2550.00
MAGAZINE
Equestrian Sports

your Kensington & Chelsea   988139
Editorial: Cascades Tower, 2 Westferry Road, London E14 8JN
Tel: 44 02031 502555
Web site: www.yourmedia.uk.com
Freq: Monthly
Circ: 5000 Not Audited
Editor: Emma Tompkins
Profile: Lifestyle magazine covering the Kensington and Chelsea areas of London. Aimed at the ABC1 population living and working within Kensington & Chelsea.
MAGAZINE
Regional

Your Kent Wedding   984159
Editorial: Pantile House, Newland Drive, Witham, Witham CM8 2AP
Tel: 44 01376 535611
Email: editor@yourkentwedding.com
Web site: yourkentwedding.com
Freq: Bi-Monthly
Circ: 10000 Not Audited
Profile: Magazine covering all aspects of weddings including venues, fashion, real weddings, honeymoons, grooms, cakes, catering, news, events, give-aways, letters and questions and answers. Aimed at brides and grooms in the Kent area.
Ad Rate: Full Page Colour £900.00
MAGAZINE
Weddings

Your Local Link   982553
Editorial: Oak Tree Farm, The Moor, Haxby, York YO32 2LH **Tel:** 44 01904 767881
Email: info@yourlocallink.co.uk
Web site: http://www.yourlocallink.co.uk/
Freq: Monthly
Circ: 89844 Not Audited
Profile: Magazine featuring community news, local events, entertainment and festivals. Aimed at people living or working in York.
Ad Rate: Full Page Colour £1200.00
MAGAZINE
Regional General Interest

Your Local Wedding Scene   995362
Editorial: Unit 12, Eventus, Sunderland Road, Market Deeping, Market Deeping PE6 8FD **Tel:** 44 01778 382762
Email: info@scenepublishing.co.uk
Web site: http://serps.website/
Freq: Semi-Annual
Circ: 15000 Not Audited
MAGAZINE
Regional General Interest, Weddings, Women's Interests

Your London Wedding   984809
Editorial: Pantile House, Newlands Drive, Witham, Witham CM8 2AP
Tel: 44 01376 514000
Email: editor@yourlondonweddingmagazine.com
Web site: www.yourlondonweddingmagazine.com
Freq: Bi-Monthly Not Audited
Editor: Georgina Cassels
Profile: Magazine covering all aspects of weddings including venues, fashion, real weddings, honeymoons, grooms, cakes, catering, news, events, give-aways, letters, questions and answer. Aimed at brides and grooms in the London area and surrounds.

Ad Rate: Full Page Colour £900.00
MAGAZINE
Weddings

your Mayfair　　986729

Editorial: Cascades Tower, 2 Westferry Road, London E14 8JN
Tel: 44 02075 151339
Email: info@yourmedialondon.com
Web site: http://www.yourmedia.uk.com
Freq: Monthly
Circ: 5000 Not Audited
Editor: Emma Tompkins
Profile: Lifestyle magazine covering the Mayfair area of London. Aimed at the ABC1 population living and working within Mayfair.
MAGAZINE
Luxury Goods, Regional General Interest

Your Move　　982568

Editorial: 36 Henry Street, Liverpool L1 5BS
Tel: 44 01517 093871
Email: post@movepublishing.co.uk
Web site: www.yourmovemagazine.com
Freq: Bi-Weekly
Circ: 50000 Not Audited
Profile: Magazine covering commercial and residential property news as well as regional general interest including lifestyle, motoring, theatre, the arts, music, days out and events. First published in 1999, the publication has an average of 90 pages per issue. Aimed at residents and visitors to Liverpool.
Ad Rate: Full Page Colour £1155.00
MAGAZINE
Property Management & Maintenance

Your North East Wedding　988611

Editorial: Pantile House, Newland Drive, Witham, Witham CM8 2AP
Tel: 44 01376 514000
Email: editor@yournortheastwedding.com
Web site: yournortheastwedding.com
Freq: Bi-Monthly
Circ: 10000 Not Audited
MAGAZINE
Weddings

Your North West Wedding

985407
Editorial: Pantile House, Newlands Drive, Witham, Witham CM8 2AP
Tel: 44 01376 514000
Email: editor@yournorthwest.wedding
Web site: www.yourmanchesterwedding. com
Freq: Bi-Monthly
Circ: 10000 Not Audited
Profile: Magazine covering all aspects of weddings including venues, fashion, real weddings, honeymoons, grooms, cakes, catering, news, events, give-aways, letters and questions and answers. Aimed at brides and grooms in the Manchester area.
Ad Rate: Full Page Mono £900.00
MAGAZINE
Weddings

Your Pet Magazine　　1101203

Web site: yourpetmag.co.uk
Freq: Bi-Monthly
MAGAZINE
Nature & Wildlife

Your South Wales Wedding

984976
Editorial: Pantile House, Newland Drive, Witham, Witham CM8 2AP
Tel: 44 01376 514000
Email: editor@yoursouthwaleswedding.com
Web site: yoursouthwaleswedding.com
Freq: Bi-Monthly
Circ: 10000 Not Audited
Profile: Magazine covering all aspects of weddings including venues, fashion, real weddings, honeymoons, grooms, cakes, catering, news, events, give-aways, letters and questions and answers. Aimed at brides and grooms in the South Wales area.
MAGAZINE
Weddings

your St. John's Wood　　988138

Editorial: Cascades Tower, 2 Westferry Road, London E14 8JN
Tel: 44 02075 151339
Email: info@yourmedialondon.com
Web site: www.yourmedia.uk.com
Freq: Monthly
Circ: 5000 Not Audited
Editor: Emma Tompkins
MAGAZINE
Regional

your Stratford City　　986670

Editorial: Cascades Tower, 2 Westferry Road, London E14 8JN
Tel: 44 02075 151339
Email: info@yourmedialondon.com
Web site: www.yourmedialondon.com
Freq: Monthly
Circ: 15000 Not Audited
Editor: Emma Tompkins
Profile: Regional lifestyle publication covering Stratford. Aimed at residents of Stratford area and distributed within the Westfield Stratford City shopping complex. This outlet covers areas within Newham Borough.
MAGAZINE
Regional General Interest

Your Surrey Wedding　　984160

Editorial: Pantile House, Newland Drive, Witham, Witham CM8 2AP
Tel: 44 01376 514000
Email: editor@yoursurrey.wedding
Web site: www.yoursurreywedding.com
Freq: Bi-Monthly
Circ: 10000 Not Audited
Profile: Magazine covering all aspects of weddings including venues, fashion, real weddings, honeymoons, grooms, cakes, catering, news, events, give-aways, letters and questions and answers. Aimed at brides and grooms in the Surrey area.
Ad Rate: Full Page Colour £900.00
MAGAZINE
Weddings

Your Sussex Wedding　　984158

Editorial: Pantile House, Newland Drive, Witham, Witham CM8 2AP
Tel: 44 01376 514000
Email: editor@your-sussex.wedding
Web site: yoursussexwedding.com
Freq: Bi-Monthly
Circ: 10000 Not Audited
Profile: Magazine covering all aspects of weddings including venues, fashion, real weddings, honeymoons, grooms, cakes, catering, news, events, give-aways, letters and questions and answers. Aimed at brides and grooms in the sussex area.
Ad Rate: Full Page Colour £900.00
MAGAZINE
Weddings

Your Thurrock　　995122

Editorial: Unit 68, Nicholls Field, Harlow
Tel: 44 07757 167689
Email: newsdesk@yourthurrock.com
Web site: www.yourthurrock.com
Freq: Daily
Circ: 45919 Cision Digital Reach
Editor: Michael Casey
MAGAZINE (ONLINE)
News & Current Affairs

Your Voice　　984322

Editorial: 2 St James' Court, Friar Gate, Derby DE1 1BT **Tel:** 44 01332 372337
Email: pressoffice@voicetheunion.org.uk
Web site: www.voicetheunion.org.uk/ yourvoice
Freq: Quarterly
Circ: 18624 Not Audited
Editor: Richard Fraser
Profile: Magazine containing news, views and advice on issues of concern to teachers, head teachers, lecturers, education support staff and child carers. Aimed at members of Voice: the union for education professionals,

chief education officers, the national press and libraries.
MAGAZINE
Disability, Education, Higher Education, Preschool, Schools & Institutions, Students

Your Wedding　　999419

Editorial: The Old Library, Church Green West, Redditch B97 4DU
Web site: yourweddingmagazine.co.uk
Freq: Annual
Circ: 20000 Not Audited
Editor: Claire Bullivant
MAGAZINE
Weddings

your West End　　996430

Editorial: Cascades Tower, 2 Westferry Road, London E14 8JN
Tel: 44 02031 502555
Email: info@yourmedialondon.com
Web site: www.yourmedialondon.com/
Freq: Monthly
Circ: 5000 Not Audited
Editor: Emma Tompkins
Profile: Lifestyle magazine for London's West End. Aimed at the A and B social demographic within the West End.
MAGAZINE
Luxury Goods, Regional General Interest

Your West Midlands Wedding

984977
Editorial: Pantile House, Newland Drive, Witham, Witham CM8 2AP
Tel: 44 01376 514000
Email: editor@yourwestmidlandswedding. com
Web site: yourwestmidlandswedding.com
Freq: Bi-Monthly Not Audited
Profile: Magazine covering all aspects of weddings including venues, fashion, real weddings, honeymoons, grooms, cakes, catering, news, events, give-aways, letters and questions and answers. Aimed at brides and grooms in the West Midlands area.
Ad Rate: Full Page Mono £900.00
MAGAZINE
Weddings

Your Yorkshire Wedding　987463

Editorial: Pantile House, Newlands Drive, Witham, Witham CM8 2AP
Tel: 44 01376 535611
Email: editor@ youryorkshireweddingmagazine.com
Web site: youryorkshireweddingmagazine. com
Freq: Bi-Monthly
Circ: 10000 Not Audited
Profile: Magazine covering weddings in Yorkshire. Covers wedding planning, bridal fashion and beauty, venues and honeymoon travel.
Ad Rate: Full Page Mono £900.00
MAGAZINE
Weddings

YourHolidayTV.com　　1073648

Tel: 44 01233 660220
Email: david@yourholidaytv.com
Web site: www.yourholidaytv.com
Freq: Daily
Circ: 12320 Cision Digital Reach
MAGAZINE (ONLINE)
Travel

Your-Hols.com　　987406

Editorial: The Reivers, Arthington Lane, Pool in Wharfdale, Otley LS21 1JZ
Email: trisha@trishaharbord.com
Web site: www.your-hols.com
Freq: Daily
Circ: 11578 Cision Digital Reach
MAGAZINE (ONLINE)
Travel

YourMoney.com　　979822

Editorial: 7th Floor, Lincoln House, 296-302 High Holborn, London WC1V 7JH
Tel: 44 02038 153670
Web site: www.yourmoney.com
Freq: Daily

Circ: 52149 Cision Digital Reach
Editor: Joanna Faith
Profile: Website covering personal finance. YOURMoney.com website shares the latest information on products including savings, investments, ISAs, insurance and in-depth financial features, news-stories, credit cards, tools and online learning applications as well as comparison tables, current accounts, personal or secured loans, pensions and what companies are the best utility providers. Aimed at consumers of financial products and intelligent, curious laypeople.
MAGAZINE (ONLINE)
Personal Finance

yourmortgage.co.uk　　979901

Editorial: 7th Floor, Lincoln House, 296-300 High Holborn, London WC1V 7JH
Tel: 44 02038 153670
Web site: www.yourmortgage.co.uk
Freq: Bi-Monthly
Circ: 14356 Cision Digital Reach
Profile: Magazine covering all aspects of the housing and mortgage markets. Includes features on home interest as well as advice on choosing the most suitable mortgage. First published in 1987. Aimed at homeowners and buyers, re-mortgagers and those interested in buying property to let.
Ad Rate: Full Page Colour £3300.00
MAGAZINE (ONLINE)
Personal Finance

Yours Magazine　　981973

Editorial: Media House, Peterborough Business Park, Peterborough PE2 6EA
Tel: 44 01733 468000
Email: yours@bauermedia.co.uk
Web site: http://www.yours.co.uk/magazine
Freq: Bi-Weekly
Circ: 251901 Not Audited
Editor: Sharon Reid
Profile: Fortnightly lifestyle magazine covering issues and interests of women over 50. It features articles on health, news, fashion and beauty, nostalgia triggered by events in the world today and campaigns on key issues. First published in 1974, the publication has an average of 148 pages per issue. Aimed at women over 50 years old.
Ad Rate: Full Page Colour £3900.00
MAGAZINE
Retirement Savings, Women's Interests

yourwellness.com　　1012356

Editorial: A4 Windsor Place, Faraday Road, Manor Royal, Crawley RH10 9TF
Tel: 44 02085 889553
Email: enquiries@yourwellness.net
Web site: www.yourwellness.com
Freq: Daily
Circ: 27082 Cision Digital Reach
MAGAZINE (ONLINE)
Alternative Medicine, Fitness & Exercise, Health & Medicine, Nutrition

Youthwork　　982168

Editorial: Premier, PO Box 17911, London SW1P 4YX **Tel:** 44 02073 161450
Email: youthwork@premier.org.uk
Web site: http://www.premieryouthwork. com/
Freq: Monthly
Circ: 6000 Not Audited
Profile: Publication featuring articles on youthwork, session planning and related information. Aimed predominantly at Christian youth workers.
Ad Rate: Full Page Mono £780.00
Ad Rate: Full Page Colour £780.00
MAGAZINE
Religion

Yumi Journal　　998254

Web site: journal.yumi.co.uk
Freq: Daily
Circ: 93 Cision Digital Reach
MAGAZINE (ONLINE)
Beauty & Grooming, Cooking & Baking, Cosmetics, Fashion, Hair

Consumer Magazines

yummymummybeauty.com

986476

Email: info@yummymummybeauty.com
Web site: www.yummymummybeauty.com
Freq: Daily
Circ: 13220 Cision Digital Reach
MAGAZINE (ONLINE)
Beauty & Grooming, Cosmetics, Hair

Yuppee

998309

Email: editor@yuppee.com
Web site: www.yuppee.com
Freq: Daily
Circ: 37613 Cision Digital Reach
MAGAZINE (ONLINE)
Dance Music, Fashion, Motorsports, Movies & Video, Pop Music, Racquet Sports, Rap & Hip Hop, Rock Music, Soccer, Travel

Zani

998001

Email: info@zani.co.uk
Web site: www.zani.co.uk/
Freq: Daily
Circ: 17318 Cision Digital Reach
Editor: Matteo Sedazzari
MAGAZINE (ONLINE)
Broadcasting, Dance Music, Entertainment, Movies & Video, Pop Music, Rap & Hip Hop, Rock Music, Soccer

ZDNet

980038

Editorial: The Warehouse, The Bower, 207-211 Old Street, London EC1V 9NR
Tel: 44 02 070211000
Email: ukeditorial@zdnet.com
Web site: http://www.zdnet.com
Freq: Daily
Circ: 11821213 Cision Digital Reach
MAGAZINE (ONLINE)
Auto Aftermarket, Computers, Data Management, Electronics, Government Technology, Industry, Internet, Mobile Communications, Security & Security Systems, Software

The Zelfs - CEASED 2015

997744

Editorial: Marlborough House, Headley Road, Grayshott, Hindhead GU26 6LG
Web site: www.thezelfs.com
Freq: Monthly Not Audited
MAGAZINE
Elementary School, Teen/Young Adult

ZERO

1101761

Email: info@zero-magazine.co.uk
Web site: www.zero-magazine.co.uk
Freq: Daily
Circ: 548 Cision Digital Reach
MAGAZINE (ONLINE)
Antiques/Collectibles, Art, Arts, Classical/Choral/Band Music, Country, Folk, Bluegrass, Dance Music, Fashion, Jazz & Blues, Literature, Music

Zero Tolerance

995897

Editorial: PO Box 6369, Rugby CV21 3PF
Tel: 44 01788 298052
Email: news@ztmag.com
Web site: www.ztmag.com
Freq: Bi-Monthly Not Audited
MAGAZINE
Rock Music

Zest For Life

1063923

Web site: www.zestforlifemag.com
Freq: Daily
Circ: 10881 Cision Digital Reach
MAGAZINE (ONLINE)
News & Current Affairs

Zing

1072206

Editorial: The Dovecote, Little Baldon, Oxford OX44 9PU **Tel:** 44 01844 278883
Web site: http://www.zingmag.net/
Freq: Quarterly
Circ: 250000 Not Audited
MAGAZINE
News & Current Affairs

Zoom Zoom

998767

Editorial: Bankside 3, 90 Southwark Street, London SE1 0SW **Tel:** 44 02037 877000
Email: zoom.in@redwoodlondon.com
Web site: www.zoomzoommag.com
Freq: 3 Times/Year

Circ: 27000000 Not Audited
MAGAZINE
Automakers

Zoopla

984941

Editorial: Union House, 182-194 Union Street, London SE1 0LH
Email: editor@zoopla.co.uk
Web site: http://www.zoopla.co.uk/discover/property-news/#FDHDCteAgVoDuxPx.97
Freq: Daily
Circ: 1370490 Cision Digital Reach
Profile: Website covering property. It covers topics on housing prices and mortgages.
MAGAZINE (ONLINE)
Commercial Real Estate, Office Design, Property Management & Maintenance, Real Estate, Residential Real Estate, Retail, Travel Industry

Zuri Magazine

995537

Editorial: Unit 125, Tudorleaf Business Centre, 2-8 Fountayne Road, London N15 4QL **Tel:** 44 02034 897320
Email: info@zurimagazine.com
Web site: www.zurimagazine.com
Freq: Quarterly
Circ: 1500 Not Audited
MAGAZINE
Beauty & Grooming, Cosmetics, Hair

Willings Volume 1
Section 5

UK Broadcast

UK Radio Stations & Networks listed A-Z

UK Television Stations & Networks listed A-Z

Index to UK Broadcast

Section Guide

RADIO

Radio Networks & Stations 476

TELEVISION

Television Networks & Stations 482

Section 5 UK Broadcast

UK Broadcast

Radio Networks & Stations

102 / 107.3 Touch Radio FM (Warwickshire, Worcestershire & Cotswolds)
Unit G4, Holly Farm Business Park, Honiley, Kenilworth CV8 1NP **Tel:** 44 01926 485600
Web site: www.102touchfm.co.uk

102.4 Wish FM
Orrell Lodge, Orrell Road, Orrell, Wigan WN5 8HJ **Tel:** 44 01942 761024
Email: news@wish-fm.com
Web site: www.wishfm.net

103.1 Central FM
The Studio, 9 Munro Road, Stirling FK7 7UU
Tel: 44 01786 577024
Email: studio@centralfm.co.uk
Web site: www.centralfm.co.uk

106 Jack FM (Oxford)
The Dumpy Building, 270 - 272 Woodstock Road, Oxford OX2 7NW
Tel: 44 01865 315980
Email: jack@jackfm.co.uk
Web site: http://www.jackfm.co.uk/

106.3 Bridge FM
St Hilary Transmitter, nr St Hilary, Cowbridge, Cardiff CF71 7DP
Tel: 44 01656 838620
Email: enquiries@bridgefm.wales
Web site: bridgefm.wales

106.9 SFM
The Latimer Studios, 1st Floor, Crescent Hall, Central Avenue, Sittingbourne ME10 4BX **Tel:** 44 01795 858037
Email: studio@sfmradio.com
Web site: http://www.sfmradio.com/

107.2 Wire FM
Orrell Lodge, Orrell Road, Wigan WN5 8HJ
Tel: 44 08447 360083
Email: news@wirefm.com
Web site: www.wirefm.com

107.6 Banbury Sound
The Ideas Centre, Holly Farm Business Park, Honiley, Warwick CV8 1NP
Tel: 44 01295 661070
Email: news@banburysound.co.uk
Web site: www.banburysound.co.uk

107.6 Capital FM Liverpool
One Park West, 33-39 Strand Street, Liverpool L1 8LT **Tel:** 44 0151 5 505800
Email: liverpool-news@thisisglobal.com
Web site: http://www.capitalfm.com/liverpool/on-air/

107.8 Radio Jackie
110 Tolworth Broadway, London KT6 7JD
Tel: 44 02082 881300
Email: studio@radiojackie.com
Web site: www.radiojackie.com

2BR
The Studios, 2A Petre Court, Accrington BB5 5HY **Tel:** 44 01254 350350
Email: news@2br.co.uk
Web site: http://www.2br.co.uk/

2BR 99.8 fm
The Studios, 2A Petre Court, Accrington, Accrington BB5 5HY **Tel:** 44 03333 444393
Email: news@2br.co.uk
Web site: www.2br.co.uk

3FM
45 Victoria Street, Douglas, Isle of Man IM1 3RS **Tel:** 44 01624 616333
Email: news@three.fm
Web site: www.three.fm

96. 2 Touch Radio FM (Coventry)
The Ideas Centre, Holly Farm Business Park, Honiley, Kenilworth CV8 1NP
Tel: 44 02476 011710
Email: coventry.studio@touchradio.co.uk
Web site: www.962touchfm.co.uk

96.2 The Revolution
Sarah Moor Studios, PO Box 962, Henshaw Street, Oldham OL1 3EN
Tel: 44 01616 216500
Email: info@revolution962.com
Web site: www.therevolution962.com

96.4 FM The Wave
P.O. Box 964, Victoria Road, Gowerton, Swansea SA4 3AB **Tel:** 44 01792 511964
Email: reception@thewave.co.uk
Web site: www.thewave.co.uk

99.9 Radio Norwich
Stanton House, 29 Yarmouth Road, Norwich NR7 0EE **Tel:** 44 01603 703300
Email: info@999radionorwich.com
Web site: www.norwich999.com

Absolute Classic Rock
One Golden Square, London W1F 9DJ
Tel: 44 02074 341215
Web site: www.absoluteclassicrock.co.uk

Absolute Radio
One Golden Square, London W1F 9DJ
Tel: 44 02074 341215
Email: newsroom@absoluteradio.co.uk
Web site: www.absoluteradio.co.uk

All About Property with Gabby Logan - Sunday (8-9pm)
Tel: 44 01613 356000
Email: logan@bbc.co.uk
Web site: http://www.bbc.co.uk/programmes/b06dbl8t

Amazing Radio
Amazing Towers, Church Street, Gateshead NE8 2AT
Email: info@amazingradio.co.uk
Web site: http://amazingradio.com

ARfm
151 Longmoor Road, Long Eaton, Long Eaton NG10 4EG **Tel:** 44 07778 949024
Email: studio@arfm.co.uk
Web site: www.arfm.co.uk

Ashbourne Radio
Ashbourne Radio, St Monica's House, Windmill Lane, Ashbourne DE6 1EY
Tel: 44 01335 346967
Email: news@highpeakradio.co.uk
Web site: http://www.ashbourneradio.co.uk/

Bailrigg FM
Fylde College, Lancaster University, Lancaster LA1 4YF **Tel:** 44 01524 593902
Email: news@bailriggfm.co.uk
Web site: www.bailriggfm.co.uk

The Bay
PO Box 969, St George's Quay, Lancaster LA1 3LD **Tel:** 44 01524 848747
Email: baynews@cnradio.com
Web site: www.thebay.co.uk

BBC Asian Network
BBC Asian Network, New Broadcasting House, London W1A 1AA
Tel: 44 02036 143660
Email: asiannetworknews@bbc.co.uk
Web site: www.bbc.co.uk/asiannetwork

BBC Coventry & Warwickshire
Priory Place, Coventry CV1 5SQ
Tel: 44 024776 539222
Email: coventry.warwickshire@bbc.co.uk
Web site: http://www.bbc.co.uk/bbccoventryandwarwickshire

BBC Essex
PO Box 765, Chelmsford, Chelmsford CM2 9XB **Tel:** 44 01245 616000
Email: essex@bbc.co.uk
Web site: www.bbc.co.uk/england/essex

BBC Hereford & Worcester
Hylton Road, Worcester WR2 5WW
Tel: 44 01905 748485
Email: bbchw@bbc.co.uk
Web site: http://www.bbc.co.uk/bbcherefordandworcester

BBC Newcastle
Broadcasting Centre, Barrack Road, Newcastle NE99 1RN **Tel:** 44 01912 324141
Email: newcastlenews@bbc.co.uk
Web site: www.bbc.co.uk/bbcnewcastle

BBC Radio 1
2nd Floor, Peel Wing, BBC Broadcasting House, Portland Place, London W1A 1AA
Tel: 44 02087 438000
Email: yourlondon@bbc.co.uk
Web site: www.bbc.co.uk/radio1

BBC Radio 1Xtra
Broadcasting House, Portland Place, London W1A 1AA **Tel:** 44 02087 438000
Web site: www.bbc.co.uk/1xtra

BBC Radio 2
Wogan House, 99 Great Portland Street, London W1A 1AA **Tel:** 44 02087 438000
Email: radio2enquiries@bbc.co.uk
Web site: www.bbc.co.uk/radio2

BBC Radio 3
New Broadcasting House, Portland Place, London W1A 1AA **Tel:** 44 02075 804468
Web site: www.bbc.co.uk/radio3

BBC Radio 4
Broadcasting House, Portland Place, London W1A 1AA **Tel:** 44 02087 438000
Web site: http://www.bbc.co.uk/radio4

BBC Radio 4 Extra
BBC Broadcasting House, Portland Place, London W1A 1AA **Tel:** 44 02087 438000
Web site: www.bbc.co.uk/radio4extra

BBC Radio 5 live
BBC Quay House, MediaCityUK, Salford M50 2QH **Tel:** 44 01613 356000
Email: 5live@bbc.co.uk
Web site: www.bbc.co.uk/5live

BBC Radio 6 Music
Western House, 99 Great Portland Street, London W1W 7NY **Tel:** 44 02075 804468
Web site: www.bbc.co.uk/6music

BBC Radio Berkshire
Caversham Park, Peppard Road, Reading RG4 8TZ **Tel:** 44 01189 464200
Email: radio.berkshire.news@bbc.co.uk
Web site: www.bbc.co.uk/england/radioberkshire

BBC Radio Bristol
Whiteladies Road, Bristol BS8 2LR
Tel: 44 01179 741111
Web site: http://www.bbc.co.uk/radiobristol

BBC Radio Cambridgeshire
Cambridge Business Park, Cowley Road, Cambridge CB4 0WZ **Tel:** 44 08459 252000
Email: cambs@bbc.co.uk
Web site: http://www.bbc.co.uk/radiocambridgeshire

BBC Radio Cornwall
Phoenix Wharf, Truro TR1 1UA
Tel: 44 01872 275421
Email: radio.cornwall@bbc.co.uk
Web site: www.bbc.co.uk/radiocornwall

BBC Radio Cumbria
Annetwell Street, Carlisle CA3 8BB
Tel: 44 01228 592444
Email: radio.cumbria@bbc.co.uk
Web site: http://www.bbc.co.uk/radiocumbria

BBC Radio Cymru
Broadcasting House, Bryn Merion, Merion Road, Bangor LL57 2BY
Tel: 44 02920 322000
Email: borecothi@bbc.co.uk
Web site: www.bbc.co.uk/radiocymru

BBC Radio Derby
56 St Helens Street, Derby DE1 3HY
Tel: 44 01332 361111
Email: radio.derby@bbc.co.uk
Web site: www.bbc.co.uk/england/radioderby

BBC Radio Devon
Broadcasting House, Seymour Road, Mannamead, Plymstock PL3 5YQ
Tel: 44 01752 234511
Email: radio.devon@bbc.co.uk
Web site: www.bbc.co.uk/devon/local_radio

BBC Radio Foyle
8 Northland Road, Londonderry BT48 7GD
Tel: 44 02871 378600
Email: radio.foyle@bbc.co.uk
Web site: www.bbc.co.uk/radiofoyle

BBC Radio Gloucestershire
London Road, Gloucester GL1 1SW
Tel: 44 01452 308585
Email: radio.gloucestershire@bbc.co.uk
Web site: www.bbc.co.uk/england/radiogloucestershire/

BBC Radio Guernsey
Broadcasting House, 4 Bulwer Avenue, St. Sampsons, Guernsey GY2 4LA
Tel: 44 01481 200600
Email: bbcguernsey@bbc.co.uk
Web site: http://www.bbc.co.uk/radioguernsey

BBC Radio Highlands & Islands
Broadcasting House, 7 Culduthel Road, Inverness IV2 4AD **Tel:** 44 01463 720720
Email: inverness.news@bbc.co.uk
Web site: http://www.bbc.co.uk/radioscotland

BBC Radio Humberside
Queens Court, Hull HU1 3RH
Tel: 44 01482 323232
Email: radio.humberside@bbc.co.uk
Web site: www.bbc.co.uk/radiohumberside

BBC Radio Jersey
18-21 Parade Road, St. Helier, Jersey JE2 3PL **Tel:** 44 01534 870000
Email: radiojersey@bbc.co.uk
Web site: http://www.bbc.co.uk/radiojersey

BBC Radio Kent
10-12 Great Hall, Mount Pleasant, Tunbridge Wells TN1 1QQ **Tel:** 44 01892 670000
Email: radio.kent@bbc.co.uk
Web site: www.bbc.co.uk/radiokent

BBC Radio Lancashire
20-26 Darwen Street, Blackburn BB2 2EA
Tel: 44 01254 262411
Email: lancsnews@bbc.co.uk
Web site: www.bbc.co.uk/england/radiolancashire

BBC Radio Leeds
Broadcasting Centre, 2 Saint Peter's Square, Leeds LS9 8AH **Tel:** 44 01132 247300
Email: radioleeds@bbc.co.uk
Web site: www.bbc.co.uk/england/radioleeds

BBC Radio Leicester
9 St Nicholas Place, Leicester LE1 5LB
Tel: 44 01162 516688
Email: radio.leicesternews@bbc.co.uk
Web site: www.bbc.co.uk/england/radioleicester

BBC Radio Lincolnshire
Newport, Lincoln LN1 3XY
Tel: 44 01522 511411
Email: radio.lincolnshire@bbc.co.uk
Web site: www.bbc.co.uk/england/radiolincolnshire

BBC Radio London
2nd Floor, Peel Wing, BBC Broadcasting House, Portland Place, London W1A 1AA
Tel: 44 02087 438000
Email: ldn-planning@bbc.co.uk
Web site: www.bbc.co.uk/radiolondon

BBC Radio Manchester
Quay House, MediaCity, Salford M50 2QH
Tel: 44 01613 356000
Email: radio.manchester@bbc.co.uk
Web site: www.bbc.co.uk/radiomanchester

BBC Radio Merseyside
31 College Lane, Liverpool L1 3DS
Tel: 44 01617 085500
Email: radio.merseyside.news@bbc.co.uk
Web site: www.bbc.co.uk/england/
radiomerseyside

BBC Radio nan Gaidheal
7 Culduthel Road, Inverness IV2 4AD
Tel: 44 01463 720720
Email: naidheachd@bbc.co.uk
Web site: www.bbc.co.uk/radionangaidheal

BBC Radio Norfolk
The Forum, Millennium Plain, Norwich NR2
1BH **Tel:** 44 01603 619331
Email: norfolknews@bbc.co.uk
Web site: http://www.bbc.co.uk/radionorfolk

BBC Radio Northampton
Broadcasting House, Abington Street,
Northampton NN1 2BH
Tel: 44 01604 737666
Email: northampton.news@bbc.co.uk
Web site: http://www.bbc.co.uk/
radionorthampton

BBC Radio Nottingham
London Road, Nottingham NG2 4UU
Tel: 44 01159 550500
Email: radio.nottingham@bbc.co.uk
Web site: http://www.bbc.co.uk/
radionottingham

BBC Radio Orkney
Castle Street, Kirwall, Orkney KW15 1DF
Email: radio.orkney@bbc.co.uk
Web site: http://www.bbc.co.uk/
radioscotland/orkney/

BBC Radio Oxford
269 Banbury Road, Summertown, Oxford
OX2 7DW **Tel:** 44 03459 311444
Email: oxford@bbc.co.uk
Web site: www.bbc.co.uk/bbcoxford

BBC Radio Scotland
40 Pacific Quay, Glasgow G51 1DA
Tel: 44 01414 226000
Web site: www.bbc.co.uk/scotland/
radioscotland

BBC Radio Scotland (Borders)
BBC Radio Scotland, Borders, Unit 1, Ettrick
Riverside, Dunsdale Road, Selkirk TD7 5EB
Tel: 44 01750 724567
Email: selkirk.news@bbc.co.uk
Web site: http://www.bbc.co.uk/
radioscotland

BBC Radio Scotland (South)
Elmbank, Lover's Walk, Dumfries DG1 1NZ
Tel: 44 01387 268008
Email: dumfries@bbc.co.uk
Web site: http://www.bbc.co.uk/news/
scotland/south_scotland

BBC Radio Scotland, North East
BBC Radio Scotland, North East,
Beechgrove Terrace, Aberdeen AB15 5ZT
Tel: 44 01224 384888
Email: news.aberdeen@bbc.co.uk
Web site: www.bbc.co.uk/radioscotland

BBC Radio Sheffield
54 Shoreham Street, Sheffield S1 4RS
Tel: 44 01142 731177
Email: radio.sheffield@bbc.co.uk
Web site: www.bbc.co.uk/england/
radiosheffield

BBC Radio Shetland
Pitt Lane, Shetland ZE1 0DW
Tel: 44 01595 694747
Email: radio.shetland@bbc.co.uk

BBC Radio Shropshire
2-4 Boscobel Drive, Shrewsbury SY1 3TT
Tel: 44 01743 248484
Email: radio.shropshire@bbc.co.uk
Web site: www.bbc.co.uk/radioshropshire

BBC Radio Solent
Broadcasting House, Havelock Road,
Southampton SO14 7PW
Tel: 44 02380 631311
Email: radio.solent@bbc.co.uk
Web site: www.bbc.co.uk/solent

BBC Radio Stoke
Cheapside, Hanley, Stoke-on-Trent ST1 1JJ
Tel: 44 01782 208080
Email: radio.stoke@bbc.co.uk
Web site: http://www.bbc.co.uk/radiostoke

BBC Radio Suffolk
Broadcasting House, St. Matthew's Street,
Ipswich IP1 3EP **Tel:** 44 01473 250000
Email: radiosuffolk@bbc.co.uk
Web site: http://www.bbc.co.uk/radiosuffolk

BBC Radio Ulster
Broadcasting House, 25-27 Ormeau Avenue,
Belfast BT2 8HQ **Tel:** 44 02890 338000
Email: ni_news@bbc.co.uk
Web site: www.bbc.co.uk/northernireland/
radioulster

BBC Radio Wales
Broadcasting House, Llantrisant Road,
Llandaff, Cardiff CF5 2YQ
Tel: 44 02920 322000
Email: newsgathering.wales@bbc.co.uk
Web site: www.bbc.co.uk/radiowales

BBC Radio York
20 Bootham Row, York YO30 7BR
Tel: 44 01904 641641
Email: northyorkshire.news@bbc.co.uk
Web site: www.bbc.co.uk/england/
radioyork

BBC Somerset
Park Street, Taunton, Taunton TA1 4DA
Tel: 44 01823 323956
Email: somerset@bbc.co.uk
Web site: http://www.bbc.co.uk/
bbcsomerset

BBC Sussex & Surrey
Broadcasting House, Queens Road,
Brighton BN1 3XB **Tel:** 44 01273 320400
Web site: http://www.bbc.co.uk/bbcsussex
Editor: Sara David

BBC Tees
Broadcasting House, Newport Road,
Middlesbrough TS1 5DG
Tel: 44 01642 225211
Email: tees.news@bbc.co.uk
Web site: www.bbc.co.uk/bbctees

BBC Three Counties Radio
BBC Three Counties, Broadcasting House -
Grove Park, Court Drive, Dunstable LU5 4GP
Tel: 44 01582 636900
Email: 3cr.news@bbc.co.uk
Web site: http://www.bbc.co.uk/
threecountiesradio

BBC Wiltshire
PO Box 1234, Swindon SN1 3RW
Tel: 44 01793 513626
Email: wiltshire@bbc.co.uk
Web site: http://www.bbc.co.uk/
bbcwiltshire

BBC WM
The Mailbox, Birmingham B1 1RF
Tel: 44 01215 676000
Email: bbcwm@bbc.co.uk
Web site: www.bbc.co.uk/wm

BBC World Service
Broadcasting House, Portland Place,
London W1A 1AA **Tel:** 44 02087 438000
Web site: www.bbc.co.uk/worldservice
Editor: Jeremy Skeet

The Beach
Radio House, 10 Oulton Road, Lowestoft
NR32 4QP **Tel:** 44 08453 451035
Email: info@thebeach.co.uk
Web site: www.thebeach.co.uk

BOB fm (Hertfordshire)
The Pump House, Knebworth Park,
Knebworth SG3 6HQ **Tel:** 44 01438 810900
Email: news@bobfm.co.uk
Web site: www.bobfm.co.uk

Bolton FM
Office 6, Bolton Market, Ashburner Street,
Bolton BL1 5TQ **Tel:** 44 01204 375408
Email: admin@boltonfm.com
Web site: www.boltonfm.com

**The Breeze (Andover,
Basingstoke and North
Hampshire)**
3 Eastgate House, Andover, Andover SP10
1EP **Tel:** 44 01264 336000
Email: andover@thebreeze.com
Web site: http://www.thebreeze.com/

**The Breeze (Bridgwater & West
Somerset)**
The Innovation Centre, Copse Road, Yeovil
BA22 8RN **Tel:** 44 01935 848488
Email: studio.bristol@thebreeze.com
Web site: http://www.thebreeze.com/
somerset/

The Breeze (Cheltenham)
2nd Floor, Normandy House, 309 High
Street, Cheltenham GL50 3HW
Tel: 44 01242 227559
Email: swnews@thebreeze.com
Web site: www.thebreeze.com/cheltenham/

The Breeze (Newbury)
Suite 2, Paddington House, Festival Place,
Basingstoke RG21 7LJ
Tel: 44 01256 694000
Email: thamesvalley-news@celador.co.uk
Web site: www.thebreeze.com/newbury/

The Breeze (South Devon)
Marble Court Business Park, Lymington
Road, Torquay, Torquay TQ1 4FB
Tel: 44 01803 321055
Email: southdevon@thebreeze.com
Web site: http://www.thebreeze.com/
southdevon/

The Breeze (South West)
County Gates, Ashton Road, Bristol BS3 2JH
Tel: 44 01179 666107
Email: swnews@thebreeze.com
Web site: www.thebreeze.com/bristol

The Breeze (Southampton)
Roman Landing, Kingsway, Southampton
SO14 1BN **Tel:** 44 08454 661107
Email: studio@thebreeze.com
Web site: http://www.thebreeze.com/
southampton/

Burn FM
University of Birmingham Guild of Students,
Edgbaston Park Rd, Edgbaston, Birmingham
B15 2TU **Tel:** 44 01212 512452
Email: stationmanager@burnfm.com
Web site: www.burnfm.com

Calon 105FM
Glyndwr University, Plas Coch Campus,
Mold Road, Wrexham LL11 2AW
Tel: 44 01978 293393
Email: info@calonfm.com
Web site: www.calonfm.com

CAM FM
Fitzwilliam College, Storey's Way,
Cambridge CB3 0DG
Email: studio@camfm.co.uk
Web site: www.camfm.co.uk

Canalside Radio 102.8 FM
Unit 2, Clarence Mill, Bollington, Bollington
SK10 5JZ **Tel:** 44 01625 576689
Email: office@thethread.org.uk
Web site: www.thethread.org.uk

Capital Birmingham
Floor 8, Eleven Brindleyplace, Birmingham
B1 2LP **Tel:** 44 01212 265700
Email: birmingham.news@capitalfm.com
Web site: www.capitalfm.com/birmingham/

Capital Cymru
The Studios, Mold Road, Wrexham LL11
4AF **Tel:** 44 02920 942900
Email: news.wales@capitalfm.com
Web site: www.capitalfm.com/cymru

Capital East Midlands
Chapel Quarter, Maid Marian Way,
Nottingham NG1 6HQ **Tel:** 44 01158 731500
Email: eastmidlands.news@capitalfm.com
Web site: http://www.capitalfm.com/
nottinghamshire/

Capital FM Scotland
Four Winds Pavilion, Pacific Quay, Glasgow
G51 1EB **Tel:** 44 01415 666106
Email: scotland.news@thisisglobal.com
Web site: www.capitalfm.com/scotland

Capital London
30 Leicester Square, London WC2H 7LA
Tel: 44 02070 548000
Email: info@thisisglobal.com
Web site: www.capitalradio.co.uk

Capital Manchester
Suite 1.1, 4 Exchange Quay, Salford,
Manchester M5 3EE **Tel:** 44 01616 624790
Email: northwest.news@capitalfm.com
Web site: http://www.capitalfm.com/
manchester

Capital North East
7th Floor, Wellbar Central, 36 Gallowgate,
Newcastle upon Tyne NE1 4TD
Tel: 44 01914 442500
Web site: www.capitalfm.com/northeast/

Capital South Coast
Whittle Avenue, Segensworth West,
Fareham, Southampton PO15 5SX
Tel: 44 01489 587600
Web site: www.capitalfm.com/southcoast/

Capital South Wales
The Red Dragon Centre, Hemingway Road,
Cardiff CF10 4DJ **Tel:** 44 02920 942900
Email: news.wales@global.com
Web site: www.capitalfm.com/southwales

Capital XTRA
29-30 Leicester Square, London WC2H 7LA
Tel: 44 02077 666000
Email: info@thisisglobal.com
Web site: http://www.capitalxtra.com/

Capital Yorkshire
Joseph's Well, Hanover Walk, Leeds LS3
1AB **Tel:** 44 01133 085100
Email: yorkshire.news@capitalfm.com
Web site: www.capitalfm.com/yorkshire

The Cat Radio
Warrington Campus, Warrington, Warrington
WA2 0DB
Web site: www.thecatradio.co.uk

CFM Radio
Atlantic House, Fletcher Way, Parkhouse,
Carlisle CA3 0LJ **Tel:** 44 01228 818964
Email: news@cfmradio.com
Web site: https://planetradio.co.uk/cfm

Chai FM

Channel 103 FM
6 Tunnell Street, St. Helier, Jersey JE2 4LU
Tel: 44 01534 888103
Email: info@channel103.com
Web site: www.channel103.com

Cheshire's Silk 106.9
Adelaide House, Adelaide Street,
Macclesfield SK10 2QS
Tel: 44 01625 269000
Email: news@silk1069.com
Web site: www.silk1069.com

Chester's Dee 106.3
2 Chantry Court, Chester CH1 4QN
Tel: 44 01244 391000
Email: news@dee1063.com
Web site: www.dee1063.com

UK Broadcast

Classic

Classic FM
30 Leicester Square, London WC2H 7LA
Tel: 44 02077 666000
Web site: www.classicfm.com

Clyde 1 FM
3 South Avenue, Clydebank Business Park,
Glasgow G81 2RX **Tel:** 44 01415 652200
Email: reception@radioclyde.com
Web site: www.clyde1.com

Clyde 2
3 South Avenue, Clydebank Business Park,
Glasgow G81 2RX **Tel:** 44 01415 652200
Email: clydenews@radioclyde.com
Web site: http://www.clyde2.com/

Colourful Radio
P O Box 194, London SW11 5WQ
Tel: 44 02034 754038
Web site: www.colourfulradio.com

Compass FM 96.4
Witham Park, Waterside South, Lincoln LN5
7JN **Tel:** 44 01472 362964
Email: news@compassfm.co.uk
Web site: www.compassfm.co.uk

**Connect 106.8 FM
(Peterborough)**
55 Headlands, Kettering, Kettering NN15
7EY **Tel:** 44 01536 513664
Email: news@connectfm.com
Web site: www.peterborough.connectfm.
com

Connect FM
55 Headlands, Kettering, Kettering NN15
7EY **Tel:** 44 01536 513664
Email: news@connectfm.com
Web site: www.connectfm.com

Cool FM
Tel: 44 02891 815555
Email: news@downtown.co.uk
Web site: www.coolfm.co.uk

Dearne FM 102 & 97.1
5 Sidings Court, White Rose Way, Doncaster
DN4 5NU **Tel:** 44 01302 341166
Email: news@dearnefm.co.uk
Web site: www.dearnefm.co.uk

Demon FM
De Montfort Students Union, Campus Centre
Building, Mill Lane, Leicester LE2 7DR
Email: info@demonfm.co.uk
Web site: www.demonfm.co.uk

Downtown Radio
Tel: 44 02891 815555
Email: news@downtown.co.uk
Web site: www.downtown.co.uk

Dragon Radio
St Hilary Transmitter, nr St Hilary, Cowbridge
CF71 7DP **Tel:** 44 02921 414110
Email: enquiries@dragonradio.wales
Web site: http://dragonradio.wales/

Dream 100 FM
Radio House, O'Brien Court, Ipswich IP6
OLW **Tel:** 44 01206 764466
Email: news@dream100.com
Web site: www.dream100.com

e24

Eagle Radio
Dolphin House, 3 North Street, Guildford
GU1 4AA **Tel:** 44 01483 300964
Email: news@964eagle.co.uk
Web site: www.964eagle.co.uk

Energy FM
PO Box 986, Douglas, Isle of Man IM99 2TB
Tel: 44 01624 611936
Email: news@energyfm.net
Web site: www.energyfm.net

Express FM

Express FM
Eldon Building, University of Portsmouth,
Winston Churchill Avenue, Portsmouth PO1
2DJ **Tel:** 44 02392 848492
Email: news@expressfm.com
Web site: www.expressfm.com

Fire Radio
Roman Landing, Kingsway, Southampton
SO14 1BN **Tel:** 44 08454 661107
Web site: www.fireradio.co.uk

FLY FM
Nottingham Trent Students Union,
Shakespeare Street, Nottingham NG1 4GH
Tel: 44 01158 486200
Email: news@flyfm.co.uk
Web site: www.flyfm.co.uk

Forge Radio
Sheffield University, Students' Union,
Western Bank, Sheffield S10 2TG
Tel: 44 01142 228646
Email: radio.manager@forgetoday.com
Web site: www.forgeradio.com

Forth 1
Forth House, Forth Street, Edinburgh EH1
3LE **Tel:** 44 01315 569255
Email: news@radioforth.com
Web site: www.forthone.com

Forth 2
Forth2, Bauer Radio, 3 South Avenue,
Clydebank G81 2RX **Tel:** 44 03332 020401
Email: news@radioforth.com
Web site: www.forth2.com

Free Radio (Birmingham)
9 Brindley Place, 4 Oozells Square,
Birmingham B1 2DJ **Tel:** 44 01215 665200
Email: news@freeradio.co.uk
Web site: www.freeradio.co.uk/birmingham

**Free Radio (Black Country &
Shropshire)**
Black Country House, Rounds Green Road,
Oldbury B69 2DG **Tel:** 44 01902 461260
Email: news@freeradio.co.uk
Web site: https://planetradio.co.uk/free/

**Free Radio (Coventry &
Warwickshire)**
9 Brindley Place, 4 Oozells Square,
Birmingham B1 2DJ **Tel:** 44 02476 868200
Email: news@freeradio.co.uk
Web site: http://www.freeradio.co.uk/
coventry

**Free Radio (Herefordshire &
Worcestershire)**
First Floor, Kirkham House, John Comyn
Drive, Worcester WR3 7NS
Tel: 44 01905 545510
Email: news@freeradio.co.uk
Web site: www.freeradio.co.uk/
herefordshire

Fresh Air
Societies' Centre, 60 Pleasance, Edinburgh
EH8 9TJ
Email: secretary@freshair.org.uk
Web site: http://www.freshair.org.uk/

Fun Kids
Greenworks, Dog and Duck Yard, Princeton
Street, London WC1R 4BH
Tel: 44 02077 397880
Email: emails@funkidslive.com
Web site: www.funkidslive.com

Gaydio
Manchester One, 53 Portland Street,
Manchester M1 3LF **Tel:** 44 08446 828301
Email: info@gaydio.co.uk
Web site: http://gaydio.co.uk/

Gem 106
City Link, Nottingham NG2 4NG
Tel: 44 01159 106100
Email: news@gem106.co.uk
Web site: http://www.gem106.co.uk/

Gold (London)

Gold (London)
30 Leicester Square, London WC2H 7LA
Tel: 44 02073 439000
Web site: www.mygoldmusic.co.uk

Gold East Midlands
30 Leicester Square, London WC2H 7LA
Tel: 44 03452 318888
Email: info@thisisglobal.com
Web site: www.mygoldmusic.co.uk

Hallam 2
Radio House, 900 Herries Road, Sheffield S6
1RH **Tel:** 44 01142 091000
Email: news@hallamfm.co.uk
Web site: http://www.hallam2.co.uk/

Hallam FM
900 Herries Road, Sheffield S6 1RH
Tel: 44 01142 091000
Email: news@hallamfm.co.uk
Web site: www.hallamfm.co.uk

Harborough FM
Unit 5, Fernie House, Fernie Road, Market
Harborough, Market Harborough LE16 7PH
Tel: 44 01858 464666
Email: info@harboroughfm.co.uk
Web site: www.harboroughfm.co.uk

Heart Cambridgeshire
Enterprise House, Vision Park, Chivers Way,
Histon, Histon CB24 9ZR
Tel: 44 01223 623800
Email: cambridgeshire.news@heart.co.uk
Web site: www.heart.co.uk/cambridge

Heart East Anglia
St George's Plain, 47-49 Colegate, Norwich,
Norwich NR3 1DB **Tel:** 44 01603 630621
Email: eastanglia.news@heart.co.uk
Web site: http://www.heart.co.uk/
eastanglia/

Heart Essex
31 Glebe Road, Chelmsford, Chelmsford
CM1 1QG **Tel:** 44 01245 524500
Email: news.essex@heart.co.uk
Web site: www.heartessex.co.uk

Heart Four Counties
4th Floor, CBX II East, Midsummer
Boulevard, Milton Keynes MK9 2EA
Tel: 44 01582 676250
Email: fcnews@heart.co.uk
Web site: www.heart.co.uk/fourcounties

Heart Gloucestershire
The Mall, Gloucester GL1 1SS
Tel: 44 01452 572400
Email: news.westcountry@heart.co.uk
Web site: www.heartgloucestershire.co.uk

Heart Hertfordshire
Unit 5, The Metro Centre, Dwight Road,
Watford WD18 9UP **Tel:** 44 01923 205480
Email: fcnews@heart.co.uk
Web site: www.heart.co.uk/hertfordshire/

Heart Kent
Radio House, John Wilson Business Park,
Whitstable, Whitstable CT5 3QX
Tel: 44 01227 772004
Email: news.kent@heart.co.uk
Web site: www.heartkent.co.uk

Heart London 106.2
30 Leicester Square, London WC2H 7LA
Tel: 44 02077 666222
Email: info@thisisglobal.com
Web site: www.heart.co.uk/london

Heart North East
7th Floor, Wellbar Central, 36 Gallowgate,
Newcastle upon Tyne NE1 4TD
Tel: 44 01914 442500
Web site: www.heart.co.uk/northeast

Heart North Wales
The Studios, Mold Road, Gwersyllt,
Wrexham LL11 4AF **Tel:** 44 01978 722286
Email: news.wales@heart.co.uk
Web site: www.heart.co.uk/northwales

Heart North West

Heart North West
Laser House, Waterfront Quays, Salford M5
3XW **Tel:** 44 01616 624700
Email: northwest.news@thisisglobal.com
Web site: www.heart.co.uk/northwest

Heart Scotland
PO Box 101, Unit 1130, Parkway Court,
Glasgow Business Park, Glasgow G69 6GA
Tel: 44 01417 811011
Web site: http://www.heart.co.uk/scotland/

Heart South Coast
Radio House, Apple Industrial Estate, Whittle
Avenue, Fareham PO15 5SX
Tel: 44 01489 587600
Email: southcoast.news@heart.co.uk
Web site: http://www.heart.co.uk/
southcoast/on-air/

Heart South West
Hawthorn House, Exeter Business Park,
Exeter EX1 3QS **Tel:** 44 01392 444444
Email: news.devon@heart.co.uk
Web site: http://www.heart.co.uk/
southwest/

Heart Sussex
Radio House, Franklin Road, Brighton BN41
1AF **Tel:** 44 01273 316900
Email: news.sussex@heart.co.uk
Web site: www.heartsussex.co.uk

Heart Thames Valley
The Chase, Calcot, Reading RG31 7RB
Tel: 44 01189 454400
Email: thamesvalley.news@heart.co.uk
Web site: www.heart.co.uk/thamesvalley

Heart Wales
Unit 1, Ty Nant Court, Morganstown, Cardiff
CF15 8LW **Tel:** 44 02920 315100
Web site: www.heart.co.uk/wales

Heart West Country
1 Passage Street, Bristol BS2 0JF
Tel: 44 01179 843200
Email: news.westcountry@heart.co.uk
Web site: www.heartbristol.co.uk

Heart West Midlands
8th Floor, 11 Brindley Place, 2 Brunswick
Square, Birmingham B1 2LP
Tel: 44 01212 265700
Email: westmids.news@heart.co.uk
Web site: www.heartwestmids.co.uk

Heart Wiltshire
Chiseldon House, Stonehill Green, Westlea,
Swindon SN5 7HB **Tel:** 44 01793 663000
Email: news.wiltshire@heart.co.uk
Web site: www.heartwilts.co.uk

Heart Yorkshire
1 Sterling Court, Capitol Business Park,
Tingley, Wakefield WF3 1EL
Tel: 44 01132 381114
Email: yorkshire.news@global.com
Web site: http://www.heart.co.uk/yorkshire/

Heartland FM
Tel: 44 01796 474000
Email: studio@heartlandfm.co.uk
Web site: www.heartlandfm.co.uk

High Peak Radio
Tel: 44 01298 813144
Email: news@highpeakradio.co.uk
Web site: www.highpeakradio.co.uk

Highveld 94.7
Tel: 44 27115 063292
Email: ravi@primedia.co.za
Web site: http://www.highveld.co.za

The Hits
Castle Quay, Castlefield, Manchester M15
4PR **Tel:** 44 03333 232113
Web site: www.thehitsradio.com

IC Radio
Beit Quad, Prince Consort Road, South
Kensington, London SW7 2BB
Email: manager@icradio.com
Web site: www.icradio.com

Ikwekwezi
Tel: 44 27124 315301
Email: mahlanguly@sabc.co.za
Web site: http://www.ikwekwezifm.co.za

Imagine FM 104.9 FM
Waterloo Place, Watson Square, Stockport
SK1 3AZ Tel: 44 01614 767340
Email: news@imaginefm.net
Web site: www.imaginefm.net

Insanity Radio
Students' Union, Royal Holloway University
of London, Egham Hill, Egham, London
TW20 0EX
Email: news@insanityradio.com
Web site: www.insanityradio.com

Island FM 104.7
12 Westerbrook, St Sampsons, Guernsey
GY2 4QQ Tel: 44 01481 242000
Email: news@islandfm.com
Web site: www.islandfm.com

Isle of Wight Radio 107 & 102
Tel: 44 01983 822557
Email: news@iwradio.co.uk
Web site: www.iwradio.co.uk

Isles FM
50 Seaforth Road, Stornoway, Isle of Lewis
HS1 2SH Tel: 44 01851 703333
Email: studio@isles.fm
Web site: www.isles.fm

JACK FM Berkshire
Radio House, Madejski Stadium, Reading
RG2 0FN Tel: 44 01189 862555
Email: news@jackfmberkshire.com
Web site: www.jackfmberkshire.com

JACK2 Oxfordshire
The Dumpy Building, 270-272 Woodstock
Road, Oxford OX2 7NW
Tel: 44 01865 315980
Email: jack2@jackfm.co.uk
Web site: http://www.jackfm2oxfordshire.
co.uk/

Jazz FM
75 - 77 Margaret Street, London W1W 8SY
Web site: http://www.jazzfm.com/

Jemm Three
Jemm Radio, PO Box 009, London TW10
9DU
Web site: www.jemmthree.com

Jozi FM
Tel: 44 27861 372346
Email: charmaine@themediaconnection.co.
za
Web site: http://www.jozifm.co.za

Juice 107.2
170 North Street, Brighton BN1 1EA
Tel: 44 01273 386107
Email: news@juicebrighton.com
Web site: www.juicebrighton.com

KCFM 99.8
Unit 3 Maritime House, Maritime Business
Park, Livingstone Road, Hessle HU13 0EG
Tel: 44 01482 333999
Email: news@kcfm.co.uk
Web site: www.kcfm.co.uk

Kerrang! Radio
One Golden Square, London W1F 9DJ
Tel: 44 02074 341215
Web site: www.kerrangradio.co.uk

Key 103
Castle Quay, Castlefield, Manchester M15
4PR Tel: 44 01612 880103
Email: news@key103.co.uk
Web site: www.key103.co.uk

Key 2
Castle Quay, Castlefield, Manchester M15
4PR Tel: 44 01612 885000
Email: news@key103.co.uk
Web site: http://www.key2radio.co.uk/

Kingdom FM
Haig House, Haig Business Park, Markinch,
Glenrothes KY7 6AQ Tel: 44 01592 753753
Email: info@kingdomfm.co.uk
Web site: www.kingdomfm.co.uk

Kiss FM (UK)
One Golden Square, London W1F 9DJ
Tel: 44 02074 341215
Web site: www.kissfmuk.com

KL.FM 96.7
18 Blackfriars Street, Kings Lynn, King's
Lynn PE30 1NN
Web site: www.klfm967.co.uk

KMFM Group
Medway House, Ginsbury Close, Sir Thomas
Longley Road, Medway City Estate, Strood,
Rochester ME2 4DU Tel: 44 01634 227800
Email: multimedianews@thekmgroup.co.uk
Web site: www.kmfm.co.uk

Lakeland Radio
Lakeland Radio, Plumgarths, Kendal, Kendal
LA8 8QJ Tel: 44 01539 737380
Email: news@lakelandradio.co.uk
Web site: www.lakelandradio.co.uk

Latitude Radio
Students' Union University of Greenwich,
Cooper Building, King William Walk, London
SE10 9JH Tel: 44 02083 317629
Email: sl405@greenwich.ac.uk
Web site: www.suug.co.uk/societies/radio/

LBC
30 Leicester Square, London WC2H 7LA
Tel: 44 02077 666400
Web site: www.lbc.co.uk

LBC London News
30 Leicester Square, London WC2H 7LA
Tel: 44 02077 666400
Email: news@lbc.co.uk
Web site: www.lbcnews1152.co.uk

Liberty Radio
199 - 201 Seven Sisters Road, London N4
3NG Tel: 44 02076 866271
Email: info@libertyradio.co.uk
Web site: www.libertyradio.co.uk

Lincs FM 102.2
Witham Park, Waterside South, Lincoln LN5
7JN Tel: 44 01522 549900
Email: news@lincsfm
Web site: www.lincsfm.co.uk

Livewire 1350 AM
Union House, University of East Anglia,
Norwich, Norwich NR4 7TJ
Tel: 44 01603 592512
Email: station.manager@livewire1350.com
Web site: www.livewire1350.com

London Greek Radio
LGR House, 437 High Road, North Finchley,
London N12 0AP Tel: 44 02083 496960
Email: news@lgr.co.uk
Web site: www.lgr.co.uk

London One Radio
25 Ashley Road, Tottenham Hale, London
N17 9LJ Tel: 44 07593 272201
Email: london1radio@gmail.com
Web site: www.londononeradio.com
Editor: Philip Baglini

Lotus FM
Tel: 44 27313 625444
Email: pillaya@sabc.co.za
Web site: http://www.lotusfm.co.za

LSRfm
Leeds University Union, Lifton Place, Leeds
LS2 9JZ
Email: info@thisislsr.com
Web site: http://thisislsr.com/

Magic Chilled
One Golden Square, London W1F 9DJ
Tel: 44 02074 341215
Email: hello@magic.co.uk
Web site: www.magicchilled.co.uk

Magic Radio (UK)
One Golden Square, London W1F 9DJ
Tel: 44 02074 341215
Email: nationalradionews@bauermedia.co.
uk
Web site: www.magic.co.uk

Manx Radio
Broadcasting House, Douglas, Isle of Man
IM1 5BW Tel: 44 01624 682600
Web site: www.manxradio.com

Mellow Magic
One Golden Square, London W1F 9DJ
Tel: 44 02074 341215
Email: nationalradionews@bauermedia.co.
uk
Web site: http://www.mellowmagic.co.uk/

Metro Radio
55 Degrees North, Pilgrim Street, Newcastle
upon Tyne NE1 6BF Tel: 44 01912 306100
Email: news@metroandmagic.com
Web site: www.metroradio.co.uk

Metro Radio 2
55 Degrees North, Pilgrim Street, Newcastle
upon Tyne NE1 6BF Tel: 44 01912 306100
Email: news@metroandmagic.com
Web site: http://www.metro2radio.co.uk/

Minster FM
PO Box 123, York YO19 5ZX
Tel: 44 01904 488888
Email: news@minsterfm.com
Web site: www.minsterfm.com

Mix 96
Friars Square Studios, Bourbon Street,
Aylesbury HP20 2PZ Tel: 44 01296 399396
Email: news@mix96.co.uk
Web site: www.mix96.co.uk

MKFM
MKFM Studios, intu Milton Keynes, 417
Saxon Gate East, Milton Keynes MK9 3DX
Tel: 44 01908 464100
Email: news@mkfm.com
Web site: www.mkfm.com

Moray Firth Radio (MFR)
PO Box 271, Inverness IV3 8UJ
Tel: 44 01463 224433
Email: news@mfr.co.uk
Web site: www.mfr.co.uk

More Radio
More Radio, The Guildbourne Centre, West
Sussex, Worthing BN11 1LZ
Tel: 44 03333 446226
Email: studio@moreradio.online
Web site: http://moreradio.online/

Motsweding
Tel: 44 27183 897104
Email: mtyalirts@sabc.co.za
Web site: http://www.motswedingfm.co.za

Munghana-Lonene

Nation Radio
Nation Radio, St Hilary Transmitter, nr St
Hilary, Cowbridge CF71 7DP
Tel: 44 02921 414100
Email: enquiries@nationradio.wales
Web site: http://nationradio.wales/

NECR
The Very Nice Shed, School Road, Kintore,
Inverurie, Inverurie AB51 0UX
Tel: 44 01467 632878
Email: news@necrfm.co.uk
Web site: www.necrfm.co.uk

Newsdesk
Splash FM, 41 Gildbourne Centre, Worthing,
Worthing BN11 1LZ Tel: 44 01903 931220
Email: news@splashfm.net
Web site: www.splashfm.net

Newsdesk
14 St Marys Walk, Hailsham BN27 1AF
Tel: 44 01323 701075
Email: news@sovereignfm.com
Web site: http://sovereignfm.com/category/
local-news/

Newsdesk
Priory Meadow Centre, Hastings TN34 1PJ
Tel: 44 01424 401078
Email: news@arrowfm.co.uk
Web site: http://arrowfm.co.uk/category/
news/

North Norfolk Radio
Breck Farm, Stody, Melton Constable NR24
2ER Tel: 44 01263 860808
Email: news@northnorfolkradio.com
Web site: www.northnorfolkradio.com

Northsound 1
Abbotswell Road, West Tullos, Aberdeen
AB12 3AJ Tel: 44 01224 337000
Email: news@northsound.co.uk
Web site: www.northsound1.co.uk

Northsound 2
Bauer Radio, 3 South Avenue, Clydebank
G81 2RX Tel: 44 01415 652200
Email: news@northsound.co.uk
Web site: www.northsound2.co.uk

Original 106 fm (Aberdeen)
Original House, Craigshaw Road, Aberdeen
AB12 3AR Tel: 44 01224 294860
Email: news@originalfm.com
Web site: www.originalfm.com

Panjab Radio
Panjab Radio House, Springfield Road,
Hayes, London UB4 0TY
Tel: 44 02088 488877
Email: info@panjabradio.co.uk
Web site: www.panjabradio.co.uk

Peak FM
Radio House, Foxwood Road, Chesterfield
S41 9RF Tel: 44 01246 269107
Web site: www.peakfm.net

Pirate FM
Pirate FM, Wilson Way, Redruth, Camborne
TR15 3XX Tel: 44 01209 314400
Email: reception@piratefm.co.uk
Web site: www.piratefm.co.uk

Planet Rock
One Golden Square, London W1F 9DJ
Tel: 44 02074 341215
Email: info@planetrock.com
Web site: www.planetrock.com

Praia FM
Tel: 44 23826 16356
Email: gccomunicacoes@yahoo.com
Web site: http://www.praiafm.biz

Premier Christian Radio
22 Chapter Street, London SW1P 4NP
Tel: 44 02073 161300
Email: studio@premier.org.uk
Web site: www.premierradio.org.uk/

Presenters
Priory Meadow Centre, Hastings, Hastings
TN34 1PJ Tel: 44 01424 401078
Email: studio@arrowfm.co.uk
Web site: www.arrowfm.co.uk

Presenters
Guildbourne Centre, Worthing, West Sussex,
Worthing BN11 1LZ Tel: 44 01903 233005
Web site: www.splashfm.net

Presenters
14 St Marys Walk, Hailsham BN27 1AF
Tel: 44 01323 701075
Email: studio@sovereignfm.com
Web site: http://sovereignfm.com/

Pulse 1
1 St James Business Park, New Augustus
Street, Bradford BD1 5LL
Tel: 44 01274 203040
Email: news@pulse.co.uk
Web site: www.pulse.co.uk

Pulse 2
1 St James Business Park, New Augustus
Street, Bradford BD1 5LL
Tel: 44 01274 203040
Email: news@pulse.co.uk
Web site: www.pulse2.co.uk/

UK Broadcast

Pulse Radio
UCLAN Student's Union, Fylde Road,
Preston PR1 2TQ **Tel:** 44 01772 8934891
Email: sumedia@uclan.ac.uk
Web site: www.uclansu.co.uk/pulseradio

Pulse Radio
LSE Student's Union, East Building,
Houghton Street, London WC2A 2AE
Email: admin@pulselse.co.uk
Web site: www.pulselse.co.uk

Pure FM
The Student Centre, Cambridge Road,
Portsmouth PO1 2EF **Tel:** 44 08458 604444
Email: live@purefm.com
Web site: www.purefm.com

Pure FM 107.8
Sanderling Building, Bird Hall Lane, Cheadle
Heath, Stockport SK3 0RF
Tel: 44 01614 745964
Email: studio@pureradio.org.uk
Web site: www.pureradio.org.uk

Purple Radio
Dunelm House, New Elvet, Durham DH1
3AN **Tel:** 44 01913 341808
Email: info@purpleradio.co.uk
Web site: www.purpleradio.co.uk

Q Radio
2nd Floor, Arena Building, 85 Ormeau Road,
Belfast BT7 1SH **Tel:** 44 02890 234967
Email: news@qonair.com
Web site: www.goqradio.com

Queen's Radio
Queen's Students' Union, University Road,
Belfast BT7 1NF **Tel:** 44 02890 971134
Email: onair@queensradio.org
Web site: www.queensradio.org

Radio 786

Radio Aire
51 Burley Road, Leeds LS3 1LR
Tel: 44 01132 835500
Email: news@radioaire.com
Web site: www.radioaire.co.uk

Radio Aire 2
51 Burley Road, Leeds LS3 1LR
Tel: 44 01612 885000
Email: news@radioaire.com
Web site: http://www.radioaire2.co.uk/

Radio Ashford
The William Harvey Hospital, Ashford,
Ashford TN24 0LZ **Tel:** 44 01233 616226
Email: news@ahbs.org.uk
Web site: http://www.radioashford.co.uk/

Radio Borders
Tweedside Park, Galashiels TD1 3TD
Tel: 44 01896 759444
Email: info@radioborders.com
Web site: www.radioborders.com

Radio Carmarthenshire
PO Box 971, Llanelli, Llanelli SA15 1YH
Tel: 44 01267 679150
Email: enquiries@radiocarmarthenshire.
wales
Web site: radiocarmarthenshire.wales

Radio Centro 97.7
Email: noticiero_elobservador@hotmail.com
Web site: http://www.radiocentro.com.ec

Radio Ceredigion
Merlin House, Parc Merlin, Glan Yr Afon
Industrial Estate, Aberystwyth SY23 3FF
Tel: 44 01970 229113
Email: enquiries@radioceredigion.wales
Web site: www.radioceredigion.com

Radio City
St Johns Beacon, 1 Houghton Street,
Liverpool L1 1RL **Tel:** 44 01514 726800
Email: news@radiocity.co.uk
Web site: www.radiocity.co.uk

Radio City 2
St Johns Beacon, 1 Houghton Street,
Liverpool L1 1RL **Tel:** 44 01514 726800
Email: news@radiocity.co.uk
Web site: http://www.radiocity2.co.uk/

Radio City Talk
St Johns Beacon, 1 Houghton Street,
Liverpool L1 1RL **Tel:** 44 01514 726800
Email: news@radiocity.co.uk
Web site: http://www.radiocitytalk.co.uk/

Radio Essex
Tel: 44 01702 455070
Email: enquiries@radioessex.com
Web site: www.radioessex.com

Radio Exe
6a Cranmere Court, Lustleigh Close, Matford
Business Park, Exeter EX2 8PW
Tel: 44 01392 823557
Email: news@radioexe.co.uk
Web site: www.radioexe.co.uk

Radio i99
Tel: 44 59342 680877
Web site: http://www.i99.com.ec

Radio Mansfield 103.2
The Media Suite, Unit 4, Brunts Business
Centre, Samuel Brunts Way, Nottingham
NG18 2AH **Tel:** 44 01623 646666
Email: info@mansfield103.co.uk
Web site: www.mansfield103.co.uk

Radio Maria
Tel: 44 26021 6221154
Email: administration.zam@radiomaria.org
Web site: http://www.radiomaria.org

Radio Paratiritis
Email: info@radioparatiritis.gr
Web site: www.radioparatiritis.gr

Radio Pembrokeshire
Unit 14, Old School Estate, Station Road,
Narberth SA67 7DU **Tel:** 44 01834 869292
Email: enquiries@radiopembrokeshire.wales
Web site: www.radiopembrokeshire.wales

Radio Plymouth
3 Crescent Avenue Mews, Plymouth PL1
3AP **Tel:** 44 01752 389535
Email: news@radioplymouth.com
Web site: www.radioplymouth.com

Radio Resonance
Tel: 44 33024 8232010
Email: radio@radio-resonance.org
Web site: www.radio-resonance.org/

Radio Scilly
Porthmellon Estate, St Mary's, Hugh Town
TR21 0JY **Tel:** 44 01720 423417
Email: studio@radioscilly.com
Web site: http://www.radioscilly.com/

Radio Universal
Tel: 44 59342 448410
Email: radiouniversalguayaquil@hotmail.com
Web site: http://es.justin.tv/
radiouniversalguayaquil

Radio Uno
Tel: 44 59342 323171
Web site: http://www.radio11q.com.ec

Radio Verulam 92.6FM
PO Box 1092, St Albans, London AL1 9QB
Tel: 44 01727 833926
Email: studio@radioverulam.com
Web site: http://www.radioverulam.com/

Radio Wave 96.5
965 Mowbray Drive, Blackpool, Blackpool
FY3 7JR **Tel:** 44 01253 650300
Email: info@thewavefm.co.uk
Web site: www.wave965.com

Radio X (UK)
30 Leicester Square, London WC2H 7LA
Tel: 44 02077 666600
Web site: www.radiox.co.uk

Radio Yorkshire
Plantagenet Media Services Limited, 1st
Floor, 247 Elland Road, Leeds LS11 8TU
Tel: 44 01133 979666
Email: news@radioyorkshire.co.uk
Web site: www.radioyorkshire.co.uk

Ram Air
University of Bradford Union of Students,
Student Central, Richmond Road, Bradford
BD7 1DP **Tel:** 44 01274 233267
Email: ramair@ubu.bradford.ac.uk
Web site: www.ramair.co.uk

Rare FM
UCL Union, 25 Gordon Street, London
WC1H 0AY
Email: rarefm@ucl.ac.uk
Web site: www.rarefm.co.uk

Rathergood Radio
Radio House, 11 Woodland Road, Darlington
Co., Durham DL3 7BJ **Tel:** 44 01325 341801
Email: news@viewtvgroup.com
Web site: www.rathergoodradio.com

raw1251AM
Students' Union Building, University of
Warwick, Coventry CV4 7AL
Web site: www.radio.warwick.ac.uk

Resonance104.4fm
144 Borough High Street, London SE1 1LB
Tel: 44 02074 071210
Email: contact@resonancefm.com
Web site: http://resonancefm.com

Ridings FM
5 Sidings Court, White Rose Way, Doncaster
DN4 5NU **Tel:** 44 01302 341166
Email: news@ridingsfm.co.uk
Web site: www.ridingsfm.co.uk

Rippel FM

RNIB Connect Radio
17 Gullane Street, Partick, Glasgow G11
6AH **Tel:** 44 01413 573518
Email: info@insightradio.co.uk
Web site: www.insightradio.co.uk

Rock FM
St Pauls Square, Preston PR1 1YE
Tel: 44 01772 477700
Web site: https://planetradio.co.uk/rock-fm/

Rock FM 2
St Pauls Square, Preston, Preston PR1 1XS
Tel: 44 01772 477700
Email: news@rockfm.co.uk
Web site: www.rockfm2.co.uk

Rother FM
5 Sidings Court, White Rose Way, Doncaster
DN4 5NU **Tel:** 44 01302 341166
Email: news@rotherfm.co.uk
Web site: www.rotherfm.co.uk

Runway Radio
F2 Sussex Manor Business Park, Crawley
RH10 9NH **Tel:** 44 01293 850905
Email: info@runwayradio.co.uk
Web site: http://www.runwayradio.co.uk/

Rutland Radio
40 Melton Road, Oakham, Oakham LE15
6AY **Tel:** 44 01572 757868
Email: news@rutlandradio.co.uk
Web site: www.rutlandradio.co.uk

Sabras Radio
Radio House, 63 Melton Road, Leicester LE4
6PN **Tel:** 44 01162 610666
Email: studio@sabrasradio.com
Web site: www.sabrasradio.com

Salford City Radio 94.4 FM
New Music, Radio House, Salford Civic
Centre, Chorley Road, Salford M27 5AW
Tel: 44 01617 932939
Email: info@salfordcityradio.org
Web site: www.salfordcityradio.org

Sam FM (Bristol)
County Gates, Ashton Road, Bristol BS3 2JH
Tel: 44 01179 666107
Email: bristol@samfm.co.uk
Web site: www.samfm.co.uk/bristol

Sam FM (South Coast)
Roman Landing, Kingsway, Southampton
SO14 1BN **Tel:** 44 08454 661107
Email: southcoast@samfm.co.uk
Web site: http://www.samfm.co.uk/
southcoast/

Sam FM Swindon
Lime Kiln Studios, Wooton Bassett, Wootton
Bassett SN4 7HF **Tel:** 44 01179 666107
Email: news@jackfmswindon.com
Web site: http://www.samfm.co.uk/
swindon/

Sansa
Email: sansa@sansa.fi
Web site: http://www.sansa.fi

Share Radio
2nd Floor, Chapter House, 22 Chapter
Street, London SW1P 4NP
Tel: 44 02077 981960
Email: newsintake@shareradio.co.uk
Web site: www.shareradio.co.uk/

Shoreditch Radio
Tel: 44 07931 478848
Email: info@shoreditchradio.co.uk
Web site: www.shoreditchradio.co.uk/

Signal 1
Stoke Road, Stoke-on-Trent ST4 2SR
Tel: 44 01782 441300
Email: news@signalradio.com
Web site: www.signal1.co.uk

Signal 107
2nd Floor Mander House, Wolverhampton
WV1 3NB **Tel:** 44 01902 571070
Email: news@signal107.co.uk
Web site: www.signal107.co.uk

Signal 2
Stoke Road, Stoke-on-Trent ST4 2SR
Tel: 44 01782 441300
Email: reception@signalradio.com
Web site: www.signal2.co.uk

Siren FM
MHT Building, University of Lincoln, Brayford
Pool, Lincoln LN6 7TS
Email: news@sirenonline.co.uk
Web site: www.sirenonline.co.uk

Sky News Radio
6 Centaurs Business Park, Grant Way,
London TW7 5QD **Tel:** 44 02070 323000
Email: radio@sky.uk
Web site: http://news.sky.com/info/radio

Smooth Extra
Laser House, Waterfront Quays, Salford M5
3XW **Tel:** 44 08450 501004
Web site: www.smoothradio.com/extra/

Smooth Radio
30 Leicester Square, London WC2H 7LA
Tel: 44 02077 666000
Web site: www.smoothradio.co.uk

Smooth Radio Bristol and Bath
30 Leicester Square, London WC1 7LA
Tel: 44 02077 666000
Web site: www.smoothradio.com/bristol/

Smooth Radio Cambridgeshire
30 Leicester Square, London WC2H 7LA
Tel: 44 02077 666000
Web site: www.smoothradio.com/
cambridgeshire/

Smooth Radio Devon
30 Leicester Square, London WC2H 7LA
Tel: 44 02077 666000
Web site: www.smoothradio.com/plymouth/

Smooth Radio Dorset & Hampshire
30 Leicester Square, London WC2H 7LA
Tel: 44 02077 666000
Web site: http://www.smoothradio.com/dorset/

Smooth Radio Essex
30 Leicester Square, London WC2H 7LA
Tel: 44 02077 666000
Web site: http://www.smoothradio.com/essex/

Smooth Radio Gloucester
30 Leicester Square, London WC1 7LA
Tel: 44 02077 666000
Web site: www.smoothradio.co.uk

Smooth Radio Herts, Beds and Bucks
30 Leicester Square, London WC1 7LA
Tel: 44 02077 666000
Web site: http://www.smoothradio.com/hertsbedsbucks

Smooth Radio Kent
30 Leicester Square, London WC1 7LA
Tel: 44 02077 666000
Web site: www.smoothradio.com/kent

Smooth Radio Norfolk
30 Leicester Square, London WC1 7LA
Tel: 44 02077 666000
Web site: www.smoothradio.com/norfolk

Smooth Radio North Wales & Cheshire
Tel: 44 02077 666000
Web site: http://www.smoothradio.com/northwales/

Smooth Radio Northamptonshire
30 Leicester Square, London WC2H 7LA
Tel: 44 02077 666000
Web site: http://www.smoothradio.com/northamptonshire/

Smooth Radio Scotland
Parkway Court, Glasgow Business Park, Glasgow G69 6GA **Tel:** 44 01417 811011
Email: scotland.news@thisisglobal.com
Web site: www.smoothradio.co.uk

Smooth Radio South Wales
30 Leicester Square, London WC1 7LA
Tel: 44 02077 666000
Web site: http://www.smoothradio.com/southwales/

Smooth Radio Suffolk
30 Leicester Square, London WC2H 7LA
Tel: 44 02077 666000
Web site: http://www.smoothradio.com/suffolk/

Smooth Radio Sussex
30 Leicester Square, London WC2H 7LA
Tel: 44 02077 666000
Web site: http://www.smoothradio.com/sussex/

Smooth Radio Thames Valley
30 Leicester Square, London WC1 7LA
Tel: 44 02077 666000
Web site: www.smoothradio.com/berkshire/

Smooth Radio Wiltshire
30 Leicester Square, London WC2H 7LA
Tel: 44 02077 666000
Web site: http://www.smoothradio.com/wiltshire/

Source Radio
CUSU, 1st Floor, The Hub, 4 Jordan Well, Coventry CV1 5QT
Web site: http://mixlr.com/source-radio/

Spark FM
The David Puttnam Media Centre, St Peters Campus, Sunderland SR6 0DD
Tel: 44 0191 5 153875
Email: info@sparksunderland.com
Web site: sparksunderland.com

Spin FM
Tel: 44 37263 07026
Email: julia@u-pop.ee
Web site: http://spinfm.upop.ee/

Spire FM
City Hall Studios, Malthouse Lane, Salisbury SP2 7QQ **Tel:** 44 01722 416644
Email: news@spirefm.co.uk
Web site: www.spirefm.co.uk

Spirit FM
9-11 Dukes Court, Bognor Road, Chichester PO19 8FX **Tel:** 44 01243 773600
Email: news@spiritfm.net
Web site: www.spiritfm.net

Sportsdesk
The Forum, Millennium Plain, Norwich NR2 1BH **Tel:** 44 01603 617411
Email: radionorfolknews@bbc.co.uk

Star Radio 107.9/1 FM
20 Mercers Row, Cambridge CB5 8HY
Tel: 44 01223 305107
Email: news@star107.co.uk
Web site: www.starradioonline.com

Stockholm College Radio 95,3

Stockholm College Radio 95,3

Storm FM
Students' Union, Bryn Haul, Victoria Drive, Bangor LL57 2EN **Tel:** 44 01248 388049
Email: enquiries@stormfm.com
Web site: www.stormfm.com

Stray FM
The Hamlet, Hornbeam Park Avenue, Harrogate HG2 8RE **Tel:** 44 01423 522972
Email: news@strayfm.com
Web site: www.strayfm.com

Sun FM
Unit 63-66T, Business & Innovation Centre, Sunderland Enterprise Park, Sunderland SR5 2TA **Tel:** 44 01915 481034
Email: news@sun-fm.com
Web site: http://www.sun-fm.com

Sunrise Radio
Sunrise House, Merrick Road, Southall, London UB2 4AT **Tel:** 44 02085 746666
Email: news@sunriseradio.com
Web site: www.sunriseradio.com

Sunrise Radio (Yorkshire)
Sunrise House, 55 Leeds Road, Little Germany, Bradford BD1 5AF
Tel: 44 01274 735043
Email: news@sunriseradio.fm
Web site: http://www.sunriseradio.fm/

Sunshine Radio 106.2, 107 & 107.8 FM
Suite 5, Penn House, Broad Street, Hereford HR4 9AP **Tel:** 44 01432 360246
Email: news@sunshineradio.co.uk
Web site: http://www.sunshineradio.co.uk/

Sunshine Radio 855 AM
Unit 11, Burway Trading Estate, Bromfield Road, Ludlow SY8 1EN
Tel: 44 01584 877855
Email: studio1@sunshineradio.co.uk
Web site: www.sunshineradio.co.uk

SURGE
Southampton University Students' Union, University of Southampton, Southampton SO17 1BJ **Tel:** 44 02380 595855
Email: studio@surgeradio.co.uk
Web site: http://www.surgeradio.co.uk

Swansea Sound
The Wave and Swansea Sound, Victoria Road, Gowerton, Swansea SA4 3AB
Tel: 44 01792 511170
Email: news@swanseasound.co.uk
Web site: www.swanseasound.co.uk

talkRADIO
18 Hatfields, London SE1 8DJ
Tel: 44 02079 597800
Email: pressreleases@talkradio.co.uk
Web site: www.talkradio.co.uk

talkSPORT
18 Hatfields, London SE1 8DJ
Tel: 44 02079 597800
Email: press.releases@talksport.co.uk
Web site: www.talksport.co.uk

talkSPORT 2
18 Hatfields, London SE1 8DJ
Tel: 44 02079 597800
Email: press.releases@talksport.co.uk
Web site: http://talksport.com/

Tameside Radio 103.6 FM
Quest Media Centre, Cavendish Mill, Bank Street, Ashton-under-Lyne OL6 7DN
Tel: 44 01613 312558
Email: info@insidetameside.com
Web site: http://www.tamesideradio.com
Editor: Nigel Skinner

Tay 2
3 South Avenue, Clydebank Business Park, Glasgow G81 2RX **Tel:** 44 01382 200800
Email: newsroom@radiotay.co.uk
Web site: http://www.tay2.co.uk/

Tay FM
6 North Isla Street, Dundee DD3 7JQ
Tel: 44 01382 423212
Email: newsroom@radiotay.co.uk
Web site: www.tayfm.co.uk

TFM 2
Castle Quay, Castlefield, Manchester M15 4PR **Tel:** 44 01612 885000
Email: news@metroandmagic.com
Web site: www.planetradio.co.uk/tfm-2/

TFM Radio
55 Degrees North, Pilgrim Street, Newcastle upon Tyne NE1 6BF **Tel:** 44 01912 306100
Email: tfmnews@tfmradio.com
Web site: www.tfmradio.co.uk

Thames Radio
Tel: 44 02070 605520
Email: enquiries@thamesradio.london
Web site: http://thamesradio.london/

Time 107.5 FM
TIME 107.5 FM, Laurie Walk, The Liberty Shopping Centre, Romford RM1 3RT
Tel: 44 01708 741075
Email: onair@time1075.net
Web site: www.time1075.net

Top Rock Radio
Email: info@toprockradio.com
Web site: www.toprockradio.com
Editor: Jim Beerman

Touch Radio 101.6 / 102.4
3 Martins Court, Telford Way, Coalville LE67 3HD **Tel:** 44 01530 278200
Email: tamworth.studio@touchradio.co.uk
Web site: www.101touchfm.co.uk

Tower FM
Orrell Lodge, Orrell Road, Orrell, Wigan WN5 8HJ **Tel:** 44 08447 360501
Email: news@towerfm.co.uk
Web site: www.towerfm.co.uk

Town 102 FM
Radio House, Orion Court, Great Blakenham, Ipswich IP6 0LW
Tel: 44 01473 530100
Email: news@town102.com
Web site: www.town102.com

Trax FM
5 Sidings Court, White Rose Way, Doncaster DN4 5NU **Tel:** 44 01302 341166
Email: news@traxfm.co.uk
Web site: www.traxfm.co.uk

U105.8 fm
UTV, Ormeau Road, Belfast BT7 1EB
Tel: 44 02890 332105
Email: news@u.tv
Web site: www.u105.com

UCB UK
Broadcast Centre, Hanchurch Lane, Stoke-on-Trent, Stone ST4 8RY
Tel: 44 01782 642000
Email: broadcasting@ucb.co.uk
Web site: www.ucb.co.uk

UK Health Radio
PO BOX 56684, London W13 3DL
Tel: 44 02032 394423
Email: info@ukhealthradio.com
Web site: http://ukhealthradio.com/

URB
University of Bath Students' Union, Norwood House, Claverton Down, Bath BA2 7AY
Tel: 44 01225 383800
Email: urb-manager@bath.ac.uk
Web site: https://www.bathstudent.com/media/1449amurb/

URF Online
Norwich House, University of Sussex, Falmer, Brighton, Brighton BN1 9QS
Tel: 44 01273 678152
Email: station.manager@urfonline.com
Web site: www.urfonline.com

URN
UoNSU, Portland Building, University Park, Nottingham NG7 2RD **Tel:** 44 01159 515522
Email: news@urn1350.net
Web site: www.urn1350.net

URY
Vanbrugh College, University of York, Heslington, York YO10 5DD
Tel: 44 01904 321350
Email: newsroom@ury.org.uk
Web site: http://www.ury.org.uk/

Viking 2
Castle Quay, Castlefield, Manchester M15 4PR **Tel:** 44 01612 885000
Email: newsdesk@vikingfm.co.uk
Web site: http://www.viking2.co.uk/

Viking FM
The Boathouse, Commercial Road, Hull HU1 2SG **Tel:** 44 01482 325141
Email: newsdesk@vikingfm.co.uk
Web site: www.planetradio.co.uk/viking/

Virgin Radio (UK)
18 Hatfields, London SE1 8DJ
Tel: 44 02079 597800
Email: press.releases@virginradio.co.uk
Web site: www.virginradio.co.uk

Vixen 101
Vixen 101, Market Weighton, Market Weighton YO43 3AH **Tel:** 44 01430 875830
Email: news@vixen101.co.uk
Web site: http://vixen101.co.uk/

Wave 102
11 Buchanan Street, Dundee DD4 6SD
Tel: 44 01382 901000
Email: news@wave102.co.uk
Web site: www.wave102.co.uk

Wave 105.2 FM
PO Box 105, Fareham, Southampton PO15 5YF **Tel:** 44 01489 481050
Email: news@wave105.com
Web site: www.wave105.com

Waves Radio Peterhead
7 Blackhouse Circle, Blackhouse Industrial Estate, Peterhead AB42 1BN
Tel: 44 01779 491012
Email: waves@wavesfm.com
Web site: www.wavesfm.com

Wessex FM
Poundbury House, Poundbury West Industrial Estate, Dorchester DT1 2PG
Tel: 44 01305 250333
Email: news@wessexfm.com
Web site: www.wessexfm.com

UK Broadcast

West FM 96.7
Ladykirk House, Ladykirk Business Park, 11
Skye Road, Prestwick KA9 2TA
Tel: 44 01292 283662
Email: news.westsound@westsound.co.uk
Web site: www.westfm.co.uk

West Sound (FM)
Unit 40, Loreburn Shopping Centre,
Dumfries DG1 2BD **Tel:** 44 01387 250999
Email: news.westsound@westsound.co.uk
Web site: www.westsoundradio.com

Wired Radio
Goldsmiths College Students Union, Dixon
Road, New Cross, London SE14 6NW
Email: info.wiredradio@gmail.com
Web site: www.wiredradio.co.uk

Xpress Radio
Cardiff University Students Union, 4th Floor,
Park Place, Cardiff CF10 3QN
Tel: 44 02920 781530
Email: stationmanager@xpressradio.co.uk
Web site: www.xpressradio.co.uk

Xpression FM
Devonshire House, Stocker Road, Exeter
EX4 4PZ **Tel:** 44 01392 723568
Email: xpressionfmstudio@gmail.com
Web site: www.xpression.fm

XS Manchester
Laser House, Waterfront Quay, Salford
Quays, Manchester M50 3XW
Tel: 44 01616 624602
Email: northwest.news@thisisglobal.com
Web site: www.xsmanchester.co.uk

Yorkshire Coast Radio
Unit 2B Newchase Business Centre, Hopper
Hill Road, Scarborough YO11 3YS
Tel: 44 01723 581700
Email: news@yorkshirecoastradio.com
Web site: www.yorkshirecoastradio.com

Your Radio FM
Carus House 201, Dumbarton Rd,
Clydebank G81 4XJ **Tel:** 44 01389 744444
Email: admin@yourradio.scot
Web site: http://www.yourradio.scot/

Television Networks & Stations

4Music
Francis House, 11 Francis Street, London
SW1P 1DE **Tel:** 44 02073 068132
Email: mpine@channel4.co.uk
Web site: www.4music.com

5*
10 Lower Thames Street, London EC3R 6EN
Tel: 44 02086 127000
Email: customerservices@channel5.com
Web site: www.channel5.com/channels/
5star

The Africa Channel
The Africa Channel International, 33-34
Gresse Street, London W1T 1QU
Tel: 44 02071 486900
Email: talk@theafricachannel.tv
Web site: http://www.theafricachannel.co.
uk/

Alibi
10 Hammersmith Grove, London W6 7AP
Tel: 44 02031 920504
Web site: alibi.uktv.co.uk

Arise News
New Zealand House, 80 Haymarket, London
SW1Y 4TQ **Tel:** 44 02073 891740
Email: info@arise.tv
Web site: http://www.arise.tv/

BBC Arabic Television
Broadcasting House, Portland Place,
London W1A 1AA **Tel:** 44 02087 438000
Email: arabicnewsgatheringplanning@bbc.
co.uk
Web site: www.bbc.com/arabic
Editor: Bassam Andari

BBC First (Belgium)
Television Centre, 101 Wood Lane, London
W12 7FA **Tel:** 44 02084 332000
Web site: www.bbceurope.com/benelux

BBC First (Netherlands)
33 Foley Street, London W1W 7TL
Web site: www.bbceurope.com/benelux/
zenders/first/

BBC Four
Broadcasting House, Portland Place,
London W1A 1AA **Tel:** 44 02087 438000
Email: press.office@bbc.co.uk
Web site: www.bbc.co.uk/bbcfour

BBC London
BBC Broadcasting House, 2nd Floor, Egton
Wing, Portland Place, London W1A 1AA
Tel: 44 02087 438000
Email: ldn-planning@bbc.co.uk
Web site: http://news.bbc.co.uk/local/
london/hi

BBC News
BBC Broadcasting House, Portland Place,
London W1A 1AA **Tel:** 44 02087 438000
Email: uknewsplan@bbc.co.uk
Web site: www.bbc.co.uk/news

BBC News Channel
BBC Broadcasting House, Portland Place,
London W1A 1AA **Tel:** 44 02087 438000
Email: uknewsplan@bbc.co.uk
Web site: http://www.bbc.co.uk/news
Editor: Jeremy Skeet

BBC Northern Ireland
Broadcasting House, Ormeau Avenue,
Belfast BT2 8HQ **Tel:** 44 02890 338000
Email: ni_news@bbc.co.uk
Web site: www.bbc.co.uk/northernireland/

BBC One
1st Floor, Dock House, MediaCityUK,
Salford M50 2LH **Tel:** 44 02087 438000
Web site: www.bbc.co.uk/bbcone
Editor: Ian Hislop

BBC One East
The Forum, Millennium Plain, Norwich NR2
1BH **Tel:** 44 01603 619331
Web site: http://www.bbc.co.uk/bbcone/
programmes/schedules/east

BBC One East Midlands
London Road, Nottingham NG2 4UU
Tel: 44 01159 550500
Web site: http://www.bbc.co.uk/bbcone/
programmes/schedules/east_midlands

BBC One North East & Cumbria
Broadcasting Centre, Barrack Road,
Newcastle upon Tyne NE99 2NE
Tel: 44 01912 321313
Email: neandcumbria@bbc.co.uk
Web site: http://www.bbc.co.uk/bbcone/
programmes/schedules/north_east

BBC One North West
Quay House, MediaCity, Salford M50 2QH
Tel: 44 01618 360030
Web site: http://www.bbc.co.uk/bbcone/
programmes/schedules/north_west
Editor: Michelle Mayman

BBC One South
Broadcasting House, 10 Havelock Road,
Southampton SO14 7PU
Tel: 44 02380 226201
Web site: http://www.bbc.co.uk/bbcone/
programmes/schedules/south

BBC One South East
The Great Hall, Mount Pleasant Road,
Tunbridge Wells TN1 1QQ
Tel: 44 01892 675580
Web site: http://www.bbc.co.uk/bbcone/
programmes/schedules/south_east

BBC One South West
Broadcasting House, Mannamead Road,
Plymouth PL3 5BD **Tel:** 44 01752 229201
Web site: http://www.bbc.co.uk/bbcone/
programmes/schedules/south_west
Editor: Sam Smith

BBC One West
Broadcasting House, Whiteladies Road,
Bristol BS8 2LR **Tel:** 44 01179 746877
Web site: http://www.bbc.co.uk/bbcone/
programmes/schedules/west
Editor: Neil Bennett

BBC One Yorks & Lincs
Queen's Court, Hull HU1 3RH
Tel: 44 01482 323232
Web site: http://www.bbc.co.uk/bbcone/
programmes/schedules/east_yorkshire

BBC One Yorkshire
2 St Peter's Square, Leeds LS9 8AH
Tel: 44 01132 247041
Web site: http://www.bbc.co.uk/bbcone/
programmes/schedules/yorkshire

BBC Scotland
Broadcasting House, 40 Pacific Quay,
Glasgow G51 1DA **Tel:** 44 01414 226000
Email: scottish.planning@bbc.co.uk
Web site: www.bbc.co.uk/scotland

BBC Two
New Broadcasting House, Portland Place,
London W1A 1AA **Tel:** 44 02087 438000
Web site: www.bbc.co.uk/bbctwo

BBC Wales
Broadcasting House, Llantrisant Road,
Llandaff, Cardiff CF5 2YQ
Tel: 44 02920 322000
Email: newsgathering.wales@bbc.co.uk
Web site: www.bbc.co.uk/wales

BBC West Midlands
Level 7, The Mailbox, Birmingham B1 1RF
Tel: 44 01215 676000
Web site: http://www.bbc.co.uk/news/
england/birmingham_and_black_country

BBC World News
New Broadcasting House, Portland Place,
London W1A 1AA **Tel:** 44 02087 438000
Email: worldplan@bbc.co.uk
Web site: www.bbc.co.uk/news/world_
radio_and_tv

BBC Worldwide
33 Foley Street, London London W1W 7TL
Tel: 44 02084 332000
Web site: www.bbcworldwide.com

**BFBS British Forces
Broadcasting Service**
Chalfont Grove, Narcot Lane, Chalfont St.
Peter, Chalfont St. Giles SL9 8TN
Tel: 44 01494 878616
Email: news@bfbs.com
Web site: www.bfbs.com

BIKE (UK)
Bike Media UK Ltd, 18th Floor, City Tower,
Basinghall Street, London EC2V 5DE
Tel: 44 02070 322338
Email: info@bikechannel.co.uk
Web site: http://www.bikechannel.co.uk/

Bloomberg Television EMEA
City Gate House, 39-45 Finsbury Square,
London EC2A 1PQ **Tel:** 44 02073 307500
Email: newsalert@bloomberg.net
Web site: www.bloomberg.com/live/europe

British Muslim TV
Tel: 44 02071 189118
Web site: www.britishmuslim.tv

Cambridge TV
15 Signet Court, Swann's Road, Cambridge
CB5 8LA **Tel:** 44 01223 750890
Email: enquiries@cambridge-tv.co.uk
Web site: www.cambridge-tv.co.uk

CBBC
Bridge House, MediaCityUK, Salford M50
2BH **Tel:** 44 01613 356000
Email: cbbc@bbc.co.uk
Web site: www.bbc.co.uk/cbbc
Editor: Lewis James

CBeebies
Bridge House, MediaCityUK, Salford M50
2BH **Tel:** 44 01613 356000
Email: cbeebies@bbc.co.uk
Web site: www.bbc.co.uk/cbeebies

Channel 4
124 Horseferry Road, London SW1P 2TX
Tel: 44 02073 964444
Web site: www.channel4.com

Channel 5
The Northern & Shell Building, 10 Lower
Thames Street, London EC3R 6EN
Tel: 44 02074 304405
Web site: www.channel5.com

CNBC International
10 Fleet Place, Limeburner Lane, London
EC4M 7QS **Tel:** 44 02076 539300
Web site: www.cnbc.com/world

CNBC uk
Web site: http://www.cnbc.com

CNN International
Turner House, 16 Great Marlborough Street,
London W1F 7HS **Tel:** 44 02076 931000
Email: cnnlondon@cnn.com
Web site: http://edition.cnn.com/

**CNN International - Connect
The World - Sunday to Thursday
(4-5pm GMT)**
Web site: www.cnn.com/connect

Community Channel
4th Floor Block A, Centre House, Wood
Lane, London W12 7SB
Tel: 44 02078 715600
Email: info@communitychannel.org
Web site: www.communitychannel.org

Cumbria TV
30 Queen Street, Ulverston, Ulverston LA12
7AF **Tel:** 44 01229 343044
Email: info@cumbriatv.net
Web site: http://www.cumbriatv.net/

Cyfra+
Tel: 44 48226 570701
Web site: http://www.cyfraplus.pl

Dave
245 Hammersmith Road, London W6 8PW
Tel: 44 02072 996200
Web site: www.dave.uktv.co.uk/

**Designed to Sparkle Jewellery
Blog - CEASED MAY 2015**
Web site: http://www.designedtosparkle.co.
uk/bridal-jewellery-blog/

Discovery Channel (U.K.)
Discovery House, Chiswick Park Building 2,
566 Chiswick High Road, London W4 5YB
Tel: 44 02088 113000
Web site: www.discoveryuk.com

E4
124-126 Horseferry Road, London SW1P
2TX
Web site: www.e4.com

Ecuavisa
Tel: 44 59342 562444
Web site: http://www.ecuavisa.com/

Estuary TV
The Grimsby Institute, Nuns Corner, Grimsby
DN34 5BQ **Tel:** 44 01472 315561
Email: info@estuary.tv
Web site: http://estuary.tv/

Eurosport
Sussex House, 2 Plane Tree Crescent,
London TW13 7HE **Tel:** 44 08456 721010
Email: se@eurosport.com
Web site: http://tv.eurosport.co.uk/
Editor: Frédéric Verdier

Extreme Sports Channel
Extreme Sports Channel, 105-109 Salusbury
Road, London NW6 6RG
Tel: 44 02073 288808
Email: onlineinfo@extreme.com
Web site: www.extreme.com

Flava
8 Chelsea Gate Studios, 115 Harwood Road,
London SW6 4QL **Tel:** 44 02073 715999
Email: info@cscmediagroup.com

FOX
10 Hammersmith Grove, London W6 7AP
Tel: 44 02077 517700
Email: foxtv.info@fox.com
Web site: http://www.foxtv.co.uk/

G.O.L.D.
245 Hammersmith Road, London W6 8PW
Web site: www.uktv.co.uk/Gold

Ginx TV
Unit 1L, Woodstock Studios, 36 Woodstock
Grove, London W12 8LE
Tel: 44 02085 766660
Email: info@ginx.tv
Web site: ginx.tv

Globetrotter Television
Globetrotter Television, 2 Fremantle Road,
Folkestone, Folkestone CT20 3PY
Tel: 44 01303 850801
Email: editor@globetrottertv.com
Web site: www.globetrottertv.com/watch_
online.html
Editor: Trevor Claringbold

Good Food Channel
245 Hammersmith Road, London W6 8PW
Tel: 44 02072 996200
Web site: www.goodfoodchannel.co.uk

H2
Westcross House, Grant Way, Isleworth,
London TW7 5QD **Tel:** 44 03331 000333
Email: feedback@aetn.co.uk
Web site: www.history.co.uk/h2

Helensburgh & Lohmond TV
The Clock Tower, East Clyde Street,
Helensburgh G84 7PA **Tel:** 44 01436 820369
Email: news@urtv.co.uk
Web site: http://www.helensburgh.tv/

HISTORY
Westcross House, Grant Way, Isleworth,
London TW7 5QD **Tel:** 44 03331 000333
Email: feedback@aetn.co.uk
Web site: www.history.co.uk/

Home
UKTV, Home, 10 Hammersmith Grove,
London W6 7AP **Tel:** 44 02072 995000
Web site: http://uktv.co.uk/home

The Horror Channel
105-109 Salusbury Road, Queen's Park,
London NW6 6RG **Tel:** 44 02073 288808
Web site: www.horrorchannel.co.uk

Horse & Country TV
Technium Springboard, Llantarnam Park,
Cwmbran, Cwmbran NP44 3AW
Tel: 44 01633 647948
Email: programmes@horseandcountry.tv
Web site: www.horseandcountry.tv

Ideal Shopping Direct Ltd
Ideal Home House, Newark Road,
Peterborough, Peterborough PE1 5WG
Tel: 44 08431 688888
Email: buying@idealshoppingdirect.co.uk
Web site: http://www.idealshoppingdirect.
co.uk/

Islam Channel
14 Bonhill Street, London EC2A 4BX
Tel: 44 02073 744511
Email: pr@islamchannel.tv
Web site: www.islamchannel.tv

It's Not Rocket Sience
Tel: 44 02071 573000
Web site: http://www.itv.com/presscentre/
ep1week7/its-not-rocket-science

ITV
The London Television Centre, Upper
Ground, London SE1 9LT
Tel: 44 02071 573000
Web site: http://www.itv.com/

ITV Anglia News
Anglia House, Rose Lane, Norwich NR1 3JG
Tel: 44 08448 816900
Email: anglianews@itv.com
Web site: www.itv.com/news/anglia
Editor: Guy Phillips

ITV Border
1 Clifford Court, Cooper Way, Parkhouse,
Carlisle CA3 0JG **Tel:** 44 08448 815888
Email: btvnews@itv.com
Web site: www.itv.com/news/border

ITV Meridian
New Cut Road, Vinters Park, Maidstone
ME14 5NZ **Tel:** 44 08448 812000
Email: itvnewsmeridian@itv.com
Web site: http://www.itv.com/meridian/
Editor: Guy Phillips

ITV News
200 Gray's Inn Road, London WC1X 8XZ
Tel: 44 02078 333000
Email: news@itn.co.uk
Web site: http://www.itv.com/news/
Editor: Guy Phillips

ITV News Central
Central Court, Gas Street, Birmingham B1
2JT **Tel:** 44 08448 814000
Email: centralnews@itv.com
Web site: www.itvlocal.com/central
Editor: Guy Phillips

ITV News Channel TV
Tel: 44 01534 480523
Email: channelnews@itv.com
Web site: http://www.itv.com/news/channel/
Editor: Gary Burgess

ITV News Granada
Orange Tower, MediaCity UK, Salford M50
2HE **Tel:** 44 01619 521000
Email: granada.reports@itv.com
Web site: www.itv.com/granada
Editor: Guy Phillips

ITV News London
200 Gray's Inn Road, London WC1X 8XZ
Tel: 44 02074 304000
Email: newsdesk@itvlondon.com
Web site: www.itv.com/news/london
Editor: Guy Phillips

ITV News West Country
Television Centre, Bath Road, Bristol BS4
3HG **Tel:** 44 08448 812307
Email: westcountry@itv.com
Web site: www.itv.com/news/westcountry
Editor: Guy Phillips

ITV Tyne Tees
ITV News Tyne Tees, Television House, The
Watermark, Gateshead NE11 9SZ
Tel: 44 08448 815153
Email: tttvnews@itv.com
Web site: www.itv.com/tynetees
Editor: Guy Phillips

ITV Wales
3 Assembly Square, Britannia Quay, Cardiff
CF10 4PL **Tel:** 44 08448 810100
Email: wales@itv.com
Web site: www.itv.com/wales

ITV Yorkshire
The Television Centre, Kirkstall Road, Leeds
LS3 1JS **Tel:** 44 01132 228700
Email: calendar@itv.com
Web site: www.itvlocal.com
Editor: Guy Phillips

ITV2
ITV Network Centre, 200 Gray's Inn Road,
London WC1X 8XZ **Tel:** 44 08448 818000
Email: itvpresscentre@itv.com
Web site: www.itv.com/itv2

itvBe
200 Gray's Inn Road, London WC1X 8XZ
Tel: 44 00440 818000
Email: itvplanning@itn.co.uk
Web site: www.itv.com/be

Kaara
Web site: http://kaara.tv/

Kanal 11
Tel: 44 37266 62450
Email: info@kanal11.ee
Web site: http://kanal11.ee

Kerrang! TV
Francis House, 11 Francis Street, London
SW1P 1DE **Tel:** 44 02072 955000
Email: feedback@kerrang.com
Web site: http://www.kerrang.com/tv/

KMTV
Medway House, Ginsbury Close, Sir Thomas
Longley Road, Rochester ME2 4DU
Tel: 44 01622 717880
Email: multimedia@thekmgroup.co.uk
Web site: http://www.kentonline.co.uk/
kmtv/

Latest TV
14-17 Manchester Street, Brighton BN2 1TF
Tel: 44 01273 818150
Email: news@thelatest.tv
Web site: http://thelatest.co.uk/brighton/
category/tv/

Levant TV
807-817, 8th Floor, Crown House, North
Circular Road, London NW10 7PN
Tel: 44 02079 986024
Email: info@levant.tv
Web site: http://levant.tv/

London Live
Northcliffe House, 2 Derry Street,
Kensington, London W8 5TT
Tel: 44 02036 150200
Email: planning@londonlive.co.uk
Web site: www.londonlive.co.uk

Made in Bristol
The Media Centre, Abbeywood Business
Park, Emma-Chris Way, Bristol BS34 7JU
Tel: 44 01179 066551
Email: news@madeinbristol.tv
Web site: www.madeinbristol.tv

Made in Cardiff
Made in Cardiff, 3rd Floor Elgin House, 106-
107 St Mary Street, Cardiff CF10 1DX
Web site: www.madeincardiff.tv

Made in Liverpool
The Television Centre, 37-45 Windsor Street,
Liverpool L8 1XE **Tel:** 44 03333 401000
Email: news@madeinliverpool.tv
Web site: www.madeinliverpool.tv

Made in Tyne & Wear
Leeds Media Centre, 21 Savile Mount, Leeds
LS7 3HZ **Tel:** 44 03333 401000
Email: news@madeintyneandwear.tv
Web site: http://www.madeintyneandwear.
tv/

Mezzo
Tel: 44 33015 6365100
Email: contact@mezzo.fr
Web site: http://www.mezzo.tv/

MoonTV.fi
Email: palaute@moontv.fi
Web site: http://moontv.fi/

MTV Base
17-29 Hawley Crescent, Camden Town,
London NW1 8TT **Tel:** 44 02035 802000
Email: pressuk@mtvne.com
Web site: www.mtv.co.uk/mtv-base

MTV Dance
17-29 Hawley Crescent, Camden Town,
London NW1 8TT **Tel:** 44 02035 802000
Email: pressuk@mtvne.com
Web site: www.mtv.co.uk/mtv-dance

MTV Hits
17-29 Hawley Crescent, Camden Town,
London NW1 8TT **Tel:** 44 02035 802000
Email: pressuk@mtvne.com
Web site: www.mtv.co.uk/mtv-hits

MTV Rocks
17-29 Hawley Crescent, Camden Town,
London NW1 8TT **Tel:** 44 02035 802000
Email: pressuk@mtvne.com
Web site: www.mtv.co.uk/channels/mtv-
rocks

Mustard TV
Prospect House, Rouen House, Norwich
NR1 1RE **Tel:** 44 01603 628311
Email: mustardproduction@archant.co.uk
Web site: www.mustardtv.co.uk

National Geographic Channel
3rd Floor, 10 Hammersmith Grove, London
W6 7AP **Tel:** 44 02031 471112
Email: ngcdutylog@fox.com
Web site: http://natgeotv.com/uk

National Geographic Wild
3rd Floor, 10 Hammersmith Grove, London
W6 7AP **Tel:** 44 02077 517700
Email: ngcdutylog@fox.com
Web site: http://natgeotv.com/uk

Nickelodeon UK
17-29 Hawley Crescent, Camden, London
NW1 8TT **Tel:** 44 02035 802000
Email: reception@nickelodeon.co.uk
Web site: www.nick.co.uk

Notts TV
Antenna Media Centre, Beck Street,
Nottingham NG1 1EQ **Tel:** 44 01158 484369
Email: news@nottstv.com
Web site: http://nottstv.com/

Peace TV
Tel: 44 02079 938470
Web site: www.peacetv.tv
Editor: Imran Yaqoob

Peretz
Tel: 44 74957 856347
Email: post@peretz.ru
Web site: http://peretz.ru

Pick
6 Centaurs Business Park, Grant Way,
Isleworth, London TW7 5QD
Tel: 44 02077 053000
Email: skyeditorial@bskyb.com

Polonia1/Polcast Television
Tel: 44 48223 378770
Email: info@polcast.tv
Web site: http://www.polonia1.pl

Polsat Sport
Tel: 44 48227 159273
Email: polsatsport@polsat.com.pl
Web site: http://www.polsatsport.pl

Radio Televisyen Brunei
Tel: 44 67312 72243111
Email: manap_hjadam@rtb.gov.bn
Web site: http://www.rtb.gov.bn

Really
10 Hammersmith Grove, London W6 7AP
Tel: 44 02072 995000
Email: feedback.uktvnetwork@bss.org
Web site: http://really.uktv.co.uk/

Reuters TV
4th Floor, Thomson Reuters Building, South
Colonnade, Canary Wharf, London E14 5EP
Tel: 44 02072 501122
Email: tvnews@reuters.com
Web site: http://www.reuters.tv/

RT UK
Millbank Tower, 16th Floor, 21-24 Millbank,
Westminster SW1P 4QP
Tel: 44 02077 982222
Email: info@rttv.ru
Web site: http://rt.com/uk/

UK Broadcast

S4C
Parc Ty Glas, Llanishen, Cardiff CF14 5DU
Tel: 44 02920 747444
Email: hello@s4c.co.uk
Web site: http://www.s4c.cymru/cy/

SABC News - New York Bureau
Web site: http://www.sabcnews.com

Scuzz
8 Chelsea Gate Studios, 115 Harwood Road,
London SW6 4QL **Tel:** 44 02073 715999
Email: info@cscmediagroup.com
Web site: https://sites.
sonypicturestelevision.com/brand.php?id=
19

Sky 1
Grant Way, London TW7 5QD
Tel: 44 03331 000333
Web site: https://www.sky.com/watch/
channel/sky-1

Sky Arts
New Horizons Court 1, Grant Way, Isleworth,
London TW7 5QD **Tel:** 44 08448 244100
Web site: www.sky.com/arts

Sky Living
New Horizons Court 1, Grant Way, Isleworth,
London TW7 5QD **Tel:** 44 03331 000333
Email: bskybpress@bskyb.com
Web site: http://www.sky.com/tv/channel/
skyliving

Sky News
Grant Way, Isleworth TW7 5QD
Tel: 44 03331 000333
Email: news.plan@sky.uk
Web site: http://news.sky.com/

Sky Sports
Grant Way, Isleworth TW7 5QD
Tel: 44 03331 000333
Email: ssn-planning@sky.uk
Web site: www.skysports.com

Sky Sports News HQ
Grant Way, Isleworth, London TW7 5QD
Tel: 44 02070 322222
Email: ssn-planning@bsky.uk
Web site: www.skysports.com/
skysportsnews

STV
Pacific Quay, Glasgow G51 1PQ
Tel: 44 01413 003000
Email: stvnews@stv.tv
Web site: www.stv.tv
Editor: Howard Simpson

SuperSport
Tel: 44 27116 866000
Email: info@supersport.co.za
Web site: http://www.supersport.com

Syfy
Universal Networks International, 1 Central
Saint Giles, St Giles High Street, London
WC2H 8NU **Tel:** 44 02036 188000
Email: syfy.team@nbcuni.com
Web site: www.syfy.com

TCM
Turner House, 16 Great Marlborough Street,
London W1F 7HS **Tel:** 44 02076 931000
Email: tcmmailuk@turner.com
Web site: http://www.tcm.com/

That's Manchester TV
Tel: 44 01616 050845
Email: news@thatsmanchester.co.uk
Web site: http://thats.tv/manchester/

That's Oxfordshire
Tel: 44 01865 570100
Email: news@thatsoxfordshire.tv
Web site: http://www.thats.tv/oxford/

That's Solent TV
Highbury, Tudor Crescent, Portsmouth PO6
2SA
Email: news@thatssolent.com
Web site: www.thats.tv

Tip TV
8-10 Grosvenor Gardens, London SW1W
0DH **Tel:** 44 02073 978506
Email: info@tiptv.co.uk
Web site: www.tiptv.co.uk
Editor: Craig Drake

Travel Channel
111 Buckingham Palace Road, London
SW1W 0SR **Tel:** 44 02075 789700
Web site: www.travelchannel.co.uk

UTV
Havelock House, Ormeau Road, Belfast BT7
1EB **Tel:** 44 02890 328122
Email: news@u.tv
Web site: http://www.itv.com/
utvprogrammes

The Vault
8 Chelsea Gate Studios, 115 Harwood Road,
London SW6 4QL **Tel:** 44 02073 715999
Email: info@cscmediagroup.com
Web site: https://ukfree.tv/channels/
channel/VAULT

Voxafrica TV UK
Voxafrica Ltd, Battersea Studio, 80
Silverthorne Road, London SW8 3HE
Tel: 44 02075 017700
Email: info@voxafrica.com
Web site: www.voxafrica.co.uk

W
10 Hammersmith Grove, London W6 7AP
Tel: 44 02031 920504
Web site: w.uktv.co.uk

Zone Club
Tel: 44 48225 470240
Email: katarzyna.sady@chellocentraleurope.
com
Web site: http://www.zoneclub.tv

Willings Volume 1
Section 6

UK Blogs

Index to UK Blogs
UK Blogs listed A-Z

Categories A-Z

UK Blogs

Categories A-Z

Architecture & Design

Armed Forces

Art

Categories A-Z

Automakers

Automotive

Aviation

Banking

Bankruptcy

Bars, Clubs & Pubs

Basketball

Beauty & Grooming

Categories A-Z

Beer

Categories A-Z

Categories A-Z

Categories A-Z

Charitable Foundations

Chemicals

Chess

Classical/Choral/Band Music

Comedy

Categories A-Z

Consumer Goods & Products

Consumer Interest

Cooking & Baking

Consumer Affairs

Consumer Electronics

Categories A-Z

Corporate Finance

Corporate Law

Corporate Management

Corporate Responsibility

Cosmetics

Categories A-Z

Country, Folk, Bluegrass

Crafts

Crafts, Hobbies, & Collecting

Credit Markets

Cricket

Crime & Violence

Criminal Law

Dance Music

Data Management

Categories A-Z

Defense & National Security

Dentistry

Derivatives

Dermatology

Diabetes

Dieting

Disability

Diseases & Conditions

Do-It-Yourself (DIY)

Driving

E-Commerce

Economics

Education

Categories A-Z

Electricity

Electronics

Elementary School

Emerging Markets

Employment

EMS/Emergency Medical Services

Energy

Categories A-Z

Equities

Estate Planning

Ethical/Moral Issues

Expatriates

Extreme/Adventure Sports

Family & Parenting

Categories A-Z

Categories A-Z

Federal Courts

Field Sports

Finance

Financial Markets

Fishing

Fitness & Exercise

Food

Food & Drug Administration

Football (American)

Categories A-Z

Categories A-Z

Categories A-Z

Section 6 UK Blogs

Categories A-Z

Internet Applications

Investment Banking

Jazz & Blues

Law

Categories A-Z

Local Entertainment Guides

Luxury Goods

Luxury Travel

Manufacturing

Marine & Boat Trade

Marketing

Categories A-Z

Martial Arts, MMA & Self-Defense

Mathematics

Media & Communications

Media Relations

Medical Technology

Medicine

Men's Interests

Mining & Quarrying

Mobile Communications

Mobile Electronics

Categories A-Z

Motorcycles

Motorsports

Movies & Video

Categories A-Z

Music

National News

Nature & Wildlife

Neurology

Categories A-Z

News

News & Current Affairs

News & Current Affairs

Northern Ireland

Nuclear Power

Nutrition

Obstetrics & Gynecology (OB/GYN)

Off-road & 4-Wheel Drive Vehicles

Office Design

Oil

Olympic Sports

Oncology

Ophthalmology & Optometry

Organic Food

Physics

Plastic/Reconstructive/Cosmetic Surgery

Plastics

Politics

Categories A-Z

Private Equity

Property Management & Maintenance

Pop Music

Preschool

Categories A-Z

Real Estate

Real Estate Law

Recruiting

Regional

Regional General Interest

Relationships

Religion

Residential Real Estate

Respiratory Diseases

Restaurant Reviews

Categories A-Z

Retail

Retirement Savings

Rock Music

Rowing

Rugby

Sales & Marketing

Schools & Institutions

Categories A-Z

Social Issues

Social Media

Software

Sports

Sports Medicine

Steel

Student Lifestyle

Students

Supply Chain Management (SCM)

Sustainable Development

Swimming/Watersports

Categories A-Z

Trucks & SUVs

Urban Planning & Development

Vegetarianism & Veganism

Veterinary Medicine

Categories A-Z

Categories A-Z

UK Blogs

UK Blogs

#Illustration Matters 996308
Email: hello@charlottemaryrose.com
Web site: charlottemaryrose.com
Freq: Daily
Circ: 806
Art, Photography

#N64Memories 1100506
Web site: http://n64memories.blogspot.co.uk/
Freq: Daily
Circ: 11306
Computer & Video Games

(Mostly) Yummy Mummy 1054175
Email: mostlyyummy@rocketmail.com
Web site: http://mostlyyummymummy.com/
Freq: Daily
Circ: 6738
Cooking & Baking, Family & Parenting, Fashion, Restaurant Reviews, Women's Interests

The (Not So) Secret Diary of a Wannabe Princess 1057618
Web site: http://www.wannabeprincess.co.uk/
Freq: Daily
Circ: 12114
Fashion, Women's Interests

*artemporary.ch 1073815
Email: artemporaryblog@gmail.com
Web site: https://artemporary.ch/
Freq: Daily
Circ: 10420
Editor: Carmela Tafaro
Art, Travel, Women's Interests

...the kathryn wheel 998380
Web site: http://thekathrynwheel.blogspot.co.uk/
Freq: Daily
Circ: 964
Art, Crafts

...To The Real. 1054517
Web site: https://tothereal.wordpress.com
Freq: Daily
Circ: 72
Education

080808 On, Now, To the Third Level 1053733
Email: 07000intune@gmail.com
Web site: http://www.080808onnowto.blogspot.co.uk/
Freq: Daily
Circ: 611
Religion

The 100 Football Grounds Club 1053827
Web site: http://100groundsclub.blogspot.co.uk/
Freq: Daily
Circ: 10056
Soccer

1000GOALS 998218
Email: 1000goals@gmail.com
Web site: www.1000goals.com
Freq: Daily
Circ: 27972
Editor: Miss Rush
Soccer

12 Books in 12 Months 1053710
Web site: http://12books12months.com/
Freq: Daily
Circ: 10174
Literature

16bits.co.uk- CEASED 2016 998433
Email: info@16bits.co.uk
Web site: http://www.16bits.co.uk/
Freq: Daily

Circ: 685
Computer & Video Games

17 Seconds 988360
Email: seventeensecondsblog@hotmail.co.uk
Web site: http://17seconds.co.uk/blog/
Freq: Daily
Circ: 9923
Classical/Choral/Band Music, Country, Folk, Bluegrass, Dance Music, Jazz & Blues, Music, Pop Music, R&B, Urban, World, Rap & Hip Hop, Rock Music

19th Hole 986722
Tel: 44 08000 436644
Email: golfblog@yourgolftravel.com
Web site: www.yourgolftravel.com/19th-hole
Freq: Daily
Circ: 120
Golf, Travel

2 boxes.co.uk 996347
Editorial: 24 Langton Place, Southfields, London SW18 5AZ
Email: sarah@2boxes.co.uk
Web site: https://2boxes.co.uk/blog/
Freq: Daily
Circ: 365
Beauty & Grooming, Cooking & Baking, Cosmetics, Fashion, Hair, Regional General Interest, Restaurant Reviews, Women's Interests

20 Jazz Funk Greats 1056317
Web site: www.20jazzfunkgreats.co.uk/wordpress
Freq: Daily
Circ: 17963
Country, Folk, Bluegrass, Jazz & Blues, Pop Music, Rock Music

20plus30 Consulting 1054592
Tel: 44 02071 930915
Email: dick@20plus30.com
Web site: http://20plus30.blogspot.co.uk/
Freq: Daily
Circ: 12616
Branding, Business, Marketing, Publishing

2Wheel Chick 1053020
Web site: http://2wheelchick.blogspot.com
Freq: Daily
Circ: 8919
Bicycles, Travel

360 en Concreto 1060999
Web site: http://www.360gradosblog.com/
Freq: Daily
Circ: 1810
Basketball, Bicycles, Billiards, Boating & Yachting, Bodybuilding, Bowling, Boxing, Building & Construction, Cricket, Equestrian Sports

38 Degrees News 998132
Editorial: Room 126, 40 Bowling Green Lane, London EC1R 0NE
Tel: 44 02079 706023
Email: emailtheteam@38degrees.org.uk
Web site: https://home.38degrees.org.uk/
Freq: Daily
Circ: 924323
National News

The 40 Year Old Domestic Goddess CEASED 988312
Web site: 40yearolddomesticgoddess.blogspot.co.uk
Freq: Daily
Circ: 6052
Family & Parenting, Women's Interests

42 Kilometros 1061698
Web site: http://blogs.eluniversal.com/eu3/Blogs/42km_index.shtml
Freq: Daily
Circ: 17653
Sports

4Ps Marketing blog 1053984
Editorial: Studio 16, 8 Hornsey Street, Islington, London N7 8EG
Tel: 44 02076 075650
Email: hello@4psmarketing.com

Web site: http://www.4psmarketing.com/blog/
Freq: Daily
Circ: 7
Advertising Industry, Branding, Marketing

5 inch and up 986942
Email: info@5inchandup.com
Web site: 5inchandup.blogspot.co.uk
Freq: Daily
Circ: 39854
Fashion

5 Things To Do Today 1052790
Email: 5thingstodotoday@gmail.com
Web site: http://5thingstodotoday.com/
Freq: Daily
Circ: 11167
Profile: Blog covering bars, restaurants, luxury hotels, fine dining, UK travel, city breaks, events, launch parties, events, things to do in London, film, music, television, theatre, art and culture.
Celebrities, Lifestyle, Men's Interests, Regional General Interest, Women's Interests

The 72 1064285
Web site: http://the72.co.uk/
Freq: Daily
Circ: 159072
Soccer

7thingsmedia Blog 1053912
Editorial: 18/20 St. John Street, London EC1M 4NX Tel: 44 02070 173190
Email: london@7thingsmedia.com
Web site: http://www.7thingsmedia.com/blog/
Freq: Daily
Circ: 11290
Advertising Industry, Branding, Data Management

891 Filmhouse/Lanterna Magicka Films 998159
Email: sean@891filmhouse.com
Web site: http://891filmhouse.blogspot.co.uk/
Freq: Daily
Circ: 1100
Movies & Video

8tokyo.com 1062012
Email: info@8tokyo.com
Web site: http://8tokyo.com
Freq: Daily
Circ: 5249
Bars, Clubs & Pubs, Comedy, Entertainment, Local Entertainment Guides, Movies & Video

92three30.com 988685
Email: admin@92three30.com
Web site: 92three30.com
Freq: Daily
Circ: 59288
Profile: Blog covering parenting, family life and children's product reviews. The blog has an archive dating back to March 2011. The outlet offers RSS (Really Simple Syndication).
Family & Parenting

991 Sleeve Notes 996911
Editorial: The Nine Nine One Building, Railway Sidings, Meopham DA13 0YS
Tel: 44 01474 815010
Email: marketing@991.com
Web site: https://sleevenotes.991.com/
Freq: Daily
Circ: 19916
Classical/Choral/Band Music, Country, Folk, Bluegrass, Dance Music, Jazz & Blues, Music, Pop Music, R&B, Urban, World, Rap & Hip Hop, Rock Music

A Baby on Board 988684
Email: ababyonboard@gmail.com
Web site: ababyonboard.com
Freq: Daily
Circ: 17663
Family & Parenting

A Beauty Junkie in London 986526
Email: jen@beautyjunkielondon.com
Web site: www.beautyjunkielondon.com
Freq: Daily
Circ: 27186
Profile: Blog covering beauty. A BEAUTY JUNKIE IN LONDON blog discusses anything from make-up and beauty buys to fashion and London lifestyle. The blog has an archive dating back to February 2009.The outlet offers RSS (Really Simple Syndication).
Beauty & Grooming, Cosmetics, Hair

A Better NHS 986856
Web site: https://abetternhs.net/
Freq: Daily
Circ: 17101
News & Current Affairs

A Bookish Redhead 1054013
Email: bookbloggeri@yahoo.co.uk
Web site: http://www.abookishredhead.co.uk/
Freq: Daily
Circ: 2409
Literature

A Bright Space 1052663
Email: info@brightspacedesign.com
Web site: http://brightspacedesign.blogspot.com
Freq: Daily
Circ: 608
Do-It-Yourself (DIY)

A Cookbook Collection 1054067
Email: acookbookcollection@gmail.com
Web site: http://acookbookcollection.com/
Freq: Daily
Circ: 11666
Cooking & Baking

A Cultured Left Foot 1053822
Email: contact@aclfarsenal.co.uk
Web site: http://www.aclfarsenal.co.uk/
Freq: Daily
Circ: 65935
Soccer

A Daisy Chain Dream 986945
Email: adaisychaindream@gmail.com
Web site: www.adaisychaindream.com
Freq: Daily
Circ: 11565
Fashion

A Diary of Injustice in Scotland 986742
Email: scottishlawreporters@gmail.com
Web site: petercherbi.blogspot.co.uk
Freq: Daily
Circ: 10116
Consumer Interest, Corporate Law, Criminal Law, Employment, Family Law, Government, Human Rights, Intellectual Property, Law, Legal Affairs

A Fashion Fix 988636
Email: afashionfix@hotmail.com
Web site: www.afashionfix.co.uk
Freq: Daily
Circ: 60802
Profile: Blog covering fashion. A Fashion Fix blog discusses anything from style and outfits to fashion events and shopping. The blog has an archive dating back to August 2013.
Fashion

A FemAle View on Beer 988530
Editorial: 4 Batson Gardens, Paignton, Paignton TQ4 5LT Tel: 44 07946 112025
Email: sophieatherton@btinternet.com
Web site: afemaleview.net
Freq: Daily
Circ: 8232
Beer

A Forte For Fashion 985585
Email: laura@aforteforfashion.co.uk
Web site: www.aforteforfashion.co.uk
Freq: Daily

Circ: 7144
Beauty & Grooming, Cosmetics, Fashion, Hair, Regional General Interest, Women's Interests

A Geordie Lost in London 997136
Editorial: 118 Emma Road, London E13 0DR
Email: ageordielostinlondon@gmail.com
Web site: https://ageordielostinlondon.co.uk/
Freq: Daily
Circ: 10618
Beauty & Grooming, Cooking & Baking, Cosmetics, Crafts, Fashion, Hair, Movies & Video, Nature & Wildlife, Regional General Interest, Restaurant Reviews

A Girl & A Beauty Blog 987049
Web site: http://agirlandabeautyblog.com/
Freq: Daily
Circ: 11884
Profile: Blog covering beauty. A GIRL & A BEAUTY BLOG discusses anything from beauty to hair products. The blog has an archive dating back to November 2010 and shares an extensive blog roll.
News & Current Affairs

A Girl Has To Eat 986504
Web site: agirlhastoeat.com
Freq: Daily
Circ: 2871
Alcohol & Spirits, Bars, Clubs & Pubs, Beer, Beverages, Cooking & Baking, Food, Grocery Stores, Organic Food, Restaurant Reviews, Vegetarianism & Veganism

A Girl, A Style 987176
Editorial: 24 Gilbert House, 6 Mill Park, Cambridge CB1 2FJ
Email: agirlastyle@hotmail.com
Web site: agirlastyle.com
Freq: Daily
Circ: 23933
Editor: Briony Whitehouse
Profile: Blog covering fashion and lifestyle. A girl, a style blog discusses anything from personal style and beauty to lifestyle. The outlet offers RSS (Really Simple Syndication).
Fashion

A glimpse of London 1054170
Email: aglimpseoflondon@gmail.com
Web site: http://www.aglimpseoflondon.com/
Freq: Daily
Circ: 7058
Cooking & Baking, Regional General Interest, Restaurant Reviews, Women's Interests

A Glug of Oil 988535
Web site: www.aglugofoil.com
Freq: Daily
Circ: 14092
Cooking & Baking

A greener life, a greener world 996806
Email: agreenerlifeagreenerworld@gmail.com
Web site: www.agreenerlifeagreenerworld.net
Freq: Daily
Circ: 15776
Alternative/Renewable Energy, Business, Corporate Responsibility, Electricity, Energy & Environment, Ethical/Moral Issues, Mining & Quarrying, Nuclear Power, Oil, Politics

A Head Full of Wishes 1052679
Editorial: 85 Studley Grange Road, London W7 2LU
Web site: http://www.fullofwishes.co.uk/
Freq: Daily
Circ: 12782
Rock Music

A Healthier Moo 1053135
Email: ahealthiermoo@googlemail.com
Web site: http://www.ahealthiermoo.co.uk
Freq: Daily

Circ: 6636
Cooking & Baking, Fitness & Exercise, Weddings

A Lady in London 987574
Web site: aladyinlondon.com
Freq: Daily
Circ: 43122
Cooking & Baking, Food, Grocery Stores, Organic Food, Regional General Interest, Restaurant Reviews, Travel, Vegetarianism & Veganism

A Life in Writing 1053616
Email: zehracranmer@gmail.com
Web site: www.zehracranmer.co.uk
Freq: Daily
Circ: 10452
Literature, Women's Interests

A Life Inside & Outside of Politics - Mark Cole 999394
Tel: 44 07817 865712
Email: johnmarkcole@gmail.com
Web site: johnmarkcole.blogspot.com
Freq: Daily
Circ: 8036
Consumer Affairs, Crime & Violence, Defense & National Security, Energy & Environment, Ethical/Moral Issues, International News, Law, National News, News & Current Affairs, Northern Ireland

A Life of Geekery 987358
Web site: http://www.alifeofgeekery.co.uk/
Freq: Daily
Circ: 8126
Cooking & Baking

A Life With Ambitions 1054449
Web site: alifewithambitions.blogspot.co.uk
Freq: Daily
Circ: 10618
Health & Medicine, Women's Interests

A Life with Frills 988565
Editorial: 66 Clunie Place, Coatbridge, Renfrew G76 7QF
Email: laurapearsonsmith.email@gmail.com
Web site: www.alifewithfrills.co.uk
Freq: Daily
Circ: 13863
Beauty & Grooming, Cosmetics, Fashion, Hair, Women's Interests

A Life... Not As Advertised
1054243
Web site: http://www.notasadvertisedblog.com/
Freq: Daily
Circ: 10474
Family & Parenting, Health & Medicine, Women's Interests

A Little Luxury for Me 988686
Web site: alittleluxuryfor.me
Freq: Daily
Circ: 10553
Women's Interests

A Little Obsessed 986069
Web site: www.alittleobsessed.co.uk
Freq: Daily
Circ: 44175
Beauty & Grooming, Cosmetics, Hair

A Lovely Planet 1068722
Email: hayley@alovelyplanet.com
Web site: www.alovelyplanet.com
Freq: Daily
Circ: 27457
Airline Inflight, Railroad, Travel

A Luxury Travel Blog 986070
Editorial: The Dedicated Partnership Ltd, Maude Street, Kendal, Kendal LA9 4QD
Web site: www.aluxurytravelblog.com
Freq: Daily
Circ: 258835
Editor: Dr Paul Johnson
Luxury Goods, Travel

A Mexican Cook 1054199
Web site: http://amexicancook.ie/
Freq: Daily

Circ: 8589
Cooking & Baking

A Model Recommends 988071
Web site: www.amodelrecommends.com
Freq: Daily
Circ: 153031
Beauty & Grooming, Cosmetics, Hair, Women's Interests

A Modern Mother 985575
Email: amodernmother@gmail.com
Web site: www.amodernmother.com
Freq: Daily
Circ: 12951
Family & Parenting

A Mother's Ramblings 987975
Email: mummy@amothersramblings.com
Web site: http://www.amothersramblings.com/
Freq: Daily
Circ: 8073
Cooking & Baking, Family & Parenting, Women's Interests

A Mountain High 1054365
Web site: http://www.amountainhigh.blogspot.com
Freq: Daily
Circ: 1674
Outdoor Recreation

A Mummy Too 987893
Web site: http://www.amummytoo.co.uk/
Freq: Daily
Circ: 84260
Cooking & Baking, Family & Parenting

A New Addition Blog 987949
Web site: anewadditionblog.co.uk
Freq: Daily
Circ: 10244
Cooking & Baking, Crafts, Do-It-Yourself (DIY), Family & Parenting, Fashion, Food, Grocery Stores, Organic Food, Restaurant Reviews, Travel

A Pentland Garden Diary 1052861
Web site: http://apentlandgarden.com/
Freq: Daily
Circ: 9761
Profile: A Pentland Garden Diary covers gardening. The blog has an archive dating back to June 2014.
Gardening, Nature & Wildlife, Organic Food

A Qiuqiu 1060979
Web site: http://aqiuqiuvip.blog.sohu.com
Freq: Daily
Circ: 5
News & Current Affairs

A Quiet Style 1053775
Email: hello@aquietstyle.co.uk
Web site: aquietstyle.co.uk
Freq: Daily
Circ: 10190
Visual Arts, Women's Interests

A Quirky Lifestyle 988550
Email: quirkylifestyle@gmail.com
Web site: http://www.quirkylifestyle.com/
Freq: Daily
Circ: 3122
Cooking & Baking, Fashion, Travel

A Rare Perspective 997445
Email: hello@rare-thoughts.com
Web site: http://www.rare-thoughts.com
Freq: Daily
Circ: 611
Relationships

A rose like this 987674
Email: aroselikethis@hotmail.co.uk
Web site: aroselikethis.blogspot.co.uk
Freq: Daily
Circ: 2840
Beauty & Grooming, Cosmetics, Fashion, Hair

A Rosie Outlook 987381
Web site: http://www.arosieoutlook.com
Freq: Daily
Circ: 31868

Profile: Blog covering fashion and lifestyle. A Rosie Outlook blog discusses anything from personal style and beauty products to hair products and lifestyle posts. The blog has an archive dating back to August 2010. The outlet offers RSS (Really Simple Syndication).
Cooking & Baking, Fashion, Women's Interests

A Running Blog - Sorelimbs
995520
Web site: http://sorelimbs.co.uk/
Freq: Daily
Circ: 1819
Fitness & Exercise, Sports

A Rush of Love 1053100
Email: arushoflove@hotmail.co.uk
Web site: http://www.arushoflove.co.uk/
Freq: Daily
Circ: 7182
Cooking & Baking, Do-It-Yourself (DIY), Family & Parenting, Travel, Weddings

A Slice of Lemon's Cake 996845
Email: lemonscakeblog@gmail.com
Web site: www.lemonscake.co.uk
Freq: Daily
Circ: 6332
Cooking & Baking, Family & Parenting, Literature

A Slice of My Life Wales 987989
Editorial: 13 Picton Street, Griffithstown, Pontypool, Pontypool NP4 5HA
Web site: asliceofmylifewales.com
Freq: Daily
Circ: 13478
Cooking & Baking, Family & Parenting, Grocery Stores, Organic Food, Regional General Interest, Vegetarianism & Veganism

A Strong Coffee 988583
Email: astrongcoffee@hotmail.com
Web site: www.astrongcoffee.co.uk
Freq: Daily
Circ: 13904
Family & Parenting

A Style Diary 987515
Email: astylediary@live.co.uk
Web site: www.astylediary.com
Freq: Daily
Circ: 9717
Profile: A Style Diary covers fashion and personal style.
Beauty & Grooming, Cosmetics, Fashion, Hair, Shopping, Women's Interests

A Tangled Web 1053062
Web site: http://www.atangledweb.org/
Freq: Daily
Circ: 8046
Politics

A Thousand Huts 1053128
Web site: thousandhuts.org
Freq: Daily
Circ: 9184
Ethical/Moral Issues, Property Management & Maintenance

A Touch of Blusher 1052549
Email: atouchofblusher@gmail.com
Web site: atouchofblusher.com
Freq: Daily
Circ: 33172
Fashion

A Very Curious Wedding 1074319
Web site: http://www.curiouswedding.co.uk/
Freq: Daily
Circ: 2578
Editor: Michelle Lyndon-Dykes
Weddings

A Wee Bit of Cooking 986509
Web site: aweebitofcooking.co.uk
Freq: Daily
Circ: 2939
Alcohol & Spirits, Bars, Clubs & Pubs, Beer, Beverages, Cooking & Baking, Food, Grocery Stores, Organic Food,

UK Blogs

Restaurant Reviews, Vegetarianism & Veganism

A Year In Redwood 1053165
Email: margaret@oldfarm.ie
Web site: http://ayearinredwood.com
Freq: Daily
Circ: 8325
Cooking & Baking, Gardening, Regional General Interest

A Yellow Brick Blog 1052920
Email: ayellowbrickblog@hotmail.com
Web site: www.ayellowbrickblog.com
Freq: Daily
Circ: 2291
Beauty & Grooming, Cosmetics, Fashion, Hair, Women's Interests

A Yorkshire Home 1053881
Web site: ayorkshirehome.com
Freq: Daily
Circ: 521
Do-It-Yourself (DIY)

A&R Factory 1074795
Tel: 44 08448 848607
Email: info@anrfactory.com
Web site: http://www.anrfactory.com/
Freq: Daily
Circ: 9911
Editor: Stefan .
Classical/Choral/Band Music, Country, Folk, Bluegrass, Dance Music, Jazz & Blues, Music, Pop Music, R&B, Urban, World, Rap & Hip Hop, Rock Music

AA cars 1053979
Web site: http://www.vcars.co.uk/news
Freq: Daily
Circ: 287
Antique & Collectible Cars, Automotive, Driving, Off-road & 4-Wheel Drive Vehicles

AAJ Press 1053476
Web site: https://aajpress.wordpress.com/
Freq: Daily
Circ: 35
Editor: Jeremy Hunt
Architecture & Design, Art

Abe Books Blog 1052620
Email: media@abebooks.com
Web site: www.abebooks.com/blog/
Freq: Daily
Circ: 33076
Literature

Abigail Ahern Blog 988398
Editorial: 127 Upper Street, Islington, London N1 1QP Tel: 44 02073 548181
Email: press@abigailahern.com
Web site: blog.abigailahern.com
Freq: Daily
Circ: 72156
Do-It-Yourself (DIY)

Abigail and the future 1053318
Email: abigailandthefuture@gmail.com
Web site: http://www.abigailandthefuture.com/
Freq: Daily
Circ: 4032
Profile: Blog covering family life. The Abigail and the FUTURE blog discusses anything from parenting and walking to recipes and family days out. The blog has an archive dating back to July 2010.
Beauty & Grooming, Cosmetics, Family & Parenting, Fashion, Hair, Regional General Interest, Weddings, Women's Interests

Abigail Edwards Blog 1052594
Email: mall@abigailedwards.com
Web site: http://www.abigailedwards.com/news/
Freq: Daily
Circ: 136
Do-It-Yourself (DIY)

ABIMARVEL 987071
Web site: www.abimarvel.com
Freq: Daily
Circ: 7689
Fashion

Absolutely Lucy 988725
Web site: www.absolutelylucy.com
Freq: Daily
Circ: 9170
Profile: Blog covering mainly lifestyle and travel; including festival, gig and event guides and product reviews.
Airline Inflight, Railroad, Theater & Performing Arts, Travel, Women's Interests

The Abundance Blog 997022
Editorial: Abundance NRG Ltd, Threshold House, 65 - 69 Shepherd's Bush Green, London W12 8TX Tel: 44 02034 758666
Email: contactus@abundancegeneration.com
Web site: https://blog.abundanceinvestment.com/
Freq: Daily
Circ: 1491
Alternative/Renewable Energy, Business, Corporate Responsibility, Equities

Abuso Emocional 1061475
Web site: http://www.abusoemocional.com/
Freq: Daily
Circ: 1787
Neurology

Acceso Directo 1061349
Web site: http://acceso-directo.com
Freq: Daily
Circ: 33152
Auto Aftermarket, Computers, Data Management, Electronics, Government Technology, Industry, Internet, Mobile Communications, Security & Security Systems, Software

The Accidental Smallholder 1053039
Web site: http://www.accidentalsmallholder.net
Freq: Daily
Circ: 56298
Gardening

The Accidental Socialite 1100776
Email: theaccidentalsocialite@gmail.com
Web site: http://theaccidentalsocialite.com/
Freq: Daily
Circ: 1342
Beauty & Grooming, Comedy, Cooking & Baking, Cosmetics, Hair, Literature, Restaurant Reviews, Travel, Women's Interests

Acrobata del Camino 1061879
Web site: http://www.acrobatadelcamino.blogspot.com
Freq: Daily
Circ: 1578
Airline Inflight, Antiques/Collectibles, Armed Forces, Art, Arts, Astrology & Parapsychology, Astronomy, Aviation, Boating & Yachting, Camping and RV Travel

Across the Arts 1054557
Email: mail@acrossthearts.co.uk
Web site: www.acrossthearts.co.uk
Freq: Daily
Circ: 5369
Antiques/Collectibles, Art, Arts, Bars, Clubs & Pubs, Comedy, Entertainment, Literature, Local Entertainment Guides, Movies & Video, Photography

ActionAid Blogs 1098940
Editorial: ActionAid UK Head Office, 33-39 Bowling Green Lane, London EC1R 0BJ
Tel: 44 02031 220561
Email: mail@actionaid.org
Web site: actionaid.org.uk
Freq: Daily
Circ: 75590
Charitable Foundations, Politics, Social Issues

Actualidad Hispana 1060914
Web site: http://actualidadhispana.blogspot.com/
Freq: Daily
Circ: 698
Americas, National News

Actually Mummy 987655
Email: mummy@actuallymummy.co.uk
Web site: actuallymummy.co.uk
Freq: Daily
Circ: 14456
Family & Parenting

Adactio 1052693
Web site: https://adactio.com/journal
Freq: Daily
Circ: 20
Internet, Mobile Communications

Adam Smith Institute 986615
Editorial: Adam Smith Institute, 23 Great Smith Street, London SW1P 3BL
Web site: adamsmith.org/blog
Freq: Daily
Circ: 421
News & Current Affairs

adambowie.com 1052595
Web site: http://www.adambowie.com/blog
Freq: Daily
Circ: 11973
Branding, Broadcasting, Football (American), Marketing, Photography, Soccer

Adamok 1052740
Email: ahoklah@gmail.com
Web site: http://www.adamok.net/
Freq: Daily
Circ: 6255
Apple, Audio Video Trade, Cameras, Computer & Video Games, Computers, Consumer Electronics, Internet, Mobile Electronics, Movies & Video, Personal Computers

Addicted to Property 1055152
Tel: 44 08450 177525
Email: info@propertydivision.co.uk
Web site: http://addictedtoproperty.co.uk/
Freq: Daily
Circ: 13339
Profile: Addicted to Property covers the property industry. The blog has an archive dating back to January 2013 and shares a short blogroll.
Property Management & Maintenance

Addiction - Addiction Blog 1003601
Web site: http://addictionblog.org/
Freq: Daily
Circ: 141771
News & Current Affairs

adeevee 999456
Email: hello@adeevee.com
Web site: www.adeevee.com
Freq: Daily
Circ: 137575
Advertising Industry

Aditi's Pen 1074205
Web site: http://www.aditispen.com/
Freq: Daily
Circ: 32206
Editor: Aditi Kaushiva
Literature, Women's Interests

Ad-lib Traveller 1054620
Web site: adlibtraveller.com
Freq: Daily
Circ: 7083
Profile: Blog covering travel. Ad-lib Traveller blog discusses anything from travel and tourism to budget travel and hotels. The blog has an archive dating back to February 2014 and shares an extensive/short blog roll.
Travel

Adliterate 1053648
Web site: http://www.adliterate.com/
Freq: Daily
Circ: 15949
Advertising Industry, Branding, Marketing

The Adoption Social 996875
Email: theadoptionsocial@gmail.com
Web site: http://www.theadoptionsocial.com
Freq: Daily

Circ: 9957
Family & Parenting

Adora Mehitabel 987401
Email: contact@adoramehitabel.com
Web site: www.adoramehitabel.co.uk
Freq: Daily
Circ: 1854
Editor: Adora Mehitabel
Fashion

Adore, reflect, sustain 995504
Editorial: 7 Birchwood Court, 25 Cobbett Road, Southampton SO18 1HJ
Tel: 44 07846 963704
Email: emmawaight@hotmail.co.uk
Web site: www.emmawaight.co.uk
Freq: Daily
Circ: 9269
Energy & Environment, Ethical/Moral Issues, Fashion, Women's Interests

Adoreabbubles 1054216
Email: adoreabbubles@hotmail.com
Web site: adoreabbubles.blogspot.ie
Freq: Daily
Circ: 1625
Beauty & Grooming, Cosmetics, Hair

Adorngirl 985591
Editorial: 46 Co-Operative House, 249 Rye Lane, London SE15 4UP
Email: adorngirl@hotmail.co.uk
Web site: https://adorngirl.com/
Freq: Daily
Circ: 14573
Profile: Blog covering fashion, beauty and lifestyle. Posts include book reviews, exhibitions, food & drink, catwalk photography and beauty review editorials.
Beauty & Grooming, Cosmetics, Fashion, Hair, Women's Interests

Adrian Swinscoe Blog 1070236
Web site: http://www.adrianswinscoe.com/
Freq: Daily
Circ: 42000
Business, Corporate Responsibility, Education, Small and Medium Business

Adventure Mummy 1052712
Email: info@adventuremummy.com
Web site: adventuremummy.com
Freq: Daily
Circ: 7929
Family & Parenting, Outdoor Recreation, Travel

Adventures Aboard AreandAre 1052570
Tel: 44 07456 001553
Email: barryandsandra@nbareandare.com
Web site: http://nbareandare.com/
Freq: Daily
Circ: 9205
Alcohol & Spirits, Beer, Marine & Boat Trade

Adventures and Play 998149
Email: adventuresofadam@hotmail.co.uk
Web site: http://adventuresandplay.com/
Freq: Daily
Circ: 6810
Family & Parenting

Adventures of a London Kiwi 1052534
Email: adventuresofalondonkiwi@gmail.com
Web site: www.adventuresofalondonkiwi.com
Freq: Daily
Circ: 13636
Profile: Blog covering travel. The Adventures of a London Kiwi blog discusses anything from travel and lifestyle to recipes and London life. The blog has an archive dating back to February 2014 and shares an extensive blog roll.
Regional General Interest, Travel, Women's Interests

Adventures of a Yorkshire Mum 1063455
Email: yorkshire_mummy@hotmail.com
Web site: http://www.adventuresofayorkshiremum.co.uk/
Freq: Daily

Circ: 9933
Profile: Blog covering motherhood. The Adventures of a Yorkshire Mum discusses anything from family fun and family recipes to parenting and product reviews. The blog has an archive dating back to April 2012.
Cooking & Baking, Family & Parenting, Travel, Women's Interests

Adventures of an Anglophile
988387
Web site: www.adventuresofananglophile. com
Freq: Daily
Circ: 6283
Profile: Blog covering fashion. The blog has an archive dating back to November 2012 and shares an short blog roll.
Fashion

Adventures with Dan
1053716
Freq: Daily
News & Current Affairs

Adventures With Words
987974
Editorial: 1 Heverfield Court, Crusoe Road, Mitcham CR4 3LG
Email: contact@adventureswithwords.com
Web site: http://www.adventureswithwords. com/
Freq: Daily
Circ: 8931
Literature

AdventurousKate.com
988344
Email: kate@adventurouskate.com
Web site: http://www.adventurouskate.com/
Freq: Daily
Circ: 612992
Travel

Adzuna Blog
1053428
Web site: https://www.adzuna.co.uk/blog/
Freq: Daily
Circ: 115284
Recruiting

Aerolineas en Argentina
1060805
Web site: http://aerar.blogspot.com/
Freq: Daily
Circ: 1327
Aviation

AFROBLUSH
987063
Web site: afroblush.com
Freq. Daily
Circ: 11058
Profile: Blog covering Pan-African culture and lifestyle including arts, fashion, food and drink.
Africa, Beauty & Grooming, Cosmetics, Fashion, Hair, Women's Interests

The Afrofilmviewer
1052652
Email: movies@geekplanetonline.com
Web site: http://afrofilmviewer.blogspot.co. uk/
Freq: Daily
Circ: 474
Entertainment, Movies & Video

The Afternoon Tea Club
997814
Email: theafternoonteaclub@hotmail.co.uk
Web site: www.theafternoonteaclub.com
Freq: Daily
Circ: 9256
Bars, Clubs & Pubs, Restaurant Reviews

The Age of Stupidity
1052690
Web site: http://theageofstupidity.blogspot. co.uk/
Freq: Daily
Circ: 521
Politics

Age UK Blog
986746
Editorial: Tavis House, 1-6 Tavistock Square, London WC1H 9NA
Web site: ageukblog.org.uk
Freq: Daily
Circ: 17037
Charitable Foundations, Geriatrics, Retirement Savings, Social Issues

Agitacion Cultural desde la Periferia
1060964
Web site: http://agitaciondesdelaperiferia. blogspot.com/
Freq: Daily
Circ: 1230
Lifestyle, Men's Interests, Regional General Interest, Women's Interests

Agnes Daisy - CEASED
988523
Web site: www.agnesdaisy.com
Freq: Daily
Circ: 916
Profile: Blog covering beauty and cosmetics. The blog has an archive dating back to January 2013 and shares an extensive blog roll.
Beauty & Grooming, Cosmetics, Fashion, Hair, Women's Interests

Agricultura Blogger
1060527
Web site: http://agriculturablogger.blogspot. com
Freq: Daily
Circ: 830
Animal Farming

Aimee Horton
1053943
Email: mrs@aimee-horton.co.uk
Web site: passthegin.co.uk
Freq: Daily
Circ: 7929
Family & Parenting

Aina's Foto
1060620
Email: aina.jerstad@hotmail.com
Web site: http://ainashobby.blogspot.com/
Freq: Daily
Circ: 1142
Photography

Ainosofia "Touch of French"
1061564
Email: ainosofia1@gmail.com
Web site: http://ainosofialla.blogspot.com/
Freq: Daily
Circ: 1875
Architecture & Design, Do-It-Yourself (DIY), Gardening, Home, Interior Design, Property Management & Maintenance, Real Estate

Air Miles Expert
1103761
Web site: http://www.airmilesexpert.com
Freq: 3 Times/Week
Circ: 10709
Airlines, Business Travel, Hotels/Motels, Luxury Travel

Akhil from Hounslow
1052759
Email: info@akhilvyas.com
Web site: http://www.akhilvyas.com/
Freq: Daily
Circ: 993
Soccer

Aksjebloggen
1061041
Tel: 44 47416 67646
Web site: http://aksjebloggen.com/
Freq: Daily
Circ: 7633
Banking, Financial Markets

Al Booth's blog
997811
Email: al@albooth.co.uk
Web site: http://www.albooth.co.uk/
Freq: Daily
Circ: 10709
Men's Interests

Al Fin y al Cabo...El Sur
1061413
Web site: http://blogs.lanacion.com.ar/el-sur/
Freq: Daily
Circ: 475
Lifestyle, Men's Interests, National News, Regional General Interest, Women's Interests

Alan in Belfast
1053412
Email: alaninbelfast@gmail.com
Web site: http://alaninbelfast.blogspot.co. uk/
Freq: Daily

Circ: 11075
Art, Literature, Northern Ireland, Politics, Regional, Religion, Theater & Performing Arts, Visual Arts

Alan's Energy Blog
997759
Editorial: 20 - 22 Southampton Street, Southampton SO15 2ED
Tel: 44 02380 231942
Email: alan@alan-whitehead.org.uk
Web site: https://alansenergyblog. wordpress.com/
Freq: Daily
Circ: 61
Alternative/Renewable Energy, Carbon Emissions & Trading, Electricity, Energy, Environment, Nuclear Power, Oil, Water & Sanitation

Alaskan in Yucatan
1061518
Web site: http://marcoyucatan.blogspot. com
Freq: Daily
Circ: 687
Airline Inflight, Railroad, Travel

Alastair Campbell Blog
1052587
Email: speaker@alastaircampbell.org
Web site: http://www.alastaircampbell.org/ blog/
Freq: Daily
Circ: 172
Branding, Charitable Foundations, Government, Marketing

Alchemy in the Kitchen
1054046
Web site: http://www.alchemyinthekitchen. ie/
Freq: Daily
Circ: 6294
Cooking & Baking, Organic Food

Alejandro Chaile
1060970
Web site: http://alejandrochaile.blogspot. com/
Freq: Daily
Circ: 521
Interior Design

Alex Donald's Multiverse
1054637
Web site: https://alexdonald.wordpress. com/
Freq: Daily
Circ: 230
Beauty & Grooming, Broadcasting, Cosmetics, Fashion, Hair, Literature, Movies & Video

Alex Dukal
1061664
Web site: http://www.alexdukal.blogspot. com
Freq: Daily
Circ: 2326
Art, Graphic Design

Alex Singleton Blog
987863
Web site: www.alexsingleton.com
Freq: Daily
Circ: 2049
News & Current Affairs

Alexa Dagmar
1061486
Email: alexadagmar@gmail.com
Web site: http://alexadagmar.com
Freq: Daily
Circ: 30102
Fashion

Alexandra Roumbas Goldtstein Blog
1054590
Email: alex@alexandragoldstein.co.uk
Web site: http://mokuska.com/
Freq: Daily
Circ: 11061
Cooking & Baking, Family & Parenting, Food, Grocery Stores, Organic Food, Pop Music, Restaurant Reviews, Theater & Performing Arts, Vegetarianism & Veganism, Visual Arts

Alexa's Attic
987889
Web site: http://www.alexasattic.com/
Freq: Daily
Circ: 10709

Profile: Blog covering beauty, cosmetics and fashion. The blog has an archive dating back to May 2013.
Beauty & Grooming, Cosmetics, Fashion, Hair

Alexfox
1054391
Web site: http://alexf0x.livejournal.com/
Freq: Daily
Circ: 116
Computer & Video Games

Alexis Marrero
1060952
Web site: http://www.alexismarrero.com/
Freq: Daily
Circ: 773
Politics

Alfombra Rosa
1061045
Web site: http://www.alfombrarosa.com
Freq: Daily
Circ: 908
Bars, Clubs & Pubs, Celebrities, Comedy, Entertainment, Local Entertainment Guides, Movies & Video

Algo sobre lo municipal
1061792
Web site: http://algomunicipal.blogspot. com/
Freq: Daily
Circ: 611
Government

Ali Gordon
1100036
Email: info@aligordon.net
Web site: http://aligordon.net/
Freq: Daily
Circ: 11343
Fashion, Fitness & Exercise, Men's Interests

Alice & Amelia - New Young Mum
1072210
Web site: http://newyoungmum.com/
Freq: Daily
Circ: 9749
Family & Parenting, Women's Interests

Alice in Weddingland Blog
999406
Email: submissions@aliceinweddingland.co. uk
Web site: www.aliceinweddingland.co.uk
Freq: Daily
Circ: 8970
Weddings

Alien on Toast
1052952
Email: sal.on.toast@gmail.com
Web site: www.alienontoast.co.uk
Freq: Daily
Circ: 8368
Cooking & Baking, Vegetarianism & Veganism

Alison Kerr's Jazz Blog
1075964
Web site: https://jazzmatters.wordpress. com/
Freq: Daily
Circ: 17
Jazz & Blues

Alison Thursby
1053166
Email: alison@alisonthursby.co.uk
Web site: http://www.alisonthursby.co.uk/
Freq: Daily
Circ: 9931
Beauty & Grooming, Cosmetics, Fashion, Hair, Women's Interests

All Aboard with Eve
1053292
Tel: 44 08004 086080
Email: evec@cruise.co.uk
Web site: http://www.cruise.co.uk/cruise-blogs/allaboardwitheve/
Freq: Daily
Circ: 128
Marine & Boat Trade, Travel

All About Hair
1053198
Web site: http://allabouthairuk.blogspot.co. uk/
Freq: Daily
Circ: 10204
Luxury Goods, Travel, Women's Interests

UK Blogs

All About The Games 985557
Editorial: The Willows, Thwaites Brow Road, Keighley BD21 4SW
Email: richard@allaboutthegames.co.uk
Web site: www.allaboutthegames.co.uk
Freq: Daily
Circ: 7244
Computer & Video Games

All Baby Advice 985806
Editorial: 1 Morgan Close, Northwood HA6 3NE
Email: allbabyadvice@yahoo.co.uk
Web site: http://www.allbabyadvice-blog.com
Freq: Daily
Circ: 15040
Family & Parenting

All Sweetness and Life. 987429
Email: allsweetnessandlife@gmail.com
Web site: all-sweetness-and-life.blogspot.com
Freq: Daily
Circ: 1257
Relationships

All That I'm Eating 988439
Email: allthatimeating@gmail.com
Web site: http://allthatimeating.co.uk
Freq: Daily
Circ: 7245
Profile: Blog covering food. ALL THAT I'M EATING blog discusses anything from food and recipes to restaurant reviews, travel and drink. The blog has an archive dating back to March 2010 and shares an short blog roll. The outlet offers RSS (Really Simple Syndication).
Cooking & Baking, Restaurant Reviews

All That Is Solid 1054149
Web site: http://averypublicsociologist.blogspot.co.uk/
Freq: Daily
Circ: 15788
Literature, Politics, Social Issues

All The Best Blog 1053453
Email: inquires@rondacarman.com
Web site: http://rondacarman.com/blog/all-the-best-blog
Freq: Daily
Luxury Goods, Women's Interests

All The Fs - SUSPENDED 2017
1053623
Web site: allthefs.com
Freq: Daily
Circ: 611
Fashion

All Things Beautiful 988945
Web site: http://allthingsbeautiful-x.blogspot.co.uk/
Freq: Daily
Circ: 7821
Profile: Blog covering beauty, cosmetics, fashion and lifestyle. The blog has an archive dating back to March 2013.
Beauty & Grooming, Cosmetics, Fashion, Hair

All Things Considered 1052623
Web site: http://allthingsconsidered.co.uk/
Freq: Daily
Circ: 10306
News & Current Affairs

All Things Nice... 1053501
Email: allthingsnice4life@gmail.com
Web site: http://www.allthingsnice4life.blogspot.co.uk/
Freq: Daily
Circ: 521
Do-It-Yourself (DIY)

AllClear Travel blog 997750
Editorial: AllClear House, 1 Redwig Court, Ashton Road, Romford RM3 8QQ
Web site: https://www.allcleartravel.co.uk/blog/
Freq: Daily
News & Current Affairs

Allergy Insight 1054389
Web site: http://foodallergyandintolerance.blogspot.co.uk/
Freq: Daily
Circ: 1700
Allergies

The Allrounder 1053640
Editorial: 119 Gideon Road, London SW11 5UU Tel: 44 07736 930229
Email: tom@theallrounder.co.uk
Web site: www.theallrounder.co.uk
Freq: Daily
Circ: 9679
Cooking & Baking, Fitness & Exercise, Nutrition, Regional General Interest, Restaurant Reviews

Allsorts & Anecdotes 1053417
Email: allsortsandanecdotes@gmail.com
Web site: allsortsandanecdotes.blogspot.co.uk
Freq: Daily
Circ: 1215
Profile: Blog covering beauty and lifestyle. Allsorts & anecdotes blog discusses anything from beauty and fashion to books and films. The blog has an archive dating back to November 2010 and shares a short blog roll.
Cosmetics, Women's Interests

allthingsIC 988100
Web site: http://www.allthingsic.com/blog/
Freq: Daily
Circ: 12384
Advertising Industry, Branding, Broadcasting, Graphic Design, Marketing, Media & Communications, Photography, Publishing

Almost Always Thinking 1053507
Web site: almostalwaysthinking.com
Freq: Daily
Circ: 1750
News & Current Affairs

Almost Zara 1053036
Web site: http://www.almostzara.com/
Freq: Daily
Circ: 6157
Audio Video Trade, Beauty & Grooming, Cameras, Consumer Electronics, Cosmetics, Fashion, Hair, Mobile Electronics, Movies & Video, Regional General Interest

Along Came Cherry 987448
Email: alongcamecherry@live.com
Web site: http://alongcamecherry.co.uk
Freq: Daily
Circ: 7937
Art, Crafts, Family & Parenting, Fashion, Travel, Women's Interests

Along Dusty Roads 1072212
Email: alongdustyroads@gmail.com
Web site: www.alongdustyroads.com
Freq: Daily
Circ: 124795
Travel

Alpine Guides Blog 1052999
Tel: 44 01138 151904
Email: info@alpine-guides.com
Web site: http://alpine-guides-blog.com/
Freq: Daily
Circ: 473
Travel, Winter Sports

Alrich Blog 1053496
Web site: https://alrich.wordpress.com/
Freq: Daily
Circ: 93
Profile: Blog covering government and politics. The Alrich Blog discusses anything from legal matters and financial affairs to politics and economics. The outlet offers RSS (Really Simple Syndication).
Law, Personal Finance, Politics

Alt1040 1061266
Web site: http://www.alt1040.com
Freq: Daily
Circ: 2347
Auto Aftermarket, Computers, Data Management, Electronics, Government

Technology, Industry, Internet, Mobile Communications, Security & Security Systems, Software

Alta Fidelidad 1061092
Web site: http://www.faustoponce.com
Freq: Daily
Circ: 6867
Bars, Clubs & Pubs, Classical/Choral/Band Music, Comedy, Country, Folk, Bluegrass, Dance Music, Entertainment, Jazz & Blues, Local Entertainment Guides, Movies & Video, Music

Alternative Eden 1053723
Email: info@alternativeeden.co.uk
Web site: www.alternativeeden.com/
Freq: Daily
Circ: 4106
Gardening

Alt-Tab 1061171
Web site: http://alt-tab.com.ar/
Freq: Daily
Circ: 6113
Auto Aftermarket, Computers, Data Management, Electronics, Government Technology, Industry, Internet, Mobile Communications, Security & Security Systems, Software

Amargado 1061856
Web site: http://elamargado.wordpress.com/
Freq: Daily
Circ: 7
Lifestyle, Men's Interests, Regional General Interest, Women's Interests

Amateur Jockeys Association of Great Britain News 1055936
Web site: http://www.amateurjockeys.org.uk/
Freq: Daily
Circ: 6483
Horse Racing

Amazing PR Blog 1053559
Editorial: Worlds End Studios, 134 Lots Road, Chelsea, London SW10 0RJ
Tel: 44 02073 520110
Email: info@amazingpr.co.uk
Web site: www.amazingpr.co.uk/blog
Freq: Daily
Circ: 277
Beauty & Grooming, Branding, Business, Cooking & Baking, Cosmetics, Fashion, Food, Grocery Stores, Hair, Marketing

Amber Rose Photography
1100165
Web site: http://amber-rosephotography.blogspot.co.uk/
Freq: Daily
Circ: 7706
Fashion, Photography

AMCR 1053231
Editorial: AMRC, Charles Darwin House 2, 107 Gray's Inn Road, London London WC1X 8TZ
Web site: amrc.org.uk/blog
Freq: Daily
Circ: 2
Charitable Foundations

Amelia Liana 987045
Email: amelia@amelialiana.com
Web site: http://liana-beauty.com
Freq: Daily
Circ: 3423
Beauty & Grooming, Cosmetics, Fashion, Hair

Amelia Liana Vlog 1095952
Email: amelia@amelialiana.com
Web site: https://www.youtube.com/user/amelialiana
Freq: Daily
Circ: 11
Beauty & Grooming, Cosmetics, Fashion, Hair, Women's Interests

The American Resident 996516
Email: theamericanresident@yahoo.co.uk
Web site: theamericanresident.com
Freq: Daily

Circ: 9757
Americas, Cooking & Baking, Do-It-Yourself (DIY), Food, Gardening, Grocery Stores, Organic Food, Restaurant Reviews, Vegetarianism & Veganism

Amigas Manualidades 1061821
Web site: http://amigasmanualidades.blogspot.com/
Freq: Daily
Circ: 1339
Crafts, Hobbies, & Collecting

Amphibia 1061494
Web site: http://www.amphibia.com.ar/
Freq: Daily
Circ: 3910
Advertising Industry, Audio Video Trade, Auto Aftermarket, Branding, Broadcasting, Cameras, Computers, Consumer Electronics, Data Management, Electronics

Amuse Your Bouche 988538
Web site: http://www.amuse-your-bouche.com/
Freq: Daily
Circ: 145104
Profile: Blog covering vegetarian food. The Amuse Your Bouche blog discusses anything from vegetarian food and recipes to cooking and baking. The outlet offers RSS (Really Simple Syndication).
Vegetarianism & Veganism

Amy Elizabeth 1053504
Email: hello@amyliz.co.uk
Web site: www.amyliz.co.uk/
Freq: Daily
Circ: 8472
Profile: Blog covering lifestyle and food. The AMY ELIZABETH blog discusses anything from recipes and fashion to book clubs and restaurants. The blog has an archive dating back to February 2012.
Cooking & Baking, Regional General Interest, Restaurant Reviews, Travel, Women's Interests

Amy Elizabeth Fashion 988367
Web site: www.amyelizabethfashion.com
Freq: Daily
Circ: 8913
Beauty & Grooming, Cosmetics, Fashion, Hair, Women's Interests

amyransom.com 996420
Web site: amyransom.com
Freq: Daily
Circ: 8024
Family & Parenting

Amzy in Wonderland 987780
Web site: http://www.amyjaynesthoughts.co.uk/
Freq: Daily
Circ: 2927
Profile: Blog covering all areas of beauty, nail care, cosmetics and beauty products.
Beauty & Grooming, Cooking & Baking, Cosmetics, Do-It-Yourself (DIY), Fashion, Hair

An [insert here] for... 1075511
Web site: https://aseasonalmovieforchristmas.wordpress.com/about/
Freq: Daily
Movies & Video

An American Girl in Chelsea
986786
Editorial: 20 Billing Road, London SW10 9UL
Email: christy@americangirlinchelsea.com
Web site: www.americangirlinchelsea.com
Freq: Daily
Circ: 10839
Americas, Beauty & Grooming, Cooking & Baking, Cosmetics, Family & Parenting, Fashion, Food, Grocery Stores, Hair, Organic Food

An Appetite For Make-up
1054559
Email: nicolacrossmanxox@gmail.com
Web site: anappetiteformakeup.blogspot.co.uk

Freq: Daily
Circ: 10439
Cosmetics

An Author's Notebook by Emma Clark Lam 996881
Web site: http://AnAuthorsNotebook.com
Freq: Daily
Circ: 10618
Family & Parenting, Literature, Regional General Interest, Women's Interests

An Essex Wife 1054351
Email: alice@anessexwife.com
Web site: http://www.projectwanderlust.co.uk/
Freq: Daily
Circ: 8769
Profile: Blog covering family life. AN ESSEX WIFE blog discusses anything from recipes and kids days out to food and travel. The blog has an archive dating back to March 2014 and shares a short blog roll.
Family & Parenting, Fashion, Restaurant Reviews, Travel, Women's Interests

An Unfamiliar Sky 987822
Web site: anunfamiliarsky.com/
Freq: Daily
Circ: 1889
Profile: Blog covering travel. AN UNFAMILIAR SKY blog discusses anything from travel and hotels to food and travel advice. The blog has an archive dating back to January 2014 and shares a short blog roll.
Travel

The Ana Mum Diary 988309
Email: amanda@theanamumdiary.co.uk
Web site: theanamumdiary.co.uk
Freq: Daily
Circ: 50239
Family & Parenting

AnaMe 1061047
Web site: http://aslaugok.com/
Freq: Daily
Circ: 10115
Classical/Choral/Band Music, Country, Folk, Bluegrass, Dance Music, Jazz & Blues, Music, Pop Music, R&B, Urban, World, Rap & Hip Hop, Rock Music

Anami Blog 1054329
Email: anamiblog@ymail.com
Web site: anamiblog.com
Freq: Daily
Circ: 8188
Do-It-Yourself (DIY), Fashion, Women's Interests

Ananyah 987814
Web site: ananyah.com
Freq: Daily
Circ: 8181
Profile: Blog covering Scottish lifestyle, restaurant reviews, recipes, entertainment and product reviews. The blog has an archive dating back to March 2006 and shares an extensive blogroll.
Cooking & Baking, Restaurant Reviews, Women's Interests

And 1 More Means Five - CEASED MAY 2017 1054482
Web site: http://and1moremeansfour.blogspot.co.uk/
Freq: Daily
Circ: 1208
Charitable Foundations, Disability, Family & Parenting

and all that Chas... 1052982
Web site: allthatchas.blogspot.co.uk
Freq: Daily
Circ: 10329
Relationships, Women's Interests

And Ruby Makes Four 998446
Email: hello@andrubymakesfour.com
Web site: http://andrubymakesfour.com/
Freq: Daily
Circ: 10182
Cooking & Baking, Do-It-Yourself (DIY), Fashion, Fitness & Exercise, Food, Grocery Stores, Nature & Wildlife, Organic

Food, Restaurant Reviews, Vegetarianism & Veganism

Andalucia Explorer 1054221
Tel: 44 34095 3564211
Email: rachel.martos@gmail.com
Web site: http://www.andaluciaexplorer.blogspot.co.uk/
Freq: Daily
Circ: 1471
Travel

ANDERZ 1095186
Web site: https://www.youtube.com/user/helenmelonworld
Freq: Daily
Circ: 3
News & Current Affairs

ANDESTOTHEAMAZON 1060982
Web site: http://www.guardian.co.uk/environment/andes-to-the-amazon
Freq: Daily
Circ: 10884
Environment, International News

Andra Loves Fashion 1052998
Email: andralovesfashion@gmail.com
Web site: http://andralovesfashion.blogspot.co.uk/
Freq: Daily
Circ: 10244
Profile: Blog covering fashion. Andra Loves Fashion blog discusses anything from outfit posts and personal style to the latest fashion trends and accessories. The blog has an archive dating back to March 2010.
Beauty & Grooming, Cosmetics, Fashion, Hair

Andrea Hegard 1053853
Web site: www.andreahegard.com
Freq: Daily
Circ: 1251
Fashion, Pop Music

Andrea's Passions 997349
Editorial: Flat 409, Colefax Building, 23 Plumbers Row, London E1 1EQ
Tel: 44 07905 811122
Web site: http://andreaspassions.com/
Freq: Daily
Circ: 8022
Airline Inflight, Cooking & Baking, Fitness & Exercise, Food, Grocery Stores, Health & Medicine, Nutrition, Organic Food, Railroad, Restaurant Reviews

Andrew Burns' blog 998089
Email: andrew.burns@edinburgh.gov.uk
Web site: http://andrewburns.blogspot.co.uk/
Freq: Daily
Circ: 10015
Politics

Andrew Isidoro - Digital Marketing Blog 1053116
Web site: andrewisidoro.co.uk/blog/
Freq: Daily
Circ: 170
Profile: Blog covering digital marketing.
Marketing

Android Phones Blog 1054486
Web site: http://www.androidphonesblog.net/
Freq: Daily
Circ: 1093
Mobile Electronics

Andy Worthington Blog 1053851
Email: andy@andyworthington.co.uk
Web site: http://www.andyworthington.co.uk/
Freq: Daily
Circ: 17961
Defense & National Security, International News, Law, Politics

Anestesia Segura Peru 1062148
Web site: http://anestesiaseguraperu.blogspot.com/
Freq: Daily
Circ: 521
Anesthesiology

Anfield HQ 997867
Email: anfieldhq96@gmail.com
Web site: http://www.anfieldhq.com/
Freq: Daily
Circ: 36272
Soccer

Anfield Online 999287
Email: response@anfield-online.co.uk
Web site: http://www.anfield-online.co.uk
Freq: Daily
Circ: 12135
Editor: John Davies
Soccer

Anfield Road 1053749
Email: web-contact@anfieldroad.com
Web site: http://www.anfieldroad.com/
Freq: Daily
Circ: 15900
Soccer

The Anfield Wrap 1053987
Editorial: Office 6:3, 1 - 27 Bridport Street, Liverpool L3 5QF
Email: theanfieldwrap@gmail.com
Web site: http://www.theanfieldwrap.com/
Freq: Daily
Circ: 149646
Soccer

angelinascasa 987704
Tel: 44 07974 243455
Web site: https://angelinascasa.com/
Freq: Daily
Circ: 11562
Profile: Blog covering beauty and travel. ANGELINASCASA blog discusses anything from vintage style and beauty to travel destinations and interior design. The outlet offers RSS (Really Simple Syndication).
Beauty & Grooming, Cosmetics, Crafts, Do-It-Yourself (DIY), Fashion, Hair, Travel, Women's Interests

Angloyankophile 996807
Email: angloyankophile@gmail.com
Web site: http://www.angloyankophile.com/
Freq: Daily
Circ: 12484
Regional General Interest, Travel

Anita Brown 3D Visualisation 1052694
Email: design_studio@hotmail.co.uk
Web site: https://anitabrown3d.com/
Freq: Daily
Circ: 8949
Do-It-Yourself (DIY), Visual Arts

Anita Davies Blog 1054939
Email: nitsa2000@hotmail.com
Web site: http://artbyanita.blogspot.co.uk/
Freq: Daily
Circ: 521
Art, Travel

The Anna Edit 986832
Web site: http://www.theannaedit.com/
Freq: Daily
Circ: 13685
Beauty & Grooming, Cosmetics, Hair, Women's Interests

Anna y su Mesa 1061490
Web site: http://annaysumesa.blogspot.com/
Freq: Daily
Circ: 1306
Cooking & Baking, Food

Annabel Karmel's Blog 986073
Editorial: 18A Pindock Mews, London W9 2PY **Tel:** 44 02072 893808
Email: enquiries@annabelkarmel.com
Web site: http://www.annabelkarmel.com/blog
Freq: Daily
Circ: 7646
Alcohol & Spirits, Bars, Clubs & Pubs, Beer, Beverages, Cooking & Baking, Family & Parenting, Food, Grocery Stores, Organic Food, Restaurant Reviews

Annabookbel 988196
Web site: http://annabookbel.net/
Freq: Daily
Circ: 15029

Profile: Annabel's House of Books covers literature, book reviews and fiction. The blog has an archive dating back to September 2008 and shares a short blogroll.
Literature

Anne's Kitchen 986978
Editorial: Anne's Kitchen, Flat 2, House 11, Block 9, St Peter's Hospital, Guildford Road, London KT16 0RL
Email: anneskitchen1@yahoo.co.uk
Web site: http://anneskitchen1.blogspot.co.uk/
Freq: Daily
Circ: 4922
Profile: Blog covering food. The ANNE'S KITCHEN blog discusses anything from cooking and recipes to cookbooks.
Cooking & Baking

Annie's Noms 997968
Web site: www.anniesnoms.com
Freq: Daily
Circ: 28918
Cooking & Baking

Anny's Adventures Blog 1104813
Web site: https://annysadventures.com/
Freq: Daily
Circ: 11335
Travel

Anorak 986074
Editorial: 330 Kingsland Road, London E8 4DA **Tel:** 44 07980 578831
Email: editor@anorak.co.uk
Web site: www.anorak.co.uk
Circ: 179434
Editor: Paul Sorene
Profile: Children's magazine covering all aspects of a child's world from fashion to stories, culture to science and sport to food. Aimed at boys and girls aged 5 to 10 years old.
Ad Rate: Full Page Mono 1000.00
Ad Rate: Full Page Colour 1000.00
Bars, Clubs & Pubs, Basketball, Bicycles, Billiards, Boating & Yachting, Bodybuilding, Bowling, Boxing, Comedy, Cricket

Another Beauty Babble 1054237
Web site: http://anotherbeautybabble.blogspot.co.uk/
Freq: Daily
Circ: 752
Beauty & Grooming, Cosmetics, Fashion, Hair, Women's Interests

Another Green World 986584
Web site: http://another-green-world.blogspot.com
Freq: Daily
Circ: 2768
Energy & Environment, Environment, Politics

Anoushka Loves 988368
Email: anoushkaloves@gmail.com
Web site: http://www.anoushkaloves.com
Freq: Daily
Circ: 33226
Profile: Blog covering beauty. ANOUSHKA LOVES discusses anything from beauty products and hair to make up, nails and diets. The blog has an archive dating back to June 2013.
Beauty & Grooming, Cosmetics, Fashion, Hair, Women's Interests

Anthony Vickers' Untypical Boro 1054392
Email: anthony.vickers@gazettemedia.co.uk
Web site: https://untypicalboro.wordpress.com/
Freq: Daily
Circ: 17
Soccer

Anthony's blog 1052730
Web site: http://antonysimpson.com
Freq: Daily
Circ: 9307
Literature, Men's Interests, Movies & Video

UK Blogs

Antiguo 1061584
Web site: http://blogs.eluniversal.com.mx/antiguo
Freq: Daily
Circ: 233
Antique & Collectible Cars

Antique Wine Company Blog
1053948
Email: info@awcfinewine.com
Web site: https://awcfinewine.com/blog/
Freq: Daily
Circ: 35
Wine/Winemaking

Antti Alanen: Film Diary 1061500
Email: antti.alanen@gmail.com
Web site: http://anttialanenfilmdiary.blogspot.co.uk/
Freq: Daily
Circ: 521
Antiques/Collectibles, Art, Arts, Internet, Literature, Movies & Video, Photography, Theater & Performing Arts, Visual Arts

Anula's Kitchen 1053699
Web site: www.anulaskitchen.com
Freq: Daily
Circ: 2518
Cooking & Baking

Anxiety United 998036
Editorial: Manor Close, Atherstone CV9 2BH
Tel: 44 07534 604121
Email: hello@anxietyunited.co.uk
Web site: http://www.anxietyunited.com/mental-health-blogs
Freq: Daily
Circ: 480
Neurology

Anyonita Nibbles Blog 988537
Email: munchies@anyonita-nibbles.com
Web site: http://www.anyonita-nibbles.co.uk
Freq: Daily
Circ: 8312
Cooking & Baking

AO Life 1052733
Email: aolife@ao.com
Web site: ao.com/life
Freq: Daily
Circ: 15061
News & Current Affairs

AOLIFE 987844
Editorial: AO Park, 5A The Parklands, Lostock, Bolton BL6 4SD
Web site: http://ao.com/life/
Freq: Daily
Circ: 15061
Cooking & Baking, Crafts, Do-It-Yourself (DIY)

Apartment Number 4 988427
Email: contact@apartmentnumber4.com
Web site: www.apartmentnumber4.com
Freq: Daily
Circ: 14020
Editor: Victoria Jackson
Fashion

Apasionados Por Los Libros
1061633
Web site: http://www.apasionados89.blogspot.com
Freq: Daily
Circ: 7873
Literature, Movies & Video

Ape to Gentleman 986423
Editorial: Scholes Mill, Old Coach Road, Tansley, Matlock, Matlock DE4 5FY
Email: contact@apetogentleman.com
Web site: www.apetogentleman.com
Freq: Daily
Circ: 56313
Beauty & Grooming, Cosmetics, Fashion, Hair, Men's Interests

Apertura Venezuela 1061994
Web site: http://www.aperturaven.blogspot.com/
Freq: Daily
Circ: 13200
Politics

Aperture Woolwich Photographic Society Blog 1056326
Editorial: Library, Shrewsbury House, Community Centre, Bushmoor Crescent, Shooters Hill, London SE18 3EG
Web site: http://aperture-wps.blogspot.co.uk/
Freq: Daily
Circ: 493
News & Current Affairs

aphrodighty 1063142
Email: aphrodighty@gmail.com
Web site: https://aphrodighty.co.uk/
Freq: Daily
Circ: 521
Bars, Clubs & Pubs, Beauty & Grooming, Comedy, Cooking & Baking, Cosmetics, Entertainment, Fashion, Fitness & Exercise, Food, Grocery Stores

Applediario 1060431
Web site: http://www.applediario.com
Freq: Daily
Circ: 29574
Apple, Auto Aftermarket, Computers, Data Management, Electronics, Government Technology, Industry, Internet, Mobile Communications, Security & Security Systems

Apple's Cosmetics 1060891
Email: contact@hkcosme.com
Web site: http://www.apple113.blogspot.com
Freq: Daily
Circ: 1604
Fashion, Food, Lifestyle, Men's Interests, Regional General Interest, Women's Interests

Apps Playground 1062736
Web site: http://appsplayground.com/
Freq: Daily
Circ: 12573
Mobile Electronics

Apuntes de Cocina 1060814
Web site: http://apuntesdecocina.com/
Freq: Daily
Circ: 10618
Cooking & Baking

Apuntes de Futbol 1061883
Web site: http://misnotasyapuntes.blogspot.com
Freq: Daily
Circ: 7790
Basketball, Bicycles, Billiards, Boating & Yachting, Bodybuilding, Bowling, Boxing, Cricket, Equestrian Sports, Extreme/Adventure Sports

ARCAM Blog 1052615
Email: support@arcam.co.uk
Web site: http://www.arcam.co.uk/advice/blog.htm
Freq: Daily
Circ: 21
Audio Video Trade

Arched Eyebrow 987828
Email: myarchedeyebrow@gmail.com
Web site: archedeyebrow.com
Freq: Daily
Circ: 9774
Fashion

Architect Your Home Blog
986076
Web site: http://architect-yourhome.com/blog
Freq: Daily
Circ: 298
Architecture & Design

Architecting IT 987450
Editorial: 1 Brookend Drive, Barton-le-Clay, Barton-le-Clay MK45 4SQ
Web site: https://blog.architecting.it/
Circ: 328
News & Current Affairs

Architecture for London 1053467
Editorial: 82 Clerkenwell Road, London EC1M 5RF

Web site: http://architectureforlondon.com/blog/
Freq: Daily
Circ: 30
Architecture & Design

Architecture with a Capital A
995732
Editorial: Capital A Architecture Ltd., 84 The Murrays, Liberton, Edinburgh EH17 8UP
Tel: 44 01312 082075
Email: project@capitala.co.uk
Web site: capitaladesign.blogspot.com
Freq: Daily
Circ: 521
Architecture & Design

Are you feeling fashionable?
1061077
Email: nadjastrange@gmail.com
Web site: http://nadjastrange.indiedays.com/
Freq: Daily
Circ: 33214
Fashion, Shopping

Arepera 1061808
Web site: http://www.arepera.com.ve/
Freq: Daily
Circ: 2117
Bars, Clubs & Pubs, Comedy, Entertainment, Lifestyle, Local Entertainment Guides, Men's Interests, Movies & Video, National News, Regional General Interest, Women's Interests

ARF_ alternativo 1061532
Web site: http://anibal-alternativo.blogspot.com/
Freq: Daily
Circ: 521
Lifestyle, Men's Interests, Regional General Interest, Women's Interests

Argentina Infomine 1061391
Tel: 44 51144 66996
Web site: http://argentina.infomine.com
Freq: Daily
Circ: 95
Mining & Quarrying

Argentina Sports 1061978
Web site: http://jorgehacosta.blogspot.com/
Freq: Daily
Circ: 578
Basketball, Bicycles, Billiards, Boating & Yachting, Bodybuilding, Bowling, Boxing, Cricket, Equestrian Sports, Extreme/Adventure Sports

Arianna's Daily 997957
Email: info@ariannainteriors.com
Web site: www.ariannasdaily.com
Freq: Daily
Circ: 8420
Do-It-Yourself (DIY), Fashion, Travel

Arkitectonia 1061009
Web site: http://www.arkitectonica.blogspot.com
Freq: Daily
Circ: 767
Architecture & Design, Building & Construction, Celebrities, International News, Urban Planning & Development

Arkitektur 6 1060976
Email: wellinge@ntnu.no
Web site: http://arkitektur6.blogspot.com
Freq: Daily
Circ: 1342
Architecture & Design, Building & Construction

Armonizando Tu Vida 1061515
Web site: http://armonizandotuvida.blogspot.com
Freq: Daily
Circ: 1067
Astrology & Parapsychology, Lifestyle, Men's Interests, Regional General Interest, Women's Interests

Arnie's Airsoft 1054501
Email: arnie@arniesairsoft.co.uk
Web site: http://arniesairsoft.co.uk/news2/
Freq: Daily

Circ: 55829
Armed Forces, Shooting/Guns

Aromas de Mama 1060870
Web site: http://recetasdecocinaaromasdemama.blogspot.com/
Freq: Daily
Circ: 685
Cooking & Baking

AROnline 986415
Editorial: 63 Pioneer Avenue, Burton Latimer, Kettering, Northampton NN15 5LJ
Email: kadams@aronline.co.uk
Web site: http://www.aronline.co.uk/blogs/
Circ: 184
Editor: Keith Adams
Antique & Collectible Cars, Automakers, Automotive, Driving, Motorcycles, Off-road & 4-Wheel Drive Vehicles, Trucks & SUVs

Around and upside down 988057
Email: hypermummy82@gmail.com
Web site: aroundandupsidedown.co.uk
Freq: Daily
Circ: 7293
Profile: Blog covering lifestyle. The Around and Upside down blog discusses anything from food recipes and motherhood to fashion and beauty. The blog has an archive dating back to November 2013.
Regional General Interest, Women's Interests

Around the World in 80 Pairs of Shoes 1053029
Email: aroundtheworldin80pairsofshoes@gmail.com
Web site: www.aroundtheworldin80pairsofshoes.com
Freq: Daily
Circ: 7557
Profile: Around the World in 80 Pairs of Shoes covers luxury travel, gluten free fine dining and shoes. The blog has an archive dating back to October 2012 and shares a short blogroll.
Travel

Arqueología Gastronómica
106200■
Web site: http://blogs.eluniversal.com/eu3/Blogs/arqga_index.shtml
Freq: Daily
Circ: 7416
Food

Arquinauta 106090■
Web site: http://www.arquinauta.com
Freq: Daily
Circ: 24777
Architecture & Design, Auto Aftermarket, Computers, Data Management, Electronics, Government Technology, Industry, Internet, Mobile Communications, Security & Security Systems

Arquitectura de Casas 106102■
Web site: http://arquitecturadecasas.blogspot.com/
Freq: Daily
Circ: 2025
Architecture & Design, Sustainable Development

Arquitectura mas Historia
10610■
Web site: http://www.arquitecturamashistoria.blogspot.com
Freq: Daily
Circ: 1193
Antiques/Collectibles, Architecture & Design, Art, Arts, Building & Construction History, Literature, Photography, Theater & Performing Arts, Visual Arts

Arquitectura y Pensamiento
10620■
Web site: http://jalbertomendoza.blogspot.com/
Freq: Daily

Circ: 752
Antiques/Collectibles, Architecture & Design, Art, Arts, Broadcasting, Literature, Photography, Regional, Regional General Interest, Theater & Performing Arts

Arquitour 1061309
Web site: http://www.arquitour.com
Freq: Daily
Circ: 24349
Architecture & Design, Urban Planning & Development

Arse 2 Mouse 1053189
Email: arse2mouse@gmail.com
Web site: http://www.arse2mouse.com/
Freq: Daily
Circ: 8475
Soccer

Arseblog 986372
Editorial: PO BOX 12036, Crumlin, Dublin
Tel: 353 01442 9879
Email: thearseblog@arseblog.com
Web site: arseblog.com
Freq: Daily
Circ: 1283191
News & Current Affairs

Arsenal Insider 987892
Email: info@arsenalinsider.com
Web site: http://www.arsenalinsider.com/
Circ: 4691
Soccer

Arsenal Vision 996614
Email: meanlean@arsenalvision.co.uk
Web site: http://www.arsenalvision.co.uk/articles.html
Freq: Daily
Circ: 136
Editor: Meansut Ozilean
Soccer

Art Babel London 987821
Tel: 44 07513 958813
Email: artbabellondon@gmail.com
Web site: artbabel-london.com/
Freq: Daily
Circ: 10618
Art, Literature, Visual Arts

Art Boreal 1060607
Web site: http://www.art-boreal.com
Freq: Daily
Circ: 687
Graphic Design, Photography

Art for interiors 1060912
Web site: http://www.nerida1.blogspot.com
Freq: Daily
Circ: 521
Art, Fashion, Lifestyle, Men's Interests, Regional General Interest, Women's Interests

Art in Cambridge 1054948
Email: picturetalk321@gmail.com
Web site: http://artincambridge.blogspot.co.uk/
Freq: Daily
Circ: 2407
Art

Art in Liverpool 986078
Editorial: Art in Liverpool, First Floor, The Courtyard, 41 Stanhope St, Liverpool L8 5RE
Email: info@artinliverpool.com
Web site: www.artinliverpool.com
Circ: 7960
Editor: Sinead Nunnes
Antiques/Collectibles, Art, Arts, Literature, Photography, Theater & Performing Arts, Visual Arts

Art is Alive 1054931
Web site: https://artisalive.co.uk/
Freq: Daily
Circ: 11861
Art, Charitable Foundations, Classical/Choral/Band Music, Country, Folk, Bluegrass, Dance Music, Jazz & Blues, Literature, Movies & Video, Music, Pop Music

Art News Blog 996884
Email: info@artnewsblog.com
Web site: http://www.artnewsblog.com/
Freq: Daily
Circ: 10086
Art

The Art of Exploring 1054354
Email: theartofexploringblog@gmail.com
Web site: http://theartofexploring.com/
Freq: Daily
Circ: 9659
Regional General Interest, Travel, Women's Interests

The Art of Living with Epilepsy 1052954
Email: jade.dolby@hotmail.co.uk
Web site: http://jade-epilepsymynewlife.blogspot.co.uk/
Freq: Daily
Circ: 737
Disability

The Art of Nature 1052809
Web site: http://artofnatureuk.blogspot.co.uk/
Freq: Daily
Circ: 973
Art, History, Nature & Wildlife, Visual Arts

Art Of The State Blog 987281
Email: contact@artofthestate.co.uk
Web site: www.artofthestate.co.uk/blog2
Freq: Daily
Circ: 263
Antiques/Collectibles, Art, Arts, Literature, Photography, Regional General Interest, Theater & Performing Arts, Visual Arts

The Art of the Torch Singer 1053506
Email: piersford@aol.com
Web site: http://cry-me-a-torch-song.com/
Freq: Daily
Circ: 9652
News & Current Affairs

Art Rabbit 988540
Web site: http://www.artrabbit.com/
Circ: 36670
Art

Art, Antiques and Luxury Design Blog 999636
Web site: http://www.art-antiques-design.com
Freq: Daily
Circ: 13740
News & Current Affairs

Art, Like Bread 1060923
Email: artlikebread@gmail.com
Web site: http://www.artlikebread.blogspot.com
Freq: Daily
Circ: 521
Art, Crafts, Do-It-Yourself (DIY)

ArtCream 1053176
Web site: http://artcre.am/
Freq: Daily
Circ: 2196
Do-It-Yourself (DIY), Women's Interests

Arte de Amasar 1060937
Web site: http://www.elartedeamasar.com/
Freq: Daily
Circ: 1540
Cooking & Baking, Food

Arte del Vino 1061373
Web site: http://www.elartedelvino.com/
Freq: Daily
Circ: 1289
Wine/Winemaking

Arte, Arte y Mas Arte 1060947
Web site: http://www.artelua.blogspot.com
Freq: Daily
Circ: 611
Art

Artefact 998034
Editorial: London College of Communication, Elephant & Castle, London SE1 6SB Tel: 44 02075 146500
Email: artefactlcc@gmail.com
Web site: http://www.artefactmagazine.com/
Freq: Daily
Circ: 15320
Student Lifestyle

Art-e-facts 1053076
Email: kalston18@gmail.com
Web site: http://artefactsobjects.blogspot.co.uk/
Freq: Daily
Circ: 1241
Antiques/Collectibles, Art, Genealogy, Photography, Visual Arts

Artequitecturas 1061178
Web site: http://www.eacontenidos.blogspot.com
Freq: Daily
Circ: 521
Architecture & Design, Bars, Clubs & Pubs, Building & Construction, Food

Artescritorio 1060796
Web site: http://artescritorio.com/
Freq: Daily
Circ: 38422
Art, Computers

Artful Kids Blog 1053044
Editorial: Suite 120, 15 Bell Street, St. Andrews KY6 9UR Tel: 44 08458 690124
Email: info@artful-kids.com
Web site: http://artful-kids.com/blog/
Freq: Daily
Circ: 233
Art, Crafts, Visual Arts

Arthur Pewty's maggot sandwich 1053839
Web site: http://arthurpewtysmaggotsandwich.blogspot.co.uk/
Freq: Daily
Circ: 894
Internet, Men's Interests, Regional

Artistas 1062038
Web site: http://do-mi-sol-artistas.blogspot.com/
Freq: Daily
Circ: 992
Art, Classical/Choral/Band Music, Country, Folk, Bluegrass, Dance Music, Jazz & Blues, Movies & Video, Music, Pop Music, R&B, Urban, World, Rap & Hip Hop

Arts End of Nowhere 998114
Web site: http://artsendofnowhere.co.uk/
Freq: Daily
Circ: 9255
Editor: Amy Smith
Airline Inflight, Art, Classical/Choral/Band Music, Comedy, Cooking & Baking, Country, Folk, Bluegrass, Dance Music, Food, Grocery Stores, Jazz & Blues

Arundel Eccentrics Antiques 1054934
Email: arundel.eccentrics@sky.com
Web site: http://arundelgal.blogspot.co.uk/
Freq: Daily
Circ: 1416
Antiques/Collectibles, Do-It-Yourself (DIY)

As easy as riding a bike 1053144
Web site: http://aseasyasridingabike.wordpress.com/
Freq: Daily
Circ: 14967
Profile: Blog covering cycling. The blog has an archive dating back to February 2011 and shares an extensive blogroll.
Bicycles

Asesor Financiero e Inversiones 1061241
Web site: http://www.asesorfinancieroeinversiones.com/
Freq: Daily

Circ: 521
Banking, Financial Markets

Ashburnham Insurance Services Blog 1053729
Tel: 44 01702 347400
Email: insure@ashburnham-insurance.co.uk
Web site: www.ashburnham-insurance.co.uk/blog
Freq: Daily
Circ: 21
Insurance

Ashtray Blog 988763
Email: blog@ecigarettedirect.co.uk
Web site: http://www.ecigarettedirect.co.uk/ashtray-blog/
Freq: Daily
Circ: 179247
Respiratory Diseases

Asiajin 1062129
Web site: http://asiajin.com
Freq: Daily
Circ: 3889
Auto Aftermarket, Computers, Data Management, Electronics, Government Technology, Industry, Internet, Mobile Communications, Security & Security Systems, Software

Asian Fashion Blog 1054259
Email: fashionspectator@gmail.com
Web site: www.asianfashionblog.co.uk/p/contact.html
Freq: Daily
Circ: 106
Fashion

Aspectus News & Insight 1052796
Editorial: Ground Floor, James House, 22 - 24 Corsham Street, London N1 6DR
Tel: 44 02072 428867
Email: info@aspectuspr.com
Web site: https://www.aspectuspr.com/news-insight/
Freq: Daily
Circ: 23
Branding, Graphic Design, Marketing

Aspiring Kennedy 1053823
Email: aspiringkennedy@gmail.com
Web site: http://www.aspiringkennedy.com/
Freq: Daily
Circ: 21180
Cooking & Baking, Restaurant Reviews, Travel

Assetz for Investors Blog 1054953
Tel: 44 08454 009000
Email: elena.rustici@assetz.co.uk
Web site: https://property.assetz.co.uk//buzz.htm
Freq: Daily
Architecture & Design, Building & Construction, Commercial Real Estate, Finance, Interior Design, Legal Affairs, Office Design, Property Management & Maintenance, Residential Real Estate, Retail

Association of Volunteer Managers 996863
Editorial: PO Box 1449, Bedford MK44 5AN
Email: info@volunteermanagers.org.uk
Web site: http://volunteermanagers.org.uk/
Freq: Daily
Circ: 8358
Charitable Foundations

Asthma UK News blog 999308
Editorial: 18 Mansell Street, London E1 8AA
Tel: 44 02077 864949
Email: mediaoffice@asthma.org.uk
Web site: https://www.asthma.org.uk/about/media/news/
Freq: Daily
Charitable Foundations

Asylum 987980
Email: johnself.asylum@googlemail.com
Web site: http://theasylum.wordpress.com/
Freq: Daily
Circ: 7862
Literature

UK Blogs

Asylum Films 1053609
Editorial: 38 Poland Street, London W1F
7LY Tel: 44 02034 178520
Email: info@asylumfilms.co.uk
Web site: http://asylumfilms.co.uk/
Freq: Daily
Circ: 3761
Advertising Industry, Branding,
Broadcasting, Movies & Video

At Home with Abby 1052976
Email: contact@athomewithabby.com
Web site: http://www.athomewithabby.com/
Freq: Daily
Circ: 8601
Do-It-Yourself (DIY), Fashion, Women's
Interests

ateliertally 988055
Web site: ateliertally.com
Freq: Daily
Circ: 6808
Graphic Design

AtFashionForte 1098941
Web site: http://atfashionforte.com/
Freq: Daily
Circ: 25742
Cooking & Baking, Fashion, Fitness &
Exercise, Nutrition, Restaurant Reviews

Atina Argentina 1061782
Web site: http://www.atinaargentina.com/
Freq: Daily
Circ: 929
National News

Atlantic Charters Blog 1053660
Email: info@atlanticcharters.co.uk
Web site: http://www.atlanticcharters.co.uk/
category/blog/
Freq: Daily
Circ: 173
Marine & Boat Trade, Travel

Atlas Deportivo 1061040
Web site: http://www.atlasdeportivo.com
Freq: Daily
Circ: 913
Basketball, Bicycles, Billiards, Boating &
Yachting, Bodybuilding, Bowling, Boxing,
Cricket, Equestrian Sports, Extreme/
Adventure Sports

Atrabilioso 1062154
Web site: http://atrabilioso.blogspot.com/
Freq: Daily
Circ: 4456
Politics

The Atresea 1052798
Web site: http://blog.artesea.co.uk/
Freq: Daily
Audio Video Trade, Cameras, Consumer
Electronics, Mobile Electronics, Movies &
Video

Atson ajatukset 1061922
Email: atso.suopanki@gmail.com
Web site: http://atson.blogspot.com
Freq: Daily
Circ: 1486
Internet, Movies & Video

Attachment Mummy 1054226
Email: lse@attachmentmummy.com
Web site: www.attachmentmummy.com
Freq: Daily
Circ: 35739
Family & Parenting

Attic 24 988150
Web site: http://attic24.typepad.com/
weblog/
Freq: Daily
Circ: 5221535
Crafts

ATTN 1053576
Web site: http://www.attnmagazine.co.uk
Freq: Daily
Circ: 14498
Classical/Choral/Band Music, Country,
Folk, Bluegrass, Dance Music, Jazz &
Blues, Music, Pop Music, R&B, Urban,
World, Rap & Hip Hop, Rock Music

Auburn Antics 988073
Email: auburnantics@gmail.com
Web site: http://www.auburnantics.co.uk/
Freq: Daily
Circ: 5236
Profile: Blog covering lifestyle. MY GINGER
BREAD JOURNEY blog discusses anything
from lifestyle and recipes to student lifestyle
and travel. The blog has an archive dating
back to January 2013.
Cooking & Baking

Audley Blog 1053442
Editorial: New Mill, New Mill Lane, Witney
OX29 9SX Tel: 44 01993 838000
Web site: https://careers.audleytravel.com/
Freq: Daily
Circ: 45170
Airline Inflight, Railroad, Travel

Augusto Giussi 1061050
Web site: http://giussi.blogspot.com/
Freq: Daily
Circ: 521
Graphic Design

Aurora Clinics Cosmetic Surgery Blog 999408
Editorial: BMI The Paddocks Clinic,
Aylesbury Road, Princes Risborough HP27
0JS Tel: 44 01844 318663
Email: info@aurora-clinics.co.uk
Web site: http://www.aurora-clinics.co.uk/
blog/
Freq: Daily
Circ: 22
Plastic/Reconstructive/Cosmetic Surgery

Autism Mumma 988324
Email: autismmumma@aol.com
Web site: www.autismmumma.com
Freq: Daily
Circ: 9542
Family & Parenting

The Autistic Naturalist 1100500
Web site: http://seanspetmonster.blogspot.
co.uk/
Freq: Daily
Circ: 805
News & Current Affairs

Auto Europe Travel Blog 1054147
Email: reservations@auto-europe.co.uk
Web site: http://blog.auto-europe.co.uk/
Freq: Daily
Circ: 39
Automotive, Driving, Off-road & 4-Wheel
Drive Vehicles, Travel

Auto Perfecto 1061928
Web site: http://elautoperfecto.blogspot.
com/
Freq: Daily
Circ: 784
Antique & Collectible Cars, Automakers,
Automotive, Driving, Motorcycles, Off-
road & 4-Wheel Drive Vehicles, Trucks &
SUVs

autoblog japan 1062009
Web site: http://jp.autoblog.com
Freq: Daily
Circ: 304173
Antique & Collectible Cars, Automakers,
Automotive, Driving, Motorcycles, Off-
road & 4-Wheel Drive Vehicles, Trucks &
SUVs

AutoeBid Blog 999208
Editorial: 1 Pancras Square, London N1C
4AG Tel: 44 08000 336022
Email: info@autoebid.com
Web site: www.autoebid.com/blog
Freq: Daily
Circ: 48
Antique & Collectible Cars, Automakers,
Automotive, Driving, Motorcycles, Off-
road & 4-Wheel Drive Vehicles, Trucks &
SUVs

Automotive Blog 986764
Email: info@automotiveblog.co.uk
Web site: automotiveblog.co.uk
Freq: Daily

Circ: 11311
Antique & Collectible Cars, Automakers,
Automotive, Driving, Off-road & 4-Wheel
Drive Vehicles

Avant Life 1069068
Editorial: Round Foundry Media Centre,
Foundry Street, Leeds LS11 5QP
Tel: 44 01133 944580
Email: avantlife@brand8pr.com
Web site: http://www.avanthomes.co.uk/
avant-life/
Freq: Daily
Circ: 147
Do-It-Yourself (DIY), Gardening, Property
Management & Maintenance

Average Film Reviews 997591
Email: nicola@averagefilmreviews.com
Web site: www.averagefilmreviews.com/
Freq: Daily
Circ: 27379
News & Current Affairs

Average Joes 987577
Email: havefun@averagejoesblog.com
Web site: http://www.averagejoes.co.uk/
Freq: Daily
Circ: 12040
Men's Interests

Aviacion Civil 1061447
Web site: http://www.aviacioncivil.com.ve/
Freq: Daily
Circ: 9752
Aviation

AWE360 Blog 1053281
Web site: https://awe365.com/
Freq: Daily
Circ: 12475
Extreme/Adventure Sports, Outdoor
Recreation, Travel

The Awesome Lady 998064
Email: theawesomeladyblog@hotmail.co.uk
Web site: http://theawesomelady.blogspot.
co.uk/
Freq: Daily
Circ: 521
Airline Inflight, Literature, Photography,
Railroad, Travel

Ayshia Armani Online 988578
Tel: 44 07429 447164
Email: info@ayshiaarmani.com
Web site: http://www.ayshiaarmanionline.
com
Freq: Daily
Circ: 10145
Africa, Beauty & Grooming, Celebrities,
Cosmetics, Fashion, Hair, Movies & Video,
Women's Interests

Azarmehr Blog 1053345
Web site: www.azarmehr.info/
Freq: Daily
Circ: 9784
Government

Azrights blog 1053306
Editorial: 81 - 83 Essex Road, London N1
2SF Tel: 44 02077 001414
Web site: http://azrights.com/media/
Freq: Daily
Circ: 77
Intellectual Property

Azucarte 1061280
Web site: http://azucararte.blogspot.com/
Freq: Daily
Circ: 521
Cooking & Baking, Food

B. Loved Weddings 997490
Email: louise@blovedblog.com
Web site: http://blovedblog.com/
Freq: Daily
Circ: 27931
Weddings

B2B Marketing Blog 1052996
Editorial: Clover House, 147-149 Farringdon
Road, London Tel: 44 02070 144920
Email: alex.clarke@b2bmarketing.net
Web site: https://www.b2bmarketing.net/
en-gb/resources/blog
Freq: Daily

Circ: 109888
Advertising Industry, Branding,
Broadcasting, Internet, Marketing

The B2B PR Blog 987248
Editorial: 27 Rathbone Street, London W1T
1NH Tel: 44 02075 806502
Email: editor@b2bprblog.com
Web site: b2bprblog.com
Freq: Daily
Circ: 7954
Editor: Heather Baker; Editor: Lauren
Mason
Profile: Blog covering business to business
public relation advice. The blog has an
archive dating back to May 2012.
Branding

B3 Designers Blog 986079
Editorial: B3 Designers, Unit 302
Metropolitan Wharf, 70 Wapping Wall,
London E1W 3SS Tel: 44 02077 298111
Email: editor@b3designers.co.uk
Web site: http://www.b3designers.co.uk/
blog/
Freq: Daily
Circ: 7
Architecture & Design, Do-It-Yourself
(DIY), Gardening, Home, Property
Management & Maintenance, Real Estate

B96 Blog 1061067
Web site: http://b96.radio.com/?s=blog
Freq: Daily
Circ: 2
Celebrities, Classical/Choral/Band Music,
Country, Folk, Bluegrass, Dance Music,
Jazz & Blues, Music, Pop Music, R&B,
Urban, World, Rap & Hip Hop, Rock Music

BA Inspiration 1062137
Email: hello@bainspiration.com
Web site: http://www.bainspiration.com
Freq: Daily
Circ: 3253
Antiques/Collectibles, Armed Forces, Art,
Arts, Astrology & Parapsychology,
Astronomy, Aviation, Boating & Yachting,
Camping and RV Travel, Cartoons

Babaduck 988551
Editorial: Retail inMotion, Suite 4 The Mall,
Beacon Court, Dublin Dublin 18
Email: babaduck@gmail.com
Web site: www.babaduck.com
Freq: Daily
Circ: 3601
News & Current Affairs

Babi Pur Blog 986690
Editorial: Babi Pur, 7 Griffin Enterprise Park,
Penrhyndeudraeth, Penrhyndeudraeth LL48
6LE Tel: 44 01766 770644
Email: marketing@babipur.co.uk
Web site: http://www.
ethicalshoppingforbabies.co.uk
Freq: Daily
Circ: 494
Ethical/Moral Issues, Family & Parenting

Baby Budgeting 986465
Web site: www.babybudgeting.co.uk
Freq: Daily
Circ: 10574
Cooking & Baking, Family & Parenting,
Personal Finance

Baby Routes 1059459
Email: babyroutes@gmail.com
Web site: http://babyroutes.co.uk
Freq: Daily
Circ: 7254
Profile: Blog covering parenthood with
travel, hiking and the great outdoors.
Family & Parenting, Outdoor Recreation,
Women's Interests

BabyBarista 986351
Editorial: 23 Hazel Avenue, Braunton EX33
2EZ
Web site: www.babybarista.com
Freq: Daily
Circ: 3842
News & Current Affairs

Babyccino Kids Blog 986707
Web site: http://babyccinokids.com/blog

Freq: Daily
Circ: 18369
Audio Video Trade, Bars, Clubs & Pubs, Cameras, Comedy, Consumer Electronics, Cooking & Baking, Crafts, Entertainment, Family & Parenting, Local Entertainment Guides

babyurbeautiful   997831
Email: babyurbeautiful@gmail.com
Web site: babyurbeautiful.blogspot.co.uk
Freq: Daily
Circ: 10502
Profile: Blog covering parenting. babyurbeautiful blog discusses anything baby products and baby beauty products. The blog has an archive dating back to June 2013.
Beauty & Grooming, Cosmetics, Family & Parenting, Hair, Women's Interests

Back Page Football   997197
Email: editor@backpagefootball.com
Web site: backpagefootball.com
Freq: Daily
Circ: 44606
News & Current Affairs

Back To The Movies   988122
Web site: http://bttm.co.uk/
Freq: Daily
Circ: 48454
Profile: Blog covering film.
Entertainment, Movies & Video

Backpacks and Bunkbeds
988034
Email: neil@backpacksandbunkbeds.co.uk
Web site: http://www.backpacksandbunkbeds.co.uk/
Freq: Daily
Circ: 69676
Travel

Backup Technology blog
1054249
Tel: 44 01133 506020
Web site: http://blog.backup-technology.com/
Freq: Daily
Circ: 3253
Auto Aftermarket, Computers, Data Management, Electronics, Government Technology, Industry, Internet, Mobile Communications, Security & Security Systems, Software

Bad PR   1053023
Email: michael.marshall@merseyskeptics.org.uk
Web site: http://badpr.co.uk
Freq: Daily
Circ: 12089
Profile: Blog covering the role and influence PR companies have in the press. The blog has an archive dating back to February 2012.
Celebrities

Baggage Reclaim   087430
Email: natalie@baggagereclaim.co.uk
Web site: www.baggagereclaim.co.uk
Freq: Daily
Circ: 126420
Relationships

Bags of Beauty   988735
Editorial: 147 Tottenham Lane, Hornsey, London N8 9BT **Tel:** 44 07580 534522
Email: susmi_patel@hotmail.com
Web site: http://www.bagsofbeauty.co.uk/
Freq: Daily
Circ: 10420
Beauty & Grooming, Cosmetics, Fashion, Hair

Bags of Love - Gift Ideas Blog
987486
Editorial: Unit 7, Space Business Park, Abbey Road, Park Royal, London NW10 7SU
Tel: 44 02089 604567
Web site: https://www.bagsoflove.co.uk/blog/
Freq: Daily
Circ: 213
Shopping

Baking Mad Blog   996434
Editorial: Western House (Block B), Lynchwood Business Park, Peterborough PE2 6FZ **Tel:** 44 01733 422400
Email: info@bakingmad.com
Web site: blog.bakingmad.com
Freq: Daily
Circ: 5
Cooking & Baking

Balanced Wellness   1053909
Tel: 44 02392 454117
Email: info@balancedwellness.co.uk
Web site: http://www.balancedwellness.co.uk/
Freq: Daily
Circ: 1548
Alternative Medicine, Health & Medicine, Nutrition

Bald Hiker   986378
Email: baldhiker@gmail.com
Web site: www.baldhiker.com
Freq: Daily
Circ: 57490
Travel

The Balkan Wargamer   1052930
Email: balkandave@googlemail.com
Web site: http://balkandave.blogspot.co.uk/
Freq: Daily
Circ: 10164
Antiques/Collectibles, Computer & Video Games, Crafts, Hobbies, & Collecting, History

The Ball Is Round   1054126
Email: tbir@gmx.com
Web site: http://theballisround.co.uk
Freq: Daily
Circ: 43647
Soccer

BALLS.ie   1053269
Email: thegaffer@balls.ie
Web site: www.balls.ie
Freq: Daily
Circ: 691816
Editor: Mark Farrelly
Basketball, Bicycles, Billiards, Boating & Yachting, Bodybuilding, Bowling, Boxing, Cricket, Equestrian Sports, Extreme/Adventure Sports

Ball-Sup - Beer Around The World
1055144
Web site: http://ball-sup.blogspot.co.uk/
Freq: Daily
Circ: 521
Beer, Cricket, Soccer, Travel

Bambella blog   988106
Web site: www.bambellablog.com
Freq: Daily
Circ: 6882
Profile: BAMBELLA blog covers fashion and lifestyle. The blog shares an extensive blogroll.
Fashion

Bambino Goodies   986080
Email: team@bambinogoodies.co.uk
Web site: www.bambinogoodies.co.uk
Circ: 16542
Family & Parenting, Fashion

Banceithin Life   1054495
Tel: 44 01974 272559
Email: escape@banceithin.com
Web site: http://banceithin.blogspot.co.uk/
Freq: Daily
Circ: 521
Travel

Band Weblogs   1053778
Email: info@bandweblogs.com
Web site: bandweblogs.com
Freq: Daily
Circ: 9237
Dance Music, Jazz & Blues, Pop Music, Rap & Hip Hop, Rock Music

Bangers & Mash   988437
Email: bangermashchat@gmail.com
Web site: http://bangers-and-mash.com
Freq: Daily
Circ: 7150

Bangs and a Bun   987143
Email: bangs@bangsandabun.com
Web site: bangsandabun.com
Freq: Daily
Circ: 12464
Editor: Muireann Carey-Campbell
Fashion, Fitness & Exercise, Women's Interests

Bao/Bread   1061709
Web site: http://baobread.wordpress.com
Freq: Daily
Circ: 55
Cooking & Baking, Food

Barahonero   1060537
Web site: http://www.barahonero.com
Freq: Daily
Circ: 652
National News, Politics

Barajitas Blog   1061905
Web site: http://www.baratijasblog.com
Freq: Daily
Circ: 1236
Auto Aftermarket, Computers, Data Management, Electronics, Government Technology, Graphic Design, Industry, Internet, Mobile Communications, Security & Security Systems

Barcos de Papel   1061790
Web site: http://barquitospapel.blogspot.com/
Freq: Daily
Circ: 1039
Crafts

The Bardathon   987567
Editorial: The University of Nottingham, University Park Campus, Nottingham NG7 2RD
Web site: blogs.nottingham.ac.uk/bardathon/
Freq: Daily
Circ: 50945
Art, Literature, Photography, Theater & Performing Arts, Visual Arts

The Barefaced Chic   1074312
Email: admin@thebarefacedchic.co.uk
Web site: http://www.thebarefacedchic.co.uk/
Freq: Daily
Circ: 8535
Editor: Michelle Lyndon-Dykes
Beauty & Grooming, Cosmetics, Fashion, Hair, Women's Interests

Barefoot Bravery   1052597
Web site: http://www.barefootbravery.com/
Freq: Daily
Circ: 1594
Beauty & Grooming, Cooking & Baking, Cosmetics, Fashion, Hair, Neurology, Regional General Interest, Restaurant Reviews, Travel, Women's Interests

Bark Time   997859
Web site: barktime.co.uk
Freq: Daily
Circ: 70113
Cooking & Baking, Family & Parenting, Women's Interests

Barkarama   987666
Editorial: Barkarama Ltd, 40 Regency Court, Brentwood, Brentwood CM14 4LU
Email: bark@barkarama.co.uk
Web site: barkarama.co.uk
Freq: Daily
Circ: 9718
Nature & Wildlife

Barkingside 21   987832
Editorial: Barkingside, Redbridge
Email: barkingside21@btinternet.com
Web site: http://barkingside21.blogspot.co.uk/
Freq: Daily
Circ: 9565
Energy & Environment, Environment

The Barnet Eye   986585
Web site: barneteye.blogspot.com
Freq: Daily
Circ: 8341
Politics, Regional

Barquisimeto.com   1060956
Web site: http://www.barquisimeto.com/
Freq: Daily
Circ: 14400
Regional General Interest

The Barrister Blog   986338
Editorial: 23 Hazel Avenue, Braunton, Braunton EX33 2EZ
Web site: www.timkevan.blogspot.com
Freq: Daily
Circ: 8751
News & Current Affairs

Bart's Bookshelf   1053731
Email: bookreviews@bartsbookshelf.co.uk
Web site: www.bartsbookshelf.co.uk
Freq: Daily
Circ: 7987
Literature

Basenotes   986508
Editorial: Basenotes.net, BCM Box 1111, London WC1N 3XX
Email: support@basenotes.net
Web site: www.basenotes.net
Circ: 381063
Profile: Basenotes.net is an online reference guide to the world of fragrances. The site features a fully searchable database of over 10,000 fragrances with over 30,000 consumer reviews and is regularly updated with industry news, fragrance articles and interviews with members of the fragrance industry.
Cosmetics

Basik Attire   1052880
Email: basikattire@gmail.com
Web site: http://basikattire.blogspot.co.uk
Freq: Daily
Circ: 1128
Profile: Blog covering fashion. BASIK ATTIRE blog discusses anything from with the latest fashion trends and personal style to fashion accessories and footwear.
Art, Fashion, Photography, Visual Arts, Women's Interests

Bass   1052557
Email: hello@kotrynabass.com
Web site: http://www.kotrynabass.com/
Freq: Daily
Circ: 11791
Profile: Blog covering lifestyle. The BASS blog discusses anything from food and fashion to travel and interior design. The blog has an archive dating back to November 2012.
Beauty & Grooming, Cooking & Baking, Cosmetics, Fashion, Hair, Travel, Women's Interests

Bath Rugby Inside Out   1052612
Web site: http://www.bathrugbyinsideout.com/
Freq: Daily
Circ: 656
Rugby

Batichango   1060660
Web site: http://www.batichango.com
Freq: Daily
Circ: 744
National News

Baul de las Costureras   1060463
Web site: http://elbauldelascostureras.blogspot.com
Freq: Daily
Circ: 732
Crafts, Hobbies, & Collecting, Fashion

BBC Introducing Blog   1054396
Web site: http://www.bbc.co.uk/blogs/introducing
Freq: Daily
Circ: 106
Country, Folk, Bluegrass, Dance Music, Pop Music, Rap & Hip Hop, Rock Music

UK Blogs

Be Bop Wino 1052754
Email: boogiewoody@hotmail.co.uk
Web site: http://bebopwinorip.blogspot.co.uk/
Freq: Daily
Circ: 611
Jazz & Blues

Be Clever With Your Cash 1094854
Web site: https://becleverwithyourcash.com/
Freq: Daily
Circ: 13481
Personal Finance

beads buttons & birds 1054527
Email: beadsbuttonsandbirds@live.co.uk
Web site: http://beadsbuttonsandbirds.blogspot.co.uk/
Freq: Daily
Circ: 2119
Crafts

Beamly TV News 1052545
Editorial: Drury House, 34 - 43 Russell Street, London WC2B 5HA
Email: hello@beamly.com
Web site: https://www.beamly.com/news
Freq: Daily
Circ: 297
Broadcasting, Movies & Video

BeansBox 1062151
Email: web@beansbox.com
Web site: http://www.beansbox.com/blog
Freq: Daily
Circ: 5
Auto Aftermarket, Computers, Data Management, Electronics, Government Technology, Industry, Internet, Mobile Communications, Security & Security Systems, Software

The Bearded Trio 988426
Email: rob@thebeardedtrio.com
Web site: http://www.thebeardedtrio.com/
Freq: Daily
Circ: 5117
Movies & Video

Beat and Byte 1061525
Web site: http://beatandbyte.com
Freq: Daily
Circ: 521
Auto Aftermarket, Classical/Choral/Band Music, Computers, Country, Folk, Bluegrass, Dance Music, Data Management, Electronics, Government Technology, Industry, Internet

The Beat That My Heart Skipped 985303
Web site: www.thebeatthatmyheartskipped.co.uk
Freq: Daily
Circ: 8667
Alcohol & Spirits, Antiques/Collectibles, Architecture & Design, Art, Arts, Bars, Clubs & Pubs, Beer, Beverages, Cooking & Baking, Do-It-Yourself (DIY)

BeatCheck 1053690
Email: info@beatcheck.co.uk
Web site: http://beatcheck.co.uk/news/
Freq: Daily
Circ: 27
Regional General Interest

Beaut Chic 1053152
Email: beautchic@gmail.com
Web site: www.beautchic.com
Freq: Daily
Circ: 10017
Cosmetics, Fashion

Beaut.ie 986082
Editorial: 26 Great Strand Street, Dublin
Tel: 353 18748 208
Email: info@beaut.ie
Web site: http://www.beaut.ie/
Freq: Daily
Circ: 152190
News & Current Affairs

The Beautiful Truth 988483
Email: thebeautifultruthie@gmail.com
Web site: www.thebeautifultruth.ie
Freq: Daily
Circ: 7757
News & Current Affairs

Beautifully Nourished 1072713
Editorial: 7 Graham Mansions, Graham Road, London E8 1EY
Email: katt-elyse@hotmail.co.uk
Web site: www.beautifullynourished.com
Freq: Weekly
Circ: 611
Beauty & Grooming, Cosmetics, Hair, Health & Medicine, Nutrition, Women's Interests

Beautifully Travelled 1074788
Email: beautifullytravelled@gmail.com
Web site: http://www.beautifullytravelled.com/
Freq: Daily
Circ: 12451
Travel

beauty & the boy 988631
Web site: beautyandtheboy.com
Freq: Daily
Circ: 7606
Profile: beauty & THE BOY blog covers beauty news.
Beauty & Grooming, Cosmetics, Hair

Beauty Aesthetic - CEASED 2015 987101
Freq: Daily
Circ: 7787
Beauty & Grooming, Cosmetics, Fashion, Hair, Women's Interests

Beauty and Rags CEASED 988495
Web site: http://www.beautyandrags.co.uk
Freq: Daily
Circ: 4069
Profile: Blog covering beauty, fashion, music and lifestyle.
Beauty & Grooming, Cosmetics, Fashion, Hair

Beauty and the Blog 986530
Email: info@beautyandtheblog.co
Web site: http://www.beautyandtheblog.co/
Freq: Daily
Circ: 7210
Beauty & Grooming, Cosmetics, Hair

Beauty and the Blonde 1054655
Email: beautyblonde@mail.com
Web site: http://beautyblondexo.blogspot.co.uk/
Freq: Daily
Circ: 521
Beauty & Grooming, Cosmetics, Fashion, Hair

Beauty and the Rest 1056760
Email: beautyshewrote@live.com
Web site: http://www.beautyandtherest.co.uk/
Freq: Daily
Circ: 2019
Beauty & Grooming, Cosmetics, Fashion, Hair

The Beauty Baker 988077
Web site: http://www.thebeautybaker.co.uk/
Freq: Daily
Circ: 9634
Profile: Blog covering fashion and beauty. The Beauty Baker discusses anything from beauty products and outfits to lifestyle and baking. The blog has an archive dating back to October 2013.
Cooking & Baking

The Beauty Dial 998171
Email: thebeautydial@live.com
Web site: thebeautydial.com
Freq: Daily
Circ: 752
Editor: Edel Cox
News & Current Affairs

Beauty Doctor 1061533
Web site: http://blog.sina.com.cn/yixuezhengxingmeirong
Freq: Daily
Circ: 25409999
Alternative Medicine, Cosmetics, Disability, Fitness & Exercise, Health & Medicine, Media Relations, Medicine, Nutrition, Patient Support, Personal Health & Wellness

The Beauty Explorer 996805
Tel: 44 07583 150056
Email: rhiannon@thebeautyexplorer.com
Web site: thebeautyexplorer.com
Freq: Daily
Circ: 521
Beauty & Grooming, Cooking & Baking, Cosmetics, Fashion, Hair, Restaurant Reviews, Travel, Women's Interests

Beauty Geek UK 998402
Email: geek@beautygeekuk.com
Web site: www.beautygeekuk.com
Freq: Daily
Circ: 24279
Beauty & Grooming, Cosmetics, Fashion, Hair, Women's Interests

Beauty H2T 1053394
Email: beautyh2t@gmail.com
Web site: http://www.beautyh2t.com/
Freq: Daily
Circ: 7505
Beauty & Grooming, Cosmetics, Fashion, Hair, Women's Interests

Beauty In My Mind 986824
Web site: www.beautyinmymind.com
Freq: Daily
Circ: 8362
Beauty & Grooming, Cosmetics, Fashion, Hair, Women's Interests

The Beauty Informer 1053021
Editorial: The Beauty Informer, 13 Mount Nod Road, Streatham Hill, London SW16 2LQ
Email: thebeautyinformer@gmail.com
Web site: www.thebeautyinformer.com
Freq: Daily
Circ: 6886
Cosmetics

Beauty King UK 1052974
Email: beautykinguk@gmail.com
Web site: www.beautykinguk.co.uk
Freq: Daily
Circ: 7750
Beauty & Grooming, Cosmetics, Fashion, Hair

Beauty of an Era 997992
Web site: www.beautyofanera.com
Freq: Daily
Circ: 10012
Beauty & Grooming, Cosmetics, Fashion, Hair, Women's Interests

The Beauty of Transport 1052589
Web site: https://thebeautyoftransport.com/
Freq: Daily
Circ: 12367
Transportation

Beauty Queen UK 1054007
Editorial: 60a Chase side, Southgate, London N14 5PA
Email: beautyqueenuk@gmail.com
Web site: http://www.beautyqueenuk.co.uk/
Freq: Daily
Circ: 152673
Profile: Blog covering beauty. Beauty Queen UK blog discusses anything from beauty to lifestyle. The blog has an archive dating back to January 2013 and shares an short blog roll. Beauty Queen UK was awarded the 'The Shine On Award' and the 'The Versatile Blogger Award'. The blog has also been nominated for the 'The Beautiful Blog Award'.
Beauty & Grooming, Cosmetics, Fashion, Hair

The Beauty Scoop! 984994
Email: info@thebeautyscoop.co.uk
Web site: www.thebeautyscoop.co.uk
Freq: Daily

Circ: 7581
Beauty & Grooming, Cosmetics, Hair

The Beauty Shortlist 987321
Email: beautyshortlist@gmail.com
Web site: thebeautyshortlist.com
Freq: Daily
Circ: 15382
Cosmetics

The Beauty Tonic 1053969
Email: info@thebeautytonic.com
Web site: http://thebeautytonic.com/
Freq: Daily
Circ: 7403
Beauty & Grooming, Cosmetics, Hair

Beauty, Bargains and Beyond 1055158
Email: beautybargainsandbeyond@sky.com
Web site: beautybargainsandbeyond.blogspot.co.uk
Freq: Daily
Circ: 8067
Beauty & Grooming, Cosmetics, Hair

BeautyBible.com 986084
Web site: http://beautybible.com/
Circ: 14678
Profile: Online magazine covering beauty information, tips, questions and answers, prize draws and exclusive offers. Aimed at women of all ages.Alternative Title: Beauty Bible
Beauty & Grooming, Cosmetics, Hair

BeautySwot 986844
Web site: www.beautyswot.com
Freq: Daily
Circ: 7308
Beauty & Grooming, Cosmetics, Hair

BeBop Spoken Here 1052793
Email: lanceliddle@gmail.com
Web site: http://lance-bebopspokenhere.blogspot.co.uk/
Freq: Daily
Circ: 2872
Jazz & Blues

Beckie Eschle 1053329
Email: beckieeschle@live.co.uk
Web site: http://www.beckieeschle.com/
Freq: Daily
Circ: 8047
Beauty & Grooming, Cosmetics, Fashion, Hair, Neurology, Women's Interests

Becky's Boudoir 1053374
Email: blog@beckysboudoir.com
Web site: beckysboudoir.com
Freq: Daily
Circ: 9209
Profile: Blog covering lingerie, fashion, beauty, women's interest and lifestyle. The blog has an archive dating back to February 2011.
Fashion, Women's Interests

Bee Happy 1052848
Email: beehappyhomeandaccessories@gmail.com
Web site: beehappyhome.blogspot.co.uk
Freq: Daily
Circ: 521
Profile: Blog covering home decorating. The blog has an archive dating back to November 2010 and shares an extensive blog roll.
Do-It-Yourself (DIY), Women's Interests

bee-it 1053518
Editorial: BEE Digital Ltd, 26-28 Hammersmith Grove, London W6 7BA
Email: hello@bee-it.co.uk
Web site: bee-it.co.uk
Freq: Daily
Circ: 14813
Education

Beekeeping 1055935
Web site: http://blog.ormskirkbeekeepers.co.uk/
Freq: Daily
Circ: 64
Profile: Publication containing reports and news on all aspects of bees and beekeeping

including disease reports, research, history, beekeeping archaeology, book reviews, honey cookery and beekeeping memorabilia. Read by members of the Devon Beekeepers Association and other beekeepers.Regular features: Bee Diseases Featuring details of diseases which affect bees.; Beekeeping Advice Featuring research into the effects of climate change, farming and other environmental factors on beekeeping.; Hint For Beginners Featuring tips and hints for starting beekeeping.
Ad Rate: Full Page Mono 32.00
Energy & Environment, Environment

Been There, Eaten That   1098967
Web site: www.beenthereeatenthat.co.uk
Freq: Daily
Circ: 9264
Cooking & Baking, Restaurant Reviews

Beer Lens   1054207
Freq: Daily
News & Current Affairs

The Beer Nut   1054410
Web site: http://thebeernut.blogspot.co.uk/
Freq: Daily
Circ: 1056
Beer

The BeerCast   1073134
Email: thebeercast@gmail.com
Web site: http://thebeercast.com/
Freq: Daily
Circ: 12069
Editor: Richard Taylor
Beer

Beermarketeer   1054930
Web site: http://beermarketeer.blogspot.co.uk/
Freq: Daily
Circ: 521
Beer

Before the Big Day   985562
Email: georgia@beforethebigday.co.uk
Web site: www.beforethebigday.co.uk
Freq: Daily
Circ: 4551
Editor: Georgia Tolley
Fashion, Weddings

BEG Bicycles blog   1052621
Tel: 44 01223 655222
Email: hello@begbicycles.com
Web site: http://www.begbicycles.com/blog/
Freq: Daily
Circ: 16
Bicycles

Behind Green Eyes   1053702
Web site: www.behindgreeneyes.com
Freq: Daily
Circ: 9027
Beauty & Grooming, Cooking & Baking, Cosmetics, Hair, Literature, Women's Interests

Beijing Boyce   1061945
Email: beijingboyce@yahoo.com
Web site: http://www.beijingboyce.com
Freq: Daily
Circ: 3995
Alcohol & Spirits, Bars, Clubs & Pubs

BeijingMan   1061957
Email: beijingman@me.com
Web site: http://beijingman.blogspot.com
Freq: Daily
Circ: 3176
Business, Small and Medium Business

Being a Mummy   988076
Email: claire@beingamummy.co.uk
Web site: beingamummy.co.uk
Freq: Daily
Circ: 8823
Family & Parenting

being little   987440
Email: beinglittle@hotmail.co.uk
Web site: http://www.beinglittle.co.uk/
Freq: Daily
Circ: 47314

Editor: Lyzi Unwin
Profile: Blog covering fashion. being little blog discusses anything from fashion and art to food, drink, lifestyle, cats and events. The blog has an archive dating back to August 2010 and shares an extensive blog roll.
Art, Fashion, Women's Interests

Being Mrs C   998214
Web site: beingmrsc.com
Freq: Daily
Circ: 9143
Cooking & Baking, Crafts, Family & Parenting

Beisbol   1062034
Web site: http://www.debeisbol.com
Freq: Daily
Circ: 1378
Bankruptcy, Company News & Appointments, Consumer Interest, Corporate Law, Criminal Law, Employment, Estate Planning, Family Law, Federal Courts, Food & Drug Administration

Beisbol 007   1061484
Web site: http://beisbol007.blogia.com/
Freq: Daily
Circ: 873
News & Current Affairs

Belelú   1060416
Tel: 44 56258 30077
Email: belelu@betazeta.com
Web site: http://www.belelu.com
Freq: Daily
Circ: 150514
Bars, Clubs & Pubs, Celebrities, Comedy, Entertainment, Fashion, Fitness & Exercise, Lifestyle, Local Entertainment Guides, Men's Interests, Movies & Video

Belfast Metalheads Reunited   1054099
Web site: http://www.belfastmetalheadsreunited.blogspot.co.uk/
Freq: Daily
Circ: 1897
Rock Music

Belize Hub   1061570
Tel: 44 50160 10315
Email: info@belizehub.com
Web site: http://www.belizehub.com
Freq: Daily
Circ: 13528
Airline Inflight, Hotels/Motels, Railroad, Travel

Bell & Smokey   1054307
Web site: bellandsmokey.com
Freq: Daily
Circ: 11232
Profile: Bell & Smokey covers fashion, interior design, art, architecture and lifestyle. The blog has an archive dating back to June 2012.
Do-It-Yourself (DIY), Fashion, Travel, Women's Interests

Bella Caledonia   988436
Editorial: PO Box 26866, Burntisland KY2 9BY
Email: bellasletters@yahoo.co.uk
Web site: http://bellacaledonia.org.uk/
Freq: Daily
Circ: 161838
Editor: Mike Small
Politics

Bellahouston Road Runners   1052918
Email: info@bellahoustonroadrunners.co.uk
Web site: www.bellahoustonroadrunners.co.uk/news/
Freq: Daily
Circ: 25
Fitness & Exercise

Belle & Boo   1054049
Email: hello@belleandboo.com
Web site: http://belleandboo.blogspot.co.uk/
Freq: Daily
Circ: 965
Crafts

Belle Du Brighton   987933
Email: bdbrighton@live.co.uk
Web site: www.belledubrighton.co.uk
Freq: Daily
Circ: 52595
Profile: Blog covering lifestyle. BELLE DU BRIGHTON blog discusses anything from lifestyle and food to fashion, beauty, photography and parenting. The blog has an archive dating back to September 2011 and shares an extensive blog roll. The outlet offers RSS (Really Simple Syndication).
Alcohol & Spirits, Bars, Clubs & Pubs, Beer, Beverages, Cooking & Baking, Family & Parenting, Food, Grocery Stores, Organic Food, Regional General Interest

Belle Jar   1064620
Freq: Daily
Editor: Louisa Ackermann
Social Issues, Women's Interests

Belle Magazine   1076646
Web site: www.bellemag.co.uk
Freq: Daily
Circ: 14973
Beauty & Grooming, Cooking & Baking, Cosmetics, Fashion, Hair, Restaurant Reviews, Travel, Women's Interests

Belleau Kitchen   986973
Editorial: Belleau Cottage, Belleau, Alford LN13 0BP
Web site: http://www.belleaukitchen.com/
Freq: Daily
Circ: 9231
Cooking & Baking, Restaurant Reviews

Belleza   1061352
Web site: http://www.webdelabelleza.com
Freq: Daily
Circ: 27249
Fashion, Fitness & Exercise, Health & Medicine

Bempton Birder   1053344
Web site: http://rugbybirder.blogspot.co.uk/
Freq: Daily
Circ: 13300
Cameras, Nature & Wildlife

Bemused Backpacker   988502
Email: bemusedbackpacker@gmail.com
Web site: http://bemusedbackpacker.com/
Freq: Daily
Circ: 11854
Profile: Blog covering budget travel and backpacking. The blog has an archive dating back to May 2013.
Travel

Ben Olivares Photography Blog   1061272
Web site: http://www.benolivares.com/blog
Freq: Daily
Circ: 39
Auto Aftermarket, Computers, Data Management, Electronics, Government Technology, Industry, Internet, Mobile Communications, Security & Security Systems, Software

Benny No Pals   997208
Web site: http://bennynopals.blogspot.co.uk/
Freq: Daily
Circ: 521
Dance Music

Berekvam   1060792
Web site: http://berekvam.com/blog/
Freq: Daily
Circ: 71
Classical/Choral/Band Music, Country, Folk, Bluegrass, Dance Music, Jazz & Blues, Music, Pop Music, R&B, Urban, World, Rap & Hip Hop, Rock Music

Berice Baby   1053583
Web site: bericebaby.co.uk
Freq: Daily
Circ: 67731
Family & Parenting, Travel, Women's Interests

Berimbau Drum   1053230
Email: berimbaudrum@yahoo.co.uk
Web site: berimbaudrum.org/
Freq: Daily
Circ: 10709
Country, Folk, Bluegrass, Jazz & Blues, Music, R&B, Urban, World, Rap & Hip Hop, Rock Music

The Berimbolo Kid - CEASED   997984
Web site: http://giorcardo1394.blogspot.co.uk/
Freq: Daily
Circ: 521
Martial Arts, MMA & Self-Defense

Berkeley PR Blog   1053686
Freq: Daily
Branding, Marketing

Berry Bros & Rudd Blog   1100579
Web site: http://bbrblog.com
Freq: Daily
Circ: 14849
Wine/Winemaking

Bertha Fréitez   1060993
Web site: http://berthafreitez.blogspot.com/
Freq: Daily
Circ: 521
Antiques/Collectibles, Art, Arts, Classical/Choral/Band Music, Country, Folk, Bluegrass, Dance Music, Jazz & Blues, Literature, Music, Photography

Bespoke Bride   988376
Email: admin@bespoke-bride.com
Web site: www.bespoke-bride.com
Freq: Daily
Circ: 43258
Weddings

Best Beginnings blog   997681
Editorial: 12 Vale Royal, London N7 9AP
Tel: 44 02074 437895
Email: info@bestbeginnings.org.uk
Web site: https://www.bestbeginnings.org.uk/Blogs/our-ceos-blog
Freq: Daily
Circ: 12911
Pediatrics

Best For Film - CEASED   986086
Web site: bestforfilm.com/film-blog/
Freq: Daily
Circ: ?
Movies & Video

Best Ski Resorts   996737
Web site: http://www.piste-maps.co.uk/Blog
Freq: Daily
Circ: 2496
Travel, Winter Sports

Bethanie Lunn Blog   997441
Email: bethanie.lunn@googlemail.com
Web site: http://bethanielunn.com/
Freq: Daily
Circ: 2871
News & Current Affairs

Better Raw   997936
Web site: betterraw.com/
Freq: Daily
Circ: 6403
News & Current Affairs

between the acts   998144
Web site: julieraby.com
Freq: Daily
Circ: 885
Entertainment, Literature, Theater & Performing Arts

Bex Howells   988931
Web site: https://bexhowells.blogspot.co.uk/
Freq: Daily
Circ: 521
Profile: Blog covering beauty, lifestyle and fashion. The blog has an archive dating back to May 2013.
Beauty & Grooming, Cosmetics, Fashion, Hair, Travel, Women's Interests

Bex Trex to teaching 1054367
Web site: http://bex-trex2teaching.blogspot.co.uk
Freq: Daily
Circ: 1319
News & Current Affairs

Bexsonn 1053997
Email: info@bexsonn.com
Web site: http://www.bexsonn.com/
Freq: Daily
Circ: 8644
Profile: Bexsonn blog covers luxury watches and whiskys. The blog has an archive dating back to January 2013.
Alcohol & Spirits, Luxury Goods

Beyond Retro Vintage Blog
994974
Editorial: 110-112 Cheshire Street, London E2 6EJ Tel: 44 02077 299001
Email: info@beyondretro.com
Web site: http://www.beyondretro.com/en/blog/
Freq: Daily
Circ: 160
Fashion

Beyond the Bathroom Scale
987065
Email: features@beyondthebathroomscale.co.uk
Web site: http://www.beyondthebathroomscale.co.uk/
Freq: Daily
Circ: 12814
Profile: Blog covering personal health, dieting, fitness and exercise. The blog has an archive dating back to April 2012.
Health & Medicine, Nutrition

Bi Blawggers International
1061245
Web site: http://blawggersinternacionales.blogspot.com/
Freq: Daily
Circ: 1430
Government

Bib&Sola 996781
Email: bibandsolablog@gmail.com
Web site: www.bibandsola.com
Freq: Daily
Circ: 1827
Regional General Interest

Biblioteca de Asterión 1061227
Web site: http://labibliotecadeasterion.blogspot.com/
Freq: Daily
Circ: 1568
Books, Literature

Bicycle-cards 1056562
Web site: http://www.bicycle-cards.co.uk/
Freq: Daily
Circ: 7747
Crafts

Bien Ahi 1061943
Web site: http://bienahi.blogspot.com/
Freq: Daily
Circ: 857
Lifestyle, Men's Interests, Regional General Interest, Women's Interests

Bien Tapatios 1061534
Web site: http://www.bientapatios.com
Freq: Daily
Circ: 1406
Antiques/Collectibles, Art, Arts, Literature, National News, Photography, Theater & Performing Arts, Visual Arts

Bien Verde 1061676
Email: bienverde@lanacion.com.ar
Web site: http://blogs.lanacion.com.ar/bien-verde/
Freq: Daily
Circ: 1661
Alternative/Renewable Energy, Environment, Sustainable Development

Bienvividos 1061285
Web site: http://blogs.lanacion.com.ar/bienvividos-calidad-de-vida/

Freq: Daily
Circ: 1
Lifestyle, Men's Interests, Neurology, Regional General Interest, Women's Interests

Bieren Fangqi, Wo Jianchi
1060935
Email: hbyrt2010@vip.sina.com
Web site: http://blog.sina.com.cn/hbhwlyrtsl
Freq: Daily
Circ: 89144
Banking, Financial Markets

Big Brother Watch 986087
Editorial: 55 Tufton Street, London SW1P 3QL Tel: 44 02073 406030
Email: info@bigbrotherwatch.org.uk
Web site: https://bigbrotherwatch.org.uk/blog/
Freq: Daily
Politics

Big Eyes Little Soles 998061
Email: contact@bigeyeslittlesoles.com
Web site: http://www.bigeyeslittlesoles.com
Freq: Daily
Circ: 9823
Cooking & Baking, Fashion, Fitness & Exercise, Food, Grocery Stores, Organic Food, Restaurant Reviews, Travel, Vegetarianism & Veganism

Big Gay Picture Show Blog
996992
Editorial: The Senate, Southernhay Gardens, Exeter EX1 1UG
Tel: 44 01392 434831
Email: enquiries@biggaypictureshow.com
Web site: http://www.biggaypictureshow.com/bgps/
Freq: Daily
Circ: 23141
Entertainment, LGBT, Movies & Video

Big Look See - CEASED 1053361
Web site: http://biglooksee.com/
Freq: Daily
Circ: 1195
News & Current Affairs

Big Red Barrel 997921
Email: management@bigredbarrel.com
Web site: http://www.bigredbarrel.com/blog/
Freq: Daily
Circ: 12757
Computer & Video Games

Big Spud 986228
Web site: www.bigspud.co.uk
Freq: Daily
Circ: 7404
Cooking & Baking, Grocery Stores

BigMae.com 1060406
Web site: http://www.bigmae.com
Freq: Daily
Circ: 13727
Elementary School, Family & Parenting, Lifestyle, Men's Interests, Preschool, Regional General Interest, Teen/Young Adult, Trading Cards & Comics, Women's Interests

The Bijou Bride 999552
Email: info@thebijoubride.com
Web site: thebijoubride.com/blog/
Freq: Daily
Circ: 93
Editor: Alexandra Merri
Weddings

The Bike Insurer 999593
Editorial: Customer Services Department, The Bike Insurer, 8 Princes Parade, Liverpool L3 1DL Tel: 44 08702 258207
Email: customer.services@thebikeinsurer.co.uk
Web site: https://www.thebikeinsurer.co.uk/motorbike-news/
Freq: Daily
Circ: 131
Motorcycles

Bikes n' stuff 1054316
Email: juliet@finalagency.com
Web site: http://www.bikes-n-stuff.com/
Freq: Daily
Circ: 9221
Profile: Blog covering cycling.
Bicycles, Extreme/Adventure Sports

bikinis and bibs 1052554
Web site: http://bikinisandbibs.co.uk/
Freq: Daily
Circ: 10729
Family & Parenting, Fashion, Luxury Goods, Travel, Women's Interests

Binary Law 986617
Web site: http://www.binarylaw.co.uk/
Freq: Daily
Circ: 9056
News & Current Affairs

Binary Moon 1052850
Web site: binarymoon.co.uk
Freq: Daily
Circ: 128146
Computer & Video Games, Graphic Design, Internet

Binny's Kitchen & Travel Diaries 1095954
Email: binnyjs@yahoo.co.uk
Web site: https://binnyskitchen.com/
Freq: Daily
Circ: 12841
Cooking & Baking, Restaurant Reviews, Travel, Women's Interests

bioBlogia 1060383
Web site: http://www.bioblogia.com
Freq: Daily
Circ: 1078
Science

Biología Estupenda 1061569
Web site: http://blogs.elcorreo.com/labiologiaestupenda/posts
Freq: Daily
Circ: 16
Science

BioMed Central blog 1054541
Editorial: Floor 6, 236 Gray's Inn Road, London WC1X 8HB
Email: blogging@biomedcentral.com
Web site: blogs.biomedcentral.com/bmcblog
Freq: Daily
Circ: 66
Science

Bip Ling Blog 1053446
Email: mooch@bipling.com
Web site: http://www.bipling.com/
Freq: Daily
Circ: 7681
Comedy, Fashion, Women's Interests

Bird and Bug Diaries 1100164
Web site: http://birdandbugdiaries.blogspot.co.uk/
Freq: Daily
Circ: 493
Nature & Wildlife

Birds on the Blog 1054377
Web site: http://birdsontheblog.co.uk/blog/
Freq: Daily
Circ: 59
Business

Birmingham Live! 998289
Email: steve@brumlive.com
Web site: http://www.brumlive.com/
Freq: Daily
Circ: 8667
Classical/Choral/Band Music, Country, Folk, Bluegrass, Dance Music, Jazz & Blues, Music, Pop Music, R&B, Urban, World, Rap & Hip Hop, Rock Music

Bishopston Mum 1054353
Email: bishopstonmum@hotmail.co.uk
Web site: http://bishopstonmum.com/
Freq: Daily
Circ: 11562
Family & Parenting

Bisous Natasha 987398
Email: contact@bisousnatasha.com
Web site: www.bisousnatasha.com
Freq: Daily
Circ: 21263
Beauty & Grooming, Cosmetics, Fashion, Hair, Photography, Travel

Bit Parade 997821
Web site: http://bitparade.co.uk/
Freq: Daily
Circ: 11562
Computer & Video Games

Bitchy Online UK 997736
Email: info@bitchyonlineuk.com
Web site: http://www.bitchyonline.com/
Freq: Daily
Circ: 9689
Broadcasting, Celebrities, Fashion, Rap & Hip Hop

Bitelia 1060988
Web site: http://www.bitelia.com
Freq: Daily
Circ: 3782
Auto Aftermarket, Computers, Data Management, Electronics, Government Technology, Industry, Internet, Mobile Communications, Security & Security Systems, Software

Bitterwallet 986569
Web site: www.bitterwallet.com
Freq: Daily
Circ: 90534
News & Current Affairs

Bixelart 1061075
Web site: http://www.bixelart.com.ve/
Freq: Daily
Circ: 474
Art, Auto Aftermarket, Computers, Data Management, Electronics, Government Technology, Industry, Internet, Mobile Communications, National News

Bizzimummy's World 997311
Tel: 44 07393 735561
Email: bizzimummy@gmail.com
Web site: www.bizzimummy.com
Freq: Daily
Circ: 12287
Family & Parenting

Black Budget Entertainment
1052801
Email: blackbudgetuk@gmail.com
Web site: http://black-budget.com/
Freq: Daily
Circ: 12369
Rap & Hip Hop

Black Marble Blog - But It Works On My PC! 1053043
Web site: blogs.blackmarble.co.uk/blogs/rfennell/default.aspx
Freq: Daily
Circ: 38650
Software

The Black Pearl Blog 1053585
Email: contact@theblackpearlblog.com
Web site: www.theblackpearlblog.com
Freq: Daily
Circ: 31426
Beauty & Grooming, Cooking & Baking, Cosmetics, Do-It-Yourself (DIY), Family & Parenting, Fashion, Hair, Restaurant Reviews, Women's Interests

Black Plastic 1056774
Web site: http://blackplastic.co.uk/
Freq: Daily
Circ: 7891
Dance Music

Blackbullion 987476
Tel: 44 08008 089533
Email: enquiries@blackbullion.co.uk
Web site: http://www.blackbullion.com/
Freq: Daily
Circ: 12449
Editor: Vivi Friedgut
Profile: Blog covering money management and financial planning for both personal and

business use. The blog has an archive dating back to November 2011.

Blazing Minds
1054098
Email: kazwebadmin@blazingminds.co.uk
Web site: http://blazingminds.co.uk/
Freq: Daily
Circ: 126663
Bars, Clubs & Pubs, Comedy, Entertainment, Local Entertainment Guides, Movies & Video

Bleeding Cool
987386
Editorial: 8 Robin Hood Lane, Kingston Vale, London SW15 3PU
Tel: 44 07801 350982
Web site: www.bleedingcool.com
Freq: Daily
Circ: 1528521
Editor: Rich Johnston
Computer & Video Games, Movies & Video

Blender and Basil
1099578
Editorial: Flat 39 Chedworth House, West Green Road, London N15 5EH
Email: blenderandbasil@gmail.com
Web site: https://blenderandbasil.com/
Freq: Daily
Circ: 10969
Alcohol & Spirits, Bars, Clubs & Pubs, Beer, Beverages, Cooking & Baking, Wine/Winemaking

Bloc de Periodista
1061210
Email: blog@blocdeperiodista.com
Web site: http://www.blocdeperiodista.com/
Freq: Daily
Circ: 11064
National News, Politics, Shopping

Blog Me Beautiful
986289
Editorial: Crackley Cottage, Sheerwater Avenue, Addlestone, London KT15 3DR
Email: blogmebeautiful@hotmail.co.uk
Web site: http://www.blog-me-beautiful.com
Freq: Daily
Circ: 9777
Beauty & Grooming, Cosmetics, Hair

Blog.SpoonGraphics
986088
Web site: https://blog.spoongraphics.co.uk/
Freq: Daily
Circ: 1901033
Editor: Chris Spooner
Antiques/Collectibles, Art, Photography, Visual Arts

Bloggerheads
1053902
Web site: http://www.bloggerheads.com
Freq: Daily
Circ: 17159
Marketing, Politics

Bloggers [heart] Books
997033
Email: bloggers-heart-books@hotmail.co.uk
Web site: http://bloggers-heart-books.blogspot.co.uk/
Freq: Daily
Circ: 1113
Literature

The Bloggers' Lounge
996524
Web site: http://www.bloggers-lounge.co.uk
Freq: Daily
Circ: 61114
News & Current Affairs

Blogging from the Pyrenees
1054009
Tel: 44 02081 235049
Email: info@hikepyrenees.co.uk
Web site: http://www.hikepyrenees.co.uk/blog/page/2/
Freq: Daily
Circ: 6076
Travel, Winter Sports

Blomma London - SUS-PENDED MARCH 2017
1053931
Web site: www.blommalondon.com/
Freq: Daily
Circ: 3242

Profile: Blog covering home decorating and lifestyle. The blog has an archive dating back to June 2014.
Do-It-Yourself (DIY)

Blonde Across the Pond
1099265
Editorial: Flat 10, 3 Singer Mews, Clapham, London SW4 6AX
Email: blondeacrossthepondcm@gmail.com
Web site: blondeacrossthepond.com
Freq: Daily
Circ: 9399
Beauty & Grooming, Cooking & Baking, Cosmetics, Do-It-Yourself (DIY), Hair, Restaurant Reviews, Travel, Wine/Winemaking

bloody hell BRENNAN
996663
Email: bloodyhellbrennan@live.com
Web site: www.bloodyhellbrennan.com
Freq: Daily
Circ: 10206
Regional General Interest

BLOOMZY
987996
Web site: http://www.bloomzy.co.uk
Freq: Daily
Circ: 10772
Profile: Blog covering lifestyle. BLOOMZY blog discusses anything from fashion and beauty to lifestyle. The outlet offers RSS (Really Simple Syndication).
Cosmetics, Fashion, Women's Interests

Blue Glass
1053387
Editorial: BlueGlass Interactive UK Ltd, 45 Leather Lane, London EC1N 7TJ
Web site: http://www.blueglass.co.uk/blog/
Freq: Daily
Circ: 69
Marketing

The Blue Guerilla
997576
Email: editor@theblueguerilla.co.uk
Web site: http://www.theblueguerilla.co.uk/
Freq: Daily
Circ: 9610
Politics

Blue Loafers
1054560
Web site: http://blueloafers.com/
Freq: Daily
Circ: 8155
Fashion

The Blue Walrus
988609
Editorial: 40 Southwell Road, London SE5 9PG
Email: staff@thebluewalrus.com
Web site: http://thebluewalrus.com/
Freq: Daily
Circ: 24143
Editor: Tim Dickinson
Classical/Choral/Band Music, Country, Folk, Bluegrass, Dance Music, Jazz & Blues, Music, Pop Music, R&B, Urban, World, Rap & Hip Hop, Rock Music

Blueberry Park
1054397
Email: karen@karenlewistextiles.com
Web site: http://blueberry-park.blogspot.co.uk/
Freq: Daily
Circ: 1700
Crafts

bluesky blog
1053022
Tel: 44 01530 518518
Email: enquiries@bluesky-world.com
Web site: http://www.bluesky-world.com/#!news/cmw2
Freq: Daily
Circ: 9332
Data Management, Environment

Blush Crafts Blog
1054668
Email: blushcrafts@gmail.com
Web site: www.blush-crafts.com
Freq: Daily
Circ: 10242
Crafts

BMW Automotive
1056315
Web site: http://bmwautomotive.co.uk
Freq: Daily
Circ: 521
Automakers, Driving

Boagworld blog
1053798
Web site: https://boagworld.com/blog
Freq: Daily
Circ: 76
Marketing

Boak and Bailey's Beer Blog
986091
Web site: boakandbailey.com
Freq: Daily
Circ: 13346
News & Current Affairs

Bobby Rabbit
1053123
Email: hello@bobbyrabbit.co.uk
Web site: www.bobbyrabbit.co.uk
Freq: Daily
Circ: 6882
Profile: Blog covering children's interiors and toys. The blog has an archive dating back to November 2012.
Do-It-Yourself (DIY)

BobfromBrockley
1052561
Web site: brockley.blogspot.co.uk
Freq: Daily
Circ: 10417
Politics

BODIE and FOU Blog
1053905
Email: leblog@bodieandfou.com
Web site: karinecandicekong.com
Freq: Daily
Circ: 23035
Do-It-Yourself (DIY), Fashion, Nutrition, Women's Interests

Bodykind
1052711
Tel: 44 08000 435566
Email: info@bodykind.com
Web site: http://blog.bodykind.com/
Freq: Daily
Circ: 19
Nutrition

Boho Weddings
987279
Editorial: 27 Rivelin Valley Road, Sheffield S6 5FE
Web site: http://www.boho-weddings.com
Freq: Daily
Circ: 45315
Fashion, Weddings

Bombay Rose
998417
Email: bombayroseblog@gmail.com
Web site: http://www.bombayrose.co.uk/
Freq: Daily
Circ: 1936
Alternative Medicine, Beauty & Grooming, Cosmetics, Fashion, Fitness & Exercise, Hair, Health & Medicine, Nutrition, Women's Interests

The Bon Vivant Journal
995742
Editorial: 78 York Street, London W1H 1DP
Tel: 44 02031 413000
Email: info@bonvivant.co.uk
Web site: http://www.bonvivant.co.uk/journal/
Freq: Daily
Circ: 7631
Editor: Emyr Thomas
Airline Inflight, Alcohol & Spirits, Bars, Clubs & Pubs, Beer, Beverages, Cooking & Baking, Food, Grocery Stores, Organic Food, Railroad

Bond Vigilantes
1053561
Email: bondvigilantes@mandg.co.uk
Web site: https://www.bondvigilantes.com/
Freq: Daily
Circ: 26876
Economics, Financial Markets

Bone White China
1053694
Email: bonewhitechina@gmail.com
Web site: bonewhitechina.co.uk
Freq: Daily
Circ: 10709
Profile: Blog covering food and lifestyle in Cambridgeshire. The blog has an archive dating back to March 2011.
Cooking & Baking, Family & Parenting, Fashion, Fitness & Exercise, Food, Grocery Stores, Nutrition, Organic Food, Regional General Interest, Restaurant Reviews

Bonjour, Blogger
996766
Editorial: 300 Badminton Road, Winterbourne, Bristol BS36 1AQ
Email: pr@bonjourblogger.com
Web site: http://www.bonjourblogger.com
Freq: Daily
Circ: 24331
Audio Video Trade, Branding, Cameras, Consumer Electronics, Electronics, Graphic Design, Marketing, Mobile Electronics, Movies & Video, Publishing

Boo & Maddie
1054154
Web site: booandmaddie.com
Freq: Daily
Circ: 8764
Do-It-Yourself (DIY), Property Management & Maintenance

Boo Roo and Tigger Too
1054106
Email: boorooandtiggertoo@gmail.com
Web site: http://www.boorooandtiggertoo.com/
Freq: Daily
Circ: 32732
Profile: Blog covering family. The Boo Roo and Tigger Too blog discusses anything from working mum life and family life.
Do-It-Yourself (DIY), Family & Parenting, Fashion, Relationships, Travel, Women's Interests

Book Angel Booktopia
1054437
Web site: bookangelbooktopia.com
Freq: Daily
Circ: 11369
Profile: Blog covering new adult and young adult fiction.
Literature

The Book Carousel
1055307
Email: thebookcarouselreviews@gmail.com
Web site: http://www.thebookcarousel.co.uk/
Freq: Daily
Circ: 521
Literature

The Book Jotter
997272
Web site: http://josbookjourney.wordpress.com/
Freq: Daily
Circ: 83
Literature

The Book Smugglers
987307
Email: contact@thebooksmugglers.com
Web site: thebooksmugglers.com
Freq: Daily
Circ: 65757
Literature

The Bookette
1053042
Email: thebookette@gmail.com
Web site: http://www.thebookette.co.uk
Freq: Daily
Circ: 3171
Literature

Bookish Magpie
1053698
Email: bookishmagpie@gmail.com
Web site: http://bookishmagpie.blogspot.co.uk/
Freq: Daily
Circ: 480
Literature

Bookmunch
1054608
Email: mrpwild@googlemail.com
Web site: https://bookmunch.wordpress.com/
Freq: Daily
Circ: 199
Editor: Peter Wild
Literature

Books, Mud and Compost. And Horses.
1052630
Email: enquiries@janebadgerbooks.co.uk
Web site: http://booksandmud.blogspot.co.uk/
Freq: Daily
Circ: 490
Literature, Regional General Interest

UK Blogs

Bookshelf 1053370
Email: alex.johnson@empathymedia.co.uk
Web site: http://www.onthebookshelf.co.uk/
Freq: Daily
Circ: 9143
Do-It-Yourself (DIY)

BookTrust blogs 988576
Editorial: Booktrust, G8 Battersea Studios,
80 Silverthorne Road, London SW8 3HE
Tel: 44 02078 018800
Email: websites@booktrust.org.uk
Web site: http://www.booktrust.org.uk/
news-and-blogs/blogs/
Freq: Daily
Circ: 18
Literature

The BOOM Moment 996065
Web site: http://theboommoment.blogspot.
co.uk/
Freq: Daily
Circ: 10709
Africa, Art, Broadcasting, Cooking &
Baking, Dance Music, Expatriates,
Fashion, Fitness & Exercise, Jazz & Blues,
Literature

The Bootcamp Pilates Blog
987316
Email: info@bootcamppilates.com
Web site: www.bootcamppilates.com/blog
Freq: Daily
Circ: 2
Profile: BOOTCAMP PILATES blog covers
healthy living, nutrition and fitness. The blog
is hosted by bootcamppilates.com.
Fitness & Exercise

Booze, Beats & Bites 988143
Editorial: 4 Irstead Road, Norwich NR5 8AR
Web site: http://www.boozebeatsbites.co.
uk/
Freq: Daily
Circ: 11861
Beer, Restaurant Reviews

Borders of Adventure 1053447
Email: bordersofadventure@gmail.com
Web site: www.bordersofadventure.com
Freq: Daily
Circ: 47406
Profile: Blog covering travel. 'The blog
focuses on adventures with a social
conscience and journeys to change
perceptions, with insight into social,
historical, political and economic factors that
shape the country. The blogger regularly
reports on misunderstood destinations, and
if travelling to a well-established or popular
destination, aims to find a different angle on
it in order to entice readers to dig a little
deeper.'
Airline Inflight, Railroad, Travel

Born Free Blog 986093
Editorial: Broadlands Business Campus,
Langhurstwood Road, Horsham RH12 4QP
Tel: 44 01403 240170
Email: info@bornfree.org.uk
Web site: bornfree.org.uk/blog/
Freq: Daily
Circ: 16
Profile: Blog covering the latest news on
animal welfare, conservation and education.
The blog has an archive dating back to
February 2007.
Charitable Foundations, Energy &
Environment

Botica del Espectaculo 1061522
Web site: http://www.boticadelespectaculo.
com/
Freq: Daily
Circ: 611
Theater & Performing Arts

Botica Pop 1061485
Web site: http://www.boticapop.com
Freq: Daily
Circ: 7852
Bars, Clubs & Pubs, Comedy,
Entertainment, Fashion, Local
Entertainment Guides, Movies & Video

Boulezian 1053060
Web site: http://boulezian.blogspot.co.uk/
Freq: Daily

Circ: 9390
Classical/Choral/Band Music

The Bourbonator 1054498
Email: thebourbonator@yahoo.co.uk
Web site: www.thebourbonator.co.uk
Freq: Daily
Circ: 611
Alcohol & Spirits, Bars, Clubs & Pubs

Box Office Football 997545
Email: mail@boxofficefootball.com
Web site: http://www.boxofficefootball.com/
category/blog/
Freq: Daily
Circ: 15
Editor: Gazza Hanafin
Soccer

The Boy and Me 986702
Email: me@theboyandme.co.uk
Web site: http://www.theboyandme.co.uk
Freq: Daily
Circ: 49138
Family & Parenting

Boy from Dagbon 987922
Email: info@boyfromdagbon.com
Web site: www.boyfromdagbon.com
Freq: Daily
Circ: 8434
Fashion

Boy Meets Fashion 1052718
Web site: http://www.boymeetsfashion.
com/
Freq: Daily
Circ: 11969
Fashion

The boy who ate the world
1054519
Web site: http://theboywhoatetheworld.
com/
Freq: Daily
Circ: 2318
Cooking & Baking, Food, Grocery Stores,
Organic Food, Restaurant Reviews,
Travel, Vegetarianism & Veganism

BPS Research Digest 996195
Web site: https://digest.bps.org.uk/
Freq: Daily
Circ: 313686
Neurology

Bradley Howard's blog 1053907
Editorial: 13th floor, 125 Old Broad Street,
London EC2N 1AR
Web site: http://www.bradbox.com/blog/
Freq: Daily
Circ: 373
Profile: Blog covering technology and its
use in business. Bradley Howard's Blog
discusses anything from technology trends
and digital media to consumer loyalty and
consumer innovation. The outlet offers RSS
(Really Simple Syndication).
Business, Industry, Internet, Mobile
Electronics

brand-e 985612
Web site: http://brand-e.biz
Freq: Daily
Circ: 43697
Editor: Steve Mullins
Branding

Branded3 Blog 1053739
Tel: 44 01132 604010
Email: contact@branded3.com
Web site: www.branded3.com/blog
Freq: Daily
Circ: 408
Branding, Marketing

Brandish - CEASED 984635
Editorial: Sutro Digital, Grand Parade, 47
Bermondsey Street, London SE1 3XT
Web site: www.brandish.tv
Freq: Daily
Circ: 11928
Men's Interests

Brandwatch Blog 1053203
Editorial: Sovereign House, Church Street,
1st Floor, Brighton BN1 1UJ
Tel: 44 01273 234290
Web site: www.brandwatch.com/blog/
Freq: Daily
Circ: 18776
Branding, Business, Marketing

Brasil Olímpico 1060652
Web site: http://brasilnaolimpiada.blogspot.
com
Freq: Daily
Circ: 475
Olympic Sports

Break Out the Skinny Girl
1074211
Email: admin@breakouttheskinnygirl.com
Web site: http://www.breakouttheskinny.
com
Freq: Daily
Circ: 1360
Health & Medicine, Nutrition

Breakfast by the Sea 1053172
Freq: Daily
Profile: Blog covering food photography.
The breakfast by the sea blog discusses
anything from food photography and food
reviews. The blog has an archive dating back
to July 2011.
News & Current Affairs

Breastfeeding Mums CEASED
996503
Web site: www.breastfeedingmums.com
Freq: Daily
Circ: 6576
Family & Parenting

Brett, the Wine Maestro 1094460
Web site: http://www.thewinemaestro.co.
uk/
Freq: Daily
Circ: 6588
Wine/Winemaking

The Brew 988638
Email: info@thebrew.me
Web site: www.thebrew.me
Freq: Daily
Circ: 8465
Editor: Tara Illingworth
Fashion, Travel, Women's Interests

Brew Geekery 995014
Editorial: 123 Hudson Apartments, Hornsey,
London N8 7RW
Web site: www.brewgeekery.com
Freq: Daily
Circ: 11671
Bars, Clubs & Pubs, Beer, Cooking &
Baking, Restaurant Reviews

Brian Micklethwait's Blog
1053101
Web site: brianmicklethwait.com
Freq: Daily
Circ: 752
Men's Interests, Politics, Regional
General Interest, Social Issues

The Brick Castle 998215
Email: thebrickcastle@gmail.com
Web site: thebrickcastle.com
Freq: Daily
Circ: 13396
Family & Parenting

Brick Dust & Glitter 997390
Editorial: 20 Shelley Drive, Lincoln LN2 4BY
Web site: http://brickdustandglitter.
blogspot.co.uk
Freq: Daily
Circ: 11112
Beauty & Grooming, Cooking & Baking,
Cosmetics, Do-It-Yourself (DIY), Family &
Parenting, Fashion, Grocery Stores, Hair,
Organic Food, Travel

Bridal Musings 998233
Email: info@bridalmusings.com
Web site: http://www.bridalmusings.com/
Freq: Daily

Circ: 618118
Weddings

BrideDeForce 987610
Editorial: Fleur De Force Ltd C/O Derek
Westaway, Westaway Motors, Boughton
Green Road, Moulton Park, Northampton
NN2 7AH
Email: bridedeforce@gmail.com
Web site: http://www.bridedeforce.com/
Freq: Daily
Circ: 10420
Weddings

Brides Up North 987271
Email: contact@bridesupnorth.co.uk
Web site: bridesupnorth.com
Freq: Daily
Circ: 25237
Weddings

Bridge of Memories 1054015
Web site: http://www.bridgeofmemories.co.
uk/
Freq: Daily
Circ: 9980
Profile: Blog covering lifestyle. A bridge of
memories blog discusses anything from
fashion and photography to travel and
lifestyle. The blog has an archive dating back
to January 2011.
Fashion, Photography, Regional General
Interest, Travel, Women's Interests

BriefBlog 1061136
Web site: http://www.briefblog.com.mx
Freq: Daily
Circ: 4821
Advertising Industry, Marketing

Bright Green 987823
Email: editors@bright-green.org
Web site: http://bright-green.org/
Freq: Daily
Circ: 18698
Energy & Environment, Environment

Bright.Bazaar 1053489
Web site: http://www.brightbazaarblog.
com/
Freq: Daily
Circ: 51239
Editor: Will Taylor
Do-It-Yourself (DIY), Fashion, Men's
Interests, Travel

BrightHouse Blog 1054508
Editorial: BrightHouse Customer Relations,
5 Hercules Way, Leavesden Park, Watford
WD25 7GS Tel: 44 08005 26069
Web site: https://www.brighthouse.co.uk/
blog
Freq: Daily
Circ: 19
Personal Finance, Shopping

Brighton Bits 1052980
Web site: http://brightonbits.blogspot.co.uk/
Freq: Daily
Circ: 521
Regional General Interest

bringingupcharlie.co.uk 985497
Email: thedotterel@gmail.com
Web site: www.bringingupcharlie.co.uk
Freq: Daily
Circ: 16627
Family & Parenting

Bristol Bites 986490
Editorial: 12 Perretts Court, Cumberland
Road, Bristol BS1 6UF
Web site: www.bristolbites.co.uk
Circ: 45420
Editor: Emily Knight
Profile: Website covering food and drink in
Bristol. Bristol Bites discusses the latest
news on restaurants, recipes, events and
deals.
Alcohol & Spirits, Bars, Clubs & Pubs,
Beer, Beverages, Cooking & Baking,
Food, Grocery Stores, Organic Food,
Restaurant Reviews, Vegetarianism &
Veganism

Bristol Eating Adventures
998090
Email: bristoleatingadventures@gmail.com
Web site: http://bristoleatingadventures.
blogspot.co.uk/
Freq: Daily
Circ: 10387
Cooking & Baking, Restaurant Reviews

Bristol Foodie
998094
Email: info@bristolfoodie.co.uk
Web site: www.bristolfoodie.co.uk
Freq: Daily
Circ: 1633
Alcohol & Spirits, Bars, Clubs & Pubs, Beer, Beverages, Cooking & Baking, Food, Grocery Stores, Organic Food, Restaurant Reviews, Vegetarianism & Veganism

Brit Decor
1053916
Web site: http://www.britdecor.co.uk/
Freq: Daily
Circ: 8547
Cooking & Baking, Do-It-Yourself (DIY)

Britain and beyond
1052603
Web site: http://anneliesemostert.blogspot.
com
Freq: Daily
Circ: 611
Cooking & Baking, Expatriates, Family & Parenting, Women's Interests

British Association for Adoption & Fostering blog
998426
Editorial: Saffron House, 6 - 10 Kirby Street, London EC1N 8TS **Tel:** 44 02074 212633
Email: press@baaf.org.uk
Web site: http://corambaaf.org.uk/blog
Freq: Daily
Circ: 31
Charitable Foundations, Family & Parenting

British Photographic History
998879
Editorial: Ground Floor Flat, 61 Great Pultney Street, Bath BA2 4DN
Tel: 44 01923 468356
Web site: http://britishphotohistory.ning.
com/
Freq: Daily
Circ: 5653918
Antiques/Collectibles, Art, Arts, Literature, Photography, Theater & Performing Arts, Visual Arts

British Style UK
1053280
Web site: britishstyleuk.com
Freq: Daily
Circ: 9047
Do-It-Yourself (DIY), Women's Interests

BritishBeautyBlogger
986094
Editorial: 6 Blackheath Rise, London SE13 7PN
Email: britishbeautyblogger@gmail.com
Web site: www.britishbeautyblogger.com
Freq: Daily
Circ: 72664
Beauty & Grooming, Cosmetics, Hair

British-born Chinese Blog
1061719
Email: burntbreadboy@yahoo.co.uk
Web site: http://british-chinese.blogspot.
com
Freq: Daily
Circ: 1045
International News

BritMums Blog
987563
Email: info@britmums.com
Web site: britmums.com
Circ: 54460
Family & Parenting, Women's Interests

Britpoplife Vlogs
1098961
Email: patstrueworld@gmail.com
Web site: https://www.youtube.com/user/
BritpopLife
Freq: Daily
Circ: 1
Family & Parenting, Relationships, Women's Interests

Brixton Blog
988263
Email: info@brixtonblog.com
Web site: http://www.brixtonblog.com/
Freq: Daily
Circ: 30199
News & Current Affairs

Brixton Pound blog
1053185
Editorial: 3 Atlantic Road, London SW9 8HX
Tel: 44 02077 333766
Email: info@brixtonpound.org
Web site: http://brixtonpound.org/blog/
Freq: Daily
Circ: 4
Regional General Interest

Broadband Genie
986095
Editorial: Carlyle House, Carlyle Road, Cambridge CB4 3DN **Tel:** 44 07411 747216
Email: editor@broadbandgenie.co.uk
Web site: www.broadbandgenie.co.uk/blog
Freq: Daily
Circ: 44
Editor: Matt Powell
Audio Video Trade, Cameras, Consumer Electronics, Mobile Electronics, Movies & Video

Brockley Central
986596
Editorial: Brockley, London
Email: nick.barron@gmail.com
Web site: http://brockleycentral.blogspot.
com
Freq: Daily
Circ: 13553
Regional General Interest, Social Issues

The Broken Line SUSPENDED
997376
Web site: http://thebrokenline.co.uk
Freq: Daily
Circ: 2370
Bicycles

Bromyard Sessions
1054385
Email: music@tonyburt.co.uk
Web site: http://www.bromyardsessions.co.
uk/
Freq: Daily
Circ: 8862
Country, Folk, Bluegrass, Jazz & Blues

The Brooke blog
998241
Editorial: The Brooke, 5th Floor Friars Bridge Court, 41 - 45 Blackfriars Road, London SE1 8NZ **Tel:** 44 02030 123456
Email: info@thebrooke.org
Web site: https://www.facebook.com/
thebrookecharity/notes
Freq: Daily
Circ: 3
Charitable Foundations

The Brown Stuff
1053806
Email: website@resilientgp.org
Web site: http://thebrownstuff.blogspot.co.
uk/
Freq: Daily
Circ: 521
Health & Medicine

The Browser
1064095
Web site: https://thebrowser.com/
Freq: Daily
Circ: 188299
National News

BTCC Crazy
1056572
Email: contact@btcccrazy.co.uk
Web site: www.btcccrazy.co.uk
Freq: Daily
Circ: 49157
Driving, Motorsports, Off-road & 4-Wheel Drive Vehicles

Bubbablue and Me
987565
Email: etustian@hotmail.com
Web site: bubbablueandme.com
Freq: Daily
Circ: 52258
Profile: Blog covering motherhood. BUBBABLUE AND ME discusses anything from family life and day's out to children's activities. The blog has an archive dating back to April 2011 The outlet offers RSS (Really Simple Syndication).
Family & Parenting, Women's Interests

Bubblegarm
986096
Email: bubblegarm@mail.com
Web site: bubblegarm.co.uk
Circ: 1779
Beauty & Grooming, Cosmetics, Family & Parenting, Hair, Women's Interests

Bucéfalo
1061556
Web site: http://www.bucefalo.com.mx
Freq: Daily
Circ: 1965
Auto Aftermarket, Bars, Clubs & Pubs, Comedy, Computers, Data Management, Electronics, Entertainment, Government Technology, Industry, Internet

Buckets & Spades
988131
Email: bucketsandspadesblog@gmail.com
Web site: www.bucketsandspadesblog.com
Freq: Daily
Circ: 41636
Advertising Industry, Branding, Fashion, Graphic Design, Marketing, Men's Interests

Budget Traveller
986381
Email: europebudgetguide@gmail.com
Web site: www.budgettraveller.org
Freq: Daily
Circ: 46267
Railroad, Travel

Bugs and Fishes
987361
Web site: bugsandfishes.blogspot.com
Freq: Daily
Circ: 6353
Crafts

Building Design Expert Blog
997200
Editorial: The Old Garage, 22 Weetwood Court, Leeds LS16 5NT
Tel: 44 01132 163357
Email: contact@buildingdesignexpert.com
Web site: http://buildingdesignexpert.com/
blog-posts/
Freq: Daily
Circ: 7492
Architecture & Design

Building Projects
999466
Tel: 44 01435 863500
Email: editorial@netmagmedia.eu
Web site: http://www.building-projects.co.
uk
Freq: Daily
Circ: 9739
Architecture & Design, Do-It-Yourself (DIY), Interior Design

Builtvisible
1053898
Editorial: 49 Tabernacle Street, London EC2A 4AA **Tel:** 44 02071 480453
Email: hello@builtvisible.com
Web site: https://builtvisible.com/blog
Freq: Daily
Circ: 58694
Branding, Data Management, Internet, Marketing

Bumbles of Rice
1052908
Email: bumblesofrice@gmail.com
Web site: bumblesofrice.com
Freq: Daily
Circ: 8039
Cooking & Baking, Family & Parenting, Women's Interests

Bump to Baby
988718
Email: alex@bump-to-baby.com
Web site: http://www.bump-to-baby.com/
Freq: Daily
Circ: 24940
Family & Parenting

Bumpkin Betty
1054056
Email: bumpkinbetty@gmail.com
Web site: bumpkinbetty.com
Freq: Daily
Circ: 6818
Beauty & Grooming, Cosmetics, Fashion, Hair, Women's Interests

BUNAC Blog
997057
Editorial: Priory House, 6 Wrights Lane, London W8 6TA **Tel:** 44 03339 997516
Email: enquiries@bunac.org.uk

Web site: http://www.bunac.org/uk/blog/
bunac-blog
Freq: Daily
Circ: 50
Charitable Foundations

Bundesliga Fanatic
997658
Email: editor@bundesligafanatic.com
Web site: http://bundesligafanatic.com/
Freq: Daily
Circ: 35981
Soccer

The Bunfight
998106
Email: thebunfight@gmail.com
Web site: thebunfight.com
Freq: Daily
Circ: 9535
Cooking & Baking

Bunni Punch
1052606
Web site: http://www.bunnipunch.co.uk/
Freq: Daily
Circ: 9175
Beauty & Grooming, Cosmetics, Fashion, Hair, Travel, Women's Interests

Bunny Kitchen
998188
Web site: bunnykitchen.com
Freq: Daily
Circ: 7053
Vegetarianism & Veganism

Burbujitas
1062072
Web site: http://burbujitaas.blogspot.com
Freq: Daily
Circ: 1479
Alumni, Careers, Disability, Education, Elementary School, Family & Parenting, Higher Education, Preschool, Schools & Institutions, Student Lifestyle

Burgers and Bruce
997700
Email: burgersandbruce@gmail.com
Web site: http://www.burgersandbruce.
com/
Freq: Daily
Circ: 3095
Profile: Blog covering food, travel and music (in particular Bruce Springsteen!). The blog has an archive dating back to July 2012 and shares a short blogroll.
Cooking & Baking, Restaurant Reviews, Rock Music, Travel

Burkatron
987602
Email: misscarolineburke@gmail.com
Web site: www.burkatron.com
Freq: Daily
Circ: 24358
Profile: Blog covering fashion. BURKATRON blog discusses anything from fashion trends and vintage style to nail art and crafts. The outlet offers RSS (Really Simple Syndication).
Beauty & Grooming, Cosmetics, Fashion, Hair, Women's Interests

Buseta de Papel
1061906
Web site: http://grupobusetadepapel.
blogspot.com/
Freq: Daily
Circ: 857
Antiques/Collectibles, Art, Arts, Literature, Photography, Theater & Performing Arts, Visual Arts

Business Advertising Blog
1054645
Web site: http://www.
businessadvertisingblog.co.uk
Freq: Daily
Circ: 912
Advertising Industry, Marketing

Business and Finance
1054430
Tel: 44 01237 7000
Web site: http://businessandfinance.com/
blog/
Freq: Daily
Circ: 44
Business, Corporate Responsibility

Business Computing World
985286
Editorial: 55 Millbrook Drive, Shenstone, Lichfield, Lichfield WS14 0JL

UK Blogs

Web site: www.businesscomputingworld.co.uk
Freq: Daily
Circ: 130775
Computers

Business Fights Poverty Blog
998131
Email: info@businessfightspoverty.org
Web site: http://businessfightspoverty.org/
Freq: Daily
Circ: 21888
Charitable Foundations

Business for Scotland
1054253
Tel: 44 01412 551415
Email: info@businessforscotland.co.uk
Web site: http://www.businessforscotland.co.uk/
Freq: Daily
Circ: 44481
Profile: Blog covering pro-independence business in Scotland. Business for Scotland discusses anything from 'making a business case for independence' and an independent economy to benefits and obstacles. The blog has an archive dating back to March 2013. The outlet offers RSS (Really Simple Syndication).
Business, Government, Politics, Scotland

Business Plus Baby
1054137
Web site: businessplusbaby.com
Freq: Daily
Circ: 22644
Business

But I'm a human not a sandwich
1061249
Email: iina.hyttinen@indiedays.com
Web site: http://butimahumannotasandwich.indiedays.com/
Freq: Daily
Circ: 38958
Fashion, Lifestyle, Men's Interests, Regional General Interest, Women's Interests

But She's A Girl
1052567
Web site: http://rousette.org.uk/blog/
Freq: Daily
Circ: 9
Audio Video Trade, Cameras, Consumer Electronics, Mobile Electronics, Movies & Video

But Why Mummy Why?
987631
Email: morgana@butwhymummywhy.com
Web site: http://coffeeworksleeprepeat.com/
Freq: Daily
Circ: 12622
Family & Parenting

Butcher, Baker, Baby
986969
Web site: www.butcherbakerblog.com
Freq: Daily
Circ: 7294
Profile: Blog covering recipes, food, cooking and baking. The blog has an archive dating back to May 2006 and shares an extensive blogroll.
Cooking & Baking, Restaurant Reviews

Buy Our Honeymoon Blog
987298
Editorial: 10 Hamilton Road, Sidcup, Bexley DA15 7HB Tel: 44 03452 240189
Email: enquiries@buy-our-honeymoon.com
Web site: https://www.buy-our-honeymoon.com/blog
Freq: Daily
Circ: 12
Profile: Blog covering honeymoon travel. The blog has an archive dating back to May 2007.
Weddings

The Buying Agent
986963
Tel: 44 08456 036110
Email: info@bdihomefinders.co.uk
Web site: thebuyingagent.wordpress.com
Freq: Daily
Circ: 7
Property Management & Maintenance

Buzzbnk's Blog
997023
Editorial: New Zealand House, 80 Haymarket, London SW1Y 4TE
Tel: 44 08000 967560
Email: hello@buzzbnk.org
Web site: blog.buzzbnk.org
Freq: Daily
Circ: 749
Business, Corporate Responsibility, Equities

Buzztrips Blog
1058920
Web site: buzztrips.co.uk
Freq: Daily
Circ: 70680
Travel

By Far The Greatest Team
998049
Email: admin@byfarthegreatestteam.com
Web site: http://www.byfarthegreatestteam.com/
Freq: Daily
Circ: 48948
Soccer

C.E. Jottings
1054468
Web site: http://paces.typepad.com/paces/
Freq: Daily
Circ: 48819
Education

Cadenasde Palabras
1061156
Web site: http://cadenasdepalabras.blogspot.com/
Freq: Daily
Circ: 1889
Literature

The Cafe Cat
988499
Web site: http://www.thecafecat.com/
Freq: Daily
Circ: 9757
Cooking & Baking

Cafe Guaguau
1061872
Web site: http://www.cafeguaguau.com
Freq: Daily
Circ: 6924
Auto Aftermarket, Computers, Data Management, Electronics, Government Technology, Industry, Internet, Mobile Communications, Security & Security Systems, Software

CAFOD Blog
986099
Editorial: Romero House, 55 Westminster Bridge Road, London SE1 7JB
Tel: 44 02077 337900
Email: cafod@cafod.org.uk
Web site: blog.cafod.org.uk
Freq: Daily
Circ: 322
Charitable Foundations

The Cake Hunter
987606
Email: iamthecakehunter@gmail.com
Web site: www.thecakehunter.co.uk
Freq: Daily
Circ: 5373
Alcohol & Spirits, Bars, Clubs & Pubs, Beer, Beverages, Cooking & Baking, Food, Grocery Stores, Organic Food, Restaurant Reviews, Vegetarianism & Veganism

Cakeyboi
988595
Email: mrcakeyboi@gmail.com
Web site: http://www.cakeyboi.com
Freq: Daily
Circ: 14206
Profile: Blog covering baked goods, baking and recipes. The blog has an archive dating back to May 2012 and shares an extensive blog roll.
Cooking & Baking

Calamity Teacher
1053821
Web site: http://calamityteacher.blogspot.co.uk/
Freq: Daily
Circ: 821
Profile: Blog covering education. Calamity Teacher blog discusses anything from education to teaching. The blog has an archive dating back to October 2012.
Careers

Caledonista
1053856
Tel: 44 01236 826666
Email: prteam@hartmannmedia.co.uk
Web site: caledonista.com
Freq: Daily
Circ: 13674
Profile: Website covering lifestyle. CALEDONISTA covers fashion, beauty, lifestyle, travel, interiors in Scotland.
Beauty & Grooming, Cosmetics, Do-It-Yourself (DIY), Fashion, Hair, Women's Interests

Calidad de Vida
1061359
Web site: http://klidaddvida.blogspot.com/
Freq: Daily
Circ: 521
Lifestyle, Men's Interests, Neurology, Regional General Interest, Women's Interests

Call Me Liz
1103796
Web site: http://www.callmeliz.co.uk/
Freq: Daily
Circ: 11890
Fashion, Shopping, Travel

Calloway Green
999186
Editorial: Calloway Green Ltd, 114A High Street, Kinver, Stourbridge DY7 6HL
Tel: 44 08450 573420
Email: info@callowaygreen.com
Web site: https://www.callowaygreen.co.uk/blog/
Freq: Daily
Circ: 55
Advertising Industry, Branding, Broadcasting, Graphic Design, Marketing, Media & Communications, Photography, Publishing

Camberwell Blog
1052781
Web site: www.camberwellonline.co.uk
Freq: Daily
Circ: 8885
Bars, Clubs & Pubs, Comedy, Entertainment, History, Local Entertainment Guides, Movies & Video

Camille Over The Rainbow
1054078
Web site: www.camilleovertherainbow.com
Freq: Daily
Circ: 36721
Profile: Blog covering fashion. CAMILLE OVER THE RAINBOW blog discusses anything from fashion shows and the latest fashion trends to fashion accessories and personal style. The blog has an archive dating back to February 2010. The outlet offers RSS (Really Simple Syndication).
Fashion, Luxury Goods, Women's Interests

Campervan Living
1053618
Web site: http://campervanliving.blogspot.co.uk/
Freq: Daily
Circ: 13010
Camping and RV Travel, Cooking & Baking, Travel

Campos de Batalla
1060955
Web site: http://blogs.eluniversal.com.mx/campo
Freq: Daily
Circ: 233
National News, Politics

Campos Eliseos
1061590
Web site: http://blogs.eluniversal.com.mx/camposeliseos/
Freq: Daily
Circ: 41856
Politics

Campr
1054633
Email: info@campr.co.uk
Web site: http://www.campr.co.uk
Freq: Daily
Circ: 521
Camping and RV Travel

CAMRGB
988142
Email: hq@camrgb.org
Web site: www.camrgb.org/blog/
Freq: Daily
Circ: 81
Profile: Blog covering beer. The blog shares an extensive blogroll.
Beer

Cancer Prevention Blog
986855
Editorial: WCRF UK, 22 Bedford Square, London WC1B 3HH Tel: 44 02073 434200
Email: wcrf@wcrf.org
Web site: http://www.wcrf-uk.org/uk/blog
Freq: Daily
Circ: 15
Profile: Blog covering cancer prevention methods as discussed by the World Cancer Research Fund (WCRF UK). The blog has an archive dating back to April 2010.
Charitable Foundations, Science

CancerIFA
1054628
Web site: http://georgeemsden.co.uk
Freq: Daily
Circ: 3021
Oncology

Canela Style
1060721
Web site: http://www.canelastyle.com/
Freq: Daily
Circ: 1535
Fashion

Canned Fashion - CEASED 2016
987072
Web site: www.cannedfashion.com
Freq: Daily
Circ: 6295
Fashion

Capitalists@Work
1053298
Web site: http://www.cityunslicker.co.uk/
Freq: Daily
Circ: 10009
Economics

Caplor blog
997760
Editorial: Caplor Farm, Hereford HR1 4PT
Tel: 44 01432 860644
Email: kika@caplor.co.uk
Web site: https://www.caplor.co.uk/
Freq: Daily
Circ: 9257
Alternative/Renewable Energy, Carbon Emissions & Trading, Electricity, Energy, Environment, Nuclear Power, Oil, Water & Sanitation

Captain Greybeard
986403
Editorial: 1 Canada Square, Canary Wharf, London E14 5AP Tel: 44 07710 740623
Web site: www.captaingreybeard.com
Freq: Daily
Circ: 9882
Airline Inflight, Railroad, Travel

Capture by Lucy
987637
Email: mama@capturebylucy.com
Web site: capturebylucy.com
Freq: Daily
Circ: 9733
Profile: Blog covering motherhood, cooking, baking, recipes and photography arts. The blog shares a short blog roll.
Family & Parenting, Photography

Car Audio Blog
1053294
Editorial: Unit 5 Spott Road, Industrial Estate, Dunbar EH42 1RS
Tel: 44 01368 860800
Web site: https://www.raysmith.co.uk/car-audio-news
Freq: Daily
Circ: 64
Antique & Collectible Cars, Audio Video Trade, Automakers, Automotive, Driving, Motorcycles, Off-road & 4-Wheel Drive Vehicles, Trucks & SUVs

Car Design Blog UK
1095951
Email: info@cardesignbloguk.com
Web site: https://cardesignbloguk.com/
Freq: Daily
Circ: 10709
Automotive, Driving

The Car Expert
987774
Editorial: 7 Heritage House, 21 Inner Park Road, London SW19 6ED
Tel: 44 07543 300719

Email: info@thecarexpert.co.uk
Web site: http://www.thecarexpert.co.uk/
Freq: Daily
Circ: 79589
Profile: Blog covering cars. The Car Expert discusses anything from buying advice and automotive news to car finance and insurance. The blog has an archive dating back to October 2011.
Automotive, Driving

Car Hire Blog 997174
Editorial: 78 York Street, London W1H 1DP
Tel: 44 08455 089845
Email: info@rhinocarhire.com
Web site: http://www.rhinocarhire.com/Car-Hire-Blog.aspx
Freq: Daily
Circ: 90
Airline Inflight, Antique & Collectible Cars, Automakers, Automotive, Driving, Motorcycles, Off-road & 4-Wheel Drive Vehicles, Railroad, Travel, Trucks & SUVs

Car News - Auto Lah 998415
Email: ahoklah@gmail.com
Web site: http://autolah.blogspot.com/
Freq: Daily
Circ: 2642
Automotive, Driving

The Car Spy 987870
Editorial: Pantiles Chambers, 85 High Street, Tunbridge Wells TN1 1XP
Tel: 44 01892 506970
Email: sales@thecarspy.net
Web site: thecarspy.wordpress.com/
Freq: Daily
Circ: 7
Editor: Mark Sekula
Profile: Blog covering cars. The Car Spy discusses anything from info on vintage and prestige car sales in the UK to buying guides.
Antique & Collectible Cars, Automakers, Automotive, Driving

Car Throttle 987858
Editorial: White Bear Yard, 2nd Floor, 144A Clerkenwell Road, London EC1R 5DF
Email: support@carthrottle.com
Web site: www.carthrottle.com/
Freq: Daily
Circ: 945940
Automotive, Driving

Cara Carmina Atelier 1061968
Web site: http://caracarmina-atelier.blogspot.com
Freq: Daily
Circ: 2355
Crafts, Photography

Caracas Bipolar 1061354
Web site: http://blogs.eluniversal.com/eu3/Blogs/ccsbp_index.shtml
Freq: Daily
Circ: 42327
National News, Politics

Caracas Ciudad de la Furia 1060826
Web site: http://caracasciuddadelafuria.blogspot.com/
Freq: Daily
Circ: 6167
Antiques/Collectibles, Art, Arts, Literature, National News, Photography, Theater & Performing Arts, Visual Arts

Caracas Refurbished 1061370
Web site: http://caracasrefurbished.wordpress.com/
Freq: Daily
Circ: 28
Architecture & Design, Basketball, Bicycles, Billiards, Boating & Yachting, Bodybuilding, Bowling, Boxing, Cricket, Equestrian Sports

CarArticles.co.uk 988588
Web site: http://www.cararticles.co.uk/
Freq: Daily
Circ: 11257
Antique & Collectible Cars, Automakers, Automotive, Driving, Motorcycles, Off-road & 4-Wheel Drive Vehicles, Trucks & SUVs

Carbon Brief 987208
Editorial: 40 Bermondsey Street, London SE1 3UD **Tel:** 44 02032 860387
Email: Info@carbonbrief.org
Web site: https://www.carbonbrief.org/
Freq: Daily
Circ: 120115
Environment, Science

Carcachita 1061319
Web site: http://lacarcachita.blogspot.com
Freq: Daily
Circ: 521
Regional General Interest

Card & Gift Network Blog 996547
Email: mail@cardandgiftblog.com
Web site: http://www.cardandgiftnetwork.com/card-and-gift-blog
Freq: Daily
Circ: 243
Crafts

Cardboard Cities 1053769
Email: hello@cardboardcities.co.uk
Web site: blog.cardboardcities.co.uk/
Freq: Daily
Circ: 5409
Crafts, Do-It-Yourself (DIY), Fashion, Visual Arts

Cardiffornia Gurl 1053175
Web site: www.cardifforniagurl.co.uk
Freq: Daily
Circ: 9787
Fashion

Carepicha Blog 1060653
Web site: http://www.h3dicho.ticoblogger.com
Freq: Daily
Auto Aftermarket, Bars, Clubs & Pubs, Comedy, Computers, Data Management, Electronics, Entertainment, Government Technology, Industry, Internet

Carey Codd Blog 1061420
Web site: http://miami.cbslocal.com/category/blogs/carey-codd
Freq: Daily
Circ: 33633
National News

Carly Rowena 1099577
Web site: www.carlyrowena.com
Freq: Daily
Circ: 35832
Profile: Carly Rowena covers fitness, fashion, healthy eating, recipes and travel. The outlet also offers a vlog.
Fitness & Exercise, Nutrition

Carly Rowena Blog 988112
Email: carlyrowena@me.com
Web site: www.carlyrowena.com/
Freq: Daily
Circ: 35832
Fitness & Exercise, Nutrition

Carly's Beauty Blog 1105191
Email: carly@carlysbeautyblog.com
Web site: http://carlysusanne.com/
Freq: Daily
Circ: 11109
Beauty & Grooming, Cosmetics, Hair

Carmin 1061610
Web site: http://artesaniascarmin.blogspot.com/
Freq: Daily
Circ: 611
Crafts, Hobbies, & Collecting

Caroline Hirons 987979
Web site: www.carolinehirons.com
Freq: Daily
Circ: 142878
News & Current Affairs

Caroline Hope Blog 988068
Tel: 44 02037 303788
Web site: www.teaandscones.co.uk/blog
Freq: Daily
Circ: 2104
Cooking & Baking

Caroline Kamp Blog 1052558
Web site: www.carolinekamp.com/blog
Freq: Daily
Circ: 4197
Do-It-Yourself (DIY)

Carrapuchiña 1062152
Web site: http://carapuchina.blogspot.com
Freq: Daily
Circ: 9605
Crafts, Fashion

Carrentals blog 1052753
Web site: http://www.carrentals.co.uk/blog
Freq: Daily
Circ: 489
Driving, Travel

The Carrot Blog 1053066
Editorial: Media Village, 131 - 151 Great Titchfield Street, London W1W 5BB
Tel: 44 02031 785048
Email: info@carrotcomms.co.uk
Web site: http://carrotcomms.co.uk/the-carrot-blog/
Freq: Daily
Circ: 3714
Marketing

Carry on Learning 1053692
Web site: http://carryonlearning.blogspot.co.uk
Freq: Daily
Circ: 1068
Profile: Blog covering teaching. Carry on Learning blog discusses anything from teaching to education. The blog has an archive dating back to April 2012 and shares an extensive blog roll. The outlet offers RSS (Really Simple Syndication).
Education

Cars & Life 987106
Editorial: Cronus Business Consultancy, 1 Victoria Sqaure, Birmingham B1 1BD
Tel: 44 07849 089727
Email: k.uygar@gmail.com
Web site: www.carsandlife.net
Freq: Daily
Circ: 10973
Profile: Cars & Life covers cars, fashion and lifestyle. This outlet offers a vlog.
Driving, Fashion, Regional General Interest

Cars UK 986314
Editorial: Potash Road, Billericay, Billericay CM11 1HG
Web site: www.carsuk.net
Circ: 54536
Editor: John Overend
Driving

Carscoops 986313
Email: info@carscoops.com
Web site: www.carscoops.com
Freq: Daily
Circ: 5244949
Driving

Carve Consulting Blog 1054224
Editorial: The Observatory, 40 Clerkenwell Close, London EC1R 0AW
Tel: 44 08450 178148
Email: team@carveconsulting.com
Web site: www.carveconsulting.com/blog
Freq: Daily
Circ: 64
Branding, Marketing

carwow 999312
Editorial: Kingsbourne House, 229 - 231 High Holborn, London WC1V 7DA
Email: hello@carwow.co.uk
Web site: https://www.carwow.co.uk/blog
Freq: Daily
Circ: 431370
Driving

Casa Costello 988581
Web site: casacostello.com
Freq: Daily
Circ: 38531
Cooking & Baking

Casa Ecológica 1060376
Web site: http://casaeco.blogspot.com

Freq: Daily
Circ: 1631
Environment

Casas de Botella 1061520
Web site: http://casasdebotellasuruguay.blogspot.com/
Freq: Daily
Circ: 761
Sustainable Development

The Case for Global Film 1052899
Web site: https://itpworld.wordpress.com/
Freq: Daily
Circ: 26770
Visual Arts

Cassiefairy 988380
Web site: Cassiefairy.com
Freq: Daily
Circ: 14211
Profile: Blog covering arts and crafts. Cassiefairy blog discusses anything from arts and crafts to knitting, fashion, food, event decorations, interior design, recipes and lifestyle. The blog has an archive dating back to May 2011 and shares an short blog roll. The outlet offers RSS (Really Simple Syndication).
Cooking & Baking, Crafts, Do-It-Yourself (DIY), Nature & Wildlife, Women's Interests

Cat Dal Interiors 1064624
Email: press@catdalinteriors.com
Web site: www.catdalinteriors.com
Freq: Daily
Circ: 1517
Do-It-Yourself (DIY)

Catalyst Energy Blog 999218
Editorial: Kathleen House, 10 James Road, Tyseley, Birmingham B11 2BA
Tel: 44 08707 107560
Email: info@catalyst-commercial.co.uk
Web site: http://www.catalyst-commercial.co.uk/energy-blog
Freq: Daily
Circ: 37
Alternative/Renewable Energy

Cate in the Kitchen 988429
Email: hello@cateinthekitchen.co.uk
Web site: https://cateinthekitchen.co.uk/
Freq: Daily
Circ: 10181
Profile: Blog covering recipes. CATE in the KITCHEN discusses anything from breakfast and dinners to desserts and cocktails. The outlet offers RSS (Really Simple Syndication).
Cooking & Baking

Cathal's Cookbook Allergy Free Cooking 1053599
Email: cathalscookbookallergyfree@gmail.com
Web site: http://cathalscookbookallergyfree.com/
Freq: Daily
Circ: 1120
Cooking & Baking

Catherine Cornelissen 1100933
Email: catherine.cornelissen@aol.com
Web site: www.catherinecornelissen.com
Freq: Daily
Circ: 521
Do-It-Yourself (DIY)

Cats and Chocolate 998179
Email: catsandchocolateblog@gmail.com
Web site: http://catsandchocolate.com/
Freq: Daily
Circ: 8930
Disability, Literature, Women's Interests

Caught by the River 1052625
Email: info@caughtbytheriver.net
Web site: http://www.caughtbytheriver.net/
Freq: Daily
Circ: 17953
Literature, Nature & Wildlife, Outdoor Recreation

CaughtOffside 986102
Editorial: Fanatix, 23 Pembridge Square, London W2 4DR
Email: editor@caughtoffside.com
Web site: www.caughtoffside.com
Freq: Daily
Circ: 321605
Soccer

Cause4 1053133
Editorial: Gun House, 1 Artillery Passage, Aldgate, London E1 7LJ
Email: enquiry@cause4.co.uk
Web site: cause4.co.uk/opinion-page
Freq: Daily
Circ: 6
Charitable Foundations

CCS Insight Blog 1052825
Tel: 44 08450 574223
Web site: ccsinsight.com/blog
Freq: Daily
Circ: 24
Internet, Mobile Communications

CDClifestyle.com 988302
Editorial: 41 Warwick Road, Earl's Court, London SW5 9UP
Email: info@cdclifestyle.com
Web site: www.cdclifestyle.com
Freq: Daily
Circ: 6975
Editor: Sam Bryan-Merrett
Luxury Goods

Celery and Cupcakes 987997
Email: celeryandcupcakes@gmail.com
Web site: http://www.celeryandcupcakes.com
Freq: Daily
Circ: 27817
Cooking & Baking

Celtic House 1057072
Web site: http://celtichouse.blogspot.co.uk/
Freq: Daily
Circ: 731
News & Current Affairs

Celtic Quick News 1053725
Email: paul@celticquicknews.co.uk
Web site: www.celticquicknews.co.uk
Freq: Daily
Circ: 125862
Soccer

Central Illustration Agency Blog 1067885
Editorial: 17b Perseverance Works, 38 Kingsland Road, London E2 8DD
Tel: 44 02032 220007
Email: info@centralillustration.com
Web site: www.centralillustration.com/blog.asp
Freq: Daily
Circ: 407
Art, Graphic Design, Visual Arts

Centre for Medical Humanities 996525
Editorial: Caedmon Building, Leazes Road, Durham DH1 1SZ **Tel:** 44 01913 348277
Email: centreformedicalhumanities@gmail.com
Web site: http://centreformedicalhumanities.org/
Freq: Daily
Circ: 16894
Health & Medicine

Centre for Public Health blog 988598
Editorial: Liverpool John Moores University, Henry Cotton Campus, Level 2, 15 - 21 Webster Street, Liverpool L3 2ET
Tel: 44 01512 314542
Email: info@cph.org.uk
Web site: http://www.cph.org.uk/
Freq: Daily
Circ: 15952
Community Care (UK), Health Administration

Centrica Blog 986103
Editorial: Millstream, Maidenhead Road, Windsor SL4 5GD

Circ: 16397
Electricity, Environment, Oil

CesArts 1062158
Web site: http://www.cesarts.blogspot.com
Freq: Daily
Circ: 790
Cooking & Baking, Food

CFCnet Blog 998408
Web site: www.cfcnet.co.uk
Freq: Daily
Circ: 48465
Soccer

CGnauta Blog 1061099
Web site: http://www.cgnauta.blogspot.com
Freq: Daily
Circ: 2319
Auto Aftermarket, Computers, Data Management, Electronics, Government Technology, Industry, Internet, Mobile Communications, Movies & Video, Security & Security Systems

Chalk Kids 998240
Email: hello@chalkkids.co.uk
Web site: chalkkids.co.uk
Freq: Daily
Circ: 8198
Editor: Stephanie Withers
Beauty & Grooming, Cooking & Baking, Cosmetics, Do-It-Yourself (DIY), Family & Parenting, Hair, Women's Interests

The Chamberlain Files 1053773
Email: chamberlain.files@rjfpa.com
Web site: http://www.thechamberlainfiles.com/
Freq: Daily
Circ: 16049
Energy & Environment, Politics, Regional, Social Issues, Transportation

Champagne & Chutney 1053363
Email: titus.rahul@gmail.com
Web site: http://www.champagneandchutney.com/
Freq: Daily
Circ: 3118
Profile: Blog covering food. CHAMPAGNE & CHUTNEY discusses anything from restaurant reviews and recipes. The blog has an archive dating back to January 2014. The outlet offers RSS (Really Simple Syndication).
Restaurant Reviews, Travel

Champagne on the Brain 996414
Web site: www.champagneonthebrain.com
Freq: Daily
Circ: 1106
Bars, Clubs & Pubs, Cooking & Baking, Driving, Restaurant Reviews, Travel, Wine/Winemaking

Chanfle's Blog 1061244
Web site: http://chanfles.com/blog
Freq: Daily
Circ: 90
Auto Aftermarket, Computers, Data Management, Electronics, Government Technology, Industry, Internet, Mobile Communications, Security & Security Systems, Software

Changing Minds, Changing Lives 1052854
Editorial: 1 London Bridge, London SE1 2SX
Tel: 44 02078 031100
Email: press@mentalhealth.org.uk
Web site: https://www.mentalhealth.org.uk/blog
Freq: Daily
Circ: 19
Profile: Blog covering mental health. The blog is hosted by the Mental Health Foundation.
Disability, Neurology

Changing Phase 1054558
Web site: http://changing-phase.blogspot.co.uk/
Freq: Daily
Circ: 9261
Profile: Blog covering education. Changing Phase discusses anything from education and languages to teaching and books. The

blog has an archive dating back to July 2009 and shares an extensive blog roll.
Education

Channel EYE 987192
Editorial: 27 Mill Street, Oxford OX2 0AJ
Web site: www.channeleye.co.uk
Circ: 16749
Editor: Mike Magee
Profile: Website covering technology. The website discusses anything from technology news, business, technology security and reviews. TechEye looks into the technology industry and investigates the business behind some of the greatest tech players in the industry such as Intel, Microsoft, Google, Cisco, Facebook, and Twitter.
Auto Aftermarket, Computers, Data Management, Electronics, Government Technology, Industry, Internet, Mobile Communications, Mobile Electronics, Security & Security Systems

Channel Mum 990646
Editorial: 42B Berkeley Road, London N8 8RU
Email: hello@channelmum.com
Web site: channelmum.com
Freq: Daily
Circ: 20702
Beauty & Grooming, Cooking & Baking, Cosmetics, Family & Parenting, Fashion, Hair

Chantelle Znideric - Personal Stylist blog 1058919
Tel: 44 01428 712245
Web site: http://personal-stylist.co.uk/blog/
Freq: Daily
Circ: 41
Fashion, Luxury Goods, Women's Interests

Charis White blog 1105202
Web site: chariswhite.com
Freq: Daily
Circ: 1052
Do-It-Yourself (DIY)

Charity Gifts Blog 999326
Email: contact@donation4charity.org
Web site: http://www.charity-gifts.org/blog/
Freq: Daily
Circ: 7
Charitable Foundations

Charles Jennings Workplace Performance 997139
Tel: 44 01962 623766
Web site: http://charles-jennings.blogspot.com/
Freq: Daily
Circ: 10069
Careers

Charli blogs 988932
Email: charli-blogs@outlook.com
Web site: charli-blogs.com
Freq: Daily
Circ: 6680
Profile: Blog covering beauty, cosmetics and lifestyle. The blog has an archive dating back to December 2010.
Beauty & Grooming, Cosmetics, Fashion, Hair, Nature & Wildlife, Women's Interests

Charlie INTEL 997731
Email: admin@charlieintel.com
Web site: www.charlieintel.com/
Freq: Daily
Circ: 629666
Computer & Video Games

Charlotte Fisher Things I do, think and buy 007280
Email: charlotte.fisher@hotmail.co.uk
Web site: www.thingsidothinkandbuy.com
Freq: Daily
Circ: 6832
Fashion

Charlotte Samantha 1052731
Email: charlottesamanthaox@gmail.com
Web site: http://charlottesamantha.co.uk/
Freq: Daily
Circ: 12821

Profile: Blog covering lifestyle, home decorating, fashion, cosmetics and beauty. The blog has an archive dating back to January 2014.
Beauty & Grooming, Cosmetics, Fashion, Hair

Charltom Wintale 1052885
Email: charltomwintale@gmail.com
Web site: http://www.charltomwintale.co.uk/
Freq: Daily
Circ: 10709
Profile: Blog covering fashion. Charltom Wintale blog discusses anything from fashion and fashion accessories to beauty and cosmetics.
Beauty & Grooming, Cosmetics, Fashion, Hair, Women's Interests

Charmed Charlee 987102
Email: charmedcharlee@hotmail.com
Web site: http://www.charmedcharlee.com/
Freq: Daily
Circ: 3171
Profile: Blog covering fashion. Charmed Charlee blog discusses anything from beauty and fashion to cosmetics and lifestyle. The blog has an archive dating back to February 2014 and shares an extensive blog roll.
Beauty & Grooming, Cosmetics, Fashion, Hair

Cheap Theatre Tickets 999498
Editorial: International House, 39 Great Windmill Street, London W1D 7LX
Tel: 44 02074 929930
Web site: cheaptheatretickets.com
Freq: Daily
Circ: 32862
Entertainment, Local Entertainment Guides

Cheapflights Travel Blog 999265
Editorial: One Alfred Place, London WC1E 7EB
Email: pr.enquiries@cheapflights.com
Web site: http://www.cheapflights.co.uk/news/
Freq: Daily
Circ: 42607
Airline Inflight, Railroad, Travel

The Checkered Flag Blogs 1058923
Email: news@thecheckeredflag.co.uk
Web site: http://www.thecheckeredflag.co.uk/category/tcf-blogs/
Freq: Daily
Circ: 256
Automotive, Driving, Motorcycles

Cheese and Biscuits 986104
Web site: www.cheesenbiscuits.blogspot.com
Freq: Daily
Circ: 8631
Alcohol & Spirits, Bars, Clubs & Pubs, Beer, Beverages, Cooking & Baking, Food, Grocery Stores, Organic Food, Restaurant Reviews, Vegetarianism & Veganism

Chef Hermes 1053448
Email: blog@chefhermes.com
Web site: http://chefhermes.com/
Freq: Daily
Circ: 1416
Cooking & Baking, Food, Grocery Stores, Organic Food, Restaurant Reviews, Vegetarianism & Veganism

Chelsea Daft 997549
Email: enquiries@chelseadaft.org
Web site: www.chelseadaft.org
Freq: Daily
Circ: 37515
Soccer

Chelsea FC Blog 987885
Email: chelseablog@gmail.com
Web site: www.chelseafcblog.com/
Freq: Daily
Circ: 24063
Soccer

Chelsea Mamma 988270
Editorial: 133 King John Avenue, Bearwood,
Bournemouth BH11 9SB
Email: chelseamamma@gmail.com
Web site: www.chelseamamma.co.uk
Freq: Daily
Circ: 94585
Family & Parenting

Chemistry blog 1053335
Tel: 44 20762 99565
Email: business@thechemistrygroup.com
Web site: http://www.thechemistrygroup.
com/chemistry-blog/
Freq: Daily
Circ: 31
Careers

Cheng Yuan 1061183
Web site: http://blog.sina.com.cn/
autochengyuan
Freq: Daily
Circ: 35639999
Automotive, Aviation, Railroad, Shipping
& Warehousing, Supply Chain
Management (SCM), Transportation

Chepe Style 1060661
Web site: http://www.chepestyle.com
Freq: Daily
Circ: 611
Antiques/Collectibles, Art, Arts, Fashion,
Literature, Photography, Regional General
Interest, Theater & Performing Arts, Visual
Arts

Cherie City 986105
Editorial: 331, Flat H, Mare Street, Hackney,
London E8 1HY
Email: cheriecity@hotmail.com
Web site: cheriecity.co.uk
Freq: Daily
Circ: 18791
Airline Inflight, Railroad, Travel

Cherished by Me 988548
Web site: cherishedbyme.com
Freq: Daily
Circ: 26168
Cooking & Baking

Cherry Menlove 986683
Tel: 44 01798 839492
Email: info@cherrymenlove.com
Web site: http://www.cherrymenlove.com
Freq: Daily
Circ: 9754
Cooking & Baking, Crafts, Do-It-Yourself
(DIY), Family & Parenting, Fitness &
Exercise, Gardening, Literature, Nutrition

Cherry Pie blog 1054369
Email: cherry@cherrypieblog.com
Web site: http://www.cherrypieblog.com/
Freq: Daily
Circ: 3980
Beauty & Grooming, Cosmetics, Hair,
Women's Interests

Cherry Poppins 997942
Email: lala@cherrypoppins.co.uk
Web site: https://www.cherrypoppins.co.uk/
Freq: Daily
Circ: 10158
Relationships

Cherry Wings 1055150
Web site: http://cherrywingscards.blogspot.
co.uk/
Freq: Daily
Circ: 872
Art, Crafts

Cherrylkd 1054629
Web site: http://cherrylkd.wordpress.com
Freq: Daily
Circ: 55
Education

The Chess Improver 996445
Web site: chessimprover.com
Freq: Daily
Circ: 7629
Chess

Chessie King 1100050
Web site: www.chessieking.com

Freq: Daily
Circ: 1889
Fashion, Fitness & Exercise, Restaurant
Reviews

Chester Fabulous Ladies 995496
Email: chester@ctcchesterandnwales.org.uk
Web site: chesterfabulousladies.blogspot.
co.uk
Freq: Daily
Circ: 1660
Bicycles

Chez Maximka 1065393
Web site: http://www.chezmaximka.
blogspot.co.uk/
Freq: Daily
Circ: 9867
Cooking & Baking, Family & Parenting,
Women's Interests

Chezdashita 1061336
Web site: http://chezdashita.blogspot.com/
Freq: Daily
Circ: 2236
Classical/Choral/Band Music, Cooking &
Baking, Country, Folk, Bluegrass, Dance
Music, Jazz & Blues, Music, Photography,
Pop Music, R&B, Urban, World, Rap & Hip
Hop

Chic Geek Diary 1052573
Email: chicgeekdiary@hotmail.co.uk
Web site: www.chicgeekdiary.com
Freq: Daily
Circ: 12676
Profile: Blog covering family, parenting,
motherhood, home decorating and lifestyle.
The blog has an archive dating back to
November 2012.
Family & Parenting, Women's Interests

Chica Tec 1061596
Web site: http://www.chicatec.com
Freq: Daily
Circ: 2865
Auto Aftermarket, Computers, Data
Management, Electronics, Government
Technology, Industry, Internet, Mobile
Communications, Security & Security
Systems, Software

Chick Lit Uncovered 997953
Email: chicklituncovered@gmail.com
Web site: http://chicklituncovered.blogspot.
co.uk/
Freq: Daily
Circ: 11125
Literature, Women's Interests

Chicklish 1053654
Web site: www.chicklish.co.uk/
Freq: Daily
Fashion, Women's Interests

**Chief Financial Analyst: Key-
nes** 1061215
Email: cannes29@sina.com
Web site: http://blog.sina.com.cn/cannes
Freq: Daily
Circ: 87434
Banking, Financial Markets

Chiguire Literario 1060806
Web site: http://www.elchiguireliterario.
com/
Freq: Daily
Circ: 9038
Computer & Video Games

Childcare is fun! 985714
Web site: http://childcareisfun.co.uk/blog/
Circ: 19
Editor: Fi Star-Stone
Family & Parenting

The Children's Society blog
988574
Editorial: The Children's Society, Edward
Rudolf House, Margery Street, London
WC1X 0JL Tel: 44 02078 414422
Email: media@childrenssociety.org.uk
Web site: http://www.childrenssociety.org.
uk/news-and-blogs/our-blog
Circ: 5
Charitable Foundations

Children's Theatre Reviews
997717
Email: flossie.waite@gmail.com
Web site: http://childrenstheatrereviews.
com/
Freq: Daily
Circ: 13418
Editor: Flossie Waite
Theater & Performing Arts

Child's i foundation 1055294
Tel: 44 03125 13226
Web site: http://www.childsifoundation.org/
Freq: Daily
Circ: 6654
Charitable Foundations

Chilean Wine 1060590
Web site: http://www.chilean-wine.com
Freq: Daily
Circ: 8361
Wine/Winemaking

ChileArq 1060571
Web site: http://www.chilearq.com
Freq: Daily
Circ: 5777
Architecture & Design, Building &
Construction, Government, Regional,
Regional General Interest

Chiltepe 1061882
Email: info@elchiltepe.com
Web site: http://www.elchiltepe.com
Freq: Daily
Circ: 799
Art, Graphic Design

China Geeks 1061377
Web site: http://chinageeks.org
Freq: Daily
Circ: 14497
International News, Social Issues

China Herald 1061548
Email: fons.tuinstra@
china-speakers-bureau.com
Web site: http://www.chinaherald.net
Freq: Daily
Circ: 3985
Economics, Politics, Social Issues

CHINA'S CHOICE 1061351
Web site: http://www.guardian.co.uk/
environment/chinas-choice
Freq: Daily
Circ: 10890
Environment, International News

**Ching-Chou Kuik's Digital
Stamps Monthly Challenge
Blog Design Team** 1056565
Web site: http://cck-digitalstamps-
challenge.blogspot.co.uk/
Freq: Daily
Circ: 589
Crafts

Chloe Adlington Blog 995085
Email: hello@chloeadlington.com
Web site: http://chloeadlington.com/blog/
Freq: Daily
Circ: 9745
Editor: Chloe Adlington
Branding, Marketing

ChloePierreLDN 996545
Email: chloepierrepr@gmail.com
Web site: http://www.chloepierre.com/
Freq: Daily
Circ: 7367
Beauty & Grooming, Cooking & Baking,
Cosmetics, Fashion, Hair, Restaurant
Reviews, Travel, Women's Interests

Chloe's Chick Lit Reviews
1054247
Email: chicklitchloe@gmail.com
Web site: http://chicklitchloe.blogspot.co.
uk/
Freq: Daily
Circ: 10361
Literature

Chloe's Way 987384
Web site: www.chloesway.com

Freq: Daily
Circ: 25079
Profile: Blog covering fashion and beauty.
CHLOE'S way blog discusses anything from
beauty buys and product reviews to fashion
and lifestyle. The blog has an archive dating
back to April 2012.
Beauty & Grooming, Cosmetics, Fashion,
Hair, Women's Interests

Chocablog 986107
Web site: www.chocablog.com
Freq: Daily
Circ: 42367
Alcohol & Spirits, Bars, Clubs & Pubs,
Beer, Beverages, Cooking & Baking,
Food, Grocery Stores, Organic Food,
Restaurant Reviews, Vegetarianism &
Veganism

Chocolate Couverture 997000
Web site: http://www.chocolatecouverture.
co.uk
Freq: Daily
Circ: 9619
Cooking & Baking

Chocolate Creative 1052602
Web site: http://chocolatecreative.blogspot.
co.uk
Freq: Daily
Circ: 3501
Profile: Blog covering interior design.
Chocolate Creative blog discusses anything
from interior design and crafts to furniture.
The blog has an archive dating back to
November 2008 and shares an extensive
blog roll.
News & Current Affairs

Chocolate Mission 986164
Web site: www.chocolatemission.net
Freq: Daily
Circ: 10087
Alcohol & Spirits, Bars, Clubs & Pubs,
Beer, Beverages, Cooking & Baking,
Food, Grocery Stores, Organic Food,
Restaurant Reviews, Vegetarianism &
Veganism

Chocolatefrog 1053993
Email: webcontact@annehoneyman.co.uk
Web site: http://chocfrog.blogspot.co.uk/
Freq: Daily
Circ: 521
Art, Crafts

Chordvine 1061961
Web site: http://www.chordvine.com
Freq: Daily
Circ: 521
Music

Chouyu Nimo 1061575
Email: loveissunny789@vip.sina.com
Web site: http://blog.sina.com.cn/
loveissunny
Freq: Daily
Circ: 26744
Bars, Clubs & Pubs, Celebrities, Comedy,
Entertainment, Lifestyle, Local
Entertainment Guides, Men's Interests,
Movies & Video, Regional General
Interest, Women's Interests

chris allen 1054631
Editorial: The Institute of Applied Social
Sciences, University of Birmingham,
Edgbaston, Birmingham B15 2TT
Tel: 44 01214 142703
Email: info@chris-allen.co.uk
Web site: https://wallscometumblingdown.
wordpress.com/
Freq: Daily
Circ: 55
Religion

Chris Legg Photography 1053834
Web site: http://www.chrislegg.net/blog/
Freq: Daily
Circ: 44
Photography

Chris Skinner's Blog 987203
Editorial: 35 New Broad Street, London
EC2M 1NH
Web site: http://thefinanser.com/
Freq: Daily

UK Blogs

Circ: 50997
Investment Banking, Personal Finance

Chris Townsend Outdoors
1052890
Email: christownsendoutdoors@gmail.com
Web site: www.christownsendoutdoors.com/
Freq: Daily
Circ: 14094
Outdoor Recreation, Travel

Chris Unitt
1052879
Web site: www.chrisunitt.co.uk/
Freq: Daily
Circ: 9263
Art, Marketing

chrissabella
996909
Email: chrissabella277@googlemail.com
Web site: http://www.chrissabella.co.uk/
Freq: Daily
Circ: 6597
Fashion

Christie
1054647
Web site: http://elancane.livejournal.com/
Freq: Daily
Circ: 9712
Social Issues

Christina Adores - CEASED 2016
996749
Editorial: 22 Knebworth House, Union Grove, London SW8 2RS
Web site: http://www.christinaadores.com/
Freq: Daily
Circ: 893
Beauty & Grooming, Cosmetics, Hair

Christmas Countdown Blog
1053527
Email: linda@christmascountdown.co.uk
Web site: http://christmascountdown.co.uk/
Freq: Daily
Circ: 10240
Audio Video Trade, Beauty & Grooming, Cameras, Consumer Electronics, Cooking & Baking, Cosmetics, Family & Parenting, Hair, Mobile Electronics, Movies & Video

Chrome & Black
1054603
Email: info@chromeandblack.com
Web site: chromeandblack.blogspot.co.uk
Freq: Daily
Circ: 10439
Visual Arts

Churumuri
1061450
Web site: http://www.churumuri.wordpress.com
Freq: Daily
Circ: 24282
Consumer Affairs, Crime & Violence, Defense & National Security, Energy & Environment, Ethical/Moral Issues, International News, Law, National News, News & Current Affairs, Northern Ireland

Ciaran's Tech Blog
1054490
Web site: http://www.coconut.ie/
Freq: Daily
Circ: 1735
Mobile Electronics

Ciberwolf
1061036
Web site: http://www.ciberwolf.com
Freq: Daily
Circ: 3345
Auto Aftermarket, Computers, Data Management, Electronics, Government Technology, Industry, Internet, Mobile Communications, Security & Security Systems, Software

Cicerone Blog
1053885
Tel: 44 01539 562069
Web site: http://blog.cicerone.co.uk/
Freq: Daily
Circ: 14633
Outdoor Recreation, Travel

Cider with Rosie
1100172
Email: enquiries@ciderwithrosie.com
Web site: http://www.ciderwithrosie.com/
Freq: Daily

Circ: 30636
Profile: Blog covering lifestyle. Cider with ROSIE blog discusses anything from life events and moments to food and recipes. The blog shares an extensive blog roll. The outlet offers RSS (Really Simple Syndication).
Regional General Interest, Women's Interests

Ciencia Amena de Arístides Bastidas
1061132
Web site: http://lacienciaamena.blogspot.com/
Freq: Daily
Circ: 471
National News, Science

Ciencia Con Una Espiral de Limón
1062019
Web site: http://cienciaconespiraldelimon.blogspot.com
Freq: Daily
Circ: 882
Cooking & Baking, Science

Ciencia Maldita
1061626
Web site: http://blogs.lanacion.com.ar/ciencia-maldita/
Freq: Daily
Circ: 27783
Science

Ciencia por Gusto
1061995
Web site: http://lacienciaporgusto.blogspot.com
Freq: Daily
Circ: 9515
Science

Ciencia Xataka
1061625
Web site: http://www.xatakaciencia.com/
Freq: Daily
Circ: 600790
Environment, Science

Ciencia y Fe
1061332
Web site: http://blogs.clarin.com/ciencia-y-fe/
Freq: Daily
Circ: 64660
Religion, Science

Cine Vertigo
1061363
Web site: http://cinevertigo.blogspot.com
Freq: Daily
Circ: 952
Bars, Clubs & Pubs, Comedy, Entertainment, Local Entertainment Guides, Movies & Video

Cine3.com
1061629
Web site: http://www.cine3.com
Freq: Daily
Circ: 42862
Movies & Video

Cinecritica
1060755
Web site: http://www.cineforochapin.blogspot.com
Freq: Daily
Circ: 548
Broadcasting, Movies & Video

Cinehouse
987945
Email: cinehouseuk@gmail.com
Web site: cinehouseuk.blogspot.co.uk/
Freq: Daily
Circ: 11418
Entertainment, Movies & Video

Cinema Chords
996791
Web site: http://cinemachords.com/
Freq: Daily
Circ: 13436
Entertainment, Movies & Video

Cinema Dial
1061787
Web site: http://cinemadial.blogspot.com/
Freq: Daily
Circ: 611
Movies & Video

Cinephonix blog
1052650
Editorial: 20 - 24 Broadwick Street, Soho, London W1F 8HT Tel: 44 02070 607151

Email: hello@cinephonix.com
Web site: http://www.cinephonix.com/blog/
Freq: Daily
Circ: 12
Music

Cinescalas
1061903
Web site: http://blogs.lanacion.com.ar/cine/
Freq: Daily
Circ: 7970
Movies & Video

Cinésthesia
1053018
Email: mikemccahill@fastmail.fm
Web site: cinesthesiac.blogspot.co.uk/
Freq: Daily
Circ: 11875
Profile: Blog covering film and DVD reviews. The blog has an archive dating back to April 2010.
Movies & Video

Cineworld Blog
981792
Editorial: 8th floor, Vantage London, Great West Road, Brentford TW8 9AG
Web site: Cineworld.co.uk/blog
Freq: Monthly
Circ: 191
Profile: Magazine featuring reviews of the latest films, star interviews and director profiles.
Ad Rate: Full Page Colour 6000.00
Movies & Video

Cinnamon Jewellery Blog
1054248
Email: spiralchick@gmail.com
Web site: http://cinnamonjewellery.blogspot.co.uk/
Freq: Daily
Circ: 611
Crafts

Cinosargo
1060387
Web site: http://www.cinosargo.bligoo.com
Freq: Daily
Circ: 27566
Art, Literature

Cippodromo
1061320
Web site: http://cippodromo.blogspot.com
Freq: Daily
Circ: 1681
Auto Aftermarket, Computers, Data Management, Electronics, Government Technology, Industry, Internet, Mobile Communications, Security & Security Systems, Software

Circle of Pine Trees
1098974
Web site: http://circleofpinetrees.com
Freq: Daily
Circ: 6492
Visual Arts

Circles of Light - Fylde
1055148
Email: circlesoflight-fylde@hotmail.co.uk
Web site: http://circlesoflight-fylde.blogspot.co.uk/
Freq: Daily
Circ: 10709
Art

Circulo de Estudio
1061710
Web site: http://circulodeestudios-centrohistorico.blogspot.com
Freq: Daily
Circ: 1809
Antiques/Collectibles, Art, Arts, History, Literature, National News, Photography, Politics, Theater & Performing Arts, Visual Arts

Ciro Urdaneta
1061269
Web site: http://blog.iws.com.ve
Freq: Daily
Circ: 95
Architecture & Design, Photography, Science

Citizenship Foundation
986109
Editorial: 50 Featherstone Street, London EC1Y 8RT Tel: 44 02075 664159
Email: info@citizenshipfoundation.org.uk
Web site: http://blog.citizenshipfoundation.org.uk/

Circ: 6645
Charitable Foundations

City Girl
1053824
Web site: http://www.citygirlblog.uk/
Freq: Daily
Circ: 7953
News & Current Affairs

City of Blackbirds
1053045
Email: hello@cityofblackbirds.com
Web site: http://cityofblackbirds.com/
Freq: Daily
Circ: 3167
Gardening, Nature & Wildlife, Photography

The City of Edinburgh Council News Blog
996250
Tel: 44 01315 294040
Email: justask@edinburgh.gov.uk
Web site: edinburgh.gov.uk/blog/newsblog
Freq: Daily
Circ: 26
Government, Scotland

Cityscape Bliss
1053290
Email: tkohutova@photographer.net
Web site: cityscape-bliss.com
Freq: Daily
Circ: 30753
Profile: CITYSCAPE BLISS lifestyle, travel and beauty. The blog has an archive dating back to November 2011.
Cooking & Baking, Cosmetics, Do-It-Yourself (DIY), Fashion, Gardening, Regional General Interest, Restaurant Reviews, Travel, Women's Interests

Ciudadana
1061842
Web site: http://laciudadana.blogspot.com/
Freq: Daily
Circ: 1120
National News, Politics

Civil Society blogs
1053807
Editorial: 15 Prescott Place, Clapham, London SW4 6BS
Email: info@civilsociety.co.uk
Web site: http://www.civilsociety.co.uk/home/featurestory/tab/blogs
Freq: Daily
Editor: Gareth Jones
Charitable Foundations

Clairejustine
988665
Email: clairejustine@live.co.uk
Web site: www.clairejustineoxox.com
Freq: Daily
Circ: 43261
Profile: Blog covering lifestyle. The Clairejustine blog discusses anything from motherhood and fashion to running and food. The blog has an archive dating back to February 2011.
Family & Parenting, Fashion

Claire's Crafty Blog
1054646
Freq: Daily
News & Current Affairs

Clamorous Voice
999621
Email: sophievduncan@gmail.com
Web site: clamorousvoice.wordpress.com
Freq: Daily
Circ: 41
Literature, Theater & Performing Arts

Clandestine Critic
1054051
Email: davidnorman@mail.com
Web site: www.clandestinecritic.co.uk
Freq: Daily
Circ: 521
Comedy, Entertainment, Local Entertainment Guides, Movies & Video

Clare with the Hair by Clare McCarthy
1098943
Editorial: No 6 Ballycasey Business Park, Ballycasey, Shannon, Co. Clare
Web site: http://clarewiththehair.com/
Freq: Daily
Circ: 10027
Beauty & Grooming, Cooking & Baking, Cosmetics, Fashion, Hair, Personal Finance, Restaurant Reviews

Class Teaching
1053758
Web site: http://classteaching.wordpress.com
Freq: Daily
Circ: 300
Profile: Blog covering education. Class Teaching blog discusses anything from education to teaching. The blog has an archive dating back to January 2012 and shares an extensive blog roll. The outlet offers RSS (Really Simple Syndication).
Education

Clear Debt
1054648
Email: enquiries@cleardebt.co.uk
Web site: www.cleardebt.co.uk/blog/
Freq: Daily
Circ: 1314

ClearBooks
986110
Editorial: Lyric House, 149 Hammersmith Road, West Kensington, London W14 0QL
Tel: 44 08448 169999
Email: support@clearbooks.co.uk
Web site: www.clearbooks.co.uk/blog
Freq: Daily
Circ: 8051
Auto Aftermarket, Computers, Data Management, Electronics, Government Technology, Industry, Internet, Mobile Communications, Security & Security Systems, Software

ClearlySo Blog
986868
Editorial: 4th Floor, 20 Old Street, London EC1V 9AB Tel: 44 02074 909520
Email: contact@clearlyso.com
Web site: https://www.clearlyso.com/category/blog/
Freq: Daily
Circ: 41
Editor: John Lloyd
Business, Charitable Foundations, Small and Medium Business

Clic Visual
1060614
Web site: http://www.clicvisual.com
Freq: Daily
Circ: 521
Auto Aftermarket, Computer & Video Games, Computers, Data Management, Electronics, Government Technology, Industry, Internet, Mobile Communications, Movies & Video

Click4quote Blog
997056
Editorial: 0 St. Peters Court, Middleborough, Colchester, Colchester CO1 1WD
Tel: 44 03308 081795
Email: enquiries@click4quote.com
Web site: www.click4quote.com/blog/
Freq: Daily
Circ: 16
Insurance

Clicony
1062131
Web site: http://blogs.eluniversal.com.mx/clicony
Freq: Daily
Circ: 1694229
Auto Aftermarket, Computers, Data Management, Electronics, Government Technology, Industry, Internet, Mobile Communications, Security & Security Systems, Software

Cliffski's Blog
998396
Web site: http://positech.co.uk/cliffsblog/
Freq: Daily
Circ: 113925
Computer & Video Games

Climb Now
1052720
Email: mail@climbnow.co.uk
Web site: http://www.climbnow.co.uk/blog
Freq: Daily
Circ: 117
Outdoor Recreation, Travel

Climb Reality
1054667
Web site: http://atouchofgnar.blogspot.co.uk/
Freq: Daily
Circ: 687
Outdoor Recreation

The Climbing Academy Blog
1053117
Tel: 44 01179 072850
Email: bristolinfo@theclimbingacademy.com
Web site: https://www.theclimbingacademy.com/blog/category/bristol/
Freq: Daily
Circ: 14
Outdoor Recreation

Climbing Frames UK Blog
1053520
Tel: 44 01284 852574
Email: info@climbingframesuk.com
Web site: https://www.selwood.com/blog/
Freq: Daily
Circ: 340
Elementary School, Family & Parenting, Preschool, Shopping

Clionautica Blog
1061458
Web site: http://clionautica.blogspot.com
Freq: Daily
Circ: 887
Politics

Clive on Learning
1053118
Email: info@morethanblended.com
Web site: http://clive-shepherd.blogspot.co.uk/
Freq: Daily
Circ: 1425
Branding, Marketing

Cloak & Swagger - CEASED 2016
985572
Web site: www.cloakandswagger.com
Circ: 521
Profile: Website covering lifestyle. The Cloak & Swagger website discusses anything from music, arts, lifestyle and fashion to urban and youth culture.
Bars, Clubs & Pubs, Comedy, Entertainment, Fashion, Lifestyle, Local Entertainment Guides, Men's Interests, Movies & Video, Regional General Interest, Women's Interests

Close Enough to Kiss
996799
Email: admin@closeenoughtokiss.co.uk
Web site: www.closeenoughtokiss.co.uk
Freq: Daily
Circ: 8935
Editor: Renee Jeffrey
Family & Parenting

Clothes Make The Man
987520
Editorial: 405 Norwood Road, West Norwood, London SE27 9BU
Web site: clothes-make-the-man.com
Freq: Daily
Circ: 10842
Fashion, Men's Interests

Clothes on Film
988339
Email: admin@clothesonfilm.com
Web site: http://clothesonfilm.com/
Freq: Daily
Circ: 40099
Fashion, Movies & Video, Photography, Theater & Performing Arts, Visual Arts

Clothes, Cameras and Coffee
1053829
Email: clothescamerasandcoffee@googlemail.com
Web site: http://clothescamerasandcoffee.blogspot.co.uk/
Freq: Daily
Circ: 7525
Fashion, Literature, Photography

Clove
986894
Editorial: Unit 12, Branksome Business Park, Bourne Valley Road, Poole BH12 1DW
Tel: 44 01202 552936
Web site: blog.clove.co.uk
Freq: Daily
Circ: 35684
Editor: Chris Ward
Mobile Electronics

Club Amantes del Vino
1061502
Web site: http://clubamantesdelvino.com/home/
Freq: Daily

Circ: 14664
Wine/Winemaking

Coach Cox
1054383
Email: russell.m.cox@gmail.com
Web site: http://www.coachcox.co.uk/
Freq: Daily
Circ: 9312
Sports

Coast Digital Blog
1054150
Editorial: 6 Beacon End Courtyard, London Road, Stanway, Colchester CO3 0NU
Tel: 44 08454 502086
Email: info@coastdigital.co.uk
Web site: http://www.coastdigital.co.uk/blog/
Freq: Daily
Circ: 2367
Marketing

Coathanger
996686
Tel: 44 02033 030654
Email: info@coathanger.net
Web site: www.coathanger.net/blog/
Freq: Daily
Circ: 28
Fashion

Cobertura Digital
1061715
Web site: http://www.coberturadigital.com
Freq: Daily
Circ: 7126
Auto Aftermarket, Computers, Data Management, Electronics, Government Technology, Industry, Internet, Mobile Communications, Security & Security Systems, Software

Cocina al Natural
1061939
Web site: http://blogs.eluniversal.com.mx/cocinaal
Freq: Daily
Circ: 233
Alcohol & Spirits, Consumer Goods & Products, Cooking & Baking, Food, Tobacco

Cocina Chilena
1060637
Email: angelicacocinachilena@gmail.com
Web site: http://comidachile.blogspot.com
Freq: Daily
Circ: 3684
Cooking & Baking, Food

Cocina de Blo
1062022
Web site: http://cocina-de-blo.blogspot.com
Freq: Daily
Circ: 2805
Cooking & Baking, Food

Cocina de Mercado
1060447
Web site: http://www.cocinademercado.blogspot.com
Freq: Daily
Circ: 652
Cooking & Baking, Food

Cocinando Con Todos Los Sentidos
1061885
Web site: http://cocinandocontodoslossentidos.blogspot.com
Freq: Daily
Circ: 611
Cooking & Baking, Food

Cocinando-te
1061088
Web site: http://blogs.clarin.com/la-insoportable-levedad-del-ser-/
Freq: Daily
Circ: 67821
Cooking & Baking, Lifestyle, Men's Interests, Regional General Interest, Women's Interests

Cocktails & Cocktalk
996132
Editorial: 90 De Frene Road, Sydenham, London SE26 4AG Tel: 44 07739 385787
Email: anthony@cocktailsandcocktalk.com
Web site: http://cocktailsandcocktalk.com/
Freq: Daily
Circ: 136916
Celebrities, LGBT, Men's Interests

Cocktails & Daydreams
1054204
Email: hello@cocktailsanddaydreams.com
Web site: www.cocktailsanddaydreams.com
Freq: Daily
Circ: 2414
Profile: Blog covering lifestyle. COCKTAILS & DAYDREAMS blog discusses anything from lifestyle, food and travel to fashion and beauty. The blog has an archive dating back to February 2012 and shares a short blog roll. The outlet offers RSS (Really Simple Syndication).
Beauty & Grooming, Cosmetics, Fashion, Hair, Women's Interests

Cocktails in Teacups
1052969
Web site: http://www.cocktailsinteacups.com/
Freq: Daily
Circ: 10217
Profile: Blog covering lifestyle. Cocktails in Teacups blog discusses anything from fashion and beauty to parenting and recipes. The blog has an archive dating back to September 2012 and shares an extensive blog roll.
Beauty & Grooming, Cooking & Baking, Cosmetics, Do-It-Yourself (DIY), Family & Parenting, Fashion, Hair, Travel, Women's Interests

Coco's Tea Party
986111
Email: cocosteaparty@gmail.com
Web site: www.cocosteaparty.com
Freq: Daily
Circ: 42998
Editor: Ella Gregory
Fashion

CODE Investing Blog
996783
Editorial: 133 Houndsditch, London EC3A 7BX Tel: 44 02032 891494
Email: contactus@crowdbnk.com
Web site: https://www.codeinvesting.com/blog/
Freq: Daily
Circ: 43
Business, Small and Medium Business

The Code Word
1052787
Editorial: 3rd Floor, Medius House, 2 Sheraton Street, London W1F 8BH
Web site: http://www.myvouchercodes.co.uk/the-code-word/
Freq: Daily
Circ: 24638
Banking, Branding, Marketing

Coethica
1053403
Email: david.connor@coethica.com
Freq: Daily
Branding, Business, Marketing

Coffee & Vanilla
986112
Web site: www.coffeeandvanilla.com
Freq: Daily
Circ: 10787
Alcohol & Spirits, Bars, Clubs & Pubs, Beer, Beverages, Cooking & Baking, Food, Grocery Stores, Organic Food, Restaurant Reviews, Vegetarianism & Veganism

Coffee Curls
1053439
Web site: http://coffeecurls.co.uk/
Freq: Daily
Circ: 10486
Family & Parenting, Women's Interests

Cold Tea & Smelly Nappies
996402
Web site: http://www.coldteaandsmellynappies.co.uk/
Freq: Daily
Circ: 6324
Family & Parenting

Colour me!
1061048
Web site: http://colourme.indiedays.com
Freq: Daily
Circ: 27452
Fashion

Colouring Without Borders
1054084
Web site: www.coloringwithoutborders.com

UK Blogs

Freq: Daily
Circ: 521
Railroad, Travel

Columna 1061232
Web site: http://lacolumna.wordpress.com
Freq: Daily
Circ: 69
National News, Politics

Come here to me 1053786
Web site: http://comeheretome.com
Freq: Daily
Circ: 12398
Alcohol & Spirits, Beer, Men's Interests, Regional General Interest, Restaurant Reviews

Comercialización Agricola 1062130
Web site: http://www.comercializacionagricola.blogspot.com
Freq: Daily
Circ: 629
Animal Farming, National News

Comfort Bites Blog 988958
Email: joromerofood@yahoo.co.uk
Web site: http://www.comfortbites.co.uk/
Freq: Daily
Circ: 8769
Cooking & Baking, Organic Food, Vegetarianism & Veganism

Cómo Bajar Rápido De Peso 1062109
Web site: http://comobajarrapidodepeso.com
Freq: Daily
Circ: 611
Nutrition

Cómo Quemar Grasa Rápidamente 1061489
Web site: http://www.comerparaperderfeliz.com
Freq: Daily
Circ: 521
Fitness & Exercise, Health & Medicine, Nutrition

Como Ser un Geek 1060788
Web site: http://www.comoserungeek.com
Freq: Daily
Circ: 3331
Auto Aftermarket, Computer & Video Games, Computers, Data Management, Electronics, Government Technology, Industry, Internet, Mobile Communications, Security & Security Systems

Compartiendo con Kachimondo 1061140
Email: kachimondo@gmail.com
Web site: http://quitarayas.blogspot.com/
Freq: Daily
Circ: 466
Classical/Choral/Band Music, Country, Folk, Bluegrass, Dance Music, Jazz & Blues, Music, Pop Music, R&B, Urban, World, Rap & Hip Hop, Rock Music

Compassion Blog 999290
Editorial: River Court, Mill Lane, Godalming, Godalming GU7 1EZ **Tel:** 44 01483 521950
Web site: http://www.ciwf.org.uk/philip-lymbery/blog/
Freq: Daily
Circ: 36978
Charitable Foundations

Complicity 996320
Email: zoe@complicity.co.uk
Web site: http://www.complicity.co.uk/blog/
Freq: Daily
Circ: 8715
Politics

Con Cafe 1061794
Web site: http://www.con-cafe.com/
Freq: Daily
Circ: 56481
Mobile Electronics

Con Ida y Vuelta 1061871
Web site: http://conidayvuelta.wordpress.com/
Freq: Daily
Circ: 11
Lifestyle, Men's Interests, Regional General Interest, Women's Interests

Concierge Angel 1099572
Email: info@conciergeangel.com
Web site: http://www.conciergeangel.com/
Freq: Daily
Circ: 15492
Cooking & Baking, Luxury Goods, Men's Interests, Restaurant Reviews, Travel, Women's Interests

The Conciousness Blog - Law firm websites, CRM & marketing 1053327
Tel: 44 01173 250200
Email: support@conscious.co.uk
Web site: http://www.conscious.co.uk/site/blog/
Freq: Daily
Circ: 7
Corporate Law, Legal Services, Marketing

confessions of a design geek 985771
Editorial: The Studio, 108 Station Road, Shalford, London GU4 8HD
Web site: http://confessionsofadesigngeek.com
Freq: Daily
Circ: 8551
Editor: Katie Treggiden
Architecture & Design, Do-It-Yourself (DIY), Gardening, Home, Property Management & Maintenance, Real Estate

Confessions of a Single Mum 996977
Email: mail@confessionsofasinglemum.co.uk
Web site: www.confessionsofasinglemum.co.uk
Freq: Daily
Circ: 19495
Family & Parenting

Confessions of a single parent pessimist 1054129
Email: info@singleparentpessimist.co.uk
Web site: http://www.singleparentpessimist.co.uk/
Freq: Daily
Circ: 7915
Profile: Blog covering single motherhood. The blog has an archive dating back to April 2013.
Cooking & Baking, Do-It-Yourself (DIY), Family & Parenting, Regional General Interest, Women's Interests

Confused Julia 988029
Email: confusedjulia@gmail.com
Web site: http://www.confusedjulia.com/
Freq: Daily
Circ: 8055
Travel

Conoce a tu Legislador 1061902
Web site: http://blogs.eluniversal.com.mx/conoce
Freq: Daily
Circ: 233
Bankruptcy, Company News & Appointments, Consumer Interest, Corporate Law, Criminal Law, Employment, Estate Planning, Family Law, Federal Courts, Food & Drug Administration

Conor's Commentary 1064059
Email: conorfryan@aol.com
Web site: http://conorfryan.blogspot.co.uk/
Freq: Daily
Circ: 490
Disability, Education, Government, Higher Education, Northern Ireland, Politics, Preschool, Schools & Institutions, Students, Travel

Conquistalo 1061208
Web site: http://www.comoconquistarlo.com

Freq: Daily
Circ: 3050
Family & Parenting, Relationships

Consensio Blog 987709
Editorial: 9 Reece Mews, South Kensington, London SW7 3HE **Tel:** 44 02033 930833
Email: enquiries@consensioholidays.co.uk
Web site: http://www.consensiochalets.co.uk/blog
Freq: Daily
Circ: 11
Travel, Winter Sports

Conservative Home 984881
Editorial: 7 Cowley Street, Westminster, London SW1P 3NB **Tel:** 44 02033 272350
Web site: conservativehome.blogs.com
Freq: Daily
Circ: 16028856
Editor: Paul Goodman
Politics

Considered 1053810
Editorial: Faculty of Education, Old Sessions House, North Holmes Road, Canterbury CT1 1QU
Email: considered@canterbury.ac.uk
Web site: www.consider-ed.org.uk
Freq: Daily
Circ: 9227
Profile: Blog covering education. The Considered blog discusses anything from education policy and research to curriculum and teacher development. The blog promotes educational discussion, debate and commentary. The blog has an archive dating back to April 2013. The outlet offers RSS (Really Simple Syndication).
Education

Constance-Victoria 1053967
Email: constance_victoria@hotmail.co.uk
Web site: constance-victoria.blogspot.co.uk
Freq: Daily
Circ: 967
Photography

Constant Gardener 1053875
Web site: sallynex.com/blog
Freq: Daily
Circ: 196
Gardening

Construction Marketers Blog 1052668
Tel: 44 01908 671707
Email: talk@pauleycreative.co.uk
Web site: http://www.pauleycreative.co.uk/blog/
Freq: Daily
Circ: 1103
Building & Construction, Marketing

Consultorio 1062056
Web site: http://psicologia-eldivan.blogspot.com/
Freq: Daily
Circ: 521
AIDS/HIV, Allergies, Cardiology, Dermatology, Diabetes, Diseases & Conditions, Gastroenterology, Hematology, Infectious Diseases, Medicine

Contadero Blog 1060899
Web site: http://contadero4.blogspot.com
Freq: Daily
Circ: 1222
Politics

Continental 996315
Editorial: 191 High Street, Yiewsley, West Drayton UB7 7XW **Tel:** 44 01895 425983
Email: marketing.uk@conti.de
Web site: http://www.continental-tyres.co.uk/car/media-services/newsroom
Freq: Daily
Circ: 14
Automakers

Conversations Overheard at the Mad Hatter's Tea Party 1061591
Web site: http://totoaguerrevere.blogspot.com/
Freq: Daily

Circ: 1990
Lifestyle, Men's Interests, Regional General Interest, Women's Interests

Conversations: The Microsoft Devices blog 999211
Editorial: 2nd floor, 35 Great Sutton Street, London EC1V 0DX **Tel:** 44 02087 980441
Email: info@republicpublishing.co.uk
Web site: http://lumiaconversations.microsoft.com//
Freq: Daily
Circ: 28903626
Mobile Electronics

Cook Sister! 986495
Email: emailcooksister@gmail.com
Web site: www.cooksister.com
Freq: Daily
Circ: 35676
Cooking & Baking

Cooking on a Bootstrap 987408
Email: jackmonroe@live.co.uk
Web site: https://cookingonabootstrap.com/
Freq: Daily
Circ: 43638
Cooking & Baking, Personal Finance

Cool Cars Blog 987860
Email: mark@coolcarsandgirls.com
Web site: http://www.coolcarsandgirls.com/
Freq: Daily
Circ: 2460
Profile: Blog covering cars. COOL CARS BLOG discusses anything from classic cars and modified cars to supercars. The outlet offers RSS (Really Simple Syndication).
Antique & Collectible Cars, Automotive, Driving

Cool Things 1053014
Email: collthings@gmail.com
Web site: http://www.collthings.co.uk/
Freq: Daily
Circ: 22921
Antiques/Collectibles, Apple, Armed Forces, Astrology & Parapsychology, Astronomy, Audio Video Trade, Aviation, Boating & Yachting, Cameras, Camping and RV Travel

Coolest Gadgets 986898
Web site: http://www.coolest-gadgets.com
Freq: Daily
Circ: 319864
Audio Video Trade, Cameras, Consumer Electronics, Mobile Electronics, Movies & Video

CoolSmartPhone 985735
Editorial: 4 Leam Drive, Burntwood, Burntwood WS7 9JG
Email: contact@coolsmartphone.com
Web site: www.coolsmartphone.com
Freq: Daily
Circ: 86397
Editor: Leigh Geary
Mobile Electronics

Coombe Mill Blog 987640
Tel: 44 01208 850344
Email: mail@coombemill.com
Web site: http://www.coombemill.com/blog/
Freq: Daily
Circ: 18903
Family & Parenting

Cooperativismo 1062144
Web site: http://blogsdelagente.com/cooperativismo
Freq: Daily
Circ: 65541
Celebrities, Politics, Social Issues

Copper Garden 987584
Email: coppergarden@live.co.uk
Web site: http://www.copper-garden.co.uk
Freq: Daily
Circ: 6756
Profile: Blog covering fashion and personal style. The blog has an archive dating back to August 2011.
Fashion

CopperGardenx Vlog 1104181
Email: coppergardon@live.oo.uk
Web site: https://www.youtube.com/user/
CopperGardenx
Freq: Daily
Circ: 1
Cosmetics, Fashion, Women's Interests

Coppola Comment 1053494
Email: francesmcoppola@gmail.com
Web site: http://www.coppolacomment.com
Freq: Daily
Circ: 48072
Profile: Blog covering finance. Coppola
Comment discusses anything from
economics and banking to welfare and the
Eurozone. The blog has an archive dating
back to February 2011 and shares an
extensive blog roll.
Classical/Choral/Band Music, Economics

The Copywriter's Crucible
1054075
Freq: Daily
News & Current Affairs

Corazón Espinado 1062027
Web site: http://www.elpoliciaco.blogspot.
com
Freq: Daily
Circ: 521
National News

Corner By Corner - CEASED
1054425
Web site: cornerbycorner.co.uk
Freq: Daily
Circ: 687
Profile: Blog covering home decorating and
family life.
Do-It-Yourself (DIY), Family & Parenting,
Literature

Corner Corto 1061662
Web site: http://cornercorto.blogspot.com/
Freq: Daily
Circ: 749
Soccer

Cornflower Books 987295
Email: kcwh@btinternet.com
Web site: www.cornflowerbooks.co.uk
Freq: Daily
Circ: 9823
Literature

Cornwall SEO 1052849
Web site: http://www.cornwallseo.com/
search/
Freq: Daily
Circ: 1104
Marketing

Coronation Street Blog 998405
Web site: www.coronationstreetupdates.
blogspot.com
Freq: Daily
Circ: 14663
Editor: Glenda Young
Broadcasting

**Corporate Law and Govern-
ance Blog** 1053976
Web site: corporatelawandgovernance.
blogspot.co.uk
Freq: Daily
Circ: 1394
Corporate Law

Corresponsal 1061453
Web site: http://www.diarioelcorresponsal.
blogia.com
Freq: Daily
Circ: 95303
National News

Corrin Creative 1052544
Web site: staceycorrin.co.uk
Freq: Daily
Circ: 10665
Do-It-Yourself (DIY), Family & Parenting

**Cosas Cositas y Cosotas con
Mesh** 1061113
Web site: http://
cosascositasycosotasconmesh.blogspot.
com
Freq: Daily
Circ: 2306
Crafts, Do-It-Yourself (DIY)

Cosme-De 1061734
Web site: http://www.cosme-de.blogspot.
com/
Freq: Daily
Circ: 1018
Cosmetics

Cosmetic Candy 986113
Web site: http://cosmetic-candy.com
Freq: Daily
Circ: 24834
Beauty & Grooming, Cosmetics, Hair

Cost Of Living 987839
Web site: www.cost-ofliving.net/
Freq: Daily
Circ: 14698
Community Care (UK), EMS/Emergency
Medical Services, Health Administration,
Healthcare Industry, Medicine, Politics

The Cosy Traveller 1054451
Web site: www.thecosytraveller.co.uk
Freq: Daily
Circ: 9660
Travel

CosyHomeBlog 985994
Email: cosyhomeblog@googlemail.com
Web site: www.cosyhomeblog.com
Freq: Daily
Circ: 6750
Editor: Rachel Newcombe
Architecture & Design, Do-It-Yourself
(DIY), Gardening, Home, Property
Management & Maintenance, Real Estate

The Cotswold Food Year 996895
Editorial: Unit 75, Oakfield Close,
Tewkesbury Business Park, Tewkesbury
GL20 8SD Tel: 44 01684 854406
Email: info@bensonscateringltd.co.uk
Web site: www.thecotswoldfoodyear.com
Freq: Daily
Circ: 2306
Cooking & Baking, Organic Food

Cottage Retreatist 1053203
Web site: http://www.cottageretreatist.com/
Freq: Daily
Circ: 1208
Profile: Blog covering frugal living, recipes,
lifestyle and dealing with debt. The blog has
an archive dating back to May 2014.
Personal Finance

Cottages & Castles Blog 1073825
Editorial: Cottages & Castles, 59 George
Street, Edinburgh EH2 2JG
Tel: 44 01738 451610
Email: holidays@cottages-and-castles.co.uk
Web site: http://www.cottages-and-castles.
co.uk/blog/
Freq: Daily
Circ: 17
Travel

Cottontails Baby 1053055
Tel: 44 01531 640886
Web site: http://blog.cottontailsbaby.co.uk/
Freq: Daily
Circ: 6
Crafts, Family & Parenting

Counselling Directory 997544
Editorial: Coliseum, Riverside Way,
Camberley GU15 3YL Tel: 44 01276 300138
Email: press@counselling-directory.org.uk
Web site: http://www.counselling-directory.
org.uk/blog
Freq: Daily
Circ: 32
Charitable Foundations

Counselling in Exeter 997239
Editorial: Room 2, Seconf Floor, 49 North
Street, Exeter EX4 3QR
Tel: 44 07917 523494

Email: awcounsellingexeter@yahoo.co.uk
Web site: http://www.
amanda.williamsonounselling.co.uk/
Freq: Daily
Circ: 10469
Health & Medicine

Country Life Property Blog
997071
Editorial: The Blue Fin Building, 110
Southwark Street, London SE1 0SU
Tel: 44 02031 484444
Web site: http://www.countrylife.co.uk/
Freq: Daily
Circ: 221686
Architecture & Design, Do-It-Yourself
(DIY), Gardening, Home, Property
Management & Maintenance, Real Estate

**Country View Crafts Chal-
lenge Blog** 1053483
Web site: http://countryviewchallenges.
blogspot.co.uk/
Freq: Daily
Circ: 1422
Crafts

Cousins Business Law Blog
1053840
Editorial: Swan House, PO Box 11543,
Birmingham B13 0ZL Tel: 44 08450 035639
Web site: http://www.business-lawfirm.co.
uk/blog/
Freq: Daily
Circ: 21
Law

Couture Blazer 1076645
Web site: https://coutureblazer.wordpress.
com/
Freq: Daily
Circ: 2
Beauty & Grooming, Cosmetics, Fashion,
Hair

Couture Girl 988507
Email: kljohnson1990@gmail.com
Web site: http://www.couture-girl.co.uk/
Freq: Daily
Circ: 47180
Beauty & Grooming, Cosmetics, Fashion,
Hair

Cowbiscuits 988934
Email: cowbiscuitsblog@gmail.com
Web site: http://www.cowbiscuits.com/
Freq: Daily
Circ: 9578
Profile: Blog covering beauty. cowbiscuits
blog discusses anything from beauty and
cosmetics to fashion and lifestyle. The blog
has an archive dating back to June 2010.
Beauty & Grooming, Cosmetics, Do-It-
Yourself (DIY), Fashion, Hair, Women's
Interests

Cozy Frog 1053078
Web site: http://cozy-frog.blogspot.co.uk/
Freq: Daily
Circ: 521
Crafts

Crack In The Road 987285
Tel: 44 07740 805066
Email: site@crackintheroad.com
Web site: www.crackintheroad.com
Freq: Daily
Circ: 13459
Editor: Ben Blackburn
Classical/Choral/Band Music, Country,
Folk, Bluegrass, Dance Music, Jazz &
Blues, Music, Pop Music, R&B, Urban,
World, Rap & Hip Hop, Rock Music

Cracked Nails and Split Ends
988051
Editorial: 1 Diprose Drive, Lowestoft,
Lowestoft NR32 4GB
Web site: www.crackednailsandsplitends.
co.uk
Freq: Daily
Circ: 16935
Profile: Cracked Nails and Split Ends covers
lifestyle, parenting, fashion, beauty, pets and
product reviews. The blog has an archive
dating back to June 2012.
Family & Parenting

Cracks y Caprichosa 1061523
Web site: http://cracksycaprichosa.
blogspot.com/
Freq: Daily
Circ: 521
Soccer

Craft Blog UK 1052891
Web site: http://www.ukcraftblog.com/
Freq: Daily
Circ: 8050
Crafts

Crafting when I can 1054923
Web site: http://poppet-craftingwhenican.
blogspot.co.uk/
Freq: Daily
Circ: 611
Crafts

Craftingallday Creations
1056770
Email: craftingallday1@yahoo.co.uk
Web site: http://craftingalldayscards.
blogspot.co.uk/
Freq: Daily
Circ: 946
Crafts

Craftingandy 1055311
Web site: http://craftingandy.blogspot.co.
uk/
Freq: Daily
Circ: 687
Art, Crafts

Crafts of Texture 1053338
Email: info@sarastexturecrafts.com
Web site: http://sarastexturecrafts.blogspot.
co.uk/
Freq: Daily
Circ: 687
Crafts

The Crafty Beeress 1058390
Web site: http://www.craftybeeress.com/
Freq: Daily
Circ: 12114
Beer, Cooking & Baking, Restaurant
Reviews

Crafty Green Poet 1053452
Email: juliet.m.wilson@gmail.com
Web site: http://craftygreenpoet.blogspot.
co.uk/
Freq: Daily
Circ: 7365
Environment, Literature

The Crafty oINK Pen 1053592
Tel: 44 01480 896885
Email: mikaelaflys@btconnect.com
Web site: http://thecraftyoinkpen.blogspot.
co.uk/
Freq: Daily
Circ: 1297
News & Current Affairs

**Crafty Ribbons Pure Inspira-
tion Blog** 1054384
Tel: 44 01258 455889
Email: info@craftyribbons.com
Web site: http://craftyribbonsinspiration.
blogspot.com/
Freq: Daily
Circ: 491
Crafts

The Crafty Wife 996323
Web site: http://craftywife.blogspot.co.uk/
Freq: Daily
Circ: 1218
Crafts

Cranky Gamers UK 995319
Email: crankytoz@gmail.com
Web site: http://www.crankygamersuk.net/
Freq: Daily
Circ: 10244
Computer & Video Games

Crash Taylor 1053272
Web site: http://www.crashtaylorblog.com
Freq: Daily
Circ: 1741
Photography

UK Blogs

Crave 1054234
Web site: www.cnet.com/uk/crave/
Freq: Daily
Circ: 40
Audio Video Trade, Cameras, Consumer Electronics, Mobile Electronics, Movies & Video

Crazy House Gaming 1053820
Web site: http://www.crazyhorsegaming.co.uk/
Freq: Daily
Circ: 972
Computer & Video Games

The crazy kitchen 988253
Email: info@thecrazykitchen.co.uk
Web site: http://www.thecrazykitchen.co.uk/
Freq: Daily
Circ: 14979
Cooking & Baking

Crazy with Twins 987625
Web site: crazywithtwins.com
Freq: Daily
Circ: 22653
Family & Parenting

Creative Applications Network Blog 987134
Editorial: Curtain House, Space 408, 134-146 Curtain Road, London EC2A 3AR
Web site: http://www.creativeapplications.net/blog/
Freq: Daily
Circ: 9
Art, Graphic Design, Software

Creative Boom 985371
Editorial: Studio A, Fourth Floor, 8 Lower Ormond Street, Manchester M1 5QF
Email: submit@creativeboom.co.uk
Web site: http://www.creativeboom.com/
Circ: 630690
Editor: Katy Cowan
Profile: The Creative Boom is an online magazine for the creative industries and covers architecture, interior design, art, graphic design, illustration, photography, travel, fashion, cars, tech and home accessories.
Antiques/Collectibles, Art, Arts, Literature, Photography, Theater & Performing Arts, Visual Arts

Creative Boys Club 1060687
Web site: http://www.creativeboysclub.com
Freq: Daily
Circ: 1412
Bars, Clubs & Pubs, Comedy, Entertainment, Local Entertainment Guides, Movies & Video

Creative Brides Blog 996399
Tel: 44 01892 655166
Email: hello@creativebrides.co.uk
Web site: www.creativebrides.co.uk/blog
Freq: Daily
Circ: 11
Weddings

Creative Intent 1052807
Tel: 44 01473 276144
Email: hello@creativeintent.co.uk
Web site: http://www.creativeintent.co.uk/blog/
Freq: Daily
Circ: 106
Computers, Internet, Marketing

The creative mind of Sylvie 1053198
Web site: http://creativemindofsylvie.blogspot.com/
Freq: Daily
Circ: 521
Crafts

The Creative Penn 988000
Web site: www.thecreativepenn.com/blog/
Freq: Daily
Circ: 13514
Literature

Creatively Inspired To Succeed 1053340
Web site: http://creativelyinspiredtosucceed.blogspot.co.uk
Freq: Daily
Circ: 611
Art, Cosmetics, Fashion, Regional General Interest, Travel, Women's Interests

The Creators Project 997764
Email: editor@thecreatorsproject.com
Web site: https://creators.vice.com/en_uk
Freq: Daily
Circ: 353056
Editor: Leander Roet
Antiques/Collectibles, Art, Arts, Bars, Clubs & Pubs, Comedy, Entertainment, Literature, Local Entertainment Guides, Movies & Video, Photography

Creditplus Blog 1074061
Tel: 44 01202 684898
Email: marketing@creditplus.co.uk
Web site: https://www.creditplus.co.uk/blog/
Freq: Daily
Circ: 36
Driving, Lending

Creepers and Cupcakes 997261
Web site: www.creepersandcupcakes.com
Freq: Daily
Circ: 9526
Beauty & Grooming, Cosmetics, Fashion, Fitness & Exercise, Hair, Nutrition, Travel, Women's Interests

Crenk 559098
Email: tips@crenk.com
Web site: http://crenk.com
Freq: Daily
Circ: 30670
Industry News, Internet Applications, Mobile Communications

The Cricket Blog 1052760
Web site: http://www.thecricketblog.com/
Freq: Daily
Circ: 6767
Cricket

The Cricket blog 1053331
Email: editor@wisdencricketer.com
Web site: http://wisdencricketer.com/blogs/
Freq: Daily
Circ: 106
Cricket

The Cricket Tier 1053992
Web site: http://thecrickettier.com/
Freq: Daily
Circ: 9193
Cricket

Cricket with Balls 1054619
Email: cricketwithballs@gmail.com
Web site: http://cricketwithballs.com/
Freq: Daily
Circ: 9511
Cricket

Crisis, Negocios y Dinero 1061604
Email: webmaster@crisisynegocio.com
Web site: http://www.crisisynegocio.com
Freq: Daily
Circ: 1166
Business, Personal Finance, Small and Medium Business

Critical Education 1053523
Email: andrewjmcgettigan@gmail.com
Web site: andrewmcgettigan.org
Freq: Daily
Circ: 11649
Alumni, Careers, Education, Student Lifestyle, Teachers

Critical Gamer 988183
Editorial: 24 Ackinduff Park, Dungannon BT70 3AU
Email: admin@criticalgamer.co.uk
Web site: http://www.criticalgamer.co.uk/
Freq: Daily

Circ: 13794
Computer & Video Games

CriticaPura 1062138
Web site: http://www.criticapura.com
Freq: Daily
Circ: 687
National News, Politics

Criticismism 988409
Email: mark@criticismism.com
Web site: http://www.criticismism.com/
Freq: Daily
Circ: 9463
Antiques/Collectibles, Art, Arts, Literature, Photography, Theater & Performing Arts, Visual Arts

Criticunder Movie 1060906
Web site: http://criticunder-movie.blogspot.com/
Freq: Daily
Circ: 521
Movies & Video

Crochetime 996827
Editorial: 108 Speer Road, London KT7 0PP
Tel: 44 07758 218005
Email: crochetime@gmail.com
Web site: crochetime.net
Freq: Daily
Circ: 8804
Crafts

Cronicas Barbituricas 1060766
Web site: http://cronicasbarbituricas.blogspot.com/
Freq: Daily
Circ: 9887
Art, Literature

Crooked Lines 1052777
Email: domgarnett@yahoo.co.uk
Web site: http://dgfishtales.blogspot.co.uk/
Freq: Daily
Circ: 2097
Fishing

The Crop Site 986249
Editorial: 5M Enterprises Ltd, Benchmark House, 8 Smithy Wood Drive, Sheffield S35 1QN
Tel: 44 01234 818180
Web site: http://www.thecropsite.com
Circ: 3015
Animal Farming, Environment

The Crowdcube Blog 997028
Editorial: The Innovation Centre, University of Exeter, Rennes Drive, Exeter EX4 4RN
Tel: 44 01392 241319
Email: support@crowdcube.com
Web site: http://blog.crowdcube.com/
Freq: Daily
Circ: 245
Business, Corporate Responsibility, Equities, Small and Medium Business

Crowdfunduk 998196
Web site: crowdfunduk.org
Freq: Daily
Circ: 8457
Charitable Foundations

Cruise Critic Blog 997546
Editorial: 7 Soho Square, London WC1D 3QB
Tel: 44 02033 203241
Email: editor@cruisecritic.co.uk
Web site: www.cruisecritic.co.uk/blog
Freq: Daily
Circ: 244
Airline Inflight, Railroad, Travel

The Cruise Line Blog 1054235
Tel: 44 08000 086677
Email: res@cruiscline.co.uk
Web site: http://www.cruiseline.co.uk/blog/
Freq: Daily
Circ: 19
Airline Inflight, Railroad, Travel

Cruise.co.uk blogs 1052906
Tel: 44 03303 038108
Email: contactus@cruise.co.uk
Web site: http://www.cruise.co.uk/
Freq: Daily
Circ: 991758
Travel

cruise1st.co.uk 1053845
Tel: 44 01618 690426
Email: editors@cruise1stblog.co.uk
Web site: http://news.cruise1st.co.uk/
Freq: Daily
Circ: 40819
Travel

Crumbs + Corkscrews 988221
Web site: http://www.crumbsandcorkscrews.co.uk/
Freq: Daily
Circ: 49178
Profile: Blog covering food, recipes and lifestyle. The blog has an archive dating back to December 2012.
Cooking & Baking, Organic Food, Restaurant Reviews

The Crumby Mummy 1053267
Web site: www.thecrumbymummy.co.uk
Freq: Daily
Circ: 46594
Profile: Blog covering motherhood. Crumby Mummy blog discusses anything from family and parenting to motherhood and baking. The outlet offers RSS (Really Simple Syndication).
Family & Parenting

Crummbs blog 997832
Editorial: 21 Waterfront House, Harry Zeital Way, London E5 9RQ
Email: hello@crummbs.co.uk
Web site: http://crummbs.co.uk/
Freq: Daily
Circ: 12777
Alcohol & Spirits, Bars, Clubs & Pubs, Beer, Beverages, Cooking & Baking, Food, Grocery Stores, Organic Food, Regional General Interest, Restaurant Reviews

Crunch Blog 999402
Editorial: Unit 11, Hove Business Centre, Fonthill Road, Hove BN3 6HA
Web site: www.crunch.co.uk/blog/
Freq: Daily
Circ: 1982
News & Current Affairs

CSAR 1057077
Email: admin@cleansheetsallround.co.uk
Web site: http://www.cleansheetsallround.co.uk/
Freq: Daily
Circ: 60624
Soccer

CSI Girls Blog 998298
Email: cosmeticsshoppingintoxication@hotmail.co.uk
Web site: http://www.thecsigirls.co.uk/
Freq: Daily
Circ: 9903
Beauty & Grooming, Cosmetics, Hair, Shopping

Cuando era Chamo 1060980
Web site: http://www.cuandoerachamo.com/
Freq: Daily
Circ: 6327
Lifestyle, Men's Interests, Regional General Interest, Women's Interests

Cuerpo Ideal 1061654
Web site: http://www.tu-cuerpo-ideal.com/blog/
Freq: Daily
Circ: 348
Fitness & Exercise, Nutrition

Cueto & Asociados 1061834
Web site: http://www.delcuetoyasoc.wordpress.com
Freq: Daily
Circ: 6
Business, Small and Medium Business

Cuidado de Plantas 1061509
Web site: http://www.cuidado-de-plantas.com
Freq: Daily
Circ: 341
Environment, Gardening

Culinary Adventures of the Spice Scribe
997019
Tel: 44 01992 767687
Web site: http://culinaryadventuresofthespicescribe.wordpress.com/
Freq: Daily
Circ: 157
Editor: Zoe Perrett
Cooking & Baking, Food, Grocery Stores, Organic Food, Restaurant Reviews, Vegetarianism & Veganism

Culpa es de la iguana
1061470
Web site: http://www.laculpaesdelaiguana.com
Freq: Daily
Circ: 611
Auto Aftermarket, Computers, Data Management, Electronics, Government Technology, Industry, Internet, Mobile Communications, National News, Politics

The Cultural Exposé
990668
Email: info@theculturalexpose.co.uk
Web site: www.theculturalexpose.co.uk
Freq: Daily
Circ: 6801
Art, Cooking & Baking, Photography, Restaurant Reviews, Theater & Performing Arts, Travel, Visual Arts

Cultural Insight
1094458
Tel: 44 02086 141500
Email: avuk-culturalinsight@grpitsrv.com
Web site: http://culturalinsight.com/
Freq: Daily
Circ: 9802
Advertising Industry, Branding, Marketing

Culture Fix
987938
Email: culturefixuk@gmail.com
Web site: www.culturefix.co.uk/
Freq: Daily
Circ: 9963
Editor: Andrew McArthur
Profile: Blog covering film and DVD reviews, music and television.
Movies & Video

The Culture Vulture
985245
Editorial: Munro House, Duke Street, Leeds LS9 8AG
Email: wearetheculturevultures@gmail.com
Web site: https://theculturevulture.co.uk/blog/
Freq: Daily
Circ: 10236
Editor: Emma Bearman
Antiques/Collectibles, Art, Arts, Bars, Clubs & Pubs, Comedy, Entertainment, Literature, Local Entertainment Guides, Movies & Video, Photography

Cumbrian Rambler
996644
Editorial: Blaw Bank, Windermere Road, Grange-over-Sands LA11 6EG
Tel: 44 07738 161943
Email: cumbrianrambler@live.co.uk
Web site: cumbrianrambler.blogspot.co.uk
Freq: Daily
Circ: 10870
Outdoor Recreation, Travel

Cupcake Crazy Gem - CEASED
988642
Web site: http://cupcakecrazygem.blogspot.com
Freq: Daily
Circ: 3054
News & Current Affairs

Curious London
987851
Web site: http://www.curious-london.co.uk
Freq: Daily
Circ: 8425
Profile: Blog covering food and drink with nightlife, bar, club, pub and restaurant reviews and event guides. The blog has an archive dating back to August 2013.
Local Entertainment Guides, Regional General Interest, Restaurant Reviews

The Curiously British Blog
1054038
Editorial: Orchard Place, 1A Thornton Avenue, Chiswick, London W4 1PL

Email: press@willowandhall.co.uk
Web site: willowandhall.co.uk/blog
Freq: Daily
Circ: 117
Profile: Blog covering British furniture and design and home decorating.
Do-It-Yourself (DIY)

Curiously Conscious
1100047
Email: curiouslyconscious@outlook.com
Web site: http://www.curiouslyconscious.com/
Freq: Daily
Circ: 26716
Beauty & Grooming, Cooking & Baking, Cosmetics, Fashion, Hair, Nutrition, Vegetarianism & Veganism

Curiously Persistent
1053380
Email: simon.kendrick@gmail.com
Web site: https://curiouslypersistent.wordpress.com/
Freq: Daily
Circ: 991
Broadcasting, Internet

Curly & Candid
999348
Email: info@curlyandcandid.co.uk
Web site: www.curlyandcandid.co.uk
Freq: Daily
Circ: 8063
Family & Parenting

Currencies Blog
1053536
Tel: 44 08003 285884
Web site: http://www.currencies.co.uk/currencies-blog
Freq: Daily
Editor: Josh Privett
Foreign Exchange Market (FOREX), Private Equity

The Curry Guy
986905
Web site: http://www.greatcurryrecipes.net/
Freq: Daily
Circ: 92865
Cooking & Baking, Restaurant Reviews

Custard Creams and London Dreams
988423
Web site: http://custardcreamsandlondondreams.com/
Freq: Daily
Circ: 8384
Profile: Blog covering London lifestyle, things to do, baking and fashion. The blog has an archive dating back to January 2013
Fashion, Women's Interests

The Custard TV
997058
Tel: 44 07521 927195
Email: lukeinthecustard@gmail.com
Web site: http://www.thecustardtv.com/p/home.html
Freq: Daily
Circ: 12847
Broadcasting

The Customer and Leadership Blog
1053563
Email: maz@thecustomerblog.co.uk
Web site: http://thecustomerblog.co.uk/
Freq: Daily
Circ: 12584
Business, Marketing

The Cut
999661
Email: press@thecutlondon.com
Web site: www.thecutlondon.com/blog
Freq: Daily
Circ: 50
Editor: Kate Baxter
Fashion

The Cutie Pie Challenge Blog
1062737
Email: happy.crafter@hotmail.com
Web site: http://cutiepiechallenge.blogspot.co.uk
Freq: Daily
Circ: 1346
Crafts

The Cutlery Chronicles
1060163
Web site: www.thecutlerychronicles.com
Freq: Daily

Circ: 9330
Cooking & Baking, Restaurant Reviews, Travel

Cwtch The Bride
996849
Email: info@cwtchthebride.com
Web site: www.cwtchthebride.com
Freq: Daily
Circ: 6486
Weddings

Cycle Bath
994992
Email: bath-cycling-campaign@yahoogroups.co.uk
Web site: http://cyclebath.org.uk/
Freq: Daily
Circ: 11384
Bicycles

CYCLECHIC Blog
1053964
Web site: www.cyclechic.co.uk/blog
Freq: Daily
Circ: 367
Bicycles

Cycling Europe
988304
Tel: 44 07970 278569
Email: office@cyclingeurope.org
Web site: http://cyclingeurope.org/
Freq: Daily
Circ: 8605
Bicycles

The Cycling Lawyer
1053464
Web site: http://thecyclingsilk.blogspot.co.uk/
Freq: Daily
Circ: 1873
Bicycles

Cycling Sports Group blog
1054233
Web site: http://www.cyclingsportsgroup.co.uk/blog
Freq: Daily
Circ: 50
Bicycles

Cycling Uphill
995511
Editorial: 29 Campbell Road, Oxford OX4 3PF
Web site: cyclinguphill.com
Freq: Daily
Circ: 35879
Bicycles

The Cynical Gardener
1053127
Email: saddingtonjoon@hotmail.com
Web site: https://thecynicalgardener.com/
Freq: Daily
Circ: 11000
Profile: Blog covering gardening. The Cynical Gardener discusses anything from plants and garden shows. The blog has an archive dating back to August 2012 and shares a short blogroll. The outlet offers RSS (Really Simple Syndication).
Gardening

D is for Dangerous
1053580
Email: hello@disfordangerous.co.uk
Web site: disfordangerous.co.uk
Freq: Daily
Circ: 672
Cosmetics, Fashion, Women's Interests

The Dabbler
988760
Email: editorial@thedabbler.co.uk
Web site: http://thedabbler.co.uk/
Freq: Daily
Circ: 18212
Editor: Andrew Nixon
Antiques/Collectibles, Art, Arts, Literature, Photography, Theater & Performing Arts, Visual Arts

The Dad Network
1053641
Email: dad@thedadnetwork.co.uk
Web site: http://www.thedadnetwork.co.uk/
Freq: Daily
Circ: 10662
Profile: Blog covering fatherhood. The Dad Network discusses anything from tips for fathers and children's activities to babies

and parenting. The blog has an archive dating back to
Computer & Video Games, Electronics, Family & Parenting, Fitness & Exercise, Nutrition

Dad Who Blogs
988255
Email: dadwhoblogs@gmail.com
Web site: dadwhoblogs.co.uk
Freq: Daily
Circ: 9778
Profile: Blog covering fatherhood. DAD WHO BLOGS discusses anything from family activities and family life to parenting and reviews. The blog has an archive dating back to April 2011. The outlet offers RSS (Really Simple Syndication).
Family & Parenting, Movies & Video

Dadams
1053182
Web site: www.dadams.co.uk
Freq: Daily
Circ: 2370
News & Current Affairs

Dadbloguk.com
987216
Email: dadbloguk@gmail.com
Web site: dadbloguk.com
Freq: Daily
Circ: 39807
Editor: John Adams
Alcohol & Spirits, Bars, Clubs & Pubs, Beer, Beverages, Cooking & Baking, Cosmetics, Family & Parenting, Fashion, Men's Interests, Wine/Winemaking

Daddacool
1052593
Web site: http://www.daddacool.co.uk
Freq: Daily
Circ: 6579
Family & Parenting, Mobile Electronics, Movies & Video

Daddy Daydream
1054411
Tel: 44 07761 350864
Email: daddydaydream@hotmail.com
Web site: http://www.daddydaydream.com/
Freq: Daily
Circ: 12902
Audio Video Trade, Cameras, Consumer Electronics, Entertainment, Family & Parenting, Men's Interests, Mobile Electronics, Movies & Video

Dadsdayoff.co.uk
1052794
Email: dadsdayoffmcr@gmail.com
Web site: http://dadsdayoff.co.uk/
Freq: Daily
Circ: 10628
Family & Parenting, Men's Interests, Regional General Interest

DaeQuest
1061788
Web site: http://daequest.com
Freq: Daily
Circ: 521
Bars, Clubs & Pubs, Classical/Choral/Band Music, Comedy, Country, Folk, Bluegrass, Dance Music, Entertainment, Jazz & Blues, Local Entertainment Guides, Movies & Video, Music

Daily Cannon
1052627
Editorial: 40 Annadale Flats, Belfast BT7 3AW Tel: 44 07874 021567
Email: info@dailycannon.com
Web site: http://dailycannon.com/
Freq: Daily
Circ: 153558
Soccer

The Daily Constitutional
988269
Editorial: 87 Messina Avenue, London NW6 4LG Tel: 44 02076 243978
Email: londonwalksblog@gmail.com
Web site: http://www.londonwalkblog.blogspot.co.uk/
Freq: Daily
Circ: 9918
Outdoor Recreation

The Daily Sail Blog
1053229
Editorial: 10 Melina Road, London W12 9HZ
Tel: 44 02087 406318
Email: james@thedailysail.com
Web site: http://www.thedailysail.com/blogs
Freq: Daily
Circ: 58

UK Blogs

Editor: James Boyd
Profile: Website covering sailing. The Daily Sail website shares the latest news, features and photographs about performance yacht and dinghy racing in the UK and abroad.
Marine & Boat Trade, Travel

DailyDOOH
986524
Web site: www.dailydooh.com
Freq: Daily
Circ: 48474
Editor: Adrian Cotterill
Advertising Industry, Branding, Broadcasting, Graphic Design, Marketing, Media & Communications, Photography, Publishing

Dainty Dollymix
997923
Email: daintydollymix@hotmail.co.uk
Web site: www.daintydollymix.com
Freq: Daily
Circ: 1735
Profile: Blog covering beauty, beauty reviews and nail art. The blog has an archive dating back to October 2009 and shares an extensive blog roll.
Beauty & Grooming, Cosmetics, Hair, Women's Interests

Daisies & Pie
1054110
Web site: www.daisiesandpie.co.uk
Freq: Daily
Circ: 12645
Cooking & Baking, Family & Parenting, Restaurant Reviews, Women's Interests

Daisies & Pies
988953
Email: wendy@daisiesandpie.co.uk
Web site: http://daisiesandpie.co.uk/
Freq: Daily
Circ: 12645
Cooking & Baking, Do-It-Yourself (DIY), Food, Grocery Stores, Organic Food, Restaurant Reviews, Vegetarianism & Veganism, Women's Interests

Daisy Fay Interiors
1053478
Web site: www.daisyfayinteriors.blogspot. co.uk/
Freq: Daily
Circ: 9478
Do-It-Yourself (DIY)

Damp Flat Books
1054947
Web site: http://dampflat.blogspot.co.uk/
Freq: Daily
Circ: 10706
Art, Crafts, Visual Arts

The Damsel Says
1054339
Email: thedamselsays@hotmail.com
Web site: thedamselsays.wordpress.com
Freq: Daily
Relationships, Women's Interests

Dan Slee Blog
986117
Web site: danslee.wordpress.com
Freq: Daily
Circ: 9814
Politics

Dan White - Digital Marketing Blog
1052688
Web site: https://www.danieljameswhite.co. uk/digital-marketing-blog/
Freq: Daily
Marketing

Dancetog
1053958
Email: opkikkertje@gmail.com
Web site: dancetog.com
Freq: Daily
Circ: 9446
Photography, Theater & Performing Arts

Dancing Dandelions
1064091
Web site: http://www.dancingdandelions.co. uk/
Freq: Daily
Circ: 9303
Bars, Clubs & Pubs, Comedy, Cooking & Baking, Do-It-Yourself (DIY), Entertainment, Family & Parenting, Local Entertainment Guides, Movies & Video, Restaurant Reviews

DANDY CLASH
987794
Web site: www.dandyclash.com
Freq: Daily
Circ: 1674
Profile: Blog covering men's lifestyle. The Dandy Clash blog discusses anything from advise and men's experiences.
Men's Interests

The Dangerous Snorkelling Club
1053074
Web site: http://snorkelclub.blogspot.co.uk/
Freq: Daily
Circ: 521
Swimming/Watersports

Dani Johanna
1053046
Email: danijohanna@hotmail.co.uk
Web site: http://www.danijohanna.co.uk/
Freq: Daily
Circ: 10830
Beauty & Grooming, Cooking & Baking, Cosmetics, Do-It-Yourself (DIY), Fashion, Hair, Pop Music, Restaurant Reviews

Daniel Merle Blog
1061652
Web site: http://blogs.lanacion.com.ar/ merle/
Freq: Daily
Circ: 4658
Photography

Daniel Santibaniez
1061394
Web site: http://danielsantibaniez.blogspot. com/
Freq: Daily
Circ: 521
Celebrities, National News

Danielle Vanier
1053865
Web site: http://www.daniellevanier.co.uk/
Freq: Daily
Circ: 11370
Profile: Blog covering fashion. DANIELLE VANIER blog discusses anything from fashion and fashion accessories to shoes. The blog has an archive dating back to October 2013.
Beauty & Grooming, Cosmetics, Fashion, Hair, Women's Interests

Danny Whatmough
1053028
Web site: http://www.dannywhatmough. com/
Freq: Daily
Circ: 2865
Branding, Internet, Marketing

Danny's Angling Blog
1053405
Email: dannysanglingblog@hotmail.co.uk
Web site: http://satonmyperch.blogspot.co. uk/
Freq: Daily
Circ: 9715
Profile: Blog covering angling. Danny's Angling Blog discusses anything from fish and equipment to angling competitions and product reviews. The blog has an archive dating back to July 2011 and shares an extensive blog roll. The outlet offers RSS (Really Simple Syndication).
Fishing

Dan's Media Digest
986118
Web site: danowen.blogspot.com
Freq: Daily
Circ: 1703
Broadcasting, Movies & Video

The Dapper Chapper
998143
Email: adam@dapperchapper.com
Web site: dapperchapper.com
Freq: Daily
Circ: 12742
Bars, Clubs & Pubs, Beauty & Grooming, Cooking & Baking, Cosmetics, Fashion, Hair, Men's Interests, Regional General Interest, Restaurant Reviews

Dark Matters
988418
Web site: http://darkmatt.blogspot.co.uk/
Freq: Daily
Circ: 10709
Computer & Video Games, Movies & Video

Dark Zero
988453
Email: team@darkzero.co.uk
Web site: http://darkzero.co.uk/
Circ: 70507
Computer & Video Games

Darktea
1054212
Web site: www.darktea.co.uk/blog/
Freq: Daily
Circ: 47159
Do-It-Yourself (DIY), Family & Parenting, Gardening

Das Weally Cool - CEASED 2017
987668
Editorial: Gorkana Group, Discovery House, 28-42 Banner Street, London EC1Y 8QE
Freq: Daily
Circ: 687
Cooking & Baking, Family & Parenting, Movies & Video

DataNews
1064494
Web site: http://www.datanews.uk/
Freq: Daily
Circ: 521
Data Management, National News

Dave MacLeod Blog
1054010
Web site: http://www.davemacleod. blogspot.co.uk/
Freq: Daily
Circ: 9397
Outdoor Recreation, Travel

Dave Plays
995521
Email: workwith@daveplays.co.uk
Web site: http://www.daveplays.co.uk/
Freq: Daily
Circ: 12000
Editor: Dave Hall
Computer & Video Games

Dave's Travel Pages
1053906
Email: dave@davestravelpages.com
Web site: davestravelpages.com
Freq: Daily
Circ: 47936
Travel

David Atkinson's Blog
996777
Editorial: 3A Handbridge, Chester CH4 7JE
Tel: 44 07974 390436
Email: atkinson.david@icloud.com
Web site: www.atkinsondavid.com
Freq: Daily
Circ: 9729
Travel

David Clapp Photography Limited
1053983
Email: info@daveclapp.co.uk
Web site: http://www.davidclapp.co.uk/blog
Freq: Daily
Circ: 26
Consumer Affairs, Entertainment, Movies & Video, Photography

David Emery Online
1053426
Email: contact@de-online.co.uk
Web site: de-online.co.uk
Freq: Daily
Circ: 8156
Men's Interests

David Hencke Blog
988088
Web site: https://davidhencke.com/
Freq: Daily
Circ: 17453
Politics

David Hepworth's blog
1053061
Email: mail@davidhepworth.com
Web site: http://whatsheonabout now. blogspot.com/
Freq: Daily
Circ: 9627
Advertising Industry, Branding, Country, Folk, Bluegrass, Jazz & Blues, Marketing, Pop Music, Rock Music

David Hernández Blog
1060390
Web site: http://www.davidhernandezblog. com
Freq: Daily

Circ: 998
Auto Aftermarket, Computers, Data Management, Electronics, Government Technology, Industry, Internet, Mobile Communications, Security & Security Systems, Software

David Higgerson Blog
986120
Web site: davidhiggerson.wordpress.com
Freq: Daily
Circ: 50879
Advertising Industry, Branding, Broadcasting, Graphic Design, Marketing, Media & Communications, Photography, Publishing

David Key blog
1054632
Tel: 44 07760 180816
Web site: http://www.ecoself.net/blog/
Freq: Daily
Circ: 84
Environment

David Naylor blog
1054393
Email: sales@bronco.co.uk
Web site: https://www.davidnaylor.co.uk/
Freq: Daily
Circ: 71428
Marketing

David Smith's EconomicsUK. com
1052559
Web site: http://www.economicsuk.com/ blog/
Freq: Daily
Circ: 6852
Economics

David Thomas' blog
1054625
Web site: http://www.mrthomasblog.com
Freq: Daily
Circ: 1266
Careers

David Thompson Blog
1053903
Web site: davidthompson.typepad.com
Freq: Daily
Circ: 36022
Social Issues

Dayana
1061751
Web site: http://www.dayanabarrionuevo. com/
Freq: Daily
Circ: 24933
Classical/Choral/Band Music, Country, Folk, Bluegrass, Dance Music, Jazz & Blues, Music, Pop Music, R&B, Urban, World, Rap & Hip Hop, Rock Music

The Daydreamer
997157
Web site: www.thedaydreamer.net
Freq: Daily
Circ: 11468
Beauty & Grooming, Cooking & Baking, Cosmetics, Fashion, Hair, Restaurant Reviews, Travel, Women's Interests

Daydreaming by Daisy
1098068
Web site: http://www.daydreamingbydaisy. com
Freq: Daily
Circ: 10322
Fashion, Fitness & Exercise, Women's Interests

Daydreams heart
1052576
Web site: http://www.daydreamsheart. blogspot.co.uk/
Freq: Daily
Circ: 10618
Cooking & Baking, Crafts, Do-It-Yourself (DIY), Fashion, Photography, Regional General Interest, Travel, Women's Interests

Dazecoop
1053258
Web site: http://www.dzecp.com/
Freq: Daily
Circ: 1120
News & Current Affairs

Dazhou's Car Talk
1061318
Web site: http://blog.sina.com.cn/ dazhoushuoche
Freq: Daily

Circ: 41249999
Antique & Collectible Cars, Automakers, Automotive, Driving, Motorcycles, Off-road & 4-Wheel Drive Vehicles, Trucks & SUVs

DB Reviews 1056322
Email: reviews.by.db@gmail.com
Web site: www.dbreviews.co.uk
Freq: Daily
Circ: 12668
Beauty & Grooming, Cosmetics, Hair, Women's Interests

DC Mobile 1060403
Web site: http://dcmobile.com.sg
Freq: Daily
Circ: 578
Cameras, Mobile Communications

DCMS blog 997822
Tel: 44 02072 116000
Email: enquiries@culture.gov.uk
Web site: http://dcmsblog.uk/
Freq: Daily
Regional General Interest, Travel

DD's Diary 1053936
Web site: www.dulwichdivorcee.com
Freq: Daily
Circ: 7184
Cooking & Baking, Fashion, Food, Grocery Stores, Organic Food, Restaurant Reviews, Vegetarianism & Veganism, Women's Interests

Dealchecker blog 986121
Editorial: Laser House, 132-140 Goswell Road, London EC1V 7DY
Email: enquiries@dealchecker.co.uk
Web site: http://www.dealchecker.co.uk/blog/
Freq: Daily
Circ: 8365
Airline Inflight, Railroad, Travel

Dear Beautiful 987444
Email: dearbeautifulboy@gmail.com
Web site: www.dearbeautifulboy.com
Freq: Daily
Circ: 9866
Family & Parenting

Dear Designer's Blog 987966
Editorial: 4 Oak Crescent, Wickford, Wickford SS11 7FF
Email: deardesigner@hotmail.co.uk
Web site: deardesigner.co.uk
Freq: Daily
Circ: 50485
Do-It-Yourself (DIY), Shopping, Women's Interests

Dearest Deer 1053952
Web site: dearestdeer.net
Freq: Daily
Circ: 7218
Profile: Blog covering fashion. Dearest Deer blog discusses anything from fashion trends and looks to food and London. The blog has an archive dating back to July 2012. The outlet offers RSS (Really Simple Syndication).
Cooking & Baking, Fashion, Regional General Interest, Restaurant Reviews, Women's Interests

Debbie Hill Blog 1053323
Email: hello@debbie-hill.co.uk
Web site: http://debbiehill.blogspot.co.uk/
Freq: Daily
Circ: 1427
Crafts, Visual Arts

Debenhams Debrief Blogs
1054184
Editorial: Regent's Place, 10 Brock Street, London NW1 3FG **Tel:** 44 08445 616161
Web site: http://www.debenhams.com/
Freq: Daily
Circ: 8853662
Beauty & Grooming, Celebrities, Charitable Foundations, Cosmetics, Do-It-Yourself (DIY), Fashion, Hair, Luxury Goods, Men's Interests, Shopping

Debtonation 1053113
Tel: 44 02033 278599
Email: portia.sale@primeeconomics.org
Web site: http://www.debtonation.org/
Freq: Daily
Circ: 6202
Banking, Bonds, Corporate Finance, Corporate Management, Credit Markets, Emerging Markets, Environment, Government, Lending, Public & Consumer Finance

Decor and Style 1053719
Email: be.curious@decorandstyle.co.uk
Web site: http://decorandstyle.co.uk
Freq: Daily
Circ: 1605
Architecture & Design, Do-It-Yourself (DIY), Women's Interests

Decorando Interiores 1061117
Web site: http://www.decorando-interiores.com
Freq: Daily
Circ: 752
Do-It-Yourself (DIY), Interior Design

Decorator's Notebook 988095
Web site: blog.decoratorsnotebook.co.uk
Freq: Daily
Circ: 18953
Profile: Blog covering home decorating and homewares. The blog shares a short blogroll.
Do-It-Yourself (DIY)

decorenvy 988468
Email: decorenvyblog@gmail.com
Web site: www.decorenvy.co.uk
Freq: Daily
Circ: 9230
Do-It-Yourself (DIY)

Deena Kakaya Blog 988541
Email: deenakakaya@gmail.com
Web site: www.deenakakaya.com
Freq: Daily
Circ: 6925
Vegetarianism & Veganism

Deep in the Light 1061344
Web site: http://blog.sina.com.cn/liangzhaohui
Freq: Daily
Circ: 41356
Antique & Collectible Cars, Automakers, Automotive, Driving, Motorcycles, Off-road & 4-Wheel Drive Vehicles, Trucks & SUVs

Deeper Blue 1054292
Email: hello@deeperblue.com
Web site: deeperblue.com
Freq: Daily
Circ: 50191
Profile: Blog covering freediving, scuba diving and spearfishing.
Swimming/Watersports

Defecito 1060795
Web site: http://www.defecito.com
Freq: Daily
Circ: 7108
Antiques/Collectibles, Architecture & Design, Art, Arts, Bars, Clubs & Pubs, Comedy, Cooking & Baking, Do-It-Yourself (DIY), Entertainment, Gardening

Defence in the media 997484
Editorial: Whitehall, London SW1A 2HB
Tel: 44 02072 189000
Web site: https://modmedia.blog.gov.uk/
Freq: Daily
Circ: 113748
Defense & National Security

degnis ft. victoria secret 1061098
Web site: http://degnis.blogspot.com/
Freq: Daily
Circ: 611
Celebrities, History, National News

DeKay's Blog 996510
Web site: http://lofi-gaming.org.uk/blog/
Freq: Daily
Circ: 198
Apple, Computer & Video Games, Personal Computers

Delhi Greens 1060861
Email: blog@delhigreens.org
Web site: http://www.delhigreens.com
Freq: Daily
Circ: 11899
Environment

Delicias del Buen Vivir 1060664
Web site: http://www.lasdeliciasdevivir.com
Freq: Daily
Circ: 1414
Cooking & Baking, Food

Delicious Doodles Challenges
1056577
Web site: http://deliciousdoodleschallenge2.blogspot.co.uk/
Freq: Daily
Circ: 483
Crafts

Delicious in Dingle 1053815
Web site: http://foodiefancies.blogspot.co.uk/
Freq: Daily
Circ: 521
Cooking & Baking, Food, Grocery Stores, Organic Food, Restaurant Reviews, Vegetarianism & Veganism

Deliciously Ella 987098
Web site: http://deliciouslyella.com/
Freq: Daily
Circ: 606932
Profile: Deliciously Ella covers clean eating, healthy eating and nutrition.
Alcohol & Spirits, Bars, Clubs & Pubs, Beer, Beverages, Cooking & Baking, Food, Grocery Stores, Organic Food, Restaurant Reviews, Vegetarianism & Veganism

Democratic Audit UK 1055293
Tel: 44 02079 556689
Web site: http://www.democraticaudit.com/
Freq: Daily
Circ: 19855
National News, Politics

Dents blog - CEASED 1054422
Web site: http://blog.dents.co.uk/
Freq: Daily
Circ: 10
Profile: Blog covering fashion accessories. The blog is hosted by Dents.co.uk. DENTS BLOG discusses anything from leather gloves and leather fashion accessories. The blog has an archive dating back to September 2009. The outlet offers RSS (Really Simple Syndication).
Fashion

Deportes a Diario 1061793
Web site: http://deportesadiario.blogspot.com/
Freq: Daily
Circ: 611
Basketball, Bicycles, Billiards, Boating & Yachting, Bodybuilding, Bowling, Boxing, Cricket, Equestrian Sports, Extreme/Adventure Sports

Descarga Online Gratis 1060485
Web site: http://www.descargaonlinegratis.com
Freq: Daily
Circ: 26131
Internet, Software

Descent World 997264
Email: hello@descent-world.co.uk
Web site: http://www.descent-world.co.uk/
Freq: Daily
Circ: 10580
Bicycles

Design Hunter 987750
Web site: http://www.designhunter.co.uk
Freq: Daily
Circ: 7430
Architecture & Design, Do-It-Yourself (DIY), Fashion, Gardening, Home, Property Management & Maintenance, Real Estate

Design Lovers Blog 997917
Web site: www.designloversblog.com

Freq: Daily
Circ: 25356
Do-It-Yourself (DIY)

Design Shack 988396
Web site: http://designshack.net/
Freq: Daily
Circ: 750567
Audio Video Trade, Cameras, Consumer Electronics, Mobile Electronics, Movies & Video

The Design Sheppard 988400
Email: stacey@thedesignsheppard.com
Web site: www.thedesignsheppard.com
Freq: Daily
Circ: 25408
Do-It-Yourself (DIY)

Designer Uncovered 996400
Editorial: 52 Little Ealing Lane, London W5 4EA **Tel:** 44 07903 171379
Web site: http://www.designeruncovered.com/
Freq: Daily
Circ: 1289
Do-It-Yourself (DIY)

Designers' Block 986675
Editorial: The Cottage, Donkleywood, Hexham NE48 1AQ **Tel:** 44 01434 240304
Email: info@ghostfurniture.co.uk
Web site: designersblock.blogspot.com
Freq: Daily
Circ: 3155
Antiques/Collectibles, Do-It-Yourself (DIY), Luxury Goods

Desmesurada 1061954
Web site: http://www.ladesmesurada.blogspot.com/
Freq: Daily
Circ: 1350
Women's Interests

Destination Delicious 988618
Email: destdelicious@gmail.com
Web site: www.destinationdelicious.com
Freq: Daily
Circ: 12113
Restaurant Reviews, Travel

Destinations Perfected 1053838
Email: alexandra@destinationsperfected.com
Web site: www.destinationsperfected.com/
Freq: Daily
Circ: 1708
Travel

Destinos Blog 1061689
Web site: http://www.destinosblog.com
Freq: Daily
Circ: 1806
Airline Inflight, Railroad, Travel

Development Truths 1098958
Web site: https://developmenttruths.wordpress.com
Freq: Daily
Circ: 7
Energy & Environment, Ethical/Moral Issues, International News

Devoted to Pink 1054105
Email: devotedtopink@hotmail.com
Web site: www.devotedtopink.com
Freq: Daily
Circ: 13616
Beauty & Grooming, Cosmetics, Fashion, Hair

Dexterous Diva 1053262
Email: hello@dexterousdiva.co.uk
Web site: dexterousdiva.co.uk/blog
Freq: Daily
Circ: 206
Profile: Blog covering content creation, blogging and social media. The blog has an archive dating back to August 2011.
Advertising Industry, Marketing

Dezeen 984176
Editorial: Dezeen Limited, Unit 10, 8 Orsman Road, London N1 5QJ **Tel:** 44 02033 271230
Email: submissions@dezeen.com
Web site: dezeen.com

UK Blogs

Circ: 504687
Architecture & Design, Do-It-Yourself
(DIY), Property Management &
Maintenance, Visual Arts

Diabetes UK Blog   986740
Editorial: Macleod House, 10 Parkway,
London NW1 7AA **Tel:** 44 03451 232399
Email: web-updates@diabetes.org.uk
Web site: blogs.diabetes.org.uk
Freq: Daily
Circ: 6598
Charitable Foundations, Diabetes, Health
& Medicine, Patient Support

diamond canopy   985132
Email: diamondcanopywinn@hotmail.com
Web site: www.diamondcanopy.com
Freq: Daily
Circ: 7500
Editor: Winnie Nip
Fashion, Lifestyle, Men's Interests,
Regional General Interest, Women's
Interests

The Diamond Store Magazine
News   1096365
Editorial: Regalian Ltd / The Diamond Store,
Suite 17410 Lower Ground Floor, 145-157 St
John Street, London EC1V 4PW
Email: info@thediamondstore.co.uk
Web site: http://news.thediamondstore.co.
uk/
Freq: Daily
Circ: 16494
Luxury Goods

Diamonds n Pearls   1052706
Web site: http://www.diamondsnpearls.co.
uk/
Freq: Daily
Circ: 10042
Profile: Blog covering fashion. Diamonds n
Pearls blog discusses anything from plus
size fashion and fashion accessories to
beauty and lifestyle. The blog has an archive
dating back to November 2010.
Beauty & Grooming, Cosmetics, Fashion,
Hair, Women's Interests

Diana es Crochet   1061276
Web site: http://www.dianaescrochet.
blogspot.com
Freq: Daily
Circ: 788
Crafts

Diary of a First Child   986487
Email: diaryofafirstchild@gmail.com
Web site: www.diaryofafirstchild.com
Freq: Daily
Circ: 965
Family & Parenting

The Diary of a Frugal Family
                    987468
Web site: frugalfamily.co.uk
Freq: Daily
Circ: 140720
Cooking & Baking, Family & Parenting,
Personal Finance

Diary of a Gig Addict   1052634
Web site: http://diaryofagigaddict.blogspot.
co.uk/
Freq: Daily
Circ: 521
Pop Music, Rock Music

The Diary of a Jewellery Lover
                    987929
Web site: www.thediaryofajewellerylover.co.
uk
Freq: Daily
Circ: 161860
Profile: The Diary of a Jewellery Lover
covers jewellery, travel, food, beauty and
homewares.
Women's Interests

The Diary of a Not So Ordinary
Boy   1053414
Web site: http://notsoordinarydiary.
wordpress.com/
Freq: Daily
Circ: 10110

Profile: Blog covering lifestyle. Diary of a Not
So Ordinary Boy blog discusses anything
from lifestyle and teaching to education,
motherhood and down's syndrome. The blog
has an archive dating back to October 2013
and shares an extensive blog roll.
Disability, Education

Diary of a Vintage Girl   1053433
Web site: http://www.diaryofavintagegirl.
com
Freq: Daily
Circ: 5399
Fashion

Diary of an SAH Stroke Survi-
vor   988379
Web site: http://diaryofansahstrokesurvivor.
wordpress.com/
Freq: Daily
Circ: 133
Profile: Blog covering stroke recovery,
stroke awareness, the NHS, social issues,
government cuts and welfare reform. The
blog has an archive dating back to April
2012 and shares an extensive blogroll.
Health & Medicine

Diary of the Dad   1053301
Web site: http://www.diaryofthedad.co.uk/
Freq: Daily
Circ: 10640
Family & Parenting

Diary of the Evans Crittens
                    997944
Web site: http://www.evans-crittens.com/
Freq: Daily
Circ: 16037
Cooking & Baking, Crafts, Family &
Parenting, Grocery Stores, Travel,
Women's Interests

Diego Mattei Blog   1061478
Web site: http://www.diegomattei.com.ar
Freq: Daily
Circ: 125313
Advertising Industry, Graphic Design

Dietitian UK   1054054
Email: priya@dietitianuk.co.uk
Web site: http://www.dietitianuk.co.uk
Freq: Daily
Circ: 9197
Cooking & Baking, Nutrition

Diets and Calories   987852
Email: caroline@dietsandcalories.com
Web site: www.dietsandcalories.com/
Freq: Daily
Circ: 27679
Profile: Blog covering diet food reviews and
dieting tips.
Cooking & Baking, Nutrition

Different Shades of Green
                    1054929
Web site: http://differentshadesofgreen.
blogspot.co.uk/
Freq: Daily
Circ: 997
Cricket

Digging the Dirt   1053183
Web site: http://www.jondickins.com/
Freq: Daily
Circ: 7859
Corporate Law

Digital Classrooms   1054217
Web site: http://www.digitalclassrooms.co.
uk
Freq: Daily
Circ: 11946
Profile: Blog covering education. digital
classrooms blog discusses anything from
education and teaching to digital learning
and primary school. The blog has an archive
dating back to November 2013 and shares
an short blog roll.
Education

Digital democracy, news,
thinking, tips & tricks   1053643
Tel: 44 11738 12989
Email: info@delib.net
Web site: http://blog.delib.net/

Freq: Daily
Circ: 411
Government Technology

Digital Diva   1053982
Email: gorkana@digital-diva.co.uk
Web site: http://www.digital-diva.co.uk/
Freq: Daily
Circ: 45488
Do-It-Yourself (DIY), Fashion, Mobile
Electronics, Restaurant Reviews, Sales &
Marketing, Travel, Women's Interests

Digital Examples   1052578
Web site: http://digital-examples.blogspot.
co.uk/
Freq: Daily
Circ: 9938
Advertising Industry, Branding, Marketing

Digital Falkon   1054177
Editorial: Grosvenor House, 20 Barrington
Road, Altrincham, Manchester WA14 1HB
Tel: 44 01618 501644
Email: info@falkondigital.com
Web site: http://www.falkondigital.com/
blog/
Freq: Daily
Circ: 44
Branding, Internet, Marketing

Digital Intelligence Today
                    779937
Web site: http://digitalintelligencetoday.com
Freq: Daily
Circ: 47451
E-Commerce, Social Media

The Digital Lifestyle   986250
Web site: thedigitallifestyle.com
Freq: Daily
Circ: 51794
Apple, Computer & Video Games,
Computers, Internet, Mobile Electronics,
Personal Computers

Digital Marketing Blog   986629
Editorial: 4th Floor, Wells Point, 79 Wells
Street, London W1T 3QN
Tel: 44 02031 999103
Web site: https://econsultancy.com/blog
Freq: Daily
Circ: 123583
Advertising Industry, Branding,
Broadcasting, Graphic Design, Marketing,
Media & Communications, Photography,
Publishing

Digital Marketing Team Blog
                    996999
Editorial: University of Bedfordshire,
University Square, Luton LU1 3JU
Tel: 44 01234 400400
Web site: http://www.deepphat.co.uk/
Freq: Daily
Circ: 10163
News & Current Affairs

Digital Media Report   1061976
Web site: http://carloscrovara.wordpress.
com/
Freq: Daily
Circ: 17
Auto Aftermarket, Computers, Data
Management, Electronics, Government
Technology, Industry, Internet, Mobile
Communications, Security & Security
Systems, Software

Digital Outbox   1052789
Email: info@digitaloutbox.com
Web site: http://digitaloutbox.com
Freq: Daily
Circ: 10558
Apple, Computer & Video Games,
Computers, Internet, Mobile Electronics,
Personal Computers

Digitaltrip Blog   1053961
Tel: 44 08443 577973
Email: info@digital-trip.co.uk
Web site: http://blog.digital-trip.com/
Freq: Daily
Circ: 6091
Airline Inflight, Business, Railroad, Travel

Dining Society   998404
Web site: diningsociety.wordpress.com
Freq: Daily
Cooking & Baking, Restaurant Reviews

DippyWrites   1073645
Email: dippywrites@gmail.com
Web site: http://www.dippywrites.com/
Freq: Daily
Circ: 9781
Beauty & Grooming, Cosmetics, Fashion,
Hair, Women's Interests

Directors Notes   988420
Email: directorsnotes@gmail.com
Web site: http://www.directorsnotes.com/
Freq: Daily
Circ: 1588
Movies & Video

Disability Rights UK   996394
Editorial: Ground Floor, CAN Mezzanine, 49
- 51 East Road, London N1 6AH
Tel: 44 02072 508181
Email: enquiries@disabilityrightsuk.org
Web site: http://disabilityrightsuk.blogspot.
co.uk/
Freq: Daily
Circ: 10477
Disability

DisabledGo News Blog   996984
Editorial: Ardent House, Gates Way,
Stevenage SG1 3HG **Tel:** 44 01438 842710
Email: media@disabledgo.com
Web site: www.disabledgo.com/blog/
Freq: Daily
Circ: 15
Charitable Foundations, Disability

Discerning Cyclist   1053794
Email: hello@thediscerningcyclist.co.uk
Web site: http://discerningcyclist.com/
Freq: Daily
Circ: 8824
Profile: The Discerning Cyclist covers
cycling, bicycles, cycling fashion and
equipment.
Bicycles, Fashion

The Discerning Man   1103179
Email: contact@thediscerningman.net
Web site: https://thediscerningman.net/
Freq: Daily
Circ: 8901
Alcohol & Spirits, Bars, Clubs & Pubs,
Beauty & Grooming, Beer, Beverages,
Cooking & Baking, Cosmetics, Fashion,
Fitness & Exercise, Hair

Discopop Directory   1054567
Email: editor@discopop.co.uk
Web site: http://blog.discopop.co.uk/
Freq: Daily
Circ: 7789
Pop Music

Discotheque Confusion   986125
Web site: www.discothequeconfusion.co.uk
Freq: Daily
Circ: 10063
Fashion, Women's Interests

Disenistica   1060475
Email: fel_salas@hotmail.com
Web site: http://www.disenistica.blogspot.
com
Freq: Daily
Circ: 1017
Art, Graphic Design

Disney Noticias Mexico   1061457
Web site: http://disneynoticiasmexico.
blogspot.com
Freq: Daily
Circ: 817
Bars, Clubs & Pubs, Comedy,
Entertainment, Local Entertainment
Guides, Movies & Video

Disney StarsMx Blog   1061016
Web site: http://disneystarsmx.blogspot.
com
Freq: Daily

Circ: 981
Bars, Clubs & Pubs, Celebrities, Comedy, Entertainment, Local Entertainment Guides, Movies & Video

Disneyrollergirl 986126
Web site: www.disneyrollergirl.net
Freq: Daily
Circ: 55330
Fashion

Disruptive Finance 1054118
Web site: http://www.disruptivefinance.co.uk
Freq: Daily
Circ: 49865
Data Management, Economics, Electronics, Industry

Disruptive Views 1054246
Email: info@disruptiveviews.com
Web site: http://disruptiveviews.com/
Freq: Daily
Circ: 15641
Advertising Industry, Branding, Broadcasting, Graphic Design, Marketing, Media & Communications, Photography, Publishing

Distilled Blog 1055942
Email: info@distilled.net
Web site: https://www.distilled.net/resources/
Freq: Daily
Circ: 11062
Branding, Marketing

Ditsy Bird Designs 1053990
Web site: http://ditsybirddesigns.blogspot.co.uk/
Freq: Daily
Circ: 10709
Art, Crafts

Dizzybrunette3 987607
Email: dizzybrunette3@gmail.com
Web site: www.dizzybrunette3.com
Freq: Daily
Circ: 10667
Beauty & Grooming, Cosmetics, Hair

dizzybrunette3 Vlog 1103791
Email: dizzybrunette3@gmail.com
Web site: https://www.youtube.com/user/dizzybrunette3
Freq: Daily
Circ: 4
Beauty & Grooming, Cosmetics, Fashion, Hair, Women's Interests

Doble Cinco 1060968
Web site: http://doble-5.blogspot.com/
Freq: Daily
Circ: 1835
Basketball, Bicycles, Billiards, Boating & Yachting, Bodybuilding, Bowling, Boxing, Cricket, Equestrian Sports, Extreme/Adventure Sports

Doctor Who News 997588
Email: submissions@doctorwhonews.net
Web site: http://www.doctorwhonews.net/
Freq: Daily
Circ: 153441
Broadcasting

The Doctor Who Site News 1055931
Email: the.doctor.who.site.global@gmail.com
Web site: http://news.thedoctorwhosite.co.uk/
Freq: Daily
Circ: 38265
Broadcasting

Doctors of the World Blog 997360
Editorial: 34th Floor, One Canada Square, London E14 5AA Tel: 44 02071 675789
Web site: https://www.doctorsoftheworld.org.uk/Pages/News/Category/news-and-blogs
Freq: Daily
Circ: 15
Health & Medicine

Does My Bum Look 40 in This? 988215
Email: doesmybumlook40@gmail.com
Web site: doesmybumlook40.blogspot.co.uk
Freq: Daily
Circ: 2268
Profile: Blog covering fashion and style. The blog has an archive dating back to February 2012.
Fashion

Doesn't Grow On Trees 990656
Editorial: 16 Coopers Close, Stratford-upon-Avon CV37 0RS
Web site: www.doesntgrowontrees.co.uk
Freq: Daily
Circ: 13123
Personal Finance

Dog-Daisy Chains 987362
Email: jmcardy@gmail.com
Web site: http://dogdaisychains.blogspot.com
Freq: Daily
Circ: 5615
Crafts

Dogs Trust Blog 986748
Editorial: 17 Wakley Street, London EC1V 7RQ Tel: 44 02078 370006
Email: pressoffice@dogstrust.org.uk
Web site: https://www.dogstrust.org.uk/news-events/blog/
Freq: Daily
Circ: 221857
Animal Farming, Charitable Foundations, Nature & Wildlife

Doing Jalsa and Showing Jilpa 1061724
Email: jalsa.jilpa@gmail.com
Web site: http://www.krishashok.wordpress.com
Freq: Daily
Circ: 2
Antiques/Collectibles, Art, Arts, Literature, Photography, Theater & Performing Arts, Visual Arts

Dolce Vanity 987043
Web site: www.dolcevanity.com
Freq: Daily
Circ: 6656
Beauty & Grooming, Cosmetics, Hair, Women's Interests

Dolly Bow Bow 987076
Email: info@dollybowbow.co.uk
Web site: http://www.dollybowbow.blogspot.co.uk/
Freq: Daily
Circ: 10135
Beauty & Grooming, Cosmetics, Fashion, Hair

Dolly bow bow Kate Murnane 1098945
Email: info@dollybowbow.co.uk
Web site: https://www.youtube.com/user/Dollybowbow
Freq: Daily
Circ: 5
Beauty & Grooming, Cosmetics, Family & Parenting, Fashion, Hair, Women's Interests

Dolly Clackett Blog 1054053
Email: thestreak@gmail.com
Web site: http://dollyclackett.blogspot.co.uk/
Freq: Daily
Circ: 2862
Crafts, Fashion

Dolly Dowsie 1054160
Web site: http://www.dollydowsie.com/
Freq: Daily
Circ: 49999
Beauty & Grooming, Cooking & Baking, Cosmetics, Do-It-Yourself (DIY), Family & Parenting, Hair

dolly mixture CEASED 985785
Web site: http://www.jacqui-dollymixture.blogspot.com
Freq: Daily

Circ: 521
Beauty & Grooming, Cosmetics, Hair

Dollybakes 988572
Email: dollybakes@gmail.com
Web site: dollybakes.co.uk
Freq: Daily
Circ: 7681
Profile: Blog covering baking. The blog has an archive dating back to February 2012.
Cooking & Baking

Dolores Fancy 1061717
Web site: http://www.doloresfancy.blogspot.com/
Freq: Daily
Circ: 2177
Celebrities, Fashion

Dolphin Mobility 1053595
Web site: http://www.dolphinlifts.co.uk
Web site: mobilityaids.blogspot.co.uk
Freq: Daily
Circ: 521
Disability

Domain Incite 1053792
Editorial: 4 Gilbert House, Usk Street, London E2 0RU Tel: 44 07504 603644
Email: info@domainincite.com
Web site: http://domainincite.com/
Freq: Daily
Circ: 97090
Internet

Domestic Goddesque CEASED 988321
Web site: domesticgoddesque.com
Freq: Daily
Circ: 9378
Family & Parenting, Women's Interests

Domesticali 996627
Web site: domesticali.typepad.com
Freq: Daily
Circ: 817186
Crafts, Women's Interests

Donal Skehan Blog 988474
Web site: www.donalskehan.com
Freq: Daily
Circ: 54372
News & Current Affairs

Donna Coulling Blog 996271
Editorial: 13 Glenilla Road, London NW3 4AJ
Web site: donnacoulling.com
Freq: Daily
Circ: 10706
News & Current Affairs

Donna Ida 996381
Editorial: 40 Elizabeth Street, London SW1W 9NZ Tel: 44 02077 925811
Email: press@donnaida.com
Web site: donnaida.com/blog
Freq: Daily
Circ: 31
Fashion

Don't Believe The Hype 1053528
Tel: 44 07734 650671
Email: dan@dontbelieve.biz
Web site: http://www.dontbelievethehype.biz/
Freq: Daily
Circ: 10012
Editor: Dan Flanagan
Classical/Choral/Band Music, Country, Folk, Bluegrass, Dance Music, Family & Parenting, Fashion, Jazz & Blues, Men's Interests, Music, Pop Music, R&B, Urban, World

Don't Cramp Our Style 987866
Web site: www.dontcrampourstyle.com
Freq: Daily
Circ: 9714
Beauty & Grooming, Cosmetics, Do-It-Yourself (DIY), Fashion, Hair

Donut Group Blogs 996907
Editorial: CityPoint, Temple Gate, Bristol BS1 6PL Tel: 44 01173 736160
Email: info@atomcontentmarketing.co.uk

Web site: http://atomcontentmarketing.co.uk/blog
Freq: Daily
Circ: 20
Business, Small and Medium Business

Dopes on the Road 995121
Email: hello@dopesontheroad.com
Web site: http://dopesontheroad.com
Freq: Daily
Circ: 10660
LGBT, Travel

Doreen's Dream 1054522
Web site: http://www.doreensdream.blogspot.co.uk/
Freq: Daily
Circ: 521
Crafts

Dorothy & Olive 988391
Email: grace@dorothyandolive.com
Web site: www.dorothyandolive.com
Freq: Daily
Circ: 2215
Profile: Blog covering fashion. dorothy and olive blog discusses anything from personal style and outfit posts tot the latest fashion trends and accessories. The blog has an archive dating back to December 2013.
Fashion

Dorsal 14 1061641
Web site: http://eldorsalcatorce.blogspot.com/
Freq: Daily
Circ: 493
Soccer

Dotmailer Blog 1053368
Editorial: No.1 London Bridge, London SE1 9BG Tel: 44 08453 379170
Web site: http://www.dotmailer.com/
Freq: Daily
Circ: 625461
Branding, Marketing

Dots & Dashes 1053766
Email: contact@dotsanddashes.co.uk
Web site: http://dotsanddashes.co.uk/
Freq: Daily
Circ: 3293
Classical/Choral/Band Music, Country, Folk, Bluegrass, Dance Music, Jazz & Blues, Music, Pop Music, R&B, Urban, World, Rap & Hip Hop, Rock Music

Dots and Spots 1053645
Email: info@dotsandspots.co.uk
Web site: http://dotsandspotsdesign.blogspot.co.uk/
Freq: Daily
Circ: 1337
Crafts

Dotty Delightful 1053841
Email: dottydelightful@gmail.com
Web site: http://www.sanctuarymoon.co.uk/
Freq: Daily
Circ: 943
Crafts, Organic Food

Doug Belshaw's Blog 1052632
Email: mail@dougbelshaw.com
Web site: http://dougbelshaw.com/blog/
Freq: Daily
Circ: 6991
Computers, Data Management, Education, Electronics, Government Technology, Higher Education, Internet, Mobile Communications, Schools & Institutions, Software

Down on the Allotment 1054220
Web site: veggies-only.blogspot.co.uk
Freq: Daily
Circ: 1592
Gardening, Organic Food, Vegetarianism & Veganism

Downs Side Up 998103
Email: downssideup@gmail.com
Web site: www.downssideup.com
Freq: Daily
Circ: 14895
Disability, Family & Parenting

UK Blogs

DPAC Blog 996164
Email: mail@dpac.uk.net
Web site: http://www.dpac.uk.net/blog/
Freq: Daily
Circ: 3
Community Care (UK), Disability, Patient
Support, Public Sector

Dr Morris' Allergy Blog 996725
Editorial: London Medical Centre bookings,
142 - 146 Harley Street, London W1G 7LE
Tel: 44 01252 851789
Email: enquiries@allergy-clinic.co.uk
Web site: http://www.allergy-clinic.co.uk/
blog/
Freq: Daily
Circ: 67
Allergies

Dr. Joseph Reddington 997021
Web site: http://joereddington.com/
Freq: Daily
Circ: 9257
Apple, Disability, Internet, Literature,
Personal Computers

Dr. Kantu News Blog 1061459
Web site: http://drkantu-opinion.blogspot.
com
Freq: Daily
Circ: 1108
National News, Politics

Dragons and Fairy Dust 987982
Web site: www.dragonsandfairydust.co.uk
Freq: Daily
Circ: 13753
Profile: Dragons and Fairy Dust covers
lifestyle, food, recipes and travel. The blog
has an archive dating back to August 2010.
Regional General Interest

Drama Queen Confessions
1053228
Web site: http://www.
dramaqueenconfessions.com/
Freq: Daily
Circ: 7856
Profile: Blog covering lifestyle, blogging,
social media, student life and fashion. The
blog has an archive dating back to May
2013.
Women's Interests

Dream Euro Trip 995083
Web site: http://www.dreameurotrip.com
Freq: Daily
Circ: 34631
Travel

Dress Me Perfect 997834
Email: team@dressmeperfect.com
Web site: www.dressmeperfect.com
Freq: Daily
Circ: 6732
Fashion

**Dress me, I'm your manne-
quin** 1054014
Web site: http://dressme-imyourmannequin.
blogspot.co.uk/
Freq: Daily
Circ: 611
Fashion, Fitness & Exercise, Women's
Interests

DressLikeA 1061402
Email: dresslikea@gmail.com
Web site: http://dresslikea.com/
Freq: Daily
Circ: 9165
News & Current Affairs

Drishtikone 1060945
Web site: http://www.drishtikone.com
Freq: Daily
Circ: 10832
Consumer Affairs, Crime & Violence,
Defense & National Security, Energy &
Environment, Ethical/Moral Issues,
International News, Law, National News,
News & Current Affairs, Northern Ireland

The Drive Blog 1053479
Web site: http://www.thedrive.co.uk/
Freq: Daily

Circ: 6090
Antique & Collectible Cars, Driving, Off-
road & 4-Wheel Drive Vehicles

Drive Blog 1053913
Email: driver@driveblog.co.uk
Web site: http://www.driveblog.co.uk/
Freq: Daily
Circ: 8442
Antique & Collectible Cars, Automakers,
Automotive, Driving, Motorcycles, Off-
road & 4-Wheel Drive Vehicles, Trucks &
SUVs

Drive Write Automotive 988064
Tel: 44 07531 159874
Email: drivewrite@yahoo.co.uk
Web site: www.drivewrite.co.uk/
Freq: Daily
Circ: 10090
Antique & Collectible Cars, Automakers,
Automotive, Driving, Motorcycles, Off-
road & 4-Wheel Drive Vehicles, Trucks &
SUVs

Drive.co.uk 1075481
Web site: www.drive.co.uk
Freq: Daily
Circ: 23149
Antique & Collectible Cars, Automakers,
Automotive, Driving, Motorcycles, Off-
road & 4-Wheel Drive Vehicles, Trucks &
SUVs

DriveBlog 986425
Editorial: Savik, Hill of Balbithan, Kintore,
Inverurie AB61 0UQ Tel: 44 01467 633667
Email: driver@driveblog.co.uk
Web site: http://www.driveblog.co.uk
Freq: Daily
Circ: 8442
Antique & Collectible Cars, Automakers,
Automotive, Driving, Motorcycles, Off-
road & 4-Wheel Drive Vehicles, Trucks &
SUVs

Driving News 996750
Web site: www.driving-news.co.uk/
Freq: Daily
Circ: 2047
Automotive, Driving

Drogadiccion Juvenil 1061166
Web site: http://drogasjovenes.blogspot.
com/
Freq: Daily
Circ: 521
Neurology

Droid Horizon 998167
Email: droidhorizon@gmail.com
Web site: droidhorizon.com
Freq: Daily
Circ: 12583
Mobile Electronics

Drømmehagen 1062113
Web site: http://drommehagen-hilde.
blogspot.com/
Freq: Daily
Circ: 892
Gardening

Droogette 1054251
Email: messycarla@hotmail.co.uk
Web site: www.droogette.com
Freq: Daily
Circ: 8064
Beauty & Grooming, Cooking & Baking,
Cosmetics, Fashion, Hair, Travel

Drop Out Diaries 1061345
Email: theboss@thedropoutdiaries.com
Web site: http://www.thedropoutdiaries.com
Freq: Daily
Circ: 6637
Airline Inflight, Food, Railroad, Travel

Duan Xian Dian Jin 1061749
Email: xwmli@yahoo.com.cn
Web site: http://jimo-stock.blog.sohu.com
Freq: Daily
Circ: 64
Financial Markets

Dublin taxi 1054287
Email: dublin2taxi@yahoo.com
Web site: http://dublintaxi.blogspot.com

Freq: Daily
Circ: 1889
Regional General Interest

Duchess of Fashion 1100581
Email: duchessoffash@gmail.com
Web site: http://duchessoffashion.co.uk/
Freq: Daily
Circ: 5026
Profile: DUCHESS OF FASHION covers
fashion and lifestyle. The blog has an archive
dating back to July 2014. The blog also
offers a vlog.
Fashion

Dulces de Queca 1061757
Web site: http://www.dulcesdequeca.com
Freq: Daily
Circ: 5179
Cooking & Baking, Food

Dundee West End 997843
Tel: 44 01382 459378
Email: fraser@frasermacpherson.org.uk
Web site: http://www.dundeewestend.com/
Freq: Daily
Circ: 7713
Politics

**Dylan Jones-Evans Blog -
SUSPENDED FEBRUARY
2017** 1054030
Web site: dylanje.blogspot.co.uk
Freq: Daily
Circ: 611
Business

Dymps and Dimes 1052977
Web site: http://www.dympsanddimes.com/
Freq: Daily
Circ: 9690
Profile: Blog covering fashion. DYMPS AND
DIMES blog discusses anything from
personal style and outfit posts to beauty and
travel. The blog has an archive dating back
to April 2013.
Beauty & Grooming, Cosmetics, Fashion,
Hair, Regional General Interest, Women's
Interests

E Turismo Viajes 1061743
Web site: http://www.eturismoviajes.com
Freq: Daily
Circ: 7801
Airline Inflight, Railroad, Travel

Early Bird Wine News 995029
Editorial: 7a White Hart Lane, Barnes,
London SW13 0PX
Email: ebwinenews@gmail.com
Web site: http://www.earlybirdwinenews.
com/
Freq: Daily
Circ: 9948
Wine/Winemaking

Easy Hiker 1053440
Email: easy.hiker57@gmail.com
Web site: easyhiker.co.uk
Freq: Daily
Circ: 13050
Outdoor Recreation, Travel

easyfundraising blog 999397
Editorial: Harmony House, 34 High Street,
Aldridge, Aldridge WS9 8LZ
Web site: easyfundraising.org.uk/blog
Freq: Daily
Circ: 25
News & Current Affairs

Eat Like A Girl 986128
Email: hello@eatlikeagirl.com
Web site: www.eatlikeagirl.com
Freq: Daily
Circ: 50780
Alcohol & Spirits, Bars, Clubs & Pubs,
Beer, Beverages, Cooking & Baking,
Food, Grocery Stores, Organic Food,
Restaurant Reviews, Vegetarianism &
Veganism

Eat Like You Love Yourself
1054525
Email: mamacook@hotmail.co.uk
Web site: http://eatlikeyouloveyourself.
blogspot.com

Freq: Daily
Circ: 9111
Cooking & Baking, Nutrition

Eat Live Breathe 1063144
Email: eatlivebreathe@gmail.com
Web site: www.eatlivebreathe.co.uk
Freq: Daily
Circ: 2642
Cooking & Baking, Do-It-Yourself (DIY),
Fitness & Exercise, Food, Grocery Stores,
Nutrition, Organic Food, Restaurant
Reviews, Vegetarianism & Veganism,
Women's Interests

Eat Travel Love 1054331
Email: eat.travel.lov3@gmail.com
Web site: www.eat-travel-love.com
Freq: Daily
Circ: 8231
Profile: Blog covering travel, food, lifestyle
and leisure activities.
Beauty & Grooming, Cosmetics, Fashion,
Hair, Restaurant Reviews, Travel

Eat, Play, Live 1052862
Email: eatplaylivewithme@gmail.com
Web site: www.eatplaylivewithme.com
Freq: Daily
Circ: 7300
Profile: Blog covering lifestyle, travel, food
and drink.
Restaurant Reviews, Travel, Women's
Interests

Eats Amazing 988568
Web site: eatsamazing.co.uk
Freq: Daily
Circ: 78178
Profile: Blog covering food. The Eats
Amazing blog discusses anything from
healthy eating and recipes to equipment
reviews and cooking. The blog has an
archive dating back to August 2012. The
outlet offers RSS (Really Simple
Syndication).
Cooking & Baking

Eatwine Blog 1060343
Web site: http://eatwineblog.com
Freq: Daily
Circ: 1754
Food, Wine/Winemaking

eBook Travel Guides Blog
1053844
Email: social@lonelyplanet.com
Web site: http://ebooktravelguide.blogspot.
co.uk/
Freq: Daily
Circ: 15256
Airline Inflight, Railroad, Travel

The Ebury Collection 987768
Email: info@theeburycollection.com
Web site: www.theeburycollection.com
Freq: Daily
Circ: 7286
Weddings

ebuyer.com blog 986129
Tel: 44 03715 213300
Email: mediaenquiries@ebuyer.com
Web site: http://www.ebuyer.com/blog/
Freq: Daily
Circ: 370
Audio Video Trade, Cameras, Consumer
Electronics, Mobile Electronics, Movies &
Video

Ecetia 1060754
Web site: http://www.ecetia.com
Freq: Daily
Circ: 10063
Auto Aftermarket, Computers, Data
Management, Electronics, Government
Technology, Industry, Internet, Mobile
Communications, Security & Security
Systems, Software

Eco Fluffy Mama 997467
Web site: http://www.ecofluffymama.com/
Freq: Daily
Circ: 14886
Family & Parenting

Eco Thrifty Living
987835
Email: ecothriftyliving@gmail.com
Web site: www.ecothriftyliving.com/
Freq: Daily
Circ: 9070
Energy & Environment, Environment,
Ethical/Moral Issues

Ecohustler
1052871
Email: ecohustler@ecohustler.co.uk
Web site: http://www.ecohustler.co.uk/
Freq: Daily
Circ: 17073
Energy & Environment

Economics Help
986693
Editorial: 29 Campbell Road, Cowley,
Oxford OX4 3PF
Email: mail@economicshelp.org
Web site: www.economicshelp.org/blog
Freq: Daily
Circ: 41499
Economics

Economoose Blog
1055146
Editorial: 140 Tabernacle Street, London
EC2A 4SD Tel: 44 0207 220987
Email: support@propertymoose.co.uk
Web site: https://propertymoose.co.uk/blog/
Freq: Daily
Circ: 22768
Architecture & Design, Building &
Construction, Business, Commercial Real
Estate, Finance, Interior Design, Legal
Affairs, Office Design, Property
Management & Maintenance, Residential
Real Estate

Ecos del Mundo
1061027
Web site: http://blog.ecosdelmundo.com/
Freq: Daily
Environment

ecoTravel Africa Blog
1053704
Tel: 44 02088 732262
Email: joanna@ecotravelafrica.co.uk
Web site: www.ecotravelafrica.co.uk/eta-
blog/4585160857
Freq: Daily
Airline Inflight, Railroad, Travel

edge-e - CEASED SEPTEM-
BER 2017
1054672
Web site: http://edge-e.blogspot.co.uk/
Freq: Daily
Circ: 1060
Profile: Blog covering lifestyle.
Cooking & Baking, Cosmetics,
Entertainment, Fashion, Restaurant
Reviews, Women's Interests

Edinburgers
1053871
Email: admin@edinburgers.co.uk
Web site: http://www.edinburgers.co.uk/
Freq: Daily
Circ: 8714
Profile: Blog covering food and drink. THE
EDINBURGERS discusses anything from
restaurant reviews and recipes to events in
Edinburgh and travel. The blog has an
archive dating back to August 2013 and
shares a short blogroll.
Alcohol & Spirits, Beer, Regional General
Interest, Restaurant Reviews, Travel,
Wine/Winemaking

Edinburgh Foody
985987
Editorial: Edinburgh Foody, 394/8 Gorgie
Road, Edinburgh EH11 2RN
Tel: 44 01314 531660
Email: caroline@edinburghfoody.com
Web site: www.edinburghfoody.com
Freq: Daily
Circ: 12845
Profile: Blog covering food. edinburgh foody
discusses anything from ingredients and
cooking to baking, restaurants and Scottish
foods. The outlet offers RSS (Really Simple
Syndication).
Alcohol & Spirits, Bars, Clubs & Pubs,
Beer, Beverages, Cooking & Baking,
Food, Grocery Stores, Organic Food,
Restaurant Reviews, Vegetarianism &
Veganism

Edinburgh Whisky Blog
987245
Email: edinburghwhisky@gmail.com
Web site: www.edinburghwhiskyblog.com

Freq: Daily
Circ: 8991
Editor: Tiger White
Alcohol & Spirits, Bars, Clubs & Pubs,
Beer, Beverages, Cooking & Baking,
Food, Grocery Stores, Organic Food,
Restaurant Reviews, Vegetarianism &
Veganism

edinburghguide.com
982828
Tel: 44 01312 080633
Web site: www.edinburghguide.com
Circ: 25827
Airline Inflight, Alcohol & Spirits, Bars,
Clubs & Pubs, Beer, Beverages, Comedy,
Entertainment, Local Entertainment
Guides, Railroad, Travel

Edspire
987627
Email: jennie@edspire.co.uk
Web site: www.edspire.co.uk
Freq: Daily
Circ: 12672
Family & Parenting

Educación y Pedablogía para
el siglo XXI
1060542
Web site: http://pedablogia.wordpress.com
Freq: Daily
Circ: 48
Disability, Education, Higher Education,
Preschool, Schools & Institutions,
Students

Educando a mis Hijos
1061339
Web site: http://www.educandoamishijos.
com/
Freq: Daily
Circ: 1402
Family & Parenting

Education Otherwise - Susan
Young
1054467
Web site: www.naht.org.uk/welcome/news-
and-media/blogs/susan-young/
Freq: Daily
Circ: 7
Education

EducationState
1053053
Email: admin@educationstate.org
Web site: http://www.educationstate.org/
Freq: Daily
Circ: 2029
Education

EEF
1053980
Web site: www.eef.org.uk/campaigning/
news-blogs-and-publications/blogs
Freq: Daily
Circ: 7159
Engineering, Manufacturing

Efemerides del Deporte
Argentino
1061342
Web site: http://efemeridesdeportivas.
blogspot.com/
Freq: Daily
Circ: 4583
Basketball, Bicycles, Billiards, Boating &
Yachting, Bodybuilding, Bowling, Boxing,
Cricket, Equestrian Sports, Extreme/
Adventure Sports

The Eggplant Emoji
1062738
Web site: eggplantemoji.com
Freq: Daily
Circ: 1569
Literature, Social Issues, Women's
Interests

Eggs On The Roof
1069075
Email: cracked@eggsontheroof.com
Web site: http://eggsontheroof.com
Freq: Daily
Circ: 5316
Cooking & Baking, Literature

EJ Style
1054179
Email: contact@ejstyle.co.uk
Web site: http://ejstyle.co.uk/
Freq: Daily
Circ: 48717
Fashion

El Economista Blog of Luis
Gonzalez
1061617
Web site: http://eleconomista.com.mx/
blogs/luis-miguel-gonzalez
Freq: Daily
Circ: 32
Economics, National News, Politics

e-Learning Stuff
987329
Email: elearningstuff@me.com
Web site: elearningstuff.net
Freq: Daily
Circ: 15751
Electronics

Electoral Reform Society
996883
Editorial: 2 - 6 Boundary Row, London SE1
8HP Tel: 44 02037 144078
Email: mediaoffice@electoral-reform.org.uk
Web site: http://www.electoral-reform.org.
uk/blog/
Freq: Daily
Circ: 264
Politics

Electronic World TV
996340
Editorial: 208 Bromford Lane, Erdington,
Birmingham B24 8DL Tel: 44 01213 273273
Email: info@electronicworldtv.co.uk
Web site: www.electronicworldtv.co.uk/
blog/
Freq: Daily
Circ: 24735
Movies & Video

Electronics Weekly Blog
996341
Editorial: 6th Floor Davis House, 2 Robert
Street, Croydon, London CR0 1QQ
Tel: 44 02082 538670
Email: tech@electronicsweekly.com
Web site: http://www.electronicsweekly.
com/blogs/
Freq: Daily
Circ: 78
Audio Video Trade, Cameras, Consumer
Electronics, Mobile Electronics, Movies &
Video

Elevatormusik
987397
Web site: www.elevatormusik.com
Freq: Daily
Circ: 11408
Cooking & Baking, Regional General
Interest, Women's Interests

The Elgin Avenue
999647
Web site: www.theelginavenue.com
Freq: Daily
Circ: 13820
Fashion

Eliana Quintero
1060851
Web site: http://www.elianaquintero.
blogspot.com
Freq: Daily
Circ: 611
Astrology & Parapsychology, Religion

Eliash
1060427
Web site: http://www.eliash.cl/blog/
Freq: Daily
Architecture & Design, Broadcasting,
Regional, Regional General Interest

elisabettawhite.com
997487
Web site: http://elisabettawhite.com/
Freq: Daily
Circ: 10022
News & Current Affairs

Eliza Flynn
987771
Editorial: 20B Highbury Park, London N5
2AB
Email: hellofitty@healthylivinglondon.com
Web site: http://elizaflynn.co.uk/
Freq: Daily
Circ: 9688
Cooking & Baking, Fitness & Exercise,
Nature & Wildlife, Nutrition, Regional
General Interest, Restaurant Reviews,
Travel

Elizabeth Baines' Blog
1054071
Email: e.baines@zen.co.uk
Web site: http://elizabethbaines.blogspot.
co.uk/
Freq: Daily

Circ: 9222
Literature

Elizabeth's Kitchen Diary
988074
Web site: http://www.
elizabethskitchendiary.co.uk/
Freq: Daily
Circ: 162501
Profile: Blog covering food. The Elizabeth's
Kitchen Diary blog discusses anything from
cooking and baking to recipes, crafts and
product reviews. The outlet offers RSS
(Really Simple Syndication).
Cooking & Baking

Ella In The Big City
1054475
Web site: ellainthebigcity.com
Freq: Daily
Circ: 10808
Beauty & Grooming, Cosmetics, Fitness &
Exercise, Hair, Nutrition, Women's
Interests

Ella La Petite Anglaise
987426
Editorial: Flat 196, Latymer Court,
Hammersmith Road, London W6 7JQ
Web site: http://www.ella-lapetiteanglaise.
com
Freq: Daily
Circ: 35445
Editor: Ella Catliff
Beauty & Grooming, Cosmetics, Fashion,
Hair, Shopping

Ella Sykes Blog
1104182
Editorial: FAO Ella Sykes, Unit 4, Block E,
Leeds Dock, Leeds LS10 1PZ
Web site: https://ellasykesblog.wordpress.
com
Freq: Daily
Circ: 26
Art, Beauty & Grooming, Cooking &
Baking, Cosmetics, Fashion, Fitness &
Exercise, Hair, Health & Medicine,
Literature, Movies & Video

Elland Occasionals
1054497
Email: rectorofelland@btinternet.com
Web site: http://ellandoccasionals.blogspot.
co.uk/
Freq: Daily
Circ: 752
Religion

Elle Yeah
987078
Email: contact@elle-yeah.com
Web site: http://www.elle-yeah.com
Freq: Daily
Circ: 6234
Editor: Elodie Russo
Profile: Blog covering fashion and lifestyle.
ELLE yeah blog discusses anything from
fashion trends and beauty to lifestyle and
home. The outlet offers RSS (Really Simple
Syndication).
Fashion

Ellie Jayden
988417
Email: ellicjaydon@hotmail.com
Web site: elliejayden.com
Freq: Daily
Circ: 9355
News & Current Affairs

Ellie Tennant Blog
1054493
Web site: ellietennant.com/blog
Freq: Daily
Circ: 157
Do-It-Yourself (DIY)

Ellies favourite things
1052872
Email: info@elliesfavouritethings.com
Web site: http://www.elliesfavouritethings.
com/
Freq: Daily
Circ: 7043
Beauty & Grooming, Cosmetics, Fashion,
Hair, Regional General Interest, Travel,
Women's Interests

Eltoria
1098946
Email: eltoriasecrets@gmail.com
Web site: http://www.eltoria.com/
Freq: Daily
Circ: 10264

UK Blogs

Profile: Blog covering beauty, cosmetics, beauty tips, fashion and fashion accessories. The blog has an archive dating back to August 2013.
Beauty & Grooming, Cosmetics, Hair, Women's Interests

Eluxe Magazine 1086850
Email: info@eluxemagazine.com
Web site: http://eluxemagazine.com/
Freq: Daily
Circ: 147367
Energy & Environment, Ethical/Moral Issues, Fashion, Luxury Goods

Em Talks 987597
Email: emtalks@gmail.com
Web site: www.emtalks.co.uk
Freq: Daily
Circ: 53631
Beauty & Grooming, Cooking & Baking, Cosmetics, Fashion, Hair, Travel, Women's Interests

emag.co.uk 988337
Editorial: 36 Commercial Road, Swindon SN1 5NS
Email: support@emag.co.uk
Web site: http://emag.co.uk/
Circ: 11228
Profile: Website covering entertainment. The EMAG.CO.UK website covers all things entertainment including celebrities, shopping, fashion, music, movies and TV.
Celebrities, Classical/Choral/Band Music, Country, Folk, Bluegrass, Dance Music, Fashion, Jazz & Blues, Movies & Video, Music, Pop Music, R&B, Urban, World

The Embedded Blog 1053032
Email: nick@flaherty.co.uk
Web site: www.embeddedblog.blogspot.com
Freq: Daily
Circ: 753
Auto Aftermarket, Computers, Data Management, Electronics, Government Technology, Industry, Internet, Mobile Communications, Security & Security Systems, Software

Embrace Scotland Blog 1052893
Tel: 44 01866 822122
Email: secretary@assc.co.uk
Web site: http://www.embracescotland.co.uk/blog/
Freq: Daily
Circ: 14030
Travel

Emergic: Rajesh Jain's Blog 1061439
Web site: http://www.emergic.org
Freq: Daily
Circ: 6497
Industry

e-Metales 1060852
Freq: Daily
Steel

Emily Canham 1098971
Email: emily@kameleon.co.uk
Web site: https://www.youtube.com/user/Butimhereforever
Freq: Daily
Circ: 6
Cosmetics, Fashion, Women's Interests

Emily Canham Vlogs 1098970
Email: emily@kameleon.co.uk
Web site: https://www.youtube.com/user/imhereforevervlogs
Freq: Daily
Circ: 6342
Cosmetics, Fashion, Women's Interests

Emily Florence Bakes 1052886
Web site: http://emilyflorencebakes.com/
Freq: Daily
Circ: 521
Alcohol & Spirits, Bars, Clubs & Pubs, Beer, Beverages, Cooking & Baking, Do-It-Yourself (DIY), Wine/Winemaking

Emily Hannah Blog 1053533
Tel: 44 02081 238042
Email: sales@emilyhannah.ltd.uk

Web site: http://www.walkingsticksonline.co.uk/blog/
Freq: Daily
Circ: 58
Disability, Fashion

Emily Jayne 996453
Editorial: 8 Worcester Road, Bromsgrove, Bromsgrove B61 7AE Tel: 44 07773 704974
Web site: http://www.emily-jayne.com
Freq: Daily
Circ: 6570
Fashion

Emily Luxton Travels 988028
Tel: 44 07888 658239
Email: hello@emilyluxton.co.uk
Web site: http://emilyluxton.co.uk/
Freq: Daily
Circ: 80973
Travel

Emily's Recipes and Reviews 1052896
Email: recipesandreviewsetc@hotmail.com
Web site: www.recipesandreviews.co.uk
Freq: Daily
Circ: 9487
Profile: Blog covering food. emily's recipes and reviews blog discusses anything from food and recipes to restaurant reviews. The blog has an archive dating back to June 2011.
Cooking & Baking

Emma & 3 987560
Web site: emmaand3.com
Freq: Daily
Circ: 25849
Education, Family & Parenting, Travel

Emma Griffiths Blog 988369
Web site: www.emmagriffy.com
Freq: Daily
Circ: 9037
Profile: Blog covering beauty products and cosmetics. The blog has an archive dating back to January 2013. This outlet also offers a vlog.
Fashion, Women's Interests

Emma in Bromley 1053540
Email: emmainbromley@gmail.com
Web site: http://www.emmainbromley.co.uk/
Freq: Daily
Circ: 8141
Family & Parenting, Women's Interests

Emma Lamb Blog 1052604
Email: emmallamb@gmail.com
Web site: http://www.emmallamb.com/blog
Freq: Daily
Circ: 8
Art, Crafts

emmagannon.co.uk 987070
Email: emmagannonuk@gmail.com
Web site: emmagannon.co.uk
Freq: Daily
Circ: 13635
Cooking & Baking, Entertainment, Fashion, Literature, Local Entertainment Guides, Movies & Video, Restaurant Reviews, Travel, Women's Interests

EmmaJayne-Designs 1054286
Web site: emmajayne-designs.co.uk
Freq: Daily
Circ: 10075
Crafts, Visual Arts

Emma's Savvy £ Savings 1052965
Tel: 44 01452 618347
Web site: http://mumssavvysavings.com/
Freq: Daily
Circ: 15240
Family & Parenting, Personal Finance

Emma's Travel Tales 1052766
Web site: emmastraveltales.co.uk
Freq: Daily
Circ: 7318
Profile: Emma's Travel Tales covers travel, destination guides and tourist activities.
Travel

Emmeline Illustration 996045
Email: hello@emmelineillustration.com
Web site: http://blog.emmelineillustration.com/
Freq: Daily
Circ: 248
Antiques/Collectibles, Art, Arts, Literature, Photography, Theater & Performing Arts, Visual Arts

Emmy's Mummy and Harry's Too 988687
Web site: www.emmysmummy.com
Freq: Daily
Circ: 29008
Family & Parenting

Emo Oil News 996342
Editorial: 197 Airport Road West, Belfast BT3 9ED Tel: 44 08454 348082
Email: info@emooil.com
Web site: http://www.emooil.com/news
Freq: Daily
Circ: 59
Oil

Emoov Blog 996343
Editorial: eMoov Limited, Fourth Floor, New North House, Ongar Road, Brentwood, Brentwood CM15 9BB Tel: 44 03331 214920
Email: press@emoov.co.uk
Web site: https://www.emoov.co.uk/news/
Freq: Daily
Circ: 126
Property Management & Maintenance

Empty Screens 988044
Email: centrefoldsandemptyscreens@live.co.uk
Web site: http://emptyscreens.com/
Freq: Daily
Circ: 1471
Editor: Jamie Neish
Entertainment, Movies & Video

En busca del equilibrio perdido 1061188
Web site: http://enbuscadelequilibrioperdido.blogspot.com
Freq: Daily
Circ: 1560
Careers, Crime & Violence, Family & Parenting, Health & Medicine, Lifestyle, Neurology, Personal Finance, Relationships

En Busca del Espacio Sospechoso 1061010
Web site: http://arquitecturatallerintegral.blogspot.com/
Freq: Daily
Circ: 521
Architecture & Design, Government, Regional, Regional General Interest

En la Pantalla Chica 1061728
Web site: http://enlapantallachica.blogspot.com/
Freq: Daily
Circ: 827
Broadcasting, Celebrities

En La Upea 1061777
Web site: http://www.enlaupea.com
Freq: Daily
Circ: 1376
National News

En sintonía con tu Ser 1061409
Web site: http://reikisintonia.blogspot.com/
Freq: Daily
Circ: 521
Careers, Crime & Violence, Family & Parenting, Health & Medicine, Lifestyle, Neurology, Personal Finance, Relationships

Enciclopedia 1060781
Web site: http://enciclopediafarmacologica.blogspot.com/
Freq: Daily
Circ: 521
Literature

Emmeline Illustration
(continued)

Encuentro con el Jazz 1060998
Web site: http://encuentroconeljazz.blogspot.com/
Freq: Daily
Circ: 521
Jazz & Blues

End Water Poverty blog 1053598
Editorial: WaterAid, 2nd Floor, 47 - 49 Durham Street, London SE11 5JD
Tel: 44 08456 000433
Email: info@endwaterpoverty.org
Web site: http://www.endwaterpoverty.org/news
Freq: Daily
Circ: 9
Charitable Foundations

EndGame 1054636
Email: info@endgame.org.uk
Web site: http://www.endgame.org.uk/
Freq: Daily
Circ: 1224
Social Issues

Energise 1053832
Email: hello@neilson.com
Web site: https://www.neilson.co.uk/do-your-thing
Freq: Daily
Circ: 7667
Travel

The Energy Saving Trust Blog 999582
Editorial: Energy Saving Trust England, 21 Dartmouth Street, London SW1H 9BP
Tel: 44 02072 220101
Email: estblog@est.org.uk
Web site: http://www.energysavingtrust.org.uk/blog
Freq: Daily
Circ: 114
Alternative/Renewable Energy, Consumer Affairs, Electricity, Energy & Environment, Sales & Marketing, Shopping

Engage 1008433
Web site: https://engageonline.wordpress.com/
Freq: Daily
Circ: 1241
Editor: David Hirsh
Regional

English for Law 1053063
Web site: http://englishforlaw.blogspot.com
Freq: Daily
Circ: 1273
Law

The English Kitchen 988372
Web site: theenglishkitchen.blogspot.co.uk
Freq: Daily
Circ: 9973
Cooking & Baking

English Mum 986505
Email: englishtowers@gmail.com
Web site: englishmum.com
Freq: Daily
Circ: 38166
Airline Inflight, Alcohol & Spirits, Bars, Clubs & Pubs, Beer, Beverages, Cooking & Baking, Family & Parenting, Food, Grocery Stores, Organic Food

English Teaching Reources 1054581
Web site: https://jwpblog.wordpress.com
Freq: Daily
Circ: 72
Alumni, Careers, Education, Student Lifestyle, Teachers

English Wedding 985553
Editorial: C/O Claire Gould, Apart-ment 1 Ling-mell Court-yard, Gos-forth Road, Seascale, Seascale CA20 1HQ
Email: info@english-wedding.com
Web site: http://www.english-wedding.com
Freq: Daily
Circ: 32586
Editor: Claire Gould
Weddings

Enjoy the Journey
1052719
Email: beth@enjoythejourney.org.uk
Web site: http://enjoythejourney.org.uk/
Freq: Daily
Circ: 6192
Profile: Blog covering travel and
backpacking. The blog has an archive dating
back to September 2011.
Travel

Entre Calzones
1061015
Web site: http://www.entrecalzones.com
Freq: Daily
Circ: 672
Fashion

Entre Grandes Cacaos
1061661
Web site: http://blogs.eluniversal.com/eu3/
Blogs/cacao_index.shtml
Freq: Daily
Circ: 17653
Celebrities, Fashion

Entre Tecnología
1061514
Web site: http://entretecnologia.blogspot.
com
Freq: Daily
Circ: 611
Auto Aftermarket, Computers, Data
Management, Electronics, Government
Technology, Industry, Internet, Mobile
Communications, Security & Security
Systems, Software

Entrometido
1061929
Web site: http://www.elentrometido.com
Freq: Daily
Circ: 795
National News, Politics

Environment and Geology
1062099
Web site: http://nitishpriyadarshi.blogspot.
com
Freq: Daily
Circ: 9699
Environment, Science

environmentalresearchweb
blog
980131
Editorial: Temple Circus, Temple Way,
Bristol BS1 6HG Tel: 44 01179 297481
Email: custserv@iop.org
Web site: environmentalresearchweb.org
Freq: Daily
Circ: 21412
Editor: Liz Kalaugher
Alternative/Renewable Energy, Carbon
Emissions & Trading, Electricity, Energy,
Environment, Nuclear Power, Oil, Water &
Sanitation

Epicurienne - CEASED JULY
2015
997747
Web site: epicurienne.co.uk
Freq: Daily
Circ: 752
Cooking & Baking

EpiphannieA
987623
Web site: http://epiphanniea.co.uk
Freq: Daily
Circ: 9852
Alcohol & Spirits, Bars, Clubs & Pubs,
Beauty & Grooming, Beer, Beverages,
Cooking & Baking, Cosmetics, Fashion,
Food, Grocery Stores

EPL Index Blog
996910
Editorial: Office 5034, PO Box 15113,
Birmingham B2 2NJ Tel: 44 08712 464951
Email: eplindex@gmail.com
Web site: http://eplindex.com/
Freq: Daily
Circ: 51076
Soccer

The Equality Trust Blog
1054342
Editorial: 18 Victoria Park Square, London
E2 9PF Tel: 44 02036 370324
Email: info@equalitytrust.org.uk
Web site: https://www.equalitytrust.org.uk/
blogs
Freq: Daily
Circ: 5
Charitable Foundations

The Equity Kicker
1053120
Web site: http://www.theequitykicker.com/
Freq: Daily
Circ: 42698
Business

Eric Joyce MP blog
997908
Editorial: 37 Church Walk, Denny FK6 6DF
Tel: 44 01324 823200
Email: eric@ericjoyce.co.uk
Web site: http://ericjoyce.co.uk/
Freq: Daily
Circ: 17123
Politics

Erna Low blog
1053423
Editorial: 9 Reece Mews, London SW7 3HE
Web site: http://www.ernalow.co.uk/blog
Freq: Daily
Circ: 169
Travel, Winter Sports

Errant Surf Blog
1053143
Tel: 44 02081 336438
Email: hello@errantsurf.com
Web site: http://blog.errantsurf.com/
Freq: Daily
Circ: 37
Swimming/Watersports

Escaparate
1061207
Email: yimmic@gmail.com
Web site: http://elblogdeyimmi.blogspot.
com/
Freq: Daily
Circ: 1797
Antiques/Collectibles, Art, Arts, Classical/
Choral/Band Music, Country, Folk,
Bluegrass, Dance Music, Jazz & Blues,
Literature, Music, National News

Escape Running
1053227
Web site: http://www.escaperunning.com/
Freq: Daily
Circ: 1801
Fitness & Exercise, Travel

The Escapologist's Daughter
988758
Email: theescapologistsdaughter@gmail.
com
Web site: http://theescapologistsdaughter.
co.uk/
Freq: Daily
Circ: 9365
Profile: Blog covering lifestyle and beauty.
Women's Interests

Escribo en tus Ojos
1061073
Web site: http://javiermirandaluque.
blogspot.com/
Freq: Daily
Circ: 992
Antiques/Collectibles, Art, Arts,
Literature, Photography, Theater &
Performing Arts, Visual Arts

Esoterica
1061727
Web site: http://www.soyesoterica.com
Freq: Daily
Circ: 33290
Personal Finance, Relationships

Espacio de Hernan Haines
1061893
Web site: http://hernanhaines.blogspot.
com/
Freq: Daily
Circ: 1161
Politics

ESPC News
1054272
Editorial: 90a George Street, Edinburgh EH2
3DF
Email: marketing@espc.com
Web site: espc.com/news
Freq: Daily
Profile: Blog covering the Scottish property
market.
Property Management & Maintenance

Espiritu Rock
1061675
Web site: http://www.espiriturock.blogspot.
com/
Freq: Daily

Circ: 968
Rock Music

eSports News UK
988669
Editorial: 11 Outwood Farm Road, Billericay,
Billericay CM11 2NA
Email: admin@leetgamesblog.com
Web site: http://www.esports-news.co.uk
Freq: Daily
Circ: 19702
Computer & Video Games

Essex Mums blog
1053593
Tel: 44 01702 330591
Web site: http://www.essexmums.org/blog/
Freq: Daily
Circ: 4196
Family & Parenting

Essie-Button
987075
Email: essiebutton@gmail.com
Web site: http://www.esteelalonde.com/
Freq: Daily
Circ: 43426
Beauty & Grooming, Cosmetics, Hair

The Establishing Shot
987946
Tel: 44 07809 232337
Email: theestablishingshot@gmail.com
Web site: www.theestablishingshot.com/
Freq: Daily
Circ: 9143
Editor: Craig Grobler
Entertainment, Movies & Video

Estado-Ley-Democracia
1061104
Web site: http://estado-ley-democracia.
blogspot.com/
Freq: Daily
Circ: 10015
Politics

ET Speaks from Home
987570
Editorial: 30 Armada Close, Lichfield WS14
0GJ Tel: 44 07921 711604
Email: etspeaksfromhome@yahoo.com
Web site: http://www.etspeaksfromhome.
co.uk/
Freq: Daily
Circ: 15005
Cooking & Baking, Crafts, Family &
Parenting, Women's Interests

Eterna Caimanera
1061627
Web site: http://lacaimana.blogspot.com/
Freq: Daily
Circ: 645
Soccer

Ethan Walker Climbing
1053837
Email: ethanwalkerclimbing@hotmail.com
Web site: http://ethanwalkerclimbing.
blogspot.co.uk
Freq: Daily
Circ: 1333
Outdoor Recreation

Ethical Superstore Blog
986321
Editorial: Follingsby Avenue, Follingsby
Park, Gateshead NE10 8HQ
Tel: 44 08450 099012
Email: enquiries@ethicalsuperstore.com
Web site: http://www.ethicalsuperstore.
com/blog/
Freq: Daily
Circ: 217
Energy & Environment

The Ethics and Insurance
Blog
996668
Web site: ethicsandinsurance.info
Freq: Daily
Circ: 611
News & Current Affairs

E-ting the World
1061977
Web site: http://www.e-tingfood.com
Freq: Daily
Circ: 7467
Food

EU Law Analysis
1053991
Web site: eulawanalysis.blogspot.co.uk
Freq: Daily

Circ: 15304
Corporate Law

euro tech news
1052939
Web site: http://eurotechnews.blogspot.co.
uk/
Freq: Daily
Circ: 521
Auto Aftermarket, Computers, Data
Management, Electronics, Government
Technology, Industry, Internet, Mobile
Communications, Security & Security
Systems, Software

Europe a la Carte
986133
Editorial: 33 Riverdene, Tweedmouth,
Berwick-upon-Tweed TD15 2JD
Web site: www.europealacarte.co.uk/blog
Freq: Daily
Circ: 46064
News & Current Affairs

EuropeBus.co.uk
1053202
Web site: http://www.europebus.co.uk/
blog/
Freq: Daily
Circ: 87
Travel

EUROPP - European Politics
and Policy
1054671
Tel: 44 02079 556909
Email: europpblog@lse.ac.uk
Web site: http://blogs.lse.ac.uk/europpblog/
Freq: Daily
Circ: 120223
Politics

Evaluate Energy
1052911
Editorial: 11-29 Fashion Street, London E1
6PX
Email: energyinfo@evaluateenergy.com
Web site: http://blog.evaluateenergy.com/
Freq: Daily
Circ: 12074
Oil

Evans Halshaw blog
997845
Web site: http://www.evanshalshaw.com/
blog/
Freq: Daily
Circ: 284
Antique & Collectible Cars, Automakers,
Automotive, Driving, Motorcycles, Off-
road & 4-Wheel Drive Vehicles, Trucks &
SUVs

Event Manager Blog
1053653
Web site: eventmanagerblog.com
Freq: Daily
Circ: 640697
Branding, Marketing

Ever So Juliet
1053954
Email: thisisjuliet@gmail.com
Web site: www.eversojuliet.com
Freq: Daily
Circ: 3030
Beauty & Grooming, Cooking & Baking,
Cosmetics, Crafts, Fashion, Hair,
Literature, Women's Interests

Every day ups and downs, a
diabetes blog
1052761
Web site: http://www.
everydayupsanddowns.co.uk/
Freq: Daily
Circ: 11037
News & Current Affairs

Everybody Plays
988184
Email: contact@everybodyplays.co.uk
Web site: http://www.everybodyplays.co.uk/
Circ: 77369
Computer & Video Games

Everyday Estée
1076751
Email: contact@esteelalonde.com
Web site: https://www.youtube.com/user/
essiebuttonvlogs
Freq: Daily
Circ: 20
Cooking & Baking, Fashion, Women's
Interests

UK Blogs

Everyday Lauren 988946
Email: everydaylauren@hotmail.com
Web site: http://www.everydaylauren.com/
Freq: Daily
Circ: 9952
Cosmetics, Women's Interests

The Everyday Man 987385
Email: mail@theeverydayman.co.uk
Web site: theeverydayman.co.uk
Freq: Daily
Circ: 74406
Men's Interests

everything in the garden's rosy 1054250
Web site: everythinginthegardensrosy.com
Freq: Daily
Circ: 10159
Gardening

Everything is Rosy 1054107
Email: everythingisrosyblog@gmail.com
Web site: everythingisrosy.com
Freq: Daily
Circ: 809
Cosmetics, Family & Parenting, Women's Interests

Everything Tech 1054080
Web site: http://www.every-thing-tech.co.uk/
Freq: Daily
Circ: 10293
Audio Video Trade, Cameras, Consumer Electronics, Mobile Electronics, Movies & Video

Everything theatre 988532
Email: info@everything-theatre.co.uk
Web site: http://everything-theatre.co.uk/
Circ: 13646
Profile: Website covering the London theatre scene.
Theater & Performing Arts

Everything's Rosie 988515
Email: everythings-rosie@hotmail.co.uk
Web site: www.everythingsrosieblog.com
Freq: Daily
Circ: 7199
Profile: Blog covering beauty and lifestyle. The blog has an archive dating back to November 2011.
Beauty & Grooming, Cosmetics, Hair, Women's Interests

Evidence Based Educational Leadership 1054944
Web site: http://evidencebasededucationalleadership.blogspot.com.au/
Freq: Daily
Circ: 10709
Education

Evonomie Digital Marketing Blog 1053516
Editorial: The Office, Pipe Hill House, Pipe Hill, Lichfield WS13 8JU
Tel: 44 01543 258522
Email: evolve@evonomie.net
Web site: http://business2businessmarketing.blogspot.co.uk/
Freq: Daily
Circ: 484
Advertising Industry, Branding, Broadcasting, Graphic Design, Marketing, Media & Communications, Photography, Publishing

Ewan McIntosh's edu.blogs.com 987327
Web site: edu.blogs.com
Freq: Daily
Circ: 10211383
News & Current Affairs

Executive Voice Blog 998249
Editorial: 2 Cob Lane Close, Digswell, Welwyn Garden City AL6 0DD
Tel: 44 08000 938464
Web site: executivevoice.co.uk/blog
Freq: Daily

Circ: 494
Education, Marketing

Exiled Preacher 1052548
Web site: exiledpreacher.blogspot.co.uk
Freq: Daily
Circ: 641
History, Literature, Religion

Exitainment 1052642
Web site: http://lightupvirginmary.blogspot.co.uk/
Freq: Daily
Circ: 611
Broadcasting

Exotic Maypole 996689
Web site: exoticmaypole.com
Freq: Daily
Circ: 10244
Women's Interests

Experience Days Blog 1052866
Editorial: Experience Days Ltd., Suite 5, 100-101 Queens Road, Brighton BN1 3XF
Email: lookafterme@experiencedays.com
Web site: http://blog.experiencedays.co.uk/
Freq: Daily
Circ: 44
Alcohol & Spirits, Audio Video Trade, Bars, Clubs & Pubs, Beauty & Grooming, Beer, Beverages, Cameras, Comedy, Consumer Electronics, Cosmetics

Experience Travel Blog 1054507
Email: hello@experiencetravelgroup.com
Web site: www.experiencetravelgroup.com/blog
Freq: Daily
Circ: 10663
Airline Inflight, Railroad, Travel

Expert Answers 996204
Editorial: 49 Brynmor Avenue, Flint CH6 5RZ
Web site: http://www.expertanswers.co.uk/blog/
Freq: Daily
Circ: 43747
Bankruptcy, Company News & Appointments, Consumer Interest, Corporate Law, Criminal Law, Employment, Estate Planning, Family Law, Federal Courts, Food & Drug Administration

Expert Dietitian blog 1054061
Email: expertdietitian@gmail.com
Web site: http://www.expertdietitian.co.uk/
Freq: Daily
Circ: 2268
Profile: Blog covering nutrition. EXPERT DIETITIAN BLOG discusses anything from nutrition and personal health to dieting. The blog has an archive dating back to March 2013.
Cooking & Baking, Nutrition

Explore 1052941
Tel: 44 01252 883748
Web site: https://www.explore.co.uk/news-and-features
Freq: Daily
Circ: 21
Airline Inflight, Railroad, Travel

Explore with Ed 1100035
Email: explorewithed@gmail.com
Web site: http://www.explorewithed.co.uk/
Freq: Daily
Circ: 12579
Cooking & Baking, Restaurant Reviews, Travel

Expression and Confession - SUSPENDED FEBRUARY 2017 996548
Email: expressionconfession@gmail.com
Web site: expressionandconfession.com
Freq: Daily
Circ: 843
Family & Parenting

ExtranetEvolution 1053435
Tel: 44 02088 581104
Email: paul.wilkinson@pwcom.co.uk
Web site: http://extranetevolution.com/

Freq: Daily
Circ: 12153
Business

F1 Fanatic 986134
Editorial: 7 Tremadoc Road, London SW4 7NF
Web site: www.f1fanatic.co.uk
Freq: Daily
Circ: 579079
Antique & Collectible Cars, Automakers, Automotive, Driving, Motorcycles, Off-road & 4-Wheel Drive Vehicles, Trucks & SUVs

Fab Food 4 All 987811
Web site: fabfood4all.co.uk
Freq: Daily
Circ: 87489
Cooking & Baking

Fabian Review Blog 986209
Editorial: 61 Petty France, Westminster, London SW1H 9EU Tel: 44 02072 274906
Email: info@fabians.org.uk
Web site: http://www.fabians.org.uk/fabian-review/
Circ: 7307
Politics

Fabric Of My Life 988397
Web site: http://fabricofmylife.co.uk/
Freq: Daily
Circ: 48635
Fashion

Fabublush 997403
Email: info@fabublush.com
Web site: http://fabublush.co.uk/
Freq: Daily
Circ: 9717
Beauty & Grooming, Cosmetics, Fashion, Hair

The Fabulous Times 1054155
Web site: thefaboustimes.com/
Freq: Daily
Circ: 7846
Profile: Blog covering fashion, food, travel, wellbeing, women in business, entertainment and blogging tips.
Do-It-Yourself (DIY), Fashion, Restaurant Reviews, Travel

Face Hunter 986136
Web site: www.facehunter.org
Freq: Daily
Circ: 31727
Fashion

Facewest Blog 1054327
Tel: 44 01943 870550
Email: sales@facewest.co.uk
Web site: http://www.facewest.co.uk/facewestblog/
Freq: Daily
Circ: 56
Outdoor Recreation

FAD - Cool Art & Stuff 987319
Editorial: Collective 37, Camden High Street, London NW1 7JE
Web site: www.fadmagazine.com
Circ: 18152
Art

FADED GLAMOUR 986412
Editorial: 175 Kennington Lane, London SE11 4EZ
Email: fg@fadedglamour.co.uk
Web site: www.fadedglamour.co.uk
Freq: Daily
Circ: 2939
Editor: Saam Das
Broadcasting, Classical/Choral/Band Music, Country, Folk, Bluegrass, Dance Music, Jazz & Blues, Movies & Video, Music, Pop Music, R&B, Urban, World, Rap & Hip Hop

Fagburn - SUSPENDED FEBRUARY 2017 1053223
Web site: http://www.fagburn.com/
Freq: Daily
Circ: 2002
Profile: Fagburn covers gay culture and gay men's portrayal in the media and in politics.

The blog has an archive dating back to April 2010 and shares an extensive blogroll.
LGBT

FAIIINT 1053790
Web site: www.faiiint.com/faiiint/
Freq: Daily
Circ: 29614
Profile: Blog covering fashion and lifestyle. FAIIINT blog discusses anything from fashion and beauty inspiration to DIY and travel. The outlet offers RSS (Really Simple Syndication).
Fashion, Women's Interests

The Fairtrade Blog 999215
Editorial: 3rd Floor, Ibex House, 42-47 Minories, London EC3N 1DY
Tel: 44 02074 407692
Email: media@fairtrade.org.uk
Web site: http://www.fairtrade.org.uk/en/media-centre/blog
Freq: Daily
Circ: 68
Charitable Foundations

Fairy Blog Mother 996790
Tel: 44 01189 585520
Web site: fairyblogmother.co.uk
Freq: Daily
Circ: 10484
Careers, Publishing

Fairy Socks 1053663
Email: joycehvernals@googlemail.com
Web site: fairysocks.blogspot.co.uk
Freq: Daily
Circ: 1075
Beauty & Grooming, Cosmetics, Hair, Women's Interests

The Fairytale Pretty Picture 988467
Editorial: 25 Link Way, Hornchurch, London RM11 3RN
Email: fairytaleprettypicture@gmail.com
Web site: http://fairytaleprettypicture.co.uk/
Freq: Daily
Circ: 8997
Profile: The Fairytale Pretty Picture covers home, interior design, fashion, lifestyle, books and DIY. The blog has an archive dating back to November 2013.
Crafts, Do-It-Yourself (DIY), Fashion, Literature

Fall Line Blog 1054452
Tel: 44 01733 293250
Web site: http://www.fall-line.co.uk/category/fall-line-blog/
Freq: Daily
Circ: 2489
Travel, Winter Sports

Fallond Stock Pick 998688
Email: fallond@fallondpicks.com
Web site: http://www.markets.fallondpicks.com/
Freq: Daily
Circ: 7241
News & Current Affairs

Familia y Flores de Bach 1061189
Web site: http://blogs.eluniversal.com/eu3/Blogs/fbach_index.shtml
Freq: Daily
Circ: 17653
Family & Parenting, Neurology

The Family Adventure Project 987642
Tel: 44 01524 782351
Web site: http://familyadventureproject.org
Freq: Daily
Circ: 23644
Airline Inflight, Railroad, Travel

Family Affairs and other matters 987918
Web site: http://www.familyaffairsandothermatters.com/
Freq: Daily
Circ: 7854
Energy & Environment, Family & Parenting, Travel

Family Budgeting 988719
Web site: family-budgeting.co.uk
Freq: Daily
Circ: 8857
Family & Parenting, Personal Finance

Family Fever 988584
Web site: myfamilyfever.co.uk
Freq: Daily
Circ: 80039
Profile: Blog covering family life and
children's activities. The blog has an archive
dating back to December 2012.
Family & Parenting

Family Four Fun 1054213
Email: familyfourfun@gmail.com
Web site: www.familyfourfun.co.uk
Freq: Daily
Circ: 10856
Family & Parenting

Family Friendly Working 1052898
Email: antonia@familyfriendlyworking.co.uk
Web site: http://www.familyfriendlyworking.
co.uk/
Freq: Daily
Circ: 46156
Business, Family & Parenting

**Family Law Blog from Family
Law in Partnership** 997569
Editorial: 1 Neal Street, Covent Garden,
London WC2H 9QL Tel: 44 02074 205000
Email: hello@flip.co.uk
Web site: www.flip.co.uk/news-blog/
Freq: Daily
Circ: 6813
Family Law

Family Law Week Blog 1054666
Tel: 44 08701 453935
Email: info@familylawweek.co.uk
Web site: http://flwblog.lawweek.co.uk/
Freq: Daily
Circ: 5706
Law

Family Lore 986339
Web site: www.familylore.co.uk
Freq: Daily
Circ: 12954
Family Law

The Family Panel 985470
Email: familypanel@yahoo.co.uk
Web site: www.familypanelreviews.co.uk
Freq: Daily
Circ: 1267
Family & Parenting

Family Travel Times 988291
Email: familytraveltimes@gmail.com
Web site: familytraveltimes.blogspot.co.uk
Freq: Daily
Circ: 5516
Profile: Family Travel Times covers family
travel and days out. The blog has an archive
dating back to June 2003.
Family & Parenting, Travel

Famous in Japan 1054938
Web site: http://famousinjapan.co.uk/
Freq: Daily
Circ: 7808
News & Current Affairs

Famous When Dead 986915
Editorial: 112-116 Old Street, London EC1V
9BG
Web site: http://fwdead.blogspot.co.uk/
Freq: Daily
Circ: 521
Art, Visual Arts

Fandom Life 1052884
Web site: http://www.fandomlife.net
Freq: Daily
Circ: 9480
Computer & Video Games, Internet,
Movies & Video

Fans Corner 997457
Web site: http://fanscorners.com/
Freq: Daily

Circ: 6515
Soccer

Fanultra 1061656
Web site: http://fanultra.posterous.com
Freq: Daily
Circ: 43
Art, Auto Aftermarket, Computers, Data
Management, Electronics, Government
Technology, Industry, Internet, Mobile
Communications, National News

Fanzine 1061093
Web site: http://elfanzinedemalbicho.
blogspot.com
Freq: Daily
Circ: 2530
Antiques/Collectibles, Art, Arts,
Literature, Photography, Theater &
Performing Arts, Visual Arts

Far From Perfect 1061037
Email: martikainen.jenni1@gmail.com
Web site: http://far-from-perfect-jenni.
blogspot.fi/
Freq: Daily
Circ: 1020
Fashion

Farm Lane Books Blog 988004
Web site: http://www.farmlanebooks.co.uk/
Freq: Daily
Circ: 3672
Literature

Farmersgirl Kitchen 986976
Email: farmersgirlkitchen@gmail.com
Web site: http://farmersgirl.blogspot.co.uk
Freq: Daily
Circ: 4463
Profile: Blog covering food. The Farmersgirl
Kitchen blog discusses anything from food
and recipes to baking. The blog has an
archive dating back to August 2007 and
shares an extensive blog roll.
Cooking & Baking

Fashion & Mash 995149
Email: info@fashionandmash.com
Web site: www.fashionandmash.com
Freq: Daily
Circ: 34742
Advertising Industry, Branding, Fashion,
Marketing, Mobile Electronics

The Fashion Ache 995134
Email: thefashionache@gmail.com
Web site: thefashionache.blogspot.com
Freq: Daily
Circ: 1060
Fashion

Fashion Bubble Gum 1061161
Email: lancyli1982@hotmail.com
Web site: http://tangotaily.blog.sohu.com
Freq: Daily
Circ: 3
Fashion

Fashion Champagne 1053408
Email: fashionchampagne@hotmail.co.uk
Web site: www.www.fashionchampagne.
com
Freq: Daily
Circ: 61
Fashion

Fashion Climate 1052815
Editorial: Flat 38, 29 Hereford Road, Notting
Hill, London W2 4TF
Web site: https://www.scarlettjosse.com/
Freq: Daily
Circ: 521
Beauty & Grooming, Cosmetics, Fashion,
Hair, Travel, Women's Interests

Fashion Daydreams 1052888
Email: reena@fashiondaydreams.com
Web site: http://www.fashiondaydreams.
com/
Freq: Daily
Circ: 9370
Fashion

Fashion Detective 986721
Web site: www.fashiondetective.co.uk
Freq: Daily

Circ: 7485
Fashion, Women's Interests

Fashion for Lunch. 1054406
Editorial: 16 Chesil Court, Bonner Road,
London E2 9JZ
Email: fashionforlunch@hotmail.com
Web site: fashionforlunch.net
Freq: Daily
Circ: 51749
Profile: Blog covering fashion and beauty.
FASHION FOR LUNCH. blog discusses
anything from fashion and lifestyle to beauty
buys and reviews.
Fashion

Fashion in M 1061169
Web site: http://fashioninm.blogspot.com
Freq: Daily
Circ: 900
Fashion

Fashion Infatuation 1076404
Email: fashioninfatuation@gmail.com
Web site: http://www.fashion-infatuation.
com/
Freq: Daily
Circ: 4392
Fashion

Fashion Influx 987594
Email: fashioninflux@gmail.com
Web site: www.fashioninflux.co.uk
Freq: Daily
Circ: 7597
Profile: Blog covering fashion. Fashion Influx
blog discusses anything from outfits and
trends to high street fashion. The blog has
an archive dating back to November 2011.
Beauty & Grooming, Cosmetics, Fashion,
Hair

Fashion is Black 996894
Web site: www.fashionisblack.co.uk
Freq: Daily
Circ: 1108
Fashion

Fashion Me Now 995022
Email: lucy@fashionmenow.co.uk
Web site: http://www.fashionmenow.co.uk/
Freq: Daily
Circ: 80881
Profile: Blog covering fashion. Fashion Me
Now blog discusses anything from beauty to
fashion. The outlet offers RSS (Really Simple
Syndication).
Fashion, Travel, Women's Interests

Fashion Mumblr 998442
Web site: www.fashionmumblr.com
Freq: Daily
Circ: 29505
Profile: Blog covering fashion and beauty.
Fashion Mumblr blog discusses anything
from personal style and the latest fashion
trends to beauty products and lifestyle
posts. The blog has an archive dating back
to August 2013.
Fashion, Travel, Women's Interests

Fashion Nomads 995106
Web site: http://fashionnomads.com/
Freq: Daily
Circ: 8400
Fashion, Women's Interests

The Fashion Police 986251
Web site: www.thefashionpolice.net
Freq: Daily
Circ: 46154
Fashion

The Fashion Samaritan 1053525
Email: info@thefashionsamaritan.com
Web site: thefashionsamaritan.com
Freq: Daily
Circ: 9878
Profile: Blog covering lifestyle, fashion and
men's interests.
Fashion

**Fashion Scout - CEASED
January 2016** 1053892
Editorial: Studio 9, 16 - 30 Provost Street,
London N1 7NG
Web site: http://www.thefashionscout.com/

Freq: Daily
Circ: 3708
Fashion

Fashion Slave 988393
Web site: www.fashionslave.co.uk
Freq: Daily
Circ: 11206
Profile: Blog covering fashion. This outlet
also offers a vlog.
Fashion

Fashioned by Love 988388
Email: fashionedbylove@yahoo.co.uk
Web site: www.fashionedbylove.co.uk
Freq: Daily
Circ: 6104
Profile: Blog covering fashion, culture,
nutrition, organic & natural beauty.
Fashion

FashionGeeksta 1061817
Email: fashiongeeksta@gmail.com
Web site: http://www.fashiongeeksta.com.
ve/
Freq: Daily
Circ: 1592
Beauty & Grooming, Cosmetics, Fashion,
Hair

Fashionicide 1053510
Email: halima@fashionicide.com
Web site: http://www.fashionicide.com/
Freq: Daily
Circ: 10009
Profile: Blog covering fashion and beauty.
The blog has an archive dating back to
September 2009.
Fashion

Fashionista Barbie 986520
Email: fashbarbie@gmail.com
Web site: www.fashionistabarbieuk.com
Freq: Daily
Circ: 14456
Fashion

Fashionistable 1052651
Web site: http://fashionistable.blogspot.co.
uk/
Freq: Daily
Circ: 1558
Fashion, Photography

Fashionistable 1054193
Web site: http://fashionistable.blogspot.co.
uk/
Freq: Daily
Circ: 1558
News & Current Affairs

Fashion-Train 986499
Email: fashion-geeek@live.com
Web site: http://fashion-train.co.uk
Freq: Daily
Circ: 8624
Fashion

Fashitects 987923
Editorial: 6 Garrick Road, Richmond,
London TW9 4JL
Email: fashitects@gmail.com
Web site: fashitects.com
Freq: Daily
Circ: 8406
Fashion, Men's Interests

Faster Future 1054336
Email: davidpcushman@gmail.com
Web site: http://fasterfuture.blogspot.co.uk/
Freq: Daily
Circ: 1330
Branding, Internet, Marketing

Fasthosts 1053960
Web site: http://blogs.fasthosts.co.uk/blog
Freq: Daily
Circ: 48
Editor: Donna Airey
Profile: Fasthosts covers business strategy,
Internet of Things, cloud, web hosting and
technology.
Internet

Fat Buddah Store Blog 1054174
Email: sales@fatbuddahstore.com
Web site: http://blog.fatbuddahstore.com/

UK Blogs

Freq: Daily
Circ: 412
Fashion

Fat Dad in Leeds - CEASED 2017
1075622
Web site: https://fatdadinleeds.com/
Freq: Daily
Circ: 737
Classical/Choral/Band Music, Cooking & Baking, Country, Folk, Bluegrass, Dance Music, Family & Parenting, Grocery Stores, Jazz & Blues, Marketing, Men's Interests, Music

Fat Girl PhD
987769
Editorial: 4 Studd Street, London N1 0QJ
Tel: 44 07450 065407
Email: fatgirlphd@gmail.com
Web site: www.fatgirlphd.com/
Freq: Daily
Circ: 1741
Profile: Blog covering healthy lifestyle. The Fat Girl PhD blog discusses anything from fitness and exercise to health eating. The blog has an archive dating back to April 2012.
Health & Medicine, Nutrition

The Fat Girl's Guide to Running
988130
Editorial: 115 Burford Whaf, 3 Cam Road, Stratford, London E15 2SQ
Email: help@toofattorun.co.uk
Web site: http://toofattorun.co.uk/blogs/
Freq: Daily
Circ: 11049
Fitness & Exercise

Father Fitness
1054424
Web site: www.fatherfitness.co.uk
Freq: Daily
Circ: 8357
Fitness & Exercise

FCO Blogs
988480
Editorial: King Charles Street, London SW1A 2AH **Tel:** 44 02070 083100
Email: newsdesk@fco.gov.uk
Web site: http://blogs.fco.gov.uk/
Freq: Daily
Circ: 233493
International News

Fear Fighting Fairey
998210
Tel: 44 07736 061711
Email: fearfighter2013@gmail.com
Web site: https://faireyclarey.com/
Freq: Daily
Circ: 10709
Cooking & Baking, Fitness & Exercise, Nutrition

Fearghal Kelly
997495
Web site: fkelly.co.uk
Freq: Daily
Circ: 9856
News & Current Affairs

Feathery Travels
1053914
Web site: featherytravels.com
Freq: Daily
Circ: 7721
Profile: Feathery Travels covers budget travel, street-art, festivals and sustainability. The blog has an archive dating back to April 2014.
Travel

February Girl
987960
Email: febgirl@hotmail.co.uk
Web site: www.febgirl.co.uk
Freq: Daily
Circ: 6396
Profile: Blog covering lifestyle. February Girl blog discusses anything from fashion and food to beauty and lifestyle. The blog has an archive dating back to February 2011.
Beauty & Grooming, Celebrities, Cooking & Baking, Cosmetics, Fashion, Hair, Theater & Performing Arts, Women's Interests

Fed Up & Drunk
996472
Editorial: Suite 1.1, Albert House, 111 Victoria Street, Bristol BS1 6AX
Tel: 44 01179 277167

Email: blogadmin@foodanddrinkguides.com
Web site: http://foodanddrinkguides.co.uk/blog/
Freq: Daily
Circ: 101
Cooking & Baking, Restaurant Reviews

Fedelosa
1061772
Web site: http://www.fedelosa.com
Freq: Daily
Circ: 3782
Auto Aftermarket, Computers, Data Management, Electronics, Government Technology, Industry, Internet, Mobile Communications, Security & Security Systems, Software

Feeding Boys
986961
Editorial: 9 Green Avenue, London W13 9RW
Web site: http://www.feedingboys.co.uk
Freq: Daily
Circ: 14220
Profile: Blog covering food. The Feeding boys and a firefighter blog discusses anything from recipes and food reviews to food competitions. The blog has an archive dating back to April 2010 and shares an extensive blog roll.
Cooking & Baking, Restaurant Reviews

FEEL MY BICEP
1053398
Web site: http://www.feelmybicep.com/
Freq: Daily
Circ: 2090
Dance Music, Jazz & Blues

Feeling Fictional
988343
Email: sarahsreviews@ymail.com
Web site: http://www.feelingfictional.com/
Freq: Daily
Circ: 10203
Literature

feeling listless
987292
Email: stuartianburns@gmail.com
Web site: http://feelinglistless.blogspot.com
Freq: Daily
Circ: 23239
Antiques/Collectibles, Art, Arts, Literature, Photography, Theater & Performing Arts, Visual Arts

Feeling Stylish
987999
Web site: www.feelingstylish.co.uk
Freq: Daily
Circ: 6410
Cosmetics, Fashion, Fitness & Exercise, Women's Interests

Feisty Tapas
997415
Email: feistytapas@gmail.com
Web site: www.feistytapas.com
Freq: Daily
Circ: 6704
Cooking & Baking

Fennel and Fern
1053910
Web site: fennelandfern.co.uk
Freq: Daily
Circ: 6655
Gardening

Feral Beryl Travels
988471
Email: jofurnival@gmail.com
Web site: http://www.feralberyltravels.com/
Freq: Daily
Circ: 10456
Travel

Fernanda Blog
1061372
Web site: http://www.milenio.com/blog/Fernanda
Freq: Daily
Circ: 42
National News, Politics

Fernando Cavia
1061499
Web site: http://www.fernandocavia.com
Freq: Daily
Circ: 862
Careers, Crime & Violence, Family & Parenting, Health & Medicine, Lifestyle, Neurology, Personal Finance, Relationships

Ferplei
1060636
Web site: http://www.ferplei.com
Freq: Daily
Circ: 53754
Basketball, Bicycles, Billiards, Boating & Yachting, Bodybuilding, Bowling, Boxing, Cricket, Equestrian Sports, Extreme/Adventure Sports

Ferraris for all
1053819
Email: ferraris@danielbenami.com
Web site: http://danielbenami.com/
Freq: Daily
Circ: 6812
Economics

The Ferret Fancier
1054103
Web site: http://ferretfancier.blogspot.co.uk/
Freq: Daily
Circ: 10709
Government, Health & Medicine

Fertility Matters
1054612
Email: katebrian@mac.com
Web site: http://fertilitymatters.org.uk/
Freq: Daily
Circ: 9416
Health & Medicine, Women's Interests

Festival Brides
997529
Email: hello@festivalbrides.co.uk
Web site: http://www.festivalbrides.co.uk/
Freq: Daily
Circ: 69360
Weddings

Fetch
1054661
Editorial: Tea Building, Unit 3.09, 56 Shoreditch High Street, London E1 6JJ
Tel: 44 02036 757020
Email: hellomarketing@wearefetch.com
Web site: http://wearefetch.com/blog/
Freq: Daily
Circ: 22
Advertising Industry, Mobile Communications

FeverBee
1052677
Web site: www.feverbee.com
Freq: Daily
Circ: 45093
Branding, Business, Corporate Responsibility, Data Management, Internet, Marketing

Fiction Bitch
1054484
Email: e.baines@zen.co.uk
Web site: http://fictionbitch.blogspot.co.uk/
Freq: Daily
Circ: 495
Literature

Fidel Ernesto Vasquez
1061390
Web site: http://fidelernestovasquez.wordpress.com/
Freq: Daily
Circ: 342
National News, Politics

Fieltro.net
1061640
Web site: http://fieltro.net/
Freq: Daily
Circ: 1429
Cooking & Baking, Crafts, Hobbies, & Collecting

Fiendishly Clever
1053395
Web site: https://fiendishlyclever.com/
Freq: Daily
Circ: 8706
News & Current Affairs

Fiesta
1060969
Web site: http://www.fiesta101.com
Freq: Daily
Circ: 33726
Shopping

FIFA Soccer blog
1053068
Web site: http://fifasoccerblog.com/
Freq: Daily
Circ: 2924
Computer & Video Games

fifi goes nom
998067
Web site: http://www.fifigoesnom.com/

Freq: Daily
Circ: 1026
Cooking & Baking

Fifi Lapin
985133
Email: fifi-lapin@hotmail.com
Web site: http://www.fifi-lapin.blogspot.com
Freq: Daily
Circ: 5475
Fashion

The Fighting Cock
998100
Email: thefightingcock@gmail.com
Web site: http://www.thefightingcock.co.uk/
Freq: Daily
Circ: 85970
Soccer

Filatelia para el Mundo
1061347
Web site: http://filateliaparaelmundo.blogspot.com/
Freq: Daily
Circ: 1052
Crafts, Hobbies, & Collecting

Film Doctor
1075500
Tel: 44 02032 903401
Email: filmgp@gmail.com
Web site: http://filmdoctor.co.uk/
Freq: Daily
Circ: 11059
Editor: Andy Wooding
Movies & Video

Film Intel
987951
Email: admin@film-intel.com
Web site: www.film-intel.com/
Freq: Daily
Circ: 7976
Editor: Sam Turner
Entertainment, Movies & Video

Film Studies For Free
988424
Email: filmstudiesff@gmail.com
Web site: http://filmstudiesforfree.blogspot.co.uk/
Freq: Daily
Circ: 7217
Movies & Video

FILMdetail
986424
Web site: www.filmdetail.com
Freq: Daily
Circ: 7767
Movies & Video

Filmonic
987562
Email: contactfilmonic@gmail.com
Web site: filmonic.com
Freq: Daily
Circ: 66297
Broadcasting, Entertainment, Local Entertainment Guides, Movies & Video

Filosofia y Mas
1061684
Web site: http://www.filosofiaymas.com
Freq: Daily
Circ: 5770
Antiques/Collectibles, Armed Forces, Astrology & Parapsychology, Astronomy, Aviation, Boating & Yachting, Camping and RV Travel, Cartoons, Casinos & Gaming, Celebrities

Finance Girl
1054435
Web site: financegirl.co.uk
Freq: Daily
Circ: 8660
Personal Finance

Financial Analyst Keynes
1061382
Email: cannes29@sina.com
Web site: http://blog.sina.com.cn/cannes
Freq: Daily
Circ: 87434
Financial Markets

Financial Blogger
999528
Web site: http://www.financialblogger.co.uk/
Freq: Daily
Circ: 3865
Personal Finance

Financial Times' Chronic Investor Blog
999264
Editorial: Number One Southwark Bridge, London SE1 9HL Tel: 44 02078 733000
Email: ic.cs@ft.com
Web site: http://www.investorschronicle.co.uk/comment/chronic-investor-blog/
Freq: Daily
Circ: 193
Editor: John Hughman
Business, Investment Banking

Find My Past
1056311
Email: support@findmypast.co.uk
Web site: https://blog.findmypast.co.uk/
Freq: Daily
Circ: 680640
Family & Parenting

Fine and dandy
1053666
Web site: www.fineanddandyblog.co.uk
Freq: Daily
Circ: 2198
Profile: Blog covering lifestyle, fashion and beauty.
Beauty & Grooming, Cosmetics, Crafts, Hair, Women's Interests

The Finest Cut
1053211
Web site: http://www.thefinestcut.co.uk/
Freq: Daily
Circ: 12840
Alcohol & Spirits, Bars, Clubs & Pubs, Beer, Beverages, Wine/Winemaking

FionaOutdoors
1053399
Email: fionaoutdoors@gmail.com
Web site: fionaoutdoors.co.uk
Freq: Daily
Circ: 14165
Bicycles, Fitness & Exercise, Outdoor Recreation

First Choice blog
1054530
Email: pressoffice@firstchoice.co.uk
Web site: http://www.firstchoice.co.uk/blog/
Freq: Daily
Circ: 274
Airline Inflight, Railroad, Travel

First Utility Blog
999374
Editorial: First Utility Limited, Point 3, Opus 40 Business Park, Haywood Road, Warwick CV34 5AH
Web site: https://www.first-utility.com/the-utility-room
Freq: Daily
Circ: 1019
Electricity, Oil

Fish Fingers for Tea
988545
Web site: fishfingersfortea.com
Freq: Daily
Circ: 1253
Profile: Blog covering food. The Fish Fingers for Tea blog discusses anything from food reviews and food recipes to budget.
Cooking & Baking

Fist Pump Fridays
1060836
Email: fistpumpfridays@gmail.com
Web site: http://fistpumpfridays.net/
Freq: Daily
Circ: 968
Classical/Choral/Band Music, Country, Folk, Bluegrass, Dance Music, Jazz & Blues, Music, Pop Music, R&B, Urban, World, Rap & Hip Hop, Rock Music

Fit Blog London
1073131
Email: fitbloglondon@gmail.com
Web site: https://fitbloglondon.com/
Freq: Daily
Circ: 521
Editor: Bethany Silcox
Fitness & Exercise, Health & Medicine, Nutrition

The Fit Londoner
1052708
Email: avhafezi@gmail.com
Web site: http://www.thefitlondoner.com/
Freq: Daily
Circ: 8244
Art, Beauty & Grooming, Cosmetics, Fitness & Exercise, Hair, Nutrition, Photography

FitBeauLife
998070
Editorial: No20 174-178 Ridley Rd, Dalston, London E8 2NH
Web site: http://fitbeaulife.com/
Freq: Daily
Circ: 722
Editor: Genevieve Sibayan
Beauty & Grooming, Cosmetics, Fitness & Exercise, Hair, Women's Interests

FitBits
1054317
Email: tesslangley@hotmail.co.uk
Web site: www.thefitbits.com
Freq: Daily
Circ: 12353
Profile: Blog covering jogging, fitness and healthy lifestyle.
Bicycles, Fitness & Exercise

Fitcetera
997988
Email: georgina@fitcetera.co.uk
Web site: fitcetera.co.uk/
Freq: Daily
Circ: 6846
Fitness & Exercise, Nutrition

Fitness Deportes
1061471
Web site: http://www.fitnessdeportes.com
Freq: Daily
Circ: 875
Basketball, Bicycles, Billiards, Boating & Yachting, Bodybuilding, Bowling, Boxing, Cricket, Equestrian Sports, Extreme/Adventure Sports

Fitness Fan
1053781
Web site: www.fitness-fan.co.uk
Freq: Daily
Circ: 2692
Fitness & Exercise

Fitness On Toast
988110
Email: fitnessontoast@gmail.com
Web site: http://fitnessontoast.com/
Freq: Daily
Circ: 35477
Editor: Faya Nilsson
Fitness & Exercise, Nutrition

Five Five Fabulous
986677
Email: hello@fivefivefabulous.com
Web site: www.fivefivefabulous.com
Freq: Daily
Circ: 13884
Fashion, Women's Interests

Fixed Gear London
1054614
Email: contact.fixedgearlondon@gmail.com
Web site: fixedgearlondon.wordpress.com
Freq: Daily
Circ: 62
Bicycles

The Fizz and Pheasant
1054299
Email: fizzandpheasant@gmail.com
Web site: https://fizzandpheasant.com/
Freq: Daily
Circ: 10709
Alcohol & Spirits, Regional General Interest, Restaurant Reviews, Travel, Wine/Winemaking

The Flaneur
986784
Email: editoral@flaneur.me.uk
Web site: flaneur.me.uk
Freq: Daily
Circ: 8579
Editor: Jonathan Powell
Profile: Blog covering art, film, TV, music, theatre, travel, sport, politics and culture. The blog has an archive dating back to May 2010.
Art, Broadcasting, Classical/Choral/Band Music, Country, Folk, Bluegrass, Dance Music, Entertainment, Fitness & Exercise, Jazz & Blues, Literature, Men's Interests

Fleet Street Fox
987224
Email: fleetstreetfox@yahoo.com
Web site: www.fleetstreetfox.com
Freq: Daily
Circ: 3239
Broadcasting, Publishing

Fleur De Force
986815
Editorial: Fleur De Force Ltd C/O Derek Westaway, Westaway Motors, Boughton

Green Road, Moulton Park, Northampton NN2 7AH
Email: fleurdeforce@gmail.com
Web site: http://www.fleurdeforce.com/
Freq: Daily
Circ: 44661
Beauty & Grooming, Cosmetics, Fashion, Hair, Women's Interests

Fleur DeForce Vlog
1076643
Email: fleurdeforce@gmail.com
Web site: https://www.youtube.com/user/FleurDeForce
Freq: Daily
Circ: 73
Beauty & Grooming, Cosmetics, Fashion, Hair, Women's Interests

Flick Filosopher
998157
Tel: 44 07412 678631
Email: maryann@flickfilosopher.com
Web site: www.flickfilosopher.com
Freq: Daily
Circ: 146218
Literature, Local Entertainment Guides, Movies & Video, Theater & Performing Arts, Visual Arts

Flickering Myth
986395
Email: editors@flickeringmyth.com
Web site: flickeringmyth.com
Freq: Daily
Circ: 1128799
Movies & Video

Flickfeast
1056570
Web site: http://flickfeast.co.uk/
Freq: Daily
Circ: 13976
Entertainment, Movies & Video

Flicks and the City
987554
Email: gorkana@flicksandthecity.com
Web site: flicksandthecity.com
Circ: 16332
Profile: Flicks and the City is an online magazine covering the latest film & TV interviews, features and reviews. The website was founded in July 2012.
Broadcasting, Local Entertainment Guides, Movies & Video

Flip Chart Fairy Tales
1052929
Web site: https://flipchartfairytales.wordpress.com/
Freq: Daily
Circ: 1867133
Business

Flo & Elle
1053455
Web site: http://floandelle.blogspot.co.uk
Freq: Daily
Circ: 493
Cooking & Baking, Fashion, Restaurant Reviews, Travel, Women's Interests

Floral Fantasies
995026
Email: helpdesk@ibas.co.uk
Web site: http://stamping-fantasies.blogspot.co.uk/
Freq: Daily
Circ: 1432
Crafts

The Floral Republic
1064492
Email: floralrepublic@hotmail.com
Web site: thefloralrepublic.com
Freq: Daily
Circ: 10779
Bars, Clubs & Pubs, Beauty & Grooming, Comedy, Cooking & Baking, Cosmetics, Entertainment, Fashion, Fitness & Exercise, Hair, Local Entertainment Guides

Florence and Mary
1053288
Email: victoriaeales@hotmail.com
Web site: http://www.florenceandmary.com/
Freq: Daily
Circ: 7877
Beauty & Grooming, Cooking & Baking, Cosmetics, Fashion, Hair, Restaurant Reviews, Travel

Florence Finds
987047
Email: hello@florencefinds.com
Web site: http://www.florencefinds.com/
Freq: Daily

Circ: 4636
Beauty & Grooming, Cooking & Baking, Cosmetics, Fashion, Hair, Travel, Women's Interests

Florence of Arabia
1098960
Web site: http://www.zahrahankir.com/
Freq: Daily
Circ: 12570
Religion, Social Issues, Women's Interests

Flower and Garden Tips
1054093
Email: admin@flower-and-garden-tips.com
Web site: flower-and-garden-tips.com/
Freq: Daily
Circ: 26237
Gardening

Flowerona
987613
Editorial: 23 Imber Park Road, Esher, London KT10 8JB
Web site: http://flowerona.com/
Freq: Daily
Circ: 25524
News & Current Affairs

Flowers & Freckles - CEASED AUGUST 2015
987961
Web site: flowersandfreckles.com
Freq: Daily
Circ: 521
Profile: Flowers & Freckles covers lifestyle, travel, personal style, beauty, food and interiors. The blog has an archive dating back to September 2011. The outlet also offers a vlog.
Fashion, Women's Interests

Flubit Blog
987230
Editorial: Metropolitan Wharf, 70 Wapping Wall, London E1W 3SS
Tel: 44 02031 377341
Email: talktous@flubit.com
Web site: blog.flubit.com
Freq: Daily
Circ: 44490
Shopping

Fluff and fripperies
987598
Email: fluffandfripperies@gmail.com
Web site: www.fluffandfripperies.com
Freq: Daily
Circ: 1965
Profile: Blog covering beauty. fluff AND fripperies blog discusses anything from lifestyle and beauty to fashion. The blog has an archive dating back to October 2010 and shares an extensive blog roll. fluff AND fripperies was awarded The Best Irish Beauty and Fashion Blog in the blog awards Ireland, and was also shortlisted as the Best International Fashion Blog in the Cosmopolitan Blog Awards.
News & Current Affairs

Flutterby Blog
998209
Tel: 353 14306 219
Email: flutterbyfashionstyling@gmail.com
Web site: www.flutteronby.ie
Freq: Daily
Circ: 521
Beauty & Grooming, Celebrities, Cosmetics, Fashion, Hair

Fluxposure Adrian Flux Insurance Blog
1052640
Web site: https://www.adrianflux.co.uk/blog/
Freq: Daily
Circ: 158704
News & Current Affairs

The Fly Away American
996328
Tel: 44 07826 285501
Email: theflyawayamerican@gmail.com
Web site: www.theflyawayamerican.com/
Freq: Daily
Circ: 12157
Travel

The Fly Away American
998019
Freq: Daily
Circ: 10230
Airline Inflight, Railroad, Travel

Flying with a Baby 1099500
Web site: http://www.flyingwithababy.com/
Freq: Daily
Circ: 11816
Family & Parenting, Travel

follow the yellow 997477
Web site: followtheyellow.co.uk
Freq: Daily
Circ: 1967
Editor: Katherine Woodfine
Antiques/Collectibles, Art, Arts,
Literature, Photography, Theater &
Performing Arts, Visual Arts

Following the Trawler 1053809
Email: thecockneyred@gmail.com
Web site: http://www.followingthetrawler.
com/
Freq: Daily
Circ: 1370
Soccer

Food & lycra 995359
Email: foodandlycra@gmail.com
Web site: foodandlycra.com
Freq: Daily
Circ: 2637
Profile: Blog covering fitness and food.
FOOD & lycra discusses anything from
running and healthy eating to recipes and
exercise. The blog has an archive dating
back to February 2013.
Fitness & Exercise, Nutrition

Food Fash Fit 1052863
Email: foodfashfit@gmail.com
Web site: foodfashfit.com
Freq: Daily
Circ: 7622
Cooking & Baking, Fashion, Fitness &
Exercise

Food I Fancy 987140
Web site: www.foodifancy.com
Freq: Daily
Circ: 6894
Cooking & Baking, Restaurant Reviews

The Food Medic 1100038
Email: hazel@thefoodmedic.co.uk
Web site: https://thefoodmedic.co.uk/
Freq: Daily
Circ: 14513
Cooking & Baking, Nutrition

The Food Sauce 1072013
Email: info@thefoodsauce.co.uk
Web site: http://thefoodsauce.co.uk/
Freq: Daily
Circ: 10981
Editor: Colin Mordi
Cooking & Baking, Restaurant Reviews

Food Stories 986140
Web site: www.helengraves.co.uk
Freq: Daily
Circ: 29838
Alcohol & Spirits, Bars, Clubs & Pubs,
Beer, Beverages, Cooking & Baking,
Food, Grocery Stores, Organic Food,
Restaurant Reviews, Vegetarianism &
Veganism

Food to Glow 1052913
Web site: kelliesfoodtoglow.com
Freq: Daily
Circ: 39518
Profile: Blog covering healthy eating
recipes. food to glow discusses anything
from cancer nutrition and healthy ingredients
to low fat and vegan recipes. The blog has
an archive dating back to February 2011 and
shares an extensive blog roll. The outlet
offers RSS (Really Simple Syndication).
Cooking & Baking, Nutrition, Organic
Food, Vegetarianism & Veganism

Food Urchin 1054514
Email: foodurchin@gmail.com
Web site: http://www.foodurchin.com/
Freq: Daily
Circ: 10201
Cooking & Baking, Restaurant Reviews

The Foodie Bugle Journal 997473
Editorial: The Foodie Bugle Shop, 2 Abbey
Street, Bath BA1 1NN Tel: 44 01793 852272
Email: info@thefoodiebugle.com
Web site: http://thefoodiebugle.com
Freq: Daily
Circ: 10136
Cooking & Baking, Restaurant Reviews

Foodie Explorers 1105197
Email: contact@foodanddrinkglasgow.co.uk
Web site: https://www.foodieexplorers.co.
uk/
Freq: Daily
Circ: 12467
Cooking & Baking, Restaurant Reviews

Foodie Quine 1058694
Web site: http://www.foodiequine.co.uk/
Freq: Daily
Circ: 13815
Editor: Claire Jessiman
Profile: Blog covering food. The FOODIE
QUINE blog discusses anything from food
and recipes to food events and food product
reviews. The blog has an archive dating back
to August 2012.
Cooking & Baking, Restaurant Reviews

Foodstinct 1053670
Email: info@foodstinct.com
Web site: http://foodstinct.com/
Freq: Daily
Circ: 9404
Profile: Blog covering food. foodstinct
discusses anything from vegetarian recipes
and restaurant reviews to cooking tips and
eating abroad. The blog has an archive
dating back to April 2012
Cooking & Baking, Restaurant Reviews,
Vegetarianism & Veganism

Foodstuff Finds 986141
Email: admin@foodstufffinds.co.uk
Web site: http://www.foodstufffinds.co.uk/
Freq: Daily
Circ: 15888
Editor: Lis Ries
Alcohol & Spirits, Bars, Clubs & Pubs,
Beer, Beverages, Cooking & Baking,
Food, Grocery Stores, Organic Food,
Restaurant Reviews, Vegetarianism &
Veganism

Foot Trails Blog 999549
Editorial: The Studio, 16 Abbey Churchyard,
George Street, Bath BA1 1LY
Tel: 44 01747 820626
Email: enquire@foottrails.co.uk
Web site: http://foottrails.co.uk/blog/
Freq: Daily
Circ: 110
Field Sports

Foot4ward 1054373
Web site: http://foot4ward.co.uk/
Freq: Daily
Circ: 10969
Fitness & Exercise, Men's Interests,
Nutrition

Football Beyond Borders 998445
Tel: 44 07738 414271
Email: info@footballbeyondborders.org
Web site: http://www.
footballbeyondborders.org/#!news/cabf
Freq: Daily
Circ: 13179
Charitable Foundations, Soccer, Teen/
Young Adult

Football Economy 1053709
Email: contact@footballeconomy.com
Web site: www.footballeconomy.com
Freq: Daily
Circ: 24216
Soccer

Football Every Day 998336
Email: alex@footballeveryday.com
Web site: http://footballeveryday.co.uk/
Freq: Daily
Circ: 12876
Editor: Alex Morgan
Soccer

The Football History Boys 988643
Email: thefootballhistoryboys@hotmail.com
Web site: http://www.
thefootballhistoryboys.com/
Freq: Daily
Circ: 10300
Soccer

The Football Ramble Blog 1054461
Email: kelly@thefootballramble.com
Web site: http://thefootballramble.com/blog
Freq: Daily
Circ: 20029
Soccer

Football Shirt Culture 1056573
Web site: www.footballshirtculture.com/
Table/Football-shirt-blog/
Freq: Daily
Circ: 6144
Soccer

Football Talk 986368
Email: admin@football-talk.co.uk
Web site: http://football-talk.co.uk
Freq: Daily
Circ: 128932
Editor: Alan McIvor
Soccer

FootballFanCast.com Football Blogs 998108
Email: editor@footballfancast.com
Web site: www.footballfancast.com/
football-blogs
Freq: Daily
Circ: 8224
Editor: Martin Crawford
Soccer

Footybunker 999433
Email: admin@footybunker.com
Web site: www.footybunker.com
Freq: Daily
Circ: 6225
Soccer

Footylatest.com 988222
Web site: http://footylatest.com/
Circ: 47992
Soccer

FootyMad 1053400
Email: info@footymad.net
Web site: http://www.footymad.net/
Freq: Daily
Circ: 399076
Soccer

For Books' Sake 985878
Email: hello@forbookssake.net
Web site: forbookssake.net
Circ: 19146
Profile: Website covering books by and for
independent women. The For Books'
Sake website covers book news, reviews and
author interviews.
Antiques/Collectibles, Art, Arts,
Literature, Photography, Theater &
Performing Arts, Visual Arts, Women's
Interests

For The Love Of Football 998038
Web site: http://fortheloveoffootballblog.
com/
Freq: Daily
Circ: 969
Editor: Mark Carruthers
Soccer

Forbidden Planet International Blog 988223
Web site: http://www.forbiddenplanet.co.uk/
blog/
Freq: Daily
Circ: 230601
Trading Cards & Comics

Forest Hill Society 988281
Email: email@foresthillsociety.com
Web site: http://www.foresthillsociety.com/
Freq: Daily

Circ: 8357
Energy & Environment, Politics, Regional
General Interest

Forever Amber 986155
Web site: foreveramber.co.uk
Freq: Daily
Circ: 85792
Beauty & Grooming, Cosmetics, Fashion,
Hair

Forever Yours, Betty 999294
Editorial: 71a Leonard Street, London EC2A
4QS
Email: hiya@foreveryoursbetty.com
Web site: http://foreveryoursbetty.com/
Freq: Daily
Circ: 7088
Profile: Blog covering fashion and lifestyle.
Forever yours, Betty blog discusses anything
from the latest fashion trends and catwalk
looks to beauty and lifestyle. The blog has an
archive dating back to July 2010 and shares
a short blog roll.
Fashion, Women's Interests

The Forgotten Flapper 1053600
Email: me_myself_andmy_mirror@hotmail.
co.uk
Web site: http://theforgottenflapper.
blogspot.co.uk/
Freq: Daily
Circ: 521
Fashion, Jazz & Blues, Theater &
Performing Arts, Travel, Women's
Interests

FormFiftyFive 986556
Email: submissions@formfiftyfive.com
Web site: www.formfiftyfive.com
Circ: 38833
Advertising Industry, Architecture &
Design, Branding, Graphic Design,
Marketing, Photography

Formula 1 a Dos Manos 1061270
Web site: http://blogs.eluniversal.com/eu3/
Blogs/F12M_index.shtml
Freq: Daily
Circ: 17649
Motorsports

Found Love Now What 1054456
Web site: http://foundlovenowwhat.com/
Freq: Daily
Circ: 6798
Profile: Blog covering expatriate living. The
Found Love NOW WHAT blog discusses
anything from travel and expatriate living to
attractions in the UK and Europe. The blog
has an archive dating back to August 2012
and shares an extensive blog roll.
Regional General Interest, Relationships,
Travel, Women's Interests

**Found now home - CEASED
2016** 1052592
Web site: http://foundnowhome.blogspot.
co.uk/
Freq: Daily
Circ: 1403
Cooking & Baking, Crafts, Do-It-Yourself
(DIY), Family & Parenting, Photography,
Regional General Interest, Travel

FourFourTweet 987432
Email: info@fourfourtweet.co.uk
Web site: www.fourfourtweet.co.uk
Freq: Daily
Circ: 11000
Soccer

Fowl Mouths Food 1052817
Editorial: 9 Longfield Crescent, London
SE26 4DU
Web site: http://www.fowlmouths.co.uk/
blog
Freq: Daily
Cooking & Baking, Restaurant Reviews,
Travel

Fox & Heather 1052618
Web site: www.foxandfeatherblog.com
Freq: Daily
Circ: 7254
Fashion, Women's Interests

Fox Socks 987380
Web site: http://foxsocks.co.uk/
Freq: Daily
Circ: 6933
News & Current Affairs

FOXY Lady Drivers Club 987865
Web site: www.foxyladydrivers.com/
foxyblog/
Freq: Daily
Circ: 156
News & Current Affairs

FPL Dugout 1054494
Web site: http://www.fpl-dugout.co.uk/
articles
Freq: Daily
Circ: 56
Soccer

FPS Prestige 988186
Email: admin@fpsprestige.com
Web site: http://www.fpsprestige.com/
Freq: Daily
Circ: 8761
Editor: Dan Thornton
Computer & Video Games

Fragrance Direct Blog 1054298
Tel: 44 01625 432565
Email: help@fragrancedirect.co.uk
Web site: http://blog.fragrancedirect.co.uk/
Freq: Daily
Circ: 69
Fashion, Luxury Goods

Frame blog 1052735
Editorial: 29 New Inn Yard, Shoreditch,
London
Email: team@moveyourframe.com
Web site: https://moveyourframe.com/blog
Freq: Daily
Circ: 7
Profile: Blog covering fitness and lifestyle.
The FRAME Blog discusses anything from
running and nutrition to food. The blog has
an archive dating back to September 2010.
Cooking & Baking, Fashion, Fitness &
Exercise, Regional General Interest

Fran Richardson Artist 1052931
Email: subscriber@franrichardson.co.uk
Web site: http://franrichardson-artist.
blogspot.com/
Freq: Daily
Circ: 848
Art

Frances Bee 1053124
Email: hello@francesbee.me
Web site: http://francesbee.me/
Freq: Daily
Circ: 8791
Fashion, Travel, Women's Interests

Frances Garrood 1052687
Web site: http://francesgarrood.blogspot.
co.uk/
Freq: Daily
Circ: 495
Literature, Regional General Interest

Franie Travels 1101934
Web site: https://franie-travels.com/
Freq: Daily
Circ: 611
Audio Video Trade, Cameras, Consumer
Electronics, Electronics, Mobile
Electronics, Movies & Video, Personal
Finance, Politics, Travel

Frankie's Weekend 996602
Web site: www.frankiesweekend.com
Freq: Daily
Circ: 8989
Cooking & Baking, Regional General
Interest, Restaurant Reviews, Women's
Interests

Frankly My Dear UK 1103180
Web site: http://www.franklymydearuk.co.
uk/
Freq: Daily
Circ: 10645
Audio Video Trade, Broadcasting,
Cameras, Consumer Electronics,
Electronics, Literature, Mobile

Electronics, Movies & Video, Pop Music,
Theater & Performing Arts

Freaky Trigger 1053277
Email: freakytrigger@gmail.com
Web site: http://freakytrigger.co.uk/
Freq: Daily
Circ: 14817
Profile: Website providing smart, informal
writing about pop culture - music, film, TV,
food and drink, books, art, science etc.
Pop Music

Freckled Elle 999297
Web site: affordabletreats.blogspot.com
Freq: Daily
Circ: 1756
Beauty & Grooming, Cosmetics, Hair

Fred Butler Style 1054094
Web site: http://fredbutlerstyle.blogspot.co.
uk
Freq: Daily
Circ: 9755
Art, Fashion, Photography, Visual Arts

Freddie Harrel 1053197
Web site: http://freddieharrel.com/
Freq: Daily
Circ: 7187
Fashion, Women's Interests

Freddy My Love 1073489
Editorial: P.O. Box - Freddy Cousin-Brown,
C/O Gleam Futures, 6th Floor, 60 Charlotte
Street, London W1T 2NU
Email: enquiries@freddymylove.co.uk
Web site: www.freddymylove.co.uk
Freq: Daily
Circ: 9666
Beauty & Grooming, Cosmetics, Fashion,
Hair

Free and Cheap London 998278
Web site: https://freeandcheaplondon.com
Freq: Daily
Circ: 11010
Antiques/Collectibles, Art, Arts, Bars,
Clubs & Pubs, Comedy, Entertainment,
Fashion, Literature, Local Entertainment
Guides, Movies & Video

Free Fitness Tips 986539
Email: enquiries@freefitnesstips.co.uk
Web site: www.freefitnesstips.co.uk
Freq: Daily
Circ: 9499
Fitness & Exercise, Nutrition

Freegle 1054503
Tel: 44 07962 449573
Email: media@ilovefreegle.org
Web site: http://www.ilovefreegle.org/blog/
Freq: Daily
Circ: 14
Charitable Foundations, Energy &
Environment, Environment

Freelance Advisor 996217
Tel: 44 03339 202817
Web site: https://www.crunch.co.uk/blog/
freelancer-advice/
Freq: Daily
Circ: 216
News & Current Affairs

The Freelance Lifestyle Blog 988016
Email: hello@emmacossey.com
Web site: http://www.freelancelifestyle.co.
uk/
Freq: Daily
Circ: 11700
Careers

Freeware 1060919
Web site: http://blogs.lanacion.com.ar/
freeware/
Freq: Daily
Circ: 56
Software

French and a bit more 1075512
Web site: http://francophile1010.blogspot.
co.uk/
Freq: Daily

Circ: 611
News & Current Affairs

French Connection - Off the Record 996404
Web site: https://www.frenchconnection.
com/blog.htm
Freq: Daily
Circ: 45
Bars, Clubs & Pubs, Beauty & Grooming,
Cooking & Baking, Cosmetics, Fashion,
Hair

French Teacher 1054319
Web site: http://frenchteachernet.blogspot.
co.uk/
Freq: Daily
Circ: 12039
Education

French Wedding Style 997482
Email: info@frenchweddingstyle.com
Web site: www.frenchweddingstyle.com
Freq: Daily
Circ: 40358
Weddings

Fresh & Fearless 1053275
Editorial: 25 Tulip Court, Alpine Road,
Queensbury, London NW9 9BS
Email: aftab@freshandfearless.co.uk
Web site: freshandfearless.co.uk
Freq: Daily
Circ: 13615
Profile: Blog covering lifestyle, fashion,
grooming, food and equine. The blog has an
archive dating back to April 2013.
Cosmetics, Fashion, Men's Interests,
Restaurant Reviews, Travel

Fresh Arsenal 998349
Email: freshfootballeditor@gmail.com
Web site: http://www.fresharsenal.com/
Freq: Daily
Circ: 33322
Soccer

Fresh Design Blog 986142
Email: freshdesignblog@gmail.com
Web site: freshdesignblog.com
Freq: Daily
Circ: 25981
Editor: Rachel Newcombe
Architecture & Design, Do-It-Yourself
(DIY), Gardening, Property Management &
Maintenance

Fresh Egg Blog 1054022
Email: socialmedia@freshegg.com
Web site: freshegg.co.uk/blog
Freq: Daily
Circ: 8750
Profile: Blog covering digital marketing, SEO
and social media.
Advertising Industry, Branding, Marketing

Freshforlife's Blog 1061568
Email: beate.rosvoll@gmail.com
Web site: http://freshforlife.wordpress.com
Freq: Daily
Circ: 17
Basketball, Bicycles, Billiards, Boating &
Yachting, Bodybuilding, Bowling, Boxing,
Cricket, Equestrian Sports, Extreme/
Adventure Sports

FreshMinds - Blog 997007
Editorial: Kingsbourne House, 229-231 High
Holborn, London WC1V 7DA
Tel: 44 02076 111000
Email: hello@freshminds.net
Web site: http://www.freshminds.net/blog/
Freq: Daily
Circ: 200
Advertising Industry, Branding,
Broadcasting, Graphic Design, Marketing,
Media & Communications, Photography,
Publishing

Freshome 986960
Email: admin@freshome.com
Web site: freshome.com
Freq: Daily
Circ: 1481198
Architecture & Design, Do-It-Yourself
(DIY), Property Management &
Maintenance

Friday is forever 1053242
Email: fridayisforever@gmail.com
Web site: http://www.fridayisforeverblog.
com/
Freq: Daily
Circ: 6569
Profile: Blog covering lifestyle, fashion and
beauty.
Beauty & Grooming, Cosmetics, Fashion,
Hair, Women's Interests

Friedmylittlebrain 1052646
Web site: http://www.friedmylittlebrain.com/
Freq: Daily
Circ: 356
Dance Music, Entertainment, Music

Friends of the Earth Green Blog 999569
Editorial: The Printworks, 1st Floor, 139
Clapham Road, London SW9 0HP
Tel: 44 02075 661649
Web site: https://www.foe.co.uk/
news_events/green_blog_26301
Freq: Daily
Circ: 174
Alternative/Renewable Energy, Carbon
Emissions & Trading, Charitable
Foundations, Electricity, Energy, Energy &
Environment, Environment, Ethical/Moral
Issues, Gardening, Mining & Quarrying

Friends of the Earth Policy and Politics Blog 996056
Editorial: The Printworks, 1st Floor, 139
Clapham Road, London SW9 0HP
Tel: 44 02075 661649
Email: webmaster@foe.co.uk
Web site: http://www.foe.co.uk/
news_events/policy_blog
Freq: Daily
Circ: 6626
Energy & Environment, Environment

Friends with Benefit 987058
Editorial: Greenwood House, 91-99 New
London Road, Chelmsford, Chelmsford CM2
0PP
Email: uk@benefitcosmetics.com
Web site: blog.benefitcosmetics.co.uk
Freq: Daily
Circ: 291
Profile: Blog covering cosmetics. The blog
has an archive dating back to July 2010.
Beauty & Grooming, Cosmetics, Hair

Frills and Spills 1053558
Email: frills.spills@gmail.com
Web site: www.frillsnspills.com
Freq: Daily
Circ: 0541
Beauty & Grooming, Cooking & Baking,
Cosmetics, Fashion, Hair

Frock and Roll 1056560
Email: hello@frock-and-roll.com
Web site: www.frock-and-roll.com/
Freq: Daily
Circ: 1965
Classical/Choral/Band Music, Country,
Folk, Bluegrass, Dance Music, Jazz &
Blues, Music, Pop Music, R&B, Urban,
World, Rap & Hip Hop, Rock Music, Visual
Arts

Frock Me I'm Famous 1052619
Email: frockmeimfamous@gmail.com
Web site: www.frockmeimfamous.com
Freq: Daily
Circ: 13648
Profile: Blog covering fashion and beauty.
FROCK ME I'M famous blog discusses
anything from fashion trends to fashion
accessories and beauty products to lifestyle
posts. The blog has an archive dating back
to October 2011. The outlet offers RSS
(Really Simple Syndication).
Cosmetics, Fashion, Travel, Women's
Interests

The Frog Blog 1053404
Email: info@ra.org
Web site: http://www.rainforest-alliance.org/
latest?types=stories
Freq: Daily

UK Blogs

Circ: 73
Consumer Affairs, Energy & Environment, Ethical/Moral Issues, International News, Politics, Regional, Social Issues

From Guate With Love 1061397
Web site: http://www.fromguatewithlove.blogspot.com
Freq: Daily
Circ: 521
Fashion, Photography

From Mamma with Love 1065158
Web site: http://www.frommammawithlove.com/
Freq: Daily
Circ: 7571
Do-It-Yourself (DIY), Family & Parenting, Travel, Women's Interests

From My Tingzijian 1061839
Email: kathy@kathrynpauli.com
Web site: http://www.kathrynpauli.com
Freq: Daily
Circ: 521
Airline Inflight, Railroad, Travel

From the Corners of the Curve 1054552
Web site: http://www.fromthecornersofthecurve.com
Freq: Daily
Circ: 7958
Profile: Blog covering plus size fashion. From the Corners of the Curve blog discusses anything from plus size fashion and lifestyle to food and beauty. The blog has an archive dating back to April 2012 and shares an extensive blog roll. The outlet offers RSS (Really Simple Syndication).
Cooking & Baking, Fashion, Regional General Interest, Restaurant Reviews, Travel, Women's Interests

Front Row Edit 997638
Web site: www.frontrowedit.co.uk
Freq: Daily
Circ: 12127
Fashion

Frontlist/Backlist 1068723
Email: emily@frontlistbacklist.co.uk
Web site: http://frontlistbacklist.co.uk
Freq: Daily
Circ: 10250
Antiques/Collectibles, Art, Arts, Cooking & Baking, Fashion, Food, Grocery Stores, Literature, Organic Food, Photography

Frozen Steel Blog 1055153
Email: frozen.steel.91@gmail.com
Web site: http://frozensteelblog.blogspot.co.uk/
Freq: Daily
Circ: 11259
Hockey, Winter Sports

Frugal Queen 987635
Web site: www.frugalqueen.co.uk
Freq: Daily
Circ: 66648
Profile: Blog covering food, lifestyle, recipes, crafts and money saving advice. The blog has an archive dating back to October 2008.
Cooking & Baking, Family & Parenting, Personal Finance

The Frugality 987485
Web site: http://www.the-frugality.com
Freq: Daily
Circ: 43529
Profile: Blog covering fashion and beauty. THE FRUGALITY blog discusses anything from style and outfits to beauty products and lifestyle. The blog has an archive dating back to December 2011.
Fashion

The Frustrated Gardener 1054325
Email: thefrustratedgardener@gmail.com
Web site: frustratedgardener.com
Freq: Daily
Circ: 9696

Profile: Blog covering gardening. The blog has an archive dating back to June 2012 and shares an extensive blogroll.
Gardening

fudzilla 997250
Email: press@fudzilla.com
Web site: http://fudzilla.com/
Freq: Daily
Circ: 440931
Editor: Mike Magee
Apple, Computer & Video Games, Mobile Communications, Mobile Electronics, Personal Computers, Telecommunications/Electronic Communications

Full Fact 987335
Editorial: 9 Warwick Court, London WC1R 5DJ Tel: 44 02033 975140
Email: team@fullfact.org
Web site: fullfact.org
Circ: 53056
Charitable Foundations, National News

Full on Learning 1054562
Web site: http://fullonlearning.com
Freq: Daily
Circ: 2878
Profile: Blog covering education. Full On Learning blog discusses anything from education and learning to teaching. The blog has an archive dating back to January 2010. The outlet offers RSS (Really Simple Syndication).
Education

Full Stride 1052684
Email: info@fullstride.co.uk
Web site: http://www.fullstride.co.uk/
Freq: Daily
Circ: 7863
Fitness & Exercise, Nutrition

Fumbling toward home 1053186
Web site: https://scottybecca.wordpress.com/about/
Freq: Daily
News & Current Affairs

Funding Circle Blog 996284
Web site: http://www.fundingcircle.com/blog/
Freq: Daily
Circ: 6875
News & Current Affairs

Fundraising Fundamentals 988675
Tel: 44 07702 952875
Email: tobinaldrich@gmail.com
Web site: https://fundraising-fundamentals.com/
Freq: Daily
Circ: 10709
Charitable Foundations

Fundraising News from SYFAB 997008
Editorial: Unit 3 - G1 Building, 6 Leeds Road, Sheffield S9 3TY
Tel: 44 01142 615141
Email: advice@syfab.org.uk
Web site: http://www.syfab.org.uk/blog.aspx
Freq: Daily
Circ: 2875
Charitable Foundations

Further Blog 1053225
Tel: 44 01603 878240
Email: info@further.co.uk
Web site: https://www.further.co.uk/blog/
Freq: Daily
Circ: 21888
Branding, Internet, Marketing

Fuss Free Flavours 986143
Web site: www.fussfreeflavours.com
Freq: Daily
Circ: 45475
Alcohol & Spirits, Bars, Clubs & Pubs, Beer, Beverages, Cooking & Baking, Food, Grocery Stores, Organic Food, Restaurant Reviews, Vegetarianism & Veganism

Futile Democracy 1053466
Email: futiledemocracy@gmail.com
Web site: https://futiledemocracy.wordpress.com/
Freq: Daily
Circ: 175
Profile: Blog covering politics. Futile Democracy blog discusses anything from US & UK politics and the British media to political history and atheism. The outlet offers RSS (Really Simple Syndication).
Politics, Religion

The Future of Law 996605
Editorial: 30 Farringdon Street, London EC4A 4HH
Web site: http://blogs.lexisnexis.co.uk/futureoflaw/
Freq: Daily
Circ: 216
Editor: Melissa Higgsmith; Editor: Sarah Plaka
Consumer Interest, Corporate Law, Criminal Law, Employment, Family Law, Government, Human Rights, Intellectual Property, Law, Legal Services

Future Pills - CEASED 2017 995110
Web site: http://futurepills.com/
Freq: Daily
Circ: 611
Health & Medicine, Medical Technology

Future Positive 996675
Editorial: 49/9 Elbe Street, Edinburgh EH6 7HP
Web site: thefuturepositive.com
Freq: Daily
Circ: 9820
News & Current Affairs

Futures 988652
Email: rebeccajlsk@gmail.com
Web site: www.ialwaysbelieveinfutures.com
Freq: Daily
Circ: 138884
Profile: Blog covering lifestyle. FUTURES blog discusses anything from lifestyle and everyday activities to motherhood. The blog has an archive dating back to January 2011 and shares an short blog roll. The outlet offers RSS (Really Simple Syndication).
Beauty & Grooming, Cosmetics, Fashion, Hair, Women's Interests

Futureversity 998737
Editorial: Ground Floor, 24-26 Fournier Street, London E1 6QE
Tel: 44 02072 477900
Email: info@futureversity.org
Web site: http://www.futureversity.org/content/1646/FV1
Freq: Daily
Circ: 90
Editor: Sarah McAlpine
Careers, Education, Student Lifestyle

Gabrielle Teare Blog 999241
Editorial: Kings Road, Chelsea, London SW3 5UW
Email: info@gabrielleteare.com
Web site: www.gabrielleteare.com/blog
Freq: Daily
Circ: 135
Fashion

Gadget Epoint News Blog 1054551
Editorial: Gadget Epoint (UK) Limited, 35 Moorfield Avenue, Denton, Manchester M34 7TF
Web site: http://www.gadgetepoint.co.uk/news/
Freq: Daily
Circ: 10
Apple, Computer & Video Games, Computers, Internet, Mobile Electronics, Personal Computers

Gadget Helpline 1054244
Tel: 44 03444 994600
Email: blog@gadgethelpline.com
Web site: http://www.gadgethelpline.com/
Freq: Daily
Circ: 34368

Editor: Jon Whitcombe
Audio Video Trade, Cameras, Consumer Electronics, Mobile Electronics, Movies & Video

Gadget Writing 1053726
Web site: http://gadgets.itwriting.com/
Freq: Daily
Circ: 13367
Audio Video Trade, Cameras, Consumer Electronics, Mobile Electronics, Movies & Video

Gadgets and Gizmos 985535
Editorial: 133 Bluebell Road, Weston-super-Mare BS22 9BX
Email: admin@gadgetsandgizmos.org
Web site: http://www.gadgetsandgizmos.org/
Freq: Daily
Circ: 12716
Audio Video Trade, Cameras, Consumer Electronics, Mobile Electronics, Movies & Video

GadgetyNews 1053929
Email: gadgetgarrett@gmail.com
Web site: http://gadgetynews.com/
Freq: Daily
Circ: 29440
Apple, Audio Video Trade, Cameras, Computer & Video Games, Computers, Consumer Electronics, Internet, Mobile Electronics, Movies & Video, Personal Computers

Galletero 1061631
Web site: http://www.elgalletero.com.mx
Freq: Daily
Circ: 1785
Auto Aftermarket, Computers, Data Management, Electronics, Government Technology, Industry, Internet, Mobile Communications, Security & Security Systems, Software

The Gallivants 1053091
Web site: http://www.thegallivants.com/
Freq: Daily
Circ: 917
Travel

The Galloping Gardener 986787
Email: thegallopinggardener@gmail.com
Web site: thegallopinggardener.blogspot.co.uk
Freq: Daily
Circ: 2409
Energy & Environment, Gardening

Gallucks 1100039
Email: info@gallucks.com
Web site: http://gallucks.com/
Freq: Daily
Circ: 14196
Fashion

Galway Public Libraries Blog 1053848
Web site: http://galwaylibrary.blogspot.co.uk/
Freq: Daily
Circ: 521
Art, Literature, Theater & Performing Arts

Game Debate 988449
Editorial: Pembroke House, 7 Brunswick Square, Bristol BS2 8PE
Email: press@game-debate.com
Web site: http://www.game-debate.com/
Circ: 2976423
Editor: Stuart Thomas
Profile: Website covering video games. The Game Debate website covers gaming reviews, system requirements and game release dates
Audio Video Trade, Cameras, Computer & Video Games, Consumer Electronics, Mobile Electronics, Movies & Video, Personal Computers

Gamebrit 986620
Email: team@gamebrit.com
Web site: www.gamebrit.com
Circ: 5834
Editor: Chris Brandrick
Profile: Website covering video games. The GAMEBRIT website discusses the latest

news and information on computer and video games.
Computer & Video Games

GameMobile.co.uk 1053828
Web site: http://www.gamemobile.co.uk/
Freq: Daily
Circ: 24602
Mobile Electronics

Games, Journalism, Other, And Books 997705
Web site: http://www.gjob.co.uk/blog/
Freq: Daily
Circ: 481
Computer & Video Games

GameShadow Blog 1053324
Email: webmaster@gameshadow.com
Web site: http://gameshadow.com/posts/
Freq: Daily
Circ: 15999
Computer & Video Games

GamezBlog 1054368
Web site: http://www.gamezblog.net/
Freq: Daily
Circ: 9829
Computer & Video Games, Personal Computers

Gamezplay 1054386
Tel: 44 01417 726745
Email: press@gamezplay.org
Web site: http://www.gamezplay.org/
Freq: Daily
Circ: 58772
Computer & Video Games

Gamified UK 1053783
Web site: gamified.uk
Freq: Daily
Circ: 28869
Profile: Blog covering gaming.
Computer & Video Games

Gap Year Escape 997540
Email: amar@gapyearescape.com
Web site: gapyearescape.com
Freq: Daily
Circ: 33734
Airline Inflight, Railroad, Travel

GARBAGELAPSAP 1061723
Email: nicholas@garbagelapsap.com
Web site: http://garbagelapsap.com/?cat=7
Freq: Daily
Circ: 521
Fashion

garbagenews.net 1060747
Freq. Daily
National News

GarçonJon.com 986886
Editorial: 53 Beacon Road, London SE13 6ED
Web site: www.garconjon.com
Freq: Daily
Circ: 8277
Fashion

Garden and Gardener 1058692
Email: gardening@mogga.com
Web site: http://www.gardenandgardener.co.uk/
Freq: Daily
Circ: 2652
Gardening

The Garden House 1057958
Email: contact@gardenhousebrighton.co.uk
Web site: www.gardenhousebrighton.co.uk
Freq: Daily
Circ: 6789
Gardening, Literature, Theater & Performing Arts

The Garden Smallholder 1052709
Email: thegardensmallholder@yahoo.co.uk
Web site: https://thegardensmallholder.wordpress.com/
Freq: Daily
Circ: 77
Profile: Blog covering gardening. The Garden Smallholder discusses anything from

allotment growing and chickens to wildlife and village life. The blog has an archive dating back to September 2008. The outlet offers RSS (Really Simple Syndication).
Cooking & Baking, Gardening, Organic Food

Gardeners' Tips 1052649
Web site: gardenerstips.co.uk/blog
Freq: Daily
Circ: 11481
Gardening

GardenVisit.com 986775
Email: gardenvisit1000@gmail.com
Web site: www.gardenvisit.com/blog
Freq: Daily
Circ: 114
Architecture & Design, Building & Construction, Do-It-Yourself (DIY), Gardening

Garen Ewing Blog 1054262
Email: webquery@rainboworchid.co.uk
Web site: http://rainboworchid.livejournal.com/
Freq: Daily
Circ: 4691
Literature

Gareth Mear Blog 1065391
Email: garethmearblog@gmail.com
Web site: http://www.garethmear.com/
Freq: Daily
Circ: 2578
Cooking & Baking, Family & Parenting, Men's Interests, Restaurant Reviews

Gary King 1053759
Email: ga.king@tavistockcollege.devon.sch.uk
Web site: http://garysking.me/
Freq: Daily
Circ: 11860
Profile: Blog covering education. Gary King blog discusses anything from education and teaching to ICT. The blog has an archive dating back to October 2012. The outlet offers RSS (Really Simple Syndication).
Education

Gas and Electric Blog 997541
Editorial: Brooklyn House, 22 The Green, Money Lane, West Drayton UB7 7PQ
Tel: 44 01895 420777
Email: info@gas-elec.co.uk
Web site: http://www.gas-elec-blog.co.uk/
Freq: Daily
Circ: 521
Alternative/Renewable Energy, Carbon Emissions & Trading, Electricity, Energy, Environment, Nuclear Power, Oil, Water & Sanitation

Gastrobaby 997065
Email: gastrobabyuk@hotmail.com
Web site: gastrobaby.co.uk
Freq: Daily
Circ: 9643
Family & Parenting

Gathered Cheer 1053102
Email: ruth@gatheredcheer.com
Web site: http://www.gatheredcheer.com/blog
Freq: Daily
Circ: 7465
Do-It-Yourself (DIY), Women's Interests

Gatsby Menswear 1052596
Web site: http://www.gatsbylifestyle.co.uk
Freq: Daily
Circ: 521
Fashion, Men's Interests

Gatwick Blog 1057074
Email: info@gatwickblog.co.uk
Web site: http://www.gatwickblog.co.uk/
Freq: Daily
Circ: 8919
Airline Inflight, Railroad, Travel

Gavin Hewitt's Europe 1053302
Editorial: BBC Broadcasting House, Portland Place, London W1A 1AA
Email: gavin.hewitt@bbc.co.uk
Web site: http://www.bbc.co.uk/news/correspondents/gavinhewitt

Freq: Daily
Circ: 18
Economics, Politics

Gay Essential 997977
Editorial: 127B Church Road, London SW13 9HR
Email: hello@gay-themed-films.com
Web site: http://gay-themed-films.com
Freq: Daily
Circ: 14019
Editor: Alexander Ryll
LGBT, Men's Interests, Movies & Video

Geek 1062139
Web site: http://elgeek.com/
Freq: Daily
Circ: 2952
Auto Aftermarket, Computers, Data Management, Electronics, Government Technology, Industry, Internet, Mobile Communications, Security & Security Systems, Software

Geek Native 1054618
Web site: www.geeknative.com/
Freq: Daily
Circ: 33225
Apple, Computer & Video Games, Computers, Internet, Movies & Video, Personal Computers

Geek-Me Up 1061732
Web site: http://www.geek-meup.com
Freq: Daily
Circ: 611
Auto Aftermarket, Computers, Data Management, Electronics, Government Technology, Industry, Internet, Mobile Communications, Security & Security Systems, Software

Geeks & Linux 1060518
Web site: http://www.glatelier.org
Freq: Daily
Circ: 32657
Internet, Software

Geeks Have Landed 1054334
Email: info@geekshavelanded.com
Web site: http://geekshavelanded.com/
Freq: Daily
Circ: 10621
Audio Video Trade, Cameras, Consumer Electronics, Mobile Electronics, Movies & Video

GeekTech 1053415
Email: thegeek@geektech.ie
Web site: http://geektech.ie
Freq: Daily
Circ: 9352
Computer & Video Games, Mobile Electronics, Personal Computers

GeekTown 1054128
Editorial: 8 Bryans Way, Cannock WS12 0HX Tel: 44 01212 884335
Web site: http://www.geektown.co.uk
Freq: Daily
Circ: 149185
Editor: Chris Brown
Broadcasting, Cartoons, Computer & Video Games, Movies & Video, Trading Cards & Comics

Geeky Gadgets 986897
Email: admin@geeky-gadgets.com
Web site: http://www.geeky-gadgets.com/
Freq: Daily
Circ: 666625
Computer & Video Games, Mobile Electronics

Gemma Hood Blog - CEASED NOVEMBER 2015 985876
Web site: https://gemmahood.wordpress.com
Freq: Daily
Alcohol & Spirits, Bars, Clubs & Pubs, Beer, Beverages, Cooking & Baking, Food, Grocery Stores, Organic Food, Restaurant Reviews, Vegetarianism & Veganism

Gemologue by Liza Urla 1098990
Editorial: 4 Montpelier Street, 255, London SW7 1EE
Email: info@gemologue.com
Web site: http://gemologue.com/
Freq: Daily
Circ: 25468
Fashion

Gente de iPad 1060893
Web site: http://www.gentedeipad.com
Freq: Daily
Circ: 1126
Apple, Electronics

Gente, Pasion y Futbol 1062132
Web site: http://gentepasionyfutbol.blogspot.com/
Freq: Daily
Circ: 521
Soccer

The Gentleman Traveller 988160
Web site: http://www.thegentlemantraveller.co.uk/
Freq: Daily
Circ: 8950
Profile: The Gentleman Traveller covers men's lifestyle, travel, food and drink.
Alcohol & Spirits, Bars, Clubs & Pubs, Beer, Beverages, Fashion, Restaurant Reviews, Travel, Wine/Winemaking

Gentlemans Butler 987190
Editorial: 275a Upper Richmond Road, London SW15 6SP Tel: 44 02087 805234
Email: info@gentlemansbutler.com
Web site: www.gentlemansbutler.com
Freq: Daily
Circ: 10145
Airline Inflight, Alcohol & Spirits, Antiques/Collectibles, Art, Arts, Bars, Clubs & Pubs, Beauty & Grooming, Beer, Beverages, Comedy

Gentlemen's Goods 987755
Editorial: 37 Croft Gardens, Ruislip, London HA4 8EY
Web site: www.gentlemensgoods.com
Freq: Daily
Circ: 9957
Editor: Chris Ford
Profile: Gentlemen's Goods covers men's interests including food, fashion, travel, cars and technology. The blog has an archive dating back to February 2010.
Alcohol & Spirits, Audio Video Trade, Bars, Clubs & Pubs, Beer, Beverages, Cameras, Consumer Electronics, Men's Interests, Mobile Electronics, Movies & Video

Geoff Barton's Pick n Mix 987339
Web site: blog.geoffbarton.co.uk
Freq: Daily
Circ: 7059
Education, Schools & Institutions

Geografía 1061174
Web site: http://lageografiaweb.blogspot.com/
Freq: Daily
Circ: 611
Science

Georgina Does 1098989
Web site: http://www.georginadoes.co.uk/
Freq: Daily
Circ: 7343
Profile: Georgina Does covers fashion, lifestyle and beauty. The blog has an archive dating back to May 2012.
Fashion, Travel, Women's Interests

Gerry Hassan blog 988438
Web site: http://www.gerryhassan.com/
Freq: Daily
Circ: 17327
Politics

Get Lippie 986311
Email: louise@getlippie.com
Web site: http://www.getlippie.com/
Freq: Daily
Circ: 8351
Cosmetics

UK Blogs

Get Movil 1061039
Web site: http://www.getmovil.com
Freq: Daily
Circ: 142875
Auto Aftermarket, Computers, Data Management, Electronics, Government Technology, Industry, Internet, Mobile Communications, Mobile Electronics, Security & Security Systems

Getintothis 1052956
Web site: http://www.getintothis.co.uk/
Freq: Daily
Circ: 54853
Classical/Choral/Band Music, Country, Folk, Bluegrass, Dance Music, Jazz & Blues, Music, Pop Music, R&B, Urban, World, Rap & Hip Hop, Rock Music

Getting stuff done 1052900
Web site: http://get-stuff-done.blogspot.co.uk/
Freq: Daily
Circ: 9532
Women's Interests

The Gibbon Bridge Hotel & Restaurant 1054379
Email: reception@gibbon-bridge.co.uk
Web site: www.gibbon-bridge.co.uk/blog
Freq: Daily
Circ: 9
Hotels/Motels

Gibbs Wyatt Stone Legal Costs Blog 1053457
Tel: 44 02036 171904
Web site: http://www.gwslaw.co.uk/blog/
Freq: Daily
Circ: 153
Legal Services

Gift Ideas Generator Blog 1052858
Email: enquiries@giftgen.co.uk
Web site: http://giftgen.blogspot.co.uk/
Freq: Daily
Circ: 521
Shopping

Giggle Beats Comedy 1057081
Web site: www.gigglebeats.co.uk/
Freq: Daily
Circ: 6772
Editor: Andrew Dipper
Comedy

Giira Yachts 1061262
Tel: 44 91982 0007559
Email: info@giirayachts.com
Web site: http://www.giirayachts.com
Freq: Daily
Circ: 687
Boating & Yachting

Gillian Lee Rose 995347
Email: gillianleerose@gmail.com
Web site: https://gillianleerose.com/
Freq: Daily
Circ: 9663
Fashion

gillianmciver 996897
Email: mail@sitespecificart.org.uk
Web site: http://blog.gillianmciver.org/
Freq: Daily
Circ: 3347
Antiques/Collectibles, Art, Arts, Literature, Photography, Theater & Performing Arts, Visual Arts

Gill's Blog 1053159
Web site: http://www.gilljameswriter.eu/
Freq: Daily
Circ: 10077
Literature

Ginger & Bread 996852
Email: gingerandbread@mail.com
Web site: gingerandbread.com
Freq: Daily
Circ: 7019
Cooking & Baking, Restaurant Reviews

Ginger Bisquite - CEASED 2016 996985
Editorial: 53 Rutland Walk, Lewisham, London
Web site: gingerbisquite.co.uk
Freq: Daily
Circ: 1060
Do-It-Yourself (DIY), Gardening, Women's Interests

Ginger Ecstasy 1053951
Email: rt.rebecca.thompson@icloud.com
Web site: www.gingerecstasy.com
Freq: Daily
Circ: 1659
Fashion

Ginger Girl Says 988037
Email: charl@gingergirlsays.com
Web site: gingergirlsays.com
Freq: Daily
Circ: 13621
Beauty & Grooming, Cosmetics, Fashion, Hair, Women's Interests

The Gingerbread House 988694
Web site: http://the-gingerbread-house.co.uk
Freq: Daily
Circ: 92487
Family & Parenting, Women's Interests

gingerbread smiles. 1053621
Email: gingerbreadsmiles@hotmail.co.uk
Web site: http://www.gingerbreadsmiles.co.uk/
Freq: Daily
Circ: 7034
Beauty & Grooming, Cooking & Baking, Cosmetics, Hair, Restaurant Reviews, Travel, Women's Interests

Gingey Bites 988526
Email: gingeybites@gmail.com
Web site: http://www.gingeybites.com
Freq: Daily
Circ: 10718
Profile: Blog covering food. The GINGEY BITES blog discusses anything from recipes and restaurants reviews. The blog has an archive dating back to June 2012.
Cooking & Baking

Gingle lists everything 988099
Email: ginglesnuff@gmail.com
Web site: ginglelistseverything.blogspot.co.uk
Freq: Daily
Circ: 1093
Profile: Blog covering London lifestyle. Gingle lists everything blog discusses anything from food and drink to London nightlife. The blog has an archive dating back to September 2011 and shares an extensive blog roll.
Regional General Interest

Gira Mundo 1060981
Web site: http://giramvndo.blogspot.com/
Freq: Daily
Circ: 900
Health & Medicine, Public Sector

Girl A La Mode 1053706
Email: charlie@girlalamode.co.uk
Web site: http://www.girlalamode.co.uk/
Freq: Daily
Circ: 7875
Fashion

Girl around Glasgow 1052710
Email: girlaroundglasgow@gmail.com
Web site: https://girlaroundglasgow.wordpress.com/
Freq: Daily
Circ: 62
Profile: Blog covering the Glasgow food scene and travel in Scotland. The blog has an archive dating back to July 2013.
Regional General Interest, Restaurant Reviews, Travel, Women's Interests

Girl Get Strong 995483
Email: pr.fitnesshealth@gmail.com
Web site: girlgetstrong.com
Freq: Daily
Circ: 346

Editor: Brad Roscoe
Fitness & Exercise, Nutrition

Girl in menswear 1052842
Email: girlinmenswear@gmail.com
Web site: http://girlinmenswear.com/
Freq: Daily
Circ: 6700
Profile: Blog covering men's fashion. The Girl in Menswear blog discusses anything from men's fashion to men's fashion events. The blog has an archive dating back to January 2013.
Fashion

The Girl in the Bowler Hat 1076647
Web site: https://amyrebair.com/
Freq: Daily
Circ: 10597
Profile: The Girl in the Bowler Hat covers fashion and lifestyle. The blog has an archive dating back to December 2012.
Beauty & Grooming, Cosmetics, Fashion, Hair, Women's Interests

Girl in the Lens 987057
Email: girlinthelensblog@gmail.com
Web site: girlinthelens.com
Freq: Daily
Circ: 6529
Fashion

Girl Meets Dress 988210
Email: enquiries@girlmeetsdress.com
Web site: http://www.girlmeetsdress.com/blog
Circ: 35
Profile: Website covering fashion. The site discusses anything from on-line rental dresses and designs to accessories and fashion designers.
Fashion

Girl Next Door Fashion 1054079
Email: girlnextdoorfashion@gmail.com
Web site: www.girlnextdoorfashion.net
Freq: Daily
Circ: 6773
Profile: Blog covering fashion. GIRL NEXT DOOR FASHION blog discusses anything from outfits and beauty to lifestyle and running. The blog has an archive dating back to December 2009.
Fashion, Women's Interests

The Girl on the Piccadilly Line 1074801
Email: piclinegirl@gmail.com
Web site: https://piclinegirl.com/
Freq: Daily
Circ: 14426
Education

Girl On The River 1054583
Web site: girlontheriver.com
Freq: Daily
Circ: 9676
Family & Parenting, Fitness & Exercise, Rowing, Women's Interests

The Girl Outdoors 988754
Email: sian.a.lewis@gmail.com
Web site: http://thegirloutdoors.co.uk/
Freq: Daily
Circ: 47328
Field Sports

Girl Racer Magazine 987859
Email: email@girlracer.co.uk
Web site: www.girlracer.co.uk
Circ: 8164
Editor: Gary Wood
Driving, Motorsports

Girl vs Globe 1052650
Web site: http://girlvsglobe.com/
Freq: Daily
Circ: 141683
Beauty & Grooming, Cosmetics, Fashion, Hair, Travel, Women's Interests

Girl with a Camera 1100045
Web site: http://girlwithacamera.co.uk/
Freq: Daily
Circ: 7947
Photography

Girls Heart Books 988001
Email: girlsheartbooks@gmail.com
Web site: http://girlsheartbooks.com/
Freq: Daily
Circ: 8342
Literature, Teen/Young Adult

Girls On The Ball 998369
Email: girlsontheball10@gmail.com
Web site: http://www.girlsontheball.com/
Freq: Daily
Circ: 10560
Soccer

The Girly Book Club Blog 999631
Editorial: SLH, 3rd Floor Portland House, Bressenden Place, London SW1E 5BH
Email: info@thegirlybookclub.com
Web site: http://girlybookclub.com/what-were-reading/
Freq: Daily
Circ: 193
Literature

GirlyGeekdom 1053140
Web site: http://girlygeekdom.com/
Freq: Daily
Circ: 8996
Audio Video Trade, Cameras, Consumer Electronics, Mobile Electronics, Movies & Video

Give As You Live 999258
Editorial: Basepoint Business Centre, Crab Apple Way, Vale Business Park, Evesham WR11 1GP Tel: 44 08700 055050
Web site: http://www.giveasyoulive.com/blog
Freq: Daily
Circ: 151
Charitable Foundations

Give Me Some Spice 1052923
Email: givemesomespice@gmail.com
Web site: http://www.givemesomespice.com/
Freq: Daily
Circ: 6142
Cooking & Baking, Food, Grocery Stores, Organic Food, Restaurant Reviews, Vegetarianism & Veganism

Gizmologia 1060892
Web site: http://www.gizmologia.com
Freq: Daily
Circ: 1775
Auto Aftermarket, Computers, Data Management, Electronics, Government Technology, Industry, Internet, Mobile Communications, Security & Security Systems, Software

The Gizzle Review 998419
Email: thegizzlereview@hotmail.co.uk
Web site: www.thegizzlereview.com/
Freq: Daily
Circ: 8824
Classical/Choral/Band Music, Country, Folk, Bluegrass, Dance Music, Entertainment, Jazz & Blues, Movies & Video, Music, Pop Music, R&B, Urban, World, Rap & Hip Hop

Glam & Glitter 1054615
Email: mail@theglamandglitter.com
Web site: theglamandglitter.com
Freq: Daily
Circ: 36884
Beauty & Grooming, Cosmetics, Fashion, Hair, Travel

The Glam Mummy 997886
Web site: theglammummy.com
Freq: Daily
Circ: 4344
Family & Parenting

Glam Rosie 1053325
Email: enquiries@glamrosie.co.uk
Web site: http://glamrosie.blogspot.co.uk/
Freq: Daily
Circ: 7037
Fashion

Glamazon Blog by Eva 997911
Web site: glamazonblog.com
Freq: Daily

Circ: 8821

Fashion, Women's Interests

Glamour in the County 1053413
Freq: Daily
News & Current Affairs

Glamoursleuth 1053364
Web site: http://www.glamoursleuth.com/
Freq: Daily
Circ: 8384
News & Current Affairs

Glasgow Food Geek 988430
Email: glasgowfoodgeek@gmail.com
Web site: glasgowfoodgeek.co.uk
Freq: Daily
Circ: 7641
Profile: Glasgow Food Geek covers the Glasgow food scene including restaurant reviews, food events and food product reviews.
Cooking & Baking, Restaurant Reviews

Glasgow Theatre Blog 988534
Email: glasgowtheatreblog@gmail.com
Web site: http://glasgowtheatreblog.com/
Freq: Daily
Circ: 12329
Theater & Performing Arts

Glasses Direct Blog 1054302
Tel: 44 01793 746601
Email: media@glassesdirect.com
Web site: https://blog.glassesdirect.co.uk/
Freq: Daily
Circ: 20623
Fashion, Health & Medicine

Gleder & Alvor 1062101
Web site: http://alvoroggleder.blogspot.com/
Freq: Daily
Circ: 1120
Disability, Education, Higher Education, Preschool, Schools & Institutions, Students

Glimmer of Hope 997878
Editorial: The Maisonette, 39 Meadow Street, Weston-super-Mare BS23 1QH
Web site: pixiedusk.livejournal.com
Freq: Daily
Circ: 12045316
Family & Parenting

Glitter Me Silly 988159
Web site: http://glittermesilly.com/
Freq: Daily
Circ: 6877
Crafts

Glitz and Glamour Makeup 998165
Web site: www.glitzandglamourmakeup.co.uk
Freq: Daily
Circ: 9342
Beauty & Grooming, Cosmetics, Hair

Global Cool - SUSPENDED APRIL 2017 986320
Editorial: 2 - 6 Cannon Street, London EC4M 6YH Tel: 44 08444 410003
Email: info@globalcool.org
Web site: globalcool.org
Circ: 8856
Energy & Environment

Global Dashboard 997148
Email: editors@globaldashboard.org
Web site: www.globaldashboard.org
Freq: Daily
Circ: 13732
Consumer Affairs, International News

Global Grasshopper 987985
Email: admin@globalgrasshopper.com
Web site: http://www.globalgrasshopper.com/
Freq: Daily
Circ: 92400
Travel

Global Justice Now Blog 1055938
Tel: 44 02078 204900
Email: offleyroad@globaljustice.org.uk
Web site: www.globaljustice.org.uk
Freq: Daily
Circ: 76376
Charitable Foundations

Global Metal Apocalypse 998160
Tel: 44 07942 088180
Email: globalmetalapocalypse@gmail.com
Web site: http://globalmetalapocalypse.weebly.com/
Freq: Daily
Circ: 15
Editor: Rhys Stevenson
Rock Music

Globocation 1053265
Email: info@globocation.com
Web site: http://www.globocation.com/
Freq: Daily
Circ: 2827
Railroad, Travel

Globopop 1061990
Web site: http://www.globopop.com
Freq: Daily
Circ: 335
Celebrities, Movies & Video

GlossyBox Blog 996221
Editorial: 13a North Audley Street, London W1K 6ZA Tel: 44 02035 981587
Email: contact@glossybox.co.uk
Web site: http://www.glossybox.co.uk/magazine/
Freq: Daily
Circ: 50
Beauty & Grooming, Cosmetics, Hair, Women's Interests

Glowology 988700
Web site: www.glowology.co.uk
Freq: Daily
Circ: 9449
Beauty & Grooming, Cosmetics, Hair, Women's Interests

Gluten Free Cuppa Tea 1053873
Web site: http://glutenfreecuppatea.co.uk/
Freq: Daily
Circ: 11375
Profile: Blog covering gluten free recipes, gluten free food and restaurant reviews. The blog has an archive dating back to October 2013.
Cooking & Baking, Nutrition, Restaurant Reviews

Gluten Free Edinburgh 996085
Editorial: 4 Eyre Place, Edinburgh EH3 5EP
Email: info@glutenfreeedinburgh.com
Web site: http://www.glutenfreeedinburgh.com/
Freq: Daily
Circ: 10611
Cooking & Baking, Grocery Stores, Organic Food, Restaurant Reviews

Go - Eat - Do 988063
Editorial: 6 Raby Drive, East Herrington, Sunderland SR3 3QE Tel: 44 01916 450885
Web site: http://go-eat-do.com
Freq: Daily
Circ: 11353
Cooking & Baking, Food, Grocery Stores, Organic Food, Restaurant Reviews, Travel, Vegetarianism & Veganism

Go Cruise With Jane 1052721
Tel: 44 02476 742135
Email: janechadwick@gocruise.co.uk
Web site: http://gocruisewithjane.co.uk/
Freq: Daily
Circ: 10288
Travel

Go Fishing With Cadbury Angling 1063271
Tel: 44 01934 875733
Email: cadburyangling@cadbury.g-l.co.uk
Web site: http://cadburyangling.blogspot.co.uk/
Freq: Daily
Circ: 521
Fishing

Go for brunch, London! 998045
Email: info@goforbrunchlondon.com
Web site: http://www.goforbrunchlondon.com
Freq: Daily
Circ: 1218
Restaurant Reviews

Go Travel with Joan Ask Joan and Road Warrior 1053789
Web site: www.joanscales.com/blog
Freq: Daily
Travel

God Is In The TV 1056578
Web site: www.godisinthetvzine.co.uk/
Freq: Daily
Circ: 51403
Profile: Website covering music. The god is in the TV website discusses anything from new music and reviews to music videos and bands.
Classical/Choral/Band Music, Country, Folk, Bluegrass, Dance Music, Jazz & Blues, Music, Pop Music, R&B, Urban, World, Rap & Hip Hop, Rock Music

GoHen Blog 997117
Editorial: 30-32 Westgate Buildings, Bath, Bath BA1 1EF Tel: 44 01225 474200
Email: hen@gohen.com
Web site: www.gohen.com/blog/
Freq: Daily
Circ: 44
Weddings

Golem XIV 1055295
Email: golemxivg@gmail.com
Web site: http://www.golemxiv.co.uk/
Freq: Daily
Circ: 13453
Banking, Personal Finance, Politics

Golfblogger.co.uk 985716
Editorial: Gordon House, 19 Crombie Acres, Westhill, Westhill AB32 6PR
Email: info@golfblogger.co.uk
Web site: www.golfblogger.co.uk
Freq: Daily
Circ: 6540
Editor: Graham Gordon
Golf

GoMo News 985370
Tel: 44 02083 932779
Email: editor@gomonews.com
Web site: http://www.gomonews.com/
Freq: Daily
Circ: 38398
Mobile Electronics

Good 4 U Blog 1053122
Editorial: Finisklin Business Park, Sligo
Tel: 353 35307 19180031
Email: laura@good4u.co.uk
Web site: www.good4u.co.uk/blog
Freq: Daily
Alternative Medicine, Cooking & Baking, Nutrition, Organic Food, Vegetarianism & Veganism

The Good Beauty Guide 1060159
Web site: http://www.thegoodbeautyguide.co.uk/
Freq: Daily
Circ: 495
Beauty & Grooming, Cosmetics, Hair, Women's Interests

Good Energy Blog 986318
Tel: 44 01249 766090
Email: enquiries@goodenergy.co.uk
Web site: www.goodenergy.co.uk/blog
Freq: Daily
Circ: 37
Alternative/Renewable Energy

Good Food Ireland 1053552
Email: info@goodfoodireland.ie
Web site: www.goodfoodireland.ie/blog
Freq: Daily
Circ: 6
Cooking & Baking, Regional General Interest

Good Golly Miss Hollie 987383
Email: goodgollymiss-hollie@hotmail.com
Web site: http://www.goodgollymisshollie.co.uk
Freq: Daily
Circ: 10187
Beauty & Grooming, Cosmetics, Fashion, Hair, Women's Interests

Good News Shared 1052657
Web site: http://goodnewsshared.com/
Freq: Daily
Circ: 20881
International News, National News

Goodness Direct 1053519
Tel: 44 01327 701579
Email: info@goodnessdirect.co.uk
Web site: http://www.goodnessdirect.co.uk/blog/
Freq: Daily
Circ: 68749
Alternative Medicine, Cooking & Baking, Nutrition, Organic Food, Vegetarianism & Veganism

Goodtrippers 998232
Email: hello@goodtrippers.co.uk
Web site: www.goodtrippers.co.uk
Freq: Daily
Circ: 4590
Energy & Environment, Ethical/Moral Issues, Nature & Wildlife, Organic Food, Travel

Gooner Talk 987879
Email: goonerchris@goonertalk.com
Web site: goonertalk.com/
Circ: 24157
Soccer

Goonerholic 1052749
Email: goonerholic@virginmedia.com
Web site: http://goonerholic.com/
Freq: Daily
Circ: 14848
Soccer

Gosh! London Blog 988260
Editorial: 1 Berwick Street, London W1F 0DR Tel: 44 02076 361011
Email: info@goshlondon.com
Web site: http://www.goshlondon.com/blog/
Freq: Daily
Circ: 17
Trading Cards & Comics

Got to Be Gourmet 1053486
Email: gottobegourmet@gmail.com
Web site: http://gottobegourmet.com/
Freq: Daily
Circ: 9409
Alcohol & Spirits, Bars, Clubs & Pubs, Beer, Beverages, Cooking & Baking, Food, Grocery Stores, Organic Food, Restaurant Reviews, Travel

The Gothic Imagination 1057069
Email: m.r.foley@stir.ac.uk
Web site: www.gothic.stir.ac.uk/category/blog/
Freq: Daily
Circ: 61
Art

Gotta keep movin' 1053006
Web site: http://gottakeepmovin.com/
Freq: Daily
Circ: 9746
Profile: Blog covering travel. Gotta Keep Movin' discusses anything from destination reviews and city guides to volunteering abroad and activity ideas.
Regional General Interest, Travel

Gourmet Urbano 1062079
Web site: http://elgourmeturbano.blogspot.com/
Freq: Daily
Circ: 16322
Bars, Clubs & Pubs, Food, Nutrition

Govan Law Centre 999315
Editorial: Orkney Street Enterprise Centre (Units 4 & 6), 18-20 Orkney Street, Glasgow G51 2BZ Tel: 44 01414 402503
Email: m@govanlc.com

UK Blogs

Web site: govanic.blogspot.com
Freq: Daily
Circ: 6374
Bankruptcy, Company News & Appointments, Consumer Interest, Corporate Law, Criminal Law, Employment, Estate Planning, Family Law, Federal Courts, Food & Drug Administration

Graeme Shimmin blog 998197
Web site: http://graemeshimmin.com/
Freq: Daily
Circ: 25059
Antiques/Collectibles, Art, Arts, Bars, Clubs & Pubs, Comedy, Entertainment, Literature, Local Entertainment Guides, Movies & Video, Photography

Graham Cluley Security News
996983
Email: press@grahamcluley.com
Web site: grahamcluley.com
Freq: Daily
Circ: 161836
News & Current Affairs

Graham Jones Blog 1054144
Tel: 44 01183 369710
Web site: grahamjones.co.uk/category/blog
Freq: Daily
Circ: 50
Psychology

Gran Chef 1061422
Web site: http://www.elgranchef.com
Freq: Daily
Circ: 401
Cooking & Baking, Nutrition

Graphique Fantastique 988116
Web site: graphiquefantastique.com
Freq: Daily
Circ: 12007
Profile: Blog covering graphic. The Graphique Fantastique blog discusses anything from graphic design to graphic events. The blog has an archive dating back to January 2009.
Graphic Design

Grassroots Football Coaching Blog 1063922
Web site: https://www.grassrootscoaching.com/blog/
Freq: Daily
Circ: 14
Editor: Simon Tann
Soccer

The Grazer 997722
Web site: http://www.the-grazer.blogspot.co.uk/
Freq: Daily
Circ: 7049
Cooking & Baking

The Great Affair Blog 1053286
Email: candacerardon@gmail.com
Web site: http://www.candaceroserardon.com/blog-2/
Freq: Daily
Circ: 41
Travel, Visual Arts

Great Drams 998168
Web site: greatdrams.com
Freq: Daily
Circ: 15326
Alcohol & Spirits

Great Stories with Heart 997520
Editorial: Wyndham Media Ltd, 27 Old Gloucester Street, London WC1N 3AX
Tel: 44 01442 862628
Email: editor@greatstorieswithheart.com
Web site: http://www.greatstorieswithheart.com/
Freq: Daily
Circ: 2671
Editor: Ian Skillicorn
Celebrities, Charitable Foundations, Women's Interests

The Great Wen 988279
Email: petershepherdwatts@hotmail.com
Web site: http://greatwen.com/

Freq: Daily
Circ: 10894
Regional General Interest

Greedy Gourmet 986147
Web site: www.greedygourmet.com
Freq: Daily
Circ: 11805
Alcohol & Spirits, Bars, Clubs & Pubs, Beer, Beverages, Cooking & Baking, Food, Grocery Stores, Organic Food, Restaurant Reviews, Vegetarianism & Veganism

Greek Love 994996
Editorial: 5A Union Road, London SW4 6JH
Email: greekloveblog@gmail.com
Web site: https://greekloveblog.com/
Freq: Daily
Circ: 521
Editor: Matt Peake
Cooking & Baking, Entertainment, LGBT, Literature, Movies & Video, Rugby, Theater & Performing Arts, Travel

Green (Living) Review 986317
Web site: greenreview.blogspot.com
Freq: Daily
Circ: 10144
Environment, Sustainable Development

Green Alliance blog 1052638
Editorial: 36 Buckingham Palace Road, London SW1W 0RE **Tel:** 44 02072 337433
Email: ga@green-alliance.org.uk
Web site: http://greenallianceblog.org.uk/
Freq: Daily
Circ: 16844
Energy & Environment, Politics

Green Construction UK 999292
Editorial: Adrian Windisch, Reading Green Party, 29 Erleigh Court Gardens, Reading RG6 1EJ
Freq: Daily
Circ: 4662
Energy & Environment, Politics

Green Diary 1054488
Web site: http://www.worldlandtrust.org/news/green-diary
Freq: Daily
Circ: 7
Energy & Environment

The Green Familia 1053554
Email: brenda@thegreenfamilia.co.uk
Web site: http://www.thegreenfamilia.com
Freq: Daily
Circ: 10282
Cooking & Baking, Environment, Organic Food, Vegetarianism & Veganism

Green Glitter UK 1052580
Email: greenglitteruk@gmail.com
Web site: greenglitter.co.uk
Freq: Daily
Circ: 702
Beauty & Grooming, Cosmetics, Ethical/Moral Issues, Fashion, Hair

Green Party Blog 986148
Editorial: 56-64 Development House, Leonard Street, London EC2A 4LT
Tel: 44 02075 490310
Email: press@greenparty.org.uk
Web site: https://www.greenparty.org.uk/
Circ: 73566
Politics

Green Pepper 1052875
Web site: http://www.greenpepper.org.uk/
Freq: Dally
Circ: 1033
Environment

Green Travel Blog 986149
Editorial: 7 - 9 North Parade Buildings, Bath BA1 1NS **Tel:** 44 01225 326888
Email: info@greentraveller.co.uk
Web site: greentraveller.co.uk/blog
Freq: Daily
Circ: 85
Airline Inflight, Railroad, Travel

Green Union 987286
Tel: 44 01769 550580
Email: info@greenunion.co.uk
Web site: http://www.greenunion.co.uk/news
Freq: Daily
Circ: 216
Weddings

Greenbanana PR + More 1053850
Email: hmlyaxley@gmail.com
Web site: https://greenbanana.wordpress.com
Freq: Daily
Circ: 13757
Branding, Marketing

Greener Leith 987837
Editorial: 36 Newhaven Road, Edinburgh EH6 5PY
Web site: greenerleith.org.uk/
Freq: Daily
Circ: 6759
Energy & Environment, Environment

The Greenpeace Blog 997074
Editorial: Greenpeace, Canonbury Villas, London N1 2PN **Tel:** 44 02078 658255
Email: info.uk@greenpeace.org
Web site: greenpeace.org.uk/blog
Freq: Daily
Editor: Damian Kahya
Alternative/Renewable Energy, Energy & Environment, Environment

Grenglish 1053701
Web site: grenglish.co.uk
Freq: Daily
Circ: 3925
Family & Parenting, Women's Interests

Grey is OK! 1098948
Web site: greyisok.blogspot.co.uk
Freq: Daily
Circ: 1177
Beauty & Grooming, Cosmetics, Hair

The Grit Doctor - SUSPENDED JANUARY 2017 988119
Web site: https://gritdoctor.wordpress.com/
Freq: Daily
Circ: 202
Profile: Blog covering fitness. THE GRIT DOCTOR discusses anything from running and motivation to marathons and gear. The blog has an archive dating back to January 2007. The outlet offers RSS (Really Simple Syndication).
Fitness & Exercise

The Grooming Guru 986389
Web site: www.groomingguru.co.uk
Freq: Daily
Circ: 9936
Beauty & Grooming, Cosmetics, Hair, Men's Interests

Grough 1054315
Email: editorial@grough.co.uk
Web site: http://www.grough.co.uk/magazine/
Freq: Daily
Circ: 48842
Field Sports, Outdoor Recreation

Grow Our Own 1053285
Web site: http://www.growourown.blogspot.co.uk/
Freq: Daily
Circ: 672
Gardening, Neurology

Growing Spaces 1052904
Web site: http://www.growingspaces.net/
Freq: Daily
Circ: 11608
Crafts, Do-It-Yourself (DIY), Regional General Interest, Travel

Growthfunders Blog 997027
Editorial: GrowthCapitalVentures Ltd t/a GrowthFunders, 15 Parsons Court, Welbury Way, Newton Aycliffe DL5 6ZE
Tel: 44 08458 057442
Email: enquiries@growthfunders.com
Web site: blog.growthfunders.com
Freq: Daily

Circ: 129
Business, Corporate Responsibility, Equities, Small and Medium Business

Grumpyishmum 988895
Editorial: 310 Bolton Road, Radcliffe, Manchester M26 3GP
Email: grumpyishmum@gmail.com
Web site: http://grumpyishmum.co.uk
Freq: Daily
Circ: 9484
Profile: Blog covering parenting, lifestyle, nature, camping, outdoors, family, craft. The blog has an archive dating back to January 2011.
Camping and RV Travel, Crafts, Education, Family & Parenting

GT Spirit 1054182
Email: contact@gtspirit.com
Web site: http://gtspirit.com/
Freq: Daily
Circ: 708948
Automotive

GTGT 1062076
Email: iamgt@126.com
Web site: http://blog.sina.com.cn/gtgt
Freq: Daily
Circ: 30244
Airline Inflight, Antique & Collectible Cars, Automakers, Automotive, Driving, Motorcycles, Off-road & 4-Wheel Drive Vehicles, Railroad, Travel, Trucks & SUVs

The Guide Dogs Blogs 999705
Editorial: The Guide Dogs for the Blind Association, Burghfield Common, Burghfield Common RG7 3YG **Tel:** 44 01189 838156
Email: socialmedia@guidedogs.org.uk
Web site: http://www.guidedogs.org.uk/news/blogs#.VZ6VUpMeq28
Freq: Daily
Charitable Foundations, Disability, Nature & Wildlife, Patient Support, Social Issues

Guido Fawkes' Blog 986150
Email: guido.fawkes@order-order.com
Web site: http://order-order.com/
Freq: Daily
Circ: 691870
Politics

Guitars and Life 997270
Email: furtheron@hotmail.co.uk
Web site: http://guitarsandlife.blogspot.co.uk/
Freq: Daily
Circ: 1250
Music

Gullwing Photography 1053603
Email: guycarpenterphoto@gmail.com
Web site: http://gullwingphotography.blogspot.co.uk/
Freq: Daily
Circ: 9621
Photography

The Gumtree blog 1053615
Web site: http://blog.gumtree.com
Freq: Daily
Circ: 26562
Broadcasting, Lifestyle, Men's Interests, Regional General Interest, Sales & Marketing, Women's Interests

Gymbags and Gladrags 987836
Web site: www.gymbagsandgladrags.com
Freq: Daily
Circ: 35328
Profile: Blog covering lifestyle, fashion, beauty, exercise and fitness. The blog has an archive dating back to January 2013.
News & Current Affairs

H is for Home 1054458
Email: hello@hisforhome.com
Web site: http://hisforhomeblog.com/#axzz3tw4CFB6N
Freq: Daily
Circ: 31176
Do-It-Yourself (DIY)

H&S Works blog 1053485
Email: editor@healthandsafety-works.com
Web site: http://www.healthandsafety-works.com/

Freq: Daily
Circ: 1511
Health & Safety

Habitat Aid Blog
1053174
Tel: 44 01749 812355
Email: info@habitataid.co.uk
Web site: https://www.habitataid.co.uk/
blog/
Freq: Daily
Circ: 13
Environment

Hackney Renters Blog
1055296
Email: hello@hackneyrenters.org
Web site: http://hackneyrenters.org/
Freq: Daily
Circ: 14014
**Property Management & Maintenance,
Residential Real Estate**

Hagen på Knatten
1060802
Web site: http://blomsterknatten.blogspot.
com
Freq: Daily
Circ: 725
Gardening

Haggerston Times
1086851
Email: haggerstontimes@gmail.com
Web site: http://www.haggerston-times.com
Freq: Daily
Circ: 10727
Editor: Edmund Ingham
Computers, Data Management, Software

Hair Advice & All Things Nice
1052947
Email: klg_hair@hotmail.co.uk
Web site: http://www.klghairadvice.com/
Freq: Daily
Circ: 6509
Hair

Hairdressing Blogs
999328
Editorial: Quadrant House, The Quadrant,
Sutton SM2 5AS **Tel:** 44 02086 523500
Email: hj@rbi.co.uk
Web site: www.hji.co.uk/static-pages/blogs-
and-experts
Freq: Daily
Circ: 9293
Beauty & Grooming, Cosmetics, Hair

HakJuNi Dot Com
1060950
Web site: http://poem23.com
Freq: Daily
Circ: 35648
**Auto Aftermarket, Computers, Data
Management, Electronics, Government
Technology, Industry, Internet, Mobile
Communications, Mobile Electronics,
Security & Security Systems**

Halcyon Velvet
1062746
Web site: http://www.halcyonvelvet.co.uk/
Freq: Daily
Circ: 7757
Fashion, Women's Interests

Halfway Hike
1053886
Web site: http://halfwayhike.com/
Freq: Daily
Circ: 9145
Profile: Blog covering hiking. The Halfway
Hike blog discusses anything from hiking
and walking to kit tests and walking events.
Outdoor Recreation

Hallam Internet Blog
1052676
Tel: 44 01159 480123
Email: info@hallaminternet.com
Web site: https://www.hallaminternet.com/
blog/
Freq: Daily
Circ: 38836
Branding, Marketing

Halsbury's Law Exchange Blog
996326
Editorial: 30 Farringdon Street, London
EC4A 4HH
Email: contact@halsburyslawexchange.co.
uk
Web site: http://www.
halsburyslawexchange.co.uk/category/
httplawexchange-lnukapps-co-ukblogblogs

Freq: Daily
Circ: 274
Editor: Sarah Plaka
Criminal Law, Government, Law

Ham and Petersham RPC
1057075
Tel: 44 02089 401366
Email: info@hprpc.co.uk
Web site: http://www.hprpc.co.uk/
Freq: Daily
Circ: 2407
Shooting/Guns

Hamburger Me
988561
Email: burgermelondon@gmail.com
Web site: www.hamburger-me.com
Freq: Daily
Circ: 7575
Profile: Blog covering burger reviews.
Restaurant Reviews

The Hampshire and Water-side Hampshire UK Blog
1053173
Email: steve@forestandwaterside.info
Web site: www.forestandwaterside.info/
Freq: Daily
Circ: 12152
**Business, Field Sports, Outdoor
Recreation, Travel**

Handbag Institute
1061403
Web site: http://web.blogs.clarin.com/wp-
content/cache/supercache/blogs.clarin.com/
lvinsti
Freq: Daily
Circ: 257771
Fashion

Handbags and Cupcakes
996706
Web site: http://www.
handbagsandcupcakes.co.uk/
Freq: Daily
Circ: 7674
**Beauty & Grooming, Cooking & Baking,
Cosmetics, Fashion, Hair, Nutrition,
Travel, Women's Interests**

Handbags to Change bags
1053030
Web site: www.handbagstochangebags.co.
uk
Freq: Daily
Circ: 4833
Profile: Blog covering motherhood.
Handbags to Change bags blog discusses
anything from motherhood and family to
parenting. The blog has an archive dating
back to June 2013.
Family & Parenting, Women's Interests

Handcrafted by Ellapu
1056328
Email: ellapu@gmail.com
Web site: http://ellapu.blogspot.co.uk/
Freq: Daily
Circ: 875
Crafts

Handpicked Media
998967
Editorial: 85a Great Portland Street, London
W1W 7JR **Tel:** 44 02076 121969
Web site: www.handpickedmedia.co.uk
Freq: Daily
Circ: 4804
News & Current Affairs

Hanna Wears
1053689
Email: hannawears@gmail.com
Web site: hannawears.com
Freq: Daily
Circ: 7131
Profile: Hanna Wears covers plus size
fashion and personal style. The blog has an
archive dating back to January 2012 and
shares an extensive blogroll.
Fashion

Hannah Gale Blog
988277
Email: hannahgale@gmail.com
Web site: hannahgale.co.uk
Freq: Daily
Circ: 152209
**Beauty & Grooming, Cosmetics, Fashion,
Hair**

Hannah Leigh blog
988469
Email: hannahleighcontact@yahoo.com
Web site: http://www.hannahleigh.co/
Freq: Daily
Circ: 10228
Fashion

Hannah Maggs
1053443
Web site: www.hannahmaggs.co.uk
Freq: Daily
Circ: 7566
Profile: Blog covering beauty. The HannaH
MaggS blog discusses anything from beauty
and lifestyle to parenting and baby products.
The blog has an archive dating back to
October 2013. The outlet offers RSS (Really
Simple Syndication).
Cosmetics, Family & Parenting

HannahMatcha
1100173
Web site: www.hannahmatcha.com
Freq: Daily
Circ: 1143
**Cameras, Cooking & Baking, Fitness &
Exercise, Women's Interests**

Hannah's Harbours
1053785
Tel: 44 01213 126084
Email: hannahw@cruise.co.uk
Freq: Daily
Marine & Boat Trade, Travel

Happening London
1054240
Email: happening.london@gmail.com
Web site: http://www.happeninglondon.co.
uk/
Freq: Daily
Circ: 10928
**Art, Bars, Clubs & Pubs, Classical/Choral/
Band Music, Comedy, Country, Folk,
Bluegrass, Dance Music, Entertainment,
Jazz & Blues, Lifestyle, Literature**

The Happiness Project London - CEASED AUGUST 2016
998128
Web site: thehappinessprojectlondon.
wordpress.com
Freq: Daily
Circ: 212
**Alcohol & Spirits, Bars, Clubs & Pubs,
Beer, Beverages, Cooking & Baking,
Food, Grocery Stores, Organic Food,
Restaurant Reviews, Vegetarianism &
Veganism**

The Happy Cake + Bake Blogger
1055157
Email: numnumcupcakes@gmail.com
Web site: http://
thehappycakeandbakeblogger.blogspot.ie/
Freq: Daily
Circ: 1387
Cooking & Baking

Happy Loves Rosie
1053915
Email: happylovesrosie@blueyonder.co.uk
Web site: www.happylovesrosie.com/
Freq: Daily
Circ: 2086
**Beauty & Grooming, Cosmetics, Fashion,
Hair**

Happy Mummy
987620
Editorial: 15 Adingtons, Halling Hill, Harlow,
London CM20 3JY
Email: maria@happymummy.co.uk
Web site: happymummy.co.uk
Freq: Daily
Circ: 9581
Profile: Blog covering motherhood,
parenting and pregnancy. The blog has an
archive dating back to September 2014.
Family & Parenting

Harder Blogger Faster
985235
Editorial: 132 - 134 Great Ancoats Street,
Manchester M4 6DE
Email: harderbloggerfaster@hotmail.com
Web site: www.harderbloggerfaster.com
Freq: Daily
Circ: 48296
Profile: Blog covering music. Harder
Blogger Faster is hosted by Vice. The blog
discusses anything from gigs and reviews to

artist interviews and downloads. The blog
has an archive dating back to June 2009.
**Classical/Choral/Band Music, Country,
Folk, Bluegrass, Dance Music, Jazz &
Blues, Music, Pop Music, R&B, Urban,
World, Rap & Hip Hop, Rock Music**

Hari Ghotra Blog
1053243
Web site: http://www.harighotra.co.uk/blog
Freq: Daily
Circ: 8
Cooking & Baking

Haringey Green Party Blog
996350
Editorial: Haringey Green Party, 47 Lea
Court, 143 Broad Lane, London N15 4QH
Email: contact@haringeygreens.org.uk
Web site: https://haringey.greenparty.org.
uk/
Freq: Daily
Circ: 31
Politics

Haringey Liberal Democrats
997018
Editorial: 62 High Street, London N8 7NX
Tel: 44 02083 478214
Email: haringey@haringeylibdems.org
Web site: http://ldharingey.nationbuilder.
com/
Freq: Daily
Circ: 328726
Politics

Harri Travels
996754
Email: harriet.constable@gmail.com
Web site: http://harritravels.com/
Freq: Daily
Circ: 10195
**Bars, Clubs & Pubs, Regional General
Interest, Travel**

Harriet Devine's Blog
988362
Web site: http://harrietdevine.typepad.com/
harriet_devines_blog/
Freq: Daily
Circ: 198997
History, Literature

Hartlepool Family
997150
Editorial: 6 Deerpool Close, Hartlepool,
Hartlepool TS24 0TD **Tel:** 44 01429 599603
Email: hartlepoolfamilyblog@gmail.com
Web site: http://www.hartlepoolfamily.com/
Freq: Daily
Circ: 10486
Family & Parenting, Women's Interests

HartoDel.com
1061577
Web site: http://www.hartodel.com
Freq: Daily
Circ: 521
**Bars, Clubs & Pubs, Basketball, Bicycles,
Billiards, Boating & Yachting,
Bodybuilding, Bowling, Boxing, Classical/
Choral/Band Music, Comedy**

Hastes Kitchen Blog
1073646
Email: enquiries@hasteskitchen.com
Web site: http://hasteskitchen.com/Index.
php/blog/
Freq: Daily
Circ: 7603
**Cooking & Baking, Vegetarianism &
Veganism**

HÅVARD TVEDTEN
1060692
Email: havard@havardtvedten.com
Web site: http://www.havardtvedten.com/
Freq: Daily
Circ: 1017
**Lifestyle, Men's Interests, Preschool,
Regional General Interest, Women's
Interests**

Hazel and Jane's allotment
1054524
Web site: http://hazelandjanesallotment.
blogspot.co.uk/
Freq: Daily
Circ: 1040
Cooking & Baking, Organic Food

HCMovieReviews
1075488
Web site: https://hcmoviereviews.
wordpress.com/

Freq: Daily
Circ: 11462
Editor: Hamish Calvert
Movies & Video

HD Warrior 1057082
Email: smallvideo@mac.com
Web site: http://www.hdwarrior.co.uk
Freq: Daily
Circ: 74986
Movies & Video

Head for Points 987919
Editorial: 2nd Floor, 1 Fore Street,
Moorgate, London EC2Y 9DT
Email: raffles@headforpoints.co.uk
Web site: www.headforpoints.com/
Freq: Daily
Circ: 652508
Editor: Robert Burgess
Travel

Headlines and Deadlines
1053566
Web site: http://alisongow.com/
Freq: Daily
Circ: 852
Publishing

Headset Press 1056569
Email: info@headsetpress.co.uk
Web site: http://www.headsetpress.co.uk/
Freq: Daily
Circ: 9305
Bicycles, Entertainment, Travel

Headspace Perspective 997205
Email: headspace-perspective@outlook.
com
Web site: www.headspace-perspective.com
Freq: Daily
Circ: 7747
News & Current Affairs

The Headwater Travel Blog
1054159
Tel: 44 01606 822578
Email: info@headwater.com
Web site: http://www.headwater.com/blog/
Freq: Daily
Circ: 7
Outdoor Recreation, Travel

**Health and Fitness Travel
Blog** 996425
Editorial: Unit 408, 4th Floor The Light Bulb,
1 Filament Walk, London SW18 4GQ
Tel: 44 02033 978891
Email: info@healthandfitnesstravel.com
Web site: www.healthandfitnesstravel.com/
blog
Freq: Daily
Circ: 30
Fitness & Exercise, Travel

The Health Cloud 997629
Editorial: Health Cloud Ltd, Caerphilly
Web site: http://www.thehealthcloud.co.uk/
Freq: Daily
Circ: 12162
News & Current Affairs

Healthier Mummy 996505
Editorial: 103 Oaklands Road, London W7
2DT
Email: carole@healthiermummy.com
Web site: healthiermummy.com
Freq: Daily
Circ: 6681
Family & Parenting, Nutrition

HealthInsightUK.org 997948
Email: editor@healthinsightuk.org
Web site: http://healthinsightuk.org/
Freq: Daily
Circ: 10121
Cardiology, Diabetes, Health & Medicine,
Nutrition

Healthy Living London 997885
Email: hellofitty@healthylivinglondon.com
Web site: http://healthylivinglondon.com/
Freq: Daily
Circ: 9935
Family & Parenting, Fitness & Exercise,
Nutrition

Healthy Miss Sofit 997067
Editorial: Anderida, Coventry Road,
Fillongley, Coventry CV7 8EQ
Email: miss.sofit.healthy@gmail.com
Web site: http://misssofit.blogspot.co.uk/
Freq: Daily
Circ: 521
Fitness & Exercise, Health & Medicine,
Nutrition

The Healthy Veggie 1054318
Email: elena@thehealthyveggie.com
Web site: http://www.thehealthyveggie.com
Freq: Daily
Circ: 6753
Profile: The Healthy Veggie covers
vegetarian recipes, outdoor adventure,
outdoor gear, kitchen appliances. camping,
hiking, climbing, travel, eco-travel, weekend
breaks and cycling.
Camping and RV Travel, Cooking &
Baking, Field Sports, Vegetarianism &
Veganism

Heard on the Wire 1052778
Web site: http://smithsocksimon.net/
Freq: Daily
Circ: 9700
Classical/Choral/Band Music, Country,
Folk, Bluegrass, Dance Music, Jazz &
Blues, Music, Pop Music, R&B, Urban,
World, Rap & Hip Hop, Rock Music

Heart Handmade UK 987091
Email: hearthandmadeuk@googlemail.com
Web site: http://www.hearthandmade.co.uk
Freq: Daily
Circ: 145721
Architecture & Design, Do-It-Yourself
(DIY), Gardening, Home, Property
Management & Maintenance, Real Estate

Heart Home Blog 997697
Editorial: 4 Oak Crescent, Wickford,
Wickford SS11 7FF
Email: info@hearthomemag.co.uk
Web site: hearthomemag.co.uk/blog/
Freq: Daily
Circ: 182
Do-It-Yourself (DIY)

Heat My Home 999198
Editorial: 44 Panton Road, Chester CH2
3HX
Email: mail@heatmyhome.co.uk
Web site: www.heatmyhome.co.uk/index.
php
Freq: Daily
Circ: 9
Editor: Stuart Lovatt
Alternative/Renewable Energy, Electricity,
Environment

Heather on her travels 986153
Editorial: 22 Henleaze Avenue, Bristol BS9
4ET Tel: 44 01179 623528
Email: heather@heatheronhertravels.com
Web site: www.heatheronhertravels.com
Freq: Daily
Circ: 45828
Airline Inflight, Railroad, Travel

The Hedge Combers 997741
Web site: hedgecombers.com
Freq: Daily
Circ: 16129
Cooking & Baking, Organic Food

Hef's Kitchen 996227
Web site: www.hefskitchen.me
Freq: Daily
Circ: 10121
Alcohol & Spirits, Bars, Clubs & Pubs,
Beer, Beverages, Cooking & Baking,
Food, Grocery Stores, Organic Food,
Restaurant Reviews, Vegetarianism &
Veganism

Heidi Likes 1053499
Web site: http://heidi-likes.blogspot.co.uk/
Freq: Daily
Circ: 6734
Beauty & Grooming, Cosmetics, Fashion,
Hair, Women's Interests

Helen Anderson 998212
Email: helenandersonenquiries@gmail.com
Web site: http://www.helenanderz.com/
Freq: Daily
Circ: 8470
Beauty & Grooming, Cosmetics, Fashion,
Hair

Helen Anderson Vlog 1095191
Email: helenandersonenquiries@gmail.com
Web site: https://www.youtube.com/user/
snakebitesparkles
Freq: Daily
Circ: 14
Beauty & Grooming, Cosmetics, Fashion,
Hair, Women's Interests

Helen Babbs Blog 1053941
Web site: https://helenbabbs.wordpress.
com/
Freq: Daily
Circ: 62
Art, Energy & Environment, Literature,
Photography, Theater & Performing Arts,
Visual Arts

Helen in Wonderlust 1053639
Web site: http://www.heleninwonderlust.co.
uk/
Freq: Daily
Circ: 73477
Profile: Blog covering travel. The Helen in
Wonderlust blog discusses anything from
travel and destinations to travel tips and
volunteering abroad. The blog has an archive
dating back to March 2014 and shares a
short blog roll.
Airline Inflight, Railroad, Travel

Helen Smith Blog 1052925
Email: emperorsclothes@btinternet.com
Web site: www.emperorsclothes.co.uk/
Freq: Daily
Circ: 6514
Literature, Theater & Performing Arts

Helene's Home 1061005
Web site: http://www.heleneshome.
blogspot.co.uk/
Freq: Daily
Circ: 1234
Classical/Choral/Band Music, Country,
Folk, Bluegrass, Dance Music, Jazz &
Blues, Music, Pop Music, R&B, Urban,
World, Rap & Hip Hop, Rock Music

Helge's fotoblogg 1060411
Email: hmro@live.no
Web site: http://helgesfotoblogg.blogspot.
com/
Freq: Daily
Circ: 823
Photography

Hello October 987580
Email: hellooctoberenquiries@gmail.com
Web site: http://www.hello-october.com/
Freq: Daily
Circ: 33728
Profile: Blog covering beauty, skincare and
cosmetics and lifestyle. The blog has an
archive dating back to August 2011 and
shares an extensive blog roll. This outlet also
offers a vlog.
Beauty & Grooming, Cosmetics, Fashion,
Hair, Women's Interests

Hello Tasha 1053761
Email: hellotasha18@hotmail.co.uk
Web site: http://www.hellotasha.co.uk/
Freq: Daily
Circ: 9727
Profile: Hello Tasha covers fashion, beauty
products and lifestyle. The blog has an
archive dating back to August 2012.
Beauty & Grooming, Cosmetics, Fashion,
Hair, Travel

HelloOctoberxo Vlog 1096042
Email: hellooctoberenquiries@gmail.com
Web site: https://www.youtube.com/user/
HelloOctoberxo
Freq: Daily
Circ: 16
Beauty & Grooming, Cosmetics, Fashion,
Hair, Women's Interests

Help Me To Save 986853
Editorial: 33 Riverdene, Berwick-upon-
Tweed TD15 2JD
Web site: helpmetosave.com
Freq: Daily
Circ: 10410
News & Current Affairs

Help me! by Marianne Power
997663
Editorial: 5 New Mile Court, London Road,
Ascot, London SL5 7EH
Email: marianne@helpmeblog.net
Web site: helpmeblog.net
Freq: Daily
Circ: 11347
Beauty & Grooming, Cosmetics, Fashion,
Hair, Men's Interests, Women's Interests

**Helping Innovate Property
(HIP) Blog** 995132
Editorial: HIP Consultant, 61 Weymouth
Drive, Washington DH4 7TQ
Tel: 44 01913 858500
Email: info@hip-consultant.co.uk
Web site: http://www.hip-consultant.co.uk/
blog
Freq: Daily
Circ: 277
Alternative/Renewable Energy,
Architecture & Design, Carbon Emissions
& Trading, Do-It-Yourself (DIY), Electricity,
Energy, Environment, Gardening, Home,
Nuclear Power

Helsbels 987871
Web site: http://helsbels.org.uk/
Freq: Daily
Circ: 7841
Bowling, Fitness & Exercise, Women's
Interests

HenryPryor.com 999488
Web site: henrypryor.com
Freq: Daily
Circ: 12511
Do-It-Yourself (DIY), Property
Management & Maintenance

Henry's Blog 1052752
Web site: http://www.henrysblog.co.uk/
Freq: Daily
Circ: 8732
Family & Parenting

Her Indoors 1052560
Web site: her-indoors.com/
Freq: Daily
Circ: 9937
Profile: Blog covering interior design. The
blog has an archive dating back to
September 2011. The outlet offers RSS
(Really Simple Syndication).
Architecture & Design, Do-It-Yourself
(DIY)

Here Come the Girls 988149
Web site: http://www.herecomethegirlsblog.
com/
Freq: Daily
Circ: 9614
Profile: Blog covering motherhood. The
Here Come The Girls blog discusses
anything from family life and recipes to kids
activities and crafts. The blog has an archive
dating back to March 2014 and shares an
extensive blog roll.
Crafts, Family & Parenting

Hermit Hideaways 1062100
Web site: http://www.hermithideaways.com
Freq: Daily
Circ: 1188
Photography

HerUni 986516
Editorial: Winchester House, 259 Old
Marylebone Road, London NW1 5RA
Email: geraldine@heruni.com
Web site: http://www.hercampus.com/
Freq: Daily
Circ: 1477661
Women's Interests

Hervia Blog 996870
Email: customerservices@hervia.com
Web site: www.hervia.com/blog

Freq: Daily
Circ: 30
Fashion

Hester Society 1054219
Editorial: Highmoor Court, Leeds LS17 6RT
Tel: 44 07846 950867
Web site: http://www.hestersociety.co.uk/
Freq: Daily
Circ: 784
Editor: Dan Hester
Airline Inflight, Alcohol & Spirits, Audio Video Trade, Bars, Clubs & Pubs, Beer, Beverages, Broadcasting, Cameras, Comedy, Consumer Electronics

Heterarchy News 1054089
Editorial: 15 Knighton Lane, Aylestone Park, Leicester LE2 8BH Tel: 44 01217 962070
Email: info@heterarchy.co.uk
Web site: http://faber.design/blog/
Freq: Daily
Architecture & Design, Interior Design

Hex Mum 999644
Editorial: Mill Farm Cottage, Mill Road, Burgh Castle, Great Yarmouth NR31 9QS
Web site: http://www.hexmumblog.com/
Freq: Daily
Circ: 10579
Family & Parenting

Hey Pesto! 1053199
Email: yvonne@heypesto.ie
Web site: http://heypesto.ie/
Freq: Daily
Circ: 9008
Cooking & Baking

Hey! Manchester 998288
Web site: http://www.heymanchester.com/
Freq: Daily
Circ: 9737
Classical/Choral/Band Music, Country, Folk, Bluegrass, Dance Music, Jazz & Blues, Music, Pop Music, R&B, Urban, World, Rap & Hip Hop, Rock Music

HeyAmyJane 987614
Email: thisdystopia13@googlemail.com
Web site: http://www.heyamyjane.com/
Freq: Daily
Circ: 10881
Profile: Blog covering beauty, make up tutorials, beauty product reviews and fashion. This outlet offers a vlog. The Camera's Lying was shortlisted for Cosmo's 'Best Beauty Vlog' and 'Best Established Fashion Blog'.
Beauty & Grooming, Cameras, Cosmetics, Fashion, Hair

HeyUGuys 986156
Editorial: 29 Prince of Wales Road, Sutton SM1 3PE
Email: mouthoff@heyuguys.co.uk
Web site: http://www.heyuguys.com/
Circ: 154999
Profile: Website covering films; test film news and reviews.
Celebrities, Movies & Video

HGVUK.com 997550
Editorial: 1 The Grange, Drumsna, Co. Leitrim Tel: 353 08723 80103
Email: info@hgvuk.com
Web site: www.hgvuk.com
Freq: Daily
Circ: 13505
News & Current Affairs

HHKMAG 1052563
Email: r.maxwell@hip-hopkings.com
Web site: http://www.hip-hopkings.com/
Freq: Daily
Circ: 10791
Profile: Blog covering UK hip hop. The blog has an archive dating back to August 2009.
Rap & Hip Hop

The Hickensian 1054058
Web site: http://hicksdesign.co.uk/journal
Freq: Daily
Circ: 138
Men's Interests

Hidden Harmonies 1060990
Email: allen@hiddenharmonies.org
Web site: http://blog.hiddenharmonies.org
Freq: Daily
Circ: 42
Antiques/Collectibles, Art, Arts, International News, Literature, Photography, Politics, Theater & Performing Arts, Visual Arts

Hide Your Arms - SUSPENDED July 2017 1053358
Email: info@hideyourarms.com
Web site: hideyourarms.com
Freq: Daily
Circ: 22279
Fashion

HiFashion 987935
Web site: www.thehifashionsite.com
Freq: Daily
Circ: 6646
Fashion

Hifi Headphones 1052696
Tel: 44 01903 768910
Email: supportdesk@hifiheadphones.co.uk
Web site: http://www.hifiheadphones.co.uk/reviews
Freq: Daily
Circ: 154
Audio Video Trade

Hijacked by Twins 998363
Email: hijackedbytwins@gmail.com
Web site: www.hijackedbytwins.com
Freq: Daily
Circ: 12002
Family & Parenting

Hiking Equipment Site 1054018
Email: contact@hikingequipmentsite.com
Web site: http://www.hikingequipmentsite.com/blogposts/
Freq: Daily
Circ: 238
Outdoor Recreation, Travel

Hilary Burrage 1054545
Web site: hilaryburrage.com
Freq: Daily
Circ: 13609
Education, International News, Politics, Social Issues

The Hillend Dabbler 1054083
Email: hillenddabbler@hotmail.co.uk
Web site: http://hillenddabbler.blogspot.co.uk/
Freq: Daily
Circ: 1781
Fishing

His Name Is Fashion - CEASED FEBRUARY 2016 1054025
Editorial: Ground Floor Flat, 61 Southwell Road, London SE5 9PF
Web site: http://www.hisnameisfashion.com/
Freq: Daily
Circ: 1804
Profile: Blog covering men's interests and men's high fashion. The blog has an archive dating back to November 2013.
Fashion

History Repeating 1056579
Web site: http://historyrepeating.org.uk/
Freq: Daily
Circ: 10333
Family & Parenting, History

Hi-Tec Inspired Blog 1054189
Editorial: Hi-Tec UK Head Office, Aviation Way, Southend-on-Sea SS2 6GH
Tel: 44 01702 561321
Web site: http://www.hi-tec.co.uk/blog
Freq: Daily
Circ: 95
Outdoor Recreation, Travel

HiTech Review 1058922
Editorial: 150 Locket Road, Harrow, London HA3 7NZ Tel: 44 02081 233324
Web site: http://www.hitechreview.com/

Freq: Daily
Circ: 25093
Editor: Sandi Benditt
Audio Video Trade, Cameras, Computer & Video Games, Consumer Electronics, Mobile Electronics, Movies & Video, Personal Computers

Hivenn 1054198
Email: hivenn@hotmail.com
Web site: www.hivenn.co.uk
Freq: Daily
Circ: 1965
Profile: Blog covering fashion and lifestyle. Hivenn blog discusses anything from personal style and photography to food and lifestyle. The outlet offers RSS (Really Simple Syndication).
Photography

HK Collection blog 995507
Editorial: 37 Staplehurst Road, Hither Green, London SE13 5ND
Tel: 44 02082 440172
Email: info@homeandkids.co.uk
Web site: http://www.blog.homeandkids.co.uk/
Freq: Daily
Circ: 1100
Do-It-Yourself (DIY), Shopping, Women's Interests

Hobby Horse 1053608
Email: griffinpainting@googlemail.com
Web site: http://paintsngluenrocknroll.blogspot.co.uk/
Freq: Daily
Circ: 633
Crafts, Hobbies, & Collecting

Hobo Internet Marketing Blog 1054398
Tel: 44 08450 940839
Email: info@hobo-web.co.uk
Web site: http://www.hobo-web.co.uk/seo-blog/
Freq: Daily
Circ: 453244
Branding, Marketing

Hold The Anchovies Please 996968
Email: holdtheanchoviesplease@yahoo.co.uk
Web site: www.holdtheanchoviesplease.com
Freq: Daily
Circ: 11871
Cooking & Baking, Restaurant Reviews

Hold Your Horses 997732
Editorial: 6 Ordell Court Road, London E3 2DS
Email: info@holdyourhorsesblog.com
Web site: www.holdyourhorsesblog.com
Freq: Daily
Circ: 784
Editor: Paul Joseph
Classical/Choral/Band Music, Country, Folk, Bluegrass, Dance Music, Jazz & Blues, Lifestyle, Men's Interests, Music, Pop Music, R&B, Urban, World, Rap & Hip Hop

HOLDUPNOW 1056571
Email: enquiries@holdupnow.com
Web site: http://holdupnow.com/
Freq: Daily
Circ: 687
Computer & Video Games, Dance Music, Fashion, Lifestyle, Men's Interests, Movies & Video, Music, Photography, Pop Music, Rap & Hip Hop

Holiday Extras Blog 1053164
Tel: 44 08000 935478
Email: hasslefree@holidayextras.com
Web site: www.holidayextras.co.uk/travel-blog.html
Freq: Daily
Circ: 51856
Airline Inflight, Railroad, Travel

Holiday Hype Blog 986271
Editorial: 2nd Floor, Dunedin House, Columbia Drive, Stockton-on-Tees TS17 6BJ
Tel: 44 08009 165189
Email: editor@hypemag.co.uk

Web site: https://www.holidayhypermarket.co.uk/hype/
Circ: 102
Travel

Holiday Parks Blog 1055302
Editorial: Amos Grove, Monkston Park, Milton Keynes MK10 9PP
Tel: 44 08445 618324
Email: enquiry@holidayparkhol.co.uk
Web site: http://www.holidayparkhol.co.uk/news/
Freq: Daily
Circ: 17
Airline Inflight, Railroad, Travel

Holiday Please Blog 1054515
Email: marketing@holidaysplease.com
Web site: http://blog.holidaysplease.co.uk/
Freq: Daily
Circ: 288
Travel

Holiday Safe Blog 1053444
Tel: 44 01732 853355
Email: website@holidaysafe.co.uk
Web site: www.holidaysafe.co.uk/blog
Freq: Daily
Circ: 57
Airline Inflight, Railroad, Travel

holidaycottages.co.uk blog 1052635
Tel: 44 01237 426263
Web site: http://www.holidaycottages.co.uk/blog
Freq: Daily
Circ: 213
Travel

Holidays Please Blog 1056768
Email: admin@holidaysplease.co.uk
Web site: http://blog.holidaysplease.co.uk/
Freq: Daily
Circ: 288
Railroad, Travel

Hollow Legs 986157
Web site: www.lizzieeatslondon.blogspot.com
Freq: Daily
Circ: 5175
Alcohol & Spirits, Bars, Clubs & Pubs, Beer, Beverages, Cooking & Baking, Food, Grocery Stores, Organic Food, Restaurant Reviews, Vegetarianism & Veganism

Holly Bobbin 1054561
Web site: www.hollybobbin.com
Freq: Daily
Circ: 9812
Crafts, Visual Arts, Women's Interests

Holly Bobbs 1053579
Web site: www.hollybobbs.co.uk
Freq: Daily
Circ: 7160
Family & Parenting

Holly Writes 1095581
Web site: http://hollywrites.com/
Freq: Daily
Circ: 521
Art, Literature, Movies & Video, Theater & Performing Arts, Travel

Home and Horizon 1053320
Email: info@homeandhorizon.com
Web site: http://www.homeandhorizon.com
Freq: Daily
Circ: 12159
Do-It-Yourself (DIY), Travel

Home Designing 986537
Email: response@home-designing.com
Web site: http://www.home-designing.com
Freq: Daily
Circ: 668040
Do-It-Yourself (DIY)

Home Gems 1054173
Email: homegems@gmail.com
Web site: www.homegems.net
Freq: Daily
Circ: 1507

UK Blogs

Editor: Rachel Newcombe
Do-It-Yourself (DIY)

The Home of K D Grace & Grace Marshall 1052806
Web site: http://kdgrace.co.uk/
Freq: Daily
Circ: 9636
Literature

The home of the Chelsea FC Blog 986253
Editorial: Chelsea Football Club, Stamford Bridge, Fulham Road, London SW6 1HS
Tel: 44 02079 582190
Web site: http://www.chelseafc.com/http://www.chelseafc.com/news/boilerplate-config/blogs.html
Freq: Daily
Circ: 1340551
Soccer

Home Truths 1052581
Web site: www.home-truths.co.uk/home-selling-blog
Freq: Daily
Circ: 116
News & Current Affairs

Homegirl London 988951
Web site: http://homegirllondon.com/
Freq: Daily
Circ: 11044
Do-It-Yourself (DIY), Women's Interests

Homemade Lure Blog 1055308
Web site: http://homeluremaking.blogspot.co.uk/
Freq: Daily
Circ: 611
News & Current Affairs

The Honest Actors' Podcast & Blog 1054264
Editorial: 240 Mitcham Lane, London SW16 6NU Tel: 44 02086 774679
Email: honestactors@gmail.com
Web site: www.inanything.com
Freq: Daily
Circ: 12770
Broadcasting, Careers, Movies & Video, Theater & Performing Arts

Honest John 986385
Editorial: Unit 4 The Courtyard, Parsons Pool, Shaftesbury SP7 8AL
Email: editor@honestjohn.co.uk
Web site: www.honestjohn.co.uk
Circ: 1900885
Editor: Keith Moody
Driving

Honest Mum 988690
Email: mum@honestmum.com
Web site: honestmum.com
Freq: Daily
Circ: 147764
Family & Parenting, Women's Interests

Honestly Healthy 988564
Editorial: 102a Chepstow Road, London W2 5QW Tel: 44 02074 713360
Email: hello@honestlyhealthyfood.com
Web site: honestlyhealthyfood.com
Freq: Daily
Circ: 48479
Nutrition

Honey Go Lightly 987955
Web site: www.honeygolightly.com
Freq: Daily
Circ: 8652
Beauty & Grooming, Cooking & Baking, Cosmetics, Fashion, Food, Grocery Stores, Hair, Organic Food, Restaurant Reviews, Vegetarianism & Veganism

Honey Pop 988521
Web site: http://honeypopkisses.com/
Freq: Daily
Circ: 9534
News & Current Affairs

The Honeyball Buzz 1053923
Tel: 44 07956 443393
Web site: http://thehoneyballbuzz.com/

Freq: Daily
Circ: 8072
Government

HoneyHype 1061460
Web site: http://joeyc.wordpress.com
Freq: Daily
Circ: 22
Fashion

Hong Kong Fashion Geek 1061762
Email: info@hkfashiongeek.com
Web site: http://www.hkfashiongeek.com
Freq: Daily
Circ: 3235
Fashion, Lifestyle, Men's Interests, Regional General Interest, Women's Interests

Hong Kong food blog 1061683
Web site: http://www.hongkongfoodblog.blogspot.com
Freq: Daily
Circ: 3030
Food

Hooked on the Music 1066388
Web site: hookedonthemusic.blogspot.co.uk
Freq: Daily
Circ: 9837
Classical/Choral/Band Music, Country, Folk, Bluegrass, Dance Music, Jazz & Blues, Music, Pop Music, R&B, Urban, World, Rap & Hip Hop, Rock Music, Women's Interests

Hookedblog 987283
Email: hookedblog@hotmail.com
Web site: www.hookedblog.co.uk
Freq: Daily
Circ: 15345
Antiques/Collectibles, Art, Arts, Literature, Photography, Theater & Performing Arts, Visual Arts

Hooting and Howling 988318
Email: hello@hootingandhowling.com
Web site: http://hootingandhowling.com/
Circ: 12859
Classical/Choral/Band Music, Country, Folk, Bluegrass, Dance Music, Jazz & Blues, Music, Pop Music, R&B, Urban, World, Rap & Hip Hop, Rock Music

Hooting Yard 1054479
Email: hooting.yard@gmail.com
Web site: http://hootingyard.org/
Freq: Daily
Circ: 6151
Literature

Hope Lies At 24 Frames Per Second 987311
Email: adam@hopelies.com
Web site: hopelies.com
Freq: Daily
Circ: 382
Movies & Video

Hope Von-Joel Stylist 1054935
Email: hopevonjoel@gmail.com
Web site: http://hopevonjoel.blogspot.co.uk/
Freq: Daily
Circ: 521
Fashion

Hopkin Looking To Curl One... 998080
Email: hltcotwitter@gmail.com
Web site: http://hltco.org/
Freq: Daily
Circ: 12967
Soccer

Hora del Pueblo 1061030
Web site: http://lahoradelpueblo.blogspot.com
Freq: Daily
Circ: 460
National News, Politics

The Horizons Tracker 996954
Email: admin@adigaskell.org
Web site: www.adigaskell.org

Freq: Daily
Circ: 41553
Business, Computers, Electronics, Internet, Mobile Communications, Small and Medium Business

Hormiga Argenta 1061765
Web site: http://lahormigargenta.blogspot.com/
Freq: Daily
Circ: 1106
Classical/Choral/Band Music, Cooking & Baking, Country, Folk, Bluegrass, Dance Music, Jazz & Blues, Lifestyle, Men's Interests, Movies & Video, Music, Pop Music

Horror Cult Films 987942
Email: contact@horrorcultfilms.co.uk
Web site: horrorcultfilms.co.uk/
Circ: 48753
Computer & Video Games, Movies & Video, Trading Cards & Comics

Horror Movies I Love 1053050
Web site: http://screamqueenarmy.blogspot.co.uk/?zx=f8e24a4e81af22cf
Freq: Daily
Circ: 521
Movies & Video

The Hostel Girl 997628
Email: thehostelgirl@outlook.com
Web site: http://thehostelgirl/
Freq: Daily
Circ: 25852
Airline Inflight, Railroad, Travel

Hostelling International Blog 1054481
Tel: 44 01707 324170
Email: info@hihostels.com
Web site: https://blog.hihostels.com//
Freq: Daily
Airline Inflight, Railroad, Travel

Hostelworld.com Travel Blog 1053264
Editorial: Charlemont Exchange, Charlemont Street, Dublin 2
Email: press@hostelworld.com
Web site: http://www.hostelworld.com/blog/
Freq: Daily
Circ: 157
Regional General Interest, Travel

Hot & Chilli 988306
Web site: www.hotandchilli.com
Freq: Daily
Circ: 11401
Profile: Blog covering travel and food.
Cooking & Baking

Hotwire Blog 1053738
Editorial: 69 Wilson Street, London EC2A 2BB Tel: 44 02076 082500
Email: alex.maclaverty@hotwirepr.com
Web site: http://www.hotwirepr.com/uk/blog-gb
Freq: Daily
Circ: 51
Branding, Marketing

House of Herby 988431
Email: houseofherby@icloud.com
Web site: houseofherby.com
Freq: Daily
Circ: 7964
Profile: Blog covering food. The HOUSE OF HERBY blog discusses anything from food reviews and restaurant reviews to cocktail.
Cooking & Baking, Restaurant Reviews

HousePriceCrash.co.uk 986671
Email: press@housepricecrash.co.uk
Web site: www.housepricecrash.co.uk
Circ: 128696
Profile: Website covering information on house prices within the UK.
Finance, Property Management & Maintenance, Residential Real Estate

Housing Energy Advisor Blog 996471
Editorial: 61 Weymouth Drive, Washington DH4 7TQ Tel: 44 01913 858500
Email: info@housingenergyadvisor.com

Web site: www.housingenergyadvisor.com/blog
Freq: Daily
Circ: 90
Alternative/Renewable Energy, Carbon Emissions & Trading, Electricity, Energy, Nuclear Power, Oil, Sustainable Development, Water & Sanitation

How Green Is Your Life 1054638
Web site: http://www.howgreenisyourlife.co.uk
Freq: Daily
Circ: 784
Do-It-Yourself (DIY), Energy & Environment

How I like my coffe 1053190
Web site: http://howilikemycoffee.blogspot.com
Freq: Daily
Circ: 3264
Family & Parenting, Health & Medicine, Literature, Women's Interests

How Not To Dismantle An Atomic Bomb 997035
Web site: http://hntdaab.co.uk/blog/
Freq: Daily
Circ: 2501
Computer & Video Games

How to Cook Good Food 988546
Web site: www.howtocookgoodfood.co.uk
Freq: Daily
Circ: 9696
Cooking & Baking

How to play house 1053567
Email: howtoplayhouse@gmail.com
Web site: https://howtoplayhouse.com/
Freq: Daily
Circ: 784
Expatriates, Women's Interests

Hoyles Fitness 1053261
Email: steve@hoylesfitness.com
Web site: hoylesfitness.com/blog
Freq: Daily
Circ: 56
Fitness & Exercise, Nutrition

The HR Headmistress' Blog 995037
Editorial: 1 Clare Stables, Vicarage Road, Stony Stratford, Milton Keynes MK11 1BN
Tel: 44 08456 448955
Web site: www.russellhrconsulting.co.uk/blog
Freq: Daily
Circ: 4804
Company News & Appointments, Education, Employment, Health & Safety, Human Resources, Recruiting

HR Transformer blog 1054261
Email: info@glassbeadconsulting.com
Web site: http://www.glassbeadconsulting.com/hr-transformer-blog
Freq: Daily
Circ: 7061
Careers

Huairen Ye Wenrou 1061642
Email: kongkongdr@126.com
Web site: http://blog.sina.com.cn/zjz
Freq: Daily
Circ: 69772
Financial Markets

Huang Hong's Blog in Ilook 1061103
Web site: http://blog.sina.com.cn/honghuang
Freq: Daily
Circ: 219500
Airline Inflight, Railroad, Relationships, Social Issues, Travel

Hubby Helps 1104364
Web site: http://www.hubbyhelps.com/
Freq: Daily
Circ: 9533
Audio Video Trade, Cameras, Consumer Electronics, Electronics, Family & Parenting, Men's Interests, Mobile Electronics, Movies & Video

Hull Echo 1099502
Editorial: 7 Sovereign Way, Kingswood, Hull HU7 3JG
Email: hullecho@gmx.co.uk
Web site: www.hullecho.com
Freq: Daily
Circ: 11500
Editor: Nicky Brockwell
Regional

The Human Cyclist 988298
Email: thehumancyclist@gmail.com
Web site: http://humancyclist.wordpress.com/
Freq: Daily
Circ: 83
Profile: Blog covering cycling. The blog has an archive dating back to August 2013.
Bicycles

Human Kinetics 996196
Editorial: 107 Bradford Road, Leeds LS28 6AT Tel: 44 01132 555665
Email: hk@hkeurope.com
Web site: http://humankinetics.me
Freq: Daily
Circ: 15486
Fitness & Exercise, Sports Medicine

The Human Mannequin 987209
Web site: thehumanmannequin.co.uk
Freq: Daily
Circ: 8847
Profile: Blog covering fashion. The Human Mannequin blog discusses anything from fashion and lifestyle to modeling. The blog has an archive dating back to December 2012 and shares a short blog roll.
Beauty & Grooming, Cooking & Baking, Cosmetics, Crafts, Do-It-Yourself (DIY), Electronics, Fashion, Hair, Luxury Goods, Nature & Wildlife

Human Sea 1052983
Email: humanseavintage@gmail.com
Web site: http://www.humanseavintage.com/
Freq: Daily
Circ: 1618
Profile: Blog covering fashion. The Human Sea blog discusses anything from vintage clothing and charity shops to homeware and fashion accessories. The blog has an archive dating back to February 2009 and shares a short blog roll. The outlet offers RSS (Really Simple Syndication).
Do-It-Yourself (DIY), Fashion, Photography, Regional General Interest, Travel, Women's Interests

Humedales de Bogotá 1061708
Web site: http://humedalesbogota.wordpress.com/
Freq: Daily
Circ: 7
Environment, Science

Hungerford Salvi Carr Blog 1055301
Tel: 44 02072 993322
Email: westend@h-s-c.co.uk
Web site: http://blog.hurford-salvi-carr.co.uk/
Freq: Daily
Circ: 251
Property Management & Maintenance

Hungry Aphrodite 996638
Editorial: 76 Ottways Lane, Ashtead, London KT21 2PW
Email: hungryaphrodite@yahoo.com
Web site: www.hungryaphrodite.com
Freq: Daily
Circ: 9834
Beauty & Grooming, Cooking & Baking, Cosmetics, Hair, Regional General Interest, Restaurant Reviews, Women's Interests

Hungry Healthy Happy 987809
Email: dannii@hungryhealthyhappy.com
Web site: www.hungryhealthyhappy.com/
Freq: Daily
Circ: 138844
Cooking & Baking, Fitness & Exercise, Nutrition, Travel

The hungry writer 998041
Editorial: The Applehouse, Aldon Manor, Aldon Lane, West Malling ME19 5PH
Email: lynne@lynnerees.com
Web site: http://www.lynnerees.com/
Freq: Daily
Circ: 9670
News & Current Affairs

HungryCityHippy 996552
Email: thehungrycityhippy@outlook.com
Web site: hungrycityhippy.co.uk
Freq: Daily
Circ: 12701
Beauty & Grooming, Cooking & Baking, Cosmetics, Environment, Hair, Restaurant Reviews, Travel

Hunting English 1053928
Web site: http://www.theconfidentteacher.com/
Freq: Daily
Circ: 16871
News & Current Affairs

Hurrah for Gin 988250
Web site: http://hurrahforgin.com
Freq: Daily
Circ: 27870
Profile: Blog covering lifestyle, motherhood, family and parenting. The blog has an archive dating back to July 2013 and shares an extensive blog roll.
News & Current Affairs

The Hush 995135
Editorial: Flat 2, Acton Apartments, 13 Branch Place, London N1 5PH
Tel: 44 07793 274172
Email: beth-roberts@hotmail.co.uk
Web site: http://thehush.me/
Freq: Daily
Circ: 521
Travel

Hybrid Hive 1075504
Email: editor@thehybridhive.com
Web site: www.thehybridhive.com
Freq: Daily
Circ: 14338
Computers, Internet, Mobile Communications

Hynd's blog 997468
Tel: 44 07903 569531
Email: stevehynd24@gmail.com
Web site: http://stevehynd.com/
Freq: Daily
Circ: 9559
Editor: Steve Hynd
International News, National News, Politics

Hypnotherapy Directory 999403
Editorial: Building 3, Riverside Way, Camberley GU15 3YL Tel: 44 01276 300138
Email: press@hypnotherapy-directory.org.uk
Web site: http://www.hypnotherapy-directory.org.uk/blog/
Freq: Daily
Circ: 7
Alternative Medicine

The Hysterectomy Association Blog 997571
Email: info@hysterectomy-association.org.uk
Web site: https://www.hysterectomy-association.org.uk/blog/
Freq: Daily
Circ: 22630
Obstetrics & Gynecology (OB/GYN)

I Am Fabulicious 986519
Tel: 44 07766 525430
Email: sarah@iamfabulicious.com
Web site: www.iamfabulicious.com
Freq: Daily
Circ: 548
Beauty & Grooming, Celebrities, Cosmetics, Hair

I CAN Communicate 997964
Editorial: 31 Angel Gate (Gate 5), Goswell Road, London EC1V 2PT
Tel: 44 02078 432510
Email: info@ican.org.uk

Web site: http://blog.ican.org.uk/
Freq: Daily
Circ: 7107
Charitable Foundations

I Covet Thee 988505
Web site: icovetthee.com
Freq: Daily
Circ: 33564
Profile: Blog covering beauty, cosmetics, make-up tutorials, beauty products and skincare. The blog has an archive dating back to April 2011 and shares an extensive blog roll. This outlet offers RSS (Really Simple Syndication).
Beauty & Grooming, Cosmetics, Fashion, Hair

I Covet Thee Vlog 1096039
Email: icovettheeenquiries@gmail.com
Web site: https://www.youtube.com/user/icovetthee
Freq: Daily
Circ: 10
Beauty & Grooming, Cosmetics, Fashion, Hair, Women's Interests

I Dress Myselff 998246
Email: psickly@gmail.com
Web site: http://idressmyselff.blogspot.com
Freq: Daily
Circ: 8965
News & Current Affairs

I Heart Beauty 1053901
Editorial: 36 Buckingham Court, 48 Kensington Park Road, London W11 3PB
Web site: iheartbeauty.net
Freq: Daily
Circ: 12065
Profile: Blog covering beauty, cosmetics, skincare, anti-ageing, haircare, nutritional supplements, cosmetic procedures. The blog has an archive dating back to September 2013.
Cosmetics

I Heart Cosmetics 986160
Email: iheartcosmetics1@gmail.com
Web site: www.iheartcosmetics.co.uk
Freq: Daily
Circ: 13861
Beauty & Grooming, Cosmetics, Hair

I J Golding Blog 1070230
Web site: http://www.ijgolding.com/
Freq: Daily
Circ: 15133
Banking, Business, Corporate Responsibility, Education, Small and Medium Business

I think I just blogged myself 1056306
Web site: http://www.ithinkijustbloggedmyself.com/
Freq: Daily
Circ: 752
Careers, Literature, Travel, Women's Interests

I Want To Read That 1054012
Email: iwanttoreadthat@btinternet.com
Web site: http://www.iwanttoreadthat.com/
Freq: Daily
Circ: 1932
Literature

I Want You To Know 987088
Email: kristabel@iwantyoutoknow.co.uk
Web site: www.iwantyoutoknow.co.uk
Freq: Daily
Circ: 53598
Fashion

I was just thinking 1099266
Web site: http://tolitasmusings.blogspot.co.uk
Freq: Daily
Circ: 1335
Entertainment, Jazz & Blues, Literature, Movies & Video, Pop Music, Rap & Hip Hop, Theater & Performing Arts, Travel

I was just thinking... 997641
Email: blestchica@gmail.com
Web site: http://tolitasmusings.blogspot.co.uk/
Freq: Daily
Circ: 1335
Antiques/Collectibles, Art, Arts, Literature, Photography, Theater & Performing Arts, Visual Arts

Iain Broome's Blog 997589
Email: hello@iainbroome.com
Web site: http://www.iainbroome.com/blog
Freq: Daily
News & Current Affairs

Iain Claridge Blog 1056581
Web site: http://www.iainclaridge.co.uk/blog/
Freq: Daily
Circ: 30552
Art, Visual Arts

Iain Dale 986159
Email: iain@iaindale.com
Web site: www.iaindale.com
Freq: Daily
Circ: 19358
Politics

Ian Fraser blog 1053037
Web site: http://www.ianfraser.org/category/blog/
Freq: Daily
Circ: 301
Banking, Business, Economics, Politics

Ian James Parsley Blog 1053957
Tel: 44 07956 045764
Email: info@ultonia.com
Web site: https://ianjamesparsley.wordpress.com/
Freq: Daily
Circ: 347
Government Technology, Public Sector

Ian Parnell Photography 1053538
Tel: 44 01142 490793
Email: ianparnellphotography@yahoo.co.uk
Web site: http://ianparnellphotography.blogspot.co.uk/
Freq: Daily
Circ: 913
Outdoor Recreation, Photography, Travel

Ian Shires 1057073
Email: shiresi@walsall.gov.uk
Web site: http://ianshires.mycouncillor.org.uk/
Freq: Daily
Circ: 78
Politics

iand.net 1053681
Web site: iand.net
Freq: Daily
Circ: 10489
Apple, Cameras, Computer & Video Games, Personal Computers

IanVisits 987352
Web site: www.ianvisits.co.uk
Freq: Daily
Circ: 93255
News & Current Affairs

Iced Gem Bakes 996904
Web site: http://www.icedgembakes.co.uk/special-diet-blog/
Freq: Daily
Cooking & Baking

Iced Jems 988628
Web site: www.icedjems.com
Freq: Daily
Circ: 3268
Profile: Blog covering baking and recipes. The blog has an archive dating back to December 2010.
Cooking & Baking

ICIS Blogs 999307
Editorial: RBI Ltd, Quadrant House, The Quadrant, London SM2 5AS
Tel: 44 02086 523335
Email: csc@icis.com
Web site: icis.com/blogs/

Freq: Daily
Circ: 25432
Alternative/Renewable Energy, Carbon Emissions & Trading, Electricity, Energy, Nuclear Power, Oil, Water & Sanitation

iCrossing 1053238
Editorial: 22 Chapter Street, 2nd Floor, London SW1P 4NP **Tel:** 44 02078 212300
Email: georgina.wright@icrossing.co.uk
Web site: www.icrossing.co.uk/uk/ideas
Freq: Daily
Circ: 30084
Advertising Industry, Branding, Data Management, Internet, Marketing

ICS Volunteer Blogs 998213
Editorial: Rougier House, 5 Rougier Street, York Y01 6HZ **Tel:** 44 01904 647799
Email: contact@internationalservice.org.uk
Web site: http://www.internationalservice.org.uk/news/volunteer-blogs.html
Freq: Daily
Circ: 930
Charitable Foundations

ICS Volunteer Blogs - Burkina Faso 1004079
Email: isburkinafaso@gmail.com
Web site: http://www.internationalservice.org.uk/work_with_us/blogs.html
Freq: Daily
Circ: 262
News & Current Affairs

ICT Evangelist 1054291
Web site: http://ictevangelist.com/
Freq: Daily
Circ: 53248
Education

Idea Idea 1061655
Web site: http://www.ideaxidea.com/
Freq: Daily
Circ: 126015
Auto Aftermarket, Computers, Data Management, Electronics, Government Technology, Industry, Internet, Mobile Communications, Security & Security Systems, Software

Ideas About Communication 1053200
Email: nedpotter@ymail.com
Web site: http://www.ned-potter.com/blog/
Freq: Daily
Circ: 6723
Advertising Industry, Branding, Business, Education, Marketing, Publishing

Ideas Arquitecturadas 1061513
Web site: http://ideas-arquitecturadas.blogspot.com
Freq: Daily
Circ: 1224
Architecture & Design, Urban Planning & Development

Ideas Matter Blog 996684
Email: info@ideasmatter.com
Web site: ideasmatter.com
Freq: Daily
Circ: 8989
Intellectual Property

Identidad Politica 1061651
Web site: http://www.identidad-politica.blogspot.com
Freq: Daily
Circ: 521
National News, Politics

Identity Designed 987309
Web site: identitydesigned.com
Freq: Daily
Circ: 42555
News & Current Affairs

Idolator 999579
Email: idolatordotcom@gmail.com
Web site: idolator.com
Freq: Daily
Circ: 319460
Pop Music

If Looks Could Kill 1056320
Editorial: 21 Young St, Edinburgh EH2 4HU
Tel: 44 01313 444638
Email: hello@iflookscouldkill.co.uk
Web site: www.iflookscouldkill.co.uk
Freq: Daily
Circ: 6275
Graphic Design, Visual Arts

IFAW Blog 997558
Editorial: 87-90 Albert Embankment, London SE1 7UD **Tel:** 44 02075 876700
Email: info-uk@ifaw.org
Web site: http://www.ifaw.org/united-kingdom/news
Freq: Daily
Circ: 22
Animal Farming, Charitable Foundations

Iglu Cruise Blog 986405
Editorial: 165 The Broadway, Wimbledon, London SW19 1NE **Tel:** 44 02085 446428
Email: editor@iglu.com
Web site: www.iglucruise.com/blog
Freq: Daily
Circ: 9563
News & Current Affairs

IgluSki Blog 996579
Editorial: 165 The Broadway, Wimbledon, London SW19 1NE **Tel:** 44 02031 316008
Email: editor@iglu.com
Web site: igluski.com/blog
Freq: Daily
Circ: 472
Travel, Winter Sports

Ignacio Serrano 1061212
Web site: http://ignacio-serrano.blogspot.com/
Freq: Daily
Circ: 521
News & Current Affairs

Ignacio Urbina 1061527
Email: info@ignaciourbina.com
Web site: http://www.di-conexiones.com
Freq: Daily
Circ: 11296
Engineering

Iguana del Ojete 1060953
Web site: http://iguanadelojete.blogspot.com
Freq: Daily
Circ: 1871
Celebrities, Social Issues

ihubbub 987232
Tel: 44 02081 336375
Email: team@ihubbbub.com
Web site: http://ihubbub.com/home-business-blog
Circ: 174
Editor: Paula Wynne
Profile: iHubbub is a social networking community to connect home businesses, freelancers, authors, remote workers and home workers.
News & Current Affairs

Illamasqua Blog 1053668
Editorial: 6-8 AMWELL STREET, London EC1R 1UQ **Tel:** 44 08449 841700
Email: freya.barry@illamasqua.com
Web site: http://www.illamasqua.com/blog/
Freq: Daily
Circ: 6227
Cosmetics, Fashion

Ilmastohuijaus 1060810
Email: hannu_tanskanen@yahoo.com
Web site: http://ilmastohuijaus.blogspot.com
Freq: Daily
Circ: 1153
Environment, Internet

Ilmastorealismia 1061639
Web site: http://ilmastorealismia.blogspot.fi/
Freq: Daily
Circ: 1850
Environment, Internet, Science

Ilmastotieto 1061294
Web site: http://ilmastotieto.wordpress.com
Freq: Daily

Circ: 48
Environment, Internet

ilovecakeandtea 988040
Email: ilovecakeandtea@hotmail.com
Web site: ilovecakeandtea.wordpress.com
Freq: Daily
Circ: 23
Profile: Blog covering the London food scene. ILOVECAKEANDTEA discusses anything from restaurants and product reviews to bars, food events and pop ups. The blog has an archive dating back to September 2011.
Bars, Clubs & Pubs, Restaurant Reviews

I'm a damn student, what do I know? 997034
Web site: www.eventmanagementstudent.com
Freq: Daily
Circ: 10246
Marketing

I'm an Airhead 1061335
Web site: http://www.henevia.com
Freq: Daily
Circ: 8710
Men's Interests

Im Chef 1060697
Web site: http://www.imchef.org/
Freq: Daily
Circ: 33496
Cooking & Baking, Food

I'm Counting UFOs 998204
Web site: imcountingufoz.com
Freq: Daily
Circ: 5569
Family & Parenting

Imágenes Urbanas 1061034
Web site: http://imagenes-urbanas.blogspot.com/
Freq: Daily
Circ: 9415
Architecture & Design, Fashion, Visual Arts, Women's Interests

Image-Restore Blog 1053450
Email: neil@image-restore.co.uk
Web site: www.image-restore.co.uk/blog
Freq: Daily
Circ: 10
Photography

Imagination Technologies Blog 1053011
Editorial: Imagination Technologies, Imagination House, Concept House & Pinnacle House, Home Park Estate, Kings Langley WD4 8LZ **Tel:** 44 01923 260511
Email: press@imgtec.com
Web site: https://www.imgtec.com/blog/
Freq: Daily
Circ: 14
Computers

The imagination tree 988322
Web site: theimaginationtree.com
Freq: Daily
Circ: 127141
Family & Parenting

Imagine Travel Blog 1053304
Tel: 44 02031 119131
Email: info@imaginetravel.com
Web site: http://blog.imaginetravel.com/
Freq: Daily
Circ: 1054
Airline Inflight, Railroad, Travel

ImALondoner 997940
Editorial: Flat 6, 55 Whytecliffe Road South, London CR8 2FF **Tel:** 44 07540 856537
Email: info@imalondoner.com
Web site: http://imalondoner.com/
Freq: Daily
Circ: 13615
Local Entertainment Guides, Men's Interests, Restaurant Reviews, Women's Interests

Immy May 998055
Editorial: Floor 4, 181 Sellincourt Road, Tooting, London SW17 9SD

Email: immymay.enquiries@gmail.com
Web site: immymay.com
Freq: Daily
Circ: 10168
Beauty & Grooming, Cooking & Baking, Cosmetics, Fashion, Hair, Organic Food, Restaurant Reviews, Travel, Women's Interests

i-motherhood 1053049
Web site: http://i-motherhood.com/
Freq: Daily
Circ: 870
Family & Parenting, Women's Interests

Imperfect Matter 987353
Email: imperfectmatter@gmail.com
Web site: www.imperfectmatter.com
Freq: Daily
Circ: 25484
Profile: Blog covering health and fitness. Imperfect Matter blog discusses anything from exercise and fitness regimes to fashion and dance. The blog has an archive dating back to February 2013. The outlet offers RSS (Really Simple Syndication).
Fitness & Exercise, Nutrition

Imperica 997109
Editorial: The River Office, Salter Brothers Yard, Folly Bridge, Oxford OX1 4LB
Tel: 44 01865 600989
Email: hello@imperica.com
Web site: imperica.com
Freq: Daily
Circ: 13132
Art, Audio Video Trade, Cameras, Consumer Electronics, Mobile Electronics, Movies & Video, Visual Arts

Implausible Blog 1063145
Email: askus@implausibleblog.com
Web site: implausibleblog.com
Freq: Daily
Circ: 3374
Airline Inflight, Cooking & Baking, Food, Grocery Stores, Lifestyle, Men's Interests, Organic Food, Railroad, Regional General Interest, Restaurant Reviews

Improving Teaching 1052792
Web site: http://improvingteaching.co.uk/
Freq: Daily
Circ: 13659
Profile: Blog covering education. IMPROVING TEACHING blog discusses anything from education and books to ethics and history. The blog has an archive dating back to August 2013.
Education

Impuestos Mexico 1061980
Web site: http://www.robnovelo.com
Freq: Daily
Circ: 36321
Banking

In a bun dance 1053675
Web site: http://ellenarnison.com/
Freq: Daily
Circ: 9940
Family & Parenting, Literature

In the Frow 987405
Email: inthefrow@live.com
Web site: http://www.inthefrow.com/
Freq: Daily
Circ: 143521
Beauty & Grooming, Cosmetics, Fashion, Hair, Women's Interests

In the Playroom 988712
Web site: intheplayroom.co.uk
Freq: Daily
Circ: 157087
Profile: Blog covering motherhood. In The Playroom blog discusses anything from play ideas and children's activities to family day's out and parenting.
Family & Parenting

In the space of reasons 1053720
Web site: http://inthespaceofreasons.blogspot.com
Freq: Daily
Circ: 8905
Neurology

Inbound Marketing blog 1053330
Editorial: Unit 13 - 15, Fazeley Studios, 191
Fazeley Street, Birmingham B5 5SE
Tel: 44 01217 534499
Web site: http://blog.tomorrow-people.com/
Freq: Daily
Circ: 366
Advertising Industry, Branding,
Broadcasting, Graphic Design, Marketing,
Media & Communications, Photography,
Publishing

Incisos 1061194
Web site: http://blogs.eluniversal.com/eu3/
Blogs/incis_index.shtml
Freq: Daily
Circ: 17622
National News, Politics

The Incredible Suit 998207
Web site: http://theincrediblesuit.blogspot.
co.uk/
Freq: Daily
Circ: 11170
Movies & Video

Indelible Pieces 988370
Email: indeliblepieces@gmail.com
Web site: www.indeliblepieces.com
Freq: Daily
Circ: 10709
Editor: Kerry Anderson
Profile: Blog covering film reviews,
television, books and lifestyle. The blog has
an archive dating back to January 2011.
Broadcasting, Literature, Movies & Video,
Regional General Interest, Travel

India Uncut Blog 1061331
Web site: http://www.indiauncut.com/iublog
Freq: Daily
Circ: 18
Bars, Clubs & Pubs, Comedy, Consumer
Affairs, Crime & Violence, Defense &
National Security, Energy & Environment,
Entertainment, Ethical/Moral Issues,
International News, Law

Indie Travel Podcast 998422
Web site: http://indietravelpodcast.com/
Freq: Daily
Circ: 39731
Travel

Individualism 1053421
Web site: http://www.individualism.co.uk/
Freq: Daily
Circ: 4310
Fashion, Men's Interests

INDSCENE 1056773
Email: contact@indscene.net
Web site: http://indscene.net/
Freq: Daily
Circ: 18204
Classical/Choral/Band Music, Country,
Folk, Bluegrass, Dance Music, Jazz &
Blues, Music, Pop Music, R&B, Urban,
World, Rap & Hip Hop, Rock Music

Influencer Relations 1053362
Web site: http://www.influencerelations.
com/
Freq: Daily
Circ: 18316
Branding, Business

Informatica XP 1061233
Web site: http://www.informaticaxp.net
Freq: Daily
Circ: 1197
Auto Aftermarket, Computers, Data
Management, Electronics, Government
Technology, Industry, Internet, Mobile
Communications, Security & Security
Systems, Software

Information Literacy Weblog
1054395
Web site: http://information-literacy.
blogspot.com
Freq: Daily
Circ: 14508
Education, Literature

Information Overlord 1052774
Web site: http://informationoverlord.co.uk/

Freq: Daily
Circ: 10103
Law, Literature

Informatorio 1061707
Web site: http://elinformatorio.blogspot.
com/
Freq: Daily
Circ: 11429
Auto Aftermarket, Business, Computers,
Data Management, Electronics,
Government Technology, Health &
Medicine, Industry, Internet, Mobile
Communications

Informed Choice 1053309
Email: hello@icfp.co.uk
Web site: http://www.icfp.co.uk/
Freq: Daily
Circ: 12027
Economics, Personal Finance

InFormed London 988737
Email: info@informedlondon.com
Web site: http://informedlondon.com/
Freq: Daily
Circ: 8081
Regional General Interest

Ingenieria y Construccion
1060478
Web site: http://www.facingyconst.
blogspot.com
Freq: Daily
Circ: 10354
Basketball, Bicycles, Billiards, Boating &
Yachting, Bodybuilding, Bowling, Boxing,
Building & Construction, Cricket,
Engineering

Ingeniero Civil 1061438
Web site: http://www.ingciv-sandrus.
blogspot.com
Freq: Daily
Circ: 521
Architecture & Design, Auto Aftermarket,
Building & Construction, Computers, Data
Management, Electronics, Government
Technology, Industry, Internet, Mobile
Communications

Inghams 987712
Editorial: Mountain House, Station Road,
Godalming, Godalming GU7 1EX
Tel: 44 01483 791045
Email: boforeyoutravel@inghams.co.uk
Web site: blog.inghams.co.uk
Freq: Daily
Circ: 875
Profile: Blog covering travel, holidays and
outdoor recreation and specialises in ski,
lakes and mountain holidays. The blog has
an archive dating back to December 2012.
Travel, Winter Sports

**Ingram Micro Mobility UK
Blog** 1053711
Tel: 44 08708 490225
Web site: http://ukblog.im-mobility.com/
Freq: Daily
Circ: 13
Mobile Electronics

Inhimillinen turhamaisuus
1061587
Email: turhamaisuus@hotmail.com
Web site: http://www.
inhimillinenturhamaisuus.com/
Freq: Daily
Circ: 1094
Fashion, Fitness & Exercise, Lifestyle,
Men's Interests, Regional General
Interest, Women's Interests

Ink On My Fingers 988161
Web site: http://pinkleart.blogspot.co.uk/
Freq: Daily
Circ: 1814
Crafts

Inmobiliaria 7 1060855
Web site: http://www.inmobiliaria7.com
Freq: Daily
Circ: 1748
Property Management & Maintenance

The Inn Way 1054576
Tel: 44 01423 871750
Email: info@teamwalking.co.uk
Web site: http://innway.blogspot.co.uk/
Freq: Daily
Circ: 10481
Outdoor Recreation, Travel

Innocent Charms Chat 1053682
Web site: http://innocentcharmschats.co.uk/
Freq: Daily
Circ: 10195
Profile: Blog covering motherhood. The
Innocent Charms Chat blog discusses
anything from motherhood and family days
out to product reviews.
Beauty & Grooming, Cosmetics, Do-It-
Yourself (DIY), Family & Parenting,
Fashion, Hair

Innovate UK Blog 1053688
Tel: 44 01793 442700
Email: pressoffice@innovateuk.gov.uk
Web site: https://innovateuk.blog.gov.uk/
Freq: Daily
Circ: 80983
Business, Government Technology,
Industry, Science

INRNG 1052804
Email: mail@inrng.com
Web site: http://inrng.com/
Freq: Daily
Circ: 93989
Bicycles

Inside Croydon 986589
Email: inside.croydon@btinternet.com
Web site: insidecroydon.com
Circ: 15708
Politics, Regional, Regional General
Interest, Social Issues

The Inside Edit 1098955
Email: hello@the-inside-edit.com
Web site: http://the-inside-edit.com/
Freq: Daily
Circ: 9773
Family & Parenting, Men's Interests,
Women's Interests

Inside The Box 1052569
Web site: insidethebox.reviews
Freq: Daily
Circ: 3802
Computer & Video Games

**Inside the mind of a bib-
liophile** 1056561
Web site: http://www.allsortsofbooks.
blogspot.co.uk/
Freq: Daily
Circ: 521
Entertainment, Literature

Inside the Travel Lab 986161
Email: web@silverfootprint.co.uk
Web site: insidethetravellab.com
Freq: Daily
Circ: 84423
Airline Inflight, Railroad, Travel

Inside the Wendy House 986477
Email: wendy_mcd83@hotmail.com
Web site: www.insidethewendyhouse.
blogspot.com
Freq: Daily
Circ: 7050
Family & Parenting

Inside View from Ireland 1054166
Web site: http://irish.typepad.com/irisheyes/
Freq: Daily
Circ: 824060
Auto Aftermarket, Computers, Data
Management, Electronics, Government
Technology, Industry, Internet, Mobile
Communications, Security & Security
Systems, Software

Inside Wiltshire 1053569
Web site: http://www.insidewiltshire.co.uk/
inside-wiltshire-news/
Freq: Daily
Circ: 399
Regional General Interest

The Inn Way — see above
Inside-Out 986506
Editorial: TopShop TopMan, Colegrave
House, 70 Berners Street, London W1T 3NL
Web site: http://www.topshop.com/blog/
Freq: Daily
Circ: 33541
Fashion, Men's Interests, Women's
Interests

**Inspiration Destination Chal-
lenge Blog** 1056584
Email: inspirationdestinationcb@gmail.com
Web site: http://
inspirationdestinationchallengeblog.
blogspot.co.uk/
Freq: Daily
Circ: 877
Crafts

Instant Ramen 1061133
Freq: Daily
Bars, Clubs & Pubs, Comedy,
Entertainment, Local Entertainment
Guides, Movies & Video

Institute for Government blog
997656
Editorial: 2 Carlton Gardens, London SW1Y
5AA Tel: 44 02077 470400
Email: enquiries@instituteforgovernment.
org.uk
Web site: http://www.
instituteforgovernment.org.uk/blog/
Freq: Daily
Circ: 74
Politics

Institute of Fundraising 988673
Editorial: Charter House, 13 - 15 Carteret
Street, London SW1H 9DJ
Tel: 44 02078 401000
Email: press@institute-of-fundraising.org.uk
Web site: http://www.institute-of-
fundraising.org.uk/blog/
Freq: Daily
Circ: 52
Charitable Foundations

Institute of Race Relations
997232
Editorial: 2 - 6 Leeke Street, Kings Cross
Road, London WC1X 9HS
Tel: 44 02078 370041
Email: news@irr.org.uk
Web site: http://www.irr.org.uk/
Freq: Daily
Circ: 19598
Politics

Insula Dulcamara 1060786
Web site: http://flordeladulcamara.blogspot.
com
Freq: Daily
Circ: 2156
Antiques/Collectibles, Art, Arts,
Literature, Photography, Theater &
Performing Arts, Visual Arts

Insulin Independent 1053463
Web site: http://www.insulinindependent.
com/
Freq: Daily
Circ: 2710
Diabetes

IntelligentHQ 998414
Email: editor@intelligenthq.com
Web site: http://www.intelligenthq.com/
Freq: Daily
Circ: 155870
Editor: Fidan Aliyeva
Business, Industry, Small and Medium
Business

IntelliHeat Blog 999309
Editorial: Unit 18 Napier Place, Stephenson
Way, Thetford IP24 3RL
Tel: 44 08451 630055
Email: contact@intelligentheat.co.uk
Web site: intelligentheat.co.uk/blog/
Freq: Daily
Circ: 36
Electricity

InterArtix 1061899
Web site: http://www.interartix.com
Freq: Daily

UK Blogs

Circ: 2725
Auto Aftermarket, Computers, Data Management, Electronics, Government Technology, Industry, Internet, Mobile Communications, Security & Security Systems, Software

Interesante
1060794
Web site: http://www.lointeresante.com
Freq: Daily
Circ: 339
Computer & Video Games, Literature

Interesting Literature
996775
Email: interestinglit2@gmail.com
Web site: interestingliterature.com/
Freq: Daily
Circ: 150149
Literature

International Adventures
995024
Editorial: INTL, 1 Hardman Street, Manchester M3 3HF
Email: landy@intladventures.com
Web site: http://www.intladventures.com/
Freq: Daily
Circ: 3858
Editor: Brad Roscoe
Travel

International Criminal Law Bureau Blog
999310
Editorial: 9 Bedford Row, London WC1R 4AZ Tel: 44 02074 892727
Email: case@internationallawbureau.com
Web site: internationallawbureau.com
Freq: Daily
Circ: 1446
Crime & Violence, Law

intheboatshed.net
1054269
Web site: intheboatshed.net
Freq: Daily
Circ: 7494
Boating & Yachting

Inthefrow Vlog
1095583
Editorial: PO Box - Victoria, Gleam Features, 60 Charlotte Street, London W1T 2NU
Email: victoria@gleamfutures.com
Web site: https://www.youtube.com/user/inthefrow
Freq: Daily
Circ: 20
Beauty & Grooming, Cosmetics, Fashion, Hair, Travel, Women's Interests

InTheKitchenWithKate
1098976
Email: kate@kameleon.co.uk
Web site: https://www.youtube.com/user/InTheKitchenWithKate
Freq: Daily
Cooking & Baking

Intoruth
1053232
Web site: http://www.intoruth.com/
Freq: Daily
Circ: 8700
Profile: IntoRuth covers lifestyle and things to do. The blog has an archive dating back to May 2009.
Do-It-Yourself (DIY), Fashion, Photography, Regional General Interest, Travel, Women's Interests

Intraskope
1061116
Web site: http://intraskope.wordpress.com
Freq: Daily
Circ: 29
Company News & Appointments, Education, Health & Safety, Human Resources, Recruiting

Intrigue Me Now...
1054028
Email: inga@intriguemenow.co.uk
Web site: www.intriguemenow.co.uk
Freq: Daily
Circ: 3684
Fashion, Women's Interests

Investor Profile
996216
Editorial: 230 Acre Lane, Northampton NN2 8DX Tel: 44 01604 211234
Email: me@investorprofile.co.uk
Web site: http://investorprofile.co.uk/blog/
Freq: Daily

Circ: 24
Investment Banking, Personal Finance

Invitaciones para Quinceañeras
1062060
Web site: http://www.invitaciones15.com
Freq: Daily
Circ: 917
Crafts, Hobbies, & Collecting, Shopping

The IPKat
1054513
Email: theipkat@gmail.com
Web site: http://ipkitten.blogspot.co.uk/
Freq: Daily
Circ: 16050
Intellectual Property

Ipso Jure
1053456
Web site: http://ipso-jure.blogspot.com
Freq: Daily
Circ: 1402
Law

Ireland's Technology blog
1053314
Email: info@irelandstechnologyblog.com
Web site: http://irelandstechnologyblog.com/
Freq: Daily
Circ: 144902
Computer & Video Games, Mobile Electronics

Irena D World
988408
Email: irenadmusic@gmail.com
Web site: www.irenadworld.com
Freq: Daily
Circ: 7719
Editor: Irena D
Profile: Blog covering fashion and music. IRENA D WORLD blog discusses anything from the latest fashion trends and personal style to fashion accessories and music. The blog has an archive dating back to February 2012.
Fashion

Irishwonder's black hat SEO blog
1053057
Freq: Daily
News & Current Affairs

Iron Views - CEASED
997661
Web site: http://www.ironviews.com/
Freq: Daily
Circ: 12763
Soccer

Irontwit
1052584
Web site: http://irontwit.creativeblogs.net/
Freq: Daily
Circ: 316
Profile: Blog covering triathlon. The Irontwit blog discusses anything from cycling and training to sports kit and Ironman competitions. The blog has an archive dating back to July 2006 and shares a short blog roll.
Fitness & Exercise

Is This Real Life?
998323
Email: isthisreallife@hotmail.co.uk
Web site: http://www.isthisreallife.co.uk/
Freq: Daily
Circ: 8643
Editor: Emma Frew
Audio Video Trade, Bars, Clubs & Pubs, Beauty & Grooming, Cameras, Celebrities, Comedy, Consumer Electronics, Cosmetics, Entertainment, Fashion

Isabella Oliver blog
1053000
Tel: 44 02074 242930
Web site: https://www.isabellaoliver.com/uk
Freq: Daily
Circ: 74232
Family & Parenting, Fashion

Ishua, Comunidad Lucanas
1061647
Web site: http://www.ishuanos.blogspot.com
Freq: Daily

Circ: 1191
Antiques/Collectibles, Art, Arts, Celebrities, Literature, Photography, Theater & Performing Arts, Visual Arts

ISIS Communications
1054304
Web site: http://isiscommunications.blogspot.co.uk/
Freq: Daily
Circ: 521
Regional General Interest

Islamia
1061974
Web site: http://www.islamiacu.blogspot.com
Freq: Daily
Circ: 14639
National News, Politics

Islay blog
1054390
Web site: http://blog.islayinfo.com
Freq: Daily
Circ: 19372
Lifestyle, Men's Interests, Regional, Regional General Interest, Travel, Women's Interests

Isopixel
1061852
Web site: http://www.isopixel.net
Freq: Daily
Circ: 109883
Auto Aftermarket, Classical/Choral/Band Music, Computers, Country, Folk, Bluegrass, Dance Music, Data Management, Electronics, Government Technology, Graphic Design, Industry

It's Round and It's White
999188
Editorial: 2 Conway Drive, Bury BL9 7QP
Email: news@itsroundanditswhite.co.uk
Web site: www.itsroundanditswhite.co.uk
Freq: Daily
Circ: 12581
Editor: Michael Bates
Soccer

itf Aviation Blog
1053642
Editorial: ITF House, 49-60 Borough Road, London SE1 1DR
Email: aviation@itf.org.uk
Web site: www.itfaviation.org
Freq: Daily
Circ: 1035
Aviation

It's A Mandy Thing
987583
Editorial: 114B Broxholm Road, West Norwood, London SE27 0BT
Tel: 44 07540 409994
Email: mandy@itsamandything.com
Web site: http://mandyceline.com/
Freq: Daily
Circ: 521
Beauty & Grooming, Cosmetics, Fashion, Hair, Men's Interests, Movies & Video, Women's Interests

It's mummy's life
1054589
Web site: http://www.itsamummyslife.com
Freq: Daily
Circ: 9000
Family & Parenting, Fitness & Exercise, Women's Interests

It's Not Easy Being Greedy
996930
Web site: itsnoteasybeinggreedy.com
Freq: Daily
Circ: 11341
Editor: Tracy Knatt
Cooking & Baking, Restaurant Reviews

its simply beauty
998172
Email: itssimplybeauty@hotmail.com
Web site: http://www.itssimplybeauty.co.uk/
Freq: Daily
Circ: 1194
Beauty & Grooming, Cosmetics, Fashion, Hair, Women's Interests

it'saLDNthing.
987060
Web site: www.itsaldnthing.com
Freq: Daily
Circ: 7456
Fashion

itsdevelopmental Blog
1053461
Web site: http://itsdevelopmental.com/
Freq: Daily
Circ: 8487
Editor: Martin Couzins
Advertising Industry, Branding, Marketing

itssimplybeauty Vlog
1104179
Email: itssimplybeauty@hotmail.com
Web site: https://www.youtube.com/user/itssimplybeauty
Freq: Daily
Circ: 1
Cosmetics, Fashion, Women's Interests

Ivan Rivera Blog
1061668
Web site: http://ivanrivera-pmp.blogspot.com
Freq: Daily
Circ: 1192
Business, Corporate Responsibility

J for Jen
999702
Editorial: Duke Studios, 1st Floor Munro House, Duke Street, Leeds LS9 8AG
Web site: http://www.jforjen.com
Freq: Daily
Circ: 35934
Fashion

J4VV4D
995142
Web site: j4vv4d.com
Freq: Daily
Circ: 13737
Industry, Internet, Security & Security Systems

Jacamo Blog
1096366
Tel: 44 08719 844000
Email: general.enquiries@jacamo.co.uk
Web site: http://www.jacamo.co.uk/blog/
Freq: Daily
Circ: 186818
Fashion

Jack Dowd's Writing Blog
1053321
Email: jackdowd@sky.com
Web site: https://jackdowdswritingblog.com/
Freq: Daily
Circ: 10618
Broadcasting, Computer & Video Games, Entertainment, Literature, Movies & Video

Jack Leslie's F1
987767
Editorial: Wren Cottage, Warrens Lane, Botesdales, Diss IP22 1BW
Tel: 44 01379 890059
Email: jackleslie1994@googlemail.com
Web site: http://www.jacksliesf1.co.uk/
Freq: Daily
Circ: 10878
Profile: Blog covering Formula 1 and motorsport. The blog has an archive dating back to July 2011 and shares a short blog roll.
Motorsports

Jackie Notman
1055937
Tel: 44 07920 461574
Freq: Daily
Circ: 10724
Alternative Medicine, Business

Jackson's Art Blog
1056310
Web site: http://www.jacksonsart.com/blog/
Freq: Daily
Circ: 102220
Profile: Blog covering art; graphic art, exhibitions and artists. The blog has an archive dating back to August 2009.
Art

Jacqui Marie Wedding Photography
1054087
Web site: http://jacqui-marie-wedding-photography.blogspot.co.uk/
Freq: Daily
Circ: 10969
Photography, Weddings

Jade in the City
1065157
Email: cityjade@outlook.com
Web site: www.cityjade.com
Freq: Daily

Circ: 521
Art, Photography, Travel, Visual Arts,
Women's Interests

Jade's Journey 996795
Web site: http://www.jadeslongjourney.co.
uk/
Freq: Daily
Circ: 6709
Family & Parenting

J'adore - CEASED 2016 1054282
Web site: j-ad0rrre.blogspot.co.uk
Freq: Daily
Circ: 1232
Cosmetics, Fashion, Nature & Wildlife,
Women's Interests

Jak Heath 988166
Email: jakheath@gmail.com
Web site: http://www.jakheath.com/
Freq: Daily
Circ: 378
Crafts

Jake Berry MP Blog 1008435
Web site: http://www.jakeberry.org
Freq: Daily
Circ: 2491
Politics

Jake Boys 1098973
Email: jake@kameleon.co.uk
Web site: https://www.youtube.com/user/
JakeBoysUK
Freq: Daily
Circ: 3
Men's Interests

Jake Boys Vlogs 1098975
Email: jake@kameleon.co.uk
Web site: https://www.youtube.com/user/
JakeBoysVlogs
Freq: Daily
Men's Interests, Relationships

Jam and Clotted Cream 986162
Web site: www.jamandclottedcream.co.uk
Freq: Daily
Circ: 13672
Alcohol & Spirits, Bars, Clubs & Pubs,
Beer, Beverages, Cooking & Baking,
Food, Grocery Stores, Organic Food,
Restaurant Reviews, Vegetarianism &
Veganism

Jam Unix Blog 1061718
Web site. http://blog.jam.net.ve/
Freq: Daily
Circ: 39
Computers

James Alexander-Sinclair
1052838
Web site: jamesalexandersinclair.com
Freq: Daily
Circ: 10191
Gardening

James Allen on F1 986163
Email: facebook@jamesallenonf1.com
Web site: www.jamesallenonf1.com
Circ: 186503
Motorsports

**James' blog: BusinessGreen
Editor's Blog** 997061
Editorial: Haymarket House, 28-29
Haymarket, London SW1Y 4RX
Web site: www.businessgreen.com/blog/
james-blog
Freq: Daily
Circ: 6585
Energy & Environment, Environment

James Hobbs Blog 988286
Tel: 44 02072 757921
Email: jameshobbs45@gmail.com
Web site: http://www.james-hobbs.co.uk/
Freq: Daily
Circ: 1162
Art

James Welsh 1094856
Email: james.32reg@gmail.com
Web site: https://www.youtube.com/
channel/UCPP291gN79ql1QZY1znOscg

Freq: Daily
Circ: 1
Beauty & Grooming, Cosmetics, Fashion,
Hair, Men's Interests

jamie goode's wine blog 986285
Tel: 44 02088 907330
Web site: www.wineanorak.com/wineblog
Freq: Daily
Circ: 43341
Wine/Winemaking

JancisRobinson.com 983689
Web site: www.JancisRobinson.com
Circ: 17704
Profile: Website covering wine news, tasting
notes and fine wine writing.
News & Current Affairs

Jane Alexander Blog 1053546
Email: jane@janealexander.org
Web site: http://exmoorjane.com/
Freq: Daily
Circ: 9483
Alternative Medicine, Health & Medicine,
Nutrition

Jane Foster Blog 1053791
Email: jane@janefoster.co.uk
Web site: www.janefosterblog.blogspot.co.
uk
Freq: Daily
Circ: 7865
Art, Crafts

Jane's London Blog 988282
Tel: 44 07941 475003
Email: jane@janeslondon.com
Web site: http://www.janeslondon.com/
Freq: Daily
Circ: 7651
Art, Regional General Interest

Janey Godley's Blog 1054371
Email: publicity@janeygodley.co.uk
Web site: http://janeygodley.blogspot.co.uk/
Freq: Daily
Circ: 1594
Comedy

Japan Economy News & Blog
1061550
Email: japaneconomynews@gmail.com
Freq: Daily
Economics

JapanBlog 1061275
Freq: Daily
Antiques/Collectibles, Art, Arts,
Literature, Photography, Theater &
Performing Arts, Visual Arts

Japon Cercano 1061806
Web site: http://blogs.eluniversal.com/eu3/
Blogs/japo_index.shtml
Freq: Daily
Circ: 6680
Lifestyle, Men's Interests, Regional
General Interest, Women's Interests

Jarabacoa Avanza 1060599
Web site: http://jarabacoaavanza.blogspot.
com
Freq: Daily
Circ: 521
Accounting, Banking, Business,
Corporate Responsibility

**Jarin blogi - biologiaa ja
maantiedettä** 1061434
Email: jari.kolehmainen@sakky.fi
Web site: http://biologi-jari.blogspot.com
Freq: Daily
Circ: 2136
Environment, Science

Jason Harry Photography

1054927
Email: info@jasonharry.com
Web site: http://jasonharryphotographer.
blogspot.co.uk/
Freq: Daily
Circ: 977
Fashion, Photography

Javi Recetas 1061125
Web site: http://www.javirecetas.com/
Freq: Daily
Circ: 3975
Cooking & Baking

Jayde Pierce Vlog 1098984
Email: teamjayde@speakanddo.com
Web site: https://www.youtube.com/
channel/UCQhwqZ33f_APooCusvTCwww
Freq: Daily
Circ: 1
Beauty & Grooming, Cosmetics, Hair

Jayne's Kitsch 998199
Tel: 44 07791 612866
Web site: http://www.jaynekitsch.co.uk/
Freq: Daily
Circ: 8393
Beauty & Grooming, Cosmetics, Fashion,
Hair, Women's Interests

Jaynes Stitching Tales 1056574
Web site: http://jaynesstitchingtales.
blogspot.co.uk/
Freq: Daily
Circ: 521
Crafts

The Jazz Breakfast 1052639
Email: peterbacon@me.com
Web site: http://thejazzbreakfast.com/feed/
Freq: Daily
Circ: 96
Jazz & Blues

Jazzabelle's Diary 987089
Email: jazzabellesdiary@hotmail.co.uk
Web site: jazzabellesdiary.blogspot.com
Freq: Daily
Circ: 7507
Fashion

JazzyVille 1053573
Web site: http://www.jazzyville.com/
Freq: Daily
Circ: 1618
Women's Interests

JB Mum of One 988721
Email: jbmumofone@yahoo.com
Web site: jbmumofone.com
Freq: Daily
Circ: 8607
Family & Parenting

JBIL 1056582
Web site: http://justbecauseilove.co.uk/
Freq: Daily
Circ: 3044
Family & Parenting, Women's Interests

JDCMB 1052605
Email: jessica.duchen@gmail.com
Web site: http://jessicamusic.blogspot.co.
uk/
Freq: Daily
Circ: 16256
Classical/Choral/Band Music, Theater &
Performing Arts

**Jean-Luc Benazet Photo-
graphy** 1053949
Freq: Daily
News & Current Affairs

The Jeans Blog 1053212
Web site: thejeansblog.com
Freq: Daily
Circ: 39318
Editor: Lorna Burford
Fashion

Jeffrey's Noise 1060809
Web site: http://www.jeffrey.co.in/blog
Freq: Daily
Circ: 20
Computers, Software

Jefrsn 1052737
Web site: http://jefrsn.com/blog
Freq: Daily
Circ: 4196
Dance Music, Fashion, Jazz & Blues,
Men's Interests, Photography, Pop Music,
R&B, Urban, World, Rap & Hip Hop

Jefusion.com 1060748
Email: gekidon05@gmail.com
Freq: Daily
Bars, Clubs & Pubs, Comedy,
Entertainment, Local Entertainment
Guides, Movies & Video

Jelly London Blog 999660
Editorial: 9-10 Charlotte Mews, London
W1T 4EF Tel: 44 02073 233307
Email: info@jellylondon.com
Web site: http://www.jellylondon.com/blog
Freq: Daily
Circ: 77
Art, Literature, Photography, Visual Arts

Jemjabella 1054231
Freq: Daily
News & Current Affairs

Jenni Ukkonen 1061826
Email: jenniukk@gmail.com
Web site: http://ellit.fi/muoti-ja-kauneus/
jenni-ukkonen/
Freq: Daily
Circ: 60045
Fashion, Lifestyle, Men's Interests,
Regional General Interest, Women's
Interests

Jennifer's Little World 988696
Web site: www.jenniferslittleworld.com
Freq: Daily
Circ: 8545
Profile: Blog covering parenting. The
Jennifer's Little World blog discusses
anything from family travel and crafts to toys
and kids days out. The blog has an archive
dating back to March 2014 and shares an
extensive blog roll.
Family & Parenting

Jennin Arkijärki 1061246
Web site: http://arkijarki.net/
Freq: Daily
Circ: 2021
Internet, Lifestyle, Men's Interests,
Regional General Interest, Women's
Interests

Jennings Motor Group Blog

996993
Editorial: Cargo Fleet Lane, Middlesbrough
TS3 8AX Tel: 44 01915 525800
Email: internetsales@jennings-ford.co.uk
Web site: http://www.jenningsmotorgroup.
co.uk/blog/
Freq: Daily
Circ: 79
Antique & Collectible Cars, Automakers,
Automotive, Driving, Motorcycles, Off-
road & 4-Wheel Drive Vehicles, Trucks &
SUVs

**Jenny Chandler I've Mostly
Been Eating** 008305
Tel: 44 01179 739421
Web site: jennychandlerblog.com
Freq: Daily
Circ: 9140
Cooking & Baking

**Jenny Eatwell's Rhubarb &
Ginger** 986948
Email: poshpaws55@googlemail.com
Web site: http://jennyeatwellsrhubarbginger.
blogspot.co.uk/
Freq: Daily
Circ: 8432
Profile: Blog covering food. The Jenny
Eatwell's Rhubarb & Ginger blog discusses
anything from recipes to food reviews. The
blog has an archive dating back to August
2010 and shares a short blog roll.
Cooking & Baking

jenography 988194
Email: jennifer@britmums.com
Web site: www.jenography.net
Freq: Daily
Circ: 11927
Travel

Jermyn Street Journal 997318
Editorial: 55 Brenthouse Rd, London E9
6QD
Web site: jermynstreetjournal.com

UK Blogs

Freq: Daily
Circ: 11768
Editor: Howard Hamilton
Art, Beauty & Grooming, Cooking &
Baking, Cosmetics, Fashion, Hair, Luxury
Goods, Men's Interests, Restaurant
Reviews

Jess Hearts Books 1054157
Email: jess2379@hotmail.com
Web site: jessheartsbooks.blogspot.co.uk
Freq: Daily
Circ: 7938
Profile: Blog covering books and book
reviews. The blog has an archive dating back
to May 2010 and shares an extensive blog
roll.
Literature

Jess who 1052979
Email: jesswhoblog@hotmail.co.uk
Web site: http://www.jesswho.co.uk/
Freq: Daily
Circ: 9058
Beauty & Grooming, Cosmetics, Do-It-
Yourself (DIY), Fashion, Hair, Regional
General Interest, Women's Interests

Jessica Loves 995357
Editorial: 7 Hurdis Road, Shirley, Solihull
B90 2DP
Web site: jessicaloves.co.uk
Freq: Daily
Circ: 10552
Beauty & Grooming, Celebrities, Cooking
& Baking, Cosmetics, Family & Parenting,
Hair, Health & Medicine, Travel,
Weddings, Women's Interests

Jessthetics 1053247
Web site: http://www.jessthetics.com/
Freq: Daily
Circ: 9320
Profile: Blog covering lifestyle. Jessthetics
blog discusses anything from DIY and food
to photography and sustainable fashion. The
blog has an archive dating back to October
2012 and shares an extensive blog roll.
News & Current Affairs

Jesus Cabello 1060777
Web site: http://jesuscabellov.blogspot.
com/
Freq: Daily
Circ: 521
Basketball, Bicycles, Billiards, Boating &
Yachting, Bodybuilding, Bowling, Boxing,
Cricket, Equestrian Sports, Extreme/
Adventure Sports

Jewels du Jour 1098992
Web site: http://www.jewelsdujour.com/
Freq: Daily
Circ: 39019
Fashion

JibberJabber UK 1053240
Email: jibberjabberuk@gmail.com
Web site: jibberjabberuk.co.uk
Freq: Daily
Circ: 8800
Cooking & Baking, Family & Parenting

Jiboneus.com 1061682
Web site: http://jiboneus.com
Freq: Daily
Circ: 975
Art, Auto Aftermarket, Classical/Choral/
Band Music, Computers, Country, Folk,
Bluegrass, Dance Music, Data
Management, Electronics, Government
Technology, Industry

Jim's Loire 1094167
Web site: http://jimsloire.blogspot.co.uk/
Freq: Daily
Circ: 9255
Wine/Winemaking

Jim's Marketing Blog 986165
Editorial: 22 High Street, Epworth,
Doncaster DN9 1ET
Web site: jimsmarketingblog.com
Freq: Daily
Circ: 144552
News & Current Affairs

Jin loves to eat 1061878
Web site: http://www.jinlovestoeat.com
Freq: Daily
Circ: 2355
Antiques/Collectibles, Art, Arts, Food,
Lifestyle, Literature, Men's Interests,
Photography, Regional General Interest,
Restaurant Reviews

Jo Eats London 1099574
Email: joeatslondon@gmail.com
Web site: http://www.joeatslondon.com/
Freq: Daily
Circ: 9345
Restaurant Reviews

Joanna Victoria 1054670
Email: joannabayford@gmail.com
Web site: http://www.joannavictoria.co.uk/
Freq: Daily
Circ: 8900
Profile: Blog covering lifestyle. The Joanna
Victoria blog discusses anything from frugal
living and book reviews to gift ideas and
living on a budget. The blog has an archive
dating back to March 2012.
Beauty & Grooming, Cosmetics, Family &
Parenting, Hair, Women's Interests

Joanne Dewberry 1053376
Web site: joannedewberry.co.uk
Freq: Daily
Circ: 54327
Business

Joe Galvin 1100168
Web site: http://joegalvin.blogspot.co.uk/
Freq: Daily
Circ: 8596
Cooking & Baking, Fashion

Joey Style 1053112
Web site: http://joeylondon.co.uk/
Freq: Daily
Circ: 8536
Profile: Blog covering fashion. JOEY STYLE
blog discusses anything from fashion and
men's fashion to women's fashion and
celebrities.
News & Current Affairs

Jog Blog 987986
Web site: http://www.jog-blog.co.uk/
Freq: Daily
Circ: 6872
Fitness & Exercise, Nutrition

Johanne Andersson 1060470
Email: johannean.blogg@hotmail.no
Web site: http://johannean.blogg.no/
Freq: Daily
Circ: 169
Fashion

JOHN ARNE RIISES BLOGG

1060714
Web site: http://www.johnarneriise.no/
Freq: Daily
Circ: 957
Basketball, Bicycles, Billiards, Boating &
Yachting, Bodybuilding, Bowling, Boxing,
Cricket, Equestrian Sports, Extreme/
Adventure Sports

John David Blake - CEASED
2017 1054635
Web site: http://johndavidblake.org
Freq: Daily
Circ: 1335
Education, Politics

John Hemming's Web Log 1053537
Web site: johnhemming.blogspot.co.uk
Freq: Daily
Circ: 9554
Politics

John Redwood's Diary 986166
Editorial: 30 Rose Street, Wokingham RG40
1XU Tel: 44 01189 629501
Email: john.redwood.mp@parliament.uk
Web site: johnredwoodsdiary.com
Freq: Daily
Circ: 20038
Politics

John Smeaton, SPUC director 1053402
Email: johnsmeaton@spuc.org.uk
Web site: spuc-director.blogspot.co.uk
Freq: Daily
Circ: 6326
Charitable Foundations, Family &
Parenting

johnbrace.com 994990
Editorial: Jenmaleo, 134 Boundary Road,
Bidston, Wirral, Birkenhead CH43 7PH
Tel: 44 01515 122500
Web site: http://johnbrace.com/
Freq: Daily
Circ: 9211
Editor: John Brace
Politics, Regional

Johnnie Moore Blog 1053751
Web site: http://johnniemoore.com/blog/
Freq: Daily
Circ: 58
Education

John's Adventures 1053946
Freq: Daily
News & Current Affairs

John's Labour Blog 986167
Email: john.gray2012@btinternet.com
Web site: http://www.johnslabourblog.org/
Freq: Daily
Circ: 10239
Politics

Joining Dots 1053508
Web site: http://joiningdots.com/blog/
Freq: Daily
Circ: 7127
News & Current Affairs

Jolopeo 1060580
Web site: http://www.jolopeo.net/v4
Freq: Daily
Circ: 521
Classical/Choral/Band Music, Country,
Folk, Bluegrass, Dance Music, Jazz &
Blues, Music, Pop Music, R&B, Urban,
World, Rap & Hip Hop, Rock Music,
Theater & Performing Arts

Jon Cronshaw 1053445
Web site: www.joncronshaw.co.uk
Freq: Daily
Circ: 767
Profile: Blog covering arts and
entertainment. The Jon Cronshaw blog
discusses anything from interviews with
musicians and art exhibitions to culture. The
blog has an archive dating back to
September 2012 and shares a short blog roll.
The outlet offers RSS (Really Simple
Syndication).
Consumer Affairs, Politics, Social Issues

Jon Slattery 986168
Email: jon.slattery369@btinternet.com
Web site: jonslattery.blogspot.com
Freq: Daily
Circ: 7278
Publishing

Jonanthan Boakes Blog 1052654
Web site: http://jonanthanboakes.blogspot.
co.uk/
Freq: Daily
Circ: 492
Computer & Video Games

Jonathan Farrington blog 1053703
Web site: http://www.jonathanfarrington.
com/
Freq: Daily
Circ: 6106
Editor: Jonathan Farrington
Business

Jonathan Fryer Blog 1052881
Web site: jonathanfryer.wordpress.com
Freq: Daily
Circ: 6780
Politics

Jonathan Savage Blog 1053204
Web site: http://www.jsavage.org.uk/
Freq: Daily
Circ: 2125
Classical/Choral/Band Music, Education,
Music

Jonathan Wallace Blog 1053932
Web site: http://jonathanwallace.blogspot.
co.uk/
Freq: Daily
Circ: 521
Politics

Jonathans blog 1053972
Web site: https://jonathansblog.co.uk/
Freq: Daily
Circ: 48595
Apple, Beer, Travel

Jonathon Porritt Blog 1054341
Web site: jonathonporritt.com/blog
Freq: Daily
Circ: 16
Energy & Environment, Environment,
Ethical/Moral Issues

jonchoo 1053539
Email: londonblogger@gmail.com
Web site: jonchoo.blogspot.co.uk
Freq: Daily
Circ: 488
Alcohol & Spirits, Cameras, Computer &
Video Games, Cooking & Baking, Mobile
Electronics, Restaurant Reviews

Jonnamaista 1061766
Email: jonnamaista@gmail.com
Web site: http://jonnamaista.blogspot.fi/
Freq: Daily
Circ: 1745
Beauty & Grooming, Cosmetics, Fashion,
Hair

Jono & Jules Do Food & Wine
1053273
Email: jono.jules@gmail.com
Web site: http://jonoandjules.com/
Freq: Daily
Circ: 789
Cooking & Baking, Food, Grocery Stores,
Organic Food, Restaurant Reviews,
Vegetarianism & Veganism, Wine/
Winemaking

Jordan Bunker 1054453
Email: jordanbunkerblog@gmail.com
Web site: http://www.jordanbunker.uk
Freq: Daily
Circ: 9561
Profile: Blog covering men's fashion and
men's lifestyle. The blog has an archive
dating back to September 2014 and shares
an extensive blogroll.
Beauty & Grooming, Cosmetics, Fashion,
Hair, Men's Interests

Jordan Publishing Blogs 1052949
Email: editor@jordanpublishing.co.uk
Web site: jordanpublishing.co.uk
Freq: Daily
Circ: 69342
Company News & Appointments,
Consumer Interest, Corporate Law,
Criminal Law, Employment, Family Law,
Government, Human Rights, Intellectual
Property, International News

Jorge Letralia 1061891
Web site: http://jorgeletralia.blogsome.com/
Freq: Daily
Circ: 381127
Lifestyle, Men's Interests, Regional
General Interest, Women's Interests

Jorgen Sundberg Blog 1054609
Tel: 44 02083 716920
Email: jorgen@linkhumans.com
Web site: http://linkhumans.com/category/
blog
Freq: Daily
Circ: 29
Branding, Internet, Marketing

Jo's Clothes 1056564
Email: josclothesblog@gmail.com
Web site: http://josclothes.co.uk/

Freq: Daily
Circ: 10082
Cooking & Baking, Cosmetics, Fashion, Health & Medicine

Jo's Kitchen 986968
Web site: www.joskitchen.co.uk
Freq: Daily
Circ: 12777
Cooking & Baking

Jose Luis Pallares 1061931
Web site: http://blogs.clarin.com/joseluispallares/
Freq: Daily
Circ: 4596
Politics

Joseph Rowntree Foundation Blog 996474
Editorial: The Homestead, 40 Water End, York YO30 6WP **Tel:** 44 01904 629241
Email: info@jrf.org.uk
Web site: jrf.org.uk/blog
Freq: Daily
Circ: 35
Charitable Foundations

Journalist On The Run 1053434
Web site: http://journalistontherun.com/
Freq: Daily
Circ: 140987
Travel

The Journey of my practice 1054297
Web site: https://globie.wordpress.com/
Freq: Daily
Circ: 2
Alternative Medicine

Journeying Beyond Breast Cancer 1053970
Email: beyondbreastcancer@live.com
Web site: http://journeyingbeyondbreastcancer.com/
Freq: Daily
Circ: 12344
Oncology

Journeys are my Diary 1054296
Web site: http://www.journeysaremydiary.com/
Freq: Daily
Circ: 7076
Profile: Blog covering lifestyle. Journeys are my Diary blog discusses anything from film and books to food. The blog has an archive dating back to January 2013.
Cooking & Baking, Fashion, Literature, Movies & Video

JOY Blog 996787
Editorial: 10-11 Bishop's Terrace, London SE11 4UE
Web site: www.joythestore.com/blog
Freq: Daily
Circ: 35
Fashion

Joy to the World 986568
Editorial: Flat 1, 62 Polthorne Grove, Plumstead, London SE18 7AS
Web site: http://joytotheworldblog.com/
Freq: Daily
Circ: 8630
Profile: Blog covering motherhood and lifestyle. Joy to The world discusses anything from children's activities and day to day life with kids to fashion and beauty. The outlet offers RSS (Really Simple Syndication).
Beauty & Grooming, Cosmetics, Family & Parenting, Fashion, Hair, Women's Interests

Joyas 1061441
Web site: http://www.joyas.name
Freq: Daily
Circ: 608
News & Current Affairs

Joyas de Titi 1061752
Web site: http://www.lasjoyasdetiti.blogspot.com
Freq: Daily

Circ: 1130
Antiques/Collectibles, Art, Arts, Crafts, Literature, Photography, Theater & Performing Arts, Visual Arts

Joyce Watson blog 1053693
Email: joyce.watson@wales.gov.uk
Web site: http://www.joycewatson.org.uk/
Freq: Daily
Circ: 1090
Politics, Wales

The Joyous Living 988749
Email: thejoyousliving@gmail.com
Web site: http://www.thejoyousliving.com/
Freq: Daily
Circ: 7323
Profile: Blog covering lifestyle, arts, books, fashion, food, music, theatre and animals.
Women's Interests

Joyzine 1054505
Web site: https://joyzineuk.wordpress.com/
Freq: Daily
Circ: 62
Dance Music, Jazz & Blues, Rap & Hip Hop

JP Festival 1053542
Web site: jpfestival.com
Freq: Daily
Circ: 14254
Field Sports

Juan de Mairena 1061797
Web site: http://demairena.blogspot.com/
Freq: Daily
Circ: 3050
Science

Juan Manuel Giaccone Presenta 1061187
Web site: http://ernestougarte.blogspot.com/
Freq: Daily
Circ: 752
Lifestyle, Men's Interests, Regional General Interest, Women's Interests

Judging Covers 1054617
Email: mail@judgingcovers.co.uk
Web site: http://judgingcovers.co.uk/
Freq: Daily
Circ: 1555
Literature

Judith's Divorce blog 1053571
Web site: http://judithsdivorceblog.blogspot.com
Freq: Daily
Circ: 1649
Relationships

JuggleMum 985826
Email: editor@jugglemum.co.uk
Web site: www.jugglemum.co.uk
Freq: Daily
Circ: 11520
Editor: Nadine Hill
Cooking & Baking, Family & Parenting, Health & Medicine, Lifestyle, Men's Interests, Personal Finance, Regional General Interest, Relationships, Restaurant Reviews, Women's Interests

Jugoweb 1060974
Web site: http://www.jugoweb.com
Freq: Daily
Circ: 1775
Auto Aftermarket, Computers, Data Management, Electronics, Government Technology, Industry, Internet, Mobile Communications, Security & Security Systems, Software

Juhlattaren kakkublogi 1061971
Email: juhlatar@gmail.com
Web site: http://juhlatar.blogspot.fi/
Freq: Daily
Circ: 993
Cooking & Baking, Food

Jules Birch blog 1053587
Email: jules@julesbirch.com
Web site: http://julesbirch.com/
Freq: Daily

Circ: 12833
Building & Construction, Politics, Residential Real Estate, Social Issues

Julia Buckley Fitness 1053842
Web site: http://juliabuckleyfitness.com/blog/
Freq: Daily
Circ: 98
Fitness & Exercise

Julia Fuentez Fashion Blog 1061670
Web site: http://juliafuentez.blogspot.com
Freq: Daily
Circ: 2496
Fashion

Julia Toivola 1061003
Email: juliablog@hotmail.com
Web site: http://mycosmo.fi/news/author/juliatoivola
Freq: Daily
Circ: 28302
Beauty & Grooming, Cosmetics, Fashion, Hair

Julian Summerhayes 998066
Tel: 44 07588 815384
Email: juliansummerhayes@gmail.com
Web site: juliansummerhayes.com
Freq: Daily
Circ: 8294
Careers

Julianne Mooney 1054415
Email: julianne.mooney@gmail.com
Web site: http://juliannemooney.com/
Freq: Daily
Circ: 2268
Regional General Interest, Travel

Junkaholique 1054358
Email: hello@junkaholique.com
Web site: http://www.junkaholique.com/
Freq: Daily
Circ: 21854
Profile: Blog covering collecting. The junkaholique blog discusses anything from vintage clothing and jewellery to camping and crafting. The blog has an archive dating back to August 2010 and shares a short blog roll.
Crafts, Do-It-Yourself (DIY), Travel

Jura Wine, Food and Travel 1094166
Web site: https://jurawine.co.uk
Freq: Daily
Circ: 7345
Cooking & Baking, Restaurant Reviews, Wine/Winemaking

Just a Normal Mummy 997971
Web site: http://justanormalmummy.blogspot.co.uk/
Freq: Daily
Circ: 6109
Family & Parenting

Just Arsenal 987887
Editorial: 37 Lombard Street, King Cross, Halifax HX1 3PA
Email: justarsenal@hotmail.co.uk
Web site: http://justarsenal.com/
Freq: Daily
Circ: 626192
Editor: Pat McLaughlin
Soccer

Just Chelsea M 995364
Editorial: 9 Evesham Road, Evesham, Evesham WR11 4TL
Email: thehazelkey@gmail.com
Web site: http://justchelseam.com/
Freq: Daily
Circ: 7989
Family & Parenting

Just Do Property Blog 986528
Editorial: Unit4 Vista Place, Coy Pond Business Park, Ingworth Road, Poole BH12 1JY **Tel:** 44 01614 428977
Email: support@justdoproperty.com
Web site: www.justdoproperty.co.uk/blog

Circ: 468
Finance, Property Management & Maintenance, Real Estate, Residential Real Estate

Just Emma 1054337
Web site: http://www.justemma.co.uk/
Freq: Daily
Circ: 7126
Beauty & Grooming, Cooking & Baking, Cosmetics, Fashion, Hair, Travel, Women's Interests

Just Football 987883
Email: just-football@live.com
Web site: www.just-football.com/
Freq: Daily
Circ: 9896
Soccer

Just Jude 1057338
Email: justjudedesigns@hotmail.co.uk
Web site: http://judith-justjude.blogspot.co.uk/
Freq: Daily
Circ: 1459
Profile: Blog covering crafts, sewing and lifestyle. The blog has an archive dating back to December 2010 and shares an extensive blog roll.
Crafts, Women's Interests

Just Julie 988381
Email: justjulieb81@gmail.com
Web site: www.justjulie.co.uk
Freq: Daily
Circ: 5583
Profile: Blog covering beauty, beauty tips and cosmetics. The blog has an archive dating back to December 2013.
Beauty & Grooming, Cosmetics, Hair

Just me Leah 1052868
Web site: http://www.xloveleahx.co.uk/
Freq: Daily
Circ: 11479
Profile: Blog covering lifestyle. JUST ME LEAH blog discusses anything from lifestyle and plus size fashion to beauty and personal health. The blog has an archive dating back to July 2010 and shares an extensive blog roll.
Beauty & Grooming, Cosmetics, Fashion, Hair, Women's Interests

Just Music I Like 1053974
Email: justmusicthatilike@gmail.com
Freq: Daily
Classical/Choral/Band Music, Country, Folk, Bluegrass, Dance Music, Music, Pop Music, R&B, Urban, World, Rock Music

Just Nice Things 986169
Editorial: 44 Hale Grove Gardens, Mill Hill, London NW7 3LP
Web site: www.just-nice-things.co.uk/
Freq: Daily
Circ: 10245
Beauty & Grooming, Cooking & Baking, Cosmetics, Fitness & Exercise, Food, Grocery Stores, Hair, Health & Medicine, Nutrition, Organic Food

Just Rach 1053503
Email: justrachblog@gmail.com
Web site: http://www.justrach.com
Freq: Daily
Circ: 3443
Profile: Blog covering lifestyle. Just Rach blog discusses anything from lifestyle and beauty to fashion. The blog has an archive dating back to August 2010.
Beauty & Grooming, Cosmetics, Do-It-Yourself (DIY), Fashion, Hair, Regional General Interest, Women's Interests

Just sing along to my stereo 1061796
Email: suvi.kylalaaso@gmail.com
Web site: http://justsingalongtomystereo.blogspot.fi
Freq: Daily
Circ: 1437
Classical/Choral/Band Music, Country, Folk, Bluegrass, Dance Music, Internet, Jazz & Blues, Music, Pop Music, R&B, Urban, World, Rap & Hip Hop, Rock Music

Justo Reclamo 1060909
Web site: http://eljustoreclamo.blogspot.
com
Freq: Daily
Circ: 1449
National News, Politics

Juventud Informada 1061123
Web site: http://juventudinformada.com.ar/
Freq: Daily
Circ: 22917
National News

Juxtabook 1053968
Tel: 44 01756 792380
Web site: juxtabook.typepad.com/books/
Freq: Daily
Circ: 176404
Literature

K Bites 1061517
Web site: http://sookyeong.wordpress.com
Freq: Daily
Circ: 28
Bars, Clubs & Pubs, Classical/Choral/
Band Music, Comedy, Country, Folk,
Bluegrass, Dance Music, Entertainment,
Jazz & Blues, Local Entertainment
Guides, Movies & Video, Music

Kabbalah 365 1061594
Web site: http://cabala365.blogspot.com
Freq: Daily
Circ: 521
Religion

Kabytes 1062048
Web site: http://www.kabytes.com/
Freq: Daily
Circ: 38996
Audio Video Trade, Cameras, Consumer
Electronics, Electronics, Internet, Mobile
Electronics, Movies & Video

Kaikki elämäni koirat 1061237
Email: annamari@saunalahti.fi
Web site: http://kaikkielamanikoirat.
blogspot.fi/
Freq: Daily
Circ: 1647
Nature & Wildlife

Kakkuviikarin vispailuja 1061573
Email: kakkuviikari@gmail.com
Web site: http://kakkuviikari.blogspot.fi/
Freq: Daily
Circ: 1366
Cooking & Baking

Kalanchoe 1054285
Email: katie@kalanchoe.co.uk
Web site: http://www.kalanchoe.co.uk/
Freq: Daily
Circ: 6432
Profile: Blog covering lifestyle, food, fashion,
beauty, travel and photography. The blog
has an archive dating back to August 2012.
Beauty & Grooming, Cooking & Baking,
Cosmetics, Fashion, Hair, Restaurant
Reviews, Travel

Kanelia ja kardemummaa
1061754
Email: kaneliajakardemummaa@live.fi
Web site: http://kaneliajakardemummaa.
blogspot.fi/
Freq: Daily
Circ: 2890
Gardening

Kara Chelsie 1054096
Editorial: 1 Hardinge Road, Kensal Rise,
London NW10 3PL
Email: karachelsie@gmail.com
Web site: http://www.karachelsie.com
Freq: Daily
Circ: 11076
Cameras, Fashion, Photography,
Restaurant Reviews, Travel, Women's
Interests

**Kara Willow - A London Life-
style Blog** 1072717
Editorial: Flat 2, 163 Balham Hill, London
SW12 9DJ
Email: contact@karawillow.com
Web site: http://www.karawillow.com

Freq: Daily
Circ: 9392
Bars, Clubs & Pubs, Comedy, Cooking &
Baking, Entertainment, Health &
Medicine, Local Entertainment Guides,
Movies & Video, Nutrition, Restaurant
Reviews, Travel

Karen Barlow 1053104
Web site: https://www.karenbarlowstylist.
co.uk/
Freq: Daily
Circ: 9660
Profile: Blog covering home decorating and
interior design. The blog has an archive
dating back to January 2011.
Do-It-Yourself (DIY)

Karen's Carry Ons 996792
Web site: http://karenscarryons.blogspot.
co.uk/
Freq: Daily
Circ: 1116
Crafts

Kari Jaquesson 1061886
Email: kari@trimtram.no
Web site: http://karijaquesson.blogg.no/
Freq: Daily
Circ: 257093
Fitness & Exercise, Health & Medicine,
Nutrition

KARLISMYUNKLE 985753
Editorial: 161 / 3 Cornell Square, London
SW8 2ES
Email: karlismyunkle@gmail.com
Web site: karlismyunkle.com
Freq: Daily
Circ: 10891
Airline Inflight, Antiques/Collectibles, Art,
Arts, Bars, Clubs & Pubs, Classical/
Choral/Band Music, Comedy, Country,
Folk, Bluegrass, Dance Music,
Entertainment

Karma Panda 1060698
Web site: http://www.karmapanda.com
Freq: Daily
Circ: 944
Literature, Nature & Wildlife, Photography

Karvapuusti 1061671
Email: marenkia@hotmail.com
Web site: http://karvapuusti.blogspot.fi/
Freq: Daily
Circ: 1403
Nature & Wildlife

Kat Got the Cream 988720
Web site: www.katgotthecream.com
Freq: Daily
Circ: 7534
Architecture & Design, Do-It-Yourself
(DIY), Fashion, Gardening, Home,
Property Management & Maintenance,
Real Estate

KatchUp 1070234
Editorial: The Lightbox, 111 Power Road,
London W4 3PY Tel: 44 02070 616321
Email: team@katchup.com
Web site: https://blog.katchup.com/
Freq: Daily
Circ: 21
Editor: Emily Birch
Cameras, Photography

Kate La Vie 986817
Email: kate@katelavie.com
Web site: http://www.katelavie.com/
Freq: Daily
Circ: 55783
Beauty & Grooming, Cosmetics, Fashion,
Hair, Women's Interests

Kate Takes 5 1053475
Email: katetakes5@gmail.com
Web site: www.katetakes5.com
Freq: Daily
Circ: 8434
Family & Parenting, Fitness & Exercise,
Travel, Women's Interests

Kate's Creative Space 1053899
Email: kate@katescreativespace.com
Web site: www.katescreativespace.com

Freq: Daily
Circ: 24746
Profile: Blog covering crafts, papercraft,
recipes and interiors.
Do-It-Yourself (DIY)

**Kath's Blog...diary of the
every day life of a crafter** 996499
Email: kathinwesthill@btinternet.com
Web site: http://kath-allthatglitter.blogspot.
co.uk/
Freq: Daily
Circ: 3231
Crafts

Kathy's Waffle 988153
Email: kathyswaffle@gmail.com
Web site: http://kathybsworlduk.blogspot.
co.uk/
Freq: Daily
Circ: 752
Crafts

Katie Cakes 1052786
Email: iheartkatiecakes@gmail.com
Web site: www.iheartkatiecakes.co.uk/
Freq: Daily
Circ: 6935
Cooking & Baking

Katie Chutzpah 987457
Email: katiechutzpah@googlemail.com
Web site: katiechutzpah.com
Freq: Daily
Circ: 1117
Beauty & Grooming, Celebrities,
Cosmetics, Entertainment, Fashion, Hair,
Luxury Goods, Restaurant Reviews,
Travel, Women's Interests

Katie Loves Cooking 1054426
Email: katielovescookinge17@gmail.com
Web site: https://katielovescooking.
wordpress.com/
Freq: Daily
Circ: 17
Cooking & Baking, Vegetarianism &
Veganism

Katie Snooks 998418
Web site: http://www.katiesnooks.com/
Freq: Daily
Circ: 8324
Beauty & Grooming, Cosmetics, Hair,
Women's Interests

Katie Snooks Vlog 1098979
Email: klsnooks@hotmail.com
Web site: https://www.youtube.com/user/
snooksy
Freq: Daily
Circ: 5
Beauty & Grooming, Cosmetics, Fashion,
Hair, Women's Interests

The Kats Paws 1068847
Email: thekatspaws@gmail.com
Web site: http://thekatspaws.com/
Freq: Daily
Circ: 10021
Beauty & Grooming, Cooking & Baking,
Cosmetics, Fashion, Hair, Regional
General Interest, Travel, Women's
Interests

Kaushal Beauty 1064931
Editorial: C/O Red Hare, Somerset House,
Strand, London WC2R 1LA
Email: kaushalmbeauty@gmail.com
Web site: http://kaushalbeauty.com/
Freq: Daily
Circ: 24097
Profile: Blog covering beauty. Kaushal
Beauty blog discusses anything from
cosmetics and beauty to beauty tips and
fashion.
Beauty & Grooming, Cosmetics, Hair

Kaushal Beauty Vlog 1076752
Editorial: C/O Red Hare, Somerset House,
Strand, London WC2R 1LA
Email: kaushalmbeauty@gmail.com
Web site: https://www.youtube.com/user/
BeautyFulfilled
Freq: Daily
Circ: 21
Beauty & Grooming, Cosmetics, Hair

Kavey Eats 986914
Editorial: Kavey Eats, 71 Hutton Grove,
North Finchley, London N12 8DS
Web site: http://www.kaveyeats.com/
Freq: Daily
Circ: 10412
Cooking & Baking, Restaurant Reviews,
Travel

Kay Sexton Blog 1053151
Web site: http://kaysexton.com/?page_id=
16
Freq: Daily
Circ: 611
News & Current Affairs

KayCeeCreates 1058392
Email: kayceecreates@outlook.com
Web site: http://www.kayceecreates.com/
Freq: Daily
Circ: 9170
Cooking & Baking, Crafts, Do-It-Yourself
(DIY), Grocery Stores, Restaurant Reviews

**Keane Ingram's Android news
and thoughts** 1053069
Web site: http://www.keanei.eu/
Freq: Daily
Circ: 491
Mobile Electronics

Kejun Feng's Art zone 1061716
Email: webmaster@jutailong.com
Web site: http://blog.sina.com.cn/fkj
Freq: Daily
Circ: 42239999
Do-It-Yourself (DIY), Engineering

Kelanjo 1054925
Web site: www.kelanjo.com/
Freq: Daily
Circ: 1222
Beauty & Grooming, Cosmetics, Fashion,
Hair, Women's Interests

Kellomies 1061672
Email: kellomies@kellomies.fi
Web site: http://www.kellomies.fi
Freq: Daily
Circ: 1712
News & Current Affairs

Kelly Prince Writes 996537
Editorial: 19 Warwick Chambers, Pater
Street, London W8 6EN
Tel: 44 07468 526857
Email: kellyprincewrites@gmail.com
Web site: http://www.kellyprincewrites.com/
Freq: Daily
Circ: 9147
Beauty & Grooming, Cooking & Baking,
Cosmetics, Fashion, Hair, Regional
General Interest, Restaurant Reviews,
Travel, Women's Interests

Kemples 988357
Web site: http://www.kemples.co.uk/
Freq: Daily
Circ: 6117
Profile: Blog covering beauty. The
KEMPLES blog discusses anything from
beauty and cosmetics to make up and
lifestyle. The blog has an archive dating back
to April 2012 and shares a short blogroll.
Beauty & Grooming, Cosmetics, Fashion,
Hair, Women's Interests

Ken Gibson's Motorpoint Blog
1063147
Editorial: Chartwell Drive, West Meadows,
Derby DE21 6BZ
Web site: https://www.motorpoint.co.uk/
motorpointpr/blog
Freq: Daily
Circ: 229
Antique & Collectible Cars, Automakers,
Automotive, Driving, Off-road & 4-Wheel
Drive Vehicles

Ken's Tech Tips 986170
Email: ken@kentechtips.com
Web site: http://kenstechtips.com/
Freq: Daily
Circ: 124461
Audio Video Trade, Cameras, Consumer
Electronics, Mobile Electronics, Movies &
Video

Willings Press Guide

Section 6: UK Blogs. Vol 1 UK & Ireland 2018

UK Blogs

Kenwood Travel 1056769
Email: info@kenwoodtravel.com
Web site: http://kenwoodtravel.co.uk/blog/
Freq: Daily
Circ: 859
Travel

Kermaruusu 1060958
Email: kermaruusu@gmail.com
Web site: http://www.kermaruusu.com/
Freq: Daily
Circ: 2979
Cooking & Baking

Kev's Snack Reviews 997718
Email: kevssnackreviews@gmail.com
Web site: kevssnackreviews.blogspot.co.uk
Freq: Daily
Circ: 10971
Cooking & Baking

Kew 1054245
Email: info@kew.org
Web site: www.kew.org/discover/blogs
Freq: Daily
Circ: 9
Gardening

Keynko 1053604
Email: keynko@gmail.com
Web site: http://keynko.com/
Freq: Daily
Circ: 6525
Crafts, Family & Parenting

Kezia Dugdale MSP blog 988440
Tel: 44 01313 486894
Web site: http://www.keziadugdale.com/
Freq: Daily
Circ: 7096
Politics

Kezzy's Crafty Journey 1053343
Web site: http://kezzyscraftyjourney.
blogspot.co.uk/
Freq: Daily
Circ: 1160
Crafts

Kia Designs Blog 986171
Editorial: Kia Designs, Studio 102, 4 Little
Portland Street, London W1W 7JB
Web site: www.kiadesigns.co.uk/kia-
designs-blog
Freq: Daily
Circ: 30
Architecture & Design, Do-It-Yourself
(DIY), Gardening, Home, Property
Management & Maintenance, Real Estate

Kian David Griffin 1050170
Email: kiangriffin@gmail.com
Web site: http://kiandavidgriffin.blogspot.ie/
Freq: Daily
Circ: 1391
Regional General Interest, Travel

KiddyCharts Blog 987453
Editorial: 10 Highfields, Saffron Walden,
Saffron Walden CB10 2AD
Email: info@kiddycharts.com
Web site: www.kiddycharts.com
Freq: Daily
Circ: 139087
Family & Parenting

Kids' Blog Club 995003
Web site: kidsblogclub.com
Freq: Daily
Circ: 8198
Family & Parenting

Kids' Craft Room 995005
Email: emma@kidscraftroom.com
Web site: http://kidscraftroom.com/
Freq: Daily
Circ: 32296
Crafts, Family & Parenting

Kids Travel 2 Blog 1053963
Tel: 44 01509 239307
Email: info@kidstravel2.com
Web site: http://blog.kidstravel2.com/
Freq: Daily
Circ: 379
Family & Parenting, Fashion

KILLER COLOURS 1060241
Email: killercolours@gmail.com
Web site: http://rodeo.net/killercolours/
Freq: Daily
Circ: 204
Beauty & Grooming, Cosmetics, Hair

KILLER COLOURS 1060501
Email: killercolours@gmail.com
Web site: http://rodeo.net/killercolours/
Freq: Daily
Circ: 204
Beauty & Grooming, Cosmetics, Hair

Kim Dellow 995547
Email: kim.dellow@gmail.com
Web site: http://www.kimdellow.co.uk/
Freq: Daily
Circ: 7542
Crafts, Do-It-Yourself (DIY)

Kim the Bookworm 996800
Email: kim@kimthebookworm.co.uk
Web site: http://www.kimthebookworm.co.
uk
Freq: Daily
Circ: 12477
Literature

**Kimb Jones Making and
Doing with WordPress** 1053462
Web site: http://kimb.me/
Freq: Daily
Circ: 6313
Computers, Internet, Software

Kine acupuntura 1060630
Web site: http://kineacupuntura.blogspot.
com/
Freq: Daily
Circ: 521
Alternative Medicine

**King & McGaw Inspiration
Blog** 1053847
Tel: 44 02033 724865
Email: marketing@kingandmcgaw.com
Web site: https://www.kingandmcgaw.com/
inspiration
Freq: Daily
Circ: 28
Art, Do-It-Yourself (DIY)

King Cricket 986172
Email: king@kingcricket.co.uk
Web site: www.kingcricket.co.uk
Freq: Daily
Circ: 10608
Cricket

King of Fuel 1003925
Email: editor@kingoffuel.com
Web site: http://www.kingoffuel.com/
Freq: Daily
Circ: 10671
Editor: Simon Tann
Antique & Collectible Cars, Automakers,
Automotive, Boating & Yachting, Driving,
Motorcycles, Off-road & 4-Wheel Drive
Vehicles, Trucks & SUVs

The King's Fund blog 1053305
Editorial: 11 - 13 Cavendish Square, London
W1G 0AN Tel: 44 02073 072400
Email: mediaoffice@kingsfund.org.uk
Web site: http://www.kingsfund.org.uk/blog
Freq: Daily
Circ: 146
Community Care (UK)

Kingsdown Roots 1052683
Web site: www.kingsdownroots.co.uk
Freq: Daily
Circ: 2637
Profile: Kingsdown Roots covers men's
fashion. The blog has an archive dating back
to December 2013 and shares an extensive
blogroll.
Fashion

Kinnemaniac 987956
Web site: http://www.kinnemaniac.com/
Freq: Daily
Circ: 11728
Profile: Blog covering movies.
KINNEMANIAC blog discusses anything

from movies and film festivals to the film
industry.
Entertainment, Movies & Video

Kip Hakes 1054564
Web site: www.kiphakes.com/category/blog
Freq: Daily
Circ: 39
Family & Parenting, Men's Interests

Kirjamatkat 1061952
Email: punahilkka84@gmail.com
Web site: https://kirjamatkat.wordpress.
com/
Freq: Daily
Circ: 48
Books, Literature

Kirkwood Golf 1057070
Web site: http://ercn86.gilliankirkwood.co.
uk/
Freq: Daily
Circ: 20
Editor: Colin Farquharson
Golf

Kirst Over The World 996890
Email: kirstovertheworld@gmail.com
Web site: http://kirstovertheworld.com/
Freq: Daily
Circ: 6935
Travel

Kirsty Norton blog 1053319
Email: yogakirsty@gmail.com
Web site: http://www.kirstynortonyoga.co.
uk/blog
Freq: Daily
Circ:
Alternative Medicine, Fitness & Exercise,
Organic Food

Kissanpäiviä sijaiskodissa
1061991
Email: myrskyhoo@gmail.com
Web site: http://moggydays.blogspot.fi/
Freq: Daily
Circ: 1647
Nature & Wildlife

Kit Me Out 996835
Tel: 44 01733 564077
Email: sales@kitmeout.com
Web site: https://www.kitmeout.com/blogs/
kitmeout-designer-clothes-fashion-blog-
amp-fashion-forum
Freq: Daily
Circ: 9295
Fashion

The Kitchen Shed 988333
Web site: thekitchenshed.co.uk
Freq: Daily
Circ: 8854
Profile: Blog covering food, recipes, healthy
eating, nutrition and vegetarian food ideas.
Cooking & Baking, Family & Parenting,
Health & Medicine

The Kitchen Shed 1052736
Email: charlie.mace@me.com
Web site: thekitchenshed.co.uk
Freq: Daily
Circ: 8854
Profile: Blog covering food, recipes, healthy
eating, nutrition and vegetarian food ideas.
Cooking & Baking, Nutrition, Organic
Food

Kitty Rambles A Lot 1052864
Email: kittyramblesalot@yahoo.co.uk
Web site: kittyramblesalot.com
Freq: Daily
Circ: 9715
Profile: Blog covering plus size fashion,
beauty and lifestyle. The blog has an archive
dating back to March 2014.
Fashion, Photography

The Kiwi Has Landed 1054537
Tel: 44 07725 332584
Email: shielsiain@gmail.com
Web site: http://www.thekiwihaslanded.
com/
Freq: Daily
Circ: 11396
Airline Inflight, Railroad, Travel

Kjøkkenfesten 1061184
Email: jorgen.helland@halogen.no
Web site: http://www.kjokkenfesten.no/
Freq: Daily
Circ: 6096
Internet, Marketing

KlairedeLys 1098942
Email: klairedelysblog@googlemail.com
Web site: www.klairedelys.com
Freq: Daily
Circ: 25958
Beauty & Grooming, Cosmetics, Hair

Klaus and Heidi 1053134
Web site: klausandheidi.com
Freq: Daily
Circ: 521
News & Current Affairs

**Knackered Mothers' Wine
Club** 988248
Email: knackeredmother@gmail.com
Web site: knackeredmotherswineclub.
blogspot.co.uk
Freq: Daily
Circ: 4040
Wine/Winemaking

KodeGeek 1061063
Web site: http://kodegeek.com
Freq: Daily
Circ: 917
Auto Aftermarket, Computers, Data
Management, Electronics, Government
Technology, Industry, Internet, Mobile
Communications, Security & Security
Systems, Software

Kokit ja Potit 1061074
Email: kokitjapotit@gmail.com
Web site: http://kokitjapotit.blogspot.fi/
Freq: Daily
Circ: 7863
Cooking & Baking, Food

Kolmen Tähden Koti 1061963
Email: marika.suomi76@gmail.com
Web site: http://www.kolmentahdenkoti.fi/
Freq: Daily
Circ: 624
Architecture & Design, Do-It-Yourself
(DIY), Gardening, Home, Property
Management & Maintenance, Real Estate

Koozai 1056767
Editorial: 53 Chandos Place, Covent
Garden, London WC2N 4HS
Tel: 44 02031 313405
Email: info@koozai.com
Web site: https://www.koozai.com/blog/
Freq: Daily
Circ: 42879
Advertising Industry, Branding, Marketing

Korea Gig Guide 1061357
Web site: http://www.koreagigguide.com
Freq: Daily
Circ: 8386
Art, Classical/Choral/Band Music,
Country, Folk, Bluegrass, Dance Music,
Jazz & Blues, Music, Pop Music, R&B,
Urban, World, Rap & Hip Hop, Rock Music

Korttipaja SannaS 1061404
Web site: http://korttipajasannas.blogspot.fi/
Freq: Daily
Circ: 2010
Crafts

Krepsemor's hage 1061095
Web site: http://krepsemor.blogspot.com
Freq: Daily
Circ: 1004
Gardening

KRLA Blog 1060641
Web site: http://www.krla870.com/blogs.
aspx
Freq: Daily
Circ:
National News, Politics

KTMY 1053762
Email: kstie@ktmy.co.uk
Web site: www.ktmy.co.uk
Freq: Daily
Circ: 9269

UK Blogs

Profile: Blog covering lifestyle and student lifestyle. The blog has an archive dating back to September 2014.
Health & Medicine, Women's Interests

Kuang Hu
1060931
Web site: http://blog.sina.com.cn/falali
Freq: Daily
Circ: 31414
Antique & Collectible Cars, Automakers, Automotive, Driving, Motorcycles, Off-road & 4-Wheel Drive Vehicles, Trucks & SUVs

Kujerruksia
1061643
Email: pigeonnaire@gmail.com
Web site: http://pigeonnaire.blogspot.fi/
Freq: Daily
Circ: 2326
Books, Movies & Video, Theater & Performing Arts

Kukkaiselämää
1061857
Email: myusualdailylife@gmail.com
Web site: http://myusualdailylife.blogspot.fi/
Freq: Daily
Circ: 2002
Gardening

Kulinaarimuruja
1061583
Email: kulinaarimuruja@gmail.com
Web site: http://valipala.blogspot.fi/
Freq: Daily
Circ: 1776
Alcohol & Spirits, Cooking & Baking, Food

Kulttuurielämää Helsingissä
1061371
Email: culturallifeofhelsinki@gmail.com
Web site: http://culturallifeofhelsinki.blogspot.fi/
Freq: Daily
Circ: 2100
Antiques/Collectibles, Art, Arts, Literature, Photography, Theater & Performing Arts, Visual Arts

Kulttuurin sekakäyttäjä
1061257
Web site: http://sekakayttoa.blogspot.fi/
Freq: Daily
Circ: 1437
Antiques/Collectibles, Art, Arts, Literature, Photography, Theater & Performing Arts, Visual Arts

Kulttuurishokki
1061505
Email: jesse.raatikainen@me.com
Freq: Daily
Antiques/Collectibles, Art, Arts, Literature, Movies & Video, Photography, Theater & Performing Arts, Visual Arts

Kuoni Travel Blog
1052591
Tel: 44 01306 856101
Web site: http://www.kuoni.co.uk/
Freq: Daily
Circ: 890832
Airline Inflight, Railroad, Travel

Kurashi
1061006
Web site: http://martinjapan.blogspot.com
Freq: Daily
Circ: 4477
Environment

Kuriositas
998129
Email: taliesyn30@aol.com
Web site: www.kuriositas.com
Freq: Daily
Circ: 47091
Editor: RJ Evans
Antiques/Collectibles, Art, Arts, Literature, Photography, Theater & Performing Arts, Visual Arts

Kwai Chi
1053424
Email: reviews@kwaichi.com
Web site: kwaichi.com
Freq: Daily
Circ: 11121
Cooking & Baking, Family & Parenting, Restaurant Reviews

Kym's Crafty Cards
986336
Editorial: The Leathermarket (13.3.1), 11-13 Weston Street, London SE1 3ER

Web site: http://kyms-crafty-cards.blogspot.co.uk/p/my-craft-room.html
Freq: Daily
Circ: 7098
Charitable Foundations, Crafts

La Belle Aventure
1054241
Email: la.belle.aventure.12@gmail.com
Web site: http://thebelleaventure.blogspot.co.uk/
Freq: Daily
Circ: 728
Cosmetics, Fashion, Women's Interests

La Concordia Blog
1053271
Tel: 44 07734 540914
Email: lesleyann@la-concordia.co.uk
Web site: http://la-concordia.co.uk/blog
Freq: Daily
Circ: 22
Airline Inflight, Railroad, Travel

labour and capital
986591
Web site: labourandcapital.blogspot.co.uk
Freq: Daily
Circ: 10116
Politics

Labour Uncut
987338
Email: editorial@labour-uncut.co.uk
Web site: http://labour-uncut.co.uk
Freq: Daily
Circ: 124096
Politics, Social Issues

LabourList
986176
Editorial: PO Box 70887, London N1P 1LL
Email: mail@labourlist.org
Web site: labourlist.org
Freq: Daily
Circ: 83820
Editor: Peter Edwards
Politics

Lado Naranja!
1060639
Web site: http://www.elladonaranja.blogspot.com
Freq: Daily
Circ: 521
Environment, Human Rights, Politics

Lady from a Tramp
1064288
Email: info@ladyfromatramp.co.uk
Web site: http://www.ladyfromatramp.co.uk/
Freq: Daily
Circ: 8706
Profile: Lady From a Tramp covers beauty, fashion, food, travel and lifestyle. The blog has an archive dating back to October 2010.
Beauty & Grooming, Cooking & Baking, Cosmetics, Family & Parenting, Fashion, Hair, Restaurant Reviews, Travel, Women's Interests

The Lady of the World
1062748
Web site: theladyoftheworld.com
Freq: Daily
Circ: 12158
Movies & Video, Women's Interests

Lady Writes
1095185
Email: info@ladywritesblog.com
Web site: http://www.ladywritesblog.com/
Freq: Daily
Circ: 12882
Beauty & Grooming, Cosmetics, Hair, Relationships, Women's Interests

LAFOTKA
1053893
Email: krista@handpickedmedia.co.uk
Web site: http://www.lafotka.com/
Freq: Daily
Circ: 9834
Profile: Blog covering fashion, style and health.
Beauty & Grooming, Cosmetics, Fashion, Hair, Nutrition, Women's Interests

Lamento de Portnoy
1061415
Web site: http://ellamentodeportnoy.blogspot.com/
Freq: Daily
Circ: 3164
Literature, Movies & Video

Lancashire Mummy
1052685
Editorial: 7 Stafford Road, Eccles, Manchester M30 9HN
Web site: https://lancashiremummy.wordpress.com/
Freq: Daily
Circ: 6
Beauty & Grooming, Cosmetics, Do-It-Yourself (DIY), Family & Parenting, Hair, Nutrition, Women's Interests

Land Matters
997673
Email: mail@andywightman.com
Web site: http://www.andywightman.com/
Freq: Daily
Circ: 16880
Politics

Landlord and BTL Blog
986177
Editorial: The Office, 5 Kendal Court, West Bridgford NG2 5HE
Email: contact@propertyhawk.co.uk
Web site: blog.propertyhawk.co.uk
Freq: Daily
Circ: 57237
Property Management & Maintenance

Landlord Blog/Life
1053303
Web site: www.propertyinvestmentproject.co.uk/blog/
Freq: Daily
Circ: 31554
Building & Construction, Interior Design, Legal Affairs, Residential Real Estate, Retail

The Landlord Law Blog
986254
Editorial: 148 Unthank Road, Norwich NR2 2RS **Tel:** 44 01603 763096
Web site: www.landlordlawblog.co.uk
Freq: Daily
Circ: 73566
Finance, Legal Affairs, Residential Real Estate

LandlordZONE Blog
986178
Editorial: Lancaster House, 70-76 Blackburn Street, Radcliffe, Manchester M26 2JW
Tel: 44 08452 604420
Web site: www.landlordzone.co.uk/news
Circ: 26
Property Management & Maintenance

The Language Business
1052747
Email: info@ie-connect.com
Web site: http://www.dblackie.blogs.com/
Freq: Daily
Circ: 208
Art, Education

Lao Cui Teahouse's Blog
1061557
Tel: 44 86138 01587069
Web site: http://blog.sina.com.cn/nanjinglaocui
Freq: Daily
Circ: 33989999
Alcohol & Spirits

Lao Sha
1061805
Web site: http://shaminnong.blog.sohu.com
Freq: Daily
Circ: 53
Financial Markets

Lapsen tahtiin
1061948
Web site: http://pienenperheenaiti.blogspot.co.uk/
Freq: Daily
Circ: 521
Elementary School, Internet, Preschool, Teen/Young Adult, Trading Cards & Comics

Larger Family Life
986483
Editorial: Larger Family Life, PO Box 645, Rochester, Rochester ME3 9XJ
Email: family@largerfamilylife.com
Web site: www.largerfamilylife.com
Freq: Daily
Circ: 21362
Profile: Blog covering large family lifestyle, pregnancy and parenting to travel, personal finance, education, recipes and home.
Education, Family & Parenting, Women's Interests

The Last Ditch
1053315
Web site: lastditch.typepad.com
Freq: Daily
Circ: 676033
Photography, Travel

Last Style of Defense
987521
Editorial: 1 Chalford Gardens, Westbury BA13 3RH
Email: laststyleofdefense@googlemail.com
Web site: www.laststyleofdefense.com
Freq: Daily
Circ: 7516
Fashion

Last Year's Girl
988323
Email: lisamarie@pixlet.net
Web site: http://lastyearsgirl.pixlet.net/
Freq: Daily
Circ: 11568
Classical/Choral/Band Music, Country, Folk, Bluegrass, Dance Music, Jazz & Blues, Music, Pop Music, R&B, Urban, World, Rap & Hip Hop, Rock Music

lastminute.com blog
986179
Editorial: Lastminute.com, Victoria Gate, Chobham Road, Woking GU21 6JD
Tel: 44 02078 664200
Web site: http://www.lastminute.com/blog/
Freq: Daily
Circ: 2261
Alcohol & Spirits, Bars, Clubs & Pubs, Beer, Beverages, Comedy, Entertainment, Local Entertainment Guides, Restaurant Reviews, Travel, Wine/Winemaking

Late for Reality
1057071
Web site: http://www.lateforreality.co.uk/
Freq: Daily
Circ: 6717
Cosmetics, Do-It-Yourself (DIY), Entertainment, Family & Parenting, Health & Medicine, Personal Finance, Relationships

Lathe
1061850
Web site: http://blog.sina.com.cn/lathe
Freq: Daily
Circ: 39269999
Antique & Collectible Cars, Automakers, Automotive, Driving, Motorcycles, Off-road & 4-Wheel Drive Vehicles, Trucks & SUVs

Latiendo en la Cueva
1061825
Web site: http://blogs.eluniversal.com/eu3/Blogs/latie_index.shtml
Freq: Daily
Circ: 17653
Lifestyle, Men's Interests, National News, Regional General Interest, Women's Interests

Laura Ashley blog
1054388
Web site: http://www.lauraashley.com/blog/
Freq: Daily
Circ: 54053
Do-It-Yourself (DIY), Fashion

Laura de Lille
1061288
Email: laurapollari@hotmail.com
Web site: http://www.lily.fi/blogit/laura-de-lille
Freq: Daily
Circ: 29385
Airline Inflight, Lifestyle, Men's Interests, Railroad, Regional General Interest, Travel, Women's Interests

Laura Let's go -matkablogi
1061605
Email: laura.a.rumbin@gmail.com
Web site: http://www.laurarumbin.com/
Freq: Daily
Circ: 2902
Airline Inflight, Railroad, Travel

Laura McInerney
1053322
Email: lauramcinerney1@gmail.com
Web site: http://lauramcinerney.com/
Freq: Daily
Circ: 14144
Editor: Laura McInerney
Profile: Blog covering education. Laura McInerney blog discusses anything from education and to education industry and

schools. The blog has an archive dating back to December 2011.
Education

Laura's Lovely Blog 1062733
Web site: http://www.laurasummers.co.uk/
Freq: Daily
Circ: 53947
Broadcasting, Literature, Social Issues, Women's Interests

Lauren Hardcastle - Being Yourself is Better 998391
Web site: laurensandrah.blogspot.co.uk
Freq: Daily
Circ: 521
Fashion, Women's Interests

Lauren Loves 1054626
Web site: http://www.laurenlovesblog.co.uk/
Freq: Daily
Circ: 8631
Beauty & Grooming, Cosmetics, Fashion, Hair

Laurence Borel blog 1053606
Email: hello@laurenceborel.com
Web site: http://www.laurenceborel.com
Freq: Daily
Circ: 6162
Branding

Laurence King News 1103016
Editorial: 361-373 City Road, 4th Floor, London EC1V 1LR
Web site: http://www.laurenceking.com/en/news/
Freq: Daily
Art, Literature, Photography, Visual Arts

Laurenella 1052722
Web site: www.laurenella.net
Freq: Daily
Circ: 8976
Profile: Blog covering fashion. Laurenella blog discusses anything from the latest fashion trends and personal style to fashion accessories and beauty buys. The blog shares an extensive blog roll.
Beauty & Grooming, Cooking & Baking, Cosmetics, Fashion, Hair, Women's Interests

Lavender and Lovage 986907
Web site: www.lavenderandlovage.com
Freq: Daily
Circ: 44714
Cooking & Baking, Restaurant Reviews

Lawrie on Gold 1074796
Email: lawrieongold@gmail.com
Web site: https://lawrieongold.com/
Freq: Daily
Circ: 8620
Mining & Quarrying

Lazy Girl Running 1053431
Email: hello@lazygirlrunning.com
Web site: http://www.lazygirlrunning.com/
Freq: Daily
Circ: 10759
Fitness & Exercise, Nutrition, Women's Interests

The Lazy Girl's Guide to Life 988094
Email: familypanel@yahoo.co.uk
Web site: https://lazygirluk.wordpress.com/
Freq: Daily
Circ: 49
Family & Parenting, Regional General Interest, Women's Interests

The LDN Diaries 987556
Editorial: 85 Gillespie Court, 9 Queensland Road, London N7 7FH
Email: contact@theldndiaries.com
Web site: http://theldndiaries.com/
Freq: Daily
Circ: 24171
Editor: Paula Holmes
Profile: Blog covering fashion, beauty and London lifestyle. The blog has an archive dating back to April 2012.
Architecture & Design, Beauty & Grooming, Cosmetics, Do-It-Yourself

(DIY), Fashion, Gardening, Hair, Home, Lifestyle, Men's Interests

LDN Fashion 986180
Editorial: LDNfashion.com, St Johns Centre, 85 Pitfield Street, London N1 6LP
Web site: www.ldnfashion.com
Freq: Daily
Circ: 17036
Fashion

LDNISTA 987506
Editorial: 14 Devonshire Place, London W1G 6HX
Email: david@ldnista.com
Web site: http://www.ldnista.com
Freq: Daily
Circ: 521
Alcohol & Spirits, Art, Bars, Clubs & Pubs, Beauty & Grooming, Beer, Beverages, Cooking & Baking, Cosmetics, Hair, Movies & Video

LDNLife 1094739
Email: editor@ldnlife.com
Web site: http://www.ldnlife.com/
Freq: Daily
Circ: 10972
Editor: Adam Clarke
Bars, Clubs & Pubs, Comedy, Entertainment, Local Entertainment Guides, Movies & Video, Restaurant Reviews

Le Blog - Hey Saturday 1098977
Email: hey@heysaturday.co
Web site: http://www.heysaturday.co/blog/
Freq: Daily
Circ: 89
Photography, Relationships

Le Blow 988484
Email: leblow@leblow.co.uk
Web site: leblow.co.uk
Circ: 9409
Profile: Website covering fashion, beauty, lifestyle, entertainment and music.
Beauty & Grooming, Cosmetics, Fashion, Hair, Women's Interests

Le Grove 988555
Email: pedro@le-grove.co.uk
Web site: http://le-grove.co.uk/
Freq: Daily
Circ: 113754
Soccer

League Football Education blog 1052645
Tel: 44 01772 326870
Email: info@lfe.org.uk
Web site: http://www.lfe.org.uk/blog/
Freq: Daily
Circ: 86
Soccer

Lean Bean Nutrition 997712
Email: leanbeannutrition@gmail.com
Web site: https://leanbeannutrition.com/
Freq: Daily
Circ: 10443
Cooking & Baking

Leapfrogg 1052860
Editorial: Second Floor, Southdown House, 130a Western Road, Brighton BN1 2LA
Tel: 44 01273 322830
Email: enquiries@leapfrogg.co.uk
Web site: http://www.leapfrogg.co.uk/froggblog/
Freq: Daily
Circ: 10
Branding, Marketing

Learn 4 Life 1054200
Web site: http://www.l4l.co.uk/
Freq: Daily
Circ: 8453
Audio Video Trade, Cameras, Consumer Electronics, Education, Mobile Electronics, Movies & Video

The Learning Geek 1054659
Web site: http://thelearninggeek.com/blog/
Freq: Daily
Circ: 184

Profile: Blog covering education. The Learning Geek blog discusses anything from education and schools to child behavior. The blog has an archive dating back to August 2013 and shares an extensive blog roll.
Education

Learning Leader 1053098
Web site: http://leadinglearner.me/
Freq: Daily
Circ: 14660
Alumni, Careers, Education, Student Lifestyle, Teachers

Learning Pool Blog 996374
Tel: 353 02071 019383
Email: hello@learningpool.com
Web site: https://www.learningpool.com/about-us/blog/
Freq: Daily
Circ: 20394
Careers, Education, Higher Education, Students

The Learning Spy 987336
Web site: learningspy.co.uk
Freq: Daily
Circ: 75597
Education, Schools & Institutions

Lee Riley (Welcome to my world...) 1054942
Web site: http://leeriley1.blogspot.co.uk/
Freq: Daily
Circ: 1531
Art, Men's Interests, Music, Rock Music, Visual Arts

Leena-muori leipoo 1061029
Email: leena-muori@suomi24.fi
Web site: http://leena-muorileipoo.vuodatus.net/
Freq: Daily
Circ: 15450
Cooking & Baking

Leena-muori leipoo 1061637
Email: leena-muori@suomi24.fi
Web site: http://leena-muorileipoo.vuodatus.net/
Freq: Daily
Circ: 15450
Cooking & Baking

Left Brain/Right Brain 996192
Web site: leftbrainrightbrain.co.uk
Freq: Daily
Circ: 16321
Disability, Neurology

Left Foot Forward 986181
Editorial: 40 Underwood Street, London N1 7JQ
Email: editor@leftfootforward.org
Web site: leftfootforward.org
Freq: Daily
Circ: 45976
Politics, Social Issues

Left Futures 987337
Web site: www.leftfutures.org
Freq: Daily
Circ: 16481
Politics, Social Issues

Left Unity 996504
Editorial: c/o Housmans, 5 Caledonian Road, London N1 9DX
Email: press@leftunity.org
Web site: http://leftunity.org/
Freq: Daily
Circ: 14183
Politics

Legal Recruitment 986745
Editorial: Ten-Percent.co.uk, Derwen Bach, Glyndwr Road, Mold CH7 5LW
Tel: 44 02071 274343
Web site: legalrecruitment.blogspot.com
Freq: Daily
Circ: 1216
Careers, Recruiting

Legos Argentina 1061028
Web site: http://legosargentina.blogspot.com/
Freq: Daily

Circ: 687
Crafts, Hobbies, & Collecting, Games, Competitions & Events

Lehtipollon leikekirja 1061115
Web site: http://lehtipollo.blogspot.fi/
Freq: Daily
Circ: 1152
Crafts

Lela London 987724
Editorial: 11 Sylvester Road, Barnsley N2 8HN
Web site: lelalondon.com
Freq: Daily
Circ: 12057
Audio Video Trade, Beauty & Grooming, Cameras, Consumer Electronics, Cooking & Baking, Cosmetics, Fashion, Food, Grocery Stores, Hair

Lemon & Oats 1070233
Editorial: 4/8 Rodney Street, Edinburgh EH4 1NG
Web site: www.lemonandoats.com
Freq: Daily
Circ: 880
Alternative Medicine, Fitness & Exercise, Health & Medicine, Nutrition

Lemontaste 1053491
Email: hello@lemonaste.com
Web site: https://thelemongrove.net/
Freq: Daily
Circ: 13649
Cooking & Baking, Luxury Goods, Restaurant Reviews, Travel

Lending Stream Blog 999388
Editorial: Wisteria Camrose House, 2A Camrose Avenue, London HA8 6EG
Tel: 44 02035 647028
Email: info@lendingstream.co.uk
Web site: www.lendingstream.co.uk/blog
Freq: Daily
Circ: 75720
Personal Finance

Leng Yan Guan Chao 1060844
Email: lengyankansh@sohu.com
Web site: http://lengyankansh.blog.sohu.com
Freq: Daily
Fashion

Leo Straniuksen blogi 1061225
Email: leo.stranius@iki.fi
Web site: http://leostranius.fi
Freq: Daily
Circ: 7295
Environment, Politics

Leonatico 1061674
Web site: http://blogs.eluniversal.com/eu3/Blogs/leon_index.shtml
Freq: Daily
Circ: 7585
News & Current Affairs

Let Me Tell You About Beer 1073135
Email: letmetellyouaboutbeer@gmail.com
Web site: www.letmetellyouaboutbeer.co.uk
Freq: Daily
Circ: 8999
Editor: Melissa Cole
Beer

Letras...Notas...Otras 1061653
Web site: http://letrasnotasotras.blogspot.com/
Freq: Daily
Circ: 521
Literature

Let's Do Something Crafty 997606
Email: jessicacherryblogs@gmail.com
Web site: http://letsdosomethingcrafty.com/
Freq: Daily
Circ: 9790
Crafts

Let's Talk Golf 996576
Web site: http://www.letstalkgolf.co.uk/
Freq: Daily

Circ: 10457
Golf

Let's Talk Mommy 997922
Web site: www.letstalkmommy.com
Freq: Daily
Circ: 42685
Family & Parenting

Letters to Monty (the ramblings of a deluded man) 1055299
Web site: http://artinacorner.blogspot.co.uk/
Freq: Daily
Circ: 856
Men's Interests

Letting a Property Blog 999342
Editorial: Suite 2, Welch House, 90 High Street, Henley-in-Arden B95 5BY
Tel: 44 03335 778888
Email: support@lettingaproperty.com
Web site: www.lettingaproperty.com/property-blog
Freq: Daily
Circ: 7917
Architecture & Design, Do-It-Yourself (DIY), Gardening, Home, Property Management & Maintenance, Real Estate

Letting Focus Blog 986182
Editorial: 107 Algernon Rd, London SE13 7AP
Web site: www.lettingfocus.com/blogs/
Freq: Daily
Circ: 245
Architecture & Design, Do-It-Yourself (DIY), Gardening, Home, Property Management & Maintenance, Real Estate

Lewis Insight 1059123
Web site: http://chrislewisinsight.com
Freq: Daily
Circ: 9022
Computers, Medical Technology

Lex Blog 1060922
Web site: http://lexmaster.blogspot.com/
Freq: Daily
Circ: 1161
Art, Graphic Design

LexisClick Blog 1054187
Editorial: 76 Shelley Road East, Boscombe, Bournemouth BH7 6HB
Tel: 44 01202 788333
Web site: http://www.lexisclick.com/blog/
Freq: Daily
Circ: 57
Branding, Internet, Marketing

Lexus Blog 996375
Editorial: Toyota (GB) PLC – Lexus Division, PO Box 814, Portsmouth PO6 9AY
Tel: 44 08451 295484
Web site: blog.lexus.co.uk
Freq: Daily
Circ: 62039
Automakers

LG Blog Chile 1060584
Web site: http://www.lgblog.cl
Freq: Daily
Circ: 56426
Auto Aftermarket, Computers, Data Management, Electronics, Government Technology, Industry, Internet, Mobile Communications, Security & Security Systems, Software

LG WALLMARK 1060219
Web site: http://www.lgwallmark.com
Freq: Daily
Circ: 10288
Internet

LG WALLMARK 1060560
Web site: http://www.lgwallmark.com
Freq: Daily
Circ: 10288
Internet

Li Chengpeng 1061693
Email: gongzuoyaoqing@sina.com
Web site: http://blog.sina.com.cn/lichengpeng
Freq: Daily

Circ: 10380030
Social Issues

Li Yang Crazy english 1061011
Email: readershome@crazyenglish.com
Web site: http://blog.sina.com.cn/lyce
Freq: Daily
Circ: 115520
Disability, Education, Higher Education, Preschool, Schools & Institutions, Students

Liberal Burblings 987341
Email: paulwalteruk@yahoo.co.uk
Web site: https://paulwalternewbury.wordpress.com
Freq: Daily
Circ: 205
Politics, Social Issues

Liberal Democrat Voice 986184
Email: voice@libdemvoice.org
Web site: libdemvoice.org
Freq: Daily
Circ: 40333
Politics

Liberal England 986185
Email: bonkers.hall@btinternet.com
Web site: liberalengland.blogspot.com/
Freq: Daily
Circ: 11756
Politics

Liberate Media Blog 986698
Editorial: 4th Floor, International House, Queens Road, Brighton BN1 3XE
Email: hello@liberatemedia.com
Web site: www.liberatemedia.com/blog
Freq: Daily
Circ: 102
Advertising Industry, Branding, Broadcasting, Graphic Design, Marketing, Media & Communications, Photography, Publishing

The Libertarian Alliance Blog 999385
Editorial: Suite 35, 2 Lansdowne Row, London W1J 6HL Tel: 44 07956 472199
Email: director@libertarian.co.uk
Web site: http://thelibertarianalliance.com/
Freq: Daily
Circ: 7727
Politics

Liberty Blog 998352
Tel: 44 02077 341234
Email: social@liberty.co.uk
Web site: http://www.liberty.co.uk/blog
Freq: Daily
Circ: 30
Fashion, Women's Interests

Liberty Blog 1053605
Editorial: Liberty House, 26 - 30 Strutton Ground, London SW1P 2HR
Tel: 44 02074 033888
Web site: https://www.liberty-human-rights.org.uk/news/blog
Freq: Daily
Circ: 2
Government, Human Rights

The Liberty Craft Blog - CEASED 997654
Web site: http://www.liberty.co.uk/blog/category/the-liberty-craft-blog/
Freq: Daily
Circ: 104219
Crafts

Liberty Online Marketing Agency Blog 1054138
Editorial: Units 1 & 2 Purbeck House, Cardiff Business Park, Llanishen, Cardiff CF14 5GJ
Email: info@libertymarketing.co.uk
Web site: http://www.libertymarketing.co.uk/blog/
Freq: Daily
Circ: 56
Branding, Internet, Marketing

LibertyLondonGirl 986186
Editorial: Garden Flat, 3 Gloucester Crescent, London NW1 7DS
Email: contact@libertylondongirl.com

Web site: www.libertylondongirl.com
Freq: Daily
Circ: 60896
Beauty & Grooming, Cosmetics, Fashion, Hair

Librarians on the loose 1054256
Web site: https://librariansontheloose.wordpress.com/
Freq: Daily
Circ: 11
News & Current Affairs

Libros que me llegan 1060918
Web site: http://loslibrosquemellegan.blogspot.com/
Freq: Daily
Circ: 845
Books, Literature

Libros y Surtidores 1061776
Web site: http://anibal-librosysurtidores.blogspot.com
Freq: Daily
Circ: 1771
Books

Liderazgo integral 1061315
Web site: http://www.liderazgo-integral.com
Freq: Daily
Circ: 521
News & Current Affairs

Liemessä 1061987
Email: jenni@jennihayrinen.com
Web site: http://liemessa.blogspot.com
Freq: Daily
Circ: 1480
Alcohol & Spirits, Consumer Goods & Products, Cooking & Baking, Food, Tobacco

The life & loves of nine-grandstudent 1054141
Email: ninegrandstudent@gmail.com
Web site: http://ninegrandstudent.co.uk
Freq: Daily
Circ: 6486
Profile: Blog covering student lifestyle. The Life & Loves of ninegrandstudent discusses anything from recipes and budgeting to beauty, lifestyle and study tips.
Beauty & Grooming, Cooking & Baking, Cosmetics, Education, Fashion, Hair, Personal Finance, Regional General Interest, Relationships, Women's Interests

Life According to Mrs Shilts 1054183
Web site: www.mrsshilts.co.uk
Freq: Daily
Circ: 49330
Family & Parenting

Life after Helsinki 2007 1062014
Web site: http://ilkar.blogspot.fi
Freq: Daily
Circ: 9442
Classical/Choral/Band Music, Country, Folk, Bluegrass, Dance Music, Jazz & Blues, Music, Pop Music, R&B, Urban, World, Rap & Hip Hop, Rock Music

Life and Times of a Student 1052852
Email: missisgoode@gmail.com
Web site: http://missisgoode.blogspot.co.uk/
Freq: Daily
Circ: 3699
Profile: Blog covering student lifestyle, university advice and leisure activities. The blog has an archive dating back to August 2012.
Education, Student Lifestyle, Women's Interests

The Life and Times of the Working Mum 999692
Editorial: Hopwood Prospect Gardens, Elm Road, Evesham WR11 3PX
Email: thelifeandtimesoftheworkingmum@gmail.com
Web site: www.thelifeandtimesoftheworkingmum.com
Freq: Daily

Circ: 2919
Family & Parenting

Life as a widower 1053767
Freq: Daily
Profile: Blog covering fatherhood. The LIFE AS A WIDOWER blog discusses anything from fatherhood and single parent. The blog has an archive dating back to January 2013.
News & Current Affairs

Life As It Is 988233
Web site: www.writinglifeasitis.blogspot.co.uk
Circ: 9321
Family & Parenting

Life at the Feeding Edge 1052795
Web site: http://www.feedingedge.co.uk/blog/
Freq: Daily
Circ: 7812
Computers, Internet

Life at the Zoo 988335
Web site: lifeatthezoo.com
Freq: Daily
Circ: 9648
News & Current Affairs

Life by Lotte 1052608
Web site: lifebylotte.com
Freq: Daily
Circ: 9694
Profile: Blog covering lifestyle. The Life by Lotte Blog discusses anything from interior design and day to day life to restaurants and culture. The blog has an archive dating back to October 2012.
Do-It-Yourself (DIY), Family & Parenting, Women's Interests

Life Daily 1052827
Email: contactlifedaily@gmail.com
Web site: http://lifedaily.co.uk/
Freq: Daily
Circ: 8468
Alcohol & Spirits, Beauty & Grooming, Cooking & Baking, Cosmetics, Family & Parenting, Hair, Restaurant Reviews, Travel, Women's Interests

Life In A Breakdown 987112
Editorial: 7 High Grange, Lichfield WS13 7DZ Tel: 44 07877 306262
Email: sarah@lifeinabreakdown.com
Web site: www.lifeinabreakdown.com
Freq: Daily
Circ: 153391
Architecture & Design, Beauty & Grooming, Cosmetics, Do-It-Yourself (DIY), Fashion, Gardening, Hair, Home, Property Management & Maintenance, Real Estate

Life in Eight 1053927
Email: gaby@lifeineight.com
Web site: lifeineight.com
Freq: Daily
Circ: 5898
Profile: Blog covering home decorating. The blog has an archive dating back to November 2012 and shares a short blog roll.
Do-It-Yourself (DIY)

Life is beautiful 1061804
Email: reetta.ekst@gmail.com
Web site: http://lifeisbeautiful.bellablogit.fi/
Freq: Daily
Circ: 11122
Beauty & Grooming, Cosmetics, Fashion, Hair

The Life of Aaliyah 996991
Email: hello@thelifeofaaliyah.com
Web site: www.thelifeofaaliyah.com
Freq: Daily
Circ: 7510
Regional General Interest

Life of Wylie 1053034
Web site: http://lifeofwylie.com
Freq: Daily
Circ: 1783
Broadcasting

Life of Yablon
987249
Tel: 44 07958 591118
Email: editor@lifeofyablon.com
Web site: www.lifeofyablon.com
Freq: Daily
Circ: 9234
Beauty & Grooming, Cooking & Baking, Cosmetics, Fashion, Hair, Shopping

Life outside London
1052865
Email: lifeoutsidelondon@gmail.com
Web site: http://lifeoutsidelondon.co.uk/
Freq: Daily
Circ: 9056
Profile: Blog covering lifestyle, pets and food. The blog has an archive dating back to August 2013.
Cooking & Baking, Literature, Photography, Regional General Interest, Relationships, Women's Interests

Life Through My Eyes
1054148
Web site: http://www.
nicolalifethroughmyeyes.com/
Freq: Daily
Circ: 8478
Beauty & Grooming, Cosmetics, Family & Parenting, Fashion, Hair, Regional General Interest

Life Twice Tasted
1054943
Web site: http://www.lifetwicetasted.
blogspot.co.uk/
Freq: Daily
Circ: 9177
Literature

Life Unexpected
1102798
Editorial: Hopwood Prospect Gardens, Elm Road, Evesham WR11 3PX
Email: lifeunexpected11@gmail.com
Web site: www.mylifeunexpected.co.uk/
Freq: Daily
Circ: 7839
Do-It-Yourself (DIY), Family & Parenting, Fitness & Exercise, Women's Interests

Life With a Lip Gloss Smile
1100043
Web site: http://lifewithalipglosssmile.com/
Freq: Daily
Circ: 10163
Profile: Blog covering fashion and beauty. The blog has an archive dating back to February 2014.
Fashion

Life with Munchers
987911
Email: hello@lifewithmunchers.com
Web site: lifewithmunchers.com
Freq: Daily
Circ: 11443
Profile: Blog covering family, parenting, lifestyle and home decorating. The blog has an archive dating back to September 2013 and shares a short blog roll.
Do-It-Yourself (DIY), Family & Parenting, Fashion

Life, Ninja Killer Cat and Everything Else...
988543
Web site: www.ninjakillercat.co.uk
Freq: Daily
Circ: 9418
Family & Parenting

life.laura.london
995348
Web site: http://lifelauralondon.com
Freq: Daily
Circ: 7994
Profile: Blog covering lifestyle. The life.laura.
london blog discusses anything from running and lifestyle. The blog has an archive dating back to December 2010.
Fitness & Exercise, Nutrition

Lifecycle
1053746
Web site: http://briangoldsmith.wordpress.
com/
Freq: Daily
Circ: 2
Bicycles, Photography

Life's Little Adventures
1094857
Web site: https://lifeslittleadventures.co.uk
Freq: Daily

Circ: 611
Cooking & Baking, Family & Parenting, Fashion, Restaurant Reviews, Travel, Women's Interests

Life's Loves
986686
Email: lifelovseditor@gmail.com
Web site: www.lifesloves.co
Freq: Daily
Circ: 10706
Cooking & Baking, Entertainment, Regional General Interest, Restaurant Reviews, Travel, Women's Interests

Lifestyle District
997032
Web site: http://www.lifestyledistrict.co.uk/
Freq: Daily
Circ: 10150
Art, Cooking & Baking, Travel

Lifestyle Maven
1053484
Email: me@lifestylemaven.co.uk
Web site: http://www.lifestylemaven.co.uk
Freq: Daily
Circ: 9325
Profile: Lifestyle Maven covers lifestyle for women in their 40s and beyond. The blog has an archive dating back to October 2014.
Beauty & Grooming, Cooking & Baking, Cosmetics, Family & Parenting, Fashion, Grocery Stores, Hair, Organic Food, Restaurant Reviews, Women's Interests

Liger
1061566
Email: info@ligerstore.com
Web site: http://blog.ligerstore.com
Freq: Daily
Circ: 4
Fashion

Light Blue Touchpaper
1053535
Email: lbt-admin@cl.cam.ac.uk
Web site: www.lightbluetouchpaper.org
Freq: Daily
Circ: 15538
Computers, Data Management, Internet, Security & Security Systems

Lightwater
998148
Web site: lightwater.wordpress.com/
Freq: Daily
Circ: 23
Politics

Lilinha Angel's World
988371
Email: lilinha_angel@yahoo.com.br
Web site: lilinhaangel.com
Freq: Daily
Circ: 13099
Family & Parenting

Lilinha Angel's World
1053279
Web site: http://lilinhaangel.com/
Freq: Daily
Circ: 13069
Bars, Clubs & Pubs, Beauty & Grooming, Cooking & Baking, Cosmetics, Family & Parenting, Fashion, Food, Hair, Restaurant Reviews

Lilla Loves
987138
Editorial: Flat 2, 11 Wilbury Avenue, Hove BN3 6HR
Web site: www.lillaloves.com
Freq: Daily
Circ: 6974
Profile: Blog covering lifestyle, fashion and beauty. The blog has an archive dating back to September 2011.
Cosmetics, Fashion, Hair, Women's Interests

Lillemor
1060769
Email: jordemodertina@gmail.com
Web site: http://lillemorblog.dk/
Freq: Daily
Circ: 1835
Elementary School, Family & Parenting, Lifestyle, Men's Interests, Preschool, Regional General Interest, Teen/Young Adult, Trading Cards & Comics, Women's Interests

Lilly Higgins
1052910
Web site: http://lillyhiggins.ie/
Freq: Daily

Circ: 7647
Cooking & Baking

Lily Doughball
988943
Web site: http://www.lilydoughball.com/
Freq: Daily
Circ: 8332
Profile: Blog covering lifestyle. Lily Doughball discusses anything from food and crafts to beauty and fashion. The blog has an archive dating back to July 2013 and shares an extensive blogroll.
News & Current Affairs

The Lily Lolo Blog
1053004
Tel: 44 01482 640619
Email: email@lilylolo.co.uk
Web site: http://www.lilylolo.co.uk/blog/
Freq: Daily
Circ: 9
Cosmetics, Fashion, Shopping

Lily Melrose
986819
Email: llymlrs@gmail.com
Web site: www.llymlrs.com
Freq: Daily
Circ: 38780
Beauty & Grooming, Cosmetics, Fashion, Hair, Women's Interests

Lily Melrose Vlog
1098956
Email: llymlrs@gmail.com
Web site: https://www.youtube.com/user/
etcllymlrs
Freq: Daily
Circ: 12
Beauty & Grooming, Cosmetics, Fashion, Hair, Women's Interests

Lily Pebbles
986820
Email: lily@lilypebbles.co.uk
Web site: http://www.lilypebbles.co.uk/
Freq: Daily
Circ: 146571
Beauty & Grooming, Cosmetics, Fashion, Hair, Women's Interests

Lily Pebbles Vlog
1096041
Editorial: PO Box Gleam Digital, 6th Floor, 60 Charlotte Street, London W1T 2NU
Email: lily@lilypebbles.co.uk
Web site: https://www.youtube.com/user/
WhatIHeartToday
Freq: Daily
Circ: 40
Beauty & Grooming, Cosmetics, Fashion, Hair, Women's Interests

Lilypod and Sweetpea
1054169
Web site: lilypodandsweetpea.com
Freq: Daily
Circ: 7285
Profile: Blog covering pregnancy. Lilypod and Sweetpea blog discusses anything from pregnancy and birth to motherhood and parenting. The blog has an archive dating back to August 2013.
Family & Parenting, Relationships, Women's Interests

The Limping Chicken
996519
Email: thelimpingchicken@gmail.com
Web site: http://limpingchicken.com/
Freq: Daily
Circ: 44602
Disability

The Linc
998978
Editorial: Brayford Pool, MHAC Building, Lincoln LN6 7TS
Email: contact@thelinc.co.uk
Web site: www.thelinc.co.uk
Freq: Daily
Circ: 13054
Editor: Angeline McCall
Bars, Clubs & Pubs, Classical/Choral/Band Music, Comedy, Country, Folk, Bluegrass, Dance Music, Entertainment, Jazz & Blues, Local Entertainment Guides, Movies & Video, Music

Linda Stuhaug
1061242
Email: linda_stuhaug@hotmail.com
Web site: http://lindastuhaug.blogg.no/
Freq: Daily
Circ: 41360
Basketball, Bicycles, Billiards, Boating & Yachting, Bodybuilding, Bowling, Boxing,

Cricket, Equestrian Sports, Extreme/Adventure Sports

Lindas Hagedrømmer
1062080
Web site: http://lindashagedrommer.
blogspot.com
Freq: Daily
Circ: 1125
Gardening

Lindy Loves
1054357
Email: lindyloves@hotmail.co.uk
Web site: http://www.lindyloves.co.uk/
Freq: Daily
Circ: 7183
Beauty & Grooming, Cooking & Baking, Cosmetics, Do-It-Yourself (DIY), Fashion, Fitness & Exercise, Hair, Nutrition, Restaurant Reviews, Travel

Line Marions treningsblogg
1061673
Email: linemarion@hotmail.com
Web site: http://www.linemarion.no/
Freq: Daily
Circ: 832
Fitness & Exercise

Linea y Forma
1061452
Web site: http://www.lineayforma.com
Freq: Daily
Circ: 26270
Fitness & Exercise, Nutrition

Linerlover's blog
1053407
Web site: http://linerlovers.wordpress.com/
Freq: Daily
Circ: 9
Marine & Boat Trade

Lines of Escape
1059604
Email: linesofescape@gmail.com
Web site: http://linesofescape.com/
Freq: Daily
Circ: 13622
Cooking & Baking, Restaurant Reviews, Travel

Lingerie Blog
1052840
Tel: 44 01212 888863
Email: jon@lingerieblog.co.uk
Web site: http://www.lingerieblog.co.uk/
Freq: Daily
Circ: 11035
Fashion, Sexual/Adult Products

Lingonews
996936
Email: stevens@id-lingoservice.eu
Web site: lingoservice.wordpress.com
Freq: Daily
Circ: 13
Literature, Theater & Performing Arts

Linpa
1061942
Email: lindaslife@live.fi
Web site: http://mysecrets-linda.blogspot.fi/
Freq: Daily
Circ: 1178
Fashion

Lips So Facto - CEASED 2016
986835
Web site: www.lipssofacto.com
Freq: Daily
Circ: 1187
Profile: Blog covering lifestyle, beauty and cosmetics.
Beauty & Grooming, Cosmetics, Hair, Women's Interests

Lipstick, Lettuce & Lycra
1052924
Email: ladylipstick@lipsticklettucelycra.co.uk
Web site: www.lipsticklettucelycra.co.uk
Freq: Daily
Circ: 10499
Cooking & Baking, Fitness & Exercise

Liquid Irish
1052729
Email: david@liquidirish.com
Web site: www.liquidirish.com
Freq: Daily
Circ: 2747
Alcohol & Spirits

UK Blogs

Liquorice Pearls 1052743
Email: liquoricepearls@gmail.com
Web site: http://www.liquoricepearls.com
Freq: Daily
Circ: 7201
Profile: Blog covering fashion and lifestyle. LIQUORICE PEARLS blog discusses anything from personal style and fashion to beauty and student life. The blog has an archive dating back to July 2009. The outlet offers RSS (Really Simple Syndication).
Beauty & Grooming, Cosmetics, Fashion, Hair

Lisa Eldridge Make Up 987118
Tel: 44 02072 212333
Web site: www.lisaeldridge.com
Freq: Daily
Circ: 617795
Beauty & Grooming, Cosmetics, Hair

Lisa Eldridge Vlog 1076648
Editorial: Lisa Eldridge Make Up / Premier Hair & Makeup, 8 Royalty Studios, 105-109 Lancaster Road, London W11 1QF
Tel: 44 02072 212333
Email: lindsay@premierhairandmakeup.com
Web site: https://www.youtube.com/user/lisaeldridgedotcom
Freq: Daily
Circ: 236
Cosmetics

Lisa Elliot Fashion Stylist 1053679
Web site: www.lisaelliottfashionstylist.blogspot.co.uk
Freq: Daily
Circ: 521
Fashion

Lisa Talbot Personal Stylist Blog 997219
Email: info@lisatalbot.co.uk
Web site: www.lisatalbot.co.uk/blog/
Freq: Daily
Circ: 2420
Fashion, Shopping

Lisa's Life 1054301
Email: lisaslife@outlook.com
Web site: lisas-life.com
Freq: Daily
Circ: 9566
Profile: Blog covering lifestyle, dogs and food. The blog has an archive dating back to April 2011.
Women's Interests

Literanova 1061859
Web site: http://www.literanova.net/index.php
Freq: Daily
Antiques/Collectibles, Art, Arts, Lifestyle, Literature, Men's Interests, Photography, Politics, Regional General Interest, Theater & Performing Arts

The Literary Adviser 1054656
Web site: https://literacyadviser.wordpress.com/
Freq: Daily
Circ: 166
Education

Little Atoms 1052641
Editorial: Little Atoms, Unit 7 Acorn Studios, 103-105 Blundell Street, London N7 9BN
Tel: 44 02034 112982
Web site: http://littleatoms.com/
Freq: Daily
Circ: 29946
Architecture & Design, Audio Video Trade, Auto Aftermarket, Cameras, Computers, Consumer Electronics, Data Management, Electronics, Government Technology, Graphic Design

The Little Beauty Guide 1060460
Email: press@thelittlebeautyguide.com
Web site: http://www.thelittlebeautyguide.com/
Freq: Daily
Circ: 1344
Beauty & Grooming, Cosmetics, Hair

Little Blog of Horrors 1060200
Editorial: 2/2, 10 Minard Road, Glasgow G41 2HN
Web site: http://www.little-blog-of-horrors.com/
Freq: Daily
Circ: 6831
Profile: Blog covering lifestyle, fashion and beauty. The blog has an archive dating back to October 2008 and shares an extensive blog roll.
Beauty & Grooming, Cosmetics, Fashion, Hair, Women's Interests

Little Cotton Rabbits 987366
Web site: www.littlecottonrabbits.typepad.co.uk
Freq: Daily
Circ: 134742
News & Current Affairs

Little Doodles 1053167
Web site: http://little-doodles.blogspot.com
Freq: Daily
Circ: 3374
Fashion, Visual Arts

Little Green Blog 986754
Web site: littlegreenblog.com
Freq: Daily
Circ: 6919
News & Current Affairs

Little Green Robot 1054308
Email: android@imagine-publishing.co.uk
Web site: littlegreenrobot.co.uk
Freq: Daily
Circ: 61563
Apple, Internet, Mobile Electronics, Personal Computers

Little green shed 1053119
Web site: http://littlegreenshedblog.co.uk/
Freq: Daily
Circ: 12083
Cooking & Baking, Crafts, Fashion, Photography, Regional General Interest, Travel, Women's Interests

Little Indie Blogs 998024
Email: littleindieblogs@gmail.com
Web site: http://littleindieblogs.blogspot.co.uk/
Freq: Daily
Circ: 11819
Rock Music

Little Lily Pad Co. 988148
Email: faq@littlelilypad.co.uk
Web site: http://www.littlelilypad.co.uk/blog/
Freq: Daily
Circ: 11402
Family & Parenting

The Little Loaf 988539
Email: thelittleloaf@gmail.com
Web site: http://www.thelittleloaf.com/
Freq: Daily
Circ: 21558
Cooking & Baking

The Little Magpie 987068
Email: enquiries@thelittlemagpie.com
Web site: http://www.thelittlemagpie.com
Freq: Daily
Circ: 10535
Profile: Blog covering fashion. The Little Magpie blog discusses anything from fashion and style to fashion accessories .The blog shares an extensive blog roll.
Airline Inflight, Fashion, Railroad, Travel

Little Miss Meat Free 1053880
Email: littlemissmeatfree@gmail.com
Web site: http://littlemissmeatfree.com/
Freq: Daily
Circ: 11632
Cooking & Baking, Vegetarianism & Veganism

Little Miss Notting Hill 987250
Email: littlemissnottinghill@gmail.com
Web site: littlemissnottinghill.com
Freq: Daily
Circ: 9015
Fashion, Women's Interests

Little Miss Winney 1098950
Email: littlemisswinney@gmail.com
Web site: http://www.littlemisswinney.com/
Freq: Daily
Circ: 10086
Beauty & Grooming, Cooking & Baking, Cosmetics, Fashion, Hair, Restaurant Reviews, Travel, Women's Interests

Little Nomad 1053662
Web site: http://the-littlenomad.blogspot.co.uk/
Freq: Daily
Circ: 7408
Profile: Blog covering travel. The LITTLE NOMAD blog discusses anything from lifestyle and food to fashion and general interest. The blog has an archive dating back to December 2011 and shares a short blog roll.
Cooking & Baking, Fashion, Photography, Travel, Women's Interests

Little one's blog 1054069
Web site: http://natalieholden-id.co.uk/
Freq: Daily
Circ: 10448
Profile: Blog covering interior design. Little One's Blog discusses anything from architecture and furniture to home accessories and inspiration. The blog has an archive dating back to August 2012.
Architecture & Design, Do-It-Yourself (DIY), Travel

Little Stuff 985779
Editorial: All4baby Ltd, 15 Manston Road, Sturminster Newton DT10 1AF
Email: info@littlestuff.co.uk
Web site: www.littlestuff.co.uk
Freq: Daily
Circ: 11077
Family & Parenting

Little Touches Details Club - Deets which Delight Blog 1073944
Tel: 44 08001 303237
Web site: https://littletouches.com/blog
Freq: Daily
Circ: 175
Travel

The little Wedding Corner 995485
Tel: 44 49045 139772312
Email: info@the-little-wedding-corner.de
Freq: Daily
News & Current Affairs

Liu Xingliang's blog 1061571
Email: xlliu@vip.163.com
Web site: http://blog.sina.com.cn/liuxingliang
Freq: Daily
Circ: 15522
Auto Aftermarket, Computers, Data Management, Electronics, Government Technology, Industry, Internet, Mobile Communications, Security & Security Systems, Software

Live Energized 986130
Editorial: Energise Water, 6-8 Bradfield Road, Wellingborough, Wellingborough NN8 4HB
Email: ross@liveenergized.com
Web site: http://liveenergized.com/
Freq: Daily
Circ: 126822
Nutrition

Live For Films 987937
Email: stuff@liveforfilms.com
Web site: http://www.liveforfilm.com/
Freq: Daily
Circ: 19920
Computer & Video Games, Entertainment, Local Entertainment Guides, Movies & Video, Trading Cards & Comics

Live Hard 988113
Email: info@livehard.co.uk
Web site: http://livehard.co.uk/
Freq: Daily
Circ: 13098
Fitness & Exercise, Nutrition

Live it. Love it. Make it. 996275
Editorial: Sew Crafty Sewing Centre, 3 High Street, Maidenhead, Maidenhead SL6 1JN
Email: liveit.loveit.makeit@gmail.com
Web site: www.liveitloveitmakeit.com
Freq: Daily
Circ: 4210
Cooking & Baking, Crafts, Do-It-Yourself (DIY), Fashion

Live Like A VIP 985119
Editorial: 541 Old Kent Road, London SE1 5EW
Email: zoe@livelikeavip.com
Web site: www.livelikeavip.com
Freq: Daily
Circ: 12976
Profile: Website covering celebrity gossip. Live Like A VIP shares the latest news on fashion, beauty, competition, celebrity spotting and interviews.
Beauty & Grooming, Celebrities, Cosmetics, Fashion, Hair

Live4Liverpool 1052822
Email: live4liverpool@snack-media.com
Web site: http://live4liverpool.com/
Freq: Daily
Circ: 27644
Soccer

Lived with Love 1053796
Email: kerrydyer03@googlemail.com
Web site: http://www.livedwithlove.com/
Freq: Daily
Circ: 10235
Cooking & Baking, Food, Grocery Stores, Organic Food, Restaurant Reviews, Vegetarianism & Veganism, Weddings, Women's Interests

LiveLifeLoveCake 1053266
Email: info@livelifelovecake.com
Web site: http://livelifelovecake.com/
Freq: Daily
Circ: 10109
Profile: Blog covering food. The livelifelovecake blog discusses anything from food and travel to restaurant reviews and global cuisine.
Cooking & Baking, Restaurant Reviews, Travel

The Liver Bird 998123
Email: lfckirstylfc@hotmail.co.uk
Web site: http://www.the-liver-bird.co.uk/
Freq: Daily
Circ: 9915
Soccer

Liverpool Cultural Champion's Blog 996818
Email: info@culture.org.uk
Web site: liverpoolculturalchampions.com
Freq: Daily
Circ: 521
Regional General Interest

Liverpool Lashes 997949
Email: liverpoollashes@yahoo.co.uk
Web site: http://www.liverpoollashes.co.uk/
Freq: Daily
Circ: 10245
Beauty & Grooming, Cosmetics, Hair, Nutrition

LIVEWIRE 999377
Editorial: Peter Benenson House, 1 Easton Street, London WC1X 0DW
Tel: 44 02074 135566
Email: press@amnesty.org
Web site: https://www.amnesty.org/en/latest/?resourceType=blogarticle&sort=date
Freq: Daily
Charitable Foundations

Living colour style 1054328
Web site: http://livingcolourstyle.com/
Freq: Daily
Circ: 9917
Crafts, Do-It-Yourself (DIY), Gardening, Women's Interests

Liz Plummer Blog 1054665
Email: liz@lizplummer.com
Web site: http://lizplummer.com/blog/
Freq: Daily

Circ: 12
Crafts, Visual Arts

Lizy's House of Cards 996840
Tel: 44 07915 698577
Email: lizyshouseofcards@mail.com
Web site: http://lizyshouseofcards.blogspot.co.uk/
Freq: Daily
Circ: 1040
Crafts

Lizzie Outside 997752
Email: lizzieoutside@icloud.com
Web site: www.lizzieoutside.co.uk
Freq: Daily
Circ: 16803
Alternative Medicine, Charitable Foundations, Cooking & Baking, Energy & Environment, Ethical/Moral Issues, Field Sports, Fitness & Exercise, Food, Grocery Stores, Health & Medicine

Lizzie's Lowdown 1058389
Email: lizzieslowdown@outlook.com
Web site: www.lizzieslowdown.com
Freq: Daily
Circ: 10709
Bars, Clubs & Pubs, Comedy, Country, Folk, Bluegrass, Entertainment, Fashion, Jazz & Blues, Local Entertainment Guides, Movies & Video, Pop Music, Rap & Hip Hop

Lizzy's Literary Life 987992
Email: lizzysiddal@yahoo.com
Web site: lizzysiddal.wordpress.com
Freq: Daily
Circ: 553
Literature

Lizzy's Literary Life 1053687
Web site: https://lizzysiddal.wordpress.com/
Freq: Daily
Circ: 553
Literature

LLI Design blog 1053451
Editorial: 8 Broadbent Close, London N6 5JW Tel: 44 02083 484800
Email: studio@llidesign.co.uk
Web site: http://blog.llidesign.co.uk/
Freq: Daily
Circ: 192
Do-It-Yourself (DIY)

Llochualandia 1061278
Web site: http://www.crowjosh.blogspot.com
Freq: Daily
Circ: 987
Auto Aftermarket, Computers, Data Management, Electronics, Government Technology, Industry, Internet, Mobile Communications, Security & Security Systems, Software

Lo Que Importa es el Riesgo 1062115
Web site: http://mipropiadecadencia.blogspot.com
Freq: Daily
Circ: 5746
Health & Medicine, Neurology, Science

Loan Ranger 997742
Editorial: Lexis House, 30 Farringdon Street, London EC4A 4HH Tel: 44 08453 701234
Email: pslbankingandfinance@lexisnexis.co.uk
Web site: http://blogs.lexisnexis.co.uk/loanranger/
Freq: Daily
Circ: 131
Banking, Tax Law

Lobster and Swan 986188
Web site: http://lobsterandswan.com/
Freq: Daily
Circ: 9719
News & Current Affairs

Local Government Chronicle Blog 999378
Editorial: 3 / 4th Floor, Telephone House, 69-77 Paul Street, London EC2A 4NQ
Email: lgcpluseditor@emap.com

Web site: www.lgcplus.com
Freq: Daily
Circ: 19317
Editor: Nick Golding
Politics

Logia Cervecera 1060939
Email: contacto@logiacervecera.com
Web site: http://www.logiacervecera.com
Freq: Daily
Circ: 1359
Beer

London & Me 995321
Web site: http://www.londonandme.org/
Freq: Daily
Circ: 1275
Fitness & Exercise, Sports

London Beauty Queen 986813
Email: hellolbq@gmail.com
Web site: www.londonbeautyqueen.com
Freq: Daily
Circ: 53420
Beauty & Grooming, Cosmetics, Fashion, Hair, Women's Interests

The London Blog 988054
Web site: http://www.thelondonblog.co/
Freq: Daily
Circ: 10420
Editor: Charlotte Clarke
Profile: The London Blog covers London lifestyle, food and drink.
Bars, Clubs & Pubs, Beauty & Grooming, Cooking & Baking, Cosmetics, Fashion, Food, Grocery Stores, Hair, Organic Food, Restaurant Reviews

London Bride Blog 987270
Web site: http://www.london-bride.com
Freq: Daily
Circ: 31308
News & Current Affairs

London Calling 996687
Email: nat@london-calling-blog.co.uk
Web site: http://www.london-calling-blog.co.uk/
Freq: Daily
Circ: 752
Regional General Interest

London Calling Blog 1054548
Email: nat@london-calling-blog.co.uk
Web site: http://www.london-calling-blog.co.uk/
Freq: Daily
Circ: 752
Neurology, Regional General Interest

The London Chatter 987692
Editorial: 18 Brompton Park Crescent, Seagrave Road, London SW6 1SN
Web site: www.thelondonchatter.com
Freq: Daily
Circ: 7951
Profile: Blog covering fashion. The London Chatter blog discusses anything from fashion and beauty to accessories and television. The blog has an archive dating back to October 2011. The outlet offers RSS (Really Simple Syndication).
News & Current Affairs

London Cyclist Blog 986189
Web site: www.londoncyclist.co.uk
Freq: Daily
Circ: 87593
Bicycles

The London Diaries 988748
Email: thelondondiaries@gmail.com
Web site: https://threepieceheart.com/
Freq: Daily
Circ: 10709
Cooking & Baking, Literature, Regional General Interest

London Eater 986190
Web site: www.londoneater.com
Freq: Daily
Circ: 25021
Alcohol & Spirits, Bars, Clubs & Pubs, Beer, Beverages, Cooking & Baking, Food, Grocery Stores, Organic Food,

Restaurant Reviews, Vegetarianism & Veganism

The London Foodie 986497
Web site: www.thelondonfoodie.co.uk
Freq: Daily
Circ: 26286
Alcohol & Spirits, Bars, Clubs & Pubs, Beer, Beverages, Cooking & Baking, Food, Grocery Stores, Organic Food, Restaurant Reviews, Vegetarianism & Veganism

London Guantanamo Campaign 1052810
Web site: http://londonguantanamocampaign.blogspot.co.uk/
Freq: Daily
Circ: 8984
News & Current Affairs

London Hotels Insight 986971
Web site: www.londonhotelsinsight.com/
Freq: Daily
Circ: 8287
Editor: Rajul Chande
Travel

London Jazz News 997247
Email: sebastian@londonjazznews.com
Web site: www.londonjazznews.com/
Freq: Daily
Circ: 16665
Editor: Sebastian Scotney
Jazz & Blues

London Living 987212
Tel: 44 02032 062000
Web site: londonliving.at
Freq: Daily
Circ: 9214
Profile: Blog covering things to do in London. London Living blog discusses anything from events and restaurant recommendations to tourist attractions. The blog has an archive dating back to February 2011 and shares an extensive blogroll. The outlet offers RSS (Really Simple Syndication).
Cooking & Baking, Local Entertainment Guides, Regional General Interest, Restaurant Reviews

London Living @ It's Your London 1054516
Web site: http://londonlivingsue.blogspot.co.uk/
Freq: Daily
Circ: 521
Regional General Interest

London Masala and Chips 988283
Web site: http://londonmasalaandchips.blogspot.co.uk/
Freq: Daily
Circ: 10038
Regional General Interest

The London Mother 1054639
Editorial: 65 Macoma Road, London SE18 2QJ
Email: hello@thelondonmother.net
Web site: http://www.thelondonmother.net/
Freq: Daily
Circ: 15434
Profile: The London Mummy Blog covers motherhood and family life.
Family & Parenting, Women's Interests

The London Mummy - an Insiders' Guide 1100580
Web site: http://www.thelondonmummy.com/
Freq: Daily
Circ: 11728
Family & Parenting, Fashion, Women's Interests

London on the Inside 987260
Editorial: Unit 11 Bayford Street Industrial Centre, Bayford Street, Hackney, London E8 3SE
Web site: londontheinside.com

Circ: 51591
Classical/Choral/Band Music, Country, Folk, Bluegrass, Dance Music, Jazz & Blues, Music, Pop Music, R&B, Urban, World, Rap & Hip Hop, Rock Music

London Pop-Ups 996785
Web site: www.londonpopups.com
Freq: Daily
Circ: 42349
Bars, Clubs & Pubs, Restaurant Reviews

London Reconnections 988262
Email: questions@londonreconnections.com
Web site: www.londonreconnections.com/
Freq: Daily
Circ: 41600
Regional General Interest

The London Review of Sandwiches 987797
Web site: londonreviewofsandwiches.wordpress.com
Freq: Daily
Circ: 134
Profile: Blog covering sandwiches in London. The blog has an archive dating back to January 2012 and shares a short blogroll.
Cooking & Baking, Restaurant Reviews

The London Sinner 987407
Email: editor@thelondonsinner.com
Web site: thelondonsinner.com
Freq: Daily
Circ: 9433
Editor: Elsa Messi
Profile: Blog covering lifestyle. The London Sinner blog discusses anything from food and drink to lifestyle and fashion. The blog has an archive dating back to February 2011. The outlet offers RSS (Really Simple Syndication).
Bars, Clubs & Pubs, Cooking & Baking, Food, Grocery Stores, Luxury Goods, Organic Food, Restaurant Reviews, Vegetarianism & Veganism, Women's Interests

London Social 101 1105388
Editorial: 3/36 Central Road, West Didsbury, Manchester
Web site: http://londonsocial101.com
Freq: Daily
Circ: 558
Alcohol & Spirits, Bars, Clubs & Pubs, Beer, Beverages, Cooking & Baking, Food, Grocery Stores, Organic Food, Regional General Interest, Restaurant Reviews

London Still 997470
Email: alexandrasilber@gmail.com
Web site: http://alexandrasilber.blogspot.co.uk/
Freq: Daily
Circ: 521
Theater & Performing Arts

London Street Foodie 1068844
Email: victoriastewartmail@yahoo.com
Web site: http://londonstreetfoodie.co.uk
Freq: Daily
Circ: 6257
Profile: Blog covering London street food. LONDON STREET FOODIE blog discusses anything from London Street food and street food stalls to street food reviews. The blog has an archive dating back to December 2011. The outlet offers RSS (Really Simple Syndication).
Cooking & Baking, Organic Food, Restaurant Reviews, Vegetarianism & Veganism

London Unattached 987591
Web site: www.london-unattached.com
Freq: Daily
Circ: 146379
Profile: Blog covering London lifestyle. The LONdON UNATTACHED blog discusses anything from food and travel to restaurant reviews.
Cooking & Baking, Regional General Interest, Travel

London Unveiled 1053589
Web site: http://londonunveiled.com
Freq: Daily

UK Blogs

Circ: 1502

Profile: Blog covering things to do in London. London Unveiled discusses anything from museums and galleries to historic buildings and gardens. The blog has an archive dating back to May 2012. The outlet offers RSS (Really Simple Syndication).

Regional General Interest, Travel

London Vision Clinic Blog
1054539

Editorial: Private Laser Eye Surgery Clinic, 138 Harley Street, London W1G 7LA
Tel: 44 02072 241005
Email: info@londonvisionclinic.com
Web site: https://www.londonvisionclinic.com/blogs/
Freq: Daily
Circ: 20998
Ophthalmology & Optometry

The London Word
984798

Email: editor@thelondonword.com
Web site: www.thelondonword.com
Circ: 377
Editor: Nick Purves
Profile: Website containing news, reviews, interviews and an entertainment guide featuring what's on in and around London.
Bars, Clubs & Pubs, Comedy, Entertainment, Local Entertainment Guides, Movies & Video, Regional General Interest

The Londoner
987041

Web site: www.thelondoner.me
Freq: Daily
Circ: 502994
Profile: Blog covering lifestyle. The blog has an archive dating back to April 2011.
Cooking & Baking, Fashion, Regional General Interest, Restaurant Reviews, Travel

LondonTheatreDirect.com
999256

Editorial: 3rd Floor, 207 Regent Street, London W1B 3HH **Tel:** 44 08455 058500
Email: hello@londontheatredirect.com
Web site: https://www.londontheatredirect.com/news
Freq: Daily
Circ: 2796
Theater & Performing Arts

Londontopia
988266

Web site: http://londontopia.net/
Circ: 91780
Profile: Website covering London lifestyle and things to do in the city including attractions, culture, events, history, music and travel.
Regional General Interest

Lorenne Blau
997269

Email: lorenne.blau@gmail.com
Web site: www.lorenneblau.com
Freq: Daily
Circ: 4713
Beauty & Grooming, Cosmetics, Fashion, Hair, Luxury Goods, Women's Interests

Lorna, literally
1053035

Email: lornaliterally@gmail.com
Web site: http://www.scaredtoast.com/
Freq: Daily
Circ: 5097
Beauty & Grooming, Cosmetics, Do-It-Yourself (DIY), Hair

Lorrie Whittington blog
1053058

Email: hello@lorriewhittington.co.uk
Web site: http://www.lorriewhittington.co.uk/news/
Freq: Daily
Circ: 3802
Art, Photography, Visual Arts

Lortemor.com
1061002

Email: lortemor@mail.com
Web site: http://lortemor.dk/
Freq: Daily
Circ: 5282
Elementary School, Family & Parenting, Lifestyle, Men's Interests, Preschool, Regional General Interest, Teen/Young

Adult, Trading Cards & Comics, Women's Interests

The lost byway
998379

Email: fugueur99@gmail.com
Web site: http://thelostbyway.com/
Freq: Daily
Circ: 8933
Outdoor Recreation

Lost Earth Adventures Blog
1053179

Editorial: 72 Gladstone Street, York YO24 4NG **Tel:** 44 01904 500094
Email: info@lostearthadventures.co.uk
Web site: https://www.lostearthadventures.co.uk/category/blog/
Freq: Daily
Circ: 238
Outdoor Recreation, Travel

Lottie Murphy
1100042

Email: lottie@lottiemurphy.com
Web site: http://www.lottiemurphy.com/
Freq: Daily
Circ: 12195
Profile: Lottie Murphy covers pilates, healthy living and fitness. This outlet also offers a vlog.
Fitness & Exercise, Women's Interests

Lottie Pearce
998183

Email: lottie.pearce@btinternet.com
Web site: www.lottiepearce.com
Freq: Daily
Circ: 11595
Fashion, Sales & Marketing, Women's Interests

Lottie's Kitchen
987099

Email: lottieslittlekitchen@live.com
Web site: http://www.lottieskitchen.co.uk/
Freq: Daily
Circ: 2409
Profile: Blog covering cooking. Lottie's Little Kitchen blog discusses anything from recipes and baking to lifestyle and travel. The blog has an archive dating back to May 2012.
Alcohol & Spirits, Bars, Clubs & Pubs, Beer, Beverages, Cooking & Baking, Food, Grocery Stores, Organic Food, Restaurant Reviews, Vegetarianism & Veganism

Lou Lou Land
997993

Email: louloulanduk@gmail.com
Web site: www.loulouland.co.uk
Freq: Daily
Circ: 8518
Beauty & Grooming, Cosmetics, Hair

Loubee Lou Blogs
1053870

Email: loubeeloublogs@gmail.com
Web site: loubeeloublogs.blogspot.co.uk
Freq: Daily
Circ: 11259
Celebrities, Cosmetics, Health & Medicine, Literature, Women's Interests

Louboutins & Lemonade
1053713

Web site: http://louboutinsnlemonade.com/
Freq: Daily
Circ: 521
Beauty & Grooming, Celebrities, Cosmetics, Fashion, Hair, Women's Interests

Louder Than War
997754

Web site: http://louderthanwar.com/blogs/
Freq: Daily
Circ: 30
Editor: Sarah Lay
Classical/Choral/Band Music, Country, Folk, Bluegrass, Dance Music, Jazz & Blues, Music, Pop Music, R&B, Urban, World, Rap & Hip Hop, Rock Music

Louise Jones Blog
1054952

Web site: http://www.biscuitsandblisters.co.uk/
Freq: Daily
Circ: 12163
Charitable Foundations, Disability, Literature, Women's Interests

Louis-Nicolas Darbon
1054326

Email: contact@louisnicolasdarbon.com
Web site: louisnicolasdarbon.freshnet.com
Freq: Daily
Circ: 4196
Art, Fashion, Photography, Visual Arts

Loulabeth
1100175

Email: loulabeth@gmail.com
Web site: www.loulabeth.co.uk
Freq: Daily
Circ: 6883
Profile: Blog covering beauty. Loulabeth blog discusses anything from beauty to beauty supplies and beauty tips. The blog has an archive dating back to September 2011. The outlet offers RSS (Really Simple Syndication).
News & Current Affairs

Love Adventure
998201

Web site: http://www.love-adventure.co.uk
Freq: Daily
Circ: 1174
Regional General Interest, Travel

Love Audrey
1053808

Email: franky@love-audrey.com
Web site: www.love-audrey.com
Freq: Daily
Circ: 8054
Women's Interests

Love Camping News Blog
1053311

Tel: 44 08455 273362
Email: info@lovecamping.co.uk
Web site: http://www.lovecamping.co.uk/news
Freq: Daily
Circ: 34
Outdoor Recreation

Love Chic Living
987587

Editorial: 53 Gertrude Road, Nottingham NG2 5BZ
Web site: lovechicliving.co.uk
Freq: Daily
Circ: 153878
Profile: Blog covering interior design. LOVE CHIC LIVING discusses anything from patterns and home accessories to furniture and inspiration. The blog has an archive dating back to February 2012 and shares an extensive blog roll.
Do-It-Yourself (DIY)

Love Cloth
987595

Email: loveclothemail@gmail.com
Web site: www.lovecloth.co.uk
Freq: Daily
Circ: 10321
Fashion, Women's Interests

Love from Lou Lou
1052691

Web site: http://www.lovefromloulou.com/
Freq: Daily
Circ: 8744
Profile: Blog covering fashion. LOVE FROM LOU LOU blog discusses anything from personal style and celebrity style to emerging talents and the latest catwalk looks. The blog has an archive dating back to June 2010.
Fashion

Love From Mummy
1053155

Web site: lovefrommummy.co.uk
Freq: Daily
Circ: 9936
Family & Parenting

Love From, Florence Grace
1054448

Web site: http://www.lovefromflorencegrace.co.uk/
Freq: Daily
Circ: 8715
Women's Interests

Love Learning
1053422

Web site: http://debrakidd.wordpress.com
Freq: Daily
Circ: 2514
Education

Love My Dress Wedding Blog
999291

Web site: www.lovemydress.net
Freq: Daily
Circ: 170809
Editor: Annabel Beeforth
Fashion, Weddings

Love Sussex Weddings
1076163

Web site: http://www.lovesussexweddings.co.uk
Freq: Daily
Circ: 5254
Women's Interests

Love to Eat to Travel
1098994

Web site: www.lovetoeattotravel.com
Freq: Daily
Circ: 11000
News & Current Affairs

Love, Life & Style by Samantha Joy
1057620

Email: info@samanthajoy.co.uk
Web site: lovelifeandstyle.co.uk
Freq: Daily
Circ: 846
Beauty & Grooming, Cooking & Baking, Cosmetics, Fashion, Hair, Health & Medicine, Nutrition, Restaurant Reviews, Travel, Weddings

LoveBrighton's Blog
999367

Editorial: Royal Pavilion, 4-5 Pavilion Buildings, Brighton BN1 1EE
Tel: 44 01273 292620
Email: media@brighton-hove.gov.uk
Web site: visitbrighton.blogspot.com
Freq: Daily
Circ: 1980
Regional General Interest, Travel

The Lovecats Inc.
1053574

Freq: Daily
News & Current Affairs

Lovell Rugby Blog
999362

Editorial: Stadium House, Aspen Way, Yalberton Industrial Estate, Paignton TQ4 7QR **Tel:** 44 01803 550767
Web site: http://offload.lovell-rugby.co.uk/
Freq: Daily
Circ: 6504
Rugby

Lovely Bicycle
1052727

Web site: http://lovelybike.blogspot.co.uk/
Freq: Daily
Circ: 9074
Bicycles

Lovely Greens
996454

Web site: http://www.lovelygreens.com/
Freq: Daily
Circ: 41864
Regional General Interest

Lovepuffin Travel Blog
1053246

Web site: http://alifeofmore.co.uk/
Freq: Daily
Circ: 9299
Profile: Lovepuffin Travel Blog covers adventure travel. The outlet also offers a vlog.
Travel

Lovereading UK Blog
995380

Editorial: Lovereading Ltd, 59 High Street, East Grinstead, East Grinstead RH19 3DD
Web site: http://blog.lovereading.co.uk/
Freq: Daily
Circ: 256
Editor: Louise Weir
Literature

The Low Carb Diabetic
1053468

Email: lowcarbdiabetic@aol.com
Web site: http://thelowcarbdiabetic.blogspot.co.uk
Freq: Daily
Circ: 14433
Diabetes, Nutrition

LRSMTH Fashion
1054171

Web site: http://www.laurarebeccasmith.com/

Freq: Daily
Circ: 10032
Fashion, Women's Interests

LSE Blogs 1054005
Editorial: Houghton Street, London WC2A 2AE
Web site: http://blogs.lse.ac.uk/
Freq: Daily
Circ: 2009113
Broadcasting, Higher Education, Publishing

Lucia Montes 1102797
Email: girlyframe@gmail.com
Web site: https://www.youtube.com/user/GirlyFrame
Freq: Daily
Circ: 1
Beauty & Grooming, Cosmetics, Fashion, Hair, Women's Interests

Lucidica 997621
Editorial: 35 Kingsland Road, Shoreditch, London E2 8AA **Tel:** 44 08444 142994
Email: service@lucidica.com
Web site: www.lucidica.com/blog
Freq: Daily
Circ: 41
Editor: Ellen Bowers
Auto Aftermarket, Computers, Data Management, Electronics, Government Technology, Industry, Internet, Mobile Communications, Security & Security Systems, Software

Lucies Loves 1100167
Email: info@luciekerley.co.uk
Web site: http://lucieloves.co.uk/
Freq: Daily
Circ: 11534
Art, Beauty & Grooming, Cooking & Baking, Cosmetics, Fashion, Fitness & Exercise, Hair, Photography, Regional General Interest, Travel

Lucy and Lydia 1073490
Editorial: C/O Gleam Futures, 6th Floor, 60 Charlotte St, London W1T 2NU
Email: lucyandlydia@gleamfutures.com
Web site: http://www.lucyandlydiablog.blogspot.co.uk/
Freq: Daily
Circ: 762
Beauty & Grooming, Cosmetics, Fashion, Hair, Pop Music, Women's Interests

Lucy Loves 1063274
Web site: lucyearnshaw.co.uk
Freq: Daily
Circ: 9246
Beauty & Grooming, Cooking & Baking, Cosmetics, Crafts, Do-It-Yourself (DIY), Fashion, Fitness & Exercise, Hair, Nutrition, Restaurant Reviews

LucyAndLydia Vlog 1098954
Editorial: Gleam Futures, 6th Floor, 60 Charlotte Street, London W1T 2NU
Email: lucyandlydia@gleamfutures.com
Web site: https://www.youtube.com/user/LucyAndLydia
Freq: Daily
Circ: 13
Beauty & Grooming, Cosmetics, Fashion, Hair, Pop Music, Women's Interests

LucyLovesYa 987962
Web site: lucylovesya.com
Freq: Daily
Circ: 7791
Profile: Blog covering fashion. LucyLovesYa blog discusses anything from fashion and beauty to music, interior design, recipes, weddings, art and crafts. The blog has an archive dating back to October 2011 and shares an short blog roll. The outlet offers RSS (Really Simple Syndication).
Cosmetics, Do-It-Yourself (DIY), Fashion

Lucy's Stash 988358
Email: hello@lucysstash.com
Web site: lucysstash.com
Freq: Daily
Circ: 21659
Profile: Blog covering nail care, nail art and nail polish. The blog has an archive dating

back to December 2010 and shares an extensive blog roll.
Beauty & Grooming, Cosmetics, Hair

Lucyy Writes 988464
Email: lucyywrites01@live.co.uk
Web site: lucyywrites01.blogspot.co.uk
Freq: Daily
Circ: 7925
Profile: Blog covering fashion, beauty, beauty supplies, cosmetics and home decorating. The blog has an archive dating back to August 2011.
Beauty & Grooming, Cosmetics, Do-It-Yourself (DIY), Fashion, Hair

Lugares Turísticos Región Lima 1060858
Web site: http://www.turismo-huacho.blogspot.com
Freq: Daily
Circ: 578
Airline Inflight, Celebrities, Railroad, Travel

Lunartik 1053040
Email: matt@lunartik.com
Web site: http://www.lunartik.com/
Freq: Daily
Circ: 6341
Crafts, Visual Arts

Lunges and Lycra 987425
Web site: http://lungesandlycra.co.uk/
Freq: Daily
Circ: 11725
Profile: Blog covering fitness. The LUNGES AND LYCRA blog discusses anything from fitness tips and running clubs to London Marathon. The blog has an archive dating back to October 2012 and shares an short blog roll.
Fashion, Fitness & Exercise, Nutrition

Luonnonkihara 1061304
Email: minna.hietakangas@kotikone.fi
Web site: https://luonnonkihara.wordpress.com/
Freq: Daily
Circ: 6878
Architecture & Design, Do-It-Yourself (DIY), Gardening, Home, Lifestyle, Men's Interests, Property Management & Maintenance, Real Estate, Regional General Interest, Women's Interests

Lussorian.com 984697
Editorial: Cedar House, Creeting Road East, Stowmarket, Stowmarket IP14 5BT
Tel: 44 02034 119111900
Email: info@orbitalmedianetwork.com
Web site: www.lussorian.com
Freq: Daily
Circ: 2871
Architecture & Design, Do-It-Yourself (DIY), Gardening, Home, Luxury Goods, Property Management & Maintenance, Real Estate

LUX FIX Studio 987489
Editorial: LUX FIX, 24th Floor, Portland House, Bressenden Place, London SW1E 5BH **Tel:** 44 02035 406180
Email: cinderella@lux-fix.com
Web site: blog.lux-fix.com
Freq: Daily
Circ: 22
Profile: Blog covering clothing and fashion. The blog has an archive dating back to March 2011 and shares a short blog roll.
Fashion, Luxury Goods

Lux Life 988651
Web site: http://www.luxlife-blog.com/
Freq: Daily
Circ: 37676
Profile: Blog covering luxury lifestyle including restaurant reviews, London life and travel. The blog has an archive dating back to August 2010 and shares a short blog roll.
Beauty & Grooming, Cosmetics, Fashion, Hair, Regional General Interest, Restaurant Reviews, Travel

The Luxe Life 987672
Editorial: 9A Hetley Road, London W12 8BA
Email: luxelife@hotmail.co.uk
Web site: http://www.the-luxelife.com/

Freq: Daily
Circ: 1665
Editor: Lucy Dachtler-Davies
Profile: Blog covering lifestyle. The Luxe Life blog discusses anything from lifestyle and fashion to beauty and travel to food. The blog has an archive dating back to November 2010 and shares a short blog roll. The outlet offers RSS (Really Simple Syndication).
Bars, Clubs & Pubs, Beauty & Grooming, Cooking & Baking, Cosmetics, Fashion, Hair, Luxury Goods, Restaurant Reviews, Travel, Women's Interests

The Luxe List (UK) 1098996
Web site: https://luxelist.me/
Freq: Daily
Circ: 11374
Beauty & Grooming, Cosmetics, Hair, Luxury Goods

luxgifts.co.uk 997511
Editorial: 33 Brookhill Close, East Barnet, London EN4 8SH
Email: press@luxgifts.co.uk
Web site: http://www.luxgifts.co.uk/
Freq: Daily
Circ: 837
Luxury Goods, Shopping

Luxury Travel Diva 1104004
Email: luxurytraveldiva1@gmail.com
Web site: luxurytraveldiva.com
Freq: Daily
Circ: 9281
Travel

Luz y Vida Express 1060790
Web site: http://bellezaysaludalnatural.blogspot.com/
Freq: Daily
Circ: 521
Alternative Medicine

LV In Love With 988923
Email: lvinlovewith@gmail.com
Web site: www.lvinlovewith.com
Freq: Daily
Circ: 1401
Profile: Blog covering beauty, make up, skin care, cosmetics and fashion. The blog has an archive dating back to May 2012.
Beauty & Grooming, Cooking & Baking, Cosmetics, Do-It-Yourself (DIY), Fashion, Food, Grocery Stores, Hair, Organic Food, Restaurant Reviews

LVB Mag 1075724
Web site: http://lvbmag.com/
Freq: Daily
Circ: 3966
Do-It-Yourself (DIY)

LWSY 996520
Editorial: 7a Crookham Road, London SW6 4EG
Email: hello@lucywillshowyou.com
Web site: www.lucywillshowyou.com
Freq: Daily
Circ: 7955
Lifestyle, Men's Interests, Regional General Interest, Women's Interests

Lydia Elise Millen 995324
Email: info@lydiaelisemillen.com
Web site: http://lydiaelisemillen.com/
Freq: Daily
Circ: 49862
Profile: Blog covering Fitness. LYDIA ELISE MILLEN blog discusses anything from fitness to fashion and personal health.
Fashion, Women's Interests

Lydia Elise Millen Vlog 1103793
Email: lydiamillen@yahoo.co.uk
Web site: https://www.youtube.com/user/lydiamillen
Freq: Daily
Circ: 442
Beauty & Grooming, Cosmetics, Fashion, Hair, Women's Interests

Lynsey the Mother Duck - The Disability Diaries 1055303
Email: lynseythemotherduck@gmail.com
Web site: lynseythemotherduck.blogspot.co.uk

Freq: Daily
Circ: 10185
Disability, Family & Parenting

Mabinogogiblog 1053570
Web site: http://greenerblog.blogspot.co.uk/
Freq: Daily
Circ: 12130
Energy & Environment, Environment, Government

Macmillan Blog 996203
Editorial: 89 Albert Embankment, London SE1 7UQ
Web site: https://community.macmillan.org.uk/blogs/
Freq: Daily
Circ: 1
News & Current Affairs

Macronomics 1052636
Web site: http://macronomy.blogspot.co.uk/
Freq: Daily
Circ: 521
Economics

Mad About The House 1052698
Web site: www.madaboutthehouse.com
Freq: Daily
Circ: 44964
Profile: Blog covering interiors, home decorating and furnishing.
Do-It-Yourself (DIY)

Mad Dog Ski 987710
Editorial: 86-90 Paul Street, London EC2A 4NE **Tel:** 44 02034 116496
Email: info@maddogski.com
Web site: http://www.maddogski.com/news-and-blogs
Freq: Daily
Circ: 10
Travel, Winter Sports

Mad Hatter's Pantry 996528
Email: madhatterspantry@gmail.com
Web site: www.madhatterspantry.co.uk
Freq: Daily
Circ: 8987
Cooking & Baking

The Mad House 988697
Email: mail@jenwalshaw.co.uk
Web site: muminthemadhouse.com
Freq: Daily
Circ: 145895
Family & Parenting

Mad News UK 997598
Email: madnewsuk@gmail.com
Web site: madnewsuk.com
Freq: Daily
Circ: 13621
Celebrities

Madam Miaow Says 988020
Email: madam.miaow@virgin.net
Web site: http://madammiaow.blogspot.co.uk/
Freq: Daily
Circ: 8601
Literature

Made By Many blog 1052997
Web site: https://madebymany.com/stories
Freq: Daily
Circ: 83
News & Current Affairs

Made with Pink 1053620
Email: madewithpink@gmail.com
Web site: http://www.madewithpink.com/
Freq: Daily
Circ: 6273
Cooking & Baking

Madeleine Loves 988716
Web site: madeleineloves.com
Freq: Daily
Circ: 9633
Beauty & Grooming, Cosmetics, Fashion, Hair

UK Blogs

Mademoiselle Poirot 1053732
Freq: Daily
Cooking & Baking, Do-It-Yourself (DIY), Photography, Visual Arts

Mademoiselle Robot 986193
Editorial - Mademoiselle Robot - Studio 34, Great Western Studios, 65 Alfred Road, London W2 5EU
Web site: www.mademoisellerobot.com
Freq: Daily
Circ: 31973
Fashion

Madhouse Family Reviews!
986486
Web site: madhousefamilyreviews.blogspot.com
Freq: Daily
Circ: 8377
Alcohol & Spirits, Bars, Clubs & Pubs, Beer, Beverages, Cooking & Baking, Family & Parenting, Food, Grocery Stores, Organic Food, Restaurant Reviews

Madizine 996937
Tel: 44 01708 700373
Email: hello@madizine.co.uk
Web site: madizine.co.uk
Freq: Daily
Circ: 10650
Fashion, Women's Interests

Magallanizate 1060897
Web site: http://blogs.eluniversal.com/eu3/Blogs/capi_index.shtml
Freq: Daily
News & Current Affairs

magCulture 997533
Editorial: 270 St John Street, London EC1V 4PE Tel: 44 02037 598022
Email: info@magculture.com
Web site: http://magculture.com/
Freq: Daily
Circ: 26581
Advertising Industry, Antiques/Collectibles, Art, Arts, Branding, Broadcasting, Graphic Design, Literature, Marketing, Media & Communications

Maghull and Lydiate 1055933
Web site: http://www.maghullandlydiateu3a.org.uk/
Freq: Daily
Circ: 918
Careers, Education, Higher Education, Schools & Institutions

Magical Penny 1053917
Email: magicalpenny@gmail.com
Web site: magicalpenny.com
Freq: Daily
Circ: 6950
Personal Finance

The Magpie Girl 1053047
Email: the.magpiegirl@gmail.com
Web site: www.themagpiegirl.com
Freq: Daily
Circ: 7251
Fashion

Magpie in the Sky 987772
Editorial: 62 Belvedere Court, 372-374 Upper Richmond Road, London SW15 6HZ
Web site: amagpieinthesky.com
Freq: Daily
Circ: 7668
Profile: Blog covering baking. A Magpie in the Sky discusses anything from cakes & recipes to running and things to do.
Cooking & Baking, Fitness & Exercise, Regional General Interest, Restaurant Reviews

Maid in London 1052937
Email: hotelworkerstogether@gmail.com
Web site: http://www.maidinlondonnow.blogspot.co.uk/
Freq: Daily
Circ: 1238
Charitable Foundations, Politics, Public Sector

Mainline Menswear 1054512
Tel: 44 01723 624264
Email: sales@mainlinemenswear.co.uk
Web site: http://www.mainlinemenswear.co.uk/blog/
Freq: Daily
Circ: 171
Fashion

Maison Cupcake 986194
Editorial: 20 Brunswick Street, Walthamstow, London E17 9NB
Web site: http://maisoncupcake.com/
Freq: Daily
Circ: 9611
Editor: Sarah Trivuncic
Cooking & Baking

Make Marketing History 1054573
Web site: http://makemarketinghistory.blogspot.co.uk/
Freq: Daily
Circ: 849
Advertising Industry, Branding, Broadcasting, Business, Marketing

Make New Tracks 998126
Tel: 44 07508 683256
Email: chrismakenewtracks@gmail.com
Web site: makenewtracks.com
Freq: Daily
Circ: 7519
Outdoor Recreation, Travel

The Make Up Fairy 987616
Email: themakeupfairypro@gmail.com
Web site: www.joannelarby.com
Freq: Daily
Circ: 7360
News & Current Affairs

Make Up to Make Out 986527
Web site: www.makeuptomakeout.co.uk
Freq: Daily
Circ: 3432
Beauty & Grooming, Cosmetics, Fashion, Hair

Make Wealth History 1054460
Email: jeremy@makewealthhistory.org
Web site: http://makewealthhistory.org/
Freq: Daily
Circ: 17491
Energy & Environment, Environment

Make, Do & Push 988683
Email: makedoandpush@gmail.com
Web site: makedoandpush.co.uk
Freq: Daily
Circ: 12513
Family & Parenting

Makelight 988285
Web site: https://makelight.com/
Freq: Daily
Circ: 11762
Crafts, Family & Parenting, Photography

Maketh-The-Man 987522
Web site: www.maketh-the-man.com
Freq: Daily
Circ: 10141
Editor: Callum Watt
Fashion, Men's Interests

Make-Up & Beauty 1053337
Email: pr@makeupandbeauty.ie
Web site: www.makeupandbeauty.ie
Freq: Daily
Circ: 6838
Beauty & Grooming, Cosmetics, Fashion, Hair

The Makeup Mole 603331
Owner: Handpicked Media
Email: christabel.draffin@gmail.com
Web site: http://www.makeupmole.com
Freq: Daily
Circ: 3565
Beauty & Grooming, Cosmetics

The Makeup Mole 1096360
Email: makeupmole@gmail.com
Web site: http://www.makeupmole.com
Freq: Daily

Circ: 3565
Beauty & Grooming, Cosmetics, Hair

Makeup Savvy 986195
Email: makeupsavvy@live.co.uk
Web site: www.makeupsavvy.co.uk
Freq: Daily
Circ: 79251
Cosmetics

Making A Mark 987293
Email: pastelsandpencils@gmail.com
Web site: makingamark.blogspot.com
Freq: Daily
Circ: 29995
Antiques/Collectibles, Art, Arts, Literature, Photography, Theater & Performing Arts, Visual Arts

Making a Scene - Creative Scene 1075506
Tel: 44 01924 437966
Email: hello@creativescene.org.uk
Web site: http://www.creativescene.org.uk/
Freq: Daily
Circ: 9049
Editor: Anna Franks
Entertainment, Local Entertainment Guides, Regional General Interest

Making It Up 987990
Email: liveotherwise@gmail.com
Web site: http://liveotherwise.co.uk/makingitup/
Freq: Daily
Circ: 12952
Profile: Blog covering beauty and cosmetics. The blog has an archive dating back to July 2014 and shares an extensive blog roll.
Literature

Making it Up 1064094
Web site: http://makingitupblog.com/
Freq: Daily
Circ: 1297
Beauty & Grooming, Cosmetics, Hair

Mallory On Travel 987523
Email: malloryontravel@gmail.com
Web site: http://malloryontravel.com/
Freq: Daily
Circ: 26057
Travel

Malt Review 995312
Editorial: 23 The Village, West Hallam, Ilkeston, West Hallam DE7 6GR
Email: maltreview@gmail.com
Web site: http://malt-review.com
Freq: Daily
Circ: 8939
Editor: Mark Newton
Alcohol & Spirits

Mama Geek 987571
Web site: mamageek.co.uk
Freq: Daily
Circ: 11661
Family & Parenting

MAMA OWL BLOG 1053817
Web site: www.mamaowl.co.uk
Freq: Daily
Circ: 6622
Family & Parenting, Women's Interests

MamaBabyBliss Blog 996241
Editorial: 14 The Chilterns, Hitchin SG4 9PP
Tel: 44 01462 632499
Email: bliss@mamababybliss.com
Web site: https://www.mamababybliss.com/blog/
Freq: Daily
Circ: 8439
Family & Parenting

Mama's Haven 997422
Web site: www.mamashaven.com
Freq: Daily
Circ: 33147
Family & Parenting

mama's V.I.B 988634
Email: mamasvib@mail.com
Web site: www.mamasvib.com
Freq: Daily

Circ: 6428
Profile: Blog covering fashion. The mama's V.I.B blog discusses anything from children's fashion and beauty to maternity fashion and shopping. The blog has an archive dating back to March 2014 and shares a short blog roll. The outlet offers RSS (Really Simple Syndication).
Beauty & Grooming, Cosmetics, Family & Parenting, Fashion, Hair, Women's Interests

Mammaful Zo 1054031
Email: mammaful@gmail.com
Web site: http://www.mammafulzo.com/
Freq: Daily
Circ: 8131
Profile: Blog covering beauty, fashion and lifestyle. The blog has an archive dating back to October 2012.
Beauty & Grooming, Cosmetics, Fashion, Hair, Women's Interests

mammasaurus 987624
Web site: www.mammasaurus.co.uk
Freq: Daily
Circ: 49979
Family & Parenting, Women's Interests

Mammywoo 995143
Email: mammywoo@me.com
Web site: misslexywoo.wordpress.com
Freq: Daily
Circ: 244
Family & Parenting

Mamta's Kitchen 996692
Web site: http://mamtaskitchen.com
Freq: Daily
Circ: 28477
Cooking & Baking

Man About Town 1100031
Web site: http://www.manabouttown.me
Freq: Daily
Circ: 10361
Profile: Magazine covering fashion, style, art, film and design. Aimed at men with a high disposable income.
Ad Rate: Full Page Mono 7000.00
Ad Rate: Full Page Colour 7000.00
News & Current Affairs

Man for Himself 987373
Editorial: 68 Vassall Road, London SW9 6HY
Email: pr@manforhimself.com
Web site: www.manforhimself.com
Freq: Daily
Circ: 42919
Fashion, Hair, Men's Interests

Man on Ledge 1074207
Web site: https://manonledge.wordpress.com
Freq: Daily
Circ: 13
Marketing, Publishing

Man Vs. Pink 1054127
Email: manvspink@gmail.com
Web site: http://manvspink.com
Freq: Daily
Circ: 11777
Profile: Blog covering fatherhood. Man vs. Pink discusses anything from being a stay at home dad and feminism to food. The blog has an archive dating back to May 2014. The outlet offers RSS (Really Simple Syndication).
Family & Parenting, Movies & Video

Manchester Fertility Blog
999330
Editorial: Amelia House, 3 Oakwood Square, Cheadle Royal Business Park, Cheadle SK8 3FS Tel: 44 01613 002730
Email: info@manchesterfertility.com
Web site: http://www.manchesterfertility.com/blog/
Freq: Daily
Circ: 67
Obstetrics & Gynecology (OB/GYN)

Manchester Mummy 998176
Email: info@manchestermummy.com
Web site: http://www.manchestermummy.com

Freq: Daily
Circ: 10050
Family & Parenting

Manchester Social 101   1105385
Editorial: 3/36 Central Road, West Didsbury, Manchester
Web site: http://mansocial.melbournesocial101.com/
Freq: Daily
Circ: 766
Alcohol & Spirits, Bars, Clubs & Pubs, Beer, Beverages, Cooking & Baking, Food, Grocery Stores, Organic Food, Regional General Interest, Restaurant Reviews

Manchester Users Network - MUN Reporter   1059603
Editorial: Users Office, Park House Hospital, Delauneys Road, Manchester M8 5RB
Tel: 44 01619 184343
Email: manchesterusersnetwork@hotmail.co.uk
Web site: http://www.manchesterusersnetwork.org.uk
Freq: Daily
Circ: 13918
Editor: Paul Reed
Community Care (UK)

MANFACE   988632
Editorial: PO Box 343, Mirfield WF13 9EE
Email: business@manface.co.uk
Web site: www.manface.uk
Freq: Daily
Circ: 12279
Beauty & Grooming, Cosmetics, Hair

Manga UK blog   1053852
Editorial: 6 Heddon Street, London W1B 4BT
Email: info@mangauk.com
Web site: http://www.mangauk.com/
Freq: Daily
Circ: 31819
Cartoons

The Man's Runway   1053878
Web site: http://www.themansrunway.co.uk/
Freq: Daily
Circ: 1297
Profile: Blog covering men's fashion. The blog has an archive dating back to July 2013.
Beauty & Grooming, Cosmetics, Fashion, Hair

Manualidades, Artcraft, Handcraft   1061659
Web site: http://www.manualidades-kinuh.blogspot.com
Freq: Daily
Circ: 521
Art, Crafts

Map to Buy   1054439
Web site: blog.maptobuy.co.uk
Freq: Daily
Circ: 50146
Lifestyle, Men's Interests, Property Management & Maintenance, Regional General Interest, Women's Interests

Mapping London   996918
Editorial: Mapping London, c/o UCL CASA, First Floor, 90 Tottenham Court Road, London W1T 4TJ
Web site: http://mappinglondon.co.uk/
Freq: Daily
Circ: 64493
News & Current Affairs

Mariam Musa   1102799
Email: mariam@wearevamp.co.uk
Web site: https://www.youtube.com/channel/UCfdgPVhm4YZXybgrRI6WcyQ
Freq: Daily
Beauty & Grooming, Cosmetics, Hair

Marianne Taylor Photography   1053079
Web site: http://www.mariannetaylorphotography.co.uk/blog
Freq: Daily

Circ: 45
Photography

Marie-Chantal Blog   1054161
Web site: mariechantalblog.com
Freq: Daily
Circ: 2912
News & Current Affairs

Marilyn Stowe Blog   999577
Editorial: Stowe Family Law, 8 Fulwood Place, Grays Inn, London WC1V 6HG
Tel: 44 02074 213300
Email: press@stowefamilylaw.co.uk
Web site: www.marilynstowe.co.uk
Freq: Daily
Circ: 31208
Family Law

Mari's Cakes   1060621
Web site: http://mariscakes.blogspot.com/
Freq: Daily
Circ: 4570
Cooking & Baking

Mari's World   986706
Web site: http://marisworld.co.uk
Freq: Daily
Circ: 12152
Family & Parenting, Women's Interests

Marisocial   1052945
Email: general.enquiries@marisota.co.uk
Web site: www.marisota.co.uk/marisocial
Freq: Daily
Circ: 48251
Fashion

Mark Horrell Blog   1053833
Web site: http://www.markhorrell.com/blog
Freq: Daily
Circ: 7148
Outdoor Recreation, Travel

Mark Lynas   1054553
Email: marklynas36@gmail.com
Web site: www.marklynas.org
Freq: Daily
Circ: 11451
Energy & Environment, Ethical/Moral Issues, Politics

Mark my words   1054229
Email: hello@borkowski.do
Web site: http://www.markborkowski.co.uk/
Freq: Daily
Circ: 11100
Advertising Industry, Branding, Marketing

Mark Pack's Blog   986196
Web site: www.markpack.org.uk
Freq: Daily
Circ: 48595
News & Current Affairs

Mark Shuttleworth Blog   1054024
Email: enquiries@markshuttleworth.com
Web site: www.markshuttleworth.com
Freq: Daily
Circ: 21984
Computers, Government Technology, Internet, Security & Security Systems, Software

Mark Thompson's Blog   986197
Email: markreckons@live.co.uk
Web site: markreckons.blogspot.com/
Freq: Daily
Circ: 8141
Politics

Mark Wadsworth Blog   1052751
Email: gmwadsworth@gmail.com
Web site: http://markwadsworth.blogspot.co.uk/
Freq: Daily
Circ: 7432
Government

Mark Warner blog   996731
Editorial: George House, 61 - 65 Kensington Church Street, London W8 4BA
Tel: 44 08448 843700
Email: marketing@markwarner.co.uk
Web site: http://www.markwarner.co.uk/blog/
Freq: Daily

Circ: 15220
Travel, Winter Sports

Mark Wilson's blog   1052948
Email: markw@markwilson.co.uk
Web site: http://www.markwilson.co.uk/blog/
Freq: Daily
Circ: 54592
Computers

The Marketing Blog   985605
Editorial: 61 Schroder Court, Englefield Green, Egham TW20 0EJ
Tel: 44 01784 434412
Web site: www.themarketingblog.co.uk
Freq: Daily
Circ: 77729
Editor: Will Corry
Advertising Industry, Branding, Broadcasting, Graphic Design, Marketing, Media & Communications, Photography, Publishing

Marketing Nerd   1055160
Email: matt@marketingnerd.co.uk
Web site: www.marketingnerd.co.uk/
Freq: Daily
Circ: 11576
Marketing

Marketing Summit   1061552
Web site: http://www.marketingsummit.blogspot.com
Freq: Daily
Circ: 1154
Advertising Industry, Branding, Broadcasting, Graphic Design, Marketing, Media & Communications, Photography, Publishing

Marketing Tom Media   1053631
Editorial: Regus House, Malthouse Avenue, Cardiff Gate Business Park, Cardiff CF23 8RU
Tel: 44 02920 263655
Email: enquiries@marketingtom.com
Web site: http://www.marketingtom.co.uk/
Freq: Daily
Circ: 9974
Computers, Industry, Marketing

The Marple Leaf   1053551
Email: themarpleleaf@gmail.com
Web site: http://www.themarpleleaf.co.uk/
Freq: Daily
Circ: 15401
Politics, Regional, Regional General Interest, Soccer

Martin Bryant blog   1053975
Freq: Daily
News & Current Affairs

Martin P Wilson   1054613
Web site: martinpwilson.wordpress.com
Freq: Daily
Circ: 68
Entertainment, LGBT, Men's Interests, Movies & Video, Regional General Interest

Mary Myatt   1054663
Email: mary@mmlearning.co.uk
Web site: http://marymyatt.com/blog
Freq: Daily
Circ: 140
Profile: Blog covering education. Mary Myatt blog discusses anything from education and schools to education curriculum. The blog has an archive dating back to August 2013. The outlet offers RSS (Really Simple Syndication).
Education

Marylebone London   996915
Editorial: 93digital Ltd, 102 Westbourne Studios, 242 Acklam Road, Portobello, London W10 5JJ
Web site: http://maryleboneonline.co.uk/
Freq: Daily
Circ: 7837
Regional General Interest, Restaurant Reviews

Marylebone Mums blog   1054283
Editorial: 6 Bryanston Mews West, London W1H 2DD
Email: marylebonemums@gmail.com

Web site: http://www.marylebonemums.com/blog
Freq: Daily
Circ: 5127
Family & Parenting

Master Graphic   1060579
Web site: http://www.xn–hablemosdediseo-crb.com
Freq: Daily
Circ: 611
Graphic Design, Internet

MATCHESFASHION.COM - The Style Report   997572
Editorial: The Shard, 32 London Bridge Street, London SE1 9SG
Tel: 44 02077 270628
Email: editorialteam@matchesfashion.com
Web site: http://www.matchesfashion.com/womens/the-style-report
Freq: Daily
Circ: 17025
Fashion

Materia Geek   1061989
Web site: http://www.materiageek.com
Freq: Daily
Circ: 611
Auto Aftermarket, Computers, Data Management, Electronics, Government Technology, Industry, Internet, Mobile Communications, National News, Security & Security Systems

MatthewWoodward.co.uk   997595
Web site: matthewwoodward.co.uk
Freq: Daily
Circ: 1359218
News & Current Affairs

Max & Mummy   1053944
Web site: www.maxandmummy.co.uk
Freq: Daily
Circ: 7946
Profile: Blog covering motherhood. MAX & MUMMY blog discusses anything from family and parenting to motherhood. The blog has an archive dating back to November 2012.
Family & Parenting, Women's Interests

Maxine Ali   1100034
Email: maxine@maxineali.com
Web site: http://maxineali.com
Freq: Daily
Circ: 10207
Cooking & Baking, Fitness & Exercise, Nutrition, Women's Interests

The May Fair Hotel Blog   995416
Web site: http://blog.themayfairhotel.co.uk/
Freq: Daily
Circ: 20
News & Current Affairs

May Petite   1051932
Email: maypetite@me.com
Web site: maypetite.blogspot.co.uk
Freq: Daily
Circ: 10446
Beauty & Grooming, Cosmetics, Fashion, Hair, Women's Interests

MayorWatch   986198
Editorial: 2nd Floor, 145-157 St John Street, London EC1V 4PY
Email: feedback@mayorwatch.co.uk
Web site: mayorwatch.co.uk
Freq: Daily
Circ: 19381
Editor: Martin Hoscik
Politics

Mazda Blog   996905
Email: contact@mazdaeur.com
Web site: http://www.mazdasocial.co.uk
Freq: Daily
Circ: 6154
Antique & Collectible Cars, Automakers, Automotive, Driving, Motorcycles, Off-road & 4-Wheel Drive Vehicles, Trucks & SUVs

UK Blogs

MBAKES 987096
Editorial: 17 Old Church Court, Bridge Road, Erith DA8 2BS
Web site: www.mbakes.com
Freq: Daily
Circ: 4131
Alcohol & Spirits, Bars, Clubs & Pubs, Beer, Beverages, Cooking & Baking, Food, Grocery Stores, Organic Food, Restaurant Reviews, Vegetarianism & Veganism

MdN Blog 1061960
Email: info@mdn.co.jp
Web site: http://mdn-mag.seesaa.net/
Freq: Daily
Circ: 3
Auto Aftermarket, Computers, Data Management, Electronics, Government Technology, Graphic Design, Industry, Internet, Mobile Communications, Security & Security Systems

me and my shadow 988218
Email: missielizzieandmyshadow@ymail.com
Web site: http://www.missielizzie-meandmyshadow.blogspot.co.uk/
Freq: Daily
Circ: 10886
Do-It-Yourself (DIY), Family & Parenting, Property Management & Maintenance

Me Firi Ghana 997590
Tel: 44 07932 896845
Email: info@mefirighana.com
Web site: www.mefirighana.com/blog
Freq: Daily
Circ: 7742
Africa

Me, My Books and I 1052901
Email: memybooksandi@yahoo.co.uk
Web site: memybooksandi.wordpress.com
Freq: Daily
Circ: 117
Literature

Me, Myself & Tottenham 998280
Email: nikhilsaglani@gmail.com
Web site: http://nikhilsaglani.com/
Freq: Daily
Circ: 10302
Soccer

Me, The Man & The Kids 986482
Email: methemanandthekids@gmail.com
Web site: www.methemanandthebaby.co.uk
Freq: Daily
Circ: 13804
Family & Parenting

Meal Planning Made Easy 997680
Web site: www.mealplanning.co.uk
Freq: Daily
Circ: 9395
Cooking & Baking

Meals Our Kids Love 995881
Email: contact@mealsourkidslove.com
Web site: http://mealsourkidslove.com/category/blog/
Freq: Daily
Circ: 234
Cooking & Baking, Family & Parenting, Food, Grocery Stores, Nutrition, Organic Food, Restaurant Reviews, Vegetarianism & Veganism

Meanmagenta Photos 1052588
Web site: http://meanmagenta-photos.blogspot.co.uk/
Freq: Daily
Circ: 521
Photography

MEB The Motor Centre Blog 996269
Editorial: 163 Tottenham Lane, Crouch End, London N8 9BT Tel: 44 02083 400656
Email: mebthemotorcentre@yahoo.co.uk
Web site: http://www.garageservicesnorthlondon.co.uk/blog/
Freq: Daily

Circ: 106
Antique & Collectible Cars, Automakers, Automotive, Driving, Motorcycles, Off-road & 4-Wheel Drive Vehicles, Trucks & SUVs

The Media Flow Blog 1052975
Tel: 44 02563 84890
Web site: http://www.themediaflow.com/blog
Freq: Daily
Circ: 18829
Branding, Internet, Marketing

Media Lens 984254
Web site: www.medialens.org
Freq: Daily
Circ: 24088
News & Current Affairs

Mediacom Beyond Advertising Blog 1053776
Editorial: 124 Theobalds Road, London WC1X 8RX Tel: 44 02071 585500
Web site: http://mediacombeyondadvertising.com/blog/
Freq: Daily
Circ: 16
Marketing

The Medium is Not Enough TV blog 988746
Web site: http://www.the-medium-is-not-enough.com/
Freq: Daily
Circ: 460
Broadcasting

Meerkatsu 998393
Email: seymouryang@gmail.com
Web site: http://meerkat69.blogspot.co.uk
Freq: Daily
Circ: 9028
Martial Arts, MMA & Self-Defense

MEF Minute 996292
Editorial: 1st Floor, 12 Great Newport Street, London, London WC2H 7JD
Email: editorial@mefmobile.org
Web site: http://mobileecosystemforum.com/mef-minute/
Freq: Daily
Circ: 106660
Mobile Electronics

Melanie's Fab Finds 1098991
Email: melaniesfabfinds@gmail.com
Web site: melaniesfabfinds.co.uk
Freq: Daily
Circ: 57166
Cooking & Baking, Family & Parenting

Mellow Mummy 986463
Email: jumblymummy@gmail.com
Web site: www.mellowmummy.co.uk
Freq: Daily
Circ: 7446
Cooking & Baking, Family & Parenting, Men's Interests, Women's Interests

The Memory Bank 1054520
Web site: http://thememorybank.co.uk/
Freq: Daily
Circ: 5336
Government, Internet

Meningitis Now Blog 999567
Editorial: Fern House, Bath Road, Stroud GL5 3TJ Tel: 44 01453 768000
Email: info@meningitisnow.org
Web site: http://www.meningitisnow.org/about-us/meet-the-team/our-team/sues-blog/
Freq: Daily
Circ: 6
Infectious Diseases

Men's Lifestyle Guide - CEASED 1053714
Web site: www.menslifestyleguide.co.uk
Freq: Daily
Circ: 2572
Beauty & Grooming, Cosmetics, Fashion, Hair, Men's Interests, Relationships

Mensos Concierge 998354
Email: info@mensosconcierge.co.uk
Web site: http://mensosconcierge.co.uk
Freq: Daily
Circ: 1222
Bars, Clubs & Pubs, Luxury Goods, Restaurant Reviews

Menswear Style 987197
Editorial: Aldgate Tower, 2 Leman Street, London E1 8FA Tel: 44 02038 084520
Email: info@menswearstyle.co.uk
Web site: www.menswearstyle.co.uk
Freq: Daily
Circ: 161896
Fashion

The Mental Elf 988378
Email: feedback@thementalelf.net
Web site: http://www.nationalelfservice.net/mental-health/
Freq: Daily
Circ: 69105
Profile: Blog covering mental health research, policy and guidance.
Health & Medicine

Mermaid Gossip 988942
Email: mermaidgossipblog@gmail.com
Web site: http://mermaidgossip.com/
Freq: Daily
Circ: 7875
Profile: Blog covering fashion, style and lifestyle. The outlet also offers a vlog.
Fashion, Regional General Interest, Women's Interests

Merrell Blog 1054042
Editorial: King's Place, 90 York Way, London N1 9AG Tel: 44 02033 762738
Email: info@merrell.eu
Web site: http://www.merrell.com/UK/en_GB/blog
Freq: Daily
Circ: 78
Outdoor Recreation, Travel, Winter Sports

The Message 1055939
Email: info@message.org.uk
Web site: www.message.org.uk
Freq: Daily
Circ: 9592
Religion

Met Uruguay 1061595
Web site: http://meteorologiauruguay.blogspot.com/
Freq: Daily
Circ: 1047
Science

Metacultura 1061820
Web site: http://blogs.eluniversal.com.mx/metacultura
Freq: Daily
Circ: 408
Antiques/Collectibles, Art, Arts, Celebrities, Literature, Photography, Theater & Performing Arts, Visual Arts

Methods of Dance 1053556
Web site: http://methodsofdance.blogspot.com
Freq: Daily
Circ: 877
Theater & Performing Arts

Metia Blog 1053950
Editorial: 101 St Martins Lane, London WC2N 4AZ
Email: info@metia.com
Web site: https://www.metia.com/blog/
Freq: Daily
Circ: 75
Branding, Marketing

Metro Girls 1061433
Web site: http://www.planetaninas.com
Freq: Daily
Circ: 2865
Elementary School, Preschool, Teen/Young Adult, Trading Cards & Comics

Metrogypsie 1054577
Editorial: 127 Booth Road, London NW9 5JU
Email: metrogypsie@gmail.com

Web site: http://www.metrogypsie.org/
Freq: Daily
Circ: 8128
Profile: Blog covering fashion and lifestyle. This outlet also offers a vlog. The blog has an archive dating back to January 2013.
Fashion, Lifestyle, Men's Interests, Regional General Interest, Women's Interests

MetropoliBlog 1061316
Web site: http://www.metropoliblog.com
Freq: Daily
Circ: 716
Celebrities, National News

Mex Files 1061767
Web site: http://mexfiles.net
Freq: Daily
Circ: 8140
Antiques/Collectibles, Art, Arts, Literature, National News, Photography, Politics, Theater & Performing Arts, Visual Arts

MexaBlog 1060948
Web site: http://mexablog.com
Freq: Daily
Circ: 336
Auto Aftermarket, Bars, Clubs & Pubs, Comedy, Computers, Data Management, Electronics, Entertainment, Government Technology, Industry, Internet

Mexicali Blog 1061139
Web site: http://www.mexicaliblog.com.mx
Freq: Daily
Circ: 1572
Antiques/Collectibles, Art, Arts, Celebrities, Literature, Photography, Theater & Performing Arts, Visual Arts

Mexican Foodie 1061936
Web site: http://www.mexicanfoodie.com
Freq: Daily
Circ: 8726
Antiques/Collectibles, Art, Arts, Cooking & Baking, International News, Literature, Photography, Theater & Performing Arts, Visual Arts

Mexicana Chic 1061482
Web site: http://www.mexicanachic.com
Freq: Daily
Circ: 521
Fashion

Mexico Bob 1061613
Web site: http://mexicobob.blogspot.com
Freq: Daily
Circ: 1771
Antiques/Collectibles, Art, Arts, Literature, Photography, Theater & Performing Arts, Visual Arts

Mexico Cooks! 1060770
Web site: http://mexicocooks.typepad.com
Freq: Daily
Circ: 4871851
Antiques/Collectibles, Art, Arts, Cooking & Baking, Food, Literature, Photography, Theater & Performing Arts, Visual Arts

Mexico Destinos 1060940
Email: info@mexicodestinos.com
Web site: http://blog.mexicodestinos.com
Freq: Daily
Circ: 87
Airline Inflight, Railroad, Travel

Mi Cocina Amateur 1061216
Email: cocinamateur@lanacion.com.ar
Web site: http://blogs.lanacion.com.ar/cocina-amateur/
Freq: Daily
Circ: 475
Cooking & Baking

Mi Opinion Deportiva 1061101
Web site: http://freddy-sports.blogspot.com/
Freq: Daily
Circ: 611
Basketball, Bicycles, Billiards, Boating & Yachting, Bodybuilding, Bowling, Boxing, Cricket, Equestrian Sports, Extreme/Adventure Sports

Mia Holt 1052933
Email: mia.holt@hotmail.com
Web site: http://miaholt.co.uk/
Freq: Daily
Circ: 9815
Cooking & Baking, Fashion, Restaurant
Reviews, Travel, Women's Interests

Mias hageliv 1061155
Email: mia.odegaard@gmail.com
Web site: http://miashage.blogspot.com/
Freq: Daily
Circ: 1111
Gardening

MIB's Instant Headache 997256
Web site: http://mibih.wordpress.com/
Freq: Daily
Circ: 49
Movies & Video

Michael 84 986500
Email: hola@michael84.co.uk
Web site: www.michael84.co.uk
Freq: Daily
Circ: 72537
Fashion

Michael Rosen's Blog 987981
Email: michael@michaelrosen.co.uk
Web site: http://michaelrosenblog.blogspot.
co.uk/
Freq: Daily
Circ: 8719
Education, Literature

Michelle Hua - Wearable Tech Fashion 1098986
Editorial: c/Manchester Science
Partnerships, BASE Flat 3, Pencroft Way,
Manchester M15 6JJ
Email: hello@madewithglove.co.uk
Web site: http://www.michellehua.co.uk/
blogs/
Freq: Daily
Circ: 226
Electronics, Fashion, Mobile Electronics

Michelle made this 1053015
Email: michellemadethis@gmail.com
Web site: http://michellemadethis.blogspot.
co.uk/
Freq: Daily
Circ: 611
Crafts

Microsoft UK Schools blog 1053978
Web site: https://blogs.msdn.microsoft.
com/ukschools/
Freq: Daily
Circ: 2606
Computers, Disability, Electronics,
Government Technology, Higher
Education, Industry, Internet, Mobile
Communications, Schools & Institutions,
Security & Security Systems

The Middle Sister 997980
Web site: http://www.themiddlesister.co.uk/
Freq: Daily
Circ: 9171
Beauty & Grooming, Broadcasting,
Cosmetics, Fashion, Hair, Literature

The middle-sized garden 900745
Tel: 44 07972 22834
Email: alexandra@themiddlesizedgarden.co.
uk
Web site: http://www.
themiddlesizedgarden.co.uk/
Freq: Daily
Circ: 12274
Profile: Blog covering gardening. The
middle-sized garden discusses anything
from gardening advice and inspiration for the
mid sized garden to plants. The blog has an
archive dating back to December 2013. The
outlet offers RSS (Really Simple
Syndication).
Gardening

Midlands Fly Fishing Blog
1052771
Email: enquiries@midlands-flyfishing.co.uk
Web site: http://www.midlands-flyfishing.co.
uk/blog

Freq: Daily
Circ: 300
Fishing

Midlands Gourmet Girl 988492
Email: midlandsgourmetgirl@gmail.com
Web site: midlandsgourmetgirl.wordpress.
com
Freq: Daily
Circ: 62
Profile: Blog covering food. The
midlandsgourmetgirl blog discusses
anything from food and restaurant reviews to
food producers and eating in the West
Midlands.
Alcohol & Spirits, Bars, Clubs & Pubs,
Beer, Beverages, Cooking & Baking,
Restaurant Reviews, Wine/Winemaking

Mighty Gadget 988884
Editorial: 1 Antrim Road, Blackpool FY2
9UR Tel: 44 01253 804513
Email: info@mightygadget.co.uk
Web site: http://mightygadget.co.uk/
Freq: Daily
Circ: 10907
Editor: James Smythe
Audio Video Trade, Cameras, Consumer
Electronics, Mobile Electronics, Movies &
Video

Migrantes 1061768
Web site: http://blogs.eluniversal.com.mx/
migrantes/
Freq: Daily
Circ: 1724
Immigration/Emigration, National News,
Politics

Miguel Ángel Santos 1061843
Web site: http://miguelangelsantos.
blogspot.com/
Freq: Daily
Circ: 1727
Banking, Economics

Mike Clark Dive Blog 1053900
Email: mike@underwater-photos.co.uk
Web site: http://mikeclarkdiveblog.blogspot.
co.uk/
Freq: Daily
Circ: 521
Nature & Wildlife, Swimming/Watersports

Mikhila.com 987459
Editorial: 36 Fewston Way, Lakeside,
Doncaster DN4 5PR
Email: mikhilamcdaid@hotmail.com
Web site: http://mikhila.com/
Freq: Daily
Circ: 11698
Beauty & Grooming, Cosmetics, Fashion,
Hair, Women's Interests

Mild Concern 988043
Email: mildconcern@googlemail.com
Web site: http://mildconcern.com/
Freq: Daily
Circ: 1051
Profile: Blog covering film. The MILD
CONCERN blog discusses anything from
film and TV reviews.
Antiques/Collectibles, Art, Arts,
Broadcasting, Literature, Movies & Video,
Photography, Theater & Performing Arts,
Visual Arts

The Mile Long Bookshelf 997228
Email: themilelongbook-shelf@hotmail.co.uk
Web site: http://www.themilelongbookshelf.
com/
Freq: Daily
Circ: 28118
Literature

Milex 1054644
Email: blogmilex@gmail.com
Web site: http://www.milexxx.com/
Freq: Daily
Circ: 6085
Fashion, Men's Interests

Milk & Honey 987077
Email: info@itsmilkandhoney.com
Web site: http://www.itsmilkandhoney.com
Circ: 11794
Women's Interests

Milk Bubble Tea 987387
Email: milkbubbleteax@gmail.com
Web site: milkbubbleteax1.blogspot.co.uk
Freq: Daily
Circ: 4415
Women's Interests

Milk Drunk Diary 997978
Email: sophia@milkdrunkdiary.com
Web site: www.milkdrunkdiary.com
Freq: Daily
Circ: 12591
Bars, Clubs & Pubs, Comedy,
Entertainment, Family & Parenting,
Fashion, Local Entertainment Guides,
Movies & Video, Women's Interests

milkteef 986816
Email: milkteef@gmail.com
Web site: www.milkteef.com
Freq: Daily
Circ: 30123
Beauty & Grooming, Cosmetics, Fashion,
Hair, Women's Interests

Mills & Reeves Blogs 1053724
Editorial: Monument Place, 24 Monument
Street, London EC3R 8AJ
Tel: 44 02076 489220
Web site: http://www.mills-reeve.com/news
Freq: Daily
Real Estate Law

Milly Naomi 987046
Email: pistachio_shoes@hotmail.com
Web site: http://www.millynaomi.com/
Freq: Daily
Circ: 12337
Beauty & Grooming, Cosmetics, Hair

Milsabores 1062041
Web site: http://www.milsabores.net/index.
php
Freq: Daily
Circ: 10833
Cooking & Baking

Mimos Culinarios 1061435
Web site: http://mimos-culinarios.blogspot.
com/
Freq: Daily
Circ: 1060
Cooking & Baking

Mind blog 999350
Editorial: 15-19 Broadway, Stratford,
London E15 4BQ Tel: 44 02085 191743
Email: media@mind.org.uk
Web site: http://www.mind.org.uk/
information-support/your-stories/
Freq: Daily
Circ: 18328
Charitable Foundations, Disability

The Mind of a Helmet Camera Cyclist 997398
Web site: http://www.magnatom.net/
Freq: Daily
Circ: 14850
Bicycles

The Mini Mes and Me 987592
Web site: www.theminimesandme.com
Freq: Daily
Circ: 42503
Cooking & Baking, Crafts, Family &
Parenting, Women's Interests

Minimalsen 1061267
Email: blog@minimalsen.dk
Web site: http://minimalsen.dk/
Freq: Daily
Circ: 783
Family & Parenting, Lifestyle, Men's
Interests, Regional General Interest,
Women's Interests

Mint Digital Blog 1054606
Editorial: Exmouth House, 3-11 Pine Street,
London EC1R 0JH
Web site: http://mintdigital.com/blog
Freq: Daily
Circ: 3
News & Current Affairs

Miradas de Foto Periodismo
1061660
Web site: http://www.vanguardia.com.mx/
blog-msierra.html
Freq: Daily
National News, Politics

Mis Fotosecuencias 1061228
Web site: http://misfotosecuencias.com.ar/
Freq: Daily
Circ: 9376
Cooking & Baking

Mis Trucos de Maquillaje
1060894
Web site: http://mistrucosdemaquillaje.
blogspot.com
Freq: Daily
Circ: 493
Beauty & Grooming, Cosmetics, Hair

Misery Guts 1052917
Email: patrick@vg247.com
Web site: http://patrickgarratt.com/
Freq: Daily
Circ: 10974
Literature

Mishka Designs 1061361
Web site: http://www.mishkadesignspv.
blogspot.com
Freq: Daily
Circ: 1860
Crafts, Weddings

Miss Geeky 987994
Web site: missgeeky.com
Freq: Daily
Circ: 7864
Apple, Audio Video Trade, Cameras,
Computer & Video Games, Computers,
Consumer Electronics, Electronics,
Internet, Literature, Mobile Electronics

Miss Mamo's World 988072
Editorial: Grafton Cottage, 117 Grafton
Street, Hull HU5 2NP
Email: missmamosworld@gmail.com
Web site: www.missmamosworld.com
Freq: Daily
Circ: 9785
Profile: Blog covering recipes. MISS
MAMO'S WORLD discusses anything from
baking and cooking to meal ideas and
beverages. The blog has an archive dating
back to December 2013. The outlet offers
RSS (Really Simple Syndication).
Cooking & Baking

Miss Mernagh 1052704
Email: info@missmernagh.com
Web site: http://missmernagh.com
Freq: Daily
Circ: 1988
Education

Miss Pond 1054300
Email: miss_pond@hotmail.com
Web site: http://misspond.com/
Freq: Daily
Circ: 9426
News & Current Affairs

Miss Thrifty 986696
Web site: http://www.miss-thrifty.co.uk
Freq: Daily
Circ: 48827
Personal Finance

Miss West End Girl 1076642
Email: hello@misswestendgirl.com
Web site: http://misswestendgirl.com/
Freq: Daily
Circ: 8748
Profile: Blog covering lifestyle, fashion,
fashion accessories and personal style. The
blog has an archive dating back to July
2010.
Cooking & Baking, Women's Interests

Missing Sleep 1053930
Web site: www.reallymissingsleep.com
Freq: Daily
Circ: 33026
Profile: Blog covering motherhood. Missing
Sleep discusses anything from children's

UK Blogs

activity ideas and family fun to product reviews.
Family & Parenting

missjengrieves.com 997147
Editorial: BBC Radio 1 Interactive Zone C, 8th Floor, New Broadcasting House, Portland Place, London W1A 1AA
Web site: missjengrieves.com
Freq: Daily
Circ: 9206
Fitness & Exercise, Health & Medicine, Nutrition, Women's Interests

MJUUUGLY's blogg! 1062024
Email: mjuuugly@gmail.com
Web site: http://mjuuugly.blogg.no/
Freq: Daily
Circ: 60521
Food, Health & Medicine, Nutrition

MMGaming 1054073
Email: contact@mmgaming.net
Web site: http://mmgaming.net/
Freq: Daily
Circ: 10307
Computer & Video Games

Mo Yan Qing Feng 1061744
Web site: http://blog.sina.com.cn/guojf
Freq: Daily
Circ: 37663
Antique & Collectible Cars, Automakers, Automotive, Driving, Motorcycles, Off-road & 4-Wheel Drive Vehicles, Trucks & SUVs

Mob76 Outlook 1053284
Web site: www.mob76outlook.com
Freq: Daily
Circ: 8499
Africa, Consumer Affairs, International News

Mobile Fun Blog 986199
Editorial: Unit 16 Network Park, Duddeston Mill Road, Birmingham B8 1AU
Tel: 44 08442 495079
Web site: http://www.mobilefun.co.uk/blog
Freq: Daily
Circ: 23927
Mobile Electronics

Mobile Monday London blog 1053180
Email: contact@mobilemonday.org.uk
Web site: http://www.mobilemonday.org.uk/
Freq: Daily
Circ: 4283
Mobile Electronics

Mobile Money Revolution 1053359
Web site: mobilemoneyrevolution.co.uk
Freq: Daily
Circ: 1647
Mobile Electronics

Mobot 996236
Email: contact@mobot.net
Web site: mobot.net
Freq: Daily
Circ: 31921
Editor: Martin James
Mobile Electronics

Moccablog 1061461
Web site: http://www.moccablog.com
Freq: Daily
Circ: 2336
Auto Aftermarket, Computers, Data Management, Electronics, Government Technology, Graphic Design, Industry, Internet, Mobile Communications, Photography

Mochachocolata Rita 1061152
Web site: http://www.mochachocolatarita.blogspot.com/
Freq: Daily
Circ: 3740
Food

MODA Blog 1053575
Email: marketing@moda-uk.co.uk
Web site: http://www.moda-uk.co.uk/
Freq: Daily

Circ: 70971
Fashion

Moda Blog 1060961
Web site: http://www.webdelamoda.com
Freq: Daily
Circ: 20279
Fashion

Moda Capital 1061553
Web site: http://modacapital.blogspot.com
Freq: Daily
Circ: 3028
Fashion

Moda Para Ellas 1061912
Web site: http://www.moda-para-ellas.com
Freq: Daily
Circ: 773
Fashion

Moda Para Ellos 1060761
Web site: http://www.moda-para-ellos.com
Freq: Daily
Circ: 1287
Fashion

Mode en Rose 1061256
Web site: http://www.lamodenrose.com
Freq: Daily
Circ: 2382
Fashion

ModeHunter 1054352
Email: info@modehunter.co.uk
Web site: http://www.modehunter.co.uk/
Freq: Daily
Circ: 8399
Fashion

Módem 1061697
Web site: http://www.elmodem.com
Freq: Daily
Circ: 2094
Auto Aftermarket, Bars, Clubs & Pubs, Comedy, Computers, Data Management, Electronics, Entertainment, Government Technology, Industry, Internet

Modern Bric-a-Brac blog 998991
Tel: 44 07752 497267
Email: modernbrickabrack@gmail.com
Web site: http://www.modernbricabrac.com/
Freq: Daily
Circ: 9765
Bars, Clubs & Pubs, Comedy, Entertainment, Local Entertainment Guides, Movies & Video, Regional General Interest

The Modern Gentleman 1052882
Web site: http://www.themitchelli.com/
Freq: Daily
Circ: 6994
Alcohol & Spirits, Fashion, Men's Interests, Wine/Winemaking

The Modern Man Blog 1053291
Web site: themodernmanblog.blogspot.co.uk
Freq: Daily
Circ: 10034
Profile: Blog covering fashion. THE MODERN MAN BLOG discusses anything from fashion and Men's interests. The blog has an archive dating back to November 2011.
Fashion, Men's Interests

Modern Mummy 1054594
Web site: http://www.modernmummy.co.uk/
Freq: Daily
Circ: 9846
Do-It-Yourself (DIY), Family & Parenting, Fashion, Women's Interests

Modernisti Kodikas 1060867
Email: modernistikodikas@gmail.com
Web site: http://divaaniblogit.fi/modernistikodikas/
Freq: Daily
Circ: 12111
Architecture & Design, Do-It-Yourself (DIY), Gardening, Home, Interior Design, Property Management & Maintenance, Real Estate

Momentum Ski 1053157
Editorial: 162 Munster Road, London SW6 6AT **Tel:** 44 02073 719111
Web site: http://momentumski.com/blog/
Freq: Daily
Circ: 2
Travel, Winter Sports

Mondomulia 988503
Editorial: Apt 3, 1 Clapham Court Terrace, London SW4 8DT
Email: mondomulia@me.com
Web site: http://mondomulia.com/
Freq: Daily
Circ: 11807
Profile: Blog covering lifestyle, restaurant reviews, cake, cooking, baking, food and photography. The blog has an archive dating back to November 2011.
Cooking & Baking, Travel

The Monetary Future 1054382
Freq: Daily
News & Current Affairs

Monevator 986200
Web site: monevator.com
Freq: Daily
Circ: 124911
Personal Finance

Money Dashboard blog 1054188
Editorial: The One Place Capital, 18 Charlotte Square, Edinburgh EH2 4DF
Email: info@moneydashboard.com
Web site: https://blog.moneydashboard.com/blog
Freq: Daily
Circ: 18893
Personal Finance

Money Is The Way 986357
Web site: http://moneyistheway.blogspot.com/
Freq: Daily
Circ: 2486
Fund Management, Hedge Funds, Private Equity

Money Moves Markets 1053170
Email: moneymovesmarkets@henderson.com
Web site: http://www.moneymovesmarkets.com/
Freq: Daily
Circ: 10013
Economics, Financial Markets

Money Sucks? 1053162
Web site: www.moneysucks.net
Freq: Daily
Circ: 12374
Profile: Blog covering money and consumer issues. The Money Sucks? blog discusses anything from personal finance and pensions to changes to government legislation and financial service providers.

Money Watch 986201
Web site: http://www.money-watch.co.uk
Freq: Daily
Circ: 9141
Personal Finance

Moneyfacts blog 1052763
Email: press@moneyfacts.co.uk
Web site: http://blog.moneyfacts.co.uk/
Freq: Daily
Circ: 35
Personal Finance

MoneyScience: Financial Blog Directory 997536
Editorial: Enterprise Development Center, Clevedon BS21 7RQ
Web site: http://www.moneyscience.com/pg/blog-directory/financial-blog-directory
Freq: Daily
Circ: 23
Bonds, Corporate Finance, Corporate Management, Credit Markets, Derivatives, Emerging Markets, Government, Lending, Public & Consumer Finance

Monos 1060902
Web site: http://monosarteimagen.blogspot.com

Freq: Daily
Circ: 521
Art, Literature, Movies & Video, National News, Politics

Monos con Navaja 1060365
Web site: http://helderbinimelis.net
Freq: Daily
Circ: 9817
Crime & Violence, Politics, Social Issues

Monsoon Spice 1054041
Email: siakrishna@gmail.com
Web site: http://www.monsoonspice.com/
Freq: Daily
Circ: 33924
Cooking & Baking

Montenegro Piensa 1061414
Web site: http://ricardomontenegro.blogspot.com/
Freq: Daily
Circ: 1608
Bankruptcy, Company News & Appointments, Consumer Interest, Corporate Law, Criminal Law, Employment, Estate Planning, Family Law, Federal Courts, Food & Drug Administration

Monty's Mortgage Blog 986202
Editorial: Coreco Group, 117-119 Houndsditch, London EC3A 7BT
Tel: 44 02072 205100
Web site: http://www.corecogroup.co.uk/montys-mortgage-blog/
Freq: Daily
Circ: 71
Finance

Mookychick 999182
Editorial: 72 Paget Avenue, London SM1 3BE
Email: editor@mookychick.co.uk
Web site: www.mookychick.co.uk
Freq: Daily
Circ: 86234
Beauty & Grooming, Cosmetics, Family & Parenting, Fashion, Hair

Moon + Forest 1056580
Email: moonandforest@gmail.com
Web site: http://www.moonandforest.co.uk/
Freq: Daily
Circ: 8370
Travel, Women's Interests

Moon to Moon 1052769
Email: moontomoon@live.co.uk
Web site: http://frommoontomoon.blogspot.co.uk/
Freq: Daily
Circ: 6002
Architecture & Design, Do-It-Yourself (DIY), Property Management & Maintenance

Moore Legal Technology's Blog 1053973
Editorial: 86 - 90 Paul Street, London EC2A 4NE **Tel:** 44 03331 222904
Email: enquiries@moorelegaltechnology.co.uk
Web site: https://www.moorelegaltechnology.co.uk/Blog
Freq: Daily
Advertising Industry, Branding, Broadcasting, Graphic Design, Marketing, Media & Communications, Photography, Publishing

moorizzla by Alya Mooro 1075492
Web site: http://www.moorizzla.com/
Freq: Daily
Circ: 9214
Dance Music, Fashion, Jazz & Blues, Rap & Hip Hop, Social Issues, Travel, Women's Interests

Moral Fibres 988955
Email: moralfibres@gmail.com
Web site: moralfibres.co.uk
Freq: Daily
Circ: 13268
Profile: Blog covering eco lifestyle. MORAL FIBRES blog discusses anything from food

and drink to travel and fashion. The blog has an archive dating back to January 2013.
News & Current Affairs

Moran Mountain 1054330
Editorial: Moran Mountain Ltd, Park Cottage, Achintee, Strathcarron IV54 8YX
Tel: 44 01520 722361
Email: martin.moran@btinternet.com
Web site: http://www.moran-mountain.co.uk/blog/
Freq: Daily
Outdoor Recreation, Travel

Mordida de Tiburon 1060758
Web site: http://blogs.eluniversal.com/eu3/Blogs/mord_index.shtml
Freq: Daily
Circ: 17653
News & Current Affairs

More (Blogger) 1061286
Web site: http://vipblog.orientalsunday.hk/yukilo
Freq: Daily
Circ: 68703
Fashion

More Than Toast 1053070
Email: hello@alicejt.com
Web site: http://morethantoast.org/
Freq: Daily
Circ: 25012
Family & Parenting, Relationships, Women's Interests

Moregeous 1053214
Web site: https://moregeous.com/
Freq: Daily
Circ: 10230
Do-It-Yourself (DIY)

MoreThanJustaCupcake-Lover 1064282
Email: morethanjustacupcakelover@gmail.com
Web site: www.morethanjustacupcakelover.co.uk
Freq: Daily
Circ: 8298
Travel, Women's Interests

MoreZoella 1066541
Web site: https://www.youtube.com/user/MoreZoella
Freq: Daily
Circ: 26
Women's Interests

Morning Glass Designs 1053473
Web site: http://www.morningglass.co.uk/news
Freq: Daily
Architecture & Design

Mortilto 1061696
Email: canabuttenschoen@yahoo.dk
Web site: http://mortilto.dk/
Freq: Daily
Circ: 1949
Elementary School, Family & Parenting, Lifestyle, Men's Interests, Preschool, Regional General Interest, Teen/Young Adult, Trading Cards & Comics, Women's Interests

Mostly Books 996929
Editorial: 36 Stert Street, Abingdon OX14 3JP **Tel:** 44 01235 525880
Email: books@mostly-books.co.uk
Web site: http://www.mostly-books.co.uk/
Freq: Daily
Circ: 6782
Literature

Mother Distracted 1066027
Web site: http://www.motherdistracted.co.uk/
Freq: Daily
Circ: 86894
Profile: Blog covering motherhood, family, parenting and lifestyle. The blog has an archive dating back to August 2012.
Family & Parenting, Women's Interests

The Mother Edit 1052944
Web site: http://www.themotheredit.com/

Freq: Daily
Circ: 11432
Beauty & Grooming, Cosmetics, Entertainment, Family & Parenting, Fashion, Hair

The Motherhood 986515
Email: contact@westlondonmum.co.uk
Web site: http://themother-hood.com/
Freq: Daily
Circ: 15474
Family & Parenting, Women's Interests

Motherhood Diaries 997368
Editorial: 120 Bunns Lane, Mill Hill, London NW7 2AP
Email: review@motherhooddiaries.com
Web site: www.motherhooddiaries.com
Freq: Daily
Circ: 9213
Family & Parenting

Motherhood Journeys 1053922
Web site: motherhoodjourneys.com
Freq: Daily
Circ: 6863
Profile: Blog covering motherhood, family life, pregnancy and children.
Family & Parenting

Motherhood: The Real Deal 1053774
Email: motherhoodtherealdeal@gmail.com
Web site: http://motherhoodtherealdeal.com/
Freq: Daily
Circ: 41295
Family & Parenting

Motherkin 1054394
Web site: http://www.motherkin.net
Freq: Daily
Circ: 548
Comedy, Family & Parenting, Preschool, Women's Interests

Mother's Always Right 1054380
Web site: http://www.mothersalwaysright.com/
Freq: Daily
Circ: 13538
Beauty & Grooming, Cooking & Baking, Cosmetics, Do-It-Yourself (DIY), Family & Parenting, Fashion, Hair, Restaurant Reviews

mothloves 000000
Email: mothloves@hotmail.com
Web site: http://www.mothloves.com/
Freq: Daily
Circ: 8957
Profile: Blog covering fashion and beauty. MOTHLOVES blog discusses anything from personal style and outfit posts to the latest fashion trends and beauty buys. The blog has an archive dating back to March 2013.
Beauty & Grooming, Cosmetics, Fashion, Hair, Women's Interests

Motivating Mum 1052671
Editorial: 8 Edgell Road, Staines TW18 2ES
Tel: 44 01784 452280
Email: debbie@motivatingmum.co.uk
Web site: http://blog.motivatingmum.co.uk/
Freq: Daily
Circ: 14014
Business, Family & Parenting

Motor Heads 987874
Web site: www.motor-heads.co.uk/
Freq: Daily
Circ: 8641
Profile: Blog covering motors. MOTOR HEADS blog discusses anything from motoring and cars to car repairs and car accessories.
Antique & Collectible Cars, Automakers, Automotive, Driving, Motorcycles, Off-road & 4-Wheel Drive Vehicles, Trucks & SUVs

Motor Range blog 997783
Editorial: 1 Northway, Maghull, Liverpool L31 5LH **Tel:** 44 08433 830333
Email: info@motorrange.co.uk
Web site: http://www.motorrange.co.uk/blog

Freq: Daily
Circ: 1538
Antique & Collectible Cars, Automakers, Automotive, Driving, Motorcycles, Off-road & 4-Wheel Drive Vehicles, Trucks & SUVs

Motor Sport Magazine Blog 997046
Editorial: 18-20 Rosemont Road, London NW3 6NE **Tel:** 44 02073 498484
Email: editorial@motorsportmagazine.co.uk
Web site: www.motorsportmagazine.com
Freq: Daily
Circ: 149090
Motorsports

Motor Trader Blog 986402
Editorial: 6th Floor, Davis House, 2 Robert Street, Croydon CR0 1QQ
Tel: 44 02082 538711
Web site: http://www.motortrader.com/blogs
Circ: 83
Editor: Curtis Hutchinson
Antique & Collectible Cars, Automakers, Automotive, Driving, Motorcycles, Off-road & 4-Wheel Drive Vehicles, Trucks & SUVs

MotorMartin 1096040
Web site: http://motormartin.com/
Freq: Daily
Circ: 13388
Automotive, Driving

Motor-Vision 988059
Email: customer.care@performancedirect.co.uk
Web site: http://www.motor-vision.co.uk/
Freq: Daily
Circ: 8573
Antique & Collectible Cars, Automakers, Automotive, Driving, Motorcycles, Off-road & 4-Wheel Drive Vehicles, Trucks & SUVs

Mouldy Fruit 1053003
Email: mouldyfruit@gmail.com
Web site: http://www.mouldyfruit.com/
Freq: Daily
Circ: 6972
Fashion

MouldyFruit Vlog 1104005
Email: mouldyfruit@gmail.com
Web site: https://www.youtube.com/user/MouldyFruit
Freq: Daily
Circ: 4112
Cosmetics

The Mountains of Instead 1053529
Web site: http://www.mountainsofinstead.com/
Freq: Daily
Circ: 1142
News & Current Affairs

Mouthing Off with Miss Mamo 997036
Editorial: Grafton Cottage, 117 Grafton Street, Hull HU5 2NP
Email: missmamosworld@gmail.com
Web site: stephaniemamo.com
Freq: Daily
Circ: 1135
Careers, Cooking & Baking, Family & Parenting, Grocery Stores, Health & Medicine, Personal Finance, Relationships

Movehut Blog 997601
Tel: 44 02082 322402
Email: news@movehut.co.uk
Web site: www.movehut.co.uk/news
Freq: Daily
Circ: 19372
Architecture & Design, Do-It-Yourself (DIY), Gardening, Home, Property Management & Maintenance, Real Estate

Movements@Manchester 1055300
Web site: http://www.movements.manchester.ac.uk/category/the-blog/

Freq: Daily
Circ: 11
Politics, Social Issues

The Movie Evangelist 987957
Email: movieevangelist@btinternet.com
Web site: https://movieevangelist.com/
Freq: Daily
Circ: 10969
Profile: Blog covering cinema.
Entertainment, Movies & Video

Movie Marker 1073943
Email: admin@moviemarker.co.uk
Web site: moviemarker.co.uk
Freq: Daily
Circ: 13546
Editor: Luke Walkley
Movies & Video

Movie Moron 986521
Email: sheridanpassell@hotmail.com
Web site: http://www.movie-moron.com
Freq: Daily
Circ: 822489
Movies & Video

Movie Talk 987952
Tel: 44 02031 483678
Email: movietalk@ipcmedia.com
Web site: http://www.whatsontv.co.uk/blog/
Freq: Daily
Circ: 157
Entertainment, Movies & Video

Movieland 1060760
Web site: http://www.blogs.hoycinema.com/movieland/posts
Freq: Daily
Movies & Video

Movies and Series 1061076
Web site: http://www.moviesandseries.com.ar/
Freq: Daily
Circ: 1154
Broadcasting, Movies & Video

Movieville 988414
Web site: http://www.movieville.org/
Freq: Daily
Circ: 548
Movies & Video

Movilandia 1060825
Web site: http://blogs.lanacion.com.ar/movilandia/
Freq: Daily
Circ: 1662
Mobile Electronics

Moving Along With The Times 996508
Email: didosdesigns@yahoo.com
Web site: http://movingalongwiththetimes.blogspot.co.uk/
Freq: Daily
Circ: 1544
Crafts

Mowbray Designs 1056563
Web site: http://mowbraydesigns.blogspot.co.uk/
Freq: Daily
Circ: 720
Crafts

Mr & Mrs T Plus 3 1073136
Editorial: Karinya, Quarry Lane, Kingsweston, Bristol BS11 0QJ
Web site: http://www.amytreasure.com/
Freq: Daily
Circ: 13174
Cooking & Baking, Do-It-Yourself (DIY), Family & Parenting, Restaurant Reviews, Women's Interests

Mr Reasonable 996853
Email: mrreasonable@outlook.com
Web site: http://reasonablenewbarnet.blogspot.co.uk/
Freq: Daily
Circ: 9511
Politics

UK Blogs

Mr X Stitch 996539
Email: artist@mrxstitch.com
Web site: http://www.mrxstitch.com/
Freq: Daily
Circ: 27935
Crafts

Mr. Boy 1053109
Email: akamrboy@gmail.com
Web site: http://karlmond.com/
Freq: Daily
Circ: 962
Profile: Blog covering men's fashion.
Fashion, Men's Interests

mrbunkeredu 1054023
Email: mrbunkeredu@gmail.com
Web site: http://mrbunkeredu.wordpress.com
Freq: Daily
Circ: 43
Profile: Blog covering education.
mrbunkeredu blog discusses anything from education to teaching. The blog has an archive dating back to October 2013 and shares an extensive blog roll.
Education, Literature

Mrlukechristian 1098951
Email: mrlukechristian@outlook.com
Web site: http://www.mrlukechristian.com
Freq: Daily
Circ: 13969
Cosmetics, Fashion, Men's Interests

Mrs O. around the world 987917
Email: ana@mrsoaroundtheworld.com
Web site: http://mrsoaroundtheworld.com/
Freq: Daily
Circ: 46221
Travel

Mrs Trefusis Takes a Taxi
1053568
Email: mrstrefusis@gmail.com
Web site: www.mrstrefusis.blogspot.co.uk
Freq: Daily
Circ: 1092
Bars, Clubs & Pubs, Literature, Restaurant Reviews

Mrs. Bargain Hunter 997187
Email: mrs@mrsbargainhunter.co.uk
Web site: http://www.mrsbargainhunter.co.uk/
Freq: Daily
Circ: 9123
Personal Finance

MrsD-Daily 985617
Email: info@puresauce.co.uk
Web site: http://www.mrsd-daily.com
Freq: Daily
Circ: 12949
Fashion

MS Power User 987481
Email: editor@wmpoweruser.com
Web site: http://mspoweruser.com/
Circ: 15644
Mobile Electronics, Personal Computers

MsMarmiteLover 987240
Email: marmitelover@mac.com
Web site: http://www.msmarmitelover.com/
Freq: Daily
Circ: 8372
Alcohol & Spirits, Bars, Clubs & Pubs, Beer, Beverages, Cooking & Baking, Food, Grocery Stores, Organic Food, Restaurant Reviews, Vegetarianism & Veganism

muddlethroughmama 1072207
Email: muddlethroughmama@gmail.com
Web site: muddlethroughmama.com
Freq: Daily
Circ: 611
Family & Parenting, Women's Interests

Muddy Stilettos 987344
Web site: www.muddystilettos.co.uk
Freq: Daily
Circ: 9076
Cooking & Baking, Shopping, Women's Interests

Muerto 1060856
Web site: http://elmuertoquehabla.blogspot.com/
Freq: Daily
Circ: 8870
Antiques/Collectibles, Armed Forces, Astrology & Parapsychology, Astronomy, Aviation, Boating & Yachting, Camping and RV Travel, Cartoons, Casinos & Gaming, Celebrities

MUFCLatest.com 988637
Email: paul@mufclatest.com
Web site: http://mufclatest.com/
Circ: 40437
Soccer

Muffins, Cupcakes y Más
1060816
Web site: http://www.muffincupcakehouse.blogspot.com
Freq: Daily
Circ: 521
Cooking & Baking

Mujer .name 1061083
Web site: http://www.mujer.name/
Freq: Daily
Circ: 916
Women's Interests

Mujer y Punto 1060349
Web site: http://www.mujerypunto.cl
Freq: Daily
Circ: 4272
Elementary School, Preschool, Teen/Young Adult, Trading Cards & Comics, Women's Interests

Mujeres Construyendo 1062017
Web site: http://www.mujeresconstruyendo1.blogspot.com
Freq: Daily
Circ: 3885
Antiques/Collectibles, Art, Arts, Auto Aftermarket, Computers, Data Management, Electronics, Government Technology, Industry, Internet

Mujeres Hoy 1061714
Web site: http://mujeres-hoy.com
Freq: Daily
Circ: 1860
Cosmetics, Health & Medicine

Multiple Mummy - CEASED
987688
Web site: multiplemummy.com
Freq: Daily
Circ: 4804
Family & Parenting

The Mum Blog 985948
Web site: www.themumblog.com
Freq: Daily
Circ: 587
Editor: Liz Jarvis
Family & Parenting

Mum in a Hurry 1053926
Email: info@muminahurry.com
Web site: muminahurry.com
Freq: Daily
Circ: 8901
Family & Parenting, Relationships, Women's Interests

Mum of Three World 996949
Email: mumofthreeworld@gmail.com
Web site: http://mumofthreeworld.blogspot.co.uk
Freq: Daily
Circ: 2066
Family & Parenting, Women's Interests

Mum on the Brink 1054359
Email: mumonthebrink@gmail.com
Web site: mumonthebrink.com
Freq: Daily
Circ: 14920
Profile: Blog covering motherhood. MUM ON THE BRINK discusses anything from family activities and travel to family gadgets and family fun.
Family & Parenting, Travel

Mumazine 996185
Web site: mumazine.com
Freq: Daily
Circ: 13172
Family & Parenting

Mumma G 1053409
Web site: www.mummagzblog.co.uk
Freq: Daily
Circ: 6736
Family & Parenting, Women's Interests

The Mummy Adventure 987447
Web site: www.themummyadventure.com
Freq: Daily
Circ: 11475
Family & Parenting

Mummy Alarm 985877
Web site: www.mummyalarm.co.uk
Freq: Daily
Circ: 13055
Profile: Blog covering motherhood. MUMMY ALARM blog discusses anything from motherhood and family to parenting. The blog has an archive dating back to January 2011 and shares a short blog roll.
Family & Parenting

Mummy B 1053432
Web site: www.mummyburgess.co.uk
Freq: Daily
Circ: 8218
Profile: Blog covering motherhood. Mummy B blog discusses anything from motherhood and parenting to weddings and home decorating. The blog has an archive dating back to April 2012.
Family & Parenting

Mummy Barrow 988257
Email: tanya@mummybarrow.com
Web site: www.mummybarrow.com
Freq: Daily
Circ: 11609
Profile: Mummy Barrow covers parenting teens, travel, food and lifestyle.
Family & Parenting, Health & Medicine

Mummy Be Beautiful 1072014
Web site: www.mummybebeautiful.com
Freq: Daily
Circ: 7972
Cooking & Baking, Family & Parenting, Health & Medicine, Nutrition, Women's Interests

Mummy Bird 1053420
Web site: http://mummybird.com/
Freq: Daily
Circ: 2887
Family & Parenting

Mummy Constant 1054443
Web site: mummyconstant.com
Freq: Daily
Circ: 8673
Profile: Mummy Constant covers motherhood, family life, recipes and gadget reviews. The blog has an archive dating back to April 2010 and shares a short blogroll
Beauty & Grooming, Cosmetics, Family & Parenting, Hair

Mummy Daddy Me 987443
Web site: mummydaddyandmemakesthree.co.uk
Freq: Daily
Circ: 82413
Do-It-Yourself (DIY), Family & Parenting, Women's Interests

Mummy do that! 1053565
Web site: mummydothat.blogspot.co.uk
Freq: Daily
Circ: 521
Profile: Blog covering motherhood. Mummy do that! blog discusses anything from family and parenting to motherhood. The blog has an archive dating back to April 2009 and shares an extensive blog roll. The outlet offers RSS (Really Simple Syndication).
Family & Parenting, Women's Interests

Mummy Endeavours 1052903
Email: hello@mummyendeavours.co.uk
Web site: mummyendeavours.co.uk
Freq: Daily
Circ: 14432
Profile: Blog covering motherhood. Mummy Endeavours blog discusses anything from family and parenting to motherhood. The blog has an archive dating back to April 2013 and the outlet offers RSS (Really Simple Syndication).
Family & Parenting, Women's Interests

Mummy Fever 988585
Email: info@mummyfever.co.uk
Web site: blog.mummyfever.co.uk
Freq: Daily
Circ: 7399
Family & Parenting

Mummy from the Heart 988689
Email: michelledpannell@gmail.com
Web site: www.mummyfromtheheart.com
Freq: Daily
Circ: 13608
Family & Parenting

Mummy Gorgeous 1057083
Editorial: Flat 1 (basement), 14 Hatherley Grove, Notting Hill, London W2 5RB
Email: hello@mummygorgeous.com
Web site: www.mummygorgeous.com
Freq: Daily
Circ: 9267
Fashion, Travel, Women's Interests

Mummy Matters 986478
Email: mummymatters@gmail.com
Web site: deepinmummymatters.com
Freq: Daily
Circ: 11938
Family & Parenting

Mummy Mishaps 986484
Email: mummymishaps@gmail.com
Web site: www.mummymishaps.blogspot.com
Freq: Daily
Circ: 1632
Profile: Blog covering motherhood, lifestyle and baked goods. The blog has an archive dating back to April 2010.
Family & Parenting

Mummy Mummy Mum! 988727
Web site: www.mummymummymum.com
Freq: Daily
Circ: 9523
Family & Parenting

Mummy Never Sleeps 988332
Email: mummyneversleeps@gmail.com
Web site: http://mummyneversleeps.co.uk/
Freq: Daily
Circ: 10658
Profile: Blog covering motherhood. Mummy Never Sleeps blog discusses anything from motherhood and parenting to lifestyle. The blog has an archive dating back to August 2012. Mummy Never Sleeps was awarded 'Funniest Post' in the SWAN UK Blog Post Awards.The outlet offers RSS (Really Simple Syndication).
Family & Parenting

Mummy to the Max 987493
Web site: mummytothemax.co.uk
Freq: Daily
Circ: 43844
Profile: Blog covering motherhood. Mummy TO THE Max blog discusses anything from motherhood and parenting to lifestyle. The blog has an archive dating back to June 2012. The outlet offers RSS (Really Simple Syndication).
Cooking & Baking, Family & Parenting, Women's Interests

Mummy vs Work 1053296
Web site: http://mummyvswork.co.uk/
Freq: Daily
Circ: 10396
Family & Parenting

Mummy Zen 1053787
Email: mummyzen@gmail.com
Web site: www.mummyzen.blogspot.co.uk
Freq: Daily
Circ: 4122
Profile: Blog covering motherhood. The Mummy Zen blog discusses anything from

motherhood and parenting tips. The blog has an archive dating back to October 2009.
Family & Parenting

Mummy's Little Monkey 986466
Web site: www.mummyslittlemonkey.
blogspot.com
Freq: Daily
Circ: 2377
Family & Parenting

Mummy's Space 1053406
Web site: http://www.mummysspace.com/
Freq: Daily
Circ: 7567
Family & Parenting

mummytravels 986732
Email: hq@mummytravels.com
Web site: http://mummytravels.com/
Freq: Daily
Circ: 41318
Profile: Mummy Travels covers family travel, including reviews, tips and destination guides. The blog has an archive dating back to February 2012. The outlet also offers a vlog.
Airline Inflight, Family & Parenting, Railroad, Travel

Mums' Days - Suspended 988227
Web site: mumsdays.com
Freq: Daily
Circ: 6506
Profile: Blog covering motherhood, family, parenting and childcare.
Family & Parenting

Mums Diary of 5 Wonderful Children 997578
Email: kirsty.21xx@live.co.uk
Web site: http://
mumsdiaryofthreewonderfulchildrenxxx.
blogspot.in/
Freq: Daily
Circ: 521
Family & Parenting

Mums Do Travel 987667
Email: gretta@mumsdotravel.com
Web site: mumsdotravel.com
Freq: Daily
Circ: 27651
Profile: Blog covering family travel.
Family & Parenting, Travel

Mum's Gone To 988292
Email: mumsgoneto@aol.com
Web site: http://www.mumsgoneto.co.uk/
Freq: Daily
Circ: 10675
Family & Parenting, Travel

MUMS THAT SLAY 999638
Editorial: 20 Harrington Road, London SE25 4LU
Email: hello@mumsthatslay
Web site: http://www.mumsthatslay.com/
Freq: Daily
Circ: 12685
Beauty & Grooming, Cosmetics, Family & Parenting, Fashion, Hair, Women's Interests

Mum's the Word 996858
Editorial: 101 Westbury Road, Southend-on-Sea, Southend-on-Sea SS2 4DL
Email: jayne@mumstheword.me
Web site: mumstheword.me
Freq: Daily
Circ: 7766
Family & Parenting

Mumstuff Blog 999623
Editorial: The Maternity Unit, 16A Pury Hill Business Park, Nr. Alderton, Towcester NN12 7LS Tel: 44 08450 090607
Web site: http://mumstuff.com/blog/
Freq: Daily
Circ: 55
Family & Parenting

Mumzy Not 999255
Editorial: Unit 11 Spitfire Business Park, 1 Hawker Road, Croydon CR0 4WD
Web site: http://www.mumzynot.com
Freq: Daily

Circ: 1625
Family & Parenting

Mundo Atleticos 1061199
Web site: http://www.mundoatleticos.com/
Freq: Daily
Circ: 652
Basketball, Bicycles, Billiards, Boating & Yachting, Bodybuilding, Bowling, Boxing, Cricket, Equestrian Sports, Extreme/ Adventure Sports

Mundo Curiosidad 1060757
Web site: http://www.mundocuriosidad.
com/
Freq: Daily
Circ: 761
Lifestyle, Men's Interests, Regional General Interest, Women's Interests

Mundo Farandulero 1061306
Web site: http://www.mundofarandulero.
com/
Freq: Daily
Circ: 521
Celebrities, Classical/Choral/Band Music, Country, Folk, Bluegrass, Dance Music, Jazz & Blues, Movies & Video, Music, Pop Music, R&B, Urban, World, Rap & Hip Hop

Mundo Gourmet 1061328
Web site: http://blogs.lanacion.com.ar/ mundo-gourmet/
Freq: Daily
Circ: 476
Food

Mundo Sonico 1061576
Web site: http://www.mundosonico.com
Freq: Daily
Circ: 1970
Bars, Clubs & Pubs, Comedy, Entertainment, Local Entertainment Guides, Movies & Video, Pop Music

Mundo Takus 1062091
Web site: http://www.mundotakus.com/
Freq: Daily
Circ: 761
Graphic Design

Mundo Videogamers 1060860
Web site: http://www.mundovideogamers.
com/
Freq: Daily
Circ: 855
Computer & Video Games

Mundos 1061622
Web site: http://www.mundos.biz
Freq: Daily
Circ: 767
Bars, Clubs & Pubs, Celebrities, Comedy, Entertainment, Local Entertainment Guides, Movies & Video

MundoTech 1061483
Web site: http://www.mundotech.net/
Freq: Daily
Circ: 79020
Auto Aftermarket, Computers, Data Management, Electronics, Government Technology, Industry, Internet, Mobile Communications, Science, Security & Security Systems

Mungolife 1062096
Email: anna@mungolife.fi
Web site: http://www.rantapallo.fi/ mungolife/
Freq: Daily
Circ: 89376
Airline Inflight, Fashion, Railroad, Travel

Muoti Mielessä 1061321
Email: malia@muotimielessa.com
Web site: http://muotimielessa.blogspot.fi/
Freq: Daily
Circ: 2840
Do-It-Yourself (DIY), Fashion

MuscleHack.com 1052826
Web site: http://www.musclehack.com/ blog/
Freq: Daily
Circ: 187
Fitness & Exercise

Music Industry Blog 1054232
Email: mark@midiaresearch.com
Web site: https://musicindustryblog.
wordpress.com/
Freq: Daily
Circ: 44352
Classical/Choral/Band Music, Country, Folk, Bluegrass, Dance Music, Jazz & Blues, Music, Pop Music, R&B, Urban, World, Rap & Hip Hop, Rock Music

Music Liberation 1053673
Email: musicliberation@hotmail.co.uk
Web site: http://musicliberation.blogspot.co.
uk/
Freq: Daily
Circ: 1484
Classical/Choral/Band Music, Country, Folk, Bluegrass, Dance Music, Jazz & Blues, Music, Pop Music, R&B, Urban, World, Rap & Hip Hop, Rock Music

Music Like Dirt 988326
Email: musiclikedirtblog@gmail.com
Web site: http://www.musiclikedirt.com/
Freq: Daily
Circ: 5051
Classical/Choral/Band Music, Country, Folk, Bluegrass, Dance Music, Jazz & Blues, Music, Pop Music, R&B, Urban, World, Rap & Hip Hop, Rock Music

The Music Manual 997967
Email: laurensmusicmanual@gmail.com
Web site: http://www.themusicmanual.co.
uk/
Freq: Daily
Circ: 10740
Classical/Choral/Band Music, Country, Folk, Bluegrass, Dance Music, Jazz & Blues, Music, Pop Music, R&B, Urban, World, Rap & Hip Hop, Rock Music

Music Matters 1054349
Web site: blogs.kent.ac.uk/music-matters
Freq: Daily
Circ: 165
Classical/Choral/Band Music

Music News Live 1054949
Email: benchallis@aol.com
Web site: http://musicnewslive.blogspot.co.
uk/
Freq: Daily
Circ: 521
Music

Musical Theatre News 986396
Web site: www.blog.musicaltheatrenews.
com
Freq: Daily
Circ: 1025
Profile: Blog covering theatre & performing arts. musical theatre news blog discusses anything from musical theatre and performing art reviews to musical theatre news and interviews. The blog has an archive dating back to October 2009 and shares a short blog roll. The outlet offers RSS (Really Simple Syndication).
News & Current Affairs

Musings from a London Mum 996274
Editorial: 73 Northview Road, London N8 7LN
Email: lm@musingsfromalondonmum.com
Web site: musingsfromalondonmum.
blogspot.co.uk
Freq: Daily
Circ: 1623
Family & Parenting, Fashion

Musings of a Mobile Marketer 1053171
Web site: www.technokitten.blogspot.co.uk
Freq: Daily
Circ: 9732
Mobile Electronics

Musings of another writer 1052637
Email: brosser24@googlemail.com
Web site: http://rebeccafinlaysonbooks.
blogspot.co.uk/
Freq: Daily

Circ: 483
Entertainment, Literature

Muslim Hands blog 996055
Editorial: 148 Gregory Boulevard, Nottingham NG7 5JE Tel: 44 01159 117222
Email: mail@muslimhands.org.uk
Web site: https://muslimhands.org.uk/latest
Freq: Daily
Charitable Foundations

must do better 1053685
Web site: http://joeybagstock.wordpress.
com
Freq: Daily
Circ: 8933
Education

Muy Geek 1061324
Web site: http://www.muygeek.com
Freq: Daily
Circ: 1335
Internet, Software

My Car Heaven 987857
Email: info@mycarheaven.com
Web site: www.mycarheaven.com/
Freq: Daily
Circ: 29010
Profile: Blog covering cars. My car heaven blog discusses anything from classic cars and supercars to hypercars.
Antique & Collectible Cars, Automotive, Driving

My City My London 1054140
Email: mycitymylondon@gmail.com
Web site: http://www.mycitymylondon.me/
Freq: Daily
Circ: 7555
Profile: Blog covering lifestyle. My City My London blog discusses anything from London and travel to fashion and food. The blog has an archive dating back to December 2013.
Cooking & Baking, Cosmetics, Family & Parenting, Fashion, Health & Medicine, Regional General Interest, Restaurant Reviews, Travel, Women's Interests

My Crafty Outlook - the jottings of craftyhazelnut 1057621
Web site: http://craftyhazelnut.blogspot.co.
uk/
Freq: Daily
Circ: 488
Crafts

My fairytale 1060230
Email: mammasiri@live.se
Web site: http://nouw.com/myfairytale
Freq: Daily
Circ: 9056
Family & Parenting, Lifestyle, Men's Interests, Obstetrics & Gynecology (OB/ GYN), Preschool, Regional General Interest, Women's Interests

My fairytale 1060438
Email: mammasiri@live.se
Web site: http://nouw.com/myfairytale
Freq: Daily
Circ: 9056
Family & Parenting, Lifestyle, Men's Interests, Obstetrics & Gynecology (OB/ GYN), Preschool, Regional General Interest, Women's Interests

My Fash Diary 999203
Web site: myfashdiary.com
Freq: Daily
Circ: 23911
Editor: Tala Samman
Cooking & Baking, Fashion, Women's Interests

My Friend's House 987551
Editorial: Rear of 53-55 North Cross Road, Dulwich, London SE22 9ET
Email: theantistylist@hotmail.com
Web site: myfriendshouse.co.uk
Freq: Daily
Circ: 9483
Do-It-Yourself (DIY), Shopping

My Funny Eye 1054442
Web site: http://myfunnyeye.blogspot.co.uk/

UK Blogs

Freq: Daily
Circ: 578
Photography

My Hidden Gems
1053449
Web site: http://www.myhiddengems.co.uk/
Freq: Daily
Circ: 3589
Travel

My Kinda Future
1053002
Tel: 44 02076 204463
Email: team@mykindafuture.com
Web site: http://www.mykindafuture.com/
blog/
Freq: Daily
Circ: 339
Education, Higher Education, Students

My Little Black Book
997912
Email: editorial@mylittleblackbook.co.uk
Web site: www.mylittleblackbook.co.uk
Freq: Daily
Circ: 11059
Careers, Women's Interests

My Little Italian Kitchen
998355
Email: info@mylittleitaliankitchen.com
Web site: http://www.mylittleitaliankitchen.com
Freq: Daily
Circ: 11709
Cooking & Baking

My Mills Baby
1053801
Web site: mymillsbaby.co.uk
Freq: Daily
Circ: 6240
Profile: Blog covering motherhood. My Mills Baby discusses anything from pregnancy and parenting to babies and product reviews. The blog has an archive dating back to September 2011.
Family & Parenting

My Moggies and Me
1105204
Email: info@mymoggies.co.uk
Web site: www.mymoggiesandme.co.uk
Freq: Daily
Circ: 48178
Nature & Wildlife

My Mummy's Pennies
1052745
Web site: www.mymummyspennies.com
Freq: Daily
Circ: 6156
Profile: Blog covering motherhood and money saving. My Mother's Pennies discusses anything from children's activities and reviews to money saving ideas and cheap family recipe ideas. The outlet offers RSS (Really Simple Syndication).
Family & Parenting, Personal Finance

My Mummy's World
995097
Email: mymummysworld@gmail.com
Web site: mymummysworld.co.uk
Freq: Daily
Circ: 52278
Family & Parenting

My Nintendo News
1102016
Web site: https://mynintendonews.com
Freq: Daily
Circ: 445137
Editor: Mark Tobin
Computer & Video Games

My Nokia Blog
986204
Web site: mynokiablog.com
Circ: 52123
Editor: Jay Montano
Mobile Electronics

My Old Man Said
988626
Email: contact@myoldmansaid.com
Web site: http://www.myoldmansaid.com/
Freq: Daily
Circ: 48117
Editor: David Michael
Soccer

My Pretty Mummy
1053872
Web site: http://www.myprettymummy.com/
Freq: Daily
Circ: 6429

Profile: Blog covering motherhood. My Pretty Mummy blog discusses anything from motherhood and family days out to parenting tips. The blog has an archive dating back to October 2011.
Family & Parenting, Fashion, Regional General Interest, Women's Interests

My Random Family Blurb
1056566
Email: myrandomblurb@aim.com
Web site: www.myrandomblurb.co.uk
Freq: Daily
Circ: 11075
Family & Parenting

My Skool
996736
Editorial: 37 Southgate Street, Winchester SO23 9EH **Tel:** 44 01962 713342
Email: team@snowskool.com
Web site: http://www.snowskool.com/blog
Freq: Daily
Circ: 12
Travel, Winter Sports

My Three and Me
1063718
Email: mythreeandme@hotmail.co.uk
Web site: mythreeandme.co.uk
Freq: Daily
Circ: 13707
Cooking & Baking, Do-It-Yourself (DIY), Family & Parenting, Nature & Wildlife, Restaurant Reviews, Women's Interests

My Two Mums
988288
Email: mytwomums@yahoo.co.uk
Web site: mytwomums.com
Circ: 12455
Profile: Blog covering parenting. My Two Mums is about 'two women in love blogging their adventures as parents'.
Family & Parenting

My Zero Waste
997556
Web site: myzerowaste.com/category/blog/
Freq: Daily
Circ: 7
Energy & Environment

MyCarNeedsA.com Blog
1095585
Tel: 44 02838 338091
Email: support@mycarneedsa.com
Web site: https://mycarneedsa.com/blog
Freq: Daily
Circ: 117
Automotive, Driving

mydaughterwontsleep
996925
Web site: mydaughterwontsleep.com
Freq: Daily
Circ: 5970
Family & Parenting

MyFashionConnect
999475
Editorial: 61 North Acre, Banstead, London SM7 2EG **Tel:** 44 01737 350659
Email: myfashionconnectglobal@blogspot.co.uk
Web site: myfashionconnectglobal.blogspot.com
Freq: Daily
Circ: 521
Fashion

MyFashionLife
986205
Web site: www.myfashionlife.com
Freq: Daily
Circ: 25239
Beauty & Grooming, Cosmetics, Fashion, Hair

MyTights Blog
998153
Tel: 44 02078 190530
Email: enquiries@mytights.com
Web site: https://www.uktights.com
Freq: Daily
Circ: 140164
Fashion

Nacion Apache
1061635
Email: nacionapache@gmail.com
Web site: http://www.nacionapache.com.ar
Freq: Daily
Circ: 2834
Lifestyle, Men's Interests, Regional General Interest, Women's Interests

Nadia PR
1074787
Editorial: 285a Kings Road, London SW3 5EW
Web site: http://www.nadia-pr.com/#!nadiapr/yt54v
Freq: Daily
Circ: 521
Art, Cooking & Baking, Fashion, Literature, Travel, Women's Interests

Nadinoo
1054652
Email: info@nadinoo.com
Web site: http://nadinoo.blogspot.co.uk/
Freq: Daily
Circ: 1652
Crafts, Fashion

Nail Your Novel
1052616
Email: rozmorriswriter@gmail.com
Web site: https://nailyournovel.wordpress.com/
Freq: Daily
Circ: 4965
Literature

The Nailasaurus
987059
Email: sammy@thenailasaurus.com
Web site: http://www.thenailasaurus.com/
Freq: Daily
Circ: 21309
Profile: Blog covering nail polish. THE NAILASAURUS blog discusses anything from nail varnish and nail care to nail art and designs. The blog has an archive dating back to April 2010.
Cosmetics

Naked PR Girl
997692
Email: nakedprgirl@gmail.com
Web site: http://nakedprgirl.com/category/blog/
Freq: Daily
Circ: 6592
Celebrities, Fashion, Marketing

Naked Security
986989
Editorial: Sophos Inc., The Pentagon, Abingdon Science Park, Abingdon OX14 3YP
Email: tips@sophos.com
Web site: http://nakedsecurity.sophos.com/
Freq: Daily
Circ: 3720367
Computers, Security & Security Systems

The Naked Trader
1054483
Web site: http://nakedtrader.co.uk/
Freq: Daily
Circ: 1155
Family & Parenting, Men's Interests, Personal Finance

nam aidsmap news
986513
Editorial: Acorn House, 314-320 Gray's Inn Road, London WC1X 8DP
Tel: 44 02078 376988
Email: info@nam.org.uk
Web site: http://www.aidsmap.com/latest-news
Freq: Daily
Circ: 115
News & Current Affairs

Namaste From Ananya
997252
Web site: http://www.namastefromananya.com/
Freq: Daily
Circ: 8075
Lifestyle, Men's Interests, Regional General Interest, Women's Interests

Nancy H Gibbs Photography
988271
Editorial: 36A Warrington Crescent, London W9 1EL
Web site: http://www.nancyhgibbsphotography.co.uk/
Freq: Daily
Circ: 6637
Profile: Blog covering lifestyle. It's a Lifestyle Thing blog discusses anything from lifestyle and fashion to travel and food.
Bars, Clubs & Pubs, Fashion, Restaurant Reviews, Travel

The Naomi Narrative
1098962
Web site: https://thenaominarrative.com/

Freq: Daily
Circ: 8915
Relationships

Narratively Speaking - CEASED 2014
987308
Web site: www.narrativelyspeaking.com
Freq: Daily
Circ: 5926
Literature

Natalie Glaze
1100174
Email: natalie@natalieglaze.com
Web site: http://www.natalieglaze.com/
Freq: Daily
Circ: 9349
Fashion, Fitness & Exercise, Organic Food, Vegetarianism & Veganism, Women's Interests

Natalie Vilen
1061528
Email: natalie.vilen@gmail.com
Web site: https://mycosmo.fi/news/author/natalievilen
Freq: Daily
Circ: 7519
Beauty & Grooming, Cosmetics, Fashion, Hair

Natascha Cox Blog
1056576
Email: connect@nataschacox.com
Web site: http://www.nataschacox.com/
Freq: Daily
Circ: 13693
Beauty & Grooming, Cosmetics, Fashion, Hair, Travel

Natinstablog
1052971
Email: info@natinstablog.com
Web site: natinstablog.com
Freq: Daily
Circ: 10165
Fashion

National Collective - CEASED 2015
998368
Web site: http://nationalcollective.com/
Freq: Daily
Circ: 13304
Politics

National Literacy Trust blog
997626
Editorial: 68 South Lambeth Road, London SW8 1RL
Freq: Daily
Circ: 65
Education

National Museums Liverpool Blog
996611
Editorial: 127 Dale Street, Liverpool L2 2JH
Tel: 44 01514 784355
Web site: blog.liverpoolmuseums.org.uk
Freq: Daily
Circ: 12707
Art

National Trust Blogs
999573
Editorial: Heelis, Kemble Drive, Swindon SN2 2NA **Tel:** 44 01793 817400
Email: press.office@nationaltrust.org.uk
Web site: nationaltrust.org.uk
Freq: Daily
Circ: 514234
Animal Farming, Camping and RV Travel, Charitable Foundations, Energy & Environment, Environment, Field Sports, Genealogy, History, Nature & Wildlife, Outdoor Recreation

Nativo Digital
1060407
Web site: http://www.nativodigital.cl
Freq: Daily
Circ: 960
Internet, Marketing

Natrural Belle
1054108
Web site: http://hairspiration.blogspot.co.uk/
Freq: Daily
Circ: 1774
Beauty & Grooming, Cosmetics, Hair

Natter Football 1052876
Email: natterfootball@gmail.com
Web site: http://natterfootball.co.uk/
Freq: Daily
Circ: 9985
Soccer

Natural Capital Partners 997539
Editorial: Natural Capital Partners, 167 Fleet Street, London EC4A 2EA
Tel: 44 02078 336000
Email: marketing@naturalcapitalpartners.com
Web site: http://www.naturalcapitalpartners.com/news-media/blog
Freq: Daily
Circ: 303
Alternative/Renewable Energy, Environment

Natural Kitchen Adventures
988558
Editorial: Flat 2, 67 Lewisham Way, London SE14 6QD
Web site: naturalkitchenadventures.com
Freq: Daily
Circ: 12651
Profile: Blog covering healthy & nutritious food, cooking, whole foods and gluten free recipes.
Cooking & Baking

Natural Nursery Blog 986674
Editorial: The Natural Nursery, Unit 2, Mayfair House, Wardrew Road, Exeter EX4 1HA Tel: 44 01392 207243
Email: info@naturalnursery.co.uk
Web site: http://www.naturalnurseryblog.co.uk
Freq: Daily
Circ: 1631
Family & Parenting, Fashion, Sales & Marketing, Shopping

The Natural Wedding Company Blog 998226
Web site: thenaturalweddingcompany.co.uk/blog/
Freq: Daily
Circ: 11276
Weddings

Naturally Cycling: Manchester
1054469
Web site: http://naturallycyclingmanchester.wordpress.com/
Freq: Daily
Circ: 48
Bicycles

Naturally Diddy 1053147
Email: diddydarling@hotmail.co.uk
Web site: http://www.naturallydiddy.com/
Freq: Daily
Circ: 1306
Profile: Blog covering beauty. Naturally Diddy blog discusses anything from beauty and cosmetics to hair and skin care. The blog has an archive dating back to April 2012.
Beauty & Grooming, Cosmetics, Hair, Nutrition, Organic Food

Naturally Good Food Blog
1056313
Email: orders@naturallygoodfood.co.uk
Web site: http://blog.naturallygoodfood.co.uk/
Freq: Daily
Circ: 5
Cooking & Baking, Organic Food, Vegetarianism & Veganism

Nature Travels 986206
Editorial: Nature Travels Ltd, 2 Leanne Business Centre, Sandford Lane, Wareham BH20 4DY Tel: 44 01929 503080
Email: admin@naturetravels.co.uk
Web site: naturetravels.wordpress.com
Freq: Daily
Circ: 27
Airline Inflight, Railroad, Travel

Naukulan Kerho 1061786
Email: naukulankerho@gmail.com
Web site: http://naukulanperhe.blogspot.fi/
Freq: Daily

Circ: 1674
Nature & Wildlife

Nayu's Reading Corner 1053665
Email: nayu@hotmail.co.uk
Web site: http://nayusreadingcorner.blogspot.co.uk/
Freq: Daily
Circ: 8551
Crafts, Literature

NCVO blog 988569
Editorial: Society Building, 8 All Saints Street, London N1 9RL
Tel: 44 02077 136161
Email: ncvo@ncvo.org.uk
Web site: http://blogs.ncvo.org.uk/
Freq: Daily
Circ: 39648
Profile: Blog covering the voluntary sector, charities, campaigning, welfare, social issues, government and policy.
Charitable Foundations

Nea Polis 1061290
Web site: http://www.neapolisblog.blogspot.com/
Freq: Daily
Circ: 548
National News, Politics, Urban Planning & Development

Nefarious Lifestyle 1052564
Email: nefariouslifestyle@gmail.com
Web site: nefariouslifestyle.co.uk
Freq: Daily
Circ: 4866
Profile: Blog covering lifestyle, digital technology and men's fashion. The blog has an archive dating back to May 2014.
Men's Interests

Neil Harding blog 1054191
Web site: http://neilharding.blogspot.co.uk
Freq: Daily
Circ: 1724
Politics

Neon London 995840
Editorial: First Floor, 78 Cathcart Road, London SW10 9DJ
Email: hello@neonlondon.uk
Web site: http://www.neonlondon.uk
Freq: Daily
Circ: 1547
Antiques/Collectibles, Art, Arts, Classical/Choral/Band Music, Country, Folk, Bluegrass, Dance Music, Jazz & Blues, Lifestyle, Literature, Men's Interests

Neovia House 1061418
Email: neoviahouse@gmail.com
Web site: http://neovias.blogspot.fi/
Freq: Daily
Circ: 1437
Architecture & Design, Do-It-Yourself (DIY), Gardening, Home, Interior Design, Internet, Property Management & Maintenance, Real Estate

Nerdgeist 1101624
Web site: https://nerdgeist.com
Freq: Daily
Circ: 10494
Editor: Jenny .
Computer & Video Games, Entertainment, Movies & Video

nerdly 986089
Email: nerdly.co.uk@gmail.com
Web site: nerdly.co.uk
Freq: Daily
Circ: 16699
Bars, Clubs & Pubs, Comedy, Entertainment, Local Entertainment Guides, Movies & Video

Nesta Crowdfunding Blog
997003
Editorial: 1 Plough Place, London EC4A 1DE
Tel: 44 02074 382500
Email: information@nesta.org.uk
Web site: www.nesta.org.uk/project/crowdfunding
Freq: Daily

Circ: 22
Business, Corporate Responsibility, Equities, Small and Medium Business

Netafull 1061295
Freq: Daily
Industry

Netmums Blog 986685
Editorial: Henry Wood House, 2 Riding House Street, London W1W 7FA
Tel: 44 02074 878253
Email: pressrelease@netmums.com
Web site: netmumsblog.com
Freq: Daily
Circ: 1859
Audio Video Trade, Beauty & Grooming, Cameras, Careers, Consumer Affairs, Consumer Electronics, Cosmetics, Do-It-Yourself (DIY), Family & Parenting, Hair

Never Ending Footsteps 996307
Email: lauren@neverendingfootsteps.com
Web site: http://www.neverendingfootsteps.com/blog/
Freq: Daily
Circ: 66
Travel

Neville Hobson 986208
Tel: 44 02075 588222
Email: hello@nevillehobson.com
Web site: www.nevillehobson.com
Freq: Daily
Circ: 28549
Advertising Industry, Branding, Broadcasting, Graphic Design, Marketing, Media & Communications, Photography, Publishing

The New Craft House 996716
Email: hello@thenewcrafthouse.com
Web site: http://thenewcrafthouse.com/blog/
Freq: Daily
Circ: 11
Crafts

New Economics Foundation Blog 1053378
Tel: 44 02078 206357
Email: press@neweconomics.org
Web site: www.neweconomics.org/blog
Freq: Daily
Circ: 49
Banking, Environment, Government

New Generation - Ski School Blog 996788
Editorial: 1st Floor, Roxburghe House, 273 - 287 Regent Street, London W1B 2HA
Tel: 44 08447 704733
Email: info@skinewgen.com
Web site: http://www.skinewgen.com/blog/
Freq: Daily
Circ: 13
Travel, Winter Sports

New Girl in Toon 998051
Email: newglrlintoon@gmail.com
Web site: http://www.newgirlintoon.co.uk/
Freq: Daily
Circ: 9582
Regional General Interest

New Mum Online 988364
Editorial: 22 Meadow Grove, Bristol BS11 9PH
Web site: www.newmumonline.co.uk
Freq: Daily
Circ: 9886
Family & Parenting

New Political Communication Unit blog 1054643
Web site: http://www.newpolcom.rhul.ac.uk/npcu-blog
Freq: Daily
Consumer Affairs, International News, National News, Politics, Social Issues

New To The Post 1054420
Email: trythis_es@mail.com
Web site: https://newtothepost.wordpress.com/
Freq: Daily

Circ: 3925
Careers, Education

NEW YORK INSPIRATION
1060194
Web site: http://www.newyorkinspiration.com/
Freq: Daily
Circ: 6208
Airline Inflight, Hotels/Motels, International News, Railroad, Shopping, Travel

NEW YORK INSPIRATION
1060619
Web site: http://www.newyorkinspiration.com/
Freq: Daily
Circ: 6208
Airline Inflight, Hotels/Motels, International News, Railroad, Shopping, Travel

News at Den 1059415
Email: admin@newsatden.co.uk
Web site: newsatden.co.uk
Freq: Daily
Circ: 74583
Editor: John Kelly
Soccer

News from the CJS Office
997013
Editorial: The Moorlands, Goathland, Whitby, Whitby YO22 5LZ
Tel: 44 01947 896007
Email: ranger@countryside-jobs.com
Web site: http://news.countryside-jobs.com
Freq: Daily
Circ: 20
Careers, Environment

The News Hub 997777
Editorial: Hikenield House, East Anton Court, Andover SP10 5RG
Email: info@the-newshub.com
Web site: https://www.the-newshub.com
Freq: Daily
Circ: 119486
International News, Politics

Newsnet.scot 997709
Web site: http://newsnet.scot
Freq: Daily
Politics

Newspaper Club 1053056
Email: newspaperclub@newspaperclub.com
Web site: http://blog.newspaperclub.com/
Freq: Daily
Circ: 14347
Crafts, Publishing

Next Green Car News 1075483
Editorial: Unit 62, Spike Island, 133 Cumberland Road, Bristol BS1 6UX
Tel: 44 01179 298855
Email: editorial@nextgreencar.com
Web site: http://www.nextgreencar.com/news/
Freq: Daily
Circ: 25
Automotive, Environment

NextGen Gaming blog 988461
Email: ben.ward@kitanamedia.com
Web site: http://nextgengamingblog.com/
Freq: Daily
Circ: 25921
Computer & Video Games

NGCards 1056761
Email: craftingallday1@yahoo.co.uk
Web site: http://ngcards.blogspot.co.uk/
Freq: Daily
Circ: 4221
Crafts

Ni Una Dieta Mas 1060929
Web site: http://blogs.eluniversal.com.mx/nidieta
Freq: Daily
Circ: 4474
Health & Medicine, Nutrition

UK Blogs

Niamh Serena 1094855
Web site: http://niamhserena.co.uk/
Freq: Daily
Circ: 11213
Beauty & Grooming, Cosmetics, Fashion, Fitness & Exercise, Hair, Health & Medicine, Nutrition, Women's Interests

Nicholas Gill Bluurb 1052843
Web site: bluurb.wordpress.com
Freq: Daily
Circ: 77
News & Current Affairs

Nick Cohen: Writing from London 1053965
Email: nick@nickcohen.net
Web site: http://nickcohen.net/
Freq: Daily
Circ: 17122
Politics, Social Issues

Nick Jordan Blog 1052648
Web site: http://www.nickjordan.co.uk/
Freq: Daily
Circ: 3095
Entertainment, Family & Parenting, Literature, Movies & Video, Music, Photography, Rock Music

Nick Pickles blog 1052770
Web site: http://www.music-photographer.co.uk/blog/
Freq: Daily
Circ: 4196
Classical/Choral/Band Music, Country, Folk, Bluegrass, Dance Music, Jazz & Blues, Music, Photography, Pop Music, R&B, Urban, World, Rap & Hip Hop, Rock Music

Nick Robinson's Newslog
986210
Editorial: BBC Westminster, 4 Millbank, London SW1P 3JQ
Web site: bbc.co.uk/news/correspondents/nickrobinson
Freq: Daily
Circ: 1246
Politics

Nick Tyrone blog 998231
Web site: http://nicktyrone.com/
Freq: Daily
Circ: 14578
Politics

Nicole Photography Blog
1052788
Email: sayhi@nicolephotography.co.uk
Web site: www.nicolephotography.co.uk/blog
Freq: Daily
Circ: 143
Photography

Niel's Doll Room 1061868
Web site: http://1-6thsensedolls.blogspot.com
Freq: Daily
Circ: 1120
Crafts, Hobbies, & Collecting

Nigel Clare blog 1054052
Web site: http://blog.nigelclare.com
Freq: Daily
Circ: 10
Profile: Blog covering lifestyle. the NIGEL CLARE blog discusses menswear and men's interest to arts, culture, design, tech and music.
Fashion, Men's Interests

Night Hawk 1054255
Web site: http://www.rogerdarlington.co.uk/nighthawk/
Freq: Daily
Consumer Affairs, Literature, Movies & Video, Politics

Nil Satis Nisi Optimum 997301
Tel: 44 07557 106108
Email: contact@nsno.co.uk
Web site: http://www.nsno.co.uk/
Freq: Daily

Circ: 71225
Soccer

Nimbus Ninety Blog 1100498
Editorial: 17 Grosvenor Gardens, London SW1W 0BD Tel: 44 02035 982237
Email: info@nimbusninety.com
Web site: http://blog.nimbusninety.com/blog
Freq: Daily
Circ: 7425
Editor: Victoria Arrington
Auto Aftermarket, Business, Computers, Data Management, Electronics, Government Technology, Industry, Internet, Mobile Communications, Security & Security Systems

Nina Ross Beauty 1102569
Email: ninarossjournal@gmail.com
Web site: https://ninarossbeauty.wordpress.com/
Freq: Daily
Circ: 61
Beauty & Grooming, Cosmetics, Hair

Nineonesix 1054151
Email: info@nineonesix.co.uk
Web site: https://nineonesix.wordpress.com/
Freq: Daily
Circ: 17
Outdoor Recreation, Travel

Niomi Smart 1053530
Editorial: 96 Leonard Street, London EC2A 4RH
Email: niomi@gleamfutures.com
Web site: http://www.niomismart.com/
Freq: Daily
Circ: 42665
Profile: Blog covering beauty, lifestyle, fashion, hotel reviews, cosmetics and restaurant reviews. The blog has an archive dating back to August 2013. This outlet offers a vlog.
Beauty & Grooming, Cooking & Baking, Cosmetics, Fashion, Hair, Regional General Interest, Restaurant Reviews, Travel, Women's Interests

Niomi Smart Vlog 1076166
Editorial: 60 Charlotte Street, London W1T 2NU
Email: niomi@gleamfutures.com
Web site: https://www.youtube.com/user/niomismart
Freq: Daily
Circ: 21
Cooking & Baking, Cosmetics, Fashion, Organic Food

Nisha Kotecha Blog 988207
Web site: nishakotecha.wordpress.com
Freq: Daily
Circ: 6498
Business, Charitable Foundations, Small and Medium Business

Nishaantishu 1053276
Web site: http://www.nishaantishu.com/
Freq: Daily
Circ: 2587
Profile: Blog covering lifestyle. The nishaantishu blog discusses anything from lifestyle and photography. The blog has an archive dating back to March 2012.
Photography, Regional General Interest, Travel, Women's Interests

Niu Dao's Blog 1061303
Email: niudao3344520@sina.com
Web site: http://blog.sina.com.cn/chenqian
Freq: Daily
Circ: 56390
Banking, Financial Markets

NLA Media Access Blog 1052607
Editorial: Wellington Gate, Church Road, Tunbridge Wells TN1 1NL
Tel: 44 01892 525273
Email: copy@nla.co.uk
Web site: http://blog.nla.co.uk/
Freq: Daily
Circ: 39
Publishing

No geek is an island 1053920
Web site: http://www.willhowells.org.uk/blog/
Freq: Daily
Movies & Video, Politics

No Love Sincerer... 1054252
Email: covfoodie@gmail.com
Web site: http://nolovesincerer.blogspot.co.uk/
Freq: Daily
Circ: 668
Cooking & Baking, Restaurant Reviews

No Rock and Roll Fun 988330
Email: simonb@gmail.com
Web site: http://xrrf.blogspot.co.uk/
Freq: Daily
Circ: 737
Classical/Choral/Band Music, Country, Folk, Bluegrass, Dance Music, Jazz & Blues, Music, Pop Music, R&B, Urban, World, Rap & Hip Hop, Rock Music

The No Sleep Gamer 1052599
Email: bggriffiths7@gmail.com
Web site: http://nosleepgamer.com/
Freq: Daily
Circ: 521
Computer & Video Games

No Volume blog 1052912
Email: hello@novolume.co.uk
Web site: http://www.novolume.co.uk/blog/
Freq: Daily
Circ: 15
Internet

Nodo9 1061284
Web site: http://www.nodo9.com
Freq: Daily
Circ: 14412
Auto Aftermarket, Computers, Data Management, Electronics, Government Technology, Industry, Internet, Mobile Communications, Security & Security Systems, Software

Nomadic Matt's Travel Blog
997570
Email: nomadicmatt@nomadicmatt.com
Web site: http://www.nomadicmatt.com/travel-blog/
Freq: Daily
Circ: 25195
Airline Inflight, Railroad, Travel

Nonstop blog 1054065
Email: info@nonstopsnow.com
Web site: http://www.nonstopsnow.com/blog
Freq: Daily
Circ: 15
Winter Sports

Nonstop Ski & Snowboard
987711
Editorial: Nonstop Office 3 & 5, 5 Argyle Street, Bath BA2 4BA Tel: 44 01225 632165
Email: info@nonstopsnow.com
Web site: nonstopsnow.com
Freq: Daily
Circ: 9218
Travel, Winter Sports

The Nordic Fit 1061462
Email: contact@thenordicfit.com
Web site: http://thenordicfit.com/
Freq: Daily
Circ: 2508
News & Current Affairs

Nordnettbloggen 1060346
Web site: http://nordnetbloggen.no/
Freq: Daily
Circ: 45585
Banking, Economics

North East Lifestyle 1052703
Web site: http://northeastlifestyle.co.uk/
Freq: Daily
Circ: 10709
Profile: Blog covering lifestyle. North East Lifestyle blog discusses anything from lifestyle and travel to fashion and beauty.

The blog has an archive dating back to November 2010.
Beauty & Grooming, Cosmetics, Fashion, Hair, Regional General Interest, Restaurant Reviews, Travel, Women's Interests

Northern Lights PR 1053386
Email: mail@northernlightspr.com
Web site: northernlightspr.com/blog
Freq: Daily
Circ: 269
Marketing

Northern Mountain Sport
1053142
Tel: 44 33067 1641409
Web site: http://www.northernmountainsport.co.uk
Freq: Daily
Circ: 2957
Travel, Winter Sports

Northern Mum 988711
Editorial: 116 Rochester Row, London SW1P 1JQ
Email: northernmum@gmail.com
Web site: www.northernmum.com
Freq: Daily
Circ: 12604
Family & Parenting

Northumberland Mam 1054238
Email: northumberlandmam@gmail.com
Web site: northumberlandmam.blogspot.co.uk
Freq: Daily
Circ: 31179
Family & Parenting

Norton's Notes 986689
Editorial: 1 Shelley Court, Harrogate HG1 3JL Tel: 44 01133 204583
Web site: chrisnorton.biz
Freq: Daily
Circ: 11646
Marketing

The Norwegian Wedding Blog
1060351
Email: norwegianweddingblog@gmail.com
Web site: http://norwegianweddingblog.blogspot.co.uk/
Freq: Daily
Circ: 493
Weddings

Not a Chimp 1054088
Email: jeremytaylor@blueyonder.co.uk
Web site: http://notachimp.blogspot.co.uk/
Freq: Daily
Circ: 548
Science

Not Another Mummy Blog* 987409
Web site: notanothermummyblog.com
Freq: Daily
Circ: 26392
Family & Parenting, Fashion, Travel, Women's Interests

Not Dressed As Lamb 1098952
Web site: www.notdressedaslamb.com
Freq: Daily
Circ: 47991
Profile: Blog covering fashion. Not Dressed As Lamb blog discusses anything from fashion and outfits to style and photography. The blog has an archive dating back to February 2014 and shares an extensive blog roll.
Fashion, Women's Interests

Not Even a Bag of Sugar 1054586
Email: notevenabagofsugar@gmail.com
Web site: http://notevena.blogspot.co.uk/
Freq: Daily
Circ: 6835
Family & Parenting

Not Just A Pretty Plate 988208
Email: notjustaprettyplate@gmail.com
Web site: notjustaprettyplate.co.uk
Freq: Daily
Circ: 521

Profile: Blog covering food. The Not Just A Pretty Plate blog discusses anything from recipes and baking to ingredients and eating out. The blog has an archive dating back to March 2013 and shares a short blog roll.

Cooking & Baking

Not My Year Off
1053772
Email: notmyyearoff@hotmail.co.uk
Web site: notmyyearoff.com
Freq: Daily
Circ: 24733

Family & Parenting

Not Such a Yummy Mummy
1053588
Email: notsuchayummymummy@yahoo.co.uk
Web site: notsuchayummymummy.wordpress.com
Freq: Daily
Circ: 100
Profile: Blog covering motherhood. Not such a yummy mummy blog discusses anything from motherhood and parenting to food and lifestyle. The blog has an archive dating back to March 2012 and shares a short blog roll. The outlet offers RSS (Really Simple Syndication).

News & Current Affairs

Not Supermum
1054279
Web site: http://www.notsupermum.com/p/about-me.html
Freq: Daily
Circ: 4

News & Current Affairs

Not Television
988329
Web site: http://www.nottelevision.net/
Freq: Daily
Circ: 10872

Theater & Performing Arts

Not Your Normal Health Blog
987796
Editorial: 31 Bells Chase, Great Baddow, Chelmsford CM2 8DS
Email: healthehelen@gmail.com
Web site: http://notyournormalhealthblog.com
Freq: Daily
Circ: 9790

Fitness & Exercise, Nutrition

Notas
1060771
Web site: http://notasdecira.blogspot.com/
Freq: Daily
Circ: 1277

Airline Inflight, Cooking & Baking, Railroad, Travel, Wine/Winemaking

Notes to Self by Cheshire Mum
1098993
Tel: 44 01625 444864
Web site: http://www.cheshiremum.co.uk/
Freq: Daily
Circ: 7763

Cooking & Baking, Do-It-Yourself (DIY), Family & Parenting, Movies & Video, Racquet Sports, Restaurant Reviews, Women's Interests

Notilogia
1060818
Web site: http://notilogia.com/
Freq: Daily
Circ: 631825

Auto Aftermarket, Computers, Data Management, Electronics, Government Technology, Industry, Internet, Mobile Communications, National News, Security & Security Systems

NotiMeridaMx
1061090
Web site: http://notimeridamx.com
Freq: Daily
Circ: 521

National News

Nouveau Blog
996475
Editorial: NBG, Nouveau House, Barnsley Road, South Elmsall, South Kirkby WF9 2HR
Tel: 44 08456 443994
Web site: http://blog.nouveaubeautygroup.com/#sthash.ZKxpKwBh.dpbs
Freq: Daily

Circ: 17

Beauty & Grooming, Cosmetics, Hair

Novedades Geek
1060374
Web site: http://www.novedadesgeek.com
Freq: Daily
Circ: 2160

Auto Aftermarket, Computers, Data Management, Electronics, Government Technology, Industry, Internet, Mobile Communications, National News, Security & Security Systems

Novel Kicks
996732
Editorial: 43 Jack Close, Chandlers Ford, Eastleigh SO53 4NU
Email: novel@novelkicks.co.uk
Web site: www.novelkicks.co.uk
Freq: Daily
Circ: 11375
Editor: Laura Parish

Literature

Novias
1062025
Web site: http://www.webdelanovia.com
Freq: Daily
Circ: 8920

Weddings

The Novice Gardener - CEASED January 2016
1054281
Web site: https://thenovicegardener.wordpress.com/
Freq: Daily
Circ: 14396
Profile: Blog covering gardening. The Novice Gardener blog discusses anything from gardening and cooking to photography. The blog has an archive dating back to March 2013.

Cooking & Baking, Gardening, Organic Food

Now We Are 40
1054190
Email: hello@nowweare40.com
Web site: nowweare40.com
Freq: Daily
Circ: 1070

Beauty & Grooming, Cosmetics, Fashion, Fitness & Exercise, Hair, Women's Interests

NSDesign Blog
1054344
Tel: 44 01415 856390
Email: info@nsdesign.net
Web site: https://www.nsdesign.co.uk/our-blog/
Freq: Daily
Circ: 398

Branding, Marketing

Nubricks Blog - Overseas Property Blog
999274
Editorial: 24 Jacks Place, Shoreditch, London E1 6NN
Email: info@nubricks.com
Web site: www.nubricks.com/blog
Freq: Daily
Circ: 7

Real Estate

Nude on Broad Street
1053019
Email: olivia.hands@hotmail.co.uk
Freq: Daily

Fashion

Nuestras Ciudades
1061512
Web site: http://www.nuestras-ciudades.blogspot.com
Freq: Daily
Circ: 9441

Alternative/Renewable Energy, Architecture & Design, Building & Construction, Carbon Emissions & Trading, Defense & National Security, Electricity, Energy, Engineering, Industry, Manufacturing

Nuestro Pais y Mas
1060787
Web site: http://nuestropaisymas.blogspot.com/
Freq: Daily
Circ: 752

Airline Inflight, Railroad, Travel

Nuestros Bebes
1061059
Web site: http://www.travesurasdebebes.blogspot.com
Freq: Daily
Circ: 1623

Family & Parenting, Lifestyle, Men's Interests, Obstetrics & Gynecology (OB/GYN), Regional General Interest, Women's Interests

Nuevo Blog de Marchetti
1061463
Web site: http://www.elnuevoblogdemarchetti.tk/
Freq: Daily
Circ: 521

Lifestyle, Men's Interests, National News, Regional General Interest, Women's Interests

Nurse Fancy Pants
1054158
Email: nursefancypants@gmail.com
Web site: http://nursefancypants.blogspot.ie/
Freq: Daily
Circ: 10728

Beauty & Grooming, Celebrities, Cosmetics, Fashion, Hair, Literature, Women's Interests

Nurture Store
1052985
Web site: nurturestore.co.uk
Freq: Daily
Circ: 155128
Profile: Blog covering children's play ideas, kids' crafts and fun activities. The blog has an archive dating back to August 2009.

Education

Nutidensmor
1061013
Email: nutidensmor@gmail.com
Web site: http://nutidensmor.dk/
Freq: Daily
Circ: 3889

Elementary School, Family & Parenting, Lifestyle, Men's Interests, Preschool, Regional General Interest, Teen/Young Adult, Trading Cards & Comics, Women's Interests

Nutmegs, seven
987037
Web site: www.nutmegsseven.co.uk
Freq: Daily
Circ: 7641
Profile: Blog covering food. The nutmegs, seven blog discusses anything from food and recipes to ingredients and eating in Oxford and Cambridge.

Cooking & Baking, Restaurant Reviews

Nutri Campeones
1061919
Web site: http://nutricampeones.blogspot.com
Freq: Daily
Circ: 2366

Cooking & Baking, Health & Medicine, Nutrition

Nutrición Tips
1060915
Web site: http://nutriciontips.blogspot.com
Freq: Daily
Circ: 1468

Fitness & Exercise, Healthcare Industry, Nutrition

Nutricion...Ni Bueno Ni Malo
1061870
Web site: http://blogs.eluniversal.com.mx/nutricion
Freq: Daily
Circ: 96

Food, Nutrition

The Nutriseed Blog
1073278
Editorial: Nutriseed Towers, Unit 5 Lanrick Road, London E14 0JP
Web site: https://www.nutriseed.uk/blogs/nutri-blog/
Freq: Daily
Circ: 909

Alternative Medicine, Cooking & Baking, Health & Medicine, Men's Interests, Nutrition, Women's Interests

Nutrition Information
1062062
Email: yayun_18@126.com
Web site: http://snowheart19.blog.sohu.com

Freq: Daily
Circ: 82

Alternative Medicine, Cosmetics, Disability, Fitness & Exercise, Food, Health & Medicine, Media Relations, Medicine, Nutrition, Patient Support

Nutritionist Resource blog
1053051
Tel: 44 08448 030244
Email: info@nutritionist-resource.org.uk
Web site: http://www.nutritionist-resource.org.uk/blog/
Freq: Daily
Circ: 14

Nutrition

The NW blog
1054372
Email: sales@networkwebcams.co.uk
Web site: http://www.networkwebcams.co.uk/blog/
Freq: Daily
Circ: 16170

Cameras

Nya Hemmet
1060252
Email: nyahemmet@metromode.se
Web site: http://nyahemmet.metromode.se/
Freq: Daily
Circ: 337

Do-It-Yourself (DIY), Interior Design

Nya Hemmet
1060562
Email: nyahemmet@metromode.se
Web site: http://nyahemmet.metromode.se/
Freq: Daily
Circ: 337

Do-It-Yourself (DIY), Interior Design

NYLON Living
988225
Email: nylonliving@btinternet.com
Web site: www.nylonliving.com
Freq: Daily
Circ: 10032
Profile: Blog covering interior design, home decorating and family travel.

Cooking & Baking, Crafts

O.R.R
1053397
Web site: http://www.orrblog.net/
Freq: Daily
Circ: 7085
Profile: Blog covering fashion. O.R.R blog discusses anything from personal style and outfit posts to the latest fashion trends and lifestyle. The outlet offers RSS (Really Simple Syndication).

Beauty & Grooming, Cooking & Baking, Cosmetics, Fashion, Hair, Photography, Women's Interests

Obsessed by Beauty
988839
Email: obsessedbybeauty@gmail.com
Web site: www.obsessedbybeauty.com
Freq: Daily
Circ: 3889

Beauty & Grooming, Cosmetics, Fashion, Hair, Women's Interests

Obson Blog
1061969
Web site: http://www.obson.wordpress.com
Freq: Daily
Circ: 6

Architecture & Design, Auto Aftermarket, Computers, Data Management, Electronics, Government Technology, Industry, Internet, Mobile Communications, Security & Security Systems

Octavo Dia
1061551
Web site: http://blogs.eluniversal.com.mx/octavo
Freq: Daily
Circ: 96

National News, Religion

Odd Socks and Pretty Frocks
1054356
Email: oddsocksandprettyfrocks@hotmail.co.uk
Web site: oddsocksandprettyfrocks.blogspot.co.uk
Freq: Daily
Circ: 7776

Women's Interests

UK Blogs

ODI Blog 986212
Editorial: 203 Blackfriars Road, London SE1
8NJ Tel: 44 02079 220300
Email: media@odi.org.uk
Web site: https://www.odi.org/opinion
Freq: Daily
Circ: 50166
Charitable Foundations

Oekonomi.no 1061944
Email: are@oekonomi.no
Web site: http://www.oekonomi.no/
Freq: Daily
Circ: 1136
Economics

Off The Post 986370
Email: offthepost@hotmail.co.uk
Web site: www.offthepost.info
Freq: Daily
Circ: 146099
Soccer

**Off the Wall Disability and
Disabled Blog** 996996
Email: admin@ableize.com
Web site: http://ableize.blogspot.co.uk/
Freq: Daily
Circ: 521
Disability

Office Genie Blog 1057946
Tel: 44 08444 155531
Email: help@officegenie.co.uk
Web site: http://www.officegenie.co.uk/blog
Freq: Daily
Circ: 20
Office Design

The Official Mini Sport Blog
996338
Editorial: Mini Sport Ltd, Thompson Street,
Padiham, Burnley BB12 7AP
Tel: 44 01282 778731
Email: sales@minisport.com
Web site: blog.minisport.com
Freq: Daily
Circ: 28
Automakers

Oh Emma 1054500
Email: emmalouisecoull@gmail.com
Web site: www.oh-emma.com
Freq: Daily
Circ: 2692
Fashion, Women's Interests

Oh My Blog 1052551
Editorial: Unit 8, Centenary Park, Coronet
Way, Manchester M50 1RE
Email: press@missguided.co.uk
Web site: http://www.missguided.co.uk/
blog/
Freq: Daily
Circ: 651
Fashion

Oh So Amelia 988308
Email: ohsoamelia@hotmail.co.uk
Web site: www.ohsoamelia.com
Freq: Daily
Circ: 118964
Family & Parenting

Oh! Grafico 1060829
Web site: http://www.ohgrafico.com
Freq: Daily
Circ: 1825
Graphic Design, Internet

Oh, the places we will go! 988301
Email: selena_jones@me.com
Web site: www.selenatheplaces.com
Freq: Daily
Circ: 7337
Profile: Blog covering travel. The Oh, the
places we will go! blog discusses anything
from travel and tourism to cruising and travel
destinations. The blog has an archive dating
back to March 2014 and shares an extensive
blog roll.
Travel

OhHay! 1053108
Email: ohhayblogs@gmail.com
Web site: ohhayblogs.blogspot.co.uk

Freq: Daily
Circ: 6610
Visual Arts

OHMS! 1062159
Web site: http://ohmmmnios.blogspot.com/
Freq: Daily
Circ: 521
Classical/Choral/Band Music, Country,
Folk, Bluegrass, Dance Music, Jazz &
Blues, Music, Pop Music, R&B, Urban,
World, Rap & Hip Hop, Rock Music

OILFIREDUP 986213
Tel: 353 07411 800041
Email: news@oilfiredup.com
Web site: http://oilfiredup.com/
Circ: 10350
News & Current Affairs

Oilholics Synonymous Report
1054650
Email: gaurav.sharma@
oilholicssynonymous.com
Web site: www.oilholicssynonymous.com
Freq: Daily
Circ: 10027
Oil

OilVoice 986214
Editorial: Acorn House, 381 Midsummer
Boulevard, Milton Keynes MK9 3HP
Web site: oilvoice.com
Circ: 99205
Environment, Oil

Ojo Científico 1061967
Web site: http://www.ojocientifico.com
Freq: Daily
Circ: 5373
Science

Old Fashioned Susie 988960
Web site: oldfashionedsusie.com
Freq: Daily
Circ: 11341
Do-It-Yourself (DIY), Fashion

Old Ladybird Books 1054642
Email: nmccar1063@aol.com
Web site: http://oldladybirdbooks.blogspot.
co.uk/
Freq: Daily
Circ: 13182
Literature

olibombbb 1104178
Email: olibombdiggity@hotmail.com
Web site: https://www.youtube.com/user/
olibombbb
Freq: Daily
Circ: 9270
Beauty & Grooming, Cosmetics, Fashion,
Hair, Women's Interests

Oliver Quinlan blog 1053971
Web site: http://www.oliverquinlan.com/
blog/
Freq: Daily
Circ: 10117
Education, Higher Education, Schools &
Institutions, Students

The Oliver's Madhouse 988307
Web site: theoliversmadhouse.co.uk
Freq: Daily
Circ: 83846
Profile: Blog covering motherhood. The
Oliver's Madhouse discusses anything from
lifestyle and family life to children's activities,
health and fitness. The blog has an archive
dating back to October 2012 and shares an
extensive blogroll.
Family & Parenting

Olivia Blogs 1098972
Web site: https://www.oliviabossert.com/
blog
Freq: Daily
Circ: 8375
Photography, Women's Interests

Ollerenshaw IT blog 1053282
Web site: http://www.siebel-tech.com/blog/
Freq: Daily
Circ: 83
Computers

Ollie & Seb's Haus 1053130
Web site: ollieandsebshaus.co.uk
Freq: Daily
Circ: 7192
Do-It-Yourself (DIY)

Oma Koti Onnenpesä 1061330
Email: omakotionnenpesa@gmail.com
Web site: http://omakotionnenpesa.
blogspot.fi/
Freq: Daily
Circ: 1277
Architecture & Design, Do-It-Yourself
(DIY), Gardening, Home, Interior Design,
Property Management & Maintenance,
Real Estate

Omenaminttu 1062102
Web site: http://omenaminttu.blogspot.fi
Freq: Daily
Circ: 1459
Food, Internet

On An Overgrown Path 988189
Email: overgrownpath@hotmail.com
Web site: http://www.overgrownpath.com/
Freq: Daily
Circ: 9285
Classical/Choral/Band Music

On Chemistry blog 1052993
Editorial: c/o BioMed Central Limited, Floor
6, 236 Gray's Inn Road, London WC1X 8HB
Tel: 44 08003 898136
Email: info@chemistrycentral.com
Web site: http://blogs.biomedcentral.com/
Freq: Daily
Circ: 27
Science

On my way 1061572
Email: hirsimakijutta@gmail.com
Web site: http://www.onmyway.fitfashion.fi
Freq: Daily
Circ: 45551
Beauty & Grooming, Cosmetics, Fashion,
Fitness & Exercise, Hair

On The Corner 1061612
Email: hola@onthecorner.com.ar
Web site: http://onthecornerstreetstyle.
blogspot.com.ar
Freq: Daily
Circ: 1018
Fashion

Once De Un Gran Mes 1060603
Web site: http://www.eldiezdeungranmes.
blogspot.com
Freq: Daily
Circ: 521
National News, Politics

Once Upon a Bookcase 1053249
Email: onceuponabookcase@gmail.com
Web site: http://www.onceuponabookcase.
co.uk/
Freq: Daily
Circ: 10921
Literature

One Bean Row 1053793
Web site: onebeanrow.com
Freq: Daily
Circ: 1697
Gardening

One Busy WAHM 1052543
Email: natalie@onebusywahm.com
Web site: http://onebusywahm.com/
Freq: Daily
Circ: 7354
Cooking & Baking, Nutrition

One Fab Day 995126
Editorial: 4 Lower Ormond Quay, Dublin 1
Tel: 353 01670 8688
Email: hello@onefabday.com
Web site: onefabday.com
Freq: Daily
Circ: 624352
Editor: Naoise McNally
News & Current Affairs

One Found Seven 1052833
Email: onefoundseven@gmail.com
Web site: https://onefoundseven.co.uk/

Freq: Daily
Circ: 10709
Profile: Blog covering creative lifestyle. The
One Found Seven blog discusses anything
from fashion and crafts to food and travel.
The blog has an archive dating back to
December 2013.
Beauty & Grooming, Cooking & Baking,
Cosmetics, Crafts, Fashion, Hair,
Restaurant Reviews, Travel, Women's
Interests

One Happy Little Crafter 1062749
Email: happy.crafter@hotmail.com
Web site: http://onehappylittlecrafter.
blogspot.co.uk/
Freq: Daily
Circ: 608
Crafts

One Inch Punch 1062051
Email: info@oneinchpunch.net
Web site: http://www.oneinchpunch.net
Freq: Daily
Circ: 12481
Bars, Clubs & Pubs, Comedy,
Entertainment, Local Entertainment
Guides, Movies & Video

One Man and His Blog 986215
Tel: 44 02079 111800
Web site: www.onemanandhisblog.com
Freq: Daily
Circ: 27171
Cameras, Photography, Publishing

One Man's Meat 1053712
Web site: conorbofin.com
Freq: Daily
Circ: 8972
Profile: Blog covering food. The One Man's
Meat blog discusses anything from food
reviews and recipes. The blog has an archive
dating back to August 2011 and shares an
extensive blog roll.
Cooking & Baking

One Nail to Rule Them All 987596
Editorial: 3 Marble Hall, Lamma Wells Road,
Holmfirth, Holme Valley HD9 2SN
Tel: 44 07889 036620
Email: onenailtorulethemall@gmail.com
Web site: http://www.onenailtorulethemall.
co.uk/
Freq: Daily
Circ: 45488
Profile: Blog covering nails and nail care.
The blog has an archive dating back to
March 2012.
Cosmetics

One Narberth 1056558
Email: info@onenarberth.co.uk
Web site: www.onenarberth.co.uk/
Freq: Daily
Circ: 1473
Editor: Ian Gravell
News & Current Affairs

One Night In Theatre 1062018
Email: onenightintheatre@gmail.com
Web site: http://onenightintheatre.blogspot.
fi/
Freq: Daily
Circ: 9807
Antiques/Collectibles, Art, Arts,
Literature, Photography, Theater &
Performing Arts, Visual Arts

One Room With A View 1075499
Web site: https://oneroomwithaview.com
Freq: Daily
Circ: 13594
Movies & Video

One Slice of Lemon 988620
Email: onesliceoflemon@gmail.com
Web site: www.onesliceoflemon.com
Freq: Daily
Circ: 8503
Profile: Blog covering lifestyle, beauty
product reviews and fashion. The blog has
an archive dating back to May 2014.
Beauty & Grooming, Cooking & Baking,
Cosmetics, Fashion, Hair, Travel

One Stop Savvy 1054428
Email: onestopsavvy@hotmail.co.uk
Web site: http://www.onestopsavvy.co.uk
Freq: Daily
Circ: 792
Profile: Blog covering beauty. ONE STOP
Savvy discusses anything from beauty
products and cosmetics to health, lifestyle
and motherhood. The blog has an archive
dating back to August 2013.
Beauty & Grooming, Cosmetics, Family &
Parenting, Fashion, Hair, Weddings,
Women's Interests

One Too Many Mornings 1054163
Web site: onetoomanymornings.co.uk/
Freq: Daily
Circ: 3030
Profile: Blog covering marketing, social
media and digital communications. The blog
has an archive dating back to May 2011 and
shares an extensive blogroll.
Marketing

OneDad3Girls - CEASED 988258
Web site: http://photalife.com/
Freq: Daily
Circ: 54794
Family & Parenting

OneSwitch 1054477
Email: info@oneswitch.org.uk
Web site: http://switchgaming.blogspot.co.
uk/
Freq: Daily
Circ: 11998
Computer & Video Games, Disability

Online Behavior 1104507
Email: info@online-behavior.com
Web site: http://online-behavior.com
Freq: No Frequency Established
Circ: 649688
Marketing, Web Site

Online Dating Help 1053072
Email: odh@onlinedatinghelp.co.uk
Web site: http://www.onlinedatinghelp.co.
uk/
Freq: Daily
Circ: 45242
Relationships

Online Journalism Blog 1052984
Web site: http://onlinejournalismblog.com/
Freq: Daily
Circ: 59842
Publishing

Online Race Driver 997066
Email: admin@onlineracedriver.com
Web site: http://www.onlineracedriver.com/
Freq: Daily
Circ: 9686
Editor: Dan Thornton
Computer & Video Games

The Online Stylist 1053816
Email: onlinestylist@me.com
Web site: www.theonlinestylist.co.uk
Freq: Daily
Circ: 48978
Fashion

Only 4 feet 9 1055147
Web site: http://only4feet9.blogspot.co.uk/
Freq: Daily
Circ: 521
Art, Fashion, Restaurant Reviews, Travel,
Women's Interests

Only Dead Fish 1053661
Web site: http://neilperkin.typepad.com/
Freq: Daily
Circ: 2680419
News & Current Affairs

Only Travel Only Blog 1054063
Web site: http://www.travelonlyblog.co.uk/
Freq: Daily
Circ: 1391
Profile: Blog covering travel. The Only Travel
Only Blog discusses anything from travel in
the Lake District and Europe to ecotourism
and food. The blog has an archive dating
back to February 2013.
Regional General Interest, Travel

Onmedica.com blog 998293
Editorial: Beechwood House, 2 - 3
Commercial Way, Christy Close, Basildon
SS15 6EF Tel: 44 01268 495600
Web site: http://www.onmedica.com/Blogs.
aspx
Freq: Daily
Circ: 2476
Medicine

Onyx Blog 996555
Tel: 44 07976 554067
Email: info@onyxsnowboarding.com
Web site: http://onyxsnowboarding.com
Freq: Daily
Circ: 3003
Travel, Winter Sports

The Ooh Tray 987947
Email: editor@theoohtray.com
Web site: www.theoohtray.com/
Freq: Daily
Circ: 10711
Editor: Ed Whitfield
Profile: Blog covering film and book
reviews.
Entertainment, Literature, Movies & Video

Ooohlalaa its Fashion 1053024
Web site: http://www.ooohlalaa-itsfashion.
com
Freq: Daily
Circ: 9671
Fashion, Women's Interests

**Open (minds, finds, con-
versations)...** 1054510
Email: antony@brilliantnoise.com
Web site: www.antonymayfield.com
Freq: Daily
Circ: 2400
Branding, Internet, Marketing

Open Culture 996817
Editorial: Open Culture, c/o World Museum
Liverpool, William Brown Street, Liverpool L3
8EN Tel: 44 01514 784928
Email: info@culture.org.uk
Web site: culture.org.uk
Freq: Daily
Circ: 10971
News & Current Affairs

Open Rights Group blog 1054624
Editorial: Open Rights Group, 12 Tileyard
Road, London N7 9AH Tel: 44 02070 961079
Email: info@openrightsgroup.org
Web site: http://www.openrightsgroup.org/
blog
Freq: Daily
Circ: 13
Data Management, Internet, Social Issues

openDemocracy.net 983303
Editorial: The Print House, 18 Ashwin Street,
London E8 3DL
Email: info@opendemocracy.net
Web site: opendemocracy.net
Circ: 193316
Editor: Rosemary Bechler
Charitable Foundations, Politics

Opinemos Hoy 1061468
Web site: http://opinemoshoy.blogspot.
com/
Freq: Daily
Circ: 521
National News

Opposable Thumbs Blog 1075814
Web site: http://opposablethumbsblog.com/
Freq: Daily
Circ: 12250
Beauty & Grooming, Cosmetics,
Electronics, Hair, Travel, Women's
Interests

Orbital Comics 1053858
Editorial: 8 Great Newport Street, London
WC2H 7JA Tel: 44 02072 400591
Email: info@orbitalcomics.com
Web site: http://www.orbitalcomics.com/
Freq: Daily
Circ: 12603
Cartoons, Trading Cards & Comics

**The Orchestra of the Age of
Enlightenment Blog** 1053458
Editorial: Kings Place, 90 York Way, London
N1 9AG Tel: 44 02072 399370
Email: info@oae.co.uk
Web site: www.oae.co.uk/category/blog
Freq: Daily
Circ: 285
Classical/Choral/Band Music

Ordinary Cycling Girl 988295
Web site: http://ordinarycyclinggirl.co.uk/
Freq: Daily
Circ: 8851
Profile: Blog covering cycling. The blog has
an archive dating back to February 2014 and
shares a short blog roll.
Bicycles

Organise My House 1052987
Email: info@stylemyhouse.co.uk
Web site: http://www.organisemyhouse.
com/category/style-decor/
Freq: Daily
Circ: 31
Profile: Blog covering interiors, home
decorating and furnishing. The blog has an
archive dating back to January 2014 and
shares a short blogroll.
Do-It-Yourself (DIY)

Organising Chaos 1053742
Web site: https://woodsiegirl.wordpress.
com/
Freq: Daily
Circ: 100
Literature

The Orient Excess 998082
Web site: http://www.orientexcess.com/
Freq: Daily
Circ: 10587
Airline Inflight, Railroad, Travel

Origami Girl's Heroics 1054090
Email: origamigirlheroics@gmail.com
Web site: http://www.origamigirlheroics.
blogspot.co.uk/
Freq: Daily
Circ: 521
Computer & Video Games, Cooking &
Baking, Crafts, Crafts, Hobbies, &
Collecting, Fashion, Literature, Weddings,
Women's Interests

Origamistas 1061628
Email: losorigamistas@gmail.com
Web site: http://losorigamistas.blogspot.
com/
Freq: Daily
Circ: 521
Crafts, Hobbies, & Collecting

Original Travel Blog 1052750
Tel: 44 02037 407867
Email: ask@originaltravel.co.uk
Web site: http://www.originaltravel.co.uk/
blog
Freq: Daily
Circ: 92
Travel

Ornamental Passions 1054092
Web site: http://ornamentalpassions.
blogspot.co.uk/
Freq: Daily
Circ: 11784
Art

Ornitorrinco en Linea 1061861
Web site: http://www.angelbc.wordpress.
com
Freq: Daily
Circ: 323
Internet, Movies & Video

Orphans of Liberty 1057086
Email: orphansofliberty@gmail.com
Web site: http://www.4liberty.org.uk/
Freq: Daily
Circ: 11833
Government, Politics

Orquidea's Arts and Crafts 1060872
Web site: http://www.orquideaartsandcraft.
blogspot.com

Freq: Daily
Circ: 687
Crafts

Orsai 1061580
Web site: http://orsai.es/blog/
Freq: Daily
Circ: 132
Lifestyle, Literature, Men's Interests,
Regional General Interest, Women's
Interests

Oslofru 1062050
Email: oslofru@gmail.com
Web site: http://oslofru.com/
Freq: Daily
Circ: 8187
Elementary School, Family & Parenting,
Lifestyle, Men's Interests, Preschool,
Regional General Interest, Teen/Young
Adult, Trading Cards & Comics, Women's
Interests

Otra Chilanga 1061479
Web site: http://laotrachilanga.blogspot.
com
Freq: Daily
Circ: 2090
Human Rights, National News, Politics

Otra Vez 1061392
Web site: http://pochogarces.blogspot.com/
Freq: Daily
Circ: 611
Cooking & Baking

Otro Blog de Diario de Oriente
1061436
Web site: http://blogs.clarin.com/
realidadespartidas/
Freq: Daily
National News

Otro Uruguay es Posible 1062140
Web site: http://pelusaradical.blogspot.
com/
Freq: Daily
Circ: 1292
Disability, Education, Environment, Higher
Education, Politics, Preschool, Schools &
Institutions, Students

Ought To Be Clowns 986216
Email: ianfoster32@gmail.com
Web site: http://oughttobeclowns.blogspot.com
Freq: Daily
Circ: 3609
Theater & Performing Arts

Our baby blog 1052989
Web site: http://www.our-baby-blog.co.uk/
Freq: Daily
Circ: 6405
Cooking & Baking, Crafts, Do-It-Yourself
(DIY), Family & Parenting, Photography

Our Big Fat Travel Adventure
1054033
Email: ourbigfattraveladventure@gmail.com
Web site: www.ourbigfattraveladventure.
com
Freq: Daily
Circ: 32252
Profile: Blog covering travel.
Travel

Our CLTR 1073282
Email: info@ourcltr.com
Web site: https://ourcltr.com/
Freq: Daily
Circ: 521
Art, Social Issues, Visual Arts

OUseful.info 1052785
Web site: http://blog.ouseful.info/
Freq: Daily
Circ: 50691
Data Management, Education

Out of My Shed 1054215
Email: outofmyshedblog@gmail.com
Web site: http://outofmyshed.co.uk/
Freq: Daily
Circ: 8377
Gardening

UK Blogs

Outdoor Chics 988663
Web site: www.outdoorchics.com
Freq: Daily
Circ: 10618
Bicycles, Extreme/Adventure Sports, Swimming/Watersports, Women's Interests

OutofOffice.com 1054072
Editorial: Clerks Court, 18 - 20 Farringdon Lane, London EC1R 3AU
Tel: 44 02071 571571
Email: darren@outofoffice.com
Web site: https://www.outofoffice.com/blog
Freq: Daily
Circ: 157
LGBT, Luxury Goods, Travel

Outside of the Boot 997827
Email: info@outsideoftheboot.com
Web site: http://outsideoftheboot.com/
Freq: Daily
Circ: 149021
Soccer

Outside Voices Blog 1054580
Editorial: 11/21 Fitzjohns Avenue, London NW3 5JY Tel: 44 02074 317730
Email: outsidevoicesblog@gmail.com
Web site: http://www.outsidevoices.co.uk/
Freq: Daily
Circ: 521
Art, Consumer Affairs, International News, Literature, National News, Photography, Theater & Performing Arts

Overcoming the Odds 1104812
Web site: https://overcomingtheoddsblog.wordpress.com/
Freq: Daily
Casinos & Gaming

Overdressed and Under-prepared 988481
Web site: overdressedunderprepared.co.uk
Freq: Daily
Circ: 2905
Fashion, Men's Interests

The Overflowing Library 987305
Email: kirstylouiseconnor@hotmail.com
Web site: www.overflowinglibrary.com
Freq: Daily
Circ: 8348
Literature

Overpass Experiences 1053454
Email: blog@wroolie.co.uk
Web site: http://www.wroolie.co.uk
Freq: Daily
Circ: 9642
Computers, Family & Parenting, Men's Interests, Mobile Electronics, Software

Ovo Energy Blog 999275
Editorial: 40 St Thomas Street, Bristol BS1 6JX Tel: 44 08005 999440
Email: hello@ovoenergy.com
Web site: http://www.ovoenergy.com/blog/
Freq: Daily
Circ: 406
Alternative/Renewable Energy

Oxfam News Blog 986712
Editorial: John Smith Drive, Oxford OX4 2JY
Tel: 44 01865 473727
Email: enquiries@oxfam.org.uk
Web site: http://www.oxfam.org.uk/blogs
Freq: Daily
Circ: 31
Charitable Foundations, Energy & Environment, Environment, Ethical/Moral Issues, Human Rights, International News, Organic Food, Politics, Social Issues, Sustainable Development

The Oxford Astrologer 996953
Email: christina@oxfordastrologer.com
Web site: http://oxford-astrologer.blogspot.com
Freq: Daily
Circ: 600
Astrology & Parapsychology

Oxford Science Blog 1054660
Tel: 44 01865 270046
Email: thomas.calver@admin.ox.ac.uk
Web site: www.ox.ac.uk/news/science-blog
Freq: Daily
Circ: 248
Education, Science

The Oxford Ski Company 996542
Editorial: 18 Thorney Leys Business Park, Witney, Witney OX28 4GE
Tel: 44 01993 899420
Email: info@oxfordski.com
Web site: http://www.oxfordski.com/inspire-me/blogs/
Freq: Daily
Circ: 5
Travel, Winter Sports

Oyster and Pearl 988552
Email: oysterpots@gmail.com
Web site: www.oysterandpearl.co.uk
Freq: Daily
Circ: 8510
Family & Parenting

P.S I love fashion 1061259
Email: psilovefashionblog@gmail.com
Web site: http://lindajuhola.com/
Freq: Daily
Circ: 31889
Fashion, Lifestyle, Men's Interests, Regional General Interest, Women's Interests

Pabellon Criollo 1061198
Web site: http://www.pabelloncriollo.com.ve/
Freq: Daily
Circ: 521
Lifestyle, Men's Interests, National News, Regional General Interest, Women's Interests

Pack Your Passport 988097
Tel: 44 07860 381659
Email: beverley@pack-your-passport.com
Web site: www.pack-your-passport.com
Freq: Daily
Circ: 40961
Profile: Blog covering travel, lifestyle, things to do and restaurants. The blog has an archive dating back to June 2011 and shares an extensive blogroll.
Travel

PAD4U Blog 999277
Editorial: PAD4U, 834 Stockport Road, Manchester M19 3AW Tel: 44 01612 572441
Email: property@pad4u.com
Web site: https://peteranthony.co.uk/blog
Freq: Daily
Circ: 16
Architecture & Design, Do-It-Yourself (DIY), Gardening, Home, Property Management & Maintenance, Real Estate

Paddle Pedal Pace 1052986
Email: paddlepedalpace@gmail.com
Web site: http://paddlepedalpace.co.uk/
Freq: Daily
Circ: 10663
Fitness & Exercise

Page to Stage Reviews 1064496
Email: pagetostagereviews@gmail.com
Web site: http://www.pagetostagereviews.com/
Freq: Daily
Circ: 9241
Editor: Zarina de Ruiter
Entertainment, Literature, Local Entertainment Guides, Theater & Performing Arts, Women's Interests

Pages by Megan 988476
Email: hello@pagesbymegan.com
Web site: www.pagesbymegan.com
Freq: Daily
Circ: 12804
Profile: Blog covering fashion. The pages by megan blog discusses anything from fashion and style to outfits and fashion accessories.
Fashion

Paige Joanna 988493
Email: paige_joanna_calvert@live.co.uk
Web site: www.paigejoanna.co.uk
Freq: Daily
Circ: 9671

Profile: Blog covering fashion. Paige Joanna blog discusses anything from fashion and beauty to crafts. The blog has an archive dating back to Febuary 2012.
Crafts, Fashion

PAIR & A SPARE 1061567
Email: apairandaspareonline@gmail.com
Web site: http://apair-andaspare.blogspot.com
Freq: Daily
Circ: 4328
Fashion

Palabras de Arena 1060864
Email: palabrasdearena@gmail.com
Web site: http://www.palabrasdearena.org
Freq: Daily
Circ: 843
International News, Literature, National News, Politics

Palabras y Escombros 1061051
Web site: http://palabrasyescombros.blogspot.com/
Freq: Daily
Circ: 1685
Literature

Palacio de Peliculas 1060596
Web site: http://www.palaciodepeliculas.net
Freq: Daily
Circ: 81217
Movies & Video

Paleo with Mrs P 1052873
Email: paleowithmrsp@gmail.com
Web site: http://paleowithmrsp.com/
Freq: Daily
Circ: 9011
Cooking & Baking, Nutrition

The Palette Pages 998161
Email: lisa@thepalettepages.com
Web site: http://www.thepalettepages.com/
Freq: Daily
Circ: 13394
Art

Palindrome Poppet 1052738
Email: palindromepoppet@yahoo.com
Web site: palindromepoppet.com/
Freq: Daily
Circ: 3203
Profile: Blog covering lifestyle. The blog has an archive dating back to July 2011.
Beauty & Grooming, Cosmetics, Fashion, Hair, Literature, Women's Interests

Paljon Melua Teatterista 1061148
Email: katri@yrtikan.net
Web site: http://paljonmeluateatterista.blogspot.fi/
Freq: Daily
Circ: 10207
Antiques/Collectibles, Art, Arts, Literature, Photography, Theater & Performing Arts, Visual Arts

Pamper and Curves 987683
Tel: 44 01516 252842
Email: perelandrabeedles@yahoo.com
Web site: http://www.pamperandcurves.com/
Freq: Daily
Circ: 7619
Profile: PAMPER AND CURVES covers plus size, rockabilly fashion. The blog has an archive dating back to May 2010.
Beauty & Grooming, Cosmetics, Crafts, Fashion, Hair

Panopticon Blog 1052780
Editorial: 11KBW, 11 King's Bench Walk, Temple, London EC4Y 7EQ
Tel: 44 02076 328500
Web site: http://panopticonblog.com/
Freq: Daily
Circ: 15614
Intellectual Property

Panorama Liberal 1060459
Web site: http://panoramaliberal.blogspot.com/
Freq: Daily

Circ: 752
Politics

The Paper Nest Dolls 1055159
Email: papernestdolls@gmail.com
Web site: http://thepapernestdolls.blogspot.co.uk/
Freq: Daily
Circ: 548
Art, Crafts

Paperhouse 1054556
Email: sarah@sarahditum.com
Web site: www.sarahditum.com
Freq: Daily
Circ: 11444
Publishing

Parent Panel 999347
Web site: www.parentpanel.co.uk
Freq: Daily
Circ: 9262
Editor: Carol Smith
Family & Parenting

Parenta Blog 999324
Editorial: Rocky Hill, Maidstone, Maidstone ME16 8PZ Tel: 44 08445 045504
Email: contact@parenta.com
Web site: http://www.parenta.com/category/childcare-news/
Freq: Daily
Circ: 16
Family & Parenting

Pargy 1054640
Email: michaela@pargy.co.uk
Web site: www.pargy.co.uk
Freq: Daily
Circ: 7242
Do-It-Yourself (DIY)

Park and Cube 987094
Editorial: G4 Olympic House, 12 Somerford Grove, London N16 7RZ
Email: hello@parkandcube.com
Web site: www.parkandcube.com
Freq: Daily
Circ: 126159
Fashion, Women's Interests

Park Life 985427
Email: park_life@me.com
Web site: http://park-life.org
Freq: Daily
Circ: 1631
Regional General Interest

Parlimentary Connections 1054366
Web site: http://www.postonline.co.uk/blog/appgifs-blog
Freq: Daily
Circ: 21
Politics

Parolan Asema 1061496
Email: info@parolanasema.fi
Web site: http://www.parolanasema.fi
Freq: Daily
Circ: 752
Architecture & Design, Do-It-Yourself (DIY), Gardening, Home, Interior Design, Property Management & Maintenance, Real Estate, Residential Real Estate

Parral Actual 1060594
Web site: http://www.parralactual.com
Freq: Daily
Circ: 9608
Advertising Industry, Branding, Broadcasting, Celebrities, Graphic Design, Marketing, Media & Communications, National News, Photography, Publishing

Passages 1057088
Web site: http://tonybayfield.blogspot.com/
Freq: Daily
Circ: 1142
Movies & Video

Passion for Flowers Blog 996859
Editorial: Balsall Common, Solihull CV7 7RE
Tel: 44 01676 529014
Web site: passionforflowers.net/our-blog/
Freq: Daily

Circ: 8

Weddings

Patch of Puddles - CEASED 2017
988653
Web site: www.patchofpuddles.co.uk
Freq: Daily
Circ: 6464
Crafts, Family & Parenting, Literature

Patchwork Harmony
988514
Email: info@patchworkharmony.co.uk
Web site: www.patchworkharmony.co.uk/blog
Freq: Daily
Circ: 6158
Crafts, Do-It-Yourself (DIY)

Patent Purple Life
987798
Tel: 44 07815 088892
Email: jo@patentpurplelife.com
Web site: www.patentpurplelife.com/
Freq: Daily
Circ: 13196
Beauty & Grooming, Cosmetics, Entertainment, Hair, Movies & Video

The Patient Gardener's Weblog
988739
Web site: http://patientgardener.wordpress.com/
Freq: Daily
Circ: 4452
Gardening

Patricia Bright
1053289
Web site: patriciabright.co.uk
Freq: Daily
Circ: 6584
Profile: Blog covering lifestyle. PATRICIA BRIGHT blog discusses anything from general lifestyle and advice to fashion and beauty. The blog has an archive dating back to April 2013. This outlet also offers a vlog. The outlet offers RSS (Really Simple Syndication).
Cosmetics, Fashion, Travel, Women's Interests

Patricia Bright Vlog
1005188
Email: patstrueworld@gmail.com
Web site: https://www.youtube.com/user/BritPopPrincess
Freq: Daily
Circ: 45
Cosmetics, Fashion, Women's Interests

Patrick Harvie MSP blog
997812
Editorial: Room 4/2, 52 St Enoch Square, Glasgow G1 4AA Tel: 44 01412 483850
Web site: https://greens.scot/msps/patrick-harvie
Freq: Daily
Politics

Paul Cairney: Politics & Public Policy
997813
Web site: http://paulcairney.wordpress.com/
Freq: Daily
Circ: 34309
Politics

Paul in London
1053383
Email: paulinlondonblogger@gmail.com
Web site: http://www.paulinlondon.com/
Freq: Daily
Circ: 9829
Theater & Performing Arts

Paul Kirtley's Blog
988293
Email: admin@paulkirtley.co.uk
Web site: http://www.paulkirtley.co.uk/
Freq: Daily
Circ: 45260
Profile: The Paul Kirtley's Blog covers outdoor recreation, camping, wilderness bushcraft and survival skills. The blog has an archive dating back to November 2010. This outlet offers a vlog.
Camping and RV Travel, Field Sports, Outdoor Recreation

PaulThomasBell.com
1098985
Email: paulthomasbell@hotmail.com
Web site: https://paulthomasbell.com/
Freq: Daily

Circ: 11548

Relationships

PC Digital
1061914
Web site: http://www.pcdigital.org
Freq: Daily
Circ: 5014
Auto Aftermarket, Computers, Data Management, Electronics, Government Technology, Industry, Internet, Mobile Communications, Security & Security Systems, Software

PC Game Reviews and News
1052800
Email: bookmoviegamereviewer@googlemail.com
Web site: http://www.pcgamereviewsandnews.com/
Freq: Daily
Circ: 1207
Computer & Video Games

Peach Trees and Bumblebees
997513
Editorial: c/o SJA 27 St John's Lane, London EC1M 4BU
Email: peachtreesandbumblebees@gmail.com
Web site: www.peachtreesandbumblebees.com
Freq: Daily
Circ: 8307
Cooking & Baking

Peak Leaders
1054027
Tel: 44 01337 860079
Email: info@peakleaders.com
Web site: http://peakleaders.com/blog/
Freq: Daily
Circ: 28
Travel, Winter Sports

Peakfan's Blog Derbyshire Cricket
1053437
Email: peakfan36@yahoo.co.uk
Web site: http://derbyshirecricket.blogspot.co.uk/
Freq: Daily
Circ: 10497
Cricket

Pebble Soup
1054091
Email: pebblesoup@gmail.com
Web site: http://www.pebblesoup.co.uk/
Freq: Daily
Circ: 8525
Cooking & Baking, Restaurant Reviews

Pedestre
1061069
Web site: http://www.ciudadpedestre.wordpress.com
Freq: Daily
Circ: 1391
Architecture & Design, Broadcasting, Building & Construction, Regional, Regional General Interest, Urban Planning & Development

Peking Duck
1062135
Web site: http://www.pekingduck.org
Freq: Daily
Circ: 9123
Airline Inflight, International News, Politics, Railroad, Travel

pelles personliga
1060202
Web site: http://pellespersonliga.se
Freq: Daily
Circ: 4905
Comedy, Lifestyle, Men's Interests, Regional General Interest, Women's Interests

pelles personliga
1060635
Web site: http://pellespersonliga.se/
Freq: Daily
Circ: 4905
Comedy, Lifestyle, Men's Interests, Regional General Interest, Women's Interests

Peluqueria
1061546
Web site: http://www.peluqueria-at.blogspot.com

Circ: 752

Hair

Penelope's Pantry
1054511
Email: penelopespantry@googlemail.com
Web site: www.penelopespantryblog.com
Freq: Daily
Circ: 7252
Cooking & Baking

Pengeblogg
1061274
Email: pengeblogg@hotmail.com
Web site: http://pengeblogg.bloggnorge.com/
Freq: Daily
Circ: 139
Financial Markets, Personal Finance

Penguin Blog
1054194
Editorial: 80 Strand, London WC2R 0RL
Web site: http://penguinblog.co.uk/
Freq: Daily
Circ: 4854
Profile: Blog covering not for profit organisations, fundraising, charity marketing, strategy and innovation. The blog has an archive dating back to July 2010 and shares a short blogroll.
Literature, Publishing

The penguin with the pointy sticks
1053477
Web site: http://bromiskelly.typepad.com/lapurplepenguin/
Freq: Daily
Circ: 64844
Crafts

Penny and Polaroids
997894
Email: pennyandpolaroids@gmail.com
Web site: www.pennyandpolaroids.com
Freq: Daily
Circ: 6542
News & Current Affairs

Penny Golightly
987470
Web site: pennygolightly.com
Freq: Daily
Circ: 12586
Personal Finance, Women's Interests

Penny Red Blog
1053158
Email: laurie.penny@gmail.com
Freq: Daily
News & Current Affairs

PennyDog Patchwork
987365
Email: kerry@penny-dog.co.uk
Web site: blog.pennydog.com
Freq: Daily
Circ: 28
Profile: Blog covering patchwork and crafts. The blog has an archive dating back to June 2008.
Crafts

PennyxxLane
1053657
Web site: pennyxxlane.com
Freq: Daily
Circ: 11566
Profile: Blog covering lifestyle, beauty, fashion and home decorating.
Beauty & Grooming, Cosmetics, Fashion, Hair, Women's Interests

Pensamiento Imaginactivo
1060493
Web site: http://www.manuelgross.bligoo.com
Freq: Daily
Circ: 290061
Fund Management, Marketing, Small and Medium Business

The Pension Playpen
1054440
Email: henry.h.tapper@gmail.com
Web site: http://henrytapper.com/
Freq: Daily
Circ: 16505
Banking, Business, Government

Peonies and Polaroids
1053216
Email: peonies@btinternet.com
Web site: http://www.peoniesandpolaroids.com/
Freq: Daily

Circ: 8499

Art, Family & Parenting, Neurology, Photography

Peony Lim
987509
Editorial: Vicarage House, 58 - 60 Kensington Church Street, London W8 4DB
Tel: 44 077/1 888777
Email: info@peonylim.com
Web site: http://www.peonylim.com/
Freq: Daily
Circ: 32059
Cooking & Baking, Do-It-Yourself (DIY), Fashion, Luxury Goods, Travel, Women's Interests

People of Print
1054068
Editorial: 17 Amhurst Terrace, London E8 2BT
Email: info@peopleofprint.com
Web site: http://www.peopleofprint.com
Freq: Daily
Circ: 28096
Profile: Blog covering graphic design and print. PEOPLE OF PRINT discusses anything from illustration and photography to 3D printing and art. The blog has an archive dating back to April 2011.
Art

The People's Movies
987936
Email: thepeoplesmovies@gmail.com
Web site: http://thepeoplesmovies.com/
Freq: Daily
Circ: 1250
Editor: Andrew McArthur
Entertainment, Local Entertainment Guides, Movies & Video

peppercorns in my pocket
1053192
Email: peppercornsinmypocket@gmail.com
Web site: http://peppercornsinmypocket.blogspot.co.uk/
Freq: Daily
Circ: 1258
Travel

The Perfect Hiding Place
1052902
Email: perfecthidingplace@live.com
Web site: theperfecthidingplace.blogspot.co.uk
Freq: Daily
Circ: 8881
Profile: Blog covering crochet. Perfect Hiding Place blog discusses anything from crochet and arts and crafts to nail art, fashion and outdoor activities. The blog has an archive dating back to Febuary 2012 and shares an extensive blog roll.
Crafts, Women's Interests

peRFect Tennis
986800
Editorial: peRFect Tennis, Tong Hall, Tong Lane, Bradford BD4 0RR
Web site: https://www.perfect-tennis.com/
Freq: Daily
Circ: 7497
Editor: Jonathan Moss
Racquet Sports

Perfectly Polished
986830
Email: perfectlypolishednails@gmail.com
Web site: http://www.perfectly-polished-nails.com
Freq: Daily
Circ: 7757
Beauty & Grooming, Cosmetics, Fashion, Hair, Women's Interests

Periodismo de Paz
1061838
Web site: http://www.periodismodepaz.org/
Freq: Daily
Circ: 6223
Politics

Permanent Style
987926
Web site: www.permanentstyle.co.uk
Freq: Daily
Circ: 74628
Fashion

Perry's
1053887
Email: social@perrys.co.uk
Web site: http://www.perrys.co.uk/car-news/category/news/

UK Blogs

Freq: Daily
Circ: 139
Antique & Collectible Cars, Automakers,
Automotive, Driving, Motorcycles, Off-
road & 4-Wheel Drive Vehicles, Trucks &
SUVs

Persolaise
1101098
Tel: 44 07944 506368
Email: persolaise@gmail.com
Web site: http://persolaise.blogspot.co.uk
Freq: Daily
Circ: 9622
Cosmetics, Men's Interests

Personas Comunes
1060832
Web site: http://personascomunes.
blogspot.com
Freq: Daily
Circ: 3122
Airline Inflight, Environment, Railroad,
Travel

PETA UK Blog
998416
Editorial: People for the Ethical Treatment of
Animals Foundation, PO Box 70315, London
N1P 2RG Tel: 44 02078 376327
Email: mediainfo-uk@peta.org.uk
Web site: blog.peta.org.uk
Freq: Daily
Circ: 89
Charitable Foundations, Energy &
Environment, Nature & Wildlife, Veterinary
Medicine

Pete Ashton's weblog
1059419
Web site: http://theculturalomnivore.co.uk/
Freq: Daily
Circ: 521
News & Current Affairs

Pete Brown's Beer Blog
998093
Web site: petebrown.blogspot.com
Freq: Daily
Circ: 10882
Alcohol & Spirits, Bars, Clubs & Pubs,
Beer, Beverages, Cooking & Baking,
Food, Grocery Stores, Organic Food,
Restaurant Reviews, Vegetarianism &
Veganism

Pete Drinks
987843
Editorial: 71 Hutton Grove, North Finchley,
London N12 8DS
Web site: https://www.petedrinks.com/
Freq: Daily
Circ: 7502
Bars, Clubs & Pubs, Beer, Cooking &
Baking, Restaurant Reviews, Wine/
Winemaking

Peter Black AM
1054491
Tel: 44 01792 536353
Email: peter.black@assembly.wales
Web site: www.peter-black.net
Freq: Daily
Circ: 10524
Politics

Peter Black Blog
1054225
Editorial: Peter Black AM, 110 Walter Road,
Swansea SA1 5QQ
Email: cllr.peter.black@swansea.gov.uk
Web site: http://peterblack.blogspot.com
Freq: Daily
Circ: 9004
Politics

Petit Moi - Big World
1056766
Email: petitmoi.bigworld@gmail.com
Web site: http://www.petitmoi-bigworld.co.
uk/
Freq: Daily
Circ: 8532
Beauty & Grooming, Cooking & Baking,
Cosmetics, Family & Parenting, Fashion,
Hair, Health & Medicine, Literature,
Women's Interests

PetrolBlog
986326
Editorial: Lake Cottage, Lydford,
Okehampton EX20 4AJ
Tel: 44 01822 820268
Email: majorgav@petrolblog.com
Web site: www.petrolblog.com
Freq: Daily

Circ: 37728
Antique & Collectible Cars, Automakers,
Automotive, Driving, Motorcycles, Off-
road & 4-Wheel Drive Vehicles, Trucks &
SUVs

Petruscosas
1060880
Web site: http://petruscosas.blogspot.com/
Freq: Daily
Circ: 521
Classical/Choral/Band Music, Country,
Folk, Bluegrass, Dance Music, Jazz &
Blues, Music, Pop Music, R&B, Urban,
World, Rap & Hip Hop, Rock Music

PG's Tips
1053332
Web site: http://pgstips.blogspot.co.uk/
Freq: Daily
Circ: 9231
Casinos & Gaming, Horse Racing, Soccer

Pharside
1054223
Web site: www.pharside.co.uk
Freq: Daily
Circ: 130709
Africa, Consumer Affairs, Cricket,
Extreme/Adventure Sports, International
News, Men's Interests, Motorsports,
Movies & Video, Regional General
Interest, Rugby

Phil Bradley's Weblog
1054651
Email: philb@philb.com
Web site: http://mdxaccountingfinance.
blogspot.co.uk/
Freq: Daily
Circ: 521
Computers, Internet

Phil on Film
1053283
Email: philipconcannon@gmail.com
Web site: www.philonfilm.net
Freq: Daily
Circ: 8350
Entertainment, Movies & Video

Phil Race Blog
1056309
Email: phil@phil-race.co.uk
Web site: http://phil-race.co.uk/
Freq: Daily
Circ: 9496
Education, Higher Education

Philip Bloom Blog
1056764
Email: help@philipbloom.net
Web site: http://philipbloom.net/blog/
Freq: Daily
Circ: 9432
Audio Video Trade, Cameras, Electronics,
Entertainment, Movies & Video,
Photography, Visual Arts

Philip John
1054205
Web site: philipjohn.co.uk
Freq: Daily
Circ: 3597
Electronics, Internet

Philip Raby
1052600
Email: mail@philipraby.co.uk
Web site: http://philipraby.co.uk/blog-2
Freq: Daily
Circ: 59
Profile: Blog covering Porsche cars. PHILIP
RABY blog discusses anything from Porsche
cars to motoring. The blog has an archive
dating back to January 2010.
Automakers

Philocalist
997727
Editorial: 508 Fresh Apartments, 138 Chapel
Street, Salford M3 6DE
Email: info@philocalist.co.uk
Web site: www.philocalist.co.uk
Freq: Daily
Circ: 9832
Beauty & Grooming, Cosmetics, Fashion,
Hair, Women's Interests

Philosophy for Life
999161
Web site: http://philosophyforlife.org/
Freq: Daily
Circ: 14216
News & Current Affairs

Phil's Salesforce Tips
1100505
Editorial: Phil Walton Consultancy, 116 Pall
Mall, London SW1Y 5ED
Tel: 44 02071 010725
Web site: http://www.
philwaltonconsultancy.co.uk/blog/
Freq: Daily
Circ: 6748
Marketing

Philsorrell
1054222
Web site: http://philsorrell.com/
Freq: Daily
Circ: 9703
Outdoor Recreation

Phones Review
986891
Email: newstips@phonesreview.co.uk
Web site: phonesreview.co.uk
Freq: Daily
Circ: 1249075
Editor: Debbie Turner
Mobile Electronics

Photography Blog
986218
Editorial: 34-44 Tunstall Road, London SW9
8DA
Email: mark@photographyblog.com
Web site: www.photographyblog.com
Freq: Daily
Circ: 669203
Editor: Mark Goldstein
Photography

Photography For Blogs
1054276
Email: emma@emmadaviesphoto.com
Web site: http://www.photographyforblogs.
com/blog/
Freq: Daily
Circ: 3347
Profile: Blog covering photography and blog
tips.
Photography

Photography News
1053883
Web site: http://photography.news/
Freq: Daily
Circ: 4872
Photography

Photography, food, Chinese medicine and marketing
1062157
Web site: http://saulkarl.blogspot.com
Freq: Daily
Circ: 611
Food

Photos by H
1057078
Web site: http://photosbyh.blogspot.co.uk/
Freq: Daily
Circ: 10439
Cameras

Pi Pediatra
1060926
Web site: http://pipediatra.blogspot.com/
Freq: Daily
Circ: 1197
Pediatrics

The Piccadilly Lane Blog
999553
Editorial: Piccadilly Lane, LCB Depot, 31
Rutland Street, Leicester LE1 1RE
Tel: 44 01162 430924
Email: hello@piccadillylane.co.uk
Web site: piccadillylane.co.uk/blog/
Freq: Daily
Circ: 3802
Crafts, Shopping

The Picky Glutton
988039
Email: pickyglutton@gmail.com
Web site: plckyglutton.com
Freq: Daily
Circ: 9779
Profile: Blog covering food. The picky
glutton blog discusses anything from
restaurant reviews and food reviews. The
blog has an archive dating back to January
2011.
Restaurant Reviews

Picturehouse
1053735
Web site: http://picturehouseblog.co.uk/
Freq: Daily

Circ: 16539
Local Entertainment Guides, Movies &
Video

Pidempi korsi
1062013
Email: pidempikorsi@gmail.com
Web site: http://pidempikorsi.tumblr.com/
Freq: Daily
Circ: 91
Vegetarianism & Veganism

Piel y Alma
1061326
Web site: http://elblogdeyimmi.blogspot.
com/
Freq: Daily
Circ: 1797
Lifestyle, Men's Interests, Regional
General Interest, Women's Interests

Piel-L Latinoamericana
1061472
Web site: http://piel-l.org/blog/
Freq: Daily
Circ: 6912
Cosmetics, Dermatology

Pieni Pilvenhattara
1062044
Email: pienipilvenhattara@luukku.com
Web site: http://pienipilvilinnani.blogspot.fi/
Freq: Daily
Circ: 1159
Architecture & Design, Do-It-Yourself
(DIY), Gardening, Home, Property
Management & Maintenance, Real Estate

Pierda Grasa Abdominal
1060600
Web site: http://pierdagrasaabdominalblog.
com/
Freq: Daily
Circ: 521
Fitness & Exercise, Nutrition

Pierre Le Cat
987790
Editorial: 6 Flower Street, Carlisle CA1 2JW
Email: pierrelecatblogger@gmail.com
Web site: http://www.pierrelecat.com/
Freq: Daily
Circ: 989
Profile: Blog covering fashion. PIERRE LE
CAT discusses anything from outfits and
jewellery to lifestyle.
Beauty & Grooming, Cosmetics, Fashion,
Hair, Shopping, Women's Interests

Pigeon Pair and Me
1054571
Web site: pigeonpairandme.com
Freq: Daily
Circ: 11893
Profile: Blog covering event guides, family
travel, child care, home decorating,
gardening, family and parenting. The blog
has an archive dating back to November
2012. This outlet offers a vlog.
Family & Parenting

Pihkala
1061448
Email: talopihkala@gmail.com
Web site: http://talopihkala.blogspot.fi/
Freq: Daily
Circ: 5880
Architecture & Design, Do-It-Yourself
(DIY), Gardening, Home, Property
Management & Maintenance, Real Estate

Pikku Punapippuri
1061955
Email: punapippuri@pikkupunapippuri.com
Web site: http://www.pikkupunapippuri.
com/
Freq: Daily
Circ: 7865
Nature & Wildlife

Pilares Básicos
1062003
Web site: http://pilaresbasicos.blogspot.
com/
Freq: Daily
Circ: 521
Celebrities, Disability, Education, Higher
Education, Preschool, Schools &
Institutions, Students

Pilgrim with a Passport
1053077
Email: journeymanjim@hotmail.com
Web site: pilgrimwithapassport.blogspot.co.
uk
Freq: Daily
Circ: 521
Travel

Pills & Pillow-Talk 996287
Web site: pillsandpillowtalk.com
Freq: Daily
Circ: 8264
Health & Medicine

Pinguicas 1061601
Web site: http://pinguicas.com/wp/
Freq: Daily
Family & Parenting, Lifestyle, Men's Interests, Obstetrics & Gynecology (OB/GYN), Regional General Interest, Women's Interests

Pink Haired Princess 997553
Email: pinkhairedprincess@hotmail.co.uk
Web site: www.pinkhairedprincess.blogspot.com
Freq: Daily
Circ: 1456
Beauty & Grooming, Cosmetics, Fashion, Hair, Women's Interests

The Pink House 1053139
Editorial: 56 Duncombe Hill, London SE23 1QB
Email: hello@pinkhouse.co.uk
Web site: www.pinkhouse.co.uk
Freq: Daily
Circ: 7849
Art, Do-It-Yourself (DIY), Restaurant Reviews

Pink Julep 987410
Editorial: 324 Upper Richmond Road, Flat 1, London SW15 6TL
Web site: pinkjulepabroad.com
Freq: Daily
Circ: 8294
Art, Beauty & Grooming, Cooking & Baking, Cosmetics, Fashion, Hair, Travel, Women's Interests

pink tentacle 1061799
Email: edo@pinktentacle.com
Web site: http://pinktentacle.com
Freq: Daily
Circ: 39144
Antiques/Collectibles, Art, Arts, Literature, Photography, Theater & Performing Arts, Visual Arts

Pink Therapy Blog 1052568
Email: admin@pinktherapy.com
Web site: pinktherapyblog.com
Freq: Daily
Circ: 1621
LGBT

Pink Wedding Days 1053756
Email: online@pinkweddingdays.co.uk
Web site: http://pinkweddingdays.blogspot.co.uk/
Freq: Daily
Circ: 9307
Profile: Blog covering civil partnerships and same sex marriage in the UK. The blog has an archive dating back to December 2010 and shares an short blog roll.
LGBT, Sexuality, Weddings

The Pink Whisk 985720
Tel: 44 01625 262743
Web site: www.thepinkwhisk.co.uk
Freq: Daily
Circ: 6536
Editor: Ruth Clemens
Alcohol & Spirits, Bars, Clubs & Pubs, Beer, Beverages, Cooking & Baking, Food, Grocery Stores, Organic Food, Restaurant Reviews, Vegetarianism & Veganism

Pinkoddy 988216
Email: pinkoddballs@hotmail.co.uk
Web site: http://pinkoddy.co.uk/blog/
Freq: Daily
Circ: 15069
Profile: Blog covering motherhood. PINKODDY blog discusses anything from motherhood and family to parenting. The blog shares and shares an extensive blog roll. The outlet offers RSS (Really Simple Syndication).
Disability, Family & Parenting, Health & Medicine

Pippa Jameson Interiors 985338
Editorial: Office 5M, 5 Bridge Street, Bishops Stortford, Bishop's Stortford CM23 2JU Tel: 44 01279 370030
Web site: pippajamesoninteriors.co.uk
Freq: Daily
Circ: 9230
Architecture & Design, Do-It-Yourself (DIY), Gardening, Home, Property Management & Maintenance, Real Estate

Pixel Health 988648
Web site: pixelhealth.net
Circ: 14081
Alternative Medicine, Audio Video Trade, Cameras, Consumer Electronics, Disability, Fitness & Exercise, Health & Medicine, Media Relations, Medicine, Mobile Electronics

The Pixie Cut 988405
Email: thepixiecut@gmail.com
Web site: www.thepixiecut.co.uk
Freq: Daily
Circ: 7594
Beauty & Grooming, Cosmetics, Fashion, Hair, Photography, Women's Interests

Pixie's Crafty Workshop 1056771
Web site: pixiescraftyworkshop.blogspot.co.uk
Freq: Daily
Circ: 940
Crafts

PixiWoo 987042
Tel: 44 02072 336425
Web site: www.pixiwoo.com
Freq: Daily
Circ: 47480
Beauty & Grooming, Cosmetics, Hair

pixiwoo Vlog 1070238
Web site: https://www.youtube.com/user/pixiwoo
Freq: Daily
Circ: 464
Beauty & Grooming, Cosmetics, Hair

Pixmedial 1060356
Web site: http://www.pixmedial.net/blog
Freq: Daily
Circ: 11
Auto Aftermarket, Computers, Data Management, Electronics, Government Technology, Industry, Internet, Mobile Communications, Security & Security Systems, Software

PJH Law Blog 996980
Editorial: 16 Wharf Road, Stamford, Stamford PE9 2EB Tel: 44 01780 757589
Email: enquiries@pjhlaw.co.uk
Web site: www.pjhlaw.co.uk/blog
Freq: Daily
Circ: 796
Employment

Plan UK Blogs 999592
Editorial: Finsgate, 5-7 Cranwood Street, London EC1V 9LH Tel: 44 02076 081311
Email: ukmedia@plan-international.org
Web site: https://plan-uk.org/blogs
Freq: Daily
Charitable Foundations, Social Issues

Planes de Ahorro y Seguros 1061218
Web site: http://plandeahorroyseguros.blogspot.com/
Freq: Daily
Circ: 521
Insurance

Planes Trains Automobiles 1054060
Email: contact@planestrainsautomobiles.co.uk
Web site: www.planestrainsautomobiles.co.uk
Freq: Daily
Circ: 1877
Automotive, Aviation, Railroad, Shipping & Warehousing, Supply Chain Management (SCM), Transportation

Planet Hugill 1052644
Web site: www.planethugill.com
Freq: Daily
Circ: 12380
Classical/Choral/Band Music

Planet Organic Blog 1053297
Email: talktous@planetorganic.com
Web site: www.planetorganic.com/blog/
Freq: Daily
Circ: 27
Organic Food

Planet Print 1054039
Email: planetprint8@gmail.com
Web site: http://planet-print.blogspot.co.uk/
Freq: Daily
Circ: 8743
Literature

Planet Property CEASED 986980
Web site: planetpropertyblog.co.uk
Freq: Daily
Circ: 842
Profile: Blog covering property and the UK housing market. The blog has an archive dating back to November 2010.
Property Management & Maintenance

Planet Veggie 986510
Web site: www.planetveggie.co.uk
Freq: Daily
Circ: 9925
Profile: Blog covering vegetarian food. The Planet Veggie blog discusses anything from vegetarian food and recipes to cookbooks and competitions. The blog has an archive dating back to January 2009 and shares a short blog roll.
Alcohol & Spirits, Bars, Clubs & Pubs, Beer, Beverages, Cooking & Baking, Food, Grocery Stores, Organic Food, Restaurant Reviews, Vegetarianism & Veganism

Plano Creativo 1060669
Web site: http://planocreativo.wordpress.com
Freq: Daily
Circ: 196
Lifestyle, Men's Interests, Neurology, Regional General Interest, Women's Interests

Plans and Presents 987778
Editorial: 69 Levernbridge Road, The Hurlet, Glasgow G53 7AB Tel: 44 07969 690832
Web site: http://www.mrspandp.com
Freq: Daily
Circ: 15142
Profile: PLANS AND PRESENTS blog covers weddings.
Weddings

Plantaliscious 1054432
Web site: http://plantaliscious.janetbruten.co.uk
Freq: Daily
Circ: 2796
Profile: Blog covering gardening. Plantaliscious discusses anything from plants and allotments to gardening advice. The blog has an archive dating back to January 2009 and shares an extensive blogroll. The outlet offers RSS (Really Simple Syndication).
Gardening

Plataforma Arquitectura 1060455
Web site: http://www.plataformaarquitectura.cl
Freq: Daily
Circ: 1161241
Architecture & Design, Building & Construction, Family & Parenting, Lifestyle, Men's Interests, Regional General Interest, Women's Interests

Plataforma Urbana 1060591
Web site: http://www.plataformaurbana.cl
Freq: Daily
Circ: 540856
Antiques/Collectibles, Art, Arts, Bars, Clubs & Pubs, Comedy, Entertainment, Literature, Local Entertainment Guides, Movies & Video, Photography

Playing by the Book 987306
Email: zoe.toft@kuvik.net
Web site: www.playingbythebook.net
Freq: Daily
Circ: 18342
Literature

PlayPennies 985730
Email: playpennies@gmail.com
Web site: www.playpennies.com
Freq: Daily
Circ: 136326
Family & Parenting

Plodding Along Nicely 995529
Web site: http://www.ploddingalongnicely.com/
Freq: Daily
Circ: 521
Profile: Plodding Along Nicely covers running and marathons. The blog has an archive dating back to February 2013 and shares a short blogroll.
Bicycles, Fitness & Exercise, Sports

Plum 1061840
Email: plumplum@163.com
Web site: http://plum.blog.sohu.com
Freq: Daily
Circ: 156
Cooking & Baking, Food, Nutrition

Plum mum 1061650
Email: signe@plummum.dk
Web site: http://plummum.dk/
Freq: Daily
Circ: 1708
Elementary School, Family & Parenting, Lifestyle, Men's Interests, Preschool, Regional General Interest, Teen/Young Adult, Trading Cards & Comics, Women's Interests

Pluma Liberal 1061277
Web site: http://www.lilianafasciani.blogspot.com/
Freq: Daily
Circ: 1043
National News, Politics

Poder y Nación 1062004
Web site: http://www.poderynacion.com
Freq: Daily
Circ: 845
Politics

The Policy Press 996974
Editorial: 1-9 Old Park Hill, Bristol BS2 0BB
Tel: 44 01179 545940
Email: pp-info@bristol.ac.uk
Web site: policypress.wordpress.com
Freq: Daily
Circ: 120468
Politics

Polish this! 1061445
Email: polishthis@gmail.com
Web site: http://www.polishthisblog.com/
Freq: Daily
Circ: 1410
Beauty & Grooming, Cosmetics, Hair

Politica de Guatemala 1061812
Web site: http://www.politicagt.com
Freq: Daily
Circ: 720
National News, Politics

Política y Politología 1061811
Web site: http://politicaypolitologia.blogspot.com
Freq: Daily
Circ: 611
Politics

Political Betting 986220
Web site: politicalbetting.com
Freq: Daily
Circ: 59341
Politics

Political Scrapbook 986221
Editorial: 40 Underwood Street, London N1 7JQ
Email: news@politicalscrapbook.net
Web site: politicalscrapbook.net
Freq: Daily

UK Blogs

Circ: 104533
Politics

politicaladvertising.co.uk
999267
Tel: 44 07525 952097
Email: pringleb@amvbbdo.com
Web site: politicaladvertising.co.uk
Freq: Daily
Circ: 12223
Politics

Polkadot Pink
1054230
Email: polkadot_pinky@hotmail.com
Web site: www.polkadot-pink.com
Freq: Daily
Circ: 11000
Profile: Blog covering fashion. Polkadot Pink blog discusses anything from fashion and beauty to book reviews, music, travel and product reviews. The blog has an archive dating back to November 2012 and shares an extensive blog roll.
Fashion, Women's Interests

POLLIANI
1060564
Email: jankapolliani@gmail.com
Web site: http://www.polliani.com/
Freq: Daily
Circ: 6465
Beauty & Grooming, Cosmetics, Fashion, Hair

Pollyanne B
1073408
Web site: http://www.pollyanneb.blogspot.co.uk/
Freq: Daily
Circ: 521
Beauty & Grooming, Cosmetics, Fashion, Hair, Women's Interests

Pommie Travels
987588
Web site: http://www.pommietravels.com/blog/
Freq: Daily
Circ: 1841
Travel

The Popcorn Muncher
988738
Email: thepopcornmuncher@gmail.com
Web site: http://thepopcornmuncher.com/
Freq: Daily
Circ: 11548
Profile: Blog covering film. THE POPCORN MUNCHER discusses anything from blockbusters and independent film to world cinema. The outlet offers RSS (Really Simple Syndication).
Movies & Video

Poppy Cross
1100041
Email: poppy.cross.co.uk@gmail.com
Web site: http://poppycross.co.uk/
Freq: Daily
Circ: 8954
Beauty & Grooming, Cooking & Baking, Cosmetics, Hair, Nutrition, Travel

Poppy Loves
987645
Email: poppyloves1@gmail.com
Web site: http://www.poppyloves.co.uk/
Freq: Daily
Circ: 69106
Women's Interests

PoppyD
997997
Web site: http://poppyd.com/
Freq: Daily
Circ: 23918
Beauty & Grooming, Cooking & Baking, Cosmetics, Fashion, Hair, Restaurant Reviews, Travel

POPSUGAR UK
986369
Editorial: 2nd Floor, Moray House, 23-31 Great Titchfield Street, London W1W 7PA
Web site: www.popsugar.co.uk
Circ: 771754
Profile: Website covering fashion. The website discusses fashion as well as lifestyle and beauty.
Celebrities, Fashion, Lifestyle, Men's Interests, Regional General Interest, Women's Interests

POPtalk
1053722
Tel: 44 08001 412404
Email: info@brainpop.co.uk

Web site: http://www.brainpop.co.uk/blog/
Freq: Daily
Circ: 99
Education

Population Matters
1054599
Tel: 44 02035 444950
Email: enquiries@populationmatters.org
Web site: http://www.populationmatters.org/2015/blog/
Freq: Daily
Circ: 1
Charitable Foundations, Community Care (UK)

Position Ignition
987367
Email: enquiries@positionignition.com
Web site: http://www.positionignition.com/blog/
Freq: Daily
Circ: 6556
Careers

Positive Letters... Inspirational Stories
1054940
Web site: http://positiveletters.blogspot.co.uk/
Freq: Daily
Circ: 9700
Literature, Travel, Women's Interests

Postcards from across the pond
1053577
Web site: http://www.pcfatp.com/
Freq: Daily
Circ: 2694
Expatriates, Literature

POTLATCH
1053730
Web site: http://potlatch.typepad.com/weblog/
Freq: Daily
Circ: 117815
Profile: Blog covering sociology. POTLATCH blog discusses anything from current affairs and politics to public issues and economics. The blog has an archive dating back to April 2013. The outlet offers RSS (Really Simple Syndication).
Economics, Politics

Pound Sterling Forecast
1053955
Web site: http://www.poundsterlingforecast.com
Freq: Daily
Circ: 39931
Personal Finance

Pousta
1060486
Web site: http://www.pousta.com
Freq: Daily
Circ: 53988
Advertising Industry, Art, Bars, Clubs & Pubs, Comedy, Entertainment, Local Entertainment Guides, Movies & Video

Pouting in Heels
988909
Web site: http://www.poutinginheels.com/
Freq: Daily
Circ: 24606
Profile: Blog covering life, love, motherhood, fashion, freelancing and women's issues. The blog has an archive dating back to February 2012 and shares an extensive blogroll. This outlet also offers a vlog.
Beauty & Grooming, Cosmetics, Crafts, Family & Parenting, Fashion, Hair, Women's Interests

Power Is A State Of Mind
996739
Editorial: 62 Vincent Avenue, Oldham OL4 2RW
Web site: http://powerisastateofmind.blogspot.co.uk/?zx=7f7c1df5b684e88c
Freq: Daily
Circ: 10709
Celebrities, Men's Interests

PR Girl State of Mind
994999
Editorial: 55 Anson Road, London NW2 3UY
Tel: 44 07961 515642
Email: andrea@prgirlstateofmind.com
Web site: http://www.prgirlstateofmind.com/
Freq: Daily
Circ: 787
Advertising Industry, Branding, Broadcasting, Graphic Design, Marketing,

---

Media & Communications, Photography, Publishing

PR Studies
1054195
Email: rbailey@pobox.com
Web site: http://prstudies.com/
Freq: Daily
Circ: 8817
Branding, Marketing

PrAACtical AAC
996522
Email: carole@praacticalaac.org
Web site: http://praacticalaac.org/
Freq: Daily
Circ: 35655
Disability

Practical Action blogs
997758
Editorial: The Schumacher Centre, Bourton on Dunsmore, Rugby CV23 9QZ
Tel: 44 01926 634510
Email: news@practicalaction.org.uk
Web site: http://practicalaction.org/blog/
Freq: Daily
Circ: 12
Charitable Foundations

Practical Ethics
997746
Web site: http://blog.practicalethics.ox.ac.uk/
Freq: Daily
Circ: 24035
Ethical/Moral Issues, National News, Religion, Social Issues

Pragmatist
1053328
Web site: http://sdj-pragmatist.blogspot.co.uk/
Freq: Daily
Circ: 10466
Consumer Affairs

Praxis Sur
1061061
Web site: http://polog.blogsome.com
Freq: Daily
Circ: 381127
Politics

The Pregnant Beauty Guide
987194
Email: pregnantbeautyguide@gmail.com
Web site: https://mum-face.com/
Circ: 9974
Beauty & Grooming, Cosmetics, Family & Parenting, Hair

Pregnantcitygirl
987813
Editorial: 37 The Ave, London NW6 7NR
Email: pr@pregnantcitygirl.com
Web site: pregnantcitygirl.com
Freq: Daily
Circ: 26579
Family & Parenting

Preston Precious
1053953
Web site: http://www.prestonprecious.com/
Freq: Daily
Circ: 6644
Family & Parenting

Pretty Big Butterflies
1054350
Email: prettybigbutterflies@gmail.com
Web site: prettybigbutterflies.com
Freq: Daily
Circ: 13997
Profile: Pretty Big Butterflies covers plus size fashion, beauty and lifestyle. The blog has an archive dating back to July 2013.
Cosmetics, Fashion, Women's Interests

Pretty Green Tea
1054312
Email: daisy@prettygreentea.com
Web site: www.prettygreentea.com
Freq: Daily
Circ: 27056
Careers, Cooking & Baking, Cosmetics, Women's Interests

Pretty Normal Me
1074065
Email: press@prettynormalme.com
Web site: http://prettynormalme.com/
Freq: Daily
Circ: 14638
Editor: Emily Clarkson
Fitness & Exercise, Nutrition, Women's Interests

Pride's Purge
987334
Email: tompridespurge@gmail.com
Web site: tompride.wordpress.com
Freq: Daily
Circ: 52170
National News, Politics

Prime
1053067
Editorial: PRIME Economics, Lafone House, Leathermarket, Weston Street, London SE1 3ER
Email: portia.sale@primeeconomics.org
Web site: www.primeeconomics.org/articles/
Freq: Daily
Circ: 37
Profile: Blog covering economy. Prime blog discusses anything from current economic policy and mainstream economics to the finance sector and 'the impact of credit on the economy and ecosystem'. The outlet offers RSS (Really Simple Syndication).
Economics, National News, Politics, Social Issues

Prime:Time
997987
Web site: primetimepr.co.uk
Freq: Daily
Circ: 11146
Branding, Marketing

Primera Clase
1062068
Web site: http://www.primera-clase.com/
Freq: Daily
Circ: 611
Airline Inflight, Defense & National Security, Engineering, Industry, Manufacturing, Marine & Boat Trade, Mining & Quarrying, National News, Paper, Plastics

Print & Pattern
988174
Email: bowiestyle@hotmail.co.uk
Web site: http://printpattern.blogspot.co.uk/
Freq: Daily
Circ: 8385
Crafts, Graphic Design

The Printsome Blog
996802
Editorial: 3rd Floor, 207 Regent Street, London W1B 4ND Tel: 44 02035 982599
Email: info@printsome.com
Web site: https://blog.printsome.com/
Freq: Daily
Circ: 57739
Fashion

Printster Blog
1054584
Tel: 44 03302 232202
Email: sales@printster.co.uk
Web site: www.printster.co.uk/blog
Freq: Daily
Circ: 137
Shopping

Private Dining Rooms Blog
1055305
Editorial: 38 Whitehall Gardens, London W3 9RD
Web site: www.privatediningrooms.co.uk
Freq: Daily
Circ: 9680
Bars, Clubs & Pubs, Hotels/Motels, Marketing, Restaurant Reviews

The Private Life Of A Girl
1053295
Web site: www.theprivatelifeofagirl.com
Freq: Daily
Circ: 43399
Profile: Blog covering beauty. THE PRIVATE LIFE OF A GIRL blog discusses anything from fashion and lifestyle to beauty. The blog has an archive dating back to May 2013.
Beauty & Grooming, Cosmetics, Fashion, Hair, Travel, Women's Interests

Product Reviews
986223
Editorial: 16 Beech Drive, Broadstairs, Broadstairs CT10 2LL
Email: generalnews@product-reviews.net
Web site: http://www.product-reviews.net
Circ: 1281932

Profile: Blog covering product reviews of cosmetics, beauty supplies, food, drink and (PR) events

Audio Video Trade, Cameras, Consumer Electronics, Mobile Electronics, Movies & Video

Professor Falken
1061531

Web site: http://professor-falken.com/
Freq: Daily
Circ: 11554
Computers, Software

Promise of Reason
1061387

Email: mail@promiseofreason.com
Web site: http://www.promiseofreason.com
Freq: Daily
Circ: 521
Politics, Social Issues

Propellernet Blog
1052836

Editorial: Castle Square House, 9 Castle Square, Brighton BN1 1EG
Tel: 44 01273 760950
Email: info@propellernet.co.uk
Web site: http://www.propellernet.co.uk/our-blog
Freq: Daily
News & Current Affairs

Property in Virginia Water
996843

Editorial: The Estate Office, 2 Station Approach, Virginia Water, London GU25 4DL
Tel: 44 01344 843000
Email: homes@bartonwyatt.co.uk
Web site: www.bartonwyatt.blogspot.co.uk
Freq: Daily
Circ: 521
Property Management & Maintenance

Property Investment & Landlord Blog
999249

Email: info@propertyinvestmentproject.co.uk
Web site: www.propertyinvestmentproject.co.uk/blog
Freq: Daily
Circ: 31554
Property Management & Maintenance

Propertynewshound
999489

Web site: propertynewshound.blogspot.com
Freq: Daily
Circ: 1285
News & Current Affairs

Protection Insurance
1053215

Web site: protection-insurance.com/
Freq: Daily
Circ: 521
Insurance, Personal Finance

Protein
1054343

Editorial: 31 New Inn Yard, Shoreditch, London EC2A 3EY
Email: info@prote.in
Web site: https://www.prote.in/
Freq: Daily
Circ: 48119
Branding, Marketing

Protesta Militar
1060857

Freq: Daily
Defense & National Security, Politics

Protz on Beer.
988949

Web site: http://protzonbeer.co.uk/news
Freq: Daily
Circ: 119
Alcohol & Spirits

Provident Blog
1059122

Web site: https://www.providentpersonalcredit.com/blog/
Freq: Daily
Circ: 8523
Personal Finance

Proyecto Sandía
1060911

Web site: http://www.proyectosandia.com.ar/
Freq: Daily
Circ: 5175
Lifestyle, Men's Interests, National News, Regional General Interest, Science, Women's Interests

Psicologa Consultora
1060767

Web site: http://psicologaconsultora.blogspot.com/
Freq: Daily
Circ: 1297
Books, Lifestyle, Literature, Men's Interests, Neurology, Regional General Interest, Women's Interests

Psicología - Malena Lede
1062007

Web site: http://psicologia-malenalede.blogspot.com/
Freq: Daily
Circ: 812
Neurology

Psicología Positiva
1061157

Web site: http://psicologiapositivauruguay.wordpress.com/
Freq: Daily
Circ: 28
Neurology

Psicologia Tecnologica
1060869

Web site: http://psicologiatecnologica.blogspot.com/
Freq: Daily
Circ: 1866
Auto Aftermarket, Computers, Data Management, Electronics, Government Technology, Industry, Internet, Mobile Communications, Neurology, Security & Security Systems

Psicologos en San Miguel
1061410

Web site: http://psicoapertura.blogspot.com/
Freq: Daily
Circ: 521
Neurology

Psicologos Peru
1061511

Web site: http://psicologosperu.blogspot.com/
Freq: Daily
Circ: 9668
Neurology

Psicomotricidad
1060865

Web site: http://www.psico-motricidad.com.ar/
Freq: Daily
Circ: 842
Neurology

Psicopedagoga Villa Antigua
1060640

Web site: http://www.psicopedagogavillaantiguacom.blogspot.com
Freq: Daily
Circ: 521
Disability, Education, Higher Education, Preschool, Schools & Institutions, Students

The Public and Health Research: Simon Denegri's Lay Review
996867

Email: info@amrc.org.uk
Web site: http://simondenegri.com/
Freq: Daily
Circ: 13758
Charitable Foundations, Medicine

Public health matters
1052959

Editorial: Public Health England, Wellington House, 133 - 155 Waterloo Road, London SE1 8UG **Tel:** 44 02076 548000
Email: phe-pressoffice@phe.gov.uk
Web site: https://publichealthmatters.blog.gov.uk/
Freq: Daily
Circ: 92619
Health & Medicine

Public Sector IT
986224

Editorial: Quadrant House, The Quadrant, Sutton SM2 5AS **Tel:** 44 02086 528642
Email: computer.weekly@rbi.co.uk
Web site: http://www.computerweekly.com/blog/Public-Sector-IT
Freq: Daily

Circ: 8299
Computers, Data Management, Internet, Mobile Communications, Software

Publicidad Creativa
1060467

Web site: http://www.lawebdelpublicista.blogspot.com
Freq: Daily
Circ: 1875
Advertising Industry, Graphic Design, Marketing

publishedmoments
1053764

Editorial: 97A Mortimer Road, Bristol BS34 7LH
Email: publishedmoments@gmail.com
Web site: http://publishedmoments.co.uk/
Freq: Daily
Circ: 8994
Literature

Pudding Lane
996855

Web site: http://www.puddinglaneblog.co.uk/
Freq: Daily
Circ: 10043
Cooking & Baking

Puerto Morelos Blog
1060821

Web site: http://www.puertomorelosblog.com
Freq: Daily
Circ: 2294
Airline Inflight, Property Management & Maintenance, Railroad, Travel

Puffin blog
1053307

Email: puffin@uk.penguingroup.com
Web site: http://blog.puffin.co.uk/
Freq: Daily
Circ: 23
Literature

Pulse Blog
999213

Editorial: 140 London Wall, Puddle Dock, London EC2Y 5DN **Tel:** 44 02079 218716
Email: feedback@pulsetoday.co.uk
Web site: http://www.pulsetoday.co.uk/news/live-blogs
Freq: Daily
Circ: 27
Editor: Nigel Praities
Health Administration, Healthcare Industry, Medicine

Punch Records
1055932

Email: rayp@punch-records.co.uk
Web site: http://punch-records.co.uk/
Freq: Daily
Circ: 14259
News & Current Affairs

PunkChyaz
987601

Email: punkchyaz@hotmail.co.uk
Web site: www.chyaz.com
Freq: Daily
Circ: 8416
Beauty & Grooming, Cosmetics, Fashion, Hair, Women's Interests

Punta del este design
1062106

Web site: http://disenosdeleste.blogspot.com/
Freq: Daily
Circ: 521
Architecture & Design, Interior Design

Punto Geek
1062032

Web site: http://www.puntogeek.com/
Freq: Daily
Circ: 146711
Auto Aftermarket, Computers, Data Management, Electronics, Government Technology, Industry, Internet, Mobile Communications, Mobile Electronics, Security & Security Systems

Punto Medio
1060820

Web site: http://blogs.clarin.com/punto-medio/
Freq: Daily
Circ: 61948
Advertising Industry, Branding, Broadcasting, Graphic Design, Marketing, Media & Communications, Photography, Publishing

Pure 360 Blog
996506

Editorial: Unit A-E, Level 3 South, New England House, New England Street, Brighton BN1 4GH **Tel:** 44 08447 042419
Email: marketing@pure360.com
Web site: pure360.com/blog
Freq: Daily
Circ: 7098
Marketing

The Pure Package Blog
999640

Editorial: Arches 38, 39 & 40, New Covent Garden Market, London SW8 5PP
Tel: 44 02077 203250
Email: info@purepackage.com
Web site: purepackage.com
Freq: Daily
Circ: 1365
Editor: Laura Birkby
Cooking & Baking, Nutrition

Pure Powder
987708

Editorial: 114 Chiswick High Road, London W4 1PU **Tel:** 44 02077 368191
Email: info@purepowder.com
Web site: http://www.purepowder.com/blog/
Freq: Daily
Circ: 89
Travel, Winter Sports

Pure Spa UK
1054097

Tel: 44 08435 071888
Email: info@purespauk.com
Web site: http://blog.purespauk.com/
Freq: Daily
Circ: 2
Fitness & Exercise

PureTravel Blog
986725

Editorial: Pure Travel, Seymour House, 30-34 Muspole Street, Norwich NR3 1DJ
Tel: 44 08452 997456
Email: enquiries@puretravel.com
Web site: www.puretravel.com/blog
Freq: Daily
Circ: 61
Travel

Purple Ella
1054597

Email: ella@purpleella.com
Web site: www.purplemum.com
Freq: Daily
Circ: 5037
Cooking & Baking, Family & Parenting, Health & Medicine, Women's Interests

Purple Persuasion
997995

Email: bipolarblogger2011@gmail.com
Web site: https://purplepersuasion.wordpress.com/
Freq: Daily
Circ: 67759
Health & Medicine

Purple Podded Peas
1053038

Web site: purplepoddedpeas.blogspot.co.uk
Freq: Daily
Circ: 8208
Art, Do-It-Yourself (DIY), Gardening

The Purple Pumpkin Blog
987808

Tel: 44 07834 872416
Email: thepurplepumpkinblog@gmail.com
Web site: thepurplepumpkinblog.co.uk/
Freq: Daily
Circ: 88676
Profile: The Purple Pumpkin Blog covers photography, travel (UK, Europe, USA + Disney), events, food, lifestyle (plus size fashion, family etc). The blog has an archive dating back to November 2011.
Cooking & Baking, Do-It-Yourself (DIY), Photography, Travel

Push Square
988179

Editorial: Unit 3, Loughborough Technology Centre, Loughborough LE11 3GE
Web site: http://www.pushsquare.com/
Circ: 261887
Editor: Sammy Barker
Profile: Website covering technology. Shares the latest news and reviews on technology and video games.
Computer & Video Games

UK Blogs

Push Start 997613
Email: pr@push-start.co.uk
Web site: http://www.push-start.co.uk/
Freq: Daily
Circ: 13005
Computer & Video Games

Push Ups and Pedicures 995490
Web site: pushupsandpedicures.com
Freq: Daily
Circ: 752
Fitness & Exercise

Pyllermor 1061313
Email: pyllermor@outlook.dk
Web site: http://www.pyllermor.dk/
Freq: Daily
Circ: 1218
Elementary School, Family & Parenting, Lifestyle, Men's Interests, Preschool, Regional General Interest, Teen/Young Adult, Trading Cards & Comics, Women's Interests

QI Biocomunicacion 1062124
Web site: http://qi-biocomunication.blogspot.com/
Freq: Daily
Circ: 641
Health & Medicine, Science

The Quackometer 999446
Web site: www.quackometer.net
Freq: Daily
Circ: 16178
News & Current Affairs

Quaequam Blog! 1053429
Email: semajmaharg@gmail.com
Web site: www.theliberati.net/quaequamblog
Freq: Daily
Circ: 4550
Politics

Qualys blog 1053333
Editorial: Qualys Ltd, 100 Brooke Drive, Green Park, Reading RG2 6UJ
Tel: 44 01189 131500
Email: info-uk@qualys.com
Web site: https://blog.qualys.com/
Freq: Daily
Circ: 450659
Auto Aftermarket, Computers, Data Management, Electronics, Government Technology, Industry, Internet, Mobile Communications, Security & Security Systems, Software

Que Biologia 1061057
Web site: http://biologiaunc.blogspot.com
Freq: Daily
Circ: 1522
Environment, Science

Que la Pases Lindo 1061172
Web site: http://www.quelapaseslindo.com.ar
Freq: Daily
Circ: 37112
Lifestyle, Men's Interests, Regional General Interest, Women's Interests

Que Tranzala Banda 1061197
Web site: http://quetranzalabanda.com
Freq: Daily
Circ: 1117
Airline Inflight, Antiques/Collectibles, Art, Arts, Bars, Clubs & Pubs, Comedy, Entertainment, Literature, Local Entertainment Guides, Movies & Video

Queer Ideas 986225
Web site: www.queerideas.co.uk
Freq: Daily
Circ: 17993
Charitable Foundations

QueryClick Blog 1052889
Editorial: 7 Castle Street, Edinburgh EH2 3AH Tel: 44 01315 567078
Email: hello@queryclick.com
Web site: http://uk.queryclick.com/en/news/
Freq: Daily
Circ: 14102
Branding, Computers, Internet, Marketing

Quick Fix Beauty 998000
Web site: http://amanda.wales/
Freq: Daily
Cosmetics

Quintessentially Travel Blog 1053553
Editorial: 29 Portland Place, London W1B 1QB Tel: 44 02070 226560
Email: info@quintessentiallytravel.com
Web site: www.quintessentiallytravel.com/en-gb/blog
Freq: Daily
Circ: 15
Airline Inflight, Railroad, Travel

The Quirky Traveller 1053341
Tel: 44 01524 735715
Web site: http://www.thequirkytraveller.com/
Freq: Daily
Circ: 43162
Travel

Quite Frankly She Said 1065608
Web site: http://www.quitefranklyshesaid.com
Freq: Daily
Circ: 28749
Profile: Blog covering lifestyle. QUITE FRANKLY SHE SAID blog discusses anything from beauty and motherhood to food. The blog has an archive dating back to September 2011.
Travel, Women's Interests

Rachel Andrew 1052921
Freq: Daily
News & Current Affairs

Rachel Lucie Blog 1052629
Web site: http://blog.rachellucie.co.uk
Freq: Daily
Circ: 262
Photography

Rachel Ogden Journalist 1053410
Email: rachelogdenjourno@gmail.com
Web site: http://rachelogden.wordpress.com/blog
Freq: Daily
Circ: 1215
Profile: Blog covering interior design. RACHEL OGDEN JOURNALIST blog discusses anything from design trends and furniture to colour schemes and DIY. The blog has an archive dating back to April 2013.
Do-It-Yourself (DIY), Interior Design, Women's Interests

Rachel Phipps 987950
Web site: www.rachelphipps.com
Freq: Daily
Circ: 6692
Editor: Rachel Phipps
Alcohol & Spirits, Bars, Clubs & Pubs, Beer, Beverages, Cooking & Baking, Food, Grocery Stores, Organic Food, Restaurant Reviews, Vegetarianism & Veganism

Rachel Wheeley Tiny Idiot 1053334
Email: rachelclarewheeley@gmail.com
Web site: http://rachelwheeley.com/
Freq: Daily
Circ: 521
Comedy, Science, Women's Interests

Rach's Place 1053921
Web site: confessionofsahm.com
Freq: Daily
Circ: 4951
Family & Parenting, Relationships, Women's Interests

Radio Clash 988327
Email: tim@radioclash.com
Web site: http://www.radioclash.com/
Freq: Daily
Circ: 8496
Dance Music

RadioKidz@LifeLog 1061646
Web site: http://www.neoearly.net

Freq: Daily
Circ: 73616
Auto Aftermarket, Classical/Choral/Band Music, Computers, Country, Folk, Bluegrass, Dance Music, Data Management, Electronics, Government Technology, Industry, Internet

Raedwald 1052748
Email: raedwalda@gmail.com
Web site: http://raedwald.blogspot.co.uk/
Freq: Daily
Circ: 12178
Politics

The Raggy Rat 996266
Email: sales@raggyrat.co.uk
Web site: http://www.raggyrat.co.uk/blog.php
Freq: Daily
Circ: 300
Crafts

Raindrops of Sapphire 987530
Email: raindropsofsapphire@gmail.com
Web site: raindropsofsapphire.com
Freq: Daily
Circ: 36263
Editor: Lorna Burford
Profile: Raindrops of Sapphire covers fashion, outfits and accessories. The blog has an archive dating back to March 2010.
Beauty & Grooming, Cosmetics, Fashion, Hair

Raining Cake 1100048
Web site: http://www.rainingcake.com/
Freq: Daily
Circ: 10064
Profile: Raining Cake covers fashion, beauty, lifestyle and hotels. The blog has an archive dating back to May 2012. The outlet also offers a vlog.
Beauty & Grooming, Cosmetics, Fashion, Hair, Travel, Women's Interests

Rainy Day Mum 988713
Web site: rainydaymum.co.uk
Freq: Daily
Circ: 89856
Family & Parenting

Raleigh International blogs 998230
Editorial: Third Floor, Dean Bradley House, 52 Horseferry Road, London SW1P 2AF
Tel: 44 02071 831270
Email: info@raleighinternational.org
Web site: http://raleighinternational.org/
Freq: Daily
Circ: 37478
Charitable Foundations

Ram Sam Saa 1061849
Email: ramsamsaa@gmail.com
Web site: http://ramsamsaa.blogspot.com
Freq: Daily
Circ: 1392
Architecture & Design, Do-It-Yourself (DIY), Elementary School, Gardening, Home, Interior Design, Lifestyle, Men's Interests, Preschool, Property Management & Maintenance

Ramblers Worldwide Holidays Blog 1053531
Tel: 44 01707 331133
Email: info@ramblersholidays.co.uk
Web site: http://news.ramblersholidays.co.uk/blog_posts
Freq: Daily
Circ: 338
Outdoor Recreation, Travel

The Rambles of Nell Monnery 986586
Email: neil@neilmonnery.co.uk
Web site: neilmonnery.co.uk
Freq: Daily
Circ: 8219
Politics

Rambling Boots 995542
Web site: http://bootsblogspot.blogspot.co.uk/
Freq: Daily

Circ: 1891
News & Current Affairs

The Ramblings of a Formerly Rock N Roll Mum 987873
Web site: www.rocknrollmum.com
Freq: Daily
Circ: 21335
Profile: Blog covering motherhood. The Ramblings of A Formerly Rock n roll Mum blog discusses anything from family life and product reviews to motherhood tips. The blog has an archive dating back to March 2012. The outlet offers RSS (Really Simple Syndication).
Family & Parenting, Women's Interests

Ramblings of a Suburban Mum 1052613
Email: ramblingsofasuburbanmummy@mail.com
Web site: http://www.realsuburbanmummy.com/
Freq: Daily
Circ: 7701
Family & Parenting

Ramblings of a Teacher 1053768
Web site: http://michaelt1979.wordpress.com
Freq: Daily
Circ: 36982
Profile: Blog covering education. Ramblings of a Teacher blog discusses anything from education to teaching. The blog has an archive dating back to January 2012. The outlet offers RSS (Really Simple Syndication).
News & Current Affairs

The Ramblings of Rebecca 996487
Tel: 44 07735 058408
Email: ramblingsofrebecca@yahoo.co.uk
Web site: readtheramblingsofrebecca.wordpress.com
Freq: Daily
Circ: 11
Travel

Random Blowe 986226
Web site: www.blowe.org.uk/
Freq: Daily
Circ: 7341
Politics

Random Jottings 988338
Email: emasl@yahoo.co.uk
Web site: http://randomjottings.typepad.com/random_jottings_of_an_ope/
Freq: Daily
Circ: 136800
Literature, Theater & Performing Arts

Random Rantings of a Tattooed Mummy 988259
Email: tatmummy@gmail.com
Web site: http://www.tattooedmummy.co.uk/
Freq: Daily
Circ: 60934
Profile: Blog covering motherhood and lifestyle. The Random Rantings of a Tattooed Mummy blog discusses anything from motherhood and family activities to family travel, festivals and camping. The blog has an archive dating back to July 2005 and shares a short blogroll.
Family & Parenting

Rapha Blogs 999514
Editorial: Rapha Racing Ltd, Imperial Works, Perren St, London NW5 3ED
Tel: 44 02074 855000
Email: enquiries@rapha.cc
Web site: http://pages.rapha.cc/features
Freq: Daily
Circ: 16098
Bicycles

Rapid Web 999329
Editorial: Rapid Web, St Albans House, St Albans Road, Stafford ST16 3DP
Tel: 44 01785 250222
Email: contact@rapidweb.biz
Web site: www.rapidweb.biz/news
Freq: Daily

Circ: 21

Advertising Industry, Branding, Broadcasting, Graphic Design, Marketing, Media & Communications, Photography, Publishing

Raspberry 1053734
Email: info@raspberry.co.uk
Web site: www.raspberry.co.uk
Freq: Daily
Circ: 3291
Crafts

Raspberrykiss 1053933
Email: contact@raspberrykiss.co.uk
Web site: www.raspberrykiss.co.uk
Freq: Daily
Circ: 12576
Cosmetics, Women's Interests

Raw Design blog 1060971
Email: rawdesignblog@hotmail.com
Web site: http://rawdesignblog.blogspot.fi
Freq: Daily
Circ: 6513
Architecture & Design, Do-It-Yourself (DIY), Gardening, Home, Interior Design, Property Management & Maintenance, Real Estate

Raw Light: Poetry and Opinion since 2005 1055151
Web site: http://rawlightblog.blogspot.co.uk/
Freq: Daily
Circ: 479
News & Current Affairs

Ray Boulger's Blog 1054489
Editorial: 5th Floor, Cutlers Exchange, 123 Houndsditch, London EC3A 7BU
Email: media@charcol.co.uk
Web site: https://www.charcol.co.uk/news-opinions/ray-boulgers-blog/
Freq: Daily
Circ: 45
Finance, Property Management & Maintenance

RE.WORK Blog 1054004
Email: hello@re-work.co
Web site: https://www.re-work.co/blog
Freq: Daily
Circ: 1667
Auto Aftermarket, Business, Computers, Data Management, Electronics, Government Technology, Industry, Internet, Mobile Communications, Science

Read and Rated 1053441
Email: lisaj.w@btinternet.com
Web site: http://readandrated.com/
Freq: Daily
Circ: 9181
Literature

Read Liverpool 997952
Web site: http://readliverpoolfc.com/
Freq: Daily
Circ: 15735
Soccer

Read Rest Relax 1054434
Email: brennanlynsey@hotmail.com
Web site: readrestrelax.com
Freq: Daily
Circ: 9765
Literature, Women's Interests

Read, Review, Repeat 1056756
Email: readreviewrepeat@live.co.uk
Web site: http://www.readreviewrepeat.co.uk/
Freq: Daily
Circ: 611
Entertainment, Literature

The Reader Online 1053270
Web site: http://blog.thereader.org.uk/
Freq: Daily
Circ: 114
Literature

Reading Away The Days 1053255
Email: readingawaythedays@yahoo.co.uk
Web site: readingawaythedays.blogspot.co.uk
Freq: Daily
Circ: 6268
Literature

Reading Matters 987301
Email: readingmatters@gmail.com
Web site: https://readingmattersblog.com/
Freq: Daily
Circ: 11481
Editor: Kim Forrester
Literature

The Reading Residence 998344
Web site: www.thereadingresidence.com
Freq: Daily
Circ: 13628
Family & Parenting

The Real Argentina 996279
Tel: 44 02074 491665
Email: info@argentowine.com
Web site: www.therealargentina.com
Freq: Daily
Circ: 25116
Americas, Cooking & Baking, Wine/Winemaking

The Real Blog 988660
Email: dcboyle@gmail.com
Web site: http://davidboyle.blogspot.co.uk/
Freq: Daily
Circ: 614
Politics, Social Issues

Real Cider 986503
Web site: http://www.real-cider.co.uk
Freq: Daily
Circ: 8537
Profile: Blog covering cider. Real Cider discusses anything from recommendations and apples to history of cider and cider making. The outlet offers RSS (Really Simple Syndication).
Alcohol & Spirits, Bars, Clubs & Pubs, Beer, Beverages, Cooking & Baking, Food, Grocery Stores, Organic Food, Restaurant Reviews, Vegetarianism & Veganism

Real Costa Rica Blog 1060724
Web site: http://www.blog.therealcostarica.com
Freq: Daily
Circ: 10050
Airline Inflight, Antiques/Collectibles, Art, Arts, Literature, Photography, Railroad, Theater & Performing Arts, Travel, Visual Arts

Real Housewife of Suffolk 1053160
Email: realhousewifeofsuffolk@gmail.com
Web site: www.realhousewifeofsuffolk.co.uk/
Freq: Daily
Circ: 5214
Family & Parenting, Health & Medicine, Women's Interests

Real Men Sow 1053966
Web site: http://www.realmensow.co.uk/
Freq: Daily
Circ: 11618
Gardening

Real Nappies for London 1054399
Editorial: The Grayston Centre, 28 Charles Square, London N1 6HT
Email: nappies@lcrn.org.uk
Web site: http://realnappiesforlondon.blogspot.co.uk/
Freq: Daily
Circ: 1359
Family & Parenting, Preschool

RealGirlRamblings 1057952
Web site: realgirlramblings.com
Freq: Daily
Circ: 7884
Family & Parenting, Men's Interests, Women's Interests

ReallyRee 986831
Email: ree@reallyree.com
Web site: http://www.reallyree.com/
Freq: Daily
Circ: 633546
Beauty & Grooming, Cosmetics, Fashion, Hair, Women's Interests

RealSoundsOK 987166
Email: realsoundsok@gmail.com
Web site: realsoundsok.blogspot.com
Freq: Daily
Circ: 548
Rock Music

Realydad 1061521
Web site: http://realydad.wordpress.com/
Freq: Daily
Circ: 11
Water & Sanitation

Reason Digital Blog 997215
Editorial: 3rd Floor, 26 Lever Street, Manchester M1 1DW Tel: 44 01616 607949
Email: hello@reasondigital.com
Web site: https://reasondigital.com/insights/
Freq: Daily
Circ: 8912
Charitable Foundations

REASONS TO CRUISE BLOG 1052656
Email: website@reasonstocruise.com
Web site: https://www.reasonstocruise.com/
Freq: Daily
Circ: 661
Editor: David Fiske
News & Current Affairs

ReBeauted 1075963
Tel: 44 01416 365283
Web site: rebeauted.com
Freq: Daily
Circ: 2065
Beauty & Grooming, Cosmetics, Hair

Rebecca McCormick's Authorial Blog 999252
Editorial: Vogue House, Hanover Square, London W1S 1JU
Email: sullenhearts@gmail.com
Web site: http://www.rebeccamccormick.co.uk/
Freq: Daily
Circ: 9850
Literature

Rebecca McMahon Blog 1053895
Tel: 44 07834 600685
Email: rebeccamcmahonmakeup@gmail.com
Web site: http://www.rebeccamcmahon.com/
Freq: Daily
Circ: 1496
Cosmetics, Fashion

Rebekah Roy Fashion Stylist 985631
Web site: http://www.fashion-stylist.net/blog/
Freq: Daily
Circ: 5834
Fashion

Recetas de Cocina 1061032
Web site: http://www.recetas-de-cocina.net
Freq: Daily
Circ: 53627
Cooking & Baking

Recetas Digitales 1061008
Web site: http://recetasdigitales.com.ar/
Freq: Daily
Circ: 611
Cooking & Baking

Recetas Simples y Deliciosas 1061875
Web site: http://www.recetassimples.com
Freq: Daily
Circ: 33084
Cooking & Baking

Recetas y Algo Mas 1062086
Web site: http://recetasdekocina.blogspot.com/
Freq: Daily
Circ: 1504
Cooking & Baking

The Recipe Resource 995539
Web site: thereciperesource.blogspot.co.uk/
Freq: Daily
Circ: 6213
News & Current Affairs

Recipes from a Normal Mum 986910
Web site: http://www.recipesfromanormalmum.com
Freq: Daily
Circ: 8805
Cooking & Baking

Recipes from a Pantry 988101
Email: recipesfromapantry@gmail.com
Web site: recipesfromapantry.com
Freq: Daily
Circ: 14021
Cooking & Baking, Food, Grocery Stores, Organic Food, Restaurant Reviews, Vegetarianism & Veganism

Recruitment Views - CEASED FEBRUARY 2016 1052724
Web site: www.recruitment-views.com
Freq: Daily
Circ: 6456
Recruiting

Recyclie 1061844
Email: katja.ulrika@gmail.com
Web site: http://recyclie.blogspot.fi/
Freq: Daily
Circ: 702
Cooking & Baking, Energy & Environment

Red Cross Blog 986736
Editorial: 44 Moorfields, London EC2Y 9AL
Tel: 44 02078 777557
Email: press@redcross.org.uk
Web site: blogs.redcross.org.uk
Freq: Daily
Circ: 5127
Charitable Foundations

Red Dog Music Blog 998292
Editorial: 1 Grassmarket, Edinburgh EH1 2HY Tel: 44 01312 298211
Email: info@reddogmusic.co.uk
Web site: http://blog.reddogmusic.co.uk/
Freq: Daily
Circ: 34694
Classical/Choral/Band Music, Country, Folk, Bluegrass, Dance Music, Jazz & Blues, Music, Pop Music, R&B, Urban, World, Rap & Hip Hop, Rock Music

The Red Ferret 986565
Email: red@redferret.net
Web site: www.redferret.net
Freq: Daily
Circ: 181043
Apple, Audio Video Trade, Auto Aftermarket, Cameras, Computer & Video Games, Computers, Consumer Electronics, Data Management, Electronics, Government Technology

Red Lips Red Hair 1053862
Email: inkivaari77@gmail.com
Web site: http://red-lips-red-hair.blogspot.co.uk/
Freq: Daily
Circ: 521
Cosmetics, Fashion, Music, Pop Music, Rock Music, Women's Interests

Red Rants 987888
Email: ianrimmer@redrants.com
Web site: http://redrants.com/
Circ: 463
Editor: Ian Rimmer
Soccer

The Red Rocket 986258
Web site: www.theredrocket.co.uk
Freq: Daily

Circ: 4590
Branding, Publishing

Red Wine Runner 1052686
Email: theredwinerunner@gmail.com
Web site: http://www.redwinerunner.co.uk/
Freq: Daily
Circ: 8347
Profile: Blog covering jogging & running.
Red Wine Runner blog discusses anything
from jogging and running to product reviews
and marathons. The blog has an archive
dating back to November 2010 and shares a
short blog roll. The outlet offers RSS (Really
Simple Syndication).
Cooking & Baking, Field Sports, Fitness &
Exercise

RedBlog 987971
Editorial: Austin Friars House, 2-6 Austin
Friars, London EC2N 2HD
Tel: 44 02072 503331
Email: redblog@redington.co.uk
Web site: blog.redington.co.uk
Freq: Daily
Circ: 2179
Insurance

**Redbows Promotional Gifts
Blog** 1053226
Editorial: Merlin Court, 24 Bryntirion Drive,
Prestatyn LL19 9NU Tel: 44 08458 386368
Email: marketing@redbows.co.uk
Web site: https://www.
promotionalgiftsstore.co.uk/blog
Freq: Daily
Circ: 2875
Marketing, Shopping

Ree ReallyRee Vlog 1104183
Email: ree@reallyree.com
Web site: https://www.youtube.com/user/
reallyree
Freq: Daily
Circ: 1
Beauty & Grooming, Cosmetics, Hair

ReeRee's blog 1052978
Editorial: 199 Kingsland Road, Shoredtich,
London E2 8AN
Email: reeree@rockalily.com
Web site: http://www.rockalily.com/blog/
Freq: Daily
Circ: 6768
Profile: ROCKALILY CUTS covers rockabilly
fashion, lifestyle, fitness and running a salon.
Fashion, Fitness & Exercise, Hair,
Women's Interests

Reflect on Film 1053977
Email: reflectionsonfilm@gmail.com
Web site: http://reflectonfilm.co.uk
Freq: Daily
Circ: 8896
Movies & Video

Reflecting English 1053114
Web site: http://reflectingenglish.wordpress.
com
Freq: Daily
Circ: 1249
Profile: Blog covering education. Reflecting
English blog discusses anything from
education and teaching to writing. The blog
has an archive dating back to October 2013.
Education

Regiosfera 1062097
Web site: http://www.regiosfera.com
Freq: Daily
Circ: 2626
Astronomy, Environment

Reich de las Mil Cervezas
1061072
Web site: http://elreichdelasmilcervezas.
blogspot.com/
Freq: Daily
Circ: 521
Classical/Choral/Band Music, Country,
Folk, Bluegrass, Dance Music, Jazz &
Blues, Music, Pop Music, R&B, Urban,
World, Rap & Hip Hop, Rock Music

Relentless Tenacity 1052845
Email: blog@totkat.org
Web site: http://www.totkat.org/

Freq: Daily
Circ: 8418
Fitness & Exercise, Nutrition

Remedy Creative Blog 997072
Editorial: 76 Calverley Road, Tunbridge
Wells, Tunbridge Wells TN1 2UJ
Tel: 44 01892 614761
Email: hello@remedycreative.com
Web site: www.remedycreative.com/blog
Freq: Daily
Circ: 16
Advertising Industry, Branding, Graphic
Design, Marketing, Photography,
Publishing

Remedy Rouge 1061429
Web site: http://remedyrouge.blogspot.com
Freq: Daily
Circ: 1060
Fashion

Ren Behan 986909
Email: info@renbehan.com
Web site: www.renbehan.com
Freq: Daily
Circ: 14019
Cooking & Baking, Restaurant Reviews

The Republik of Mancunia
987891
Email: admin@therepublikofmancunia.com
Web site: therepublikofmancunia.com/
Freq: Daily
Circ: 49183
Profile: Blog covering Manchester United
Football Club. The blog has an archive
dating back to May 2006 and shares a short
blogroll.
Soccer

Reputation Matters 1053908
Web site: http://www.reputations.org.uk/
Freq: Daily
Circ: 9319
Profile: Blog covering reputation
management for online. Reputation Matters
discusses anything from managing company
and brand reputation online to managing
personal and professional information online,
and removing negative content online. The
blog has an archive dating back to February
2014.
Branding, Marketing

Resourcing Solutions blog
999214
Tel: 44 01189 320100
Email: info@resourcing-solutions.com
Web site: http://www.resourcing-solutions.
com/blog-news/blog
Freq: Daily
Circ: 801
Alternative/Renewable Energy, Public
Sector, Railroad

Restaurants and Food in Cork
1052782
Web site: http://www.corkbilly.com/
Freq: Daily
Circ: 11174
Alcohol & Spirits, Bars, Clubs & Pubs,
Beer, Beverages, Cooking & Baking,
Grocery Stores, Organic Food, Restaurant
Reviews, Wine/Winemaking

The Restored Kitchen 996899
Web site: www.therestoredkitchen.com
Freq: Daily
Circ: 9165
Cooking & Baking, Photography

RESULTS 1056772
Editorial: RESULTS UK Head Office, 31-33
Bondway, London SW8 1SJ
Web site: http://www.results.org.uk/blog
Freq: Daily
Circ: 13
Charitable Foundations

Rethink Blog 997053
Editorial: 89 Albert Embankment, London
SE1 7TP Tel: 44 02078 403138
Email: info@rethink.org
Web site: https://www.rethink.org/news-
views
Freq: Daily

Circ: 242
Charitable Foundations, Neurology

Retirement Investing Today
1052914
Email: contact.retirementinvesting@gmail.
com
Web site: http://www.
retirementinvestingtoday.com/
Freq: Daily
Circ: 24015
Personal Finance

Retro Chick 986955
Editorial: 49 Lindley Street, Norwich NR1
2HF
Email: hello@retrochick.co.uk
Web site: www.retrochick.co.uk
Freq: Daily
Circ: 111644
Fashion

Return on Digital Blog 1054550
Editorial: Ground Floor, The Tower, Deva
Centre, Trinity Way, Manchester M3 7BF
Tel: 44 08453 142100
Email: results@returnondigital.com
Web site: https://return.co/blog/
Freq: Daily
Circ: 23
Branding, Internet, Marketing

Rev Stan's Theatre Blog 988529
Email: rightrevstan@gmail.com
Web site: http://theatre.revstan.com/
Freq: Daily
Circ: 5337
Theater & Performing Arts

Review Avenue 998208
Web site: http://www.review-avenue.co.uk/
Freq: Daily
Circ: 666
Movies & Video

Reviewed by the Bride 997618
Editorial: 81 Lower Saltram, Plymstock,
Plymouth, Plymstock PL9 7PW
Web site: reviewedbythebride.blogspot.co.
uk
Freq: Daily
Circ: 521
News & Current Affairs

Revista Proyecta 1060965
Web site: http://revistaproyecta.wordpress.
com/
Freq: Daily
Architecture & Design, Celebrities,
National News

Revitalize Fitness 1056763
Email: aimee@revitalizefitness.co.uk
Web site: http://revitalizefitness.co.uk/blog/
Freq: Daily
Circ: 136
Fitness & Exercise

Revolución del Pensamiento
1060975
Web site: http://juanmanuelgiaccone.
blogspot.com/
Freq: Daily
Circ: 521
Economics, Politics

Revolutionary Measures 1053612
Email: chris@measuresconsulting.com
Web site: https://measuresconsulting.
wordpress.com
Freq: Daily
Circ: 29
Marketing

Reyqui Blog 1061619
Web site: http://www.reyqui.com
Freq: Daily
Circ: 611
Auto Aftermarket, Computers, Data
Management, Electronics, Government
Technology, Industry, Internet, Mobile
Communications, Movies & Video,
Security & Security Systems

Rhian Westbury (Blog) 1086843
Email: rhian.westbury@ntlworld.com
Web site: http://www.rhianwestbury.co.uk/

Freq: Daily
Circ: 62870
Rock Music, Women's Interests

Rhiannon Ashlee Vlog 1098957
Editorial: PO Box 538, Tunbridge Wells TN2
9TN
Email: amplify@greenlightdigital.com
Web site: https://www.youtube.com/user/
FashionRocksMySocks
Freq: Daily
Circ: 6
Beauty & Grooming, Cosmetics, Fashion,
Hair, Women's Interests

Rhyme & Ribbons 1053962
Web site: rhymeandribbons.com
Freq: Daily
Circ: 8822
Profile: Blog covering travel. The Rhyme &
Ribbons blog discusses anything from travel
and expatriate living to food and crafts. The
blog has an archive dating back to March
2014 and shares a short blog roll.
Cooking & Baking, Travel, Women's
Interests

Richard Aucock 1053715
Web site: www.richardaucock.com
Freq: Daily
Circ: 1765
Antique & Collectible Cars, Automakers,
Automotive, Driving, Motorcycles, Off-
road & 4-Wheel Drive Vehicles, Trucks &
SUVs

Richard Branson Blog - Virgin
1052907
Web site: www.virgin.com/richard-branson
Freq: Daily
Circ: 399049
Aviation, International News, Social
Issues

Richard Kermode blog 1052765
Tel: 44 07817 761813
Email: info@richardkermode.co.uk
Web site: http://www.richardkermode.co.
uk/blog/
Freq: Daily
Circ: 468
Outdoor Recreation

**Richard Peters Photography
Blog** 1052797
Email: info@richardpeters.co.uk
Web site: http://www.richardpeters.co.uk/
blog/
Freq: Daily
Circ: 40102
Photography

Richard Stacy 1054044
Email: stacyconsulting@googlemail.com
Web site: richardstacy.com
Freq: Daily
Circ: 11672
News & Current Affairs

richardtech 1101208
Email: inbox@richardtech.net
Web site: richardtech.net
Freq: Daily
Circ: 11007
Electronics, Mobile Electronics

Ride UK BMX 1056312
Email: cleggy@rideukbmx.com
Web site: http://rideukbmx.com
Freq: Daily
Circ: 31941
Profile: Magazine covering all aspects of
BMX riding including bicycle freestyle, dirt
jumping and street riding. The publication
also covers worldwide events, interviews,
riders, road trips, bike tests and product
reviews. First published in 1992, the
publication has an average of 196 pages per
issue. Aimed at BMX riders between 10 to 30
years old.
Bicycles

Riding Storms 1074786
Web site: ridingstorms.wordpress.com
Freq: Daily
Circ: 392
Women's Interests

Right by the Medway - John Ward
1063411
Web site: http://wwwjohn-m-ward.blogspot.co.uk/
Freq: Daily
Circ: 10226
Politics

The Right Human
1052927
Email: vmistiaen@ntlworld.com
Web site: www.therighthuman.blogspot.co.uk
Freq: Daily
Circ: 521
Consumer Affairs, Energy & Environment, International News, Politics, Social Issues

Rightmove Property Blog
1054047
Editorial: Rightmove PLC, 4th Floor, 33 Soho Square, London W1D 3QU
Email: press@rightmove.co.uk
Web site: http://www.rightmove.co.uk/news/
Freq: Daily
Circ: 22712
Architecture & Design, Building & Construction, Commercial Real Estate, Finance, Interior Design, Legal Affairs, Office Design, Property Management & Maintenance, Residential Real Estate, Retail

RIMMA - matkablogi
1061000
Email: rimma.blogging@gmail.com
Web site: http://www.rimmablog.com
Freq: Daily
Circ: 1463
Airline Inflight, Outdoor Recreation, Railroad, Travel

Rina
1060572
Web site: http://rina-melconian.blogspot.com/
Freq: Daily
Circ: 873
Bars, Clubs & Pubs, Comedy, Crafts, Hobbies, & Collecting, Entertainment, Graphic Design, Local Entertainment Guides, Movies & Video

Rincón de Edy
1061632
Web site: http://www.edy.com.mx
Freq: Daily
Circ: 9559
Auto Aftermarket, Bars, Clubs & Pubs, Basketball, Bicycles, Billiards, Boating & Yachting, Bodybuilding, Bowling, Boxing, Comedy

Rincon de las Manualidades de Siry
1001027
Web site: http://siry-manualidades.blogspot.com/
Freq: Daily
Circ: 801
Crafts

Rincon de Yoga
1062122
Web site: http://www.rincondeyoga.com.ar/
Freq: Daily
Circ: 521
Fitness & Exercise

Rincon del Vinotinto
1061876
Web site: http://tolima1954.blogspot.com/
Freq: Daily
Circ: 521
Soccer

Rincon Tecnologico
1061135
Web site: http://www.elrincontecnologico.com
Freq: Daily
Circ: 644
Auto Aftermarket, Computers, Data Management, Electronics, Government Technology, Industry, Internet, Mobile Communications, National News, Security & Security Systems

Rinniboo
1100503
Web site: http://www.rinniboo.com/
Freq: Daily
Circ: 1463
Cosmetics, Electronics, Fashion, Mobile Electronics, Women's Interests

Risk, Health and Safety Solutions Blog
1053610
Tel: 44 03335 770248
Email: info@rhssltd.co.uk
Web site: http://rhssltd.blogspot.co.uk/
Freq: Daily
Circ: 521
Health & Medicine

RM Education blog
1052799
Tel: 44 08450 700300
Email: pr@rm.com
Web site: http://www.rm.com/blog
Freq: Daily
Circ: 28
Disability, Education, Higher Education, Preschool, Schools & Institutions, Students

RMR Proyectos
1061780
Web site: http://rmrarq.blogspot.com/
Freq: Daily
Circ: 1416
Architecture & Design, Building & Construction, Regional, Regional General Interest

Road Cycling Blogs
999358
Editorial: Factory Media Ltd, 2 Tun Yard, Peardon Street, London SW8 3HT
Tel: 44 02073 329700
Email: timothy.john@factorymedia.com
Web site: www.roadcyclinguk.com/blogs
Freq: Daily
Circ: 15842
Bicycles

Rob Edwards Blog
988217
Web site: http://www.robedwards.com/
Freq: Daily
Circ: 7599
Alternative/Renewable Energy, Energy & Environment, Environment

Rob Ryan Blog
1054218
Editorial: Ryantown HQ, 5 – 6 Teesdale Yard, Teesdale Street, London E2 6QE
Email: info@robryanstudio.com
Web site: http://robryanstudio.com/category/blog
Freq: Daily
Circ: 6
Crafts, Visual Arts

Robert Kyriakides's Weblog
986315
Editorial: 37 Queen Anne Street, London W1G 9JB
Web site: robertkyriakides.wordpress.com
Freq: Daily
Circ: 17
Alternative/Renewable Energy, Energy & Environment, Environment

Rock and Blog
1061121
Web site: http://blogs.eluniversal.com.mx/rockandblog
Freq: Daily
Circ: 408
Classical/Choral/Band Music, Country, Folk, Bluegrass, Dance Music, Jazz & Blues, Music, Pop Music, R&B, Urban, World, Rap & Hip Hop, Rock Music

Rock del Uruguay
1061690
Web site: http://www.rockdeluruguay.com/
Freq: Daily
Circ: 1203
Rock Music

Rock My Style
987793
Web site: rockmystyle.co.uk
Freq: Daily
Circ: 9015
Profile: Blog covering fashion, beauty, home interiors, culinary ideas and travel.
Beauty & Grooming, Cooking & Baking, Cosmetics, Crafts, Do-It-Yourself (DIY), Fashion, Hair, Regional General Interest, Restaurant Reviews, Women's Interests

Rock My Wedding
987272
Email: info@rockmywedding.co.uk
Web site: www.rockmywedding.co.uk
Freq: Daily
Circ: 176673
Fashion, Weddings

Rock 'n Roll Times
1061630
Web site: http://www.rocknrolltimesyouraccount.blogspot.com
Freq: Daily
Circ: 1135
Classical/Choral/Band Music, Country, Folk, Bluegrass, Dance Music, Jazz & Blues, Music, Pop Music, R&B, Urban, World, Rap & Hip Hop, Rock Music

Rock Paper Shotgun
988177
Email: contact@rockpapershotgun.com
Web site: http://www.rockpapershotgun.com/
Freq: Daily
Circ: 3811739
Computer & Video Games, Personal Computers

Rock Rock Blog
1061254
Email: rockrockblog@gmail.com
Web site: http://www.rockrockblog.com
Freq: Daily
Circ: 903
Bars, Clubs & Pubs, Comedy, Entertainment, Local Entertainment Guides, Movies & Video, Rock Music

Rocket Bobs Cycle Works
1053994
Tel: 44 07714 205576
Email: info@rocketbobs.biz
Web site: http://rocketbobs.blogspot.co.uk/
Freq: Daily
Circ: 548
Motorcycles

RockettStGeorge Blog
998951
Editorial: Unit 12, Old Kiln Works, Ditchling Industrial Estate, Hassocks BN6 8SG
Tel: 44 01444 253391
Email: contact@rockettstgeorge.co.uk
Web site: https://rockettstgeorge.me/
Freq: Daily
Circ: 10532
Architecture & Design, Do-It-Yourself (DIY), Gardening, Home, Property Management & Maintenance, Real Estate

Rodando Cine
1061298
Web site: http://www.rodandocine.com
Freq: Daily
Circ: 6933
Bars, Clubs & Pubs, Comedy, Entertainment, Local Entertainment Guides, Movies & Video

Romanian Mum Blog
1053805
Web site: http://romanianmum.com/
Freq: Daily
Circ: 0746
Family & Parenting

Roobla
987940
Editorial: The Admiral's Office, Chatham, Chatham ME4 4TZ
Email: talk@roobla.com
Web site: http://roobla.com/
Freq: Daily
Circ: 12990
Profile: Blog covering reviews of film, computer games, TV and gadgets.
Broadcasting, Classical/Choral/Band Music, Computer & Video Games, Country, Folk, Bluegrass, Dance Music, Jazz & Blues, Movies & Video, Music, Pop Music, R&B, Urban, World

Room to Bloom - CEASED NOVEMBER 2016
1053995
Web site: www.room-to-bloom.com/blog
Freq: Daily
Circ: 11834
Profile: Blog covering interiors and home decoration of children's spaces. The blog has an archive dating back to December 2011 and shares a short blogroll.
Do-It-Yourself (DIY)

RosaClavelRosa
1061778
Web site: http://rosaclavelrosa.blogspot.com
Freq: Daily
Circ: 929
Fashion

Rosanna Pierce
1098980
Email: rpiercemakeup@gmail.com
Web site: https://www.youtube.com/user/RPierceMakeup
Freq: Daily
Circ: 1188
Cosmetics, Fashion, Women's Interests

The ROSEGARDEN IN MALEVIK
1060181
Email: rosor.eu@telia.com
Web site: http://www.maleviksrosentradgard.blogspot.com/
Freq: Daily
Circ: 3076
Crafts, Do-It-Yourself (DIY), Gardening

The ROSEGARDEN IN MALEVIK
1060700
Email: rosor.eu@telia.com
Web site: http://www.maleviksrosentradgard.blogspot.com/
Freq: Daily
Circ: 3076
Crafts, Do-It-Yourself (DIY), Gardening

Roses and Rolltops
1053129
Web site: www.rosesandrolltops.co.uk
Freq: Daily
Circ: 9546
Profile: Blog covering lifestyle, baking, travel and interiors.
Do-It-Yourself (DIY)

Rosie Glow
1053177
Email: rosie-glow@live.co.uk
Web site: rosie-glow.co.uk
Freq: Daily
Circ: 11549
Profile: Blog covering fashion. Rosie glow blog discusses anything from fashion and art to design and photography. The blog has an archive dating back to September 2010 and shares an extensive blog roll.
News & Current Affairs

Rosie Reads Romance
1052936
Email: rosiereadsromance@gmail.com
Web site: http://rosiereadsromance.blogspot.co.uk/
Freq: Daily
Circ: 521
Literature

Rosiepink
1053148
Email: rosiepink@btinternet.com
Web site: http://rosiepink.typepad.co.uk/
Freq: Daily
Circ: 72611
Crafts

Ross Hewitt Ski Blog
996634
Web site: https://rosshewitt.net/
Freq: Daily
Circ: 1022
Outdoor Recreation, Winter Sports

Rostros de la Justicia
1061720
Web site: http://blogs.eluniversal.com.mx/justicia
Freq: Daily
Circ: 233
Bankruptcy, Company News & Appointments, Consumer Interest, Corporate Law, Criminal Law, Employment, Estate Planning, Family Law, Federal Courts, Food & Drug Administration

Rotafolio Hiperlocal
1061742
Web site: http://rotafolio.wordpress.com/
Freq: Daily
Circ: 11
Advertising Industry, Branding, Broadcasting, Graphic Design, Marketing, Media & Communications, Photography, Publishing

Rotten Otter - CEASED AUGUST 2016
1054026
Web site: http://www.rottenotter.com/
Freq: Daily
Circ: 2125
Profile: Blog covering beauty. Rotten Otter blog discusses anything from lifestyle and

UK Blogs

cosmetics to skincare and beauty. The blog has an archive dating back to August 2009.
Beauty & Grooming, Cosmetics, Fashion, Hair

Rough Version 1053854
Email: fgavin@gmail.com
Web site: http://roughversion.blogspot.co.uk/
Freq: Daily
Circ: 2059
Art, Literature, Photography, Theater & Performing Arts, Visual Arts

Round the north we go 1054082
Web site: http://www.merseytart.com/
Freq: Daily
Circ: 10230
Railroad

Routenote.com Blog 1053683
Tel: 44 01872 870688
Web site: http://routenote.com/blog/
Freq: Daily
Circ: 243
Classical/Choral/Band Music, Country, Folk, Bluegrass, Dance Music, Jazz & Blues, Music, Pop Music, R&B, Urban, World, Rap & Hip Hop, Rock Music

Rowe Running 1053607
Web site: http://rowerunning.co.uk/
Freq: Daily
Circ: 1507
Fitness & Exercise, Sports

The Royal Mint Blog 999684
Tel: 44 01443 222111
Web site: blog.royalmint.com
Freq: Daily
Circ: 9575
Antiques/Collectibles, Economics, Sales & Marketing

Royston Cartoon Blog 1052895
Email: roystonrobertson@gmail.com
Web site: http://www.roystoncartoons.com/
Freq: Daily
Circ: 8401
Visual Arts

The RSPB Community 999578
Editorial: The Lodge, Potton Road, Sandy SG19 2DL Tel: 44 01767 681577
Email: pressoffice@rspb.org.uk
Web site: http://www.rspb.org.uk/community/ourwork/b/default.aspx
Freq: Daily
Circ: 5
Charitable Foundations, Energy & Environment, Environment, Nature & Wildlife

RSPCA Insights 999360
Editorial: Wilberforce Way, Southwater, Horsham, Southwater RH13 9RS
Tel: 44 03001 230244
Email: press@rspca.org.uk
Web site: blogs.rspca.org.uk/insights
Freq: Daily
Circ: 28904
Profile: Blog covering animal welfare and animal protection, including everything from pets and horses to wildlife conservation. As it is a charity organisation it also covers fundraising and raising awareness. The blog has an archive dating back to February 2012.
Charitable Foundations

The Rubbish Diet Blog 996901
Web site: www.therubbishdiet.org.uk
Freq: Daily
Circ: 9507
Cooking & Baking

The Rugby Blog 986259
Editorial: 64 Kimber Road, London SW18 4PP
Web site: www.therugbyblog.com
Freq: Daily
Circ: 8565
Editor: Jamie Hosie
Rugby

Run & Relax 1052805
Tel: 44 07811 868851
Email: info@runninggirl.co.uk

Web site: http://www.runninggirl.co.uk/
Freq: Daily
Circ: 1568
Fitness & Exercise

Run my own way 1054474
Web site: http://runmyownway.wordpress.com/
Freq: Daily
Circ: 18
Profile: Blog covering running. Run Your Own Way blog discusses anything from running and jogging to product reviews and events. The blog has an archive dating back to July 2010. The outlet offers RSS (Really Simple Syndication).
Sports

Run To Win 1053259
Web site: https://yellowrunner.wordpress.com/
Freq: Daily
Circ: 13
Fitness & Exercise

The Runner Beans 988602
Web site: http://www.therunnerbeans.com/
Freq: Daily
Circ: 12490
Profile: Blog covering fitness. The runner beans blog discusses anything from running races and exercise to recipes and travel. The blog has an archive dating back to January 2011.
Fitness & Exercise

The Running Bug 985573
Email: editorial@therunningbug.co.uk
Web site: http://therunningbug.co.uk/rbblogs/default.aspx
Circ: 21
Profile: Website covering running. The running bug website shares the latest news on running events, advice on training and information on running gear.
Fitness & Exercise, Health & Medicine, Nutrition

Running Cupcake 1053890
Email: emailme@runningcupcake.co.uk
Web site: http://runningcupcake.co.uk/
Freq: Daily
Circ: 7225
Fitness & Exercise, Nutrition

Running OK in the UK - CEASED August 2016 995339
Web site: http://runningokintheuk.blogspot.co.uk/
Freq: Daily
Circ: 889
Fitness & Exercise, Sports

Runs Like a Dog 1052834
Email: irunlikeadog@gmail.com
Web site: http://runslikeadog.wordpress.com
Freq: Daily
Circ: 29
Fitness & Exercise

Rupert's Read 986587
Editorial: 17 Merton Road, Norwich NR2 3TT Tel: 44 01603 219294
Email: ruperttread@fastmail.co.uk
Web site: rupertread.org
Freq: Daily
Circ: 1107
Energy & Environment, Environment, Politics

Ruth Crilly Vlog 1098944
Web site: https://www.youtube.com/user/AModelRecommends
Freq: Daily
Circ: 34
Beauty & Grooming, Cosmetics, Hair, Women's Interests

Ruth Writes 1101515
Web site: https://ruth-writes.co.uk/
Freq: Daily
Circ: 8987
Alcohol & Spirits, Bars, Clubs & Pubs, Beauty & Grooming, Beer, Beverages, Cooking & Baking, Cosmetics, Hair, Restaurant Reviews, Wine/Winemaking

Ryan147.com - CEASED NOVEMBER 2016 1054407
Web site: http://ryan147.com/
Freq: Daily
Circ: 8654
Billiards, Classical/Choral/Band Music, Country, Folk, Bluegrass, Dance Music, Jazz & Blues, Music, Pop Music, R&B, Urban, World, Rap & Hip Hop, Rock Music

Saborearte Entusiasma 1061079
Web site: http://saboreartentusiasma.blogspot.com
Freq: Daily
Circ: 1251
Antiques/Collectibles, Art, Arts, Food, Literature, Photography, Theater & Performing Arts, Visual Arts

Sadiq Khan For London 1054401
Email: london@labour.org.uk
Web site: http://www.sadiq.london/
Freq: Daily
Circ: 36426
Government

Saijis 1061488
Email: saija.ritamaki@hotmail.fi
Web site: http://saijis.blogspot.fi/
Freq: Daily
Circ: 1170
Beauty & Grooming, Cosmetics, Fashion, Hair

sailboat. 986840
Email: sailorjennie@googlemail.com
Web site: www.sailorjennie.com
Freq: Daily
Circ: 7489
Beauty & Grooming, Cosmetics, Fashion, Hair, Women's Interests

Sailing Logic blog 1053201
Tel: 44 02380 330999
Email: info@sailinglogic.co.uk
Web site: http://blog.sailinglogic.co.uk
Freq: Daily
Circ: 30
Swimming/Watersports

Salads and Sequins 1053515
Email: tamzin_sparkles@hotmail.co.uk
Web site: http://www.saladandsequins.com/
Freq: Daily
Circ: 7312
Cooking & Baking, Fitness & Exercise, Nutrition, Organic Food

Sally's 1061809
Email: countrysally@wippies.com
Web site: http://countrysally.blogspot.fi/
Freq: Daily
Circ: 1299
Architecture & Design, Do-It-Yourself (DIY), Gardening, Home, Interior Design, Property Management & Maintenance, Real Estate

Salon del Mal 1060375
Web site: http://www.salondelmal.com
Freq: Daily
Circ: 93293
Bars, Clubs & Pubs, Comedy, Computer & Video Games, Entertainment, Local Entertainment Guides, Movies & Video

Salon Rojo 1061962
Web site: http://blogs.eluniversal.com.mx/salonrojo
Freq: Daily
Circ: 1724
Bars, Clubs & Pubs, Comedy, Entertainment, Local Entertainment Guides, Movies & Video

Sal's Snippets 1054569
Web site: http://salssnippets.blogspot.co.uk/
Freq: Daily
Circ: 521
Art, Cooking & Baking, Do-It-Yourself (DIY), Gardening, Restaurant Reviews, Women's Interests

Saltrock blog 998443
Editorial: Saltrock House, Velator, Braunton EX33 2DX Tel: 44 01271 815306

Email: info@saltrock.com
Web site: http://www.saltrock.com/blog/
Freq: Daily
Circ: 20
Swimming/Watersports

Salud en Notas 1061430
Web site: http://saludennotas.blogspot.com/
Freq: Daily
Circ: 762
Alternative Medicine, Disability, Fitness & Exercise, Health & Medicine, Media Relations, Medicine, Nutrition, Patient Support, Personal Health & Wellness, Psychology

Salud para todos 1061263
Web site: http://salud-para-todo-el-mundo.blogspot.com/
Freq: Daily
Circ: 521
Health & Medicine

Saluddatos 1060575
Web site: http://saluddatos.blogspot.com/
Freq: Daily
Circ: 611
Alternative Medicine, Disability, Fitness & Exercise, Health & Medicine, Media Relations, Medicine, Nutrition, Patient Support, Personal Health & Wellness, Psychology

SAM 1053522
Email: hello@imsamsquire.co.uk
Web site: imsamsquire.com
Freq: Daily
Circ: 16170
Fashion, Men's Interests

Samantha Maria Vlog 1076159
Editorial: Sammi, Gleam, 96 Leonard Street, London EC2A 4RH
Email: sammi@gleamfutures.com
Web site: https://www.youtube.com/user/beautycrush
Freq: Daily
Circ: 36996
Beauty & Grooming, Cosmetics, Fashion, Hair

SamanthaMariaOfficial 987073
Web site: http://www.samanthamariaofficial.com/
Freq: Daily
Circ: 43753
Beauty & Grooming, Cosmetics, Fashion, Hair, Women's Interests

SamanthaMariaVlogs 1076754
Editorial: Sammi, Gleam, 96 Leonard Street, London EC2A 1PQ
Email: sammi@gleamfutures.com
Web site: https://www.youtube.com/user/TheSammiMariaShow
Freq: Daily
Circ: 2
Beauty & Grooming, Cosmetics, Hair, Women's Interests

Same Difference 988052
Email: samedifferenceone@hotmail.co.uk
Web site: http://samedifference1.com/
Freq: Daily
Circ: 52379
Editor: Sarah Ismail
Disability

The Same Old Chic 1060492
Web site: http://www.thesameoldchic.com
Freq: Daily
Circ: 9522
Beauty & Grooming, Cosmetics, Fashion, Hair, Women's Interests

Samizdata 1053572
Email: reply@samizdata.com
Web site: http://www.samizdata.net/
Freq: Daily
Circ: 60813
Ethical/Moral Issues, Government, National News, Politics, Science

Sammy Jean Blog 1056321
Web site: http://sammyjeancrafts.blogspot.co.uk/

Freq: Daily
Circ: 1333
Crafts

The Samosa 1053184
Email: info@thesamosa.org.uk
Web site: www.thesamosa.co.uk
Freq: Daily
Circ: 7916
Profile: Blog covering politics. The Samosa blog discusses anything from human rights and world politics to social issues and culture.
Consumer Affairs, International News, Politics, Religion, Social Issues

Samphire and Salsify 988641
Web site: http://www.samphireandsalsify.com/
Freq: Daily
Circ: 12326
Profile: Blog covering food. The Samphire and Salsify blog discusses anything from food recipes and restaurant reviews.
Restaurant Reviews

Samuel Jing Blog 987925
Web site: blog.samueljing.com
Freq: Daily
Circ: 6545
Fashion

San Rafael 1061934
Web site: http://www.sanrafaeltemaspediatricos.com/
Freq: Daily
Circ: 494
Pediatrics

Sanctuary Blog 1061560
Email: admin@sanctuaryasia.com
Web site: http://www.sanctuaryasia.com/index.php?option=com_myblog&Itemid=52
Freq: Daily
Circ: 6
Environment

Sandhya's Kitchen 1100170
Email: sandhyaskitchen@yahoo.com
Web site: http://sandhyahariharan.co.uk/
Freq: Daily
Circ: 12084
Cooking & Baking, Vegetarianism & Veganism

Sands Media Serviocs 1053737
Tel: 44 07977 186408
Email: petersandssms@gmail.com
Web site: http://sandsmediaservices.blogspot.co.uk/
Freq: Daily
Circ: 12293
Advertising Industry, Branding, Broadcasting, Graphic Design, Marketing, Media & Communications, Photography, Publishing

Sandy Teje 1061909
Web site: http://lostejidoodocandra.blogspot.com/
Freq: Daily
Circ: 714
Crafts

SANE blog 997686
Editorial: St. Mark's Studios, 14 Chillingworth Road, Islington, London N7 8QJ Tel: 44 02038 051751
Email: mediateam@sane.org.uk
Web site: http://www.sane.org.uk/how_you_can_help/blogging/
Freq: Daily
Circ: 265
Charitable Foundations

SanNails 1062136
Email: mysannails@gmail.com
Web site: http://sannails.blogspot.fi/
Freq: Daily
Circ: 1269
Cosmetics

Sarah + Laura 1053754
Email: sarahpluslaura@gmail.com
Web site: http://sarahpluslaura.blogspot.co.uk/
Freq: Daily

Circ: 10158
Profile: Blog covering lesbian relationship and lifestyle. The blog has an archive dating back to July 2011.
Cooking & Baking, LGBT, Travel, Weddings

Sarah Akwisombe 1053897
Email: yo@sarahakwisombe.com
Web site: http://www.sarahakwisombe.com/blog
Freq: Daily
Circ: 44
Profile: Blog covering interior design. SARAH AKWISOMBE discusses anything from colour schemes and furniture to home accessories. The blog has an archive dating back to March 2014.
Do-It-Yourself (DIY)

Sarah Graham 1052575
Editorial: 7 Otter Close, London E15 2PZ
Email: contact@sarah-graham.co.uk
Web site: http://sarah-graham.co.uk/blog
Freq: Daily
Circ: 6418
Profile: Blog covering feminism. Sarah Graham blog discusses anything from social issues and culture to women in journalism and in the media. The blog has an archive dating back to August 2011 and shares an extensive blogroll. The outlet offers RSS (Really Simple Syndication).
Health & Medicine, Social Issues

Sarah Louise Ryan 1098978
Web site: http://www.sarahlouiseryan.com/
Freq: Daily
Circ: 9578
Relationships

Sarah Woo. 997696
Email: lady@sarahwoo.co.uk
Web site: www.sarahwoo.co.uk
Freq: Daily
Circ: 9291
Fashion, Fitness & Exercise, Health & Medicine, Women's Interests

Sarah's Flowers Blog 1054641
Tel: 44 01217 223436
Email: sales@sarahsflowers.co.uk
Web site: www.sarahsflowers.co.uk/blog
Freq: Daily
Circ: 292
Weddings

The Sardine Tin 1053959
Web site: http://www.thesardinetin.com/
Freq: Daily
Circ: 5014
Family & Parenting, Women's Interests

Sartorialee 1054314
Email: sartorialee@englandmail.com
Web site: sartorialee.wordpress.com
Freq: Daily
Circ: 9
Fashion

The sassy She 998816
Editorial: SASSY HQ, 50 Taranto Road, Southampton, Southampton SO16 5PN
Tel: 44 07525 665284
Email: lisa@thesassyshe.com
Web site: http://www.thesassyshe.com/blog/
Freq: Daily
Circ: 11
Beauty & Grooming, Celebrities, Cosmetics, Fashion, Hair, Shopping, Teen/Young Adult, Women's Interests

satsumaloans.co.uk Tools and Tips 1104593
Editorial: 1 Godwin Street, Bradford BD1 2SU
Web site: https://www.satsumaloans.co.uk/tools-and-tips
Freq: Daily
Circ: 20188
Editor: Andrew Halliday
News & Current Affairs

Satyameva Jayate 1061353
Email: jai.dharma@gmail.com
Web site: http://www.satyameva-jayate.org

Freq: Daily
Circ: 8381
Antiques/Collectibles, Art, Arts, Consumer Affairs, Crime & Violence, Defense & National Security, Energy & Environment, Ethical/Moral Issues, International News, Law

Save the Children UK 986229
Editorial: 1 St John's Lane, London EC1M 4AR Tel: 44 02070 126841
Email: media@savethechildren.org.uk
Web site: blogs.savethechildren.org.uk/blogs-by-blogger/
Freq: Daily
Circ: 1
Charitable Foundations, Community Care (UK)

Savidge Reads 987304
Editorial: 17 Heathbank Road, Devonshire Park, Wirral CH42 7LD
Email: savidgereads@gmail.com
Web site: http://savidgereads.wordpress.com
Freq: Daily
Circ: 7576
Literature

Saving Sally 1053371
Email: sally@saving-sally.co.uk
Web site: http://www.saving-sally.co.uk/
Freq: Daily
Circ: 899
Profile: Blog covering personal finance. Sally Saving discusses anything from budgeting and money saving tips to loans and debt.
Personal Finance

The Savvy Scot 987469
Email: mail@savvyscot.com
Web site: savvyscot.com
Freq: Daily
Circ: 46956
Fitness & Exercise, Travel

Scarlett Entertainment & Events 997624
Web site: http://www.scarlettentertainment.com/latest-news
Freq: Daily
Circ: 33
News & Current Affairs

SCARPA Team 1053517
Tel: 44 01912 960212
Email: info@mountainboot.co.uk
Web site: www.scarpa.co.uk/scarpa-team/
Freq: Daily
Circ: 53
Outdoor Recreation, Travel

Scenes From The Battleground 1053013
Web site: teachingbattleground.wordpress.com
Freq: Daily
Circ: 18888
Education

The School's News Service 1052928
Tel: 44 01536 399000
Email: sales@hamilton-house.com
Web site: www.blog.schools.co.uk/
Freq: Daily
Circ: 27
Education

Science blog - CRUK 986230
Editorial: Angel Building, 407 St John Street, London EC1V 4AD Tel: 44 02034 698300
Email: newsfeed@cancer.org.uk
Web site: scienceblog.cancerresearchuk.org/
Freq: Daily
Circ: 87432
Charitable Foundations, Oncology

Science Fiction and Fantasy Blog 1053601
Email: williams@quarryhs.co.uk
Web site: http://sciencefictionfantasy.blogspot.co.uk/
Freq: Daily

Circ: 521
Literature, Movies & Video, Science Fiction

Science Fiction Galaxies 1062120
Email: wangk1026@foxmail.com
Web site: http://blog.sina.com.cn/sfw
Freq: Daily
Circ: 51728
Airline Inflight, Auto Aftermarket, Computers, Data Management, Electronics, Fashion, Government Technology, Industry, Internet, Mobile Communications

The Science of Appearance 988705
Web site: http://www.thescienceofappearance.com/
Freq: Daily
Circ: 8637
Profile: Blog covering men's lifestyle and fashion.
Men's Interests

Sci-Fi Drama Queen 998903
Editorial: 1 Fonthill Villas, 2B Fonthill Road, London N4 3HX Tel: 44 07590 714914
Email: scifidramaqueen@gmail.com
Web site: scifidramaqueen.com
Freq: Daily
Circ: 9382
Bars, Clubs & Pubs, Comedy, Entertainment, Local Entertainment Guides, Movies & Video

Sci-MX Nutrition Blog 1052585
Tel: 44 01452 656010
Email: customerservices@sci-mx.co.uk
Web site: http://www.sci-mx.co.uk/blog/
Freq: Daily
Circ: 87
Fitness & Exercise

Scoope Mag 1096364
Email: scoopemag@hotmail.co.uk
Web site: https://scoopemag.wordpress.com/
Freq: Daily
Circ: 299
Dance Music, Fashion, Jazz & Blues, Pop Music, Rap & Hip Hop, Restaurant Reviews, Theater & Performing Arts

Scope Blog 986744
Editorial: 6 Market Road, London N7 9PW
Tel: 44 02076 197200
Email: pressoffice@scope.org.uk
Web site: http://blog.scope.org.uk/
Freq: Daily
Circ: 11406
Charitable Foundations, Community Care (UK), Disability, Patient Support

SCOT goes POP! 988443
Email: icehouse.250@gmail.com
Web site: http://scotgoespop.blogspot.co.uk/
Freq: Daily
Circ: 61525
Profile: Blog covering Scottish Politics. SCOT goes POP! discusses anything from the Scottish referendum and Scottish independence to election polls. The blog has an archive dating back to April 2008 and shares an extensive blogroll. The outlet offers RSS (Really Simply Syndication).
Politics

Scotland Votes 997941
Tel: 44 01315 566649
Web site: http://www.scotlandvotes.com/blog
Freq: Daily
Circ: 39
Politics

Scott Country Blog 1052867
Web site: http://www.scottcountryblog.blogspot.co.uk/
Freq: Daily
Circ: 15
Field Sports, Regional General Interest

Scott Matthewman 1053465
Web site: http://matthewman.net/
Freq: Daily

Circ: 3420
Broadcasting, Theater & Performing Arts

Scottish Council for Voluntary Organisations Blog   999189
Tel: 44 01314 748045
Email: enquiries@scvo.org.uk
Web site: www.scvo.org.uk/blog/
Freq: Daily
Circ: 7
Charitable Foundations, Politics

Scottish Law Reporter   986363
Email: scottishlawreporter@gmail.com
Web site: scottishlaw.blogspot.com
Freq: Daily
Circ: 7821
Scotland

Scottish Mum   986704
Email: scottishmum@gmail.com
Web site: http://scottishmum
Freq: Daily
Circ: 33273
Family & Parenting

Scottish Outlander   1053760
Web site: scottishoutlander.co.uk
Freq: Daily
Circ: 4463
Editor: Lindsay McWilliams
Profile: Blog covering lifestyle.
Cooking & Baking, Do-It-Yourself (DIY), Fashion, Nature & Wildlife, Regional General Interest, Restaurant Reviews, Travel, Women's Interests

Scottish Rugby Blog   986231
Web site: www.scottishrugbyblog.co.uk
Freq: Daily
Circ: 13173
Rugby

Scotzine   987884
Tel: 44 07870 401013
Email: editor@scotzine.com
Web site: www.scotzine.com/
Circ: 11880
Editor: Andy Muirhead
Profile: Website covering sports. The SCOTZINE website shares the latest news and information on football.
Soccer

ScrapFriends & Family   1060782
Web site: http://scrapfriendsfamily.blogspot.com/
Freq: Daily
Circ: 987
Crafts

Screen Relish   1074066
Web site: http://www.screenrelish.com/
Freq: Daily
Circ: 131648
Movies & Video

Screenwriter   1053894
Tel: 44 01675 8000
Web site: http://www.irishtimes.com/blogs/screenwriter/
Freq: Daily
Circ: 1165
Entertainment, Movies & Video

Sea Angels   1053382
Web site: http://sea-angels.blogspot.co.uk/
Freq: Daily
Circ: 731
Do-It-Yourself (DIY)

Sea That Sparkles   1061988
Email: seathatsparkles@gmail.com
Web site: http://www.seathatsparkles.com/
Freq: Daily
Circ: 2065
Fashion, Food, Lifestyle, Men's Interests, Regional General Interest, Women's Interests

Searching for Spice   997314
Editorial: 71 York Gardens, Walton on Thames, London KT12 3EN
Email: searchingforspice@hotmail.co.uk
Web site: searchingforspice.com
Freq: Daily

Circ: 13227
Cooking & Baking

Seashells & Sunflowers   1061154
Web site: http://www.seashellsandsunflowers.com
Freq: Daily
Circ: 3057
Airline Inflight, Railroad, Travel

SEATCupra.net   999305
Email: administrator@seatcupra.net
Web site: www.seatcupra.net
Freq: Daily
Circ: 125783
Automakers

Sebastian Gonzalvo   1061592
Web site: http://sebastiangonzalvo.blogspot.com/
Freq: Daily
Circ: 1862
National News

Seccion Aurea   1061828
Web site: http://www.carmenes.org
Freq: Daily
Circ: 1126
Advertising Industry, Graphic Design

Second Time Mummy   1048923
Web site: http://secondtimemummy.com
Circ: 1328
News

Secret Food Tours Recommendations   1068724
Tel: 44 02088 632146
Email: tony.levene@gmail.com
Web site: http://secretfoodtours.com/recommendations
Freq: Daily
Circ: 5886
Cooking & Baking, Food, Grocery Stores, Organic Food, Restaurant Reviews, Vegetarianism & Veganism

Secret London   1053416
Editorial: Fever, Interchange Triangle, Camden Market, Chalk Farm Road, London NW1 8AB
Email: hello@secretldn.com
Web site: secretldn.com
Freq: Daily
Circ: 602367
Alcohol & Spirits, Bars, Clubs & Pubs, Beer, Beverages, Comedy, Entertainment, Local Entertainment Guides, Movies & Video, Regional General Interest, Restaurant Reviews

Secret Style File   997481
Editorial: 21 Edinburgh Close, Pinner HA5 1JR Tel: 44 07932 051661
Email: secretstylefile@gmail.com
Web site: www.secretstylefile.com
Freq: Daily
Circ: 8994
Beauty & Grooming, Cosmetics, Fashion, Hair

Secret Victorianist   996462
Tel: 44 07590 834901
Email: secretvictorianist@gmail.com
Web site: www.secretvictorianist.com
Freq: Daily
Circ: 8697
Literature

Secret Wedding Blog   996353
Email: hello@secretweddingblog.com
Web site: secretweddingblog.com
Freq: Daily
Circ: 23849
Weddings

Secretos del Abuelo   1061223
Web site: http://www.lossecretosdelabuelo.com/
Freq: Daily
Circ: 611
Alternative Medicine

Secretstylist   1061297
Web site: http://secretstylist.blogspot.com
Freq: Daily

Circ: 470
Fashion

Sediment   985869
Email: cjandpk@gmail.com
Web site: http://sedimentblog.blogspot.co.uk/
Freq: Daily
Circ: 12282
Profile: Sediment blog covers wine.
Alcohol & Spirits, Bars, Clubs & Pubs, Beer, Beverages, Cooking & Baking, Food, Grocery Stores, Organic Food, Restaurant Reviews, Vegetarianism & Veganism

Seduccion   1061836
Web site: http://seduccionstark.blogspot.com/
Freq: Daily
Circ: 875
Careers, Crime & Violence, Family & Parenting, Health & Medicine, Lifestyle, Personal Finance, Relationships

Seedrs Blog   996286
Editorial: 201 Borough High Street, London SE1 1JA
Web site: https://www.seedrs.com/learn/blog
Freq: Daily
Circ: 60
Business, Corporate Responsibility, Equities, Small and Medium Business

Seeds and Stitches   1052538
Email: seedsandstitches@gmail.com
Web site: http://www.seedsandstitches.com/
Freq: Daily
Circ: 6698
Art, Crafts, Do-It-Yourself (DIY), Family & Parenting

Seenit blog   997391
Editorial: 57-59 Beak Street, London W1F 9SJ
Email: info@seenit.io
Web site: http://seenit.io/blog
Freq: Daily
Circ: 4
Advertising Industry, Graphic Design, Marketing, Mobile Electronics, Photography

Segundas Lecturas   1061201
Web site: http://segundaslecturas.blogspot.com
Freq: Daily
Circ: 801
International News, Politics

Selfish Mother   996630
Editorial: 8 Beira Street, London SW12 9LJ
Web site: www.SelfishMother.com
Freq: Daily
Circ: 26648
News & Current Affairs

Self-sufficient in Suburbia   1053802
Web site: self-sufficientinsuburbia.blogspot.com
Freq: Daily
Circ: 687
Cooking & Baking, Organic Food

Selina Lake blog   1054340
Email: stylist@selinalake.co.uk
Web site: http://selinalake.blogspot.co.uk/
Freq: Daily
Circ: 3835
Do-It-Yourself (DIY)

Selina Wears   986944
Web site: www.selinawears.com
Freq: Daily
Circ: 1219650
Editor: Selina Jervis
Fashion

SellMyMobile.com Blog   999190
Editorial: Spear House, Cobbett Road, Burntwood WS7 3GL Tel: 44 08715 661691
Web site: www.sellmymobile.com/blog/
Freq: Daily

Circ: 51149
Mobile Electronics

Sempre Inter   998382
Email: nima@sempreinter.com
Web site: http://www.sempreinter.com/
Freq: Daily
Circ: 626299
Editor: Nima Tavallaey Roodsari
Soccer

Semsee's Sparkly Scribblings   988172
Email: semsee@ymail.com
Web site: http://semsee.blogspot.co.uk/
Freq: Daily
Circ: 521
Crafts

SenSpa Blog   1053721
Tel: 44 01590 624467
Email: relax@senspa.co.uk
Web site: http://blog.senspa.co.uk/
Freq: Daily
Circ: 11
Alternative Medicine, Fitness & Exercise, Nutrition

Sentado Frente al Mundo   1061930
Email: sentadofrentealmundo@gmail.com
Web site: http://sentado-frente-al-mundo.blogspot.com/
Freq: Daily
Circ: 1489
Lifestyle, Men's Interests, Regional General Interest, Women's Interests

SEOno   1098988
Web site: http://seono.co.uk/
Freq: Daily
Circ: 45894
Marketing

Seoul Eats   1061795
Web site: http://www.seouleats.com
Freq: Daily
Circ: 26814
Food, Restaurant Reviews

Séptimo Sentido   1061562
Web site: http://septimosentido.blogspot.com
Freq: Daily
Circ: 488
Antiques/Collectibles, Art, Arts, Classical/Choral/Band Music, Country, Folk, Bluegrass, Dance Music, Jazz & Blues, Literature, Movies & Video, Music

Serendipity Reviews   987973
Web site: www.serendipityreviews.co.uk/
Freq: Daily
Circ: 9619
Editor: Vivienne Dacosta
Literature

Serenity You   988536
Email: serenityyou@hotmail.co.uk
Web site: www.serenityyou.com
Freq: Daily
Circ: 47777
Family & Parenting

Sergio Space   1061366
Web site: http://www.sergioelbio.blogspot.com
Freq: Daily
Circ: 578
National News, Politics

Seti   1060624
Web site: http://www.seti.cl
Freq: Daily
Circ: 3073
Astronomy, Science

Seven Colored Map Diary   1062083
Email: cmap777@gmail.com
Web site: http://blog.sina.com.cn/qiseditu
Freq: Daily
Circ: 141620
Airline Inflight, Photography, Railroad, Travel

Seven Miles of Steel Thistles
089006
Web site: http://steelthistles.blogspot.co.uk/
Freq: Daily
Circ: 8138
Literature

Sew create it
1054946
Web site: http://janeweston.blogspot.com/
Freq: Daily
Circ: 3215
Crafts, Photography

Sew Justine Sew
1052953
Email: justine-mullins@sky.com
Web site: http://sewjustinesew.blogspot.co.uk/
Freq: Daily
Circ: 1857
Crafts

Sew, Incidentally...
1052934
Email: sew.incidentally@yahoo.com
Web site: http://sew-incidentally.blogspot.co.uk/
Freq: Daily
Circ: 7947
Crafts, Fashion

Sex & London City
988275
Web site: http://www.sexandloncity.co.uk/
Circ: 8281
Beauty & Grooming, Cosmetics, Fashion, Hair, Relationships

Sex Drugs and Bacon Rolls
988751
Editorial: Unit 14, Jacks Place, London E1 6NN
Email: foodblog@hotmail.co.uk
Web site: http://sexdrugsandbaconrolls.wordpress.com
Freq: Daily
Circ: 2
Profile: Blog covering food. The Sex Drugs and Bacon Rolls blog discusses anything from food and restaurant reviews.
Alcohol & Spirits, Bars, Clubs & Pubs, Beer, Beverages, Cooking & Baking, Food, Grocery Stores, Organic Food, Restaurant Reviews, Vegetarianism & Veganism

Shabby Chick
998245
Email: andreamynard@yahoo.co.uk
Web site: http://www.shabbychick.me.uk/
Freq: Daily
Circ: 6162
Airline Inflight, Cooking & Baking, Food, Grocery Stores, Organic Food, Railroad, Regional General Interest, Restaurant Reviews, Travel, Vegetarianism & Veganism

The Shakespeare Blog
999637
Email: shakespearesbeagle@yahoo.co.uk
Web site: theshakespeareblog.com
Freq: Daily
Circ: 16213
Literature

Shanghai Eye
1061529
Web site: http://www.shanghaieye.net
Freq: Daily
Circ: 1047
Antiques/Collectibles, Art, Arts, Literature, Photography, Theater & Performing Arts, Visual Arts

Shaolin Tiger
1053064
Freq: Daily
News & Current Affairs

The Share Centre Blog
996432
Editorial: PO Box 2000, Aylesbury HP21 8ZB Tel: 44 01296 439256
Email: pressoffice@share.co.uk
Web site: https://www.share.com/blog/
Freq: Daily
Circ: 50435
Bonds, Economics, Emerging Markets, Financial Markets, Investment Banking

Share Sleuth
986687
Editorial: 2 West Regent Street, Glasgow G2 1RW Tel: 44 01412 06399

Web site: http://www.iii.co.uk/news-opinion/blog/share-sleuth
Freq: Daily
Circ: 71607
News & Current Affairs

Sharking for Chips & Drinks
1073643
Web site: http://sharkingforchipsanddrinks.com
Freq: Daily
Circ: 11884
Restaurant Reviews

She by SMD
1098953
Editorial: 14 Douglas Muir Grds, Milngavie, Glasgow G62 7RZ
Web site: www.shebysmd.com
Freq: Daily
Circ: 10072
Beauty & Grooming, Cosmetics, Fashion, Hair, Lifestyle, Men's Interests, Regional General Interest, Women's Interests

She Dreams
1056323
Web site: http://www.shedreams.co.uk/
Freq: Daily
Circ: 7619
Beauty & Grooming, Cosmetics, Entertainment, Fashion, Hair

She Gets Around
1054064
Web site: http://shegetsaround.co.uk/
Freq: Daily
Circ: 10550
Travel

She Goes Wear
994975
Editorial: 1 Hammersmith Broadway, London W6 9DL
Web site: shegoeswear.com
Freq: Daily
Circ: 7970
Beauty & Grooming, Cosmetics, Fashion, Hair, Women's Interests

She Loves To Read - CEASED 2016
996351
Web site: http://shelovestoread.weebly.com/
Freq: Daily
Circ: 20
Literature

She Might be Loved
1053745
Email: georgina@shemightbeloved.com
Web site: http://www.shemightbeloved.com/
Freq: Daily
Circ: 13808
Profile: Blog covering lifestyle, plus size fashion and beauty. The blog has an archive dating back to June 2013.
Beauty & Grooming, Cooking & Baking, Cosmetics, Fashion, Hair, Travel, Women's Interests

She Reads Novels
987970
Email: shereadsnovels@gmail.com
Web site: http://shereadsnovels.wordpress.com/
Freq: Daily
Circ: 354
Profile: Blog covering literature. She Reads Novels discusses anything from historical fiction and classics to fantasy and science fiction. The blog has an archive dating back to October 2009 and shares an extensive blogroll. The outlet offers RSS (Really Simple Syndication).
Literature

She Wears Fashion
988706
Email: shewearsfashion@gmail.com
Web site: www.shewearsfashion.com
Freq: Daily
Circ: 39592
Women's Interests

Shed blog
1052791
Freq: Daily
Do-It-Yourself (DIY), Gardening

Shedworking
1054509
Web site: http://www.shedworking.co.uk/
Freq: Daily

Circ: 44903
Architecture & Design, Building & Construction, Do-It Yourself (DIY), Property Management & Maintenance, Residential Real Estate, Sustainable Development

Shelley Makes
1075501
Web site: https://shelleymakes.com/
Freq: Daily
Circ: 134
Editor: Shelley George
Art, Crafts

Shelter policy blog
986747
Editorial: 88 Old Street, London EC1V 9HU
Tel: 44 02075 052162
Email: press_office@shelter.org.uk
Web site: blog.shelter.org.uk
Freq: Daily
Circ: 260677
Profile: Blog covering charity and social policy with regards to housing issues in the UK. The blog has an archive dating back to January 2012 and shares an extensive blog roll.
Charitable Foundations, Social Issues

Shenzhen Noted
1060983
Web site: http://maryannodonnell.wordpress.com
Freq: Daily
Circ: 55
Social Issues

Shepherds Walks
1053532
Tel: 44 01669 621044
Email: info@shepherdswalks.co.uk
Web site: http://shepherdswalks.co.uk/blog
Freq: Daily
Circ: 60
Outdoor Recreation, Travel

The Shift - Le Miami's Insider Edit
1059121
Web site: http://www.lemiami.com/the-shift/
Freq: Daily
Circ: 34
Editor: Katie Sharples; Editor: Olivia Squire
Luxury Goods, Travel, Women's Interests

Shiny Nail Art
1061921
Email: shinynailartblogi@gmail.com
Web site: http://shiny-nailart.blogspot.com
Freq: Daily
Circ: 1997
Beauty & Grooming, Cosmetics, Hair, Internet

Shiny New Books
995530
Email: info@shinynewbooks.co.uk
Web site: http://shinynewbooks.co.uk/
Freq: Daily
Circ: 15118
Literature

shinyshiny
983290
Editorial: Sutro Digital, Grand Parade, 47 Bermondsey Street, London SE1 3XT
Tel: 44 07885 836842
Email: chris@shinymedia.com
Web site: www.shinyshiny.tv
Freq: Daily
Circ: 73873
Apple, Audio Video Trade, Cameras, Computer & Video Games, Computers, Consumer Electronics, Internet, Mobile Electronics, Movies & Video, Personal Computers

Shipmonk
1053252
Email: dave@davecmonk.com
Web site: http://shipmonk.co.uk/
Freq: Daily
Circ: 10379
Profile: Blog covering cruises. The SHIPMONK blog discusses anything from cruises and cruise ships to destinations and cruising news. The blog has an archive dating back to March 2013.
News & Current Affairs

Shiraz Socialist
1053373
Email: voltairespriest@gmail.com
Web site: https://shirazsocialist.wordpress.com
Freq: Daily

Circ: 7099
International News, National News, Politics, Social Issues

Shirley's Wardrobe
1054363
Freq: Daily
Profile: Blog covering fashion. SHIRLEY'S WARDROBE blog discusses anything from the latest fashion trends and personal style to beauty and shopping. The blog has an archive dating back to January 2009. The outlet offers RSS (Really Simple Syndication).
News & Current Affairs

Shirls Gardenwatch
986791
Email: shirl@shirlsgardenwatch.co.uk
Web site: blog.shirlsgardenwatch.co.uk
Freq: Daily
Gardening, Nature & Wildlife

SHLYNSBIN
987104
Web site: www.shlynsbin.com
Freq: Daily
Circ: 903
Beauty & Grooming, Cosmetics, Hair

The Shoe Snob
1052905
Editorial: Timothy Everest, 35 Bruton Place, London W1J 6NS
Web site: http://www.theshoesnobblog.com/
Freq: Daily
Circ: 118121
Fashion

Shoeperwoman
986232
Web site: www.shoeperwoman.com
Freq: Daily
Circ: 42834
Fashion

Shonagh Scott Vlog
1096369
Email: info@showme-makeup.co.uk
Web site: https://www.youtube.com/user/smiles2310
Freq: Daily
Circ: 4
Beauty & Grooming, Cosmetics, Hair

ShopSafe
1052579
Tel: 44 01912 325684
Email: graham@shopsafe.co.uk
Web site: http://blog.shopsafe.co.uk/news/
Freq: Daily
Circ: 19
Business, Shopping

ShopStyle Blog
1054070
Web site: http://www.shopstyle.co.uk/blog
Freq: Daily
Circ: 1065
Fashion

Shotgun Korea
1060936
Web site: http://shotgunkorea.wordpress.com
Freq: Daily
Circ: 28
Alumni, Careers, Disability, Education, Higher Education, Preschool, Schools & Institutions, Student Lifestyle, Students, Teachers

The SHOWstudio Blog
986260
Editorial: SHOWstudio, 19 Motcomb St, Belgravia, London SW1X 8LB
Tel: 44 02072 357680
Email: feedback@showstudio.com
Web site: www.showstudio.com/blog
Circ: 88
Editor: Lou Stoppard
Fashion

Shreddelicious
1066387
Web site: http://www.shreddelicious.com/
Freq: Daily
Circ: 15133
Music, Rock Music

The Shrieking Violet
998409
Email: natalie.rose.bradbury@googlemail.com
Web site: theshriekingviolets.blogspot.com
Freq: Daily
Circ: 9235
Art

UK Blogs

Shy Strange Manic 1053126
Email: shystrangemanic@gmail.com
Web site: http://www.shystrangemanic.
com/
Freq: Daily
Circ: 9476
Beauty & Grooming, Cosmetics, Fashion,
Hair, Literature, Women's Interests

Side Street Style 988693
Email: sidestreetstyleblog@gmail.com
Web site: www.sidestreetstyle.com
Freq: Daily
Circ: 53804
Profile: Blog covering lifestyle, parenting,
interiors and travel. The blog has an archive
dating back to August 2009 and shares an
extensive blogroll.
Fashion, Women's Interests

sidepodcast Blog 996466
Web site: http://sidepodcast.com/blog
Freq: Daily
Circ: 31
Editor: Christine Blachford
News & Current Affairs

Siempre Natural 1061519
Web site: http://siempre-natural.blogspot.
com/
Freq: Daily
Circ: 521
Alternative Medicine

Signos 1061667
Web site: http://signos-contexto.blogspot.
com
Freq: Daily
Circ: 1275
Government

Silla Chic 1061064
Web site: http://lasillachic.blogspot.com/
Freq: Daily
Circ: 1319
Crafts, Hobbies, & Collecting, Do-It-
Yourself (DIY), Interior Design

SilverSpoon London 997668
Editorial: 1308, 20 Palace Street, London
SW1E 5BB
Web site: http://www.silverspoonlondon.co.
uk/
Freq: Daily
Circ: 89664
Profile: Blog covering London lifestyle.
SILVERSPOON LONDON blog discusses
anything from the London food scene and
London events to luxury travel. The blog has
an archive dating back to January 2014. The
outlet offers RSS (Really Simple
Syndication).
Cooking & Baking, Food, Grocery Stores,
Organic Food, Restaurant Reviews,
Travel, Vegetarianism & Veganism,
Women's Interests

Silversprite 1054104
Web site: http://www.silversprite.com
Freq: Daily
Circ: 3900
Computer & Video Games

SilverTiger 1052681
Web site: https://tigergrowl.wordpress.com/
Freq: Daily
Circ: 100
Regional General Interest

Simon Antrobus' blog 996866
Editorial: 67-69 Cowcross Street, London
EC1M 6PU Tel: 44 02070 172747
Email: pressoffice@addaction.org.uk
Web site: http://www.addaction.org.uk/blog
Freq: Daily
Circ: 3
Charitable Foundations

Simon Lovell Blog 1053131
Tel: 44 01225 446875
Email: simon@simonlovell.co.uk
Web site: http://www.simonlovell.co.uk/
Freq: Daily
Circ: 9666
Branding, Business, Fitness & Exercise,
Marketing

Simon May Blog 1053310
Email: mail@mygeekout.com
Web site: http://simon-may.com/
Freq: Daily
Circ: 26211
News & Current Affairs

Simon Wakeman Blog 986688
Editorial: 57 Oaks Park, Rough Common,
Canterbury CT2 9DP
Web site: simonwakeman.com
Freq: Daily
Circ: 6890
Advertising Industry, Branding, Graphic
Design, Marketing

Simonblog 1060934
Web site: http://www.simonblog.com
Freq: Daily
Circ: 55554
Auto Aftermarket, Computers, Data
Management, Electronics, Government
Technology, Industry, Internet, Mobile
Communications, Security & Security
Systems, Software

Simon's JamJar 1100049
Email: hello@simonsjamjar.com
Web site: http://www.simonsjamjar.com/
Freq: Daily
Circ: 7603
Travel

Simon's SQL Blog 1053560
Web site: http://sqlblogcasts.com/blogs/
simons/default.aspx
Freq: Daily
Circ: 14791
Computers, Data Management, Internet

simple thoughts 1052988
Web site: david.deltaflow.com
Freq: Daily
Circ: 5
Religion

Simple y Llano 1061381
Web site: http://www.simpleyllano.com
Freq: Daily
Circ: 521
Auto Aftermarket, Computers, Data
Management, Electronics, Government
Technology, Graphic Design, Industry,
Internet, Mobile Communications,
Security & Security Systems

Simply Cooked 1053471
Email: simplycookedblog@gmail.com
Web site: http://simplycooked.blogspot.co.
uk/
Freq: Daily
Circ: 688
Cooking & Baking, Restaurant Reviews

Simply Hike 1052624
Email: info@simplyhike.co.uk
Web site: https://www.simplyhike.co.uk/
blog/
Freq: Daily
Circ: 6534
Outdoor Recreation

Simply Oloni 988455
Email: itsoloni@gmail.com
Web site: http://simplyoloni.com/
Freq: Daily
Circ: 16443
Profile: Blog covering sex, love &
relationships. The blog has an archive dating
back to August 2008.
Relationships, Women's Interests

Simply Splendiferous 1053846
Email: splediferousblog@btinternet.com
Web site: http://simplysplendiferous.com/
Freq: Daily
Circ: 6948
Art, Cooking & Baking, Visual Arts

simply.food 988556
Email: simplysensationalfood@gmail.com
Web site: www.simplysensationalfood.com
Freq: Daily
Circ: 11803
Vegetarianism & Veganism

Simplyscuba Blog 1053676
Email: customercare@simplyscuba.com
Web site: https://www.simplyscuba.com/
blog/
Freq: Daily
Circ: 164
Swimming/Watersports, Travel

Simply-Woman.com 983763
Email: editor@simply-woman.com
Web site: http://www.simply-woman.com
Circ: 7540
Editor: Sarah Saunders
Airline Inflight, Bars, Clubs & Pubs,
Beauty & Grooming, Celebrities, Comedy,
Cosmetics, Entertainment, Fashion, Hair,
Local Entertainment Guides

Sim's Life Blog 996498
Email: sim@simslife.co.uk
Web site: www.simslife.co.uk
Freq: Daily
Circ: 9970
Family & Parenting, Fitness & Exercise,
Nutrition

Single Parent Dad 1054055
Email: contactspd@gmail.com
Web site: http://singleparentdad.blogspot.
co.uk/
Freq: Daily
Circ: 1954
Family & Parenting

Siskot Kokkaa 1062077
Email: siskotkokkaa@gmail.com
Web site: http://siskotkokkaa.blogspot.com
Freq: Daily
Circ: 2017
Alcohol & Spirits, Consumer Goods &
Products, Cooking & Baking, Food,
Tobacco

Sistema Bach 1061004
Web site: http://sistemabach.blogspot.com/
Freq: Daily
Circ: 611
Alternative Medicine

sisterhood (and all that) 996898
Web site: http://www.dontbuyherflowers.
com/sisterhoodandallthat/
Freq: Daily
Circ: 143
Family & Parenting, Relationships

Sisustus ja Sepustus 1061935
Web site: http://sisustusjasepustus.
indiedays.com/
Freq: Daily
Circ: 24580
Architecture & Design, Cooking & Baking,
Do-It-Yourself (DIY), Gardening, Home,
Interior Design, Property Management &
Maintenance, Real Estate

Sisustusblogi 1060772
Email: info@sisustusblogi.fi
Web site: http://sisustusblogi.fi
Freq: Daily
Circ: 1866
Architecture & Design, Do-It-Yourself
(DIY), Gardening, Home, Interior Design,
Property Management & Maintenance,
Real Estate

SiteVisibility 1053498
Editorial: King Place Suite, 3 King Place,
Brighton BN1 1GA Tel: 44 01273 733433
Web site: http://www.sitevisibility.co.uk/
blog/category/theblog/
Freq: Daily
Circ: 80
Internet, Marketing

six out of ten 987243
Email: sixoutoftenmag@gmail.com
Web site: www.sixoutoften.co.uk
Freq: Daily
Circ: 44659
Profile: Blog covering travel, lifestyle, food,
drink, hotels, budget, luxury, days out,
beauty and fashion. The blog has an archive
dating back to March 2013.
Travel, Women's Interests

Sixt Car Hire Blog 1054563
Tel: 44 08444 993399
Email: reservations@sixt.com
Web site: http://www.sixtblog.co.uk/
Freq: Daily
Circ: 1676
Automakers, Automotive, Driving, Off-
road & 4-Wheel Drive Vehicles

The Sixth Axis 988180
Email: pr@thesixthaxis.com
Web site: http://www.thesixthaxis.com/
Circ: 199439
Computer & Video Games

Skamasle 1060565
Web site: http://www.skamasle.com
Freq: Daily
Circ: 26880
Auto Aftermarket, Computers, Data
Management, Electronics, Government
Technology, Industry, Internet, Mobile
Communications, Security & Security
Systems, Software

The Ski Blog - Chalets Direct
996683
Email: info@chaletsdirect.com
Web site: skiblog.chaletsdirect.com
Freq: Daily
Circ: 21
Travel, Winter Sports

Ski Buzz 987702
Tel: 44 08712 369501
Email: contact@crystalholidays.co.uk
Web site: www.ski-buzz.co.uk
Freq: Daily
Circ: 9625
Winter Sports

Ski Club Blog 996659
Editorial: 57-63 Church Road, London
SW19 5SB Tel: 44 02084 102000
Email: skiers@skiclub.co.uk
Web site: http://skiclubgb.wordpress.com/
Freq: Daily
Circ: 2
Travel, Winter Sports

Ski Independence blog 1052922
Editorial: 21 Logie Mill, Edinburgh EH7 4HG
Email: marketing@ski-i.com
Web site: http://www.ski-i.com/blog
Freq: Daily
Circ: 16
Winter Sports

The Skiing Department 998217
Email: info@snow.guide
Web site: http://blog.
themountaindepartment.com/
Freq: Daily
Circ: 33
Editor: Robert Stewart
Winter Sports

The Skin and Beauty Blog 998017
Email: theskinandbeautyblog@gmail.com
Web site: www.theskinandbeautyblog.com
Freq: Daily
Circ: 6363
Beauty & Grooming, Cosmetics, Hair

Skin Deep Blog 987189
Email: contact@skindeepbeautyblog.com
Web site: www.skindeepbeautyblog.com
Freq: Daily
Circ: 9736
Beauty & Grooming, Cosmetics, Hair

Skineable 1061105
Web site: http://www.skineable.com
Freq: Daily
Circ: 3828
Electronics, Graphic Design, Internet

The Skinny Doll 998348
Email: theskinnydoll@gmail.com
Web site: http://www.theskinnydoll.com/
Freq: Daily
Circ: 8176
News & Current Affairs

The Skint Dad Blog 988033
Web site: skintdad.co.uk

Freq: Daily
Circ. 141071
Profile: Blog covering personal finance for parents looking to save money, make money and manage money. The blog has an archive dating back to August 2013. 'The Skint Dad blog's mantra is all about spending less, without living without. It covers budgeting, cheap meals, money saving, money making and other personal finance topics.'
Family & Parenting, Personal Finance

The Skint Sailor 1057617
Email: skintsailor@yahoo.co.uk
Web site: theskintsaiilor.blogspot.co.uk
Freq: Daily
Circ: 578
Boating & Yachting

Skittish Library 998267
Email: skittishlibrary@outlook.com
Web site: http://skittishlibrary.co.uk/
Freq: Daily
Circ: 10203
Antiques/Collectibles, Art, Arts, Literature, Photography, Theater & Performing Arts, Visual Arts

Skiworld Blog 987713
Editorial: 3 Vencourt Place, London W6 9NU
Tel: 44 08444 930430
Email: admin@skiworld.co.uk
Web site: www.skiworld.co.uk/blog/
Freq: Daily
Circ: 92
Profile: Blog covering skiing.
Travel, Winter Sports

Sky Blues blog 997962
Email: neil@skybluesblog.co.uk
Web site: http://www.skybluesblog.co.uk/
Freq: Daily
Circ: 11557
Soccer

Slimmedcartree 1053691
Email: corinne@skinnedcartree.com
Web site: http://slimmedcartree.com/
Freq: Daily
Circ: 33074
Fitness & Exercise, Nutrition

Slinky By Tuesday 988178
Web site: slinkybytuesday.blogspot.co.uk
Freq: Daily
Circ: 521
Profile: Slinky By Tuesday blog covers weight loss, nutrition and fitness.
Nutrition

The Slog 1054654
Web site: https://hat4uk.wordpress.com/
Freq: Daily
Circ: 60984
Politics, Social Issues

Sloth Boogie 988341
Editorial: Another Kind Studio, Unit G13 Olympic House, 12 Somerford Grove, London N16 7RZ
Email: patrick@slothboogie.com
Web site: http://www.slothboogie.com/
Freq: Daily
Circ: 26484
Dance Music

The Slow Lane 1059416
Tel: 44 01653 617001
Web site: http://www.inntravel.co.uk/slow
Freq: Daily
Circ: 56
News & Current Affairs

Slugger O'Toole 986234
Email: editor@sluggerotoole.com
Web site: sluggerotoole.com
Freq: Daily
Circ: 54631
Politics

Slummy Single Mummy 1052643
Web site: http://slummysinglemummy.com/
Freq: Daily
Circ: 49035
Family & Parenting

The SMALL BUSINESS BLOG 986637
Web site: http://sme-blog.com
Freq: Daily
Circ: 29423
Business

Small Business Heroes 987320
Tel: 44 02075 806502
Email: editor@smallbusinessheroes.co.uk
Web site: smallbusinessheroes.co.uk
Circ: 13387
Editor: Lauren Mason
Profile: Website covering small business. The SMALL BUSINESS HEROES website shares the latest news and information on small business and entrepreneurship in the UK. "Its features, profiles and advice sections are aimed at offering straight-talking insight into life as a UK SME owner, providing a resource for all types of small businesses."
Business, Small and Medium Business

Small Crazy 1053095
Email: y@smallcrazy.com
Web site: www.smallcrazy.com
Freq: Daily
Circ: 4366
Fashion, Travel, Women's Interests

Small Luxury Hotels of the World Blog 1053945
Tel: 44 08000 482314
Email: reservation@slh.com
Web site: http://blog.slh.com/
Freq: Daily
Circ: 15
Airline Inflight, Railroad, Travel

The Small Places 1052940
Web site: http://thesmallplaces.wordpress.com
Freq: Daily
Circ: 10619
Law, Social Issues

The Smallest Smallholding 906709
Web site: www.smallestsmallholding.com
Freq: Daily
Circ: 1555
News & Current Affairs

The Smart Girl's Travel Guide 1054203
Email: johnny@onestep4ward.com
Web site: http://www.thesmartgirlstravelguide.com/
Freq: Daily
Circ: 6018
Railroad, Travel

Smart Insights 1052577
Email: alexander.clark@smartinsights.com
Web site: http://www.smartinsights.com/blog/
Freq: Daily
Circ: 1133041
Advertising Industry, Branding, Marketing

The Smart Leisure Guide 997660
Editorial: Flat 4, 15 Leslie Place, Edinburgh EH4 1NF **Tel:** 44 01313 432116
Web site: http://smartleisureguide.wordpress.com/
Freq: Daily
Airline Inflight, Railroad, Travel

Smart Traffic 1053107
Email: enquiries@smart-traffic.co.uk
Web site: smart-traffic.co.uk/blog/
Freq: Daily
Circ: 297
Marketing

SMB Bearings blog 1052897
Tel: 44 01993 842555
Email: accounts@smbbearings.com
Web site: http://smbbearings.blogspot.co.uk/
Freq: Daily
Circ: 752
Extreme/Adventure Sports

Smells Like Fashion 897873
Email: smellslikefashion.blog@gmail.com
Web site: http://www.smellslikefashion.com
Freq: Daily
Circ: 3222
Beauty & Grooming, Fashion, Lifestyle

Smells Like Fashion 1065159
Email: smellslikefashion.blog@gmail.com
Web site: http://www.smellslikefashion.com/en/
Freq: Daily
Circ: 830
Cosmetics, Fashion, Women's Interests

SMP 988428
Editorial: c/o Elemental Communications Limited, Lincoln House, 75 Brokesley Street, London E3 4QJ
Web site: www.socialmediaportal.com
Circ: 40227
Audio Video Trade, Cameras, Consumer Electronics, Mobile Electronics, Movies & Video

Smudgetikka 986720
Editorial: 38 Kirkley Road, London SW19 3AY
Email: smudgetikka@gmail.com
Web site: www.smudgetikka.com
Freq: Daily
Circ: 36186
Fashion

Snoman 1053026
Tel: 44 02081 338899
Email: snoman@sno.co.uk
Web site: https://www.sno.co.uk/blog/
Freq: Daily
Circ: 875
Travel, Winter Sports

Snookerbacker 1053081
Email: snookerbacker@ymail.com
Web site: http://www.snookerbacker.com/
Freq: Daily
Circ: 27158
Billiards

Snow Guide 1053708
Email: info@snow.guide
Web site: http://blog.themountaindepartment.com
Freq: Daily
Circ: 37
Winter Sports

Snowboard Blog 996730
Editorial: 26-28 Reading Road South, Fleet, Fleet GU52 7QL **Tel:** 44 01252 612223
Email: info@thesnowboardshop.co.uk
Web site: http://www.thesnowboardshop.co.uk/blog/
Freq: Daily
Circ: 18
Winter Sports

Snowing Indoors 1100171
Email: em@snowingindoors.com
Web site: http://www.snowingindoors.com/
Freq: Daily
Circ: 6737
Family & Parenting

SNUFFELDYRETS LILLE VER-DEN 1061549
Web site: http://snuffeldyret.blogspot.com
Freq: Daily
Circ: 900
Gardening

Snug Corner 1054936
Email: snugscorner@gmail.com
Web site: http://www.snugcorner.co.uk
Freq: Daily
Circ: 1060
Beauty & Grooming, Cosmetics, Fashion, Hair, Health & Medicine, Nutrition, Women's Interests

So Little Time for Books 1052716
Email: solittletimeforbooks@googlemail.com
Web site: http://solittletimeforbooks.blogspot.co.uk/
Freq: Daily
Circ: 5023
Literature

So Many Lovely Things 987998
Email: somanylovelythings@gmail.com
Web site: somanylovelythings.com
Freq: Daily
Circ: 9504
Profile: Blog covering beauty, product reviews, make-up, skincare, nail care, fashion, shoes and accessories. The blog shares an extensive blog roll.
Cosmetics, Fashion, Women's Interests

So Sue Me 998184
Email: suzanne@sosueme.ie
Web site: sosueme.ie
Freq: Daily
Circ: 44517
News & Current Affairs

So what's up?! 1061311
Email: christian.brosstad@gmail.com
Web site: http://christianbrosstad.com
Freq: Daily
Circ: 10051
Internet

So Wrong It's Nom 1053651
Editorial: 3 Ripon Road, London N176PP
Email: hello@sowrongitsnom.com
Web site: http://sowrongitsnom.com/
Freq: Daily
Circ: 11108
Cooking & Baking, Restaurant Reviews

So You're Getting Married 987287
Web site: http://www.soyouregettingmarried.com/
Freq: Daily
Circ: 8046
Weddings

Sobre la Marcha 1062057
Web site: http://blogs.eluniversal.com/eu3/Blogs/smarc_index.shtml
Freq: Daily
Circ: 17653
Politics

Sobre Notebooks 1062071
Web site: http://www.sobrenotebooks.com.ar
Freq: Daily
Circ: 917
Personal Computers, Software

The Sociable 1053696
Email: info@sociable.co
Web site: http://sociable.co/
Freq: Daily
Circ: 49706
Computer & Video Games, Government Technology, Internet, Mobile Electronics

Social Beautify 987967
Email: info@socialbeautify.co.uk
Web site: www.socialbeautify.co.uk
Freq: Daily
Circ: 7958
Profile: Blog covering beauty, beauty tips and cosmetics. The blog has an archive dating back to May 2011. This outlet offers a vlog.
Beauty & Grooming, Cosmetics, Fashion, Hair

Social Bookshelves 1053224
Web site: www.socialbookshelves.com
Freq: Daily
Circ: 14859
Literature

Social Finance 1052946
Editorial: Social Finance Ltd, 131-151 Great Titchfield Street, London W1W 5BB
Email: info@socialfinance.org.uk
Web site: http://www.socialfinance.org.uk/resources/blogs/
Freq: Daily
Circ: 1

The Social Issue 987326
Tel: 44 07788 474253
Email: saba@sabasalman.com
Web site: thesocialissue.com
Freq: Daily
Circ: 9299
Social Issues

UK Blogs

Social Media London Blog
1070069
Web site: http://socialmedialondon.co.uk/category/blog/
Freq: Daily
Circ: 108
Editor: Laurence Hebberd
Marketing

Socialist Health Association Blog
987988
Editorial: 22 Blair Road, Manchester M16 8NS Tel: 44 01612 861926
Email: admin@sochealth.co.uk
Web site: www.sochealth.co.uk/home/blog/
Circ: 29
Health & Medicine, Politics

Socialist Unity
986236
Web site: socialistunity.com
Freq: Daily
Circ: 12217
News & Current Affairs

SocioLingo Africa
1054280
Web site: www.sociolingo.com
Freq: Daily
Circ: 8127
News & Current Affairs

Sociología Contemporánea
1061322
Web site: http://www.sociologiac.net
Freq: Daily
Circ: 10827
Auto Aftermarket, Computers, Data Management, Electronics, Government Technology, Industry, Internet, Mobile Communications, Science, Security & Security Systems

sockertjocken.se
1060180
Web site: http://sockertjocken.se
Freq: Daily
Circ: 1422
Alternative Medicine, Disability, Fitness & Exercise, Health & Medicine, Media Relations, Medicine, Nutrition, Patient Support, Personal Health & Wellness, Psychology

sockertjocken.se
1060668
Web site: http://sockertjocken.se
Freq: Daily
Circ: 1422
Alternative Medicine, Disability, Fitness & Exercise, Health & Medicine, Media Relations, Medicine, Nutrition, Patient Support, Personal Health & Wellness, Psychology

Sofa Stories
1103015
Web site: http://sofastories.co.uk/
Freq: Daily
Circ: 900
Family & Parenting, Women's Interests

Soft-Libre
1061018
Web site: http://www.elsoftwarelibre.wordpress.com
Freq: Daily
Circ: 55
Computers, Software

Software Utilitario Gratis para PC
1061206
Web site: http://blogs.clarin.com/utilitarios-pc/
Freq: Daily
Circ: 70506
Software

Softwarelogia
1061704
Web site: http://www.softwarelogia.com
Freq: Daily
Circ: 11839
Auto Aftermarket, Computers, Data Management, Electronics, Government Technology, Industry, Internet, Mobile Communications, Security & Security Systems, Software

Solamente Futbol
1060726
Web site: http://www.solamentefutbol.cl
Freq: Daily

Circ: 11448
Soccer

The Soldiers' Charity blog
996121
Web site: https://www.soldierscharity.org/
Freq: Daily
Circ: 19129
News & Current Affairs

Solitary Walker
1054020
Web site: http://www.solitary-walker.blogspot.co.uk/
Freq: Daily
Circ: 548
Outdoor Recreation, Travel

Solo Noche
1061476
Web site: http://www.solonoche.com
Freq: Daily
Circ: 1344
Bars, Clubs & Pubs, Celebrities, Classical/Choral/Band Music, Comedy, Country, Folk, Bluegrass, Dance Music, Entertainment, Jazz & Blues, Local Entertainment Guides, Movies & Video

Sólo Trucos
1060354
Web site: http://www.solotrucos.org
Freq: Daily
Circ: 1238
Internet

Some Superfluous Opinions
1060874
Email: starlened@gmail.com
Web site: http://somesuperfluousopinions.blogspot.fi/
Freq: Daily
Circ: 1653
Theater & Performing Arts

SomersF1 - The technical side of Formula One
1096035
Email: somersf1@gmail.com
Web site: http://www.somersf1.co.uk
Freq: Daily
Circ: 47732
Automakers, Automotive, Driving, Motorsports

Something I Like
1053388
Web site: somethingilike.com
Freq: Daily
Circ: 1633
Profile: Blog covering food, recipes, baking, travel, sports and lifestyle.
Fitness & Exercise, Restaurant Reviews, Travel

Some-thingdefinitelyhappened
1069067
Email: carrie-ann@somethingdefinitelyhappened.com
Web site: http://somethingdefinitelyhappened.com
Freq: Daily
Circ: 10420
Fashion

Somewhere in the between
1052816
Email: joemortimer.words@gmail.com
Web site: http://wordsbyjoemortimer.com/blog
Freq: Daily
Circ: 6543
Travel

Sommeliers y Punto
1061681
Web site: http://sommeliersypunto.blogspot.com
Freq: Daily
Circ: 1785
Antiques/Collectibles, Art, Arts, Food, Literature, Movies & Video, Photography, Theater & Performing Arts, Visual Arts, Wine/Winemaking

Song, By Toad Blog
988347
Web site: http://songbytoad.com/
Freq: Daily
Circ: 10409
Classical/Choral/Band Music, Country, Folk, Bluegrass, Dance Music, Jazz &

Blues, Music, Pop Music, R&B, Urban, World, Rap & Hip Hop, Rock Music

Sonja Lewis
1053312
Web site: http://mojo.gorkana.com/#/journalists/1041834
Freq: Daily
Expatriates, Regional General Interest, Travel, Women's Interests

Soothed in the City
998281
Email: info@soothedinthecity.com
Web site: http://www.soothedinthecity.com/
Freq: Daily
Circ: 10955
Travel

Sophia Meola
988359
Email: sophiameola@hotmail.co.uk
Web site: http://www.sophiameola.co.uk/
Freq: Daily
Circ: 8589
Profile: Blog covering beauty. The Sophia Meola blog discusses anything from beauty and fashion to lifestyle and shopping. The blog has an archive dating back to July 2012.
Beauty & Grooming, Cosmetics, Fashion, Hair, Women's Interests

Sophie etc
1100033
Email: blog@sophieetc.com
Web site: http://www.sophieetc.com/
Freq: Daily
Circ: 7783
Profile: Blog covering fashion. Sophie etc blog discusses anything from fashion and fashion accessories to beauty and cosmetics. The blog has an archive dating back to and shares an extensive blog roll.
Cooking & Baking, Fashion, Restaurant Reviews, Women's Interests

Sophie in the Sticks
988957
Email: sophieinthesticks@gmail.com
Web site: http://www.sophieinthesticks.co.uk/
Freq: Daily
Circ: 9015
Profile: Blog covering fashion. Sophie in the Sticks blog discusses anything from fashion and photography to food, fitness and lifestyle. The blog has an archive dating back to December 2011 and shares an extensive blog roll.
Cooking & Baking, Fashion, Fitness & Exercise, Food, Grocery Stores, Organic Food, Photography, Regional General Interest, Restaurant Reviews, Vegetarianism & Veganism

Sophie Louise
1052758
Web site: keepcalmlookpretty.blogspot.co.uk
Freq: Daily
Circ: 521
Editor: Sophie Cockett
Beauty & Grooming, Cosmetics, Fashion, Hair, Women's Interests

Sophie Robinson Interiors Blog
1053482
Web site: http://www.sophierobinson.co.uk
Freq: Daily
Circ: 8056
Do-It-Yourself (DIY)

Sophie Rosie
1053656
Email: hellosophierosie@gmail.com
Web site: www.sophierosie.com
Freq: Daily
Circ: 10354
Fashion, Women's Interests

Sophie's Suitcase
988892
Tel: 44 07881 635372
Email: sophiessuitcase@outlook.com
Web site: http://sophiessuitcase.com/
Freq: Daily
Circ: 12271
Profile: Blog covering travel, holiday activities and destination guides. The blog has an archive dating back to July 2012.
Travel

Sorry About The Mess
996688
Email: chloebridge@gmail.com
Web site: http://sorry-about-the-mess.co.uk

Freq: Daily
Circ: 7848
Family & Parenting

Soulthing
1061862
Web site: http://soulthingmusic.blogspot.com
Freq: Daily
Circ: 521
Classical/Choral/Band Music, Country, Folk, Bluegrass, Dance Music, Jazz & Blues, Music, Pop Music, R&B, Urban, World, Rap & Hip Hop, Rock Music

Soundbite Culture
996946
Email: jonathan.campbell@hotmail.co.uk
Web site: www.soundbiteculture.com
Freq: Daily
Circ: 10422
Editor: Jonathan Campbell
Literature, Movies & Video, Pop Music

Sounds and Colours
996782
Email: info@soundsandcolours.com
Web site: http://www.soundsandcolours.com/
Freq: Daily
Circ: 19898
Art, International News, Literature, Movies & Video, Photography, R&B, Urban, World, Theater & Performing Arts, Visual Arts

Sounds Good To Me Too
1054293
Email: soundsgoodtometoo@gmail.com
Web site: http://soundsgoodtometoo.com/
Freq: Daily
Circ: 2124
Profile: Blog covering music.
Classical/Choral/Band Music, Country, Folk, Bluegrass, Dance Music, Jazz & Blues, Music, Pop Music, R&B, Urban, World, Rap & Hip Hop, Rock Music

The Source
997184
Editorial: PO Box 4805, Worthing BN11 9QW
Freq: Daily
Circ: 5211
Electricity, Oil

South London Blog
997050
Email: hello@southlondonblog.co.uk
Web site: http://www.southlondonblog.co.uk/
Freq: Daily
Circ: 9516
Editor: Natalie De Luca
Regional General Interest, Restaurant Reviews

South Molton St Style
987038
Web site: www.southmoltonststyle.com
Freq: Daily
Circ: 8658
Profile: Blog covering fashion and lifestyle. The South Molton St Style discusses anything from outfits and fashion trends to travel and food. The blog has an archive dating back to March 2011 and shares an extensive blog roll.
Fashion

Southerly
1054011
Editorial: Unit 3-4, Berrytime Studios, 190-192 Queenstown Road, London SW8 3NR
Tel: 44 02033 974971
Email: info@hellosoutherly.com
Web site: http://www.hellosoutherly.com/blog
Freq: Daily
Circ: 43
Branding, Marketing

The Southerner
988956
Email: becca@thesoutherner.co.uk
Web site: http://www.thesoutherner.co.uk/
Freq: Daily
Circ: 1348
Profile: Blog covering lifestyle. The SOUTHERNER blog discusses anything from travel and food.
Cooking & Baking, Food, Grocery Stores, Organic Food, Restaurant Reviews, Travel, Vegetarianism & Veganism, Women's Interests

The Spa Man
987234

Editorial: 60 Norton Gardens, London SW16 4TB
Web site: www.thespaman.co.uk
Circ: 9985
Profile: Website covering spas. SPA MAN website looks at the spa industry, wellness, health, male grooming and fitness.
Airline Inflight, Beauty & Grooming, Cosmetics, Hair, Railroad, Travel

Space for the Butterflies
988151

Email: cariemay21@gmail.com
Web site: http://spaceforthebutterflies.com/
Freq: Daily
Circ: 7469
Profile: Blog covering family, parenting, motherhood and lifestyle. The blog has an archive dating back to February 2006.
Crafts

Spacehive Blog
997004

Editorial: 30 Marsh Wall, London E14 9FY
Email: info@spacehive.com
Web site: https://www.spacehive.com/
Freq: Daily
Circ: 17673
Business, Equities, Small and Medium Business

Spaghetti Traveller
1054029

Editorial: 1A, 64 Brunswick place, Hove BN3 1NB
Web site: www.spaghettitraveller.com
Freq: Daily
Circ: 7508
Editor: Tom Bourlet
Travel

Spain Williams Family Law Specialists
999314

Editorial: The Old Cart Shed, Worten Lower Yard, Great Chart, Ashford TN23 3BU
Tel: 44 03334 051070
Email: info@spainwilliams.com
Web site: https://www.spainwilliams.com/blog
Freq: Daily
Circ: 9
Family Law

Spamloco
1062141

Web site: http://spamloco.net/
Freq: Daily
Circ: 104376
Internet, Security & Security Systems

Spark Inside
998269

Editorial: Suite 128, 15 - 17 Caledonian Road, London N1 9DX Tel: 44 02034 680706
Email: info@sparkinside.org
Web site: http://www.sparkinside.org/
Freq: Daily
Circ: 8500
Charitable Foundations

Sparkles and Stretchmarks Blog
987242

Editorial: 39 Buller Road, Newton Abbot, Newton Abbot TQ12 1AB
Email: hayley@sparklesandstretchmarks.com
Web site: http://www.sparklesandstretchmarks.com/
Freq: Daily
Circ: 40145
Beauty & Grooming, Cosmetics, Family & Parenting, Fashion, Hair

SpeakThinkBlog
1059294

Editorial: 12 Links Yard, London E1 5LX
Tel: 44 02073 751253
Email: enquiries@speakmedia.co.uk
Web site: speakthinkblog.speakmedia.co.uk
Freq: Daily
Circ: 26
Marketing

Speckyboy Design Magazine
999352

Editorial: 10 Moray Park Place, Culloden, Inverness IV2 7NG
Email: mail@speckyboy.com
Web site: www.speckyboy.com
Freq: Daily
Circ: 841421

Editor: Sufyan bin Uzayr
Graphic Design

Spectrum of Life - Parenting with a hint of autism
986705

Email: savvymum4@googlemail.com
Web site: www.savette.com
Freq: Daily
Circ: 7896
Disability, Family & Parenting

The Speculative Scotsman
1054202

Email: thespeculativescotsman@googlemail.com
Web site: http://scotspec.blogspot.co.uk/
Freq: Daily
Circ: 4686
Literature

Speed Communications blog
1052803

Editorial: 30 Park Street, London SE1 9EQ
Tel: 44 02078 423200
Web site: http://speedcommunications.com/blog/
Freq: Daily
Circ: 8
Advertising Industry, Branding, Broadcasting, Graphic Design, Marketing, Media & Communications, Photography, Publishing

Speedmonkey
997901

Tel: 44 07713 115183
Email: matthew.hubbard@btinternet.com
Web site: http://www.speedmonkey.co.uk/
Freq: Daily
Circ: 9246
Antique & Collectible Cars, Automakers, Automotive, Driving, Motorcycles, Off-road & 4-Wheel Drive Vehicles, Trucks & SUVs

Speirs
1054502

Web site: www.speirs.org/
Freq: Daily
Circ: 13965
News & Current Affairs

Spence and Partners Blog
1052675

Tel: 44 02074 955505
Web site: http://www.spenceandpartners.co.uk/blog/
Freq: Daily
Circ: 52
Banking, Business, Government

Spencer Media
1054402

Email: david@spencermedia.co.uk
Web site: http://www.spencermedia.co.uk/blog
Freq: Daily
Circ: 5736
Profile: Blog covering lifestyle. SPENCER MEDIA blog discusses anything from lifestyle and events to sports.
Broadcasting

SpiderGroup Blog
1053700

Tel: 44 01179 330572
Email: info@spidergroup.co.uk
Web site: http://www.spidergroup.com/blog/
Freq: Daily
Circ: 8913
Computers, Data Management, Electronics, Industry, Internet, Mobile Communications, Security & Security Systems, Software

The Spine
1052582

Email: thespineblog@gmail.com
Web site: http://davidwaywell.blogspot.in/
Freq: Daily
Circ: 521
Art, Politics, Visual Arts

Spinwatch
1054102

Tel: 44 07973 424015
Web site: http://spinwatch.org/index.php/blog
Freq: Daily
Circ: 37
Energy & Environment, Politics, Social Issues

Spirit of Mirko
987901

Email: spiritofmirko@gmail.com
Web site: http://spiritofmirko.com/
Freq: Daily
Circ: 8866
Soccer

Spitalfields Life
987310

Email: spitalfieldslife@gmail.com
Web site: spitalfieldslife.com
Freq: Daily
Circ: 56734
Regional General Interest

Spittoon
986238

Web site: http://www.spittoon.biz/
Freq: Daily
Circ: 13350
Wine/Winemaking

Splodz Blogz
987902

Tel: 44 07876 567734
Email: zoe@splodzblogz.co.uk
Web site: splodzblogz.co.uk/
Freq: Daily
Circ: 11408
Editor: Zoe Homes
Profile: Splodz Blogz covers outdoor recreation, adventure, travel and experiences. The blog has an archive dating back to January 2010.
Alcohol & Spirits, Bars, Clubs & Pubs, Beer, Beverages, Cooking & Baking, Fashion, Food, Grocery Stores, Organic Food, Restaurant Reviews

Spoke + Co
1099576

Email: enquiries@spokeandco.co.uk
Web site: http://www.spokeandco.co.uk
Freq: Daily
Circ: 8216
Fashion, Travel, Women's Interests

Spoons on Trays
996645

Web site: http://www.spoonsontrays.com/
Freq: Daily
Circ: 11000
Art, Literature, Theater & Performing Arts

Sports Betting Blog
1053208

Web site: www.sports-betting-blog.co.uk/
Freq: Daily
Circ: 1956
Horse Racing

Sports Coach UK Blog
1054662

Tel: 44 01132 744802
Web site: http://www.sportscoachuk.org/blog
Freq: Daily
Circ: 84
Basketball, Bicycles, Billiards, Boating & Yachting, Bodybuilding, Bowling, Boxing, Cricket, Equestrian Sports, Extreme/Adventure Sports

Sports Nutrition Vlog
986239

Editorial: 41 Malvern Road, London E8 3LP
Email: contact@sportsnutritionvlog.com
Web site: www.sportsnutritionvlog.com
Freq: Daily
Circ: 2675
Nutrition

Spotify (UK)
999253

Editorial: Fourth Floor, 25 Argyll Street, London W1F 7TU
Email: press@spotify.com
Web site: http://news.spotify.com/uk/
Freq: Daily
Circ: 386
Audio Video Trade, Classical/Choral/Band Music, Country, Folk, Bluegrass, Dance Music, Jazz & Blues, Mobile Electronics, Music, Pop Music, R&B, Urban, World, Rap & Hip Hop

Spreadsheet Journalism
1053205

Web site: http://spreadsheetjournalism.com/
Freq: Daily
Circ: 8124
Software

The Spring Blog
1054376

Web site: http://soundsfromthespring.blogspot.co.uk/

Freq: Daily
Circ: 767
News & Current Affairs

Springwise
990463

Editorial: 19-20 Great Sutton Street, London EC1V 0DR
Email: info@springwise.com
Web site: www.springwise.com
Circ: 434561
Business

Spy Review
525009

Web site: http://www.spyreview.co.uk
Freq: Daily
Circ: 4040
Security & Security Systems

SQL Blog
1054057

Email: admin@sqlblog.com
Web site: http://sqlblog.com/blogs/jamie_thomson/default.aspx
Freq: Daily
Circ: 17851
Computers, Data Management, Internet

Squawka Blog
996570

Editorial: 38-40 Commercial Road, London E1 1LN Tel: 44 02034 273731
Email: info@squawka.com
Web site: www.squawka.com/
Freq: Daily
Circ: 1232017
Soccer

The Squeaky Door
1053667

Email: juliette@juliettesaumande.com
Web site: http://juliettesaumande.blogspot.co.uk/
Freq: Daily
Circ: 521
Literature, Visual Arts

Squibb Vicious
987670

Email: squibbvicious@gmail.com
Web site: http://squibbvicious.com/
Freq: Daily
Circ: 8158
Profile: Blog covering lifestyle, food, fashion and travel.
Beauty & Grooming, Cooking & Baking, Cosmetics, Fashion, Hair, Regional General Interest, Restaurant Reviews, Travel

Squirrel's nuts
1053073

Email: autumntrees@gmail.com
Web site: http://squirrel-nuts.blogspot.com/
Freq: Daily
Circ: 1507
Crafts

SR Nutrition
1054574

Tel: 44 07814 414541
Email: info@srnutrition.co.uk
Web site: http://www.srnutrition.co.uk/blog
Freq: Daily
Circ: 18
Profile: Blog covering nutrition. SR Nutrition blog discusses anything from nutrition and healthy recipes to personal health and children's nutrition. The blog has an archive dating back to August 2011.
Nutrition

SRBank Blogg
1060837

Web site: http://blogg.sr-bank.no/
Freq: Daily
Circ: 32070
Economics, Personal Finance

St. Mungo's Broadway blog
998376

Editorial: Griffin House, 161 Hammersmith Road, London W6 8BS
Tel: 44 02087 625500
Email: info@mungos.org
Web site: http://blog.mungos.org/
Freq: Daily
Circ: 134
Charitable Foundations

Stack of Marking
1053986

Web site: https://stackofmarking.wordpress.com/
Freq: Daily

UK Blogs

Circ: 394

Profile: Blog covering education. Stack of Marking blog discusses anything from education and to schools and the curriculum. The blog has an archive dating back to April 2013.

Education

The Stag Company
999551

Editorial: 4th Floor Hanover House, 118 Queens Road, Brighton BN1 3XG
Tel: 44 01273 225070
Email: suppliers@henheaven.co.uk
Web site: http://www.thestagcompany.com
Freq: Daily
Circ: 23254
Weddings

StagWeb blog
997105

Tel: 44 08451 305225
Email: theantler@stagweb.co.uk
Web site: http://www.stagweb.co.uk/blog/
Freq: Daily
Circ: 117
Weddings

Stamping by H
1057090

Web site: http://stampingbyh.blogspot.co.uk/
Freq: Daily
Circ: 7786
Crafts

Stamping Ground
988152

Web site: http://stamping-ground.blogspot.co.uk/
Freq: Daily
Circ: 1680
Crafts

Stand-Out.net Fashion Blog
999257

Editorial: Stand-Out.net, 4 Featherby Way, Rochford SS4 1LD Tel: 44 02031 891883
Email: sales@stand-out.net
Web site: http://www.stand-out.net/blog
Freq: Daily
Circ: 29270
Fashion

Stargazer - CEASED 2017
1055143

Web site: http://stargazersusie.blogspot.co.uk/
Freq: Daily
Circ: 752
Cooking & Baking, Entertainment, Restaurant Reviews, Travel

Stealstylist
1052839

Web site: http://www.stealstylist.com/
Freq: Daily
Circ: 4845
Beauty & Grooming, Cosmetics, Fashion, Hair, Regional General Interest, Women's Interests

Stefanie Grace blog
988770

Email: stefaniegraceblog@gmail.com
Web site: http://stefaniegrace.com/
Freq: Daily
Circ: 10145
Cooking & Baking, Expatriates, Fitness & Exercise, Restaurant Reviews, Travel

Stella Harasek
1061984

Email: stella@stellaharasek.com
Web site: http://www.stellaharasek.com/
Freq: Daily
Circ: 3966
Alcohol & Spirits, Beauty & Grooming, Cosmetics, Do-It-Yourself (DIY), Fashion, Food, Hair, Lifestyle, Literature, Men's Interests

Step Up Club
1054546

Web site: step-up-club.net
Freq: Daily
Circ: 11247
Careers, Women's Interests

Step Up Your Sex Life
1098964

Email: stepupyoursexlife@gmail.com
Web site: https://stepupyoursexlife.com/
Freq: Daily
Circ: 611
Relationships

StepChange MoneyAware
996514

Editorial: Wade House, Merrion Centre, Leeds LS2 8NG Tel: 44 08001 381111
Email: moneyaware@stepchange.org
Web site: http://moneyaware.co.uk/
Freq: Daily
Circ: 80941
Charitable Foundations, Personal Finance

Steph and The Spaniels
1053664

Email: stephandthespaniels@googlemail.com
Web site: www.stephandthespaniels.com/
Freq: Daily
Circ: 10583
Profile: Blog covering lifestyle. STEPHANIE Dreams blog discusses anything from fashion and personal style to lifestyle posts. The blog has an archive dating back to December 2009.
Beauty & Grooming, Cosmetics, Fashion, Hair, Travel

Stephanie Burgis Blog
1052955

Web site: http://www.stephanieburgis.com/blog/
Freq: Daily
Circ: 39
Entertainment, Literature, Science Fiction

Stephanie's Marketing World
1054941

Web site: http://stephanieclarkmarketing.blogspot.co.uk
Freq: Daily
Circ: 521
Branding, Marketing

Stephen Tall Blog
987912

Web site: http://stephentall.org/
Freq: Daily
Circ: 12504
Politics

Stephen Waddington Blog
1053697

Web site: wadds.co.uk
Freq: Daily
Circ: 73986
Marketing

Steve Beasant Blog
988015

Editorial: 51 Columbia Road, Grimsby DN32 8EA Tel: 44 01472 314183
Email: s.beasant@gmail.com
Web site: http://stevebeasant.4mp.org.uk/
Freq: Daily
Circ: 88
Politics

Steve Booker
987831

Email: hello@stevebooker.co.uk
Web site: www.stevebooker.co.uk
Freq: Daily
Circ: 62740
Profile: Blog covering men's fashion and lifestyle. The Steve Booker blog discusses anything from style and accessories to gadgets and music. The blog has an archive dating back to September 2013.
Cooking & Baking, Fashion, Men's Interests

Steven Aitchison Blog
1054499

Tel: 44 01698 267676
Email: enquiries@stevenaitchison.co.uk
Web site: www.stevenaitchison.co.uk/blog
Freq: Daily
Circ: 1239425
Business, Personal Finance, Relationships

The Steven Aspinall Archive
998185

Web site: http://thestevenaspinallarchive.com/
Freq: Daily
Circ: 10618
Art, Photography, Visual Arts

Sticky Fingers
987894

Web site: www.thestickyfingersblog.com
Freq: Daily
Circ: 9403
Family & Parenting

Stines treningsblogg
1061561

Email: stine_tk@hotmail.no
Web site: http://stinean.blogg.no/
Freq: Daily
Circ: 10954
Fitness & Exercise

Stinkyink Blog
986240

Editorial: Unit 9, Alveley Industrial Estate, Bridgnorth, Bridgnorth WV15 6HG
Tel: 44 08444 144141
Web site: www.stinkyinkshop.co.uk/blog/
Freq: Daily
Circ: 47
Editor: Matthew Bird

Stitch and Bear Food Blog
988563

Email: stitchandbearblog@gmail.com
Web site: www.stitchandbear.com
Freq: Daily
Circ: 8435
News & Current Affairs

The Stitch Sharer
997116

Email: thestitchsharer@hotmail.co.uk
Web site: www.thestitchsharer.com
Freq: Daily
Circ: 9097
Crafts, Fashion

Stitchworks
1052562

Web site: http://stitchworks-jackie.blogspot.co.uk/
Freq: Daily
Circ: 521
Crafts

Stockbridge Online
1056308

Email: enquiries@stc-nyorks.co.uk
Web site: www.stockbridgeonline.co.uk
Freq: Daily
Circ: 2249
Gardening, Science

Stop Crying Your Heart Out
1053153

Email: scyhodotcom@gmail.com
Web site: http://stopcryingyourheartoutnews.blogspot.co.uk/
Freq: Daily
Circ: 12970
Pop Music, Rock Music

Stories My Suitcase Could Tell
996672

Email: workwithkathryn@gmail.com
Web site: http://storiesmysuitcasecouldtell.com/
Freq: Daily
Circ: 11328
Travel

The Story of a Girl Who Lives Above Her Means
987389

Web site: http://www.astoryofagirl.com/
Freq: Daily
Circ: 6350
Profile: Blog covering fashion, beauty, food and lifestyle. The blog has an archive dating back to February 2010 and shares an extensive blog roll.
Beauty & Grooming, Cosmetics, Fashion, Hair

Story of Mum
997574

Email: pippa@storyofmum.com
Web site: storyofmum.com
Freq: Daily
Circ: 8701
Family & Parenting, Women's Interests

The Stovax & Gazco Blog
999529

Editorial: Faloon Road, Sowton Industrial Estate, Exeter, Exeter EX2 7LF
Tel: 44 01392 474000
Web site: stovax.com/blog/
Freq: Daily
Circ: 36
Interior Design, Manufacturing

Strange Attractor
1054445

Web site: http://charman-anderson.com/
Freq: Daily
Circ: 8020
Marketing, Publishing

Strangeness & Charm
1054227

Email: strangenessblog@gmail.com
Web site: http://strangenessandcharm.co.uk
Freq: Daily
Circ: 8352
Profile: Blog covering lifestyle. STRANGENESS & CHARM blog discusses anything from beauty and fashion to lifestyle. The blog has an archive dating back to September 2009 and shares an extensive blog roll.
Cosmetics, Fashion, Women's Interests

Strategic HCM Blog
996865

Tel: 44 01344 420512
Email: info@strategic-hcm.com
Web site: http://strategic-hcm.blogspot.com
Freq: Daily
Circ: 11163
Company News & Appointments, Education, Employment, Health & Safety, Human Resources, Recruiting

Strategist: Xu Wenming
1060853

Email: xwmlj168@163.com
Web site: http://blog.sina.com.cn/jimolicai
Freq: Daily
Circ: 41928
Banking, Financial Markets

Stratford-upon-Avon Theatre Review Blog
996357

Email: bwthornton20@yahoo.com
Web site: stratford-upon-avon-theatre.blogspot.co.uk
Freq: Daily
Circ: 13937
Entertainment, Local Entertainment Guides, Movies & Video, Theater & Performing Arts

Strat-Talking
998056

Web site: strat-talking.com
Freq: Daily
Circ: 8379
Advertising Industry, Branding, Marketing

Strawberry Blonde Beauty Blog
987048

Email: strawberryblondebeauty@gmail.com
Web site: www.strawberryblondebeauty.com
Freq: Daily
Circ: 9503
Beauty & Grooming, Cosmetics, Hair

Streaming
1061998

Web site: http://blogs.lanacion.com.ar/streaming/
Freq: Daily
Circ: 137
Auto Aftermarket, Computers, Data Management, Electronics, Government Technology, Industry, Internet, Mobile Communications, Security & Security Systems, Software

Street Art News
1053393

Email: contact@streetartnews.net
Web site: streetartnews.net
Freq: Daily
Circ: 102702
Profile: Blog covering urban and street art.
Art, Visual Arts

Street Eats
997737

Email: hello@streeteatslondon.com
Web site: http://streeteatslondon.com/
Freq: Daily
Circ: 11255
Cooking & Baking, Food, Grocery Stores, Organic Food, Regional General Interest, Restaurant Reviews, Vegetarianism & Veganism

Street Gentry
1053849

Email: team@streetgentry.co.uk
Web site: http://streetgentry.co.uk
Freq: Daily
Circ: 2595
Profile: Blog covering men's fashion and lifestyle. The Street Gentry blog discusses anything from men's fashion design and men's accessories to men's groom.
Fashion, Men's Interests

Stressed Rach 1053308
Web site: http://stressedrach.co.uk/
Freq: Daily
Circ: 66975
Beauty & Grooming, Cosmetics, Family & Parenting, Hair, Women's Interests

Stressy Mummy 987561
Web site: www.stressymummy.com
Freq: Daily
Circ: 11265
Profile: Blog covering motherhood and lifestyle. STRESSY MUMMY discusses anything from children's activities and children's product reviews to parenting tales and recipes. The outlet offers RSS (Really Simple Syndication).
Cooking & Baking, Family & Parenting, Women's Interests

Stretford End 996327
Email: strettyrant@googlemail.com
Web site: www.stretford-end.com/
Freq: Daily
Circ: 12771
Soccer

Striking Mum 1053509
Email: kateonthinice@gmail.com
Web site: kateonthinice.com
Freq: Daily
Circ: 11473
Family & Parenting, Women's Interests

STRUPAG 996997
Web site: www.strupag.com
Freq: Daily
Circ: 6876
Family & Parenting

Stu n Dumplings 1053876
Email: stundumplings@gmail.com
Web site: http://www.stundumplings.co.uk
Freq: Daily
Circ: 652
Fishing, Men's Interests, Outdoor Recreation, Regional General Interest, Swimming/Watersports, Travel

Stuart Bruce Blog 997990
Tel: 44 02032 391093
Web site: stuartbruce.biz
Freq: Daily
Circ: 12128
Advertising Industry, Branding, Broadcasting, Graphic Design, Marketing, Media & Communications, Photography, Publishing

Stuart Jeffery's Blog 987834
Editorial: 82 Buckland Road, Maidstone ME16 0SD Tel: 44 07970 436029
Email: sjeffery@fastmail.com
Web site: http://www.stuartjeffery.net/
Freq: Daily
Circ: 10047
Energy & Environment, Politics

Stuck in a Book 988204
Email: simondavidthomas@yahoo.co.uk
Web site: http://www.stuckinabook.com
Freq: Daily
Circ: 9304
Literature

Studded Kisses 988600
Email: studdedkisses@hotmail.com
Web site: www.studdedkissesblog.co.uk
Freq: Daily
Circ: 12838
Profile: Blog covering fashion. STUDDED KISSES discusses anything from outfits and shoes to high street labels. The blog has an archive dating back to March 2012.
Regional General Interest

The Student Blogger 987764
Web site: www.thestudentblogger.co.uk
Freq: Daily
Circ: 10070
Profile: Blog covering lifestyle. The Student Blogger blog discusses anything from lifestyle and university to fashion and food. The blog has an archive dating back to October 2013. The outlet offers RSS (Really Simple Syndication).
Education, Students

Stuff & Nonsense Blog 1054572
Editorial: Op UG, Ffordd William Morgan, St. Asaph Business Park, St. Asaph LL17 0JD
Tel: 44 01745 851848
Email: feb2017@stuffandnonsense.co.uk
Web site: stuffandnonsense.co.uk/blog
Freq: Daily
Circ: 248
Advertising Industry, Branding, Graphic Design, Marketing

Styl.sh 997267
Editorial: 17 Seymour Place, London W1H 5BF
Email: help@buymywardrobe.com
Web site: www.styl.sh
Freq: Daily
Circ: 1799
Fashion

style & the bride 996222
Web site: www.styleandthebride.co.uk
Freq: Daily
Circ: 13746
Fashion, Weddings

Style & Then Some 986626
Email: styleandthensome@gmail.com
Web site: https://styleandthensome.wordpress.com/
Freq: Daily
Circ: 92
Beauty & Grooming, Cosmetics, Fashion, Hair, Men's Interests, Women's Interests

Style at every age 1054165
Web site: http://www.styleateveryage.com
Freq: Daily
Circ: 4415
Fashion

Style blog for him 1052779
Tel: 44 02031 090388
Email: events@nhjstyle.com
Web site: http://www.nhjstyle.com/style-blog-for-him/
Freq: Daily
Circ: 9
Fashion

The Style Box 987394
Web site: www.thestylebox.com
Freq: Daily
Circ: 6440
Profile: Blog covering lifestyle, fashion, travel and motherhood. The blog has an archive dating back to November 2010.
Cooking & Baking, Family & Parenting, Fashion, Travel

Style Bubble 986242
Editorial: Flat 3, 20a Denwell Road, London N7 7BL
Email: susie@stylebubble.co.uk
Web site: www.stylebubble.co.uk
Freq: Daily
Circ: 108766
Fashion

Style Clip 1061495
Web site: http://www.winnyli.com
Freq: Daily
Circ: 521
Fashion

Style Insider 1053459
Web site: www.riverisland.com/styleinsider/blog
Freq: Daily
Circ: 263
Fashion

Style Journal 1054538
Editorial: Unit 3, 17-18 Clere Street, London EC2A 4LJ
Web site: www.shopological.com/article
Freq: Daily
Circ: 459528
Beauty & Grooming, Cosmetics, Fashion, Hair, Women's Interests

Style Junkie 1053935
Web site: http://www.stylejunkie.co.uk/
Freq: Daily
Circ: 1026
Profile: Blog covering fashion. STYLE JUNKIE blog discusses anything from

fashion and style to fashion accessories and trends. The blog has an archive dating back to September 2011 and shares an extensive blog roll.
Fashion

The Style King 986603
Editorial: 240 East Carriage House, Royal Carriage Mews, London SE18 6GL
Web site: www.thestyleking.com
Circ: 7617
Fashion

Style Made Simple 1059293
Web site: stylemadesimple.co.uk
Freq: Daily
Circ: 4768
Crafts, Do-It-Yourself (DIY), Women's Interests

Style Matters 1075967
Web site: https://alisonkerr.wordpress.com/
Freq: Daily
Circ: 7
Fashion

Style Me Curvy 996211
Email: stylemecurvy@gmail.com
Web site: http://www.stylemecurvy.net/
Freq: Daily
Circ: 10338
Fashion

Style Me Sunday 995138
Web site: stylemesunday.blogspot.com
Freq: Daily
Circ: 611
Family & Parenting, Fashion

The Style Rawr! 987093
Email: contact@thestylerawr.com
Web site: www.thestylerawr.com
Freq: Daily
Circ: 7946
Fashion

Style Slicker 985828
Web site: www.styleslicker.com
Freq: Daily
Circ: 11758
Fashion

Style Vampyre 1056559
Web site: http://stylevampyre.blogspot.co.uk/
Freq: Daily
Circ: 521
News & Current Affairs

Style with Friends 1054566
Email: stylewithfriends@gmail.com
Web site: http://www.stylewithfriends.co.uk/
Freq: Daily
Circ: 7504
Profile: Blog covering fashion. Style with Friends blog discusses anything from fashion to friendship. The blog has an archive dating back to December 2012. The outlet offers RSS (Really Simple Syndication).
Fashion

Style, Space and Stuff 1054305
Email: sstansbridge@gmail.com
Web site: www.stylespaceandstuff.blogspot.co.uk/
Freq: Daily
Circ: 1437
Cooking & Baking, Cosmetics, Do-It-Yourself (DIY), Food, Grocery Stores, Organic Food, Restaurant Reviews, Vegetarianism & Veganism

StyleBomb 995514
Web site: stylebomb.net
Freq: Daily
Circ: 1195
Beauty & Grooming, Cosmetics, Fashion, Hair, Travel

StyleHaul 996088
Tel: 44 13235 103829
Email: info@stylehaul.com
Web site: http://www.stylehaul.com/
Freq: Daily
Circ: 33285
Men's Interests, Women's Interests

StyleInkHK 1061253
Email: info@styleinkhk.com
Web site: http://www.styleinkhk.com
Freq: Daily
Circ: 1068
Fashion

STYLESUZI 986953
Email: stylesuzi@hotmail.co.uk
Web site: stylesuzi.com
Freq: Daily
Circ: 25090
Fashion

StyleSuzi Vlog 1096036
Email: stylesuzi@hotmail.co.uk
Web site: https://www.youtube.com/user/StyleSuzi
Freq: Daily
Circ: 8
Beauty & Grooming, Cosmetics, Fashion, Hair, Women's Interests

Styling the Way Forward 988129
Email: stylingthewayforward@hotmail.com
Web site: http://stwfblog.com
Freq: Daily
Circ: 9982
Profile: Blog covering lifestyle, fashion, travel and cosmetics. The blog has an archive dating back to December 2012.
Beauty & Grooming, Cosmetics, Fashion, Hair, Women's Interests

The Stylist and the Wardrobe 999412
Web site: http://thestylistandthewardrobe.com/
Freq: Daily
Circ: 8614
Do-It-Yourself (DIY), Fashion, Women's Interests

Stylitz 1053717
Email: alicja71@hotmail.com
Web site: stylitz.com
Freq: Daily
Circ: 11562
Profile: Blog covering fashion. Stylitz blog discusses anything from style and fashion inspirations to the latest fashion news and exhibitions. The outlet offers RSS (Really Simple Syndication).
Fashion

Stylonylon 987483
Editorial: 23 Comberton Road, London E5 9PU
Email: stylonylon@gmail.com
Web site: stylonylon.com
Freq: Daily
Circ: 39292
Beauty & Grooming, Cooking & Baking, Cosmetics, Fashion, Hair, Photography, Shopping, Travel

Su Yan Tian Shi 1061692
Web site: http://www.plainfaceangel.blogspot.com
Freq: Daily
Circ: 1866
Fashion, Food, Lifestyle, Men's Interests, Regional General Interest, Women's Interests

SubScribe 1006615
Email: editor@sub-scribe.co.uk
Web site: www.sub-scribe.co.uk
Freq: Daily
Circ: 14844
Consumer Affairs, Publishing

Sue Atkins The Parenting Expert Blog 1052870
Editorial: GLEN HOUSE, 22 GLENTHORNE ROAD, London W6 0NG
Email: angelica.tziotis@dcdmedia.co.uk
Web site: http://www.sueatkinsparentingcoach.com/sues-blog/
Freq: Daily
Circ: 49
Family & Parenting

Sue's Handmade Cards 1063457
Web site: http://crafty-moone.blogspot.co.uk/
Freq: Daily

UK Blogs

Circ: 521
News & Current Affairs

Suffolktradingstandards's Blog
996417
Editorial: Landmark House, 8 Egerton Road, Ipswich IP1 5PF Tel: 44 01473 264859
Email: tradingstandards@suffolk.gov.uk
Web site: http://suffolktradingstandards.wordpress.com/
Freq: Daily
Circ: 16031
Consumer Affairs

Sugar Pink Food
996667
Tel: 44 01392 660080
Web site: www.latoyah.co.uk
Freq: Daily
Circ: 7216
Cooking & Baking, Grocery Stores, Restaurant Reviews

Sugar, Darling?
998192
Email: nancy@sugar-darling.com
Web site: http://www.sugar-darling.com/
Freq: Daily
Circ: 10772
Cooking & Baking, Cosmetics, Fashion, Shopping, Women's Interests

Suggestive Digestive
1054549
Email: catherinemcgee2@gmail.com
Web site: http://suggestivedigestive.com/
Freq: Daily
Circ: 1504
Profile: Blog covering lifestyle, fashion, beauty, food and travel. The blog has an archive dating back to April 2012.
Cosmetics, Fashion, Restaurant Reviews, Travel

Suklaapossu
1062065
Web site: http://suklaapossu.blogspot.fi/
Freq: Daily
Circ: 1087
Cooking & Baking

The Sunday Girl
986814
Email: thesundaygirlblog@yahoo.co.uk
Web site: www.thesundaygirl.com
Freq: Daily
Circ: 59813
Profile: Blog covering lifestyle, fashion and beauty. The blog has an archive dating back to March 2013.
Beauty & Grooming, Cosmetics, Fashion, Hair, Women's Interests

Super Adventures in Gaming
997614
Web site: superadventuresingaming.blogspot.co.uk/
Freq: Daily
Circ: 10709
Computer & Video Games

Super Luchas
1060751
Web site: http://superluchas.net
Freq: Daily
Circ: 614729
Bars, Clubs & Pubs, Basketball, Bicycles, Billiards, Boating & Yachting, Bodybuilding, Bowling, Boxing, Comedy, Cricket

SuperBreak blog
1052802
Editorial: Eboracum Way, York YO31 7RE
Tel: 44 01904 420443
Email: internet@superbreak.com
Web site: http://blog.superbreak.com/
Freq: Daily
Circ: 6090
Airline Inflight, Railroad, Travel

Superdrug Blog
987205
Editorial: Garden Floor, 16 Connaught Place, London W2 2ES
Tel: 44 02074 207000
Web site: www.superdrug.com/blog
Freq: Daily
Circ: 33
Beauty & Grooming, Cosmetics, Hair

Supergolden Bakes
988245
Email: supergolden88@gmail.com
Web site: www.supergoldenbakes.com
Freq: Daily

Circ: 47793
Cooking & Baking

Sur Cultural
1061636
Web site: http://www.surcultural.info
Freq: Daily
Circ: 656
Celebrities, Disability, Education, Higher Education, Preschool, Schools & Institutions, Students

Sur Piensa
1061058
Web site: http://ferledesma.blogspot.com
Freq: Daily
Circ: 784
Celebrities, National News

Surangi Style
1075503
Web site: http://www.surangi-style.com/
Freq: Daily
Circ: 11844
News & Current Affairs

Surf Nation
1054214
Web site: http://www.surfnation.co.uk/
Freq: Daily
Circ: 7579
Swimming/Watersports

The Surrey Edit
998102
Email: surreyedit@gmail.com
Web site: http://surreyedit.com/
Freq: Daily
Circ: 983
Regional General Interest

Surrey Mummy
1072209
Email: info@surreymummy.com
Web site: http://surreymummy.com/
Freq: Daily
Circ: 36107
Family & Parenting

Susan K Mann
987618
Email: email@susankmann.com
Web site: susankmann.com
Freq: Daily
Circ: 14440
Family & Parenting

Sussex Guide - Ceased
997259
Web site: http://www.sussex.org.uk/
Freq: Daily
Circ: 1269
Regional General Interest

Sussex Mummy Reviews
1054630
Email: info@sussexmummy.co.uk
Web site: http://sussexmummy.co.uk/index/
Freq: Daily
Circ: 2919
Family & Parenting, Fashion, Women's Interests

Sustainable Cities, Sustainable World
1052990
Tel: 44 07578 685978
Web site: http://sustainablecitiessustainableworld.blogspot.co.uk/
Freq: Daily
Circ: 9576
Alternative/Renewable Energy, Environment

Suuntana maailma
1061428
Email: suuntanamaailma@gmail.com
Web site: http://www.suuntanamaailma.com/
Freq: Daily
Circ: 2288
Airline Inflight, Railroad, Travel

Suzann Pettersen
1002082
Web site: http://suzanngolf.com/blog/
Freq: Daily
Circ: 251
Golf

Suzanne's Cards
1056757
Email: suzannescards@aol.com
Web site: http://suzannescards.blogspot.co.uk/
Freq: Daily
Circ: 548
Crafts

The Swag Guide
1096368
Email: bloggers@theswagguide.com
Web site: theswagguide.com
Freq: Daily
Circ: 1161
Fitness & Exercise, Nutrition, Women's Interests

Swaroop C H
1061243
Web site: http://www.swaroopch.com
Freq: Daily
Circ: 39985
Computers, Data Management, Internet

Sweeping The Nation
997950
Email: sweepingthenation@dsl.pipex.com
Web site: http://sweepingthenation.blogspot.co.uk/
Freq: Daily
Circ: 7706
Classical/Choral/Band Music, Country, Folk, Bluegrass, Dance Music, Jazz & Blues, Music, Pop Music, R&B, Urban, World, Rap & Hip Hop, Rock Music

Sweet Dreams Beauty
997999
Email: sweetdreamsblog1@gmail.com
Web site: http://www.sweetdreamsbeauty.co.uk/
Freq: Daily
Circ: 7667
Beauty & Grooming, Cosmetics, Fashion, Hair, Women's Interests

Sweetie Sal
987803
Email: sweetiesal@hotmail.com
Web site: www.sweetiesal.com
Freq: Daily
Circ: 7850
Profile: Sweetie Sal covers lifestyle, beauty and fashion. The blog has an archive dating back to February 2012.
Beauty & Grooming, Cooking & Baking, Cosmetics, Fashion, Hair, Restaurant Reviews, Women's Interests

The Swelle Life
985787
Email: denise@theswellelife.com
Web site: www.theswellelife.com
Freq: Daily
Circ: 3436
Alcohol & Spirits, Architecture & Design, Bars, Clubs & Pubs, Beer, Beverages, Cooking & Baking, Do-It-Yourself (DIY), Fashion, Food, Gardening

Swinny.net
986244
Web site: swinny.net
Freq: Daily
Circ: 9438
Alternative/Renewable Energy, Electricity, Water & Sanitation

Switched On Art
1052935
Email: info@switchedonart.com
Web site: http://www.switchedonart.com/
Freq: Daily
Circ: 841
Art

Swoon Worthy
987845
Email: swoonworthypr@gmail.com
Web site: www.swoonworthy.co.uk
Freq: Daily
Circ: 76415
Do-It-Yourself (DIY)

Sympathy for the moon
1053031
Email: hello@davidthorpe.info
Web site: http://sympathyftm.blogspot.co.uk/
Freq: Daily
Circ: 10520
Consumer Affairs, Crime & Violence, Defense & National Security, Energy & Environment, Ethical/Moral Issues, International News, Law, National News, Politics, Social Issues

t*rexes and tiaras
1052919
Web site: www.trexesandtiaras.com
Freq: Daily
Circ: 7329
Profile: Blog covering lifestyle. T*rexes and tiaras blog discusses anything from fashion and shoes to books and lifestyle. The blog

---

has an archive dating back to October 2009 and shares an extensive blog roll.
Women's Interests

Taber Holidays blog
1054496
Editorial: PO Box 176, Tofts House, Tofts Road, Cleckheaton BD19 3WX
Tel: 44 01274 875199
Email: office@taberhols.co.uk
Web site: https://www.scandinaviaonly.co.uk/blog/
Freq: Daily
Circ: 14
Travel

Table for Two
1056316
Web site: http://blogs.xs4all.co.uk/tablefortwo/
Freq: Daily
Circ: 2796
Cooking & Baking, Food, Grocery Stores, Organic Food, Restaurant Reviews, Vegetarianism & Veganism

The Tailored
1052586
Email: team@thetailored.co.uk
Web site: thetailored.co.uk
Freq: Daily
Circ: 521
Driving, Fashion, Men's Interests, Off-road & 4-Wheel Drive Vehicles

Take on the Road
1053278
Web site: www.takeontheroad.com
Freq: Daily
Circ: 1718
Airline Inflight, Railroad, Travel

TAKE ONE
987941
Web site: http://www.takeonecff.com/
Freq: Daily
Circ: 12036
Editor: Rosy Hunt
Profile: Blog covering arthouse and festival cinema.
Entertainment, Movies & Video, Theater & Performing Arts, Visual Arts

Take to the Road
1096038
Email: hello@taketotheroad.co.uk
Web site: www.taketotheroad.co.uk
Freq: Daily
Circ: 55394
Antique & Collectible Cars, Driving

Tales from the Reading Room
988203
Email: litlove1@yahoo.co.uk
Web site: http://litlove.wordpress.com/
Freq: Daily
Circ: 3775
Profile: Blog covering literature and book reviews. Tales from the Reading Room discusses anything from fiction and memoirs. The blog has an archive dating back to April 2006 and shares an extensive blogroll. The outlet offers RSS (Really Simple Syndication).
Literature

The Tales of Annie Bean
996046
Email: talesofanniebean@gmail.com
Web site: www.talesofanniebean.com
Freq: Daily
Circ: 10936
Editor: Annie Bean
Profile: Blog covering lifestyle. The Tales Of annie Bean blog discusses anything from fashion and beauty to music reviews.
Bicycles, Cooking & Baking, Fitness & Exercise, Women's Interests

Tales of Sonny & Luca
1052783
Email: sonnyandluca@gmail.com
Web site: www.sonnyandluca.co.uk
Freq: Daily
Circ: 7849
Family & Parenting

Talis Blog
1053521
Editorial: Talis Education Limited, 48 Frederick Street, Birmingham B1 3HN
Tel: 44 01213 742740
Web site: http://talis.com/blog/
Freq: Daily
Circ: 45
Careers, Education

Talita Kum!　1061078
Web site: http://talitakummaria.blogspot.com/
Freq: Daily
Circ: 611
Literature

Talk Money Blog　986245
Tel: 44 01606 784973
Web site: talkmoneyblog.co.uk
Freq: Daily
Circ: 4723
Personal Finance

Talking THFC　998383
Email: talkingthfc.enquiries@live.com
Web site: http://talkingthfc.wordpress.com/
Freq: Daily
Circ: 2
Soccer

Talking Transplants　997806
Email: talkingtransplants@gmail.com
Web site: http://talkingtransplants.blogspot.co.uk/
Freq: Daily
Circ: 521
News & Current Affairs

Tall Skinny Kiwi　1053718
Email: tallskinnykiwi@gmail.com
Web site: http://tallskinnykiwi.typepad.com
Freq: Daily
Circ: 3011284
Travel

Tall, Curvy Mummas　1053254
Web site: http://tallcurvymumma.wordpress.com
Freq: Daily
Circ: 22
Profile: Blog covering plus size fashion and beauty.
Beauty & Grooming, Cosmetics, Fashion, Hair

Taller la Otra　1061219
Web site: http://tallerlaotra.blogspot.com
Freq: Daily
Circ: 8470
Antiques/Collectibles, Art, Arts, Lifestyle, Literature, Men's Interests, National News, Photography, Politics, Regional General Interest

Talon-ted Lex　1098983
Email: talontedlex@hotmail.co.uk
Web site: http://talontedlex.co.uk/
Freq: Daily
Circ: 13692
Cosmetics

Tamar Blog　1052856
Editorial: 10 Barley Mow Passage, London W4 4PH Tel: 44 02089 957878
Email: why@tamar.com
Web site: http://blog.tamar.com/
Freq: Daily
Circ: 4064
Advertising Industry, Branding, Internet, Marketing

Tamarind and Thyme　986246
Email: tamarindandthyme@gmail.com
Web site: tamarindandthyme.wordpress.com/
Freq: Daily
Circ: 18261
News & Current Affairs

Tami Bee　1053584
Web site: www.tami-bee.com
Freq: Daily
Circ: 9656
Fashion, Women's Interests

Taming Twins　998206
Web site: http://tamingtwins.com/
Freq: Daily
Circ: 12765
Cooking & Baking, Crafts

Tammy Tour Guide　997435
Web site: tammytourguide.wordpress.com
Freq: Daily

Circ: 7
Airline Inflight, Railroad, Travel

Tanglemouse Cards　1056759
Web site: http://tanglemousecards.blogspot.co.uk/
Freq: Daily
Circ: 3057
Crafts

Tanya Burr　987200
Web site: www.tanyaburr.co.uk
Freq: Daily
Circ: 171945
Profile: Blog covering beauty and lifestyle. The blog has an archive dating back to March 2011. This outlet also offers a vlog. The fundamentals of working with vloggers are the same as with traditional journalists at traditional media outlets:
Beauty & Grooming, Cosmetics, Fashion, Hair, Women's Interests

Tanya Burr Vlog　1069615
Web site: https://www.youtube.com/user/pixi2woo
Freq: Daily
Circ: 251
Beauty & Grooming, Cosmetics, Fashion, Hair, Women's Interests

Tarde O Temprano　1061841
Web site: http://www.tardeotemprano.net
Freq: Daily
Circ: 6365
Bars, Clubs & Pubs, Comedy, Entertainment, Fashion, Local Entertainment Guides, Movies & Video, Photography

tartanmouth　1053025
Web site: tartanmouth.blogspot.co.uk
Freq: Daily
Circ: 9961
Profile: Blog covering lifestyle, fashion, beauty, travel, food and books. The blog has an archive dating back to January 2014.
Literature, Women's Interests

Tarun Taikakakut　1061913
Email: taikakakut@luukku.com
Web site: http://taikakakut.blogspot.fi/
Freq: Daily
Circ: 1701
Cooking & Baking

Tashi Skervin　1053763
Email: tashi@tashiskervin.com
Web site: tashiskervin.com
Freq: Daily
Circ: 9586
Beauty & Grooming, Cosmetics, Fitness & Exercise, Hair, Travel, Women's Interests

Tastes Like Glitter　987055
Email: bicky@tasteslikeglitter.com
Web site: http://www.tasteslikeglitter.com
Circ: 2411
Cosmetics

Tate　988718
Editorial: 20 John Islip Street, Millbank, London SW1P 4RG Tel: 44 02078 878730
Email: pressoffice@tate.org.uk
Web site: http://www.tate.org.uk/art
Circ: 13352
Art

The Tattooed Book　998150
Editorial: Greylings, Church Street, Rudgwick, Rudgwick RH12 3EE
Tel: 44 07713 631327
Email: thetattooedbook@yahoo.co.uk
Web site: http://thetattooedbook.blogspot.co.uk/
Freq: Daily
Circ: 1034
Literature

Tattooed Tea Lady　988027
Web site: http://www.tattooedtealady.com/
Circ: 26628
News & Current Affairs

TATTOOLOGIST　1060244
Email: naridyard@gmail.com
Web site: http://tattoologist.nataliehanks.com/

Freq: Daily
Circ: 25516
Fashion

TATTOOLOGIST　1060412
Email: naridyard@gmail.com
Web site: http://tattoologist.nataliehanks.com/
Freq: Daily
Circ: 25516
Fashion

Tax Research UK　986247
Editorial: The Old Orchard, Bexwell Road, Downham Market, Downham Market PE38 9LJ Tel: 44 01353 665405
Web site: www.taxresearch.org.uk/Blog/
Freq: Daily
Circ: 47762
Personal Finance, Politics

TaxAssist Accountants　999497
Tel: 44 08000 523555
Email: info@taxassist.co.uk
Web site: http://www.taxassist.co.uk/resources/news-archive
Freq: Daily
Circ: 10
Accounting, Tax Law

Taxpayers' Alliance Blog　986248
Editorial: 55 Tufton Street, London SW1P 3QL Tel: 44 02079 981450
Email: info@taxpayersalliance.com
Web site: www.taxpayersalliance.com
Freq: Daily
Circ: 29630
Politics

Taylor Hearts Travel　988769
Email: char@taylorheartstravel.com
Web site: http://taylorheartstravel.com/
Freq: Daily
Circ: 25396
Profile: Taylor Hearts Travel covers 'stylish, unique and exciting travel'. The blog also offers a vlog.
News & Current Affairs

Taylor James Blog　1053514
Editorial: 45 - 47 Underwood Street, London N1 7LG Tel: 44 02077 394488
Email: press@taylorjames.com
Web site: http://www.taylorjames.com/blog/
Freq: Daily
Circ: 2
Graphic Design

Tea Party Beauty　988959
Editorial: 43 Willowdale, Middleton, Leeds LS10 4FN
Email: teapartybeauty@gmail.com
Web site: http://www.teapartybeauty.com/
Freq: Daily
Circ: 48063
Profile: Blog covering beauty. TEA PARTY BEAUTY blog discusses anything from beauty products and reviews to fashion and lifestyle. The blog has an archive dating back to April 2013 and shares an extensive blog roll.
Beauty & Grooming, Cosmetics, Hair

Tea Party with Alice　1060418
Email: teapartywithalice@live.com
Web site: teapartywithalice.com
Freq: Daily
Circ: 8595
Profile: Blog covering beauty. TEA PARTY WITH ALICE blog discusses anything from beauty and fashion to lifestyle. The blog has an archive dating back to January 2013.
Beauty & Grooming, Cosmetics, Hair, Women's Interests

Tea Toast Fashion　1053268
Email: teatoastfashionblog@gmail.com
Web site: http://teatoastfashion.blogspot.co.uk/
Freq: Daily
Circ: 9157
Beauty & Grooming, Cameras, Cosmetics, Fashion, Hair, Regional General Interest, Women's Interests

Tea with Me and Friends　988226
Email: teawithmeandfriends@gmail.com
Web site: http://teawithmeandfriends.blogspot.co.uk
Freq: Daily
Circ: 8693
Profile: Blog covering afternoon tea. Tea With Me And Friends blog discusses anything from afternoon tea and tea to English tea rooms and baked goods. The blog has an archive dating back to June 2013 and shares an short blog roll. Tea With Me And Friends was shortlisted for the 'UK Blog Awards'.
Bars, Clubs & Pubs, Restaurant Reviews

Tea&Co　1062030
Web site: http://www.teaandco.com
Freq: Daily
Circ: 672
Alcohol & Spirits

Teacher Geek　1052916
Web site: http://createinnovateexplore.com/
Freq: Daily
Circ: 6186
Education

Teacher Toolkit　1052741
Web site: https://www.teachertoolkit.co.uk/
Freq: Daily
Circ: 18453
Education

Teaching Ideas Blog　1054257
Email: news@teachingideas.com
Web site: teachingideas.co.uk
Freq: Daily
Circ: 216884
Education

Teaching Science　1054176
Email: teachingofscience@gmail.com
Web site: https://teachingofscience.wordpress.com/
Freq: Daily
Circ: 122
Profile: Blog covering education, science, ICT and teaching. The blog has an archived dating back to May 2008 and shares an extensive blog roll.
Education

Teaching Science - Science Ideas - CEASED September 2016　1054578
Web site: www.scittscience.co.uk/
Freq: Daily
Circ: 12818
News & Current Affairs

Teaching: Leading Learning　1053377
Web site: http://chrishildrew.wordpress.com
Freq: Daily
Circ: 68
Profile: Blog covering education. Teaching: Leading Learning blog discusses anything from education to teaching.The blog has an archive dating back to December 2012 and shares an extensive blog roll. The outlet offers RSS (Really Simple Syndication).
Education

Team Honk　997249
Web site: http://teamhonk.org/
Freq: Daily
Circ: 4838
Charitable Foundations, Family & Parenting

Tearfund Blog　996443
Editorial: 100 Church Road, Teddington TW11 8QE Tel: 44 02089 779144
Email: enquiries@tearfund.org
Web site: http://www.tearfund.org/en/blog/
Freq: Daily
Circ: 41261
Charitable Foundations, Social Issues

teawithonesugarplease　1053470
Web site: http://teawithonesugarplease.blogspot.co.uk/
Freq: Daily

UK Blogs

Circ: 1789
Family & Parenting, Regional General Interest, Shopping

Tech Trends 1065156
Web site: http://alicebonasio.com/blog/
Freq: Daily
Circ: 173
Computers, Data Management, Education, Electronics, Government Technology, Higher Education, Industry, Internet, Mobile Communications, Software

TechblooG 1060399
Web site: http://www.techbloog.com
Freq: Daily
Circ: 1209
Auto Aftermarket, Computers, Data Management, Electronics, Government Technology, Industry, Internet, Mobile Communications, Security & Security Systems, Software

TechDigest 981678
Editorial: 4th Floor, 17 Old Court Place, London W8 4PL Tel: 44 02030 060455
Web site: www.techdigest.tv
Freq: Daily
Circ: 73341
Apple, Audio Video Trade, Cameras, Computer & Video Games, Computers, Consumer Electronics, Internet, Mobile Electronics, Movies & Video, Personal Computers

TechHim 1060776
Web site: http://www.techhim.com
Freq: Daily
Circ: 5639
Internet, Mobile Communications

TechHub 1053132
Editorial: 20 Ropemaker Street, London EC2Y 9AR Tel: 44 02074 900764
Email: hello@techhub.com
Web site: https://blog.techhub.com/
Freq: Daily
Circ: 33987
Industry

Techie Talk 1057085
Web site: www.techietalk.co.uk/
Freq: Daily
Circ: 49282
Apple, Audio Video Trade, Cameras, Consumer Electronics, Internet, Mobile Electronics, Movies & Video, Personal Computers

Technocracia 1062089
Web site: http://www.technocracia.com
Freq: Daily
Circ: 14347
Auto Aftermarket, Computers, Data Management, Electronics, Government Technology, Industry, Internet, Mobile Communications, Security & Security Systems, Software

TechnoLlama Blog 1054355
Web site: http://www.technollama.co.uk/
Freq: Daily
Circ: 16095
Intellectual Property

Technology Blogged 1053634
Email: write@technologyblogged.com
Web site: http://www.technologyblogged.com/
Freq: Daily
Circ: 33273
Audio Video Trade, Cameras, Consumer Electronics, Mobile Electronics, Movies & Video

Technology Enhanced Learning Blog 1052714
Web site: http://www.dontwasteyourtime.co.uk/
Freq: Daily
Circ: 13961
News & Current Affairs

Technology Resourcing Blog 1052887
Tel: 44 01483 302211
Email: info@tech-res.co.uk
Web site: http://tech-res.co.uk/blog/
Freq: Daily
Circ: 84
Recruiting

technorumors 1054457
Email: info@technorumors.com
Web site: http://www.technorumors.com/
Freq: Daily
Circ: 10725
Audio Video Trade, Cameras, Consumer Electronics, Mobile Electronics, Movies & Video

Techraze 1061497
Web site: http://www.techraze.com
Freq: Daily
Circ: 118184
Auto Aftermarket, Computer & Video Games, Computers, Data Management, Electronics, Government Technology, Industry, Internet, Mobile Communications, Security & Security Systems

TechSling 1053918
Email: contact@techsling.com
Web site: http://www.techsling.com/
Freq: Daily
Circ: 159861
Apple, Computer & Video Games, Computers, Internet, Mobile Electronics, Personal Computers

Techtastico 1061864
Web site: http://www.techtastico.com
Freq: Daily
Circ: 88896
Auto Aftermarket, Computer & Video Games, Computers, Data Management, Electronics, Government Technology, Industry, Internet, Mobile Communications, Security & Security Systems

TechUK Blog 1053137
Editorial: 10 St Bride Street, London EC4A 4AD Tel: 44 02073 312000
Email: info@techuk.org
Web site: http://www.techuk.org/
Freq: Daily
Circ: 46229
Auto Aftermarket, Computers, Data Management, Electronics, Government Technology, Industry, Internet, Mobile Communications, Security & Security Systems, Software

Tecneira 1060612
Web site: http://colunas.epocanegocios.globo.com/tecneira
Freq: Daily
Circ: 53
Auto Aftermarket, Computers, Data Management, Electronics, Government Technology, Industry, Internet, Mobile Communications, Security & Security Systems, Software

Tecno Gente 1061221
Web site: http://www.tecnogente.info/
Freq: Daily
Circ: 3544
Lifestyle, Men's Interests, Regional General Interest, Women's Interests

TecnoArk 1060496
Web site: http://www.tecnoark.com
Freq: Daily
Circ: 2535
Auto Aftermarket, Computers, Data Management, Electronics, Government Technology, Industry, Internet, Mobile Communications, National News, Science

TecnoArquitectura 1060525
Web site: http://www.tecnoarquitectura.com
Freq: Daily
Circ: 608
Architecture & Design, Auto Aftermarket, Computers, Data Management, Electronics, Government Technology, Industry, Internet, Mobile

Communications, Security & Security Systems

Tecnodatum 1061869
Web site: http://www.tecnodatum.com
Freq: Daily
Circ: 7555
Auto Aftermarket, Computers, Data Management, Electronics, Government Technology, Industry, Internet, Marketing, Mobile Communications, National News

TecnoDiva 1061465
Web site: http://www.tecnodiva.com
Freq: Daily
Circ: 6674
Auto Aftermarket, Computers, Data Management, Electronics, Government Technology, Industry, Internet, Mobile Communications, National News, Security & Security Systems

TecnoLatino 1060505
Web site: http://www.tecnolatino.com
Freq: Daily
Circ: 36425
Auto Aftermarket, Computers, Data Management, Electronics, Government Technology, Industry, Internet, Mobile Communications, Security & Security Systems, Software

Tecnoweb Studio 1061738
Web site: http://www.tecnowebstudio.com
Freq: Daily
Circ: 41817
Auto Aftermarket, Computers, Data Management, Electronics, Government Technology, Industry, Internet, Mobile Communications, Security & Security Systems, Software

Ted El Mecanico 1061884
Web site: http://tedelmecanico.com/
Freq: Daily
Circ: 4015
Classical/Choral/Band Music, Country, Folk, Bluegrass, Dance Music, Jazz & Blues, Music, Pop Music, R&B, Urban, World, Rap & Hip Hop, Rock Music

Teen Librarian 1054657
Email: editor@teenlibrarian.co.uk
Web site: http://teenlibrarian.co.uk/
Freq: Daily
Circ: 15941
Education, Higher Education, Literature, Schools & Institutions, Students, Teen/Young Adult, Trading Cards & Comics

Tehidy Holiday Park Blog 1054582
Tel: 44 01209 216489
Email: holiday@tehidy.co.uk
Web site: http://www.tehidy.co.uk/Blog/
Freq: Daily
Circ: 306
Outdoor Recreation, Travel

Teippitarha 1061979
Email: janina@teippitarha.fi
Web site: http://teippitarha.blogspot.fi
Freq: Daily
Circ: 1785
Crafts

TekCrispy 1061745
Web site: http://www.tekcrispy.com
Freq: Daily
Circ: 17731
Auto Aftermarket, Computers, Data Management, Electronics, Government Technology, Industry, Internet, Mobile Communications, Security & Security Systems, Software

Telco2.0 1054132
Email: contact@telco2.net
Web site: http://www.telco2.net/blog/
Freq: Daily
Circ: 402
Auto Aftermarket, Computers, Data Management, Electronics, Government Technology, Industry, Internet, Mobile Communications, Security & Security Systems, Software

Telling Tech Tales 1053638
Web site: tellingtechtales.com
Freq: Daily
Circ: 521
Auto Aftermarket, Computers, Data Management, Electronics, Government Technology, Industry, Internet, Mobile Communications, Security & Security Systems, Software

Temporary:Secretary 987092
Email: blog@temporary-secretary.com
Web site: http://www.temporary-secretary.com/
Freq: Daily
Circ: 27881
Profile: Blog covering fashion and beauty, reviews and beauty supplies. The blog has an archive dating back to August 2008.
Beauty & Grooming, Cooking & Baking, Cosmetics, Fashion, Hair, Women's Interests

Tennis Blog UK 1054145
Email: info.uk@tennisplanet.com
Web site: tennisbloguk.blogspot.co.uk
Freq: Daily
Circ: 767
Racquet Sports

Tenoch 1061226
Web site: http://tenoch.scimexico.com
Freq: Daily
Circ: 182
Auto Aftermarket, Computers, Data Management, Electronics, Government Technology, Industry, Internet, Mobile Communications, Science, Security & Security Systems

Tent Sniffing for Beginners 997276
Email: tentsniffer@gmail.com
Web site: http://www.tentsandfestivals.co.uk/
Freq: Daily
Circ: 8558
Camping and RV Travel

Tepilo Blog 997011
Editorial: 3 The Plough Brewery, 516 Wandsworth Road, London SW8 3JX
Tel: 44 08443 878377
Email: press@tepilo.com
Web site: http://www.tepilo.com/blog/
Freq: Daily
Circ: 47
Architecture & Design, Property Management & Maintenance

Terapeuta Holistico 1061678
Web site: http://terapeutaholistico.com/
Freq: Daily
Circ: 521
Alternative Medicine

Terapias Alternativas 1061271
Web site: http://terapiasvegetales.blogspot.com/
Freq: Daily
Circ: 9688
Alternative Medicine

Terrys Fabrics 1053770
Email: blog@terrysfabrics.co.uk
Web site: http://www.terrysfabrics.co.uk/blog/
Freq: Daily
Circ: 76867
Do-It-Yourself (DIY)

Textos en su Tinta 1061835
Web site: http://textosensutinta.blogspot.com/
Freq: Daily
Circ: 1028
Art, Cooking & Baking, Literature

Thankfifi 988297
Editorial: 1-1, 18 Royal Terrace, Glasgow G3 7NY Tel: 44 07587 141059
Email: thankfifi@gmail.com
Web site: http://www.thankfifi.com
Freq: Daily
Circ: 10254
Profile: Blog covering fashion. Thankfifi blog discusses anything from outfits and trends to

food and places. The blog has an archive dating back to August 2011. The outlet offers RSS (Really Simple Syndication).
Alcohol & Spirits, Beauty & Grooming, Cooking & Baking, Cosmetics, Fashion, Hair

That 1980s Sports Blog 1052590
Email: that1980ssportsblog@gmail.com
Web site: that1980ssportsblog.blogspot.co.uk
Freq: Daily
Circ: 10541
Basketball, Bicycles, Billiards, Boating & Yachting, Bodybuilding, Bowling, Boxing, Cricket, Equestrian Sports, Extreme/ Adventure Sports

That Adventurer 988765
Email: thatadventurerblog@gmail.com
Web site: http://www.thatadventurer.co.uk/
Freq: Daily
Circ: 12735
Profile: THAT ADVENTURER covers adventure and outdoor travel activities and stylish accommodation offerings across the World.
News & Current Affairs

That Girl's Got an Appetite
998224
Email: thatgirlsgotanappetite@gmail.com
Web site: http://thatgirlsgotanappetite.com
Freq: Daily
Circ: 1106
Cooking & Baking, Food, Grocery Stores, Organic Food, Restaurant Reviews, Vegetarianism & Veganism

That Grape Juice 986431
Email: freshness@thatgrapejuice.net
Web site: http://thatgrapejuice.net/
Freq: Daily
Circ: 187117
Editor: Sam Ajilore
Celebrities, Rap & Hip Hop

That Is Beyond 1052981
Email: thatisbeyond@gmail.com
Web site: https://thatisbeyond.com/
Freq: Daily
Circ: 10420
Beauty & Grooming, Cosmetics, Fashion, Hair, Men's Interests

That Jesse Bloke Reads 1052566
Email: editor@books4teens.co.uk
Web site: http://www.thatjessebloke.co.uk/
Freq: Daily
Circ: 6654
Literature

That Lancashire Lass 988893
Editorial: 310 Bolton Road, Radcliffe, Radcliffe M26 3GP
Email: eyuplass@thatlancashirelass.com
Web site: www.thatlancashirelass.com
Freq: Daily
Circ: 7889
Profile: Blog covering motherhood, family, parenting, food and lifestyle. The blog has an archive dating back to April 2014.
Camping and RV Travel, Education, Family & Parenting, Travel

That New Dress 1062735
Email: enquiries@thatnewdress.com
Web site: http://www.thatnewdress.com/
Freq: Daily
Circ: 6878
Art, Beauty & Grooming, Cooking & Baking, Cosmetics, Do-It-Yourself (DIY), Fashion, Hair, Health & Medicine, Local Entertainment Guides, Movies & Video

That Pommie Girl 1064933
Web site: www.thatpommiegirl.com
Freq: Daily
Circ: 22787
Profile: Blog covering fashion. The That Pommie Girl blog discusses anything from fashion and style tips to fashion accessories and outfits. The blog has an archive dating back to September 2013.
Beauty & Grooming, Cosmetics, Fashion, Hair, Nutrition

That's Crafty Challenge Blog
1054669
Email: laura@thatscrafty.co.uk
Web site: http://thatscraftychallenges.blogspot.in/
Freq: Daily
Circ: 611
Crafts

That's So Yesterday 986949
Email: vintagechicuk@yahoo.com
Web site: thatssoyestreday.blogspot.com
Freq: Daily
Circ: 4481
Profile: Blog covering lifestyle. That's So Yesterday blog discusses anything from fashion and beauty to lifestyle. The blog has an archive dating back to November 2008.
Fashion

The Drum 1095286
Web site: http://www.thedrum.com
Circ: 1191890
News

Theatre Breaks Blog 988038
Tel: 44 02032 871808
Email: kingsley.deplume@theatrebreaks.com
Web site: http://www.theatrebreaks.co.uk/blog/
Circ: 3
Theater & Performing Arts

Theatre, Books and Movies
998155
Web site: theatrebooksandmovies.com
Freq: Daily
Circ: 2724
News & Current Affairs

THEbatzuk 1061539
Web site: http://www.thebatzuk.org
Freq: Daily
Circ: 12693
Auto Aftermarket, Classical/Choral/Band Music, Computers, Country, Folk, Bluegrass, Dance Music, Data Management, Electronics, Government Technology, Industry, Internet

TheBookPeople.co.uk blog
1053835
Tel: 44 03456 023030
Web site: http://www.thebookpeople.co.uk/blog/
Freq: Daily
Circ: 199
Literature

TheEntertainmentWebsite.com
997320
Editorial: Flat 31, 4 Earnshaw Street, London WC2H 8AJ **Tel:** 44 02072 404769
Email: admin@theentertainmentwebsite.com
Web site: http://theentertainmentwebsite.com/
Freq: Daily
Circ: 10630
Entertainment, Movies & Video, Theater & Performing Arts

TheFloatingRumShack.com blog
988922
Editorial: 10 Priestley Court, High Wycombe, High Wycombe HP13 7WZ
Email: thefloatingrumshack@gmail.com
Web site: http://thefloatingrumshack.com/content/
Freq: Daily
Circ: 406
Alcohol & Spirits

TheFonecast 1054604
Email: info@thefonecast.com
Web site: thefonecast.com
Freq: Daily
Circ: 1582
Mobile Electronics

theinsider.se 1060203
Email: erik.liden@insiderfonder.se
Web site: http://theinsider.se
Freq: Daily
Circ: 9443
Banking, Fund Management

theinsider.se 1060608
Email: erik.liden@insiderfonder.se
Web site: http://theinsider.se
Freq: Daily
Circ: 9443
Banking, Fund Management

them apples 986498
Web site: http://www.them-apples.co.uk
Freq: Daily
Circ: 56960
Alcohol & Spirits, Bars, Clubs & Pubs, Beer, Beverages, Cooking & Baking, Food, Grocery Stores, Organic Food, Restaurant Reviews, Vegetarianism & Veganism

Theme Park Trader 1102568
Web site: http://www.themeparktrader.com
Freq: Daily
Circ: 13906
Regional General Interest, Travel

the-northernlight.com 1061217
Email: the-northernlight@hotmail.com
Web site: http://the-northernlight.com/
Freq: Daily
Circ: 6770
Fashion

Therapy Directory blog 1054506
Tel: 44 08448 030245
Email: info@therapy-directory.org.uk
Web site: http://www.therapy-directory.org.uk/blog/
Freq: Daily
Circ: 7
Alternative Medicine

Therese Fischer 1060237
Email: info@theresefischer.com
Web site: http://nyheter24.se/modette/theresefischer/
Freq: Daily
Circ: 30
Beauty & Grooming, Cosmetics, Fashion, Hair

Therese Fischer 1060391
Email: info@theresefischer.com
Web site: http://nyheter24.se/modette/theresefischer/
Freq: Daily
Circ: 30
Beauty & Grooming, Cosmetics, Fashion, Hair

Therese Johaug 1060512
Web site: http://www.theresejohaug.no/
Freq: Daily
Circ: 2868
Lifestyle, Men's Interests, Regional General Interest, Winter Sports, Women's Interests

The-Room 995477
Web site: http://www.the-room.co.nz/
Freq: Daily
Circ: 1342
Editor: Rachel Cunningham
Beauty & Grooming, Cosmetics, Fashion, Hair, Travel, Women's Interests

These City Days 1052968
Web site: www.thesecitydays.co.uk
Freq: Daily
Circ: 8463
Profile: Blog covering lifestyle. These City Days blog discusses anything from well-being and beauty to hobbies. The blog has an archive dating back to June 2013.
Beauty & Grooming, Cooking & Baking, Cosmetics, Crafts, Hair, Women's Interests

Thesweetspot.dk 1060960
Email: laura@reformliving.dk
Web site: http://thesweetspot.dk/
Freq: Daily
Circ: 4567
Do-It-Yourself (DIY)

Think Left 997134
Email: admin@think-left.org
Web site: think-left.org
Freq: Daily

Circ: 12346
Politics, Social Issues

Think What You Like 1054197
Web site: http://thinkwhatyoulike.com/
Freq: Daily
Circ: 652
Beauty & Grooming, Cosmetics, Fitness & Exercise, Hair, Nutrition, Travel, Women's Interests

Thinker's blog 1061736
Email: sfskz@sina.com
Web site: http://blog.sina.com.cn/sfskz
Freq: Daily
Circ: 22532
Antique & Collectible Cars, Antiques/ Collectibles, Art, Arts, Automakers, Automotive, Bars, Clubs & Pubs, Comedy, Driving, Entertainment

thinking liberal 996321
Email: matthew@thinkingliberal.co.uk
Web site: http://thinkingliberal.co.uk/
Freq: Daily
Circ: 8728
Politics

thinkmoney news & advice
999382
Editorial: Think Park, Mosley Road, Trafford Park, Manchester M17 1FQ
Email: contactus@thinkmoney.com
Web site: http://www.thinkmoney.co.uk/news-advice/
Freq: Daily
Circ: 235
Personal Finance

Thinly Spread 988351
Web site: thinlyspread.co.uk
Freq: Daily
Circ: 12623
Family & Parenting, Women's Interests

Third Force News Blog 1054471
Editorial: Third Force News, Mansfield Traquair Centre, 15 Mansfield Place, Edinburgh EH3 6BB
Email: tfn@scvo.org.uk
Web site: http://thirdforcenews.org.uk/blogs
Freq: Daily
Circ: 105
Editor: Susan Smith
Charitable Foundations, Consumer Affairs, Energy & Environment, Ethical/ Moral Issues, National News, Politics, Regional, Science, Scotland, Social Issues

Thirty Something London 988458
Email: info@thirtysomethinglondon.com
Web site: www.thirtysomethinglondon.com
Freq: Daily
Circ: 10705
Profile: Blog covering dating, single life and bar reviews. The blog has an archive dating back to January 2013.
Men's Interests, Relationships

This City Life 1054450
Web site: http://thiscitylife.co.uk/
Freq: Daily
Circ: 6924
Regional General Interest, Travel

This Cotswold Girl 1063273
Email: hello@thiscotswoldgirl.com
Web site: http://thecotswoldguide.co.uk/
Freq: Daily
Circ: 1507
Cooking & Baking, Food, Grocery Stores, Organic Food, Regional General Interest, Restaurant Reviews, Vegetarianism & Veganism, Women's Interests

This Enchanted Pixie 988559
Email: thisenchantedpixie@hotmail.com
Web site: thisenchantedpixie.org
Freq: Daily
Circ: 19798
Cooking & Baking, Family & Parenting, Fashion

This Girl Thrives 988477
Email: lydiarosesmyth@gmail.com
Web site: http://www.thisgirlthrives.co.uk/

UK Blogs

Freq: Daily
Circ: 3264
Beauty & Grooming, Cosmetics, Fashion, Hair

This Is Entertainment 999166
Tel: 44 07922 080181
Web site: jamesmparry.wordpress.com/
Freq: Daily
Circ: 3247
Bars, Clubs & Pubs, Comedy, Entertainment, Local Entertainment Guides, Movies & Video

This is Life 1054294
Web site: http://www.angelathisislife.com/
Freq: Daily
Circ: 11143
Profile: Blog covering family. This is Life blog discusses anything from family and parenting to motherhood and lifestyle. The blog has an archive dating back to October 2009 and shares a short blog roll.
Beauty & Grooming, Cooking & Baking, Cosmetics, Crafts, Family & Parenting, Fashion, Hair, Travel

This is my Classroom 1053401
Web site: http://thisismyclassroom.wordpress.com
Freq: Daily
Circ: 54
Profile: Blog covering education. This is my classroom blog discusses anything education and teaching to primary school mathematics and literacy. The blog has an archive dating back to August 2012 and shares an extensive blog roll.
Education

This is Teral 996273
Editorial: 321 Hither Green Lane, Lewisham, London SE13 6TJ
Email: teralatilan@gmail.com
Web site: www.thisisteral.com
Freq: Daily
Circ: 12139
Beauty & Grooming, Cosmetics, Fashion, Hair, Women's Interests

This little house 1054459
Email: thislittlehouse1@gmail.com
Web site: http://www.thislittlehouse.co.uk/
Freq: Daily
Circ: 7826
Profile: This Little House covers family life, parenting, family travel and DIY. The blog has an archive dating back to February 2013.
Crafts, Do-It-Yourself (DIY), Family & Parenting, Fashion

This Mummy Loves 986678
Email: thismummyloves@gmail.com
Web site: http://thismummyloves.com/
Freq: Daily
Circ: 17852
Family & Parenting, Women's Interests

This Particular. 988071
Web site: http://www.thisparticularblog.com/
Freq: Daily
Circ: 2168
Profile: Blog covering lifestyle. This Particular. discusses anything food and beauty to lifestyle. The blog has an archive dating back to January 2014 and shares a short blogroll. The outlet offers RSS (Really Simple Syndication).
Cooking & Baking, Food, Grocery Stores, Organic Food, Regional General Interest, Restaurant Reviews, Vegetarianism & Veganism

This Ridiculous World 1061598
Email: thisridiculousworld@gmail.com
Web site: http://thisridiculousworld.com
Freq: Daily
Circ: 2386
Social Issues

This Woman's Word 987788
Email: dani@thiswomansword.com
Web site: thiswomansword.com
Freq: Daily
Circ: 10372

Profile: Blog covering fitness and exercise. THIS WOMAN'S WORD blog discusses anything from fitness and nutrition to personal health. The blog has an archive dating back to November 2012. The blog was a finalist in the Individual Health category at the UK Blog Awards.
Beauty & Grooming, Cooking & Baking, Cosmetics, Fitness & Exercise, Hair, Nutrition, Regional General Interest, Restaurant Reviews, Women's Interests

thisisme 1063454
Web site: http://thisismeblog.com/
Freq: Daily
Circ: 1121
Family & Parenting, Travel, Women's Interests

Thomson blog 998424
Editorial: Crawley Business Quarter, Fleming Way, Crawley RH10 9QL
Tel: 44 01293 645700
Email: corporate.communications@tuitravel.com
Web site: www.thomson.co.uk/blog/
Freq: Daily
Circ: 10801
Airline Inflight, Railroad, Travel

Thoroughly Modern Milly 987517
Editorial: Flat 37, Mundania Court, London SE22 0NQ
Email: milly@thoroughlymodernmilly.com
Web site: www.thoroughlymodernmilly.com
Circ: 11363
Editor: Milly Kenny-Ryder
Profile: Website covering lifestyle. The Thoroughly Modern Milly websites discusses anything from art and music to food, beauty, fashion, theater and travel. The Thoroughly Modern Milly was originally a blog and began in April 2010, and then launched into an online magazine in February 2012.
Art, Beauty & Grooming, Cooking & Baking, Cosmetics, Fashion, Hair, Pop Music, R&B, Urban, World, Theater & Performing Arts, Travel

Thou Shalt Not Covet 1060199
Email: tsncblog@hotmail.co.uk
Web site: http://thoushaltnotcovet.net/
Freq: Daily
Circ: 79683
Profile: Blog covering beauty, make-up, nail art, fashion, jewellery, lifestyle and travel. The blog has an archive dating back to February 2013 and shares an extensive blog roll. The outlet offers RSS (Really Simple Syndication).
Art, Cooking & Baking, Fashion, Photography, Restaurant Reviews, Visual Arts, Women's Interests

Thought Scratchings 997846
Web site: http://thoughtscratchings.com/
Freq: Daily
Circ: 9795
Literature

Thoughts on Chinese Car Industry 1061427
Web site: http://blog.sina.com.cn/mushi1667
Freq: Daily
Circ: 34649999
Antique & Collectible Cars, Automakers, Automotive, Aviation, Driving, Motorcycles, Off-road & 4-Wheel Drive Vehicles, Railroad, Shipping & Warehousing, Supply Chain Management (SCM)

Thoughts on Film 988412
Web site: http://thoughtsonfilm.co.uk/
Freq: Daily
Circ: 8414
Movies & Video

Threadnoodle 1055297
Email: threadnoodle@hotmail.co.uk
Web site: http://threadnoodle.blogspot.co.uk/
Freq: Daily
Circ: 578
Art, Crafts

Three blog 1054598
Editorial: Three Press Office, Hutchison 3G UK Ltd., Star House, 20 Grenfell Road, Maidenhead SL6 1EX **Tel:** 44 07454 959715
Email: three@mww.com
Web site: http://www.three.co.uk/hub/
Freq: Daily
Circ: 139
Mobile Electronics

Three Monsters and Me 1054462
Web site: www.twomonstersandme.com
Freq: Daily
Circ: 4764
Cooking & Baking, Family & Parenting, Health & Medicine, Women's Interests

Three Thousand Versts of Loneliness 1053169
Email: owen.polley@talk21.com
Web site: http://threethousandversts.blogspot.co.uk/
Freq: Daily
Circ: 11562
Defense & National Security, International News, Northern Ireland, Politics, Regional

ThumbelinaLillie 988363
Email: info@thumbelinalillie.com
Web site: www.thumbelinalillie.com
Freq: Daily
Circ: 11562
Fashion

Thunder & Threads 987586
Web site: thunderandthreads.com
Freq: Daily
Circ: 6556
Fashion

Thyme & Honey 1054487
Web site: http://www.thymeandhoney.co.uk/
Freq: Daily
Circ: 1113
Cooking & Baking, Restaurant Reviews, Travel

Tickle Your Fancy 1061329
Email: sara.tickle@gmail.com
Web site: http://www.lily.fi/blogit/tickle-your-fancy
Freq: Daily
Circ: 67308
Fashion

Tidy Away Today 987585
Email: tidyawaytoday@yahoo.co.uk
Web site: www.tidyawaytoday.co.uk
Freq: Daily
Circ: 11046
Editor: Antonia Ludden
Do-It-Yourself (DIY)

Tidy Design 999194
Editorial: Office 2, 17 Pembroke Road, Portsmouth PO1 2NT **Tel:** 44 02392 861839
Email: support@tidydesign.com
Web site: www.tidydesign.com/blog
Freq: Daily
Circ: 82
Graphic Design

Tigerlilly Quinn 988164
Web site: http://www.tigerlillyquinn.com
Freq: Daily
Circ: 41517
Profile: Blog covering lifestyle. Tigerlilly Quinn discusses anything from fashion and interior design and motherhood to life. The blog has an archive dating back to January 2010. The outlet offers RSS (Really Simple Syndication).
Do-It-Yourself (DIY), Family & Parenting, Fashion

Tikichris 988261
Web site: http://tikichris.com/
Freq: Daily
Circ: 16510
Regional General Interest, Travel

Tilly Jayne 1052535
Web site: www.tillyjayne.com
Freq: Daily

Three Three blog 1054598

Circ: 7351
Fashion

Tim Anderson's ITWriting 1052726
Web site: http://www.itwriting.com/blog/
Freq: Daily
Circ: 39274
Audio Video Trade, Cameras, Consumer Electronics, Mobile Electronics, Movies & Video

Tim Forrest's E & A blog 998428
Web site: https://tfeanda.com/
Freq: Daily
Circ: 9483
Antiques/Collectibles, Art

Tim Nash 1053369
Web site: https://timnash.co.uk/
Freq: Daily
Circ: 69743
Internet

Time to Craft 996427
Email: cheryl@timetocraft.co.uk
Web site: http://timetocraft.co.uk/
Freq: Daily
Circ: 7394
Crafts

Time2Gossip 987231
Editorial: 31 Cowley Crescent, Hersham, Walton-on-Thames KT12 5RH
Email: time2gossip@gmail.com
Web site: http://www.time2gossip.co.uk/
Freq: Daily
Circ: 8798
Editor: Fiona Kay Dunne
Audio Video Trade, Beauty & Grooming, Cameras, Consumer Electronics, Cosmetics, Electronics, Fashion, Hair, Mobile Electronics, Movies & Video

Timebank 986268
Editorial: Royal London House, 22-25 Finsbury Square, London EC2A 1DX
Tel: 44 02031 110700
Email: helpdesk@timebank.org.uk
Web site: timebank.org.uk/blog
Freq: Daily
Circ: 3
Charitable Foundations

Timera Energy 997858
Editorial: Heron Tower, 110 Bishopsgate, London EC2N 4AY **Tel:** 44 02079 610805
Email: info@timera-energy.com
Web site: http://www.timera-energy.com/our-insights/blog/
Freq: Daily
Circ: 142
Carbon Emissions & Trading, Electricity, Oil

Tin Box Traveller 1063928
Web site: http://tinboxtraveller.co.uk
Freq: Daily
Circ: 15412
Family & Parenting, Travel

Tinies Blog 996210
Editorial: Bedford House - Fulham Green, 69-79 Fulham High Street, Fulham, London SW6 3JW **Tel:** 44 02073 848657
Email: info@tinies.com
Web site: http://www.tinies.com/blog/
Freq: Daily
Circ: 6
Community Care (UK), Health Administration, Preschool, Recruiting

Tink Jayne 988422
Email: tinkerbelljayne@googlemail.com
Web site: www.allabouttink.co.uk
Freq: Daily
Circ: 8286
Profile: Tink Jayne covers lifestyle, travel, beauty, style, food, events and personal health. The blog has an archive dating back to December 2010.
Lifestyle, Men's Interests, Regional General Interest, Women's Interests

Tinman London 1054313
Web site: http://www.tinmanlondon.com/
Freq: Daily

Circ: 10928
Profile. Blog covering lifestyle, The tinman london blog discusses anything from general lifestyle and music.
Dance Music, Fashion, Lifestyle, Men's Interests, Pop Music, Rap & Hip Hop, Regional General Interest, Women's Interests

Tinned Tomatoes 986911
Email: tinnedtomatoes@googlemail.com
Web site: http://www.tinnedtomatoes.com
Freq: Daily
Circ: 42785
Vegetarianism & Veganism

Tiny Bird Heart 1053391
Email: tinybirdheart@live.com
Web site: tinybirdheart.com/
Freq: Daily
Circ: 9817
Profile: Blog covering lifestyle, fashion, food, pets and travel.
Cooking & Baking, Family & Parenting, Fashion, Travel

Tiny Twisst 987612
Email: tinytwisst@gmail.com
Web site: www.tinytwisst.com
Freq: Daily
Circ: 7114
Profile: Blog covering fashion. TINY TWISST blog discusses anything from outfit posts and picks of the week to beauty posts to DIY features. The blog has an archive dating back to March 2012. The outlet offers RSS (Really Simple Syndication).
Fashion, Women's Interests

Tip Top Toppers Things 996497
Email: tiptoptoppers@btinternet.com
Web site: http://tiptoptoppers.blogspot.co.uk/
Freq: Daily
Circ: 846
Crafts

Tips for Travellers 988724
Web site: http://www.tipsfortravellers.com/
Freq: Daily
Circ: 11473
Airline Inflight, Railroad, Travel

Tired Mummy of Two 988606
Editorial: 102 Shillingford Road, Manchester M18 7TN
Email: info@tiredmummyoftwo.co.uk
Web site: www.tiredmummyoftwo.co.uk
Freq: Daily
Circ: 10032
Family & Parenting, Women's Interests

TM Blog 988092
Editorial: 4 Pentonville Road, Islington, London N1 9HF Tel: 44 02073 163372
Email: blog@ticketmaster.co.uk
Web site: blog.ticketmaster.co.uk/
Freq: Daily
Circ: 768
Profile: Blog covering live events and music.
Basketball, Billiards, Bowling, Boxing, Classical/Choral/Band Music, Country, Folk, Bluegrass, Cricket, Dance Music, Entertainment, Football (American)

To Become Mum 1052572
Email: tobecomemum@gmail.com
Web site: tobecomemum.co.uk
Freq: Daily
Circ: 9105
Profile: Blog covering motherhood, family, lifestyle, food, books, home decorating and parenting. The blog has an archive dating back to November 2012.
Cosmetics, Family & Parenting, Women's Interests

To Each Its Own 1061565
Web site: http://www.sakshijuneja.com/blog
Freq: Daily
Circ: 67
Antiques/Collectibles, Art, Arts, Bars, Clubs & Pubs, Comedy, Consumer Affairs, Crime & Violence, Defense & National Security, Energy & Environment, Entertainment

To Limbo and Beyond 1053743
Freq: Daily
News & Current Affairs

To quote 1060221
Web site: http://www.toquote.se
Freq: Daily
Circ: 1420
News & Current Affairs

To quote 1060649
Web site: http://www.toquote.se
Freq: Daily
Circ: 1420
News & Current Affairs

To The Days Like This 1053826
Web site: www.tothedayslikethis.com
Freq: Daily
Circ: 6193
Profile: Blog covering travel. The to the days like this blog discusses anything from travel and food to expatriate living and lifestyle. The blog has an archive dating back to March 2014 and shares a short blog roll.
Travel

Toast & Butter 999370
Web site: http://toastandbutter.net/
Freq: Daily
Circ: 10211
Alcohol & Spirits, Bars, Clubs & Pubs, Beer, Beverages, Cooking & Baking, Food, Grocery Stores, Organic Food, Restaurant Reviews, Vegetarianism & Veganism

Today I'm Wearing Blog 987169
Editorial: Northcliffe House, 2 Derry Street, London W8 5TT Tel: 44 02036 151314
Email: editorial@todayimwearing.com
Web site: https://www.todayimwearing.com/
Circ: 2526
Editor: Lottie Kay
Fashion

Toddlebabes 1053586
Email: toddleinfo@toddlebabes.co.uk
Web site: www.toddlebabes.co.uk
Freq: Daily
Circ: 4213
Family & Parenting

The Tofu Diaries 997986
Email: thetofudiaries@gmail.com
Web site: http://natalietamara.co.uk/
Freq: Daily
Circ: 65855
Profile: Blog covering vegetarian food, recipes, lifestyle and travel. The blog has an archive dating back to January 2014.
Airline Inflight, Cooking & Baking, Food, Grocery Stores, Organic Food, Railroad, Restaurant Reviews, Travel, Vegetarianism & Veganism

tofugu.com 1060839
Web site: http://tofugu.com
Freq: Daily
Circ: 624541
Antiques/Collectibles, Art, Arts, Literature, Photography, Theater & Performing Arts, Visual Arts

tokyomango.com 1061419
Email: mango@tokyomango.com
Web site: http://tokyomango.com
Freq: Daily
Circ: 26414
Bars, Clubs & Pubs, Comedy, Entertainment, Local Entertainment Guides, Movies & Video

Tom Francis Regrets This Already 1053740
Web site: http://www.pentadact.com/
Freq: Daily
Circ: 1652
Apple, Computer & Video Games, Computers, Internet, Movies & Video, Personal Computers

Tom Hall Travel 1053939
Web site: http://tomhalltravel.com/
Freq: Daily

Circ: 611
Regional General Interest, Travel

Tom Watson MP 986269
Editorial: Tom Watson MP, Terry Duffy House, Thomas Street, West Bromwich B70 6NT Tel: 44 01215 691904
Email: watsont@parliament.uk
Web site: http://www.tom-watson.co.uk
Freq: Daily
Circ: 5137
Politics

Tom's Bike Trip 988299
Web site: http://tomsbiketrip.com/
Freq: Daily
Circ: 40452
News & Current Affairs

The Torch: Entertainment Guide 998421
Tel: 44 07976 759908
Web site: http://thetorchentertainmentguide.com/
Freq: Daily
Circ: 10255
Apple, Computer & Video Games, Computers, Internet, Personal Computers

Torie Jayne 1052892
Email: toriejayne@gmail.com
Web site: http://toriejayne.com
Freq: Daily
Circ: 11193
Cooking & Baking, Crafts, Do-It-Yourself (DIY)

Total BioPharma 987267
Editorial: Terrapinn Holdings Ltd, 4th Floor, Welken House, 10-11 Charterhouse Square, London EC1M 6EH Tel: 44 02076 087030
Email: enquiry.uk@terrapinn.com
Web site: http://www.totalbiopharma.com/
Freq: Daily
Circ: 11970
Health & Medicine

Total Customer 987262
Editorial: Terrapinn Holdings Ltd, 4th Floor, Welken House, 10-11 Charterhouse Square, London EC1M 6EH Tel: 44 02076 087030
Email: enquiry.uk@terrapinn.com
Web site: http://www.totalcustomer.org/
Freq: Daily
Circ: 4025
Advertising Industry, Branding, Broadcasting, Graphic Design, Marketing, Media & Communications, Photography, Publishing

Total Fitness 1060835
Email: mail@nina-furseth.com
Web site: http://www.nina-furseth.com/
Freq: Daily
Circ: 2927
Fitness & Exercise

Total Flanker 987908
Email: totalflanker-blog@yahoo.co.uk
Web site: http://www.totalflanker.co.uk/
Freq: Daily
Circ: 521
Rugby

Total Pro Sports 997255
Email: icisicmedia@gmail.com
Web site: http://www.totalprosports.com/
Freq: Daily
Circ: 3657266
Basketball, Bicycles, Billiards, Boating & Yachting, Bodybuilding, Bowling, Boxing, Cricket, Equestrian Sports, Extreme/Adventure Sports

The Totality 1054375
Web site: www.the-totality.com/
Freq: Daily
Circ: 2671
Profile: Blog covering lifestyle. THE TOTALITY blog discusses anything from film reviews and men's fashion to culture. The blog has an archive dating back to August 2012.
Cooking & Baking, Food, Grocery Stores, Men's Interests, Movies & Video, Organic Food, Restaurant Reviews, Vegetarianism & Veganism

Totaljobs.com blog 997452
Editorial: Holden House, 57 Rathbone Place, London W1T 1JU
Tel: 44 03330 145111
Email: totaljobsteam@redconsultancy.com
Web site: http://blog.totaljobs.com/
Freq: Daily
Circ: 2339716
Careers

Totsy's Place 1053578
Tel: 44 01253 735355
Email: headoffice@talkingtots.info
Web site: http://totsy.typepad.com/
Freq: Daily
Circ: 1294190
Family & Parenting, Preschool, Schools & Institutions

Touchscreens & Beau-tyqueens 1060566
Web site: http://touchscreensandbeautyqueens.com
Freq: Daily
Circ: 3560
Profile: Blog covering beauty. touchscreens & beautyqueens discusses anything from beauty products and nails to outfits and lifestyle.
Beauty & Grooming, Cosmetics, Hair

ToUChstone Blog 986582
Editorial: Congress House, Great Russell Street, London WC1B 3LS
Tel: 44 02076 364030
Email: info@tuc.org.uk
Web site: touchstoneblog.org.uk
Freq: Daily
Circ: 21092
Employment

Tourdust 996424
Editorial: Tourdust Ltd., 67 Akeman Street, Tring, Tring HP23 6AF Tel: 44 02037 335274
Email: help@tourdust.com
Web site: www.tourdust.com/blog
Freq: Daily
Circ: 33
Travel

Toxylicious blog 988947
Email: toxycat100@aol.com
Web site: http://toxylicious.blogspot.co.uk/
Freq: Daily
Circ: 10709
Profile: Blog covering beauty, technology, fashion and lifestyle. The blog shares an extensive blog roll.
Audio Video Trade, Beauty & Grooming, Cameras, Consumer Electronics, Cosmetics, Fashion, Hair, Mobile Electronics, Movies & Video, Women's Interests

Toybuzz 985811
Editorial: 6 Fairacre Close, Thornhill, Cardiff CF14 9HR
Email: contact@toybuzz.co.uk
Web site: www.toybuzz.co.uk
Freq: Daily
Circ: 1306
Toys

Toyota Blog 997551
Editorial: Toyota (GB) PLC, PO Box 814, Portsmouth PO6 9AY Tel: 44 08447 016202
Web site: blog.toyota.co.uk
Freq: Daily
Circ: 663477
Automakers

TPreview 995519
Email: contact@tpreview.co.uk
Web site: http://www.tpreview.co.uk/
Freq: Daily
Circ: 11160
Editor: Tom Souter
Computer & Video Games

Track Days Blog 996995
Editorial: Digital House, Threshelfords Business Park, Inworth Road, Colchester CO5 9SE Tel: 44 01376 809001
Email: info@trackdays.co.uk
Web site: https://www.trackdays.co.uk/news/
Freq: Daily

UK Blogs

Urban Pixxels 1052674
Web site: http://www.urbanpixxels.com/
Freq: Daily
Circ: 9006
Profile: Blog covering lifestyle, travel, photography and food from the point of view of a Dutch expatriate living in London.
Cooking & Baking, Photography, Regional General Interest, Restaurant Reviews, Travel, Women's Interests

Urban Splash Blog 1053250
Email: headoffice@urbansplash.co.uk
Web site: urbansplash.co.uk/blog
Freq: Daily
Circ: 2
Property Management & Maintenance, Sales & Marketing

Urban Travel Blog 1054043
Email: duncan@urbantravelblog.com
Web site: www.urbantravelblog.com
Freq: Daily
Circ: 40071
Travel

Urban Vox 1053550
Web site: http://www.urbanvox.net
Freq: Daily
Circ: 7496
Bars, Clubs & Pubs, Lifestyle, Men's Interests, Regional General Interest, Women's Interests

Urbanknit blog 988714
Email: contact@urbanknit.com
Web site: http://www.urbanknit.com/blog/
Freq: Daily
Circ: 72
Crafts, Fashion, Women's Interests

Urbansocial Dating Blog 1098982
Email: webmaster@urbansocial.com
Web site: http://www.urbansocial.com/blog/
Freq: Daily
Circ: 137
Men's Interests, Relationships, Women's Interests

Ursula Rose Blog 1070430
Web site: http://ursula-rose.com
Freq: Daily
Circ: 968
Family & Parenting

The Used Car Guy 1096037
Editorial: 2 Chester Way, Banbury, Oxford OX16 0NS
Email: contact@theusedcarguy.co.uk
Web site: http://theusedcarguy.co.uk/
Freq: Daily
Circ: 63931
Antique & Collectible Cars, Automakers, Automotive, Driving

Used Cars NI Blog 1053217
Editorial: 30 University Street, Belfast BTZ 1FZ Tel: 44 02890 324065
Web site: http://blog.usedcarsni.com/
Freq: Bi-Weekly
Circ: 55091
Automotive

Utelier blog 997669
Email: info@utelier.com
Web site: http://blog.utelier.com/
Freq: Daily
Circ: 214
News & Current Affairs

Utterly Luxury 996364
Editorial: 12 Emily Hall Gardens, Baildon BD17 5BG Tel: 44 07960 271779
Web site: www.utterlyluxury.com
Freq: Daily
Circ: 521
Do-It-Yourself (DIY), Travel

Utterly Scrummy Food for Families 986947
Email: utterlyscrumptious@gmail.com
Web site: http://utterlyscrummy.blogspot.co.uk/
Freq: Daily
Circ: 8013
Cooking & Baking, Grocery Stores

Val's Kitchen 1053293
Email: valskitcheninfo@gmail.com
Web site: www.valskitchen.com
Freq: Daily
Circ: 7222
Cooking & Baking, Restaurant Reviews

Valuable Content 1053317
Tel: 44 01179 290414
Email: info@valuablecontent.co.uk
Web site: http://www.valuablecontent.co.uk/
Freq: Daily
Circ: 14285
Branding, Computers, Graphic Design, Internet, Marketing

Vanessa Jackman 985629
Web site: www.vanessajackman.blogspot.com/
Freq: Daily
Circ: 11863
Fashion

Veg Plotting 986790
Email: vegplotting@gmail.com
Web site: vegplotting.blogspot.co.uk
Freq: Daily
Circ: 9762
Editor: Michelle Chapman
Gardening, Organic Food

The Vegetarian Experience 997237
Web site: http://www.thevegetarianexperience.co.uk/
Freq: Daily
Circ: 7814
Vegetarianism & Veganism

Veggie Desserts 988104
Web site: veggiedesserts.co.uk
Freq: Daily
Circ: 72609
Profile: Blog covering vegetable desserts.
Vegetarianism & Veganism

Veggie Runners 1054570
Email: hello@veggierunners.com
Web site: http://www.veggierunners.com/
Freq: Daily
Circ: 8422
Profile: Blog covering jogging & running. Veggie Runners blog discusses anything from jogging and running to vegetarianism and recipes. The blog has an archive dating back to May 2012 and shares a short blog roll. The outlet offers RSS (Really Simple Syndication).
Cooking & Baking, Fitness & Exercise, Nutrition, Sports, Vegetarianism & Veganism

Velcro Dog 996518
Web site: velcrodog.co.uk
Freq: Daily
Circ: 1643
Nature & Wildlife

The Veloce Blog 1054309
Tel: 44 01305 260068
Email: info@veloce.co.uk
Web site: http://velocenews.blogspot.co.uk/
Freq: Daily
Circ: 521
Antique & Collectible Cars, Automakers, Automotive, Driving, Luxury Goods, Motorcycles, Off-road & 4-Wheel Drive Vehicles, Trucks & SUVs

VéloCityGirl 987087
Email: jools@velocitygirl.co.uk
Web site: http://velocitygirl.co.uk/
Freq: Daily
Circ: 12328
Profile: Blog covering cycling. Vélo-City-Girl discusses anything from cycling and cycling fashion to fashion and lifestyle. The blog has an archive dating back to March 2010 and shares an extensive blog roll. Vélo-City-Girl was shortlisted for the 'Cosmopolitan Blog Awards' for lifestyle blog and was a finalist for the 'Total Women's Cycling Awards'.
Bicycles, Women's Interests

Velovoice 1052739
Web site: http://velovoice.blogspot.co.uk

Freq: Daily
Circ: 1605
Profile: Velovoice covering cycling, bicycles and mountain biking. The blog has an archive dating back to May 2011 and shares an extensive blogroll.
Bicycles

Verbs & Pixels 997703
Editorial: Greylings, Church Street, Rudgwick, Rudgwick RH12 3EE
Tel: 44 07713 631327
Email: contact@verbsandpixels.com
Web site: http://verbsandpixels.com/
Freq: Daily
Circ: 752
Broadcasting, Computer & Video Games, Literature, Movies & Video

Verily Victoria Vocalises 998091
Web site: vevivos.com
Freq: Daily
Circ: 49713
Airline Inflight, Family & Parenting, Railroad, Travel, Women's Interests

Vertical Leap Blog 1054289
Editorial: 33 Cavendish Square, London W1G 0PW Tel: 44 08451 232753
Email: info@vertical-leap.uk
Web site: https://www.vertical-leap.uk/blog/
Freq: Daily
Circ: 102
Advertising Industry, Branding, Broadcasting, Graphic Design, Marketing, Media & Communications, Photography, Publishing

Vertical Veg 1052851
Web site: http://www.verticalveg.org.uk
Freq: Daily
Circ: 10500
Profile: Blog covering growing your own food in containers and small space.
Do-It-Yourself (DIY), Gardening, Organic Food

Very Berry Handmade 1054101
Email: veryberryhandmade@gmail.com
Web site: http://veryberryhandmade.co.uk/
Freq: Daily
Circ: 6815
Crafts, Family & Parenting, Gardening

The Very Blog 1052972
Tel: 44 03448 222321
Web site: http://blog.very.co.uk/
Freq: Daily
Circ: 17236
Fashion

The Very Simon G 985240
Editorial: 13 Chiltern Close, Bushey, Potters Bar WD234PZ
Email: theverysimong@hotmail.co.uk
Web site: www.theverysimong.com
Freq: Daily
Circ: 11946
Fashion

Vex in the City 986278
Email: yinka@vexinthecity.com
Web site: www.vexinthecity.com
Freq: Daily
Circ: 13068
Beauty & Grooming, Cosmetics, Hair

vialaporte 997188
Editorial: Unit B, 27 St John's Lane, London EC1M 4BU
Email: info@vialaporte.com
Web site: vialaporte.com
Freq: Daily
Circ: 1067
Editor: Vincent Laporte
Restaurant Reviews

Vicky's FlipFlop Travels 988504
Email: vicky@vickyflipfloptravels.com
Web site: http://vickyflipfloptravels.com/
Freq: Daily
Circ: 133915
Travel

Victoria Sponge, Pease Pudding 987069
Email: victoriaspongepeasepudding@gmail.com
Web site: http://victoriaspongepeasepudding.com/
Freq: Daily
Circ: 7031
Profile: Blog covering food. Victoria Sponge, Pease Pudding blog discusses anything from food to Baking. The blog has an archive dating back to October 2011.
Cooking & Baking

View from the West Stand 1052609
Email: mattsimpson23@yahoo.com
Web site: http://www.leytonorientblog.com/
Freq: Daily
Circ: 12111
Soccer

Views From An Urban Lake 997844
Editorial: Townlands Crescent, Wolverton Mill, Milton Keynes MK12 5GS
Web site: http://www.viewsfromanurbanlake.co.uk/
Freq: Daily
Circ: 8141
Nature & Wildlife

Vinspire 997238
Email: vinspireuk@gmail.com
Web site: www.vinspireuk.com
Freq: Daily
Circ: 9958
Alcohol & Spirits, Bars, Clubs & Pubs, Beer, Beverages, Wine/Winemaking

vInspired Blog 999845
Editorial: 5th floor, Dean Bradley House, 52 Horseferry Road, London SW1P 2AF
Tel: 44 02079 607000
Email: pressoffice@vinspired.com
Web site: https://vinspired.com/blog
Freq: Daily
Circ: 3
Careers, Charitable Foundations, Teen/Young Adult

Vintage Brighton 1075494
Email: vintagebrighton@gmail.com
Web site: www.vintagebrighton.com
Freq: Daily
Circ: 10211
News & Current Affairs

Vintage Eye 1053788
Tel: 44 07880 550025
Email: editor@vintageeye.com
Web site: http://michellehatchermedia.com/
Freq: Daily
Circ: 10709
Editor: Michelle Hatcher
Antique & Collectible Cars, Fashion

Vintage Folly 987090
Email: rachelvf@live.co.uk
Web site: http://www.vintagefolly.com
Freq: Daily
Circ: 8295
Profile: Blog covering food, crafts, books, home decorating, beauty, clothing, vintage glamour and family.
Women's Interests

Vintage Frills 1053005
Email: vintagefrillsblog@gmail.com
Web site: vintage-frills.com/
Freq: Daily
Circ: 9793
Profile: VINTAGE FRILLS blog covers fashion, beauty and lifestyle.
Antiques/Collectibles, Beauty & Grooming, Cooking & Baking, Cosmetics, Fashion, Hair, Literature, Sales & Marketing, Women's Interests

Vintage Travel Blog 1053168
Tel: 44 01954 261431
Email: holidays@vintagetravel.co.uk
Web site: www.vintagetravel.co.uk/blog/
Freq: Daily
Travel

Vintage Vixen 1053541
Web site: http://vintagevixen.blogspot.com
Freq: Daily
Circ: 7760
Fashion

Violet Daffodils 1053260
Web site: violetdaffodils.com/
Freq: Daily
Circ: 6840
Profile: Blog covering lifestyle, travel, beauty, art, computer games and fashion. The blog has an archive dating back to April 2012.
Computer & Video Games, Fashion, Travel, Women's Interests

VIP SKI 996741
Editorial: 140 - 142 Wandsworth High Street, London SW19 4JJ
Tel: 44 02088 751957
Email: ski@vip-chalets.com
Web site: http://www.vip-chalets.com/blog
Freq: Daily
Circ: 10
Travel, Winter Sports

VIPXO 987830
Email: vipxoblog@gmail.com
Web site: www.vipxo.co.uk
Freq: Daily
Circ: 7961
Profile: Blog covering fashion and beauty. VIPXO blog discusses anything from personal style and the latest fashion trends to beauty buys and product reviews. The blog has an archive dating back to January 2009. The outlet offers RSS (Really Simple Syndication).
Beauty & Grooming, Cosmetics, Fashion, Hair

Virgin Holidays Blog 996293
Editorial: The Galleria, Station Road, Crawley RH10 1WW Tel: 44 01293 744228
Email: press.office@virginholidays.co.uk
Web site: https://www.virginholidays.co.uk/blog
Freq: Daily
Circ: 1738 I
Travel

Virgos & Kisses 1054360
Email: virgosandkisses@gmail.com
Web site: http://www.virgosandkisses.com
Freq: Daily
Circ: 7602
Profile: Blog covering fashion and lifestyle. VIRGOS & KISSES blog discusses anything from fashion and photography to film and lifestyle. The blog has an archive dating back to April 2013.
Beauty & Grooming, Cosmetics, Fashion, Hair, Regional General Interest, Women's Interests

Vision 7 Blog 1061999
Web site: http://vision7blog.blogspot.com/
Freq: Daily
Circ: 1394
Advertising Industry, Branding, Broadcasting, Business, Graphic Design, Marketing, Media & Communications, Photography, Publishing, Small and Medium Business

VisionMobile Blog 1053041
Editorial: 90 Long Acre, London WC2E 9RZ
Tel: 44 08450 038742
Email: hello@visionmobile.com
Web site: http://www.visionmobile.com/blog/
Freq: Daily
Circ: 293
Mobile Electronics

Visit Belfast 1054074
Editorial: 9 Donegall Square North, Belfast BT1 5GJ
Email: info@visitbelfast.com
Web site: http://visitbelfast.com/
Freq: Daily
Circ: 18357
Profile: Website covering tourism. The Visit Belfast website shares the latest tourism news in Belfast.
Travel

Visit Lancashire Blog 1054260
Tel: 44 01772 426459
Email: info@visitlancashire.com
Web site: http://blog.visitlancashire.com/
Freq: Daily
Circ: 21
Regional General Interest

Visit Northumberland Blog 1053562
Tel: 44 01670 794520
Email: info@northumberlandtourism.co.uk
Web site: http://visitnorthumberland.com/blog
Freq: Daily
Circ: 128
Travel

VisitEngland Blog 995454
Editorial: Sanctuary Buildings, 20 Great Smith Street, London SW1P 3BT
Tel: 44 02075 781400
Email: editorial@visitengland.org
Web site: https://www.visitengland.com/blog
Freq: Daily
Circ: 113
Editor: Katie Rowe
Airline Inflight, Railroad, Travel

Visordown blog 997538
Editorial: Immediate Media Company LTD, Vineyard House, 44 Brook Green, London W6 7BT
Email: webeditor@visordown.com
Web site: www.visordown.com/blogs
Freq: Daily
Circ: 107
Motorcycles

Vistage UK Blog 1052732
Tel: 44 01489 770200
Email: karin.simonsen@vistage.co.uk
Web site: http://blog.vistage.co.uk/
Freq: Daily
Circ: 20294
Branding, Business, Marketing

Visual Culture Blog 997153
Email: marcus.bohr@network.rca.ac.uk
Web site: visualcultureblog.com
Freq: Daily
Circ: 3052
Photography

Vitality Health Life Site 1074209
Web site: magazine.vitality.co.uk
Freq: Daily
Circ: 403907
Fitness & Exercise, Health & Medicine, Nutrition

Viva Live Music 996406
Editorial: 2 Cob Lane Close, Digswell, Welwyn Garden City AL6 0DD
Tel: 44 08000 938464
Email: enquiries@vivalivemusic.co.uk
Web site: http://vivalivemusic.co.uk/blog/
Freq: Daily
Circ: 81
Music

Vivatramp 987382
Web site: http://www.vivatramp.co.uk/
Freq: Daily
Circ: 10857
Profile: Blog covering books and liefstyle. Vivatramp blog discusses anything from book reviews and creative writing to outfit posts and lifestyle. The blog has an archive dating back to June 2010.
News & Current Affairs

ViviannaDoesMakeup Vlog 1098947
Email: anna@viviannadoesmakeup.com
Web site: https://www.youtube.com/user/ViviannaDoesMakeup
Freq: Daily
Circ: 42
Cosmetics, Fashion, Women's Interests

Vodafone Social 987374
Web site: http://blog.vodafone.co.uk/
Freq: Daily
Circ: 1574132
Mobile Electronics, Shopping

Vogueaholic 1061965
Web site: http://im-a-vogueaholic.blogspot.com
Freq: Daily
Circ: 911
Fashion

The Voguish Vagabond 1053649
Email: avantengarde@gmail.com
Web site: thevoguishvagabond.com/contact
Freq: Daily
Circ: 22
Profile: The Voguish Vagabond covers men's fashion. The blog has an archive dating back to January 2014.
Fashion

Volatile Fiction 997689
Editorial: 159 Knaves Hill, Leighton Buzzard LU7 2SL
Web site: volatilefiction.wordpress.com
Freq: Daily
Circ: 77
Cosmetics

Vox Political 988594
Web site: http://voxpoliticalonline.com/
Freq: Daily
Circ: 61710
Profile: Blog covering politics. Vox Political blog discusses anything from government policy and laws to economics and current affairs. The blog has an archive dating back to December 2011 and shares a short blog roll.
Politics

The Voyage - CEASED 2016 996848
Web site: http://thefamilyvoyage.blogspot.co.uk/
Freq: Daily
Circ: 611
Health & Medicine

vr360 Things to do in Orlando 1054236
Email: info@vr360homes.co.uk
Web site: http://www.vr360homes.com/blog
Freq: Daily
Circ: 76
Real Estate, Travel

Vulpes Libris 987964
Email: bookfoxes@gmail.com
Web site: http://vulpeslibris.wordpress.com/
Freq: Daily
Circ: 2304
Literature

WILD & GRIZZLY 1052762
Email: wildandgrizzly@gmail.com
Web site: www.wildandgrizzly.com
Freq: Daily
Circ: 25684
Cooking & Baking, Do-It-Yourself (DIY), Family & Parenting, Fashion, Travel, Women's Interests

Walhez.com 1062066
Web site: http://www.walhez.com
Freq: Daily
Circ: 347
Auto Aftermarket, Computers, Data Management, Electronics, Government Technology, Industry, Internet, Mobile Communications, Security & Security Systems, Software

Walking Class Hero - Ramblers 996540
Email: ramblers@ramblers.org.uk
Web site: http://www.ramblers.org.uk/news/blogs/meet-our-bloggers/walking-class-hero.aspx
Freq: Daily
Circ: 1
Outdoor Recreation

Walking Randomly 601848
Web site: http://www.walkingrandomly.com
Freq: 3 Times/Week
Circ: 33162
Computer Programming, Linux, Mathematics, Physics, Software

Walking the blog 1053555
Web site: http://charleshawes.veddw.com
Freq: Daily
Circ: 188
Profile: walking the blog covers Welsh lifestyle.
Outdoor Recreation

Walking with Angels 1054441
Email: walkingwithangels@live.co.uk
Web site: www.walkingwithangels.co.uk
Freq: Daily
Circ: 6108
Family & Parenting

Walks And Walking 996950
Editorial: Lydon House, Queen Mary Avenue, London E18 2FQ
Tel: 44 07912 664473
Email: walksuk@gmail.com
Web site: www.walksandwalking.com
Freq: Daily
Circ: 7532
Outdoor Recreation

Waltzingmouse Makes Blog 996354
Email: claire.brennan1@ntlworld.com
Web site: http://waltzingmouse.blogspot.co.uk/
Freq: Daily
Circ: 846
Crafts

Wander with Laura 1052678
Editorial: 14 Loomsway, Wirral, Liverpool CH61 4UD
Email: contact@wanderwithlaura.com
Web site: http://wanderwithlaura.com/
Freq: Daily
Circ: 7982
Beauty & Grooming, Cooking & Baking, Cosmetics, Fashion, Hair, Travel

Wandering Mee 1054610
Email: mee@wanderingmee.com
Web site: http://www.wanderingmee.com/
Freq: Daily
Circ: 1683
Railroad, Travel

Wanderlust Daydreaming 998329
Editorial: GreenPig Studios, Ynysmeurig Road, Aberoynon CF45 4SU
Email: wanderlustdaydreaming@gmail.com
Web site: http://www.wanderlustdaydreaming.co.uk/
Freq: Daily
Circ: 9541
Beauty & Grooming, Cosmetics, Fashion, Hair, Women's Interests

wantthatwedding 987284
Web site: http://www.wantthatwedding.co.uk/
Freq: Daily
Circ: 63925
Weddings

The Wardrobe 1052926
Email: thewardrobe@cadandthedandy.co.uk
Web site: http://www.cadandthedandy.co.uk/blog/
Freq: Daily
Circ: 2
Fashion

Warrantywise Blog 1060238
Editorial: 5 Petre Court, Petre Road, Accrington BB5 5HY
Web site: www.warrantywise.co.uk/blog
Freq: Daily
Circ: 78
Automotive, Driving, Insurance, Personal Finance

Warren Knight Blog 1098987
Web site: http://www.warrenknight.co.uk/blog/
Freq: Daily
Circ: 193
Marketing

UK Blogs

Warriorwomen 1054492
Email: warriorwomenblog@gmail.com
Web site: http://www.warriorwomen.co.uk
Freq: Daily
Circ: 7644
Bicycles, Sports

Was This In The Plan? 987842
Web site: http://www.wasthisintheplan.co.uk/
Freq: Daily
Circ: 11248
Profile: Blog covering parenting. Was this in the Plan? blog discusses anything from parenting lifestyle to motherhood. The blog has an archive dating back to November 2008.
Disability, Family & Parenting, Health & Medicine

The Washerwoman 1053831
Web site: http://thewasherwoman.blogspot.co.uk/
Freq: Daily
Circ: 821
Crafts

Watch Anish 1054125
Email: watchanish@gmail.com
Web site: http://www.watchanish.com/
Freq: Daily
Circ: 36790
Editor: Anish Bhatt
Fashion, Luxury Goods

The Watchers Film Show blog 1054086
Email: thewatchersfilmshow@gmail.com
Web site: http://www.thewatchersfilmshowblog.blogspot.co.uk/
Freq: Daily
Circ: 9939
Entertainment, Movies & Video

Watching You Grow 986252
Web site: watchingyougrow.co.uk
Freq: Daily
Circ: 7829
Family & Parenting, Women's Interests

Water Painted Dreams 1054478
Web site: www.waterpainteddreams.com
Freq: Daily
Circ: 10187
Profile: Blog covering lifestyle. Water Painted Dreams blog discusses anything from books and beauty to crafts.
Literature, Women's Interests

Wave to Mummy 1095189
Email: wavetomummy@gmail.com
Web site: http://www.wavetomummy.com
Freq: Daily
Circ: 10276
Beauty & Grooming, Cosmetics, Do-It-Yourself (DIY), Family & Parenting, Fashion, Hair, Photography, Regional General Interest, Travel, Women's Interests

The Way of the Web 1054579
Web site: http://www.thewayoftheweb.net/blog/
Freq: Daily
Circ: 2
Editor: Dan Thornton
Internet, Marketing

WCRS Blog 1052874
Tel: 44 02031 286000
Email: chris.boyton@wcrs.com
Web site: http://www.wcrs.com/
Freq: Daily
Circ: 14762
Advertising Industry, Branding, Broadcasting, Graphic Design, Marketing

We Are Scamp Blog 999517
Editorial: 2 Windermere Avenue, London NW6 6LN Tel: 44 02036 332469
Email: hello@wearescamp.co.uk
Web site: http://www.wearescamp.co.uk/blogs/we-are-scamp-blog
Freq: Daily
Circ: 33
Family & Parenting, Fashion, Shopping

We Are Twinset 1072202
Email: wearetwinset@gmail.com
Web site: http://www.wearetwinset.com
Freq: Daily
Circ: 8697
Fashion, Women's Interests

We don't eat anything with a face 1053253
Email: faceless.food@yahoo.com
Web site: http://wedonteatanythingwithaface.blogspot.co.uk
Freq: Daily
Circ: 7314
Cooking & Baking, Restaurant Reviews, Vegetarianism & Veganism

We Fell in Love Blog 1052847
Email: features@wefellinlove.co.uk
Web site: wefellinlove.co.uk/blog
Freq: Daily
Weddings

We Know Gamers 998400
Email: liban-ali@weknowgamers.net
Web site: http://www.weknowgamers.net/
Freq: Daily
Circ: 12587
Computer & Video Games

We Love Food, It's All We Eat 987840
Email: welovefood@btinternet.com
Web site: http://www.welovefood-itsallweeat.com
Freq: Daily
Circ: 10739
Cooking & Baking, Restaurant Reviews, Travel

We Love Home 1012917
Email: hello@welovehomeblog.com
Web site: http://welovehomeblog.com
Freq: Daily
Circ: 10445
Home Decorating & Décor, Interior Design

We Make Money Not Art 1053524
Email: user@ctrl.it
Web site: we-make-money-not-art.com
Freq: Daily
Circ: 35092
Art, Visual Arts

We Plug Good Music 1054290
Email: info@wepluggoodmusic.com
Web site: http://www.wepluggoodmusic.com/
Freq: Daily
Circ: 10466
Dance Music, Jazz & Blues, Music, Pop Music, R&B, Urban, World, Rap & Hip Hop

We The Food Snobs 987854
Email: wefoodsnobs@wethefoodsnobs.com
Web site: wethefoodsnobs.com
Freq: Daily
Circ: 12750
Profile: Blog covering food. WE THE FOOD SNOBS blog discusses anything from food recipes and restaurant reviews. The blog has an archive dating back to October 2012.
Alcohol & Spirits, Cooking & Baking, Restaurant Reviews

WE.Sky's BLOG 1062149
Email: weskylixiaofeng@qq.com
Web site: http://blog.sina.com.cn/lixiaofeng
Freq: Daily
Circ: 89182
Computer & Video Games

Weather to Ski 996543
Tel: 44 02031 513154
Email: info@weathertoski.co.uk
Web site: http://www.weathertoski.co.uk/our-blog/
Freq: Daily
Circ: 150
Travel, Winter Sports

Web Analytics World 1054275
Tel: 44 01698 744590
Email: info@webanalyticsworld.net
Web site: webanalyticsworld.net
Freq: Daily
Circ: 132567

Editor: Brian Kane
Internet

Web Master 1061043
Email: info@elwebmaster.com
Web site: http://www.elwebmaster.com
Freq: Daily
Circ: 112368
Advertising Industry, Branding, Broadcasting, Graphic Design, Internet, Marketing, Media & Communications, Photography, Publishing

WebEden blog 1053419
Email: info@webeden.org
Web site: http://www.webeden.co.uk/blog/
Freq: Daily
Circ: 50
Internet, Software

The Webmaster 998242
Editorial: 8 Rose Walk, Wisbech, Wisbech PE13 1SG Tel: 44 01223 969674
Email: jonathan@thewebmaster.com
Web site: https://www.thewebmaster.com/
Freq: Daily
Circ: 14795
Internet

WebRetailer Blog 1054540
Email: support@webretailer.com
Web site: http://www.webretailer.com/lean-commerce/#/
Freq: Daily
Auto Aftermarket, Business, Internet

The Wedding Affair Blog 997141
Editorial: Cottingham Lea, Back Lane, Easingwold, York YO61 3BW
Tel: 44 08432 898504
Email: enquiries@theweddingaffair.co.uk
Web site: http://theweddingaffair.co.uk/
Freq: Daily
Circ: 9315
Editor: Chris Hogg; Editor: Lisa Hogg
Weddings

The Wedding Fair Blog 1053342
Editorial: Ocean Media Group Ltd, One Canada Square, Canary Wharf, London E14 5AP Tel: 44 08448 740787
Web site: http://theweddingfairs.com/blog
Freq: Daily
Circ: 330
Weddings

The Wedding Fairy blog 997775
Web site: http://theweddingfairy.tv/wedding-fairy-blog/
Freq: Daily
Circ: 20
Weddings

Wedding Hour Blog 1054446
Editorial: Belfield, North Garth Lane, Sheriff Hutton, York YO60 6SF
Tel: 44 01904 236345
Email: enquiries@theweddingaffair.co.uk
Web site: http://theweddingaffair.co.uk/
Freq: Daily
Circ: 9010
Weddings

The Wedding of My Dreams Blog 997509
Editorial: Hill Top Barn, 7 Home Farm, Meriden Road, Berkswell, Coventry CV7 7SL
Tel: 44 08446 931449
Email: info@theweddingofmydreams.co.uk
Web site: http://blog.theweddingofmydreams.co.uk/
Freq: Daily
Circ: 33669
Weddings

Wedding Sparrow 995346
Web site: http://weddingsparrow.com/
Freq: Daily
Circ: 9929
Editor: Sara Russell
Weddings

Wedges & Weights 988114
Email: wedgesandweights@gmail.com
Web site: https://www.wedgesandweights.com/blog/

Freq: Daily
Profile: Blog covering fitness and exercise. Wedges & Weights discusses anything from workouts and nutrition advice to fitness advice and motivation.
Fitness & Exercise, Health & Medicine, Nutrition

Wednesday's Creative Inspirations Challenge Blog 1056775
Email: cinspirations@hotmail.com
Web site: http://cinspirations.blogspot.co.uk/
Freq: Daily
Circ: 1002
Crafts

Week Woman 1053027
Web site: https://weekwoman.wordpress.com/
Freq: Daily
Circ: 72795
Women's Interests

Weekend Wonders 1052610
Web site: http://www.weekend-wonders.com/
Freq: Daily
Circ: 521
Fashion, Women's Interests

Weight Loss Guru 525862
Web site: http://www.weightlossguru.com/blog
Freq: Weekly
Circ: 67
Dieting, Health & Medicine, Nutrition

Welcome to my world 1053425
Web site: http://www.mmcgrath.co.uk
Freq: Daily
Circ: 8621
Economics, Government Technology, Literature, Movies & Video, Politics

Welcome to Optimism 1054431
Editorial: 16 Hanbury Street, London E1 6QR Tel: 44 02071 947000
Web site: http://wklondon.typepad.com/
Freq: Daily
Circ: 1042951
Advertising Industry, Branding, Marketing

Well I Guess This Is Growing Up 1052883
Web site: welliguessthisisgrowingup.co.uk
Freq: Daily
Circ: 8992
Do-It-Yourself (DIY), Family & Parenting, Women's Interests

Wellicious Blog 1053146
Editorial: First Floor, 18 - 24 Westbourne Grove, London W2 5RH
Tel: 44 02072 213300
Email: press@wellicious.com
Web site: http://www.wellicious.com/wellblog
Freq: Daily
Circ: 20
Fitness & Exercise

The Well-Travelled Postcard 1052742
Email: contact@thewell-travelledpostcard.com
Web site: thewell-travelledpostcard.com
Freq: Daily
Circ: 24761
Profile: Blog covering travel. The WELL-TRAVELLED POSTCARD blog discusses anything from travel and hotels to festivals and working abroad. The blog has an archive dating back to February 2014 and shares a short blog roll.
Airline Inflight, Railroad, Travel

Welsh Hills Again 1053274
Web site: welshhillsagain.blogspot.co.uk
Freq: Daily
Circ: 1875
Property Management & Maintenance, Regional General Interest

WEMBLEY MATTERS 999445
Editorial: c/o 23 Sultcroft Close, Wembley, London HA9 9JJ
Web site: wembleymatters.blogspot.com
Freq: Daily
Circ: 11334
Energy & Environment, Ethical/Moral Issues, Politics, Regional, Social Issues, Transportation

We're Going on an Adventure 998186
Web site: www.goingonanadventure.co.uk
Freq: Daily
Circ: 87175
Family & Parenting

West Egg 1053597
Email: info.westegg@gmail.com
Web site: http://westegg-interiors.blogspot.co.uk/
Freq: Daily
Circ: 8139
Do-It-Yourself (DIY), Travel

West End Whingers 986281
Web site: westendwhingers.wordpress.com
Freq: Daily
Circ: 299
Theater & Performing Arts

West End Wilma 988520
Editorial: PO Box 73609, London SE13 9EE
Email: wilma@westendwilma.com
Web site: http://www.westendwilma.com/category/blog/
Freq: Daily
Circ: 785
Theater & Performing Arts

West End Wilma - DUPLICATE 1053680
Web site: http://www.westendwilma.com
Freq: Daily
Circ: 16261
Entertainment, Theater & Performing Arts

West Ham blog 1052894
Web site: http://www.westhamblog.co.uk
Freq: Daily
Circ: 1864
Soccer

West Ham Till I Die 1052775
Web site: www.westhamtillidie.com
Freq: Daily
Circ: 42834
Soccer

WestEndTheatre.com 998109
Email: editor@westendtheatre.com
Web site: http://www.westendtheatre.com/category/blog/
Freq: Daily
Circ: 77
Theater & Performing Arts

Westminster Walks Blog 1054374
Web site: http://westminsterwalks.london/blog/
Freq: Daily
Outdoor Recreation

Wex Blog 996629
Editorial: Wex Photographic, Unit B Frenbury Estate, Drayton High Road, Norwich NR6 5DP Tel: 44 01603 486413
Email: pr@wex.co.uk
Web site: www.wexphotographic.com/blog/
Freq: Daily
Circ: 310
Cameras, Photography

What Allergy? 988709
Web site: http://whatallergy.com/
Freq: Daily
Circ: 36919
Allergies

What Are You Wearing Today 1060413
Email: fredrikdelange@gmail.com
Web site: http://waywtblog.com/
Freq: Daily
Circ: 842
News & Current Affairs

What do i know? 1053942
Email. kathyflake@yahoo.com
Web site: http://whatdoiknow.typepad.com
Freq: Daily
Circ: 2558697
Regional General Interest, Women's Interests

What DVD 1052647
Tel: 44 07979 232027
Web site: http://www.whatdvd.net
Freq: Daily
Circ: 1292
Movies & Video

What Emma Did 998315
Editorial: 187 Ashton Road East, Failsworth, Failsworth M35 9PP
Email: editor@whatemmadid.com
Web site: www.whatemmadid.com
Freq: Daily
Circ: 27975
Beauty & Grooming, Cosmetics, Fashion, Hair, Women's Interests

What Goes Around 1053594
Web site: http://stopdoingdumbthingstocustomers.com/
Freq: Daily
Circ: 10534
Art, Marketing

What I Ate Today And Why 1054210
Web site: whatiatetodayandwhy.co.uk
Freq: Daily
Circ: 521
Profile: Blog covering food. WHAT I ATE TODAY AND WHY blog discusses anything from food to travel. The blog has an archive dating back to December 2012.
Cooking & Baking, Travel

What Kate Baked... and Baby 988065
Web site: www.whatkatebaked.com
Freq: Daily
Circ: 8053
Cooking & Baking

What Lauren Did Today 1054311
Email: whatlaurendidtoday@gmail.com
Web site: whatlaurendidtoday.blogspot.co.uk
Freq: Daily
Circ: 9017
Profile: Blog covering lifestyle and books.
Beauty & Grooming, Cosmetics, Hair, Literature, Women's Interests

What Lottie Loves 1053161
Tel: 44 07583 429367
Web site: http://www.themummyblogger.co.uk/
Freq: Daily
Circ: 8597
Women's Interests

What Movie This Week 987954
Email: thesloth@whatmoviethisweek.com
Web site: http://whatmoviethisweek.com/
Freq: Daily
Circ: 1149
Editor: Ruth Sloss
Entertainment, Movies & Video

What Olivia Did 987097
Web site: www.whatoliviadid.com
Freq: Daily
Circ: 46317
Fashion

What Row Chose 1054332
Web site: http://rowbowsclothes.blogspot.co.uk/
Freq: Daily
Circ: 9691
Fashion

What She Wears 1054634
Tel: 353 08766 99103
Email: editor@whatshewears.ie
Web site: http://www.whatshewears.ie/
Freq: Daily
Circ: 1456

Editor: Anne Marie Boyhan
Fashion, Shopping

What Should I Have for Dinner Tonight? 1052811
Web site: http://what-should-i-have-for-dinner-tonight.blogspot.co.uk/
Freq: Daily
Circ: 988
Cooking & Baking

What the Job is this? 997132
Email: whatthejobisthis@gmail.com
Web site: whatthejobisthis.com
Freq: Daily
Circ: 1505
Careers

What the Redhead Said 1053938
Web site: whattheredheadsaid.com
Freq: Daily
Circ: 49368
Family & Parenting

What Would Sophie Do 1052943
Web site: https://whatwouldsophiedo.wordpress.com/
Freq: Daily
Circ: 2
Cosmetics, Regional General Interest, Travel, Women's Interests

What's Good? Online 988125
Editorial: 18 Soho Square, London W1D 3QL Tel: 44 02070 258022
Email: info@whatsgoodonline.co.uk
Web site: http://www.whatsgoodonline.co.uk/
Circ: 1785
Bars, Clubs & Pubs, Broadcasting, Comedy, Dance Music, Entertainment, Fashion, Jazz & Blues, Local Entertainment Guides, Movies & Video, Pop Music

What's Katie Doing? 997897
Email: katiebhughes@aol.com
Web site: whatskatiedoing.blogspot.co.uk
Freq: Daily
Circ: 2204
Regional General Interest, Travel

Wheels for Women 1095730
Web site: http://www.wheelsforwomen.ie
Freq: Daily
Circ: 13725
Automotive, Driving

When in Wonderland 1054143
Web site: http://wheninwonderland.blogspot.co.uk/
Freq: Daily
Circ: 10709
Profile: Blog covering fashion and lifestyle. When in Wonderland blog discusses anything from personal style and outfit posts to music and travel. The blog has an archive dating back to February 2011.
Fashion

When I've Got Time 995497
Editorial: 113 Finsbury Park Road, Upper Floor Flat, London N4 2JU
Email: whenivegottime@gmail.com
Web site: www.whenivegottime.com
Freq: Daily
Circ: 10709
Cooking & Baking, Restaurant Reviews, Travel, Women's Interests

Where is Harriet 1053705
Email: whereisharriet@hotmail.co.uk
Web site: http://www.whereisharriet.net/
Freq: Daily
Circ: 4000
Fashion, Women's Interests

Where Worlds Collide 997226
Email: tim@kalyr.com
Web site: http://www.kalyr.com/weblog/
Freq: Daily
Classical/Choral/Band Music, Computer & Video Games, Country, Folk, Bluegrass, Dance Music, Jazz & Blues, Music, Politics, Pop Music, R&B, Urban, World, Railroad

Where's Mollie? 988070
Web site: http://wheresmollie.com/
Freq: Daily
Circ: 14686
Profile: Blog covering lifestyle, fashion, travel and things to do in London. This outlet offers a vlog.
Cooking & Baking, Fashion, Food, Grocery Stores, Organic Food, Regional General Interest, Restaurant Reviews, Vegetarianism & Veganism

Where's Runnicles? 988022
Email: admin@wheresrunnicles.com
Web site: http://www.wheresrunnicles.com/
Freq: Daily
Circ: 7034
Antiques/Collectibles, Art, Arts, Classical/Choral/Band Music, Literature, Photography, Theater & Performing Arts, Visual Arts

Where's the Benefit? 999537
Email: wheresthebenefit@gmail.com
Web site: wheresthebenefit.blogspot.com/
Freq: Daily
Circ: 8347
Politics, Social Issues

Whiitelist by Simi Lindgren 1095957
Email: whitelistbymrsl@outlook.com
Web site: http://www.whiitelist.com/
Freq: Daily
Circ: 6899
Beauty & Grooming, Cosmetics, Family & Parenting, Fashion, Hair, Travel, Women's Interests

Whimsical Mumblings 1052938
Email: whimsicalmumblings@ymail.com
Web site: http://www.whimsicalmumblings.co.uk/
Freq: Daily
Circ: 13068
Beauty & Grooming, Cosmetics, Do-It-Yourself (DIY), Entertainment, Family & Parenting, Hair, Movies & Video, Personal Finance, Women's Interests

Whimsical Wonderland Weddings 986283
Email: lou@whimsicalwonderlandweddings.com
Web site: www.whimsicalwonderlandweddings.com
Freq: Daily
Circ: 38822
Weddings

Whiskey for Aftershave 1054601
Email: whiskeyaftershave@yahoo.co.uk
Web site: http://whiskeyforaftershave.com
Freq: Daily
Circ: 3164
Family & Parenting

Whisky Co. 1074311
Editorial: 26 Barony Street, Edinburgh EH3 6NY
Email: info@thewhiskyco.co.uk
Web site: www.thewhiskyco.co.uk
Freq: Daily
Circ: 2957
Alcohol & Spirits, Travel

The White Company Blog 1053300
Editorial: 1 Derry Street, London W8 5HY
Tel: 44 02073 616888
Email: press@thewhitecompany.com
Web site: http://blog.thewhitecompany.com/
Freq: Daily
Circ: 248265
Do-It-Yourself (DIY)

White Journal 1054142
Web site: http://www.thewhitejournal.co.uk/
Freq: Daily
Circ: 8957
Profile: Blog covering lifestyle. The White Journal blog discusses anything from lifestyle and fashion to interiors.
Cooking & Baking, Crafts, Do-It-Yourself (DIY), Photography, Travel

UK Blogs

White Label Media 1053071
Editorial: 16 High Holborn, London WC1V 6BX
Email: sayhello@whitelabelglobal.com
Web site: http://whitelabelglobal.com/blog
Freq: Daily
Circ: 4240
Advertising Industry, Branding, Broadcasting, Graphic Design, Marketing, Media & Communications, Photography, Publishing

The White List 1054295
Email: contact@the-white-list.co.uk
Web site: the-white-list.co.uk
Freq: Daily
Circ: 2718
Fashion, Men's Interests, Restaurant Reviews, Travel

White Sun of the Desert 1054321
Web site: http://www.desertsun.co.uk/blog/
Freq: Daily
Circ: 1078
Oil

White. Blog 1053379
Freq: Daily
Circ: 6996
Advertising Industry, Branding, Marketing

The Whiteboard Blog 1053105
Web site: http://www.whiteboardblog.co.uk/
Freq: Daily
Circ: 84404
Apple, Education, Internet, Personal Computers

Who Ate all the Pies 986284
Email: psoren@gmail.com
Web site: www.whoateallthepies.tv
Circ: 355369
Editor: Paul Sorene
Profile: Website covering football. WHO ATE ALL THE PIES website discusses anything from the latest news on English and South American Leagues to gossips about WAGs and transfers rumors.
Soccer

Who Can Fix My Car Blog 1053241
Email: team@whocanfixmycar.com
Web site: whocanfixmycar.com/blog
Freq: Daily
Antique & Collectible Cars, Automakers, Automotive, Driving, Motorcycles, Off-road & 4-Wheel Drive Vehicles, Trucks & SUVs

Who is blogging? at the Blue-coat 996610
Editorial: School Lane, Liverpool L1 3BX
Tel: 44 01517 025324
Email: info@thebluecoat.org.uk
Web site: www.thebluecoat.org.uk/blog/index/who-is-blogging
Freq: Daily
Circ: 47
Art

The whole world is a play-ground 997203
Email: thewholeworldisaplayground@gmail.com
Web site: http://www.thewholeworldisaplayground.com/
Freq: Daily
Circ: 35046
News & Current Affairs

Wholeheartedly Healthy 988708
Editorial: 6 Farnham Close, Newton Hall, Durham DH1 5FL Tel: 44 07791 257393
Email: hello@lauraagarwilson.com
Web site: http://wholeheartedlyhealthy.com/
Freq: Daily
Circ: 38373
Nutrition

Wholesome Ireland 997303
Email: wholesomecook@gmail.com
Web site: wholesomeireland.com
Freq: Daily
Circ: 10426
News & Current Affairs

Who's The Mummy? 1054077
Web site: whosthemummy.co.uk
Freq: Daily
Circ: 58620
Family & Parenting, Travel

WhoScored.com 997217
Email: info@whoscored.com
Web site: http://www.whoscored.com/
Freq: Daily
Circ: 5286914
Soccer

Wide Sea No Anchor 997779
Email: widesea.noanchor@gmail.com
Web site: http://wideseanoanchor.com/
Freq: Daily
Circ: 6401
Airline Inflight, Railroad, Travel

The Width of a Post 997306
Email: Widthofapost@gmail.com
Web site: http://widthofapost.com/
Freq: Daily
Circ: 11809
Editor: Jason McKeown
Soccer

Wife, Mum, Student Bum 988320
Web site: http://www.wifemumstudentbum.com/
Freq: Daily
Circ: 5596
Profile: Blog covering motherhood and lifestyle. The blog has an archive dating back to September 2012.
Family & Parenting, Women's Interests

Wiggle blog 996515
Editorial: 3 Optima, Northarbour Spur, Portsmouth PO6 3TU
Web site: http://blog.wiggle.com
Freq: Daily
Circ: 25152
Bicycles

The Wild Eye 997909
Editorial: 44 Hamsey Crescent, Lewes BN7 1NP
Email: matt@thewildeye.co.uk
Web site: http://www.thewildeye.co.uk/blog/
Freq: Daily
Circ: 60
Movies & Video

Wild South London 1100501
Email: mrpenrose@live.co.uk
Web site: https://wildsouthlondon.wordpress.com/
Freq: Daily
Circ: 35
Nature & Wildlife, Outdoor Recreation, Regional General Interest

The Wild Swans 1053650
Web site: www.thewild-swans.com
Freq: Daily
Circ: 8455
Profile: Blog covering men's fashion, men's lifestyle and travel. The blog has an archive dating back to December 2011.
Fashion

Wild Tide 1052701
Email: wildtideblog@gmail.com
Web site: http://wildtide.co.uk/
Freq: Daily
Circ: 10119
Profile: Blog covering food, music, outdoor recreation, water sports, fitness, technology, clothing and style. The blog has an archive dating back to July 2013 and shares a short blogroll.
Camping and RV Travel, Men's Interests, Nature & Wildlife, Outdoor Recreation, Regional General Interest, Travel

Wild Webmink 1054345
Web site: http://webmink.com/
Freq: Daily
Circ: 8325
Audio Video Trade, Cameras, Consumer Electronics, Electronics, Mobile Electronics, Movies & Video

Wildfire Tech PR blog 1052950
Tel: 44 02084 088000
Web site: http://blog.emlwildfire.com/
Freq: Daily
Circ: 63
Profile: Blog covering PR and technology.
Advertising Industry, Auto Aftermarket, Branding, Broadcasting, Computers, Data Management, Electronics, Government Technology, Graphic Design, Industry

The Wildlife Channel 1100502
Email: ecaton93@gmail.com
Web site: https://thewildlifechannel.co.uk/
Freq: Daily
Circ: 10479
Energy & Environment

Wildlife Gadget Man 997975
Tel: 44 01473 712076
Web site: http://wildlifegadgetman.com
Freq: Daily
Circ: 7138
Cameras, Nature & Wildlife

Wilfredo Jordan Blog 1060759
Web site: http://www.wilfredojordan.blogspot.com
Freq: Daily
Circ: 9884
Auto Aftermarket, Computers, Data Management, Electronics, Government Technology, Industry, Internet, Mobile Communications, National News, Politics

Willgen Blog 996339
Tel: 44 01664 823821
Email: enquiries@willgen.co.uk
Web site: http://www.willgen.co.uk/blog/
Freq: Daily
Alternative/Renewable Energy, Carbon Emissions & Trading, Electricity, Energy, Environment, Nuclear Power, Oil, Water & Sanitation

Wilson Leaves Leicester 996615
Editorial: Chaucer 6, iQ Salford, Seaford Road, Salford M6 6FN
Web site: wilsonleavesleicester.wordpress.com/
Freq: Daily
Circ: 6
Regional General Interest

Wind is my direction 1060798
Email: fanyiren@foxmail.com
Web site: http://blog.sina.com.cn/gavinfan
Freq: Daily
Circ: 113874
Airline Inflight, Railroad, Travel

Windows 32 Bits 1060490
Web site: http://www.windows32bits.com
Freq: Daily
Circ: 521
Auto Aftermarket, Building & Construction, Computers, Data Management, Electronics, Government Technology, Industry, Internet, Mobile Communications, Security & Security Systems

Wine & Olives 988462
Email: info@wineandolives.co.uk
Web site: wineandolives.co.uk
Freq: Daily
Circ: 10022
Profile: Blog covering food, Edinburgh restaurant reviews, recipes and lifestyle. The blog has an archive dating back to August 2011.
Alcohol & Spirits, Bars, Clubs & Pubs, Beer, Beverages, Cooking & Baking, Food, Grocery Stores, Organic Food, Restaurant Reviews, Vegetarianism & Veganism

The Wine and Accessories Blog 1052628
Web site: https://www.barrelsandbottles.co.uk/blogs/barrelsblog
Freq: Daily
Circ: 20
News & Current Affairs

The Wine Sleuth 1053193
Email: denisemedrano@gmail.com
Web site: thewinesleuth.co.uk

Freq: Daily
Circ: 12852
Wine/Winemaking

Wine Spice + + 1052932
Tel: 44 02077 244606
Email: we@hpwines.co.uk
Web site: http://wineforspicewarrenedwardes.blogspot.co.uk/
Freq: Daily
Circ: 10618
Wine/Winemaking

The Wing to Heaven 1053736
Web site: https://thewingtoheaven.wordpress.com/
Freq: Daily
Circ: 14936
Profile: Blog covering education. The Wing to Heaven blog discusses anything from education and education policy to schools. The blog has an archive dating back to December 2011. The outlet offers RSS (Really Simple Syndication).
Education

Wings Over Scotland 988593
Web site: http://wingsoverscotland.com/
Freq: Daily
Circ: 644724
Editor: Stuart Campbell
Scotland

Winstonsdad's Blog 987963
Email: winstonsdad@live.co.uk
Web site: http://winstonsdad.wordpress.com/
Freq: Daily
Circ: 2275
Literature

WirelessDuniya 1061735
Web site: http://www.wirelessduniya.com
Freq: Daily
Circ: 41070
Mobile Communications, Mobile Electronics

Wise Words 1054362
Email: monazwise@gmail.com
Web site: www.wisewords.ie
Freq: Daily
Circ: 7758
Cooking & Baking

WishWishWish 985134
Editorial: 23 Wood Street, High Barnet, London EN5 4BE
Web site: wishwishwish.net
Freq: Daily
Circ: 163678
Fashion

With happy hearts 1052601
Web site: http://www.withhappyhearts.com/
Freq: Daily
Circ: 521
Cooking & Baking, Family & Parenting, Women's Interests

Witterings 1054254
Web site: http://fantasybob.blogspot.com
Freq: Daily
Circ: 468
Cricket

Witty Dawn UK 1053674
Web site: http://audreyscat.blogspot.co.uk/
Freq: Daily
Circ: 1155
Profile: Blog covering arts and crafts. WITTY DAWN UK discusses anything from arts and crafts to sewing, vintage fabric, fashion and furniture. The blog has an archive dating back to July 2010 and shares an extensive blog roll.
Crafts, Do-It-Yourself (DIY), Fashion

WitWitWoo 1054621
Web site: http://witwitwoo.com/
Freq: Daily
Circ: 12051
Family & Parenting, Travel, Women's Interests

Wiwibloggs 997810
Editorial: 17 Zenoria Street, First Floor (R),
London SL22 8HH
Email: wiwi.bloggs@gmail.com
Web site: http://wiwibloggs.com/
Freq: Daily
Circ: 98673
Broadcasting

Wolf's Gaming Blog 995021
Web site: http://wolfsgamingblog.com/
Freq: Daily
Circ: 569
Computer & Video Games

The Women's Room 985264
Email: amanda@thewomensroomblog.com
Web site: www.thewomensroomblog.com
Freq: Daily
Circ: 26013
Profile: WOMEN'S ROOM blog covers
feminism and women's interest.
Fashion, Lifestyle, Men's Interests,
Regional General Interest, Women's
Interests

The Women's Room 1052915
Web site: thewomensroom.org.uk/blog
Freq: Daily
Circ: 2
Profile: WOMEN'S ROOM blog covers
feminism and women's interest.
Politics, Social Issues

Wonderful You 987404
Email: wonderful.you@hotmail.co.uk
Web site: http://blog.wonderful~you.com/
Freq: Daily
Circ: 2618
Beauty & Grooming, Cosmetics, Fashion,
Hair

Wood and Luxe 1076167
Web site: http://woodandluxe.com
Freq: Daily
Circ: 8777
Alternative Medicine, Health & Medicine,
Nutrition, Travel

Woodborough House Blog 999363
Editorial: 21 Reading Road, Pangbourne,
Reading, Pangbourne RG8 7LR
Tel: 44 01183 214068
Email: info@woodboroughhouse.com
Web site: http://www.woodboroughhouse.
com/blog/
Freq: Daily
Circ: 68
Dentistry

Worcester Park Blog 988273
Email: mail@worcesterparkblog.org.uk
Web site: http://www.worcesterparkblog.
org.uk/
Freq: Daily
Circ: 10160
Regional General Interest

The Word Den 1057953
Web site: http://theworddden.blogspot.co.uk/
Freq: Daily
Circ: 8833
Literature

Wordarts 1053427
Email: catherine@wordarts.co.uk
Web site: http://wordarts.blogspot.co.uk/
Freq: Daily
Circ: 10226
Literature

Words & Riddims 997809
Email: wordsandriddims@gmail.com
Web site: http://www.wordsandriddims.
com/
Freq: Daily
Circ: 10246
R&B, Urban, World

**Wordsworth and Romanti-
cism** 998346
Editorial: Dove Cottage, Grasmere LA22
9SH Tel: 44 01839 435544
Email: enquiries@wordsworth.org.uk
Web site: https://wordsworth.org.uk/blog/

Freq: Daily
Circ: 204
Literature

Working Mum on the Verge
1053313
Email: carol.workingmum@googlemail.com
Web site: http://workingmumonverge.
blogspot.co.uk/
Freq: Daily
Circ: 521
Family & Parenting

The Working Traveller 1054347
Web site: http://www.the-working-traveller.
com/
Freq: Daily
Circ: 40194
Travel

**The World According to
Charlotte Coster** 988731
Web site: http://www.charlottecoster.
blogspot.co.uk/
Freq: Daily
Circ: 9587
Profile: Blog covering university life, poetry
and lifestyle. The blog has an archive dating
back to August 2012.
Women's Interests

The World and Then Some
987516
Email: ellerosewilliams@gmail.com
Web site: www.theworldandthensome.com
Freq: Daily
Circ: 32469
Editor: Elle-Rose Williams
News & Current Affairs

World Coal Association Blog
1053874
Editorial: 5th Floor, Heddon House, 149 -
151 Regent Street, London W1B 4JD
Tel: 44 02078 510052
Email: media@worldcoal.org
Web site: http://www.worldcoal.org/news-
opinion-cat/blog
Freq: Daily
Circ: 326
Mining & Quarrying

World First blog 1054185
Tel: 44 03459 080161
Email: info@world-first.co.uk
Web site: http://blog.world-first.co.uk/
Freq: Daily
Circ: 51730
Insurance, Travel

World Land Trust News 996480
Editorial: Blyth House, Bridge Street,
Halesworth IP19 8AB Tel: 44 01986 874422
Email: info@worldlandtrust.org
Web site: www.worldlandtrust.org/news/
latest-news
Freq: Daily
Circ: 3
Charitable Foundations, Energy &
Environment

World of Faz 988416
Email: worldoffazstyle@gmail.com
Web site: http://www.worldoffaz.com/
Freq: Daily
Circ: 10414
Cooking & Baking, Fashion, Fitness &
Exercise, Nutrition, Restaurant Reviews

World of Joy 997582
Email: hazelsworldofjoy@gmail.com
Web site: hazelsworldofjoy.blogspot.co.uk
Freq: Daily
Circ: 7394
Crafts, Fashion

The World of Kitsch 999583
Email: kitschandink@me.com
Web site: http://theworldofkitsch.com/
Freq: Daily
Circ: 10997
Antiques/Collectibles, Shopping

World Vision UK Blog 995402
Editorial: World Vision UK, Opal Drive, Fox
Milne, Milton Keynes MK15 0ZR
Tel: 44 02078 023461
Email: info@worldvision.org.uk
Web site: http://www.worldvision.org.uk/
news-and-views/
Freq: Daily
Circ: 16
Charitable Foundations, Social Issues

The World Wide Wardrobe
1096370
Email: info@theworldwidewardrobe.com
Web site: http://www.
theworldwidewardrobe.com/
Freq: Daily
Circ: 10155
Fashion

Worldstores Group Blogs
1054528
Web site: http://www.worldstores.co.uk
Freq: Daily
Circ: 911124
Architecture & Design, Cooking & Baking,
Do-It-Yourself (DIY), Gardening, Property
Management & Maintenance, Restaurant
Reviews, Travel

Worshipblues 1054180
Email: questions@worshipblues.com
Web site: http://www.worshipblues.com
Freq: Daily
Circ: 9552
Beauty & Grooming, Cooking & Baking,
Cosmetics, Do-It-Yourself (DIY), Fashion,
Hair, Men's Interests, Travel, Women's
Interests

WRC Blog 997555
Email: news@wrc.com
Web site: www.wrc.com
Freq: Daily
Circ: 465349
Motorsports

Write Like No One's Watching
988254
Email: writelikenooneswatching@gmail.com
Web site: writelikenooneswatching.com
Freq: Daily
Circ: 8133
Family & Parenting

Writing about dance 996661
Tel: 44 07818 245074
Email: nicholas.minns@gmail.com
Web site: http://writingaboutdance.com/
Freq: Daily
Circ: 13099
Theater & Performing Arts

Writing From The Tub 1054019
Email: carly@writingfromthetub.co.uk
Web site: http://writingfromthetub.co.uk/
Freq: Daily
Circ: 7841
Profile: Writing from the tub covers novel
writing, fiction and book reviews. The blog
has an archive dating back to April 2009.
Literature

Writing, fatshion, me 1054954
Email: sullenhearts@gmail.com
Web site: http://sullen-hearts.blogspot.co.
uk/
Freq: Daily
Circ: 2763
Fashion, Women's Interests

Wry Mummy 997227
Web site: wrymummy.blogspot.co.uk
Freq: Daily
Circ: 5936
Family & Parenting

WTF1 blog 997676
Web site: http://wtf1.co.uk/
Freq: Daily
Circ: 171123
Motorsports

WWF UK Blog 986724
Editorial: The Living Planet Centre, Rufford
House, Brewery Road, London GU21 4LL
Tel: 44 01483 412383
Email: info@wwf.org.uk
Web site: http://blogs.wwf.org.uk/
Freq: Daily
Circ: 1275
Profile: Blog covering animal welfare,
wildlife conservation and animal protection.
The blog is hosted by WWF, a registered
charity.
Alternative/Renewable Energy, Animal
Farming, Charitable Foundations,
Economics, Energy & Environment,
Environment, Ethical/Moral Issues, Nature
& Wildlife, Organic Food, Politics

www.salmandean.com 995124
Editorial: Flat 8, 73 Warren Road, London
E4 6QR
Email: salmandean101@gmail.com
Web site: www.salmandean.com
Freq: Daily
Circ: 7680
Editor: Salman Dean
Fashion, Hair, Health & Medicine, Men's
Interests, Nutrition, Travel

X 997537
Freq: Daily
Circ: 240726
Energy & Environment, Environment

Xombie Dirge 996635
Tel: 44 07979 521423
Email: xombiedirge@googlemail.com
Web site: http://xombiedirge.com/
Freq: Daily
Circ: 34124
Art, Cartoons, Literature, Movies & Video,
Science Fiction, Visual Arts

YA Love Magazine 1057089
Email: admin@yalovemag.com
Web site: http://yalovemag.com/
Freq: Daily
Circ: 9799
Literature

Yapp Brothers 986286
Editorial: Yapp Brothers Ltd, The Old
Brewery, Water Street, Warminster BA12
6DY Tel: 44 01747 860423
Email: sales@yapp.co.uk
Web site: www.yapp.co.uk/blog
Freq: Daily
Circ: 163
Wine/Winemaking

Yasmin Chopin 1054146
Email: ycld@yasminchopin.com
Web site: yasminchopin.com
Freq: Daily
Circ: 7904
Do-It-Yourself (DIY)

year of the yes 995463
Email: admin@yearoftheyes.com
Web site: yearoftheyes.com
Freq: Daily
Circ: 4799
Careers, Cooking & Baking, Education,
Literature, Restaurant Reviews, Travel,
Women's Interests

Yellow Days - CEASED 2015
987593
Web site: www.catsyellowdays.com
Freq: Daily
Circ: 6795
Profile: Blog covering motherhood. Yellow
Days blog discusses anything from
motherhood and family to parenting and
lifestyle. The blog has an archive dated back
to July 2011. The outlet offers RSS (Really
Simple Syndication).
Family & Parenting

Yes, Please 1057948
Web site: yespleaseblog.co
Freq: Daily
Circ: 11906
Cooking & Baking, Luxury Goods,
Restaurant Reviews, Travel, Women's
Interests

UK Blogs

Yet another t-girl blog 1053797
Freq: Daily
News & Current Affairs

Yin&Yang Blog 987289
Web site: yinnyang.co.uk
Freq: Daily
Circ: 6021
Antiques/Collectibles, Art, Arts, Classical/
Choral/Band Music, Country, Folk,
Bluegrass, Dance Music, Fashion, Jazz &
Blues, Lifestyle, Literature

Yogadoo 1098969
Email: helloyogadoo@gmail.com
Web site: http://yogadoo.co.uk/journal/
Freq: Daily
Circ: 143
Fitness & Exercise

Yorkshire Dad 988056
Editorial: 12 Highbank Grove, Harrogate,
Harrogate HG2 7LN
Email: yorkshiredad@live.com
Web site: yorkshiredad.co.uk
Freq: Daily
Circ: 10463
Family & Parenting

Yorkshire Dales Food 986263
Editorial: Church End Farm, Kirkby Malham,
Skipton, Skipton BD23 4BU
Web site: https://yorkshiredalesfood.co.uk/
Freq: Daily
Circ: 10705
Cooking & Baking, Regional General
Interest

Yorkshire Pudd 987738
Email: info@yorkshirepudd.co.uk
Web site: http://www.yorkshirepudd.co.uk
Freq: Daily
Circ: 11470
Profile: Blog covering food. The
YORKSHIRE PUDD blog discusses anything
from food and catering to restaurant reviews.
The blog has an archive dating back to April
2012. The outlet offers RSS (Really Simple
Syndication).
Cooking & Baking, Restaurant Reviews

You Baby Me Mummy 1100504
Email: youbabymemummy@gmail.com
Web site: http://youbabymemummy.com/
Freq: Daily
Circ: 141503
Profile: You Baby Me Mummy covers
motherhood, child care, family and
parenting. The blog has an archive dating
back to August 2012 and shares a short blog
roll.
Family & Parenting

YouGen Blog 986287
Editorial: Meadway, Cotford, Sidbury,
Sidmouth EX10 0SH Tel: 44 01908 699999
Email: yougen@nef.org.uk
Web site: www.yougen.co.uk/blog/
Freq: Daily
Circ: 7151
Alternative/Renewable Energy

Young Money Blog 988192
Web site: http://youngmoneyblog.co.uk/
Freq: Daily

Circ: 13848
Personal Finance

Your Boyhood 1061293
Web site: http://www.yourboyhood.com
Freq: Daily
Circ: 1590
Fashion

Your Industry News Blog 986606
Editorial: INTERKAB House, Links Place,
Aberdeen AB11 5DY Tel: 44 01224 582902
Email: info@yourindustrynews.com
Web site: http://www.yourindustrynews.
com/blog/
Freq: Daily
Circ: 5440
Alternative/Renewable Energy,
Chemicals, Defense & National Security,
Mining & Quarrying, Nuclear Power, Oil,
Steel, Telecommunications/Electronic
Communications

You're not from round here.
988723
Email: helpfulmummy@hotmail.com
Web site: http://www.helpfulmum.com/
Freq: Daily
Circ: 8897
Family & Parenting

**You're reading Mia Smith's
blogroll** 1053326
Web site: http://dispensabl095.livejournal.
com
Freq: Daily
Audio Video Trade, Government
Technology, Mobile Electronics, Security
& Security Systems

YouthNet Blog 986713
Editorial: 50 Featherstone Street, London
EC1Y 8RT Tel: 44 02072 505716
Email: media@youthnet.org
Web site: http://www.youthnet.org/news/
Freq: Daily
Circ: 38
Careers, Charitable Foundations,
Community Care (UK), Education, Social
Issues, Teen/Young Adult

Yummei 1054035
Web site: http://www.yummei.com
Freq: Daily
Circ: 7651
Profile: Blog covering food. The YUMMEI
blog discusses anything from food and
restaurant reviews to recipes and travel. The
blog has an archive dating back to January
2012.
Cooking & Baking, Regional General
Interest, Restaurant Reviews, Travel,
Women's Interests

Yutaka Blog 1086847
Web site: http://www.yutaka.co/en/blog
Freq: Daily
Circ: 52
Cooking & Baking

Zancada 1060444
Web site: http://www.zancada.com/
Freq: Daily

Circ: 46983
Elementary School, Fashion, Lifestyle,
Men's Interests, Preschool, Regional
General Interest, Teen/Young Adult,
Trading Cards & Comics, Women's
Interests

Zavor Digital 1060577
Web site: http://www.zavordigital.com/blog
Freq: Daily
Circ: 36
Auto Aftermarket, Computers, Data
Management, Electronics, Government
Technology, Industry, Internet, Marketing,
Mobile Communications, Security &
Security Systems

zavvi blog 1053163
Email: social@zavvi.com
Web site: http://www.zavvi.com/blog/
Freq: Daily
Circ: 37260
Editor: Thomas Pitts
Computer & Video Games, Movies &
Video

Zelo Street 998111
Email: timfenton@btinternet.com
Web site: http://zelo-street.blogspot.co.uk/
Freq: Daily
Circ: 38612
Politics, Religion

Zenith Holidays 1053646
Editorial: Bombers Cottage, Dwelly Lane,
Edenbridge TN8 6QF Tel: 44 02031 377678
Web site: http://www.zenithholidays.co.uk/
blog/
Freq: Daily
Circ: 7
Travel, Winter Sports

The Zest Blog 988035
Editorial: Nelson House, Old Pharmacy
Yard, Church Street, Dereham NR19 1DJ
Tel: 44 01362 853938
Email: info@economycarhire.com
Web site: https://www.zestcarrental.com/
blog/
Circ: 1194
Travel

Zoe Amar 988677
Tel: 44 07764 498168
Email: zoe@zoeamar.com
Web site: http://zoeamar.com/blog/
Freq: Daily
Circ: 25
Profile: Blog covering charities, marketing
and social media. The blog has an archive
dating back to December 2011.
News & Current Affairs

Zoe Bee 1052744
Web site: www.zoebee.co.uk
Freq: Daily
Circ: 10249
Profile: Blog covering book reviews,
lifestyle, travel and food. The blog has an
archive dating back to January 2014 and
shares an extensive blog roll.
Women's Interests

Zoë Harcombe's Blog 996534
Email: press@theobesityepidemic.org
Web site: www.zoeharcombe.com/blog/
Freq: Daily
Circ: 1539
Nutrition

Zoe London 986812
Web site: www.zoelondon.me
Freq: Daily
Circ: 55908
Beauty & Grooming, Cosmetics, Fashion,
Hair, Women's Interests

Zoe London Vlog 1103635
Web site: https://www.youtube.com/user/
thelondonlipgloss
Freq: Daily
Circ: 775
Beauty & Grooming, Cosmetics, Fashion,
Hair, Women's Interests

Zoella 987061
Editorial: 6th floor, 60 Charlotte Street,
London W1T 2NU
Web site: http://www.zoella.co.uk
Freq: Daily
Circ: 885260
Beauty & Grooming, Cosmetics, Fashion,
Hair, Women's Interests

Zoella Vlog 1066390
Web site: https://www.youtube.com/user/
zoella280390
Freq: Daily
Circ: 6140
Beauty & Grooming, Cosmetics, Fashion,
Hair, Women's Interests

Zona Gamex 1061746
Web site: http://zonagamex.net/
Freq: Daily
Circ: 1154
Computer & Video Games

Zona Selecta 1061937
Web site: http://www.zonaselecta.com
Freq: Daily
Circ: 3200
Bars, Clubs & Pubs, Celebrities, Comedy,
Entertainment, Industry, Local
Entertainment Guides, Movies & Video,
National News, Personal Finance

ZonaFull 1061158
Web site: http://www.zonafull.org
Freq: Daily
Circ: 1184
Auto Aftermarket, Computers, Data
Management, Electronics, Government
Technology, Industry, Internet, Mobile
Communications, Security & Security
Systems, Software

Zoopla Property News 997016
Editorial: Zoopla Property Group, Harlequin
Building, 65 Southwark Street, London SE1
0HR Tel: 44 02076 204719
Email: editor@zoopla.co.uk
Web site: http://www.zoopla.co.uk/
discover/property-news/
#PIKPZ1s253eYBp7g.97
Freq: Daily
Circ: 24563
Property Management & Maintenance

Willings Volume 1
Section 7

UK News Services & Syndicates

UK News Services & Syndicates

UK News Services & Syndicates

and international magazines, radio and websites.

Airline Industry Information
M2 Editorial, Amadeus House, 27b Floral Street, London WC2E 9DP
Tel: 44 02070 470200
Email: editorial@m2.com
Web site: www.m2.com/m2/web/publication.php/aii
Profile: Airline Industry Information is an email newsletter which provides information on the airline industry, travel and related events. Airline Industry Information newsletter is hosted by M2 Communications, media services company.

Alamy Live News
6-8 West Central, 127 Olympic Avenue, Milton Park, Abingdon OX14 4SA
Tel: 44 01235 844690
Email: news@alamy.com
Web site: www.alamy.com/news

Alliance News
Blackfriars Foundry, Unit 301, 154-156 Blackfriars Road, London SE1 8EN
Tel: 44 02071 990340
Email: newsroom@alliancenews.com
Web site: www.alliancenews.com

Allstar Picture Library
20 Clifton Street, Scarborough, Scarborough YO12 7SR **Tel:** 44 01723 367264
Email: admin@allstarpl.com
Web site: www.allstarpl.com

Alpha Press
PO Box 71891, London N1P 2RE
Tel: 44 02072 537705
Email: picture.desk@alphapress.com
Web site: www.alphapress.com

Apex News & Pictures
The Studio, 3, The Firs, Kennford, Exeter EX6 7TZ **Tel:** 44 01392 824024
Email: pictures@apexnewspix.com
Web site: www.apexnewspix.com

APM Health Europe
6-14 Underwood Street, London N1 7JQ
Tel: 44 02073 242320
Email: editorial@apmnews.com
Web site: www.apmhealtheurope.com
Profile: Website covering pharmaceutical and healthcare market news.

Argus Media
Argus House, 175 St John Street, London EC1V 4LW **Tel:** 44 02077 804200
Email: london@argusmedia.com
Web site: www.argusmedia.com

Argus Media - Argus Coal Daily Market Service
Web site: http://www.argusmedia.com/Coal/Argus-Coal-Daily

Asset TV
6-7 Waterside, Station Road, Harpenden AL5 4US **Tel:** 44 01582 764000
Email: hello@asset.tv
Web site: www.asset.tv

Astrid
Web site: www.astridmedia.co.uk

Axonn Media
Metropolitan Wharf, 70 Wapping Wall, London E1W 3SS
Web site: www.axonn.co.uk
Editor: Ian Dunt

BANG Showbiz
28 Holmes Road, London NW5 3AB
Tel: 44 02074 287500
Web site: bangshowbiz.com
Profile: Material accepted: Entertainment news, entertainment features, celebrity interview opportunities, music news, film news, royal news and features. Serves: National and regional newspapers, national

Barcroft Media
Studio 14, Shoreditch Stables, 138 Kingsland Road, London E2 8DY
Tel: 44 02070 331031
Web site: www.barcroftmedia.com

Bournemouth News & Picture Service
Unit 1, First Floor, 40-44 Holdenhurst Road, Bournemouth BH8 8AD
Tel: 44 01202 558833
Email: news@bnps.co.uk
Web site: www.bnps.co.uk
Profile: Material accepted: All general news, features and photographic material from central southern England. Serves: National and provincial press, radio and TV throughout Dorset, Hampshire, Wiltshire and Devon. Apple-Picture transmission.

Camera Press
21 Queen Elizabeth Street, London SE1 2PD
Tel: 44 02073 781300
Email: info@camerapress.com
Web site: www.camerapress.com
Profile: International picture agency specialising in celebrities and members of the Royal Family. Also covers art, science, travel, lifestyle, events and offbeat issues. Serves: Worldwide.

Capital Pictures
85 Randolph Avenue, Maida Vale, London W9 1DL **Tel:** 44 02071 933606
Email: sales@capitalpictures.com
Web site: www.capitalpictures.com
Profile: Material accepted: Photographs and information regarding photo-calls and photo opportunities. Serves: UK and worldwide. Phil Loftus is the Managing Director to whom press releases should be addressed.

Car and Driving
The Old Hay Barn, Field Place Estate, Byfleets Lane, Broadbridge Heath, Horsham RH12 3PB **Tel:** 44 01403 289154
Email: info@caranddriving.com
Web site: www.caranddriving.com/new/main.jsp?u=public
Profile: Material accepted: All aspects of motoring. Serves: Motoring publications and websites in the UK.

Car Enthusiast Editorial Agency
Email: editorial@carenthusiast.com
Web site: www.carenthusiast.com

Caters News Agency
Queensgate, 121 Suffolk Street Queensway, Birmingham B1 1LX **Tel:** 44 01216 161100
Email: news@catersnews.com
Web site: www.catersnews.com
Profile: Material accepted: News of events in the West Midlands. Serves: National newspapers and magazines.

Cavendish Press
Albert House, 17 Bloom Street, Manchester M1 3HZ **Tel:** 44 01612 371066
Email: newsdesk@cavendish-press.co.uk
Web site: www.cavendish-press.co.uk
Profile: Material accepted: General news, showbusiness, entertainment, celebrity, leisure, travel, food and wine, business, computing and legal issues for Manchester and the North West. Serves: North West. Alternative Co. Name: CP Media

The Central Scotland News Agency
Tel: 44 01786 462423
Email: csnews@btconnect.com

Centre Press
Tel: 44 01417 746969
Email: centrenews@hemedia.co.uk
Web site: http://swns.com

CMU
Kemp House, 152 City Road, London EC1V 2NX **Tel:** 44 02070 999050
Email: musicnews@unlimitedmedia.co.uk
Web site: www.completemusicupdate.com/
Editor: Andy Malt
Profile: Website covering music. theCMUwebsite.com shares the latest news on the music industry, musicians, artists, bands, festivals, releases, reviews and gossip.

Company Secretary's Review
LexisNexis, Lexis House, 30 Farringdon Street, London EC4A 4HH
Tel: 44 08453 701234
Web site: lexisweb.co.uk/guides/sources/company-secretary-s-review

Content Media
60-62 Comercial, London E1 6LT
Tel: 44 02071 937699
Email: info@contentmedia.co.uk
Web site: www.contentmedia.co.uk
Editor: Mak Rahmdel

Cover Media
18 Vine Hill, London EC1R 5DZ
Tel: 44 02033 973000
Email: info@covermg.com
Web site: www.covermg.com

Deadline News
The Bond Building, 29 Breadalbane Street, Edinburgh EH6 5JW **Tel:** 44 01315 612233
Email: info@deadlinenews.co.uk
Web site: www.deadlinenews.co.uk
Profile: Material accepted: News, pictures and features covering Scotland and the UK. Serves: UK national and regional newspapers, broadcast media and magazines. Previous Co. Name: Deadline Scotland

DNA Publishing Ltd
141 Blandford Road, Poole, Poole BH15 4AT
Email: info@dnapublishing.co.uk
Web site: www.dnapublishing.co.uk

Dragon News and Picture Agency
14 Brynymor Road, Swansea SA1 4JQ
Tel: 44 01792 464800
Email: mail@dragon-pictures.com
Web site: www.dragon-pictures.com
Editor: Bob Arthur

Eastnews Press Agency
Tel: 44 01255 502140
Email: newsdesk@eastnews.co.uk
Web site: http://www.eastnews.co.uk/page1/index.html

Englemed Health News
52 Perry Avenue, Birmingham B42 2NE
Email: newsroom@englemed.co.uk
Web site: www.englemed.co.uk

Entertainment News
Entertainment News, 7digital Group PLC, 69 Wilson Street, London EC2A 2BB
Tel: 44 02070 997777
Email: newsroom@entertainmentnews.co.uk
Web site: http://about.7digital.com/company/entertainment-news
Profile: Report detailing information on events taking place in the next nine months.

Essex News and Pictures
Email: news@essexnewsandpictures.co.uk
Web site: http://www.eastnews.co.uk/page1/index.html

etfExpress
First Floor, Liberation Station, St Helier, St. Helier JE2 3AS **Tel:** 44 01534 719780
Email: editorial@globalfundmedia.com
Web site: www.etfexpress.com

Excalibur Press
Email: excaliburbelfast@gmail.com
Web site: http://excaliburpress.co.uk/

F Stop Press Ltd
Tel: 44 01335 418365
Email: info@fstoppress.com
Web site: www.fstoppress.com

Feats Press
Tel: 44 01273 831138
Email: info@featspress.com
Web site: www.featspress.com

Feature World
238a London Road, St. Albans AL1 1JQ
Email: alison@featureworld.co.uk
Web site: www.featureworld.co.uk

FENS Information
FENS Information, Tower Point, 44 North Road, Brighton BN1 1YR
Tel: 44 01273 666351
Email: uk@fensintl.com
Web site: www.fensinformation.com

Ferrari Press Agency
2b Westmount Road, Eltham, London SE9 1JD **Tel:** 44 02082 942333
Email: news@ferraripress.com
Web site: www.ferraripress.com
Profile: Material accepted: National and local news, features and pictures. Serves: National newspapers and magazines.

Fit For Print
3rd Floor, 207 Regent Street, London W1B 3HH **Tel:** 44 02076 272635
Email: info@fitforprint.co.uk
Web site: www.fitforprint.co.uk

Foresight News
Wells Point, 79 Wells Street, London W1T 3QN **Tel:** 44 02079 704299
Email: editorial@foresightnews.com
Web site: www.foresightnews.com

freelancejournalist.co.uk
39 Romilly Road, London N4 2QY
Tel: 44 02073 591200
Email: info@freelancejournalist.co.uk
Web site: www.freelancejournalist.co.uk

GAP Interiors
The Old School Hall, Little Tey Road, Feering, Colchester CO5 9RP
Web site: www.gapinteriors.com

Getty Images
101 Bayham Street, London NW1 0AG
Tel: 44 08003 767981
Web site: www.gettyimages.com

Global Listings
Fifth Floor, 10 Lloyds Avenue, London EC3N 3AJ **Tel:** 44 02077 024436
Email: editorial.department@globallistings.info
Web site: www.globallistings.info

globalmtn-i.com
D'Arblay House, 16 D'Arblay Street, London W1F 8EA **Tel:** 44 02074 371331
Email: editorial@mtn-i.com
Web site: www.globalmtn-i.com

Goff Photos
54 High Street, Selsey, Chichester PO20 0RD **Tel:** 44 01243 606595
Email: info@goffphotos.com
Web site: www.goffphotos.com

The Good Content Company
Web site: www.goodcontentcompany.com

Guzelian
Cathedral House, 26-28 Church Bank, Little Germany, Bradford BD1 4DZ
Tel: 44 01274 737222
Email: pictures@guzelian.co.uk
Web site: www.guzelian.co.uk
Profile: News and feature photography agency serving UK national newspapers and worldwide markets. Full service of editorial and public relations photography. Material accepted: All national press releases and picture ideas.

Haymarket Network
Teddington Studios, Broom Road Teddington, Slough TW11 9PG
Tel: 44 02082 675013
Email: info@haymarketnetwork.com
Web site: www.haymarketnetwork.com

Hayters Teamwork
47 Dean Street, London W1D 5BE
Tel: 44 02071 836727
Email: sport@hayters.com
Web site: http://hayters.com/

Heart Features
Tel: 44 01227 807650
Email: christabel@heartfeatures.co.uk
Web site: http://www.heartfeatures.co.uk/

HOT Features
HOT Features Ltd, 28 Harvey Road, London N8 9PA **Tel:** 44 02083 483464
Email: info@hotfeatures.co.uk
Web site: www.hotfeatures.co.uk

HotSpot Media
Branston Court, Branston Street, Birmingham B18 6BA **Tel:** 44 01215 511004
Email: features@hotspotmedia.co.uk
Web site: www.hotspotmedia.co.uk

i-Images
Tower Bridge Studios, 12 - 18 Sampson Street, London E1W 1NA
Tel: 44 02085 061486
Email: picturedesk@i-images.co
Web site: www.i-images.co

Inò
Vine Court, Portsmouth Road, Godalming GU8 5HJ **Tel:** 44 01483 419822
Email: inc@incword.com
Web site: http://inccontent.com/

Independent Media News
Grosvenor House, 197 Shenley Road, Borehamwood, London WD6 1AR
Tel: 44 02077 179696
Email: news@imngroup.com
Web site: http://www.imncontent.com/

India Press Agency (IPA)
Tel: 44 91112 334648
Email: indiapressagency@gmail.com
Web site: http://www.ipanewspack.com

Industry Today (UK)
18 Boiler House, Electric Wharf, Coventry CV1 4JU **Tel:** 44 08701 994044
Email: support@industrytoday.co.uk
Web site: www.industrytoday.co.uk

INS News Agency
145 Wharfedale Road, Winnersh Triangle, Reading RG41 5RB **Tel:** 44 01189 440600
Email: newsdesk@insnews.co.uk
Web site: www.insnews.co.uk
Editor: Neil Hyde

Institutional Asset Manager
First Floor, Liberation Station, St Helier, Jersey JE2 3AS **Tel:** 44 01534 719780
Email: editorial@globalfundmedia.com
Web site: www.institutionalassetmanager.co.uk

Interview Hub
Tel: 44 01273 933533
Email: bespoke@interviewhub.co.uk

JMA Jewish Media Agency
Tel: 44 01618 201619
Email: editor@jewishmediaagency.com
Web site: http://jewishmediaagency.com/

The Jourdan Agency
145-157 St. John Street, London EC1V 4PY
Tel: 44 02078 132520
Email: info@jourdanagency.com
Web site: jourdanagency.com

Lancaster & Crowther Sports Agency
Suite 102, 315 Chiswick High Road, Chiswick, London W4 4HH
Tel: 44 02082 306127
Email: lancasterandcrowther@yahoo.co.uk
Web site: http://www.lancastercrowther.com/

London at Large
Kemp House, 152-160 City Road, London EC1V 2DW **Tel:** 44 02072 757667
Email: newsbreaks@londonatlarge.com
Web site: www.londonatlarge.com
Profile: Material accepted: Forward planning service covering arts, entertainment, music, fashion, people, events, press launches, conferences, photo calls, premieres, launches, clubs, television, theatre, books, music, sport, film releases, general and regional news and events. Serves: Nationwide and international.

M&Y News Agency
65 Osborne Road, Portsmouth PO5 3LS
Tel: 44 02392 820311
Web site: www.mynewsagency.co.uk

M2 PressWIRE
M2 Editorial, Amadeus House, 27b Floral Street, London WC2E 9DP
Tel: 44 02070 470200
Email: editorial@m2.com
Web site: www.m2.com/group

Medavia
25-27 Stokes Croft, Bristol BS1 3PY
Tel: 44 01179 733730
Email: contact@medavia.co.uk
Web site: www.medavia.co.uk

Media Bounty
Unit G, 11 Bell Yard Mews, 175 Dermondooy Street, London SE1 3TN
Tel: 44 02072 602600
Email: hello@mediabounty.com
Web site: www.mediabounty.com

The Media Eye
4B Prowse Place, London NW1 9PH
Tel: 44 02075 536060
Email: enquiries@themediaeye.com
Web site: www.themediaeye.com

Media Genie
26 Hythe Quay, Colchester CO2 8JB
Email: genie@mediagenie.co.uk
Web site: www.mediagenie.co.uk
Editor: Paul Wagland

Mercury Press and Media
Suite 308, QD Business Centre, Norfolk Street, Liverpool L1 0BG
Tel: 44 01517 096707
Email: editorial@mercurypress.co.uk
Web site: www.mercurypress.co.uk

mni
23 Austin Friars, 2nd Floor, London EC2N 2QP **Tel:** 44 02035 862248
Email: editorial@marketnews.com
Web site: https://mninews.marketnews.com

Monitor Picture Library
The Forge, Roydon, Harlow CM19 5HH
Tel: 44 01279 792700
Email: info@monitorpicturelibrary.com
Web site: www.monitorpicturelibrary.com

Motoring Research
Harpenden Hall, Southdown Road, Harpenden, Harpenden AL5 1TE
Tel: 44 01582 761625
Email: contact@motoringresearch.com
Web site: http://www.motoringresearch.com

National News
31a Great Sutton Street, London EC1V 0NA
Tel: 44 02076 843000
Email: news@nationalnews.co.uk
Web site: swns.com
Profile: Material accepted: All press releases. Serves: UK.

newsflare
Newsflare Limited, Fanshaw House, Fanshaw Street, London N1 6HX
Tel: 44 08432 895191
Email: contact@newsflare.com
Web site: http://www.newsflare.com

Newsline Media
Unit 4, 21 Mid Stocket Road, Aberdeen AB15 5JL **Tel:** 44 01224 594000
Email: news@newsline-media.com
Web site: www.newsline-media.com

NewsNow.co.uk
The Euston Office, 1 Euston Square, 40 Melton Street, London NW1 2FD
Tel: 44 08458 388890
Email: info@newsnow.co.uk
Web site: www.newsnow.co.uk

North News & Pictures
69 Grainger Street, Newcastle upon Tyne NE1 5JE **Tel:** 44 01912 330223
Email: news@northnews.co.uk
Web site: http://www.northnews.co.uk/

Northstar
Northdown House, 11-21 Northdown Street, London N1 9BN **Tel:** 44 02078 337410
Email: info@contactnorthstar.com
Web site: www.thisisnorthstar.com

Nouvelle d'Europe (UK Edition)
40 Craven Street, London WC2N 5NG
Tel: 44 02073 891730
Email: uk-ed@oushinet.com
Web site: www.oushinet.com

Page One Photography
Unit 1, The Glade Business Centre, Forum Road, Nottingham NG5 9RW
Tel: 44 01159 818880
Email: pictures@pageonephotography.co.uk
Web site: www.pageonephotography.co.uk
Profile: Material accepted: National news and photographs. Serves: Midlands.

Panos Pictures
Unit K Reliance Wharf, Hertford Road, London N1 5EW **Tel:** 44 02039 228382
Email: pics@panos.co.uk
Web site: www.panos.co.uk

Parliament Today
Press Gallery, House of Commons, London SW1A 0AA **Tel:** 44 02032 710064
Email: enquiries@parliamenttoday.com
Web site: parliamenttoday.com

Photoshot
29-31 Saffron Hill, London EC1N 8SW
Tel: 44 02074 216000
Email: sales@photoshot.com
Web site: www.photoshot.com
Editor: Martin Ballans

Press Association
PA News Centre, 292 Vauxhall Bridge Road, London SW1V 1AE **Tel:** 44 02079 637000
Email: copy@pressassociation.com
Web site: www.pressassociation.com
Profile: Material accepted: Financial, commercial, parliamentary, general news and features. Alternative Co. Name: Press Association Email system does not accept attachments, all material must be sent as open text. Plain text emails only. Press releases should be addressed to the News Desk.

The Press People
Mariners Wharf, 8 Holyrood Street, London SE1 2EL **Tel:** 44 02079 408949
Email: hello@presspeople.co.uk
Web site: www.presspeople.co.uk

Private Equity Wire
First Floor, Liberation Station, St Helier, St. Helier JE2 3AS **Tel:** 44 01534 719780
Email: editorial@globalfundmedia.com
Web site: www.privateequitywire.co.uk

Property Funds World
First Floor, Liberation Station, St Helier, St. Helier JE2 3AS **Tel:** 44 01534 719780
Email: editorial@globalfundmedia.com
Web site: www.propertyfundsworld.com

Raconteur Media
6th Floor, 38-40 Commercial Road, London E1 1LN **Tel:** 44 02038 773800
Email: info@raconteur.net
Web site: www.raconteur.net

Radio NewsHub
Tel: 44 08000 096007
Email: news@radionewshub.com
Web site: http://radionewshub.com/

Redspy
2 Shad Thames, London SE1 2YU
Web site: www.redspy.co.uk

Redwood (London)
Bankside 3, 90 Southwark Street, London SE1 0SW **Tel:** 44 02077 470700
Email: info@redwoodlondon.com
Web site: www.redwoodlondon.com

Ross Parry Agency Ltd
40 Back Ford St, Farsley, Pudsey LS28 5LD
Tel: 44 01132 361842
Email: newsdesk@rossparry.co.uk
Web site: www.rossparry.co.uk
Profile: Material accepted: General news, sport, features and photographs from Yorkshire and The Humber. Serves: National newspapers and magazines.

Saltire News and Sport
Tel: 44 01312 254153
Email: desk@saltirenews.com

Sax Rohmer Ltd
Tel: 44 01273 930202
Email: contact@saxrohmer.co.uk
Web site: http://saxrohmer.tumblr.com/

Science Media Centre
215 Euston Road, London NW1 2BE
Web site: www.sciencemediacentre.org

Scottish News Agency
Avian House, 87 Brook Street, Dundee DD5 1DJ **Tel:** 44 01382 427035
Email: newsdesk@scottishnews.com
Web site: www.scottishnews.com
Editor: Kieran Findlay

Profile: Material accepted: News and sport in Scotland. Regular features on construction, housing and tourism in Scotland. Serves: The Scottish press and several UK websites.

Sell My Story (sellmystory.co.uk)
25-27 Stokes Croft, Bristol BS1 3PY
Tel: 44 01179 833730
Email: contact@medavia.co.uk
Web site: www.sellmystory.co.uk

Shutterstock
Third Floor, Counting House Hays Galleria, 51-57 Tooley Street, London SE1 2QN
Email: mediaalerts@shutterstock.com
Web site: http://www.shutterstock.com

Slipcase
14 Bedford Square, London WC1B 3JA
Tel: 44 02034 095411
Email: info@myslipcase.co.uk
Web site: http://www.slipcase.com/

SNTV
IMG Studios, 5 Longwalk Road, Stockley Park, London UB11 1FE
Tel: 44 02033 145770
Email: planning@sntv.com
Web site: www.sntv.com

Solent News and Photo Agency
23 Mitchell Point, Ensign Way, Southampton S031 4RF **Tel:** 44 02380 458800
Email: info@solentnews.co.uk
Web site: www.solentnews.co.uk

Somerset News Service
3 Lewis Road, Taunton TA2 6DU

Specialist News Services
c/o Encore, Barnard's Inn, 86 Fetter Lane, London EC4A 1EN
Email: desk@snsnews.co.uk
Web site: www.specialistnews.co.uk

Splash News and Picture Agency
1st FL, Suite B, 1-3 Grosvenor Place, London SW1X 7HJ **Tel:** 44 08709 342666
Email: splashuk@splashnews.com
Web site: www.splashnews.com

Sports Media
16 Linen House, 253 Kilburn Lane, London W10 4BQ
Email: jonny.gould@sportsmedia.co.uk
Web site: www.sportsmedia.co.uk

Sportsbeat
247, The Broadway, London SW19 1SD
Tel: 44 08704 450156
Web site: www.sportsbeat.co.uk
Profile: Material accepted: All sports news, pictures, results and features. Serves: Worldwide for pictures and television.

Sportsline Media
Email: contact@sportslinemedia.co.uk
Web site: http://www.sportslinemedia.co.uk/

StockMarketWire
Thames House, 18 Park Street, London SE1 9ER **Tel:** 44 02073 787131
Email: editorial@stockmarketwire.com
Web site: www.stockmarketwire.com

Strand News
226, Strand, London WC2R 1BA
Tel: 44 02073 531300
Web site: www.strandnews.co.uk

STYLE LDN
Email: info@styleldn.com
Web site: www.styleldn.com

SWNS
The Media Centre, Abbey Wood Park, Filton, Bristol BS34 7JU **Tel:** 44 01179 066500
Email: editorial@swns.com
Web site: www.swns.com
Editor: Andrew Young

SWNS Digital
3rd Floor Office, 31 Great Sutton Street, London EC1V 0NA **Tel:** 44 02071 383041
Email: editorial@swns.com
Web site: http://www.digitalhub.media/
Editor: Jack Peat

UK News Services & Syndicates

Talk to the Press
Floor 3, 31 Great Sutton Street, Clerkenwell,
London EC1V 0NA **Tel:** 44 08449 632475
Email: message@talktothepress.com
Web site: talktothepress.co.uk

TravelMole
Email: ukeditor@travelmole.com
Web site: http://www.travelmole.com/

Trinity Mirror Shared Content Unit
Trinity Mirror Regionals, One Canada
Square, Canary Wharf, London E14 5AP
Tel: 44 02072 933000
Web site: www.trinitymirror.com/

University World News
9 Newbury Street, London EC1A 7HU
Email: editorial@universityworldnews.com
Web site: www.universityworldnews.com

Viva Press
13 Beaconsfield Villas, Brighton BN1 6HA
Tel: 44 01273 566708
Email: enquiries@viva-press.com
Web site: http://www.viva-press.com

Wales News Service
Jones Court, Womanby Street, Cardiff CF10
1BR **Tel:** 44 02920 666366
Email: news@walesnews.com
Web site: www.walesnews.com

Wardle Whittell Agency
1 Clayton Park Square, Jesmond, Newcastle
Upon Tyne, Newcastle upon Tyne NE2 4DP
Email: hello@wwa-sport.com
Web site: http://wwa-sport.com
Editor: Ian Winrow
Profile: The Wardle Whittell Agency is a
freelance agency whose staff cover football.
It provides editorial comment, match reports,
features and other content to the UK's
national newspapers, news syndicates,
broadcasters and media companies. It was
founded in Newcastle in 1984 by John
Wardle.

Wealth Adviser
First Floor, Liberation Station, St Helier,
Jersey JE2 3AS **Tel:** 44 01534 719780
Email: editorial@globalfundmedia.com
Web site: www.wealthadviser.co

WENN (World Entertainment News Network)
35 Kings Exchange, Tileyard Road, London
N7 9AH **Tel:** 44 02076 072757
Email: newsdesk@wenn.com
Web site: www.wenn.com

West Coast News
Renaissance House, Parracombe,
Barnstaple, Barnstaple EX31 4QH
Tel: 44 01598 763296
Email: newsdesk@westcoast-news.co.uk
Web site: http://www.westcoast-news.co.
uk/index.html?_ret_=return

Profile: Material accepted: General news
stories and features from the South West of
England. Serves: National press.

WireImage
101 Bayham Street, London NW1 0AG
Tel: 44 02075 795759
Email: ukentertainment@wireimage.com
Web site: www.wireimage.com
Profile: WireImage is a photo news service
featuring photos covering the entertainment
industry, including film, music and fashion. It
is a part of Getty Images.

Work Work Work
Web site: http://www.workworkwork.co/

Zone
Western Transit Shed, 12-13 Stable Street,
London N1C 4AB **Tel:** 44 02036 978600
Email: hello@zonedigital.com
Web site: www.thisiszone.com
Editor: Chris Gibbons

Willings Volume 1
Section 8

Ireland

Newspapers Index
Daily Newspaper listed A-Z by title
Regional, Local & Weekly Newspapers listed A-Z by title
Newspapers (Online) listed A-Z by title
Periodicals Index
Periodicals listed A-Z
Radio Networks & Stations listed A-Z
Television Stations & Networks listed A-Z
News Services & Syndicates listed A-Z

Non-Nationals

National & Regional Daily Newspapers

Irish Daily Star
980838

Editorial: Irish Daily Star, Independent House, 27-32 Talbot Street, Dublin Dublin 1
Tel: 353 14993 400
Email: news@thestar.ie
Web site: www.thestar.ie
Freq: Daily
Circ: 50732 Not Audited
Editor: Gerard Colleran
Profile: The Irish Daily Star is a daily newspaper covering all the latest news, current affairs, international news, celebrities, entertainment, showbiz and sport. The paper was first published on 29th February 1988.
Ad Rate: Full Page Mono €17690.00
Ad Rate: Full Page Colour €20330.00

Irish Examiner
980751

Editorial: City Quarter, Lapps Quay, Cork
Tel: 353 21427 2722
Email: news@examiner.ie
Web site: http://www.irishexaminer.com/
Freq: Daily
Circ: 30090 Not Audited
Profile: The Irish Examiner is a daily newspaper covering news, current affairs, sports and business. The newspaper was first published in 1841.
Ad Rate: Full Page Mono €17400.00
Ad Rate: Full Page Colour €20100.00

Irish Independent
980164

Editorial: Independent House, 27 - 32 Talbot Street, Dublin 1 **Tel:** 353 01705 5333
Email: info@independent.ie
Web site: www.independent.ie
Freq: Daily
Circ: 97104 Not Audited
Editor: Cormac Bourke; **Editor:** Fionnan Sheahan
Profile: The Irish Independent is a daily national newspaper and covers news, current affairs, sports and general features.
Ad Rate: Full Page Mono ,.......... €15347.00
Ad Rate: Full Page Colour €20085.00

The Irish Times
979835

Editorial: PO Box 74, 24-28 Tara Street, Dublin 2 **Tel:** 353 01675 8000
Email: newsdesk@irishtimes.com
Web site: www.irishtimes.com
Freq: Daily
Circ: 66251 Not Audited
Profile: The Irish Times is a daily newspaper covering news, current affairs, sports and general features. The newspaper was first published in 1859.
Ad Rate: Full Page Mono €27190.00
Ad Rate: Full Page Colour €34000.00

NATIONALIST AND MUNSTER ADVERTISER
1095134

The Sunday Business Post
980861

Editorial: Hambledon House, 19/26 Pembroke Street Lower, Dublin 2
Tel: 353 01602 6000
Email: sbpost@iol.ie
Web site: www.businesspost.ie
Freq: Weekly
Circ: 30244 Not Audited
Editor: Ian Kehoe
Profile: The Sunday Business Post is a weekly national newspaper and covers business, economics, finance, politics, news and current affairs.
Ad Rate: Full Page Mono €13600.00
Ad Rate: Full Page Colour €18600.00

Sunday Independent (Ireland)
980836

Editorial: 27-32 Talbot Street, Dublin
Tel: 353 01705 5333

Email: snews@independent.ie
Web site: www.independent.ie
Freq: Weekly
Circ: 191594 Not Audited
Editor: Cormac Bourke

Sunday World
980837

Editorial: Independent House, 27-32 Talbot Street, Dublin **Tel:** 353 01884 8900
Email: news@sundayworld.com
Web site: www.sundayworld.com
Freq: Weekly
Circ: 149652 Not Audited
Editor: Jack Gleeson; **Editor:** Colm Macginty

Regional & Local Weekly Newspapers

The Anglo Celt
998459

Editorial: Station House, Cavan H12 DA52
Tel: 353 04943 31100
Web site: www.anglocelt.ie
Freq: Weekly Not Audited
Editor: Linda O'Reilly

The Argus (Ireland)
994676

Editorial: Partnership Court, Park Street, Dundalk **Tel:** 353 04293 89700
Email: editorial@argus.ie
Web site: www.argus.ie
Freq: Weekly
Circ: 9307 Not Audited

Bray People
983771

Editorial: Channing House, Upper Row Street, Co. Wexford, Ireland
Tel: 353 05391 40100
Email: front.office@peoplenews.ie
Web site: www.independent.ie/regionals/braypeople
Freq: Weekly
Circ: 4000 Not Audited
Profile: This is the online version of the Bray People, a weekly, local newspaper covering all the latest on local news, sport, entertainment and lifestyle in Bray, County Wicklow.

Carlow People
983807

Editorial: Channing House, Upper Row Street, Co. Wexford **Tel:** 353 59914 1877
Web site: http://www.carlowpeople.ie/
Freq: Weekly
Circ: 10000 Not Audited
Profile: This is the online version of the Carlow People, a weekly, local newspaper published on Tuesdays, covering all the latest on local news, entertainment, lifestyle and sport in Carlow and the surrounding area.

Clare Champion
983798

Editorial: Barrack Street, Ennis, Co. Clare
Tel: 353 65682 8105
Email: editor@clarechampion.ie
Web site: www.clarechampion.ie
Freq: Weekly
Circ: 16000 Not Audited
Editor: Austin Hobbs
Profile: The Clare Champion is a weekly local newspaper covering all the latest on local news, arts and sport for in Ennis and the surrounding area.
Ad Rate: Full Page Mono €5088.00
Ad Rate: Full Page Colour €5724.00

Clare People Series
1101751

Editorial: Mill Road, Ennis, Co. Clare
Tel: 353 06568 95500
Email: info@clarepeople.ie
Web site: www.clarepeople.com
Freq: Weekly
Circ: 8753 Not Audited

The Connacht Tribune
987180

Editorial: 15 Market Street, Galway
Tel: 353 91530 222
Email: news@ctribune.ie
Web site: www.connachttribune.ie
Freq: Weekly
Circ: 22000 Not Audited
Profile: Weekly newspaper published every Thursday. It covers news, events and sports issues for County Galway in Ireland. Brendan Carroll is the Editor to whom press releases should be addressed.
Ad Rate: Full Page Mono €7776.00
Ad Rate: Full Page Colour €9720.00

Connaught Telegraph
983796

Editorial: No. 1 Main street/Market Street, Castlebar, Co. Mayo F23 EY18
Tel: 353 94902 1711
Email: info@con-telegraph.ie
Web site: http://www.con-telegraph.ie
Freq: Weekly
Circ: 19000 Not Audited
Profile: The Connaught Telegraph is a weekly local newspaper covering all the latest on local news, sport and history from the West of Ireland.
Ad Rate: Full Page Mono €5616.00
Ad Rate: Full Page Colour €6912.00

Cork Independent
984772

Editorial: Northpoint House, Northpoint Business Park, Blackpool, Cork
Tel: 353 02142 88566
Email: editor@corkindependent.com
Web site: www.corkindependent.com
Freq: Weekly
Circ: 15143 Not Audited
Editor: Wendy Good
Profile: Online version of the Cork Independent newspaper covering local news and sports for the surrounding area.

The Corkman
983803

Editorial: The Spa, Mallow, Co. Cork
Tel: 353 22423 94
Email: newsdesk@corkman.ie
Web site: http://www.independent.ie/regionals/corkman/
Freq: Weekly
Circ: 8000 Not Audited
Editor: Brendan Malone
Profile: The Corkman is a weekly local newspaper published on Thursdays covering all the latest local news, entertainment, lifestyle and sport from Avondhu, North Cork and Muskerry.
Ad Rate: Full Page Mono €2240.00
Ad Rate: Full Page Colour €2464.00

The Donegal News
981663

Editorial: St. Anne's Court, High Road, Letterkenny Co. Donegal
Tel: 353 07491 21014
Email: editor@donegalnews.com
Web site: www.donegalnews.com
Freq: 2 Times/Week
Circ: 9448 Not Audited
Editor: Columba Gill

Douglas Post
998666

Editorial: St Patrick Mills, Douglas West, Cork **Tel:** 353 08944 08242
Web site: www.douglaspost.ie
Freq: Weekly
Circ: 10000 Not Audited
Editor: George Thompson

Drogheda Independent
983785

Editorial: 9 Shop Street, Drogheda, County Louth **Tel:** 353 41987 6800
Email: editorial@drogheda-independent.ie
Web site: www.independent.ie/regionals/droghedaindependent
Freq: Weekly
Circ: 6852 Not Audited
Editor: Hubert Murphy
Profile: This is the online version of the Drogheda Independent, a weekly, local newspaper covering all the latest news, sport, entertainment and lifestyle for the surrounding areas.

Drogheda Leader
984271

Editorial: 35 Laurence Street, Drogheda, County Louth **Tel:** 353 41983 6100
Email: news@droghedaleader.ie

Web site: www.droghedaleader.ie
Freq: Weekly
Circ: 24000 Not Audited
Editor: Gordon Hatch
Profile: This is the online version of the Drogheda Leader, a weekly, local newspaper covering all the latest on local news in Drogheda and the surrounding villages in County Louth and Meath.

Dublin Gazette Newspapers
1060357

Editorial: Second Floor, Heritage House, Dundrum Office Park, Dundrum, Dublin 14
Tel: 353 01601 0240
Email: info@gazettegroup.com
Web site: www.gazettegroup.com
Freq: Weekly
Circ: 52958 Not Audited

Dublin People
985836

Editorial: 80-83 Omni Park Shopping Centre, Santry, Dublin Dublin 9
Tel: 353 01862 1611
Email: news@dublinpeople.com
Web site: http://www.dublinpeople.com/news/northsidewest
Freq: Weekly
Circ: 120000 Not Audited
Editor: Neil Fetherson; **Editor:** Jack Gleeson; **Editor:** Pat O'Rourke
Profile: Website for the Dublin People newspapers the Northside People and the Southside People, covering local news, sports and events for Dublin.

Dundalk Democrat
999100

Editorial: 7 Crowe Street, Dundalk, County Louth **Tel:** 353 04293 34058
Email: editor@dundalkdemocrat.ie
Web site: http://www.dundalkdemocrat.ie/
Freq: Weekly
Circ: 5539 Not Audited
Editor: David Lynch
Profile: Website of the Dundalk Democrat (town edition) and Dundalk Democrat (county edition), covering the latest in local news, sports and leisure from Dundalk and the surrounding area.

The Enniscorthy Echo
986828

Editorial: Slaney Place, Enniscorthy, County Wexford **Tel:** 353 05392 59900
Email: editor@theecho.ie
Web site: www.wexfordecho.ie
Freq: Weekly Not Audited
Editor: Tom Mooney
Profile: The Enniscorthy Echo is a weekly, local newspaper published on Tuesdays covering all the latest on local news and sport in Enniscorthy and the surrounding area.
Ad Rate: Full Page Mono €2912.00
Ad Rate: Full Page Colour €3584.00

Enniscorthy Guardian
998625

Editorial: Channing House, Upper Row Street, Co. Wexford **Tel:** 353 53914 0100
Email: front.office@peoplenews.ie
Web site: http://www.independent.ie/regionals/enniscorthyguardian/
Freq: Weekly
Circ: 3000 Not Audited

The Evening Echo
984221

Editorial: Evening Echo, Linn Dubh, Assumption Road, Cork
Tel: 353 02142 72722
Email: echoeditorial@eecho.ie
Web site: www.eveningecho.ie
Freq: Daily
Circ: 10270 Not Audited
Editor: Maurice Gubbins
Profile: The Evening Echo is an Irish evening newspaper covering regional news, lifestyle, sports and entertainment listings for the region of County Cork in Ireland. The newspaper was first published in 1892.
Ad Rate: Full Page Mono €4600.00
Ad Rate: Full Page Colour €5520.00

Galway Advertiser
983797

Editorial: 41-42 Eyre Square, Galway
Tel: 353 91530 900
Email: news@galwayadvertiser.ie
Web site: http://www.advertiser.ie/galway
Freq: Weekly

Regional & Local Weekly Newspapers

Circ: 28854 Not Audited
Profile: Website for local paper the Galway Advertiser covering the latest local news and events from Galway city and county.

Galway City Tribune 987987
Editorial: 15 Market Street, Galway
Tel: 353 09153 6222
Email: news@ctribune.ie
Web site: www.connachttribune.ie
Freq: Weekly
Circ: 22000 Not Audited
Profile: The Galway City Tribune is a weekly, local newspaper published on Fridays, covering all the latest on local news, sport and lifestyle in Galway City. Regular features: Entertainment, Lifestyle, Motoring, Property, Sport.
Ad Rate: Full Page Mono €8569.00
Ad Rate: Full Page Colour €8569.00

Galway Independent 1098995
Editorial: Independent House, Galway Retail Park, Headford Road, Galway
Tel: 353 09156 9000
Email: editor@galwayindependent.com
Web site: http://www.galwayindependent.com/
Freq: Weekly
Profile: Website for local paper the Galway Independent covering the latest local news and events from Galway city and county.

The Gorey Echo 986827
Editorial: Slaney Place, Enniscorthy, County Wexford **Tel:** 353 05392 59900
Email: editor@theecho.ie
Web site: www.wexfordecho.ie
Freq: Weekly Not Audited
Editor: Tom Mooney
Profile: The Gorey Echo is a weekly, local newspaper published on Tuesdays covering all the latest on local news and sport in Gorey and the surrounding area.
Ad Rate: Full Page Mono €2912.00
Ad Rate: Full Page Colour €3584.00

Gorey Guardian 999020
Editorial: Channing House, Upper Row Street, Co. Wexford **Tel:** 353 05391 40100
Email: front.office@peoplenews.ie
Web site: www.independent.ie/regionals/goreyguardian/
Freq: Weekly
Circ: 5500 Not Audited

Herald 980839
Editorial: Independent House, 27-32 Talbot Street, Dublin 1 **Tel:** 353 01705 5333
Email: hnews@herald.ie
Web site: www.herald.ie
Freq: Daily
Circ: 44085 Not Audited
Editor: Shane Doran

Inish Times 984238
Editorial: 33 Main Street, Buncrana, Co Donegal **Tel:** 353 07493 41055
Email: editor@inishtimes.com
Web site: http://www.donegalnow.com/inish-times
Freq: Weekly
Circ: 3565 Not Audited
Profile: The Inish Times is a weekly, local newspaper published on Tuesdays, covering all the latest on local news in the Inishowen area.
Ad Rate: Full Page Mono €1300.00
Ad Rate: Full Page Colour €1600.00

The Irish Catholic 995998
Tel: 353 16874 020
Email: news@irishcatholic.ie
Web site: www.irishcatholic.ie
Freq: Weekly
Circ: 90000 Not Audited
Profile: Weekly religious newspaper specialising in news, comment and analysis on events both inside and outside the Catholic Church.
Ad Rate: Full Page Mono €2000.00
Ad Rate: Full Page Colour €2400.00

Kerry's Eye 983780
Editorial: 22 Ashe Street, Tralee, Co. Kerry
Tel: 353 66714 9200
Email: news@kerryseye.com
Web site: www.kerryseye.com
Freq: Weekly
Circ: 25000 Not Audited
Editor: Colin Lacey
Profile: Kerry's Eye is a weekly, local newspaper covering all the latest on local news and sport in Kerry, Cork, Limerick and the surrounding areas. The paper is published on Thursdays.
Ad Rate: Full Page Mono €3200.00
Ad Rate: Full Page Colour €3500.00

Kilkenny People 984803
Editorial: 34 High Street, Kilkenny
Tel: 353 05677 21015
Email: editor@kilkennypeople.ie
Web site: www.kilkennypeople.ie
Freq: Weekly
Circ: 10591 Not Audited
Editor: Brian Keyes
Profile: Website of the Kilkenny People, a local paper circulated in County Kilkenny, Ireland, covering local news, sports and entertainment.

Leinster Express 984801
Editorial: Dublin Road, Portlaoise
Tel: 353 05786 21666
Email: editor@leinsterexpress.ie
Web site: www.leinsterexpress.ie
Freq: Weekly
Circ: 11070 Not Audited
Editor: Pat Somers
Profile: Website of The Leinster Express, a weekly newspaper featuring news, sports and leisure from County Laois, Ireland.

Leinster Leader 984802
Editorial: 19 South Main Street, Naas, Co. Kildare **Tel:** 353 45897 302
Email: editor@leinsterleader.ie
Web site: www.leinsterleader.ie
Freq: Weekly
Circ: 10000 Not Audited
Profile: The Leinster Leader is a weekly local newspaper covering local news and sports for the surrounding area. The paper is available on Tuesdays.
Ad Rate: Full Page Mono €5145.00
Ad Rate: Full Page Colour €6208.00

The Limerick Leader 984207
Editorial: 54 O'Connell Street, Limerick
Tel: 353 06121 4500
Email: news@limerickleader.ie
Web site: www.limerickleader.ie
Freq: Daily
Circ: 13420 Not Audited
Editor: Eugene Phelan
Profile: The Limerick Leader is a local newspaper covering local news, sports and lifestyle for the surrounding area. Established 1889.
Ad Rate: Full Page Colour €3000.00

The Limerick Post 985327
Editorial: 97 Henry Street, Henry Street, Limerick **Tel:** 353 06141 3322
Email: news@limerickpost.ie
Web site: www.limerickpost.ie
Freq: Weekly
Circ: 15891 Not Audited
Profile: Online version of the Limerick Post newspaper covering local news and sports for the surrounding area.

Mayo Advertiser 985220
Editorial: Chapel Street, Castlebar, Co. Mayo **Tel:** 353 09490 35010
Email: news@mayoadvertiser.ie
Web site: www.advertiser.ie/mayo
Freq: Daily
Circ: 21000 Not Audited

The Mayo News 983782
Editorial: The Fairgreen, Westport, Co. Mayo **Tel:** 353 98253 11
Email: editor@mayonews.ie
Web site: www.mayonews.ie
Freq: Weekly
Circ: 10229 Not Audited
Editor: Michael Duffy
Profile: Online version of the Mayo News newspaper covering local news for the surrounding area.

Meath Chronicle 984180
Editorial: Market Square, Navan, Co. Meath C15 A078 **Tel:** 353 04690 79600
Email: info@meathchronicle.ie
Web site: www.meathchronicle.ie
Freq: Weekly
Circ: 10373 Not Audited
Editor: Gavan Becton
Profile: Online version of the Meath Chronicle newspaper covering local news and sports for the surrounding area.

The Munster Express 983809
Editorial: 37 The Quay, Waterford
Tel: 353 05187 2141
Email: news@munster-express.ie
Web site: http://www.munster-express.ie
Freq: 2 Times/Week
Circ: 5389 Not Audited
Profile: Online version of the Munster Express newspaper covering local news, sports, entertainments and business for the surrounding area.

The Nationalist (Tipperary) 983788
Editorial: Queen Street, Clonmel, Co. Tipperary **Tel:** 353 05261 72500
Email: editor@nationalist.ie
Web site: http://www.nationalist.ie/
Freq: Weekly
Circ: 12736 Not Audited
Editor: Michael Haverin

The Nationalist Series 983781
Editorial: Hanover House, Hanover, Carlow
Tel: 353 59917 0100
Email: news@carlow-nationalist.ie
Web site: www.carlow-nationalist.ie
Freq: Weekly
Circ: 8783 Not Audited
Editor: Conal O'Boyle; **Editor:** Barbara Sheridan

Nenagh Guardian 983800
Editorial: 13 Summerhill, Nenagh, Co. Tipperary **Tel:** 353 67312 14
Email: editorial@nenaghguardian.ie
Web site: http://www.nenaghguardian.ie/
Freq: Weekly
Circ: 6000 Not Audited
Editor: Garry Cotter
Profile: The Nenagh Guardian is a weekly local newspaper that circulates in North Tipperary, Ireland and is based in Nenagh, County Tipperary.
Ad Rate: Full Page Mono €2510.00
Ad Rate: Full Page Colour €3110.00

The New Ross Echo 986829
Editorial: 4 Mary Street, New Ross, County Wexford **Tel:** 353 05144 5062
Email: editor@theecho.ie
Web site: www.wexfordecho.ie
Freq: Weekly Not Audited
Editor: Tom Mooney
Profile: The New Ross Echo is a weekly, local newspaper published on Tuesdays covering all the latest on local news and sport in New Ross and the surrounding area.
Ad Rate: Full Page Mono €2912.00
Ad Rate: Full Page Colour €3584.00

New Ross Standard 983808
Editorial: Channing House, Upper Row Street, Co. Wexford **Tel:** 353 53914 0100
Email: front.office@peoplenews.ie
Web site: ww.independent.ie/regionals/newrossstandard
Freq: Weekly
Circ: 5781 Not Audited
Editor: Jim Hayes
Profile: The New Hoss Standard is a weekly local newspaper covering local news for the surrounding area.
Ad Rate: Full Page Mono €1823.00
Ad Rate: Full Page Colour €1823.00

North County Leader 983914
Editorial: Leader House, North Street, Swords, Co. Dublin **Tel:** 353 18400 200
Email: news@northcountyleader.ie
Web site: www.northcountyleader.ie
Freq: Weekly
Circ: 39000 Not Audited
Profile: The North County Leader is a local newspaper covering all the latest news and issues in the area.
Ad Rate: Full Page Colour €3969.00

The Northern Standard 985773
Editorial: The Diamond, Monaghan Town, Co. Monaghan **Tel:** 353 04782 188
Email: newsdesk@northern-standard.ie
Web site: www.northernstandard.ie
Freq: Weekly
Circ: 13500 Not Audited
Editor: Peter Hughes
Profile: The Northern Standard is a weekly local newspaper covering local news and sports for the surrounding area. The newspaper is published on a Thursday.The Northern Standard was first published in 1839. The outlet offers RSS (Really Simple Syndication).
Ad Rate: Full Page Mono €5597.00
Ad Rate: Full Page Colour €7038.00

Offaly Independent 984111
Editorial: c/o 11 Sean Costello St, Athlone, Co. Westmeath **Tel:** 353 05793 26756
Email: news@offalyindependent.ie
Web site: www.offalyindependent.ie
Freq: Weekly Not Audited
Editor: Tadhg Carey
Profile: The Offaly Independent is a free newspaper published on Fridays covering Tullamore and the surrounding areas in County Offaly.
Ad Rate: Full Page Mono €2112.00
Ad Rate: Full Page Colour €2669.00

Roscommon Herald 984231
Tel: 353 07196 62004
Email: editor@roscommonherald.com
Web site: www.roscommonherald.com
Freq: Weekly
Circ: 8324 Not Audited
Editor: Christina McHugh
Profile: The Roscommon Herald is a weekly local newspaper covering local news for the surrounding area.
Ad Rate: Full Page Mono €2700.00
Ad Rate: Full Page Colour €3110.00

Sligo Weekender 984319
Editorial: 4 Teeling Street, Sligo
Tel: 353 71917 4900
Email: info@sligoweekender.ie
Web site: http://www.sligoweekender.ie/
Freq: Weekly
Circ: 6000 Not Audited
Editor: Robert Cullen
Profile: Website for Sligo Weekender covering the latest local news and events from County Sligo and North Mayo.

The Southern Star 984771
Editorial: Ilen Street, Skibbereen, Co. Cork
Tel: 353 02821 200
Email: editorial@southernstar.ie
Web site: www.southernstar.ie
Freq: Weekly
Circ: 12000 Not Audited
Editor: Con Downing
Profile: Website for local paper the Southern Star, covering the latest local news and events from Cork.

Tirconaill Tribune 983802
Editorial: Main Street, Milford, Donegal
Tel: 353 04915 3600
Email: tribune15@gmail.com
Freq: Weekly
Circ: 6800 Not Audited
Editor: John McAteer
Profile: Headquartered at Milford, The Tirconaill Tribune is a local newspaper which circulates in County Donegal, Ireland. John McAteer is the Editor to whom all press releases should be addressed.Press Day: Wednesday
Ad Rate: Full Page Mono €550.00
Ad Rate: Full Page Colour €1000.00

Tullamore Tribune 983792
Editorial: William Street, Tullamore, Co. Offaly **Tel:** 353 57932 1152
Email: editor@tullamoretribune.ie
Web site: www.tullamoretribune.ie
Freq: Weekly
Circ: 12000 Not Audited

Editor: Gerard Scully
Profile: The Tullamore Tribune is a weekly paper published every Wednesday covering the latest local news and events from the town of Tullamore and the surrounding County Offaly.

Waterford News & Star   983867

Editorial: Gladstone House, Gladstone Street, Waterford **Tel:** 353 05187 4951
Email: editor@waterford-news.com
Web site: www.waterford-news.ie
Freq: Weekly
Circ: 8500 Not Audited
Editor: Mary Frances Ryan

Waterford Today   997525

Editorial: 36 Mayor's Walk, Waterford
Tel: 353 05185 4135
Email: news@waterford-today.ie
Web site: http://www.waterford-today.ie
Freq: Weekly
Circ: 17100 Not Audited
Editor: Paddy Gallagher
Profile: Newspaper containing information about Waterford and the surrounding area.
Ad Rate: Full Page Mono €1900.00
Ad Rate: Full Page Colour €2375.00

West Cork Times   996372

Tel: 353 27627 38
Email: news@westcorktimes.com

Web site: westcorktimes.com
Freq: Bi-Weekly
Circ: 10000 Not Audited

Western People   983789

Editorial: Tone Street, Ballina, Co. Mayo
Tel: 353 09660 999
Email: newsdesk@westernpeople.ie
Web site: www.westernpeople.ie
Freq: Weekly
Circ: 11000 Not Audited
Editor: James Laffey
Profile: This is the online version of the Western People, a weekly, local newspaper published on Tuesdays covering all the latest on local news and sport in Mayo, Sligo, Galway and Roscommon.

The Westmeath Examiner   983794

Editorial: Blackhall Place, Mullingar, Co. Westmeath N91 V2NT **Tel:** 353 04493 46700
Email: editor@westmeathexaminer.ie
Web site: www.westmeathexaminer.ie
Freq: Weekly
Circ: 7284 Not Audited
Editor: Brian O'Loughlin
Profile: Online version of the Westmeath Examiner newspaper covering local news and sports for the surrounding area.

The Westmeath Independent   990221

Editorial: Westmeath Independent, Sean Costello Street, Athlone, Co. Westmeath
Tel: 353 09064 34300
Email: editor@westmeathindependent.ie
Web site: www.westmeathindependent.ie
Freq: Weekly
Circ: 7726 Not Audited
Editor: Tadhg Carey
Profile: The Westmeath Independent is a weekly, local newspaper published on Wednesdays covering all the latest on local news, entertainment and sport in Westmeath and the surrounding areas of Longford, Offaly (Kings), Galway and Roscommon.
Ad Rate: Full Page Mono €4576.00
Ad Rate: Full Page Colour €4576.00

The Wexford Echo   983786

Editorial: 17 Selskar Street, Wexford
Tel: 353 05391 42948
Email: editor@theecho.ie
Web site: www.wexfordecho.ie
Freq: Weekly Not Audited
Editor: Tom Mooney
Profile: The Wexford Echo is a weekly, local newspaper published on Tuesdays covering all the latest on local news and sport in Wexford and the surrounding area.
Ad Rate: Full Page Mono €2912.00
Ad Rate: Full Page Colour €3584.00

Wexford People   983795

Editorial: Channing House, Upper Row Street, Co. Wexford **Tel:** 050 06001 40100
Email: wexfordpeople@peoplenews.ie
Web site: www.wexfordpeople.ie
Freq: Weekly
Circ: 10868 Not Audited
Editor: Jim Hayes
Profile: This is the online version of the Wexford People, a weekly, local newspaper published on Tuesdays, covering all the latest on local news, entertainment, lifestyle and sport in Wexford and the surrounding area.

Wicklow People   983799

Editorial: Channing House, Upper Row Street, County Wexford **Tel:** 353 04046 7004
Email: front.office@peoplenews.ie
Web site: http://www.independent.ie/regionals/wicklowpeople/
Freq: Weekly
Circ: 10050 Not Audited
Editor: David Tucker
Profile: This is the online version of the Wicklow People, a weekly, local newspaper published on Tuesdays, covering all the latest on local news, entertainment, lifestyle and sport in Wicklow and the surrounding area.

Periodicals Index

Periodicals

Accountancy Ireland
983039

Editorial: Chartered Accountants House, 47-49 Pearse Street, Dublin D02 YN40
Tel: 353 01637 7392
Email: hello@accountancyireland.ie
Web site: www.accountancyireland.ie
Freq: Bi-Monthly
Circ: 26337 Not Audited
Profile: Journal of the Institute of Chartered Accountants in Ireland covers accountancy, business and management, taxation, information technology, general news, leisure and lifestyle. Read by all members and students of The Institute of Chartered Accountants in Ireland and all members of the Institute of Accounting Technicians in Ireland.
Ad Rate: Full Page Colour €2800.00
MAGAZINE
Accounting

AgriLand
1052655

Tel: 353 35301 4498103
Email: editor@agriland.ie
Web site: www.agriland.ie
Freq: Daily
Circ: 35533 Cision Digital Reach
MAGAZINE (ONLINE)
Animal Farming

An Fear Rua - The GAA Unplugged
998883

Editorial: Clowanstown, Co. Meath
Email: liamcahill@indigo.ie
Web site: www.anfearrua.ie
Freq: Daily
Circ: 1710 Cision Digital Reach
Editor: Liam Cahill
MAGAZINE (ONLINE)
Field Sports

Architecture Ireland
984888

Editorial: 9 Sandyford Office Park, Sandyford, Dublin Dublin 18
Tel: 353 01295 8115
Email: derek@architectureireland.ie
Web site: www.architectureireland.ie
Freq: Bi-Monthly Not Audited
Editor: Sandra O'Connell
Profile: Official journal of the Royal Institute of the Architects of Ireland. First published in 1980, the publication has an average of 72 pages per issue. Aimed at architects, builders and government officials.
Ad Rate: Full Page Mono €1925.00
Ad Rate: Full Page Colour €2785.00
MAGAZINE
Architecture & Design

Biotechnology Ireland
985317

Editorial: The Plaza, East Point Business Park, Dublin **Tel:** 353 01808 2668
Email: client.service@enterprise-ireland.com
Web site: www.enterprise-ireland.com/en/events/associated-events/bioconnect-ireland.html
Freq: Daily
Circ: 45540 Cision Digital Reach
MAGAZINE (ONLINE)
Biotechnology

BreakingNews.ie
1053989

Editorial: Linn Dubh, Assumption Road, Blackpool, Cork T23 RCH6
Tel: 353 02148 02214
Email: desk@breakingnews.ie
Web site: http://www.breakingnews.ie
Freq: Daily

Circ: 2139055 Cision Digital Reach
MAGAZINE (ONLINE)
Business, Computer & Video Games, Golf, Horse Racing, International News, Movies & Video, National News, Rugby, Soccer

Build Your Own House and Home
984531

Editorial: 3rd Floor, New Market House, New Market Square, Dublin
Tel: 353 01473 5040
Email: editor@houseandhome.ie
Web site: www.houseandhome.ie
Freq: Annual
Circ: 15000 Not Audited
MAGAZINE
Architecture & Design, Do-It-Yourself (DIY)

Business & Finance
981504

Editorial: Unit 1A, Waters Edge, Charlotte Quay, Dublin Dublin 4
Tel: 353 01237 7000
Web site: www.businessandfinance.ie
Freq: Bi-Monthly
Circ: 14676 Not Audited
Profile: Magazine covering all aspects of business, finance, economic policy and related political events in Ireland, Northern Ireland, the UK and Europe. Read by company managers, top company executives and general public.
Ad Rate: Full Page Colour €3945.00
MAGAZINE
Banking, Business

Business Plus
983040

Editorial: 30 Morehampton Road, Dublin Dublin 4 **Tel:** 353 01660 8400
Email: info@businessplus.ie
Web site: www.bizplus.ie
Freq: Monthly
Circ: 10498 Not Audited
Editor: Nick Mulcahy
Profile: Magazine providing information about Irish companies and developments of interest to them. Includes articles on entrepreneurs, quoted companies, fund-raising, IT, e-business, shares, investments, health, wine and cars. Aimed at SME owner managers and managers within large companies.
Ad Rate: Full Page Colour €3240.00
MAGAZINE
Business, Corporate Responsibility

CANCER PROFESSIONAL
986964

Editorial: 25 Adelaide Street, Dun Laoghaire, Co. Dublin
Tel: 353 01280 3967
Email: info@medmedia.ie
Web site: www.medmedia.ie/publications/titles.html
Freq: Quarterly
Circ: 3000 Not Audited
Editor: Eimear Vize
MAGAZINE
Oncology

Cara magazine
998721

Editorial: Unit 3, Block 3, Harbour Square, Dun Laoghaire, Co Dublin
Tel: 353 01280 8415
Email: info@image.ie
Web site: http://www.image.ie/
Freq: Bi-Monthly Not Audited
Editor: Lucy White
Profile: In-flight magazine from Aer Lingus covering fashion, beauty and health, travel, the arts and lifestyle. Read by travellers on Aer Lingus flights.
Ad Rate: Full Page Colour €5495.00
MAGAZINE
Airline Inflight

Caravan Cruise
985507

Editorial: D'Alton Street, Claremorris, Co. Mayo **Tel:** 353 09493 72819
Email: info@caravancruise.ie
Web site: www.caravancruise.ie
Freq: Monthly
Circ: 6000 Not Audited
MAGAZINE
Camping and RV Travel

Checkout Ireland
981284

Editorial: Adelaide Hall, 3 Adelaide Street, Dun Laoghaire, Co Dublin
Tel: 353 01230 0322
Email: editor@checkout.ie
Web site: www.checkout.ie
Freq: Monthly
Circ: 5408 Not Audited
Editor In Chief: Stephen Wynne-Jones
Profile: Website covering all matters relating to the Irish grocery and drinks trade. Aimed at independent retailers, food and drink manufacturers and off licenses.
MAGAZINE
Food, Retail Management

Click Magazine (Ireland)
998822

Editorial: Blue Lake House, Brookfield Terrace, Blackrock, Co. Dublin
Tel: 353 01487 7836
Email: editor@clickonline.com
Web site: http://clickonline.com
Freq: Monthly
Circ: 15000 Not Audited
MAGAZINE
Audio Video Trade, Cameras, Computer & Video Games, Consumer Electronics, Electronics, Mobile Electronics, Movies & Video

Comic Buzz
999333

Editorial: 135 Grace Park Heights, Dublin
Email: hello@comicbuzz.com
Web site: http://comicbuzz.com
Circ: 15112 Cision Digital Reach
MAGAZINE (ONLINE)
Apple, Cartoons, Computer & Video Games, Computers, Internet, Personal Computers

Confetti
982421

Editorial: 3rd Floor, New Market House, New Market Square, Dublin
Tel: 353 14735 040
Email: editor@confetti.ie
Web site: www.confetti.ie
Freq: Quarterly
Circ: 15000 Not Audited
Editor: Laura Cunningham
Profile: Magazine covering all aspects of wedding planning, including articles on venues, dresses, beauty, health and honeymoons.
Ad Rate: Full Page Colour €2200.00
MAGAZINE
Weddings

Consumer Choice Magazine
998860

Editorial: 26 Upper Pembroke Street, Dublin **Tel:** 353 01637 3961
Email: cai@thecai.ie
Web site: www.consumerassociation.ie
Freq: Monthly
Circ: 10000 Not Audited
MAGAZINE
Alcohol & Spirits, Books, Consumer Goods & Products, Cosmetics, Fashion, Food, Gardening, Hair, Office Supplies, Retail

The Consumers Association of Ireland
987183

Editorial: 26 Upper Pembroke Street, Dublin **Tel:** 353 01637 3961
Email: cai@thecai.ie
Web site: www.thecai.ie

Freq: Daily
Circ: 7769 Cision Digital Reach
MAGAZINE (ONLINE)
Charitable Foundations

Digital Times (Ireland)
990603

Editorial: Unit 4A CRDS Building, Dundrum Business Park, Dundrum Road, Dublin Dublin 14 **Tel:** 353 01299 3839
Email: hello@digitaltimes.ie
Web site: www.digitaltimes.ie
Freq: Daily
Circ: 5765 Cision Digital Reach
Editor: Stephen Conmy
MAGAZINE (ONLINE)
Marketing

Drinks Industry Ireland
985298

Editorial: 55 Spruce Avenue, Stillorgan Industrial Estate, Dublin Dublin 18
Tel: 353 01294 7766
Email: drinksinireland@gmail.com
Web site: www.drinksindustryireland.ie
Freq: Monthly
Circ: 4000 Not Audited
Editor: Pat Nolan
Profile: Magazine covering the drinks industry in Ireland including news on developments, interviews with decision makers and features on the latest trends. Aimed at brewers, distillers, hotel, pub, night club and off-licence managers and retailers.
Ad Rate: Full Page Colour €2500.00
MAGAZINE
Alcohol & Spirits

Dublin Live
1068965

Editorial: Floor 4, Park House, Dublin 7
Tel: 353 18299 613
Email: news@dublinlive.ie
Web site: http://www.dublinlive.ie/
Freq: Daily
Circ: 19077 Cision Digital Reach
Editor: Alana Fearon
MAGAZINE (ONLINE)
Regional General Interest

Dublin Review of Books
995715

Editorial: 17 D'Olier Street, Dublin
Tel: 353 86600 5526
Email: info@drb.ie
Web site: www.drb.ie
Freq: Quarterly
Circ: 16152 Cision Digital Reach
MAGAZINE (ONLINE)
Literature

Easy Food
981805

Editorial: First Floor, Barker House, Church Road, Co Wicklow Co. Wicklow
Tel: 353 01255 7566
Email: editoreasyfood@zahrapublishing.com
Web site: www.easyfood.ie
Freq: Monthly
Circ: 17534 Not Audited
Editor: Dee Laffan
MAGAZINE
Cooking & Baking, Food, Grocery Stores, Organic Food, Restaurant Reviews, Vegetarianism & Veganism

Easy Parenting
987083

Editorial: First Floor, Zoe House, Co Wicklow Co Wicklow **Tel:** 353 12878 636
Web site: www.easyparenting.ie
Freq: Bi-Monthly
Circ: 7130 Not Audited
Editor: Emma Parkin
MAGAZINE
Family & Parenting

Education (IE)
981542

Editorial: 168 Ardlea Road, Artane, Dublin Dublin 5 **Tel:** 353 01832 9246
Email: education@clubi.ie

Web site: www.educationmagazine.ie
Freq: Quarterly
Circ: 20000 Not Audited
Editor: Niall Gormley
MAGAZINE
Schools & Institutions

Engineers Journal 1051157
Email: editor@engineersjournal.ie
Web site: www.engineersjournal.ie
Freq: Daily
Circ: 43751 Cision Digital Reach
Editor: Mary Anne Carrigan
Profile: Magazine focusing on
engineering projects in all fields including
biomedical, chemical and process,
electrical, electronics, ICT, infrastructure
both civil and structural, mechanical and
manufacturing.
Ad Rate: Full Page Colour €2730.00
MAGAZINE (ONLINE)
Engineering

entertainment.ie 982863
Editorial: 26 Great Strand Street, Dublin
1 Tel: 353 01874 8208
Email: info@entertainment.ie
Web site: www.entertainment.ie
Freq: Daily
Circ: 2147886 Cision Digital Reach
MAGAZINE (ONLINE)
Bars, Clubs & Pubs, Comedy,
Entertainment, Local Entertainment
Guides, Movies & Video

eumom.ie 996511
Editorial: 101 Monkstown Road,
Blackrock, Co. Dublin
Tel: 353 12805 050
Email: info@eumom.ie
Web site: http://www.eumom.ie/
Freq: Daily
Circ: 61323 Cision Digital Reach
MAGAZINE (ONLINE)
Family & Parenting

**European Supermarket
Magazine** 985542
Editorial: 3 Adelaide Street, Dun
Laoghaire, Dublin Tel: 353 01230 0322
Email: ctovo@esmmagazine.com
Web site: www.esmmagazine.com
Freq: Bi-Monthly
Circ: 9000 Not Audited
Editor In Chief: Stephen Wynne-Jones
MAGAZINE
Food

EuroTimes 981185
Tel: 353 01209 1100
Email: eurotimes@eurotimes.org
Web site: www.eurotimes.org
Freq: Monthly
Circ: 46515 Not Audited
Profile: Magazine focusing on the
practice of ophthalmology in Europe.
Featuring coverage of scientific
congresses and events worldwide.
Ad Rate: Full Page Colour €7750.00
MAGAZINE
Ophthalmology & Optometry

EVOKE.ie 998374
Editorial: 3rd Floor Embassy House,
Herbert Park Lane, Ballsbridge, Dublin
D4 Tel: 353 01256 0800
Email: info@evoke.ie
Web site: http://evoke.ie/
Freq: Daily
Circ: 117614 Cision Digital Reach
MAGAZINE (ONLINE)
Celebrities, National News, Regional
General Interest

Excite UK 996382
Editorial: 11/12 Hogan Place, Dublin 2
Web site: www.excite.co.uk

Freq: Daily
Circ: 124888 Cision Digital Reach
MAGAZINE (ONLINE)
Antique & Collectible Cars,
Architecture & Design, Automakers,
Automotive, Bars, Clubs & Pubs,
Beauty & Grooming, Celebrities,
Comedy, Cosmetics, Do-It-Yourself
(DIY)

Farmers Journal 983730
Editorial: Irish Farm Centre, Dublin
Dublin 12 Tel: 353 01419 9500
Email: edit@farmersjournal.ie
Web site: www.farmersjournal.ie
Freq: Weekly
Circ: 63430 Not Audited
Editor: Justin McCarthy
Profile: Newspaper covering all aspects
of Agriculture, food and rural living.
Ad Rate: Full Page Mono €10584.00
Ad Rate: Full Page Colour €16200.00
MAGAZINE
Animal Farming

Finance Dublin 1050388
Editorial: Fintel House, 6 The Mall,
Beacon Court, Dublin Dublin 18
Tel: 353 01293 0566
Email: editorial@financedublin.com
Web site: www.financedublin.com
Freq: Monthly Not Audited
Editor: Ken O'Brien
MAGAZINE
Banking, Bonds, Commodities,
Corporate Finance, Corporate
Management, Credit Markets,
Derivatives, Economics, Emerging
Markets, Equities

Fleet Transport 984810
Editorial: D'Alton Street, Claremorris,
Co. Mayo Tel: 353 09493 72819
Email: enquiries@fleet.ie
Web site: www.fleet.ie
Freq: Monthly
Circ: 8500 Not Audited
Profile: Magazine covering all aspects of
fleet management and transport
including cars, buses, coaches, vans,
utility vehicles, trailers, maritime fleets,
news, views and road tests. Aimed at
road transport operators and decision
makers.
Ad Rate: Full Page Colour €1950.00
MAGAZINE
Automotive, Aviation, Railroad,
Shipping & Warehousing, Supply Chain
Management (SCM), Transportation

**Food & Drink Business
Europe** 985493
Editorial: 51 Parkwest Enterprise Centre,
Nangor Road, Dublin
Tel: 353 01612 0880
Web site: http://www.fdbusiness.com/
about/
Freq: Monthly
Circ: 24900 Not Audited
Editor: Mike Rohan
MAGAZINE
Alcohol & Spirits, Food

Food & Wine (Ireland) 999034
Editorial: Rosemount House, Dundrum
Road, Dundrum, Dublin 14
Tel: 353 01240 5300
Web site: http://foodwine.net/
Freq: Monthly
Circ: 7560 Not Audited
Editor: Miriam Atkins
MAGAZINE
Cooking & Baking, Food, Grocery
Stores, Organic Food, Restaurant
Reviews, Vegetarianism & Veganism,
Wine/Winemaking

Footwear in Ireland 1054209
Editorial: Castle House, Main Street,
Rathfarnham, Dublin
Tel: 353 35301 2836782
Email: mail@futuramagazine.ie
Web site: www.futuramagazine.ie/fw.
html
Freq: Quarterly
Circ: 3000 Not Audited
Editor: Alexander Fitzgerald
Profile: Footwear in Ireland covers
footwear for men, women and children.
Includes leather goods, accessories,
handbags, jewellery and travel goods.
Ad Rate: Full Page Colour €2195.00
MAGAZINE
News & Current Affairs

Fora.ie 1075816
Editorial: Level 4, Latin Hall, Golden
Lane, Dublin 8
Email: news@fora.ie
Web site: https://fora.ie/
Freq: Daily
Circ: 1544 Cision Digital Reach
Editor: Peter Bodkin
MAGAZINE (ONLINE)
Business, Corporate Responsibility,
Small and Medium Business

Futura 985396
Editorial: Castle House, Main Street,
Rathfarnham, Dublin
Tel: 353 35301 2836782
Email: mail@futuramagazine.ie
Web site: www.futuramagazine.ie
Freq: Monthly
Circ: 4800 Not Audited
Profile: Launched in 1963, Futura is a
fashion trade magazine for womenswear
buyers in Ireland. Includes national
business updates from around the
country, international news, latest
collections from top-selling brands,
essential event guide, showtalk.
Ad Rate: Full Page Colour €2195.00
MAGAZINE
Fashion

Gadgets.ie 1100046
Web site: http://gadgets.ie/
Freq: Daily
Circ: 4221 Cision Digital Reach
MAGAZINE (ONLINE)
Audio Video Trade, Cameras,
Consumer Electronics, Electronics,
Mobile Electronics, Movies & Video

Galway Now 984219
Editorial: Unit 2, 1st Floor, Galway
Technology Park, Galway
Tel: 353 09138 4350
Email: editor@goldenegg.ie
Web site: www.goldenegg.ie
Freq: Monthly
Circ: 10000 Not Audited
MAGAZINE
Women's Interests

GCN (Gay Community News) 984147
Editorial: The Skylab Building, 2
Exchange Street Upper, Dublin 8
Tel: 353 01675 5025
Email: editor@gcn.ie
Web site: http://theoutmost.com/
Freq: Monthly
Circ: 9925 Not Audited
Editor: Brian Finnegan
MAGAZINE
LGBT, Sexuality

Gig Listings 1071356
Email: listings@hotpress.ie Not Audited
MAGAZINE
News & Current Affairs

The Gloss Magazine 999041
Editorial: The Courtyard, 40 Main Street,
Blackrock, Co Dublin
Tel: 353 01275 5130
Email: theglossmagazine@gmail.com
Web site: www.thegloss.ie
Freq: Monthly
Circ: 72011 Not Audited
Editor: Sarah McDonnell
MAGAZINE
Women's Interests

Go Rail 985496
Editorial: 13 Trinity St, Dublin
Tel: 353 12411 500
Email: info@hotpress.ie
Web site: www.hotpress.com
Freq: Quarterly
Circ: 400000 Not Audited
MAGAZINE
Railroad

Golf Digest Ireland 983915
Editorial: Unit E7 Calmount Office Park,
Ballymount, Dublin Dublin 12
Tel: 353 01419 9604
Email: info@golfdigest.ie
Web site: www.golfdigestevents.ie
Freq: Monthly
Circ: 103000 Not Audited
Profile: Magazine covering golf news,
tips and techniques, instruction from top
players and equipment reviews. With
exclusive tuition in every issue from Tiger
Woods, Phil Mickelson and Butch
Harmon plus others.
Ad Rate: Full Page Colour €2700.00
MAGAZINE
Golf

Guts Magazine 1053750
Email: gutsdublin@gmail.com
Web site: www.thisisguts.com
Freq: Bi-Monthly
Circ: 8961 Cision Digital Reach
Editor: Roisin Agnew
MAGAZINE (ONLINE)
Art, Careers, Crime & Violence, Family
& Parenting, Health & Medicine,
Literature, Relationships

Health & Safety Review 086018
Editorial: 123 Ranelagh, Dublin 6
Tel: 353 01497 2711
Email: shane@irn.ie
Web site: www.healthandsafetyreview.ie
Freq: Monthly Not Audited
Editor: Herbert Mulligan
MAGAZINE
Health Administration

Health Manager 996407
Editorial: 78 Furze Road, Sandyford,
Dublin D18 YW2 Tel: 353 01297 4070
Email: info@hmi.ie
Web site: http://www.healthmanager.ie
Freq: Bi-Monthly
Circ: 12277 Cision Digital Reach
MAGAZINE (ONLINE)
Health Administration

Her 1052547
Editorial: Her.ie, The Distillery Building,
Fumbally Court, Fumbally Lane, Dublin 8
Tel: 353 01669 6950
Email: editorial@her.ie
Web site: http://www.her.ie/
Freq: Daily
Circ: 740515 Cision Digital Reach
MAGAZINE (ONLINE)
Women's Interests

HGV Ireland 985054
Editorial: No.1 The Grange, Drumsna,
Co. Leitrim Tel: 353 08723 80103
Email: info@hgvireland.com
Web site: http://hgvireland.com

Periodicals

Freq: Daily
Circ: 13146 Cision Digital Reach
MAGAZINE (ONLINE)
Automotive, Railroad, Shipping &
Warehousing, Supply Chain
Management (SCM), Transportation

Hospitality Ireland 983743
Editorial: Adelaide Hall, 3 Adelaide
Street, Dun Laoghaire, Co Dublin
Tel: 353 01236 5880
Email: info@hospitality-ireland.com
Web site: www.hospitalityireland.com/
Freq: Bi-Monthly
Circ: 7500 Not Audited
Editor: Emily Hourican
Profile: Magazine for the Irish food
service and on-trade drinks industry.
Ad Rate: Full Page Colour €2895.00
MAGAZINE
Bars, Clubs & Pubs, Hotels/Motels

hospitalityenews.com 985656
Editorial: 61 The Headlands, Putland
Road, Bray, Co. Wicklow
Tel: 353 12042 844
Web site: http://www.hospitalityenews.
ie/
Freq: Daily
Circ: 9466 Cision Digital Reach
Editor: Frank Corr
MAGAZINE (ONLINE)
Bars, Clubs & Pubs, Hotels/Motels

Hot Press 982104
Editorial: 13 Trinity Street, Dublin Dublin
2 Tel: 353 12411 500
Email: info@hotpress.ie
Web site: www.hotpress.com
Freq: Bi-Weekly
Circ: 18736 Not Audited
Editor: Niall Stokes
Profile: Magazine featuring popular
music, movies, current affairs, fashion,
comedy, sport, sex and popular culture.
Includes news, reviews and interviews.
Ad Rate: Full Page Mono €3300.00
Ad Rate: Full Page Colour €4500.00
MAGAZINE
Rock Music

Hotel & Catering Review 981145
Editorial: Old Stone Building, Blackhall
Green, Dublin Tel: 353 01432 2200
Email: maeve.martin@
ashvillemediagroup.com
Web site: www.hotelandcateringreview.
ie
Freq: Monthly
Circ: 6500 Not Audited
Editor: Maeve Martin
MAGAZINE
Bars, Clubs & Pubs, Food, Hotels/
Motels

Hotel & Restaurant Times
988211
Editorial: H&R House, Carton Court,
Maynooth, Co. Kildare
Tel: 353 01628 5447
Email: editorial@
hotelandrestauranttimes.ie
Web site: www.hotelandrestauranttimes.
ie/
Freq: Bi-Monthly
Circ: 3500 Not Audited
Profile: Magazine containing information
about the hotel, restaurant and hospitality
industry in Ireland. Read by hoteliers,
restaurateurs, caterers, interior designers
and architects.
MAGAZINE
Bars, Clubs & Pubs, Hotels/Motels

House and Home 984145
Editorial: 256 Media, 2nd Floor The Mill,
Greenmount Avenue, Harold's Cross,
Dublin Dublin 6W Tel: 353 14735 040

Web site: www.houseandhome.ie
Freq: Bi-Monthly
Circ: 15631 Not Audited
Editor: Anna Shelswell-White
MAGAZINE
Do-It-Yourself (DIY)

House and Home (Ireland)
1054066
Editorial: Second Floor, The Mill,
Greenmount Avenue, Dublin 6W
Freq: Bi-Monthly
Circ: 16212 Not Audited
MAGAZINE
Do-It-Yourself (DIY), Gardening

IdentiGEN 997129
Editorial: Unit 2, Trinity Enterprise
Centre, Pearse Street, Dublin
Tel: 353 01677 0221
Email: info@identigen.com
Web site: www.identigen.com
Freq: Daily
Circ: 982 Cision Digital Reach
MAGAZINE (ONLINE)
News & Current Affairs

IMAGE (Ireland) 982371
Editorial: Unit 3, Block 3 Harbour
Square, Crofton Road, Dun Laoghaire,
Co. Dublin Tel: 353 01280 8415
Email: info@image.ie
Web site: www.image.ie
Freq: Monthly
Circ: 22691 Not Audited
Editor: Rosie McMeel
MAGAZINE
Women's Interests

Image Interiors & Living 981846
Editorial: Unit 3, Block 3 Harbour
Square, Crofton Road, Dun Laoghaire,
Co Dublin Tel: 353 01271 9600
Email: info@image.ie
Web site: www.image.ie/interiors
Freq: Bi-Monthly
Circ: 17175 Not Audited
Editor: Amanda Kavanagh
Profile: Magazine covering all aspects of
homes and interiors.
Ad Rate: Full Page Colour €3400.00
MAGAZINE
Do-It-Yourself (DIY)

InBusiness Magazine 1006762
Editorial: Old Stone Building, Blackhall
Green, Blackhall Place, Dublin Dublin 7
Tel: 353 01432 2205
Email: info@chambers.ie
Web site: http://inbusinessireland.com/
Freq: Quarterly
Circ: 200000 Not Audited
MAGAZINE
Business, Corporate Responsibility

Industrial Relation News (IRN)
995734
Editorial: 123 Ranelagh, Dublin
Tel: 353 01497 2711
Web site: www.irn.ie
Freq: Weekly Not Audited
Editor: Brian Sheehan
MAGAZINE
Company News & Appointments,
Education, Health & Safety, Human
Resources, Recruiting

Inis Magazine 1054937
Editorial: 17 North Great George's
Street, Dublin D01 R2F1
Tel: 353 01872 7475
Web site: http://www.
childrensbooksireland.ie/inis
Freq: 3 Times/Year Not Audited
MAGAZINE
Teen/Young Adult

**International Journal of
Adhesion & Adhesives** 983469
Editorial: Brook Vale Plasa, East Park,
Shannon Tel: 353 61709 600
Web site: http://www.journals.elsevier.
com/international-journal-of-adhesion-
and-adhesives/
Freq: Bi-Monthly Not Audited
Profile: Journal publishing original
research on adhesion and the
development of adhesives, methods of
testing, test data, new adhesive
materials, sealants, design of bonded
joints and manufacturing technology.
Read by adhesion scientists, chemists,
civil design, mechanical engineers and
manufacturers of adhesives and
dispensing equipment.
Ad Rate: Full Page Mono €835.00
Ad Rate: Full Page Colour €1815.00
MAGAZINE
Manufacturing

International Living 1069074
Editorial: 42 Elysium House, Ballytruckle,
Waterford Tel: 353 05130 9400
Email: editor@internationalliving.com
Web site: www.internationalliving.com
Freq: Monthly Not Audited
Profile: Magazine covering investment,
lifestyle, real-estate and general
information on buying property
worldwide outside the USA and the cost
of living and healthcare. Also includes
practical information on living overseas.
Aimed at Americans looking to buy
property or start a new life outside the
United States of America.
Ad Rate: Full Page Colour €2000.00
MAGAZINE
Airline Inflight, Men's Interests,
Railroad, Retirement Savings, Travel,
Women's Interests

InTouch 981527
Editorial: INTO Head Office, Vere Foster
House, 35 Parnell Square, Dublin
Tel: 353 01804 7700
Email: editor@into.ie
Web site: www.into.ie
Freq: Bi-Monthly Not Audited
Editor: Peter Mullan
MAGAZINE
Disability, Education, Higher
Education, Preschool, Schools &
Institutions, Students

InTouch Rugby 996465
Tel: 353 02868 641633
Email: info@intouchrugby.com
Web site: www.intouchrugby.com
Freq: Daily
Circ: 32832 Cision Digital Reach
Editor: Garry Watters
MAGAZINE (ONLINE)
Rugby

Ireland Afloat 982208
Editorial: 2 Lower Glenageary Road, Dun
Laoghaire County Dublin
Tel: 353 01284 6161
Web site: www.afloat.ie
Freq: Bi-Monthly
Circ: 8000 Not Audited
Editor: David O'Brien
MAGAZINE
Boating & Yachting

Ireland of The Welcomes 982339
Editorial: Rosemount House, Dundrum
Road, Dumdrum, Dublin
Tel: 353 01240 5300
Web site: www.irelandofthewelcomes.
com
Freq: Bi-Monthly
Circ: 25511 Not Audited
Profile: Magazine celebrating the history,
culture and lifestyle of Ireland.

Ad Rate: Full Page Colour €3200.00
MAGAZINE
Travel

Irish Arts Review 984323
Editorial: 15 Harcourt Terrace, Dublin
Tel: 353 01676 6711
Email: editorial@irishartsreview.com
Web site: www.irishartsreview.com
Freq: Quarterly
Circ: 9000 Not Audited
Editor: John Mulcahy
Profile: Journal on arts in Ireland,
features painting, sculpture, architecture
and decorative arts.
Ad Rate: Full Page Colour €4000.00
MAGAZINE
Antiques/Collectibles, Art,
Photography, Visual Arts

Irish Brides 982423
Editorial: Crannagh House, 198
Rathfarnham Road, Dublin 14
Tel: 353 01884 8901
Email: info@irishbrides.ie
Web site: www.irishbrides.ie
Freq: Quarterly
Circ: 7000 Not Audited
Editor: Jillian Bolger
MAGAZINE
Weddings

Irish Broker Magazine 983042
Editorial: 136 Baldoyle Industrial Estate,
Baldoyle, Dublin Tel: 353 01839 5060
Email: info@iba.ie
Web site: www.iba.ie
Freq: Monthly
Circ: 5000 Not Audited
Profile: Magazine covering the insurance
industry including life insurance,
pensions and mortgages.
MAGAZINE
Insurance

Irish Building 987600
Editorial: Windsor Mews, Summerhill
Parade, Sandycove, Co. Dublin A96
D6Y6 Tel: 353 01442 9264
Web site: www.irishbuildingmagazine.ie
Freq: Bi-Monthly
Circ: 14690 Cision Digital Reach
MAGAZINE (ONLINE)
Building & Construction

**Irish Construction Industry
Magazine** 984122
Tel: 353 08741 84353
Web site: www.irishconstruction.com
Freq: Bi-Monthly
Circ: 3200 Not Audited
Profile: Magazine covering all aspects of
the Irish construction industry. Aimed at
construction industry professionals.
Ad Rate: Full Page Colour €900.00
MAGAZINE
Building & Construction

Irish Country Magazine 986965
Editorial: Irish Farm Centre, Bluebell,
Dublin 12 Tel: 353 14199 500
Email: info@irishcountrymagazine.ie
Web site: http://www.
irishcountrymagazine.ie
Freq: Monthly
Circ: 24309 Not Audited
Editor: Jennifer Stevens
Profile: Magazine covering lifestyle. The
IRISH COUNTRY MAGAZINE shares the
latest news on interior design and
fashion.
MAGAZINE
Women's Interests

Irish Farmers Monthly 985106
Tel: 353 01709 600
Email: info@ifpmedia.com
Web site: www.irishfarmersmonthly.com

Freq: Monthly
Circ: 23400 Not Audited
Profile: Magazine covering news, business advice and research within the agricultural industry.
Ad Rate: Full Page Colour €3100.00
MAGAZINE
Animal Farming

The Irish Field   982038
Editorial: Irish Farm Centre, Bluebell, Dublin 12 **Tel:** 353 01405 1100
Email: editorial@theirishfield.ie
Web site: www.theirishfield.ie
Freq: Weekly
Circ: 50000 Not Audited
Profile: Newspaper focusing on Irish and international horse racing, breeding and sport horses.
Ad Rate: Full Page Colour €5650.00
MAGAZINE
Equestrian Sports, Horse Racing

Irish Film and Television Network   1069612
Editorial: 3rd Floor, 17-19 Lower Hatch Street, Dublin **Tel:** 353 01905 3595
Email: news@iftn.ie
Web site: www.iftn.ie
Freq: Daily
Circ: 63993 Cision Digital Reach
MAGAZINE (ONLINE)
Broadcasting

Irish Food Magazine   987181
Editorial: 31 Deansgrange Road, Blackrock, Dublin **Tel:** 353 12893 305
Web site: www.irishfoodmagazine.com
Freq: Monthly Not Audited
Editor: Oonagh O'Mahony
MAGAZINE
Food

The Irish Garden   981967
Editorial: Unit 55 Spruce Avenue, Stillorgan Industrial Estate, Sandyford, Dublin A94 N125 **Tel:** 353 01294 7777
Email: info@garden.ie
Web site: www.garden.ie
Freq: Monthly
Circ: 8094 Not Audited
Editor: Gerry Daly
Profile: Magazine focusing on gardening. Also contains articles on lifestyle and issues with particular relevance to Ireland.
Ad Rate: Full Page Colour €2890.00
MAGAZINE
Gardening

Irish Golfer Magazine   1063146
Editorial: Golf House, Buckley's Lane, Main Sreet Leixlip, Co. Kildare
Tel: 353 01503 6090
Email: info@matchplaymedia.ie
Web site: www.irishgolfer.ie
Freq: Monthly
Circ: 11599 Not Audited
MAGAZINE
Golf

Irish Greyhound Review   982034
Editorial: P.O.Box 7993, Dun Laoghaire County Dublin **Tel:** 353 12804 481
Email: walshmgt@eircom.net
Freq: Annual
Circ: 12000 Not Audited
Editor: Michael Fortune
MAGAZINE
Games, Competitions & Events

Irish Journal of Medical Science   988834
Web site: link.springer.com/journal/11845
Freq: Quarterly Not Audited

Profile: Official journal of the Royal Academy of Medicine in Ireland. Covers medical and allied topics. Aimed at doctors, consultants and students world-wide.
Ad Rate: Full Page Colour €1270.00
MAGAZINE
Biotechnology, Medical Technology, Medicine, Science

Irish Marketing Journal   984233
Editorial: 45 Upper Mount Street, Dublin
Tel: 353 01661 1660
Email: info@adworld.ie
Web site: www.irishmarketingjournal.ie
Freq: Monthly
Circ: 6000 Not Audited
Profile: Magazine covering marketing, media and advertising affairs in Ireland. Aimed at marketing and managing directors of Ireland's top companies, advertising agency personnel, media companies, state bodies and other marketing and advertising sector workers.
Ad Rate: Full Page Colour €3120.00
MAGAZINE
Advertising Industry, Marketing

The Irish Medical Journal
    988835
Tel: 353 01676 7273
Web site: www.imj.ie/
Freq: Monthly Not Audited
Editor: Dr John Murphy
Profile: Journal of the Irish Medical Association of Ireland that aims to educate medical students and postgraduates through scientific research, review articles and updates on contemporary clinical practices while providing an ongoing forum for medical debate.
MAGAZINE
Healthcare Industry, Medicine, Nursing/Nurses

Irish Medical Times   981188
Editorial: Unit 2, First Floor, Merchants Hall, 25 Merchants Quay, Dublin 8
Tel: 353 01817 6300
Email: editor@imt.ie
Web site: www.imt.ie
Freq: Weekly
Circ: 6750 Not Audited
Editor: Dara Gantly
Profile: Journal containing news and information on developments in medicine. Aimed at doctors.Pictures only accepted in digital format as high resolution JPEGs. Regular features: Analysis; Clinical; Interview; Lifestyle; News; Opinion; Special Report
Ad Rate: Full Page Colour €2250.00
MAGAZINE
Medicine

Irish Pharmacist   986467
Editorial: 7 Upper Leeson Street, Dublin 4 **Tel:** 353 01441 0024
Web site: www.greencrosspublishing.ie/publication.aspx?contentid=4
Freq: Monthly
Circ: 2089 Not Audited
Editor: Pat Kelly
Profile: Magazine with news and comment plus clinical and business articles relating to both community and hospital pharmacy in Ireland and worldwide. Aimed at community and hospital pharmacists.
MAGAZINE
Pharmaceuticals

Irish Pharmacy News   998174
Tel: 353 01669 0562
Email: editorial@ipnirishpharmacynews.ie
Web site: www.pharmacynewsireland.com/index.html

Freq: Monthly Not Audited
MAGAZINE
Healthcare Industry, Pharmaceuticals

Irish Pharmacy Retailer   1008767
Editorial: Unit 7, Greenhills Business Park, Greenhills Road, Dublin 12
Tel: 353 01462 6429
Email: news@irishpharmacyretailer.com
Web site: www.irishpharmacyretailer.com
Freq: Bi-Monthly
Circ: 3000 Not Audited
Editor: Lucy Earley
MAGAZINE
Pharmaceuticals

Irish Printer   984272
Editorial: Old Stone Building, Blackhall Green, Blackhall Place, Dublin
Tel: 353 01432 2200
Email: maeve.martin@ashvillemediagroup.com
Web site: www.irishprinter.ie
Freq: Bi-Monthly
Circ: 1472 Not Audited
Editor: Maeve Martin
Profile: Magazine covering the printing industry including features on technology, management, equipment, companies and events, market sector reports, trends in industry, business law and finance. Aimed at the printing and graphic arts industry.
Ad Rate: Full Page Colour €2120.00
MAGAZINE
Publishing

Irish Tatler   982373
Editorial: Rosemount House, Dundrum Road, Dundrum, Dublin
Tel: 353 01240 5300
Web site: http://www.irishtatler.com/
Freq: Monthly
Circ: 21056 Not Audited
Editor: Shauna O'Halloran
Profile: Glossy women's magazine focussing on style, beauty, social issues, relationships, interiors, food and travel.
Ad Rate: Full Page Colour €3060.00
MAGAZINE
Women's Interests

Irish Tatler Man   985704
Editorial: Rosemount House, Dundrum Road, Dundrum, Dublin
Tel: 353 01240 5300
Email: info@harmonia.ie
Web site: www.harmonia.ie
Freq: Quarterly
Circ: 5215 Not Audited
Editor: Alexander Fitzgerald
Profile: The Irish Tatler Man is a quarterly Irish men's lifestyle and health magazine owned by Harmonia, Ltd. It provides the latest information covering style, fashion, grooming, health and fitness, gadgets, travel, celebrity interviews and lifestyle. It also features sports, motors, relationship issues food & drink, events calender guide, finance, culture, music, film and book reviews. First published in 2010.
Ad Rate: Full Page Colour €3060.00
MAGAZINE
Men's Interests

Irish Travel Trade News   984187
Editorial: C4 Nutgrove Office Park, Nutgrove Avenue, Rathfarnham, Dublin 14 **Tel:** 353 35301 2164222
Email: michael.flood@advantagegroup.com
Web site: www.irishtraveltradenews.com
Freq: Bi-Monthly
Circ: 2200 Not Audited
Editor: Michael Flood
Profile: Magazine focusing on travel and tourism. Aimed at travel professionals throughout Ireland, Europe and the USA.
Ad Rate: Full Page Mono €1640.00

Ad Rate: Full Page Colour €2390.00
MAGAZINE
Travel

Irish Wedding Diary   1063141
Editorial: Rear 177 Rathgar Road, Rathmines Park, Rathmines, Dublin 6
Tel: 353 01498 3211
Email: info@irishweddingdiary.ie
Web site: www.irishweddingdiary.ie
Freq: Quarterly
Circ: 5515 Not Audited
Editor: Paul McCormack
Profile: Magazine covering all aspects of weddings including, fashion, beauty, honeymoons, venues, car hire, photography and flowers. Aimed at brides and grooms to be.
Ad Rate: Full Page Colour €1800.00
MAGAZINE
Weddings

irishhealth.com   986917
Editorial: 25 Adelaide Street, Dun Laoghaire, Co. Dublin
Email: ihadmin@medmedia.ie
Web site: www.irishhealth.com
Freq: Daily
Circ: 51261 Cision Digital Reach
Editor: Niall Hunter
MAGAZINE (ONLINE)
Alternative Medicine, Health & Medicine

The Journal of Music   985283
Editorial: The Journal of Music, An Spidéal, Conamara, Co. Galway
Tel: 353 08682 41309
Email: editor@journalofmusic.com
Web site: www.journalofmusic.com
Freq: Daily
Circ: 31252 Cision Digital Reach
Editor: Benedict Schlepper-Connolly
MAGAZINE (ONLINE)
Classical/Choral/Band Music, Country, Folk, Bluegrass, Jazz & Blues, Pop Music

Licensing World   983199
Editorial: Old Stone Building, Blackhall Green, Dublin **Tel:** 353 01432 2200
Email: maeve.martin@ashvillemediagroup.com
Web site: www.licensingworld.ie
Freq: Quarterly Not Audited
Editor: Maeve Martin
Profile: Magazine for the licensed trade. Aimed at managers of pubs, drinks companies, off licences, nightclubs and restaurants.
Ad Rate: Full Page Colour €2750.00
MAGAZINE
Bars, Clubs & Pubs

Life and Fitness Magazine
    1105195
Editorial: Curraghgraigue, Borrisoleigh, Co. Tipperary **Tel:** 353 05045 1945
Email: info@lifeandfitnessmag.ie
Web site: www.lifeandfitnessmag.ie
Freq: Daily
Circ: 11004 Cision Digital Reach
Editor: Derry O'Donnell
MAGAZINE (ONLINE)
Fitness & Exercise, Regional General Interest

The Market (Irish)   1008764
Editorial: The Plaza, East Point Business Park, Dublin **Tel:** 353 01727 2000
Email: the.market@enterprise-ireland.com
Web site: www.the-market.ie
Freq: Quarterly
Circ: 5500 Not Audited
Editor: Mary Sweetman
MAGAZINE
Business, Corporate Responsibility

Periodicals

Marketing.ie
983416
Editorial: 1 Albert Park, Sandycove, Dublin Tel: 353 12807 735
Email: cullen@marketing.ie
Web site: www.marketing.ie
Freq: Bi-Monthly
Circ: 3000 Not Audited
Editor: Michael Cullen
MAGAZINE
Advertising Industry, Branding, Broadcasting, Graphic Design, Marketing, Media & Communications, Photography, Publishing

Maternity
1054263
Editorial: Old Stone Building, Blackhall Green, Dublin 7 Tel: 353 01432 2200
Email: info@ashville.com
Web site: www.ashville.com
Freq: Annual
Circ: 65000 Not Audited
Editor: Penny Gray
MAGAZINE
Family & Parenting

Maternity & Infant
983910
Editorial: Old Stone Building, Blackhall Green, Dublin Tel: 353 01432 2200
Email: editorial@infant.ie
Web site: www.infant.ie
Freq: Bi-Monthly
Circ: 15025 Not Audited
Editor: Penny Gray
Profile: Magazine covering advice, expert opinion, parenting, questions and answers, fashion, competitions and tips. Aimed at Irish mums-to-be and parents of pre-school and school age children. Previous title: Infant
Ad Rate: Full Page Colour €3400.00
MAGAZINE
Family & Parenting

Medical Independent
986464
Editorial: 7 Upper Leeson Street, Dublin 4 Tel: 353 01441 0024
Web site: www.medicalindependent.ie
Freq: Bi-Monthly
Circ: 6315 Not Audited
MAGAZINE
Medicine

Menswear in Ireland
1052614
Editorial: Castle House, Main Street, Rathfarnham, Dublin
Tel: 353 35301 2836782
Email: mail@futuramagazine.ie
Web site: www.futuramagazine.ie/mw.html
Freq: Monthly
Circ: 4300 Not Audited
Editor: Alexander Fitzgerald
Profile: Menswear in Ireland was launched in 1997. Published five times annually in January, February, July, August, October/November and December. Covers national and international fashion news, trend analysis and collection reports, interviews, the latest from international trade shows, and current issues in menswear retailing.
Ad Rate: Full Page Colour €2195.00
MAGAZINE
Fashion

Motley Magazine
999510
Editorial: 54 College Road, Cork
Tel: 353 02149 03000
Email: editor@motley.ie
Web site: www.motley.ie
Freq: Monthly
Circ: 2500 Not Audited
MAGAZINE
Student Lifestyle

The Movie Bit
996797
Tel: 353 08776 19791
Email: news@themoviebit.com

Web site: www.themoviebit.com
Freq: Daily
Circ: 29306 Cision Digital Reach
MAGAZINE (ONLINE)
Entertainment, Movies & Video

Movies.ie
996872
Email: info@movies.ie
Web site: www.movies.ie
Freq: Daily
Circ: 24602 Cision Digital Reach
Editor: Vincent Donnelly
MAGAZINE (ONLINE)
Entertainment, Local Entertainment Guides, Movies & Video

MyHome.ie
1103017
Editorial: The Irish Times Building, 24-28 Tara Street, Dublin Tel: 353 01827 9400
Email: enquiries@myhome.ie
Web site: http://www.myhome.ie/
Freq: Daily
Circ: 2014785 Cision Digital Reach
Editor: James Rogers
MAGAZINE (ONLINE)
Real Estate

Naturally Good Health
999509
Editorial: Dept AA1571, PO BOX 4214, Dublin Tel: 353 01279 810080
Email: info@targetpublishing.com
Web site: www.naturallygoodhealth.ie
Freq: Quarterly
Circ: 100000 Not Audited
Editor: Rachel Symonds
MAGAZINE
Alternative Medicine, Nutrition

Nursing in General Practice
996837
Editorial: 7 Adelaide Court, Adelaide Road, Dublin 2 Tel: 353 01418 9799
Web site: www.greencrosspublishing.ie/publication.aspx?contentid=5
Freq: Bi-Monthly
Circ: 6104 Not Audited
MAGAZINE
Nursing/Nurses

Oh Baby!
999664
Tel: 353 02122 90204
Email: info@ohbaby.ie
Web site: www.ohbaby.ie
Freq: Quarterly
Circ: 20000 Not Audited
MAGAZINE
Family & Parenting

Oncology News
986723
Tel: 353 02882 897023
Email: patricia@oncologynews.biz
Web site: http://www.oncologynews.biz/index.html
Freq: Bi-Monthly Not Audited
Editor: Denys Wheatley
Profile: Magazine providing journal reviews of oncology related publications. Each review is a doctor's own summary of an original paper. It features lead articles on topical issues, interviews with leading figures, book reviews of the latest oncology related books, and news from conferences and events in the field. Aimed at cancer care professionals.
MAGAZINE
Oncology

Passive House Plus (Irish Edition)
984324
Editorial: Blackrock, PO Box 9688, Co. Dublin Tel: 353 01210 7513
Email: info@passivehouseplus.ie
Web site: passivehouseplus.ie
Freq: Bi-Monthly
Circ: 6468 Not Audited
Editor: Jeff Colley

Profile: Magazine focused on building and upgrading to the world's leading low energy standard - passive house and promotes the viability of sustainable construction and development in the UK and Ireland. Covers energy efficiency, renewable energy, indoor air quality, water usage and the environmental impact of materials.
MAGAZINE
Building & Construction, Sustainable Development

PetrolWorld
998746
Email: editor@petrolworld.com
Web site: www.petrolworld.com
Freq: Quarterly Not Audited
Editor: Derek Owens
MAGAZINE
Oil

The Phoenix (Ireland)
998628
Editorial: 44 Lower Baggot Street, Dublin Tel: 353 16611 062
Email: goldhawk@thephoenix.ie
Web site: www.thephoenix.ie
Freq: Bi-Weekly
Circ: 13273 Not Audited
Editor: Paddy Prendiville
MAGAZINE
International News, Northern Ireland

Plan Magazine
1005567
Tel: 353 01831 3448
Email: info@planonline.ie
Web site: http://planonline.ie/
Freq: Bi-Monthly
Circ: 2800 Not Audited
MAGAZINE
Architecture & Design, Building & Construction, Commercial Real Estate, Finance, Urban Planning & Development

Poetry Ireland Review
988649
Tel: 353 01678 9815
Email: publications@poetryireland.ie
Web site: poetryireland.ie/publications/poetry-review.html
Freq: 3 Times/Year
Circ: 1200 Not Audited
Profile: Magazine covering the best of Irish and International poetry and translation. Interviews with established and emerging poets. Essays and features. Reviews new collections and anthologies. This outlet can be reached via mail at: 32 Kildare St Dublin, Ireland, ZIP Code: 2. Aimed at anyone with an interest in poetry.
MAGAZINE
Literature

Pregnancy & Parenting
982408
Editorial: 22 Mariner's Point, Greenhills Road, Wicklow Town, Co Wicklow
Tel: 353 04043 2563
Email: info@pregnancyandparentingmagazine.ie
Web site: n/a
Freq: Quarterly
Circ: 15000 Not Audited
Editor: Suzanne Gallagher
MAGAZINE
Family & Parenting

RapidMicroBiology.com
986920
Editorial: Derryduff Enterprise Park, Rosscarbery, Co. Cork
Tel: 353 23883 1884
Email: info@rapidmicrobiology.com
Web site: rapidmicrobiology.com
Freq: Daily
Circ: 10358 Cision Digital Reach
Editor: Sue Brockman
MAGAZINE (ONLINE)
Science

RDS Test
1055310
Editorial: 4th Floor, Bishops Square, Redmonds Hill, Dublin 2
Email: test@test.com
Freq: Monthly
MAGAZINE
News & Current Affairs

Renovate Your House and Home
984236
Editorial: 3rd Floor, New Market House, New Market Square, Dublin
Tel: 353 01473 5040
Email: editor@houseandhome.ie
Web site: www.houseandhome.ie
Freq: Quarterly
Circ: 15000 Not Audited
Profile: Magazine covering all aspects of renovating your home and features on real home renovations.
Ad Rate: Full Page Colour €2850.00
MAGAZINE
Do-It-Yourself (DIY)

Retail News
981301
Editorial: 14 Upper Fitzwilliam Street, Dublin Tel: 353 01678 5165
Email: info@retailnews.ie
Web site: www.retailnews.ie
Freq: Monthly
Circ: 6580 Not Audited
Editor: John Walshe
Profile: Magazine covering the grocery sector.
Ad Rate: Full Page Colour €3125.00
MAGAZINE
Retail Management

RSVP
985544
Editorial: Morrison House, Morrison Island, Cork Tel: 353 02149 49701
Email: info@rsvpmagazine.ie
Web site: www.rsvpmagazine.ie
Freq: Monthly
Circ: 28415 Not Audited
Editor: Paula Lenihan
Profile: Magazine covering celebrity and showbiz news. It features fashion, beauty, travel and health articles.
MAGAZINE
Celebrities

RTÉ Guide
983413
Editorial: Donnybrook, Dublin
Tel: 353 01208 3111
Email: rteguide@rte.ie
Web site: http://www.rte.ie/rteguide/
Freq: Weekly
Circ: 48089 Not Audited
Editor: Catherine Lee
MAGAZINE
Bars, Clubs & Pubs, Comedy, Entertainment, Fashion, Lifestyle, Local Entertainment Guides, Men's Interests, Movies & Video, Regional General Interest, Women's Interests

RugbyRep
1105199
Tel: 353 02868 641633
Email: gary@rugbyrep.com
Web site: rugbyrep.com
Freq: Daily
Circ: 12683 Cision Digital Reach
Editor: Garry Watters
MAGAZINE (ONLINE)
Rugby

Salon Magazine
986735
Editorial: Unit 7, Greenhills Business Park, Greenhills Road, Dublin 12
Tel: 353 01414 9475
Email: chris@exigome.com
Web site: www.salonmagazine.ie/
Freq: Bi-Monthly
Circ: 5000 Not Audited
Editor: Lucy Earley
MAGAZINE
Cosmetics, Hair

SeniorTimes 1075618
Editorial: Unit 1, 15 Oxford Lane,
Ranelagh, Dublin Tel: 353 01496 9028
Email: info@slp.ie
Web site: www.seniortimes.ie
Freq: Bi-Monthly
Circ: 20000 Not Audited
MAGAZINE
Retirement Savings

Shelf Life 983821
Editorial: 55 Spruce Avenue, Stillorgan
Industrial Estate, Sandyford, Dublin
Tel: 353 01294 7777
Email: info@mediateam.ie
Web site: www.shelflife.ie
Freq: Monthly
Circ: 7535 Not Audited
Editor: Gillian Hamill
MAGAZINE
Alcohol & Spirits, Food, Retail
Management

SiliconRepublic.com 984857
Editorial: Digital Exchange, Crane Street,
The Digital Hub, Dublin
Tel: 353 01625 1444
Email: info@siliconrepublic.com
Web site: www.siliconrepublic.com
Freq: Daily
Circ: 704756 Cision Digital Reach
Editor: John Kennedy
MAGAZINE (ONLINE)
Audio Video Trade, Auto Aftermarket,
Cameras, Computers, Consumer
Electronics, Data Management,
Electronics, Government Technology,
Industry, Internet

The Skipper 1006436
Tel: 353 08682 39608
Email: editorial@maramedia.ie
Web site: www.maramedia.ie/the-
skipper-home
Freq: Monthly
Circ: 5000 Not Audited
Editor: Niall Duffy
Profile: Newspaper representing the
commercial fishing, fish processing and
aquaculture industries throughout
Ireland. Aimed at commercial fishing and
aquaculture industry personnel, marine
academics and students.
Ad Rate: Full Page Mono €1200.00
Ad Rate: Full Page Colour €1450.00
MAGAZINE
Animal Farming, Marine & Boat Trade

Social & Personal 984330
Editorial: 19 Nassau Street, Dublin
Dublin 2 Tel: 353 01633 3993
Email: info@socialandpersonal.ie
Web site: www.socialandpersonal.ie
Freq: Monthly
Circ: 22737 Not Audited
Editor: Alexandra McKeever
Profile: Magazine focusing on general
lifestyle issues. Includes interviews with
celebrities and features on home
decoration, fashion, parties and people.
Aimed at women aged 24 years old and
above.
Ad Rate: Full Page Colour €2500.00
MAGAZINE
Fashion, Men's Interests, Women's
Interests

Social & Personal Weddings
984425
Editorial: 19 Nassau Street, Dublin
Dublin 2 Tel: 353 01633 3993
Email: weddings@socialandpersonal.ie
Web site: www.
socialandpersonalweddings.ie
Freq: Quarterly
Circ: 4886 Not Audited
Editor: Alexandra McKeever

Profile: Magazine covering all aspects of
weddings including women's and men's
fashion, venues and honeymoons.
Ad Rate: Full Page Colour €2100.00
MAGAZINE
Weddings

STELLAR Magazine 984825
Editorial: 5th Floor, Haymarket House,
Smithfield, Dublin Tel: 353 01687 7444
Email: info@stellar.ie
Web site: www.stellar.ie
Freq: Monthly
Circ: 16509 Not Audited
Editor: Kirstie McDermott
MAGAZINE
Beauty & Grooming, Cosmetics,
Fashion, Hair, Women's Interests

Storyful.com 985650
Editorial: Ferry House, 48 Lower Mount
Street, Dublin Tel: 353 15370 300
Email: editor@storyful.com
Web site: www.storyful.com
Freq: Daily
Circ: 101582 Cision Digital Reach
MAGAZINE (ONLINE)
Banking, Business, National News,
Politics, Small and Medium Business

Taipei Show Daily 1068962
Editorial: 28 Llewellyn Way,
Rathfarnham, Dublin
Tel: 353 08728 44374
Email: info@bikeshowdaily.com
Web site: http://www.taipeishowdaily.
com/index.php
Freq: Annual
Circ: 18000 Not Audited
MAGAZINE
Bicycles, Fitness & Exercise

TechCentral.ie 984637
Editorial: Media House, South County
Business Park, Leopardstown, Dublin
Tel: 353 01294 7777
Email: info@mediateam.ie
Web site: http://www.techcentral.ie/
Freq: Daily
Circ: 56652 Cision Digital Reach
MAGAZINE (ONLINE)
Auto Aftermarket, Computers, Data
Management, Electronics,
Government Technology, Industry,
Internet, Mobile Communications,
Security & Security Systems, Software

TechPro 981702
Editorial: 55 Spruce Avenue, Stillorgan
Industrial Estate, Sandyford, Dublin A94
N125 Tel: 353 01294 7777
Email: info@mediateam.ie
Web site: http://www.techcentral.ie/
category/pro/
Freq: Monthly
Circ: 7000 Not Audited
Profile: Magazine with information about
IT products, news, technology,
networking and trends. Aiming to provide
its readership with Irish-specific trade
and product information, the publication
contains industry and company
newsbriefs covering developments,
contracts, deals, strategies, and events.
Ad Rate: Full Page Colour €4500.00
MAGAZINE
Computers

That Health Site 997014
Editorial: Barrack Street, Bantry, Cork
Tel: 353 27556 58
Email: home@starbrydge.com
Web site: http://thathealthsite.com/
Freq: Daily
Circ: 10618 Cision Digital Reach
MAGAZINE (ONLINE)
Alternative Medicine, Health &
Medicine, Nutrition, Obstetrics &
Gynecology (OB/GYN), Sexual Health

thejournal.ie 987466
Editorial: 4th floor, Golden Lane, Latin
Hall, Dublin 8
Email: news@thejournal.ie
Web site: http://www.thejournal.ie/
Freq: Daily
Circ: 1896120 Cision Digital Reach
Editor: Susan Daly
MAGAZINE (ONLINE)
Consumer Affairs, Crime & Violence,
Defense & National Security, Energy &
Environment, Ethical/Moral Issues,
International News, Law, National
News, News & Current Affairs,
Northern Ireland

Totally Dublin 985398
Editorial: 60 Merrion Square, Dublin
Tel: 353 01687 0695
Email: editor@totallydublin.ie
Web site: totallydublin.ie
Freq: Monthly
Circ: 50000 Not Audited
MAGAZINE
Bars, Clubs & Pubs, Classical/Choral/
Band Music, Comedy, Country, Folk,
Bluegrass, Dance Music,
Entertainment, Jazz & Blues, Lifestyle,
Local Entertainment Guides, Men's
Interests

Travel Extra 983922
Tel: 353 01295 7418
Email: info@travelextra.ie
Web site: www.travelextra.ie
Freq: Monthly
Circ: 3150 Not Audited
Editor: Eoghan Corry
Profile: Magazine focusing on travel,
holidays and entertainment in Ireland.
Ad Rate: Full Page Colour €2750.00
MAGAZINE
Travel

Trinity News 981780
Editorial: Dublin University Publications,
House 6, Trinity College, Dublin 2
Tel: 353 18962 335
Email: editor@trinitynews.ie
Web site: www.trinitynews.ie
Freq: Bi-Monthly Not Audited
Profile: Independent student newspaper
of Trinity College, Dublin.
MAGAZINE
Student Lifestyle

TV NOW! 982357
Editorial: TVNow magazine, 5th Floor
Haymarket House, Smithfield, Dublin
Email: info@tvnowmagazine.ie
Web site: n/a
Freq: Weekly
Circ: 23008 Not Audited
Editor: Deborah Mcgee
Profile: TV listings magazine containing
features on soaps, celebrities, fashion,
beauty and health.
Ad Rate: Full Page Colour €3650.00
MAGAZINE
Broadcasting, Entertainment, Local
Entertainment Guides

U Magazine 982380
Editorial: Rosemount House, Dundrum
Road, Dundrum, Dublin
Tel: 353 01240 5300
Email: umagazine@harmonia.ie
Web site: www.umagazine.ie
Freq: Bi-Weekly
Circ: 24134 Not Audited
Editor: Aisling O'Toole
MAGAZINE
Women's Interests

Upstairs Downstairs 985319
Editorial: 45 Maunsells Park, Taylors Hill,
Galway Tel: 353 91588 359
Email: info@upstairsdownstairsltd.com

Web site: www.
upstairsdownstairsonline.com
Freq: Bi-Monthly Not Audited
Editor: Ann Leyden
Profile: Magazine containing articles on
the home, gardening, products, services
and ideas.
Ad Rate: Full Page Colour €1350.00
MAGAZINE
Architecture & Design, Do-It-Yourself
(DIY), Gardening, Property
Management & Maintenance

Veterinary Ireland Journal
987184
Editorial: 31 Deansgrange Road,
Blackrock, Co. Dublin
Tel: 353 01289 3305
Web site: http://www.
veterinaryirelandjournal.com/
Freq: Monthly
Circ: 2300 Not Audited
Editor: Miriam Atkins
Profile: Journal focusing on all aspects
of veterinary science with a special
emphasis on the Irish veterinary
profession. Read by veterinary surgeons.
Ad Rate: Full Page Colour €2100.00
MAGAZINE
Veterinary Medicine

Village 1076164
Editorial: 6 Ormond Quay Upper, Dublin
Tel: 353 01873 5824
Email: editor@villagemagazine.ie
Web site: www.villagemagazine.ie
Freq: Monthly
Circ: 8700 Not Audited
Editor: Michael Smith
Profile: Local news magazine covering
health, beauty, fashion, motoring, travel,
lifestyle, entertainment, restaurants and
property.
Ad Rate: Full Page Colour €550.00
MAGAZINE
Politics

VIP Magazine 982382
Editorial: Haymarket House, Smithfield
Square, Dublin Tel: 353 01687 7444
Email: info@vipmagazine.ie
Web site: http://vipmagazine.ie/
Freq: Monthly
Circ: 24435 Not Audited
Profile: Magazine containing news,
interviews and photo sessions with Irish
celebrities. Includes coverage of
weddings, births and celebrations.
Ad Rate: Full Page Colour €4300.00
MAGAZINE
Celebrities

WellnessCentral 1076748
Editorial: NDRC, 8 Crane St, Dublin
Tel: 353 08575 58203
Email: darryl@wellnesscentral.co.uk
Web site: http://www.wellnesscentral.co.
uk/
Freq: Daily
Circ: 11308 Cision Digital Reach
MAGAZINE (ONLINE)
Beauty & Grooming, Cooking &
Baking, Cosmetics, Fitness &
Exercise, Food, Grocery Stores, Hair,
Nutrition, Organic Food, Restaurant
Reviews

Woman's Way 982440
Editorial: Rosemount House, Dundrum
Road, Dundrum, Dublin
Tel: 353 01240 5300
Email: womansway@gmail.com
Web site: http://womansway.ie/
Freq: Weekly
Circ: 20711 Not Audited
Editor: Áine Toner
Profile: Magazine featuring articles on
fashion, cookery, beauty, real life, short
stories, travel, celebrity interviews, soaps

and TV, interiors, gardening, health, special features and interviews.
Ad Rate: Full Page Colour €3600.00
MAGAZINE
Women's Interests

Women Mean Business   983455
Editorial: 2nd Floor, Pardigm House, Dundrum Office Park, Dublin Dublin 14
Tel: 353 35312 964025
Email: ed@womenmeanbusiness.com
Web site: www.womenmeanbusiness.com

Freq: Daily
Circ: 14978 Cision Digital Reach
MAGAZINE (ONLINE)
Business

World of Irish Nursing and Midwifery   986912
Editorial: 17 Adelaide Street, Dun Laoghaire Co. Dublin
Tel: 353 01280 3967
Email: nursing@medmedia.ie

Web site: http://www.medmedia.ie/publications/titles.html
Freq: Monthly
Circ: 40000 Not Audited
MAGAZINE
Nursing/Nurses, Obstetrics & Gynecology (OB/GYN)

Xposé   987108
Editorial: First Floor, Zoe House, Church Road, Greystones, County Wicklow
Tel: 353 01255 7566

Email: editor@xposemag.ie
Web site: www.zahramediagroup.com
Freq: Monthly
Circ: 16016 Not Audited
Profile: Magazine covering showbiz and celebrity news. It features the latest catwalk looks, style tips from industry experts and how to recreate celebrity looks on a budget.
MAGAZINE
Beauty & Grooming, Celebrities, Cosmetics, Fashion, Hair, Women's Interests

Broadcast

Radio Networks & Stations

98FM
South Block, The Malt House, Grand Canal
Quay, Dublin Dublin 2 **Tel:** 353 14398 800
Email: news@98fm.com
Web site: www.98fm.ie

Clare FM
Abbeyfield Centre, Francis Street, County
Clare **Tel:** 353 06568 28888
Email: info@clarefm.ie
Web site: www.clarefm.ie

Cork's 96FM
Broadcasting House, St Patrick's Place,
Cork T23 E183 **Tel:** 353 02145 51596
Email: news@96fm.ie
Web site: www.96fm.ie

Dublin South FM
5th Floor, Dundrum Town Centre, Sandyford
Road, Dublin Dublin 16 **Tel:** 353 01296 0939
Email: info@dublinsouthfm.ie
Web site: www.dublinsouthfm.ie

East Coast FM
Radio Centre, Killarney road, Bray, Co.
Wicklow **Tel:** 353 12724 700
Email: mail@eastcoast.fm
Web site: www.eastcoast.fm

FM104
Macken House, Mayor Street Upper, North
Wall, Dublin **Tel:** 353 16797 104
Email: info@fm104.ie
Web site: www.fm104.ie

Galway Bay FM
Sandy Road, Galway, Ireland
Tel: 353 09177 0000
Email: news@galwaybayfm.ie
Web site: www.galwaybayfm.ie

Highland Radio
Pine Hill, Letterkenny, Co. Donegal
Tel: 353 07912 5000
Email: enquiries@highlandradio.com
Web site: www.highlandradio.com

KCLR 96fm
Broadcast Centre, Leggettsrath Business
Park, Carlow Road, Kilkenny
Tel: 353 18909 09696
Email: news@kclr96fm.com
Web site: www.kclr96fm.com

Kfm
Kfm Broadcast Centre, M7 Business Park,
Newhall, Naas, Co. Kildare
Tel: 353 04589 8999
Email: news@kfmradio.com
Web site: www.kfmradio.com

Limerick's Live 95FM
Unit 5-6 Richmond Court, Dock Road,
Limerick **Tel:** 353 06146 1900
Email: news@live95fm.ie
Web site: www.live95fm.ie

LMFM Radio
Rathmullan Road, Drogheda, Co. Louth PO
Box 958 **Tel:** 353 41983 2000
Email: info@lmfm.ie
Web site: www.lmfm.ie

Midlands 103
Tindle House, Axis Business Park,
Tullamore, Co. Offaly **Tel:** 353 05793 51333
Email: info@midlandsradio.fm
Web site: http://www.midlands103.com/

MidWest Radio
Clare street, Ballyhaunis, Co. Mayo
Tel: 353 81830 0055
Email: studio@midwestradio.ie
Web site: http://www.midwestradio.ie

Newstalk
5th Floor, Marconi House, Digges Lane,
Dublin D02 TD60 **Tel:** 353 01644 5100
Email: newsroom@newstalk.ie
Web site: http://www.newstalk.com

Radio Dublino
Tel: 353 01867 1190
Email: info@radiodublino.com
Web site: www.radiodublino.com

Radio Kerry
Maine Street, Tralee, Co. Kerry
Tel: 353 66719 3666
Email: info@radiokerry.ie
Web site: www.radiokerry.ie

Red FM
University Technological Centre, Curraheen
Rd, Bishopstown, Cork
Tel: 353 02148 65500
Email: news@redfm.ie
Web site: www.redfm.ie

RTÉ 2FM
Donnybrook, Dublin Dublin 4
Tel: 353 01208 3111
Email: newsdesk@rte.ie
Web site: www.rte.ie/2fm

RTÉ Lyric FM
Cornmarket Square, Limerick
Tel: 353 61207 300
Email: lyric@rte.ie
Web site: www.rte.ie/lyricfm

RTÉ Radio One
Donnybrook, Dublin Dublin 4
Tel: 353 12083 111
Email: info@rte.ie
Web site: http://www.rte.ie/radio1/
Editor: Shane Mcelhatton

Shannonside FM
Unit 1E, Master Tech Business Park, Athlone
Road, Longford **Tel:** 353 04333 49317
Email: news@shannonside.ie
Web site: www.shannonside.ie

South East Radio
South East Radio, Custom House Quay,
Wexford **Tel:** 353 53914 5200
Email: info@southeastradio.ie
Web site: www.southeastradio.ie

SPIN 1038
Level 3 South Block, The Malt House, Grand
Canal Quay, Dublin 2 **Tel:** 353 16564 600
Email: info@spin1038.com
Web site: www.spin1038.com

Spirit Radio
Radio Centre, Kilarney Road, Bray, Co.
Wicklow **Tel:** 353 12724 760
Email: info@spiritradio.ie
Web site: www.spiritradio.ie

Sunshine 106.8 FM
Sunshine 106.8, 2nd Floor, Castleforbes
House, Dublin D01 A8N0
Tel: 353 01865 2140
Email: mail@sunshineradio.ie
Web site: http://www.sunshineradio.ie/

Tipp FM
Premier Broadcast Centre, Gurtnafleur
Business Park, Clonmel, Co. Tipperary
Tel: 353 05261 25299
Email: reception@tippfm.com
Web site: www.tippfm.com

Today FM
Marconi House, Digges Lane, Dublin
Tel: 353 18507 15100
Email: live@todayfm.com
Web site: www.todayfm.com

WLR FM
Broadcast Centre, Ardkeen, Waterford,
Waterford X91 C4VN **Tel:** 353 05187 2248
Email: news@wlrfm.com
Web site: www.wlrfm.com

XXX
Marconi House, Digges Lane, Dublin 2

Television Networks & Stations

RTÉ Television
Donnybrook, Dublin **Tel:** 353 01208 3111
Email: newsdesk@rte.ie
Web site: www.rte.ie/tv/
Editor: Paul Edward Cunningham

UTV Ireland
Macken House, Mayor Street Upper, Dublin
1 **Tel:** 353 01819 8709
Email: news@utv.ie
Web site: www.utvireland.ie

News Services & Syndicates

Business World (Ireland)
5 Saint Andrew Street, Dublin 2
Tel: 353 01679 9500
Email: newsdesk@businessworld.ie
Web site: https://www.businessworld.ie

Willings Volume 1
Section 9

Master Index

I - Global Intelligence for the CIO

Artsbeat

The Blackcountryman

Concrete Engineering International

Destination Weddings & Honeymoons Abroad

Entertainment Technology

Fitcetera

Horse & Hound

International Rental News

J

KCLR 96fm

Logistics Handling

M

Miss Geeky

Nickelodeon UK

Performance French Cars

Q

SanNails

South Wales Guardian

Teen Librarian

Van Fleet World

The World of Fine Wine

The World of Hospitality

X

Y

Z